Advanced
Financial
Accounting

Advanced Financial Accounting

Seventh Edition

Richard E. Baker
Northern Illinois University

Valdean C. Lembke
University of Iowa

Thomas E. King
Southern Illinois University Edwardsville

Cynthia G. Jeffrey
Iowa State University

Boston   Burr Ridge, IL   Dubuque, IA   Madison, WI   New York   San Francisco   St. Louis
Bangkok   Bogotá   Caracas   Kuala Lumpur   Lisbon   London   Madrid   Mexico City
Milan   Montreal   New Delhi   Santiago   Seoul   Singapore   Sydney   Taipei   Toronto

The **McGraw·Hill** Companies

ADVANCED FINANCIAL ACCOUNTING
International Edition 2008

Portions of **FASB Statement No.52**, "Foreign Currency Translation," copyright by the
Financial Accounting Standards Board, 401 Merritt 7, PO Box 5116, Norwalk, CT 06856-
5116, U.S.A., are reproduced with permission. Complete copies of this document are available
from the FASB.

Material from the Uniform CPA Examination and Unofficial Answers, Copyright 1969, 1970,
1972, 1973, 1974, 1975, 1976, 1977, 1978, 1979, 1980, 1981, 1982, 1983, 1984, 1985, 1986,
1987, 1988, 1989, 1990, 1991, 1992, 1993, 1994, 1995, 1996, 1997, 1998, by the American
Institute of Certified Public Accountants, is reprinted (or adapted) with permission.

Material from the Certified Management Accountants Examination, Copyright 1974, 1975,
1976, 1977, 1979, 1980, 1981, 1982, 1983, 1984, 1985, 1986, 1987, 1988, 1989, by the
Institute of Certified Management Accountants, is reprinted (or adapted) with permission.

10 09 08 07 06 05 04 03 02 01
20 09 08 07
CTF   BJE

When ordering this title, use ISBN: 978-007-125913-2 or MHID: 007-125913-9

Printed in Singapore

www.mhhe.com

About the Authors

Richard E. Baker

Richard E. Baker is a member of the faculty at Northern Illinois University. His academic recognitions include being named the Ernst & Young Distinguished Professor of Accountancy at Northern Illinois University. In addition, he was recognized as an inaugural University Presidential Teaching Professor, the highest teaching recognition of his university. He received his B.S. degree from the University of Wisconsin—River Falls and his MBA and Ph.D. from the University of Wisconsin—Madison. His activities in the American Accounting Association have been continuous over many years and include serving on the AAA's Executive Committee as the Director of Education of the AAA; as a member of the AAA's Council as the Chair of the Teaching and Curriculum Section; and previously as the President of the Midwest Region. His lengthy service to the Federation of Schools of Accountancy (FSA) includes the offices of the President, the Vice President, and the Secretary. Many of his extensive professional or academic organization committee service efforts have involved research in assessing teaching and learning outcomes, designing innovative curriculum models, developing meaningful measurement criteria for evaluating accounting programs, and continually integrating new electronic technology into the accounting classroom. Professor Baker has served as an Associate Editor for *Issues in Accounting Education* and previously served as a reviewer for this journal for several years. He also has served as an Associate Editor of *Advances in Accounting Education*. He has received numerous teaching awards at both the undergraduate and graduate levels and has been selected as the Illinois CPA Society's Outstanding Accounting Educator. His most recent published research studies have concentrated on ways to make the learning/teaching experience as effective as possible. Other published research includes studies in financial reporting and mergers and acquisitions. Professor Baker's major teaching areas include advanced financial accounting, financial theory, and international business management. He is a CPA and has taught advanced financial accounting topics in CPA Examination review courses.

Valdean C. Lembke

Valdean C. Lembke has been a faculty member in the Department of Accounting at the University of Iowa for many years. He received his B.S. degree from Iowa State University and his MBA and Ph.D. from the University of Michigan. He has internal audit and public accounting experience. He has been active in the American Accounting Association, including service as President of the Midwest Region and Book Review Editor for *Issues in Accounting Education*. He was twice named recipient of the Gilbert P. Maynard Excellence in Accounting Instruction award. Professor Lembke has been actively involved in service to the Department of Accounting. He served two terms as department head and has been head of the Professional Program in Accounting. Professor Lembke has authored or coauthored articles in journals such as *The Accounting Review;* the *Journal of Accounting, Auditing and Finance;* the *Journal of Accountancy;* and the *Internal Auditor.* He also coauthored *Financial Accounting: A Decision-Making Approach,* an introductory accounting text, and a chapter on business combinations and consolidated financial statements in the *Accountant's Encyclopedia.* His teaching has been primarily in undergraduate and graduate coursework in financial accounting and in governmental and not-for-profit accounting. He has taught advanced financial accounting on a continuing basis.

Thomas E. King

Thomas E. King is a member of the faculty of the School of Business at Southern Illinois University Edwardsville. He received his B.S. degree from California State University, Northridge, and his MBA and Ph.D. from the University of California, Los Angeles. He is a CPA and received an Elijah Watt Sells Award and the Illinois gold medal for his scores on the Uniform CPA Examination. He has a number of years of business and consulting experience and has taught for more than 30 years. Professor King coauthored with Valdean Lembke the chapter on business combinations and consolidated financial statements in the *Accountant's Encyclopedia,* and he has authored or coauthored numerous articles appearing in journals such as *The Accounting Review; Accounting Horizons;* the *Journal of Accountancy;* the *Journal of Accounting, Auditing and Finance;* the *Journal of Accounting Education;* and *Financial Executive.* He also coauthored *Financial Accounting: A Decision-Making Approach,* an introductory accounting text. Professor King has served on the editorial boards of *Advances in Accounting* and *Advances in Accounting Education* for a number of years. He has completed two terms on the Board of Governors of the St. Louis Chapter of the Institute of Internal Auditors, and he has been active in the Financial Executives Institute, the Institute of Management Accountants, and the Illinois CPA Society. Professor King has taught advanced financial accounting, along with other financial accounting courses.

Cynthia G. Jeffrey

Cynthia G. Jeffrey is an Associate Professor of Accounting in the College of Business at Iowa State University. She received her B.S. and M.S. at Iowa State University and her Ph.D. from the University of Minnesota. She is a CPA and a member of the AICPA, the American Accounting Association, and the Canadian Academic Accounting Association. Professor Jeffrey received the Graduate Teaching Award from Iowa State University in 2005 and was recognized as Teacher of the Year in 2000. She was Director of the Master of Accounting program from its inception in 1999 until 2004. Professor Jeffrey has authored or coauthored articles in journals such as *The Accounting Review,* the *Journal of Accounting, Auditing and Finance, Business Ethics Quarterly, Behavioral Research in Accounting, The International Journal of Accounting,* the *Asia-Pacific Journal of Accounting,* and *Issues in Accounting Education.* Professor Jeffrey is the editor of *Research on Professional Responsibility and Ethics in Accounting.* She teaches both graduate and undergraduate courses and her major teaching areas are financial accounting, financial accounting theory, and international accounting.

Preface

The seventh edition of *Advanced Financial Accounting* is a comprehensive and highly illustrated presentation of the accounting and reporting principles used in a variety of business entities. Every day, the business press carries stories about the merger and acquisition mania, the complexities of modern business entities and new organizational structures for conducting business, accounting scandals related to complex business transactions, the foreign activities of multinational firms, the operations of governmental and nonprofit entities, and other topics typically included in advanced accounting. Accountants must know how to deal with the accounting and reporting ramifications of these issues.

OVERVIEW

The seventh edition of *Advanced Financial Accounting* continues to provide strong coverage of advanced accounting topics, as well as integrated coverage based on continuous case examples. The text is highly illustrated with complete presentations of worksheets, schedules, and financial statements so that students can see the development of each topic. The inclusion of all recent FASB and GASB pronouncements and the continuing deliberations of the authoritative bodies provides a current and contemporary text for students preparing for the CPA Examination and current practice. In the chapters covering consolidation subsequent to the date of combination, three alternative methods of accounting for the parent's investment in the subsidiary are presented in each chapter (basic equity) and appendices (cost and fully adjusted equity) to provide the opportunity for exploring the differences in the methods and seeing that the consolidated financial statements are the same regardless of the method the parent company uses to account for the investment. The chapters dealing with global operations include a comprehensive discussion of accounting for foreign currency derivatives and other financial instruments and arrangements used in today's business arena. The governmental and not-for-profit chapters include all recent important pronouncements and developments in those areas.

KEY FEATURES

The key strengths of this book are its clear and readable discussions of concepts and the detailed demonstrations of these concepts through illustrations and explanations. The many favorable responses to earlier editions from both students and instructors confirm our beliefs that clear presentation and comprehensive illustrations are essential to learning the sophisticated topics in an advanced accounting course. Key features of the seventh edition include:

- **A building block approach based on a strong conceptual foundation.** For each major topic area, students are provided with a thorough conceptual understanding before advancing to the procedures. The discussion begins with the fundamental concepts and why they are important. These fundamentals are then illustrated, giving students a basic example before progressing. Once this conceptual foundation is established, the complexities are layered gradually in successive steps. The authors developed this methodology through years of teaching advanced accounting. Many adopters have commented favorably on the effectiveness of this approach.

- **The use of a continuous case for each major subject matter area.** The comprehensive case of Peerless Products Corporation and its subsidiary, Special Foods Inc., has been continued in the for-profit chapters. For the governmental chapters, the Sol City case has been used to facilitate the development of governmental accounting and reporting concepts and procedures. Using a continuous case provides several benefits. First, students need only become familiar with one set of data and can then move more quickly through the subsequent discussions and illustrations without having to absorb a new set of data. Second, the case adds realism to the study of advanced accounting and permits students to see the effects of each successive step on the financial reports of a company. Finally, comparing and contrasting alternative methods using a continuous case allows students to evaluate different methods and outcomes more readily.

- **Extensive illustrations of key concepts.** The book is heavily illustrated with complete, not partial, workpapers, financial statements, and other computations and comparisons useful for demonstrating each topic. The illustrations are cross-referenced to the relevant text discussion. In the consolidations portion of the text, the focus is on the basic equity method of accounting for an investment in a subsidiary. However, two other methods—the cost method and the fully adjusted equity method—are fully discussed and illustrated in chapter appendices. Workpaper entries presented in the consolidations chapters are separately identified with an (E) and are shaded to differentiate them clearly from book entries. The extensive use of illustrations makes the learning process more efficient by allowing students to see quickly and readily the applications of the concepts. In addition, the illustrations reinforce understanding of the concepts by demonstrating the effects on the financial statements. In this manner, students understand that the many workpaper procedures typically covered in advanced accounting are the means to a desired end, not the end themselves.

- **Comprehensive coverage with significant flexibility.** The subject matter of advanced accounting is expanding at an unprecedented rate. New topics are being added, and traditional topics require more extensive coverage. Flexibility is therefore essential in an advanced accounting text. Most one-term courses are unable to cover all the topics included in this text. In recognition of time constraints, this text is structured to provide the most efficient use of the time available. The self-contained units of subject matter allow for substantial flexibility in sequencing the course materials. In addition, individual chapters are organized to allow for opportunities to go into greater depth on some topics through the use of the "Additional Considerations" sections. Several chapters include appendices containing discussions of alternative accounting procedures or illustrations of procedures or concepts that are of a supplemental nature.

- **Contemporary topical coverage.** Today's dynamic business environment requires accountants to continually learn about new types of transactions, new technologies available to the profession, and new requirements and standards for accounting and financial reporting. This textbook integrates the most recent professional standards and includes cases and examples from current practice. For example, because of the importance of the Sarbanes-Oxley Act, coverage of SOX has been extended in this edition. Due to the significance, and notoriety, of special-purpose entities (SPEs) in recent years, coverage of this important topic has been included. Discussion of the FASB's interpretation relating to variable-rate interest entities (VIEs) is included and illustrated along with a discussion and illustration of the consolidation of VIEs. The text also includes a discussion of the FASB's deliberations and proposals relating to business combinations and important consolidation issues, such as the treatment of noncontrolling interests and full recognition of fair values and goodwill (entity approach). While the textbook reflects contemporary professional issues, it also continues to provide updated discussion and extensive illustrations of the continuing conceptual foundations for each of the topics. Students are presented with an abundance of current information and learning opportunities to see that the topics in their advanced financial accounting are a significant part of today's profession of accountancy.

- **Extensive end-of-chapter materials.** A large number of questions, cases, exercises, and problems at the end of each chapter provides students an opportunity to solidify their understanding of the chapter material and assess their mastery of the subject matter. The end-of-chapter materials progress from simple, focused exercises to more complex, integrated problems. Cases provide opportunities for extending thought and for gaining exposure to different sources of accounting-related information. These cases include Financial Accounting Research System (FARS) database searches, company data using the Internet, and Kaplan CPA Review simulations. The AICPA has identified five skills to be examined as part of the CPA exam: (*a*) analysis, (*b*) judgment, (*c*) communication, (*d*) research, and (*e*) understanding. The end-of-chapter materials provide abundant opportunities for students to enhance those skills with realistic and real-world applications of advanced financial accounting topics.

ORGANIZATION: THE STORY OF PEERLESS PRODUCTS CORPORATION AND SPECIAL FOODS INC.

This textbook presents the complete story of a company, Peerless Products Corporation, from its beginning, through its growth to a multinational consolidated entity, and finally to its end. At each stage of the entity's development, including the acquisition of a subsidiary, Special Foods Inc., the textbook presents comprehensive examples and discussions of the accounting and financial reporting issues that accountants face. In this edition, discussions tied to the Peerless continuous case are easily identified by the company logos in the margin:

The following description explains how the text is organized and how continuing examples are used to demonstrate many of the topics:

Business Combinations, Intercorporate Equity Investments, and Consolidation Concepts

Chapters 1 and 2 of the textbook introduce the issues of complex organizational structures and accounting for business combinations and intercorporate equity investments. Chapter 3 provides a conceptual foundation for the study of consolidated financial statements.

Consolidation of Wholly Owned Subsidiaries

Chapter 4 initiates the story of Peerless Products Corporation, which purchases all of the stock of Special Foods Inc. and maintains Special Foods as a subsidiary. The consolidation workpaper is presented, with a discussion of both a simple workpaper as of the date of combination and a three-part workpaper for consolidation subsequent to acquisition. Basic consolidation procedures for consolidation at the date of combination and subsequent to combination are presented. The preparation of consolidated financial statements for Peerless Products and its wholly owned subsidiary Special Foods is illustrated for two years of combined operations.

Consolidation of Less-than-Wholly Owned Subsidiaries

Chapter 5 builds on the consolidation concepts introduced in Chapters 3 and 4 with an examination of the complexities added by a parent acquiring less than 100 percent ownership of a subsidiary. The consolidation of less-than-wholly owned subsidiaries is illustrated for two years of operations by assuming that Peerless Products acquires 80 percent of Special Foods' stock.

Intercompany Transactions

As is common for affiliated companies, Peerless Products and Special Foods engage in a number of intercompany transactions. Chapters 6, 7, and 8 discuss intercorporate transfers of services, noncurrent assets, and inventory, as well as intercompany debt transactions.

Complex Ownership Issues

Chapter 9 examines the special consolidation problems that arise from complex ownership structures. Included are the accounting issues that arise if: (1) Special Foods issues preferred stock, (2) Peerless decreases its percentage ownership in Special Foods by selling some of its stock investment in Special Foods to a party outside the consolidated entity or increases its ownership percentage by acquiring additional stock of Special Foods, (3) Special Foods purchases a subsidiary of its own, (4) Special Foods acquires some of Peerless Products' stock, and (5) Special Foods issues stock dividends.

Consolidation Reporting Issues

Chapter 10 completes the discussion of consolidated reporting by presenting several additional consolidation issues encountered by Peerless and Special Foods. First, the preparation of a consolidated cash flow statement is discussed and illustrated for Peerless Products and Special Foods. Second, the impact of interim acquisitions on consolidated financial statements is examined. Third, the chapter discusses tax considerations related to consolidated entities. The chapter concludes with a discussion of the computation of consolidated earnings per share.

Multinational Accounting

Chapters 11 and 12 present the accounting and reporting issues that arise when Peerless enters the multinational business environment. First, Peerless extends its sales to international customers and begins dealing in foreign currency transactions. To manage its risk, Peerless uses forward exchange contracts and other financial derivatives for hedging purposes. Comprehensive appendices are presented that discuss using the time value of derivatives and accounting for other forms of derivatives. In Chapter 12, Peerless acquires a subsidiary located in Germany. The German company reports its operations in euros, and Peerless must translate the subsidiary's trial balance into U.S. dollars to consolidate the operations of its German subsidiary.

Segment and Interim Reporting

Chapter 13 discusses segment reporting requirements and examines the segment and related disclosures that Peerless must make in its consolidated financial statements. Interim financial reporting also is discussed in this chapter and is illustrated with Peerless's interim reports.

SEC Reporting

Chapter 14 presents a discussion of the issues that Peerless must understand if it wishes to "go public" and issue stock or debt in the capital markets. The Securities and Exchange Commission has many specific rules, procedures, and reporting requirements that companies must follow if their securities are going to trade publicly. Coverage of the Sarbanes-Oxley Act is presented in this chapter so that students can gain some insight into this significant act.

Partnership Accounting

Chapters 15 and 16 step back in chronology to review the origins of Peerless Products. The process begins with C. Alt starting a software development business. Alt then forms a partnership with Blue, and, after operating for a year, the two partners bring Cha into the partnership because they need her business expertise. Accounting issues associated with partnership accounting are presented in these two chapters. After operating the partnership for several years, the partners incorporate their business under the name of Peerless Products Corporation.

Governmental and Nonprofit Accounting

Chapters 17 and 18 present the accounting and financial reporting for Sol City, the city in which Peerless Products is located. C. Alt serves on the city council, and the chapters present the accounting information needed by Alt to represent his constituents. Chapter 19 presents the accounting and financial reporting requirements for Sol City University and Sol City Community Hospital, along with several other nonprofit agencies located in Sol City.

Corporations in Financial Difficulty

Chapter 20 closes the story of Peerless Products and Special Foods. Because of the poor health of C. Alt, the consolidated entity experiences a variety of financial problems. Attempts are made to restructure its debt and to reorganize with the help of a court-appointed receiver. However, the company has too many financial problems and is forced to enter into bankruptcy.

Supplemental Chapters

The text's Website at www.mhhe.com/baker7e contains two supplemental chapters. The first, Accounting for Branch Operations, presents illustrations and discusses the issues of accounting and reporting for home offices and branches. The second supplemental chapter, Estates and Trusts, presents the accounting for C. Alt's estate by Blue, the administrator of the estate and also the first partner brought into the Peerless Products partnership. These chapters include end-of-chapter material for which solutions may be obtained online by instructors.

CHANGES FOR THE SEVENTH EDITION

Each of the chapters in the text has been revised to include comprehensive discussion and full illustration of relevant FASB and GASB standards. In addition, end-of-chapter materials have been revised to best illustrate and explore prior and new standards.

1. **Reorganization of consolidation foundation material.** The consolidation materials in the first section of the book have been extensively reorganized. The discussion of different theories of consolidation in Chapter 3 has been streamlined and a numerical example has been added to illustrate the effects of the different theories, including the FASB's proposed standards on combinations and consolidations. Because most subsidiaries are wholly owned, consolidation procedures for wholly owned subsidiaries are discussed before adding the complexity of less-than-wholly owned subsidiaries. Thus, Chapter 4 deals with the consolidation of wholly owned subsidiaries both at the date of acquisition and beyond. Most of the important aspects of consolidation are discussed in Chapter 4 in the context of wholly owned subsidiaries. Chapter 5 then builds on this foundation to discuss consolidation of majority-owned subsidiaries.

2. **Illustrations of proposed FASB standards on consolidation and combinations.** The FASB currently is moving toward the completion of projects proposing major changes in accounting for business combinations and the presentation of consolidated financial statements. Although the proposed standards are not yet finalized, they will, if adopted, have a significant impact on future practice. The FASB's proposals are included in the text in several ways. First, brief coverage of the proposed standards is integrated throughout the text when relevant topics are discussed. Second, a more detailed discussion of the proposed standards is provided in a separate section in Chapters 1, 3, and 5. Third, numerical examples are provided to illustrate the effects of implementing the proposed standards. For example, in Chapter 5, a full workpaper illustration of the preparation of consolidated financial statements under the proposed standards is presented. This illustration is extended on the text's Website, and additional illustrations are presented as well (www.mhhe.com/baker7e). End-of-chapter materials relating to the proposed standards have been included in the text.

3. **Increased coverage of the Sarbanes-Oxley Act.** The Sarbanes-Oxley Act (SOX) has had a profound impact on auditing and corporate governance. Chapter 14 provides an extensive overview and discussion of SOX, providing a background essential for accountants. Cases have been added for students to gain additional understanding of SOX.

4. **Integration of the Revised Uniform Partnership Act.** The model Revised Uniform Partnership Act (RUPA), or a significant adaptation, has now been adopted in about 40 states. Additional states are in the process of evaluating the impact of the RUPA on their states to determine which parts of the model RUPA they might adopt. Chapters 15 and 16 discuss and illustrate the essential provisions of RUPA.

5. **Increased focus on governmental and not-for-profit financial statements and disclosures.** Chapters 17 and 18 (on governmental entities) and Chapter 19 (on not-for-profit entities) have been updated to include recent GASB and FASB standards, and the discussion and end-of-chapter materials have been enhanced to provide students with more opportunities to understand how the accounting and reporting standards affect the financial statements and other elements of the entities' annual reports.

6. **More real-world examples throughout the text.** Additional real-world examples have been added throughout the chapters to illustrate the topics and to show students that the topics covered are important for accountants to understand and be able to apply in the dynamic business environment. These examples make it "real" for students.

7. **End-of-chapter materials have been significantly restructured.**

   - *New cases:* Real-world cases included in the end-of-chapter materials have been updated and a number of new ones added throughout the text. These cases provide students with a sense of relevancy, an opportunity to engage in online research, and a chance to practice formal writing.

   - *Kaplan CPA Review simulations:* Also introduced are a number of simulations of advanced financial accounting issues that use the framework by Kaplan CPA Review. Students can work the simulations online to gain experience on the presentation and operation of simulations that appear on the computerized CPA exam.

   - *Supplemental problems:* Some of the longer, more complex problems in some of the chapters have been moved to the textbook's Website (www.mhhe.com/baker7e) and are now presented as Supplemental Problems. Advanced financial accounting classes that wish to intensively explore the accounting and reporting requirements of a chapter's topics can access the Website and download this problem material. By moving some of the longer problems to the Website, the authors created space to add more real-world research cases, which are becoming increasingly important for advanced financial accounting courses.

RETAINED FEATURES

The features that provided the strength of earlier editions have been retaned in the seventh edition:

1. The comprehensive continuous case approach has been retained because it provides students with the ability to see how each successive step affects the financial reporting model of an entity. The Peerless Products and Special Foods case is robust and serves as a foundation for the building block approach used throughout the text.

2. Although each chapter has been revised to reflect recent FASB and GASB standards, as well as to refine and focus the discussion and presentations, extensive efforts were made to ensure retention of the clear writing style that faculty and students have valued very highly in previous editions.

3. The full coverage of the FASB and GASB standards that have direct applicability to the topics in advanced financial accounting has been continued.

4. Cases at the end of each chapter requiring students to write essay-type responses reflecting alternative viewpoints or justifying a specific accounting choice have been retained and updated. Students are asked to explain their reasoning and often are asked to use library or Internet research tools and materials in support of their answers. These cases require students to go beyond the computational level in addressing the topics in advanced financial accounting.

5. The study guide for the text is written by the authors of the text to ensure full integration and compatible presentation of the topics. The study guide for the seventh edition has

been revised to reflect all the updates and enhancements in the textbook as a result of the new GASB and FASB standards, and every effort has been made to provide a terrific learning tool for students.

6. Because advanced financial accounting is often taken by students who plan to take the CPA Examination, numerous end-of-chapter materials are provided in the formats used for testing on the CPA Examination. A wide variety of multiple-choice questions and cases requiring database research and written presentations is provided.

SUPPLEMENTS

This text is accompanied by a full ancillary program with items designed to enhance the learning process. Supplemental materials are available from McGraw-Hill/Irwin.

For the Student

Study Guide (0073210889)

Written by the authors of the text, the study guide contains summaries of the key concepts presented in each chapter and provides self-diagnostic and review materials in the form of objective-type and fill-in-the-blank questions, as well as both short and comprehensive exercises and problems. The solutions are provided so that achievement levels can be assessed readily and topics that need further review can be identified.

Online Learning Center (URL: www.mhhe.com/baker7e), Student Edition

- *Learning Objectives:* The online material for each chapter begins with the learning objective for that chapter. Students gain an overview of the importance to accountants of the topics covered in each chapter.
- *Online Quizzes:* Prepared by Amy Kaiser, interactive quizzes give students a variety of multiple-choice and true/false questions related to each chapter for self-evaluation.
- *Excel Worksheets:* Prepared by Harlan Fuller, these worksheets for use with Excel are provided to facilitate completion of problems requiring numerous mechanical computations. Available only online.
- *Check Figures:* Prepared by the text authors, a list of answers is provided separately for many of the end-of-chapter materials in the text. Available only online.
- *Microsoft PowerPoint Slides®:* Authored by Alex Clifford, copies of the Microsoft PowerPoint Slides® are available by chapter to facilitate note-taking and review.
- *Supplemental Problems:* Additional problem materials for many of the chapters are available online to enhance students' learning of the topics in the chapters. These supplemental problems tend to be longer and present a more comprehensive fact situation in order to broaden students' understanding of the topics in the chapters.
- *Supplemental Chapters:* Two chapters are available online for students wishing extended learning in regard to: (*a*) accounting for home office and branch operations; and (*b*) accounting and reporting for estates and trusts. Cases, exercises, and problems are also available for these two chapters.
- *PowerWeb:* This feature is a unique Website that extends the learning experience beyond the core textbook and includes the following learning aids:
  - ➤ Current readings.
  - ➤ Study tips and self-quizzes.
  - ➤ Links to related sites.
  - ➤ Web research guides.
  - ➤ Access to Northern Light Search Engine, providing Internet access to additional articles.

For the Instructor

Instructor's Resource CD-ROM (0073210897)

Only for instructors, this CD combines all instructor resource teaching supplements into one easy-to-use format:

- *Solutions Manual:* Created by the authors, solutions are provided for all questions, cases, exercises, and problems in the text. Solutions are carefully explained and logically presented. Answers for many of the multiple-choice questions include computations and explanations. Instructors can prepare transparencies directly from the solutions manual.

- *Instructor's Resource Manual:* Prepared by Beth Woods, the instructor's resource manual includes chapter outlines, additional examples, teaching suggestions, and other materials to assist instructors in making the most effective use of the text.

- *Test Bank:* Authored by Leonard Stokes, this comprehensive collection of both conceptual and procedural test items has been revised. The material is organized by chapter and includes a large variety of multiple-choice questions, exercises, and problems that can be used to measure student achievement in each chapter's topics. The test items are closely coordinated with the text to ensure consistency.

Online Learning Center (URL: www.mhhe.com/baker7e), *Instructor Edition*

- Instructor supplements such as the *Solutions Manual, Instructor's Resource Manual,* and *Microsoft PowerPoint Slides*® are available in downloadable form and are password protected.

- *Supplemental Problems:* Downloadable additional exercises and problems are provided for many chapters in both the Student Edition and the Instructor Edition. Instructors can assign these additional exercises and problems to broaden their students' understanding of the topics in the chapters. The Instructor Edition includes downloadable solutions to those supplemental exercises and problems.

- *Supplemental Chapters:* Two chapters are available online: (*a*) accounting for home office and branch operations; and (*b*) accounting and reporting for estates and trusts. Cases, exercises, and problems are also available for these two chapters and the Instructor Edition includes solutions to those end-of-chapter items.

- *Instructor Updates:* The Online Learning Center contains timely discussions and illustrations of major accounting or financial reporting issues under deliberation by standard-setting bodies. Instructors can choose to download these updates and share them with their students.

- *PowerWeb* delivers to instructors and students the latest news and developments pertinent to the course:

  ➢ Access to current articles related to advanced financial accounting.

  ➢ Updates.

  ➢ Links to related sites.

  ➢ Web research guide.

  ➢ Access to Northern Light Search Engine, providing Internet access to additional articles.

- *Online Course Support* provides course content cartridges available for course Websites to support online class delivery when using products such as WebCT or Blackboard.

- *Page-Out* is McGraw-Hill's Course Management System that provides a "point and click" course Website tool.

Acknowledgments

This text includes the thoughts and contributions of many individuals, and we wish to express our sincere appreciation to them. First, and foremost, we thank all the students in our advanced accounting classes, from whom we have learned so much. In many respects, this text is an outcome of the learning experiences we have shared with our students. Second, we wish to thank the many outstanding teachers we have had in our own educational programs, from whom we learned the joy of learning. We are indebted to our colleagues in advanced accounting for helping us reach our goal of writing the best possible advanced financial accounting text. We appreciate the many valuable comments and suggestions from the instructors who used earlier editions of the text. Their comments and suggestions have contributed to making this text a more effective learning tool. We especially wish to thank: C. Richard Baker, Adelphi University; Jean C. Bedard; Mark Bettner, Bucknell University; Bruce Bradford, Fairfield University; Bobby Carmichael, Texas A&M; Charles Christianson, Luther College; Steve Czarsty, Mary Washington College; David Doran, Pennsylvania State University, Erie; John Engstrom, Northern Illinois University; Wayne Higley, Buena Vista College; Sharron Hoffmans, University of Texas, El Paso; James Hopkins, Morningside College; Gordon Hosch, University of New Orleans; David Karmon, Central Michigan University; Aubrey Kosson; James Lahey, Northern Illinois University; May H. Lo, Western New England College; Mary Maury, St. John's University; Ralph McQuade, Jr., Bentley College; David Meeting, Cleveland State University; Philip Meyer, Boston University; Jon Nance, Southwest Missouri State University; Scott Newman, Western State College of Colorado; Larry Prober, Rider University; Terence Reilly, Albright College; Max Rexroad, Illinois State University; Andrew Rosman, University of Connecticut; Eugene Rozanski, Illinois State University; Norlin Reuschhoff, University of Notre Dame; Victoria Rymer, University of Maryland at College Park; Nancy Starnes, Southern Illinois University, Edwardsville; Pam Smith, Northern Illinois University; James Stice, Brigham Young University; Mack Tennyson, University of Charleston; Stuart Webster, University of Wyoming; and Scott Whisenant, University of Houston.

We also wish to thank John R. Simon, Northern Illinois University, for his assistance in revising the end-of-chapter material in several chapters of the text. Appreciation is expressed to Wendy A. Duffy for her development of FARS cases for several of the chapters. We also thank Lisa Enfinger for her work in accuracy checking, as well as the supplements authors: Leonard Stokes, for the creation of the Test Bank; Harlan Fuller, for creation of the Excel Templates; Alex Clifford, for development of the Microsoft PowerPoint Slides®; Amy Kaiser, for creation of the Online Quizzes; and Beth Woods, for creation of the Instructor's Resource Manual. Typing assistance was provided by Margaret Berg, Northern Illinois University. We especially want to thank Lois Lembke for her many efforts on our Solutions Manual.

We are grateful for the assistance and direction of the McGraw-Hill/Irwin team: Stewart Mattson, Steve DeLancey, Dan Wiencek, Robin Reed, Megan McFarlane, Harvey Yep, Gina Hangos, Jess Kosic, Susan Lombardi, Ira Roberts, Matthew Baldwin, and Christine Vaughan, who all worked hard to champion our book through the production process.

Permission has been received from the Institute of Certified Management Accountants of the Institute of Management Accountants to use questions and/or unofficial answers from past CMA examinations. We appreciate the cooperation of the American Institute of Certified Public Accountants for providing permission to adapt and use materials from past Uniform CPA Examinations. We also thank Kaplan CPA Review for providing its online framework for advanced financial accounting students so they might gain important experience with the types of simulations included on the Uniform CPA Examination.

Above all, we extend our deepest appreciation to our families, who continue to provide the encouragement and support necessary for this project.

Richard E. Baker
Valdean C. Lembke
Thomas E. King
Cynthia G. Jeffrey

Brief Contents

Contents

Chapter One

Intercorporate Acquisitions and Investments in Other Entities

The business environment in the United States is perhaps the most dynamic and vibrant in the world. Each day, new companies and new products enter the marketplace, and others are forced to leave or to change substantially in order to survive. In this setting, existing companies often find it necessary to combine their operations with those of other companies or to establish new operating units in emerging areas of business activity.

In recent years, the business world has witnessed many corporate acquisitions and combinations, often involving some of the nation's largest and best-known companies. Some of these combinations have captured the attention of the public because of the personalities involved, the daring strategies employed, and the huge sums of money at stake.

Recent business practice has also experienced the creation of numerous less traditional types of enterprise structures and new, sometimes novel, entities for carrying out the enterprise's operating and financing activities. The creation of new structures and special entities is often a response to today's current operating environment, with its abundant operating risks, global considerations, and tax complexities. In some cases, however, as evidenced by recent lawsuits, criminal investigations, congressional actions, and corporate bankruptcies, the legitimacy of the use of some of these structures and special entities has been questioned.

Overall, today's business environment is one of the most exciting and challenging in history, being characterized by rapid change and exceptional complexity. In this environment, regulators, such as the Securities and Exchange Commission (SEC), Financial Accounting Standards Board (FASB), and Public Company Accounting Oversight Board (PCAOB), are scrambling to respond to the rapid-paced changes in a manner that ensures the continued usefulness of accounting reports to reflect economic reality.

A number of accounting and reporting issues arise when two or more companies join under common ownership or a company creates a complex organizational structure involving any of a variety of forms of new financing or operating entities. The first 10 chapters of this text focus on a number of these issues. Chapter 1 lays the foundation by describing some of the factors that have led to corporate expansion and some of the types of complex organizational structures and relationships that have evolved. Then the chapter deals explicitly with the accounting and reporting issues related to formal business combinations. Chapter 2 focuses on investments in the common stock of other companies and on selected other types of investments in and relationships with other entities. The next eight chapters systematically develop the reporting procedures used by related companies when one controls the others and they present *consolidated financial statements* that portray the related companies as if they were actually a single company.

THE DEVELOPMENT OF COMPLEX BUSINESS STRUCTURES

Today's business environment is complex. The complexity arises from doing business across different states and countries, each with its own laws and risks, the intricacies of tax provisions, the myriad of exceedingly complex business transactions and financial instruments, and various other factors. The simple business setting in which one company has two or three manufacturing plants and produces products for a local or regional market is much less common now than it was several decades ago. As companies grow in size, and as a response to the complex business environment, they often develop complex organizational and ownership structures.

Enterprise Expansion

Most business enterprises seek to expand as a means of survival and profitability. Both the owners and managers of a business enterprise have an interest in seeing a company grow in size. This size often allows economies of scale to exist with regard to production and distribution. By expanding into new markets or acquiring other companies already in those markets, companies can develop new earning potential and those in cyclical industries can add greater stability to earnings through diversification. For example, Boeing, a company very strong in commercial aviation, acquired McDonnell Douglas, a company weak in commercial aviation but very strong in military aviation and other defense and space applications. When orders for commercial airliners plummeted following a precipitous decline in air travel, increased defense spending, partially related to the war in Iraq, helped level out Boeing's earnings.

Corporate management often is rewarded with higher salaries as company size increases. In addition, prestige frequently increases with the size of a company and with a reputation for the successful acquisition of other companies. As a result, corporate management often finds it personally advantageous to increase company size. For instance, Bernard Ebbers started his telecommunications career as the head of a small discount long-distance telephone service company and built it into one of the world's largest corporations, WorldCom. In the process, Ebbers became well known for his acquisition prowess and became tremendously wealthy—until WorldCom (now MCI) was racked by accounting scandals and declared bankruptcy and Ebbers was sentenced to prison.

Organizational Structure and Business Objectives

Complex organizational structures often evolve to help achieve a business's objectives, such as increasing profitability or reducing risk. For example, many companies establish subsidiaries to conduct certain business activities. A *subsidiary* is a corporation that is controlled by another corporation, referred to as a *parent company*, usually through majority ownership of its common stock. Because a subsidiary is a separate legal entity, the parent's risk associated with the subsidiary's activities is limited. Companies often transfer their receivables to subsidiaries or special-purpose entities that use the receivables as collateral for bonds issued to other entities (securitization). External parties may hold partial or complete ownership of those entities, allowing the transferring company to share its risk associated with the receivables. In some situations, tax benefits may be realized by conducting certain activities through a separate entity. Bank of America, for example, established a subsidiary to which it transferred bank-originated loans and was able to save $418 million in quarterly taxes.[1]

Organizational Structure, Acquisitions, and Ethical Considerations

In some cases, corporate managers have used complex organizational structures to manipulate financial reporting and to enrich themselves. Many major corporations, taking advantage of loopholes or laxness in financial reporting requirements, have used subsidiaries or other entities to borrow large amounts of money without reporting the debt on their balance

---

[1] "PNC Shakes Up Banking Sector; Investors Exit," *The Wall Street Journal*, January 30, 2002, p. C2.

sheets. Some companies have created special entities that have then been used to manipulate profits.

The term "special-purpose entity" has become well known in recent years because of the egregious abuse of these entities by companies such as Enron. A *special-purpose entity* (SPE) is, in general, a financing vehicle that is not a substantive operating entity, usually one created for a single specified purpose. An SPE may be in the form of a corporation, trust, or partnership. Enron Corp., one of the world's largest companies prior to its collapse in 2001, established many SPEs, at least some of which were intended to manipulate financial reporting. Some of Enron's SPEs apparently were created primarily to hide debt while others were used to create fictional transactions or to convert borrowings into reported revenues.

One of the major topics discussed in this chapter is accounting for mergers and acquisitions, an area that can lend itself to manipulation. Historically, it has been one of the most difficult and troublesome areas of financial reporting. In addition to the complexities of combining the financial information of two previously independent companies, many issues arise relating to the treatment of acquisition-related costs and values. These accounting issues require numerous estimates, assumptions, and judgments that significantly affect future financial reporting for the companies involved. While professional judgment is important throughout financial reporting, judgments about fair presentation can be particularly difficult when accounting for mergers and acquisitions.

Arthur Levitt, former chairman of the SEC, highlighted some of these potential problems in his speech "The Numbers Game," delivered September 28, 1998. Levitt feared that in their zeal to meet Wall Street earnings targets, companies were misusing accounting estimates and techniques. He worried that illusion, rather than integrity, was driving financial reports. His concern was that a lack of trust in financial reporting has the potential for undermining the efficient functioning of our capital markets.

One issue on which Levitt focused was "creative acquisition accounting" or "merger magic." A method of accounting for business combinations that sometimes created earnings and, in the view of many, provided misleading financial reporting subsequent to the combination, pooling of interests, has been eliminated by the FASB. However, Levitt pointed out that other areas of manipulation remain in accounting for mergers and acquisitions. For instance, the SEC has been concerned about accounting for in-process research and development (IPR&D) costs. According to **FASB Interpretation No. 4**, "Applicability of FASB Statement No. 2 to Business Combinations Accounted for by the Purchase Method," IPR&D is required to be written off when purchased in a business combination. Many companies have assigned a large portion of the acquisition cost of an acquired company to in-process research and development and immediately charged the full amount off to expense, freeing reporting in future periods from the burden of those costs. However, the appropriate amount to assign to IPR&D is difficult to evaluate because of the lack of a widely accepted model for valuing IPR&D. SEC scrutiny of this issue seems to have lessened the amount of IPR&D charge-offs. Overall, the frequency and size of merger transactions, and the complexity of acquisition accounting, make the potential impact on financial statements critically important.

The public outrage surrounding the massive losses suffered by Enron's creditors, investors, and employees focused attention on SPEs and on weaknesses in accounting and the accounting profession. Because of the Enron scandal and massive accounting failures at other major corporations, Congress, the SEC, and the FASB have taken actions to strengthen the financial reporting process and to clarify the rules relating to special entities and relationships. Of particular note here is that the FASB issued a new pronouncement relating to SPEs, or more specifically, what the FASB refers to as "variable interest entities"; this topic is discussed in Chapter 3. In addition, the FASB is in the process of issuing a series of pronouncements having to do with reporting issues associated with different organizational structures and relationships (e.g., intercorporate investments in common stock and consolidated financial statements). These issues will be discussed in later chapters.

BUSINESS EXPANSION AND FORMS OF ORGANIZATIONAL STRUCTURE

Historically, businesses have expanded by internal growth through new product development and expansion of existing product lines into new markets. In recent decades, however, many companies have chosen to expand by combining with or acquiring other companies. Either approach may lead to a change in organizational structure.

Expansion from Within

As companies expand from within, they often find it advantageous to conduct their expanded operations through new subsidiaries or other entities, such as partnerships, joint ventures, or special entities. In most of these situations, an identifiable segment of the company's existing assets is transferred to the new entity, and, in exchange, the transferring company receives equity ownership.

Companies may be motivated to establish new subsidiaries or other entities for a variety of reasons. Broadly diversified companies may place unrelated operations in separate subsidiaries to establish clear lines of control and facilitate the evaluation of operating results. In some cases, an entity that specializes in a particular type of activity or has its operations in a particular country may qualify for special tax incentives. Of particular importance in some industries is the fact that a separate legal entity may be permitted to operate in a regulatory environment without subjecting the entire entity to regulatory control. Also, by creating a separate legal entity, a parent company may be able to protect itself from exposing the entire company's assets to legal liability that may stem from a new product line or entry into a higher risk form of business activity.

Companies might also establish new subsidiaries or other entities, not as a means of expansion, but as a means of disposing of a portion of their existing operations through outright sale or a transfer of ownership to existing shareholders or others. In some cases, companies have used this approach in disposing of a segment of operations that no longer fits well with the overall mission of the company. In other cases, the approach has been used as a means of disposing of unprofitable operations or to gain regulatory or shareholder approval of a proposed merger with another company. A *spin-off* occurs when the ownership of a newly created or existing subsidiary is distributed to the parent's stockholders without their surrender of any of their stock in the parent company. A *split-off* occurs when the subsidiary's shares are exchanged for shares of the parent, thereby leading to a reduction in the outstanding shares of the parent company. Although a transfer of ownership to one or more unrelated parties normally results in a taxable transaction, properly designed transfers of ownership to existing shareholders generally qualify as nontaxable exchanges.

Expansion through Business Combinations

Many times companies find that entry into new product areas or geographic regions is more easily accomplished by acquiring or combining with other companies than through internal expansion. For example, SBC Communications, a major telecommunications company and one of the "Baby Bells," significantly increased its service area by combining with Pacific Telesis and Ameritech and, ultimately, acquiring AT&T (and adopting its name).

A *business combination* occurs when two or more companies join under common control. The concept of *control* relates to the ability to direct policies and management. Traditionally, control over a company has been gained by acquiring a majority of the company's common stock. However, the diversity of financial and operating arrangements employed in recent years also raises the possibility of gaining control with less than majority ownership or, in some cases, with no ownership at all.

The types of business combinations found in today's business environment and the terms of the combination agreements are as diverse as the firms involved. Companies enter into various types of formal and informal arrangements that may have at least some of the characteristics of a business combination. Most companies tend to avoid recording informal agreements on their books because of the potential difficulty of enforcing them. In fact, some types of informal arrangements, such as those aimed at fixing prices or apportioning potential customers, are illegal. Formal agreements generally are enforceable and are more likely to be recognized on the books of the participants.

Informal Arrangements

Informal arrangements take many different forms. A simple gentlemen's agreement may be all that is needed to establish an amiable long-term relationship in a joint business venture. In other cases, companies with complementary products or services develop implicit working relationships. For example, a building contractor might always use a particular electrical or plumbing subcontractor. Some companies form *strategic alliances* for working together on a somewhat more formal basis. For example, Washington Mutual, the country's largest thrift organization, formed a strategic alliance with SAFECO Corporation to distribute SAFECO annuities through Washington Mutual's multistate branch network, and Continental Airlines and Northwest Airlines entered a strategic agreement for route sharing. Companies that partially depend on each other may use interlocking directorates, in which one or more members serve on the boards of directors of both companies, as a means of providing a degree of mutual direction without taking formal steps to join together.

The informality and freedom that make informal arrangements workable also are strong factors against combining financial statements and treating the companies as if they were a single entity. Another key factor in most informal arrangements is the continuing separation of ownership and the ease with which the informal arrangements can be terminated. Without some type of combined ownership, the essentials of a business combination generally are absent.

Formal Agreements

Formal business combinations usually are accompanied by written agreements. These agreements specify the terms of the combination, including the form of the combined company, the consideration to be exchanged, the disposition of outstanding securities, and the rights and responsibilities of the participants. Consummation of such an agreement requires recognition on the books of one or more of the companies that are a party to the combination.

In some cases, a formal agreement may be equivalent in substance to a business combination, yet different in form. For example, a company entering into an agreement to lease all of another company's assets for a period of several decades is, in effect, acquiring the other company. Similarly, an operating agreement giving to one company full management authority over the operations of another company for an extended period of time may be viewed as a means of effecting a business combination. In spite of the substance of these types of agreements, they usually are not treated as business combinations from an accounting perspective.

Frequency of Business Combinations

Very few major companies function as single legal entities in our modern business environment. Virtually all major companies have at least one subsidiary, with more than a few broadly diversified companies having several hundred subsidiaries. In some cases, subsidiaries are created to incorporate separately part of the ongoing operations previously conducted within the parent company. Other subsidiaries are acquired through business combinations.

Business combinations are a continuing and frequent part of the business environment. A merger boom occurred in the 1960s. This period was characterized by frantic and, in some cases, disorganized merger binges, resulting in creation of a large number of conglomerates, or companies operating in many different industries. Because many of the resulting companies lacked coherence in their operations, they often were less successful than anticipated, and many of the acquisitions of the 1960s have since been sold or abandoned. In the 1980s, the number of business combinations again increased. That period saw many leveraged buyouts, but the resulting debt has plagued many of those companies over the years.

The number of business combinations through the 1990s dwarfed previous merger booms, with all records for merger activity shattered. This pace continued into the new century, with a record-setting $3.3 trillion in deals closed in 2000.[2] However, with the downturn in the economy in the early 2000s, the number of mergers declined significantly. Many companies put their expansion plans on hold, and a number of the mergers that did occur were aimed at survival. Toward the middle of 2003, merger activity again increased and has accelerated significantly into the last half of the decade. During one period of less than 100 hours in 2006, "around $110 billion in acquisition deals were sealed worldwide in sectors ranging from natural gas, to copper, to mouthwash to steel, linking investors and industrialists from India, to Canada, to Luxembourg to the U.S."[3] Clearly, business combinations will continue to be an important area of business activity into the foreseeable future.

During the past 10 years, business combinations have been common in telecommunications, defense, banking and financial services, information technology, energy and natural resources, entertainment, pharmaceuticals, and manufacturing. Some of the world's largest companies and best-known names have been involved in recent major acquisitions, such as Procter & Gamble, Gillette, Citicorp, Bank of America, AT&T, Whirlpool, Sprint, Verizon, Adobe Systems, Chrysler, Daimler-Benz, ConocoPhillips, British Petroleum, and Exxon.

Complex Organizational Structures

While a parent-subsidiary structure has been standard for major corporations for a number of decades, more complex structures have started to become common in recent years. Many companies now conduct at least part of their operations through entities other than subsidiaries. For instance, corporate joint ventures and partnerships are commonly found in energy development and distribution, construction, motion picture production, and various other industries. Cingular, for instance, the largest provider of mobile wireless communications in the United States, is a joint venture between AT&T and BellSouth. As is discussed in Chapter 3, special-purpose and variable interest entities, including trusts, have gained widespread use as financing vehicles. The adoption of less traditional, innovative organizational structures provides many challenges for financial reporting.

Organizational Structure and Financial Reporting

When companies expand or change their organizational structure by acquiring other companies or through internal division, the new structure must be examined to determine the appropriate financial reporting procedures. Several approaches are possible, depending on the circumstances:

1. **Merger** A business combination in which the acquired company's assets and liabilities are combined with those of the acquiring company results in no additional organizational components. Thus, financial reporting is based on the original organizational structure.

2. **Controlling ownership** A business combination in which the acquired company remains as a separate legal entity with a majority of its common stock owned by the purchasing company leads to a parent–subsidiary relationship. Accounting standards normally require that the financial statements of the parent and subsidiary be consolidated for general-purpose reporting so the companies appear as a single company. The treatment is the same if the subsidiary is created rather than purchased. The treatment is also the same when the other entity is unincorporated and the investor company has control and majority ownership.[4]

3. **Noncontrolling ownership** The purchase of a less-than-majority interest in another corporation does not usually result in a business combination or controlling situation. A similar situation arises when a company creates another entity and holds less than a controlling position in it or purchases a less-than-controlling interest in an existing

[2] Dennis K. Berman and Jason Singer, "Big Mergers Are Making a Comeback as Companies, Investors Seek Growth," *The Wall Street Journal*, November 5, 2005, p. A1.

[3] Dennis K. Berman and Jason Singer, "Blizzard of Deals Heralds an Era of Megamergers," *The Wall Street Journal*, June 27, 2006, p. A1.

[4] Majority ownership is generally a sufficient but not a necessary condition for the indicated treatment. Unlike the corporate case, percentage ownership does not fully describe the nature of a beneficial interest in a partnership. Investments in partnerships are discussed in later chapters.

partnership. In its financial statements, the investor company reports its interest in the investee as an investment with the specific method of accounting for the investment dictated by the circumstances.

4. **Other beneficial interest** One company may have a beneficial interest in another entity even without a direct ownership interest. The beneficial interest may be defined by the agreement establishing the entity or by an operating or financing agreement. When the beneficial interest is based on factors other than percentage ownership, the reporting rules may be complex and depend on the circumstances. In general, a company that has the ability to make decisions significantly affecting the results of another entity's activities or is expected to receive a majority of the other entity's profits and losses is considered to be that entity's *primary beneficiary*. Normally, that entity's financial statements would be consolidated with those of the primary beneficiary.

These different situations, and the related accounting and reporting procedures, will be discussed throughout the first 10 chapters of the text. The primary focus will be on the first three situations, especially the purchase of all or part of another company's stock. The discussion of the fourth situation will be limited because of its complexity and the diversity of possible arrangements.

CREATING BUSINESS ENTITIES

Companies that choose to conduct a portion of their operations through separate business entities usually do so through corporate subsidiaries, corporate joint ventures, or partnerships. The ongoing accounting and reporting for investments in corporate joint ventures and subsidiaries are discussed in Chapters 2 through 10. Ongoing accounting for investments in partnerships is discussed in Chapter 2, and accounting for partnerships themselves is discussed in Chapters 15 and 16. This section discusses the origination of these entities when the parent or investor creates them rather than purchases an interest in an existing corporation or partnership.

When a company transfers assets or operations to another entity that it has created, a vast number of variations in the types of entities and the types of agreements between the creating company and the created entity is possible. Accordingly, it is impossible to establish a single set of rules and procedures that will suffice in all situations. The discussion here focuses on the most straightforward and quite common cases in which the transferring company creates a subsidiary or partnership that it owns and controls, including cases in which the company intends to transfer ownership to its stockholders. The more complex situations will be reserved for later discussion.

In these simple cases, the company transfers assets, and perhaps liabilities, to an entity that the company has created and controls and in which it holds majority ownership. The company transfers assets and liabilities to the created entity at book value, and the transferring company recognizes an ownership interest in the newly created entity equal to the book value of the net assets transferred. Recognition of fair values of the assets transferred in excess of their carrying values on the books of the transferring company normally is not appropriate in the absence of an arm's-length transaction. Thus, no gains or losses are recognized on the transfer by the transferring company. However, if the value of an asset transferred to a newly created entity has been impaired prior to the transfer and its fair value is less than the carrying value on the transferring company's books, the transferring company should recognize an impairment loss and transfer the asset to the new entity at the lower fair value.

The created entity begins accounting for the transferred assets and liabilities in the normal manner based on their book values at the time of transfer. Subsequent financial reporting involves consolidating the created entity's financial statements with those of the parent company. Overall, the consolidated financial statements appear the same as if the transfer had not taken place.

As an illustration of a created entity, assume that Allen Company creates a subsidiary, Blaine Company, and transfers the following assets to Blaine in exchange for all 100,000 shares of Blaine's $2 par common stock:

Item	Cost	Book Value
Cash		$ 70,000
Inventory	$ 50,000	50,000
Land	75,000	75,000
Building	100,000	80,000
Equipment	250,000	160,000
		$435,000

Allen records the transfer with the following entry:[5]

(1)	Investment in Blaine Company Common Stock	435,000	
	Accumulated Depreciation	110,000	
	Cash		70,000
	Inventory		50,000
	Land		75,000
	Building		100,000
	Equipment		250,000

$110,000 = (\$100,000 - \$80,000) + (\$250,000 - \$160,000)$

Blaine Company records the transfer of assets and the issuance of stock at the book value of the assets transferred, as follows:

(2)	Cash	70,000	
	Inventory	50,000	
	Land	75,000	
	Building	100,000	
	Equipment	250,000	
	Accumulated Depreciation		110,000
	Common Stock, $2 par		200,000
	Additional Paid-In Capital		235,000

If Blaine Company had been created as a partnership rather than a corporation, the accounting would be similar. Assume that Allen invests the same assets as in the corporate case and an unrelated company, Chaney Corp., invests $65,000 cash for a 10 percent share of Blaine's profits and losses, with Allen operating and controlling the partnership. Allen Company records its investment as in entry (1), with a debit to Investment in Blaine Partnership replacing its investment in Blaine's common stock. Blaine records the receipt of assets from Allen and Chaney as follows:

(3)	Cash	135,000	
	Inventory	50,000	
	Land	75,000	
	Building	100,000	
	Equipment	250,000	
	Accumulated Depreciation		110,000
	Capital, Allen Company		435,000
	Capital, Chaney Corp.		65,000

[5] Journal entries used in the text to illustrate the various accounting procedures are numbered sequentially within individual chapters for easy reference. Each journal entry number appears only once in a chapter.

BUSINESS COMBINATIONS

A business combination involves joining under common control two or more previously separate businesses. Business combinations can take one of several different forms and can be effected in different ways.

Forms of Business Combinations

The three primary legal forms of business combinations are illustrated in Figure 1–1. A ***statutory merger*** is a type of business combination in which only one of the combining companies survives and the other loses its separate identity. The acquired company's assets and liabilities are transferred to the acquiring company, and the acquired company is dissolved, or ***liquidated***. The operations of the previously separate companies are carried on in a single legal entity following the merger.

A ***statutory consolidation*** is a business combination in which both the combining companies are dissolved and the assets and liabilities of both companies are transferred to a newly created corporation. The operations of the previously separate companies are carried on in a single legal entity, and neither of the combining companies remains in existence after a statutory consolidation. In many situations, however, the resulting corporation is new in form only, and in substance it actually is one of the combining companies reincorporated with a new name.

FIGURE 1–1
Types of Business Combinations

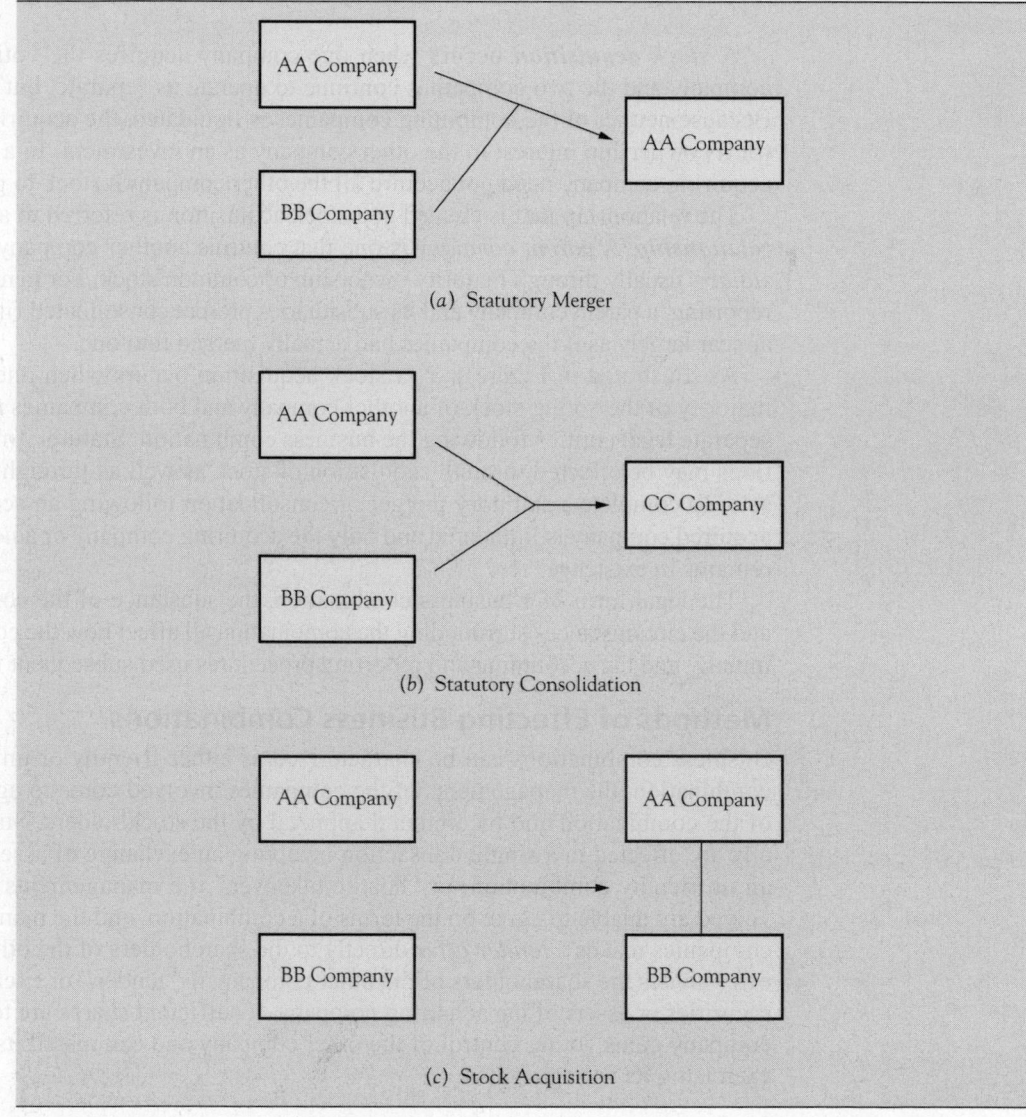

(*a*) Statutory Merger

(*b*) Statutory Consolidation

(*c*) Stock Acquisition

FIGURE 1–2
Determining the
Type of Business
Combination

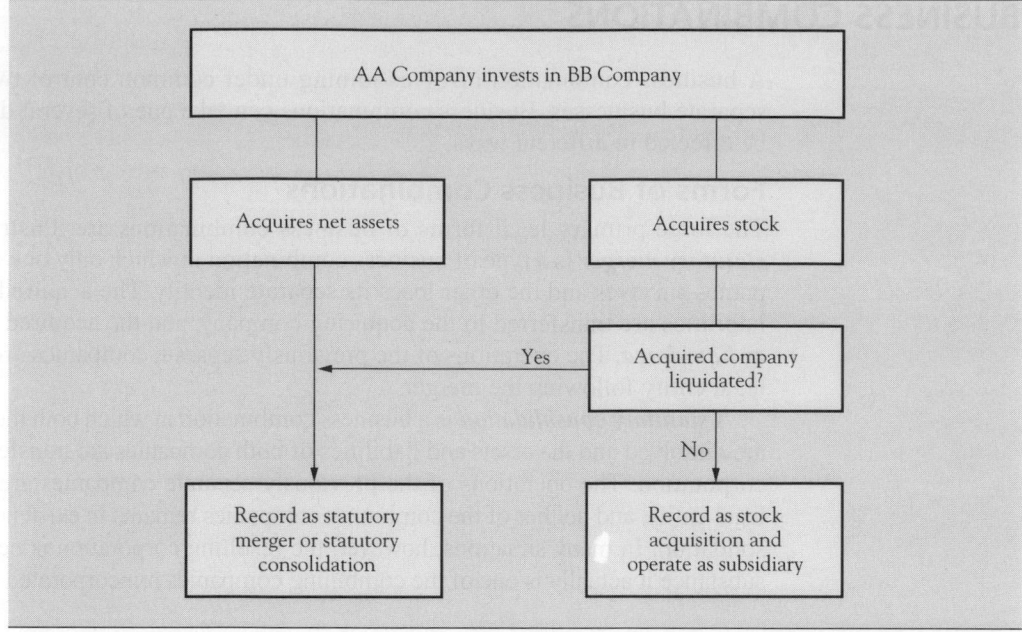

A *stock acquisition* occurs when one company acquires the voting shares of another company and the two companies continue to operate as separate, but related, legal entities. Because neither of the combining companies is liquidated, the acquiring company accounts for its ownership interest in the other company as an investment. In a stock acquisition, the acquiring company need not acquire all the other company's stock to gain control.

The relationship that is created in a stock acquisition is referred to as a *parent–subsidiary relationship*. A *parent company* is one that controls another company, referred to as a *subsidiary,* usually through majority ownership of common stock. For general-purpose financial reporting, a parent company and its subsidiaries present consolidated financial statements that appear largely as if the companies had actually merged into one.

As illustrated in Figure 1–2, a stock acquisition occurs when one company acquires a majority of the voting stock of another company and both companies remain in existence as separate legal entities following the business combination. Statutory mergers and consolidations may be effected through acquisition of stock as well as through acquisition of net assets. To complete a statutory merger or consolidation following an acquisition of stock, the acquired company is liquidated and only the acquiring company or a newly created company remains in existence.

The legal form of a business combination, the substance of the combination agreement, and the circumstances surrounding the combination all affect how the combination is recorded initially and the accounting and reporting procedures used subsequent to the combination.

Methods of Effecting Business Combinations

Business combinations can be characterized as either friendly or unfriendly. In a friendly combination, the managements of the companies involved come to agreement on the terms of the combination and recommend approval by the stockholders. Such combinations usually are effected in a single transaction involving an exchange of assets or voting shares. In an unfriendly combination, or "hostile takeover," the managements of the companies involved are unable to agree on the terms of a combination, and the management of one of the companies makes a *tender offer* directly to the shareholders of the other company. A tender offer invites the shareholders of the other company to "tender," or exchange, their shares for securities or assets of the acquiring company. If sufficient shares are tendered, the acquiring company gains voting control of the other company and can install its own management by exercising its voting rights.

The specific procedures to be used in accounting for a business combination depend on whether the combination is effected through an acquisition of assets or an acquisition of stock.

Acquisition of Assets

Sometimes one company acquires another company's assets through direct negotiations with its management. The agreement also may involve the acquiring company's assuming the other company's liabilities. Combinations of this sort take forms (*a*) or (*b*) in Figure 1–1. The selling company generally distributes to its stockholders the assets or securities received in the combination from the acquiring company and liquidates, leaving only the acquiring company as the surviving legal entity.

The acquiring company accounts for the combination by recording each asset acquired, each liability assumed, and the consideration given in exchange.

Acquisition of Stock

A business combination effected through a stock acquisition does not necessarily have to involve the acquisition of all of a company's outstanding voting shares. For one company to gain control over another through stock ownership, a majority (i.e., more than 50 percent) of the outstanding voting shares usually is required. An acquisition of less than a majority of the outstanding voting shares typically is not regarded as a business combination. When a single stockholder holds a majority of the voting stock, the remaining shares are referred to as the **minority interest** or **noncontrolling interest**.

In those cases when control of another company is acquired and both companies remain in existence as separate legal entities following the business combination, the stock of the acquired company is recorded on the books of the acquiring company as an investment and subsequently is accounted for as an intercorporate investment. Alternatively, the acquired company may be liquidated and its assets and liabilities transferred to the acquiring company or a newly created company. To do so, all or substantially all of the acquired company's voting stock must be obtained. An acquisition of stock and subsequent liquidation of the acquired company is equivalent to an acquisition of assets.

Valuation of Business Entities

All parties involved in a business combination must believe they have an opportunity to benefit before they will agree to participate. Determining whether a particular combination proposal is advantageous can be difficult. Both the value of a company's assets and its future earning potential are important in assessing the value of the company. Also, the tax aspects must be considered. For example, one factor that may increase the value of a potential acquiree is the existence of accumulated net operating losses that can be used under U.S. tax law to shelter future income from taxes.

Value of Individual Assets and Liabilities

The value of a company's individual assets and liabilities is usually determined by appraisal. For some items, the value may be determined with relative ease, such as investments that are traded actively in the securities markets, or short-term payables. For other items, the appraisal may be much more subjective, such as the value of land located in an area where there have been few recent sales. In addition, certain intangibles typically are not reported on the balance sheet. For example, the costs of developing new ideas, new products, and new production methods normally are expensed as research and development costs in the period incurred.

Current liabilities often are viewed as having fair values equal to their book values because they will be paid at face amount within a short time. Long-term liabilities, however, must be valued based on current interest rates if different from the effective rates at the issue dates of the liabilities. For example, if $100,000 of 10-year, 6 percent bonds, paying interest annually, had been issued at par three years ago, and the current market rate of interest for the same type of security is 10 percent, the value of the liability currently is computed as follows:

Present value for 7 years at 10% of principal payment of $100,000 ($100,000 × .51316)	$51,316
Present value at 10% of 7 interest payments of $6,000 ($6,000 × 4.86842)	29,211
Present value of bond	$80,527

Although accurate assessments of the value of assets and liabilities may be difficult, they form an important part of the overall determination of the value of an enterprise.

Value of Potential Earnings

In many cases, assets operated together as a group have a value that exceeds the sum of their individual values. This "going-concern value" makes it desirable to operate the assets as an ongoing entity rather than sell them individually. A company's earning power as an ongoing enterprise is of obvious importance in valuing that company.

There are different approaches to measuring the value of a company's future earnings. Sometimes companies are valued based on a multiple of their current earnings. For example, if Bargain Company reports earnings of $35,000 for the current year, the company's value based on a multiple of 10 times current earnings is $350,000. The appropriate multiple to use is a matter of judgment and is based on factors such as the riskiness and variability of the earnings and the anticipated degree of growth.

Another method of valuing a company is to compute the present value of the anticipated future net cash flows generated by the company. This requires assessing the amount and timing of future cash flows and discounting them back to the present value at the discount rate determined to be appropriate for the type of enterprise. For example, if Bargain Company is expected to generate cash flows of $35,000 for each of the next 25 years, the present value of the firm at a discount rate of 10 percent is $317,696, computed as follows:

Annual cash flow generated	$ 35,000
Present value factor for an annuity of 25 annual payments at 10%	× 9.07704
Present value of future earnings	$ 317,696

Estimating the potential for future earnings requires numerous assumptions and estimates. Not surprisingly, the buyer and seller often have difficulty agreeing on the value of a company's expected earnings.

Valuation of Consideration Exchanged

When one company acquires another, a value must be placed on the consideration given in the exchange. Little difficulty is encountered when cash is used in an acquisition, but valuation may be more difficult when securities are exchanged, particularly new untraded securities or securities with unusual features. For example, General Motors completed an acquisition a number of years ago using a new Series B common stock that paid dividends based on subsequent earnings of the acquired company rather than on the earnings of General Motors as a whole. Some companies have used non-interest-bearing bonds (zero coupon bonds), which have a fair value sufficiently below par value to compensate the holder for interest. Other companies have used various types of convertible securities. Unless these securities, or others that are considered equivalent, are being traded in the market, estimates of their value must be made. The approach generally followed is to use the value of some similar security with a determinable market value and adjust for the estimated value of the differences in the features of the two securities.

ACCOUNTING FOR BUSINESS COMBINATIONS

The purchase of an ongoing business is essentially the same as the purchase of any other asset or group of assets. When an asset is purchased, consideration is given in exchange for the ownership rights to the item acquired. Similarly, when a business is purchased, consideration is given in exchange for the ownership rights relinquished by the owners of the acquired company. At the time an asset is purchased, the buyer records the asset at the cost incurred in acquiring that asset. The cost generally is determined based on the fair value of the asset acquired or the fair value of the consideration given. If a collection of assets is purchased for a single lump-sum purchase price, the total cost must be allocated to the individual assets acquired based on their fair values. The same principles apply to the purchase of an ongoing business as apply to the purchase of individual assets or groups of assets.

FASB Statement No. 141, "Business Combinations" (FASB 141), specifies the currently accepted procedures for accounting for business combinations, although the FASB is in the process of revising **FASB 141. FASB 157**, "Fair Value Measurements" (FASB 157) provides a framework for applying fair value measurements in accounting.

Determining the Purchase Price

In accounting for a business combination under current standards, the purchaser considers all costs associated with acquiring the other company's net assets or stock as part of the total purchase price. The value of the consideration given to the owners of the acquired company normally constitutes the largest part of the total cost, but other costs also may be significant. There are three types of other costs that may be incurred in effecting a business combination: direct costs, costs of issuing securities, and indirect and general costs.

All direct costs associated with purchasing another company are treated as part of the total cost of the acquired company. For example, finders' fees often are paid to firms specializing in locating companies that meet the particular needs of the acquiring company. In addition, business combinations often result in substantial accounting, legal, and appraisal fees. Currently, all of these costs are capitalized as part of the total purchase price of the acquired company.

Those costs incurred in issuing common or preferred stock in connection with a business combination should be treated as a reduction in the issue price of the securities rather than as an addition to the purchase price of the acquired company. Such costs include listing fees, audit and legal fees related to stock registration, and brokers' commissions. Costs incurred in issuing bonds or other debt securities as part of a business combination should be accounted for as bond issue costs and amortized over the term of the bonds.

All indirect and general costs related to a business combination or to the issuance of securities in a combination should be expensed as incurred. For example, the salary costs of accountants on the acquiring company's staff would be expensed, even though some of their time was spent on matters related to the combination.

To illustrate the treatment of the costs incurred in a business combination, assume that on January 1, 20X1, Point Corporation purchases all the assets and liabilities of Sharp Company in a statutory merger by issuing to Sharp 10,000 shares of $10 par common stock. The shares issued have a total market value of $600,000. Point incurs legal and appraisal fees of $40,000 in connection with the combination and stock issue costs of $25,000. The total purchase price is equal to the value of the shares issued by Point plus the additional costs incurred related to the acquisition of assets:

Fair value of stock issued	$600,000
Other acquisition costs	40,000
Total purchase price	$640,000

The stock issued by Point to effect the combination is valued at its fair value minus the issue costs:

Fair value of stock issued	$600,000
Stock issue costs	(25,000)
Recorded amount of stock	$575,000

Recently, the FASB proposed that all direct costs incurred in a business combination should be expensed as incurred. Under the FASB's new approach, an acquired company will be valued at its fair value. No costs associated with bringing about the combination will be capitalized. This requirement is not yet effective but is expected in the near future.

Combination Effected through Purchase of Net Assets

When one company acquires the net assets of another in a business combination, the acquiring company records on its books the individual assets and liabilities acquired in the combination and the consideration given in exchange. Once the total purchase price of an acquisition has been determined, it must be assigned to the individual assets and liabilities acquired. Each identifiable asset and liability acquired is valued at its fair value at the date of combination. Any amount of the purchase price in excess of the fair value of the identifiable assets and liabilities acquired is viewed as the price paid for *goodwill*. In theory, goodwill is the excess earning power of the acquired company; in practice, goodwill represents the premium paid to acquire control.

In the Sharp Company acquisition, the total purchase price was computed to be $640,000. Assume the book values and fair values of Sharp's individual assets and liabilities given in Figure 1–3. When transferred to Point, these individual assets and liabilities must be recorded on its books at their fair values at the date of the business combination.

The relationship between the total purchase price paid for Sharp's net assets, the fair value of its net assets, and the book value of its net assets is illustrated in the following diagram:

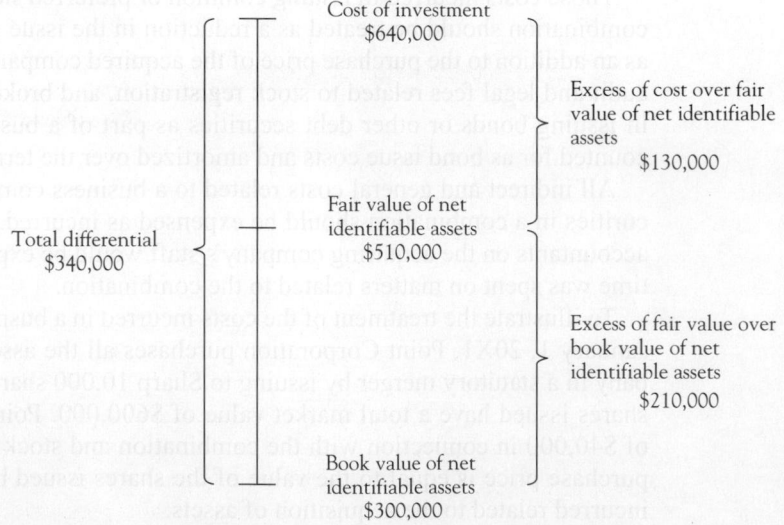

The $40,000 of other acquisition costs associated with the combination and the $25,000 of stock issue costs normally would be incurred before the time that Point receives Sharp's assets. To facilitate accumulating these amounts before recording the combination, Point may record them in separate temporary "suspense" accounts as incurred:

FIGURE 1–3
Sharp Company Balance Sheet Information, December 31, 20X0

Assets, Liabilities, and Equities	Book Value	Fair Value
Cash and Receivables	$ 45,000	$ 45,000
Inventory	65,000	75,000
Land	40,000	70,000
Buildings and Equipment	400,000	350,000
Accumulated Depreciation	(150,000)	
Patent		80,000
Total Assets	$400,000	$620,000
Current Liabilities	$100,000	110,000
Common Stock ($5 par)	100,000	
Additional Paid-In Capital	50,000	
Retained Earnings	150,000	
Total Liabilities and Equities	$400,000	
Fair Value of Net Assets		$510,000

(4)	Deferred Merger Costs	40,000	
	Cash		40,000
	Record costs related to purchase of Sharp Company.		

(5)	Deferred Stock Issue Costs	25,000	
	Cash		25,000
	Record costs related to issuance of common stock.		

On the date of combination, Point records the combination with the following entry:

(6)	Cash and Receivables	45,000	
	Inventory	75,000	
	Land	70,000	
	Buildings and Equipment	350,000	
	Patent	80,000	
	Goodwill	130,000	
	Current Liabilities		110,000
	Common Stock		100,000
	Additional Paid-In Capital		475,000
	Deferred Merger Costs		40,000
	Deferred Stock Issue Costs		25,000
	Record purchase of Sharp Company.		

Entry (6) records all of Sharp's individual assets and liabilities, both tangible and intangible, on Point's books at their fair values on the date of combination. The fair value of Sharp's net assets recorded is $510,000 ($620,000 − $110,000). The $130,000 difference between the total purchase price of $640,000 ($600,000 + $40,000), as computed earlier, and the fair value of Sharp's net assets is recorded as goodwill.

In recording the business combination, Sharp's book values are not relevant to Point; only the fair values are recorded. Because a change in ownership has occurred, the basis of accounting used by the acquired company is not relevant to the purchaser. Consistent with this view, accumulated depreciation recorded by Sharp on its buildings and equipment is not relevant to Point and is not recorded. In other words, the assets and liabilities acquired are recorded by the purchaser in the same way as if there were no business combination and they were purchased as a group for a lump-sum purchase price.

The costs incurred in bringing about the merger are recorded in a separate temporary account entitled Deferred Merger Costs until the transfer of assets to Point is recorded. Because the merger costs are considered part of the total purchase price, the temporary account must be closed with entry (6) and these costs assigned, along with the remainder of the purchase price, to the net assets recorded. Similarly, the stock issue costs are recorded in a temporary account and then treated as a reduction in the proceeds received from the issuance of the stock by reducing the amount of additional paid-in capital recorded. Thus, the stock issued is recorded at its $600,000 fair value less the $25,000 of issue costs, with the $100,000 par value recorded in the common stock account and the remaining $475,000 recorded as additional paid-in capital.

Temporary accounts normally are used to accumulate the merger and stock issue costs because numerous individual costs often are incurred at different times before a business combination. Merger costs incurred after a combination is recorded may be debited directly to goodwill, and stock issue costs incurred subsequently are charged against additional paid-in capital.

Entries Recorded by Acquired Company

On the date of the combination, Sharp records the following entry to recognize receipt of the Point shares and the transfer of all individual assets and liabilities to Point:

(7)	Investment in Point Stock	600,000	
	Current Liabilities	100,000	
	Accumulated Depreciation	150,000	
	Cash and Receivables		45,000
	Inventory		65,000
	Land		40,000
	Buildings and Equipment		400,000
	Gain on Sale of Net Assets		300,000
	Record transfer of assets to Point Corporation.		

Sharp recognizes the fair value of Point Corporation shares at the time of the exchange and records a gain of $300,000. The distribution of Point shares and the liquidation of Sharp are recorded on Sharp's books with the following entry:

(8)	Common Stock	100,000	
	Additional Paid-In Capital	50,000	
	Retained Earnings	150,000	
	Gain on Sale of Net Assets	300,000	
	Investment in Point Stock		600,000
	Record distribution of Point Corporation stock.		

Recording Goodwill

Goodwill is viewed in accounting as the total of all those factors that permit a company to earn above-average profits. As with any asset, goodwill is valued based on its original cost to the purchaser when objectively determinable. Because expenditures for "self-developed" goodwill often are not distinguishable from current operating costs, such expenditures are required to be expensed as incurred. When goodwill is purchased in connection with a business combination, however, the amount of the expenditure is viewed as objectively determinable and is capitalized. The cost of goodwill purchased is measured as the excess of the total purchase price over the fair value of the net identifiable assets acquired. The goodwill recorded when Point purchases Sharp Company is valued at $130,000, the difference between the total purchase price of $640,000 and the $510,000 fair value of Sharp's net identifiable assets.

Subsequent Accounting for Goodwill

Once goodwill has been recorded in a business combination, it must be accounted for in accordance with **FASB Statement No. 142**, "Goodwill and Other Intangible Assets" (FASB 142). Goodwill is carried forward at the original amount, without amortization, unless it becomes impaired. Goodwill must be tested for impairment at least annually, at the same time each year, and more frequently if events that are likely to impair the value of the goodwill occur.

The process of testing goodwill for impairment is complex. It involves examining potential goodwill impairment by each of the company's reporting units, where a reporting unit is an operating segment[6] or a component of an operating segment that is a business for which management regularly reviews financial information from that component. When goodwill arises in a business combination, it must be assigned to individual reporting units. The goodwill is assigned to units that are expected to benefit from the combination, even if no other assets or liabilities of the acquired company are assigned to those units. To test for the impairment of goodwill, the fair value of the reporting unit is compared with its carrying amount. If the fair value of the reporting unit exceeds its carrying amount, the goodwill of that reporting unit is considered unimpaired. On the other hand, if the carrying amount of the reporting unit exceeds its fair value, an impairment of the reporting unit's goodwill is implied.

The amount of the reporting unit's goodwill impairment is measured as the excess of the carrying amount of the unit's goodwill over the implied value of its goodwill. The implied value of its goodwill is determined as the excess of the fair value of the reporting unit over the fair value of its net assets excluding goodwill. Goodwill impairment losses are recognized in income from continuing operations or income before extraordinary gains and losses.

As an example of goodwill impairment, assume that Reporting Unit A is assigned $100,000 of goodwill arising from a recent business combination. The following assets and liabilities are assigned to Reporting Unit A:

Item	Carrying Amount	Fair Value
Cash and receivables	$ 50,000	$ 50,000
Inventory	80,000	90,000
Equipment	120,000	150,000
Goodwill	100,000	
Total assets	$350,000	$290,000
Current payables	(10,000)	(10,000)
Net assets	$340,000	$280,000

By summing the carrying amounts of the assets and subtracting the carrying amount of the payables, the carrying amount of the reporting unit, including the goodwill, is determined to be $340,000. If the fair value of the reporting unit is estimated to be $360,000, no impairment of goodwill is indicated. On the other hand, if the fair value of the reporting unit is estimated to be $320,000, a second comparison must be made to determine the amount of any impairment loss. The implied value of Reporting Unit A's goodwill is determined by deducting the $280,000 fair value of the net assets, excluding goodwill, from the unit's $320,000 fair value. The $40,000 difference ($320,000 − $280,000) represents Reporting Unit A's implied goodwill. The impairment loss is measured as the excess of the carrying amount of the unit's goodwill ($100,000) over the implied value of the goodwill ($40,000), or $60,000. This goodwill impairment loss is combined with any impairment losses from other reporting units to determine the total impairment loss to be reported by the company

---

[6] An operating segment is defined in *Financial Accounting Standards Board Statement No. 131*, "Disclosures about Segments of an Enterprise and Related Information," June 1997.

as a whole. Goodwill is written down by the amount of the impairment loss. Once written down, goodwill may not be written up for recoveries.

Negative Goodwill

Sometimes the purchase price of an acquired company is less than the fair value of the net identifiable assets acquired. This difference often is referred to as ***negative goodwill***.

The existence of negative goodwill might be viewed as implying that the acquired company should be liquidated because the assets and liabilities are worth more individually than together as an ongoing enterprise. On the other hand, the view usually adopted in practice is that the acquisition represents a ***bargain purchase***.

Under **FASB 141**, any excess of the fair value of acquired net assets over the cost of the acquired entity (negative goodwill) is to be used to reduce the amounts that otherwise would have been assigned to the acquired assets except financial assets other than equity-method investments, assets to be sold, deferred tax assets, prepaid postretirement benefit assets, and any other current assets.[7] Any amount remaining after reducing these acquired assets to zero would be recognized as an extraordinary gain.

To illustrate the treatment of negative goodwill, assume that Point Corporation purchases all of Sharp Company's assets and liabilities at a total cost of $460,000 rather than the $640,000 assumed previously. In this case, the relationship between the total purchase price paid for the stock of Sharp, the fair value of Sharp's net assets, and the book value of Sharp's net assets is illustrated in the following diagram:

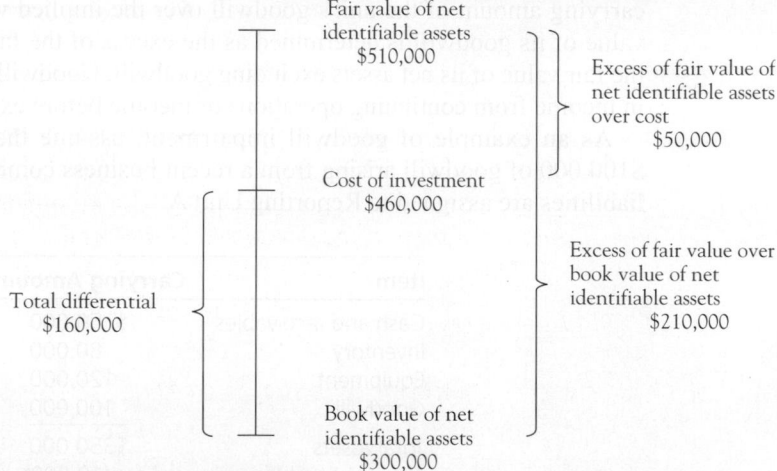

The fair values of Sharp's assets and liabilities total $510,000. The $510,000 total fair value of the net identifiable assets acquired exceeds the $460,000 purchase price by $50,000. This $50,000 of negative goodwill is apportioned as follows:

Item	Book Value	Fair Value	Reduction	Amount Recorded
Cash and Receivables	$ 45,000	$ 45,000		$ 45,000
Inventory	65,000	75,000		75,000
Land	40,000	70,000	70/500 × $50,000 = $ 7,000	63,000
Buildings and Equipment (net)	250,000	350,000	350/500 × 50,000 = 35,000	315,000
Patent		80,000	80/500 × 50,000 = 8,000	72,000
Total Identifiable Assets	$400,000	$620,000	$50,000	$570,000
Current Liabilities	100,000	110,000		110,000
Net Identifiable Assets	$300,000	$510,000		$460,000

[7] *Financial Accounting Standards Board Statement No. 141*, "Business Combinations," June 2001, para. 44.

Recently, the FASB concluded that a change in the approach to accounting for negative goodwill is warranted. The FASB's proposal, if adopted, would require recognition as a gain in the period of acquisition of any negative goodwill remaining after valuing the assets and liabilities acquired at their fair values.

Combination Effected through Purchase of Stock

Many business combinations are effected by purchasing the voting stock of another company rather than by acquiring its net assets. In such a situation, the acquired company continues to exist, and the purchasing company records an investment in the common stock of the acquired company rather than the individual assets and liabilities. As with the purchase of the assets and liabilities, the cost of the investment is based on the total value of the consideration given in purchasing the shares, together with any additional costs incurred in bringing about the combination. For example, if Point Corporation (*a*) exchanges 10,000 shares of its stock with a total market value of $600,000 for all of Sharp Company's shares and (*b*) incurs merger costs of $40,000 and stock issue costs of $25,000, previously recorded in deferred charge accounts, Point records the following entry upon receipt of the Sharp stock:

(9)	Investment in Sharp Stock	640,000	
	Common Stock		100,000
	Additional Paid-In Capital		475,000
	Deferred Merger Costs		40,000
	Deferred Stock Issue Costs		25,000
	Record purchase of Sharp Company stock.		

When a business combination is effected through an acquisition of stock, the acquired company may continue to operate as a separate company, or it may lose its separate identity and be merged into the acquiring company. The accounting and reporting procedures for intercorporate investments in common stock when the acquired company continues in existence are discussed in the next nine chapters. If the acquired company is liquidated and its assets and liabilities are transferred to the acquiring company, the dollar amounts recorded would be identical to those in entry (6).

Financial Reporting Subsequent to a Business Combination

Financial statements prepared subsequent to a business combination reflect the combined entity only from the date of combination. When a combination occurs during a fiscal period, income earned by the acquired company prior to the combination is not reported in the income statement of the combined enterprise. If the combined company presents comparative financial statements that include statements for periods before the combination, those statements include only the activities and financial position of the acquiring company, not those of the acquired company.

To illustrate financial reporting subsequent to a business combination, assume the following information for Point Corporation and Sharp Company:

	20X0	20X1
Point Corporation:		
Separate income (excluding any income from Sharp)	$300,000	$300,000
Shares outstanding, December 31	30,000	40,000
Sharp Company:		
Net income	$ 60,000	$ 60,000

Point Corporation acquires all of Sharp Company's stock at book value on January 1, 20X1, by issuing 10,000 shares of common stock. Subsequently, Point Corporation presents comparative financial statements for the years 20X0 and 20X1. The net income and earnings per share that Point presents in its comparative financial statements for the two years are as follows:

20X0:	
Net Income	$300,000
Earnings per Share ($300,000/30,000 shares)	$10.00
20X1:	
Net Income ($300,000 + $60,000)	$360,000
Earnings per Share ($360,000/40,000 shares)	$9.00

If Point Corporation had purchased Sharp Company in the middle of 20X1 instead of at the beginning, Point would include only Sharp's earnings subsequent to acquisition in its 20X1 income statement. If Sharp earned $25,000 in 20X1 before acquisition by Point and $35,000 after the combination, Point would report total net income for 20X1 of $335,000 ($300,000 + $35,000).

Any goodwill that a company records must be reported as a separate line item in the balance sheet. A goodwill impairment loss that occurs during the period must be reported as a separate line item within income from continuing operations in the income statement unless the loss relates to discontinued operations, in which case the loss is reported in the income statement within the discontinued operations section.

Disclosure Requirements

A number of disclosures are required following a business combination to provide to financial statement readers information about the combination and the expected effects of the combination on subsequent operating results. **FASB 141** requires the following disclosures, among others, in the notes to the financial statements in periods in which material business combinations occur:[8]

1. Identification of the acquired company and the percentage ownership acquired.
2. The main reasons for the acquisition and a description of the factors that led to the recognition of goodwill.
3. The period for which the operations of the acquired company are included in the operating statement of the combined entity.
4. The cost of the acquired company and the amount and value of any ownership interests issued.
5. The existence of any contingencies associated with the acquisition.
6. The amount of any purchased research and development written off during the period.

The notes to the financial statements also must disclose additional information relating to intangible assets in the period in which a business combination is completed if the amounts assigned to goodwill or other intangible assets acquired are significant in relation to the total cost of the acquired entity. For intangible assets subject to amortization, disclosures include the total amount assigned to such assets, the amount of any significant residual value, and the weighted-average amortization period. For intangibles not subject to amortization, the amount assigned to such assets must be disclosed. Also, the total amount of goodwill and the amount deductible for tax purposes must be disclosed, along with the amount of goodwill by reportable segment for those companies required to disclose segment information under **FASB 131**.

Furthermore, note disclosures must include pro forma operating information for the period in which the business combination occurred as if the combination had occurred at the beginning of the period, and for the immediately preceding period if comparative financial statements are presented, as if the combination had occurred at the beginning of that period.

[8] From *FASB Statement No. 141*, "Business Combinations," June 2001, para. 51–55.

ADDITIONAL CONSIDERATIONS IN ACCOUNTING FOR BUSINESS COMBINATIONS

Two primary methods of accounting for business combinations have been found in practice over the years. Several years ago, the FASB limited the accounting methods to just one. Now, the FASB is in the process of modifying the accounting procedures for business combinations again.

Accounting and Reporting Methods

For more than half a century, two methods of accounting for business combinations, *purchase* and *pooling of interests*, were acceptable in practice. In 2001, however, the FASB issued **Statement No. 141**, "Business Combinations" (FASB 141), which eliminated pooling of interests as an acceptable method of accounting for business combinations. Thus, all business combinations are now accounted for using the purchase method. Over the decades, however, many business combinations have been accounted for as poolings, and the effects of these poolings will be found in financial statements for years to come. Accountants, therefore, need at least a general knowledge of pooling of interests accounting even though it no longer is an acceptable method.

The central idea underlying purchase accounting for business combinations is the same idea underlying the purchase of any asset or group of assets—a change in ownership. Throughout accounting, a change in ownership is an event that calls for a change in the basis of accounting. As with any purchase transaction in accounting, the purchase of an ongoing business results in a change in ownership from the seller to the purchaser, and the purchaser's accounting is based on the fair value of the assets and liabilities acquired, not on the seller's book values.

The central idea underlying pooling of interests accounting was opposite that of purchase accounting—a continuity of ownership. This method assumed that the owners of the combining companies became the owners of the combined company. Continuity of ownership required that poolings be effected only by one company issuing its common stock to acquire the assets or stock of another company. Because the ownership did not change, the premise of pooling was that no change in the basis of accounting was warranted. Thus, the book values of both companies were carried forward. Although purchase accounting recognizes goodwill when the purchase price exceeds the fair value of the net assets acquired, pooling accounting did not record goodwill because no purchase price, only a carry-forward of book values, was recognized. Furthermore, pooling resulted in carrying forward the retained earnings of all combining companies while purchase accounting deals with the purchase of assets and liabilities but recognizes that retained earnings cannot be purchased. A difference between purchase and pooling could also be seen in the presentation of comparative financial statements. Because pooling was based on the premise of continuity of ownership, comparative statements presented subsequent to a pooling for periods prior to the combination treated the combined companies as if they had always been combined. Although pooling is no longer acceptable, prior poolings must still be treated in this manner in extended financial presentations.

The large number of combinations treated as poolings was the result of management's preference for that method in many cases. Management often preferred the pooling method because, by not writing up fixed assets to higher fair values, depreciation charges were lower under pooling than under purchase accounting and income was higher. Also, prior to issuance of **FASB 142** in 2001, goodwill was required to be amortized. To avoid the amortization of goodwill and the resulting negative effect, often significant, on income under purchase accounting, many companies chose to structure their combinations as poolings. Management, in addition, was often able to create earnings under pooling that otherwise would not have been reported, and, because of the carry-forward of the acquired company's retained earnings, the combined company sometimes gained additional dividend flexibility. Further, the pooling of interests method hid the value of the consideration given in the business combination, shielding management from stockholder criticism in those cases in which management had overpaid for acquisitions, a not uncommon occurrence.

Proposed Changes from the FASB

The FASB has proposed significant changes in accounting for business combinations, and these proposed standards are expected to be implemented in the near future for new combinations. The new standards would not be retroactive. While some of the proposed changes have been mentioned earlier in the chapter, this section summarizes the most significant changes:

1. An acquired company will be valued at its fair value rather than a value based only on the value of the consideration given. Individual assets will be valued at their fair values at the date of combination. Goodwill will be calculated as the difference between the fair value of the acquired company and the fair value of its net identifiable assets.

2. In a stock acquisition, if the acquiring company acquires less than 100 percent of the other company's stock, the acquired company will nevertheless be valued at its full fair value on the date of combination, as will the individual assets and liabilities of the acquired company in consolidated financial statements. The portion of the fair value increment and goodwill recognized that is not attributable to the acquiring company will be allocated in the consolidated financial statements to the remaining stockholders of the acquired company, the noncontrolling interest. (Examples of this full-fair-value/full-goodwill approach are provided in the discussion of consolidated financial statements in Chapters 3 and 5.)

3. Acquisition-related costs will not be viewed as part of the consideration exchanged and will be expensed as incurred. Stock issue costs will be deducted from paid-in capital, as is currently the case.

4. In a bargain purchase (negative-goodwill case), where the fair value of the acquiring company's interest in the acquired company exceeds the fair value of the consideration given for that interest, the goodwill that otherwise would have been recognized from the combination will be reduced by the amount of the excess. If that goodwill is reduced to zero, any remaining amount of the excess will be recognized as a gain attributable to the acquirer. As an example, assume that Palor Company acquires 75 percent of Noble Company's common stock for $225,000 cash. At the time, Noble reports assets with a book value of $400,000 and a fair value of $510,000 and liabilities with a book value and fair value of $190,000. The management of Palor estimates that the fair value of Noble is $360,000. In this situation, Palor has paid less than 75 percent of the fair value of Noble's net assets [$225,000 versus $240,000 ($320,000 × .75)]. Consolidated financial statements prepared immediately following the acquisition will report Noble's assets ($510,000) and liabilities ($190,000) at their fair values. A $15,000 gain on the bargain purchase will be reported for the excess of Palor's share of the fair value of Noble's net assets ($240,000) over the purchase price ($225,000). The amount reported for the noncontrolling interest at the date of acquisition will be $80,000 ($320,000 × .25).

5. Separate valuation accounts related to assets required to be recognized at fair value will not be recognized.

6. An acquiring company will revalue to fair value any of the acquired company's stock already held at the acquisition date and recognize a gain or loss on the revaluation. As an example, assume that Palor Company acquires 35 percent of Noble Company's common shares and uses the equity method to account for its investment. Palor subsequently acquires an additional 40 percent of Noble's shares for $144,000 when the management of Palor estimates the total fair value of Noble to be $360,000. The equity-method carrying value of the original shares on Palor's books is $98,000 at the time the additional shares are acquired. The total recorded amount of Palor's investment in Noble will be $270,000 ($360,000 × .75). Palor will report a gain of $28,000 [($360,000 × .35) − $98,000] on the original shares previously carried under the equity method.

Additional proposed changes related to consolidated financial statements are discussed in Chapters 3 and 5.

Summary of Key Concepts

Business combinations and complex organizational structures are an important part of the global business scene. Many companies add organizational components by creating new corporations or partnerships through which to carry out a portion of their operations. In other cases, companies may enter into business combinations to acquire other companies through which to further their objectives.

When a company creates another corporation or a partnership through a transfer of assets, the book values of those assets are transferred to the new entity and no gain or loss is recognized. The creating company and the new entity will combine their financial statements for general-purpose financial reporting to appear as if they were a single company as long as the creating company continues to control the new entity.

Business combinations occur when previously separate companies join together under common control. There are three types of formal business combinations: (*a*) statutory mergers, where one of the combining companies loses its separate legal identity and the other company continues with the assets and liabilities of both companies; (*b*) statutory consolidations, where both combining companies join to form a new company; and (*c*) stock acquisitions, where both combining companies maintain their separate existence, with one company owning the common stock of the other.

The procedures used to account for a business combination are similar to those used to account for any purchase of an asset or group of assets. The purchasing company records the assets and liabilities acquired at their fair values. Any excess of the purchase price over the fair value of the net assets acquired is recorded as the intangible asset goodwill. Once recorded, the goodwill is not amortized but must be tested for impairment at least annually. If goodwill is impaired, it is written down and a loss recognized for the amount of the impairment. For financial reporting, the business combination is given effect as of the date of combination.

An alternative method of accounting for business combinations called "pooling of interests" was acceptable for many years in addition to the current procedures. This method was based on the idea of a continuity of ownership and resulted in the book values of the combining companies being carried forward rather than the change in the basis of accounting appropriate when ownership changes. The FASB eliminated the pooling method in 2001, but so many poolings occurred in the years prior to that method's elimination that pooling accounting will be in evidence for years to come. The FASB has proposed new standards of accounting for business combinations that are expected to be implemented in the near future.

Key Terms

bargain purchase, *14*	negative goodwill, *18*	special-purpose entity, *3*
business combination, *4*	noncontrolling interest, *11*	spin-off, *4*
consolidated financial statements, *1*	parent company, *2*	split-off, *4*
	parent–subsidiary relationship, *10*	statutory consolidation, *9*
control, *4*		statutory merger, *9*
goodwill, *14*	pooling of interests, *21*	stock acquisition, *10*
liquidated, *9*	primary beneficiary, *7*	subsidiary, *2*
minority interest, *11*	purchase, *21*	tender offer, *10*

Questions

Q1-1 What types of circumstances would encourage management to establish a complex organizational structure?

Q1-2 How would the decision to dispose of a segment of operations using a split-off rather than a spin-off impact the financial statements of the company making the distribution?

Q1-3 Why did companies such as Enron find the use of special-purpose entities to be advantageous?

Q1-4 Describe each of the three legal forms that a business combination might take.

Q1-5 What basis of accounting normally is used in recording the assets and liabilities transferred to a new wholly owned subsidiary?

Q1-6 How might the concept of beneficial ownership impact the reporting of an interest in another company?

Q1-7* Why did corporate management often prefer pooling of interests treatment in recording business combinations?

*Indicates that the item relates to "Additional Consideration."

Q1-8* What would be the balance sheet and income statement impacts of recording a business combination as a purchase rather than a pooling of interests?

Q1-9 How does goodwill arise in a business combination? Under what conditions is it recorded?

Q1-10 When a business combination occurs after the beginning of the year, the income earned by the acquired company between the beginning of the year and the date of combination is excluded from the net income reported by the combined company for the year. Why?

Q1-11 What is the maximum balance in retained earnings that can be reported by the combined entity following a business combination?

Q1-12 What factors may make it attractive for a company to complete a business combination by acquiring the stock of another company and operating it as a subsidiary?

Q1-13 How does negative goodwill arise in a business combination? How is it normally treated for financial reporting purposes?

Q1-14 When is goodwill considered impaired following a business combination?

Q1-15 How is the amount of additional paid-in capital determined when recording a business combination?

Q1-16 How are prior-period financial statement data of the acquired company reported by the combined company following a business combination? Why?

Q1-17 Which of the costs incurred in completing a business combination are capitalized under current standards?

Q1-18 Which of the costs incurred in completing a business combination should be treated as a reduction of additional paid-in capital?

Q1-19* When less than 100 percent ownership of a company is acquired, how will the valuation of assets and liabilities of the acquired company differ from current accounting practice under the changes proposed by the FASB? How will the valuation of goodwill change?

Q1-20* When the acquiring company in a business combination pays less than the fair value of the identifiable net assets of the acquiree, how will the treatment of negative goodwill be changed under the FASB's proposed standard?

Q1-21* Under the FASB's proposed standard, what conditions would result in the acquiring company in a business combination recognizing a gain on shares of the acquiree's stock already held at the date of combination?

Cases

C1-1 Reporting Alternatives and International Harmonization

Understanding

Accounting procedures for business combinations differ among countries. In most countries, pooling of interests accounting is unacceptable while accounting standards in some countries permit goodwill to be written off directly against stockholders' equity at the time of a business combination treated as a purchase.

Required

a. Over the years, many U.S. companies complained they were at a disadvantage when competing against foreign companies in purchasing other business enterprises because, unlike U.S. companies, most foreign companies did not need to capitalize goodwill. Why were U.S. companies opposed to capitalizing goodwill?

b. Should U.S. companies care about accounting standards other than those that are generally accepted in the United States? Explain.

C1-2 Assignment of Acquisition Costs

Research FARS

Troy Company notified Kline Company's shareholders that it was interested in purchasing controlling ownership of Kline and offered to exchange one share of Troy's common stock for each share of Kline Company submitted by July 31, 2003. At the time of the offer, Troy's shares were trading for $35 per share and Kline's shares were trading at $28. Troy acquired all of the shares of Kline prior

*Indicates that the item relates to "Additional Consideration."

to December 31, 2003, and transferred the assets and liabilities of Kline to its books. In addition to issuing its shares, Troy paid a finder's fee of $200,000, stock registration and audit fees of $60,000, legal fees of $90,000 for transferring Kline's assets and liabilities to Troy, and $370,000 in legal fees to settle litigation brought by Kline's shareholders who alleged that the offering price was below the per share fair value of Kline's net assets.

Troy is currently negotiating to purchase Lad Company through an exchange of common stock and expects to incur additional costs comparable to those involved in the acquisition of Kline.

Required

Troy Company's vice-president of finance has asked you to review the current accounting literature, including authoritative pronouncements and exposure drafts by the FASB and other appropriate bodies, and prepare a memo reporting the required treatment of the additional costs at the time Kline Company was acquired, the current requirements for reporting the additional costs of acquiring Lad Company, and any proposed changes in the treatment of those costs. Support your recommendations with citations and quotations from the authoritative financial reporting standards or other literature.

C1-3   **Evaluation of Merger**

Research

There are many reasons a company acquires another company, and the acquisition often has a significant impact on the financial statements. In 2005, 3M Corporation acquired CUNO Incorporated. Obtain a copy of the 3M 10-K filing for 2005. The 10-K reports the annual results for a company and is often available on the Investor Relations section of a company's Website. It is also available on the SEC's Website at www.SEC.gov.

Required

Use the 10-K for 2005 to find the answers to the following questions about 3M's acquisition of CUNO Inc. (*Hint*: You can search on the term CUNO once you have accessed the 10-K online.)

a. Provide at least one reason why 3M acquired CUNO.

b. How was the acquisition funded?

c. What was the impact of the CUNO acquisition on net accounts receivable?

d. What was the impact of the CUNO acquisition on inventories?

C1-4   **Business Combinations**

Analysis

A merger boom comparable to those of the 1960s and mid-1980s occurred in the 1990s and into the new century. The merger activity of the 1960s was associated with increasing stock prices and heavy use of pooling of interests accounting. The mid-1980s activity was associated with a number of leveraged buyouts and acquisitions involving junk bonds. Merger activity in the early 1990s, on the other hand, appeared to involve primarily purchases with cash and standard debt instruments. By the mid-1990s, however, many business combinations were being effected through exchanges of stock.

a. Which factors do you believe were the most prominent in encouraging business combinations in the 1990s? Which of these was the most important? Explain why.

b. If a major review of the tax laws were undertaken, would it be wise or unwise public policy to establish greater tax incentives for corporate mergers? Propose three incentives that might be used.

c. If the FASB were interested in encouraging more mergers, what action should it take with regard to revising or eliminating existing accounting standards? Explain.

d. Why were so many of the business combinations in the middle and late 1990s effected through exchanges of stock?

C1-5   **Determination of Goodwill Impairment**

Research
FARS

Plush Corporation purchased 100 percent of Common Corporation's common stock on January 1, 20X3, and paid $450,000. The fair value of Common's identifiable net assets at that date was $430,000. By the end of 20X5, the fair value of Common, which Plush considers to be a reporting unit, had increased to $485,000; however, Plush's external auditor made a passing comment to the company's chief accountant that Plush may need to recognize impairment of goodwill on one or more of its investments.

Required

Prepare a memo to Plush's chief accountant indicating the tests used in determining whether goodwill has been impaired. Include in your discussion one or more possible conditions under which Plush may be required to recognize impairment of goodwill on its investment in Common Corporation. In preparing your memo, review the current accounting literature, including authoritative pronouncements of the FASB and other appropriate bodies. Support your discussion with citations and quotations from the applicable literature.

C1-6

Risks Associated with Acquisitions

Analysis

Not all business combinations are successful, and many entail substantial risk. Acquiring another company may involve a number of different types of risk. Obtain a copy of the 10-K report for Google, Inc., for the year ended December 31, 2005, available at the SEC's Website (www.sec.gov). The report can also be accessed through Yahoo Finance or the company's Investor Relations page.

Required

On page 34 of the 10-K report, Google provides information to investors about its motivation for acquiring companies and the possible risks associated with such acquisitions. Briefly discuss the risks that Google sees inherent in potential acquisitions.

C1-7

Numbers Game

Communication

Arthur Levitt's speech, "The Numbers Game," is available on the SEC's Website at http://www.sec.gov/news/speech/speecharchive/1998/spch220.txt. Read the speech, and then answer the following questions.

Required

a. Briefly explain what motivations Levitt discusses for earnings management.

b. What specific techniques for earnings management does Levitt discuss?

c. According to Levitt, why is the issue of earnings management important?

C1-8

Companies Built through Business Combinations: MCI and Citigroup

Analysis

Some companies grow large through internal expansion. Other companies rise to be among the largest in their industries through a series of business combinations. Two major companies that have followed the latter route are MCI (previously MCI WorldCom Inc.) and Citigroup Inc.

Required

a. What are the primary businesses of MCI and Citigroup?

b. Trace major acquisitions of both companies and provide a brief history of how the two companies reached their current positions. What consideration (e.g., cash, stock) was used in their acquisitions? What was the apparent strategy in the growth of the two companies?

c. Who are Sanford Weill and Bernard Ebbers? What roles have they played in the growth of MCI and Citigroup, and what is their current status?

C1-9

Leveraged Buyouts

Analysis

A type of acquisition that was not discussed in the chapter is the *leveraged buyout*. Many experts argue that a leveraged buyout (LBO) is not a type of business combination but rather just a restructuring of ownership. Yet some would see an LBO as having many of the characteristics of a business combination. The number of LBOs in recent years has grown dramatically and, therefore, accounting for these transactions is of increased importance.

Required

a. What is a leveraged buyout? How does an LBO compare with a management buyout (MBO)?

b. What authoritative pronouncements, if any, deal with leveraged buyouts?

c. Is a leveraged buyout a type of business combination? Explain.

d. What is the major issue in determining the proper basis for an interest in a company purchased through a leveraged buyout?

Exercises

E1-1   Multiple-Choice Questions on Complex Organizations

Select the correct answer for each of the following questions.

1. Growth in the complexity of the U.S. business environment:
   a. Has led to increased use of partnerships to avoid legal liability.
   b. Has led to increasingly complex organizational structures as management has attempted to achieve its business objectives.
   c. Has encouraged companies to reduce the number of operating divisions and product lines so they may better control those they retain.
   d. Has had no particular impact on the organizational structures or the way in which companies are managed.

2. Which of the following is not an appropriate reason for establishing a subsidiary?
   a. The parent wishes to protect existing operations by shifting new activities with greater risk to a newly created subsidiary.
   b. The parent wishes to avoid subjecting all of its operations to regulatory control by establishing a subsidiary that focuses its operations in regulated industries.
   c. The parent wishes to reduce its taxes by establishing a subsidiary that focuses its operations in areas where special tax benefits are available.
   d. The parent wishes to be able to increase its reported sales by transferring products to the subsidiary at the end of the fiscal year.

3. Which of the following actions is likely to result in recording goodwill on Randolph Company's books?
   a. Randolph acquires Penn Corporation in a business combination recorded as a merger.
   b. Randolph purchases a majority of Penn's common stock in a business combination and continues to operate it as a subsidiary.
   c. Randolph distributes ownership of a newly created subsidiary in a distribution considered to be a spin-off.
   d. Randolph distributes ownership of a newly created subsidiary in a distribution considered to be a split-off.

4. When an existing company creates a new subsidiary and transfers a portion of its assets and liabilities to the new entity:
   a. The new entity records both the assets and liabilities it received at fair values.
   b. The new entity records both the assets and liabilities it received at the carrying values of the original company.
   c. The original company records a gain or loss on the difference between its carrying values and the fair values of the assets transferred to the new entity.
   d. The original company records the difference between the carrying values and the fair values of the assets transferred to the new entity as goodwill.

5. When a company assigns goodwill to a reporting unit acquired in a business combination, it must:
   a. Record an impairment loss if the fair value of the net identifiable assets held by a reporting unit decreases.
   b. Record an impairment loss if the fair value of the reporting unit decreases.
   c. Record an impairment loss if the carrying value of the reporting unit is less than the fair value of the reporting unit.
   d. Record an impairment loss if the fair value of the reporting unit is less than its carrying value and the carrying value of goodwill is more than the implied value of its goodwill.

E1-2   Multiple-Choice Questions on Recording Business Combinations [AICPA Adapted]

Select the correct answer for each of the following questions.

1. Goodwill represents the excess of the cost of an acquired company over the:

    a. Sum of the fair values assigned to identifiable assets acquired less liabilities assumed.

    b. Sum of the fair values assigned to tangible assets acquired less liabilities assumed.

    c. Sum of the fair values assigned to intangible assets acquired less liabilities assumed.

    d. Book value of an acquired company.

2. In a business combination, costs of registering equity securities to be issued by the acquiring company are a(n):

    a. Expense of the combined company for the period in which the costs were incurred.

    b. Direct addition to stockholders' equity of the combined company.

    c. Reduction of the otherwise determinable fair value of the securities.

    d. Addition to goodwill.

3. Which of the following is the appropriate basis for valuing fixed assets acquired in a business combination carried out by exchanging cash for common stock?

    a. Historical cost.

    b. Book value.

    c. Cost plus any excess of purchase price over book value of assets acquired.

    d. Fair value.

4. In a business combination, the appraisal value of the identifiable assets acquired exceeds the acquisition price. The excess appraisal value should be reported as a:

    a. Deferred credit.

    b. Reduction of the values assigned to current assets and a deferred credit for any unallocated portion.

    c. Pro rata reduction of the values assigned to current and noncurrent assets and a deferred credit for any unallocated portion.

    d. No answer listed is correct.

5. On June 30, 20X2, Pane Corporation exchanged 150,000 shares of its $20 par value common stock for all of Sky Corporation's common stock. At that date, the fair value of Pane's common stock issued was equal to the book value of Sky's net assets. Both corporations continued to operate as separate businesses, maintaining accounting records with years ending December 31. Information from separate company operations follows:

	Pane	Sky
Retained earnings, Dec. 31, 20X1	$3,200,000	$925,000
Net income, 6 months ended June 30, 20X2	800,000	275,000
Dividends paid, March 25, 20X2	750,000	—

What amount of retained earnings would Pane report in its June 30, 20X2, consolidated balance sheet?

    a. $5,200,000.

    b. $4,450,000.

    c. $3,525,000.

    d. $3,250,000.

6. A and B Companies have been operating separately for five years. Each company has a minimal amount of liabilities and a simple capital structure consisting solely of voting common stock. A Company, in exchange for 40 percent of its voting stock, acquires 80 percent of the common stock of B Company. This is a "tax-free" stock-for-stock (type B) exchange for tax purposes. B Company assets have a total net fair market value of $800,000 and a total net book value of

$580,000. The fair market value of the A stock used in the exchange is $700,000. The goodwill on this acquisition would be:

a. Zero.

b. $60,000.

c. $120,000.

d. $236,000.

E1-3 Multiple-Choice Questions on Reported Balances [AICPA Adapted]

Select the correct answer for each of the following questions.

1. On December 31, 20X3, Saxe Corporation was merged into Poe Corporation. In the business combination, Poe issued 200,000 shares of its $10 par common stock, with a market price of $18 a share, for all of Saxe's common stock. The stockholders' equity section of each company's balance sheet immediately before the combination was:

	Poe	Saxe
Common Stock	$3,000,000	$1,500,000
Additional Paid-In Capital	1,300,000	150,000
Retained Earnings	2,500,000	850,000
	$6,800,000	$2,500,000

In the December 31, 20X3, consolidated balance sheet, additional paid-in capital should be reported at:

a. $950,000.

b. $1,300,000.

c. $1,450,000.

d. $2,900,000.

2. On January 1, 20X1, Rolan Corporation issued 10,000 shares of common stock in exchange for all of Sandin Corporation's outstanding stock. Condensed balance sheets of Rolan and Sandin immediately before the combination follow:

	Rolan	Sandin
Total Assets	$1,000,000	$500,000
Liabilities	$ 300,000	$150,000
Common Stock ($10 par)	200,000	100,000
Retained Earnings	500,000	250,000
Total Liabilities and Equities	$1,000,000	$500,000

Rolan's common stock had a market price of $60 per share on January 1, 20X1. The market price of Sandin's stock was not readily ascertainable. Rolan's investment in Sandin's stock will be stated in Rolan's balance sheet immediately after the combination in the amount of:

a. $100,000.

b. $350,000.

c. $500,000.

d. $600,000.

3. On February 15, 20X1, Reed Corporation paid $1,500,000 for all of Cord Inc.'s issued and outstanding common stock. The book values and fair values of Cord's assets and liabilities on February 15, 20X1, were as follows:

	Book Value	Fair Value
Cash	$ 160,000	$ 160,000
Receivables	180,000	180,000
Inventory	290,000	270,000
Property, plant, and equipment	870,000	960,000
Liabilities	(350,000)	(350,000)
Net worth	$1,150,000	$1,220,000

What is the amount of goodwill resulting from the business combination?

a. $0.

b. $70,000.

c. $280,000.

d. $350,000.

4. On April 1, 20X2, Jack Company paid $800,000 for all of Ann Corporation's issued and outstanding common stock. Ann's recorded assets and liabilities on April 1, 20X2, were as follows:

Cash	$ 80,000
Inventory	240,000
Property and equipment (net of accumulated depreciation of $320,000)	480,000
Liabilities	(180,000)

On April 1, 20X2, Ann's inventory was determined to have a fair value of $190,000 and the property and equipment had a fair value of $560,000. What is the amount of goodwill resulting from the business combination?

a. $0.

b. $50,000.

c. $150,000.

d. $180,000.

5. Action Corporation issued nonvoting preferred stock with a fair market value of $4,000,000 in exchange for all the outstanding common stock of Master Corporation. On the date of the exchange, Master had tangible net assets with a book value of $2,000,000 and a fair value of $2,500,000. In addition, Action issued preferred stock valued at $400,000 to an individual as a finder's fee in arranging the transaction. As a result of this transaction, Action should record an increase in net assets of:

a. $2,000,000.

b. $2,500,000.

c. $2,900,000.

d. $4,400,000.

E1-4 Multiple-Choice Questions Involving Account Balances

Select the correct answer for each of the following questions.

1. Topper Company established a subsidiary and transferred equipment with a fair value of $72,000 to the subsidiary. Topper had purchased the equipment with an expected life of 10 years 4 years earlier for $100,000 and has used straight-line depreciation with no expected residual value. At the time of the transfer, the subsidiary should record:

 a. Equipment at $72,000 and no accumulated depreciation.

 b. Equipment at $60,000 and no accumulated depreciation.

 c. Equipment at $100,000 and accumulated depreciation of $40,000.

 d. Equipment at $120,000 and accumulated depreciation of $48,000.

2. Lead Corporation established a new subsidiary and transferred to it assets with a cost of $90,000 and a book value of $75,000. The assets had a fair value of $100,000 at the time of transfer. The transfer will result in:

 a. A reduction of net assets reported by Lead Corporation of $90,000.

 b. A reduction of net assets reported by Lead Corporation of $75,000.

 c. No change in the reported net assets of Lead Corporation.

 d. An increase in the net assets reported by Lead Corporation of $25,000.

3. Tear Company, a newly established subsidiary of Stern Corporation, received assets with an original cost of $260,000, a fair value of $200,000, and a book value of $140,000 from the parent in exchange for 7,000 shares of Tear's $8 par value common stock. Tear should record:

 a. Additional paid-in capital of $0.

 b. Additional paid-in capital of $84,000.

 c. Additional paid-in capital of $144,000.

 d. Additional paid-in capital of $204,000.

4. Grout Company reports assets with a carrying value of $420,000 (including goodwill with a carrying value of $35,000) assigned to an identifiable reporting unit. The fair value of the net assets held by the reporting unit is currently $350,000, and the fair value of the reporting unit is $395,000. At the end of the current period, Grout should report goodwill of:

 a. $45,000.

 b. $35,000.

 c. $25,000.

 d. $10,000.

5. Twill Company has a reporting unit with the fair value of its net identifiable assets of $500,000. The carrying value of the reporting unit's net assets on Twill's books is $575,000, which includes $90,000 of goodwill. The fair value of the reporting unit is $560,000. Twill should report impairment of goodwill of:

 a. $60,000.

 b. $30,000.

 c. $15,000.

 d. $0.

E1-5   Asset Transfer to Subsidiary

Pale Company was established on January 1, 20X1. Along with other assets, it immediately purchased land for $80,000, a building for $240,000, and equipment for $90,000. On January 1, 20X5, Pale transferred these assets, cash of $21,000, and inventory costing $37,000 to a newly created subsidiary, Bright Company, in exchange for 10,000 shares of Bright's $6 par value stock. Pale uses straight-line depreciation and useful lives of 40 years and 10 years for the building and equipment, respectively, with no estimated residual values.

Required

 a. Give the journal entry that Pale recorded when it transferred the assets to Bright.

 b. Give the journal entry that Bright recorded for the receipt of assets and issuance of common stock to Pale.

E1-6   Creation of New Subsidiary

Lester Company transferred the following assets to a newly created subsidiary, Mumby Corporation, in exchange for 40,000 shares of its $3 par value stock:

	Cost	Book Value
Cash	$ 40,000	$ 40,000
Accounts Receivable	75,000	68,000
Inventory	50,000	50,000
Land	35,000	35,000
Buildings	160,000	125,000
Equipment	240,000	180,000

Required

a. Give the journal entry in which Lester recorded the transfer of assets to Mumby Corporation.

b. Give the journal entry in which Mumby recorded the receipt of assets and issuance of common stock to Lester.

E1-7 Balance Sheet Totals of Parent Company

Foster Corporation established Kline Company as a wholly owned subsidiary. Foster reported the following balance sheet amounts immediately before and after it transferred assets and accounts payable to Kline Company in exchange for 4,000 shares of $12 par value common stock:

	Amount Reported			
	Before Transfer		**After Transfer**	
Cash		$ 40,000		$ 25,000
Accounts Receivable		65,000		41,000
Inventory		30,000		21,000
Investment in Kline Company				66,000
Land		15,000		12,000
Depreciable Assets	$180,000		$115,000	
Accumulated Depreciation	75,000	105,000	47,000	68,000
Total Assets		$255,000		$233,000
Accounts Payable		$ 40,000		$ 18,000
Bonds Payable		80,000		80,000
Common Stock		60,000		60,000
Retained Earnings		75,000		75,000
Total Liabilities and Equities		$255,000		$233,000

Required

a. Give the journal entry that Foster recorded when it transferred its assets and accounts payable to Kline.

b. Give the journal entry that Kline recorded upon receipt of the assets and accounts payable from Foster.

E1-8 Creation of Partnership

Glover Corporation entered into an agreement with Renfro Company to establish G&R Partnership. Glover agreed to transfer the following assets to G&R for 90 percent ownership, and Renfro agreed to transfer $50,000 cash to the partnership for 10 percent ownership.

	Cost	Book Value
Cash	$ 10,000	$ 10,000
Accounts Receivable	19,000	19,000
Inventory	35,000	35,000
Land	16,000	16,000
Buildings	260,000	200,000
Equipment	210,000	170,000

Required

a. Give the journal entry that Glover recorded at the time of its transfer of assets to G&R.

b. Give the journal entry that Renfro recorded at the time of its transfer of cash to G&R.

c. Give the journal entry that G&R recorded upon the receipt of assets from Glover and Renfro.

E1-9   Stock Acquisition

McDermott Corporation has been in the midst of a major expansion program. Much of its growth had been internal, but in 20X1 McDermott decided to continue its expansion through the acquisition of other companies. The first company acquired was Tippy Inc., a small manufacturer of inertial guidance systems for aircraft and missiles. On June 10, 20X1, McDermott issued 17,000 shares of its $25 par common stock for all 40,000 of Tippy's $10 par common shares. At the date of combination, Tippy reported additional paid-in capital of $100,000 and retained earnings of $350,000. McDermott's stock was selling for $58 per share immediately prior to the combination. Subsequent to the combination, Tippy operated as a subsidiary of McDermott.

Required

Present the journal entry or entries that McDermott would make to record the business combination with Tippy.

E1-10   Balances Reported Following Combination

Elm Corporation and Maple Company have announced terms of an exchange agreement under which Elm will issue 8,000 shares of its $10 par value common stock to acquire all of Maple Company's assets. Elm shares currently are trading at $50, and Maple $5 par value shares are trading at $18 each. Historical cost and fair value balance sheet data on January 1, 20X2, are as follows:

	Elm Corporation		Maple Company	
Balance Sheet Item	Book Value	Fair Value	Book Value	Fair Value
Cash and Receivables	$150,000	$150,000	$ 40,000	$ 40,000
Land	100,000	170,000	50,000	85,000
Buildings and Equipment (net)	300,000	400,000	160,000	230,000
Total Assets	$550,000	$720,000	$250,000	$355,000
Common Stock	$200,000		$100,000	
Additional Paid-In Capital	20,000		10,000	
Retained Earnings	330,000		140,000	
Total Equities	$550,000		$250,000	

Required

What amount will be reported immediately following the business combination for each of the following items in the combined company's balance sheet?

a. Common Stock.

b. Cash and Receivables.

c. Land.

d. Buildings and Equipment (net).

e. Goodwill.

f. Additional Paid-In Capital.

g. Retained Earnings.

E1-11   Goodwill Recognition

Spur Corporation reported the following balance sheet amounts on December 31, 20X1:

Balance Sheet Item	Historical Cost	Fair Value
Cash and Receivables	$ 50,000	$ 40,000
Inventory	100,000	150,000
Land	40,000	30,000
Plant and Equipment	400,000	350,000
Less: Accumulated Depreciation	(150,000)	
Patent		130,000
Total Assets	$440,000	$700,000
Accounts Payable	$ 80,000	$ 85,000
Common Stock	200,000	
Additional Paid-In Capital	20,000	
Retained Earnings	140,000	
Total Liabilities and Equities	$440,000	

Required

Blanket purchased Spur Corporation's assets and liabilities for $670,000 cash on December 31, 20X1. Give the entry that Blanket made to record the purchase.

E1-12 Negative Goodwill

Musial Corporation used debentures with a par value of $580,000 to acquire 100 percent of Sorden Company's net assets on January 1, 20X2. On that date, the fair value of the bonds issued by Musial was $564,000, and the following balance sheet data were reported by Sorden:

Balance Sheet Item	Historical Cost	Fair Value
Cash and Receivables	$ 55,000	$ 50,000
Inventory	105,000	200,000
Land	60,000	100,000
Plant and Equipment	400,000	300,000
Less: Accumulated Depreciation	(150,000)	
Goodwill	10,000	
Total Assets	$480,000	$650,000
Accounts Payable	$ 50,000	$ 50,000
Common Stock	100,000	
Additional Paid-In Capital	60,000	
Retained Earnings	270,000	
Total Liabilities and Equities	$480,000	

Required

Give the journal entry that Musial recorded at the time of exchange.

E1-13 Impairment of Goodwill

Mesa Corporation purchased Kwick Company's net assets and assigned goodwill of $80,000 to Reporting Division K. The following assets and liabilities are assigned to Reporting Division K:

	Carrying Amount	Fair Value
Cash	$ 14,000	$ 14,000
Inventory	56,000	71,000
Equipment	170,000	190,000
Goodwill	80,000	
Accounts Payable	30,000	30,000

Required

Determine the amount of goodwill to be reported for Division K and the amount of goodwill impairment to be recognized, if any, if Division K's fair value is determined to be:

a. $340,000.

b. $280,000.

c. $260,000.

E1-14 Assignment of Goodwill

Double Corporation purchased Simple Company for $450,000 on January 1, 20X4. On that date, Simple's identifiable net assets had a fair value of $390,000. The assets acquired in the purchase of Simple are considered to be a separate reporting unit of Double. The carrying value of Double's investment at December 31, 20X4, is $500,000.

Required

Determine the amount of goodwill impairment, if any, that should be recognized at December 31, 20X4, if the fair value of the net assets (excluding goodwill) at that date is $440,000 and the fair value of the reporting unit is determined to be:

a. $530,000.

b. $485,000.

c. $450,000.

E1-15 Goodwill Assigned to Reporting Units

Groft Company purchased Strobe Company's net assets and assigned them to four separate reporting units. Total goodwill of $186,000 is assigned to the reporting units as indicated:

	Reporting Unit			
	A	B	C	D
Carrying value of investment	$700,000	$330,000	$380,000	$520,000
Goodwill included in carrying value	60,000	48,000	28,000	50,000
Fair value of net identifiable assets at year-end	600,000	300,000	400,000	500,000
Fair value of reporting unit at year-end	690,000	335,000	370,000	585,000

Required

Determine the amount of goodwill that Groft should report at year-end. Show how you computed it.

E1-16 Goodwill Measurement

Washer Company has a reporting unit resulting from an earlier business combination. The reporting unit's current assets and liabilities are:

	Carrying Amount	Fair Value
Cash	$ 30,000	$ 30,000
Inventory	70,000	100,000
Land	30,000	60,000
Buildings	210,000	230,000
Equipment	160,000	170,000
Goodwill	150,000	
Notes Payable	100,000	100,000

Required

Determine the amount of goodwill to be reported and the amount of goodwill impairment, if any, if the fair value of the reporting unit is determined to be:

a. $580.000.

b. $540,000.

c. $500,000.

d. $460,000.

E1-17 Computation of Fair Value

Grant Company acquired all of Bedford Corporation's assets and liabilities on January 1, 20X2, in a business combination. At that date, Bedford reported assets with a book value of $624,000 and liabilities of $356,000. Grant noted that Bedford had $40,000 of research and development costs on its books at the acquisition date that did not appear to be of value. Grant also determined that patents developed by Bedford had a fair value of $120,000 but had not been recorded by Bedford. Except for buildings and equipment, Grant determined the fair value of all other assets and liabilities reported by Bedford approximated the recorded amounts. In recording the transfer of assets and liabilities to its books, Grant recorded goodwill of $93,000. Grant paid $517,000 to acquire Bedford's assets and liabilities. If the book value of Bedford's buildings and equipment was $341,000 at the date of acquisition, what was their fair value?

E1-18 Computation of Shares Issued and Goodwill

Dunyain Company acquired Allsap Corporation on January 1, 20X1, through an exchange of common shares. All of Allsap's assets and liabilities were immediately transferred to Dunyain, which reported total par value of shares outstanding of $218,400 and $327,600 and additional paid-in capital of $370,000 and $650,800 immediately before and after the business combination, respectively.

a. Assuming that Dunyain's common stock had a market value of $25 per share at the time of exchange, what number of shares was issued?

b. What is the par value per share of Dunyain's common stock?

c. Assuming that Allsap's identifiable assets had a fair value of $476,000 and its liabilities had a fair value of $120,000, what amount of goodwill did Dunyain record at the time of the business combination?

E1-19 Combined Balance Sheet

The following balance sheets were prepared for Adam Corporation and Best Company on January 1, 20X2, just before they entered into a business combination:

Item	Adam Corporation Book Value	Adam Corporation Fair Value	Best Company Book Value	Best Company Fair Value
Cash and Receivables	$150,000	$150,000	$ 90,000	$ 90,000
Inventory	300,000	380,000	70,000	160,000
Buildings and Equipment	600,000	430,000	250,000	240,000
Less: Accumulated Depreciation	(250,000)		(80,000)	
Total Assets	$800,000	$960,000	$330,000	$490,000
Accounts Payable	$ 75,000	$ 75,000	$ 50,000	$ 50,000
Notes Payable	200,000	215,000	30,000	35,000
Common Stock:				
$8 par value	180,000			
$6 par value			90,000	
Additional Paid-In Capital	140,000		55,000	
Retained Earnings	205,000		105,000	
Total Liabilities and Equities	$800,000		$330,000	

Adam acquired all of Best Company's assets and liabilities on January 1, 20X2, in exchange for its common shares. Adam issued 8,000 shares of stock to complete the business combination.

Required

Prepare a balance sheet of the combined company immediately following the acquisition, assuming the market price of Adam's shares was:

a. $60 at the date of issue.

b. $48 at the date of issue.

E1-20 Recording a Business Combination

The following financial statement information was prepared for Blue Corporation and Sparse Company at December 31, 20X2:

Balance Sheets
December 31, 20X2

	Blue Corporation		Sparse Company	
Cash		$ 140,000		$ 70,000
Accounts Receivable		170,000		110,000
Inventory		250,000		180,000
Land		80,000		100,000
Buildings and Equipment	$ 680,000		$ 450,000	
Less: Accumulated Depreciation	(320,000)	360,000	(230,000)	220,000
Goodwill		70,000		20,000
Total Assets		$1,070,000		$700,000
Accounts Payable		$ 70,000		$195,000
Bonds Payable		320,000		100,000
Bond Premium				10,000
Common Stock		120,000		150,000
Additional Paid-In Capital		170,000		60,000
Retained Earnings		390,000		185,000
Total Liabilities and Equities		$1,070,000		$700,000

Blue and Sparse agreed to combine as of January 1, 20X3. To effect the merger, Blue paid finder's fees of $30,000 and legal fees of $24,000. Blue also paid $15,000 of audit fees related to the issuance of stock, stock registration fees of $8,000, and stock listing application fees of $6,000.

At January 1, 20X3, book values of Sparse Company's assets and liabilities approximated market value except for inventory with a market value of $200,000, buildings and equipment with a market value of $350,000, and bonds payable with a market value of $105,000. All assets and liabilities were immediately recorded on Blue's books.

Required
Give all journal entries that Blue recorded assuming:

a. Blue issued 40,000 shares of $8 par value common stock to acquire all of Sparse's assets and liabilities in a business combination. Blue common stock was trading at $14 per share on January 1, 20X3.

b. Blue issued 8,000 shares of $10 par value preferred stock to acquire all of Sparse's assets and liabilities in a business combination. Blue preferred stock was determined to have a market value of $50 per share at the time of issue.

E1-21 **Reporting Income**

On July 1, 20X2, Alan Enterprises merged with Cherry Corporation through an exchange of stock and the subsequent liquidation of Cherry. Alan issued 200,000 shares of its stock to effect the combination. The book values of Cherry's assets and liabilities were equal to their fair values at the date of combination, and the value of the shares exchanged was equal to Cherry's book value. Information relating to income for the companies is as follows:

	20X1	Jan. 1–June 30, 20X2	July 1–Dec. 31, 20X2
Net Income:			
Alan Enterprises	$4,460,000	$2,500,000	$3,528,000
Cherry Corporation	1,300,000	692,000	—

Alan Enterprises had 1,000,000 shares of stock outstanding prior to the combination.

Required
Compute the net income and earnings-per-share amounts that would be reported in Alan's 20X2 comparative income statements for both 20X2 and 20X1.

E1-22* **Acquisition of Net Assets**

Sun Corporation concluded the fair value of Tender Company was $60,000 and paid that amount to acquire its net assets. Tender reported assets with a book value of $55,000 and fair value of $71,000 and liabilities with a book value and fair value of $20,000 on the date of combination. Sun also paid $4,000 to a search firm for finder's fees related to the acquisition.

Required

Give the journal entries to be made by Sun to record its investment in Tender and its payment of the finder's fees, assuming the FASB proposal for accounting for business combinations is adopted.

E1-23* **Reporting Goodwill**

Samper Company reported the book value of its net assets at $160,000 when Public Corporation acquired 100 percent ownership. The fair value of Samper's net assets was determined to be $190,000 and the fair value of the company was estimated at $310,000 on that date.

Required

Using the FASB proposed standard for business combinations, determine the amount of goodwill to be reported in consolidated financial statements presented immediately following the combination and the amount at which Public will record its investment in Samper if the amount paid by Public is:

a. $310,000.

b. $196,000.

c. $150,000.

Problems

P1-24 **Assets and Accounts Payable Transferred to Subsidiary**

Tab Corporation decided to establish Collon Company as a wholly owned subsidiary by transferring some of its existing assets and liabilities to the new entity. In exchange, Collon issued Tab 30,000 shares of $6 par value common stock. The following information is provided on the assets and accounts payable transferred:

	Cost	Book Value	Fair Value
Cash	$ 25,000	$ 25,000	$ 25,000
Inventory	70,000	70,000	70,000
Land	60,000	60,000	90,000
Buildings	170,000	130,000	240,000
Equipment	90,000	80,000	105,000
Accounts Payable	45,000	45,000	45,000

Required

a. Give the journal entry that Tab recorded for the transfer of assets and accounts payable to Collon.

b. Give the journal entry that Collon recorded for the receipt of assets and accounts receivable from Tab.

P1-25 **Creation of New Subsidiary**

Eagle Corporation established a subsidiary to enter into a new line of business considered to be substantially more risky than Eagle's current business. Eagle transferred the following assets and accounts payable to Sand Corporation in exchange for 5,000 shares of $10 par value stock of Sand:

	Cost	Book Value
Cash	$ 30,000	$ 30,000
Accounts Receivable	45,000	40,000
Inventory	60,000	60,000
Land	20,000	20,000
Buildings and Equipment	300,000	260,000
Accounts Payable	10,000	10,000

Required

a. Give the journal entry that Eagle recorded for the transfer of assets and accounts payable to Sand.

b. Give the journal entry that Sand recorded for receipt of the assets and accounts payable from Eagle.

P1-26   Incomplete Data on Creation of Subsidiary

Thumb Company created New Company as a wholly owned subsidiary by transferring assets and accounts payable to New in exchange for its common stock. New recorded the following entry when it received the assets and accounts payable:

Cash	3,000	
Accounts Receivable	16,000	
Inventory	27,000	
Land	9,000	
Buildings	70,000	
Equipment	60,000	
Accounts Payable		14,000
Accumulated Depreciation—Buildings		21,000
Accumulated Depreciation—Equipment		12,000
Common Stock		40,000
Additional Paid-In Capital		98,000

Required

a. What was Thumb's book value of the total assets transferred to New Company?

b. What amount did Thumb report as its investment in New after the transfer?

c. What number of shares of $5 par value stock did New issue to Thumb?

d. What impact did the transfer of assets and accounts payable have on the amount reported by Thumb as total assets?

e. What impact did the transfer of assets and accounts payable have on the amount that Thumb and the consolidated entity reported as shares outstanding?

P1-27   Establishing a Partnership

Krantz Company and Dull Corporation decided to form a partnership. Krantz agreed to transfer the following assets and accounts payable to K&D Partnership in exchange for 60 percent ownership:

	Cost	Book Value
Cash	$ 10,000	$ 10,000
Inventory	30,000	30,000
Land	70,000	70,000
Buildings	200,000	150,000
Equipment	120,000	90,000
Accounts Payable	50,000	50,000

Dull agreed to contribute cash of $200,000 to K&D Partnership.

Required

a. Give the journal entries that K&D recorded for its receipt of assets and accounts payable from Krantz and Dull.

b. Give the journal entries that Krantz and Dull recorded for their transfer of assets and accounts payable to K&D Partnership.

P1-28   Balance Sheet Data for Companies Establishing a Partnership

Good Corporation and Nevall Company formed G&W Partnership in which Good received 75 percent ownership and Nevall received 25 percent ownership. The following assets were transferred by Good and Nevall:

	Good Corporation		Nevall Company	
	Cost	**Book Value**	**Cost**	**Book Value**
Cash	$ 21,000	$21,000	$ 3,000	$ 3,000
Inventory	4,000	4,000	25,000	25,000
Land	15,000	15,000		
Buildings	100,000	70,000		
Equipment	60,000	40,000	36,000	22,000

Required

a. Give the journal entry that Good recorded for its transfer of assets to G&W Partnership.

b. Give the journal entry that Nevall recorded for its transfer of assets to G&W Partnership.

c. Give the journal entry that G&W recorded for its receipt of assets from Good and Nevall.

P1-29 Journal Entries to Record a Business Combination

On January 1, 20X2, Frost Company acquired all of TKK Corporation's assets and liabilities by issuing 24,000 shares of its $4 par value common stock. At that date, Frost shares were selling at $22 per share. Historical cost and fair value balance sheet data for TKK at the time of acquisition were as follows:

Balance Sheet Item	Historical Cost	Fair Value
Cash and Receivables	$ 28,000	$ 28,000
Inventory	94,000	122,000
Buildings and Equipment	600,000	470,000
Less: Accumulated Depreciation	(240,000)	
Total Assets	$482,000	$620,000
Accounts Payable	$ 41,000	$ 41,000
Notes Payable	65,000	63,000
Common Stock ($10 par value)	160,000	
Retained Earnings	216,000	
Total Liabilities and Equities	$482,000	

Frost paid legal fees for the transfer of assets and liabilities of $14,000. Frost also paid audit fees of $21,000 and listing application fees of $7,000, both related to the issuance of new shares.

Required

Prepare the journal entries made by Frost to record the business combination.

P1-30 Recording Business Combinations

Taylor Corporation exchanged shares of its $2 par common stock for all of Mark Company's assets and liabilities in a planned merger. Immediately prior to the combination, Mark's assets and liabilities were as follows:

Assets	
Cash and Equivalents	$ 41,000
Accounts Receivable	73,000
Inventory	144,000
Land	200,000
Buildings	1,520,000
Equipment	638,000
Accumulated Depreciation	(431,000)
Total Assets	$2,185,000

Liabilities and Equities

Accounts Payable	$ 35,000
Short-Term Notes Payable	50,000
Bonds Payable	500,000
Common Stock ($10 par)	1,000,000
Additional Paid-In Capital	325,000
Retained Earnings	275,000
Total Liabilities and Equities	$2,185,000

Immediately prior to the combination, Taylor reported $250,000 additional paid-in capital and $1,350,000 retained earnings. The fair values of Mark's assets and liabilities were equal to their book values on the date of combination except that Mark's buildings were worth $1,500,000 and its equipment was worth $300,000. Costs associated with planning and completing the business combination totaled $38,000, and stock issue costs totaled $22,000. The market value of Taylor's stock at the date of combination was $4 per share.

Required

Prepare the journal entries that would appear on Taylor's books to record the combination if Taylor issued the following number of shares in the combination:

a. 400,000 shares.
b. 900,000 shares.

P1-31 **Business Combination with Goodwill**

Anchor Corporation paid cash of $178,000 to acquire Zink Company's net assets on February 1, 20X3. The balance sheet data for the two companies and fair value information for Zink immediately before the business combination were:

Balance Sheet Item	Anchor Corporation Book Value	Zink Company Book Value	Zink Company Fair Value
Cash	$240,000	$ 20,000	$ 20,000
Accounts Receivable	140,000	35,000	35,000
Inventory	170,000	30,000	50,000
Patents	80,000	40,000	60,000
Buildings and Equipment	380,000	310,000	150,000
Less: Accumulated Depreciation	(190,000)	(200,000)	
Total Assets	$820,000	$235,000	$315,000
Accounts Payable	$ 85,000	$ 55,000	$ 55,000
Notes Payable	150,000	120,000	120,000
Common Stock:			
$10 par value	200,000		
$6 par value		18,000	
Additional Paid-In Capital	160,000	10,000	
Retained Earnings	225,000	32,000	
Total Liabilities and Equities	$820,000	$235,000	

Required

a. Give the journal entry recorded by Anchor Corporation when it purchased Zink's net assets.
b. Prepare a balance sheet for Anchor immediately following the acquisition.
c. Give the journal entry to be recorded by Anchor if it purchases all of Zink's common stock for $178,000.

P1-32 Negative Goodwill

Eagle Company purchased Lark Corporation's net assets on January 3, 20X2, for $565,000 cash. In addition, $5,000 of direct costs were incurred in consummating the combination. At the time of acquisition, Lark reported the following historical cost and current market data:

Balance Sheet Item	Book Value	Fair Value
Cash and Receivables	$ 50,000	$ 50,000
Inventory	100,000	150,000
Buildings and Equipment (net)	200,000	300,000
Patent	—	200,000
Total Assets	$350,000	$700,000
Accounts Payable	$ 30,000	$ 30,000
Common Stock	100,000	
Additional Paid-In Capital	80,000	
Retained Earnings	140,000	
Total Liabilities and Equities	$350,000	

Required

Give the journal entry or entries with which Eagle recorded its purchase of Lark's net assets.

P1-33 Computation of Account Balances

Aspro Division is considered to be an individual reporting unit of Tabor Company. Tabor acquired the division by issuing 100,000 shares of its common stock with a market price of $7.60 each. Tabor management was able to identify assets with fair values of $810,000 and liabilities of $190,000 at the date of acquisition. At the end of the first year, the reporting unit had assets with a fair value of $950,000, and the fair value of the reporting entity was $930,000. Tabor's accountants concluded it must recognize impairment of goodwill in the amount of $30,000 at the end of the first year.

Required

a. Determine the fair value of the reporting unit's liabilities at the end of the first year. Show your computation.

b. If the reporting unit's liabilities at the end of the period had been $70,000, what would the fair value of the reporting unit had to have been to avoid recognizing an impairment of goodwill? Show your computation.

P1-34 Goodwill Assigned to Multiple Reporting Units

The fair values of assets and liabilities held by three reporting units and other information related to the reporting units owned by Rover Company are as follows:

	Reporting Unit		
	A	B	C
Cash and Receivables	$ 30,000	$ 80,000	$ 20,000
Inventory	60,000	100,000	40,000
Land	20,000	30,000	10,000
Buildings	100,000	150,000	80,000
Equipment	140,000	90,000	50,000
Accounts Payable	40,000	60,000	10,000
Fair Value of Reporting Unit	400,000	440,000	265,000
Carrying Value of Investment	420,000	500,000	290,000
Goodwill Included in Carrying Value	70,000	80,000	40,000

Required

a. Determine the amount of goodwill that Rover should report in its current financial statements.

b. Determine the amount, if any, that Rover should report as impairment of goodwill for the current period.

P1-35   Journal Entries

On January 1, 20X3, More Products Corporation issued 12,000 shares of its $10 par value stock to acquire the net assets of Light Steel Company. Underlying book value and fair value information for the balance sheet items of Light Steel at the time of acquisition follow:

Balance Sheet Item	Book Value	Fair Value
Cash	$ 60,000	$ 60,000
Accounts Receivable	100,000	100,000
Inventory (LIFO basis)	60,000	115,000
Land	50,000	70,000
Buildings and Equipment	400,000	350,000
Less: Accumulated Depreciation	(150,000)	—
Total Assets	$520,000	$695,000
Accounts Payable	$ 10,000	$ 10,000
Bonds Payable	200,000	180,000
Common Stock ($5 par value)	150,000	
Additional Paid-In Capital	70,000	
Retained Earnings	90,000	
Total Liabilities and Equities	$520,000	

Light Steel shares were selling at $18 and More Products shares were selling at $50 just before the merger announcement. Additional cash payments made by More Products in completing the acquisition were:

Finder's fee paid to firm that located Light Steel	$10,000
Audit fee for stock issued by More Products	3,000
Stock registration fee for new shares of More Products	5,000
Legal fees paid to assist in transfer of net assets	9,000
Cost of SEC registration of More Products shares	1,000

Required

Prepare all journal entries to record the business combination on More Products' books.

P1-36   Purchase at More Than Book Value

Ramrod Manufacturing acquired all the assets and liabilities of Stafford Industries on January 1, 20X2, in exchange for 4,000 shares of Ramrod's $20 par value common stock. Balance sheet data for both companies just before the merger are given as follows:

Balance Sheet Items	Ramrod Manufacturing		Stafford Industries	
	Book Value	Fair Value	Book Value	Fair Value
Cash	$ 70,000	$ 70,000	$ 30,000	$ 30,000
Accounts Receivable	100,000	100,000	60,000	60,000
Inventory	200,000	375,000	100,000	160,000
Land	50,000	80,000	40,000	30,000
Buildings and Equipment	600,000 }	540,000	400,000 }	350,000
Less: Accumulated Depreciation	(250,000)		(150,000)	
Total Assets	$770,000	$1,165,000	$480,000	$630,000
Accounts Payable	$ 50,000	$ 50,000	$ 10,000	$ 10,000
Bonds Payable	300,000	310,000	150,000	145,000
Common Stock:				
$20 par value	200,000			
$5 par value			100,000	
Additional Paid-In Capital	40,000		20,000	
Retained Earnings	180,000		200,000	
Total Liabilities and Equities	$770,000		$480,000	

Ramrod shares were selling for $150 on the date of acquisition.

Required

Prepare the following:

a. Journal entries to record the acquisition on Ramrod's books.

b. A balance sheet for the combined enterprise immediately following the business combination.

P1-37 Business Combination

Following are the balance sheets of Boogie Musical Corporation and Toot-Toot Tuba Company as of December 31, 20X5.

BOOGIE MUSICAL CORPORATION
Balance Sheet
December 31, 20X5

Assets		Liabilities and Equities	
Cash	$ 23,000	Accounts Payable	$ 48,000
Accounts Receivable	85,000	Notes Payable	65,000
Allowance for Uncollectible Accounts	(1,200)	Mortgage Payable	200,000
Inventory	192,000	Bonds Payable	200,000
Plant and Equipment	980,000	Capital Stock ($10 par)	500,000
Accumulated Depreciation	(160,000)	Premium on Capital Stock	1,000
Other Assets	14,000	Retained Earnings	118,800
Total Assets	$1,132,800	Total Liabilities and Equities	$1,132,800

TOOT-TOOT TUBA COMPANY
Balance Sheet
December 31, 20X5

Assets		*Liabilities and Equities*	
Cash	$ 300	Accounts Payable	$ 8,200
Accounts Receivable	17,000	Notes Payable	10,000
Allowance for Uncollectible Accounts	(600)	Mortgage Payable	50,000
Inventory	78,500	Bonds Payable	100,000
Plant and Equipment	451,000	Capital Stock ($50 par)	100,000
Accumulated Depreciation	(225,000)	Premium on Capital Stock	150,000
Other Assets	25,800	Retained Earnings	(71,200)
Total Assets	$347,000	Total Liabilities and Equities	$347,000

In preparation for a possible business combination, a team of experts from Boogie Musical made a thorough examination and audit of Toot-Toot Tuba. They found that Toot-Toot's assets and liabilities were correctly stated except that they estimated uncollectible accounts at $1,400. The experts also estimated the market value of the inventory at $35,000 and the market value of the plant and equipment at $500,000. The business combination took place on January 1, 20X6, and on that date Boogie Musical acquired all the assets and liabilities of Toot-Toot Tuba. On that date, Boogie's common stock was selling for $55 per share.

Required
Record the combination on Boogie's books assuming that Boogie issued 9,000 of its $10 par common shares in exchange for Toot-Toot's assets and liabilities.

P1-38 **Combined Balance Sheet**

Bilge Pumpworks and Seaworthy Rope Company agreed to merge on January 1, 20X3. On the date of the merger agreement, the companies reported the following data:

Balance Sheet Items	Bilge Pumpworks Book Value	Bilge Pumpworks Fair Value	Seaworthy Rope Company Book Value	Seaworthy Rope Company Fair Value
Cash and Receivables	$ 90,000	$ 90,000	$ 20,000	$ 20,000
Inventory	100,000	150,000	30,000	42,000
Land	100,000	140,000	10,000	15,000
Plant and Equipment	400,000		200,000	
Less: Accumulated Depreciation	(150,000)	300,000	(80,000)	140,000
Total Assets	$540,000	$680,000	$180,000	$217,000
Current Liabilities	$ 80,000	$ 80,000	$ 20,000	$ 20,000
Capital Stock	200,000		20,000	
Capital in Excess of Par Value	20,000		5,000	
Retained Earnings	240,000		135,000	
Total Liabilities and Equities	$540,000		$180,000	

Bilge Pumpworks has 10,000 shares of its $20 par value shares outstanding on January 1, 20X3, and Seaworthy has 4,000 shares of $5 par value stock outstanding. The market values of the shares are $300 and $50, respectively.

Required

a. Bilge issues 700 shares of stock in exchange for all of Seaworthy's net assets. Prepare a balance sheet for the combined entity immediately following the merger.

b. Prepare the stockholders' equity section of the combined company's balance sheet, assuming Bilge acquires all of Seaworthy's net assets by issuing:

1. 1,100 shares of common.
2. 1,800 shares of common.
3. 3,000 shares of common.

P1-39   Incomplete Data Problem

On January 1, 20X2, End Corporation acquired all of Cork Corporation's assets and liabilities by issuing shares of its common stock in a business combination recorded as a purchase. Partial balance sheet data for the companies prior to the business combination and immediately following the combination are as follows:

	End Corp. Book Value	Cork Corp. Book Value	Combined Entity
Cash	$ 40,000	$ 10,000	$ 50,000
Accounts Receivable	60,000	30,000	88,000
Inventory	50,000	35,000	96,000
Buildings and Equipment (net)	300,000	110,000	430,000
Goodwill			?
Total Assets	$450,000	$185,000	$?
Accounts Payable	$ 32,000	$ 14,000	$ 46,000
Bonds Payable	150,000	70,000	220,000
Bond Premium	6,000		6,000
Common Stock, $5 par	100,000	40,000	126,000
Additional Paid-In Capital	65,000	28,000	247,000
Retained Earnings	97,000	33,000	?
Total Liabilities and Equities	$450,000	$185,000	$?

Required

a. What number of shares did End issue to acquire Cork's assets and liabilities?

b. What was the market value of the shares issued by End?

c. What was the fair value of the inventory held by Cork at the date of combination?

d. What was the fair value of the net assets held by Cork at the date of combination?

e. What amount of goodwill, if any, will be reported by the combined entity immediately following the combination?

f. What balance in retained earnings will the combined entity report immediately following the combination?

g. If the depreciable assets held by Cork had an average remaining life of 10 years at the date of acquisition, what amount of depreciation expense will be reported on those assets in 20X2?

P1-40 **Incomplete Data Following Purchase**

On January 1, 20X1, Alpha Corporation acquired all of Bravo Company's assets and liabilities by issuing shares of its $3 par value stock to the owners of Bravo Company in a business combination. Alpha also made a cash payment to Banker Corporation as a finder's fee. Partial balance sheet data for Alpha and Bravo, before the cash payment and issuance of shares, and a combined balance sheet following the business combination are as follows:

	Alpha Corporation	Bravo Company		Combined Entity
	Book Value	Book Value	Fair Value	Combined Entity
Cash	$ 65,000	$ 15,000	$ 15,000	$ 56,000
Accounts Receivable	105,000	30,000	30,000	135,000
Inventory	210,000	90,000	?	320,000
Buildings and Equipment (net)	400,000	210,000	293,000	693,000
Goodwill				?
Total Assets	$780,000	$345,000	$448,000	$?
Accounts Payable	$ 56,000	$ 22,000	$ 22,000	$ 78,000
Bonds Payable	200,000	120,000	120,000	320,000
Common Stock	96,000	70,000		117,000
Additional Paid-In Capital	234,000	42,000		577,000
Retained Earnings	194,000	91,000		?
Total Liabilities and Equities	$780,000	$345,000	$142,000	$?

Required

a. What number of its $5 par value shares did Bravo have outstanding at January 1, 20X1?

b. Assuming that all of Bravo's shares were issued when the company was started, what was the price per share received at the time of issue?

c. How many shares of Alpha were issued at the date of combination?

d. What was the market value of Alpha's shares issued at the date of combination?

e. What amount of cash did Alpha pay to Banker as a finder's fee?

f. What was the fair value of Bravo's inventory at the date of combination?

g. What was the fair value of Bravo's net assets at the date of combination?

h. What amount of goodwill, if any, will be reported in the combined balance sheet following the combination?

P1-41 **Comprehensive Business Combination Problem**

Integrated Industries Inc. entered into a business combination agreement with Hydrolized Chemical Corporation (HCC) to ensure an uninterrupted supply of key raw materials and to realize certain economies from combining the operating processes and the marketing efforts of the two companies. Under the terms of the agreement, Integrated issued 180,000 shares of its $1 par common stock in exchange for all of HCC's assets and liabilities. The Integrated shares then were distributed to HCC's shareholders, and HCC was liquidated.

Immediately prior to the combination, HCC's balance sheet appeared as follows, with fair values also indicated:

	Book Values	Fair Values
Assets		
Cash	$ 28,000	$ 28,000
Accounts Receivable	258,000	251,500
Less: Allowance for Bad Debts	(6,500)	
Inventory	381,000	395,000
Long-Term Investments	150,000	175,000
Land	55,000	100,000
Rolling Stock	130,000	63,000
Plant and Equipment	2,425,000	2,500,000
Less: Accumulated Depreciation	(614,000)	
Patents	125,000	500,000
Special Licenses	95,800	100,000
Total Assets	$3,027,300	$4,112,500
Liabilities		
Current Payables	$ 137,200	$ 137,200
Mortgages Payable	500,000	520,000
Equipment Trust Notes	100,000	95,000
Debentures Payable	1,000,000	950,000
Less: Discount on Debentures	(40,000)	
Total Liabilities	$1,697,200	$1,702,200
Stockholders' Equity		
Common Stock ($5 par)	600,000	
Additional Paid-In Capital from Common Stock	500,000	
Additional Paid-In Capital from		
Reirement of Preferred Stock	22,000	
Retained Earnings	220,100	
Less: Treasury Stock (1,500 shares)	(12,000)	
Total Liabilities and Equity	$3,027,300	

Immediately prior to the combination, Integrated's common stock was selling for $14 per share. Integrated incurred direct costs of $135,000 in arranging the business combination and $42,000 of costs associated with registering and issuing the common stock used in the combination.

Required

a. Prepare all journal entries that Integrated should have entered on its books to record the business combination.

b. Present all journal entries that should have been entered on HCC's books to record the combination and the distribution of the stock received.

P1-42* **Acquisition in Multiple Steps**

Deal Corporation issued 4,000 shares of its $10 par value stock with a market value of $85,000 to acquire 85 percent ownership of Mead Company on August 31, 20X3. The fair value of Mead was determined to be $100,000 on that date. Deal had earlier purchased 15 percent of Mead's shares for $9,000 and used the cost method in accounting for its investment in Mead. Deal later paid appraisal fees of $3,500 and stock issue costs of $2,000 incurred in completing the acquisition of the additional shares.

Required

Give the journal entries to be recorded by Deal in completing the acquisition of the additional shares of Mead under the requirements outlined in the FASB exposure draft on business combinations.

P1-43* **Negative Goodwill**

Using the data presented in E1-12, determine the amount Musical Corporation would record as a gain on revaluation of subsidiary shares and prepare the journal entries Musial would record at the time of the exchange under the FASB's proposed requirements for business combinations.

Reporting Intercorporate Interests

Companies often acquire ownership or other interests in other companies through a variety of arrangements and for a variety of reasons. Some companies invest in other companies simply to earn a favorable return by taking advantage of potentially profitable situations. However, companies can have many other reasons for acquiring interests in other entities, including to (1) gain control over other companies, (2) enter new market or product areas through companies established in those areas, (3) ensure a supply of raw materials or other production inputs, (4) ensure a customer for production output, (5) gain economies associated with greater size, (6) diversify, (7) gain new technology, (8) lessen competition, and (9) limit risk. Examples of intercorporate investments include IBM's acquisition of a sizable portion of Intel's stock to ensure a supply of computer components, AT&T's purchase of the stock of McCaw Cellular Communications to gain a foothold in the cellular phone market, and Texaco's acquisition of Getty Oil's stock to acquire oil and gas reserves.

Accounting for intercorporate ownership investments and various types of interests in other companies can differ in a number of respects from accounting for other types of investments. This chapter presents the accounting and reporting procedures for investments in common stock and for selected other types of interests in different entities.

ACCOUNTING FOR INVESTMENTS IN COMMON STOCK

The method used to account for investments in common stock depends on the level of influence or control that the investor is able to exercise over the investee. The level of influence is the primary factor determining whether the investor and investee will present consolidated financial statements or the investor will report the investment in common stock in its balance sheet using either the cost method (adjusted to market value, if appropriate) or the equity method. Figure 2–1 summarizes the relationship between methods used to report intercorporate investments in common stock and levels of ownership and influence.

Consolidation involves combining for financial reporting the individual assets, liabilities, revenues, and expenses of two or more related companies as if they were part of a single company. This process includes the elimination of all intercompany ownership and activities. Consolidation normally is appropriate when one company, referred to as the *parent*, controls another company, referred to as a *subsidiary*. The specific requirements for consolidation are discussed in Chapter 3. A subsidiary that is not consolidated with the parent is referred to as an *unconsolidated subsidiary* and is shown as an investment on the parent's balance sheet. Under current accounting standards, most subsidiaries are consolidated.

The *equity method* is used for external reporting when the investor exercises *significant influence* over the operating and financial policies of the investee and consolidation is not appropriate. The equity method may not be used in place of consolidation when consolidation is appropriate, and therefore its primary use is in reporting nonsubsidiary investments. This method is used most often when one company holds between 20 and 50 percent of another company's common stock. Under the equity method, the investor recognizes income

FIGURE 2–1   **Financial Reporting Basis by Level of Common Stock Ownership**

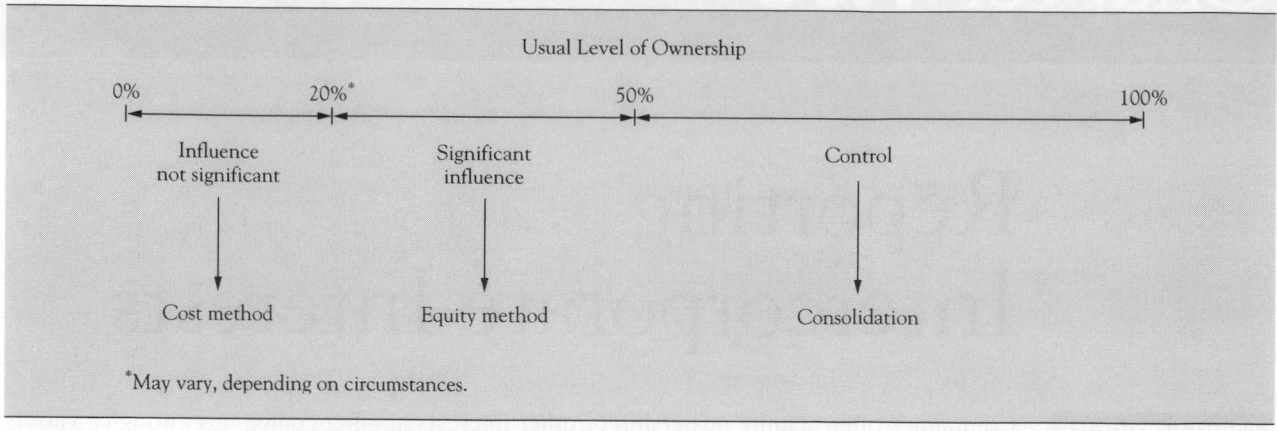

*May vary, depending on circumstances.

from the investment as the investee earns the income. Instead of combining the individual assets, liabilities, revenues, and expenses of the investee with those of the investor, as in consolidation, the investment is reported as one line in the investor's balance sheet, and income recognized from the investee is reported as one line in the investor's income statement. The investment represents the investor's share of the investee's net assets, and the income recognized is the investor's share of the investee's net income.

The ***cost method*** is used for reporting investments in equity securities when both consolidation and equity-method reporting are inappropriate. If cost-method equity securities have readily determinable fair values, they must be adjusted to market value at year-end under **FASB Statement 115**.[1] Under the cost method, the investor recognizes income from the investment when the income is distributed by the investee as dividends.

Coca-Cola's balance sheet provides a good example of the financial reporting of cost and equity investments:

	December 31	
	2005	**2004**
Investments		
Equity-method investments:		
Coca-Cola Enterprises Inc.	**$1,731**	$1,569
Coca-Cola Hellenic Bottling Company S.A.	**1,039**	1,067
Coca-Cola FEMSA, S.A. de C.V.	**982**	792
Coca-Cola Amatil Limited	**748**	736
Other, principally bottling companies	**2,062**	1,733
Cost-method investments, principally bottling companies	**360**	355
Total Investments	**$6,922**	$6,252

Under normal circumstances, companies using the cost or equity method for financial reporting purposes also use that method in accounting for the investment on their books. When consolidated statements are prepared for financial reporting purposes, the parent still must account for the investment on its books using either the cost or equity method even though the intercorporate investment and related income must be eliminated in preparing the consolidated statements. A survey of 900 companies conducted by the authors indicated that both the cost and equity methods were being used by companies in accounting for

[1] *Financial Accounting Standards Board Statement No. 115,* "Accounting for Certain Investments in Debt and Equity Securities," May 1993. Because the provisions of **FASB 115** are normally discussed in Intermediate Accounting, detailed coverage is not provided here. Note, however, that equity investments accounted for using the cost method are accounted for as discussed in this chapter, with the provisions of **FASB 115** applied as end-of-period adjustments. **FASB 115** is not applicable to equity-method investments.

their investments in consolidated subsidiaries. The preparation of consolidated financial statements is discussed in Chapters 3 through 10.

THE COST METHOD

Intercorporate investments accounted for by the cost method are carried by the investor at historical cost. Income is recorded by the investor as dividends are declared by the investee. The cost method is used when the investor lacks the ability either to control or to exercise significant influence over the investee. The inability of an investor to exercise either control or significant influence over an investee may result from the size of the investment, usually at common stock ownership levels of less than 20 percent. In some situations, other factors, such as the bankruptcy of the investee, prevent the investor from exercising control or significant influence regardless of the size of the investment.

Accounting Procedures under the Cost Method

The cost method is consistent with the treatment normally accorded noncurrent assets. At the time of purchase, the investor records its investment in common stock at the total cost incurred in making the purchase. Subsequently, the carrying amount of the investment remains unchanged under the cost method; the investment continues to be carried at its original cost until the time of sale. Income from the investment is recognized by the investor as dividends are declared by the investee. Once the investee declares a dividend, the investor has a legal claim against the investee for a proportionate share of the dividend, and realization of the income is considered certain enough to be recognized. Recognition of investment income before a dividend declaration is considered inappropriate because the investee's income is not available to the owners until a dividend is declared.

To illustrate the cost method, assume that ABC Company purchases 20 percent of XYZ Company's common stock for $100,000 at the beginning of the year but does not gain significant influence over XYZ. During the year, XYZ has net income of $60,000 and pays dividends of $20,000. ABC Company records the following entries relating to its investment in XYZ:

(1)	Investment in XYZ Company Stock	100,000	
	Cash		100,000
	Record purchase of XYZ Company stock.		
(2)	Cash	4,000	
	Dividend Income		4,000
	Record dividend income from XYZ Company:		
	$20,000 × .20		

Note that ABC records only its share of the distributed earnings of XYZ and makes no entry regarding the undistributed portion. The carrying amount of the investment remains at its original cost of $100,000.

Declaration of Dividends in Excess of Earnings since Acquisition

A special treatment is required under the cost method in situations in which an investor holds common stock in a company that declares dividends in excess of the income it has earned since the investor acquired its stock. The dividends received are viewed first as representing earnings of the investee from the purchase date of the investment to the declaration date of the dividend. All dividends declared by the investee in excess of its earnings since acquisition by the investor are viewed by the investor as *liquidating dividends*. The investor's share of these liquidating dividends is treated as a return of capital, and the investment account balance is reduced by that amount. Blocks of an investee's stock acquired at different times should be treated separately for purposes of computing liquidating dividends.

Liquidating Dividends Illustrated

To illustrate the computation of liquidating dividends received by the investor, assume that Investor Company purchases 10 percent of the common stock of Investee Company on January 2, 20X1. The annual income and dividends of Investee, the amount of dividend income recognized by Investor each year under the cost method, and the reduction of the carrying amount of Investor's investment in Investee when appropriate are as follows:

	Investee Company			Investor Company		
Year	Net Income	Dividends	Cumulative Undistributed Income	Cash Received	Dividend Income	Reduction of Investment
20X1	$100,000	$ 70,000	$30,000	$ 7,000	$ 7,000	
20X2	100,000	120,000	10,000	12,000	12,000	
20X3	100,000	120,000	–0–	12,000	11,000	$1,000
20X4	100,000	120,000	–0–	12,000	10,000	2,000
20X5	100,000	70,000	30,000	7,000	7,000	

Investor Company records its 10 percent share of Investee's dividend as income in 20X1 because the income of Investee exceeds its dividend. In 20X2, Investee's dividend exceeds earnings for the year, but the cumulative dividends declared since January 2, 20X1, the date Investor acquired Investee's stock, do not exceed Investee's earnings since that date. Hence, Investor again records its 10 percent share of the dividend as income. By the end of 20X3, dividends declared by Investee since January 2, 20X1, total $310,000, while Investee's income since that date totals only $300,000. Thus, from Investor's point of view, $10,000 of the 20X3 dividend represents a return of capital while the remaining $110,000 represents a distribution of earnings. Investor's share of each amount is 10 percent. The entry to record the 20X3 dividend on Investor's books is:

(3)	Cash	12,000	
	Investment in Investee Company Stock		1,000
	Dividend Income		11,000
	Record receipt of 20X3 dividend from Investee Company:		
	$12,000 = $120,000 × .10		
	$1,000 = ($310,000 − $300,000) × .10		
	$11,000 = ($120,000 − $10,000) × .10		

Once the investor has recorded a liquidating dividend, the comparison in future periods between cumulative earnings and dividends of the investee should be based on the date of the last liquidating dividend rather than the date the investor acquired the investee's stock. In the example, Investor Company records liquidating dividends in 20X3 and 20X4. In years after 20X4, Investor compares earnings and dividends of Investee from the date of the most recent liquidating dividend in 20X4 rather than comparing from January 2, 20X1. All the dividend paid in 20X5 is considered by Investor to be a distribution of earnings.

Liquidating Dividends following Switch from Equity Method

If the investor previously carried the investment using the equity method and, because of the sale of a portion of the investment, switches to the cost method, the date of the switch in methods replaces the date of acquisition as the reference date for distinguishing liquidating dividends. From that point forward, the investor should compare earnings and dividends of the investee starting at the date of the switch to the cost method.

Investee's View of Liquidating Dividends

Dividends received by an investor in excess of earnings since acquisition, while viewed as liquidating dividends by the investor, usually are not liquidating dividends from the investee's point of view. This type of dividend might occur, for example, when an investee's stock is acquired shortly before a dividend is declared. The investee does not consider a dividend to be a liquidating dividend unless the investee's retained earnings is insufficient or the investee specifically declares a liquidating dividend for all common shareholders.

Acquisition at Interim Date

The acquisition of an investment at other than the beginning or end of a fiscal period generally does not create any major problems when the cost method is used in accounting for the investment. The only potential difficulty involves determining whether some part of the payment received by the investor is a liquidating dividend when the investee declares a dividend soon after the investor purchases stock in the investee. In this situation, the investor must estimate the amount of the investee's earnings for the portion of the period during which the investor held the investee's stock and may record dividend income only on that portion.

Changes in the Number of Shares Held

Changes in the number of investment shares resulting from stock dividends, stock splits, or reverse splits receive no formal recognition in the accounts of the investor. The carrying value of the investment before the stock dividend or split becomes the carrying amount of the new, greater or lesser number of shares. Purchases and sales of shares, of course, do require journal entries but do not result in any unusual difficulties under the cost method.

Purchases of Additional Shares

A purchase of additional shares of a stock already held is recorded at cost in the same way as an initial purchase of shares. The investor's new percentage ownership of the investee then is calculated, and other evidence, if available, is evaluated to determine whether the total investment still should be carried at cost or if the investor should switch to the equity method. When the additional shares give the investor the ability to exercise significant influence over the investee, the equity method should be applied retroactively from the date of the original investment, as illustrated later in this chapter.

Sales of Shares

If all or part of an intercorporate investment in stock is sold, the transaction is accounted for in the same manner as the sale of any other noncurrent asset. A gain or loss on the sale is recognized for the difference between the proceeds received and the carrying amount of the investment sold.

If shares of the stock have been purchased at more than one price, a determination must be made at the time of sale as to which of the shares have been sold. The specific shares sold may be identified through segregation, numbered stock certificates, or other means. When specific identification is impractical, either a FIFO or weighted-average cost flow assumption may be used; however, the weighted-average method seldom is used in practice because it is not acceptable for tax purposes.

THE EQUITY METHOD

The equity method of accounting for intercorporate investments in common stock is intended to reflect the investor's changing equity or interest in the investee. This method is a rather curious one in that the balance in the investment account generally does not reflect either cost or market value, and it does not necessarily represent a pro rata share of the investee's book value. Instead, the investment is recorded at the initial purchase price and adjusted each period for the investor's share of the investee's profits or losses and the dividends declared by the investee.

Use of the Equity Method

APB Opinion No. 18 (as amended), "The Equity Method of Accounting for Investments in Common Stock" (APB 18), requires that the equity method be used for reporting investments in common stock of the following:[2]

1. Corporate joint ventures. A *corporate joint venture* is a corporation owned and operated by a small group of businesses, none of which owns a majority of the joint venture's common stock.

2. Companies in which the investor's voting stock interest gives the investor the "ability to exercise significant influence over operating and financial policies" of that company.

The second condition is the broader of the two and establishes the "significant influence" criterion. Because assessing the degree of influence may be difficult in some cases, **APB 18** establishes a 20 percent rule.[3] In the absence of evidence to the contrary, an investor holding 20 percent or more of an investee's voting stock is presumed to have the ability to exercise significant influence over the investee. On the other hand, an investor holding less than 20 percent of an investee's voting stock is presumed not to have the ability to exercise significant influence in the absence of evidence to the contrary.

In most cases, an investment of 20 to 50 percent in another company's voting stock is reported under the equity method. Notice, however, that the 20 percent rule does not apply if other evidence is available that provides a better indication of the ability or inability of the investor to significantly influence the investee.

Regardless of the level of ownership, the equity method is not appropriate if the investor's influence is limited by circumstances other than stock ownership, such as bankruptcy of the investee or severe restrictions placed on the availability of a foreign investee's earnings or assets by a foreign government.

Investor's Equity in the Investee

Under the equity method, the investor records its investment at the original cost. This amount is adjusted periodically for changes in the investee's stockholders' equity occasioned by the investee's profits, losses, and dividend declarations. The effect of the investee's income, losses, and dividends on the investor's investment account and other accounts can be characterized in the following way:

Reported by Investee	Effect on Investor's Accounts
Net income	Record income from investment Increase investment account
Net loss	Record loss from investment Decrease investment account
Dividend declaration	Record asset (cash or receivable) Decrease investment account

Recognition of Income

Under the equity method, the investor's income statement includes the investor's proportionate share of the investee's income or loss each period. The carrying amount of the investment is adjusted by the same amount to reflect the change in the net assets of the investee resulting from the investee's income.

---

[2] *Accounting Principles Board Opinion No. 18*, "The Equity Method of Accounting for Investments in Common Stock," March 1971, para. 16.
[3] Ibid., para. 17.

To illustrate, assume ABC Company acquires significant influence over XYZ Company by purchasing 20 percent of the common stock of the XYZ Company at the beginning of the year. XYZ reports income of $60,000 for the year. ABC records its $12,000 share of XYZ's income with the following entry:

(4)	Investment in XYZ Company Stock	12,000	
	Income from Investee		12,000
	Record income from investment in XYZ Company:		
	$60,000 × .20		

This entry may be referred to as the ***equity accrual*** and normally is made as an adjusting entry at the end of the period. If the investee reports a loss for the period, the investor recognizes its share of the loss and reduces the carrying amount of the investment by that amount.

Because of the ability to exercise significant influence over the policies of the investee, realization of income from the investment is considered to be sufficiently ensured to warrant recognition by the investor as the income is earned by the investee. This differs from the case in which the investor does not have the ability to significantly influence the investee and the investment must be reported using the cost method; in that case, income from the investment is recognized only upon declaration of a dividend by the investee.

Recognition of Dividends

Dividends from an investment are not recognized as income under the equity method because the investor's share of the investee's income is recognized as it is earned by the investee. Instead, such dividends are viewed as distributions of previously recognized income that already has been capitalized in the carrying amount of the investment. The investor must consider investee dividends declared as a reduction in its equity in the investee and, accordingly, reduce the carrying amount of its investment. In effect, all dividends from the investee are treated as liquidating dividends under the equity method. Thus, if ABC Company owns 20 percent of XYZ Company's common stock and XYZ declares and pays a $20,000 dividend, the following entry is recorded on the books of ABC to record its share of the dividend:

(5)	Cash	4,000	
	Investment in XYZ Company Stock		4,000
	Record receipt of dividend from XYZ: $20,000 × .20		

Carrying Amount of the Investment

Because the investment account on the investor's books under the equity method is adjusted for the investor's share of the investee's income or losses and dividends, the carrying amount of the investment usually is not the same as the original cost to the investor. Only if the investee pays dividends in the exact amount of its earnings will the carrying amount of the investment subsequent to acquisition be equal to its original cost. If the earnings of the investee subsequent to investment by the investor exceed the investee's dividends during that time, the carrying amount of the investment will be greater than its original cost. On the other hand, if the investee's dividends exceed its income, the carrying amount of the investment will be less than its original cost.

To illustrate the change in the carrying amount of the investment under the equity method, assume that after ABC acquires 20 percent of XYZ's common stock for $100,000, XYZ earns income of $60,000 and pays dividends of $20,000. The carrying amount of the investment starts with the original cost of $100,000 and is increased by ABC's share of XYZ's income, which is $12,000. The carrying amount is reduced by ABC's share of XYZ's dividends, which is $4,000. Thus, the carrying amount of the investment at the end of the period is $108,000 ($100,000 + $12,000 − $4,000). The investment account on ABC's books appears as follows:

Investment in XYZ Common Stock			
Original cost	100,000		
Equity accrual		Dividends	
($60,000 × .20)	12,000	($20,000 × .20)	4,000
Ending balance	108,000		

The $8,000 increase in the investment account represents ABC's 20 percent share of XYZ's undistributed earnings ($60,000 − $20,000) for the period.

Acquisition at Interim Date

When an investment is purchased, the investor begins accruing income from the investee under the equity method at the date of acquisition. No income earned by the investee before the date of acquisition of the investment may be accrued by the investor. When the purchase occurs between balance sheet dates, the amount of income earned by the investee from the date of acquisition to the end of the fiscal period may need to be estimated by the investor in recording the equity accrual.

To illustrate, assume that ABC acquires 20 percent of XYZ's common stock on October 1 for $109,000. XYZ earns income of $60,000 uniformly throughout the year and pays dividends of $20,000 on December 20. The carrying amount of the investment is increased by $3,000, which represents ABC's share of XYZ's net income earned between October 1 and December 31, and is decreased by $4,000 as a result of dividends received at year end:

Investment in XYZ Common Stock			
Original cost	109,000		
Equity accrual		Dividends	
($60,000 × ¼ ×.20)	3,000	($20,000 × .20)	4,000
Ending balance	108,000		

Difference between Cost of Investment and Underlying Book Value

When one corporation buys the common stock of another, the purchase price normally is based on the market price of the shares acquired rather than the book values of the investee's assets and liabilities. As a result, there often is a difference between the cost of the investment to the investor and the book value of the investor's proportionate share of the underlying net assets of the investee. This difference is referred to as a ***differential***.

There are several reasons that the cost of an investment might exceed the book value of the underlying net assets and give rise to a positive differential. One reason is that the investee's assets may be worth more than their book values. Another reason could be the existence of unrecorded goodwill associated with the excess earning power of the investee. In either case, the portion of the differential pertaining to each asset of the investee, including goodwill, must be ascertained. When the equity method is applied, that portion of the differential pertaining to limited-life assets of the investee, including identifiable intangibles, must be amortized over the remaining economic lives of those assets. Any portion of the differential that represents goodwill (referred to as *equity-method goodwill*) is not amortized or written off because of impairment. However, an impairment loss on the investment itself should be recognized if it suffers a decline in value that is other than temporary.

Amortization or Write-Off of the Differential

When the equity method is used, each portion of the differential must be treated in the same manner as the investee treats the assets or liabilities to which the differential relates. Thus, any portion of the differential related to depreciable or amortizable assets of the investee should be amortized over the remaining time that the cost of the asset is being allocated by the investee. Amortization of the differential associated with depreciable or amortizable assets of the investee is necessary on the investor's books to reflect the decline in the future benefits the investor expects from that portion of the investment cost associated with those assets. The investee recognizes the reduction in service potential of assets with limited lives as depreciation or amortization expense based on the amount it has invested in those assets. This reduction, in turn, is recognized by the investor through its share of the investee's net income. When the cost of the investor's interest in the investee's assets is greater than the investee's cost (as reflected in a positive differential), the additional cost must be amortized as well.

The approach to amortizing the differential that is most consistent with the idea of reflecting all aspects of the investment in just one line on the balance sheet and one line on the income statement is to reduce the income recognized by the investor from the investee and the balance of the investment account:

Income from Investee	XXX	
Investment in Common Stock of Investee		XXX

The differential represents the amount paid by the investor in excess of the book value of the investment and is included in the investment amount. Hence, the amortization or reduction of the differential involves the reduction of the investment account. At the same time, the investor's net income must be reduced by an equal amount to recognize that a portion of the amount paid for the investment has expired.

Treatment of the Differential Illustrated

To illustrate the equity method when the cost of the investment exceeds the book value of the underlying net assets, assume that Ajax Corporation purchases 40 percent of the common stock of Barclay Company on January 1, 20X1, for $200,000. Barclay has net assets on that date with a book value of $400,000 and fair value of $465,000. Ajax's share of the book value of Barclay's net assets at acquisition is $160,000 ($400,000 × .40). A $40,000 differential is computed as follows:

Cost of investment to Ajax	$ 200,000
Book value of Ajax's share of Barclay's net assets	(160,000)
Differential	$ 40,000

The $65,000 excess of the fair value over the book value of Barclay's net assets consists of a $15,000 increase in the value of Barclay's land and a $50,000 increase in the value of Barclay's equipment. Ajax's 40 percent share of the increase in the value of Barclay's assets is as follows:

	Total Increase	Ajax's 40% Share
Land	$15,000	$ 6,000
Equipment	50,000	20,000
	$65,000	$26,000

Thus, $26,000 of the differential is assigned to land and equipment, with the remaining $14,000 attributed to goodwill. The allocation of the differential can be illustrated as follows:

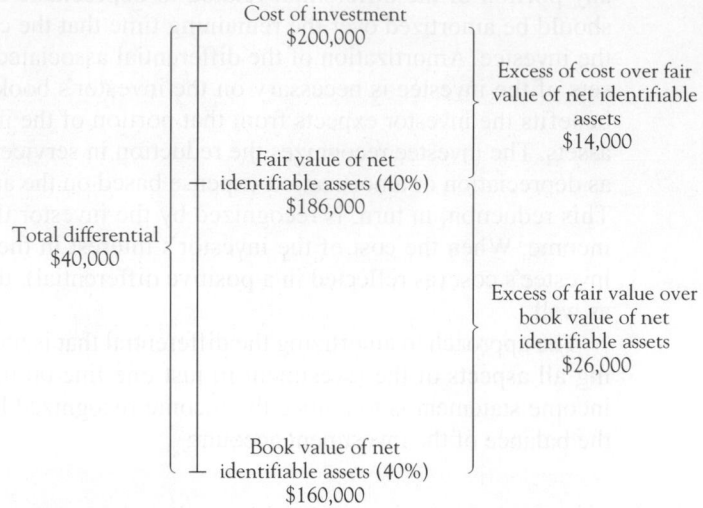

Cost of investment
$200,000

Excess of cost over fair value of net identifiable assets
$14,000

Fair value of net identifiable assets (40%)
$186,000

Total differential
$40,000

Excess of fair value over book value of net identifiable assets
$26,000

Book value of net identifiable assets (40%)
$160,000

Although the differential relates to assets of Barclay, the additional cost incurred by Ajax to acquire a claim on the assets of Barclay is reflected in Ajax's investment in Barclay. No separate differential account is established, and no separate accounts are recorded on Ajax's books to reflect the apportionment of the differential to specific assets of Ajax. Similarly, no separate expense account is established on Ajax's books. Amortization or write-off of the differential is accomplished by reducing Ajax's investment account and the income Ajax recognizes from its investment in Barclay.

Because land has an unlimited economic life, the portion of the differential related to land is not amortized. The $20,000 portion of the differential related to Barclay's equipment is amortized over the equipment's remaining life. If the equipment's remaining life is five years, Ajax's annual amortization of the differential is $4,000 ($20,000 ÷ 5).

Beginning in 1970, financial reporting standards required that goodwill be amortized over its useful life, not to exceed 40 years. In 2001, however, the FASB issued **Statement No. 142**, "Goodwill and Other Intangible Assets," under which equity method goodwill is neither amortized nor written off. That portion of the differential remains imbedded in the investment account. Thus, in this example, the only amortization of the differential is the $4,000 related to Barclay's equipment.

Barclay declares dividends of $20,000 during 20X1 and at year-end reports net income of $80,000 for the year. Using the equity method, Ajax records the following entries on its books during 20X1:

(6)	Investment in Barclay Stock	200,000	
	Cash		200,000
	Record purchase of Barclay stock.		
(7)	Cash	8,000	
	Investment in Barclay Stock		8,000
	Record dividend from Barclay: $20,000 × .40		
(8)	Investment in Barclay Stock	32,000	
	Income from Investee		32,000
	Record equity-method income: $80,000 × .40		

(9)	Income from Investee	4,000	
	Investment in Barclay Stock		4,000
	Amortize purchase differential related to equipment.		

With these entries, Ajax recognizes $28,000 of income from Barclay and adjusts its investment in Barclay to an ending balance of $220,000.

The amortization on Ajax's books of the portion of the differential related to Barclay's equipment is the same ($4,000) for each of the first five years (20X1 through 20X5). This amortization stops after 20X5 because this portion of the differential is fully amortized after five years.

Notice that no special accounts are established on the books of the investor with regard to the differential or the amortization of the differential. The only two accounts involved are "Income from Investee" and "Investment in Barclay Stock." As the Investment in Barclay Stock account is amortized, the differential between the carrying amount of the investment and the book value of the underlying net assets decreases.

Disposal of Differential-Related Assets

Although the differential is included on the books of the investor as part of the investment account, it relates to specific assets of the investee. Thus, if the investee disposes of any asset to which the differential relates, that portion of the differential must be removed from the investment account on the investor's books. When this is done, the investor's share of the investee's gain or loss on disposal of the asset must be adjusted to reflect the fact that the investor paid more for its proportionate share of that asset than did the investee. For example, if in the previous illustration Barclay Company sells the land to which $6,000 of Ajax's differential relates, Ajax does not recognize a full 40 percent of the gain or loss on the sale. Assume that Barclay originally had purchased the land in 20X0 for $75,000 and sells the land in 20X2 for $125,000. Barclay recognizes a gain on the sale of $50,000, and Ajax's share of that gain is 40 percent, or $20,000. The portion of the gain actually recognized by Ajax, however, must be adjusted as follows because of the amount in excess of book value paid by Ajax for its investment in Barclay:

Ajax's share of Barclay's reported gain	$20,000
Portion of Ajax's differential related to the land	(6,000)
Gain to be recognized by Ajax	$14,000

Thus, if Barclay reports net income (including gain on sale of land) of $150,000 for 20X2, Ajax records the following entries (disregarding dividends and amortization of the differential relating to equipment):

(10)	Investment in Barclay Stock	60,000	
	Income from Investee		60,000
	Record equity-method income: $150,000 × .40		

(11)	Income from Investee	6,000	
	Investment in Barclay Stock		6,000
	Remove differential related to Barclay's land sold.		

The same approach applies when dealing with a limited-life asset. The unamortized portion of the original differential relating to the asset sold is removed from the investment account, and the investor's share of the investee's income is adjusted by that amount.

Note that the investor does not separately report its share of ordinary gains or losses included in the investee's net income, such as the gain on the sale of the fixed asset or the write-off of the unamortized purchase differential. Consistent with the idea of using only a single line in the income statement to report the impact of the investee's activities on the investor, all such items are included in the Income from Investee account. Current standards do require the investor to report its share of an investee's extraordinary gains and losses, prior-period adjustments, and elements of other comprehensive income, if material to the investor, as separate items in the same manner as the investor reports its own.

Impairment of Investment Value

As with many assets, accounting standards require that equity-method investments be written down if their value is impaired. If the market value of the investment declines materially below its equity-method carrying amount, and the decline in value is considered other than temporary, the carrying amount of the investment should be written down to the market value and a loss recognized. The new lower value serves as a starting point for continued application of the equity method. Subsequent recoveries in the value of the investment may not be recognized.

Changes in the Number of Shares Held

Some changes in the number of common shares held by an investor are handled easily under the equity method, but others require a bit more attention. A change resulting from a stock dividend, split, or reverse split is treated in the same way as under the cost method. No formal accounting recognition is required on the books of the investor. On the other hand, purchases and sales of shares do require formal recognition.

Purchases of Additional Shares

A purchase of additional shares of a common stock already held by an investor and accounted for using the equity method simply involves adding the cost of the new shares to the investment account and applying the equity method in the normal manner from the date of acquisition forward. The new and old investments in the same stock are combined for financial reporting purposes. Income accruing to the new shares can be recognized by the investor only from the date of acquisition forward.

To illustrate, assume that ABC Company purchases 20 percent of XYZ Company's common stock on January 2, 20X1, and another 10 percent on July 1, 20X1, and that the stock purchases are at book value. If XYZ earns income of $25,000 from January 2 to June 30 and earns $35,000 from July 1 to December 31, the total income recognized in 20X1 by ABC from its investment in XYZ is $15,500, computed as follows:

Income, January 2 to June 30: $25,000 × .20	$ 5,000
Income, July 1 to December 31: $35,000 × .30	10,500
Income from investment, 20X1	$15,500

If XYZ declares and pays a $10,000 dividend on January 15 and again on July 15, ABC reduces its investment account by $2,000 ($10,000 × .20) on January 15 and by $3,000 ($10,000 × .30) on July 15.

When an investment in common stock is carried using the cost method and purchases of additional shares give the investor the ability to significantly influence the investee, a retroactive switch from the cost method to the equity method is required. This change to the equity method must be applied retroactively to the date of the first acquisition of the investee's stock.

To illustrate a change to the equity method, assume that Aron Corporation purchases 15 percent of Zenon Company's common stock on January 2, 20X1, and another 10 percent on January 2, 20X4. Furthermore, assume that Aron switches to the equity method on

January 2, 20X4, because it gains the ability to significantly influence Zenon. Given the following income and dividend data for Zenon, and assuming the purchases of stock are at book value, the investment income figures reported by Aron originally and as restated are as follows:

	Zenon		Investment Income Reported by Aron	
Year	Net Income	Dividends	Originally under Cost[a]	Restated under Equity[b]
20X1	$15,000	$10,000	$1,500	$2,250
20X2	18,000	10,000	1,500	2,700
20X3	22,000	10,000	1,500	3,300
	$55,000	$30,000	$4,500	$8,250

[a]15 percent of Zenon's dividends for the year.
[b]15 percent of Zenon's net income for the year.

Thus, in Aron's 20X4 financial report, the comparative statements for 20X1, 20X2, and 20X3 are restated to include Aron's 15 percent share of Zenon's profit and to exclude from income Aron's share of dividends recognized under the cost method. In addition, the investment account and retained earnings of Aron are restated as if the equity method had been applied from the date of the original acquisition. This restatement is accomplished on Aron's books with the following journal entry on January 2, 20X4:

(12)	Investment in Zenon Company Stock	3,750	
	Retained Earnings		3,750
	Restate investment account from cost to equity method:		
	$8,250 − $4,500		

In 20X4, if Zenon reports net income of $30,000, Aron's investment income is $7,500 (25 percent of Zenon's net income).

Sales of Shares

The sale of all or part of an investment in common stock carried using the equity method is treated the same as the sale of any noncurrent asset. First, the investment account is adjusted to the date of sale for the investor's share of the investee's current earnings. Then, a gain or loss is recognized for the difference between the proceeds received and the carrying amount of the shares sold.

If only part of the investment is sold, the investor must decide whether to continue using the equity method to account for the remaining shares or to change to the cost method. The choice is based on evidence available after the sale as to whether the investor still is able to exercise significant influence over the investee. If the equity method no longer is appropriate after the date of sale, the carrying value of the remaining investment is treated as the cost of that investment, and the cost method is applied in the normal manner from the date of sale forward. No retroactive restatement of the investment to actual cost is made.

THE COST AND EQUITY METHODS COMPARED

Some of the key features of the cost and equity methods are summarized and compared in Figure 2–2.

The cost method of accounting for intercorporate investments is consistent with the historical cost basis for most other assets. This method is subject to the usual criticisms leveled against

FIGURE 2–2
Summary Comparison of the Cost and Equity Methods

Item	Cost Method	Equity Method
Recorded amount of investment at date of acquisition	Original cost	Original cost
Usual carrying amount of investment subsequent to acquisition	Original cost	Original cost increased (decreased) by investor's share of investee's income (loss) and decreased by investor's share of investee's dividends and by amortization or write-off of the differential
Differential	Not amortized or written off	Amortized or written down if related to limited-life assets of investee or assets disposed of
Income recognition by investor	Investor's share of investee's dividends declared from earnings since acquisition	Investor's share of investee's earnings since acquisition, whether distributed or not, reduced by any amortization or write-off of the differential
Investee dividends from earnings since acquisition by investor	Income	Reduction of investment
Investee dividends in excess of earnings since acquisition by investor	Reduction of investment	Reduction of investment

historical cost. In particular, questions arise as to the relevance of reporting the purchase price of an investment acquired some years earlier. The cost method does conform more closely to the traditional accounting and legal views of the realization of income in that the investee's earnings are not available to the investor until transferred as dividends. Income based on dividend distributions sometimes can be manipulated, however. The significant influence criterion, which must be met to use the equity method, takes into consideration that the declaration of dividends by the investee can be influenced by the investor. Recognizing equity-method income from the investee without regard to investee dividends provides protection against manipulating the investor's net income by influencing investee dividend declarations.

On the other hand, the equity method is criticized because the asset valuation departs from historical cost but stops short of a market value approach. Instead, the carrying amount of the investment is composed of a number of components and is not similar to the valuation of any other assets.

Over the years there has been considerable criticism of the use of the equity method as a substitute for the consolidation of certain types of subsidiaries. Although the equity method has been viewed as a "one-line consolidation," the amount of detail reported is considerably different under the equity method than with consolidation. For example, an investor would report the same equity-method income from the following two investees even though their income statements are quite different in composition:

	Investee 1	Investee 2
Sales	$50,000	$ 500,000
Operating Expenses	(30,000)	(620,000)
Operating Income (Loss)	$20,000	$(120,000)
Gain on Sale of Land		140,000
Net Income	$20,000	$ 20,000

Similarly, an investment in the stock of another company is reported under the equity method as a single amount in the balance sheet of the investor regardless of the asset and capital structure of the investee. In the past, some companies borrowed heavily through unconsolidated subsidiaries and reported their investments in the subsidiaries using the equity method. Because the debt was not reported in these situations, concerns were raised over the use of the equity method to facilitate "off-balance sheet" financing.

As a result of these concerns, the Financial Accounting Standards Board eliminated the use of the equity method for reporting investments in subsidiaries by requiring the consolidation of virtually all majority-owned subsidiaries. The FASB is expected in the future to study the use of the equity method for investments in corporate joint ventures and other types of investees.

INTERESTS OTHER THAN INVESTMENTS IN COMMON STOCK

Increasingly in recent years, companies have developed interests in other entities that are not represented by investments in common stock. Such interests may involve equity investments in partnerships, or the interests might reflect no ownership at all. Because of the diversity and complexity of these types of arrangements, the accounting rules, if they exist at all, are often complex or, in some cases, not well specified.

Investments in Partnerships

FASB pronouncements generally relate to corporations rather than partnerships. Thus, companies holding equity investments in partnerships generally have more flexibility but less guidance in reporting their investments.

Equity investments in partnerships do not provide the clear-cut measures found with common stock investments. An investment in the common stock of a corporation almost always provides for a proportionate share of profits, a proportionate share of distributions, a proportionate claim on net assets, and proportionate voting rights. The same is not true of equity investments in partnerships. A partner contributing a specified share of the partnership's capital may have a different share of profits (but not necessarily the same share of losses), a different proportion of distributions (drawing rights), and a greater or lesser degree of control than indicated by the capital share. For partnerships, all of these ownership rights are determined by the partnership agreement (or state law) rather than by percentage ownership. Thus, the convenient measures available to determine the financial reporting methods for investments in common stock are not available for investments in partnerships.

Companies with ownership investments in partnerships choose one of several methods of reporting those investments:

1. Cost method
2. Equity method
3. Pro rata consolidation
4. Consolidation

Reporting Methods Illustrated

As an illustration of the methods of accounting for ownership investments in partnerships, assume that on January 1, 20X5, Albers Company invests $200,000 for a 40 percent share of initial capital of AB Partnership and a 40 percent share of the profits and losses. For the year 20X5, Albers reports the following, excluding its investment in AB Partnership:

Revenues, 20X5	$ 700,000
Expenses, 20X5	400,000
Assets, 12/31/20X5 (excluding investment in AB)	1,000,000
Liabilities, 12/31/20X5	300,000

Also assume that the AB Partnership reports $80,000 of revenues and $50,000 of expenses; no amounts are distributed to or withdrawn by the partners. The financial statements for AB Partnership and Albers Company's financial statements under several possible reporting alternatives are presented in Figure 2–3 on page 64.

FIGURE 2–3   **Reporting Alternatives for Equity Interests in Partnerships**

Balance Sheet

	AB Partnership	Albers Company Consolidated Balance Sheet			
		Cost Method	Equity Method	Pro Rata Consolidation	Full Consolidation
Assets	$630,000	$1,000,000	$1,000,000	$ 1,252,000[a]	$ 1,630,000[b]
Investment in AB Partnership		200,000	212,000[c]		
	$630,000	$1,200,000	$1,212,000	$ 1,252,000	$ 1,630,000
Liabilities	$100,000	$ 300,000	$ 300,000	$ 340,000[d]	$ 400,000[e]
Interest of Outside Partner					318,000[f]
Owners' Equity	530,000[g]	900,000	912,000[h]	912,000[h]	912,000[h]
	$630,000	$1,200,000	$1,212,000	$ 1,252,000	$ 1,630,000

[a] $1,252,000 = $1,000,000 + ($630,000 × .40)
[b] $1,630,000 = $1,000,000 + $630,000
[c] $212,000 = $200,000 + ($30,000 × .40)
[d] $340,000 = $300,000 + ($100,000 × .40)
[e] $400,000 = $300,000 + $100,000
[f] $318,000 = $530,000 × .60
[g] Capital, Albers Company $212,000
    Capital, Outside Partner $318,000
[h] $912,000 = $900,000 + ($30,000 × .40)

Income Statement

	AB Partnership	Consolidated Income Statement			
		Cost Method	Equity Method	Pro Rata Consolidation	Full Consolidation
Revenues	$80,000	$700,000	$700,000	$732,000[a]	$780,000[b]
Expenses	(50,000)	(400,000)	(400,000)	(420,000)[c]	(450,000)[d]
Income from Partnership			12,000[e]		
Income to Outside Partner					(18,000)[f]
Net Income	$30,000[g]	$300,000	$312,000	$312,000	$312,000

[a] $732,000 = $700,000 + ($80,000 × .40)
[b] $780,000 = $700,000 + $80,000
[c] $420,000 = $400,000 + ($50,000 × .40)
[d] $450,000 = $400,000 + $50,000
[e] $12,000 = $30,000 × .40
[f] $18,000 = $30,000 × .60
[g] Allocation of income:
    Albers (40%) $12,000
    Outside Partner (60%) $18,000

The cost and equity methods of accounting for investments in partnerships are applied largely in the same manner as for investments in common stock. In the AB Partnership example, no income is distributed by the partnership (withdrawn by the partners), and, accordingly, the investor recognizes no income from the partnership under the cost method. The equity method is more generally used in accounting for partnership interests, and the investor recognizes its share of partnership income even though the income is not withdrawn from the partnership.

Authoritative bodies generally view pro rata consolidation as an unacceptable reporting method for investments in other corporations (e.g., corporate joint ventures). Nevertheless, pro rata consolidation has been used in practice to at least a small degree to account for certain investments in common stock and to a greater degree to account for investments in partnerships and unincorporated joint ventures (e.g., two or three partners with nearly equal investments or profit shares). This method involves combining the investor's proportionate share of the partnership's assets, liabilities, revenues, and expenses with those of the investor. This approach provides the same overall results as the equity method (e.g., same net income and net assets), but the details within the financial statements differ.

Full consolidation of a partnership with one of the partners has not been widespread in practice. This method involves combining the full amount of the partnership's assets, liabilities, revenues, and expenses with the like items of one of the partners. Because the consolidating partner has only a partial claim on the income and net assets of the partnership, the claim of the outside partner(s) must be recognized in the consolidated income statement and balance sheet, as indicated in Figure 2–3. Also as shown in Figure 2–3, full consolidation leads to the same overall results as the equity method and pro rata consolidation. However, while net income (after deducting income to outside partners) and net assets (after deducting the claim of outside partners) are the same under each of the three methods, the details of the financial statements differ.

Standards for Reporting Partnership Interests

The method of reporting partnership interests can have a significant effect on the financial statements, especially for companies that conduct a large portion of their activities through partnerships (such as some construction companies). The cost method provides little information relating to the partnership investment and, thus, is generally not an appropriate method to use. The equity method can hide partnership debt and disguise the type of income earned by the partnership because, in effect, the partnership assets and liabilities are netted against one another and the partner's share is reported as a single line in the balance sheet; similarly, all of the partnership's income and expense items are combined and the partner's share of income is reported as a single line in the income statement.

Both pro rata consolidation, especially for unincorporated joint ventures, and full consolidation have received significant support for reporting partnership interests. Unfortunately, partnership arrangements relating to control, veto power, share of profits and losses, distribution of different types of assets, responsibility for partnership debt, and other factors are often so complex and varied that establishing standards for reporting partnership interests has been extremely difficult. The FASB is continuing to grapple with issues surrounding the reporting of interests in partnerships and joint ventures. One step the FASB has taken is to issue **Interpretation No. 46**, "Consolidation of Variable Interest Entities, an interpretation of **ARB No. 51**." While this pronouncement does not address accounting for partnership interests directly, its provisions do apply in some instances. Specifically, the interpretation establishes standards for when certain types of entities should be consolidated by a particular investor. This topic is discussed in Chapter 3.

Nonequity Interests in Other Entities

In some situations, a company may have a nonownership interest in another entity, which might be a corporation, partnership, or trust. For example, a company might share in the profits of another entity through an operating agreement without having an ownership interest. In another common situation, a company might sell assets to another entity and provide some type of guarantee with respect to those assets, the debt of the other entity, or the return to be received by the owners of the entity. Because of the diversity of the types of arrangements found in practice, no standards exist to cover all potential situations. Some existing standards may have an indirect bearing on various aspects of nonownership interests, such as the FASB's requirement to report guarantees at fair value. The FASB's pronouncements on variable interest entities and certain types of special-purpose entities are applicable in some cases to nonownership interests. Variable interest entities and special-purpose entities are discussed in Chapter 3.

ADDITIONAL CONSIDERATIONS RELATING TO THE EQUITY METHOD

Determination of Significant Influence

The general rule established in **APB 18** is that the equity method is appropriate when the investor, by virtue of its common stock interest in an investee, is able to exercise significant influence over the operating and financial policies of the investee. In the absence of other evidence, common stock ownership of 20 percent or more is viewed as indicating that the investor is able to exercise significant influence over the investee. However, the APB also stated a number of factors that could constitute other evidence of the ability to exercise significant influence:[4]

1. Representation on board of directors.
2. Participation in policy making.
3. Material intercompany transactions.
4. Interchange of managerial personnel.
5. Technological dependency.
6. Size of investment in relation to concentration of other shareholdings.

Conversely, the FASB provides in **FASB Interpretation No. 35** some examples of evidence that an investor is unable to exercise significant influence over an investee.[5] These situations include legal or regulatory challenges to the investor's influence by the investee, agreement by the investor to give up important shareholder rights, concentration of majority ownership among a small group of owners who disregard the views of the investor, and unsuccessful attempts by the investor to obtain information from the investee or representation on the investee's board of directors.

Unrealized Intercompany Profits

The equity method as applied under **APB 18** often is referred to as a *one-line consolidation* because (*a*) the investor's income and stockholders' equity are the same as if the investee were consolidated and (*b*) all equity method adjustments are made through the investment and related income accounts, which are reported in only a single line in the balance sheet and a single line in the income statement.[6] The view currently taken in consolidation is that intercompany sales do not result in the realization of income until the intercompany profit is confirmed in some way, usually through a transaction with an unrelated third party. For example, if a parent company sells inventory to a subsidiary at a profit, that profit cannot be recognized in the consolidated financial statements until it is confirmed by resale of the inventory to an external party. Because profits from sales to related companies are viewed from a consolidated perspective as being unrealized until there is a resale to unrelated parties, such profits must be eliminated when preparing consolidated financial statements.

The consolidated financial statements are not the only ones affected, however, because **APB 18** requires that the income of an investor that reports an investment using the equity method must be the same as if the investee were consolidated. Therefore, the investor's equity-method income from the investee must be adjusted for unconfirmed profits on intercompany sales as well. The term for the application of the equity method that includes the adjustment for unrealized profit on sales to affiliates is *fully adjusted equity method*.

---

[4] **APB 18**, para. 17.

[5] *Financial Accounting Standards Board Interpretation No. 35*, "Criteria for Applying the Equity Method of Accounting for Investments in Common Stock," May 1981, para. 4.

[6] Although **APB 18** established the requirement for an equity-method investor's income and stockholders' equity to be the same as if the investee were consolidated, the FASB's recent decision to not permit the write-off of equity-method goodwill may lead to differences in situations in which such goodwill has been impaired.

Adjusting for Unrealized Intercompany Profits

An intercompany sale normally is recorded on the books of the selling affiliate in the same manner as any other sale, including the recognition of profit. In applying the equity method, any intercompany profit remaining unrealized at the end of the period must be deducted from the amount of income that otherwise would be reported.

Under the one-line consolidation approach, the income recognized from the investment and the carrying amount of the investment are reduced to remove the effects of the unrealized intercompany profits. In future periods when the intercompany profit actually is realized, the entry is reversed.

Unrealized Profit Adjustments Illustrated

To illustrate the adjustment for unrealized intercompany profits under the equity method, assume that Palit Corporation owns 40 percent of the common stock of Label Manufacturing. During 20X1, Palit sells inventory to Label for $10,000; the inventory originally cost Palit $7,000. Label resells one-third of the inventory to outsiders during 20X1 and retains the other two-thirds in its ending inventory. The amount of unrealized profit is computed as follows:

Total intercompany profit	$10,000 − $7,000 = $3,000
Unrealized portion	$3,000 × ⅔ = $2,000

Assuming that Label reports net income of $60,000 for 20X1 and declares no dividends, the following entries are recorded on Palit's books at the end of 20X1:

December 31, 20X1

(13)	Investment in Label Manufacturing Stock	24,000	
	Income from Label Manufacturing		24,000
	Record equity-method income:		
	$60,000 × .40		
(14)	Income from Label Manufacturing	2,000	
	Investment in Label Manufacturing Stock		2,000
	Remove unrealized intercompany profit.		

If all the remaining inventory is sold in 20X2, the following entry is made on Palit's books at the end of 20X2 to record the realization of the previously unrealized intercompany profit:

December 31, 20X2

(15)	Investment in Label Manufacturing Stock	2,000	
	Income from Label Manufacturing		2,000
	Recognize realized intercompany profit.		

Additional Requirements of APB 18

APB 18, the governing pronouncement dealing with equity-method reporting, includes several additional requirements:

1. The investor's share of the investee's extraordinary items and prior-period adjustments should be reported as such by the investor, if material.
2. If an investor's share of investee losses exceeds the carrying amount of the investment, the equity method should be discontinued once the investment has been reduced to zero.

No further losses are to be recognized by the investor unless the investor is committed to provide further financial support for the investee or unless the investee's imminent return to profitability appears assured. If, after the equity method has been suspended, the investee reports net income, the investor again should apply the equity method, but only after the investor's share of net income equals its share of losses not previously recognized.

3. Preferred dividends of the investee should be deducted from the investee's net income if declared or, whether declared or not, if the preferred stock is cumulative, before the investor computes its share of investee earnings.

APB 18 also includes a number of required financial statement disclosures. When using the equity method, the investor must disclose:

1. The name and percentage ownership of each investee.
2. The investor's accounting policies with respect to its investments in common stock, including the reasons for any departures from the 20 percent criterion established by **APB 18**.
3. The amount and accounting treatment of any differential.
4. The aggregate market value of each identified nonsubsidiary investment where a quoted market price is available.
5. Either separate statements for or summarized information as to assets, liabilities, and results of operations of corporate joint ventures of the investor, if material in the aggregate.

Investor's Share of Other Comprehensive Income

When an investor uses the equity method to account for its investment in another company, the investor's comprehensive income should include its proportionate share of each of the amounts reported as "Other Comprehensive Income" by the investee. For example, assume that Ajax Corporation purchases 40 percent of the common stock of Barclay Company on January 1, 20X1. For the year 20X1, Barclay reports net income of $80,000 and comprehensive income of $115,000, which includes other comprehensive income (in addition to net income) of $35,000. This other comprehensive income (OCI) reflects an unrealized $35,000 gain (net of tax) resulting from an increase in the fair value of an investment in stock classified as available-for-sale under the criteria established by **FASB 115**. In addition to recording the normal equity-method entries, Ajax recognizes its proportionate share of the unrealized gain on available-for-sale securities reported by Barclay during 20X1 with the following entry:

(16)	Investment in Barclay Stock	14,000	
	Unrealized Gain on Investments of Investee (OCI)		14,000
	Recognize share of investee's unrealized gain on available-for-sale securities.		

Entry (16) has no effect on Ajax's net income for 20X1, but it does increase Ajax's other comprehensive income, and thus its total comprehensive income, by $14,000. Ajax will make a similar entry at the end of each period for its proportionate share of any increase or decrease in Barclay's accumulated unrealized holding gain.

Tax Allocation Procedures

Intercompany income accruals and dividend transfers must be taken into consideration in computing income tax expense for the period. The impact depends on the level of ownership and the filing status of the companies. Because corporations generally are permitted to deduct 80 percent of the dividends received (100 percent if at least 80 percent of all voting stock is owned), they are taxed at relatively low effective tax rates (20 percent times the marginal tax rate) on those dividends.

When an investor and an investee file a consolidated tax return, intercompany dividends and income accruals are eliminated in determining taxable income. Deferred tax accruals, therefore, are not needed even though temporary differences occur between the recognition of investment income by the investor and realization through dividend transfers from the investee. Consolidated tax returns may be filed when an investor owns at least 80 percent of a subsidiary's stock and elects to file a consolidated return. Otherwise, an investor and investee must file separate returns.

If an investor and an investee file separate tax returns, the investor is taxed on the dividends received from the investee rather than on the amount of investment income reported. The amount of tax expense reported in the income statement of the investor each period should be based on income from the investor's own operations as well as on income recognized from its intercompany investments. **FASB Statement No. 109**, "Accounting for Income Taxes" (FASB 109), specifies those situations in which additional deferred tax accruals are required as a result of temporary differences in the recognition of income for financial reporting purposes and that used in determining taxable income.

Tax Expense under the Cost Method

If the investor reports its investment using the cost method, income tax expense recorded by the investor on the investment income and the amount of taxes actually paid both are based on dividends received from the investee. No interperiod income tax allocation is required under the cost method because the income is recognized in the same period for both financial reporting and tax purposes; there are no temporary differences.

Tax Expense under the Equity Method

If the investment is reported using the equity method and separate tax returns are filed, the investor reports its share of the investee's income in the income statement but reports only its share of the investee's dividends in the tax return. When the amount of the investee's dividends is different from its earnings, a temporary difference arises and interperiod tax allocation is required for the investor. In this situation, deferred income taxes must be recognized on the difference between the equity-method income reported by the investor in its income statement and the dividend income reported in its tax return. Current accounting standards generally require that the investor's reported income tax expense be computed as if all the investment income recognized by the investor under the equity method actually had been received. Thus, the investor's tax expense is recorded in excess of the taxes actually paid when the investee's earnings are greater than its dividends and normally is recorded at less than taxes actually paid when dividends are greater than earnings.

The requirements for computing the investor's income tax expense on income from intercorporate investments in common stock are summarized in Figure 2–4.

Treatment of Income Taxes Illustrated

As an example of the treatment of income taxes related to intercorporate investments in which the investor and investee each file separate tax returns, assume that T Company owns 20 percent of the common stock of S Company. S reports net income of $100,000 (after deducting its income taxes) for 20X1 and declares dividends of $30,000. T reports income

FIGURE 2–4
Investor Income Tax Expense Computation

Type of Investee	Computation of Investor's Income Tax Expense Related to Income from Investee
Equity-method investees	Ordinary tax rate × (investor's share of investee net income − dividend deduction)[a]
Cost-method investees	Ordinary tax rate × (dividends received − dividend deduction)

[a]Need not accrue taxes if the earnings will be distributed in a tax-free transfer or if there is evidence that the earnings of a foreign subsidiary or foreign corporate joint venture are to be reinvested permanently.

before taxes of $500,000 from its own operations, not including any investment income. Assume that T's effective combined federal and state tax rate is 40 percent. T computes its income taxes payable as follows:

Separate operating income	$500,000
Dividend income: $30,000 × .20	6,000
Total income	$506,000
Dividend deduction: $6,000 × .80	(4,800)
Taxable income	$501,200
Effective tax rate	× .40
Income taxes payable	$200,480

The income tax expense to be reported in T's 20X1 income statement and the deferred tax liability to be reported in T's year-end balance sheet are computed as follows:

	Reporting Method	
	Cost	**Equity**
Computation of T's reported accounting income before taxes		
Separate operating income	$500,000	$500,000
Income from investee	6,000	20,000
Income before taxes	$506,000	$520,000
Computation of tax expense		
Income before taxes	$506,000	$520,000
Income not taxable:		
($6,000 × .80)	(4,800)	
($20,000 × .80)		(16,000)
Taxable income per books	$501,200	$504,000
Income tax rate	× .40	× .40
Income tax expense	$200,480	$201,600
Computation of deferred tax liability		
Taxable income per books	$501,200	$504,000
Taxable income per tax return	(501,200)	(501,200)
Temporary difference	$ 0	$ 2,800
Income tax rate		× .40
Deferred tax liability	$ 0	$ 1,120

The journal entry on T's books to record income tax expense for 20X1 under equity-method reporting is:

(17)	Income Tax Expense	201,600	
	Income Taxes Payable		200,480
	Deferred Tax Liability		1,120
	Record income tax expense for 20X1: $1,120 = $2,800 × .40		

Notice that if the investor carries its investment at cost, interperiod tax allocation is not required because the only difference between accounting and taxable income is due to the dividend deduction, which is not a temporary difference. If, however, the investment is carried using the equity method, the investor recognizes its proportionate share of investee income but pays taxes only on the dividends received. A portion of the difference between the equity-method income recognized and the dividends received is viewed as a temporary difference, and the investor's income tax expense for financial reporting purposes is based on its income taxes actually payable for the year plus the tax effects of any temporary differences.

Accounting for Investments in Subsidiaries

Companies are free to adopt whatever procedures they wish in accounting for investments in controlled subsidiaries on their books. Because investments in consolidated subsidiaries are eliminated when consolidated statements are prepared, the consolidated statements are not affected by the procedures used to account for the investments on the parent's books.

In practice, companies follow three different approaches in accounting for their consolidated subsidiaries:

1. Fully adjusted equity method.
2. Modified version of the equity method.
3. Cost method.

Several modified versions of the equity method are found in practice, and all usually are referred to as the ***modified equity method***. Some companies apply the equity method without making adjustments for unrealized intercompany profits and the amortization of the differential. Others adjust for the amortization of the differential but omit the adjustments for unrealized intercompany profits. This latter approach is referred to in this text as the ***basic equity method*** and is used through many of the later chapters on consolidations. While modified versions of the equity method are not acceptable for financial reporting purposes, they may provide some clerical savings for the parent if used on the books when consolidation of the subsidiary is required.

Summary of Key Concepts	Ownership of intercorporate investments in common stock can lead to the preparation of consolidated financial statements or to use of the equity method or cost method (adjusted to market, if necessary) for financial reporting purposes. Consolidation generally is appropriate if one entity controls the investee, usually through majority ownership of the investee's voting stock. The equity method is required when an investor has sufficient stock ownership in an investee to significantly influence the operating and financial policies of the investee but owns less than a majority of the investee's stock. In the absence of other evidence, ownership of 20 percent or more of an investee's voting stock is viewed as giving the investor the ability to exercise significant influence over the investee. The cost method is used when consolidation and the equity method are not appropriate, usually when the investor is unable to exercise significant influence over the investee. If the cost method is used in reporting an investment in common stock and the common stock is marketable, an adjustment to market is required for financial reporting purposes.

The cost method is similar to the approach used in accounting for other noncurrent assets. The investment is carried at its original cost to the investor. Consistent with the realization concept, income from the investment is recognized when distributed by the investee in the form of dividends.

The equity method is unique in that the carrying value of the investment is adjusted periodically to reflect the investor's changing equity in the underlying investee. Income from the investment is recognized by the investor under the equity method as the investee reports the income rather than when it is distributed.

Key Terms

basic equity method, *71*	equity method, *49*	parent, *49*
consolidation, *49*	fully adjusted equity	significant influence, *49*
corporate joint venture, *54*	method, *66*	subsidiary, *49*
cost method, *50*	liquidating dividends, *51*	unconsolidated subsidiary, *49*
differential, *56*	modified equity method, *71*	
equity accrual, *55*	one-line consolidation, *66*	

Questions	Q2-1	What types of investments in common stock normally are accounted for using (*a*) the equity method and (*b*) the cost method?
	Q2-2	How is the ability to significantly influence the operating and financial policies of a company normally demonstrated?
	Q2-3	When is equity-method reporting considered inappropriate even though sufficient common shares are owned to allow the exercise of significant influence?
	Q2-4	When will the balance in the intercorporate investment account be the same under the cost method and the equity method?
	Q2-5	Describe an investor's treatment of an investee's prior-period dividends and earnings when the investor acquires significant influence through a purchase of additional stock.
	Q2-6	From the point of view of an investor in common stock, what is a liquidating dividend? Is a liquidating dividend viewed in the same way by the investee?
	Q2-7	What effect does a liquidating dividend have on the balance in the investment account under the cost method and the equity method?
	Q2-8	When is the carrying value of the investment account reduced under equity-method reporting?
	Q2-9	What is a corporate joint venture? How should an investment in the common stock of a corporate joint venture normally be reported?
	Q2-10	What is a differential? How is a differential treated by an investor in computing income from an investee under (*a*) cost-method and (*b*) equity-method reporting?
	Q2-11	How is the receipt of a dividend recorded under the equity method? Under the cost method?
	Q2-12	Turner Manufacturing Corporation owns 40 percent of the common shares of Straight Lace Company. If Straight Lace reports net income of $100,000 for 20X5, what factors may cause Turner to report less than $40,000 of income from the investee?
	Q2-13	What types of complexities arise in applying the equity method to accounting for an investment in a partnership?
	Q2-14	In what types of situations could it be appropriate to use equity-method reporting even though the investor does not hold voting common stock of the investee?
	Q2-15*	When must tax allocation procedures be used in recording income tax expense under the equity method?
	Q2-16*	Will the expected amount of deferred income taxes be larger under the cost method or the equity method? Explain.
	Q2-17*	How does the fully adjusted equity method differ from the basic equity method?
	Q2-18*	Explain the concept of a one-line consolidation.
	Q2-19*	What is the basic equity method? When might a company choose to use the basic equity method rather than the fully adjusted equity method?
	Q2-20*	How are extraordinary items of the investee disclosed by the investor under equity-method reporting?

Cases

C2-1

Choice of Accounting Method

Understanding

Slanted Building Supplies purchased 32 percent of the voting shares of Flat Flooring Company in March 20X3. On December 31, 20X3, the officers of Slanted Building Supplies indicated they needed advice on whether to use the equity method or cost method in reporting their ownership in Flat Flooring.

Required

a. What factors should be considered in determining whether equity-method reporting is appropriate?

b. Which of the two methods is likely to show the larger reported contribution to Slanted's earnings in 20X4? Explain.

*Indicates that the item relates to "Additional Considerations."

c. Why might the use of the equity method become more appropriate as the percentage of ownership increases?

C2-2 Intercorporate Ownership

Research FARS

Most Company purchased 90 percent of the voting common stock of Port Company on January 1, 20X4, and 15 percent of the voting common stock of Adams Company on July 1, 20X4. In preparing the financial statements for Most Company at December 31, 20X4, you discover that Port Company purchased 10 percent of the common stock of Adams Company in 20X2 and continues to hold those shares. Adams Company reported net income of $200,000 for 20X4 and paid a dividend of $70,000 on December 20, 20X4.

Required

Most Company's chief accountant instructs you to review the current accounting literature, including pronouncements of the FASB and other appropriate bodies, and prepare a memo discussing whether the cost or equity method should be used in reporting the investment in Adams Company in Most's consolidated statements prepared at December 31, 20X4. Support your recommendations with citations and quotations from the authoritative financial reporting standards or other literature.

C2-3 Application of the Equity Method

Research FARS

Forth Company owned 85,000 of Brown Company's 100,000 shares of common stock until January 1, 20X2, at which time it sold 70,000 of the shares to a group of seven investors, each of whom purchased 10,000 shares. On December 3, 20X2, Forth received a dividend of $9,000 from Brown. Forth continues to purchase a substantial portion of Brown's output under a contract that runs until the end of 20X9. Because of this arrangement, Forth is permitted to place two of its employees on the board of directors of Brown.

Required

Forth Company's controller is not sure whether the company should use the cost or equity method in accounting for its investment in Brown Company. The controller asked you to review the relevant accounting literature and prepare a memo containing your recommendations. Support your recommendations with citations and quotations from the appropriate authoritative financial reporting standards or other literature.

C2-4 Complex Organizational Structures

Analysis

Major companies often have very complex organizational structures, sometimes consisting of different types of entities. Some organizational structures include combinations of corporations, partnerships, and perhaps other types of entities. Complex organizational structures often present challenges for financial reporting.

Required

a. What type of entity is Atlas America, Inc. (i.e., corporation, partnership, trust)? What is the company's business?

b. Atlas America lists a number of subsidiaries in its Form 10-K filed with the SEC (in separate Exhibit No. 21.1). What types of entities are included among the subsidiaries? How does the company report its subsidiaries and interests in energy partnerships?

c. What type of entity is Atlas Pipeline Partners? What types of entities are its subsidiaries? What arrangement is there for the management of Atlas Pipeline Partners?

d. Does Atlas Pipeline Partners present separate or consolidated financial statements? What type of entity is NOARK Pipeline System, and what is Atlas Pipeline's relationship to NOARK? How is NOARK reflected in Atlas Pipeline's financial statements?

C2-5 Evaluating Investments

Understanding

Major companies often have investments in a number of other entities. The types of entities, ownership shares, and circumstances may differ considerably for these various investments, thus leading to different reporting methods for the different investments. The Dow Chemical Company is a company with numerous investments in other corporations, joint ventures, and partnerships.

Required

a. Approximately how many subsidiaries (10, 50, or more than 100) does Dow Chemical have? What is Dow's consolidation policy?

b. For what types of entities does Dow use the equity-method of reporting? What is the highest percentage ownership for affiliates actually owned by Dow and reported using the equity method? Exclusive of Dow Corning, MEGlobal, Equipolymers, and EQUATE Petrochemical, what was the total differential associated with Dow's equity-method investments at December 31, 2005? What was the nature of the differential relating to MEGlobal, Equipolymers, and EQUATE Petrochemical?

c. What method does Dow use to evaluate the goodwill of subsidiaries for impairment?

d. An investment that suffers a significant decline in value that is judged as being other than temporary must be written down to its fair value and a loss recognized. Did Dow Chemical experience such a loss in the past with respect to any of its partnership or joint venture investments? Explain.

C2-6 Reporting Significant Investments in Common Stock

Analysis

The reporting treatment for investments in common stock depends on the level of ownership and the ability to influence policies of the investee. The reporting treatment may even change over time as ownership levels or other factors change. When investees are not consolidated, the investments typically are reported in the Investments section of the investor's balance sheet. However, the investor's income from those investments is not always easy to find in the investor's income statement.

Required

a. Harley-Davidson, Inc., holds an investment in the common stock of Buell Motorcycle Company. How did Harley-Davidson report this investment before 1998? How does it report the investment now? Why did Harley change its method of reporting its investment in Buell?

b. Chevron owns both common and preferred shares of Dynegy Inc. How does Chevron report its investment in Dynegy Inc. common stock? How does it report its investment in Dynegy preferred stock?

c. Prior to 1999, where did PepsiCo report its share of the net income or loss of its unconsolidated affiliates over which it exercised significant influence but not control? What rationale might be given for this treatment? How does PepsiCo now report this type of income?

d. Does Sears have any investments in companies that it accounts for using the equity method? Where are these investments reported in the balance sheet, and where is the income from these investments reported in the income statement?

Exercises

E2-1 Multiple-Choice Questions on Use of Cost and Equity Methods [AICPA Adapted]

Select the correct answer for each of the following questions.

1. Peel Company received a cash dividend from a common stock investment. Should Peel report an increase in the investment account if it uses the cost method or equity method of accounting?

	Cost	Equity
a.	No	No
b.	Yes	Yes
c.	Yes	No
d.	No	Yes

2. In 20X0, Neil Company held the following investments in common stock:

- 25,000 shares of B&K Inc.'s 100,000 outstanding shares. Neil's level of ownership gives it the ability to exercise significant influence over the financial and operating policies of B&K.
- 6,000 shares of Amal Corporation's 309,000 outstanding shares.

During 20X0, Neil received the following distributions from its common stock investments:

November 6	$30,000 cash dividend from B&K
November 11	$1,500 cash dividend from Amal
December 26	3 percent common stock dividend from Amal
	The closing price of this stock was $115 per share.

What amount of dividend revenue should Neil report for 20X0?

    a. $1,500.

    b. $4,200.

    c. $31,500.

    d. $34,200.

3. What is the most appropriate basis for recording the acquisition of 40 percent of the stock in another company if the acquisition was a noncash transaction?

    a. At the book value of the consideration given.

    b. At the par value of the stock acquired.

    c. At the book value of the stock acquired.

    d. At the fair value of the consideration given.

4. An investor uses the equity method to account for investments in common stock. The purchase price implies a fair value of the investee's depreciable assets in excess of the investee's net asset carrying values. The investor's amortization of the excess:

    a. Decreases the investment account.

    b. Decreases the goodwill account.

    c. Increases the investment revenue account.

    d. Does not affect the investment account.

5. A corporation exercises significant influence over an affiliate in which it holds a 40 percent common stock interest. If its affiliate completed a fiscal year profitably but paid no dividends, how would this affect the investor corporation?

    a. Result in an increased current ratio.

    b. Result in increased earnings per share.

    c. Increase several turnover ratios.

    d. Decrease book value per share.

6. An investor in common stock received dividends in excess of the investor's share of investee's earnings subsequent to the date of the investment. How will the investor's investment account be affected by those dividends under each of the following methods?

	Cost Method	Equity Method
a.	No effect	No effect
b.	Decrease	No effect
c.	No effect	Decrease
d.	Decrease	Decrease

7. An investor uses the cost method to account for an investment in common stock. A portion of the dividends received this year was in excess of the investor's share of investee's earnings subsequent to the date of investment. The amount of dividend revenue that should be reported in the investor's income statement for this year would be:

    a. Zero.

    b. The total amount of dividends received this year.

    c. The portion of the dividends received this year that was in excess of the investor's share of investee's earnings subsequent to the date of investment.

    d. The portion of the dividends received this year that was not in excess of the investor's share of investee's earnings subsequent to the date of investment.

E2-2 **Multiple-Choice Questions on Intercorporate Investments**
Select the correct answer for each of the following questions.

1. Companies often acquire ownership in other companies using a variety of ownership arrangements. Equity-method reporting should be used by the investor whenever:

    a. The investor purchases voting common stock of the investee.

    b. The investor has significant influence over the operating and financing decisions of the investee.

    c. The investor purchases goods and services from the investee.

    d. The carrying value of the investment is less than the market value of the investee's shares held by the investor.

2. The carrying amount of an investment should be written down by the investor if:

    a. The carrying amount of the investment is more than the market value of the shares held, and the decline is considered to be temporary.

    b. The carrying amount of the investment is less than the market value of the shares held, and the increase is considered to be temporary.

    c. The carrying amount of the investment is more than the market value of the shares held, and the decline is considered to be other than temporary.

    d. The carrying amount of the investment is less than the market value of the shares held, and the increase is considered to be other than temporary.

3. An investment in a partnership potentially may be reported using:

    a. Cost method.

    b. Equity method.

    c. Full consolidation.

    d. All of the above.

4. Prescott Company holds a 40 percent interest in G&K Partnership, which has operated profitably since its formation and has made no distributions of earnings to its owners. Prescott's total assets at the end of the fourth year of ownership will be highest if it uses:

    a. Full consolidation.

    b. Pro rata consolidation.

    c. Equity-method reporting.

    d. Cost-method reporting.

5. Using equity-method reporting for investments in partnerships as opposed to investments in corporations:

    a. May be more difficult because factors other than the percent of assets contributed to the partnership may determine whether the equity method is appropriate.

    b. Is more difficult to apply because partnerships generally do not follow generally accepted accounting principles in recording everyday transactions.

    c. Is easier because the dollar amounts typically are much smaller.

    d. Is easier because corporations must pay income taxes and partnerships do not.

E2-3 **Multiple-Choice Questions on Applying Equity Method [AICPA Adapted]**
Select the correct answer for each of the following questions.

1. Green Corporation owns 30 percent of the outstanding common stock and 100 percent of the outstanding noncumulative nonvoting preferred stock of Axel Corporation. In 20X1, Axel declared

dividends of $100,000 on its common stock and $60,000 on its preferred stock. Green exercises significant influence over Axel's operations. What amount of dividend revenue should Green report in its income statement for the year ended December 31, 20X1?

    a. $0.

    b. $30,000.

    c. $60,000.

    d. $90,000.

2. On January 2, 20X3, Kean Company purchased 30 percent interest in Pod Company for $250,000. On this date, Pod's stockholders' equity was $500,000. The carrying amounts of Pod's identifiable net assets approximated their fair values, except for equipment whose fair value exceeded its carrying amount by $200,000 and had an expected remaining useful life of 15 years at January 2, 20X3. Pod reported net income of $100,000 for 20X3 and paid no dividends. Kean accounts for this investment using the equity method. In its December 31, 20X3, balance sheet, what amount should Kean report as its investment in Pod?

    a. $210,000.

    b. $220,000.

    c. $270,000.

    d. $276,000.

3. On January 1, 20X8, Mega Corporation acquired 10 percent of the outstanding voting stock of Penny Inc. On January 2, 20X9, Mega gained the ability to exercise significant influence over Penny's financial and operating decisions by acquiring an additional 20 percent of Penny's outstanding stock. The two purchases were made at prices proportionate to the value assigned to Penny's net assets, which equaled their carrying amounts. For the years ended December 31, 20X8 and 20X9, Penny reported the following:

	20X8	20X9
Dividends Paid	$200,000	$300,000
Net Income	600,000	650,000

In 20X9, what amounts should Mega report as current year investment income and as an adjustment, before income taxes, to 20X8 investment income?

	20X9 Investment Income	Adjustment to 20X8 Investment Income
a.	$195,000	$160,000
b.	$195,000	$100,000
c.	$195,000	$ 40,000
d.	$105,000	$ 40,000

4. Investor Inc. owns 40 percent of Alimand Corporation. During the calendar year 20X5, Alimand had net earnings of $100,000 and paid dividends of $10,000. Investor mistakenly recorded these transactions using the cost method rather than the equity method of accounting. What effect would this have on the investment account, net earnings, and retained earnings, respectively?

    a. Understate, overstate, overstate.

    b. Overstate, understate, understate.

    c. Overstate, overstate, overstate.

    d. Understate, understate, understate.

5. A corporation using the equity method of accounting for its investment in a 40 percent-owned investee, which earned $20,000 and paid $5,000 in dividends, made the following entries:

Investment in Investee	8,000	
Equity in Earnings of Investee		8,000
Cash	2,000	
Dividend Revenue		2,000

What effect will these entries have on the investor's statement of financial position?

a. Financial position will be fairly stated.

b. Investment in the investee will be overstated, retained earnings understated.

c. Investment in the investee will be understated, retained earnings understated.

d. Investment in the investee will be overstated, retained earnings overstated.

E2-4 Cost versus Equity Reporting

Roller Corporation purchased 20 percent ownership of Steam Company on January 1, 20X5, for $70,000. On that date, the book value of Steam's reported net assets was $200,000. The excess over book value paid is attributable to depreciable assets with a remaining useful life of 10 years. Net income and dividend payments of Steam in the following periods were:

Year	Net Income	Dividends
20X5	$20,000	$ 5,000
20X6	40,000	15,000
20X7	20,000	35,000

Required

Prepare journal entries on Roller Corporation's books relating to its investment in Steam Company for each of the three years, assuming it accounts for the investment using (*a*) the cost method and (*b*) the equity method.

E2-5 Cost versus Equity Reporting

Winston Corporation purchased 40 percent of the stock of Fullbright Company on January 1, 20X2, at underlying book value. The companies reported the following operating results and dividend payments during the first three years of intercorporate ownership:

	Winston Corporation		Fullbright Company	
Year	Operating Income	Dividends	Net Income	Dividends
20X2	$100,000	$ 40,000	$70,000	$30,000
20X3	60,000	80,000	40,000	60,000
20X4	250,000	120,000	25,000	50,000

Required

Compute the net income reported by Winston for each of the three years, assuming it accounts for its investment in Fullbright using (*a*) the cost method and (*b*) the equity method.

E2-6 Acquisition Price

Phillips Company bought 40 percent ownership in Jones Bag Company on January 1, 20X1, at underlying book value. In 20X1, 20X2, and 20X3, Jones Bag reported net income of $8,000, $12,000, $20,000, and dividends of $15,000, $10,000, and $10,000, respectively. The balance in Phillips Company's investment account on December 31, 20X3, was $54,000.

Required

In each of the following independent cases, determine the amount that Phillips paid for its investment in Jones Bag stock assuming that Phillips accounted for its investment using the (*a*) cost method and (*b*) equity method.

E2-7   Investment Income

Ravine Corporation purchased 30 percent ownership of Valley Industries for $90,000 on January 1, 20X6, when Valley had capital stock of $240,000 and retained earnings of $60,000. The following data were reported by the companies for the years 20X6 through 20X9:

Year	Operating Income, Ravine Corporation	Net Income, Valley Industries	Dividends Declared Ravine	Dividends Declared Valley
20X6	$140,000	$30,000	$ 70,000	$20,000
20X7	80,000	50,000	70,000	40,000
20X8	220,000	10,000	90,000	40,000
20X9	160,000	40,000	100,000	20,000

Required

a. What net income would Ravine Corporation have reported for each of the years, assuming Ravine accounts for the intercorporate investment using (1) the cost method and (2) the equity method?

b. Give all appropriate journal entries for 20X8 that Ravine made under both the cost and the equity methods.

E2-8   Impairment of Investment Value

Port Company purchased 30,000 of the 100,000 outstanding shares of Sund Company common stock on January 1, 20X2, for $180,000. The purchase price was equal to the book value of the shares purchased. Sund reported net income of $40,000, $30,000, and $5,000 for 20X2, 20X3, and 20X4, respectively. It paid a dividend of $25,000 in 20X2, but paid no dividends in 20X3 and 20X4. Due to the expiration of patent rights, Sund's net income for 20X4 declined substantially and it expected relatively large operating losses in 20X5 and beyond. In December 20X4 Sund's shares suffered a decline in value that is apparently other than temporary. The shares were trading at $4.50 each on December 31, 20X4.

Required

Compute the amounts Port Company should report as the carrying values of its investment in Sund Company at December 31, 20X2, 20X3, and 20X4.

E2-9   Alternative Reporting for Investment in Partnership

Moss Company invested $90,000 in TF Partnership on January 1, 20X1, for a 45 percent share of its profits and losses. At December 31, 20X2, Moss reported total assets of $510,000 (excluding its investment in TF) and liabilities of $40,000, and TF reported total assets of $250,000 and liabilities of $30,000.

Required

Present the balance sheets for Moss Company at December 31, 20X2, assuming they are prepared using the following reporting alternatives for its investment in TF Partnership:

a. Cost method.

b. Equity method.

c. Pro rata consolidation.

d. Consolidation.

E2-10   Differential Assigned to Patents

Power Corporation purchased 35 percent of the common stock of Snow Corporation on January 1, 20X2, by issuing 15,000 shares of its $6 par value common stock. The market price of Power's shares at the date of issue was $24. Snow reported net assets with a book value of $980,000 on that date. The amount paid in excess of the book value of Snow's net assets was attributed to the increased value of patents held by Snow with a remaining useful life of eight years. Snow reported net income of $56,000 and paid dividends of $20,000 in 20X2 and reported a net loss of $44,000 and paid dividends of $10,000 in 20X3.

Required

Assuming that Power Corporation uses the equity method in accounting for its investment in Snow Corporation, prepare all journal entries for Power for 20X2 and 20X3.

E2-11 Differential Assigned to Copyrights

Best Corporation acquired 25 percent of the voting common stock of Flair Company on January 1, 20X7, by issuing bonds with a par value and fair value of $170,000 and making a cash payment of $26,000. At the date of acquisition, Flair reported assets of $740,000 and liabilities of $140,000. The book values and fair values of Flair's net assets were equal except for land and copyrights. Flair's land had a fair value $16,000 greater than its book value. All of the remaining purchase price was attributable to the increased value of Flair's copyrights with a remaining useful life of eight years. Flair Company reported a loss of $88,000 in 20X7 and net income of $120,000 in 20X8. Flair paid dividends of $24,000 each year.

Required

Assuming that Best Corporation uses the equity method in accounting for its investment in Flair Company, prepare all journal entries for Best for 20X7 and 20X8.

E2-12 Purchase Differential Attributable to Depreciable Assets

Capital Corporation purchased 40 percent of Cook Company's stock on January 1, 20X4, for $136,000. On that date, Cook reported net assets of $300,000 valued at historical cost and $340,000 stated at fair value. The difference was due to the increased value of buildings with a remaining life of 10 years. During 20X4 and 20X5 Cook reported net income of $10,000 and $20,000 and paid dividends of $6,000 and $9,000, respectively.

Required

Assuming that Capital Corporation uses (*a*) the equity method and (*b*) the cost method in accounting for its ownership of Cook Company, give the journal entries that Capital recorded in 20X4 and 20X5.

E2-13 Investment Income

Brindle Company purchased 25 percent of Monroe Company's voting common stock for $162,000 on January 1, 20X4. At that date, Monroe reported assets of $690,000 and liabilities of $230,000. The book values and fair values of Monroe's assets were equal except for land, which had a fair value $30,000 greater than book value, and equipment, which had a fair value $80,000 greater than book value. The remaining economic life of all depreciable assets at January 1, 20X4, was five years. The amount of the differential assigned to goodwill is not amortized. Monroe reported net income of $68,000 and paid dividends of $34,000 in 20X4.

Required

Compute the amount of investment income to be reported by Brindle for 20X4.

E2-14 Income from Investee

Spone Corporation purchased 40 percent of Hall Corporation's voting common stock on January 1, 20X8, for $133,400. Hall reported net income of $55,000 for 20X8 and paid dividends of $25,000 on December 30, 20X8. At the date of acquisition, Hall reported assets of $345,000 and liabilities of $105,000. A total of $24,000 of the purchase differential was assigned to buildings with a remaining economic life of 10 years at January 1, 20X8. In addition, $8,000 of the purchase differential was assigned to equipment with a remaining economic life of five years at January 1, 20X8. The amount of the differential assigned to goodwill is not amortized.

Required

Compute the amount of investment income to be reported by Spone for 20X8.

E2-15 Determination of Purchase Price

Branch Corporation purchased 30 percent of Hardy Company's common stock on January 1, 20X5, and paid $28,000 above book value. The full amount of the additional payment was attributed to amortizable assets with a life of eight years remaining at January 1, 20X5. During 20X5 and 20X6, Hardy reported net income of $110,000 and $20,000 and paid dividends of $50,000 and $40,000, respectively. Branch uses the equity method in accounting for its investment in Hardy and reported a balance in its investment account of $161,000 on December 31, 20X6.

Required

Compute the amount paid by Branch to purchase Hardy shares.

E2-16 **Computation of Purchase Price**

Scott Company purchased 30 percent of the ownership of Earnest Enterprises on January 1, 20X2, at underlying book value. In 20X2 Earnest reported net income of $60,000 and paid dividends of $15,000 and in 20X3 reported a loss of $40,000 and paid dividends of $35,000. Scott uses the equity method in accounting for its investment in Earnest and reported a balance in its investment account of $135,000 on December 31, 20X3.

Required

Compute the amount paid by Scott Company to purchase the shares of Earnest Enterprises.

E2-17 **Correction of Error**

During review of the adjusting entries to be recorded on December 31, 20X8, Grand Corporation discovered that it had inappropriately been using the cost method in accounting for its investment in Case Products Corporation. Grand purchased 40 percent ownership of Case Products on January 1, 20X6, for $56,000, at which time Case Products reported retained earnings of $60,000 and capital stock outstanding of $40,000. The purchase differential was attributable to patents with a life of eight years. Income and dividends of Case Products were:

Year	Net Income	Dividends
20X6	$40,000	$15,000
20X7	60,000	20,000
20X8	80,000	20,000

Required

Give the correcting entry required on December 31, 20X8, to properly report the investment under the equity method, assuming the books have not been closed. Case Products' dividends were declared in early November and paid in early December each year.

E2-18 **Purchase Differential Assigned to Land and Equipment**

Rod Corporation purchased 30 percent ownership of Stafford Corporation on January 1, 20X4, for $65,000, which was $10,000 above the underlying book value. Half the additional amount was attributable to an increase in the value of land held by Stafford, and half was due to an increase in the value of equipment. The equipment had a remaining economic life of five years on January 1, 20X4. During 20X4, Stafford reported net income of $40,000 and paid dividends of $15,000.

Required

Give the journal entries that Rod Corporation recorded during 20X4 related to its investment in Stafford Corporation, assuming Rod uses the equity method in accounting for its investment.

E2-19 **Equity Entries with Positive and Negative Goodwill**

Turner Corporation reported the following balances at January 1, 20X9:

Item	Book Value	Fair Value
Cash	$ 45,000	$ 45,000
Accounts Receivable	60,000	60,000
Inventory	120,000	130,000
Buildings and Equipment	300,000	240,000
Less: Accumulated Depreciation	(150,000)	
Total Assets	$375,000	$475,000
Accounts Payable	$ 75,000	$ 75,000
Common Stock ($10 par value)	100,000	
Additional Paid-In Capital	30,000	
Retained Earnings	170,000	
Total Liabilities and Equities	$375,000	

On January 1, 20X9, Chad Corporation purchased 40 percent of Turner's stock. All tangible assets had a remaining economic life of 10 years at January 1, 20X9. Both companies use the FIFO inventory method. Turner reported net income of $40,000 in 20X9 and paid dividends of $8,000. Chad uses the equity method in accounting for its investment in Turner.

Required
Give all journal entries that Chad recorded during 20X9 with respect to its investment assuming:

a. Chad paid $175,000 for the ownership of Turner on January 1, 20X9. The amount of the differential assigned to goodwill is not amortized.

b. Chad paid $140,000 for the ownership of Turner on January 1, 20X9.

E2-20 Income Reporting

Grandview Company purchased 40 percent of the stock of Spinet Corporation on January 1, 20X8, at underlying book value. Spinet recorded the following income for 20X9:

Income before Extraordinary Gain	$60,000
Extraordinary Gain	30,000
Net Income	$90,000

Required
Prepare all journal entries on Grandview's books for 20X9 to account for its investment in Spinet.

E2-21* Investee with Preferred Stock Outstanding

Reden Corporation purchased 45 percent of Montgomery Company's common stock on January 1, 20X9, at underlying book value of $288,000. Montgomery's balance sheet contained the following stockholders' equity balances:

Preferred Stock ($5 par value, 50,000 shares issued and outstanding)	$250,000
Common Stock ($1 par value, 150,000 shares issued and outstanding)	150,000
Additional Paid-In Capital	180,000
Retained Earnings	310,000
Total Stockholders' Equity	$890,000

Montgomery's preferred stock is cumulative and pays a 10 percent annual dividend. Montgomery reported net income of $95,000 for 20X9 and paid a total dividend of $40,000.

Required
Give the journal entries recorded by Reden Corporation for 20X9 related to its investment in Montgomery Company common stock.

E2-22* Other Comprehensive Income Reported by Investee

Callas Corporation paid $380,000 to acquire 40 percent ownership of Thinbill Company on January 1, 20X9. The amount paid was equal to underlying book value. During 20X9, Thinbill reported operating income of $45,000, an increase of $10,000 in the market value of trading securities held for the year, and an increase of $20,000 in the market value of available-for-sale securities held for the year. Thinbill paid dividends of $9,000 on December 10, 20X9.

Required
Give all journal entries that Callas Corporation recorded in 20X9, including closing entries at December 31, 20X9, associated with its investment in Thinbill Company.

E2-23* Other Comprehensive Income Reported by Investee

Baldwin Corporation purchased 25 percent of Gwin Company's common stock on January 1, 20X8, at underlying book value. In 20X8 Gwin reported a net loss of $20,000 and paid dividends of $10,000, and in 20X9 the company reported net income of $68,000 and paid dividends of $16,000. Gwin also purchased marketable securities classified as available-for-sale on February 8, 20X9, and reported an increase of $12,000 in their fair value at December 31, 20X9. Baldwin reported a balance of $67,000 in its investment in Gwin at December 31, 20X9.

Required
Compute the amount paid by Baldwin Corporation to purchase the shares of Gwin Company.

E2-24*   **Deferred Income Taxes**

Denbow Corporation reported a deferred tax liability of $37,800 in its balance sheet dated December 31, 20X1. Denbow's only temporary difference resulted from its use of the equity method to report its 25 percent investment in Crabapple Industries, acquired at underlying book value on December 31, 20X0. During 20X1, Denbow received a dividend of $25,000 from Crabapple, the first dividend ever paid by the company. The dividend qualified for the 80 percent dividend deduction. Denbow's effective tax rate is 45 percent.

Required

Compute Crabapple's net income for 20X1.

Problems   **P2-25**   **Multiple-Choice Questions on Applying the Equity Method [AICPA Adapted]**

Select the correct answer for each of the following questions.

1. On July 1, 20X3, Barker Company purchased 20 percent of Acme Company's outstanding common stock for $400,000 when the fair value of Acme's net assets was $2,000,000. Barker does not have the ability to exercise significant influence over Acme's operating and financial policies. The following data concerning Acme are available for 20X3:

	Twelve Months Ended December 31, 20X3	Six Months Ended December 31, 20X3
Net income	$300,000	$160,000
Dividends declared and paid	190,000	100,000

   In its income statement for the year ended December 31, 20X3, how much income should Barker report from this investment?

   a. $20,000.
   b. $32,000.
   c. $38,000.
   d. $60,000.

2. On January 1, 20X3, Miller Company purchased 25 percent of Wall Corporation's common stock; no goodwill resulted from the purchase. Miller appropriately carries this investment at equity, and the balance in Miller's investment account was $190,000 on December 31, 20X3. Wall reported net income of $120,000 for the year ended December 31, 20X3, and paid dividends on its common stock totaling $48,000 during 20X3. How much did Miller pay for its 25 percent interest in Wall?

   a. $172,000.
   b. $202,000.
   c. $208,000.
   d. $232,000.

3. On January 1, 20X7, Robohn Company purchased for cash 40 percent of Lowell Company's 300,000 shares of voting common stock for $1,800,000 when 40 percent of the underlying equity in Lowell's net assets was $1,740,000. The payment in excess of underlying equity was assigned to amortizable assets with a remaining life of six years. The amortization is not deductible for income tax reporting. As a result of this transaction, Robohn has the ability to exercise significant influence over Lowell's operating and financial policies. Lowell's net income for the year ended December 31, 20X7, was $600,000. During 20X7, Lowell paid $325,000 in dividends to its shareholders. The income reported by Robohn for its investment in Lowell should be:

   a. $120,000.
   b. $130,000.
   c. $230,000.
   d. $240,000.

4. In January 20X0, Farley Corporation acquired 20 percent of Davis Company's outstanding common stock for $800,000. This investment gave Farley the ability to exercise significant influence

over Davis. The book value of the acquired shares was $600,000. The excess of cost over book value was attributed to an identifiable intangible asset, which was undervalued on Davis's balance sheet and which had a remaining economic life of 10 years. For the year ended December 31, 20X0, Davis reported net income of $180,000 and paid cash dividends of $40,000 on its common stock. What is the proper carrying value of Farley's investment in Davis on December 31, 20X0?

a. $772,000.

b. $780,000.

c. $800,000.

d. $808,000.

P2-26 **Amortization of Purchase Differential**

Ball Corporation purchased 30 percent of Krown Company's common stock on January 1, 20X5, by issuing preferred stock with a par value of $50,000 and a market price of $120,000. The following amounts relate to Krown's balance sheet items at that date:

	Book Value	Fair Value
Cash and Receivables	$200,000	$200,000
Buildings and Equipment	400,000	360,000
Less: Accumulated Depreciation	(100,000)	
Total Assets	$500,000	
Accounts Payable	$ 50,000	50,000
Bonds Payable	200,000	200,000
Common Stock	100,000	
Retained Earnings	150,000	
Total Liabilities and Equities	$500,000	

Krown purchased buildings and equipment on January 1, 20X0, with an expected economic life of 20 years. No change in overall expected economic life occurred as a result of the acquisition of Ball's stock. The amount paid in excess of the fair value of Krown's reported net assets is attributed to unrecorded copyrights with a remaining useful life of eight years. During 20X5, Krown reported net income of $40,000 and paid dividends of $10,000.

Required

Give all journal entries to be recorded on Ball Corporation's books during 20X5, assuming it uses the equity method in accounting for its ownership of Krown Company.

P2-27 **Computation of Account Balances**

Easy Chair Company purchased 40 percent ownership of Stuffy Sofa Corporation on January 1, 20X1, for $150,000. Stuffy Sofa's balance sheet at the time of acquisition was as follows:

STUFFY SOFA CORPORATION

Balance Sheet

January 1, 20X1

Cash		$ 30,000	Current Liabilities	$ 40,000
Accounts Receivable		120,000	Bonds Payable	200,000
Inventory		80,000	Common Stock	200,000
Land		150,000	Additional	
Buildings and Equipment	$300,000		Paid-In Capital	40,000
Less: Accumulated			Retained Earnings	80,000
Depreciation	(120,000)	180,000		
Total Assets		$560,000	Total Liabilities and Equities	$560,000

During 20X1 Stuffy Sofa Corporation reported net income of $30,000 and paid dividends of $9,000. The fair values of Stuffy Sofa's assets and liabilities were equal to their book values at the date of acquisition, with the exception of buildings and equipment, which had a fair value $35,000 above book value. All buildings and equipment had remaining lives of five years at the time of the business combination. The amount attributed to goodwill as a result of its purchase of Stuffy Sofa shares is not amortized.

Required

a. What amount of investment income will Easy Chair Company record during 20X1 under equity-method accounting?

b. What amount of income will be reported under the cost method?

c. What will be the balance in the investment account on December 31, 20X1, under (1) cost-method and (2) equity-method accounting?

P2-28   Retroactive Recognition

Idle Corporation has been acquiring shares of Fast Track Enterprises at book value for the last several years. Data provided by Fast Track included the following:

	20X2	20X3	20X4	20X5
Net Income	$40,000	$60,000	$40,000	$50,000
Dividends	20,000	20,000	10,000	20,000

Fast Track declares and pays its annual dividend on November 15 each year. Its net book value on January 1, 20X2, was $250,000. Idle purchased shares of Fast Track on three occasions:

Date	Percent of Ownership Purchased	Amount Paid
January 1, 20X2	10%	$25,000
July 1, 20X3	5	15,000
January 1, 20X5	10	34,000

Required

Give the journal entries to be recorded on Idle's books in 20X5 related to its investment in Fast Track.

P2-29   Multistep Acquisition

Jackson Corporation purchased shares of Phillips Corporation in the following sequence:

Date	Number of Shares Purchased	Amount Paid
January 1, 20X6	1,000 shares	$25,000
January 1, 20X8	500 shares	15,000
January 1, 20X9	2,000 shares	70,000

The book value of Phillips's net assets at January 1, 20X6, was $200,000. Each year since Jackson first purchased shares, Phillips has reported net income of $70,000 and paid dividends of $20,000. The amount paid in excess of the book value of Phillips's net assets was attributed to the increase in the value of identifiable intangible assets with a remaining life of five years at the date the shares of Phillips were purchased. Phillips has had 10,000 shares of voting common stock outstanding throughout the four-year period.

Required

Give the journal entries recorded on Jackson Corporation's books in 20X9 related to its investment in Phillips Corporation.

P2-30 **Investment in Joint Venture**

Tye Corporation invested in an unincorporated joint venture and elected to use pro rata consolidation in preparing its financial statements. For the year ended December 31, 20X3, Tye reported income of $52,000 from its separate operations and net income of $60,000. The joint venture reported assets of $293,000 and liabilities of $45,000 on January 1, 20X3, and assets of $330,000 and liabilities of $50,000 on December 31, 20X3. It made no distributions to owners during the year.

Required

a. Determine the percentage ownership of the joint venture held by Tye.

b. If Tye reports total assets (excluding its investment in the unincorporated joint venture) of $700,000 at December 31, 20X3, what amount of total assets will Tye report in its balance sheet on that date?

P2-31 **Investment in Partnership**

Down Corporation paid $84,000 to acquire 30 percent of the ownership of DF Partnership and shares in its profits and losses at 30 percent. DF Partnership did not make any distribution to its owners during 20X4. At December 31, 20X4, Down and DF reported the following amounts when Down used the equity method in accounting for its investment in DF:

	Down Corporation	DF Partnership
Assets (other than investments)	$800,000	$380,000
Investment in DF Partnership	105,000	
Liabilities	175,000	30,000
Owners' Equity	730,000	350,000
Sales Revenue for 20X4	500,000	400,000
Expenses for 20X4	345,000	370,000

Required

Present the balance sheets at December 31, 20X4, and income statements for 20X4 for Down Corporation, assuming they are prepared using the following reporting alternatives for Down's investment in DF Partnership:

a. Cost method.

b. Equity method.

c. Pro rata consolidation.

d. Consolidation.

P2-32 **Complex Differential**

Essex Company issued common shares with a par value of $50,000 and a market value of $165,000 in exchange for 30 percent ownership of Tolliver Corporation on January 1, 20X2. Tolliver reported the following balances on that date:

TOLLIVER CORPORATION
Balance Sheet
January 1, 20X2

	Book Value	Fair Value
Assets		
Cash	$ 40,000	$ 40,000
Accounts Receivable	80,000	80,000
Inventory (FIFO basis)	120,000	150,000
Land	50,000	65,000
Buildings and Equipment	500,000	
Less: Accumulated Depreciation	(240,000)	320,000
Patent		25,000
Total Assets	$550,000	$680,000

(continued)

Liabilities and Equities

Accounts Payable	$ 30,000	$ 30,000
Bonds Payable	100,000	100,000
Common Stock	150,000	
Additional Paid-In Capital	20,000	
Retained Earnings	250,000	
Total Liabilities and Equities	$550,000	

The estimated economic life of the patents held by Tolliver is 10 years. The buildings and equipment are expected to last 12 more years on average. Tolliver paid dividends of $9,000 during 20X2 and reported net income of $80,000 for the year.

Required

Compute the amount of investment income (loss) reported by Essex from its investment in Tolliver for 20X2 and the balance in the investment account on December 31, 20X2, assuming the equity method is used in accounting for the investment.

P2-33 **Equity Entries with Differential**

On January 1, 20X0, Hunter Corporation issued 6,000 of its $10 par value shares to acquire 45 percent of the shares of Arrow Manufacturing. Arrow Manufacturing's balance sheet immediately before the acquisition contained the following items:

ARROW MANUFACTURING
Balance Sheet
January 1, 20X0

	Book Value	Fair Value
Assets		
Cash and Receivables	$ 30,000	$ 30,000
Land	70,000	80,000
Buildings and Equipment (net)	120,000	150,000
Patent	80,000	80,000
Total Assets	$300,000	
Liabilities and Equities		
Accounts Payable	$ 90,000	90,000
Common Stock	150,000	
Retained Earnings	60,000	
Total Liabilities and Equities	$300,000	

On the date of the stock acquisition, Hunter's shares were selling at $35, and Arrow Manufacturing's buildings and equipment had a remaining economic life of 10 years. The amount of the differential assigned to goodwill is not amortized.

In the two years following the stock acquisition, Arrow Manufacturing reported net income of $80,000 and $50,000 and paid dividends of $20,000 and $40,000, respectively. Hunter used the equity method in accounting for its ownership of Arrow Manufacturing.

Required

a. Give the entry recorded by Hunter Corporation at the time of acquisition.

b. Give the journal entries recorded by Hunter during 20X0 and 20X1 related to its investment in Arrow Manufacturing.

c. What balance will be reported in Hunter's investment account on December 31, 20X1?

P2-34 **Equity Entries with Differential**

Ennis Corporation acquired 35 percent of Jackson Corporation's stock on January 1, 20X8, by issuing 25,000 shares of its $2 par value common stock. Jackson Corporation's balance sheet immediately before the acquisition contained the following items:

JACKSON CORPORATION
Balance Sheet
January 1, 20X8

	Book Value	Fair Value
Assets		
Cash and Receivables	$ 40,000	$ 40,000
Inventory (FIFO basis)	80,000	100,000
Land	50,000	70,000
Buildings and Equipment (net)	240,000	320,000
Total Assets	$410,000	$530,000
Liabilities and Equities		
Accounts Payable	$ 70,000	$ 70,000
Common Stock	130,000	
Retained Earnings	210,000	
Total Liabilities and Equities	$410,000	

Shares of Ennis were selling at $8 at the time of the acquisition. On the date of acquisition, the remaining economic life of buildings and equipment held by Jackson was 20 years. The amount of the differential assigned to goodwill is not amortized. For the year 20X8, Jackson reported net income of $70,000 and paid dividends of $10,000.

Required

a. Give the journal entries recorded by Ennis Corporation during 20X8 related to its investment in Jackson Corporation.

b. What balance will Ennis report as its investment in Jackson at December 31, 20X8?

P2-35 **Additional Ownership Level**

Balance sheet and income and dividend data for Amber Corporation, Blair Corporation, and Carmen Corporation at January 1, 20X3, were as follows:

Account Balances	Amber Corporation	Blair Corporation	Carmen Corporation
Cash	$ 70,000	$ 60,000	$ 20,000
Accounts Receivable	120,000	80,000	40,000
Inventory	100,000	90,000	65,000
Fixed Assets (net)	450,000	350,000	240,000
Total Assets	$740,000	$580,000	$365,000
Accounts Payable	$105,000	$110,000	$ 45,000
Bonds Payable	300,000	200,000	120,000
Common Stock	150,000	75,000	90,000
Retained Earnings	185,000	195,000	110,000
Total Liabilities and Equity	$740,000	$580,000	$365,000
Income from Operations in 20X3	$220,000	$100,000	
Net Income for 20X3			$ 50,000
Dividends Declared and Paid	60,000	30,000	25,000

On January 1, 20X3, Amber Corporation purchased 40 percent of the voting common stock of Blair Corporation by issuing common stock with a par value of $40,000 and fair value of $130,000. Immediately after this transaction, Blair purchased 25 percent of the voting common stock of Carmen Corporation by issuing bonds payable with a par value and market value of $51,500.

On January 1, 20X3, the book values of Blair's net assets were equal to their fair values except for equipment that had a fair value $30,000 greater than book value and patents that had a fair value $25,000 greater than book value. At that date the equipment had a remaining economic life of eight years and the patents had a remaining economic life of five years. The book values of Carmen's assets were equal to their fair values except for inventory that had a fair value $6,000 in excess of book value and was accounted for on a FIFO basis.

Required

a. Compute the net income reported by Amber Corporation for 20X3, assuming the equity method is used by Amber and Blair in accounting for their intercorporate investments.

b. Give all journal entries recorded by Amber relating to its investment in Blair during 20X3.

P2-36 Correction of Error

Hill Company paid $164,000 to acquire 40 percent ownership of Dale Company on January 1, 20X2. Net book value of Dale's assets on that date was $300,000. Book values and fair values of net assets held by Dale were the same except for equipment and patents. Equipment held by Dale had a book value of $70,000 and fair value of $120,000. All of the remaining purchase price was attributable to the increased value of patents with a remaining useful life of eight years. The remaining economic life of all depreciable assets held by Dale was five years.

Dale Company's net income and dividends for the three years immediately following the purchase of shares were:

Year	Net Income	Dividends
20X2	$40,000	$15,000
20X3	60,000	20,000
20X4	70,000	25,000

The computation of Hill's investment income for 20X4 and entries in its investment account since the date of purchase were as follows:

		20X4 Investment Income
Pro rata income accrual ($70,000 × .40)		$28,000
Amortize patents ($44,000 ÷ 8 years)	$5,500	
Dividends received ($25,000 × .40)		10,000
20X4 investment income		$32,500

Investment in Dale Company		
1/1/X2 purchase price	$164,000	
20X2 income accrual	16,000	
Amortize patents		$5,500
20X3 income accrual	24,000	
Amortize patents		5,500
20X4 income accrual	28,000	
Amortize patents		5,500
12/31/X4 balance	$215,500	

Before making closing entries at the end of 20X4, Hill's new controller reviewed the reports and was convinced that both the balance in the investment account and the investment income that Hill reported for 20X4 were in error.

Required

Prepare a correcting entry, along with supporting computations, to properly state the balance in the investment account and all related account balances at the end of 20X4.

P2-37* **Other Comprehensive Income Reported by Investee**

Dewey Corporation owns 30 percent of the common stock of Jimm Company, which it purchased at underlying book value on January 1, 20X5. Dewey reported a balance of $245,000 for its investment in Jimm Company on January 1, 20X5, and $276,800 at December 31, 20X5. During 20X5, Dewey and Jimm Company reported operating income of $340,000 and $70,000, respectively. Jimm received dividends from investments in marketable equity securities in the amount of $7,000 during 20X5. It also reported an increase of $18,000 in the market value of its portfolio of trading securities and an increase in the value of its portfolio of securities classified as available-for-sale. Jimm paid dividends of $20,000 in 20X5. Ignore income taxes in determining your solution.

Required

a. Assuming that Dewey uses the equity method in accounting for its investment in Jimm, compute the amount of income from Jimm recorded by Dewey in 20X5.

b. Compute the amount added to the investment account during 20X5.

c. Compute the amount reported by Jimm as other comprehensive income in 20X5.

d. If all of Jimm's other comprehensive income arose solely from its investment in available-for-sale securities purchased on March 10, 20X5, for $130,000, what was the market value of those securities at December 31, 20X5?

P2-38* **Equity-Method Income Statement**

Wealthy Manufacturing Company purchased 40 percent of the voting shares of Diversified Products Corporation on March 23, 20X4. On December 31, 20X8, Wealthy Manufacturing's controller attempted to prepare income statements and retained earnings statements for the two companies using the following summarized 20X8 data:

	Wealthy Manufacturing	Diversified Products
Net Sales	$850,000	$400,000
Cost of Goods Sold	670,000	320,000
Other Expenses	90,000	25,000
Dividends Paid	30,000	10,000
Retained Earnings, 1/1/X8	420,000	260,000

Wealthy Manufacturing uses the equity method in accounting for its investment in Diversified Products. The controller was also aware of the following specific transactions for Diversified Products in 20X8, which were not included in the preceding data:

1. On June 30, 20X8, Diversified incurred a $5,000 extraordinary loss from a volcanic eruption near its Greenland facility.

2. Diversified sold its entire Health Technologies division on September 30, 20X8, for $375,000. The book value of Health Technologies division's net assets on that date was $331,000. The division incurred an operating loss of $15,000 in the first nine months of 20X8.

3. On January 1, 20X8, Diversified switched from FIFO inventory costing to the weighted-average method. Had Diversified always used the weighted-average method, prior years' income would have been lower by $20,000.

4. During 20X8, Diversified sold one of its delivery trucks after it was involved in an accident and recorded a gain of $10,000.

Required

a. Prepare an income statement and retained earnings statement for Diversified Products for 20X8.

b. Prepare an income statement and retained earnings statement for Wealthy Manufacturing for 20X8.

P2-39* **Computing Income Tax Expense**

Swan Products Inc. owns 25 percent of Computech Computer Company's common stock, purchased December 28, 20X3, at book value. During the three years subsequent to the acquisition of its stock by Swan Products, Computech reported the following net income and dividends:

	20X4	20X5	20X6
Net Income	$20,000	$ 8,000	$40,000
Dividends	4,000	10,000	12,000

Swan has an effective income tax rate of 40 percent. All dividends it received from Computech qualify for the 80 percent dividend deduction.

Required

a. Compute the amount of income tax expense that Swan should have reported in its income statement for each of the three years with respect to its investment in Computech, assuming that Swan reports its investment using (1) the cost method and (2) the equity method.

b. Present all journal entries related to its investment in Computech, including income tax effects, that Swan should have recorded for each of the three years, assuming Swan accounts for its investment using the cost method.

c. Present all journal entries related to its investment in Computech, including income tax effects, that Swan should have recorded for each of the three years, assuming Swan accounts for its investment using the equity method.

Chapter **Three**

The Reporting Entity and Consolidated Financial Statements

Today, nearly all major corporations prepare consolidated financial statements. While people often think of the world's corporate giants as being single companies, closer examination reveals that each actually is composed of a number of separate companies. For example, General Motors Corporation and Ford Motor Company both own dozens of other companies. The Walt Disney Company is famous for spectacular theme parks and immortal cartoon characters, but it also owns many subsidiaries that include the following businesses: Miramax Films, Touchstone Pictures, Buena Vista Home Entertainment, Hollywood Records, the ABC Television Network and ABC Radio Networks, ESPN, many local television and radio stations, and Disney Cruise Line. Similarly, Time Warner Inc. owns more than 1,500 subsidiaries, including America Online, MapQuest, Moviefone, Time Warner Cable (which owns many subsidiaries), Turner Broadcasting (which owns many subsidiaries), Warner Bros. Entertainment, Warner Bros. Television, New Line Cinema, Warner Home Entertainment, DC Comics, Home Box Office, the Atlanta Braves (professional baseball), Time, and CNN (Cable News Network). General Motors, Ford, The Walt Disney Company, and Time Warner each present consolidated financial statements, as do nearly all corporations that are publicly held.

Consolidated financial statements present the financial position and results of operations for a *parent* (controlling entity) and one or more *subsidiaries* (controlled entities) as if all the individual entities actually were a single company or entity. Consolidation is required when a corporation owns a majority of another corporation's outstanding common stock. As discussed later in the chapter, consolidation also may be appropriate in certain other situations, and not all units subject to consolidation need necessarily be corporations or even business (for profit) enterprises.

Two companies are considered to be *related companies* or *affiliates* when one controls the other or both are under the common control of another entity. Consolidated financial statements are generally considered to be more useful than the separate financial statements of the individual companies when the companies are related. The accounting principles applied in the preparation of consolidated financial statements are the same accounting principles applied in preparing separate-company financial statements. The process of preparing consolidated financial statements involves bringing together the separate financial statements of related companies as if the related companies were actually a single company.

Any business combination results in one of two situations: either (1) the net assets of one or both of the combining companies are transferred to a single company (a merger or statutory consolidation) or (2) the combining companies each remain as *separate legal entities* (a stock acquisition). In the first case, no consolidation questions arise because only a single corporation emerges from the business combination. The financial statements of the resulting reporting entity are those of a single corporation. The matter of consolidated financial statements arises in the second instance because of the existence of two or more legally separate but related companies. A similar situation also arises if a company creates rather than purchases a subsidiary. Whether the subsidiary is acquired or created, each individual company maintains its own accounting records, but consolidated statements are needed to present the companies together as a single economic entity for general-purpose financial reporting.

USEFULNESS OF CONSOLIDATED FINANCIAL STATEMENTS

Consolidated financial statements are presented primarily for those parties having a long-run interest in the parent company, including the parent's shareholders, creditors, and other resource providers. Consolidated statements often provide the only means of obtaining a clear picture of the total resources of the combined entity that are under the parent's control and the results of employing those resources. Especially when the number of related companies is substantial, consolidated statements may provide the only means of conveniently summarizing the vast amount of information relating to the individual companies and how the positions and operations of the individual companies affect the overall consolidated entity.

Current and prospective stockholders of the parent company are usually more interested in the consolidated financial statements than those of the individual companies because the well-being of the parent company is affected by the operations of its subsidiaries. When subsidiaries are profitable, profits accrue to the parent, and, similarly, the parent cannot escape the ill effects of unprofitable subsidiaries. By examining the consolidated statements, owners and potential owners are better able to assess the effectiveness with which management employs all the resources under its control.

The parent's long-term creditors also find the consolidated statements useful because the effects of subsidiary operations on the overall health and future of the parent are relevant to their decisions. In addition, although the parent and its subsidiaries are separate companies, the parent's creditors have an indirect claim on the subsidiaries' assets. The parent's short-term creditors, however, even though they also have an indirect claim on the subsidiaries' assets, are usually more interested in the parent's immediate solvency rather than its long-term profitability. Accordingly, they tend to rely more on the parent's separate financial statements, especially the balance sheet.

The parent company's management has a continuing need for current information both about the combined operations of the consolidated entity and about the individual companies forming the consolidated entity. For example, individual subsidiaries might have substantial volatility in their operations, and not until operating results and balance sheets are combined can the manager understand the overall impact of the activities for the period. On the other hand, information about individual companies within the consolidated entity may also be useful. For example, it may allow a manager to offset a cash shortfall in one subsidiary with excess cash from another without resorting to costly outside borrowing. The parent company's management may be particularly concerned with the consolidated financial statements because top management generally is evaluated, and sometimes compensated, based on the overall performance of the entity as reflected in the consolidated statements.

The creditors and any outside stockholders of subsidiaries generally are most interested in the separate financial statements of those subsidiaries. Subsidiary resource providers have no claim on the parent company unless the parent has provided guarantees or entered into other arrangements for the benefit of the subsidiaries.

LIMITATIONS OF CONSOLIDATED FINANCIAL STATEMENTS

While consolidated financial statements are useful, their limitations also must be kept in mind. Some information is lost any time data sets are aggregated; this is particularly true when the information involves an aggregation across companies that have substantially different operating characteristics.

Some of the more important limitations of consolidated financial statements are as follows:

1. Because the operating results and financial position of individual companies included in the consolidation are not disclosed, the poor performance or position of one or more companies may be hidden by the good performance and position of others.

2. Not all the consolidated retained earnings balance is necessarily available for dividends of the parent because a portion may represent the parent's share of undistributed subsidiary earnings. Similarly, because the consolidated statements include the subsidiary's assets, not all assets shown are available for dividend distributions of the parent company.

3. Because financial ratios based on the consolidated statements are calculated on aggregated information, they are not necessarily representative of any single company in the consolidation, including the parent.

4. Similar accounts of different companies that are combined in the consolidation may not be entirely comparable. For example, the length of operating cycles of different companies may vary, causing receivables of similar length to be classified differently.

5. Additional information about individual companies or groups of companies included in the consolidation often is necessary for a fair presentation; such additional disclosures may require voluminous footnotes.

SUBSIDIARY FINANCIAL STATEMENTS

Some financial statement users may be interested in the separate financial statements of individual subsidiaries, either instead of or in addition to consolidated financial statements. While the parent company's management is concerned with the entire consolidated entity as well as individual subsidiaries, the creditors, preferred stockholders, and noncontrolling common stockholders of subsidiary companies are most interested in the separate financial statements of the subsidiaries in which they have an interest. Because subsidiaries are legally separate from their parents, a subsidiary's creditors and stockholders generally have no claim on the parent and the subsidiary's stockholders do not share in the parent's profits. Therefore, consolidated financial statements usually are of little use to those interested in obtaining information about the assets, capital, or income of individual subsidiaries.

CONSOLIDATED FINANCIAL STATEMENTS: CONCEPTS AND STANDARDS

Consolidated financial statements are intended to provide a meaningful representation of the overall position and activities of a single economic entity comprising a number of related companies. Current consolidation standards have been established by **Accounting Research Bulletin No. 51**, "Consolidated Financial Statements" (ARB 51), issued in 1959, and **FASB Statement No. 94**, "Consolidation of All Majority-Owned Subsidiaries" (FASB 94), issued in 1987. Under current standards, subsidiaries must be consolidated unless the parent is precluded from exercising control. When consolidation of a subsidiary is not appropriate, the subsidiary is reported as an intercorporate investment.

Traditional View of Control

Over the years, the single most important criterion for determining when an individual subsidiary should be consolidated has been that of control. **ARB 51** indicates that consolidated financial statements normally are appropriate for a group of companies when one company "has a controlling financial interest in the other companies." It also states that "the usual condition for a controlling financial interest is ownership of a majority voting interest. . . ." In practice, control has been determined by the proportion of voting shares of a company's stock owned directly or indirectly by another company. This criterion was formalized by

FASB 94, which requires consolidation of all majority-owned subsidiaries unless the parent is unable to exercise control.

Although majority ownership is the most common means of acquiring control, a company may be able to direct the operating and financing policies of another with less than majority ownership, such as when the remainder of the stock is widely held. **FASB 94** does not preclude consolidation with less than majority ownership, but such consolidations have seldom been found in practice.

Indirect Control

The traditional view of control includes both direct and indirect control. ***Direct control*** typically occurs when one company owns a majority of another company's common stock. ***Indirect control*** or *pyramiding* occurs when a company's common stock is owned by one or more other companies that are all under common control. Examples of indirect control of Z Company by P Company include the following ownership situations:

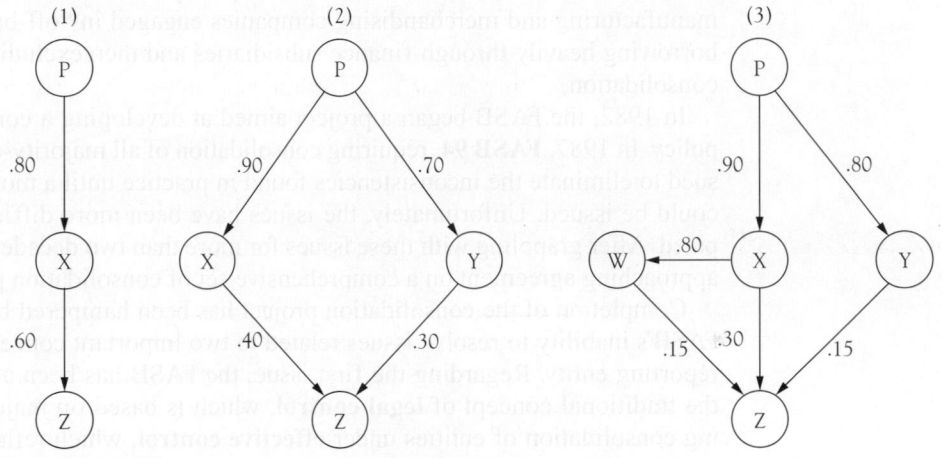

In (1), P owns 80 percent of X, which owns 60 percent of Z.

In (2), P owns 90 percent of X and 70 percent of Y; X owns 40 percent of Z; Y owns 30 percent of Z.

In (3), P owns 90 percent of X and 80 percent of Y; X owns 80 percent of W and 30 percent of Z; Y owns 15 percent of Z; W owns 15 percent of Z.

In each case, P's control over Z is indirect because it is gained by controlling other companies that control Z.

Ability to Exercise Control

Under certain circumstances, a subsidiary's majority stockholders may not be able to exercise control even though they hold more than 50 percent of its outstanding voting stock. This might occur, for instance, if the subsidiary was in legal reorganization or in bankruptcy; while the parent might hold majority ownership, control would rest with the courts or a court-appointed trustee. Similarly, if the subsidiary was located in a foreign country and that country had placed restrictions on the subsidiary that prevented the remittance of profits or assets back to the parent company, consolidation of that subsidiary would not be appropriate because of the parent's inability to control important aspects of the subsidiary's operations.

Differences in Fiscal Periods

A difference in the fiscal periods of a parent and subsidiary should not preclude consolidation of that subsidiary. Often the subsidiary's fiscal period, if different from the parent's, is changed to coincide with that of the parent. Another alternative is to adjust the financial statement data of the subsidiary each period to place the data on a basis consistent with the fiscal period of the parent. Both the Securities and Exchange Commission and current accounting standards permit the consolidation of a subsidiary's financial statements without adjusting the fiscal period of the subsidiary if that period does not differ from the parent's by more than three months and if recognition is given to intervening events that have a material effect on financial position or results of operations.

Changing Concept of the Reporting Entity

For nearly three decades, **ARB 51** served without significant revision as the primary source of consolidation policy. Over those years, many changes occurred in the business environment, including widespread diversification of companies and the increased emphasis on financial services by manufacturing and merchandising companies such as General Electric and Harley-Davidson.

In addition, the criteria used in determining whether to consolidate specific subsidiaries were subject to varying interpretations. Companies exercised great latitude in selecting which subsidiaries to consolidate and which to report as intercorporate investments. The lack of consistency in consolidation policy became of increasing concern as many manufacturing and merchandising companies engaged in "off-balance sheet financing" by borrowing heavily through finance subsidiaries and then excluding those subsidiaries from consolidation.

In 1982, the FASB began a project aimed at developing a comprehensive consolidation policy. In 1987, **FASB 94**, requiring consolidation of all majority-owned subsidiaries, was issued to eliminate the inconsistencies found in practice until a more comprehensive standard could be issued. Unfortunately, the issues have been more difficult to resolve than anticipated. After grappling with issues for more than two decades, the FASB finally may be approaching agreement on a comprehensive set of consolidation policies and procedures.

Completion of the consolidation project has been hampered by, among other things, the FASB's inability to resolve issues related to two important concepts: (1) control and (2) the reporting entity. Regarding the first issue, the FASB has been attempting to move beyond the traditional concept of **legal control**, which is based on majority ownership, to requiring consolidation of entities under **effective control**, which reflects an ability to direct the policies of another entity even though majority ownership is lacking. Such a view of control would likely result in the consolidation of some companies in which little, or even no, ownership was held, and could also result in the consolidation of entities other than corporations, such as partnerships and trusts. In regard to the second issue, the FASB has attempted to define the reporting entity, which would go a long way toward resolving the issue of when to prepare consolidated statements and what entities should be included. Unfortunately, the FASB has found that both issues are so complex that they are not easily resolved. Thus, the FASB has moved on with attempting to establish consolidation standards without first resolving these issues, even though the FASB still plans to attempt their resolution.

In 2005, the FASB issued an exposure draft of a new standard on consolidated financial statements.[1] The proposed standard sets ownership of a majority voting interest as the usual condition for consolidation. In this regard, the proposed standard is consistent with **ARB 51**. However, the FASB's related exposure draft on business combinations indicates that exceptions to simple reliance on majority ownership will be more frequent than in current practice.

OVERVIEW OF THE CONSOLIDATION PROCESS

The consolidation process adds together the financial statements of two or more legally separate companies, creating a single set of financial statements. The following chapters discuss the specific procedures used to produce consolidated financial statements in considerable detail. An understanding of the procedures is important because they facilitate the accurate and efficient preparation of consolidated statements. However, the focus should

[1] *Financial Accounting Standards Board Proposed Statement of Financial Accounting Standards,* "Consolidated Financial Statements, Including Accounting and Reporting of Noncontrolling Interests in Subsidiaries," June 30, 2005, 72 pp.

continue to be on the end product, the financial statements. The procedures are intended to produce financial statements that appear as if the consolidated companies are actually a single company.

The separate financial statements of the companies involved serve as the starting point each time consolidated statements are prepared. These separate statements are added together, after some adjustments and eliminations, to generate consolidated statements. The adjustments and eliminations relate to intercompany transactions and holdings. While the individual companies within a consolidated entity may legitimately report sales and receivables or payables to one another, the consolidated entity as a whole must report only transactions with parties outside the consolidated entity and receivables from or payables to external parties. Thus, the adjustments and eliminations required as part of the consolidation process aim at ensuring that the consolidated financial statements are presented as if they were the statements of a single enterprise.

After all the consolidation procedures have been applied, the preparer should review the resulting statements and ask: "Do these statements appear as if the consolidated companies were actually a single company?" To answer this question, two other questions must be answered:

1. Are items included in the statements that would not appear, or that would be stated at different amounts, in the statements of a single company?

2. Do any items not appear in these statements that would appear if the consolidated entity were actually a single company?

These questions are answered based not on a knowledge of consolidation procedures, but on a thorough knowledge of generally accepted accounting principles. If the statements are not equivalent to those of a single company, additional procedures must be completed to provide statements as they would be presented by a single reporting entity.

THE CONSOLIDATION PROCESS ILLUSTRATED

The basic concepts that apply to the preparation of consolidated financial statements are illustrated in the following example. The focus of the example is on the balance sheet, but the concepts apply equally to the other financial statements as well. Assume that on January 1, 20X1, Popper Company purchases at book value all of Sun Corporation's common stock. At the end of 20X1, the balance sheets of the two companies appear as follows:

Balance Sheets December 31, 20X1		
	Popper	Sun
Assets		
Cash	$ 5,000	$ 3,000
Receivables (net)	84,000	30,000
Inventory	95,000	60,000
Fixed Assets (net)	375,000	250,000
Other Assets	25,000	15,000
Investment in Sun Stock	300,000	
Total Assets	$884,000	$358,000
Liabilities and Equities		
Short-Term Payables	$ 60,000	$ 8,000
Long-Term Payables	200,000	50,000
Common Stock	500,000	200,000
Retained Earnings	124,000	100,000
Total Liabilities and Equities	$884,000	$358,000

Additional information regarding Popper and Sun is as follows:

1. Popper uses the basic equity method to account for its investment in Sun. The investment account is carried at the book value of Sun's net assets and is adjusted for Popper's share of Sun's earnings and dividends.
2. Sun owes Popper $1,000 on account at the end of the year.
3. Sun purchases $6,000 of inventory from Popper during 20X1. The inventory originally cost Popper $4,000. Sun still holds all the inventory at the end of the year.

The Consolidated Entity

The following diagram can be helpful in understanding the consolidated entity:

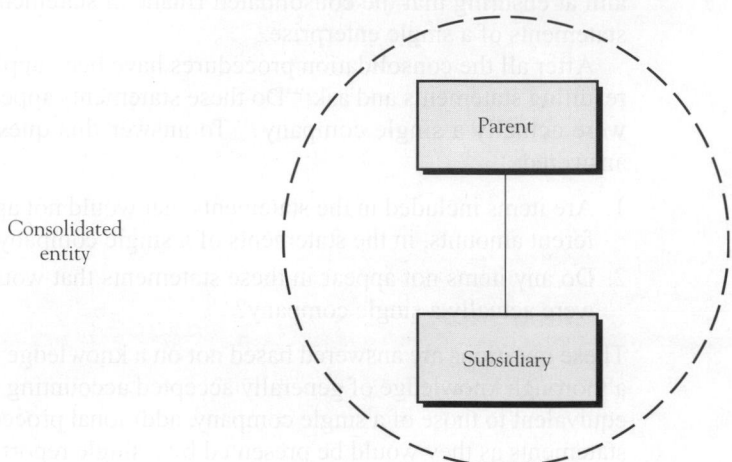

The boxes representing the parent and the subsidiary indicate legal entities. Transactions are recorded in the accounts of these legal entities. The dashed circular line can be viewed as defining the consolidated entity, which encompasses both the parent and the subsidiary. This consolidated entity has no legal existence but is considered to have economic reality.

Transactions or ownership relations that cross over the dashed line can be viewed as involving outsiders and are properly reflected in the consolidated financial statements. Those transactions or relations that are entirely within the consolidated entity are not reflected in the consolidated financial statements because they do not involve outsiders. Instead, they are viewed as occurring within a single accounting entity and, therefore, do not qualify for inclusion in the consolidated statements.

The consolidated balance sheet for Popper and Sun appears in Figure 3–1, along with the computations used in deriving the balances reported. The like accounts from the parent and subsidiary financial statements are added together and then adjusted, when appropriate, to remove the effects of intercompany ownership and transactions. For example, the totals reported for cash, fixed assets, other assets, and long-term payables in this example are derived by simply adding together the amounts reported by the two companies. An adjustment is required to reduce receivables (net) and short-term payables for intercompany debt. Similarly, inventory and retained earnings are adjusted to remove the write-up in carrying value that occurred when Sun purchased the inventory from Popper. For corporate ownership, only the stockholders' equity balances of Popper, as the parent company, are included in the consolidated balance sheet. A discussion of the rationale for each of the adjustments is presented in the sections that follow.

In the Popper and Sun example, several items need to be given special attention to ensure that the consolidated financial statements appear as if they are the statements of a single company:

1. Intercorporate stockholdings.
2. Intercompany receivables and payables.
3. Intercompany sales.

FIGURE 3–1
Consolidated
Balance Sheet

POPPER COMPANY
Consolidated Balance Sheet
December 31, 20X1

Assets		Liabilities and Equities	
Cash	$ 8,000[a]	Short-Term Payables	$ 67,000[f]
Receivables (net)	113,000[b]	Long-Term Payables	250,000[g]
Inventory	153,000[c]		
Fixed Assets (net)	625,000[d]	Common Stock	500,000[h]
Other Assets	40,000[e]	Retained Earnings	122,000[i]
Total Assets	$939,000	Total Liabilities and Equities	$939,000

The consolidated balances were obtained as follows:
[a] Cash: $5,000 + $3,000 = $8,000
[b] Receivables (net): $84,000 + $30,000 − $1,000 = $113,000
[c] Inventory: $95,000 + $60,000 − $2,000 = $153,000
[d] Fixed Assets (net): $375,000 + $250,000 = $625,000
[e] Other Assets: $25,000 + $15,000 = $40,000
[f] Short-Term Payables: $60,000 + $8,000 − $1,000 = $67,000
[g] Long-Term Payables: $200,000 + $50,000 = $250,000
[h] Common Stock: $500,000 + $200,000 − $200,000 = $500,000
[i] Retained Earnings: $124,000 + $100,000 − $100,000 − $2,000 = $122,000

Intercorporate Stockholdings

In the example given, Popper Company's common stock is held by those outside the consolidated entity and is properly viewed as the common stock of the entire entity. Sun's common stock, on the other hand, is held entirely within the consolidated entity and is not stock outstanding from a consolidated viewpoint. These relationships are illustrated as follows:

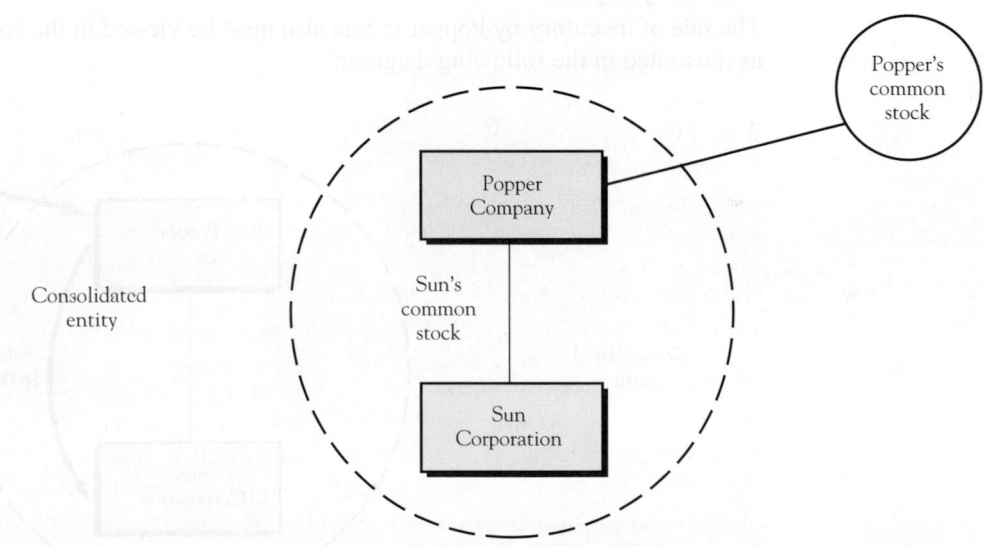

Because a company cannot report in its financial statements an investment in itself, Sun's common stock and Popper's investment in that stock both must be eliminated. Popper's common stock remains as the common stock of the consolidated entity.

Only Popper Company's retained earnings is included in the consolidated balance sheet shown in Figure 3–1. Sun's retained earnings is not reported in the consolidated balance sheet because it relates to an ownership interest held entirely within the consolidated entity. Popper's retained earnings, on the other hand, represents a claim of the parent's shareholders, viewed as the residual owners of the consolidated entity. Popper's retained earnings (less the unrealized intercompany profit) indicates the amount of undistributed past earnings of the consolidated entity accruing to the stockholders of the parent company and, therefore, is reported as consolidated retained earnings.

Intercompany Receivables and Payables

The intercompany receivable/payable can be viewed as follows:

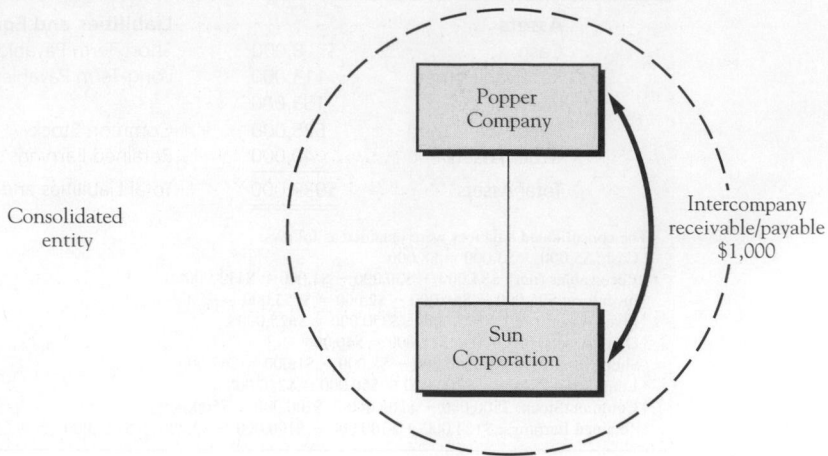

A single company cannot owe itself money. While as separate companies Popper properly reports a $1,000 trade receivable from Sun and Sun properly reports a $1,000 trade payable to Popper, such a receivable/payable does not exist from a consolidated viewpoint. Therefore, the $1,000 is eliminated from both receivables and payables in preparing the consolidated balance sheet.

Intercompany Sales

The sale of inventory by Popper to Sun also must be viewed in the context of a single entity, as illustrated in the following diagram:

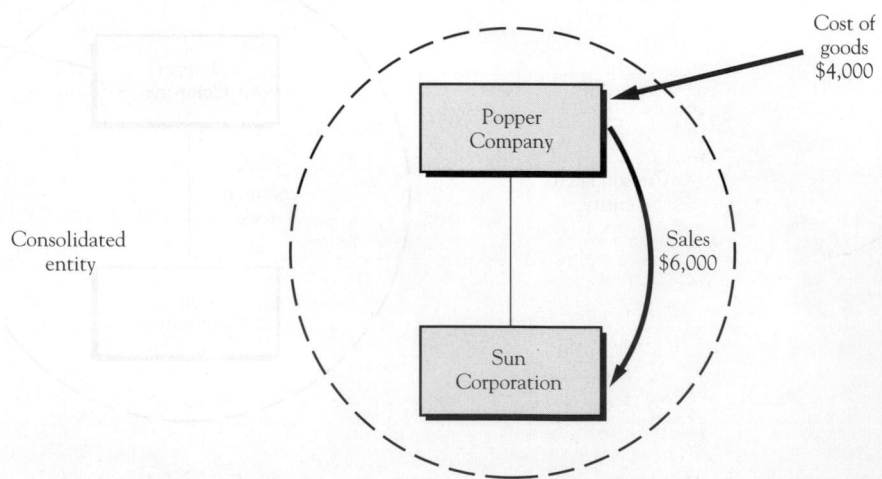

A single company may not recognize a profit and write up its inventory simply because the inventory is transferred from one department or division to another. This also applies to intercompany sales within a consolidated entity. In this example, the intercompany inventory remaining at the end of the period ($6,000) must be restated to its original cost to the consolidated entity, the $4,000 paid by Popper. Similarly, the $2,000 profit recognized on the intercompany sale and included in Popper's retained earnings may not be included in the consolidated amounts. Therefore, both the inventory and the consolidated retained earnings must be reduced by the $2,000 unrealized intercompany profit when preparing the consolidated balance sheet. In preparing a consolidated income statement, the $6,000 intercompany sale would have to be removed from the combined revenues of Popper and Sun because it does not represent a sale to an external party.

Difference between Cost and Book Value

In the current example, Popper purchased its investment in Sun's stock at book value. In reality, the purchase price of a subsidiary usually differs from the book value of the shares acquired. This differential is treated in the same way in preparing consolidated financial statements as for a merger, discussed in Chapter 1. If Popper had paid more for its investment in Sun than the book value of the shares acquired (a debit differential), the excess would be allocated in consolidation to specific assets and liabilities of Sun or to goodwill.

Single-Entity Viewpoint

The various adjustments discussed in this simplified example illustrate the type of thinking involved in the preparation of consolidated financial statements. To understand each of the adjustments needed in preparing consolidated statements, the reader should focus on (1) identifying the treatment accorded a particular item by each of the separate companies and (2) identifying the amount that would appear in the financial statements with respect to that item if the consolidated entity were actually a single company.

Mechanics of the Consolidation Process

A worksheet is used to facilitate the process of combining and adjusting the account balances involved in a consolidation. The parent company and each subsidiary maintains its own set of books. No set of books exists for the consolidated entity. Instead, the balances of the accounts are taken at the end of each period from the books of the parent and each subsidiary and entered in the consolidation workpaper.

A consolidation workpaper for the preparation of Popper Company's consolidated balance sheet appears in Figure 3–2. The account balances for Popper and Sun, taken from their separate books, are listed in the first two columns beside one another so the amounts for each asset, liability, and equity item may be added across to obtain the consolidated balances.

FIGURE 3–2
Consolidated Balance Sheet Workpaper

			POPPER COMPANY AND SUBSIDIARY Consolidated Balance Sheet Workpaper December 31, 20X1		
	Popper	Sun	**Eliminations**		
Item	Company	Corporation	Debit	Credit	Consolidated
Cash	5,000	3,000			8,000
Receivables (net)	84,000	30,000		(a) 1,000	113,000
Inventory	95,000	60,000		(b) 2,000	153,000
Fixed Assets (net)	375,000	250,000			625,000
Other Assets	25,000	15,000			40,000
Investment in Sun Stock	300,000			(c) 300,000	
	884,000	358,000			939,000
Short-Term Payables	60,000	8,000	(a) 1,000		67,000
Long-Term Payables	200,000	50,000			250,000
Common Stock	500,000	200,000	(c) 200,000		500,000
Retained Earnings	124,000	100,000	(c) 100,000		
			(b) 2,000		122,000
	884,000	358,000	303,000	303,000	939,000

Elimination entries:
(a) Eliminate intercompany receivable/payable.
(b) Eliminate unrealized intercompany profit included in ending inventory against consolidated retained earnings.
(c) Eliminate intercorporate investment against subsidiary's stockholders' equity.

When simply adding the amounts from the two companies leads to a consolidated figure different from the amount that would appear if the two companies were actually one, the combined amount must be adjusted to the desired figure. This is done through the preparation of *eliminating entries*. Separate debit and credit columns are provided for the eliminating entries in the workpaper in Figure 3–2. The final column in the workpaper presents the amounts to appear in the consolidated balance sheet. These amounts are obtained by summing across each line and including the effects of each debit or credit elimination or adjustment. The consolidated amounts then appear in the consolidated balance sheet as in Figure 3–1.

The following chapters discuss consolidation workpapers and eliminating entries in more detail. The consolidation procedures and workpapers are important because they facilitate the preparation of the consolidated statements, help ensure clerical accuracy, and provide a trail for the verification of the account balances in the consolidated statements. At this point, however, the reader should focus on understanding what numbers appear in the financial statements when adopting a single-entity viewpoint rather than concentrating on specific procedures or workpaper techniques.

NONCONTROLLING INTEREST

A parent company does not always own 100 percent of a subsidiary's outstanding common stock. The parent may have acquired less than 100 percent of a company's stock in a business combination, or it may originally have held 100 percent but sold or awarded some shares to others. For the parent to consolidate the subsidiary, only a controlling interest is needed. Those shareholders of the subsidiary other than the parent are referred to as "noncontrolling" or "minority" shareholders. The claim of these shareholders on the income and net assets of the subsidiary is referred to as the *noncontrolling interest* or the *minority interest*.

The noncontrolling shareholders clearly have a claim on the subsidiary's assets and earnings through their stock ownership. Because all of the subsidiary's assets, liabilities, and earnings normally are included in the consolidated statements, the noncontrolling shareholders' claim on these items must be reported. The noncontrolling shareholders' claim on the subsidiary's net assets has been shown most commonly between liabilities and stockholders' equity in the consolidated balance sheet. A few companies have reported the noncontrolling interest with liabilities, although it clearly does not meet the legal or accounting definition of a liability. The portion of the subsidiary net income assigned to the noncontrolling interest normally has been deducted from earnings available to all shareholders to arrive at consolidated net income in the consolidated income statement. Although this assignment of income does not meet the definition of an expense, it normally has been accorded this expense-type treatment. For example, Century Telephone generally has referred to the minority interest's share of income as an expense in the notes to its consolidated financial statements.

In uncomplicated situations, the amount of noncontrolling interest is a simple proportionate share of the relevant subsidiary amounts. For example, if a subsidiary has net income of $150,000 and the noncontrolling shareholders own 10 percent of the subsidiary's common stock, their share of income is $15,000 ($150,000 × .10). Similarly, if the subsidiary's only stockholders' equity accounts are common stock of $600,000 and retained earnings of $200,000, the total noncontrolling interest, reflecting the noncontrolling shareholders' claim on the net assets of the subsidiary, is computed as follows:

Subsidiary common stock	$600,000
Subsidiary retained earnings	200,000
Book value of subsidiary	$800,000
Noncontrolling stockholders' proportionate share	× .10
Noncontrolling interest	$ 80,000

Several different consolidation theories that affect the computation and treatment of the noncontrolling interest have been proposed. These theories are discussed briefly later in the chapter.

COMBINED FINANCIAL STATEMENTS

Financial statements sometimes are prepared for a group of companies when no one company in the group owns a majority of the common stock of any other company in the group. Financial statements that include a group of related companies without including the parent company or other owner are referred to as *combined financial statements*.

Combined financial statements are commonly prepared when an individual, rather than a corporation, owns or controls a number of companies and wishes to include them all in a single set of financial statements. In some cases, a parent company may prepare financial statements that include only its subsidiaries, not the parent. In other cases, a parent may prepare financial statements for its subsidiaries by operating group, with all the subsidiaries engaged in a particular type of operation, or those located in a particular geographical region, reported together.

The procedures used to prepare combined financial statements are essentially the same as those used in preparing consolidated financial statements. All intercompany receivables and payables, intercompany transactions, and unrealized intercompany profits and losses must be eliminated in the same manner as in the preparation of consolidated statements. Although no parent company is included in the reporting entity, any intercompany ownership, and the associated portion of stockholders' equity, must be eliminated in the same way as the parent's investment in a subsidiary is eliminated in preparing consolidated financial statements. The remaining stockholders' equity of the companies in the reporting entity is divided into the portions accruing to the controlling and noncontrolling interests.

SPECIAL-PURPOSE AND VARIABLE INTEREST ENTITIES

While consolidation standards pertaining to related corporations have at times lacked clarity and needed updating, consolidation standards relating to partnerships or other types of entities such as trusts have been virtually nonexistent. Even corporate consolidation standards have not been adequate in situations in which other relationships such as guarantees and operating agreements overshadow the lack of a significant ownership element. As a result, companies such as Enron have taken advantage of the lack of standards to avoid reporting debt or losses by hiding them in special entities that were not consolidated. Although many companies have used special entities for legitimate purposes, financial reporting has not always captured the economic substance of the relationships. Only in the past few years have consolidation standards for these special entities started to provide some uniformity in the financial reporting for corporations having relationships with such entities.

ARB 51 established consolidation standards in terms of one company controlling another and set majority voting interest as the usual condition leading to consolidation. Similarly, **FASB 94** requires consolidation for majority-owned subsidiaries. In recent years, however, new types of relationships have been established between corporations and other entities that often are difficult to characterize in terms of voting, controlling, or ownership interests. Such entities often are structured to provide financing and/or control through forms other than those used by traditional operating companies. Some entities have no governing boards, or they may have boards or managers with only a limited ability to direct the entity's activities. Such entities may be governed instead by their incorporation or partnership documents, or by other agreements or documents. Some entities may have little equity investment, and the equity investors may have little or no control over the entity. For these special types of entities, **ARB 51** does not provide a clear basis for consolidation.

These special types of entities have generally been referred to as *special-purpose entities (SPEs)*. In general, SPEs are corporations, trusts, or partnerships created for a single specified purpose. They usually have no substantive operations and are used only for financing purposes. SPEs have been used for several decades for asset securitization, risk sharing, and taking advantage of tax statutes. Prior to 2003, no comprehensive reporting framework had been established for SPEs. Several different pronouncements from various bodies dealt with selected issues or types of SPEs, but the guidance provided by these issuances was incomplete, vague, and not always correctly interpreted in practice.

Off-Balance Sheet Financing

Imagine that Genergy, Inc., needs $1 billion to finance building a gas pipeline in central Asia. Potential investors may want their risk/reward exposure limited to the pipeline without other aspects of Genergy's business. They might also want the pipeline to be a self-supporting independent entity with cash flows that are separate from Genergy's other business activities, and they may want to eliminate the possibility that Genergy will sell the pipeline. These objectives might be achieved by forming an SPE or what the FASB refers to as a *variable interest entity (VIE),* with a charter that specifies these limited operating activities.

Once the VIE is established, the pipeline assets and the debt used to finance the pipeline may be, under certain circumstances, excluded from Genergy's balance sheet. In this manner, Genergy has achieved *off-balance sheet financing* of the pipeline. As long as the VIE is not consolidated, Genergy's financial statements will not reflect the assets, liabilities, cash flows, revenues, and expenses associated with owning and operating the pipeline. Further, any transactions between Genergy and the pipeline entity are not eliminated in preparing Genergy's financial statements.

Some estimates have indicated that well over half of American companies use some type of off-balance sheet financing, involving perhaps trillions of dollars. These transactions are often facilitated by the use of some type of special entity, such as a VIE. There is concern that VIEs can be motivated either by a genuine business purpose, such as risk sharing among investors and isolation of project risk from company risk, or by a desire to meet specific financial reporting goals that may or may not be supported by the underlying economic substance of the transactions.

Companies might prefer to keep debt and the related assets financed by that debt off the balance sheet for a number of reasons, but the main one often has to do with making the company appear better to investors. One effect is to reduce the company's leverage and debt/equity ratios. Net income also may be increased as neither the interest on the debt nor the depreciation on the related assets is included in expenses. Further, the smaller asset base, because the assets are not shown on the balance sheet, combined with the higher net income produces a higher calculated return on assets.

Several means of keeping debt and related assets off of a company's balance sheet have become common in practice. A company may lease assets from a third party such as a VIE, which borrows the money to buy the assets. Careful engineering of the lease terms so that it qualifies for treatment as an operating rather than a capital lease avoids recognition of the asset and lease obligation. Another possibility is for a company to sell assets such as accounts receivable outright rather than borrowing against them. A third option found with increasing frequency is for a company to create a new VIE and transfer both assets and liabilities to it. This not only allows the sponsoring corporation to remove the asset and related debt from its balance sheet, but the company also may be able to recognize a gain on the disposal of the asset.

Complex organizational structures increase the need for accounting standards aimed at ensuring that financial statements reflect the economic substance of those structures and the related transactions. However, the very complexity of these organizational structures makes the development of these standards a challenging endeavor.

Qualifying Special-Purpose Entities

Certain types of SPEs that are widely used for servicing financial assets and meet very restrictive conditions established by **FASB Statement No. 140** are referred to as *qualifying SPEs.* Although the conditions are complex, in general they require that the SPE be "demonstrably distinct from the transferor," its activities be significantly limited, and it hold only certain types of financial assets.[2] For example, a finance-type company making many car loans, such as GMAC, might sell all of the car loans to an SPE especially established for the purpose. The SPE would then issue bonds (collateralized asset obligations) to the public using the car loans as collateral. The SPE would collect the payments on the car loans and make the payments on the bonds. While the SPE would have a significant amount of long-term debt, it might have little or no equity ownership. If the conditions of **FASB 140** are met, this type of SPE is not consolidated by the transferor of assets to the SPE.

Variable Interest Entities

In January 2003, the FASB issued **FASB Interpretation No. 46**, *Consolidation of Variable Interest Entities,* an interpretation of **ARB No. 51**, with a revised version issued in December 2003[3] (FIN 46R). For clarification, the interpretation uses the term *variable interest entities* to encompass SPEs and any other entities falling within its conditions. This pronouncement does not apply to entities that are considered qualifying SPEs under **FASB No. 140**.

A *variable interest entity (VIE)* is a legal structure used for business purposes, usually a corporation, trust, or partnership, that either (1) does not have equity investors that have voting rights and share in all of the entity's profits and losses or (2) has equity investors that do not provide sufficient financial resources to support the entity's activities. In a variable interest entity, specific agreements may limit the extent to which the equity investors, if any, share in the entity's profits or losses, and the agreements may limit the control that equity investors have over the entity's activities. For the equity investment to be considered sufficient financial support for the entity's activities (condition 2), it must be able to absorb the entity's expected future losses. A total equity investment that is less than 10 percent of the entity's total assets is, in general, considered to be insufficient by itself to allow the entity to finance its activities, and an investment of more than 10 percent might be needed, depending on the circumstances.

A typical variable interest entity might be created (or sponsored) by a corporation for a particular purpose, such as purchasing the sponsoring company's receivables or leasing facilities to the sponsoring company. The sponsoring company may acquire little or no stock (or other equity interest) in the VIE. Instead, the sponsoring company may enlist another party to purchase most or all of the common stock. The majority of the VIE's capital, however, normally comes from borrowing. Because lenders may be reluctant to lend (at least at reasonable interest rates) to an entity with only a small amount of equity, the sponsoring company often guarantees the VIE's loans. Thus, the sponsoring company may have little or no equity investment in the VIE, but the loan guarantees represent a type of interest in the VIE.

A corporation having an interest in a VIE cannot simply rely on its percentage stock ownership, if any, to determine whether to consolidate the entity. Instead each party having a variable interest in the VIE must determine the extent to which it shares in the VIE's expected profits and losses. **FIN 46R** (para. 2c) defines a *variable interest* in a VIE as a contractual, ownership (with or without voting rights), or other money-related interest in an entity that changes with changes in the fair value of the entity's net assets exclusive of variable interests. In other words, variable interests increase with the VIE's profits and decrease with its losses. The VIE's variable interests will absorb portions of the losses, if they occur, or receive portions of the residual returns.

Variable interests may be of a number of different types. The designation of several common types of interests in a VIE are as follows:

[2] *Financial Accounting Standards Board Statement No. 140,* "Accounting for Transfers and Servicing of Financial Assets and Extinguishments of Liabilities," September 2000, para. 35.
[3] *Financial Accounting Standards Board Interpretation No. 46 (revised December 2003),* "Consolidation of Variable Interest Entities, an interpretation of **ARB No. 51**," December 2003.

Type of Interest	Variable Interest?
Common stock, with no special features or provisions	Yes
Common stock, with loss protection or other provisions	Maybe
Senior debt	Usually not
Subordinated debt	Yes
Loan or asset guarantees	Yes

Common stock that places the owners' investment at risk is a variable interest. In some cases, certain common stock may have, by agreement, special provisions that protect the investor against losses or provide a fixed return. These special types of shares may not involve significant risk on the part of the investor and might, depending on the provisions, result in an interest that is not a variable interest. Senior debt usually carries a fixed return and is protected against loss by subordinated interests. Subordinated debt represents a variable interest because, if the entity's cash flows are insufficient to pay off the subordinated debt, the holders of that debt will sustain losses. They do not have the same protection against loss that holders of the senior debt have. Parties that guarantee the value of assets or liabilities can sustain losses if they are called on to make good on their guarantees, and, therefore, the guarantees represent variable interests.

The nature of each party's variable interest determines whether consolidation by that party is appropriate. An enterprise that will absorb a majority of the VIE's expected losses, receive a majority of the VIE's expected residual returns, or both, is called the ***primary beneficiary*** of the variable interest entity. The primary beneficiary must consolidate the VIE. If the entity's profits and losses are divided differently, the enterprise absorbing a majority of the losses will consolidate the VIE.

As an example of the financial reporting determinations that must be made by parties having an interest in a VIE, suppose that Young Company and Zebra Corporation, both financially stable companies, create YZ Corporation to lease equipment to Young and other companies. Zebra purchases all of YZ's common stock. Young guarantees Zebra a 7 percent dividend on its stock, agrees to absorb all of YZ's losses, and, in addition, guarantees fixed-rate bank loans that are made to YZ. All profits in excess of the 7 percent payout to Zebra are split evenly between Young and Zebra.

In this case, the bank loans are not variable interests because they carry a fixed interest rate and are guaranteed by Young, a company capable of honoring the guarantee. Common stock of a VIE is a variable interest if the investment is at risk. In this case, Zebra's investment is not at risk, but it does share in the profits of YZ, and the amount of profits is not fixed. Therefore, the common stock is a variable interest. However, Zebra will not consolidate YZ because Zebra does not share in the losses, all of which Young will bear. Young would consolidate YZ because Young's guarantees represent a variable interest and it will absorb a majority (all) of the losses.

If consolidation of a VIE is appropriate, the amounts to be consolidated with those of the primary beneficiary are based on fair values at the date the enterprise first becomes the primary beneficiary. However, assets and liabilities transferred to a VIE by its primary beneficiary are valued at their book values, with no gain or loss recognized on the transfer. Subsequent to the initial determination of consolidation values, a VIE is accounted for in consolidated financial statements in accordance with **ARB 51** in the same manner as if it were consolidated based on voting interests. Intercompany balances and transactions are eliminated so the resulting consolidated financial statements appear as if there were just a single entity. These procedures are consistent with those used when consolidating parent and subsidiary corporations. Appendix 3A presents a simple illustration of the consolidation of a VIE.

ADDITIONAL CONSIDERATIONS—
DIFFERENT APPROACHES TO CONSOLIDATION

The previous sections gave a brief overview of the concepts, issues, and procedures to be discussed in Chapters 4 through 10. Before these matters are covered in detail in subsequent chapters, this section addresses the various theories underlying the consolidation process.

Several different accounting theories have been suggested that might serve as a basis for preparing consolidated financial statements. The choice of theory can have a significant impact on the consolidated financial statements in cases when the parent company owns less than 100 percent of the subsidiary's common stock. This discussion focuses on three alternative theories of consolidation: (1) proprietary, (2) parent company, and (3) entity. The proprietary and entity theories may be viewed as falling near opposite ends of a spectrum, with the parent company theory falling somewhere in between:

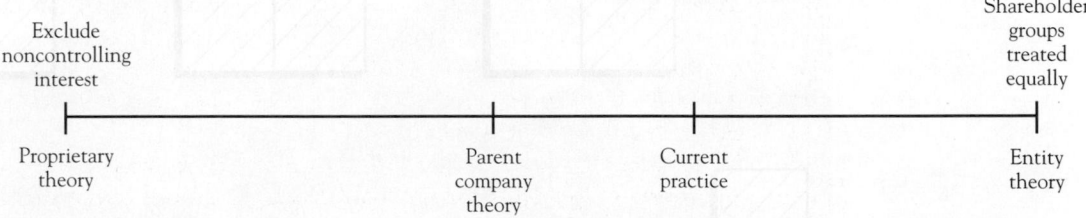

While the accounting profession has adopted no one of the three theories in its entirety, the consolidation procedures traditionally used in practice come closest to the parent company approach. The FASB, however, has indicated its intention to move to the entity theory in the near future.

Theories of Consolidation

The ***proprietary theory*** of accounting views the firm as an extension of the owners. The firm's assets, liabilities, revenues, and expenses are viewed as those of the owners themselves. When applied to consolidated financial statements, the proprietary concept results in a ***pro rata consolidation*** in which the parent company consolidates only its proportionate share of a less-than-wholly owned subsidiary's assets, liabilities, revenues, and expenses.

The ***parent company theory*** is perhaps better suited to the modern corporation and the preparation of consolidated financial statements than is the proprietary approach. The parent company theory recognizes that the parent has the ability to effectively control all of the assets and liabilities of a majority-owned subsidiary, not just a proportionate share, even though the parent does not actually own the subsidiary's assets or have any obligation for its liabilities. The consolidated financial statements include all of the subsidiary's assets, liabilities, revenues, and expenses. Separate recognition is given in the consolidated balance sheet to the noncontrolling interest's claim on the subsidiary's net assets and in the consolidated income statement to the earnings assigned to the noncontrolling shareholders.

As a general ownership theory, the ***entity theory*** focuses on the firm as a separate economic entity rather than on the ownership rights of the shareholders. Emphasis under the entity approach is on the consolidated entity itself, with the controlling and noncontrolling shareholders viewed as two separate groups, each having an equity in the consolidated entity. Neither of the two groups is emphasized over the other or over the consolidated entity. Accordingly, all of the assets, liabilities, revenues, and expenses of a less-than-wholly owned subsidiary are included in the consolidated financial statements, with no special treatment accorded either the controlling or noncontrolling interest.

FIGURE 3–3
Recognition of Subsidiary Net Assets

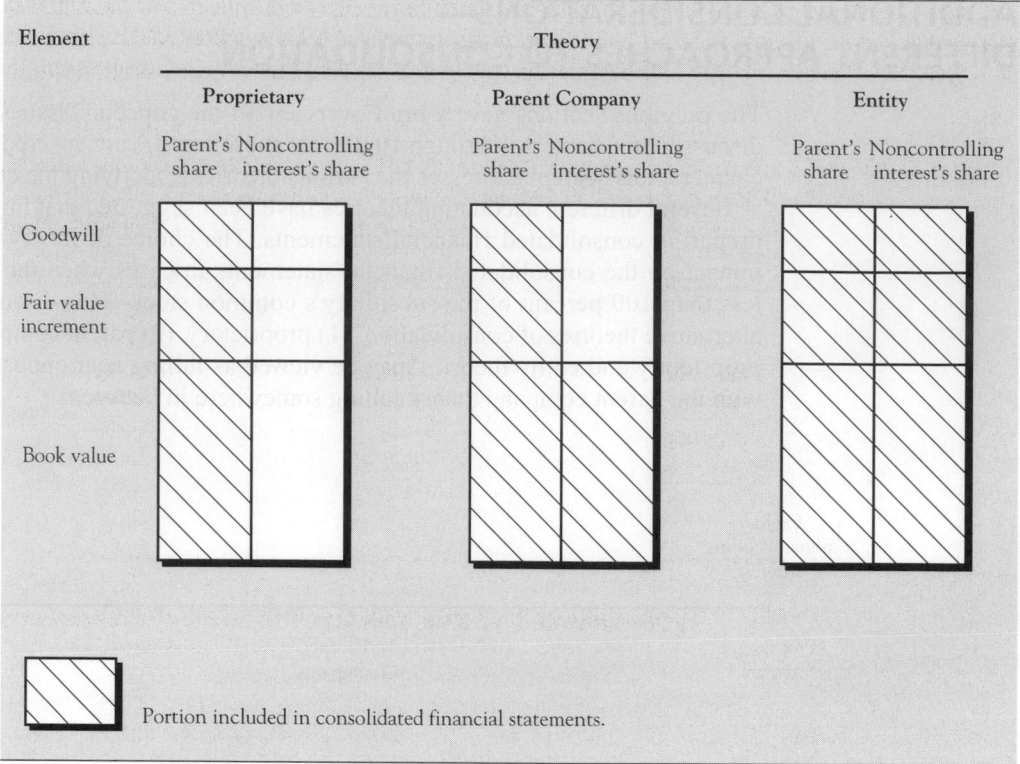

Comparison of Alternative Theories

Figure 3–3 provides a comparison of the amounts included in a consolidated balance sheet (lined areas) for a parent and less-than-wholly owned subsidiary under the different approaches to consolidation. With the proprietary theory, only the parent's share of a subsidiary's assets and liabilities is included in the consolidated balance sheet, with the amount based on the fair values of those assets and liabilities on the date majority ownership in the subsidiary is acquired. Goodwill is included for the excess of the purchase price over the fair value of the parent's share of the subsidiary's net identifiable assets. The portion of the subsidiary's identifiable assets and liabilities claimed by the noncontrolling interest is excluded from the consolidated balance sheet, as is any implied goodwill assignable to the noncontrolling interest.

The parent company approach includes all of the subsidiary's assets and liabilities in the consolidated balance sheet, as can be seen from the lined areas in Figure 3–3. However, only the parent's share of any fair value increment and goodwill is included. As a result, subsidiary assets are included at their full fair values only when the parent purchases full ownership of the subsidiary. The noncontrolling shareholder's claim is reported in the consolidated balance sheet based on a proportionate share of the book value of the subsidiary's net assets.

All subsidiary assets and liabilities are also included in the consolidated balance sheet under the equity approach. However, the amounts included are based on the full fair values at the date of combination, and the full amount of any goodwill is included regardless of the percentage ownership held by the parent. The amount of noncontrolling interest reported in the consolidated balance sheet is based on a proportionate share of the total amount of subsidiary net assets, including goodwill.

Figure 3–4 provides a comparison of amounts included in the consolidated income statement under the different approaches when a less-than-wholly owned subsidiary is consolidated. In general, the income statement treatment is consistent with the balance sheet treatment shown in Figure 3–3 under each theory. As can be seen from the lined areas, the proprietary theory results in consolidation of just the parent's share of the revenues, expenses, and net income of the subsidiary. On the other hand, both the parent company and entity theories result in consolidation of all of the subsidiary's revenues and expenses, regardless of degree of majority ownership. Under the parent company theory, however, the noncontrolling interest's share of income is deducted to arrive at consolidated net income.

FIGURE 3–4
Recognition of
Subsidiary Income

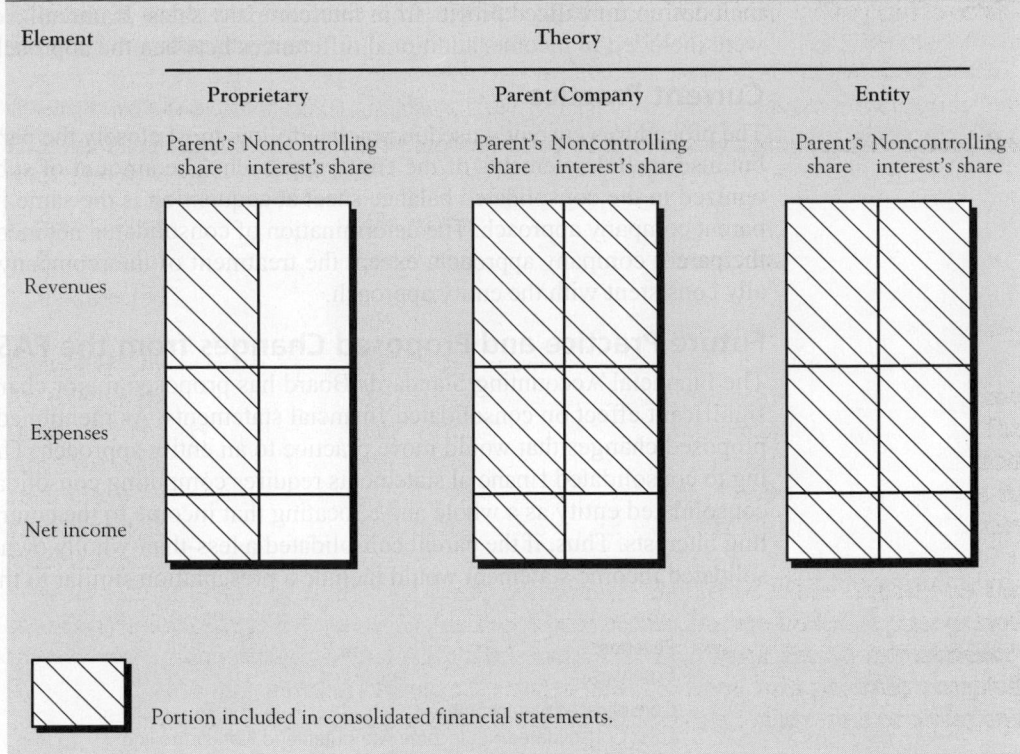

FIGURE 3–5 provides a numerical comparison of the different consolidation approaches. The example assumes that P Company acquires 80 percent of the stock of S Company on January 1, 20X1, for $96,000. On that date, S Company holds assets with a book value of $100,000 and fair value of $120,000. The $20,000 fair value increment relates entirely to S Company's buildings and equipment, with a remaining life of 10 years. Straight-line depreciation is used. For the year 20X1, P Company reports income from its own operations of $200,000, and S Company reports net income of $30,000. The example assumes the income

FIGURE 3–5 Illustration of the effects of different approaches to the preparation of consolidated financial statements

Item	Theory			Current Accounting Practice
	Proprietary	Parent Company	Entity	
Value of subsidiary net assets recognized at acquisition:				
Book value:				
$100,000 × .80	$ 80,000			
$100,000 × 1.00		$100,000	$100,000	$100,000
Fair value increment:				
$20,000 × .80	16,000	16,000		16,000
$20,000 × 1.00			20,000	
Total net assets	$ 96,000	$116,000	$120,000	$116,000
Amount of noncontrolling interest recognized at acquisition		$ 20,000	$ 24,000	$ 20,000
Amount of fair value increment amortized	$ 1,600	$ 1,600	$ 2,000	$ 1,600
Consolidated net income	$222,400[a]	$222,400[a]	$228,000[b]	$222,400[a]
Income assigned to noncontrolling interest		$ 6,000[c]	$ 5,600[d]	$ 6,000[c]

[a]$222,400 = $200,000 + ($30,000 × .80) − $1,600[*]
[b]$228,000 = $200,000 + $30,000 − $2,000[*]
[c]$6,000 = $30,000 × .20
[d]$5,600 = ($30,000 − $2,000) × .20
[*]Amortization of fair value increment using straight-line basis over 10 years.

includes no unrealized profits from intercompany sales. If unrealized intercompany profits were included in income, additional differences between the approaches could be seen.

Current Practice

The procedures currently used in practice follow most closely the parent company approach but also include elements of the entity approach. The amount of subsidiary net assets recognized in the consolidated balance sheet at acquisition is the same in practice as under the parent company approach. The determination of consolidated net income in practice follows the parent company approach, except the treatment of intercompany transactions is generally consistent with the entity approach.

Future Practice and Proposed Changes from the FASB

The Financial Accounting Standards Board has proposed major changes that would have a significant effect on consolidated financial statements. As mentioned earlier, the FASB has proposed changes that would move practice to an entity approach. The exposure draft relating to consolidated financial statements requires computing consolidated net income for the consolidated entity as a whole and allocating that income to the controlling and noncontrolling interests. Thus, if the parent consolidated a less-than-wholly owned subsidiary, the consolidated income statement would include a presentation similar to the following:

Revenues	$1,800,000
Expenses	(800,000)
Consolidated Net Income	$1,000,000
Less: Consolidated Net Income Attributable to Noncontrolling Interest in Subsidiary	(75,000)
Consolidated Net Income Attributable to Controlling Interest	$ 925,000

Although this type of presentation still focuses somewhat on the controlling interest, it treats the noncontrolling interest's share of income as an allocation of consolidated net income rather than a deduction to arrive at consolidated net income.

The FASB's exposure draft would also resolve the current confusion in practice about where to report the noncontrolling interest in the balance sheet by requiring the noncontrolling interest to be treated as an ownership interest in the balance sheet as well as the income statement. The exposure draft requires the noncontrolling interest to be reported in the consolidated balance sheet in the stockholders' equity section, in a manner similar to the following:

Equity:	
Controlling Interest	
Common Stock	$10,000,000
Additional Paid-In Capital	50,000,000
Retained Earnings	30,000,000
Total Controlling Interest	$90,000,000
Noncontrolling Interest in Subsidiary	5,000,000
Total Equity	$95,000,000

Other specific proposed changes relating to consolidated financial statements are discussed briefly in Chapter 5. The changes proposed by the FASB with respect to business combinations, discussed in Chapter 1, also need to be considered in connection with the preparation of consolidated financial statements. The FASB's exposure draft on business combinations[4] requires recognition, as of the date of combination, of the full fair value increment associated with the assets and liabilities acquired in a business combination, along with the full amount of implied

---

[4] *Financial Accounting Standards Board Proposed Statement of Financial Accounting Standards,* "Business Combinations," June 30, 2005 (Norwalk, Connecticut), 215 pp.

goodwill, including the portion related to the noncontrolling interest. This requirement is consistent with the entity theory. It would not be applied retroactively to previous acquisitions.

To illustrate, suppose that Piranha Company purchases 80 percent of Sardine Company's common stock for $550,000. Sardine's overall fair value is estimated at $687,500. Sardine's net assets have a book value of $500,000 and a fair value of $600,000. Piranha's net assets after the combination, excluding its investment in Sardine, have a book value of $2,000,000. The amounts to be reported in the consolidated balance sheet immediately after the acquisition under the approach currently used in practice and the FASB's proposed approach would be as follows:

	Current Practice	FASB Approach
Net Assets	$2,580,000	$2,600,000
Goodwill	70,000	87,500

In current practice, the amount assigned to the consolidated entity's net assets is the book value of the parent's net assets ($2,000,000) plus the full book value of the subsidiary's net assets ($500,000) plus the parent's share of the increase in value of the subsidiary's net assets ($100,000 × .80). Goodwill in current practice is computed as the excess of the purchase price ($550,000) over the parent's share of the fair value of the subsidiary's net assets ($600,000 × .80). Under the FASB's proposed approach, the net assets would be valued at the book value of the parent's net assets ($2,000,000) plus the full fair value of the subsidiary's net assets at the date of combination ($600,000). Goodwill of $87,500 would be computed as the difference between Sardine's overall fair value ($687,500) and the fair value of its net assets ($600,000). Goodwill of $87,500 would be computed as the difference between Sardine's overall fair value ($687,500) and the fair value of its net assets ($600,000).

Summary of Key Concepts

Consolidated financial statements present the financial position and results of operations of a parent and one or more subsidiaries as if they were actually a single company. As a result, a group of legally separate companies is portrayed as a single economic entity by the consolidated financial statements. All indications of intercorporate ownership and the effects of all intercompany transactions are excluded from the consolidated statements. The basic approach to the preparation of consolidated financial statements is to combine the separate financial statements of the individual consolidating companies and then to eliminate or adjust those items that would not appear, or that would appear differently, if the companies actually were one.

Current consolidation standards require that the consolidated financial statements include all companies under common control unless control is questionable. Consolidated financial statements are prepared primarily for those with a long-run interest in the parent company, especially the parent's stockholders and long-term creditors. While consolidated financial statements allow interested parties to view a group of related companies as a single economic entity, such statements have some limitations. In particular, information about the characteristics and operations of the individual companies within the consolidated entity is lost in the process of combining financial statements.

New types of business arrangements have proved troublesome for financial reporting. In particular, special types of entities, called *special-purpose entities* and *variable interest entities,* have been used to hide or transform various types of transactions, in addition to being used for many legitimate purposes such as risk sharing. Often these entities were disclosed only through vague notes to the financial statements. Reporting standards now require that the party that is the primary beneficiary of a variable interest entity consolidate that entity.

Several different theories or approaches underlie the preparation of consolidated financial statements, and the approach used can significantly affect the consolidated statements when the subsidiaries are not wholly owned. The proprietary and entity theories can be viewed as lying at opposite ends of a spectrum, with the parent company theory in the middle. Current practice tends to fall closest to the parent company theory, with some characteristics of the entity theory. The FASB is in the process of issuing two new pronouncements that will move practice toward the entity theory. The FASB is in the process of issuing two new pronouncements that will move practice toward the entity theory.

Key Terms

affiliates, *92*
combined financial
    statements, *103*
consolidated financial
    statements, *92*
direct control, *95*
effective control, *96*
eliminating entries, *102*
entity theory, *107*

indirect control, *95*
legal control, *96*
minority interest, *102*
noncontrolling interest, *102*
parent, *92*
parent company theory, *107*
primary beneficiary, *106*
proprietary theory, *107*
pro rata consolidation, *107*

related companies, *92*
separate legal entities, *92*
special-purpose entities
    (SPEs), *103*
subsidiaries, *92*
variable interest entity
    (VIE), *105*

Appendix 3A Consolidation of Variable Interest Entities

The standards for determining whether a party with an interest in a variable interest entity (VIE) should consolidate the VIE were discussed earlier in the chapter. Once a party has determined that it must consolidate a VIE, the consolidation procedures are similar to those used when consolidating a subsidiary. As an illustration, assume that Ignition Petroleum Company joins with Mammoth Financial Corporation to create a special corporation, Exploration Equipment Company, that would lease equipment to Ignition and other companies. Ignition purchases 10 percent of Exploration's stock for $1,000,000, and Mammoth purchases the other 90 percent for $9,000,000. Profits are to be split equally between the two owners, but Ignition agrees to absorb the first $500,000 of annual losses. Immediately after incorporation, Exploration borrows $120,000,000 from a syndicate of banks, and Ignition guarantees the loan. Exploration then purchases plant, equipment, and supplies for its own use and equipment for lease to others. The balance sheets of Ignition and Exploration appear as follows just prior to the start of Exploration's operations:

Item	Ignition	Exploration
Cash and Receivables	$100,000,000	$ 23,500,000
Inventory and Supplies	50,000,000	200,000
Equipment Held for Lease		105,000,000
Investment in Exploration Equipment Co.	1,000,000	
Plant and Equipment (net)	180,000,000	1,350,000
Total Assets	$331,000,000	$130,050,000
Accounts Payable	$ 900,000	$ 50,000
Bank Loans Payable	30,000,000	120,000,000
Common Stock Issued and Outstanding	200,000,000	10,000,000
Retained Earnings	100,100,000	
Total Liabilities and Equity	$331,000,000	$130,050,000

Both Ignition and Mammoth hold variable interests in Exploration. Ignition's variable interests include both its common stock and its guarantees. Ignition is the primary beneficiary of Exploration because it shares equally in the profits with Mammoth but must absorb a larger share of the expected losses than Mammoth, both through its profit and loss sharing agreement with Mammoth and its loan guarantee. Accordingly, Ignition must consolidate Exploration.

Ignition's consolidated balance sheet that includes Exploration appears as in Figure 3–6. The balances in Exploration's asset and liability accounts are added to the balances of Ignition's like accounts. Ignition's investment in Exploration is eliminated against the common stock of Exploration, and Exploration's remaining common stock is labeled as noncontrolling interest and reported between liabilities and equity or within the equity section of the consolidated balance sheet.

FIGURE 3–6
Balance Sheet
Consolidating a
Variable Interest
Entity

IGNITION PETROLEUM COMPANY
Consolidated Balance Sheet

Assets

Cash and Receivables	$123,500,000
Inventory and Supplies	50,200,000
Equipment Held for Lease	105,000,000
Plant and Equipment (net)	181,350,000
Total Assets	$460,050,000

Liabilities

Accounts Payable	$ 950,000	
Bank Loans Payable	150,000,000	
Total Liabilities		$150,950,000

Stockholders' Equity

Common Stock	$200,000,000	
Retained Earnings	100,100,000	
Noncontrolling Interest	9,000,000	
Total Stockholders' Equity		309,100,000
Total Liabilities and Stockholders' Equity		$460,050,000

Questions

Q3-1 What is the basic idea underlying the preparation of consolidated financial statements?

Q3-2 How might consolidated statements help an investor assess the desirability of purchasing shares of the parent company?

Q3-3 Are consolidated financial statements likely to be more useful to the owners of the parent company or to the noncontrolling owners of the subsidiaries? Why?

Q3-4 What is meant by "parent company"? When is a company considered to be a parent?

Q3-5 Are consolidated financial statements likely to be more useful to the creditors of the parent company or the creditors of the subsidiaries? Why?

Q3-6 Why is ownership of a majority of the common stock of another company considered important in consolidation?

Q3-7 What major criteria must be met before a company is consolidated?

Q3-8 When is consolidation considered inappropriate even though the parent holds a majority of the voting common shares of another company?

Q3-9 How has reliance on legal control as a consolidation criterion led to off-balance sheet financing?

Q3-10 What types of entities are referred to as *special-purpose entities*, and how have they generally been used?

Q3-11 How does a variable interest entity typically differ from a traditional corporate business entity?

Q3-12 What characteristics are normally examined in determining whether a company is a primary beneficiary of a variable interest entity?

Q3-13 What is meant by "indirect control"? Give an illustration.

Q3-14 What means other than majority ownership might be used to gain control over a company? Can consolidation occur if control is gained by other means?

Q3-15 Why must intercompany receivables and payables be eliminated when consolidated financial statements are prepared?

Q3-16 Why are subsidiary shares not reported as stock outstanding in the consolidated balance sheet?

Q3-17 What must be done if the fiscal periods of the parent and its subsidiary are not the same?

Q3-18 What is the noncontrolling interest in a subsidiary?

Q3-19 What is the difference between consolidated and combined financial statements?

Q3-20* How does the proprietary theory of consolidation differ from current accounting practice?

Q3-21* How does the entity theory of consolidation differ from current accounting practice?

Q3-22* Which theory of consolidation is closest to current accounting practice?

*Indicates that the item relates to "Additional Considerations."

Q3-23* Under the FASB's proposed standard for consolidated financial statements, how is the definition of consolidated net income changed in those cases in which the parent owns less than 100 percent of the subsidiary's stock?

Q3-24* How will the FASB's proposed standards for business combinations and consolidated financial statements change the dollar amount reported in the consolidated balance sheet for noncontrolling interest?

Q3-25* How will the FASB's proposed standards for business combinations and consolidated financial statements change the amount reported as goodwill when the parent owns less than 100 percent of a subsidiary's stock?

Cases

C3-1 Computation of Total Asset Values

Understanding

A reader of Gigantic Company's consolidated financial statements received from another source copies of the financial statements of the individual companies included in the consolidation. He is confused by the fact that the total assets in the consolidated balance sheet differ rather substantially from the sum of the asset totals reported by the individual companies.

Required

Will this relationship always be true? What factors may cause this difference to occur?

C3-2 Accounting Entity [AICPA Adapted]

Understanding

The concept of the accounting entity often is considered to be the most fundamental of accounting concepts, one that pervades all of accounting.

Required

a. (1) What is an accounting entity? Explain.
   (2) Explain why the accounting entity concept is so fundamental that it pervades all of accounting.

b. For each of the following, indicate whether the entity concept is applicable; discuss and give illustrations.
   (1) A unit created by or under law.
   (2) The product-line segment of an enterprise.
   (3) A combination of legal units.
   (4) All the activities of an owner or a group of owners.
   (5) The economy of the United States.

C3-3 Recognition of Fair Value and Goodwill

Research FARS

March Corporation purchased 65 percent of Ember Corporation's ownership on January 1, 20X3, for $708,500 and allocated $84,500 of the purchase price to goodwill. The $97,500 paid by March for the excess of fair value over book value of Ember's net assets was assigned to depreciable assets with a remaining useful life of 10 years at January 1, 20X3.

Recent FASB actions have pointed toward the recognition of 100 percent of the fair value of the assets and liabilities held by the acquired company and 100 percent of the implied goodwill.

Required

Analyze the impact of adopting the FASB proposal on March's consolidated financial statements prepared at December 31, 20X3, and prepare a memo describing the current reporting requirements and those proposed by the FASB. Include in your memo citations to and quotations from the appropriate accounting literature.

C3-4 Joint Venture Investment

Research FARS

Dell Computer Corp. and CIT Group, Inc., established Dell Financial Services L.P. (DFS) as a joint venture to provide financing services for Dell customers. While Dell owns 70 percent of the equity of DFS and CIT owns 30 percent, the two companies have equal votes on the board of directors. In the event that DFS incurs losses, they will be allocated entirely to CIT. Net income of DFS is allocated 70 percent to Dell and 30 percent to CIT after CIT has recovered any losses. CIT

*Indicates that the item relates to "Additional Considerations."

regularly purchases receivables from DFS at a premium, a portion of which DFS securitizes. CIT has recourse against DFS for any delinquencies. Both Dell and CIT have said they have no plans to consolidate DFS.

Required

You have been assigned to the audit team of PricewaterhouseCoopers that currently audits Dell Computer and have been asked to provide a memo to the company describing the conditions under which consolidation of a variable interest entity normally is required. You are also asked to provide your conclusions as to whether Dell, CIT, neither company, or both should consolidate DFS. Include in your discussion citations to or quotations from the relevant financial reporting standards and information from the reports of Dell and CIT.

C3-5 **Need for Consolidation [AICPA Adapted]**

Analysis

Sharp Company will acquire 90 percent of Moore Company in a business combination. The total consideration has been agreed on, but the nature of Sharp's payment has not. It is expected that on the date the business combination is to be consummated, the fair value will exceed the book value of Moore's assets minus liabilities. Sharp desires to prepare consolidated financial statements that will include Moore's financial statements.

Required

a. Explain how the amount of goodwill is determined.

b. From a theoretical standpoint, why should consolidated financial statements be prepared?

c. From a theoretical standpoint, what is usually the first necessary condition to be met before consolidated financial statements can be prepared?

C3-6 **What Company Is That?**

Analysis

Many well-known products and names come from companies that may be less well known or may be known for other reasons. In some cases, an obscure parent company may have well-known subsidiaries, and often familiar but diverse products may be produced under common ownership.

Required

a. Viacom is not necessarily a common name easily identified because it operates through numerous subsidiaries, but its brand names are seen every day. What are some of the well-known brand names from Viacom's subsidiaries? What changes occurred in its organizational structure in 2006? Who is Sumner Redstone?

b. ConAgra Foods, Inc., is one of the world's largest food processors and distributors. Although it has relatively few subsidiaries with well-known names, it produces hundreds of products familiar to those who shop in supermarkets. What are some of ConAgra's well-known subsidiary companies? What are some of the well-known products produced by ConAgra and its subsidiaries? What are ConAgra's four major business segments? Which segment accounts for the largest dollar volume of sales to unaffiliated customers?

C3-7 **Subsidiaries and Core Businesses**

Analysis

During previous merger booms, a number of companies acquired many subsidiaries that often were in businesses unrelated to the acquiring company's central operations. In many cases, the acquiring company's management was unable to manage effectively the many diverse types of operations found in the numerous subsidiaries. More recently, many of these subsidiaries have been sold or, in a few cases, liquidated so the parent companies could concentrate on their core businesses.

Required

a. In 1986, General Electric acquired nearly all of the common stock of the large brokerage firm Kidder, Peabody Inc. Unfortunately, the newly acquired subsidiary's performance was very poor. What ultimately happened to this subsidiary of General Electric?

b. What major business has Sears, Roebuck been in for many decades? What other businesses was it in during the 1980s and early 1990s? What were some of its best-known subsidiaries during that time? Does Sears still own those subsidiaries? What additional acquisitions have occurred?

c. PepsiCo is best known as a soft-drink company. What well-known subsidiaries did PepsiCo own during the mid-1990s? Does PepsiCo still own them?

d. When a parent company and its subsidiaries are in businesses that are considerably different in nature, such as retailing and financial services, how meaningful are their consolidated financial statements in your opinion? Explain. How might financial reporting be improved in such situations?

C3-8 **International Consolidation Issues**

Research

The International Accounting Standards Board (IASB) is charged with developing a set of high-quality standards and encouraging their adoption globally. Standards promulgated by the IASB are called International Financial Reporting Standards (IFRS). The European Union (EU) requires statements prepared using IFRS for all companies that list on the EU stock exchanges. While the United States does not yet accept IFRS, the SEC has indicated that it is working toward allowing international companies that list on U.S. exchanges to use IFRS for financial reporting in the United States.

The differences between U.S. GAAP and IFRS are described in many different publications. For example, PricewaterhouseCoopers has a publication available for download on its Website (http://www.pwc.com/extweb/pwcpublications.nsf/docid/74d6c09e0a4ee610802569a1003354c8) entitled "Similarities and Differences—A Comparison of IFRS and U.S. GAAP" that provides a topic-based comparison. Based on the information in this publication or others, answer the following questions about the preparation of consolidated financial statements.

Required

a. Under U.S. GAAP, consolidated financial statements must be prepared for the parent and all majority-owned subsidiaries, with an exception only if the parent is unable to exercise control over a subsidiary. What is required by IFRS?

b. Under U.S. GAAP, negative goodwill is used to reduce on a pro rata basis the values assigned to the identifiable assets acquired other than current assets, financial instruments, assets to be sold, prepaid pension assets, and deferred taxes (as discussed in Chapter 1). Any negative goodwill remaining is recognized as an extraordinary gain. What is the treatment of negative goodwill required under IFRS?

c. U.S. GAAP requires a two-step process to evaluate goodwill for potential impairment (as discussed in Chapter 1). What is required by IFRS with respect to goodwill impairment?

C3-9 **Off-Balance Sheet Financing and VIEs**

Understanding

A variable interest entity (VIE) is a structure frequently used for off-balance sheet financing. VIEs have become quite numerous in recent years and have been the subject of some controversy.

Required

a. Briefly explain what is meant by off-balance sheet financing.

b. What are three techniques used to keep debt off the balance sheet?

c. What are some legitimate uses of VIEs?

d. How can VIEs be used to manage earnings to meet financial reporting goals? How does this relate to the importance of following the intent of the guidelines for consolidations?

C3-10 **Alternative Accounting Methods**

Analysis

The use of proportionate or pro rata consolidation generally has not been acceptable in the United States. Normally, a significant investment in the common stock of another company must either be fully consolidated or reported using the equity method.

Required

a. What method does Amerada Hess use to account for its investments in affiliates and joint ventures?

b. What method does EnCana Corporation use to account for its investments in jointly controlled ventures? In what country is EnCana based? Does this make a difference?

c. What method does Centex Corporation use to account for its investments in affiliates? Is its treatment of Centex Construction Products Inc. in accordance with generally accepted accounting principles? How might this treatment be justified?

d. Should the method used to account for investments in affiliates be different depending on whether the affiliate is a corporation or an unincorporated partnership? Explain.

Exercises **E3-1** **Multiple-Choice Questions on Consolidation Overview [AICPA Adapted]**

Select the correct answer for each of the following questions.

1. When a parent–subsidiary relationship exists, consolidated financial statements are prepared in recognition of the accounting concept of:

   a. Reliability.

   b. Materiality.

   c. Legal entity.

   d. Economic entity.

2. Consolidated financial statements are typically prepared when one company has a controlling interest in another unless:

   a. The subsidiary is a finance company.

   b. The fiscal year-ends of the two companies are more than three months apart.

   c. Circumstances prevent the exercise of control.

   d. The two companies are in unrelated industries, such as real estate and manufacturing.

3. Penn Inc., a manufacturing company, owns 75 percent of the common stock of Sell Inc., an investment company. Sell owns 60 percent of the common stock of Vane Inc., an insurance company. In Penn's consolidated statements, should consolidation accounting or equity-method accounting be used for Sell and Vane?

   a. Consolidation used for Sell and equity method used for Vane.

   b. Consolidation used for both Sell and Vane.

   c. Equity method used for Sell and consolidation used for Vane.

   d. Equity method used for both Sell and Vane.

4. Shep Company has a receivable from its parent, Pep Company. Should this receivable be separately reported on Shep's balance sheet and in Pep's consolidated balance sheet?

	Shep's Balance Sheet	Pep's Consolidated Balance Sheet
a.	Yes	No
b.	Yes	Yes
c.	No	No
d.	No	Yes

5. Which of the following is the best theoretical justification for consolidated financial statements?

   a. In form the companies are one entity; in substance they are separate.

   b. In form the companies are separate; in substance they are one entity.

   c. In form and substance the companies are one entity.

   d. In form and substance the companies are separate.

E3-2 **Multiple-Choice Questions on Variable Interest Entities**

Select the correct answer for each of the following questions.

1. Special-purpose entities generally:

   a. Have a much larger portion of assets financed by equity shareholders than do companies such as General Motors.

   b. Have relatively large amounts of preferred stock and convertible securities outstanding.

   c. Have a much smaller portion of their assets financed by equity shareholders than do companies such as General Motors.

   d. Pay out a relatively high percentage of their earnings as dividends to facilitate the sale of additional shares.

2. Variable interest entities may be established as:

    a. Corporations.

    b. Trusts.

    c. Partnerships.

    d. All of the above.

3. An enterprise that will absorb a majority of a variable interest entity's expected losses is called the:

    a. Primary beneficiary.

    b. Qualified owner.

    c. Major facilitator.

    d. Critical management director.

4. In determining whether or not a variable interest entity is to be consolidated, the FASB focused on:

    a. Legal control.

    b. Effective control.

    c. Frequency of intercompany transfers.

    d. Proportionate size of the two entities.

5. A qualified special-purpose entity:

    a. Must always be consolidated.

    b. Meets the criteria to be exempted from consolidation.

    c. Permits consolidation of only those activities of the special-purpose entity that are related to the activities of the transferor.

    d. Permits proportionate consolidation based on the proportion of ownership held by the transferor.

E3-3 Multiple-Choice Questions on Consolidated Balances [AICPA Adapted]

Select the correct answer for each of the following questions.

1. Par Corporation owns 60 percent of Sub Corporation's outstanding capital stock. On May 1, 20X8, Par advanced Sub $70,000 in cash, which was still outstanding at December 31, 20X8. What portion of this advance should be eliminated in the preparation of the December 31, 20X8, consolidated balance sheet?

    a. $70,000.

    b. $42,000.

    c. $28,000.

    d. $0.

Items 2 and 3 are based on the following:

On January 2, 20X8, Pare Company purchased 75 percent of Kidd Company's outstanding common stock. Selected balance sheet data at December 31, 20X8, are as follows:

	Pare Company	Kidd Company
Total Assets	$420,000	$180,000
Liabilities	$120,000	$ 60,000
Common Stock	100,000	50,000
Retained Earnings	200,000	70,000
	$420,000	$180,000

2. In Pare's December 31, 20X8, consolidated balance sheet, what amount should be reported as minority interest in net assets?

   a. $0.

   b. $30,000.

   c. $45,000.

   d. $105,000.

3. In its consolidated balance sheet at December 31, 20X8, what amount should Pare report as common stock outstanding?

   a. $50,000.

   b. $100,000.

   c. $137,500.

   d. $150,000.

4. At the time Hyman Corporation became a subsidiary of Duane Corporation, Hyman switched depreciation of its plant assets from the straight-line method to the sum-of-the-years'-digits method used by Duane. As to Hyman, this change was a:

   a. Change in an accounting estimate.

   b. Correction of an error.

   c. Change of accounting principle.

   d. Change in the reporting entity.

5. Consolidated statements are proper for Neely Inc., Randle Inc., and Walker Inc., if:

   a. Neely owns 80 percent of the outstanding common stock of Randle and 40 percent of Walker; Randle owns 30 percent of Walker.

   b. Neely owns 100 percent of the outstanding common stock of Randle and 90 percent of Walker; Neely bought the Walker stock one month before the foreign country in which Walker is based imposed restrictions preventing Walker from remitting profits to Neely.

   c. Neely owns 100 percent of the outstanding common stock of Randle and Walker; Walker is in legal reorganization.

   d. Neely owns 80 percent of the outstanding common stock of Randle and 40 percent of Walker; Reeves Inc. owns 55 percent of Walker.

E3-4   Multiple-Choice Questions on Consolidation Overview [AICPA Adapted]

Select the correct answer for each of the following questions.

1. Consolidated financial statements are typically prepared when one company has:

   a. Accounted for its investment in another company by the equity method.

   b. Accounted for its investment in another company by the cost method.

   c. Significant influence over the operating and financial policies of another company.

   d. The controlling financial interest in another company.

2. Aaron Inc. owns 80 percent of the outstanding stock of Belle Inc. Compare the consolidated net earnings of Aaron and Belle (X) and Aaron's net earnings if it does not consolidate Belle (Y).

   a. X is greater than Y.

   b. X is equal to Y.

   c. X is less than Y.

   d. Cannot be determined.

3. On October 1, X Company acquired for cash all of Y Company's outstanding common stock. Both companies have a December 31 year-end and have been in business for many years. Consolidated net income for the year ended December 31 should include net income of:

  a. X Company for three months and Y Company for three months.

  b. X Company for 12 months and Y Company for 3 months.

  c. X Company for 12 months and Y Company for 12 months.

  d. X Company for 12 months, but no income from Y Company until Y Company distributes a dividend.

 4. Ownership of 51 percent of the outstanding voting stock of a company would usually result in:

  a. The use of the cost method.

  b. The use of the lower-of-cost-or-market method.

  c. A pooling of interests.

  d. A consolidation.

E3-5 Balance Sheet Consolidation

On January 1, 20X3, Guild Corporation reported total assets of $470,000, liabilities of $270,000, and stockholders' equity of $200,000. At that date, Bristol Corporation reported total assets of $190,000, liabilities of $135,000, and stockholders' equity of $55,000. Following lengthy negotiations, Guild paid Bristol's existing shareholders $55,000 in cash for 100 percent of the voting common shares of Bristol.

Required

Immediately after Guild purchased the Bristol shares:

a. What amount of total assets did Guild report in its balance sheet?

b. What amount of total assets was reported in the consolidated balance sheet?

c. What amount of total liabilities was reported in the consolidated balance sheet?

d. What amount of stockholders' equity was reported in the consolidated balance sheet?

E3-6 Balance Sheet Consolidation with Intercompany Transfer

Potter Company purchased 100 percent of the voting common shares of Stately Corporation by issuing bonds with a par value and fair value of $135,000 to Stately's existing shareholders. Immediately prior to the acquisition, Potter reported total assets of $510,000, liabilities of $320,000, and stockholders' equity of $190,000. At that date, Stately reported total assets of $350,000, liabilities of $215,000, and stockholders' equity of $135,000. Included in Stately's liabilities was an account payable to Potter in the amount of $15,000, which Potter included in its accounts receivable.

Required

Immediately after Potter purchased Stately's shares:

a. What amount of total assets did Potter report in its balance sheet?

b. What amount of total assets was reported in the consolidated balance sheet?

c. What amount of total liabilities was reported in the consolidated balance sheet?

d. What amount of stockholders' equity was reported in the consolidated balance sheet?

E3-7 Intercompany Transfers

Route Manufacturing purchased 80 percent of the stock of Hampton Mines Inc. in 20X3. In preparing the consolidated financial statements at the end of 20X5, Route's controller discovered that Route had purchased $75,000 of raw materials from Hampton Mines during the year and that the parent company had not paid for the last purchase of $12,000. All the inventory purchased was still on hand at year-end. Hampton Mines had spent $50,000 in producing the items sold to Route.

Required

a. What effect, if any, will failure to eliminate or adjust for these items have on total current assets reported in the consolidated balance sheet on December 31, 20X5?

b. What effect, if any, will failure to eliminate or adjust for these items have on the consolidated entity's net working capital?

c. What effect, if any, will failure to eliminate or adjust for these items have on the computation of income when the inventory is sold in the following period?

E3-8   Subsidiary Acquired for Cash

Fineline Pencil Company purchased 100 percent of Smudge Eraser Corporation's stock on January 2, 20X3, for $150,000 cash. Summarized balance sheet data for the companies on December 31, 20X2, are as follows:

	Fineline Pencil Company		Smudge Eraser Corporation	
	Book Value	Fair Value	Book Value	Fair Value
Cash	$200,000	$200,000	$ 50,000	$ 50,000
Other Assets	400,000	650,000	120,000	180,000
Total Debits	$600,000		$170,000	
Current Liabilities	$100,000	100,000	$ 80,000	80,000
Common Stock	300,000		50,000	
Retained Earnings	200,000		40,000	
Total Credits	$600,000		$170,000	

Required

Prepare a consolidated balance sheet immediately following the acquisition.

E3-9   Subsidiary Acquired with Bonds

Byte Computer Corporation purchased 100 percent of Nofail Software Company's stock on January 2, 20X3, by issuing bonds with a par value of $140,000 and a fair value of $150,000 in exchange for the shares. Summarized balance sheet data presented for the companies just before the acquisition are as follows:

	Byte Computer Corporation		Nofail Software Company	
	Book Value	Fair Value	Book Value	Fair Value
Cash	$200,000	$200,000	$ 50,000	$ 50,000
Other Assets	400,000	650,000	120,000	180,000
Total Debits	$600,000		$170,000	
Current Liabilities	$100,000	100,000	$ 80,000	80,000
Common Stock	300,000		50,000	
Retained Earnings	200,000		40,000	
Total Credits	$600,000		$170,000	

Required

Prepare a consolidated balance sheet immediately following the acquisition.

E3-10   Subsidiary Acquired by Issuing Preferred Stock

Byte Computer Corporation purchased 100 percent of Nofail Software Company's common stock on January 2, 20X3, by issuing preferred stock with a par value of $6 per share and a market value of $10 per share. A total of 15,000 shares of preferred stock was issued. Balance sheet data for the two companies immediately before the business combination are presented in E3-9.

Required

Prepare a consolidated balance sheet for the companies immediately after Byte obtains ownership of Nofail by issuing the preferred stock.

E3-11   Reporting for a Variable Interest Entity

Gamble Company convinced Conservative Corporation that the two companies should establish Simpletown Corporation to build a new gambling casino in Simpletown Corner. Although chances for the casino's success were relatively low, a local bank loaned $140,000,000 to the new corporation, which built the casino at a cost of $130,000,000. Conservative purchased 100 percent of the initial capital stock offering for $5,600,000, and Gamble agreed to supply 100 percent of the management and guarantee the bank loan. Gamble also guaranteed a 20 percent return to Conservative on its investment for the first 10 years. Gamble will receive all profits in excess of the 20 percent return to Conservative. Immediately after the casino's construction, Gamble reported the following amounts:

Cash	$ 3,000,000
Buildings and Equipment	240,600,000
Accumulated Depreciation	10,100,000
Accounts Payable	5,000,000
Bonds Payable	20,300,000
Common Stock	103,000,000
Retained Earnings	105,200,000

The only disclosure that Gamble currently provides in its financial reports about its relationships to Conservative and Simpletown is a brief footnote indicating that a contingent liability exists on its guarantee of Simpletown Corporation's debt.

Required

Prepare a balance sheet in good form for Gamble immediately following the casino's construction.

E3-12 ### Consolidation of a Variable Interest Entity

Teal Corporation is the primary beneficiary of a variable interest entity with total assets of $500,000, liabilities of $470,000, and owners' equity of $30,000. Because Teal owns 25 percent of the VIE's voting stock, it reported a $7,500 investment in the VIE in its balance sheet. Teal reported total assets of $190,000 (including its investment in the VIE), liabilities of $80,000, common stock of $15,000, and retained earnings of $95,000 in its balance sheet.

Required

Prepare a condensed balance sheet in good form for Teal, taking into consideration that it is the primary beneficiary of the variable interest entity.

E3-13 ### Computation of Subsidiary Net Income

Frazer Corporation owns 70 percent of Messer Company's stock. In the 20X9 consolidated income statement, the noncontrolling interest was assigned $18,000 of income.

Required

What amount of net income did Messer Company report for 20X9?

E3-14 ### Incomplete Consolidation

Belchfire Motors' accountant was called away after completing only half of the consolidated statements at the end of 20X4. The data left behind included the following:

Item	Belchfire Motors	Premium Body Shop	Consolidated
Cash	$ 40,000	$ 20,000	$ 60,000
Accounts Receivable	180,000	30,000	200,000
Inventory	220,000	50,000	270,000
Buildings and Equipment (net)	300,000	290,000	590,000
Investment in Premium Body Shop	150,000		
Total Debits	$890,000	$390,000	$1,120,000
Accounts Payable	$ 30,000	$ 40,000	
Bonds Payable	400,000	200,000	
Common Stock	200,000	100,000	
Retained Earnings	260,000	50,000	
Total Credits	$890,000	$390,000	

Required

a. Belchfire Motors purchased shares of Premium Body Shop at underlying book value on January 1, 20X1. What portion of the ownership of Premium Body Shop does Belchfire apparently hold?

b. Compute the consolidated totals for each of the remaining balance sheet items.

E3-15 Noncontrolling Interest

Sanderson Corporation purchased 70 percent of Kline Corporation's common stock on January 1, 20X7, for $294,000 in cash. The stockholders' equity accounts of the two companies at the date of purchase are:

	Sanderson Corporation	Kline Corporation
Common Stock ($10 par value)	$ 400,000	$ 180,000
Additional Paid-In Capital	222,000	65,000
Retained Earnings	358,000	175,000
Total Stockholders' Equity	$ 980,000	$ 420,000

Required

a. What amount will be assigned to the noncontrolling interest on January 1, 20X7, in the consolidated balance sheet?

b. Prepare the stockholders' equity section of Sanderson and Kline's consolidated balance sheet as of January 1, 20X7.

c. Sanderson purchased ownership of Kline to ensure a constant supply of electronic switches, which it purchases regularly from Kline. Why might Sanderson not feel compelled to purchase all of Kline's shares?

E3-16 Computation of Consolidated Net Income

Ambrose Corporation owns 75 percent of Kroop Company's common stock, acquired at underlying book value on January 1, 20X4. The income statements for Ambrose and Kroop for 20X4 include the following amounts:

	Ambrose Corporation	Kroop Company
Sales	$528,000	$150,000
Dividend Income	9,000	
Total Income	$537,000	$150,000
Less: Cost of Goods Sold	$380,000	$ 87,000
Depreciation Expense	32,000	20,000
Other Expenses	66,000	23,000
Total Expenses	$478,000	$130,000
Net Income	$ 59,000	$ 20,000

Ambrose uses the cost method in accounting for its ownership of Kroop. Kroop paid dividends of $12,000 in 20X4.

Required

a. What amount should Ambrose report in its income statement as income from its investment in Kroop using equity-method accounting?

b. What amount of income should be assigned to noncontrolling interest in the consolidated income statement for 20X4?

c. What amount should Ambrose report as consolidated net income for 20X4?

d. Why should Ambrose not report consolidated net income of $79,000 ($59,000 + $20,000) for 20X4?

E3-17 **Computation of Subsidiary Balances**

Tall Corporation purchased 75 percent of Light Corporation's voting common stock on January 1, 20X2, at underlying book value. Noncontrolling interest was assigned income of $8,000 in Tall's consolidated income statement for 20X2 and a balance of $65,500 in Tall's consolidated balance sheet at December 31, 20X2. Light reported retained earnings of $70,000 and additional paid-in capital of $40,000 on January 1, 20X2. Light did not pay dividends or issue stock in 20X2.

Required

a. Compute the amount of net income reported by Light for 20X2.

b. Prepare the stockholders' equity section of Light's balance sheet at December 31, 20X2.

E3-18 **Subsidiary Acquired at Net Book Value**

Banner Corporation purchased all of Dwyer Company's common stock at underlying book value and uses the equity method in accounting for its investment. Balance sheet information provided by the companies at December 31, 20X8, is as follows:

	Banner Corporation	Dwyer Company
Cash	$ 40,000	$ 20,000
Accounts Receivable	120,000	70,000
Inventory	180,000	90,000
Fixed Assets (net)	350,000	240,000
Investment in Dwyer Company Stock	170,000	
Total Debits	$860,000	$420,000
Accounts Payable	$ 65,000	$ 30,000
Notes Payable	350,000	220,000
Common Stock	150,000	90,000
Retained Earnings	295,000	80,000
Total Credits	$860,000	$420,000

Required

Prepare a consolidated balance sheet for Banner at December 31, 20X8.

E3-19* **Applying Alternative Accounting Theories**

Noway Manufacturing owns 75 percent of Positive Piston Corporation's stock. During 20X9, Noway and Positive Piston reported sales of $400,000 and $200,000 and expenses of $280,000 and $160,000, respectively.

Required

Compute the amount of total revenue, total expenses, and net income to be reported in the 20X9 consolidated income statement under the following alternative approaches:

a. Proprietary theory.

b. Parent company theory.

c. Entity theory.

d. Current accounting practice.

E3-20* **Measurement of Goodwill**

Rank Corporation purchased 60 percent of Fresh Company's stock on December 31, 20X4. In preparing the consolidated financial statements at December 31, 20X4, goodwill of $240,000 was reported. The goodwill is attributable to Rank's purchase of Fresh shares, and the parent company approach was used in determining the amount of goodwill reported.

Required

Determine the amount of goodwill to be reported under each of the following consolidation alternatives:

a. Proprietary theory.

b. Entity theory.

c. Current accounting practice.

E3-21* Valuation of Assets under Alternative Accounting Theories

Garwood Corporation purchased 75 percent of Zorn Company's voting common stock on January 1, 20X4. At the time of acquisition, Zorn reported buildings and equipment at book value of $240,000; however, an appraisal indicated a fair value of $290,000.

Required

If consolidated statements are prepared, determine the amount at which buildings and equipment will be reported using the following consolidation alternatives:

a. Entity theory.

b. Parent company theory.

c. Proprietary theory.

d. Current accounting practice.

E3-22* Reported Income under Alternative Accounting Theories

Placer Corporation purchased 80 percent of Billings Company's voting common stock on January 1, 20X4, at underlying book value. Placer and Billings reported total revenue of $410,000 and $200,000 and total expenses of $320,000 and $150,000, respectively, for the year ended December 31, 20X4.

Required

Determine the amount of total revenue, total expense, and net income to be reported in the consolidated income statement for 20X4 under the following consolidation alternatives:

a. Entity theory.

b. Parent company theory.

c. Proprietary theory.

d. Current accounting practice.

E3-23* Acquisition of Majority Ownership

Lang Company reports net assets with a book value of $120,000 and fair value of $170,000. The overall fair value of Lang is determined to be $200,000 when Pace Corporation purchases 75 percent ownership for $150,000. Pace reports net assets with a book value of $520,000 and a fair value of $640,000 at that time, excluding its investment in Lang.

Required

Compute the amounts that would be reported immediately after the combination under (1) current accounting practice and (2) the FASB's new proposed standards for each of the following:

a. Net identifiable assets.

b. Goodwill.

c. Noncontrolling interest.

E3-24* Consolidated Net Income

Blank Company and Gem Corporation reported revenues of $600,000 and $300,000, respectively, for 20X8. The companies reported operating expenses of $450,000 and $180,000, respectively. Blank owns 70 percent of Gem's common shares, purchased at book value.

Required

a. Prepare an abbreviated income statement for the consolidated entity under (1) current reporting practice and (2) the FASB proposed standards.

b. Assume that Blank purchased its 70 percent share of Gem for an amount $14,000 over book value rather than at book value. All of the difference relates to a $20,000 excess of fair value over book value of Gem's depreciable assets having a remaining useful life of 10 years from the date of combination. By what amount would the income assigned to the noncontrolling interest be different than had the acquisition been at book value under (1) current reporting standards and (2) the FASB's proposed standards?

Problems

P3-25 Multiple-Choice Questions on Consolidated and Combined Financial Statements [AICPA Adapted]

Select the correct answer for each of the following questions.

1. What is the theoretically preferred method of presenting a noncontrolling interest in a consolidated balance sheet?

   a. As a separate item within the liability section.

   b. As a deduction from (contra to) goodwill from consolidation, if any.

   c. By means of notes or footnotes to the balance sheet.

   d. As a separate item within the stockholders' equity section.

2. Presenting consolidated financial statements this year when statements of individual companies were presented last year is:

   a. The correction of an error.

   b. An accounting change that should be reported prospectively.

   c. An accounting change that should be reported by restating the financial statements of all prior periods presented.

   d. Not an accounting change.

3. A subsidiary, acquired for cash in a business combination, owned equipment with a market value in excess of book value as of the date of combination. A consolidated balance sheet prepared immediately after the acquisition would treat this excess as:

   a. Goodwill.

   b. Plant and equipment.

   c. Retained earnings.

   d. Deferred credit.

4. When combined financial statements are prepared for a group of related companies, intercompany transactions and intercompany profits or losses should be eliminated when the group is composed of:

	Commonly Controlled Companies	Unconsolidated Subsidiaries
a.	No	No
b.	No	Yes
c.	Yes	Yes
d.	Yes	No

5. Mr. Cord owns four corporations. Combined financial statements are being prepared for these corporations, which have intercompany loans of $200,000 and intercompany profits of $500,000. What amount of these intercompany loans and profits should be included in the combined financial statements?

	Intercompany	
	Loans	Profits
a.	$200,000	$0
b.	$200,000	$500,000
c.	$0	$0
d.	$0	$500,000

P3-26 Intercompany Sales

Knight Corporation owns 100 percent of Spahn Company's voting shares. During 20X6, Spahn purchased inventory items for $20,000 and sold them to Knight for $50,000. Knight continues to hold the items in inventory on December 31, 20X6. Sales for the two companies during 20X6 totaled $300,000, and total cost of goods sold was $200,000.

Required

a. If no adjustment is made to eliminate the intercorporate sale when a consolidated income statement is prepared for 20X6, by what amount will consolidated net income be overstated or understated?

b. Prepare a consolidated income statement for 20X6 without any adjustment for the intercorporate sale.

c. Prepare a consolidated income statement for 20X6 adjusted for the intercorporate sale.

d. What items in the consolidated income statements are different in parts *b* and *c?*

P3-27   Intercompany Inventory Transfer

River Products Corporation purchases all its inventory from its wholly owned subsidiary, Clayborn Corporation. In 20X2, Clayborn produced inventory at a cost of $10,000 and sold it to River Products for $25,000. The parent held all the items in inventory on January 1, 20X3. During 20X3, River Products sold all the units for $55,000.

Required

Assuming the companies had no other transactions during either year, indicate the appropriate amounts to be reported in the consolidated financial statements for the following items:

a. Inventory on January 1, 20X3.

b. Cost of goods sold for 20X2.

c. Cost of goods sold for 20X3.

d. Sales for 20X2.

e. Sales for 20X3.

P3-28   Determining Net Income of Consolidated Entity

Placer Corporation purchased 75 percent of Murdokk Enterprises' common stock on January 1, 20X1, for $20,000 more than underlying book value. The excess payment is assigned to increased value of equipment, which had a remaining life of eight years at the date of the business combination. Placer reported net income of $110,000 and paid dividends of $30,000 in 20X1. Murdokk reported net income of $24,000 and paid dividends of $14,000 in 20X1. Placer accounts for its ownership of Murdokk using the cost method.

Required

Determine the amount of consolidated net income to be reported for 20X1 for Placer and its subsidiary.

P3-29   Determining Net Income of Parent Company

Tally Corporation and its subsidiary reported consolidated net income of $164,300 for 20X2. Tally had purchased 60 percent of the common shares of its subsidiary at underlying book value. Noncontrolling interest was assigned income of $15,200 in the consolidated income statement for 20X2.

Required

Determine the amount of separate operating income reported by Tally for 20X2.

P3-30   Consolidation of a Variable Interest Entity

On December 28, 20X3, Stern Corporation and Ram Company established S&R Partnership, with cash contributions of $10,000 and $40,000, respectively. The partnership's purpose is to purchase from Stern accounts receivable that have an average collection period of 80 days and hold them to collection. The partnership borrows cash from Midtown Bank and purchases the receivables without recourse but at an amount equal to the expected percent to be collected, less a financing fee of 3 percent of the gross receivables. Stern and Ram hold 20 percent and 80 percent of the ownership of the partnership, respectively, and Stern guarantees both the bank loan made to the partnership and a 15 percent annual return on the investment made by Ram. Stern receives any income in excess of the 15 percent return guaranteed to Ram. The partnership agreement provides Stern total control over the partnership's activities. On December 31, 20X3, Stern sold $8,000,000 of accounts receivable to the partnership. The partnership immediately borrowed $7,500,000 from the bank and paid Stern $7,360,000. Prior to the sale, Stern had established a $400,000 allowance for uncollectibles on the receivables sold to the partnership. The balance sheets of Stern and S&R immediately after the sale of receivables to the partnership contained the following:

	Stern Corporation	S&R Partnership
Cash	$7,960,000	$ 190,000
Accounts Receivable	4,200,000	8,000,000
Allowance for Uncollectible Accounts	(210,000)	(400,000)
Other Assets	5,400,000	
Prepaid Finance Charges	240,000	
Investment in S&R Partnership	10,000	
Accounts Payable	950,000	
Deferred Revenue		240,000
Bank Notes Payable		7,500,000
Bonds Payable	9,800,000	
Common Stock	700,000	
Retained Earnings	6,150,000	
Capital, Stern Corporation		10,000
Capital, Ram Company		40,000

Required

Assuming that Stern is S&R's primary beneficiary, prepare a consolidated balance sheet in good form for Stern at January 1, 20X4.

P3-31   Reporting for Variable Interest Entities

Purified Oil Company and Midwest Pipeline Corporation established Venture Company to conduct oil exploration activities in North America to reduce their dependence on imported crude oil. Midwest Pipeline purchased all 20,000 shares of the newly created company for $10 each. Purified Oil agreed to purchase all of Venture's output at market price, guarantee up to $5,000,000 of debt for Venture, and absorb all losses if the company proved unsuccessful. Purified and Midwest agreed to share equally the profits up to $80,000 per year and to allocate 70 percent of those in excess of $80,000 to Purified and 30 percent to Midwest.

Venture immediately borrowed $3,000,000 from Second National Bank and purchased land, drilling equipment, and supplies to start its operations. Following these asset purchases, Venture and Purified Oil reported the following balances:

	Venture Company	Purified Oil Company
Cash	$ 230,000	$ 410,000
Drilling Supplies	420,000	
Accounts Receivable		640,000
Equipment (net)	1,800,000	6,700,000
Land	900,000	4,200,000
Accounts Payable	150,000	440,000
Bank Loans Payable	3,000,000	8,800,000
Common Stock	200,000	560,000
Retained Earnings		2,150,000

The only disclosure that Purified Oil currently provides in its financial statements with respect to its relationship with Midwest Pipeline and Venture is a brief note indicating that a contingent liability exists on the guarantee of Venture Company debt.

Required

Assuming that Venture is considered to be a variable interest entity and Purified Oil is the primary beneficiary, prepare a balance sheet in good form for Purified Oil.

P3-32   Consolidated Income Statement Data

Slender Products Corporation purchased 80 percent ownership of LoCal Bakeries on January 1, 20X3, for $40,000 more than its portion of LoCal's underlying book value. The full additional payment is assigned to depreciable assets with an eight-year economic life. Income statement data for the two companies for 20X3 included the following:

	Slender Products		LoCal Bakeries	
Sales		$300,000		$200,000
Cost of Goods Sold	$200,000		$130,000	
Depreciation Expense	40,000	(240,000)	30,000	(160,000)
Income before Income from Subsidiary		$ 60,000		
Net Income				$ 40,000

During 20X3, Slender Products purchased a special imported yeast for $35,000 and resold it to LoCal for $50,000. LoCal did not resell any of the yeast before year-end.

Required

Determine the amounts to be reported for each of the following items in the consolidated income statement for 20X3:

a. Sales.

b. Investment income from LoCal Bakeries.

c. Cost of goods sold.

d. Depreciation expense.

P3-33   **Incomplete Company and Consolidated Data**

Beryl Corporation purchased 100 percent of Stargel Enterprises' common stock on December 31, 20X4. At that date, the book values and fair values of Stargel's identifiable assets and liabilities were identical. Balance sheet data for the individual companies and the consolidated entity on January 1, 20X5, are as follows:

	Beryl Corporation	Stargel Enterprises	Consolidated Entity
Cash	$ 60,000	$ 35,000	$ 95,000
Accounts Receivable	90,000	50,000	130,000
Inventory	120,000	90,000	?
Land	70,000	50,000	105,000
Buildings and Equipment	340,000	220,000	560,000
Less: Accumulated Depreciation	(180,000)	(90,000)	(270,000)
Investment in Stargel Enterprises Stock	110,000		
Goodwill			30,000
Total Assets	$610,000	$355,000	$?
Accounts Payable	$ 75,000	$ 55,000	$?
Wages Payable	30,000	20,000	50,000
Notes Payable	250,000	200,000	450,000
Common Stock	?	30,000	100,000
Retained Earnings	155,000	50,000	140,000
Total Liabilities and Stockholders' Equity	$610,000	$355,000	$?

Required

a. Assuming there were no inventory transactions between the companies, what balance for inventory should be reported in the consolidated balance sheet?

b. What amount did Beryl pay to acquire Stargel? Was this amount equal to, greater than, or less than underlying book value? How do you know?

c. Beryl sold land it had purchased 12 years earlier for $10,000 to Stargel immediately after it acquired Stargel. At what price did Beryl sell the land to Stargel? How do you know?

d. What balance will be reported as accounts payable in the consolidated balance sheet?

e. What is the par value of Beryl's common stock outstanding at January 1, 20X5?

P3-34   Consolidation Following Intercompany Sale of Equipment

Potash Company owns 100 percent of Bortz Corporation's common stock, which it acquired on December 31, 20X4, at underlying book value. Potash uses the equity method in accounting for its investment in Bortz. On December 31, 20X6, Potash sold equipment with a book value of $85,000 to Bortz for $110,000. Bortz made immediate payment of $93,000 and will pay the remainder on March 15, 20X7. Balance sheet data on January 1, 20X7, are as follows:

	Potash Company	Bortz Corporation
Cash	$ 50,000	$ 35,000
Accounts Receivable	110,000	60,000
Merchandise Inventory	95,000	75,000
Equipment (net)	230,000	105,000
Investment in Bortz Corporation Stock	140,000	
Total Assets	$625,000	$275,000
Accounts Payable	$ 82,000	$ 28,000
Notes Payable	200,000	107,000
Common Stock	180,000	50,000
Additional Paid-In Capital		25,000
Retained Earnings	163,000	65,000
Total Liabilities and Stockholders' Equity	$625,000	$275,000

Required

Prepare a consolidated balance sheet for Potash as of January 1, 20X7.

P3-35   Parent Company and Consolidated Amounts

Quoton Corporation purchased 80 percent of Tempro Company's common stock on December 31, 20X5, at underlying book value. Tempro provided the following trial balance data at December 31, 20X5:

	Debit	Credit
Cash	$ 28,000	
Accounts Receivable	65,000	
Inventory	90,000	
Buildings and Equipment (net)	210,000	
Cost of Goods Sold	105,000	
Depreciation Expense	24,000	
Other Operating Expenses	31,000	
Dividends Declared	15,000	
Accounts Payable		$ 33,000
Notes Payable		120,000
Common Stock		90,000
Retained Earnings		130,000
Sales		195,000
Total	$568,000	$568,000

Required

a. How much did Quoton pay to purchase its shares of Tempro?

b. If consolidated financial statements are prepared at December 31, 20X5, what amount will be assigned to the noncontrolling interest in the consolidated balance sheet?

c. If Quoton reported income of $143,000 from its separate operations for 20X5, what amount of consolidated net income will be reported for 20X5?

d. If Quoton had purchased its ownership of Tempro on January 1, 20X5, at underlying book value and Quoton reported income of $143,000 from its separate operations for 20X5, what amount of consolidated net income would be reported for 20X5?

P3-36 **Parent Company and Consolidated Balances**

Exacto Company reported net assets of $260,000 on January 1, 20X5, and reported the following net income and dividends for the years indicated:

Year	Net Income	Dividends
20X5	$35,000	$12,000
20X6	45,000	20,000
20X7	30,000	14,000

True Corporation purchased 75 percent of Exacto's common stock on January 1, 20X5, and reported a balance of $259,800 in its investment account on December 31, 20X7. True assigned the excess of the purchase price over book value of the shares acquired to equipment with an economic life of 10 years remaining at January 1, 20X5.

Required

a. What amount in excess of book value did True pay when it purchased Exacto's shares?

b. What amount will be added to buildings and equipment when the consolidated balance sheet is prepared at December 31, 20X7?

c. What amount will be added to accumulated depreciation when the consolidated balance sheet is prepared at December 31, 20X7?

d. What amount will be assigned to the noncontrolling shareholders in the consolidated balance sheet prepared at December 31, 20X7?

P3-37 **Indirect Ownership**

Purple Corporation recently attempted to expand by purchasing ownership in Green Company. The following ownership structure was reported on December 31, 20X9:

Investor	Investee	Percentage of Ownership Held
Purple Corporation	Green Company	70
Green Company	Orange Corporation	10
Orange Corporation	Blue Company	60
Green Company	Yellow Company	40

The following income from operations (excluding investment income) and dividend payments were reported by the companies during 20X9:

Company	Operating Income	Dividends Paid
Purple Corporation	$ 90,000	$60,000
Green Company	20,000	10,000
Orange Corporation	40,000	30,000
Blue Company	100,000	80,000
Yellow Company	60,000	40,000

Required

Compute the amount of consolidated net income reported for 20X9.

P3-38 **Comprehensive Problem: Consolidated Financial Statements**

Bishop Enterprises purchased 100 percent of Mangle Manufacturing Company's common shares on January 1, 20X7, for $1,250,000, a price that was $55,000 in excess of the book value of the shares acquired. All of the excess of the cost over book value was related to goodwill except for $25,000 related to equipment with a five-year remaining life at the date of combination.

Balance sheets for the two companies as of December 31, 20X7, were as follows:

	Bishop Enterprises	Mangle Manufacturing
Cash	$ 71,000	$ 33,000
Receivables (net)	431,000	122,000
Inventory	909,000	370,000
Investment in Mangle Stock (at cost)	1,250,000	—
Land	510,000	100,000
Buildings (net)	1,303,000	250,000
Equipment (net)	1,528,000	475,000
Total Assets	$6,002,000	$1,350,000
Current Payables	$ 227,000	$ 95,000
Bonds Payable	500,000	—
Common Stock	1,000,000	500,000
Additional Paid-In Capital	3,550,000	400,000
Retained Earnings	725,000	355,000
Total Liabilities and Equity	$6,002,000	$1,350,000

For the year 20X7, the separate income statements of Bishop and Mangle included, among other items, the following:

	Bishop Enterprises	Mangle Manufacturing
Sales Revenue	$8,325,000	$2,980,000
Cost of Goods Sold	5,150,000	2,010,000
Depreciation Expense	302,000	85,000

The only intercompany transaction during 20X7 was the sale of inventory at year-end from Bishop to Mangle. Bishop originally purchased the goods for $34,000 and sold them to Mangle for $45,000 on account. Mangle still had all of the goods in its inventory at year-end but had not yet paid for them.

Required

Indicate the amount at which Bishop and its subsidiary would report each of the following items in the 20X7 consolidated financial statements:

a. Cash.

b. Receivables (net).

c. Inventory.

d. Investment in Mangle Stock.

e. Equipment (net).

f. Goodwill.

g. Current Payables.

h. Common Stock (par).

i. Sales Revenue.

j. Cost of Goods Sold.

k. Depreciation Expense.

P3-39* ### Balance Sheet Amounts under Alternative Accounting Theories

Parsons Corporation purchased 75 percent ownership of Tumble Company on December 31, 20X7, for $210,000. Summarized balance sheet amounts for the companies on December 31, 20X7, prior to the purchase, were as follows:

	Parsons Corporation	Tumble Company Book Value	Tumble Company Fair Value
Cash and Inventory	$300,000	$ 80,000	$ 80,000
Buildings and Equipment (net)	400,000	120,000	180,000
Total Assets	$700,000	$200,000	$260,000
Common Stock	$380,000	$ 90,000	
Retained Earnings	320,000	110,000	
Total Liabilities and Stockholders' Equity	$700,000	$200,000	

Required

If consolidated financial statements are prepared, determine the amounts that would be reported as cash and inventory, buildings and equipment (net), and goodwill using the following consolidation alternatives:

a. Proprietary theory.

b. Parent company theory.

c. Entity theory.

d. Current accounting practice.

P3-40* ### Reported Balances

Roof Corporation acquired 80 percent of the stock of Gable Company by issuing shares of its common stock with a value of $192,000. At that time, the fair value of Gable was estimated to be $240,000 and the fair value of its identifiable assets and liabilities was $310,000 and $95,000, respectively. Gable's assets and liabilities had book values of $220,000 and $95,000, respectively.

Required

Compute the amounts to be reported immediately after the combination under (1) current reporting standards and (2) the FASB's proposed standards:

a. Investment in Gable reported by Roof.

b. The increase in identifiable assets of the combined entity.

c. The increase in total liabilities of the combined entity.

d. Goodwill for the combined entity.

e. Noncontrolling interest reported in the consolidated balance sheet.

P3-41* ### Acquisition Price

Darwin Company holds assets with a fair value of $120,000 and a book value of $90,000 and liabilities with a book value and a fair value of $25,000. The fair value of Darwin as an entity was determined to be $135,000 at the date Brad Corporation purchased 60 percent ownership.

Required

a. What amount did Brad pay for the shares if no goodwill and no gain on a bargain purchase were reported under current reporting standards?

b. What amount did Brad pay for the shares if goodwill of $18,000 was reported under current reporting standards?

c. What amount did Brad pay for the shares if goodwill of $40,000 were to be reported under the FASB's proposed new standards?

d. What balance would be assigned the noncontrolling interest in the consolidated balance sheet if goodwill of $27,000 were to be reported for the the combined entity under the FASB's proposed standards?

Chapter **Four**

Consolidation of Wholly Owned Subsidiaries

Consolidated and unconsolidated financial statements are prepared using the same generally accepted accounting principles. The unique aspect of consolidated statements is that they bring together the operating results and financial positions of two or more separate legal entities into a single set of statements for the economic entity as a whole. To accomplish this, the consolidation process includes procedures that eliminate all effects of intercorporate ownership and intercompany transactions.

This chapter and the next provide a thorough introduction to the process of preparing consolidated financial statements. Then, using these chapters as a foundation and following a building-block approach, Chapters 6 through 10 deal with intercorporate transfers and other consolidation issues.

CONSOLIDATION PROCEDURES

Consolidation procedures, including the use of a consolidation workpaper, are established to bring together the accounts of a parent and its subsidiaries so they appear as a single entity. The starting point for preparing consolidated financial statements is the books of the separate consolidating companies. Because the consolidated entity has no books, all amounts in the consolidated financial statements originate on the books of the parent or a subsidiary or in the consolidation workpaper.

The term *subsidiary* has been defined as "an entity . . . in which another entity known as its *parent* holds a controlling financial interest."[1] A parent company may hold all or less than all of a corporate subsidiary's common stock, but at least majority ownership is normally required for the presentation of consolidated financial statements. Most, but not all, corporate subsidiaries are wholly owned by their parents.

Because most subsidiaries are wholly owned, this chapter begins the in-depth examination of consolidation procedures by focusing on the procedures for wholly owned subsidiaries. The chapter begins with basic consolidation procedures applied to the preparation of a consolidated balance sheet immediately following the establishment of a parent–subsidiary relationship, and it introduces the use of a simple consolidation workpaper for the balance sheet only. It then moves to the preparation of a full set of consolidated financial statements in subsequent periods and the use of a three-part workpaper designed to facilitate the preparation of a consolidated income statement, retained earnings statement, and balance sheet. Chapter 5 extends the discussion by dealing with the preparation of consolidated financial statements for less-than-wholly owned subsidiaries.

[1]*Financial Accounting Standards Board Proposed Statement of Financial Accounting Standards*, "Consolidated Financial Statements, Including Accounting and Reporting of Noncontrolling Interests in Subsidiaries," June 30, 2005, para. 5g.

FIGURE 4–1
Format for
Consolidation
Workpaper

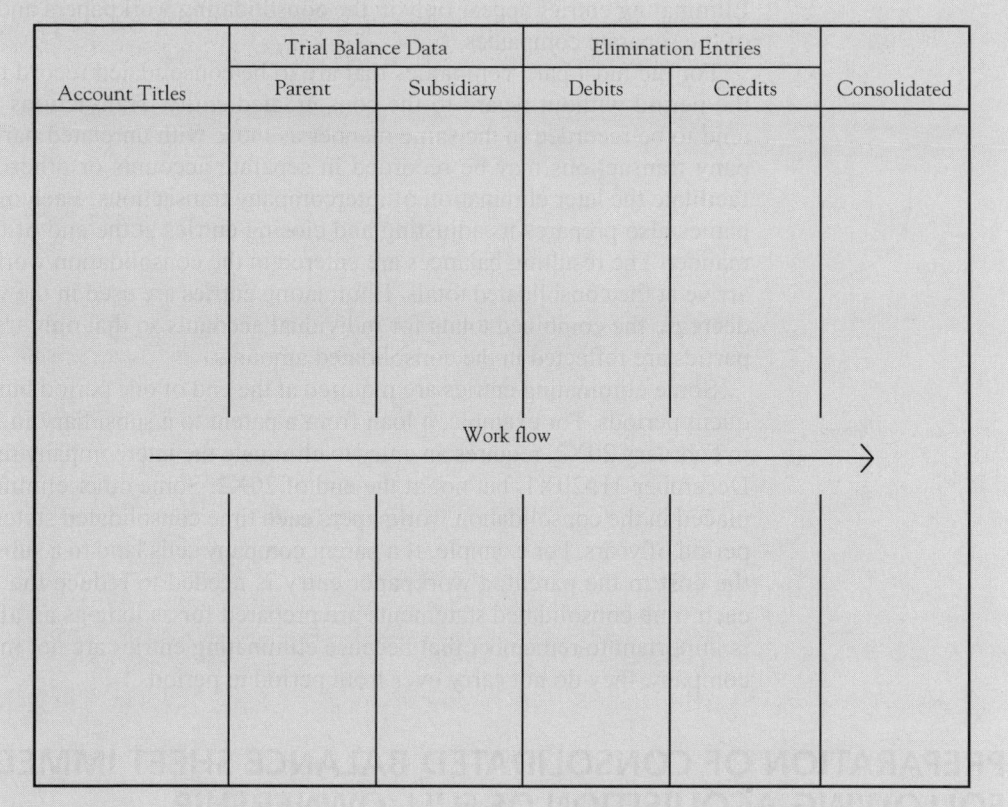

Account Titles	Trial Balance Data		Elimination Entries		Consolidated
	Parent	Subsidiary	Debits	Credits	

Work flow ⟶

CONSOLIDATION WORKPAPERS

The *consolidation workpaper* provides a mechanism for efficiently combining the accounts of the separate companies involved in the consolidation and for adjusting the combined balances to the amounts that would be reported if all consolidating companies were actually a single company. Keep in mind that no set of books exists for the consolidated entity. The parent and its subsidiaries, as separate legal and accounting entities, maintain their own books. When consolidated financial statements are prepared, the account balances are taken from the separate books of the parent and each subsidiary and placed in the consolidation workpaper. The consolidated statements are prepared, after adjustments and eliminations, from the amounts in the consolidation workpaper.

Workpaper Format

The basic form of a consolidation workpaper is shown in Figure 4–1. The titles of the accounts of the consolidating companies are listed in the first column of the workpaper. The account balances from the books or trial balances of the individual companies are listed in the next set of columns, with a separate column for each company included in the consolidation. Entries are made in the columns labeled Elimination Entries to adjust or eliminate balances so that the resulting amounts are those that would appear in the financial statements if all the consolidating companies actually formed a single company. The balances in the last column are obtained by summing all amounts algebraically across the workpaper by account. These are the balances that appear in the consolidated financial statements.

Nature of Eliminating Entries

Eliminating entries are used in the consolidation workpaper to adjust the totals of the individual account balances of the separate consolidating companies to reflect the amounts that would appear if all the legally separate companies were actually a single company.

Eliminating entries appear only in the consolidating workpapers and do not affect the books of the separate companies.

For the most part, companies that are to be consolidated record their transactions during the period without regard to the consolidated entity. Transactions with related companies tend to be recorded in the same manner as those with unrelated parties, although intercompany transactions may be recorded in separate accounts or other records may be kept to facilitate the later elimination of intercompany transactions. Each of the consolidating companies also prepares its adjusting and closing entries at the end of the period in the normal manner. The resulting balances are entered in the consolidation workpaper and combined to arrive at the consolidated totals. Eliminating entries are used in the workpaper to increase or decrease the combined totals for individual accounts so that only transactions with external parties are reflected in the consolidated amounts.

Some eliminating entries are required at the end of one period but not at the end of subsequent periods. For example, a loan from a parent to a subsidiary in December 20X1, repaid in February 20X2, requires an entry to eliminate the intercompany receivable and payable on December 31, 20X1, but not at the end of 20X2. Some other eliminating entries need to be placed in the consolidation workpapers each time consolidated statements are prepared for a period of years. For example, if a parent company sells land to a subsidiary for $5,000 above the cost to the parent, a workpaper entry is needed to reduce the land amount by $5,000 each time consolidated statements are prepared for as long as an affiliate holds the land. It is important to remember that because eliminating entries are not made on the books of any company, they do not carry over from period to period.

PREPARATION OF CONSOLIDATED BALANCE SHEET IMMEDIATELY FOLLOWING ACQUISITION OF FULL OWNERSHIP

The simplest consolidation setting occurs when the financial statements of related companies are consolidated immediately after a parent–subsidiary relationship is established through a business combination or creation of a new subsidiary. A series of examples follows to illustrate the preparation of a consolidated balance sheet in various situations that might arise following a business combination. In each example, Peerless Products Corporation purchases all or part of the common stock of Special Foods Inc. on January 1, 20X1, and immediately prepares a consolidated balance sheet. The separate balance sheets of the two companies immediately before the combination appear in Figure 4–2.

FIGURE 4–2
Balance Sheets of Peerless Products and Special Foods, January 1, 20X1, Immediately before Combination

	Peerless Products	Special Foods
Assets		
Cash	$ 350,000	$ 50,000
Accounts Receivable	75,000	50,000
Inventory	100,000	60,000
Land	175,000	40,000
Buildings and Equipment	800,000	600,000
Accumulated Depreciation	(400,000)	(300,000)
Total Assets	$1,100,000	$500,000
Liabilities and Stockholders' Equity		
Accounts Payable	$ 100,000	$100,000
Bonds Payable	200,000	100,000
Common Stock	500,000	200,000
Retained Earnings	300,000	100,000
Total Liabilities and Equity	$1,100,000	$500,000

In the discussion that follows, all journal entries and workpaper eliminating entries are numbered sequentially throughout the chapter. Eliminating entries appearing in the workpapers are also discussed in the text of the chapter. To avoid confusing the eliminating entries with journal entries that appear on the separate books of the parent or subsidiary, all workpaper eliminating entries appearing in the text are shaded and designated by an entry number preceded by an E.

Full Ownership Purchased at Book Value

In the first example, Peerless purchases all of Special Foods' outstanding common stock for $300,000. On the date of combination, the fair values of Special Foods' individual assets and liabilities are equal to their book values shown in Figure 4–2. Because Peerless acquires all of Special Foods' common stock and because Special Foods has only the one class of stock outstanding, the total book value of the shares acquired equals the total stockholders' equity of Special Foods ($200,000 + $100,000). The purchase price of $300,000 is equal to the book value of the shares acquired. This ownership situation can be characterized as follows:

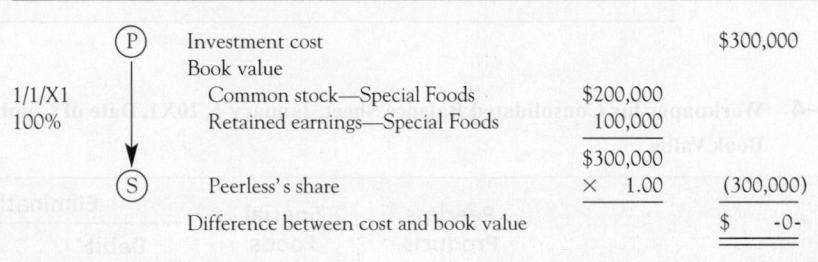

	Investment cost		$300,000
	Book value		
1/1/X1	Common stock—Special Foods	$200,000	
100%	Retained earnings—Special Foods	100,000	
		$300,000	
	Peerless's share	× 1.00	(300,000)
	Difference between cost and book value		$ -0-

Peerless records the stock acquisition on its books with the following entry on the date of combination:

January 1, 20X1

(1)	Investment in Special Foods Stock	300,000	
	Cash		300,000
	Record purchase of Special Foods stock.		

The separate financial statements of Peerless and Special Foods immediately after the combination appear in Figure 4–3. Special Foods' balance sheet in Figure 4–3 is the same as in Figure 4–2, but Peerless's balance sheet has changed to reflect the $300,000 reduction in cash and the recording of the investment in Special Foods stock for the same amount. Note that the $300,000 of cash was paid to the former stockholders of Special Foods and not to the company itself. Accordingly, that cash is no longer in the consolidated entity.

Consolidation Workpaper

The workpaper for the preparation of a consolidated balance sheet immediately following the acquisition is presented in Figure 4–4. The first two columns of the workpaper in Figure 4–4 are the account balances taken from the books of Peerless and Special Foods, as shown in Figure 4–3. The balances of like accounts are placed side by side so that they may be added together. If more than two companies were to be consolidated, a separate column would be included in the workpaper for each additional subsidiary.

The accounts are placed in the workpaper so that those having debit balances are in the upper half of the workpaper and those having credit balances are in the lower half. Total debit items must equal total credit items for each of the companies and for the consolidated totals.

FIGURE 4–3
Balance Sheets of Peerless Products and Special Foods, January 1, 20X1, Immediately after Combination

	Peerless Products	Special Foods
Assets		
Cash	$ 50,000	$ 50,000
Accounts Receivable	75,000	50,000
Inventory	100,000	60,000
Land	175,000	40,000
Buildings and Equipment	800,000	600,000
Accumulated Depreciation	(400,000)	(300,000)
Investment in Special Foods Stock	300,000	
Total Assets	$1,100,000	$500,000
Liabilities and Stockholders' Equity		
Accounts Payable	$ 100,000	$100,000
Bonds Payable	200,000	100,000
Common Stock	500,000	200,000
Retained Earnings	300,000	100,000
Total Liabilities and Equity	$1,100,000	$500,000

FIGURE 4–4 **Workpaper for Consolidated Balance Sheet, January 1, 20X1, Date of Combination; 100 Percent Purchase at Book Value**

Item	Peerless Products	Special Foods	Eliminations Debit	Eliminations Credit	Consolidated
Cash	50,000	50,000			100,000
Accounts Receivable	75,000	50,000			125,000
Inventory	100,000	60,000			160,000
Land	175,000	40,000			215,000
Buildings and Equipment	800,000	600,000			1,400,000
Investment in Special Foods Stock	300,000			(2) 300,000	
Total Debits	1,500,000	800,000			2,000,000
Accumulated Depreciation	400,000	300,000			700,000
Accounts Payable	100,000	100,000			200,000
Bonds Payable	200,000	100,000			300,000
Common Stock	500,000	200,000	(2) 200,000		500,000
Retained Earnings	300,000	100,000	(2) 100,000		300,000
Total Credits	1,500,000	800,000	300,000	300,000	2,000,000

Elimination entry:

(2) Eliminate investment balance and stockholders' equity of Special Foods.

(*Note:* Elimination entries are keyed to those in the text; all entries are numbered sequentially throughout the chapter.)

The two columns labeled Eliminations in Figure 4–4 are used to adjust the amounts reported by the individual companies to the amounts appropriate for the consolidated statement. All eliminations made in the workpapers are made in double-entry form; the debit amounts of each entry must equal the credit amounts. All parts of the same eliminating entry are keyed with the same number or other symbol so that whole entries can be identified. When the workpaper is completed, total debits entered in the Debit Eliminations column must equal total credits entered in the Credit Eliminations column. After the appropriate eliminating entries have been entered in the Eliminations columns, summing algebraically across the individual accounts provides the consolidated totals.

Investment Elimination Entry

The only eliminating entry in the workpaper in Figure 4–4 is one needed to eliminate the Investment in Special Foods Stock account and the subsidiary's stockholders' equity accounts. This is accomplished through entry E(2) in the workpaper:

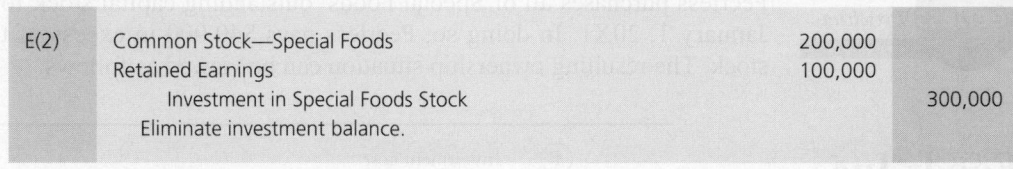

E(2)	Common Stock—Special Foods	200,000	
	Retained Earnings	100,000	
	Investment in Special Foods Stock		300,000
	Eliminate investment balance.		

Remember that this entry is made in the consolidation workpaper, not on the books of either the parent or the subsidiary, and is presented here in general journal form only for instructional purposes.

The investment account must be eliminated because, from a single entity viewpoint, a company cannot hold an investment in itself. The subsidiary's stock and the related stockholders' equity accounts must be eliminated because the subsidiary's stock is held entirely within the consolidated entity and none represents claims by outsiders.

From a somewhat different viewpoint, the investment account on the parent's books can be thought of as a single account representing the parent's investment in the net assets of the subsidiary, a so-called *one-line consolidation*. In a full consolidation, the subsidiary's individual assets and liabilities are combined with those of the parent. Including both the net assets of the subsidiary, as represented by the balance in the investment account, and the subsidiary's individual assets and liabilities would double count the same set of assets. Therefore, the investment account is eliminated and not carried to the consolidated balance sheet.

The Consolidated Balance Sheet

The consolidated balance sheet presented in Figure 4–5 is prepared directly from the last column of the consolidation workpaper in Figure 4–4. The total debit and credit balances shown on the balance sheet differ from the debit and credit totals given in the workpaper because contra asset accounts are included with the credits in the workpaper but are offset against the related assets in the consolidated balance sheet. Because no operations occurred between the date of combination and the preparation of the consolidated balance sheet, the stockholders' equity section of the consolidated balance sheet is identical to that of Peerless in Figure 4–2.

Full Ownership Purchased at More than Book Value

A company's stock price is influenced by many factors, including net asset values, enterprise earning power, and general market conditions. When one company purchases another, there

FIGURE 4–5 Consolidated Balance Sheet, January 1, 20X1, Date of Combination; 100 Percent Purchase at Book Value

PEERLESS PRODUCTS CORPORATION AND SUBSIDIARY Consolidated Balance Sheet January 1, 20X1					
Assets			Liabilities		
Cash		$ 100,000	Accounts Payable		$ 200,000
Accounts Receivable		125,000	Bonds Payable		300,000
Inventory		160,000			
Land		215,000	Stockholders' Equity		
Buildings and Equipment	$1,400,000		Common Stock		500,000
Accumulated Depreciation	(700,000)	700,000	Retained Earnings		300,000
Total Assets		$1,300,000	Total Liabilities and Equity		$1,300,000

is no reason to expect that the purchase price necessarily will be equal to the acquired stock's book value. The process used to prepare the consolidated balance sheet is complicated only slightly when 100 percent of a company's stock is purchased at a price different from its book value.

To illustrate the purchase of a subsidiary at a price higher than book value, assume that Peerless purchases all of Special Foods' outstanding capital stock for $340,000 in cash on January 1, 20X1. In doing so, Peerless pays $40,000 in excess of the book value of that stock. The resulting ownership situation can be viewed as follows:

	(P)	Investment cost		$340,000
		Book value		
1/1/X1		Common stock—Special Foods	$200,000	
100%		Retained earnings—Special Foods	100,000	
			$300,000	
	(S)	Peerless's share	× 1.00	(300,000)
		Differential		$ 40,000

Peerless records the stock acquisition with the following entry:

January 1, 20X1

(3)	Investment in Special Foods Stock	340,000	
	Cash		340,000
	Record purchase of Special Foods stock.		

In a business combination, the purchase price must be allocated to the assets and liabilities acquired. Therefore, the full amount paid by Peerless must be assigned to specific assets and liabilities or to goodwill when preparing consolidated financial statements.

The workpaper procedures used in adjusting to the proper consolidated amounts follow a consistent pattern. The first eliminating entry prepared involves the elimination of the parent's investment account balance and each of the subsidiary's stockholders' equity accounts. When the purchase price is above the book value of the stock acquired, the first eliminating entry includes a debit to a workpaper clearing account to balance the entry. This clearing account is referred to as the ***purchase differential***, or just *differential*. The differential represents the difference between the cost of the investment as recorded on the parent's books and the book value of the shares acquired based on the stockholders' equity accounts of the subsidiary.

The workpaper entry to eliminate Peerless's investment account and the stockholders' equity accounts of Special Foods is as follows:

E(4)	Common Stock—Special Foods	200,000	
	Retained Earnings	100,000	
	Differential	40,000	
	Investment in Special Foods Stock		340,000
	Eliminate investment balance.		

The balance assigned to Differential in this initial eliminating entry is subsequently cleared from that account through one or more additional workpaper entries. These additional workpaper entries adjust the various account balances to reflect the fair values of the subsidiary's assets and liabilities at the time the parent acquired the subsidiary and to establish goodwill, if appropriate.

Treatment of a Positive Differential

There are several reasons that the purchase price of a company's stock might exceed the stock's book value:

1. Errors or omissions on the books of the subsidiary.
2. Excess of fair value over the book value of the subsidiary's net identifiable assets.
3. Existence of goodwill.

Errors or Omissions on the Books of the Subsidiary

An examination of an acquired company's books may reveal material errors. In some cases, the acquired company may have expensed rather than capitalized assets or, for other reasons, omitted them from the books. An acquired company that previously had been closely held may not have followed generally accepted accounting principles in maintaining its accounting records. In some cases, there may simply have been inadequate recordkeeping.

Where such errors or omissions exist, corrections should be made directly on the subsidiary's books as of the date of acquisition. These corrections are treated as prior-period adjustments in accordance with **FASB Statement No. 16**, "Prior Period Adjustments" (FASB 16). Once the subsidiary's books are stated in accordance with generally accepted accounting principles, that portion of the differential attributable to the errors or omissions will no longer exist.

Excess of Fair Value over Book Value of Subsidiary's Net Identifiable Assets

The fair value of a company's assets is an important factor in the overall determination of the company's purchase price. In many cases, the fair value of an acquired company's net assets exceeds the book value. Consequently, the purchase price may exceed the book value of the stock acquired. The procedures used in preparing the consolidated balance sheet should lead to reporting all of the acquired company's assets and liabilities based on their fair values on the date of combination. This valuation may be accomplished in one of two ways: (1) the assets and liabilities of the subsidiary may be revalued directly on the books of the subsidiary or (2) the accounting basis of the subsidiary may be maintained and the revaluations made each period in the consolidation workpaper.

Revaluing the assets and liabilities on the subsidiary's books generally is the simplest approach if all of the subsidiary's common stock is acquired. On the other hand, it generally is not appropriate to revalue the assets and liabilities on the subsidiary's books if there is a significant noncontrolling interest in that subsidiary. From a noncontrolling shareholder's point of view, the subsidiary is a continuing company, and the basis of accounting should not change. More difficult to resolve is the situation in which the parent acquires all of the subsidiary's common stock but continues to issue separate financial statements of the subsidiary to holders of the subsidiary's bonds or preferred stock. Revaluing the assets and liabilities of the subsidiary directly on the subsidiary's books is referred to as ***push-down accounting*** and is discussed later in this chapter.

When the assets and liabilities are revalued directly on the subsidiary's books, that portion of the differential then no longer exists. However, if the assets and liabilities are not revalued on the subsidiary's books, an entry to revalue those assets and allocate the differential is needed in the consolidation workpaper each time consolidated financial statements are prepared, for as long as the related assets are held.

In the example introduced earlier, Peerless Products acquired all of Special Foods' stock for $340,000, giving rise to a $40,000 debit differential. In a consolidated balance sheet prepared immediately after acquisition, the investment elimination entry appearing in the consolidation workpaper is (as given earlier):

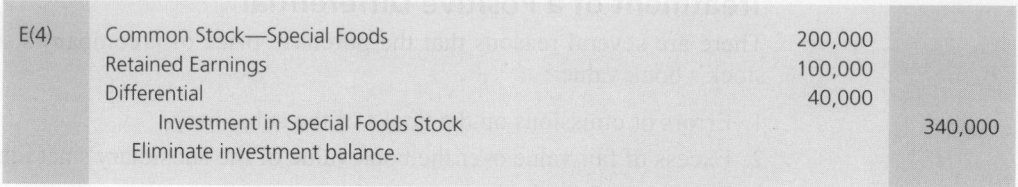

E(4)	Common Stock—Special Foods	200,000	
	Retained Earnings	100,000	
	Differential	40,000	
	Investment in Special Foods Stock		340,000
	Eliminate investment balance.		

If the fair value of Special Foods' land is determined to be $40,000 more than its book value, and all other assets and liabilities have fair values equal to their book values, the entire amount of the differential is allocated to the subsidiary's land. This allocation of the differential is made in the consolidation workpaper with the following entry:

E(5)	Land	40,000	
	Differential		40,000
	Assign differential to land.		

The consolidation workpaper reflecting the allocation of the differential to the subsidiary's land is illustrated in Figure 4–6. The workpaper is based on the data in Figure 4–2 and a purchase price of $340,000 for the Special Foods stock.

The amounts reported in the consolidated balance sheet are those in the Consolidated column of the workpaper in Figure 4–6. Land is included in the consolidated balance sheet at $255,000, the amount carried on Peerless's books ($175,000) plus the amount carried on Special Foods' books ($40,000) plus the differential reflecting the increased value of Special Foods' land ($40,000).

This example is sufficiently simple that the assignment of the differential to land could be made directly in eliminating entry E(4) rather than through the use of the differential

FIGURE 4–6 **Workpaper for Consolidated Balance Sheet, January 1, 20X1, Date of Combination; 100 Percent Purchase at More than Book Value**

Item	Peerless Products	Special Foods	Eliminations Debit	Eliminations Credit	Consolidated
Cash	10,000	50,000			60,000
Accounts Receivable	75,000	50,000			125,000
Inventory	100,000	60,000			160,000
Land	175,000	40,000	(5) 40,000		255,000
Buildings and Equipment	800,000	600,000			1,400,000
Investment in Special Foods Stock	340,000			(4) 340,000	
Differential			(4) 40,000	(5) 40,000	
Total Debits	1,500,000	800,000			2,000,000
Accumulated Depreciation	400,000	300,000			700,000
Accounts Payable	100,000	100,000			200,000
Bonds Payable	200,000	100,000			300,000
Common Stock	500,000	200,000	(4) 200,000		500,000
Retained Earnings	300,000	100,000	(4) 100,000		300,000
Total Credits	1,500,000	800,000	380,000	380,000	2,000,000

Elimination entries:
(4) Eliminate investment balance and stockholders' equity of Special Foods.
(5) Assign differential to land.

clearing account. In practice, however, the differential often relates to more than a single asset, and the allocation of the differential may be considerably more complex than in this example. The possibilities for clerical errors are reduced in complex situations by making two separate entries rather than one complicated entry.

Existence of Goodwill

If a company purchases a subsidiary at a price in excess of the total of the fair values of the subsidiary's net identifiable assets, the additional amount generally is considered to be a payment for the excess earning power of the acquired company, referred to as *goodwill*. Thus, once the subsidiary's identifiable assets are restated to their fair values, any remaining debit differential normally is allocated to goodwill.

If, in the example of Peerless and Special Foods, the fair values of Special Foods' assets and liabilities are equal to their book values, and the $40,000 differential is considered a payment for goodwill, the following elimination entry is needed in the consolidation workpaper:

E(6)	Goodwill	40,000	
	Differential		40,000
	Assign differential to goodwill.		

The consolidation workpaper would appear as in Figure 4–6 except that elimination entry E(6) would replace elimination entry E(5). Goodwill, which does not appear on the books of either Peerless or Special Foods, would appear at $40,000 in the consolidated balance sheet prepared immediately after acquisition.

In the past, some companies have included in goodwill the portion of the purchase price related to certain identifiable intangible assets. This treatment is not acceptable, and the portion of the purchase price related to an intangible asset that arises from a contractual or legal right or is separable from the entity must be allocated to that asset.

Illustration of Treatment of Debit Differential

In many situations, the differential relates to a number of different assets and liabilities. As a means of illustrating the allocation of the differential to various assets and liabilities, assume that the book values and fair values of Special Foods' assets and liabilities are as shown in Figure 4–7. The inventory and land have fair values in excess of their book values, while the buildings and equipment are worth less than their book values.

FIGURE 4–7
Balance Sheet for Special Foods Inc., January 1, 20X1, Date of Combination

		Book Value	Fair Value	Difference between Fair Value and Book Value
Cash		$ 50,000	$ 50,000	
Accounts Receivable		50,000	50,000	
Inventory		60,000	75,000	$15,000
Land		40,000	100,000	60,000
Buildings and Equipment	$ 600,000			
Accumulated Depreciation	(300,000)	300,000	290,000	(10,000)
		$500,000	$565,000	
Accounts Payable		$100,000	$100,000	
Bonds Payable		100,000	135,000	(35,000)
Common Stock		200,000		
Retained Earnings		100,000		
		$500,000	$235,000	$30,000

Bond prices fluctuate as interest rates change. In this example, the value of Special Foods' bonds payable is higher than the book value. This indicates that the nominal interest rate on the bonds is higher than the current market rate of interest, and, therefore, investors are willing to pay a price higher than par for the bonds. In determining a purchase price for Special Foods, Peerless must recognize that it is assuming a liability that pays an interest rate higher than the current market rate and will pay a lower price for Special Foods than if the liability carried a lower interest rate. The resulting consolidated financial statements, therefore, should recognize the fair values rather than the book values of Special Foods' liabilities.

Assume that Peerless Products acquires all of Special Foods' capital stock for $400,000 on January 1, 20X1, by issuing $100,000 of 9 percent bonds and paying cash of $300,000. The resulting ownership situation can be pictured as follows:

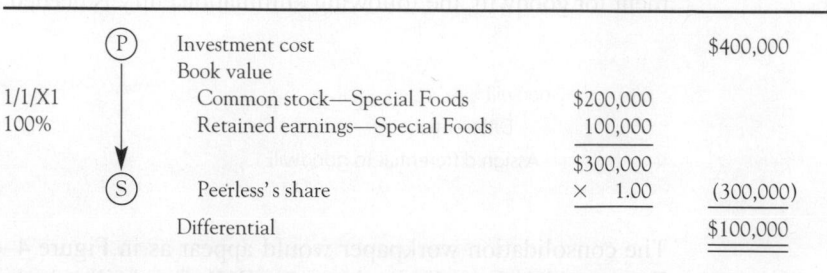

	Investment cost		$400,000
	Book value		
1/1/X1	Common stock—Special Foods	$200,000	
100%	Retained earnings—Special Foods	100,000	
		$300,000	
	Peerless's share	× 1.00	(300,000)
	Differential		$100,000

Peerless records the investment on its books with the following entry:

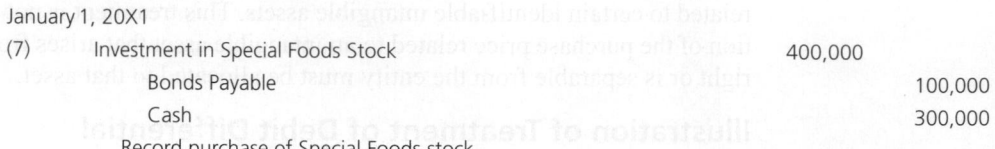

January 1, 20X1			
(7)	Investment in Special Foods Stock	400,000	
	Bonds Payable		100,000
	Cash		300,000
	Record purchase of Special Foods stock.		

The relationship between the total purchase price paid for the stock of Special Foods, the fair value of Special Foods' net assets, and the book value of Special Foods' net assets is as follows:

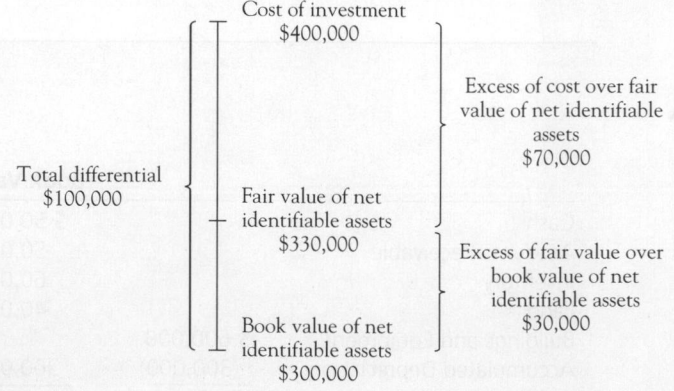

The total $400,000 purchase price exceeds by $100,000 the book value of Special Foods' net assets (assets of $500,000 less liabilities of $200,000). Thus, the total purchase differential is $100,000. The total fair value of the net identifiable assets acquired in the combination is $330,000 ($565,000 − $235,000), based on the data in Figure 4–7. The amount by which the total purchase price of $400,000 exceeds the $330,000 fair value of the net identifiable assets is $70,000, and that amount is assigned to goodwill in the consolidated balance sheet.

FIGURE 4–8   Workpaper for Consolidated Balance Sheet, January 1, 20X1, Date of Combination; 100 Percent Purchase at More than Book Value

Item	Peerless Products	Special Foods	Eliminations Debit	Eliminations Credit	Consolidated
Cash	50,000	50,000			100,000
Accounts Receivable	75,000	50,000			125,000
Inventory	100,000	60,000	(9) 15,000		175,000
Land	175,000	40,000	(9) 60,000		275,000
Buildings and Equipment	800,000	600,000		(9) 10,000	1,390,000
Goodwill			(9) 70,000		70,000
Investment in Special Foods Stock	400,000			(8) 400,000	
Differential			(8) 100,000	(9) 100,000	
Total Debits	1,600,000	800,000			2,135,000
Accumulated Depreciation	400,000	300,000			700,000
Accounts Payable	100,000	100,000			200,000
Bonds Payable	300,000	100,000			400,000
Premium on Bonds Payable				(9) 35,000	35,000
Common Stock	500,000	200,000	(8) 200,000		500,000
Retained Earnings	300,000	100,000	(8) 100,000		300,000
Total Credits	1,600,000	800,000	545,000	545,000	2,135,000

Elimination entries:
(8) Eliminate investment balance and stockholders' equity of Special Foods.
(9) Assign differential.

The eliminations entered in the consolidation workpaper in preparing the consolidated balance sheet immediately after the combination are:

E(8)	Common Stock—Special Foods	200,000	
	Retained Earnings	100,000	
	Differential	100,000	
	Investment in Special Foods Stock		400,000
	Eliminate investment balance.		
E(9)	Inventory	15,000	
	Land	60,000	
	Goodwill	70,000	
	Buildings and Equipment		10,000
	Premium on Bonds Payable		35,000
	Differential		100,000
	Assign differential.		

These entries are reflected in the workpaper in Figure 4–8. While entry E(9) is somewhat more complex than those in the previous examples, there is no conceptual difference. In each case, the end result is a consolidated balance sheet with the subsidiary's assets and liabilities valued at their fair values at the date of combination.

Full Ownership Purchased at Less than Book Value

There have been numerous cases of companies with common stock trading in the market at prices less than book value. Often the companies are singled out as prime acquisition targets. When one company acquires the stock of another at less than book value, possible explanations for the negative, or credit, differential may include:

1. Errors or omissions on the books of the subsidiary.
2. Excess of book value over the fair value of the subsidiary's net identifiable assets.

3. Diminution of previously recorded goodwill.
4. Bargain purchase.

Errors or Omissions on the Subsidiary's Books

As in the case of a debit differential, errors or omissions on the subsidiary's books should be corrected directly on those books. Often this involves recognizing previously unrecorded liabilities incurred by the subsidiary. Once these corrections are made on the subsidiary's books, that portion of the differential will no longer exist.

Excess of Book Value over Fair Value of Subsidiary's Net Identifiable Assets

Because in a business combination all assets and liabilities of the acquired company are to be valued based on their fair values as of the date of combination, adjustments are needed for any of the acquired company's assets and liabilities carried at amounts other than their current fair values. Assets with fair values less than their book values are written down on the subsidiary's books if push-down accounting is used or if the asset values are impaired as of the date of combination and accounting standards require recognition of an impairment loss. Otherwise, the assets are revalued in the consolidation workpaper.

Diminution of Previously Recorded Goodwill

If the subsidiary has goodwill carried on its books from a previous business combination, the credit differential may indicate that goodwill no longer exists. If that is determined to be the case, the goodwill should be written off the subsidiary's books.

Bargain Purchase

In some cases the reason for a credit differential may not be clear. One possibility is the existence of "negative goodwill," indicating that the subsidiary's net assets are worth less as a going concern than if they were sold individually. Another view is that the acquiring company simply made a *bargain purchase*. This view assumes that for whatever reason (e.g., forced sale, general stock market conditions), the subsidiary was acquired at a price below its estimated value.

When an unallocated credit differential exists, the FASB requires that this *negative goodwill* be allocated proportionately against the amounts that otherwise would be assigned to all of the acquired assets other than cash and cash equivalents, trade receivables, inventory, financial instruments reported at fair value, assets to be disposed of by sale, and deferred tax assets. Any remaining negative goodwill would be recognized as an extraordinary gain. Note that liabilities and most current assets are not assigned a portion of an unallocated credit differential because other valuation principles take precedence with respect to these items. In particular, most liabilities are valued at the fixed amount of the claims or their present values, while current assets typically have readily determinable net realizable values.

Illustration of Treatment of Credit Differential

Using the example of Peerless Products and Special Foods, assume the book values and fair values of Special Foods' assets and liabilities on January 1, 20X1, are as shown in Figure 4–9. Peerless purchases all of Special Foods' stock for $260,000. The resulting ownership situation is as follows:

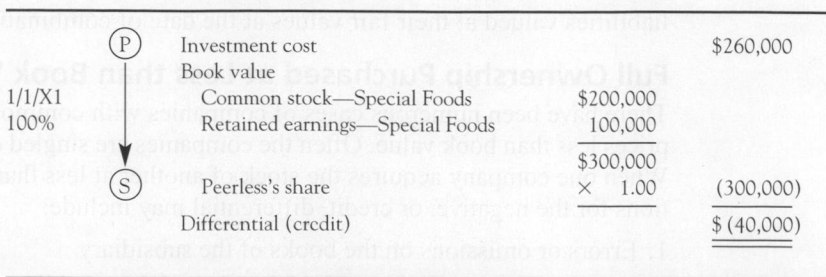

	Investment cost		$260,000
	Book value		
1/1/X1	Common stock—Special Foods	$200,000	
100%	Retained earnings—Special Foods	100,000	
		$300,000	
	Peerless's share	× 1.00	(300,000)
	Differential (credit)		$ (40,000)

FIGURE 4–9
Balance Sheet for Special Foods Inc., January 1, 20X1, Date of Combination

		Book Value	Fair Value	Difference between Fair Value and Book Value
Cash		$ 50,000	$ 50,000	
Accounts Receivable		50,000	50,000	
Inventory		60,000	60,000	
Land		40,000	45,000	$ 5,000
Buildings and Equipment	$ 600,000			
Accumulated Depreciation	(300,000)	300,000	280,000	(20,000)
		$500,000	$485,000	
Accounts Payable		$100,000	$100,000	
Bonds Payable		100,000	100,000	
Common Stock		200,000		
Retained Earnings		100,000		
		$500,000	$200,000	$(15,000)

Peerless records its investment in Special Foods with the following entry on its books:

January 1, 20X1

(10)	Investment in Special Foods Stock	260,000	
	Cash		260,000
	Record purchase of Special Foods stock.		

The relationship between the total purchase price of the investment, the fair value of Special Foods' net assets, and the book value of Special Foods' net assets can be shown as follows:

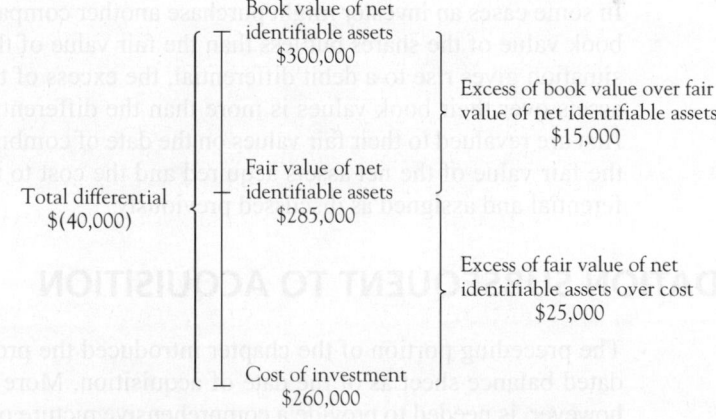

If a consolidated balance sheet is prepared immediately after the combination, the following elimination entries are made in the consolidation workpaper:

E(11)	Common Stock—Special Foods	200,000	
	Retained Earnings	100,000	
	Investment in Special Foods Stock		260,000
	Differential		40,000
	Eliminate investment balance.		

E(12)	Land	5,000	
	Differential	15,000	
	Buildings and Equipment		20,000
	Assign differential to bring land and buildings and equipment of Special Foods to fair values.		
E(13)	Differential	25,000	
	Land		3,462
	Buildings and Equipment		21,538
	Assign remaining credit differential.		

The purchase price ($260,000) of Special Foods' stock is $40,000 less than its book value ($300,000), resulting in a credit differential as shown in eliminating entry E(11). The assets are revalued to their fair values in eliminating entry E(12), leaving a $25,000 unallocated credit differential. This remaining credit differential is allocated in eliminating entry E(13) against Special Foods' noncurrent assets in proportion to their fair values. The differential allocations in workpaper entries E(12) and E(13) are computed as follows:

Item	Book Value	Initial Adjustment to Fair Value	Fair Value	Allocation Ratio		Unallocated Differential		Allocated Reduction
Land	$ 40,000	$ 5,000	$ 45,000	45/325	×	$(25,000)	=	$ (3,462)
Buildings and Equipment	300,000	(20,000)	280,000	280/325	×	(25,000)	=	(21,538)
Totals	$340,000	$(15,000)	$325,000					$(25,000)

Ownership Purchased at More than Book Value and Less than Fair Value

In some cases an investor might purchase another company's stock at a price higher than the book value of the shares but less than the fair value of the underlying net assets. While this situation gives rise to a debit differential, the excess of the fair value of the subsidiary's net assets over their book values is more than the differential. In consolidation, the net assets first are revalued to their fair values on the date of combination. Then the difference between the fair value of the net assets acquired and the cost to the parent is treated as a credit differential and assigned as discussed previously.

CONSOLIDATION SUBSEQUENT TO ACQUISITION

The preceding portion of the chapter introduced the procedures used to prepare a consolidated balance sheet as of the date of acquisition. More than a consolidated balance sheet, however, is needed to provide a comprehensive picture of the consolidated entity's activities following acquisition. As with a single company, the set of basic financial statements for a consolidated entity consists of a balance sheet, an income statement, a statement of changes in retained earnings, and a statement of cash flows.

This portion of the chapter presents the procedures used to prepare a consolidated balance sheet, income statement, and retained earnings statement subsequent to the date of combination. The preparation of a consolidated statement of cash flows is discussed in Chapter 10.

The discussion that follows first deals with the important concepts of consolidated net income and consolidated retained earnings, followed by a description of the workpaper format used to facilitate the preparation of a full set of consolidated financial statements. The specific procedures used to prepare consolidated financial statements subsequent to the date of combination are then discussed.

This and subsequent chapters focus on procedures for consolidation when the parent company accounts for its investment in subsidiary stock using the equity method. If the parent accounts for its investment using the cost method, the general approach to the preparation of consolidated financial statements is the same, but the specific procedures differ somewhat. Consolidation procedures using the cost method are discussed in Appendix 5A. Regardless of the method the parent uses to account for its subsidiary investment, however, the consolidated statements will be the same because the investment and related accounts are eliminated in the consolidation process.

The approach followed to prepare a complete set of consolidated financial statements subsequent to a business combination is quite similar to that used to prepare a consolidated balance sheet as of the date of combination. However, in addition to the assets and liabilities, the revenues and expenses of the consolidating companies must be combined. As the accounts are combined, eliminations must be made in the consolidation workpaper so that the consolidated financial statements appear as if they are the financial statements of a single company.

Because consolidation subsequent to a subsidiary's acquisition involves changes that take place over time, the resulting financial statements rest heavily on the concepts of consolidated net income and consolidated retained earnings. The consolidation approach that has traditionally been used in practice in the United States and Canada is essentially the parent company approach, which emphasizes the income and retained earnings of the consolidated entity accruing to the parent.

Consolidated Net Income

All revenues and expenses of the individual consolidating companies arising from transactions with nonaffiliated companies are included in the consolidated income statement. The amount reported as *consolidated net income* is that part of the total enterprise's income that is assigned to the parent company's shareholders. When all subsidiaries are wholly owned by the parent, all income of the parent and its subsidiaries accrues to the parent company's shareholders. In this case, consolidated net income is the difference between consolidated revenues and expenses.

Consolidated net income is computed by adding the parent's proportionate share of the income of all subsidiaries, adjusted for any differential write-off or goodwill impairment, to the parent's income from its own separate operations (parent's net income less investment income from the subsidiaries under either the cost or equity method). Intercorporate investment income included in the parent's net income must be eliminated in computing consolidated net income to avoid double counting. The computation of consolidated net income is basically the same as computing the parent's equity-method net income, and the two amounts are normally equal in the absence of several special items, discussed later.

In simple cases with only wholly owned subsidiaries, consolidated net income is equal to the parent's income from its own separate operations plus the net income of all subsidiaries, adjusted for any differential write-off. To illustrate the computation of consolidated net income, assume that Push Corporation purchases all of the stock of Shove Company at book value. During 20X1, Shove reports net income of $25,000, while Push reports net income of $125,000, including equity-method income from Shove of $25,000. Consolidated net income for 20X1 is computed as follows:

Push's net income	$125,000
Less: Equity-method income from Shove	(25,000)
Push's share of Shove's net income (100%)	25,000
Consolidated net income	$125,000

Consolidated Retained Earnings

Consolidated retained earnings must be measured on a basis consistent with that used in determining consolidated net income. *Consolidated retained earnings* is that portion of the consolidated enterprise's undistributed earnings accruing to the parent company shareholders. As with a single company, ending consolidated retained earnings is equal to the beginning consolidated retained earnings balance plus consolidated net income, less consolidated dividends.

Only those dividends paid to the owners of the consolidated entity can be included in the consolidated retained earnings statement. Because the owners of the parent company are considered to be the owners of the consolidated entity, only dividends paid by the parent company to its shareholders are treated as a deduction in the consolidated retained earnings statement; dividends of the subsidiary are not included.

Computing Consolidated Retained Earnings

Consolidated retained earnings is computed by adding together the parent's retained earnings from its own operations (excluding any income from consolidated subsidiaries recognized by the parent) and the parent's proportionate share of the net income of each subsidiary since the date of acquisition, adjusted for differential write-off and goodwill impairment. This is the same approach used to compute the parent's retained earnings when the parent accounts for consolidated subsidiaries using the equity method on its books. In the absence of unrealized profits from intercompany transactions and goodwill impairment, consolidated retained earnings and the parent's equity-method retained earnings are normally equal.

If the parent accounts for subsidiaries using the equity method on its books, the retained earnings of each subsidiary is completely eliminated when the subsidiary is consolidated. This is necessary because (1) retained earnings cannot be purchased, and so subsidiary retained earnings at the date of a business combination cannot be included in the combined company's retained earnings; (2) the parent's share of the subsidiary's income since acquisition is already included in the parent's equity-method retained earnings; and (3) the noncontrolling interest's share (if any) of the subsidiary's retained earnings is not included in consolidated retained earnings.

Computation of Consolidated Retained Earnings Illustrated

In the simple example given earlier, assume that Push's January 1, 20X1, retained earnings balance is $400,000 and Shove's is $250,000. During 20X1, Shove reports $25,000 of net income and declares $10,000 of dividends. Push reports $100,000 of separate operating earnings plus $25,000 of equity-method income from its 100 percent interest in Shove; Push declares dividends of $30,000. Based on this information, the retained earnings balances for Push and Shove on December 31, 20X1, are computed as follows:

	Push	Shove
Balance, January 1, 20X1	$400,000	$250,000
Net income, 20X1	125,000	25,000
Dividends declared in 20X1	(30,000)	(10,000)
Balance, December 31, 20X1	$495,000	$265,000

Consolidated retained earnings is computed by first determining the parent's retained earnings from its own operations. This computation involves removing from the parent's retained earnings the $25,000 of subsidiary income since acquisition recognized by the parent, leaving $470,000 ($495,000 − $25,000) of retained earnings resulting from the parent's own operations. The parent's 100 percent share of the subsidiary's net income since the date of acquisition is then added to this number, resulting in consolidated retained earnings of $495,000. This number is the same as the parent's equity-method retained earnings.

Workpaper Format

Several different workpaper formats for preparing consolidated financial statements are used in practice. One of the most widely used formats is the three-part workpaper, consisting of one part for each of three basic financial statements: the income statement, the statement of retained earnings, and the balance sheet.

FIGURE 4–10   **Format for Comprehensive Three-Part Consolidation Workpaper**

Item	Trial Balance Data		Elimination Entries		Consolidated
	Parent	Subsidiary	Debits	Credits	
Credit Accounts: Revenues Gains Debit Accounts: Contra Revenues Expenses Losses Net Income			INCOME STATEMENT SECTION		
Beginning Retained Earnings Add: Net Income Deduct: Dividends Ending Retained Earnings			RETAINED EARNINGS STATEMENT SECTION		

Debit Accounts:
 Assets
 Contra Liabilities
Credit Accounts:
 Contra Assets
 Liabilities
 Stockholders' Equity:
  Capital Stock
  Paid-In Capital
  Retained Earnings
			BALANCE SHEET SECTION		

Figure 4–10 presents the format for the comprehensive three-part consolidation workpaper. The columns are the same as those for the balance sheet workpaper discussed earlier in this chapter. The final column in the workpaper contains the totals of each line summed algebraically across and is the basis for preparing the consolidated financial statements.

The top portion of the workpaper is used in preparing the consolidated income statement. All income statement accounts with credit balances are listed first, with those having debit balances listed next. When the income statement portion of the workpaper is completed, a total for each column is entered at the bottom of the income statement portion of the workpaper. The bottom line in this part of the workpaper shows the parent's net income, the subsidiary's net income, the totals of the debit and credit eliminations for this section of the workpaper, and consolidated net income. The entire bottom line is carried down to the retained earnings statement portion of the workpaper immediately below.

The retained earnings statement section of the workpaper is in the same format as a retained earnings statement. Net income and the other totals from the bottom line of the income statement portion of the workpaper are brought down from above. Similarly, the final line in the retained earnings statement section of the workpaper is carried down in its entirety to the balance sheet section.

The bottom portion of the workpaper reflects the balance sheet amounts at the end of the period. Debits and credits are separated in the same manner as in the consolidated balance sheet workpaper presented earlier. The retained earnings amounts appearing in the balance sheet section of the workpaper are the totals carried forward from the bottom line of the retained earnings statement section.

The series of examples appearing in the following sections of this chapter demonstrate the use of the comprehensive three-part consolidation workpaper.

CONSOLIDATION SUBSEQUENT TO ACQUISITION— 100 PERCENT OWNERSHIP PURCHASED AT BOOK VALUE

Each of the consolidated financial statements is prepared as if it is taken from a single set of books that is being used to account for the overall consolidated entity. There is, of course, no set of books for the consolidated entity, and as in the preparation of the consolidated balance sheet, the consolidation process starts with the data recorded on the books of the individual consolidating companies. The account balances from the books of the individual companies are placed in the three-part workpaper, and entries are made to eliminate the effects of intercorporate ownership and transactions.

To view the process of consolidation subsequent to acquisition, assume that on January 1, 20X1, Peerless Products Corporation purchases all of the common stock of Special Foods Inc. for its underlying book value of $300,000. At that time, Special Foods has $200,000 of common stock outstanding and retained earnings of $100,000. The resulting ownership situation is as follows:

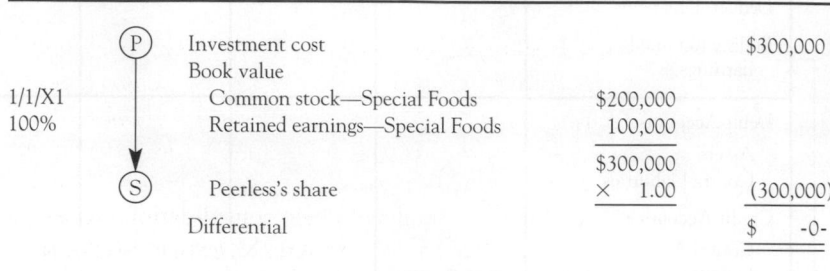

Peerless accounts for its investment in Special Foods stock using the equity method. Information about Peerless and Special Foods as of the date of combination and for the years 20X1 and 20X2 appears in Figure 4–11.

Year of Combination

On January 1, 20X1, Peerless records its purchase of Special Foods common stock with the following entry:

January 1, 20X1

(14)	Investment in Special Foods Stock	300,000	
	Cash		300,000
	Record purchase of Special Foods stock.		

FIGURE 4–11
Selected Information about Peerless Products and Special Foods on January 1, 20X1, and for the Years 20X1 and 20X2

	Peerless Products	Special Foods
Common Stock, January 1, 20X1	$500,000	$200,000
Retained Earnings, January 1, 20X1	300,000	100,000
20X1:		
Separate Operating Income, Peerless	140,000	
Net Income, Special Foods		50,000
Dividends	60,000	30,000
20X2:		
Separate Operating Income, Peerless	160,000	
Net Income, Special Foods		75,000
Dividends	60,000	40,000

During 20X1, Peerless records operating earnings of $140,000, excluding its income from investing in Special Foods, and declares dividends of $60,000. Special Foods reports 20X1 net income of $50,000 and declares dividends of $30,000.

Parent Company Entries

Peerless records its 20X1 income and dividends from Special Foods under the equity method with the following entries:

(15)	Cash	30,000	
	Investment in Special Foods Stock		30,000
	Record dividends from Special Foods:		
	$30,000 × 1.00		
(16)	Investment in Special Foods Stock	50,000	
	Income from Subsidiary		50,000
	Record equity-method income:		
	$50,000 × 1.00		

Consolidation Workpaper—Year of Combination

After all appropriate entries, including year-end adjustments, have been made on the books of Peerless and Special Foods, a consolidation workpaper is prepared as in Figure 4–12. The adjusted account balances from the books of Peerless and Special Foods are placed in the first two columns of the workpaper. Then all amounts that reflect intercorporate transactions or ownership are eliminated in the consolidation process.

The distinction between journal entries recorded on the books of the individual companies and the eliminating entries recorded only on the consolidation workpaper is an important one. Book entries affect balances on the books and the amounts that are carried to the consolidation workpaper; workpaper eliminating entries affect only those balances carried to the consolidated financial statements in the period. As mentioned previously, the eliminating entries presented in this text are identified with an "E" prefix to the left of the journal entry number whenever they are shown outside the workpaper.

In this example, the accounts that must be eliminated because of intercorporate ownership are the stockholders' equity accounts of Special Foods, including dividends declared, Peerless's investment in Special Foods stock, and Peerless's income from Special Foods. While these accounts can be eliminated in a single entry, two entries often are used to avoid the complexity of a single, large entry.

The first eliminating entry, E(17), removes both the investment income reflected in the parent's income statement and the parent's portion of any dividends declared by the subsidiary during the period:

E(17)	Income from Subsidiary	50,000	
	Dividends Declared		30,000
	Investment in Special Foods Stock		20,000
	Eliminate income from subsidiary.		

Under the equity method, the parent recognized on its separate books its share (100 percent) of the subsidiary's income. In the consolidated income statement, however, the individual revenue and expense accounts of the subsidiary are combined with those of the parent. Income recognized by the parent from all consolidated subsidiaries, therefore, must be eliminated to avoid double counting. The subsidiary's dividends paid to the parent company must be eliminated when consolidated statements are prepared so that only dividend declarations related to the parent's shareholders are treated as dividends of the consolidated entity.

FIGURE 4–12 **December 31, 20X1, Equity-Method Workpaper for Consolidated Financial Statements, Year of Combination; 100 Percent Purchase at Book Value**

Item	Peerless Products	Special Foods	Eliminations Debit	Eliminations Credit	Consolidated
Sales	400,000	200,000			600,000
Income from Subsidiary	50,000		(17) 50,000		
Credits	450,000	200,000			600,000
Cost of Goods Sold	170,000	115,000			285,000
Depreciation and Amortization	50,000	20,000			70,000
Other Expenses	40,000	15,000			55,000
Debits	(260,000)	(150,000)			(410,000)
Net Income, carry forward	190,000	50,000	50,000		190,000
Retained Earnings, January 1	300,000	100,000	(18) 100,000		300,000
Net Income, from above	190,000	50,000	50,000		190,000
	490,000	150,000			490,000
Dividends Declared	(60,000)	(30,000)		(17) 30,000	(60,000)
Retained Earnings, December 31, carry forward	430,000	120,000	150,000	30,000	430,000
Cash	210,000	75,000			285,000
Accounts Receivable	75,000	50,000			125,000
Inventory	100,000	75,000			175,000
Land	175,000	40,000			215,000
Buildings and Equipment	800,000	600,000			1,400,000
Investment in Special Foods Stock	320,000			(17) 20,000	
				(18) 300,000	
Debits	1,680,000	840,000			2,200,000
Accumulated Depreciation	450,000	320,000			770,000
Accounts Payable	100,000	100,000			200,000
Bonds Payable	200,000	100,000			300,000
Common Stock	500,000	200,000	(18) 200,000		500,000
Retained Earnings, from above	430,000	120,000	150,000	30,000	430,000
Credits	1,680,000	840,000	350,000	350,000	2,200,000

Elimination entries:
(17) Eliminate income from subsidiary.
(18) Eliminate beginning investment balance.

The investment account is credited for the difference between investment income and the parent's portion of subsidiary dividends. This difference represents the net change in the investment account for the period. The investment account balance increased by $20,000 during 20X1. Entering a $20,000 credit to the investment account in the workpaper takes the account balance back to the $300,000 balance at the beginning of the period.

The second eliminating entry removes the intercorporate ownership claim and stockholders' equity accounts of the subsidiary as of the beginning of the period:

E(18)	Common Stock—Special Foods	200,000	
	Retained Earnings, January 1	100,000	
	Investment in Special Foods Stock		300,000
	Eliminate beginning investment balance.		

This entry credits the investment account for its balance at the beginning of the period and, together with entry E(17), fully eliminates the balance of the investment account at the end of the period. Note that the parent's investment in the stock of a consolidated subsidiary never appears in the consolidated balance sheet.

Common stock and retained earnings are debited in entry E(18) for the balances in the accounts at the beginning of the period. Ending retained earnings never is adjusted directly when a three-part workpaper is prepared. Instead, the three components of ending retained earnings are eliminated individually: the beginning retained earnings balance is eliminated by entry E(18) in the retained earnings statement portion of the workpaper, and income (from the subsidiary) and dividends are eliminated by entry E(17).

Workpaper Relationships

Both of the eliminating entries are entered in Figure 4–12 and the amounts totaled across and down to complete the workpaper. Some specific points to recognize with respect to the full workpaper are as follows:

1. Each of the first two sections of the workpaper "telescopes" into the section below in a logical progression. As part of the normal accounting cycle, net income is closed to retained earnings, and retained earnings is reflected in the balance sheet. Similarly, in the consolidation workpaper, the net income is carried into the retained earnings statement section of the workpaper, and the ending retained earnings line is carried into the balance sheet section of the workpaper. Note that in both cases the entire line, including total eliminations, is carried forward.

2. Double-entry bookkeeping requires total debits to equal total credits for any single eliminating entry and for the workpaper as a whole. Because some eliminating entries extend to more than one section of the workpaper, however, the totals of the debit and credit eliminations are not likely to be equal in either of the first two sections of the workpaper. The totals of all debits and credits at the bottom of the balance sheet section are equal because the cumulative balances from the two upper sections are carried forward to the balance sheet section.

3. In the balance sheet portion of the workpaper, total debit balances must equal total credit balances for each company and the consolidated entity.

4. When (1) the parent uses the equity method of accounting for the investment, (2) there are no unrealized profits from intercorporate transactions, and (3) no impairment of goodwill has occurred, consolidated net income should equal the parent's net income and consolidated retained earnings should equal the parent's retained earnings. This means the existing balance in subsidiary retained earnings must be eliminated to avoid double counting.

5. Certain other clerical safeguards are incorporated into the workpaper. The amounts reflected in the bottom line of the income statement section, when summed (algebraically) across, must equal the number reported as consolidated net income. Similarly, the amounts in the last line of the retained earnings statement section must equal consolidated retained earnings when summed across.

Second and Subsequent Years of Ownership

The consolidation procedures employed at the end of the second and subsequent years are basically the same as those used at the end of the first year. Adjusted trial balance data of the individual companies are used as the starting point each time consolidated statements are prepared because no separate books are kept for the consolidated entity. An additional check is needed in each period following acquisition to ensure that the beginning balance of consolidated retained earnings shown in the completed workpaper equals the balance reported at the end of the prior period. In all other respects the eliminating entries and workpaper are comparable with those shown for the first year.

Parent Company Entries

Consolidation two years after acquisition is illustrated by continuing the example of Peerless Products and Special Foods, based on the data in Figure 4–11. Peerless's separate income from its own operations for 20X2 is $160,000, and its dividends total $60,000. Special Foods reports net income of $75,000 in 20X2 and pays dividends of $40,000. Equity-method entries recorded by Peerless in 20X2 are as follows:

(19)	Cash	40,000	
	Investment in Special Foods Stock		40,000
	Record dividends from Special Foods:		
	$40,000 × 1.00		

(20)	Investment in Special Foods Stock	75,000	
	Income from Subsidiary		75,000
	Record equity-method income:		
	$75,000 × 1.00		

With these entries, the balance in the investment account reported by Peerless increases from $320,000 on January 1, 20X2, to $355,000 on December 31, 20X2, and reported net income of Peerless totals $235,000 ($160,000 + $75,000).

Consolidation Workpaper—Second Year Following Combination

The workpaper to prepare consolidated statements for 20X2 is illustrated in Figure 4–13. Entry E(21) eliminates Peerless's 20X2 income from Special Foods and the dividend payment made to Peerless by Special Foods. The credit to the investment account in entry E(21) removes the change in the investment account recorded by Peerless during the period:

E(21)	Income from Subsidiary	75,000	
	Dividends Declared		40,000
	Investment in Special Foods Stock		35,000
	Eliminate income from subsidiary.		

The second workpaper entry eliminates the beginning balance in the investment account and the stockholders' equity accounts of the subsidiary at the beginning of 20X2:

E(22)	Common Stock—Special Foods	200,000	
	Retained Earnings, January 1	120,000	
	Investment in Special Foods Stock		320,000
	Eliminate beginning investment balance.		

Because the parent purchased all of the subsidiary's common stock at book value and is accounting for the investment using the equity method, the balance in its investment account is equal to the stockholders' equity of the subsidiary. The full balance of the subsidiary's retained earnings must be eliminated each period. Special Foods' retained earnings of

FIGURE 4–13 December 31, 20X2, Equity-Method Workpaper for Consolidated Financial Statements, Second Year Following Combination; 100 Percent Purchase at Book Value

Item	Peerless Products	Special Foods	Eliminations Debit	Eliminations Credit	Consolidated
Sales	450,000	300,000			750,000
Income from Subsidiary	75,000		(21) 75,000		
Credits	525,000	300,000			750,000
Cost of Goods Sold	180,000	160,000			340,000
Depreciation and Amortization	50,000	20,000			70,000
Other Expenses	60,000	45,000			105,000
Debits	(290,000)	(225,000)			(515,000)
Net Income, carry forward	235,000	75,000	75,000		235,000
Retained Earnings, January 1	430,000	120,000	(22) 120,000		430,000
Net Income, from above	235,000	75,000	75,000		235,000
	665,000	195,000			665,000
Dividends Declared	(60,000)	(40,000)		(21) 40,000	(60,000)
Retained Earnings, December 31, carry forward	605,000	155,000	195,000	40,000	605,000
Cash	245,000	85,000			330,000
Accounts Receivable	150,000	80,000			230,000
Inventory	180,000	90,000			270,000
Land	175,000	40,000			215,000
Buildings and Equipment	800,000	600,000			1,400,000
Investment in Special Foods Stock	355,000			(21) 35,000 (22) 320,000	
Debits	1,905,000	895,000			2,445,000
Accumulated Depreciation	500,000	340,000			840,000
Accounts Payable	100,000	100,000			200,000
Bonds Payable	200,000	100,000			300,000
Common Stock	500,000	200,000	(22) 200,000		500,000
Retained Earnings, from above	605,000	155,000	195,000	40,000	605,000
Credits	1,905,000	895,000	395,000	395,000	2,445,000

Elimination entries:
(21) Eliminate income from subsidiary.
(22) Eliminate beginning investment balance.

$100,000 on the date of combination cannot be purchased by Peerless and therefore must be excluded from consolidated retained earnings. Further, the $20,000 increase in Special Foods' retained earnings during 20X1 already is reflected in Peerless's retained earnings as a result of using the equity method.

After placement of entries E(21) and E(22) in the consolidation workpaper, the workpaper is completed in the normal manner as shown in Figure 4–13. All workpaper relationships discussed in conjunction with Figure 4–12 continue in the second year as well. The beginning consolidated retained earnings balance for 20X2, as shown in Figure 4–13, should be compared with the ending consolidated retained earnings balance for 20X1, as shown in Figure 4–12, to ensure that they are the same.

Consolidated Net Income and Retained Earnings

In the consolidation workpapers illustrated in Figures 4–12 and 4–13, consolidated net income for 20X1 and 20X2 appears as the last number in the income statement section of the workpapers in the Consolidated column on the far right. The numbers can be computed as follows:

	20X1	20X2
Peerless's net income	$190,000	$235,000
Peerless's equity income from Special Foods	(50,000)	(75,000)
Special Foods' net income	50,000	75,000
Consolidated net income	$190,000	$235,000

In this simple illustration, consolidated net income is the same as the parent's equity-method net income. Had the parent used the cost method to account for its investment in Special Foods, the consolidated net income would not be the same as the parent's net income.

In Figures 4–12 and 4–13, consolidated retained earnings is the last figure in the retained earnings statement section of the workpapers, in the Consolidated column. Consolidated retained earnings is equal to the beginning balance of consolidated retained earnings plus consolidated net income, less dividends declared on the parent's common stock. It also can be computed as follows:

	20X1	20X2
Peerless's beginning retained earnings from its own operations	$300,000	$380,000
Peerless's income from its own operations	140,000	160,000
Peerless's income from Special Foods since acquisition (cumulative)	50,000	125,000
Peerless's dividends declared	(60,000)	(60,000)
Consolidated retained earnings	$430,000	$605,000

As with income, consolidated retained earnings is the same as the parent's equity-method retained earnings in simple cases.

CONSOLIDATION SUBSEQUENT TO ACQUISITION—100 PERCENT OWNERSHIP PURCHASED AT MORE THAN BOOK VALUE

In many cases an investment in another company is purchased at an amount in excess of the book value of the shares acquired. The excess of the purchase price over the book value of the net identifiable assets purchased must be allocated to those assets and liabilities acquired, including any purchased goodwill. If this revaluation is not accomplished on the separate books of the subsidiary through the use of push-down accounting, as illustrated in Appendix 4A, it must be made in the consolidation workpaper each time consolidated statements are prepared. In addition, if the revaluations relate to assets or liabilities that must be depreciated, amortized, or otherwise written off, appropriate entries must be made in the consolidation workpaper to reduce consolidated net income accordingly.

When an investor company accounts for an investment using the equity method, as illustrated in Chapter 2, it records the amount of differential viewed as expiring during the period as a reduction of the income recognized from the investee. In consolidation, the purchase differential is assigned to the appropriate asset and liability balances, and consolidated income is adjusted for the amounts expiring during the period by assigning them to the related expense items (e.g., depreciation expense).

Year of Combination

To illustrate the purchase of total ownership at an amount greater than book value, assume that Peerless Products purchases all of Special Foods' common stock on January 1, 20X1, for $387,500. The purchase price includes cash of $300,000 and a 60-day note for $87,500 (paid at maturity during 20X1). At the date of combination, Special Foods is holding the assets and liabilities shown in Figure 4–2. The resulting ownership situation is as follows:

(P)	Investment cost			$387,500
	Book value			
1/1/X1	Common stock—Special Foods	$200,000		
100%	Retained earnings—Special Foods	100,000		
		$300,000		
(S)	Peerless's share	× 1.00		(300,000)
	Differential			$ 87,500

The total book value of Special Foods stock on the date of combination is $300,000. The difference between the total purchase price of $387,500 and the book value of the shares acquired is $87,500.

On the date of combination, all of Special Foods' assets and liabilities have fair values equal to their book values, except as follows:

	Book Value	Fair Value	Fair Value Increment
Inventory	$ 60,000	$ 65,000	$ 5,000
Land	40,000	50,000	10,000
Buildings and Equipment	300,000	360,000	60,000
	$400,000	$475,000	$75,000

Of the $87,500 total differential, $75,000 relates to identifiable assets of Special Foods. The remaining $12,500 is attributable to goodwill. The apportionment of the differential appears as follows:

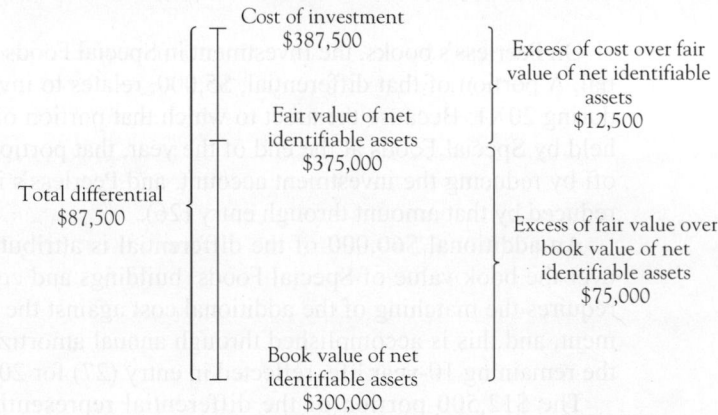

All the inventory to which the differential relates is sold during 20X1; none is left in ending inventory. The buildings and equipment have a remaining economic life of 10 years from the date of combination, and straight-line depreciation is used. At the end of 20X1, Peerless's management determines that the goodwill acquired in the combination with Special Foods has been impaired. Management determines that a $3,000 goodwill impairment loss should be recognized in the consolidated income statement.

For the first year immediately after the date of combination, 20X1, Peerless Products earns income from its own separate operations of $140,000 and pays dividends of $60,000. Special Foods reports net income of $50,000 and pays dividends of $30,000.

Parent Company Entries

During 20X1, Peerless makes the normal equity-method entries on its books to record its purchase of Special Foods stock and its income and dividends from Special Foods:

(23)	Investment in Special Foods Stock	387,500	
	Cash		300,000
	Notes Payable		87,500
	Record purchase of Special Foods stock.		
(24)	Cash	30,000	
	Investment in Special Foods Stock		30,000
	Record dividends from Special Foods.		
(25)	Investment in Special Foods Stock	50,000	
	Income from Subsidiary		50,000
	Record equity-method income.		

Entries (24) and (25) are the same as if Peerless had acquired its investment at underlying book value. In addition, however, entries are needed on Peerless's books to recognize the write-off of the differential:

(26)	Income from Subsidiary	5,000	
	Investment in Special Foods Stock		5,000
	Adjust income for differential related to inventory sold.		
(27)	Income from Subsidiary	6,000	
	Investment in Special Foods Stock		6,000
	Amortize differential related to buildings and equipment.		

On Peerless's books, the Investment in Special Foods Stock account includes the differential. A portion of that differential, $5,000, relates to inventory of Special Foods that is sold during 20X1. Because the asset to which that portion of the differential relates is no longer held by Special Foods at the end of the year, that portion of the differential must be written off by reducing the investment account, and Peerless's income from Special Foods must be reduced by that amount through entry (26).

An additional $60,000 of the differential is attributable to the excess of the fair value over the book value of Special Foods' buildings and equipment. Use of the equity method requires the matching of the additional cost against the income recognized from the investment, and this is accomplished through annual amortization of $6,000 ($60,000 ÷ 10) over the remaining 10-year life, reflected in entry (27) for 20X1.

The $12,500 portion of the differential representing equity-method goodwill is not adjusted. Although the goodwill will be written down and a goodwill impairment loss recognized when preparing consolidated financial statements, the FASB has indicated that no equity-method adjustment should be made to reflect this impairment of goodwill. Thus, the parent's equity-method net income (and retained earnings) will be different than

FIGURE 4–14 December 31, 20X1, Equity-Method Workpaper for Consolidated Financial Statements, Year of Combination; 100 Percent Purchase at More than Book Value

Item	Peerless Products	Special Foods	Eliminations Debit	Eliminations Credit	Consolidated
Sales	400,000	200,000			600,000
Income from Subsidiary	39,000		(28) 39,000		
Credits	439,000	200,000			600,000
Cost of Goods Sold	170,000	115,000	(30) 5,000		290,000
Depreciation and Amortization	50,000	20,000	(31) 6,000		76,000
Goodwill Impairment Loss			(32) 3,000		3,000
Other Expenses	40,000	15,000			55,000
Debits	(260,000)	(150,000)			(424,000)
Net Income, carry forward	179,000	50,000	53,000		176,000
Retained Earnings, January 1	300,000	100,000	(29) 100,000		300,000
Net Income, from above	179,000	50,000	53,000		176,000
	479,000	150,000			476,000
Dividends Declared	(60,000)	(30,000)		(28) 30,000	(60,000)
Retained Earnings, December 31, carry forward	419,000	120,000	153,000	30,000	416,000
Cash	122,500	75,000			197,500
Accounts Receivable	75,000	50,000			125,000
Inventory	100,000	75,000			175,000
Land	175,000	40,000	(30) 10,000		225,000
Buildings and Equipment	800,000	600,000	(30) 60,000		1,460,000
Investment in Special Foods Stock	396,500			(28) 9,000	
				(29) 387,500	
Goodwill			(30) 12,500	(32) 3,000	9,500
Differential			(29) 87,500	(30) 87,500	
Debits	1,669,000	840,000			2,192,000
Accumulated Depreciation	450,000	320,000		(31) 6,000	776,000
Accounts Payable	100,000	100,000			200,000
Bonds Payable	200,000	100,000			300,000
Common Stock	500,000	200,000	(29) 200,000		500,000
Retained Earnings, from above	419,000	120,000	153,000	30,000	416,000
Credits	1,669,000	840,000	523,000	523,000	2,192,000

Elimination entries:
  (28) Eliminate income from subsidiary.
  (29) Eliminate beginning investment balance.
  (30) Assign beginning differential.
  (31) Amortize differential related to buildings and equipment.
  (32) Write down goodwill for impairment.

consolidated net income (and retained earnings) when an impairment of goodwill has occurred.

Consolidation Workpaper—Year of Combination

After the subsidiary income accruals are entered on Peerless's books, the adjusted trial balance data of the consolidating companies are entered in the three-part consolidation workpaper as shown in Figure 4–14.

The first two workpaper entries eliminate the subsidiary income and dividends recorded by Peerless and eliminate the investment account and the stockholders' equity accounts of Special Foods:

E(28)	Income from Subsidiary	39,000	
	Dividends Declared		30,000
	Investment in Special Foods Stock		9,000
	Eliminate income from subsidiary.		
E(29)	Common Stock—Special Foods	200,000	
	Retained Earnings, January 1	100,000	
	Differential	87,500	
	Investment in Special Foods Stock		387,500
	Eliminate beginning investment balance.		

Entry E(28) removes the net effect of the income accrual recorded by the parent during 20X1 in entries (25), (26), and (27) and removes the dividends declared by the subsidiary during the period, as recorded in entry (24). The second elimination entry, E(29), removes the stockholders' equity balances of the subsidiary and the investment account of the parent as of the beginning of the period. Because the purchase price of the investment exceeded its book value, a purchase differential appears as the balancing figure in this entry. The differential established in this entry represents the unamortized amount as of the beginning of the period. Because the combination occurred on the first day of 20X1, the amount equals the differential on the date of combination, $87,500. As before, the differential account serves as a clearing account in the workpaper and is entered in the balance sheet portion of the workpaper at the bottom of the asset section.

Three additional eliminating entries are needed in the workpaper in Figure 4–14 to allocate and write down the differential:

E(30)	Cost of Goods Sold	5,000	
	Land	10,000	
	Buildings and Equipment	60,000	
	Goodwill	12,500	
	Differential		87,500
	Assign beginning differential.		
E(31)	Depreciation Expense	6,000	
	Accumulated Depreciation		6,000
	Amortize differential related to buildings and equipment:		
	$60,000 \div 10$ years		
E(32)	Goodwill Impairment Loss	3,000	
	Goodwill		3,000
	Write down goodwill for impairment.		

Entry E(30) assigns the original amount of the differential to the appropriate asset and expense accounts based on the fair value differences computed previously.

Because all inventory on hand on the date of combination has been sold during the year, the $5,000 of differential applicable to inventory is allocated directly to cost of goods sold. The cost of goods sold recorded on the books of Special Foods is correct for that company's separate financial statements. However, the cost of the inventory to the consolidated entity is viewed as being $5,000 higher, and this additional cost must be included in consolidated cost of goods sold.

No workpaper entry is needed in future periods with respect to the inventory because the inventory has been expensed and no longer is on the subsidiary's books. The portion of the differential related to the inventory no longer exists on Peerless's books after 20X1 because it is removed from the investment account by entry (26).

The differential assigned to depreciable assets in entry E(30) must be charged to depreciation expense over the remaining lives of those assets. From a consolidated viewpoint, the parent's additional payment is part of the total cost of the depreciable assets. Depreciation already is recorded on the subsidiary's books based on the original cost of the assets to the subsidiary, and these amounts are carried to the consolidation workpaper as depreciation expense. Depreciation on the additional cost of those assets to the consolidated entity is entered in the consolidation workpaper through entry E(31).

The difference between the $387,500 total purchase price paid by Peerless and the $375,000 fair value of Special Foods' net identifiable assets is assumed to be payment for the excess earning power of Special Foods. This difference is entered in the workpaper in Figure 4–14 with entry E(30) as goodwill of $12,500. The $3,000 impairment of this goodwill is recognized with eliminating entry E(32). Although goodwill is not amortized, it must be written down when its value is impaired. This entry reduces the amount of goodwill to be reported in the consolidated balance sheet and establishes a loss to be reported in the consolidated income statement.

A distinction must be made between journal entries recorded on the parent's books under equity-method reporting and the eliminating entries needed in the workpaper to prepare the consolidated financial statements. The eliminating entry to record depreciation expense in the workpaper is needed even though Peerless amortizes the purchase differential on its books at the end of 20X1 with entry (27). The entry on Peerless's books alters the balance in its investment account and the amount of income recognized from Special Foods. However, both account balances are eliminated in the consolidation process, thereby removing any effect of entry (27) on the consolidated totals. Consequently, consolidated income does not reflect the amortization of the differential unless eliminating entry (31) is made.

Once the appropriate eliminating entries are placed in the consolidation workpaper in Figure 4–14, the workpaper is completed by summing each row across, taking into consideration the debit or credit effect of the eliminations.

Consolidated Net Income and Retained Earnings

As can be seen from the workpaper, consolidated net income for 20X1 is $176,000 and consolidated retained earnings on December 31, 20X1, is $416,000. These amounts can be computed as shown in Figure 4–15. Note that both consolidated net income and retained earnings are reduced by the write-off of the purchase differential and the impairment of goodwill.

FIGURE 4–15
Consolidated Net Income and Retained Earnings, 20X1; 100 Percent Purchase at More than Book Value

Consolidated net income, 20X1:	
Peerless's separate operating income	$140,000
Special Foods' net income	50,000
Write-off of differential related to inventory sold during 20X1	(5,000)
Amortization of differential related to buildings and equipment in 20X1	(6,000)
Goodwill impairment loss	(3,000)
Consolidated net income, 20X1	$176,000
Consolidated retained earnings, December 31, 20X1:	
Peerless's retained earnings on date of combination, January 1, 20X1	$300,000
Peerless's separate operating income, 20X1	140,000
Special Foods' 20X1 net income	50,000
Write-off of differential related to inventory sold during 20X1	(5,000)
Amortization of differential related to buildings and equipment in 20X1	(6,000)
Goodwill impairment loss	(3,000)
Dividends declared by Peerless, 20X1	(60,000)
Consolidated retained earnings, December 31, 20X1	$416,000

Second Year of Ownership

The consolidation procedures employed at the end of the second year, and in periods thereafter, are basically the same as those used at the end of the first year. Consolidation two years after acquisition is illustrated by continuing the example used for 20X1. During 20X2, Peerless Products earns income from its own separate operations of $160,000 and pays dividends of $60,000; Special Foods reports net income of $75,000 and pays dividends of $40,000. No further impairment of the goodwill acquired in the business combination occurs during 20X2.

Parent Company Entries

Peerless Products records the following entries on its separate books during 20X2:

(33)	Cash	40,000	
	Investment in Special Foods Stock		40,000
	Record dividends from Special Foods.		
(34)	Investment in Special Foods Stock	75,000	
	Income from Subsidiary		75,000
	Record equity-method income.		
(35)	Income from Subsidiary	6,000	
	Investment in Special Foods Stock		6,000
	Amortize differential related to buildings and equipment.		

Entry (35) to record the 20X2 amortization of the purchase differential related to buildings and equipment is identical to entry (27) recorded by Peerless in 2001 because the straight-line method is used.

The changes in the parent's investment account for 20X1 and 20X2 can be summarized as follows:

	20X1		20X2	
Balance at start of year		$387,500		$396,500
Income from subsidiary:				
Parent's accrual of subsidiary's income	$50,000		$75,000	
Differential write-off for inventory sold	(5,000)			
Amortization of differential	(6,000)		(6,000)	
		39,000		69,000
Less: Dividends received from subsidiary		(30,000)		(40,000)
Balance at end of year		$396,500		$425,500

Consolidation Workpaper—Second Year Following Combination

The workpaper to prepare a complete set of consolidated financial statements for the year 20X2 is illustrated in Figure 4–16. Eliminating entries at the end of 20X2 are similar to those at the end of 20X1.

The first workpaper entry, E(36), eliminates Peerless's income from Special Foods and Special Foods' dividends for 20X2:

E(36)	Income from Subsidiary	69,000	
	Dividends Declared		40,000
	Investment in Special Foods Stock		29,000
	Eliminate income from subsidiary.		

FIGURE 4–16 December 31, 20X2, Equity-Method Workpaper for Consolidated Financial Statements, Second Year Following Combination; 100 Percent Purchase at More than Book Value

Item	Peerless Products	Special Foods	Eliminations Debit	Eliminations Credits	Consolidated
Sales	450,000	300,000			750,000
Income from Subsidiary	69,000		(36) 69,000		
Credits	519,000	300,000			750,000
Cost of Goods Sold	180,000	160,000			340,000
Depreciation and Amortization	50,000	20,000	(39) 6,000		76,000
Other Expenses	60,000	45,000			105,000
Debits	(290,000)	(225,000)			521,000
Net Income, carry forward	229,000	75,000	75,000		229,000
Retained Earnings, January 1	419,000	120,000	(37) 120,000		
			(40) 3,000		416,000
Net Income, from above	229,000	75,000	75,000		229,000
	648,000	195,000			645,000
Dividends Declared	(60,000)	(40,000)		(36) 40,000	(60,000)
Retained Earnings, December 31, carry forward	588,000	155,000	198,000	40,000	585,000
Cash	157,500	85,000			242,500
Accounts Receivable	150,000	80,000			230,000
Inventory	180,000	90,000			270,000
Land	175,000	40,000	(38) 10,000		225,000
Buildings and Equipment	800,000	600,000	(38) 60,000		1,460,000
Investment in Special Foods Stock	425,500			(36) 29,000	
				(37) 396,500	
Goodwill			(38) 12,500	(40) 3,000	9,500
Differential			(37) 76,500	(38) 76,500	
Debits	1,888,000	895,000			2,437,000
Accumulated Depreciation	500,000	340,000		(38) 6,000	
				(39) 6,000	852,000
Accounts Payable	100,000	100,000			200,000
Bonds Payable	200,000	100,000			300,000
Common Stock	500,000	200,000	(37) 200,000		500,000
Retained Earnings, from above	588,000	155,000	198,000	40,000	585,000
Credits	1,888,000	895,000	557,000	557,000	2,437,000

Elimination entries:
(36) Eliminate income from subsidiary.
(37) Eliminate beginning investment balance.
(38) Assign beginning differential.
(39) Amortize differential related to buildings and equipment.
(40) Adjust for 20X1 impairment of goodwill.

The net credit to the investment account of $29,000 represents the increase in the account balance during the period and takes the account balance back to the amount on January 1, 20X2, the beginning of the second year.

Entry E(37) eliminates the balances in Peerless's investment account and Special Foods' stockholders' equity accounts as of the beginning of the period:

E(37)	Common Stock—Special Foods	200,000	
	Retained Earnings, January 1	120,000	
	Differential	76,500	
	Investment in Special Foods Stock		396,500
	Eliminate beginning investment balance.		

Together, entries E(36) and E(37) fully eliminate the ending balance in the parent's investment account.

Entry E(37) also establishes the purchase differential as of the beginning of 20X2. The differential at the beginning of 20X1, the date of combination, was $87,500 and was reduced by the amounts written off during 20X1. During 20X1, Peerless wrote off the $5,000 of the differential related to the inventory sold in 20X1 and amortized $6,000 of the differential related to buildings and equipment. Thus, the unamortized balance of the differential at the beginning of 20X2 is $76,500 ($87,500 − $5,000 − $6,000).

In the consolidation workpaper, allocation of the purchase differential in 20X2 is different from the allocation in the first year in several respects:

1. No allocation is made to inventory or cost of goods sold.
2. The balance in the Goodwill account in 20X2 should be only $9,500 because of the $3,000 write-off of goodwill in 20X1 to reflect an impairment loss. However, because the purchase differential was not written down on Peerless's books to reflect the goodwill impairment and goodwill is not amortized (in accordance with the FASB's requirements), the original $12,500 amount of goodwill is established in the workpaper. The prior-period impairment is then recognized in a separate entry.
3. Accumulated depreciation must be entered in the workpaper to reflect the additional depreciation on the buildings and equipment taken in the 20X1 consolidation workpaper. This should be part of the 20X2 consolidated total, but it does not automatically carry forward from the previous year's workpaper.

Entry E(38) assigns the January 1, 20X2, purchase differential:

E(38)	Land	10,000	
	Buildings and Equipment	60,000	
	Goodwill	12,500	
	Differential		76,500
	Accumulated Depreciation		6,000
	Assign beginning differential.		

Because each year's workpaper is prepared from the trial balance data reported by the separate companies, not from the previous year's workpaper, the $6,000 of additional accumulated depreciation entered in the consolidation workpaper at the end of 20X1 does not automatically carry over to the 20X2 workpaper. Thus, the workpaper entry to allocate the differential each time also must establish the additional accumulated depreciation for all prior years on any differential amounts assigned to depreciable assets.

The 20X2 depreciation of the portion of the differential assigned to buildings and equipment is given in entry E(39):

E(39)	Depreciation Expense	6,000	
	Accumulated Depreciation		6,000
	Amortize differential related to buildings and equipment:		
	$60,000 ÷ 10 years		

FIGURE 4–17
Consolidated Net Income and Retained Earnings, 20X2; 100 Percent Purchase at More than Book Value

Consolidated net income, 20X2:	
Peerless's separate operating income	$160,000
Special Foods' net income	75,000
Amortization of differential related to buildings and equipment in 20X2	(6,000)
Consolidated net income, 20X2	$229,000
Consolidated retained earnings, December 31, 20X2:	
Consolidated retained earnings, December 31, 20X1	$416,000
Peerless's separate operating income, 20X2	160,000
Special Foods' 20X2 net income	75,000
Amortization of differential related to buildings and equipment in 20X2	(6,000)
Dividends declared by Peerless, 20X2	(60,000)
Consolidated retained earnings, December 31, 20X2	$585,000

The amount of additional depreciation expense each period remains the same from year to year unless (1) a depreciation method other than straight-line is used, (2) some of the underlying assets are sold, or (3) some of the assets become fully depreciated.

Entry E(40) corrects the beginning consolidated retained earnings and the goodwill balance for the impairment loss recognized in the 20X1 consolidated income statement:

E(40)	Retained Earnings, January 1	3,000	
	Goodwill		3,000
	Adjust for 20X1 impairment of goodwill.		

Because the purchase differential on Peerless's books is not written down under the equity method to reflect the 20X1 impairment of goodwill, the differential established in the 20X2 workpaper through entry E(37) includes the full $12,500 differential originally representing goodwill. Also, because the impairment loss did not affect Peerless's equity-method net income, and Peerless's retained earnings becomes consolidated retained earnings, beginning consolidated retained earnings will be overstated unless it is reduced by the amount of the prior period's impairment loss. Thus, both beginning consolidated retained earnings and goodwill must be reduced each period in the consolidated workpaper for the 20X1 impairment.

Consolidated Net Income and Retained Earnings

The computation of 20X2 consolidated net income and consolidated retained earnings at the end of 20X2 is shown in Figure 4–17.

INTERCOMPANY RECEIVABLES AND PAYABLES

All forms of intercompany receivables and payables need to be eliminated when consolidated financial statements are prepared. From a single-company viewpoint, a company cannot owe itself money. If a company owes an affiliate $1,000 on account, one company carries a $1,000 receivable on its separate books, and the other has a payable for the same amount. When consolidated financial statements are prepared, the following elimination entry is needed in the consolidation workpaper:

E(41)	Accounts Payable	1,000	
	Accounts Receivable		1,000
	Eliminate intercompany receivable/payable.		

If no eliminating entry is made, both the consolidated assets and liabilities are overstated by an equal amount.

If the intercompany receivable/payable bears interest, all accounts related to the intercompany claim must be eliminated in the preparation of consolidated statements, including the receivable/payable, interest income, interest expense, and any accrued interest on the intercompany claim. Other forms of intercorporate claims, such as bonds, are discussed in subsequent chapters. In all cases, failure to eliminate these claims can distort consolidated balances. As a result, the magnitude of debt of the combined entity may appear to be greater than it is, working capital ratios may be incorrect, and other types of comparisons may be distorted.

PUSH-DOWN ACCOUNTING

The term *push-down accounting* refers to the practice of revaluing the assets and liabilities of a purchased subsidiary directly on that subsidiary's books at the date of acquisition. If this practice is followed, the revaluations are recorded once on the purchased subsidiary's books at the date of acquisition and, therefore, are not made in the consolidation workpapers each time consolidated statements are prepared.

Those who favor push-down accounting argue that the change in the subsidiary's ownership in an acquisition is reason for adopting a new basis of accounting for the subsidiary's assets and liabilities, and this new basis of accounting should be reflected directly on the subsidiary's books. This argument is most persuasive when the subsidiary is wholly owned and is consolidated or has its separate financial statements included with the statements of the parent.

On the other hand, when a subsidiary has a significant noncontrolling interest or the subsidiary has bonds or preferred stock held by the public, push-down accounting may be inappropriate. The use of push-down accounting in the financial statements issued to the noncontrolling shareholders or to those holding bonds or preferred stock results in a new basis of accounting even though, from the perspective of those statement users, the entity has not changed. From their viewpoint, push-down accounting results in the revaluation of the assets and liabilities of a continuing enterprise, a practice that normally is not acceptable.

SEC Staff Accounting Bulletin No. 54 requires push-down accounting whenever a business combination results in the acquired subsidiary becoming substantially wholly owned. The staff accounting bulletin encourages but does not require the use of push-down accounting in situations in which the subsidiary is less than wholly owned or the subsidiary has outstanding debt or preferred stock held by the public.

The revaluation of assets and liabilities on a subsidiary's books involves making an entry to debit or credit each asset and liability account to be revalued, with the balancing entry to a revaluation capital account. Once the revaluations are made on the books of the subsidiary, the new book values of the subsidiary's assets, including goodwill, are equal to the acquisition cost of the subsidiary. Thus, no differential arises in the consolidation process. The investment elimination entry in a consolidation workpaper prepared immediately after acquisition of a subsidiary and revaluation of its assets on its books might appear as follows:

E(42)	Capital Stock—Subsidiary	XXX	
	Retained Earnings	XXX	
	Revaluation Capital	XXX	
	Investment in Subsidiary Stock		XXX
	Eliminate investment balance.		

Note that the Revaluation Capital account is eliminated in preparing consolidated statements. A more detailed example of push-down accounting is given in Appendix 4A.

Summary of Key Concepts

Consolidated financial statements present the financial position and results of operations of two or more separate legal entities as if they were a single company. A consolidated balance sheet prepared on the date a parent acquires a subsidiary appears the same as if the acquired company had been merged into the parent.

A consolidation workpaper provides a means of efficiently developing the data needed to prepare consolidated financial statements. The workpaper includes a separate column for the trial balance data of each of the consolidating companies, a debit and a credit column for the elimination entries, and a column for the consolidated totals that appear in the consolidated financial statements. A three-part consolidation workpaper facilitates preparation of a consolidated income statement, retained earnings statement, and balance sheet, and it includes a section for each statement. Eliminating entries are needed in the workpaper to remove the effects of intercompany ownership and intercompany transactions so the consolidated financial statements appear as if the separate companies are actually one. Workpaper eliminating entries are needed to (1) eliminate the parent's subsidiary investment and the subsidiary's stockholders' equity accounts, (2) eliminate the subsidiary's income recognized by the parent during the period and the subsidiary's dividends declared, (3) assign any differential to specific assets and liabilities, (4) amortize or write off a portion of the differential, if appropriate, and (5) eliminate intercompany receivables and payables.

Consolidated net income is computed in simple cases for a parent and a wholly owned subsidiary as the total of the parent's income from its own operations and the subsidiary's net income, adjusted for the write-off of differential, if appropriate. In this situation, consolidated retained earnings is computed as the total of the parent's retained earnings, excluding any income from the subsidiary, plus the subsidiary's cumulative net income since acquisition.

When a subsidiary is acquired for an amount greater than its book value, some parents may prefer to assign the purchase differential to individual assets and liabilities directly on the books of the subsidiary at the time of acquisition, thereby eliminating the need for revaluation entries in the consolidation workpaper each period. This procedure is called push-down accounting.

Key Terms

bargain purchase, *146*
consolidated net income, *149*
consolidated retained
    earnings, *149*

consolidation workpaper, *135*
eliminating entries, *135*
goodwill, *143*
parent, *134*

purchase differential, *140*
push-down accounting, *141*
subsidiary, *134*

Appendix 4A Push-Down Accounting Illustrated

When a subsidiary is acquired in a business combination, its assets and liabilities must be revalued to their fair values as of the date of combination for consolidated reporting. If *push-down accounting* is employed, the revaluations are made as of the date of combination directly on the books of the subsidiary and no eliminating entries related to the differential are needed in the workpapers.

The following example illustrates the consolidation process when assets and liabilities are revalued directly on a subsidiary's books rather than using consolidation workpaper entries to accomplish the revaluation. Assume that Peerless Products purchases all of Special Foods' common stock on January 1, 20X1, for $370,000 cash. The purchase price is $70,000 in excess of the book value of Special Foods stock, with $10,000 of the differential related to land and $60,000 related to buildings and equipment having a remaining life of 10 years. Peerless accounts for its investment in Special Foods stock using the equity method.

Peerless records the acquisition of stock on its books with the following entry:

January 1, 20X1

(43)	Investment in Special Foods Stock	370,000	
	Cash		370,000
	Record purchase of Special Foods stock.		

In contrast to a workpaper revaluation, the use of push-down accounting involves the revaluation of the assets on the separate books of Special Foods and alleviates the need for revaluation entries in the consolidation workpaper each period. If push-down accounting is used to revalue Special Foods' assets, the following entry is made directly on Special Foods' books:

	January 1, 20X1		
(44)	Land	10,000	
	Buildings and Equipment	60,000	
	Revaluation Capital		70,000
	Revalue assets to reflect fair values at date of combination.		

This entry increases the amount at which the land and the buildings and equipment are shown in Special Foods' separate financial statements and gives rise to a revaluation capital account that is shown in the stockholders' equity section of Special Foods' balance sheet. Special Foods records $6,000 additional depreciation on its books to reflect the amortization over 10 years of the $60,000 write-up of buildings and equipment. This additional depreciation decreases Special Foods' reported net income for 20X1 from $50,000 to $44,000.

On its books, Peerless records its income and dividends from Special Foods:

(45)	Cash	30,000	
	Investmnt in Special Foods Stock		30,000
	Record dividends from Special Foods.		
(46)	Investment in Special Foods Stock	44,000	
	Income from Subsidiary		44,000
	Record equity-method income.		

The equity-method income recorded by Peerless in entry (46) is less than had push-down accounting not been employed because Special Foods' income is reduced by the additional depreciation on the write-up of the buildings and equipment recorded on Special Foods' books. Because the revaluation is recorded on Special Foods' books, the book value of the stock purchased by Peerless equals the purchase price. Therefore, no differential exists, and Peerless need not record any amortization associated with the investment. The net amount of income from Special Foods recorded by Peerless is the same regardless of whether or not push-down accounting is employed.

Figure 4–18 shows the consolidation workpaper prepared at the end of 20X1 and includes the effects of revaluing Special Foods' assets. Note that Special Foods' Land and its Buildings and Equipment have been increased by $10,000 and $60,000, respectively. Also note the Revaluation Capital account in Special Foods' stockholders' equity.

Because the revaluation was accomplished directly on the books of Special Foods, only the two investment elimination entries are needed in the workpaper illustrated in Figure 4–18:

E(47)	Income from Subsidiary	44,000	
	Dividends Declared		30,000
	Investment in Special Foods Stock		14,000
	Eliminate income from subsidiary.		
E(48)	Common Stock—Special Foods	200,000	
	Retained Earnings, January 1	100,000	
	Revaluation Capital	70,000	
	Investment in Special Foods Stock		370,000
	Eliminate beginning investment balance.		

FIGURE 4–18 December 31, 20X1, Equity-Method Workpaper for Consolidated Financial Statements, Year of Combination; 100 Percent Purchase at More than Book Value; Push-Down Accounting

Item	Peerless Products	Special Foods	Eliminations Debit	Eliminations Credit	Consolidated
Sales	400,000	200,000			600,000
Income from Subsidiary	44,000		(47) 44,000		
Credits	444,000	200,000			600,000
Cost of Goods Sold	170,000	115,000			285,000
Depreciation and Amortization	50,000	26,000			76,000
Other Expenses	40,000	15,000			55,000
Debits	(260,000)	(156,000)			(416,000)
Net Income, carry forward	184,000	44,000	44,000		184,000
Retained Earnings, January 1	300,000	100,000	(48) 100,000		300,000
Net Income, from above	184,000	44,000	44,000		184,000
	484,000	144,000			484,000
Dividends Declared	(60,000)	(30,000)		(47) 30,000	(60,000)
Retained Earnings, December 31, carry forward	424,000	114,000	144,000	30,000	424,000
Cash	140,000	75,000			215,000
Accounts Receivable	75,000	50,000			125,000
Inventory	100,000	75,000			175,000
Land	175,000	50,000			225,000
Buildings and Equipment	800,000	660,000			1,460,000
Investment in Special Foods Stock	384,000			(47) 14,000	
				(48) 370,000	
Debits	1,674,000	910,000			2,200,000
Accumulated Depreciation	450,000	326,000			776,000
Accounts Payable	100,000	100,000			200,000
Bonds Payable	200,000	100,000			300,000
Common Stock	500,000	200,000	(48) 200,000		500,000
Retained Earnings, from above	424,000	114,000	144,000	30,000	424,000
Revaluation Capital		70,000	(48) 70,000		
Credits	1,674,000	910,000	414,000	414,000	2,200,000

Elimination entries:
(47) Eliminate income from subsidiary.
(48) Eliminate beginning investment balance.

Questions

Q4-1 How does an eliminating entry differ from an adjusting entry?

Q4-2 What is the term *differential* used to indicate?

Q4-3 What is negative goodwill? How is it reported in the consolidated balance sheet?

Q4-4 How is it possible for there to be a positive purchase differential but negative goodwill on a purchase of the stock of another company?

Q4-5 What portion of the balances of subsidiary stockholders' equity accounts are included in the consolidated balance sheet?

Q4-6 What portion of the book value of the net assets held by a subsidiary at acquisition is included in the consolidated balance sheet?

Q4-7 What portion of the fair value of a subsidiary's net assets normally is included in the consolidated balance sheet following a business combination?

Q4-8 What is the justification for using a differential clearing account in preparing consolidated statements?

Q4-9 What happens to the purchase differential in the consolidation workpaper prepared as of the date of combination? How is it reestablished so that the proper balances can be reported the following year?

Q4-10 Explain why consolidated financial statements become increasingly important when the purchase differential is very large.

Q4-11 How does the elimination process change when consolidated statements are prepared after—rather than at—the date of acquisition?

Q4-12 What are the three parts of the consolidation workpaper, and what sequence is used in completing the workpaper parts?

Q4-13 How are a subsidiary's dividend declarations reported in the consolidated retained earnings statement?

Q4-14 Give a definition of *consolidated net income*.

Q4-15 How is consolidated net income computed in a consolidation workpaper?

Q4-16 Give a definition of *consolidated retained earnings*.

Q4-17 How is the amount reported as consolidated retained earnings determined?

Q4-18 Why is the beginning retained earnings balance for each company entered in the three-part consolidation workpaper rather than just the ending balance?

Q4-19 When Ajax was preparing its consolidation workpaper, the differential was properly assigned to buildings and equipment. What additional entry generally must be made in the workpaper?

Q4-20 What determines whether the balance assigned to the differential remains constant or decreases each period?

Q4-21 What does the term *push-down accounting* mean?

Q4-22 Under what conditions is push-down accounting considered appropriate?

Q4-23 What happens to the differential when push-down accounting is used following a business combination?

Cases

C4-1 Need for Consolidation Process

Communication

At a recent staff meeting, the vice president of marketing appeared confused. The controller had assured him that the parent company and each of the subsidiary companies had properly accounted for all transactions during the year. After several other questions, he finally asked, "If it has been done properly, then why must you spend so much time and make so many changes to the amounts reported by the individual companies when you prepare the consolidated financial statements each month? You should be able to just add the reported balances together."

Required

Prepare an appropriate response to help the controller answer the marketing vice president's question.

C4-2 Account Presentation

Research FARS

Prime Company has been expanding rapidly and is now an extremely diversified company for its size. It currently owns three companies with manufacturing facilities, two companies primarily in retail sales, a consumer finance company, and two natural gas pipeline companies. This has led to some conflict between the company's chief accountant and its treasurer. The treasurer advocates presenting no more than five assets and three liabilities on its balance sheet. The chief accountant has resisted combining balances from substantially different subsidiaries and has asked for your assistance.

Required

Review the appropriate authoritative pronouncements or other relevant accounting literature to see what guidance is provided and prepare a memo to the chief accountant with your findings. Include citations to and quotations from the most relevant references. Include in your memo at least two examples of situations in which it may be inappropriate to combine similar appearing accounts of two subsidiaries.

C4-3 Consolidating an Unprofitable Subsidiary

Research FARS

Amazing Chemical Corporation's president had always wanted his own yacht and crew and concluded that Amazing Chemical should diversify its investments by purchasing an existing boatyard and repair facility on the lake shore near his summer home. He could then purchase a yacht and have a convenient place to store it and have it repaired. Although the board of directors was never formally asked to approve this new venture, the president moved forward with optimism and a rather substantial amount of corporate money to purchase full ownership of the boatyard, which had lost rather significant amounts of money each of the five prior years and had never reported a profit for the original owners.

Not surprisingly, the boatyard continued to lose money after Amazing Chemical purchased it, and the losses grew larger each month. Amazing Chemical, a very profitable chemical company, reported net income of $780,000 in 20X2 and $850,000 in 20X3 even though the boatyard reported net losses of $160,000 in 20X2 and $210,000 in 20X3 and was fully consolidated.

Required

Amazing Chemical's chief accountant has become concerned that members of the board of directors or company shareholders will accuse him of improperly preparing the consolidated statements. The president does not plan to tell anyone about the losses, which do not show up in the consolidated income statement that the chief accountant prepared. You have been asked to prepare a memo to the chief accountant indicating the way to include subsidiaries in the consolidated income statement and to provide citations to or quotations from the authoritative accounting literature that would assist the chief accountant in dealing with this matter. You have also been asked to search the accounting literature to see whether any reporting requirements require disclosure of the boatyard in notes to the financial statements or in management's discussion and analysis.

C4-4 Assigning a Purchase Differential

Analysis

Ball Corporation's owners recently offered to sell 60 percent of their ownership to Timber Corporation for $450,000. Timber's business manager was told that Ball's book value was $300,000, and she estimates the fair value of its net assets at approximately $600,000. Ball has relatively old equipment and manufacturing facilities and uses a LIFO basis for inventory valuation of some items and a FIFO basis for others.

Required

If Timber accepts the offer and purchases Ball, what difficulties are likely to be encountered in assigning the purchase differential?

C4-5 Negative Retained Earnings

Understanding

Although Sloan Company had good earnings reports in 20X5 and 20X6, it had a negative retained earnings balance on December 31, 20X6. Jacobs Corporation purchased 80 percent of Sloan's common stock on January 1, 20X7.

Required

a. Explain how Sloan's negative retained earnings balance is reflected in the consolidated balance sheet immediately following the acquisition.

b. Explain how the existence of negative retained earnings changes the consolidation workpaper entries.

c. Can goodwill be recorded if Jacobs pays more than book value for Sloan's shares? Explain.

C4-6 Balance Sheet Reporting Issues

Judgment

Crumple Car Rentals is planning to expand into the western part of the United States and needs to acquire approximately 400 additional automobiles for rental purposes. Because Crumple's cash reserves were substantially depleted in replacing the bumpers on existing automobiles with new "fashion plate" bumpers, the expansion funds must be acquired through other means. Crumple's management has identified three options:

1. Issue additional debt.
2. Create a wholly owned leasing subsidiary that would borrow the money with a guarantee for payment from Crumple. The subsidiary would then lease the cars to the parent.

3. Create a trust that would borrow the money with a guarantee for repayment from Crumple and lease the cars to it. In the event of liquidation, the residual value of the trust would go to the Historical Preservation Society of Pleasantville.

The acquisition price of the cars is approximately the same under all three alternatives.

Required

a. You have been asked to compare and contrast the three alternatives from the perspective of:
   (1) The impact on Crumple's consolidated balance sheet.
   (2) Their legal ramifications.
   (3) The ability to control the maintenance, repair, and replacement of automobiles.
b. You are to consider any alternatives that might be used in acquiring the required automobiles.
c. You are to select the preferred alternative and show why it is the best choice.

Exercises

E4-1 Multiple-Choice Questions on Consolidation Process

Select the most appropriate answer for each of the following questions.

1. Goodwill is:

   a. Seldom reported because it is too difficult to measure.
   b. Reported when more than book value is paid in purchasing another company.
   c. Reported when the fair value of the payment made in the purchase is greater than the fair value of the net identifiable assets acquired.
   d. Generally smaller for small companies and increases in amount as the companies acquired increase in size.

2. [AICPA Adapted] Wright Corporation includes several subsidiaries in its consolidated financial statements. In its December 31, 20X2, trial balance, Wright had the following intercompany balances before eliminations:

	Debit	Credit
Current receivable due from Main Company	$ 32,000	
Noncurrent receivable from Main Company	114,000	
Cash advance to Corn Corporation	6,000	
Cash advance from King Company		$ 15,000
Intercompany payable to King Company		101,000

In its December 31, 20X2, consolidated balance sheet, what amount should Wright report as intercompany receivables?

   a. $152,000.
   b. $146,000.
   c. $36,000.
   d. $0.

3. Beni Corporation purchased 100 percent of Carr Corporation's outstanding capital stock for $430,000 cash. Immediately before the purchase, the balance sheets of both corporations reported the following:

	Beni	Carr
Assets	$2,000,000	$750,000
Liabilities	$ 750,000	$400,000
Common Stock	1,000,000	310,000
Retained Earnings	250,000	40,000
Liabilities and Stockholders' Equity	$2,000,000	$750,000

At the date of purchase, the fair value of Carr's assets was $50,000 more than the aggregate carrying amounts. In the consolidated balance sheet prepared immediately after the purchase, the consolidated stockholders' equity should amount to:

a. $1,680,000.

b. $1,650,000.

c. $1,600,000.

d. $1,250,000.

Items 4 and 5 are based on the following information:

Nugget Company's balance sheet on December 31, 20X6, was as follows:

Assets		Liabilities and Stockholders' Equity	
Cash	$ 100,000	Current Liabilities	$ 300,000
Accounts Receivable	200,000	Long-Term Debt	500,000
Inventories	500,000	Common Stock (par $1 per share)	100,000
Property, Plant, and Equipment (net)	900,000	Additional Paid-In Capital	200,000
		Retained Earnings	600,000
		Total Liabilities and	
Total Assets	$1,700,000	Stockholders' Equity	$1,700,000

On December 31, 20X6, Gold Company purchased all of Nugget's outstanding common stock for $1,500,000 cash. On that date, the fair (market) value of Nugget's inventories was $450,000, and the fair value of Nugget's property, plant, and equipment was $1,000,000. The fair values of all other assets and liabilities of Nugget were equal to their book values.

4. As a result of Gold's acquisition of Nugget, the consolidated balance sheet of Gold and Nugget should reflect goodwill in the amount of:

a. $500,000.

b. $550,000.

c. $600,000.

d. $650,000.

5. Assuming that the balance sheet of Gold (unconsolidated) on December 31, 20X6, reflected retained earnings of $2,000,000, what amount of retained earnings should be shown in the December 31, 20X6, consolidated balance sheet of Gold and its new subsidiary, Nugget?

a. $2,000,000.

b. $2,600,000.

c. $2,800,000.

d. $3,150,000.

E4-2   Multiple-Choice Questions on Consolidation [AICPA Adapted]

Select the correct answer for each of the following questions.

1. On January 1, 20X1, Prim Inc. acquired all of Scrap Inc.'s outstanding common shares for cash equal to the stock's book value. The carrying amounts of Scrap's assets and liabilities approximated their fair values, except that the carrying amount of its building was more than fair value. In preparing Prim's 20X1 consolidated income statement, which of the following adjustments would be made?

a. Decrease depreciation expense and recognize goodwill amortization.

b. Increase depreciation expense and recognize goodwill amortization.

c. Decrease depreciation expense and recognize no goodwill amortization.

d. Increase depreciation expense and recognize no goodwill amortization.

2. The first examination of Rudd Corporation's financial statements was made for the year ended December 31, 20X8. The auditor found that Rudd had purchased another company on January 1, 20X8, and had recorded goodwill of $100,000 in connection with this purchase. Although a friend of the auditor believes the goodwill will last no more than five years, Rudd's

management has found no impairment of goodwill during 20X8. In its 20X8 financial statements, Rudd should report:

	Amortization Expense	Goodwill
a.	$ 0	$100,000
b.	$100,000	$ 0
c.	$ 20,000	$ 80,000
d.	$ 0	$ 0

3. Consolidated financial statements are being prepared for a parent and its four subsidiaries that have intercompany loans of $100,000 and intercompany profits of $300,000. How much of these intercompany loans and profits should be eliminated?

	Intercompany	
	Loans	Profits
a.	$ 0	$ 0
b.	$ 0	$300,000
c.	$100,000	$ 0
d.	$100,000	$300,000

4. On April 1, 20X8, Plum Inc. paid $1,700,000 for all of Long Corp.'s issued and outstanding common stock. On that date, the costs and fair values of Long's recorded assets and liabilities were as follows:

	Cost	Fair Value
Cash	$ 160,000	$ 160,000
Inventory	480,000	460,000
Property, plant and equipment (net)	980,000	1,040,000
Liabilities	(360,000)	(360,000)
Net assets	$1,260,000	$1,300,000

In Plum's March 31, 20X9, consolidated balance sheet, what amount of goodwill should be reported as a result of this business combination?

a. $360,000.

b. $396,000.

c. $400,000.

d. $440,000.

E4-3 Basic Elimination Entry

On December 31, 20X3, Broadway Corporation reported common stock outstanding of $200,000, additional paid-in capital of $300,000, and retained earnings of $100,000. On January 1, 20X4, Johe Company acquired control of Broadway in a business combination.

Required

Give the eliminating entry that would be needed in preparing a consolidated balance sheet immediately following the combination if Johe purchased all of Broadway's outstanding common stock for $600,000.

E4-4 Eliminating Entries with Differential

On June 10, 20X8, Tower Corporation purchased 100 percent of Brown Company's common stock. Summarized balance sheet data for the two companies immediately after the stock purchase are as follows:

Item	Tower Corp.	Brown Company Book Value	Brown Company Fair Value
Cash	$ 15,000	$ 5,000	$ 5,000
Accounts Receivable	30,000	10,000	10,000
Inventory	80,000	20,000	25,000
Buildings and Equipment (net)	120,000	50,000	70,000
Investment in Brown Stock	100,000		
Total	$345,000	$85,000	$110,000
Accounts Payable	$ 25,000	$ 3,000	$ 3,000
Bonds Payable	150,000	25,000	25,000
Common Stock	55,000	20,000	
Retained Earnings	115,000	37,000	
Total	$345,000	$85,000	$ 28,000

Required

a. Give the eliminating entries required to prepare a consolidated balance sheet immediately after the purchase of Brown Company shares.

b. Explain how eliminating entries differ from other types of journal entries recorded in the normal course of business.

E4-5 **Balance Sheet Consolidation**

Reed Corporation purchased 100 percent of Thorne Corporation's voting common stock on December 31, 20X4, for $395,000. At the date of combination, Thorne reported the following:

Cash	$120,000	Current Liabilities	$ 80,000
Inventory	100,000	Long-Term Liabilities	200,000
Buildings (net)	420,000	Common Stock	120,000
		Retained Earnings	240,000
Total	$640,000	Total	$640,000

At December 31, 20X4, the book values of Thorne's net assets and liabilities approximated their fair values, except for buildings, which had a fair value of $20,000 less than book value, and inventories, which had a fair value $36,000 more than book value.

Required

Reed Corporation wishes to prepare a consolidated balance sheet immediately following the business combination. Give the eliminating entry or entries needed to prepare a consolidated balance sheet at December 31, 20X4.

E4-6 **Eliminating Entries with Negative Goodwill**

Snow Corporation purchased all of Conger Corporation's voting shares on January 1, 20X2, for $365,000. At that time Conger reported common stock outstanding of $80,000 and retained earnings of $130,000. The book values of Conger's assets and liabilities approximated their fair values, except for land, which had a book value of $80,000 and a fair value of $100,000, and buildings, which had a book value of $220,000 and a fair value of $400,000. Land and buildings are the only noncurrent assets that Conger holds.

Required

a. Compute the amount of negative goodwill at the date of acquisition.

b. Give the eliminating entry or entries required immediately following the acquisition to prepare a consolidated balance sheet.

E4-7 Balance Sheet Workpaper

Simon Corporation purchased 100 percent of Faith Corporation's common stock on December 31, 20X2, for $150,000. Data from the balance sheets of the two companies included the following amounts as of the date of acquisition:

Item	Simon Corporation	Faith Corporation
Cash	$ 65,000	$ 18,000
Accounts Receivable	87,000	37,000
Inventory	110,000	60,000
Buildings and Equipment (net)	220,000	150,000
Investment in Faith Corporation Stock	150,000	
Total Assets	$632,000	$265,000
Accounts Payable	$ 92,000	$ 35,000
Notes Payable	150,000	80,000
Common Stock	100,000	60,000
Retained Earnings	290,000	90,000
Total Liabilities and Stockholders' Equity	$632,000	$265,000

At the date of the business combination, the book values of Faith's net assets and liabilities approximated fair value.

Required

a. Give the eliminating entry or entries needed to prepare a consolidated balance sheet immediately following the business combination.

b. Prepare a consolidated balance sheet workpaper.

E4-8 Balance Sheet Workpaper with Differential

Simon Corporation purchased 100 percent of Faith Corporation's common stock on December 31, 20X2, for $189,000. Data from the balance sheets of the two companies included the following amounts as of the date of acquisition:

Item	Simon Corporation	Faith Corporation
Cash	$ 26,000	$ 18,000
Accounts Receivable	87,000	37,000
Inventory	110,000	60,000
Buildings and Equipment (net)	220,000	150,000
Investment in Faith Corporation Stock	189,000	
Total Assets	$632,000	$265,000
Accounts Payable	$ 92,000	$ 35,000
Notes Payable	150,000	80,000
Common Stock	100,000	60,000
Retained Earnings	290,000	90,000
Total Liabilities and Stockholders' Equity	$632,000	$265,000

At the date of the business combination, Faith's net assets and liabilities approximated fair value except for inventory, which had a fair value of $84,000 and buildings and equipment (net), which had a fair value of $165,000.

Required

a. Give the eliminating entry or entries needed to prepare a consolidated balance sheet immediately following the business combination.

b. Prepare a consolidation balance sheet workpaper.

E4-9 Workpaper for Wholly Owned Subsidiary

Gold Enterprises purchased 100 percent of Premium Builders' stock on December 31, 20X4. Balance sheet data for Gold and Premium on January 1, 20X5, are as follows:

	Gold Enterprises	Premium Builders
Cash and Receivables	$ 80,000	$ 30,000
Inventory	150,000	350,000
Buildings and Equipment (net)	430,000	80,000
Investment in Premium Stock	167,000	
Total Assets	$827,000	$460,000
Current Liabilities	$100,000	$110,000
Long-Term Debt	400,000	200,000
Common Stock	200,000	140,000
Retained Earnings	127,000	10,000
Total Liabilities and Stockholders' Equity	$827,000	$460,000

At the date of the business combination, Premium's cash and receivables had a fair value of $28,000, inventory had a fair value of $357,000, and buildings and equipment had a fair value of $92,000.

Required

a. Give all eliminating entries needed to prepare a consolidated balance sheet on January 1, 20X5.

b. Complete a consolidated balance sheet workpaper.

c. Prepare a consolidated balance sheet in good form.

E4-10 Computation of Consolidated Balances

Astor Corporation's balance sheet at January 1, 20X7, reflected the following balances:

Cash and Receivables	$ 80,000	Accounts Payable	$ 40,000
Inventory	120,000	Income Taxes Payable	60,000
Land	70,000	Bonds Payable	200,000
Buildings and Equipment (net)	480,000	Common Stock	250,000
		Retained Earnings	200,000
Total Assets	$750,000	Total Liabilities and Stockholders' Equity	$750,000

Phel Corporation, which had just entered into an active acquisition program, purchased 100 percent of Astor's common stock on January 2, 20X7, for $576,000. A careful review of the fair value of Astor's assets and liabilities indicated the following:

	Book Value	Fair Value
Inventory	$120,000	$140,000
Land	70,000	60,000
Buildings and Equipment (net)	480,000	550,000

Required

Compute the appropriate amount to be included in the consolidated balance sheet immediately following the acquisition for each of the following items:

a. Inventory.

b. Land.

c. Buildings and Equipment (net).

d. Goodwill.

e. Investment in Astor Corporation.

E4-11 **Multiple-Choice Questions on Balance Sheet Consolidation**

Top Corporation purchased 100 percent of Sun Corporation's common stock on December 31, 20X2. Balance sheet data for the two companies immediately following the acquisition follow:

Item	Top Corporation	Sun Corporation
Cash	$ 49,000	$ 30,000
Accounts Receivable	110,000	45,000
Inventory	130,000	70,000
Land	80,000	25,000
Buildings and Equipment	500,000	400,000
Less: Accumulated Depreciation	(223,000)	(165,000)
Investment in Sun Corporation Stock	198,000	
Total Assets	$844,000	$405,000
Accounts Payable	$ 61,500	$ 28,000
Taxes Payable	95,000	37,000
Bonds Payable	280,000	200,000
Common Stock	150,000	50,000
Retained Earnings	257,500	90,000
Total Liabilities and Stockholders' Equity	$844,000	$405,000

At the date of the business combination, the book values of Sun's net assets and liabilities approximated fair value except for inventory, which had a fair value of $85,000, and land, which had a fair value of $45,000.

Required

For each question below, indicate the appropriate total that should appear in the consolidated balance sheet prepared immediately after the business combination.

1. What amount of inventory will be reported?
   a. $70,000.
   b. $130,000.
   c. $200,000.
   d. $215,000.

2. What amount of goodwill will be reported?
   a. $0.
   b. $23,000.
   c. $43,000.
   d. $58,000.

3. What amount of total assets will be reported?
   a. $84,400.
   b. $1,051,000.
   c. $1,109,000.
   d. $1,249,000.

4. What amount of total liabilities will be reported?
   a. $265,000.
   b. $436,500.
   c. $701,500.
   d. $1,249,000.

5. What amount of consolidated retained earnings will be reported?
   a. $547,500.
   b. $397,500.

  c. $347,500.

  d. $257,500.

6. What amount of total stockholders' equity will be reported?

  a. $407,500.

  b. $547,500.

  c. $844,000.

  d. $1,249,000.

E4-12   Consolidation Entries for Wholly Owned Subsidiary

Trim Corporation purchased 100 percent of Round Corporation's voting common stock on January 1, 20X2, for $400,000. At that date, Round reported the following summarized balance sheet data:

Assets	$700,000	Accounts Payable	$100,000
		Bonds Payable	200,000
		Common Stock	120,000
		Retained Earnings	280,000
Total	$700,000	Total	$700,000

Round reported net income of $80,000 for 20X2 and paid dividends of $25,000.

Required

a. Give the journal entries recorded by Trim Corporation during 20X2 on its books if Trim accounts for its investment in Round using the equity method.

b. Give the eliminating entries needed at December 31, 20X2, to prepare consolidated financial statements.

E4-13   Basic Consolidation Entries for Fully Owned Subsidiary

Amber Corporation reported the following summarized balance sheet data on December 31, 20X6:

Assets	$600,000	Liabilities	$100,000
		Common Stock	300,000
		Retained Earnings	200,000
Total	$600,000	Total	$600,000

On January 1, 20X7, Purple Company purchased 100 percent of Amber's stock for $500,000. Amber reported net income of $50,000 for 20X7 and paid dividends of $20,000.

Required

a. Give the journal entries recorded by Purple on its books during 20X7 if it accounts for its investment in Amber using the equity method.

b. Give the eliminating entries needed on December 31, 20X7, to prepare consolidated financial statements.

E4-14   Wholly Owned Subsidiary with Differential

Canton Corporation is a wholly owned subsidiary of Winston Corporation. Winston acquired ownership of Canton on January 1, 20X3, for $28,000 above Canton's reported net assets. At that date, Canton reported common stock outstanding of $60,000 and retained earnings of $90,000. The purchase differential is assigned to equipment with an economic life of seven years at the date of the business combination. Canton reported net income of $30,000 and paid dividends of $12,000 in 20X3.

Required

a. Give the journal entries recorded by Winston Corporation during 20X3 on its books if Winston accounts for its investment in Canton using the equity method.

b. Give the eliminating entries needed at December 31, 20X3, to prepare consolidated financial statements.

E4-15 **Basic Consolidation Workpaper**

Blake Corporation acquired 100 percent of Shaw Corporation's voting shares on January 1, 20X3, at underlying book value. Blake uses the equity method in accounting for its investment in Shaw. Adjusted trial balances for Blake and Shaw on December 31, 20X3, are as follows:

Item	Blake Corporation		Shaw Corporation	
	Debit	Credit	Debit	Credit
Current Assets	$145,000		$105,000	
Depreciable Assets (net)	325,000		225,000	
Investment in Shaw Corporation Stock	170,000			
Depreciation Expense	25,000		15,000	
Other Expenses	105,000		75,000	
Dividends Declared	40,000		10,000	
Current Liabilities		$ 50,000		$ 40,000
Long-Term Debt		100,000		120,000
Common Stock		200,000		100,000
Retained Earnings		230,000		50,000
Sales		200,000		120,000
Income from Subsidiary		30,000		
	$810,000	$810,000	$430,000	$430,000

Required

a. Give all eliminating entries required on December 31, 20X3, to prepare consolidated financial statements.

b. Prepare a three-part consolidation workpaper as of December 31, 20X3.

E4-16 **Basic Consolidation Workpaper for Second Year**

Blake Corporation acquired 100 percent of Shaw Corporation's voting shares on January 1, 20X3, at underlying book value. Blake uses the equity method in accounting for its investment in Shaw. Adjusted trial balances for Blake and Shaw on December 31, 20X4, are as follows:

Item	Blake Corporation		Shaw Corporation	
	Debit	Credit	Debit	Credit
Current Assets	$210,000		$150,000	
Depreciable Assets (net)	300,000		210,000	
Investment in Shaw Corporation Stock	190,000			
Depreciation Expense	25,000		15,000	
Other Expenses	150,000		90,000	
Dividends Declared	50,000		15,000	
Current Liabilities		$ 70,000		$ 50,000
Long-Term Debt		100,000		120,000
Common Stock		200,000		100,000
Retained Earnings		290,000		70,000
Sales		230,000		140,000
Income from Subsidiary		35,000		
	$925,000	$925,000	$480,000	$480,000

Required

a. Give all eliminating entries required on December 31, 20X4, to prepare consolidated financial statements.

b. Prepare a three-part consolidation workpaper as of December 31, 20X4.

E4-17   **Consolidation Workpaper with Differential**

Kennelly Corporation purchased all of Short Company's common shares on January 1, 20X5, for $180,000. On that date, the book value of the net assets reported by Short was $150,000. The entire purchase differential was assigned to depreciable assets with a six-year remaining economic life from January 1, 20X5.

The adjusted trial balances for the two companies on December 31, 20X5, are as follows:

Item	Kennelly Corporation Debit	Kennelly Corporation Credit	Short Company Debit	Short Company Credit
Cash	$ 15,000		$ 5,000	
Accounts Receivable	30,000		40,000	
Inventory	70,000		60,000	
Depreciable Assets (net)	325,000		225,000	
Investment in Short Company Stock	195,000			
Depreciation Expense	25,000		15,000	
Other Expenses	105,000		75,000	
Dividends Declared	40,000		10,000	
Accounts Payable		$ 50,000		$ 40,000
Notes Payable		100,000		120,000
Common Stock		200,000		100,000
Retained Earnings		230,000		50,000
Sales		200,000		120,000
Income from Subsidiary		25,000		
	$805,000	$805,000	$430,000	$430,000

Kennelly uses the equity method in accounting for its investment in Short. Short declared and paid dividends on December 31, 20X5.

Required

a. Prepare the eliminating entries needed as of December 31, 20X5, to complete a consolidation workpaper.

b. Prepare a three-part consolidation workpaper as of December 31, 20X5.

E4-18   **Consolidation Workpaper for Subsidiary**

Land Corporation purchased 100 percent of Growth Company's voting stock on January 1, 20X4, at underlying book value. Land uses the equity method in accounting for its ownership of Growth. On December 31, 20X4, the trial balances of the two companies are as follows:

Item	Land Corporation Debit	Land Corporation Credit	Growth Company Debit	Growth Company Credit
Current Assets	$ 238,000		$150,000	
Depreciable Assets (net)	500,000		300,000	
Investment in Growth Company Stock	190,000			
Depreciation Expense	25,000		15,000	
Other Expenses	150,000		90,000	
Dividends Declared	50,000		15,000	
Accumulated Depreciation		$ 200,000		$ 90,000
Current Liabilities		70,000		50,000
Long-Term Debt		100,000		120,000
Common Stock		200,000		100,000
Retained Earnings		318,000		70,000
Sales		230,000		140,000
Income from Subsidiary		35,000		
	$1,153,000	$1,153,000	$570,000	$570,000

Required

a. Give all eliminating entries required on December 31, 20X4, to prepare consolidated financial statements.

b. Prepare a three-part consolidation workpaper as of December 31, 20X4.

E4-19 Push-Down Accounting

Jefferson Company purchased all of Louis Corporation's common shares on January 2, 20X3, for $789,000. At the date of combination, Louis's balance sheet appeared as follows:

Assets		Liabilities	
Cash and Receivables	$ 34,000	Current Payables	$ 25,000
Inventory	165,000	Notes Payable	100,000
Land	60,000	Stockholders' Equity	
Buildings (net)	250,000	Common Stock	200,000
Equipment (net)	320,000	Additional Capital	425,000
		Retained Earnings	79,000
Total	$829,000	Total	$829,000

The fair values of all of Louis's assets and liabilities were equal to their book values except for its fixed assets. Louis's land had a fair value of $75,000; the buildings, a fair value of $300,000; and the equipment, a fair value of $340,000.

Jefferson Company decided to employ push-down accounting for the acquisition of Louis Corporation. Subsequent to the combination, Louis continued to operate as a separate company.

Required

a. Record the purcase of Louis's stock on Jefferson's books.

b. Present any entries that would be made on Louis's books related to the business combination, assuming push-down accounting is used.

c. Present, in general journal form, all elimination entries that would appear in a consolidation workpaper for Jefferson and its subsidiary prepared immediately following the combination.

Problems

P4-20 Assignment of Differential in Workpaper

Teresa Corporation purchased all the voting shares of Sally Enterprises on January 1, 20X4. Balance sheet amounts for the companies on the date of acquisition were as follows:

	Teresa Corporation	Sally Enterprises
Cash and Receivables	$ 40,000	$ 20,000
Inventory	95,000	40,000
Land	80,000	90,000
Buildings and Equipment	400,000	230,000
Investment in Sally Enterprises	290,000	
Total Debits	$905,000	$380,000
Accumulated Depreciation	$175,000	$ 65,000
Accounts Payable	60,000	15,000
Notes Payable	100,000	50,000
Common Stock	300,000	100,000
Retained Earnings	270,000	150,000
Total Credits	$905,000	$380,000

Sally Enterprises' buildings and equipment were estimated to have a market value of $175,000 on January 1, 20X4. All other items appeared to have market values approximating current book values.

Required

a. Complete a consolidated balance sheet workpaper for January 1, 20X4.

b. Prepare a consolidated balance sheet in good form.

P4-21 **Computation of Consolidated Balances**

Retail Records Inc. purchased all of Decibel Studios' voting shares on January 1, 20X2, for $280,000. Retail's balance sheet immediately after the combination contained the following balances:

RETAIL RECORDS INC.
Balance Sheet
January 1, 20X2

Cash and Receivables	$120,000	Accounts Payable	$ 75,000
Inventory	110,000	Taxes Payable	50,000
Land	70,000	Notes Payable	300,000
Buildings and Equipment (net)	350,000	Common Stock	400,000
Investment in Decibel Stock	280,000	Retained Earnings	105,000
Total Assets	$930,000	Total Liabilities and Stockholders' Equity	$930,000

Decibel's balance sheet at acquisition contained the following balances:

DECIBEL STUDIOS
Balance Sheet
January 1, 20X2

Cash and Receivables	$ 40,000	Accounts Payable	$ 90,000
Inventory	180,000	Notes Payable	250,000
Buildings and Equipment (net)	350,000	Common Stock	100,000
Goodwill	30,000	Additional Paid-In Capital	200,000
		Retained Earnings	(40,000)
Total Assets	$600,000	Total Liabilities and Stockholders' Equity	$600,000

On the date of combination, the inventory held by Decibel had a fair value of $170,000, and its buildings and recording equipment had a value of $375,000. Goodwill reported by Decibel resulted from a purchase of Sound Stage Enterprises in 20X1. Sound Stage was liquidated and its assets and liabilities were brought onto Decibel's books.

Required

Compute the balances to be reported in the consolidated balance sheet immediately after the acquisition for:

a. Inventory.

b. Buildings and Equipment (net).

c. Investment in Decibel Stock.

d. Goodwill.

e. Common Stock.

f. Retained Earnings.

P4-22 **Balance Sheet Consolidation [AICPA Adapted]**

Case Inc. acquired all Frey Inc.'s outstanding $25 par common stock on December 31, 20X3, in exchange for 40,000 shares of its $25 par common stock. Case's common stock closed at $56.50 per share on a national stock exchange on December 31, 20X3. Both corporations continued to operate as separate businesses maintaining separate accounting records with years ending December 31.

On December 31, 20X4, after year-end adjustments and the closing of nominal accounts, the companies had condensed balance sheet accounts as follows:

	Case	Frey
Assets		
Cash	$ 825,000	$ 330,000
Accounts and Other Receivables	2,140,000	835,000
Inventories	2,310,000	1,045,000
Land	650,000	300,000
Depreciable Assets (net)	4,575,000	1,980,000
Investment in Frey Inc.	2,680,000	
Long-Term Investments and Other Assets	865,000	385,000
Total Assets	$14,045,000	$4,875,000
Liabilities and Stockholders' Equity		
Accounts Payable and Other Current Liabilities	$ 2,465,000	$1,145,000
Long-Term Debt	1,900,000	1,300,000
Common Stock, $25 Par Value	3,200,000	1,000,000
Additional Paid-In Capital	2,100,000	190,000
Retained Earnings	4,380,000	1,240,000
Total Liabilities and Stockholders' Equity	$14,045,000	$4,875,000

Additional Information

1. Case uses the equity method of accounting for its investment in Frey.
2. On December 31, 20X3, Frey's assets and liabilities had fair values equal to the book balances with the exception of land, which had a fair value of $550,000. Frey had no land transactions in 20X4.
3. On June 15, 20X4, Frey paid a cash dividend of $4 per share on its common stock.
4. On December 10, 20X4, Case paid a cash dividend totaling $256,000 on its common stock.
5. On December 31, 20X3, immediately before the combination, the stockholders' equities were:

	Case	Frey
Common Stock	$2,200,000	$1,000,000
Additional Paid-In Capital	1,660,000	190,000
Retained Earnings	3,166,000	820,000
	$7,026,000	$2,010,000

6. The 20X4 net income amounts according to the separate books of Case and Frey were $890,000 (exclusive of equity in Frey's earnings) and $580,000, respectively.

Required

Prepare a consolidated balance sheet workpaper for Case and its subsidiary, Frey, for December 31, 20X4. A formal consolidated balance sheet is not required.

P4-23 Consolidated Balance Sheet

Thompson Company spent $240,000 to buy all of Lake Corporation's stock on January 1, 20X2. The balance sheets of the two companies on December 31, 20X3, showed the following amounts:

	Thompson Company	Lake Corporation
Cash	$ 30,000	$ 20,000
Accounts Receivable	100,000	40,000
Land	60,000	50,000
Buildings and Equipment	500,000	350,000
Less: Accumulated Depreciation	(230,000)	(75,000)
Investment in Lake Corporation	252,000	
	$712,000	$385,000
Accounts Payable	$80,000	$ 10,000
Taxes Payable	40,000	70,000
Notes Payable	100,000	85,000
Common Stock	200,000	100,000
Retained Earnings	292,000	120,000
	$712,000	$385,000

Lake reported retained earnings of $100,000 at the date of acquisition. The difference between the purchase price and underlying book value is assigned to buildings and equipment with a remaining economic life of 10 years from the date of acquisition.

Required

a. Give the appropriate eliminating entry or entries needed to prepare a consolidated balance sheet as of December 31, 20X3.

b. Prepare a consolidated balance sheet workpaper as of December 31, 20X3.

P4-24 **Comprehensive Problem: Consolidation in Subsequent Period**

Thompson Company spent $240,000 to buy all Lake Corporation's stock on January 1, 20X2. On December 31, 20X4, the trial balances of the two companies were as follows:

Item	Thompson Company Debit	Thompson Company Credit	Lake Corporation Debit	Lake Corporation Credit
Cash	$ 74,000		$ 42,000	
Accounts Receivable	130,000		53,000	
Land	60,000		50,000	
Buildings and Equipment	500,000		350,000	
Investment in Lake Corporation Stock	268,000			
Cost of Services Provided	470,000		130,000	
Depreciation Expense	35,000		18,000	
Other Expenses	57,000		60,000	
Dividends Declared	30,000		12,000	
Accumulated Depreciation		$ 265,000		$ 93,000
Accounts Payable		71,000		17,000
Taxes Payable		58,000		60,000
Notes Payable		100,000		85,000
Common Stock		200,000		100,000
Retained Earnings		292,000		120,000
Service Revenue		610,000		240,000
Income from Subsidiary		28,000		
	$1,624,000	$1,624,000	$715,000	$715,000

Lake Corporation reported retained earnings of $100,000 at the date of acquisition. The difference between the purchase price and underlying book value is assigned to buildings and equipment with a remaining economic life of 10 years from the date of acquisition. At December 31, 20X4, Lake owed Thompson $2,500 for services provided.

Required

a. Give all journal entries recorded by Thompson with regard to its investment in Lake during 20X4.

b. Give all eliminating entries required on December 31, 20X4, to prepare consolidated financial statements.

c. Prepare a three-part consolidation workpaper as of December 31, 20X4.

P4-25   Consolidated Balances [AICPA Adapted]

The separate condensed balance sheets and income statements of Purl Corporation and its wholly owned subsidiary, Scott Corporation, are as follows:

Balance Sheets
December 31, 20X0

	Purl	Scott
Current Assets		
Cash	$ 80,000	$ 60,000
Accounts Receivable (net)	140,000	25,000
Inventories	90,000	50,000
Total Current Assets	$ 310,000	$135,000
Property, Plant & Equipment (net)	625,000	280,000
Investment in Scott (equity method)	390,000	
Total Assets	$1,325,000	$415,000
Current Liabilities		
Accounts Payable	$ 160,000	$ 95,000
Accrued Liabilities	110,000	30,000
Total Current Liabilities	$ 270,000	$125,000
Stockholders' Equity		
Common Stock ($10 par)	$300,000	$ 50,000
Additional Paid-In Capital		10,000
Retained Earnings	755,000	230,000
Total Stockholders' Equity	1,055,000	290,000
Total Liabilities and Stockholders' Equity	$1,325,000	$415,000

Income Statement
Year Ended December 31, 20X0

	Purl	Scott
Sales	$2,000,000	$750,000
Cost of Goods Sold	(1,540,000)	(500,000)
Gross Margin	$ 460,000	$250,000
Operating Expenses	(260,000)	(150,000)
Operating Income	$ 200,000	$100,000
Equity in Earnings of Scott	60,000	
Income Before Taxes	$ 260,000	$100,000
Provision for Income Taxes	(60,000)	(30,000)
Net Income	$ 200,000	$ 70,000

Additional Information

- On January 1, 20X0, Purl purchased for $360,000 all of Scott's $10 par, voting common stock. On January 1, 20X0, the fair value of Scott's assets and liabilities equaled their carrying amount of $410,000 and $160,000, respectively, except that the fair values of certain items identifiable in Scott's inventory were $10,000 more than their carrying amounts and Scott held unrecorded copyrights with a fair value of $100,000 and a remaining useful life of 10 years. The inventory items were still on hand at December 31, 20X0.

- During 20X0, Purl and Scott paid cash dividends of $100,000 and $30,000, respectively. For tax purposes, Purl receives the 100 percent exclusion for dividends received from Scott.

- There were no intercompany transactions, except for Purl's receipt of dividends from Scott and Purl's recording of its share of Scott's earnings. Both Purl and Scott paid income taxes at the rate of 30 percent.

In the December 31, 20X0, consolidated financial statements of Purl and its subsidiary:

1. Total current assets should be:
   a. $455,000.
   b. $445,000.
   c. $310,000.
   d. $135,000.

2. Total assets should be:
   a. $1,740,000.
   b. $1,450,000.
   c. $1,350,000.
   d. $1,325,000.

3. Total retained earnings should be:
   a. $985,000.
   b. $825,000.
   c. $795,000.
   d. $755,000.

4. Net income should be:
   a. $270,000.
   b. $200,000.
   c. $190,000.
   d. $170,000.

5. Copyright amortization expense should be:
   a. $20,000.
   b. $10,000.
   c. $6,000.
   d. $0.

P4-26   Intercorporate Receivables and Payables

Kim Corporation acquired 100 percent of Normal Company's outstanding shares on January 1, 20X7. Balance sheet data for the two companies immediately after the purchase follow:

	Kim Corporation	Normal Company
Cash	$ 70,000	$ 35,000
Accounts Receivable	90,000	65,000
Inventory	84,000	80,000
Buildings and Equipment	400,000	300,000
Less: Accumulated Depreciation	(160,000)	(75,000)
Investment in Normal Company Stock	305,000	
Investment in Normal Company Bonds	50,000	
Total Assets	$839,000	$405,000

(continued)

(continued)

	Kim Corporation	Normal Company
Accounts Payable	$ 50,000	$ 20,000
Bonds Payable	200,000	100,000
Common Stock	300,000	150,000
Capital in Excess of Par		140,000
Retained Earnings	289,000	(5,000)
Total Liabilities and Equities	$839,000	$405,000

As indicated in the parent company balance sheet, Kim purchased $50,000 of Normal's bonds from the subsidiary immediately after it purchased the stock. An analysis of intercompany receivables and payables also indicates that the subsidiary owes the parent $10,000. On the date of combination, the book values and fair values of Normal's assets and liabilities were the same.

Required

a. Give all eliminating entries needed to prepare a consolidated balance sheet for January 1, 20X7.

b. Complete a consolidated balance sheet workpaper.

c. Prepare a consolidated balance sheet in good form.

P4-27 ### Comprehensive Problem: Consolidation of Subsidiary

On January 2, 20X8, Primary Corporation purchased 100 percent of Street Company's outstanding common stock. In exchange for Street's stock, Primary issued bonds payable with a par and fair value of $650,000 directly to the selling stockholders of Street. The two companies continued to operate as separate entities subsequent to combination.

Immediately prior to the combination, the book values and fair values of the companies' assets and liabilities were as follows:

	Primary		Street	
	Book Value	Fair Value	Book Value	Fair Value
Cash	$ 12,000	$ 12,000	$ 9,000	$ 9,000
Receivables	41,000	39,000	31,000	30,000
Allowance for Bad Debts	(2,000)		(1,000)	
Inventory	86,000	89,000	68,000	72,000
Land	55,000	200,000	50,000	70,000
Buildings and Equipment	960,000	650,000	670,000	500,000
Accumulated Depreciation	(411,000)		(220,000)	
Patent				40,000
Total Assets	$741,000	$990,000	$607,000	$721,000
Current Payables	$ 38,000	$ 38,000	$ 29,000	$ 29,000
Bonds Payable	200,000	210,000	100,000	90,000
Common Stock	300,000		200,000	
Additional Paid-In Capital	100,000		130,000	
Retained Earnings	103,000		148,000	
Total Liabilities and Equity	$741,000		$607,000	

At the date of combination, Street owed Primary $6,000 plus accrued interest of $500 on a short-term note. Both companies have properly recorded these amounts.

Required

a. Record the business combination on the books of Primary Corporation.

b. Present in general journal form all elimination entries needed in a workpaper to prepare a consolidated balance sheet immediately following the business combination on January 2, 20X8.

c. Prepare and complete a consolidated balance sheet workpaper as of January 2, 20X8, immediately following the business combination.

d. Present a consolidated balance sheet for Primary and its subsidiary as of January 2, 20X8.

P4-28 **Consolidation Workpaper at End of First Year of Ownership**

Mill Corporation acquired 100 percent ownership of Roller Company on January 1, 20X8, for $128,000. At that date, the fair value of Roller's buildings and equipment was $20,000 more than book value. Buildings and equipment are depreciated on a 10-year basis. Although goodwill is not amortized, the management of Mill concluded at December 31, 20X8, that goodwill involved in its purchase of Roller shares had been impaired and the correct carrying value was $2,500.

Trial balance data for Mill and Roller on December 31, 20X8, are as follows:

Item	Mill Corporation Debit	Mill Corporation Credit	Roller Company Debit	Roller Company Credit
Cash	$ 19,500		$ 21,000	
Accounts Receivable	70,000		12,000	
Inventory	90,000		25,000	
Land	30,000		15,000	
Buildings and Equipment	350,000		150,000	
Investment in Roller Co. Stock	134,000			
Cost of Goods Sold	125,000		110,000	
Wage Expense	42,000		27,000	
Depreciation Expense	25,000		10,000	
Interest Expense	12,000		4,000	
Other Expenses	13,500		5,000	
Dividends Declared	30,000		16,000	
Accumulated Depreciation		$145,000		$ 40,000
Accounts Payable		45,000		16,000
Wages Payable		17,000		9,000
Notes Payable		150,000		50,000
Common Stock		200,000		60,000
Retained Earnings		102,000		40,000
Sales		260,000		180,000
Income from Subsidiary		22,000		
	$941,000	$941,000	$395,000	$395,000

Required

a. Give all eliminating entries needed to prepare a three-part consolidation workpaper as of December 31, 20X8.

b. Prepare a three-part consolidation workpaper for 20X8 in good form.

P4-29 **Consolidation Workpaper at End of Second Year of Ownership**

Mill Corporation acquired 100 percent ownership of Roller Company on January 1, 20X8, for $128,000. At that date, the fair value of Roller's buildings and equipment was $20,000 more than book value. Buildings and equipment are depreciated on a 10-year basis. Although goodwill is not amortized, the management of Mill concluded at December 31, 20X8, that goodwill involved in its purchase of Roller shares had been impaired and the correct carrying value was $2,500. No additional impairment occurred in 20X9.

Trial balance data for Mill and Roller on December 31, 20X9, are as follows:

Item	Mill Corporation Debit	Mill Corporation Credit	Roller Company Debit	Roller Company Credit
Cash	$ 45,500		$ 32,000	
Accounts Receivable	85,000		14,000	
Inventory	97,000		24,000	
Land	50,000		25,000	
Buildings and Equipment	350,000		150,000	
Investment in Roller Co. Stock	148,000			
Cost of Goods Sold	145,000		114,000	
Wage Expense	35,000		20,000	
Depreciation Expense	25,000		10,000	
Interest Expense	12,000		4,000	
Other Expenses	23,000		16,000	
Dividends Declared	30,000		20,000	
Accumulated Depreciation		$ 170,000		$ 50,000
Accounts Payable		51,000		15,000
Wages Payable		14,000		6,000
Notes Payable		150,000		50,000
Common Stock		200,000		60,000
Retained Earnings		136,500		48,000
Sales		290,000		200,000
Income from Subsidiary		34,000		
	$1,045,500	$1,045,500	$429,000	$429,000

Required

a. Give all eliminating entries needed to prepare a three-part consolidation workpaper as of December 31, 20X9.

b. Prepare a three-part consolidation workpaper for 20X9 in good form.

c. Prepare a consolidated balance sheet, income statement, and retained earnings statement for 20X9.

P4-30   ## Comprehensive Problem: Wholly Owned Subsidiary

Power Corporation acquired 100 percent ownership of Upland Products Company on January 1, 20X1, for $200,000. On that date Upland reported retained earnings of $50,000 and had $100,000 of common stock outstanding. Power has used the equity method in accounting for its investment in Upland.

Trial balance data for the two companies on December 31, 20X5, are as follows:

Item	Power Corporation Debit	Power Corporation Credit	Upland Products Company Debit	Upland Products Company Credit
Cash and Receivables	$ 43,000		$ 65,000	
Inventory	260,000		90,000	
Land	80,000		80,000	
Buildings and Equipment	500,000		150,000	
Investment in Upland Products Stock	235,000			
Cost of Goods Sold	120,000		50,000	
Depreciation Expense	25,000		15,000	
Inventory Losses	15,000		5,000	
Dividends Declared	30,000		10,000	
Accumulated Depreciation		$ 205,000		$105,000
Accounts Payable		60,000		20,000

(continued)

Notes Payable	200,000	50,000
Common Stock	300,000	100,000
Retained Earnings	318,000	90,000
Sales	200,000	100,000
Income from Subsidiary	25,000	
	$1,308,000 $1,308,000	$465,000 $465,000

Additional Information

1. On the date of combination, the fair value of Upland's depreciable assets was $50,000 more than book value. The purchase differential assigned to depreciable assets should be written off over the following 10-year period.
2. There was $10,000 of intercorporate receivables and payables at the end of 20X5.

Required

a. Give all journal entries that Power recorded during 20X5 related to its investment in Upland.
b. Give all eliminating entries needed to prepare consolidated statements for 20X5.
c. Prepare a three-part workpaper as of December 31, 20X5.

P4-31 Comprehensive Problem: Differential Apportionment

Jersey Corporation purchased 100 percent of Lime Company on January 1, 20X7, for $203,000. The trial balances for the two companies on December 31, 20X7, included the following amounts:

Item	Jersey Corporation Debit	Jersey Corporation Credit	Lime Company Debit	Lime Company Credit
Cash	$ 82,000		$ 25,000	
Accounts Receivable	50,000		55,000	
Inventory	170,000		100,000	
Land	80,000		20,000	
Buildings and Equipment	500,000		150,000	
Investment in Lime Company Stock	240,000			
Cost of Goods Sold	500,000		250,000	
Depreciation Expense	25,000		15,000	
Other Expenses	75,000		75,000	
Dividends Declared	50,000		20,000	
Accumulated Depreciation		$ 155,000		$ 75,000
Accounts Payable		70,000		35,000
Mortgages Payable		200,000		50,000
Common Stock		300,000		50,000
Retained Earnings		290,000		100,000
Sales		700,000		400,000
Income from Subsidiary		57,000		
	$1,772,000	$1,772,000	$710,000	$710,000

Additional Information

1. On January 1, 20X7, Lime reported net assets with a book value of $150,000. A total of $20,000 of the purchase price is applied to goodwill, which was not impaired in 20X7.
2. Lime's depreciable assets had an estimated economic life of 11 years on the date of combination. The difference between fair value and book value of tangible assets is related entirely to buildings and equipment.
3. Jersey used the equity method in accounting for its investment in Lime.
4. Detailed analysis of receivables and payables showed that Lime owed Jersey $16,000 on December 31, 20X7.

Required

a. Give all journal entries recorded by Jersey with regard to its investment in Lime during 20X7.

b. Give all eliminating entries needed to prepare a full set of consolidated financial statements for 20X7.

c. Prepare a three-part consolidation workpaper as of December 31, 20X7.

P4-32A **Push-Down Accounting**

On December 31, 20X6, Greenly Corporation and Lindy Company entered into a business combination in which Greenly acquired all of Lindy's common stock for $935,000. At the date of combination, Lindy had common stock outstanding with a par value of $100,000, additional paid-in capital of $400,000, and retained earnings of $175,000. The fair values and book values of all Lindy's assets and liabilities were equal at the date of combination, except for the following:

	Book Value	Fair Value
Inventory	$ 50,000	$ 55,000
Land	75,000	160,000
Buildings	400,000	500,000
Equipment	500,000	570,000

The buildings had a remaining life of 20 years, and the equipment was expected to last another 10 years. In accounting for the business combination, Greenly decided to use push-down accounting on Lindy's books.

During 20X7, Lindy earned net income of $88,000 and paid a dividend of $50,000. All of the inventory on hand at the end of 20X6 was sold during 20X7. During 20X8, Lindy earned net income of $90,000 and paid a dividend of $50,000.

Required

a. Record the purchase of Lindy's stock on Greenly's books on December 31, 20X6.

b. Record any entries that would be made on December 31, 20X6, on Lindy's books related to the business combination if push-down accounting is employed.

c. Present all eliminating entries that would appear in the workpaper to prepare a consolidated balance sheet immediately after the combination.

d. Present all entries that Greenly would record during 20X7 related to its investment in Lindy if Greenly uses the equity method of accounting for its investment.

e. Present all eliminating entries that would appear in the workpaper to prepare a full set of consolidated financial statements for the year 20X7.

f. Present all eliminating entries that would appear in the workpaper to prepare a full set of consolidated financial statements for the year 20X8.

Kaplan CPA Review

KAPLAN

CPA EDUCATION

Kaplan CPA Review Simulation on Comprehensive Consolidation Procedures

Access to the online CPA Simulation can be attained by visiting the text's Website: www.mhhe.com/baker7e

Situation

On January 1, Year One, Big Corporation purchases for $700,000 in cash all of the outstanding voting stock of Little Corporation. It was the first such purchase for either company. On the day prior to the transaction, Big and Little reported assets of $2 million and $800,000, liabilities of $900,000 and $330,000, contributed capital of $300,000 and $100,000, and retained earnings of $800,000 and $370,000, respectively. Unless otherwise stated, assume Little Corporation holds a building with a book value of $200,000 but a fair value of $300,000. The building has a 10-year remaining life. All of Little's other assets and liabilities are fairly valued in its financial records.

Topics Covered in the Simulation

a. Computation of consolidated assets.

b. Goodwill measurement.

c. Computation of consolidated expenses.

d. Allocation of purchase differentials.

e. Equity-method reporting.

f. Valuation of other intangibles.

g. Determining when control exists.

h. Testing for goodwill impairment.

Chapter **Five**

Consolidation of Less-than-Wholly Owned Subsidiaries

A controlling financial interest in a subsidiary is required for a parent to consolidate that subsidiary. In practice, this means that only majority ownership is required for consolidation, not total ownership. Consolidated financial statements often include one or more subsidiaries that are less than wholly owned by the parent. The stockholders who own the shares of the subsidiary not held by the parent are referred to collectively as the *noncontrolling interest* or *minority interest*.

All of a subsidiary's assets, liabilities, revenues, and expenses are included in consolidated financial statements whether or not that subsidiary is wholly owned. The parent's percentage ownership of a subsidiary does not affect the portion of the subsidiary's financial statement amounts included in the consolidated statements—100 percent must be included. Because of this, whenever a parent company holds less than total ownership of a subsidiary, the claim of the noncontrolling shareholders must be reflected in the consolidated financial statements. The noncontrolling interest's share of subsidiary income is usually deducted at the bottom of the income statement to obtain consolidated net income. The noncontrolling interest's claim on the net assets of the subsidiary is usually shown in the balance sheet between liabilities and stockholders' equity, although it also might be shown at the bottom of the stockholders' equity section.

EFFECT OF A NONCONTROLLING INTEREST

When a subsidiary is less than wholly owned, the general approach to consolidation is the same as discussed in Chapter 4, but the consolidation procedures must be modified slightly to recognize the noncontrolling interest. Also, the computation of consolidated net income and retained earnings must allow for the claim of the noncontrolling interest.

Consolidated Net Income

As in Chapter 4, *consolidated net income* is that portion of the enterprise's total income that accrues to the parent company's stockholders. Consolidated net income is computed by adding the parent's proportionate share of the income of all subsidiaries, adjusted for any differential write-off or goodwill impairment, to the parent's income from its own separate operations (parent's net income less income from the subsidiaries included in net income). When a subsidiary is less than wholly owned, a portion of its income accrues to its noncontrolling shareholders and is excluded from consolidated net income. A subsidiary's income available to common stockholders is divided between the parent and noncontrolling stockholders based on their relative common stock ownership of the subsidiary. For example, if a parent owns 80 percent of a subsidiary's common stock and the subsidiary earns $100,000 of income, $80,000 accrues to the parent and is included in consolidated net income and the remaining $20,000 is allocated to the noncontrolling interest. Note that the noncontrolling shareholders in a particular subsidiary only have a proportionate claim on the income of that subsidiary and not on the income of the parent or any other subsidiary.

Computation of consolidated net income might proceed in either of two ways. An additive approach might be used by adding the parent's share of the subsidiary's net income to the parent's income from its own operations, similar to the computation of the parent's net income using the equity method. An alternative is to use a residual approach, as is used in the consolidation workpaper, by subtracting the noncontrolling interest's share of the subsidiary's net income from the sum of the parent's separate income and the subsidiary's net income. The only difference in the two approaches is in the order of computation, and both provide the same result.

To illustrate the computation of consolidated net income, assume that Push Corporation owns 80 percent of the stock of Shove Company, which was purchased at book value. During 20X1, Shove reports net income of $25,000, while Push reports earnings of $100,000 from its own operations and equity-method investment income of $20,000. Consolidated net income for 20X1 is computed as follows:

Additive Computation:		
Separate operating income of Push		$100,000
Net income of Shove	$ 25,000	
Push's proportionate share	× .80	20,000
Consolidated net income		$120,000
Residual Computation:		
Net income of Push		$120,000
Less: Income from subsidiary		(20,000) $100,000
Net income of Shove		25,000
		$125,000
Less: Income to noncontrolling interest	$ 25,000	
	× .20	(5,000)
Consolidated net income		$120,000

Consolidated Retained Earnings

Consolidated retained earnings is that portion of the consolidated entity's undistributed earnings accruing to the parent's stockholders. It is calculated by adding the parent's share of the subsidiary's cumulative net income since acquisition to the parent's retained earnings from its own operations (excluding any income from the subsidiary included in retained earnings).

As an illustration of the computation of consolidated retained earnings when a noncontrolling interest exists, assume that Push purchases 80 percent of the stock of Shove on January 1, 20X1, and accounts for its investment in Shove using the equity method. Net income and dividends are as follows for Push and Shove during the two years following acquisition:

	Push	Shove
Retained earnings, January 1, 20X1	$400,000	$250,000
Net income, 20X1	120,000	25,000
Dividends, 20X1	(30,000)	(10,000)
Retained earnings December 31, 20X1	$490,000	$265,000
Net income, 20X2	148,000	35,000
Dividends, 20X2	(30,000)	(10,000)
Retained earnings, December 31, 20X2	$608,000	$290,000

Consolidated retained earnings at December 31, 20X2, two years after the date of combination, is computed as follows:

Push's retained earnings, December 31, 20X2	$608,000
Equity accrual from Shove since acquisition ($25,000 + $35,000) × .80	(48,000)
Push's retained earnings from its own operations, December 31, 20X2	$560,000
Push's share of Shove's net income since acquisition $60,000 × .8	48,000
Consolidated retained earnings, December 31, 20X2	$608,000

Several important points can be noted from the example. First, the subsidiary's retained earnings is not combined with that of the parent. Only the parent's share of the subsidiary's cumulative net income since the date of combination is included. Second, consolidated retained earnings is equal to the parent's retained earnings in this example because the parent uses the equity method to account for its investment in the subsidiary. If the parent accounted for the investment using the cost method, the parent's retained earnings and consolidated retained earnings would differ. Finally, the cumulative income from the subsidiary recognized by the parent on its books must be removed from the parent's retained earnings to arrive at retained earnings from the parent's own operations so that all or part (depending on whether the equity or cost method is used) of the same income will not be included twice.

Workpaper Format

The same three-part workpaper described in Chapter 4 can be used when consolidating less-than-wholly owned subsidiaries, with only minor modifications. The workpaper must allow for including the noncontrolling interest's claim on the income and assets of the subsidiaries. The noncontrolling interest's claim on the income of a subsidiary, calculated as the noncontrolling shareholders' proportionate share of the subsidiary's net income, is deducted at the bottom of the workpaper's income statement section to arrive at consolidated net income. The noncontrolling interest's claim on the subsidiary's net assets, computed as the noncontrolling interest's proportionate share of the subsidiary's stockholders' equity, is added at the bottom of the workpaper's credit portion of the balance sheet section. The noncontrolling interest's claims on both income and net assets are entered in the workpaper through eliminating entries and then carried over to the Consolidated column. As discussed in Chapter 4, the amounts in the Consolidated column are used to prepare the consolidated financial statements.

PREPARATION OF CONSOLIDATED BALANCE SHEET IMMEDIATELY FOLLOWING ACQUISITION OF CONTROLLING OWNERSHIP

The consolidation process for a majority-owned subsidiary is the same as for a wholly owned subsidiary except the claims of the noncontrolling or minority interest must be included. The example of Peerless Products Corporation and Special Foods Inc. from Chapter 4 will serve as a basis for illustrating consolidation procedures when less than full ownership of a subsidiary is held. Assume that on January 1, 20X1, Peerless purchases 80 percent of the common stock of Special Foods for $310,000 cash. The ownership situation can be characterized as follows:

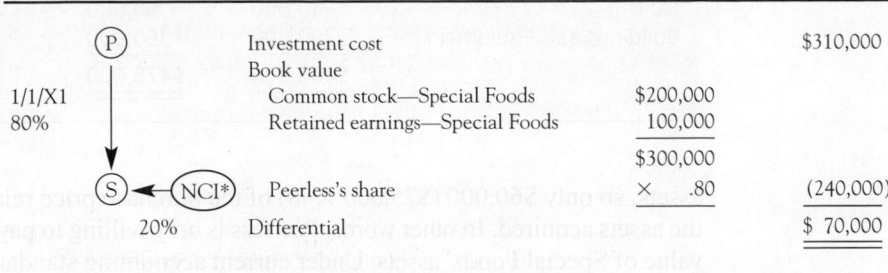

| | Investment cost | | $310,000 |

* Noncontrolling interest

Peerless records the purchase on its books with the following entry:

(1)	Investment in Special Foods Stock	310,000	
	Cash		310,000
	Record purchase of Special Foods stock.		

The balance sheets of Peerless and Special Foods appear immediately after acquisition as in Figure 5–1. The fair values of all of Special Foods' assets and liabilities are equal to their book values except as shown in Figure 5–2.

The total book value of Special Foods' stock is $300,000 (Special Foods' total stockholders' equity). Because Peerless purchases only 80 percent of Special Foods' stock, the book value of the shares purchased is $240,000 ($300,000 × .80). The total purchase price paid by Peerless is $310,000, resulting in a purchase differential of $70,000 for the difference between the purchase price and book value of the shares acquired ($310,000 − $240,000). As can be seen from Figure 5–2, Special Foods' assets have fair values that are $75,000 in excess of their book values. However, Peerless has only an 80 percent claim on Special Foods'

FIGURE 5–1
Balance Sheets of Peerless Products and Special Foods, January 1, 20X1, Immediately after Combination

	Peerless Products	Special Foods
Assets		
Cash	$ 40,000	$ 50,000
Accounts Receivable	75,000	50,000
Inventory	100,000	60,000
Land	175,000	40,000
Buildings and Equipment	800,000	600,000
Accumulated Depreciation	(400,000)	(300,000)
Investment in Special Foods Stock	310,000	
Total Assets	$1,100,000	$500,000
Liabilities and Stockholders' Equity		
Accounts Payable	$ 100,000	$100,000
Bonds Payable	200,000	100,000
Common Stock	500,000	200,000
Retained Earnings	300,000	100,000
Total Liabilities and Equity	$1,100,000	$500,000

FIGURE 5–2
Values of Select Assets of Special Foods

	Book Value	Fair Value	Fair Value Increment	Peerless' 80% Portion
Inventory	$ 60,000	$ 65,000	$ 5,000	$ 4,000
Land	40,000	50,000	10,000	8,000
Buildings and Equipment	300,000	360,000	60,000	48,000
	$400,000	$475,000	$75,000	$60,000

assets, so only $60,000 ($75,000 × .8) of the purchase price relates to the increased value of the assets acquired. In other words, Peerless is only willing to pay for its share of the increased value of Special Foods' assets. Under current accounting standards, only the parent's share of the excess of the fair value of the acquired assets over their book value is recognized.

With $60,000 of the differential allocated to Peerless' identifiable assets, the remaining $10,000 ($70,000 − $60,000) is viewed as being attributable to goodwill. As with the fair value increment related to Special Foods' identifiable assets, only the parent's share of the implied goodwill is recognized. The total differential can be viewed as follows:

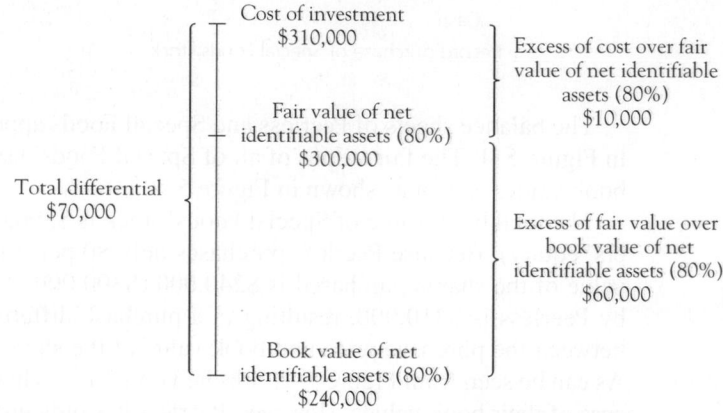

If a consolidated balance sheet is prepared immediately after the combination of Peerless and Special Foods, the consolidation workpaper appears as in Figure 5–3. The following eliminating entries are included in the workpaper:

E(2)	Common Stock—Special Foods	200,000	
	Retained Earnings	100,000	
	Differential	70,000	
	Investment in Special Foods Stock		310,000
	Noncontrolling Interest		60,000
	Eliminate investment balance and establish noncontrolling interest.		
E(3)	Inventory	4,000	
	Land	8,000	
	Buildings and Equipment	48,000	
	Goodwill	10,000	
	Differential		70,000
	Assign differential.		

The first workpaper entry eliminates Peerless' investment account and the stockholders' equity accounts of Special Foods. This entry also establishes the noncontrolling shareholders' claim on the subsidiary's assets in the workpaper. This $60,000 amount is computed as the

FIGURE 5–3 **Workpaper for Consolidated Balance Sheet, January 1, 20X1, Date of Combination; 80 Percent Purchase at More than Book Value**

Item	Peerless Products	Special Foods	Eliminations Debit	Eliminations Credit	Consolidated
Cash	40,000	50,000			90,000
Accounts Receivable	75,000	50,000			125,000
Inventory	100,000	60,000	(3) 4,000		164,000
Land	175,000	40,000	(3) 8,000		223,000
Buildings and Equipment	800,000	600,000	(3) 48,000		1,448,000
Goodwill			(3) 10,000		10,000
Investment in Special Foods Stock	310,000			(2) 310,000	
Differential			(2) 70,000	(3) 70,000	
Total Debits	1,500,000	800,000			2,060,000
Accumulated Depreciation	400,000	300,000			700,000
Accounts Payable	100,000	100,000			200,000
Bonds Payable	200,000	100,000			300,000
Common Stock	500,000	200,000	(2) 200,000		500,000
Retained Earnings	300,000	100,000	(2) 100,000		300,000
Noncontrolling Interest				(2) 60,000	60,000
Total Credits	1,500,000	800,000	440,000	440,000	2,060,000

Elimination entries:
(2) Eliminate investment balance and stockholders' equity of Special Foods; establish noncontrolling interest.
(3) Assign differential.

noncontrolling shareholders' 20 percent proportionate share of Special Foods' $300,000 book value. Note that the amount of the noncontrolling interest is unaffected by the acquisition price paid by Peerless and the existence of a differential.

The $60,000 noncontrolling interest amount is not taken from the books of either the parent or the subsidiary; it enters the workpaper only through eliminating entry E(2). This entry is an example of an eliminating entry that does more than just eliminate balances carried over from the books of the separate companies; it establishes a new item in the workpaper. The noncontrolling interest is placed in the workpaper at the bottom of the credit portion of the workpaper shown in Figure 5–3 and is carried across to the Consolidated column.

Entry E(2) also gives rise to a $70,000 differential in the workpaper because of the excess of the purchase price included in the investment account over Peerless's share of the book value of Special Foods. Entry E(3) allocates that differential to Special Foods' identifiable assets based on the amounts in Figure 5–2. It also assigns the $10,000 remaining amount of the differential to goodwill.

Once the eliminating entries are placed in the workpaper, each row is summed across to get the consolidated totals. Note that the asset amounts included in the Consolidated column, and thus in the consolidated balance sheet, consist of book values for Peerless' assets, plus book values for Special Foods' assets, plus the parent's share of the fair value increments for the subsidiary's assets, plus the parent's share of implied goodwill. When the subsidiary is less than wholly owned, the subsidiary's assets are not reported at their full fair values at the date of combination but at their book values plus the parent's share of the fair value increments.

CONSOLIDATION SUBSEQUENT TO ACQUISITION OF CONTROLLING OWNERSHIP

Consolidation subsequent to acquisition involves the preparation of a complete set of consolidated financial statements, as discussed in Chapter 4. To continue the illustration from the previous section beyond the date of acquisition, assume Peerless Products and Special

FIGURE 5–4
Income and Dividend Information about Peerless Products and Special Foods for the Years 20X1 and 20X2

	Peerless Products	Special Foods
20X1:		
Separate operating income, Peerless	140,000	
Net income, Special Foods		50,000
Dividends	60,000	30,000
20X2:		
Separate operating income, Peerless	160,000	
Net income, Special Foods		75,000
Dividends	60,000	40,000

Foods report the income and dividends shown in Figure 5–4. With respect to the assets to which the $70,000 purchase differential relates, assume that all of the inventory is sold during 20X1, the buildings and equipment have a remaining economic life of 10 years from the date of combination, and straight-line depreciation is used. Further, assume that management determines at the end of 20X1 that the goodwill is impaired and should be written down by $2,500. Finally, assume that Peerless accounts for its investment in Special Foods using the equity method.

Year of Combination

The business combination of Peerless Products and Special Foods occurs at the beginning of 20X1. Accordingly, Peerless recognizes income and dividends from Special Foods for the entire year, and the consolidated statements portray the two companies as if they were one entity for the entire year. The procedures are basically the same as those in Chapter 4 except the parent claims only its share of the subsidiary's income and dividends, and the consolidation procedures must allow for the claims of the noncontrolling shareholders.

Parent Company Entries

During 20X1, Peerless Products makes the normal entry on its books to record its purchase of Special Foods stock. Peerless also makes the usual equity-method entries to record income and dividends from its subsidiary, but, unlike in Chapter 4, Peerless must share Special Foods' income and dividends with the subsidiary's other stockholders. Accordingly, Peerless recognizes only its proportionate share of Special Foods' net income and dividends. Peerless records the following entries during 20X1:

(4)	Investment in Special Foods Stock	310,000	
	Cash		310,000
	Record purchase of Special Foods stock.		
(5)	Cash	24,000	
	Investment in Special Foods Stock		24,000
	Record dividends from Special Foods:		
	$30,000 × .80		
(6)	Investment in Special Foods Stock	40,000	
	Income from Subsidiary		40,000
	Record equity-method income:		
	$50,000 × .80		

In addition, Peerless must write off a portion of the purchase differential with the following entries:

(7)	Income from Subsidiary	4,000	
	Investment in Special Foods Stock		4,000
	Adjust income for differential related to inventory sold.		

(8)	Income from Subsidiary	4,800	
	Investment in Special Foods Stock		4,800
	Amortize differential related to buildings and equipment:		
	$48,000 ÷ 10 years		

Special Foods' inventory to which $4,000 of the differential relates was sold during the year. Therefore, that portion of the differential must be written off by taking it out of the investment account, and the parent's income from the subsidiary must be reduced. Also, the $48,000 additional cost of the investment related to the increased value of Special Foods' buildings and equipment must be amortized at $4,800 per year ($48,000 ÷ 10) over the remaining 10-year life with entry (8).

The $10,000 portion of the differential related to goodwill is not adjusted on the parent's books. Even though the goodwill of the consolidated entity is impaired, current standards dictate against writing down the investment account unless the value of the investment declines significantly and the decline is judged as being other than temporary.

Consolidation Workpaper—Year of Combination

After the subsidiary income accruals are entered on Peerless's books, the adjusted trial balance data of the consolidating companies are entered in the three-part consolidation workpaper as shown in Figure 5–5.

The first three workpaper entries eliminate the subsidiary income and dividends recorded by Peerless, eliminate the investment account and the stockholders' equity accounts of Special Foods, and establish the noncontrolling interest:

E(9)	Income from Subsidiary	31,200	
	Dividends Declared		24,000
	Investment in Special Foods Stock		7,200
	Eliminate income from subsidiary.		
E(10)	Income to Noncontrolling Interest	10,000	
	Dividends Declared		6,000
	Noncontrolling Interest		4,000
	Assign income to noncontrolling interest.		
E(11)	Common Stock—Special Foods	200,000	
	Retained Earnings, January 1	100,000	
	Differential	70,000	
	Investment in Special Foods Stock		310,000
	Noncontrolling Interest		60,000
	Eliminate beginning investment balance.		

Entry E(9) removes the net effect of the income accrual recorded by the parent during 20X1 in entries (6), (7), and (8) and removes the parent's portion of dividends declared by the subsidiary during the period, as recorded in entry (5). Elimination entry E(10) places the noncontrolling interest's share of subsidiary income ($50,000 × .20) in the workpaper, eliminates the noncontrolling interest's share of subsidiary dividends ($30,000 × .20), and recognizes the increase in the noncontrolling interest during 20X1. The $4,000 increase in the claim of the noncontrolling shareholders for the period is included in the balance assigned to the noncontrolling interest in the bottom portion of the balance sheet section of the workpaper. Note that the amount of income assigned to the noncontrolling interest in entry E(10) is based on the net income of Special Foods only and is not affected by any write-off of the differential.

FIGURE 5–5 December 31, 20X1, Equity-Method Workpaper for Consolidated Financial Statements, Year of Combination; 80 Percent Purchase at More than Book Value

Item	Peerless Products	Special Foods	Eliminations Debit		Credit		Consolidated
Sales	400,000	200,000					600,000
Income from Subsidiary	31,200		(9)	31,200			
Credits	431,200	200,000					600,000
Cost of Goods Sold	170,000	115,000	(12)	4,000			289,000
Depreciation and Amortization	50,000	20,000	(13)	4,800			74,800
Goodwill Impairment Loss			(14)	2,500			2,500
Other Expenses	40,000	15,000					55,000
Debits	(260,000)	(150,000)					(421,300)
							178,700
Income to Noncontrolling Interest			(10)	10,000			(10,000)
Net Income, carry forward	171,200	50,000		52,500			168,700
Retained Earnings, January 1	300,000	100,000	(11)	100,000			300,000
Net Income, from above	171,200	50,000		52,500			168,700
	471,200	150,000					468,700
Dividends Declared	(60,000)	(30,000)			(9)	24,000	
					(10)	6,000	(60,000)
Retained Earnings, December 31, carry forward	411,200	120,000		152,500		30,000	408,700
Cash	194,000	75,000					269,000
Accounts Receivable	75,000	50,000					125,000
Inventory	100,000	75,000					175,000
Land	175,000	40,000	(12)	8,000			223,000
Buildings and Equipment	800,000	600,000	(12)	48,000			1,448,000
Investment in Special Foods Stock	317,200				(9)	7,200	
					(11)	310,000	
Goodwill			(12)	10,000	(14)	2,500	7,500
Differential			(11)	70,000	(12)	70,000	
Debits	1,661,200	840,000					2,247,500
Accumulated Depreciation	450,000	320,000			(13)	4,800	774,800
Accounts Payable	100,000	100,000					200,000
Bonds Payable	200,000	100,000					300,000
Common Stock	500,000	200,000	(11)	200,000			500,000
Retained Earnings, from above	411,200	120,000		152,500		30,000	408,700
Noncontrolling Interest					(10)	4,000	
					(11)	60,000	64,000
Credits	1,661,200	840,000		488,500		488,500	2,247,500

Elimination entries:
(9) Eliminate income from subsidiary.
(10) Assign income to noncontrolling interest.
(11) Eliminate beginning investment balance.
(12) Assign beginning differential.
(13) Amortize differential related to buildings and equipment.
(14) Write down goodwill for impairment.

The third elimination entry, E(11), removes the stockholders' equity balances of the subsidiary and the investment account of the parent as of the beginning of the period and establishes the amount of the noncontrolling shareholders' claim as of the beginning of the period. Because the purchase price of the investment exceeded its book value, a purchase differential appears as the balancing figure in this entry. The differential established in this entry represents the unamortized amount as of the beginning of the period. Because the combination occurred on the first day of 20X1, the amount equals the differential on the date of combination, $70,000. As in Chapter 4, the differential account serves as a clearing account in the workpaper and is entered in the balance sheet portion of the workpaper at the bottom of the asset section.

Noncontrolling interest is credited for $60,000 ($300,000 × .20) in entry E(11), representing 20 percent of Special Foods' stockholders' equity at the beginning of the year. The noncontrolling interest totals $64,000 at the end of the period as a result of elimination entries E(10) and E(11). The amount assigned to the noncontrolling interest is based on the underlying book value of the subsidiary's net assets and is not affected by the amount the parent paid in purchasing the subsidiary's stock.

Three additional eliminating entries are needed in the workpaper in Figure 5–5 to allocate and write down the differential:

E(12)	Cost of Goods Sold	4,000	
	Land	8,000	
	Buildings and Equipment	48,000	
	Goodwill	10,000	
	Differential		70,000
	Assign beginning differential.		
E(13)	Depreciation Expense	4,800	
	Accumulated Depreciation		4,800
	Amortize differential related to buildings and equipment:		
	$48,000 ÷ 10 years		
E(14)	Goodwill Impairment Loss	2,500	
	Goodwill		2,500
	Write down goodwill for impairment.		

Entry E(12) assigns the original amount of the differential to the appropriate asset and expense accounts based on the fair value differences shown in Figure 5–2.

Because all inventory on hand on the date of combination has been sold during the year, the $4,000 of differential applicable to inventory is allocated directly to cost of goods sold. The cost of the inventory to the consolidated entity is viewed as being $4,000 higher than the cost to the subsidiary, and this additional cost must be included in consolidated cost of goods sold.

The differential assigned to depreciable assets in entry E(12) must be charged to depreciation expense over the remaining lives of those assets. From a consolidated viewpoint, the parent's additional payment is part of the total cost of the depreciable assets. Depreciation already is recorded on the subsidiary's books based on the original cost of the assets to the subsidiary, and these amounts are carried to the consolidation workpaper as depreciation expense. Depreciation on the additional cost of those assets to the consolidated entity is entered in the consolidation workpaper through entry E(13).

The difference between the $310,000 total purchase price paid by Peerless and the $300,000 fair value of Peerless's share of the net identifiable assets acquired is assumed to be payment for the excess earning power of Special Foods. This difference is entered in the workpaper with entry E(12) as goodwill of $10,000. The impairment in the value of the goodwill during 20X1 is recognized with eliminating entry E(14). Although goodwill is not amortized, it must be written down when its value is impaired. This entry reduces the amount of goodwill to be reported in the consolidated balance sheet and establishes a loss to be reported in the consolidated income statement.

FIGURE 5–6
Consolidated Net Income and Retained Earnings, 20X1; 80 Percent Purchase at More than Book Value

Consolidated net income, 20X1:	
Peerless's separate operating income	$140,000
Peerless's share of Special Foods' net income: $50,000 × .80	40,000
Write-off of differential related to inventory sold during 20X1	(4,000)
Amortization of differential related to buildings and equipment in 20X1	(4,800)
Goodwill impairment loss	(2,500)
Consolidated net income, 20X1	$168,700
Consolidated retained earnings, December 31, 20X1:	
Peerless's retained earnings on date of combination, January 1, 20X1	$300,000
Peerless's separate operating income, 20X1	140,000
Peerless's share of Special Foods' 20X1 net income: $50,000 × .80	40,000
Write-off of differential related to inventory sold during 20X1	(4,000)
Amortization of differential related to buildings and equipment in 20X1	(4,800)
Goodwill impairment loss	(2,500)
Dividends declared by Peerless, 20X1	(60,000)
Consolidated retained earnings, December 31, 20X1	$408,700

The distinction between journal entries recorded on the parent's books under the equity method and the eliminating entries in the consolidation workpaper is important. Even though Peerless amortizes the differential related to Special Foods' buildings and equipment on its books with entry (8), eliminating entry E(13) is still needed in the workpaper to record depreciation expense. All effects of Peerless's subsidiary income accrual, including the effects of entry (8), are eliminated in the workpaper by entry E(9). Consequently, eliminating entry E(13) is required for consolidated net income to reflect the amortization of the additional cost of Special Foods' buildings and equipment to the consolidated entity.

Once the appropriate eliminating entries are placed in the consolidation workpaper in Figure 5–5, the workpaper is completed by summing each row across, taking into consideration the debit or credit effect of the eliminations.

Consolidated Net Income and Retained Earnings

As can be seen from the workpaper in Figure 5–5, consolidated net income for 20X1 is $168,700 and consolidated retained earnings on December 31, 20X1, is $408,700. These amounts can be computed as shown in Figure 5–6. Note that both consolidated net income and retained earnings are reduced by the write-off of the purchase differential and the impairment of goodwill. Because the goodwill impairment is recognized in consolidated net income but not in the parent's equity-method income, consolidated net income and retained earnings are less than those of the parent.

Second Year of Ownership

The equity-method and consolidation procedures employed during the second and subsequent years of ownership are the same as in the first year and are illustrated by continuing the Peerless Products and Special Foods example through 20X2. No further impairment of the goodwill arising from the business combination occurs in 20X2.

Parent Company Entries

Peerless Products records the following entries on its separate books during 20X2:

(15)	Cash	32,000	
	Investment in Special Foods Stock		32,000
	Record dividends from Special Foods:		
	$40,000 × .80		

(16)	Investment in Special Foods Stock	60,000	
	Income from Subsidiary		60,000
	Record equity-method income:		
	$75,000 × .80		

(17)	Income from Subsidiary	4,800	
	Investment in Special Foods Stock		4,800
	Amortize differential related to buildings and equipment.		

The changes in the parent's investment account for 20X1 and 20X2 can be summarized as follows:

		20X1		20X2
Balance at start of year		$310,000		$317,200
Income from subsidiary:				
Parent's share of subsidiary's income	$40,000		$60,000	
Differential write-off for inventory sold	(4,000)			
Amortization of differential	(4,800)		(4,800)	
		31,200		55,200
Less: Dividends received from subsidiary		(24,000)		(32,000)
Balance at end of year		$317,200		$340,400

Consolidation Workpaper—Second Year Following Combination

The workpaper to prepare a complete set of consolidated financial statements for the year 20X2 is illustrated in Figure 5–7. Eliminating entries at the end of 20X2 are similar to those at the end of 20X1.

The first workpaper entry, eliminates Peerless's income from Special Foods and Peerless's share of Special Foods' dividends for 20X2:

E(18)	Income from Subsidiary	55,200	
	Dividends Declared		32,000
	Investment in Special Foods Stock		23,200
	Eliminate income from subsidiary.		

The net credit to the investment account of $23,200 represents the increase in the account balance during the period and takes the account balance back to the amount on January 1, 20X2, the beginning of the second year.

The amount of subsidiary income assigned to the noncontrolling shareholders in 20X2 is $15,000 ($75,000 × .20), and this amount enters the workpaper through entry E(19):

E(19)	Income to Noncontrolling Interest	15,000	
	Dividends Declared		8,000
	Noncontrolling Interest		7,000
	Assign income to noncontrolling interest.		

The $15,000 of subsidiary income assigned to the noncontrolling interest is subtracted to arrive at consolidated net income in the income statement portion of the workpaper. Entry E(19) also includes a credit to Dividends Declared to eliminate the noncontrolling interest's

FIGURE 5–7 December 31, 20X2, Equity-Method Workpaper for Consolidated Financial Statements, Second Year Following Combination; 80 Percent Purchase at More than Book Value

Item	Peerless Products	Special Foods	Eliminations Debit		Eliminations Credit		Consolidated
Sales	450,000	300,000					750,000
Income from Subsidiary	55,200		(18)	55,200			
Credits	505,200	300,000					750,000
Cost of Goods Sold	180,000	160,000					340,000
Depreciation and Amortization	50,000	20,000	(22)	4,800			74,800
Other Expenses	60,000	45,000					105,000
Debits	(290,000)	(225,000)					(519,800)
							230,200
Income to Noncontrolling Interest			(19)	15,000			(15,000)
Net Income, carry forward	215,200	75,000		75,000			215,200
Retained Earnings, January 1	411,200	120,000	(20)	120,000			
			(23)	2,500			408,700
Net Income, from above	215,200	75,000		75,000			215,200
	626,400	195,000					623,900
Dividends Declared	(60,000)	(40,000)			(18)	32,000	
					(19)	8,000	(60,000)
Retained Earnings, December 31, carry forward	566,400	155,000		197,500		40,000	563,900
Cash	221,000	85,000					306,000
Accounts Receivable	150,000	80,000					230,000
Inventory	180,000	90,000					270,000
Land	175,000	40,000	(21)	8,000			223,000
Buildings and Equipment	800,000	600,000	(21)	48,000			1,448,000
Investment in Special Foods Stock	340,400				(18)	23,200	
					(20)	317,200	
Goodwill			(21)	10,000	(23)	2,500	7,500
Differential			(20)	61,200	(21)	61,200	
Debits	1,866,400	895,000					2,484,500
Accumulated Depreciation	500,000	340,000			(21)	4,800	
					(22)	4,800	849,600
Accounts Payable	100,000	100,000					200,000
Bonds Payable	200,000	100,000					300,000
Common Stock	500,000	200,000	(20)	200,000			500,000
Retained Earnings, from above	566,400	155,000		197,500		40,000	563,900
Noncontrolling Interest					(19)	7,000	
					(20)	64,000	71,000
Credits	1,866,400	895,000		524,700		524,700	2,484,500

Elimination entries:
(18) Eliminate income from subsidiary.
(19) Assign income to noncontrolling interest.
(20) Eliminate beginning investment balance.
(21) Assign beginning differential.
(22) Amortize differential related to buildings and equipment.
(23) Adjust for 20X1 impairment of goodwill.

portion of Special Foods' dividends. Entries E(18) and E(19) together totally eliminate the dividends of Special Foods. The $7,000 difference between the noncontrolling stockholders' share of subsidiary income and dividends represents the increase in the noncontrolling interest for 20X2 and is placed in the balance sheet portion of the workpaper.

Entry E(20) eliminates the balances in Peerless's investment account and Special Foods' stockholders' equity accounts as of the beginning of the period:

E(20)	Common Stock—Special Foods	200,000	
	Retained Earnings, January 1	120,000	
	Differential	61,200	
	Investment in Special Foods Stock		317,200
	Noncontrolling Interest		64,000
	Eliminate beginning investment balance.		

Together, entries E(18) and E(20) fully eliminate the ending balance in the parent's investment account. The noncontrolling interest is credited for its proportionate share of the subsidiary's book value at the beginning of the period ($320,000 × .20). This amount is added to the 20X2 increase in noncontrolling interest established in entry E(19), and the total is reported in the consolidated balance sheet.

Entry E(20) also establishes in the workpaper the purchase differential as of the beginning of 20X2. The differential at the beginning of 20X1, the date of combination, was $70,000, but it was reduced in 20X1 by amounts written off: $4,000 for inventory sold and $4,800 of amortization related to Special Foods' buildings and equipment. The remaining balance of the differential at the beginning of 20X2 is $61,200 ($70,000 − $4,000 − $4,800). Entry E(21) assigns the January 1, 20X2, differential:

E(21)	Land	8,000	
	Buildings and Equipment	48,000	
	Goodwill	10,000	
	Differential		61,200
	Accumulated Depreciation		4,800
	Assign beginning differential.		

Keep in mind that each year's workpaper is prepared from the trial balance data reported by the separate companies, not from the previous year's workpaper. The $4,800 of accumulated depreciation entered in the consolidation workpaper at the end of 20X1 does not automatically carry over to the 20X2 workpaper. Therefore, the workpaper entry to allocate the differential each time also must establish the additional accumulated depreciation for all prior years on any differential amounts assigned to depreciable assets.

The 20X2 depreciation of the portion of the differential assigned to buildings and equipment is given in entry E(22):

E(22)	Depreciation Expense	4,800	
	Accumulated Depreciation		4,800
	Amortize differential related to buildings and equipment:		
	$48,000 ÷ 10 years		

Entry E(23) corrects the beginning consolidated retained earnings and the goodwill balance for the impairment loss recognized in the 20X1 consolidated income statement:

E(23)	Retained Earnings, January 1	2,500	
	Goodwill		2,500
	Adjust for 20X1 impairment of goodwill.		

FIGURE 5–8
Consolidated Net Income and Retained Earnings, 20X2; 80 Percent Purchase at More than Book Value

Consolidated net income, 20X2:	
Peerless's separate operating income	$160,000
Peerless's share of Special Foods' net income: $75,000 × .80	60,000
Amortization of differential related to buildings and equipment in 20X2	(4,800)
Consolidated net income, 20X2	$215,200
Consolidated retained earnings, December 31, 20X2:	
Consolidated retained earnings, December 31, 20X1	$408,700
Peerless's separate operating income, 20X2	160,000
Peerless's share of Special Foods' 20X2 net income: $75,000 × .80	60,000
Amortization of differential related to buildings and equipment in 20X2	(4,800)
Dividends declared by Peerless, 20X2	(60,000)
Consolidated retained earnings, December 31, 20X2	$563,900

Because the purchase differential on Peerless's books is not written down under the equity method to reflect the 20X1 impairment of goodwill, the differential established in the 20X2 workpaper through entry E(20) includes the full $10,000 differential originally representing goodwill. Also, because the impairment loss did not affect Peerless's equity-method net income, and Peerless's retained earnings becomes consolidated retained earnings, beginning consolidated retained earnings will be overstated unless it is reduced by the amount of the prior period's impairment loss. Thus, both beginning consolidated retained earnings and goodwill must be reduced each period in the consolidation workpaper for the 20X1 impairment.

Consolidated Net Income and Retained Earnings

The computation of 20X2 consolidated net income and consolidated retained earnings at the end of 20X2 is shown in Figure 5–8.

Consolidated Financial Statements

A consolidated income statement and retained earnings statement for the year 20X2 and a consolidated balance sheet as of December 31, 20X2, are presented in Figure 5–9.

DISCONTINUANCE OF CONSOLIDATION

A previously consolidated subsidiary is excluded from consolidation if it no longer meets the criteria for consolidation, usually because the parent can no longer exercise control over the subsidiary (e.g., the subsidiary is in bankruptcy). In such cases, the subsidiary also does not qualify for reporting using the equity method, and the parent must report its investment in the subsidiary under the cost method. When an accounting change of this sort occurs, the financial statements subsequent to the change are viewed as the statements of a different entity. **FASB Statement No. 154**, "Accounting Changes and Error Corrections," requires that the change in reporting entity be applied retrospectively to reflect the new entity. Thus, the financial statements of periods prior to the change presented for comparative purposes are restated to exclude the subsidiary from consolidation and include the parent's investment reported under the cost method. In addition, the financial statements for the period of change must disclose the nature of the change, the reason for it, and the effects on income, other comprehensive income, and related per share amounts for all periods presented.

TREATMENT OF OTHER COMPREHENSIVE INCOME

FASB Statement No. 130, "Reporting Comprehensive Income" (FASB 130), established a new category for financial reporting, *other comprehensive income*, which includes all revenues, expenses, gains, and losses that under generally accepted accounting principles are

FIGURE 5–9   **Consolidated Financial Statements for Peerless Products Corporation and Special Foods Inc., 20X2**

PEERLESS PRODUCTS CORPORATION AND SUBSIDIARY
Consolidated Income Statement
For the Year Ended December 31, 20X2

Sales		$ 750,000
Cost of Goods Sold		(340,000)
Gross Margin		$ 410,000
Expenses:		
Depreciation and Amortization	$ 74,800	
Other Expenses	105,000	
Total Expenses		(179,800)
		$ 230,200
Income to Noncontrolling Interest		(15,000)
Consolidated Net Income		$ 215,200

PEERLESS PRODUCTS CORPORATION AND SUBSIDIARY
Consolidated Retained Earnings Statement
For the Year Ended December 31, 20X2

Consolidated Retained Earnings, January 1, 20X2	$408,700
Consolidated Net Income, 20X2	215,200
Dividends Declared, 20X2	(60,000)
Consolidated Retained Earnings, December 31, 20X2	$563,900

PEERLESS PRODUCTS CORPORATION AND SUBSIDIARY
Consolidated Balance Sheet
December 31, 20X2

Assets			Liabilities		
Cash		$ 306,000	Accounts Payable	$200,000	
Accounts Receivable		230,000	Bonds Payable	300,000	
Inventory		270,000			$ 500,000
Land		223,000	Noncontrolling Interest		71,000
Buildings and Equipment	$1,448,000		Stockholders' Equity		
Accumulated Depreciation	(849,600)		Common Stock	$500,000	
		598,400	Retained Earnings	563,900	
Goodwill		7,500			1,063,900
Total		$1,634,900	Total		$1,634,900

excluded from net income.[1] Comprehensive income is the sum of net income and other comprehensive income. **FASB 130** permits several different options for reporting comprehensive income, but the consolidation process is the same regardless of the reporting format.

Other comprehensive income accounts are temporary accounts that are closed at the end of each period. Instead of being closed to Retained Earnings as revenue and expense accounts are, other comprehensive income accounts are closed to a special stockholders' equity account, Accumulated Other Comprehensive Income.

Modification of the Consolidation Workpaper

When a parent or subsidiary has recorded other comprehensive income, the consolidation workpaper normally includes an additional section for other comprehensive income. This section of the workpaper facilitates computation of the amount of other comprehensive income to be reported, the portion, if any, of other comprehensive income to be assigned to the noncontrolling interest, and the amount of accumulated other comprehensive income to be

[1] Other comprehensive income elements include foreign currency translation adjustments, unrealized gains and losses on certain derivatives and investments in certain types of securities, and certain minimum pension liability adjustments.

reported in the consolidated balance sheet. Although this extra section of the workpaper for comprehensive income could be placed after the income statement section of the standard workpaper, the format used here is to place it at the bottom of the workpaper. If neither the parent nor any subsidiary reports other comprehensive income, the section can be omitted from the workpaper. When other comprehensive income is reported, the workpaper is prepared in the normal manner, with the additional section added to the bottom. The only modification within the standard workpaper is an additional stockholders' equity account included in the balance sheet portion of the workpaper for the cumulative effects of the other comprehensive income.

To illustrate the consolidation process when a subsidiary reports other comprehensive income, assume that during 20X2 Special Foods purchases $20,000 of investments classified as available-for-sale. By December 31, 20X2, the fair value of the securities increases to $30,000. Other than the effects of accounting for Special Foods' investment in securities, the financial statement information reported by Peerless Products and Special Foods at December 31, 20X2, is identical to that presented in Figure 5–7.

Adjusting Entry Recorded by Subsidiary

At December 31, 20X2, Special Foods recognizes the increase in the fair value of its available-for-sale securities by recording the following adjusting entry:

(24)	Investment in Available-for-Sale Securities	10,000	
	Unrealized Gain on Investments (OCI)		10,000
	Record increase in fair value of available-for-sale securities.		

The unrealized gain is not included in the subsidiary's net income but is reported by the subsidiary as an element of other comprehensive income (OCI).

Adjusting Entry Recorded by Parent Company

In 20X2, Peerless records all its normal entries [(15) through (17)] relating to its investment in Special Foods as if the subsidiary had not reported other comprehensive income. In addition, at December 31, 20X2, Peerless products separately recognizes its proportionate share of the subsidiary's unrealized gain from the increase in the value of the available-for-sale securities:

(17a)	Investment in Special Foods Stock	8,000	
	Other Comprehensive Income from Subsidiary—Unrealized		
	Gain on Investments (OCI)		8,000
	Record Peerless's proportionate share of the increase in value of available-for-sale securities held by subsidiary.		

Consolidation Workpaper—Second Year following Combination

The workpaper to prepare a complete set of consolidated financial statements for the year 20X2 is illustrated in Figure 5–10. In the workpaper, Peerless's balance in the Investment in Special Foods Stock account is greater than the balance in Figure 5–7 because of entry (17a), and Peerless's $8,000 proportionate share of Special Foods' unrealized gain is included in the separate section of the workpaper for comprehensive income (Other Comprehensive Income from Subsidiary—Unrealized Gain on Investments). Special Foods' trial balance has been changed to reflect (1) the reduction in the cash balance resulting from the investment acquisition, (2) the investment in available-for-sale securities, and (3) an unrealized gain of $10,000 on the investment.

Consolidation Procedures

Eliminating entries E(18) through E(23) were used in preparing the consolidation workpaper for 20X2 presented in Figure 5–7. When other comprehensive income is introduced, the

FIGURE 5–10 **December 31, 20X2, Comprehensive Income Illustration, Second Year Following Combination; 80 Percent Purchase at More than Book Value**

Item	Peerless Products	Special Foods	Eliminations Debit	Eliminations Credit	Consolidated
Sales	450,000	300,000			750,000
Income from Subsidiary	55,200		(18) 55,200		
Credits	505,200	300,000			750,000
Cost of Goods Sold	180,000	160,000			340,000
Depreciation and Amortization	50,000	20,000	(22) 4,800		74,800
Other Expenses	60,000	45,000			105,000
Debits	(290,000)	(225,000)			(519,800)
					230,200
Income to Noncontrolling Interest			(19) 15,000		(15,000)
Net Income, carry forward	215,200	75,000	75,000		215,200
Retained Earnings, January 1	411,200	120,000	(20) 120,000		
			(23) 2,500		408,700
Net Income, from above	215,200	75,000	75,000		215,200
	626,400	195,000			623,900
Dividends Declared	(60,000)	(40,000)		(18) 32,000	
				(19) 8,000	(60,000)
Retained Earnings, December 31, carry forward	566,400	155,000	197,500	40,000	563,900
Cash	221,000	65,000			286,000
Accounts Receivable	150,000	80,000			230,000
Inventory	180,000	90,000			270,000
Land	175,000	40,000	(21) 8,000		223,000
Buildings and Equipment	800,000	600,000	(21) 48,000		1,448,000
Investment in AFS Securities		30,000			30,000
Investment in Special Foods Stock	348,400			(18) 23,200	
				(20) 317,200	
				(25) 8,000	
Goodwill			(21) 10,000	(23) 2,500	7,500
Differential			(20) 61,200	(21) 61,200	
Debits	1,874,400	905,000			2,494,500
Accumulated Depreciation	500,000	340,000		(21) 4,800	
				(22) 4,800	849,600
Accounts Payable	100,000	100,000			200,000
Bonds Payable	200,000	100,000			300,000
Common Stock	500,000	200,000	(20) 200,000		500,000
Retained Earnings, from above	566,400	155,000	197,500	40,000	563,900
Accumulated Other Comprehensive Income, from below	8,000	10,000	10,000		8,000
Noncontrolling Interest				(19) 7,000	
				(20) 64,000	
				(26) 2,000	73,000
Credits	1,874,400	905,000	534,700	534,700	2,494,500
Other Comprehensive Income:					
OCI from Subsidiary—Unrealized Gain on Investments	8,000		(25) 8,000		
Unrealized Gain on Investments		10,000			10,000
Other Comprehensive Income to Noncontrolling Interest			(26) 2,000		(2,000)
Accumulated Other Comprehensive Income, January 1					
Accumulated Other Comprehensive Income, December 31, carry up	8,000	10,000	10,000		8,000

Elimination entries:
(18) Eliminate income from subsidiary.
(19) Assign income to noncontrolling interest.
(20) Eliminate beginning investment balance.
(21) Assign beginning differential.
(22) Amortize differential related to buildings and equipment.
(23) Adjust for 20X1 impairment of goodwill.
(25) Eliminate other comprehensive income from subsidiary.
(26) Assign other comprehensive income to noncontrolling interest.

parent's income from its subsidiary is eliminated in the normal manner with entry E(18), and a proportionate share of the subsidiary's income is allocated to the noncontrolling interest with entry E(19); both of these entries are as shown in Figure 5–7. Entry E(20) in Figure 5–7 eliminates the beginning balances of the investment account and the beginning stockholders' equity balances of the subsidiary. Although this entry remains unchanged in this example, it would have included the elimination of the beginning balance of the subsidiary's accumulated Other Comprehensive Income if the subsidiary had had a balance as of the beginning of the period because that account is properly included in the subsidiary's stockholders' equity; further, a portion of the balance of that account would have been allocated to the beginning noncontrolling interest, as with the other stockholders' equity accounts of the subsidiary.

Eliminating entries E(21) through E(23) dealing with the differential also are unchanged from Figure 5–7. However, two additional entries are needed for the treatment of the subsidiary's other comprehensive income. First, the proportionate share of the subsidiary's other comprehensive income recorded by the parent with entry (17a) must be eliminated to avoid double counting the subsidiary's other comprehensive income. Thus, entry (17a) is reversed in the workpaper:

E(25)	Other Comprehensive Income from Subsidiary—Unrealized		
	Gain on Investments (OCI)	8,000	
	Investment in Special Foods Stock		8,000
	Eliminate other comprehensive income from subsidiary.		

Second, a proportionate share of the subsidiary's other comprehensive income must be allocated to the noncontrolling interest, just as is done with the subsidiary's net income:

E(26)	Other Comprehensive Income to Noncontrolling Interest	2,000	
	Noncontrolling Interest		2,000
	Assign other comprehensive income to noncontrolling interest.		

Thus, the amount of other comprehensive income reported in the consolidated financial statements equals the parent's 80 percent share of the subsidiary's $10,000 of other comprehensive income; the remaining $2,000 is included in the noncontrolling interest.

While consolidated net income is the same in Figure 5–10 as in Figure 5–7, the other comprehensive income section of the workpaper in Figure 5–10 gives explicit recognition to the unrealized gain on available-for-sale securities held by Special Foods. This permits recognition in the consolidated financial statements under any of the alternative formats permitted by the FASB. Consolidated financial statements are presented in Figure 5–11.

Consolidation Workpaper—Comprehensive Income in Subsequent Years

Each year following 20X2, Special Foods will adjust the unrealized gain on investments on its books for the change in fair value of the available-for-sale securities. For example, if Special Foods' investment increased in value by an additional $5,000 during 20X3, Special Foods would increase by $5,000 the carrying amount of its investment in securities and recognize as an element of 20X3's other comprehensive income an unrealized gain of $5,000. Under equity-method recording, Peerless would increase its Investment in Special Foods Stock account and record its $4,000 share of the subsidiary's other comprehensive income.

The eliminating entries required to prepare the consolidation workpaper at December 31, 20X3, would include the normal eliminating entries corresponding to E(18), E(19), and E(21) through E(23). In addition, the normal investment elimination entry corresponding to E(20) would be expanded to eliminate the subsidiary's $10,000 beginning Accumulated Other Comprehensive Income balance and to increase the noncontrolling interest by its proportionate share of the subsidiary's beginning Accumulated Other Comprehensive Income

FIGURE 5–11
Consolidated
Financial
Statements for
Peerless Products
Corporation
and Special
Foods Inc., 20X2,
Including Other
Comprehensive
Income

PEERLESS PRODUCTS CORPORATION AND SUBSIDIARY
Consolidated Statement of Income
For the Year Ended December 31, 20X2

Sales		$750,000
Cost of Goods Sold		(340,000)
Gross Margin		$410,000
Expenses:		
Depreciation and Amortization	$ 74,800	
Other Expenses	105,000	
Total Expenses		(179,800)
		$230,200
Income to Noncontrolling Interest		(15,000)
Consolidated Net Income		$215,200

PEERLESS PRODUCTS CORPORATION AND SUBSIDIARY
Consolidated Statement of Comprehensive Income
For the Year Ended December 31, 20X2

Consolidated Net Income		$215,200
Other Comprehensive Income:		
Unrealized Gain on Investments Held by Subsidiary	$10,000	
Other Comprehensive Income to Noncontrolling Interest	(2,000)	
Other Comprehensive Income to Controlling Interest		8,000
Consolidated Comprehensive Income		$223,200

PEERLESS PRODUCTS CORPORATION AND SUBSIDIARY
Consolidated Statement of Financial Position
December 31, 20X2

Assets		
Cash		$ 286,000
Accounts Receivable		230,000
Inventory		270,000
Investment in Available-for-Sale Securities		30,000
Land		223,000
Buildings and Equipment	$1,448,000	
Accumulated Depreciation	(849,600)	
		598,400
Goodwill		7,500
Total Assets		$1,644,900
Liabilities		
Accounts Payable	$ 200,000	
Bonds Payable	300,000	
Total Liabilities		$ 500,000
Noncontrolling Interest		73,000
Stockholders' Equity		
Common Stock	$ 500,000	
Retained Earnings	563,900	
Accumulated Other Comprehensive Income	8,000	
Total Stockholders' Equity		1,071,900
Total Liabilities and Stockholders' Equity		$1,644,900

amount ($10,000 × .20). Two additional eliminating entries corresponding to E(25) and E(26) also would be needed:

E(25a)	Other Comprehensive Income from Subsidiary—Unrealized		
	Gain on Investments (OCI)	4,000	
	Investment in Special Foods Stock		4,000
	Eliminate other comprehensive income from subsidiary.		
E(26a)	Other Comprehensive Income to Noncontrolling Interest	1,000	
	Noncontrolling Interest		1,000
	Assign other comprehensive income to noncontrolling interest.		

ADDITIONAL CONSIDERATIONS

Now that the basic consolidation procedures have been discussed, several additional items must be considered to provide completeness and clarity. The discussion in this section relates to the treatment of several different accounts in consolidation and also briefly addresses the impact on consolidated financial statements of the FASB's new exposure drafts relating to business combinations and consolidated financial statements.

Subsidiary Valuation Accounts at Acquisition

The consolidation treatment of a subsidiary's various valuation accounts depends on the particular type of account. The discussion that follows assumes that push-down accounting is not employed.

A subsidiary's accumulated depreciation on the date of acquisition theoretically should be eliminated in the preparation of consolidated financial statements. When fixed assets are acquired, whether in a business combination or otherwise, the seller's accumulated depreciation on the assets is never transferred to the purchaser's books. Thus, the subsidiary's depreciable assets at the date of combination theoretically should be valued in the consolidated balance sheet at their fair values at that date and accumulated depreciation recognized only for depreciation subsequent to the combination. In consolidation, this would involve offsetting the subsidiary's accumulated depreciation at the date of combination against the asset amounts in the workpaper each period. This offset would have no effect on the net asset amount, and therefore, as a practical matter, most companies simply combine the accumulated depreciation amounts of the parent and subsidiary when preparing consolidated financial statements.

Accounts receivable normally are valued in the balance sheet at net realizable value through the use of the allowance for uncollectible accounts to bring the full legal amount of the receivable down to the actual amount expected to be collected. Thus, if the receivable balance and allowance are both correctly stated on the subsidiary's books, those amounts should be brought into the consolidated balance sheet. However, the FASB's new exposure draft takes the view that the receivables of the subsidiary at the date of combination should be valued in the consolidated balance sheet at their fair values on that date without a valuation account.

If a subsidiary is holding investment securities at the date of combination, those securities must be revalued to fair value. A valuation account associated with the subsidiary's available-for-sale securities at the date of combination should be eliminated against the related accumulated unrealized gain or loss account. Only unrealized gains and losses on the subsidiary's available-for-sale securities subsequent to the combination should be combined with the parent's allowance and included in the consolidated balance sheet.

A subsidiary may have long-term debt outstanding at the date of acquisition, and that debt must be valued at its fair value at the date of combination. If the fair value is different than the book value, the difference is recognized through a discount or premium account associated with the debt, as discussed in Chapter 1. The adjustment to a debt discount or premium account is made each period in the workpaper when consolidated financial statements are prepared. An adjustment to interest expense also is needed because the adjustment to the discount or premium must be amortized each period in the workpaper. The amortization, in turn, results in a smaller adjustment to the subsidiary's discount or premium in future periods.

Negative Retained Earnings of Subsidiary at Acquisition

A parent company may purchase a subsidiary with a negative or debit balance in its retained earnings account. An accumulated deficit of a subsidiary at acquisition causes no special problems in the consolidation process. The normal investment elimination entry is made in the consolidation workpaper except that the debit balance in the subsidiary's Retained Earnings account is eliminated with a credit entry. Thus, the investment elimination entry appears as follows:

E(27)	Capital Stock—Subsidiary	XXX	
	Differential	XXX	
	Retained Earnings		XXX
	Investment in Subsidiary		XXX
	Eliminate investment balance.		

Other Stockholders' Equity Accounts

The discussion of consolidated statements up to this point has dealt with companies having stockholders' equity consisting only of retained earnings and a single class of capital stock issued at par. Typically, companies have more complex stockholders' equity structures, often including preferred stock and various types of additional contributed capital. The treatment of preferred stock in the consolidation process is discussed in Chapter 9.

In general, all stockholders' equity accounts accruing to the common shareholders receive the same treatment as common stock and are eliminated at the time common stock is eliminated. The proportionate amounts of the noncontrolling shareholders' interests in those accounts are combined as part of the noncontrolling interest in the consolidated balance sheet.

Subsidiary's Disposal of Differential-Related Assets

The disposal of an asset usually has income statement implications. If the asset is held by a subsidiary and is one to which a differential is assigned in the consolidation workpaper, both the parent's equity-method income and consolidated net income are affected. The portion of the remaining differential at the time of sale that relates to the asset sold must be written off by the parent under the equity method as a reduction in both the income from the subsidiary and the investment account. In consolidation, the portion of the differential related to the asset sold is treated as an adjustment to consolidated income.

Inventory

Any inventory-related differential is assigned to inventory for as long as the subsidiary holds the inventory units. In the period in which the inventory units are sold, the inventory-related differential is assigned to Cost of Goods Sold, as illustrated previously in Figure 5–5.

The inventory costing method used by the subsidiary determines the period in which the differential cost of goods sold is recognized. When the subsidiary uses FIFO inventory costing, the inventory units on hand on the date of combination are viewed as being the first units sold after the combination. Therefore, the differential normally is assigned to cost of goods sold in the period immediately after the combination. When the subsidiary uses LIFO inventory costing, the inventory units on the date of combination are viewed as remaining in the subsidiary's inventory. Only if the inventory level drops below its level at the date of combination is a portion of the differential assigned to cost of goods sold.

Fixed Assets

A purchase differential related to land held by a subsidiary is added to the Land balance in the consolidation workpaper each time a consolidated balance sheet is prepared. If the subsidiary sells the land to which the differential relates, the differential is treated in the consolidation workpaper as an adjustment to the gain or loss on the sale of the land in the period of the sale.

To illustrate, assume that on January 1, 20X1, Bright purchases all the common stock of Star at $10,000 more than book value. All the differential relates to land that Star had purchased earlier for $25,000. So long as Star continues to hold the land, the $10,000 differential is assigned to Land in the consolidation workpaper. If Star sells the land to an unrelated company for $40,000, the following entry is recorded on Star's books:

(28)	Cash	40,000	
	Land		25,000
	Gain on Sale of Land		15,000
	Record sale of land.		

While a gain of $15,000 is appropriate for Star to report, the land cost the consolidated entity $35,000 ($25,000 + $10,000). Therefore, the consolidated enterprise must report a gain of only $5,000. To reduce the $15,000 gain reported by Star to the $5,000 gain that should be reported by the consolidated entity, the following elimination is included in the consolidation workpaper for the year of the sale:

E(29)	Gain on Sale of Land	10,000	
	Differential		10,000
	Assign beginning differential.		

If, instead, Star sells the land for $32,000, the $7,000 ($32,000 − $25,000) gain recorded by Star is eliminated, and a loss of $3,000 ($32,000 − $35,000) is recognized in the consolidated income statement. The eliminating entry in this case is:

E(30)	Gain on Sale of Land	7,000	
	Loss on Sale of Land	3,000	
	Differential		10,000
	Assign beginning differential.		

When the equity method is used on the parent's books, the parent must adjust the carrying amount of the investment and its equity-method income in the period of the sale to write off the differential, as discussed in Chapter 2. Thereafter, the $10,000 differential no longer exists.

The sale of differential-related equipment is treated in the same manner as land except that the amortization for the current and previous periods must be considered.

Changes Proposed by the FASB

As discussed in Chapters 1 and 3, the FASB has proposed significant changes in accounting for business combinations and the presentation of consolidated financial statements. Several of the most important proposals directly affecting consolidated financial statements are discussed in this section, with an illustration presented in Appendix 5B. Note that the new standards would not be applied retroactively to business combinations that occurred or subsidiaries that were acquired prior to the effective date of the new standards, so current subsidiaries would continue to be reflected in the consolidated financial statements as previously discussed.

In general, the criteria for when consolidated financial statements should be presented and which companies should be consolidated are the same as under current standards. The proposed standards are broader, requiring consolidation of certain entities that currently might be excluded from consolidation, such as trusts and nonprofit entities, and they permit the consolidation of less-than-majority owned companies in some cases. However, the specific criteria to be applied in these cases have not been clarified.

One of the most significant changes relates to the acquisition of less-than-wholly owned subsidiaries, discussed and illustrated in Chapters 1 and 3. The proposed standard on business combinations requires acquired companies, and all of their assets and liabilities, to be valued at their fair values at the date of combination, regardless of the percentage ownership acquired by the parent. As discussed earlier in this chapter, the acquisition of a less-than-wholly owned subsidiary under current standards results in the recognition in the consolidated financial statements of only the parent's share of any fair-value increment related to the net assets acquired and the parent's share of any implied goodwill arising from the combination. Under the FASB's proposal, goodwill would be computed as the difference between the fair value of the acquired company as a whole and the fair value of its net identifiable assets. This can be contrasted with the current approach of measuring goodwill as the difference between the purchase price of the acquired company and the fair value of the parent's share of the acquired company's net identifiable assets. Because the amount of the noncontrolling interest in a less-than-wholly owned subsidiary at the date of combination would be based on the total fair value of the subsidiary under the new standards, rather than on the book value, it generally would be larger than under current standards.

Chapter 3 pointed out that the FASB has adopted an entity approach to consolidated financial statements in its proposed standards and accordingly requires a specific treatment for the noncontrolling interest that is different from the approach most frequently used in practice currently. As illustrated in Chapter 3, the proposal requires calculating consolidated net income without deducting income assigned to the noncontrolling interest, and then income attributable to the noncontrolling interest is deducted to arrive at income attributable to the controlling interest. Consistent with this treatment, the proposal calls for the noncontrolling interest's claim on the net assets of the subsidiary to be reported in the stockholders' equity section of the consolidated balance sheet.

Preparation of a consolidation workpaper giving effect to the requirements of the proposed standards is illustrated in Appendix 5B.

Summary of Key Concepts

The procedures and workpaper for consolidating less-than-wholly owned subsidiaries are the same as discussed in Chapter 4 for wholly owned subsidiaries, with several modifications. When the parent purchases its majority investment in a subsidiary and pays more than the book value of the shares acquired, the differential relates only to the parent's interest. Thus, the assets of the subsidiary are valued, not at full fair value as with a 100 percent acquisition, but at the book value of those assets plus the parent's share of the fair value increment. In addition, only the parent's share of goodwill implied by the purchase price is recognized in the consolidated financial statements.

In the consolidation of a less-than-wholly owned subsidiary, the claims of the noncontrolling shareholders on the income and net assets of the subsidiary must be recognized, and these claims are entered in the consolidation workpaper through eliminating entries. Consolidated net income is the sum of the parent's income for the period from its own operations and its proportionate share of the subsidiary's net income, adjusted for any amortization or write-off of the differential. Consolidated retained earnings is equal to the parent's cumulative income from its own operations for all periods plus the parent's proportionate share of the subsidiary's net income since acquisition, adjusted for any amortization or write-off of the differential, minus all of the parent's cumulative dividends.

When a subsidiary has other comprehensive income for the period, the parent's proportionate share is recognized in consolidated comprehensive income. Other comprehensive income of the subsidiary can be accommodated in a three-part workpaper by adding an additional section at the bottom.

Key Terms

Appendix **5A** Consolidation and the Cost Method

Not all parent companies use the equity method to account for their subsidiary investments that are to be consolidated. The choice of the cost or equity method has no effect on the consolidated financial statements. This is so because the balance in the parent's investment account, the parent's income from the subsidiary, and related items are eliminated in preparing the consolidated statements. Thus, the parent is free to use on its separate books either the cost method or some version of the equity method in accounting for investments in subsidiaries that are to be consolidated.

Although the parent's net income and retained earnings under the equity method usually equal the consolidated amounts, this equality usually does not exist when the cost method is used. Because the cost method uses different parent-company entries than the equity method, it also requires different eliminating entries in preparing the consolidation workpaper. Keep in mind that the consolidated financial statements appear the same regardless of whether the parent uses the cost or the equity method on its separate books.

CONSOLIDATION—YEAR OF COMBINATION

To illustrate the preparation of consolidated financial statements when the parent company carries its investment in the subsidiary using the cost method, the Peerless Products and Special Foods example is used once again. Assume that Peerless purchases 80 percent of the common stock of Special Foods on January 1, 20X1, for $310,000. The purchase price is $70,000 in excess of the book value of the stock acquired. Of the total differential, $8,000 relates to land, $48,000 relates to buildings and equipment having a remaining life of 10 years from the date of combination, $4,000 relates to inventory that is sold during 20X1, and $10,000 relates to goodwill that is reduced by a $2,500 impairment loss in 20X1 and remains constant thereafter. All other data are the same as presented in Figures 5–1 and 5–4.

Parent Company Cost-Method Entries

When the cost method is used, only two journal entries are recorded by Peerless during 20X1 related to its investment in Special Foods. Entry (31) records Peerless's purchase of Special Foods stock; entry (32) recognizes dividend income based on the $24,000 ($30,000 × .80) of dividends received during the period:

(31)	Investment in Special Foods Stock	310,000	
	Cash		310,000
	Record purchase of Special Foods stock.		
(32)	Cash	24,000	
	Dividend Income		24,000
	Record dividends from Special Foods:		
	$30,000 × .80		

No entries are made on the parent's books to amortize or write off the portion of the purchase differential that expires during 20X1, as would be done under the equity method.

Consolidation Workpaper—Year of Combination

The workpaper to prepare consolidated financial statements for December 31, 20X1, is shown in Figure 5–12. The trial balance data for Peerless and Special Foods included in the workpaper in Figure 5–12 differ from those presented in Figure 5–5 only by the effects of using the cost method rather than the equity method on Peerless's books.

FIGURE 5–12 December 31, 20X1, Cost-Method Workpaper for Consolidated Financial Statements, Year of Combination; 80 Percent Purchase at More than Book Value

Item	Peerless Products	Special Foods	Eliminations Debit		Eliminations Credit		Consolidated
Sales	400,000	200,000					600,000
Dividend Income	24,000		(33)	24,000			
Credits	424,000	200,000					600,000
Cost of Goods Sold	170,000	115,000	(36)	4,000			289,000
Depreciation and Amortization	50,000	20,000	(37)	4,800			74,800
Goodwill Impairment Loss			(37)	2,500			2,500
Other Expenses	40,000	15,000					55,000
Debits	(260,000)	(150,000)					(421,300)
							178,700
Income to Noncontrolling Interest			(34)	10,000			(10,000)
Net Income, carry forward	164,000	50,000		45,300			168,700
Retained Earnings, January 1	300,000	100,000	(35)	100,000			300,000
Net Income, from above	164,000	50,000		45,300			168,700
	464,000	150,000					468,700
Dividends Declared	(60,000)	(30,000)			(33)	24,000	
					(34)	6,000	(60,000)
Retained Earnings, December 31, carry forward	404,000	120,000		145,300		30,000	408,700
Cash	194,000	75,000					269,000
Accounts Receivable	75,000	50,000					125,000
Inventory	100,000	75,000					175,000
Land	175,000	40,000	(36)	8,000			223,000
Buildings and Equipment	800,000	600,000	(36)	48,000			1,448,000
Investment in Special Foods Stock	310,000				(35)	310,000	
Goodwill			(36)	10,000	(37)	2,500	7,500
Differential			(35)	70,000	(36)	70,000	
Debits	1,654,000	840,000					2,247,500
Accumulated Depreciation	450,000	320,000			(37)	4,800	774,800
Accounts Payable	100,000	100,000					200,000
Bonds Payable	200,000	100,000					300,000
Common Stock	500,000	200,000	(35)	200,000			500,000
Retained Earnings, from above	404,000	120,000		145,300		30,000	408,700
Noncontrolling Interest					(34)	4,000	
					(35)	60,000	64,000
Credits	1,654,000	840,000		481,300		481,300	2,247,500

Elimination entries:
(33) Eliminate dividend income from subsidiary.
(34) Assign income to noncontrolling interest.
(35) Eliminate investment balance at date of acquisition.
(36) Assign differential at date of acquisition.
(37) Amortize differential and reduce goodwill for impairment.

Five eliminating entries are used to prepare the consolidation workpaper:

E(33)	Dividend Income	24,000	
	Dividends Declared		24,000
	Eliminate dividend income from subsidiary.		

E(34)	Income to Noncontrolling Interest	10,000	
	Dividends Declared		6,000
	Noncontrolling Interest		4,000
	Assign income to noncontrolling interest.		
E(35)	Common Stock—Special Foods	200,000	
	Retained Earnings, January 1	100,000	
	Differential	70,000	
	Investment in Special Foods Stock		310,000
	Noncontrolling Interest		60,000
	Eliminate investment balance at date of acquisition.		
E(36)	Cost of Goods Sold	4,000	
	Land	8,000	
	Buildings and Equipment	48,000	
	Goodwill	10,000	
	Differential		70,000
	Assign differential at date of acquisition.		
E(37)	Depreciation Expense	4,800	
	Goodwill Impairment Loss	2,500	
	Accumulated Depreciation		4,800
	Goodwill		2,500
	Amortize differential related to buildings and equipment ($4,800) and reduce goodwill for impairment ($2,500).		

Entry E(33) eliminates the dividend income recorded by Peerless during the period along with Special Foods' dividend declaration related to the stockholdings of Peerless. Entry E(34) assigns income to the noncontrolling shareholders ($50,000 × .20) and eliminates their portion of the subsidiary dividends ($30,000 × .20). This entry is the same as under the equity method and is not affected by the method used on the parent's books.

Entry E(35) eliminates the balances in the stockholders' equity accounts of Special Foods and the balance in Peerless's investment account as of the date of combination. A differential clearing account is established, representing the $70,000 purchase differential at that date. Entry E(36) assigns the differential to the appropriate expense and asset categories. Entry E(37) recognizes the additional depreciation related to the portion of the differential assigned to buildings and equipment. This entry also establishes in the workpaper the loss from the impairment of the goodwill included in the differential and reduces the goodwill by the amount of the impairment.

The investment elimination entry, E(35), is the same as the corresponding entry made when using the equity method. This occurs only in the year of acquisition because the balances eliminated are those at the beginning of the year, the date of combination. The balances on the date of combination are the same regardless of the method used to account for the investment subsequent to the combination. In all subsequent years, the investment elimination entries differ.

Under the cost method, Peerless's 20X1 net income and ending retained earnings are $4,700 lower than the consolidated totals in Figure 5–12. This occurs because, using the cost method, Peerless did not include in income its percentage share of the undistributed net income of Special Foods ($20,000 × .80), nor did Peerless reduce its income for the write-off of the portion of the purchase differential assigned to inventory sold during 20X1 ($4,000) or the amortization of the differential relating to buildings and equipment ($4,800). Also, a $2,500 goodwill impairment loss was recognized in consolidation but not by Peerless. Consolidated retained earnings in the workpaper includes both the parent's retained earnings and the parent's share of the undistributed earnings of the subsidiary since acquisition.

CONSOLIDATION—SECOND YEAR OF OWNERSHIP

Consolidation differences between cost-method accounting and equity-method accounting tend to be more evident in the second year of ownership. To see this, assume that Peerless earns income from its own separate operations of $160,000 during 20X2 and pays dividends of $60,000; Special Foods reports net income of $75,000 for 20X2 and pays dividends of $40,000.

Parent Company Cost-Method Entry

Only a single entry is recorded by the parent in 20X2 in relation to its subsidiary investment:

(38)	Cash	32,000	
	Dividend Income		32,000
	Record dividends from Special Foods:		
	$40,000 × .80		

Consolidation Workpaper—Second Year Following Combination

The trial balance data for Peerless and Special Foods are entered in the consolidation workpaper at December 31, 20X2, as shown in Figure 5–13.

The first two elimination entries are similar to those used in the first year. Entry E(39) eliminates the dividend income from Special Foods recorded by Peerless and the dividend declaration of Special Foods related to Peerless's investment:

E(39)	Dividend Income	32,000	
	Dividends Declared		32,000
	Eliminate dividend income from subsidiary.		

Entry E(40) assigns to the noncontrolling shareholders their share of the subsidiary's income ($75,000 × .20) and eliminates the noncontrolling interest's portion of subsidiary dividends ($40,000 × .20):

E(40)	Income to Noncontrolling Interest	15,000	
	Dividends Declared		8,000
	Noncontrolling Interest		7,000
	Assign income to noncontrolling interest.		

Under the cost method, the parent company has not recognized its portion of the undistributed earnings of the subsidiary on the parent company's books. Therefore, the parent company's retained earnings at the beginning of the second period is less than consolidated retained earnings, and the investment account balance reported by the parent is less than its proportionate share of the subsidiary's net assets at that date. The approach used in completing the consolidation workpaper in Figure 5–13 is to eliminate the balances reported by the parent company under the cost method and to carry the parent's portion of the increase in the subsidiary's retained earnings across to the Consolidated column.

Because the balance in the parent's investment account usually remains constant under the cost method, the investment elimination entry also remains constant. Entry E(41) eliminates the balance in Peerless's investment account and the balances in the stockholders' equity accounts of Special Foods as they existed at the date of combination:

E(41)	Common Stock—Special Foods	200,000	
	Retained Earnings, January 1	100,000	
	Differential	70,000	
	Investment in Special Foods Stock		310,000
	Noncontrolling Interest		60,000
	Eliminate investment balance at date of acquisition.		

This entry is exactly the same as investment elimination entry E(35) made in the first year. The investment elimination entry continues to be the same in each subsequent year unless there is a change in ownership level or a change in the number of subsidiary shares outstanding or unless the subsidiary declares dividends in excess of earnings since acquisition by the parent.

FIGURE 5–13   December 31, 20X2, Cost-Method Workpaper for Consolidated Financial Statements, Second Year Following Combination; 80 Percent Purchase at More than Book Value

Item	Peerless Products	Special Foods	Eliminations Debit	Eliminations Credit	Consolidated
Sales	450,000	300,000			750,000
Dividend Income	32,000		(39) 32,000		
Credits	482,000	300,000			750,000
Cost of Goods Sold	180,000	160,000			340,000
Depreciation and Amortization	50,000	20,000	(44) 4,800		74,800
Other Expenses	60,000	45,000			105,000
Debits	(290,000)	(225,000)			(519,800)
					230,200
Income to Noncontrolling Interest			(40) 15,000		(15,000)
Net Income, carry forward	192,000	75,000	51,800		215,200
Retained Earnings, January 1	404,000	120,000	(41) 100,000		
			(42) 4,000		
			(43) 11,300		408,700
Net Income, from above	192,000	75,000	51,800		215,200
	596,000	195,000			623,900
Dividends Declared	(60,000)	(40,000)		(39) 32,000	
				(40) 8,000	(60,000)
Retained Earnings, December 31, carry forward	536,000	155,000	167,100	40,000	563,900
Cash	221,000	85,000			306,000
Accounts Receivable	150,000	80,000			230,000
Inventory	180,000	90,000			270,000
Land	175,000	40,000	(43) 8,000		223,000
Buildings and Equipment	800,000	600,000	(43) 48,000		1,448,000
Investment in Special Foods Stock	310,000			(41) 310,000	
Goodwill			(43) 7,500		7,500
Differential			(41) 70,000	(43) 70,000	
Debits	1,836,000	895,000			2,484,500
Accumulated Depreciation	500,000	340,000		(43) 4,800	
				(44) 4,800	849,600
Accounts Payable	100,000	100,000			200,000
Bonds Payable	200,000	100,000			300,000
Common Stock	500,000	200,000	(41) 200,000		500,000
Retained Earnings, from above	536,000	155,000	167,100	40,000	563,900
Noncontrolling Interest				(40) 7,000	
				(41) 60,000	
				(42) 4,000	71,000
Credits	1,836,000	895,000	500,600	500,600	2,484,500

Elimination entries:
(39) Eliminate dividend income from subsidiary.
(40) Assign income to noncontrolling interest.
(41) Eliminate investment balance at date of acquisition.
(42) Assign undistributed prior earnings of subsidiary to noncontrolling interest.
(43) Assign differential remaining at beginning of year.
(44) Amortize differential related to buildings and equipment.

Another workpaper entry is needed to establish the proper balance for noncontrolling share-holders in the consolidated balance sheet. Entry E(40) assigns to the noncontrolling shareholders their share of the increase in the stockholders' equity of the subsidiary during 20X2. Entry E(41) assigns to the noncontrolling shareholders their share of the subsidiary's stockholders' equity as of the date of combination, January 1, 20X1. An additional entry is needed to assign to the noncontrol-ling shareholders their share of the increase in the subsidiary's stockholders' equity that occurred between the date of combination and the beginning of the current period. This increase is computed as follows:

Balance in retained earnings of Special Foods on January 1, 20X2	$120,000
Balance in retained earnings of Special Foods at acquisition	(100,000)
Undistributed earnings	$ 20,000
Noncontrolling interest's share	× .20
Increase assignable to noncontrolling interest	$ 4,000

Entry E(42) assigns to the noncontrolling interest its share of the increase in the stockholders' equity of Special Foods that occurred between the date of combination and the beginning of the current period:

E(42)	Retained Earnings, January 1	4,000	
	Noncontrolling Interest		4,000
	Assign undistributed prior earnings of subsidiary to noncontrolling interest.		

A comparable computation and eliminating entry are necessary each time consolidated statements are prepared.

The final two entries in the consolidation workpaper are related to the differential:

E(43)	Land	8,000	
	Buildings and Equipment	48,000	
	Goodwill	7,500	
	Retained Earnings, January 1	11,300	
	Differential		70,000
	Accumulated Depreciation		4,800
	Assign differential remaining at beginning of year.		
E(44)	Depreciation Expense	4,800	
	Accumulated Depreciation		4,800
	Amortize differential related to buildings and equipment.		

Entry E(43) assigns the original amount of the purchase differential so that the subsidiary's asset and contra asset accounts are brought to their appropriate consolidated balances as of the beginning of 20X2. Entry E(44) amortizes for 20X2 the portion of the differential related to buildings and equipment.

The assignment of the differential in entry E(43) reflects the reduction in goodwill as a result of the $2,500 impairment loss in 20X1. In addition, Accumulated Depreciation is increased for the $4,800 of additional depreciation taken in the 20X1 consolidation workpaper.

Under the cost method, the parent does not recognize the amortization or write-off of the dif-ferential on its own books. As a result, beginning retained earnings reported by the parent must be reduced by the cumulative write-off of the differential recognized in the consolidated financial state-ments for all prior years to bring it into agreement with the Retained Earnings balance reported for the consolidated entity at the end of the prior year. Keep in mind that entries made in previous years' consolidation workpapers do not carry over to the current year. Therefore, entry E(43) is needed to reduce consolidated retained earnings by the amount of the differential write-off in 20X1, consisting of the following:

Amount related to inventory sold in 20X1	$ 4,000
Additional depreciation of buildings and equipment	4,800
Goodwill impairment loss	2,500
Reduction in beginning retained earnings	$11,300

Consolidated Retained Earnings

Consolidated Retained Earnings on January 1, 20X2, is derived in the consolidation workpaper by combining the parent's Retained Earnings and the subsidiary's Retained Earnings with the debits and credits from the various eliminating entries. The January 1, 20X2, $408,700 balance computed in this manner is equal to the December 31, 20X1, balance shown in Figure 5–12.

The beginning balance of the subsidiary's Retained Earnings is not fully eliminated under the cost method because the parent's Retained Earnings does not include undistributed earnings of the subsidiary since acquisition. As a result, some portion of subsidiary Retained Earnings must be carried across and included in consolidated Retained Earnings.

Consolidated retained earnings on December 31, 20X2, can be reconciled with the balances reported by Peerless and Special Foods, as follows:

Retained earnings of Peerless, December 31, 20X2	$536,000
Retained earnings of Special Foods, December 31, 20X2	155,000
Total	$691,000
Deduct the following:	
Special Foods' retained earnings at acquisition, January 1, 20X1	(100,000)
Noncontrolling interest's share of Special Foods' undistributed earnings since acquisition [($20,000 + $35,000) × .20]	(11,000)
Write-off of differential for 20X1 ($4,000 + $4,800 + $2,500)	(11,300)
Write-off of differential for 20X2	(4,800)
Consolidated retained earnings, December 31, 20X2	$563,900

Appendix **5B** Illustration of the FASB's Proposed Changes

The case of Peerless Products and Special Foods used throughout the chapter can be used to illustrate the impact of the FASB's proposed changes in accounting for business combinations and the presentation of consolidated financial statements. Assume once again that Peerless purchases 80 percent of the common stock of Special Foods on January 1, 20X1, for $310,000. The balance sheets of Peerless and Special Foods immediately after the combination appear as in Figure 5–1.

On the date of combination, Special Foods reports net assets having a book value of $300,000. After careful examination, Peerless's management determines the fair value of Special Foods' net assets to be $375,000 and the fair value of Special Foods as a whole to be $387,500. The $75,000 fair value increment is assigned to inventory ($5,000), land ($10,000), and buildings and equipment ($60,000), as shown in Figure 5–2. The $12,500 of goodwill ($387,500 − $375,000) is assigned proportionately to Peerless (80 percent) and the noncontrolling shareholders (20 percent).

PARENT COMPANY ENTRIES

Special Foods reports net income of $50,000 in 20X1 and pays dividends of $30,000. All of the inventory to which the $5,000 differential relates is sold during 20X1. The buildings and equipment have a remaining economic life of 10 years from the date of combination, and straight-line depreciation is used. At the end of 20X1, Peerless's management determines that the goodwill established at the time of the combination has been impaired and recognition of a $3,125 goodwill impairment loss is warranted. The goodwill impairment is judged as relating proportionately to the goodwill assigned to the controlling and noncontrolling shareholders.

During 20X1, Peerless records the following entries on its books to account for its investment in Special Foods stock under the equity method:

(45)	Investment in Special Foods stock	310,000	
	Cash		310,000
	Record purchase of Special Foods stock.		

(46)	Cash	24,000	
	Investment in Special Foods stock		24,000
	Record dividends from Special Foods: $30,000 × .80		

(47)	Investment in Special Foods stock	40,000	
	Income from Subsidiary		40,000
	Record equity-method income: $50,000 × .80		

(48)	Income from Subsidiary	4,000	
	Investment in Special Foods stock		4,000
	Adjust income for purchase differential related to inventory sold: $5,000 × .80		

(49)	Income from Subsidiary	4,800	
	Investment in Special Foods stock		4,800
	Amortize purchase differential related to buildings and equipment.		

These entries are the same as entries (4) through (8) shown previously under current standards.

CONSOLIDATION WORKPAPER

At the end of 20X1, Peerless prepares consolidated financial statements based on the consolidation workpaper presented in Figure 5–14. Most of the eliminating entries in Figure 5–14 differ from those in Figure 5–5 because the FASB's proposed standards require recognizing the full fair values of the subsidiary's assets and liabilities rather than just the parent's share of the fair value increment. In addition, the proposed standards require recognition of the full amount of goodwill based on the difference between the fair value of the acquired company and the fair value of its net identifiable assets, rather than computing goodwill as the excess of the purchase price over the parent's share of the fair value of the subsidiary's net identifiable assets.

The first eliminating entry in the workpaper, E(50), eliminates Peerless' income from Special Foods recognized on its books under the equity method, Peerless's share of Special Foods dividends, and the change in the investment account during the year on Peerless' books. This entry is the same as E(9) under current standards:

E(50)	Income from Subsidiary	31,200	
	Dividends Declared		24,000
	Investment in Special Foods stock		7,200
	Eliminate income from subsidiary.		

The next elimination entry assigns income to the noncontrolling interest:

E(51)	Income to Noncontrolling Interest	7,175	
	Dividends Declared		6,000
	Noncontrolling Interest		1,175
	Assign income to noncontrolling interest.		

FIGURE 5–14 December 31, 20X1, Equity-Method Workpaper for Consolidated Financial Statements under Proposed Accounting Standards, Year of Combination; 80 Percent Purchase at More than Book Value

Item	Peerless Products	Special Foods	Eliminations Debit	Eliminations Credit	Consolidated
Sales	400,000	200,000			600,000
Income from Subsidiary	31,200		(50) 31,200		
Credits	431,200	200,000			600,000
Cost of Goods Sold	170,000	115,000	(53) 5,000		290,000
Depreciation and Amortization	50,000	20,000	(54) 6,000		76,000
Goodwill Impairment Loss			(55) 3,125		3,125
Other Expenses	40,000	15,000			55,000
Debits	(260,000)	(150,000)			(424,125)
Consolidated Net Income					175,875
Income to Noncontrolling Interest			(51) 7,175		(7,175)
Income to Controlling Interest, carry forward	171,200	50,000	52,500		168,700
Retained Earnings, January 1	300,000	100,000	(52) 100,000		300,000
Income, from above	171,200	50,000	52,500		168,700
	471,200	150,000			468,700
Dividends Declared	(60,000)	(30,000)		(50) 24,000	
				(51) 6,000	(60,000)
Retained Earnings, December 31 carry forward	411,200	120,000	152,500	30,000	408,700
Cash	194,000	75,000			269,000
Accounts Receivable	75,000	50,000			125,000
Inventory	100,000	75,000			175,000
Land	175,000	40,000	(53) 10,000		225,000
Buildings and Equipment	800,000	600,000	(53) 60,000		1,460,000
Investment in Special Foods Stock	317,200			(50) 7,200	
				(52) 310,000	
Goodwill			(53) 12,500	(55) 3,125	9,375
Entity Differential			(52) 87,500	(53) 87,500	
Debits	1,661,200	840,000			2,263,375
Accumulated Depreciation	450,000	320,000		(54) 6,000	776,000
Accounts Payable	100,000	100,000			200,000
Bonds Payable	200,000	100,000			300,000
Common Stock	500,000	200,000	(52) 200,000		500,000
Retained Earnings, from above	411,200	120,000	152,500	30,000	408,700
Noncontrolling Interest				(51) 1,175	
				(52) 77,500	78,675
Credits	1,661,200	840,000	522,500	522,500	2,263,375

Elimination entries:
(50) Eliminate income from subsidiary.
(51) Assign income to noncontrolling interest.
(52) Eliminate beginning investment balance.
(53) Assign beginning entity differential.
(54) Amortize entity differential related to buildings and equipment.
(55) Write down goodwill for impairment.

This entry is similar to E(10), but the amounts are different because the noncontrolling shareholders are viewed, under the proposed standards, as having a claim on the increase in the fair value of Special Foods' assets, including goodwill. The total entity differential is the difference between the fair value of Special Foods on the date of combination and the book value of its net assets ($387,500 − $300,000). While the noncontrolling interest's claim includes 20 percent of this amount, it must also bear the burden of its share of any write-offs of this entity differential. Accordingly, the noncontrolling interest's share of Special Foods' income is computed as follows:

Net income reported by Special Foods	$50,000
Less entity differential assigned to inventory sold in period	(5,000)
Depreciation of entity differential assigned to buildings and equipment	(6,000)
Impairment of goodwill	(3,125)
Special Foods' adjusted income	$35,875
Noncontrolling owners' proportionate share	× .20
Income assigned to noncontrolling shareholders	$ 7,175

Entry E(52) eliminates Peerless's beginning investment balance and Special Foods' beginning stockholders' equity balances, and it assigns 20 percent of the total fair value of Special Foods ($387,500) to the noncontrolling interest:

E(52)			
	Common Stock—Special Foods	200,000	
	Retained Earnings, January 1	100,000	
	Entity Differential	87,500	
	Investment in Special Foods Stock		310,000
	Noncontrolling Interest		77,500
	Eliminate beginning investment balance.		

The amount assigned to the noncontrolling interest in entry E(52) is greater than the amount in entry E(11) under current standards because it is based on the fair value rather than book value of Special Foods. Entry E(52) also establishes the differential in the workpaper. This differential is referred to here as the *entity differential* to distinguish it from the *purchase differential* that arises under current standards. The entity differential is the difference on the date of combination between the fair value of the subsidiary and its book value, whereas the purchase differential is the difference between the purchase price paid by the parent and the book value of the subsidiary's shares acquired by the parent. Because the entity differential relates to the subsidiary as a whole, it results in an increase in the noncontrolling interest by a proportionate share of the differential. Thus, the noncontrolling interest is established in the workpaper with entry E(52) at an amount that is $17,500 ($87,500 × .20) higher than the amount in entry E(11) under current standards.

The next three eliminating entries all have to do with the entity differential that was established in the workpaper with entry E(52):

E(53)			
	Cost of Goods Sold	5,000	
	Land	10,000	
	Buildings and Equipment	60,000	
	Goodwill	12,500	
	Entity Differential		87,500
	Assign beginning entity differential.		
E(54)			
	Depreciation Expense	6,000	
	Accumulated Depreciation		6,000
	Amortize entity differential related to buildings and equipment: $60,000 ÷ 10		
E(55)			
	Goodwill Impairment Loss	3,125	
	Goodwill		3,125
	Write down goodwill for impairment.		

Eliminating entry E(53) allocates the entity differential, adding the fair value increment as of the date of combination to Special Foods' assets and entering goodwill in the workpaper. Entry E(54) recognizes the depreciation of that portion of the entity differential related to Special Foods' buildings and equipment. Entry E(55) recognizes in the workpaper the goodwill impairment loss incurred during 20X1 and reduces goodwill by that amount.

Once all of the eliminating entries are entered in the consolidation workpaper, it can be completed in the normal manner. Several points should be noted from the workpaper in Figure 5–14:

1. All of the entries related to the differential and the noncontrolling interest are based on the fair value of the subsidiary at the date of combination, not the book value, and, therefore, the amounts differ from those in Figure 5–5.

2. Consolidated net income appears as a subtotal toward the bottom of the income statement section of the workpaper and is computed as the difference between the debit and credit items in that section; it is not the last item in that section of the workpaper. Consolidated net income is allocated to the two ownership groups by deducting the income to the noncontrolling interest to arrive at consolidated net income allocated to the controlling interest, the last figure in the consolidated column in that section of the workpaper.

3. Unlike consolidated net income, consolidated retained earnings includes only the portion of the entity's undistributed earnings accruing to the controlling interest. Accordingly, the retained earnings statement section of the workpaper is the same as in Figure 5–5.

4. Asset amounts in the consolidated column of the balance sheet section of the workpaper are greater than in Figure 5–5 because they are based on the full fair value of Special Foods' assets at the date of combination. The noncontrolling interest shown at the bottom of the consolidated column is greater than in Figure 5–5 because it includes the noncontrolling interest's share of Special Foods' fair value at the date of combination rather than on the book value. This noncontrolling interest amount can be calculated as follows:

Book value of Special Foods' net assets, December 31, 20X1		$320,000
Noncontrolling stockholders' share		× .20
Book value of noncontrolling interest, December 31, 20X1		$ 64,000
Entity differential, January 1, 20X1	$87,500	
Changes in entity differential, 20X1:		
Goodwill impairment loss	(3,125)	
Cost of goods sold	(5,000)	
Additional depreciation	(6,000)	
Entity differential remaining at December 31, 20X1	$73,375	
Noncontrolling stockholders' share	× .20	14,675
Total noncontrolling interest, December 31, 20X1		$ 78,675

Questions

Q5-1 Where is the balance assigned to the noncontrolling interest reported in the consolidated balance sheet?

Q5-2 Why must a noncontrolling interest be reported in the consolidated balance sheet?

Q5-3 How does the introduction of noncontrolling shareholders change the consolidation workpaper?

Q5-4 How is the amount assigned to the noncontrolling interest in the consolidated balance sheet normally determined?

Q5-5 What portion of consolidated retained earnings is assigned to the noncontrolling interest in the consolidated balance sheet?

Q5-6 When the parent pays more than book value in acquiring majority ownership, how is the balance assigned to the noncontrolling interest in the consolidated balance sheet determined?

Q5-7 When majority ownership is acquired, what portion of the fair value of assets held by the subsidiary at acquisition is reported in the consolidated balance sheet?

Q5-8 When majority ownership is acquired, what portion of the goodwill reported in the consolidated balance sheet is assigned to the noncontrolling interest?

Q5-9 How is the income assigned to the noncontrolling interest normally computed?

Q5-10 How is income assigned to the noncontrolling interest shown in the consolidation workpaper?

Q5-11 How are dividends paid by a subsidiary to noncontrolling shareholders treated in the consolidation workpaper?

Q5-12 Does a noncontrolling shareholder have access to any information other than the consolidated financial statements to determine how well the subsidiary is doing? Explain.

Q5-13 How do other comprehensive income elements reported by a subsidiary affect the consolidated financial statements?

Q5-14 What portion of other comprehensive income reported by a subsidiary is included in the consolidated statement of comprehensive income as accruing to parent company shareholders?

Q5-15* What effect does a negative retained earnings balance on the subsidiary's books have on consolidation procedures?

Q5-16* What type of adjustment must be made in the consolidation workpaper if a differential is assigned to land and the subsidiary disposes of the land in the current period?

Q5-17A Why are eliminating entries in the consolidation workpaper different when the parent accounts for its investment in a subsidiary using the cost method rather than the equity method? What is the major difference in eliminating entries?

Q5-18B When majority ownership is purchased at an amount greater than book value, how will the amounts reported in the consolidated balance sheet change under the FASB's proposed new standards for business combinations and consolidated financial statements?

Q5-19B When majority ownership is acquired at an amount greater than book value, how will the amounts reported as consolidated net income change under the FASB's proposed new standards for business combinations and consolidated financial statements?

Q5-20B How do the consolidation eliminating entries change when majority ownership is purchased at an amount greater than book value under the FASB's proposed new standards for business combinations and consolidated financial statements?

Cases

C5-1 **Consolidation Workpaper Preparation**

The newest clerk in the accounting office recently entered trial balance data for the parent company and its subsidiaries on the new company microcomputer. After a few minutes of additional work needed to eliminate the intercompany investment account balances, he expressed his satisfaction at having completed the consolidation workpaper for 20X5. In reviewing the printout of the consolidation workpaper, other employees raised several questions, and you are asked to respond.

Required

Analysis Indicate whether each of the following items can be answered by looking at the data in the consolidation workpaper (indicate why or why not):

a. Is it possible to tell if the parent is using the equity method in recording its ownership of each subsidiary?

b. Is it possible to tell if the correct amount of consolidated net income has been reported?

c. One of the employees thought the parent company had paid well above the fair value of net assets for a subsidiary purchased on January 1, 20X5. Is it possible to tell by reviewing the consolidation workpaper?

d. Is it possible to determine from the workpaper the percentage ownership of a subsidiary held by the parent?

C5-2 **Consolidated Income Presentation**

Research Standard Company has a relatively high profit margin on its sales, and Jewel Company has a substan-
FARS tially lower profit margin. Standard holds 55 percent of Jewel's common stock and includes Jewel in its consolidated statements. Standard and Jewel reported sales of $100,000 and $60,000, respectively,

*Indicates that the item relates to "Additional Considerations."

in 20X4. Sales increased to $120,000 and $280,000 for the two companies in 20X5. The average profit margins of the two companies remained constant over the two years at 60 percent and 10 percent, respectively.

Standard's treasurer was aware that the subsidiary was awarded a major new contract in 20X5 and anticipated a substantial increase in net income for the year. She was disappointed to learn that consolidated net income had increased by only 38 percent even though sales were 2.5 times higher than in 20X4. She is not trained in accounting and does not understand the fundamental processes used in preparing Standard's consolidated income statement.

Required

As a member of the accounting department, you have been asked to prepare a memo to the treasurer explaining how consolidated net income is computed and the procedures used to allocate income to the parent company and to the subsidiary's minority shareholders. Include in your memo citations to or quotations from the authoritative literature. To assist the treasurer in gaining a better understanding, prepare an analysis showing the amounts actually reported and those that would have been reported as consolidated net income if Standard had owned 100 percent of Jewel's stock. Clearly explain why the amounts differ.

C5-3 **Pro Rata Consolidation**

Research
FARS

Rose Corporation and Krome Company established a joint venture to manufacture components for both companies' use on January 1, 20X1, and have operated it quite successfully for the past four years. Rose and Krome both contributed 50 percent of the equity when the joint venture was created. Rose purchases roughly 70 percent of the output of the joint venture and Krome purchases 30 percent. Rose and Krome have equal numbers of representatives on the joint venture's board of directors and participate equally in its management. Joint venture profits are distributed at year-end on the basis of total purchases by each company.

Required

Rose has been using the equity method to report its investment in the joint venture; however, Rose's financial vice president believes that each company should use pro rata consolidation. As a senior accountant at Rose, you have been asked to prepare a memo discussing those situations in which pro rata consolidation may be appropriate and to offer your recommendation as to whether Rose should continue to use the equity method or switch to pro rata consolidation. Include in your memo citations of and quotations from the authoritative literature to support your arguments.

C5-4 **Elimination Procedures**

A new employee has been given responsibility for preparing the consolidated financial statements of Sample Company. After attempting to work alone for some time, the employee seeks assistance in gaining a better overall understanding of the way in which the consolidation process works.

Required

You have been asked to provide assistance in explaining the consolidation process.

Communication
a. Why must the eliminating entries be entered in the consolidation workpaper each time consolidated statements are prepared?

b. How is the beginning-of-period noncontrolling interest balance determined?

c. How is the end-of-period noncontrolling interest balance determined?

d. Which of the subsidiary's account balances must always be eliminated?

e. Which of the parent company's account balances must always be eliminated?

C5-5 **Revised Reporting Standards**

Analysis

Revised reporting standards for goodwill and other aspects of business combinations as well as consolidation standards dealing with variable interest entities and noncontrolling interests have been adopted within the last several years or are in the proposal stage.

Required

a. Curtiss-Wright Corporation adopted SFAS No. 142 on January 1, 2002, and no longer amortizes goodwill. By what amounts did goodwill increase in 2001 and 2002, and what amounts were reported at December 31, 2001, and 2002? What percent of Curtiss-Wright's total assets does goodwill represent at December 31, 2002? How does this compare to other companies?

b. The financial statements of Fox Television Holdings are consolidated with those of the Fox Entertainment Group, Inc., even though the Fox Entertainment Group, Inc., does not own any of the common stock of Fox Television Holdings. On what factors does Fox Entertainment Group, Inc., base its decision to consolidate?

Exercises

E5-1 Multiple-Choice Questions on Consolidation Process

Select the most appropriate answer for each of the following questions.

1. If A Company purchases 80 percent of the stock of B Company on January 1, 20X2, immediately after the acquisition:

   a. Consolidated retained earnings will be equal to the combined retained earnings of the two companies.
   b. Goodwill will be reported in the consolidated balance sheet.
   c. A Company's additional paid-in capital may be reduced to permit the carryforward of B Company retained earnings.
   d. Consolidated retained earnings and A Company retained earnings will be the same.

2. Which of the following is incorrect?

   a. The noncontrolling shareholders' claim on the subsidiary's net assets is based on the book value of the subsidiary's net assets.
   b. Only the parent's portion of the difference between book value and fair value of the subsidiary's assets is assigned to those assets.
   c. Goodwill represents the difference between the book value of the subsidiary's net assets and the amount paid by the parent to buy ownership.
   d. Total assets reported by the parent generally will be less than total assets reported on the consolidated balance sheet.

3. Which of the following statements is correct?

   a. Foreign subsidiaries do not need to be consolidated if they are reported as a separate operating group under segment reporting.
   b. Consolidated retained earnings does not include the noncontrolling interest's claim on the subsidiary's retained earnings.
   c. The noncontrolling shareholders' claim should be adjusted for changes in the fair value of the subsidiary assets but should not include goodwill.
   d. Consolidation is expected any time the investor holds significant influence over the investee.

4. [AICPA Adapted] At December 31, 20X9, Grey Inc. owned 90 percent of Winn Corporation, a consolidated subsidiary, and 20 percent of Carr Corporation, an investee in which Grey cannot exercise significant influence. On the same date, Grey had receivables of $300,000 from Winn and $200,000 from Carr. In its December 31, 20X9, consolidated balance sheet, Grey should report accounts receivable from its affiliates of:

   a. $500,000.
   b. $340,000.
   c. $230,000.
   d. $200,000.

Items 5 and 6 are based on the following information:
   Deer Company acquired 70 percent of Elk Corporation's outstanding stock. Deer's separate balance sheet immediately after the acquisition and the consolidated balance sheet are as follows:

	Deer	Consolidated
Current Assets	$106,000	$146,000
Investment in Elk (cost)	100,000	
Goodwill		8,100
Fixed Assets (net)	270,000	370,000
	$476,000	$524,100
Current Liabilities	$ 15,000	$ 28,000
Capital Stock	350,000	350,000
Noncontrolling Interest		35,100
Retained Earnings	111,000	111,000
	$476,000	$524,100

Ten thousand dollars of the excess payment for the investment in Elk was ascribed to undervaluation of its fixed assets; the balance of the excess payment was ascribed to goodwill. Elk's current assets included a $2,000 receivable from Deer that arose before they became related on an ownership basis.

The following two items relate to Elk's separate balance sheet prepared at the time Deer acquired its 70 percent interest in Elk.

5. What was the total of the current assets on Elk's separate balance sheet at the time Deer acquired its 70 percent interest?

 a. $38,000.

 b. $40,000.

 c. $42,000.

 d. $104,000.

6. What was the total stockholders' equity on Elk's separate balance sheet at the time Deer acquired its 70 percent interest?

 a. $64,900.

 b. $70,000.

 c. $100,000.

 d. $117,000.

E5-2 **Multiple-Choice Questions on Consolidation [AICPA Adapted]**
Select the correct answer for each of the following questions.

1. A 70 percent owned subsidiary company declares and pays a cash dividend. What effect does the dividend have on the retained earnings and minority interest balances in the parent company's consolidated balance sheet?

 a. No effect on either retained earnings or minority interest.

 b. No effect on retained earnings and a decrease in minority interest.

 c. Decreases in both retained earnings and minority interest.

 d. A decrease in retained earnings and no effect on minority interest.

2. How is the portion of consolidated earnings to be assigned to the noncontrolling interest in consolidated financial statements determined?

 a. The parent's net income is subtracted from the subsidiary's net income to determine the noncontrolling interest.

 b. The subsidiary's net income is extended to the noncontrolling interest.

 c. The amount of the subsidiary's earnings recognized for consolidation purposes is multiplied by the noncontrolling interest's percentage of ownership.

 d. The amount of consolidated earnings on the consolidated workpapers is multiplied by the noncontrolling interest percentage on the balance sheet date.

3. On January 1, 20X5, Post Company purchased an 80 percent investment in Stake Company. The acquisition cost was equal to Post's equity in Stake's net assets at that date. On January 1, 20X5,

Post and Stake had retained earnings of $500,000 and $100,000, respectively. During 20X5, Post had net income of $200,000, which included its equity in Stake's earnings, and declared dividends of $50,000; Stake had net income of $40,000 and declared dividends of $20,000. There were no other intercompany transactions between the parent and subsidiary. On December 31, 20X5, what should the consolidated retained earnings be?

  a. $650,000.
  b. $666,000.
  c. $766,000.
  d. $770,000.

Items 4 and 5 are based on the following information:
  On January 1, 20X8, Ritt Corporation purchased 80 percent of Shaw Corporation's $10 par common stock for $975,000. On this date, the carrying amount of Shaw's net assets was $1,000,000. The fair values of Shaw's identifiable assets and liabilities were the same as their carrying amounts except for plant assets (net), which were $100,000 in excess of the carrying amount. For the year ended December 31, 20X8, Shaw had net income of $190,000 and paid cash dividends totaling $125,000.

4. In the January 1, 20X8, consolidated balance sheet, the amount of goodwill reported should be:

  a. $0.
  b. $75,000.
  c. $95,000.
  d. $175,000.

5. In the December 31, 20X8, consolidated balance sheet, the amount of noncontrolling interest reported should be:

  a. $200,000.
  b. $213,000.
  c. $220,000.
  d. $233,000.

E5-3 Eliminating Entries with Differential

On June 10, 20X8, Brown Corporation purchased 60 percent of Amber Company's common stock. Summarized balance sheet data for the two companies immediately after the stock purchase are as follows:

Item	Brown Corp. Book Value	Amber Company Book Value	Amber Company Fair Value
Cash	$ 15,000	$ 5,000	$ 5,000
Accounts Receivable	30,000	10,000	10,000
Inventory	80,000	20,000	25,000
Buildings and Equipment (net)	120,000	50,000	70,000
Investment in Amber Stock	60,000		
Total	$305,000	$85,000	$110,000
Accounts Payable	$ 25,000	$ 3,000	$ 3,000
Bonds Payable	150,000	25,000	25,000
Common Stock	55,000	20,000	
Retained Earnings	75,000	37,000	
Total	$305,000	$85,000	$ 28,000

Required

a. Give the eliminating entries required to prepare a consolidated balance sheet immediately after the purchase of Amber Company shares.

b. Explain how eliminating entries differ from other types of journal entries recorded in the normal course of business.

E5-4 Consolidation with Minority Interest

Elder Corporation purchased 75 percent of Dynamic Corporation's voting common stock on December 31, 20X4, for $388,000. At the date of combination, Dynamic reported the following:

Current Assets	$220,000	Current Liabilities	$ 80,000
Long-Term Assets (net)	420,000	Long-Term Liabilities	200,000
		Common Stock	120,000
		Retained Earnings	240,000
Total	$640,000	Total	$640,000

At December 31, 20X4, the book values of Dynamic's net assets and liabilities approximated their fair values, except for buildings, which had a fair value of $80,000 more than book value, and inventories, which had a fair value of $36,000 more than book value.

Required

Elder Corporation wishes to prepare a consolidated balance sheet immediately following the business combination. Give the eliminating entry or entries needed to prepare a consolidated balance sheet at December 31, 20X4.

E5-5 Workpaper for Majority-Owned Subsidiary

Glitter Enterprises purchased 60 percent of Lowtide Builders' stock on December 31, 20X4. Balance sheet data for Glitter and Lowtide on January 1, 20X5, are as follows:

	Glitter Enterprises	Lowtide Builders
Cash and Receivables	$ 80,000	$ 30,000
Inventory	150,000	350,000
Buildings and Equipment (net)	430,000	80,000
Investment in Lowtide Stock	90,000	
Total Assets	$750,000	$460,000
Current Liabilities	$100,000	$110,000
Long-Term Debt	400,000	200,000
Common Stock	200,000	140,000
Retained Earnings	50,000	10,000
Total Liabilities and Stockholders' Equity	$750,000	$460,000

Required

a. Give all eliminating entries needed to prepare a consolidated balance sheet on January 1, 20X5.
b. Complete a consolidated balance sheet workpaper.
c. Prepare a consolidated balance sheet in good form.

E5-6 Multiple-Choice Questions on Balance Sheet Consolidation

Planter Corporation purchased 70 percent of Silk Corporation's common stock on December 31, 20X2. Balance sheet data for the two companies immediately following the acquisition follow:

Item	Planter Corporation	Silk Corporation
Cash	$ 49,000	$ 30,000
Accounts Receivable	110,000	45,000
Inventory	130,000	70,000
Land	80,000	25,000
Buildings and Equipment	500,000	400,000
Less: Accumulated Depreciation	(223,000)	(165,000)
Investment in Silk Corporation Stock	145,500	
Total Assets	$791,500	$405,000

(continued)

Accounts Payable	$ 61,500	$ 28,000
Taxes Payable	95,000	37,000
Bonds Payable	280,000	200,000
Common Stock	150,000	50,000
Retained Earnings	205,000	90,000
Total Liabilities and Stockholders' Equity	$791,500	$405,000

At the date of the business combination, the book values of Silk's net assets and liabilities approximated fair value except for inventory, which had a fair value of $85,000, and land, which had a fair value of $45,000.

Required

For each question below, indicate the appropriate total that should appear in the consolidated balance sheet prepared immediately after the business combination.

1. What amount of inventory will be reported?

   a. $179,000.

   b. $200,000.

   c. $210,500.

   d. $215,000.

2. What amount of goodwill will be reported?

   a. $0.

   b. $23,000.

   c. $29,500.

   d. $47,500.

3. What amount of total assets will be reported?

   a. $1,196,500.

   b. $1,098,500.

   c. $1,086,000.

   d. $1,051,000.

4. What amount of total liabilities will be reported?

   a. $265,000.

   b. $436,500.

   c. $622,000.

   d. $701,500.

5. What amount will be reported as noncontrolling interest?

   a. $42,000.

   b. $48,000.

   c. $106,500.

   d. $148,500.

6. What amount of consolidated retained earnings will be reported?

   a. $295,000.

   b. $268,000.

   c. $232,000.

   d. $205,000.

7. What amount of total stockholders' equity will be reported?

   a. $355,000.

   b. $397,000.

   c. $453,000.

   d. $495,000.

E5-7 Basic Consolidation Entries for Majority-Owned Subsidiary

Farmstead Company reported the following summarized balance sheet data on December 31, 20X8:

Assets	$350,000	Accounts Payable	$ 50,000
		Common Stock	100,000
		Retained Earnings	200,000
Total	$350,000	Total	$350,000

On January 1, 20X9, Horrigan Corporation purchased 70 percent of Farmstead's stock for $210,000. Farmstead reported net income of $20,000 for 20X9 and paid dividends of $5,000.

Required

a. Give the equity-method journal entries recorded by Horrigan on its books during 20X9 related to its ownership of Farmstead.

b. Give the eliminating entries needed on December 31, 20X9, to prepare consolidated financial statements.

E5-8 Majority-Owned Subsidiary with Differential

Canton Corporation is a majority-owned subsidiary of Winston Corporation, which acquired 75 percent ownership of it on January 1, 20X3, for $133,500. At that date, Canton reported common stock outstanding of $60,000 and retained earnings of $90,000. The purchase differential is assigned to equipment with an economic life of seven years at the date of the business combination. Canton reported net income of $30,000 and paid dividends of $12,000 in 20X3.

Required

a. Give the journal entries recorded by Winston during 20X3 on its books if it accounts for its investment in Canton using the equity method.

b. Give the eliminating entries needed at December 31, 20X3, to prepare consolidated financial statements.

E5-9 Differential Assigned to Amortizable Asset

Franklin Corporation acquired 90 percent of Lancaster Company's voting common stock on January 1, 20X1, for $486,000. At the time of the combination, Lancaster reported common stock outstanding of $120,000 and retained earnings of $380,000. The book value of Lancaster's net assets approximated market value except for patents that had a market value of $40,000 more than their book value. The patents had a remaining economic life of five years at the date of the business combination. Lancaster reported net income of $60,000 and paid dividends of $20,000 during 20X1.

Required

a. What balance did Franklin report as its investment in Lancaster at December 31, 20X1, assuming Franklin uses the equity method in accounting for its investment?

b. Give the eliminating entry or entries needed to prepare consolidated financial statements at December 31, 20X1.

E5-10 Consolidation after One Year of Ownership

Steadry Corporation purchased 80 percent of Lowe Corporation's stock on January 1, 20X2. At that date Lowe reported retained earnings of $80,000 and had $120,000 of stock outstanding. The fair value of its equipment and buildings was $32,000 more than the book value.

Steadry paid $190,000 to acquire the Lowe shares. The remaining economic life for all Lowe's depreciable assets was eight years on the date of combination. The amount of the differential assigned to goodwill is not amortized. Lowe reported net income of $40,000 in 20X2 and declared no dividends.

Required

a. Give the eliminating entries needed to prepare a consolidated balance sheet immediately after Steadry purchased Lowe stock.

b. Give all eliminating entries needed to prepare a full set of consolidated financial statements for 20X2.

E5-11 Computation of Income Reported by Subsidiary

Blithe Company purchased 60 percent of Spirit Company's stock for $100,000 on January 1, 20X6, when Spirit reported $120,000 of common stock outstanding and retained earnings of $25,000. On December 31, 20X8, Blithe reported its investment in Spirit at $126,100 using equity-method accounting for its investment. Blithe received dividends from Spirit totaling $15,000 over the three-year period. The purchase differential is amortized over 10 years.

Required

Determine the amount of net income reported by Spirit over the three-year period.

E5-12 Consolidation Following Three Years of Ownership

Boxwell Corporation purchased 60 percent of Conway Company ownership on January 1, 20X7, for $277,500. Conway reported the following net income and dividend payments:

Year	Net Income	Dividends Paid
20X7	$45,000	$25,000
20X8	55,000	35,000
20X9	30,000	10,000

On January 1, 20X7, Conway had $250,000 of $5 par value common stock outstanding and retained earnings of $150,000. At that date, Conway held land with a book value of $22,500 and a market value of $30,000 and equipment with a book value of $320,000 and a market value of $360,000. The remainder of the purchase price was attributable to an increase in the value of patents, which had a remaining useful life of 10 years. All depreciable assets held by Conway at the date of acquisition had a remaining economic life of six years.

Required

a. Prepare the eliminating entries needed at January 1, 20X7, to prepare a consolidated balance sheet.

b. Compute the balance reported by Boxwell as its investment in Conway at January 1, 20X9.

c. Prepare the journal entries recorded by Boxwell with regard to its investment in Conway during 20X9.

d. Prepare the eliminating entries needed at December 31, 20X9, to prepare a three-part consolidation workpaper.

E5-13 Multiple-Choice Questions on Consolidated Balances

Farrow Corporation acquired 70 percent of the stock of Rand Company on January 1, 20X7, for $300,000. Other relevant data are as follows:

	Farrow	Rand
Common stock outstanding	$200,000	$250,000
Retained earnings, January 1, 20X7	240,000	150,000
Net income for 20X7		40,000
Operating income, excluding investment income	180,000	
Dividends declared	35,000	10,000

The excess of purchase price over book value was assigned to depreciable assets with a remaining economic life of five years.

Required

Select the correct answer for each of the following:

1. What amount of investment income will Farrow report for 20X7 on its investment in Rand?

    a. $36,000.

    b. $28,000.

    c. $25,200.

    d. $24,000.

2. What amount of consolidated net income will be reported for 20X7?

   a. $220,000.

   b. $216,000.

   c. $208,000.

   d. $204,000.

3. What amount of income will be assigned to the noncontrolling interest in the 20X7 consolidated income statement?

   a. $66,000.

   b. $12,000.

   c. $10,800.

   d. $9,000.

4. What amount will be reported as dividend payments by the consolidated entity for 20X7?

   a. $45,000.

   b. $42,000.

   c. $38,000.

   d. $35,000.

5. What amount will be reported as common stock outstanding in the consolidated balance sheet prepared at December 31, 20X7?

   a. $200,000.

   b. $275,000.

   c. $375,000.

   d. $450,000.

6. What amount will be reported in the consolidated balance sheet prepared at December 31, 20X7, as the balance in retained earnings?

   a. $240,000.

   b. $390,000.

   c. $409,000.

   d. $589,000.

7. What amount will Farrow show as its investment in Rand at December 31, 20X7?

   a. $300,000.

   b. $317,000.

   c. $314,000.

   d. $328,000.

E5-14 **Consolidation Workpaper for Majority-Owned Subsidiary**

Proud Corporation purchased 80 percent of Stergis Company's voting stock on January 1, 20X3, at underlying book value. Proud uses the equity method in accounting for its ownership of Stergis during 20X3. On December 31, 20X3, the trial balances of the two companies are as follows:

Item	Proud Corporation		Stergis Company	
	Debit	Credit	Debit	Credit
Current Assets	$173,000		$105,000	
Depreciable Assets	500,000		300,000	
Investment in Stergis Company Stock	136,000			
Depreciation Expense	25,000		15,000	
Other Expenses	105,000		75,000	
Dividends Declared	40,000		10,000	

(continued)

Accumulated Depreciation	$175,000		$ 75,000
Current Liabilities	50,000		40,000
Long-Term Debt	100,000		120,000
Common Stock	200,000		100,000
Retained Earnings	230,000		50,000
Sales	200,000		120,000
Income from Subsidiary	24,000		
	$979,000	$979,000	$505,000	$505,000

Required

a. Give all eliminating entries required as of December 31, 20X3, to prepare consolidated financial statements.

b. Prepare a three-part consolidation workpaper.

c. Prepare a consolidated balance sheet, income statement, and retained earnings statement for 20X3.

E5-15   Consolidation Workpaper for Majority-Owned Subsidiary for Second Year

Proud Corporation purchased 80 percent of Stergis Company's voting stock on January 1, 20X3, at underlying book value. Proud uses the equity method in accounting for its ownership of Stergis. On December 31, 20X4, the trial balances of the two companies are as follows:

	Proud Corporation		Stergis Company	
Item	**Debit**	**Credit**	**Debit**	**Credit**
Current Assets	$235,000		$150,000	
Depreciable Assets (net)	500,000		300,000	
Investment in Stergis Company Stock	152,000			
Depreciation Expense	25,000		15,000	
Other Expenses	150,000		90,000	
Dividends Declared	50,000		15,000	
Accumulated Depreciation		$ 200,000		$ 90,000
Current Liabilities		70,000		50,000
Long-Term Debt		100,000		120,000
Common Stock		200,000		100,000
Retained Earnings		284,000		70,000
Sales		230,000		140,000
Income from Subsidiary		28,000		
	$1,112,000	$1,112,000	$570,000	$570,000

Required

a. Give all eliminating entries required on December 31, 20X4, to prepare consolidated financial statements.

b. Prepare a three-part consolidation workpaper as of December 31, 20X4.

E5-16   Preparation of Stockholders' Equity Section with Other Comprehensive Income

Tollway Corporation purchased 75 percent of Stem Corporation's common stock on January 1, 20X8, for $435,000. At that date, Stem reported common stock outstanding of $300,000 and retained earnings of $200,000. The purchase differential is assigned to other intangible assets and amortized over 10 years. Tollway and Stem reported the following data for 20X8 and 20X9:

	Stem Corporation			Tollway Corporation	
Year	Net Income	Comprehensive Income	Dividends Paid	Operating Income	Dividends Paid
20X8	$40,000	$50,000	$15,000	$120,000	$70,000
20X9	60,000	65,000	30,000	140,000	70,000

Required

a. Compute consolidated net income for 20X8 and 20X9.

b. Compute consolidated comprehensive income for 20X8 and 20X9.

c. Assuming that Tollway reported capital stock outstanding of $320,000 and retained earnings of $430,000 at January 1, 20X8, prepare the stockholders' equity section of the consolidated balance sheet at December 31, 20X8 and 20X9.

E5-17   Eliminating Entries for Subsidiary with Other Comprehensive Income

Palmer Corporation purchased 70 percent of Krown Corporation's ownership on January 1, 20X8, for $140,000. At that date Krown reported capital stock outstanding of $120,000 and retained earnings of $80,000. During 20X8, Krown reported net income of $30,000 and comprehensive income of $36,000 and paid dividends of $25,000.

Required

a. Present all entries that Palmer would have recorded in accounting for its investment in Krown during 20X8.

b. Present all eliminating entries needed at December 31, 20X8, to prepare a complete set of consolidated financial statements for Palmer Corporation and its subsidiary.

E5-18*   Consolidation of Subsidiary with Negative Retained Earnings

General Corporation purchased 80 percent of Strap Company's voting common stock on January 1, 20X4, for $138,000. Strap's balance sheet at the date of acquisition contained the following balances:

STRAP COMPANY
Balance Sheet
January 1, 20X4

Cash	$ 20,000	Accounts Payable	$ 35,000
Accounts Receivable	35,000	Notes Payable	180,000
Land	90,000	Common Stock	100,000
Building and Equipment	300,000	Additional Paid-In Capital	75,000
Less: Accumulated Depreciation	(85,000)	Retained Earnings	(30,000)
Total Assets	$360,000	Total Liabilities and Stockholders' Equity	$360,000

At the date of acquisition, the reported book values of Strap's assets and liabilities approximated fair value.

Required

Give the eliminating entry or entries needed to prepare a consolidated balance sheet immediately following the business combination.

E5-19*   Complex Assignment of Differential

On December 31, 20X4, Holly Corporation purchased 90 percent of Brinker Inc.'s common stock for $888,000, a price $240,000 in excess of the book value of the shares acquired. Of the $240,000 differential, $5,000 related to the increased value of Brinker's inventory, $75,000 related to the increased value of its land, $60,000 related to the increased value of its equipment, and $50,000 was associated with a change in the value of its notes payable due to increasing interest rates. Brinker's equipment had a remaining life of 15 years from the date of combination. The amount of the differential assigned to goodwill is not amortized. Brinker sold all inventory it held at the end of 20X4 during 20X5; the land to which the differential related also was sold during the year for a large gain. The amortization of the differential relating to Brinker's notes payable was $7,500 for 20X5.

At the date of combination, Brinker reported retained earnings of $120,000, common stock outstanding of $500,000, and premium on common stock of $100,000. For the year 20X5, it reported net income of $68,000, but paid no dividends. Holly accounts for its investment in Brinker using the equity method.

Required

a. Present all entries that Holly would have recorded during 20X5 with respect to its investment in Brinker.

b. Present all elimination entries that would have been included in the workpaper to prepare a full set of consolidated financial statements for the year 20X5.

E5-20A **Basic Cost-Method Workpaper**

Blake Corporation purchased 100 percent of Shaw Corporation's voting shares on January 1, 20X3, at underlying book value. Blake uses the cost method in accounting for its investment in Shaw. Shaw's retained earnings, as shown in the 20X3 trial balance, was $50,000 on January 1, 20X3. On December 31, 20X3, the trial balance data for the two companies are as follows:

Item	Blake Corporation Debit	Blake Corporation Credit	Shaw Corporation Debit	Shaw Corporation Credit
Current Assets	$145,000		$105,000	
Depreciable Assets (net)	325,000		225,000	
Investment in Shaw Corporation Stock	150,000			
Depreciation Expense	25,000		15,000	
Other Expenses	105,000		75,000	
Dividends Declared	40,000		10,000	
Current Liabilities		$ 50,000		$ 40,000
Long-Term Debt		100,000		120,000
Common Stock		200,000		100,000
Retained Earnings		230,000		50,000
Sales		200,000		120,000
Dividend Income		10,000		
	$790,000	$790,000	$430,000	$430,000

Required

a. Give all eliminating entries needed to prepare a three-part consolidation workpaper as of December 31, 20X3.

b. Prepare the workpaper in good form.

E5-21A **Cost-Method Workpaper in Subsequent Period**

The trial balances for Blake Corporation and Shaw Corporation as of December 31, 20X4, follow:

Item	Blake Corporation Debit	Blake Corporation Credit	Shaw Corporation Debit	Shaw Corporation Credit
Current Assets	$170,000		$110,000	
Depreciable Assets (net)	300,000		210,000	
Investment in Shaw Corporation Stock	150,000			
Depreciation Expense	25,000		15,000	
Other Expenses	250,000		160,000	
Dividends Declared	20,000		15,000	

(continued)

(continued)

Item	Blake Corporation Debit	Blake Corporation Credit	Shaw Corporation Debit	Shaw Corporation Credit
Current Liabilities		$ 30,000		$ 20,000
Long-Term Debt		100,000		120,000
Common Stock		200,000		100,000
Retained Earnings		270,000		70,000
Sales		300,000		200,000
Dividend Income		15,000		
	$915,000	$915,000	$510,000	$510,000

Blake purchased 100 percent ownership of Shaw on January 1, 20X3, at a cost of $150,000. Shaw reported $50,000 of retained earnings at acquisition. Blake uses the cost method in accounting for its investment in Shaw.

Required

a. Give all eliminating entries required to prepare a full set of consolidated statements for 20X4.

b. Prepare a three-part consolidation workpaper in good form as of December 31, 20X4.

E5-22A   Cost-Method Consolidation for Majority-Owned Subsidiary

Lintner Corporation purchased 80 percent of Knight Company's voting stock on January 1, 20X6, at underlying book value. Lintner uses the cost method in accounting for its investment in Knight. Knight reported $50,000 of retained earnings at the time of acquisition. Trial balance data for the two companies on December 31, 20X7, are as follows:

Item	Lintner Corporation Debit	Lintner Corporation Credit	Knight Company Debit	Knight Company Credit
Current Assets	$ 183,000		$ 80,000	
Depreciable Assets	500,000		300,000	
Investment in Knight Company Stock	120,000			
Depreciation Expense	25,000		15,000	
Other Expenses	251,000		155,000	
Dividends Declared	25,000		20,000	
Accumulated Depreciation		$ 200,000		$ 90,000
Accounts Payable		120,000		110,000
Common Stock		200,000		100,000
Retained Earnings		268,000		70,000
Sales		300,000		200,000
Dividend Income		16,000		
	$1,104,000	$1,104,000	$570,000	$570,000

Required

a. Prepare eliminating entries as of December 31, 20X7, for a full set of consolidated statements.

b. Prepare a three-part consolidation workpaper as of December 31, 20X7.

c. Prepare a consolidated income statement, balance sheet, and retained earnings statement for 20X7.

E5-23B   Computation of Consolidated Balances

Slim Corporation's balance sheet at January 1, 20X7, reflected the following balances:

Cash and Receivables	$ 80,000	Accounts Payable	$ 40,000
Inventory	120,000	Income Taxes Payable	60,000
Land	70,000	Bonds Payable	200,000
Buildings and Equipment (net)	480,000	Common Stock	250,000
		Retained Earnings	200,000
Total Assets	$750,000	Total Liabilities and Stockholders' Equity	$750,000

Ford Corporation entered into an active acquisition program and purchased 80 percent of Slim's common stock on January 2, 20X7, for $470,000. The fair value of Slim as a whole at that date was determined to be $587,500. A careful review of the fair value of Slim's assets and liabilities indicated the following:

	Book Value	Fair Value
Inventory	$120,000	$140,000
Land	70,000	60,000
Buildings and Equipment (net)	480,000	550,000

Goodwill is assigned proportionately to Ford and the noncontrolling shareholders.

Required

Consistent with the proposed FASB recommendations illustrated in Appendix 5B, compute the appropriate amount to be included in the consolidated balance sheet immediately following the acquisition for each of the following items:

a. Inventory.

b. Land.

c. Buildings and Equipment (net).

d. Goodwill.

e. Investment in Slim Corporation.

f. Noncontrolling Interest.

E5-24B   ### Balance Sheet Workpaper

Power Company owns 90 percent of Pleasantdale Dairy's stock. The balance sheets of the two companies immediately after the Pleasantdale acquisition showed the following amounts:

	Power Company	Pleasantdale Dairy
Cash and Receivables	$ 130,000	$ 70,000
Inventory	210,000	90,000
Land	70,000	40,000
Buildings and Equipment (net)	390,000	220,000
Investment in Pleasantdale Stock	270,000	
Total Assets	$1,070,000	$420,000
Current Payables	$ 80,000	$ 40,000
Long-Term Liabilities	200,000	100,000
Common Stock	400,000	60,000
Retained Earnings	390,000	220,000
Total Liabilities and Stockholders' Equity	$1,070,000	$420,000

The fair value of Pleasantdale as a whole at the date of acquisition was determined to be $300,000. The full amount of the increase over book value is assigned to land held by Pleasantdale. At the date of acquisition, Pleasantdale owed Power $8,000 plus $900 accrued interest. Pleasantdale had recorded the accrued interest, but Power had not.

Required

Prepare and complete a consolidated balance sheet workpaper consistent with the proposed FASB recommendations illustrated in Appendix 5B.

E5-25B   ### Majority-Owned Subsidiary Purchased at Greater than Book Value

Zenith Corporation purchased 70 percent of Down Corporation's common stock on December 31, 20X4, for $102,200. The fair value of Down as a whole at that date was determined to be $146,000. Data from the balance sheets of the two companies included the following amounts as of the date of acquisition:

Item	Zenith Corporation	Down Corporation
Cash	$ 50,300	$ 21,000
Accounts Receivable	90,000	44,000
Inventory	130,000	75,000
Land	60,000	30,000
Buildings and Equipment	410,000	250,000
Less: Accumulated Depreciation	(150,000)	(80,000)
Investment in Down Corporation Stock	102,200	
Total Assets	$692,500	$340,000
Accounts Payable	$152,500	$ 35,000
Mortgage Payable	250,000	180,000
Common Stock	80,000	40,000
Retained Earnings	210,000	85,000
Total Liabilities and Stockholders' Equity	$692,500	$340,000

At the date of the business combination, the book values of Down's assets and liabilities approximated fair value except for inventory, which had a fair value of $81,000, and buildings and equipment, which had a fair value of $185,000. At December 31, 20X4, Zenith reported accounts payable of $12,500 to Down, which reported an equal amount in its accounts receivable.

Required

a. Consistent with the proposed FASB recommendations illustrated in Appendix 5B, give the eliminating entry or entries needed to prepare a consolidated balance sheet immediately following the business combination.

b. Prepare a consolidated balance sheet workpaper.

c. Prepare a consolidated balance sheet in good form.

Problems

P5-26 Majority-Owned Subsidiary Purchased at Book Value

Cameron Corporation purchased 70 percent of Darla Corporation's common stock on December 31, 20X4, for $87,500. Data from the balance sheets of the two companies included the following amounts as of the date of acquisition:

Item	Cameron Corporation	Darla Corporation
Cash	$ 65,000	$ 21,000
Accounts Receivable	90,000	44,000
Inventory	130,000	75,000
Land	60,000	30,000
Buildings and Equipment	410,000	250,000
Less: Accumulated Depreciation	(150,000)	(80,000)
Investment in Darla Corporation Stock	87,500	
Total Assets	$692,500	$340,000
Accounts Payable	$152,500	$ 35,000
Mortgage Payable	250,000	180,000
Common Stock	80,000	40,000
Retained Earnings	210,000	85,000
Total Liabilities and Stockholders' Equity	$692,500	$340,000

At the date of the business combination, the book values of Darla Corporation's assets and liabilities approximated fair value. At December 31, 20X4, Cameron reported accounts payable of $12,500 to Darla, which reported an equal amount in its accounts receivable.

Required

a. Give the eliminating entry or entries needed to prepare a consolidated balance sheet immediately following the business combination.

b. Prepare a consolidated balance sheet workpaper.

c. Prepare a consolidated balance sheet in good form.

P5-27 Majority-Owned Subsidiary Purchased at Greater than Book Value

Cameron Corporation purchased 70 percent of Darla Corporation's common stock on December 31, 20X4, for $102,200. Data from the balance sheets of the two companies included the following amounts as of the date of acquisition:

Item	Cameron Corporation	Darla Corporation
Cash	$ 50,300	$ 21,000
Accounts Receivable	90,000	44,000
Inventory	130,000	75,000
Land	60,000	30,000
Buildings and Equipment	410,000	250,000
Less: Accumulated Depreciation	(150,000)	(80,000)
Investment in Darla Corporation Stock	102,200	
Total Assets	$692,500	$340,000
Accounts Payable	$152,500	$ 35,000
Mortgage Payable	250,000	180,000
Common Stock	80,000	40,000
Retained Earnings	210,000	85,000
Total Liabilities and Stockholders' Equity	$692,500	$340,000

At the date of the business combination, the book values of Darla's assets and liabilities approximated fair value except for inventory, which had a fair value of $81,000, and buildings and equipment, which had a fair value of $185,000. At December 31, 20X4, Cameron reported accounts payable of $12,500 to Darla, which reported an equal amount in its accounts receivable.

Required

a. Give the eliminating entry or entries needed to prepare a consolidated balance sheet immediately following the business combination.

b. Prepare a consolidated balance sheet workpaper.

c. Prepare a consolidated balance sheet in good form.

P5-28 Comprehensive Problem: Consolidation of Majority-Owned Subsidiary

On January 2, 20X8, B. N. Counter Corporation purchased 75 percent of Ticken Tie Company's outstanding common stock. In exchange for Ticken Tie's stock, B. N. Counter issued bonds payable with a par and fair value of $500,000 directly to the selling stockholders of Ticken Tie. The two companies continued to operate as separate entities subsequent to the combination.

Immediately prior to the combination, the book values and fair values of the companies' assets and liabilities were as follows:

	B. N. Counter		Ticken Tie	
	Book Value	Fair Value	Book Value	Fair Value
Cash	$ 12,000	$ 12,000	$ 9,000	$ 9,000
Receivables	41,000	39,000	31,000	30,000
Allowance for Bad Debts	(2,000)		(1,000)	
Inventory	86,000	89,000	68,000	72,000
Land	55,000	200,000	50,000	70,000
Buildings and Equipment	960,000	650,000	670,000	500,000
Accumulated Depreciation	(411,000)		(220,000)	
Patent				40,000
Total Assets	$741,000	$990,000	$607,000	$721,000

(continued)

(continued)

	B. N. Counter		Ticken Tie	
	Book Value	**Fair Value**	**Book Value**	**Fair Value**
Current Payables	$ 38,000	$ 38,000	$ 29,000	$29,000
Bonds Payable	200,000	210,000	100,000	90,000
Common Stock	300,000		200,000	
Additional Paid-In Capital	100,000		130,000	
Retained Earnings	103,000		148,000	
Total Liabilities and Equity	$741,000		$607,000	

At the date of combination, Ticken Tie owed B. N. Counter $6,000 plus accrued interest of $500 on a short-term note. Both companies have properly recorded these amounts.

Required

a. Record the business combination on the books of B. N. Counter Corporation.

b. Present in general journal form all elimination entries needed in a workpaper to prepare a consolidated balance sheet immediately following the business combination on January 2, 20X8.

c. Prepare and complete a consolidated balance sheet workpaper as of January 2, 20X8, immediately following the business combination.

d. Present a consolidated balance sheet for B. N. Counter and its subsidiary as of January 2, 20X8.

P5-29   Incomplete Data

Thorne Corporation purchased controlling ownership of Skyler Corporation on December 31, 20X3, and a consolidated balance sheet was prepared immediately. Partial balance sheet data for the two companies and the consolidated entity at that date follow:

THORNE CORPORATION AND SKYLER CORPORATION
Balance Sheet Data
December 31, 20X3

Item	Thorne Corporation	Skyler Corporation	Consolidated Entity
Cash	$ 60,500	$ 35,000	$ 95,500
Accounts Receivable	98,000	?	148,000
Inventory	105,000	80,000	191,500
Buildings and Equipment	400,000	340,000	766,000
Less: Accumulated Depreciation	(215,000)	(140,000)	(355,000)
Investment in Skyler Corporation Stock	?		
Goodwill			9,000
Total Assets	$620,000	$380,000	$855,000
Accounts Payable	$115,000	$ 46,000	$146,000
Wages Payable	?	?	94,000
Notes Payable	200,000	110,000	310,000
Common Stock	120,000	75,000	?
Retained Earnings	115,000	125,000	?
Noncontrolling Interest			70,000
Total Liabilities and Equities	$?	$380,000	$855,000

During 20X3, Thorne provided engineering services to Skyler and has not yet been paid for them. There were no other receivables or payables between Thorne and Skyler at December 31, 20X3.

Required

a. What is the amount of unpaid engineering services at December 31, 20X3, on work done by Thorne for Skyler?

b. What balance in accounts receivable did Skyler report at December 31, 20X3?

c. What amounts of wages payable did Thorne and Skyler report at December 31, 20X3?

d. What percentage of Skyler's shares were purchased by Thorne?

e. What amounts of capital stock and retained earnings must be reported in the consolidated balance sheet?

f. What amount did Thorne pay to acquire the Skyler shares?

P5-30 Ownership Balances

Penn Corporation acquired 75 percent of Eastland Company's voting common stock on January 1, 20X2, for $648,000. The purchase differential was assigned to equipment with a remaining economic life of eight years at the date of acquisition. On that date, Eastland reported the following stockholders' equity balances:

Common Stock, $10 par value	$300,000
Additional Paid-In Capital	180,000
Retained Earnings	320,000

Penn Corporation reported retained earnings of $485,000 at January 1, 20X2, and operating income of $65,000, $80,000, and $50,000 in 20X2, 20X3, and 20X4, respectively. Penn and Eastland paid dividends of $30,000 and $20,000, respectively, each of the three years. Eastland had 30,000 shares of common stock outstanding throughout the three-year period. In the consolidated balance sheet prepared at December 31, 20X4, noncontrolling interest was reported at $227,500.

Required

a. Compute the balance in Retained Earnings reported by Eastland Company on December 31, 20X4.

b. Compute the balance in the investment account reported by Penn on December 31, 20X4, assuming it uses the equity method in accounting for its ownership of Eastland.

c. Compute the balance in consolidated retained earnings on December 31, 20X4.

P5-31 Income and Retained Earnings

Quill Corporation purchased 70 percent of North Company's stock on January 1, 20X9, for $105,000. The companies reported the following stockholders' equity balances immediately after the acquisition:

	Quill Corporation	North Company
Common Stock	$120,000	$ 30,000
Additional Paid-In Capital	230,000	80,000
Retained Earnings	290,000	40,000
Total	$640,000	$150,000

Quill and North reported 20X9 operating incomes of $90,000 and $35,000 and dividend payments of $30,000 and $10,000, respectively.

Required

a. Compute the amount reported as net income by each company for 20X9, assuming Quill uses equity-method accounting for its investment in North.

b. Compute consolidated net income for 20X9.

c. Compute the reported balance in retained earnings at December 31, 20X9, for both companies.

d. Compute consolidated retained earnings at December 31, 20X9.

e. How would the computation of consolidated retained earnings at December 31, 20X9, change if Quill uses the cost method in accounting for its investment in North?

P5-32 Consolidation Workpaper at End of First Year of Ownership

Power Corporation acquired 75 percent of Best Company's ownership on January 1, 20X8, for $96,000. At that date, the fair value of Best's buildings and equipment was $20,000 more than book value. Buildings and equipment are depreciated on a 10-year basis. Although goodwill is not amortized, the management of Power concluded at December 31, 20X8, that goodwill involved in its purchase of Best shares had been impaired and the correct carrying value was $2,500.

Trial balance data for Power and Best on December 31, 20X8, are as follows:

Item	Power Corporation		Best Company	
	Debit	Credit	Debit	Credit
Cash	$ 47,500		$ 21,000	
Accounts Receivable	70,000		12,000	
Inventory	90,000		25,000	
Land	30,000		15,000	
Buildings and Equipment	350,000		150,000	
Investment in Best Co. Stock	100,500			
Cost of Goods Sold	125,000		110,000	
Wage Expense	42,000		27,000	
Depreciation Expense	25,000		10,000	
Interest Expense	12,000		4,000	
Other Expenses	13,500		5,000	
Dividends Declared	30,000		16,000	
Accumulated Depreciation		$145,000		$ 40,000
Accounts Payable		45,000		16,000
Wages Payable		17,000		9,000
Notes Payable		150,000		50,000
Common Stock		200,000		60,000
Retained Earnings		102,000		40,000
Sales		260,000		180,000
Income from Subsidiary		16,500		
	$935,500	$935,500	$395,000	$395,000

Required

a. Give all eliminating entries needed to prepare a three-part consolidation workpaper as of December 31, 20X8.

b. Prepare a three-part consolidation workpaper for 20X8 in good form.

P5-33 **Consolidation Workpaper at End of Second Year of Ownership**

Power Corporation acquired 75 percent of Best Company's ownership on January 1, 20X8, for $96,000. At that date, the fair value of Best's buildings and equipment was $20,000 more than book value. Buildings and equipment are depreciated on a 10-year basis. Although goodwill is not amortized, the management of Power concluded at December 31, 20X8, that goodwill involved in its purchase of Best shares had been impaired and the correct carrying value was $2,500. No additional impairment occurred in 20X9.

Trial balance data for Power and Best on December 31, 20X9, are as follows:

Item	Power Corporation		Best Company	
	Debit	Credit	Debit	Credit
Cash	$ 68,500		$ 32,000	
Accounts Receivable	85,000		14,000	
Inventory	97,000		24,000	
Land	50,000		25,000	
Buildings and Equipment	350,000		150,000	
Investment in Best Co. Stock	111,000			

(continued)

Cost of Goods Sold	145,000		114,000	
Wage Expense	35,000		20,000	
Depreciation Expense	25,000		10,000	
Interest Expense	12,000		4,000	
Other Expenses	23,000		16,000	
Dividends Declared	30,000		20,000	
Accumulated Depreciation		$ 170,000		$ 50,000
Accounts Payable		51,000		15,000
Wages Payable		14,000		6,000
Notes Payable		150,000		50,000
Common Stock		200,000		60,000
Retained Earnings		131,000		48,000
Sales		290,000		200,000
Income from Subsidiary		25,500		
	$1,031,500	$1,031,500	$429,000	$429,000

Required

a. Give all eliminating entries needed to prepare a three-part consolidation workpaper as of December 31, 20X9.

b. Prepare a three-part consolidation workpaper for 20X9 in good form.

c. Prepare a consolidated balance sheet, income statement, and retained earnings statement for 20X9.

P5-34 Comprehensive Problem: Majority-Owned Subsidiary

Pillar Corporation acquired 80 percent ownership of Stanley Wood Products Company on January 1, 20X1, for $160,000. On that date Stanley reported retained earnings of $50,000 and had $100,000 of common stock outstanding. Pillar has used the equity method in accounting for its investment in Stanley.

Trial balance data for the two companies on December 31, 20X5, are as follows:

Item	Pillar Corporation Debit	Pillar Corporation Credit	Stanley Wood Products Company Debit	Stanley Wood Products Company Credit
Cash and Receivables	$ 81,000		$ 65,000	
Inventory	260,000		90,000	
Land	80,000		80,000	
Buildings and Equipment	500,000		150,000	
Investment in Stanley Wood Products Stock	188,000			
Cost of Goods Sold	120,000		50,000	
Depreciation Expense	25,000		15,000	
Inventory Losses	15,000		5,000	
Dividends Declared	30,000		10,000	
Accumulated Depreciation		$ 205,000		$105,000
Accounts Payable		60,000		20,000
Notes Payable		200,000		50,000
Common Stock		300,000		100,000
Retained Earnings		314,000		90,000
Sales		200,000		100,000
Income from Subsidiary		20,000		
	$1,299,000	$1,299,000	$465,000	$465,000

Additional Information

1. On the date of combination, the fair value of Stanley's depreciable assets was $50,000 more than book value. The purchase differential assigned to depreciable assets should be written off over the following 10-year period.
2. There was $10,000 of intercorporate receivables and payables at the end of 20X5.

Required

a. Give all journal entries that Pillar recorded during 20X5 related to its investment in Stanley.
b. Give all eliminating entries needed to prepare consolidated statements for 20X5.
c. Prepare a three-part workpaper as of December 31, 20X5.

P5-35 **Comprehensive Problem: Differential Apportionment**

Bigelow Corporation purchased 80 percent of Granite Company on January 1, 20X7, for $173,000. The trial balances for the two companies on December 31, 20X7, included the following amounts:

Item	Bigelow Corporation Debit	Bigelow Corporation Credit	Granite Company Debit	Granite Company Credit
Cash	$ 38,000		$ 25,000	
Accounts Receivable	50,000		55,000	
Inventory	240,000		100,000	
Land	80,000		20,000	
Buildings and Equipment	500,000		150,000	
Investment in Granite Company Stock	202,000			
Cost of Goods Sold	500,000		250,000	
Depreciation Expense	25,000		15,000	
Other Expenses	75,000		75,000	
Dividends Declared	50,000		20,000	
Accumulated Depreciation		$ 155,000		$ 75,000
Accounts Payable		70,000		35,000
Mortgages Payable		200,000		50,000
Common Stock		300,000		50,000
Retained Earnings		290,000		100,000
Sales		700,000		400,000
Income from Subsidiary		45,000		
	$1,760,000	$1,760,000	$710,000	$710,000

Additional Information

1. On January 1, 20X7, Granite reported net assets with a book value of $150,000. A total of $20,000 of the purchase price is applied to goodwill, which was not impaired in 20X7.
2. Granite's depreciable assets had an estimated economic life of 11 years on the date of combination. The difference between fair value and book value of tangible assets is related entirely to buildings and equipment.
3. Bigelow used the equity method in accounting for its investment in Granite.
4. Detailed analysis of receivables and payables showed that Granite owed Bigelow $16,000 on December 31, 20X7.

Required

a. Give all journal entries recorded by Bigelow with regard to its investment in Granite during 20X7.
b. Give all eliminating entries needed to prepare a full set of consolidated financial statements for 20X7.
c. Prepare a three-part consolidation workpaper as of December 31, 20X7.

P5-36   **Comprehensive Problem: Differential Apportionment in Subsequent Period**

Bigelow Corporation purchased 80 percent of Granite Company on January 1, 20X7, for $173,000. The trial balances for the two companies on December 31, 20X8, included the following amounts:

Item	Bigelow Corporation Debit	Bigelow Corporation Credit	Granite Company Debit	Granite Company Credit
Cash	$ 59,000		$ 31,000	
Accounts Receivable	83,000		71,000	
Inventory	275,000		118,000	
Land	80,000		30,000	
Buildings and Equipment	500,000		150,000	
Investment in Granite Company Stock	215,000			
Cost of Goods Sold	490,000		310,000	
Depreciation Expense	25,000		15,000	
Other Expenses	62,000		100,000	
Dividends Declared	45,000		25,000	
Accumulated Depreciation		$ 180,000		$ 90,000
Accounts Payable		86,000		30,000
Mortgages Payable		200,000		70,000
Common Stock		300,000		50,000
Retained Earnings		385,000		140,000
Sales		650,000		470,000
Income from Subsidiary		33,000		
	$1,834,000	$1,834,000	$850,000	$850,000

Additional Information

1. On January 1, 20X7, Granite reported net assets with a book value of $150,000. A total of $20,000 of the purchase price is applied to goodwill. At December 31, 20X8, Bigelow management reviewed the amount attributed to goodwill and concluded goodwill was impaired and should be reduced to $6,000.
2. Granite's depreciable assets had an estimated economic life of 11 years on the date of combination. The difference between fair value and book value of tangible assets is related entirely to Buildings and Equipment.
3. Bigelow used the equity method in accounting for its investment in Granite.
4. Detailed analysis of receivables and payables showed that Bigelow owed Granite $9,000 on December 31, 20X8.

Required

a. Give all journal entries recorded by Bigelow with regard to its investment in Granite during 20X8.

b. Give all eliminating entries needed to prepare a full set of consolidated financial statements for 20X8.

c. Prepare a three-part consolidation workpaper as of December 31, 20X8.

P5-37   **Analyzing Consolidated Data**

Buckman Corporation and Eckel Mining Company reported the following balance sheet data as of December 31, 20X3:

BUCKMAN CORPORATION
Balance Sheet
December 31, 20X3

Current Assets	$ 81,000	Current Liabilities	$ 70,000
Long-Term Assets (net)	400,000	Bonds Payable	100,000
Investment in Eckel Mining Company	120,000	Common Stock	200,000
		Retained Earnings	231,000
Total	$601,000	Total	$601,000

ECKEL MINING COMPANY
Balance Sheet
December 31, 20X3

Current Assets	$ 50,000	Current Liabilities	$ 30,000
Long-Term Assets (net)	200,000	Bonds Payable	50,000
		Common Stock	100,000
		Retained Earnings	70,000
Total	$250,000	Total	$250,000

Buckman purchased controlling ownership of Eckel on January 1, 20X3. The amount Buckman paid in excess of book value relates to production patents held by Eckel. Buckman uses the equity method in accounting for its ownership in Eckel. Since Buckman has more than 50 percent ownership of Eckel, it prepared consolidated statements for 20X3 as follows:

BUCKMAN CORPORATION AND SUBSIDIARY
Consolidated Balance Sheet
December 31, 20X3

Current Assets	$ 91,000	Current Liabilities	$ 60,000
Long-Term Assets (net)	600,000	Bonds Payable	150,000
Patents	18,000	Noncontrolling Interest	68,000
		Common Stock	200,000
		Retained Earnings	231,000
Total	$709,000	Total	$709,000

BUCKMAN CORPORATION AND SUBSIDIARY
Consolidated Income Statement
For the Year Ended December 31, 20X3

Sales		$400,000
Cost of Goods Sold	$260,000	
Other Expenses	57,000	(317,000)
		$ 83,000
Income to Noncontrolling Interest		(12,000)
Consolidated Net Income		$ 71,000

The patents are amortized over a 10-year life.

Required

a. What percentage of Eckel Mining's common stock does Buckman hold?

b. Was the stock purchase made at underlying book value or at some other amount? If at another amount, how much more or less than book value was paid?

c. What amount of net income did Eckel Mining report for 20X3?

d. If Eckel Mining paid dividends of $10,000 in 20X3, (1) what was the balance of the noncontrolling interest on January 1, 20X3, and (2) what amount did Buckman pay to purchase the Eckel Mining shares on January 1, 20X3?

e. Were there any intercompany receivables or payables on December 31, 20X3? If so, what amount?

P5-38 Subsidiary with Other Comprehensive Income in Year of Acquisition

Amber Corporation acquired 60 percent ownership of Sparta Company on January 1, 20X8, at underlying book value. Trial balance data at December 31, 20X8, for Amber and Sparta are as follows:

Item	AMBER CORPORATION Debit	AMBER CORPORATION Credit	SPARTA COMPANY Debit	SPARTA COMPANY Credit
Cash	$ 27,000		$ 8,000	
Accounts Receivable	65,000		22,000	
Inventory	40,000		30,000	
Buildings and Equipment	500,000		235,000	
Investment in Row Company Securities			40,000	
Investment in Sparta Company	108,000			
Cost of Goods Sold	150,000		110,000	
Depreciation Expense	30,000		10,000	
Interest Expense	8,000		3,000	
Dividends Declared	24,000		15,000	
Accumulated Depreciation		$140,000		$ 85,000
Accounts Payable		63,000		20,000
Bonds Payable		100,000		50,000
Common Stock		200,000		100,000
Retained Earnings		208,000		60,000
Other Comprehensive Income from Subsidiary (OCI)—Unrealized Gain on Investments		6,000		
Unrealized Gain on Investments (OCI)				10,000
Sales		220,000		148,000
Income from Subsidiary		15,000		
	$952,000	$952,000	$473,000	$473,000

Additional Information

Sparta purchased stock of Row Company on January 1, 20X8, for $30,000 and classified the investment as available-for-sale securities. The value of Row's securities increased to $40,000 at December 31, 20X8.

Required

a. Give all eliminating entries needed to prepare a three-part consolidation workpaper as of December 31, 20X8.

b. Prepare a three-part consolidation workpaper for 20X8 in good form.

c. Prepare a consolidated balance sheet, income statement, and statement of comprehensive income for 20X8.

P5-39 ### Subsidiary with Other Comprehensive Income in Year Following Acquisition

Amber Corporation acquired 60 percent ownership of Sparta Company on January 1, 20X8, at underlying book value. Trial balance data at December 31, 20X9, for Amber and Sparta are as follows:

Item	Amber Corporation Debit	Amber Corporation Credit	Sparta Company Debit	Sparta Company Credit
Cash	$ 18,000		$ 11,000	
Accounts Receivable	45,000		21,000	
Inventory	40,000		30,000	
Buildings and Equipment	585,000		257,000	
Investment in Row Company Securities			44,000	
Investment in Sparta Company	116,400			
Cost of Goods Sold	170,000		97,000	
Depreciation Expense	30,000		10,000	
Interest Expense	8,000		3,000	
Dividends Declared	40,000		20,000	

(continued)

(continued)

Item	Amber Corporation Debit	Amber Corporation Credit	Sparta Company Debit	Sparta Company Credit
Accumulated Depreciation		$ 170,000		$ 95,000
Accounts Payable		75,000		24,000
Bonds Payable		100,000		50,000
Common Stock		200,000		100,000
Retained Earnings		231,000		70,000
Accumulated Other Comprehensive Income		6,000		10,000
Other Comprehensive Income from Subsidiary (OCI)—Unrealized Gain on Investments		2,400		
Unrealized Gain on Investments (OCI)				4,000
Sales		250,000		140,000
Income from Subsidiary		18,000		
	$1,052,400	$1,052,400	$493,000	$493,000

Additional Information

Sparta purchased stock of Row Company on January 1, 20X8, for $30,000 and classified the investment as available-for-sale securities. The value of Row's securities increased to $40,000 and $44,000, respectively, at December 31, 20X8, and 20X9.

Required

a. Give all eliminating entries needed to prepare a three-part consolidation workpaper as of December 31, 20X9.

b. Prepare a three-part consolidation workpaper for 20X9 in good form.

P5-40A Cost-Method Workpaper with Differential

Trial balance data for Light Corporation and Star Company on December 31, 20X5, are as follows:

Item	Light Corporation Debit	Light Corporation Credit	Star Company Debit	Star Company Credit
Cash	$ 37,000		$ 20,000	
Accounts Receivable	50,000		30,000	
Inventory	70,000		60,000	
Buildings and Equipment	300,000		240,000	
Investment in Star Company Stock (at cost)	220,000			
Cost of Goods Sold	210,000		85,000	
Depreciation Expense	25,000		20,000	
Other Expenses	23,000		25,000	
Dividends Declared	20,000		10,000	
Accumulated Depreciation		$105,000		$ 65,000
Accounts Payable		40,000		20,000
Taxes Payable		70,000		55,000
Common Stock		200,000		150,000
Retained Earnings, January 1		230,000		50,000
Sales		300,000		150,000
Dividend Income		10,000		
	$955,000	$955,000	$490,000	$490,000

Light purchased all of Star's shares on January 1, 20X5, for $220,000. The full purchase differential is assigned to goodwill. At December 31, 20X5, the management of Light reviewed the amount attributed to goodwill and concluded goodwill had been impaired and should be reported at $8,000. Light uses the cost method in accounting for its investment in Star.

Required

Present all eliminating entries needed to prepare consolidated financial statements for the year 20X5, and prepare a three-part consolidation workpaper in good form as of December 31, 20X5.

P5-41A   Cost-Method Consolidation in Subsequent Period

Trial balance data for Light Corporation and Star Company on December 31, 20X6, are as follows:

Item	Light Corporation		Star Company	
	Debit	Credit	Debit	Credit
Cash	$ 46,000		$ 30,000	
Accounts Receivable	55,000		40,000	
Inventory	75,000		65,000	
Buildings and Equipment	300,000		240,000	
Investment in Star Company (at cost)	220,000			
Cost of Goods Sold	270,000		135,000	
Depreciation Expense	25,000		20,000	
Other Expenses	21,000		10,000	
Dividends Declared	20,000		20,000	
Accumulated Depreciation		$ 130,000		$ 85,000
Accounts Payable		20,000		30,000
Taxes Payable		50,000		35,000
Common Stock		200,000		150,000
Retained Earnings, January 1		262,000		60,000
Sales		350,000		200,000
Dividend Income		20,000		
	$1,032,000	$1,032,000	$560,000	$560,000

Light purchased all of Star's shares on January 1, 20X5, for $220,000. Star's retained earnings balance at the date of acquisition was $50,000. The full purchase differential is assigned to goodwill. At December 31, 20X5, the management of Light reviewed the amount attributed to goodwill and concluded goodwill had been impaired and should be reported at $8,000. No further impairment occurred during 20X6. Light uses the cost method in accounting for its investment in Star.

Required

Present all eliminating entries needed to prepare consolidated financial statements for the year 20X6, and prepare a three-part consolidation workpaper in good form as of December 31, 20X6.

P5-42A   Cost-Method Consolidation of Majority-Owned Subsidiary

Rapid Delivery Corporation was created on January 1, 20X2, and quickly became successful. On January 1, 20X6, the owner sold 80 percent of the stock to Samuelson Company at underlying book value. Samuelson has continued to operate the subsidiary as a separate legal entity and uses the cost method in recording investment income.

Trial balance data for the two companies on December 31, 20X6, consist of the following:

Item	Samuelson Company		Rapid Delivery Corporation	
	Debit	Credit	Debit	Credit
Cash and Receivables	$ 141,000		$ 80,000	
Inventory	240,000		100,000	
Land	80,000		20,000	
Buildings and Equipment	500,000		150,000	
Investment in Rapid Delivery Stock	120,000			
Cost of Goods Sold	500,000		250,000	
Depreciation Expense	25,000		15,000	
Wage Expense	45,000		35,000	
Other Expenses	30,000		40,000	
Dividends Declared	50,000		20,000	

(continued)

(continued)

Item	Samuelson Company Debit	Samuelson Company Credit	Rapid Delivery Corporation Debit	Rapid Delivery Corporation Credit
Accumulated Depreciation		$ 155,000		$ 75,000
Accounts Payable		70,000		35,000
Notes Payable		200,000		50,000
Common Stock		300,000		50,000
Retained Earnings		290,000		100,000
Sales		700,000		400,000
Dividend Income		16,000		
	$1,731,000	$1,731,000	$710,000	$710,000

Rapid Delivery's retained earnings on the date of acquisition was $100,000.

Required

Samuelson's controller has asked you to prepare a three-part consolidation workpaper in good form and to prepare a consolidated income statement, balance sheet, and statement of changes in retained earnings for the year 20X6.

P5-43A ## Comprehensive Cost-Method Consolidation Problem

Pillar Corporation acquired 80 percent ownership of Stanley Wood Products Company on January 1, 20X1, for $160,000. On that date Stanley reported retained earnings of $50,000 and had $100,000 of common stock outstanding. Pillar has used the cost method in recording its investment in Stanley.

Trial balance data for the two companies on December 31, 20X5, are as follows:

Item	Pillar Corporation Debit	Pillar Corporation Credit	Stanley Wood Products Company Debit	Stanley Wood Products Company Credit
Cash and Receivables	$ 81,000		$ 65,000	
Inventory	260,000		90,000	
Land	80,000		80,000	
Buildings and Equipment	500,000		150,000	
Investment in Stanley Wood Products Stock	160,000			
Cost of Goods Sold	120,000		50,000	
Depreciation Expense	25,000		15,000	
Inventory Losses	15,000		5,000	
Dividends Declared	30,000		10,000	
Accumulated Depreciation		$ 205,000		$105,000
Accounts Payable		60,000		20,000
Notes Payable		200,000		50,000
Common Stock		300,000		100,000
Retained Earnings		298,000		90,000
Sales		200,000		100,000
Dividend Income		8,000		
	$1,271,000	$1,271,000	$465,000	$465,000

Additional Information

1. On the date of combination, the fair value of Stanley's depreciable assets was $50,000 more than book value. The purchase differential assigned to depreciable assets should be written off over the following 10-year period.
2. There was $10,000 of intercorporate receivables and payables at the end of 20X5.

Required

a. Give all journal entries that Pillar recorded during 20X5 related to its investment in Stanley.

b. Give all eliminating entries needed to prepare consolidated statements for 20X5.

c. Prepare a three-part consolidation workpaper as of December 31, 20X5.

P5-44B **Majority-Owned Subsidiary with Differential**

Amber Corporation is a majority-owned subsidiary of Polar Company, which acquired 75 percent ownership of Amber on January 1, 20X3, for $133,500. At that date, Amber reported common stock outstanding of $60,000 and retained earnings of $90,000. The fair value of Amber as a whole was determined to be $178,000 at acquisition. The book values and fair values of Amber's assets and liabilities were equal, except for equipment, which had increased $28,000 in value and had an economic life of seven years at the date of the business combination. Amber reported net income of $30,000 and paid dividends of $12,000 in 20X3.

Required

a. Give the journal entries recorded by Polar during 20X3 on its books if it accounts for its investment in Amber using the equity method.

b. Consistent with the proposed FASB recommendations illustrated in Appendix 5B, give the eliminating entries needed at December 31, 20X3, to prepare consolidated financial statements.

P5-45B **Consolidation Workpaper at End of First Year of Ownership**

Using the information provided in P5-32, prepare a solution incorporating the proposed FASB recommendations illustrated in Appendix 5B. Assume the fair value of Best Company as a whole was $128,000 at acquisition and that goodwill and goodwill impairment were assigned proportionately to Power Corporation and the noncontrolling shareholders of Best Company. (Note that Power Corporation does not adjust its Income from Subsidiary for goodwill impairment under the basic equity method.)

P5-46B **Comprehensive Problem: Differential Apportionment**

Using the information provided in P5-35, but ignoring the amount of goodwill given, prepare a solution incorporating the proposed FASB recommendations illustrated in Appendix 5B. Assume the fair value of Granite Company as a whole was $216,250 and the fair vale of its net identifiable assets was $191,250 at acquisition. Goodwill is assigned proportionately to Bigelow Corporation and the noncontrolling shareholders of Granite Company.

Chapter Six

Intercompany Transfers of Services and Noncurrent Assets

A parent company and its subsidiaries often engage in a variety of transactions among themselves. For example, manufacturing companies often have subsidiaries that develop raw materials or produce components to be included in the products of affiliated companies. Some companies sell consulting or other services to affiliated companies. A number of major retailers, such as J. C. Penney Company, transfer receivables to their credit subsidiaries in return for operating cash. United States Steel Corporation and its subsidiaries engage in numerous transactions with one another, including sales of raw materials, fabricated products, and transportation services. Such transactions often are critical to the operations of the overall consolidated entity. These transactions between related companies are referred to as *intercompany* or *intercorporate transfers*.

The central idea of consolidated financial statements is that they report on the activities of the consolidating affiliates as if the separate affiliates actually constitute a single company. Because single companies are not permitted to reflect internal transactions in their financial statements, consolidated entities also must exclude from their financial statements the effects of transactions that are totally within the consolidated entity.

Building on the basic consolidation procedures presented in earlier chapters, this chapter and the next two deal with the effects of intercompany transfers. This chapter deals with intercompany services and sales of fixed assets, and Chapters 7 and 8 discuss intercompany sales of inventory and intercompany debt transfers.

OVERVIEW OF THE CONSOLIDATED ENTITY

The consolidated entity is an aggregation of a number of different companies. The financial statements prepared by the individual affiliates are consolidated into a single set of financial statements representing the financial position and operating results of the entire economic entity as if it were a single company.

Figure 6–1 illustrates a consolidated entity with each of the affiliated companies engaging in both intercompany transfers and transactions with external parties. From a consolidated viewpoint, only transactions with parties outside the economic entity are included in the income statement. Thus, the arrows crossing the perimeter of the consolidated entity in Figure 6–1 represent transactions that are included in the operating results of the consolidated entity for the period. Transfers between the affiliated companies, shown in Figure 6–1 as those arrows not crossing the boundary of the consolidated entity, are equivalent to transfers between operating divisions of a single company and are not reported in the consolidated statements.

Elimination of Intercompany Transfers

All aspects of intercompany transfers must be eliminated in preparing consolidated financial statements so that the statements appear as if they were those of a single company.

FIGURE 6–1
Transactions
of Affiliated
Companies

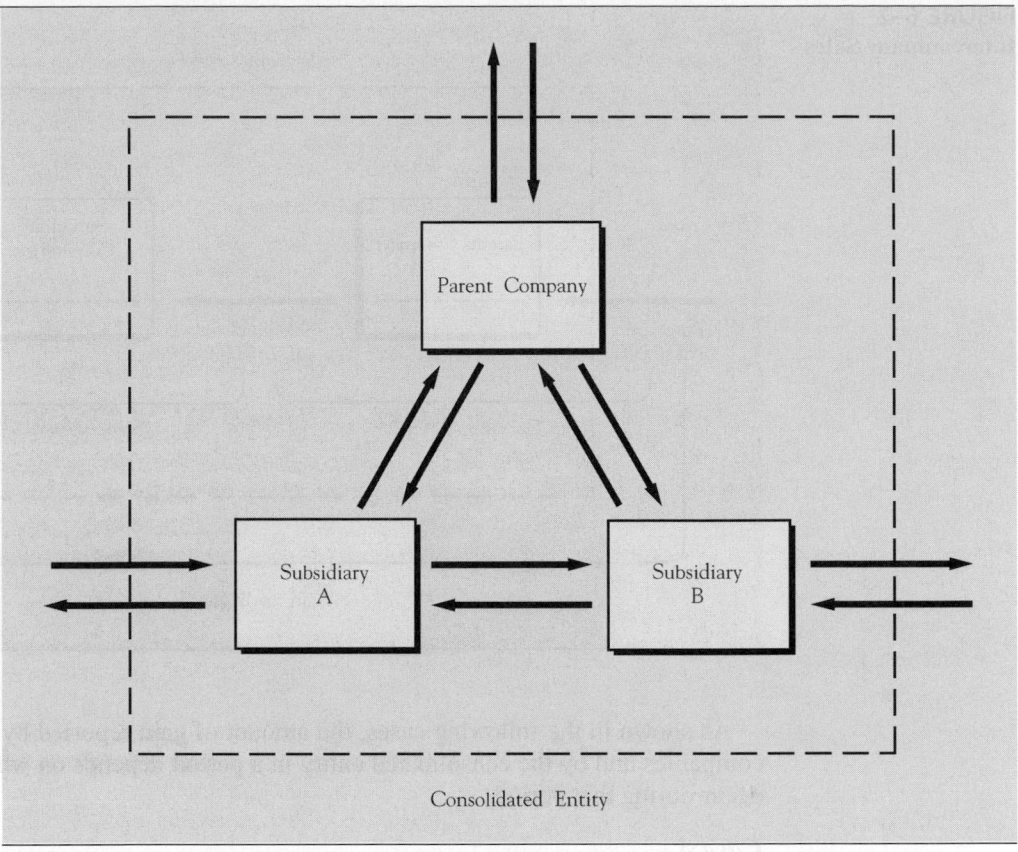

Accounting Research Bulletin No. 51, "Consolidated Financial Statements" (ARB 51), mentions open account balances, security holdings, sales and purchases, and interest and dividends as examples of the intercompany balances and transactions that must be eliminated.[1]

No distinction is made between wholly owned and less-than-wholly owned subsidiaries with regard to the elimination of intercompany transfers. The focus in consolidation is on the single-entity concept rather than on the percentage of ownership. Once the conditions for consolidation are met, a company becomes part of a single economic entity, and all transactions with related companies become internal transfers that must be eliminated fully, regardless of the level of ownership held.

Elimination of Unrealized Profits and Losses

Companies usually record transactions with affiliates on the same basis as transactions with nonaffiliates, including recognition of profits and losses. Profit or loss from selling an item to a related party normally is considered realized at the time of the sale from the selling company's perspective, but the profit is not considered realized for consolidation purposes until confirmed, usually through resale to an unrelated party. This unconfirmed profit from an intercompany transfer is referred to as ***unrealized intercompany profit***.

The following illustrations provide an overview of the intercompany sale process using land as an example. Figure 6–2 shows a series of transactions involving a parent company and its subsidiary. Land first is purchased by Parent Company from an unrelated party, then sold to a subsidiary of Parent Company, and finally sold by the subsidiary to an unrelated party. The three transactions, and the amounts, are as follows:

T1—Purchase by Parent Company from outsider for $10,000.

T2—Sale from Parent Company to Subsidiary Corporation for $15,000.

T3—Sale from Subsidiary Corporation to outsider for $25,000.

[1] *Accounting Research Bulletin No. 51*, "Consolidated Financial Statements," August 1959, para. 6.

FIGURE 6–2
Intercompany Sales

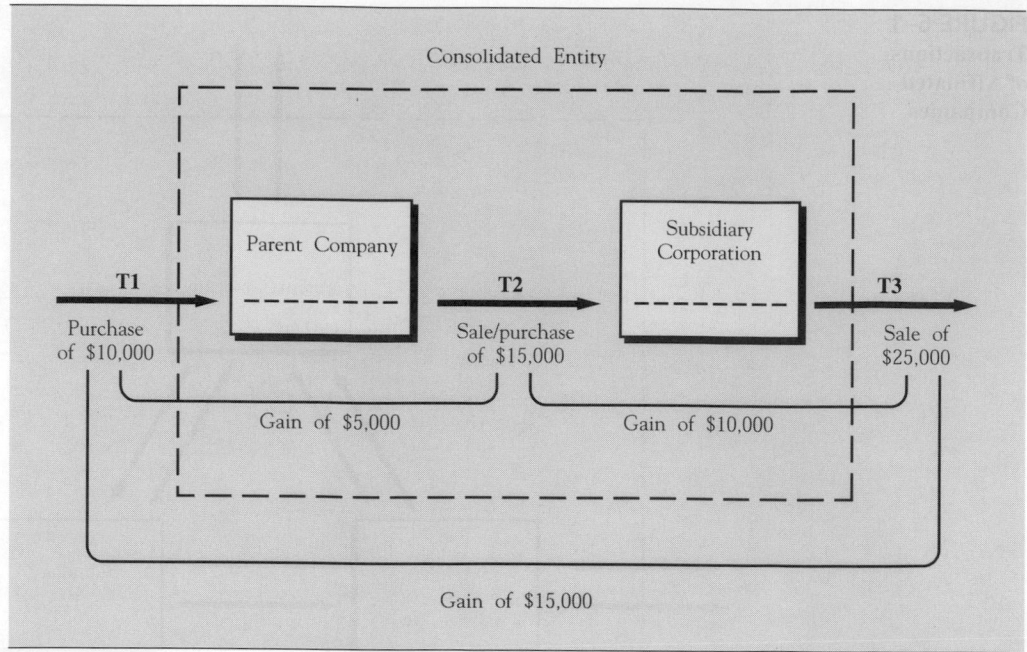

As shown in the following cases, the amount of gain reported by each of the individual companies and by the consolidated entity in a period depends on which of the transactions occur during that period.

Case A

All three transactions are completed in the same accounting period. The gain amounts reported on the transactions are:

Parent Company	$ 5,000 ($15,000 − $10,000)
Subsidiary Corporation	10,000 ($25,000 − $15,000)
Consolidated Entity	15,000 ($25,000 − $10,000)

The gain reported by each of the entities is considered to be realized because the land is resold to an unrelated party during the period. The total gain reported by the consolidated entity is the difference between the $10,000 price paid by the consolidated entity and the $25,000 price at which the consolidated entity sold the land to an outsider. This $15,000 gain is reported in the consolidated income statement. From a consolidated viewpoint, the sale from Parent Company to Subsidiary Corporation, transaction T2, is an internal transaction and is not reported in the consolidated financial statements.

Case B

Only transaction T1 is completed during the current period. The gain amounts reported on the transactions are:

Parent Company	$-0-
Subsidiary Corporation	-0-
Consolidated Entity	-0-

No sale has been made by either of the affiliated companies, and no gains are reported or realized. The land is reported both in Parent Company's balance sheet and in the consolidated balance sheet at its cost to Parent, which also is the cost to the consolidated entity.

Case C

Only transactions T1 and T2 are completed during the current period. The gain amounts reported on the transactions are:

Parent Company	$5,000 ($15,000 − $10,000)
Subsidiary Corporation	-0-
Consolidated Entity	-0-

The $5,000 gain reported by Parent Company is considered unrealized from a consolidated point of view and is not reported in the consolidated income statement because the land has not been resold to a party outside the consolidated entity. The land is carried on the books of Subsidiary Corporation at $15,000, the cost to Subsidiary. From a consolidated viewpoint, the land is overvalued by $5,000 and must be reported at its $10,000 cost to the consolidated entity.

Case D

Only transaction T3 is completed during the current period, T1 and T2 having occurred in a prior period. The gain amounts reported on the transactions in the current period are:

Parent Company	$ -0-
Subsidiary Corporation	10,000 ($25,000 − $15,000)
Consolidated Entity	15,000 ($25,000 − $10,000)

Subsidiary recognizes a gain equal to the difference between its selling price of $25,000 and cost of $15,000 while the consolidated entity reports a gain equal to the difference between its selling price of $25,000 and cost of $10,000.

From a consolidated viewpoint, the sale of an asset wholly within the consolidated entity involves only a change in the location of the asset and does not represent the culmination of the earning process. To culminate the earning process with respect to the consolidated entity, a sale must be made to a party external to the consolidated entity. The key to deciding when to report a transaction in the consolidated financial statements is to visualize the consolidated entity and determine whether a particular transaction occurs totally within the consolidated entity, in which case its effects must be excluded from the consolidated statements, or involves outsiders and thus constitutes a transaction of the consolidated entity.

INTERCOMPANY TRANSFERS OF SERVICES

Related companies frequently purchase services from one another. These services may be of many different types; intercompany purchases of consulting, engineering, marketing, and maintenance services are common.

When one company purchases services from a related company, the purchaser typically records an expense and the seller records a revenue. When consolidated financial statements are prepared, both the expense and revenue must be eliminated. For example, if the parent sells consulting services to the subsidiary for $50,000, the parent would recognize $50,000 of consulting revenue on its books and the subsidiary would recognize $50,000 of consulting expense. In the consolidation workpaper, an eliminating entry would be needed to reduce both consulting revenue (debit) and consulting expense (credit) by $50,000. Because the revenue and expense are equal and both are eliminated, income is unaffected by the elimination. Even though income is not affected, the elimination is still important, however, because otherwise both revenues and expenses are overstated.

Generally, a simplistic approach is taken in eliminating intercompany transfers of services by assuming that the services benefit the current period and, therefore, any intercompany profit on the services becomes realized within the period of transfer. Accordingly, no eliminating entries relating to the current period's transfer of services are needed in future periods because the intercompany profit is considered realized in the transfer period.

Usually the assumption that the profit on intercompany sales of services is realized in the period of sale is a realistic assumption. In some cases, however, realization of intercompany profit on the services does not occur in the period the services are provided and the amounts are significant. For example, if the parent company charges a subsidiary for architectural services to design a new manufacturing facility for the subsidiary, the subsidiary would include that cost in the capitalized cost of the new facility. From a consolidated point of view, however, any profit the parent recognized on the intercompany sale of services (revenue over the cost of providing the service) would have to be eliminated from the reported cost of the new facility until the intercompany profit became realized. Realization would be viewed as occurring over the life of the facility. Thus, eliminating entries would be needed each year similar to those illustrated later in the chapter for intercompany transfers of fixed assets.

INTERCOMPANY TRANSFERS OF LAND

When intercorporate transfers of noncurrent assets occur, adjustments often are needed in the preparation of consolidated financial statements for as long as the assets are held by the acquiring company. The simplest example of an intercorporate asset transfer is the intercorporate sale of land.

Overview of the Profit Elimination Process

When land is transferred between related companies at book value, no special adjustments or eliminations are needed in preparing the consolidated statements. If, for example, a company purchases land for $10,000 and sells it to its subsidiary for $10,000, the asset continues to be valued at the $10,000 original cost to the consolidated entity:

Parent			Subsidiary		
Cash	10,000		Land	10,000	
Land		10,000	Cash		10,000

Because the seller records no gain or loss, both income and assets are stated correctly from a consolidated viewpoint.

Land transfers at more or less than book value do require special treatment in the consolidation process. The selling entity's gain or loss must be eliminated because the land is still held by the consolidated entity, and no gain or loss may be reported in the consolidated financial statements until the land is sold to a party outside the consolidated entity. Likewise, the land must be reported at its original cost in the consolidated financial statements as long as it is held within the consolidated entity, regardless of which affiliate holds the land.

As an illustration, assume that Peerless Products Corporation acquires land for $20,000 on January 1, 20X1, and sells the land to its subsidiary, Special Foods Incorporated, on July 1, 20X1, for $35,000, as follows:

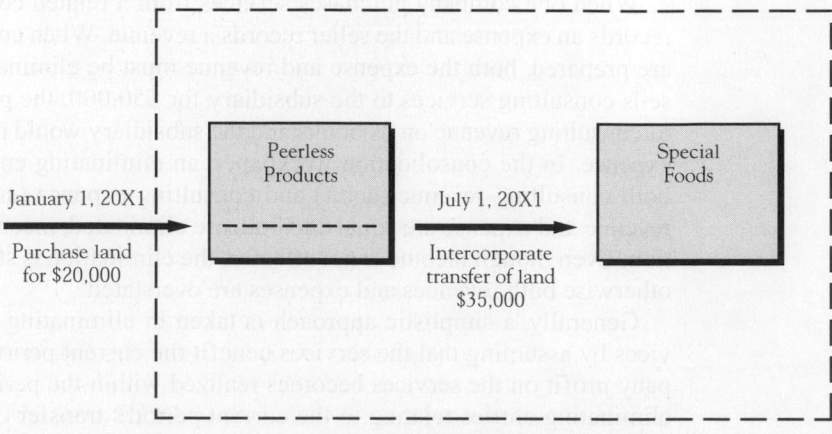

Consolidated Entity

Peerless records the purchase of the land and its sale to Special Foods with the following entries:

January 1, 20X1

(1)	Land	20,000	
	Cash		20,000
	Record purchase of land.		

July 1, 20X1

(2)	Cash	35,000	
	Land		20,000
	Gain on Sale of Land.		15,000
	Record sale of land to Special Foods.		

Special Foods records the purchase of the land from Peerless as follows:

July 1, 20X1

(3)	Land	35,000	
	Cash		35,000
	Record purchase of land from Peerless.		

The intercorporate transfer causes the seller to recognize a $15,000 gain and the carrying value of the land to increase by the same amount. Neither of these amounts may be reported in the consolidated financial statements because the $15,000 intercompany gain is unrealized from a consolidated viewpoint. The land has not been sold to a party outside the consolidated entity but only transferred within; consequently, the land must continue to be reported at its original cost to the consolidated entity. The gain must be eliminated in the preparation of consolidated financial statements and the land restated from the $35,000 recorded on Special Foods' books to its original cost of $20,000. This is accomplished with the following eliminating entry in the consolidation workpaper prepared at the end of 20X1:

E(4)	Gain on Sale of Land	15,000	
	Land		15,000
	Eliminate unrealized gain on sale of land.		

Assignment of Unrealized Profit Elimination

A gain or loss on an intercompany transfer is recognized by the selling affiliate and ultimately accrues to the stockholders of that affiliate. When a sale is from a parent to a subsidiary, referred to as a ***downstream sale***, any gain or loss on the transfer accrues to the parent company's stockholders. When the sale is from a subsidiary to its parent, an ***upstream sale***, any gain or loss accrues to the subsidiary's stockholders. If the subsidiary is wholly owned, all gain or loss ultimately accrues to the parent company as the sole stockholder. If, however, the selling subsidiary is not wholly owned, the gain or loss on the upstream sale is apportioned between the parent company and the noncontrolling shareholders.

Generally, gains and losses are not considered realized by the consolidated entity until a sale is made to an external party. Unrealized gains and losses are eliminated in preparing consolidated financial statements against the interests of those shareholders who recognized the gains and losses in the first place: the shareholders of the selling affiliate. Therefore, the direction of the sale determines which shareholder group absorbs the elimination of unrealized intercompany gains and losses. Specifically, unrealized intercompany gains and losses are eliminated in the following ways:

Sale	Elimination
Downstream (parent to subsidiary)	Against controlling interest
Upstream (subsidiary to parent):	
Wholly owned subsidiary	Against controlling interest
Majority-owned subsidiary	Proportionately against controlling and noncontrolling interests

As an illustration, assume that Purity Company owns 75 percent of the common stock of Southern Corporation. Purity reports operating income from its own activities, excluding any investment income from Southern, of $100,000; Southern reports net income of $60,000. Included in the income of the selling affiliate is an unrealized gain of $10,000 on the intercompany transfer of an asset. If the sale is a downstream transfer, all unrealized profit is eliminated from the controlling interest's share of income when consolidated statements are prepared. Thus, consolidated net income is computed as follows:

Purity's separate income		$100,000
Less: Unrealized intercompany profit on downstream asset sale		(10,000)
Purity's separate realized income		$ 90,000
Purity's share of Southern's income:		
Southern's net income	$60,000	
Purity's proportionate share	× .75	45,000
Consolidated net income		$135,000

If, instead, the intercompany transfer is from subsidiary to parent, the unrealized profit on the upstream sale is eliminated proportionately from the interests of the controlling and noncontrolling shareholders. In this situation, consolidated net income is computed as follows:

Purity's separate income		$100,000
Purity's share of Southern's realized income:		
Southern's net income	$60,000	
Less: Unrealized intercompany profit on upstream asset sale	(10,000)	
Southern's realized income	$50,000	
Purity's proportionate share	× .75	37,500
Consolidated net income		$137,500

Consolidated net income is $2,500 higher in the upstream case because 25 percent of the unrealized profit elimination is deducted from the noncontrolling interest rather than deducting the full amount from the controlling interest as in the downstream case.

Note that unrealized intercompany gains and losses are always fully eliminated in preparing consolidated financial statements. The existence of a noncontrolling interest in a selling subsidiary affects only the allocation of the eliminated unrealized gain or loss and not the amount eliminated.

Income to Noncontrolling Interest

The income assigned to the noncontrolling interest is the noncontrolling interest's proportionate share of the subsidiary's income realized in transactions with parties external to the consolidated entity. Income assigned to the noncontrolling interest in the downstream example is computed as follows:

Southern's net income	$60,000
Proportionate share to noncontrolling interest	× .25
Income assigned to noncontrolling interest	$15,000

Income assigned to the noncontrolling interest in the upstream example is computed as follows:

Southern's net income	$60,000
Less: Unrealized gain on upstream asset sale	(10,000)
Southern's realized net income	$50,000
Proportionate share to noncontrolling interest	× .25
Income assigned to noncontrolling interest	$12,500

In the downstream example, the $10,000 of unrealized intercompany profit is recognized on the parent company's books; therefore, the noncontrolling interest is not affected by the unrealized gain on the downstream intercompany transaction. The entire $60,000 of the subsidiary's income is realized in transactions with parties external to the consolidated entity. In the upstream example, the subsidiary's income includes $10,000 of unrealized intercompany profit. The amount of the subsidiary's income realized in transactions with external parties is only $50,000 ($60,000 less $10,000 of unrealized intercompany profit).

Downstream Sale

To illustrate more fully the treatment of unrealized intercompany profits, assume the following with respect to the Peerless and Special Foods example used previously:

1. Peerless Products Corporation purchases 80 percent of Special Foods Inc.'s stock on December 31, 20X0, at the stock's book value of $240,000.

2. On July 1, 20X1, Peerless sells land to Special Foods for $35,000. Peerless had originally purchased the land on January 1, 20X1, for $20,000. Special Foods continues to hold the land through 20X1 and subsequent years.

3. During 20X1, Peerless reports separate income of $155,000, consisting of income from regular operations of $140,000 and a $15,000 gain on the sale of land; Peerless declares dividends of $60,000. Special Foods reports net income of $50,000 and declares dividends of $30,000.

4. Peerless accounts for its investment in Special Foods using the basic equity method, under which it records its share of Special Foods' net income and dividends but does not adjust for unrealized intercompany profits.

Peerless records the sale of the land and the resulting gain of $15,000 ($35,000 − $20,000) with entry (2), given previously. Special Foods records the purchase of the land for $35,000 with entry (3).

Basic Equity-Method Entries—20X1

During 20X1, Peerless records its share of income and dividends from Special Foods with the usual entries under the basic equity method:

(5)	Cash	24,000	
	Investment in Special Foods Stock		24,000
	Record dividends from Special Foods:		
	$30,000 × .80		

(6)	Investment in Special Foods Stock	40,000	
	Income from Subsidiary		40,000
	Record equity-method income:		
	$50,000 × .80		

On December 31, 20X1, the investment account on Peerless's books appears as follows:

	Investment in Special Foods Stock				
	Original cost	240,000			
(6)	Equity accrual		(5)	Dividends	
	($50,000 × .80)	40,000		($30,000 × .80)	24,000
	Balance, 12/31/X1	256,000			

Consolidation Workpaper—20X1

The consolidation workpaper used in preparing consolidated financial statements for 20X1 is shown in Figure 6–3. The normal workpaper entries are included:

E(7)	Income from Subsidiary	40,000	
	Dividends Declared		24,000
	Investment in Special Foods Stock		16,000
	Eliminate income from subsidiary.		

E(8)	Income to Noncontrolling Interest	10,000	
	Dividends Declared		6,000
	Noncontrolling Interest		4,000
	Assign income to noncontrolling interest.		
	$10,000 = $50,000 × .20		
	$6,000 = $30,000 × .20		

E(9)	Common Stock—Special Foods	200,000	
	Retained Earnings, January 1	100,000	
	Investment in Special Foods Stock		240,000
	Noncontrolling Interest		60,000
	Eliminate beginning investment balance.		

Entry E(7) eliminates the changes in Peerless's investment account for the year, the income from Special Foods recognized by Peerless in entry (6), and Peerless's share of Special Foods' dividends recognized in entry (5). Entry E(8) assigns a share of Special Foods' income to the noncontrolling stockholders ($50,000 × .20) and eliminates their share of Special Foods' dividends. Income assigned to the noncontrolling interest is not affected by the unrealized intercompany gain because the transfer was a downstream sale. Entry E(9) eliminates Peerless's beginning investment balance and the beginning stockholders' equity amounts of Special Foods and establishes the noncontrolling interest as of the beginning of the year.

FIGURE 6–3   **December 31, 20X1, Consolidation Workpaper, Period of Intercompany Sale; Downstream Sale of Land**

Item	Peerless Products	Special Foods	Eliminations Debit	Eliminations Credit	Consolidated
Sales	400,000	200,000			600,000
Gain on Sale of Land	15,000		(10) 15,000		
Income from Subsidiary	40,000		(7) 40,000		
Credits	455,000	200,000			600,000
Cost of Goods Sold	170,000	115,000			285,000
Depreciation and Amortization	50,000	20,000			70,000
Other Expenses	40,000	15,000			55,000
Debits	(260,000)	(150,000)			(410,000)
					190,000
Income to Noncontrolling Interest			(8) 10,000		(10,000)
Net Income, carry forward	195,000	50,000	65,000		180,000
Retained Earnings, January 1	300,000	100,000	(9) 100,000		300,000
Net Income, from above	195,000	50,000	65,000		180,000
	495,000	150,000			480,000
Dividends Declared	(60,000)	(30,000)		(7) 24,000	
				(8) 6,000	(60,000)
Retained Earnings, December 31, carry forward	435,000	120,000	165,000	30,000	420,000
Cash	299,000	40,000			339,000
Accounts Receivable	75,000	50,000			125,000
Inventory	100,000	75,000			175,000
Land	155,000	75,000		(10) 15,000	215,000
Buildings and Equipment	800,000	600,000			1,400,000
Investment in Special Foods Stock	256,000			(7) 16,000	
				(9) 240,000	
Debits	1,685,000	840,000			2,254,000
Accumulated Depreciation	450,000	320,000			770,000
Accounts Payable	100,000	100,000			200,000
Bonds Payable	200,000	100,000			300,000
Common Stock	500,000	200,000	(9) 200,000		500,000
Retained Earnings, from above	435,000	120,000	165,000	30,000	420,000
Noncontrolling Interest				(8) 4,000	
				(9) 60,000	64,000
Credits	1,685,000	840,000	365,000	365,000	2,254,000

Elimination entries:
(7) Eliminate income from subsidiary.
(8) Assign income to noncontrolling interest.
(9) Eliminate beginning investment balance.
(10) Eliminate unrealized gain on downstream sale of land.

One additional entry is needed to eliminate the unrealized gain on the intercompany sale of the land:

E(10)	Gain on sale of Land	15,000	
	Land		15,000
	Eliminate unrealized gain on downstream sale of land.		

Because the land still is held within the consolidated entity, the $15,000 gain recognized on Peerless's books must be eliminated in the consolidation workpaper so that it does not appear in the consolidated income statement. Similarly, the land must appear in the consolidated balance sheet at its $20,000 original cost to the consolidated entity and, therefore, must be reduced from the $35,000 amount carried on Special Foods' books.

Consolidated Net Income

The 20X1 consolidated net income is computed as follows:

Peerless's separate income		$155,000
Less: Unrealized intercompany profit on downstream land sale		(15,000)
Peerless's separate realized income		$140,000
Peerless's share of Special Foods' income:		
Special Foods' net income	$50,000	
Peerless's proportionate share	× .80	40,000
Consolidated net income, 20X1		$180,000

Noncontrolling Interest

The noncontrolling stockholders' share of the income of the consolidated entity is limited to their proportionate share of the subsidiary's income. Special Foods' net income for 20X1 is $50,000, and the noncontrolling stockholders' ownership interest is 20 percent. Therefore, income of $10,000 ($50,000 × .20) is allocated to the noncontrolling interest.

As shown in Figure 6–3, the total noncontrolling interest at the end of 20X1 is $64,000, which represents the noncontrolling stockholders' proportionate share of the total book value of the subsidiary:

Book value of Special Foods, December 31, 20X1:	
Common stock	$200,000
Retained earnings	120,000
Total book value	$320,000
Noncontrolling stockholders' proportionate share	× .20
Noncontrolling interest, December 31, 20X1	$ 64,000

The noncontrolling interest is unaffected by the unrealized gain on the downstream sale.

Upstream Sale

An upstream sale results in the recording of intercompany profits on the subsidiary's books. If the profits are unrealized from a consolidated viewpoint, they must not be included in the consolidated financial statements. The unrealized intercompany profits are eliminated from the consolidation workpaper in the same manner as in the downstream case. However, the profit elimination reduces both the controlling and the noncontrolling interests in proportion to their ownership.

The treatment of an upstream sale may be illustrated with the same example used to illustrate a downstream sale. In this case, Special Foods recognizes a $15,000 gain from selling the land to Peerless in addition to the $50,000 of income earned from its regular operations; thus, Special Foods' net income for 20X1 is $65,000. Peerless's separate income is $140,000 and comes entirely from its normal operations.

The upstream sale from Special Foods to Peerless is as follows:

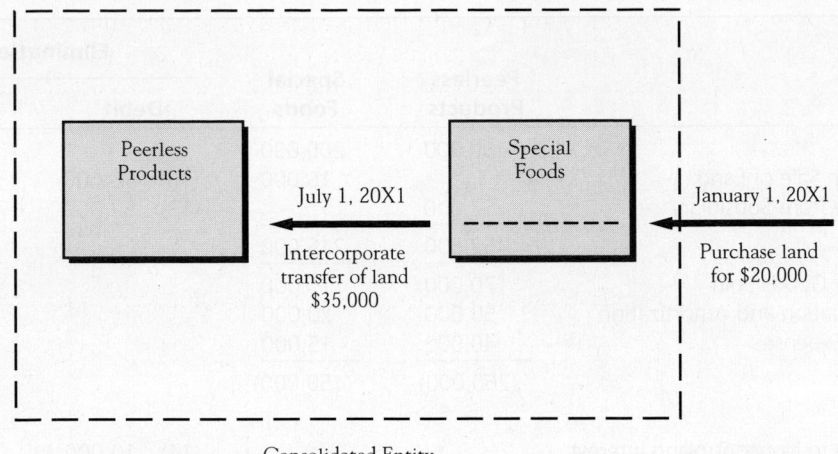

Consolidated Entity

Basic Equity-Method Entries—20X1

During 20X1, Peerless records the normal entries under the basic equity method, reflecting its share of Special Foods' income and dividends:

(11)	Cash	24,000	
	Investment in Special Foods Stock		24,000
	Record dividends from Special Foods:		
	$30,000 × .80		
(12)	Investment in Special Foods Stock	52,000	
	Income from Subsidiary		52,000
	Record equity-method income:		
	$65,000 × .80		

Note that Peerless's equity accrual in entry (12) includes its share of both Special Foods' operating income and Special Foods' gain on the transfer of the land.

The investment account on Peerless's books appears as follows at the end of 20X1:

Investment in Special Foods Stock			
Original cost	240,000		
(12) Equity accrual		(11) Dividends	
($65,000 × .80)	52,000	($30,000 × .80)	24,000
Balance, 12/31/X1	268,000		

Consolidation Workpaper—20X1

The consolidation workpaper prepared at the end of 20X1 appears in Figure 6–4. The four eliminating entries needed to prepare consolidated statements in the upstream case are nearly identical with those in the downstream case:

E(13)	Income from Subsidiary	52,000	
	Dividends Declared		24,000
	Investment in Special Foods Stock		28,000
	Eliminate income from subsidiary.		

FIGURE 6–4   December 31, 20X1, Consolidation Workpaper, Period of Intercompany Sale; Upstream Sale of Land

Item	Peerless Products	Special Foods	Eliminations Debit	Credit	Consolidated
Sales	400,000	200,000			600,000
Gain on Sale of Land		15,000	(16) 15,000		
Income from Subsidiary	52,000		(13) 52,000		
Credits	452,000	215,000			600,000
Cost of Goods Sold	170,000	115,000			285,000
Depreciation and Amortization	50,000	20,000			70,000
Other Expenses	40,000	15,000			55,000
Debits	(260,000)	(150,000)			(410,000)
					190,000
Income to Noncontrolling Interest			(14) 10,000		(10,000)
Net Income, carry forward	192,000	65,000	77,000		180,000
Retained Earnings, January 1	300,000	100,000	(15) 100,000		300,000
Net Income, from above	192,000	65,000	77,000		180,000
	492,000	165,000			480,000
Dividends Declared	(60,000)	(30,000)		(13) 24,000	
				(14) 6,000	(60,000)
Retained Earnings, December 31, carry forward	432,000	135,000	177,000	30,000	420,000
Cash	229,000	110,000			339,000
Accounts Receivable	75,000	50,000			125,000
Inventory	100,000	75,000			175,000
Land	210,000	20,000		(16) 15,000	215,000
Buildings and Equipment	800,000	600,000			1,400,000
Investment in Special Foods Stock	268,000			(13) 28,000	
				(15) 240,000	
Debits	1,682,000	855,000			2,254,000
Accumulated Depreciation	450,000	320,000			770,000
Accounts Payable	100,000	100,000			200,000
Bonds Payable	200,000	100,000			300,000
Common Stock	500,000	200,000	(15) 200,000		500,000
Retained Earnings, from above	432,000	135,000	177,000	30,000	420,000
Noncontrolling Interest				(14) 4,000	
				(15) 60,000	64,000
Credits	1,682,000	855,000	377,000	377,000	2,254,000

Elimination entries:
(13) Eliminate income from subsidiary.
(14) Assign income to noncontrolling interest.
(15) Eliminate beginning investment balance.
(16) Eliminate unrealized gain on upstream sale of land.

E(14)	Income to Noncontrolling Interest	10,000	
	Dividends Declared		6,000
	Noncontrolling Interest		4,000
	Assign income to noncontrolling interest:		
	$10,000 = ($65,000 − $15,000) × .20$		
	$6,000 = $30,000 × .20$		

E(15)	Common Stock—Special Foods	200,000	
	Retained Earnings, January 1	100,000	
	Investment in Special Foods Stock		240,000
	Noncontrolling Interest		60,000
	Eliminate beginning investment balance.		
E(16)	Gain on Sale of Land	15,000	
	Land		15,000
	Eliminate unrealized gain on upstream sale of land.		

The only difference between these elimination entries and those in the downstream example is in entry E(13). This difference results from the subsidiary's reporting $65,000 as its income in the upstream example rather than the $50,000 reported in the downstream example, with the additional $15,000 being the gain on the sale of the land.

Entry E(14), which assigns income to the noncontrolling interest, is the same as in the downstream example. The assignment of income to the controlling and noncontrolling interests is based on the subsidiary's realized income, which is the same in both cases, $50,000.

The only procedural difference in the upstream and downstream elimination process is that unrealized intercompany profits of the subsidiary from upstream sales are eliminated proportionately against the controlling and noncontrolling interests while unrealized intercompany profits of the parent from downstream sales are eliminated totally against the controlling interest. Thus, in the downstream example, the entire $15,000 unrealized intercompany gain was eliminated against the controlling interest's share of income to derive consolidated net income. In the upstream case, $3,000 of the unrealized intercompany gain is subtracted from the noncontrolling stockholders' share of income. The noncontrolling stockholders' share of the subsidiary's total net income is $13,000 ($65,000 × .20) but is reduced by their $3,000 ($15,000 × .20) share of the unrealized gain on the intercompany sale.

Particularly note that the elimination of the unrealized intercompany profit is the same for the upstream case in entry E(16) as for the downstream case in entry E(10). The full amount of the unrealized intercompany profit, $15,000 in this example, is always eliminated. The only difference between the upstream and downstream cases involves how the income reduction for unrealized profit is allocated between the controlling and noncontrolling interests.

Consolidated Net Income

When intercompany profits that are unrealized from a consolidated point of view are included in the income of a subsidiary, consolidated net income and the noncontrolling stockholders' share of income both must be adjusted for the unrealized profits. Consolidated net income for 20X1 is computed as follows:

Peerless's separate income		$140,000
Peerless's share of Special Foods' realized income:		
Special Foods' net income	$65,000	
Less: Unrealized intercompany profit on upstream land sale	(15,000)	
Special Foods' realized income	$50,000	
Peerless's proportionate share	× .80	40,000
Consolidated net income, 20X1		$180,000

This amount appears in the workpaper in Figure 6–4 as the result of the income eliminations and the assignment of income to the noncontrolling interest:

Peerless's net income		$192,000
Special Foods' net income		65,000
		$257,000
Eliminations:		
Peerless's income from Special Foods	$52,000	
Unrealized gain on sale of land	15,000	
		(67,000)
		$190,000
Noncontrolling stockholders' share of income		(10,000)
Consolidated net income, 20X1		$180,000

Consolidated net income in this year is the same whether or not there is an intercompany sale because the gain is unrealized. The unrealized gain must be eliminated fully, with consolidated net income based only on the realized income of the two affiliates.

Noncontrolling Interest

The income assigned to the noncontrolling shareholders is computed as their proportionate share of the realized income of Special Foods, as follows:

Special Foods' net income	$65,000
Less: Unrealized intercompany profit on upstream land sale	(15,000)
Special Foods' realized income	$50,000
Proportionate share to noncontrolling interest	× .20
Income to noncontrolling interest	$10,000

Total noncontrolling interest is computed as the noncontrolling stockholders' proportionate share of the stockholders' equity of Special Foods, excluding unrealized gains and losses. On December 31, 20X1, noncontrolling interest totals $64,000, computed as follows:

Book value of Special Foods, December 31, 20X1:	
Common stock	$200,000
Retained earnings	135,000
Total book value	$335,000
Unrealized intercompany gain on upstream land sale	(15,000)
Realized book value of Special Foods	$320,000
Noncontrolling stockholders' proportionate share	× .20
Noncontrolling interest, December 31, 20X1	$ 64,000

Eliminating Unrealized Profits after the First Year

In the period in which unrealized profits arise from an intercorporate sale, workpaper eliminating entries are used in the consolidation process to remove the gain or loss recorded by the seller and to adjust the reported amount of the asset back to the price originally paid by the selling affiliate. Each period thereafter while the asset is held by the purchasing affiliate, the reported asset balance and the shareholder claims of the selling affiliate are adjusted to remove the effects of the unrealized gain or loss. Income in those subsequent periods is not affected.

In the case of a downstream sale, the parent recognizes the entire profit on the intercompany transfer and includes it in its retained earnings in subsequent years. Therefore, the following eliminating entry is needed in the consolidation workpaper each year after the year of the downstream sale of the land, for as long as the subsidiary holds the land:

E(17)	Retained Earnings, January 1	15,000	
	Land		15,000
	Eliminate unrealized gain on prior-period downstream sale of land.		

This entry reduces beginning consolidated retained earnings and the reported balance of the land to exclude the unrealized intercompany gain.

In the upstream case, the subsidiary recognizes the intercompany profit. The parent recognizes its proportionate share of the gain, and that amount is included in the parent's beginning retained earnings in subsequent years. In the consolidation workpaper prepared in years subsequent to the intercompany transfer while the land is held by the parent, the unrealized intercompany gain is eliminated from the reported balance of the land and proportionately from the subsidiary ownership interests with the following entry:

E(18)	Retained Earnings, January 1	12,000	
	Noncontrolling Interest	3,000	
	Land		15,000
	Eliminate unrealized gain on prior-period upstream sale of land.		

Thus, in periods subsequent to an upstream intercompany transfer, consolidated retained earnings is reduced by the parent's share of the unrealized intercompany gain, and the noncontrolling interest is reduced by the remainder. All other elimination entries are made as if there is no unrealized intercompany gain.

Subsequent Disposition of Asset

Unrealized profits on intercompany sales of assets are viewed as being realized at the time the assets are resold to external parties. For consolidation purposes, the gain or loss recognized by the affiliate selling to the external party must be adjusted for the previously unrealized intercompany gain or loss. While the seller's reported profit on the external sale is based on that affiliate's cost, the gain or loss reported by the consolidated entity is based on the cost of the asset to the consolidated entity, which is the cost incurred by the affiliate that purchased the asset originally from an outside party.

When previously unrealized intercompany profits are realized, the effects of the profit elimination process must be reversed. At the time of realization, the full amount of the deferred intercompany profit is added back into the consolidated income computation and assigned to the shareholder interests from which it originally was eliminated.

To illustrate the treatment of unrealized intercompany profits once the transferred asset is resold, assume that Peerless purchases land from an outside party for $20,000 on January 1, 20X1, and sells the land to Special Foods on July 1, 20X1, for $35,000. Special

Foods subsequently sells the land to an outside party on March 1, 20X5, for $45,000, as follows:

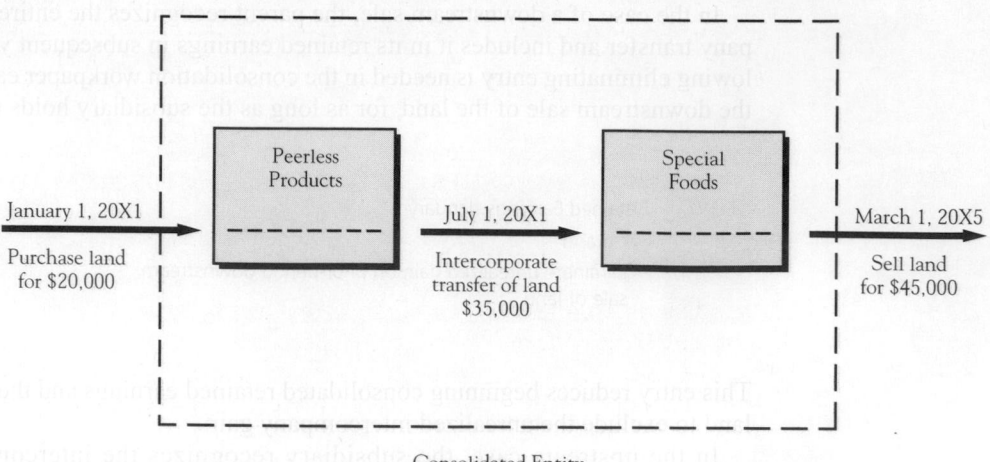

Consolidated Entity

Special Foods recognizes a gain on the sale to the outside party of $10,000 ($45,000 − $35,000). From a consolidated viewpoint, however, the gain is $25,000, the difference between the price at which the land left the consolidated entity ($45,000) and the price at which the land entered the consolidated entity ($20,000) when purchased originally by Peerless.

In the consolidation workpaper, the land no longer needs to be reduced by the unrealized intercompany gain because the gain now is realized and the consolidated entity no longer holds the land. Instead, the $10,000 gain recognized by Special Foods on the sale of the land to an outsider must be adjusted to reflect a total gain for the consolidated entity of $25,000. Thus, the following eliminating entry is made in the consolidation workpaper prepared at the end of 20X5:

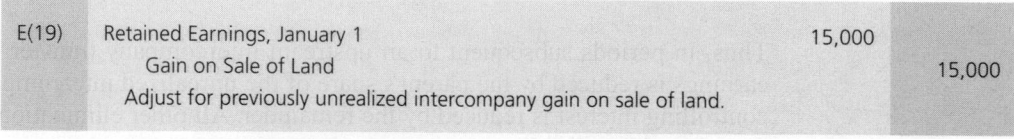

E(19)	Retained Earnings, January 1	15,000	
	Gain on Sale of Land		15,000
	Adjust for previously unrealized intercompany gain on sale of land.		

In addition to adjusting the gain, this entry reduces beginning consolidated retained earnings by the amount of the unrealized intercompany gain previously recognized by Peerless. All other elimination entries are the same as if there were no unrealized intercompany profits at the beginning of the period.

No additional consideration need be given the intercompany transfer in periods subsequent to the external sale. From a consolidated viewpoint, all aspects of the transaction are complete, and the profit is realized once the sale to an external party occurs.

In the example, if the sale to the external party had been made by Peerless following an upstream intercompany transfer from Special Foods, the workpaper treatment would be the same as in the case of the downstream transfer except that the debit in elimination entry E(19) would be prorated between beginning Retained Earnings ($12,000) and Noncontrolling Interest ($3,000) based on the relative ownership interests. In addition, the income assigned to the noncontrolling interest in the workpaper would be based on the subsidiary's realized net income. Because the $15,000 intercompany gain becomes realized during the year through an exchange with an external party, the subsidiary's realized net income includes the subsidiary's reported net income plus the intercompany gain.

INTERCOMPANY TRANSFERS OF DEPRECIABLE ASSETS

Unrealized intercompany profits on a depreciable or amortizable asset are viewed as being realized gradually over the remaining economic life of the asset as it is used by the purchasing affiliate in generating revenue from unaffiliated parties. In effect, a portion of the unrealized gain or loss is realized each period as benefits are derived from the asset and its service potential expires.

The amount of depreciation recognized on a company's books each period on an asset purchased from an affiliate is based on the intercorporate transfer price. From a consolidated viewpoint, however, depreciation must be based on the cost of the asset to the consolidated entity, which is the asset's cost to the related company that originally purchased it from an outsider. Eliminating entries are needed in the consolidation workpaper to restate the asset, associated accumulated depreciation, and depreciation expense to the amounts that would appear in the financial statements if there had been no intercompany transfer. Because the intercompany sale takes place totally within the consolidated entity, the consolidated financial statements must appear as if the intercompany transfer had never occurred.

Downstream Sale

The example of Peerless Products and Special Foods is modified to illustrate the downstream sale of a depreciable asset. Assume that Peerless sells equipment to Special Foods on December 31, 20X1, for $7,000, as follows:

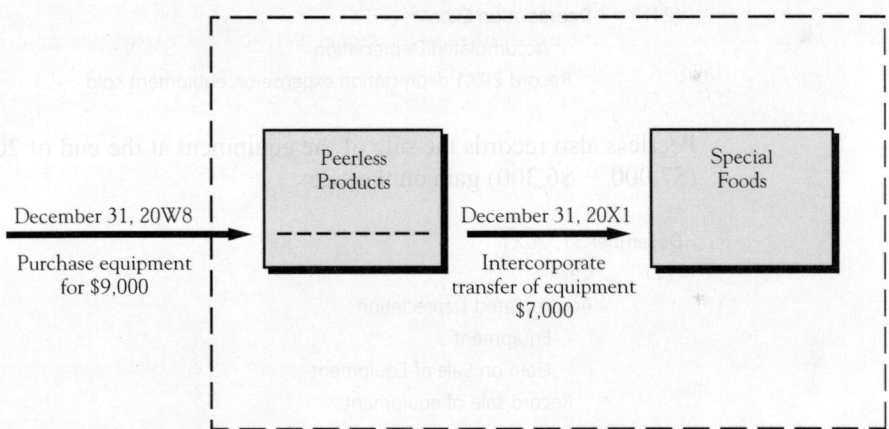

December 31, 20W8
Purchase equipment for $9,000

Peerless Products

December 31, 20X1
Intercorporate transfer of equipment $7,000

Special Foods

Consolidated Entity

The equipment originally cost Peerless $9,000 when purchased on December 31, 20W8, three years before December 31, 20X1, and is being depreciated over a total life of 10 years using straight-line depreciation with no residual value. The book value of the equipment immediately before the sale by Peerless is computed as follows:

Original cost to Peerless		$9,000
Accumulated depreciation on December 31, 20X1:		
Annual depreciation ($9,000 ÷ 10 years)	$900	
Number of years	× 3	
		(2,700)
Book value on December 31, 20X1		$6,300

The gain recognized by Peerless on the intercompany sale of the equipment is:

Sale price of the equipment	$7,000
Book value of the equipment	(6,300)
Gain on sale of the equipment	$ 700

Separate-Company Entries—20X1

Special Foods records the purchase of the equipment at its cost:

December 31, 20X1

(20)	Equipment	7,000	
	Cash		7,000
	Record purchase of equipment.		

Special Foods does not depreciate the equipment during 20X1 because the equipment is purchased at the very end of 20X1.

Peerless must record depreciation on the equipment for 20X1 because it held the asset until the end of the year:

December 31, 20X1

(21)	Depreciation Expense	900	
	Accumulated Depreciation		900
	Record 20X1 depreciation expense on equipment sold.		

Peerless also records the sale of the equipment at the end of 20X1 and recognizes the $700 ($7,000 − $6,300) gain on the sale:

December 31, 20X1

(22)	Cash	7,000	
	Accumulated Depreciation	2,700	
	Equipment		9,000
	Gain on Sale of Equipment		700
	Record sale of equipment.		

In addition, Peerless records the normal basic equity-method entries to recognize its share of Special Foods' income and dividends for 20X1:

(23)	Cash	24,000	
	Investment in Special Foods Stock		24,000
	Record dividends from Special Foods:		
	$30,000 × .80		

(24)	Investment in Special Foods Stock	40,000	
	Income from Subsidiary		40,000
	Record equity-method income:		
	$50,000 × .80		

Consolidation Workpaper—20X1

The workpaper to prepare consolidated financial statements at the end of 20X1 appears in Figure 6–5. The first three elimination entries in the workpaper are the normal entries to (1) eliminate the income and dividends from Special Foods recognized by Peerless and the change in the investment account for the year, (2) assign income to the noncontrolling

FIGURE 6–5 **December 31, 20X1, Consolidation Workpaper, Period of Intercompany Sale; Downstream Sale of Equipment**

Item	Peerless Products	Special Foods	Eliminations		Consolidated
			Debit	Credit	
Sales	400,000	200,000			600,000
Gain on Sale of Equipment	700		(28) 700		
Income from Subsidiary	40,000		(25) 40,000		
Credits	440,700	200,000			600,000
Cost of Goods Sold	170,000	115,000			285,000
Depreciation and Amortization	50,000	20,000			70,000
Other Expenses	40,000	15,000			55,000
Debits	(260,000)	(150,000)			(410,000)
					190,000
Income to Noncontrolling Interest			(26) 10,000		(10,000)
Net Income, carry forward	180,700	50,000	50,700		180,000
Retained Earnings, January 1	300,000	100,000	(27) 100,000		300,000
Net Income, from above	180,700	50,000	50,700		180,000
	480,700	150,000			480,000
Dividends Declared	(60,000)	(30,000)		(25) 24,000	
				(26) 6,000	(60,000)
Retained Earnings, December 31, carry forward	420,700	120,000	150,700	30,000	420,000
Cash	271,000	68,000			339,000
Accounts Receivable	75,000	50,000			125,000
Inventory	100,000	75,000			175,000
Land	175,000	40,000			215,000
Buildings and Equipment	791,000	607,000	(28) 2,000		1,400,000
Investment in Special Foods Stock	256,000			(25) 16,000	
				(27) 240,000	
Debits	1,668,000	840,000			2,254,000
Accumulated Depreciation	447,300	320,000		(28) 2,700	770,000
Accounts Payable	100,000	100,000			200,000
Bonds Payable	200,000	100,000			300,000
Common Stock	500,000	200,000	(27) 200,000		500,000
Retained Earnings, from above	420,700	120,000	150,700	30,000	420,000
Noncontrolling Interest				(26) 4,000	
				(27) 60,000	64,000
Credits	1,668,000	840,000	352,700	352,700	2,254,000

Elimination entries:
(25) Eliminate income from subsidiary.
(26) Assign income to noncontrolling interest.
(27) Eliminate beginning investment balance.
(28) Eliminate unrealized gain on downstream sale of equipment.

interest, and (3) eliminate the stockholders' equity accounts of Special Foods and the investment account as of the beginning of the year:

E(25)	Income from Subsidiary	40,000	
	Dividends Declared		24,000
	Investment in Special Foods Stock		16,000
	Eliminate income from subsidiary.		

E(26)	Income to Noncontrolling Interest	10,000	
	Dividends Declared		6,000
	Noncontrolling Interest		4,000
	Assign income to noncontrolling interest:		
	$10,000 = $50,000 × .20		
E(27)	Common Stock—Special Foods	200,000	
	Retained Earnings, January 1	100,000	
	Investment in Special Foods Stock		240,000
	Noncontrolling Interest		60,000
	Eliminate beginning investment balance.		

An additional workpaper entry is needed to eliminate the unrealized intercompany gain on the sale of the equipment from consolidated net income and to restate the equipment to the amounts that would appear in the consolidated statements if there had been no intercompany sale. The amounts in the trial balances of the parent and subsidiary include the effects of the intercompany transfer and need to be adjusted in the consolidation workpaper to the balances immediately before the transfer:

	Amounts from Trial Balances	Elimination	Consolidated Amounts
Buildings and equipment	$7,000	$2,000	$9,000
Accumulated depreciation	-0-	(2,700)	(2,700)
Gain on sale of equipment	(700)	700	-0-

Thus, the following entry is needed in the workpaper:

E(28)	Buildings and Equipment	2,000	
	Gain on Sale of Equipment	700	
	Accumulated Depreciation		2,700
	Eliminate unrealized gain on downstream sale of equipment.		

As a result of this entry, the equipment, stated at $7,000 on Special Foods' books, is reported in the consolidated balance sheet at $9,000 ($7,000 + $2,000), its original cost to Peerless. While Special Foods has not depreciated the equipment, elimination entry E(28) provides for $2,700 of accumulated depreciation ($900 × 3), the amount that would have been shown on Peerless's books had the equipment not been sold. Entry E(28) also eliminates the $700 intercompany gain that is unrealized and cannot appear when Peerless and Special Foods are viewed together as a single entity. The overall effect of entry E(28) is to report exactly the same numbers in the consolidated financial statements as if the parent company had continued to own the equipment and there had been no intercompany transfer.

Separate-Company Entries—20X2

During 20X2, Special Foods begins depreciating the $7,000 cost of the equipment acquired from Peerless Products over its remaining life of seven years using straight-line depreciation. The resulting depreciation is $1,000 per year ($7,000 ÷ 7 years):

(29)	Depreciation Expense	1,000	
	Accumulated Depreciation		1,000
	Record depreciation expense for 20X2.		

This amount is $100 more per year than the depreciation that would have been recorded each year if Peerless had continued to hold the equipment.

Peerless records its normal equity-method entries for 20X2 to reflect its share of Special Foods' $74,000 income and dividends of $40,000:

(30)	Cash	32,000	
	Investment in Special Foods Stock		32,000
	Record dividends from Special Foods:		
	$40,000 × .80		
(31)	Investment in Special Foods Stock	59,200	
	Income from Subsidiary		59,200
	Record equity-method income:		
	$74,000 × .80		

Special Foods' net income is only $74,000 in 20X2 because it has been reduced by the $1,000 of depreciation on the transferred asset. Accordingly, Peerless's share of that income is $59,200 ($74,000 × .80).

The investment account on Peerless's books appears as follows:

Investment in Special Foods Stock				
Original cost	240,000			
(24) 20X1 equity accrual		(23) 20X1 dividends		
($50,000 × .80)	40,000	($30,000 × .80)	24,000	
Balance, 12/31/X1	256,000			
(31) 20X2 equity accrual		(30) 20X2 dividends		
($74,000 × .80)	59,200	($40,000 × .80)	32,000	
Balance, 12/31/X2	283,200			

Consolidation Workpaper—20X2

The consolidation workpaper for 20X2 is presented in Figure 6–6. The trial balance amounts from the basic example have been adjusted to reflect the intercompany asset sale. The first three elimination entries are the normal entries to eliminate income and dividends from the subsidiary, the investment account, and the stockholders' equity accounts of the subsidiary, and to establish the noncontrolling interest in the workpaper:

E(32)	Income from Subsidiary	59,200	
	Dividends Declared		32,000
	Investment in Special Foods Stock		27,200
	Eliminate income from subsidiary.		
E(33)	Income to Noncontrolling Interest	14,800	
	Dividends Declared		8,000
	Noncontrolling Interest		6,800
	Assign income to noncontrolling interest:		
	$14,800 = $74,000 × .20		
E(34)	Common Stock—Special Foods	200,000	
	Retained Earnings, January 1	120,000	
	Investment in Special Foods Stock		256,000
	Noncontrolling Interest		64,000
	Eliminate beginning investment balance.		

FIGURE 6–6 December 31, 20X2, Consolidation Workpaper, Next Period following Intercompany Sale; Downstream Sale of Equipment

Item	Peerless Products	Special Foods	Eliminations Debit		Eliminations Credit		Consolidated
Sales	450,000	300,000					750,000
Income from Subsidiary	59,200		(32)	59,200			
Credits	509,200	300,000					750,000
Cost of Goods Sold	180,000	160,000					340,000
Depreciation and Amortization	49,100	21,000			(36)	100	70,000
Other Expenses	60,000	45,000					105,000
Debits	(289,100)	(226,000)					(515,000)
							235,000
Income to Noncontrolling Interest			(33)	14,800			(14,800)
Net Income, carry forward	220,100	74,000		74,000		100	220,200
Retained Earnings, January 1	420,700	120,000	(34)	120,000			
			(35)	700			420,000
Net Income, from above	220,100	74,000		74,000		100	220,200
	640,800	194,000					640,200
Dividends Declared	(60,000)	(40,000)			(32)	32,000	
					(33)	8,000	(60,000)
Retained Earnings, December 31, carry forward	580,800	154,000		194,700		40,100	580,200
Cash	298,000	78,000					376,000
Accounts Receivable	150,000	80,000					230,000
Inventory	180,000	90,000					270,000
Land	175,000	40,000					215,000
Buildings and Equipment	791,000	607,000	(35)	2,000			1,400,000
Investment in Special Foods Stock	283,200				(32)	27,200	
					(34)	256,000	
Debits	1,877,200	895,000					2,491,000
Accumulated Depreciation	496,400	341,000	(36)	100	(35)	2,700	840,000
Accounts Payable	100,000	100,000					200,000
Bonds Payable	200,000	100,000					300,000
Common Stock	500,000	200,000	(34)	200,000			500,000
Retained Earnings, from above	580,800	154,000		194,700		40,100	580,200
Noncontrolling Interest					(33)	6,800	
					(34)	64,000	70,800
Credits	1,877,200	895,000		396,800		396,800	2,491,000

Elimination entries:
(32) Eliminate income from subsidiary.
(33) Assign income to noncontrolling interest.
(34) Eliminate beginning investment balance.
(35) Eliminate unrealized gain on equipment.
(36) Eliminate excess depreciation.

Entry E(33) assigns the noncontrolling interest its full 20 percent of the $74,000 reported income of Special Foods, given that the unrealized profits are on the books of the parent.

In addition to the normal elimination entries, entry E(35) is needed to eliminate the effects of the 20X1 intercompany transaction as of the beginning of 20X2:

E(35)	Buildings and Equipment	2,000	
	Retained Earnings, January 1	700	
	Accumulated Depreciation		2,700
	Eliminate unrealized gain on equipment.		

Entry E(35) restates the balance of the equipment to $9,000 ($7,000 + $2,000), the original cost to the consolidated entity when purchased by Peerless. Accumulated depreciation on the equipment is credited for $2,700. This is the amount at which accumulated depreciation would have been stated as of January 1, 20X2, if the asset had not been transferred to Special Foods:

Depreciation per year ($9,000 ÷ 10 years)	$ 900
Number of years to December 31, 20X1	× 3
Accumulated depreciation, December 31, 20X1	$2,700

Entry E(35) also reduces beginning retained earnings by the amount of intercompany profit unrealized at the beginning of the year. The full amount of the unrealized gain is included in Peerless's beginning retained earnings. If this amount were reported in consolidated retained earnings, the balance would be overstated because the gain has not been realized from a consolidated viewpoint.

One additional eliminating entry is needed in the December 31, 20X2, consolidation workpaper. Special Foods started depreciating the transferred asset at the beginning of 20X2 and recorded depreciation of $1,000 ($7,000 ÷ 7 years) on its separate books. From a consolidated point of view, however, the depreciation expense for 20X2 should be based on the $6,300 ($9,000 − $2,700) remaining book value of the equipment on Peerless's books immediately before the transfer. This $6,300 is allocated over the remaining seven-year life of the equipment, resulting in depreciation of $900 per year ($6,300 ÷ 7 years) from a consolidated perspective. Therefore, consolidated depreciation expense and the associated accumulated depreciation must be reduced by $100 from the amount recorded by Special Foods:

E(36)	Accumulated Depreciation	100	
	Depreciation Expense		100
	Eliminate excess depreciation.		

Note that this entry increases consolidated net income by $100. The $700 unrealized gain on the intercorporate sale is viewed as being realized at $100 per year over the seven years following the transfer. After seven years, the intercompany gain will be fully realized, and no further eliminations of depreciation or retained earnings will be needed.

Separating entries (35) and (36) is purely a matter of preference. Some prefer to combine the two entries and establish the consolidated balances at the end of the year in a single entry:

E(36a)	Buildings and Equipment	2,000	
	Retained Earnings, January 1	700	
	Depreciation Expense		100
	Accumulated Depreciation		2,600

The $2,600 credit to Accumulated Depreciation represents the difference between the $3,600 ($900 × 4 years) amount at which consolidated accumulated depreciation should be stated on December 31, 20X2, and the $1,000 amount at which accumulated depreciation is stated on Special Foods' books.

Once all the eliminating entries have been made in the workpaper, the adjusted balances exclude the effects of the intercorporate transfer:

	Subsidiary Trial Balance	Elimination	Consolidated Amounts
Buildings and Equipment	$7,000	$2,000	$9,000
Accumulated Depreciation	(1,000)	(2,600)	(3,600)
Depreciation Expense	1,000	(100)	900

Consolidated Net Income and Retained Earnings

Computation of consolidated net income for 20X2 must include an adjustment for the realization of profit on the 20X1 sale of equipment to Special Foods:

Peerless's separate income		$160,900
Partial realization of intercompany gain on downstream sale of equipment		100
Peerless's separate realized income		$161,000
Peerless's share of Special Foods' income:		
Special Foods' net income	$74,000	
Peerless's proportionate share	× .80	59,200
Consolidated net income, 20X2		$220,200

Because Peerless does not adjust its investment income from Special Foods for unrealized gains and losses, Peerless's retained earnings includes the unrealized intercompany gain and therefore exceeds the amount that should be reported as consolidated retained earnings. Accordingly, consolidated retained earnings at December 31, 20X2, can be computed by subtracting the remaining unrealized intercompany gain from Peerless's retained earnings:

Peerless's retained earnings, December 31, 20X2		$580,800
Less: Unrealized 20X1 intercompany gain	$700	
20X2 partial realization of gain	(100)	(600)
Consolidated retained earnings, December 31, 20X2		$580,200

Noncontrolling Interest

Income allocated to the noncontrolling stockholders in 20X2 is equal to their proportionate share of the subsidiary's realized and reported income. Special Foods' net income for 20X2 is $74,000, and the noncontrolling interest's 20 percent share is $14,800 ($74,000 × .20).

The total noncontrolling interest at the end of 20X2 is $70,800, equal to the noncontrolling stockholders' proportionate share of the total book value of the subsidiary:

Book value of Special Foods, December 31, 20X2:	
Common stock	$200,000
Retained earnings	154,000
Total book value	$354,000
Noncontrolling stockholders' proportionate share	× .20
Noncontrolling interest, December 31, 20X2	$ 70,800

Consolidation in Subsequent Years

The consolidation procedures in subsequent years are quite similar to those in 20X2. As long as Special Foods continues to hold and depreciate the equipment, consolidation procedures must include:

1. Restating the asset and accumulated depreciation balances.
2. Adjusting depreciation expense for the year.
3. Reducing beginning retained earnings by the amount of the intercompany gain unrealized at the beginning of the year.

For example, selected entries from the December 31, 20X3, consolidation workpaper for Peerless Products and Special Foods are as follows:

E(37)	Buildings and Equipment	2,000	
	Retained Earnings, January 1	600	
	Accumulated Depreciation		2,600
	Eliminate unrealized gain on equipment.		
E(38)	Accumulated Depreciation	100	
	Depreciation Expense		100
	Eliminate excess depreciation.		

These entries are the same as entries E(35) and E(36) for 20X2, except that an additional $100 of the intercompany gain is considered realized by the end of 20X2. Therefore, the reduction of beginning retained earnings in entry E(37) is for $600, the $700 original amount of the intercompany gain less the $100 portion of the gain considered realized in 20X2.

The credit to Accumulated Depreciation in entry E(37) is $100 less than in entry E(35) for 20X2 because Special Foods credited $100 more to Accumulated Depreciation on its books in 20X2 than was appropriate for consolidated reporting. Because this amount is brought into the workpaper, the restatement of the beginning accumulated depreciation in entry E(37) is $100 less than in the previous year:

Accumulated depreciation that would have been recorded by Peerless as of December 31, 20X2, if asset had not been transferred [($9,000 ÷ 10) × 4]	$3,600
Accumulated depreciation recorded by Special Foods as of December 31, 20X2 [($7,000 ÷ 7) × 1]	(1,000)
Workpaper adjustment to accumulated depreciation	$2,600

Both the debit to beginning Retained Earnings and the credit to Accumulated Depreciation will decrease by $100 each year until the asset is fully depreciated and the intercompany gain is fully recognized.

Change in Estimated Life of Asset upon Transfer

When a depreciable asset is transferred between companies, a change in the remaining estimated economic life may be appropriate. For example, the acquiring company may use the asset in a different type of production process, or the frequency of use may change. When a change in the estimated life of a depreciable asset occurs at the time of an intercorporate transfer, the treatment is no different than if the change occurred while the asset remained on the books of the transferring affiliate. The new remaining useful life is used as a basis for depreciation both by the purchasing affiliate and for purposes of preparing consolidated financial statements.

Upstream Sale

The treatment of unrealized profits arising from upstream intercompany sales is identical to that of downstream sales except that the unrealized profit, and subsequent realization, must be allocated between the controlling and noncontrolling interests. The case of an upstream sale can be illustrated using the same example as for the downstream sale. Assume that Special Foods sells equipment to Peerless Products for $7,000 on December 31, 20X1, and reports total income for 20X1 of $50,700 ($50,000 + $700), including the $700 gain on the sale of the equipment. Special Foods originally purchased the equipment for $9,000 three years before the intercompany sale.[2] The book value of the equipment at the date of sale is as follows:

Original cost to Special Foods		$9,000
Accumulated depreciation on December 31, 20X1:		
Annual depreciation ($9,000 ÷ 10 years)	$900	
Number of years	× 3	
		(2,700)
Book value on December 31, 20X1		$6,300

Separate-Company Entries—20X1

Special Foods records depreciation on the equipment for the year and the sale of the equipment to Peerless on December 31, 20X1, with the following entries:

December 31, 20X1

(39)	Depreciation Expense	900	
	Accumulated Depreciation		900
	Record 20X1 depreciation expense on equipment sold.		

(40)	Cash	7,000	
	Accumulated Depreciation	2,700	
	Equipment		9,000
	Gain on Sale of Equipment		700
	Record sale of equipment.		

Peerless records the purchase of the equipment from Special Foods with the following entry:

December 31, 20X1

(41)	Equipment	7,000	
	Cash		7,000
	Record purchase of equipment.		

In addition, Peerless records the following basic equity-method entries to recognize its share of Special Foods' reported income and dividends:

(42)	Cash	24,000	
	Investment in Special Foods Stock		24,000
	Record dividends from Special Foods:		
	$30,000 × .80		

(43)	Investment in Special Foods Stock	40,560	
	Income from Subsidiary		40,560
	Record equity-method income:		
	($50,000 + $700) × .80		

[2] To avoid additional complexity, the equipment's fair value is assumed to be equal to its book value on the date of combination. There is, therefore, no purchase differential related to the equipment.

Consolidation Workpaper—20X1

The consolidation workpaper for 20X1 is presented in Figure 6–7. It is the same as that presented in Figure 6–5 except where modified to reflect the upstream sale of the equipment.

Four eliminating entries appear in the consolidation workpaper for 20X1:

E(44)	Income from Subsidiary	40,560	
	Dividends Declared		24,000
	Investment in Special Foods Stock		16,560
	Eliminate income from subsidiary.		
E(45)	Income to Noncontrolling Interest	10,000	
	Dividends Declared		6,000
	Noncontrolling Interest		4,000
	Assign income to noncontrolling interest:		
	$10,000 = ($50,700 − $700) × .20		
E(46)	Common Stock—Special Foods	200,000	
	Retained Earnings, January 1	100,000	
	Investment in Special Foods Stock		240,000
	Noncontrolling Interest		60,000
	Eliminate beginning investment balance.		
E(47)	Buildings and Equipment	2,000	
	Gain on Sale of Equipment	700	
	Accumulated Depreciation		2,700
	Eliminate unrealized gain on upstream sale of equipment.		

Entry E(44) is the normal workpaper entry to eliminate the income and dividends from Special Foods recorded by Peerless and is based on the amounts recorded by Peerless on its books during 20X1. Entry E(45) assigns income to the noncontrolling shareholders based on their share of Special Foods' realized income, computed as follows:

Net income of Special Foods for 20X1	$50,700
Unrealized gain on intercompany sale	(700)
Realized net income of Special Foods for 20X1	$50,000
Noncontrolling stockholders' proportionate share	× .20
Income to noncontrolling interest, 20X1	$10,000

In the upstream case, the elimination of unrealized profits is allocated against both Peerless Products and the noncontrolling shareholders, both being owners of Special Foods. Assigning income of $10,000 to the noncontrolling interest in the Figure 6–7 workpaper leaves $180,000 as consolidated net income. Thus, consolidated net income is equal to Peerless's income from its own separate operations plus Peerless's share of Special Foods' realized net income:

Peerless's separate operating income	$140,000
Peerless's share of Special Foods' realized income	
[($50,700 − $700) × .80]	40,000
Consolidated net income, 20X1	$180,000

FIGURE 6–7 **December 31, 20X1, Consolidation Workpaper, Period of Intercompany Sale;**
Upstream Sale of Equipment

Item	Peerless Products	Special Foods	Eliminations Debit	Eliminations Credit	Consolidated
Sales	400,000	200,000			600,000
Gain on Sale of Equipment		700	(47) 700		
Income from Subsidiary	40,560		(44) 40,560		
Credits	440,560	200,700			600,000
Cost of Goods Sold	170,000	115,000			285,000
Depreciation and Amortization	50,000	20,000			70,000
Other Expenses	40,000	15,000			55,000
Debits	(260,000)	(150,000)			(410,000)
					190,000
Income to Noncontrolling Interest			(45) 10,000		(10,000)
Net Income, carry forward	180,560	50,700	51,260		180,000
Retained Earnings, January 1	300,000	100,000	(46) 100,000		300,000
Net Income, from above	180,560	50,700	51,260		180,000
	480,560	150,700			480,000
Dividends Declared	(60,000)	(30,000)		(44) 24,000	
				(45) 6,000	(60,000)
Retained Earnings, December 31, carry forward	420,560	120,700	151,260	30,000	420,000
Cash	257,000	82,000			339,000
Accounts Receivable	75,000	50,000			125,000
Inventory	100,000	75,000			175,000
Land	175,000	40,000			215,000
Buildings and Equipment	807,000	591,000	(47) 2,000		1,400,000
Investment in Special Foods Stock	256,560			(44) 16,560	
				(46) 240,000	
Debits	1,670,560	838,000			2,254,000
Accumulated Depreciation	450,000	317,300		(47) 2,700	770,000
Accounts Payable	100,000	100,000			200,000
Bonds Payable	200,000	100,000			300,000
Common Stock	500,000	200,000	(46) 200,000		500,000
Retained Earnings, from above	420,560	120,700	151,260	30,000	420,000
Noncontrolling Interest				(45) 4,000	
				(46) 60,000	64,000
Credits	1,670,560	838,000	353,260	353,260	2,254,000

Elimination entries:
  (44) Eliminate income from subsidiary.
  (45) Assign income to noncontrolling interest.
  (46) Eliminate beginning investment balance.
  (47) Eliminate unrealized gain on upstream sale of equipment.

Eliminating entries E(46) and E(47) are identical to those used in the downstream case. Entry E(46) is not affected by the transfer. Entry E(47) is not affected by the direction of the sale in the period in which the sale occurs.

Separate-Company Books—20X2

In the year following the intercorporate transfer, Special Foods reports net income of $75,900 (with the $900 of depreciation expense on the transferred asset now excluded).

Peerless records the normal basic equity-method entries on its books to recognize its share of Special Foods' 20X2 income and dividends. At the end of 20X2, the investment account on Peerless's books appears as follows:

Investment in Special Foods Stock				
	Original cost	240,000		
(43)	20X1 equity accrual		(42) 20X1 dividends	
	($50,700 × .80)	40,560	($30,000 × .80)	24,000
	Balance, 12/31/X1	256,560		
	20X2 equity accrual		20X2 dividends	
	($75,900 × .80)	60,720	($40,000 × .80)	32,000
	Balance, 12/31/X2	285,280		

Consolidation Elimination Entries—20X2

The consolidation workpaper for 20X2 is presented in Figure 6–8. The elimination entries used in the preparation of consolidated financial statements for 20X2 are as follows:

E(48)	Income from Subsidiary	60,720	
	Dividends Declared		32,000
	Investment in Special Foods Stock		28,720
	Eliminate income from subsidiary:		
	$60,720 = $75,900 × .80		
E(49)	Income to Noncontrolling Interest	15,200	
	Dividends Declared		8,000
	Noncontrolling Interest		7,200
	Assign income to noncontrolling interest:		
	$15,200 = ($75,900 + $100) × .20		
E(50)	Common Stock—Special Foods	200,000	
	Retained Earnings, January 1	120,700	
	Investment in Special Foods Stock		256,560
	Noncontrolling Interest		64,140
	Eliminate beginning investment balance:		
	$256,560 = ($200,000 + $120,700) × .80		
	$64,140 = ($200,000 + $120,700) × .20		
E(51)	Buildings and Equipment	2,000	
	Retained Earnings, January 1	560	
	Noncontrolling Interest	140	
	Accumulated Depreciation		2,700
	Eliminate unrealized gain on upstream sale of equipment.		
E(52)	Accumulated Depreciation	100	
	Depreciation Expense		100
	Eliminate excess depreciation.		

The second-year elimination entries differ little between the upstream and downstream cases except that the amount of unrealized intercompany gain at the beginning of the period is allocated proportionally between the controlling interest (retained earnings) and the noncontrolling interest in entry E(51); it was allocated entirely to the controlling interest in

FIGURE 6–8 **December 31, 20X2, Consolidation Workpaper, Next Period following Intercompany Sale; Upstream Sale of Equipment**

Item	Peerless Products	Special Foods	Eliminations Debit	Eliminations Credit	Consolidated
Sales	450,000	300,000			750,000
Income from Subsidiary	60,720		(48) 60,720		
Credits	510,720	300,000			750,000
Cost of Goods Sold	180,000	160,000			340,000
Depreciation and Amortization	51,000	19,100		(52) 100	70,000
Other Expenses	60,000	45,000			105,000
Debits	(291,000)	(224,100)			(515,000)
					235,000
Income to Noncontrolling Interest			(49) 15,200		(15,200)
Net Income, carry forward	219,720	75,900	75,920	100	219,800
Retained Earnings, January 1	420,560	120,700	(50) 120,700		
			(51) 560		420,000
Net Income, from above	219,720	75,900	75,920	100	219,800
	640,280	196,600			639,800
Dividends Declared	(60,000)	(40,000)		(48) 32,000	
				(49) 8,000	(60,000)
Retained Earnings, December 31, carry forward	580,280	156,600	197,180	40,100	579,800
Cash	284,000	92,000			376,000
Accounts Receivable	150,000	80,000			230,000
Inventory	180,000	90,000			270,000
Land	175,000	40,000			215,000
Buildings and Equipment	807,000	591,000	(51) 2,000		1,400,000
Investment in Special Foods Stock	285,280			(48) 28,720	
				(50) 256,560	
Debits	1,881,280	893,000			2,491,000
Accumulated Depreciation	501,000	336,400	(52) 100	(51) 2,700	840,000
Accounts Payable	100,000	100,000			200,000
Bonds Payable	200,000	100,000			300,000
Common Stock	500,000	200,000	(50) 200,000		500,000
Retained Earnings, from above	580,280	156,600	197,180	40,100	579,800
Noncontrolling Interest			(51) 140	(49) 7,200	
				(50) 64,140	71,200
Credits	1,881,280	893,000	399,420	399,420	2,491,000

Elimination entries:
(48) Eliminate income from subsidiary.
(49) Assign income to noncontrolling interest.
(50) Eliminate beginning investment balance.
(51) Eliminate unrealized gain on upstream sale of equipment.
(52) Eliminate excess depreciation.

entry E(35) for the downstream case. The $700 unrealized gain on the upstream sale was eliminated proportionally against both the controlling and the noncontrolling interests at the end of 20X1. Therefore, elimination of the unrealized gain at the beginning of 20X2 must be treated as a reduction of both consolidated retained earnings and the noncontrolling interest.

The difference in the annual depreciation recorded by the purchasing affiliate, Peerless in this case, and the amount that would have been recorded by the selling affiliate, Special Foods, is $100:

Depreciation recorded by Peerless ($7,000 ÷ 7 years)	$1,000
Depreciation that would have been recorded by Special Foods if asset had not been transferred ($9,000 ÷ 10 years)	(900)
	$ 100

Entry E(52) adjusts depreciation expense and accumulated depreciation for this difference and has the effect of increasing total income by $100.

The $100 increase in income is viewed as resulting from the realization of a portion of the gain on the intercompany transfer. The $700 unrealized gain is considered realized at $100 per year over the seven-year period following the intercorporate transfer. As $100 of the gain is realized each year, the controlling interest is increased by $80, its 80 percent share, and the noncontrolling interest is increased by $20, its 20 percent share. Entry E(49) allocates a proportionate share of Special Foods' income to the noncontrolling interest and is based on Special Foods' reported income ($75,900) plus the portion of the intercompany gain considered realized during 20X2 ($100). The remaining $80 of realized gain accrues to the controlling interest and increases consolidated net income.

Entry E(50) is the normal entry to eliminate the investment account and subsidiary stockholders' equity balances as of the beginning of the year. The entry also assigns to the noncontrolling interest a pro rata portion of the subsidiary stockholders' equity balances ($320,700 × .20) as of the beginning of the year. This amount ($64,140), however, is greater than the actual amount assigned to the noncontrolling interest at the end of last period (see Figure 6–7). This increase is attributed to the $140 noncontrolling stockholders' share of the unrealized intercompany profit at the beginning of the period ($700 × .20). Entry E(51) reduces the noncontrolling interest by a proportionate share of the unrealized intercompany profit at the beginning of the year, and the two entries together establish the correct beginning balance of the noncontrolling interest.

Consolidated Net Income

Peerless Products' separate income for 20X2 is $159,000 after deducting an additional $1,000 for the depreciation on the transferred asset. Consolidated net income for 20X2 can be computed as follows:

Peerless's separate operating income			$159,000
Peerless's share of Special Foods' realized income:			
Special Foods' net income	$75,900		
Partial realization of intercompany gain on upstream sale	100		
Special Foods' realized income	$76,000		
Peerless's proportionate share	× .80		60,800
Consolidated net income, 20X2			$219,800

Noncontrolling Interest

The noncontrolling interest's share of income is $15,200 for 20X2, computed as the noncontrolling stockholders' proportionate share of the realized income of Special Foods ($76,000 × .20). Total noncontrolling interest is computed as the noncontrolling stockholders' proportionate share of the stockholders' equity of Special Foods, excluding unrealized gains and losses. On December 31, 20X2, the noncontrolling interest totals $71,200, computed as follows:

Book value of Special Foods, December 31, 20X2:	
Common Stock	$200,000
Retained earnings ($120,700 + $75,900 − $40,000)	156,600
Total book value	$356,600
Unrealized 20X1 intercompany gain on upstream sale	(700)
Intercompany gain realized in 20X2	100
Realized book value of Special Foods	$356,000
Noncontrolling stockholders' share	× .20
Noncontrolling interest, December 31, 20X2	$ 71,200

Asset Transfers before Year-End

In cases in which an intercorporate asset transfer occurs during a period rather than at the end, a portion of the intercompany gain or loss is considered realized in the period of the transfer. When this occurs, the workpaper eliminating entries at the end of the year must include an adjustment of depreciation expense and accumulated depreciation. The amount of this adjustment is equal to the difference between the depreciation recorded by the purchaser and that which would have been recorded by the seller during the portion of the year elapsing after the intercorporate sale.

If, for example, the upstream sale of equipment from Special Foods to Peerless occurred on January 1, 20X1, rather than on December 31, 20X1, an additional eliminating entry identical to E(52) would be needed in the consolidation workpaper prepared for December 31, 20X1.

INTERCOMPANY TRANSFERS OF AMORTIZABLE ASSETS

Production rights, patents, and other types of intangible assets may be sold to affiliated enterprises. Accounting for intangible assets usually differs from accounting for tangible assets in that amortizable intangibles normally are reported at the remaining unamortized balance without the use of a contra account. Other than netting the accumulated amortization on an intangible asset against the asset cost, the intercompany sale of intangibles is treated the same in consolidation as the intercompany sale of tangible assets.

Summary of Key Concepts

Transactions between affiliated companies within a consolidated entity must be viewed as if they occurred within a single company. Under generally accepted accounting principles, the effects of transactions that are internal to an enterprise may not be included in external accounting reports. Therefore, the effects of all transactions between companies within the consolidated entity must be eliminated in preparing consolidated financial statements.

The elimination of intercompany transactions must include the removal of unrealized intercompany profits. When one company sells an asset to an affiliate within the consolidated entity, any intercompany profit is not considered realized until confirmed by subsequent events. If the asset has an unlimited life, as with land, the unrealized intercompany gain or loss is realized at the time the asset is resold to a party outside the consolidated entity. If the asset has a limited life, the unrealized intercompany gain or loss is considered to be realized over the remaining life of the asset as the asset is used and depreciated or amortized.

Consolidation procedures relating to unrealized gains and losses on intercompany transfers of assets involve workpaper adjustments to restate the assets and associated accounts, such as accumulated depreciation, to the balances that would be reported if there had been no intercompany transfer. In the period of transfer, the income assigned to the shareholders of the selling affiliate must be reduced by their share of the unrealized intercompany profit. If the sale is a downstream sale, the unrealized intercompany gain or loss is eliminated against the controlling interest. When an upstream sale occurs, the unrealized intercompany gain or loss is eliminated proportionately against the controlling and noncontrolling interests.

Key Terms	downstream sale, *265*	unrealized intercompany	upstream sale, *265*
	intercompany transfers, *260*	profit, *261*	
	intercorporate transfers, *260*		

Appendix 6A Intercompany Transfers of Noncurrent Assets— Fully Adjusted Equity Method and Cost Method

A parent company may account for a subsidiary using any of several methods. So long as the subsidiary is to be consolidated, the method of accounting for the subsidiary on the parent's books will have no impact on the consolidated financial statements. While the primary focus of Chapter 6 is on consolidation following use of the basic equity method on the parent's books, two other methods are used in practice with some frequency as well. These methods are the fully adjusted equity method and the cost method.

FULLY ADJUSTED EQUITY METHOD

A company that chooses to account for an investment using the fully adjusted equity method records its proportionate share of subsidiary income and dividends in the same manner as under the basic equity method. In addition, the investor's share of any unrealized profits from intercompany transactions is removed from the parent's income in the period of intercompany sale by reducing both the investment account and the income recognized from the investee. When the intercompany profits subsequently are realized, the investor increases both the investment account and the income recognized from the investee. With these adjustments, parent company net income normally equals consolidated net income.

To illustrate this, assume the same facts as in the upstream sale of equipment discussed previously and reflected in Figure 6–7. Special Foods sells equipment to Peerless Products for $7,000 on December 31, 20X1, and reports total income for 20X1 of $50,700, including the $700 gain on the sale of the equipment. Special Foods originally purchased the equipment for $9,000 three years before the intercompany sale. Both companies use straight-line depreciation.

As illustrated previously, Special Foods records 20X1 depreciation on the equipment and the gain on the December 31, 20X1, sale of the equipment to Peerless with the following entries:

```
December 31, 20X1
(53)    Depreciation Expense                                        900
            Accumulated Depreciation                                        900
        Record 20X1 depreciation expense on equipment sold.


(54)    Cash                                                      7,000
        Accumulated Depreciation                                  2,700
            Equipment                                                     9,000
            Gain on Sale of Equipment                                       700
        Record sale of equipment.
```

Peerless records the purchase of the equipment from Special Foods with the following entry:

```
December 31, 20X1
(55)    Equipment                                                 7,000
            Cash                                                          7,000
        Record purchase of equipment.
```

Fully Adjusted Equity-Method Entries—20X1

In applying the fully adjusted equity method, Peerless recognizes its 80 percent share of Special Foods' income and dividends for 20X1 in the same way as under the basic equity method:

(56)	Cash	24,000	
	Investment in Special Foods Stock		24,000
	Record dividends from Special Foods:		
	$30,000 × .80		

(57)	Investment in Special Foods Stock	40,560	
	Income from Subsidiary		40,560
	Record equity-method income:		
	$50,700 × .80		

An additional entry is needed under the fully adjusted equity method to reduce income by Peerless's proportionate share of the $700 unrealized intercompany gain:

(58)	Income from Subsidiary	560	
	Investment in Special Foods Stock		560
	Remove unrealized gain on sale of equipment: $700 × .80		

This entry is consistent with the idea of a "one-line consolidation" and ensures that the parent's equity-method net income is equal to consolidated net income.

Entries (57) and (58) together record total income from Special Foods of $40,000. This amount is equal to Peerless's share of the realized net income of Special Foods, computed as follows:

Reported net income of Special Foods for 20X1	$50,700
Unrealized gain on intercompany sale	(700)
Realized net income of Special Foods for 20X1	$50,000
Peerless's proportionate share	× .80
Peerless's income from Special Foods, 20X1	$40,000

Because the intercompany sale is an upstream sale, only the parent's share of the unrealized gain is deducted in deriving equity-method net income. If the sale were downstream, the full $700 amount of the unrealized gain would be deducted in entry (58).

After the equity-method adjustments for December 31, 20X1, the investment account has a balance of $256,000:

Original purchase price of Special Foods stock	$240,000
Peerless's proportionate share of Special Foods' income ($50,700 × .80)	40,560
Peerless's share of Special Foods' dividends ($30,000 × .80)	(24,000)
Peerless's share of unrealized gain ($700 × .80)	(560)
Balance of investment account, December 31, 20X1	$256,000

Note that at the end of 20X1, Peerless's income and the investment account both are lower than had the basic equity method been used to account for the investment in Special Foods. The $560 difference is equal to Peerless's share of the unrealized intercompany gain ($700 × .80).

Consolidation Workpaper—20X1

The consolidation workpaper prepared as of December 31, 20X1, is presented in Figure 6–9. It is the same as that presented in Figure 6–7, except where modified to reflect use of the fully adjusted equity method.

Four eliminating entries appear in the consolidation workpaper prepared as of December 31, 20X1:

E(59)	Income from Subsidiary	40,000	
	Dividends Declared		24,000
	Investment in Special Foods Stock		16,000
	Eliminate income from subsidiary.		
E(60)	Income to Noncontrolling Interest	10,000	
	Dividends Declared		6,000
	Noncontrolling Interest		4,000
	Assign income to noncontrolling interest:		
	$10,000 = ($50,700 − $700) × .20		
E(61)	Common Stock—Special Foods	200,000	
	Retained Earnings, January 1	100,000	
	Investment in Special Foods Stock		240,000
	Noncontrolling Interest		60,000
	Eliminate beginning investment balance.		
E(62)	Buildings and Equipment	2,000	
	Gain on Sale of Equipment	700	
	Accumulated Depreciation		2,700
	Eliminate unrealized gain on upstream sale of equipment.		

All these entries are the same as those in Figure 6–7 prepared following use of the basic equity method, except for entry E(59). This entry eliminates the income recorded by Peerless under the equity method and differs from entry E(44) in Figure 6–7 by the amount of the unrealized profit adjustment recorded by Peerless with entry (58). The remainder of the workpaper is completed the same way as when the basic equity method is used.

Although entry (58) removed a pro rata share of the unrealized gain from the income reported on Peerless's books, it did not eliminate the gain from consolidated net income. Entry (58) changes only the amount of income from the subsidiary recognized by Peerless and the balance in the investment account. These balances, in turn, are eliminated by entries E(59) and E(61). The gain account entered on Special Foods' books at the time the equipment is sold is unaffected by the entries recorded by Peerless and, therefore, carries over to the consolidation workpaper unless eliminated. Entry E(62) is needed to prevent the gain from appearing in the consolidated income statement.

Note that in the workpaper shown in Figure 6–9, the parent's net income is equal to consolidated net income and the parent's retained earnings is equal to consolidated retained earnings.

Fully Adjusted Equity-Method Entries—20X2

In 20X2, Peerless records its share of Special Foods' $75,900 income and $40,000 of dividends with the following entries:

(63)	Cash	32,000	
	Investment in Special Foods Stock		32,000
	Record dividends from Special Foods:		
	$40,000 × .80		
(64)	Investment in Special Foods Stock	60,720	
	Income from Subsidiary		60,720
	Record equity-method income:		
	$75,900 × .80		

FIGURE 6–9 December 31, 20X1, Fully Adjusted Equity-Method Consolidation Workpaper, Period of Intercompany Sale; Upstream Sale of Equipment

Item	Peerless Products	Special Foods	Eliminations Debit	Eliminations Credit	Consolidated
Sales	400,000	200,000			600,000
Gain on Sale of Equipment		700	(62) 700		
Income from Subsidiary	40,000		(59) 40,000		
Credits	440,000	200,700			600,000
Cost of Goods Sold	170,000	115,000			285,000
Depreciation and Amortization	50,000	20,000			70,000
Other Expenses	40,000	15,000			55,000
Debits	(260,000)	(150,000)			(410,000)
					190,000
Income to Noncontrolling Interest			(60) 10,000		(10,000)
Net Income, carry forward	180,000	50,700	50,700		180,000
Retained Earnings, January 1	300,000	100,000	(61) 100,000		300,000
Net Income, from above	180,000	50,700	50,700		180,000
	480,000	150,700			480,000
Dividends Declared	(60,000)	(30,000)		(59) 24,000	
				(60) 6,000	(60,000)
Retained Earnings, December 31, carry forward	420,000	120,700	150,700	30,000	420,000
Cash	257,000	82,000			339,000
Accounts Receivable	75,000	50,000			125,000
Inventory	100,000	75,000			175,000
Land	175,000	40,000			215,000
Buildings and Equipment	807,000	591,000	(62) 2,000		1,400,000
Investment in Special Foods Stock	256,000			(59) 16,000	
				(61) 240,000	
Debits	1,670,000	838,000			2,254,000
Accumulated Depreciation	450,000	317,300		(62) 2,700	770,000
Accounts Payable	100,000	100,000			200,000
Bonds Payable	200,000	100,000			300,000
Common Stock	500,000	200,000	(61) 200,000		500,000
Retained Earnings, from above	420,000	120,700	150,700	30,000	420,000
Noncontrolling Interest				(60) 4,000	
				(61) 60,000	64,000
Credits	1,670,000	838,000	352,700	352,700	2,254,000

Elimination entries:
(59) Eliminate income from subsidiary.
(60) Assign income to noncontrolling interest.
(61) Eliminate beginning investment balance.
(62) Eliminate unrealized gain on upstream sale of equipment.

Peerless records an additional entry under the fully adjusted equity method to increase income for the partial realization of the unrealized intercompany gain:

(65)	Investment in Special Foods Stock	80	
	Income from Subsidiary		80
	Recognize portion of gain on sale of equipment:		
	($700 ÷ 7 years) × .80		

The gain on the 20X1 intercompany transfer is viewed as being realized over a seven-year period. The $100 of intercompany gain realized each year is equal to the difference between the amount of depreciation recorded by Peerless ($1,000) and the amount that would have been recorded by Special Foods had there been no intercompany transfer ($900). Because depreciation expense will be adjusted in the preparation of consolidated financial statements to the amount that would have been reported if there had been no intercompany transfer, total income in the workpaper will be increased by $100. This increase will be allocated between the controlling and noncontrolling interests in the upstream case, leading to an increase of $80 ($100 × .80) in consolidated net income.

Entry (65) adds to Peerless's equity-method income a proportionate share of the part of the gain considered realized during 20X2. Recall that Peerless's 20X1 income was reduced by a proportionate share of the unrealized gain. Therefore, Peerless's portion of the realized part of the gain ($100 × .80) is put back into its income and the investment account in 20X2. Consistent with the idea of a one-line consolidation, entry (65) makes Peerless's fully adjusted equity-method net income equal to consolidated net income.

Consolidation Workpaper—20X2

The consolidation workpaper for 20X2 is shown in Figure 6–10. The following elimination entries are included in the workpaper:

E(66)	Income from Subsidiary	60,800	
	Dividends Declared		32,000
	Investment in Special Foods Stock		28,800
	Eliminate income from subsidiary:		
	$60,800 = ($75,900 + $100) × .80		
E(67)	Income to Noncontrolling Interest	15,200	
	Dividends Declared		8,000
	Noncontrolling Interest		7,200
	Assign income to noncontrolling interest:		
	$15,200 = ($75,900 + $100) × .20		
E(68)	Common Stock—Special Foods	200,000	
	Retained Earnings, January 1	120,700	
	Investment in Special Foods Stock		256,560
	Noncontrolling Interest		64,140
	Eliminate beginning investment balance:		
	$256,560 = ($200,000 + $120,700) × .80		
	$64,140 = ($200,000 + $120,700) × .20		
E(69)	Buildings and Equipment	2,000	
	Investment in Special Foods Stock	560	
	Noncontrolling Interest	140	
	Accumulated Depreciation		2,700
	Eliminate unrealized gain on upstream sale of equipment.		
E(70)	Accumulated Depreciation	100	
	Depreciation Expense		100
	Eliminate excess depreciation.		

These entries are the same as the eliminating entries used following application of the basic equity method, with two differences. First, entry E(66) eliminates Special Foods' income and dividends recognized by Peerless. Because the 20X2 income recognized by Peerless under the fully adjusted equity method includes Peerless's share of the realized 20X1 intercompany gain, which is not included when using the basic equity method, the income elimination is $80 ($100 × .80) higher following use of the fully adjusted equity method.

FIGURE 6–10 December 31, 20X2, Fully Adjusted Equity-Method Consolidation Workpaper, Next Period following Intercompany Sale; Upstream Sale of Equipment

Item	Peerless Products	Special Foods	Eliminations Debit	Eliminations Credit	Consolidated
Sales	450,000	300,000			750,000
Income from Subsidiary	60,800		(66) 60,800		
Credits	510,800	300,000			750,000
Cost of Goods Sold	180,000	160,000			340,000
Depreciation and Amortization	51,000	19,100		(70) 100	70,000
Other Expenses	60,000	45,000			105,000
Debits	(291,000)	(224,100)			(515,000)
					235,000
Income to Noncontrolling Interest			(67) 15,200		(15,200)
Net Income, carry forward	219,800	75,900	76,000	100	219,800
Retained Earnings, January 1	420,000	120,700	(68) 120,700		420,000
Net Income, from above	219,800	75,900	76,000	100	219,800
	639,800	196,600			639,800
Dividends Declared	(60,000)	(40,000)		(66) 32,000	
				(67) 8,000	(60,000)
Retained Earnings, December 31, carry forward	579,800	156,600	196,700	40,100	579,800
Cash	284,000	92,000			376,000
Accounts Receivable	150,000	80,000			230,000
Inventory	180,000	90,000			270,000
Land	175,000	40,000			215,000
Buildings and Equipment	807,000	591,000	(69) 2,000		1,400,000
Investment in Special Foods Stock	284,800		(69) 560	(66) 28,800	
				(68) 256,560	
Debits	1,880,800	893,000			2,491,000
Accumulated Depreciation	501,000	336,400	(70) 100	(69) 2,700	840,000
Accounts Payable	100,000	100,000			200,000
Bonds Payable	200,000	100,000			300,000
Common Stock	500,000	200,000	(68) 200,000		500,000
Retained Earnings, from above	579,800	156,600	196,700	40,100	579,800
Noncontrolling Interest			(69) 140	(67) 7,200	
				(68) 64,140	71,200
Credits	1,880,800	893,000	399,500	399,500	2,491,000

Elimination entries:
(66) Eliminate income from subsidiary.
(67) Assign income to noncontrolling interest.
(68) Eliminate beginning investment balance.
(69) Eliminate unrealized gain on upstream sale of equipment.
(70) Eliminate excess depreciation.

The second difference is in entry E(69). When the basic equity method is used, the parent's share of the intercompany gain unrealized at the beginning of 20X2 is included in its retained earnings and must be eliminated when consolidating. This was accomplished in the basic equity illustration through entry E(51). When the fully adjusted equity method is used, however, the parent's share of the unrealized gain is deducted from income on the parent's books in the year of the intercompany transfer and subsequently is not included in retained earnings. Therefore, no additional elimination of retained earnings is needed.

Replacing the debit to Retained Earnings in entry E(51) is a debit to the investment account in entry E(69). Because the investment account is reduced at the same time that the unrealized income is deducted from the parent's income, eliminating entry E(68), which credits the investment account for an amount equal to the parent's proportionate share of the beginning subsidiary stockholders' equity balances, eliminates an amount greater than the actual beginning investment account balance. The additional amount is equal to the parent's share of the intercompany gain unrealized at the beginning of the year. Entry E(69) debits the investment account for that amount, and the two entries together, E(68) and E(69), fully eliminate the beginning balance of the investment.

All other eliminations are the same under both the basic and the fully adjusted equity methods.

COST METHOD

When using the cost method of accounting for an investment in a subsidiary, the parent records dividends received from the subsidiary during the period as income. No entries are made under the cost method to record the parent's share of undistributed subsidiary earnings, amortize differential, or remove unrealized intercompany profits.

To illustrate consolidation following an intercompany sale of equipment when the parent accounts for its subsidiary investment using the cost method, assume the same facts as in the previous illustrations of an upstream sale.

Consolidation Workpaper—20X1

The workpaper illustrated in Figure 6–11 is used in preparing consolidated financial statements for 20X1 following the upstream sale of equipment to Peerless by Special Foods. The following elimination entries appear in the workpaper, assuming Peerless uses the cost method to account for its investment:

E(71)	Dividend Income	24,000	
	Dividends Declared		24,000
	Eliminate dividend income from subsidiary:		
	$30,000 × .80		
E(72)	Income to Noncontrolling Interest	10,000	
	Dividends Declared		6,000
	Noncontrolling Interest		4,000
	Assign income to noncontrolling interest:		
	$10,000 = ($50,700 − $700) × .20		
E(73)	Common Stock—Special Foods	200,000	
	Retained Earnings, January 1	100,000	
	Investment in Special Foods Stock		240,000
	Noncontrolling Interest		60,000
	Eliminate investment balance at date of acquisition.		
E(74)	Buildings and Equipment	2,000	
	Gain on Sale of Equipment	700	
	Accumulated Depreciation		2,700
	Eliminate unrealized gain on upstream sale of equipment.		

Entry E(71) eliminates Peerless's share of Special Foods' 20X1 dividends. All other eliminating entries are the same as under the basic equity method in the year of acquisition.

FIGURE 6–11 December 31, 20X1, Cost-Method Consolidation Workpaper, Period of Intercompany Sale; Upstream Sale of Equipment

Item	Peerless Products	Special Foods	Eliminations Debit	Eliminations Credit	Consolidated
Sales	400,000	200,000			600,000
Gain on Sale of Equipment		700	(74) 700		
Dividend Income	24,000		(71) 24,000		
Credits	424,000	200,700			600,000
Cost of Goods Sold	170,000	115,000			285,000
Depreciation and Amortization	50,000	20,000			70,000
Other Expenses	40,000	15,000			55,000
Debits	(260,000)	(150,000)			(410,000)
					190,000
Income to Noncontrolling Interest			(72) 10,000		(10,000)
Net Income, carry forward	164,000	50,700	34,700		180,000
Retained Earnings, January 1	300,000	100,000	(73) 100,000		300,000
Net Income, from above	164,000	50,700	34,700		180,000
	464,000	150,700			480,000
Dividends Declared	(60,000)	(30,000)		(71) 24,000	
				(72) 6,000	(60,000)
Retained Earnings, December 31, carry forward	404,000	120,700	134,700	30,000	420,000
Cash	257,000	82,000			339,000
Accounts Receivable	75,000	50,000			125,000
Inventory	100,000	75,000			175,000
Land	175,000	40,000			215,000
Buildings and Equipment	807,000	591,000	(74) 2,000		1,400,000
Investment in Special Foods Stock	240,000			(73) 240,000	
Debits	1,654,000	838,000			2,254,000
Accumulated Depreciation	450,000	317,300		(74) 2,700	770,000
Accounts Payable	100,000	100,000			200,000
Bonds Payable	200,000	100,000			300,000
Common Stock	500,000	200,000	(73) 200,000		500,000
Retained Earnings, from above	404,000	120,700	134,700	30,000	420,000
Noncontrolling Interest				(72) 4,000	
				(73) 60,000	64,000
Credits	1,654,000	838,000	336,700	336,700	2,254,000

Elimination entries:
(71) Eliminate dividend income from subsidiary.
(72) Assign income to noncontrolling interest.
(73) Eliminate investment balance at date of acquisition.
(74) Eliminate unrealized gain on upstream sale of equipment.

Consolidation Workpaper—20X2

The consolidation workpaper prepared for December 31, 20X2, is presented in Figure 6–12. The following eliminating entries are needed in the workpaper:

E(75)	Dividend Income	32,000	
	Dividends Declared		32,000
	Eliminate dividend income from subsidiary:		
	$40,000 × .80		

FIGURE 6–12   December 31, 20X2, Cost-Method Consolidation Workpaper, Next Period following Intercompany
Sale; Upstream Sale of Equipment

Item	Peerless Products	Special Foods	Eliminations Debit		Eliminations Credit		Consolidated
Sales	450,000	300,000					750,000
Dividend Income	32,000		(75)	32,000			
Credits	482,000	300,000					750,000
Cost of Goods Sold	180,000	160,000					340,000
Depreciation and Amortization	51,000	19,100			(80)	100	70,000
Other Expenses	60,000	45,000					105,000
Debits	(291,000)	(224,100)					(515,000)
							235,000
Income to Noncontrolling Interest			(76)	15,200			(15,200)
Net Income, carry forward	191,000	75,900		47,200		100	219,800
Retained Earnings, January 1	404,000	120,700	(77)	100,000			
			(78)	4,140			
			(79)	560			420,000
Net Income, from above	191,000	75,900		47,200		100	219,800
	595,000	196,600					639,800
Dividends Declared	(60,000)	(40,000)			(75)	32,000	
					(76)	8,000	(60,000)
Retained Earnings, December 31, carry forward	535,000	156,600		151,900		40,100	579,800
Cash	284,000	92,000					376,000
Accounts Receivable	150,000	80,000					230,000
Inventory	180,000	90,000					270,000
Land	175,000	40,000					215,000
Buildings and Equipment	807,000	591,000	(79)	2,000			1,400,000
Investment in Special Foods Stock	240,000				(77)	240,000	
Debits	1,836,000	893,000					2,491,000
Accumulated Depreciation	501,000	336,400	(80)	100	(79)	2,700	840,000
Accounts Payable	100,000	100,000					200,000
Bonds Payable	200,000	100,000					300,000
Common Stock	500,000	200,000	(77)	200,000			500,000
Retained Earnings, from above	535,000	156,600		151,900		40,100	579,800
Noncontrolling Interest			(79)	140	(76)	7,200	
					(77)	60,000	
					(78)	4,140	71,200
Credits	1,836,000	893,000		354,140		354,140	2,491,000

Elimination entries:
(75) Eliminate dividend income from subsidiary.
(76) Assign income to noncontrolling interest.
(77) Eliminate investment balance at date of acquisition.
(78) Assign undistributed prior earnings of subsidiary to noncontrolling interest.
(79) Eliminate unrealized gain on upstream sale of equipment.
(80) Eliminate excess depreciation.

E(76)	Income to Noncontrolling Interest	15,200	
	Dividends Declared		8,000
	Noncontrolling Interest		7,200
	Assign income to noncontrolling interest:		
	$15,200 = ($75,900 + $100) \times .20$		

E(77)	Common Stock—Special Foods	200,000	
	Retained Earnings, January 1	100,000	
	Investment in Special Foods Stock		240,000
	Noncontrolling Interest		60,000
	Eliminate investment balance at date of acquisition.		
E(78)	Retained Earnings, January 1	4,140	
	Noncontrolling Interest		4,140
	Assign undistributed prior earnings of subsidiary to noncontrolling interest: ($120,700 − $100,000) × .20		
E(79)	Buildings and Equipment	2,000	
	Retained Earnings, January 1	560	
	Noncontrolling Interest	140	
	Accumulated Depreciation		2,700
	Eliminate unrealized gain on upstream sale of equipment.		
E(80)	Accumulated Depreciation	100	
	Depreciation Expense		100
	Eliminate excess depreciation.		

Entry E(75) eliminates Peerless's share of Special Foods' dividends. Entry E(76) assigns income to the noncontrolling interest in the normal manner, taking into consideration a proportionate share of the $100 of intercompany gain considered realized during 20X2. The investment elimination entry normally does not change under the cost method because the carrying amount of the investment does not change. Therefore, entry E(77) is the same as the investment elimination entry in 20X1. However, an additional entry, E(78), is needed to assign a proportionate share of Special Foods' undistributed prior years' income since the date of combination to the noncontrolling interest [($50,700 − $30,000) × .20]. The portion of beginning retained earnings that is neither eliminated nor assigned to the noncontrolling interest carries over in the workpaper to the Consolidated column as the beginning balance of consolidated retained earnings.

Entries E(79) and E(80) eliminate the effects of the intercompany transfer and are the same as when consolidation follows use of the basic equity method.

Questions

Q6-1   When are profits on intercorporate sales considered to be realized? Explain.

Q6-2   What is an upstream sale? Which company may have unrealized profits on its books in an upstream sale?

Q6-3   What dollar amounts in the consolidated financial statements will be incorrect if intercompany services are not eliminated?

Q6-4   How are unrealized profits on current-period intercorporate sales treated in preparing the income statement for (*a*) the selling company and (*b*) the consolidated entity?

Q6-5   How are unrealized profits treated in the consolidated income statement if the intercorporate sale occurred in a prior period and the transferred item is sold to a nonaffiliate in the current period?

Q6-6   How are unrealized intercorporate profits treated in the consolidated statements if the intercorporate sale occurred in a prior period and the profits have not been realized by the end of the current period?

Q6-7   What is a downstream sale? Which company may have unrealized profits on its books in a downstream sale?

Q6-8   What portion of the unrealized intercorporate profit is eliminated in a downstream sale? In an upstream sale?

Q6-9   How is the effect of unrealized intercorporate profits on consolidated net income different between an upstream and a downstream sale?

Q6-10   Unrealized profits from a prior-year upstream sale were realized in the current period. What effect will this event have on income assigned to the noncontrolling interest in the consolidated income statement for the current period?

Q6-11   A subsidiary sold a depreciable asset to the parent company at a profit in the current period. Will the income assigned to the noncontrolling interest in the consolidated income statement for the current period be more than, less than, or equal to a proportionate share of the reported net income of the subsidiary? Why?

Q6-12   A subsidiary sold a depreciable asset to the parent company at a profit of $1,000 in the current period. Will the income assigned to the noncontrolling interest in the consolidated income statement for the current period be more if the intercorporate sale occurs on January 1 or on December 31? Why?

Q6-13   If a company sells a depreciable asset to its subsidiary at a profit on December 31, 20X3, what account balances must be eliminated or adjusted in preparing the consolidated income statement for 20X3?

Q6-14   If the sale in the preceding question occurs on January 1, 20X3, what additional account will require adjustment in preparing the consolidated income statement?

Q6-15   In the period in which an intercorporate sale occurs, how do the consolidation eliminating entries differ when unrealized profits pertain to an intangible asset rather than a tangible asset?

Q6-16   When is unrealized profit on an intercompany sale of land considered realized? When is profit on an intercompany sale of equipment considered realized? Why do the treatments differ?

Q6-17   In the elimination of a prior-period unrealized intercorporate gain on depreciable assets, why does the debit to Retained Earnings decrease over time?

Q6-18A   A parent company may use on its books one of several different methods of accounting for its ownership of a subsidiary: (*a*) cost method, (*b*) basic equity method, or (*c*) fully adjusted equity method. How will the choice of method affect the reported balance in the investment account when there are unrealized intercorporate profits on the parent's books at the end of the period?

Cases

C6-1   Correction of Elimination Procedures

Plug Corporation purchased 60 percent of Coy Company's common stock approximately 10 years ago. On January 1, 20X2, Coy sold equipment to Plug for $850,000 and recorded a $150,000 loss on the sale. Coy had purchased the equipment for $1,200,000 on January 1, 20X0, and was depreciating it on

Research   a straight-line basis over 12 years with no assumed residual value.

FARS   In preparing Plug's consolidated financial statements for 20X2, its chief accountant increased the reported amount of the equipment by $150,000 and eliminated the loss on the sale of equipment recorded by Coy. No other eliminations or adjustments related to the equipment were made.

Required

As a member of the audit firm Gotcha and Gotcha, you have been asked, after reviewing Plug's consolidated income statement, to prepare a memo to Plug's controller detailing the elimination procedures that should be followed in transferring equipment between subsidiary and parent. Include citations to or quotations from the authoritative literature to support your recommendations. Your memo should include the correct eliminating entry and explain why each debit and credit is needed.

C6-2   Elimination of Intercorporate Services

Dream Corporation owns 90 percent of Classic Company's common stock and 70 percent of Plain Company's stock. Dream provides legal services to each subsidiary and bills it for 150 percent of the cost of the services provided. During 20X3, Classic recorded legal expenses of $80,000 when it paid

Research   Dream for legal assistance in an unsuccessful patent infringement suit against another company, and

FARS   Plain recorded legal expenses of $150,000 when it paid Dream for legal work associated with the purchase of additional property in Montana to expand an existing strip mine owned by Plain. In preparing the consolidated statements at December 31, 20X3, no eliminations were made for intercompany services. When asked why no entries had been made to eliminate the intercompany services, Dream's chief accountant replied that intercompany services are not mentioned in the company accounting manual and can be ignored.

Required

Prepare a memo detailing the appropriate treatment of legal services provided by Dream to Plain and Classic during 20X3. Include citations to or quotations from authoritative accounting standards to support your recommendations. In addition, provide the eliminating entries at December 31, 20X3, and 20X4, needed as a result of the services provided in 20X3, and explain why each debit or credit is necessary.

C6-3 Noncontrolling Interest

Understanding

Current reporting standards require the consolidated entity to include all the revenues, expenses, assets, and liabilities of the parent and its subsidiaries in the consolidated financial statements. When the parent does not own all of a subsidiary's shares, various rules and procedures exist with regard to the assignment of income and net assets to noncontrolling shareholders and the way in which the noncontrolling interest is to be reported.

Required

a. How is the amount of income assigned to noncontrolling shareholders in the consolidated income statement computed if there are no unrealized intercorporate profits on the subsidiary's books?

b. How is the amount reported for the noncontrolling interest in the consolidated balance sheet computed if there are no unrealized intercorporate profits on the subsidiary's books?

c. What effect do unrealized intercorporate profits have on the computation of income assigned to the noncontrolling interest if the profits arose from a transfer of (1) land or (2) equipment?

d. Are the noncontrolling shareholders of a subsidiary likely to find the amounts assigned to them in the consolidated financial statements useful? Explain.

C6-4 Intercompany Sale of Services

Analysis

Diamond Manufacturing Company regularly purchases janitorial and maintenance services from its wholly owned subsidiary, Schwartz Maintenance Services Inc. Schwartz bills Diamond monthly at its regular rates for the services provided, with the services consisting primarily of cleaning, groundskeeping, and small repairs. The cost of providing the services that Schwartz sells consists mostly of salaries and associated labor costs that total about 60 percent of the amount billed. Diamond issues consolidated financial statements annually.

Required

a. When Diamond prepares consolidated financial statements, what account balances of Diamond and Schwartz related to the intercompany sale of services must be adjusted or eliminated in the consolidation workpaper? What impact do these adjustments or eliminations have on consolidated net income?

b. In the case of intercompany sales of services at a profit, at what point in time are the intercompany profits considered to be realized? Explain.

C6-5 Intercompany Profits

Analysis

Companies have many different practices for pricing transfers of goods and services from one affiliate to another. Regardless of the approaches used for internal decision making and performance evaluation or for tax purposes, all intercompany profits, unless immaterial, are supposed to be eliminated when preparing consolidated financial statements until confirmed through transactions with external parties.

Required

a. Century Telephone Enterprises Inc. provides certain services to its subsidiaries, and some of its service subsidiaries provide services and materials to Century's telephone subsidiaries. How are these transactions billed among the affiliates? Are intercompany profits eliminated when consolidated financial statements are prepared? Explain.

b. Verizon Communications also is in the telephone business, although it is larger and more diversified than Century Telephone. How does it treat intercompany profits for consolidation?

c. Harley-Davidson operates in two business areas: (1) motorcycles and related products and (2) financial services. Does Harley eliminate all effects of intercompany transactions when preparing consolidated financial statements? Explain. What effect does its treatment have on consolidated net income?

Exercises

E6-1 Multiple-Choice Questions on Intercompany Transfers [AICPA Adapted]

For each question, select the single best answer.

1. Water Company owns 80 percent of Fire Company's outstanding common stock. On December 31, 20X9, Fire sold equipment to Water at a price in excess of Fire's carrying amount, but less than its original cost. On a consolidated balance sheet at December 31, 20X9, the carrying amount of the equipment should be reported at:

   a. Water's original cost.

   b. Fire's original cost.

   c. Water's original cost less Fire's recorded gain.

   d. Water's original cost less 80 percent of Fire's recorded gain.

2. Company J acquired all of Company K's outstanding common stock in exchange for cash. The acquisition price exceeds the fair value of net assets acquired. How should Company J determine the amounts to be reported for the plant and equipment and long-term debt acquired from Company K?

	Plant and Equipment	Long-Term Debt
a.	K's carrying amount	K's carrying amount
b.	K's carrying amount	Fair value
c.	Fair value	K's carrying amount
d.	Fair value	Fair value

3. Port Inc. owns 100 percent of Salem Inc. On January 1, 20X2, Port sold delivery equipment to Salem at a gain. Port had owned the equipment for two years and used a five-year straight-line depreciation rate with no residual value. Salem is using a three-year straight-line depreciation rate with no residual value for the equipment. In the consolidated income statement, Salem's recorded depreciation expense on the equipment for 20X2 will be decreased by:

   a. 20 percent of the gain on the sale.

   b. 33⅓ percent of the gain on the sale.

   c. 50 percent of the gain on the sale.

   d. 100 percent of the gain on the sale.

4. On January 1, 20X0, Poe Corporation sold a machine for $900,000 to Saxe Corporation, its wholly owned subsidiary. Poe paid $1,100,000 for this machine, which had accumulated depreciation of $250,000. Poe estimated a $100,000 salvage value and depreciated the machine using the straight-line method over 20 years, a policy that Saxe continued. In Poe's December 31, 20X0, consolidated balance sheet, this machine should be included in fixed-asset cost and accumulated depreciation as:

	Cost	Accumulated Depreciation
a.	$1,100,000	$300,000
b.	$1,100,000	$290,000
c.	$ 900,000	$ 40,000
d.	$ 850,000	$ 42,500

5. Scroll Inc., a wholly owned subsidiary of Pirn Inc., began operations on January 1, 20X1. The following information is from the condensed 20X1 income statements of Pirn and Scroll:

	Pirn	Scroll
Sales	$500,000	$300,000
Cost of Goods Sold	(350,000)	(270,000)
Gross Profit	$150,000	$ 30,000
Depreciation	(40,000)	(10,000)
Other Expenses	(60,000)	(15,000)
Income from Operations	$ 50,000	$ 5,000
Gain on Sale of Equipment to Scroll	12,000	
Income before Taxes	$ 62,000	$ 5,000

Equipment purchased by Scroll from Pirn for $36,000 on January 1, 20X1, is depreciated using the straight-line method over four years. What amount should be reported as depreciation expense in Pirn's 20X1 consolidated income statement?

   a. $50,000.

   b. $47,000.

   c. $44,000.

   d. $41,000.

E6-2 **Multiple-Choice Questions on Intercompany Transactions**

Select the correct answer for each of the following questions.

1. Upper Company holds 60 percent of Lower Company's voting shares. During the preparation of consolidated financial statements for 20X5, the following eliminating entry was made:

Retained Earnings, January 1	10,000	
Land		10,000

Which of the following statements is correct?

   a. Upper Company purchased land from Lower Company during 20X5.

   b. Upper Company purchased land from Lower Company before January 1, 20X5.

   c. Lower Company purchased land from Upper Company during 20X5.

   d. Lower Company purchased land from Upper Company before January 1, 20X5.

2. Middle Company holds 60 percent of Bottom Corporation's voting shares. Bottom has developed a new type of production equipment that appears to be quite marketable. It spent $40,000 in developing the equipment; however, Middle agreed to purchase the production rights for the machine for $100,000. If the intercompany sale occurred on January 1, 20X2, and the production rights are expected to have value for five years, at what amount should the rights be reported in the consolidated balance sheet for December 31, 20X2?

   a. $0.

   b. $32,000.

   c. $80,000.

   d. $100,000.

Questions 3 through 6 are based on the following information:

On January 1, 20X4, Gold Company purchased a computer with an expected economic life of five years. On January 1, 20X6, Gold sold the computer to Silver Corporation and recorded the following entry:

Cash	39,000	
Accumulated Depreciation	16,000	
Computer Equipment		40,000
Gain on Sale of Equipment		15,000

Silver Corporation holds 60 percent of Gold's voting shares. Gold reported net income of $45,000, and Silver reported income from its own operations of $85,000 for 20X6. There is no change in the estimated economic life of the equipment as a result of the intercorporate transfer.

3. In the preparation of the 20X6 consolidated income statement, depreciation expense will be:

   a. Debited for $5,000 in the eliminating entries.

   b. Credited for $5,000 in the eliminating entries.

   c. Debited for $13,000 in the eliminating entries.

   d. Credited for $13,000 in the eliminating entries.

4. In the preparation of the 20X6 consolidated balance sheet, computer equipment will be:

   a. Debited for $1,000.

   b. Debited for $15,000.

   c. Credited for $24,000.

   d. Debited for $40,000.

5. Income assigned to the noncontrolling interest in the 20X6 consolidated income statement will be:

   a. $12,000.

   b. $14,000.

   c. $18,000.

   d. $52,000.

6. Consolidated net income for 20X6 will be:

   a. $103,000.

   b. $106,000.

   c. $112,000.

   d. $130,000.

E6-3   Elimination Entries for Land Transfer

Huckster Corporation purchased land on January 1, 20X1, for $20,000. On June 10, 20X4, it sold the land to its subsidiary, Lowly Corporation, for $30,000. Huckster owns 60 percent of Lowly's voting shares.

Required

a. Give the workpaper eliminating entries needed to remove the effects of the intercompany sale of land in preparing the consolidated financial statements for 20X4 and 20X5.

b. Give the workpaper eliminating entries needed on December 31, 20X4 and 20X5, if Lowly had initially purchased the land for $20,000 and then sold it to Huckster on June 10, 20X4, for $30,000.

E6-4   Intercompany Services

Power Corporation owns 75 percent of Swift Company's stock. Swift provides health care services to its employees and those of Power. During 20X2, Power recorded $45,000 as health care expense for medical care given to its employees by Swift. Swift's costs incurred in providing the services to Power were $32,000.

Required

a. By what amount will consolidated net income change when the intercompany services are eliminated in preparing Power's consolidated statements for 20X2?

b. What would be the impact of eliminating the intercompany services on consolidated net income if Power owned 100 percent of Swift's stock rather than 75 percent? Explain.

c. If in its consolidated income statement for 20X2 Power had reported total health care costs of $70,000, what was the cost to Swift of providing health care services to its own employees?

E6-5   Elimination Entries for Intercompany Services

On January 1, 20X5, Block Corporation started using a wholly owned subsidiary to deliver all its sales overnight to its customers. During 20X5, Block recorded delivery service expense of $76,000 and made payments of $58,000 to the subsidiary.

Required

Give the workpaper eliminating entries related to the intercompany services needed on December 31, 20X5, to prepare consolidated financial statements.

E6-6 Elimination Entries for Depreciable Asset Transfer: Year-End Sale

Pam Corporation holds 70 percent ownership of Northern Enterprises. On December 31, 20X6, Northern paid Pam $40,000 for a truck that Pam had purchased for $45,000 on January 1, 20X2. The truck was considered to have a 15-year life from January 1, 20X2, and no residual value. Both companies depreciate equipment using the straight-line method.

Required

a. Give the workpaper eliminating entry or entries needed on December 31, 20X6, to remove the effects of the intercompany sale.

b. Give the workpaper eliminating entry or entries needed on December 31, 20X7, to remove the effects of the intercompany sale.

E6-7 Transfer of Land

Bowen Corporation owns 70 percent of Roan Corporation's voting common stock. On March 12, 20X2, Roan sold land it had purchased for $140,000 to Bowen for $185,000. Bowen plans to build a new warehouse on the property in 20X3.

Required

a. Give the workpaper eliminating entries to remove the effects of the intercompany sale of land in preparing the consolidated financial statements at December 31, 20X2 and 20X3.

b. Give the workpaper eliminating entries needed at December 31, 20X3 and 20X4, if Bowen had initially purchased the land for $150,000 and sold it to Roan on March 12, 20X2, for $180,000.

E6-8 Transfer of Depreciable Asset at Year-End

Frazer Corporation purchased 60 percent of Minnow Corporation's voting common stock on January 1, 20X1, at underlying book value. On December 31, 20X5, Frazer received $210,000 from Minnow for a truck Frazer had purchased on January 1, 20X2, for $300,000. The truck is expected to have a 10-year useful life and no salvage value. Both companies depreciate trucks on a straight-line basis.

Required

a. Give the workpaper eliminating entry or entries needed at December 31, 20X5, to remove the effects of the intercompany sale.

b. Give the workpaper eliminating entry or entries needed at December 31, 20X6, to remove the effects of the intercompany sale.

E6-9 Transfer of Depreciable Asset at Beginning of Year

Frazer Corporation purchased 60 percent of Minnow Corporation's voting common stock on January 1, 20X1, at underlying book value. On January 1, 20X5, Frazer received $245,000 from Minnow for a truck Frazer had purchased on January 1, 20X2, for $300,000. The truck is expected to have a 10-year useful life and no salvage value. Both companies depreciate trucks on a straight-line basis.

Required

a. Give the workpaper eliminating entry or entries needed at December 31, 20X5, to remove the effects of the intercompany sale.

b. Give the workpaper eliminating entry or entries needed at December 31, 20X6, to remove the effects of the intercompany sale.

E6-10 Sale of Equipment to Subsidiary in Current Period

On January 1, 20X7, Wainwrite Corporation sold to Lance Corporation equipment it had purchased for $150,000 and used for eight years. Wainwrite recorded a gain of $14,000 on the sale. The equipment has a total useful life of 15 years and is depreciated on a straight-line basis. Wainwrite holds 70 percent of Lance's voting common shares.

Required

a. Give the journal entry made by Wainwrite on January 1, 20X7, to record the sale of equipment.

b. Give the journal entries recorded by Lance during 20X7 to record the purchase of equipment and year-end depreciation expense.

c. Give the eliminating entry or entries related to the intercompany sale of equipment needed at December 31, 20X7, to prepare a full set of consolidated financial statements.

d. Give the eliminating entry or entries related to the equipment required at January 1, 20X8, to prepare a consolidated balance sheet only.

E6-11   Upstream Sale of Equipment in Prior Period

Baywatch Industries purchased 80 percent ownership of Tubberware Corporation on January 1, 20X0, at underlying book value. On January 1, 20X6, Baywatch paid Tubberware $270,000 to acquire equipment that Tubberware had purchased on January 1, 20X3, for $300,000. The equipment is expected to have no scrap value and is depreciated over a 15-year useful life.

Baywatch reported operating earnings of $100,000 for 20X8 and paid dividends of $40,000. Tubberware reported net income of $40,000 and paid dividends of $20,000 in 20X8.

Required

a. Compute the amount reported as consolidated net income for 20X8.

b. By what amount would consolidated net income change if the equipment sale had been a downstream sale rather than an upstream sale?

c. Give the eliminating entry or entries required to eliminate the effects of the intercompany sale of equipment in preparing a full set of consolidated financial statements at December 31, 20X8.

E6-12   Elimination Entries for Midyear Depreciable Asset Transfer

Albion Corporation holds 90 percent ownership of Andrews Company. On July 1, 20X3, Albion sold equipment that it had purchased for $30,000 on January 1, 20X1, to Andrews for $28,000. The equipment's original six-year estimated total economic life remains unchanged. Both companies use straight-line depreciation. The equipment's residual value is considered negligible.

Required

a. Give the eliminating entry or entries in the consolidation workpaper prepared as of December 31, 20X3, to remove the effects of the intercompany sale.

b. Give the eliminating entry or entries in the consolidation workpaper prepared as of December 31, 20X4, to remove the effects of the intercompany sale.

E6-13   Consolidated Net Income Computation

Verry Corporation owns 75 percent of Spawn Corporation's voting common stock. Verry reported income from its separate operations of $90,000 and $110,000 in 20X4 and 20X5, respectively. Spawn reported net income of $60,000 and $40,000 in 20X4 and 20X5, respectively.

Required

a. Compute consolidated net income for 20X4 and 20X5 if Verry sold land with a book value of $95,000 to Spawn for $120,000 on June 30, 20X4.

b. Compute consolidated net income for 20X4 and 20X5 if Spawn sold land with a book value of $95,000 to Verry for $120,000 on June 30, 20X4.

E6-14   Elimination Entries for Intercompany Transfers

Speedy Delivery Service purchased at book value 80 percent of the voting shares of Acme Real Estate Company. On January 1, 20X3, the date of purchase, Acme Real Estate reported common stock of $300,000 and retained earnings of $100,000. During 20X3 Speedy Delivery provided courier services for Acme Real Estate in the amount of $15,000. Also during 20X3, Acme Real Estate purchased land for $1,000. It sold the land to Speedy Delivery Service for $26,000 so that Speedy Delivery could build a new transportation center. Speedy Delivery reported $65,000 of operating income from its delivery operations in 20X3. Acme Real Estate reported net income of $40,000 and paid dividends of $10,000 in 20X3.

Required

a. Compute consolidated net income for 20X3.

b. Give all journal entries recorded by Speedy Delivery Service related to its investment in Acme Real Estate assuming Speedy uses the basic equity method in accounting for the investment.

c. Give all eliminating entries required in preparing a consolidation workpaper as of December 31, 20X3.

E6-15   Sale of Building to Parent in Prior Period

Turner Company purchased 70 percent of Split Company's stock approximately 20 years ago. On December 31, 20X8, Turner purchased a building from Split for $300,000. Split had purchased the building on January 1, 20X1, at a cost of $400,000 and used straight-line depreciation on an expected life of 20 years. The asset's total estimated economic life is unchanged as a result of the intercompany sale.

Required

a. What amount of depreciation expense on the building will Turner report for 20X9?

b. What amount of depreciation expense would Split have reported for 20X9 if it had continued to own the building?

c. Give the eliminating entry or entries needed to eliminate the effects of the intercompany building transfer in preparing a full set of consolidated financial statements at December 31, 20X9.

d. What amount of income will be assigned to the noncontrolling interest in the consolidated income statement for 20X9 if Split reports net income of $40,000 for 20X9?

e. Assume that Split reports assets with a book value of $350,000 and liabilities of $150,000 at January 1, 20X9, and reports net income of $40,000 and dividends of $15,000 for 20X9. What amount will be assigned to the noncontrolling interest in the consolidated balance sheet at December 31, 20X9?

E6-16 Intercompany Sale at a Loss

Parent Company holds 90 percent of Sunway Company's voting common shares. On December 31, 20X8, Parent recorded a loss of $16,000 on the sale of equipment to Sunway. At the time of the sale, the equipment's estimated remaining economic life was eight years.

Required

a. Will consolidated net income be increased or decreased when eliminating entries associated with the sale of equipment are made at December 31, 20X8? By what amount?

b. Will consolidated net income be increased or decreased when eliminating entries associated with the sale of equipment are made at December 31, 20X9? By what amount?

E6-17 Eliminating Entries following Intercompany Sale at a Loss

Brown Corporation holds 70 percent of Transom Company's voting common stock. On January 1, 20X2, Transom paid $300,000 to acquire a building with a 15-year expected economic life. Transom uses straight-line depreciation for all depreciable assets. On December 31, 20X7, Brown purchased the building from Transom for $144,000. Brown reported income, excluding investment income from Transom, of $125,000 and $150,000 for 20X7 and 20X8, respectively. Transom reported net income of $15,000 and $40,000 for 20X7 and 20X8, respectively.

Required

a. Give the appropriate eliminating entry or entries needed to eliminate the effects of the intercompany sale of the building in preparing consolidated financial statements for 20X7.

b. Compute the amount to be reported as consolidated net income for Brown for 20X7.

c. Give the appropriate eliminating entry or entries needed to eliminate the effects of the intercompany sale of the building in preparing consolidated financial statements for 20X8.

d. Compute the amount to be reported as consolidated net income for Brown for 20X8.

E6-18 Multiple Transfers of Asset

Swanson Corporation purchased land from Clayton Corporation for $240,000 on December 20, 20X3. This purchase followed a series of transactions between Swanson-controlled subsidiaries. On February 7, 20X3, Sullivan Corporation purchased the land from a nonaffiliate for $145,000. It sold the land to Kolder Company for $130,000 on October 10, 20X3, and Kolder sold the land to Clayton for $180,000 on November 27, 20X3. Swanson has control of the following companies:

Subsidiary	Level of Ownership	20X3 Net Income
Sullivan Corporation	80 percent	$120,000
Kolder Company	70 percent	60,000
Clayton Corporation	90 percent	80,000

Swanson reported income from its separate operations of $150,000 for 20X3.

Required

a. At what amount should the land be reported in the consolidated balance sheet as of December 31, 20X3?

b. What amount of gain or loss on sale of land should be reported in the consolidated income statement for 20X3?

c. What amount should be reported as consolidated net income for 20X3?

d. Give any elimination entries related to the land that should appear in the workpaper used to prepare consolidated financial statements for 20X3.

E6-19 **Elimination Entry in Period of Transfer**

Blank Corporation owns 60 percent of Grand Corporation's voting common stock. On December 31, 20X4, Blank paid Grand $276,000 for dump trucks Grand had purchased on January 1, 20X2. Both companies use straight-line depreciation. The eliminating entry included in preparing consolidated financial statements at December 31, 20X4, was:

Trucks	24,000	
Gain on Sale of Trucks	36,000	
Accumulated Depreciation		60,000

Required

a. What amount was paid by Grand to purchase the trucks on January 1, 20X2?

b. What was the economic life of the trucks on January 1, 20X2?

c. Give the workpaper eliminating entry needed in preparing the consolidated financial statements at December 31, 20X5.

E6-20 **Elimination Entry Computation**

Stern Manufacturing purchased an ultrasound drilling machine with a remaining 10-year economic life from a 70 percent owned subsidiary for $360,000 on January 1, 20X6. Both companies use straight-line depreciation. The subsidiary recorded the following entry when it sold the machine to Stern:

Cash	360,000	
Accumulated Depreciation	150,000	
Equipment		450,000
Gain on Sale of Equipment		60,000

Required

Give the workpaper elimination entry or entries needed to remove the effects of the intercorporate sale of equipment when consolidated financial statements are prepared as of (*a*) December 31, 20X6, and (*b*) December 31, 20X7.

E6-21 **Using the Eliminating Entry to Determine Account Balances**

Pastel Corporation acquired controlling interest of Somber Corporation in 20X5 at underlying book value. In preparing a consolidated balance sheet workpaper at January 1, 20X9, Pastel's controller included the following eliminating entry:

Equipment	53,500	
Retained Earnings	9,450	
Noncontrolling Interest	1,050	
Accumulated Depreciation		64,000

A note at the bottom of the consolidation workpaper at January 1, 20X9, indicates the equipment was purchased from a nonaffiliate on January 1, 20X1, for $120,000 and was sold to an affiliate on December 31, 20X8. The equipment is being depreciated on a 15-year straight-line basis. Somber reported stock outstanding of $300,000 and retained earnings of $200,000 at January 1, 20X9. Somber reported net income of $25,000 and paid dividends of $6,000 for 20X9.

Required

a. What percentage ownership of Somber Corporation does Pastel hold?

b. Was the parent or subsidiary the owner prior to the intercorporate sale of equipment? Explain.

c. What was the intercompany transfer price of the equipment on December 31, 20X8?

d. What amount of income will be assigned to the noncontrolling interest in the consolidated income statement for 20X9?

e. Assuming Pastel and Somber report depreciation expense of $15,000 and $9,000, respectively, for 20X9, what depreciation amount will be reported in the consolidated income statement for 20X9?

f. Give all eliminating entries needed at December 31, 20X9, to prepare a complete set of consolidated financial statements.

E6-22   Intercompany Sale of Services

Norgaard Corporation is provided management consulting services by its 75 percent owned subsidiary, Bline Inc. During 20X3, Norgaard paid Bline $123,200 for its services. For the year 20X4, Bline billed Norgaard $138,700 for such services and collected all but $6,600 by year-end. Bline's labor cost and other associated costs for the employees providing services to Norgaard totaled $91,000 in 20X3 and $112,000 in 20X4. Norgaard reported $2,342,000 of income from its own separate operations for 20X4, and Bline reported net income of $631,000.

Required

a. Present all elimination entries related to the intercompany sale of services that would be needed in the consolidation workpaper used to prepare a complete set of consolidated financial statements for 20X4.

b. Compute consolidated net income for 20X4.

E6-23A   Fully Adjusted Equity Method and Cost Method

Newtime Products purchased 65 percent of TV Sales Company's stock at underlying book value on January 1, 20X3. At that time, TV Sales reported shares outstanding of $300,000 and retained earnings of $100,000. During 20X3, TV Sales reported net income of $50,000 and paid dividends of $5,000. In 20X4, TV Sales reported net income of $70,000 and paid dividends of $20,000.

The following transactions occurred between Newtime Products and TV Sales in 20X3 and 20X4:

1. TV Sales sold camera equipment to Newtime for a $40,000 profit on December 31, 20X3. The equipment had a five-year estimated economic life remaining at the time of intercompany transfer and is depreciated on a straight-line basis.

2. Newtime sold land costing $30,000 to TV Sales on June 30, 20X4, for $41,000.

Required

a. Assuming that Newtime uses the fully adjusted equity method to account for its investment in TV Sales:

   (1) Give the journal entries recorded on Newtime's books in 20X4 related to its investment in TV Sales.

   (2) Give all eliminating entries needed to prepare a consolidation workpaper for 20X4.

b. Assuming that Newtime uses the cost method to account for its investment in TV Sales:

   (1) Give the journal entries recorded on Newtime's books in 20X4 related to its investment in TV Sales.

   (2) Give all eliminating entries needed to prepare a consolidation workpaper for 20X4.

Problems   P6-24   Computation of Consolidated Net Income

Petime Corporation owns 90 percent of United Grain Company. Petime paid $9,000 in excess of underlying book value to purchase United's shares and is amortizing the balance over a 10-year period. During 20X4, United sold land to Petime at a $7,000 profit. United Grain reported net income of $19,000 and paid dividends of $4,000 in 20X4. Petime reported income, exclusive of its income from United Grain, of $34,000 and paid dividends of $15,000 in 20X4.

Required

a. Compute consolidated net income for 20X4.

b. By what amount would 20X4 consolidated net income increase or decrease if the sale of land had been from Petime to United Grain, and the gain on the sale of land had been included in Petime's $34,000 income?

P6-25   Subsidiary Net Income

Lander Corporation purchased 75 percent of Toll Corporation's voting common shares for $350,000 on January 1, 20X4, when Toll reported common stock outstanding of $150,000 and retained earnings of $270,000. The purchase differential is amortized over 10 years. On December 31, 20X4, Toll sold a building to Lander and recorded a gain of $20,000. Income assigned to the noncontrolling shareholders in the 20X4 consolidated income statement was $17,500.

Required

a. Compute the amount of net income Toll reported for 20X4.

b. Compute the amount reported as consolidated net income if Lander reported operating income of $234,000 for 20X4.

P6-26   Consolidated Net Income

Forest Corporation purchased 70 percent of Part Company's voting common stock on January 1, 20X2, for $294,000. At the time, Part reported common stock outstanding of $150,000 and retained earnings of $220,000. Forest is amortizing the excess paid over underlying book value over a 10-year period. Forest reported income, exclusive of its income from Part, of $83,000 and paid dividends of $40,000 during 20X4. Part reported net income of $30,000 and paid dividends of $8,000 during 20X4.

Required

a. Compute consolidated net income for 20X4 assuming that Part sold land it had purchased for $21,000 to Forest for $29,000 on January 31, 20X4.

b. Compute consolidated net income for 20X4 assuming that Forest sold land it had purchased for $21,000 to Part for $29,000 on January 31, 20X4.

P6-27   Transfer of Asset from One Subsidiary to Another

Pelts Company holds a total of 70 percent of Bugle Corporation and 80 percent of Cook Products Corporation stock. Bugle purchased a warehouse with an expected life of 20 years on January 1, 20X1, for $40,000. On January 1, 20X6, it sold the warehouse to Cook Products for $45,000.

Required

Complete the following table showing selected information that would appear in the separate 20X6 income statements and balance sheets of Bugle Corporation and Cook Products Corporation and in the 20X6 consolidated financial statements.

	Bugle Corporation	Cook Products Corporation	Consolidated Entity
Depreciation expense			
Fixed assets—warehouse			
Accumulated depreciation			
Gain on sale of warehouse			

P6-28   Consolidated Eliminating Entry

In preparing its consolidated financial statements at December 31, 20X7, the following eliminating entry was included in the consolidation workpaper of Master Corporation:

Buildings	140,000	
Gain on Sale of Building	28,000	
Depreciation Expense		2,000
Accumulated Depreciation		166,000

Master owns 60 percent of Rakel Corporation's voting common stock. On January 1, 20X7, Rakel sold Master a building it had purchased for $600,000 on January 1, 20X1, and depreciated on a 20-year straight-line basis. Master recorded depreciation for 20X7 using straight-line depreciation and the same useful life and residual value as Rakel.

Required

a. What amount did Master pay Rakel for the building?

b. What amount of accumulated depreciation did Rakel report at January 1, 20X7, prior to the sale?

c. What annual depreciation expense did Rakel record prior to the sale?

d. What expected residual value did Rakel use in computing its annual depreciation expense?

e. What amount of depreciation expense did Master record in 20X7?

f. If Rakel reported net income of $80,000 for 20X7, what amount of income will be assigned to the noncontrolling interest in the consolidated income statement for 20X7?

g. If Rakel reported net income of $65,000 for 20X8, what amount of income will be assigned to the noncontrolling interest in the consolidated income statement for 20X8?

P6-29 **Multiple-Choice Questions**

Select the correct answer for each of the following questions.

1. In the preparation of a consolidated income statement:

   a. Income assigned to noncontrolling shareholders always is computed as a pro rata portion of the reported net income of the consolidated entity.

   b. Income assigned to noncontrolling shareholders always is computed as a pro rata portion of the reported net income of the subsidiary.

   c. Income assigned to noncontrolling shareholders in the current period is likely to be less than a pro rata portion of the reported net income of the subsidiary in the current period if the subsidiary had an unrealized gain on an intercorporate sale of depreciable assets in the preceding period.

   d. Income assigned to noncontrolling shareholders in the current period is likely to be more than a pro rata portion of the reported net income of the subsidiary in the current period if the subsidiary had an unrealized gain on an intercorporate sale of depreciable assets in the preceding period.

2. When a 90 percent owned subsidiary records a gain on the sale of land to an affiliate during the current period and the land is not resold before the end of the period:

   a. The full amount of the gain will be excluded from consolidated net income.

   b. Consolidated net income will be increased by the full amount of the gain.

   c. A proportionate share of the unrealized gain will be excluded from income assigned to noncontrolling interest.

   d. The full amount of the unrealized gain will be excluded from income assigned to noncontrolling interest.

3. During 20X5, Subsidiary Corporation sells land to Parent Corporation and records a gain of $15,000 on the sale. Subsidiary reports 20X5 net income of $55,000. Parent holds 60 percent of the voting shares of Subsidiary. Parent plans to build a new general headquarters on the land in 20X7. If no adjustment is made for unrealized profits in preparing the consolidated financial statements as of December 31, 20X5:

   a. Consolidated net income will be overstated by $15,000.

   b. Consolidated retained earnings will be overstated by $15,000.

   c. Income assigned to the noncontrolling interest in the consolidated income statement will be overstated by $9,000.

   d. Consolidated net income will be overstated by $9,000.

   e. Both answers a and b are correct.

4. Minor Company sold land to Major Company on November 15, 20X4, and recorded a gain of $30,000 on the sale. Major owns 80 percent of Minor's common shares. Which of the following statements is correct?

   a. A proportionate share of the $30,000 must be treated as a reduction of income assigned to the noncontrolling interest in the consolidated income statement unless the land is resold to a nonaffiliate in 20X4.

   b. The $30,000 will not be treated as an adjustment in computing income assigned to the noncontrolling interest in the consolidated income statement in 20X4 unless the land is resold to a nonaffiliate in 20X4.

   c. In computing consolidated net income it does not matter whether the land is or is not resold to a nonaffiliate before the end of the period; the $30,000 will not affect the computation of consolidated net income in 20X4 because the profits are on the subsidiary's books.

   d. Minor's trial balance as of December 31, 20X4, should be adjusted to remove the $30,000 gain since the gain is not yet realized.

5. Lewis Company owns 80 percent of Tomassini Corporation's stock. You are told that Tomassini has sold equipment to Lewis and that the following eliminating entry is needed to prepare consolidated statements for 20X9:

Equipment	20,000	
Gain on Sale of Equipment	40,000	
Depreciation Expense		5,000
Accumulated Depreciation		55,000

Which of the following is incorrect?

    a. The parent paid $40,000 in excess of the subsidiary's carrying amount to acquire the asset.

    b. From a consolidated viewpoint, depreciation expense as Lewis recorded it is overstated.

    c. The asset transfer occurred in 20X9 before the end of the year.

    d. Consolidated net income will be reduced by $40,000 when this entry is used as an eliminating entry.

P6-30 **Intercompany Services Provided to Subsidiary**

During 20X4, Plate Company paid its employees $80,000 for work done in helping its wholly owned subsidiary build a new office building that was completed on December 31, 20X4. Plate recorded the $110,000 payment from the subsidiary for the work done as service revenue. The subsidiary included the payment in the cost of the building and is depreciating the building over 25 years with no assumed residual value.

Required

Present the eliminating entries needed at December 31, 20X4 and 20X5, to prepare Plate's consolidated financial statements.

P6-31 **Consolidated Net Income with Intercorporate Transfers**

In its 20X7 consolidated income statement, Skekel Development Company reported consolidated net income of $921,000 and $45,000 of income assigned to the 30 percent noncontrolling interest in its only subsidiary, Subsidence Mining, Inc. During the year, Subsidence had sold a previously mined parcel of land to Skekel for a new housing development; the sales price to Skekel was $500,000, and the land had a carrying amount at the time of sale of $560,000. At the beginning of the previous year, Skekel had sold excavation and grading equipment to Subsidence for $240,000; the equipment had a remaining life of six years as of the date of sale and a book value of $210,000. The equipment originally had cost $350,000 when Skekel purchased it on January 2, 20X2. The equipment never was expected to have any salvage value.

Skekel had purchased its investment in Subsidence 12 years earlier for a price $300,000 in excess of the book value of the shares acquired; all the excess over the book value was attributable to intangible assets with a remaining life of 20 years from the date of combination. Both parent and subsidiary use straight-line amortization and depreciation.

Required

    a. Present the journal entry made by Skekel to record the sale of equipment in 20X6 to Subsidence.

    b. Present all elimination entries related to the intercompany transfers of land and equipment that should appear in the consolidation workpaper used to prepare a complete set of consolidated financial statements for 20X7.

    c. Compute Subsidence's 20X7 net income.

    d. Compute Skekel's 20X7 income from its own separate operations, excluding any investment income from its investment in Subsidence Mining.

P6-32 **Computation of Retained Earnings following Multiple Transfers**

Great Company purchased 80 percent of Meager Corporation's common stock on January 1, 20X4, for $280,000. Great's corporate controller has lost the consolidation files for the past three years and has asked you to compute the proper retained earnings balances for the consolidated entity at January 1, 20X8, and December 31, 20X8. The controller has been able to determine the following:

1. The book value of Meager's net assets at January 1, 20X4, was $290,000 and the fair value of its net assets was $325,000. This difference was due to an increase in the value of equipment. All depreciable assets had a remaining life of 10 years at the date of combination. At December 31, 20X8, Great's management reviewed the amount attributed to goodwill as a result of its purchase of Meager common stock and concluded an impairment loss of $14,000 should be recognized in 20X8.

2. Great uses the basic equity method in accounting for its investment in Meager.

3. Meager has reported net income of $30,000 and paid dividends of $20,000 each year since Great purchased its ownership.

4. Great reported retained earnings of $450,000 in its December 31, 20X7, balance sheet. For 20X8, Great reported operating income of $65,000 and paid dividends of $45,000.

5. Meager sold land costing $40,000 to Great for $56,000 on December 31, 20X7.

6. On January 1, 20X6, Great sold depreciable assets with a remaining useful life of 10 years to Meager and recorded a $22,000 gain on the sale.

Required

Compute the appropriate amounts to be reported as consolidated retained earnings at January 1, 20X8, and December 31, 20X8.

P6-33 Preparation of Consolidated Balance Sheet

Lofton Company owns 60 percent of Temple Corporation's voting shares, purchased on May 17, 20X1, at book value. The companies' permanent accounts on December 31, 20X6, contained the following balances:

	Lofton Company	Temple Corporation
Cash and Receivables	$101,000	$ 20,000
Inventory	80,000	40,000
Land	150,000	90,000
Buildings and Equipment	400,000	300,000
Investment in Temple Corporation Stock	150,000	
	$881,000	$450,000
Accumulated Depreciation	$135,000	$ 85,000
Accounts Payable	90,000	25,000
Notes Payable	200,000	90,000
Common Stock	100,000	200,000
Retained Earnings	356,000	50,000
	$881,000	$450,000

On January 1, 20X2, Lofton paid $100,000 for equipment with a 10-year expected total economic life. The equipment was depreciated on a straight-line basis with no residual value. Temple purchased the equipment from Lofton on December 31, 20X4, for $91,000.

Temple sold land it had purchased for $30,000 on February 23, 20X4, to Lofton for $20,000 on October 14, 20X5.

Required

a. Prepare a consolidated balance sheet workpaper in good form as of December 31, 20X6.

b. Prepare a consolidated balance sheet as of December 31, 20X6.

P6-34 Consolidation Workpaper with Intercompany Transfers

Mist Company purchased 65 percent of Blank Corporation's voting common stock on June 20, 20X2, at underlying book value. The balance sheets and income statements for the companies at December 31, 20X4, are as follows:

MIST COMPANY AND BLANK CORPORATION
Balance Sheets
December 31, 20X4

Item	Mist Company	Blank Corp.
Cash	$ 32,500	$ 22,000
Accounts Receivable	62,000	37,000
Inventory	95,000	71,000
Land	40,000	15,000
Buildings and Equipment (net)	200,000	125,000
Investment in Blank Corp. Stock	110,500	
Total Assets	$540,000	$270,000
Accounts Payable	$ 35,000	$ 20,000
Bonds Payable	180,000	80,000
Common Stock, $5 par value	100,000	60,000
Retained Earnings	225,000	110,000
Total Liabilities and Stockholders' Equity	$540,000	$270,000

MIST COMPANY AND BLANK CORPORATION
Combined Income and Retained Earnings Statements
Year Ended December 31, 20X4

Item	Mist Company		Blank Corp.	
Sales and Service Revenue		$286,500		$128,500
Gain on Sale of Land		4,000		
Gain on Sale of Building				13,200
Income from Subsidiary		19,500		
		$310,000		$141,700
Cost of Goods and Services Sold	$160,000		$75,000	
Depreciation Expense	22,000		19,000	
Other Expenses	76,000	(258,000)	17,700	(111,700)
Net Income		$ 52,000		$ 30,000
Dividends Paid		(25,000)		(5,000)
Change in Retained Earnings		$ 27,000		$ 25,000

Additional Information

1. Mist uses the basic equity method in accounting for its investment in Blank.
2. During 20X4, Mist charged Blank $24,000 for consulting services to Blank during the year. The services cost Mist $17,000.
3. On January 1, 20X4, Blank sold Mist a building for $13,200 above its carrying value on Blank's books. The building had a 12-year remaining economic life at the time of transfer.
4. On June 14, 20X4, Mist sold land it had purchased for $3,000 to Blank for $7,000. Blank continued to hold the land at December 31, 20X4.

Required

a. Give all eliminating entries needed to prepare a full set of consolidated financial statements for 20X4.
b. Prepare a consolidation workpaper for 20X4.
c. Prepare the 20X4 consolidated balance sheet, income statement, and retained earnings statement.

P6-35 **Consolidation Workpaper in Year of Intercompany Transfer**

Prime Company holds 80 percent of Lane Company's stock, acquired on January 1, 20X2, for $160,000. On the acquisition date, Lane reported retained earnings of $50,000 and had $100,000 of common stock outstanding. Prime uses the basic equity method in accounting for its investment in Lane.

Trial balance data for the two companies on December 31, 20X6, are as follows:

Item	Prime Company		Lane Company	
	Debit	**Credit**	**Debit**	**Credit**
Cash and Accounts Receivable	$ 113,000		$ 35,000	
Inventory	260,000		90,000	
Land	80,000		80,000	
Buildings and Equipment	500,000		150,000	
Investment in Lane Company Stock	232,000			
Cost of Goods Sold	140,000		60,000	
Depreciation and Amortization	25,000		15,000	
Other Expenses	15,000		5,000	
Dividends Declared	30,000		5,000	
Accumulated Depreciation		$ 205,000		$ 45,000
Accounts Payable		60,000		20,000
Bonds Payable		200,000		50,000
Common Stock		300,000		100,000
Retained Earnings		338,000		105,000
Sales		240,000		120,000
Gain on Sale of Equipment		20,000		
Income from Subsidiary		32,000		
Total	$1,395,000	$1,395,000	$440,000	$440,000

Additional Information

1. At the date of combination, the book values and fair values of all separably identifiable assets of Lane were the same. At December 31, 20X6, the management of Prime reviewed the amount attributed to goodwill as a result of its purchase of Lane stock and concluded an impairment loss of $25,000 should be recognized in 20X6.

2. On January 1, 20X5, Lane sold land that had cost $8,000 to Prime for $18,000.

3. On January 1, 20X6, Prime sold to Lane equipment that it had purchased for $75,000 on January 1, 20X1. The equipment has a total economic life of 15 years and was sold to Lane for $70,000. Both companies use straight-line depreciation.

4. There was $7,000 of intercompany receivables and payables on December 31, 20X6.

Required

a. Give all eliminating entries needed to prepare a consolidation workpaper for 20X6.

b. Prepare a three-part workpaper for 20X6 in good form.

c. Prepare a consolidated balance sheet, income statement, and retained earnings statement for 20X6.

P6-36   Intercorporate Sales in Prior Years

On January 1, 20X5, Pond Corporation purchased 80 percent of Skate Company's stock by issuing common stock with a fair value of $180,000. At that date, Skate reported retained earnings of $100,000. The balance sheets for Pond and Skate at January 1, 20X8, and December 31, 20X8, and income statements for 20X8 were reported as follows:

	20X8 Balance Sheet Data			
	Pond Corporation		**Skate Company**	
	January 1	**December 31**	**January 1**	**December 31**
Cash	$ 40,400	$ 68,400	$ 10,000	$ 47,000
Accounts Receivable	120,000	130,000	60,000	65,000
Interest and Other Receivables	40,000	45,000	8,000	10,000
Inventory	100,000	140,000	50,000	50,000
Land	50,000	50,000	22,000	22,000
Buildings and Equipment	400,000	400,000	240,000	240,000
Accumulated Depreciation	(150,000)	(185,000)	(70,000)	(94,000)
Investment in Skate Company Stock	211,000	224,000		
Investment in Tin Co. Bonds	135,000	134,000		
Total Assets	$946,400	$1,006,400	$320,000	$340,000
Accounts Payable	$ 60,000	$ 65,000	$ 16,500	$ 11,000
Interest and Other Payables	40,000	45,000	7,000	12,000
Bonds Payable	300,000	300,000	100,000	100,000
Bond Discount			(3,500)	(3,000)
Common Stock	150,000	150,000	30,000	30,000
Additional Paid-In Capital	155,000	155,000	20,000	20,000
Retained Earnings	241,400	291,400	150,000	170,000
Total Liabilities and Equities	$946,400	$1,006,400	$320,000	$340,000

	20X8 Income Statement Data	
	Pond Corporation	**Skate Company**
Sales	$450,000	$ 250,000
Income from Subsidiary	21,000	
Interest Income	14,900	
Total Revenue	$485,900	$ 250,000

(continued)

Cost of Goods Sold	$285,000		$136,000	
Other Operating Expenses	50,000		40,000	
Depreciation Expense	35,000		24,000	
Interest Expense	24,000		10,500	
Miscellaneous Expenses	11,900	(405,900)	9,500	(220,000)
Net Income		$ 80,000		$ 30,000

Additional Information

1. In 20X2 Skate developed a patent for a high-speed drill bit that Pond planned to market more extensively. In accordance with generally accepted accounting standards, Skate charges all research and development costs to expense in the year the expenses are incurred. At January 1, 20X5, the estimated market value of the patent rights was estimated to be $50,000. Pond believes the patent will be of value for the next 20 years. The remainder of the purchase differential is assigned to buildings and equipment, which also had a 20-year estimated economic life at January 1, 20X5. All of Skate's other assets and liabilities identified by Pond at the date of acquisition had book values and fair values that were relatively equal.

2. On December 31, 20X7, Pond sold a building to Skate for $65,000 that it had purchased for $125,000 and depreciated on a straight-line basis over 25 years. At the time of sale, Pond reported accumulated depreciation of $75,000 and a remaining life of 10 years.

3. On July 1, 20X6, Skate sold land that it had purchased for $22,000 to Pond for $35,000. Pond is planning to build a new warehouse on the property prior to the end of 20X9.

4. Both Pond and Skate paid dividends in 20X8.

Required

a. Give all eliminating entries required to prepare a three-part consolidation working paper at December 31, 20X8.

b. Prepare a three-part workpaper for 20X8 in good form.

P6-37 ### Intercorporate Sale of Land and Depreciable Asset

Champion Corporation purchased 70 percent of Morris Company's voting common stock for $154,500 on January 1, 20X3, when Morris reported common stock outstanding of $100,000 and retained earnings of $85,000. At that date Morris held buildings and equipment with a fair value $25,000 more than book value and a 10-year remaining life. The additional payment in excess of book value is assigned to a copyright held by Morris with a five-year life at the date of acquisition.

Trial balances for Champion and Morris on December 31, 20X5, are as follows:

	Champion Corporation		Morris Company	
	Debit	**Credit**	**Debit**	**Credit**
Cash	$ 20,250		$ 58,000	
Accounts Receivable	65,000		70,000	
Interest and Other Receivables	30,000		10,000	
Inventory	150,000		180,000	
Land	80,000		60,000	
Buildings and Equipment	315,000		240,000	
Bond Discount			15,000	
Investment in Morris Company Stock	172,750			
Cost of Goods Sold	375,000		110,000	
Depreciation Expense	25,000		10,000	
Interest Expense	24,000		33,000	
Other Expense	28,000		17,000	
Dividends Declared	30,000		5,000	

(continued)

(continued)

	Champion Corporation		Morris Company	
	Debit	**Credit**	**Debit**	**Credit**
Accumulated Depreciation—				
Buildings and Equipment		$ 120,000		$ 60,000
Accounts Payable		61,000		28,000
Other Payables		30,000		20,000
Bonds Payable		250,000		300,000
Common Stock		150,000		100,000
Additional Paid-In Capital		30,000		
Retained Earnings		178,000		100,000
Sales		450,000		190,400
Other Income		28,250		
Gain on Sale of Equipment				9,600
Income from Subsidiary		17,750		
Total	$1,315,000	$1,315,000	$808,000	$808,000

Champion sold land it had purchased for $21,000 to Morris on September 20, 20X4, for $32,000. Morris plans to use the land for future plant expansion. On January 1, 20X5, Morris sold equipment to Champion for $91,600. Morris purchased the equipment on January 1, 20X3, for $100,000 and depreciated it on a 10-year basis, including an estimated residual value of $10,000. The residual value and estimated economic life of the equipment remained unchanged as a result of the transfer and both companies use straight-line depreciation.

Required

a. Compute the amount of unamortized purchase differential at January 1, 20X5.

b. Prepare a reconciliation between the balance in the Investment in Morris Company Stock account reported by Champion at December 31, 20X5, and the underlying book value of net assets reported by Morris at that date.

c. Give all eliminating entries needed to prepare a full set of consolidated financial statements at December 31, 20X5, for Champion and Morris.

d. Prepare a three-part workpaper for 20X5 in good form.

P6-38 **Consolidation Workpaper in Year following Intercompany Transfer**

Prime Company holds 80 percent of Lane Company's stock, acquired on January 1, 20X2, for $160,000. On the date of acquisition, Lane reported retained earnings of $50,000 and $100,000 of common stock outstanding. Prime uses the basic equity method in accounting for its investment in Lane.

Trial balance data for the two companies on December 31, 20X7, are as follows:

	Prime Company		Lane Company	
Item	**Debit**	**Credit**	**Debit**	**Credit**
Cash and Accounts Receivable	$ 151,000		$ 55,000	
Inventory	240,000		100,000	
Land	100,000		80,000	
Buildings and Equipment	500,000		150,000	
Investment in Lane Company Stock	240,000			
Cost of Goods Sold	160,000		80,000	
Depreciation and Amortization	25,000		15,000	
Other Expenses	20,000		10,000	
Dividends Declared	60,000		35,000	
Accumulated Depreciation		$ 230,000		$ 60,000
Accounts Payable		60,000		25,000
Bonds Payable		200,000		50,000
Common Stock		300,000		100,000
Retained Earnings		420,000		140,000
Sales		250,000		150,000
Income from Subsidiary		36,000		
Total	$1,496,000	$1,496,000	$525,000	$525,000

Additional Information

1. At the date of combination, the book values and fair values of all of Lane's separably identifiable assets were the same. At December 31, 20X6, the management of Prime reviewed the amount attributed to goodwill as a result of its purchase of Lane stock and recognized an impairment loss of $25,000. No further impairment occurred in 20X7.

2. On January 1, 20X5, Lane sold land that had cost $8,000 to Prime for $18,000.

3. On January 1, 20X6, Prime sold to Lane equipment that it had purchased for $75,000 on January 1, 20X1. The equipment has a total 15-year economic life and was sold to Lane for $70,000. Both companies use straight-line depreciation.

4. Intercorporate receivables and payables total $4,000 on December 31, 20X7.

Required

a. Prepare a reconciliation between the balance in Prime's Investment in Lane Company Stock account reported on December 31, 20X7, and the book value of Lane.

b. Prepare all workpaper eliminating entries needed as of December 31, 20X7, and complete a three-part consolidation workpaper for 20X7.

P6-39 Incomplete Data

Partial trial balance data for Phantom Corporation, Shadow Company, and the consolidated entity at December 31, 20X7, are as follows:

Item	Phantom Corporation	Shadow Company	Consolidated Entity
Cash	$ 66,500	$ 25,000	$ 91,500
Accounts Receivable	(d)	35,000	126,000
Inventory	160,000	75,000	235,000
Buildings and Equipment	345,000	150,000	(i)
Land	70,000	90,000	153,000
Investment in Shadow Company Stock	(f)		
Cost of Goods Sold	230,000	195,000	425,000
Depreciation Expense	45,000	10,000	52,000
Amortization Expense			(e)
Miscellaneous Expense	18,000	15,000	33,000
Dividends Declared	25,000	20,000	25,000
Income to Noncontrolling Interest			(l)
Copyrights			5,000
Total Debits	**$1,190,500**	**$615,000**	**$1,671,200**
Accumulated Depreciation	$ 180,000	$ 80,000	$ (j)
Accounts Payable	25,000	85,000	101,000
Common Stock	100,000	50,000	(a)
Additional Paid-In Capital	(b)	70,000	140,000
Retained Earnings	380,000	80,000	(k)
Income from Subsidiary	15,500		
Sales	343,000	(c)	593,000
Gain on Sale of Land	(g)		(h)
Noncontrolling Interest			82,800
Total Credits	**$1,190,500**	**$615,000**	**$1,671,200**

Additional Information

1. Phantom Corporation purchased 60 percent ownership of Shadow Company on January 1, 20X4, for $105,000. Shadow reported retained earnings of $30,000 on January 1, 20X4. The purchase differential is assigned to copyrights that are being amortized over a six-year life.

2. On August 13, 20X7, Phantom sold land to Shadow for $28,000. Phantom also has accounts receivable from Shadow on services performed prior to the end of 20X7.

3. Shadow sold equipment it had purchased for $60,000 on January 1, 20X4, to Phantom on January 1, 20X6, for $45,000. The equipment is depreciated on a straight-line basis and had a total expected useful life of five years when Shadow purchased it. No change in life expectancy resulted from the intercompany transfer.

Required

Compute the dollar amount for each of the balances identified by a letter.

P6-40 **Intercompany Sale of Equipment at a Loss in Prior Period**

Block Corporation was created on January 1, 20X0, to develop computer software. On January 1, 20X5, Foster Company purchased 90 percent of Block's common stock at underlying book value. Trial balances for Foster and Block on December 31, 20X9, follow:

	Foster Company		Block Corporation	
	Debit	**Credit**	**Debit**	**Credit**
Cash	$ 82,000		$ 32,400	
Accounts Receivable	80,000		90,000	
Other Receivables	40,000		10,000	
Inventory	200,000		130,000	
Land	80,000		60,000	
Buildings and Equipment	500,000		250,000	
Investment in Block Corporation Stock	216,000			
Cost of Goods Sold	500,000		250,000	
Depreciation Expense	45,000		15,000	
Other Expense	95,000		75,000	
Dividends Declared	40,000		20,000	
Accumulated Depreciation		$ 155,000		$ 75,000
Accounts Payable		63,000		35,000
Other Payables		95,000		20,000
Bonds Payable		250,000		200,000
Bond Premium				2,400
Common Stock		210,000		50,000
Additional Paid-In Capital		110,000		
Retained Earnings		235,000		150,000
Sales		680,000		385,000
Other Income		26,000		15,000
Income from Subsidiary		54,000		
Total	$1,878,000	$1,878,000	$932,400	$932,400

On January 1, 20X7, Block sold equipment to Foster for $48,000. Block had purchased the equipment for $90,000 on January 1, 20X5, and was depreciating it on a straight-line basis with a 10-year expected life and no anticipated scrap value. The equipment's total expected life is unchanged as a result of the intercompany sale.

Required

a. Give all eliminating entries required to prepare a three-part consolidated working paper at December 31, 20X9.

b. Prepare a three-part workpaper for 20X9 in good form.

P6-41 **Comprehensive Problem: Intercorporate Transfers**

Rossman Corporation holds 75 percent of the common stock of Schmid Distributors Inc., purchased on December 31, 20X1, for $2,340,000. At the date of acquisition, Schmid reported common stock with a par value of $1,000,000, additional paid-in capital of $1,350,000, and retained earnings of $620,000. The differential at acquisition was attributable to the following items:

Inventory (sold in 20X2)	$ 22,500
Land	40,000
Goodwill	50,000
Total Differential	$112,500

During 20X2, Rossman sold to Schmid at a gain of $23,000 a piece of land that it had purchased several years before; Schmid continues to hold the land. In 20X6, Rossman and Schmid entered into a five-year contract under which Rossman provides management consulting services to Schmid on a continuing basis; Schmid pays Rossman a fixed fee of $80,000 per year for these services. At December 31, 20X8, Schmid owed Rossman $20,000 as the final 20X8 quarterly payment under the contract.

On January 2, 20X8, Rossman purchased from Schmid for $250,000 equipment that Schmid was then carrying at $290,000. Schmid had purchased that equipment on December 27, 20X2, for $435,000. The equipment is expected to have a total 15-year life and no salvage value. The amount of the differential assigned to goodwill is not amortized.

At December 31, 20X8, trial balances for Rossman and Schmid appeared as follows:

Item	Rossman Corporation Debit	Rossman Corporation Credit	Schmid Distributors Inc. Debit	Schmid Distributors Inc. Credit
Cash	$ 50,700		$ 38,000	
Current Receivables	101,800		89,400	
Inventory	286,000		218,900	
Investment in Schmid Stock	2,970,000			
Land	400,000		1,200,000	
Buildings and Equipment	2,400,000		2,990,000	
Cost of Goods Sold	2,193,000		525,000	
Depreciation and Amortization	202,000		88,000	
Other Expenses	1,381,000		227,000	
Dividends Declared	50,000		20,000	
Accumulated Depreciation		$ 1,105,000		$ 420,000
Current Payables		86,200		76,300
Bonds Payable		1,000,000		200,000
Common Stock		100,000		1,000,000
Additional Paid-In Capital		1,272,000		1,350,000
Retained Earnings, January 1		1,497,800		1,400,000
Sales		4,801,000		985,000
Other Income or Loss		90,000	35,000	
Income from Subsidiary		82,500		
Total	$10,034,500	$10,034,500	$5,431,300	$5,431,300

As of December 31, 20X8, Schmid had declared but not yet paid its fourth-quarter dividend of $5,000. Both companies use straight-line depreciation and amortization. Rossman uses the basic equity method to account for its investment in Schmid.

Required

a. Compute the amount of the differential as of January 1, 20X8.

b. Verify the balance in Rossman's Investment in Schmid Stock account as of December 31, 20X8.

c. Present all elimination entries that would appear in a three-part consolidation workpaper as of December 31, 20X8.

d. Prepare and complete a three-part workpaper for the preparation of consolidated financial statements for 20X8.

P6-42A   **Fully Adjusted Equity Method**
On December 31, 20X7, Prime Company recorded the following entry on its books to adjust its investment in Lane Company from the basic equity method to the fully adjusted equity method:

Retained Earnings	26,000	
Income from Subsidiary		2,000
Investment in Lane Company Stock		24,000

Required

a. Adjust the data reported by Prime in the trial balance in Problem P6-38 for the effects of the adjusting entry presented above.

b. Prepare the journal entries that would have been recorded on Prime's books during 20X7 if it had always used the fully adjusted equity method.

c. Prepare all eliminating entries needed to complete a consolidation workpaper as of December 31, 20X7, assuming Prime has used the fully adjusted equity method.

d. Complete a three-part consolidation workpaper as of December 31, 20X7.

P6-43A   Cost Method

The trial balance data presented in Problem P6-38 can be converted to reflect use of the cost method by inserting the following amounts in place of those presented for Prime Company:

Investment in Lane Company Stock	$160,000
Retained Earnings	348,000
Income from Subsidiary	-0-
Dividend Income	28,000

Required

a. Prepare the journal entries that would have been recorded on Prime's books during 20X7 under the cost method.

b. Prepare all eliminating entries needed to complete a consolidation workpaper as of December 31, 20X7, assuming Prime has used the cost method.

c. Complete a three-part consolidation workpaper as of December 31, 20X7.

Chapter **Seven**

Intercompany Inventory Transactions

Inventory transactions are the most common form of intercompany exchange. Conceptually, the elimination of inventory transfers between related companies is no different than for other types of intercompany transactions. All revenue and expense items recorded by the participants must be eliminated fully in preparing the consolidated income statement, and all profits and losses recorded on the transfers are deferred until the items are sold to a nonaffiliate.

The recordkeeping process for intercompany transfers of inventory may be more complex than for other forms of transfers. There often are many different types of inventory items, and some may be transferred from affiliate to affiliate. Also, the problems of keeping tabs on which items have been resold and which items are still on hand are greater in the case of inventory transactions because part of a shipment may be sold immediately by the purchasing company and other units may remain on hand for several accounting periods. Nevertheless, the consolidation procedures relating to inventory transfers are quite similar to those discussed in Chapter 6 relating to fixed assets.

GENERAL OVERVIEW

The workpaper eliminating entries used in preparing consolidated financial statements must eliminate fully the effects of all transactions between related companies. When there have been intercompany inventory transactions, eliminating entries are needed to remove the revenue and expenses related to the intercompany transfers recorded by the individual companies. The eliminations ensure that only the historical cost of the inventory to the consolidated entity is included in the consolidated balance sheet when the inventory is still on hand and is charged to cost of goods sold in the period the inventory is resold to nonaffiliates.

Transfers at Cost

Merchandise sometimes is sold to related companies at the seller's cost or carrying value. When an intercorporate sale includes no profit or loss, the balance sheet inventory amounts at the end of the period require no adjustment for consolidation because the purchasing affiliate's inventory carrying amount is the same as the cost to the transferring affiliate and the consolidated entity. At the time the inventory is resold to a nonaffiliate, the amount recognized as cost of goods sold by the affiliate making the outside sale is the cost to the consolidated entity.

Even when the intercorporate sale includes no profit or loss, however, an eliminating entry is needed to remove both the revenue from the intercorporate sale and the related cost of goods sold recorded by the seller. This avoids overstating these two accounts. Consolidated net income is not affected by the eliminating entry when the transfer is made at cost because both revenue and cost of goods sold are reduced by the same amount.

Transfers at a Profit or Loss

Companies use many different approaches in setting intercorporate transfer prices. In some companies, the sale price to an affiliate is the same as the price to any other customer. Some companies routinely mark up inventory transferred to affiliates by a certain percentage of cost. Other companies have elaborate transfer pricing policies designed to encourage internal sales. Regardless of the method used in setting intercorporate transfer prices, the elimination process must remove the effects of such sales from the consolidated statements.

When intercompany sales include profits or losses, the workpaper eliminations needed for consolidation in the period of transfer must adjust accounts in both the consolidated income statement and balance sheet:

Income statement: Sales and cost of goods sold. The sales revenue from the intercompany sale and the related cost of goods sold recorded by the transferring affiliate must be removed.

Balance sheet: Inventory. The profit or loss on the intercompany sale must be removed so the inventory is reported at the cost to the consolidated entity.

The resulting financial statements appear as if the intercompany transfer had not occurred.

Effect of Type of Inventory System

Most companies use either a perpetual or a periodic inventory control system to keep track of inventory and cost of goods sold. Under a perpetual inventory system, a purchase of merchandise is debited directly to the Inventory account; a sale requires a debit to Cost of Goods Sold and a credit to Inventory for the cost of the item. When a periodic system is used, a purchase of merchandise is debited to a Purchases account rather than to Inventory, and no entry is made to recognize cost of goods sold until the end of the accounting period.

The choice between periodic and perpetual inventory systems results in different entries on the books of the individual companies and, therefore, slightly different workpaper eliminating entries in preparing consolidated financial statements. Because most companies use perpetual inventory systems, the discussion in the chapter focuses on the consolidation procedures used in connection with perpetual inventories.

DOWNSTREAM SALE OF INVENTORY

For consolidation purposes, profits recorded on an intercorporate inventory sale are recognized in the period in which the inventory is resold to an unrelated party. Until the point of resale, all intercorporate profits must be deferred. Consolidated net income must be based on the realized income of the transferring affiliate. Because intercompany profits from downstream sales are on the parent's books, consolidated net income and the overall claim of parent company shareholders must be reduced by the full amount of the unrealized profits.

When a company sells an inventory item to an affiliate, one of three situations results: (1) the item is resold to a nonaffiliate during the same period, (2) the item is resold to a nonaffiliate during the next period, or (3) the item is held for two or more periods by the purchasing affiliate. The continuing example of Peerless Products Corporation and Special Foods Inc. is used to illustrate the consolidation process under each of the alternatives. As in Chapter 6, assume that Peerless Products purchases 80 percent of the common stock of Special Foods on December 31, 20X0, for its book value of $240,000.

As an illustration of the effects of a downstream sale, assume that on March 1, 20X1, Peerless buys inventory for $7,000 and resells it to Special Foods for $10,000 on April 1. Peerless records the following entries on its books:

March 1, 20X1			
(1)	Inventory	7,000	
	Cash		7,000
	Purchase of inventory.		

		April 1, 20X1		
(2)	Cash		10,000	
	Sales			10,000
	Sale of inventory to Special Foods.			

(3)	Cost of Goods Sold		7,000	
	Inventory			7,000
	Cost of inventory sold to Special Foods.			

Special Foods records the purchase of the inventory from Peerless with the following entry:

		April 1, 20X1		
(4)	Inventory		10,000	
	Cash			10,000
	Purchase of inventory from Peerless.			

Resale in Period of Intercorporate Transfer

To illustrate consolidation when inventory is sold to an affiliate and then resold to a nonaffiliate during the same period, assume that on November 5, 20X1, Special Foods sells the inventory purchased from Peerless to Nonaffiliated Corporation for $15,000, as follows:

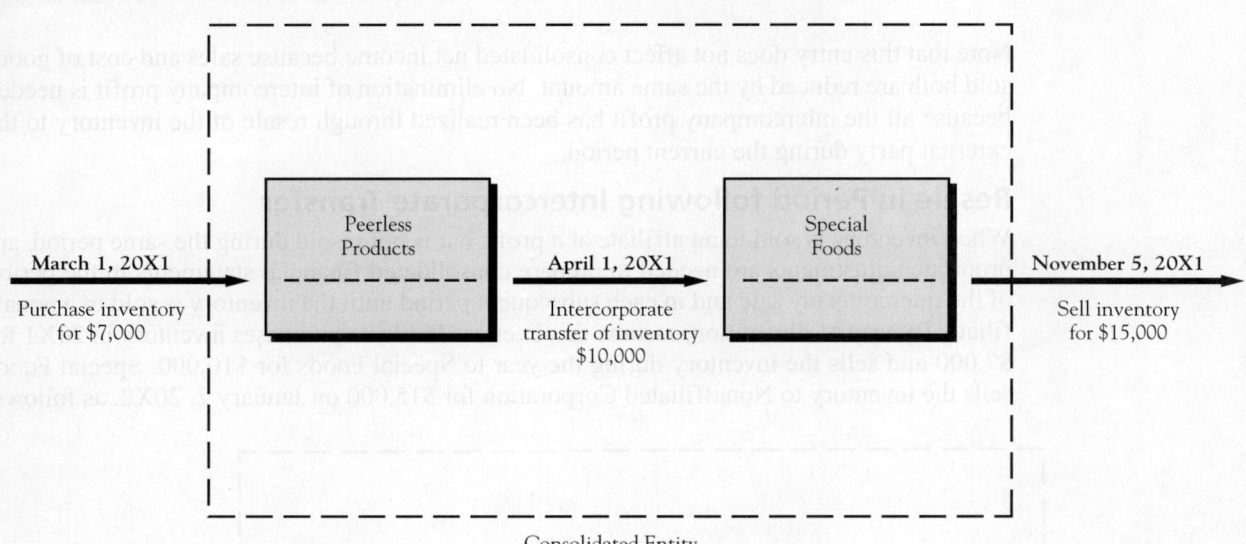

Consolidated Entity

Special Foods records the sale to Nonaffiliated with the following entries:

		November 5, 20X1		
(5)	Cash		15,000	
	Sales			15,000
	Sale of inventory to Nonaffiliated.			

(6)	Cost of Goods Sold		10,000	
	Inventory			10,000
	Cost of inventory sold to Nonaffiliated.			

A review of all entries recorded by the individual companies indicates that incorrect balances will be reported in the consolidated income statement if the effects of the intercorporate sale are not removed:

Item	Peerless Products	Special Foods	Unadjusted Totals	Consolidated Amounts
Sales	$10,000	$15,000	$25,000	$15,000
Cost of Goods Sold	(7,000)	(10,000)	(17,000)	(7,000)
Gross Profit	$ 3,000	$ 5,000	$ 8,000	$ 8,000

Although consolidated gross profit is correct even if no adjustments are made, the totals for sales and cost of goods sold derived by simply adding the amounts on the books of Peerless and Special Foods are overstated for the consolidated entity. The selling price of the inventory to Nonaffiliated Corporation is $15,000, and the original cost to Peerless Products is $7,000. Thus, gross profit of $8,000 is correct from a consolidated viewpoint, but consolidated sales and cost of goods sold should be $15,000 and $7,000, respectively, rather than $25,000 and $17,000. In the consolidation workpaper, the amount of the intercompany sale must be eliminated from both sales and cost of goods sold to correctly state the consolidated totals:

E(7)	Sales	10,000	
	Cost of Goods Sold		10,000
	Eliminate intercompany inventory sale.		

Note that this entry does not affect consolidated net income because sales and cost of goods sold both are reduced by the same amount. No elimination of intercompany profit is needed because all the intercompany profit has been realized through resale of the inventory to the external party during the current period.

Resale in Period following Intercorporate Transfer

When inventory is sold to an affiliate at a profit but is not resold during the same period, appropriate adjustments are needed to prepare consolidated financial statements in the period of the intercompany sale and in each subsequent period until the inventory is sold to a nonaffiliate. By way of illustration, assume that Peerless Products purchases inventory in 20X1 for $7,000 and sells the inventory during the year to Special Foods for $10,000. Special Foods sells the inventory to Nonaffiliated Corporation for $15,000 on January 2, 20X2, as follows:

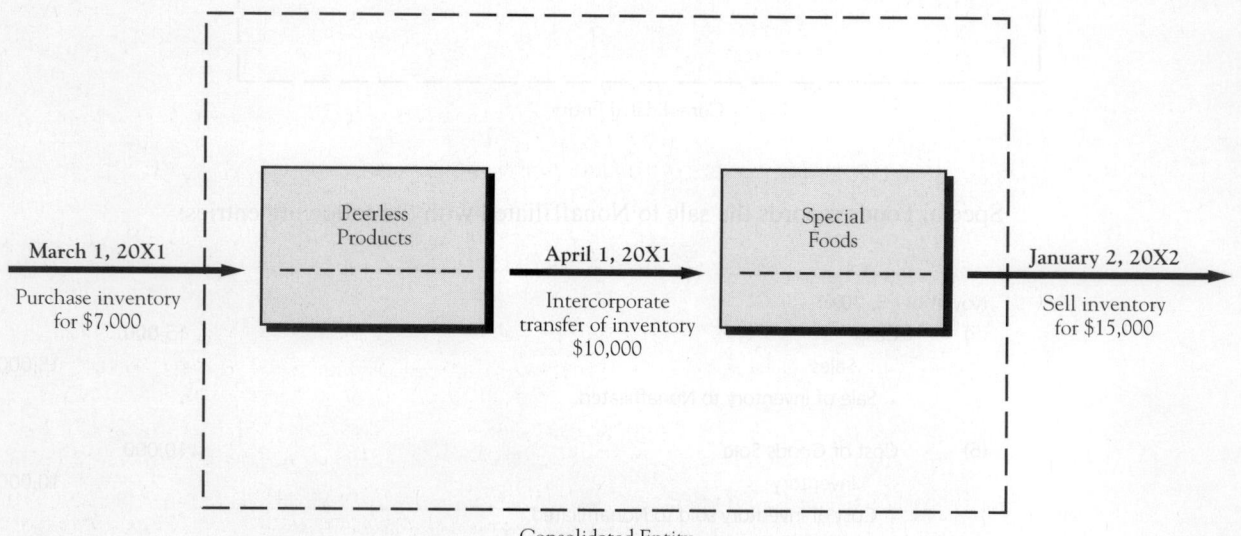

Consolidated Entity

During 20X1, Peerless records the purchase of the inventory and the sale to Special Foods with journal entries (1) through (3), given previously; Special Foods records the purchase of the inventory from Peerless with entry (4). In 20X2, Special Foods records the sale of the inventory to Nonaffiliated with entries (5) and (6), given earlier.

Basic Equity-Method Entries—20X1

Using the basic equity method, Peerless records its share of Special Foods' income and dividends for 20X1 in the normal manner:

(8)	Cash	24,000	
	Investment in Special Foods Stock		24,000
	Record dividends from Special Foods:		
	$30,000 × .80		
(9)	Investment in Special Foods Stock	40,000	
	Income from Subsidiary		40,000
	Record equity-method income:		
	$50,000 × .80		

As a result of these entries, the ending balance of the investment account is $256,000 ($240,000 + $40,000 − $24,000).

Consolidation Workpaper—20X1

The consolidation workpaper prepared at the end of 20X1 appears in Figure 7–1. Four elimination entries are included in the workpaper:

E(10)	Income from Subsidiary	40,000	
	Dividends Declared		24,000
	Investment in Special Foods Stock		16,000
	Eliminate income from subsidiary.		
E(11)	Income to Noncontrolling Interest	10,000	
	Dividends Declared		6,000
	Noncontrolling Interest		4,000
	Assign income to noncontrolling interest.		
	$10,000 = $50,000 × .20		
E(12)	Common Stock—Special Foods	200,000	
	Retained Earnings, January 1	100,000	
	Investment in Special Foods Stock		240,000
	Noncontrolling Interest		60,000
	Eliminate beginning investment balance.		
E(13)	Sales	10,000	
	Cost of Goods Sold		7,000
	Inventory		3,000
	Eliminate intercompany downstream sale of inventory.		

Only entry E(13) relates to the elimination of unrealized inventory profits; the other entries are the type normally found in the workpaper.

Entry E(10) is based on entries (8) and (9) on Peerless's books and eliminates both Peerless's share of Special Foods' income and dividends and the change in the investment account for the period. The noncontrolling interest is not affected by the downstream inventory transfer and is assigned a pro rata portion ($50,000 × .20) of the net income of Special

FIGURE 7–1   December 31, 20X1, Consolidation Workpaper, Period of Intercompany Sale;
Downstream Inventory Sale

Item	Peerless Products	Special Foods	Eliminations Debit		Eliminations Credit		Consolidated
Sales	400,000	200,000	(13)	10,000			590,000
Income from Subsidiary	40,000		(10)	40,000			
Credits	440,000	200,000					590,000
Cost of Goods Sold	170,000	115,000			(13)	7,000	278,000
Depreciation and Amortization	50,000	20,000					70,000
Other Expenses	40,000	15,000					55,000
Debits	(260,000)	(150,000)					(403,000)
							187,000
Income to Noncontrolling Interest			(11)	10,000			(10,000)
Net Income, carry forward	180,000	50,000		60,000		7,000	177,000
Retained Earnings, January 1	300,000	100,000	(12)	100,000			300,000
Net Income, from above	180,000	50,000		60,000		7,000	177,000
	480,000	150,000					477,000
Dividends Declared	(60,000)	(30,000)			(10)	24,000	
					(11)	6,000	(60,000)
Retained Earnings, December 31, carry forward	420,000	120,000		160,000		37,000	417,000
Cash	264,000	75,000					339,000
Accounts Receivable	75,000	50,000					125,000
Inventory	100,000	75,000			(13)	3,000	172,000
Land	175,000	40,000					215,000
Buildings and Equipment	800,000	600,000					1,400,000
Investment in Special Foods Stock	256,000				(10)	16,000	
					(12)	240,000	
Debits	1,670,000	840,000					2,251,000
Accumulated Depreciation	250,000	220,000					470,000
Accounts Payable	100,000	100,000					200,000
Bonds Payable	400,000	200,000					600,000
Common Stock	500,000	200,000	(12)	200,000			500,000
Retained Earnings, from above	420,000	120,000		160,000		37,000	417,000
Noncontrolling Interest					(11)	4,000	
					(12)	60,000	64,000
Credits	1,670,000	840,000		360,000		360,000	2,251,000

Elimination entries:
(10) Eliminate income from subsidiary.
(11) Assign income to noncontrolling interest.
(12) Eliminate beginning investment balance.
(13) Eliminate intercompany downstream sale of inventory.

Foods in workpaper entry E(11). This entry also eliminates the noncontrolling stockholders' share of Special Foods' dividends ($30,000 × .20) and establishes the $4,000 increase in the noncontrolling interest for the period due to the excess of Special Foods' net income over its dividends [($50,000 − $30,000) × .20]. Entry E(12) eliminates the beginning balances of Special Foods' stockholders' equity accounts and Peerless's investment account, and also establishes the amount of the noncontrolling interest at the beginning of the period. The intercompany inventory sale has no effect on this entry because the entry eliminates balances as of the beginning of the year while the intercompany transaction occurred during the year.

Entry E(13) is needed to eliminate the effects of the intercompany sale of inventory. The journal entries recorded by Peerless Products and Special Foods in 20X1 on their separate books will result in an overstatement of consolidated gross profit for 20X1 and the consolidated inventory balance at year-end unless the amounts are adjusted in the consolidation workpaper. The amounts resulting from the intercompany inventory transactions from the separate books of Peerless Products and Special Foods, and the appropriate consolidated amounts, are as follows:

Item	Peerless Products	Special Foods	Unadjusted Totals	Consolidated Amounts
Sales	$10,000	$ -0-	$10,000	$ -0-
Cost of Goods Sold	(7,000)	$ -0-	(7,000)	-0-
Gross Profit	$ 3,000	$ -0-	$ 3,000	$ -0-
Inventory	$ -0-	$10,000	$10,000	$7,000

Eliminating entry E(13) corrects the unadjusted totals to the appropriate consolidated amounts. Both Sales and Cost of Goods Sold taken from the trial balance of Peerless Products are reduced in preparing the consolidated income statement. In doing so, income is reduced by the difference of $3,000 ($10,000 − $7,000). In addition, ending inventory reported on Special Foods' books is stated at the intercompany exchange price rather than the historical cost to the consolidated entity. Until resold to an external party by Special Foods, the inventory must be reduced by the amount of unrealized intercompany profit each time consolidated statements are prepared.

Consolidated Net Income—20X1

Consolidated net income for 20X1 is shown as $177,000 in the Figure 7–1 workpaper. This amount is verified as follows:

Peerless's separate operating income		$140,000
Less: Unrealized intercompany profit on downstream inventory sale		(3,000)
Peerless's separate realized income		$137,000
Peerless's share of Special Foods' income:		
Special Foods' net income	$50,000	
Peerless's proportionate share	× .80	40,000
Consolidated net income, 20X1		$177,000

Basic Equity-Method Entries—20X2

During 20X2, Special Foods receives $15,000 when it sells to Nonaffiliated Corporation the inventory that it had purchased for $10,000 from Peerless in 20X1. Also, Peerless records its pro rata portion of Special Foods' net income and dividends for 20X2 with the normal basic equity-method entries:

(14)	Cash	32,000	
	Investment in Special Foods Stock		32,000
	Record dividends from Special Foods:		
	$40,000 × .80		
(15)	Investment in Special Foods Stock	60,000	
	Income from Subsidiary		60,000
	Record equity-method income:		
	$75,000 × .80		

Investment Account Balance

The investment account on Peerless's books appears as follows:

Investment in Special Foods Stock			
Original cost	240,000		
(9) 20X1 Equity accrual		(8) 20X1 Dividends	
($50,000 × .80)	40,000	($30,000 × .80)	24,000
Balance, 12/31/X1	256,000		
(15) 20X2 Equity accrual		(14) 20X2 Dividends	
($75,000 × .80)	60,000	($40,000 × .80)	32,000
Balance, 12/31/X1	284,000		

Consolidation Workpaper—20X2

The consolidation workpaper prepared at the end of 20X2 is shown in Figure 7–2. Four elimination entries are needed:

E(16)	Income from Subsidiary	60,000	
	Dividends Declared		32,000
	Investment in Special Foods Stock		28,000
	Eliminate income from subsidiary.		
E(17)	Income to Noncontrolling Interest	15,000	
	Dividends Declared		8,000
	Noncontrolling Interest		7,000
	Assign income to noncontrolling interest.		
	$15,000 = $75,000 × .20		
E(18)	Common Stock—Special Foods	200,000	
	Retained Earnings, January 1	120,000	
	Investment in Special Foods Stock		256,000
	Noncontrolling Interest		64,000
	Eliminate beginning investment balance.		
E(19)	Retained Earnings, January 1	3,000	
	Cost of Goods Sold		3,000
	Eliminate beginning inventory profit.		

Entry E(16) eliminates the effects of basic equity-method entries (14) and (15) recorded by Peerless Products during 20X2. Entry E(17) assigns the noncontrolling shareholders their share of income ($75,000 × .20) and establishes in the workpaper the 20X2 increase in the claim of the noncontrolling shareholders on Special Foods' net assets. Because the sale is downstream, the amount of income assigned to noncontrolling shareholders and the balance of the noncontrolling interest are not affected by the intercompany profit. Entry E(18) eliminates Special Foods' beginning stockholders' equity balances and Peerless's beginning investment balance, and it establishes the beginning noncontrolling interest with a balance equal to 20 percent of Special Foods' book value.

Entry E(19) is needed to adjust cost of goods sold to the proper consolidated balance and to reduce beginning retained earnings. The unrealized intercompany profit included in Special Foods' beginning inventory was charged to Cost of Goods Sold when Special Foods sold the inventory during the period. Thus, consolidated cost of goods sold will be overstated for

FIGURE 7–2   **December 31, 20X2, Consolidation Workpaper, Next Period following Intercompany Sale; Downstream Inventory Sale**

Item	Peerless Products	Special Foods	Eliminations Debit	Eliminations Credit	Consolidated
Sales	450,000	300,000			750,000
Income from Subsidiary	60,000		(16) 60,000		
Credits	510,000	300,000			750,000
Cost of Goods Sold	180,000	160,000		(19) 3,000	337,000
Depreciation and Amortization	50,000	20,000			70,000
Other Expenses	60,000	45,000			105,000
Debits	(290,000)	(225,000)			(512,000)
					238,000
Income to Noncontrolling Interest			(17) 15,000		(15,000)
Net Income, carry forward	220,000	75,000	75,000	3,000	223,000
Retained Earnings, January 1	420,000	120,000	(18) 120,000		
			(19) 3,000		417,000
Net Income, from above	220,000	75,000	75,000	3,000	223,000
	640,000	195,000			640,000
Dividends Declared	(60,000)	(40,000)		(16) 32,000	
				(17) 8,000	(60,000)
Retained Earnings, December 31, carry forward	580,000	155,000	198,000	43,000	580,000
Cash	291,000	85,000			376,000
Accounts Receivable	150,000	80,000			230,000
Inventory	180,000	90,000			270,000
Land	175,000	40,000			215,000
Buildings and Equipment	800,000	600,000			1,400,000
Investment in Special Foods Stock	284,000			(16) 28,000	
				(18) 256,000	
Debits	1,880,000	895,000			2,491,000
Accumulated Depreciation	300,000	240,000			540,000
Accounts Payable	100,000	100,000			200,000
Bonds Payable	400,000	200,000			600,000
Common Stock	500,000	200,000	(18) 200,000		500,000
Retained Earnings, from above	580,000	155,000	198,000	43,000	580,000
Noncontrolling Interest				(17) 7,000	
				(18) 64,000	71,000
Credits	1,880,000	895,000	398,000	398,000	2,491,000

Elimination entries:
(16) Eliminate income from subsidiary.
(17) Assign income to noncontrolling interest.
(18) Eliminate beginning investment balance.
(19) Eliminate beginning inventory profit.

20X2 if it is reported in the consolidated income statement at the unadjusted total from the books of Peerless and Special Foods:

Item	Peerless Products	Special Foods	Unadjusted Totals	Consolidated Amounts
Sales	$ -0-	$15,000	$15,000	$15,000
Cost of Goods Sold	-0-	(10,000)	(10,000)	(7,000)
Gross Profit	$ -0-	$ 5,000	$ 5,000	$ 8,000

Unlike the period in which the intercompany transfer occurs, no adjustment to sales is required in a subsequent period when the inventory is sold to a nonaffiliate. The amount reported by Special Foods reflects the sale outside the economic entity and is the appropriate amount to be reported for consolidation. By removing the $3,000 of intercorporate profit from Cost of Goods Sold in entry E(19), the original acquisition price paid by Peerless Products is reported, and $8,000 of gross profit is correctly reported in the consolidated income statement.

Elimination entry E(19) also reduces the beginning balance of retained earnings by the amount of the intercompany profit unrealized at the beginning of 20X2. Because Peerless had recognized all the intercompany profit on the downstream sale in 20X1 and it is included in Peerless's beginning retained earnings balance, beginning consolidated retained earnings will be overstated if the full balance reported by Peerless is carried to the consolidated financial statements. Entry E(19) results in the reporting of beginning consolidated retained earnings and cost of goods sold for the year as if there had been no unrealized intercompany profit at the beginning of the year.

Once the sale is made to an external party, the transaction is complete and no adjustments or eliminations related to the intercompany transaction are needed in future periods.

Consolidated Net Income—20X2

Consolidated net income for 20X2 is shown as $223,000 in the Figure 7–2 workpaper. This amount is verified as follows:

Peerless's separate operating income		$160,000
Realization of deferred intercompany profit		3,000
Peerless's separate realized income		$163,000
Peerless's share of Special Foods' income:		
Special Foods' net income	$75,000	
Peerless's proportionate share	× .80	60,000
Consolidated net income, 20X2		$223,000

Inventory Held Two or More Periods

Companies may carry the cost of inventory purchased from an affiliate for more than one accounting period. For example, the cost of an item may be in a LIFO inventory layer and would be included as part of the inventory balance until the layer is liquidated. Prior to liquidation, an eliminating entry is needed in the consolidation workpaper each time consolidated statements are prepared to restate the inventory to its cost to the consolidated entity. For example, if Special Foods continues to hold the inventory purchased from Peerless Products, the following eliminating entry is needed in the consolidation workpaper each time a consolidated balance sheet is prepared for years following the year of intercompany sale, for as long as the inventory is held:

E(20)	Retained Earnings, January 1	3,000	
	Inventory		3,000
	Eliminate beginning inventory profit.		

No income statement adjustments are needed in the periods following the intercorporate sale until the inventory is resold to parties external to the consolidated entity.

UPSTREAM SALE OF INVENTORY

When an upstream sale of inventory occurs and the inventory is resold by the parent to a nonaffiliate during the same period, all the parent's equity-method entries and the eliminating entries in the consolidation workpaper are identical to those in the downstream case.

When the inventory is not resold to a nonaffiliate before the end of the period, workpaper eliminating entries are different from the downstream case only by the apportionment of the unrealized intercompany profit to both the controlling and noncontrolling interests. The intercompany profit in an upstream sale is recognized by the subsidiary and shared between the controlling and noncontrolling stockholders of the subsidiary. Therefore, the elimination of the unrealized intercompany profit must reduce the interests of both ownership groups each period until the profit is confirmed by resale of the inventory to a nonaffiliated party.

An upstream sale can be illustrated using the same example as used for the downstream sale. Assume an intercompany sale of inventory from Special Foods to Peerless Products, as follows:

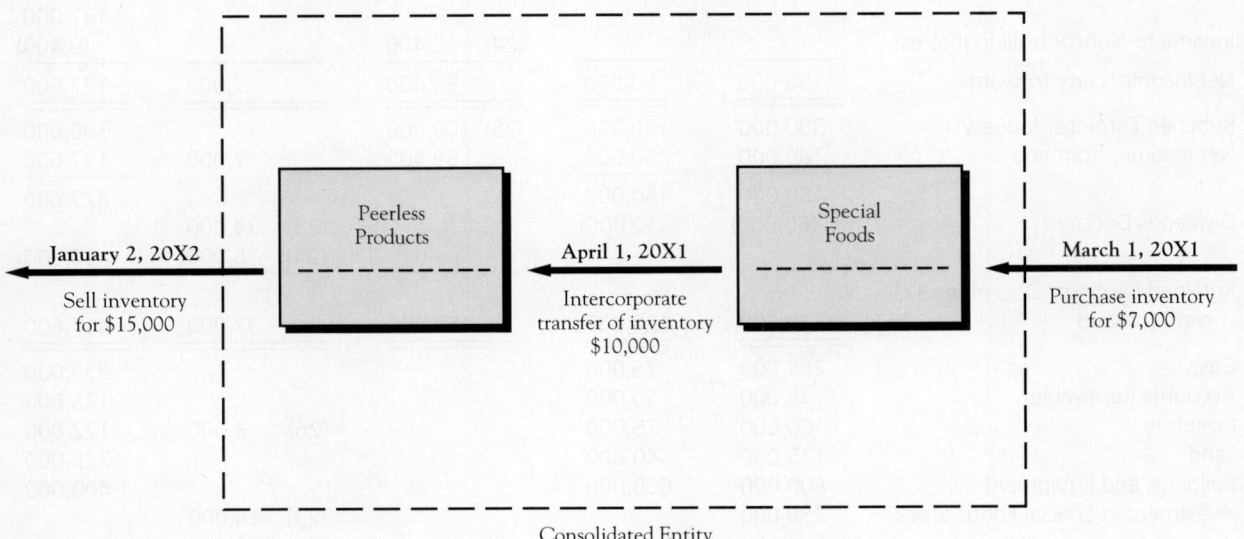

Consolidated Entity

Special Foods purchases the inventory on March 1, 20X1, for $7,000 and sells it to Peerless for $10,000 during the same year. Peerless holds the inventory until January 2 of the following year, at which time Peerless sells it to Nonaffiliated Corporation for $15,000.

Basic Equity-Method Entries—20X1

Peerless Products records the following basic equity-method entries in 20X1:

(21)	Cash	24,000	
	Investment in Special Foods Stock		24,000
	Record dividends from Special Foods:		
	$30,000 × .80		
(22)	Investment in Special Foods Stock	40,000	
	Income from Subsidiary		40,000
	Record equity-method income:		
	$50,000 × .80		

These entries are the same as in the illustration of the downstream sale.

Consolidation Workpaper—20X1

The workpaper for the preparation of the 20X1 consolidated financial statements is shown in Figure 7–3. Four eliminating entries are included in the workpaper:

FIGURE 7–3 December 31, 20X1, Consolidation Workpaper, Period of Intercompany Sale; Upstream Inventory Sale

Item	Peerless Products	Special Foods	Eliminations Debit	Eliminations Credit	Consolidated
Sales	400,000	200,000	(26) 10,000		590,000
Income from Subsidiary	40,000		(23) 40,000		
Credits	440,000	200,000			590,000
Cost of Goods Sold	170,000	115,000		(26) 7,000	278,000
Depreciation and Amortization	50,000	20,000			70,000
Other Expenses	40,000	15,000			55,000
Debits	(260,000)	(150,000)			(403,000)
					187,000
Income to Noncontrolling Interest			(24) 9,400		(9,400)
Net Income, carry forward	180,000	50,000	59,400	7,000	177,600
Retained Earnings, January 1	300,000	100,000	(25) 100,000		300,000
Net Income, from above	180,000	50,000	59,400	7,000	177,600
	480,000	150,000			477,600
Dividends Declared	(60,000)	(30,000)		(23) 24,000	
				(24) 6,000	(60,000)
Retained Earnings, December 31, carry forward	420,000	120,000	159,400	37,000	417,600
Cash	264,000	75,000			339,000
Accounts Receivable	75,000	50,000			125,000
Inventory	100,000	75,000		(26) 3,000	172,000
Land	175,000	40,000			215,000
Buildings and Equipment	800,000	600,000			1,400,000
Investment in Special Foods Stock	256,000			(23) 16,000	
				(25) 240,000	
Debits	1,670,000	840,000			2,251,000
Accumulated Depreciation	250,000	220,000			470,000
Accounts Payable	100,000	100,000			200,000
Bonds Payable	400,000	200,000			600,000
Common Stock	500,000	200,000	(25) 200,000		500,000
Retained Earnings, from above	420,000	120,000	159,400	37,000	417,600
Noncontrolling Interest				(24) 3,400	
				(25) 60,000	63,400
Credits	1,670,000	840,000	359,400	359,400	2,251,000

Elimination entries:
(23) Eliminate income from subsidiary.
(24) Assign income to noncontrolling interest.
(25) Eliminate beginning investment balance.
(26) Eliminate intercompany upstream sale of inventory.

E(23)	Income from Subsidiary	40,000	
	Dividends Declared		24,000
	Investment in Special Foods Stock		16,000
	Eliminate income from subsidiary.		
E(24)	Income to Noncontrolling Interest	9,400	
	Dividends Declared		6,000
	Noncontrolling Interest		3,400
	Assign income to noncontrolling interest:		
	$9,400 = ($50,000 − $3,000) × .20		

E(25)	Common Stock—Special Foods	200,000	
	Retained Earnings, January 1	100,000	
	Investment in Special Foods Stock		240,000
	Noncontrolling Interest		60,000
	Eliminate beginning investment balance.		
E(26)	Sales	10,000	
	Cost of Goods Sold		7,000
	Inventory		3,000
	Eliminate intercompany upstream sale of inventory.		

All workpaper eliminating entries in the year of the intercorporate transfer are the same in the upstream case as in the downstream case except for entry E(24). Because the intercompany profit recognized by Special Foods on the upstream sale was shared by both the controlling and noncontrolling interests, both must be reduced by the unrealized profit elimination. Income assigned to the noncontrolling interest in entry E(24) is based on the realized income of Special Foods ($50,000 − $3,000) and, therefore, is reduced by the noncontrolling stockholders' share of the unrealized intercompany profit.

Because the unrealized profit elimination is allocated proportionately between the controlling and noncontrolling interests in the upstream case, the income assigned to the noncontrolling shareholders is $600 ($3,000 × .20) less in Figure 7–3 for the upstream case than in Figure 7–1 for the downstream case. Accordingly, consolidated net income is $600 higher. All other consolidated income statement amounts are identical in the two cases.

Consolidated Net Income—20X1

Consolidated net income for 20X1 is shown in the workpaper as $177,600 after deducting the noncontrolling stockholders' share of income. This amount may be verified as follows:

Peerless's separate operating income		$140,000
Peerless's share of Special Foods' income:		
Special Foods' net income	$50,000	
Less: Unrealized intercompany profit on upstream inventory sale	(3,000)	
Special Foods' realized income	$47,000	
Peerless's proportionate share	× .80	37,600
Consolidated net income, 20X1		$177,600

Basic Equity-Method Entries—20X2

Peerless recognizes its share of Special Foods' income and dividends for 20X2 with the normal basic equity-method entries:

(27)	Cash	32,000	
	Investment in Special Foods Stock		32,000
	Record dividends from Special Foods:		
	$40,000 × .80		
(28)	Investment in Special Foods Stock	60,000	
	Income from Subsidiary		60,000
	Record equity-method income:		
	$75,000 × .80		

As in the downstream illustration, the investment account balance at the end of 20X2 is $284,000.

Consolidation Workpaper—20X2

The consolidation workpaper used to prepare consolidated financial statements at the end of 20X2 appears in Figure 7–4. The workpaper includes the following elimination entries:

E(29)	Income from Subsidiary	60,000	
	Dividends Declared		32,000
	Investment in Special Foods Stock		28,000
	Eliminate income from subsidiary.		
E(30)	Income to Noncontrolling Interest	15,600	
	Dividends Declared		8,000
	Noncontrolling Interest		7,600
	Assign income to noncontrolling interest:		
	$15,600 = ($75,000 + $3,000) \times .20$		
E(31)	Common Stock—Special Foods	200,000	
	Retained Earnings, January 1	120,000	
	Investment in Special Foods Stock		256,000
	Noncontrolling Interest		64,000
	Eliminate beginning investment balance.		
E(32)	Retained Earnings, January 1	2,400	
	Noncontrolling Interest	600	
	Cost of Goods Sold		3,000
	Eliminate beginning inventory profit:		
	$2,400 = $3,000 \times .80$		
	$600 = $3,000 \times .20$		

Entry E(30) assigns income of $15,600 [($75,000 + $3,000) \times .20]$ to the noncontrolling stockholders based on the realized net income of the subsidiary. The income assigned to the noncontrolling interest consists of a proportionate share of both the $75,000 reported net income of Special Foods and the $3,000 of intercompany inventory profit realized in 20X2.

Workpaper entry E(32) deals explicitly with the elimination of the inventory profit on the upstream sale. In the preparation of the 20X1 consolidated financial statements, the unrealized profit was deducted proportionately from consolidated net income and the income assigned to the noncontrolling interest. The unrealized profit at the beginning of 20X2 is apportioned against both controlling and noncontrolling shareholders in entry E(32). As in the downstream case, Cost of Goods Sold must be credited in the consolidation workpaper to reflect the original cost to the consolidated entity ($7,000) of the inventory sold.

Consolidated Net Income—20X2

Consolidated net income for 20X2 is shown as $222,400 in the Figure 7–4 workpaper. This amount is verified as follows:

Peerless's separate operating income		$160,000
Peerless's share of Special Foods' income:		
Special Foods' net income	$75,000	
Realized intercompany profit on upstream inventory sale	3,000	
Special Foods' realized income	$78,000	
Peerless's proportionate share	$\times$ .80	62,400
Consolidated net income, 20X2		$222,400

FIGURE 7–4   December 31, 20X2, Consolidation Workpaper, Next Period following Intercompany Sale; Upstream Inventory Sale

Item	Peerless Products	Special Foods	Eliminations Debit	Eliminations Credit	Consolidated
Sales	450,000	300,000			750,000
Income from Subsidiary	60,000		(29) 60,000		
Credits	510,000	300,000			750,000
Cost of Goods Sold	180,000	160,000		(32) 3,000	337,000
Depreciation and Amortization	50,000	20,000			70,000
Other Expenses	60,000	45,000			105,000
Debits	(290,000)	(225,000)			(512,000)
					238,000
Income to Noncontrolling Interest			(30) 15,600		(15,600)
Net Income, carry forward	220,000	75,000	75,600	3,000	222,400
Retained Earnings, January 1	420,000	120,000	(31) 120,000		
			(32) 2,400		417,600
Net Income, from above	220,000	75,000	75,600	3,000	222,400
	640,000	195,000			640,000
Dividends Declared	(60,000)	(40,000)		(29) 32,000	
				(30) 8,000	(60,000)
Retained Earnings, December 31, carry forward	580,000	155,000	198,000	43,000	580,000
Cash	291,000	85,000			376,000
Accounts Receivable	150,000	80,000			230,000
Inventory	180,000	90,000			270,000
Land	175,000	40,000			215,000
Buildings and Equipment	800,000	600,000			1,400,000
Investment in Special Foods Stock	284,000			(29) 28,000	
				(31) 256,000	
Debits	1,880,000	895,000			2,491,000
Accumulated Depreciation	300,000	240,000			540,000
Accounts Payable	100,000	100,000			200,000
Bonds Payable	400,000	200,000			600,000
Common Stock	500,000	200,000	(31) 200,000		500,000
Retained Earnings, from above	580,000	155,000	198,000	43,000	580,000
Noncontrolling Interest			(32) 600	(30) 7,600	
				(31) 64,000	71,000
Credits	1,880,000	895,000	398,600	398,600	2,491,000

Elimination entries:
(29) Eliminate income from subsidiary.
(30) Assign income to noncontrolling interest.
(31) Eliminate beginning investment balance.
(32) Eliminate beginning inventory profit.

ADDITIONAL CONSIDERATIONS

The frequency of intercompany inventory transfers and the varied circumstances under which they may occur raise a number of additional implementation issues. Several of these are discussed briefly in this section.

Sale from One Subsidiary to Another

Transfers of inventory often occur between companies that are under common control or ownership. When one subsidiary sells merchandise to another subsidiary, the eliminating entries are identical to those presented earlier for sales from a subsidiary to its parent. The full amount of any unrealized intercompany profit is eliminated, with the profit elimination allocated proportionately against the ownership interests of the selling subsidiary.

As an illustration, assume that Peerless Products owns 90 percent of the outstanding stock of Super Industries in addition to its 80 percent interest in Special Foods. If Special Foods sells inventory at a $3,000 profit to Super Industries for $10,000 and Super Industries holds all of the inventory at the end of the period, the following elimination entry is among those needed in the consolidation workpaper prepared at the end of the period:

E(33)	Sales	10,000	
	Cost of Goods Sold		7,000
	Inventory		3,000
	Eliminate intercompany sale of inventory.		

The $3,000 elimination of unrealized intercompany profit is allocated proportionately between the two shareholder groups of the selling affiliate. Thus, consolidated net income is reduced by Peerless's 80 percent share of the intercompany profit, or $2,400, and Special Foods' noncontrolling interest is reduced by its 20 percent share, or $600.

Costs Associated with Transfers

When one affiliate transfers inventory to another, some additional cost, such as freight, is often incurred in the transfer. This cost should be treated in the same way as if the affiliates were operating divisions of a single company. If the additional cost would be inventoried in transferring the units from one location to another within the same company, that treatment also would be appropriate for consolidation.

Lower of Cost or Market

A company might write down inventory purchased from an affiliate under the lower-of-cost-or-market rule if the market value at the end of the period is less than the intercompany transfer price. Such a situation can be illustrated by assuming that a parent company purchases inventory for $20,000 and sells it to its subsidiary for $35,000. The subsidiary still holds the inventory at year-end and determines that its market value (replacement cost) is $25,000 at that time.

The subsidiary writes the inventory down from $35,000 to its lower market value of $25,000 at the end of the year and records the following entry:

(34)	Loss on Decline in Value of Inventory	10,000	
	Inventory		10,000
	Write down inventory to market value.		

While this entry revalues the inventory to $25,000 on the subsidiary's books, the appropriate valuation from a consolidated viewpoint is the $20,000 original cost of the inventory to the parent. Therefore, the following eliminating entry is needed in the consolidation workpaper:

E(35)	Sales	35,000	
	Cost of Goods Sold		20,000
	Inventory		5,000
	Loss on Decline in Value of Inventory		10,000
	Eliminate intercompany sale of inventory.		

The inventory loss recorded by the subsidiary must be eliminated because the $20,000 inventory valuation for consolidation purposes is below the $25,000 market value of the inventory.

Sales and Purchases before Affiliation

Sometimes companies that have sold inventory to one another later join together in a business combination. The consolidation treatment of profits on inventory transfers that occurred before the business combination depends on whether the companies were at that time independent and the sale transaction was the result of arm's-length bargaining. As a general rule, the effects of transactions that are not the result of arm's-length bargaining must be eliminated. However, the combining of two companies does not necessarily mean that their prior transactions with one another were not conducted at arm's length. The circumstances surrounding the prior transactions, such as the price and quantity of units transferred, would have to be examined.

In the absence of evidence to the contrary, companies that have joined together in a business combination are viewed as having been separate and independent prior to the combination. Thus, if the prior sales were the result of arm's-length bargaining, they are viewed as transactions between unrelated parties. Accordingly, no elimination or adjustment is needed in preparing consolidated statements subsequent to the combination, even if an affiliate still holds the inventory.

Summary of Key Concepts

Consolidated financial statements are prepared for the consolidated entity as if it were a single company. Therefore, the effects of all transactions between companies within the entity must be eliminated in preparing consolidated financial statements.

The treatment of intercompany inventory transactions is similar to the treatment of intercompany transfers of noncurrent assets discussed in Chapter 6. Each time consolidated statements are prepared, all effects of intercompany transactions occurring during that period, and the effects of unrealized profits from transactions in prior periods, must be eliminated. For intercompany inventory transactions, the intercompany sale and cost of goods sold must be eliminated. In addition, the intercompany profit may not be recognized in consolidation until it is confirmed by resale of the inventory to an external party. Unrealized intercompany profits must be eliminated fully and are allocated proportionately against the stockholder groups of the selling affiliate. If inventory containing unrealized intercompany profits is sold during the period, consolidated cost of goods sold must be adjusted to reflect the actual cost to the consolidated entity of the inventory sold; if the inventory is still held at the end of the period, it must be adjusted to its actual cost to the consolidated entity.

Appendix 7A   Intercompany Inventory Transactions—Fully Adjusted Equity Method and Cost Method

Consolidation procedures following use of first the fully adjusted equity method and then the cost method are illustrated with the example of the upstream sale of inventory presented earlier. Assume that Special Foods purchases inventory for $7,000 in 20X1 and, in the same year, sells the inventory to Peerless Products for $10,000. Peerless Products sells the inventory to external parties in 20X2. Both companies use perpetual inventory control systems.

FULLY ADJUSTED EQUITY METHOD

The journal entries on Peerless's books and the elimination entries in the consolidation workpaper are the same under the fully adjusted equity method as under the basic equity method except for differences related to unrealized intercompany profits. When using the fully adjusted equity method, the parent reduces its income and the balance of the investment account for its share of unrealized intercompany profits that arise during the period. Subsequently, the parent increases its income and the carrying amount of the investment account when the intercompany profits are realized through transactions with external parties.

Fully Adjusted Equity-Method Entries—20X1

In 20X1, Peerless Products records the normal equity-method entries reflecting its share of Special Foods' income and dividends, and an additional entry to reduce income and the investment account by the parent's share of the unrealized intercompany profit arising during the year:

(36)	Cash	24,000	
	Investment in Special Foods Stock		24,000
	Record dividends from Special Foods: $30,000 × .80		
(37)	Investment in Special Foods Stock	40,000	
	Income from Subsidiary		40,000
	Record equity-method income:		
	$50,000 × .80		
(38)	Income from Subsidiary	2,400	
	Investment in Special Foods Stock		2,400
	Remove unrealized profit on upstream sale of inventory: $3,000 × .80		

Entry (38) is used under the fully adjusted equity method to reduce the parent's income and the investment account by the parent's share of unrealized profits and, consequently, to bring the parent's net income into agreement with consolidated net income.

Consolidation Elimination Entries—20X1

Four eliminating entries are needed in the workpaper to prepare consolidated financial statements for 20X1:

E(39)	Income from Subsidiary	37,600	
	Dividends Declared		24,000
	Investment in Special Foods Stock		13,600
	Eliminate income from subsidiary.		
E(40)	Income to Noncontrolling Interest	9,400	
	Dividends Declared		6,000
	Noncontrolling Interest		3,400
	Assign income to noncontrolling interest:		
	$9,400 = ($50,000 − $3,000) × .20		
E(41)	Common Stock—Special Foods	200,000	
	Retained Earnings, January 1	100,000	
	Investment in Special Foods Stock		240,000
	Noncontrolling Interest		60,000
	Eliminate beginning investment balance.		
E(42)	Sales	10,000	
	Cost of Goods Sold		7,000
	Inventory		3,000
	Eliminate intercompany upstream sale of inventory.		

All these workpaper entries are the same as those following use of the basic equity method except for entry E(39). Because the parent's recorded income from Special Foods is $2,400 less under the fully adjusted equity method than under the basic equity method, the elimination of that income in entry E(39) is for the lesser amount. Similarly, the increase in the investment account on the parent's books during 20X1 under the fully adjusted equity method is reduced by the parent's share of the unrealized intercompany profit, and that difference is reflected in elimination entry E(39).

Fully Adjusted Equity-Method Entries—20X2

With resale of the inventory to an external party in 20X2, the parent company recognizes its portion of the $3,000 of deferred inventory profit in addition to its pro rata portion of the reported net income of the subsidiary:

(43)	Cash	32,000	
	Investment in Special Foods Stock		32,000
	Record divicends from Special Foods:		
	$40,000 × .80		
(44)	Investment in Special Foods Stock	60,000	
	Income from Subsidiary		60,000
	Record equity-method income:		
	$75,000 × .80		
(45)	Investment in Special Foods Stock	2,400	
	Income from Subsidiary		2,400
	Recognize deferred profit on upstream sale of inventory:		
	$3,000 × .80		

Once the inventory is sold to a nonaffiliate, the intercompany profit is considered realized by the consolidated entity and is included in consolidated net income. Peerless records entry (45) to bring its equity-method net income into agreement with consolidated net income.

Consolidation Elimination Entries—20X2

Workpaper eliminating entries needed for the preparation of consolidated financial statements at the end of 20X2 are as follows:

E(46)	Income from Subsidiary	62,400	
	Dividends Declared		32,000
	Investment in Special Foods Stock		30,400
	Eliminate income from subsidiary.		
E(47)	Income to Noncontrolling Interest	15,600	
	Dividends Declared		8,000
	Noncontrolling Interest		7,600
	Assign income to noncontrolling interest:		
	$15,600 = ($75,000 + $3,000) × .20		
E(48)	Common Stock—Special Foods	200,000	
	Retained Earnings, January 1	120,000	
	Investment in Special Foods Stock		256,000
	Noncontrolling Interest		64,000
	Eliminate beginning investment balance.		
E(49)	Investment in Special Foods Stock	2,400	
	Noncontrolling Interest	600	
	Cost of Goods Sold		3,000
	Eliminate beginning inventory profit.		

Peerless's equity-method income and share of Special Foods' dividends are eliminated in entry E(46). Just as the equity-method entries on the parent's books include the parent's share of the realized inventory profit, income assigned to noncontrolling shareholders for 20X2 in entry E(47) must include 20 percent of both the $75,000 reported net income of Special Foods and the $3,000 deferred intercompany inventory profit realized in 20X2. Thus, income assigned to the noncontrolling interest in the 20X2 income statement is $15,600 [($75,000 + $3,000) × .20].

Entry E(48) is the normal workpaper entry to eliminate the beginning balances of the subsidiary's stockholders' equity accounts and the investment account. The credit to the investment account is for Peerless's share of the book value of Special Foods. Because Peerless reduced the balance of the investment account in 20X1 with entry (38) to remove unrealized intercompany profits, entry E(48) credits the investment account for $2,400 more than its beginning balance.

Workpaper entry E(49) deals explicitly with the elimination of the inventory profit on the upstream sale. Cost of Goods Sold is credited in the consolidation workpaper to reflect the original cost to the consolidated entity ($7,000) of the inventory sold. The unrealized profit at the beginning of the period is allocated against both controlling and noncontrolling shareholders. The parent's share of the unrealized intercompany profit already has been removed from its beginning retained earnings by entry (38) in 20X1. This entry reduced Peerless's income and ending retained earnings for 20X1 and brought Peerless's retained earnings into agreement with consolidated retained earnings on December 31, 20X1. Thus, Peerless's 20X2 beginning retained earnings is equal to consolidated retained earnings at the beginning of 20X2 and may be included in the 20X2 consolidation workpaper without additional adjustment.

The debit to the investment account for $2,400 in entry E(49) is needed because entry E(48) over-eliminates the investment account owing to the reduction by entry (38). Together, entries E(46), E(48), and E(49) fully eliminate the balance in the investment account.

COST METHOD

When using the cost method, the parent records dividends received from the subsidiary as income but makes no adjustments with respect to undistributed income of the subsidiary or unrealized intercompany profits. As an example of consolidation following an upstream intercompany sale of inventory when the parent accounts for its investment in the subsidiary using the cost method, assume the same facts as in previous illustrations dealing with an upstream sale.

Consolidation Elimination Entries—20X1

The following eliminating entries are needed in the workpaper used to prepare consolidated financial statements for 20X1:

E(50)	Dividend Income	24,000	
	Dividends Declared		24,000
	Eliminate dividend income from subsidiary:		
	$30,000 × .80		
E(51)	Income to Noncontrolling Interest	9,400	
	Dividends Declared		6,000
	Noncontrolling Interest		3,400
	Assign income to noncontrolling interest:		
	$9,400 = ($50,000 − $3,000) × .20		
E(52)	Common Stock—Special Foods	200,000	
	Retained Earnings, January 1	100,000	
	Investment in Special Foods Stock		240,000
	Noncontrolling Interest		60,000
	Eliminate investment balance at date of acquisition.		
E(53)	Sales	10,000	
	Cost of Goods Sold		7,000
	Inventory		3,000
	Eliminate intercompany upstream sale of inventory.		

These eliminating entries are the same as those following use of the basic equity method, except for entry E(50). This entry eliminates the parent's dividend income from Special Foods rather than its share of Special Foods' net income.

Consolidation Elimination Entries—20X2

Elimination entries needed in the consolidation workpaper prepared at the end of 20X2 are as follows:

E(54)	Dividend Income	32,000	
	Dividends Declared		32,000
	Eliminate dividend income from subsidiary:		
	$40,000 × .80		
E(55)	Income to Noncontrolling Interest	15,600	
	Dividends Declared		8,000
	Noncontrolling Interest		7,600
	Assign income to noncontrolling interest:		
	$15,600 = ($75,000 + $3,000) × .20		
E(56)	Common Stock—Special Foods	200,000	
	Retained Earnings, January 1	100,000	
	Investment in Special Foods Stock		240,000
	Noncontrolling Interest		60,000
	Eliminate investment balance at date of acquisition.		
E(57)	Retained Earnings, January 1	4,000	
	Noncontrolling Interest		4,000
	Assign undistributed prior earnings of subsidiary		
	to noncontrolling interest: $20,000 × .20		
E(58)	Retained Earnings, January 1	2,400	
	Noncontrolling Interest	600	
	Cost of Goods Sold		3,000
	Eliminate beginning inventory profit.		

Entries E(55) and E(58) are the same as those following the use of the basic equity method. Entry E(54) eliminates the dividend income recorded by Peerless in 20X2. Entry E(56) eliminates the balances at the date of combination of Special Foods' stockholders' equity accounts and the investment account. This entry is the same each year. Because this entry does not change, it assigns to the noncontrolling stockholders only their share of Special Foods' book value at the date of combination. Therefore, entry E(57) is needed to assign to the noncontrolling interest a proportionate share of the undistributed earnings of Special Foods from the date of combination to the beginning of the current year.

Questions

Q7-1   Why must inventory transfers to related companies be eliminated in preparing consolidated financial statements?

Q7-2   Why is there need for an eliminating entry when an intercompany inventory transfer is made at cost?

Q7-3   Distinguish between an upstream sale of inventory and a downstream sale. Why is it important to know whether a sale is upstream or downstream?

Q7-4   How do unrealized intercompany profits on a downstream sale of inventory made during the current period affect the computation of consolidated net income?

Q7-5   How do unrealized intercompany profits on an upstream sale of inventory made during the current period affect the computation of consolidated net income?

Q7-6   Will the elimination of unrealized intercompany profits on an upstream sale or on a downstream sale in the current period have a greater effect on income assigned to the noncontrolling interest? Why?

Q7-7   What is the basic eliminating entry needed when inventory is sold to an affiliate at a profit and is resold to an unaffiliated party before the end of the period? (Assume both affiliates use perpetual inventory systems.)

Q7-8   What is the basic eliminating entry needed when inventory is sold to an affiliate at a profit and is not resold before the end of the period? (Assume both affiliates use perpetual inventory systems.)

Q7-9   How is the amount to be reported as cost of goods sold by the consolidated entity determined when there have been intercorporate sales during the period?

Q7-10   How is the amount to be reported as consolidated retained earnings determined when there have been intercorporate sales during the period?

Q7-11   How is the amount of consolidated retained earnings assigned to the noncontrolling interest affected by unrealized inventory profits at the end of the year?

Q7-12   How do unrealized intercompany inventory profits from a prior period affect the computation of consolidated net income when the inventory is resold in the current period? Is it important to know if the sale was upstream or downstream? Why, or why not?

Q7-13   How will the elimination of unrealized intercompany inventory profits recorded on the parent's books affect consolidated retained earnings?

Q7-14   How will the elimination of unrealized intercompany inventory profits recorded on the subsidiary's books affect consolidated retained earnings?

Q7-15*   Is an inventory sale from one subsidiary to another treated in the same manner as an upstream sale or a downstream sale? Why?

Q7-16*   Par Company regularly purchases inventory from Eagle Company. Recently, Par Company purchased a majority of the voting shares of Eagle Company. How should it treat inventory profits recorded by Eagle Company before the day of acquisition? Following the day of acquisition?

Cases

C7-1

Judgment

Measuring Cost of Goods Sold

Shortcut Charlie usually manages to develop some simple rule to handle even the most complex situations. In providing for the elimination of the effects of inventory transfers between the parent company and a subsidiary or between subsidiaries, Shortcut started with the following rules:

1. When the buyer continues to hold the inventory at the end of the period, credit cost of goods sold for the amount recorded as cost of goods sold by the company that made the intercompany sale.

2. When the buyer resells the inventory before the end of the period, credit cost of goods sold for the amount recorded as cost of goods sold by the company that made the intercompany sale plus the profit recorded by that company.

3. Debit sales for the total amount credited in rule 1 or 2 above.

One of the new employees is seeking some assistance in understanding how the rules work and why.

Required

a. Explain why rule 1 is needed when consolidated statements are prepared.

b. Explain what is missing from rule 1, and prepare an alternative or additional statement for the elimination of unrealized profit when the purchasing affiliate does not resell to an unaffiliated company in the period in which it purchases inventory from an affiliate.

c. Does rule 2 lead to the correct result? Explain your answer.

d. The rules do not provide assistance in determining how much profit was recorded by either of the two companies. Where should the employee look to determine the amount of profit referred to in rule 2?

*Indicates that the item relates to "Additional Considerations."

C7-2   ## Inventory Values and Intercompany Transfers

Research
FARS

Water Products Corporation has been supplying high-quality bathroom fixtures to its customers for several decades and uses a LIFO inventory system. Rapid increases in the cost of fixtures have resulted in inventory values substantially below current replacement cost. To bring its inventory carrying costs up to more reasonable levels, Water Products sold its entire inventory to Plumbers Products Corporation and purchased an entirely new supply of inventory items from Growinkle Manufacturing. Water Products owns common stock of both Growinkle and Plumbers Products.

Water Products' external auditor immediately pointed out that under some ownership levels of these two companies, Water Products could accomplish its goal and under other levels it could not.

Required

Prepare a memo to Water Products' president describing the effects of intercompany transfers on the valuation of inventories and discuss the effects that different ownership levels of Growinkle and Plumbers Products would have on the success of Water Products' plan. Include citations to or quotations from the authoritative accounting literature to support your position.

C7-3   ## Intercompany Inventory Transfers

Research
FARS

On December 20, 20X2, Evert Corporation paid Frankle Company $180,000 for inventory that Frankle had purchased for $240,000. Frankle had not previously recognized a loss and reduced the inventory's carrying value because the drop in prices was considered temporary. A resurgence in demand for the product occurred in early 20X3, and Evert sold the entire inventory for $310,000.

Evert owns 90 percent of Frankle's stock. Evert prepared consolidated financial statements at December 31, 20X2 and 20X3, but failed to make adjustments to the reported data provided by Evert and Frankle for the intercorporate sale.

Required

Prepare a memo to Evert's treasurer describing the required treatment of intercorporate sales of inventory. Include citations to or quotations from the authoritative accounting literature to support your position. You should include in your memo an analysis of the effects that eliminating the intercompany transfer would have had on Evert's reported revenues and expenses for 20X2 and 20X3 and on its balance sheet accounts at December 31, 20X2 and 20X3.

C7-4   ## Unrealized Inventory Profits

Understanding

Morrison Company owns 80 percent of Bloom Corporation's stock. The companies frequently engage in intercompany inventory transactions.

Required

Name the conditions that would make it possible for each of the following statements to be true. Treat each statement independently.

a. Income assigned to the noncontrolling interest in the consolidated income statement for 20X3 is greater than a pro rata share of the reported net income of Bloom.

b. Income assigned to the noncontrolling interest in the consolidated income statement for 20X3 is greater than a pro rata share of Bloom's reported net income, but consolidated net income is reduced as a result of the elimination of intercompany inventory transfers.

c. Cost of goods sold reported in the income statement of Morrison is greater than consolidated cost of goods sold for 20X3.

d. Consolidated inventory is greater than the amounts reported by the separate companies.

C7-5   ## Eliminating Inventory Transfers

Analysis

Ready Building Products has six subsidiaries that sell building materials and supplies to the public and to the parent and other subsidiaries. Because of the invoicing system Ready uses, it is not possible to keep track of which items have been purchased from related companies and which have been bought from outside sources. Due to the nature of the products purchased, there are substantially different profit margins on different product groupings.

Required

a. If no effort is made to eliminate intercompany sales for the period or unrealized profits at year-end, what elements of the financial statements are likely to be misstated?

b. What type of control system would you recommend to Ready's controller to provide the information needed to make the required eliminating entries?

c. Would it matter if the buyer and seller used different inventory costing methods (FIFO, LIFO, or weighted average)? Explain.

d. Assume you believe that the adjustments for unrealized profit would be material. How would you go about determining what amounts must be eliminated at the end of the current period?

C7-6 **Intercompany Profits and Transfers of Inventory**

Many companies transfer inventories from one affiliate to another. Often the companies have integrated operations in which one affiliate provides the raw materials, another manufactures finished products, *Analysis* another distributes the products, and perhaps another sells the products at retail. In other cases, various affiliates may be established for selling the company's products in different geographic locations, especially in different countries. Often tax considerations also have an effect on intercompany transfers.

Required

a. Are Xerox Corporation's intercompany transfers significant? How does Xerox treat intercompany transfers for consolidation purposes?

b. How does ExxonMobil Corporation price its products for intercompany transfers? Are these transfers significant? How does ExxonMobil treat intercompany profits for consolidation purposes?

c. What types of intercompany and intersegment sales does Ford Motor Company have? Are they significant? How are they treated for consolidation?

Exercises **E7-1** **Multiple-Choice Questions on Intercompany Inventory Transfers [AICPA Adapted]**

Select the correct answer for each of the following questions.

1. Perez Inc. owns 80 percent of Senior Inc. During 20X2, Perez sold goods with a 40 percent gross profit to Senior. Senior sold all of these goods in 20X2. For 20X2 consolidated financial statements, how should the summation of Perez and Senior income statement items be adjusted?

   a. Sales and cost of goods sold should be reduced by the intercompany sales.

   b. Sales and cost of goods sold should be reduced by 80 percent of the intercompany sales.

   c. Net income should be reduced by 80 percent of the gross profit on intercompany sales.

   d. No adjustment is necessary.

2. Parker Corporation owns 80 percent of Smith Inc.'s common stock. During 20X1, Parker sold inventory to Smith for $250,000 on the same terms as sales made to third parties. Smith sold all of the inventory purchased from Parker in 20X1. The following information pertains to Smith and Parker's sales for 20X1:

	Parker	Smith
Sales	$1,000,000	$700,000
Cost of Sales	400,000	350,000
Gross Profit	$ 600,000	$350,000

What amount should Parker report as cost of sales in its 20X1 consolidated income statement?

   a. $750,000.

   b. $680,000.

   c. $500,000.

   d. $430,000.

Items 3 and 4 are based on the following information:

Nolan owns 100 percent of the capital stock of both Twill Corporation and Webb Corporation. Twill purchases merchandise inventory from Webb at 140 percent of Webb's cost. During 20X0, Webb sold merchandise that had cost it $40,000 to Twill. Twill sold all of this merchandise to unrelated customers for $81,200 during 20X0. In preparing combined financial statements for 20X0, Nolan's bookkeeper disregarded the common ownership of Twill and Webb.

3. What amount should be eliminated from cost of goods sold in the combined income statement for 20X0?

   a. $56,000.
   b. $40,000.
   c. $24,000.
   d. $16,000.

4. By what amount was unadjusted revenue overstated in the combined income statement for 20X0?

   a. $16,000.
   b. $40,000.
   c. $56,000.
   d. $81,200.

5. Clark Company had the following transactions with affiliated parties during 20X2:

   - Sales of $60,000 to Dean Inc., with $20,000 gross profit. Dean had $15,000 of this inventory on hand at year-end. Clark owns a 15 percent interest in Dean and does not exert significant influence.
   - Purchases of raw materials totaling $240,000 from Kent Corporation, a wholly owned subsidiary. Kent's gross profit on the sales was $48,000. Clark had $60,000 of this inventory remaining on December 31, 20X2.

   Before eliminating entries, Clark had consolidated current assets of $320,000. What amount should Clark report in its December 31, 20X2, consolidated balance sheet for current assets?

   a. $320,000.
   b. $317,000.
   c. $308,000.
   d. $303,000.

6. Selected data for two subsidiaries of Dunn Corporation taken from the December 31, 20X8, pre-closing trial balances are as follows:

	Banks Co. (Debits)	Lamm Co. (Credits)
Shipments to Banks	$ —	$150,000
Shipments from Lamm	200,000	—
Intercompany Inventory Profit on Total Shipments		50,000

   Additional data relating to the December 31, 20X8, inventory are as follows:

Inventory acquired by Banks from outside parties	$175,000
Inventory acquired by Lamm from outside parties	250,000
Inventory acquired by Banks from Lamm	60,000

   At December 31, 20X8, the inventory reported on the combined balance sheet of the two subsidiaries should be:

   a. $425,000.
   b. $435,000.
   c. $470,000.
   d. $485,000.

**E7-2 Multiple-Choice Questions on the Effects of Inventory Transfers
[AICPA Adapted]**

Select the correct answer for each of the following questions.

1. During 20X3, Park Corporation recorded sales of inventory costing $500,000 to Small Company, its wholly owned subsidiary, on the same terms as sales made to third parties. At December 31, 20X3, Small held one-fifth of these goods in its inventory. The following information pertains to Park and Small's sales for 20X3:

	Park	Small
Sales	$2,000,000	$1,400,000
Cost of Sales	800,000	700,000
Gross Profit	$1,200,000	$ 700,000

In its 20X3 consolidated income statement, what amount should Park report as cost of sales?

 a. $1,000,000.
 b. $1,060,000.
 c. $1,260,000.
 d. $1,500,000.

Items 2 through 6 are based on the following information:

Selected information from the separate and consolidated balance sheets and income statements of Pard Inc. and its subsidiary, Spin Company, as of December 31, 20X8, and for the year then ended is as follows:

	Pard	Spin	Consolidated
Balance Sheet Accounts			
Accounts Receivable	$ 26,000	$ 19,000	$ 39,000
Inventory	30,000	25,000	52,000
Investment in Spin	67,000	—	—
Patents	—	—	30,000
Minority Interest	—	—	10,000
Stockholders' Equity	154,000	50,000	154,000
Income Statement Accounts			
Revenues	$200,000	$140,000	$308,000
Cost of Goods Sold	150,000	110,000	231,000
Gross Profit	$ 50,000	$ 30,000	$ 77,000
Equity in Earnings of Spin	11,000	—	—
Amortization of Patents	—	—	2,000
Net Income	36,000	20,000	40,000

Additional information

- During 20X8, Pard sold goods to Spin at the same markup on cost that Pard uses for all sales. At December 31, 20X8, Spin had not paid for all of these goods and still held 37.5 percent of them in inventory.
- Pard acquired its interest in Spin on January 2, 20X5. Pard's policy is to amortize patents by the straight-line method.

2. What was the amount of intercompany sales from Pard to Spin during 20X8?

 a. $3,000.
 b. $6,000.
 c. $29,000.
 d. $32,000.

3. At December 31, 20X8, what was the amount of Spin's payable to Pard for intercompany sales?

    a. $3,000.
    b. $6,000.
    c. $29,000.
    d. $32,000.

4. In Pard's consolidated balance sheet, what was the carrying amount of the inventory that Spin purchased from Pard?

    a. $3,000.
    b. $6,000.
    c. $9,000.
    d. $12,000.

5. What is the percent of minority interest ownership of Spin?

    a. 10 percent.
    b. 20 percent.
    c. 25 percent.
    d. 45 percent.

6. Over how many years has Pard chosen to amortize patents?

    a. 15 years.
    b. 19 years.
    c. 23 years.
    d. 40 years.

E7-3   Multiple-Choice Questions—Consolidated Income Statement

Select the correct answer for each of the following questions.

Blue Company purchased 60 percent ownership of Kelly Corporation in 20X1. On May 10, 20X2, Kelly purchased inventory from Blue for $60,000. Kelly sold all of the inventory to an unaffiliated company for $86,000 on November 10, 20X2. Blue produced the inventory sold to Kelly for $47,000. The companies had no other transactions during 20X2.

1. What amount of sales will be reported in the 20X2 consolidated income statement?

    a. $51,600.
    b. $60,000.
    c. $86,000.
    d. $146,000.

2. What amount of cost of goods sold will be reported in the 20X2 consolidated income statement?

    a. $36,000.
    b. $47,000.
    c. $60,000.
    d. $107,000.

3. What amount will be reported as consolidated net income for 20X2?

    a. $13,000.
    b. $26,000.
    c. $28,600.
    d. $39,000.

E7-4   Multiple-Choice Questions—Consolidated Balances

Select the correct answer for each of the following questions.

Lorn Corporation purchased inventory from Dresser Corporation for $120,000 on September 20, 20X1, and resold 80 percent of the inventory to unaffiliated companies prior to December 31, 20X1, for $140,000. Dresser produced the inventory sold to Lorn for $75,000. Lorn owns 70 percent of Dresser's voting common stock. The companies had no other transactions during 20X1.

1. What amount of sales will be reported in the 20X1 consolidated income statement?

    a. $98,000.
    b. $120,000.
    c. $140,000.
    d. $260,000.

2. What amount of cost of goods sold will be reported in the 20X1 consolidated income statement?

    a. $60,000.
    b. $75,000.
    c. $96,000.
    d. $120,000.
    e. $171,000.

3. What amount of consolidated net income will be reported for 20X1?

    a. $20,000.
    b. $30,800.
    c. $44,000.
    d. $45,000.
    e. $69,200.
    f. $80,000.

4. What inventory balance will be reported by the consolidated entity on December 31, 20X1?

    a. $15,000.
    b. $16,800.
    c. $24,000.
    d. $39,000.

E7-5   Multiple-Choice Questions—Consolidated Income Statement

Select the correct answer for each of the following questions.

Showtime Corporation holds 80 percent of the stock of Movie Productions Inc. During 20X4, Showtime purchased an inventory of snack bar items for $40,000 and resold $30,000 to Movie Productions for $48,000. Movie Productions Inc. reported sales of $67,000 in 20X4 and had inventory of $16,000 on December 31, 20X4. The companies held no beginning inventory and had no other transactions in 20X4.

1. What amount of cost of goods sold will be reported in the 20X4 consolidated income statement?

    a. $20,000.
    b. $30,000.
    c. $32,000.
    d. $52,000.
    e. $62,000.

2. What amount of net income will be reported in the 20X4 consolidated income statement?

    a. $12,000.
    b. $18,000.
    c. $40,000.
    d. $47,000.
    e. $53,000.

3. What amount of income will be assigned to the noncontrolling interest in the 20X4 consolidated income statement?

    a. $7,000.
    b. $8,000.
    c. $9,400.
    d. $10,200.
    e. $13,400.

E7-6   Realized Profit on Intercompany Sale

Nordway Corporation purchased 90 percent of Olman Company's voting shares of stock in 20X1. During 20X4, Nordway purchased 40,000 Playday doghouses for $24 each and sold 25,000 of the doghouses to Olman for $30 each. Olman sold all of the doghouses to retail establishments prior to December 31, 20X4, for $45 each. Both companies use perpetual inventory systems.

Required

a. Give the journal entries Nordway recorded for the purchase of inventory and resale to Olman Company in 20X4.

b. Give the journal entries Olman recorded for the purchase of inventory and resale to retail establishments in 20X4.

c. Give the workpaper eliminating entry(ies) needed in preparing consolidated financial statements for 20X4 to remove all effects of the intercompany sale.

E7-7   Sale of Inventory to Subsidiary

Nordway Corporation purchased 90 percent of Olman Company's voting shares of stock in 20X1. During 20X4, Nordway purchased 40,000 Playday doghouses for $24 each and sold 25,000 of the doghouses to Olman for $30 each. Olman sold 18,000 of the doghouses to retail establishments prior to December 31, 20X4, for $45 each. Both companies use perpetual inventory systems.

Required

a. Give all journal entries Nordway recorded for the purchase of inventory and resale to Olman Company in 20X4.

b. Give the journal entries Olman recorded for the purchase of inventory and resale to retail establishments in 20X4.

c. Give the workpaper eliminating entry(ies) needed in preparing consolidated financial statements for 20X4 to remove the effects of the intercompany sale.

E7-8   Inventory Transfer between Parent and Subsidiary

Karlow Corporation owns 60 percent of Draw Company's voting shares. During 20X3, Karlow produced 25,000 computer desks at a cost of $82 each and sold 10,000 desks to Draw for $94 each. Draw sold 7,000 of the desks to unaffiliated companies for $130 each prior to December 31, 20X3, and sold the remainder in early 20X4 for $140 each. Both companies use perpetual inventory systems.

Required

a. What amounts of cost of goods sold did Karlow and Draw record in 20X3?

b. What amount of cost of goods sold must be reported in the consolidated income statement for 20X3?

c. Give the workpaper eliminating entry or entries needed in preparing consolidated financial statements at December 31, 20X3, relating to the intercorporate sale of inventory.

d. Give the workpaper eliminating entry or entries needed in preparing consolidated financial statements at December 31, 20X4, relating to the intercorporate sale of inventory.

e. Give the workpaper eliminating entry or entries needed in preparing consolidated financial statements at December 31, 20X4, relating to the intercorporate sale of inventory if Draw had produced the computer desks at a cost of $82 each and sold 10,000 desks to Karlow for $94 each in 20X3, with Karlow selling 7,000 desks to unaffiliated companies in 20X3 and the remaining 3,000 in 20X4.

E7-9   Income Statement Effects of Unrealized Profit

Holiday Bakery owns 60 percent of Farmco Products Company's stock. During 20X8, Farmco produced 100,000 bags of flour, which it sold to Holiday Bakery for $900,000. On December 31, 20X8, Holiday had 20,000 bags of flour purchased from Farmco Products on hand. Farmco prices its sales at cost plus 50 percent of cost for profit. Holiday, which purchased all its flour from Farmco in 20X8, had no inventory on hand on January 1, 20X8.

Holiday Bakery reported income from its baking operations of $400,000, and Farmco Products reported net income of $150,000 for 20X8.

Required

a. Compute the amount reported as cost of goods sold in the 20X8 consolidated income statement.

b. Give the workpaper eliminating entry or entries required to remove the effects of the intercompany sale in preparing consolidated statements at the end of 20X8.

c. Compute the amount reported as consolidated net income for 20X8.

E7-10 **Prior-Period Unrealized Inventory Profit**

Holiday Bakery owns 60 percent of Farmco Products Company's stock. On January 1, 20X9, inventory reported by Holiday included 20,000 bags of flour purchased from Farmco at $9 per bag. By December 31, 20X9, all the beginning inventory purchased from Farmco Products had been baked into products and sold to customers by Holiday. There were no transactions between Holiday and Farmco during 20X9.

Both Holiday Bakery and Farmco Products price their sales at cost plus 50 percent markup for profit. Holiday reported income from its baking operations of $300,000, and Farmco reported net income of $250,000 for 20X9.

Required

a. Compute the amount reported as cost of goods sold in the 20X9 consolidated income statement for the flour purchased from Farmco in 20X8.

b. Give the eliminating entry or entries required to remove the effects of the unrealized profit in beginning inventory in preparing the consolidation workpaper as of December 31, 20X9.

c. Compute the amount reported as consolidated net income for 20X9.

E7-11 **Computation of Consolidated Income Statement Data**

Bass Company purchased 60 percent of Cooper Company's voting shares for $260,000 on January 1, 20X2. Cooper reported total stockholders' equity of $400,000 at the time of acquisition. The purchase differential is assigned to patents with an expected economic life of 10 years from the date of combination.

During 20X5, Bass purchased inventory for $20,000 and sold the full amount to Cooper Company for $30,000. On December 31, 20X5, Cooper's ending inventory included $6,000 of items purchased from Bass. Also in 20X5, Cooper purchased inventory for $50,000 and sold the units to Bass for $80,000. Bass included $20,000 of its purchase from Cooper in ending inventory on December 31, 20X5.

Summary income statement data for the two companies revealed the following:

	Bass Company	Cooper Company
Sales	$ 400,000	$ 200,000
Income from Subsidiary	25,000	
	$ 425,000	$ 200,000
Cost of Goods Sold	$ 250,000	$ 120,000
Other Expenses	70,000	35,000
Total Expenses	$(320,000)	$(155,000)
Net Income	$ 105,000	$ 45,000

Required

a. Compute the amount to be reported as sales in the 20X5 consolidated income statement.

b. Compute the amount to be reported as cost of goods sold in the 20X5 consolidated income statement.

c. What amount of income will be assigned to the noncontrolling shareholders in the 20X5 consolidated income statement?

d. What amount of consolidated net income will be reported for 20X5?

E7-12 **Sale of Inventory at a Loss**

The price of high-quality burnwhistles fluctuates substantially from month to month. As a result, it is not uncommon for a company that deals in burnwhistles to report a substantial gain in one period, followed by a substantial loss in the following period. The price of burnwhistles was relatively high during the first three months of 20X8, declined substantially for the next four months, and then recovered nicely by year-end. On February 6, 20X8, Trent Company purchased burnwhistles for $400,000 and sold them to Gord Corporation on July 10, 20X8, for $300,000. Gord held its purchase for several months before selling 60 percent to nonaffiliates for $360,000 in late November. The remaining units were held at year-end and are expected to be sold in early 20X9 for approximately $240,000. Gord owns 75 percent of the stock of Trent Company.

Required

a. Give the journal entries Trent and Gord recorded during 20X8 related to the initial purchase, intercorporate sale, and resale of inventory.

b. What amount should be reported as cost of goods sold in the 20X8 consolidated income statement?

c. If Gord reported operating income of $230,000 and Trent reported net income of $80,000, what amount of consolidated net income should Gord report for 20X8?

d. Give the workpaper eliminating entry or entries needed in preparing consolidated financial statements for 20X8 to remove all effects of the intercompany transfer.

E7-13   Intercompany Sales

Hollow Corporation purchased 70 percent of Surg Corporation's voting stock on May 18, 20X1, at underlying book value. The companies reported the following data with respect to intercompany sales in 20X4 and 20X5:

Year	Purchased by	Purchase Price	Sold to	Sale Price	Unsold at End of Year	Year Sold to Unaffilliated Co.
20X4	Surg Corp.	$120,000	Hollow Corp.	$180,000	$ 45,000	20X5
20X5	Surg Corp.	90,000	Hollow Corp.	135,000	30,000	20X6
20X5	Hollow Corp.	140,000	Surg Corp.	280,000	110,000	20X6

Hollow reported operating income (excluding income from its investment in Surg) of $160,000 and $220,000 in 20X4 and 20X5, respectively. Surg reported net income of $90,000 and $85,000 in 20X4 and 20X5, respectively.

Required

a. Compute consolidated net income for 20X4.

b. Compute the inventory balance reported in the consolidated balance sheet at December 31, 20X5, for the transactions shown.

c. Compute the amount included in consolidated cost of goods sold for 20X5 relating to the transactions shown.

d. Compute consolidated net income for 20X5.

E7-14   Consolidated Balance Sheet Workpaper

The December 31, 20X8, balance sheets for Doorst Corporation and its 70 percent owned subsidiary Hingle Company contained the following summarized amounts:

DOORST CORPORATION AND HINGLE COMPANY
Balance Sheets
December 31, 20X8

	Doorst Corporation	Hingle Company
Cash and Receivables	$ 98,000	$ 40,000
Inventory	150,000	100,000
Buildings and Equipment (net)	310,000	280,000
Investment in Hingle Company Stock	280,000	
Total Assets	$838,000	$420,000

(continued)

(continued)

	Doorst Corporation	Hingle Company
Accounts Payable	$ 70,000	$ 20,000
Common Stock	200,000	150,000
Retained Earnings	568,000	250,000
Total Liabilities and Equity	$838,000	$420,000

Doorst purchased the shares of Hingle Company at book value on January 1, 20X7. On December 31, 20X8, Doorst's balance sheet contains inventory items purchased from Hingle for $95,000. The items cost Hingle $55,000 to produce. In addition, Hingle's inventory contains goods it purchased from Doorst for $25,000 that Doorst had produced for $15,000.

Required

a. Prepare all eliminating entries needed to complete a consolidated balance sheet workpaper as of December 31, 20X8.

b. Prepare a consolidated balance sheet workpaper as of December 31, 20X8.

E7-15* Multiple Transfers between Affiliates

Klon Corporation owns 70 percent of Brant Company's stock and 60 percent of Torkel Company's stock. During 20X8, Klon sold inventory purchased in 20X7 for $100,000 to Brant for $150,000. Brant then sold the inventory at its cost of $150,000 to Torkel. Prior to December 31, 20X8, Torkel sold $90,000 of inventory to a nonaffiliate for $120,000 and held $60,000 in inventory at December 31, 20X8.

Required

a. Give the journal entries recorded by Klon, Brant, and Torkel during 20X8 relating to the intercorporate sale and resale of inventory.

b. What amount should be reported in the 20X8 consolidated income statement as cost of goods sold?

c. What amount should be reported in the December 31, 20X8, consolidated balance sheet as inventory?

d. Give the eliminating entry needed at December 31, 20X8, to remove the effects of the inventory transfers.

E7-16 Inventory Sales

Herb Corporation holds 60 percent ownership of Spice Company. Each year, Spice purchases large quantities of a gnarl root used in producing health drinks. Spice purchased $150,000 of roots in 20X7 and sold $40,000 of these purchases to Herb for $60,000. By the end of 20X7, Herb had resold all but $15,000 of its purchase from Spice. Herb generated $90,000 on the sale of roots to various health stores during the year.

Required

a. Give the journal entries recorded by Herb and Spice during 20X7 relating to the initial purchase, intercorporate sale, and resale of gnarl roots.

b. Give the workpaper eliminating entries needed as of December 31, 20X7, to remove all effects of the intercompany transfer in preparing the 20X7 consolidated financial statements.

E7-17 Prior-Period Inventory Profits

Home Products Corporation sells a broad line of home detergent products. Home Products owns 75 percent of the stock of Level Brothers Soap Company. During 20X8, Level Brothers sold soap products to Home Products for $180,000, which it had produced for $120,000. Home Products sold $150,000 of its purchase from Level Brothers in 20X8 and the remainder in 20X9. In addition, Home Products purchased $240,000 of inventory from Level Brothers in 20X9 and resold $90,000 of the items before year-end. Level Brothers' cost to produce the items sold to Home Products in 20X9 was $160,000.

Required

a. Give all workpaper eliminating entries needed for December 31, 20X9, to remove the effects of the intercompany inventory transfers in 20X8 and 20X9.

b. Compute the amount of income assigned to noncontrolling shareholders in the 20X8 and 20X9 consolidated income statements if Level Brothers reported net income of $350,000 for 20X8 and $420,000 for 20X9.

Problems

P7-18   Consolidated Income Statement Data

Sweeny Corporation owns 60 percent of Bitner Company's shares. Partial 20X2 financial data for the companies and consolidated entity were as follows:

	Sweeny Corporation	Bitner Company	Consolidated Totals
Sales	$550,000	$450,000	$820,000
Cost of Goods Sold	310,000	300,000	420,000
Inventory, Dec. 31	180,000	210,000	375,000

On January 1, 20X2, Sweeny's inventory contained items purchased from Bitner for $75,000. The cost of the units to Bitner was $50,000. All intercorporate sales during 20X2 were made by Bitner to Sweeny.

Required

a. What amount of intercorporate sales occurred in 20X2?

b. How much unrealized intercompany profit existed on January 1, 20X2? On December 31, 20X2?

c. Give the workpaper eliminating entries relating to inventory and cost of goods sold needed to prepare consolidated financial statements for 20X2.

d. If Bitner reports net income of $90,000 for 20X2, what amount of income is assigned to the noncontrolling interest in the 20X2 consolidated income statement?

P7-19   Unrealized Profit on Upstream Sales

Carroll Company sells all its output at 25 percent above cost. Pacific Corporation purchases all its inventory from Carroll. Selected information on the operations of the companies over the past three years is as follows:

	Carroll Company		Pacific Corporation	
Year	Sales to Pacific Corp.	Net Income	Inventory, Dec. 31	Operating Income
20X2	$200,000	$100,000	$ 70,000	$150,000
20X3	175,000	90,000	105,000	240,000
20X4	225,000	160,000	120,000	300,000

Pacific purchased 60 percent of the ownership of Carroll on January 1, 20X1, at underlying book value.

Required

Compute consolidated net income and income assigned to the noncontrolling interest for 20X2, 20X3, and 20X4.

P7-20   Net Income of Consolidated Entity

Stem Corporation purchased 70 percent of Crown Corporation's voting stock on January 1, 20X2, for $465,000. At that date, Crown reported common stock outstanding of $200,000 and retained earnings of $350,000. The purchase differential is assigned to buildings with an expected life of 20 years from the date of combination.

On December 31, 20X4, Stem had $25,000 of unrealized profits on its books from inventory sales to Crown, and Crown had $40,000 of unrealized profit on its books from inventory sales to Stem. All inventory held at December 31, 20X4, was sold during 20X5.

On December 31, 20X5, Stem had $14,000 of unrealized profit on its books from inventory sales to Crown, and Crown had unrealized profit on its books of $55,000 from inventory sales to Stem.

Stem reported income from its separate operations (excluding income on its investment in Crown and amortization of purchase differential) of $118,000 in 20X5, and Crown reported net income of $65,000.

Required

Compute consolidated net income for 20X5.

P7-21　Correction of Eliminating Entries

In preparing the consolidation workpaper for Bolger Corporation and its 60 percent owned subsidiary, Feldman Company, the following eliminating entries were proposed by Bolger's bookkeeper:

E(1)	Cash	80,000	
	Accounts Payable		80,000
	To eliminate the unpaid balance for intercorporate inventory sales in 20X5.		
E(2)	Cost of Goods Sold	12,000	
	Income from Subsidiary		12,000
	To eliminate unrealized inventory profits at December 31, 20X5.		
E(3)	Income from Subsidiary	140,000	
	Sales		140,000
	To eliminate intercompany sales for 20X5.		

Bolger's bookkeeper recently graduated from Oddball University, and while the dollar amounts recorded are correct, he had some confusion in determining which accounts needed adjustment. All intercorporate sales in 20X5 were from Feldman to Bolger, and Feldman sells inventory at cost plus 40 percent of cost. Bolger uses the basic equity method in accounting for its ownership in Feldman.

Required

a. What percentage of the intercompany inventory transfer was resold prior to the end of 20X5?

b. Give the appropriate eliminating entries needed at December 31, 20X5, to prepare consolidated financial statements.

P7-22　Incomplete Data

Keller Corporation acquired 75 percent of the ownership of Tropic Company on January 1, 20X1. The purchase differential paid by Keller is assigned to buildings and equipment and expensed over 10 years. Financial statement data for the two companies and the consolidated entity at December 31, 20X6, are as follows:

KELLER CORPORATION AND TROPIC COMPANY
Balance Sheet Data
December 31, 20X6

Item	Keller Corporation	Tropic Company	Consolidated Entity
Cash	$ 67,000	$ 45,000	$ 112,000
Accounts Receivable	?	55,000	145,000
Inventory	125,000	90,000	211,000
Buildings and Equipment	400,000	240,000	670,000
Less: Accumulated Depreciation	(180,000)	(110,000)	(?)
Investment in Tropic Company	?		
Total Assets	$?	$320,000	$?
Accounts Payable	$ 86,000	$ 20,000	$ 89,000
Other Payables	?	8,000	?
Notes Payable	250,000	120,000	370,000
Common Stock	120,000	60,000	120,000
Retained Earnings	180,000	112,000	177,000
Noncontrolling Interest			42,000
Total Liabilities and Equity	$?	$320,000	$?

KELLER CORPORATION AND TROPIC COMPANY
Income Statement Data
For the Year Ended December 31, 20X6

Item	Keller Corporation	Tropic Company	Consolidated Entity
Sales	$420,000	$260,000	$650,000
Income from Subsidiary	27,000		
Total Income	$447,000	$260,000	$650,000
Cost of Goods Sold	$310,000	$170,000	$445,000
Depreciation Expense	20,000	25,000	48,000
Interest Expense	25,000	9,500	34,500
Other Expenses	22,000	15,500	37,500
Total Expenses	($377,000)	($220,000)	($565,000)
			$ 85,000
Income to Noncontrolling Interest			(9,000)
Net Income	$ 70,000	$ 40,000	$ 76,000

Required

a. What amount of purchase differential did Keller pay in acquiring its ownership of Tropic?

b. What amount should be reported as accumulated depreciation for the consolidated entity at December 31, 20X6?

c. If Tropic reported retained earnings of $30,000 on January 1, 20X1, what amount did Keller pay to acquire its ownership in Tropic?

d. What balance does Keller report as its investment in Tropic at December 31, 20X6?

e. What amount of intercorporate sales of inventory occurred in 20X6?

f. What amount of unrealized inventory profit exists at December 31, 20X6?

g. Assuming that all unrealized profits on intercompany inventory sales at January 1, 20X6, were on Keller's books, were the inventory sales during 20X6 upstream or downstream? How do you know?

h. Give the eliminating entry used in eliminating intercompany inventory sales during 20X6.

i. Assuming all unrealized profits on intercompany inventory sales at January 1, 20X6, were on Keller's books, what was the amount of unrealized profit at January 1, 20X6?

j. What balance in accounts receivable did Keller report at December 31, 20X6?

P7-23 Eliminations for Upstream Sales

Clean Air Products owns 80 percent of the stock of Superior Filter Company, which it acquired at underlying book value on August 30, 20X6. Summarized trial balance data for the two companies as of December 31, 20X8, are as follows:

	Clean Air Products		Superior Filter Company	
	Debit	Credit	Debit	Credit
Cash and Accounts Receivable	$ 145,000		$ 90,000	
Inventory	220,000		110,000	
Buildings and Equipment (net)	270,000		180,000	
Investment in Superior Filter Stock	280,000			
Cost of Goods Sold	175,000		140,000	
Depreciation Expense	30,000		20,000	
Current Liabilities		$ 150,000		$ 30,000
Common Stock		200,000		90,000
Retained Earnings		488,000		220,000
Sales		250,000		200,000
Income from Subsidiary		32,000		
Total	$1,120,000	$1,120,000	$540,000	$540,000

On January 1, 20X8, Clean Air's inventory contained filters purchased for $60,000 from Superior Filter, which had produced the filters for $40,000. In 20X8, Superior Filter spent $100,000 to produce additional filters, which it sold to Clean Air for $150,000. By December 31, 20X8, Clean Air had sold all filters that had been on hand January 1, 20X8, but continued to hold in inventory $45,000 of the 20X8 purchase from Superior Filter.

Required

a. Prepare all eliminating entries needed to complete a consolidation workpaper for 20X8.

b. Compute consolidated net income for 20X8.

c. Compute the balance assigned to the noncontrolling interest in the consolidated balance sheet as of December 31, 20X8.

P7-24 **Multiple Inventory Transfers**

Ajax Corporation purchased at book value 70 percent of Beta Corporation's ownership and 90 percent of Cole Corporation's ownership in 20X5. There are frequent intercompany transfers among the companies. Activity relevant to 20X8 follows:

Year	Producer	Production Cost	Buyer	Transfer Price	Unsold at End of Year	Year Sold
20X7	Beta Corporation	$24,000	Ajax Corporation	$30,000	$10,000	20X8
20X7	Cole Corporation	60,000	Beta Corporation	72,000	18,000	20X8
20X8	Ajax Corporation	15,000	Beta Corporation	35,000	7,000	20X9
20X8	Beta Corporation	63,000	Cole Corporation	72,000	12,000	20X9
20X8	Cole Corporation	27,000	Ajax Corporation	45,000	15,000	20X9

For the year ended December 31, 20X8, Ajax reported $80,000 of income from its separate operations (excluding income from intercorporate investments), Beta reported net income of $37,500, and Cole reported net income of $20,000.

Required

a. Compute the amount to be reported as consolidated net income for 20X8.

b. Compute the amount to be reported as inventory in the December 31, 20X8, consolidated balance sheet for the preceding items.

c. Compute the amount to be reported as income assigned to noncontrolling shareholders in the 20X8 consolidated income statement.

P7-25 **Consolidation with Inventory Transfers and Other Comprehensive Income**

On January 1, 20X1, Priority Corporation purchased 90 percent of Tall Corporation's common stock at underlying book value. Priority uses the equity method in accounting for its investment in Tall. The stockholders' equity section of Tall at January 1, 20X5, contained the following balances:

Common Stock ($5 par)	$ 400,000
Additional Paid-In Capital	200,000
Retained Earnings	790,000
Accumulated Other Comprehensive Income	10,000
Total	$1,400,000

During 20X4, Tall sold goods costing $30,000 to Priority for $45,000, and Priority resold 60 percent prior to year-end. It sold the remainder in 20X5. Also in 20X4, Priority sold inventory items costing $90,000 to Tall for $108,000. Tall resold $60,000 of its purchases in 20X4 and the remaining $48,000 in 20X5.

In 20X5, Priority sold additional inventory costing $30,000 to Tall for $36,000, and Tall resold $24,000 of it prior to year-end. Tall sold inventory costing $60,000 to Priority in 20X5 for $90,000, and Priority resold $48,000 of its purchase by December 31, 20X5.

Priority reported 20X5 income of $240,000 from its separate operations and paid dividends of $150,000. Tall reported 20X5 net income of $90,000 and comprehensive income of $110,000. Tall reported other comprehensive income of $10,000 in 20X4. In both years, other comprehensive income arose from an increase in the market value of securities classified as available-for-sale. Tall paid dividends of $60,000 in 20X5.

Required

a. Compute the balance in the investment account reported by Priority at December 31, 20X5.

b. Compute the amount of investment income reported by Priority on its investment in Tall for 20X5.

c. Compute the amount of income assigned to noncontrolling shareholders in the 20X5 consolidated income statement.

d. Compute the balance assigned to noncontrolling shareholders in the consolidated balance sheet prepared at December 31, 20X5.

e. Priority and Tall report inventory balances of $120,000 and $100,000, respectively, at December 31, 20X5. What amount should be reported as inventory in the consolidated balance sheet at December 31, 20X5?

f. Compute the amount reported as consolidated net income for 20X5.

g. Prepare the eliminating entries needed to complete a consolidation workpaper as of December 31, 20X5.

P7-26 **Multiple Inventory Transfers between Parent and Subsidiary**

Proud Company and Slinky Company both produce and purchase equipment for resale each period and frequently sell to each other. Since Proud Company holds 60 percent ownership of Slinky Company, Proud's controller compiled the following information with regard to intercompany transactions between the two companies in 20X5 and 20X6:

Year	Produced by	Sold to	Percent Resold to Nonaffiliate in 20X5	Percent Resold to Nonaffiliate in 20X6	Cost to Produce	Sale Price to Affiliate
20X5	Proud Company	Slinky Company	60%	40%	$100,000	$150,000
20X5	Slinky Company	Proud Company	30	50	70,000	100,000
20X6	Proud Company	Slinky Company		90	40,000	60,000
20X6	Slinky Company	Proud Company		25	200,000	240,000

Required

a. Give the eliminating entries required at December 31, 20X6, to eliminate the effects of the inventory transfers in preparing a full set of consolidated financial statements.

b. Compute the amount of cost of goods sold to be reported in the consolidated income statement for 20X6.

P7-27 **Consolidation following Inventory Transactions**

Bell Company purchased 60 percent ownership of Troll Corporation on January 1, 20X1, for $83,000. On that date, Troll reported common stock outstanding of $100,000 and retained earnings of $20,000. The purchase differential is assigned to land to be used as a future building site. Bell uses the equity method in accounting for its ownership of Troll. On December 31, 20X2, the trial balances of the two companies are as follows:

Item	Bell Company Debit	Bell Company Credit	Troll Corporation Debit	Troll Corporation Credit
Cash and Accounts Receivable	$ 69,200		$ 51,200	
Inventory	60,000		55,000	
Land	40,000		30,000	
Buildings and Equipment	520,000		350,000	
Investment in Troll Corporation Stock	113,000			
Cost of Goods Sold	99,800		61,000	
Depreciation Expense	25,000		15,000	
Interest Expense	6,000		14,000	
Dividends Declared	40,000		10,000	

(continued)

(*continued*)

Item	Bell Company Debit	Bell Company Credit	Troll Corporation Debit	Troll Corporation Credit
Accumulated Depreciation		$175,000		$ 75,000
Accounts Payable		68,800		41,200
Bonds Payable		80,000		200,000
Bond Premium		1,200		
Common Stock		200,000		100,000
Retained Earnings		230,000		50,000
Sales		200,000		120,000
Income from Subsidiary		18,000		
	$973,000	$973,000	$586,200	$586,200

Troll sold inventory costing $25,500 to Bell for $42,500 in 20X1. Bell resold 80 percent of the purchase in 20X1 and the remainder in 20X2. Troll sold inventory costing $21,000 to Bell in 20X2 for $35,000, and Bell resold 70 percent prior to December 31, 20X2. In addition, Bell sold inventory costing $14,000 to Troll for $28,000 in 20X2, and Troll resold all but $13,000 of its purchase prior to December 31, 20X2.

Required

a. Record the journal entry or entries for 20X2 on Bell's books related to its investment in Troll Corporation, using the basic equity method.

b. Prepare the elimination entries needed to complete a consolidated workpaper for 20X2.

c. Prepare a three-part consolidation workpaper for 20X2.

P7-28   **Consolidation Workpaper**

Crow Corporation purchased 70 percent of West Company's voting common stock on January 1, 20X5, for $291,200. On that date, the book value of West's net assets was $380,000, and their book values were equal to their fair values, except for land that had a fair value $14,000 greater than book value. The amount attributed to goodwill as a result of the purchase of West shares is not amortized.

CROW CORPORATION AND WEST COMPANY
Trial Balance Data
December 31, 20X9

Item	Crow Corporation Debit	Crow Corporation Credit	West Company Debit	West Company Credit
Cash and Receivables	$ 81,300		$ 85,000	
Inventory	200,000		110,000	
Land, Buildings, and Equipment (net)	270,000		250,000	
Investment in West Company Stock	315,700			
Cost of Goods and Services	200,000		150,000	
Depreciation Expense	40,000		30,000	
Dividends Declared	35,000		5,000	
Sales and Service Revenue		$ 300,000		$200,000
Income from Subsidiary		14,000		
Accounts Payable		60,000		30,000
Common Stock		200,000		150,000
Retained Earnings		568,000		250,000
Total	$1,142,000	$1,142,000	$630,000	$630,000

On January 1, 20X9, Crow's inventory contained unrealized intercompany profits recorded by West in the amount of $30,000. West's inventory on that date contained $15,000 of unrealized intercompany profits recorded on Crow's books. Both companies sold their ending 20X8 inventories to unrelated companies in 20X9.

During 20X9, West sold inventory costing $37,000 to Crow for $62,000. Crow held all inventory purchased from West during 20X9 on December 31, 20X9. Also during 20X9, Crow sold goods costing $54,000 to West for $90,000. West continues to hold $20,000 of its purchase from Crow on December 31, 20X9.

On January 1, 20X6, Crow paid $95,000 to West for equipment purchased by West on January 1, 20X1, for $120,000. The total estimated economic life of 15 years for the equipment remains unchanged.

Required

a. Prepare all eliminating entries needed to complete a consolidation workpaper as of December 31, 20X9.

b. Prepare a consolidation workpaper as of December 31, 20X9.

c. Prepare a reconciliation between the balance in retained earnings reported by Crow on December 31, 20X9, and consolidated retained earnings.

P7-29 **Computation of Consolidated Totals**

Bunker Corporation owns 80 percent of Harrison Company's stock. At the end of 20X8, Bunker and Harrison reported the following partial operating results and inventory balances:

	Bunker Corporation	Harrison Company
Total sales	$660,000	$510,000
Sales to Harrison Company	140,000	
Sales to Bunker Corporation		240,000
Net income		20,000
Operating income (excluding investment income from Harrison)	70,000	
Inventory on hand, December 31, 20X8, purchased from:		
Harrison Company	48,000	
Bunker Corporation		42,000

Bunker regularly prices its products at cost plus a 40 percent markup for profit. Harrison prices its sales at cost plus a 20 percent markup. The total sales reported by Bunker and Harrison include both intercompany sales and sales to nonaffiliates.

Required

a. What amount of sales will be reported in the consolidated income statement for 20X8?

b. What amount of cost of goods sold will be reported in the 20X8 consolidated income statement?

c. What amount of consolidated net income will be reported for 20X8?

d. What balance will be reported for inventory in the consolidated balance sheet for December 31, 20X8?

P7-30 **Intercompany Transfer of Inventory and Land**

Hart Corporation purchased 70 percent of Bock Company's voting common shares on January 1, 20X2, for $94,000. At that date, Bock had $80,000 of common stock outstanding and retained earnings of $20,000. The excess of the amount paid over underlying book value is assigned to buildings and equipment, which had a fair value $20,000 greater than book value and a remaining 10-year life, and to patents, which had a remaining life of five years at the date of the business combination. Trial balances for the companies as of December 31, 20X3, are as follows:

Item	Hart Corporation Debit	Credit	Bock Company Debit	Credit
Cash and Accounts Receivable	$ 29,900		$ 21,600	
Inventory	165,000		35,000	
Land	80,000		40,000	
Buildings and Equipment	340,000		260,000	
Investment in Bock Company Stock	115,200			
Cost of Goods Sold	186,000		79,800	
Depreciation Expense	20,000		15,000	
Interest Expense	16,000		5,200	
Dividends Declared	30,000		15,000	

(continued)

(continued)

	Hart Corporation		Bock Company	
Item	Debit	Credit	Debit	Credit
Accumulated Depreciation		$140,000		$ 80,000
Accounts Payable		92,400		35,000
Bonds Payable		200,000		100,000
Bond Premium				1,600
Common Stock		120,000		80,000
Retained Earnings		142,000		50,000
Sales		260,000		125,000
Other Income		13,600		
Income from Subsidiary		14,100		
	$982,100	$982,100	$471,600	$471,600

On December 31, 20X2, Bock purchased inventory for $32,000 and sold it to Hart for $48,000. Hart resold $27,000 of the inventory during 20X3 and had the remaining balance in inventory at December 31, 20X3.

During 20X3, Bock sold inventory purchased for $60,000 to Hart for $90,000, and Hart resold all but $24,000 of its purchase. On March 10, 20X3, Hart sold inventory purchased for $15,000 to Bock for $30,000. Bock sold all but $7,600 of the inventory prior to December 31, 20X3.

During 20X2, Bock sold land it had purchased for $22,000 to Hart for $37,000. Hart plans to build a warehouse on the property in the near future.

Required

a. Give all eliminating entries needed to prepare a full set of consolidated financial statements at December 31, 20X3, for Hart and Bock.

b. Prepare a three-part consolidation workpaper for 20X3.

P7-31 Consolidation Using Financial Statement Data

Direct Sales Corporation purchased 60 percent of Concerto Company's stock on January 1, 20X3, for $24,000 in excess of the underlying book value. The difference relates to goodwill. At December 31, 20X6, Direct Sales management reviewed the amount attributed to goodwill and concluded that goodwill had been impaired. The correct carrying value at December 31, 20X6, is $12,000.

Balance sheet data for January 1, 20X6, and December 31, 20X6, and income statement data for 20X6 for the two companies are as follows:

DIRECT SALES CORPORATION AND CONCERTO COMPANY
Balance Sheet Data
January 1, 20X6

Item	Direct Sales Corporation		Concerto Company	
Cash	$ 9,800		$ 10,000	
Accounts Receivable	60,000		50,000	
Inventory	100,000		80,000	
Total Current Assets		$169,800		$140,000
Land		70,000		20,000
Buildings and Equipment	$300,000		$200,000	
Less: Accumulated Depreciation	(140,000)	160,000	(70,000)	130,000
Investment in Concerto Company Stock		144,000		
Total Assets		$543,800		$290,000
Accounts Payable		$ 30,000		$ 20,000
Bonds Payable		120,000		70,000
Common Stock	$100,000		$ 50,000	
Retained Earnings	293,800	393,800	150,000	200,000
Total Liabilities and Stockholders' Equity		$543,800		$290,000

DIRECT SALES CORPORATION AND CONCERTO COMPANY
Balance Sheet Data
December 31, 20X6

Item	Direct Sales Corporation		Concerto Company	
Cash	$ 26,800		$ 35,000	
Accounts Receivable	80,000		40,000	
Inventory	120,000		90,000	
Total Current Assets		$226,800		$165,000
Land		70,000		20,000
Buildings and Equipment	$340,000		$200,000	
Less: Accumulated Depreciation	(165,000)	175,000	(85,000)	115,000
Investment in Concerto Company Stock		153,000		
Total Assets		$624,800		$300,000
Accounts Payable		$ 80,000		$ 15,000
Bonds Payable		120,000		70,000
Common Stock	$100,000		$ 50,000	
Retained Earnings	324,800	424,800	165,000	215,000
Total Liabilities and Stockholders' Equity		$624,800		$300,000

DIRECT SALES CORPORATION AND CONCERTO COMPANY
Income Statement Data
Year Ended December 31, 20X6

Item	Direct Sales Corporation		Concerto Company	
Sales		$400,000		$200,000
Income from Subsidiary		21,000		
		$421,000		$200,000
Cost of Goods Sold	$280,000		$120,000	
Depreciation and Amortization Expense	25,000		15,000	
Other Expenses	35,000	(340,000)	30,000	(165,000)
Net Income		$ 81,000		$ 35,000

In 20X4, Concerto purchased a piece of land for $35,000 and later in the year sold it to Direct Sales for $45,000. Direct Sales is still using the land in its operations.

On January 1, 20X6, Direct Sales held inventory purchased from Concerto for $48,000. During 20X6, Direct Sales purchased an additional $90,000 of goods from Concerto and held $54,000 of its purchases on December 31, 20X6. Concerto sells inventory to the parent at 20 percent above cost.

Concerto also purchases inventory from Direct Sales Corporation. On January 1, 20X6, Concerto held inventory purchased from Direct Sales for $14,000, and on December 31, 20X6, it held inventory purchased from Direct Sales for $7,000. Concerto's total purchases from Direct Sales Corporation were $22,000 in 20X6. Direct Sales Corporation sells items to Concerto Company at 40 percent above cost.

During 20X6, Direct Sales paid dividends of $50,000, and Concerto paid dividends of $20,000.

Required

a. Prepare all eliminating entries needed to complete a consolidation workpaper as of December 31, 20X6.

b. Prepare a three-part consolidation workpaper as of December 31, 20X6.

P7-32 **Intercorporate Transfers of Inventory and Equipment**

Block Corporation was created on January 1, 20X0, to develop computer software. On January 1, 20X5, Foster Company purchased 90 percent of Block's common stock at underlying book value. Trial balances for Foster and Block on December 31, 20X9, are as follows:

	20X9 Trial Balance Data			
	Foster Company		**Block Corporation**	
Item	Debit	Credit	Debit	Credit
Cash	$ 187,000		$ 57,400	
Accounts Receivable	80,000		90,000	
Other Receivables	40,000		10,000	
Inventory	137,000		130,000	
Land	80,000		60,000	
Buildings and Equipment	500,000		250,000	
Investment in Block Corporation Stock	238,500			
Cost of Goods Sold	593,000		270,000	
Depreciation Expense	45,000		15,000	
Other Expenses	95,000		75,000	
Dividends Declared	40,000		20,000	
Accumulated Depreciation		$ 155,000		$ 75,000
Accounts Payable		63,000		35,000
Other Payables		95,000		20,000
Bonds Payable		250,000		200,000
Bond Premium				2,400
Common Stock		210,000		50,000
Additional Paid-In Capital		110,000		
Retained Earnings		248,500		165,000
Sales		815,000		415,000
Other Income		26,000		15,000
Income from Subsidiary		63,000		
Total	$2,035,500	$2,035,500	$977,400	$977,400

On January 1, 20X7, Block sold equipment to Foster for $48,000. Block had purchased the equipment for $90,000 on January 1, 20X5; it was depreciated on a straight-line basis with an expected life of 10 years and no anticipated scrap value. The equipment's total expected life is unchanged as a result of the intercompany transfer.

During 20X9, Block produced inventory for $20,000 and sold it to Foster for $30,000. Foster resold 60 percent of the inventory in 20X9. Also in 20X9, Foster sold inventory purchased from Block in 20X8. It had cost Block $60,000 to produce the inventory, and Foster purchased it for $75,000.

Required

a. What amount of cost of goods sold will be reported in the 20X9 consolidated income statement?

b. What inventory balance will be reported in the December 31, 20X9, consolidated balance sheet?

c. What amount of income will be assigned to noncontrolling shareholders in the 20X9 consolidated income statement?

d. What amount will be assigned to noncontrolling interest in the consolidated balance sheet prepared at December 31, 20X9?

e. What amount of retained earnings will be reported in the consolidated balance sheet at December 31, 20X9?

f. Give all eliminating entries required to prepare a three-part consolidation workpaper at December 31, 20X9.

g. Prepare a three-part consolidation workpaper at December 31, 20X9.

P7-33   Consolidated Balance Sheet Workpaper [AICPA Adapted]

The December 31, 20X6, condensed balance sheets of Pine Corporation and its 90 percent owned subsidiary, Slim Corporation, are presented in the accompanying worksheet.

Additional Information:

- Pine's investment in Slim was purchased for $1,200,000 cash on January 1, 20X6, and is accounted for by the basic equity method.

- At January 1, 20X6, Slim's retained earnings amounted to $600,000, and its common stock amounted to $200,000.

- Slim declared a $1,000 cash dividend in December 20X6, payable in January 20X7.

- As of December 31, 20X6, Pine had not recorded any portion of Slim's 20X6 net income or dividend declaration.

- Slim borrowed $100,000 from Pine on June 30, 20X6, with the note maturing on June 30, 20X7, at 10 percent interest. Correct accruals have been recorded by both companies.

- During 20X6, Pine sold merchandise to Slim at an aggregate invoice price of $300,000, which included a profit of $60,000. At December 31, 20X6, Slim had not paid Pine for $90,000 of these purchases, and 5 percent of the total merchandise purchased from Pine still remained in Slim's inventory.

- Pine's excess cost over book value of its investment in Slim has appropriately been identified as goodwill. At December 31, 20X6, Pine's management reviewed the amount attributed to goodwill and found no evidence of impairment.

Required

Complete the accompanying workpaper for Pine and its subsidiary, Slim, at December 31, 20X6.

PINE CORPORATION AND SUBSIDIARY
Consolidated Balance Sheet Workpaper
December 31, 20X6

	Pine Corporation	Slim Corporation	Adjustments and Eliminations Debit	Adjustments and Eliminations Credit	Consolidated
Assets					
Cash	75,000	15,000			
Accounts and Other Current Receivables	410,000	120,000			
Merchandise Inventory	920,000	670,000			
Plant and Equipment, Net	1,000,000	400,000			
Investment in Slim	1,200,000				
Totals	3,605,000	1,205,000			
Liabilities and Stockholders' Equity:					
Accounts Payable and Other Current Liabilities	140,000	305,000			
Common Stock ($10 par)	500,000	200,000			
Retained Earnings	2,965,000	700,000			
Totals	3,605,000	1,205,000			

P7-34   Comprehensive Worksheet Problem

Randall Corporation acquired 80 percent of Sharp Company's voting shares on January 1, 20X4, for $280,000 in cash and marketable securities. At acquisition, Sharp reported net assets of $300,000. Trial balances for the two companies on December 31, 20X7, are as follows:

	Randall Corporation		Sharp Company	
Item	Debit	Credit	Debit	Credit
Cash	$ 130,300		$ 10,000	
Accounts Receivable	80,000		70,000	
Inventory	170,000		110,000	
Buildings and Equipment	600,000		400,000	
Investment in Sharp Company Stock	304,000			
Cost of Goods Sold	416,000		202,000	
Depreciation and Amortization	30,000		20,000	
Other Expenses	24,000		18,000	
Dividends Declared	50,000		25,000	
Accumulated Depreciation		$ 310,000		$120,000
Accounts Payable		100,000		15,200
Bonds Payable		300,000		100,000
Bond Premium				4,800
Common Stock		200,000		100,000
Additional Paid-In Capital				20,000
Retained Earnings		345,900		215,000
Sales		500,000		250,000
Other Income		20,400		30,000
Income from Subsidiary		28,000		
	$1,804,300	$1,804,300	$855,000	$855,000

Additional Information

a. The purchase differential is appropriately assigned to buildings and equipment that had a remaining 10-year economic life at the date of combination.

b. Randall and Sharp regularly purchase inventory from each other. During 20X6, Sharp sold inventory costing $40,000 to Randall Corporation for $60,000, and Randall resold 60 percent of the inventory in 20X6 and 40 percent in 20X7. Also in 20X6, Randall sold inventory costing $20,000 to Sharp for $26,000. Sharp resold two-thirds of the inventory in 20X6 and one-third in 20X7.

c. During 20X7, Sharp sold inventory costing $30,000 to Randall for $45,000, and Randall sold items purchased for $9,000 to Sharp for $12,000. Before the end of the year, Randall resold one-third of the inventory it purchased from Sharp in 20X7. Sharp continues to hold all the units purchased from Randall during 20X7.

d. Randall sold equipment originally purchased for $75,000 to Sharp for $50,000 on December 31, 20X5. Accumulated depreciation over the 12 years of use before the intercorporate sale was $45,000. The estimated remaining life at the time of transfer was eight years. Straight-line depreciation is used by both companies.

e. Sharp owes Randall $10,000 on account on December 31, 20X7.

Required

a. Prepare the 20X7 journal entries recorded on Randall's books related to its investment in Sharp if Randall uses the basic equity method.

b. Prepare all eliminating entries needed to complete a consolidation workpaper as of December 31, 20X7.

c. Prepare a three-part consolidation workpaper as of December 31, 20X7.

d. Prepare, in good form, a consolidated income statement, balance sheet, and retained earnings statement for 20X7.

P7-35 **Comprehensive Consolidation Workpaper; Equity Method [AICPA Adapted]**

Fran Corporation acquired all outstanding $10 par value voting common stock of Brey Inc. on January 1, 20X9, in exchange for 25,000 shares of its $20 par value voting common stock. On December 31, 20X8, Fran's common stock had a closing market price of $30 per share on a national stock exchange. The acquisition was appropriately accounted for as a purchase. Both companies continued to operate as separate business entities maintaining separate accounting records with years ending December 31. Fran accounts for its investment in Brey stock using the equity method without adjusting for unrealized intercompany profits.

On December 31, 20X9, the companies had condensed financial statements as follows:

	Fran Corporation		Brey Inc.	
	Dr	(Cr)	Dr	(Cr)
Income Statement				
Net Sales		$(3,800,000)		$(1,500,000)
Equity in Brey's Income		(181,000)		
Gain on Sale of Warehouse		(30,000)		
Cost of Goods Sold	2,360,000		870,000	
Operating Expenses (including depreciation)	1,100,000		440,000	
Net Income		$ (551,000)		$ (190,000)
Retained Earnings Statement				
Balance, 1/1/X9		$ (440,000)		$ (156,000)
Net Income		(551,000)		(190,000)
Dividends Paid			40,000	
Balance, 12/31/X9		$ (991,000)		$ (306,000)
Balance Sheet				
Assets:				
Cash	$ 570,000		$ 150,000	
Accounts Receivable (net)	860,000		350,000	
Inventories	1,060,000		410,000	
Land, Plant, and Equipment	1,320,000		680,000	
Accumulated Depreciation	(370,000)		(210,000)	
Investment in Brey	891,000			
Total Assets	$ 4,331,000		$ 1,380,000	
Liabilities and Stockholders' Equity:				
Accounts Payable and Accrued Expenses		$(1,340,000)		$ (594,000)
Common Stock		(1,700,000)		(400,000)
Additional Paid-In Capital		(300,000)		(80,000)
Retained Earnings		(991,000)		(306,000)
Total Liabilities and Equity		$(4,331,000)		$(1,380,000)

Additional Information

There were no changes in the Common Stock and Additional Paid-In Capital accounts during 20X9 except the one necessitated by Fran's acquisition of Brey.

At the acquisition date, the fair value of Brey's machinery exceeded its book value by $54,000. The excess cost will be amortized over the estimated average remaining life of six years. The fair values of all of Brey's other assets and liabilities were equal to their book values. At December 31, 20X9, Fran's management reviewed the amount attributed to goodwill as a result of its purchase of Brey's common stock and concluded an impairment loss of $35,000 should be recognized in 20X9.

On July 1, 20X9, Fran sold a warehouse facility to Brey for $129,000 cash. At the date of sale, Fran's book values were $33,000 for the land and $66,000 for the undepreciated cost of the building.

Based on a real estate appraisal, Brey allocated $43,000 of the purchase price to the land and $86,000 to the building. Brey is depreciating the building over its estimated five-year remaining useful life by the straight-line method with no salvage value.

During 20X9, Fran purchased merchandise from Brey at an aggregate invoice price of $180,000, which included a 100 percent markup on Brey's cost. At December 31, 20X9, Fran owed Brey $86,000 on these purchases, and $36,000 of this merchandise remained in Fran's inventory.

Required

Develop and complete a consolidation workpaper that would be used to prepare a consolidated income statement and a consolidated retained earnings statement for the year ended December 31, 20X9, and a consolidated balance sheet as of December 31, 20X9. List the accounts in the workpaper in the same order as they are listed in the financial statements provided. Formal consolidated statements are not required. Ignore income tax considerations. Supporting computations should be in good form.

P7-36A **Fully Adjusted Equity Method**

On December 31, 20X7, Randall Corporation recorded the following entry on its books to adjust from the basic equity method to the fully adjusted equity method for its investment in Sharp Company stock:

Retained Earnings	25,900	
Income from Subsidiary	100	
Investment in Sharp Company Stock		26,000

Required

a. Adjust the data reported by Randall in the trial balance contained in Problem P7-34 for the effects of the preceding adjusting entry.

b. Prepare the journal entries that would have been recorded on Randall's books during 20X7 under the fully adjusted equity method.

c. Prepare all eliminating entries needed to complete a consolidation workpaper at December 31, 20X7, assuming Randall has used the fully adjusted equity method.

d. Complete a three-part consolidation workpaper as of December 31, 20X7.

P7-37A **Cost Method**

The trial balance data presented in Problem P7-34 can be converted to reflect use of the cost method by inserting the following amounts in place of those presented for Randall Corporation:

Investment in Sharp Company Stock	$280,000
Retained Earnings	329,900
Income from Subsidiary	-0-
Dividend Income	20,000

Required

a. Prepare the journal entries that would have been recorded on Randall's books during 20X7 under the cost method.

b. Prepare all eliminating entries needed to complete a consolidation workpaper as of December 31, 20X7, assuming Randall uses the cost method.

c. Complete a three-part consolidation workpaper as of December 31, 20X7.

Intercompany Indebtedness

One advantage of having control over other companies is that management has the ability to transfer resources from one legal entity to another as needed by the individual companies. Companies often find it beneficial to lend excess funds to affiliates and to borrow from affiliates when cash shortages arise. The borrower often benefits from lower borrowing rates, less restrictive credit terms, and the informality and lower debt issue costs of intercompany borrowing relative to public debt offerings. The lending affiliate may benefit by being able to invest excess funds in a company about which it has considerable knowledge, perhaps allowing it to earn a given return on the funds invested while incurring less risk than if it invested in unrelated companies. Also, the combined entity may find it advantageous for the parent company or another affiliate to borrow funds for the entire enterprise rather than having each affiliate going directly to the capital markets.

CONSOLIDATION OVERVIEW

Figure 8–1 illustrates two types of intercompany debt transfers. A **direct intercompany debt transfer** involves a loan from one affiliate to another without the participation of an unrelated party, as in Figure 8–1(*a*). Examples include a trade receivable/payable arising from an intercompany sale of inventory on credit and the issuance of a note payable by one affiliate to another in exchange for operating funds.

An **indirect intercompany debt transfer** involves the issuance of debt to an unrelated party and the subsequent purchase of the debt instrument by an affiliate of the issuer. For example, in Figure 8–1(*b*), Special Foods borrows funds by issuing a debt instrument, such as a note or a bond, to Nonaffiliated Corporation. The debt instrument subsequently is purchased from Nonaffiliated Corporation by Special Foods' parent, Peerless Products. Thus, Peerless Products acquires the debt of Special Foods indirectly through Nonaffiliated Corporation.

All account balances arising from intercorporate financing arrangements must be eliminated when consolidated statements are prepared. The consolidated financial statements portray the consolidated entity as a single company. Therefore, in Figure 8–1, transactions that do not cross the boundary of the consolidated entity are not reported in the consolidated financial statements. Although in illustration (*a*) Special Foods borrows funds from Peerless, the consolidated entity as a whole does not borrow, and the intercompany loan is not reflected in the consolidated financial statements.

In illustration (*b*), Special Foods borrows funds from Nonaffiliated Corporation. Because this transaction is with an unrelated party and crosses the boundary of the consolidated entity, it is reflected in the consolidated financial statements. In effect, the consolidated entity is borrowing from an outside party, and the liability is included in the consolidated balance sheet. When Peerless purchases Special Foods' debt instrument from Nonaffiliated, this transaction also crosses the boundary of the consolidated entity. In effect, the consolidated entity repurchases its debt and needs to report the purchase as a debt retirement. As with

FIGURE 8–1 Intercompany Debt Transactions

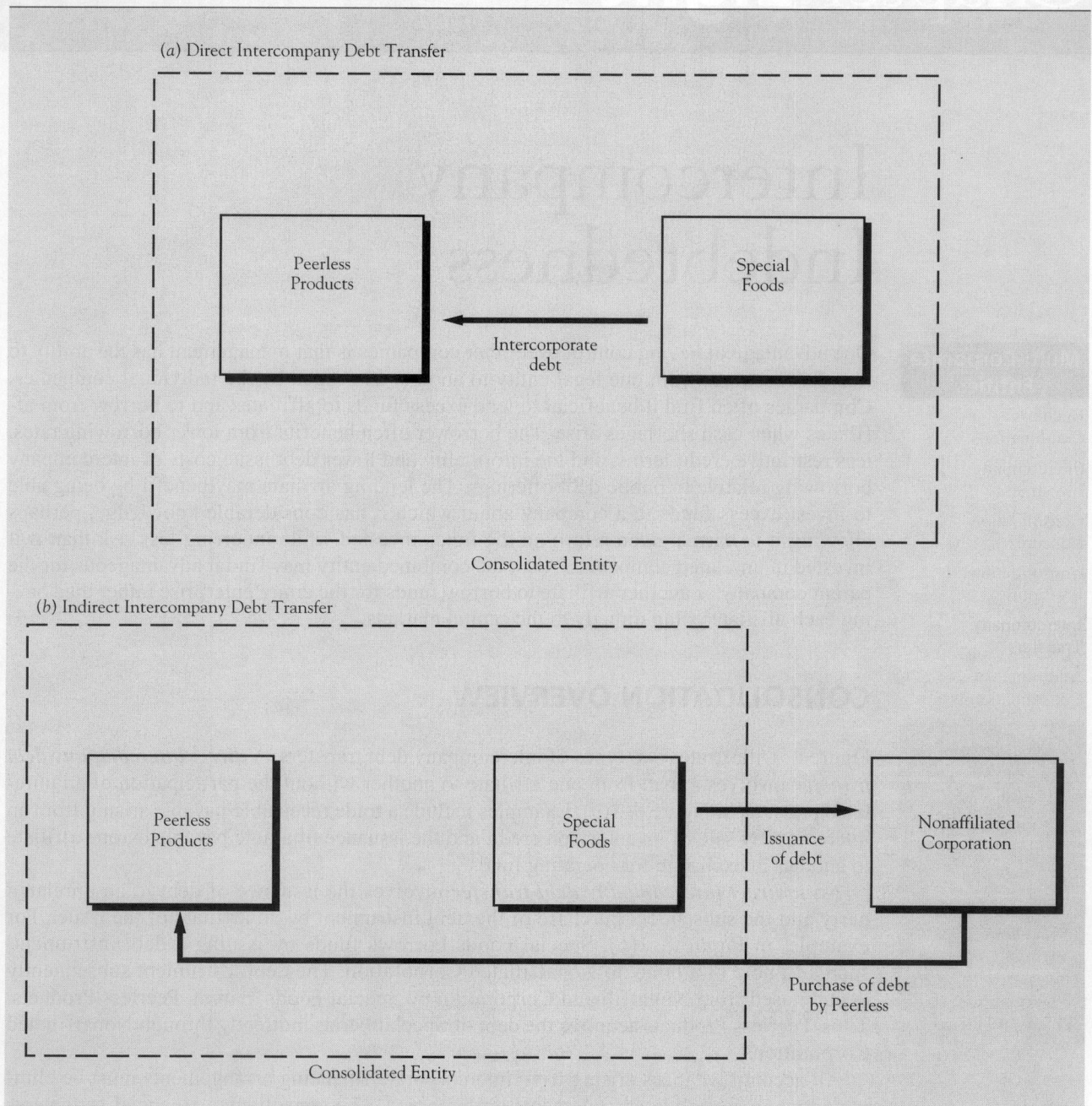

(a) Direct Intercompany Debt Transfer

Peerless Products

Special Foods

Intercorporate debt

Consolidated Entity

(b) Indirect Intercompany Debt Transfer

Peerless Products

Special Foods

Nonaffiliated Corporation

Issuance of debt

Purchase of debt by Peerless

Consolidated Entity

most retirements of debt before maturity, a purchase of an affiliate's bonds usually gives rise to a gain or loss on the retirement; the gain or loss is reported in the consolidated income statement even though it does not appear in the separate income statement of either affiliate.

This chapter discusses the procedures used to prepare consolidated financial statements when intercorporate indebtedness arises from either direct or indirect debt transfers. Although the discussion focuses on bonds, the same concepts and procedures also apply to notes and other types of intercorporate indebtedness.

BOND SALE DIRECTLY TO AN AFFILIATE

When one company sells bonds directly to an affiliate, all effects of the intercompany indebtedness must be eliminated in preparing consolidated financial statements. A company cannot report an investment in its own bonds or a bond liability to itself. Thus, when the consolidated entity is viewed as a single company, all amounts associated with the intercorporate indebtedness must be eliminated, including the investment in bonds, the bonds payable, any unamortized discount or premium on the bonds, the interest income and expense on the bonds, and any accrued interest receivable and payable.

Transfer at Par Value

When a note or bond payable is sold directly to an affiliate at par value, the entries recorded by the investor and the issuer should be mirror images of each other. To illustrate, assume that on January 1, 20X1, Special Foods borrows $100,000 from Peerless Products by issuing to Peerless $100,000 par value, 12 percent, 10-year bonds. This transaction is represented by Figure 8–1(*a*). During 20X1, Special Foods records interest expense on the bonds of $12,000 ($100,000 × .12), and Peerless records an equal amount of interest income.

In the preparation of consolidated financial statements for 20X1, two elimination entries are needed in the consolidation workpaper to remove the effects of the intercompany indebtedness:

E(1)	Bonds Payable	100,000	
	Investment in Special Foods Bonds		100,000
	Eliminate intercorporate bond holdings.		
E(2)	Interest Income	12,000	
	Interest Expense		12,000
	Eliminate intercompany interest.		

These entries eliminate from the consolidated statements the bond investment and associated income recorded on Peerless's books and the liability and related interest expense recorded on Special Foods' books. The resulting statements appear as if the indebtedness does not exist, which from a consolidated viewpoint it does not.

Note that these entries have no effect on consolidated net income because they reduce interest income and interest expense by the same amount. Eliminating entries E(1) and E(2) are required at the end of each period for as long as the intercorporate indebtedness continues. If any interest had accrued on the bonds at year-end, that too would have to be eliminated.

Transfer at a Discount or Premium

When the coupon or nominal interest rate on a bond is different from the yield demanded by those who lend funds, a bond sells at a discount or premium. In such cases, the amount of bond interest income or expense recorded no longer equals the cash interest payments. Instead, interest income and expense amounts are adjusted for the amortization of the discount or premium.

As an illustration of the treatment of intercompany bond transfers at other than par, assume that on January 1, 20X1, Peerless Products purchases $100,000 par value, 12 percent, 10-year bonds from Special Foods for $90,000. Interest on the bonds is payable on January 1 and July 1. The interest expense recognized by Special Foods and the interest income recognized by Peerless each year include straight-line amortization of the discount, as follows:

Cash interest ($100,000 × .12)	$12,000
Amortization of discount ($10,000 ÷ 20 semiannual interest periods) × 2 periods	1,000
Interest expense or income	$13,000

Half of these amounts are recognized in each of the two interest payment periods during a year. Although the interest method of amortization usually is required for amortizing discounts and premiums, the straight-line method is acceptable when it does not depart materially from the interest method and when transactions are between parent and subsidiary companies or between subsidiaries of a common parent.

Entries by the Debtor

Special Foods records the issuance of the bonds on January 1 at a discount of $10,000. It recognizes interest expense on July 1, when the first semiannual interest payment is made, and on December 31, when interest is accrued for the second half of the year. The amortization of the bond discount causes interest expense to be greater than the cash interest payment and causes the balance of the discount to decrease. Special Foods records the following entries related to the bonds during 20X1:

January 1, 20X1

(3)	Cash	90,000	
	Discount on Bonds Payable	10,000	
	Bonds Payable		100,000
	Issue bonds to Peerless Products.		

July 1, 20X1

(4)	Interest Expense	6,500	
	Discount on Bonds Payable		500
	Cash		6,000
	Semiannual payment of interest.		

December 31, 20X1

(5)	Interest Expense	6,500	
	Discount on Bonds Payable		500
	Interest Payable		6,000
	Accrue interest expense at year-end.		

Entries by the Bond Investor

Peerless Products records the purchase of the bonds and the interest income derived from the bonds during 20X1 with the following entries:

January 1, 20X1

(6)	Investment in Special Foods Bonds	90,000	
	Cash		90,000
	Purchase of bonds from Special Foods.		

July 1, 20X1

(7)	Cash	6,000	
	Investment in Special Foods Bonds	500	
	Interest Income		6,500
	Receive interest on bond investment.		

December 31, 20X1

(8)	Interest Receivable	6,000	
	Investment in Special Foods Bonds	500	
	Interest Income		6,500
	Accrue interest income at year-end.		

The amortization of the discount by Peerless increases interest income to an amount greater than the cash interest payment and causes the balance of the bond investment account to increase.

Elimination Entries at Year-End

The December 31, 20X1, bond-related amounts taken from the books of Peerless Products and Special Foods and the appropriate consolidated amounts are as follows:

Item	Peerless Products	Special Foods	Unadjusted Totals	Consolidated Amounts
Bonds Payable	-0-	$(100,000)	$(100,000)	-0-
Discount on Bonds Payable	-0-	9,000	9,000	-0-
Interest Payable	-0-	(6,000)	(6,000)	-0-
Investment in Bonds	$ 91,000	-0-	91,000	-0-
Interest Receivable	6,000	-0-	6,000	-0-
Interest Expense	-0-	$ 13,000	$ 13,000	-0-
Interest Income	$(13,000)	-0-	(13,000)	-0-

All account balances relating to the intercorporate bond holdings must be eliminated in the preparation of consolidated financial statements. Toward that end, the consolidation work-paper prepared on December 31, 20X1, includes the following eliminating entries related to the intercompany bond holdings:

E(9)	Bonds Payable	100,000	
	Investment in Special Foods Bonds		91,000
	Discount on Bonds Payable		9,000
	Eliminate intercorporate bond holdings.		
E(10)	Interest Income	13,000	
	Interest Expense		13,000
	Eliminate intercompany interest.		
E(11)	Interest Payable	6,000	
	Interest Receivable		6,000
	Eliminate intercompany interest receivable/payable.		

Entry E(9) eliminates the bonds payable and associated discount against the investment in bonds. The book value of the bond liability on Special Foods' books and the investment in bonds on Peerless's books will be the same so long as both companies amortize the discount in the same way.

Entry E(10) eliminates the bond interest income recognized by Peerless during 20X1 against the bond interest expense recognized by Special Foods. Because the interest for the second half of 20X1 was accrued but not paid, an intercompany receivable/payable exists at the end of the year. Entry E(11) eliminates the interest receivable against the interest payable.

Consolidation at the end of 20X2 requires elimination entries similar to those at the end of 20X1. Because $1,000 of the discount is amortized each year, the bond investment balance on Peerless's books increases to $92,000 ($90,000 + $1,000 + $1,000). Similarly, the bond discount on Special Foods' books decreases to $8,000, resulting in an effective bond liability of $92,000. The consolidation elimination entries related to the bonds at the end of 20X2 are as follows:

E(12)	Bonds Payable	100,000	
	Investment in Special Foods Bonds		92,000
	Discount on Bonds Payable		8,000
	Eliminate intercorporate bond holdings.		

E(13)	Interest Income	13,000	
	Interest Expense		13,000
	Eliminate intercompany interest.		
E(14)	Interest Payable	6,000	
	Interest Receivable		6,000
	Eliminate intercompany interest receivable/payable.		

BONDS OF AFFILIATE PURCHASED FROM A NONAFFILIATE

A more complex situation occurs when bonds that were issued to an unrelated party are acquired later by an affiliate of the issuer. From the viewpoint of the consolidated entity, an acquisition of an affiliate's bonds retires the bonds at the time they are purchased. The bonds no longer are held outside the consolidated entity once they are purchased by another company within the consolidated entity, and they must be treated as if repurchased by the debtor. Acquisition of the bonds of an affiliate by another company within the consolidated entity is referred to as **constructive retirement**. Although the bonds actually are not retired, they are treated as if they were retired in preparing consolidated financial statements.

When a constructive retirement occurs, the consolidated income statement for the period reports a gain or loss on debt retirement based on the difference between the carrying value of the bonds on the books of the debtor and the purchase price paid by the affiliate in acquiring the bonds. Neither the bonds payable nor the purchaser's investment in the bonds is reported in the consolidated balance sheet because the bonds are no longer considered outstanding.

Purchase at Book Value

In the event that a company purchases an affiliate's debt from an unrelated party at a price equal to the liability reported by the debtor, the elimination entries required in preparing the consolidated financial statements are identical to those used in eliminating a direct intercorporate debt transfer. In this case, the total of the bond liability and the related premium or discount reported by the debtor equal the balance in the investment account shown by the bondholder, and the interest income reported by the bondholder each period equals the interest expense reported by the debtor. All of these amounts need to be eliminated to avoid misstating the accounts in the consolidated financial statements.

Purchase at an Amount Less than Book Value

Continuing movement in the level of interest rates and the volatility of other factors influencing the securities markets make it unlikely that a company's bonds will sell after issuance at a price identical to their book value. When the price paid to acquire the bonds of an affiliate differs from the liability reported by the debtor, a gain or loss is reported in the consolidated income statement in the period of constructive retirement. In addition, the bond interest income and interest expense reported by the two affiliates subsequent to the purchase must be eliminated in preparing consolidated statements. Interest income reported by the investing affiliate and interest expense reported by the debtor are not equal in this case because of the different bond carrying amounts on the books of the two companies. The difference in the bond carrying amounts is reflected in the amortization of the discount or premium and, in turn, causes interest income and expense to differ.

As an example of consolidation following the purchase of an affiliate's bonds at less than book value, assume that Peerless Products Corporation purchases 80 percent of the common stock of Special Foods Inc. on December 31, 20X0, for its underlying book value of $240,000. In addition, the following conditions occur:

1. On January 1, 20X1, Special Foods issues 10-year, 12 percent bonds payable with a par value of $100,000; the bonds are issued at 102. Nonaffiliated Corporation purchases the bonds from Special Foods.

2. The bonds pay interest on June 30 and December 31.

3. Both Peerless Products and Special Foods amortize bond discount and premium using the straight-line method.

4. On December 31, 20X1, Peerless Products purchases the bonds from Nonaffiliated for $91,000.

5. Special Foods reports net income of $50,000 for 20X1 and $75,000 for 20X2. Special Foods declares dividends of $30,000 in 20X1 and $40,000 in 20X2.

6. Peerless earns $140,000 in 20X1 and $160,000 in 20X2 from its own separate operations. Peerless declares dividends of $60,000 in both 20X1 and 20X2.

The bond transactions of Special Foods and Peerless appear as follows:

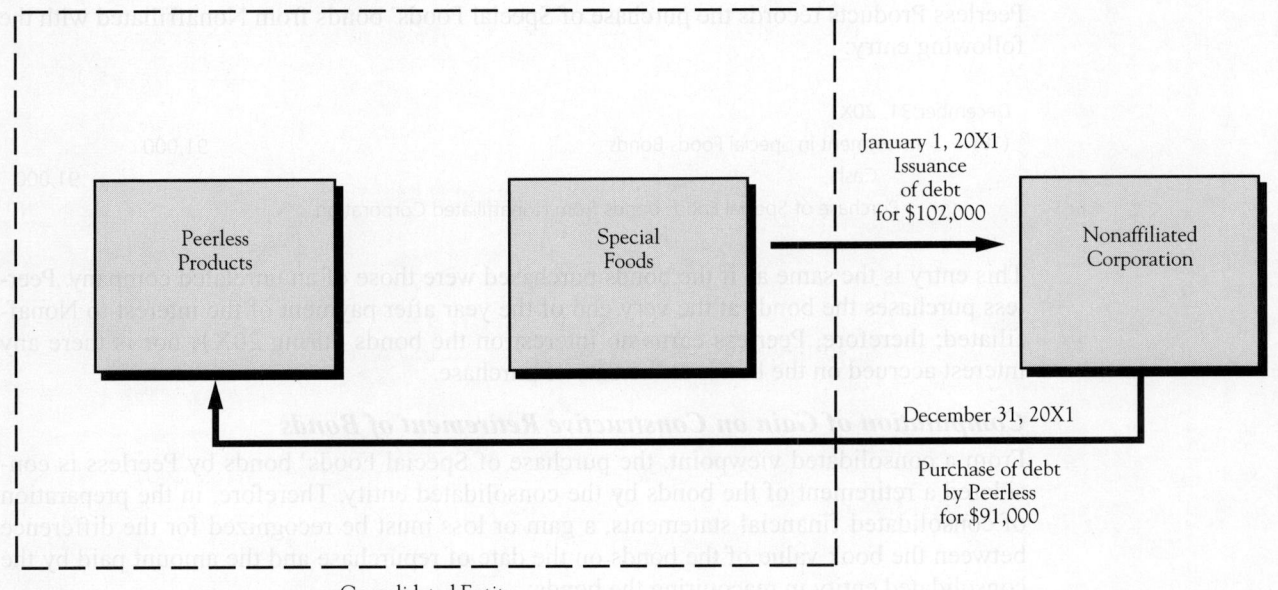

Bond Liability Entries—20X1

Special Foods records the following entries related to its bonds during 20X1:

January 1, 20X1			
(15)	Cash	102,000	
	Bonds Payable		100,000
	Premium on Bonds Payable		2,000
	Sale of bonds to Nonaffiliated.		
June 30, 20X1			
(16)	Interest Expense	5,900	
	Premium on Bonds Payable	100	
	Cash		6,000
	Semiannual payment of interest:		
	$5,900 = $6,000 − $100		
	$100 = $2,000 ÷ 20 interest periods		
	$6,000 = $100,000 × .12 × 6/12		
December 31, 20X1			
(17)	Interest Expense	5,900	
	Premium on Bonds Payable	100	
	Cash		6,000
	Semiannual payment of interest.		

Entry (15) records the issuance of the bonds to Nonaffiliated Corporation for $102,000. Entries (16) and (17) record the payment of interest and the amortization of the bond premium at each of the two interest payment dates during 20X1. Total interest expense for 20X1 is $11,800 ($5,900 × 2), and the book value of the bonds on December 31, 20X1, is as follows:

Book value of bonds at issuance	$102,000
Amortization of premium, 20X1	(200)
Book value of bonds, December 31, 20X1	$101,800

Bond Investment Entries—20X1

Peerless Products records the purchase of Special Foods' bonds from Nonaffiliated with the following entry:

December 31, 20X1

(18)	Investment in Special Foods Bonds	91,000	
	Cash		91,000
	Purchase of Special Foods bonds from Nonaffiliated Corporation.		

This entry is the same as if the bonds purchased were those of an unrelated company. Peerless purchases the bonds at the very end of the year after payment of the interest to Nonaffiliated; therefore, Peerless earns no interest on the bonds during 20X1, nor is there any interest accrued on the bonds at the date of purchase.

Computation of Gain on Constructive Retirement of Bonds

From a consolidated viewpoint, the purchase of Special Foods' bonds by Peerless is considered a retirement of the bonds by the consolidated entity. Therefore, in the preparation of consolidated financial statements, a gain or loss must be recognized for the difference between the book value of the bonds on the date of repurchase and the amount paid by the consolidated entity in reacquiring the bonds:

Book value of Special Foods' bonds, December 31, 20X1	$101,800
Price paid by Peerless to purchase bonds	(91,000)
Gain on constructive retirement of bonds	$ 10,800

This gain is included in the consolidated income statement as a gain on the retirement of bonds.

Assignment of Gain on Constructive Retirement

Four approaches have been used in practice for assigning the gain or loss on the constructive retirement of the bonds of an affiliate to the shareholders of the participating companies. Depending upon the method selected, the gain or loss may be assigned to any of the following:

1. The affiliate issuing the bonds.
2. The affiliate purchasing the bonds.
3. The parent company.
4. The issuing and purchasing companies, based on the difference between the carrying amounts of the bonds on their books at the date of purchase and the par value of the bonds.

No compelling reasons seem to exist for choosing one of these methods over the others, and in practice the choice often is based on expediency and lack of materiality. The FASB's approach is to assign the gain or loss to the issuing company. In previous chapters, gains and losses on intercompany transactions were viewed as accruing to the shareholders of the selling affiliate. When this approach is applied in the case of intercorporate debt transactions, gains and losses arising from the intercompany debt transactions are viewed as accruing to the shareholders of the selling or issuing affiliate. In effect, the purchasing affiliate is viewed as acting on behalf of the issuing affiliate by acquiring the bonds.

An important difference exists between the intercompany gains and losses discussed in previous chapters and the gains and losses arising from intercorporate debt transactions. Gains and losses from intercorporate transfers of assets are recognized by the individual affiliates and are eliminated in consolidation. Gains and losses from intercorporate debt transactions are not recognized by the individual affiliates but must be included in consolidation.

When the subsidiary is the issuing affiliate, the gain or loss on constructive retirement of the bonds is viewed as accruing to the subsidiary's shareholders. Thus, the gain or loss is apportioned between consolidated net income and the noncontrolling interest based on the relative ownership interests in the common stock. If the parent is the issuing affiliate, the entire gain or loss on the constructive retirement accrues to the controlling interest, and none is apportioned to the noncontrolling interest.

As a result of the interest income and expense entries recorded annually by the companies involved, the constructive gain or loss is recognized over the remaining term of the bond issue; accordingly, the total amount of the unrecognized gain or loss decreases each period and is fully amortized at the time the bond matures. Thus, no permanent gain or loss is assigned to the debtor company's shareholders.

Basic Equity-Method Entries—20X1

In addition to recording the bond investment with entry (18), Peerless records the following basic equity-method entries during 20X1 to account for its investment in Special Foods stock:

(19)	Cash	24,000	
	Investment in Special Foods Stock		24,000
	Record dividends from Special Foods:		
	$30,000 \times .80$		

(20)	Investment in Special Foods Stock	40,000	
	Income from Subsidiary		40,000
	Record equity-method income:		
	$50,000 \times .80$		

These entries result in a $256,000 balance in the investment account at the end of 20X1.

Consolidation Workpaper—20X1

The December 31, 20X1, workpaper to prepare consolidated financial statements for Peerless Products and Special Foods is presented in Figure 8–2. The following eliminating entries are included in the workpaper:

E(21)	Income from Subsidiary	40,000	
	Dividends Declared		24,000
	Investment in Special Foods Stock		16,000
	Eliminate income from subsidiary.		
E(22)	Income to Noncontrolling Interest	12,160	
	Dividends Declared		6,000
	Noncontrolling Interest		6,160
	Assign income to noncontrolling interest:		
	$12,160 = (\$50,000 + \$10,800) \times .20$		

FIGURE 8–2 December 31, 20X1, Consolidation Workpaper; Repurchase of Bonds at Less than Book Value

Item	Peerless Products	Special Foods	Eliminations Debit	Eliminations Credit	Consolidated
Sales	400,000	200,000			600,000
Income from Subsidiary	40,000		(21) 40,000		
Gain on Bond Retirement				(24) 10,800	10,800
Credits	440,000	200,000			610,800
Cost of Goods Sold	170,000	115,000			285,000
Depreciation and Amortization	50,000	20,000			70,000
Other Expenses	20,000	3,200			23,200
Interest Expense	20,000	11,800			31,800
Debits	(260,000)	(150,000)			(410,000)
					200,800
Income to Noncontrolling Interest			(22) 12,160		(12,160)
Net Income, carry forward	180,000	50,000	52,160	10,800	188,640
Retained Earnings, January 1	300,000	100,000	(23) 100,000		300,000
Net Income, from above	180,000	50,000	52,160	10,800	188,640
	480,000	150,000			488,640
Dividends Declared	(60,000)	(30,000)		(21) 24,000	
				(22) 6,000	(60,000)
Retained Earnings, December 31, carry forward	420,000	120,000	152,160	40,800	428,640
Cash	173,000	76,800			249,800
Accounts Receivable	75,000	50,000			125,000
Inventory	100,000	75,000			175,000
Land	175,000	40,000			215,000
Buildings and Equipment	800,000	600,000			1,400,000
Investment in Special Foods Bonds	91,000			(24) 91,000	
Investment in Special Foods Stock	256,000			(21) 16,000	
				(23) 240,000	
Debits	1,670,000	841,800			2,164,800
Accumulated Depreciation	450,000	320,000			770,000
Accounts Payable	100,000	100,000			200,000
Bonds Payable	200,000	100,000	(24) 100,000		200,000
Premium on Bonds Payable		1,800	(24) 1,800		
Common Stock	500,000	200,000	(23) 200,000		500,000
Retained Earnings, from above	420,000	120,000	152,160	40,800	428,640
Noncontrolling Interest				(22) 6,160	
				(23) 60,000	66,160
Credits	1,670,000	841,800	453,960	453,960	2,164,800

Elimination entries:
(21) Eliminate income from subsidiary.
(22) Assign income to noncontrolling interest.
(23) Eliminate beginning investment balance.
(24) Eliminate intercompany bond holdings.

E(23)	Common Stock—Special Foods	200,000	
	Retained Earnings, January 1	100,000	
	Investment in Special Foods Stock		240,000
	Noncontrolling Interest		60,000
	Eliminate beginning investment balance.		
E(24)	Bonds Payable	100,000	
	Premium on Bonds Payable	1,800	
	Investment in Special Foods Bonds		91,000
	Gain on Bond Retirement		10,800
	Eliminate intercorporate bond holdings.		

Workpaper entry E(21) eliminates the changes in the investment account during 20X1, the parent's share of the subsidiary's net income, and the dividends recognized by Peerless during the year. Income of $12,160 is assigned to the noncontrolling interest in entry E(22), computed as follows:

Net income of Special Foods	$50,000
Gain on constructive retirement of bonds	10,800
Realized net income of Special Foods	$60,800
Noncontrolling stockholders' share	× .20
Noncontrolling interest's share of income	$12,160

The gain on the constructive retirement of the bonds is attributed to the shareholders of the issuing company, Special Foods. Therefore, a proportionate share of the gain ($10,800 × .20) is assigned to the noncontrolling interest along with a proportionate share of Special Foods' reported net income. If Peerless had been the issuing affiliate, all of the gain would be included in consolidated net income and none would be allocated to the noncontrolling interest.

Entry E(22) also eliminates the noncontrolling interest's share of Special Foods' dividends declared during 20X1 and recognizes the increase in the noncontrolling interest's claim on the subsidiary's net assets. Entry E(23) eliminates Peerless's investment account and the stockholders' equity balances of Special Foods at the beginning of the year, and it establishes in the workpaper the amount of the noncontrolling interest at the beginning of the year.

The final entry in the workpaper, E(24), eliminates the intercompany bond holdings and recognizes the gain on constructive retirement of the bonds. The appropriate consolidated balances and the amounts recorded on the books of Peerless and Special Foods are as follows:

Item	Peerless Products	Special Foods	Unadjusted Totals	Consolidated Amounts
Bonds Payable	-0-	$(100,000)	$(100,000)	-0-
Premium on Bonds Payable	-0-	(1,800)	(1,800)	-0-
Investment in Bonds	$91,000	-0-	91,000	-0-
Interest Expense	-0-	$11,800	$11,800	$11,800
Interest Income	-0-	-0-	-0-	-0-
Gain on Bond Retirement	-0-	-0-	-0-	(10,800)

Special Foods' bonds payable and Peerless's investment in Special Foods' bonds cannot appear in the consolidated balance sheet because the bond holdings involve parties totally within the single economic entity. Note that the gain recognized on the constructive retirement of the bonds does not appear on the books of either Peerless or Special Foods because the bonds still are outstanding from the perspective of the separate companies. From the viewpoint of the consolidated entity, the bonds are retired at the end of 20X1, and a gain must be entered in the consolidation workpaper so that it appears in the consolidated income statement.

No eliminations are needed with respect to interest income or interest expense in preparing the consolidated statements for December 31, 20X1. Because Peerless purchased the bonds at the end of the year, no interest income is recorded by Peerless until 20X2. The interest expense of $11,800 ($12,000 − $200) recorded by Special Foods is viewed appropriately as interest expense of the consolidated entity because the bonds were held by an unrelated party during all of 20X1.

Consolidated Net Income—20X1

Consolidated net income of $188,640 is shown in the workpaper in Figure 8–2. This amount is verified as follows:

Peerless's separate operating income		$140,000
Peerless's share of Special Foods' income:		
Special Foods' net income	$50,000	
Gain on constructive retirement of bonds	10,800	
Special Foods' realized income	$60,800	
Peerless's proportionate share	× .80	48,640
Consolidated net income, 20X1		$188,640

Consolidated net income is $8,640 higher ($10,800 × .80) than it would have been had Peerless not purchased the bonds.

Noncontrolling Interest—December 31, 20X1

Total noncontrolling interest on December 31, 20X1, includes a proportionate share of both the reported book value of Special Foods and the gain on constructive bond retirement. The balance of the noncontrolling interest on December 31, 20X1, is computed as follows:

Book value of Special Foods, December 31, 20X1:		
Common stock		$200,000
Retained earnings		120,000
Total reported book value		$320,000
Gain on constructive retirement of bonds		10,800
Realized book value of Special Foods		$330,800
Noncontrolling stockholders' share		× .20
Noncontrolling interest, December 31, 20X1		$ 66,160

Bond Liability Entries—20X2

Special Foods records interest on its bonds during 20X2 with the following entries:

June 30, 20X2			
(25)	Interest Expense	5,900	
	Premium on Bonds Payable	100	
	Cash		6,000
	Semiannual payment of interest.		
December 31, 20X2			
(26)	Interest Expense	5,900	
	Premium on Bonds Payable	100	
	Cash		6,000
	Semiannual payment of interest.		

Bond Investment Entries—20X2

Peerless Products accounts for its investment in Special Foods' bonds in the same way as if the bonds were those of a nonaffiliate. The $91,000 purchase price paid by Peerless reflects a $9,000 ($100,000 − $91,000) discount from the par value of the bonds. This discount is amortized over the nine-year remaining term of the bonds at $1,000 per year ($9,000 ÷ 9 years), or $500 per six-month interest payment period. Peerless's entries to record interest income for 20X2 are as follows:

	June 30, 20X2			
(27)	Cash		6,000	
	Investment in Special Foods Bonds		500	
		Interest Income		6,500
	Record receipt of bond interest.			

	December 31, 20X2			
(28)	Cash		6,000	
	Investment in Special Foods Bonds		500	
		Interest Income		6,500
	Record receipt of bond interest.			

This $13,000 of interest income is earned by Peerless in addition to its $160,000 of separate operating income for 20X2.

Subsequent Recognition of Gain on Constructive Retirement

In the year of the constructive bond retirement, 20X1, the entire $10,800 gain on the retirement was recognized in the consolidated income statement but not on the books of either Peerless or Special Foods. The total gain on the constructive bond retirement in 20X1 was equal to the sum of the discount on Peerless's bond investment and the premium on Special Foods' bond liability at the time of the constructive retirement:

Peerless's discount on bond investment	$ 9,000
Special Foods' premium on bond liability	1,800
Total gain on constructive retirement of bonds	$10,800

This can be visualized as in the following figure:

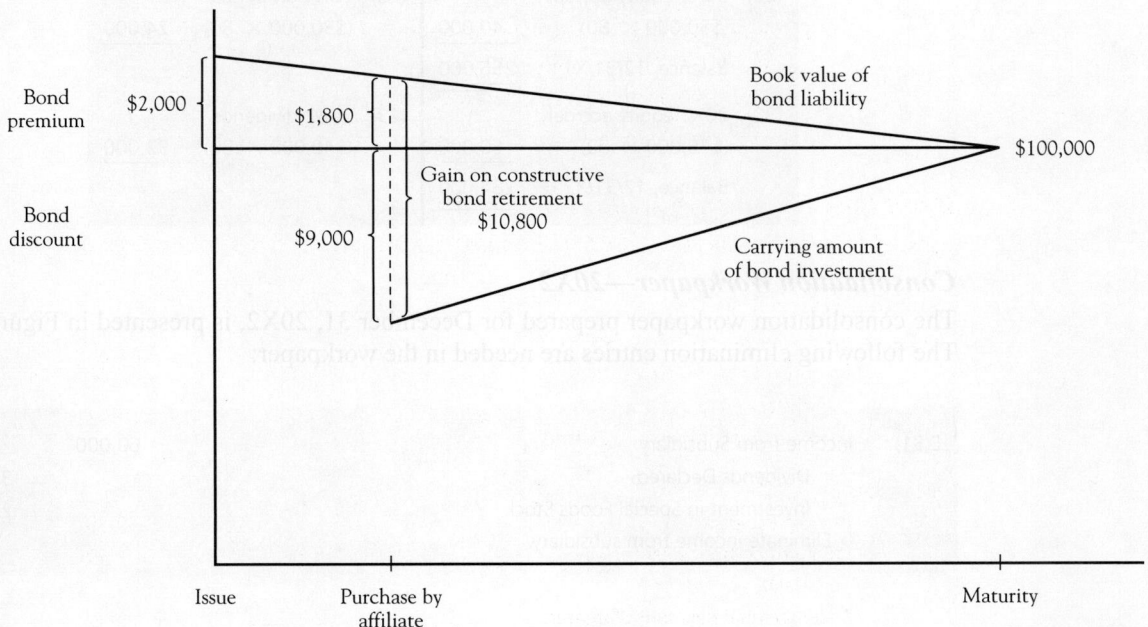

In each year subsequent to 20X1, both Peerless and Special Foods recognize a portion of the constructive gain as they amortize the discount on the bond investment and the premium on the bond liability:

Peerless's amortization of discount on bond investment ($9,000 ÷ 9 years)	$1,000
Special Foods' amortization of premium on bonds payable ($1,800 ÷ 9 years)	200
Annual increase in combined incomes of separate companies	$1,200

Thus, the $10,800 gain on constructive bond retirement, previously recognized in the consolidated income statement, is recognized on the books of Peerless and Special Foods at the rate of $1,200 each year. Over the remaining nine-year term of the bonds, Peerless and Special Foods will recognize the full $10,800 gain ($1,200 × 9).

Basic Equity-Method Entries—20X2

In addition to the entries related to its investment in Special Foods' bonds, Peerless records the following entries during 20X2 under the basic equity method:

(29)	Cash	32,000	
	Investment in Special Foods Stock		32,000
	Record dividends from Special Foods:		
	$40,000 × .80		
(30)	Investment in Special Foods Stock	60,000	
	Income from Subsidiary		60,000
	Record equity-method income:		
	$75,000 × .80		

Investment Account—20X2

At the end of 20X2, Peerless's account for its investment in the common stock of Special Foods appears as follows:

Investment in Special Foods Stock					
	Original cost	240,000			
(20)	20X1 equity accrual		(19)	20X1 dividends	
	($50,000 × .80)	40,000		($30,000 × .80)	24,000
	Balance, 12/31/X1	256,000			
(30)	20X2 equity accrual		(29)	20X2 dividends	
	($75,000 × .80)	60,000		($40,000 × .80)	32,000
	Balance, 12/31/X2	284,000			

Consolidation Workpaper—20X2

The consolidation workpaper prepared for December 31, 20X2, is presented in Figure 8–3. The following elimination entries are needed in the workpaper:

E(31)	Income from Subsidiary	60,000	
	Dividends Declared		32,000
	Investment in Special Foods Stock		28,000
	Eliminate income from subsidiary.		

FIGURE 8–3 December 31, 20X2, Consolidation Workpaper; Next Year following Repurchase of Bonds at Less than Book Value

Item	Peerless Products	Special Foods	Eliminations Debit	Eliminations Credit	Consolidated
Sales	450,000	300,000			750,000
Interest Income	13,000		(34) 13,000		
Income from Subsidiary	60,000		(31) 60,000		
Credits	523,000	300,000			750,000
Cost of Goods Sold	180,000	160,000			340,000
Depreciation and Amortization	50,000	20,000			70,000
Other Expenses	40,000	33,200			73,200
Interest Expense	20,000	11,800		(34) 11,800	20,000
Debits	(290,000)	(225,000)			(503,200)
					246,800
Income to Noncontrolling Interest			(32) 14,760		(14,760)
Net Income, carry forward	233,000	75,000	87,760	11,800	232,040
Retained Earnings, January 1	420,000	120,000	(33) 120,000	(34) 8,640	428,640
Net Income, from above	233,000	75,000	87,760	11,800	232,040
	653,000	195,000			660,680
Dividends Declared	(60,000)	(40,000)		(31) 32,000	
				(32) 8,000	(60,000)
Retained Earnings, December 31, carry forward	593,000	155,000	207,760	60,440	600,680
Cash	212,000	86,600			298,600
Accounts Receivable	150,000	80,000			230,000
Inventory	180,000	90,000			270,000
Land	175,000	40,000			215,000
Buildings and Equipment	800,000	600,000			1,400,000
Investment in Special Foods Bonds	92,000			(34) 92,000	
Investment in Special Foods Stock	284,000			(31) 28,000	
				(33) 256,000	
Debits	1,893,000	896,600			2,413,600
Accumulated Depreciation	500,000	340,000			840,000
Accounts Payable	100,000	100,000			200,000
Bonds Payable	200,000	100,000	(34) 100,000		200,000
Premium on Bonds Payable		1,600	(34) 1,600		
Common Stock	500,000	200,000	(33) 200,000		500,000
Retained Earnings, from above	593,000	155,000	207,760	60,440	600,680
Noncontrolling Interest				(32) 6,760	
				(33) 64,000	
				(34) 2,160	72,920
Credits	1,893,000	896,600	509,360	509,360	2,413,600

Elimination entries:
(31) Eliminate income from subsidiary.
(32) Assign income to noncontrolling interest.
(33) Eliminate beginning investment balance.
(34) Eliminate intercompany bond holdings.

E(32)	Income to Noncontrolling Interest	14,760	
	Dividends Declared		8,000
	Noncontrolling Interest		6,760
	Assign income to noncontrolling interest:		
	$14,760 = ($75,000 − $1,200) × .20		
E(33)	Common Stock—Special Foods	200,000	
	Retained Earnings, January 1	120,000	
	Investment in Special Foods Stock		256,000
	Noncontrolling Interest		64,000
	Eliminate beginning investment balance.		
E(34)	Bonds Payable	100,000	
	Premium on Bonds Payable	1,600	
	Interest Income	13,000	
	Investment in Special Foods Bonds		92,000
	Interest Expense		11,800
	Retained Earnings, January 1		8,640
	Noncontrolling Interest		2,160
	Eliminate intercorporate bond holdings:		
	$1,600 = $2,000 − $200 − $200		
	$13,000 = ($100,000 × .12) + $1,000		
	$92,000 = $91,000 + $1,000		
	$11,800 = ($100,000 × .12) − $200		
	$8,640 = $10,800 × .80		
	$2,160 = $10,800 × .20		

Entry E(31) eliminates the net effect of the 20X2 equity-method entries recorded on Peerless's books. Entry E(32) assigns income to the noncontrolling interest, as follows:

Net income of Special Foods, 20X2	$75,000
Less: 20X1 gain on constructive retirement of debt recognized in 20X2 by affiliates:	
Amortization of Peerless's bond discount	(1,000)
Amortization of Special Foods' bond premium	(200)
Income as a basis for apportionment	$73,800
Noncontrolling interest's proportionate share	× .20
Noncontrolling interest's share of income	$14,760

In 20X1, the gain on the constructive retirement of the bonds was included in consolidated net income and in the computation of income assigned to noncontrolling shareholders. As the gain is recognized on the books of the two affiliates through their amortization of the bond discount and premium, its effect must be eliminated from consolidated net income and from the amount of income assigned to the noncontrolling interest in entry E(32).

Entry E(33) is the normal entry to eliminate the 20X2 beginning balances of Special Foods' stockholders' equity accounts and the beginning balance of Peerless's Investment in Special Foods Stock account and to establish the amount of the noncontrolling interest at the beginning of 20X2. Entry E(33) establishes the beginning amount of the noncontrolling interest as if there were no constructive gain. The entries to the investment account and to noncontrolling interest are based on each shareholder group's proportionate share of the book value of Special Foods at the beginning of the period:

Book value of Special Foods, January 1, 20X2:	
Common stock	$200,000
Retained earnings	120,000
Total book value	$320,000
Controlling interest's share of book value ($320,000 × .80)	$256,000
Noncontrolling interest's share of book value ($320,000 × .20)	64,000
Total assigned	$320,000

The impact of the constructive gain on the beginning noncontrolling interest balance and on the beginning consolidated retained earnings balance is reflected in entry E(34) in the workpaper. Entry E(34) increases the beginning balance of consolidated retained earnings by Peerless's $8,640 share ($10,800 × .80) of the gain on constructive retirement of the bonds that has not been recorded on the books of the affiliates as of the beginning of the period. Similarly, the noncontrolling interest is increased by its $2,160 proportionate share ($10,800 × .20) of the unrecorded gain. Because the gain on constructive retirement of the bonds was recognized in the 20X1 consolidated income statement but not on the separate books of Peerless and Special Foods, the beginning balances of consolidated retained earnings and the noncontrolling interest will be understated unless the gain amount is added into the workpaper in 20X2 and apportioned to each.

Entry E(34) also eliminates all aspects of the intercorporate bond holdings, including (1) Peerless's investment in bonds, (2) Special Foods' bonds payable and the associated premium, (3) Peerless's bond interest income, and (4) Special Foods' bond interest expense. The amounts related to the bonds from the books of Peerless and Special Foods and the appropriate consolidated amounts are as follows:

Item	Peerless Products	Special Foods	Unadjusted Totals	Consolidated Amounts
Bonds Payable	-0-	$(100,000)	$(100,000)	-0-
Premium on Bonds Payable	-0-	(1,600)	(1,600)	-0-
Investment in Bonds	$ 92,000	-0-	92,000	-0-
Interest Expense	-0-	$ 11,800	$ 11,800	-0-
Interest Income	$(13,000)	-0-	(13,000)	-0-

All balances related to the intercompany bond holdings are eliminated in entry E(34) so that none of the unadjusted totals appear in the consolidated financial statements.

Consolidated Net Income—20X2

Consolidated net income of $232,040 is shown in the workpaper in Figure 8–3. This amount is verified as follows:

Peerless's separate income		$173,000
Peerless's share of Special Foods' income:		
Special Foods' net income	$75,000	
Peerless's amortization of bond discount	(1,000)	
Special Foods' amortization of bond premium	(200)	
Income as a basis for apportionment	$73,800	
Peerless's proportionate share	× .80	59,040
Consolidated net income, 20X2		$232,040

Noncontrolling Interest—December 31, 20X2

Total noncontrolling interest on December 31, 20X2, includes a proportionate share of both the reported book value of Special Foods and the portion of the gain on constructive bond retirement not yet recognized by the affiliates:

Book value of Special Foods, December 31, 20X2:		
Common stock		$200,000
Retained earnings		155,000
Total book value		$355,000
Gain on constructive retirement of bonds	$10,800	
Less: Portion recognized by affiliates during 20X2	(1,200)	
Constructive gain not yet recognized by affiliates		9,600
Realized book value of Special Foods		$364,600
Noncontrolling stockholders' share		× .20
Noncontrolling interest, December 31, 20X2		$ 72,920

Bond Elimination Entry in Subsequent Years

In years after 20X2, the workpaper entry to eliminate the intercompany bonds and to adjust for the gain on constructive retirement of the bonds is similar to entry E(34). The unamortized bond discount and premium decrease each year by $1,000 and $200, respectively. As of the beginning of 20X3, $9,600 of the gain on the constructive retirement of the bonds remains unrecognized by the affiliates, computed as follows:

Gain on constructive retirement of bonds		$10,800
Less: Portion recognized by affiliates during 20X2:		
Peerless's amortization of bond discount	$1,000	
Special Foods' amortization of bond premium	200	
Total gain recognized by affiliates		(1,200)
Unrecognized gain on constructive retirement of bonds, January 1, 20X3		$ 9,600

In the bond elimination entry in the consolidation workpaper prepared at the end of 20X3, this amount is allocated between beginning retained earnings and the noncontrolling interest:

E(35)			
	Bonds Payable	100,000	
	Premium on Bonds Payable	1,400	
	Interest Income	13,000	
	Investment in Special Foods Bonds		93,000
	Interest Expense		11,800
	Retained Earnings, January 1		7,680
	Noncontrolling Interest		1,920
	Eliminate intercorporate bond holdings:		
	$1,400 = $2,000 − $200 − $200 − $200		
	$13,000 = ($100,000 × .12) + $1,000		
	$93,000 = $91,000 + $1,000 + $1,000		
	$11,800 = ($100,000 × .12) − $200		
	$7,680 = ($10,800 − $1,200) × .80		
	$1,920 = ($10,800 − $1,200) × .20		

Purchase at an Amount Greater than Book Value

When an affiliate's bonds are purchased from a nonaffiliate at an amount greater than their book value, the consolidation procedures are virtually the same as previously illustrated except that a loss is recognized on the constructive retirement of the debt. For example, assume that Special Foods issues 10-year, 12 percent bonds on January 1, 20X1, at par of $100,000. The bonds are purchased from Special Foods by Nonaffiliated Corporation, which sells the bonds to Peerless Products on December 31, 20X1, for $104,500. Special Foods recognizes $12,000 ($100,000 × .12) of interest expense each year. Peerless recognizes interest income of $11,500 in each year after 20X1, computed as follows:

Annual cash interest payment ($100,000 × .12)	$12,000
Less: Amortization of premium on bond investment ($4,500 ÷ 9 years)	(500)
Interest income	$11,500

Because the bonds were issued at par, the carrying amount on Special Foods' books remains at $100,000. Thus, once Peerless purchases the bonds from Nonaffiliated Corporation for $104,500, a loss on the constructive retirement must be recognized in the consolidated income statement for $4,500 ($104,500 − $100,000). The bond elimination entry in the consolidation workpaper prepared at the end of 20X1 removes the bonds payable and the bond investment and recognizes the loss on the constructive retirement:

E(36)			
	Bonds Payable	100,000	
	Loss on Bond Retirement	4,500	
	Investment in Special Foods Bonds		104,500
	Eliminate intercorporate bond holdings.		

In subsequent years, Peerless amortizes the premium on the bond investment, reducing interest income and the bond investment balance by $500 each year. This, in effect, recognizes a portion of the loss on the constructive retirement. When consolidated statements are prepared, the amount of the loss on constructive retirement that has not been recognized by the separate affiliates at the beginning of the period is allocated proportionately against the ownership interests of the issuing affiliate. The bond elimination entry needed in the consolidation workpaper prepared at the end of 20X2 is as follows:

E(37)			
	Bonds Payable	100,000	
	Interest Income	11,500	
	Retained Earnings, January 1	3,600	
	Noncontrolling Interest	900	
	Investment in Special Foods Bonds		104,000
	Interest Expense		12,000
	Eliminate intercorporate bond holdings:		
	$11,500 = ($100,000 × .12) − $500		
	$3,600 = $4,500 × .80		
	$900 = $4,500 × .20		
	$104,000 = $104,500 − $500		
	$12,000 = $100,000 × .12		

Similarly, the following entry is needed in the consolidation workpaper at the end of 20X3:

E(38)	Bonds Payable	100,000	
	Interest Income	11,500	
	Retained Earnings, January 1	3,200	
	Noncontrolling Interest	800	
	Investment in Special Foods Bonds		103,500
	Interest Expense		12,000
	Eliminate intercorporate bond holdings:		
	$3,200 = ($4,500 − $500) × .80		
	$800 = ($4,500 − $500) × .20		
	$103,500 = $104,500 − $500 − $500		

Summary of Key Concepts

The effects of intercompany debt transactions must be eliminated completely in preparing consolidated financial statements, just as with other types of intercompany transactions. Only debt transactions between the consolidated entity and unaffiliated parties are reported in the consolidated statements.

When one affiliate issues bonds that are purchased directly by another affiliate, the bonds are viewed from a consolidated point of view as never having been issued. Thus, all aspects of the intercompany bond holding are eliminated in consolidation. Items requiring elimination include (1) the bond investment from the purchasing affiliate's books, (2) the bond liability and any associated discount or premium from the issuer's books, (3) the interest income recognized by the investing affiliate and the interest expense recognized by the issuer, and (4) any intercompany interest receivable/payable as of the date of the consolidated statements.

When a company purchases the bonds of an affiliate from a nonaffiliate, the bonds are treated in consolidation as if they had been issued and subsequently repurchased by the consolidated entity. If the price paid by the purchasing affiliate is different from the issuer's book value of the bonds, a gain or loss from retirement of the bonds is recognized in the consolidated income statement. In addition, all aspects of the intercompany bond holding are eliminated because the bonds are treated as if the consolidated entity had retired them.

Key Terms

| constructive retirement, *376* | direct intercompany debt transfer, *371* | indirect intercompany debt transfer, *371* |

Appendix **8A** Intercompany Indebtedness—Fully Adjusted Equity Method and Cost Method

Consolidation procedures following use of (1) the fully adjusted equity method and (2) the cost method are illustrated with the example of the intercompany bond transaction presented earlier. Assume that Special Foods issues bonds with a par value of $100,000 and a term of 10 years to Nonaffiliated Corporation for $102,000 on January 1, 20X1. Peerless Products purchases the bonds from Nonaffiliated Corporation on December 31, 20X1, for $91,000.

FULLY ADJUSTED EQUITY METHOD

The accounting procedures under the fully adjusted equity method are the same as under the basic equity method except that the parent (1) adjusts its income and the investment account by its proportionate share of the gain or loss on the constructive retirement of the bonds in the year of repurchase and (2) adjusts for the implicit recognition of the gain or loss by it and its subsidiary as they amortize the discount and premium in subsequent years.

The 20X1 gain on the constructive retirement in this illustration is $10,800, computed as follows:

Book value of Special Foods' bonds, December 31, 20X1 ($102,000 − $200)	$101,800
Price paid by Peerless to purchase bonds	(91,000)
Gain on constructive retirement of bonds	$ 10,800

Fully Adjusted Equity-Method Entries—20X1

Peerless records the following entries under the fully adjusted equity method during 20X1 to account for its investment in Special Foods stock:

(39)	Cash	24,000	
	Investment in Special Foods Stock		24,000
	Record dividends from Special Foods:		
	$30,000 × .80		
(40)	Investment in Special Foods Stock	40,000	
	Income from Subsidiary		40,000
	Record equity-method income:		
	$50,000 × .80		
(41)	Investment in Special Foods Stock	8,640	
	Income from Subsidiary		8,640
	Recognize income from bond retirement:		
	($101,800 − $91,000) × .80		

Entry (41) adjusts equity-method net income by a proportionate share of the gain on the constructive retirement of Special Foods' bonds. Although the gain itself is not recognized by Peerless, its net income under the fully adjusted equity method must equal consolidated net income. In keeping with the concept of a one-line consolidation, Peerless's share of the gain on constructive retirement of Special Foods' bonds is included in its share of income from Special Foods.

Entries (39), (40), and (41) record income from Special Foods of $48,640 and increase the carrying amount of the investment on Peerless's books to $264,640 as of December 31, 20X1.

Consolidation Elimination Entries—20X1

The December 31, 20X1, workpaper to prepare consolidated financial statements for Peerless Products and Special Foods contains the following eliminating entries:

E(42)	Income from Subsidiary	48,640	
	Dividends Declared		24,000
	Investment in Special Foods Stock		24,640
	Eliminate income from subsidiary.		
E(43)	Income to Noncontrolling Interest	12,160	
	Dividends Declared		6,000
	Noncontrolling Interest		6,160
	Assign income to noncontrolling interest:		
	$12,160 = ($50,000 + $10,800) × .20		
E(44)	Common Stock—Special Foods	200,000	
	Retained Earnings, January 1	100,000	
	Investment in Special Foods Stock		240,000
	Noncontrolling Interest		60,000
	Eliminate beginning investment balance.		

E(45)	Bonds Payable	100,000	
	Premium on Bonds Payable	1,800	
	Investment in Special Foods Bonds		91,000
	Gain on Bond Retirement		10,800
	Eliminate intercorporate bond holdings.		

Fully Adjusted Equity-Method Entries—20X2

In addition to the entries related to its investment in Special Foods' bonds, Peerless records the following entries during 20X2 under the fully adjusted equity method:

(46)	Cash	32,000	
	Investment in Special Foods Stock		32,000
	Record dividends from Special Foods:		
	$40,000 × .80		

(47)	Investment in Special Foods Stock	60,000	
	Income from Subsidiary		60,000
	Record equity-method income:		
	$75,000 × .80		

(48)	Income from Subsidiary	960	
	Investment in Special Foods Stock		960
	Adjust for portion of gain on constructive		
	bond retirement recognized:		
	($10,800 ÷ 9) × .80		

Entry (48) adjusts for Peerless's portion of the gain on the constructive bond retirement recognized on the separate books of Peerless and Special Foods during 20X2 as a result of the excess of Peerless's $13,000 interest income accrual over Special Foods' $11,800 charge to interest expense. Whereas neither Peerless nor Special Foods recognized any of the gain from the constructive bond retirement on its separate books in 20X1, Peerless adjusted its equity-method income from Special Foods for its 80 percent share of the $10,800 gain, $8,640. Therefore, as Peerless and Special Foods recognize the gain over the remaining term of the bonds, Peerless must reverse its 20X1 entry for its share of the gain. This adjustment is needed to avoid double counting Peerless's share of the gain. Thus, the original adjustment of $8,640 is reversed by $960 ($8,640 ÷ 9 years) each year. This is accomplished in 20X2 through entry (48).

The amount of entry (48) also equals Peerless's 80 percent share of the difference in interest expense and interest income to be eliminated in consolidation:

Elimination of Peerless's interest income	$13,000
Elimination of Special Foods' interest expense	(11,800)
Net reduction in income	$ 1,200
Peerless's proportionate share	× .80
Reduction in consolidated net income	$ 960

When the bond interest expense and bond interest income are eliminated in the preparation of consolidated financial statements, consolidated net income is reduced by $960. Entry (48) adjusts Peerless's equity-method income to equal consolidated net income.

Peerless's account relating to its investment in Special Foods' common stock appears as follows at the end of 20X2:

Investment in Special Foods Stock					
	Original cost	240,000			
(40)	20X1 equity accrual		(39)	20X1 dividends	
	($50,000 × .80)	40,000		($30,000 × .80)	24,000
(41)	Gain on constructive bond retirement				
	($10,800 × .80)	8,640			
	Balance, 12/31/X1	264,640			
(47)	20X2 equity accrual		(46)	20X2 dividends	
	($75,000 × .80)	60,000		($40,000 × .80)	32,000
			(48)	Recognized portion of constructive gain	
				($8,640 ÷ 9 years)	960
	Balance, 12/31/X2	291,680			

Consolidation Elimination Entries—20X2

The following elimination entries are needed in the workpaper to prepare consolidated financial statements for 20X2:

E(49)
Income from Subsidiary	59,040	
Dividends Declared		32,000
Investment in Special Foods Stock		27,040
Eliminate income from subsidiary.		

E(50)
Income to Noncontrolling Interest	14,760	
Dividends Declared		8,000
Noncontrolling Interest		6,760
Assign income to noncontrolling interest:		
$14,760 = ($75,000 − $1,200) × .20		

E(51)
Common Stock—Special Foods	200,000	
Retained Earnings, January 1	120,000	
Investment in Special Foods Stock		256,000
Noncontrolling Interest		64,000
Eliminate beginning investment balance.		

E(52)
Bonds Payable	100,000	
Premium on Bonds Payable	1,600	
Interest Income	13,000	
Investment in Special Foods Bonds		92,000
Interest Expense		11,800
Investment in Special Foods Stock		8,640
Noncontrolling Interest		2,160
Eliminate intercorporate bond holdings:		
$1,600 = $2,000 − $200 − $200		
$13,000 = ($100,000 × .12) + $1,000		
$92,000 = $91,000 + $1,000		
$11,800 = ($100,000 × .12) − $200		
$8,640 = $10,800 × .80		
$2,160 = $10,800 × .20		

COST METHOD

Preparation of consolidated financial statements when the cost method has been used is illustrated with the same example employed for the fully adjusted equity method. Peerless recognizes dividend income of $24,000 ($30,000 × .80) in 20X1 and $32,000 ($40,000 × .80) in 20X2 under the cost method. Peerless makes no adjustments with respect to Special Foods' undistributed earnings or the gain on the constructive bond retirement.

Consolidation Elimination Entries—20X1

The following eliminating entries are needed in the consolidation workpaper prepared at the end of 20X1, following use of the cost method:

E(53)	Dividend Income	24,000	
	Dividends Declared		24,000
	Eliminate dividend income from subsidiary: $30,000 × .80		
E(54)	Income to Noncontrolling Interest	12,160	
	Dividends Declared		6,000
	Noncontrolling Interest		6,160
	Assign income to noncontrolling interest:		
	$12,160 = ($50,000 + $10,800) × .20		
E(55)	Common Stock—Special Foods	200,000	
	Retained Earnings, January 1	100,000	
	Investment in Special Foods Stock		240,000
	Noncontrolling Interest		60,000
	Eliminate investment balance at date of acquisition.		
E(56)	Bonds Payable	100,000	
	Premium on Bonds Payable	1,800	
	Investment in Special Foods Bonds		91,000
	Gain on Bond Retirement		10,800
	Eliminate intercorporate bond holdings.		

Consolidation Elimination Entries—20X2

Elimination entries needed in the consolidation workpaper at the end of 20X2 are as follows:

E(57)	Dividend Income	32,000	
	Dividends Declared		32,000
	Eliminate dividend income from subsidiary: $40,000 × .80		
E(58)	Income to Noncontrolling Interest	14,760	
	Dividends Declared		8,000
	Noncontrolling Interest		6,760
	Assign income to noncontrolling interest:		
	$14,760 = ($75,000 − $1,200) × .20		
E(59)	Common Stock—Special Foods	200,000	
	Retained Earnings, January 1	100,000	
	Investment in Special Foods Stock		240,000
	Noncontrolling Interest		60,000
	Eliminate investment balance at date of acquisition.		

E(60)	Retained Earnings, January 1	4,000	
	Noncontrolling Interest		4,000
	Assign undistributed prior earnings of subsidiary to noncontrolling interest: $20,000 × .20		
E(61)	Bonds Payable	100,000	
	Premium on Bonds Payable	1,600	
	Interest Income	13,000	
	Investment in Special Foods Bonds		92,000
	Interest Expense		11,800
	Retained Earnings, January 1		8,640
	Noncontrolling Interest		2,160
	Eliminate intercorporate bond holdings:		
	$1,600 = $2,000 − $200 − $200		
	$13,000 = ($100,000 × .12) + $1,000		
	$92,000 = $91,000 + $1,000		
	$11,800 = ($100,000 × .12) − $200		
	$8,640 = $10,800 × .80		
	$2,160 = $10,800 × .20		

Questions

Q8-1   When is a gain or loss on bond retirement included in the consolidated income statement?

Q8-2   What is meant by a constructive bond retirement in a multi-corporate setting? How does a constructive bond retirement differ from an actual bond retirement?

Q8-3   When a bond issue has been placed directly with an affiliate, what account balances will be stated incorrectly in the consolidated statements if the intercompany bond ownership is not eliminated in preparing the consolidation workpaper?

Q8-4   When an affiliate's bonds are purchased from a nonaffiliate during the period, what balances will be stated incorrectly in the consolidated financial statements if the intercompany bond ownership is not eliminated in preparing the consolidation workpaper?

Q8-5   For a multi-corporate entity, how is the recognition of gains or losses on bond retirement changed when emphasis is placed on the economic entity rather than the legal entity?

Q8-6   When a parent company sells land to a subsidiary at more than book value, the consolidation eliminating entries at the end of the period include a debit to the gain on the sale of land. When a parent purchases the bonds of a subsidiary from a nonaffiliate at less than book value, the eliminating entries at the end of the period contain a credit to a gain on bond retirement. Why are these two situations not handled in the same manner in the consolidation workpaper?

Q8-7   What is the effect of eliminating intercompany interest income and interest expense on consolidated net income when there has been a direct sale of bonds to an affiliate? Why?

Q8-8   What is the effect of eliminating intercompany interest income and interest expense on consolidated net income when a loss on bond retirement has been reported in a prior year's consolidated financial statements as a result of a constructive retirement of an affiliate's bonds? Why?

Q8-9   If an affiliate's bonds are purchased from a nonaffiliate at the beginning of the current year, how can the amount of the gain or loss on constructive retirement be computed by looking at the two companies' year-end trial balances?

Q8-10   When the parent company purchases a subsidiary's bonds from a nonaffiliate for more than book value, what income statement accounts will be affected in preparing consolidated financial statements? What will be the effect of the purchase on consolidated net income? Explain.

Q8-11   When a subsidiary purchases the bonds of its parent from a nonaffiliate for less than book value, what will be the effect on consolidated net income?

Q8-12 How is the amount of income assigned to the noncontrolling interest affected by the direct placement of a subsidiary's bonds with the parent company?

Q8-13 How is the amount of income assigned to the noncontrolling interest affected when the parent purchases the bonds of its subsidiary from an unaffiliated company for less than book value?

Q8-14 How would the relationship between interest income recorded by a subsidiary and interest expense recorded by the parent be expected to change when a direct placement of the parent's bonds with the subsidiary is compared with a constructive retirement in which the subsidiary purchases the bonds of the parent from a nonaffiliate?

Q8-15 A subsidiary purchased bonds of its parent company from a nonaffiliate in the preceding period, and a gain on bond retirement was reported in the consolidated income statement as a result of the purchase. What effect will that event have on the amount of consolidated net income reported in the current period?

Q8-16 A parent company purchased its subsidiary's bonds from a nonaffiliate in the preceding year, and a loss on bond retirement was reported in the consolidated income statement. How will income assigned to the noncontrolling interest be affected in the year following the constructive retirement?

Q8-17 A parent purchases a subsidiary's bonds directly from the subsidiary. The parent later sells the bonds to a nonaffiliate. From a consolidated viewpoint, what occurs when the parent sells the bonds? Is a gain or loss reported in the consolidated income statement when the parent sells the bonds? Why?

Q8-18 Shortly after a parent company purchased its subsidiary's bonds from a nonaffiliate, the subsidiary retired the entire issue. How is the gain or loss on bond retirement reported by the subsidiary treated for consolidation purposes?

Cases

C8-1 **Recognition of Retirement Gains and Losses**

Analysis

Bradley Corporation sold bonds to Flood Company in 20X2 at 90. At the end of 20X4, Century Corporation purchased the bonds from Flood at 105. Bradley then retired the full bond issue on December 31, 20X7, at 101. Century holds 80 percent of Bradley's voting stock. Neither Century nor Bradley owns stock of Flood Company.

Required

a. Indicate how each of the three bond transactions should be recorded by the companies involved.

b. Indicate when, if at all, the consolidated entity headed by Century should recognize a gain or loss on bond retirement, and indicate whether a gain or a loss should be recognized.

c. Will income assigned to Bradley's noncontrolling shareholders be affected by the bond transactions? If so, in which years?

C8-2 **Borrowing by Variable Interest Entities**

Research FARS

Hydro Corporation needed to build a new production facility. Because it already had a relatively high debt ratio, the company decided to establish a joint venture with Rich Corner Bank. This arrangement permitted the joint venture to borrow $30,000,000 for 20 years on a fixed interest rate basis at an interest rate nearly 2 percent less than Hydro would have paid if it had borrowed the money. Rich Corner Bank purchased 100 percent of the joint venture's equity for $200,000, and Hydro provided a guarantee of the debt to the bond holders and a guarantee to Rich Corner Bank that it would earn a 20 percent annual return on its investment.

On completion of the production facility, Hydro entered into a 10-year lease with the joint venture for use of the new facility. Due to the lease agreement terms, Hydro has reported the lease as an operating lease. Hydro does not report an investment in the joint venture because it holds no equity interest.

Required

As a senior member of Hydro's accounting staff, you have been asked to investigate the financial reporting standards associated with accounting for variable interest entities and determine whether Hydro's reporting is appropriate. Prepare a memo to Hydro's president stating your findings and conclusions and analyzing the impact on Hydro's financial statements if the current reporting procedures are inappropriate. Include citations to or quotations from the authoritative accounting literature in support of your findings and conclusions.

C8-3 Subsidiary Bond Holdings

Research FARS

Farflung Corporation has in excess of 60 subsidiaries worldwide. It owns 65 percent of the voting common stock of Micro Company and 80 percent of the shares of Eagle Corporation. Micro sold $400,000 par value first mortgage bonds at par value on January 2, 20X0, to Independent Company. No intercorporate ownership exists between Farflung and its subsidiaries and Independent.

On December 31, 20X4, Independent determined the need for cash for other purposes and sold the Micro bonds to Eagle for $424,000. Farflung's accounting department was not aware of the bond purchase by Eagle and included the Micro Company bonds among its long-term liabilities in the consolidated balance sheet prepared at December 31, 20X4.

Required

In reviewing the financial statements of Farflung and its subsidiaries at December 31, 20X5, you discovered Eagle Corporation's investment in Micro's bonds and immediately brought it to the attention of Farflung's financial vice president. You have been asked to prepare a memo to the financial vice president detailing the appropriate reporting treatment when intercorporate bond ownership occurs in this way and to provide recommendations as to the actions, if any, Farflung should take in preparing its consolidated statements at December 31, 20X5. Include in your memo citations to or quotations from applicable authoritative accounting standards in support of your position.

C8-4 Interest Income and Expense

Understanding

Snerd Corporation's controller is having difficulty explaining the impact of several of the company's intercorporate bond transactions.

Required

a. Snerd receives interest payments in excess of the amount of interest income it records on its investment in Snort bonds. Did Snerd purchase the bonds at par value, at a premium, or at a discount? How can you tell?

b. The 20X3 consolidated income statement reported a gain on the retirement of a subsidiary's bonds. If Snerd purchased the bonds from a nonaffiliate at par value:

   (1) Were the subsidiary's bonds originally sold at a premium or a discount? How can you tell?

   (2) Will the annual interest payments received by Snerd be more or less than the interest expense recorded by the subsidiary? Explain.

   (3) How is the difference between the interest income recorded by Snerd and the interest expense recorded by the subsidiary treated in preparing consolidated financial statements at the end of each period?

C8-5 Intercompany Debt

Analysis

Intercompany debt, both long-term and short-term, arises frequently. In some cases, intercorporate borrowings may arise because one affiliate can borrow at a cheaper rate than others, and lending to other affiliates may reduce the overall cost of borrowing. In other cases, intercompany receivables/payables arise because of intercompany sales of goods or services or other types of intercompany transactions.

Required

a. What major problem might arise with intercompany debt between a domestic parent and a foreign subsidiary or between subsidiaries in different countries? How has Hershey Foods dealt with this problem?

b. Did Hershey Foods' intercompany loans arise because of direct loans or because of intercompany sales of goods and services on credit?

Exercises

E8-1 Bond Sale from Parent to Subsidiary

Lamar Corporation owns 60 percent of Humbolt Corporation's voting shares. On January 1, 20X2, Lamar Corporation sold $150,000 par value 6 percent first mortgage bonds to Humbolt for $156,000. The bonds mature in 10 years and pay interest semiannually on January 1 and July 1.

Required

a. Prepare the journal entries for 20X2 for Humbolt related to its ownership of Lamar's bonds.

b. Prepare the journal entries for 20X2 for Lamar related to the bonds.

c. Prepare the workpaper eliminating entries needed on December 31, 20X2, to remove the effects of the intercorporate ownership of bonds.

E8-2 Computation of Transfer Price

Nettle Corporation sold $100,000 par value, 10-year, first mortgage bonds to Timberline Corporation on January 1, 20X5. The bonds, which bear a nominal interest rate of 12 percent, pay interest semiannually on January 1 and July 1. The entry to record interest income by Timberline Corporation on December 31, 20X7, was as follows:

Interest Receivable	6,000	
Interest Income		5,750
Investment in Nettle Corporation Bonds		250

Timberline Corporation owns 65 percent of the voting stock of Nettle Corporation, and consolidated statements are prepared on December 31, 20X7.

Required

a. What was the original purchase price of the bonds to Timberline Corporation?

b. What is the balance in Timberline's bond investment account on December 31, 20X7?

c. Give the workpaper eliminating entry or entries needed to remove the effects of the intercompany ownership of bonds in preparing consolidated financial statements for 20X7.

E8-3 Bond Sale at Discount

Wood Corporation owns 70 percent of Carter Company's voting shares. On January 1, 20X3, Carter sold bonds with a par value of $600,000 at 98. Wood purchased $400,000 par value of the bonds; the remainder was sold to nonaffiliates. The bonds mature in five years and pay an annual interest rate of 8 percent. Interest is paid semiannually on January 1 and July 1.

Required

a. What amount of interest expense should be reported in the 20X4 consolidated income statement?

b. Give the journal entries recorded by Wood during 20X4 with regard to its investment in Carter bonds.

c. Give all workpaper eliminating entries needed to remove the effects of the intercorporate bond ownership in preparing consolidated financial statements for 20X4.

E8-4 Evaluation of Intercorporate Bond Holdings

Stellar Corporation purchased bonds of its subsidiary from a nonaffiliate during 20X6. Although Stellar purchased the bonds at par value, a loss on bond retirement is reported in the 20X6 consolidated income statement as a result of the purchase.

Required

a. Were the bonds originally sold by the subsidiary at a premium or a discount? Explain.

b. Will the annual interest payments received by Stellar be more or less than the interest expense recorded by the subsidiary each period? Explain.

c. As a result of the entry recorded at December 31, 20X7, to eliminate the effects of the intercompany bond holding, will consolidated net income be increased or decreased? Explain.

E8-5 Multiple-Choice Questions

Select the correct answer for each of the following questions.

1. [AICPA Adapted] Wagner, a holder of a $1,000,000 Palmer Inc. bond, collected the interest due on March 31, 20X8, and then sold the bond to Seal Inc. for $975,000. On that date, Palmer, a 75 percent owner of Seal, had a $1,075,000 carrying amount for this bond. What was the effect of Seal's purchase of Palmer's bond on the retained earnings and minority interest amounts reported in Palmer's March 31, 20X8, consolidated balance sheet?

Retained Earnings	Minority Interest
a. $100,000 increase	No effect
b. $75,000 increase	$25,000 increase
c. No effect	$25,000 increase
d. No effect	$100,000 increase

2. **[AICPA Adapted]** P Company purchased term bonds at a premium on the open market. These bonds represented 20 percent of the outstanding class of bonds issued at a discount by S Company, P's wholly owned subsidiary. P intends to hold the bonds to maturity. In a consolidated balance sheet, the difference between the bond carrying amounts of the two companies would be:

   a. Included as a decrease to retained earnings.

   b. Included as an increase in retained earnings.

   c. Reported as a deferred debit to be amortized over the remaining life of the bonds.

   d. Reported as a deferred credit to be amortized over the remaining life of the bonds.

The following information relates to questions 3–6:

Kruse Corporation holds 60 percent of the voting common shares of Gary's Ice Cream Parlors. On January 1, 20X6, Gary's purchased $50,000 par value, 10 percent, first mortgage bonds of Kruse from Cane for $58,000. Kruse originally issued the bonds to Cane on January 1, 20X4, for $53,000. The bonds have a 10-year maturity from the date of issue.

Gary's reported net income of $20,000 for 20X6, and Kruse reported income (excluding income from ownership of Gary's stock) of $40,000.

3. What amount of interest expense does Kruse record annually?

   a. $4,000.

   b. $4,700.

   c. $5,000.

   d. $10,000.

4. What amount of interest income does Gary's Ice Cream Parlors record for 20X6?

   a. $4,000.

   b. $5,000.

   c. $9,000.

   d. $10,000.

5. What gain or loss on the retirement of bonds should be reported in the 20X6 consolidated income statement?

   a. $2,400 gain.

   b. $5,600 gain.

   c. $5,600 loss.

   d. $8,000 loss.

6. What amount of consolidated net income should be reported for 20X6?

   a. $47,100.

   b. $52,000.

   c. $54,400.

   d. $60,000.

E8-6 Multiple-Choice Questions

On January 1, 20X4, Passive Heating Corporation paid $104,000 for $100,000 par value, 9 percent bonds of Solar Energy Corporation. Solar had issued $300,000 of the 10-year bonds on January 1, 20X2, for $360,000. Passive previously had purchased 80 percent of the common stock of Solar on January 1, 20X1, at underlying book value.

Passive reported operating income (excluding income from subsidiary) of $50,000, and Solar reported net income of $30,000 for 20X4.

Required

Select the correct answer for each of the following questions.

1. What amount of interest expense should be included in the 20X4 consolidated income statement?
   a. $14,000.
   b. $18,000.
   c. $21,000.
   d. $27,000.

2. What amount of gain or loss on bond retirement should be included in the 20X4 consolidated income statement?
   a. $4,000 gain.
   b. $4,000 loss.
   c. $12,000 gain.
   d. $16,000 loss.

3. Income assigned to the noncontrolling interest in the 20X4 consolidated income statement should be:
   a. $6,000.
   b. $8,100.
   c. $8,400.
   d. $16,000.

E8-7 Constructive Retirement at End of Year

Able Company issued $600,000 of 9 percent first mortgage bonds on January 1, 20X1, at 103. The bonds mature in 20 years and pay interest semiannually on January 1 and July 1. Prime Corporation purchased $400,000 of Able's bonds from the original purchaser on December 31, 20X5, for $397,000. Prime owns 60 percent of Able's voting common stock.

Required

a. Prepare the workpaper elimination entry or entries needed to remove the effects of the intercorporate bond ownership in preparing consolidated financial statements for 20X5.

b. Prepare the workpaper elimination entry or entries needed to remove the effects of the intercorporate bond ownership in preparing consolidated financial statements for 20X6.

E8-8 Constructive Retirement at Beginning of Year

Able Company issued $600,000 of 9 percent first mortgage bonds on January 1, 20X1, at 103. The bonds mature in 20 years and pay interest semiannually on January 1 and July 1. Prime Corporation purchased $400,000 of Able's bonds from the original purchaser on January 1, 20X5, for $396,800. Prime owns 60 percent of Able's voting common stock.

Required

a. Prepare the workpaper elimination entry or entries needed to remove the effects of the intercorporate bond ownership in preparing consolidated financial statements for 20X5.

b. Prepare the workpaper elimination entry or entries needed to remove the effects of the intercorporate bond ownership in preparing consolidated financial statements for 20X6.

E8-9 Retirement of Bonds Sold at a Discount

Farley Corporation owns 70 percent of Snowball Enterprises's stock. On January 1, 20X1, Farley sold $1,000,000 par value 7 percent, 20-year, first mortgage bonds to Kling Corporation at 97. On January 1, 20X8, Snowball purchased $300,000 par value of the Farley bonds directly from Kling for $296,880.

Required

Prepare the eliminating entry needed at December 31, 20X8, to remove the effects of the intercorporate bond ownership in preparing consolidated financial statements.

E8-10 Loss on Constructive Retirement

Apple Corporation holds 60 percent of Shortway Publishing Company's voting shares. Apple issued $500,000 of 10 percent bonds with a 10-year maturity on January 1, 20X2, at 90. On January 1, 20X8,

Shortway purchased $100,000 of the Apple bonds for $108,000. Partial trial balances for the two companies on December 31, 20X8, are as follows:

	Apple Corporation	Shortway Publishing Company
Investment in Shortway Publishing Company Stock	$141,000	
Investment in Apple Corporation Bonds		$106,000
Bonds Payable	500,000	
Discount on Bonds Payable	15,000	
Interest Expense	55,000	
Interest Income		8,000
Interest Payable	25,000	
Interest Receivable		5,000

Required

Prepare the workpaper eliminating entry or entries needed on December 31, 20X8, to remove the effects of the intercorporate bond ownership in preparing consolidated financial statements.

E8-11   **Determining the Amount of Retirement Gain or Loss**

Online Enterprises owns 95 percent of Downlink Corporation. On January 1, 20X1, Downlink issued $200,000 of five-year bonds at 115. Annual interest of 12 percent is paid semiannually on January 1 and July 1. Online purchased $100,000 of the bonds on August 31, 20X3, at par value. The following balances are taken from the separate 20X3 financial statements of the two companies:

	Online Enterprises	Downlink Corporation
Investment in Downlink Corporation Bonds	$100,000	
Interest Income	4,000	
Interest Receivable	6,000	
Bonds Payable		$200,000
Bond Premium		12,000
Interest Expense		18,000
Interest Payable		12,000

Required

a. Compute the amount of interest expense that should be reported in the consolidated income statement for 20X3.

b. Compute the gain or loss on constructive bond retirement that should be reported in the 20X3 consolidated income statement.

c. Prepare the consolidation workpaper eliminating entry or entries as of December 31, 20X3, to remove the effects of the intercorporate bond ownership.

E8-12   **Evaluation of Bond Retirement**

Bundle Company issued $500,000 par value 10-year bonds at 104 on January 1, 20X3, which Mega Corporation purchased. The coupon rate on the bonds is 11 percent. Interest payments are made semiannually on July 1 and January 1. On July 1, 20X6, Parent Company purchased $200,000 par value of the bonds from Mega for $192,200. Parent owns 70 percent of Bundle's voting shares.

Required

a. What amount of gain or loss will be reported in Bundle's 20X6 income statement on the retirement of bonds?

b. Will a gain or loss be reported in the 20X6 consolidated financial statements for Parent for the constructive retirement of bonds? What amount will be reported?

c. How much will Parent's purchase of the bonds change consolidated net income for 20X6?

d. Prepare the workpaper eliminating entry or entries needed to remove the effects of the intercorporate bond ownership in preparing consolidated financial statements at December 31, 20X6.

e. Prepare the workpaper eliminating entry or entries needed to remove the effects of the intercorporate bond ownership in preparing consolidated financial statements at December 31, 20X7.

f. If Bundle reports net income of $50,000 for 20X7, what amount of income will be assigned to the noncontrolling interest in the consolidated income statement?

E8-13 Elimination of Intercorporate Bond Holdings

Stang Corporation issued to Bradley Company $400,000 par value, 10-year bonds with a coupon rate of 12 percent on January 1, 20X5, at 105. The bonds pay interest semiannually on July 1 and January 1. On January 1, 20X8, Purple Corporation purchased $100,000 of the bonds from Bradley for $104,900.

Purple owns 65 percent of the voting common shares of Stang and prepares consolidated financial statements.

Required

a. Prepare the workpaper eliminating entry or entries needed to remove the effects of the intercorporate bond ownership in preparing consolidated financial statements for 20X8.

b. Assuming that Stang reports net income of $20,000 for 20X8, compute the amount of income assigned to noncontrolling shareholders in the 20X8 consolidated income statement.

c. Prepare the workpaper eliminating entry or entries needed to remove the effects of the intercorporate bond ownership in preparing consolidated financial statements for 20X9.

Problems P8-14 Consolidation Workpaper with Sale of Bonds to Subsidiary

Porter Company purchased 60 percent ownership of Temple Corporation on January 1, 20X1, at underlying book value. On that date, Porter sold $80,000 par value, 8 percent five-year bonds directly to Temple for $82,000. The bonds pay interest annually on December 31. Porter uses the basic equity method in accounting for its ownership of Temple. On December 31, 20X2, the trial balances of the two companies are as follows:

Item	Porter Company Debit	Porter Company Credit	Temple Corporation Debit	Temple Corporation Credit
Cash and Accounts Receivable	$ 80,200		$ 40,000	
Inventory	120,000		65,000	
Buildings and Equipment	500,000		300,000	
Investment in Temple Corporation Stock	102,000			
Investment in Porter Company Bonds			81,200	
Cost of Goods Sold	99,800		61,000	
Depreciation Expense	25,000		15,000	
Interest Expense	6,000		14,000	
Dividends Declared	40,000		10,000	
Accumulated Depreciation		$175,000		$ 75,000
Accounts Payable		68,800		41,200
Bonds Payable		80,000		200,000
Bond Premium		1,200		
Common Stock		200,000		100,000
Retained Earnings		230,000		50,000
Sales		200,000		114,000
Interest Income				6,000
Income from Subsidiary		18,000		
	$973,000	$973,000	$586,200	$586,200

Required

a. Record the journal entry or entries for 20X2 on Porter's books related to its investment in Temple.

b. Record the journal entry or entries for 20X2 on Porter's books related to its bonds payable.

c. Record the journal entry or entries for 20X2 on Temple's books related to its investment in Porter's bonds.

d. Prepare the elimination entries needed to complete a consolidated workpaper for 20X2.

e. Prepare a three-part consolidated workpaper for 20X2.

P8-15 Consolidation Workpaper with Sale of Bonds to Parent

Mega Corporation purchased 90 percent of Tarp Company's voting common shares on January 1, 20X2, at underlying book value. Mega also purchased $100,000 of 6 percent, five-year bonds directly from Tarp on January 1, 20X2, for $104,000. The bonds pay interest annually on December 31. The trial balances of the companies as of December 31, 20X4, are as follows:

Item	Mega Corporation Debit	Mega Corporation Credit	Tarp Company Debit	Tarp Company Credit
Cash and Receivables	$ 22,000		$ 36,600	
Inventory	165,000		75,000	
Buildings and Equipment	400,000		240,000	
Investment in Tarp Company Stock	121,500			
Investment in Tarp Company Bonds	101,600			
Cost of Goods Sold	86,000		79,800	
Depreciation Expense	20,000		15,000	
Interest Expense	16,000		5,200	
Dividends Declared	30,000		20,000	
Accumulated Depreciation		$140,000		$ 80,000
Current Payables		92,400		35,000
Bonds Payable		200,000		100,000
Bond Premium				1,600
Common Stock		120,000		80,000
Retained Earnings		242,000		50,000
Sales		140,000		125,000
Interest Income		5,200		
Income from Subsidiary		22,500		
	$962,100	$962,100	$471,600	$471,600

Required

a. Record the journal entry or entries for 20X4 on Mega's books related to its investment in Tarp Common stock.

b. Record the journal entry or entries for 20X4 on Mega's books related to its investment in Tarp Company bonds.

c. Record the journal entry or entries for 20X4 on Tarp's books related to its bonds payable.

d. Prepare the elimination entries needed to complete a consolidated workpaper for 20X4.

e. Prepare a three-part consolidated workpaper for 20X4.

P8-16 Direct Sale of Bonds to Parent

On January 1, 20X1, Elm Corporation paid Morton Advertising $122,000 to acquire 70 percent of Vincent Company stock. Elm also paid $45,000 to acquire $50,000 par value, 8 percent 10-year bonds directly from Vincent on that date. Interest payments are made on January 1 and July 1. The stock purchase price was $45,000 above book value and resulted from an increase in the value of depreciable assets held by Vincent. The assets had an estimated remaining economic life of 15 years on January 1, 20X1.

The trial balances for the two companies as of December 31, 20X3, are as follows:

Item	Elm Corporation Debit	Elm Corporation Credit	Vincent Company Debit	Vincent Company Credit
Cash and Current Receivables	$ 24,500		$ 46,000	
Inventory	170,000		70,000	
Land, Buildings, and Equipment (net)	320,000		180,000	
Investment in Vincent Bonds	46,500			
Investment in Vincent Stock	155,000			
Discount on Bonds Payable			7,000	
Operating Expenses	198,500		161,000	
Interest Expense	27,000		9,000	
Dividends Declared	60,000		10,000	
Current Liabilities		$ 35,000		$ 33,000
Bonds Payable		300,000		100,000
Common Stock		100,000		50,000
Retained Earnings		244,000		100,000
Sales		300,000		200,000
Interest Income		4,500		
Income from Subsidiary		18,000		
Total	$1,001,500	$1,001,500	$483,000	$483,000

On July 1, 20X2, Vincent sold land that it had purchased for $17,000 to Elm for $25,000. Elm continues to hold the land at December 31, 20X3.

Required

a. Record the journal entries for 20X3 on Elm's books related to its investment in Vincent's stock and bonds.

b. Record the entries for 20X3 on Vincent's books related to its bond issue.

c. Prepare elimination entries needed to complete a consolidation workpaper for 20X3.

d. Prepare a three-part consolidation workpaper for 20X3.

P8-17 **Information Provided in Eliminating Entry**

Gross Corporation issued $500,000 par value, 10-year bonds at 104 on January 1, 20X1, which Independent Corporation purchased. On July 1, 20X5, Rupp Corporation purchased $200,000 of Gross bonds from Independent. The bonds pay 9 percent interest annually on December 31. The preparation of consolidated financial statements for Gross and Rupp at December 31, 20X7, required the following eliminating entry:

Bonds Payable	200,000	
Premium on Bonds Payable	2,400	
Interest Income	18,600	
Investment in Gross Corporation Bonds		198,200
Interest Expense		17,200
Retained Earnings, January 1		4,200
Noncontrolling Interest		1,400

Required

With the information given, answer each of the following questions. Show how you derived your answer.

a. Is Gross or Rupp the parent company? How do you know?

b. What percentage of the subsidiary's ownership does the parent hold?

c. What amount did Rupp pay when it purchased the bonds on July 1, 20X5?

d. Was a gain or a loss on bond retirement included in the 20X5 consolidated income statement? What amount was reported?

e. If 20X7 consolidated net income of $70,000 would have been reported without the preceding eliminating entry, what amount will actually be reported?

f. Will income to noncontrolling interest reported in 20X7 increase or decrease as a result of the preceding eliminating entry? By what amount?

g. Prepare the eliminating entry needed to remove the effects of the intercorporate bond ownership in completing a three-part consolidation workpaper at December 31, 20X8.

P8-18 Prior Retirement of Bonds

Amazing Corporation purchased $100,000 par value bonds of its subsidiary, Broadway Company, on December 31, 20X5, from Lemon Corporation. The 10-year bonds bear a 9 percent coupon rate and were originally sold by Broadway on January 1, 20X3, to Lemon. Interest is paid annually on December 31. Amazing owns 85 percent of the stock of Broadway.

In preparing the consolidation workpaper at December 31, 20X6, Amazing's controller made the following entry to eliminate the effects of the intercorporate bond ownership:

Bonds Payable	100,000	
Interest Income	8,600	
Retained Earnings, January 1	5,355	
Noncontrolling Interest	945	
Investment in Broadway Company Bonds		102,400
Discount on Bonds Payable		3,000
Interest Expense		9,500

Required

With the information given, answer the following questions:

a. What amount did Amazing pay when it purchased Broadway's bonds?

b. Prepare the journal entry made by Broadway in 20X6 to record its interest expense for the year.

c. Prepare the journal entry made by Amazing in 20X6 to record its interest income on the Broadway bonds that it holds.

d. Prepare the eliminating entry to remove the effects of the intercorporate bond ownership in completing a three-part consolidation workpaper at December 31, 20X5.

e. Broadway reported net income of $60,000 and $80,000 for 20X5 and 20X6, respectively. Amazing reported income from its separate operations of $120,000 and $150,000 for 20X5 and 20X6, respectively. What amount of net income was reported for the consolidated entity in each of the two years?

P8-19 Incomplete Data

Ballard Corporation purchased 70 percent of Condor Company's voting shares on January 1, 20X4, at underlying book value. On that date it also purchased $100,000 par value, 12 percent Condor bonds, which had been issued on January 1, 20X1, with a 10-year maturity.

During preparation of the consolidated financial statements for December 31, 20X4, the following eliminating entry was made in the workpaper:

Bonds Payable	100,000	
Bond Premium	6,000	
Loss on Bond Retirement	3,500	
Interest Income	?	
Investment in Condor Company Bonds		109,000
Interest Expense		?

Required

a. What price did Ballard pay to purchase the Condor bonds?

b. What was the carrying amount of the bonds on Condor's books on the date of purchase?

c. If Condor reports net income of $30,000 in 20X5, what amount of income should be assigned to the noncontrolling interest in the 20X5 consolidated income statement?

P8-20 Balance Sheet Eliminations

Bath Corporation purchased 80 percent of Stang Brewing Company's stock on January 1, 20X1, at underlying book value. On that date, Stang issued $300,000 par value, 8 percent, 10-year bonds to Sidney Malt Company. Bath subsequently purchased $100,000 of the bonds from Sidney Malt for $102,000 on January 1, 20X3. Interest is paid semiannually on January 1 and July 1.

Summarized balance sheets for Bath and Stang as of December 31, 20X4, follow:

BATH CORPORATION
Balance Sheet
December 31, 20X4

Cash and Receivables	$122,500	Accounts Payable	$ 40,000
Inventory	200,000	Bonds Payable	400,000
Buildings and Equipment (net)	320,000	Common Stock	200,000
Investment in Stang Brewing:		Retained Earnings	320,000
Bonds	101,500		
Stock	216,000		
Total Assets	$960,000	Total Liabilities and Owners' Equity	$960,000

STANG BREWING COMPANY
Balance Sheet
December 31, 20X4

Cash and Receivables	$124,000	Accounts Payable	$ 28,000
Inventory	150,000	Bonds Payable	300,000
Buildings and Equipment (net)	360,000	Bond Premium	36,000
		Common Stock	100,000
		Retained Earnings	170,000
Total Assets	$634,000	Total Liabilities and Owners' Equity	$634,000

At December 31, 20X4, Stang holds $42,000 of inventory purchased from Bath, and Bath holds $26,000 of inventory purchased from Stang. Stang and Bath sell at cost plus markups of 30 percent and 40 percent, respectively.

Required

a. Prepare all elimination entries needed on December 31, 20X4, to complete a consolidation balance sheet workpaper.

b. Prepare a consolidated balance sheet workpaper.

c. Prepare a consolidated balance sheet in good form.

P8-21 **Computations Relating to Bond Purchase from Nonaffiliate**

Bliss Perfume Company issued $300,000 of 10 percent bonds on January 1, 20X2, at 110. The bonds mature 10 years from issue and have semiannual interest payments on January 1 and July 1. Parsons Corporation owns 80 percent of Bliss Perfume stock. On April 1, 20X4, Parsons purchased $100,000 par value of Bliss Perfume bonds in the securities markets.

Partial trial balances for the two companies on December 31, 20X4, are as follows:

	Parsons Corporation	Bliss Perfume Company
Investment in Bliss Perfume Company Bonds	$105,600	
Interest Income	6,900	
Interest Receivable	5,000	
Bonds Payable		$300,000
Bond Premium		21,000
Interest Expense		27,000
Interest Payable		15,000

Required

a. What was the purchase price of the Bliss Perfume bonds to Parsons?

b. What amount of gain or loss on bond retirement should be reported in the consolidated income statement for 20X4?

c. Prepare the necessary workpaper eliminating entries as of December 31, 20X4, to remove the effects of the intercorporate bond ownership.

P8-22   Computations following Parent's Acquisition of Subsidiary Bonds

Mainstream Corporation holds 80 percent of Offenberg Company's voting shares, acquired on January 1, 20X1, at underlying book value. On January 1, 20X4, Mainstream purchased Offenberg bonds with a par value of $40,000. The bonds pay 10 percent interest annually on December 31 and mature on December 31, 20X8. Mainstream uses the basic equity method in accounting for its ownership in Offenberg. Partial balance sheet data for the two companies on December 31, 20X5, are as follows:

	Mainstream Corporation	Offenberg Company
Investment in Offenberg Company stock	$120,000	
Investment in Offenberg Company Bonds	42,400	
Interest Income	3,200	
Bonds Payable		$100,000
Bond Premium		11,250
Interest Expense		6,250
Common Stock	300,000	100,000
Retained Earnings, December 31, 20X5	500,000	50,000

Required

a. Compute the gain or loss on bond retirement reported in the 20X4 consolidated income statement.

b. Prepare the eliminating entry needed to remove the effects of the intercorporate bond ownership in completing the consolidation workpaper for 20X5.

c. What balance should be reported as consolidated retained earnings on December. 31, 20X5?

P8-23   Consolidation Workpaper—Year of Retirement

Tyler Manufacturing purchased 60 percent of the ownership of Brown Corporation stock on January 1, 20X1, at underlying book value. Tyler also purchased $50,000 of Brown bonds at par value on December 31, 20X3. Brown sold the bonds on January 1, 20X1, at 120; they have a stated interest rate of 12 percent. Interest is paid semiannually on June 30 and December 31.

On December 31, 20X1, Brown sold to Tyler for $30,000 a building with a remaining life of 15 years. Brown purchased the building 10 years earlier for $40,000. It is being depreciated based on a 25-year expected life.

Trial balances for the two companies on December 31 20X3, are as follows:

Item	Tyler Manufacturing Debit	Tyler Manufacturing Credit	Brown Corporation Debit	Brown Corporation Credit
Cash	$ 68,000		$ 55,000	
Accounts Receivable	100,000		75,000	
Inventory	120,000		110,000	
Investment in Brown Bonds	50,000			
Investment in Brown Stock	102,000			
Depreciable Assets (net)	360,000		210,000	
Interest Expense	20,000		20,000	
Operating Expenses	302,200		150,000	
Dividends Declared	40,000		10,000	
Accounts Payable		$ 94,200		$ 52,000
Bonds Payable		200,000		200,000
Bond Premium				28,000
Common Stock		300,000		100,000
Retained Earnings		150,000		50,000
Sales		400,000		200,000
Income from Subsidiary		18,000		
Total	$1,162,200	$1,162,200	$630,000	$630,000

Required

a. Prepare a consolidation workpaper for 20X3, in good form.

b. Prepare a consolidated balance sheet, income statement, and statement of changes in retained earnings for 20X3.

P8-24 Consolidation Workpaper—Year after Retirement

Bennett Corporation owns 60 percent of the stock of Stone Container Company, which it acquired at book value in 20X1. On December 31, 20X3, Bennett purchased $100,000 par value bonds of Stone. Stone originally issued the bonds at par value. The bonds' coupon rate is 9 percent. Interest is paid semiannually on June 30 and December 31. Trial balances for the two companies on December 31, 20X4, are as follows:

Item	Bennett Corporation Debit	Bennett Corporation Credit	Stone Container Company Debit	Stone Container Company Credit
Cash	$ 61,600		$ 20,000	
Accounts Receivable	100,000		80,000	
Inventory	120,000		110,000	
Other Assets	340,000		250,000	
Investment in Stone Container Bonds	106,000			
Investment in Stone Container Stock	126,000			
Interest Expense	20,000		18,000	
Other Expenses	368,600		182,000	
Dividends Declared	40,000		10,000	
Accounts Payable		$ 80,000		$ 50,000
Bonds Payable		200,000		200,000
Common Stock		300,000		100,000
Retained Earnings		214,200		70,000
Sales		450,000		250,000
Interest Income		8,000		
Income from Subsidiary		30,000		
Total	$1,282,200	$1,282,200	$670,000	$670,000

All interest income recognized by Bennett is related to its investment in Stone bonds.

Required

a. Prepare a consolidation workpaper for 20X4 in good form.

b. Prepare a consolidated balance sheet, income statement, and retained earnings statement for 20X4.

P8-25 Intercorporate Inventory and Debt Transfers

Lance Corporation purchased 75 percent of Avery Company's common stock at underlying book value on January 1, 20X3. Trial balances for Lance and Avery on December 31, 20X7, are as follows:

	20X7 Trial Balance Data			
Item	Lance Corporation Debit	Lance Corporation Credit	Avery Company Debit	Avery Company Credit
Cash	$ 37,900		$ 48,800	
Accounts Receivable	110,000		105,000	
Other Receivables	30,000		15,000	
Inventory	167,000		120,000	
Land	90,000		40,000	
Buildings and Equipment	500,000		250,000	
Investment in Avery Company:				
Bonds	78,800			
Stock	183,000			
Cost of Goods Sold	620,000		240,000	

(continued)

Depreciation Expense	45,000		15,000	
Interest and Other Expenses	35,000		22,000	
Dividends Declared	50,000		24,000	
Accumulated Depreciation		$ 155,000		$ 75,000
Accounts Payable		118,000		35,000
Other Payables		40,000		20,000
Bonds Payable		250,000		200,000
Bond Premium				4,800
Common Stock		250,000		50,000
Additional Paid-In Capital		40,000		
Retained Earnings		291,700		170,000
Sales		750,000		320,000
Interest and Other Income		16,000		5,000
Income from Subsidiary		36,000		
Total	$1,946,700	$1,946,700	$879,800	$879,800

During 20X7, Lance resold inventory purchased from Avery in 20X6. It had cost Avery $44,000 to produce the inventory, and Lance purchased it for $59,000. In 20X7, Lance purchased inventory for $40,000 and sold it to Avery for $60,000. At December 31, 20X7, Avery continued to hold $27,000 of the inventory.

Avery issued $200,000 of 8 percent, 10-year bonds on January 1, 20X4, at 104. Lance purchased $80,000 of the bonds from one of the original owners for $78,400 on December 31, 20X5. Both companies use straight-line write-off of premiums and discounts. Interest is paid annually on December 31.

Required

a. What amount of cost of goods sold will be reported in the 20X7 consolidated income statement?

b. What inventory balance will be reported in the December 31, 20X7, consolidated balance sheet?

c. Prepare the journal entry to record interest expense for Avery for 20X7.

d. Prepare the journal entry to record interest income for Lance for 20X7.

e. What amount will be assigned to noncontrolling interest in the consolidated balance sheet prepared at December 31, 20X7?

f. Prepare all eliminating entries needed at December 31, 20X7, to complete a three-part consolidation workpaper.

g. Prepare a consolidation workpaper for 20X7 in good form.

P8-26   **Intercorporate Bond Holdings and Other Transfers**

On January 1, 20X5, Pond Corporation purchased 75 percent of Skate Company's stock at underlying book value. The balance sheets for Pond and Skate at January 1, 20X8, and December 31, 20X8, and income statements for 20X8 were reported as follows:

	20X8 Balance Sheets			
	Pond Corporation		**Skate Company**	
	January 1	**December 31**	**January 1**	**December 31**
Cash	$ 57,600	$ 53,100	$ 10,000	$ 47,000
Accounts Receivable	130,000	176,000	60,000	65,000
Interest and Other Receivables	40,000	45,000	8,000	10,000
Inventory	100,000	140,000	50,000	50,000
Land	50,000	50,000	22,000	22,000
Buildings and Equipment	400,000	400,000	240,000	240,000
Accumulated Depreciation	(150,000)	(185,000)	(70,000)	(94,000)
Investment in Skate Company:				
Stock	150,000	165,000		
Bonds	42,800	42,400		
Investment in Tin Co. Bonds	135,000	134,000		
Total Assets	$955,400	$1,020,500	$320,000	$340,000

(continued)

(*continued*)

	Pond Corporation		Skate Company	
	January 1	December 31	January 1	December 31
Accounts Payable	60,000	65,000	16,500	11,000
Interest and Other Payables	40,000	45,000	7,000	12,000
Bonds Payable	300,000	300,000	100,000	100,000
Bond Discount			(3,500)	(3,000)
Common Stock	150,000	150,000	30,000	30,000
Additional Paid-In Capital	155,000	155,000	20,000	20,000
Retained Earnings	250,400	305,500	150,000	170,000
Total Liabilities and Equities	$955,400	$1,020,500	$320,000	$340,000

	20X8 Income Statements			
	Pond Corporation		Skate Company	
Sales		$450,000		$250,000
Income from Subsidiary		22,500		
Interest Income		18,500		
Total Revenue		491,000		250,000
Cost of Goods Sold	$285,000		$136,000	
Other Operating Expenses	50,000		40,000	
Depreciation Expense	35,000		24,000	
Interest Expense	24,000		10,500	
Miscellaneous Expenses	11,900	405,900	9,500	220,000
Net Income		$ 85,100		$ 30,000

Additional Information

1. Pond sold a building to Skate for $65,000 on December 31, 20X7. Pond had purchased the building for $125,000 and was depreciating it on a straight-line basis over 25 years. At the time of sale, Pond reported accumulated depreciation of $75,000 and a remaining life of 10 years.
2. On July 1, 20X6, Skate sold land that it had purchased for $22,000 to Pond for $35,000. Pond is planning to build a new warehouse on the property prior to the end of 20X9.
3. Skate issued $100,000 par value, 10-year bonds with a coupon rate of 10 percent on January 1, 20X5, at $95,000. On December 31, 20X7, Pond purchased $40,000 par value of Skate's bonds for $42,800. Both companies amortize bond premiums and discounts on a straight-line basis. Interest payments are made on July 1 and January 1.
4. Pond and Skate paid dividends of $30,000 and $10,000, respectively, in 20X8.

Required

a. Prepare all eliminating entries needed at December 31, 20X8, to complete a three-part consolidation workpaper.

b. Prepare a three-part workpaper for 20X8 in good form.

P8-27   **Comprehensive Multiple-Choice Questions**

Blackwood Enterprises owns 80 percent of Grange Corporation's voting stock. Blackwood had purchased the shares on January 1, 20X4, for $234,500, at which time Grange reported common stock outstanding of $200,000 and retained earnings of $50,000. The book values of all Grange's assets were equal to their market values, except for buildings with a fair value $30,000 more than book value at the date of combination. The buildings had an expected 10-year remaining economic life from the date of combination. On December 31, 20X6, Blackwood's management reviewed the amount attributed to goodwill as a result of its purchase of Grange common stock and concluded that an impairment loss of $7,500 should be recorded in 20X6.

The following trial balances were prepared by the companies on December 31, 20X6:

Item	Blackwood Enterprises Debit	Blackwood Enterprises Credit	Grange Corporation Debit	Grange Corporation Credit
Cash	$ 194,220		$183,000	
Inventory	200,000		180,000	
Buildings and Equipment	500,000		400,000	
Investment in Grange Corporation Bonds	106,400			
Investment in Grange Corporation Stock	287,300			
Cost of Goods Sold	220,000		140,000	
Depreciation and Amortization	50,000		30,000	
Interest Expense	24,000		16,000	
Other Expenses	16,000		14,000	
Dividends Declared	20,000		15,000	
Accumulated Depreciation		$ 250,000		$180,000
Current Liabilities		100,000		50,000
Bonds Payable		400,000		200,000
Bond Premium				8,000
Common Stock		300,000		200,000
Retained Earnings		202,400		100,000
Sales		300,000		240,000
Other Income		35,920		
Income from Subsidiary		29,600		
Total	$1,617,920	$1,617,920	$978,000	$978,000

Blackwood purchases much of its inventory from Grange. The inventory Blackwood held on January 1, 20X6, contained $2,000 of unrealized intercompany profit. During 20X6, Grange sold goods costing $50,000 to Blackwood for $70,000. Blackwood resold the inventory held at the beginning of the year and 70 percent of the inventory it purchased in 20X6 prior to the end of the year. The inventory remaining at the end of 20X6 was sold in 20X7.

On January 1, 20X6, Blackwood purchased from Kirkwood Corporation $100,000 par value bonds of Grange Corporation. Kirkwood had purchased the 10-year bonds on January 1, 20X1. The coupon rate is 9 percent, and interest is paid annually on December 31.

Required

Select the correct answer for each of the following questions.

1. What should be the total amount of inventory reported in the consolidated balance sheet as of December 31, 20X6?

   a. $360,000.

   b. $374,000.

   c. $375,200.

   d. $380,000.

2. What amount of cost of goods sold should be reported in the 20X6 consolidated income statement?

   a. $288,000.

   b. $294,000.

   c. $296,000.

   d. $360,000.

3. What amount of interest income did Blackwood Enterprises record from its investment in Grange Corporation bonds during 20X6?

    a. $7,400.

    b. $7,720.

    c. $9,000.

    d. $10,600.

4. What amount of interest expense should be reported in the 20X6 consolidated income statement?

    a. $24,000.

    b. $32,000.

    c. $33,000.

    d. $40,000.

5. What is the unamortized balance of the purchase differential as of January 1, 20X6?

    a. $19,200.

    b. $29,700.

    c. $32,100.

    d. $34,500.

6. What amount of depreciation and amortization should be reported in the 20X6 consolidated income statement?

    a. $77,600.

    b. $80,000.

    c. $82,400.

    d. $83,450.

7. What amount of gain or loss on bond retirement should be included in the 20X6 consolidated income statement?

    a. $2,400.

    b. $3,000.

    c. $4,000.

    d. $6,400.

8. What amount of income should be assigned to the noncontrolling interest in the 20X6 consolidated income statement?

    a. $6,720.

    b. $7,200.

    c. $8,000.

    d. $8,400.

9. What amount should be assigned to the noncontrolling interest in the consolidated balance sheet as of December 31, 20X6?

    a. $63,200.

    b. $63,320.

    c. $63,800.

    d. $65,000.

10. What amount of goodwill, if any, should be reported in the consolidated balance sheet as of December 31, 20X6?

    a. $0.

    b. $3,000.

    c. $10,500.

    d. $27,000.

P8-28   **Comprehensive Problem: Intercorporate Transfers**

Berry Manufacturing Company purchased 90 percent of Bussman Corporation's outstanding common stock on December 31, 20X5, for $1,150,000. On that date, Bussman reported common stock of $500,000, premium on common stock of $280,000, and retained earnings of $420,000. The fair values of all of Bussman's assets and liabilities were equal to their book values on the date of combination, except for land, which was worth more than its book value. Berry estimated that its 90 percent share of the increase in the value of Bussman's land was $30,000.

On April 1, 20X6, Berry issued at par $200,000 of 10 percent bonds directly to Bussman; interest on the bonds is payable March 31 and September 30. On January 2, 20X7, Berry purchased all of Bussman's outstanding 10-year, 12 percent bonds from an unrelated institutional investor at 98. The bonds originally had been issued on January 2, 20X1, for 101. Interest on the bonds is payable December 31 and June 30.

Since the date it was acquired by Berry Manufacturing, Bussman has sold inventory to Berry on a regular basis. The amount of such intercompany sales totaled $64,000 in 20X6 and $78,000 in 20X7, including a 30 percent gross profit. All inventory transferred in 20X6 had been resold by December 31, 20X6, except inventory for which Berry had paid $15,000 and did not resell until January 20X7. All inventory transferred in 20X7 had been resold at December 31, 20X7, except merchandise for which Berry had paid $18,000.

At December 31, 20X7, trial balances for Berry and Bussman appeared as follows:

Item	Berry Manufacturing Debit	Berry Manufacturing Credit	Bussman Corporation Debit	Bussman Corporation Credit
Cash	$ 41,500		$ 29,000	
Current Receivables	112,500		85,100	
Inventory	301,000		348,900	
Investment in Bussman Stock	1,249,000			
Investment in Bussman Bonds	985,000			
Investment in Berry Bonds			200,000	
Land	1,231,000		513,000	
Buildings and Equipment	2,750,000		1,835,000	
Cost of Goods Sold	2,009,000		430,000	
Depreciation and Amortization	195,000		85,000	
Other Expenses	643,000		206,000	
Dividends Declared	50,000		40,000	
Accumulated Depreciation		$1,210,000		$ 619,000
Current Payables		98,000		79,000
Bonds Payable		200,000		1,000,000
Premium on Bonds Payable				3,000
Common Stock		1,000,000		500,000
Premium on Common Stock		700,000		280,000
Retained Earnings, January 1		3,033,000		470,000
Sales		3,101,000		790,000
Other Income		135,000		31,000
Income from Subsidiary		90,000		
Total	$9,567,000	$9,567,000	$3,772,000	$3,772,000

As of December 31, 20X7, Bussman had declared but not yet paid its fourth-quarter dividend of $10,000. Both Berry and Bussman use straight-line depreciation and amortization, including the amortization of bond discount and premium. On December 31, 20X7, Berry's management reviewed the amount attributed to goodwill as a result of its purchase of Bussman common stock and concluded that an impairment loss in the amount of $25,000 had occurred during 20X7. Berry uses the basic equity method to account for its investment in Bussman.

Required

a. Compute the amount of the differential as of January 1, 20X7.

b. Compute the balance of Berry's Investment in Bussman Stock account as of January 1, 20X7.

c. Compute the gain or loss on the constructive retirement of Bussman's bonds that should appear in the 20X7 consolidated income statement.

d. Compute the income that should be assigned to the noncontrolling interest in the 20X7 consolidated income statement.

e. Compute the total noncontrolling interest as of December 31, 20X6.

f. Present all elimination entries that would appear in a three-part consolidation workpaper as of December 31, 20X7.

g. Prepare and complete a three-part workpaper for the preparation of consolidated financial statements for 20X7.

P8-29A **Fully Adjusted Equity Method**

On December 31, 20X4, Bennett Corporation recorded the following entry on its books to adjust its investment in Stone Container Company stock from the basic equity method to the fully adjusted equity method:

Retained Earnings	4,200	
Income from Subsidiary		600
Investment in Stone Container Company Stock		3,600

Required

a. Adjust the data reported by Bennett in the trial balance contained in Problem P8-24 for the effects of the preceding adjusting entry.

b. Prepare the journal entries that would have been recorded on Bennett's books during 20X4 under the fully adjusted equity method.

c. Prepare all eliminating entries needed to complete a consolidation workpaper as of December 31, 20X4, assuming Bennett has used the fully adjusted equity method.

d. Complete a three-part consolidation workpaper as of December 31, 20X4.

P8-30A **Cost Method**

The trial balance data presented in Problem P8-24 can be converted to reflect use of the cost method by inserting the following amounts in place of those presented for Bennett Corporation:

Investment in Stone Container Stock	$ 75,000
Retained Earnings	187,200
Income from Subsidiary	-0-
Dividend Income	6,000

Stone reported retained earnings of $25,000 on the date Bennett purchased 60 percent of the stock.

Required

a. Prepare the journal entries that would have been recorded on Bennett's books during 20X4 under the cost method.

b. Prepare all eliminating entries needed to complete a consolidation workpaper as of December 31, 20X4, assuming Bennett uses the cost method.

c. Complete a three-part consolidation workpaper as of December 31, 20X4.

Kaplan CPA Review

KAPLAN

CPA EDUCATION

Kaplan CPA Review Simulation on Basic Consolidation Procedures

Access to the online CPA Simulation can be attained by visiting the text's Website: www.mhhe.com/Baker7e.

Situation

Giant Company acquired all of the outstanding common stock of Tiny Corporation 4 years ago for $240,000 more than book value. This excess was assigned equally to a building (10-year life), inventory (sold within 1 year), and goodwill. On its separate financial statements for the current year, Giant reported sales of $900,000, cost of goods sold of $500,000, and operating expenses of $200,000. No investment income was included in these figures. On its separate financial statements for the current year, Tiny reported sales of $500,000, cost of goods sold of $200,000, and operating expenses of $100,000. Both companies paid dividends of $20,000 this year and reported positive current ratios of above 1-to-1.

Topics Covered in the Simulation

a. Intercompany inventory transfers.

b. Intercompany equipment transfers.

c. Intercompany land transfers.

d. Intercompany loans.

e. Equity-method reporting.

f. Push-down accounting.

g. Reporting noncontrolling interest (minority interest).

h. Negative goodwill.

Consolidation Ownership Issues

Only simple ownership situations have been presented in the preceding illustrations of consolidations. In practice, however, relatively complex ownership structures are often found. For example, a subsidiary may have preferred stock outstanding in addition to its common stock, and in some cases a parent may acquire shares of both a subsidiary's common and preferred stock. Other times, one or more subsidiaries may acquire stock of the parent or of other related companies. Sometimes the parent's ownership claim on a subsidiary may change through its purchase or sale of subsidiary shares or through stock transactions of the subsidiary.

The discussion in this chapter is intended to provide a basic understanding of some of the consolidation problems arising from complex ownership situations commonly encountered in practice. The following topics are discussed:

1. Subsidiary preferred stock outstanding.
2. Changes in the parent's ownership interest in the subsidiary.
3. Multiple ownership levels.
4. Reciprocal or mutual ownership.
5. Subsidiary stock dividends.

SUBSIDIARY PREFERRED STOCK OUTSTANDING

Many companies have more than one type of stock outstanding. Each type of security typically serves a particular function, and each has a different set of rights and features. Preferred stockholders normally have preference over common shareholders with respect to dividends and the distribution of assets in a liquidation. The right to vote usually is withheld from preferred shareholders, so preferred stock ownership normally does not convey control, regardless of the number of shares owned.

Because a subsidiary's preferred shareholders do have a claim on the net assets of the subsidiary, special attention must be given to that claim in the preparation of consolidated financial statements.

Consolidation with Subsidiary Preferred Stock Outstanding

During preparation of consolidated financial statements, the amount of subsidiary stockholders' equity accruing to preferred shareholders must be determined before dealing with the elimination of the intercompany common stock ownership. If the parent holds some of the subsidiary's preferred stock, its portion of the preferred stock interest must be eliminated. Any portion of the subsidiary's preferred stock interest not held by the parent is assigned to the noncontrolling interest.

As an illustration of the preparation of consolidated financial statements with subsidiary preferred stock outstanding, recall the following information from the example

of Peerless Products Corporation and Special Foods Incorporated used in previous chapters:

1. Peerless Products purchases 80 percent of Special Foods' common stock on December 31, 20X0, at its book value of $240,000 and accounts for the investment using the basic equity method.
2. Peerless Products earns income from its own operations of $140,000 in 20X1 and declares dividends of $60,000.
3. Special Foods reports net income of $50,000 in 20X1 and declares common dividends of $30,000.

Also assume that on January 1, 20X1, Special Foods issues $100,000 of 12 percent preferred stock at par value, none of which is purchased by Peerless. The regular $12,000 preferred dividend is paid in 20X1.

Allocation of Special Foods' Net Income

Of the total $50,000 of net income reported by Special Foods for 20X1, $12,000 ($100,000 × .12) is assigned to the preferred shareholders as their current dividend. Peerless Products records its share of the remaining amount, computed as follows:

Special Foods' net income, 20X1	$50,000
Less: Preferred dividends ($100,000 × .12)	(12,000)
Special Foods' income accruing to common shareholders	$38,000
Peerless's proportionate share	× .80
Peerless's income from Special Foods	$30,400

Income assigned to the noncontrolling interest for 20X1 is the total of Special Foods' preferred dividends and the noncontrolling common stockholders' 20 percent share of Special Foods' $38,000 of income remaining after preferred dividends are deducted:

Preferred dividends of Special Foods	$12,000
Income assigned to Special Foods' noncontrolling common shareholders ($38,000 × .20)	7,600
Income to noncontrolling interest	$19,600

Consolidation Workpaper

The workpaper to prepare consolidated financial statements at the end of 20X1 appears in Figure 9–1. The following elimination entries are included in the workpaper:

E(1)	Income from Subsidiary	30,400	
	Dividends Declared—Common		24,000
	Investment in Special Foods Common		6,400
	Eliminate income from subsidiary.		
E(2)	Income to Noncontrolling Interest	19,600	
	Dividends Declared—Preferred		12,000
	Dividends Declared—Common		6,000
	Noncontrolling Interest		1,600
	Assign income to noncontrolling interest.		

FIGURE 9–1 December 31, 20X1, Consolidation Workpaper, First Year following Combination; 80 Percent Purchase at Book Value

Item	Peerless Products	Special Foods	Eliminations Debit	Eliminations Credit	Consolidated
Sales	400,000	200,000			600,000
Income from Subsidiary	30,400		(1) 30,400		
Credits	430,400	200,000			600,000
Cost of Goods Sold	170,000	115,000			285,000
Depreciation and Amortization	50,000	20,000			70,000
Other Expenses	40,000	15,000			55,000
Debits	(260,000)	(150,000)			(410,000)
					190,000
Income to Noncontrolling Interest			(2) 19,600		(19,600)
Net Income, carry forward	170,400	50,000	50,000		170,400
Retained Earnings, January 1	300,000	100,000	(3) 100,000		300,000
Net Income, from above	170,400	50,000	50,000		170,400
	470,400	150,000			470,400
Dividends Declared: Preferred		(12,000)		(2) 12,000	
Common	(60,000)	(30,000)		(1) 24,000	
				(2) 6,000	(60,000)
Retained Earnings, December 31, carry forward	410,400	108,000	150,000	42,000	410,400
Cash	264,000	163,000			427,000
Accounts Receivable	75,000	50,000			125,000
Inventory	100,000	75,000			175,000
Land	175,000	40,000			215,000
Buildings and Equipment	800,000	600,000			1,400,000
Investment in Special Foods Common	246,400			(1) 6,400	
				(3) 240,000	
Debits	1,660,400	928,000			2,342,000
Accumulated Depreciation	250,000	220,000			470,000
Accounts Payable	100,000	100,000			200,000
Bonds Payable	400,000	200,000			600,000
Preferred Stock		100,000	(4) 100,000		
Common Stock	500,000	200,000	(3) 200,000		500,000
Retained Earnings, from above	410,400	108,000	150,000	42,000	410,400
Noncontrolling Interest				(2) 1,600	
				(3) 60,000	
				(4) 100,000	161,600
Credits	1,660,400	928,000	450,000	450,000	2,342,000

Elimination entries:
 (1) Eliminate income from subsidiary.
 (2) Assign income to noncontrolling interest.
 (3) Eliminate beginning investment in common stock.
 (4) Eliminate subsidiary preferred stock.

E(3)	Common Stock—Special Foods	200,000	
	Retained Earnings, January 1	100,000	
	Investment in Special Foods Common		240,000
	Noncontrolling Interest		60,000
	Eliminate beginning investment in common stock.		
E(4)	Preferred Stock—Special Foods	100,000	
	Noncontrolling Interest		100,000
	Eliminate subsidiary preferred stock.		

In consolidation, the $12,000 preferred dividend is treated as income assigned to the noncontrolling interest. Because Peerless holds none of Special Foods' preferred stock, all of it is classified as part of the noncontrolling interest.

Subsidiary Preferred Stock Held by Parent

Occasionally a parent company holds preferred stock of a subsidiary in addition to its investment in the subsidiary's common stock. Because the preferred stock held by the parent is within the consolidated entity, it must be eliminated when consolidated financial statements are prepared. Likewise, any income from the preferred stock recorded by the parent also must be eliminated.

As an illustration of the treatment of subsidiary preferred stock held by the parent, assume that Peerless Products purchases 60 percent of Special Foods' $100,000 par value, 12 percent preferred stock for $60,000 when issued on January 1, 20X1. During 20X1, dividends of $12,000 are declared on the preferred stock. Peerless recognizes $7,200 ($12,000 × .60) of dividend income from its investment in Special Foods' preferred stock, and the remaining $4,800 ($12,000 × .40) is paid to the holders of the other preferred shares.

In consolidation, the total income assigned to the noncontrolling interest includes the portion of the preferred dividend paid on the shares not held by Peerless:

Noncontrolling interest's share of preferred dividends ($12,000 × .40)	$ 4,800
Income assigned to Special Foods' noncontrolling common shareholders ($38,000 × .20)	7,600
Income to noncontrolling interest	$12,400

The eliminating entries needed in the consolidation workpaper prepared at the end of 20X1 are as follows:

E(5)	Income from Subsidiary	30,400	
	Dividends Declared—Common		24,000
	Investment in Special Foods Common		6,400
	Eliminate income from subsidiary:		
	$30,400 = ($50,000 − $12,000) × .80		
E(6)	Dividend Income—Preferred	7,200	
	Dividends Declared—Preferred		7,200
	Eliminate dividend income from subsidiary preferred: $12,000 × .60		
E(7)	Income to Noncontrolling Interest	12,400	
	Dividends Declared—Preferred		4,800
	Dividends Declared—Common		6,000
	Noncontrolling Interest		1,600
	Assign income to noncontrolling interest:		
	$12,400 = $4,800 + $7,600		
	$4,800 = $12,000 × .40		

E(8)	Common Stock—Special Foods	200,000	
	Retained Earnings, January 1	100,000	
	Investment in Special Foods Common		240,000
	Noncontrolling Interest		60,000
	Eliminate beginning investment in common stock.		
E(9)	Preferred Stock—Special Foods	100,000	
	Investment in Special Foods Preferred		60,000
	Noncontrolling Interest		40,000
	Eliminate subsidiary preferred stock.		

Several points should be noted regarding these elimination entries:

1. Peerless's 60 percent share of Special Foods' preferred stock is eliminated against the preferred stock investment account. The remaining preferred stock is included in the noncontrolling interest.

2. Peerless's dividend income from its investment in Special Foods' preferred stock is eliminated against its share of Special Foods' dividends declared.

3. The income assigned to the noncontrolling interest includes income of Special Foods accruing to both preferred and common shareholders other than Peerless Products. Similarly, the total noncontrolling interest includes Special Foods' stockholders' equity amounts accruing to both preferred and common stockholders other than Peerless.

Subsidiary Preferred Stock with Special Provisions

Many different features of preferred stocks are found in practice. For example, most preferred stocks are cumulative, a few are participating, and many are callable at some price other than par value. When a subsidiary with preferred stock outstanding is consolidated, the provisions of the preferred stock agreement must be examined to determine the portion of the subsidiary's stockholders' equity to be assigned to the preferred stock interest.

A cumulative dividend provision provides some degree of protection for preferred shareholders by requiring the company to pay both current and omitted past preferred dividends before any dividend can be given to common shareholders. If a subsidiary has cumulative preferred stock outstanding, an amount of income equal to the current year's preferred dividend is assigned to the preferred stock interest in consolidation whether or not the preferred dividend is declared. When dividends are in arrears on a subsidiary's cumulative preferred stock, recognition is given in consolidation to the claim of the preferred shareholders by assigning to the preferred stock interest an amount of subsidiary retained earnings equal to the passed dividends. On the other hand, when a subsidiary's preferred stock is noncumulative, the subsidiary has no obligation to pay undeclared dividends. Consequently, no special consolidation procedures are needed with respect to undeclared dividends on noncumulative subsidiary preferred stock.

Preferred stock participation features allow the preferred stockholders to receive a share of income distribution that exceeds the preferred stock base dividend rate. Although few preferred stocks are participating, many different types of participation arrangements are possible. Once the degree of participation has been determined, the appropriate share of subsidiary income and net assets is assigned to the preferred stock interest in the consolidated financial statements.

Many preferred stocks are callable, often at prices that exceed the par value. The amount to be paid to retire a subsidiary's callable preferred stock under the preferred stock agreement is viewed as the preferred stockholders' claim on the subsidiary's assets, and that amount of subsidiary stockholders' equity is assigned to the preferred stock interest in preparing the consolidated balance sheet.

Illustration of Subsidiary Preferred Stock with Special Features

To examine the consolidation treatment of subsidiary preferred stock with the most common special features, assume that Special Foods issues $100,000 par value, 12 percent preferred stock on January 1, 20X0, and that the stock is cumulative, nonparticipating, and callable at 105. No dividends are declared on the preferred stock during 20X0. On December 31, 20X0, Peerless Products purchases 80 percent of Special Foods' common stock for $240,000, and on January 1, 20X1, Peerless purchases 60 percent of the preferred stock for $61,000. The following are the stockholders' equity accounts of Special Foods on December 31, 20X0:

Preferred Stock	$100,000
Common Stock	200,000
Retained Earnings	100,000
Total Stockholders' Equity	$400,000

The amount assigned to the preferred stock interest in the preparation of a consolidated balance sheet on January 1, 20X1, is computed as follows:

Par value of Special Foods' preferred stock	$100,000
Call premium	5,000
Dividends in arrears for 20X0	12,000
Total preferred stock interest, January 1, 20X1	$117,000

This amount is apportioned between Peerless and the noncontrolling shareholders:

Peerless's share of preferred stock interest ($117,000 × .60)	$ 70,200
Noncontrolling stockholders' share of preferred stock interest ($117,000 × .40)	46,800
Total preferred stock interest, January 1, 20X1	$117,000

Because the preferred stock interest exceeds the par value of the preferred stock by $17,000, the portion of Special Foods' retained earnings accruing to the common shareholders is reduced by that amount. Therefore, Special Foods' common stockholders have a total claim on the company's net assets as follows:

Common stock	$200,000
Retained earnings ($100,000 − $17,000)	83,000
Total common stock interest, January 1, 20X1	$283,000

Special Foods' common stock interest is apportioned between Peerless Products and the noncontrolling shareholders in the following manner:

Peerless's share of common stock interest ($283,000 × .80)	$226,400
Noncontrolling stockholders' share of common stock interest ($283,000 × .20)	56,600
Total common stock interest, January 1, 20X1	$283,000

Eliminating entries needed in the consolidation workpaper to prepare a consolidated balance sheet as of January 1, 20X1, are as follows:

E(10)	Common Stock—Special Foods	200,000	
	Retained Earnings	83,000	
	Differential	13,600	
	Investment in Special Foods Common		240,000
	Noncontrolling Interest		56,600
	Eliminate investment in common stock:		
	$83,000 = $100,000 − $17,000		
	$13,600 = $240,000 − ($283,000 × .80)		
	$56,600 = $283,000 × .20		
E(11)	Preferred Stock—Special Foods	100,000	
	Retained Earnings	17,000	
	Investment in Special Foods Preferred		61,000
	Additional Paid-In Capital		9,200
	Noncontrolling Interest		46,800
	Eliminate subsidiary preferred stock:		
	$17,000 = $117,000 − $100,000		
	$9,200 = ($117,000 × .60) − $61,000		
	$46,800 = $117,000 × .40		

The following points should be noted with respect to eliminating entries E(10) and E(11):

1. Only the $83,000 portion of Special Foods' retained earnings relating to the common stock interest is eliminated in entry E(10). The remaining $17,000 of retained earnings related to the preferred stock interest is eliminated in entry E(11).

2. Because Peerless's share of Special Foods' common stock interest is $226,400 ($283,000 × .80) and the cost of the investment was $240,000, a $13,600 differential arises in consolidation. This differential is assigned to the appropriate assets and liabilities in the workpaper.

3. The total noncontrolling interest on January 1, 20X1, consists of both preferred and common stock interests, as follows:

Preferred stock interest ($117,000 × .40)	$ 46,800
Common stock interest ($283,000 × .20)	56,600
Total noncontrolling interest, January 1, 20X1	$103,400

4. The difference between the cost of Peerless's investment in Special Foods' preferred stock and the underlying claim on Special Foods' net assets is computed as follows:

Claim on Special Foods' net assets ($117,000 × .60)	$70,200
Cost of preferred stock investment	(61,000)
Difference	$ 9,200

From a consolidated viewpoint, Peerless's purchase of the preferred stock is considered a retirement of a noncontrolling ownership interest by the consolidated entity. Because this retirement occurred at less than book value and gains and losses are not recognized on capital transactions, this excess is considered to be additional paid-in capital of the consolidated entity and is credited to that account in entry E(11).

CHANGES IN PARENT COMPANY OWNERSHIP

Although preceding chapters have treated the parent company's subsidiary ownership interest as remaining constant over time, in actuality ownership levels sometimes vary. Changes in ownership levels may result from either the parent's or the subsidiary's actions. The parent company can change ownership ratios by purchasing or selling shares of the subsidiary in transactions with unaffiliated companies. A subsidiary can change the parent's ownership percentage by selling additional shares to or repurchasing shares from unaffiliated parties or through stock transactions with the parent (if the subsidiary is less than wholly owned).

Parent's Purchase of Additional Shares from Nonaffiliate

A parent company may purchase the common stock of a subsidiary at different points in time. When consolidated statements are prepared, the cost of each block of stock purchased is compared with the stock's book value at the date of purchase and the difference is treated as part of the purchase differential to be assigned.

Purchases of additional shares of an investee's common stock were discussed in the context of accounting for intercorporate investments in Chapter 2. Additional effects of multiple purchases of a subsidiary's stock on the consolidation process are illustrated in the following example.

Assume that on January 1, 20X0, Special Foods has $200,000 of common stock outstanding and retained earnings of $60,000. During 20X0, 20X1, and 20X2, Special Foods reports the following information:

Period	Net Income	Dividends	Ending Book Value
20X0	$40,000	-0-	$300,000
20X1	50,000	$30,000	320,000
20X2	75,000	40,000	355,000

Peerless Products purchases its 80 percent interest in Special Foods in several blocks, as follows:

Purchase Date	Ownership Percentage Purchased	Cost	Book Value	Differential
January 1, 20X0	20	$ 56,000	$ 52,000	$ 4,000
December 31, 20X0	10	35,000	30,000	5,000
January 1, 20X2	50	185,000	160,000	25,000
	80	$276,000	$242,000	$34,000

All of the differential relates to land held by Special Foods. Note that Peerless does not gain control of Special Foods until January 1, 20X2.

The investment account on Peerless's books will include the following amounts:

20X0	
Purchase shares (January 1)	$ 56,000
Equity-method income ($40,000 × .20)	8,000
Purchase of shares (December 31)	35,000
Balance in investment account (December 31)	$ 99,000

(continued)

(continued)

20X1		
Equity-method income ($50,000 × .30)		15,000
Dividends received ($30,000 × .30)		(9,000)
Balance in investment account (December 31)		$105,000
20X2		
Purchase of shares (January 1)		185,000
Equity-method income ($75,000 × .80)		60,000
Dividends received ($40,000 × .80)		(32,000)
Balance in investment account (December 31)		$318,000

Because Peerless Products gains control of Special Foods on January 1, 20X2, consolidated statements are prepared for the year 20X2. The consolidation workpaper prepared at the end of the year includes the following elimination entries:

E(12)	Income from Subsidiary	60,000	
	Dividends Declared		32,000
	Investment in Special Foods Stock		28,000
	Eliminate income from subsidiary.		
E(13)	Income to Noncontrolling Interest	15,000	
	Dividends Declared		8,000
	Noncontrolling Interest		7,000
	Assign income to noncontrolling shareholders:		
	$15,000 = $75,000 × .20		
	$8,000 = $40,000 × .20		
	$7,000 = $15,000 − $8,000		
E(14)	Common Stock—Special Foods	200,000	
	Retained Earnings, January 1	120,000	
	Land	34,000	
	Investment in Special Foods Stock		290,000
	Noncontrolling Interest		64,000
	Eliminate beginning investment balance:		
	$290,000 = $105,000 + $185,000		
	$64,000 = $320,000 × .20		

Entry E(12) eliminates the income from Special Foods recognized by Peerless during 20X2. Entry E(13) assigns income to the noncontrolling shareholders and eliminates their share of Special Foods' dividends based on the 20 percent noncontrolling ownership interest held during 20X2. Entry E(14) eliminates the beginning stockholders' equity balances of Special Foods, establishes the noncontrolling interest as of the beginning of the year, and eliminates the beginning investment account balance of Peerless.

In the event that a purchase of additional shares is made during the period, the eliminating entries are altered so that consolidated net income includes only the earnings accruing to the parent company for the portion of the period in which the parent owned the additional shares. Consolidation procedures for interim acquisitions are illustrated in Chapter 10.

Parent's Sale of Subsidiary Shares to Nonaffiliate

A gain or loss normally occurs and is recorded on the seller's books when a company disposes of all or part of an investment. **APB 18** deals explicitly with sales of stock of an investee, requiring recognition of a gain or loss on the difference between the selling price and the carrying amount of the stock.[1] A question arises, however, when the shares sold are those of a subsidiary and the subsidiary continues to qualify for consolidation. When a parent sells some of the shares of a subsidiary but continues to hold a controlling interest, the issue is whether the gain or loss on the sale of shares should be carried to the consolidated income statement or eliminated in consolidation.

Recognizing a gain or loss in the consolidated income statement on a sale of subsidiary shares while continuing to consolidate the subsidiary seems inconsistent with the concept of a single economic entity. From a consolidated viewpoint, the subsidiary shares become part of the noncontrolling interest outstanding at the point they are sold to a nonaffiliate. If no gains or losses are recognized when a single company issues stock, none should be recognized when a company within a consolidated entity issues stock. The difference between the carrying value on the parent's books before the sale and the sale price is conceptually better represented in the consolidated financial statements as an adjustment to additional paid-in capital rather than as a gain or loss. This also has been the FASB's view for the past decade, although it has yet to be incorporated into an official pronouncement. However, this treatment is required in the FASB's proposed new standard for consolidated financial statements.

As an illustration of the sale of subsidiary stock to a nonaffiliate, assume that on December 31, 20X0, Special Foods has 20,000 common shares outstanding with a total par value of $200,000 and retained earnings of $100,000. On that date, Peerless acquires an 80 percent interest in Special Foods by purchasing 16,000 shares of its $10 par common stock at book value of $240,000 ($300,000 × .80). Special Foods reports net income of $50,000 for 20X1 and pays dividends of $30,000. On January 1, 20X2, Peerless sells 1,000 shares of its Special Foods common stock to a nonaffiliate for $19,000, leaving it with a 75 percent interest (15,000 ÷ 20,000) in Special Foods. On the date of sale, Special Foods has total stockholders' equity of $320,000, consisting of common stock of $200,000 and retained earnings of $120,000.

Difference between Carrying Amount and Sale Price of Investment

The equity-method carrying amount of Peerless's investment in Special Foods on the date of sale reflects Peerless's share of Special Foods' 20X1 net income and dividends, as follows:

Cost of investment, December 31, 20X0	$240,000
Peerless's share of Special Foods' 20X1 net income ($50,000 × .80)	40,000
Peerless's share of Special Foods' 20X1 dividends ($30,000 × .80)	(24,000)
Investment balance, January 1, 20X2	$256,000

Because no differential exists, the balance of the investment account equals 80 percent of the total stockholders' equity of Special Foods on January 1, 20X1.

Peerless records the sale of the Special Foods stock with the following entry:

January 1, 20X2			
(15)	Cash	19,000	
	Investment in Special Foods Stock		16,000
	Gain on Sale of Investment		3,000
	Record sale of investment:		
	$16,000 = $256,000 × 1/16		

---

[1] *Accounting Principles Board Opinion No. 18,* "The Equity Method of Accounting for Investments in Common Stock," March 1971, para. 19(f).

Peerless recognizes a gain of $3,000 on the sale for the difference between the $16,000 carrying amount of the shares ($256,000 × ¹⁄₁₆) and the selling price of $19,000.

Consolidation Workpaper 20X2

If recognition of the gain on the sale of the stock is considered appropriate in the consolidated income statement, no adjustment is needed in preparing consolidated statements for December 31, 20X2, or in the periods that follow. On the other hand, excluding the gain from the consolidated income statement is more consistent with the view of a single economic entity. In that case, the gain is eliminated and additional paid-in capital is established in the December 31, 20X2, consolidation workpaper with the following entry:

E(16)	Gain on Sale of Investment	3,000	
	Additional Paid-In Capital		3,000
	Eliminate gain on transaction involving subsidiary stock.		

This entry treats the stock transaction as the issuance of stock by the consolidated entity to the noncontrolling interest.

The consolidation workpaper prepared as of December 31, 20X2, is shown in Figure 9–2. In addition to entry E(16), the workpaper includes the normal entries to eliminate a 75 percent investment in Special Foods:

E(17)	Income from Subsidiary	56,250	
	Dividends Declared		30,000
	Investment in Special Foods Stock		26,250
	Eliminate income from subsidiary:		
	$56,250 = $75,000 × .75		
	$30,000 = $40,000 × .75		
	$26,250 = $56,250 − $30,000		
E(18)	Income to Noncontrolling Interest	18,750	
	Dividends Declared		10,000
	Noncontrolling Interest		8,750
	Assign income to noncontrolling interest:		
	$18,750 = $75,000 × .25		
	$10,000 = $40,000 × .25		
	$8,750 = $18,750 − $10,000		
E(19)	Common Stock—Special Foods	200,000	
	Retained Earnings, January 1	120,000	
	Investment in Special Foods Stock		240,000
	Noncontrolling Interest		80,000
	Eliminate beginning investment in common stock:		
	$240,000 = $320,000 × .75		
	$80,000 = $320,000 × .25		

Entry E(17) eliminates Peerless's 75 percent share of Special Foods' income and dividends. Entry E(18) assigns income to the noncontrolling stockholders based on their 25 percent ownership interest.

FIGURE 9–2   December 31, 20X2, Consolidation Workpaper, Second Year following Combination; 75 Percent Ownership, Purchased at Book Value

Item	Peerless Products	Special Foods	Eliminations Debit	Eliminations Credit	Consolidated
Sales	450,000	300,000			750,000
Gain on Sale of Investment	3,000		(16) 3,000		
Income from Subsidiary	56,250		(17) 56,250		
Credits	509,250	300,000			750,000
Cost of Goods Sold	180,000	160,000			340,000
Depreciation and Amortization	50,000	20,000			70,000
Other Expenses	60,000	45,000			105,000
Debits	(290,000)	(225,000)			(515,000)
					235,000
Income to Noncontrolling Interest			(18) 18,750		(18,750)
Net Income, carry forward	219,250	75,000	78,000		216,250
Retained Earnings, January 1	420,000	120,000	(19) 120,000		420,000
Net Income, from above	219,250	75,000	78,000		216,250
	639,250	195,000			636,250
Dividends Declared	(60,000)	(40,000)		(17) 30,000	
				(18) 10,000	(60,000)
Retained Earnings, December 31, carry forward	579,250	155,000	198,000	40,000	576,250
Cash	308,000	85,000			393,000
Accounts Receivable	150,000	80,000			230,000
Inventory	180,000	90,000			270,000
Land	175,000	40,000			215,000
Buildings and Equipment	800,000	600,000			1,400,000
Investment in Special Foods Stock	266,250			(17) 26,250	
				(19) 240,000	
Debits	1,879,250	895,000			2,508,000
Accumulated Depreciation	300,000	240,000			540,000
Accounts Payable	100,000	100,000			200,000
Bonds Payable	400,000	200,000			600,000
Common Stock	500,000	200,000	(19) 200,000		500,000
Additional Paid-In Capital				(16) 3,000	3,000
Retained Earnings, from above	579,250	155,000	198,000	40,000	576,250
Noncontrolling Interest				(18) 8,750	
				(19) 80,000	88,750
Credits	1,879,250	895,000	398,000	398,000	2,508,000

Elimination entries:
(16) Eliminate gain on transaction involving subsidiary stock.
(17) Eliminate income from subsidiary.
(18) Assign income to noncontrolling interest.
(19) Eliminate beginning investment in common stock.

The balance in Peerless's investment account shown in the consolidation workpaper is $266,250. This amount is the result of the following entries in the investment account:

Investment in Special Foods Stock				
Original cost	240,000			
20X1 equity accrual ($50,000 × .80)	40,000		20X1 dividends ($30,000 × .80)	24,000
Balance, 12/31/X1	256,000			
		(15)	Sale of 1,000 shares ($256,000 × ¹⁄₁₆)	16,000
20X2 equity accrual ($75,000 × .75)	56,250		20X2 dividends ($40,000 × .75)	30,000
Balance, 12/31/X2	266,250			

The amount of Peerless's investment eliminated in entry E(19) is the balance at the beginning of 20X2 immediately after Peerless sold the 1,000 shares; this amount equals Peerless's 75 percent share of the $320,000 beginning book value of Special Foods. Entries E(17) and E(19) together eliminate the total investment balance reported by Peerless on December 31, 20X2.

The amount assigned to the noncontrolling interest in entry E(19) is 25 percent of Special Foods' beginning book value. The total noncontrolling interest established in entries E(18) and E(19) together is $88,750, equal to 25 percent of Special Foods' $355,000 book value on December 31, 20X2.

Consolidation Subsequent to 20X2

In preparing consolidated financial statements each year after 20X2, a workpaper entry similar to E(16) is needed to reestablish the $3,000 increase in additional paid-in capital. Because the gain recognized by Peerless in 20X2 has been closed to Retained Earnings, beginning retained earnings must be reduced to eliminate the effects of the gain. The entry included in the consolidation workpaper each year after 20X2 is as follows:

E(20)	Retained Earnings, January 1	3,000	
	Additional Paid-In Capital		3,000
	Eliminate effects of gain on transaction involving subsidiary stock.		

Subsidiary's Sale of Additional Shares to Nonaffiliate

Additional funds are generated for the consolidated enterprise when a subsidiary sells new shares to parties outside the economic entity. A sale of additional shares to an unaffiliated party increases the subsidiary's total shares outstanding and, consequently, reduces the percentage ownership held by the parent company. At the same time, the dollar amount assigned to the noncontrolling interest in the consolidated financial statements increases. The resulting amounts of the controlling and noncontrolling interests are affected by two factors:

1. The number of shares sold to nonaffiliates.
2. The price at which the shares are sold to nonaffiliates.

Difference between Book Value and Sale Price of Subsidiary Shares

If the sale price of new shares equals the book value of outstanding shares, there is no change in the existing shareholders' claim. If the subsidiary's stockholders' equity is viewed as a pie, the overall size of the pie increases. The parent's share of the pie decreases, but the size of the parent's slice remains the same because of the increase in the overall size of the pie.

The eliminating entries used in consolidation simply are changed to recognize the increase in the claim of the noncontrolling shareholders and the corresponding increase in the stockholders' equity balances of the subsidiary.

Most sales, however, do not occur at book value. When the sale price and book value are not the same, all common shareholders are assigned a pro rata portion of the difference. In this situation, the book value of the subsidiary's shares held by the parent changes even though the number remains constant. The size of both the pie and the parent's share of it change; the size of the parent's slice changes because the increase in the pie's size and the decrease in the parent's share do not exactly offset one another.

The change in book value of the shares held by the parent company can be reported in the consolidated statements in one of two ways under current reporting standards:

1. An adjustment to paid-in capital.
2. A gain or loss in the consolidated income statement.

Although support for both alternatives can be found in the accounting literature, the FASB has recommended that the acquisition of treasury stock or the issuance of additional shares by the subsidiary be treated as transactions in the equity of the consolidated entity with no gain or loss recognized.

From a consolidated viewpoint, a subsidiary's sale of additional shares to unaffiliated parties and a parent's sale of subsidiary shares are similar transactions: in both cases the consolidated entity sells shares to the noncontrolling interest. Because the participants in a consolidation are regarded as members of a single economic entity, the sale of subsidiary shares to the noncontrolling interest should be treated in the same way regardless of whether the parent or the subsidiary sells the shares. The recognition of a gain or loss on such a transaction seems inappropriate because the sale of stock to unaffiliated parties by the consolidated entity is a capital transaction from a single-entity viewpoint.

Illustration of Sale of Subsidiary Stock to Nonaffiliate

To examine the sale of additional shares by a subsidiary to a nonaffiliate, assume that Peerless Products acquires an 80 percent interest in Special Foods by purchasing 16,000 shares of Special Foods' $10 par common stock on December 31, 20X0, at book value of $240,000. Special Foods has only common stock outstanding. All other information is the same as that used previously. On January 1, 20X2, Special Foods sells 5,000 additional shares of stock to nonaffiliates for $20 per share, a total of $100,000. After the sale, Special Foods has 25,000 shares outstanding, and Peerless has a 64 percent interest (16,000 ÷ 25,000) in Special Foods.

The January 1, 20X2, sale of additional shares results in the following change in Special Foods' balance sheet:

	Before Sale	Following Sale
Common Stock, $10 par value	$200,000	$250,000
Additional Paid-In Capital		50,000
Retained Earnings	120,000	120,000
Total Stockholders' Equity	$320,000	$420,000

The book value of Peerless's investment in Special Foods changes as a result of the sale of additional shares as follows:

	Before Sale	Following Sale
Special Foods' total stockholders' equity	$320,000	$420,000
Peerless's proportionate share	× .80	× .64
Book value of Peerless's investment in Special Foods	$256,000	$268,800

Note that, while Peerless's ownership percentage decreases from 80 percent to 64 percent, the book value of Peerless's investment increases by $12,800. The increase in book value occurs because the $20 selling price of the additional shares exceeds the $16 ($320,000 ÷ 20,000 shares) book value of the outstanding shares before the sale:

Selling price of additional shares	$ 20
Book value of shares before sale ($320,000 ÷ 20,000 shares)	(16)
Excess of selling price over book value	$ 4
Number of shares sold	× 5,000
Excess book value added	$20,000
Peerless's proportionate share	× .64
Increase in Peerless's equity	$12,800

The increase in Peerless's equity in the net assets of Special Foods may be recorded on Peerless's books with the following entry:

(21)	Investment in Special Foods Stock	12,800	
	Additional Paid-In Capital		12,800
	Record increase in equity in subsidiary resulting from subsidiary sale of shares.		

Consistent with the FASB recommendation, the approach used here avoids recognizing a gain or loss because the change results from the capital transactions of a related company.

The investment elimination entry needed to prepare a consolidated balance sheet on January 1, 20X2, immediately after the sale of the additional shares, is as follows:

E(22)	Common Stock—Special Foods	250,000	
	Additional Paid-In Capital—Special Foods	50,000	
	Retained Earnings, January 1	120,000	
	Investment in Special Foods Stock		268,800
	Noncontrolling Interest		151,200
	Eliminate investment in common stock:		
	$268,800 = $420,000 × .64		
	$151,200 = $420,000 × .36		

Additional paid-in capital recorded by Special Foods from the sale of the additional shares is eliminated in the preparation of consolidated financial statements, as are all of the subsidiary's stockholders' equity accounts. The noncontrolling interest's share of the increase in the book value of Special Foods' stock resulting from the sale of additional shares is reflected in the balance of the noncontrolling interest in the consolidated balance sheet. The $151,200 balance of the noncontrolling interest is 36 percent of the $420,000 total book value of Special Foods after the sale of the additional shares. Peerless's $12,800 share of the increase in Special Foods' book value is included in the consolidated balance sheet by carrying over the additional paid-in capital recorded by Peerless in entry (21).

Sale of Subsidiary Stock at Less than Book Value

A sale of stock by a subsidiary to a nonaffiliate at less than existing book value has an effect opposite to that just illustrated. The parent company's claim is diminished as a result of selling additional shares at less than existing book value. A reduction in the book value of the shares held by the parent normally is treated as a debit to Additional Paid-In Capital and a credit to the investment account. In the absence of the Additional Paid-In Capital account, retained earnings is reduced.

Subsidiary's Sale of Additional Shares to Parent

A sale of additional shares directly from a less-than-wholly owned subsidiary to its parent increases the parent's ownership percentage. If the sale is at a price equal to the book value of the existing shares, the increase in the parent's investment account equals the increase in the stockholders' equity of the subsidiary. The net book value assigned to the noncontrolling interest remains unchanged. In preparing consolidated financial statements, the normal elimination entries are made based on the parent's new ownership percentage.

When the parent purchases shares directly from a subsidiary at an amount other than the book value of the subsidiary's shares already outstanding, a differential is measured as the difference between the price paid and the resulting increase in the total underlying book value of all shares owned by the parent. This increase in book value includes both the amount assigned to the new shares just acquired from the subsidiary and the increase or decrease in the book value of shares previously held by the parent. In preparing consolidated financial statements, the differential thus determined is treated in the same manner as a differential arising on a purchase from a nonaffiliate. However, because the parent may be able to influence the purchase price of the shares in this case, the amount of differential may or may not have an obvious connection to changes in the value of identifiable assets or liabilities and must be reviewed carefully in determining how it is to be assigned.

As an illustration of the sale of additional shares from a subsidiary to its parent, assume that in the example of Peerless Products and Special Foods, Peerless purchases in the market 16,000 shares of Special Foods $10 par common stock at book value of $240,000 on December 31, 20X0, giving Peerless an 80 percent interest. By December 31, 20X1, the equity-method carrying amount of the investment on Peerless's books is $256,000. On January 1, 20X2, Peerless purchases an additional 5,000 shares of common directly from Special Foods for $20 per share. This additional $100,000 investment gives Peerless a total ownership interest in Special Foods of 84 percent (21,000 ÷ 25,000).

The subsidiary's sale of additional shares to the parent results in the following change in Special Foods' balance sheet:

	Before Sale	Following Sale
Common Stock, $10 par value	$200,000	$250,000
Additional Paid-In Capital		50,000
Retained Earnings	120,000	120,000
Total Stockholders' Equity	$320,000	$420,000

The book value of Peerless's investment in Special Foods changes as a result of the sale of additional shares, as follows:

	Before Sale	Following Sale
Special Foods' total stockholders' equity	$320,000	$420,000
Peerless's proportionate share	× .80	× .84
Book value of Peerless's investment in Special Foods	$256,000	$352,800

If Special Foods' stockholders' equity is viewed as a pie, the size of both the pie and Peerless's percentage share of it increase. Therefore, the size of Peerless's slice of the pie increases by $96,800.

The new book value per share of Special Foods' stock is $16.80 ($420,000 ÷ 25,000 shares) as compared with the $16.00 ($320,000 ÷ 20,000 shares) book value before the sale of additional shares. The book value is higher because the price Peerless paid for the additional shares is more than the stock's previous book value.

Because Peerless paid a price for the additional shares that is in excess of their book value, a differential arises, as follows:

Price paid by Peerless for additional shares		$100,000
Increase in book value of Peerless's investment:		
Book value following acquisition ($420,000 × .84)	$352,800	
Book value before acquisition ($320,000 × .80)	(256,000)	
Increase in book value		(96,800)
Differential		$ 3,200

The investment elimination entry needed to prepare a consolidated balance sheet immediately following the sale of additional shares to Peerless on January 1, 20X2, is as follows:

E(23)	Common Stock—Special Foods	250,000	
	Additional Paid-In Capital	50,000	
	Retained Earnings, January 1	120,000	
	Differential	3,200	
	Investment in Special Foods Stock		356,000
	Noncontrolling Interest		67,200
	Eliminate investment in common stock:		
	$356,000 = $256,000 + $100,000		
	$67,200 = $420,000 × .16		

The balance eliminated from Peerless's investment account equals the previous balance of $256,000 plus the $100,000 cost of the additional shares. The amount of the noncontrolling interest is established at 16 percent of the $420,000 book value of Special Foods.

Subsidiary's Purchase of Shares from Nonaffiliate

Sometimes a subsidiary purchases treasury shares from noncontrolling shareholders. Noncontrolling shareholders frequently find they have little opportunity for input into the subsidiary's activities and operations and often are willing sellers. The parent company may prefer not to be concerned with outside shareholders and may direct the subsidiary to reacquire any noncontrolling shares that become available.

Although the parent is not a direct participant when a subsidiary purchases treasury stock from noncontrolling shareholders, the parent's equity in the net assets of the subsidiary may change as a result of the transaction. When this occurs, the amount of the change must be recognized in preparing the consolidated statements.

For example, assume that Peerless Products owns 80 percent of Special Foods' 20,000 shares of $10 par common stock, which it purchased on January 1, 20X1, for $240,000. On January 1, 20X2, Special Foods purchases 1,000 treasury shares from a nonaffiliate for $20 per share. Peerless's interest in Special Foods increases to 84.21 percent (16,000 ÷ 19,000) as a result of Special Foods' reacquisition of shares, and the noncontrolling interest decreases to 15.79 percent (3,000 ÷ 19,000). The stockholders' equity of Special Foods before and after the reacquisition of shares is as follows:

	Before Purchase	Following Purchase
Common Stock, $10 par value	$200,000	$200,000
Retained Earnings	120,000	120,000
Total	$320,000	$320,000
Less: Treasury Stock		(20,000)
Total Stockholders' Equity	$320,000	$300,000

The underlying book value of Special Foods' shares held by Peerless changes as a result of the stock reacquisition, as follows:

	Before Purchase	Following Purchase
Special Foods' total stockholders' equity	$320,000	$300,000
Peerless's proportionate share	× .80	× .8421
Book value of Peerless's investment in Special Foods	$256,000	$252,630

The reacquisition of shares by Special Foods at an amount higher than book value results in a decrease in the book value of Peerless's investment of $3,370 ($256,000 − $252,630). Peerless recognizes the decrease with the following entry:

(24)	Retained Earnings	3,370	
	Investment in Special Foods Stock		3,370
	Record decrease in equity in subsidiary from subsidiary stock reacquisition.		

As with the sale of additional shares to a nonaffiliate, an adjustment to additional paid-in capital seems to be the most appropriate way of recognizing the change in the parent's equity in the net assets of the subsidiary. Peerless reduces retained earnings in this situation because it has no additional paid-in capital on its books.

The investment elimination entry needed in a consolidation workpaper prepared immediately after the stock reacquisition on January 1, 20X2, is as follows:

E(25)	Common Stock—Special Foods	200,000	
	Retained Earnings, January 1	120,000	
	Treasury Stock		20,000
	Investment in Special Foods Stock		252,630
	Noncontrolling Interest		47,370
	Eliminate investment in common stock:		
	$252,630 = $256,000 − $3,370		
	$47,370 = $300,000 × .1579		

Note that this entry eliminates all of the common stockholders' equity balances of the subsidiary, including the treasury stock.

Subsidiary's Purchase of Shares from Parent

A subsidiary can reduce the number of shares it has outstanding through purchases from the parent as well as from noncontrolling shareholders. In practice, stock repurchases from the parent occur infrequently. A parent reducing its ownership interest in a subsidiary usually does so by selling some of its holdings to nonaffiliates to generate additional funds.

When a subsidiary reacquires some of its shares from its parent, the parent records a gain or loss on the difference between the selling price and the change in the carrying amount of its investment. Some question exists as to whether a transaction of this type between a parent and its subsidiary can be regarded as arm's length; consequently, reporting the gain or loss in the parent's income statement can be questioned. From a consolidated viewpoint, when a subsidiary reacquires its shares from the parent, the transaction represents an internal transfer and does not give rise to a gain or loss.

As an example of the reacquisition of a subsidiary's shares from its parent, assume that Peerless Products purchases in the market 16,000 of Special Foods' 20,000 shares of $10 par common stock on December 31, 20X0, at book value of $240,000. On January 1, 20X2, Special Foods repurchases 4,000 shares from Peerless at $20 per share, leaving Peerless with a 75 percent interest (12,000 ÷ 16,000) in Special Foods. The stockholders' equity of Special Foods before and after the reacquisition of shares is as follows:

	Before Purchase	Following Purchase
Common Stock, $10 par value	$200,000	$200,000
Retained Earnings	120,000	120,000
Total	$320,000	$320,000
Less: Treasury Stock		(80,000)
Total Stockholders' Equity	$320,000	$240,000

The carrying amount of Peerless's investment in Special Foods' stock equals the underlying book value of the shares in this example. The book value of the shares changes as a result of the reacquisition, as follows:

	Before Purchase	Following Purchase
Special Foods' total stockholders' equity	$320,000	$240,000
Peerless's proportionate share	× .80	× .75
Book value of Peerless's investment in Special Foods	$256,000	$180,000

Peerless records the sale of 25 percent (4,000 ÷ 16,000) of its investment in Special Foods with the following entry:

January 1, 20X2		
(26) Cash	80,000	
Investment in Special Foods Stock		76,000
Gain on Sale of Investment		4,000
Record sale of investment:		
$80,000 = $20 × 4,000 shares		
$76,000 = $256,000 − $180,000		
$4,000 = $80,000 − $76,000		

The new carrying value of the investment is $180,000 ($256,000 − $76,000). Because there is no differential in this case, this amount equals 75 percent of Special Foods' total stockholders' equity of $240,000 following the reacquisition. The $76,000 decrease in the carrying value includes both the reduction resulting from the decrease in the number of shares held and the reduction in the book value of those shares still held.

During preparation of consolidated financial statements for 20X2, the gain must be reclassified as additional paid-in capital, and the stockholders' equity balances of Special Foods, including the treasury stock, must be eliminated. The following eliminating entries are included, along with the other usual entries, in a consolidation workpaper prepared as of December 31, 20X2:

E(27)	Gain on Sale of Investment	4,000	
	Additional Paid-In Capital		4,000
	Eliminate gain on transaction involving subsidiary stock.		
E(28)	Common Stock—Special Foods	200,000	
	Retained Earnings, January 1	120,000	
	Treasury Stock		80,000
	Investment in Special Foods Stock		180,000
	Noncontrolling Interest		60,000
	Eliminate investment in common stock:		
	$180,000 = $240,000 \times .75$		
	$60,000 = $240,000 \times .25$		

COMPLEX OWNERSHIP STRUCTURES

Current reporting standards call for preparing consolidated financial statements when one company has direct or indirect control over another. The discussion to this point has focused on a simple, direct parent–subsidiary relationship. Many companies, however, have substantially more complex organizational schemes.

Figure 9–3 shows three different types of ownership structures. A **direct ownership** situation of the type discussed in preceding chapters is shown in Figure 9–3(*a*); the parent has controlling interest in each of the subsidiaries. In the **multilevel ownership** case shown in Figure 9–3(*b*), the parent has only **indirect control** over the company controlled by its subsidiary. The eliminating entries used in preparing consolidated financial statements in this situation are similar to those used in a simple ownership situation, but careful attention must be given to the sequence in which the data are brought together.

Figure 9–3(*c*) reflects **reciprocal ownership** or **mutual holdings**. With reciprocal ownership, the parent owns a majority of the subsidiary's common stock and the subsidiary holds some of the parent's common shares. If mutual shareholdings are ignored in the preparation of consolidated financial statements, some reported amounts may be materially overstated.

Multilevel Ownership and Control

In many cases, companies establish multiple corporate levels through which they carry out diversified operations. For example, a company may have a number of subsidiaries, one of which is a retailer. The retail subsidiary may in turn have a finance subsidiary, a real estate subsidiary, an insurance subsidiary, and perhaps other subsidiaries. This means that when consolidated statements are prepared, they include companies in which the parent has only an indirect investment along with those in which it holds direct ownership.

The complexity of the consolidation process increases as additional ownership levels are included. The amount of income and net assets to be assigned to the controlling and noncontrolling shareholders, and the amount of unrealized profits and losses to be eliminated, must be determined at each level of ownership.

When a number of different levels of ownership exist, the first step normally is to consolidate the bottom, or most remote, subsidiaries with the companies at the next higher level. This sequence is continued up through the ownership structure until the subsidiaries owned

FIGURE 9–3 **Alternative Ownership Structures**

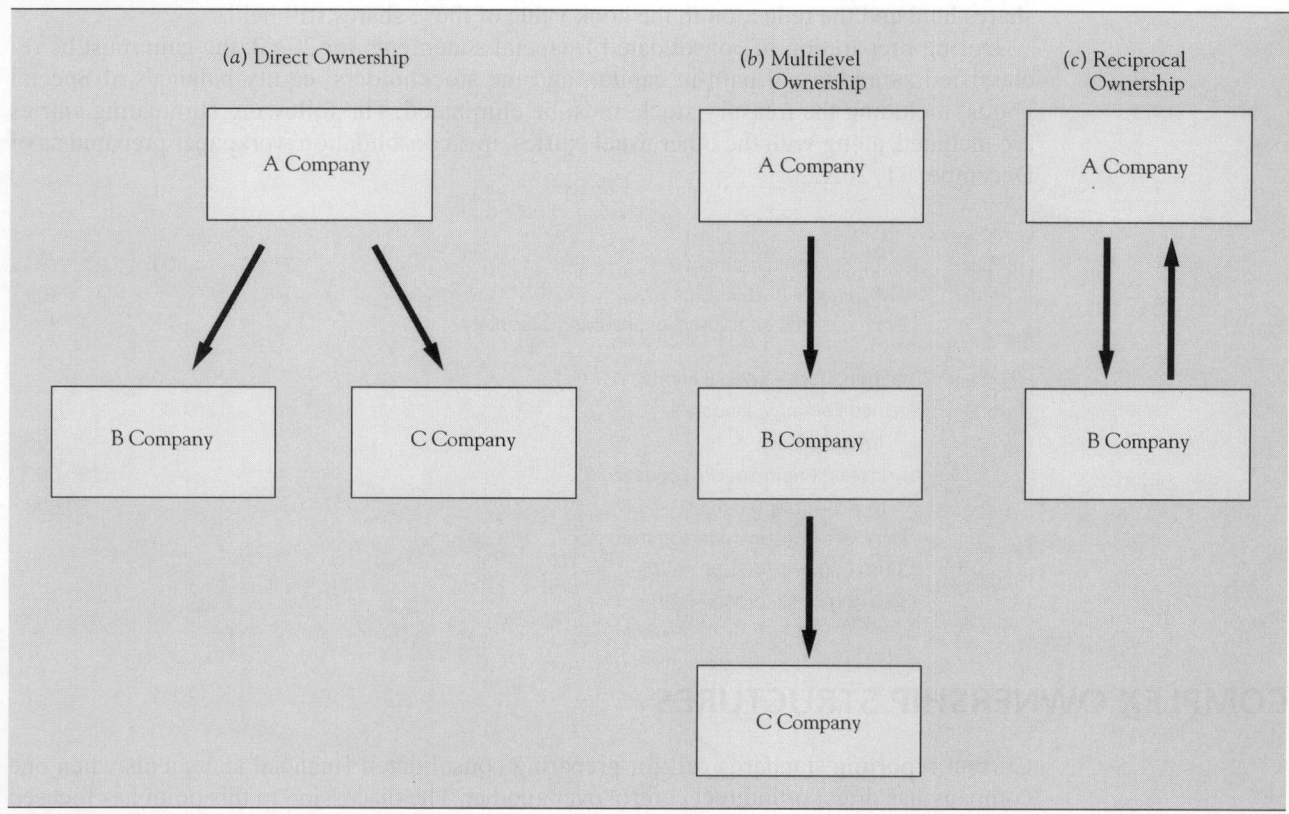

(a) Direct Ownership

A Company

B Company   C Company

(b) Multilevel Ownership

A Company

B Company

C Company

(c) Reciprocal Ownership

A Company

B Company

directly by the parent company are consolidated with it. Income is apportioned between the controlling and noncontrolling shareholders of the companies at each level.

As an illustration of consolidation when multiple ownership levels exist, assume the following:

1. Peerless Products purchases 80 percent of Special Foods' common stock on December 31, 20X0, at book value of $240,000.

2. Special Foods purchases 90 percent of Bottom Company's common stock on January 1, 20X1, at book value of $162,000. On the date of acquisition, Bottom has common stock of $100,000 and retained earnings of $80,000.

3. During 20X1, Bottom reports net income of $10,000 and declares dividends of $8,000; Special Foods reports separate operating income of $50,000 and declares dividends of $30,000.

All other data are the same as in the Peerless Products–Special Foods examples used throughout previous chapters. The ownership structure is as follows:

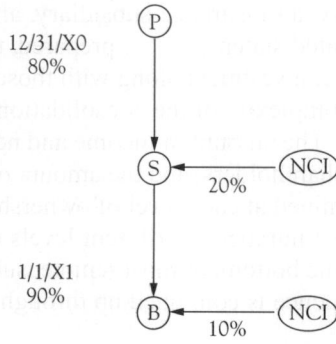

Computation of Net Income

In the case of a three-tiered structure involving a parent company, its subsidiary, and the subsidiary's subsidiary, the parent company's equity-method net income is computed by first adding an appropriate portion of the income of the bottom subsidiary to the separate earnings of the parent's subsidiary and then adding an appropriate portion of that total to the parent's separate earnings. Consolidated net income can be computed in the same way.

Peerless's net income is computed as follows:

	Peerless Products	Special Foods	Bottom Company	Noncontrolling Interest
Operating income	$140,000	$50,000	$10,000	
Income from:				
Bottom Company		9,000		$ 1,000
Special Foods	47,200			11,800
Net income	$187,200	$59,000	$10,000	$12,800

Consolidated net income equals Peerless's equity-method net income and can be verified by totaling the operating incomes of the three companies and deducting the noncontrolling interest:

Operating income:		
Peerless Products		$140,000
Special Foods		50,000
Bottom Company		10,000
Total separate income		$200,000
Noncontrolling interest in:		
Bottom Company ($10,000 × .10)	$ 1,000	
Special Foods ($59,000 × .20)	11,800	
Total noncontrolling interest		(12,800)
Consolidated net income		$187,200

Consolidation Workpaper

The 20X1 workpaper used in consolidating Peerless Products, Special Foods, and Bottom Company is shown in Figure 9–4.

The eliminations related to Special Foods' investment in Bottom Company are entered first:

E(29)	Income from Bottom Company	9,000	
	Dividends Declared		7,200
	Investment in Bottom Company Stock		1,800
	Eliminate income from Bottom Company:		
	$9,000 = $10,000 × .90		
	$7,200 = $8,000 × .90		
	$1,800 = $9,000 − $7,200		

E(30)	Income to Noncontrolling Interest	1,000	
	Dividends Declared		800
	Noncontrolling Interest		200
	Assign income to noncontrolling shareholders of Bottom Company:		
	$1,000 = $10,000 × .10		
	$800 = $8,000 × .10		
	$200 = $1,000 − $800		

FIGURE 9–4 December 31, 20X1, Consolidation Workpaper, First Year following Combination; Direct and Indirect Holdings

Item	Peerless Products	Special Foods	Bottom Company	Eliminations Debit	Eliminations Credit	Consolidated
Sales	400,000	200,000	150,000			750,000
Income from Bottom Company		9,000		(29) 9,000		
Income from Special Foods	47,200			(32) 47,200		
Credits	447,200	209,000	150,000			750,000
Cost of Goods Sold	170,000	115,000	80,000			365,000
Depreciation and Amortization	50,000	20,000	35,000			105,000
Other Expenses	40,000	15,000	25,000			80,000
Debits	(260,000)	(150,000)	(140,000)			(550,000)
						200,000
Income to Noncontrolling Interest				(30) 1,000		
				(33) 11,800		(12,800)
Net Income, carry forward	187,200	59,000	10,000	69,000		187,200
Retained Earnings, January 1	300,000	100,000	80,000	(31) 80,000		
				(34) 100,000		300,000
Net Income, from above	187,200	59,000	10,000	69,000		187,200
	487,200	159,000	90,000			487,200
Dividends Declared	(60,000)	(30,000)	(8,000)		(29) 7,200	
					(30) 800	
					(32) 24,000	
					(33) 6,000	(60,000)
Retained Earnings, December 31, carry forward	427,200	129,000	82,000	249,000	38,000	427,200
Cash	264,000	20,200	25,000			309,200
Accounts Receivable	75,000	50,000	30,000			155,000
Inventory	100,000	75,000	40,000			215,000
Land	175,000	40,000	50,000			265,000
Buildings and Equipment	800,000	600,000	75,000			1,475,000
Investment in Bottom Company Stock		163,800			(29) 1,800	
					(31) 162,000	
Investment in Special Foods Stock	263,200				(32) 23,200	
					(34) 240,000	
Debits	1,677,200	949,000	220,000			2,419,200
Accumulated Depreciation	250,000	220,000	20,000			490,000
Accounts Payable	100,000	100,000	18,000			218,000
Bonds Payable	400,000	300,000				700,000
Common Stock	500,000	200,000	100,000	(31) 100,000		
				(34) 200,000		500,000
Retained Earnings, from above	427,200	129,000	82,000	249,000	38,000	427,200
Noncontrolling Interest					(30) 200	
					(31) 18,000	
					(33) 5,800	
					(34) 60,000	84,000
Credits	1,677,200	949,000	220,000	549,000	549,000	2,419,200

Elimination entries:
(29) Eliminate income from Bottom Company.
(30) Assign income to noncontrolling shareholders of Bottom Company.
(31) Eliminate investment in Bottom Company stock.
(32) Eliminate income from Special Foods.
(33) Assign income to noncontrolling shareholders of Special Foods.
(34) Eliminate investment in Special Foods stock.

E(31)	Common Stock—Bottom Company	100,000	
	Retained Earnings, January 1	80,000	
	Investment in Bottom Company Stock		162,000
	Noncontrolling Interest		18,000
	Eliminate investment in Bottom Company Stock:		
	$162,000 = $180,000 \times .90$		
	$18,000 = $180,000 \times .10$		

Next, the eliminations related to Peerless's investment in Special Foods are entered in the workpaper:

E(32)	Income from Special Foods	47,200	
	Dividends Declared		24,000
	Investment in Special Foods Stock		23,200
	Eliminate income from Special Foods:		
	$47,200 = $59,000 \times .80$		
	$24,000 = $30,000 \times .80$		
	$23,200 = $47,200 - $24,000$		
E(33)	Income to Noncontrolling Interest	11,800	
	Dividends Declared		6,000
	Noncontrolling Interest		5,800
	Assign income to noncontrolling shareholders of Special Foods:		
	$11,800 = $59,000 \times .20$		
	$6,000 = $30,000 \times .20$		
	$5,800 = $11,800 - $6,000$		
E(34)	Common Stock—Special Foods	200,000	
	Retained Earnings, January 1	100,000	
	Investment in Special Foods Stock		240,000
	Noncontrolling Interest		60,000
	Eliminate investment in Special Foods stock:		
	$240,000 = $300,000 \times .80$		
	$60,000 = $300,000 \times .20$		

Order of Acquisition

In the preceding example, Peerless acquired its investment in Special Foods before Special Foods acquired its investment in Bottom Company. If, however, Special Foods had already owned its interest in Bottom Company when Peerless purchased its interest in Special Foods, a portion of Bottom Company's undistributed income since its acquisition would have accrued to Special Foods. So long as Special Foods accounts for its investment in Bottom Company using the equity method, no special problems arise; the normal consolidation procedures are followed. However, if Special Foods uses the cost method in accounting for its investment in Bottom Company, a workpaper conversion to the equity method must be made so that Special Foods' retained earnings at the date of the combination includes the appropriate share of Bottom Company's earnings since acquisition and so that the differential is correctly determined.

Unrealized Intercompany Profits

When intercompany sales occur between multilevel affiliates, unrealized intercompany profits must be eliminated against the appropriate ownership interests. The most convenient way of doing this is to compute the amount of realized income each company contributes before apportioning income between controlling and noncontrolling interests.

For example, the realized income accruing to the ownership interests of each affiliate is computed in the following manner given the unrealized profit amounts indicated:

	Peerless Products	Special Foods	Bottom Company	Noncontrolling Interest
Operating income	$140,000	$50,000	$10,000	
Unrealized profit	(5,000)	(10,000)	(3,000)	
Realized operating profit	$135,000	$40,000	$ 7,000	
Income from:				
Bottom Company		6,300		$ 700
Special Foods	37,040			9,260
Realized net income	$172,040	$46,300	$ 7,000	$9,960

Consolidated net income equals the $172,040 realized net income listed for Peerless Products. The normal workpaper entries to eliminate unrealized intercompany profits, as discussed in Chapters 6 and 7, are entered in the workpaper for each company involved.

Reciprocal or Mutual Ownership

A reciprocal relationship exists when two companies hold stock in each other. Reciprocal relationships are relatively rare in practice, and their accounting impact is often immaterial.

There are two different approaches to the treatment of reciprocal relationships. The **treasury stock method** is used most frequently in practice and treats shares of the parent held by a subsidiary as if they had been repurchased by the parent. The **entity approach** views the parent and subsidiary as a single entity with income shared between the different ownership groups, explicitly taking into consideration the reciprocal relationship.

Treasury Stock Method

Under the treasury stock method, purchases of a parent's stock by a subsidiary are treated in the same way as if the parent had repurchased its own stock and was holding it in the treasury. The subsidiary normally accounts for the investment in the parent's stock using the cost method because such investments usually are small and almost never confer the ability to significantly influence the parent.

Income assigned to the noncontrolling interest in the subsidiary usually is based on the subsidiary's net income, which includes the dividend income from the investment in the parent. The parent, however, normally bases its equity-method share of the subsidiary's income on the subsidiary's income, excluding the dividend income from the parent.

As an example of the treasury stock method, assume the following:

1. Peerless Products purchases 80 percent of Special Foods' common stock on December 31, 20X0, at book value of $240,000.

2. Special Foods purchases 10 percent of Peerless's common stock on January 1, 20X1, at book value of $80,000.

3. For 20X1, the two companies report the following separate operating income and dividends:

	Operating Income	Dividends
Peerless Products	$140,000	$60,000
Special Foods	50,000	30,000
Total operating income	$190,000	

The reciprocal ownership relationship between Peerless and Special Foods is as follows:

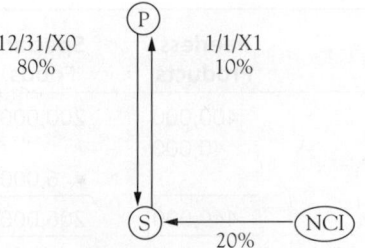

Special Foods records the purchase of its investment in Peerless's common stock with the following entry:

January 1, 20X1

(35)	Investment in Peerless Products Stock	80,000	
	Cash		80,000
	Record purchase of Peerless Products stock.		

Because it does not gain the ability to significantly influence Peerless, Special Foods accounts for the investment using the cost method. During 20X1, Special Foods records the receipt of dividends from Peerless with the following entry:

(36)	Cash	6,000	
	Dividend Income		6,000
	Record dividend income from Peerless:		
	$60,000 \times .10$		

The consolidation workpaper prepared at the end of 20X1, shown in Figure 9–5, includes the following eliminating entries:

E(37)	Dividend Income	6,000	
	Dividends Declared		6,000
	Eliminate dividend income from Peerless.		
E(38)	Income from Subsidiary	40,000	
	Dividends Declared		24,000
	Investment in Special Foods Stock		16,000
	Eliminate income from subsidiary.		
E(39)	Income to Noncontrolling Interest	11,200	
	Dividends Declared		6,000
	Noncontrolling Interest		5,200
	Assign income to noncontrolling interest.		
E(40)	Treasury Stock	80,000	
	Investment in Peerless Products Stock		80,000
	Reclassify investment in Peerless stock as treasury stock.		
E(41)	Common Stock—Special Foods	200,000	
	Retained Earnings, January 1	100,000	
	Investment in Special Foods Stock		240,000
	Noncontrolling Interest		60,000
	Eliminate investment in Special Foods stock.		

FIGURE 9–5 **December 31, 20X1, Treasury Stock-Method Workpaper for First Year following Combination; 80 Percent Purchase at Book Value**

Item	Peerless Products	Special Foods	Eliminations		Consolidated
			Debit	**Credit**	
Sales	400,000	200,000			600,000
Income from Subsidiary	40,000		(38) 40,000		
Dividend Income		6,000	(37) 6,000		
Credits	440,000	206,000			600,000
Cost of Goods Sold	170,000	115,000			285,000
Depreciation and Amortization	50,000	20,000			70,000
Other Expenses	40,000	15,000			55,000
Debits	(260,000)	(150,000)			(410,000)
					190,000
Income to Noncontrolling Interest			(39) 11,200		(11,200)
Net Income, carry forward	180,000	56,000	57,200		178,800
Retained Earnings, January 1	300,000	100,000	(41) 100,000		300,000
Net Income, from above	180,000	56,000	57,200		178,800
	480,000	156,000			478,800
Dividends Declared	(60,000)	(30,000)		(37) 6,000	
				(38) 24,000	
				(39) 6,000	(54,000)
Retained Earnings, December 31, carry forward	420,000	126,000	157,200	36,000	424,800
Cash	264,000	1,000			265,000
Accounts Receivable	75,000	50,000			125,000
Inventory	100,000	75,000			175,000
Land	175,000	40,000			215,000
Buildings and Equipment	800,000	600,000			1,400,000
Investment in Special Foods Stock	256,000			(38) 16,000	
				(41) 240,000	
Investment in Peerless Products Stock		80,000		(40) 80,000	
Debits	1,670,000	846,000			2,180,000
Accumulated Depreciation	450,000	320,000			770,000
Accounts Payable	100,000	100,000			200,000
Bonds Payable	200,000	100,000			300,000
Common Stock	500,000	200,000	(41) 200,000		500,000
Retained Earnings, from above	420,000	126,000	157,200	36,000	424,800
Noncontrolling Interest				(39) 5,200	
				(41) 60,000	65,200
Treasury Stock			(40) 80,000		(80,000)
Credits	1,670,000	846,000	437,200	437,200	2,180,000

Elimination entries:
(37) Eliminate dividend income from Peerless.
(38) Eliminate income from subsidiary.
(39) Assign income to noncontrolling interest.
(40) Reclassify investment in Peerless stock as treasury stock.
(41) Eliminate investment in Special Foods stock.

Eliminating entry E(40) reclassifies Special Foods' investment in Peerless stock as if it were treasury stock. All of Peerless's common stock is shown in the consolidated balance sheet as outstanding. The treasury stock is shown at cost as an $80,000 deduction from total stockholders' equity, just as treasury stock is shown in a single company's balance sheet at cost. Note that entry E(37) reduces the amount shown in the consolidated retained earnings statement as dividends paid to those outside the consolidated entity.

The remaining entries needed in the 20X1 consolidation workpaper are the normal entries to eliminate Peerless's investment in Special Foods and income from Special Foods that Peerless recognizes. The income from Special Foods recognized by Peerless is based on Special Foods' separate income, excluding dividend income from Peerless. Therefore, the income elimination is for $40,000, Peerless's 80 percent share of Special Foods' separate operating income of $50,000.

Note that the parent's equity-method income and consolidated net income may not be equal under this approach. Peerless's income is computed as follows:

Peerless's separate operating income	$140,000
Peerless's share of Special Foods' operating income ($50,000 × .80)	40,000
Peerless's net income	$180,000

Consolidated net income is computed as follows:

Peerless's separate operating income		$140,000
Special Foods' separate operating income		50,000
Total separate income		$190,000
Less noncontrolling interest:		
Special Foods' net income ($50,000 + $6,000)	$56,000	
Noncontrolling stockholders' share	× .20	
		(11,200)
Consolidated net income		$178,800

The difference occurs because the $6,000 of Peerless's dividends paid to Special Foods is considered when computing the noncontrolling interest but not when computing the parent's net income.

There is some question about the appropriate amount of income to assign to the noncontrolling interest under the treasury stock approach and, therefore, the amount of consolidated net income. Income assigned to the noncontrolling interest normally is computed as the noncontrolling stockholders' proportionate share of the subsidiary's net income. In the computation shown, the subsidiary's net income includes dividend income from Special Foods' investment in Peerless. The noncontrolling interest is credited with its full share of subsidiary net income.

Entity Approach

The entity approach to dealing with reciprocal stock holdings, often referred to as the traditional or conventional approach, is more consistent with the entity theory of consolidation than is the treasury stock method. Under this approach, the total of the separate incomes of the consolidating companies is viewed as the total income of the consolidated entity and is apportioned between the controlling and noncontrolling shareholders. In assigning income to the shareholder groups, recognition is given to the reciprocal nature of the relationship created when a subsidiary acquires shares of the parent company. A set of simultaneous equations normally is used in computing a reciprocal income total for each company. The resulting amounts then are used in apportioning income to the controlling and noncontrolling interests.

The balance sheet presentation under the entity approach is quite different than under the treasury stock method. The parent's shares held by the subsidiary are not reported as treasury stock; instead, the balance in the subsidiary's investment in the parent is eliminated in the same manner as the parent's investment in the common stock of the subsidiary. A proportionate amount of the parent's common stock, additional paid-in capital, and retained earnings is eliminated against the subsidiary's investment account in preparing the consolidated statements.

The apportionment of income under the entity approach is illustrated with the same example used to illustrate the treasury stock method. Total income assigned to each of the two companies equals the company's separate operating income plus its share of the other company's total income. For example, let

$$P = \text{Peerless Products' total income}$$
$$S = \text{Special Foods' total income}$$

The total incomes of Peerless and Special Foods can be stated as follows:

$$P = \$140,000 + .80S$$
$$S = \$50,000 + .10P$$

Total income assigned to each of the two companies can be determined by solving these equations simultaneously:

$$P = \$140,000 + .80S$$
$$P = \$140,000 + .80(\$50,000 + .10P)$$
$$P = \$140,000 + \$40,000 + .08P$$
$$.92P = \$180,000$$
$$P = \underline{\$195,652}$$
$$S = \$50,000 + .10P$$
$$S = \$50,000 + .10(\$195,652)$$
$$S = \$50,000 + \$19,565$$
$$S = \underline{\$69,565}$$

These income figures serve as a basis for determining the amount of income to be assigned to the controlling and noncontrolling interests. However, none of the computed totals can be reported without adjustment because an affiliate holds some portion of each company's shares. The balances assigned are based on the portion of ownership held by shareholders outside the consolidated entity:

Consolidated net income:		
Peerless's income	$195,652	
Proportion of shares held outside consolidated entity	× .90	
		$176,087
Income to noncontrolling interest:		
Special Foods' income	$ 69,565	
Proportion of shares held by noncontrolling stockholders	× .20	
		13,913
Total income assigned		$190,000

Note that consolidated net income is not the amount of income assigned to Peerless; rather, it is the assigned amount adjusted for the percentage of total shares held by the consolidated entity's stockholders. That is, 90 percent of Peerless's shares is held by those deemed to be the stockholders of the consolidated entity, and the other 10 percent is held within the consolidated entity.

The total of the amounts reported as consolidated net income and income assigned to noncontrolling shareholders of the consolidated subsidiaries always should equal the sum of the separate operating incomes of the individual companies:

Reported operating income:	
Peerless Products	$140,000
Special Foods	50,000
Total income reported	$190,000

SUBSIDIARY STOCK DIVIDENDS

Subsidiary dividends payable in shares of the subsidiary's common stock require slight changes in the elimination entries used in preparing consolidated financial statements. Because stock dividends are issued proportionally to all common stockholders, the relative interests of the controlling and noncontrolling stockholders do not change as a result of the stock dividend. The investment's carrying amount on the parent's books also is unaffected by a stock dividend. On the other hand, the stockholders' equity accounts of the subsidiary do change, although total stockholders' equity does not. The stock dividend represents a permanent capitalization of retained earnings, thus decreasing retained earnings and increasing capital stock and, perhaps, additional paid-in capital.

In the preparation of consolidated financial statements for the period in which a stock dividend is declared by the subsidiary, the stock dividend declaration must be eliminated along with the increased common stock and increased additional paid-in capital, if any. The stock dividend declared cannot appear in the consolidated retained earnings statement because only the parent's dividends are viewed as dividends of the consolidated entity.

In subsequent years, the balances in the subsidiary's stockholders' equity accounts are eliminated in the normal manner. Keep in mind that stock dividends do not change the total stockholders' equity of a company; they only realign the individual accounts within stockholders' equity. Therefore, the full balances of all the subsidiary's stockholders' equity accounts must be eliminated in consolidation, as is the usual procedure, even though amounts have been shifted from one account to another.

Illustration of Subsidiary Stock Dividends

As an illustration of the treatment of a subsidiary's stock dividend, assume that in the Peerless Products and Special Foods example, Special Foods declares a 25 percent stock dividend in 20X1 on its $200,000 of common stock and elects to capitalize the par value of the shares. Special Foods records the stock dividend with the following entry:

(42)	Stock Dividends Declared	50,000	
	Common Stock		50,000
	Record 25 percent stock dividend:		
	$200,000 × .25		

The investors make only a memo entry to record the receipt of the stock dividend.

When consolidated financial statements are prepared at the end of 20X1, the normal elimination entries are made in the workpaper. If the subsidiary had declared no stock dividend, the entry for eliminating the investment account and subsidiary stockholders' equity balances at the beginning of the period would have been:

E(43)	Common Stock—Special Foods	200,000	
	Retained Earnings, January 1	100,000	
	Investment in Special Foods Stock		240,000
	Noncontrolling Interest		60,000
	Eliminate beginning investment balance.		

With the subsidiary having declared the stock dividend, all elimination entries are the same except for the investment elimination entry. Entry E(43) is altered as follows:

E(44)	Common Stock—Special Foods	250,000	
	Retained Earnings, January 1	100,000	
	Investment in Special Foods Stock		240,000
	Noncontrolling Interest		60,000
	Stock Dividends Declared		50,000
	Eliminate beginning investment balance:		
	$250,000 = $200,000 + $50,000		
	$50,000 = $200,000 \times .25		

Note that although the common stock balance has increased by the $50,000 amount of the stock dividend, the elimination of retained earnings is not changed in the year of the stock dividend because dividends declared have not been closed to retained earnings; only the beginning balance of retained earnings is eliminated. Just as with other dividends of the subsidiary, stock dividends must be eliminated because they are not viewed as dividends of the consolidated entity.

Impact on Subsequent Periods

At the end of 20X1, the stock dividend declaration is closed into the subsidiary's Retained Earnings account and does not separately appear in the financial statements of future periods. The stock dividend results in a common stock balance $50,000 higher and a retained earnings balance $50,000 lower on the subsidiary's books than if there had been no stock dividend. The investment elimination entry in the consolidation workpaper must reflect these changed balances.

Thus, assume that the appropriate investment elimination entry on December 31, 20X2, is as follows if Special Foods declares no stock dividend:

E(45)	Common Stock—Special Foods	200,000	
	Retained Earnings, January 1	120,000	
	Investment in Special Foods Stock		256,000
	Noncontrolling Interest		64,000
	Eliminate beginning investment balance.		

The following entry would replace entry E(45) in the consolidation workpaper prepared as of December 31, 20X2, if Special Foods had declared the stock dividend during 20X1:

E(46)	Common Stock—Special Foods	250,000	
	Retained Earnings, January 1	70,000	
	Investment in Special Foods Stock		256,000
	Noncontrolling Interest		64,000
	Eliminate beginning investment balance.		

Entry E(46) is identical to entry E(45) except that the elimination of common stock is $50,000 higher and the elimination of retained earnings is $50,000 lower, reflecting the differences in the balances of those accounts due to the stock dividend.

Summary of Key Concepts

A number of stockholders' equity issues arise in the preparation of consolidated financial statements. When subsidiaries have preferred stock outstanding, any of the preferred stock held by the parent must be eliminated because it is held within the consolidated entity. The remaining preferred stock is treated as part of the noncontrolling interest. In the assessment of the preferred shareholders' claim, consideration must be given to all the features of the preferred stock, including cumulative dividends in arrears, dividend participation features, and retirement premiums.

Transactions involving subsidiary common stock may affect the percentage ownership of the controlling shareholders. Although existing accounting standards permit some degree of diversity in practice, the concept of a single economic entity implies that transactions involving subsidiary stock should be viewed as equity transactions of the consolidated entity. Thus, no gains or losses should be reported in the consolidated income statement on such transactions. For example, a gain or loss recognized by a parent on a sale of subsidiary shares back to the subsidiary should be eliminated in preparing consolidated statements because the transfer is entirely within the consolidated entity.

The organizational structure of some consolidated entities may be more complex than just a parent and one or more subsidiaries. In some cases, subsidiaries hold controlling interests in other companies, thus giving the parent an indirect interest. Consolidation proceeds from the lowest level to the highest in these cases. In a relatively few cases, a subsidiary may own common shares of its parent. Usually those common shares are treated as treasury stock in consolidated financial statements.

Stock dividends declared by a subsidiary result in only minor changes in the eliminations needed to prepare consolidated financial statements. In the year the stock dividend is declared, the stock dividend declaration and the higher balance of the common stock must be eliminated in preparing consolidated statements. In subsequent years, the investment elimination entry reflects the higher amount of the subsidiary's common stock and the lower amount of retained earnings.

Key Terms

direct ownership, *435*
entity approach, *440*
indirect control, *435*
multilevel ownership, *435*
mutual holdings, *435*
reciprocal ownership, *435*
treasury stock method, *440*

Questions

Q9-1 How does the consolidation process deal with preferred stock of a subsidiary?

Q9-2 What portion of subsidiary preferred stock outstanding is reported as part of the noncontrolling interest in the consolidated balance sheet?

Q9-3 Why are subsidiary preferred dividends paid to nonaffiliates normally deducted from earnings in arriving at consolidated net income? When is it not appropriate to deduct subsidiary preferred dividends in computing consolidated net income?

Q9-4 How does a call feature on subsidiary preferred stock affect the claim of the noncontrolling interest reported in the consolidated balance sheet?

Q9-5 Explain how the existence of a subsidiary's preferred shares might affect the amount of goodwill reported following the purchase of the subsidiary.

Q9-6 A parent company sells common shares of one of its subsidiaries to a nonaffiliate for more than their carrying value on the parent's books. How should the parent company report the sale? How should the sale be reported in the consolidated financial statements?

Q9-7 A subsidiary sells additional shares of its common stock to a nonaffiliate at a price that is higher than the previous book value per share. How does the sale benefit the existing shareholders?

Q9-8 A parent company purchases additional common shares of one of its subsidiaries from a nonaffiliate at $10 per share above underlying book value. Explain how this purchase is reflected in the consolidated financial statements for the year.

Q9-9 How are treasury shares held by a subsidiary reported in the consolidated financial statements?

Q9-10 What is indirect ownership? How does one company gain control of another through indirect ownership?

Q9-11 Explain how a reciprocal ownership arrangement between two subsidiaries could lead the parent company to overstate its income if no adjustment is made for the reciprocal relationship.

Q9-12 How will parent company shares held by a subsidiary be reflected in the consolidated balance sheet when the treasury stock method is used?

Q9-13 How does the entity approach differ from the treasury stock method in computing consolidated net income when there is reciprocal ownership between the parent and the subsidiary?

Q9-14 Parent Company holds 80 percent ownership of Subsidiary Company, and Subsidiary Company owns 90 percent of the stock of Tiny Corporation. What effect will $100,000 of unrealized intercompany profits on Tiny's books on December 31, 20X5, have on the amount of consolidated net income reported for the year?

Q9-15 Snapper Corporation holds 70 percent ownership of Bit Company, and Bit holds 60 percent ownership of Slide Company. Should Slide be consolidated with Snapper Corporation? Why?

Q9-16 What effect will a subsidiary's 15 percent stock dividend have on the consolidated financial statements?

Q9-17 What effect will a subsidiary's 15 percent stock dividend have on the elimination entries used in preparing a consolidated balance sheet at the end of the year in which the dividend is distributed?

Q9-18 When multilevel affiliations exist, explain why it generally is best to prepare consolidated financial statements by completing the eliminating entries for companies furthest from parent company ownership first and completing the eliminating entries for those owned directly by the parent company last.

Cases

C9-1

Analysis

Effect of Subsidiary Preferred Stock

Snow Corporation issued common stock with a par value of $100,000 and preferred stock with a par value of $80,000 on January 1, 20X5, when the company was created. Klammer Corporation acquired a controlling interest in Snow on January 1, 20X6.

Required
What does Klammer's controller need to know about the preferred stock to determine consolidated net income for 20X6?

C9-2

*Research
FARS*

Presentation of Noncontrolling Interest

The management of Deep Company is unsure of the amount it must report as noncontrolling interest in its consolidated balance sheet at December 31, 20X4, and its income statement for 20X4. Deep holds 6,000 of the 60,000 shares of Brown Company's $20 par value preferred stock outstanding. The preferred shares have a stated annual dividend rate of 10 percent and are cumulative. These shares also have a $4 per share redemption premium. Deep also holds 24,000 of the 40,000 outstanding shares of Brown's voting common stock. For the year ended December 31, 20X4, Brown reported net income of $200,000 and paid its preferred dividends on schedule.

Deep's treasurer reported to the press that the company had realized $120,000 ($200,000 × .60) of investment income from its investment in the common stock of Brown Company and $12,000 (6,000 shares × $20 × .10) of dividend income on its investment in Brown's preferred stock.

Required
As a member of Deep's accounting staff, prepare a memo to the treasurer that discusses the procedures by which Deep must compute income on its investment in Brown's common and preferred stocks and total income assigned to noncontrolling shareholders in the Deep Company consolidated income statement. Explain why the amounts reported by the treasurer are incorrect and provide a computation of the correct amounts for the year. Your discussion should include citations to or quotations from applicable authoritative accounting pronouncements in support of your conclusions.

C9-3

*Research
FARS*

Sale of Subsidiary Shares

Book Corporation purchased 90,000 shares of Lance Company at underlying book value of $3 per share on June 30, 20X1. On January 1, 20X5, Lance reported its net book value as $400,000 and continued to have 100,000 shares of common stock outstanding. On that date, Book sold 30,000 shares of Lance to Triple Corporation for $5.60 per share. Book uses the equity method in accounting for its investment in Lance and recorded a gain on sale of investments of $48,000 in its consolidated income statement for 20X5.

Required

Book's vice president of finance, Robert Reader, has asked you to prepare a memo addressed to him presenting the alternative ways to record the difference between the carrying value and sale price of the shares that are sold and your recommendations on the preferred reporting alternative. Citations to or quotations from the relevant authoritative accounting literature, including the most recent FASB recommendations or requirements, should be included in providing the basis of support for your recommendations.

C9-4 **Sale of Subsidiary Shares**

Analysis Hardcore Mining Company acquired 88 percent of the common stock of Mountain Trucking Company on January 1, 20X2, at a cost of $30 per share. On December 31, 20X7, when the book value of Mountain Trucking stock was $70 per share, Hardcore sold one-quarter of its investment in Mountain Trucking to Basic Manufacturing Company for $90 per share.

Required

What effect will the sale have on the 20X7 consolidated financial statements of Hardcore Mining if (*a*) Basic Manufacturing is an unrelated company and (*b*) Hardcore Mining holds 60 percent of Basic's voting shares?

C9-5 **Reciprocal Ownership**

Judgment Strong Manufacturing Company holds 94 percent ownership of Thorson Farm Products and 68 percent ownership of Kenwood Distributors. Thorson has excess cash at the end of 20X4 and is considering buying shares of its own stock, shares of Strong, or shares of Kenwood.

Required

If Thorson wishes to take the action that will be best for the consolidated entity, what factors must it consider in making its decision? How can it maximize consolidated net income?

Exercises **E9-1** **Multiple-Choice Questions on Preferred Stock Ownership**

Blank Corporation prepared the following summarized balance sheet on January 1, 20X1:

Assets	$150,000	Liabilities	$ 20,000
		Preferred Stock	30,000
		Common Stock	40,000
		Retained Earnings	60,000
Total Assets	$150,000	Total Liabilities and Equities	$150,000

Required

Select the correct answer for each of the following questions.

1. Shepard Company purchases 80 percent of Blank Corporation's common shares for $90,000. The amount reported as noncontrolling interest in the consolidated balance sheet is:

   a. $20,000.
   b. $26,000.
   c. $30,000.
   d. $50,000.

2. Shepard Company purchases 80 percent of Blank Corporation's common shares for $90,000 and 70 percent of Blank's preferred shares for $21,000. The amount reported as noncontrolling interest in Shepard's consolidated balance sheet is:

   a. $9,000.
   b. $20,000.
   c. $29,000.
   d. $50,000.

3. Shepard Company purchases 80 percent of Blank Corporation's common shares for $90,000 and 70 percent of Blank's preferred shares for $21,000 on January 1, 20X1. If Shepard's retained earnings is $150,000 on December 31, 20X0, the consolidated retained earnings reported immediately after the stock purchases is:

   a. $48,000.
   b. $150,000.
   c. $198,000.
   d. $210,000.

4. Shepard Company purchases 80 percent of Blank Corporation's common shares for $90,000 and 70 percent of Blank's preferred shares for $21,000 on January 1, 20X1. Shepard has no preferred shares outstanding. The amount of preferred stock reported in the consolidated balance sheet immediately after the stock purchases is:

   a. $0.
   b. $9,000.
   c. $21,000.
   d. $30,000.

E9-2 Multiple-Choice Questions on Multilevel Ownership

Musical Corporation purchases 80 percent of Dustin Corporation's common shares on January 1, 20X2. On January 2, 20X2, Dustin purchases 60 percent of Rustic Corporation's common stock. Information on company book values on the date of purchase and operating results for 20X2 is as follows:

Company	Book Value	Purchase Price	20X2 Operating Income
Musical Corporation	$800,000		$100,000
Dustin Corporation	300,000	$240,000	80,000
Rustic Corporation	200,000	120,000	50,000

Required

Select the correct answer for each of the following questions.

1. Consolidated net income for 20X2 is:

   a. $180,000.
   b. $188,000.
   c. $194,000.
   d. $234,000.

2. The amount of 20X2 income assigned to the noncontrolling interest of Rustic Corporation is:

   a. $0.
   b. $20,000.
   c. $30,000.
   d. $50,000.

3. The amount of 20X2 income assigned to the noncontrolling interest of Dustin Corporation is:

   a. $10,000.
   b. $16,000.
   c. $22,000.
   d. $26,000.

4. The amount of income assigned to the noncontrolling interest in the 20X2 consolidated income statement is:

   a. $20,000.
   b. $22,000.
   c. $42,000.
   d. $46,000.

5. Assume that Dustin pays $160,000, rather than $120,000, to purchase 60 percent of Rustic's common stock. If the purchase differential is amortized over 10 years, the effect on 20X2 consolidated net income will be a decrease of:

    a. $0.

    b. $2,400.

    c. $3,200.

    d. $4,000.

E9-3 Acquisition of Preferred Shares

The summarized balance sheet of Separate Company on January 1, 20X3, contained the following amounts:

Total Assets	$350,000	Total Liabilities	$ 50,000
		Preferred Stock	100,000
		Common Stock	50,000
		Retained Earnings	150,000
Total Assets	$350,000	Total Liabilities and Equities	$350,000

On January 1, 20X3, Joint Corporation purchased 70 percent of the common shares and 60 percent of the preferred shares of Separate Company at underlying book value.

Required

Give the workpaper elimination entries needed to prepare a consolidated balance sheet immediately following the purchase of shares by Joint.

E9-4 Reciprocal Ownership [AICPA Adapted]

Pride Corporation owns 80 percent of Simba Corporation's outstanding common stock. Simba, in turn, owns 10 percent of Pride's outstanding common stock.

Required

a. What percent of the dividends paid by Simba is reported as dividends declared in the consolidated financial statements?

b. What percent of the dividends paid by Pride is reported as dividends declared in the consolidated retained earnings statement?

E9-5 Subsidiary with Preferred Stock Outstanding

Clayton Corporation purchased 75 percent of the common stock and 40 percent of the preferred stock of Topple Company on January 1, 20X6, for $270,000 and $80,000, respectively. At the time of purchase, Topple's balance sheet contained the following balances:

Preferred Stock ($10 par value)	$200,000
Common Stock ($5 par value)	150,000
Retained Earnings	210,000
Total Stockholders' Equity	$560,000

Required

Give the eliminating entries needed to prepare a consolidated balance sheet immediately after Clayton purchased the Topple shares.

E9-6 Subsidiary with Preferred Stock Outstanding

Clayton Corporation purchased 75 percent of the common stock and 40 percent of the preferred stock of Topple Company on January 1, 20X6, for $270,000 and $80,000, respectively. At the time of purchase, Topple's balance sheet contained the following balances:

Preferred Stock ($10 par value)	$200,000
Common Stock ($5 par value)	150,000
Retained Earnings	210,000
Total Stockholders' Equity	$560,000

For the year ended December 31, 20X6, Topple reported net income of $70,000 and paid dividends of $50,000. The preferred stock is cumulative and pays an annual dividend of 8 percent.

Required

a. Prepare the journal entries recorded by Clayton for its investments in Topple during 20X6.

b. Present the eliminating entries needed to prepare the consolidated financial statements for Clayton Corporation as of December 31, 20X6.

E9-7 Preferred Dividends and Call Premium

On January 1, 20X2, Fischer Corporation purchased 90 percent of the common shares and 60 percent of the preferred shares of Culbertson Company at underlying book value. Culbertson's balance sheet at the time of purchase contained the following balances:

Total Assets	$860,000	Total Liabilities	$ 80,000
		Preferred Stock	100,000
		Common Stock	300,000
		Retained Earnings	380,000
Total Assets	$860,000	Total Liabilities and Equities	$860,000

The preferred shares are cumulative with regard to dividends. The shares have a 12 percent annual dividend rate and are five years in arrears on January 1, 20X2. All of the $10 par value preferred shares are callable at $12 per share after December 31, 20X0. During 20X2, Culbertson reported net income of $70,000 and paid no dividends.

Required

a. Compute Culbertson's contribution to consolidated net income for 20X2.

b. Compute the amount of income to be assigned to the noncontrolling interest in the 20X2 consolidated income statement.

c. Compute the portion of Culbertson's retained earnings assignable to its preferred shareholders on January 1, 20X2.

d. Compute the book value of the common stock on January 1, 20X2.

e. Compute the amount to be reported as the noncontrolling interest in the consolidated balance sheet on January 1, 20X2.

E9-8 Multilevel Ownership

Grasper Corporation owns 70 percent of Latent Corporation's common stock and 25 percent of Dally Corporation's common stock. In addition, Latent owns 40 percent of Dally's stock. In 20X6, Grasper, Latent, and Dally reported operating income of $90,000, $60,000, $40,000 and paid dividends of $45,000, $30,000, and $10,000, respectively.

Required

a. What amount of consolidated net income will Grasper report for 20X6?

b. What amount of income will be assigned to noncontrolling interest in the 20X6 consolidated income statement?

c. What amount will be reported as dividends declared in Grasper's 20X6 consolidated retained earnings statement?

E9-9 Eliminating Entries for Multilevel Ownership

Promise Enterprises purchased 90 percent of Brown Corporation's voting common stock on January 1, 20X3, for $315,000. Immediately after Promise acquired its ownership, Brown purchased 60 percent of Tann Company's stock for $120,000. During 20X3, Promise reported operating income of $200,000 and paid dividends of $80,000. Brown reported operating income of $120,000 and paid dividends of $50,000. Tann reported net income of $40,000 and paid dividends of $15,000. At January 1, 20X3, the stockholders' equity sections of the balance sheets of the companies were as follows:

	Promise Enterprises	Brown Corporation	Tann Company
Common Stock	$200,000	$150,000	$100,000
Additional Paid-In Capital	160,000	60,000	60,000
Retained Earnings	360,000	140,000	40,000
Total Stockholders' Equity	$720,000	$350,000	$200,000

Required

a. Prepare the journal entries recorded by Brown for its investment in Tann during 20X3.

b. Prepare the journal entries recorded by Promise for its investment in Brown during 20X3.

c. Prepare the eliminating entries related to Brown's investment in Tann and Promise's investment in Brown that are needed in preparing consolidated financial statements for Promise and its subsidiaries at December 31, 20X3.

E9-10   Reciprocal Ownership

Grower Supply Corporation holds 85 percent of Schultz Company's voting common stock. At the end of 20X4, Schultz purchased 30 percent of Grower Supply's stock. Schultz records dividends received from Grower Supply as dividend income. In 20X5, Grower Supply and Schultz reported income from their separate operations of $112,000 and $50,000 and paid dividends of $70,000 and $30,000, respectively.

Required

Compute the amounts reported as consolidated net income and income assigned to the noncontrolling interest for 20X5 under (a) the treasury stock method and (b) the entity approach.

E9-11   Consolidated Balance Sheet with Reciprocal Ownership

Talbott Company purchased 80 percent of Short Company's stock on January 1, 20X8, at underlying book value. On December 31, 20X9, Short purchased 10 percent of Talbott's stock. Balance sheets for the two companies on December 31, 20X9, are as follows:

TALBOTT COMPANY
Condensed Balance Sheet
December 31, 20X9

Cash	$ 78,000	Accounts Payable	$ 90,000
Accounts Receivable	120,000	Bonds Payable	400,000
Inventory	150,000	Common Stock	300,000
Buildings and Equipment (net)	400,000	Retained Earnings	310,000
Investment in Short Company			
Common Stock	352,000		
Total Assets	$1,100,000	Total Liabilities and Equities	$1,100,000

SHORT COMPANY
Condensed Balance Sheet
December 31, 20X9

Cash	$ 39,000	Accounts Payable	$ 60,000
Accounts Receivable	80,000	Bonds Payable	100,000
Inventory	120,000	Common Stock	200,000
Buildings and Equipment (net)	300,000	Retained Earnings	240,000
Investment in Talbott Company			
Common Stock	61,000		
Total Assets	$600,000	Total Liabilities and Equities	$600,000

Required

Assuming that the treasury stock method is used in reporting Talbott's shares held by Short, prepare a consolidated balance sheet workpaper and consolidated balance sheet for December 31, 20X9.

E9-12 **Subsidiary Stock Dividend**

Lake Company reported the following summarized balance sheet data as of December 31, 20X2:

Cash	$ 30,000	Accounts Payable	$ 50,000
Accounts Receivable	80,000	Common Stock	100,000
Inventory	90,000	Retained Earnings	200,000
Buildings and Equipment	270,000		
Less: Accumulated Depreciation	(120,000)		
Total Assets	$350,000	Total Liabilities and Equities	$350,000

Lake issues 4,000 additional shares of its $10 par value stock to its shareholders as a stock dividend on April 20, 20X3. The market price of Lake's shares at the time of the stock dividend is $40. Lake reports net income of $25,000 and pays a $10,000 cash dividend in 20X3. Lindale Company purchased 70 percent of Lake's common shares at book value on January 1, 20X1, and uses the basic equity method in accounting for its investment in Lake.

Required

a. Give the journal entries recorded by Lake and Lindale at the time the stock dividend is declared and distributed.

b. Give the workpaper elimination entries needed to prepare consolidated financial statements for 20X3.

c. Give the workpaper elimination entry needed to prepare a consolidated balance sheet on January 1, 20X4.

E9-13 **Sale of Subsidiary Shares by Parent**

Stable Home Builders Inc. purchased 80 percent of the stock of Acme Concrete Works on January 1, 20X3, for $360,000. Acme Concrete's balance sheet contained the following amounts at the time of the combination:

Cash	$ 30,000	Accounts Payable	$ 50,000
Accounts Receivable	65,000	Bonds Payable	300,000
Inventory	15,000	Common Stock	200,000
Construction Work in Progress	470,000	Retained Earnings	250,000
Other Assets (net)	220,000		
Total Assets	$800,000	Total Liabilities and Equities	$800,000

During each of the next three years, Acme Concrete reported net income of $50,000 and paid dividends of $20,000. On January 1, 20X5, Stable sold 4,000 of the Acme $10 par value shares for $120,000 in cash. Stable used the basic equity method in accounting for its ownership of Acme.

Required

a. Compute the balance in the investment account reported by Stable on January 1, 20X5, before its sale of shares.

b. Prepare the entry recorded by Stable when it sold the Acme shares.

c. Prepare the appropriate elimination entries to complete a full consolidation workpaper for 20X5.

E9-14 **Purchase of Additional Shares from Nonaffiliate**

Weal Corporation purchased 60 percent of Modern Products Company's shares on December 31, 20X7, for $240,000 and 20 percent on January 1, 20X9, for $96,000. Summarized balance sheets for Modern on the dates indicated are as follows:

	December 31		
	20X7	**20X8**	**20X9**
Cash	$ 40,000	$ 70,000	$ 90,000
Accounts Receivable	50,000	90,000	120,000
Inventory	70,000	100,000	160,000
Buildings and Equipment (net)	340,000	320,000	300,000
Total Assets	$500,000	$580,000	$670,000
Accounts Payable	$ 50,000	$100,000	$140,000
Bonds Payable	100,000	100,000	100,000
Common Stock	150,000	150,000	150,000
Retained Earnings	200,000	230,000	280,000
Total Liabilities and Equities	$500,000	$580,000	$670,000

Modern paid dividends of $20,000 in each of the three years. Weal uses the basic equity method in accounting for its investment in Modern and amortizes all purchase differentials over 10 years against the related investment income. All differentials are assigned to patents in the consolidated financial statements.

Required

a. Compute the balance in Weal's Investment in Modern Products Company Stock account on December 31, 20X8.

b. Compute the balance in Weal's Investment in Modern Products Company Stock account on December 31, 20X9.

c. Prepare the eliminating entries needed as of December 31, 20X9, to complete a three-part consolidation workpaper.

E9-15 Repurchase of Shares by Subsidiary from Nonaffiliate

Blatant Advertising Corporation acquired 60 percent of Quinn Manufacturing Company's shares on December 31, 20X1, at underlying book value of $180,000. Quinn's balance sheet on January 1, 20X7, contained the following balances:

Cash	$ 80,000	Accounts Payable	$ 60,000
Accounts Receivable	100,000	Bonds Payable	240,000
Inventory	160,000	Common Stock	100,000
Buildings and Equipment	700,000	Additional Paid-In Capital	150,000
Less: Accumulated Depreciation	(240,000)	Retained Earnings	250,000
Total Assets	$800,000	Total Liabilities and Equities	$800,000

On January 1, 20X7, Quinn purchased 2,000 of its own $10 par value common shares from Nonaffiliated Corporation for $42 per share.

Required

a. Compute the change in the book value of the shares held by Blatant Advertising as a result of the repurchase of shares by Quinn Manufacturing.

b. Give the entry to be recorded on Blatant Advertising's books to recognize the change in the book value of the shares it holds.

c. Give the eliminating entry needed in preparing a consolidated balance sheet immediately following the purchase of shares by Quinn.

E9-16 Sale of Shares by Subsidiary to Nonaffiliate

Browne Corporation purchased 11,000 shares of Schroeder Corporation on January 1, 20X3, at book value. On December 31, 20X8, Schroeder reported these balance sheet amounts:

Cash	$ 80,000	Accounts Payable	$ 50,000
Accounts Receivable	120,000	Bonds Payable	100,000
Inventory	200,000	Common Stock	150,000
Buildings and Equipment	600,000	Additional Paid-In Capital	50,000
Less: Accumulated Depreciation	(250,000)	Retained Earnings	400,000
Total Assets	$750,000	Total Liabilities and Equities	$750,000

On January 1, 20X9, Schroeder issued an additional 5,000 shares of its $10 par value common stock to Nonaffiliated Company for $80 per share.

Required

a. Compute the change in book value of the shares held by Browne as a result of Schroeder's issuance of additional shares.

b. Give the entry to be recorded on Browne's books to recognize the change in book value of the shares it holds, assuming the change in book value is to be treated as an adjustment to additional paid-in capital.

c. Record the eliminating entry needed to prepare a consolidated balance sheet immediately after Schroeder's issuance of additional shares.

Problems P9-17 Multiple-Choice Questions on Preferred Stock Ownership

Stacey Corporation owns 80 percent of the common shares and 70 percent of the preferred shares of Upland Company, all purchased at underlying book value on January 1, 20X2. The balance sheets of Stacey and Upland immediately after the acquisition contained these balances:

	Stacey Corporation	Upland Company
Cash and Receivables	$150,000	$ 80,000
Inventory	200,000	100,000
Buildings and Equipment (net)	250,000	220,000
Investment in Upland Preferred Stock	70,000	
Investment in Upland Common Stock	200,000	
Total Assets	$870,000	$400,000
Liabilities	$220,000	$ 50,000
Preferred Stock		100,000
Common Stock	300,000	200,000
Retained Earnings	350,000	50,000
Total Liabilities and Equities	$870,000	$400,000

The preferred stock issued by Upland pays a 10 percent dividend and is cumulative. For 20X2 Upland reports net income of $30,000 and pays no dividends. Stacey reports income from its separate operations of $100,000 and pays dividends of $40,000 during 20X2.

Required

Select the correct answer for each of the following questions.

1. Total noncontrolling interest reported in the consolidated balance sheet as of January 1, 20X2, is:
   a. $30,000.
   b. $50,000.
   c. $70,000.
   d. $80,000.

2. Income assigned to the noncontrolling interest in the 20X2 consolidated income statement is:

   a. $6,000.

   b. $7,000.

   c. $9,000.

   d. $14,000.

3. Consolidated net income for 20X2 is:

   a. $116,000.

   b. $123,000.

   c. $124,000.

   d. $130,000.

4. Excluding the noncontrolling interest, total stockholders' equity reported in the consolidated balance sheet as of January 1, 20X2, is:

   a. $650,000.

   b. $750,000.

   c. $850,000.

   d. $900,000.

5. Preferred stock outstanding reported in the consolidated balance sheet as of January 1, 20X2, is:

   a. $0.

   b. $30,000.

   c. $70,000.

   d. $100,000.

P9-18 **Multilevel Ownership with Purchase Differential**

Purple Corporation owns 80 percent of Corn Corporation's common stock. It purchased the shares on January 1, 20X1, for $520,000. At the date of acquisition, Corn reported common stock outstanding of $400,000 and retained earnings of $200,000. The excess of purchase price over Purple's proportionate share of the book value of Corn's net assets is assigned to a trademark with a life of five years. Each year since acquisition, Corn has reported income from operations of $60,000 and paid dividends of $25,000.

Corn purchased 70 percent ownership of Bark Company on January 1, 20X3, for $405,000. At January 1, 20X3, Bark reported common stock outstanding of $250,000 and retained earnings of $300,000. In 20X3, Bark reported net income of $30,000 and paid dividends of $20,000. The purchase differential is assigned to buildings and equipment with an economic life of 10 years at the date of acquisition.

Required

a. Prepare the journal entries recorded by Corn for its investment in Bark during 20X3.

b. Prepare the journal entries recorded by Purple for its investment in Corn during 20X3.

c. Prepare the eliminating entries related to Corn's investment in Bark and Purple's investment in Corn needed to prepare consolidated financial statements for Purple and its subsidiaries at December 31, 20X3.

P9-19 **Subsidiary Stock Dividend**

Pound Manufacturing Corporation prepared the following balance sheet as of January 1, 20X8:

Cash	$ 40,000	Accounts Payable	$ 50,000
Accounts Receivable	90,000	Bonds Payable	200,000
Inventory	180,000	Common Stock	100,000
Buildings and Equipment	500,000	Additional Paid-In Capital	70,000
Less: Accumulated Depreciation	(110,000)	Retained Earnings	280,000
Total Assets	$700,000	Total Liabilities and Equities	$700,000

The company is considering a 2-for-1 stock split, a stock dividend of 4,000 shares, or a stock dividend of 1,500 shares on its $10 par value common stock. The current market price per share of Pound stock on January 1, 20X8, is $50. Quick Sales Corporation acquired 68 percent of Pound's common shares on January 1, 20X4, at underlying book value.

Required

Give the investment elimination entry required to prepare a consolidated balance sheet at the close of business on January 1, 20X8, for each of the alternative transactions under consideration by Pound Manufacturing.

P9-20 **Subsidiary Preferred Stock Outstanding**

Emerald Corporation purchased 10,500 shares of the common stock and 800 shares of the 8 percent preferred stock of Pert Company on December 31, 20X4, at underlying book value. Pert reported the following balance sheet amounts on January 1, 20X5:

Cash	$ 30,000	Accounts Payable	$ 20,000
Accounts Receivable	70,000	Bonds Payable	100,000
Inventory	120,000	Preferred Stock	200,000
Buildings and Equipment	600,000	Common Stock	150,000
Less: Accumulated Depreciation	(150,000)	Retained Earnings	200,000
Total Assets	$670,000	Total Liabilities and Equities	$670,000

Pert's preferred stock is $100 par value, and its common stock is $10 par value. The preferred dividends are cumulative and are two years in arrears on January 1, 20X5. Pert reports net income of $34,000 for 20X5 and pays no dividends.

Required

a. Present the workpaper eliminating entries needed to prepare a consolidated balance sheet on January 1, 20X5.

b. Assuming that Emerald reported income from its separate operations of $80,000 in 20X5, compute the amount of consolidated net income and the amount of income to be assigned to noncontrolling shareholders in the 20X5 consolidated income statement.

P9-21 **Ownership of Subsidiary Preferred Stock**

Presley Pools Inc. purchased 60 percent of the common stock of Jacobs Jacuzzi Company on December 31, 20X6, for $1,800,000. All of the excess of the cost of the investment over the book value of the shares acquired was attributable to goodwill. On December 31, 20X7, the management of Presley Pools reviewed the amount attributed to goodwill and concluded an impairment loss of $26,000 should be recognized in 20X7. On January 2, 20X7, Presley purchased 20 percent of the outstanding preferred shares of Jacobs for $42,000.

In its 20X6 annual report, Jacobs reported the following stockholders' equity balances at the end of the year:

Preferred Stock (10 percent, $100 par)	$ 200,000
Premium on Preferred Stock	5,000
Common Stock	500,000
Additional Paid-In Capital—Common	800,000
Retained Earnings	1,650,000
Total Stockholders' Equity	$3,155,000

The preferred stock is cumulative and has a liquidation value equal to its call price of $101 per share. Because of cash flow problems, Jacobs declared no dividends during 20X6, the first time it had missed a preferred dividend. With the improvement in operations during 20X7, Jacobs declared the current stated preferred dividend as well as preferred dividends in arrears; Jacobs also declared a common dividend for 20X7 of $10,000. Jacobs's reported net income for 20X7 was $280,000.

Required

a. Compute the amount of the preferred stockholders' claim on Jacobs Jacuzzi's assets on December 31, 20X6.

b. Compute the December 31, 20X6, book value of the Jacobs common shares purchased by Presley.

c. Compute the amount of goodwill associated with Presley's purchase of Jacobs common stock at the date of acquisition.

d. Compute the amount of income that should be assigned to the noncontrolling interest in the 20X7 consolidated income statement.

e. Compute the amount of income from its subsidiary that Presley should have recorded during 20X7 using the basic equity method.

f. Compute the total amount that should be reported as noncontrolling interest in the December 31, 20X7, consolidated balance sheet.

g. Present all elimination entries that should appear in a consolidation workpaper to prepare a complete set of 20X7 consolidated financial statements for Presley Pools and its subsidiary.

P9-22 Consolidation Workpaper with Subsidiary Preferred Stock

Brown Company owns 90 percent of the common stock and 60 percent of the preferred stock of White Corporation, both acquired at underlying book value on January 1, 20X1. Trial balances for the companies on December 31, 20X6, are as follows:

	Brown Company		White Corporation	
	Debit	Credit	Debit	Credit
Cash	$ 58,000		$100,000	
Accounts Receivable	80,000		120,000	
Dividends Receivable	9,000			
Inventory	100,000		200,000	
Buildings and Equipment (net)	360,000		270,000	
Investment in White Corporation:				
Preferred Stock	120,000			
Common Stock	364,500			
Cost of Goods Sold	280,000		170,000	
Depreciation and Amortization	40,000		30,000	
Other Expenses	131,000		20,000	
Dividends Declared:				
Preferred Stock			15,000	
Common Stock	60,000		10,000	
Accounts Payable		$ 100,000		$ 70,000
Bonds Payable		300,000		
Dividends Payable				15,000
Preferred Stock				200,000
Common Stock		200,000		100,000
Retained Earnings		435,000		250,000
Sales		500,000		300,000
Dividend Income		9,000		
Income from Subsidiary		58,500		
Total	$1,602,500	$1,602,500	$935,000	$935,000

White Corporation's preferred shares pay a 7.5 percent annual dividend and are cumulative. Preferred dividends for 20X6 were declared on December 31, 20X6, and are to be paid January 1, 20X7.

Required

a. Prepare the eliminating entries needed to complete a full consolidation workpaper for 20X6.
b. Prepare a consolidation workpaper as of December 31, 20X6.

P9-23 Subsidiary Stock Transactions

Apex Corporation acquired 75 percent of Beta Company's common stock on May 15, 20X3, at underlying book value. Beta's balance sheet on December 31, 20X6, contained these amounts:

Cash	$ 75,000	Accounts Payable	$ 30,000
Accounts Receivable	50,000	Bonds Payable	200,000
Inventory	125,000	Common Stock ($10 par)	100,000
Buildings and Equipment	700,000	Additional Paid-In Capital	80,000
Less: Accumulated Depreciation	(220,000)	Retained Earnings	320,000
Total Assets	$730,000	Total Liabilities and Equities	$730,000

During 20X7, Apex earned operating income of $90,000, and Beta reported net income of $45,000. Neither company declared any dividends during 20X7.

Beta is considering repurchasing 1,000 of its outstanding shares as treasury stock for $68 each.

Required

a. Assuming Beta purchases the shares from Nonaffiliated Company on January 1, 20X7:

    (1) Compute the effect on the book value of the shares held by Apex.

    (2) Give the entry on Apex's books to record the change in the book value of its investment in Beta's shares.

    (3) Prepare the eliminating entries needed on December 31, 20X7, to complete a consolidation workpaper.

b. Assuming Beta purchases the shares directly from Apex on January 1, 20X7:

    (1) Compute the effect on the book value of the shares held by Apex.

    (2) Give the entry on Apex's books to record its sale of Beta shares to Beta.

    (3) Prepare the eliminating entries needed on December 31, 20X7, to complete a consolidation workpaper.

P9-24 **Sale of Subsidiary Shares**

Penn Corporation purchased 80 percent ownership of ENC Company on January 1, 20X2, at underlying book value. On January 1, 20X4, Penn sold 2,000 shares of ENC's stock for $60,000 to American School Products. Trial balances for the companies on December 31, 20X4, contain the following data:

	Penn Corporation		ENC Company	
	Debit	**Credit**	**Debit**	**Credit**
Cash	$ 30,000		$ 35,000	
Accounts Receivable	70,000		50,000	
Inventory	120,000		100,000	
Buildings and Equipment	650,000		230,000	
Investment in ENC Company	162,000			
Cost of Goods Sold	210,000		100,000	
Depreciation Expense	20,000		15,000	
Other Expenses	21,000		25,000	
Dividends Declared	15,000		10,000	
Accumulated Depreciation		$ 170,000		$ 95,000
Accounts Payable		50,000		20,000
Bonds Payable		200,000		30,000
Common Stock ($10 par)		200,000		100,000
Additional Paid-In Capital		50,000		20,000
Retained Earnings		320,000		130,000
Sales		280,000		170,000
Gain on Sale of ENC Company Stock		10,000		
Income from Subsidiary		18,000		
Total	$1,298,000	$1,298,000	$565,000	$565,000

ENC's net income was earned evenly throughout the year. Both companies declared and paid their dividends on December 31, 20X4. Penn uses the basic equity method in accounting for its investment in ENC.

Required

a. Prepare the elimination entries needed to complete a full consolidation workpaper for 20X4.

b. Prepare a consolidation workpaper for 20X4.

P9-25 Sale of Shares by Subsidiary to Nonaffiliate

Craft Corporation held 80 percent of Delta Corporation's outstanding common shares on December 31, 20X2. Balance sheets for the two companies on that date follow:

CRAFT CORPORATION
Balance Sheet
December 31, 20X2

Cash	$ 50,000	Accounts Payable	$ 70,000
Accounts Receivable	90,000	Mortgages Payable	250,000
Inventory	180,000	Common Stock	300,000
Buildings and Equipment	700,000	Additional Paid-In Capital	180,000
Less: Accumulated Depreciation	(200,000)	Retained Earnings	500,000
Investment in Delta Corporation	480,000		
Total Assets	$1,300,000	Total Liabilities and Equities	$1,300,000

DELTA CORPORATION
Balance Sheet
December 31, 20X2

Cash	$ 50,000	Accounts Payable	$ 70,000
Accounts Receivable	120,000	Taxes Payable	80,000
Inventory	200,000	Common Stock	200,000
Buildings and Equipment	600,000	Additional Paid-In Capital	50,000
Less: Accumulated Depreciation	(220,000)	Retained Earnings	350,000
Total Assets	$750,000	Total Liabilities and Equities	$750,000

On January 1, 20X3, Delta issued 4,000 additional shares of its $10 par value common stock to Nonaffiliated Corporation for $45 per share. Craft recorded the change in the book value of its Delta shares as an adjustment to its investment in Delta and an adjustment to its additional paid-in capital.

Required

a. Give the workpaper elimination entry needed in preparing a consolidated balance sheet as of January 1, 20X3, immediately following the sale of shares by Delta.

b. Prepare a consolidated balance sheet workpaper as of the close of business on January 1, 20X3.

c. Prepare a consolidated balance sheet as of the close of business on January 1, 20X3.

P9-26 Sale of Additional Shares to Parent

Shady Lane Manufacturing Company holds 75 percent of Tin Products Corporation's common stock. The balance sheets of the two companies for January 1, 20X1, are as follows:

SHADY LANE MANUFACTURING COMPANY
Balance Sheet
January 1, 20X1

Cash	$ 227,500	Accounts Payable	$ 50,000
Accounts Receivable	60,000	Bonds Payable	400,000
Inventory	100,000	Common Stock	200,000
Buildings and Equipment	600,000	Additional Paid-In Capital	50,000
Less: Accumulated Depreciation	(150,000)	Retained Earnings	400,000
Investment in Tin Products	262,500		
Total Assets	$1,100,000	Total Liabilities and Equities	$1,100,000

TIN PRODUCTS CORPORATION
Balance Sheet
January 1, 20X1

Cash	$ 60,000	Accounts Payable	$ 50,000
Accounts Receivable	100,000	Bonds Payable	300,000
Inventory	180,000	Common Stock ($10 par)	100,000
Buildings and Equipment	600,000	Additional Paid-In Capital	50,000
Less: Accumulated Depreciation	(240,000)	Retained Earnings	200,000
Total Assets	$700,000	Total Liabilities and Equities	$700,000

On January 2, 20X1, Shady Lane purchased an additional 2,500 shares of common stock directly from Tin Products for $150,000. Any purchase differential is assigned to buildings and equipment.

Required

a. Prepare the eliminating entry needed to complete a consolidated balance sheet workpaper immediately following the issuance of additional shares to Shady Lane.

b. Prepare a consolidated balance sheet workpaper immediately following the issuance of additional shares to Shady Lane.

P9-27 **Complex Ownership Structure**

First Boston Corporation purchased 80 percent of the common stock of Gulfside Corporation on January 1, 20X5. Gulfside holds 60 percent of the voting shares of Paddock Company, and Paddock owns 10 percent of the stock of First Boston. All purchases were made at underlying book value. During 20X7, income from the separate operations of First Boston, Gulfside, and Paddock was $44,000, $34,000, and $50,000, respectively, and dividends of $30,000, $20,000, and $10,000, respectively, were paid. The companies use the cost method of accounting for intercorporate investments and, accordingly, record dividends received as other (nonoperating) income.

Required

Compute the amount of consolidated net income and the income to be assigned to the noncontrolling shareholders of Gulfside and Paddock for 20X7 using (a) the entity approach and (b) the treasury stock method.

Chapter **Ten**

Additional Consolidation Reporting Issues

The financial statements of a consolidated entity must be prepared in conformity with generally accepted accounting principles in the same manner as for any individual enterprise. Standards of reporting and presentation are no different for a consolidated entity than for a single-corporate entity. This chapter discusses the following general financial reporting topics as they relate to consolidated financial statements:

1. The consolidated statement of cash flows.
2. Consolidation following an interim acquisition.
3. Consolidation tax considerations.
4. Consolidated earnings per share.

CONSOLIDATED STATEMENT OF CASH FLOWS

Consolidated entities, as with individual companies, must present a *statement of cash flows* when they issue a complete set of financial statements. A consolidated statement of cash flows is similar to a statement of cash flows prepared for a single-corporate entity and is prepared in basically the same manner.

Preparation of a Consolidated Cash Flow Statement

A consolidated statement of cash flows is typically prepared after the consolidated income statement, retained earnings statement, and balance sheet. Rather than being included in the three-part consolidation workpaper, the consolidated cash flow statement is prepared from the information in the other three statements. When an indirect approach is used in preparing the statement, with consolidated net income as the starting point, consolidated net income must be adjusted for all items that affect consolidated net income and the cash of the consolidated entity differently. Preparation of a consolidated statement of cash flows requires only a few adjustments (such as those for depreciation and amortization resulting from the write-off of a purchase differential) beyond those used in preparing a cash flow statement for an individual company.

As in the other consolidated financial statements, all transfers between affiliates should be eliminated in preparing the consolidated statement of cash flows. Although the sale or purchase of assets is a source or use of cash to an individual company, if such activities occur entirely within the consolidated entity, they should not be included in the statement of cash flows. Unrealized profits on intercompany transfers are eliminated in preparing the consolidated balance sheet and income statement, and therefore no additional elimination of unrealized intercompany profits is needed in preparing the statement of cash flows.

When there is a noncontrolling interest, the income assigned to the noncontrolling stockholders is treated as an adjustment in deriving the amount of cash generated from operating activities. Income assigned to the noncontrolling interest is deducted in computing consolidated net income but does not represent an outflow of cash. Therefore, income assigned to the noncontrolling interest is added back to consolidated net income in the consolidated statement of cash flows to derive the cash flow from operating activities.

Receipts from and payments to noncontrolling shareholders usually are included in the consolidated cash flow statement as cash flows related to financing activities. For example, dividend payments to noncontrolling shareholders normally are included along with dividend payments to parent company shareholders as a use of cash. A sale of additional shares to noncontrolling shareholders or a repurchase of shares from them is considered to be a transaction with a nonaffiliate and is reported as a source or use of cash.

Consolidated Cash Flow Statement Illustrated

As an example of the preparation of a consolidated cash flow statement, assume the following:

1. Peerless Products purchases 80 percent of Special Foods common stock on December 31, 20X0, for $66,000 above book value.

2. Of the $66,000 differential at acquisition, $8,000 is assigned to land, $48,000 to equipment with a 10-year remaining life, and $10,000 to goodwill. Management determines that the goodwill is impaired by the end of 20X1, and a $2,500 write-down is warranted; the value of the goodwill remains constant thereafter.

3. During 20X2, Peerless pays dividends of $60,000; Special Foods reports net income of $75,000 and pays dividends of $40,000.

4. During 20X2, Peerless sells land that it had purchased in 20X1 for $40,000 to a nonaffiliate for $70,000.

5. Special Foods purchases additional equipment from an unrelated company at the end of 20X2 for $100,000.

Consolidated balance sheet information as of December 31, 20X1 and 20X2, follows:

	December 31	
	20X1	**20X2**
Cash	$ 269,000	$ 276,000
Accounts Receivable	125,000	230,000
Inventories	175,000	270,000
Land	223,000	183,000
Buildings and Equipment	1,448,000	1,548,000
Goodwill	7,500	7,500
Total Debits	$2,247,500	$2,514,500
Accumulated Depreciation	$ 774,800	$ 849,600
Accounts Payable	200,000	230,000
Bonds Payable	300,000	300,000
Common Stock	500,000	500,000
Retained Earnings	408,700	563,900
Noncontrolling Interest	64,000	71,000
Total Credits	$2,247,500	$2,514,500

The consolidated income statement for 20X2 is as follows:

Sales		$720,000
Gain on Sale of Land		30,000
		$750,000
Less: Cost of Goods Sold	$340,000	
Depreciation Expense	74,800	
Other Expenses	105,000	(519,800)
Income Available to All Shareholders		$230,200
Income to Noncontrolling Interest		(15,000)
Consolidated Net Income		$215,200

FIGURE 10–1 Workpaper for Peerless Products and Subsidiary Consolidated Statement of Cash Flows, 20X2

Item	Balance 1/1/X2	Debits	Credits	Balance 12/31/X2
Cash	269,000	7,000 (a)		276,000
Accounts Receivable	125,000	105,000 (b)		230,000
Inventory	175,000	95,000 (c)		270,000
Land	223,000		40,000 (d)	183,000
Buildings and Equipment	1,448,000	100,000 (e)		1,548,000
Goodwill	7,500			7,500
	2,247,500			2,514,500
Accumulated Depreciation	774,800		74,800 (f)	849,600
Accounts Payable	200,000		30,000 (g)	230,000
Bonds Payable	300,000			300,000
Common Stock	500,000			500,000
Retained Earnings	408,700	60,000 (h)	215,200 (i)	563,900
Noncontrolling Interest	64,000	8,000 (j)	15,000 (k)	71,000
	2,247,500	375,000	375,000	2,514,500
Cash Flows from Operating Activities:				
Net Income		215,200 (i)		
Depreciation Expense		74,800 (f)		
Income to Noncontrolling Interest		15,000 (k)		
Gain on Sale of Land			30,000 (d)	
Increase in Accounts Receivable			105,000 (b)	
Increase in Inventory			95,000 (c)	
Increase in Accounts Payable		30,000 (g)		
Cash Flows from Investing Activities:				
Acquisition of Equipment			100,000 (e)	
Sale of Land		70,000 (d)		
Cash Flows from Financing Activities:				
Dividends to Parent Company Shareholders			60,000 (h)	
Dividends to Noncontrolling Shareholders			8,000 (j)	
Increase in Cash			7,000 (a)	
		405,000	405,000	

(a) Increase in cash balance.
(b) Increase in accounts receivable.
(c) Increase in inventory.
(d) Sale of land.
(e) Purchase of buildings and equipment.
(f) Depreciation charges for 20X2.
(g) Increase in accounts payable.
(h) Peerless dividends, $60,000.
(i) Consolidated net income, $215,200.
(j) Special Foods dividends to noncontrolling interest ($40,000 × .20).
(k) Income to noncontrolling interest ($75,000 × .20).

A workpaper to prepare a consolidated statement of cash flows is presented in Figure 10–1. Although a number of different workpaper formats may be used in preparing statements of cash flows, the workpaper for preparing a consolidated statement of cash flows is no different from that used for a single-corporate entity. The essential workpaper entries can be seen in Figure 10–1. The consolidated statement of cash flows is prepared from the bottom portion of the workpaper.

Peerless's consolidated statement of cash flows for 20X2 is shown in Figure 10–2. The statement is similar to one that would be prepared for a single company. However, two items unique to consolidated statements are included in Figure 10–2. First, income assigned to the noncontrolling interest is added back to cash generated from operating activities because it was subtracted to arrive at consolidated net income but did not reduce the cash generated from operations. Second, dividends paid to noncontrolling shareholders result in an

FIGURE 10–2
Consolidated
Statement of
Cash Flows for
the Year Ended
December 31, 20X2

PEERLESS PRODUCTS CORPORATION AND SUBSIDIARY		
Consolidated Statement of Cash Flows		
For the Year Ended December 31, 20X2		
Cash Flows from Operating Activities:		
Consolidated Net Income		$ 215,200
Noncash Expenses, Revenues, Losses, and Gains included in Income:		
Depreciation Expense		74,800
Income Assigned to Noncontrolling Interest		15,000
Gain on Sale of Land		(30,000)
Increase in Accounts Receivable		(105,000)
Increase in Inventory		(95,000)
Increase in Accounts Payable		30,000
Net Cash Provided by Operating Activities		$105,000
Cash Flows from Investing Activities:		
Acquisition of Equipment	$(100,000)	
Sale of Land	70,000	
Net Cash Used in Investing Activities		(30,000)
Cash Flows from Financing Activities:		
Dividends Paid:		
To Parent Company Shareholders	$ (60,000)	
To Noncontrolling Shareholders	(8,000)	
Net Cash Used in Financing Activities		(68,000)
Net Increase in Cash		$ 7,000
Cash at Beginning of Year		269,000
Cash at End of Year		$276,000

outflow of cash even though they are not shown as dividends declared in the consolidated retained earnings statement. Although not viewed as distributions of consolidated retained earnings, dividends to the noncontrolling shareholders use cash in reducing the noncontrolling interest.

Consolidated Cash Flow Statement—Direct Method

Although nearly all major companies use the indirect method of presenting a cash flow statement, as illustrated in the previous example, critics have argued that the direct method is less confusing and more useful. Authoritative bodies have generally expressed a preference for the direct method even though they have not required its use.

Using the same information as in the illustration of the indirect method, Figure 10–3 shows a workpaper for the preparation of a consolidated cash flow statement using the direct method. The only section of the cash flow statement affected by the difference in approaches is the operating activities section. Under the indirect approach, as in Figure 10–2, the operating activities section starts with net income and, to derive cash provided by operating activities, adjusts for all items affecting cash and net income differently. Under the direct approach in Figure 10–3, the operating activities section of the statement shows the actual cash flows. In this example, the only cash flows related to operations are as follows:

Cash Flows from Operating Activities:	
Cash Received from Customers	$615,000
Cash Paid to Suppliers	(510,000)
Net Cash Provided by Operating Activities	$105,000

The final number in this section is the same under both approaches, but this method provides a clearer picture of cash flows related to operations than does the indirect approach. Cash received from customers equals the sales revenue ($720,000) from the consolidated

FIGURE 10–3 **Workpaper for Peerless Products and Subsidiary Consolidated Statement of Cash Flows—Direct Method, 20X2**

Item	Balance 1/1/X2	Debits	Credits	Balance 12/31/X2
Cash	269,000	7,000 (a)		276,000
Accounts Receivable	125,000	105,000 (b)		230,000
Inventory	175,000	95,000 (c)		270,000
Land	223,000		40,000 (d)	183,000
Buildings and Equipment	1,448,000	100,000 (e)		1,548,000
Goodwill	7,500			7,500
	2,247,500			2,514,500
Accumulated Depreciation	774,800		74,800 (f)	849,600
Accounts Payable	200,000		30,000 (c)	230,000
Bonds Payable	300,000			300,000
Common Stock	500,000			500,000
Retained Earnings	408,700	60,000 (g)	215,200 (h)	563,900
Noncontrolling Interest	64,000	8,000 (i)	15,000 (j)	71,000
	2,247,500	375,000	375,000	2,514,500
Sales	720,000		720,000 (b)	
Gain on Sale of Land	30,000		30,000 (d)	
	750,000			
Cost of Goods Sold	340,000	340,000 (c)		
Depreciation Expense	74,800	74,800 (f)		
Other Expenses	105,000	105,000 (c)		
Income to Noncontrolling Interest	15,000	15,000 (j)		
	534,800			
Net Income	215,200	215,200 (h)		
		750,000	750,000	

Cash Flows from Operating Activities:				
Cash Received from Customers		615,000 (b)		
Cash Paid to Suppliers			510,000 (c)	
Cash Flows from Investing Activities:				
Acquisition of Equipment			100,000 (e)	
Sale of Land		70,000 (d)		
Cash Flows from Financing Activities:				
Dividends to Parent Company Shareholders			60,000 (g)	
Dividends to Noncontrolling Shareholders			8,000 (i)	
Increase in Cash			7,000 (a)	
		685,000	685,000	

(a) Increase in cash balance.
(b) Payments received from customers.
(c) Payments to suppliers.
(d) Sale of land.
(e) Acquisition of equipment.
(f) Depreciation charges for 20X2.
(g) Peerless dividends, $60,000.
(h) Consolidated net income, $215,200.
(i) Special Foods dividends to noncontrolling interest ($40,000 × .20).
(j) Income to noncontrolling interest ($75,000 × .20).

income statement minus the increase in accounts receivable ($105,000). Cash paid to suppliers equals cost of goods sold ($340,000), plus other expenses ($105,000), plus the increase in inventory ($95,000), minus the increase in accounts payable ($30,000). The remainder of the cash flow statement is the same under both approaches except that a separate reconciliation of operating cash flows and net income is required under the direct approach.

CONSOLIDATION FOLLOWING AN INTERIM ACQUISITION

When one company purchases another company's common stock, the subsidiary is viewed as being part of the consolidated entity only from the time the stock is acquired. Consequently, when a subsidiary is purchased during a fiscal period rather than at the beginning or end, the results of the subsidiary's operations are included in the consolidated statements only for the portion of the year that the stock is owned by the parent.

The results of operations for a subsidiary purchased during the fiscal period are included in the consolidated income statement in one of two ways:

1. Include in the consolidated income statement the revenue and expenses of the subsidiary as if it had been acquired at the beginning of the fiscal period, and deduct the parent's share of the subsidiary's preacquisition earnings at the bottom of the consolidated income statement.

2. Include in the consolidated income statement only the subsidiary's revenue earned and expenses incurred subsequent to the date of combination.

Although the FASB has proposed requiring the second alternative, **ARB 51** allows both. However, **ARB 51** expresses a preference for the first alternative because it better indicates the level of activity of the current economic entity and provides better comparisons with future periods. This alternative is found most often in practice and is illustrated here.

To better understand consolidation following an interim acquisition, assume that on July 1, 20X1, Peerless Products purchases 80 percent of Special Foods' common stock for its underlying book value of $246,400.

Special Foods reports income and dividends for 20X1 as follows:

	Before Combination (January 1 to June 30)	After Combination (July 1 to December 31)
Net Income	$20,000	$30,000
Dividends	12,000	18,000

The book value of Special Foods' stock acquired by Peerless on July 1, 20X1, is computed as follows:

Book value of Special Foods on January 1, 20X1:	
Common stock	$200,000
Retained earnings	100,000
	$300,000
Net income, January 1 to June 30, 20X1	20,000
Dividends, January 1 to June 30, 20X1	(12,000)
Book value of Special Foods on July 1, 20X1	$308,000
Peerless's ownership interest	× .80
Book value on July 1, 20X1, of shares acquired by Peerless	$246,400

The ownership situation on July 1, 20X1, is as follows:

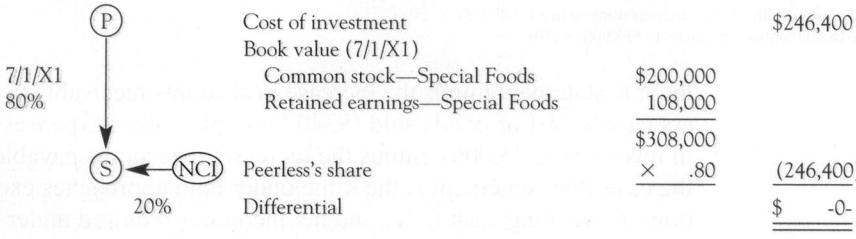

Cost of investment		$246,400
Book value (7/1/X1)		
7/1/X1 Common stock—Special Foods	$200,000	
80% Retained earnings—Special Foods	108,000	
	$308,000	
Peerless's share	× .80	(246,400)
20% Differential		$ -0-

Parent Company Entries

Peerless records the purchase of Special Foods stock with the following entry:

July 1, 20X1

(1)	Investment in Special Foods Stock	246,400	
	Cash		246,400
	Record purchase of Special Foods stock.		

During the second half of 20X1, Peerless records its share of Special Foods' income and dividends under the equity method:

(2)	Cash	14,400	
	Investment in Special Foods Stock		14,400
	Record dividends from Special Foods:		
	$18,000 \times .80$		
(3)	Investment in Special Foods Stock	24,000	
	Income from Subsidiary		24,000
	Record equity-method income:		
	$30,000 \times .80$		

Consolidation Workpaper

The consolidation workpaper reflecting the interim acquisition of Special Foods stock during 20X1 is presented in Figure 10–4. The trial balance of Special Foods for 20X1 is the same as used previously in Figure 5–5. The trial balance for Peerless is the same as in Figure 5–5 except that the amount of Peerless's cash reflects the interim purchase, as does the income from Special Foods recognized by Peerless.

The elimination entries in the consolidation workpaper prepared as of December 31, 20X1, are as follows:

E(4)	Income from Subsidiary	24,000	
	Dividends Declared		14,400
	Investment in Special Foods Stock		9,600
	Eliminate income from subsidiary.		
E(5)	Income to Noncontrolling Interest	10,000	
	Dividends Declared		6,000
	Noncontrolling Interest		4,000
	Assign income to noncontrolling interest.		
E(6)	Common Stock—Special Foods	200,000	
	Retained Earnings, January 1	100,000	
	Preacquisition Subsidiary Income	16,000	
	Dividends Declared		9,600
	Investment in Special Foods Stock		246,400
	Noncontrolling Interest		60,000
	Eliminate beginning investment balance:		
	$16,000 = $20,000 \times .80$		
	$9,600 = $12,000 \times .80$		

Entry E(4) eliminates the income from Special Foods that Peerless has recognized since the date of combination ($30,000 \times .80$), Peerless's share of Special Foods' dividends declared since the date of combination ($18,000 \times .80$), and the change in Peerless's

FIGURE 10–4 December 31, 20X1, Equity-Method Workpaper for Consolidated Financial Statements, Year of Combination; 80 Percent Purchase at Book Value; Interim Acquisition

Item	Peerless Products	Special Foods	Eliminations Debit	Eliminations Credit	Consolidated
Sales	400,000	200,000			600,000
Income from Subsidiary	24,000		(4) 24,000		
Credits	424,000	200,000			600,000
Cost of Goods Sold	170,000	115,000			285,000
Depreciation and Amortization	50,000	20,000			70,000
Other Expenses	40,000	15,000			55,000
Debits	(260,000)	(150,000)			(410,000)
					190,000
Preacquisition Subsidiary Income			(6) 16,000		(16,000)
Income to Noncontrolling Interest			(5) 10,000		(10,000)
Net Income, carry forward	164,000	50,000	50,000		164,000
Retained Earnings, January 1	300,000	100,000	(6) 100,000		300,000
Net Income, from above	164,000	50,000	50,000		164,000
	464,000	150,000			464,000
Dividends Declared	(60,000)	(30,000)		(4) 14,400	
				(5) 6,000	
				(6) 9,600	(60,000)
Retained Earnings, December 31, carry forward	404,000	120,000	150,000	30,000	404,000
Cash	248,000	75,000			323,000
Accounts Receivable	75,000	50,000			125,000
Inventory	100,000	75,000			175,000
Land	175,000	40,000			215,000
Buildings and Equipment	800,000	600,000			1,400,000
Investment in Special Foods Stock	256,000			(4) 9,600	
				(6) 246,400	
Debits	1,654,000	840,000			2,238,000
Accumulated Depreciation	450,000	320,000			770,000
Accounts Payable	100,000	100,000			200,000
Bonds Payable	200,000	100,000			300,000
Common Stock	500,000	200,000	(6) 200,000		500,000
Retained Earnings, from above	404,000	120,000	150,000	30,000	404,000
Noncontrolling Interest				(5) 4,000	
				(6) 60,000	64,000
Credits	1,654,000	840,000	350,000	350,000	2,238,000

Elimination entries:
   (4) Eliminate income from subsidiary.
   (5) Assign income to noncontrolling interest.
   (6) Eliminate beginning investment balance.

investment account since the date of combination. Entry E(5) assigns the noncontrolling interest's share of Special Foods' income for the entire year to the noncontrolling interest, eliminates the noncontrolling interest's share of dividends declared by Special Foods during 20X1, and enters the increase in the noncontrolling interest during the year. The amounts assigned to the noncontrolling interest are not affected by whether the combination takes place at the beginning of the year or during the year.

Entry E(6) eliminates Peerless's investment account balance as of the date of combination. It also eliminates Special Foods' stockholders' equity balances as of the beginning of 20X1 and establishes the amount of the noncontrolling interest as of the beginning of the year. Note that computations relating to the noncontrolling interest consider the entire year 20X1, but those involving the controlling shareholders deal only with the period subsequent to the date of combination.

Entry E(6) also eliminates the dividends declared prior to combination that relate to the Special Foods shares purchased by Peerless on July 1, 20X1. All $30,000 of dividends declared by the subsidiary during 20X1 must be eliminated because none represents dividends paid by the consolidated entity. Entry E(4) eliminates the $14,400 paid to the parent company between July 1, 20X1, and December 31, 20X1. E(5) eliminates the $6,000 paid to the stockholders who did not sell their shares to the parent and who, therefore, are included as noncontrolling stockholders for the entire year. Entry E(6) eliminates the remaining $9,600 of subsidiary dividends paid between January 1, 20X1, and July 1, 20X1, to the stockholders of Special Foods who sold their ownership interests to Peerless on July 1, 20X1.

Entry E(6) also establishes $16,000 of *preacquisition subsidiary income*. This represents the income between January 1, 20X1, and July 1, 20X1, that accrued to the previous stockholders of Special Foods who sold their shares to Peerless on July 1, 20X1. This preacquisition income may not be recognized as income of the consolidated entity because it represents income of Special Foods earned prior to the combination date. Because all of Special Foods' revenue and expenses for the entire year 20X1 are included in the consolidated income statement, the preacquisition earnings accruing to the shares purchased by Peerless on July 1, 20X1, must be deducted to obtain consolidated net income.

The consolidated income statement for the year of the interim acquisition is prepared as if the combination had taken place at the beginning of the year, and the controlling stockholders' percentage times Special Foods' preacquisition earnings is deducted, along with the income accruing to the noncontrolling interest, at the bottom of the consolidated income statement:

PEERLESS PRODUCTS CORPORATION AND SUBSIDIARY
Consolidated Income Statement
For the Year Ended December 31, 20X1

Sales		$600,000
Cost of Goods Sold		(285,000)
Gross Margin		$315,000
Expenses:		
Depreciation and Amortization	$70,000	
Other Expenses	55,000	
Total Expenses		(125,000)
		$190,000
Preacquisition Subsidiary Income		(16,000)
Income to Noncontrolling Interest		(10,000)
Consolidated Net Income		$164,000

The controlling shareholders' income is the same under this approach as if Special Foods' books had been closed immediately before the combination and a new fiscal period started on the date of combination. If the books had been closed, Special Foods' preacquisition earnings and dividends would have been closed into Retained Earnings. The resulting interim balance of the Retained Earnings account would serve as the beginning balance in making the investment elimination entry. As in the normal investment elimination entry, the subsidiary's retained earnings at the beginning of the period, which is the date of combination in this case, would be eliminated.

CONSOLIDATION INCOME TAX ISSUES

A parent company and its subsidiaries may file a ***consolidated income tax return***, or they may choose to file separate returns. For a subsidiary to be eligible to be included in a consolidated tax return, at least 80 percent of its stock must be held by the parent company or another company included in the consolidated return.

A major advantage of filing a consolidated return is the ability to offset the losses of one company against the profits of another. In addition, dividends and other transfers between the affiliated companies are not taxed. Thus, tax payments on profits from intercompany transfers can be delayed until the intercompany profits are realized through transactions with nonaffiliates. When separate returns are filed, the selling company is required to pay tax on the intercompany profits it has recognized, whether or not the profits are realized from a consolidated viewpoint. Filing a consolidated return also may make it possible to avoid limits on the use of certain items such as foreign tax credits and charitable contributions.

An election to file a consolidated income tax return carries with it some limitations. Once an election is made to include a subsidiary in the consolidated return, the company cannot file separate tax returns in the future unless it receives approval from the Internal Revenue Service. The subsidiary's tax year also must be brought into conformity with the parent's tax year. In addition, preparing a consolidated tax return can become quite difficult when numerous companies are involved and complex ownership arrangements exist between the companies.

The income tax aspects associated with equity-method reporting for unconsolidated investees were discussed in Chapter 2. Two consolidation financial reporting issues relating to income taxes are discussed in this chapter:

1. Allocation of income tax amounts from a consolidated tax return to the individual companies.
2. Tax effects of unrealized intercompany profit eliminations.

Allocation of Tax Expense When a Consolidated Return Is Filed

A consolidated tax return portrays the companies included in the return as if they actually were a single legal entity. All intercorporate transfers of goods and services and intercompany dividends are eliminated and a single income tax figure is assessed when a consolidated return is prepared.

Consolidated companies sometimes need to prepare separate financial statements for noncontrolling shareholders and creditors. Because only a single income tax amount is determined for the consolidated entity when a consolidated tax return is filed, income tax expense must be assigned to the individual companies included in the return in some manner. The way in which the consolidated income tax amount is allocated to the individual companies can affect the amounts reported in the income statements of both the separate companies and the consolidated entity. When a subsidiary is less than 100 percent owned by the parent, income tax expense assigned to the subsidiary reduces proportionately the income assigned to the parent and the noncontrolling interest. Therefore, as a larger part of the tax expense is assigned to such a subsidiary, the income to noncontrolling interest becomes smaller and consolidated net income becomes larger.

Although no authoritative pronouncements specify the assignment of consolidated income tax expense to the individual companies included in the consolidated tax return, a reasonable approach is to allocate consolidated income tax expense among the companies on the basis of their relative contributions to income before taxes. As an example, assume that Peerless Products owns 80 percent of the stock of Special Foods, purchased at book value, and the two companies elect to file a consolidated tax return for 20X1. Peerless Products reports operating earnings before taxes of $140,000, excluding income from Special Foods, and Special Foods reports income before taxes of $50,000. If the corporate tax rate is 40 percent, consolidated income taxes are $76,000 ($190,000 × .40). Tax expense of $56,000 is assigned to Peerless Products, and $20,000 is assigned to Special Foods, determined as follows:

Peerless Products: ($140,000/$190,000) × $76,000 = $56,000	
Special Foods: ($50,000/$190,000) × $76,000 = 20,000	
Consolidated tax expense	$76,000

Income assigned to the noncontrolling interest is computed as follows:

Special Foods' income before tax	$50,000
Income tax expense assigned to Special Foods	(20,000)
Special Foods' net income	$30,000
Noncontrolling stockholders' proportionate share	× .20
Income assigned to noncontrolling interest	$ 6,000

The consolidated income statement for 20X1 shows the following amounts:

Consolidated Operating Income	$190,000
Less: Income Tax Expense	(76,000)
Income Available to All Shareholders	$114,000
Less: Income Assigned to Noncontrolling Interest	(6,000)
Consolidated Net Income	$108,000

Other allocation bases may be preferred when affiliates have significantly different tax characteristics, such as when only one of the companies qualifies for special tax exemptions or credits.

Tax Effects of Unrealized Intercompany Profit Eliminations

The income tax effects of unrealized intercompany profit eliminations depend on whether the companies within the consolidated entity file a consolidated tax return or separate tax returns.

Unrealized Profits When a Consolidated Return Is Filed

Intercompany transfers are eliminated in computing both consolidated net income and taxable income when a consolidated tax return is filed. Only sales outside the consolidated entity are recognized both for tax and for financial reporting purposes. Because profits are taxed in the same period they are recognized for financial reporting purposes, no *temporary differences* arise, and no additional tax accruals are needed in preparing the consolidated financial statements.

Unrealized Profits When Separate Returns Are Filed

When each company within a consolidated entity files a separate income tax return, that company is taxed individually on the profits from intercompany sales. The focus in separate tax returns is on the transactions of the separate companies, and no consideration is given to whether the intercompany profits are realized from a consolidated viewpoint. Thus, the profit from an intercompany sale is taxed when the intercompany transfer occurs, without waiting for confirmation through sale to a nonaffiliate. For consolidated financial reporting purposes, however, unrealized intercompany profits must be eliminated. While the separate company may pay income taxes on the unrealized intercompany profit, the tax expense must be eliminated when the unrealized intercompany profit is eliminated in the preparation of consolidated financial statements. This difference in the timing of the income tax expense recognition results in the recording of *deferred income taxes*.

For example, if Special Foods sells inventory costing $23,000 to Peerless Products for $28,000, and none is resold before year-end, the entry to eliminate the intercorporate transfer when consolidated statements are prepared is:

E(7)	Sales	28,000	
	Cost of Goods Sold		23,000
	Inventory		5,000
	Eliminate intercompany upstream sale of inventory.		

Income assigned to Special Foods' shareholders is reduced by $5,000 as a result of entry E(7). An adjustment to tax expense also is required in preparing consolidated statements if Special Foods files a separate tax return. With a 40 percent corporate income tax rate, eliminating entry E(8) adjusts income tax expense of the consolidated entity downward by $2,000 ($5,000 × .40) to reflect the reduction of reported profits:

E(8)	Deferred Tax Asset	2,000	
	Income Tax Expense		2,000
	Eliminate tax expense on unrealized intercompany profit.		

The debit to the deferred tax asset in entry E(8) reflects the tax effect of a temporary difference between the income reported in the consolidated income statement and that reported in the separate tax returns of the companies within the consolidated entity. Consistent with the treatment accorded other temporary differences, this tax effect normally is carried to the consolidated balance sheet as an asset. If the intercompany profit is expected to be recognized in the consolidated income statement in the next year, the deferred taxes are classified as current.

Unrealized Profit in Separate Tax Return Illustrated

For purposes of illustrating the treatment of income taxes when Peerless and Special Foods file separate tax returns, assume the following information:

1. Peerless owns 80 percent of Special Foods' common stock, purchased at book value.
2. During 20X1, Special Foods purchases inventory for $23,000 and sells it to Peerless for $28,000. Peerless continues to hold all of the inventory at the end of 20X1.
3. The effective combined federal and state tax rate for both Peerless and Special Foods is 40 percent.

Although Special Foods' trial balance includes $50,000 of income before taxes and tax expense of $20,000 ($50,000 × .40), consolidated net income and income assigned to noncontrolling shareholders are based on realized net income of $27,000, computed as follows:

Special Foods' net income	$30,000
Add back income tax expense	20,000
Special Foods' income before taxes	$50,000
Unrealized profit on upstream sale	(5,000)
Special Foods' realized income before taxes	$45,000
Income taxes on realized income (40%)	(18,000)
Special Foods' realized net income	$27,000
Special Foods' realized net income assigned to:	
Controlling interest ($27,000 × .80)	$21,600
Noncontrolling interest ($27,000 × .20)	5,400
Special Foods' realized net income	$27,000

If Peerless accounts for its investment in Special Foods using the basic equity method, the eliminating entries needed for the preparation of a consolidation workpaper as of December 31, 20X1, are as follows:

E(9)	Income from Subsidiary	24,000	
	Dividends Declared		24,000
	Eliminate income from subsidiary:		
	$30,000 × .80		
E(10)	Income to Noncontrolling Interest	5,400	
	Noncontrolling Interest	600	
	Dividends Declared		6,000
	Assign income to noncontrolling interest:		
	$5,400 = $27,000 × .20		
	$600 = $6,000 − $5,400		
	$6,000 = $30,000 × .20		
E(11)	Common Stock—Special Foods	200,000	
	Retained Earnings, January 1	100,000	
	Investment in Special Foods Stock		240,000
	Noncontrolling Interest		60,000
	Eliminate beginning investment balance.		
E(12)	Sales	28,000	
	Cost of Goods Sold		23,000
	Inventory		5,000
	Eliminate intercompany upstream sale of inventory.		
E(13)	Deferred Tax Asset	2,000	
	Income Tax Expense		2,000
	Eliminate tax expense on unrealized intercompany profit:		
	$5,000 × .40		

Entries E(9), E(10), and E(11) are the normal entries to eliminate the dividends declared and beginning stockholders' equity accounts of the subsidiary, the parent's investment account, and income from the subsidiary recognized by the parent and to establish the noncontrolling interest. As entry E(9) indicates, Special Foods distributed its entire 20X1 reported net income as dividends. Thus, the balance of the investment account remains at the original cost. Because the realized net income of Special Foods ($27,000) was less than dividends paid ($30,000), entry E(10) contains a debit to noncontrolling interest indicating a reduction in the claim of the noncontrolling shareholders during the period. Entries E(12) and E(13) eliminate the effects of the intercompany transaction, establish the tax effects of the temporary difference, and reduce consolidated net income by the unrealized intercompany profit net of taxes.

Another temporary difference normally would be included in the consolidated balance sheet and in the computation of consolidated income tax expense. In addition to temporary differences arising from unrealized profits, differences normally exist between subsidiary net income and dividend distributions. Peerless pays income taxes for the period based on its reported dividends from Special Foods but includes in consolidated net income for financial reporting its proportionate share of Special Foods' realized net income. This difference between the amount of income reported in the consolidated income statement and the amount reported in the tax return is considered a temporary difference, and deferred taxes normally must be recognized on this difference. In this example, Special Foods distributes all of its income as dividends, and the only temporary difference relates to the unrealized intercompany profit.

Subsequent Profit Realization When Separate Returns Are Filed

When unrealized intercompany profits at the end of one period subsequently are recognized in another period, the tax effects of the temporary difference must again be considered.

If income taxes were ignored, eliminating entry E(14) would be used in preparing consolidated statements as of December 31, 20X2, assuming that Special Foods had $5,000 of unrealized inventory profit on its books on January 1, 20X2, and the inventory was resold in 20X2:

E(14)	Retained Earnings, January 1	4,000	
	Noncontrolling Interest	1,000	
	Cost of Goods Sold		5,000
	Eliminate beginning inventory profit.		

On the other hand, if the 40 percent tax rate is considered, eliminating entry E(15) is used in place of entry E(14):

E(15)	Retained Earnings, January 1	2,400	
	Noncontrolling Interest	600	
	Income Tax Expense	2,000	
	Cost of Goods Sold		5,000
	Eliminate beginning inventory profit:		
	$2,400 = ($5,000 − $2,000) × .80		
	$600 = ($5,000 − $2,000) × .20		
	$2,000 = $5,000 × .40		

Unrealized profit of $3,000 rather than $5,000 is apportioned between the controlling and noncontrolling shareholders in this case. Tax expense of $2,000 is recognized for financial reporting purposes in 20X2 even though the $5,000 of intercompany profit was reported on Special Foods' separate tax return and the $2,000 of taxes was paid on the profit in 20X1. Entry E(15) recognizes the tax expense in the consolidated income statement in the same year as the income is recognized from a consolidated viewpoint. No workpaper adjustment to the Deferred Tax Asset account is needed at the end of 20X2 because the deferred tax asset was entered only in the consolidation workpaper at the end of 20X1, but not on the books of either company; it does not carry over to 20X2.

CONSOLIDATED EARNINGS PER SHARE

In general, *consolidated earnings per share* is calculated in the same way as earnings per share is calculated for a single corporation. Basic consolidated EPS equals consolidated net income available to the parent's common stockholders (i.e., after deducting any preferred dividends of the parent) divided by the weighted-average number of the parent's common shares outstanding during the period.

The computation of diluted consolidated EPS is more complicated. A subsidiary's contribution to the diluted EPS number may be different from its contribution to consolidated net income because of different underlying assumptions. Both the percentage of ownership held within the consolidated entity and the total amount of subsidiary income available to common shareholders may be different. In the computation of EPS, the parent's percentage of ownership frequently is changed when a subsidiary's convertible bonds and preferred stock are treated as common stock and the subsidiary's options and warrants are treated as if they had been exercised. In addition, income available to common shareholders of the subsidiary changes when bonds and preferred stock are treated as common stock for purposes of computing EPS. Interest expense or preferred dividends, if already deducted, must be added back in computing income available to common shareholders when the securities are considered to be common stock.

Computation of Diluted Consolidated Earnings per Share

Consolidated net income normally is the starting point in the computation of diluted consolidated EPS. It then is adjusted for the effects of parent and subsidiary dilutive securities. The following formulation can be used in computing diluted consolidated EPS:

$$
\text{Diluted consolidated EPS} = \frac{\left(\begin{array}{c}\text{Consolidated net income}\end{array} \pm \begin{array}{c}\text{Adjustment for parent securities}\end{array} - \left(\begin{array}{c}\text{Percent ownership held by parent}\end{array} \times \begin{array}{c}\text{Income available to common shareholders of subsidiary}\end{array}\right)\right) + \left(\begin{array}{c}\text{Shares held by parent}\end{array} \times \begin{array}{c}\text{Subsidiary diluted EPS}\end{array}\right)}{\begin{array}{c}\text{Weighted average of parent company shares outstanding}\end{array} + \begin{array}{c}\text{Shares of parent to be issued if dilutive securities are converted and options exercised}\end{array}}
$$

This formula shows the adjustments to consolidated net income and the parent's common shares outstanding that are needed in computing diluted consolidated EPS. In general, securities of the parent company that are convertible or exercisable into parent company shares must be included as shares outstanding if they are dilutive. When convertible bonds are treated as common stock and the additional shares are added in the denominator, the after-tax interest savings must be added back into the numerator. Dividends on preferred stock that continues to be classified as preferred stock are deducted from the numerator, and no deduction is made for dividends on preferred stock considered to be common stock.

The two other adjustments in the numerator relate to the amount of subsidiary income to be included in computing diluted consolidated EPS. First, the parent's portion of the subsidiary's income available to common shareholders is deducted so that an adjusted income number can be substituted. The amount deducted from consolidated net income is computed by multiplying the parent's ownership percentage of subsidiary common shares outstanding times the subsidiary's income after preferred dividends have been deducted. The subsidiary's contribution to diluted consolidated EPS is determined by multiplying the subsidiary's number of shares held by the parent and other affiliates (or the number of shares that would be held after exercise or conversion of other subsidiary securities held) times the diluted EPS computed for the subsidiary. In this way, the effect of the subsidiary's dilutive securities is considered in computing diluted consolidated EPS.

Occasionally, a subsidiary is permitted to issue rights, warrants, or options to purchase the parent's common stock or to issue a security convertible into the parent's common stock. Such rights, warrants, and options of the subsidiary are treated in the same way as if the parent had issued them.

Subsidiary bonds or preferred stock convertible into the parent's common stock are treated in a slightly different manner. If the securities are treated as if converted, income available to common shareholders of the subsidiary is increased as a result of the reduction in interest expense, net of tax, or preferred dividends. The parent's portion of the earnings increase is included in the diluted consolidated EPS computation through the subsidiary EPS component. The number of parent company shares into which the security is convertible is added to the denominator of the diluted consolidated EPS computation.

Computation of Consolidated Earnings per Share Illustrated

As an illustration of the computation of consolidated earnings per share for Peerless Products and Special Foods, assume the following:

1. Peerless Products purchases 80 percent of the stock of Special Foods on December 31, 20X0, at book value.

2. Both Special Foods and Peerless Products have effective income tax rates of 40 percent and file a consolidated tax return.

3. Special Foods has 20X1 income before taxes of $50,000, an allocated share of consolidated income taxes of $20,000, and net income of $30,000.

4. Consolidated net income for 20X1 is $108,000, computed as follows:

Peerless's separate operating income	$140,000
Special Foods' income before taxes	50,000
Total entity income before taxes	$190,000
Consolidated income taxes (40%)	(76,000)
Total entity income after taxes	$114,000
Less: Income to noncontrolling shareholders ($30,000 × .20)	(6,000)
Consolidated net income	$108,000

5. Peerless's capital structure consists of 100,000 shares of $5 par value common stock and 10,000 shares of $10 par, 10 percent convertible preferred stock. The preferred stock is convertible into 25,000 shares of Peerless's common.

6. Special Foods has 20,000 shares of $10 par value common stock and $100,000 of 6 percent convertible bonds outstanding. The bonds, issued at par, are convertible into 4,000 shares of Special Foods' common stock.

7. On January 1, 20X1, Special Foods grants its officers options to purchase 9,000 shares of common stock of Peerless Products at $26 per share at any time during the five years following the date of the grant. None is exercised during 20X1. The average market price of Peerless's common stock during 20X1 is $29 per share.

Special Foods' Earnings per Share

Before consolidated EPS can be calculated, the EPS total for each subsidiary must be computed. Basic and diluted EPS for Special Foods for 20X1 differ because Special Foods has dilutive convertible bonds outstanding.

Basic and diluted EPS for Special Foods for 20X1 are computed as follows:

	Basic	Diluted
Special Foods' net income	$30,000	$30,000
Interest effect of assumed conversion of bonds, net of taxes ($100,000 × .06) × (1 − .40)		3,600
Income accruing to common shares	$30,000	$33,600
Weighted-average common shares outstanding in 20X1	20,000	20,000
Additional shares from assumed bond conversion		4,000
Weighted-average shares and share equivalents	20,000	24,000
Earnings per share:		
$30,000 / 20,000 shares	$ 1.50	
$33,600 / 24,000 shares		$ 1.40

FIGURE 10–5
Computation of
Peerless Products
and Subsidiary
Consolidated
Earnings per Share
for 20X1

	Basic Earnings per Share	Diluted Earnings per Share
Numerator		
Consolidated net income	$108,000	$108,000
Less: Peerless's share of Special Foods' net income ($30,000 × .80)		(24,000)
Add: Peerless's share of Special Foods' income based on EPS ($1.40 × 16,000 shares)		22,400
Less: Preferred dividends	(10,000)	
Total	$ 98,000	$106,400
Denominator		
Weighted-average shares outstanding	100,000	100,000
Assumed exercise of stock options[a]		931
Preferred stock assumed converted		25,000
Total	100,000	125,931
Earnings per Share		
$98,000 / 100,000 shares	$.98	
$106,400 / 125,931 shares		$.84

[a]Treasury stock method of assuming exercise of stock options:

Shares issued		9,000
Shares repurchased:		
Proceeds from issuing shares (9,000 shares × $26)	$234,000	
Repurchase price per share	÷ $29	
Shares repurchased		(8,069)
Increase in shares outstanding		931

The assumed conversion of the bonds reduces Special Foods' diluted EPS from $1.50 to 1.40.

Consolidated Earnings per Share

Consolidated earnings per share for 20X1 is $.98 based on weighted-average common shares outstanding and $.84 assuming full dilution. The computations are shown in Figure 10–5, with diluted EPS based on the formula presented earlier.

For diluted EPS, consolidated net income of $108,000 is reduced by Peerless's $24,000 ($30,000 × .80) proportionate share of Special Foods' net income. Special Foods' contribution to diluted earnings per share is then added back. A total of $22,400 ($1.40 × 16,000 shares) is added for diluted EPS. If Peerless also had purchased a portion of Special Foods' convertible bonds, an equivalent number of shares would be added to Peerless's holdings in computing the amount added back for diluted EPS. The amount of subsidiary earnings added back into the numerator also can be computed by multiplying the revised ownership ratio times the revised earnings contribution. Earnings available to Special Foods' common shareholders in computing diluted EPS increases to $33,600 ($30,000 + $3,600) with the assumed bond conversion, and the number of shares outstanding increases by 4,000. As a result, the revised ownership ratio is reduced to $66\frac{2}{3}$ percent (16,000 shares ÷ 24,000 shares). The earnings contribution computed in this manner is $22,400 ($33,600 × $.66\frac{2}{3}$).

Peerless's preferred stock is treated as preferred stock in computing basic EPS, and preferred dividends are deducted in determining the income accruing to common shareholders in the numerator. In computing diluted EPS, the preferred stock is treated as common stock outstanding because it is convertible and dilutive. Therefore, no dividends are deducted in the numerator, and 25,000 shares of common are added into the denominator.

Stock options for 9,000 shares of parent company stock can be exercised at any time and must be reflected in the computation of diluted EPS. As computed in Figure 10–5 using the treasury stock method, an additional 931 shares are added to the denominator in computing diluted EPS.

Summary of Key Concepts

In addition to an income statement, balance sheet, and statement of retained earnings, a full set of consolidated financial statements must include a consolidated statement of cash flows. The consolidated statement of cash flows is prepared from the other three consolidated statements in the same way as the statement of cash flows is prepared for a single company. However, certain additional adjustments are needed. For example, income assigned to the noncontrolling interest reduces consolidated net income but does not use cash; it therefore must be added back to net income in deriving cash generated from operating activities. Also, dividends to noncontrolling shareholders must be included as a financing use of cash because they do require the use of cash even though they are not viewed as dividends of the consolidated entity.

When a subsidiary is purchased at an interim date during the year, the consolidation procedures must ensure that income earned by the subsidiary before it was part of the consolidated entity is not included in the basis for calculating consolidated net income. The approach used most frequently is to include the subsidiary's revenues and expenses for the entire year and then deduct its preacquisition earnings.

Two major financial reporting issues related to income taxes arise in consolidation. The first is concerned with how to allocate income tax expense to individual companies included in a consolidated income tax return. One approach is to allocate the total tax based on the contributions of the individual companies to the total entity income. The issue is important because the allocation impacts the separate financial statements and the amounts assigned to the noncontrolling interests in the consolidated statements. The second tax issue involves the income tax effects of intercorporate transactions. For consolidating companies filing separate tax returns, income tax expense is recognized in the consolidated income statement when the associated transaction is recognized by the consolidated entity, not necessarily when it is reported by an individual company. If an intercompany gain or loss is included in an individual company's tax return in a different period from the one in which it is included in the consolidated income statement, deferred income taxes should be recognized on the temporary difference.

Consolidated earnings per share is calculated largely in the same way as for a single company. The numerator of the basic EPS computation is based on earnings available to the holders of the parent's common stock, and the denominator is the weighted-average number of the parent's common shares outstanding during the period. Diluted consolidated EPS assumes both the parent's and subsidiary's dilutive securities are converted, and special adjustments to consolidated net income may be needed to reflect the effect of the assumed conversion on the amount of subsidiary income to include in the EPS numerator.

Key Terms

consolidated earnings per share, *476*	deferred income taxes, *473*	temporary differences, *473*
consolidated income tax return, *472*	preacquisition subsidiary income, *471*	
	statement of cash flows, *463*	

Questions

Q10-1 Why not simply add a fourth part to the three-part consolidation workpaper to permit preparation of a consolidated cash flow statement?

Q10-2 Why is income that is assigned to the noncontrolling interest added back to consolidated net income to compute net cash flow from operating activities in a consolidated statement of cash flows?

Q10-3 Why are dividend payments to noncontrolling shareholders treated as an outflow of cash in the consolidated cash flow statement but not included as dividends paid in the consolidated retained earnings statement?

Q10-4 Why are payments to suppliers not shown in the statement of cash flows when the indirect method is used in presenting cash flows from operating activities?

Q10-5 Why are changes in inventory balances not shown in the statement of cash flows when the direct method is used in presenting the cash flows from operating activities?

Q10-6 Are sales included in the consolidation workpaper in computing cash flows from operating activities when the indirect method or direct method is used?

Q10-7 How is an increase in inventory included in the amounts reported as cash flows from operating activities under (*a*) the indirect method and (*b*) the direct method?

Q10-8 Why do companies that file consolidated tax returns often choose to allocate tax expense to the individual affiliates?

Q10-9 How do unrealized profits on intercompany transfers affect the amount reported as income tax expense in the consolidated financial statements?

Q10-10 How do interperiod income tax allocation procedures affect consolidation eliminating entries in the period in which unrealized intercompany profits arise?

Q10-11 How do interperiod income tax allocation procedures affect consolidation eliminating entries in the period in which intercompany profits unrealized as of the beginning of the period are realized?

Q10-12 How does the use of interperiod tax allocation procedures affect the amount of income assigned to noncontrolling shareholders in the period in which unrealized intercompany profits are recorded by the subsidiary?

Q10-13 Why is it not possible simply to add together the separately computed earnings per share amounts of individual affiliates in deriving consolidated earnings per share?

Q10-14 How are dividends that are paid to the parent's preferred shareholders and to the subsidiary's preferred shareholders treated in computing consolidated earnings per share?

Q10-15 What factors may cause a subsidiary's income contribution to consolidated earnings per share to be different from its contribution to consolidated net income?

Q10-16 When a convertible bond of a subsidiary is treated as common stock in computing the subsidiary's diluted earnings per share, how is the interest on the bond treated in the computation of diluted consolidated earnings per share?

Q10-17 How are rights, warrants, and options of subsidiary companies treated in the computation of consolidated earnings per share?

Q10-18 What effect does the presence of a noncontrolling interest have on the computation of consolidated earnings per share?

Cases

C10-1 The Effect of Security Type on Earnings per Share

Judgment

Stage Corporation has both convertible preferred stock and convertible debentures outstanding at the end of 20X3. The annual cash payment to the preferred shareholders and to the bondholders is the same, and the two issues convert into the same number of common shares.

Required

a. If both issues are dilutive and are converted into common stock, which issue will cause the larger reduction in basic earnings per share when converted? Why?

b. If both issues are converted into common stock, which issue will cause the larger increase in consolidated net income when converted?

c. If the preferred shares remain outstanding, what conditions must exist for them to be excluded entirely from the computation of basic earnings per share?

d. Stage is a subsidiary of Prop Company. How will these securities affect the earnings per share reported for the consolidated enterprise?

C10-2 Evaluating Consolidated Statements

Research FARS

Cowl Company has been reporting losses for the last three years and has been unable to pay its bills from cash generated from its operations. On December 31, 20X4, Cowl's president instructed its treasurer to transfer a large amount of cash to Cowl from Plum Corporation, which is 80 percent owned by Cowl. It appears Cowl will not return to profitability in the near future and may never be able to repay Plum. Cowl's treasurer is concerned that, although cash will appear to be unchanged in the consolidated financial statements, the subsidiary has much less cash than it previously held and Plum's minority shareholders might learn about the transfer and initiate a lawsuit or other action against Cowl's management.

Required

As a member of Cowl's accounting department, you have been asked to determine whether information on the transfer will be shown in the consolidated cash flow statement or other financial statements and to search the FASB's pronouncements and those of other authoritative bodies to see whether information germane to the minority shareholders of a subsidiary must be disclosed in cases such as this. Prepare a memo indicating your findings, and include citations to or quotations from relevant authoritative pronouncements.

C10-3   ### Earnings per Share

Research
FARS

Major Corporation has 100,000 shares of $10 par value common stock outstanding and no preferred stock outstanding. Minor Corporation has 50,000 shares of $5 par value common stock and 20,000 shares of $20 par value preferred stock outstanding. The preferred shares pay an annual dividend of $2 each and are cumulative. In addition, each preferred share can be converted into five shares of Minor's common stock at any time prior to December 31, 20X9. For the year ended December 31, 20X4, Major reported operating earnings of $170,000, and Minor reported net income of $130,000. Major owns 60 percent of Minor's common shares and 30 percent of its preferred stock.

Major's chief accountant has no experience in computing earnings per share and has concluded Major's primary and diluted EPS for 20X4 is $2.36.

Required

As a senior staff member of Major's accounting department, you have been asked to prepare a memo to the chief accountant that includes the computations needed to determine basic and diluted earnings per share for the consolidated entity. In your memo include citations to or quotations from the authoritative accounting literature in support of the procedures you use.

C10-4   ### Income Tax Expense

Understanding

Johnson Corporation purchased 100 percent ownership of Freelance Company at book value on March 3, 20X2. Johnson, which makes frequent inventory purchases from Freelance, uses the equity method in accounting for its investment in Freelance. Both companies are subject to 40 percent income tax rates and file separate tax returns.

Required

a. When will an inventory transfer cause consolidated income tax expense to be higher than the amount paid?

b. When tax payments are higher than tax expense, how is the overpayment reported in the consolidated financial statements?

c. What types of transfers other than inventory transfers will cause consolidated income tax expense to be less than income taxes paid?

d. What types of transfers other than inventory transfers will cause consolidated income tax expense to be more than income taxes paid?

C10-5   ### Consolidated Cash Flows

Analysis

The consolidated cash flows from operations of Jones Corporation and its subsidiary Short Manufacturing for 20X2 decreased quite substantially from 20X1 despite the fact that consolidated net income increased slightly in 20X2.

Required

a. What factors included in the computation of consolidated net income may explain this difference between cash flows from operations and net income?

b. How might a change in credit terms extended by Short Manufacturing explain a part of the difference?

c. How would an inventory write-off affect cash flows from operations?

d. How would a write-off of uncollectible accounts receivable affect cash flows from operations?

e. How does the preparation of a statement of cash flows differ for a consolidated entity compared with a single corporate entity?

Exercises

E10-1   Analysis of Cash Flows

In its consolidated cash flow statement for the year ended December 31, 20X2, Lamb Corporation reported operating cash inflows of $284,000, financing cash outflows of $230,000, and $80,000 for investing cash outflows, and an ending cash balance of $57,000. Lamb purchased 70 percent of Mint Company's common stock on March 12, 20X1, at book value. Mint reported net income of $30,000, paid dividends of $10,000 in 20X2, and is included in Lamb's consolidated statements. Lamb paid dividends of $45,000 in 20X2. The indirect method is used in computing cash flow from operations.

Required

a. What was the consolidated cash balance at January 1, 20X2?

b. What amount was reported as dividends paid in the cash flow from financing activities section of the statement of cash flows?

c. What adjustment to consolidated net income was made as a result of Lamb's ownership of Mint in deriving cash flow from operations?

d. If the other adjustments to reconcile consolidated net income and cash provided by operations resulted in an increase of $77,000, what amount was reported as consolidated net income for 20X2?

E10-2   Statement of Cash Flows

Becon Corporation's controller has just finished preparing a consolidated balance sheet, income statement, and statement of changes in retained earnings for the year ended December 31, 20X4. Becon owns 60 percent of Handy Corporation's stock, which it purchased on May 7, 20X1. You have been provided with the following information:

Consolidated net income for 20X4 was $243,000.

Handy reported net income of $70,000 for 20X4.

Becon paid dividends of $25,000 in 20X4.

Handy paid dividends of $15,000 in 20X4.

Becon issued common stock on April 7, 20X4, for a total of $150,000.

Consolidated wages payable increased by $7,000 in 20X4.

Consolidated depreciation expense for the year was $21,000.

Consolidated accounts receivable decreased by $32,000 in 20X4.

Bonds payable of Becon with a book value of $204,000 were retired for $200,000 on December 31, 20X4.

Consolidated amortization expense on patents was $13,000 for 20X4.

Becon sold land that it had purchased for $142,000 to a nonaffiliate for $134,000 on June 10, 20X4.

Consolidated accounts payable decreased by $12,000 during 20X4.

Total purchases of equipment by Becon and Handy during 20X4 were $295,000.

Consolidated inventory increased by $16,000 during 20X4.

There were no intercompany transfers between Becon and Handy in 20X4 or prior years except for Handy's payment of dividends. Becon uses the indirect method in preparing its cash flow statement.

Required

a. What amount of income was assigned to the noncontrolling interest in the consolidated income statement for 20X4?

b. What amount of dividends was paid to the noncontrolling interest during 20X4?

c. What amount will be reported as net cash provided by operating activities for 20X4?

d. What amount will be reported as net cash used in investing activities for 20X4?

e. What amount will be reported as net cash used in financing activities for 20X4?

f. What was the change in cash balance for the consolidated entity for 20X4?

E10-3 **Computation of Operating Cash Flows**

Toggle Company reported sales of $310,000 and cost of goods sold of $180,000 for 20X2. During 20X2, Toggle's accounts receivable increased by $17,000, inventory decreased by $8,000, and accounts payable decreased by $21,000.

Required

Compute the amounts to be reported by Toggle as cash received from customers, cash payments to suppliers, and cash flows from operating activities for 20X2.

E10-4 **Consolidated Operating Cash Flows**

Power Corporation owns 75 percent of Turk Company's stock; no intercompany purchases or sales were made in 20X4. For the year, Power and Turk reported sales of $300,000 and $200,000 and cost of goods sold of $160,000 and $95,000, respectively. Power's inventory increased by $35,000, but Turk's decreased by $15,000. Power's accounts receivable increased by $28,000 and its accounts payable decreased by $17,000 during 20X4. Turk's accounts receivable decreased by $10,000 and its accounts payable increased by $4,000.

Required

Using the direct method of computing cash flows from operating activities, compute the following:

a. Cash received from customers.

b. Cash payments to suppliers.

c. Cash flows from operating activities.

E10-5 **Preparation of Statement of Cash Flows**

The accountant for Consolidated Enterprises Inc. has just finished preparing a consolidated balance sheet, income statement, and statement of changes in retained earnings for 20X3. The accountant has asked for assistance in preparing a statement of cash flows for the consolidated entity. Consolidated Enterprises holds 80 percent of the stock of Separate Way Manufacturing. The following items are proposed for inclusion in the consolidated cash flow statement:

Decrease in accounts receivable	$ 23,000
Increase in accounts payable	5,000
Increase in inventory	15,000
Increase in bonds payable	120,000
Equipment purchased	380,000
Common stock repurchased	35,000
Depreciation reported for current period	73,000
Gain recorded on sale of equipment	8,000
Book value of equipment sold	37,000
Goodwill impairment loss	3,000
Sales	900,000
Cost of goods sold	368,000
Dividends paid by parent	60,000
Dividends paid by subsidiary	30,000
Consolidated net income for the year	450,000
Income assigned to the noncontrolling interest	14,000

Required

Prepare in good form a statement of cash flows for Consolidated Enterprises Inc. using the indirect method of computing cash flows from operations.

E10-6 **Direct Method Cash Flow Statement**

Using the data presented in E10-5, prepare a statement of cash flows for Consolidated Enterprises Inc. using the direct method of computing cash flows from operating activities.

E10-7 **Analysis of Consolidated Cash Flow Statement**

The following 20X2 consolidated statement of cash flows is presented for Acme Printing Company and its subsidiary, Jones Delivery:

ACME PRINTING COMPANY AND SUBSIDIARY
Consolidated Statement of Cash Flows
For the Year Ended December 31, 20X2

Cash Flows from Operating Activities:		
Consolidated Net Income	$ 120,000	
Noncash Items Included in Income:		
Depreciation Expense	45,000	
Amortization of Patents	1,000	
Amortization of Bond Premium	(2,000)	
Income to Noncontrolling Interest	10,000	
Loss on Sale of Equipment	23,000	
Decrease in Inventory	20,000	
Increase in Accounts Receivable	(12,000)	
Net Cash Provided by Operating Activities		$205,000
Cash Flows from Investing Activities:		
Purchase of Buildings	$(150,000)	
Sale of Equipment	60,000	
Net Cash Used in Investing Activities		$ (90,000)
Cash Flows from Financing Activities:		
Dividends Paid:		
To Acme Printing Shareholders	$ (50,000)	
To Noncontrolling Shareholders	(6,000)	
Sale of Bonds	100,000	
Repurchase of Acme Printing Stock	(120,000)	
Net Cash Used in Financing Activities		(76,000)
Net Increase in Cash		$ 39,000

Acme Printing purchased 60 percent of the voting shares of Jones in 20X1 for $40,000 above book value.

Required

a. Determine Jones's net income for 20X2.

b. Determine the amount of dividends paid by Jones in 20X2.

c. Explain why the amortization of bond premium is treated as a deduction from net income in arriving at net cash flows from operating activities.

d. Explain why an increase in accounts receivable is treated as a deduction from net income in arriving at net cash flows from operating activities.

e. Explain why dividends to noncontrolling stockholders are not shown as a dividend payment in the retained earnings statement but are shown as a distribution of cash in the consolidated cash flow statement.

f. Did the loss on the sale of equipment included in the consolidated statement of cash flows result from a sale to an affiliate or a nonaffiliate? How do you know?

E10-8   Midyear Acquisition

Yarn Manufacturing Corporation issued stock with a par value of $67,000 and a market value of $503,500 to purchase 95 percent of Spencer Corporation stock on August 30, 20X1. On January 1, 20X1, Spencer reported the following stockholders' equity balances:

Common Stock ($10 par value)	$150,000
Additional Paid-In Capital	50,000
Retained Earnings	300,000
Total Stockholders' Equity	$500,000

Spencer reported net income of $60,000 in 20X1, earned uniformly throughout the year, and declared and paid dividends of $10,000 on June 30 and $25,000 on December 31, 20X1. Yarn accounts for its investment in Spencer Corporation using the basic equity method.

Yarn reported retained earnings of $400,000 on January 1, 20X1, and had 20X1 income of $140,000 from its separate operations. Yarn paid dividends of $80,000 on December 31, 20X1.

Required

a. Compute consolidated retained earnings as of January 1, 20X1, as it would appear in comparative consolidated financial statements presented at the end of 20X1.

b. Compute consolidated net income reported for 20X1.

c. Compute consolidated retained earnings as of December 31, 20X1.

d. Give the December 31, 20X1, balance of Yarn Manufacturing's investment in Spencer Corporation.

E10-9 Purchase of Shares at Midyear

Highbeam Corporation paid $319,500 to purchase 90 percent ownership of Copper Company on April 1, 20X2. On January 1, 20X2, Copper reported these stockholders' equity balances:

Common Stock	$160,000
Additional Paid-In Capital	40,000
Retained Earnings	150,000
Total Stockholders' Equity	$350,000

Copper's operating results and dividend payments for 20X2 were as follows:

	January 1 to March 31	April 1 to December 31
Sales	$90,000	$250,000
Total expenses	(80,000)	(220,000)
Net income	$10,000	$ 30,000
Dividends paid	$ 5,000	$ 15,000

Highbeam uses the equity method in recording its investment in Copper.

Required

a. Prepare the journal entries that Highbeam recorded in 20X2 for its investment in Copper.

b. Give the workpaper eliminating entries needed at December 31, 20X2, to prepare consolidated financial statements.

E10-10 Tax Deferral on Gains and Losses

Springdale Corporation holds 75 percent of the voting shares of Holiday Services Company. During 20X7 Springdale sold inventory costing $60,000 to Holiday Services for $90,000, and Holiday Services resold one-third of the inventory in 20X7. Also in 20X7, Holiday Services sold land with a book value of $140,000 to Springdale for $240,000, and Springdale continues to hold the land. The companies file separate tax returns and are subject to a 40 percent tax rate.

Required

Give the eliminating entries relating to the intercorporate sale of inventories and land to be entered in the consolidation workpaper prepared at the end of 20X7.

E10-11 Unrealized Profits in Prior Year

Springdale Corporation holds 75 percent of the voting shares of Holiday Services Company. During 20X7 Springdale sold inventory costing $60,000 to Holiday Services for $90,000, and Holiday Services resold one-third of the inventory in 20X7. The remaining inventory was resold in 20X8. Also in 20X7, Holiday Services sold land with a book value of $140,000 to Springdale for $240,000. Springdale continues to hold the land at the end of 20X8. The companies file separate tax returns and are subject to a 40 percent tax rate.

Required

Give the eliminating entries relating to the intercorporate sale of inventories and land needed in the consolidation workpaper at the end of 20X8. Assume that Springdale uses the basic equity method in accounting for its investment in Holiday Services.

E10-12 **Allocation of Income Tax Expense**

Winter Corporation owns 80 percent of Ray Guard Corporation's stock and 90 percent of Block Company's stock. The companies file a consolidated tax return each year and in 20X5 paid a total tax of $80,000. Each company is involved in a number of intercompany inventory transfers each period. Information on the companies' activities for 20X5 is as follows:

Company	20X5 Reported Operating Income	20X4 Intercompany Profit Realized in 20X5	20X5 Intercompany Profit Not Realized in 20X5
Winter Corporation	$100,000	$40,000	$10,000
Ray Guard Corporation	50,000		20,000
Block Company	30,000	20,000	10,000

Required

a. Determine the amount of income tax expense that should be assigned to each company.

b. Compute consolidated net income for 20X5. (*Note:* Winter Corporation does not record income tax expense on income from subsidiaries because a consolidated tax return is filed.)

E10-13 **Effect of Preferred Stock on Earnings per Share**

Amber Corporation holds 70 percent of Newtop Company's voting common shares but none of its preferred shares. Summary balance sheets for the companies on December 31, 20X1, are as follows:

	Amber Corporation	Newtop Company
Cash	$ 14,000	$ 30,000
Accounts Receivable	40,000	50,000
Inventory	110,000	80,000
Buildings and Equipment	280,000	200,000
Less: Accumulated Depreciation	(130,000)	(60,000)
Investment in Newtop Company	126,000	
Total Assets	$440,000	$300,000
Accounts Payable	$ 70,000	$ 70,000
Wages Payable	40,000	
Preferred Stock	100,000	50,000
Common Stock ($10 par value)	120,000	100,000
Retained Earnings	110,000	80,000
Total Liabilities and Owners' Equity	$440,000	$300,000

Neither of the preferred issues is convertible. Amber's preferred pays a 9 percent annual dividend, and Newtop's preferred pays a 10 percent dividend. Newtop reported net income of $45,000 and paid a total of $20,000 of dividends in 20X1. Amber reported income from its separate operations of $59,000 and paid total dividends of $45,000 in 20X1.

Required

Compute 20X1 consolidated earnings per share. Ignore any tax consequences.

E10-14 **Effect of Convertible Bonds on Earnings per Share**

Crystal Corporation owns 60 percent of Evans Company's common shares. Balance sheet data for the companies on December 31, 20X2, are as follows:

	Crystal Corporation	Evans Company
Cash	$ 85,000	$ 30,000
Accounts Receivable	80,000	50,000
Inventory	120,000	100,000
Buildings and Equipment	700,000	400,000
Less: Accumulated Depreciation	(240,000)	(80,000)
Investment in Evans Company Stock	150,000	
Total Assets	$895,000	$500,000
Accounts Payable	$145,000	$ 50,000
Bonds Payable	250,000	200,000
Common Stock ($10 par value)	300,000	100,000
Retained Earnings	200,000	150,000
Total Liabilities and Owners' Equity	$895,000	$500,000

The bonds of Crystal Corporation and Evans Company pay annual interest of 8 percent and 10 percent, respectively. Crystal's bonds are not convertible. Evans's bonds can be converted into 10,000 shares of its company stock anytime after January 1, 20X1. An income tax rate of 40 percent is applicable to both companies. Evans reports net income of $30,000 for 20X2 and pays dividends of $15,000. Crystal reports income from its separate operations of $45,000 and pays dividends of $25,000.

Required

Compute basic and diluted earnings per share for the consolidated entity for 20X2.

E10-15 **Effect of Convertible Preferred Stock on Earnings per Share**

Eagle Corporation holds 80 percent of Standard Company's common shares. The companies report the following balance sheet data for December 31, 20X1:

	Eagle Corporation	Standard Company
Cash	$ 50,000	$ 40,000
Accounts Receivable	80,000	60,000
Inventory	140,000	90,000
Buildings and Equipment	700,000	300,000
Less: Accumulated Depreciation	(280,000)	(140,000)
Investment in Standard Company Stock	160,000	
Total Assets	$850,000	$350,000
Accounts Payable	$120,000	$ 50,000
Taxes Payable	80,000	
Preferred Stock ($10 par value)	200,000	100,000
Common Stock:		
$10 par value	100,000	
$5 par value		50,000
Retained Earnings	350,000	150,000
Total Liabilities and Owners' Equity	$850,000	$350,000

An 8 percent annual dividend is paid on the Eagle preferred stock and a 12 percent dividend is paid on the Standard preferred stock. The preferred shares of Eagle are not convertible. Standard's preferred shares can be converted into 15,000 shares of common stock at any time. For 20X1, Standard reports net income of $45,000 and pays total dividends of $20,000, and Eagle reports income from its separate operations of $60,000 and pays total dividends of $35,000.

Required

Compute basic and diluted earnings per share for the consolidated entity for 20X1.

Problems P10-16 Direct Method Computation of Cash Flows

Car Corporation owns 70 percent of the voting common stock of Bus Company. At December 31, 20X1, the companies reported the following:

	Car Corporation	Bus Company
Sales, 20X1	$400,000	$240,000
Cost of goods sold, 20X1	235,000	105,000
Increase (decrease) in 20X1:		
Inventory	(22,000)	16,000
Accounts receivable	9,000	(2,000)
Accounts payable	(31,000)	15,000

During 20X1 Bus sold inventory costing $70,000 to Car for $100,000, and Car resold 40 percent of the inventory prior to December 31, 20X1. No intercompany inventory transactions occurred prior to 20X1, nor did intercompany receivables and payables exist at December 31, 20X1.

Required

Using the direct method, prepare the cash flows from operating activities section of the consolidated statement of cash flows for 20X1 in good form.

P10-17 Preparing a Statement of Cash Flows

Metal Corporation acquired 75 percent ownership of Ocean Company on January 1, 20X1. Consolidated balance sheets at January 1, 20X3, and December 31, 20X3, are as follows:

Item	Jan. 1, 20X3	Dec. 31, 20X3
Cash	$ 68,500	$ 100,500
Accounts Receivable	82,000	97,000
Inventory	115,000	123,000
Land	45,000	55,000
Buildings and Equipment	515,000	550,000
Less: Accumulated Depreciation	(186,500)	(223,000)
Patents	5,000	4,000
	$644,000	$ 706,500
Accounts Payable	$ 61,000	$ 66,000
Wages Payable	26,000	20,000
Notes Payable	250,000	265,000
Common Stock ($10 par value)	150,000	150,000
Retained Earnings	130,000	174,500
Noncontrolling Interest	27,000	31,000
	$644,000	$ 706,500

The consolidated income statement for 20X3 contained the following amounts:

Sales		$490,000
Cost of Goods Sold	$259,000	
Wage Expense	55,000	
Depreciation Expense	36,500	
Interest Expense	16,000	
Amortization Expense	1,000	
Other Expenses	39,000	(406,500)
		$ 83,500
Income to Noncontrolling Interest		(9,000)
Consolidated Net Income		$ 74,500

Metal and Ocean paid dividends of $30,000 and $20,000, respectively, in 20X3.

Required

a. Prepare a workpaper to develop a consolidated statement of cash flows for 20X3 using the indirect method of computing cash flows from operations.

b. Prepare a consolidated statement of cash flows for 20X3.

P10-18   Preparing a Statement of Cash Flows—Direct Method

Required

Using the data presented in P10-17:

a. Prepare a workpaper to develop a consolidated statement of cash flows for 20X3 using the direct method of computing cash flows from operations.

b. Prepare a consolidated statement of cash flows for 20X3.

P10-19   Consolidated Statement of Cash Flows

Traper Company holds 80 percent ownership of Arrow Company. The consolidated balance sheets as of December 31, 20X3, and December 31, 20X4, are as follows:

	Dec. 31, 20X3	Dec. 31, 20X4
Cash	$ 83,000	$ 181,000
Accounts Receivable	210,000	175,000
Inventory	320,000	370,000
Land	190,000	160,000
Buildings and Equipment	850,000	980,000
Less: Accumulated Depreciation	(280,000)	(325,000)
Goodwill	40,000	28,000
Total Assets	$1,413,000	$1,569,000
Accounts Payable	$ 52,000	$ 74,000
Interest Payable	45,000	30,000
Bonds Payable	400,000	500,000
Bond Premium	18,000	16,000
Noncontrolling Interest	40,000	44,000
Common Stock	300,000	300,000
Additional Paid-In Capital	70,000	70,000
Retained Earnings	488,000	535,000
Total Liabilities and Owners' Equity	$1,413,000	$1,569,000

The 20X4 consolidated income statement contained the following amounts:

Sales		$600,000
Cost of Goods Sold	$375,000	
Depreciation Expense	45,000	
Interest Expense	69,000	
Loss on Sale of Land	20,000	
Goodwill Impairment Loss	12,000	(521,000)
		$ 79,000
Income to Noncontrolling Interest		(7,000)
Consolidated Net Income		$ 72,000

Traper purchased its investment in Arrow on January 1, 20X2, for $190,000. At that time, Arrow reported net assets of $150,000. A total of $40,000 of the purchase differential was assigned to goodwill. The remainder of the differential was assigned to equipment with a remaining life of 20 years from the date of combination.

Traper sold $100,000 of bonds on December 31, 20X4, to assist in generating additional funds. Arrow reported net income of $35,000 for 20X4 and paid dividends of $15,000. Traper reported 20X4 equity-method net income of $80,000 and paid dividends of $25,000.

Required

a. Prepare a workpaper to develop a consolidated statement of cash flows for 20X4 using the indirect method of computing cash flows from operations.

b. Prepare a consolidated statement of cash flows for 20X4.

P10-20   Consolidated Statement of Cash Flows—Direct Method

Required
Using the data presented in P10-19:

a. Prepare a workpaper to develop a consolidated statement of cash flows for 20X4 using the direct method of computing cash flows from operations.

b. Prepare a consolidated statement of cash flows for 20X4.

P10-21   Consolidated Statement of Cash Flows

Sun Corporation was created on January 1, 20X2, and quickly became successful. On January 1, 20X6, its owner sold 80 percent of the stock to Weatherbee Company at underlying book value. Weatherbee continued to operate the subsidiary as a separate legal entity and used the equity method in accounting for its investment in Sun. The following consolidated financial statements have been prepared as of December 31, 20X6:

WEATHERBEE COMPANY AND SUBSIDIARY
Consolidated Balance Sheets

	January 1, 20X6	December 31, 20X6
Cash	$ 54,000	$ 75,000
Accounts Receivable	121,000	111,000
Inventory	230,000	360,000
Land	95,000	100,000
Buildings and Equipment	800,000	650,000
Less: Accumulated Depreciation	(290,000)	(230,000)
Total Assets	$1,010,000	$1,066,000
Accounts Payable	$ 90,000	$ 105,000
Bonds Payable	300,000	250,000
Noncontrolling Interest	30,000	38,000
Common Stock	300,000	300,000
Retained Earnings	290,000	373,000
Total Liabilities and Owners' Equity	$1,010,000	$1,066,000

WEATHERBEE COMPANY AND SUBSIDIARY
Consolidated Income Statement
Year Ended December 31, 20X6

Sales	$1,070,000
Gain on Sale of Equipment	30,000
	$1,100,000
Cost of Goods Sold	$ 750,000
Depreciation Expense	40,000
Other Expenses	150,000
Total Expenses	$ (940,000)
	$ 160,000
Income to Noncontrolling Interest	(12,000)
Consolidated Net Income	$ 148,000

WEATHERBEE COMPANY AND SUBSIDIARY
Consolidated Retained Earnings Statement
Year Ended December 31, 20X6

Balance, January 1, 20X6	$290,000
20X6 Net Income	148,000
	$438,000
Dividends Paid in 20X6	(65,000)
Balance, December 31, 20X6	$373,000

During 20X6, Sun reported net income of $60,000 and paid dividends of $20,000; Weatherbee reported net income of $148,000 and paid dividends of $65,000. There were no intercompany transfers during the period.

Required

Prepare a workpaper for a consolidated statement of cash flows for 20X6 using the indirect method of computing cash flows from operations.

P10-22 Consolidated Statement of Cash Flows—Direct Method

Required

Using the data presented in P10-21, prepare a workpaper to develop a consolidated statement of cash flows using the direct method for computing cash flows from operations.

P10-23 Consolidated Statement of Cash Flows [AICPA Adapted]

Following are the consolidated balance sheet accounts of Brimer Inc. and its subsidiary, Dore Corporation, as of December 31, 20X6 and 20X5.

	20X6	20X5	Net Increase (Decrease)
Assets			
Cash	$ 313,000	$ 195,000	$118,000
Marketable Equity Securities, at cost	175,000	175,000	-0-
Allowance to Reduce Marketable			
Equity Securities to Market	(13,000)	(24,000)	11,000
Accounts Receivable, net	418,000	440,000	(22,000)
Inventories	595,000	525,000	70,000
Land	385,000	170,000	215,000
Plant and Equipment	755,000	690,000	65,000
Accumulated Depreciation	(199,000)	(145,000)	(54,000)
Goodwill, net	57,000	60,000	(3,000)
Total Assets	$2,486,000	$2,086,000	$400,000
Liabilities and Stockholders' Equity			
Current Portion of Long-Term Note	$ 150,000	$ 150,000	$ -0-
Accounts Payable and Accrued Liabilities	595,000	474,000	121,000
Note Payable, Long-Term	300,000	450,000	(150,000)
Deferred Income Taxes	44,000	32,000	12,000
Minority Interest in Net Assets of Subsidiary	179,000	161,000	18,000
Common Stock, par $10	580,000	480,000	100,000
Additional Paid-In Capital	303,000	180,000	123,000
Retained Earnings	335,000	195,000	140,000
Treasury Stock, at cost	-0-	(36,000)	36,000
Total Liabilities and Stockholders' Equity	$2,486,000	$2,086,000	$400,000

Additional Information

1. On January 20, 20X6, Brimer issued 10,000 shares of its common stock for land having a fair value of $215,000.

2. On February 5, 20X6, Brimer reissued all of its treasury stock for $44,000.

3. On May 15, 20X6, Brimer paid a $58,000 cash dividend on its common stock.

4. On August 8, 20X6, equipment was purchased for $127,000.

5. On September 30, 20X6, equipment was sold for $40,000. The equipment cost $62,000 and had a carrying amount of $34,000 on the date of sale.

6. On December 15, 20X6, Dore paid a cash dividend of $50,000 on its common stock.

7. A goodwill impairment loss of $3,000 was recognized in 20X6.

8. Deferred income taxes represent temporary differences relating to the use of accelerated depreciation methods for income tax reporting and the straight-line method for financial reporting.

9. Net income for 20X6 was as follows:

Consolidated net income	$198,000
Dore Corporation	110,000

10. Brimer owns 70 percent of its subsidiary, Dore. There was no change in the ownership interest in Dore during 20X5 and 20X6. There were no intercompany transactions other than the dividend paid to Brimer Inc. by its subsidiary.

Required
Prepare a consolidated statement of cash flows for Brimer Inc. and its subsidiary for the year ended December 31, 20X6, using the indirect method.

P10-24 **Statement of Cash Flows Prepared from Consolidation Workpaper**

Detecto Corporation purchased 60 percent of Strand Company's outstanding shares on January 1, 20X1, for $24,000 more than book value. The full amount of the excess payment is considered related to patents and is being amortized over an eight-year period. In 20X1, Strand purchased a piece of land for $35,000 and later in the year sold it to Detecto for $45,000. Detecto is still holding the land as an investment. During 20X3, Detecto bonds with a value of $100,000 were exchanged for equipment valued at $100,000.

On January 1, 20X3, Detecto held inventory purchased previously from Strand for $48,000. During 20X3, Detecto purchased an additional $90,000 of goods from Strand and held $54,000 of this inventory on December 31, 20X3. Strand sells merchandise to the parent at cost plus a 20 percent markup.

Strand also purchases inventory items from Detecto. On January 1, 20X3, Strand held inventory it had previously purchased from Detecto for $14,000, and on December 31, 20X3, it held goods it purchased from Detecto for $7,000 during 20X3. Strand's total purchases from Detecto in 20X3 were $22,000. Detecto sells inventory to Strand at cost plus a 40 percent markup.

The consolidated balance sheet at December 31, 20X2, contained the following amounts:

	Debit	Credit
Cash	$ 92,000	
Accounts Receivable	135,000	
Inventory	140,000	
Land	75,000	
Buildings and Equipment	400,000	
Patents	18,000	
Accumulated Depreciation		$210,000
Accounts Payable		114,200
Bonds Payable		90,000
Noncontrolling Interest		72,800
Common Stock		100,000
Retained Earnings		273,000
Totals	$860,000	$860,000

The consolidation workpaper below was prepared on December 31, 20X3. All eliminating entries and adjustments have been entered properly in the workpaper. Detecto accounts for its investment in Strand using the basic equity method.

Required

a. Prepare a workpaper for a consolidated statement of cash flows for 20X3 using the indirect method.

b. Prepare a consolidated statement of cash flows for 20X3.

DETECTO CORPORATION AND STRAND COMPANY
Consolidation Workpaper
December 31, 20X3

Item	Detecto Corporation	Strand Company	Eliminations Debit	Eliminations Credit	Consolidated
Sales	400,000	200,000	(8) 22,000		
			(9) 90,000		488,000
Income from Subsidiary	18,000		(1) 18,000		
Credits	418,000	200,000			488,000
Cost of Goods Sold	280,000	120,000		(6) 4,000	
				(7) 8,000	
				(8) 20,000	
				(9) 81,000	287,000
Amortization Expense			(4) 3,000		3,000
Depreciation Expense	25,000	15,000			40,000
Other Expenses	35,000	30,000			65,000
Debits	(340,000)	(165,000)			(395,000)
					93,000
Income to Noncontrolling Interest			(2) 13,600		(13,600)
Net Income, carry forward	78,000	35,000	146,600	113,000	79,400
Retained Earnings, January 1	287,800	150,000	(3) 150,000		
			(5) 6,000		
			(6) 4,000		
			(7) 4,800		273,000
Net Income, from above	78,000	35,000	146,600	113,000	79,400
	365,800	185,000			352,400
Dividends Declared	(50,000)	(20,000)		(1) 12,000	
				(2) 8,000	(50,000)
Retained Earnings, December 31, carry forward	315,800	165,000	311,400	133,000	302,400
Cash	26,800	35,000			61,800
Accounts Receivable	80,000	40,000			120,000
Inventory	120,000	90,000		(8) 2,000	
				(9) 9,000	199,000
Land	70,000	20,000		(5) 10,000	80,000
Buildings and Equipment	340,000	200,000			540,000
Investment in Strand Company Stock	144,000			(1) 6,000	
				(3) 138,000	
Differential			(3) 18,000	(4) 18,000	
Patents			(4) 15,000		15,000
Debits	780,800	385,000			1,015,800
Accumulated Depreciation	165,000	85,000			250,000
Accounts Payable	80,000	15,000			95,000
Bonds Payable	120,000	70,000			190,000
Common Stock	100,000	50,000	(3) 50,000		100,000
Retained Earnings, from above	315,800	165,000	311,400	133,000	302,400
Noncontrolling interest			(5) 4,000	(2) 5,600	
			(7) 3,200	(3) 80,000	78,400
Credits	780,800	385,000	401,600	401,600	1,015,800

P10-25 Midyear Purchase of Controlling Interest

Blase Company operates on a calendar-year basis, reporting its results of operations quarterly. For the first quarter of 20X1, Blase reported net income of $60,000 and paid a dividend of $10,000. On April 1, Starstruck Theaters Inc. purchased 85 percent of Blase's common stock for $750,000; Blase had 100,000 shares of $1 par common stock outstanding, originally issued at $6 per share. Any cost over the book value of the shares acquired by Starstruck Theaters is related to goodwill. On December 31, 20X1, the management of Starstruck Theaters reviewed the amount attributed to goodwill as a result of its purchase of Blase common stock and concluded that goodwill was not impaired.

Blase's retained earnings statement for the full year 20X1 appears as follows:

Retained Earnings, January 1, 20X1	$150,000
Net Income	175,000
Dividends	(40,000)
Retained Earnings, December 31, 20X1	$285,000

Starstruck Theaters accounts for its investment in Blase using the equity method.

Required

a. Present all entries that Starstruck Theaters would have recorded in accounting for its investment in Blase during 20X1.

b. Present all eliminating entries needed in a workpaper to prepare a complete set of consolidated financial statements for the year 20X1.

P10-26 Consolidation Involving a Midyear Purchase

Buster Products Corporation acquired 90 percent ownership of Sanford Company on October 20, 20X2, through an exchange of voting shares in a transaction recorded as a purchase. Buster Products issued 8,000 shares of its $10 par stock to acquire 27,000 shares of Sanford's $5 par stock. The market value of shares issued by Buster was $247,500. Trial balances of the two companies on December 31, 20X2, are as follows:

	Buster Products Corporation		Sanford Company	
	Debit	**Credit**	**Debit**	**Credit**
Cash	$ 85,000		$ 50,000	
Accounts Receivable	100,000		60,000	
Inventory	150,000		100,000	
Buildings and Equipment	400,000		340,000	
Investment in Sanford Stock	252,000			
Cost of Goods Sold	305,000		145,000	
Depreciation Expense	25,000		20,000	
Other Expense	14,000		25,000	
Dividends Declared	40,000		30,000	
Accumulated Depreciation		$ 105,000		$ 65,000
Accounts Payable		40,000		50,000
Taxes Payable		70,000		55,000
Bonds Payable		250,000		100,000
Common Stock		200,000		150,000
Additional Paid-in Capital		167,500		
Retained Earnings		135,000		100,000
Sales		390,000		250,000
Income from Subsidiary		13,500		
Totals	$1,371,000	$1,371,000	$770,000	$770,000

In 20X2, Sanford reported net income of $45,000 before its acquisition by Buster Products and $15,000 after acquisition. Sanford paid dividends of $20,000 in April and $10,000 in November of 20X2. Buster Products paid dividends of $40,000 in 20X2. Buster Products uses the equity method in accounting for its investment in Sanford.

Required

a. Give all journal entries recorded by Buster Products during 20X2 that relate to its investment in Sanford.

b. Give the workpaper elimination entries needed on December 31, 20X2, to prepare consolidated financial statements.

c. Prepare a three-part consolidation workpaper as of December 31, 20X2.

P10-27 Tax Allocation in Consolidated Balance Sheet

Acme Powder Corporation purchased 70 percent of Brown Company's stock on December 31, 20X7, at underlying book value. The two companies' balance sheets on December 31, 20X9, are as follows:

ACME POWDER CORPORATION AND BROWN COMPANY
Balance Sheets
December 31, 20X9

	Acme Powder Corporation	Brown Company
Cash	$ 44,400	$ 20,000
Accounts Receivable	120,000	60,000
Inventory	170,000	120,000
Land	90,000	30,000
Buildings and Equipment	500,000	300,000
Less: Accumulated Depreciation	(180,000)	(80,000)
Investment in Brown Company Stock	280,000	
Total Assets	$1,024,400	$450,000
Accounts Payable	$ 70,000	$ 20,000
Wages Payable	80,000	30,000
Bonds Payable	200,000	
Common Stock	100,000	150,000
Retained Earnings	574,400	250,000
Total Liabilities and Equities	$1,024,400	$450,000

On December 31, 20X9, Acme Powder holds inventory purchased from Brown for $70,000. Brown's cost of producing the merchandise was $50,000. Brown also had purchased inventory from Acme. Brown's ending inventory contains $85,000 of purchases that had cost Acme Powder $60,000 to produce.

On December 30, 20X9, Brown sold equipment to Acme Powder for $90,000. Brown had purchased the equipment for $120,000 several years earlier. At the time of sale to Acme, the equipment had a book value of $40,000. The two companies file separate tax returns and are subject to a 40 percent tax rate. Acme Powder does not record tax expense on its share of Brown's undistributed earnings.

Required

a. Complete a consolidated balance sheet workpaper as of December 31, 20X9.

b. Prepare a consolidated balance sheet as of December 31, 20X9.

P10-28 Computations Involving Tax Allocation

Broom Manufacturing used cash to purchase 75 percent of the voting stock of Satellite Industries on January 1, 20X3, at underlying book value. Broom accounts for its investment in Satellite using the basic equity method.

Broom had no inventory on hand on January 1, 20X5. During 20X5 Broom purchased $300,000 of goods from Satellite and had $100,000 remaining on hand at the end of 20X5. Satellite normally prices its items so that their cost is 70 percent of sale price. On January 1, 20X5, Satellite held inventory that it purchased from Broom for $50,000. Broom's cost of producing the items was $30,000. Satellite sold all of the merchandise in 20X5 and made no inventory purchases from Broom during 20X5.

On July 15, 20X5, Satellite sold land that it had purchased for $240,000 to Broom for $360,000. The companies file separate tax returns and have a 40 percent income tax rate. Broom does not record tax expense on its portion of the undistributed earnings of Satellite. Tax expense recorded by Broom in 20X5 with regard to its investment in Satellite is based on dividends received from Satellite in 20X5. In computing taxable income, 80 percent of intercorporate dividend payments are exempt from tax.

Satellite reported net income of $190,000 for 20X5 and net assets of $900,000 on December 31, 20X5. Broom's reported income before investment income from Satellite and income tax expense was $700,000 for 20X5. Satellite and Broom paid dividends of $150,000 and $400,000, respectively, in 20X5.

Required

a. Give the journal entries recorded on Broom's books during 20X5 to reflect its ownership of Satellite.

b. Compute consolidated net income for 20X5.

c. Compute the income assigned to the noncontrolling interests in the 20X5 consolidated income statement.

d. Compute the amount assigned to the noncontrolling interest in the consolidated balance sheet prepared as of December 31, 20X5.

P10-29 Workpaper Involving Tax Allocation

Hardtack Bread Company holds 70 percent of the common shares of Custom Pizza Corporation. Trial balances for the two companies on December 31, 20X7, are as follows:

Item	Hardtack Bread Company Debit	Hardtack Bread Company Credit	Custom Pizza Corporation Debit	Custom Pizza Corporation Credit
Cash	$ 35,800		$ 56,000	
Accounts Receivable	130,000		40,000	
Inventory	220,000		60,000	
Land	60,000		20,000	
Buildings and Equipment	450,000		400,000	
Patents	70,000			
Investment in Custom Pizza				
Common Stock	158,200			
Cost of Goods Sold	435,000		210,000	
Depreciation and Amortization	40,000		20,000	
Tax Expense	44,000		24,000	
Other Expenses	11,400		10,000	
Dividends Declared	20,000		10,000	
Accumulated Depreciation		$ 150,000		$160,000
Accounts Payable		40,000		30,000
Wages Payable		70,000		20,000
Bonds Payable		200,000		100,000
Deferred Income Taxes		120,000		40,000
Common Stock ($10 par value)		100,000		50,000
Retained Earnings		374,200		150,000
Sales		580,000		300,000
Income from Subsidiary		25,200		
Gain on Sale of Equipment		15,000		
Total	$1,674,400	$1,674,400	$850,000	$850,000

At the beginning of 20X7, Hardtack held inventory purchased from Custom Pizza containing unrealized profits of $10,000. During 20X7, Hardtack purchased $120,000 of inventory from Custom Pizza and on December 31, 20X7, had goods on hand containing $25,000 of unrealized intercompany profit. On December 31, 20X7, Hardtack sold equipment to Custom Pizza for $65,000. Hardtack had purchased the equipment for $150,000 and had accumulated depreciation of $100,000 on it at the time of sale. The companies file separate tax returns and are subject to a 40 percent income tax rate on all taxable income. Intercompany dividends are 80 percent exempt from taxation.

Required

a. Prepare all eliminating entries needed as of December 31, 20X7, to prepare consolidated financial statements for Hardtack Bread Company and its subsidiary.

b. Prepare a three-part consolidation workpaper for 20X7.

P10-30 Earnings per Share with Convertible Securities

Branch Manufacturing Corporation owns 80 percent of the common shares of Short Retail Stores. The companies' balance sheets as of December 31, 20X4, were as follows:

	Branch Manufacturing Corporation	Short Retail Stores
Cash	$ 50,000	$ 30,000
Accounts Receivable	100,000	80,000
Inventory	260,000	120,000
Land	90,000	60,000
Buildings and Equipment	500,000	300,000
Less: Accumulated Depreciation	(220,000)	(120,000)
Investment in Short Retail Stores Stock	120,000	
Total Assets	$900,000	$470,000
Accounts Payable	$ 40,000	$ 20,000
Bonds Payable	300,000	200,000
Preferred Stock ($10 par value)	200,000	100,000
Common Stock:		
$10 par value	150,000	
$5 par value		100,000
Retained Earnings	210,000	50,000
Total Liabilities and Equity	$900,000	$470,000

The 8 percent preferred stock of Short Retail is convertible into 12,000 shares of common stock, and Short's 10 percent bonds are convertible into 8,000 shares of common stock. Short Retail reported net income of $49,200 for 20X4 and paid dividends of $30,000.

Branch Manufacturing has 11 percent preferred stock and 12 percent bonds outstanding, neither of which is convertible. Branch Manufacturing reported after-tax income, excluding investment income from Short Retail, of $100,000 in 20X4 and paid dividends of $60,000. The companies file separate tax returns and are subject to a 40 percent income tax.

Required

Compute basic and diluted earnings per share for the consolidated entity.

P10-31 Comprehensive Earnings per Share

Mighty Corporation holds 80 percent of Longfellow Company's common stock. The following balance sheet data are presented for December 31, 20X7:

	Mighty Corporation	Longfellow Company
Cash	$ 100,000	$ 90,000
Accounts Receivable	150,000	220,000
Inventory	300,000	300,000
Land	100,000	290,000
Buildings and Equipment	2,250,000	900,000
Less: Accumulated Depreciation	(850,000)	(250,000)
Investment in Longfellow Company Stock	600,000	
Total Assets	$2,650,000	$1,550,000

(continued)

Accounts Payable	$ 200,000	$ 100,000
Bonds Payable	800,000	500,000
Preferred Stock ($100 par value)		200,000
Common Stock ($10 par value)	1,000,000	400,000
Retained Earnings	650,000	350,000
Total Liabilities and Equities	$2,650,000	$1,550,000

Longfellow reported net income of $115,000 in 20X7 and paid dividends of $60,000. Its bonds have an annual interest rate of 8 percent and are convertible into 30,000 common shares. Its preferred shares pay an 11 percent annual dividend and convert into 20,000 shares of common stock. In addition, Longfellow has warrants outstanding for 10,000 shares of common stock at $8 per share. The 20X7 average price of Longfellow common shares was $40.

Mighty reported income of $300,000 from its own operations for 20X7 and paid dividends of $200,000. Its 10 percent bonds convert into 25,000 shares of its common stock. The companies file separate tax returns and are subject to income taxes of 40 percent.

Required

Compute basic and diluted earnings per share for the consolidated entity for 20X7.

Chapter Eleven

Multinational Accounting: Foreign Currency Transactions and Financial Instruments

Many companies, large and small, depend on international markets for supplies of goods and for sales of their products and services. Every day the business press carries stories about the effects of export and import activity on the U.S. economy and the large flows of capital among the world's major countries. Also reported are changes in the exchange rates of the major currencies of the world, such as, "The dollar weakened today against the yen." This chapter and Chapter 12 discuss the accounting issues associated with companies that operate internationally.

A company operating in international markets is subject to normal business risks such as lack of demand for its products in the foreign marketplace, labor strikes, and transportation delays in getting its products to the foreign customer. In addition, the U.S. entity may incur foreign currency risks whenever it conducts transactions in other currencies. For example, if a U.S. company acquires a machine on credit from a Swiss manufacturer, the Swiss company may require payment in Swiss francs (SFr). This means the U.S. company must eventually use a foreign currency broker or a bank to exchange U.S. dollars for Swiss francs to pay for the machine. In the process, the U.S. company may experience foreign currency gains or losses from fluctuations in the value of the U.S. dollar relative to the Swiss franc.

The topic of foreign exchange markets is one of the most important and often misunderstood subjects in international business. It provides the framework for international business and influences both the form and the content of international business activities. Multinational enterprises (MNEs) entering into international transactions must agree on which currency will be used. Factors that affect this decision include familiarity with the foreign currency, the potential for gains and losses from changes in exchange rates, nationalistic pride, and practicality.

MNEs transact in a variety of currencies as a result of their export and import activities. There are approximately 150 different currencies around the world, but most international trade has been settled in six major currencies that have shown stability and general acceptance over time: the U.S. dollar, the British pound, the Canadian dollar, the Japanese yen, the Swiss franc, and the European euro.

The European euro (symbol €) is a relatively new currency introduced in 1999 to members of the European Union (EU) that wished to participate in a common currency. By 2002, euro notes and coins were introduced to be used in everyday trade. The EU is an organization of democratic member states from the European continent. The Union has grown over time and as of 2006 is composed of 25 member countries: Belgium, France, Germany, Italy, Luxembourg, the Netherlands, Denmark, Ireland, the United Kingdom, Greece, Portugal, Spain, Austria, Finland, Sweden, Cyprus, Czech Republic, Estonia, Hungary, Latvia, Lithuania, Malta, Poland, Slovakia and Slovenia. Bulgaria and Romania are expected to accede to the EU in 2007. In addition, Croatia, Turkey and Macedonia have applied for accession. The EU is a dominant economic force, rivaling the United States, and the euro is now as familiar to companies doing international business as the U.S. dollar.

The EU is one of several regional groupings, and these groupings are becoming increasingly important. Two other major groupings are North America and Asia. Growth has been rapid within each bloc, while growing more slowly with trading partners outside the blocs. The North American Free Trade Agreement (NAFTA) was approved by the U.S. Congress in 1993 and created a free-trade area of Canada, the United States, and Mexico, a market that exceeds 420 million people. Over time, the agreement will result in the elimination of tariffs (taxes) on goods shipped between these three countries. The East Asia Economic Group (EAEG) is composed of more than 600 million persons from the Pacific Rim countries. The agreements among EAEG members tend to focus on formalizing trade arrangements in Pacific Asia rather than on standardizing production quality as is the focus of many of the agreements within the European Union.

Currency names and symbols often reflect a country's nationalistic pride and history. For example, the U.S. dollar receives its name from a variation of the German word *Taler,* the name of a silver piece that was first minted in 1518 and became the chief coin of Europe and the new world. Some historians argue that the dollar symbol ($) is derived from a capital letter *U* superimposed over a capital letter *S*. The greenback as we know it today was first printed in 1862, in the midst of the Civil War, and now is issued by the 12 Federal Reserve banks scattered across the United States. The U.S. dollar can be identified in virtually every corner of the world because it has become one of the most widely traded currencies.

THE ACCOUNTING ISSUES

Accountants must be able to record and report transactions involving exchanges of U.S. dollars and foreign currencies. *Foreign currency transactions* of a U.S. company include sales, purchases, and other transactions giving rise to a transfer of foreign currency or the recording of receivables or payables that are *denominated*—that is, numerically specified to be settled—in a foreign currency. Because financial statements of virtually all U.S. companies are prepared using the U.S. dollar as the reporting currency, transactions denominated in other currencies must be restated to their U.S. dollar equivalents before they can be recorded in the U.S. company's books and included in its financial statements. This process of restating foreign currency transactions to their U.S. dollar equivalent values is termed *translation*.

In addition, many large U.S. corporations have multinational operations, such as foreign-based subsidiaries or branches. For example, a U.S. auto manufacturer may have manufacturing subsidiaries in Canada, Mexico, Spain, and Great Britain. The foreign subsidiaries prepare their financial statements in the currency of their countries; for example, the Mexican subsidiary reports its operations in pesos. The foreign currency amounts in the financial statements of these subsidiaries have to be translated, that is, restated, into their U.S. dollar equivalents, before they can be consolidated with the financial statements of the U.S. parent company that uses the U.S. dollar as its reporting currency unit.

This chapter presents the accounting procedures for recording and reporting foreign transactions. Chapter 12 presents the procedures for combining or consolidating a foreign entity with a U.S. parent company. **FASB Statement No. 52**, "Foreign Currency Translation" (FASB 52), issued in 1981, serves as the primary guide for accounting for accounts receivable and accounts payable foreign currency–denominated transactions that require payment or receipt of foreign currency. **FASB Statement No. 133**, "Accounting for Derivative Instruments and Hedging Activities" (FASB 133), issued in 1998, guides the accounting for financial instruments specified as derivatives for the purpose of hedging certain items.

FOREIGN CURRENCY EXCHANGE RATES

Before 1972, most major currencies were valued on the basis of a gold standard whereby their international values were fixed per ounce of gold. However, in 1972, most countries signed an agreement to permit the values of their currencies to "float" based on the supply and demand for them. The resulting *foreign currency exchange rates* between currencies are established daily by foreign exchange brokers who serve as agents for individuals or countries wishing to deal in foreign currencies. Some countries, such as China, maintain an official fixed rate of currency exchange and have established fixed exchange rates for dividends remitted outside the country. These official rates may be changed at any time, and companies doing business abroad should contact the foreign country's government to ensure that the companies are in compliance with any currency exchange restrictions.

The Determination of Exchange Rates

A country's currency is much like any other commodity, and exchange rates change because of a number of economic factors affecting the supply of and demand for a nation's currency. For example, if a nation is experiencing high levels of inflation, the purchasing power of its currency decreases. This reduction in the value of a currency is reflected by a decrease in the positioning of that country's currency relative to other nations' currencies. Other factors causing exchange rate fluctuations are a nation's balance of payments, changes in a country's interest rate and investment levels, and the stability and process of governance. For example, if the United States had a higher average interest rate than that in Great Britain, the international investment community might seek to invest in the United States, thus increasing the demand for U.S. dollars relative to British pounds. The dollar would increase in value relative to the pound because of the increased demand. Exchange rates are determined daily and published in several sources, including *The Wall Street Journal*. Figure 11–1 presents an example of a typical daily business press report for selected foreign exchange rates. The rates illustrated in the table are current as of June 2006. Updated exchange rates may be obtained from most business publications and from many metropolitan newspapers.

Direct versus Indirect Exchange Rates

As indicated in Figure 11–1, the relative value of one currency to another may be expressed in two different ways: either *directly* or *indirectly*.

Direct Exchange Rate

The direct exchange rate (DER) is the number of *local currency units (LCUs)* needed to acquire one *foreign currency unit (FCU)*. From the viewpoint of a U.S. entity, the direct exchange rate can be viewed as the U.S. dollar cost of one foreign currency unit. The direct exchange rate ratio is expressed as follows, with the LCU, the U.S. dollar, in the numerator:

$$\text{DER} = \frac{\text{U.S. dollar–equivalent value}}{1\,\text{FCU}}$$

The direct exchange rate is used most often in accounting for foreign operations and transactions because the foreign currency–denominated accounts must be translated to their U.S. dollar equivalent values. For example, if $1.20 can acquire €1 (1 European euro), the direct exchange rate of the dollar versus the European euro is $1.20, as follows:

$$\frac{\$1.20}{\text{€1}} = \$1.20$$

FIGURE 11–1 **Foreign Exchange Rates for Selected Major Currencies as of June, 2006**

Country	Currency	Direct Exchange Rate (U.S. dollar equivalent)	Indirect Exchange Rate (currency per U.S. dollar)
Argentina	peso	0.3243	3.0835
Australia	dollar	0.7431	1.346
Bahrain	dinar	2.6525	0.377
Brazil	real	0.4409	2.2679
Canada	dollar	0.8918	1.1213
1-month forward		0.8914	1.1218
3-months forward		0.8933	1.1194
6-months forward		0.8954	1.1168
Chile	peso	0.0018	555.56
China	yuan renminbi	0.1247	8.0192
Colombia	peso	0.0004	2500
Czech Republic	koruna	0.0448	22.3214
Denmark	krone	0.1694	5.9031
Ecuador	U.S. dollar	1	1
Egypt	pound	0.1733	5.77
Hong Kong	dollar	0.1288	7.764
India	rupee	0.0218	45.8716
Indonesia	rupiah	0.0001	10000
Israel	shekel	0.223	4.4843
Japan	yen	0.0087	114.9425
1-month forward		0.0088	113.6364
3-months forward		0.0089	112.3596
6-months forward		0.009	111.1111
Malaysia	ringgit	0.2727	3.667
Mexico	peso	0.0875	11.4286
Philippines	peso	0.0188	53.1915
Russia	ruble	0.0371	26.9542
South Korea	won	0.001	1000
Sweden	krona	0.1369	7.3046
Switzerland	franc	0.8101	1.2344
1-month forward		0.819	1.221
3-months forward		0.8216	1.2171
6-months forward		0.827	1.2092
Taiwan	dollar	0.0308	32.4675
Thailand	bhat	0.026	38.4615
U.K.	pound	1.84	0.5435
1-month forward		1.8425	0.5427
3-months forward		1.8448	0.542
6-months forward		1.8481	0.5411
Venezuela	bolivar	0.0005	2000
SDR		1.4839	0.6739
Euro		1.2639	0.7912

Indirect Exchange Rate

The indirect exchange rate (IER) is the reciprocal of the direct exchange rate. From the viewpoint of a U.S. entity, the indirect exchange rate is:

$$IER = \frac{1\,FCU}{U.S.\,dollar-equivalent\,value}$$

For the European euro example, the indirect exchange rate is:

$$\frac{€1}{\$1.20} = €0.8333$$

Another way to express this is:

$$\text{IER} = \frac{\text{Number of foreign currency units}}{\$1}$$

$$= \frac{€0.8333}{\$1}$$

Thus, the indirect exchange rate of €0.8333 = $1 shows the number of foreign currency units that may be obtained for 1 U.S. dollar. The business press and people who travel outside the United States often use the indirect exchange rate.

Note that the direct and indirect rates are inversely related and that both state the same economic relationships between two currencies. For example, if the indirect exchange rate is given, the direct exchange rate may be computed by simply inverting the indirect exchange rate. If given the indirect exchange rate of €0.8333 (€0.8333 / $1), the direct exchange rate can be computed as ($1 / €0.8333) = $1.20. If given the direct exchange rate of $1.20, the indirect exchange rate can be computed as (€1 / $1.20) = €0.8333. Again, the currency in the numerator identifies the direction of the exchange rate. In practice, a slight difference might exist in the inverse relationship because of brokers' commissions or small differences in demand for the two currencies.

Some persons identify the direct exchange rate as *American terms* to indicate that it is U.S. dollar–based and represents an exchange rate quote from the perspective of a person in the United States. The indirect exchange rate is sometimes identified as *European terms* to indicate the direct exchange rate from the perspective of a person in Europe, which means the exchange rate shows the number of units of the European's local currency units per one U.S. dollar. A guide to help remember the difference in exchange rates is to note that the U.S. dollar is the numerator for the direct rate or American terms (the foreign currency unit is in the denominator), and the foreign currency unit is in the numerator for the indirect rate or European terms (with the U.S. dollar in the denominator). The *terms currency* is the numerator and the *base currency* is the denominator in the exchange rate ratio. The numerator is the key to the identification of the rate.

Changes in Exchange Rates

A change in an exchange rate is referred to as a *strengthening* or *weakening* of one currency against another. For example, the exchange rate of the U.S. dollar versus the euro changed as follows:

	January 2005	July 2005	January 2006	July 2006
Direct exchange rate (U.S. dollar–equivalent of 1 euro)	$1.35	$1.20	$1.18	$1.28
Indirect exchange rate (Euro per 1 U.S. dollar)	€0.74	€0.83	€0.85	€0.78

Strengthening of the U.S. Dollar—Direct Exchange Rate Decreases

Between January 1, 2005, and July 1, 2005, the direct exchange rate decreased from $1.35 = €1 to $1.20 = €1, indicating that it took less U.S. currency ($) to acquire 1 European euro (€). In other words, the cost of 1 euro was $1.35 on January 1 but decreased to $1.20 on July 1. This means that the value of the U.S. currency rose relative to the euro. This is termed a *strengthening* of the dollar versus the euro. Alternatively, looking at the indirect exchange rate, 1 U.S. dollar could acquire 0.74 European euros on January 1, but it could acquire more euros, 0.83, on July 1. Thus, the relative value of the dollar versus the euro was greater on July 1 than on January 1.

Think of the strengthening of the U.S. dollar as:

- Taking less U.S. currency to acquire one foreign currency unit.
- One U.S. dollar acquiring more foreign currency units.

Imports from Europe were less expensive for U.S. consumers on July 1 than on January 1 because of the strengthening of the dollar. For example, assume that a European manufacturer is selling a German-made automobile for €25,000. To determine the U.S. dollar–equivalent value of the €25,000 on January 1, the following equation is used:

$$\begin{matrix} \textbf{U.S. dollar–} \\ \textbf{equivalent value} \end{matrix} = \begin{matrix} \textbf{Foreign currency} \\ \textbf{units} \end{matrix} \times \begin{matrix} \textbf{Direct exchange} \\ \textbf{rate} \end{matrix}$$
$$\$33{,}750 \qquad = \qquad €25{,}000 \qquad \times \qquad \$1.35$$

Between January 1 and July 1, the direct exchange rate decreased as the dollar strengthened relative to the euro. On July 1, the U.S. dollar equivalent value of the €25,000 is:

$$\begin{matrix} \textbf{U.S. dollar–} \\ \textbf{equivalent value} \end{matrix} = \begin{matrix} \textbf{Foreign currency} \\ \textbf{units} \end{matrix} \times \begin{matrix} \textbf{Direct exchange} \\ \textbf{rate} \end{matrix}$$
$$\$30{,}000 \qquad = \qquad €25{,}000 \qquad \times \qquad \$1.20$$

Although a strengthening of the dollar is favorable for U.S. companies purchasing goods from another country, it adversely affects U.S. companies selling products in that country. Following a strengthening of the dollar, U.S. exports to Europe are more expensive for European customers. For example, assume a U.S. manufacturer is selling a U.S.–made machine for $10,000. To determine the foreign currency (euro) equivalent value of the $10,000 on January 1, the following equation is used:

$$\begin{matrix} \textbf{Foreign currency} \\ \textbf{equivalent value} \end{matrix} = \begin{matrix} \textbf{U.S. dollar} \\ \textbf{units} \end{matrix} \times \begin{matrix} \textbf{Indirect exchange} \\ \textbf{rate} \end{matrix}$$
$$€7{,}400 \qquad = \qquad \$10{,}000 \qquad \times \qquad €0.74$$

On July 1, after a strengthening of the dollar, the machine would cost the European customer €8,300, as follows:

$$\begin{matrix} \textbf{Foreign currency} \\ \textbf{equivalent value} \end{matrix} = \begin{matrix} \textbf{U.S. dollar} \\ \textbf{units} \end{matrix} \times \begin{matrix} \textbf{Indirect exchange} \\ \textbf{rate} \end{matrix}$$
$$€8{,}300 \qquad = \qquad \$10{,}000 \qquad \times \qquad €0.83$$

This substantial increase in cost could lead the European customer to decide not to acquire the machine from the U.S. company. Thus, a U.S. company's international sales can be seriously affected by changes in foreign currency exchange rates.

Weakening of the U.S. Dollar—Direct Exchange Rate Increases

Between July 1, 2005, and July 1, 2006, the direct exchange rate increased from $1.20 = €1 to $1.28 = €1, indicating that it took more U.S. currency to acquire 1 euro. On July 1, 2005, a euro cost $1.20, but on July 1, 2006, the relative cost for 1 euro increased to $1.28. This means that the value of the U.S. currency dropped relative to the euro, termed a *weakening* of the dollar against the euro. Another way to view this change is to note that the indirect exchange rate decreased, indicating that on July 1, 2006, 1 dollar acquired fewer euros than it did on July 1, 2005. On July 1, 2005, 1 U.S. dollar could acquire 0.83 euros,

FIGURE 11–2
Relationships between Currencies and Exchange Rates

	January, 2005	July, 2005	July, 2006
Direct exchange rate ($ / €)	$1.35	$1.20	$1.28
Indirect exchange rate (€ / $)	€0.74	€0.83	€0.78

Between January 1, 2005, and July 1, 2005—strengthening of the U.S. dollar:
  Direct rate decreases
    Dollar strengthens (takes less U.S. currency to acquire 1 euro)
  Indirect rate increases
    Euro weakens (takes more euros to acquire 1 U.S. dollar)
  Imports into U.S. normally increase in quantity
    Foreign goods imported into U.S. less expensive in dollars ($1 can acquire more)
  Exports from U.S. normally decrease in quantity
    U.S.–made exports more expensive (takes more euros to acquire goods)

Between July 1, 2005, and July 1, 2006—weakening of the U.S. dollar:
  Direct rate increases
    Dollar weakens (takes more U.S. currency to acquire 1 euro)
  Indirect rate decreases
    Euro strengthens (takes fewer euros to acquire 1 U.S. dollar)
  Imports into U.S. normally decrease in quantity
    Foreign goods imported into U.S. more expensive in dollars
  Exports from U.S. normally increase in quantity
    U.S.–made exports less expensive in euros

but on July 1, 2006, 1 U.S. dollar could acquire fewer euros, 0.78, indicating that the relative value of the dollar dropped between July 1, 2005, and July 1, 2006.

Think of the weakening of the U.S. dollar as:

- Taking more U.S. currency to acquire one foreign currency unit.
- One U.S. dollar acquiring fewer foreign currency units.

The relationships between currencies, imports, and exports is summarized in Figure 11–2.

During the latter part of the 1970s, the dollar consistently weakened against other major currencies because of several factors, including the high inflation the United States experienced. This weakening did help the U.S. balance of trade because it reduced the quantity of then more expensive imports, while making U.S.–made goods less expensive in other countries. In the first half of the 1980s, the dollar consistently strengthened relative to other currencies. Not only was the U.S. economy strong and producing goods more efficiently but also high interest rates attracted large foreign investment in the U.S. capital markets. A stronger dollar added to the foreign trade deficit by making imports less expensive and U.S.–made goods more expensive on the world market. Beginning in 1986 and continuing through the early 1990s, the dollar again weakened relative to the major international currencies. In the latter 1990s, the dollar generally strengthened because of the robustness of the U.S. economy, but in the early 2000s, the dollar again weakened because of the high trade deficit and the sluggish U.S. economy.

These changes in the international value of the dollar affect any consumer acquiring imported goods. A weakening dollar means that imports become more expensive while a strengthening dollar means that imports become less expensive. One reason the U.S. government may let the dollar weaken is to reduce the trade deficits. U.S. exporters can sell their goods more easily overseas, thus boosting their profitability. Imports should decrease because of the higher relative prices of the foreign-made goods, thus enhancing the demand for domestic-made goods within the United States. If the dollar weakens too far, overseas investors reduce their demand for dollar-dominated U.S. assets such as U.S. stocks and bonds. The reduced investment demand may require an increase in bond interest rates to offset overseas investors' reduction in bond returns due to the weakening dollar. An increase in interest rates may reduce economic investment within the United States. Finally a weakening dollar means that foreign travel becomes more expensive because of the reduction in the dollar's purchasing power. Thus, the U.S. government's management of the value of the dollar is a balancing act to achieve the needs of both U.S. businesses and U.S. consumers.

Spot Rates versus Current Rates

FASB 52 refers to the use of both spot rates and current rates for measuring the currency used in international transactions. The *spot rate* is the exchange rate for immediate delivery of currencies. The *current rate* is defined simply as the spot rate on the entity's balance sheet date.

Forward Exchange Rates

A third exchange rate is the rate on future, or forward, exchanges of currencies. Figure 11–1 shows these exchange rates for the major international currencies for one month, three months, and six months forward. Active dealer markets in *forward exchange contracts* are maintained for companies wishing to either receive or deliver major international currencies. The forward rate on a given date is not the same as the spot rate on the same date. Expectations about the relative value of currencies are built into the forward rate. The difference between the forward rate and the spot rate on a given date is called the *spread*. The spread gives information about the perceived strengths or weaknesses of currencies. For instance, assume the spot rate for the French franc is $0.1486 and the 30-day forward rate is $0.1387. The spread is the difference between these two numbers, or $0.0099. Because the forward rate is less than the spot rate, the expectation is that the dollar will strengthen against the franc in the next 30 days. The actual spot rate when the contract is due in 30 days may be higher or lower than the forward rate. By entering into the forward contract, the U.S. company gives up the chance of receiving a better exchange rate but also avoids the possibility of an exchange rate loss. This reduces the risk for the U.S. company.

For example, a U.S. company may have a liability in British pounds due in 30 days. Rather than wait 30 days to buy the pounds and risk having the dollar weaken in value relative to the pound, the company can go to a foreign exchange dealer and enter into a one-month forward exchange contract at the forward exchange rate in effect on the contract date. The United States has approximately 2,000 foreign exchange dealer institutions of which about 200 are market making, large banks such as Citibank, Chase Manhattan Bank, and Bank of America, which do the greatest volume of foreign exchange activity. The contract enables the buyer to receive British pounds from an exchange broker 30 days from the contract date at a price fixed now by the contract.

The next section of the chapter presents the accounting for import and export transactions and for forward exchange contracts.

FOREIGN CURRENCY TRANSACTIONS

As defined earlier, foreign currency transactions are economic activities denominated in a currency other than the entity's recording currency. These transactions include the following:

1. Purchases or sales of goods or services (imports or exports), the prices of which are stated in a foreign currency.
2. Loans payable or receivable in a foreign currency.
3. Purchase or sale of foreign currency forward exchange contracts.
4. Purchase or sale of foreign currency units.

One party in a foreign exchange transaction must exchange its own currency for another country's currency. Some persons use a shorthand to refer to foreign exchange transactions by using just the letters FX. This book uses the longer, more generally used description, which is *foreign exchange.*

For financial statement purposes, transactions denominated in a foreign currency must be translated into the currency the reporting company uses. Additionally, at each balance sheet date—interim as well as annual—account balances denominated in a currency other than the entity's reporting currency must be adjusted to reflect changes in exchange rates during the period since the last balance sheet date or since the foreign currency transaction date if it occurred during the period. This adjustment restates the foreign currency–denominated accounts to their U.S. dollar–equivalent values as of the balance sheet date. The adjustment in equivalent U.S. dollar values is a ***foreign currency transaction gain or loss*** for the entity when exchange rates have changed. For example, assume that a U.S. company acquires €5,000 from its bank on January 1, 20X1, for use in future purchases from German companies. The direct exchange rate is $1.20 = €1; thus the company pays the bank $6,000 for €5,000, as follows:

U.S. dollar – equivalent value = Foreign currency units × Direct exchange rate

$$\$6,000 \qquad = \qquad €5,000 \qquad × \qquad \$1.20$$

The following entry records this exchange of currencies:

January 1, 20X1			
(1)	Foreign Currency Units (€)	6,000	
	Cash		6,000

The parenthetical notation (€) is used here after the debit account to indicate that the asset is European euros, but for accounting purposes it is recorded and reported at its U.S. dollar–equivalent value. This translation to the U.S. equivalent value is required in order to add the value of the foreign currency units to all of the company's other accounts that are reported in dollars.

On July 1, 20X1, the exchange rate is $1.100 = €1 as represented in the following time line:

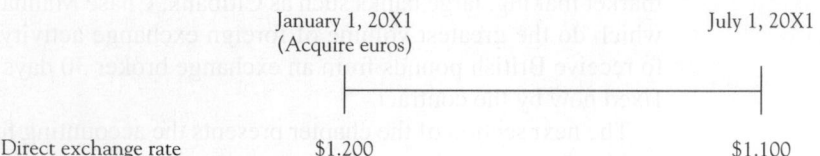

January 1, 20X1 (Acquire euros)		July 1, 20X1
Direct exchange rate	$1.200	$1.100

The direct exchange rate has decreased, reflecting that the U.S. dollar has strengthened. On July 1, it takes less U.S. currency to acquire 1 euro than it did on January 1. If the dollar has strengthened, the euro has weakened. By holding the euros during a weakening of the euro relative to the dollar, the company experiences a foreign currency transaction loss, as follows:

Equivalent dollar value of €5.000 on January 1:	
€5.000 × $1.200	$6,000
Equivalent dollar value of €5.000 on July 1:	
€5.000 × $1.100	5,500
Foreign currency transaction loss	$ 500

If the U.S. company prepares financial statements on July 1, the following adjusting entry is required:

July 1, 20X1

(2)	Foreign Currency Transaction Loss	500	
	Foreign Currency Units (€)		500

The foreign currency transaction loss is the result of a foreign currency transaction and is included in this period's income statement, usually as a separate item under "Other Income or Loss." Some accountants use the account title Exchange Loss instead of the longer title Foreign Currency Transaction Loss. In this book, the longer, more descriptive account title is used to communicate fully the source of the loss. The Foreign Currency Units account is reported on the balance sheet at a value of $5,500, its equivalent U.S. dollar value on that date.

In the previous examples, the U.S. company used the U.S. dollar as its primary currency for performing its major financial and operating functions, that is, as its *functional currency*. Also, the U.S. company prepared its financial statements in U.S. dollars, its *reporting currency*. Any transactions denominated in currencies other than the U.S. dollar require translation to their equivalent U.S. dollar values. Generally, the majority of a business's cash transactions take place in the *local currency* of the country in which the entity operates. The U.S. dollar is the functional currency for virtually all companies based in the United States. A company operating in Germany would probably use the euro as its functional currency. *In this chapter, the local currency is assumed to be the entity's functional and reporting currency.* The few exceptions to this general case are discussed in Chapter 12.

Illustrations of various types of foreign currency transactions are given in the sections that follow. Note that different exchange rates are used to value selected foreign currency transactions, depending on a number of factors such as management's reason for entering the foreign currency transaction, the nature of the transaction, and the timing of the transaction.

Foreign Currency Import and Export Transactions

Payables and receivables that arise from transactions with foreign-based entities and that are denominated in a foreign currency must be measured and recorded by the U.S. entity in the currency used for its accounting records—the U.S. dollar. The relevant exchange rate for settlement of a transaction denominated in a foreign currency is the spot exchange rate on the date of settlement. At the time the transaction is settled, payables or receivables denominated in foreign currency units must be adjusted to their current U.S. dollar–equivalent value. If financial statements are prepared before the foreign currency payables or receivables are settled, their account balances must be adjusted to their U.S. dollar–equivalent values as of the balance sheet date, using the current rate on the balance sheet date.

An overview of the required accounting for an import or export transaction denominated in a foreign currency, assuming the company does *not* use forward contracts, is as follows:

1. *Transaction date.* Record the purchase or sale transaction at the U.S. dollar–equivalent value using the spot direct exchange rate on this date.
2. *Balance sheet date.* Adjust the payable or receivable to its U.S. dollar–equivalent, end-of-period value using the current direct exchange rate. Recognize any exchange gain or loss for the change in rates between the transaction and balance sheet dates.
3. *Settlement date.* First adjust the foreign currency payable or receivable for any changes in the exchange rate between the balance sheet date (or transaction date if transaction occurs after the balance sheet date) and the settlement date, recording any exchange gain or loss as required. Then record the settlement of the foreign currency payable or receivable.

This adjustment process is required because the FASB adopted what is called the *two-transaction approach,* which views the purchase or sale of an item as a separate transaction from the foreign currency commitment. By adopting the two-transaction approach to foreign currency transactions, the FASB established the general rule that foreign currency exchange

FIGURE 11–3 **Comparative U.S. Company Journal Entries for Foreign Purchase Transaction Denominated in Dollars versus Foreign Currency Units**

If Denominated in U.S. Dollars			If Denominated in Japanese Yen		
October 1, 20X1 (Date of Purchase)					
Inventory	14,000		Inventory	14,000	
Accounts Payable		14,000	Accounts Payable (¥)		14,000
			$14,000 = ¥2,000,000 × $.0070 spot rate		
December 31, 20X1 (Balance Sheet Date)					
No entry			Foreign Currency Transaction Loss	2,000	
			Accounts Payable (¥)		2,000
			Adjust payable denominated in foreign currency to current U.S. dollar equivalent and recognize exchange loss:		
			$ 16,000 = ¥2,000,000 × $.0080 Dec. 31 spot rate		
			−14,000 = ¥2,000,000 × $.0070 Oct. 1 spot rate		
			$ 2,000 = ¥2,000,000 × ($.0080 − $.0070)		
April 1, 20X2 (Settlement Date)					
			Accounts Payable (¥)	800	
			Foreign Currency Transaction Gain		800
			Adjust payable denominated in foreign currency to current U.S. dollar equivalent and recognize exchange gain:		
			$ 15,200 = ¥2,000,000 × $.0076 Apr. 1 spot rate		
			−16,000 = ¥2,000,000 × $.0080 Dec. 31 spot rate		
			$ 800 = ¥2,000,000 × ($.0076 − $.0080)		
			Foreign Currency Units (¥)	15,200	
			Cash		15,200
			Acquire FCU to settle debt:		
			$15,200 = ¥2,000,000 × $.0076 April 1 spot rate		
Accounts Payable	14,000		Accounts Payable (¥)	15,200	
Cash		14,000	Foreign Currency Units (¥)		15,200

gains or losses resulting from the revaluation of assets or liabilities denominated in a foreign currency must be recognized currently in the income statement of the period in which the exchange rate changes. A few exceptions to this general rule are allowed and are discussed later in this chapter.

Illustration of Foreign Purchase Transaction

Figure 11–3 illustrates the journal entries used to measure and record a purchase of goods from a foreign supplier denominated either in the entity's local currency or in a foreign currency. On the left side of Figure 11–3, the transaction is denominated in U.S. dollars, the recording and reporting currency of the U.S. company; on the right side, the transaction is denominated in Japanese yen (¥). The U.S. company is subject to a foreign currency transaction gain or loss only if the transaction is denominated in the foreign currency. If the foreign transaction is denominated in U.S. dollars, no special accounting problems exist and no currency rate adjustments are necessary.

The following information describes the case:

1. On October 1, 20X1, Peerless Products, a U.S. company, acquired goods on account from Tokyo Industries, a Japanese company, for $14,000, or 2,000,000 yen.

2. Peerless Products prepared financial statements at its year-end of December 31, 20X1.

3. Settlement of the payable was made on April 1, 20X2.

The direct spot exchange rates of the U.S. dollar equivalent value of 1 yen were as follows:

Date	Direct Exchange Rate
October 1, 20X1 (transaction date)	$.0070
December 31, 20X1 (balance sheet date)	.0080
April 1, 20X2 (settlement date)	.0076

A time line may help to clarify the relationships between the dates and the economic events, as follows:

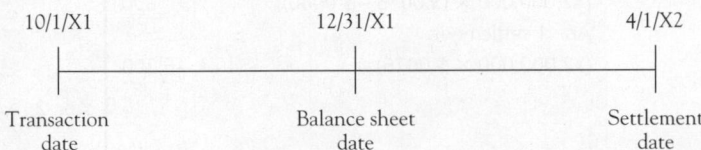

10/1/X1	12/31/X1	4/1/X2
Transaction date	Balance sheet date	Settlement date

Accounts relating to transactions denominated in yen are noted by the parenthetical symbol for the yen (¥) after the account title. As you proceed through the example, you should especially note the assets and liabilities denominated in the foreign currency and the adjustment needed to reflect their current values by use of the U.S. dollar–equivalent rate of exchange.

Key Observations from Illustration

If the purchase contract is denominated in dollars, the foreign entity (Tokyo Industries) bears the foreign currency exchange risk. If the transaction is denominated in yen, the U.S. company (Peerless Products Corporation) is exposed to exchange rate gains and losses. The accounts relating to liabilities denominated in foreign currency units must be valued at the spot rate, with any foreign currency transaction gain or loss recognized in the period's income. The purchase contract includes specification of the denominated currency as the two parties agreed.

On October 1, 20X1, the purchase is recorded on the books of Peerless Products. The U.S. dollar–equivalent value of 2,000,000 yen on this date is $14,000 (¥ 2,000,000 × $.0070).

On December 31, 20X1, the balance sheet date, the payable denominated in foreign currency units must be adjusted to its current U.S. dollar–equivalent value. The direct exchange rate has increased since the date of purchase, indicating that the U.S. dollar has weakened relative to the yen. Therefore, on December 31, 20X1, $16,000 is required to acquire 2,000,000 yen (¥ 2,000,000 × $.0080), whereas, on October 1, 20X1, only $14,000 was required to obtain 2,000,000 yen (¥ 2,000,000 × $.0070). This increase in the exchange rate requires the recognition of a $2,000 foreign currency transaction loss if the transaction is denominated in yen, the foreign currency unit. No entry is made if the transaction is denominated in U.S. dollars because Peerless has a liability for $14,000 regardless of the changes in exchange rates.

The payable is settled on April 1, 20X2. If the payable is denominated in U.S. dollars, no adjustment is necessary and the liability is extinguished by payment of $14,000. However, assets and liabilities denominated in foreign currency units must again be adjusted to their present U.S. dollar–equivalent values. The dollar has strengthened between December 31, 20X1, and April 1, 20X2, as shown by the decrease in the direct exchange rate. In other words, fewer dollars are needed to acquire 2,000,000 yen on April 1, 20X2, than on December 31, 20X1. Accounts Payable is adjusted to its current dollar value, and an $800 foreign currency transaction gain [¥ 2,000,000 × ($.0076 − $.0080)] is recognized for the change in rates since the balance sheet date. Peerless acquires 2,000,000 yen, paying an exchange broker the spot exchange rate of $15,200 (¥ 2,000,000 × $.0076). Finally, Peerless extinguishes its liability denominated in yen by paying Tokyo Industries the 2,000,000 yen.

Understanding the revaluations may be easier by viewing the process within the perspective of a T-account. The following T-account posts the entries in Figure 11–3:

Accounts Payable (¥)		
	20X1	
	Oct. 1 14,000 (¥2,000,000 × $.0070)	
	Dec. 31 2,000 [¥2,000,000 × ($.0080 − $.0070)]	
	Dec. 31 16,000 Balance (¥2,000,000 × $.0080)	
20X2		
Apr. 1		
[¥2,000,000 × ($.0076 − $.0080)] 800		
Apr. 1 settlement		
(¥2,000,000 × $.0076) 15,200		
	Apr. 2 -0- Balance	

Some accountants combine the revaluation and settlement entries into one entry. Under this alternative approach, the following entries would be made on April 1, 20X2, the settlement date, instead of the entries presented for that date in Figure 11–3:

	April 1, 20X2		
(3)	Foreign Currency Units (¥)	15,200	
	Cash		15,200
	Acquire foreign currency		
(4)	Accounts Payable (¥)	16,000	
	Foreign Currency Transcation Gain		800
	Foreign Currency Units (¥)		15,200
	Settle foreign currency payable and recognize gain from change in exchange rates since December 31, 20X1.		

The final account balances resulting from the preceding one-entry approach and the two-entry approach used in Figure 11–3 are the same.

In summary, if the transaction is denominated in U.S. dollars, Peerless Products has no foreign currency exchange exposure; Tokyo Industries bears the risk of foreign currency exposure. If the transaction is denominated in yen, however, Peerless has a foreign currency exchange risk. The assets and liabilities denominated in foreign currency units must be valued at their U.S. dollar–equivalent values and a foreign currency transaction gain or loss must be recognized on that period's income statement.

MANAGING INTERNATIONAL CURRENCY RISK WITH FOREIGN CURRENCY FORWARD EXCHANGE FINANCIAL INSTRUMENTS

Companies need to manage business risks. Derivative instruments are an important tool in managing risk. Companies operating internationally are subject not only to normal business risks but also to additional risks from changes in currency exchange rates. Therefore, multinational enterprises (MNEs) often use derivative instruments, including foreign currency–denominated forward exchange contracts, foreign currency options, and foreign currency futures, to manage risk associated with foreign currency transactions.

The accounting for derivatives and hedging activities is guided by three standards. **FASB Statement No. 133**, "Accounting for Derivative Instruments and Hedging Activities" (FASB 133), defined derivatives and established the general rule of recognizing all derivatives as either assets or liabilities in the balance sheet and measuring those financial instruments at fair value. **FASB Statement No. 138**, "Accounting for Certain Derivative Instruments and Certain Hedging Activities" (FASB 138), provided several amendments of importance to multinational entities. **FASB Statement No. 149**, "Amendment of Statement 133 on Derivative Instruments and Hedging Activities (FASB 149) considered a number of specific implementation issues.

A *financial instrument* is cash, evidence of ownership, or a contract that both (1) imposes on one entity a contractual obligation to deliver cash or another instrument and (2) conveys to the second entity that contractual right to receive cash or another financial instrument. Examples include cash, stock, notes payable and receivable, and many financial contracts.

A *derivative* is a financial instrument or other contract whose value is "derived from" some other item that has a variable value over time. An example of a derivative is a foreign currency forward exchange contract whose value is derived from changes in the foreign currency exchange rate over the contract's term. Note that not all financial instruments are derivatives.

The specific definition of a derivative is a financial instrument or contract possessing all of the following characteristics:

1. The financial instrument must contain one or more underlyings and one or more notional amounts, which specify the terms of the financial instrument.

    a. An **underlying** is any financial or physical variable that has observable or objectively verifiable changes. Currency exchange rates, commodity prices, index of prices or rates, days of winter warming, or other variables including the occurrence or nonoccurrence of a specified event such as the scheduled payment under a contract are examples of an underlying.

    b. A **notional amount** is the number of currency units, shares, bushels, pounds, or other units specified in the financial instrument.

2. The financial instrument or other contract requires no initial net investment or an initial net investment that is smaller than required for other types of contracts expected to have a similar response to changes in market factors. Many derivative instruments require no initial net investment or only a small investment for the time value of the contract (as discussed later in this chapter).

3. The contract terms: (*a*) require or permit net settlement, (*b*) provide for the delivery of an asset that puts the recipient in an economic position not substantially different from net settlement, or (*c*) allow for the contract to be readily settled net by a market or other mechanism outside the contract. For example, a forward contract requires the delivery of a specified number of shares of stock, but there is an option market mechanism that offers a ready opportunity to sell the contract or to enter into an offsetting contract.

Occasionally, a financial instrument may have an embedded derivative that must be separated, or bifurcated, from its host contract. An example of an embedded derivative is a company's issuing debt that includes regular interest as well as a potential premium payment based on the future price of a commodity such as crude oil. In this case, the contingent payment feature is a derivative. Another example is the debt agreement that specifies a principal, but whose interest rate is based on the U.S. LIBOR (London Interbank Offered Rate), which is a variable rate. In this case, the interest is the embedded derivative because its value, which is derived from the market, is variable.

Derivatives Designated as Hedges

Derivatives may be designated to hedge or reduce risks. Some companies obtain derivatives that are not designated as hedges but as speculative financial instruments. For example, a company may enter into a forward exchange contract that does not have any offsetting intent. In this case, the gain or loss on the derivative is recorded in periodic earnings.

FASB 133 provided specific requirements for classifying a derivative as a hedge. Hedge accounting offsets the gain (loss) on the hedged item with the loss (gain) on the hedging instrument. Hedges are applicable to (1) foreign currency exchange risk in which currency exchange rates change over time, (2) interest rate risks, particularly for companies owing variable rate debt instruments, and (3) commodity risks whose future commodity prices may be quite different from spot prices.

For a derivative instrument to qualify as a hedging instrument, the following two criteria must be met:

1. Sufficient documentation must be provided at the beginning of the hedge term to identify the objective and strategy of the hedge, the hedging instrument and the hedged item, and how the hedge's effectiveness will be assessed on an ongoing basis.

2. The hedge must be highly effective throughout its term. Effectiveness is measured by evaluating the hedging instrument's ability to generate changes in fair value that offset the changes in value of the hedged item. This effectiveness must be tested at the time the hedge is entered into, every three months thereafter, and each time financial statements are prepared. Effectiveness is viewed as the derivative instrument's ability to offset changes in the fair value or cash flows of the hedged item within the range between 80 and 125 percent of the change in value of the hedged item.

Derivatives that meet the requirements for a hedge and are designated as such by the company's management are accounted for in accordance with **FASB 133** and **FASB 138**, as follows:

1. *Fair value hedges* are designated to hedge the exposure to potential changes in the fair value of (*a*) a recognized asset or liability such as available-for-sale investments or (*b*) an unrecognized firm commitment for which a binding agreement exists, such as to buy or sell inventory. The net gains and losses on the hedged asset or liability and the hedging instrument are recognized in current earnings on the statement of income. An example of a fair value hedge is presented in Appendix 11B using an option contract to hedge available-for-sale securities.

2. *Cash flow hedges* are designated to hedge the exposure to potential changes in the anticipated cash flows, either into or out of the company, for (*a*) a recognized asset or liability such as future interest payments on variable-interest debt or (*b*) a forecasted cash transaction such as a forecasted purchase or sale. A forecasted cash transaction is a transaction that is expected to occur but for which there is not yet a firm commitment. Thus, a forecasted transaction has no present rights to future benefits or a present liability for future obligations. **FASB 133** specifies that a derivative must be valued at its current fair market value. For cash flow hedges, changes in the fair market value of a derivative are separated into an effective portion and an ineffective portion. The net gain or loss on the effective portion of the hedging instrument should be reported in other comprehensive income. The gain or loss on the ineffective portion is reported in current earnings on the statement of income.

   The effective portion is defined as the part of the gain (or loss) on the hedging instrument that offsets a loss (or gain) on the hedged item. This portion of the change in the derivative's fair market value is related to the intrinsic value from changes in the underlying. Any remaining gain (or loss) on the hedging instrument is defined as the ineffective portion. This portion of the change in the derivative's fair market value is related to the time value of the derivative and reduces to zero at the derivative's expiration date. An example of determining the effective versus the ineffective portion of a change in value of a derivative is presented in Appendix 11B with regard to a cash flow hedge using an option to hedge an anticipated purchase of inventory.

3. *Foreign currency hedges* are hedges in which the hedged item is denominated in a foreign currency. Note that the incremental risk being hedged in a foreign currency hedge

is the change in fair value or the change in cash flows attributable to the changes in the foreign currency exchange rates. The following types of hedges of foreign currency risk may be designated by the entity:

a. A *fair value hedge* of a firm commitment to enter into a foreign currency transaction, such as a binding agreement to purchase equipment from a foreign manufacturer with the payable due in the foreign currency or a recognized foreign currency–denominated asset or liability (including an available-for-sale security). Just as with hedge accounting for firm commitments not involving foreign currency commitments in item (1) above, the gain or loss on the foreign currency hedging derivative and the offsetting loss or gain on the foreign currency–hedged item are recognized currently in earnings on the statement of income.

b. A *cash flow hedge* of a forecasted foreign currency transaction, such as a probable future foreign currency sale, the forecasted functional currency–equivalent cash flows associated with a recognized asset or liability, or a forecasted intercompany transaction. Just as with accounting for hedges of forecasted transactions not involving foreign currency commitments in item (2) above, the effective portion of the gain or loss on the foreign currency hedging derivative instrument is recognized as a component of other comprehensive income. The ineffective portion of the gain or loss is recognized currently in earnings.

Cash flow hedges are used when all variability in the hedged item's functional currency–equivalent cash flows are eliminated by the effect of the hedge. Cash flow hedges with a derivative based only on changes in the exchange rates cannot be designated, for example, for a variable-rate foreign currency–denominated asset or liability because some of the cash flow variability is not covered with that specific hedge. However, foreign currency–denominated forward contracts can be used as cash flow hedges of foreign currency–denominated assets or liabilities that are fixed in terms of the number of foreign currency units.

c. A hedge of a net investment in a foreign operation. A derivative designated as hedging this type of foreign currency exposure has its gain or loss reported in other comprehensive income as part of the cumulative translation adjustment, as will be discussed in Chapter 12.

Forward Exchange Contracts

For the reporting year ended October 2005, the Foreign Exchange Committee of the New York Federal Reserve Board reported that the average daily volume in foreign exchange instruments totaled $440 billion, and the average daily volume in over-the-counter foreign exchange options totaled $37 billion.[1] The Chicago Mercantile Exchange (CME) is the world's largest and most diverse regulated foreign exchange trading market. The CME is an international marketplace that brings together buyers and sellers on its CME Globex electronic trading platform and on its trading floors. In 2005, over 84 million foreign exchange contracts with a notional value of $10.2 trillion traded at the CME.[2] In May 2006, CME foreign exchange products averaged a record 501,000 contracts per day, up 69 percent from the year earlier; electronic foreign exchange products set a monthly record of 451,000 contracts per day, an increase of 90 percent from the previous year.[3]

Companies operating internationally often enter into forward exchange contracts with foreign currency brokers for the exchange of different currencies at specified future dates at specified rates. Forward exchange contracts are acquired from foreign currency brokers. Typically, these contracts are written for one of the major international currencies. They are available for virtually any time period up to 12 months forward, but most are for relatively shorter time periods, usually between 30 and 180 days. Forward exchange contracts can be entered into to receive foreign currency or to deliver foreign currency at a specified date

[1] http://www.newyorkfed.org/fxc/2006/fxc012306.pdf, accessed July 11, 2006.
[2] http://cme.mediaroom.com/file.php/60/FXfactq206.pdf, accessed July 11, 2006.
[3] http://www.cme.com/about/press/cn/06-76May06Volume18770.html, accessed July 11, 2006.

in the future (the expiration date). The forward exchange rate differs from the spot rate because of the different economic factors involved in determining a future versus spot rate of exchange. For hedging transactions, if the forward rate is more than the spot rate, the difference between the forward and spot rate is termed *premium on the forward exchange contract;* that is, the foreign currency is selling at a premium in the forward market. If the forward rate is less than the spot rate, the difference is a *discount on the forward exchange contract;* that is, the foreign currency is selling at a discount in the forward market.

FASB 133 establishes a basic rule of fair value for accounting for forward exchange contracts. Changes in the fair value are recognized in the accounts, but the specific accounting for the change depends on the purpose of the hedge. For forward exchange contracts, the basic rule is to use the forward exchange rate to value the forward contract.

Multinational entities often use foreign currency forward contract derivatives. These contracts may be designated as hedging instruments or may not fulfill all the requirements for a hedge and would thus not be hedging instruments. The cases discussed in the next sections of this chapter illustrate the following:

Case 1: This case presents the most common use of foreign currency forward contracts, which is to manage a part of the foreign currency exposure from accounts payable or accounts receivable denominated in a foreign currency. Note that the company has entered into a foreign currency forward contract but that the contract does not qualify for or the company does not designate the forward contract as a hedging instrument. Thus, the forward contract is not a designated hedge but can offset most, if not all, foreign currency risks. The forward contract is valued using the forward rate, and changes in the market value of the forward contract are recognized currently in earnings on the statement of income. The foreign currency account payable or account receivable is revalued using the spot rate in accordance with **FASB 52**.

Case 2: This case presents the accounting for an unrecognized firm commitment to enter into a foreign currency transaction, which is accounted for as a fair value hedge. A firm commitment exists because of a binding agreement for the future transaction that meets all requirements for a firm commitment. The hedge is against the possible changes in fair value of the firm commitment (e.g., the inventory to be purchased or the equipment to be acquired) from changes in the foreign currency exchange rates.

Case 3: This case presents the accounting for a forecasted foreign currency–denominated transaction, which is accounted for as a cash flow hedge of the possible changes in future cash flows. The forecasted transaction is *probable* but not a *firm* commitment. Thus, the transaction has not yet occurred nor is it assured; the company is *anticipating* a *possible* future foreign currency transaction. Because the foreign currency hedge is against the impact of changes in the foreign currency exchange rates used to predict the possible future foreign currency–denominated cash flows, it is accounted for as a cash flow hedge. **FASB 138** allows for the continuation of a cash flow hedge after the purchase or sale transaction occurs until settlement of the foreign currency–denominated account payable or receivable arising from the transaction. Alternatively, at the time the company enters into a binding agreement for the transaction that had been forecasted, the hedge can be changed to a fair value hedge, but any other comprehensive income recognized on the cash flow hedge to that date is not reclassified until the earnings process is completed.

Case 4: This case presents the accounting for foreign currency forward contracts used to speculate in foreign currency markets. These transactions are not hedging transactions. The foreign currency forward contract is revalued periodically to its fair value using the forward exchange rate for the remainder of the contract term. The gain or loss on the revaluation is recognized currently in earnings on the statement of income.

A time line of the possible points at which a company uses foreign currency contracts follows. Note that a company may use just one foreign currency forward contract during the time between each event and the final settlement of the foreign currency payable or receivable or may use more than one foreign currency forward contract during the time span presented. For example, a company could use one forward contract between the time of the forecast of the future transaction and the time it signs a binding agreement, or it could just continue with one forward contract the entire time between the date of the forecast and the final settlement.

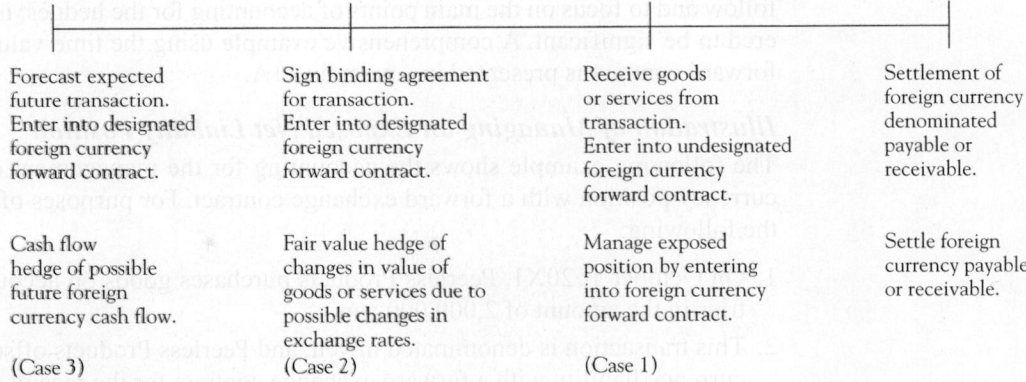

Forecast expected future transaction. Enter into designated foreign currency forward contract.	Sign binding agreement for transaction. Enter into designated foreign currency forward contract.	Receive goods or services from transaction. Enter into undesignated foreign currency forward contract.	Settlement of foreign currency denominated payable or receivable.
Cash flow hedge of possible future foreign currency cash flow.	Fair value hedge of changes in value of goods or services due to possible changes in exchange rates.	Manage exposed position by entering into foreign currency forward contract.	Settle foreign currency payable or receivable.
(Case 3)	(Case 2)	(Case 1)	

Thus, the accounting for the hedge is based on the purpose for which the hedge, in this case a foreign currency forward contract, is entered into.

The following four cases illustrate the accounting for the major uses of forward exchange contracts.

Case 1: Managing an Exposed Foreign Currency Net Asset or Liability Position: Not a Designated Hedging Instrument

A company that has more trade receivables or other assets denominated in a foreign currency than liabilities denominated in that currency incurs a foreign currency risk from its *exposed net asset position*. Alternatively, the company has an *exposed net liability position* if liabilities denominated in a foreign currency exceed receivables denominated in that currency.

The most common use of forward exchange contracts is for *managing an exposed foreign currency position, either a net asset or a net liability position*. Entering into a foreign currency forward contract balances a foreign exchange payable with a receivable in the same foreign currency, thus offsetting the risk of foreign exchange fluctuations. For example, a U.S. company acquiring goods from a Swiss company may be required to make payment in Swiss francs. If the transaction is denominated in Swiss francs, the U.S. company is exposed to the effects of changes in exchange rates between the dollar and the Swiss franc. To protect itself from fluctuations in the value of the Swiss franc, the U.S. company can enter into a forward exchange contract to receive francs at the future settlement date. The U.S. company then uses these francs to settle its foreign currency commitment arising from the foreign purchase transaction.

Alternatively, a U.S. company could have a receivable denominated in a foreign currency that it could also manage with a forward exchange contract. In this case, the U.S. company contracts to *deliver* foreign currency units to the forward exchange broker at a future date in exchange for U.S. dollars.

FASB 133 specifies the general rule that the relevant exchange rate for measuring the fair value of a forward exchange contract is the *forward exchange rate* at each valuation date. Note that **FASB 52** specifies that the foreign currency–denominated account receivable or account payable from the exchange transaction is valued by using the *spot rate* at the valuation date. Forward contracts must be adjusted for changes in the fair value of the forward contract. Because of the two different currency exchange rates used—the spot and the forward—a difference normally exists between the amount of gain and loss. This difference should not be large but does create some volatility in the income stream.

Time Value of Future Cash Flows from Forward Contracts

One other item of note is that **FASB 133** requires the recognition of an interest factor if interest is significant. Thus, when interest is significant, companies should use the *present value* of the expected future net cash flows to value the forward contract. By using the present value, the company explicitly recognizes the time value of money. For the examples that follow and to focus on the main points of accounting for the hedges, interest was not considered to be significant. A comprehensive example using the time value of money to value a forward contract is presented in Appendix 11A.

Illustration of Managing an Exposed Net Liability Position

The following example shows the accounting for the management of an exposed foreign currency position with a forward exchange contract. For purposes of this example, assume the following:

1. On October 1, 20X1, Peerless Products purchases goods on account from Tokyo Industries in the amount of 2,000,000 yen.

2. This transaction is denominated in yen, and Peerless Products offsets its exposed foreign currency liability with a forward exchange contract for the receipt of 2,000,000 yen from a foreign exchange broker.

3. The term of the forward exchange contract equals the six-month credit period extended by Tokyo Industries.

4. December 31 is the year-end of Peerless Products, and the payable is settled on April 1, 20X2.

The relevant direct exchange rates are as follows:

| | U.S. Dollar–Equivalent Value of 1 Yen | |
Date	Spot Rate	Forward Exchange Rate
October 1, 20X1 (transaction date)	$.0070	$.0075 (180 days)
December 31, 20X1 (balance sheet date)	.0080	.0077 (90 days)
April 1, 20X2 (settlement date)	.0076	

A time line for these transactions is as follows:

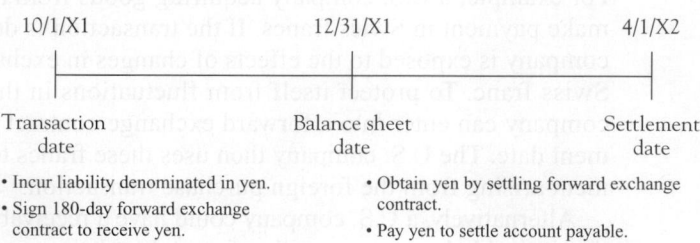

The following entries record the events for this illustration.

October 1, 20X1

(5)	Inventory	14,000	
	Accounts Payable (¥)		14,000
	Purchase inventory on account		
	$14,000 = ¥2,000,000 × $.0070 Oct. 1 spot rate		
(6)	Foreign Currency Receivable from Exchange Broker (¥)	15,000	
	Dollars Payable to Exchange Broker ($)		15,000
	Purchase forward contract to receive 2,000,000 yen:		
	$15,000 = ¥2,000,000 × $.0075 forward rate		

These entries record the purchase of inventory on credit, which is denominated in yen, and the signing of a six-month forward exchange contract to receive 2,000,000 yen in

FIGURE 11–4
T-Accounts for the
Illustration of the
Management of
an Exposed
Net Liability

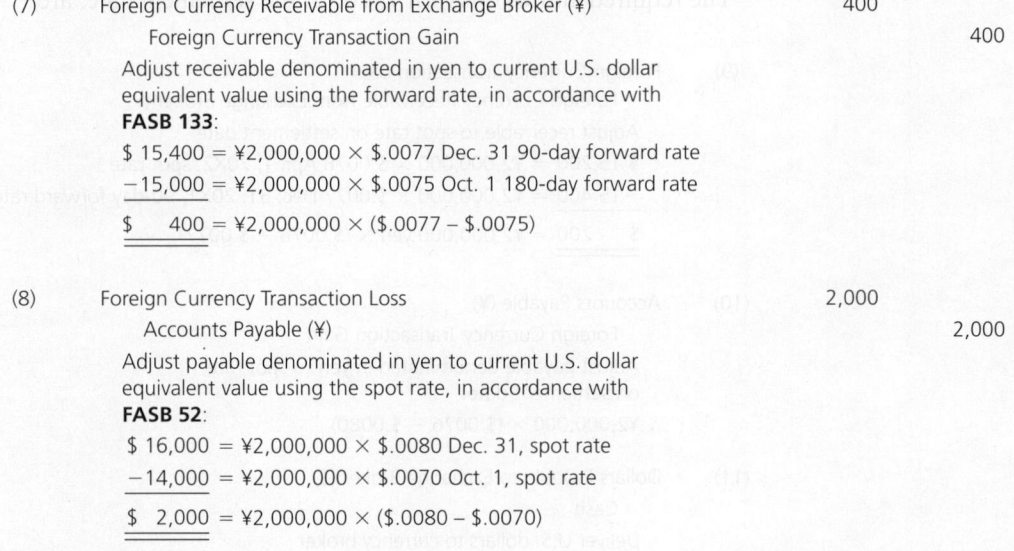

exchange for $15,000 (¥2,000,000 × $.0075 forward rate). The amount payable to the exchange broker is denominated in U.S. dollars, whereas the receivable from the broker is denominated in yen. The entries for the transaction, the adjusting journal entries for the balance sheet date valuations, and the settlements of the forward contract and the accounts payable are posted to T-accounts in Figure 11–4.

The required adjusting entries on December 31, 20X1, Peerless's fiscal year-end, are:

(7)   Foreign Currency Receivable from Exchange Broker (¥) 400
      Foreign Currency Transaction Gain 400

    Adjust receivable denominated in yen to current U.S. dollar
    equivalent value using the forward rate, in accordance with
    FASB 133:

    $ 15,400 = ¥2,000,000 × $.0077 Dec. 31 90-day forward rate
    −15,000 = ¥2,000,000 × $.0075 Oct. 1 180-day forward rate

    $ 400 = ¥2,000,000 × ($.0077 − $.0075)

(8)   Foreign Currency Transaction Loss 2,000
      Accounts Payable (¥) 2,000

    Adjust payable denominated in yen to current U.S. dollar
    equivalent value using the spot rate, in accordance with
    FASB 52:

    $ 16,000 = ¥2,000,000 × $.0080 Dec. 31, spot rate
    −14,000 = ¥2,000,000 × $.0070 Oct. 1, spot rate

    $ 2,000 = ¥2,000,000 × ($.0080 − $.0070)

Note that the foreign currency–denominated account payable is valued by using the spot rate. This is the valuation requirement specified in **FASB 52**. The forward exchange contract is valued using the forward exchange rate for the remainder of the forward contract. This valuation basis is required by **FASB 133**. The direct exchange spot rate has increased between October 1, 20X1, the date of the foreign currency transaction, and December 31, 20X1, the balance sheet date. As previously illustrated, this means that the U.S. dollar has weakened relative to the yen because it takes more U.S. currency to acquire 1 yen at year-end (¥1 = $.0080) than at the initial date of the purchase transaction (¥1 = $.0070), and a U.S. company with a liability in yen experiences an exchange loss. The U.S. dollar–equivalent values of the foreign currency–denominated accounts at October 1, 20X1, and December 31, 20X1, follow:

Accounts	U.S. Dollar–Equivalent Values of Foreign Currency–Denominated Accounts		Foreign Currency Transaction Gain (Loss)
	October 1, 20X1 (Transaction Date)	December 31, 20X1 (Balance Sheet Date)	
Foreign Currency Receivable from Exchange Broker (¥)	$15,000 (a)	$15,400 (b)	$ 400
Accounts Payable (¥)	14,000 (c)	16,000 (d)	(2,000)

(a) ¥2,000,000 × $.0075 October 1, 180-day forward rate
(b) ¥2,000,000 × $.0077 December 31, 90-day forward rate
(c) ¥2,000,000 × $.0070 October 1, spot rate
(d) ¥2,000,000 × $.0080 December 31, spot rate

On October 1, the U.S. dollar–equivalent value of the foreign currency receivable from the broker is $15,000. Because of the increase in the forward exchange rate of the yen relative to the dollar (i.e., the weakening of the dollar versus the yen), the U.S. dollar–equivalent value of the foreign currency receivable on December 31, 20X1, increases to $15,400, resulting in a foreign currency transaction gain of $400. For the U.S. company, the U.S. dollar–equivalent value of the liability has increased to $16,000, resulting in a $2,000 foreign currency transaction loss. Because of the differing valuation requirements of the forward contract and the exposed liability, the exchange gain of the accounts payable (¥) is not necessarily an exact offset of the exchange loss on the foreign currency receivable (¥).

The required entries on April 1, 20X2, the settlement date, are:

(9)	Foreign Currency Transaction Loss	200	
	Foreign Currency Receivable from Exchange Broker (¥)		200

Adjust receivable to spot rate on settlement date:

$ 15,200 = ¥2,000,000 × $.0076 Apr. 1, 20X2, spot rate
−15,400 = ¥2,000,000 × $.0077 Dec. 31, 20X1, 90-day forward rate

$ 200 = ¥2,000,000 yen × ($.0076 − $.0077)

(10)	Accounts Payable (¥)	800	
	Foreign Currency Transaction Gain		800

Adjust payable denominated in yen to spot rate on settlement date:
¥2,000,000 × ($.0076 − $.0080)

(11)	Dollars Payable to Exchange Broker ($)	15,000	
	Cash		15,000

Deliver U.S. dollars to currency broker as specified in forward contract.

(12)	Foreign Currency Units (¥)	15,200	
	Foreign Currency Receivable from Exchange Broker (¥)		15,200

Receive ¥2,000,000 from exchange broker; valued at Apr. 1, 20X2, spot rate:
$15,200 = ¥2,000,000 × $.0076

(13)	Accounts Payable (¥)	15,200	
	Foreign Currency Units (¥)		15,200

Pay 2,000,000 yen to Tokyo Industries, Inc., in settlement of liability denominated in yen.

The direct exchange spot rate has decreased from the $.0080 rate on the balance sheet date to $.0076 on April 1, 20X2, the settlement date, indicating that the U.S. dollar has strengthened relative to the yen. Fewer dollars are needed to acquire the same number of yen on the settlement date than were needed on the balance sheet date. The forward exchange contract becomes due on April 1, 20X2, and is now valued at the current spot rate. The difference between the 90-day forward rate on December 31, 20X1, and the spot rate at the date of the completion of the forward rate results in the loss of $200. The U.S. dollar equivalent values of the foreign currency–denominated accounts on December 31, 20X1, and April 1, 20X2, follow:

	U.S. Dollar–Equivalent Values of Foreign Currency–Denominated Accounts		Foreign Currency Transaction Gain (Loss)
Accounts	December 31, 20X1 (Balance Sheet Date)	April 1, 20X2 (Settlement Date)	
Foreign Currency			
Receivable from Exchange Broker (¥)	$15,400 (a)	$15,200 (b)	$(200)
Accounts Payable (¥)	16,000 (c)	15,200 (d)	800

(a) ¥2,000,000 yen × $.0077 December 31, 90-day forward rate
(b) ¥2,000,000 yen × $.0076 April 1, 20X2, spot rate
(c) ¥2,000,000 yen × $.0080 December 31, spot rate
(d) ¥2,000,000 yen × $.0076 April 1, 20X2 spot rate

On December 31, 20X1, the U.S. dollar–equivalent value of the foreign currency receivable from the broker is $15,400. Because the yen weakened relative to the dollar, the foreign currency receivable on April 1, 20X2, is lower in U.S. dollar–equivalent value, and an exchange loss of $200 is recognized. The U.S. dollar–equivalent value of the foreign currency account payable is $16,000 on December 31, 20X1, but because the yen weakened (i.e., the dollar strengthened) during the period from December 31, 20X1, to April 1, 20X2, the U.S. dollar–equivalent value of the payable decreases to $15,200 on April 1, 20X2. This results in an $800 foreign currency transaction gain during this period.

Note that the total net foreign exchange transactions loss for the two years combined is $1,000 [20X1: $(2,000) plus $400; 20X2: $800 less $(200)]. This is the effect of the forward contract premium on October 1, 20X1, being taken into the earnings stream. Note the premium was for the difference between the forward rate ($.0075) and the spot rate ($.0070) at the date the forward contract was signed. At the April 1, 20X2, completion date, both of the foreign currency–denominated accounts are valued at the spot rate. Thus, the ¥2,000,000 × ($.0070 − $.0075) premium is the net effect on earnings over the term of the forward contract. The two accounts denominated in foreign currency start at different valuations but end using the same spot rate at the end of the term of the forward contract.

The forward exchange contract offsets the foreign currency liability position. On April 1, 20X2, Peerless pays the $15,000 forward contract price to the exchange broker and receives the 2,000,000 yen, which it then uses to extinguish its account payable to Tokyo Industries. Note that after settlement, all account balances in Figure 11–4 are reduced to zero.

If Peerless Products had a foreign currency receivable, it could also manage its exposed net asset position by acquiring a forward exchange contract to deliver foreign currency to the exchange broker. In this case, the forward currency payable to the exchange broker is denominated in the foreign currency. The forward exchange contract is settled when Peerless gives the broker the foreign currency units it has received from its customer. The foreign currency is then exchanged for U.S. dollars at the agreed-upon contractual rate from the forward exchange contract. The assets and liabilities denominated in foreign currency units must be revalued to their U.S. dollar–equivalent values in the same manner as for the import illustration. Recall that, for valuation purposes, **FASB 133** requires the use of the forward exchange rate for forward contracts, and **FASB 52** requires the use of spot rates for exposed net asset or liability accounts arising from foreign currency transactions.

Formal Balance Sheets Reporting Net Amounts for Forward Exchange Contracts

FASB 133 requires the recognition of all derivatives in the statement of financial position (the balance sheet) at net fair value. This means that the balance sheet presents the net of the forward contract receivable from the exchange broker against the dollars payable to the exchange broker. Some companies account for the forward exchange contract with only memorandum entries, using the philosophy that the contract is simply for the exchange of one currency for another. The underlying exposed accounts receivable or accounts payable denominated in foreign currency units are still presented. For example, a formal balance sheet prepared on October 1, 20X1, after the transactions recorded in entries (5) and (6), reports the following net amounts:

Assets		Liabilities	
Inventory	$14,000	Accounts Payable (¥)	$14,000

Under the net method of reporting the forward exchange contract, the gain or loss on the change in the value of the forward exchange contract must be recorded and reported in the balance sheet. The balance sheet prepared on December 31, 20X1, after posting entries (7) and (8) includes the following:

Assets		Liabilities and Equity	
Forward Exchange Contract (¥) (at net fair value)	$400	Accounts Payable (¥)	$16,000
		Retained Earnings (for net exchange loss)	(1,600)

Note that under the net approach to reporting, the forward exchange contract is valued at net fair value. The $2,000 foreign currency transaction loss on the account payable denominated in yen is partially offset with the $400 foreign currency transaction gain for the forward contract receivable in yen.

The net balance sheet presented on April 1, 20X2, immediately after entry (10) but before the settlement of the forward exchange contract and the accounts payable, is:

Assets		Liabilities and Equity	
Forward Exchange Contract (¥) (at net fair value)	$200	Accounts Payable (¥)	$15,200
		Retained Earnings (for amount of the premium)	(1,000)

The forward exchange contract is then settled by paying the exchange broker the $15,000 in U.S. dollars as initially contracted for in the forward exchange contract, receiving the 2,000,000 yen now valued at $15,200 and closing the net forward exchange contract for the difference of the $200.

The net approach is required for reporting derivative forward exchange contracts on the balance sheet. Nevertheless, we believe that recording both sides of the forward exchange contracts in the account maintains a full record of each side of the transaction.

Case 2: Hedging an Unrecognized Foreign Currency Firm Commitment: A Foreign Currency Fair Value Hedge

A company may expose itself to foreign currency risk *before* a purchase or sale transaction occurs. For example, a company may sign a noncancelable order to purchase goods from a foreign entity in the future to be paid for in the foreign currency. By agreeing to a purchase price in the present for a future purchase, the company has accepted an *identifiable foreign currency commitment* although the purchase has not yet occurred; that is, the purchase contract is still executory (unrecognized). The company will not have a liability obligation until after delivery of the goods, but it is exposed to changes in currency exchange rates before the transaction date (the date of delivery of the goods).

FASB 133 specified the accounting requirements for the use of forward exchange contracts **hedging unrecognized foreign currency firm commitments**. The company can separate the commitment into its financial instrument (the obligation to pay yen) and nonfinancial asset (the right to receive inventory) aspects. The forward contract taken out is then a hedge of the changes in the fair value of the firm commitment for the foreign currency risk being hedged. A hedge of a firm commitment comes under the accounting for fair value hedges, and the forward contract is to be valued at its fair value.

It is interesting to note the different accounting treatment of a hedge of a forecasted transaction (cash flow hedge) versus that for a hedge of an unrecognized foreign currency firm commitment (fair value hedge). A *forecasted* transaction is *anticipated* but not *guaranteed*. The forecasted transaction may actually occur as anticipated, but a hedge of a forecasted transaction is accounted for as a cash flow hedge with the effective portion of the change in the hedge's fair value recognized in other comprehensive income. On the other hand, a firm commitment is an agreement with an unrelated party that is binding and usually legally enforceable. The agreement has the following characteristics:

1. The agreement specifies all significant terms such as the quantity, the fixed price, and the timing of the transaction. The price may be denominated in either the entity's functional currency or in a foreign currency.
2. The agreement must contain a penalty provision sufficiently large to make performance of the agreement probable.

A forecasted transaction may become a firm commitment if an agreement having these listed characteristics is made between the parties. Any cash flow hedge of the forecasted transaction may be changed to a fair value hedge when the firm commitment agreement is made. However, any amounts recorded in other comprehensive income under the cash flow hedge are not reclassified into earnings until the initially forecasted transaction impacts earnings.

FASB 131 provides for management of an enterprise to select the basis by which the effectiveness of the hedge will be measured. Management may select the forward exchange rate, the spot rate, or the intrinsic value for measuring effectiveness. The examples used in this chapter use the forward rate, which is consistent with the general rule of valuing forward exchange contracts as specified in **FASB 133**. The measure of the change in fair value of the forward contract uses the forward exchange rate for the remainder of the term and then, if interest is significant, the change in the forward rates is discounted to reflect the time value of money. The entries for a hedge of an identifiable foreign currency commitment are presented in the following illustration.

Illustration of Hedging an Unrecognized Foreign Currency Firm Commitment

For illustration purposes, the import transaction between Peerless Products and Tokyo Industries used throughout this chapter is extended with the following information:

1. On August 1, 20X1, Peerless contracts to purchase special-order goods from Tokyo Industries. Their manufacture and delivery will take place in 60 days (on October 1, 20X1). The contract price is 2,000,000 yen, to be paid by April 1, 20X2, which is 180 days after delivery.
2. On August 1, Peerless hedges its foreign currency payable commitment with a forward exchange contract to receive 2,000,000 yen in 240 days (the 60 days until delivery plus

180 days of credit period). The future rate for a 240-day forward contract is $.0073 to 1 yen. The purpose of this 240-day forward exchange contract is twofold. First, for the 60 days from August 1, 20X1, until October 1, 20X1, the forward exchange contract is a hedge of an identifiable foreign currency commitment. For the 180-day period from October 1, 20X1, until April 1, 20X2, the forward exchange contract is a hedge of a foreign currency exposed net liability position.

The relevant exchange rates for this example are as follows:

	U.S. Dollar–Equivalent Value of 1 Yen	
Date	Spot Rate	Forward Exchange Rate
August 1, 20X1	$.0065	$.0073 (240 days)
October 1, 20X1	.0070	.0075 (180 days)

A time line for the transactions follows:

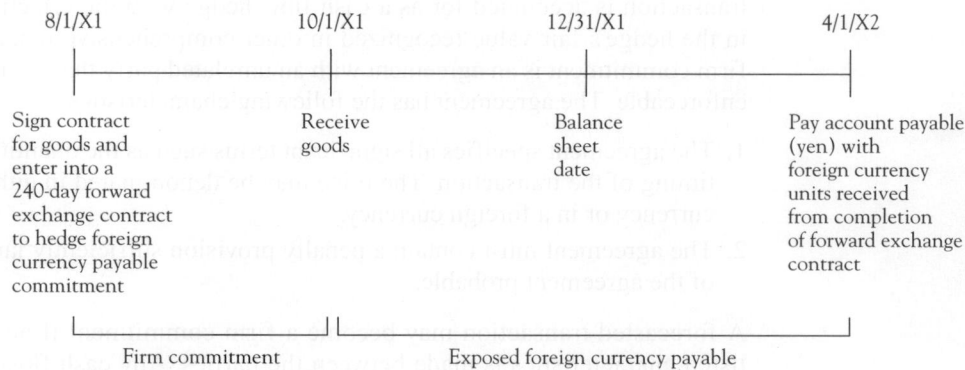

On August 1, 20X1, the company determines the value of its commitment to pay yen for the future accounts payable using the forward exchange rate. However, the payable is not recorded on August 1 because the exchange transaction has not yet occurred; the payable is maintained in memorandum form only. The forward exchange contract must be valued at its fair value. At the time the company enters into the forward exchange contract, the contract has no net fair value because the $14,600 foreign currency receivable equals the $14,600 dollars payable under the contract. The subsequent changes in the fair value of the forward contract are measured using the forward rate and then, if interest is significant, discounted to reflect the time value of money. For purposes of this illustration, we assume that interest is not significant and that hedge effectiveness is measured with reference to the change in the forward exchange rates.

August 1, 20X1

(14)	Foreign Currency Receivable from Exchange Broker (¥)	14,600	
	Dollars Payable to Exchange Broker ($)		14,600
	Sign forward exchange contract for receipt of 2,000,000 yen in 240 days:		
	$14,600 = ¥2,000,000 × $.0073 Aug. 1, 240-day forward rate		

On October 1, 20X1, the forward exchange contract is revalued to its fair value in accordance with **FASB 133**. The accounts payable in yen are recorded at the time the inventory is received.

October 1, 20X1

(15)	Foreign Currency Receivable from Exchange Broker (¥)	400	
	Foreign Currency Transaction Gain		400

Adjust forward contract to fair value, using
the forward rate at this date, and recognize gain:

$ 15,000 = ¥2,000,000 × $.0075 Oct. 1, 180-day forward rate

−14,600 = ¥2,000,000 × $.0073 Aug. 1, 240-day forward rate

$ 400 = ¥2,000,000 × $($.0075 − $.0073)

(16)	Foreign Currency Transaction Loss	400	
	Firm Commitment		400

To record the loss on the financial instrument
aspect of the firm commitment:

$ 15,000 = ¥2,000,000 × $.0075 Oct. 1, 180-day forward rate

−14,600 = ¥2,000,000 × $.0073 Aug. 1, 240-day forward rate

$ 400 = ¥2,000,000 × $($.0075 − $.0073)

The Firm Commitment account is a temporary account for the term of the unrecognized firm commitment. If it has a debit balance, it is shown in the assets section of the balance sheet; when it has a credit balance, as in this example, it is shown in the liability section of the balance sheet:

Assets		Liabilities and Equity	
Forward Exchange Contract (¥) (at net fair value)	$400	Firm Commitment	$400

Note that the $400 foreign currency transaction gain is offset against the $400 foreign currency transaction loss, resulting in no net effect on earnings.

The next entry records the receipt of the inventory and the recognition of the accounts payable in yen. Note that the temporary account, Firm Commitment, is closed against the purchase price of the inventory. The accounts payable are valued at the spot exchange rate in accordance with **FASB 52**.

(17)	Inventory	13,600	
	Firm Commitment	400	
	Accounts Payable(¥)		14,000

Record accounts payable at spot rate
and record inventory purchase:

$14,000 = ¥2,000,000 × $.0070 Oct. 1, spot rate

Key Observations from Illustration

The August 1, 20X1, entry records the signing of the forward exchange contract that is used to hedge the identifiable foreign currency commitment arising from the noncancelable purchase agreement. In entries (15) and (16), the forward contract and the underlying hedged foreign currency payable commitment are both revalued to their current value, and the $400 gain on the forward contract offsets the $400 loss on the foreign currency payable commitment. Entry (17) records the accounts payable in yen at the current spot rate and records the $400 inventory net that resulted from the recognition of the $400 loss on the financial instrument aspect of the firm commitment in entry (16).

FIGURE 11–5   **Comparison of Journal Entries: Hedge of an Unrecognized Firm Commitment**

Forward Exchange Contract (Use forward exchange rate)			Hedge of an Unrecognized Firm Commitment (Use forward exchange rate)		
August 1, 20X1. Recognize forward exchange contract valued at forward rate.					
(14) Foreign Currency Receivable (¥)	14,600				
Dollars Payable to Exchange Broker		14,600			
October 1, 20X1. Revalue foreign currency receivable and firm commitment hedge using forward rate.					
(15) Foreign Currency Receivable (¥)	400		(16) Foreign Currency Transaction Loss	400	
Foreign Currency Transaction Gain		400	Firm Commitment		400
			Economic Management of an Exposed Foreign Currency Payable (Use spot exchange rate)		
October 1, 20X1. Receive inventory, close firm commitment, and recognize foreign currency accounts payable.					
			(17) Inventory	13,600	
			Firm Commitment	400	
			Accounts Payable (¥)		14,000
December 31, 20X1. Revalue forward contract using forward rate, and accounts payable in yen using spot rate.					
(7) Foreign Currency Receivable (¥)	400		(8) Foreign Currency Transaction Loss	2,000	
Foreign Currency Transaction Gain		400	Accounts Payable (¥)		2,000
April 1, 20X2. Revalue forward contract at its termination to spot rate, and accounts payable in yen to spot rate.					
(9) Foreign Currency Transaction Loss	200		(10) Accounts Payable (¥)	800	
Foreign Currency Receivable (¥)		200	Foreign Currency Transaction Gain		800
April 1, 20X2. Deliver $14,600 in U.S. dollars to exchange broker, receiving yen. Use yen to settle accounts payable.					
(11) Dollars Payable to Exchange Broker	14,600				
Cash		14,600			
(12) Foreign Currency Units (¥)	15,200		(13) Accounts Payable (¥)	15,200	
Foreign Currency Receivable (¥)		15,200	Foreign Currency Units (¥)		15,200

At this point, the company has an exposed net liability position, which is hedged with a forward exchange contract, and the subsequent accounting follows the accounting for an exposed foreign currency liability position as presented previously in Case 1. Figure 11–5 presents a side-by-side comparison of the journal entries for the forward contract and the unrecognized firm commitment, which are valued at the forward exchange rates. The exposed foreign currency–denominated account payable is recognized at the time the company receives the inventory and is valued using the spot exchange rate.

Case 3: Hedging a Forecasted Foreign Currency Transaction: A Foreign Currency Cash Flow Hedge

It is interesting to note the different accounting treatment of a hedge of a forecasted transaction as a cash flow hedge versus that of an identifiable foreign currency commitment as a fair value hedge. A forecasted transaction is anticipated but not guaranteed. The forecasted transaction may actually occur as anticipated, but a hedge of a forecasted transaction is accounted for as a cash flow hedge with the effective portion of the change in fair value of the hedging instrument recognized in other comprehensive income. This type of hedge is against the changes in possible future cash flow that may result from changes in the foreign currency exchange rate. A forecasted transaction may become a firm commitment if the parties make a binding agreement. Prior to **FASB 138**, an entity could designate a forward foreign currency contract as a cash flow hedge if the purpose of the contract was offsetting forecasted cash flows, including transactions such as forecasted purchases or sales. Changes in the fair value of the cash flow hedge would be recognized as part of other comprehensive income.

When the forecasted transaction became a firm commitment, the forward contract would be redesignated as a fair value hedge, and changes in the fair value of the contract would then be recognized in earnings. Any amount recorded in other comprehensive income under the cash flow hedge would not be reclassified into earnings until the initially forecasted transaction impacted earnings. If the forecasted foreign currency transaction did not occur and was not expected to occur in the future, the amount recorded in other comprehensive income would be reclassified into earnings. The forward rate was used to value the forward contract and the spot rate was used to value the account receivable or payable resulting from the transaction.

FASB 138 allows management the additional option of designating the forward contract as a cash flow hedge from the time the contract is initially made until the final settlement of the payable or receivable, rather than requiring that the contract be redesignated as a fair value hedge when the forecasted transaction becomes a firm commitment. Changes in the value of the forward contract are measured using the forward exchange rate, while changes in the account payable or receivable are measured using the spot exchange rate. However, **FASB 138** requires that other comprehensive income from the forward contract revaluation be offset for any foreign exchange gain or loss on the account receivable or payable. Any remaining component of other comprehensive income is taken into the earnings stream only on final completion of the earnings process. Note that the forward contract must meet the requirements of a hedging instrument under the provisions of **FASB 133**, including the designation and tests of effectiveness.

FASB 138 allows management to: (1) designate the forward contract as a cash flow hedge while it is a forecasted transaction and then redesignate it as a fair value hedge for the remainder of the contract, or (2) designate the forward contract as a cash flow hedge for the entire period of time from the initial forecasting of the transaction through the eventual settlement of the receivable or payable. However, most companies regularly hedge their foreign currency receivables and payables and are likely to declare the forward contract as a continuing cash flow hedge in order to fully offset any gains or losses on changes in the fair value of the forward contract.

The following example is based on the data in Case 2 but adds the following assumption: the purchase of inventory is forecasted in August, but there is not a binding agreement for this purchase. Peerless Products Corporation enters into the 240-day forward exchange contract as a designated hedge against the future cash flows from the forecasted transaction, including the foreign currency–denominated accounts payable that would result from the purchase. Figure 11–6 presents the entries for this case, assuming that the hedge is designated as a cash flow hedge when the transaction is forecasted and then redesignated as a fair value hedge when the transaction occurs and the inventory is purchased. Figure 11–6 presents the entries for this case by bringing into the illustration Case 1 entries that would not change and noting the entries that would change with a *C* behind the entry number. Note that the entry on October 1 records the effect of the change in value of the forward contract as a component of Other Comprehensive Income.

Figure 11–7 presents the entries for this case assuming the hedge is designated as a cash flow hedge and remains as such between inception in August and final settlement in April. Figure 11–7 presents the entries for this case by bringing into the illustration Case 1 entries that would not change and noting the entries that would change with a letter *C* behind the entry number. Note the major differences in accounting for the forward contract as a cash flow hedge here versus as a fair value hedge in Case 2 are (1) the effective portion of the revaluation of the forward exchange contract is recorded in Other Comprehensive Income, (2) no firm commitment account exists under a forecasted transaction, (3) no revaluation of the forward contract receivable is required on October 1 and the inventory is recorded at its equivalent U.S. dollar cost determined at the spot rate, (4) there is an offset against Other Comprehensive Income to fully match the foreign currency transaction gain or loss recognized on the exposed foreign currency account payable, and (5) the $600 remaining balance in Other Comprehensive Income after the foreign currency payable is paid on April 1, 20X2,

FIGURE 11–6 **Journal Entries for Cash Flow Hedge Redesignated as Fair Value Hedge When a Forecasted Transaction Becomes a Transaction**

Entries for Forward Contract (Use forward exchange rate)		Entries for Foreign Currency Account Payable (Use spot rate)	
August 1, 20X1. Acquire forward exchange contract valued at forward rate.			
(14) Foreign Currency Receivable (¥)	14,600		
Dollars Payable to Exchange Broker	14,600		
October 1, 20X1. Receive inventory that was a forecasted transaction and recognize the foreign currency accounts payable at the spot rate. Change designation from a cash flow hedge to a fair value hedge; bring the forward contract to fair value as of this date.			
(15C) Foreign Currency Receivable (¥)	400	(17C) Inventory	14,000
Other Comprehensive Income	400	Accounts Payable (¥)	14,000
¥2,000,000 × ($.0075 − $.0073)			
December 31, 20X1. Revalue the forward contract to year-end fair values using the change in the forward rate since October 1 and recognize gain or loss in net income. Revalue accounts payable in yen using the spot rate.			
(7) Foreign Currency Receivable (¥)	400	(8) Foreign Currency Transaction Loss	2,000
Foreign Currency Transaction Gain	400	Accounts Payable (¥)	2,000
¥2,000,000 × ($.0077 − $.0075)			
April 1, 20X2. Revalue the forward contract using the spot rate at the termination of the contract and accounts payable in yen using the spot rate. Offset transaction gain on payable against other comprehensive income.			
(9) Foreign Currency Transaction Loss	200	(10) Accounts Payable (¥)	800
Foreign Currency Receivable (¥)	200	Foreign Currency Transaction Gain	800
¥2,000,000 × ($.0076 − $.0077)			
April 1, 20X2. Deliver $14,600 in U.S. dollars to the exchange broker and receive yen. Use yen to settle accounts payable.			
(11) Dollars Payable to Exchange Broker	14,600		
Cash	14,600		
(12) Foreign Currency Units (¥)	15,200	(13) Accounts Payable (¥)	15,200
Foreign Currency Receivable	15,200	Foreign Currency Units (¥)	15,200
Assumed sale of inventory and culmination of earnings process of other comprehensive income from forward contract.			
(C) Cost of Goods Sold	600	Cost of Goods Sold	14,000
Other Comprehensive Income	600	Inventory	14,000

is finally reclassified into cost of goods sold at the time the inventory is sold, which is the culmination of the earnings process related to the cash flow hedge.

Case 4: Speculation in Foreign Currency Markets

An entity may also decide to speculate in foreign currency as with any other commodity. For example, a U.S. company expects that the dollar will strengthen against the Swiss franc, that is, that the direct exchange rate will decrease. In this case, the U.S. company might *speculate with a forward exchange contract* to sell francs for future delivery, expecting to be able to purchase them at a lower price at the time of delivery.

The economic substance of this foreign currency speculation is to expose the investor to foreign exchange risk for which the investor expects to earn a profit. The exchange rate for valuing accounts related to speculative foreign exchange contracts is the forward rate for the remaining term of the forward contract. The gain or loss on a speculative forward contract is computed by determining the difference between the forward exchange rate on the date of contract (or on the date of a previous valuation) and the forward exchange rate available for the remaining term of the contract. The forward exchange rate is used to value the forward contract.

FIGURE 11–7 **Journal Entries for Cash Flow Hedge of a Forecasted Transaction**

Entries for Forward Contract		Entries for Foreign Currency Account Payable	
(Use forward exchange rate)		(Use spot rate)	

August 1, 20X1. Acquire forward exchange contract valued at forward rate.

(14) Foreign Currency Receivable (¥)	14,600		
Dollars Payable to Exchange Broker		14,600	

October 1, 20X1. Receive inventory that was a forecasted transaction and recognize the foreign currency accounts payable at the spot rate.

(No revaluation of foreign currency receivable required at this date)		(17C) Inventory	14,000	
		Accounts Payable (¥)		14,000

December 31, 20X1. Revalue the forward contract to year-end fair value using the change in the forward rate since August 1 and recognize the effective portion of the change in value as other comprehensive income. Revalue accounts payable in yen using the spot rate. Then, in accordance with **FASB 133**, reclassify a portion of the other comprehensive income to equally offset the foreign currency transaction loss recognized on the foreign currency payable that was remeasured using the spot exchange rate in accordance with **FASB 52**.

(7C) Foreign Currency Receivable (¥)	800		(8) Foreign Currency Transaction Loss	2,000	
Other Comprehensive Income		800	Accounts Payable (¥)		2,000
(¥2,000,000 × ($.0077 − $.0073))					
(C) Other Comprehensive Income	2,000				
Foreign Currency Transaction Gain		2,000			
To offset loss on account payable.					

April 1, 20X2. Revalue the forward contract at its termination using the spot rate and accounts payable in yen using the spot rate. Offset transaction gain on payable against other comprehensive income.

9(C) Other Comprehensive Income	200		(10) Accounts Payable (¥)	800	
Foreign Currency Receivable (¥)		200	Foreign Currency Transaction Gain		800
(C) Foreign Currency Transaction Loss	800				
Other Comprehensive Income		800			
To offset gain on account payable.					

April 1, 20X2. Deliver $14,600 in U.S. dollars to the exchange broker and receive yen. Use yen to settle accounts payable.

(11) Dollars Payable to Exchange Broker	14,600				
Cash		14,600			
(12) Foreign Currency Units (¥)	15,200		(13) Accounts Payable (¥)	15,200	
Foreign Currency Receivable (¥)		15,200	Foreign Currency Units (¥)		15,200

Assumed sale of inventory and culmination of earnings process of other comprehensive income from forward contract.

(C) Cost of Goods Sold	600		(C) Cost of Goods Sold	14,000	
Other Comprehensive Income		600	Inventory		14,000

Illustration of Speculation with Forward Contract

The following example illustrates the accounting for a U.S. company entering into a speculative forward exchange contract in Swiss francs (SFr), a currency in which the company has no receivables, payables, or commitments.

1. On October 1, 20X1, Peerless Products entered into a 180-day forward exchange contract to deliver SFr 4,000 at a forward rate of $.74 = SFr 1, when the spot rate was $.73 = SFr 1. Thus, the forward contract was to deliver SFr 4,000 and receive $2,960 (SFr 4,000 × $.74).

2. On December 31, 20X1, the balance sheet date, the forward rate for a 90-day forward contract was $.78 = SFr 1, and the spot rate for francs was $.75 = SFr 1.

3. On April 1, 20X2, the company acquired SFr 4,000 in the open market and delivered the francs to the broker, receiving the agreed-upon forward contract price of $2,960. At this date, the spot rate was $.77 = SFr 1.

A summary of the direct exchange rates for this illustration follows.

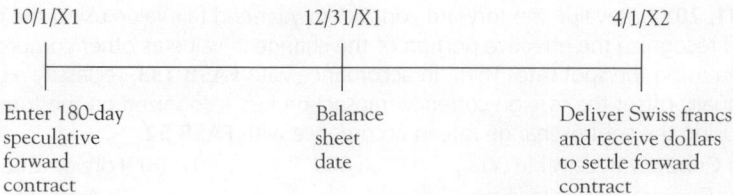

	U.S. Dollar–Equivalent of 1 Franc	
Date	Spot Rate	Forward Rate
October 1, 20X1	$.73	$.74 (180 days)
December 31, 20X1	.75	.78 (90 days)
April 1, 20X2	.77	

A time line of the economic events is as follows:

10/1/X1	12/31/X1	4/1/X2
Enter 180-day speculative forward contract	Balance sheet date	Deliver Swiss francs and receive dollars to settle forward contract

The entries for these transactions are as follows:

October 1, 20X1

(18)	Dollars Receivable from Exchange Broker ($)	2,960	
	Foreign Currency Payable to Exchange Broker (SFr)		2,960

Enter into speculative forward exchange contract:
$2,960 = SFr 4,000 × $.74, the 180-day forward rate

December 31, 20X1

(19)	Foreign Currency Transaction Loss	160	
	Foreign Currency Payable to Exchange Broker (SFr)		160

Recognize speculation loss on forward contract
for difference between initial 180-day forward
rate and forward rate for remaining term
to maturity of contract of 90 days:
$160 = SFr 4,000 × ($.78 − $.74)

April 1, 20X2

(20)	Foreign Currency Payable to Exchange Broker (SFr)	40	
	Foreign Currency Transaction Gain		40

Revalue foreign currency payable to spot rate
at end of term of forward contract:
$40 = SFr 4,000 × ($.78 − $.77)

(21)	Foreign Currency Units (SFr)	3,080	
	Cash		3,080

Acquire foreign currency units (SFr) in
open market when spot rate is $.77 = SFr1:
$3,080 = SFr 4,000 × $.77 spot rate

(22)	Foreign Currency Payable to Exchange Broker (SFr)	3,080	
	Foreign Currency Units (SFr)		3,080

Deliver foreign currency units to exchange
broker in settlement of forward contract:
$3,080 = SFr 4,000 × $.77 spot rate

(23)	Cash	2,960	
	Dollars Receivable from Exchange Broker ($)		2,960

Receive U.S. dollars from exchange broker as contracted.

Key Observations from Illustration

The October 1 entry records the forward contract payable of 4,000 Swiss francs to the exchange broker. The payable is denominated in a foreign currency but must be translated into U.S. dollars used as the reporting currency of Peerless Products. For speculative contracts, the forward exchange contract accounts are valued to fair value by using the forward exchange rate for the remaining contract term.

The December 31 entry adjusts the payable denominated in foreign currency to its appropriate balance at the balance sheet date. The payable, Foreign Currency Payable to Exchange Broker, is adjusted for the increase in the forward exchange rate from October 1, 20X1. The foreign currency transaction loss is reported on the income statement, usually under "Other Income (Loss)."

Entry (20), the first April 1 entry, revalues the foreign currency payable to its current U.S. dollar–equivalent value using the spot rate of exchange and recognizes the speculation gain. Entry (21) shows the acquisition of the 4,000 francs in the open market at the spot rate of $.77 = SFr 1. These francs will be used to settle the foreign currency payable to the exchange broker. The next two entries on this date, (22) and (23), recognize the settlement of the forward contract with the delivery of the 4,000 francs to the exchange broker and the receipt of the $2,960 agreed to when the contract was signed on October 1, 20X1. The $40 foreign currency transaction gain is the difference between the value of the foreign currency contract on December 31 using the forward rate and the value of the foreign currency units on April 1 using the spot rate.

Note that the company has speculated and lost because the dollar actually weakened against the Swiss franc. The net loss on the speculative forward contract was $120, which is the difference between the $160 loss recognized in 20X1 and the $40 gain recognized in 20X2.

Although this example shows a delivery of foreign currency units with a forward exchange contract, a company may also arrange a future contract for the receipt of foreign currency units. In this case, the October 1 entry is as follows:

October 1, 20X1

(24)	Foreign Currency Receivable from Exchange Broker (SFr)	2,960	
	Dollars Payable to Exchange Broker ($)		2,960
	Sign forward exchange contract for future receipt of foreign currency units:		
	$2,960 = SFr 4,000 × $.74		

The remainder of the accounting is similar to that of a delivery contract except that the company records an exchange gain on December 31 because it has a receivable denominated in a foreign currency that has now strengthened relative to the dollar.

Foreign Exchange Matrix

The relationships between changes in exchange rates and the resulting exchange gains and losses are summarized in Figure 11–8. For example, if a company has an account receivable denominated in a foreign currency, the exposed net monetary asset position results in the recognition of an exchange gain if the direct exchange rate increases but an exchange loss if the exchange rate decreases. If a company offsets an asset denominated in a foreign currency with a liability also denominated in that currency, the company has protected itself from any changes in the exchange rate because any gain is offset by an equal exchange loss.

ADDITIONAL CONSIDERATIONS

A Note on Measuring Hedge Effectiveness

FASB 133 states that, at the beginning of each hedging transaction, a company must define the method it will use to measure the effectiveness of the hedge. *Effectiveness* means that there will be an approximate offset, within the range of 80 to 125 percent, of the changes in the fair value of the cash flows or changes in fair value to the risk being hedged. Effectiveness must be assessed at least every three months and when the company reports financial

FIGURE 11–8 Foreign Exchange Matrix

Transactions or Accounts Denominated in Foreign Currency Units	Direct Exchange Rate Changes	
	Exchange Rate Increases (dollar has weakened)	Exchange Rate Decreases (dollar has strengthened)
Net monetary asset position, for example: (1) Foreign Currency Units (2) Accounts Receivable (3) Foreign Currency Receivable from Exchange Broker	EXCHANGE GAIN	EXCHANGE LOSS
Net monetary liability position, for example: (1) Accounts Payable (2) Bonds Payable (3) Foreign Currency Payable to Exchange Broker	EXCHANGE LOSS	EXCHANGE GAIN

statements or earnings. A company may elect to choose from several different measures for assessing hedge effectiveness. The examples to this point in the chapter use the change in forward rates, but a company may use the change in spot prices or change in intrinsic value. The ***intrinsic value of a derivative*** is the value related to the changes in value of the underlying item. The ***time value of a derivative*** is related to the value assigned to the opportunity to hold the derivative open for a period of time. The time value expires over the term of the derivative and is zero at the derivative's maturity date. If the company uses spot prices for measuring hedge effectiveness, any difference between the spot price and the forward price is excluded from the assessment of hedge effectiveness and is included currently in earnings.

Interperiod Tax Allocation for Foreign Currency Gains (Losses)

Temporary differences in the recognition of foreign currency gains or losses between tax accounting and GAAP accounting require interperiod tax allocation. Generally, the accrual method of recognizing the effects of changes in exchange rates in the period of change differs from the general election for recognizing exchange gains for tax purposes in the period of actual conversion of the foreign currency–denominated item. The temporary difference is recognized in accordance with **FASB Statement No. 109**, "Accounting for Income Taxes" (FASB 109).

Hedges of a Net Investment in a Foreign Entity

In the earlier discussions of the use of forward exchange contracts as a hedging instrument, the exchange risks from transactions denominated in a foreign currency could be offset. This same concept is applied by U.S. companies that view a net investment in a foreign entity as a long-term commitment that exposes them to foreign currency risk. A number of balance sheet management tools are available for a U.S. company to hedge its net investment in a foreign affiliate. Management may use forward exchange contracts, other foreign currency commitments, or certain intercompany financing arrangements, including intercompany transactions. For example, a U.S. parent company could borrow 10,000 British pounds to hedge against an equivalent net asset position of its British subsidiary. Any effects of exchange rate fluctuations between the pound and the dollar would be offset by the investment in the British subsidiary and the loan payable.

FASB 133 specifies that for derivative financial instruments designated as a hedge of the foreign currency exposure of a net investment in a foreign operation, the portion of the change in fair value equivalent to a foreign currency transaction gain or loss should be reported in other comprehensive income. That part of other comprehensive income resulting from a hedge of a net investment in a foreign operation then becomes part of the cumulative translation adjustment in accumulated other comprehensive income. Chapter 12 presents both the translation adjustment portion of other comprehensive income and accumulated other comprehensive income.

Summary of Key Concepts

Virtually all companies have foreign transactions. The general rule is that accounts resulting from transactions denominated in foreign currency units must be valued and reported at their equivalent U.S. dollar values. Forward exchange contracts typically use the forward rate for determining current fair value. These accounts must be adjusted to recognize the effects of changes in the exchange rates. For fair value hedges, the gain or loss is taken into current earnings. For cash flow hedges, the gain or loss is taken to other comprehensive income for the period.

Key Terms

cash flow hedges, *514*
current rate, *507*
derivative, *513*
fair value hedges, *514*
financial instrument, *513*
foreign currency exchange rate, *502*
foreign currency hedges, *514*
foreign currency transaction gain or loss, *508*
foreign currency transactions, *501*

foreign currency unit (FCU), *502*
forward exchange contract, *507*
functional currency, *509*
hedging unrecognized foreign currency firm commitments, *523*
intrinsic value of a derivative, *532*
local currency, *509*
local currency unit (LCU), *502*

managing an exposed foreign currency position—either a net asset or a net liability position, *517*
notional amount, *513*
reporting currency, *509*
speculate with a forward exchange contract, *528*
spot rate, *507*
spread, *507*
time value of a derivative, *532*
underlying, *513*

Appendix 11A Illustration of Valuing Forward Exchange Contracts with Recognition for the Time Value of Money

This illustration uses the exemple of a hedge of an identifiable, unrecognized foreign currency commitment from the chapter to illustrate the present value of the forward exchange contract and hedge.

1. On August 1, 20X1, Peerless Products Corporation contracts to purchase special-order goods from Tokyo Industries. The manufacture and delivery of the goods will take place in 60 days (on October 1, 20X1). The contract price is 2,000,000 yen to be paid by April 1, 20X2, which is 180 days after delivery.

2. On August 1, 20X1, Peerless Products hedges its foreign currency payable commitment with a forward exchange contract to receive 2,000,000 yen in 240 days (the 60 days until delivery plus 180 days of credit period). The future rate for a 240-day forward contract is $.0073 to 1 yen. The purpose of this 240-day forward exchange contract is twofold. First, for the 60 days from August 1, 20X1, until October 1, 20X1, the forward exchange contract is a hedge of an identifiable foreign currency commitment. For the 180-day period from October 1, 20X1, until April 1, 20X2, the forward exchange contract is a hedge of a foreign currency–exposed net liability position.

3. Peerless uses a discount interest rate of 10 percent to present value the expected future cash flows from forward exchange contracts.

4. Peerless measures the effectiveness of hedges of identifiable, unrecognized firm commitments based on changes in the forward exchange rate.

The relevant exchange rates for this example are as follows:

| | U.S. Dollar–Equivalent Value of 1 Yen | |
Date	Spot Rate	Forward Exchange Rate
August 1, 20X1	$.0065	$.0073 (240 days)
October 1, 20X1	.0070	.0075 (180 days)
December 31, 20X1 (balance sheet date)	.0080	.0077 (90 days)
April 1, 20X2 (settlement date)	.0076	

A time line for transactions follows.

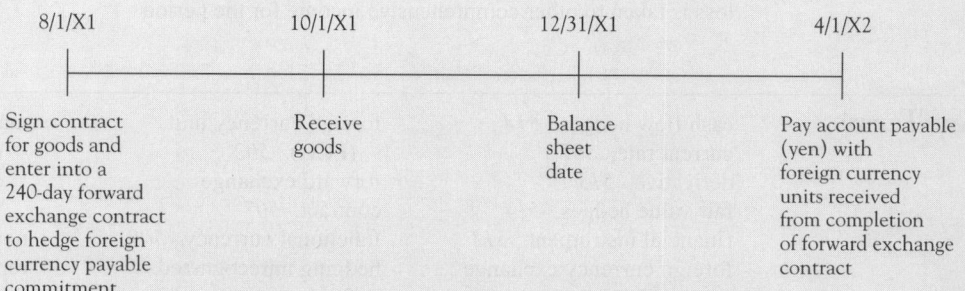

8/1/X1	10/1/X1	12/31/X1	4/1/X2
Sign contract for goods and enter into a 240-day forward exchange contract to hedge foreign currency payable commitment	Receive goods	Balance sheet date	Pay account payable (yen) with foreign currency units received from completion of forward exchange contract

The computation of hedge effectiveness is performed using the changes in the forward exchange rate in accordance with the general requirements of **FASB 133** and the company's specific policies regarding measurement of effectiveness of the hedge by using the forward exchange rates.

| | Change in the Fair Value of | | |
	Forward Contract Based on Changes in Forward Rate Gain (Loss)	Firm Commitment Based on Changes in Forward Rate Gain (Loss)	Effectiveness Ratio for the Period
October 1, 20X1	$380(a)	$(380)	1.00
December 31, 20X1	400(b)	No longer applicable because firm commitment was completed on October 1, 20X1.	
April 1, 20X2	(180)(c)		

(a) $380 = [($.0075 − $.0073) × ¥2,000,000] for the $400 cumulative, undiscounted gain from the change in the forward rates and then discounted at a 10 percent annual rate for the six-month period from October 1, 20X1, to April 1, 20X2, the completion date of the forward contract: NPV (.05, 400) = $380.95, rounded.
(b) $400 = [($.0077 − $.0073) × ¥2,000,000] for the $800 cumulative, undiscounted gain from the change in the forward rates since entering the forward contract and then (1) discounted at a 10 percent annual rate for the three-month period from December 31, 20X1, to April 1, 20X2, NPV (.025,800) = $780.49, rounded; and then (2) subtract prior recognition of $380 reported for October 1, 20X1, in (a).
(c) $(180) = [($.0076 − $.0073) × ¥2,000,000] for the $600 cumulative gain from the change in the forward rate since entering the forward contract on August 1, 20X1, to the spot rate on April 1, 20X2, the completion of the forward contract; then subtract the prior recognition of $780 gain recognized previously in (a) and (b). This results in a loss of $(180) in the current period.

The amounts in the following entry on August 1, 20X1, are not present valued because the entry is a memorandum-type entry and because the interest factor will be taken into earnings through the changes in the fair value of the forward contract. Note that at the date of signing the forward contract, the net fair value of the forward contract is zero because the receivable and payable are equal to each other.

August 1, 20X1

(25)	Foreign Currency Receivable from Exchange Broker (¥)	14,600	
	Dollars Payable to Exchange Broker ($)		14,600

Sign forward exchange contract for receipt of 2,000,000 yen in 240 days:
$14,600 = ¥2,000,000 × $.0073 Aug. 1, 240-day forward rate

On October 1, 20X1, the forward exchange contract will be revalued to its net fair value, recognizing the time value of money by using the present value of the expected future net cash flow from the forward contract. The temporary liability account, Firm Commitment, is also recorded at this time. Net present values can easily be computed using an electronic spreadsheet such as Excel and the Net Present Value (NPV) function.

October 1, 20X1

(26)	Foreign Currency Receivable from Exchange Broker (¥)	380	
	Foreign Currency Transaction Gain		380

Adjust forward contract to net fair value,
using the present value of the change in the forward rates.
[Item (a) in the hedge effectiveness illustration.]

(27)	Foreign Currency Transaction Loss	380	
	Firm Commitment		380

To record the loss on the financial instrument aspect
of the firm commitment, using the present value of the
change in the forward exchange rates. [Same amount as
item (a) for this example because the effectiveness of the
hedge on the firm commitment is assessed using the change
in the forward exchange rates.]

On October 1, 20X1, the discounted net fair value of the forward contract is $380.

The next entry is to record the receipt of the inventory and the recognition of the accounts payable in yen. Note that the temporary account, Firm Commitment, is closed against the purchase price of the inventory.

(28)	Inventory	13,620	
	Firm Commitment	380	
	Accounts Payable (¥)		14,000

Record accounts payable at spot rate and the inventory
purchase, closing the temporary liability account:
$14,000 = ¥2,000,000 × $.0070 Oct. 1 spot rate

The required adjusting entries on December 31, 20X1, Peerless's fiscal year-end, are:

(29)	Foreign Currency Receivable from Exchange Broker (¥)	400	
	Foreign Currency Transaction Gain		400

Adjust forward contract to net fair value, using the
present value of the change in the forward rates.
[Item (b) in the hedge effectiveness illustration.]

(30)	Foreign Currency Transaction Loss	2,000	
	Accounts Payable (¥)		2,000

Adjust payable denominated in yen to current U.S. dollar–
equivalent value: $2,000 = ¥2,000,000 × ($.0080 − $.0070).
No interest factor is used for this revaluation; thus,
no present value computation is made.

On December 31, 20X1, the discounted net fair value of the forward contract is $780. The first required entry on April 1, 20X2, the settlement date, is:

(31)	Foreign Currency Transaction Loss	180	
	Foreign Currency Receivable from Exchange Broker (¥)		180

Adjust forward contract for the change in the forward rate to the
spot rate on settlement date: [Item (c) in the hedge effectiveness illustration.]

$ .0076 spot rate on 4/1/X2, the end of the forward contract

−.0073 forward rate on 8/1/X1, the beginning of the forward contract

$ .0003 × ¥2,000,000 = $ 600 cumulative change from 8/1/X1

−780 gains previously recognized

$(180) reduction (loss) this period

Note that at this point, the net foreign currency transaction gain on just the forward contract is $600. This is the difference between the time value of the forward contract (the $1,600 premium on the forward contract—$.0073 forward rate less $.0065 spot rate—when the forward contract was signed on August 1, 20X1, which is taken into earnings over the term of the forward contract) and the intrinsic value of the forward contract (the $2,200 difference between the spot rate of $.0065 on August 1, 20X1, and the spot rate of $.0076 on the forward contract completion date of April 1, 20X2). Another way to compute the net gain over the term of the forward contract is to compare the forward rate at the date the contract is signed ($.0073) and the spot rate at the date the contract is completed ($.0076). The net gain is $600 [¥2,000,000 × ($.0073 − $.0076)].

The following April 1, 20X2, entries complete the forward contract and the payment of the accounts payable that was denominated as ¥2,000,000.

(32)	Accounts Payable (¥)	800	
	Foreign Currency Transaction Gain		800

Adjust payable denominated in yen to spot rate
on settlement date. No interest factor for this item.
$800 = ¥2,000,000 × ($.0076 − $.0080)

(33)	Dollars Payable to Exchange Broker ($)	14,600	
	Cash		14,600

Deliver U.S. dollars to currency broker
as specified in forward contract.

(34)	Foreign Currency Units (¥)	15,200	
	Foreign Currency Receivable from Exchange Broker (¥)		15,200

Receive ¥2,000,000 from exchange broker;
valued at Apr. 1, 20X2, spot rate:
$15,200 = ¥2,000,000 × $.0076

(35)	Accounts Payable (¥)	15,200	
	Foreign Currency Units (¥)		15,200

Pay 2,000,000 yen to Tokyo Industries, Inc.,
in settlement of liability denominated in yen.

Appendix **11B** Use of Other Financial Instruments by Multinational Companies

This chapter detailed the accounting for forward exchange contracts that were used to hedge exposed asset or liability positions or to hedge foreign currency commitments, or that were entered into for speculative purposes. Many multinational enterprises (MNEs) typically use financial instruments other than forward contracts to manage the risks associated with international transactions. A general definition of a financial instrument is that it is cash, stock, or a contract that imposes a contractual obligation to deliver or receive cash or another financial instrument to another entity. Examples of financial instruments are receivables/payables, bonds, shares of stock, foreign currency forward contracts, futures contracts, options, and financial swaps. A derivative financial instrument is when the value of a financial instrument is derived from some other item such as a contract valued on an index of stock values or futures contracts in which the value is determined by contemporary and predicted economic events. The other derivative financial instruments most often used by MNEs are futures, options, and swaps.

Accounting standard setters have had the daunting task of obtaining a consensus on the accounting, reporting, and disclosing of financial instruments. The FASB first placed the financial instrument project on its agenda in 1986 and has since continued to work on this project. Along the way, it issued **FASB Statement No. 105**, "Disclosure of Information about Financial Instruments with Off-Balance Sheet Risk" (FASB 105), **FASB Statement No. 107**, "Disclosures about Fair Value of Financial Instruments" (FASB 107), and **FASB Statement No. 119**, "Disclosure about Derivative Financial Instruments and Fair Value of Financial Instruments" (FASB 119). In 1998, the FASB issued **FASB Statement No. 133**, "Accounting for Derivative Instruments and Hedging Activities" (FASB 133). **FASB 133** supersedes **FASB Statement No. 80**, "Accounting for Future Contracts" (FASB 80), **FASB 105**, and **FASB 119**. In 1999, the FASB issued **FASB 137**, which delayed the implementation date of **FASB 133** for one year, until June 15, 2000, but **FASB 137** did not change any of **FASB 133**'s requirements.

FASB 133 specified four major decisions underlying the logic of the standard: (1) derivatives are assets or liabilities and should be reported in the financial statements, (2) fair value is the most relevant measure for financial instruments and the only relevant measure for derivatives, and adjustment to the carrying amount of hedged items should reflect offsetting changes in their fair value while the hedge is in effect, (3) only items that are assets or liabilities should be reported as such in the financial statements, and (4) special accounting for items designated as being hedged should be provided only for qualifying transactions, and an aspect of qualification should be an assessment of offsetting changes in fair values or cash flows. Thus, **FASB 133** has a general rule of fair value, requires the recognition of gains and losses for the changes in fair value, and limits the applications of hedge accounting. It defines *fair value* as the amount at which an asset (liability) could be bought (incurred) or sold (settled) in a current transaction between willing parties. Quoted market prices are typically the best evidence of fair value. In addition, **FASB 133** amended **FASB 107** to include specific disclosures about concentrations of credit risk of all financial instruments and encouraged disclosure about the market risk of all financial instruments. *Credit risk* is the loss that might occur if a party to the contract involving the entity fails to perform. *Market risk* is the loss that might occur from future changes in market prices that would impair the value of the financial instrument.

FASB Statement No. 138, "Accounting for Certain Derivative Instruments and Certain Hedging Activities: An Amendment of FASB Statement No. 133" (FASB 138), issued in 2000, amended four smaller items in **FASB 133** in response to technical concerns raised by practitioners and preparers of the financial statements: (1) it broadened the application of the normal purchases and sales exception so that fewer of these contracts requiring delivery of nonfinancial assets would need to be accounted for as derivatives, (2) it redefined the interest rate risk to permit a benchmark risk-free interest rate to be the hedged risk, (3) it permitted hedging recognized foreign currency–denominated assets or liabilities with either cash flow or fair value hedges but still requires the foreign currency–denominated asset or liability to be valued according to the provisions of **FASB 52**, and (4) it broadened the ability to hedge with intercompany derivatives.

FASB Statement No. 149, "Amendment of Statement 133 on Derivative Instruments and Hedging Activities" (FASB 149), issued in 2003, presented a series of modifications resulting from implementation issues related to the definition of a derivative. **FASB 149** clarified several definitional issues but did not change the basic concepts presented in **FASB 133**.

This appendix supplements the chapter by presenting a brief overview of futures, options, and swaps. It first gives brief definitions and descriptions. Next, it presents several examples of accounting for a hedge with a futures contract, a hedge with an option contract, and an interest-rate swap. Finally, it presents a description of the disclosure requirements that currently apply. A discussion of the detailed mechanics and risk ramifications of transactions that utilize these instruments is beyond the coverage of an advanced financial accounting textbook.

DEFINITIONS AND DESCRIPTIONS

A *derivative financial instrument* is an instrument whose value is based on or "derived from" the value of something else (an underlying). That underlying can be the value of another financial instrument, a commodity, an index, an asset, or a debt instrument. Because the derivative financial instrument has a value that is linked to the underlying, it makes the derivative a useful hedging instrument to offset the change in value of the hedged item. Examples of derivative financial instruments include futures, forward, swap, and option contracts; interest-rate caps; and fixed-rate loan commitments.

Forward and Futures Contracts

A forward contract is an agreement between a buyer and a seller that requires the delivery of some commodity at a specified future date at a price agreed to today (the exercise price). As presented in the chapter, foreign currency forward contracts are typically made with dealers of foreign exchange, and the contract is fulfilled at the end of the contract term by the exchanges of the currencies between the company and the dealer. Changes in the underlying market value of the foreign currency are recognized by the company holding the forward contract. The net fair value of a forward contract when it is written is zero because neither party pays anything and neither party receives anything. The contract is executory at this point. During the term of the forward contract, the net fair value changes based on the difference between a newly written forward contract for the remaining term and the original forward contract. At expiration, the forward contract's net fair value is the difference between the spot price and the original forward rate.

Futures are very similar to forward contracts except futures have standardized contract terms, they are traded on organized exchanges, and traders must realize any losses or gains on each and every trading day. Futures are contracts between two parties—a buyer and a seller—to buy or sell something at a specified future date, which is termed the *expiration date.* The contract trades on a futures exchange such as the Chicago Board of Trade (CBOT) or the Chicago Mercantile Exchange (CME). Futures contracts are actively traded in a number of commodities including grains and oilseeds, livestock and meat, food and fiber, and metals and energy. It is even possible to enter into futures contracts on foreign currencies. Companies trading in futures contracts are normally required to place cash in their margin accounts held by the brokerage exchange or a *clearing house,* and the gain (loss) on the futures contract is then added (subtracted) from the company's margin account. This margin account is settled daily for the changes in contract value. Margin accounts are maintained at some percentage (typically 2 to 5 percent) of the contract amount. Most investors do not expect to actually exchange the futures contract for the optioned item—the futures contract is simply an investment vehicle to ride the value curve of the optioned item—and they use a *closing transaction* to settle the future contract. If a company is the purchaser of a futures contract, it is said to "go long" in a position. If a company contracts to sell with a futures contract, it is said to "go short." Futures contracts are sometimes referred to as *liquid forward contracts* because futures trade separately. The accounting for futures contracts is quite similar to accounting for foreign currency forward contracts.

Both futures and forward contracts are obligations to deliver a specified amount at a specified point in time. There is a potential for a gain under favorable circumstances and a potential for a loss under unfavorable circumstances. As presented in Chapter 11, not only the losses but also the gains are minimized by using foreign currency forward contracts. Forward contracts are commonly used for hedging foreign currency transactions because the forward contracts can be customized as to duration and amounts. Futures contracts are standardized as to duration and amount but are more readily accessible because of their wide acceptance in a futures exchange arena.

Option Contracts

An option contract between two parties—the buyer and the seller—gives the buyer (option holder) the right, but not the obligation, to purchase from or sell something to the option seller (option writer) at a date in the future at a price agreed to at the time the option contract is exchanged. Options can be written on a large variety of commodities such as grains, food and fibers, petroleum, livestock, metals, interest rates, and various foreign currencies. The option buyer pays the seller some amount of money, typically termed the "premium," for this right. An option to buy something is referred to as a "call"; an option to sell something is called a "put." Options trade on organized markets similar to the stock market. Exchanges on which options trade are the Chicago Board Options Exchange (CBOE), the Philadelphia Stock Exchange (PHLX), the American Stock Exchange (AMEX), and the Pacific Stock Exchange (PSE).

An option contract can give the buyer future control over a large number of shares or other items at the nominal cost of the option. This ability of the option for future control is the *time value* of the option. Over the option's term, the time value decreases to zero at the option's expiration date. Changes in the time value of the option are always taken to current earnings. The party selling the right is the writer; the party buying the right is the holder. The option holder has the right to exercise or not exercise the option. The holder of the option would not exercise the right embedded in the option if by doing so it would result in a loss. The option writer, however, is subject to risk because the option holder could exercise the option, forcing the writer to deliver under terms that are not favorable to the writer. An option's *intrinsic value* is directly related to the change in underlying value of the hedged item. The change in intrinsic value of a fair value hedge is taken to current earnings. The change in the effective portion of intrinsic value of a cash flow hedge is taken to other comprehensive income. An example of an option used as a hedge is presented later in this appendix.

The option is sold with a *strike price,* the price at which the holder has the option to buy or sell the item. If an investor holds a call option to purchase one share of Peerless Products stock for $5 a share from the writer, the holder may exercise that option when the market share price exceeds the strike price. If the market price is $6 a share, the holder will save $1 by exercising the option and purchasing the stock for $5. If the holder wishes to turn the savings into a cash profit, the investor would sell the share of stock, purchased for $5, on the market for $6. Alternatively, the holder of the option could directly sell the option for $1, its intrinsic value. When the market price is more than the strike price, the option to buy is "in the money." When the market price is less than the strike price, the option to buy is "out of the money."

If an investor is the holder of a put option to sell one share of Peerless Products for $5 a share to the writer, the holder will exercise that option when the share price is below the strike price. If the market price is $4 a share, the holder will make $1 by exercising the sell option at $5 per share rather than selling the share on the open market at $4 per share. When the market price is less than the option price, the option to sell is "in the money."

For the Peerless Products stock example, a summary of the relationship between the option type and the term used to describe the difference between the current market price of the underlying and the option's strike price is as follows:

Option	Current Market Price Equals the Option's Strike Price ($5 = $5)	Current Market Price Is More than the Option's Strike Price ($6 > $5)	Current Market Price Is Less than the Option's Strike Price ($4 < $5)
Call (buy)	At the money	In the money	Out of the money
Put (sell)	At the money	Out of the money	In the money

Options are typically purchased for a fee that is usually a small percentage of the optioned item's current value (e.g., 1 to 7 percent). The option's terms stipulate whether the option can be exercised at any time during the option period or only at the end of the exercise period. The minimum value of a put option is zero because a put option need not be exercised. Therefore, a put option can never have a negative value, and the maximum loss of the holder of a put option is the premium initially paid for the option.

Figure 11–9 presents an overview of the major features of forwards, futures, and options.

Swaps

A *swap* is an arrangement by which two parties exchange cash flows over a period of time. Swaps can be designed to swap currencies, interest rates, or commodities. The two most common types of financial swaps used by companies are (1) currency swaps and (2) interest rate swaps. An example of a currency swap is Peerless Products Corporation's sale of products in Great Britain for which it receives pounds sterling. Another company located in London, England, sells products in the United States for which it receives U.S. dollars. A currency swap would occur, for example, if Peerless (a U.S. company) agrees that the periodic currency flows in pounds sterling from its Great Britain operations will be forwarded to its counterparty in Great Britain, and the dollar sales in the United States by the London company will be forwarded to Peerless, the U.S. company. At the end of each period, the two companies agree to settle up for any differences in the notional amount of the swap at the end of the period. Thus, both parties to this currency swap avoid dealing in other than their local currencies and avoid foreign currency exchange costs.

Another example of a swap is an interest-rate swap in which two parties agree to exchange the interest payments on a stated amount of principal (also called the "notional amount"). Typically, the swap is an exchange of a variable (floating) rate interest and a fixed-rate interest. For example, Peerless may issue variable-rate debt but wish to fix its interest rates because it believes the variable rate may increase. Peerless may enter into a contract with a counterparty who has a fixed-rate bond but who is looking for a variable-rate interest because that company assumes the interest rates may

FIGURE 11–9
Features of
Forwards, Futures,
and Options

Type of Derivative	Features
Forwards	• Contracted through a dealer, usually a bank • Possibly customized to meet contracting company's terms and needs • Typically no margin deposit required • Must be completed either with the underlying's future delivery or net cash settlement
Futures	• Traded on an exchange and acquired through an exchange broker • Cannot be customized; for a specific amount at a specific date • Often company required to open a margin account with a small deposit so daily changes in futures value can be posted to the account • Usually settled with a net cash amount prior to maturity date; not expected to be completed by the underlying's future delivery
Options	• Traded on a variety of exchanges • Acquired on a large variety of commodities and major foreign currencies • Issued in two types, put (sell) and call (buy) • Option premium (fee) paid by the option holder to the writer (counterparty) for that right • Taker's or holder's loss limited to a maximum of the premium paid but virtually unlimited potential profit if underlying market moves in the option holder's desired direction • Grantor (counterparty or writer) offered potential to earn a maximum of the option premium and to lose a virtually unlimited amount if underlying market moves in the opposite direction than desired

decrease. Often the contract includes a financial intermediary to which net settlement payments are made and which charges a nominal fee for its services. Sometimes the counterparty is a dealer, which is a bank or an investment banking firm, that makes a market in swaps and other interest-rate derivatives. The notional amount (principal) is specified as the same for both parties, and Peerless fixes the interest rate on its notional amount while the counterparty obtains the variable rate it was seeking. Note that the debt is not being extinguished and any fees paid to arrange the swap should be treated as debt issuance costs that are amortized over the term of the debt. Each company is still responsible for its actual interest payment to its creditor. The swap is merely an agreement for the net periodic settlement of the difference between the two interest rates and is done solely between the two companies that contracted for the interest swap. The simple swap of fixed- versus variable-interest rates is sometimes referred to as a *plain vanilla swap* or a *generic swap*. An interest rate swap is presented later in this appendix.

An overview of the accounting for the three major types of hedges is presented in Figure 11–10. Review this figure before proceeding to the examples.

EXAMPLE OF THE USE OF AN OPTION TO HEDGE AN ANTICIPATED PURCHASE OF INVENTORY: A CASH FLOW HEDGE

Assume that Peerless Products plans in 90 days to purchase 30,000 bushels of wheat that currently have a value of $75,000 (30,000 bushels × $2.50 spot price per bushel). Also assume that Peerless wants to lock in the value of the anticipated future purchase.

Peerless purchases a call option on wheat futures to hedge against a price change in the anticipated purchase of the inventory. If the price of wheat increases, the profit on the purchased call option will offset the higher price that Peerless would have to pay for the wheat. If the price of wheat decreases, Peerless loses the premium it paid for the call option but can then buy the wheat at a lower price.

On November 1, 20X1, Peerless purchases call options for a February 1, 20X2, call (90 days in the future) at a call price of $2.50. Peerless pays a premium of $.05 per bushel, for a total cost of $1,500

FIGURE 11–10   Overview of Three Types of Hedges

Type of Hedge	Basic Criteria	Recognition and Measurement
Fair value hedge	A hedge of the derivative instrument's exposure to changes in the fair value of an asset or liability, or of an unrecognized firm commitment.	Gain or loss on the hedging instrument, as well as the related loss or gain on the hedged item, should be recognized currently in earnings.
Cash flow hedge	Hedge the derivative instrument's exposure to variability in expected future cash flows of a recognized asset or liability, or of a forecasted transaction, that is attributable to a particular risk.	Gain or loss on the effective portion of hedge (e.g., the intrinsic value) is deferred and reported as a component of other comprehensive income. Any gain or loss on the derivative that is not offset by cash flow losses and gains on the hedged forecasted transaction (i.e., ineffective, including the time value of the option) is recognized currently in earnings.
Foreign currency hedge	A hedge of the foreign currency exposure of: 1. An unrecognized firm commitment 2. An available-for-sale security 3. A forecasted transaction 4. A net investment in a foreign operation	The recognition and measurement differ by type of hedge: 1. This is a foreign currency fair value hedge 2. This is a foreign currency fair value hedge 3. This is a foreign currency cash flow hedge 4. The gain or loss on the effective portion of the hedging derivative on a net investment in a foreign operative shall be reported as part of the translation adjustment component of other comprehensive income.

(30,000 bushels × $.05). The call options are for a notional amount of 30,000 bushels of wheat. Peerless specifies that the derivative qualifies for cash flow hedge accounting. It is a cash flow hedge because the option is hedging a forecasted, or planned, future transaction involving cash flows. Note that this example shows the entire $1,500 as the time value of the option; in other words, it sets a futures price equal to the current market price. This type of contract is sometimes termed "at the money," meaning it specifies the futures price of the underlying at the current market price. Thus, the value of the contract when it is signed is only with regard to the *time value* of the expectation that the actual future price of the commodity will differ from the current market price.

An overview of this hedge follows:

Hedging instrument	Call option on wheat futures
Hedged item	Forecasted purchase of wheat
Type of hedge	Cash flow hedge
Underlying	Price of a bushel of wheat
Notional amount	30,000 bushels of wheat
Time value at origin of hedge	$1,500, at the money
Valuation of call option	Fair value
If underlying increases in value	Call option increases in value
If underlying decreases in value	Call option decreases in value

Gain or loss on hedge:

Effective portion	To Other Comprehensive Income; related to change in intrinsic value of hedge
Ineffective portion	To current earnings; related to change in time value of hedge

The entry to record the purchase of the call options is as follows:

November 1, 20X1

(36)	Purchased Call Options	1,500	
	Cash		1,500

To record the purchase of call options for 30,000 bushels of wheat at $2.50 per bushel in 90 days. The options are at the money; therefore, the $1,500 is all time value.

The fair market information for this example follows:

Fair Value Computations			
	November 1, 20X1	December 31, 20X1	February 1, 20X2
Bushel of wheat	$ 2.50	$ 2.60	$ 2.58
Total: 30,000 bushels			
Call Option:			
Option market value	$1,500	$3,700	$2,400
(from market information)			
Less: Intrinsic value:			
[Number of bushels ×			
(Market price − Strike price)]			
[30,000 bushels × ($2.50 − $2.50)]	-0-		
[30,000 bushels × ($2.60 − $2.50)]		(3,000)	
[30,000 bushels × ($2.58 − $2.50)]			(2,400)
Time value remaining	$1,500	$ 700	$ -0-

Note that for a cash flow hedge, the change in the intrinsic value (effective portion) is recognized in Other Comprehensive Income, and the change in the time value (ineffective portion) is recognized in current earnings.

At December 31, 20X1, the price of wheat increases to $2.60 per bushel. The *intrinsic value* is the change in value of the options due to the change in market value of the underlying. For cash flow hedges, the change in a derivative's intrinsic value is recorded in other comprehensive income. On December 31, the intrinsic value of the options is $3,000 (30,000 bushels × $.10 increase).

FASB 133 requires that hedging instruments be revalued to fair value at each balance sheet date. The change in value of the options is due to two factors: the change in the intrinsic value and the reduction of the time value. An option's time value decreases over its term and is zero when the options expire. At December 31, 20X1, the fair market value of the options is $3,700, meaning that the option's remaining time value is valued by the market at $700 ($3,700 fair value less $3,000 intrinsic value). **FASB 133** specifies that the $800 ($1,500 initial amount − $700 remaining) reduction in the time value portion of a derivative is recognized as part of current earnings. Entry (37) records the change in the value of the options to value them at their fair value at the balance sheet date.

December 31, 20X1

(37)	Purchased Call Options	2,200	
	Loss on Hedge Activity	800	
	Other Comprehensive Income		3,000

To revalue the options to their fair market value, recognizing the reduction in time value and the increase in intrinsic value:

$2,200 = $3,700 current fair value of options less $1,500 balance on November 1
$800 = ($1,500 − $700 remaining) reduction in time value of options
$3,000 = 30,000 bushels × $.10 increase in intrinsic value

Note that the increase in intrinsic value is recorded in Other Comprehensive Income pending the completion of the forecasted inventory transaction. The Other Comprehensive Income account is used to "store" the intrinsic value gains or losses on cash flow hedges until they are reclassified into earnings when the hedged transaction affects earnings.

At February 1, 20X2, the end of the 90 days, the price of wheat is $2.58 per bushel. The decrease in the intrinsic value of the call options is recorded as follows:

February 1, 20X2

| (38) | Other Comprehensive Income | 600 | |
| | Purchased Call Options | | 600 |

To record the other comprehensive income, deferring the earning recognition of the loss on the purchased call options:
$600 = 30,000 bushels × ($2.58 − $2.60)

The next entry (39) recognizes the expiration of the remaining amount ($700) of the time value of the purchased call option because the option has now expired. **FASB 133** specifies that the change in the time value portion of a derivative be recognized in current earnings.

February 1, 20X2

| (39) | Loss on Hedge Activity | 700 | |
| | Purchased Call Options | | 700 |

To recognize the loss of the $700 remaining time value of the purchased call options that have now expired.

Peerless now decides to sell the contracts for their intrinsic value of $2,400 [30,000 bushels × ($2.58 − $2.50 call price)]. In addition, Peerless acquires the 30,000 bushels of wheat at the current market price of $2.58 per bushel. The next entry records the sale of the purchased call options at their current market price.

February 1, 20X2

| (40) | Cash | 2,400 | |
| | Purchased Call Options | | 2,400 |

To record the sale of the call options.

Peerless now purchases the 30,000 bushels of wheat at the current market price of $2.58 per bushel.

February 1, 20X2

| (41) | Wheat Inventory | 77,400 | |
| | Cash | | 77,400 |

Finally, Peerless later sells the wheat at a price of $100,000 and records the sale as well as the reclassification of the other comprehensive income resulting from the purchased call options. Note that the other comprehensive income is taken into income only when the underlying item enters the income stream.

| (42) | Cash | 100,000 | |
| | Sale | | 100,000 |

To record the sale of the 30,000 bushels of wheat.

| (43) | Cost of Goods Sold | 77,400 | |
| | Wheat Inventory | | 77,400 |

To recognize the cost of the wheat sold.

| (44) | Other Comprehensive Income—Reclassification | 2,400 | |
| | Cost of Goods Sold. | | 2,400 |

To reclassify into earnings the other comprehensive income from the cash flow hedge.

The reduction of the cost of goods sold increases net income for the period. The earning process for the other comprehensive income was the sale of the wheat. The hedge was successful. Peerless has a gain of $2,400 less the $1,500 it paid for the time value of the call options.

EXAMPLE OF AN OPTION CONTRACT TO HEDGE AVAILABLE-FOR-SALE SECURITIES: A FAIR VALUE HEDGE

Assume that on January 1, 20X1, Peerless purchases 100 shares of Special Foods stock at a cost of $25 per share. The company classifies these as available-for-sale securities because it does not intend to sell them in the near term. To protect itself from a decrease in the value of the investment, on December 31, 20X1, the company purchases, for a $300 premium, an at-the-money put option (i.e., option price is current market price), which gives it the right but not the obligation to sell 100 shares of Special Foods at $30 per share. The option expires on December 31, 20X3. The fair value of the investment and the option follow:

Fair Value Computations			
	December 31		
	20X1	**20X2**	**20X3**
Special Foods shares:			
Per share	$ 30	$ 29	$ 26
Total (100 shares)	3,000	2,900	2,600
Put option:			
Market value (*a*)	$ 300	$ 340	$ 400
Less: Intrinsic value (*b*)	(-0-)	(100)	(400)
Time value (*c*)	$ 300	$ 240	$ -0-

(*a*) Market value is obtained from the current market price. There is a variety of option pricing models, such as the Black-Scholes model, to estimate the value of these options.
(*b*) Intrinsic value is the difference between the current market price and the option price times the number of shares. It is easy to compute at any point in the life of the option. For example, the intrinsic value on December 31, 20X2, is ($30 option price − $29 current market price) × 100 shares.
(*c*) The time value of the option reflects the effect of discounting the expected future cash flows and a portion for the expected volatility in the price of the underlying asset. A simple way to compute the value is that it is the difference between the option's market value and its intrinsic value.

Note that the time value at December 31, 20X1, is for the entire option price because the option was purchased for the current market price. The time value decreases to zero at the end of the option because no time element remains at that expiration point and the market value of the option is then based solely on its intrinsic value. Peerless exercises the option just before its expiration on December 31, 20X3, and delivers the Special Foods shares to the option writer.

Peerless determines the hedge effectiveness based on the changes in the option's intrinsic value. This is an acceptable method for determining effectiveness using options because of the ultimate value of the option being based on the price of the underlying asset in this example, the stock of Special Foods.

Hedge Effectiveness Analysis			
Date	**Change in Option's Intrinsic Value (Gain) Loss**	**Change in Value of Special Foods Shares (Gain) Loss**	**Effectiveness Ratio for Period**
December 31, 20X2	$(100)	$100	1.00
December 31, 20X3	$(300)	$300	1.00

An overview of this hedge is:

Hedging instrument	Put option on Special Foods stock
Hedged item	100 shares of Special Foods stock
Type of hedge	Fair value hedge
Underlying	Price of a share of Special Foods stock
Notional amount	100 shares of Special Foods stock
Time value at origin of hedge	$300, at the money
Valuation of put option	Fair value
If underlying increases in value	Put option decreases in value
If underlying decreases in value	Put option increases in value

Gain or loss on hedge:

Effective portion	To current earnings; related to change in intrinsic value of hedge
Ineffective portion	To current earnings; related to change in time value of hedge

The entries for this example follow:

January 1, 20X1

(45)	Available-for-Sale Securities	2,500	
	Cash		2,500

Acquire 100 shares of Special Foods stock
at a price of $25 per share.

December 31, 20X1

(46)	Available-for-Sale Securities	500	
	Other Comprehensive Income		500

Mark to market of $30 the Special Foods stock
and recognize the other comprehensive income
in accordance with **FASB 115**:
$500 = ($30 − $25) × 100 shares

(47)	Put Option	300	
	Cash		300

Purchase put option, at the money,
to sell 100 shares of Special Foods at $30.
This $300 is the time value of the option.

Note that **FASB 133** amends **FASB 115** and requires the gain or loss on an available-for-sale security designated as a hedged item to be recognized in current earnings during the period. In entry (46), the marked-to-market value for the available-for-sale securities was recognized in other comprehensive income, in accordance with **FASB 115**. As can be seen in entry (48), once available-for-sale securities are hedged in a fair value hedge, the gain or loss on marking to market must be taken to earnings for the period.

(48)	Loss on Hedge Activity	100	
	Available-for-Sale Securities		100

Record decrease in fair value for the Special Foods
stock in accordance with **FASB 133**:
$100 = ($30 − $29) × 100 shares

FASB 133 specifies that the change in intrinsic value of fair value hedges be recognized currently in net earnings of the period. This is different from cash flow hedges in which the changes in intrinsic value were taken to other comprehensive income. Therefore, entry (49) recognizes the increase in the intrinsic value of this fair value hedge as a gain that will be closed to Retained Earnings.

December 31, 20X2

(49)	Put Option	100	
	Gain on Hedge Activity		100

Record increase in the intrinsic value of the put option.

(50)	Loss on Hedge Activity	60	
	Put Option		60

To record in earnings the ineffective portion of the change in
the fair value of the put options (i.e., the change in the time value).
$60 = $300 initial time value − $240 remaining time value

The entries for December 31, 20X3, continue the valuation process.

December 31, 20X3

(51)	Loss on Hedge Activity	300	
	Available-for-Sale Securities		300
	Mark to market of $26 the Special Foods stock and recognize the loss in earnings: $300 = ($26 − $29) × 100 shares		
(52)	Put Option	300	
	Gain on Hedge Activity		300
	Record the increase in the intrinsic value of the put option.		
(53)	Loss on Hedge Activity	240	
	Put Option		240
	Record in earnings the ineffective portion of the change in fair value of the put option (i.e., the change in the time value).		

Entry (53) eliminates the remainder of the option's time value which was initially $300. Entry (50) took $60 of the time value of the option against earnings of 20X2. Entry (53) takes the remainder into earnings of 20X3 because at the end of the option period, no time value remains. The only value of the put option at its term date is its intrinsic value.

(54)	Cash	3,000	
	Put Option		400
	Available-for-Sale Securities		2,600
	Exercise the put option and delivery of the securities at a price of $30 per share.		
(55)	Other Comprehensive Income	500	
	Realized Gain on Sale of Securities		500
	Reclassify the other comprehensive income on Special Foods stock that was recorded on Dec. 31, 20X1, to earnings because the securities have now been sold. $100 = ($30 − 2 $29) × 100 shares		

It is also important to note that **FASB 133** does not permit hedge accounting for hedges of trading securities. **FASB 115** requires that trading securities be marked to market with the gain or loss reported in net earnings for the period. Therefore, any gains or losses on financial instruments that are planned to hedge the risks of holding trading securities are always taken to net earnings for the period.

An overview of the journal entries made for the hedged available-for-sale securities and for the hedging put option is presented in Figure 11–11.

EXAMPLE OF AN INTEREST-RATE SWAP TO HEDGE VARIABLE-RATE DEBT: A CASH FLOW HEDGE

Assume that on June 30, 20X1, Peerless borrows $5,000,000 of three-year, variable-rate debt with interest payments equal to the six-month U.S.$LIBOR (London Interbank Offered Rate) for the prior six months. The debt is not prepayable. The company then enters into a three-year interest-rate swap with First Bank to convert the debt's variable rate to a fixed rate. The swap agreement specifies that Peerless will pay interest at a fixed rate of 7.5 percent and receive interest at a variable rate equal to the six-month U.S.$LIBOR rate based on the notional amount of $5,000,000. Both the debt and the swap require interest to be paid semiannually on June 30 and December 31. Peerless specifies the swap as a cash flow hedge. A schematic of the swap relationships is presented in Figure 11–12.

FIGURE 11–11   Journal Entries for a Fair Value Hedge of Available-for-Sale Securities

| Entries for Available-for-Sale Securities (hedged item) | | | Entries for Put Option Contract (hedging instrument) | | |

January 1, 20X1. Acquire 100 shares of Special Foods stock as available-for-sale security.
| (45) Available-for-Sale Securities | 2,500 | | | | |
| Cash | | 2,500 | | | |

December 31, 20X1. Revalue available-for-sale securities to market value in accordance with **FASB 115** and purchase put option for current market price of underlying.
| (46) Available-for-Sale Securities | 500 | | (47) Put Option | 300 | |
| Other Comprehensive Income | | 500 | Cash | | 300 |

December 31, 20X2. Revalue available-for-sale securities in accordance with **FASB 133** and adjust put option to current market value for increases in $100 intrinsic value and $60 reduction in time value of option.
(48) Loss on Hedge Activity	100		(49) Put Option	100	
Available-for-Sale Securities		100	Gain on Hedge Activity		100
			(50) Loss on Hedge Activity	60	
			Put Option		60

December 31, 20X3. Revalue available-for-sale securities and adjust put option to current market value for the $300 increase in intrinsic value and the $240 reduction in time value of the option.
(51) Loss on Hedge Activity	300		(52) Put Option	300	
Available-for-Sale Securities		300	Gain on Hedge Activity		300
			(53) Loss on Hedge Activity	240	
			Put Option		240

December 31, 20X3. Exercise put option and deliver 100 shares of stock at a $30 per share price. Reclassify other comprehensive income recognized in (46) on available-for-sale securities now sold.
(54) Cash	3,000				
Put Option		400			
Available-for-Sale Securities		2,600			
(55) Other Comprehensive Income	500				
Realized Gain on Sale of Securities		500			

FIGURE 11–12
Fixed for Variable Interest-Rate Swap on $5,000,000 Notional Amount

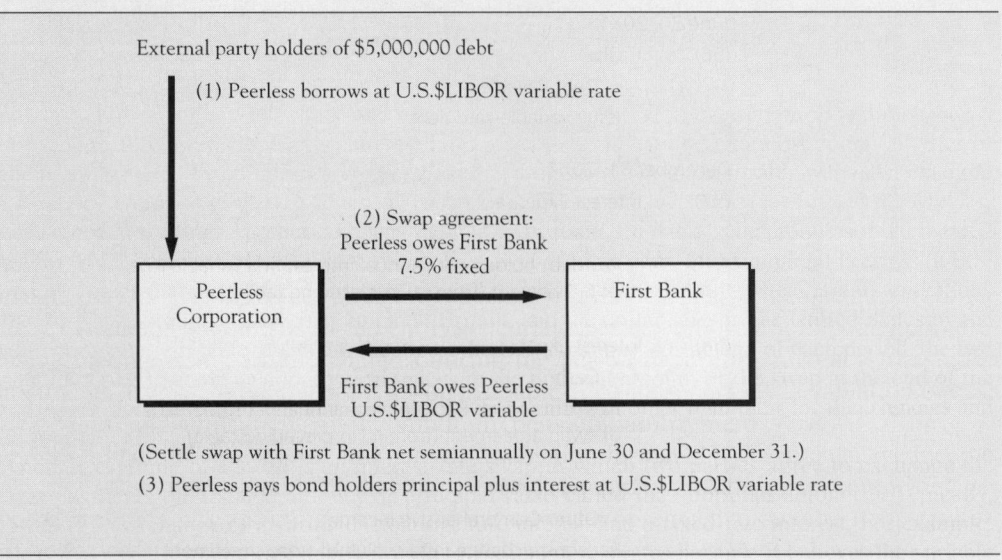

External party holders of $5,000,000 debt

(1) Peerless borrows at U.S.$LIBOR variable rate

(2) Swap agreement:
Peerless owes First Bank
7.5% fixed

Peerless Corporation   First Bank

First Bank owes Peerless
U.S.$LIBOR variable

(Settle swap with First Bank net semiannually on June 30 and December 31.)

(3) Peerless pays bond holders principal plus interest at U.S.$LIBOR variable rate

The six-month U.S.$LIBOR rate and the market value of the swap agreement, as determined by a swap broker, follow for the first year of the swap agreement:

Date	Six-Month U.S. $LIBOR Rate	Swap Agreement Fair Value Asset (Liability)
June 30, 20X1	6.0%	$ -0-
December 31, 20X1	7.0	165,000
June 30, 20X2	5.5	(70,000)

Note that Peerless must still pay the variable interest to the holders of the $5,000,000 debt. The interest-rate swap is just between Peerless and First Bank. The estimate of the fair value of the swap agreement was obtained from a broker-dealer of interest-rate swap agreements. Note that the value of the swap agreement to Peerless is positive if it believes that the variable rate will rise to higher than the fixed rate, but the swap agreement's value to Peerless is negative if it believes that the variable rate will remain lower than the fixed rate. Peerless's payments on the variable-rate debt and the net payments to First Bank on the interest-rate swap agreement are presented for the initial two semiannual periods:

	Interest Payments	
	December 31, 20X1	June 30, 20X2
Variable-rate interest payment	$150,000 (a)	$175,000 (b)
Interest-rate swap net payment	37,500 (c)	12,500
Total cash payment	$187,500 (d)	$187,500

(a) $150,000 = $5,000,000 × .06 × 6/12 months
(b) $175,000 = $5,000,000 × .07 × 6/12 months
(c) $37,500 = net payment required to First Bank for difference between variable and fixed interest rates
(d) $187,500 = $5,000,000 × .075 fixed rate × 6/12 months

Peerless recognizes interest expense based on the two factors of the variable rate plus the net payment or receipt from the swap agreement. In essence, Peerless has an interest expense equal to 7.5 percent of the notional amount of $5,000,000.

The entries to account for the first year of the interest-rate swap follow:

June 30, 20X1

(56)	Cash	5,000,000	
	Debt Payable		5,000,000
	Issue variable-rate debt.		

December 31, 20X1

(57)	Interest Expense	150,000	
	Cash		150,000
	Pay debt holders semiannual interest at a variable rate of 6.0 percent (from [a] in preceding table).		

(58)	Interest Expense	37,500	
	Cash		37,500
	Payment to First Bank for semiannual net settlement of swap agreement (from [c] in preceding table).		

(59)	Swap Agreement	165,000	
	Other Comprehensive Income		165,000
	Recognize change in fair value of swap agreement to other comprehensive income because the swap is a cash flow hedge.		

June 30, 20X2

(60)	Interest Expense	175,000	
	Cash		175,000
	Pay debt holders semiannual interest at a		
	variable rate of 7.0 percent (from [b] in preceding table).		

(61)	Interest Expense	12,500	
	Cash		12,500
	Payment to First Bank for semiannual		
	net settlement of swap agreement		

(62)	Other Comprehensive Income	235,000	
	Swap Agreement		235,000
	Recognize decrease in fair value of swap agreement		
	from $165,000 asset to $(70,000) liability to		
	Other Comprehensive Income because the		
	swap is a cash flow hedge.		

The swap agreement is reported on the balance sheet at its fair value. The amounts accumulated in Other Comprehensive Income are indirectly recognized in Peerless's earnings as periodic settlements of the payments required under the swap agreement are made, and the fair value of the swap agreement reaches zero at the end of the term of the agreement.

REPORTING AND DISCLOSURE REQUIREMENTS: DISCLOSURES ABOUT FAIR VALUE OF FINANCIAL INSTRUMENTS

FASB Statement No. 107, "Disclosures about Fair Value of Financial Instruments" (FASB 107), required disclosure of information pertaining to all financial instruments. This standard is the first to require information with respect to the current fair value of the financial instruments. Estimating fair value is of great practical difficulty because many financial instruments do not have a readily traded market from which to determine their value. Estimation methods are permitted, but if no estimation can be made, the reasons for the impracticality must be disclosed.

FASB 107 does not permit the fair values of derivatives to be netted or aggregated with nonderivative financial instruments. The required disclosures are as follows:

1. The fair value based on quoted market prices. If fair value is not quoted, then a practical estimation is allowed.
2. Information relevant to the fair value such as carrying value, effective interest rate, maturity, and reasons why it is not practical to estimate, if such is the case.
3. Distinction between instruments held for trading or nontrading purposes.

FASB 133 added a number of disclosures regarding derivatives and financial instruments. The company holding or issuing derivatives must disclose both its objectives for holding or issuing the instruments and the face or contract amount of the derivatives. The company must also distinguish between derivatives designated as fair value hedges, as cash flow hedges, as hedges of the foreign currency exposure of a net investment in a foreign operation, and all other derivatives. Specific disclosures are required for each type of hedge, but generally the company must disclose the purpose of the activity, the amount of any gains or losses recognized during the period (either in earnings or in other comprehensive income), and where those gains or losses and related assets and liabilities are reported in the statement of income and statement of financial position.

Companies operating internationally have increased risks when transacting in more than one currency. For that reason, a number of financial instruments are used in order to manage the increased risk. Chapter 11 presented the most commonly used financial instrument, the foreign currency forward exchange contract. This appendix briefly discussed several of the other major financial instruments used by multinational companies. It is certain that increased sophistication of the types of risk management tools will continue to occur in the business arena, and accountants must continue their efforts to understand and account for these instruments.

Questions

Q11-1   Explain the difference between indirect and direct exchange rates.

Q11-2   What is the direct exchange rate if a U.S. company receives $1.3623 in Canadian currency in exchange for $1.00 in U.S. currency?

Q11-3   The U.S. dollar strengthened against the European euro. Will imports from Europe into the United States be more expensive or less expensive in U.S. dollars? Explain.

Q11-4   Differentiate between a foreign transaction and a foreign currency transaction. Give an example of each.

Q11-5   What types of economic factors affect currency exchange rates? Give an example of a change in an economic factor that results in a weakening of the local currency unit versus a foreign currency unit.

Q11-6   How are assets and liabilities denominated in a foreign currency measured on the transaction date? On the balance sheet date?

Q11-7   When are foreign currency transaction gains or losses recognized in the financial statements? Where are these gains or losses reported in the financial statements?

Q11-8   Sun Company, a U.S. corporation, has an account payable of $200,000 denominated in Canadian dollars. If the direct exchange rate increases, will Sun experience a foreign currency transaction gain or loss on this payable?

Q11-9   What are some ways a U.S. company can manage the risk of changes in the exchange rates for foreign currencies?

Q11-10   Distinguish between an exposed net asset position and an exposed net liability position.

Q11-11   Explain why a difference usually exists between a currency's spot rate and forward rate. Give two reasons this difference is usually positive when a company enters into a contract to receive foreign currency at a future date.

Q11-12   A forward exchange contract may be used (*a*) to manage an exposed foreign currency position, (*b*) to hedge an identifiable foreign currency commitment, (*c*) to hedge a forecasted foreign currency transaction, or (*d*) to speculate in foreign currency markets. What are the main differences in accounting for these four uses?

Q11-13   How—if at all—should the following items be reported on the financial statements?

    a. Foreign Currency Receivable from Broker
    b. Foreign Currency Transaction Loss
    c. Foreign Currency Transaction Gain
    d. Dollars Payable to Exchange Broker
    e. Premium on Forward Contract
    f. Foreign Currency Units
    g. Accounts Payable (denominated in a foreign currency)

Cases

C11-1   **Effects of Changing Exchange Rates**

Analysis

Since the early 1970s, the U.S. dollar has both increased and decreased in value against other currencies such as the Japanese yen, the Swiss franc, and the British pound. The value of the U.S. dollar, as well as the value of currencies of other countries, is determined by the balance between the demand for and the supply of the currency on the foreign exchange markets. A drop in the value of the U.S. dollar has a widespread impact not only on consumers and businesses that deal with their counterparts overseas but also on consumers and businesses that operate solely within the United States.

Required

a. Identify the factors that influence the demand for and supply of the U.S. dollar on the foreign exchange markets.

b. Explain the effect a drop in value of the U.S. dollar in relation to other currencies on the foreign exchange markets has on:

    (1) The sales of a U.S. business firm that exports part of its output to foreign countries.

    (2) The costs of a U.S. business firm that imports from foreign countries part of the inputs used in the manufacture of its products.

c. Explain why and how consumers and business firms that operate solely within the United States are affected by the drop in value of the U.S. dollar in relation to other currencies on the foreign exchange markets.

C11-2 **Reporting a Foreign Currency Transaction on the Financial Statements [AICPA Adapted]**

Judgment

On November 30, 20X5, Bow Company received goods with a cost denominated in pounds. During December 20X5, the dollar's value declined relative to the pound. Bow believes that the original exchange rate will be restored by the time payment is due in 20X6.

Required

a. State how Bow should report the impact, if any, of the changes in the exchange rate of the dollar and the pound on its 20X5 financial statements.

b. Explain why the reporting is appropriate.

C11-3 **Changing Exchange Rates**

Research

Using the library or electronic resources, obtain and or prepare charts of the monthly average direct exchange rates for the past two years for the U.S. dollar versus (1) the Japanese yen, (2) the European euro, (3) the British pound, and (4) the Mexican peso. Your four charts should each have time on the horizontal axis and the direct exchange rate on the horizontal axis.

Questions for Discussion

a. Has the dollar strengthened or weakened during this time against each of the currencies?

b. What major economic or political factors could have caused the changes in the four foreign currencies' exchange rates versus the U.S. dollar?

c. Select one major factor from part (*b*) for each currency and present an argument showing how a change in that factor could cause the change in the exchange rate.

C11-4 **Accounting for Foreign Currency–Denominated Accounts Payable**

Mardi Gras Corporation operates a group of specialty shops throughout the southeastern United States. The shops have traditionally stocked and sold kitchen and bath products manufactured in the United States. This year, Mardi Gras has established a business relationship with a manufacturing company in Lucerne, Switzerland, to purchase a line of luxury bath products to sell in its shops. As part of the business arrangement, payments by Mardi Gras are due 30 days after receipt of the merchandise, whose cost is quoted and payable in Swiss francs.

Research
FARS

Mardi Gras records the purchases in inventory when it receives the merchandise and records a liability to the Swiss company, using the exchange rate for Swiss francs on the date the inventory purchase is recorded. When payment is made, Mardi Gras debits or credits to inventory any difference between the liability previously recorded and the dollar amount required to settle the liability in Swiss francs. Mardi Gras uses a perpetual inventory system and the FIFO method of inventory costing and can easily trace these adjustments to the specific inventory purchased.

Required

Obtain the most current accounting standards on accounting for foreign currency transactions. You can obtain access to accounting standards through the Financial Accounting Research System (FARS), from your library, or from some other source. As a staff accountant with the public accounting firm that audits Mardi Gras' annual financial statements, write a memo to Marie Lamont, the manager in charge of the audit, discussing the client's accounting for its transactions with the Swiss company. Support any recommendations with citations and quotations from the authoritative financial reporting standards.

C11-5 **Accounting for Foreign Currency Forward Contracts**

Avanti Corporation is a small Midwestern company that manufactures wooden furniture. Tim Martin, Avanti's president, has decided to expand operations significantly and has entered into a contract with a German company to purchase specialty equipment for the expansion in manufacturing capacity. The contract fixes the price of the equipment at 4.5 million euros, and the equipment will be delivered in five months with payment due 30 days after delivery.

Research
FARS

Tim is concerned that the value of the euro versus the U.S. dollar could increase during the six months between the date of the contract and the date of payment, thus increasing the effective price of the equipment to Avanti. Lindsay Williams, Avanti's treasurer, has suggested that the company enter into a forward contract to purchase 4.5 million euros in six months, thereby locking in an exchange rate for euros. Tim likes the idea of eliminating the uncertainty over the exchange rate for euros but is concerned about the effects of the forward contract on Avanti's financial statements. Because Avanti has not had previous experience with foreign currency transactions, Lindsay is unsure of what the financial statement effects are.

Required

Obtain the most current accounting standards on accounting for foreign currency forward contracts. You can obtain access to accounting standards through the Financial Accounting Research System (FARS), from your library, or from some other source. Lindsay has asked you, as her assistant, to research the accounting for a foreign currency forward contract. Write a memo to her reporting on the results of your research. Support your recommendations with citations and quotations from the authoritative financial reporting standards.

C11-6B   ### Accounting for Hedges of Available-for-Sale Securities

Rainy Day Insurance Company maintains an extensive portfolio of bond investments classified as available-for-sale securities under FASB 115. The bond investments have a variety of fixed interest rates and have maturity dates ranging from 1 to 15 years. Rainy Day acquired the bonds with the expectation that it could hold them until maturity or sell them any time that funds are required for unusually high insurance claims.

Research
FARS

   Because of the large dollar amount invested, Rainy Day is concerned about fluctuations in interest rates that affect the fair value of its bond portfolio. One of Rainy Day's investment professionals has proposed that the company invest in an interest rate futures contract to hedge its exposure to interest rate changes. Changes in the fair value of the futures contract would offset changes in the bond portfolio's fair value. If Rainy Day applies hedge accounting under FASB 133, the income statement effect of changes in the fair value of the derivative would be offset by recording in earnings the changes in the fair value of the bond portfolio attributable to the hedged (interest rate) risk.

Required

Obtain the most current accounting standards on accounting for hedges of available-for-sale securities. You can obtain access to accounting standards through the Financial Accounting Research System (FARS), from your library, or from some other source. Rainy Day's CFO, Mark Becker, has asked you, as an accountant in Rainy Day's investment division, to determine whether hedge accounting can be used in the scenario proposed. Write a memo to Mark, reporting on the results of your research. Support your recommendations with citations and quotations from the authoritative financial reporting standards.

Exercises   **E11-1**   ### Exchange Rates

Suppose the direct foreign exchange rates in U.S. dollars are:

   1 British pound = $1.60
   1 Canadian dollar = $.74

Required

a. What are the indirect exchange rates for the British pound and the Canadian dollar?

b. How many pounds must a British company pay to purchase goods costing $8,000 from a U.S. company?

c. How many U.S. dollars must be paid for a purchase costing 4,000 Canadian dollars?

E11-2   ### Changes in Exchange Rates

Upon arrival at the international airport in the country of Canteberry, Charles Alt exchanged $200 of U.S. currency into 1,000 florins, the local currency unit. Upon departure from Canteberry's international airport on completion of his business, he exchanged his remaining 100 florins into $15 of U.S. currency.

Required

a. Determine the currency exchange rates for each of the cells in the following matrix for Charles Alt's business trip to Canteberry.

b. Discuss and illustrate whether the U.S. dollar strengthened or weakened relative to the florin during Charles's stay in Canteberry.

c. Did Charles experience a foreign currency transaction gain or a loss on the 100 florins he held during his visit to Canteberry and converted to U.S. dollars at the departure date? Explain your answer.

	Arrival Date	Departure Date
Direct exchange rate		
Indirect exchange rate		

E11-3 Basic Understanding of Foreign Exposure

The Hi-Stakes Company has a number of importing and exporting transactions. Importing activities result in payables, and exporting activities result in receivables. (LCU represents the local currency unit of the foreign entity.)

Required

a. If the direct exchange rate increases, does the dollar weaken or strengthen relative to the other currency? If the indirect exchange rate increases, does the dollar weaken or strengthen relative to the other currency?

b. Indicate in the following table whether Hi-Stakes will have a foreign currency transaction gain (G), loss (L), or not be affected (NA) by changes in the direct or indirect exchange rates for each of the four situations presented.

Transaction	Settlement Currency	Direct Exchange Rate		Indirect Exchange Rate	
		Increases	**Decreases**	**Increases**	**Decreases**
Importing	Dollar	_____	_____	_____	_____
Importing	LCU	_____	_____	_____	_____
Exporting	Dollar	_____	_____	_____	_____
Exporting	LCU	_____	_____	_____	_____

E11-4 Account Balances

Merchant Company had the following foreign currency transactions:

1. On November 1, 20X6, Merchant sold goods to a company located in Munich, Germany. The receivable was to be settled in European euros on February 1, 20X7, with the receipt of €250,000 by Merchant Company.

2. On November 1, 20X6, Merchant purchased machine parts from a company located in Berlin, Germany. Merchant is to pay €125,000 on February 1, 20X7.

The direct exchange rates are as follows:

November 1, 20X6	€1 = $.60
December 31, 20X6	€1 = $.62
February 1, 20X7	€1 = $.58

Required

a. Prepare T-accounts for the following five accounts related to these transactions: Foreign Currency Units (€), Accounts Receivable (€), Accounts Payable (€), Foreign Currency Transaction Loss, and Foreign Currency Transaction Gain.

b. Within the T-accounts you have prepared, appropriately record the following items:

1. The November 1, 20X6, export transaction (sale).
2. The November 1, 20X6, import transaction (purchase).

3. The December 31, 20X6, year-end adjustment required of the foreign currency–denominated receivable of €250,000.

4. The December 31, 20X6, year-end adjustment required of the foreign currency–denominated payable of €125,000.

5. The February 1, 20X7, adjusting entry to determine the U.S. dollar–equivalent value of the foreign currency receivable on that date.

6. The February 1, 20X7, adjusting entry to determine the U.S. dollar–equivalent value of the foreign currency payable on that date.

7. The February 1, 20X7, settlement of the foreign currency receivable.

8. The February 1, 20X7, settlement of the foreign currency payable.

E11-5 **Determining Year-End Account Balances for Import and Export Transactions**

Delaney Inc. has several transactions with foreign entities. Each transaction is denominated in the local currency unit of the country in which the foreign entity is located. For each of the following independent cases, determine the December 31, 20X2, year-end balance in the appropriate accounts for the case. Write "NA" for "not applicable" in the space provided in the following chart if that account is not relevant to the specific case.

Case 1. On November 12, 20X2, Delaney purchased goods from a foreign company at a price of LCU 40,000 when the direct exchange rate was 1 LCU = $.45. The account has not been settled as of December 31, 20X2, when the exchange rate has decreased to 1 LCU = $.40.

Case 2. On November 28, 20X2, Delaney sold goods to a foreign entity at a price of LCU 20,000 when the direct exchange rate was 1 LCU = $1.80. The account has not been settled as of December 31, 20X2, when the exchange rate has increased to 1 LCU = $1.90.

Case 3. On December 2, 20X2, Delaney purchased goods from a foreign company at a price of LCU 30,000 when the direct exchange rate was 1 LCU = $.80. The account has not been settled as of December 31, 20X2, when the exchange rate has increased to 1 LCU = $.90.

Case 4. On December 12, 20X2, Delaney sold goods to a foreign entity at a price of LCU 2,500,000 when the direct exchange rate was 1 LCU = $.003. The account has not been settled as of December 31, 20X2, when the exchange rate has decreased to 1 LCU = $.0025.

Required

Provide the December 31, 20X2, year-end balances on Delaney's records for each of the following applicable items:

	Accounts Receivable	Accounts Payable	Foreign Currency Transaction Exchange Loss	Foreign Currency Transaction Exchange Gain
Case 1	_____	_____	_____	_____
Case 2	_____	_____	_____	_____
Case 3	_____	_____	_____	_____
Case 4	_____	_____	_____	_____

E11-6 **Transactions with Foreign Companies**

Harris Inc. had the following transactions:

1. On May 1, Harris purchased parts from a Japanese company for a U.S. dollar equivalent value of $8,400 to be paid on June 20. The exchange rates were:

May 1	1 yen = $.0070
June 20	1 yen = .0075

2. On July 1, Harris sold products to a Brazilian customer for a U.S. dollar equivalent of $10,000, to be received on August 10. Brazil's local currency unit is the real. The exchange rates were:

July 1	1 real = $.20
August 10	1 real = .22

Required

a. Assume that the two transactions are denominated in U.S. dollars. Prepare the entries required for the dates of the transactions and their settlement in U.S. dollars.

b. Assume that the two transactions are denominated in the applicable local currency units of the foreign entities. Prepare the entries required for the dates of the transactions and their settlement in the local currency units of the Japanese company (yen) and the Brazilian customer (real).

E11-7 Foreign Purchase Transaction

On December 1, 20X1, Rone Imports, a U.S. company, purchased clocks from Switzerland for 15,000 francs (SFr), to be paid on January 15, 20X2. Rone's fiscal year ends on December 31, and its reporting currency is the U.S. dollar. The exchange rates are:

December 1, 20X1	1 SFr = $.70
December 31, 20X1	1 SFr = .66
January 15, 20X2	1 SFr = .68

Required

a. In which currency is the transaction denominated?

b. Prepare journal entries for Rone to record the purchase, the adjustment on December 31, and the settlement.

E11-8 Adjusting Entries for Foreign Currency Balances

Chocolate De-lites imports and exports chocolate delicacies. Some transactions are denominated in U.S. dollars and others in foreign currencies. A summary of accounts receivable and accounts payable on December 31, 20X6, before adjustments for the effects of changes in exchange rates during 20X6, follows:

Accounts receivable:	
In U.S. dollars	$164,000
In 475,000 Egyptian pounds (E£)	$ 73,600
Accounts payable:	
In U.S. dollars	$ 86,000
In 21,000,000 yen (¥)	$175,300

The spot rates on December 31, 20X6, were:

E£1 = $.176

¥1 = $.0081

The average exchange rates during the collection and payment period in 20X7 are:

E£1 = $.18

¥1 = $.0078

Required

a. Prepare the adjusting entries on December 31, 20X6.

b. Record the collection of the accounts receivable in 20X7.

c. Record the payment of the accounts payable in 20X7.

d. What was the foreign currency gain or loss on the accounts receivable transaction denominated in E£ for the year ended December 31, 20X6? For the year ended December 31, 20X7? Overall for this transaction?

e. What was the foreign currency gain or loss on the accounts receivable transaction denominated in ¥? For the year ended December 31, 20X6? For the year ended December 31, 20X7? Overall for this transaction?

f. What was the combined foreign currency gain or loss for both transactions? What could Chocolate De-lites have done to reduce the risk associated with the transactions denominated in foreign currencies?

E11-9 Purchase with Forward Exchange Contract

Merit & Family purchased engines from Canada for 30,000 Canadian dollars on March 10, with payment due on June 8. Also, on March 10, Merit acquired a 90-day forward contract to purchase 30,000 Canadian dollars of C$1 = $.58. The forward contract was acquired to manage Merit & Family's exposed net liability position in Canadian dollars, but it was not designated as a hedge. The spot rates were:

March 10	C$1 = $.57
June 8	C$1 = $.60

Required

Prepare journal entries for Merit & Family to record the purchase of the engines, entries associated with the forward contract, and entries for the payment of the foreign currency payable.

E11-10 Purchase with Forward Exchange Contract and Intervening Fiscal Year-End

Pumped Up Company purchased equipment from Switzerland for 140,000 francs on December 16, 20X7, with payment due on February 14, 20X8. On December 16, 20X7, Pumped Up also acquired a 60-day forward contract to purchase francs at a forward rate of SFr 1 = $.67. On December 31, 20X7, the forward rate for an exchange on February 14, 20X8, is SFr 1 = $.695. The spot rates were:

December 16, 20X7	1 SFr = $.68
December 31, 20X7	1 SFr = .70
February 14, 20X8	1 SFr = .69

Part I

Assume that the forward contract is not designated as a hedge but is entered into to manage the company's foreign currency–exposed accounts payable.

a. Prepare journal entries for Pumped Up to record the purchase of equipment, all entries associated with the forward contract, the adjusting entries on December 31, 20X7, and entries to record the revaluations and payment on February 14, 20X8.

b. What was the effect on the statement of income of the foreign currency transactions, including both the accounts payable and the forward contract, for the year ended December 31, 20X7?

c. What was the overall effect on the statement of income of these transactions from December 16, 20X7, to February 14, 20X8?

Part II

Now assume the forward contract is designated as a cash flow hedge of the variability of the future cash flows from the foreign currency account payable. The company uses the forward exchange rate to assess effectiveness.

Required

Prepare journal entries for Pumped Up to record the purchase of equipment, all entries associated with the forward contract, the adjusting and reclassification entries on December 31, 20X7, and entries to record the revaluations and payment on February 14, 20X8.

E11-11 Foreign Currency Transactions [AICPA Adapted]

Select the correct answer for each of the following questions.

1. Dale Inc., a U.S. company, bought machine parts from a German company on March 1, 20X1, for 30,000 euros, when the spot rate for euros was $.4895. Dale's year-end was March 31, when the spot rate was $.4845. On April 20, 20X1, Dale paid the liability with 30,000 euros acquired at a rate of $.4945. Dale's income statements should report a foreign exchange gain or loss for the years ended March 31, 20X1 and 20X2 of:

	20X1	20X2
a.	$0	$0
b.	$0	$150 loss
c.	$150 loss	$0
d.	$150 gain	$300 loss

2. Marvin Company's receivable from a foreign customer is denominated in the customer's local currency. This receivable of 900,000 local currency units (LCU) has been translated into $315,000 on Marvin's December 31, 20X5, balance sheet. On January 15, 20X6, the receivable was collected in full when the exchange rate was 3 LCU to $1. The journal entry Marvin should make to record the collection of this receivable is:

	Debit	Credit
a. Foreign Currency Units	300,000	
Accounts Receivable		300,000
b. Foreign Currency Units	300,000	
Exchange Loss	15,000	
Accounts Receivable		315,000
c. Foreign Currency Units	300,000	
Deferred Exchange Loss	15,000	
Accounts Receivable		315,000
d. Foreign Currency Units	315,000	
Accounts Receivable		315,000

3. On July 1, 20X1, Black Company lent $120,000 to a foreign supplier, evidenced by an interest-bearing note due on July 1, 20X2. The note is denominated in the borrower's currency and was equivalent to 840,000 local currency units (LCU) on the loan date. The note principal was appropriately included at $140,000 in the receivables section of Black's December 31, 20X1, balance sheet. The note principal was repaid to Black on the July 1, 20X2, due date when the exchange rate was 8 LCU to $1. In its income statement for the year ended December 31, 20X2, what amount should Black include as a foreign currency transaction gain or loss on the note principal?

    a. $0.

    b. $15,000 loss.

    c. $15,000 gain.

    d. $35,000 loss.

4. If 1 Canadian dollar can be exchanged for 90 cents of U.S. currency, what fraction should be used to compute the indirect quotation of the exchange rate expressed in Canadian dollars?

    a. 1.10/1.

    b. 1/1.10.

    c. 1/.90.

    d. .90/1.

5. On July 1, 20X4, Bay Company borrowed 1,680,000 local currency units (LCU) from a foreign lender evidenced by an interest-bearing note due on July 1, 20X5, which is denominated in the currency of the lender. The U.S. dollar equivalent of the note principal was as follows:

Date	Amount
7/1/X4 (date borrowed)	$210,000
12/31/X4 (Bay's year-end)	240,000
7/1/X5 (date repaid)	280,000

In its income statement for 20X5, what amount should Bay include as a foreign exchange gain or loss on the note principal?

    a. $70,000 gain.

    b. $70,000 loss.

    c. $40,000 gain.

    d. $40,000 loss.

6. An entity denominated a sale of goods in a currency other than its functional currency. The sale resulted in a receivable fixed in terms of the amount of foreign currency to be received. The exchange rate between the functional currency and the currency in which the transaction was denominated changed. The effect of the change should be included as a:

   a. Separate component of stockholders' equity whether the change results in a gain or a loss.

   b. Separate component of stockholders' equity if the change results in a gain, and as a component of income if the change results in a loss.

   c. Component of income if the change results in a gain, and as a separate component of stockholders' equity if the change results in a loss.

   d. Component of income whether the change results in a gain or a loss.

7. An entity denominated a December 15, 20X6, purchase of goods in a currency other than its functional currency. The transaction resulted in a payable fixed in terms of the amount of foreign currency, and was paid on the settlement date, January 20, 20X7. The exchange rates between the functional currency and the currency in which the transaction was denominated changed at December 31, 20X6, resulting in a loss that should:

   a. Not be reported until January 20, 20X7, the settlement date.

   b. Be included as a separate component of stockholders' equity at December 31, 20X6.

   c. Be included as a deferred charge at December 31, 20X6.

   d. Be included as a component of income from continuing operations for 20X6.

E11-12 Sale in Foreign Currency

Marko Company sold spray paint equipment to Spain for 5,000,000 pesetas (P) on October 1, with payment due in six months. The exchange rates were:

October 1, 20X6	1 peseta = $.0068
December 31, 20X6	1 peseta = .0078
April 1, 20X7	1 peseta = .0076

Required

a. Did the dollar strengthen or weaken relative to the peseta during the period from October 1 to December 31? Did it strengthen or weaken between January 1 and April 1 of the next year?

b. Prepare all required journal entries for Marko as a result of the sale and settlement of the foreign transaction, assuming that its fiscal year ends on December 31.

c. Did Marko have an overall net gain or net loss from its foreign currency exposure?

E11-13 Sale with Forward Exchange Contract

Alman Company sold pharmaceuticals to a Swedish company for 200,000 kronor (SKr) on April 20, with settlement to be in 60 days. On the same date, Alman entered into a 60-day forward contract to sell 200,000 SKr at a forward rate of 1 SKr = $.167 in order to manage its exposed foreign currency receivable. The forward contract is not designated as a hedge. The spot rates were:

April 20	SKr 1 = $.170
June 19	SKr 1 = .165

Required

a. Record all necessary entries related to the foreign transaction and the forward contract.

b. Compare the effects on net income of Alman's use of the forward exchange contract versus the effects if Alman had not used a forward exchange contract.

E11-14 Foreign Currency Transactions [AICPA Adapted]

Choose the correct answer for each of the following questions.

1. On November 15, 20X3, Chow Inc., a U.S. company, ordered merchandise FOB shipping point from a German company for 200,000 euros. The merchandise was shipped and invoiced on

December 10, 20X3. Chow paid the invoice on January 10, 20X4. The spot rates for euros on the respective dates were:

November 15, 20X3	$.4955
December 10, 20X3	.4875
December 31, 20X3	.4675
January 10, 20X4	.4475

In Chow's December 31, 20X3, income statement, the foreign exchange gain is:

a. $9,600.

b. $8,000.

c. $4,000.

d. $1,600.

2. Stees Corporation had the following foreign currency transactions during 20X2. First, it purchased merchandise from a foreign supplier on January 20, 20X2, for the U.S. dollar equivalent of $90,000. The invoice was paid on March 20, 20X2, at the U.S. dollar equivalent of $96,000. Second, on July 1, 20X2, Stees borrowed the U.S. dollar equivalent of $500,000 evidenced by a note that was payable in the lender's local currency on July 1, 20X4. On December 31, 20X2, the U.S. dollar equivalents of the principal amount and accrued interest were $520,000 and $26,000, respectively. Interest on the note is 10 percent per annum. In Stees's 20X2 income statement, what amount should be included as a foreign exchange loss?

a. $0.

b. $6,000.

c. $21,000.

d. $27,000.

3. On September 1, 20X1, Cott Corporation received an order for equipment from a foreign customer for 300,000 local currency units (LCU) when the U.S. dollar equivalent was $96,000. Cott shipped the equipment on October 15, 20X1, and billed the customer for 300,000 LCU when the U.S. dollar equivalent was $100,000. Cott received the customer's remittance in full on November 16, 20X1, and sold the 300,000 LCU for $105,000. In its income statement for the year ended December 31, 20X1, Cott should report a foreign exchange gain of:

a. $0.

b. $4,000.

c. $5,000.

d. $9,000.

4. On April 8, 20X3, Trul Corporation purchased merchandise from an unaffiliated foreign company for 10,000 units of the foreign company's local currency. Trul paid the bill in full on March 1, 20X4, when the spot rate was $.45. The spot rate was $.60 on April 8, 20X3, and was $.55 on December 31, 20X3. For the year ended December 31, 20X4, Trul should report a transaction gain of:

a. $1,500.

b. $1,000.

c. $500.

d. $0.

5. On October 1, 20X5, Stevens Company, a U.S. company, contracted to purchase foreign goods requiring payment in pesos one month after their receipt in Stevens's factory. Title to the goods passed on December 15, 20X5. The goods were still in transit on December 31, 20X5. Exchange rates were 1 dollar to 22 pesos, 20 pesos, and 21 pesos on October 1, December 15, and December 31, 20X5, respectively. Stevens should account for the exchange rate fluctuations in 20X5 as

a. A loss included in net income before extraordinary items.

b. A gain included in net income before extraordinary items.

c. An extraordinary gain.

d. An extraordinary loss.

6. On October 2, 20X5, Louis Co., a U.S. company, purchased machinery from Stroup, a German company, with payment due on April 1, 20X6. If Louis's 20X5 operating income included no foreign exchange gain or loss, then the transaction could have

   a. Resulted in an extraordinary gain.

   b. Been denominated in U.S. dollars.

   c. Caused a foreign currency gain to be reported as a contra account against machinery.

   d. Caused a foreign currency translation gain to be reported as a separate component of stockholders' equity.

7. Cobb Co. purchased merchandise for 300,000 pounds from a vendor in London on November 30, 20X5. Payment in British pounds was due on January 30, 20X6. The exchange rates to purchase 1 pound were as follows:

	November 30, 20X5	December 31, 20X5
Spot rate	$1.65	$1.62
30-day rate	1.64	1.59
60-day rate	1.63	1.56

   In its December 31, 20X5, income statement, what amount should Cobb report as a foreign exchange gain?

   a. $12,000.

   b. $9,000.

   c. $6,000.

   d. $0.

E11-15   **Sale with Forward Contract and Fiscal Year-End**
Jerber Electronics Inc. sold electrical equipment to a Dutch company for 50,000 guilders (G) on May 14, with collection due in 60 days. On the same day, Jerber entered into a 60-day forward contract to sell 50,000 guilders at a forward rate of G 1 = $.541. The forward contract is not designated as a hedge. Jerber's fiscal year ends on June 30. The forward rate on June 30 for an exchange on July 13 is G 1 = $.530. The spot rates follow:

May 14	G 1 = $.530
June 30	G 1 = .534
July 13	G 1 = .525

Required

   a. Prepare journal entries for Jerber to record (1) the sale of equipment, (2) the forward contract, (3) the adjusting entries on June 30, (4) the July 13 collection of the receivable, and (5) the July settlement of the forward contract.

   b. What was the effect on the income statement in the fiscal year ending June 30?

   c. What was the overall effect on the income statement from this transaction?

   d. What would have been the overall effect on income if the forward contract had not been acquired?

E11-16A   **Hedge of a Purchase (Commitment without and with Time Value of Money Considerations)**
On November 1, 20X6, Smith Imports Inc. contracted to purchase teacups from England for 30,000 pounds (£). The teacups were to be delivered on January 30, 20X7, with payment due on March 1, 20X7. On November 1, 20X6, Smith entered into a 120-day forward contract to receive 30,000 pounds at a forward rate of £ 1 = $1.59. The forward contract was acquired to hedge the financial component of the foreign currency commitment.

Additional Information for the Exchange Rate

1. Assume the company uses the forward rate in measuring the forward exchange contract and for measuring hedge effectiveness.
2. Spot and exchange rates follow:

Date	Spot Rate	Forward Rate for March 1, 20X7
November 1, 20X6	£1 = $1.61	£1 = $1.59
December 31, 20X6	£1 = 1.65	£1 = 1.62
January 30, 20X7	£1 = 1.59	£1 = 1.60
March 1, 20X7	£1 = 1.585	

Required

a. What is Smith's net exposure to changes in the exchange rate of pounds for dollars between November 1, 20X6, and March 1, 20X7?

b. Prepare all journal entries from November 1, 20X6, through March 1, 20X7, for the purchase of the subassemblies, the forward exchange contract, and the foreign currency transaction. Assume Smith's fiscal year ends on December 31, 20X6.

Requirement (c) requires information from Appendix 11A.

c. Assume that interest is significant and the time value of money is considered in valuing the forward contract and hedged commitment. Use a 12 percent annual interest rate. Prepare all journal entries from November 1, 20X6, through March 1, 20X7, for the purchase of the subassemblies, the forward exchange contract, and the foreign currency transaction. Assume Smith's fiscal year ends on December 31, 20X7.

E11-17 Gain or Loss on Speculative Forward Exchange Contract

On December 1, 20X1, Sycamore Company acquired a 90-day speculative forward contract to sell 120,000 European euros (€) at a forward rate of €1 = $.58. The rates are as follows:

Date	Spot Rate	Forward Rate for March 1
December 1, 20X1	€1 = $.60	€1 = $.58
December 31, 20X1	€1 = .59	€1 = .56
March 1, 20X2	€1 = .57	

Required

a. Prepare a schedule showing the effects of this speculation on 20X1 income before income taxes.

b. Prepare a schedule showing the effects of this speculation on 20X2 income before income taxes.

E11-18 Speculation in a Foreign Currency

Nick Andros of Streamline Company suggested that the company speculate in foreign currency as a partial hedge against its operations in the cattle market, which fluctuates like a commodity market. On October 1, 20X1, Streamline bought a 180-day forward contract to purchase 50,000,000 yen (¥) at a forward rate of ¥1 = $.0075 when the spot rate was $.0070. Other exchange rates were as follows:

Date	Spot Rate	Forward Rate for March 31, 20X2
December 31, 20X1	$.0073	$.0076
March 31, 20X2	.0072	

Required

a. Prepare all journal entries related to Streamline Company's foreign currency speculation from October 1, 20X1, through March 31, 20X2, assuming the fiscal year ends on December 31, 20X1.

b. Did Streamline Company gain or lose on its purchase of the forward contract? Explain.

E11-19   Forward Exchange Transactions [AICPA Adapted]

Select the correct answer for each of the following questions.

1. The following information applies to Denton Inc.'s sale of 10,000 foreign currency units under a forward contract dated November 1, 20X5, for delivery on January 31, 20X6:

	11/1/X5	12/31/X5
Spot rates	$0.80	$0.83
30-day forward rate	0.79	0.82
90-day forward rate	0.78	0.81

Denton entered into the forward contract to speculate in the foreign currency. In its income statement for the year ended December 31, 20X5, what amount of loss should Denton report from this forward contract?

a. $400.

b. $300.

c. $200.

d. $0.

2. On September 1, 20X5, Johnson Inc. entered into a foreign exchange contract for speculative purposes by purchasing 50,000 European euros for delivery in 60 days. The rates to exchange U.S. dollars for euros follow:

	9/1/X5	9/30/X5
Spot rate	$.75	$.70
30-day forward rate	.73	.72
90-day forward rate	.74	.73

In its September 30, 20X5, income statement, what amount should Johnson report as foreign exchange loss?

a. $2,500.

b. $1,500.

c. $1,000.

d. $500.

Items 3 through 5 are based on the following:

On December 12, 20X5, Dahl Company entered into three forward exchange contracts, each to purchase 100,000 francs in 90 days. The relevant exchange rates are as follows:

	Spot Rate	Forward Rate for March 12, 20X6
December 12, 20X5	$.88	$.90
March 31, 20X2	.98	.93

3. Dahl entered into the first forward contract to manage the foreign currency risk from a purchase of inventory in November 20X5, payable in March 20X6. The forward contract is not designated

as a hedge. At December 31, 20X5, what amount of foreign currency transaction gain should Dahl include in income from this forward contract?

a. $0.

b. $3,000.

c. $5,000.

d. $10,000.

4. Dahl entered into the second forward contract to hedge a commitment to purchase equipment being manufactured to Dahl's specifications. At December 31, 20X5, what amount of foreign currency transaction gain should Dahl include in income from this forward contract?

a. $0.

b. $3,000.

c. $5,000.

d. $10,000.

5. Dahl entered into the third forward contract for speculation. At December 31, 20X5, what amount of foreign currency transaction gain should Dahl include in income from this forward contract?

a. $0.

b. $3,000.

c. $5,000.

d. $10,000.

Problems P11-20 Multiple-Choice Questions on Foreign Currency Transactions

Jon-Jan Restaurants purchased green rice, a special variety of rice, from China for 100,000 renminbi on November 1, 20X8. Payment is due on January 30, 20X9. On November 1, 20X8, the company also entered into a 90-day forward contract to purchase 100,000 renminbi. The forward contract is not designated as a hedge. The rates were as follows:

Date	Spot Rate	Forward Rate
November 1, 20X8	$.120	$.126 (90 days)
December 31, 20X8	.124	.129 (30 days)
January 30, 20X9	.127	

Required

Select the correct answer for each of the following questions.

1. The entry on November 1, 20X8, to record the forward contract includes a:

a. Debit to Foreign Currency Receivable from Exchange Broker, 100,000 renminbi.

b. Debit to Foreign Currency Receivable from Exchange Broker, $12,600.

c. Credit to Premium on Forward Contract, $600.

d. Credit to Dollars Payable to Exchange Broker, $12,600.

2. The entries on December 31, 20X8, include a:

a. Debit to Financial Expense, $300.

b. Credit to Foreign Currency Payable to Exchange Broker, $300.

c. Debit to Foreign Currency Receivable from Exchange Broker, $300.

d. Debit to Foreign Currency Receivable from Exchange Broker, $12,600.

3. The entries on January 30, 20X9, include a:

a. Debit to Dollars Payable to Exchange Broker, $12,000.

b. Credit to Cash, $12,600.

c. Credit to Premium on Forward Contract, $600.

d. Credit to Foreign Currency Receivable from Exchange Broker, $12,600.

4. The entries on January 30, 20X9, include a:

   a. Debit to Financial Expense, $400.

   b. Debit to Dollars Payable to Exchange Broker, $12,600.

   c. Credit to Foreign Currency Units (renminbi), $12,600.

   d. Debit to Foreign Currency Payable to Exchange Broker, $12,700.

5. The entries on January 30, 20X9, include a:

   a. Debit to Foreign Currency Units (renminbi), $12,700.

   b. Debit to Dollars Payable to Exchange Broker, $12,700.

   c. Credit to Foreign Currency Transaction Gain, $100.

   d. Credit to Foreign Currency Receivable from Exchange Broker, $12,600.

P11-21 **Foreign Sales**

Tex Hardware sells many of its products overseas. The following are some selected transactions.

1. Tex sold electronic subassemblies to a firm in Denmark for 120,000 Danish krones (Dkr) on June 6, when the exchange rate was Dkr 1 = $.1750. Collection was made on July 3, when the rate was Dkr 1 = $.1753.

2. On July 22, Tex sold copper fittings to a company in London for 30,000 pounds (£), with payment due on September 20. Also, on July 22, Tex entered into a 60-day forward contract to sell 30,000 pounds at a forward rate of £ 1 = $1.630. The spot rates follow:

July 22	£1 = $1.580
September 20	£1 = $1.612

3. Tex sold storage devices to a Canadian firm for C$70,000 (Canadian dollars) on October 11, with payment due on November 10. On October 11, Tex entered into a 30-day forward contract to sell Canadian dollars at a forward rate of C$1 = $.730. The forward contract is not designated as a hedge. The spot rates were as follows:

October 11	C$1 = $.7350
November 10	C$1 = $.7320

Required

Prepare journal entries to record Tex's foreign sales of its products, use of forward contracts, and settlements of the receivables.

P11-22 **Foreign Currency Transactions**

Globe Shipping, a U.S. company, is an importer and exporter. The following are some transactions with foreign companies.

1. Globe sold blue jeans to a South Korean importer on January 15 for $7,400, when the exchange rate was KRW 1 = $.185. Collection, in dollars, was made on March 15, when the exchange rate was $.180.

2. On March 8, Globe purchased woolen goods from Ireland for 7,000 pounds (IR£). The exchange rate was IR£1 = $1.68 on March 8, but the rate was $1.66 when payment was made on May 1.

3. On May 12, Globe signed a contract to purchase toys made in Taiwan for 80,000 Taiwan dollars (NT$). The toys were to be delivered 80 days later on August 1, and payment was due on September 9, which was 40 days after delivery. On May 12, Globe also entered into a 120-day undesignated forward contract to buy 80,000 Taiwan dollars at a forward rate of NT$1 = $.0376. On August 1, the forward rate for a September 9 exchange is NT $1 = $.0378. The spot rates were as follows:

May 12	NT$1 = $.0370
August 1	NT$1 = .0375
September 9	NT$1 = .0372

4. Globe sold microcomputers to a German enterprise on June 6 for 150,000 euros. Payment was due in 90 days, on September 4. On July 6, Globe entered into a 60-day undesignated forward contract to sell 150,000 euros at a forward rate of €1 = $.580. The spot rates follow:

June 6	€1 = $.600
July 6	€1 = .590
September 4	€1 = .585

Required

Prepare all necessary journal entries for Globe to account for the foreign transactions, including the sales and purchases of inventory, forward contracts, and settlements.

P11-23A **Comprehensive Problem: Four Uses of Forward Exchange Contracts without and with Time Value of Money Considerations**

On December 1, 20X1, Micro World, Inc., entered into a 120-day forward contract to purchase 100,000 Australian dollars (A$). Micro World's fiscal year ends on December 31. The direct exchange rates follow:

Date	Spot Rate	Forward Rate for March 31, 20X2
December 1, 20X1	$.600	$.609
December 31, 20X1	.610	.612
January 30, 20X2	.608	.605
March 31, 20X2	.602	

Required

Prepare all journal entries for Micro World, Inc., for the following *independent* situations:

a. The forward contract was to manage the foreign currency risks from the purchase of furniture for 100,000 Australian dollars on December 1, 20X1, with payment due on March 31, 20X2. The forward contract is not designated as a hedge.

b. The forward contract was to hedge a firm commitment agreement made on December 1, 20X1, to purchase furniture on January 30, with payment due on March 31, 20X2. The derivative is designated as a fair value hedge.

c. The forward contract was to hedge an anticipated purchase of furniture on January 30. The purchase took place on January 30, with payment due on March 31, 20X2. The derivative is designated as a cash flow hedge. The company uses the forward exchange rate to measure hedge effectiveness.

d. The forward contract was for speculative purposes only.

Requirement (e) uses the material in Appendix 11A.

e. Assume that interest is significant and the time value of money is considered in valuing the forward contract. Use a 12 percent annual interest rate. Prepare all journal entries required if, as in requirement (a), the forward contract was to manage the foreign currency–denominated payable from the purchase of furniture for 100,000 Australian dollars on December 1, 20X1, with payment due on March 31, 20X2.

P11-24 **Foreign Purchases and Sales Transactions and Hedging**
Part I

Maple Company had the following export and import transactions during 20X5:

1. On March 1, Maple sold goods to a Canadian company for 30,000 Canadian dollars (C$), receivable on May 30. The spot rates for marks were C$1 = $.65 on March 1 and C$1 = $.68 on May 30.

2. On July 1, Maple signed a contract to purchase equipment from a Japanese company for 500,000 yen. The equipment was manufactured in Japan during August and was delivered to Maple on August 30, with payment due in 60 days on October 29. The spot rates for yen were ¥1 = $.102

on July 1, ¥1 = $.104 on August 30, and ¥1 = $.106 on October 29. The 60-day forward exchange rate on August 30, 20X5, was ¥1 = $.1055.

3. On November 16, Maple purchased inventory from a London company for 10,000 pounds, payable on January 15, 20X6. The spot rates for pounds were £1 = $1.65 on November 16, £1 = $1.63 on December 31, and £1 = $1.64 on January 15, 20X6. The forward rate on December 31, 20X5, for a January 15, 20X6, exchange was £1 = $1.645.

Required

a. Prepare journal entries to record Maple's import and export transactions during 20X5 and 20X6.

b. What amount of foreign currency transaction gain or loss would Maple report on its income statement for 20X5?

Part II

Assume that Maple used forward contracts to manage the foreign currency risks of all of its export and import transactions during 20X5.

1. On March 1, 20X5, Maple, anticipating a weaker Canadian dollar on the May 30, 20X5, settlement date, entered into a 90-day forward contract to sell 30,000 Canadian dollars at a forward exchange rate of C$1 = $.64. The forward contract was not designated as a hedge.

2. On July 1, 20X5, Maple, anticipating a strengthening of the yen on the October 29, 20X5, settlement date, entered into a 120-day forward contract to purchase 500,000 yen at a forward exchange rate of ¥1 = $.105. The forward contract was designated as a fair value hedge of a firm commitment.

3. On November 16, 20X5, Maple, anticipating a strengthening of the pound on the January 15, 20X6, settlement date, entered into a 60-day undesignated forward exchange contract to purchase 10,000 pounds at a forward exchange rate of £1 = $1.67.

Required

a. Prepare journal entries to record Maple's foreign currency activities during 20X5 and 20X6.

b. What amount of foreign currency transaction gain or loss would Maple report on its income statement for 20X5, if Parts I and II of this problem were combined?

c. What amount of foreign currency transaction gain or loss would Maple report on its statement of income for 20X6, if Parts I and II of this problem were combined?

P11-25 **Understanding Foreign Currency Transactions**

Dexter Inc. had the following items in its unadjusted and adjusted trial balances at December 31, 20X5:

	Trial Balances	
	Unadjusted	**Adjusted**
Accounts Receivable (denominated in Australian dollars)	$42,000	$41,700
Dollars Receivable from Exchange Broker	40,600	?
Foreign Currency Receivable from Exchange Broker	82,000	81,000
Accounts Payable (denominated in South Korean wons)	80,000	?
Dollars Payable to Exchange Broker	?	?
Foreign Currency Payable to Exchange Broker	40,600	?

Additional Information

1. On December 1, 20X5, Dexter sold goods to a company in Australia for 70,000 Australian dollars. Payment in Australian dollars is due on January 30, 20X6. On the transaction date, Dexter entered into a 60-day forward contract to sell 70,000 Australian dollars on January 30, 20X6. The 30-day forward rate on December 31, 20X5, was A$1 = $.57.

2. On October 2, 20X5, Dexter purchased equipment from a South Korean company for 400,000 South Korean wons (KRW), payable on January 30, 20X6. On the transaction date, Dexter entered into a 120-day forward contract to purchase 400,000 South Korean wons on January 30, 20X6. On December 31, 20X5, the spot rate was KRW = $.2020.

Required

Using the information contained in the trial balances, answer each of the following questions:

a. What was the indirect exchange rate for Australian dollars on December 1, 20X5? What was the indirect exchange rate on December 31, 20X5?

b. What is the balance in the account Foreign Currency Payable to Exchange Broker in the adjusted trial balance?

c. When Dexter entered into the 60-day forward contract to sell 70,000 Australian dollars, what was the direct exchange rate for the 60-day forward contract?

d. What is the amount of Dollars Receivable from Exchange Broker in the adjusted trial balance?

e. What was the indirect exchange rate for South Korean wons on October 2, 20X5? What was the indirect exchange rate on December 31, 20X5?

f. What is the balance in the account Dollars Payable to Exchange Broker in both the unadjusted and the adjusted trial balance columns?

g. When Dexter entered into the 120-day forward contract to purchase 400,000 South Korean wons, what was the direct exchange rate for the 120-day forward contract?

h. What was the Accounts Payable balance at December 31, 20X5?

P11-26   **Matching Key Terms**

Match the items in the left-hand column with the descriptions/explanations in the right-hand column.

Items	Descriptions/Explanations
1. Direct exchange rate	A. Exchange rate for immediate delivery of currencies.
2. Indirect exchange rate	B. Imports and exports whose prices are stated in a foreign
3. Managing an exposed net asset position	currency.
	C. The primary currency used by a company for performing
4. Spot rates	its major financial and operating functions.
5. Current rates	D. U.S. companies prepare their financial statements in
6. Foreign currency transaction gain	U.S. dollars.
	E. 1 European euro equals $.65.
7. Foreign currency transaction loss	F. A forward contract is entered into when receivables denominated in European euros exceed payables
8. Foreign currency transactions	denominated in that currency.
	G. Accounts that are fixed in terms of foreign currency units.
9. Hedging a firm commitment	H. 1 U.S. dollar equals 99 Japanese yen.
	I. Spot rate on the entity's balance sheet date.
10. Functional currency	J. In an export or import transaction, the date that foreign
11. Speculating in a foreign currency	currency units are received or paid, respectively.
	K. A forward contract is entered into when payables
12. Managing an exposed net liability position	denominated in British pounds exceeds receivables denominated in that currency.
13. Settlement date	L. Reported when receivables are denominated in European
14. Denominated	euros and the euro strengthens compared to the U.S. dollar.
15. Reporting currency	M. A forward contract is entered into on May 1 that hedges an import transaction to occur on July 1.
	N. Forward contract in which no hedging is intended.
	O. Reported when payables are denominated in Swiss francs and the franc strengthens compared to the U.S. dollar.

P11-27B   **Multiple-Choice Questions on Derivatives and Hedging Activities**

Select the correct answer for each of the following questions.

1. According to FASB 133, which of the following is not an underlying?

   a. A security price.

   b. A monthly average temperature.

   c. The price of a barrel of oil.

   d. The number of foreign currency units.

2. The intrinsic value of a cash flow hedge has increased since the last balance sheet date. Which of the following accounting treatments is appropriate for this increase in value?

   a. Do not record the increase in the value because it has not been realized in an exchange transaction.

   b. Record the increase in value to current earnings.

   c. Record the increase to Other Comprehensive Income.

   d. Record the increase in a deferred income account.

3. The requirements for a derivative instrument include all but which of the following?

   a. Has one or more underlyings.

   b. Has one or more notional amounts.

   c. Requires an initial net investment equal to that required for other types of contracts that would be expected to have a similar response to changes in market factors.

   d. Requires or permits net settlement.

4. A decrease in the intrinsic value of a fair value hedge is accounted for as:

   a. A decrease of current earnings.

   b. Not recorded because the exchange transaction has not yet occurred.

   c. A decrease of other comprehensive income.

   d. A liability to be offset with subsequent increases in the fair value of the hedge.

5. Changes in the fair value of the effective portion of a hedging financial instrument are recognized as a part of current earnings of the period for which of the following:

	Cash Flow Hedge	**Fair Value Hedge**
a.	Yes	Yes
b.	No	Yes
c.	Yes	No
d.	No	No

6. According to FASB 133, for which of the following is hedge accounting not allowed?

   a. A forecasted purchase or sale.

   b. Available-for-sale securities.

   c. Trading securities.

   d. An unrecognized firm commitment.

P11-28B **A Cash Flow Hedge: Use of an Option to Hedge an Anticipated Purchase**

Mega Company believes the price of oil will increase in the coming months. Therefore, it decides to purchase call options on oil as a price-risk-hedging device to hedge the expected increase in prices on an anticipated purchase of oil.

On November 30, 20X1, Mega purchases call options for 10,000 barrels of oil at $30 per barrel at a premium of $2 per barrel, with a March 1, 20X2, call date. The following is the pricing information for the term of the call:

Date	Spot Price	Futures Price (for March 1, 20X2, delivery)
November 30, 20X1	$30	$31
December 31, 20X1	31	32
March 1, 20X2	33	

The information for the change in the fair value of the options follows:

Date	Time Value	Intrinsic Value	Total Value
November 30, 20X1	$20,000	$ -0-	$20,000
December 31, 20X1	6,000	10,000	16,000
March 1, 20X2		30,000	30,000

On March 1, 20X2, Mega sells the options at their value on that date and acquires 10,000 barrels of oil at the spot price. On June 1, 20X2, Mega sells the oil for $34 per barrel.

Required

a. Prepare the journal entry required on November 30, 20X1, to record the purchase of the call options.

b. Prepare the adjusting journal entry required on December 31, 20X1, to record the change in time and intrinsic value of the options.

c. Prepare the entries required on March 1, 20X2, to record the expiration of the time value of the options, the sale of the options, and the purchase of the 10,000 barrels of oil.

d. Prepare the entries required on June 1, 20X2, to record the sale of the oil and any other entries required as a result of the option.

P11-29B **A Fair Value Hedge: Use of an Option to Hedge Available-for-Sale Securities**

On November 3, 20X2, PRD Corporation acquired 100 shares of JRS Company at a cost of $12 per share. PRD classifies them as available-for-sale securities. On this same date, PRD decides to hedge against a possible decline in the value of the securities by purchasing, at a cost of $100, an at-the-money put option to sell the 100 shares at $12 per share. The option expires on March 3, 20X3. The fair values of the investment and the options follow:

	November 3, 20X2	December 31, 20X2	March 3, 20X3
JRS Company shares			
Per share:	$ 12	$ 11	$ 10.50
Put Option (100 shares)			
Market value	$100	$140	$150
Intrinsic value	-0-	100	150
Time value	$100	$ 40	$ -0-

Required

a. Prepare the entries required on November 3, 20X2, to record the purchase of the JRS stock and the put options.

b. Prepare the entries required on December 31, 20X2, to record the change in intrinsic value and time value of the options, as well as the revaluation of the available-for-sale securities.

c. Prepare the entries required on March 3, 20X3, to record the exercise of the put option and the sale of the securities at that date.

P11-30B **Matching Key Terms—Hedging and Derivatives**

Match the items in the left-hand column with the descriptions/explanations in the right-hand column.

Items	Descriptions/Explanations
1. Put option	A. Hedge of the exposure to changes in the fair value of a recognized asset or liability or an unrecognized firm commitment.
2. Notional amount	
3. Intrinsic value	
4. Underlying	B. Hedge of the exposure to variable cash flows of a forecasted transaction.
5. Gains or losses on cash flow hedges	
	C. Derivative instrument that is part of a host contract.
6. Foreign currency hedge	D. Specified interest rate, security price, or other variable.
	E. Number of currency units, shares, bushels, or other units specified in the contract.
7. Fair value hedge	
8. Call option	F. Recognized in current earnings in the period of the change in value.
9. Effectiveness	
10. Time value	G. Recognized in Other Comprehensive Income in the period of the change in value.
11. Gains or losses on fair value hedges	
	H. Measure of the extent to which the derivative offsets the changes in the fair values or cash flows of the hedged item.

(continued)

(continued)

Items		Descriptions/Explanations
12. Cash flow hedge	I.	Hedge of the net investment in foreign operations.
13. Interest rate swap	J.	Conversion of a company's fixed-rate debt to a variable-rate debt.
14. Bifurcation		
15. Embedded derivative	K.	Option that provides the right to acquire an underlying at an exercise or strike price.
	L.	Option that provides the right to sell an underlying at an exercise or strike price.
	M.	Value of an option due to the spread between the current market price of the hedged item and the option's strike price.
	N.	Value of an option due to the opportunity to exercise the option over the term of the option period.
	O.	Process of separating the value of an embedded derivative from its host contract.

P11-31 Determining Financial Statement Amounts

Kiwi Painting Company engages in a number of foreign currency transactions in euros (€). For each of the following independent transactions, determine the dollar amount to be reported in the December 31, 2004, financial statements for the items presented in the following requirements. The relevant direct exchange rates for the euro follow:

	September 1, 2004	November 30, 2004	December 31, 2004
Spot rate	$0.95	$1.05	$0.98
Forward rate for exchange on February 1, 2005	0.97	1.03	1.01

These are the independent transactions:

1. Kiwi entered into a forward exchange contract on September 1, 2004, to be settled on February 1, 2005, to hedge a firm foreign currency commitment to purchase inventory on November 30, 2004, with payment due on February 1, 2005. The forward contract was for 20,000 euros, the agreed-upon cost of the inventory. The derivative is designated as a fair value hedge of the firm commitment.

2. Kiwi entered into a forward exchange contract on September 1, 2004, to be settled on February 1, 2005, to hedge a forecasted purchase of inventory on November 30, 2004. The inventory was purchased on November 30 with payment due on February 1, 2005. The forward contract was for 20,000 euros, the expected cost of the inventory. The derivative is designated as a cash flow hedge to be continued through to payment of the euro-denominated account payable.

3. Kiwi entered into a forward contract on November 30, 2004, to be settled on February 1, 2005, to manage the financial currency exposure of a euro-denominated accounts payable in the amount of 20,000 euros from the purchase of inventory on that date. The payable is due on February 1, 2005. The forward contract is not designated as a hedge.

4. Kiwi entered into a forward contract on September 1, 2004, to speculate on the possible changes in exchange rates between the euro and the U.S. dollar between September 1, 2004, and February 1, 2005. The forward contract is for speculation purposes and is not a hedge.

Required

Enter the dollar amount that would be shown for each of the following items as of December 31, 2004. Compute the statement amounts net. For example, if the transaction generated both a foreign currency exchange gain and a loss, specify just the net amount that would be reported in the financial statements. If no amount would be reported for an item, enter NA for Not Applicable in the space.

	Transaction			
	1	2	3	4
Forward contract receivable	_____	_____	_____	_____
Inventory	_____	_____	_____	_____
Accounts payable (€)	_____	_____	_____	_____
Foreign currency exchange gain (loss), net	_____	_____	_____	_____
Other comprehensive income gain (loss), net	_____	_____	_____	_____

Chapter Twelve

Multinational Accounting: Translation of Foreign Entity Statements

When a U.S. multinational company prepares its financial statements for reporting to its stockholders, it must include its foreign-based operations measured in U.S. dollars and reported using U.S. GAAP. These foreign operations may be subsidiaries, branches, or investments of the U.S. company. This chapter presents the translation of the financial statements of a foreign business entity into U.S. dollars, a restatement that is necessary before the statements can be combined or consolidated with the U.S. company's statements, which are already reported in dollars.

Accountants preparing financial statements must consider both the differences in accounting principles and the differences in currencies used to measure the foreign entity's operations. For example, a British subsidiary of a U.S. company provides the parent statements measured in British pounds sterling, using the British system of accounting, which is different from U.S. accounting methods and measures. The U.S. parent company must typically perform the following steps in the translation and consolidation of the British subsidiary:

1. Receive the British subsidiary's financial statements, which are reported in pounds sterling.

2. Restate the statements to conform to U.S. generally accepted accounting principles.

3. Translate the statements measured in pounds sterling into their equivalent U.S. dollar amounts. Each foreign entity account balance must be individually translated into its U.S. dollar equivalent, as follows:

$$\begin{array}{ccc} \text{Account measured} & & \text{Account measured} \\ \text{in foreign} & \times \quad \text{exchange} \quad = & \text{in U.S. dollar–} \\ \text{currency units} & \text{rate} & \text{equivalent value} \end{array}$$

4. Consolidate the translated subsidiary's accounts, which are now measured in dollars, with the parent company's accounts.

DIFFERENCES IN ACCOUNTING PRINCIPLES

Methods used to measure economic activity differ around the world. A country's economic, legal, educational, and political systems; stages of technological development or sophistication; culture and tradition; and various other socioeconomic factors all influence the development of accounting standards and the accounting profession in that nation. These differences have led to significant diversity in accounting standards from one nation to another. The lack of a uniform set of accounting standards creates problems for companies, preparers, and users. Some countries develop their accounting principles based on the information needs of the taxing authorities. Other countries have accounting principles designed to meet the needs of the central government economic planners. U.S. accounting standards focus on the information needs of the common stockholder or the creditors.

Another major financial reporting model is in the process of being developed by the International Accounting Standards Board (IASB). The IASB has a mandate to establish a set of international financial reporting standards and to encourage adoption of those standards globally. There are 14 members of the IASB, of whom 12 are full-time members (i.e., employed only by the IASB). The IASB requires that its membership be composed of the following: five former auditors, three former preparers of accounts, three former users of accounts, and one academic. The remaining two members may have any of these or other backgrounds.

The IASB promulgates International Financial Reporting Standards (IFRSs). Prior to the formation of the IASB, International Accounting Standards (IASs) were issued by the International Accounting Standards Committee. IASs were issued between 1973 and 2001. The IASB adopted all IASs and continued their development, calling new standards IFRSs. Although IASs are no longer produced, they are still in effect unless replaced by an IFRS. IFRSs are used in many countries around the world, including Singapore, Hong Kong, Russia, Australia, and South Africa. The European Commission has required all publicly listed companies in the European Union (EU) to provide their consolidated financial statements using IFRSs beginning with the year 2005. Prior to 2005 there were around 350 publicly listed companies that used IFRSs; as of 2005, the number has grown to around 7,000. The IASB Website presents a list of the countries that require or allow IFRSs for securities filings in that country.

When measured by market capitalization, U.S. GAAP is used by more than half of the world's companies. IFRSs are now also relatively widely used, given their adoption by the European Union and others. Many feel that a single set of high-quality global accounting standards would improve investor confidence in the market and serve to increase market efficiency by allowing investors to draw better comparisons among investment options from different countries.

The existence of multiple models of accounting standards has significant implications for U.S. firms. For those multinational firms with subsidiaries and branches outside of the United States, it is necessary to prepare financial statements using the financial reporting standards where each business unit is located and then translate these statements to U.S. GAAP to allow preparation of consolidated financial statements. Additionally, if U.S. companies choose to list on stock exchanges outside of the U.S., either in addition to listing on U.S. exchanges or in lieu of such listings, these companies need to prepare financial statements under the financial reporting standards required by the non-U.S exchange. Because of this, there is significant interest in minimizing the differences between U.S. GAAP and IFRS. Convergence would lower costs for issuers, since they would not have to incur the cost of preparing financial statements using different sets of accounting standards.

The FASB is working with the IASB to improve the quality of reporting standards and to "converge" the two sets of standards. In September 2002, the FASB issued "the Norwalk Agreement" in which both the FASB and the IASB pledged to work together both to improve the quality of their financial reporting standards and to converge the standards by working to minimize the differences between them. This convergence effort focuses both on the evaluation of existing standards and guidance for implementing current standards and new standards as they are developed. PricewaterhouseCoopers offers a publication on its Website entitled *Similarities and Differences—A Comparison of IFRS and U.S. GAAP* that provides a topic-based comparison. This publication can be accessed on the Web at http://www.pwc.com/extweb/pwcpublications.nsf/docid/74d6c09e0a4ee610802569a1003354c8.

Other countries are also working to converge their standards with IFRS. For example, Nippon Keidanren (Japan Business Federation), a comprehensive economic organization born in May 2002 by amalgamation of Keidanren (Japanese Federation of Economic

Organizations) and Nikkeiren (Japanese Federation of Employers' Associations) with 1306 member companies, including 91 of foreign ownership, 129 industrial organizations, and 47 regional employers' associations, supports efforts in Japan to accelerate the convergence of accounting standards and to seek mutual recognition of standards in Japan, the United States, and Europe.

Currently, the SEC requires that domestic companies prepare their financial statements under U.S. GAAP. Foreign issuers that do not use U.S. GAAP must reconcile their financial statements to U.S. GAAP and file this reconciliation on a Form 20-F. Foreign issuers, of course, also have the option of preparing their financial statements under U.S. GAAP and some do report on this basis. One goal of convergence is to eliminate the need for this reconciliation. In 2005, the SEC issued a "roadmap" describing preliminary conditions that would be necessary before this could happen. The SEC's position is that the strength of U.S. GAAP is in part due to its development and use over many decades, allowing standards to be tested and refined. Because of its widespread use, both the strengths and weaknesses of U.S. GAAP are well known. While IFRSs also constitute a comprehensive set of accounting standards, they have only existed for a few years. The SEC believes it is necessary to assess the consistency and faithfulness of IFRS interpretation and application before allowing the use of these standards without reconciliation. The SEC believes that it may be possible to eliminate the requirement for the reconciliation schedule for companies using IFRSs by 2009.

If convergence efforts are successful, it is anticipated that there will be a uniform set of international financial reporting standards that "harmonize" the best from U.S. GAAP and the IASB's IFRSs. The New York Stock Exchange, working with the International Organization of Securities Commissions (IOSCO), has continued to promote the resolution of differences in accounting and financial reporting rules, particularly between the two largest standard-setting groups, the FASB and the IASB. It is anticipated that eventually one set of international financial reporting standards will be used by companies listed on any of the major stock exchanges of the world.

A number of international firms gain access to U.S. securities markets via American Depository Receipts (ADRs), which are essentially derivative instruments representing shares of a non-U.S. company. ADRs are traded on the NYSE and other U.S. exchanges. About 15 percent of the total companies listed on the NYSE are foreign companies. The ADRs are issued by a depository bank, such as J. P. Morgan or Citibank, which holds the actual shares of the foreign company's stock. Thus, the ADRs are a security that represents the shares of a non-U.S. company. Foreign companies' ADRs traded on U.S. exchanges must be registered with the U.S. SEC, and these companies must annually file a Form 20-F to reconcile the information to U.S. GAAP.

DETERMINING THE FUNCTIONAL CURRENCY

Imagine that you received 100 British pounds sterling in payment on an account in your London subsidiary on December 31, 20X1, and deposited it a London bank. Assume that at the end of 20X1 the exchange rate is $1.80. To report the deposit on your 20X1 balance sheet stated in dollars, you would translate the deposit at the current rate and you would report an asset of $180. At the end of 20X2, assume you still have the 100 pounds sterling in the bank, but now the exchange rate is $1.70. To report the deposit on your 20X2 balance sheet, if you use the exchange rate at the end of 20X2, this amount would now translate into $170 and you would have an imbalance, also referred to as a *translation adjustment*, of $10 to deal with. If you translated at the historical rate, you would still translate into $180 and there would be no imbalance. Which is the correct exchange rate to use?

Date	Currency on Deposit	Current Exchange Rate	Dollar Equivalent
12/31/20X1	£100	$1.80	$180
12/31/20X2	100	1.70	170

Two major issues that must be addressed when financial statements are translated from a foreign currency into U.S. dollars are:

1. Which exchange rate should be used to translate foreign currency balances to domestic currency?

2. How should translation gains and losses be accounted for? Should they be included in income?

There are three possible exchange rates that may be used in converting foreign currency values to the U.S. dollar. The ***current rate*** is the exchange rate at the end of the trading day on the balance sheet date. The ***historical rate*** is the exchange rate that existed when an initial transaction took place, such as the exchange rate on the date an asset was acquired or a liability incurred. The ***average rate*** for the period is usually a simple average for a period of time and is usually the exchange rate used to measure revenues and expenses. Translation methods may employ a single rate or multiple rates. The translation adjustment created by the application of these exchange rates also must be reflected in the financial statements, either as a component of net income or a component of comprehensive income. The disposition of the translation adjustment will be discussed later in this chapter.

FASB Statement No. 52, "Foreign Currency Translation" (FASB 52) provides specific guidelines for translating a foreign currency into U.S. dollars to allow preparation of consolidated financial statements measured, or denominated, in dollars. The purpose of **FASB 52** is to present results that are directionally sympathetic to the real economic effects of exchange rate movements. Additionally, **FASB 52** seeks to preserve financial results and relationships in the foreign financial statements through the translation process. For instance, if the gross margin on sales is positive when measured in the foreign currency, it should still be positive when sales and cost of goods sold are translated into dollars. The FASB adopted the concept of the ***functional currency***, which is defined as "the currency of the primary economic environment in which the entity operates; normally that is the currency of the environment in which an entity primarily generates and receives cash."[1] The functional currency is used to differentiate between two types of foreign operations, those that are self-contained and integrated into a local environment, and those that are an extension of the parent and integrated with the parent. A U.S. company may have foreign affiliates in many different countries. Each affiliate must be analyzed to determine its individual functional currency.

Figure 12–1 presents the six indicators that must be assessed to determine an entity's functional currency: cash flows, sales prices, sales markets, expenses, financing, and intercompany transactions. If a foreign affiliate uses the local currency for most of its transactions, and if the cash generated is not regularly physically returned to the parent in the U.S., the local currency is usually the functional currency. Also, the foreign affiliate usually has active sales markets in its own country and obtains financing from local sources.

Some foreign-based entities, however, use a functional currency different from the local currency: For example, a U.S. company subsidiary in Venezuela may conduct virtually all of its business in Brazil, or a branch or a subsidiary of a U.S. company operating in Britain may well use the U.S. dollar as its major currency although it maintains its accounting records in British pounds sterling. The following factors indicate that the U.S. dollar is the functional currency for the British subsidiary: Most of its cash transactions are in U.S. dollars; its major sales markets are in the United States; production components are generally obtained from the United States; and the U.S. parent is primarily responsible for financing the British subsidiary.

The FASB adopted the functional currency approach after considering the following objectives of the translation process:

a. Provide information that is generally compatible with the expected economic effects of a rate change on an enterprise's cash flows and equity.

b. Reflect in consolidated statements the financial results and relationships of the individual consolidated entities as measured in their functional currencies in conformity with U.S. generally accepted accounting principles.[2]

---

[1] *Financial Accounting Standards Board Statement No. 52*, "Foreign Currency Translation," 1981, para. 5.
[2] *FASB 52*, para. 4.

FIGURE 12–1 Functional Currency Indicators

Indicator	Factors Indicating Foreign Currency (Local Currency) Is the Functional Currency	Factors Indicating U.S. Dollar (Parent's Currency) Is the Functional Currency
Cash flows	Primarily in foreign currency and do not affect parent's cash flows	Directly impact the parent's current cash flows and are readily available to the parent company
Sales prices	Primarily determined by local competition or local government regulation; not generally responsive to changes in exchange rates	Responsive to short-term changes in exchange rates and worldwide competition
Sales markets	Active local sales markets for company's products; possibly, significant amounts of exports	Sales markets mostly in parent's country, or sales contracts are denominated in parent's currency
Expenses	Labor, materials, and other costs are primarily local costs	Production components generally obtained from the parent company's country
Financing	Primarily obtained from, and denominated in, local currency units; entity's operations generate funds sufficient to service financing needs	Primarily from the parent, or other dollar-denominated financing
Intercompany transactions and arrangements	Few intercompany transactions with parent	Frequent intercompany transactions with parent, or foreign entity is an investment or financing arm for the parent

The functional currency approach requires the foreign entity to translate all of its transactions into its functional currency. If an entity has transactions denominated in other than its functional currency, the foreign transactions must be adjusted to their equivalent functional currency value before the company may prepare financial statements.

Functional Currency Designation in Highly Inflationary Economies

An exception to the criteria for selecting a functional currency is specified when the foreign entity is located in countries such as Argentina and Peru, which have experienced severe inflation. Severe inflation is defined as inflation exceeding 100 percent over a three-year period.[3] The FASB concluded that the volatility of hyperinflationary currencies distorts the financial statements if the local currency is used as the foreign entity's functional currency. Therefore, in cases of operations located in highly inflationary economies, the reporting currency of the U.S. parent—the U.S. dollar—should be used as the foreign entity's functional currency. This exception prevents unrealistic asset values and income statement charges if the hyperinflation is ignored and normal translation procedures are used. For example, assume that a foreign subsidiary constructed a building that cost 1,000,000 pesos when the exchange rate was \$.05 = 1 peso. Further assume that because of hyperinflation in the foreign subsidiary's country, the exchange rate becomes \$.00005 = 1 peso. The translated values of the building at the time it was constructed and after the hyperinflation follow:

Amount (pesos)	Date of Construction		After Hyperinflation	
	Rate	Translated Amount	Rate	Translated Amount
1,000,000	\$.05	\$50,000	\$.00005	\$50

The translated values after the hyperinflation do not reflect the building's market value or historical cost. Thus, the FASB required the use of the U.S. dollar as the functional currency in cases of hyperinflation to give some stability to the financial statements.

[3] *FASB 52*, para. 11.

Once a foreign affiliate's functional currency is chosen, it should be used consistently. However, if changes in economic circumstances necessitate a change in the designation of the foreign affiliate's functional currency, the accounting change should be treated as a change in estimate: current and prospective treatment only, no restatement of prior periods.

TRANSLATION VERSUS REMEASUREMENT OF FOREIGN FINANCIAL STATEMENTS

Two different methods are used to restate foreign entity statements to U.S. dollars: (1) the *translation* of the foreign entity's functional currency statements into U.S. dollars and (2) the *remeasurement* of the foreign entity's statements into the functional currency of the entity. After remeasurement, the statements must then be translated if the functional currency is *not* the U.S. dollar. No additional work is needed if the functional currency is the U.S. dollar.

Translation is the most common method used and is applied when the local currency is the foreign entity's functional currency. This is the normal case in which, for example, a U.S. company's French subsidiary uses the euro as its recording and functional currency. The subsidiary's statements must be translated from euros into U.S. dollars. To translate the financial statements, the company will use the current rate, which is the exchange rate on the balance sheet date, to convert the local currency balance sheet account balances into U.S. dollars. Any translation adjustment that occurs is a component of comprehensive income. Because revenues and expenses are assumed to occur uniformly over the period, revenues and expenses on the income statement are translated using the average rate for the reporting period. This translation method is called the *current rate method*.

Remeasurement is the restatement of the foreign entity's financial statements from the local currency that the entity used into the foreign entity's functional currency. Remeasurement is required only when the functional currency is different from the currency used to maintain the books and records of the foreign entity. For example, a relatively self-contained Canadian sales branch of a U.S. company may use the U.S. dollar as its functional currency but may select the Canadian dollar as its recording and reporting currency. Of course, if the Canadian branch uses the U.S. dollar for both its functional and reporting currency, no translation or remeasurement is necessary: Its statements are already measured in U.S. dollars and are ready to be combined with the U.S. home office statements.

The method used to remeasure the financial statements from the local currency to the functional currency is called the *temporal method*. Monetary assets and liabilities are those that represent rights to receive or obligations to pay a fixed number of foreign currency units in the future. Under the temporal method, the current rate is usually used to translate these monetary amounts to the functional currency. Nonmonetary items include fixed assets, long-term investments, and inventories. These items are usually translated at the historical rate that existed when the assets were originally purchased or the liability originally incurred. Revenues and expenses on the income statement are translated using the average rate for the reporting period. Any imbalance that occurs because of the application of the temporal method is included in the calculation of net income on the income statement.

The application of the temporal method converts a foreign currency to the functional currency. If the functional currency is the U.S. dollar, no additional adjustments are needed. If the functional currency is something other than the U.S. dollar, the current rate method must be applied to restate the financial information in U.S. dollars.

One application of remeasurement is for affiliates located in countries experiencing hyperinflation. For example, an Argentinian subsidiary of a U.S. parent records and reports its financial statements in the local currency, the Argentine peso. However, because the Argentine economy experiences inflation exceeding 100 percent over a three-year period, the U.S. dollar is specified as the functional currency for reporting purposes and the subsidiary's statements must then be remeasured from Argentine pesos into U.S. dollars.

The following table presents an overview of the methods a U.S. company would use to restate a foreign affiliate's financial statements in U.S. dollars.

Currency in Which the Foreign Affiliate's Books and Records Are Maintained	Functional Currency	Restatement Method
Local currency (i.e., currency of the country in which the foreign entity is located)	Local currency	Translate to U.S. dollars using current exchange rates
Local currency	U.S. dollar (such as required in hyperinflationary economies)	Remeasure from local currency to U.S. dollar
Local currency	Third country's currency (Not LCU or U.S. dollar)	First, remeasure from the local currency into the functional currency, then translate from functional currency to U.S. dollars
U.S. dollar	U.S. dollar	No restatement is necessary; already in U.S. dollars

The conceptual reasons for the two different methods, translation and remeasurement, come from a consideration of the primary objective of the translation process: to provide information that shows the expected impact of exchange rate changes on the U.S. company's cash flows and equity. Foreign affiliates fall into two groups. Those in the first group are relatively self-contained entities that generate and spend local currency units. The local currency is the functional currency for this group of entities. These foreign affiliates may reinvest the currency they generate or may distribute funds to their home office or parent company in the form of dividends. Exchange rate changes do not directly affect the U.S. parent company's cash flows. Rather, the rate changes affect the foreign affiliate's net assets (assets minus liabilities) and, therefore, the U.S. parent company's net investment in the entity.

The second group of foreign affiliates is made up of entities that are an extension of the U.S. company. These affiliates operate in a foreign country but are directly affected by changes in exchange rates because they depend on the U.S. economy for sales markets, production components, or financing. For this group, the U.S. dollar is the functional currency. There is a presumption that the effect of exchange rate changes on the foreign affiliate's net assets will directly affect the U.S. parent company's cash flows, so the exchange rate adjustments are reported in the U.S. parent's income.

Translation and remeasurement include different adjustment procedures and may result in significantly different consolidated financial statements. Both methods are illustrated in this chapter.

TRANSLATION OF FUNCTIONAL CURRENCY STATEMENTS INTO THE REPORTING CURRENCY OF THE U.S. COMPANY

Most business entities transact and record business activities in the local currency. Therefore, the local currency of the foreign entity is its functional currency. The translation of the foreign entity's statement into U.S. dollars is a relatively straightforward process.

The FASB believes that the underlying economic relationships presented in the foreign entity's financial statements should not be distorted or changed during the translation process from the foreign entity's functional currency into the currency of the U.S. parent. For example, if the foreign entity's functional currency statements report a current ratio of 2:1 and a gross margin of 60 percent of sales, these relationships should pass through the translation process into the U.S. parent's reporting currency. It is important to be able to evaluate the performance of the foreign entity's management with the same economic measures used to operate the foreign entity. To maintain the economic relationships in the functional currency statements, the account balances must be translated by a comparable exchange rate.

The translation is made by using the current exchange rate for *all* assets and liabilities. This rate is the spot rate on the balance sheet date. The income statement items—revenue, expenses, gains, and losses—should be translated at the exchange rate on the dates on which the underlying transactions occurred, although for practical purposes an average exchange rate for the period may be used for these items with the assumption that revenues and expenses are recognized evenly over the period. However, if a material gain or loss results from a specific event, the exchange rate on the date of the event rather than the average exchange rate should be used to translate the transaction results.

The stockholders' equity accounts, other than retained earnings, are translated at historical exchange rates. The appropriate historical rate is the rate on the latter of the date the parent company acquired the investment in the foreign entity or the date the subsidiary had the stockholders' equity transaction. This is necessary to complete the elimination of the parent company's investment account against the foreign subsidiary's capital accounts in the consolidation process. The subsidiary's translated retained earnings are carried forward from the previous period with additions for this period's income and deductions for dividends declared during the period. Dividends are translated at the exchange rate on the date of declaration. It is interesting to observe that if the foreign entity has not paid its declared dividend by the end of its fiscal period, it has a dividends payable account that is translated at the current rate. Nevertheless, the dividend deduction from Retained Earnings is translated using the exchange rate on the date of dividend declaration.

In summary, the translation of the foreign entity's financial statements from its functional currency into the reporting currency of the U.S. company is made as follows:

Income statement accounts:	
Revenue and expenses	Generally, average exchange rate for period covered by statement
Balance sheet accounts:	
Assets and liabilities	Current exchange rate on balance sheet date
Stockholders' equity	Historical exchange rates

Because various rates are used to translate the foreign entity's individual accounts, the trial balance debits and credits after translation are not equal. The balancing item to make the translated trial balance debits equal the credits is called the *translation adjustment*.

Financial Statement Presentation of Translation Adjustment

The translation adjustment resulting from the translation process is part of the entity's comprehensive income for the period. **FASB Statement No. 130**, "Reporting Comprehensive Income" (FASB 130), issued in June 1997, defined comprehensive income to include all changes in equity during a period except those resulting from investments by owners and distributions to owners. *Comprehensive income* includes net income and *"other comprehensive income"* items that are part of the changes in the net assets of a business enterprise from nonowner sources (e.g., not additional capital investments and dividends) during a period. **FASB 130** requires the reporting of comprehensive income as part of the primary financial statements of the entity. The major items comprising the other comprehensive income items are the changes during the period in foreign currency translation adjustments, unrealized gains or losses on available-for-sale securities, revaluation of cash flow hedges, and adjustments in the minimum pension liability item.

FASB 130 allows for several alternative presentation formats for comprehensive income. The single-statement, combined income approach first presents the items composing net income and then has a section presenting the other comprehensive income items. An alternative, two-statement presentation first presents the computation of net income on one statement and then a related statement that begins with net income and reconciles to comprehensive income by reporting the other comprehensive income items separately. A third alternative, used by many companies, is just to present the items composing other comprehensive income in a schedule of accumulated other comprehensive income in the consolidated statement of shareholders' equity. An entity may present the components of other comprehensive income items net of tax or show the aggregate tax effects related to the total other comprehensive income items as one amount.

Each period's other comprehensive income (OCI) is closed to accumulated other comprehensive income (AOCI), which is displayed separately from other stockholders' equity items (e.g., capital stock, additional paid-in capital, and retained earnings). An appropriate title, such as *"Accumulated Other Comprehensive Income,"* is used to describe this stockholders' equity item. The statement of changes in stockholders' equity opens with the accumulated balance of the other comprehensive income items at the beginning of the period, then includes the change in the translation adjustment and the additional other comprehensive income items during the period that were included in the period's comprehensive income, and ends with the accumulated other comprehensive income balance at the end of the period. The accumulated ending balance of the other comprehensive income items is then reported in the entity's balance sheet as part of the stockholders' equity section, usually after retained earnings. The discussion of the disclosure requirements presented later in this chapter demonstrates the financial statements for the Peerless Products Corporation example presented in the chapter.

Illustration of Translation and Consolidation of a Foreign Subsidiary

In Chapter 11, the examples illustrated the effects of a dollar that was strengthening against the euro during 20X1. In the examples for the remainder of this chapter, the dollar weakens against the euro during 20X1. Thus, in Chapters 11 and 12, changes in exchange rates in both directions will have been illustrated.

To examine the consolidation of a foreign subsidiary, assume the following facts:

1. On January 1, 20X1, Peerless, a U.S. company, purchased 100 percent of the outstanding capital stock of German Company, a firm located in Berlin, Germany, for $66,000, which is $6,000 above book value. (The proof of the differential is shown at the end of the next section of the chapter.) The excess of cost over book value is attributable to a patent amortizable over 10 years. Balance sheet accounts in a trial balance format for both companies immediately *before* the acquisition are presented in Figure 12–2.
2. The local currency for German Company is the euro (€), which is also its functional currency.
3. On October 1, 20X1, the subsidiary declared and paid dividends of €6,250.
4. The subsidiary received $4,200 in a sales transaction with a U.S. company when the exchange rate was $1.20 = €1. The subsidiary still has this foreign currency on December 31, 20X1.

FIGURE 12–2
Balance Sheet Accounts for the Two Companies on January 1, 20X1 (Immediately before Acquisition of 100 percent of German Company's Stock by Peerless Products, a U.S. Company)

	Peerless Products	German Company
Cash	$ 350,000	€ 2,500
Receivables	75,000	10,000
Inventory	100,000	7,500
Land	175,000	-0-
Plant and Equipment	800,000	50,000
Total Debits	$1,500,000	€70,000
Accumulated Depreciation	$ 400,000	€ 5,000
Accounts Payable	100,000	2,500
Bonds Payable	200,000	12,500
Common Stock	500,000	40,000
Retained Earnings, 12/31/X0	300,000	10,000
Total Credits	$1,500,000	€70,000

5. Relevant direct spot exchange rates ($/€1) are:

Date	Rate
January 1, 20X1	$1.20
October 1, 20X1	1.36
December 31, 20X1	1.40
20X1 average	1.30

Date-of-Acquisition Translation Workpaper

Figure 12–3 presents the translation of German Company's trial balance on January 1, 20X1. This illustration assumes that the subsidiary's books and records are maintained in European euros, the subsidiary's functional currency.

The translation of the subsidiary's trial balance from the functional currency (€) into dollars, the U.S. parent's reporting currency, is made using the *current rate method.* Under purchase accounting, the subsidiary's stockholders' equity accounts are translated using the current rate on the date of the parent company's purchase of the subsidiary's stock.

The entry made by Peerless Products to record the purchase of 100 percent of German Company's stock is:

January 1, 20X1

(1)	Investment in German Company Stock	66,000	
	Cash		66,000
	Purchase of German Company stock.		

The differential on January 1, 20X1, the date of acquisition, is computed as follows:

1/1/X1	(P)	Investment cost		$66,000
100%		Book value of investment:		
		Common stock	$48,000	
		Retained earnings	12,000	
		Total	$60,000	
	(G)	Percent of German Company's stock acquired by Peerless Corporation	× 1.00	
		Book value acquired by Peerless Corporation		(60,000)
		Differential (excess of cost over book value) attributable to patent		$ 6,000

FIGURE 12–3
Workpaper to Translate Foreign Subsidiary on January 1, 20X1 (Date of Acquisition) Functional Currency Is the European Euro

Item	Trial Balance, €	Exchange Rate, $/€	Trial Balance, $
Cash	2,500	1.20	3,000
Receivables	10,000	1.20	12,000
Inventory	7,500	1.20	9,000
Plant and Equipment	50,000	1.20	60,000
Total Debits	70,000		84,000
Accumulated Depreciation	5,000	1.20	6,000
Accounts Payable	2,500	1.20	3,000
Bonds Payable	12,500	1.20	15,000
Common Stock	40,000	1.20	48,000
Retained Earnings	10,000	1.20	12,000
Total Credits	70,000		84,000

Note: $1.20 is direct exchange rate on January 1, 20X1.

A graphic representation of the acquisition is as follows:

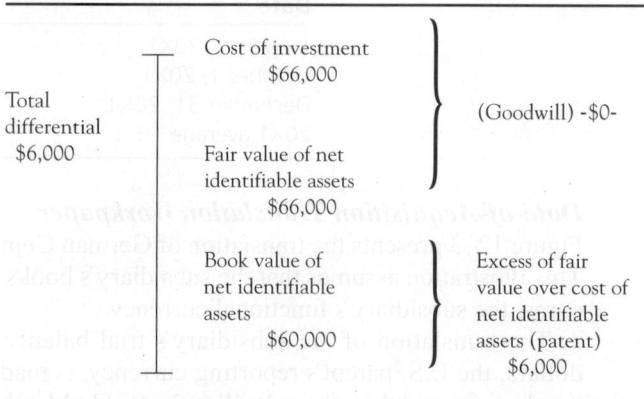

Date-of-Acquisition Consolidated Balance Sheet

The consolidated balance sheet workpaper for Peerless Products and its German subsidiary on January 1, 20X1, is presented in Figure 12–4. The consolidation process is identical to the date-of-acquisition consolidations presented in Chapter 4. The eliminating entries are as follows:

E(2)	Common Stock—German Company	48,000	
	Retained Earnings	12,000	
	Differential	6,000	
	Investment in German Company Stock		66,000
	Eliminate investment balance.		
E(3)	Patent	6,000	
	Differential		6,000
	Assign differential.		

FIGURE 12–4 January 1, 20X1, Workpaper for Consolidated Balance Sheet, Date of Acquisition
100 Percent Purchase at More than Book Value

	Peerless Products	German Company	Eliminations Debit	Eliminations Credit	Consolidated
Cash	$ 284,000	$ 3,000			$ 287,000
Receivables	75,000	12,000			87,000
Inventory	100,000	9,000			109,000
Land	175,000				175,000
Plant and Equipment	800,000	60,000			860,000
Investment in German Co. Stock	66,000			(2) 66,000	
Differential			(2) 6,000	(3) 6,000	
Patent			(3) 6,000		6,000
Total Debits	$1,500,000	$84,000			$1,524,000
Accumulated Depreciation	400,000	6,000			406,000
Accounts Payable	100,000	3,000			103,000
Bonds Payable	200,000	15,000			215,000
Common Stock	500,000	48,000	(2) 48,000		500,000
Retained Earnings	300,000	12,000	(2) 12,000		300,000
Total Credits	$1,500,000	$84,000	72,000	72,000	$1,524,000

FIGURE 12–5
December 31, 20X1, Translation of Foreign Subsidiary's Trial Balance
European Euro Is the Functional Currency

Item	Balance, €	Exchange Rate	Balance, $
Cash	10,750	1.40	15,050
Foreign Currency Units	3,000	1.40	4,200
Receivables	10,500	1.40	14,700
Inventory	5,000	1.40	7,000
Plant and Equipment	50,000	1.40	70,000
Cost of Goods Sold	22,500	1.30	29,250
Operating Expenses	14,500	1.30	18,850
Foreign Currency Transaction Loss	500	1.30	650
Dividends Paid	6,250	1.36	8,500
Total Debits	123,000		168,200
Accumulated Depreciation	7,500	1.40	10,500
Accounts Payable	3,000	1.40	4,200
Bonds Payable	12,500	1.40	17,500
Common Stock	40,000	1.20	48,000
Retained Earnings (1/1)	10,000	(a)	12,000
Sales	50,000	1.30	65,000
Total	123,000		157,200
Accumulated Other Comprehensive Income—Translation Adjustment			11,000
Total Credits			168,200

(a) From the January 1, 20X1, translation workpaper.

Subsequent to Date of Acquisition

The accounting subsequent to the date of acquisition is very similar to the accounting used for domestic subsidiaries. The major differences are due to the effects of changes in the exchange rates of the foreign currency.

Translation of Foreign Subsidiary's Postacquisition Trial Balance
Figure 12–5 illustrates the translation of German Company's December 31, 20X1, trial balance.

Note the account Foreign Currency Units in the trial balance of the German subsidiary. This account represents the $4,200 of U.S. dollars held by the subsidiary. Because this account is denominated in a currency other than the subsidiary's reporting currency, German Company made an adjusting journal entry to revalue the account from the amount originally recorded using the exchange rate on the date the company received the currency to that amount's equivalent exchange value at the end of the year.

The subsidiary made the following entry on its books when it received the U.S. dollars:

(4)	Foreign Currency Units ($)	€3,500	
	Sales		€3,500

Record sales and receipt of 4,200 U.S. dollars
at spot exchange rate on date of receipt:
€3,500 = $4,200/$1.20 exchange rate

At the end of the period, the subsidiary adjusted the foreign currency units (the U.S. dollars) to the current exchange rate ($1.40 = €1) by making the following entry:

(5)	Foreign Currency Transaction Loss	€500	
	Foreign Currency Units ($)		€500

Adjust account denominated in foreign
currency units to current exchange rate:

$4,200/$1.40	€3,000
Less: Preadjusted balance	(3,500)
Foreign currency transaction loss	€ (500)

The foreign currency transaction loss is a component of the subsidiary's net income, and the Foreign Currency Units account is classified as a current asset on the subsidiary's balance sheet. The subsidiary's net income consists of the following elements:

Sales	€50,000
Cost of Goods Sold	(22,500)
Operating Expenses	(14,500)
Foreign Currency Transaction Loss	(500)
Net Income	€12,500

Because the European euro is the foreign entity's functional currency, the subsidiary's statements must be translated into U.S. dollars using the current rate method. The assets and liabilities are translated using the current exchange rate at the balance sheet date ($1.40), the income statement accounts are translated using the average rate for the period ($1.30), and the stockholders' equity accounts are translated using the appropriate historical exchange rates ($1.20 and $1.36). The dividends are translated at the October 1 rate ($1.36), which was the exchange rate on the date the dividends were declared. The example assumes the dividends were paid on October 1, the same day they were declared. If the dividends had not been paid by the end of the year, the liability dividends payable would be translated at the current exchange rate of $1.40 = €1.

One of the analytical features provided by the current rate method is that many of the ratios management uses to manage the foreign subsidiary are the same in U.S. dollars as they are in the foreign currency unit. This relationship is true for the assets and liabilities of the balance sheet and the revenue and expenses of the income statement because the translation for these accounts uses the same exchange rate—the current rate for the assets and liabilities, and the average exchange rate for the income statement accounts. Thus, the *scale* of these accounts has changed but not their *relative amounts* within their respective statements. This relationship is not true when the ratio includes numbers from both the income statement and the balance sheet or when a stockholders' equity account is included with an asset or liability. The following table illustrates the relative relationships within the financial statements using the data in Figure 12–5:

	Measured in €	Measured in U.S. Dollars
Current ratio:		
Current assets	€29,250	$40,950
Current liabilities	€ 3,000	$ 4,200
Current ratio	9.75	9.75
Cost of goods sold as a percentage of sales:		
Cost of goods sold	€22,500	$29,250
Sales	€50,000	$65,000
Percent	45%	45%

The translation adjustment in Figure 12–5 arises because the investee's assets and liabilities are translated at the current rate, whereas other rates are used for the stockholders' equity and income statement account balances. Although the translation adjustment may be thought of as a balancing item to make the trial balance debits equal the credits, the effects of changes in the exchange rates during the period should be calculated to prove the accuracy of the translation process. This proof for 20X1, the acquisition year, is provided in Figure 12–6.

The proof begins with determination of the effect of changes in the exchange rate on the beginning investment and on the elements that alter the beginning investment. Note that only events affecting the stockholders' equity accounts will change the net assets investment. In this example, the changes to the investment account occurred from income of €12,500 and dividends of €6,250. No changes occurred in the stock outstanding during the year. The beginning net investment is translated using the exchange rate at the beginning of the year.

FIGURE 12–6
Proof of Translation Adjustment as of December 31, 20X1
European Euro Is the Functional Currency

PEERLESS PRODUCTS AND SUBSIDIARY
Proof of Translation Adjustment
Year Ended December 31, 20X1

	€	Translation Rate	$
Net assets at beginning of year	50,000	1.20	60,000
Adjustment for changes in net assets position during year:			
Net income for year	12,500	1.30	16,250
Dividends paid	(6,250)	1.36	(8,500)
Net assets translated at:			
Rates during year			67,750
Rates at end of year	56,250	1.40	78,750
Change in other comprehensive income— translation adjustment during year (net increase)			11,000
Accumulated other comprehensive income— translation adjustment, 1/1			-0-
Accumulated other comprehensive income— translation adjustment, 12/31 (credit)			11,000

The income and dividends are translated using the exchange rate at the date the transactions occurred. The income was earned evenly over the year; thus the average exchange rate for the period is used to translate income. The ending net assets position is translated using the exchange rate at the end of the year. The cumulative translation adjustment at the beginning of the year is zero in this example because the subsidiary was acquired on January 1, 20X1.

The Accumulated Other Comprehensive Income—Translation Adjustment account has a credit balance because the spot exchange rate at the end of the first period of ownership is higher than the exchange rate at the beginning of the period or the average for the period. If the exchange rate had decreased during the period, the translation adjustment would have had a debit balance. Another way of determining whether the accumulated translation adjustment has a debit or credit balance is to use balance sheet logic. For example, the subsidiary's translated balance sheet at the beginning of the year would be:

Translated Balance Sheet, 1/1/X1			
Net assets	$60,000	Common stock	$60,000

The translated balance sheet at the end of the year would be:

Translated Balance Sheet, 12/31/X1			
Net assets	$78,750	Common stock	$60,000
		Retained earnings (net income less dividends)	7,750
		Accumulated other comprehensive income— translation adjustment	11,000
Total	$78,750	Total	$78,750

Note that the $11,000 is a credit balance in order to make the balance sheet "balance."

Entries on Parent Company's Books Entries on the parent company's books are made to recognize the dollar equivalent values of the parent's share of the subsidiary's income, amortization of the excess of cost over book value, a cumulative translation adjustment for the parent's differential, and the dividends received from the foreign subsidiary. In addition, the parent company must recognize its share of the translation adjustment arising from the translation of the subsidiary's financial statements. The periodic change in the parent company's translation adjustment from the foreign investment is reported as a component of the parent company's other comprehensive income.

The entries that Peerless Products makes to account for its investment in German Company follow. Peerless Products received the dividend on October 1, 20X1, and immediately converted it to U.S. dollars as follows:

October 1, 20X1

(6)	Cash	8,500	
	Investment in German Company Stock		8,500
	Dividend received from foreign subsidiary:		
	€6,250 × $1.36 exchange rate		

December 31, 20X1

(7)	Investment in German Company Stock	16,250	
	Income from Subsidiary		16,250
	Equity in net income of foreign subsidiary:		
	€12,500 × $1.30 average exchange rate		
(8)	Investment in German Company Stock	11,000	
	Other Comprehensive Income—Translation Adjustment		11,000
	Parent's share of change in translation adjustment from		
	translation of subsidiary's accounts: $11,000 × 1.00		

If some time passed between the declaration and payment of dividends, the parent company would record dividends receivable from the foreign subsidiary on the declaration date. This account would be denominated in a foreign currency and would be adjusted to its current exchange rate on the balance sheet date and on the payment date, just like any other account denominated in a foreign currency. Any foreign transaction gain or loss resulting from the adjustment procedure would be included in the parent's income for the period.

The Differential The allocation and amortization of the excess of cost over book value require special attention in the translation of a foreign entity's financial statements. The differential does not exist on the foreign subsidiary's books; it is part of the parent's investment account. However, the translated book value of the foreign subsidiary is a major component of the investment account on the parent's books and is directly related to a foreign-based asset. **FASB 52** requires that the allocation and amortization of the difference between the investment cost and its book value be made in terms of the functional currency of the foreign subsidiary and that these amounts then be translated at the appropriate exchange rates on the workpaper balance sheet date. The periodic amortization affects the income statement and is therefore measured at the average exchange rate used to translate other income statement accounts. On the other hand, the remaining unamortized balance of the differential is reported in the balance sheet and is translated at the current exchange rate used for balance sheet accounts. The effect of this difference in rates is shown in the parent company's translation adjustment as a revision of part of the parent's original investment in the subsidiary.

Peerless Products amortizes the patent over a 10-year period. The patent amortization follows.

	European Euros	Translation Rate	U.S. Dollars
Income Statement			
Differential at beginning of year	€5,000	1.20	$6,000
Amortization this period (€5,000/10 years)	(500)	1.30	(650)
Remaining balances	€4,500		$5,350

(continued)

Balance Sheet

Remaining balance on 12/31/X1 translated at year-end exchange rates	€4,500	1.40	$6,300
Difference to other comprehensive income— translation adjustment (credit)			$ 950

Another way to view the differential adjustment of $950 is that it adjusts the parent company's differential, which is currently part of the investment account, to the amount necessary to prepare the consolidated balance sheet. In this example, if no differential adjustment is made, the patent on the consolidated balance sheet would be $5,350, which is incorrect. Because the balance sheet must report the patent translated at the end-of-period exchange rate of $6,300, the differential adjustment is made to properly report the amount in the consolidated balance sheet. Thus, the adjustment may be thought of as an adjustment necessary to obtain the correct amount of the differential to prepare the consolidated balance sheet. Depending on the direction of the changes in the exchange rate, the differential adjustment could be a debit or credit amount. In this case, the differential must be increased from $5,350 to $6,300, necessitating a debit of $950 to the investment account and a corresponding credit to the Other Comprehensive Income—Translation Adjustment account.

Entry (9) recognizes the amortization of the patent for the period. Entry (10) records the portion of the translation adjustment on the increase in the differential for the investment in the foreign subsidiary.

(9)	Income from Subsidiary	650	
	Investment in German Company Stock		650
	Amortization of patent:		
	$650 = €500 × $1.30 average exchange rate		
(10)	Investment in German Company Stock	950	
	Other Comprehensive Income—Translation Adjustment		950
	Recognize translation adjustment on increase in differential.		

It is important to note that the $950 translation adjustment from the differential is attributed solely to the parent company. Noncontrolling Interest is not assigned any portion of this translation adjustment. This $950 translation adjustment is attributable to the excess of cost paid over the book value of the assets and therefore is added to the differential, which is a component of the investment in the foreign subsidiary, thereby resulting in a debit to the investment account on the parent company's books.

The December 31, 20X1, balance in the Investment in German Company Stock account is $85,050, as shown in the following T-account. The numbers in parentheses are the corresponding journal entry numbers from the text.

Investment in German Company Stock					
(1)	Purchase price	66,000			
			(6)	Dividends	8,500
(7)	Equity income	16,250			
(8)	Share of subsidiary's translation adjustment	11,000			
			(9)	Amortization of differential	650
(10)	Translation adjustment on differential	950			
	Balance, 12/31/X1	85,050			

Note that the $11,950 Other Comprehensive Income—Translation Adjustment account balance in the parent company's books is composed of its share of the translation adjustment from translating the subsidiary's trial balance ($11,000) plus the parent company's adjustment ($950) due to the differential it paid for the investment.

During the parent company's closing entries process, the following two entries would be included to separately close net income from the subsidiary and the other comprehensive income arising from its investment in the subsidiary.

(11)	Income from Subsidiary	15,600	
	Retained Earnings		15,600
	To close net income from subsidiary:		
	$15,600 = $16,250 − $650		

(12)	Other Comprehensive Income—Translation Adjustment	11,950	
	Accumulated Other Comprehensive Income—		
	Translation Adjustment		11,950
	To close other comprehensive income resulting from the		
	investment in the German subsidiary:		
	$11,950 = $11,000 + $950		

Subsequent Consolidation Workpaper The consolidation workpaper is prepared after the translation process is completed. The process of consolidation is the same as for a domestic subsidiary, except for two major differences: (1) The parent company will record its share of the translation adjustment arising from the translation of the foreign subsidiary's accounts; as presented in entry (8) for this example, the parent owns 100 percent of the subsidiary, but, in cases of a less-than-wholly owned subsidiary, the noncontrolling interest would be assigned its percentage share of the translation adjustment, and (2) as shown previously, the patent amortization for the period is translated at the income statement rate (average for the period), whereas the ending patent balance is translated at the balance sheet rate (current exchange rate). As shown in entry (10), a translation adjustment must be computed on the differential and assigned as part of the parent company's investment in the foreign subsidiary.

The workpaper is presented in Figure 12–7. The trial balance for German Company is obtained from the translated amounts computed earlier in Figure 12–5. The workpaper entries follow in journal entry form. These entries are *not* made on either company's books; they are only in the workpaper elimination columns.

E(13)	Income from Subsidiary	15,600	
	Dividends Declared		8,500
	Investment in German Company Stock		7,100
	Eliminate income from subsidiary:		
	$15,600 = $16,250 equity share − $650 amortization		

E(14)	Other Comprehensive Income—Translation Adjustment	11,000	
	Investment in German Co. Stock		11,000
	To eliminate the other comprehensive income from the		
	subsidiary that had been recorded by the parent.		

E(15)	Common Stock—German Co.	48,000	
	Retained Earnings, January 1, 20X1	12,000	
	Accumulated Other Comprehensive Income, January 1, 20X1	0	
	Differential	6,000	
	Investment in German Co. Stock		66,000
	Eliminate beginning-of-period investment balance.		

E(16)	Differential	950	
	Investment in German Co. Stock		950
	Eliminate end-of-period differential adjustment that		
	was recorded in investment account.		

FIGURE 12–7   December 31, 20X1, Consolidation Workpaper, Prepared after Translation of Foreign Statements

Item	Peerless Products	German Company	Eliminations Debit	Eliminations Credit	Consolidated
Sales	400,000	65,000			465,000
Income from Subsidiary	15,6000		(13) 15,600		
Credits	415,600	65,000			465,000
Cost of Goods Sold	170,000	29,250			199,250
Operating Expenses	90,000	18,850	(18) 650		109,500
Foreign Currency Transaction Loss		650			650
Debits	(260,000)	(48,750)			(309,400)
Net Income, carry forward	155,600	16,250	16,250		155,600
Retained Earnings, 1/1	300,000	12,000	(15) 12,000		300,000
Net Income, from above	155,600	16,250	16,250		155,600
	455,600	28,250			455,6000
Dividends Declared	(60,000)	(8,500)		(13) 8,500	(60,000)
Retained Earnings, 12/31	395,600	19,750	28,250	8,500	395,600
Cash	422,500	15,050			437,550
Dollars Held by Subsidiary		4,200			4,200
Receivables	75,000	14,700			89,700
Inventory	100,000	7,000			107,000
Land	175,000				175,000
Plant and Equipment	800,000	70,000			870,000
Investment in German Co. Stock	85,050			(13) 7,100	
				(14) 11,000	
				(15) 66,000	
				(16) 950	
Differential			(15) 6,000	(17) 6,950	
			(16) 950		
Patent			(17) 6,950	(18) 650	6,300
Debits	1,657,550	110,950			1,689,750
Accumulated Depreciation	450,000	10,500			460,500
Accounts Payable	100,000	4,200			104,200
Bonds Payable	200,000	17,500			217,500
Common Stock	500,000	48,000	(15) 48,000		500,000
Retained Earnings, from above	395,600	19,750	28,250	8,500	395,600
Accumulated Other Comprehensive Income, from below	11,950	11,000	11,000		11,950
Credits	1,657,550	110,950	101,150	101,150	1,689,750
Accumulated Other Comp. Income, 1/1	0	0	(15) 0		0
Other Comp. Income— Translation Adj.	11,950	11,000	(14) 11,000		11,950
Accumulated Other Comp. Income, 12/31, (credit) carry up	11,950	11,000	11,000	0	11,950

Key to eliminations:

(13) Eliminate net income from subsidiary.

(14) Eliminate parent company's share of other comprehensive income from change in translation adjustment.

(15) Eliminate beginning investment account balance.

(16) Eliminate translation adjustment to differential.

(17) Assign differential to patent.

(18) Amortize patent.

E(17)	Patent	6,950	
	Differential		6,950
	Assign differential, including periodic adjustment of $950, to patent:		
	$6,950 = $6,000 + $950 differential adjustment		
E(18)	Operating Expenses—Amortization of Patent	650	
	Patent		650
	Amortize patent:		
	$650 = €500 × $1.30		

When the parent company uses the equity method and no intercompany revenue transactions occur, the parent's net income and retained earnings equal the consolidated net income and consolidated retained earnings. This makes it possible to verify the amounts reported on the consolidated financial statements.

Noncontrolling Interest of a Foreign Subsidiary

Most U.S. companies prefer to own 100 percent of their foreign subsidiaries. Doing so provides for more efficient management of the subsidiary and no requirement to prepare separate financial statements of the subsidiary for a noncontrolling interest. If a foreign subsidiary was less-than-wholly owned, however, the noncontrolling interest would be computed and accounted for just as it was beginning in Chapter 4 of this text. The only difference is the allocation of the translation adjustment that arises from the translation of the foreign subsidiary's trial balance accounts. Thus, for example, if Peerless had an 80 percent interest in German Company and another investor owned a 20 percent noncontrolling interest, the noncontrolling interest would be allocated its percentage share of the translation adjustment through the elimination entry process. The noncontrolling interest on the consolidated balance sheet at year-end would include its share of the accumulated other comprehensive income from the translation adjustment, as follows:

Common stock ($48,000 × .20)		$ 9,600
Retained earnings:		
Beginning retained earnings ($12,000 × .20)	$2,400	
Add: Net income ($16,250 × .20)	3,250	
Less: Dividends ($8,500 × .20)	(1,700)	
Total retained earnings		3,950
Accumulated other comprehensive income— translation adjustment ($11,000 × .20)		2,200
Total noncontrolling interest		$15,750

REMEASUREMENT OF THE BOOKS OF RECORD INTO THE FUNCTIONAL CURRENCY

A second method of restating foreign affiliates' financial statements in U.S. dollars is remeasurement. Although remeasurement is not as commonly used as translation, some situations in which the functional currency of the foreign affiliate is not its local currency exist. Remeasurement is similar to translation in that its goal is to obtain equivalent U.S. dollar values for the foreign affiliate's accounts so they may be combined or consolidated with the U.S. company's statements. The exchange rates used for remeasurement, however, are different from those used for translation, resulting in different dollar values for the foreign affiliate's accounts.

The FASB provided examples of several situations requiring remeasurement:[4]

1. A foreign sales branch or subsidiary of a U.S. manufacturer that primarily takes orders from foreign customers for U.S.-manufactured goods, that bills and collects from foreign customers, and that might have a warehouse to provide for timely delivery of the product to those foreign customers. In substance, this foreign operation may be the same as the export sales department of a U.S. manufacturer.

2. A foreign division, branch, or subsidiary that primarily manufactures a subassembly shipped to a U.S. plant for inclusion in a product that is sold to customers located in the United States or in different parts of the world.

3. A foreign shipping subsidiary that primarily transports ore from a U.S. company's foreign mines to the United States for processing in a U.S. company's smelting plants.

4. A foreign subsidiary that is primarily a conduit for euro borrowings to finance operations in the United States.

In most cases, the foreign affiliate may be thought of as a direct production or sales arm of the U.S. company, but it uses the local currency to record and report its operations. In addition, foreign entities located in highly inflationary economies, defined as economies having a cumulative three-year inflation rate exceeding 100 percent, must use the dollar as their functional currency, and their statements are remeasured into U.S. dollars. Many South American countries have experienced hyperinflation, with some countries having annual inflation rates in excess of 100 percent. If the foreign affiliate uses the U.S. dollar as both its functional and its reporting currency, no remeasurement is necessary because its operations are already reported in U.S. dollars.

The remeasurement process should produce the same end result as if the foreign entity's transactions had been initially recorded in dollars. For this reason, certain transactions and account balances are restated to their U.S. dollar equivalents using a historical exchange rate, the spot exchange rate at the time the transaction originally occurred. The remeasurement process divides the balance sheet into monetary and nonmonetary accounts. Monetary assets and liabilities, such as cash, short-term or long-term receivables, and short-term or long-term payables, have their amounts fixed in terms of the units of currency. These accounts are subject to gains or losses from changes in exchange rates. Nonmonetary assets are accounts such as inventories and plant and equipment, which are not fixed in relation to monetary units.

The monetary accounts are remeasured using the current exchange rate. The appropriate historical exchange rate is used to remeasure nonmonetary balance sheet account balances and related revenue, expense, gain, and loss account balances. A list of the accounts to be remeasured with the appropriate historical exchange rate is provided in Figure 12–8.[5]

Because of the variety of rates used to remeasure the foreign currency trial balance, the debits and credits of the U.S. dollar–equivalent trial balance will probably not be equal. In this case, the balancing item is a ***remeasurement gain or loss***, which is included in the period's income statement.

Statement Presentation of Remeasurement Gain or Loss

Any exchange gain or loss arising from the remeasurement process is included in the current period income statement, usually under "Other Income." Various account titles are used, such as Foreign Exchange Gain (Loss), Currency Gain (Loss), Exchange Gain (Loss), or Remeasurement Gain (Loss). The title Remeasurement Gain (Loss) is used here because it is most descriptive of the source of the item. The remeasurement gain or loss is included in the period's income because if the transactions had originally been recorded in U.S. dollars, the exchange gains and losses would have been recognized this period as part of the adjustments required for valuation of foreign transactions denominated in a foreign currency. Upon completion of the remeasurement process, the foreign entity's financial statements are

---

[4] These examples were provided in the exposure draft of **FASB 52** but were not included in its final draft. The FASB did not want the examples to limit remeasurement to those cases in which the U.S. dollar is the functional currency.
[5] **FASB 52,** para. 48.

FIGURE 12–8

Accounts to Be Remeasured Using Historical Exchange Rates

Source: *FASB 52*, para. 48.

Marketable securities:
   Equity securities
   Debt securities not intended to be held until maturity
Inventories
Prepaid expenses such as insurance, advertising, and rent
Property, plant, and equipment
Accumulated depreciation on property, plant, and equipment
Patents, trademarks, licenses, and formulas
Goodwill
Other intangible assets
Deferred charges and credits, except deferred income taxes and policy acquisition costs for
   life insurance companies
Deferred income
Common stock
Preferred stock carried at issuance price
Revenue and expenses related to nonmonetary items, for example:
   Cost of goods sold
   Depreciation of property, plant, and equipment
   Amortization of intangible items such as patents, licenses, etc.
   Amortization of deferred charges or credits, except deferred income taxes and policy
      acquisition costs for life insurance companies

presented as they would have been had the U.S. dollar been used to record the transactions in the local currency as they occurred.

Illustration of Remeasurement of a Foreign Subsidiary

German Company again is used, this time to present remeasurement of financial statements. The only difference between the previous example of translation and the current example is that the foreign subsidiary's functional currency is now assumed to be the U.S. dollar rather than the European euro. German Company maintains its books and records in euros to provide required reports to the German government. Because the dollar is the functional currency, German Company's financial statements will be remeasured into dollars. Once the foreign affiliate's statements are remeasured, the consolidation process is the same as for a domestic subsidiary.

Remeasurement of Foreign Subsidiary's Postacquisition Trial Balance

The subsidiary's trial balance must be remeasured from the European euro into the U.S. dollar as shown in Figure 12–9. The current exchange rate is used to remeasure the monetary accounts, and the appropriate historical exchange rates are used for each of the nonmonetary accounts.

Three items need special attention. First, the plant and equipment is remeasured using the historical rate on the date the parent company acquired the foreign subsidiary. If the subsidiary purchases any additional plant or equipment after the parent has acquired the subsidiary's stock, the additional plant or equipment will be remeasured using the exchange rate on the date of the purchase of the additional plant. The same cautionary note is applicable for the other nonmonetary items. It is important to maintain a record of the subsidiary's acquisition or disposition of nonmonetary assets and equities after the foreign subsidiary's stock is acquired to ensure use of the proper exchange rates to remeasure these items. Recall that the business combination was accounted for as a purchase; therefore, the appropriate historical rate is the spot rate on the date the parent purchased the foreign subsidiary's stock. If the combination had been accounted for as a pooling, the appropriate historical spot rates would be the rates on the dates the subsidiary originally issued the stock and acquired the nonmonetary assets, not the later date on which the parent company acquired the subsidiary's stock.

Second, the cost of goods sold consists of transactions that occurred at various exchange rates. The beginning inventory was acquired when the rate was $1.20 = €1. Inventory purchases were made at different times during the year, so the average rate of $1.30 was used

FIGURE 12–9
December 31, 20X1, Remeasurement of the Foreign Subsidiary's Trial Balance
U.S. Dollar Is the Functional Currency

Item	Balance, €	Exchange Rate	Balance, $
Cash	10,750	1.40	15,050
Foreign Currency Units	3,000	1.40	4,200
Receivables	10,500	1.40	14,700
Inventory	5,000	1.38	6,900
Plant and Equipment	50,000	1.20	60,000
Cost of Goods Sold	22,500	(a)	28,100
Operating Expenses	14,500	(b)	18,600
Foreign Currency Transaction Loss	500	1.30	650
Dividends Paid	6,250	1.36	8,500
Total Debits	123,000		156,700
Accumulated Depreciation	7,500	1.20	9,000
Accounts Payable	3,000	1.40	4,200
Bonds Payable	12,500	1.40	17,500
Common Stock	40,000	1.20	48,000
Retained Earnings	10,000	(c)	12,000
Sales	50,000	1.30	65,000
Total	123,000		155,700
Remeasurement Gain			1,000
Total Credits			156,700

	In Euros	Exchange Rate	In Dollars
(a) Cost of Goods Sold:			
Beginning Inventory	7,500	1.20	9,000
Purchases	20,000	1.35	26,000
Goods Available	27,500		35,000
Less: Ending Inventory	(5,000)	1.38	(6,900)
Cost of Goods Sold	22,500		28,100
(b) Operating Expenses:			
Cash Expenses	12,000	1.35	15,600
Depreciation Expense	2,500	1.20	3,000
	14,500		18,600

(c) Carry forward from January 1, 20X1, workpaper.

for the remeasurement exchange rate. For purposes of illustration, the example assumes that ending inventory was acquired when the direct exchange rate was $1.38 = €1 and the FIFO inventory method is used.

Third, the operating expenses are also incurred at different exchange rates. The depreciation expense is remeasured at $1.20 = €1 because it is associated with a nonmonetary account, Plant and Equipment, which is remeasured at the historical exchange rate of $1.20 = €1. The average exchange rate is used to remeasure the remaining operating expenses because they are assumed to be incurred evenly throughout the period.

The remeasurement gain is recognized in this period's income statement. The remeasurement exchange gain is a balancing item to make total debits and total credits equal, but it can be proved by analyzing changes in the monetary items during the period. The subsequent consolidation workpaper and the proof of the remeasurement exchange gain are shown in the "Additional Considerations" section at the end of this chapter.

Summary of Translation versus Remeasurement

When the functional currency is the dollar, the nonmonetary items on the balance sheet are remeasured using historical exchange rates. In this example, the direct exchange rate has increased during the period; therefore, the nonmonetary accounts are lower when remeasured than when translated. A summary of the differences between the translation and remeasurement methods is presented in Figure 12–10.

FIGURE 12–10 **Summary of the Translation and Remeasurement Processes**

Item	Translation Process	Remeasurement Process
Foreign entity's functional currency	Local currency unit	U.S. dollar
Method used	Current rate method	Monetary-nonmonetary method
Income statement accounts:		
Revenue	Weighted-average exchange rate	Weighted-average exchange rate, except revenue related to nonmonetary items (historical exchange rate)
Expenses	Weighted-average exchange rate	Weighted-average exchange rate, except costs related to nonmonetary items (historical exchange rate)
Balance sheet accounts:		
Monetary accounts	Current exchange rate	Current exchange rate
Nonmonetary accounts	Current exchange rate	Historical exchange rate
Stockholders' equity capital accounts	Historical exchange rate	Historical exchange rate
Retained earnings	Prior-period balance plus income less dividends	Prior-period balance plus income less dividends
Exchange rate adjustments arising in process	Translation adjustment accumulated in stockholders' equity	Remeasurement gain or loss included in period's income statement

FOREIGN INVESTMENTS AND UNCONSOLIDATED SUBSIDIARIES

Most companies consolidate their foreign subsidiaries in conformity with **FASB Statement No. 94**, "Consolidation of All Majority-Owned Subsidiaries" (FASB 94). In some cases these operations are not consolidated, because of criteria that apply to foreign subsidiaries. Generally, a parent company consolidates a foreign subsidiary, except when one of the following conditions becomes so severe that the U.S. company owning a foreign company may not be able to exercise the necessary level of economic control over the foreign subsidiary's resources and financial operations to warrant consolidation:

1. Restrictions on foreign exchange in the foreign country.
2. Restrictions on transfers of property in the foreign country.
3. Other governmentally imposed uncertainties.

An unconsolidated foreign subsidiary is reported as an investment on the U.S. parent company's balance sheet. The U.S. investor company must use the equity method if it has the ability to exercise "significant influence" over the investee's financial and operating policies. If the equity method cannot be applied, the cost method is used to account for the foreign investment, recognizing income only as dividends are received.

When the equity method is used for an unconsolidated foreign subsidiary, the investee's financial statements are either remeasured or translated, depending on the determination of the functional currency. If remeasurement is used, the foreign entity's statements are remeasured in dollars and the investor records its percentage of the investee's income and makes necessary amortizations or impairments of any differential. A shortcut approach is available for translation: Multiply the foreign affiliate's net income measured in foreign currency units by the average exchange rate during the period and then recognize the parent company's percentage share of the translated net income. In addition, the investor must recognize its share of the translation adjustment arising from the translation of the foreign entity's financial statements. The investor's share of the translation adjustment from its foreign investees is reported on the investor's balance sheet as a separate component of stockholders' equity and as an adjustment of the carrying value of the investment account. The entries on the investor's books are the same under the equity method whether the subsidiary is consolidated or reported as an unconsolidated investment.

Liquidation of a Foreign Investment

The translation adjustment account is directly related to a company's investment in a foreign entity. If the investor sells a substantial portion of its stock investment, **FASB Interpretation No. 37**, "Accounting for Translation Adjustments upon Sale of Part of an Investment in a Foreign Entity" (FIN 37), requires that the pro rata portion of the accumulated translation adjustment account attributable to that investment be included in computing the gain or loss on the disposition of the investment. For example, if the parent company sold off 30 percent of its investment in a foreign subsidiary, 30 percent of the related cumulative translation adjustment would be removed from the translation adjustment account and included in determining the gain or loss on the disposition of the foreign investment.

HEDGE OF A NET INVESTMENT IN A FOREIGN SUBSIDIARY

FASB 133 permits hedging of a net investment in foreign subsidiaries. For example, Peerless has a net investment of €50,000 in its German subsidiary for which it paid $66,000. Peerless could decide to hedge all, some, or none of this investment by accepting a liability in euros. Peerless could hedge its net asset investment by contracting for a forward exchange contract to sell euros, or the company could incur a euro-based liability. **FASB 133** states that the gain or loss on the effective portion of a hedge of a net investment is taken to other comprehensive income as part of the translation adjustment. However, the amount of offset to comprehensive income is limited to the translation adjustment for the net investment. For example, if the forward exchange rate is used to measure effectiveness, the amount of offset is limited to the change in spot rates during the period. Any excess on the ineffective portion of the hedge must be recognized currently in earnings.

For example, on January 1, 20X1, Peerless decides to hedge the portion of its investment that it just made in German Company that is related to the book value of German Company's net assets. Peerless is unsure whether the direct exchange rate for euros will increase or decrease for the year and wishes to hedge its net asset investment. On January 1, 20X1, Peerless's 100 percent ownership share of German Company's net assets is equal to €50,000 (€40,000 capital stock plus €10,000 retained earnings). Peerless borrows €50,000, at a 5 percent rate of interest to hedge its equity investment in German Company, and the principal and interest are due and payable on January 1, 20X2.

The entries on Peerless's books to account for this hedge of a net investment follow:

	January 1, 20X1		
(19)	Cash	60,000	
	Loan Payable (€)		60,000
	Borrow a euro-denominated loan to hedge		
	net investment in German subsidiary:		
	$60,000 = €50,000 × $1.20 spot rate		
	December 31, 20X1		
(20)	Other Comprehensive Income	10,000	
	Loan Payable (€)		10,000
	Revalue foreign currency–denominated		
	payable to end-of-period spot rate:		
	$10,000 = €50,000 × ($1.40 − $1.20)		
(21)	Interest Expense	3,250	
	Foreign Currency Transaction Loss	250	
	Interest Payable (€)		3,500
	Accrue interest expense and payable on euro loan:		
	$3,250 = €50,000 × .05 interest × $1.30 average exchange rate		
	$3,500 = €50,000 × .05 interest × $1.40 ending spot rate		

(22)	Accumulated Other Comprehensive Income—		
	Translation Adjustment	10,000	
	Profit and Loss Summary (or Retained Earnings)	250	
	Foreign Currency Transaction Loss		250
	Other Comprehensive Income		10,000
	Close nominal accounts related to hedge of net investment in foreign subsidiary.		

Then, when the principal and interest are paid on January 1, 20X2, the following entry is made:

January 1, 20X2			
(23)	Interest Payable (€)	3,500	
	Loan Payable (€)	70,000	
	Cash		73,500
	Pay principal and interest due on euro-denominated hedge:		
	$70,000 = $60,000 + $10,000		

During 20X1, Peerless hedged a portion of its net asset investment in the foreign subsidiary. The dollar weakened against the euro (the direct exchange rate increased) and Peerless recognized a gain on a net asset investment in euros and a loss on a liability payable in euros. Without this hedge of the net investment, Peerless would have reported a $11,950 credit balance in the cumulative translation portion of accumulated other comprehensive income ($11,950 = $11,000 + $950 differential adjustment). With the hedge of its net investment, Peerless will report just $1,950 ($11,950 − $10,000 effect of hedge) as its change in the cumulative translation adjustment for 20X1. Thus, Peerless has balanced a portion of its net exposure on its January 1, 20X1, net asset investment in German Company.

Note also that the amount of the offset to other comprehensive income is limited to the effective portion of the hedge based on the revaluation of the net assets. Any excess, in this case the $250 loss on the revaluation of the interest payable in entry (21), is taken directly to current earnings on the income statement.

DISCLOSURE REQUIREMENTS

FASB 52 requires the aggregate foreign transaction gain or loss included in income to be se parately disclosed in the income statement or in an accompanying note. This includes gains or losses recognized from foreign currency transactions, forward exchange contracts, and any remeasurement gain or loss. If not disclosed as a one-line item on the income statement, this disclosure is usually a one-sentence footnote summarizing the company's foreign operations.

Under the translation method, the periodic change in the translation adjustment is reported as an element of other comprehensive income, as required by **FASB 130**. Figure 12–11 presents the two-statement approach to displaying comprehensive income. The consolidated statement of comprehensive income presents the detail of the parent's other comprehensive income of $11,950. Figure 12–12 presents the statement of changes in equity that reconciles all of the elements of stockholders' equity. The balance sheet would then display the capital stock, retained earnings, and accumulated other comprehensive income in the stockholders' equity section. In addition, **FASB 52** requires footnote disclosure of exchange rate changes that occur after the balance sheet date and their effect on unsettled foreign currency transactions, if significant.

ADDITIONAL CONSIDERATIONS IN ACCOUNTING FOR FOREIGN OPERATIONS AND ENTITIES

This section covers special topics in accounting for multinational enterprises. Although many of these additional considerations are very technical, study of this section will complement your understanding of the many issues of accounting for foreign entities.

FIGURE 12–11
Two-Statement Approach to Display Comprehensive Income

PEERLESS PRODUCTS AND SUBSIDIARY Consolidated Statement of Income Year Ended December 31, 20X1	
Sales	$465,000
Cost of Goods Sold	(199,250)
Gross Profit	265,750
Operating Expenses	(109,500)
Foreign Currency Transaction Loss	(650)
Consolidated Net Income to Controlling Interest	$155,600

PEERLESS PRODUCTS AND SUBSIDIARY Consolidated Statement of Comprehensive Income Year Ended December 31, 20X1	
Consolidated Net Income to Controlling Interest	$155,600
Other Comprehensive Income:	
Foreign Currency Translation Adjustment	$ 11,950
Comprehensive Income to Controlling Interest	$167,550

Remeasurement Case: Subsequent Consolidation Workpaper

The consolidation workpaper for the remeasurement case is presented in Figure 12–13. The accounts for German Company are obtained from the remeasured accounts computed in Figure 12–9. The remeasurement gain is included in the German subsidiary's trial balance because the source of this account is the remeasurement of the subsidiary's accounts.

The Income from Subsidiary account can be proved as follows:

Income from Subsidiary			
		Parent's share of subsidiary income: ($18,650 × 1.00)	18,650
Amortization of patent ($6,000 / 10 years)	600		
		Balance, 12/31/X1	18,050

FIGURE 12–12   **Consolidated Statement of Changes in Stockholders' Equity**

PEERLESS PRODUCTS AND SUBSIDIARY Consolidated Statement of Changes in Equity Year Ended December 31, 20X1					
	Total	**Comprehensive Income**	**Retained Earnings**	**Accumulated Other Comprehensive Income**	**Capital Stock**
Beginning Balance	$800,000		$300,000	$ -0-	$500,000
Comprehensive Income:					
Net Income	155,600	$155,600	155,600		
Other Comprehensive Income:					
Foreign Currency Translation Adjustment	11,950	11,950		11,950	
Comprehensive Income		$167,550			
Dividends Declared on Common Stock	(60,000)		(60,000)		
Ending Balance	$907,550		$395,600	$11,950	$500,000

FIGURE 12–13 **December 31, 20X1, Consolidation Workpaper, Prepared after Remeasurement of Foreign Statements**

Item	Peerless Products	German Company	Eliminations Debit	Eliminations Credit	Consolidated
Sales	400,000	65,000			465,000
Remeasurement Gain		1,000			1,000
Income from Subsidiary	18,050		(24) 18,050		
Credits	418,050	66,000			466,000
Cost of Goods Sold	170,000	28,100			198,100
Operating Expenses	90,000	18,600	(27) 600		109,200
Foreign Currency Transaction Loss		650			650
Debits	(260,000)	(47,350)			(307,950)
Net Income, carry forward	158,050	18,650	18,650		158,050
Retained Earnings, 1/1	300,000	12,000	(25) 12,000		300,000
Net Income, from above	158,050	18,650	18,650		158,050
	458,050	30,650			458,050
Dividends Declared	(60,000)	(8,500)		(24) 8,500	(60,000)
Retained Earnings, 12/31	398,050	22,150	30,650	8,500	398,050
Cash	422,500	15,050			437,550
Dollars Held by Subsidiary		4,200			4,200
Receivables	75,000	14,700			89,700
Inventory	100,000	6,900			106,900
Land	175,000				175,000
Plant and Equipment	800,000	60,000			860,000
Investment in German Co. Stock	75,520			(24) 9,550	
				(25) 66,000	
Differential			(25) 6,000	(26) 6,000	
Patent			(26) 6,000	(27) 600	5,400
Debits	1,648,050	100,850			1,678,750
Accumulated Depreciation	450,000	9,000			459,000
Accounts Payable	100,000	4,200			104,200
Bonds Payable	200,000	17,500			217,500
Common Stock	500,000	48,000	(25) 48,000		500,000
Retained Earnings, from above	398,050	22,150	30,650	8,500	398,050
Credits	1,648,050	100,850	90,650	90,650	1,678,050

Elimination entries:
(24) Eliminate income and dividends from subsidiary.
(25) Eliminate beginning investment account balance.
(26) Assign beginning differential to patent.
(27) Amortize patent.

In the consolidated income statement, the Remeasurement Gain account is usually offset against the foreign currency transaction loss account, generating, in this example, a net gain of $350 ($1,000 − $650). This gain is reported in the other income section of the income statement.

The remaining consolidation process is identical to the process for a domestic subsidiary. Note that the $5,400 patent shown on the consolidated balance sheet is the unamortized portion of the initial $6,000 amount ($5,400 = $6,000 − $600). No special adjustments are required for the patent when using the remeasurement process.

The eliminating entries are as follows:

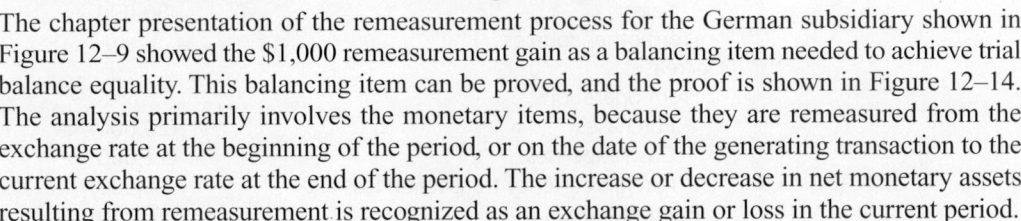

E(24)	Income from Subsidiary	18,050	
	Dividends Declared		8,500
	Investment in German Co. Stock		9,550
	Eliminate income from subsidiary.		
E(25)	Common Stock—German Co.	48,000	
	Retained Earnings, January 1, 20X1	12,000	
	Differential	6,000	
	Investment in German Co. Stock		66,000
	Eliminate beginning-of-period investment balance.		
E(26)	Patent	6,000	
	Differential		6,000
	Assign differential to patent.		
E(27)	Operating Expenses—Amortization of Patent	600	
	Patent		600
	Amortize patent.		

A comparison of Figures 12–7 and 12–13 shows that the foreign subsidiary's reported income differs between translation and remeasurement. The primary reason that subsidiary income is approximately 15 percent higher when the dollar is the functional currency ($18,650 versus $16,250 under translation) is that the U.S. dollar weakened against the European euro during the year. This results in a remeasurement gain for the subsidiary because it was transacting in the stronger currency (the euro) during the period. Furthermore, the subsidiary's cost of goods sold and operating expenses are remeasured at a lower exchange rate, resulting in a higher income.

Proof of Remeasurement Exchange Gain

The chapter presentation of the remeasurement process for the German subsidiary shown in Figure 12–9 showed the $1,000 remeasurement gain as a balancing item needed to achieve trial balance equality. This balancing item can be proved, and the proof is shown in Figure 12–14. The analysis primarily involves the monetary items, because they are remeasured from the exchange rate at the beginning of the period, or on the date of the generating transaction to the current exchange rate at the end of the period. The increase or decrease in net monetary assets resulting from remeasurement is recognized as an exchange gain or loss in the current period.

Schedule 1 presents the net monetary positions at the beginning and end of the year. The €11,250 change in the net monetary position is the change from a net liability opening balance of €2,500 to a net monetary asset position ending balance of €8,750. Schedule 2 presents the detailed effects of exchange rate changes on the foreign entity's net monetary position during this period. The beginning net monetary position is included using the exchange rate at the beginning of the year. Then all increases and decreases in the net monetary accounts are added or deducted using the exchange rates at the time the transactions occurred. Other sources of increases or decreases in the monetary accounts would include financing and investing transactions such as purchases of plant or equipment, issuance of long-term debt, or selling stock. The computed net monetary position at the end of the year using the transaction date exchange rates ($11,250) is then compared with the year-end net monetary position using the year-end exchange rate ($12,250). Because of the increasing exchange rate, the net asset position at the year-end was higher when remeasured using the December 31, 20X1, exchange rate of $1.40. This means that the U.S. dollar–equivalent value of the net monetary assets at the end of the year increased from $11,250 to $12,250 and that a remeasurement gain of $1,000 should be recognized. If the U.S. dollar–equivalent

FIGURE 12–14
**Proof of the
Remeasurement
Exchange Gain
for the Year Ended
December 31, 20X1**
Functional Currency
Is the U.S. Dollar

Proof of Remeasurement Gain
Remeasurement of German Company
For Year Ended December 31, 20X1

Schedule 1
Statement of Net Monetary Positions

	End of Year	Beginning of Year
Monetary assets:		
Cash	€10,750	€ 2,500
Foreign currency units	3,000	-0-
Receivables	10,500	10,000
Total	€24,250	€12,500
Less: Monetary equities:		
Accounts payable	€ 3,000	€ 2,500
Bonds payable	12,500	12,500
Total	€15,500	€15,000
Net monetary liabilities		€(2,500)
Net monetary assets	€ 8,750	
Increase in net monetary assets during year	€11,250	

Schedule 2
Analysis of Changes in Monetary Accounts

	€	Exchange Rate	U.S. $
Exposed net monetary liability position, 1/1	(2,500)	1.20	(3,000)
Adjustments for changes in net monetary position during year:			
Increases:			
From operations:			
Sales	50,000	1.30	65,000
From other sources	-0-		-0-
Decreases:			
From operations:			
Purchases	(20,000)	1.30	(26,000)
Cash expenses	(12,000)	1.30	(15,600)
Foreign currency transaction loss	(500)	1.30	(650)
From dividends	(6,250)	1.36	(8,500)
From other uses	-0-		-0-
Net monetary position prior to remeasurement at year-end rates			11,250
Exposed net monetary asset position, 12/31	8,750	1.40	12,250
Remeasurement gain			1,000

value of the December 31, 20X1, exposed net monetary assets position, as remeasured with the December 31 exchange rate, would have been lower than the computed value of $11,250, then a remeasurement loss would have been recognized for the reduction in the U.S. dollar–equivalent value of the net assets.

Statement of Cash Flows

The statement of cash flows is a link between two balance sheets. Individual companies have some latitude and flexibility in preparing the statement of cash flows. A general rule is that accounts reported in the statement of cash flows should be restated in U.S. dollars using the same rates as used for balance sheet and income statement purposes. Because the average exchange rate is used in the income statement and the ending spot exchange rate (current rate) is used in the balance sheet, a balancing item for the differences in exchange rates appears in the statement of cash flows. This balancing item can be analyzed and traced to the specific accounts that generate the difference, but it does not affect the net change in the cash flow for the period.

Lower-of-Cost-or-Market Inventory Valuation under Remeasurement

The application of the lower-of-cost-or-market rule to inventories requires special treatment when the recording currency is not the entity's functional currency and, therefore, the foreign entity's financial statements must be remeasured into the functional currency. The historical cost of inventories must first be remeasured using historical exchange rates to determine the functional currency historical cost value. Then these remeasured costs are compared with the market value of the inventories translated using the current rate. The final step is to compare the cost and market, now both in the functional currency, and to recognize any appropriate write-downs to market. The comparison is made in functional currency values, not local or recording currency values; therefore, it is possible to have a write-down appear in the functional currency statements but not on the subsidiary's books, or on the subsidiary's books but not in the consolidated statements.

To illustrate the application of the lower-of-cost-or-market method, assume that a German subsidiary acquired €5,000 of inventory when the direct exchange rate was $1.38 = €1. At the end of the year, the direct exchange rate had decreased to $1.20 = €1. The estimated net realizable value of the inventory (ceiling) is €5,500; its replacement cost is €5,000; and the net realizable value less a normal profit margin (floor) is €4,000. The valuation of the inventory is first specified in the local currency unit (euro), and then evaluated after remeasurement into its functional currency, the U.S. dollar, using the end-of-period exchange rate, as follows:

	€	Exchange	U.S. $
Historical cost	€5,000	$1.38	$6,900
Net realizable value (ceiling)	€5,500	$1.20	$6,600
Replacement cost	5,000	1.20	6,000
Net realizable value less normal profit (floor)	4,000	1.20	4,800

The market value of the inventory is €5,000, or $6,000 in U.S. dollars. Note that the subsidiary recorded no write-down because the historical cost of the inventory was the same as market. However, the comparison in functional currency (U.S. dollar) values shows that the U.S. parent requires a $900 write-down to write the inventory down from its functional currency historical cost of $6,900 to its functional currency market value of $6,000.

Intercompany Transactions

A U.S. parent or home office may have many intercompany sales or purchases transactions with its foreign affiliate that create intercompany receivables or payables. The process of translating receivables or payables denominated in a foreign currency was discussed in Chapter 11. For example, assume that a U.S. company has a foreign currency–denominated receivable from its foreign subsidiary. The U.S. company would first revalue the foreign currency–denominated receivable to its U.S. dollar equivalent value as of the date of the financial statements. After the foreign affiliate's statements have been translated or remeasured, depending on the foreign affiliate's functional currency, the intercompany payable and receivable should be at the same U.S. dollar value and can be eliminated.

FASB 52 provides an exception when the intercompany foreign currency transactions will not be settled within the foreseeable future. These intercompany transactions may be considered part of the net investment in the foreign entity. The translation adjustments on these long-term receivables or payables are deferred and accumulated as part of the cumulative translation account. For example, a U.S. parent company may loan its German subsidiary $10,000 for which the parent does not expect repayment for the foreseeable future. Under the translation method, the dollar-denominated loan payable account of the subsidiary would first be adjusted for the effects of any changes in exchange rates during the period. Any exchange gain or loss adjustment relating to this intercompany note should be classified as part of the cumulative translation adjustment account in stockholders' equity, not in the subsidiary's net income for the period. The same result would occur whether the long-term intercompany financing was denominated in U.S. dollars or the local currency—in our example, the euro. Thus, where financing is regarded as part of the long-term investment in the foreign entity, any exchange gain or loss adjustments on that financing are accumulated in the cumulative translation adjustment account in stockholders' equity.

A particularly interesting problem arises when unrealized intercompany profits occur from transactions between the parent and foreign subsidiary. The problem is how to eliminate the profit across currencies that are changing in value relative to each other. For example, assume that the parent, Peerless Products Corporation, made a downstream sale of inventory to its German subsidiary. The goods cost the parent $10,000 but were sold to the subsidiary for €10,000 when the exchange rate was $1.30 = €1, resulting in an intercompany profit of $3,000 ($13,000 − $10,000). The goods are still in the subsidiary's inventory at the end of the year when the current exchange rate is $1.40 = €1. The relevant facts are summarized as follows:

	Measured in U.S. Dollars	Measured in European Euros
Initial inventory transfer date ($1.30 = €1):		
Selling price (€10,000 × $1.30)	$13,000	€10,000
Cost to parent	(10,000)	
Intercompany profit	$ 3,000	
Balance sheet date ($1.40 = €1):		
Inventory translation ($14,000 = €10,000 × $1.40)	$14,000	€10,000

There are two issues here:

1. At what amount should the ending inventory be shown on the consolidated balance sheet—the original intercompany transfer price of $13,000 (€10,000 × $1.30), the present equivalent exchange value of $14,000 (€10,000 × $1.40 current exchange rate), or some other amount?

2. What amount should be eliminated for the unrealized intercompany gain—the original intercompany profit of $3,000 or the balance sheet date exchange equivalent of the intercompany profit of $4,000 ($14,000 present exchange value less $10,000 original cost to parent)?

FASB 52 provides the following guidance to answer these questions.[6]

> The elimination of intercompany profits that are attributable to sales or other transfers between entities that are consolidated, combined, or accounted for by the equity method in the enterprise's financial statements shall be based on the exchange rates at the dates of the sales or transfers. The use of reasonable approximations or averages is permitted.

Therefore, for the example, the eliminating entry for the intercompany profit is:

E(28)	Cost of Goods Sold	3,000	
	Ending Inventory		3,000
	Elimination of unrealized intercompany profit based on exchange rates of date of transfer.		

[6] *FASB 52*, para. 25.

The inventory is shown on the consolidated balance sheet at $11,000, which is a $1,000 increase over the initial cost to the parent company. This increase will result in a corresponding increase in a credit to the translation adjustment component of stockholders' equity. The FASB has stated that changes in exchange rates occurring *after* the date of the intercompany transaction are independent of the initial inventory transfer.

Income Taxes

Interperiod tax allocation is required whenever temporary differences exist in the recognition of revenue and expenses for income statement purposes and for tax purposes. Exchange gains and losses from foreign currency transactions require the recognition of a deferred tax if they are included in income but not recognized for tax purposes in the same period.

A deferral is required for the portion of the translation adjustment related to the subsidiary's undistributed earnings that are included in the parent's income. **APB Opinion No. 23**, "Accounting for Income Taxes—Special Areas" (APB 23), presumes that a temporary difference exists for the undistributed earnings of a subsidiary unless the earnings are indefinitely reinvested in it. Deferred taxes need not be recognized if the undistributed earnings will be indefinitely reinvested in the subsidiary. However, if the parent expects eventually to receive the presently undistributed earnings of a foreign subsidiary, deferred tax recognition is required, and the tax entry recorded by the parent should include a debit to Other Comprehensive Income rather than to additional income tax, as follows:

(29)	Other Comprehensive Income—Translation Adjustment	X,XXX	
	Deferred Taxes Payable		X,XXX

Translation When a Third Currency Is the Functional Currency

There may be a few cases in which the foreign subsidiary maintains its books and records in the local currency unit but has a third currency as its functional currency. For example, assume that our subsidiary, German Company, maintains its records in its local currency, the euro. If the subsidiary conducts many of its business activities in the Swiss franc, management may conclude that the Swiss franc is the subsidiary's functional currency. If the entity's books and records are *not* expressed in its functional currency, the following two-step process must be used:

1. Remeasure the subsidiary's financial statements into the functional currency. In our example, the financial statements expressed in euros would be remeasured into Swiss francs. The remeasurement process would be the same as illustrated earlier in the chapter. The statements would now be expressed in the entity's functional currency, the Swiss franc.
2. The statements expressed in Swiss francs are then translated into U.S. dollars using the translation process illustrated in the chapter.

As indicated, this occurrence is not common in practice but is a consideration for foreign subsidiaries that have very significant business activities in a currency other than the currency of the country in which the subsidiary is physically located. This discussion indicates that it is important first to determine the foreign entity's functional currency before beginning the translation process.

Summary of Key Concepts

The restatement of a foreign affiliate's financial statements in U.S. dollars may be made using the translation or remeasurement method, depending on the foreign entity's functional currency. Most foreign affiliates' statements are translated using the current rate method because the local currency unit is typically the functional currency. If the U.S. dollar is the functional currency, remeasurement is used to convert the foreign entity's statements from the local currency into dollars. The choice of functional currency affects the valuations of the foreign entity's accounts reported on the consolidated financial statements.

Because translation or remeasurement is performed with different exchange rates applied to balance sheet and income statement accounts, a balancing item called a "translation adjustment" or "remeasurement gain or loss" is created in the process. The translation adjustment is proportionally divided between the parent company and the noncontrolling interest. The parent company's share, adjusted for the effects from the differential paid for the investment, is reported as a component of other comprehensive income and then accumulated in the stockholders' equity section of the consolidated balance sheet. The noncontrolling interest's share is a direct adjustment to noncontrolling interest reported in the consolidated balance sheet. The remeasurement gain or loss is reported in the consolidated statement of income.

Key Terms

Accumulated Other
  Comprehensive
  Income, *580*
average rate, *575*
comprehensive income, *579*
current rate, *575*

current rate method, *577*
functional currency, *575*
historical rate, *575*
other comprehensive
  income, *579*
remeasurement, *577*

remeasurement gain
  or loss, *591*
temporal method, *577*
translation, *577*
translation adjustment, *579*

Questions

Q12-1 Define the following terms: (*a*) local currency unit, (*b*) recording currency, and (*c*) reporting currency.

Q12-2 What factors are used to determine a reporting entity's functional currency? Provide at least one example for which a company's local currency may not be its functional currency.

Q12-3 Some accountants are seeking to harmonize international accounting standards. What is meant by the term *harmonize?* How might harmonization result in better financial reporting for a U.S. parent company with many foreign investments?

Q12-4 A Canadian-based subsidiary of a U.S. parent uses the Canadian dollar as its functional currency. Describe the methodology for translating the subsidiary's financial statements into the parent's reporting currency.

Q12-5 A U.S. company has a foreign sales branch located in Spain. The Spanish branch has selected the U.S. dollar for its functional currency. Describe the methodology for remeasuring the branch's financial statements into the U.S. company's reporting currency.

Q12-6 Discuss the accounting treatment and disclosure of translation adjustments. When does the translation adjustment account have a debit balance? When does it have a credit balance?

Q12-7 Where is the remeasurement gain or loss shown in the consolidated financial statements?

Q12-8 When the functional currency is the foreign affiliate's local currency, why are the stockholders' equity accounts translated at historical exchange rates? How is retained earnings computed?

Q12-9 Comment on the following statement: "The use of the current exchange rate method of translating a foreign affiliate's financial statements allows for an assessment of foreign management by the same ratio criteria used to manage the foreign affiliate."

Q12-10 A U.S. company paid more than book value in acquiring a foreign affiliate. How is this excess reported in the consolidated balance sheet and income statement in subsequent periods when the functional currency is the local currency unit of the foreign affiliate?

Q12-11 What is the logic behind the parent company's recognizing on its books its share of the translation adjustment arising from the translation of its foreign subsidiary?

Q12-12 Are all foreign subsidiaries consolidated? Why or why not?

Q12-13 Describe the accounting for a foreign investment that is not consolidated with the U.S. company.

Q12-14 Describe the basic problem of eliminating intercompany transactions with a foreign affiliate.

Cases

C12-1 **Determining a Functional Currency**

Judgment

Following are descriptions of several independent situations.

1. Rockford Company has a subsidiary in Argentina. The subsidiary does not have much debt because of the high interest costs resulting from the average annual inflation rate exceeding 100 percent.

Most of its sales and expense transactions are denominated in Argentinian pesos, and the subsidiary attempts to minimize its receivables and payables. Although the subsidiary owns a warehouse, the primary asset is inventory that it receives from Rockford. The Argentinian government requires all companies located in Argentina to provide the central government with a financial report using the Argentinian system of accounts and government-mandated forms for financial statements.

2. JRB International located in Dallas, Texas, is the world's largest manufacturer of electronic stirrups. The company acquires the raw materials for its products from around the world and begins the assembly process in Dallas. It then sends the partially completed units to its subsidiary in Mexico for assembly completion. Mexico has been able to hold its inflation rate under 100 percent over the last three years. The subsidiary is required to pay its employees and local vendors in Mexican pesos. The parent company provides all financing for the Mexican subsidiary, and the subsidiary sends all of its production back to the warehouse in Dallas, from which it is shipped as orders are received. The subsidiary provides the Mexican government with financial statements.

3. Huskie Inc. maintains a branch office in Great Britain. The branch office is fairly autonomous because it must find its own financing, set its own local marketing policies, and control its own costs. The branch receives weekly shipments from Huskie Inc., which it then conveys to its customers. The pound sterling is used to pay the subsidiary's employees and to pay for the weekly shipments.

4. Hola Company has a foreign subsidiary located in a rural area of Switzerland, right next to the Swiss–French border. The subsidiary hires virtually all its employees from France and makes most of its sales to companies in France. The majority of its cash transactions are maintained in the European euro. However, it is required to pay local property taxes and sales taxes in Swiss francs and to provide annual financial statements to the Swiss government.

Required

For each of these independent cases, determine:

a. The foreign entity's reporting currency in which its books and records are maintained.

b. The foreign entity's functional currency.

c. The process to be used to restate the foreign entity's financial statements into the reporting currency of the U.S.–based parent company.

C12-2 Principles of Consolidating and Translating Foreign Accounts [AICPA Adapted]

Petie Products Company was incorporated in Wisconsin in 20X0 as a manufacturer of dairy supplies and equipment. Since incorporating, Petie has doubled in size about every three years and is now considered one of the leading dairy supply companies in the country.

Understanding During January 20X4, Petie established a subsidiary, Cream Ltd., in the emerging nation of Kolay. Petie owns 90 percent of the outstanding capital stock of Cream; Kolay citizens hold the remaining 10 percent of Cream's outstanding capital stock, as Kolay law requires. The investment in Cream, accounted for by Petie using the equity method, represents about 18 percent of Petie's total assets at December 31, 20X7, the close of the accounting period for both companies.

Required

a. What criteria should Petie use in determining whether it would be appropriate to prepare consolidated financial statements with Cream Ltd. for the year ended December 31, 20X7? Explain.

b. Independent of your answer to part a, assume it has been appropriate for Petie and Cream to prepare consolidated financial statements for each year, 20X4 through 20X7. Before they can be prepared, the individual account balances in Cream's December 31, 20X7, adjusted trial balance must be translated into dollars. The kola (K) is the subsidiary's functional currency. For each of the following 10 accounts, taken from Cream's adjusted trial balance, specify what exchange rate (e.g., average exchange rate for 20X7, current exchange rate on December 31, 20X7) should be used to translate the account balance into dollars and explain why that rate is appropriate. Number your answers to correspond with these accounts.

(1) Cash in Kolay National Bank.

(2) Trade Accounts Receivable (all from 20X7 revenue).

(3) Supplies Inventory (all purchased during the last quarter of 20X7).

(4) Land purchased in 20X4.

(5) Short-Term Note Payable to Kolay National Bank.

   (6) Capital Stock (no par or stated value and all issued in January 20X4).

   (7) Retained Earnings, January 1, 20X7.

   (8) Sales Revenue.

   (9) Depreciation Expense (on buildings).

   (10) Salaries Expense.

C12-3 **Translating and Remeasuring Financial Statements of Foreign Subsidiaries [AICPA Adapted]**

Communication

Wahl Company's 20X5 consolidated financial statements include two wholly owned subsidiaries, Wahl Company of Australia (Wahl A) and Wahl Company of France (Wahl F). Functional currencies are the U.S. dollar for Wahl A and the European euro for Wahl F.

Required

a. What are the objectives of translating a foreign subsidiary's financial statements?

b. How are gains and losses arising from the translation or remeasurement of each subsidiary's financial statements measured and reported in Wahl's consolidated financial statements?

c. FASB Statement No. 52 identifies several economic indicators to be considered both individually and collectively in determining the functional currency for a consolidated subsidiary. List three of these indicators.

d. What exchange rate is used to incorporate each subsidiary's equipment cost, accumulated depreciation, and depreciation expense in Wahl's consolidated financial statements?

C12-4 **Translation Adjustment and Comprehensive Income**

Analysis

Dundee Company owns 100 percent of a subsidiary located in Ireland. The parent company uses the Irish pound as the subsidiary's functional currency. At the beginning of the year, the debit balance in Accumulated Other Comprehensive Income—Translation Adjustment account, which was the only item in accumulated other comprehensive income, was $80,000. The subsidiary's translated trial balance at the end of the year is as follows:

	Debit	Credit
Cash	$ 50,000	
Receivables	24,700	
Inventories	60,300	
Property, Plant, and Equipment (net)	328,000	
Cost of Sales	285,000	
Operating Expenses (including depreciation)	140,000	
Dividends	12,000	
Current Payables		$ 16,000
Long-Term Payables		181,000
Capital Stock		100,000
Retained Earnings (1/1 balance)		135,000
Sales		560,000
Accumulated Other Comprehensive Income—Translation Adjustment	92,000	
	$992,000	$992,000

Required

a. Prepare the subsidiary's statement of income, ending in net income, for the year.

b. Prepare the subsidiary's statement of comprehensive income for the year.

c. Prepare a year-end balance sheet for the subsidiary.

d. FASB 130 allows for alternative operating statement displays of the other comprehensive income items. Discuss the major differences between the one-statement format of the Statement of Income and Comprehensive Income versus the two-statement format of the Statement of Income with a separate Statement of Comprehensive Income.

C12-5 Changes in the Cumulative Translation Adjustment Account

The following footnote was abstracted from a recent annual report of Johnson & Johnson Company:

Understanding

Footnote 7: Foreign Currency Translation

For translation of its international currencies, the Company has determined that the local currencies of its international subsidiaries are the functional currencies except those in highly inflationary economies, which are defined as those which have had compound cumulative rates of inflation of 100% or more during the last three years.

In consolidating international subsidiaries, balance sheet currency effects are recorded as a separate component of stockholders' equity. This equity account includes the results of translating all balance sheet assets and liabilities at current exchange rates, except those located in highly inflationary economies, principally Brazil, which are reflected in operating results. These translation adjustments do not exist in terms of functional cash flows; such adjustments are not reported as part of operating results since realization is remote unless the international businesses were sold or liquidated.

An analysis of the changes during 20X3 and 20X2 in the separate component of stock-holders' equity for foreign currency translation adjustments follows (with debit amounts in parentheses):

(Dollars in Millions)	20X3	20X2
Balance at beginning of year	$(146)	$ 134
Change in translation adjustments	(192)	(280)
Balance at end of year	$(338)	$(146)

Required

a. What is the main point of the footnote?

b. How is the footnote related to the concepts covered in the chapter?

c. List some possible reasons the company's translation adjustment decreased from a $134 million credit balance at the end of 20X1 to a $338 million debit balance at the end of 20X3.

d. Assume that the translated stockholders' equities of the foreign subsidiaries, other than the cumulative translation adjustment, remained constant from 20X1 through 20X3 at a balance of $500 million. What were the translated balances in the net assets (assets minus liabilities) of the foreign subsidiaries in each of the three years? What factors might cause the changes in the balances of the net assets over the three-year period?

e. How would changes in the local currency unit's exchange rate in the countries in which the company has subsidiaries affect the cumulative translation adjustment?

f. How could you verify the actual causal factors for the changes in the cumulative translation adjustment of Johnson & Johnson Company for the years presented? Be specific!

C12-6 Pros and Cons of Foreign Investment

Many larger U.S. companies have significant investments in foreign operations. For example, McDonald's Corporation, the food service company, obtains 47 percent of its consolidated revenues and 44 percent of its operating income from, and has 45 percent of its invested assets in, non-U.S. locations. Unisys, the information systems company, obtains 51 percent of its consolidated revenues and 65 percent of its operating income from, and has 40 percent of its invested assets in, non-U.S. locations. Foreign operations impose additional types of operating risks to companies, including the risks from changes in the exchange rates for currencies, statutory acts by the foreign governments, and producing and marketing goods in an environment outside the United States.

Judgment

With the passage of the North American Free Trade Agreement (NAFTA), more companies are confronted with the decision of whether or not to expand their production and marketing investments to Canada and Mexico.

Required

Using NAFTA as a discussion focus, address the following questions.

a. Explain why a U.S. company might find it advantageous to increase its production capacity of its subsidiaries in Mexico. Describe some circumstances under which it would be disadvantageous for a U.S. company to increase its investment in production subsidiaries located in Mexico.

b. In your opinion, would an increase in U.S. companies' investments in Mexico and Canada be good or bad for U.S. consumers?

c. What are some possible solutions to the possible problem of an increase in the U.S. unemployment rate if U.S. companies shift their production facilities to non-U.S. locations? Select one and discuss the pros and cons of that possible solution.

d. What conclusion can you draw from the attempts of the U.S. government to decrease barriers to international trade and investment? In your opinion, is this a good effort on the part of the government, or do you feel this effort should be changed?

C12-7   Determining an Entity's Functional Currency

Maxima Corporation, a U.S. company, manufactures lighting fixtures and ceiling fans. Eight years ago, it set up a subsidiary in Mexico to manufacture three of its most popular ceiling fan models. When the subsidiary, Luz Maxima, was set up, it did business exclusively with Maxima, receiving shipments of materials from U.S. suppliers selected by Maxima and selling all of its production to Maxima. Maxima's management made a determination that its subsidiary's functional currency was the U.S. dollar.

*Research
FARS*

During the past five years changes in Luz Maxima's operations have occurred. The subsidiary has developed relationships with suppliers within Mexico and is obtaining a significant percentage of its materials requirements from these suppliers. In addition, Luz Maxima has expanded its production by introducing a new product line marketed within Mexico and Central America. These products now make up a substantial percentage of the subsidiary's sales. Luz Maxima obtained long-term debt financing and a line of credit from several Mexican banks to expand its operations.

Prior to the preparation of Maxima's consolidated financial statements for the current year, Luz Maxima's financial statements, reported in Mexican pesos, must be converted into U.S. dollars. Maxima's CFO, Garry Parise, is concerned that Luz Maxima's functional currency may no longer be the U.S. dollar and that remeasurement of its financial statements may not be appropriate.

Required

Obtain the most current accounting standards on determining an entity's functional currency. You can obtain access to accounting standards through the Financial Accounting Research System (FARS), from your library, or from some other source. Garry has asked you, as an accountant in the controller's department, to research the functional currency issue. Write a memo to him, reporting on the results of your research. Support your recommendations with citations and quotations from the authoritative financial reporting standards.

C12-8   Accounting for the Translation Adjustment

Sonoma Company has owned 100 percent of the outstanding common stock of Valencia Corporation, a Spanish subsidiary, for the past 15 years. The Spanish company's functional currency is the peso, and its financial statements are translated into U.S. dollars prior to consolidation.

*Research
FARS*

In the current year, Sonoma has sold 30 percent of Valencia's voting common stock to a nonaffiliated company. Sonoma's controller, Renee Voll, has calculated a gain on the sale of this portion of its investment in Valencia. The consolidated balance sheet at the end of last year contained a debit balance cumulative translation adjustment related to the Spanish subsidiary. Voll believes that the decrease in Sonoma's share of Valencia's translation adjustment will be automatically included in other comprehensive income as the year-end translation adjustment is calculated and that Sonoma's share is included in the consolidated financial statements. However, she has asked you, as an accountant in her department, to research the accounting for the translation adjustment as a result of the sale of a part of the investment in the Spanish subsidiary.

Required

Obtain the most current accounting standards on accounting for the translation adjustment resulting from translating the trial balance of a foreign affiliate. You can obtain access to accounting standards through the Financial Accounting Research System (FARS), from your library, or from some other source. Write a memo to Renee reporting on the results of your research. Support your recommendations with citations and quotations from the authoritative financial reporting standards.

Exercises **E12-1** **Multiple-Choice Questions on Translation and Remeasurement [AICPA Adapted]**
For each of the seven cases presented below, work the case twice and select the best answer. First assume that the foreign currency is the functional currency; then assume that the U.S. dollar is the functional currency.

1. Certain balance sheet accounts in a foreign subsidiary of Shaw Company on December 31, 20X1, have been restated in United States dollars as follows:

	Restated at	
	Current Rates	Historical Rates
Accounts Receivable, Current	$100,000	$110,000
Accounts Receivable, Long-Term	50,000	55,000
Prepaid Insurance	25,000	30,000
Patents	40,000	45,000
Total	$215,000	$240,000

What total should be included in Shaw's balance sheet for December 31, 20X1, for the above items?

   a. $215,000.
   b. $225,000.
   c. $230,000.
   d. $240,000.

2. A wholly owned foreign subsidiary of Nick Inc. has certain expense accounts for the year ended December 31, 20X4, stated in local currency units (LCU) as follows:

	LCU
Depreciation of Equipment (related assets were purchased January 1, 20X2)	120,000
Provision for Uncollectible Accounts	80,000
Rent	200,000

The exchange rates at various dates were as follows:

	Dollar Equivalent of 1 LCU
January 1, 20X2	$.50
December 31, 20X4	.40
Average, 20X4	.44

What total dollar amount should be included in Nick's statement of income to reflect the preceding expenses for the year ended December 31, 20X4?

   a. $160,000.
   b. $168,000.
   c. $176,000.
   d. $183,200.

3. Linser Corporation owns a foreign subsidiary with 2,600,000 local currency units (LCU) of property, plant, and equipment before accumulated depreciation on December 31, 20X4. Of this amount, 1,700,000 LCU were acquired in 20X2 when the rate of exchange was 1.5 LCU = $1, and

900,000 LCU were acquired in 20X3 when the rate of exchange was 1.6 LCU = $1. The rate of exchange in effect on December 31, 20X4, was 1.9 LCU = $1. The weighted average of exchange rates that were in effect during 20X4 was 1.8 LCU = $1. Assuming that the property, plant, and equipment are depreciated using the straight-line method over a 10-year period with no salvage value, how much depreciation expense relating to the foreign subsidiary's property, plant, and equipment should be charged in Linser's statement of income for 20X4?

a. $144,444.

b. $162,000.

c. $169,583.

d. $173,333.

4. On January 1, 20X1, Pat Company formed a foreign subsidiary. On February 15, 20X1, Pat's subsidiary purchased 100,000 local currency units (LCU) of inventory. Of the original inventory purchased on February 15, 20X1, 25,000 LCU made up the entire inventory on December 31, 20X1. The exchange rates were 2.2 LCU = $1 from January 1, 20X1, to June 30, 20X1, and 2 LCU = $1 from July 1, 20X1, to December 31, 20X1. The December 31, 20X1, inventory balance for Pat's foreign subsidiary should be restated in U.S. dollars in the amount of:

a. $10,500.

b. $11,364.

c. $11,905.

d. $12,500.

5. At what rates should the following balance sheet accounts in the foreign currency financial statements be restated into U.S. dollars?

	Equipment	Accumulated Depreciation of Equipment
a.	Current	Current
b.	Current	Average for year
c.	Historical	Current
d.	Historical	Historical

6. A credit-balancing item resulting from the process of restating a foreign entity's financial statement from the local currency unit to U.S. dollars should be included as a (an):

a. Separate component of stockholders' equity.

b. Deferred credit.

c. Component of income from continuing operations.

d. Extraordinary item.

7. A foreign subsidiary of the Bart Corporation has certain balance sheet accounts on December 31, 20X2. Information relating to these accounts in U.S. dollars is as follows:

	Restated at	
	Current Rates	Historical Rates
Marketable Securities	$ 75,000	$ 85,000
Inventories, carried at average cost	600,000	700,000
Refundable Deposits	25,000	30,000
Goodwill	55,000	70,000
	$755,000	$885,000

What total should be included in Bart's balance sheet on December 31, 20X2, as a result of the preceding information?

a. $755,000.

b. $780,000.

  c. $870,000.

  d. $880,000.

E12-2   Multiple-Choice Questions on Translation and Foreign Currency Transactions [AICPA Adapted]

The following information should be used for questions 1, 2, and 3. Select the best answers under each of two alternative assumptions: (*a*) the LCU is the functional currency and the translation method is appropriate or (*b*) the U.S. dollar is the functional currency and the remeasurement method is appropriate.

1. Refer to the preceding requirements. Gate Inc. had a credit adjustment of $30,000 for the year ended December 31, 20X2, from restating its foreign subsidiary's accounts from their local currency units into U.S. dollars. Additionally, Gate had a receivable from a foreign customer payable in the customer's local currency. On December 31, 20X1, this receivable for 200,000 local currency units (LCU) was correctly included in Gate's balance sheet at $110,000. When the receivable was collected on February 15, 20X2, the U.S. dollar equivalent was $120,000. In Gate's 20X2 consolidated statement of income, how much should be reported as foreign exchange gain in computing net income?

   a. $0.

   b. $10,000.

   c. $30,000.

   d. $40,000.

2. Refer to the preceding requirements. Bar Corporation had a realized foreign exchange loss of $13,000 for the year ended December 31, 20X2, and must also determine whether the following items will require year-end adjustment:

   (1) Bar had a $7,000 credit resulting from the restatement in dollars of the accounts of its wholly owned foreign subsidiary for the year ended December 31, 20X2.

   (2) Bar had an account payable to an unrelated foreign supplier payable in the supplier's local currency. The U.S. dollar–equivalent of the payable was $60,000 on the October 31, 20X2, invoice date and $64,000 on December 31, 20X2. The invoice is payable on January 30, 20X3.

   What amount of the net foreign exchange loss in computing net income should be reported in Bar's 20X2 consolidated statement of income?

   a. $6,000.

   b. $10,000.

   c. $13,000.

   d. $17,000.

3. Refer to the preceding requirements. The balance in Simpson Corp.'s foreign exchange loss account was $15,000 on December 31, 20X2, before any necessary year-end adjustment relating to the following:

   (1) Simpson had a $20,000 debit resulting from the restatement in dollars of the accounts of its wholly owned foreign subsidiary for the year ended December 31, 20X2.

   (2) Simpson had an account payable to an unrelated foreign supplier, payable in the supplier's local currency on January 27, 20X3. The U.S. dollar–equivalent of the payable was $100,000 on the November 28, 20X2, invoice date, and $106,000 on December 31, 20X2.

   In Simpson's 20X2 consolidated income statement, what amount should be included as foreign exchange loss in computing net income?

   a. $41,000.

   b. $35,000.

   c. $21,000.

   d. $15,000.

4. When remeasuring foreign currency financial statements into the functional currency, which of the following items would be remeasured using an historical exchange rate?

   a. Inventories carried at cost.

   b. Trading securities carried at market values.

   c. Bonds payable.

   d. Accrued liabilities.

5. A foreign subsidiary's functional currency is its local currency, which has not experienced significant inflation. The weighted-average exchange rate for the current year would be the appropriate exchange rate for translating:

	Sales to Customers	Wages Expense
a.	No	No
b.	Yes	Yes
c.	No	Yes
d.	Yes	No

6. The functional currency of Dahl Inc.'s subsidiary is the European euro. Dahl borrowed euros as a partial hedge of its investment in the subsidiary. In preparing consolidated financial statements, Dahl's debit balance of its translation adjustment exceeded its exchange gain on the borrowing. How should the translation adjustment and the exchange gain be reported in Dahl's consolidated financial statements?

a. The translation adjustment should be netted against the exchange gain, and the excess translation adjustment should be reported in the stockholders' equity section of the balance sheet.

b. The translation adjustment should be netted against the exchange gain, and the excess translation adjustment should be reported in the statement of income in computing net income.

c. The translation adjustment is reported as a component of other comprehensive income and then accumulated in the stockholders' equity section of the balance sheet, and the exchange gain should be reported in the statement of income in computing net income.

d. The translation adjustment should be reported in the statement of income, and the exchange gain should be reported separately in the stockholders' equity section of the balance sheet.

E12-3   Matching Key Terms

Match the descriptions of terms on the left with the terms on the right. Some terms may be used once, more than once, or not at all.

Descriptions of Terms	Terms
1. The group that has attempted to harmonize the world's many different accounting methods.	A. Financial Accounting Standards Board
2. The currency of the primary economic environment in which the entity operates.	B. Remeasurement gain or loss
3. The functional currency for a U.S. subsidiary located in a country with > 100 percent inflation over the last three years.	C. Translation adjustment
4. Translation of all assets and liabilities of a foreign subsidiary using the foreign exchange rate at the balance sheet date.	D. Current rate method
5. Restatement of the fixed assets and inventories of a foreign subsidiary into U.S. dollars using historical exchange rates.	E. Remeasurement method
6. Inclusion of this gain or loss on the U.S. company's statement of income as part of net income.	F. U.S. dollar
7. The item that balances the debits and credits of the foreign subsidiary's adjusted trial balance in U.S. dollars, assuming the functional currency is the currency of the foreign subsidiary's country.	G. Functional currency
8. The item that balances the debits and credits of the foreign subsidiary's adjusted trial balance in U.S. dollars, assuming the functional currency is the U.S. dollar.	H. International Accounting Standards Board
9. Translation of the statement of income accounts of a foreign subsidiary using the average exchange rate for the year.	I. International Managerial Accounting Society
10. Restatement of depreciation expense and cost of goods sold of a foreign subsidiary using historical exchange rates.	J. Functional currency indicators
11. An analysis of a foreign subsidiary's cash flows, sales prices, sales markets, expenses, and financing.	K. Historical rate method
12. The periodic change in this item reported as a component of other comprehensive income.	L. Cumulative transaction gain or loss

E12-4 **Multiple-Choice Questions on Translation and Remeasurement**
Use the following information for questions 1, 2, and 3.

Bartell Inc., a U.S. company, acquired 90 percent of the common stock of a Malaysian company on January 1, 20X5, for $160,000. The net assets of the Malaysian subsidiary amounted to 680,000 ringitts (RM) on the date of acquisition. On January 1, 20X5, the book values of the Malaysian subsidiary's identifiable assets and liabilities approximated their fair values. Exchange rates at various dates during 20X5 follow:

January 1	RM 1 = $.21
December 31	RM 1 = $.24
Average for 20X5	RM 1 = $.22

1. Refer to the preceding information. On January 1, 20X5, how much goodwill was acquired by Bartell?
   a. $17,200.
   b. $31,480.
   c. $11,400.
   d. $25,360.

2. Refer to the preceding information. Assume that Bartell acquired $10,500 of goodwill on January 1, 20X5, and the goodwill suffered a 10 percent impairment loss in 20X5. If the functional currency is the Malaysian ringgit, how much goodwill impairment loss should be reported on Bartell's consolidated statement of income for 20X5?
   a. $1,050.
   b. $1,200.
   c. $1,100.
   d. $1,175.

3. Refer to the preceding information but now assume that the U.S. dollar is the functional currency. How much goodwill impairment loss should be reported on Bartell's consolidated statement of income in this situation?
   a. $1,050.
   b. $1,200.
   c. $1,100.
   d. $1,175.

Use the following information for questions 4, 5, 6, and 7.

Mondell Inc., a U.S. company, acquired 100 percent of the common stock of a German company on January 1, 20X5, for $402,000. The German subsidiary's net assets amounted to 300,000 euros on the date of acquisition. On January 1, 20X5, the book values of its identifiable assets and liabilities approximated their fair values. As a result of an analysis of functional currency indicators, Mondell determined that the euro was the functional currency. On December 31, 20X5, the German subsidiary's adjusted trial balance, translated into U.S. dollars, contained $12,000 more debits than credits. The German subsidiary reported income of 25,000 euros for 20X5 and paid a cash dividend of 5,000 euros on November 30, 20X5. Included on the German subsidiary's income statement was depreciation expense of 2,500 euros. Mondell uses the basic equity method of accounting for its investment in the German subsidiary and determined that goodwill in the first year had an impairment loss of 10 percent of its initial amount. Exchange rates at various dates during 20X5 follow:

January 1	€1 = $1.20
November 30	€1 = 1.30
December 31	€1 = 1.32
Average for 20X5	€1 = 1.24

4. Refer to the preceding information. What amount should Mondell record as "income from subsidiary" based on the German subsidiary's reported net income?
   a. $31,000.
   b. $31,100.

    c. $33,000.

    d. $30,000.

5. Refer to the preceding information. The receipt of the dividend will result in:

    a. A credit to the investment account for $6,200.

    b. A debit to the income from subsidiary account for $6,600.

    c. A credit to the investment account for $6,600.

    d. A credit to the investment account for $6,500.

6. Refer to the preceding information. On Bartell's consolidated balance sheet at December 31, 20X5, what amount should be reported for the goodwill acquired on January 1, 20X5?

    a. $37,660.

    b. $37,800.

    c. $41,580.

    d. $39,880.

7. Refer to the preceding information. In the stockholders' equity section of Bartell's consolidated balance sheet at December 31, 20X5, Bartell should report the translation adjustment as a component of other comprehensive income of:

    a. $12,000.

    b. $15,920.

    c. $13,400.

    d. $8,080.

E12-5 Translation

On January 1, 20X1, Popular Creek Corporation organized RoadTime Company as a subsidiary in Switzerland with an initial investment cost of Swiss francs (SFr) 60,000. RoadTime's December 31, 20X1, trial balance in SFr is as follows:

	Debit	Credit
Cash	SFr 7,000	
Accounts Receivable (net)	20,000	
Receivable from Popular Creek	5,000	
Inventory	25,000	
Plant and Equipment	100,000	
Accumulated Depreciation		SFr 10,000
Accounts Payable		12,000
Bonds Payable		50,000
Common Stock		60,000
Sales		150,000
Cost of Goods Sold	70,000	
Depreciation Expense	10,000	
Operating Expense	30,000	
Dividends Paid	15,000	
Total	SFr 282,000	SFr 282,000

Additional Information

1. The receivable from Popular Creek is denominated in Swiss francs. Popular Creek's books show a $4,000 payable to RoadTime.

2. Purchases of inventory goods are made evenly during the year. Items in the ending inventory were purchased November 1.

3. Equipment is depreciated by the straight-line method with a 10-year life and no residual value. A full year's depreciation is taken in the year of acquisition. The equipment was acquired on March 1.

4. The dividends were declared and paid on November 1.

5. Exchange rates were as follows:

January 1	SFr1 = $.73
March 1	SFr1 = .74
November 1	SFr1 = .77
December 31	SFr1 = .80
20X1 Average	SFr1 = .75

6. The Swiss franc is the functional currency.

Required
Prepare a schedule translating the December 31, 20X1, trial balance from Swiss francs to dollars.

E12-6   **Proof of Translation Adjustment**
Refer to the data in Exercise 12-5.

Required
a. Prepare a proof of the translation adjustment computed in Exercise 12-5.
b. Where is the translation adjustment reported on Popular Creek's consolidated financial statements and its foreign subsidiary?

E12-7   **Remeasurement**
Refer to the data in Exercise 12-5, but assume that the dollar is the functional currency for the foreign subsidiary.

Required
Prepare a schedule remeasuring the December 31, 20X1, trial balance from Swiss francs to dollars.

E12-8*   **Proof of Remeasurement Gain (Loss)**
Refer to the data in Exercises 12-5 and 12-7.

Required
a. Prepare a proof of the remeasurement gain or loss computed in Exercise 12-7.
b. How should this remeasurement gain or loss be reported on Popular Creek's consolidated financial statements and the financial statements of its foreign subsidiary?

E12-9   **Translation with Strengthening U.S. Dollar**
Refer to the data in Exercise 12-5, but now assume that the exchange rates were as follows:

January 1	SFr1 = $.80
March 1	SFr1 = .77
November 1	SFr1 = .74
December 31	SFr1 = .73
20X1 Average	SFr1 = .75

The receivable from Popular Creek Corporation is denominated in Swiss francs. Popular Creek's books show a $3,650 payable to RoadTime.

Assume the Swiss franc is the functional currency.

Required
a. Prepare a schedule translating the December 31, 20X1, trial balance from Swiss francs to dollars.
b. Compare the results of Exercise 12-5, in which the dollar is weakening against the Swiss franc during 20X1, with the results in this exercise (E12-9), in which the dollar is strengthening against the Swiss franc during 20X1.

*Indicates that the item relates to "Additional Considerations."

E12-10 **Remeasurement with Strengthening U.S. Dollar**

Refer to the data in Exercise 12-5, but now assume that the exchange rates were as follows:

January 1	SFr1 = $.80
March 1	SFr1 = .77
November 1	SFr1 = .74
December 31	SFr1 = .73
20X1 Average	SFr1 = .75

The receivable from Popular Creek is denominated in Swiss francs. Its books show a $3,650 payable to RoadTime.

Assume that the U.S. dollar is the functional currency.

Required

a. Prepare a schedule remeasuring the December 31, 20X1, trial balance from Swiss francs to dollars.

b. Compare the results of Exercise 12-7, in which the dollar weakens against the Swiss franc during 20X1, with the results in this exercise (E12-10), in which the dollar strengthened against the Swiss franc during 20X1.

E12-11 **Remeasurement and Translation of Cost of Goods Sold**

Duff Company is a subsidiary of Rand Corporation and is located in Madrid, Spain, where the currency is the Spanish peseta (P). Data on Duff's inventory and purchases are as follows:

Inventory, January 1, 20X7	P220,000
Purchases during 20X7	P846,000
Inventory, December 31, 20X7	P180,000

The beginning inventory was acquired during the fourth quarter of 20X6, and the ending inventory was acquired during the fourth quarter of 20X7. Purchases were made evenly over the year. Exchange rates were as follows:

Fourth quarter of 20X6	P1 = $0.0070
January 1, 20X7	P1 = $0.0075
Average during 20X7	P1 = $0.0080
Fourth quarter of 20X7	P1 = $0.0082
December 31, 20X7	P1 = $0.0085

Required

a. Show the remeasurement of cost of goods sold for 20X7, assuming that the U.S. dollar is the functional currency.

b. Show the translation of cost of goods sold for 20X7, assuming that the Spanish peseta is the functional currency.

E12-12 **Equity-Method Entries for a Foreign Subsidiary**

Thames Company is located in London, England. The local currency is the British pound (£). On January 1, 20X8, Dek Company purchased an 80 percent interest in Thames for $400,000, which resulted in an excess of cost-over-book value of $48,000 due solely to a trademark having a remaining life of 10 years. Dek uses the equity method to account for its investment.

Dek's December 31, 20X8, trial balance has been translated into U.S. dollars, requiring a translation adjustment debit of $6,400. Thames's net income translated into U.S. dollars is $60,000. It declared and paid a £15,000 dividend on May 1, 20X8.

Relevant exchange rates are as follows:

January 1, 20X8	£1 = $1.60
Average for 20X8	£1 = $1.63
May 1, 20X8	£1 = $1.64
December 31, 20X8	£1 = $1.65

Required

a. Record the dividend received by Dek from Thames.

b. Prepare the entries to record Dek's equity in the net income of Thames and the parent's share of the translation adjustment.

c. Show a calculation of the differential reported on the consolidated balance sheet of December 31, 20X8, and the translation adjustment from differential.

d. Record the amortization of the trademark on Dek's books.

e. Calculate the amount of the translation adjustment reported on the statement of comprehensive income as an element of other comprehensive income.

E12-13 **Effects of a Change in the Exchange Rate—Translation and Other Comprehensive Income**

Bentley Company owns a subsidiary in India whose balance sheets in rupees (R) for the last two years follow:

	December 31, 20X6	December 31, 20X7
Assets:		
Cash	R 100,000	R 80,000
Receivables	450,000	550,000
Inventory	680,000	720,000
Fixed Assets, net	1,000,000	900,000
Total Assets	R2,230,000	R2,250,000
Equities:		
Current Payables	R 260,000	R 340,000
Long-Term Debt	1,250,000	1,100,000
Common Stock	500,000	500,000
Retained Earnings	220,000	310,000
Total Equities	R2,230,000	R2,250,000

Bentley formed the subsidiary on January 1, 20X6, when the exchange rate was 30 rupees for 1 U.S. dollar. The exchange rate for 1 U.S. dollar on December 31, 20X6, and December 31, 2007, had increased to 35 rupees and 40 rupees, respectively. Income is earned evenly over the year, and the subsidiary declared no dividends during its first two years of existence.

Required

a. Present both the direct and the indirect exchange rate for the rupees for the three dates of (1) January 1, 20X6, (2) December 31, 20X6, and (3) December 31, 20X7. Did the dollar strengthen or weaken in 20X6 and in 20X7?

b. Prepare the subsidiary's translated balance sheet as of December 31, 20X6, assuming the rupee is the subsidiary's functional currency.

c. Prepare the subsidiary's translated balance sheet as of December 31, 20X7, assuming the rupee is the subsidiary's functional currency.

d. Compute the amount that 20X7's other comprehensive income would include as a result of the translation.

E12-14 **Computation of Gain or Loss on Sale of Asset by Foreign Subsidiary**

On December 31, 20X2, your company's Mexican subsidiary sold land at a selling price of 3,000,000 pesos. The land had been purchased for 2,000,000 pesos on January 1, 20X1, when the exchange rate was 10 pesos to 1 U.S. dollar. The exchange rate for 1 U.S. dollar was 11 pesos on December 31, 20X1, and 12 pesos on December 31, 20X2. Assume that the subsidiary had no other assets and no liabilities during the two years that it owned the land.

Required

a. Prepare all entries regarding the purchase and sale of the land that would be made on the books of the Mexican subsidiary whose reporting currency is the Mexican peso.

b. Determine the amount of the gain or loss on the transaction that would be reported on the subsidiary's remeasured statement of income in U.S. dollars, assuming the U.S. dollar is the functional currency. Determine the amount of the remeasurement gain or loss that would be reported on the remeasured statement of income in U.S. dollars.

c. Determine the amount of the gain or loss on the transaction that would be reported on the subsidiary's translated statement of income in U.S. dollars, assuming the Mexican peso is the functional currency. Determine the amount of the other comprehensive income that would be reported on the consolidated statement of other comprehensive income for 20X2.

E12-15* **Intercompany Transactions**

Hawk Company sold inventory to United Ltd., an English subsidiary. The goods cost Hawk $8,000 and were sold to United for $12,000 on November 27, payable in British pounds. The goods are still on hand at the end of the year on December 31. The British pound (£) is the functional currency of the English subsidiary. The exchange rates follow:

November 27	£1 = $1.60
December 31	£1 = 1.70

Required

a. At what dollar amount is the ending inventory shown in the trial balance of the consolidated workpaper?

b. What amount is eliminated for the unrealized intercompany gross profit, and at what amount is the inventory shown on the consolidated balance sheet?

Problems P12-16 Parent Company Journal Entries and Translation

On January 1, 20X1, Par Company purchased all the outstanding stock of North Bay Company, located in Canada, for $120,000. On January 1, 20X1, the direct exchange rate for the Canadian dollar (C$) was C$1 = $.80. North Bay's book value on January 1, 20X1, was C$90,000. The fair value of North Bay's plant and equipment was C$10,000 more than book value, and the plant and equipment is being depreciated over 10 years, with no salvage value. The remainder of the differential is attributable to a trademark, which will be amortized over 10 years.

During 20X1, North Bay earned C$20,000 in income and declared and paid C$8,000 in dividends. The dividends were declared and paid in Canadian dollars when the exchange rate was C$1 = $.75. On December 31, 20X1, Par continues to hold the Canadian currency received from the dividend. On December 31, 20X1, the direct exchange rate is C$1 = $.70. The average exchange rate during 20X1 was C$1 = $.75. Management has determined that the Canadian dollar is the appropriate functional currency for North Bay Company.

Required

a. Prepare a schedule showing the differential allocation and amortization for 20X1. The schedule should present both Canadian dollars and U.S. dollars.

b. Par uses the basic equity method to account for its investment. Provide the entries that it would record in 20X1 for its investment in North Bay for the following items:

   (1) Purchase of investment in North Bay.
   (2) Equity accrual for Par's share of North Bay's income.
   (3) Recognition of dividend declared and paid by North Bay.
   (4) Amortization of differential.
   (5) Recognition of translation adjustment on differential.

c. Prepare a schedule showing the proof of the translation adjustment for North Bay as a result of the translation of the subsidiary's accounts from Canadian dollars to U.S. dollars. Then provide the entry that Par would record for its share of the translation adjustment resulting from the translation of the subsidiary's accounts.

d. Provide the entry required by Par to restate the C$8,000 in the Foreign Currency Units account into its year-end U.S. dollar equivalent value.

P12-17 **Translation, Journal Entries, Consolidated Comprehensive Income, and Stockholders' Equity**

On January 1, 20X5, Taft Company acquired all of the outstanding stock of Vikix, Inc., a Norwegian company, at a cost of $151,200. Vikix's net assets on the date of acquisition were 700,000 kroner (NKr). On January 1, 20X5, the book and fair values of the Norwegian subsidiary's identifiable assets and liabilities approximated their fair values except for property, plant, and equipment and patents acquired. The fair value of Vikix's property, plant, and equipment exceeded its book value by $18,000. The remaining useful life of Vikix's equipment at January 1, 20X5 was 10 years. The remainder of the differential was attributable to a patent having an estimated useful life of 5 years. Vikix's trial balance on December 31, 20X5, in kroner, follows:

	Debits	Credits
Cash	NKr 150,000	
Accounts Receivable (net)	200,000	
Inventory	270,000	
Property, Plant, and Equipment	600,000	
Accumulated Depreciation		NKr 150,000
Accounts Payable		90,000
Notes Payable		190,000
Common Stock		450,000
Retained Earnings		250,000
Sales		690,000
Cost of Goods Sold	410,000	
Operating Expenses	100,000	
Depreciation Expense	50,000	
Dividends Paid	40,000	
Total	NKr1,820,000	NKr1,820,000

Additional Information

1. Vikix uses the FIFO method for its inventory. The beginning inventory was acquired on December 31, 20X4, and ending inventory was acquired on December 15, 20X5. Purchases of NKr420,000 were made evenly throughout 20X5.

2. Vikix acquired all of its property, plant, and equipment on July 1, 20X3, and uses straight-line depreciation.

3. Vikix's sales were made evenly throughout 20X5, and its operating expenses were incurred evenly throughout 20X5.

4. The dividends were declared and paid on July 1, 20X5.

5. Taft's income from its own operations was $275,000 for 20X5, and its total stockholders' equity on January 1, 20X5, was $3,500,000. Taft declared $100,000 of dividends during 20X5.

6. Exchange rates were as follows:

July 1, 20X3	NKr1 = $.15
December 30, 20X4	NKr1 = $.18
January 1, 20X5	NKr1 = $.18
July 1, 20X5	NKr1 = $.19
December 15, 20X5	NKr1 = $.205
December 31, 20X5	NKr1 = $.21
Average for 20X5	NKr1 = $.20

Required

a. Prepare a schedule translating the trial balance from Norwegian kroner into U.S. dollars. Assume the kroner is the functional currency.

b. Assume that Taft uses the basic equity method. Record all journal entries that relate to its investment in the Norwegian subsidiary during 20X5. Provide the necessary documentation and support for the amounts in the journal entries, including a schedule of the translation adjustment related to the differential.

c. Prepare a schedule that determines Taft's consolidated comprehensive income for 20X5.

d. Compute Taft's total consolidated stockholders' equity at December 31, 20X5.

P12-18   Remeasurement, Journal Entries, Consolidated Net Income, and Stockholders' Equity

Refer to the information in Problem 12-17. Assume the U.S. dollar is the functional currency, not the kroner.

Required

a. Prepare a schedule remeasuring the trial balance from Norwegian kroner into U.S. dollars.

b. Assume that Taft uses the basic equity method. Record all journal entries that relate to its investment in the Norwegian subsidiary during 20X5. Provide the necessary documentation and support for the amounts in the journal entries.

c. Prepare a schedule that determines Taft's consolidated net income for 20X5.

d. Compute Taft's total consolidated stockholders' equity at December 31, 20X5.

P12-19   Proof of Translation Adjustment

Refer to the information presented in Problem 12-17 and your answer to part *a* of Problem 12-17.

Required

Prepare a schedule providing a proof of the translation adjustment.

P12-20*   Remeasurement Gain or Loss

Refer to the information given in Problem 12-17 and your answer to part *a* of Problem 12-18.

Required

Prepare a schedule providing a proof of the remeasurement gain or loss. For this part of the problem, assume that the Norwegian subsidiary had the following monetary assets and liabilities at January 1, 20X5:

Monetary Assets	
Cash	NKr 10,000
Accounts Receivable (net)	140,000

Monetary Liabilities	
Accounts Payable	NKr 70,000
Notes Payable	140,000

On January 1, 20X5, the Norwegian subsidiary has a net monetary liability position of NKr60,000.

P12-21 Translation and Calculation of Translation Adjustment

On January 1, 20X4, Alum Corporation acquired DaSilva Company, a Brazilian subsidiary, by purchasing all the common stock at book value. DaSilva's trial balances on January 1, 20X4, and December 31, 20X4, expressed in Brazilian reals (BRL), follow:

	January 1, 20X4		December 31, 20X4	
	Debit	**Credit**	**Debit**	**Credit**
Cash	BRL 62,000		BRL 57,700	
Accounts Receivable (net)	83,900		82,000	
Inventories	95,000		95,000	
Prepaid Insurance	5,600		2,400	
Plant and Equipment	250,000		350,000	
Accumulated Depreciation		BRL 67,500		BRL 100,000
Intangible Assets	42,000		30,000	
Accounts Payable		20,000		24,000
Income Taxes Payable		30,000		27,000
Interest Payable		1,000		1,100
Notes Payable		20,000		20,000
Bonds Payable		120,000		120,000
Common Stock		80,000		80,000
Additional Paid-In Capital		150,000		150,000
Retained Earnings		50,000		50,000
Sales				500,000
Cost of Goods Sold			230,000	
Insurance Expense			3,200	
Depreciation Expense			32,500	
Amortization Expense			12,000	
Operating Expense			152,300	
Dividends Paid			25,000	
Total	BRL538,500	BRL538,500	BRL1,072,100	BRL1,072,100

Additional Information

1. DaSilva uses FIFO inventory valuation. Purchases were made uniformly during 20X4. Ending inventory for 20X4 is composed of units purchased when the exchange rate was $.25.

2. The insurance premium for a two-year policy was paid on October 1, 20X3.

3. Plant and equipment were acquired as follows:

Date	Cost
January 1, 20X1	BRL 200,000
July 10, 20X2	50,000
April 7, 20X4	100,000

4. Plant and equipment are depreciated using the straight-line method and a 10-year life, with no residual value. A full month's depreciation is taken in the month of acquisition.

5. The intangible assets are patents acquired on July 10, 20X2, at a cost of BRL60,000. The estimated life is five years.

6. The common stock was issued on January 1, 20X1.

7. Dividends of BRL 10,000 were declared and paid on April 7. On October 9, BRL15,000 of dividends were declared and paid.

8. Exchange rates were as follows:

January 1, 20X1	BRL1 = $.45
July 10, 20X2	BRL1 = .40
October 1, 20X3	BRL1 = .34
January 1, 20X4	BRL1 = .30
April 7, 20X4	BRL1 = .28
October 9, 20X4	BRL1 = .23
December 31, 20X4	BRL1 = .20
20X4 average	BRL1 = .25

Required

a. Prepare a schedule translating the December 31, 20X4, trial balance of DaSilva from reals to dollars.

b. Prepare a schedule calculating the translation adjustment as of the end of 20X4. The net assets on January 1, 20X4, were BRL 280,000.

P12-22*   **Remeasurement and Proof of Remeasurement Gain or Loss**

Refer to the information in Problem 12-21. Assume that the dollar is the functional currency.

Required

a. Prepare a schedule remeasuring the December 31, 20X4, trial balance of DaSilva Company from reals to dollars.

b. Prepare a schedule providing a proof of the remeasurement gain or loss.

P12-23   **Translation**

Alamo Inc. purchased 80 percent of the outstanding stock of Western Ranching Company, located in Australia, on January 1, 20X3. The purchase price in Australian dollars (A$) was A$200,000, and A$40,000 of the differential was allocated to plant and equipment, which is amortized over a 10-year period. The remainder of the differential was attributable to a patent. Alamo Inc. amortizes the patent over 10 years. Western Ranching's trial balance on December 31, 20X3, in Australian dollars is as follows:

	Debits	Credits
Cash	A$ 44,100	
Accounts Receivable (net)	72,000	
Inventory	86,000	
Plant and Equipment	240,000	
Accumulated Depreciation		A$ 60,000
Accounts Payable		53,800
Payable to Alamo Inc.		10,800
Interest Payable		3,000
12% Bonds Payable		100,000
Premium on Bonds		5,700
Common Stock		90,000
Retained Earnings		40,000
Sales		579,000
Cost of Goods Sold	330,000	
Depreciation Expense	24,000	
Operating Expenses	131,500	
Interest Expense	5,700	
Dividends Paid	9,000	
Total	A$942,300	A$942,300

Additional Information

1. Western Ranching uses average cost for cost of goods sold. Inventory increased by A$20,000 during the year. Purchases were made uniformly during 20X3. The ending inventory was acquired at the average exchange rate for the year.
2. Plant and equipment were acquired as follows:

Date	Cost
January 20X1	A$180,000
January 1, 20X3	60,000

3. Plant and equipment are depreciated using the straight-line method and a 10-year life, with no residual value.
4. The payable to Alamo is in Australian dollars. Alamo's books show a receivable from Western Ranching of $6,480.
5. The 10-year bonds were issued on July 1, 20X3, for A$106,000. The premium is amortized on a straight-line basis. The interest is paid on April 1 and October 1.
6. The dividends were declared and paid on April 1.
7. Exchange rates were as follows:

January 20X1	A$1 = $.93
August 20X1	A$1 = $.88
January 1, 20X3	A$1 = $.70
April 1, 20X3	A$1 = $.67
July 1, 20X3	A$1 = $.64
December 31, 20X3	A$1 = $.60
20X3 average	A$1 = $.65

Required

a. Prepare a schedule translating the December 31, 20X3, trial balance of Western Ranching from Australian dollars to U.S. dollars.
b. Prepare a schedule providing a proof of the translation adjustment.

P12-24 **Parent Company Journal Entries and Translation**

Refer to the information given in Problem 12-23 for Alamo and its subsidiary, Western Ranching. Assume that the Australian dollar (A$) is the functional currency and that Alamo uses the basic equity method for accounting for its investment in Western Ranching.

Required

a. Prepare the entries that Alamo would record in 20X3 for its investment in Western Ranching. Your entries should include the following:

   (1) Record the initial investment on January 1, 20X3.

   (2) Record the dividend received by the parent company.

   (3) Recognize the parent company's share of the equity income of the subsidiary.

   (4) Record the amortizations of the differential.

   (5) Recognize the translation adjustment required by the parent from the adjustment of the differential.

   (6) Recognize the parent company's share o f the translation adjustment resulting from the translation of the subsidiary's accounts.

b. Provide the necessary documentation and support for the amounts recorded in the journal entries, including a schedule of the translation adjustment related to the differential.

P12-25 **Consolidation Workpaper after Translation**

Refer to the information given in Problems 12-23 and 12-24 for Alamo and its subsidiary, Western Ranching. Assume that the Australian dollar (A$) is the functional currency and that Alamo uses the basic equity method for accounting for its investment in Western Ranching. A December 31, 20X3, trial balance for Alamo Inc. follows. Use this translated trial balance for completing this problem.

Item	Debit	Credit
Cash	$ 38,000	
Accounts Receivable (net)	140,000	
Receivable from Western Ranching	6,480	
Inventory	128,000	
Plant and Equipment	500,000	
Investment in Western Ranching	152,064	
Cost of Goods Sold	600,000	
Depreciation Expense	28,000	
Operating Expenses	204,000	
Interest Expense	2,000	
Dividends Declared	50,000	
Translation Adjustment	22,528	
Accumulated Depreciation		$ 90,000
Accounts Payable		60,000
Interest Payable		2,000
Common Stock		500,000
Retained Earnings, January 1, 20X3		179,656
Sales		1,000,000
Income from Subsidiary		39,416
Total	$1,871,072	$1,871,072

Required

a. Prepare a set of eliminating entries, in general journal form, for the entries required to prepare a comprehensive consolidation workpaper (including other comprehensive income) as of December 31, 20X3.

b. Prepare a comprehensive consolidation workpaper as of December 31, 20X3.

P12-26* **Remeasurement**

Refer to the information in Problem 12-23. Assume the U.S. dollar is the functional currency.

Required

a. Prepare a schedule remeasuring the December 31, 20X3, trial balance of Western Ranching from Australian dollars to U.S. dollars.

b. Prepare a schedule providing a proof of the remeasurement gain or loss. The subsidiary's net monetary liability position on January 1, 20X3, was A$80,000.

P12-27 **Parent Company Journal Entries and Remeasurement**

Refer to the information given in Problems 12-23 and 12-26* for Alamo and its subsidiary, Western Ranching. Assume that the U.S. dollar is the functional currency and that Alamo uses the basic equity method for accounting for its investment in Western Ranching.

Required

a. Prepare the entries that Alamo would record in 20X3 for its investment in Western Ranching. Your entries should do the following:

(1) Record the initial investment on January 1, 20X3.

(2) Record the dividend received by the parent company.

(3) Recognize the parent company's share of the equity income from the subsidiary.

(4) Record the amortizations of the differential.

b. Provide the necessary documentation and support for the amounts recorded in the journal entries.

P12-28*   **Consolidation Workpaper after Remeasurement**

Refer to the information given in Problems 12-23 and 12-27 for Alamo and its subsidiary, Western Ranching. Assume that the U.S. dollar is the functional currency and that Alamo uses the basic equity method for accounting for its investment in Western Ranching. A December 31, 20X3, trial balance for Alamo follows. Use this remeasured trial balance for completing this problem.

Item	Debit	Credit
Cash	$ 38,000	
Accounts Receivable (net)	140,000	
Receivable from Western Ranching	6,480	
Inventory	128,000	
Plant and Equipment	500,000	
Investment in Western Ranching	178,544	
Cost of Goods Sold	600,000	
Depreciation Expense	28,000	
Operating Expenses	204,000	
Interest Expense	2,000	
Dividends Declared	50,000	
Accumulated Depreciation		$ 90,000
Accounts Payable		60,000
Interest Payable		2,000
Common Stock		500,000
Retained Earnings, January 1, 20X3		179,656
Sales		1,000,000
Income from Subsidiary		43,368
Total	$1,875,024	$1,875,024

Required

a. Prepare a set of eliminating entries, in general journal form, for the entries required to prepare a three-part consolidation workpaper as of December 31, 20X3.

b. Prepare a three-part consolidation workpaper as of December 31, 20X3.

P12-29   **Foreign Currency Remeasurement [AICPA Adapted]**

On January 1, 20X1, Kiner Company formed a foreign subsidiary that issued all of its currently outstanding common stock on that date. Selected accounts from the balance sheets, all of which are shown in local currency units, are as follows:

	December 31	
	20X2	**20X1**
Accounts Receivable (net of allowance for uncollectible accounts of 2,200 LCU on December 31, 20X2, and 2,000 LCU on December 31, 20X1)	LCU 40,000	LCU 35,000
Inventories, at cost	80,000	75,000
Property, Plant, and Equipment (net of allowance for accumulated depreciation of 31,000 LCU on December 31, 20X2, and 14,000 LCU on December 31, 20X1)	163,000	150,000
Long-Term Debt	100,000	120,000
Common Stock, authorized 10,000 shares, par value 10 LCU per share; issued and outstanding, 5,000 shares on December 31, 20X2, and December 31, 20X1	50,000	50,000

Additional Information

1. Exchange rates are as follows:

January 1, 20X1–July 31, 20X1	2 LCU = $1
August 1, 20X1–October 31, 20X1	1.8 LCU = $1
November 1, 20X1–June 30, 20X2	1.7 LCU = $1
July 1, 20X2–December 31, 20X2	1.5 LCU = $1
Average monthly rate for 20X1	1.9 LCU = $1
Average monthly rate for 20X2	1.6 LCU = $1

2. An analysis of the accounts receivable balance is as follows:

	20X2	20X1
Accounts Receivable:		
Balance at beginning of year	LCU 37,000	
Sales (36,000 LCU per month in 20X2 and 31,000 LCU per month in 20X1)	432,000	LCU 372,000
Collections	(423,600)	(334,000)
Write-offs (May 20X2 and December 20X1)	(3,200)	(1,000)
Balance at end of year	LCU 42,200	LCU 37,000

	20X2	20X1
Allowance for Uncollectible Accounts:		
Balance at beginning of year	LCU 2,000	
Provision for uncollectible accounts	3,400	LCU 3,000
Write-offs (May 20X2 and December 20X1)	(3,200)	(1,000)
Balance at end of year	LCU 2,200	LCU 2,000

3. An analysis of inventories, for which the first-in, first-out inventory method is used, follows:

	20X2	20X1
Inventory at beginning of year	LCU 75,000	
Purchases (June 20X2 and June 20X1)	335,000	LCU375,000
Goods available for sale	LCU410,000	LCU375,000
Inventory at end of year	(80,000)	(75,000)
Cost of goods sold	LCU330,000	LCU300,000

4. On January 1, 20X1, Kiner's foreign subsidiary purchased land for 24,000 LCU and plant and equipment for 140,000 LCU. On July 4, 20X2, additional equipment was purchased for 30,000 LCU. Plant and equipment is being depreciated on a straight-line basis over a 10-year period, with no residual value. A full year's depreciation is taken in the year of purchase.

5. On January 15, 20X1, 7 percent bonds with a face value of 120,000 LCU were issued. These bonds mature on January 15, 20X7, and the interest is paid semiannually on July 15 and January 15. The first interest payment was made on July 15, 20X1.

Required

Prepare a schedule remeasuring the selected accounts into U.S. dollars for December 31, 20X1, and December 31, 20X2, respectively, assuming the U.S. dollar is the functional currency for the foreign subsidiary. The schedule should be prepared using the following form:

Item	Balance in LCU	Appropriate Exchange Rate	Remeasured into U.S. Dollars
December 31, 20X1:			
Accounts Receivable (net)			
Inventories			
Property, Plant, and Equipment (net)			
Long-Term Debt			
Common Stock			
December 31, 20X2:			
Accounts Receivable (net)			
Inventories			
Property, Plant, and Equipment (net)			
Long-Term Debt			
Common Stock			

P12-30 Foreign Currency Translation

Refer to the information in Problem 12-29 for Kiner Company and its foreign subsidiary.

Required

Prepare a schedule translating the selected accounts into U.S. dollars as of December 31, 20X1, and December 31, 20X2, respectively, assuming that the local currency unit is the foreign subsidiary's functional currency.

P12-31 Matching Key Terms

Match the items in the left-hand column with the descriptions/explanations in the right-hand column.

Items	Descriptions/Explanations
1. Current exchange rate	A. Method used to restate a foreign entity's financial statement when the local currency unit is the functional currency.
2. Foreign entity goodwill under translation	
3. Increase in the translation adjustment for the year	
4. Other comprehensive income— translation adjustment	B. Method used to restate a foreign entity's financial statements when the U.S. dollar is the functional currency.
5. Translation	C. Currency of the environment in which an entity primarily generates and expends cash.
6. Historical exchange rate	
7. Foreign entity goodwill under remeasurement	D. Is always the local currency unit of the foreign entity.
8. Remeasurement	E. Exchange rate at the end of the period.
9. A decrease in the translation adjustment for the year	F. Exchange rate at the date of the asset acquisition or at the date of dividend declaration.
10. Functional currency	G. Average exchange rate during the period.
	H. Periodic change in the cumulative translation adjustment.
	I. Method under which goodwill must be adjusted to the current exchange rate at the balance sheet date.
	J. Method under which goodwill is restated using the historical exchange rate.
	K. Increase of the exchange rate during the year.
	L. Decrease of the exchange rate during the year.

P12-32

Translation Choices

The U.S. parent company is preparing its consolidated financial statements for December 31, 20X4. The foreign company's local currency (LCU) is the functional currency. Information is presented in Data Set A and Data Set B.

Data Set A:

	Exchange Rate	Date
1.	LCU .74	June 16, 20X1: date foreign company purchased
2.	LCU .80	January 1, 20X4: beginning of current year
3.	LCU .87	March 31, 20X4
4.	LCU .86	June 12, 20X4
5.	LCU .85	Average for year 20X4
6.	LCU .84	November 1, 20X4
7.	LCU .83	December 31, 20X4: end of current year
8.	No translation rate is applied	

Data Set B:

a. Accounts receivable outstanding from sales on March 31, 20X4.
b. Sales revenue earned during year.
c. Dividends declared on November 1, 20X4.
d. Ending inventory balance from acquisitions through the year.
e. Equipment purchased on March 31, 20X4.
f. Depreciation expense on equipment.
g. Common stock outstanding.
h. Dividends payable from dividends declared on June 12, 20X4.
i. Accumulated Other Comprehensive Income balance from prior fiscal year.
j. Bond payable issued January 1, 20X4.
k. Interest expense on the bond payable.

Required

a. Select the appropriate exchange rate from the amounts presented in Data Set A to prepare the translation worksheet for each of the accounts presented in Data Set B.

b. Determine the direct exchange rate for January 1, 20X4.

c. Determine whether the U.S. dollar strengthened or weakened during 20X4.

P12-33

Proof of Translation Adjustment

MaMi Co. Ltd. located in Mexico City is a wholly owned subsidiary of Special Foods, a U.S. company. At the beginning of the year, MaMi's condensed balance sheet was reported in Mexican pesos (MXP) as follows:

Assets	3,425,000	Liabilities	2,850,000
		Stockholders' Equity	575,000

During the year, the company earned income of MXP270,000 and on November 1 declared dividends of MXP150,000. The Mexican peso is the functional currency. Relevant exchange rates between the peso and the U.S. dollar follow:

January 1 (beginning of year)	$.0870
Average for year	.0900
November 1	.0915
December 31 (end of year)	.0930

Required

a. Prepare a proof of the translation adjustment, assuming that the beginning credit balance of the accumulated other comprehensive income—translation adjustment was $3,250.

b. Did the U.S. dollar strengthen or weaken against the Mexican peso during the year?

Kaplan CPA Review

KAPLAN

CPA EDUCATION

Please visit the text Website for the online CPA Simulation: www.mhhe.com/baker7e.

Situation: The Texas Corporation located in San Antonio, has transactions both in the United States and in Mexico. The U.S. dollar is its functional currency. In addition, this company has a wholly owned subsidiary (Mexico, Inc.) located in Mexico. Consolidated financial statements are being prepared for year 1. The currency exchange rates are as follows for the current year (year 1M):

January 1, year 1	1 peso equals $0.088
Average for year 1	1 peso equals $0.090
November 1, year 1	1 peso equals $0.092
December 31, year 1	1 peso equals $0.094
December 31, year 1	1 peso equals $0.095
January 31, year 2	1 peso equals $0.098

Topics to be covered in simulation:

- Sale to an unrelated company in Mexico.
- Purchase of equipment from an unrelated company in Mexico.
- Impact of the designation of the functional currency as the dollar or the peso.
- Translation of expenses from the peso to the dollar, assuming the peso is the functional currency.
- Translation of expenses from the peso to the dollar, assuming the dollar is the functional currency.
- Translation of fixed assets.
- Translation of liabilities.
- Translation adjustment.
- Functional currency.
- Forward exchange contracts.

Chapter **Thirteen**

Segment and Interim Reporting

REPORTING FOR SEGMENTS

Diversification into new products and multinational markets during the 1960s and early 1970s created the need for disaggregated information about the individual segments or components of an enterprise. This information need was addressed by the Accounting Principles Board, the Financial Executives Institute, the Institute of Management Accountants, the Securities Exchange Commission, and, finally, the Financial Accounting Standards Board.

Large, diversified companies can be viewed as a portfolio of assets operated as divisions or subsidiaries, often multinational in scope. The various components of a large company may have different profit rates, different degrees and types of risk, and different opportunities for growth. A major issue for accountants is how to develop and disclose the information necessary to reflect these essential differences. The following discussion presents the accounting standards for reporting an entity's operating components, foreign operations, and major customers.

SEGMENT REPORTING ACCOUNTING ISSUES

In 1967, the APB issued **APB Statement No. 2**, "Disclosure of Supplemental Financial Information by Diversified Companies (APB 2)," which recommended voluntary disclosure of segment information. In 1969, the SEC required line-of-business reporting in registration statements of new stock issues and in 1970 extended this requirement to Form 10-K, the report filed annually by all publicly held companies. Using extensive research reports prepared by the Institute of Management Accountants[1] and the Financial Executives Institute,[2] the FASB issued **FASB Statement No. 14**, "Financial Reporting for Segments of a Business Enterprise" (FASB 14), in December 1976. This pronouncement required the supplemental disclosure of revenue, profits, assets, and other information for selected industry segments of an entity as well as disclosures about its foreign operations.

Preparers of financial statements believed that **FASB 14** required significant additional accounting costs because companies had to analyze their financial operations by industrial lines of business, although that was not how most businesses were organized. Furthermore, financial analysts and other financial statement users stated that, although information about segments was essential for full analysis of a company, the standards in **FASB 14** were inadequate.

---

[1] M. Backer and R. McFarland, *External Reporting for Segments of a Business,* Institute of Management Accountants (New York, 1968).
[2] R. Mautz, *Financial Reporting by Diversified Companies,* Financial Executives Research Foundation (New York, 1968).

The FASB joined with the Canadian Institute of Chartered Accountants (CICA) to study the information needs for disaggregated disclosures. Also, the AICPA formed the Special Committee on Financial Reporting ("The Jenkins Committee," named after its chairman, Ed Jenkins), which recommended in 1994 that the FASB assign its highest priority to improving segment reporting. In June 1997, the FASB published **FASB Statement No. 131**, "Disclosures about Segments of an Enterprise and Related Information" (FASB 131). Although some aspects of the disclosure criteria from **FASB 14** were continued, **FASB 131** took a *management approach* to the definition of segments. The standard focuses on financial information that an enterprise's financial decision makers use to evaluate the entity's operating segments. Thus, **FASB 131** required that financial information be provided about segments that correspond to the internal organization structure of the entity as used by the company's chief operating decision maker in deciding how to allocate resources and assessing performance. These components are termed *operating segments*. Thus, the financial statements report disaggregated information on the same organizational basis as the company's internal decision makers use.

FASB 131 defines an operating segment as having three characteristics:

1. The component unit's business activities generate revenue and incur expenses, including any revenue or expenses in transactions with other business units of the company.

2. The component unit's operating results are regularly reviewed by the entity's chief operating decision maker, who then determines the resources to be assigned to the segment and evaluates its performance.

3. Separate financial information is available for the component unit.

Generally, the corporate headquarters is not a separate operating segment. Also, the company may choose to aggregate several individual operating segments that have very similar economic characteristics (i.e., products and services, production processes, type or class of customer, methods used to distribute products or provide for services). Management may also believe that the aggregation will provide more meaningful information to the users of the financial statements.

Whenever the issue of defining the income for a segment of an enterprise arises, one problem is the allocation of costs to specific segments. For example, should a segment's income include directly traceable costs only, or should it also include an allocation of common costs, such as companywide advertising or a central purchasing department? One accounting researcher has stated that all allocations are arbitrary, that is, not completely verifiable with empirical evidence, and therefore, net income after deducting any allocated costs is arbitrary.[3] In **FASB 131**, the FASB stated that the allocations of revenues and costs should be included for a reported segment only if they are included in the segment's profit or loss that the chief operating decision maker uses. Also, only those assets included in the measure of the segment's assets that the chief operating decision maker uses shall be reported for that segment. Thus, the FASB again is striving to align the segments' external financial disclosures with the internal reporting used by the company's management to make resource allocations and other decisions regarding the operating segments.

INFORMATION ABOUT OPERATING SEGMENTS

Many entities are diversified across several lines of business. Each line may be subject to unique competitive factors and may react differently to changes in the economic environment. For example, a large company such as Johnson & Johnson operates in several major lines: consumer, pharmaceutical, and professional. Its products include disposable contact lenses, baby products, surgical products, antibody therapies, and cold and flu medications. A conglomerate may operate in several consumer markets, each with different characteristics. In addition, a company is exposed to different risks in each of the markets in which

---

[3] A. Thomas, *The Allocation Problem: Part Two,* American Accounting Association (Sarasota, FL, 1974).

it acquires its factors of production. Consolidated statements present all of these heterogeneous factors in a single-entity context. The purpose of segment reporting is to allow financial statement users to look behind the consolidated totals to the individual components that constitute the entity.

Defining Reportable Segments

The process of determining separately *reportable operating segments*, that is, segments for which separate supplemental disclosures must be made, is based on management's specification of those operating segments that are used internally for evaluating the enterprise's financial position and operating performance.

Ten Percent Quantitative Thresholds

The FASB specified three *10 percent significance rules* to determine which of the operating segments shall have separately reported information. The separate disclosures are required for segments meeting at least one of the following tests:

1. The segment's revenue, including both external sales and intersegment sales or transfers, is 10 percent or more of the total revenues from external sales plus intersegment transactions of all operating segments.
2. The absolute value of the segment's profit or loss is 10 percent or more of the greater, in absolute value, of (*a*) the total profit of all operating segments that did not report a loss, or (*b*) the total loss of all operating segments that did report a loss.
3. The segment's assets are 10 percent or more of the total assets of all operating segments.

Note that the revenue test includes intersegment sales or transfers. The FASB found that the full impact of a particular segment on the entire enterprise should be measured. Also, the FASB believed that the definition of an operating segment should include components of an enterprise that sell primarily or exclusively to other components of the enterprise. Information about these "vertically integrated" operations provide insight into the production and operations of the enterprise.

FASB 131 states that the segment disclosure should include the reportable segments' measures of profit or loss. Thus, the report shall be the same as used for internal decision-making purposes. Some companies may allocate operating expenses arising from shared facilities such as a common warehouse. Other companies may allocate items such as interest costs, income taxes, or income from equity investments to specific segments. Whatever is used for internal decision-making purposes to measure the operating segment's profit or loss shall be reported in the external disclosure.

Although an enterprise is required to report the assets of the separately reportable operating segments, **FASB 131** also allows companies to report their segments' liabilities if the company finds that the fuller disclosure would be meaningful. The assets to be reported are those used by the chief operating decision maker in making decisions about the segment and might include intangible assets such as goodwill or other intangibles. If commonly used assets are allocated to the segments, then these should be included in the reported amounts. The assets might also include financing items such as investments in equity securities or intersegment loans. The key point is that the revenues, profit or loss, and assets should be reported on the same basis as used for internal decision-making purposes.

If the total external revenue of the separately reportable operating segments is less than 75 percent of the total consolidated revenue, then management must select and disclose information about additional operating segments until at least 75 percent of consolidated revenue is included in reportable segments. The choice of which additional operating segments to report is left to management.

Information about the operating segments that are not separately reportable is combined and disclosed in an "All Other" category. The sources of the revenue in the All Other category must be described, but the level of disclosure for this category is significantly less than for the separately reportable segments. Again, note that the corporate headquarters (or corporate administration) is not typically included as an operating segment of an enterprise.

FIGURE 13–1
Consolidated
Financial Statements
for Peerless Products
Corporation and
Subsidiary

PEERLESS PRODUCTS CORPORATION AND SUBSIDIARY
Consolidated Statement of Income and Retained Earnings
Year Ended December 31, 20X1

Revenues:		
Sales		$572,000
Income from Investment in Barclay		32,000
Expenses and Deductions:		
Cost of Goods Sold		(267,000)
Depreciation and Amortization		(70,000)
Other Expenses		(15,000)
Interest Expense		(30,000)
Income to Noncontrolling Interest		(10,000)
Income Taxes		(62,000)
Net Income		$150,000
Retained Earnings, January 1		300,000
Less: Dividends		(60,000)
Retained Earnings, December 31		$390,000

PEERLESS PRODUCTS CORPORATION AND SUBSIDIARY
Consolidated Balance Sheet
December 31, 20X1

Cash		$ 131,000
Accounts Receivable		125,000
Inventory		165,000
Investment in Barclay Stock		184,000
Land		215,000
Building and Equipment	$1,400,000	
Less: Accumulated Depreciation	(770,000)	630,000
Total Assets		$1,450,000
Accounts Payable		$ 200,000
Bonds Payable		300,000
Noncontrolling Interest		60,000
Common Stock		500,000
Retained Earnings		390,000
Total Liabilities and Stockholders' Equity		$1,450,000

Illustration of 10 Percent Tests

Figure 13–1 represents the consolidated financial statements for Peerless Products Corporation and Special Foods Inc. Information for the example is as follows:

1. Peerless owns 80 percent of Special Foods' common stock. Special Foods reports a profit of $50,000 for 20X1 and pays dividends of $30,000. The December 31, 20X1, balances in Special Foods' stockholders' equity accounts total $300,000, of which the noncontrolling interest is 20 percent.

2. Peerless acquires 40 percent of Barclay Company stock on January 1, 20X1, for a cost of $160,000, which is equal to the book value of the stock on that date. The equity method is used to account for this investment. Barclay Company earns $80,000 in profit during 20X1 and pays $20,000 in dividends. This investment is managed by the corporate office and is not assigned to any operating segment.

Segment disclosure provides a breakdown of the consolidated totals into their constituent parts. The items that appear in the consolidated statements and must be disaggregated are sales of $572,000 and total assets of $1,450,000. In the segment analysis, segment profit is also used; however, this figure is not usually presented directly on the consolidated income statement and is computed separately.

Figure 13–2 is a workpaper used to perform the disaggregation from the consolidated totals into the various operating segments. Figure 13–2 also includes additional data necessary for preparing the annual report footnote disclosure presented later in this chapter.

Additional information for this illustration is as follows:

1. The consolidated entity of Peerless Products and Special Foods comprises five different operating segments as well as a central corporate administration. The operating segments are defined by management as Food Products, Plastic and Packaging, Consumer and Commercial, Health and Scientific, and Chemicals.

2. On January 1, 20X1, the Food Products segment of Special Foods issues a $100,000, 12 percent note payable to the Plastic and Packaging segment of Peerless Products. The intercompany interest is $12,000 for the year and is properly eliminated from the consolidated statements.

3. Each operating segment makes sales to unaffiliated customers. In addition, $28,000 of intersegment sales are made during the year by the Food Products, the Plastic and Packaging, and the Consumer and Commercial segments. The cost of these intersegment sales is $18,000. These goods are still in the ending inventories of the purchasing operating segments, and the unrealized inventory profit of $10,000 must be eliminated from both cost of goods sold and inventories in preparing the consolidated financials. Specific revenue information is presented in Figure 13–2.

4. Figure 13–2 also presents the profit and loss information for each segment as it is defined by the entity. The entity uses a concept it terms "controllable earnings" to measure segment performance. As defined by the company, controllable earnings includes interest revenue and interest expense in the entity's definition of segment profit or loss. Therefore, interest is reported on a segment basis. Depreciation is separately reported because if depreciation, depletion, or amortization expenses are included in the measure of segment profit or loss, **FASB 131** requires that these cost elements be disclosed separately to provide information to financial statement users to approximate the cash flow for each segment.

5. A computer costing $30,000 is acquired during the year. The computer is used for production scheduling and control and is being depreciated by the straight-line method over a period of three years ($30,000 ÷ 3 years = $10,000 per year). The annual expense of this computer is allocated on the basis of use, which the computer itself monitors. These allocated costs are shown in Figure 13–2 immediately below the other costs for each operating segment.

6. The intersegment interest expense from the intercompany note is attributable to the Food Products segment, and the intercompany interest income is earned by the Plastic and Packaging segment.

7. The company's policy on determining segment performance does not include income from the investment in any of its operating segment's profit or loss. Rather, this item is assigned to corporate administration. This information is collected in the workpaper to reconcile the consolidated totals.

8. The assets section of Figure 13–2 presents the assets for the operating segments as well as for the corporate administration center. Included in the segments' assets is an allocation of the $20,000 book value ($30,000 less $10,000 of accumulated depreciation) of the production computer. Note also that the intersegment notes are assigned to a specific segment for internal decision-making purposes, but these notes are eliminated in the preparation of the consolidated financials.

The specific significance tests that Peerless Products and its subsidiary must use to determine separately reportable operating segments are as follows:

Ten Percent Revenue Test The first 10 percent test is applied to each operating segment's total revenue as a percentage of the combined revenue of all segments before

FIGURE 13–2 Workpaper to Analyze Peerless Products and Subsidiary's Operating Segments

PEERLESS PRODUCTS CORPORATION AND SPECIAL FOODS INC.
Segmental Disclosure Workpaper

Item	Operating Segments: Food Products	Operating Segments: Plastic and Packaging	Operating Segments: Consumer and Commercial	Operating Segments: Health and Scientific	Operating Segments: Chemicals	Corporate Administration	Combined	Intersegment Eliminations	Consolidated
Revenue:									
Sales to unaffiliated customers	317,000	95,000	41,000	86,000	33,000		572,000		572,000
Intersegment sales	6,000	18,000	4,000				28,000	(28,000)	
Total revenue	323,000	113,000	45,000	86,000	33,000		600,000	(28,000)	572,000
Profit:									
Directly traceable operating costs	(103,000)	(31,000)	(63,000)	(55,000)	(37,000)		(289,000)	18,000	(271,000)
Depreciation of segment's assets	(7,000)	(4,000)	(5,000)	(6,000)	(4,000)		(26,000)		(26,000)
Allocated depreciation	(3,000)	(1,000)	(2,000)	(3,000)	(1,000)		(10,000)		(10,000)
Other items:									
Interest revenue—intersegment		12,000					12,000	(12,000)	
Interest expense—to unaffiliates		(30,000)					(30,000)		(30,000)
Interest expense—intersegment	(12,000)						(12,000)	12,000	
Segment profit (loss)	198,000	59,000	(25,000)	22,000	(9,000)		245,000	(10,000)	235,000
General corporate expenses						(45,000)	(45,000)		(45,000)
Income from equity investment						32,000	32,000		32,000
Income from continuing operations, before taxes	198,000	59,000	(25,000)	22,000	(9,000)	(13,000)	232,000	(10,000)	222,000
Assets:									
Operating segments:									
Segment (other than intersegment)	411,000	275,000	100,000	310,000	80,000		1,176,000	(10,000)	1,166,000
Intersegment notes		100,000					100,000	(100,000)	
Total of operating segments	411,000	375,000	100,000	310,000	80,000		1,276,000	(110,000)	1,166,000
General corporate						100,000	100,000		100,000
Equity investments						184,000	184,000		184,000
Total assets	411,000	375,000	100,000	310,000	80,000	284,000	1,560,000	(110,000)	1,450,000
Total expenditures made during year for long-term assets	48,000	21,000	10,000	29,000	12,000		120,000		

elimination of intersegment transfers and sales. If an operating segment's total revenue is 10 percent or more of the combined revenue of all segments, then the segment is separately reportable and supplementary disclosures must be provided for it in the annual report.

The 10 percent revenue tests are applied as follows:

Segment	Segment Revenue	Percent of Combined Revenue of $600,000	Reportable Segment
Food Products	$323,000	53.8%	Yes
Plastic and Packaging	113,000	18.8	Yes
Consumer and Commercial	45,000	7.5	No
Health and Scientific	86,000	14.3	Yes
Chemicals	33,000	5.5	No
Total	$600,000	100.0%*	

*Unrounded percents for segments total to 100 percent.

The revenue test shows that the following operating segments are separately reportable: Food Products, Plastic and Packaging, and Health and Scientific. A common shortcut is to compute 10 percent of the denominator of the test (for Peerless and its subsidiary, $600,000 × .10) and then compare each segment's total revenue with that fraction. In this case, reportable segments are those with $60,000 or more in total revenue.

Ten Percent Profit (Loss) Test The profit or loss test is the second test to determine which operating segments are separately reportable. The test is to determine whether a segment's profit or loss is equal to or greater than 10 percent of the absolute value of either the combined operating profits or the combined operating losses of the segments, whichever is greater.

Because two segments had operating losses for the year, separate tabulations are made, as follows:

Segment	Segment Profits	Segment Losses
Food Products	$198,000	
Plastic and Packaging	59,000	
Consumer and Commercial		$(25,000)
Health and Scientific	22,000	
Chemicals		(9,000)
Total	$279,000	$(34,000)

The greater absolute total is the $279,000 of profits. This amount becomes the denominator for the 10 percent operating profit or loss test. Because this test is based on absolute amounts, all numbers are treated as positive numbers. The test data follow:

Segment	Profit (Loss)	Percent of Test Amount of $279,000	Separately Reportable
Food Products	$198,000	71.0%	Yes
Plastic and Packaging	59,000	21.1	Yes
Consumer and Commercial	(25,000)	9.0	No
Health and Scientific	22,000	7.9	No
Chemicals	(9,000)	3.2	No

The Food Products and Plastic and Packaging segments are separately reportable using the profit or loss test.

Assets Test The last of the tests to determine whether a segment is separately reportable is the 10 percent assets test. Note that the items composing each segment's assets are defined by management, as used for internal decision-making purposes. Management may include intangibles, receivables, and even intercompany items, as defined by the management. Assume that Peerless's management defines the segment assets to include intercompany items such as the intercompany notes. Recognize that it really is up to the management to define what is, and what is not, included in each of the definitions of segment profit or loss and the segment assets.

The combined assets of all operating segments ($1,276,000) are used for this test. The difference of $110,000 between the combined assets of the operating segments ($1,276,000) and the amount included ($1,166,000) in the consolidated assets is due to (*a*) the $10,000 unrealized intercompany profit from intersegment inventory transactions that has not been realized in sales to third parties, and (*b*) the $100,000 of intersegment notes. These intercompany amounts must be eliminated in the consolidation process.

The 10 percent significance rule is applied to segment assets as follows:

Segment	Segment Assets	Percent of Test Amount of $1,276,000	Separately Reportable
Food Products	$ 411,000	32.2%	Yes
Plastic and Packaging	375,000	29.4	Yes
Consumer and Commercial	100,000	7.8	No
Health and Scientific	310,000	24.3	Yes
Chemicals	80,000	6.3	No
Total	$1,276,000	100.0%	

The Food Products, Plastic and Packaging, and Health and Scientific operating segments are separately reportable using the 10 percent assets test; that is, their assets are equal to or greater than 10 percent of the combined assets of the operating segments ($127,600 = $1,276,000 × .10).

Figure 13–3 summarizes the results of the three tests. Recall that a segment is separately reportable if it meets any one of the three 10 percent tests. The following segments are separately reportable under the three tests: Food Products, Plastic and Packaging, and Health and Scientific. The remaining segments, Consumer and Commercial and Chemicals, are not separately reportable under any of the three tests. Specific segment information must therefore be reported in the annual report for the three separately reportable segments, and summary information for the remaining two nonreportable segments must be combined under the heading "All Other."

FIGURE 13–3
Summary of Reportable Industry Segments: 10 Percent Tests

	Food Products	Plastic and Packaging	Consumer and Commercial	Health and Scientific	Chemicals
Revenue test	Yes	Yes	No	Yes	No
Operating profit (loss) test	Yes	Yes	No	No	No
Identifiable assets test	Yes	Yes	No	Yes	No

Comprehensive Disclosure Test

After determining which of the segments is reportable under any of the three 10 percent tests, the company must apply a comprehensive test. The comprehensive test is the **75 percent consolidated revenue test**.

Seventy-Five Percent Consolidated Revenue Test

The total revenue from external sources by all separately reportable operating segments must equal at least 75 percent of the total consolidated revenue. The reporting company must identify additional operating segments as reportable until this test is met. Peerless Products and Special Foods, with three reportable segments, compute the 75 percent test as follows:

Sales to unaffiliated customers by reportable segments:		
Food Products	$317,000	
Plastic and Packaging	95,000	
Health and Scientific	86,000	
Total of reportable segments		$498,000
Consolidated revenue		$572,000
Reportable segments' percentage of consolidated revenue ($498,000 ÷ $572,000)		87.1%

Because this percentage is equal to or greater than 75 percent, no further operating segments must be separately reported. Had the percentage been less than 75 percent, additional individual operating segments would have been required to be treated as reportable until the 75 percent test was met.

Other Considerations

A practical limit of about 10 segments is used as an upper limit on the number of reportable segments because above that number, the supplemental information may become overly detailed. A company having more than about 10 reportable segments should consider aggregating the most closely related segments. Peerless Products and Special Foods have just three reportable segments.

In addition, companies must exercise judgment to determine the individual segments to be reported. For example, a segment may meet or fail a specific test because of some unusual situation, such as an abnormally high profit or loss on a one-time contract. The concept of interperiod comparability should be followed in deciding whether or not the segment should be disclosed in the current period. Companies should separately report segments that have been reported in prior years but fail the current period's significance tests because of abnormal occurrences. Similarly, companies need not separately report a segment that has met a 10 percent test on a one-time basis only because of abnormal circumstances. A company is required, however, to indicate why a reportable segment is not disclosed.

Finally, if a segment becomes reportable in the current period but has not been reported separately in earlier periods, the prior years' comparative segment disclosures, which are included in the current year's annual report, should be restated to obtain comparability of financial data.

Reporting Segment Information

The specific disclosures required for each reportable segment are defined in **FASB 131**. In segment reporting, the following quantitative and descriptive information must be disclosed for *each* segment determined to be separately reportable:

1. *General information.* Information must be disclosed regarding: (*a*) how the company identifies each separately reportable segment, including information about the company's

organizational structure (i.e., whether the company organizes along product lines, geographic areas, or some other organizational factor), and (*b*) the types of products or services from which each reportable segment earns its revenues.

2. *Amounts for each separately reportable segment.* Segment disclosures must include amounts for: (*a*) each segment's profit or loss and the measurement procedures used to determine the profit or loss, including how the company accounts for intersegment transactions, and (*b*) each segment's assets.

3. *Measures of segment profit or loss.* Each of the following must be disclosed if it is used to measure the segment profit or loss reviewed by the company's chief operating decision maker: (*a*) revenues from external sales, (*b*) revenues from transactions with other operating segments of the company, (*c*) interest revenue, (*d*) interest expense, (*e*) depreciation and amortization expense, (*f*) equity in the income of investees accounted for by the equity method, (*g*) income tax expense or benefit, (*h*) extraordinary items, and (*i*) other significant noncash items.

4. *Segment assets.* The following information on each separately reportable segment's assets must be disclosed if it is included in the computation of segment assets reviewed by the company's chief operating decision maker: (*a*) the amount of investment in equity-method investees, and (*b*) the total expenditures for increases to long-term productive assets through the capital budget, since these expenditures often indicate which segments the company is building for the future.

5. *Reconciliations to consolidated totals.* Finally, the segment disclosures must include reconciliations between the reportable segments' total revenues, total profits or losses, and total assets and the related consolidated totals for those items. If the company decides to disclose liabilities for each reportable segment, a reconciliation is also required between the reportable segments' total liabilities and the consolidated total liabilities.

Companies are allowed to present these disclosures in separate schedules or in the footnotes. Most companies present footnote disclosures with accompanying schedules. An example of a commonly used disclosure format is presented in Figure 13–4 for Peerless Products and Special Foods. The figure presents the information on the operating segments used in the example and only the current year's data. In practice, however, companies provide comparative data for at least two prior fiscal periods together with the current period's information.

FASB 131 specified that segment disclosures must also be made in interim statements such as the quarterly financial statements. The interim reports must disclose the following about each reportable segment: (1) revenues from external customers, (2) intersegment revenues, (3) a measure of segment profit or loss, (4) total assets for which there has been a material change from the most recent annual report, (5) any differences from the most recent annual report in the definition of operating segments or in how segment profit or loss is computed, and (6) a reconciliation of the total of segment profit or loss to the entity's consolidated totals.

ENTERPRISEWIDE DISCLOSURES

The focus in **FASB 131** is to provide financial statement users with information by which they may determine the risks and potential returns of an entity, using the same basis of information aggregation as used by the company's management. Certainly, the risks of doing business in one country may be quite different from the risks of doing business in another country. Today's large multinational entities have operations in many countries and foreign markets. In addition, a company that obtains a significant percentage of its revenue from just one customer has a different risk profile than a company that has many smaller customers. Thus, **FASB 131** established what it termed ***enterprisewide disclosure*** standards to provide users more information about the risks of the company. These enterprisewide disclosures are typically made in a footnote to the financial statements.

FIGURE 13–4 **Required Footnote Disclosures for Peerless Products Corporation and Subsidiary's Operating Segments**

Footnote X
Information about the Company's Operations in Different Operating Segments

| Item | Operating Segments | | | | |
	Food Products	Plastics and Packaging	Health and Scientific	All Others	Combined
Revenue to unaffiliated customers	317,000	95,000	86,000	74,000	572,000
Intersegment revenue	6,000	18,000		4,000	28,000
Interest revenue—-intersegment		12,000			12,000
Interest expense—unaffiliated		30.000			30,000
Interest expense—intersegment	12,000				12,000
Depreciation	10,000	5,000	9,000	12,000	36,000
Segment profit (loss)	198,000	59,000	22,000	(34,000)	245,000
Segment assets	411,000	375,000	310,000	180,000	1,276,000
Expenditures for segment assets	48,000	21,000	29,000	22,000	120,000

Reconciliation of Reportable Segment Revenue to Consolidated Revenue

Total revenues for reportable segments	$ 522,000
Other revenues	78,000
Elimination of intersegment revenues	(28,000)
Total consolidated revenues	$ 572,000

Reconciliation of Reportable Segment Profit and Loss to Consolidated Profit or Loss

Total profit and loss for reportable segments	$ 279,000
Other profits or loss	(34,000)
Elimination of intersegment profit	(10,000)
General corporate expense	(45,000)
Income from equity investment	32,000
Income before income taxes and extraordinary items	$ 222,000

Reconciliation of Reportable Segment Assets to Consolidated Assets

Total assets for reportable segments	$1,096,000
Other assets	180,000
Elimination of intersegment profits in assets	(10,000)
Intersegment notes	(100,000)
General corporate assets	100,000
Equity investments	184,000
Consolidated total assets	$1,450,000

Information about Products and Services

Three categories of required information are included under enterprisewide disclosures. The first is that the company is required to report the revenues from external customers for each major product and service, or each group of similar products and services, unless it is impracticable for it to do so. The reason for this requirement is that the company may have organized its operating segments on a basis different from its product lines. However, if the company does establish its operating segments by product line, then the segment disclosures discussed earlier in this chapter meet this first, enterprisewide disclosure requirement.

Information about Geographic Areas

The second category is information about the geographic areas in which the company operates. The company must report the following unless it is impracticable for it to do so:

1. Revenues from external customers attributed to the company's home country of domicile (the United States for U.S. firms) and the revenue from external customers attributed to

all foreign countries in which the enterprise generates revenues. If revenues from external customers generated in an individual country are material, then the revenues for that country shall also be separately disclosed.

2. Long-lived productive assets located in the entity's home country of domicile and the total assets located in all foreign countries in which the entity holds assets. As with revenue, if assets in an individual foreign country are material, then the amount of assets held in that specific country shall also be disclosed separately.

FASB 131 defines the long-term assets as excluding financial instruments, long-term customer relationships of a financial institution, mortgage or other servicing rights, deferred policy acquisition costs, and deferred tax assets. The FASB believes that companies typically maintain accounting records on a country-by-country basis because of the political, economic, and other specific factors that differ across countries. Thus, if the company generates a material amount of revenue in a specific country or has made a material long-lived asset investment in a specific country, this information should be readily available for management to include in the enterprisewide disclosures. Although **FASB 131** specified no materiality threshold for specific country disclosures, the 10 percent guideline for disaggregated disclosures seems to have gained acceptance.

Note that the revenues for the geographic information are those only to unaffiliated, external customers. Intersegment revenues are not included. The assets are only those long-lived, productive assets and exclude current assets and several types of noncurrent assets as specified by **FASB 131**. All companies must disclose domestic versus total foreign revenues and long-lived assets unless it is impracticable to do so. For purposes of the following disclosure, assume that $840,000 of the total consolidated assets of $1,450,000 are determined to be long-lived, productive assets meeting the specifications of **FASB 131**. Separate country disclosures would be provided for material amounts. Assume that Peerless uses a 10 percent materiality threshold for assessing its foreign operations. Therefore, separate disclosure is presented for any country having greater than or equal to 10 percent of the consolidated revenue or the total long-lived assets. An example of the footnote disclosure that could be made by Peerless Products follows:

Geographic Information		
	Revenue	**Long-Lived Asset**
United States	$380,000	$471,000
Total Foreign	192,000	369,000
Total	$572,000	$840,000
Significant Countries:		
Canada	$116,000	$220,000
Mexico	28,000	102,000

The company must also disclose the basis for attributing revenues from external customers to the individual countries. For example, one method may be to assign revenues based on the location of the customer.

Information about Major Customers

The third and final category of enterprisewide disclosures required by **FASB 131** is information about major customers. An important issue is how to define an individual customer. For applying the disclosure test, each of the following is considered to be an individual customer: any single customer (including a group of customers or companies under common control), the federal government, a state government, a local government, or a foreign government. Materiality is not defined for this disclosure, but again, the

10 percent guideline seems to have gained the support of practice. The disclosures include the amount of revenue from each significant customer and the identity of the segment or segments reporting the revenues. The names of the individual customers need not be disclosed. The following is an example of the type of footnote disclosure that Peerless Products could use:

> Revenues from one customer of the Food Products segment represent approximately $64,000 of the company's consolidated revenues.

This concludes the discussion of segment reporting. The remainder of the chapter presents another major area of financial disclosure: interim financial reporting.

INTERIM FINANCIAL REPORTING

Interim reports, which cover a time period of less than one year, provide timely information on the operating progress of the entity throughout the year. Interim reports can be for a week, a month, a quarter, or for several quarters. Many companies prepare monthly financial statements for internal management purposes. Publicly held companies are required to publish quarterly reports and the rapid stock market reaction to the public release of quarterly information indicates that investors and other financial statement users look closely at these reports. The quarterly report is, in many ways, a smaller version of the annual report. It includes an abbreviated statement of income, balance sheet, statement of cash flows, and selected footnotes and other disclosures for the quarter being reported, as well as comparative data for prior quarters.

Form 10-Q is the SEC's quarterly report and, for most companies, this quarterly report must be filed within 35 days after the end of each of the first three quarters. The annual report may be used in place of the interim report for the fourth quarter. The 35-day requirement is for publicly owned companies classified as "accelerated filers," which are companies with at least $75 million in aggregate market value that have been subject to the periodic and annual reporting requirements for at least one year, including the filing of at least one annual report. Most companies traded on the major stock exchanges are in the accelerated filers category. Those companies not meeting the accelerated filers criteria have 45 days after the end of each of the first three quarters to file their quarterly reports.

The SEC does not require quarterly financial statements to be audited, but selected quarterly financial data must be reported in a footnote in the annual financial report. This annual disclosure requirement means that the independent registered public accounting firm performing the company's annual audit must review the company's quarterly reports made during the fiscal year and note any errors or restatements. Because of the wide use of interim reports, including monthly and quarterly reports, accountants must be aware of the principles and procedures used in preparing these reports.

THE FORMAT OF THE QUARTERLY FINANCIAL REPORT

Quarterly financial reports generally contain the following items:

1. An income statement for the most recent quarter of the current fiscal period and a comparative income statement for the same quarter for the prior fiscal year.
2. Income statements for the cumulative year-to-date time period and for the corresponding period of the prior fiscal year.
3. A condensed balance sheet at the end of the current quarter and a condensed balance sheet at the end of the prior fiscal year. However, companies should include the balance sheet as of the end of the corresponding interim period of the previous year if it is necessary for an understanding of the impact of seasonal fluctuations on the company's financial condition.
4. A statement of cash flows as of the end of the current cumulative year-to-date period and for the same time span for the prior year.

5. Footnotes that update those in the last annual report. These interim footnotes include summaries of material changes in measurement or major economic events that have occurred since the end of the most recent fiscal year.

6. A report by management analyzing and discussing the results for the latest interim period.

ACCOUNTING ISSUES

Interim reporting presents accountants with several technical and conceptual measurement issues. Most of these center on the accounting concept of periodicity and the division of the annual period into interim periods. Note that interim reporting includes financial statements for any period less than one year, including monthly reports, quarterly reports, or any other portion of an annual period.

The use of quarterly reports to provide timely information is a fairly recent development. Many firms began publishing quarterly reports voluntarily in the late 1940s. These early reports raised substantive accounting issues because no standards existed to guide their presentation. Some firms' first three quarterly reports suggested a significant profit for the year, and then arbitrary and questionable fourth-quarter adjustments reconciled to an actual loss for the year. The lack of established guidelines led to experimentation with a variety of cost allocations among periods, resulting in unrealistic patterns of quarterly income. It was not until 1973, when the Accounting Principles Board issued **APB Opinion No. 28**, "Interim Financial Reporting" (APB 28), that guidelines were finally standardized.

Discrete versus Integral View of Interim Reporting

Two divergent views of interim reporting were held before the release of **APB 28**. The *discrete theory of interim reporting* views each interim period as a basic accounting period to be evaluated as if it were an annual accounting period. Any end-of-period adjustments and deferrals are determined using the same accounting principles used for the annual report.

The *integral theory of interim reporting* views an interim period as an installment of an annual period. Under this view, recognition and adjustment of certain income or expense items may be affected by judgments about the expected results of the entire year's operations. For example, expenses that normally would be charged to operations in one period for annual accounting purposes could be deferred and expensed in several interim periods based on an allocation using sales volume, production levels, or some other basis.

To examine the differences between these two theories, assume that Peerless Products Corporation incurred a $20,000 cost at the beginning of the second quarter of its fiscal year for an advertising campaign intended to generate sales revenue for the remainder of the year. Under the discrete view, the entire $20,000 must be charged against income in the second quarter. Under the integral view, however, the advertising cost could initially be recorded as a deferred cost and expensed over the second, third, and fourth interim periods. The allocation to the individual periods could be made on the basis of the sales volume generated or some other appropriate basis. Under the integral view, one interim period would not bear the entire expense that benefits more than one interim period.

Both views were applied in practice, and it was up to the Accounting Principles Board to settle the conflict. The integral view was selected as the primary theory for interim reporting, although some modifications of this theory were made so that reports would conform closely to the results of operations for the year.

Accounting Pronouncements on Interim Reporting

APB 28 standardized the preparation and reporting of interim income statements. The opinion defines the income elements and the measurement of costs on an interim basis. The opinion also provides guidance for the annual report footnote summarizing the published interim disclosures and explaining any adjustments required to make the interim figures total the annual figures. This conformance to the annual report increases the reliability of the published interim statements and brings interim reporting under the view of the external auditors who review the footnotes in the annual report as part of the audit.

FASB Statement No. 154, "Accounting Changes and Error Corrections" (FASB 154), issued in 2005, replaced **APB Opinion No. 20**, "Accounting Changes (APB 20), and **FASB Statement No. 3**, "Reporting Accounting Changes in Interim Financial Statements (FASB 3). **FASB 154** specifies that a change in an accounting principle made in an interim period is reported using the retrospective application to the prechange interim periods for the direct effects of the change. The financial statements for the earliest period presented, either annual or interim, are adjusted for the effects of the change at that point in time and all subsequent financial statements, again both annual and interim, are adjusted for the newly adopted accounting principle. A change in estimate in an interim period is reported currently and prospectively, and no prior periods are restated. A change in entity in an interim period requires retrospective application.

FASB Interpretation No. 18, "Accounting for Income Taxes in Interim Periods" (FIN 18), amended **APB 28**. This interpretation tackles the difficult problems of measuring the tax provision for interim reports when the actual tax expense is based on annual income. The interpretation allows estimates and judgments in order to obtain a reasonable relationship between the reported interim operating income and the related income tax provision. Examples of accounting for taxes in interim statements are presented later in this chapter.

REPORTING STANDARDS FOR INTERIM INCOME STATEMENTS

The form of the interim income statement is the same as the form of the annual income statement. Some differences exist in the measurement of specific components of income because of the shorter time period. In general, the accounting standards used for interim statements are the same as those used for the annual statements, although **APB 28** provides an abundance of technical assistance to measure and report on an interim basis. Figure 13–5 presents an overview of the major accounting principles used for the interim income statement. The technical requirements relevant to interim reporting are discussed in the following sections.

Revenue

One of the most significant elements of the interim income statement is revenue from sales. Investors wish to assess the entity's revenue-generating capability, so they compare revenue of the current interim period with revenue of the corresponding interim period of prior years. The measurement basis used to determine revenue earned in an interim period should be the same as that used for the full fiscal year.

Thus, revenue must be recognized and reported in the period in which earned and cannot be deferred to other periods to present a more stable revenue stream. Revenue from seasonal businesses, such as in agriculture, food products, wholesale or retail outlets, and amusements, cannot be manipulated to eliminate seasonal trends.

The APB considered the issue of seasonality to be very important. Businesses that experience material seasonal variations in their revenue are encouraged to supplement their interim reports with information for 12-month periods ending at the interim date for the current and preceding years. Such disclosures reduce the possibility that users of the reports might make unwarranted inferences about the annual results from an interim report with material seasonal variation.

Cost of Goods Sold and Inventory

Cost of goods sold is generally the largest single expense on the interim statement of income. A general rule is that interim cost of goods sold should be computed with the direct and allocated cost elements on the same basis as used to compute the annual cost of goods sold. However, **APB 28** does permit the following practical modifications to this general rule:

1. *Use estimated gross profit rates*. Estimated gross profit rates may be used to compute the interim cost of goods sold. Thus, a physical inventory count does not need to be made in each interim.

2. *LIFO temporary liquidations*. Due to seasonality and other factors, companies using the LIFO method of inventory valuation sometimes have temporary liquidations of the

FIGURE 13–5 **Overview of Interim Income Statement Accounting Principles**

Revenue	Recognize as earned during an interim period on same basis as used for annual reporting.
Cost of goods sold	Product costs for interim period recognized on same basis as used for annual reporting, except for interims:
	• Estimated gross profit rates may be used to determine interim cost of goods sold.
	• Temporary liquidations of LIFO-base inventories are charged to cost of goods sold using expected replacement cost of the items.
	• Lower-of-cost-or-market valuation method allows for loss recoveries for increases in market prices in later interim periods of the same fiscal year.
	• Standard cost systems should use same procedures as for annual reporting except that price variances or volume or capacity variances expected to be absorbed by end of the year should be deferred.
All other costs and expenses	Expense as incurred or allocated among interim periods' expenses based on benefits received or other systematic and rational basis.
Income taxes	Based on estimated annual effective tax rate, with recognition of tax benefits of an operating loss if benefits are assured beyond a reasonable doubt; second and subsequent quarters are based on changes in cumulative amount of tax computed, including changes in estimates.
Disposal of a component of the entity, or extraordinary, unusual, infrequently occurring, and contingent items	Recognize in interim period in which they occur.
Accounting changes:	
1. Change in accounting principle	Retrospective application to all prechange interim periods reported.
2. Change in an accounting estimate	Apply to current and prospective interim periods only.
3. Change in a reporting entity	Retrospective application to all prechange interim periods reported.

LIFO-base inventory during one or more interim periods. These temporary liquidations are expected to be replenished by the end of the fiscal year. In these cases, the interim cost of goods sold is charged for the expected replacement cost of the liquidated inventory, not the LIFO historical cost of the inventory. If, by the end of the year, the LIFO inventory base is not replaced, then the liquidated inventory is charged to cost of goods sold at its LIFO cost base.

3. *Lower-of-cost-or-market valuations.* Inventory losses from decreases in market value below cost are recognized in the period of the decline. Recoveries of market price in subsequent interim periods should be recognized in the period of recovery as recoveries of losses that were recognized in prior interim periods of that fiscal year. No gains are recognized for increases of market value above cost. Temporary market price declines that are expected to be reversed by the end of the fiscal year do not have to be recognized in the interim period because no loss is expected for the full fiscal year.

4. *Standard cost systems.* Manufacturers that use standard cost systems to compute cost of goods sold and ending inventory should use the same procedures for determining variances for an interim period as are used for the fiscal year. However, variances that are anticipated to be absorbed by the end of the fiscal year are usually not included in computing interim income.

Illustration of Temporary LIFO Liquidation

The reason that the interim treatment of LIFO inventory liquidations differs from the annual treatment of LIFO liquidations is that the inventory is expected to be replaced by the end of the fiscal year. Interim income for the period of the temporary liquidation would be overstated if cost of goods sold were charged with the lower LIFO inventory costs in a time of rising prices. The following example illustrates this point.

1. During the third quarter of its fiscal year, Special Foods experienced a temporary liquidation of 2,000 units in its LIFO base owing to seasonal fluctuations. The LIFO unit cost is $25. The liquidation is normal, and the company plans to replace the liquidated inventory during the early part of the next (fourth) interim period.

2. The estimated replacement cost of the inventory is $35 per unit.

The entry in the third interim period to account for the temporary inventory liquidation is:

(1)			
	Cost of Goods Sold	70,000	
	Inventory		50,000
	Excess of Replacement Cost over LIFO		
	Cost of Inventory Liquidated		20,000
	Record temporary LIFO inventory liquidation:		
	$70,000 = 2,000 units × $35		
	$50,000 = 2,000 units × $25 LIFO cost		

The interim income statement presents cost of goods sold at the expected replacement cost. The Excess of Replacement Cost over LIFO Cost of Inventory Liquidated should be shown as a current liability on the interim balance sheet, although some accountants net this against the inventory reported on the interim balance sheet.

When the inventory is replaced at $36 per unit during the fourth quarter, the following entry is made:

(2)			
	Cost of Goods Sold	2,000	
	Inventory	50,000	
	Excess of Replacement Cost over		
	LIFO Cost of Inventory Liquidated	20,000	
	Accounts Payable		72,000
	Record replacement of LIFO inventory liquidation:		
	$50,000 = 2,000 × $25 LIFO cost		
	$72,000 = 2,000 × $36		

The actual replacement price of $36 is different from the estimated replacement price of $35. The difference is an adjustment to cost of goods sold in the replacement period. The third quarter's interim report is not retroactively restated. If the liquidated inventory is not replaced by the end of the fiscal year, the liability account is written off to Cost of Goods Sold, decreasing the reported annual cost of goods sold to its correct amount.

Illustration of Market Write-Down and Recovery

The following example illustrates the use of the lower-of-cost-or-market (LCM) method for interim reports:

1. At the beginning of its fiscal year, Peerless Products has 10,000 units of inventory on hand with a FIFO cost of $10 each.

2. No additional purchases are made during the year.

3. The sales and market values at the end of each quarter during the fiscal year are as follows:

Quarter	Units Sold in Quarter	Unit Market Values at End of Quarter
1	2,000	$ 7
2	2,000	6
3	2,000	7
4	2,000	11

FIGURE 13–6
Interim Lower-of-Cost-or-Market Analysis of the Inventory Account of Peerless Products Corporation

Quarter	Item	Units	Inventory Unit Price	Inventory Dollars
	Balance, beginning of year	10,000	$10	$100,000
1	Inventory sold, first quarter	(2,000)	$10	(20,000)
	Adjustment to market: [8,000 units × ($10 − $7)]	8,000	(3)	(24,000)
	Balance, end of first quarter	8,000	$ 7	$ 56,000
2	Inventory sold, second quarter	(2,000)	$ 7	(14,000)
	Adjustment to market: [6,000 units × ($7 − $6)]	6,000	(1)	(6,000)
	Balance, end of second quarter	6,000	$ 6	$ 36,000
3	Inventory sold, third quarter	(2,000)	$ 6	(12,000)
	Market price recovery: [4,000 units × ($6 − $7)]	4,000	1	4,000
	Balance, end of third quarter	4,000	$ 7	$ 28,000
4	Inventory sold, fourth quarter	(2,000)	$ 7	(14,000)
	Market price recovery: [2,000 units × ($7 − $10)]	2,000	3	6,000
	Balance, end of fourth quarter	2,000	$10(a)	$ 20,000

(a) Note that although market value is $11, inventory valuation cannot exceed cost.

Peerless is not certain of the causes of the reductions in market value and considers them to be permanent; therefore, it recognizes the reductions in the quarters in which they occur. *No recognition is required* if the reductions are anticipated to be temporary, with recovery by year-end.

Figure 13–6 presents the calculations needed to adjust Peerless's inventory account to the lower of cost or market. At the end of the first quarter, the ending inventory of the quarter is written down by $24,000, and a loss is recognized on the interim income statement. Many companies report this write-down as part of their cost of goods sold because it is associated with inventory. By the end of the second quarter, a write-down of $6,000 of the ending inventory is required. The third-quarter interim report shows a loss recovery of $4,000 due to an increase in inventory replacement costs. Note that this is a recovery of valuation losses recognized in prior quarters. In quarter 4, the $11 market price is $1 higher than the initial cost of the inventory. A $6,000 loss recovery on the fourth-quarter ending inventory of the 2,000 units is recognized to bring the inventory valuation from $7 per unit to its original cost of $10 per unit. Note that the inventory may not be valued at an amount in excess of cost.

A graphical representation of the market prices during the year is presented in Figure 13–7. Note that after decreasing during the first two quarters, the market price increases during the third and fourth quarters. At year-end, the price is $11 per unit, which is above the initial cost for the inventory.

Another way to view the effects of the write-downs is to compute the amount that would be reported in each quarter's cost of goods sold. This amount would include the costs assigned to the goods sold during the quarter plus the effects of any inventory write-downs and less the effects of any recoveries of losses recognized in prior interim periods. These market adjustments are normally treated as adjustments of cost of goods sold to represent

FIGURE 13–7
Graph of Market
Prices of Inventory

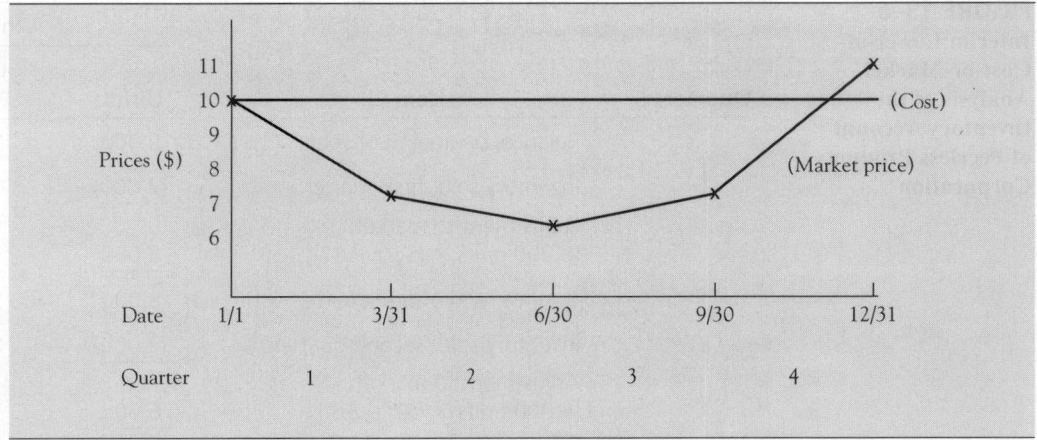

all the product costs in one location on the income statement. The following table shows the computation of cost of goods sold for each quarter:

Quarter	Costs Assigned to Goods Sold	Ending Inventory Write-Down to Market (or Loss Recovery)	Total
1	2,000 units × $10	8,000 units × $3	$44,000
2	2,000 units × $7	6,000 units × $1	20,000
3	2,000 units × $6	(4,000 units × $1)	8,000
4	2,000 units × $7	(2,000 units × $3)	8,000

If the reductions in market value in quarters 1 and 2 were considered temporary, no write-downs would need to be recognized and therefore no loss recoveries would be recognized in quarters 3 and 4. The total of the cost of goods sold reported for the interims must reconcile to the amount reported on the annual financial statements. Note that the year-end market price ($11) is higher than the market price at the beginning of the year ($10). On the annual statement:

$$8,000 \text{ units} \times \$10 \text{ unit price} = \$80,000$$

On the interim statements:

Quarter 1	$44,000
Quarter 2	20,000
Quarter 3	8,000
Quarter 4	8,000
Total	$80,000

To be able to focus on the main points of the example, it was assumed that no additional inventory was acquired during the year. Of course, in actual practice, most companies make continuous inventory acquisitions. These purchases would be added to inventory at whatever cost flow method the company uses. The lower-of-cost-or-market valuation method would be applied at the end of each quarter in the same manner as in the example, and the losses or loss recoveries would be recognized.

All Other Costs and Expenses

The integral view adopted by the APB is evident when dealing with interim period costs. The general principle is that costs and expenses should be charged to interim income in the interim period in which they are incurred. Some costs and expenses however, are allocated among the interim periods based on an estimate of time used, benefit received, or activity level of the interim period, as part of the estimated amount for the full fiscal year.

The choice between immediate recognition of the expenditure on the interim period's income statement and deferral and allocation to several periods' interim income statements is based on a subjective evaluation of the periods that benefit from the expenditure. Although most expenditures are charged to the interim period in which they are incurred, the following descriptions illustrate when an expenditure may be deferred and allocated to several interim periods:

1. Some companies concentrate their major equipment repairs in a plant shut-down time in one interim period. For interim reporting these repair costs should be deferred (prepaid asset) or accrued (estimated liability) and allocated to repair expense in each of the interim periods that benefit from the repair costs.
2. Property taxes should be deferred or accrued in each interim period rather than recognized fully as an expense of the interim period in which they are paid.
3. Major advertising campaign costs should be allocated to the interim periods that benefit from them rather than recognized solely in the interim period in which they are incurred. A typical allocation procedure is to estimate the anticipated sales volume for each of the interim periods that will benefit from the advertising campaign. Generally, the total advertising costs are expensed for determining annual income and no deferral is made beyond the fiscal year-end.

Note that a company can accrue probable and estimable costs in earlier interim periods than the period in which the cash is paid. For example, Peerless has a management policy of closing its main production plant each August for a two-week painting and repairs period. On January 1 the company estimates that a total of $60,000 will be incurred for this plant rehabilitation effort and that it will benefit all four quarters of the year. The company will allocate this cost to each quarter, even the two quarters preceding the actual shutdown. In this case, an accrual for the repair expense will be made in the first and second quarters. When the actual cost is incurred in the third quarter, the accrual liability will be eliminated, but the repair expense will still be shown for each quarter. The remaining repair expense for the year will then be allocated to the third and fourth quarters. The key point is that the repair expense can be allocated to each quarter that benefits, even though the cash flow for the item does not occur until a late quarter in the fiscal year. Accruals (estimated liabilities) and deferrals (prepaid assets) are used for these applications.

Illustration of Deferral and Allocation of Advertising Costs

On April 1, the beginning of the second quarter of Peerless Products and Subsidiary's consolidated fiscal year, a $20,000 cost was incurred for an advertising campaign expected to benefit the last three quarters of the current year. Consolidated sales for the second, third, and fourth quarters are expected to total $400,000. In this case, Peerless determined that the advertising campaign would not benefit the first quarter; therefore, no advertising expense was accrued in the first quarter ending March 31, and the only advertising expenditure during the year is the $20,000 incurred on April 1.

The $20,000 cost is recorded as a prepaid asset when incurred and then charged to Advertising Expense in each of the interim periods benefited, as shown in Figure 13–8. The allocation base selected is the quarterly sales in the periods benefited as a percentage of the estimated total sales for the period of benefit.

At the beginning of the third quarter (July 1), $15,000 of advertising cost remains in Prepaid Advertising. If actual quarterly sales differ from the estimated amounts, the allocation

FIGURE 13–8
Accounting for Advertising Costs that Benefit More than One Interim Period

Date	Quarterly Sales	Debit Advertising Expense	Credit Prepaid Advertising	Balance in Prepaid Advertising
April 1				$20,000
June 30	$100,000	$ 5,000(a)	$ 5,000	15,000(b)
September 30	100,000	5,000	5,000	10,000
December 31	200,000	10,000	10,000	-0-
Totals	$400,000	$20,000	$20,000	

(a) $5,000 = ($100,000 / $400,000) × $20,000.
(b) $15,000 = $20,000 − $5,000.

procedure is revised for the change in estimate. For example, if on September 30, management determines the consolidated sales for the third quarter, ending on September 30, to be $120,000 and estimates that fourth-quarter sales will be $180,000, then the remaining balance of $15,000 in Prepaid Advertising is allocated to the third quarter as follows:

$$\$6,000 = \frac{\$120,000}{\$300,000} \times \$15,000$$

The fourth quarter is charged for any remaining balance in the Prepaid Advertising account.

Accounting for Income Taxes in Interim Periods

The *interim income tax* computation poses a particularly troublesome problem for accountants because the actual tax burden is computed on income for the entire fiscal year. In addition, temporary differences between tax accounting and GAAP accounting require the recognition of deferred taxes. Nevertheless, the interim tax provision is a significant item and requires estimates and a number of subjective evaluations based on the anticipated annual tax. The first step is to determine the effective annual tax rate for use in computing the interim income tax provision.

Estimating the Effective Annual Tax Rate

Estimates are a normal part of the accounting cycle, and the interim income tax provision is based on an estimate of the effective annual tax rate on income from continuing operations. The estimated annual tax rate includes all anticipated tax credits, state income taxes, foreign income taxes, capital gains taxes, and other tax planning efforts that are expected for the full fiscal period. The estimate is updated each interim period and the interim tax provision or benefit is then determined.

Items such as unusual or infrequent events, discontinued operations, and extraordinary items are not included in the estimate because the statement of income reports these separately along with their related net-of-tax effects. Also, extraordinary items often have specific tax treatments different from operating income. For example, a fire loss of a building may involve depreciation recapture and other capital loss tax considerations.

Differences between Book and Tax Income There typically will be differences between the amount of operating income computed for financial statement (book) purposes and the operating income computed for tax purposes. The two major categories of differences are discussed in **FASB Statement 109**, Accounting for Income Taxes" (FASB 109), and are often covered extensively in intermediate financial accounting classes.

The first category is most often referred to as "permanent" or nontemporary differences. Permanent differences are not included in determining the amount of taxable income for a period. Examples of these permanent differences include:

1. Life insurance premiums paid by the company on executive policies for which the company is the beneficiary (not tax deductible).

2. Proceeds of life insurance collected (not tax includible).

3. Dividends received deduction on portion of dividends received on U.S. corporation stock investments (not tax includible).

4. Interest income received on state or local government bonds that is classified as not taxable (not tax includible).

5. Certain types of fines or court penalties designated as not tax deductible.

These items are included in the determination of financial statement income (book), but they are not included in the computation of taxable income. Thus, book income is adjusted for these items in order to determine the taxable income for the interim period.

The second category of differences is usually referred to as "temporary" differences. Temporary differences between the recognition of a transaction for book versus tax income result in deferred taxes. For example, a revenue may be recognized for tax either before or after the period in which it is recognized for book purposes. Or, an expense may be recognized for tax purposes in a period different from that used for book purposes. Examples of temporary differences include:

1. Rent collected in advance (reported on tax return in period collected but as revenue on books in period earned).

2. Estimated expenses and losses (reported on books at time of accrual but on tax return in period paid).

3. Accelerated depreciation on tax return and straight-line depreciation on the income statement (difference of depreciation expense on books versus tax).

4. Revaluing inventory to lower-of-cost-or-market on financial statements (loss shown on books in period of write-down but on tax return in period sold).

The deferred tax asset or deferred tax liability created by these temporary differences is reported on the balance sheet. The income tax expense shown on the income statement is the sum of the income tax actually payable in the period plus (or minus for a deferred tax asset) the amount of the tax deferral for the period.

The reporting process is illustrated next.

Illustration of Estimating Effective Annual Tax Rate

Figure 13–9 illustrates the computation of the tax rate. While proceeding through the example, note the adjustments, such as the differences between tax accounting and GAAP accounting, necessary to determine the annual rate. Following are data for the illustration:

1. Peerless Products and its subsidiary expect to earn $225,000 consolidated income from continuing operations for the 20X1 fiscal year.

FIGURE 13–9
Estimation of Effective Annual Tax Rate

	Estimated Annual Amounts
Income from continuing operations	$225,000
Adjust for permanent differences:	
Add premiums on key officers' life insurance	2,000
Deduct dividends received exclusion	(27,000)
Estimated annual taxable income	$200,000
Combined federal and state income taxes	× 38%
Estimated annual taxes before tax credits	$ 76,000
Deduct business tax credit	(22,000)
Estimated income taxes for year	$ 54,000
Divide by estimated annual income from continuing operations	$225,000
Estimated effective annual tax rate on continuing operations ($54,000 ÷ $225,000)	24%

2. Permanent differences between accounting income and tax income are expected to be $2,000 for premiums paid for life insurance carried by the company on key officers (company is beneficiary) and an exclusion of $27,000 for dividends received from investments in stocks of other companies.

3. The combined federal and state income tax rate is estimated to be 38 percent (30 percent federal and 8 percent state), and the company expects to be eligible for a $22,000 business tax credit related to new job development expenditures and employee retraining costs.

The estimated effective tax rate of 24 percent computed in Figure 13–9 is used to determine the income tax provision for the first quarter. Assuming that the first-quarter earnings were $20,000, the following entry records the tax provision:

(3)	Income Tax Expense	4,800	
	Income Taxes Payable		4,800
	Record first-quarter tax provision:		
	$4,800 = $20,000 × .24 effective tax rate		

Updating the Estimated Annual Rate in Subsequent Interim Periods

Assume that second-quarter actual earnings are $25,000, for a cumulative total for the year to date of $45,000 ($20,000 + $25,000). The consolidated entity must first recompute its estimate of its effective annual tax rate based on the updated information it has at the end of the second quarter, such as additional differences between taxable and accounting income or a better estimate of projected annual earnings. Assuming the new estimated effective annual tax rate is 34 percent because of changes in the estimated amount of the available business tax credit and other changes in estimates, this rate replaces the 24 percent rate used at the end of the first quarter.

The new estimated tax rate is used to compute the estimated year-to-date income tax provision at the end of the second interim period, as follows:

Actual cumulative income for first two quarters	
($20,000 + $25,000)	$45,000
Updated estimated effective annual tax rate	× 34%
Cumulative income tax provision (expense)	$15,300
Less: Income tax provision made in first quarter	(4,800)
Income tax provision required in second quarter	$10,500

Peerless Products and its subsidiary report an income tax expense of $10,500 on the second-quarter consolidated income statement. The tax provision is cumulative, and the first-quarter provision is *not* retroactively restated for the change in the estimate of the annual tax rate.

The example does not include any temporary differences between accounting income and taxable income that result in deferred taxes. Temporary differences generally do not affect the estimate of the tax provision. Instead, the recognition of any temporary difference is normally made in the entry to record the tax provision and associated tax liability. For example, if $2,000 of the second-quarter income of $25,000 is due to a temporary difference in which accounting income is higher than tax income, the following entry is made to recognize the provision and deferral:

(4)	Income Tax Expense	10,500	
	Deferred Tax Liability		680
	Income Taxes Payable		9,820
	Record second-quarter tax provision:		
	$10,500 = Income taxes payable plus deferred tax liability		
	$ 680 = Computation of deferred tax liability effect from temporary		
	difference between tax and book income		

Losses and Operating Loss Carrybacks and Carryforwards

Accountants face an interesting problem when a company has a year-to-date loss as of the end of an interim period. Normally, an operating loss creates a tax benefit (that is, reduces tax payable) because the loss can be carried back against the operating income shown in previous years and the company may file a claim for a refund of taxes paid in prior years. After the carryback portion of an operating loss is depleted, any remaining operating loss is carried forward against future operating income. These carryback and carryforward provisions, however, apply only to annual results, not to interim results.

These and other special tax problems are discussed in **FIN 18**. The first part of the interpretation deals with the numerous alternative income trends possible, such as an operating loss for year to date but income anticipated for the year, or operating income for year to date but loss expected for the year. The possible combinations of interim and annual results are too numerous to show here, but one special case is covered. This special case is the determination of the tax benefit for a company with a year-to-date operating loss but with the expectation of an annual income. The issue is how to determine and report the income tax for the interim periods.

FASB Statement No. 109, "Accounting for Income Taxes" (FASB 109), also addresses the issue of accounting for income taxes in an interim period. **FASB 109** affirms the general rule that the realization of a tax benefit must be assured beyond a reasonable doubt before the benefit may be recognized in the financial statements. For interim reporting purposes, the most common reason for allowing the recognition of a tax benefit for a company with a year-to-date operating loss is that the company has had consistent seasonal trends in income during the year. Thus, the company has generally had income in the later interim periods that has offset the losses in the earlier interim periods. **FASB Interpretation No. 48**, "Accounting for Uncertainty in Income Taxes: An Interpretation of FASB Statement No. 109" (FIN 48), established a more-likely-than-not criteria of having a likelihood of more than 50 percent as the threshold for beyond a reasonable doubt. Therefore, a company with an operating loss in the early interim periods, with consistent experience of seasonality and income for the year, can recognize a tax benefit of a to-date operating loss in the early interim periods. If the realization of a tax benefit of an interim operating loss is not assured by the end of the fiscal period, the company cannot show any tax benefit on the interim statements.

Illustration of Interim Operating Loss

Figure 13–10 presents the computation of the tax or benefit that should be shown on the interim statements if a company experiences a year-to-date loss but anticipates an annual income. For example, assume that the consolidated entity of Peerless Products Corporation and Special Foods Inc. has an actual first-quarter loss of $40,000 but expects an annual income of $222,000. The estimated annual tax rate is 24 percent. The consolidated entity has a normal seasonal variation of losses in the first quarter followed by profits in subsequent

FIGURE 13–10
Interim Analysis When Tax Benefit of Operating Loss Is Assured

Reporting Period	Continuing Income (Loss) before Taxes — Reporting Period	Year to Date	Estimated Effective Annual Tax Rate, %	Tax (Benefit) — Year to Date (a)	Less Previously Provided	Reported in Period
First quarter	$ (40,000)	$ (40,000)	24.0%	$ (9,600)		$ (9,600)
Second quarter	$ 20,000	(20,000)	34.0	(6,800)	$ (9,600)	2,800
Third quarter	80,000	60,000	34.0	20,400	(6,800)	27,200
Fourth quarter	162,000	222,000	27.9(b)	62,000	20,400	41,600
Fiscal year	$222,000					$62,000

(a) Year to date: Year-to-date continuing income (loss) × Updated estimated effective annual tax rate.
(b) Rounded off.

FIGURE 13–11
Interim Analysis When Operating Loss Benefit Is Not Assured

Reporting Period	Continuing Income (Loss) before Taxes		Estimated Effective Annual Tax Rate, %	Tax (Benefit)		
	Reporting Period	Year to Date		Year to Date (a)	Less Previously Provided	Reported in Period
First quarter	$ (40,000)	$(40,000)	24.0%	$ -0-		$ -0-
Second quarter	$ 20,000	(20,000)	34.0	$ -0-	$ -0-	$ -0-
Third quarter	80,000	60,000	34.0	20,400	$ -0-	20,400
Fourth quarter	162,000	222,000	27.9	62,000	20,400	41,600
Fiscal year	$222,000					$62,000

(a) Year to date: Year-to-date continuing income (loss) × Updated estimated effective annual tax rate.

quarters. Therefore, the tax benefit of the operating loss of $9,600 ($40,000 × .24) is assured beyond a reasonable doubt, and the tax benefit is shown in the loss quarter.

A partial income statement for the first quarter follows. Note how the tax benefit reduces the reported net loss:

PEERLESS PRODUCTS AND SPECIAL FOODS
Partial Interim Consolidated Income Statement
First Quarter Ended March 31, 20X1

Operating Loss before Income Tax Effect	$(40,000)
Less: Tax Benefit of Operating Loss	9,600
Net Loss	$(30,400)

At the end of 20X1, Peerless Products and Subsidiary computed its actual annual income tax provision for 20X1 as $62,000. The year-to-date tax provision in the fourth quarter should equal the total actual annual provision, and the amount of tax reported in the fourth quarter is the balance necessary to reach the amount of the annual provision. Therefore, the actual annual income tax rate on continuing income for 20X1 was 27.9 percent ($62,000 annual tax provision ÷ $222,000 annual income from continuing operations before the deduction for income to noncontrolling interest).

If the realizability of the tax benefit from the operating loss is not assured beyond a reasonable doubt, no tax benefit should be shown. This case is presented in Figure 13–11. Note that the actual annual provisions are identical; the differences are in the interim presentations.

Disposal of a Component of the Entity or Extraordinary, Unusual, Infrequently Occurring, and Contingent Items

APB 28 requires the measurement and reporting of major nonoperating items on the same bases as used to prepare the annual report. Extraordinary items, discontinued operations, and unusual and infrequently occurring items should be reported in the interim period in which they occur and not allocated to the other interim periods of the year. The materiality test for extraordinary items should be based on the estimate of income for the entire fiscal year. The materiality test for discontinued operations and unusual and infrequent transactions should be based on the operating income of the interim period in which the discontinued operations are first reported.

Contingencies or other major uncertainties that could affect the company also must be disclosed on the same basis as that used in the annual report. This disclosure is required to provide information on items that might affect the fairness of the interim report. The procedures for measuring and reporting contingencies in both interim and annual reports are presented in **FASB Statement No. 5**, "Accounting for Contingencies" (FASB 5).

ACCOUNTING CHANGES IN INTERIM PERIODS

FASB Statement No. 154, "Accounting Changes and Error Corrections" (FASB 154), specified three categories of accounting changes, as follows: (*a*) change in an accounting principle, (*b*) change in an accounting estimate, and (*c*) change in a reporting entity. The statement noted that a correction of an error in previously issued financial statements is not an accounting change and the entity must restate all prior financial statements presented to correct the error(s) in those financials. The standard does not alter the transition provisions presented in existing pronouncements for applying changes in specific accounting requirements covered in an existing standard.

Change in an Accounting Principle (Retrospective Application)

A change in accounting principle may be made by an entity only if the change is required by a new accounting standard, or if the company can justify that the new accounting principle is preferable to the old accounting principle. A change from a generally accepted accounting principle to another generally accepted accounting principle for measurement or valuation purposes requires that the *retrospective application* process be applied to all prior periods' financial statements, including the financial statements for interim periods. Only the direct effects of the change in accounting principle, including any related tax effects, are included in the retrospective application to the prior periods. However, accounting for changes in the method of depreciation, amortization, or depletion for long-lived, nonfinancial assets, such as from the straight-line to the accelerated method of depreciation for equipment, are accounted for as a change in estimate effected by a change in accounting principle. Changes in accounting estimates are discussed in the next section of this chapter.

Retrospective Application

Direct effects are those adjustments necessary to make the change in accounting principle in the immediately affected assets or liabilities. Indirect effects are those affecting current or future cash flows that result from making the change in accounting principle. These indirect effects are reported in the period the change is made. An adjusted balance sheet to reflect the retrospective application of the new accounting principle is provided for the earliest period presented. All financial statements for each subsequent annual and interim period are adjusted for the effects of the change in accounting principle. For example, if a company makes a change from the weighted-average method to the FIFO method of accounting for inventories in the current year, the company would retrospectively apply the FIFO method to all prior periods for which financial statements are provided. The beginning inventory amount for the earliest period presented would be adjusted to reflect the new accounting principle, with a corresponding adjustment to retained earnings, and the new method would be reflected in all subsequent financial statements presented.

If the cumulative amount of the effect of the change can be determined, but it is impracticable to determine its period-by-period effects, the company should report the cumulative amount of the change on the financial statements as of the beginning of the earliest period practicable and then revise the subsequent financial statements presented. However, if a company wishes to make an accounting change in principle in an interim period and the entity is not able to determine the effects of the change on the previous interim periods of the current fiscal year, the entity must wait until the beginning of a subsequent fiscal year to make the change in accounting principle.

Change in an Accounting Estimate (Current and Prospective Application)

Changes in accounting estimates are the result of new information that becomes available to the entity. These changes are reported on a current and prospective basis only; that is, the changes are reported only in the current period in which the change is made and in the future periods affected by the change. Previously issued financial statements are *not* adjusted. An example of a change in accounting estimate is a change in the method of computing the allowance for uncollectibles of accounts receivable because more recent information indicates the prior provisions were inadequate.

Changes in Depreciation, Amortization, or Depletion

FASB 154 requires a change in the method of depreciation, amortization, or depletion of long-lived, nonfinancial assets because of new information, such as current usage patterns that differ from expectations, to be accounted for as a change in accounting estimate effected by a change in accounting principle. The current and prospective application is used to report this change and prior financial statements are not restated.

Change in a Reporting Entity (Retrospective Application)

A change in reporting entity requires a retrospective application to all prior periods presented to reflect the new reporting entity. The primary examples of changes in reporting entity are: (*a*) presenting consolidated or combined financial statements rather than individual statements for the separate entities, (*b*) changing the specific subsidiaries that comprise the consolidated entity for which consolidated financials are presented, and (*c*) changing the entities that are included in combined financial statements.

An entity making an accounting change is also required to make a number of disclosures in the period of the change. Included in these disclosures are the effect of the change on income from continuing operations and net income. In the case of a change in accounting principle, the entity must also disclose the nature and justification for the change and the cumulative effect of the change on retained earnings or other components of equity as of the beginning of the earliest period presented.

Summary of Key Concepts	Segment disclosures about an entity's components' operations and foreign areas in which an entity operates provide information about the different risks and profitability of each of the individual components that the entity comprises. These additional disclosures are useful in assessing past performance and prospects of future performance. A critical issue is the definition of a segment. The FASB allows management the flexibility it needs to disaggregate its operations but imposes several significance tests to determine which segments are separately reportable.

Interim reports must be issued by publicly held corporations so users of the information can assess corporate performance and make predictions about results for the annual fiscal period. The major issues are the measurement and disclosure problems of breaking down the annual reporting period into smaller parts. The FASB has selected the integral theory of interim reporting, which views an interim period as an integral part of an annual period. Many of the technical problems revolve around cost of goods sold and income taxes. Estimates based on expected annual results are allowed when determining both of these costs. Even with the estimation and measurement problems, interim reports are primary disclosure vehicles that are quickly and carefully evaluated by investors and other users of financial statements. |

Key Terms

discrete theory of interim reporting, *643*	interim income tax, *650*	75 percent consolidated revenue test, *638*
enterprisewide disclosure, *639*	interim reports, *642*	10 percent significance rules, *632*
integral theory of interim reporting, *643*	management approach, *631*	
	reportable operating segments, *632*	

Questions

Q13-1 How might information on a company's operations in different industries be helpful to investors?

Q13-2 What is the relationship between the FASB's requirements for segment-based disclosures and a company's profit centers?

Q13-3 What are the three 10 percent significance tests used to determine reportable segments under FASB 131? Give the numerator and denominator for each of the tests.

Q13-4   Specifically, what items are in the determination of a segment's profit or loss?

Q13-5   A company has 10 industry segments, of which the largest five account for 80 percent of the combined revenues of the company. What considerations are important in determining the number of segments that are separately reportable? How are the remaining segments reported?

Q13-6   Only two materiality tests are used to determine separately reportable foreign operations. What are these two tests? Why isn't the third test, the profit or loss test, used to assess foreign operations?

Q13-7   What information must be disclosed about a company's major customers? Are the names of customers disclosed?

Q13-8   How can interim reports be used by investors to identify a company's seasonal trends?

Q13-9   Distinguish between the discrete and integral views of interim reporting. Which view is used in APB Opinion No. 28?

Q13-10   How is revenue recognized on an interim basis?

Q13-11   Describe the basic rules for computing cost of goods sold and inventory on an interim basis. In what circumstances are estimates permitted to determine costs?

Q13-12   How does the application of the lower-of-cost-or-market valuation method for inventories differ between interim statements and annual statements?

Q13-13   How might the accounting for an advertising campaign expenditure of $200,000 in the first quarter of a company's fiscal year differ between the integral theory and the discrete theory of interim reporting?

Q13-14   Describe the process of updating the estimate of the effective annual tax rate in the second quarter of a company's fiscal year.

Q13-15   How is the tax benefit of an interim period's operating loss treated if the future realizability of the tax benefit is *not* assured beyond a reasonable doubt?

Q13-16   How are extraordinary items reported on an interim basis?

Q13-17   The Maness Company made a change in accounting for its inventories during the third quarter of its fiscal year. The company switched from the LIFO method to the average cost method. Describe the reporting of this accounting change on prior interim financial statements and on the third quarter's interim financial statements.

Cases

C13-1   ### Segment Disclosures [CMA Adapted]

Chemax Inc. manufactures a wide variety of pharmaceuticals, medical instruments, and other related medical supplies. Eighteen months ago the company developed and began to market a new product line of antihistamine drugs under various trade names. Sales and profitability of this product line during the current fiscal year greatly exceeded management's expectations. The new product line will account for 10 percent of the company's total sales and 12 percent of the company's operating income for the fiscal year ending June 30, 20X0. Management believes sales and profits will be significant for several years.

Judgment

Chemax is concerned that its market share and competitive position may suffer if it discloses the volume and profitability of its new product line in its annual financial statements. Management is not sure how FASB 131 applies in this case.

Required

a. What is the purpose of requiring segment information in financial statements?

b. Identify and explain the factors that should be considered when attempting to decide how products should be grouped to determine a single business segment.

c. What options, if any, does Chemax Inc. have with the disclosure of its new antihistamine product line? Explain your answer.

C13-2   ### Matching Revenue and Expenses for Interim Periods

Understanding

Periodic reporting adds complexity to accounting by requiring estimates, accruals, deferrals, and allocations. Interim reporting creates even greater difficulties in matching revenue and expenses.

Required

a. Explain how revenue, product costs, gains, and losses should be recognized for interim periods.

b. Explain how determination of cost of goods sold and inventory differs for interim period reports versus annual reports.

c. Explain the interim accounting treatment of period costs such as depreciation.

d. Explain the treatment of the following items for interim financial statements:

 (1) Long-term contracts

 (2) Advertising

 (3) Seasonal revenue

 (4) Flood loss

 (5) Annual major repairs and maintenance to plant and equipment during the last two weeks in December

---

C13-3

Segment Disclosures in the Financial Statements [CMA Adapted]

Analysis

Bennett Inc. is a publicly held corporation whose diversified operations have been separated into five industry segments. Bennett is in the process of preparing its annual financial statements for the year ended December 31, 20X5. The following information has been collected for the preparation of the segment reports required by FASB 131.

BENNETT INC.
Selected Data
For the Year Ended December 31, 20X5
(in thousands)

Item	Power Tools	Fastening Systems	Household Products	Plumbing Products	Security Systems
Sales to Unaffiliated Customers	$32,000	$ 4,500	$ 4,800	$3,000	$2,000
Intersegment Sales	10,000	5,500	200	1,000	—
Total Revenue	42,000	10,000	5,000	4,000	2,000
Cost of Goods Sold	30,000	8,000	4,500	3,100	1,700
Operating Profit	4,500	1,000	(600)	700	(100)
Net Income	2,600	800	(750)	(100)	(200)
Segment Assets	50,000	23,000	17,000	6,000	4,000

Required

a. Determine which of the operating segments are reportable segments for Bennett. Your determination should include all required tests and the results of those tests for each of Bennett's five segments.

b. The reportable segments determined in (*a*) must represent a substantial portion of Bennett's total operations when taken together. Describe how to determine whether a substantial portion of Bennett's operations are explained by its segment information.

C13-4

Determining Industry and Geographic Segments

Research

A major producer of cereal breakfast foods had been reporting in its annual reports just one dominant product line (cereals) in only the U.S. domestic geographic area. The company had no other separately reportable segments. For several years, the U.S. company had a Canadian subsidiary that produced a variety of pasta. In 20X5, one brand of pasta, "Healthcare," suddenly became very popular with the health-conscious public in both the United States and Canada, and the Canadian subsidiary more than tripled its sales and profits within the year.

The management of the U.S. parent company did not want to disclose to its competitors how profitable the Canadian subsidiary was because the company wanted to maintain its strong economic position without more competition.

You have been able to determine the following (in millions):

	Cereal Products	Pasta Products
Net sales	$3,885	$834
Operating profit	445	151
Segment assets	1,565	147

All cereal product operations are located in the United States, and all pasta product operations are located in Canada. The Standard Industrial Classification (SIC) number is 2043 for cereal products, and 2098 for the Canadian subsidiary's pasta products. (The Standard Industrial Classification Index is prepared by the U.S. Office of Management and Budget and is used widely to define a company's major industrial groups.)

Required

a. Why would management be reluctant to disclose information about very successful—and very unsuccessful—operations in the segmental disclosure footnote in the annual report?

b. Present both theoretical and applied arguments for including the pasta products segment with the cereal products segment as one internal operating segment, thus not requiring separate disclosure under FASB 131. How does the fact that the pasta products have suddenly become popular affect the disclosure requirements under FASB 131?

c. Present the requirements under FASB 131 for reporting the cereal products and pasta products by geographic area. Must the Canadian operations be disclosed separately in a geographic disclosure footnote?

C13-5 Segment Reporting

The manager you work for has asked you to perform some research to determine what types of information public companies are providing on their Internet home pages. The public company you work for is considering establishing its own home page. In particular, the manager wants you to note how these companies describe their products and services on their home pages. After researching the home pages, the manager wants you to review each company's Form 10-K by using the Electronic Data Gathering, Analysis, and Retrieval Database (EDGAR). While looking at the Form 10-Ks, the manager wants you to observe how the companies describe the segments of their business. For example, are the segments as described in the Form 10-K similar to the products and services mentioned on the same company's home page?

Research

Required

a. Using an Internet search engine, find a home page of a *public company*. (*Hint:* A helpful search term is "Company Home Pages.") Then write a brief summary about what you find on the company's home page discussing the following:

(1) What type of information is provided related to the company's products or services?

(2) What other information is listed on the home page?

b. Using the EDGAR database, locate the most recent Form 10-K for the company you selected. (*Note:* The Electronic Data Gathering, Analysis, and Retrieval Database [EDGAR] collects and maintains the forms that are required to be filed by public companies to the U.S. Securities and Exchange Commission [SEC].) (*Hint:* The Internet URL for the EDGAR Database is http://www.sec.gov/edgarhp.htm.)

(1) Review the Form 10-K and locate the segment disclosure information. Print off this segment information.

(2) Write a brief report summarizing what you find in the company's Form 10-K regarding segment disclosures. Include the following information:

(a) Describe the company's segments as displayed in the Form 10-K. Discuss on what basis the segments are presented.

(b) Discuss which segment(s) has (have) the highest revenues, is (are) the most profitable, and has (have) the most assets.

C13-6   **Interim Reporting**

Research

The company you work for is considering going public. Your current position is within the external financial reporting group. The manager you work for wants you to review some public company quarterly reports, Form 10-Qs, to see what type of information is disclosed. The manager does not want you to perform technical research to determine what the exact reporting requirements are for the Form 10-Q but to understand generally what information other companies seem to be supplying in their Form 10-Qs.

Required

a. Determine the name of two public companies you would like to use in your review of Form 10-Qs. (*Hint:* There are various ways to determine the public companies you want to research. For example, you could use an Internet search engine to find a home page of a *public* company. A helpful search term is "Company Home Pages." Another method would be to select public companies you already know of or you find through the use of a newspaper or periodical.)

b. Using the EDGAR database, locate the most recent Form 10-Qs for the two companies you selected. (*Hint:* The Internet URL for the SEC's home page is http://www.sec.gov/. The SEC provides a company search engine for its EDGAR database. Alternatively, some persons prefer to use Edgarscan at http://edgarscan.pwcglobal.com to access and use the SEC's EDGAR database.) In addition, for one of these companies, locate the Form 10-Q for the same period in the prior year. Prepare a one- to two-page summary after performing the following analysis:

   (1) Take one company's recent Form 10-Q and write a brief summary of the contents of the Form 10-Q. Discuss how the Form 10-Q information compares with the information you know is included in a Form 10-K, which is the annual report to the SEC.

   (2) Review the same company's Form 10-Q from the previous year, and discuss the similarities and differences you notice in the Form 10-Qs for different time periods.

   (3) Review the other company's Form 10-Q from the current year, and provide a discussion of the similarities and differences you notice in the Form 10-Qs for different companies.

C13-7   **Defining Segments for Disclosure**

Randy Rivera, CFO of Stanford Corporation, a manufacturer of packaged retail food products, has reviewed the company's segment disclosures for the current year. In the first draft of the disclosures, the company reports information about four segments: cheese, snacks and crackers, pizza, and desserts and confectionery. He has suggested that the segment disclosures be expanded to include additional segments.

Research
FARS

Randy notes that the cereals segment, included in the segment disclosures last year, is not included in the current year. Although the cereals segment reported a loss for the current year and suffered a significant decline in revenues as a result of a prolonged labor dispute, he believes that Stanford should continue to provide information about this segment. In addition, Stanford recently introduced a new product line, sports beverages. This operating segment is expected to expand rapidly and is highly profitable. Randy believes that shareholders would view this profitability positively if the sports beverage segment were included in the segment disclosures.

The accountant who prepared the segment information has reviewed the segment data with Randy. Revenues of the cereals segment and the sports beverage segment account for 9 percent and 6 percent of combined revenues of all segments, respectively. Each segment's assets are approximately 8 percent of the combined assets of all segments. The cereals segment was the only segment to record a loss, which amounted to 5 percent of the combined profit of all segments reporting profits. The sports beverage segment profit was 9 percent of this total.

After reviewing the data, Randy still believes that the inclusion of the two segments would improve the segment disclosures and has asked you to research the appropriateness of his suggestion.

Required

Obtain the most current accounting standards on accounting for segments. You can obtain access to accounting standards through the Financial Accounting Research System (FARS), from your library, or from some other source. Write a memo to Randy responding to his suggestion that the segment disclosures be expanded to include the cereals and sports beverage segments. Support your recommendations with citations and quotations from the authoritative financial reporting standards.

C13-8   **Income Tax Provision in Interim Periods**

Andrea Meyers, a supervisor in the controller's department at Vanderbilt Company, is reviewing the calculation of the income tax provision to be included in the financial statements for the first quarter of 20X5. She is questioning the estimate of the effective tax rate expected to be applicable for fiscal year 20X5 because this estimated rate is significantly lower than Vanderbilt's actual effective tax rate for 20X4.

Research
FARS

Bob Graber, who prepared the income tax calculation, explains to Andrea that the estimate of the effective annual tax rate reflects the anticipated enactment of a new business energy tax credit that will provide substantial tax benefits to Vanderbilt. This energy tax credit has the approval of the president, has been passed by the House of Representatives, and is under consideration in the Senate. It is expected to be enacted no later than the third quarter of 20X5, and its benefits should be available beginning with 20X5 tax returns.

Required

Obtain the most current accounting standards for interim reporting. You can obtain access to accounting standards through the Financial Accounting Research System (FARS), from your library, or from some other source. Andrea has asked you, an accountant in the controller's department, to research the computation of the estimated effective annual tax rate for interim reporting. Write a memo to her reporting on the results of your research. Support your recommendations with citations and quotations from the authoritative financial reporting standards.

C13-9   **Questions about Interim Reporting**

Required

Application

Prepare a brief answer to each of the following questions about interim reporting, assuming the company is preparing its Form 10-Q for the third quarter of its fiscal year.

1. How many different income statements would the company present? Describe the reporting periods presented in the income statements.

2. How would the company report a change in accounting principle for depreciation of its building that was made effective the first day of the third quarter? The change was made as a result of an accounting study that concluded that the estimated future benefits from the equipment will be different from those previously expected.

3. How many different balance sheets would the company present? What is the balance sheet date (as of what date) for each balance sheet?

4. Must interim financial statements filed with the SEC be audited by an independent public accountant who would provide an audit opinion on those statements? Explain your answer.

5. Is a company required to present segment information in the interim report? If yes, are the interim segment disclosures different from the annual segment disclosures? Explain your answers.

6. Within what period of time after the end of the quarter must a Form 10-Q be filed with the SEC?

7. May a company use one accounting method for computing interim total revenues and a different accounting method for computing its annual total revenues?

8. Is the company required to physically count its ending inventory each quarter so that it can accurately determine its ending inventory for the balance sheet and its cost of goods sold for the income statement? Explain how ending inventory is computed for interim reporting.

9. The company shuts down each year for two weeks during its third quarter in order to retool its manufacturing lines for the next year's products. Can the company allocate the costs of retooling incurred in its third quarter to the other three quarters (I, II, and IV) during the year? If yes, explain how this allocation would be made.

10. How would the company report a change in accounting principle from the completed contract method of revenue recognition to the percentage-of-completion method of revenue recognition on its long-term construction contracts? The change was made on the last day of the third quarter.

11. The company had assumed during the first two quarters of the year that it would receive a material income tax credit from the federal government. However, during the third quarter the company was informed that it would not be receiving the expected tax credit this year. The company had included the estimated tax credit in the computation of its income tax rate for the first two quarters of the year. Should the company retroactively restate the first two quarters of tax expense because of the change in information received in the third quarter? Explain your answer.

Exercises

E13-1 Reportable Segments

Amalgamated Products has seven operating segments. Data on the segments are as follows:

Segments	Revenues	Segment Profit (Loss)	Segment Assets
Electronics	$ 42,000	$ (8,600)	$ 73,000
Bicycles	105,000	30,400	207,000
Sporting Goods	53,000	(4,900)	68,000
Home Appliances	147,000	23,000	232,000
Gas and Oil Equipment	186,000	11,700	315,000
Glassware	64,000	(19,100)	96,000
Hardware	178,000	38,600	194,000
Total	$775,000	$71,100	$1,185,000

Included in the $105,000 revenue of the Bicycles segment are sales of $25,000 made to the Sporting Goods segment.

Required

a. Which segments are separately reportable?

b. Do the separately reportable segments include a sufficient portion of total revenue? Explain.

E13-2 Multiple-Choice Questions on Segment Reporting [AICPA Adapted]

Select the correct answer for each of the following questions.

1. Barbee Corporation discloses supplementary operating segment information for its two reportable segments. Data for 20X5 are available as follows:

	Segment E	Segment W
Sales	$750,000	$250,000
Traceable operating expenses	325,000	130,000

Additional 20X5 expenses are as follows:

Indirect operating expenses	$120,000

Appropriately selected common indirect operating expenses are allocated to segments based on the ratio of each segment's sales to total sales. The 20X5 operating profit for Segment E was:

a. $260,000.

b. $335,000.

c. $395,000.

d. $425,000.

2. The viewpoint used to determine segmental disclosures in annual reports is called the:

a. Segment approach.

b. Portfolio approach.

c. Economic entity approach.

d. Management approach.

3. Dutko Company has three lines of business, each of which is a significant industry segment. Company sales aggregated $1,800,000 in 20X6, of which Segment 3 contributed 60 percent. Traceable costs were $600,000 for Segment 3 from a total of $1,200,000 for the company as a

whole. In addition, $350,000 of common costs are allocated in the ratio of a segment's income before common costs to the total income before common costs. For Segment 3 Dutko should report a 20X6 segment profit of:

a. $200,000.

b. $270,000.

c. $280,000.

d. $480,000.

e. None of the above.

4. Stein Company is a diversified company that discloses supplemental financial information on its industry segments. The following information is available for 20X2:

	Sales	Traceable Costs	Allocable Costs
Segment A	$400,000	$225,000	
Segment B	300,000	240,000	
Segment C	200,000	135,000	
Totals	$900,000	$600,000	$150,000

Allocable costs are assigned based on the ratio of a segment's income before allocable costs to total income before allocable costs. This is an appropriate method of allocation. The segment profit for Segment B for 20X2 is:

a. $0.

b. $10,000.

c. $30,000.

d. $50,000.

e. None of the above.

5. Selected data for a segment of a business enterprise are to be reported separately in accordance with FASB 131 when the revenue of the segment exceeds 10 percent of the:

a. Combined net income of all segments reporting profits.

b. Total revenue obtained in transactions with outsiders.

c. Total revenue of all the enterprise's industry segments.

d. Total combined revenue of all segments reporting profits.

6. Kimber Company operates in four different industries, each of which is appropriately regarded as a reportable segment. Total sales for 20X2 for all segments combined were $1,000,000. Sales for Segment 2 were $400,000, and the traceable costs were $150,000. Total common costs for all segments combined were $500,000. Kimber allocates common costs based on the ratio of a segment's sales to total sales, an appropriate method of allocation. The segment profit to be reported for Segment 2 for 20X2 is:

a. $50,000.

b. $125,000.

c. $200,000.

d. $250,000.

e. None of the above.

7. The following information pertains to Reding Corporation for the year ended December 31, 20X6.

Sales to unaffiliated customers	$2,000,000
Intersegment sales of products similar to those sold to unaffiliated customers	600,000

All of Reding's segments are engaged solely in manufacturing operations. Reding has a reportable segment if that segment's revenue exceeds:

a. $264,000.

b. $260,000.

c. $204,000.

d. $200,000.

8. Snow Corporation's revenue for the year ended December 31, 20X2, was as follows:

Consolidated revenue per income statement	$1,200,000
Intersegment sales	180,000
Intersegment transfers	60,000
Combined revenue of all industry segments	$1,440,000

Snow has a reportable operating segment if that segment's revenue exceeds:

a. $6,000.

b. $24,000.

c. $120,000.

d. $144,000.

9. Porter Corporation is engaged solely in manufacturing operations. The following data (consistent with prior years' data) pertain to the industries in which operations were conducted for the year ended December 31, 20X5:

Industry Segment	Total Revenue	Segment Profit	Assets at 12/31/X5
A	$10,000,000	$1,750,000	$20,000,000
B	8,000,000	1,400,000	17,500,000
C	6,000,000	1,200,000	12,500,000
D	3,000,000	550,000	7,500,000
E	4,250,000	675,000	7,000,000
F	1,500,000	225,000	3,000,000
Totals	$32,750,000	$5,800,000	$67,500,000

In its segment information for 20X5, how many reportable segments does Porter have?

a. Three.

b. Four.

c. Five.

d. Six.

10. Boecker is a multidivisional corporation that has both intersegment sales and sales to unaffiliated customers. Boecker should report segment financial information for each segment meeting which of the following criteria?

a. Segment profit or loss is 10 percent or more of consolidated profit or loss.

b. Segment profit or loss is 10 percent or more of combined profit or loss of all company segments.

c. Segment revenue is 10 percent or more of combined revenue of all company segments.

d. Segment revenue is 10 percent or more of consolidated revenue.

Use the following information for questions 11 and 12.

Ward Corporation, a publicly owned corporation, is subject to the requirements for segment reporting. In its income statement for the year ending December 31, 20X5, Ward reported revenues of

$50,000,000, operating expenses of $47,000,000, and net income of $3,000,000. Operating expenses included payroll costs of $15,000,000. Ward's combined assets of all industry segments at December 31, 20X5, were $40,000,000.

11. In its 20X5 financial statements, Ward should disclose major customer data if sales to any single customer amount to at least:

   a. $300,000.

   b. $1,500,000.

   c. $4,000,000.

   d. $5,000,000.

12. In its 20X5 financial statements, Ward should disclose foreign revenues in a specific country if revenues from foreign operations in that country are at least:

   a. $5,000,000.

   b. $4,700,000.

   c. $4,000,000.

   d. $1,500,000.

E13-3 Multiple-Choice Questions on Interim Reporting [AICPA Adapted]

Select the correct answer for each of the following questions.

1. In considering interim financial reporting, how did the Accounting Principles Board conclude that such reporting should be viewed?

   a. As a "special" type of reporting that need not follow generally accepted accounting principles.

   b. As useful only if activity is evenly spread throughout the year so that estimates are unnecessary.

   c. As reporting for a basic accounting period.

   d. As reporting for an integral part of an annual period.

2. Which of the following is an inherent difficulty in determining the results of operations on an interim basis?

   a. Cost of sales reflects only the amount of product expense allocable to revenue recognized as of the interim date.

   b. Depreciation on an interim basis is a partial estimate of the actual annual amount.

   c. Costs expensed in one interim period may benefit other periods.

   d. Revenue from long-term construction contracts accounted for by the percentage-of-completion method is based on annual completion, and interim estimates may be incorrect.

3. Which of the following reporting practices is permissible for interim financial reporting?

   a. Use of the gross profit method for interim inventory pricing.

   b. Use of the direct costing method for determining manufacturing inventories.

   c. Deferral of unplanned variances under a standard cost system until the following year.

   d. Deferral of nontemporary inventory market declines until year-end.

4. On January 1, 20X2, Harris Inc. paid $40,000 property taxes on its plant for the calendar year 20X2. In March 20X2, Harris made $120,000 annual major repairs to its machinery. These repairs will benefit the entire calendar year's operations. How should these expenses be reflected in Harris's quarterly income statements?

		Three Months Ended		
	March 31, 20X2	June 30, 20X2	September 30, 20X2	December 31, 20X2
a.	$ 22,000	$46,000	$46,000	$46,000
b.	40,000	40,000	40,000	40,000
c.	70,000	30,000	30,000	30,000
d.	160,000	-0-	-0-	-0-

5. Wenger Company experienced an inventory loss from market decline of $420,000 in April 20X2. The company recorded this loss in April 20X2 after its March 31, 20X2, quarterly report was issued. None of this loss was recovered by the end of the year. How should this loss be reflected in Wenger's quarterly income statements?

		Three Months Ended		
	March 31, 20X2	June 30, 20X2	September 30, 20X2	December 31, 20X2
a.	$ -0-	$ -0-	$ -0-	$420,000
b.	-0-	140,000	140,000	140,000
c.	-0-	420,000	-0-	-0-
d.	105,000	105,000	105,000	105,000

6. A company that uses the last-in, first-out (LIFO) method of inventory costing finds, at an interim reporting date, that there has been a partial liquidation of the base-period inventory level. The decline is considered temporary, and the base inventory will be replaced before year-end. The amount shown as inventory on the interim reporting date should:

   a. Not consider the LIFO liquidation, and cost of sales for the interim reporting period should include the expected cost of replacement of the liquidated LIFO base.

   b. Be shown at the actual level, and cost of sales for the interim reporting period should reflect the decrease in LIFO base-period inventory level.

   c. Not consider the LIFO liquidations, and cost of sales for the interim reporting period should reflect the decrease in LIFO base-period inventory level.

   d. Be shown at the actual level, and the decrease in inventory level should not be reflected in the cost of sales for the interim reporting period.

7. During the second quarter of 20X5, Camerton Company sold a piece of equipment at a $12,000 gain. What portion of the gain should Camerton report in its income statement for the second quarter of 20X5?

   a. $12,000.

   b. $6,000.

   c. $4,000.

   d. $0.

8. On March 15, 20X1, Burge Company paid property taxes of $180,000 on its factory building for calendar year 20X1. On April 1, 20X1, Burge made $300,000 in unanticipated repairs to its plant equipment. The repairs will benefit operations for the remainder of the calendar year. What total amount of these expenses should be included in Burge's quarterly income statement for the three months ended June 30, 20X1?

   a. $75,000.

   b. $145,000.

   c. $195,000.

   d. $345,000.

9. SRB Company had an inventory loss from a market price decline that occurred in the first quarter. The loss was not expected to be restored in the fiscal year. However, in the third quarter the inventory had a market price recovery that exceeded the first-quarter decline. For interim financial reporting, the dollar amount of net inventory should:

   a. Decrease in the first quarter by the amount of the market price decline and increase in the third quarter by the amount of the market price recovery.

   b. Decrease in the first quarter by the amount of the market price decline and increase in the third quarter by the amount of the decrease in the first quarter.

   c. Not be affected in the first quarter and increase in the third quarter by the amount of the market price recovery that exceeded the amount of the market price decline.

   d. Not be affected in either the first quarter or the third quarter.

10. For external reporting purposes, it is appropriate to use estimated gross profit rates to determine the cost of goods sold for:

	Interim Financial Reporting	Year-End Financial Reporting
a.	Yes	Yes
b.	Yes	No
c.	No	Yes
d.	No	No

11. On June 30, 20X5, Park Corporation incurred a $100,000 net loss from disposal of a business component. Also, on June 30, 20X5, Park paid $40,000 for property taxes assessed for the calendar year 20X5. What amount of the preceding items should be included in the determination of Park's net income or loss for the six-month interim period ended June 30, 20X5?

    a. $140,000.

    b. $120,000.

    c. $90,000.

    d. $70,000.

E13-4 **Temporary LIFO Liquidation**

During June, Kissick Hardware, which uses a perpetual inventory system, sold 920 units from its LIFO-base inventory, which had originally cost $12 per unit. The replacement cost is expected to be $21 per unit. Kissick is reducing inventory levels and expects to replace only 640 of these units by December 31, the end of the fiscal year.

Required

a. Prepare the entry in June to record the sale of the 920 units.

b. Prepare the entry for the replacement of the 640 units in August at an actual cost of $19.80 per unit.

E13-5 **Inventory Write-Down and Recovery**

Comeback Company, a calendar-year entity, had 9,000 medical instruments in its beginning inventory for 20X2. On December 31, 20X1, the instruments had been adjusted down to $10.20 per unit from an actual average cost of $10.55 per unit. It was the lower of average cost or market. No additional units were purchased during 20X2. The following additional information is provided for 20X2:

Quarter	Date	Inventory (units)	Replacement Cost
1	March 31, 20X2	8,000	$10.10
2	June 30, 20X2	7,500	10.35
3	September 30, 20X2	6,000	9.90
4	December 31, 20X2	4,000	10.00

Required

Determine the cost of goods sold for each quarter, and verify the total cost of goods sold by computing annual cost of goods sold on a lower-of-cost-or-market basis.

E13-6 **Multiple-Choice Questions on Income Taxes at Interim Dates [AICPA Adapted]**

Select the correct answer for each of the following questions.

1. According to APB Opinion No. 28, "Interim Financial Reporting," income tax expense in an income statement for the first interim period of an enterprise's fiscal year should be computed by:

    a. Applying the estimated income tax rate for the full fiscal year to the pretax accounting income for the interim period.

    b. Applying the estimated income tax rate for the full fiscal year to the taxable income for the interim period.

    c. Applying the statutory income tax rate to the pretax accounting income for the interim period.

    d. Applying the statutory income tax rate to the taxable income for the interim period.

2. Neil Company, which has a fiscal year ending January 31, had the following pretax accounting income and estimated effective annual income tax rates for the first three quarters of the year ended January 31, 20X2:

Quarter	Pretax Accounting Income	Estimated Effective Annual Income Tax Rate at End of Quarter, %
First	$60,000	40%
Second	70,000	40
Third	40,000	45

Neil's income tax expenses in its interim income statement for the third quarter are:

    a. $18,000.

    b. $24,500.

    c. $25,500.

    d. $76,500.

    e. None of the above.

3. Beckett Corporation expects to sustain an operating loss of $100,000 for the full year ending December 31, 20X3. Beckett operates entirely in one jurisdiction, where the tax rate is 40 percent. Anticipated tax credits for 20X3 total $10,000. No permanent differences are expected. Realization of the full tax benefit of the expected operating loss and realization of anticipated tax credits are assured beyond any reasonable doubt because they will be carried back. For the first quarter ended March 31, 20X3, Beckett reported an operating loss of $20,000. How much of a tax benefit should Beckett report for the interim period ended March 31, 20X3?

    a. $0.

    b. $8,000.

    c. $10,000.

    d. $12,500.

    e. None of the above.

4. The computation of a company's third-quarter provision for income taxes should be based on earnings:

    a. For the quarter at an expected effective annual income tax rate.

    b. For the quarter at the statutory rate.

    c. To date at an expected effective annual income tax rate less prior quarters' provisions.

    d. To date at the statutory rate less prior quarters' provisions.

5. During the first quarter of 20X5, Stahl Company had income before taxes of $200,000, and its effective income tax rate was 15 percent. Stahl's 20X4 effective annual income tax rate was 30 percent, but Stahl expects its 20X5 effective annual income tax rate to be 25 percent. In its first-quarter interim income statement, what amount of income tax expense should Stahl report?

    a. $0.

    b. $30,000.

    c. $50,000.

    d. $60,000.

6. Which of the following items will result in the recognition of a deferred tax asset or liability in the second quarter of 2007 for Nelson Company:

    a. The portion of dividends received this quarter on an investment in stock of a U.S. corporation that qualifies for the dividend exclusion.

    b. A provision of an expected loss from a lawsuit that is finally settled in 2008.

    c. Expenses related to the acquisition of a municipal bond whose income is not taxable for income tax purposes.

    d. Life insurance payments made on policies for executives for which the company is the beneficiary.

E13-7 **Significant Foreign Operations**

Information about the domestic and foreign operations of Radon Inc. is as follows:

	Geographic Area					
	United States	Britain	Brazil	Israel	Australia	Total
Sales to unaffiliated customers	$364,000	$252,000	$72,000	$58,000	$47,000	$ 793,000
Interarea sales between affiliates	38,000	19,000	6,000			63,000
Total revenue	$402,000	$271,000	$78,000	$58,000	$47,000	$ 856,000
Profit	34,500	22,500	11,300	3,200	4,500	76,000
Long-lived assets	509,000	439,000	93,000	66,000	75,000	1,182,000

Required

Prepare schedules showing appropriate tests to determine which countries are material, using a 10 percent materiality threshold.

E13-8 **Major Customers**

Sales by Knight Inc. to major customers are as follows:

Customer	Sales	Reporting Segment
State of Illinois	$2,700,000	Computer hardware
Cook County, Illinois	3,500,000	Computer software
U.S. Treasury Department	3,900,000	Service contract
U.S. Department of Defense	2,200,000	Service contract
Bank of England	4,650,000	Computer software
Philips NV	2,850,000	Computer hardware
Honda	5,400,000	Computer hardware

Required

If worldwide sales total $43,000,000 for the year, which of Knight's customers should be disclosed as major customers?

E13-9 **Estimated Annual Tax Rate**

Supra, Inc., estimates total federal and state tax rates to be 40 percent. Expected annual pretax earnings from continuing operations are $1,200,000. Differences between tax income and financial statement income are expected to be the following:

Dividend exclusion for dividends received on the company's stock investments	$70,000
Tax exempt income received	20,000
Premiums for life insurance on officers for which the company is the beneficiary	12,000

A business tax credit of $40,000 should be available.

    Supra's first quarter pretax earnings are $170,000 which includes an extraordinary loss of $30,000 before any tax effect of the extraordinary loss.

Required

a. Estimate Supra's effective combined federal and state tax rate on income from continuing operations for the year.

b. Prepare the entry to record the tax provision for the income from continuing operations for the first quarter.

E13-10 Operating Loss Tax Benefits

Tem Technology has a first-quarter operating loss of $100,000 and expects the following income for the other three quarters:

Second quarter	$ 80,000
Third quarter	160,000
Fourth quarter	400,000

Tem estimated the effective annual tax rate at 40 percent at the end of the first quarter and changed it to 45 percent at the end of the third quarter. The company has a normal seasonal pattern of losses in the first quarter and income in the other quarters.

Required

Prepare a schedule computing the tax or tax benefits that should be shown on the interim statements.

E13-11 Industry Segment and Geographic Area Revenue Tests

Symbiotic Chemical Company has four major industry segments and operates both in the U.S. domestic market and in several foreign markets. Information about its revenue from the specific industry segments and its foreign activities for the year 20X2 is as follows:

Sales to Unaffiliated Customers (in thousands)			
Industry Segment	**Domestic**	**Foreign**	**Total**
Ethical Drugs	$300		$300
Nonprescription Drugs	325	$100	425
Generic Drugs	125	245	370
Industrial Chemicals	70		70

Sales to Affiliated Customers (in thousands)			
Industry Segment	**Domestic**	**Foreign**	**Total**
Ethical Drugs	$20		$ 20
Nonprescription Drugs	50	$40	90
Generic Drugs	40	60	100
Industrial Chemicals	10		10

All of the foreign revenues of the Nonprescription Drugs segment, both to unaffiliated and intersegment customers, were attributable to a Taiwanese division of the company. This division operated exclusively in Taiwan except for a $10,000 sale from the division to a U.S. subsidiary of the company. All other foreign operations of the company take place exclusively within the country of Mexico.

Required

a. Determine which of the company's operating segments are separately reportable under the revenue test for segment reporting.

b. Determine which of the foreign countries are separately reportable under the revenue test for reporting foreign operations using a 10 percent materiality threshold.

c. Prepare a schedule for disclosing the company's revenue by industry segment for 20X2.

d. Prepare a schedule for disclosing the company's revenue by geographic area for 20X2.

E13-12 Different Reporting Methods for Interim Reports [CMA Adapted]

Following are seven independent cases on how accounting facts might be reported on an individual company's interim financial reports.

1. Bean Company was reasonably certain it would have an employee strike in the third quarter. As a result, the company shipped heavily during the second quarter but plans to defer the recognition of the sales in excess of the normal sales volume. The deferred sales will be recognized as sales in the third quarter when the strike is in progress. Bean management thinks this is more nearly representative of normal second- and third-quarter operations.

2. Green Inc. takes a physical inventory at year-end for annual financial statement purposes. Inventory and cost of sales reported in the interim quarterly statements are based on estimated gross profit rates because a physical inventory would result in a cessation of operations.

3. ER Company is planning to report one-fourth of its annual pension expense each quarter.

4. Fair Corporation wrote down inventory to reflect the lower of cost or market in the first quarter of 20X1. At year-end, the market price exceeds the original acquisition cost of this inventory. Consequently, management plans to write the inventory back up to its original cost as a year-end adjustment.

5. Carson Company realized a large gain on the sale of investments at the beginning of the second quarter. The company wants to report one-third of the gain in each of the remaining quarters.

6. Ring Corporation has estimated its annual audit fee. Management plans to prorate this expense equally over all four quarters.

7. Mega Corporation made a change in the depreciation of its warehouse building during the third quarter of 20X1. The change was from the accelerated method to the straight-line method to better match the depreciation expense to the current levels of usage of the warehouse. The company plans to use the cumulative effect approach to present the effects of the change as of the beginning of the third quarter.

Required

For the seven cases, state whether the method proposed for interim reporting is acceptable under generally accepted accounting principles applicable to interim financial data. Support each answer with a brief explanation.

Problems P13-13 Segment Reporting Workpaper and Schedules

West Corporation reported the following consolidated data for 20X2:

Sales	$ 810,000
Consolidated income before taxes	128,000
Total assets	1,200,000

Data reported for West's four operating divisions are as follows:

	Division A	Division B	Division C	Division D
Sales to outsiders	$280,000	$130,000	$340,000	$60,000
Intersegment sales	60,000		18,000	12,000
Traceable costs	245,000	90,000	290,000	82,000
Assets	400,000	105,000	500,000	75,000

Intersegment sales are priced at cost, and all goods have been subsequently sold to nonaffiliates. Some joint production costs are allocated to the divisions based on total sales. These joint costs were $45,000 in 20X2. The company's corporate center had $20,000 of general corporate expenses and $120,000 of assets that the chief operating decision maker did not use in decision making regarding the operating segments.

Required

Each of the following items is unrelated to the others.

a. The divisions are industry segments.

(1) Prepare a segmental disclosure worksheet for the company.

(2) Prepare schedules showing which segments are reportable.

b. Assume that each division operates in an individual geographic area and Division A is in the domestic area and the other divisions each operate in a separate foreign country. Assume that one-half of the assets in each geographic area represent long-lived, productive assets as defined in FASB 131. Prepare schedules showing which geographic areas are reportable using a 10 percent materiality threshold.

c. Determine the amount of sales to an outside customer that would cause that outside customer to be classified as a major customer under the criteria of FASB 131.

P13-14   **Segment Reporting Workpaper and Schedules**

Calvin Inc. has operating segments in five different industries: apparel, building, chemical, furniture, and machinery. Data for the five segments for 20X1 are as follows:

	Apparel	Building	Chemical	Furniture	Machinery
Sales to nonaffiliates	$870,000	$750,000	$55,000	$95,000	$180,000
Intersegment sales			5,000	15,000	140,000
Cost of goods sold	480,000	450,000	42,000	78,000	150,000
Selling expenses	160,000	40,000	10,000	20,000	30,000
Other traceable					
expenses	40,000	30,000	6,000	12,000	18,000
Allocated general					
corporate expenses	80,000	75,000	7,000	13,000	25,000
Other information:					
Segment assets	610,000	560,000	80,000	90,000	140,000
Depreciation expense	60,000	50,000	10,000	11,000	25,000
Capital expenditures	20,000	30,000			15,000

Additional Information

1. The corporate headquarters had general corporate expenses totaling $235,000. For internal reporting purposes, $200,000 of these expenses were allocated to the divisions based on their cost of goods sold. The other corporate expenses are not used in segmental decision making by the chief operating decision maker.

2. The company has an intercorporate transfer pricing policy that all intersegment sales shall be priced at cost. All intersegment sales were sold to outsiders by December 31, 20X1.

3. Corporate headquarters had assets of $125,000 that were not used in segmental decision making by the chief operating decision maker.

4. The depreciation expense (listed in the section titled, "Other information") has already been added into cost of goods sold in accordance with the company's cost measurement policies.

Required

a. Prepare a segmental disclosure workpaper for Calvin Inc.

b. Prepare schedules to show which segments are separately reportable.

c. Prepare the information about the company's operations in different industry segments as required by FASB 131.

d. Would there be any differences in the specification of reportable segments if the building segment had $460,000 in assets instead of $560,000, and the furniture segment had $190,000 in assets instead of $90,000? Justify your answer by preparing a schedule showing the percentages for each of the three 10 percent segment tests for each of the five segments using these new amounts for segment assets.

P13-15   **Interim Income Statement**

Chris Inc. has accumulated the following information for its second-quarter income statement for 20X2:

Sales	$850,000
Cost of goods sold	420,000
Operating expenses	230,000

Additional Information

1. First-quarter income before taxes was $100,000, and the estimated effective annual tax rate was 40 percent. At the end of the second quarter, expected annual income is $600,000, and a dividend exclusion of $30,000 and a business tax credit of $15,000 are anticipated. The combined state and federal tax rate is 50 percent.

2. The $420,000 cost of goods sold is determined by the LIFO method and includes 7,500 units from the base layer at a cost of $12 per unit. However, you have determined that these units are expected to be replaced at a cost of $26 per unit.

3. The operating expenses of $230,000 include a $60,000 factory rearrangement cost incurred in April. You have determined that the second quarter will receive about 25 percent of the benefits from this project, with the remainder benefiting the third and fourth quarters.

Required

a. Calculate the expected effective annual tax rate at the end of the second quarter for Chris Inc.

b. Prepare the income statement for the second quarter of 20X2. Your solution should include a computation of income tax (or benefit) with the following headings:

Interim Period	Operating Income (Loss before Taxes)		Estimated Effective Annual Tax Rate	Tax (Benefit)		
	Current Period	Year to Date		Year to Date	Less Previously Provided	Reported in This Period

P13-16 Interim Income Statement

At the end of the second quarter of 20X1, Malta Corporation assembled the following information:

1. The first quarter resulted in a $90,000 loss before taxes. During the second quarter, sales were $1,200,000; purchases were $650,000; and operating expenses were $320,000.

2. Cost of goods sold is determined by the FIFO method. The inventory at the end of the first quarter was reduced by $4,000 to a lower-of-cost-or-market figure of $78,000. During the second quarter, replacement costs recovered, and by the end of the period, market value exceeded the ending inventory cost by $1,250.

3. The ending inventory is estimated by the gross profit method. The estimated gross profit rate is 46 percent.

4. At the end of the first quarter, the effective annual tax rate was estimated at 45 percent. At the end of the second quarter, expected annual income is $600,000. An investment tax credit of $15,000 and dividends received deduction of $75,000 are expected for the year. The combined state and federal tax rate is 40 percent.

5. The tax benefits from operating losses are assured beyond a reasonable doubt. Prior years' income totaling $50,000 is available for operating loss carrybacks.

Required

a. Calculate the expected effective annual tax rate at the end of the second quarter for Malta Corporation.

b. Prepare the income statement for the second quarter of 20X1. Your solution should include a computation of income tax (or benefit) for the first and second quarters.

P13-17 Evaluating Foreign Operations

For many years, Clark Company operated exclusively in the United States, but recently it expanded its operations to the Pacific Rim countries of New Zealand, Singapore, and Australia. After a modest beginning in these countries, recent successes have resulted in an increased level of operations in each country. Operating information (in thousands of U.S. dollars) for the company's domestic and foreign operations follows.

	United States	New Zealand	Singapore	Australia
Sales to unaffiliated	$2,500	$320	$ 60	$120
Interarea sales	100		10	
Operating expenses	1,820	290	70	30
Long-lived assets	2,200	280	140	80

In addition, common costs of $120,000 are to be allocated to operations on the basis of the ratio of an area's sales to nonaffiliates to total company sales to nonaffiliates.

Required

a. Determine the profit or loss for each geographic segment.

b. Discuss the general reporting requirements related to the company's geographic areas.

c. Determine which, if any, of the three individual foreign geographic segments is separately reportable, using a 10 percent materiality threshold.

P13-18 **Interim Accounting Changes**

During the third quarter of its 20X7 fiscal year, Press Company is considering the different methods of reporting accounting changes on its interim segements. Preliminary data are available for the third quarter of 20X7, ending on September 30, 20X7, prior to any adjustments required for any accounting changes. The company's tax rate is 40 percent of income. Selected interim data for the company, in thousands of dollars, follow:

Quarter Ended	Net Sales	Gross Profit	Earnings from Operations, Before Tax	Net Earnings
20X7:				
March 31	$388	$133	$27	$16.2
June 30	406	135	30	18.0
September 30 (preliminary)	428	151	32	19.2
20X6:				
March 31	394	139	27	16.2
June 30	416	151	32	19.2
September 30	403	148	31	18.6
December 31	385	134	31	18.6

Required

For each of the following *independent* cases, present the comparative interim financial data for the company for the three quarters of 20X7 and the comparative data for 20X6, assuming that in a meeting on the last day of the third quarter of 20X7, the company decides to make the specified accounting change.

a. The company decides to change from the FIFO method of accounting for inventory to the LIFO method. The accounting department has prepared the following schedule of data, in thousands of dollars, showing the cost of goods sold each quarter under the LIFO method. The selected interim data presented above are based on the FIFO method. The accounting department has determined that there will be no difference in cost of goods sold prior to January 1, 20X6.

Quarter Ended	LIFO
20X7:	
March 31	$265
June 30	283
September 30	291
20X6:	
March 31	267
June 30	278
September 30	280
December 31	260

b. The company decides to switch from the straight-line method of depreciation to the accelerated method of depreciation because of a change in the estimated future benefits from the asset. The company has determined that the accumulated depreciation would have been $42,000 higher as of January 1, 20X6, if the accelerated method has been used. The depreciation expense determined under the two methods is presented below:

Quarter Ended	Depreciation Expense—Accelerated Method	Depreciation Expense—Straight-Line Method
20X7:		
March 31	$45	$45
June 30	44	45
September 30	42	45
20X6:		
March 31	50	40
June 30	48	40
September 30	47	40
December 31	45	40

c. The company decides to change its method of accounting for recognizing sales revenue on its long-term contracts. The company had been using the completed contract method, but changed to the percentage-of-completion method. The accounting department has prepared an analysis of the sales and gross profit recognition under each of the two methods, in thousands of dollars, as follows:

Quarter Ended	Completed Contract Sales	Completed Contract Gross Profit	Percentage-of-Completion Sales	Percentage-of-Completion Gross Profit
20X7:				
March 31	$ 80	$ 20	$60	$30
June 30	-0-	-0-	55	30
September 30	100	50	70	40
20X6:				
March 31	-0-	-0-	60	40
June 30	150	100	40	20
September 30	-0-	-0-	50	30
December 31	60	40	50	30

P13-19 ## Segment Disclosures in the Financial Statements

Multiplex Inc., a public company whose stock is traded on a national stock exchange, reported the following information on its consolidated financial statements for 20X5:

From the consolidated income statement:	
Sales revenues	$564,000,000
Rental revenues	34,000,000
Income before income taxes	65,000,000
Income taxes	20,000,000
From the consolidated balance sheet:	
Total assets	$475,000,000

Multiplex management determined that it had the following operating segments during 20X5: (1) car rental, (2) aerospace, (3) communications, (4) health and fitness products, and (5) heavy equipment manufacturing. The company assembled the following information for these industry segments for 20X5 (dollar amounts stated in millions):

Item	Car Rental	Aerospace	Communications	Health/ Fitness	Heavy Equipment
Sales		$204	$60	$50	$250
Rentals	$34				
Intersegment sales	5				25
Cost of goods sold		141			177
Selling expenses	16	42	29	23	37
Other traceable expenses	4	8	11	5	10
Allocation of common costs	2	7	2	2	7
Assets	20	107	70	80	195
Other information:					
Depreciation expense (included above)	4	15	4	5	25
Capital expenditures	3	30		15	40

Additional Information

1. The corporate headquarters had general corporate expenses totaling $33,000,000 and assets of $25,000,000 (the chief operating decision maker used neither piece of information in defining operating segment performance).

2. The $5,000,000 of intersegment sales of the car rental segment consisted of car rentals to the aerospace ($2,000,000) and communications ($3,000,000) segments. The intersegment sales of $25,000,000 of the heavy equipment segment were made to the aerospace segment. The aerospace segment is using the equipment in its manufacturing operations. The heavy equipment segment realized a profit of $8,000,000 from this sale. At December 31, 20X5, $7,000,000 of this profit was unrealized from a consolidated viewpoint.

3. At December 31, 20X5, there were no intercompany receivables or payables related to the intersegment car rentals. However, the heavy equipment segment had a $15,000,000 receivable from the intersegment sale to the aerospace segment. The company's policy is to include intersegment receivables in a segment's assets for purposes of evaluating segment performance.

Required

a. Prepare schedules for each of the three 10 percent tests: (1) the revenue test, (2) the profit or loss test, and (3) the assets test. Each schedule should indicate which of Multiplex's industry segments are reportable segments for 20X5.

b. Indicate whether Multiplex's reportable segments meet the 75 percent revenue test.

c. Prepare the information about the company's operations in different industry segments as required by FASB 131.

P13-20 ### Reporting Operations in Different Countries

Watson Inc., a multinational company, has operating divisions in France, Mexico, and Japan as well as in the United States. The company reported the following information on its consolidated financial statements for 20X5:

From the consolidated income statement:	
Sales revenues	$856,000,000
Net income	60,000,000
From the consolidated balance sheet:	
Total assets	$750,000,000

The following additional information was assembled for Watson's domestic and international operations for 20X5 (dollars stated in millions):

Item	Domestic	France	Mexico	Japan
Sales to unaffiliated customers	$430	$300	$36	$90
Intracompany sales between				
geographic areas	50			10
Operating profit	7	40	2	18
General corporate expenses	30			
Long-lived assets	235	160	29	81

Additional Information

1. The domestic intracompany sales of $50,000,000 were made to Watson's French division. A total gross profit of $20,000,000 was realized by Watson's domestic operations on these sales. At December 31, 20X5, $10,000,000 of the total gross profit was unrealized from a consolidated viewpoint. At December 31, 20X5, Watson's French division owed domestic $15,000,000 related to these sales.

2. The intracompany sales made by Watson's Japanese division were made to Watson's Mexican division. The Japanese division realized a gross profit of $2,000,000 on the sales. At December 31, 20X5, all of the goods sold to the Mexican division remained in its inventory. At December 31, 20X5, the Japanese division had an $8,000,000 receivable related to these sales.

Required

a. Determine whether Watson Inc. must separately report its foreign operations.

b. Determine which of the three individual foreign geographic segments is separately reportable, using a 10 percent materiality threshold.

c. Prepare the information about the company's domestic and foreign operations as required by FASB 131.

P13-21 Matching Key Terms

Match the terms on the left side with the descriptions on the right. A description may be used once, more than once, or not at all.

Terms	Descriptions of Terms
1. Management approach	A. Based on all assets used by management to assess that business unit's performance.
2. Reportable operating segment	
3. 10 percent revenue test for segments	B. Not computed until tax is paid.
4. Revenue test for material foreign country disclosure	C. Each interim period viewed as an installment of an annual period.
5. Asset test for reportable operating segments	D. Includes intercorporate sales and transfers.
6. Asset test for material foreign country disclosure	E. Annual statutory tax rate.
	F. Based on long-lived assets used in that business unit only.
7. Comprehensive segment disclosure test	G. Values cost of goods sold at the LIFO cost of the goods sold.
8. Enterprisewide disclosures	
9. Discrete theory of interim reporting	H. Values cost of goods sold at the expected costs of replacements.
10. Integral theory of interim reporting	
11. Recovery of prior write-down for interim inventory valuations	I. Requires sales to unaffiliated units for separately disclosed segments to be greater than or equal to 75 percent of total consolidated revenue.
12. Interim LIFO liquidations to be replaced by year end	J. Segment that must meet each of the three 10 percent segment significance tests.
13. Effective annual tax rate	K. Product revenues, geographic areas, and information about major customers.
	L. Basis of defining segments for financial statements.
	M. Views each interim period as a basic accounting period, similar to an annual accounting period.
	N. Recovery allowed by APB 28.
	O. Based on sales to unaffiliated entities only.
	P. Not permitted under APB 28.
	Q. Estimate of the income tax that will actually be paid for the year.
	R. Segment that has met at least one of the three 10 percent segment significance tests.

Supplemental Problems for this chapter are available as part of the *Online Learning Center* on the textbook's Website.

Chapter **Fourteen**

SEC Reporting

Multi-Corporate Entities

Multinational Entities

Reporting Requirements

Segment and Interim Reporting

SEC Reporting

Partnerships

Not-for-Profit and Governmental Entities

Corporations in Financial Difficulty

Multi-Corporate Entities

Multinational Entities

Reporting Requirements

Segment and Interim Reporting

SEC Reporting

Partnerships

Not-for-Profit and Governmental Entities

Corporations in Financial Difficulty

Since its creation in 1934, the Securities and Exchange Commission (SEC) has had a significant impact on the capital formation process by which companies obtain capital from investors. The SEC is an independent federal agency responsible for regulating securities markets in which stocks and bonds of the major companies trade and for the "full and fair disclosure" of financial information so investors may make informed investment decisions. The ability of companies to raise capital in the stock markets and the hundreds of millions of shares that are traded daily both indicate the SEC's success in maintaining an effective marketplace for companies issuing securities and for investors seeking capital investments.

If our example company, Peerless Products Corporation, decides to issue securities on a stock exchange (i.e., go public), the process begins with the company filing a registration statement, usually a Form S-1, with the Securities and Exchange Commission. Once approved by the SEC, Peerless would then make an initial public offering (IPO) of its securities. To remain publicly traded, Peerless would be required to meet a number of SEC filing requirements, including annual and interim reports to the SEC. This chapter presents an overview of the SEC and the laws and regulations that a publicly held company must follow.

HISTORY OF SECURITIES REGULATION

The need for regulation has gone hand in hand with the offering of securities to the general public. In the thirteenth century, King Edward I of England established a Court of Aldermen to regulate security trades in London. In the latter part of the eighteenth century, England's Parliament passed several acts, termed the Bubble Acts, to control questionable security schemes that had become popular. In 1790, the New York Stock Exchange was created to serve as a clearinghouse for securities trades between members of the exchange. The need for additional sources of capital paralleled the advent of the industrial revolution and the growth of commerce in the United States. Some individuals took advantage of this situation and offered securities of fictitious companies for sale to the general public or used financial reports that were not factual about the offering company's financial picture. In 1911, because of the lack of any federal security regulatory laws, several states began passing what were called "blue sky laws" to regulate the offering of securities by companies made up only of "blue sky," that is, which did not have a sound financial base.

The era of the 1920s was one of heavy stock speculation by many individuals. Business executives, cabdrivers, and assembly-line workers all wanted to participate in the many stock opportunities that existed at that time. Unfortunately, a number of abuses were occurring in the marketplace. For example, certain speculators sought to manipulate selected stock prices by issuing untrue press releases about companies' operations or managements. Companies were not required to be audited, and some of them issued false and misleading financial statements. Investors were using excessive amounts of margin; that is, they were borrowing heavily to invest in stocks. Some employees of companies were using inside information—information that had not been released to the public—to purchase or sell their company's stock for personal advantage.

679

The month of October 1929 is often viewed as the beginning of the Great Depression. Stock prices plunged to record lows within just a few weeks as panic took over the market. It became obvious that some form of federal regulation was necessary to restore confidence in the stock market. The Federal Securities Acts of 1933 and 1934 were part of President Franklin D. Roosevelt's New Deal legislation. The Securities Act of 1933 regulated the initial distribution of security issues by requiring companies to make "full and fair" disclosure of their financial affairs before their securities could be offered to the public. The Securities Exchange Act of 1934 required all companies whose stocks were traded on a stock exchange to periodically update their financial information. In addition, the 1934 act created the Securities and Exchange Commission and assigned it the responsibility of administering both the 1933 and 1934 acts.

The SEC has the legal responsibility to regulate trades of securities and to determine the types of financial disclosures that a publicly held company must make. Although the SEC has the ultimate legal authority to establish the disclosure requirements, it has worked closely with the accounting profession to prescribe the accounting principles and standards used to measure and report companies' financial conditions and results of operations. The SEC's role is to ensure full and fair disclosure; it does not guarantee the investment merits of any security. Stock markets still operate on a *caveat emptor* ("Let the buyer beware") basis. The SEC has consistently taken the position that investors must have the necessary information to make their own assessments of the risk and return attributes of a security.

The present role of the SEC is particularly complex. In 1935, its first year of full activity, only 284 new securities were registered for sale to the general public. Now the number of new securities being registered for sale is more than 5,000 per year. The SEC also regulates more than 10,000 securities brokers and dealers and must monitor stock exchange volumes often surpassing a billion shares a day.

ELECTRONIC DATA GATHERING, ANALYSIS, AND RETRIEVAL (EDGAR) SYSTEM

The SEC continues to work to facilitate the registration and filing process and has developed an electronic filing system known as EDGAR (Electronic Data Gathering, Analysis, and Retrieval). Under this system, firms electronically file directly by using computers, facilitating the data transfer and making public data more quickly available. EDGAR filings may be found on the World Wide Web, under the SEC's home page (www.sec.gov) within 24 hours of filing. All public companies are now required to use EDGAR, although some hardship exemptions are allowed for smaller firms.

The SEC believes that EDGAR is accomplishing its primary purpose of increasing the efficiency and fairness of the securities markets by expediting the receipt, acceptance, dissemination, and analysis of time-sensitive data filed with the SEC. Any individual with access to the World Wide Web can easily download and print the documents from EDGAR, which has become an important data source for corporate researchers, investors, and all other participants in the securities markets.

INTERNATIONAL HARMONIZATION OF ACCOUNTING STANDARDS FOR PUBLIC OFFERINGS

In the late 1980s, the Securities and Exchange Commission urged the International Organization of Securities Commissions (IOSCO) to increase its efforts to narrow the alternative accounting treatments allowed for international accounting standards. The SEC is examining the possibility of designating a set of accounting standards that could be used by overseas companies wishing to enter the U.S. capital market. Currently, foreign registrants must reconcile their financial reports to U.S. GAAP. The U.S.'s accounting principles are often more restrictive than those in other countries.

The worldwide economy has a number of major securities exchanges in which firms can seek equity capital. The SEC seeks to preserve the international prestige of the U.S. capital markets by providing a wider forum for international firms. With the encouragement of the SEC and the IOSCO, the International Accounting Standards Board (IASB) is working with the Financial Accounting Standards Board (FASB) to develop a uniform set of accounting and financial reporting standards that could be used by all companies seeking financing through any of the world's major stock markets, including those of the United States. While the IASB and FASB continue their work, the SEC has formed a number of mutual agreements for cross-border filings, for example, to allow registrants to use domestically prepared financial statements for U.S. firms filing in Canadian capital markets and for Canadian firms filing in U.S. capital markets. However, these mutual agreements are only a stepping-stone to the eventual acceptance of standardized accounting for securities offerings in any of the major international securities exchanges.

SECURITIES AND EXCHANGE COMMISSION

Organizational Structure of the Commission

The SEC's five commissioners are appointed by the president of the United States with the advice and consent of the Senate. Figure 14–1 is an organizational chart of the Commission showing the four separate divisions and the major offices of the 18 that must report directly to the Commission. The four divisions, and their primary responsibilities, are as follows:

1. *Division of Corporation Finance.* Develops and administers the disclosure requirements for the securities acts and reviews all registration statements and other issue-oriented disclosures. This is the division with which accountants are most familiar because all registration forms are submitted to it.

2. *Division of Enforcement.* Directs the SEC's enforcement actions. This division has several options for enforcement ranging from persuasion to administrative proceedings to litigation. An administrative proceeding often is used to gather evidence and present findings on a specific issue, such as a significant shareholder not filing proper reports with the SEC. Many of the administrative proceedings result in a consent action by a registrant, stock market participant, or professional practicing before the SEC in which the party accepts the judgment of the SEC. Litigation is used for serious infractions of the laws administered by the SEC, such as when a securities broker engages in the fraudulent

FIGURE 14–1
Organizational Structure of the Securities and Exchange Commission

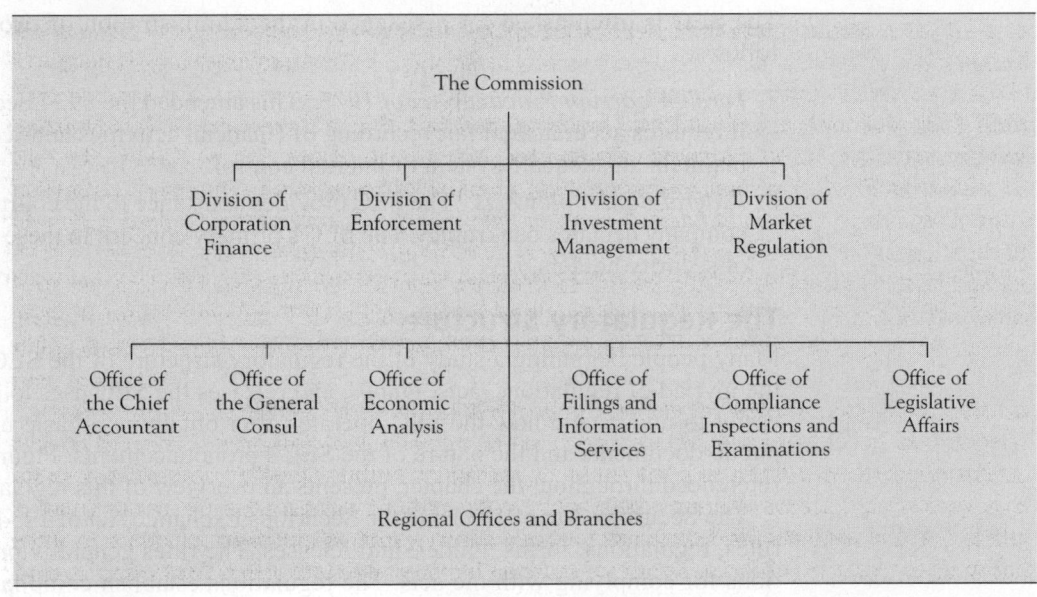

sale of securities. Litigation can result in injunctions to discontinue actions as well as civil or criminal sanctions.

3. *Division of Investment Management.* Regulates investment advisers and investment companies.

4. *Division of Market Regulation.* Regulates national securities exchanges, brokers, and dealers of securities.

Several offices support these divisions, of which one of the most important for accountants is the Office of the Chief Accountant. This office assists the Commission by studying current accounting issues and preparing position papers for the SEC to consider. The other major offices listed offer the Commission advice on a variety of economic and regulatory matters.

Laws Administered by the SEC

In addition to the Securities Acts of 1933 and 1934, the SEC is responsible for administering other laws established to regulate companies or individuals involved with the securities markets. The laws are as follows:

1. *Public Utility Holding Company Act of 1935.* This prohibits artificial pyramids of capital in public utilities and allows the SEC to restructure those "holding companies" whose only purpose is to concentrate the stock voting power in a few individuals.

2. *Trust Indenture Act of 1939.* This requires a trustee to be appointed for sales of bonds, debentures, and other debt securities of public corporations, thus bringing in a bonded expert to administer the debt.

3. *Investment Company Act of 1940.* This controls companies such as mutual funds that invest funds for the public. These companies must be audited annually, with the auditor reporting directly to the SEC.

4. *Investment Advisors Act of 1940.* This requires complete disclosure of information about investment advisers, including their backgrounds, business affiliations, and bases for compensation.

5. *Securities Investor Protection Act of 1970.* This created the Securities Investor Protection Corporation (SIPC), an entity responsible for insuring investors from possible losses if an investment house enters bankruptcy. A small fee is added to the cost of each stock trade to cover the costs of the SIPC.

6. *Sarbanes-Oxley Act of 2002.* This created the Public Company Accounting Oversight Board (PCAOB) and created a number of responsibilities for audit committees of publicly held companies and for public accounting firms.

The SEC is often asked for assistance in the administration of two other major laws, as follows:

7. *Foreign Corrupt Practices Act of 1977.* This amended the 1934 Securities Exchange Act. It requires accurate and fair recording of financial activities and requires management to maintain an adequate system of internal control.

8. *Federal Bankruptcy Acts.* The SEC provides assistance to the courts when a publicly held company declares bankruptcy. The SEC's primary concern in these cases is the protection of security holders.

The Regulatory Structure

Many people beginning a study of the regulatory structure of the SEC are overwhelmed by the myriad of regulations, acts, guides, and releases the SEC uses to perform its tasks. It is easier to understand how the SEC operates after obtaining a basic understanding of these public documents and the nature of the SEC's pronouncements. Figure 14–2, which will be referenced throughout the chapter, presents an overview of this regulatory structure.

The Securities Act of 1933 and the Securities Exchange Act of 1934 are broken down into rules, regulations, forms, guides, and releases. The rules generally provide specific definitions for complying with the acts. The regulations establish compliance requirements; for

FIGURE 14–2   **The Regulatory Structure**

Item	Contents
Securities Act of 1933	Statute regulating initial registration and sale of securities.
Securities Act rules	Basic definitions of Securities Act terms such as *offers, distribution, participation,* and *accredited investor.*
Securities Act regulations	Detailed requirements of registration. At the present time there are six regulations (Regulations A, B, C, D, E, F), of which two (A and D) specify exemptions from registration requirements for small or private stock offerings.
Securities Act forms	Content of registration forms. The most frequently used forms are Form 1-A for small offerings of securities and Forms S-1, S-2, and S-3, which are general registration forms.
Securities Act industry guides	Specifications of additional disclosures required in registration statements of companies in special industries such as oil and gas, banking, and real estate.
Securities Act releases (SRs)	Announcements amending or adopting new rules, guides, forms, or policies under the 1933 act. Approximately 6,000 releases have been published. These are noted with a prefix; for example, for release number 6,000, Release 33-6000.
Securities Exchange Act of 1934	Regulation of security trading and requirements for periodic reports by publicly held companies.
Exchange Act rules	Specific reporting requirements of over-the-counter securities, special reports required by stockholders who own 5 percent or more of a company's outstanding stock, and prohibition of manipulative and deceptive devices or contrivances.
Exchange Act forms	Specification of the content of periodic reports. The most commonly used forms are Form 10-K (annual report), Form 10-Q (quarterly report), and Form 8-K (current events report).
Exchange Act industry guides	Additional periodic reporting requirements of companies in specialized industries such as electric and gas utilities, oil and gas, and banking.
Securities Exchange Act releases (SRs)	Announcements of amendments or adoptions of new rules, guides, forms, or policy statements pertaining to the 1934 act. More than 15,000 have been issued, identified with a prefix; for example, for number 15,000, Release 34-15000.
Regulation S-X (Reg. S-X)	Articles specifying the form and content of financial disclosures: financial statements, schedules, footnotes, reports of accountants, and pro forma disclosures.
Regulation S-K (Reg. S-K)	Articles specifying disclosure rules of nonfinancial items to be included in registration statements, annual reports, and proxy statements. Major items are descriptions of business, management's discussion and analysis, disagreements with accountants, and required information about new stock issues.
Accounting and Auditing Enforcement Releases (AAERs)	Announcements of enforcement actions involving accountants practicing before the SEC. Includes discussion of the findings and opinions (including sanctions against the accountants involved) of enforcement hearings held by the Commission. *AAER No. 1* is a codification of all enforcement topics previously included in the Accounting Series Releases.
Staff Accounting Bulletins (SABs)	New or revised administrative practices and interpretations used by the Commission's staff in reviewing financial statements.

example, the regulations of the 1933 act detail specific reporting requirements for special cases such as small companies. The forms specify the format of the reports to be made under each of the acts. The guides provide specified additional disclosure requirements for selected industries such as oil and gas, and banks. The releases are used for amendments or adoptions of new requirements under the acts.

Two major regulations, **Regulation S-X** and **Regulation S-K**, govern the preparation of financial statements and associated disclosures made in reports to the SEC. Specifically,

Regulation S-X presents the rules for preparing financial statements, footnotes, and the auditor's report. Regulation S-K covers all nonfinancial items, such as management's discussion and analysis of the company's operations and financial position.

The SEC needed some reporting vehicle to inform accountants about changes made in disclosure requirements, regulatory changes in the auditor–client relationship, and the results of enforcement actions taken against participants in the financial disclosure or securities trading process. Before 1982, the SEC used Accounting Series Releases (ASRs) for this purpose and had issued 307 ASRs covering a wide range of topics. In 1982, these ASRs were classified as covering either financial accounting topics or enforcement actions. Regulatory actions of the SEC are now provided on the SEC's Website. Those governing reporting and financial accounting requirements are identified by a release number that begins with the number of the securities act being changed or amended (e.g., Release No. 33-8545, Release No. 34-51293, and so on).

The *Accounting and Auditing Enforcement Releases (AAERs)* present the results of enforcement actions taken against accountants, brokers, and other participants in the filing process. Most of these actions result from the filing of a false or misleading statement. The SEC can use administrative proceedings, in which case the hearings take place before an administrative law judge (ALJ) who is independent of the Commission. Both the SEC and the defendant are allowed to present evidence. The administrative law judge then issues a report which includes the findings of fact and a recommended sanction, such as barring a person from further participation in auditing publicly traded companies or from employment as a broker or a member of management of a publicly traded company. In more serious cases, the SEC may file a complaint with a federal court seeking injunctions prohibiting illegal acts or practices, or other court orders seeking civil monetary penalties or other forms of sanctions.

An interesting example of a civil action is presented in Litigation Release No. 17588, on June 27, 2002. It is also identified as Accounting and Auditing Release No. 1585. The title of the release is, "SEC Charges WorldCom with $3.8 Billion Fraud. Commission Action Seeks Injunction, Money Penalties, Prohibitions on Destroying Documents and Making Extraordinary Payments to WorldCom Affiliates, and the Appointment of a Corporate Monitor." This litigation release presents the initial SEC action against WorldCom for its massive accounting fraud in which the company capitalized and deferred, rather than properly expensing, approximately $3.8 billion of costs. This fraud eventually led to the bankruptcy of WorldCom and the indictments of several of the company's top management.

The *Staff Accounting Bulletins (SABs)* allow the Commission's staff to make announcements on technical issues with which it is concerned as a result of reviews of SEC filings. The SABs are not formal actions of the Commission; nevertheless, most preparers do follow these bulletins because they represent the views of the staff that will be reviewing their companies' filings.

A recent example of a Staff Accounting Bulletin is SAB No. 101, "Revenue Recognition in Financial Statements," issued in 1999. SAB No. 101 focused on the several revenue recognition procedures the SEC staff found inconsistently applied by registrants. One special item was the discussion of revenue recognition by the "New Economy" Internet firms. These companies focus on revenue growth, and many do not report any positive income. Analysts and stock market investors gauge these companies based on their revenue growth. For example, Company A, an Internet company, may offer another company's products (Company T) on Company A's Website. Customers place their orders and provide a credit card number to A's Internet site. Company A then forwards the order to Company T, which ships the goods to the customer. The goods normally cost $200, for which Company A receives $20 for facilitating the sale. The question is this: Can Company A record the entire $200 gross sale and a $180 cost of goods sold to report its profit of $20, or should Company A record just the net $20 sales commission as its revenue? SAB No. 101 states that the revenue should be reported on the net basis, not the gross basis that the SEC staff believes inflates both the reported revenue and cost of goods sold. As viewed by the SEC staff, Company A did not take title to the goods, did not incur the risks and rewards of ownership of the goods, and was only an agent or broker for Company T for which it received a commission or fee.

The 1933 and 1934 securities acts provided the SEC with broad regulatory powers to determine the accounting and reporting standards for publicly traded companies. The SEC has generally relied on the accounting profession to establish accounting standards through creation and support for a standard-making body, for example, the APB and the FASB. The cooperation between the SEC and the FASB has worked with varying levels of success. The FASB is sensitive to the changes in the business world and attempts to react quickly to these changes by promulgating new accounting standards when needed. The SEC, however, continues to fulfill its responsibility by issuing releases on subjects that it believes must be addressed.

ISSUING SECURITIES: THE REGISTRATION PROCESS

Companies wishing to sell debt or stock securities in interstate offerings to the general public are generally required by the Securities Act of 1933 to register those securities with the SEC. The registration process requires extensive disclosure about the company, its management, and the intended use of the proceeds from the issue. The registrant must also provide audited financial statements. The basic financial statements required in the annual report are: (1) two years of balance sheets, (2) three years of statements of income, (3) three years of statements of cash flows, and (4) three years of statements of shareholders' equity. Prior years' statements are presented on a comparative basis with those for the current period. In addition, the SEC requires at least five years of selected financial information presenting key numbers from the four basic financial statements.

A number of types of securities and securities transactions are exempt from the need to be registered under the 1933 act. Although the SEC may exempt these from full registration requirements, the antifraud provisions of the securities acts still apply to all offerings. The exempt securities are commercial paper (i.e., notes) with a maturity of nine months or less; intrastate issues in which the securities are offered and sold only within one state; securities exchanged by an issuer exclusively with its existing shareholders with no commission charged (e.g., a stock split or a stock dividend issued by a corporation); issuances of securities by governments, banks, savings and loan associations, farmers, co-ops, and common carriers regulated by the Interstate Commerce Commission; and securities of nonprofit religious, educational, or charitable organizations. Small issues under the SEC's *Regulation A* for issuances up to $5,000,000 within a 12-month period can be exempt if there is a notice filed with the SEC and an "offering circular" containing financial and other information provided to the persons to whom the offer is made (the financial statements in the offering circular do not have to be audited). Thus, some required disclosures of financial statements and other financial information fall under Regulation A.

Regulation D of the SEC presents three important exemptions from full registration requirements for private placements (i.e., not offered to the general public) of securities, as follows:

1. Rule 504 of Regulation D exempts small issuances up to $1,000,000 within a 12-month period to any number of investors. No specific disclosures are required, but the offerer must send a notice of the offering to the SEC within 15 days of the first sale of the securities.
2. Rule 505 of Regulation D exempts issuances up to $5,000,000 within a 12-month period. The sales can be made to up to 35 "unaccredited investors" and to an unlimited number of "accredited investors." Accredited investors include banks, credit unions, insurance companies, partnerships and corporations, and individuals having a net worth exceeding $1,000,000 or individual income of $200,000 for the two most recent years. Unaccredited investors are persons who do not meet the income or net worth requirements. An unaccredited investor who purchases the securities must be supplied with audited balance

sheets along with other financial statements. If the sales are only to accredited investors, no disclosures are required. Under Rule 505, the SEC must be notified within 15 days of the first sale, and the issuer must restrict the purchasers' rights to resell the securities, generally for a period of two years. The securities typically state the nature of their restriction and that they have not been registered with the SEC.

3. Rule 506 of Regulation D allows private placements of an unlimited amount of securities and applies, in general, the same rules of Rule 505 except the maximum of 35 unaccredited investors must be sophisticated investors who have knowledge and experience in financial affairs.

The offering process usually begins with the selection of an investment banker, also called an "underwriter," who assists the company in the registration process by providing marketing information and ultimately directing the distribution of the securities. The underwriting agreement is a contract between the company and the underwriter and specifies such items as the underwriter's responsibilities and the final disposition of any unsold securities remaining at the end of the public offering. In some cases, the underwriter agrees to purchase any remaining securities; in others, the company is required to withdraw any unsold securities. An offering team includes the company, the underwriter, the company's independent accountant, the company's legal counsel, and experts such as appraisers or engineers who may be required. Typically, the underwriter requires a "comfort letter" from the accountant to indicate that the company has fulfilled all the accounting requirements in the registration process.

The Registration Statement

The process of public offerings of securities begins with the preparation of the registration statement. The company must select 1 from among approximately 20 different forms the SEC currently has for registering securities. The most common are *Form S-1*, *Form S-2*, and *Form S-3*. Others are required when registering stock option plans, foreign issues, limited issuances under Regulation D, and special types of offerings. Form S-1 is the most comprehensive registration statement; Form S-2 is an abbreviated form for present registrants who have other publicly traded stock; Form S-3 is a brief form available for large, established registrants whose stock has been trading for several years.

Form S-1 has two different levels of disclosure. Part I, often referred to as the "prospectus," is intended primarily for investors and includes the basic information package as well as information about the intended use of the proceeds, a description of the securities being offered, and the plan of distribution, including the name of the principal underwriter. Filings for bond issues must include summary information about the ratio of earnings to fixed charges so investors are informed about some of the financial risk the new bond issue adds to the company. Part II of Form S-1 includes more detailed information, such as a list of the expenses of issuing and distributing the new security, additional information about directors and officers, and additional financial statement schedules. The registration statement must be signed by the principal executive, financial, and accounting officers, as well as a majority of the company's board of directors. The company then submits its registration statement to an SEC review by the Division of Corporation Finance.

SEC Review and Public Offering

The SEC seeks to provide potential investors full and fair disclosure of all material information necessary for assessing the securities' risk and return expectations. The SEC does not, however, guarantee the value of the stock or bond security.

Most first-time registrants receive a "customary review," which is a thorough examination by the SEC and may result in acceptance or, alternatively, a *comment letter* specifying the deficiencies that must be corrected before the securities may be offered for sale. Established companies that already have stock widely traded generally are subject to a summary review or a cursory review. Once the registration statement becomes effective, the company may begin selling securities to the public. This review period is 20 days unless the company receives a comment letter from the SEC.

Between the time the registration statement is presented to the SEC and its effective date, the company may issue a ***preliminary prospectus***, referred to as a *red herring prospectus,* which provides tentative information to investors about an upcoming issue. The name "red herring" comes from the red ink used on the cover of this preliminary prospectus, indicating that it is not an offering statement and that the securities being discussed are not yet available for sale. In addition, the company generally prepares a "tombstone ad" in the business press to inform investors of the upcoming offering. These ads are bordered in black ink, hence the title.

The time period between the initial decision to offer securities and the actual sale may not exceed 120 days. In the interim, many factors can affect the stock market and decrease the company's ability to obtain capital. In 1982, the SEC devised the ***shelf registration*** rule for large, established companies with other issues of stock already actively traded. These companies may file a registration statement with the SEC for a stock issue that may be "brought off the shelf " and, with the aid of an underwriter, updated within a very short time, usually two to three days. A shelf registration is limited to 10 percent of the company's currently outstanding stock but allows large companies to select the optimal time to sell their stock.

Accountants' Legal Liability in the Registration Process

Accountants play a key role in the preparation of the registration statement. The company's own accountants prepare the initial financial disclosures, which are then audited by the company's independent accountants. The 1933 act created a very broad legal liability for all participants in the registration process, and this legal exposure is particularly high for accountants because financial disclosures make up the majority of the registration statement. Under section 11 of the 1933 act, accountants are liable for any materially false or misleading information *to the effective date* of the registration statement. The underwriters handling the sale of the securities often require a "comfort letter" from the registrant's public accountants for the period between the filing date and the effective date. This comfort letter provides additional evidence that the public accountant has not found any adverse financial changes since the filing date. Plaintiffs suing the accountant are not required to show they relied on the registration statement, only that the statement was wrong at the effective date! Accountants have a "due diligence" defense, the result of interpretations by the courts as to what is generally required in a reasonable investigation of the company's financial position; however, the broad legal exposure causes many anxieties for accountants involved with the offering of securities.

PERIODIC REPORTING REQUIREMENTS

The Securities Exchange Act of 1934 regulates the trading of securities and imposes reporting requirements on companies whose securities trade on one of the stock exchanges. Companies with more than $10 million in assets and whose securities are held by more than 500 persons must file annual and other periodic reports as updates on their economic activities. The three basic forms used for this updating are Form 10-K, Form 10-Q, and Form 8-K.

Form 10-K is the annual filing to the SEC. In 2002, the SEC changed the filing deadlines of the Form 10-K for "accelerated filers," which are defined as those companies having at least $75 million in aggregate market value that have been subject to the periodic and annual reporting requirements for at least one year, including the filing of at least one annual report. Accelerated filers must file their Form 10-K within 60 days after the end of the company's fiscal year. Small businesses, and others who do not meet the requirements for an accelerated filer, have until 90 days after the end of their fiscal years.

Form 10-K has four parts and the general format is similar to the company's annual report to shareholders (ARS). Parts I, II, and III include the management's discussion and analysis, the audited financial statements and footnotes, the report by management on the internal control structure and the assessment of the effectiveness of those controls, the auditor's opinion, and at least five years of condensed financial information disclosures. Some of this information is sometimes "incorporated by reference" to other annual reports to shareholders (ARS) or other filings made to the SEC. Also included must be a statement signed by the CEO and CFO that certifies that the financials and disclosures contained in the report are appropriate and that those financial statements and disclosures fairly present, in all material respects, the operations and the financial condition of the issuer.

Part IV of the Form 10-K contains additional schedules and exhibits. Form 10-K differs from the annual report to shareholders by providing specific information relevant to the security holders, such as descriptions of any matters submitted to a vote of security holders; discussion of any disagreements with external auditors; management compensation and major ownership blocks; and schedules detailing selected asset and liability accounts, including accounts receivable, property, plant, and equipment, the company's investments in other enterprises, and indebtedness of the company and its affiliates. The SEC also requires disclosure in the annual report as to where investors can obtain access to a company's SEC periodic filings, including whether the company provides access to its filings on its Website, free of charge, as soon as possible after the filings are made to the SEC.

Form 10-Q is the quarterly report to the SEC. Accelerated filers must file a Form 10-Q within 35 days after the end of each of their first three quarters. No Form 10-Q is filed for the fourth quarter because that is when the Form 10-K is filed. Those companies not classified as accelerated filers must file within 45 days after the end of each of their first three quarters.

Part I of Form 10-Q includes comparative financial statements prepared in accordance with **APB 28**; these interim statements need not be audited. Essentially, the company provides financial statements for the most recent quarter, cumulative statements from the beginning of the fiscal period, and comparative statements for the equivalent quarters in the preceding fiscal year. Selected data from the interim statements must also be disclosed in a footnote in the company's annual report, and the independent auditors do, on an ex post basis, review the previously issued interims for the year as part of the year-end, annual audit.

Part II of Form 10-Q is an update on significant matters occurring since the last quarter. These include new legal proceedings, changes in the rights of securities, defaults on senior securities, increases or decreases in the number of securities outstanding, and other materially important events affecting security holders.

Form 8-K is used to disclose unscheduled material events. In 2004, the SEC issued final rules that increased the number of reportable items to be disclosed by Form 8-K filings and also accelerated the timing of the filing requirement. Companies must file a Form 8-K within four business days of the occurrence of a "triggering event." Many of the 19 triggering events involve the company's board of directors, or an authorizing officer of the company, making a commitment or conclusion regarding one or more of the reportable items. A number of these events involve accountants and it is important that accountants understand which events require a Form 8-K filing. Because of the expansion of the number of reportable items, the SEC reorganized Form 8-K items into nine topical sections, each with a subnumbering system used for specific items in that section.

1. *Registrant's Business and Operations.* The three reportable events in this section are: (1.01) entry into a material agreement; (1.02) termination of a material agreement; and (1.03) the bankruptcy or receivership of the company.

2. *Financial Information.* This section contains the following six items: (2.01) the completion of the acquisition or disposition of assets; (2.02) the public announcement of material results of operations and financial condition; (2.03) the creation of a direct financial obligation under an off-balance sheet arrangement; (2.04) an event that accelerates or increases a direct financial obligation under an off-balance sheet arrangement; (2.05) costs associated with exit or disposal activities when the board commits the company to an exit or disposal of a material part of the business; and (2.06) material impairments of a company's assets.

3. *Securities and Trading Markets.* The three items in this section are: (3.01) notice of delisting or failure to satisfy a continuing listing rule; (3.02) an unregistered sale of equity securities; and (3.03) material modifications to the rights of security holders.

4. *Matters Related to Accountants and Financial Statements.* The two items in this section are: (4.01) changes in the registrant's certifying accountant; and (4.02) nonreliance on previously issued financial statements or a related audit report.

5. *Corporate Governance and Management.* The six items in this section are: (5.01) changes in control of the registrant; (5.02) the departure of directors or principal officers, or the election or appointment of principal officers; (5.03) amendments to the articles of incorporation or bylaws, including any change in the registrant's fiscal year; (5.04) the temporary suspension of trading under the registrant's employee benefit plans; (5.05) amendments to the registrant's code of ethics, or waiver of a provision of the code of ethics; and (5.06) a change in shell company status. A shell company has very limited operations and holds only minor amounts of assets. The company is essentially a legal shell under which other companies operate.

6. *Asset-based Securities.* This section requires disclosure of material items related to asset-backed securities such as a bond issue. Disclosures are required for a change of servicer or trustee of the security; a change in the credit enhancement or other external support for the securities; or a failure to make a distribution required by the security agreement.

7. *Regulation FD.* (Item 7.01) This section requires filing a Form 8-K to broadly report material information that is being provided to securities analysts, selected institutional investors, or others. Regulation FD seeks to eliminate the informational advantages of having access to officers or other management members through public channels. For example, if the CEO of a registrant spoke to a group of financial analysts at a lunch meeting during which the general future of the company and its industry was discussed, the company would file a Form 8-K disclosing the meeting and include major informational items presented by the CEO.

8. *Other Events.* (Item 8.01) This section is unstructured and flexible to allow management to disclose items it believes may be of material importance to security holders.

9. *Financial Statements and Exhibits.* (Item 9.01) This section includes a listing of the financial statements, pro forma financial information, and exhibits required to be filed as part of Form 8-K.

For changes in the registrant's certifying accountant (Item 4.01), Form 8-K must include the following: the date the former auditor resigned or was dismissed, a statement describing and fully discussing any material disagreements with the former auditors over accounting or auditing standards over the past 24 months, a statement stating whether the former auditor's opinion was qualified in any way for the past two years and describing the nature of any qualification, and a letter from the former auditor as an exhibit to Form 8-K that states whether the former auditor agrees or disagrees with the facts as stated in the Form 8-K, as presented by the registrant.

Another SEC form with which accountants should be familiar is Schedule 13D. This schedule is filed by any person or group of persons who acquire a beneficial ownership of more than 5 percent of a class of registered equity securities and must be filed within 10 days after such an acquisition. *Beneficial ownership* is defined as directly or indirectly having the power to vote the shares or investment power to sell the security. In addition, anytime there are material changes in the facts set forth in the schedule, the investor must file an amendment on Schedule 13D. Thus, any investor making an acquisition of 5 percent or more of any class of equity securities of a publicly held company must promptly report the investment to the SEC.

Proxy statements are materials submitted to shareholders for votes on corporate matters such as the election of directors, changes in the corporate charter, issuance of new securities or modification of outstanding securities, or plans for a major business combination. In many cases, voting on these matters takes place at the annual meeting but it may also occur at a special meeting. A proxy card soliciting the shareholder's vote is often in the form of a checkoff ballot that management encourages the shareholder to return to be voted at the meeting. The proxy solicitation materials must include the specific proposals being presented to the shareholders, accompanied by supporting statements of facts and circumstances to explain the proposals. The materials also include information about the committees of the board of directors and executive compensation and share ownership. If there will be an election of directors, the SEC also requires that the registrant's annual report to shareholders be included with the proxy materials. An increasing number of companies are using the Internet to provide their proxy materials, annual report, and proxy cards to shareholders who request the electronic form. The company must send out printed materials to all other shareholders. A copy of a registrant's proxy statement is available on the SEC's EDGAR database of filings for that company under the title "DEF 14A" to identify it as the definitive, or final, proxy statement filed under Section 14A of the Securities Exchange Act of 1934.

Individual shareholders or a group of shareholders may sometimes use proxy solicitations for proposals that are opposed by management. Rule 14-8 of the Securities Exchange Act of 1934 presents detailed rules and regulations that must be met in order to have these shareholder proposals included on a company's proxy card and included along with any supporting statements in the proxy statement. The rules are quite specific with regard to who is eligible to submit a proposal, the content and subject matter of a proposal, and deadlines for submitting a proposal. At times, the business press carries news of proxy battles between management and nonmanagement groups, in which each side is soliciting shareholders' support.

Accountants' Legal Liability in Periodic Reporting

The 1934 Securities Exchange Act provides for a limited level of legal exposure from involvement in the preparation and filing of periodic reports. Civil liability is imposed for filing materially false or misleading statements. The accountant's liability for registration statements under the 1933 act extends to the date the registration becomes effective. Plaintiffs suing accountants under the 1934 act must show that a periodic report contains a misleading material fact and that they suffered a loss because they relied on that report. Accountants are provided with due diligence defenses to combat any lawsuits brought under the 1934 act.

FOREIGN CORRUPT PRACTICES ACT OF 1977

In the mid-1970s, Congress held a number of public hearings that brought to light the payment of millions of dollars in bribes to high government officials of other countries by U.S.–based companies seeking to win defense or consumer product contracts. Alarmed by the size and scope of these activities, Congress passed the ***Foreign Corrupt Practices Act of 1977 (FCPA)*** as a major amendment to the Securities Exchange Act of 1934. The FCPA has two major sections: Part I prohibits foreign bribes, and Part II requires publicly held companies to maintain an adequate system of internal control and accurate records.

Under Part I, individuals associated with U.S. companies are prohibited from bribing foreign governmental or political officials for the purpose of securing a contract or otherwise increasing the company's business. Small compensating or agents' fees to lower-level civil servants are allowed if the purpose of these fees is to facilitate a transaction that is already in process, such as to obtain shipping permits or to acquire local licenses in a foreign country. Both civil and criminal sanctions can be imposed on individuals making foreign bribes.

Part II of the FCPA has had a significant impact on both corporate accountants and independent auditors. This part requires all public companies, whether operating internationally or not, to keep detailed records that accurately and fairly reflect their financial transactions and to develop and maintain an adequate internal control system. An internal control system should ensure that all major transactions are fully authorized, that transactions are properly recorded and reported, that the company's assets are safeguarded, and that management's policies are properly carried out.

Although the FCPA was not specific about the types of internal controls necessary, it defined the following as important aspects of a good internal control system: (1) strong budgetary controls, (2) an objective internal audit function that helps develop, document, and then monitor the control system, (3) an active audit committee of nonmanagement members of the company's board of directors, and (4) a review of the internal control system by the independent auditors. The FCPA allows for the development of "tailored" control procedures that best serve the company. In addition, the FCPA indicated that the cost of an internal control procedure should not outweigh its benefit to the firm.

The FCPA also had a significant effect on independent auditors by requiring them to evaluate a company's internal controls and to communicate any material weaknesses in those controls to the company's top management and board of directors. The total impact of the FCPA is still unclear. Subsequent proposals offered by the SEC itself have somewhat softened the foreign bribery section of the act; however, Part II of the FCPA, dealing with internal control, certainly increased the interest of companies in maintaining strong internal control systems.

SARBANES-OXLEY ACT OF 2002

A major law affecting auditors and publicly traded companies was signed into law on July 30, 2002. The proposed law gained impetus after the revelations about accounting and financial mismanagement at Enron, WorldCom, and others. Named after its two sponsors, Senator Paul Sarbanes and Congressman Michael Oxley, the *Sarbanes-Oxley Act* (broadly known as SOX) has a number of major implications for accountants. Its supporters hoped that the act would minimize corporate governance accounting and financial reporting abuses and help restore investor confidence in the financial reports of publicly traded companies. The following discussion summarizes the major sections of the Sarbanes-Oxley Act.

Title I: Public Company Accounting Oversight Board

Section 101 of Title I of the act established a new accounting oversight board to regulate accounting firms and be responsible for establishing or modifying auditing and attestation standards. The *Public Company Accounting Oversight Board (PCAOB)* is administered by the SEC, which is responsible for appointing its five full-time members. Many accountants use the shorthand of "Peek-A-Boo" to refer to the PCAOB. Two board members must be or must have been CPAs; however, the other three cannot have been CPAs. The PCAOB chair may be a CPA but that person must not have practiced accounting during the five years prior to being appointed as chair. The board's funding includes mandatory fees from public companies. Accounting firms with publicly held audit clients must be registered with the PCAOB and are subject to continuing quality inspections for compliance to the requirements of the act.

The PCAOB has the authority to establish or to adopt standards for audit firm quality controls. The range of its authority includes auditing and related attestation standards, quality control, ethics, independence, and other areas necessary to protect the public interest. The board also manages the regular inspection of the registered accounting firms' operations and auditing processes. Any accounting firm that does not cooperate can be prohibited from auditing public companies. If the PCAOB finds any violations of its standards, that accounting firm can be referred to the SEC and possibly to the Department of Justice for prosecution.

Title II: Auditor Independence

A major change brought about by the Sarbanes-Oxley Act prohibits auditors from offering certain nonaudit services to their audit clients. These services include information systems design and implementations, appraisals or valuation services, internal audits, human resources services, legal or expert services not related to audit services, and bookkeeping services. Tax services provided by an auditor for a publicly held company require preapproval of the company's audit committee. Thus, accounting firms must determine whether they wish to provide a company with audit or nonaudit services; they cannot provide both to the same company.

Title II requires that both the lead audit partner and the audit review partner for publicly held companies be rotated at least every five years. To avoid a conflict of interest, the company's CEO, controller, CFO, chief accounting officer, or person in an equivalent position cannot have been employed by the company's audit firm during the one-year period preceding the audit.

Title III: Corporate Responsibility

Title III specifies that *audit committees* be composed of nonmangement members of a company's board of directors. Generally, the chair of the audit committee has financial experience. The Sarbanes-Oxley Act requires the auditor to report directly to, and have its work overseen by, the company's audit committee, not the company's management. The audit committee is responsible for the appointment, compensation, and oversight of the work of the public accounting firm employed by the company. Furthermore, the audit committee must approve all services provided by the auditor, and the auditor must report the following additional information to the audit committee: critical accounting policies and practices, alternative treatments within GAAP that have been discussed with the company's management, accounting disagreements between the auditor and management, and any other important issues arising between the auditor and management.

Section 302 of the act requires both the CEO and the CFO of each publicly traded company to provide a signed statement to accompany each annual and quarterly financial report. These two officers are required to certify that the financial statements and disclosures fairly present, in all material respects, the operations and conditions of the issuer. Furthermore, their signed statement must include declarations that they are responsible for establishing and maintaining internal controls and that these controls have been evaluated as to their effectiveness within 90 days prior to the report.

In the case of accounting restatements due to the material noncompliance of the issuer, the CEO and CFO must forfeit bonuses and incentive compensation provided on the basis of the incorrect accounting information.

Title IV: Enhanced Financial Disclosures

Financial reports filed with the SEC must reflect all material correcting adjustments that have been identified by the registered accounting firm and also all material off-balance sheet transactions and relationships that may have a material effect on the financial status of the issuer. Section 402 prohibits a company from making personal loans to any director or executive officer. However, consumer credit companies may make home improvement and consumer credit loans to its officers if these loans are made on the same terms as those made to the general public.

A major requirement of the Sarbanes-Oxley Act is specified in Section 404, which requires that each annual filing of a stock issuer must contain an *internal control report* by management that reports on the existence and effectiveness of the company's internal control over financial reporting. A company's internal control over financial reporting is a process designed to provide reasonable assurance of the reliability of the financial reporting and preparation of financial statements for external purposes in accordance with generally accepted accounting principles. In May 2003, the SEC released rules (Release No. 33-8238) that established specific requirements for the content of this report. Management's internal control report must include the following items: (*a*) a statement that management is responsible for establishing and maintaining an adequate system; (*b*) the identification of the framework used to evaluate the internal controls; (*c*) a statement as to whether or not the internal control is effective as of year-end; (*d*) the disclosure of any material weaknesses in the internal control system; and (*e*) a statement that the company's external auditors have issued an audit report on management's assessment of its internal controls. The independent auditors also must report on the reliability of management's assessment of internal controls over financial reporting.

In May 2005, the Securities and Exchange Commission released a statement on the first year's implementation of Section 404 and felt that there were significant start-up costs from this new requirement. However, the SEC feels that benefits have been produced from Section 404's requirements and that the Section 404 implementation process will become more efficient over time. The annual filings of publicly held companies now include both the management report on internal control over financial reporting and the expanded independent auditor's report on its assessment of that internal control system. The auditor's report must include a statement attesting to the assessment made by management on the company's internal control structures, including specific notes about any significant defects or material noncompliance found on the basis of that testing.

Title V: Analyst Conflicts of Interest

Research analysts and brokers and dealers must report if they hold securities in any company for which they prepare a research report, if any compensation was received from the company that was the subject of a research report, and if a company that is the subject of a research report was a client of the broker or dealer.

Title VI: Commission Resources and Authority

Title VI increased the funding for the SEC and also increased the SEC's disciplinary and litigation authority over auditors, attorneys, brokers and dealers, and others who practice in the securities markets and who have engaged in illegal, unethical, or improper professional conduct.

Title VII: Studies and Reports

The GAO and SEC are charged with conducting various studies, including the factors leading to the consolidation of public accounting firms since 1989 and the impacts of that consolidation, the role of credit rating agencies in the securities markets, and whether investment banks and financial advisers assisted public companies in earnings manipulation and obfuscation of financial conditions.

Title VIII: Corporate and Criminal Fraud Accountability

The act established severe penalties for anyone who destroys records, commits securities fraud, or fails to report fraud. The penalty for willfully failing to maintain all audit or review workpapers for at least five years is a felony punishable by up to 10 years. Section 802 of the act specifies that persons destroying documents in a federal or bankruptcy investigation are punishable by up to 20 years. The criminal penalty for securities fraud was increased to 25 years.

The statute of limitations for the discovery of fraud was increased to two years from the date of discovery and five years after the actual fraud. Previously, it had been only one year from the date of discovery and three years after the actual fraud. Section 806 provides "whistleblower protection" to employees of the company or the accounting firm who lawfully assist in an investigation of fraud or other criminal conduct by federal regulators, Congress, or supervisors.

Title IX: White-Collar Crime Penalty Enhancements

This title increases the minimum penalty for mail and wire fraud from 5 to 10 years, makes it a crime to tamper with a record or impede any official proceeding, and allows the SEC to prohibit anyone convicted of securities fraud from being an officer or director of any publicly traded company. In addition, this section of SOX includes criminal liability up to five years for corporate officers who fail to certify financial reports or who willfully certify financial statements knowing they do not comply with the act.

Title X: Sense of Congress Regarding Corporate Tax Returns

Congress felt that the federal income tax return of a corporation should be signed by the chief executive officer.

Title XI: Corporate Fraud and Accountability

This section increased the penalties for persons using deceptive devices, engaging in fraudulent transactions, or otherwise acting to impede an official proceeding. It also increased the penalties for violations of the Securities Exchange Act of 1934 up to $25 million and up to 20 years in prison.

The Sarbanes-Oxley Act will have a significant impact on financial reporting, auditing, and corporate governance. The SEC continues to develop the implementation guidelines for various sections of the act, and, therefore, the daily business and accounting press will have continued coverage of the act. The complete act is linked on the SEC's Website (www.sec.gov).

DISCLOSURE REQUIREMENTS

Virtually every SEC accounting release reminds registrants of the commitment to full and fair disclosure of financial information needed by investors. The SEC has taken the lead in requiring management to provide its analysis of the company's operations.

Management Discussion and Analysis

The *management discussion and analysis (MD&A)* of a company's financial condition and results of operations is part of the basic information package (BIP) required in all major filings with the SEC. The SEC has taken the leadership role in requiring management to analyze and discuss the financial statements for investors, and this discussion often extends to four or more pages of the annual report. The financial statements are, after all, management's expressions of the economic consequences of their decisions made during the period. Management has the clearest picture of the company's financial environment. A key element in the MD&A is a view that looks both historically and forward at the company's liquidity and solvency. The SEC recognizes that investors are particularly concerned with a company's ability to generate adequate amounts of cash to meet short-term and long-term cash needs.

The MD&A is continually being monitored by the SEC because the Commission believes the information presented in the MD&A is important for investors. In response to the requirement in section 401 of the Sarbanes-Oxley Act and new section 13(j) of the Securities Exchange Act of 1934, the SEC examined the items listed in its MD&A rules. With Release No. 33-8182, the SEC revised the list of required items in the MD&A, effective April 7, 2003. The items now required in the MD&A are:

1. *Liquidity*. Identify trends, commitments, events, or uncertainties that are reasonably likely to materially change the registrant's liquidity. Indicate the course of action that is proposed to remedy any deficiency identified. Also, identify and describe the internal and external sources of liquidity, with a brief discussion of any material unused sources of liquid assets.

2. *Capital resources*. Discuss material commitments for capital expenditures, their general purposes, and the expected sources of funds to fulfill those commitments. Also discuss trends and expected material changes in the mix of equity, debt, and any off-balance sheet financing arrangements.

3. *Results of operations*. Describe and discuss unusual or infrequent events or transactions affecting revenues, expenses, and the reported income from continuing operations. Discuss trends or expectations of material impacts on future revenues and expenses. For material increases in net sales, discuss the impact of an increase in price versus the impact of an increase in volume and discuss the impact of the introduction of new products. Then, for each of the most recent three years, discuss the impact of inflation and changing prices on net sales and revenue and on income from continuing operations.

4. *Off-balance sheet arrangements*. A separately identified section that includes discussion of off-balance sheet arrangements that have or are likely to have a material effect on the company's financial condition, changes in financial condition, results of

operations, liquidity, capital expenditures, or capital resources. Required disclosures for these off-balance sheet arrangements include the nature and business purpose of the arrangements, the impact of the arrangements on revenues, expenses, and cash flows, and a description of events or other items that would materially change the benefits of the arrangement and the actions the company has taken or would take if those circumstances were to occur.

5. *Tabular disclosure of contractual obligations.* A table in the following format shall be provided, listing the aggregated amount of each type of contractual obligations, (if present):

Contractual Obligations	Payments Due by Period				
	Total	Less than 1 Year	1–3 Years	3–5 Years	More than 5 Years
Long-term debt obligations					
Capital lease obligations					
Operating lease obligations					
Purchase obligations for goods or services					
Other long-term liabilities reflected on the registrant's balance sheet under GAAP					
Total					

The MD&A should cover the financial statements and other statistical data for the most recent three-year time span and make year-to-year comparisons of material changes in the line items. Management should attempt to explain the cause(s) of the material changes. Section 401 of the Sarbanes-Oxley Act specifies the required disclosure of material off-balance sheet transactions, arrangements, and obligations in each annual and each quarterly report. The MD&A in the quarterly reports should be viewed as updating the annual information. Thus, the MD&A in quarterly reports is generally much shorter in length than that in the annual report.

Pro Forma Disclosures

Pro forma disclosures are essentially "what-if" financial presentations often taking the form of summarized financial statements. Pro forma statements are used to show the effects of major transactions that occur after the end of the fiscal period or that have occurred during the year but are not fully reflected in the company's historical cost financial statements. The SEC requires these to be presented whenever the company has made a significant business combination or disposition, a corporate reorganization, an unusual asset exchange, or a restructuring of existing indebtedness. A pro forma condensed income statement presented in the footnotes shows the impact of the transaction on the company's income from continuing operations, thereby helping investors to focus on the specific effects of the major transaction. The pro forma balance sheet includes all adjustments reflecting the full impact of the transaction. Investors therefore have (1) the historical cost primary financial statements, and (2) the pro forma statements, which more fully present and illustrate the effects of the transaction on the company's financial condition.

Summary of Key Concepts

Since its creation in 1934, the SEC has played a significant role in the development of financial disclosures necessary for investor confidence in the capital formation process. The Commission has consistently worked for full and fair disclosure of information it considers necessary so investors can assess the risks and returns of companies wishing to offer their securities to the public. The SEC has taken the leadership in a myriad of reporting issues, predominantly in reporting liquidity and solvency measures, thereby ensuring that investors have access to a management narrative of the company's performance.

Although the SEC has the statutory responsibility to develop and maintain accounting principles used for financial reporting, it has permitted the rule-making bodies of the accounting profession to take the initiative in establishing accounting principles and reporting standards. The cooperation has worked with varying success over the years. The SEC has shown its willingness and capacity to assume the lead in those areas in which it feels the private sector is not moving rapidly enough. It is expected that this arrangement will continue in the future.

Key Terms

Accounting and Auditing
  Enforcement Releases
  (AAERs), *684*
audit committees, *692*
comment letter, *686*
Foreign Corrupt Practices Act
  of 1977 (FCPA), *690*
internal control report, *692*
management discussion and
  analysis (MD&A), *694*
periodic reporting forms:
  Form 10-K, Form 10-Q,
  Form 8-K, *687–688*

preliminary prospectus, *687*
pro forma disclosures, *695*
proxy statements, *689*
Public Company Accounting
  Oversight Board
  (PCAOB), *691*
registration statements:
  Form S-1, Form S-2,
  Form S-3, *686*
Regulation A, *685*
Regulation D, *685*
Regulation S-K, *683*
Regulation S-X, *683*

Sarbanes-Oxley Act, *691*
shelf registration, *687*
Staff Accounting Bulletins
  (SABs), *684*

Questions

Q14-1 What is the basis of the SEC's legal authority to regulate accounting principles?

Q14-2 Which securities act—1933 or 1934—regulates the initial registration of securities? Which regulates the periodic reporting of publicly traded companies?

Q14-3 Which division of the SEC receives the registration statements of companies wishing to make public offerings of securities? Which division investigates individuals or firms that may be in violation of a security act?

Q14-4 Which law requires that companies maintain accurate accounting records and an adequate system of internal control? What is meant by an "adequate system of internal control"?

Q14-5 What does Regulation S-X cover? What is included in Regulation S-K?

Q14-6 What types of public offerings of securities are exempted from the comprehensive registration requirements of the SEC?

Q14-7 When must a company use a Form S-1 registration form? In what circumstances may a company use a Form S-3 registration form?

Q14-8 Define the following terms, which are part of the SEC terminology: (*a*) customary review, (*b*) comment letter, (*c*) red herring prospectus, (*d*) shelf registration.

Q14-9 What is included in Form 10-K? When must a 10-K be filed with the SEC?

Q14-10 Must interim reports submitted to the SEC be audited? What is the role of the public accountant in the preparation of Form 10-Q?

Q14-11 What types of items that specifically involve the accounting function are reported on Form 8-K?

Q14-12 What is a proxy? What must be included in the proxy material submitted to security holders?

Q14-13 Describe Parts I and II of the Foreign Corrupt Practices Act. What is the impact of this act on companies and public accountants?

Q14-14 What types of information must be disclosed in the management discussion and analysis?

Q14-15 Describe the major requirements of the Sarbanes-Oxley Act of 2002.

Cases

C14-1 **Objectives of Securities Acts [CMA Adapted]**

Research

During the late 1920s, approximately 55 percent of all personal savings in the United States were used to purchase securities. Public confidence in the business community was extremely high as stock values doubled and tripled in short periods of time. The road to wealth was believed to be through the stock market, and everyone who was able participated. Thus, the public was severely affected when the Dow Jones Industrial Average fell 89 percent between 1929 and 1933. The public outcry arising from this decline in stock prices motivated the passage of major federal laws regulating the securities industry.

Required

a. Describe the investment practices of the 1920s that contributed to the erosion of the stock market.

b. Explain the basic objectives of each of the following:
   (1) Securities Act of 1933.
   (2) Securities Exchange Act of 1934.

c. More legislation has resulted from abuses in the securities industry. Explain the provisions of the Foreign Corrupt Practices Act of 1977.

C14-2 Roles of SEC and FASB [CMA Adapted]

The development of accounting theory and practice has been influenced directly and indirectly by many organizations and institutions. Two of the most important institutions have been the Financial Accounting Standards Board (FASB) and the Securities and Exchange Commission (SEC).

Understanding

The FASB is an independent body established in 1972. It is composed of seven persons who represent public accounting and fields other than public accounting.

The SEC is a governmental regulatory agency created in 1934 to administer the Securities Act of 1933 and the Securities Exchange Act of 1934. These acts and the creation of the SEC resulted from the widespread collapse of business and the securities markets in the early 1930s.

Required

a. What official role does the SEC have in the development of financial accounting theory and practice?

b. What is the interrelationship between the FASB and the SEC with respect to the development and establishment of financial accounting theory and practice?

C14-3 Information Content of Proxy

The proxy contains an abundance of information believed by the SEC to be necessary for stockholders to make an informed vote on the items the company presents for their voting consideration. This case provides opportunities to analyze the proxy of a publicly held company and to survey the types of information presented in the proxy.

Application

Required

Using EDGAR or another source, obtain the most recent proxy for Caterpillar Inc. or a different company specified by your instructor. Answer the following questions regarding the information presented in the proxy.

a. Summarize the proposals that are being placed before the shareholders for their voting consideration and state the board of directors' recommendation on each proposal.

b. List and briefly describe the duties of each of the standing committees of the board of directors.

c. For the most recent year presented in your proxy, what was the total annual compensation received by the chairman and CEO of the company?

The remaining questions ask about information presented in the annual financial report that accompanies the proxy statement.

d. Summarize the information presented in Management's Report on Internal Control Over Financial Reporting.

e. What does the Report of Independent Registered Public Accounting Firm include with regard to its evaluation of the company's internal control over financial reporting?

f. Identify the categories and major information content presented in the Management's Discussion and Analysis.

C14-4 Proxy Solicitations [CMA Adapted]

The Securities and Exchange Commission has the authority to regulate proxy solicitations. This authority is derived from the Securities Exchange Act of 1934 and is closely tied to the disclosure objective of this act. Regulations established by the SEC require corporations to mail a proxy statement to each shareholder shortly before the annual shareholder meeting.

Understanding

Required

a. Explain the purpose of proxy statements.

b. Identify four types of events or actions for which proxy statements normally are solicited.

C14-5 **Registration Process [CMA Adapted]**

Bandex Inc. has been in business for 15 years. The company has compiled a record of steady but not spectacular growth. Bandex's engineers have recently perfected a product that has an application in the small computer market. Initial orders have exceeded the company's capacity and the decision has been made to expand.

Research

Bandex has financed past growth from internally generated funds, and since the initial stock offering 15 years ago, no further shares have been sold. Bandex's finance committee has been discussing methods of financing the proposed expansion. Both short-term and long-term notes were ruled out because of high interest rates. Mel Greene, the chief financial officer, said, "It boils down to either bonds, preferred stock, or additional common stock." Alice Dexter, a consultant employed to help in the financing decision, stated, "Regardless of your choice, you will have to file a registration statement with the SEC."

Bob Schultz, Bandex's chief accountant for the past five years, stated, "I've coordinated the filing of all the periodic reports required by the SEC—10-Ks, 10-Qs, and 8-Ks. I see no reason I can't prepare a registration statement also."

Required

a. Identify the circumstances under which a firm must file a registration statement with the Securities and Exchange Commission (SEC).

b. Explain the objectives of the registration process required by the Securities Act of 1933.

c. Identify and explain the SEC publications that Bob Schultz would use to guide him in preparing the registration statement.

C14-6 **Form 8-K [CMA Adapted]**

Jerford Company is a well-known manufacturing company with several wholly owned subsidiaries. The company's stock is traded on the New York Stock Exchange, and the company files all appropriate reports with the Securities and Exchange Commission. Jerford's financial statements are audited by a public accounting firm. Jerford Company changed independent auditors during 20X6. Consequently, the financial statements were certified by a different public accounting firm in 20X6 than in 20X5.

Communication

Required

What information is Jerford responsible for filing with the SEC with respect to this change in auditors? Explain your answer completely. (*Hint:* Item 304 of Regulation S-K provides guidance on reporting a change in auditor.)

C14-7 **Form 8-K [CMA Adapted]**

The purpose of the Securities Act of 1933 is to regulate the initial offering of a firm's securities by ensuring that investors are given full and fair disclosure of all pertinent information about the firm. The Securities Exchange Act of 1934 was passed to regulate the trading of securities on secondary markets and to eliminate abuses in the trading of securities after their initial distribution. To accomplish these objectives, the 1934 act created the Securities and Exchange Commission. Under the auspices of the SEC, public companies must not only register their securities but must also periodically prepare and file Forms 8-K, 10-K, and 10-Q.

Understanding

Required

a. With regard to Form 8-K, discuss:

    (1) The purpose of the report.

    (2) The timing of the report.

    (3) The format of the report.

    (4) The role of financial statements in the filing of the report.

b. Identify five circumstances under which the SEC requires the filing of Form 8-K.

c. Discuss how the filing of Form 8-K fosters the purpose of the SEC.

d. Does the SEC pass judgment on securities based on information contained in periodic reports? Explain your answer.

C14-8 Audit Committees [CMA Adapted]

Understanding

An early event leading to the establishment of audit committees as a regular subcommittee of boards of directors occurred in 1940 as part of the consent decree relative to the McKesson-Robbins scandal. (A consent decree is the formal statement issued in an enforcement action when a person agrees to terms of a disciplinary nature without admitting to the allegations in the complaint.) An audit committee composed of outside directors was required as part of the consent decree.

Title III of the Sarbanes-Oxley Act of 2002 specifies requirements for the membership of the audit committee and its authority. The Sarbanes-Oxley Act must be followed by all publicly traded firms.

Required

a. Explain the role of the audit committee, as specified by the Sarbanes-Oxley Act, with regard to the annual audit conducted by the company's external auditors.

b. Discuss the relationship that should exist between the audit committee and a company's internal audit staff.

c. Explain why the members of the audit committee should be outside (independent of management) board members.

C14-9 SEC

Research

The company that employs you is a U.S. publicly traded corporation that manufactures chemicals. You are in the external financial reporting department, and your position requires that you keep current on all the new accounting requirements. While you realize that Staff Accounting Bulletins (SABs) are not formal SEC actions, periodically you like to review the new SABs to see if any are relevant to your company.

Today you decided to perform some research and ascertain if any new SABs have been issued. In addition, your boss, the manager in charge of the department, recently mentioned something to you about the SEC's Division of Enforcement. You do not know a lot about this particular division; however, because you will be doing some SEC research today anyway, you have decided you will find out more about the SEC's Division of Enforcement.

Required

a. Prepare a one-page memo summarizing a recent SAB.

b. Research the SEC's Division of Enforcement. Answer or perform the following:

    (1) What year was the division formed?

    (2) Discuss various actions the division may take.

    (3) Prepare a one-paragraph summary of a recent litigation proceeding.

    (4) Prepare a one-paragraph summary of a recent administrative proceeding.

C14-10 EDGAR Database

Research

Currently, you are an experienced senior working at a public accounting firm. For the upcoming busy season you received a new client, a publicly traded corporation. The manager on this client is someone you have not worked with before. You hope to impress this manager because you hear that she strongly supports those seniors who work for her if she considers them to be excellent employees. At the end of this busy season, you will be up for promotion to manager and would like her support.

Next week you have an internal planning meeting with the manager. Today you will be working in the office, and you have decided to devote the day to performing some background reading to become acquainted with this client. When you get to the office today, you learn that the manager is at a client location and unreachable. Since you will not be able to get any background information on your client from her today, you decide you will get information alternatively using the Internet.

Required

a. Using either the SEC's browser or Edgarscan (at edgarscan.pwcglobal.com), select a company from the EDGAR database with a name beginning with the first letter of your last name. The company selected will be your new client as discussed above. (*Hint:* It may be helpful to determine the company through use of *The Wall Street Journal* or other business periodical.)

b. Prepare a one- or two-page summary listing the types of reports made to the SEC by your client over the last year. Include a brief description of the contents of each of these reports. Select one of the reports and print the first page of that report.

C14-11　**Discovery Case**

Research

This case provides learning opportunities using available databases and/or the Internet to obtain contemporary information about the topics in advanced financial accounting. Note that the Internet is dynamic and any specific Website listed may change its address. In that case, use a good search engine to locate the current address for the Website.

Required

Find two recent articles on the Sarbanes-Oxley Act of 2002. Then review and summarize the major information items reported in the articles. Prepare a one- to two-page report presenting your summary.

One search process could be to use a good search engine and search the Internet for the two articles. Another search process could be to access a business articles index such as that for *The Wall Street Journal.* Locate your two articles and then obtain the articles through your library. A third search process could be to use a database of business articles such as ABI/INFORM® or LEXIS-NEXIS® to find your two articles.

Exercises　**E14-1**　**Organization Structure and Regulatory Authority of the SEC [CMA Adapted]**
Select the correct answer for each of the following questions.

1. Two interesting and important topics concerning the SEC are the role it plays in the development of accounting principles and the impact it has had and will continue to have on the accounting profession and business in general. Which of the following statements about the SEC's authority on accounting practice is false?

   a. The SEC has the statutory authority to regulate and to prescribe the form and content of financial statements and other reports it receives.

   b. Regulation S-X of the SEC is the principal source of the form and content of financial statements to be included in registration statements and financial reports filed with the Commission.

   c. The SEC has little if any authority over disclosures in corporate annual reports mailed to shareholders with proxy solicitations. The type of information disclosed and the format to be used are left to the discretion of management.

   d. If the Commission disagrees with some presentation in the registrant's financial statements but the principles used by the registrant have substantial authoritative support, the SEC often accepts footnotes to the statements in lieu of correcting the statements to the SEC view, provided the SEC has not previously expressed its opinion on the matter in published material.

2. The Securities and Exchange Commission was established in 1934 to help regulate the U.S. securities market. Which of the following statements is true about the SEC?

   a. The SEC prohibits the sale of speculative securities.

   b. The SEC regulates securities offered for public sale.

   c. Registration with the SEC guarantees the accuracy of the registrant's prospectus.

   d. The SEC's initial influences and authority have diminished in recent years as the stock exchanges have become more organized and better able to police themselves.

   e. The SEC's powers are broad with respect to enforcement of its reporting requirements as established in the 1933 and 1934 acts but narrow with respect to new reporting requirements because these require confirmation by Congress.

3. The Securities and Exchange Commission is organized into several divisions and principal offices. The organization unit that reviews registration statements, annual reports, and proxy statements filed with the Commission is:

   a. The Office of the Chief Accountant.

   b. The Division of Corporation Finance.

   c. The Division of Enforcement.

   d. The Division of Market Regulation.

   e. The Office of the Comptroller.

4. Regulation S-X:

   a. Specifies the information that can be incorporated by reference from the annual report into the registration statement filed with the SEC.

    b. Specifies the regulation and reporting requirements of proxy solicitations.

    c. Provides the basis for generally accepted accounting principles.

    d. Specifies the general form and content requirements of financial statements filed with the SEC.

    e. Provides explanations and clarifications of changes in accounting or auditing procedures used in reports filed with the SEC.

5. Which of the following is not a purpose of the Securities Exchange Act of 1934?

    a. To establish federal regulation over securities exchanges and markets.

    b. To prevent unfair practices on securities exchanges and markets.

    c. To discourage and prevent the use of credit in financing excessive speculation in securities.

    d. To approve the securities of corporations which are to be traded publicly.

    e. To control unfair use of information by corporate insiders.

6. Regulation S-K disclosure requirements of the SEC deal with the company's business, properties, and legal proceedings; selected five-year summary financial data; management's discussion and analysis of financial condition and results of operations; and:

    a. The form and content of the required financial statements.

    b. The requirements for filing interim financial statements.

    c. Unofficial interpretations and practices regarding securities laws disclosure requirements.

    d. Supplementary financial information such as quarterly financial data and information on the effects of changing prices.

    e. The determination of the proper registration statement form to be used in any specific public offering of securities.

E14-2 Registration of New Securities [CMA Adapted]

Select the correct answer for each of the following questions.

1. In the registration and sales of new securities issues, the SEC:

    a. Endorses the investment merit of a security by allowing its registration to "go effective."

    b. Provides a rating of the investment quality of the security.

    c. May not allow the registration to "go effective" if it judges the security's investment risk to be too great.

    d. Allows all registrations to "go effective" if the issuing company's external accountant is satisfied that disclosures and representations are not misleading.

    e. Does not make any guarantees regarding the material accuracy of the registration statement.

2. The 1933 Securities Act provides for a 20-day waiting period between the filing and the effective date of the registration. During this waiting period the registrant is prohibited from:

    a. Preparing any amendments to the registration statement.

    b. Announcing the prospective issue of the securities being registered.

    c. Accepting offers to purchase the securities being registered from potential investors.

    d. Placing an advertisement indicating by whom orders for the securities being registered will be accepted.

    e. Issuing a prospectus in preliminary form.

3. Before turning over the proceeds of a securities offering to a registrant, the underwriters frequently require a "comfort letter" from the public accountant. The purpose of the comfort letter is:

    a. To remove the public distrust of a red herring by converting the letter into a prospectus.

    b. To find out if the public accountant found any adverse financial change between the date of audit and the effective date of the securities offering.

    c. To gain comfort from the public accountant's audit of the stub-period financial statements contained in the registration statement.

    d. To meet SEC regulations requiring the public accountant to give an opinion as an expert on the financial statements of the registrant.

    e. To conform to New York Stock Exchange (NYSE) member requirements that a comfort letter from a public accountant be obtained before public sale of securities.

E14-3 **Reporting Requirements of the SEC [CMA Adapted]**

Select the correct answer for each of the following questions.

1. Form 10-K is filed with the SEC to update the information a company supplied when filing a registration statement under the Securities and Exchange Act of 1934. Form 10-K is a report that is filed:

   a. Annually within 60 days of the end of a company's fiscal year.
   b. Semiannually within 30 days of the end of a company's second and fourth fiscal quarters.
   c. Quarterly within 45 days of the end of each quarter.
   d. Monthly within 2 weeks of the end of each month.
   e. Within 15 days of the occurrence of significant events.

2. Regulation S-X disclosure requirements of the SEC deal with:

   a. Changes in and disagreements with accountants on accounting and financial disclosure.
   b. Management's discussion and analysis of the financial condition and the results of operations.
   c. The requirements for filing interim financial statements and pro forma financial information.
   d. Summary information, risk factors, and the ratio of earnings to fixed charges.
   e. Information concerning recent sales of unregistered securities.

3. Form 10-Q is filed with the SEC to keep both investors and experts apprised of a company's operations and financial position. Form 10-Q is a report that is filed within:

   a. 90 days after the end of the fiscal year covered by the report.
   b. 35 days after the end of each of the first three quarters of each fiscal year.
   c. 90 days after the end of an employee stock purchase plan fiscal year.
   d. 15 days after the occurrence of a significant event.
   e. 60 days after the end of the fiscal year covered by the report.

4. A significant event affecting a company registered under the Securities and Exchange Act of 1934 should be reported on:

   a. Form 10-K.
   b. Form 10-Q.
   c. Form S-1.
   d. Form 8-K.
   e. Form 11-K.

5. Within 4 days after the occurrence of any event that is of material importance to the stockholders, a company must file a Form 8-K information report with the SEC to disclose the event. An example of the type of event required to be disclosed is:

   a. A salary increase to the officers.
   b. A contract to continue to employ the same certified public accounting firm as in the prior year.
   c. A change in projected earnings per share from $12.00 to $12.11 per share.
   d. The purchase of bank certificates of deposit.
   e. The acquisition of a large subsidiary other than in the ordinary course of business.

6. Form 8-K must generally be submitted to the SEC within 4 days after the occurrence of a significant event. Which one of the following is not an event that would be reported by Form 8-K?

   a. The replacement of the registrant company's external auditor.
   b. A change in accounting principle.
   c. The resignation of one of the directors of the registrant company.
   d. A significant acquisition or disposition of assets.
   e. A change in control of the registrant company.

7. Which one of the following items is not required to be included in a company's periodic 8-K report filed with the SEC when significant events occur?

   a. Acquisition or disposition of a significant amount of assets.

   b.   Instigation or termination of material legal proceedings other than routine litigation incidental to the business.

   c.   Change in certifying public accountant.

   d.   Election of new vice president of finance to replace the retiring incumbent.

   e.   Default in the payment of principal, interest, or sinking fund installment.

E14-4   Corporate Governance [CMA Adapted]

Select the correct answer for each of the following questions.

1.   A major impact of the Foreign Corrupt Practices Act of 1977 is that registrants subject to the Securities Exchange Act of 1934 are required to:

   a.   Keep records that reflect the transactions and dispositions of assets and maintain a system of internal accounting controls.

   b.   Provide access to records by authorized agencies of the federal government.

   c.   Record all correspondence with foreign nations.

   d.   Prepare financial statements in accordance with international accounting standards.

   e.   Produce full, fair, and accurate periodic reports on foreign commerce, foreign political party affiliations, or both.

2.   The requirements of the Foreign Corrupt Practices Act of 1977 to devise and maintain an adequate system of internal accounting control is assigned in the act to the:

   a.   Chief financial officer.

   b.   Board of directors.

   c.   Director of internal auditing.

   d.   Company's external auditor.

   e.   Company as a whole with no designation of specific persons or positions.

3.   Shareholders may ask or allow others to enter their vote at a shareholders' meeting that they are unable to attend. The document furnished to shareholders to provide background information for their vote is a:

   a.   Registration statement.

   b.   Proxy statement.

   c.   10-K report.

   d.   Prospectus.

4.   Formation and meaningful utilization of an audit committee of the board of directors is required of publicly traded companies that are subject to the rules of the:

   a.   Securities and Exchange Commission.

   b.   Financial Accounting Standards Board.

   c.   National Association of Securities Dealers.

   d.   American Institute of Certified Public Accountants.

5.   An external auditor's involvement with a Form 10-Q that is being prepared for filing with the SEC would most likely consist of:

   a.   An audit of the financial statements included in Form 10-Q.

   b.   A compilation report on the financial statements included in Form 10-Q.

   c.   Issuing a comfort letter that covers stub-period financial data.

   d.   Issuing an opinion on the internal controls under which the Form 10-Q data were developed.

   e.   A review of the interim financial statements included in Form 10-Q.

E14-5   Application of Securities Act of 1933 [AICPA Adapted]

Various Enterprises Corporation is a medium-size conglomerate listed on the American Stock Exchange. It is constantly in the process of acquiring small corporations and invariably needs additional money. Among its diversified holdings is a citrus grove that it purchased eight years ago as an investment. The grove's current fair market value is in excess of $2 million. Various also owns 800,000 shares of Resistance Corporation, which it acquired in the open market over a period of years. These shares represent a 17 percent minority interest in Resistance and are worth approximately $2.5 million. Various does its short-term financing with a consortium of banking institutions. Several of these loans are maturing; in addition to renewing these loans, it wishes to increase its short-term debt from $3 to $4 million.

Because of these factors, Various is considering resorting to one or all of the following alternatives to raise additional working capital.

1. An offering of 500 citrus grove units at $5,000 per unit. Each unit would give the purchaser a 0.2 percent ownership interest in the citrus grove development. Various would furnish management and operation services for a fee under a management contract, and net proceeds would be paid to the unit purchasers. The offering would be confined almost exclusively to the state in which the groves are located or in the adjacent state in which Various is incorporated.

2. An increase in the short-term borrowing by $1 million from the banking institution that currently provides short-term funds. The existing debt would be consolidated, extended, and increased to $4 million and would mature over a nine-month period. This would be evidenced by a short-term note.

3. Sale of the 17 percent minority interest in Resistance in the open market through its brokers over a period of time and in such a way as to minimize decreasing the value of the stock. The stock is to be sold in an orderly manner in the ordinary course of the broker's business.

Required

In separate paragraphs discuss the impact of the registration requirements of the Securities Act of 1933 on each of the proposed alternatives.

E14-6 **Federal Securities Acts [AICPA Adapted]**
Select the correct answer for each of the following questions.

1. Which of the following statements concerning the prospectus required by the Securities Act of 1933 is correct?

   a. The prospectus is a part of the registration statement.

   b. The prospectus should enable the SEC to pass on the merits of the securities.

   c. The prospectus must be filed after an offer to sell.

   d. The prospectus is prohibited from being distributed to the public until the SEC approves the accuracy of the facts embodied therein.

2. Which of the following securities would be regulated by the provisions of the Securities Act of 1933?

   a. Securities issued by not-for-profit, charitable organizations.

   b. Securities guaranteed by domestic governmental organizations.

   c. Securities issued by savings and loan associations.

   d. Securities issued by insurance companies.

3. Which of the following securities is exempt from registration under the Securities Act of 1933?

   a. Shares of nonvoting common stock, provided their par value is less than $1.

   b. A class of stock given in exchange for another class by the issuer to its existing stockholders without the issuer paying a commission.

   c. Limited partnership interests sold for the purpose of acquiring funds to invest in bonds issued by the United States.

   d. Corporate debentures that were previously subject to an effective registration statement, provided they are convertible into shares of common stock.

4. Pix Corp. is making a $6,000,000 stock offering. Pix wants the offering exempt from registration under the Securities Act of 1933. Which of the following provisions of the act would Pix have to comply with for the offering to be exempt?

   a. Regulation A.

   b. Regulation D, Rule 504.

   c. Regulation D, Rule 505.

   d. Regulation D, Rule 506.

5. An offering made under the provisions of Regulation A of the Securities Act of 1933 requires that the issuer:

   a. File an offering circular with the SEC.

   b. Sell only to accredited investors.

    c. Provide investors with the prior four years' audited financial statements.

    d. Provide investors with a proxy registration statement.

6. Integral Corp. has assets in excess of $4 million, has 350 stockholders, and has issued common and preferred stock. Integral is subject to the reporting provisions of the Securities Exchange Act of 1934. For its 2000 fiscal year, Integral filed the following with the SEC: quarterly reports, an annual report, and a periodic report listing newly appointed officers of the corporation. Integral did not notify the SEC of stockholder "short swing" profits; did not report that a competitor made a tender offer to Integral's stockholders; and did not report changes in the price of its stock as sold on the New York Stock Exchange. Under SEC reporting requirements, which of the following was Integral required to do?

    a. Report the tender offer to the SEC.

    b. Notify the SEC of stockholder "short swing" profits.

    c. File the periodic report listing newly appointed officers.

    d. Report the changes in the market price of its stock.

7. Which of the following factors, by itself, requires a corporation to comply with the reporting requirements of the Securities Exchange Act of 1934?

    a. Six hundred employees.

    b. Shares listed on a national securities exchange.

    c. Total assets of $2 million.

    d. Four hundred holders of equity securities.

8. Which of the following persons is *not* an insider of a corporation subject to the Securities Exchange Act of 1934 registration and reporting requirements?

    a. An attorney for the corporation.

    b. An owner of 5 percent of the corporation's outstanding debentures.

    c. A member of the board of directors.

    d. A stockholder who owns 10 percent of the outstanding common stock.

Chapter **Fifteen**

Partnerships: Formation, Operation, and Changes in Membership

The number of partnerships in the United States has been estimated to be between 1.5 and 2.0 million, second only to sole proprietorships, which number in excess of 15 million businesses. In contrast, there are about 1 million corporations in the United States. Accountants are often called on to aid in the formation and operation of partnerships to ensure proper measurement and valuation of the partnership's transactions. This chapter focuses on the formation and operation of partnerships, including accounting for the addition of new partners and the retirement of a present partner. Chapter 16 presents the accounting for the termination and liquidation of partnerships.

Partnerships are a popular form of business because they are easy to form and they allow several individuals to combine their talents and skills in a particular business venture. In addition, partnerships provide a means of obtaining more equity capital than a single individual can obtain and allow the sharing of risks for rapidly growing businesses.

Accounting for partnerships requires recognition of several important factors. First, from an accounting viewpoint, the partnership is a separate business entity. The Internal Revenue Code, however, views the partnership form as a conduit only, not separable from the business interests of the individual partners. Therefore, several differences exist between tax and financial accounting for specific events, such as the value assigned to assets contributed in the formation of the partnership. This chapter presents the generally accepted accounting principles of partnership accounting. A brief discussion of the tax aspects of a partnership is presented in Appendix 15A to this chapter.

Second, although many partnerships account for their operations using accrual accounting, some partnerships use the cash basis or modified cash basis of accounting. These alternatives are allowed because the partnership records are maintained for the partners and must reflect their information needs. The partnership's financial statements are usually prepared only for the partners but occasionally for the partnership's creditors. Unlike publicly traded corporations, most partnerships are not required to have annual audits of their financial statements. Although many partnerships adhere to generally accepted accounting principles (GAAP), deviations from GAAP are found in practice. The specific needs of the partners should be the primary criteria for determining the accounting policies to be used for a specific partnership.

NATURE OF PARTNERSHIP ENTITY

The partnership form of business has several unique elements because of its legal and accounting status. The following section describes the major characteristics that distinguish the partnership form of organization.

Legal Regulation of Partnerships

Each state regulates the partnerships that are formed in it. Accountants advising partnerships must be familiar with partnership laws because these laws describe many of the rights of each partner and of creditors during the creation, operation, and liquidation of the partnership. Each state tends to begin with a uniform or model act and then modifies it to fit that state's business culture and history. The Uniform Partnership Act of 1914 served for many years as the model for defining the rights and responsibilities of the partners to each other and to the creditors of the partnership. In 1994 the National Conference of Commissioners on Uniform State Laws (NCCUSL) approved the first major revision of the model act to better reflect current business practices while also retaining many of the valuable provisions of the original act. This 1994 revision was titled the Revised Uniform Partnership Act (RUPA). During the next three years the NCCUSL continued to make small revisions of the model act and in 1997 it approved the final model as the **Uniform Partnership Act of 1997 (UPA 1997)**. Most states have now adopted the more recent model partnership act and it will be used for discussion and illustration in this and the next chapter on partnerships.

Definition of a Partnership

Section 202 of the UPA 1997 states that, ". . . the association of two or more persons to carry on as co-owners of a business for profit forms a partnership . . ." This definition encompasses three distinct factors:

1. *Association of two or more persons.* The "persons" are usually individuals; however, they may also be corporations or other partnerships.
2. *To carry on as co-owners.* This means that each partner has the apparent authority, unless restricted by the partnership agreement, to act as an agent of the partnership for transactions in the ordinary course of business of the kind carried on by the partnership. These transactions can legally bind the partnership to third parties.
3. *Business for profit.* A partnership may be formed to perform any legal business, trade, profession, or other service. However, the partnership must attempt to make a profit; therefore, not-for-profit entities, such as fraternal groups, may not organize as partnerships.

Formation of a Partnership

A primary advantage of the partnership form of entity is ease of formation. The agreement to form a partnership may be as informal as a handshake or as formal as a many-paged partnership agreement. Each partner must agree to the formation agreement, and partners are strongly advised to have a formal written agreement to avoid potential problems that may arise during the operation of the business. It is usually true that if the potential partners cannot agree on the various operating aspects before a partnership is formed, many future disputes may arise that could cause severe management problems and that might seriously imperil the operations of the partnership.

The partnership agreement should include the following items:

1. The name of the partnership and the names of the partners.
2. The type of business to be conducted by the partnership and the duration of the partnership agreement.
3. The initial capital contribution of each partner and the method by which to account for future capital contributions.
4. A complete specification of the profit or loss distribution, including salaries, interest on capital balances, bonuses, limits on withdrawals in anticipation of profits, and the percentages used to distribute any residual profit or loss.
5. Procedures used for changes in the partnership, such as admission of new partners and the retirement of a partner.
6. Other aspects of operations the partners decide on, such as the management rights of each partner, election procedures, and accounting methods.

Each partner should sign the partnership agreement to indicate acceptance of the terms. A carefully prepared partnership agreement can eliminate many of the more common types of problems and disputes that may arise in the partnership's future operations.

Other Major Characteristics of Partnerships

After a state adopts the provisions of the UPA 1997, all partnerships formed in that state are regulated by the act. For partnerships that do not have a formal partnership agreement, the act provides the legal framework that governs the relationships among the partners and the rights of creditors of the partnership; in essence, the UPA 1997 becomes the partnership agreement for those partnerships that do not have one. The following presents the sections of the UPA 1997 applicable to the formation and operation of a partnership. Chapter 16 will present the sections of the UPA 1997 applicable to the dissolution and liquidation of a partnership.

1. *Partnership agreement.* The UPA 1997 governs in those partnership relations that are not specifically presented in the partnership agreement; thus, the UPA 1997 is used by the courts when there is no partnership agreement. There are several provisions of the UPA 1997 that are not waivable by partnership agreement. For example, a partnership may not restrict a partner's rights of access to the partnership's books and records, eliminate the obligations of partners for good faith and fair dealing with the other partners and the partnership, restrict any rights of third parties under the act, or reduce any legal rights of individual partners.

2. *Partnership as a separate entity.* A partnership is a separate business entity distinct from its partners. This **entity concept** means that a partnership can sue or be sued and that partnership property belongs to the partnership and not to any individual partner. Thus, there is no new partnership entity when there is a membership change in the partners (a new partner is admitted or a partner leaves the partnership).

3. *Partner is an agent of the partnership.* Each partner is an agent of the partnership for transactions of the kind carried on in the ordinary course of the partnership business, unless the partner did not have the authority to act for the partnership in that specific matter and the third party knew or had received a notification that the partner lacked authority. This agency relationship among the partners is very important. If the partnership determines that only specific partners shall have the authority for specific business transactions, then the partnership must make third parties aware of the limitations of authority of other partners. This notice should be in a public form either as a formal filing of a statement of partnership authority (discussed in the next point) or in direct communications with third parties. Otherwise, third parties may presume a partner has the authority to act as an agent for the partnership in those normal business transactions of the type engaged in for the business in which the partnership operates.

4. *Statement of partnership authority.* A **Statement of Partnership Authority** describes the partnership and identifies the specific authority of partners to transact specific types of business on behalf of the partnership. This voluntary statement is filed with the secretary of the state. The statement is a notice of any limitations on the rights of specific partners to enter into specific types of transactions. Partnerships should file these statements particularly for partnership transactions in real estate. The act states that a filed statement of partnership authority is sufficient constructive notice to third parties for partnership real estate transactions, but it is not necessarily sufficient notice for other types of partnership transactions.

5. *Partner's liability is joint and several.* All partners are liable jointly and severally for all obligations of the partnership unless otherwise provided by law. In the event a partnership fails and its assets are not sufficient to pay its obligations, partners are required to make contributions to the partnership in the proportion to which they share partnership losses. If a partner fails to make a contribution of the amount required, then all other partners must contribute in the proportion to which those partners share partnership losses. Partnership creditors must first be satisfied from partnership assets and additional partner contributions are classified as partnership assets. If a partnership creditor takes legal action against an individual partner for a partnership obligation, the partnership creditor does not have any superior rights to the partner's individual assets. In this case, the partnership creditor joins with the other personal creditors.

6. *Partner's rights and duties.* Each partner is to have a capital account presenting the amount of that partner's contributions to the partnership, net of any liabilities, and the partner's share of the partnership profits or losses, less any distributions. The partner is entitled to an equal share of the profits or losses unless otherwise agreed to in the partnership agreement. New partners can be admitted only with the consent of all of the partners. Each partner has a right of access to the partnership's books and records, and each partner has a duty to act for the partnership in good faith and fair dealing.

7. *Partner's transferable interest in the partnership.* Under the entity approach to a partnership stated in the act, a partner is not a co-owner of any partnership property. This means that the only **transferable interest** of a partner is the partner's share of the profits and losses of the partnership and the right to receive distributions, including any liquidating distribution. A partner may not transfer any rights of management or authority to transact any of the partnership's business operations. Thus the partner's individual creditors may not attach any of the partnership's assets but a partner's personal creditor may obtain a legal judgment for attachment of the partner's transferable interest.

8. *Partner's dissociation.* A **partner's dissociation** means that the partner can no longer act on behalf of the partnership. A partner is dissociated from a partnership when any of the following events occurs: (*a*) the partner gives notice to the partnership of the partner's express will to withdraw as a partner; (*b*) the partner is expelled from the partnership in accordance with the partnership agreement, typically because the partner has violated some part of the partnership agreement or it becomes unlawful for the partnership to continue business with that partner; (*c*) by one of several judicial determinations (such as the partner committing a material breach of the partnership agreement, or the partner engaging in serious conduct that materially and adversely affects the partnership), (*d*) the partner becoming a debtor in bankruptcy, or (*e*) the partner's death.

Types of Limited Partnerships

Many persons view the possibility of personal liability for a partnership's obligations as a major disadvantage of the general partnership form of business. For this reason, sometimes people become limited partners in one of the several limited partnership forms. A limited partnership (LP) is different from a limited liability partnership (LLP), or a limited liability limited partnership (LLLP). The variations are based on the degree of liability shield provided to the partners.

Limited partnerships (LP)   In a limited partnership (LP), there is at least one general partner and one or more limited partners. The general partner is personally liable for the obligations of the partnership and has management responsibility. Limited partners are liable only to the extent of their capital contribution but do not have any management authority. The Uniform Limited Partnership Act of 2001 (ULPA 2001) is the model legal act used to regulate limited partnerships and has been adopted in many states. Accounting for the investment in a limited partnership is based on an evaluation of control. Typically, the general partner has the necessary elements of operational control of the limited partnership and will consolidate the investment on the general partner's books. The limited partners typically use the equity method to account for their investments. However, in 2005, the Emerging Issues Task Force (EITF) reached consensus in **EITF Issue No. 04-05,** "Determining Whether a General Partner, or the General Partners as a Group, Controls a Limited Partnership or Similar Entity When the Limited Partners Have Certain Rights" (EITF 04-05). The EITF examined cases in which the limited partners have either (*a*) the ability to dissolve the limited partnership or to remove the general partners without cause (the so-called "kick-out right"), or (*b*) have substantive participating rights to be actively engaged in the significant decisions of the limited partnership's business. In these two cases, the presumption of control by the general partners could be overcome and then each of the general partners would account for its investment in the limited partnership using the equity method of accounting. The identifier, LP or Limited Partnership, must be included in the name or identification of the limited partnership.

Limited Liability Partnerships (LLP)   A limited liability partnership (LLP) is one in which each partner has some degree of liability shield. There are no general or limited partners in an

LLP; thus each partner has the rights and duties of a general partner, but limited legal liability. A partner in a limited liability partnership is not personally liable for a partnership obligation. However, several states have defined that each partner in an LLP is fully liable for the obligations of the partnership, though not for acts of professional negligence or malpractice committed by other partners. Some legal support for the LLP came as a result of the fact that most professional service partnerships, such as accounting firms, have significant amounts of insurance to cover judgments in lawsuits and other losses from offering services. A limited liability partnership must identify itself as such by adding the LLP letters behind the name of the partnership in all correspondence or other means of identification of the firm. Virtually all large public accounting firms are LLPs. This designation has not changed the nature of accounting services provided to clients and has been generally accepted in the business market.

Limited Liability Limited Partnership (LLLP) In most states, a limited partnership may elect to become a limited liability limited partnership. In an LLLP, each partner is liable only for the business obligations of the partnership, and not for acts of malpractice or other wrongdealing by the other partners in the normal course of the partnership's business. The ULPA 2001 includes the regulatory guidance for LLLPs. The advantage of an LLLP is that general partners, even though responsible for management of the partnership, have no personal liability for partnership obligations, similar to the shield provided to limited partners. The identifier "LLLP" or the phrase "limited liability limited partnership" must be included in the name or identification of the entity.

ACCOUNTING FOR THE FORMATION OF A PARTNERSHIP

At the formation of a partnership, it is necessary to assign a proper value to the noncash assets and liabilities contributed by the partners. An item contributed by a partner becomes partnership property. The partnership must clearly distinguish between capital contributions and loans made to the partnership by individual partners. Loan arrangements should be evidenced by promissory notes or other legal documents necessary to show that a loan arrangement exists between the partnership and an individual partner. Also, it is important to clearly distinguish between tangible assets that are owned by the partnership and those specific assets that are owned by individual partners but are used by the partnership. Accurate records of the partnership's tangible assets must be maintained.

The contributed assets should be valued at their fair values, which may require appraisals or other valuation techniques. Liabilities assumed by the partnership should be valued at the present value of the remaining cash flows.

The individual partners must agree to the percentage of equity that each will have in the net assets of the partnership. Generally, the capital balance is determined by the proportionate share of each partner's capital contribution. For example, if A contributes 70 percent of the net assets in a partnership with B, then A will have a 70 percent capital share and B will have a 30 percent capital share. In recognition of intangible factors, such as a partner's special expertise or necessary business connections, however, partners may agree to any proportional division of capital. Therefore, before recording the initial capital contribution, all partners must agree on the valuation of the net assets and on each partner's capital share.

Illustration of Accounting for Partnership Formation

The following illustration is used as the basis for the remaining discussion in this chapter. Alt, a sole proprietor, has been developing software for several types of computers. The business has the following account balances as of December 31, 20X0:

Cash	$ 3,000	Liabilities	$10,000
Inventory	7,000	Alt, Capital	15,000
Equipment	20,000		
Less Accumulated			
Depreciation	(5,000)		
Total Assets	$25,000	Total Liabilities and Capital	$25,000

Alt needs additional technical assistance to meet the increasing sales and offers Blue an interest in the business. Alt and Blue agree to form a partnership. Alt's business is audited, and its net assets are appraised. The audit and appraisal disclose that $1,000 of liabilities has not been recorded, inventory has a market value of $9,000, and the equipment has a fair value of $19,000.

Alt and Blue prepare and sign a partnership agreement that includes all significant operating policies. Blue will contribute $10,000 cash for a one-third capital interest. The AB Partnership is to acquire all of Alt's business and assume its debts.

The entry to record the initial capital contribution on the partnership's books is:

January 1, 20X1			
(1)	Cash	13,000	
	Inventory	9,000	
	Equipment	19,000	
	Liabilities		11,000
	Alt, Capital		20,000
	Blue, Capital		10,000

Formation of AB Partnership by capital contributions of Alt and Blue.

Key Observations from Illustration

Note that the partnership is an accounting entity separate from each of the partners and that the assets and liabilities are recorded at their market values at the time of contribution. No accumulated depreciation is carried forward from the sole proprietorship to the partnership. All liabilities are recognized and recorded.

The partnership's capital is $30,000. This is the sum of the individual partners' capital accounts and is the value of the partnership's assets less liabilities. The fundamental accounting equation—assets less liabilities equals capital—is used often in partnership accounting. Blue is to receive a one-third capital interest in the partnership with a contribution of $10,000. In this case, his capital interest equals his capital contribution.

Each partner's capital amount recorded does not necessarily have to equal his or her capital contribution. The partners could decide to divide the total capital equally regardless of the source of the contribution. For example, although Alt contributed $20,000 of the $30,000 partnership capital, he could agree to $15,000 as his initial capital balance and permit Blue the remaining $15,000 as a capital credit. On the surface this may not seem to be a reasonable action by Alt, but it is possible that Blue has some particularly important business experience needed by the partnership and Alt agrees to the additional credit to Blue in recognition of his experience and skills. The key point is that the partners may allocate the capital contributions in any manner they desire. The accountant must be sure that all partners agree to the allocation and then record it accordingly.

ACCOUNTING FOR OPERATIONS OF A PARTNERSHIP

A partnership provides services or sells products in pursuit of profit. These transactions are recorded in the appropriate journals and ledger accounts. Many partnerships use accrual accounting and generally accepted accounting principles to maintain their books because GAAP results in better measures of income than alternative accounting methods such as the cash basis or modified cash basis. Partnership financial statements are prepared for the partners and occasionally for partnership creditors. Some partnerships may deviate from GAAP accounting to simplify recordkeeping or to reflect current asset values for an ongoing partnership. Although most partnerships are not audited, in the event an audit is made of a partnership that does not follow GAAP, the partnership's financial statements will not receive a "clean" or unqualified opinion because of its departures from GAAP. Accountants often encourage the use of GAAP for financial statement purposes because the partners may then compare the partnership's financial statements with those of other business entities; if a creditor requires audited financial statements as a condition for a loan to the partnership, the partnership's statements are not restricted from receiving an unqualified audit opinion.

Partners' Accounts

The partnership may maintain several accounts for each partner in its accounting records. These *partners' accounts* are as follows:

Capital Accounts

The initial investment of a partner, any subsequent capital contributions, profit or loss distributions, and any withdrawals of capital by the partner are ultimately recorded in the partner's capital account. Each partner has one capital account, which usually has a credit balance. On occasion, a partner's capital account may have a debit balance, called a *deficiency* or sometimes termed a *deficit,* which occurs because the partner's share of losses and withdrawals exceeds his or her capital contribution and share of profits. A deficiency is usually eliminated by additional capital contributions. The balance in the capital account represents the partner's share of the partnership's net assets.

Drawing Accounts

Partners generally make withdrawals of assets from the partnership during the year in anticipation of profits. A separate drawing account often is used to record the periodic withdrawals and is then closed to the partner's capital account at the end of the period. For example, the following entry is made in the AB Partnership's books for a $3,000 cash withdrawal by Blue on May 1, 20X1:

May 1, 20X1			
(2)	Blue, Drawing	3,000	
	Cash		3,000
	Withdrawal of $3,000 by Blue.		

Noncash drawings should be valued at their market values at the date of the withdrawal. A few partnerships make an exception to the rule of market value for partners' withdrawals of inventory. They record withdrawals of inventory at cost, thereby not recording a gain or loss on these drawings.

Loan Accounts

The partnership may look to its present partners for additional financing. Any loans between a partner and the partnership should always be accompanied by proper loan documentation such as a promissory note. A loan from a partner is shown as a payable on the partnership's books, the same as any other loan. Unless all partners agree otherwise, the partnership is obligated to pay interest on the loan to the individual partner. Note that interest is *not* required to be paid on capital investments unless the partnership agreement states that capital interest is to be paid. The partnership records interest on loans as an operating expense. Alternatively, the partnership may lend money to a partner, in which case it records a loan receivable from the partner. Again, unless all partners agree otherwise, these loans should bear interest, and the interest income should be recognized on the partnership's income statement. The following entry is made to record a $4,000, 10 percent, one-year loan from Alt to the partnership on July 1, 20X1:

July 1, 20X1			
(3)	Cash	4,000	
	Loan Payable to Alt		4,000
	Sign loan agreement with partner Alt.		

The loan payable to Alt is reported in the partnership's balance sheet. A loan from a partner is a related-party transaction for which separate footnote disclosure is required, and it must be reported as a separate balance sheet item, not included with other liabilities.

ALLOCATING PROFIT OR LOSS TO PARTNERS

Profit or loss is allocated to the partners at the end of each period in accordance with the partnership agreement. If no partnership agreement exists, section 401 of the UPA 1997 declares that all partners are to share profits and losses equally. Virtually all partnerships have a profit or loss allocation agreement. The agreement must be followed precisely, and if it is unclear, the accountant should make sure that all partners agree to the profit or loss distribution. Many problems and later arguments can be avoided by carefully specifying the profit or loss distribution in the articles of copartnership.

A wide range of *profit distribution plans* is found in the business world. Some partnerships have straightforward distribution plans; others have extremely complex ones. It is the accountant's responsibility to distribute the profit or loss according to the partnership agreement regardless of how simple or complex that agreement is. Profit distributions are similar to dividends for a corporation: These distributions should not be included on the partnership's income statement regardless of how the profit is distributed. Profit distributions are recorded directly into the partner's capital accounts, not treated as expense items.

Most partnerships use one or more of the following distribution methods:

1. Preselected ratio.
2. Interest on capital balances.
3. Salaries to partners.
4. Bonuses to partners.

Preselected ratios are usually the result of negotiations between the partners. Ratios for profit distributions may be based on the percentage of total partnership capital, time and effort invested in the partnership, or a variety of other factors. Smaller partnerships often split profits evenly among the partners. In addition, some partnerships have different ratios if the firm suffers a loss rather than earns a profit. The partnership form of business allows a wide selection of profit distribution ratios to meet the partners' individual desires.

Distributing partnership income based on interest on capital balances recognizes the contribution of the partners' capital investments to the partnership's profit-generating capacity. This interest on capital is generally not an expense of the partnership; it is a distribution of profits. If one or more of the partners' services are important to the partnership, the profit distribution agreement may provide for salaries or bonuses. Again, these salaries paid to partners are generally a form of profit distribution, not an expense of the partnership. Occasionally, the distribution process may depend on the size of the profit or may differ if the partnership has a loss for the period. For example, salaries to partners might be paid only if revenue exceeds expenses by a certain amount. The accountant must carefully read the partnership agreement to determine the precise profit distribution plan for the specific circumstances at the time.

The profit or loss distribution is recorded with a closing entry at the end of each period. The revenue and expenses are closed into an income summary account or directly into the partners' capital accounts. In the following examples, an income summary account is used, the balance of which is net income or net loss after the revenue and expense accounts are closed and before the income or loss is distributed to the partners' capital accounts.

Illustrations of Profit Allocation

During 20X1, the AB Partnership earns $45,000 of revenue and incurs $35,000 in expenses, leaving a profit of $10,000 for the year. Alt maintains a capital balance of $20,000 during the year, but Blue's capital investment varies during the year as follows:

Date	Debit	Credit	Balance
January 1			$10,000
May 1	$3,000		7,000
September 1		$500	7,500
November 1	1,000		6,500
December 31			6,500

The debits of $3,000 and $1,000 are recorded in Blue's drawing account; the additional investment is credited to his capital account.

Arbitrary Profit Sharing Ratio

Alt and Blue could agree to share profits in a ratio unrelated to their capital balances or to any other operating feature of the partnership. For example, the partners might agree to share profits or losses in the ratio of 60 percent to Alt and 40 percent to Blue. Some partnership agreements specify this ratio as 3:2. The following schedule illustrates how the net income is distributed using a 3:2 profit sharing ratio:

	Alt	Blue	Total
Profit sharing percentage	60%	40%	100%
Net income			$10,000
Allocate 60:40	$6,000	$4,000	(10,000)
Total	$6,000	$4,000	$ -0-

This schedule shows how net income is distributed to the partners' capital accounts. The actual distribution is accomplished by closing the Income Summary account. In addition, the drawing accounts are closed to the capital accounts at the end of the period.

December 31, 20X1				
(4)	Blue, Capital		4,000	
	Blue, Drawing			4,000
	Close Blue's drawing account.			
(5)	Revenue		45,000	
	Expenses			35,000
	Income Summary			10,000
	Close revenue and expenses.			
(6)	Income Summary		10,000	
	Alt, Capital			6,000
	Blue, Capital			4,000
	Distribute profit in accordance with partnership agreement.			

Interest on Capital Balances

The partnership agreement may provide for interest to be credited on the partners' capital balances as part of the distribution of profits. The rate of interest is often a stated percentage, but some partnerships use an interest rate that is determined by reference to current U.S. Treasury rates or current money market rates.

As stated earlier, interest calculated on partners' capital is generally a form of profit distribution. The calculation is made after net income is determined in order to decide how to distribute the income.

Particular caution must be exercised whenever interest on capital balances is included in the profit distribution plan. For example, the amount of the distribution can be significantly different depending on whether the interest is computed on beginning capital balances, ending capital balances, or average capital balances for the period. Most provisions for interest on capital specify that a weighted-average capital should be used. This method explicitly recognizes the time span for which each capital level is maintained during the period. For example, Blue's weighted-average capital balance for 20X1 is computed as follows:

Date	Debit	Credit	Balance	Months Maintained	Months Times Dollar Balance
January 1			$10,000	4	$40,000
May 1	$3,000		7,000	4	28,000
September 1		$500	7,500	2	15,000
November 1	1,000		6,500	2	13,000
Total				12	$96,000
Average capital ($96,000 ÷ 12 months)					$ 8,000

If Alt and Blue agreed to allow interest of 15 percent on the weighted-average capital balances with any remaining profit to be distributed in the 60:40 ratio, the distribution of the $10,000 profit would be calculated as follows:

	Alt	Blue	Total
Profit percentage	60%	40%	100%
Average capital	$20,000	$8,000	
Net income			$10,000
Interest on average capital (15%)	$ 3,000	$1,200	(4,200)
Residual income			$ 5,800
Allocate 60:40	3,480	2,320	(5,800)
Total	$ 6,480	$3,520	$ -0-

Salaries

Salaries to partners are generally included as part of the profit distribution plan to recognize and compensate for differing amounts of personal services partners provide to the business.

Section 401 of the UPA 1997 states that a partner is not entitled to compensation for services performed for the partnership except for reasonable compensation for services in winding up the business of the partnership. Some partnership agreements, however, do specify a management fee to be paid to a partner who provides very specific administration responsibilities.

A general precept of partnership accounting is that salaries to partners are not operating expenses but are part of the profit distribution plan. This precept is closely related to the proprietary concept of owner's equity. According to the proprietary theory, the proprietor invests capital and personal services in pursuit of income. The earnings are a result of those two investments. The same logic applies to the partnership form of organization. Some partners invest capital while others invest personal time. Those who invest capital are typically rewarded with interest on their capital balances; those who invest personal time are rewarded with salaries. However, both interest and salaries are a result of the respective investments and are used not in the determination of income but in the determination of the proportion of income to credit to each partner's capital account. An interesting question arises if the partnership experiences losses. Can salaries to the partners during the year be treated as a distribution of profits? Although any amounts actually paid to partners during the year are really drawings made in anticipation of profits, the agreed salary amounts usually are added to the loss and that total is then distributed to the partners' capital accounts. Caution should be exercised if the partnership experiences a loss during the year. Some partnership agreements specify different distributions for profit than for losses. The accountant must be especially careful to follow precisely the partnership agreement when distributing the period's profit or loss to the partners.

To examine partnership salaries, assume that the partnership agreement provides for salaries of $2,000 to Alt and $5,000 to Blue. Any remainder is to be distributed in the profit and loss–sharing ratio of 60:40 percent. The profit distribution is calculated as follows:

	Alt	Blue	Total
Profit percentage	60%	40%	100%
Net income			$10,000
Salary	$2,000	$5,000	(7,000)
Residual income			$ 3,000
Allocate 60:40	1,800	1,200	(3,000)
Total	$3,800	$6,200	$ -0-

Bonuses

Bonuses are sometimes used as a means of providing additional compensation to partners who have provided services to the partnership. Bonuses are typically stated as a percentage of income either before or after the bonus. Sometimes the partnership agreement requires a minimum income to be earned before a bonus is calculated. The bonus is easily calculated by deriving and solving an equation. For example, a bonus of 10 percent of income in excess of $5,000 is to be credited to Blue's capital account before distributing the remaining profit. In Case 1, the bonus is computed as a percentage of income *before* subtracting the bonus. In Case 2, the bonus is computed as a percentage of income *after* subtracting the bonus.

Case 1:

$$\text{Bonus} = X\%(\text{NI} - \text{MIN})$$

where: $X\%$ = The bonus percentage

NI = Net income before bonus

MIN = Minimum amount of income before bonus

$$\text{Bonus} = .10(\$10,000 - \$5,000) = \$500$$

Case 2:

$$\text{Bonus} = X\%(\text{NI} - \text{MIN} - \text{Bonus})$$
$$= .10(\$10,000 - \$5,000 - \text{Bonus})$$
$$= .10(\$5,000 - \text{Bonus})$$
$$= \$500 - .10\,\text{Bonus}$$
$$1.10\,\text{Bonus} = \$500$$
$$\text{Bonus} = \$454.55$$

The distribution of net income based on Case 2 is calculated as follows:

	Alt	Blue	Total
Profit percentage	60%	40%	100%
Net income			$10,000
Bonus to partner		$ 455	(455)
Residual income			$ 9,545
Allocate 60:40	$5,727	3,818	(9,545)
Total	$5,727	$4,273	$ -0-

Multiple Bases of Profit Allocation

A partnership agreement may describe a combination of several allocation procedures to be used to distribute profit. For example, the profit and loss agreement of the AB Partnership specifies the following allocation method:

1. Interest of 15 percent on weighted-average capital balances.
2. Salaries of $2,000 for Alt and $5,000 for Blue.
3. A bonus of 10 percent to be paid to Blue on partnership income exceeding $5,000 before subtracting the bonus, partners' salaries, and interest on capital balances.
4. Any residual to be allocated in the ratio of 60 percent to Alt and 40 percent to Blue.

The partnership agreement should also contain a provision to specify the allocation process in the event that partnership income is not sufficient to satisfy all allocation procedures. Some partnerships specify a profit distribution to be followed to whatever extent is possible. Most agreements specify that the entire process is to be completed and any remainder is to be allocated in the profit and loss ratio as illustrated in the following schedule:

	Alt	Blue	Total
Profit percentage	60%	40%	100%
Average capital	$20,000	$8,000	
Net income:			$10,000
Step 1:			
Interest on average capital (15 percent)	$ 3,000	$1,200	(4,200)
Remaining after step 1			$ 5,800
Step 2:			
Salary	2,000	5,000	(7,000)
Deficiency after step 2			$ (1,200)
Step 3:			
Bonus		500	(500)
Deficiency after step 3			$ (1,700)
Step 4:			
Allocate 60:40	(1,020)	(680)	1,700
Total	$ 3,980	$6,020	$ -0-

In this case, the first two distribution steps created a deficiency. The AB Partnership agreement provided that the entire profit distribution process must be completed and any deficiency distributed in the profit and loss ratio. A partnership agreement could specify that the profit distribution process stop at any point in the event of an operating loss or the creation of a deficiency. Again, it is important for the accountant to have a thorough knowledge of the partnership agreement before beginning the profit distribution process.

Special Profit Allocation Methods

Some partnerships distribute net income on the basis of other criteria. For example, most public accounting partnerships distribute profit on the basis of partnership "units." A new partner acquires a certain number of units, and additional units are assigned by a firmwide compensation committee for obtaining new clients, for providing the firm with specific areas of industrial expertise, for serving as a local office's managing partner, or for accepting a variety of other responsibilities.

Other partnerships may devise profit distribution plans that reflect the earnings of the partnership. For example, some medical or dental partnerships allocate profit on the basis of billed services. Other criteria may be number or size of clients, years of service with the firm, or the partner's position within the firm. An obvious advantage of the partnership form of organization is the flexibility it allows partners for the distribution of profits.

PARTNERSHIP FINANCIAL STATEMENTS

A partnership is a separate reporting entity for accounting purposes, and the three financial statements—income statement, balance sheet, and statement of cash flows—typically are prepared for the partnership at the end of each reporting period. Interim statements may also be prepared to meet the partners' information needs. In addition to the three basic financial statements, a *statement of partners' capital* is usually prepared to present the changes in the partners' capital accounts for the period. The statement of partners' capital for the AB Partnership for 20X1 under the multiple-base profit distribution plan illustrated in the prior section follows:

	AB PARTNERSHIP **Statement of Partners' Capital** **For the Year Ended December 31, 20X1**		
	Alt	**Blue**	**Total**
Balance, January 1, 20X1	$20,000	$10,000	$30,000
Add: Additional investment		500	500
Net income distribution	3,980	6,020	10,000
	$23,980	$16,520	$40,500
Less: Withdrawal		(4,000)	(4,000)
Balance, December 31, 20X1	$23,980	$12,520	$36,500

CHANGES IN MEMBERSHIP

Changes in the membership of a partnership occur with the addition of new partners or the dissociation of present partners. New partners are often a primary source of additional capital or needed business expertise. The legal structure of a partnership requires that the *admission of a new partner* be subject to the unanimous approval of the present partners. Furthermore, public announcements are typically made about new partner additions so that third parties transacting business with the partnership are aware of the partnership change. Section 306 of the Uniform Partnership Act of 1997 states that a person admitted as a new partner of an existing partnership is not personally liable for any partnership obligation incurred before the new partner was admitted.

The retirement or withdrawal of a partner from a partnership is a dissociation of that partner. A partner's dissociation does not necessarily mean a dissolution and winding up of the partnership. Many partnerships continue in business and, under section 701 of the UPA 1997, the partnership may purchase the dissociated partner's interest at a *buyout price*. The buyout price is the estimated amount if (1) the assets were sold for a price equal to the greater of the liquidation value or the value based on a sale of the entire business as a going concern without the dissociated partner, and (2) the partnership was wound up at that time, with payment of all the partnership's creditors and termination of the business. Partners who simply wish to leave a partnership may be liable to the partnership for damages to the partnership caused by a wrongful dissociation. A wrongful dissociation occurs when the dissociation is in breach of an express provision of the partnership agreement or, for partnerships formed for a definite term or specific undertaking, before the term or undertaking has been completed. There are also some events that require judicial dissolution and winding up of the partnership. These will be discussed in Chapter 16.

General Concepts to Account for a Change in Membership in the Partnership

The Partnership as an Entity Separate from the Individual Partners and the Use of GAAP

The Uniform Partnership Act of 1997 clearly defines a partnership as an entity separate from the individual partners. As such, the partnership entity does not change because of the addition or withdrawal of an individual partner. This is similar to the concept of the entity for the corporate form of business, in which the business is not necessarily revalued each time there is a change in stockholders.

Some partnerships choose to comply with generally accepted accounting principles (GAAP) in their accounting and financial reporting. These partnerships follow the same standards established by the FASB and other regulatory bodies as public companies. Often venture capital firms or other credit suppliers may require that the private partnership company comply with GAAP so that the partnership's financials can be compared with those of other public companies. Venture capital firms have a goal of eventually taking their investees public. Thus, if a partnership follows GAAP and is audited by external auditors, the partnership can receive an audit opinion stating that it is in conformity with generally accepted accounting principles.

A partnership following GAAP and defining its company as an entity separate from the individual partners would account for a change in membership in the same manner as a corporate entity would account for changes in its investors. Additional investments would be recognized at their fair values along with the related increase in the company's total capital.

GAAP does not provide guidance for revaluing net assets that increase in value with a change in partnership membership. However, there are a few situations under GAAP for which a reduction in value of specific net assets may be recognized when there is a change in partnership membership. For example, **FASB Statement No. 142**, "Goodwill and Other Intangible Assets" (FASB 142), presents procedures for recognizing impairments of currently held goodwill. **FASB Statement No. 144**, "Accounting for the Impairment of Disposal of Long-Lived Assets" (FASB 144), presents the accounting standards for recognizing impairment losses on long-lived assets. However, there are no GAAP standards that provide for increases in the value of tangible assets or recognition of new goodwill, solely due to a change in partnership membership.

The Partnership as an Aggregate of Partners' Interests and the Use of Non-GAAP Accounting

The partners in a private company may choose to follow non-GAAP accounting methods that meet their specific information needs. In this case, the company may still be audited by external auditors, but the audit opinion would distinctly state that non-GAAP accounting principles were used in preparing the financial statements. These partnerships may not receive an "unqualified" audit opinion.

Many partnerships use the transactions surrounding the change of partnership members as an opportunity for revaluing the partnership's existing assets and liabilities or for recording previously unrecognized goodwill. These practices of ***net asset revaluation*** or ***goodwill recognition*** are not in compliance with GAAP. Partnerships using these non-GAAP methods argue that revaluing assets at the time of the change in partnership membership states fully the true economic condition of the partnership at the time of the change in membership and assigns the changes in asset and liability values and goodwill to the partners who have been managing the business during the time the changes in value occurred. Some accountants believe this revaluation is necessary to value properly each partner's present equity in the partnership. Because so many partnerships do revalue net assets or recognize goodwill at the time of a change in partnership membership, the following sections of this chapter discuss these non-GAAP methods of accounting for changes in the partnership membership.

This chapter also discusses the ***bonus method*** sometimes agreed upon by the partners when there is a change in the partnership membership. The bonus method does not change the net capital of the partnership beyond the amount invested by the new partner. Rather, the bonus method assigns partners' capital interests based on the agreement of the partners, and it is often based on the value of the new partner's investment. In some cases, the current partners assign some of their capital to a new partner; in other cases, a new partner agrees to assign a portion of his or her capital interest to the prior partners. Thus, the bonus method does not violate GAAP because partners may legally assign any or all of their transferable partnership capital interest to other partners. Partners in private companies have free choice as to how they may account for changes in partnership membership. As noted, a private partnership may use either GAAP or non-GAAP methods, based on the information needs of the partners.

New Partner Purchases an Interest

An individual may acquire a partnership interest directly from one or more of the present partners. In this type of transaction, cash or other assets are exchanged outside the partnership, and the only entry necessary on the partnership's books is a reclassification of the total capital of the partnership.

A concept used with some frequency is book value. The **book value of a partnership** is simply the total amount of the capital, which is also the amount of net assets (total assets minus total liabilities). Book value is important because it serves as a basis for asset and liability revaluations or goodwill recognition.

For purposes of this discussion, assume that after operations and partners' withdrawals during 20X1 and 20X2, AB Partnership has a book value of $30,000 and profit percentages on January 1, 20X3, as follows:

	Capital Balance	Profit Percentage
Alt	$20,000	60
Blue	10,000	40
Total	$30,000	100

The following information describes the case:

1. On January 1, 20X3, Alt and Blue invite Cha to become a partner in their business. The resulting partnership will be called the ABC Partnership.
2. Cha purchases a one-fourth interest in the partnership capital directly from Alt and Blue for a total cost of $9,000, paying $5,900 to Alt and $3,100 to Blue. Cha will have a capital credit of $7,500 ($30,000 × .25) in a proportionate reclassification from Alt and Blue's capital accounts.
3. Cha will be entitled to a 25 percent interest in the profits or losses of the partnership. The remaining 75 percent interest will be divided between Alt and Blue in their old profit ratio of 60:40 percent. The resulting profit and loss percentages after the admission of Cha follow:

Partner	Profit Percentage
Alt	45 (75% of .60)
Blue	30 (75% of .40)
Cha	25
Total	100

In this example, Cha's 25 percent share of partnership profits or losses is the same as her one-fourth capital interest. These two percentage shares do not have to be the same. As described earlier in the chapter, a partner's capital interest may change over time because of profit distributions, withdrawals, or additional investments in capital. Furthermore, Cha could have acquired her entire capital interest directly from either partner. It is not necessary that a new partner directly purchasing an interest do so in a proportionate reclassification from each of the prior partners.

The transaction is between Cha and the individual partners and is not reflected on the partnership's books. The only entry in this case is to reclassify the partnership capital. Both Alt and Blue provide one-fourth of their capital to Cha, as follows:

January 1, 20X3				
(7)	Alt, Capital		5,000	
	Blue, Capital		2,500	
	Cha, Capital			7,500
	Reclassify capital to new partner:			
	From Alt: $5,000 = $20,000 \times .25$			
	From Blue: $2,500 = $10,000 \times .25$			

In this case the capital credit to Cha is only $7,500, although $9,000 is paid for the one-fourth interest. The $9,000 payment implies that the fair value of the partnership is $36,000, calculated as follows:

$$\$9,000 = \text{Fair value} \times .25$$

$$\$36,000 = \text{Fair value}$$

The partnership's book value is $30,000 before Cha's investment. The payment of $9,000 is made directly to the individual partners, and it does not become part of the partnership's assets. The $6,000 difference between the partnership's fair value and its new book value could be due to understated assets or to unrecognized goodwill.

Alt and Blue could use the evidence from Cha's acquisition to revalue the partnership's assets and fully reflect the changes in values that have taken place before the admission of Cha. Failure to do so could result in Cha's sharing proportionately in the increases in value when the increases are realized. For example, if the partnership has land that is undervalued by $6,000 that it sells after Cha is admitted to the partnership, Cha will share in the gain on the sale according to the profit ratio. To avoid this possible problem, some partnerships revalue the assets at the time a new partner is admitted even if the new partner purchases the partnership interest directly from the present partners. In this case, Alt and Blue could recognize the increase in the value of the land immediately before the admission of Cha and properly allocate the increase to their capital accounts in their 60:40 profit ratio, as follows:

(8)	Land		6,000	
	Alt, Capital			3,600
	Blue, Capital			2,400
	Revaluation of land before admission of new partner:			
	To Alt: $3,600 = $6,000 \times .60$			
	To Blue: $2,400 = $6,000 \times .40$			

Note that the partnership's total resulting capital is $36,000 ($30,000 prior plus the $6,000 revaluation). The transfer of a one-fourth capital credit to Cha is recorded as follows:

(9)	Alt, Capital		5,900	
	Blue, Capital		3,100	
	Cha, Capital			9,000
	Reclassify capital to new partner:			
	$5,900 = $23,600 \times .25$			
	$3,100 = $12,400 \times .25$			
	$9,000 = $36,000 \times .25$			

The partnership's accountant should ensure that sufficient evidence exists for any revaluation of assets and liabilities to prevent valuation abuses. Corroborating evidence such as appraisals or an extended period of excess earnings helps support asset valuations.

New Partner Invests in Partnership

A new partner may acquire a share of the partnership by investing in the business. In this case, the partnership receives the cash or other assets. Three cases are possible when a new partner invests in a partnership:

Case 1. The new partner's investment equals the new partner's proportion of the partnership's book value.

Case 2. The investment is for *more* than the new partner's proportion of the partnership's book value. This indicates that the partnership's prior net assets are undervalued on the books or that unrecorded goodwill exists.

Case 3. The investment is for *less* than the new partner's proportion of the partnership's book value. This suggests that the partnership's prior net assets are overvalued on its books or that the new partner may be contributing goodwill in addition to other assets.

The first step in determining how to account for the admission of a new partner is to compute the ***new partner's proportion of the partnership's book value*** as follows:

$$
\begin{pmatrix} \text{New partner's} \\ \text{proportion of} \\ \text{the partnership's} \\ \text{book value} \end{pmatrix} = \begin{pmatrix} \text{Prior} \\ \text{capital of} \\ \text{present} \\ \text{partners} \end{pmatrix} + \begin{pmatrix} \text{Investment} \\ \text{of new} \\ \text{partner} \end{pmatrix} \times \begin{pmatrix} \text{Percentage} \\ \text{of capital} \\ \text{to new} \\ \text{partner} \end{pmatrix}
$$

The new partner's proportion of the partnership's book value is compared with the amount of the investment the new partner made to determine the procedures to be followed in accounting for his or her admission. Figure 15–1 presents an overview of the three cases presented above. Step 1 is to compare the new partner's investment with his or her proportion of the partnership's book value. Note that this is done before any revaluations or recognition of goodwill. Step 2 is to determine the specific admission method. Three different methods are

FIGURE 15–1 **Overview of Accounting for Admission of a New Partner**

Step 1: Compare Proportionate Book Value and Investment of New Partner	*Step 2: Alternative Methods to Account for Admission*	*Key Observations*
Investment cost > Book value (Case 2)	1. Revalue net assets up to market value and allocate to prior partners. 2. Record unrecognized goodwill and allocate to prior partners. 3. Assign bonus to prior partners.	• Prior partners receive asset valuation increase, goodwill, or bonus indicated by the excess of new partner's investment over book value of the capital share initially assignable to new partner. • Recording asset valuation increase or prior partners' goodwill increases total resulting partnership capital.
Investment cost = Book value (Case 1)	1. No revaluations, bonus, or goodwill.	• No additional allocations necessary because new partner will receive a capital share equal to the amount invested. • Total resulting partnership capital equals prior partners' capital plus investment of new partner.
Investment cost < Book value (Case 3)	1. Revalue net assets down to market value and allocate to prior partners. 2. Recognize goodwill brought in by new partner. 3. Assign bonus to new partner.	• Prior partners are assigned the reduction of asset values occurring before admission of the new partner. Alternatively, new partner is assigned goodwill or bonus as part of admission incentive. • Recording asset valuation decrease reduces total resulting capital, while recording new partner's goodwill increases total resulting capital.

available to the partnership to account for the admission of a new partner when a difference exists between the new partner's investment and his or her proportion of the partnership's book value. The three methods are: (1) revalue net assets, (2) recognize goodwill, or (3) use the bonus method. Under the revaluation of net assets and goodwill recognition methods, the historical cost bases of the partnership's net assets are adjusted during the admission of the new partner. Some partners object to this departure from historical cost and prefer to use the bonus method, which uses capital interest transfers among the partners to align the total resulting capital of the partnership. Under the bonus method, net assets remain at their historical cost bases to the partnership. The choice of method of accounting for the admission of a new partner is up to the partners.

Several parallels exist between accounting for the admission of a new partner and accounting for an investment in the stock of another company. If a new partner pays more than book value, the excess of cost over book value, that is, the positive differential, may be due to unrecognized goodwill or to undervalued assets—the same cases as in accounting for the differential for stock investments. If book value equals the investment cost, then no differential exists, indicating that the book values of the net assets equal their fair values. If the new partner's investment is less than the proportionate book value, that is, an excess of book value over cost exists, the assets of the partnership may be overvalued. Therefore, the only concept unique to partnership accounting is the use of the bonus method. Figure 15–1 serves as a guide through the following discussion.

The AB Partnership example presented earlier is again used to illustrate the three cases. A review of the major facts for this example follows:

1. The January 1, 20X3, capital of the AB Partnership is $30,000. Alt's balance is $20,000, and Blue's balance is $10,000. Alt and Blue share profits in the ratio of 60:40.
2. Cha is invited into the partnership. Cha will have a one-fourth capital interest and a 25 percent share of profits. Alt and Blue will share the remaining 75 percent of profits in the ratio of 60:40, resulting in Alt having a 45 percent share of any profits and Blue having a 30 percent share.

Case 1. Investment Equals Proportion of the Partnership's Book Value

The total book value of the partnership before the admission of the new partner is $30,000, and the new partner, Cha, is buying a one-fourth capital interest for $10,000.

The amount of a new partner's investment is often the result of negotiations between the prior partners and the prospective partner. As with any acquisition or investment, the investor must determine its market value. In the case of a partnership, the prospective partner attempts to ascertain the market value and earning power of the partnership's net assets. The new partner's investment is then a function of the percentage of partnership capital being acquired. In this case, Cha must believe that the $10,000 investment required is a fair price for a one-fourth interest in the resulting partnership; otherwise, she would not make the investment.

After the amount of investment is agreed on, it is possible to calculate the new partner's proportionate book value. For a $10,000 investment, Cha will have a one-fourth interest in the partnership, as follows:

Investment in partnership	$10,000
New partner's proportionate book value:	
($30,000 + $10,000) × .25	(10,000)
Difference (Investment = Book value)	$ -0-

Because the amount of the investment ($10,000) equals the new partner's 25 percent proportionate book value ($10,000 = $40,000 × .25), there is an implication that the net assets are fairly valued. Total resulting capital equals the prior partners' capital ($30,000) plus the new partner's tangible investment ($10,000). Note that the capital credit assigned to the new partner is her share of the total resulting capital of the partnership after her admission as partner. The entry on the partnership's books is:

January 1, 20X3		
(10) Cash	10,000	
Cha, Capital		10,000
Admission of Cha for one-fourth interest upon investment of $10,000.		

The following schedule presents the key concepts in Case 1:

	Prior Capital	New Partner's Tangible Investment	New Partner's Proportion of Partnership's Book Value (25%)	Total Resulting Capital	New Partner's Share of Total Resulting Capital (25%)
Case 1					
New partner's investment equals proportionate book value	$30,000	$10,000	$10,000		
No revaluations, bonus, or goodwill				$40,000	$10,000

Case 2. New Partner's Investment More than Proportion of the Partnership's Book Value

In some cases, a new partner may invest more in an existing partnership than his or her proportionate share of the partnership's book value. This means that the new partner perceives some value in the partnership that the books of account do not reflect.

For example, assume Cha invests $11,000 for a one-fourth capital interest in the ABC Partnership. The first step is to compare the new partner's investment with the new partner's proportionate book value, as follows:

Investment in partnership	$11,000
New partner's proportionate book value: ($30,000 + $11,000) × .25	(10,250)
Difference (Investment > Book value)	$ 750

Cha has invested $11,000 for an interest with a book value of $10,250, thus paying an excess of $750 over the present book value.

Generally, an excess of investment over the respective book value of the partnership interest indicates that the partnership's prior net assets are undervalued or that the partnership has some unrecorded goodwill. Three alternative accounting treatments exist in this case:

1. *Revalue net assets upward.* Under this alternative:
   a. Book values of net assets are increased to their market values.
   b. The prior partners' capital accounts are increased for their respective shares of the increase in the book values of the net assets.
   c. The partnership's total resulting capital reflects the prior capital balances plus the amount of asset revaluation plus the new partner's investment.
2. *Record unrecognized goodwill.* With this method:
   a. Unrecognized goodwill is recorded.

b. The prior partners' capital accounts are increased for their respective shares of the goodwill.

c. The partnership's total resulting capital reflects the prior capital balances plus the goodwill recognized plus the new partner's investment.

3. *Use bonus method.* Essentially, the bonus method is a transfer of capital balances among the partners. This method is used when the partners do not wish to record adjustments in asset and liability accounts or recognize goodwill. Under this method:

a. The prior partners' capital accounts are increased for their respective shares of the bonus paid by the new partner.

b. The partnership's total resulting capital reflects the prior capital balances plus the new partner's investment.

The partnership may use any one of the three alternatives. The decision is usually a result of negotiations between the prior partners and the prospective partner. Some accountants criticize the revaluation of net assets or recognition of goodwill because it results in a marked departure from the historical cost principle and differs from the accepted accounting principles in **FASB Statement No. 142**, "Goodwill and Other Intangible Assets" (FASB 142), which prohibits corporations from recognizing goodwill that has not been acquired by purchase. Accountants who use the goodwill or asset revaluation methods argue that the goal of partnership accounting is to state fairly the relative capital equities of the partners, and this may require different accounting procedures from those used in corporate entities.

The accountant's function is to ensure that any estimates used in the valuation process are based on the best evidence available. Subjective valuations that could impair the fairness of the presentations made in the partnership's financial statements should be avoided or minimized.

Illustration of Revaluation of Net Assets Approach

Assume that Cha paid a $750 excess ($11,000 − $10,250) over her proportionate book value because the partnership owns land with a book value of $4,000 but a recent appraisal indicates the land has a market value of $7,000. The prior partners decide to use the admission of the new partner to recognize the increase in the land's value and to assign this increase to the capital accounts of the prior partners. The increase in land value is allocated to the partners' capital accounts in the profit and loss ratio that existed during the time of the increase. Alt's capital is increased by $1,800 (60 percent of the $3,000 increase), and Blue's capital is increased by $1,200 (40 percent of the $3,000). The partnership makes the following entry for the revaluation of the land:

(11)	Land	3,000	
	Alt, Capital		1,800
	Blue, Capital		1,200
	Revalue partnership land to market value.		

Cha's $11,000 investment brings the partnership's total resulting capital to $44,000, as follows:

Prior capital of AB Partnership	$30,000
Revaluation of land to market value	3,000
Cha's investment	11,000
Total resulting capital of ABC Partnership	$44,000

Cha is acquiring a one-fourth interest in the total resulting capital of the ABC Partnership. Her capital credit, after revaluing the land, is calculated as follows:

$$\text{New partner's share of total resulting capital} = (\$30,000 + \$3,000 + \$11,000) \times .25 = \$11,000$$

The entry to record the admission of Cha into the partnership follows:

(12)	Cash	11,000	
	Cha, Capital		11,000
	Admission of Cha for one-fourth capital interest in ABC Partnership.		

When the land is eventually sold, Cha will participate in the gain or loss calculated on the basis of the new $7,000 book value, which is the land's market value at the time of her admission into the partnership. The entire increase in the land value before Cha's admission belongs to the prior partners.

Illustration of Goodwill Recognition An entering partner may be paying an excess because of unrecognized goodwill, indicated by the partnership's high profitability. Some partnerships use the change in membership as an opportunity to record unrecognized goodwill created by the prior partners. Recording unrecognized goodwill is used for partnership accounting to establish appropriate capital equity among the partners. As noted earlier, this is an exception to the general rule established in **FASB 142**, but the partners' information needs and the specific purposes of the partnership's financial statements can serve to justify the exception.

Generally, the amount of goodwill is determined by negotiations between the prior and prospective partners and is based on estimates of future earnings. For example, the prior and new partners may agree that, due to the prior partners' efforts, the partnership has superior earnings potential and that $3,000 of goodwill should be recorded to recognize this fact. The new partner's negotiated investment cost will be based partly on the earnings potential of the partnership. Alternatively, goodwill may be estimated from the amount of the new partner's investment. For example, in this case, Cha is investing $11,000 for a one-fourth interest; therefore, she must believe the total resulting partnership capital is $44,000 ($11,000 × 4). The estimated goodwill is $3,000:

Step 1	
25% of estimated total resulting capital	$11,000
Estimated total resulting capital ($11,000 ÷ .25)	$44,000
Step 2	
Estimated total resulting capital	$44,000
Total net assets not including goodwill	
($30,000 prior plus $11,000 invested by Cha)	(41,000)
Estimated goodwill	$ 3,000

Another way to view the creation of goodwill at the time of a new partner's admission is to use a T-account form for the partnership's balance sheet. Any additional net assets, such as recognizing goodwill, must be balanced with additional capital, as follows:

		Balance Sheet		
Prior to admission of new partner Cha	Net assets	$30,000	Partners' capital	$30,000
New partner's cash investment	Cash	11,000	New tangible capital	11,000
Capital prior to recognizing goodwill		$41,000		$41,000
Estimated new goodwill	Goodwill	3,000	Capital from goodwill	3,000
Total resulting capital	Net assets	$44,000	Total resulting capital	$44,000

Once the new ABC Partnership's total resulting capital is estimated ($44,000), the new goodwill ($3,000) is the balance sheet balancing difference between the tangible capital

($41,000), which includes the new partner's cash investment and the estimated total resulting capital of ABC Partnership ($44,000).

The unrecorded goodwill is recorded, and the prior partners' capital accounts are credited for the increase in assets. The adjustments to the capital accounts are in the profit and loss ratio that existed during the periods the goodwill was developed. This increased Alt's capital by 60 percent of the goodwill and Blue's by 40 percent. The entries to record goodwill and the admission of Cha are as follows:

(13)	Goodwill	3,000	
	Alt, Capital		1,800
	Blue, Capital		1,200
	Recognize unrecorded goodwill.		
(14)	Cash	11,000	
	Cha, Capital		11,000
	Admission of Cha to partnership for a		
	one-fourth capital interest: $44,000 × .25		

Another reason for recording goodwill is that the new partner may want her capital balance to equal the amount of investment made. The investment is based on the market value of the partnership, and for this equality to occur, the partnership must restate its prior net assets to their fair values.

It is important to note that the $11,000 credit to Cha's capital account is one-fourth of the total resulting capital of ABC Partnership of $44,000 as follows:

$$\frac{\text{New partner's share of}}{\text{total resulting capital}} = (\$30,000 + \$3,000 + \$11,000) \times .25 = \$11,000$$

In future periods, any impairment loss of goodwill will be charged against partnership earnings before net income is distributed to the partners. Consequently, Cha's future profit distribution may be affected by the goodwill recognized at the time of her admission into the partnership.

Illustration of Bonus Method Some partnerships are averse to recognizing asset revaluations or unrecorded goodwill when a new partner is admitted. Instead, they record a portion of the new partner's investment as a bonus to the existing partners to align the capital balances properly at the time of the new partner's admission. In this case, the $750 excess paid by Cha is a bonus allocated to the prior partners in their profit and loss ratio of 60 percent to Alt and 40 percent to Blue. ABC Partnership's total resulting capital consists of $30,000 prior capital of Alt and Blue plus the $11,000 investment of Cha. No additional capital is recognized by revaluing assets. The value of the capital credit acquired by the new partner is calculated as:

$$\frac{\text{New partner's share of}}{\text{total resulting capital}} = (\$30,000 + \$11,000) \times .25 = \$10,250$$

The entry to record the admission of Cha under the bonus method is as follows:

(15)	Cash	11,000	
	Alt, Capital		450
	Blue, Capital		300
	Cha, Capital		10,250
	Admission of Cha with bonus to Alt and Blue.		

Cha may dislike the bonus method because her capital balance is $750 less than her investment in the partnership. This is a disadvantage of the bonus method.

The following schedule presents the key concepts for Case 2:

	Prior Capital	New Partner's Tangible Investment	New Partner's Proportion of Partnership's Book Value (25%)	Total Resulting Capital	New Partner's Share of Total Resulting Capital (25%)
Case 2					
New partner's investment greater than proportionate book value	$30,000	$11,000	$10,250		
1. Revalue assets by increasing land $3,000				$44,000	$11,000
2. Recognize $3,000 goodwill for prior partners				$44,000	$11,000
3. Bonus of $750 to prior partners				$41,000	$10,250

Case 3. New Partner's Investment Less than Proportion of the Partnership's Book Value

It is possible that a new partner may pay less than his or her proportionate share of the partnership's book value. For example, assume Cha invests $8,000 for a one-fourth capital interest in the ABC Partnership. The first step is to compare the new partner's investment with the new partner's proportionate book value, as follows:

Investment in partnership	$ 8,000
New partner's proportionate book value:	
($30,000 + $8,000) × .25	(9,500)
Difference (Investment < Book value)	$(1,500)

The fact that Cha's investment is less than the book value of a one-fourth interest in the partnership indicates that the partnership has overvalued net assets or the prior partners recognize that Cha is contributing additional value in the form of expertise or skills she possesses that are needed by the partnership. In this case, Cha is investing $8,000 in cash and an additional amount that may be viewed as goodwill.

As with Case 2, in which the investment is more than the book value acquired, there are three alternative approaches to account for the differential when the investment is less than the book value acquired. The three approaches are as follows:

1. *Revalue net assets downward.* Under this alternative:
   a. Book values of net assets are decreased to recognize the reduction in their values.
   b. The prior partners' capital accounts are decreased for their respective share of the decrease in the values of the net assets.
   c. The partnership's total resulting capital reflects the prior capital balances less the amount of the net asset valuation write-down plus the new partner's investment.

2. *Recognize goodwill brought in by the new partner.* In this approach:
   a. Goodwill or other intangible benefits brought in by the new partner are recorded and included in the new partner's capital account.
   b. The prior partners' capital accounts remain unchanged.

c. The partnership's total resulting capital reflects the prior capital balances plus the new goodwill brought in plus the new partner's tangible investment.

3. *Use bonus method.* Under the bonus method:

   a. The new partner is assigned a bonus from the prior partners' capital accounts, which are decreased for their respective shares of the bonus paid to the new partner.

   b. The partnership's total resulting capital reflects the prior capital balances plus the new partner's investment.

Illustration of Revaluation of Net Assets Approach Assume that the reason Cha paid only $8,000 for a one-fourth interest in the partnership is that inventory currently recorded at a book value of $14,000 has a fair market value of only $8,000 because of the obsolescence of several items. The partners agree to write down the inventory to its fair value before the new partner's admission. The write-down is allocated to the prior partners in the profit and loss ratio that existed during the period of the inventory decline: 60 percent to Alt and 40 percent to Blue. The write-down is recorded as follows:

(16)	Alt, Capital	3,600	
	Blue, Capital	2,400	
	Inventory		6,000
	Revalue inventory to market.		

Note that the partnership's total capital has now been reduced from $30,000 to $24,000 as a result of the $6,000 write-down. The value of Cha's share of total resulting capital of the ABC Partnership, *after the write-down,* is calculated as follows:

$$\text{New partner's share of total resulting capital} = (\$24,000 + \$8,000) \times .25 = \$8,000$$

The entry to record the admission of Cha as a partner in the ABC Partnership is:

(17)	Cash	8,000	
	Cha, Capital		8,000
	Admission of Cha to partnership.		

Cha's recorded capital credit is equal to her investment because the total partnership capital of $32,000 ($24,000 + $8,000) now represents the partnership's fair value.

Illustration of Recording Goodwill for New Partner The prior partners may offer Cha a one-fourth capital interest in the ABC Partnership for an $8,000 investment because Cha has essential business experience, skills, customer contacts, reputation, or other ingredients of goodwill that she will bring into the partnership. The amount of goodwill brought in by the new partner is usually determined through negotiations between the prior partners and the prospective partner. For example, Alt, Blue, and Cha may agree that Cha's abilities will generate excess earnings for the resulting ABC Partnership. They agree that Cha should be given $2,000 of goodwill recognition when she joins the partnership in recognition of her anticipated excess contribution to the partnership's future earnings. The negotiated goodwill is recognized and added to her tangible investment to determine the amount of capital credit.

Alternatively, the amount of goodwill brought in by the new partner may be estimated from the amount of the total capital being retained by the prior partners. In this case, the prior partners are retaining a 75 percent interest in the partnership and allowing the new partner a 25 percent capital interest. The dollar amount of the prior partners' 75 percent interest is $30,000. Cha's investment of $8,000 plus goodwill makes up the remaining

25 percent. The amount of goodwill that Cha brought into the partnership is determined as follows:

Step 1	
75% of estimated total resulting capital	$30,000
Estimated total resulting capital ($30,000 ÷ .75)	$40,000
Step 2	
Estimated total resulting capital	$40,000
Total net assets not including goodwill	
($30,000 + $8,000)	(38,000)
Estimated goodwill	$ 2,000

Note that the goodwill estimate for the new partner is made using the information from the prior partners' interests. In Case 2, the estimate of goodwill to the prior partners was made using the information from the new partner's investment. The reason for this difference is that the best available information should be used for the goodwill estimates. If the new partner's goodwill is being estimated, it is not logical to use the new partner's tangible investment to estimate the total investment made by the new partner, including goodwill. That is circular reasoning that involves using a number to estimate itself. Furthermore, when goodwill is being assigned to the prior partners, it is not logical to use the existing capital of the prior partners to estimate their goodwill. A useful phrase to remember how to estimate goodwill is to use the opposite partner's information for the estimate:

> Use new partner to estimate goodwill to prior partners; use prior partners to estimate goodwill to new partner.

The entry to record the admission of Cha into the ABC Partnership is:

(18)			
	Cash	8,000	
	Goodwill	2,000	
	Cha, Capital		10,000
	Admission of Cha to partnership.		

Note that the ABC Partnership's total resulting capital is now $40,000, with Alt and Blue together having a 75 percent interest and Cha having a 25 percent interest.

Illustration of Bonus Method Cha's admission as a new partner with a one-fourth interest in the ABC Partnership for an investment of only $8,000 may be accounted for by recognizing a bonus given to Cha from the prior partners. The $1,500 bonus is the difference between the new partner's $9,500 book value and her $8,000 investment. The prior partners' capital accounts are reduced by $1,500 in their profit and loss ratio of 60 percent for Alt and 40 percent for Blue, and Cha's capital account is credited for $9,500, as follows:

(19)			
	Cash	8,000	
	Alt, Capital	900	
	Blue, Capital	600	
	Cha, Capital		9,500
	Admission of Cha to partnership.		

Note that the amount of the capital credit assigned to the new partner is her share of the total resulting capital, as follows:

$$\text{New partner's share of total resulting capital} = (\$30,000 + \$8,000) \times .25 = \$9,500$$

The following schedule presents the key concepts for Case 3:

	Prior Capital	New Partner's Tangible Investment	New Partner's Proportion of Partnership's Book Value (25%)	Total Resulting Capital	New Partner's Share of Total Resulting Capital (25%)
Case 3					
New partner's investment less than proportionate book value	$30,000	$8,000	$9,500		
1. Revalue assets by decreasing inventory by $6,000				$32,000	$ 8,000
2. Recognize goodwill of $2,000 for new partner				$40,000	$10,000
3. Bonus of $1,500 to new partner				$38,000	$ 9,500

Summary and Comparison of Accounting for Investment of New Partner

Figure 15–2 presents the entries made in each of the three cases discussed. In addition, the capital balance of each of the three partners immediately after the admission of Cha is presented to the right of the journal entries.

The following summarizes the alternative methods of accounting for the investment of a new partner:

Case 1. New partner's investment equals *his or her proportion of the partnership's book value.*

1. The new partner's capital credit equals his or her investment.
2. This case recognizes no goodwill or bonus.

Case 2. New partner's investment is more than *his or her proportion of the partnership's book value.*

1. The revaluation of an asset or recognition of goodwill increases the partnership's total resulting capital. The increase is allocated to the prior partners in their profit and loss ratio.
2. After recognition of the asset revaluation or unrecorded goodwill, the new partner's capital credit equals his or her investment and his or her percentage of the total resulting capital.
3. Under the bonus method, the partnership's total resulting capital is the sum of the prior partnership's capital plus the investment by the new partner. The capital credit recorded for the new partner is less than the investment but equals his or her percentage of the resulting partnership capital.

Case 3. New partner's investment is less than *his or her proportion of the partnership's book value.*

1. Under the revaluation of assets approach, the write-down of the assets reduces the prior partners' capital in their profit and loss ratio. The new partner's capital is then credited for the amount of the investment.
2. Under the goodwill method, goodwill is assigned to the new partner, and the total resulting capital of the partnership is increased. The new partner's capital is credited for his or her percentage interest in the total resulting capital of the partnership.
3. The bonus method results in a transfer of capital from the prior partners to the new partner. The new partnership's total resulting capital equals the prior capital plus the new partner's investment. The new partner's capital credit is more than the investment made but equals his or her percentage of the total resulting capital.

FIGURE 15–2
Summary of
Accounting for
Investment of New
Partner: Journal
Entries and Capital
Balances after
Admission of New
Partner

Case 1: New partner's investment equals proportionate book value. Cha invests $10,000 cash for one-fourth capital interest.

Cash	10,000		Alt	$20,000
Cha, Capital		10,000	Blue	10,000
			Cha	10,000
			Total	$40,000

Case 2: New partner's investment is greater than proportionate book value. Cha invests $11,000 cash for one-fourth capital interest.

(a) Revalue net assets: (upward)

Land	3,000		Alt	$21,800
Alt, Capital		1,800	Blue	11,200
Blue, Capital		1,200	Cha	11,000
Cash	11,000		Total	$44,000
Cha, Capital		11,000		

(b) Recognize goodwill for prior partners:

Goodwill	3,000		Alt	$21,800
Alt, Capital		1,800	Blue	11,200
Blue, Capital		1,200	Cha	11,000
Cash	11,000		Total	$44,000
Cha, Capital		11,000		

(c) Bonus to prior partners:

Cash	11,000		Alt	$20,450
Alt, Capital		450	Blue	10,300
Blue, Capital		300	Cha	10,250
Cha, Capital		10,250	Total	$41,000

Case 3: New partner's investment is less than proportionate book value. Cha invests $8,000 cash for a one-fourth capital interest.

(a) Revalue net assets: (downward)

Alt, Capital	3,600		Alt	$16,400
Blue, Capital	2,400		Blue	7,600
Inventory		6,000	Cha	8,000
Cash	8,000		Total	$32,000
Cha, Capital		8,000		

(b) Recognize goodwill for new partner:

Cash	8,000		Alt	$20,000
Goodwill	2,000		Blue	10,000
Cha, Capital		10,000	Cha	10,000
			Total	$40,000

(c) Bonus to new partner:

Cash	8,000		Alt	$19,100
Alt, Capital	900		Blue	9,400
Blue, Capital	600		Cha	9,500
Cha, Capital		9,500	Total	$38,000

Determining a New Partner's Investment Cost

In the previous sections, the amount of the new partner's contribution has been provided. In some instances, accountants are asked to determine the amount of cash investment the new partner should be asked to contribute. The basic principles of partnership accounting provide the means to solve this question. For example, let's continue the basic example of partners Alt and Blue wishing to admit Cha as a new partner. The prior partnership capital was $30,000, and the partners wish to invite Cha into the partnership for a one-fourth interest.

Assume that the prior partners, Alt and Blue, agree that the partnership's assets should be revalued up by $3,000 to recognize the increase in value of the land held by the partnership. The question is how much Cha, the new partner, should be asked to invest for her one-fourth interest.

When determining the new partner's investment cost, it is important to note the total resulting capital of the partnership and the percentage of ownership interest retained by the prior partners. In this example, the prior partners retain a three-fourth interest in the resulting partnership, for which their 75 percent capital interest is $33,000, the $30,000 of prior capital plus the $3,000 from the revaluation of the land, as follows:

75% of total resulting capital	$33,000
Total resulting capital (100%)	$44,000
Less prior partners' capital	(33,000)
Cash contribution required of new partner	$11,000

Note that this is simply another way to evaluate the admission process as discussed in the net asset revaluation illustration under Case 2.

In some cases, the bonus amount may be determined prior to the determination of the cash contribution required from the new partner. For example, assume that Alt and Blue agree to give Cha a bonus of $1,500 for joining the partnership. The following schedule determines the amount of cash investment required of Cha, the new partner:

Prior capital of Alt and Blue	$30,000
Less bonus given to Cha upon admission	(1,500)
Capital retained by Alt and Blue (75%)	$28,500
Total resulting capital	
($28,500 ÷ .75)	$38,000
Less prior partners' capital	(28,500)
Capital credit required of new partner	$ 9,500
Less bonus to new partner from prior partners	(1,500)
Cash contribution required of new partner	$ 8,000

This second example is another way to view the bonus-to-new-partner method under Case 3 as presented. The key is to determine the amount of capital that the prior partners will retain for their percentage share in the partnership's total resulting capital after admitting the new partner. The new partner's cash contribution can be computed simply by determining the amount of the capital credit that will be assigned to him or her and then recognizing any bonuses that will be used to align the capital balances.

Dissociation of a Partner from the Partnership

When a partner retires or withdraws from a partnership, that partner is dissociated from the partnership. In most cases, the partnership purchases the dissociated partner's interest in the partnership for a buyout price. Section 701 of the UPA 1997 states that the buyout price is the estimated amount if (1) the assets of the partnership were sold at a price equal to the greater of the liquidation value or the value based on a sale of the entire business as a going concern without the dissociated partner, and (2) the partnership was wound up at that time, with all partnership obligations settled. Note that goodwill may be included in the valuation. The partnership must pay interest to the dissociated partner from the date of dissociation to the date of payment. In cases of wrongful dissociation, the partnership may sue the partner for damages the wrongful dissociation causes the partnership.

In the case in which the partnership agrees to the dissociation and it is not wrongful, the accountant can aid in the computation of the buyout price. It is especially important to determine all existing liabilities on the dissociation date. The partnership agreement may include other procedures to use in the case of a partner dissociation, such as the specifics of valuation, the process of the acquisition of the dissociated partner's transferable value, and other aspects of the change in membership process.

Some partnerships have an audit performed when a change in partners is made. This audit establishes the existence of and the accuracy of the book values of the assets and liabilities. On occasion, accounting errors are found during an audit. Errors should be corrected and the partners' capital accounts adjusted based on the profit and loss ratio that existed in the period in which the errors were made. For example, if an audit disclosed that three years ago depreciation expense was charged for $4,000 less than it should have been, the error is corrected retroactively, and the partners' capital accounts are charged with their respective shares of the adjustment based on their profit and loss ratio of three years ago.

Generally, the continuing partners buy out the retiring partner either by making a direct acquisition or by having the partnership acquire the retiring partner's interest. If the continuing partners directly acquire the retiring partner's interest, the only entry on the partnership's books is to record the reclassification of capital among the partners. If the partnership acquires the retiring partner's interest, the partnership must record the reduction of total partnership capital and the corresponding reduction of assets paid to the retiring partner. Computation of the buyout price when a partner dissociates from the partnership can take the form of three possible scenarios. These are discussed next.

1. Buyout Price Equal to Partner's Capital Credit

Assume Alt retires from the ABC Partnership when his capital account has a balance of $55,000 after recording all increases in the partnership's net assets including income earned up to the date of the retirement. All partners agree to $55,000 as the buyout price of Alt's partnership interest. The entry made by the ABC Partnership is:

(20)	Alt, Capital	55,000	
	Cash		55,000
	Retirement of Alt.		

If the partnership is unable to pay the total of $55,000 to Alt at the time of retirement, it must recognize a liability for the remaining portion.

2. Buyout Price Greater than Partner's Capital Credit

Assume Alt has a capital credit of $55,000 and all the partners agree to a buyout price of $65,000. Most partnerships would account for the $10,000 payment above Alt's capital credit ($65,000 paid − $55,000) as a capital adjustment bonus to Alt from the capital accounts of the remaining partners. In this case, the $10,000 would be allocated against the capital accounts of Blue and Cha in their profit ratio. Blue has a 30 percent interest, and Cha has a 25 percent interest in the net income of the ABC Partnership. The sum of their respective shares is 55 percent (30 percent + 25 percent), and their relative profit percentages, rounded to the nearest percentage, are 55 percent for Blue and 45 percent for Cha, computed as follows:

	Prior Profit Percentage	Remaining Profit Percentage
Alt	45	0
Blue	30	55 (30/55)
Cha	25	45 (25/55)
Total	100	100

The entry to record the retirement of Alt is:

(21)	Alt, Capital	55,000	
	Blue, Capital	5,500	
	Cha, Capital	4,500	
	Cash		65,000
	Retirement of Alt.		

The $10,000 bonus paid to Alt is allocated to Blue and Cha in their respective profit ratios. Blue is charged for 55 percent, and Cha is charged for the remaining 45 percent.

Occasionally, a partnership uses the retirement of a partner to record unrecognized goodwill. In this case, the partnership may record the retiring partner's share only, or it may impute the entire amount of goodwill based on the retiring partner's profit percentage. If it imputes total goodwill, the remaining partners also receive their respective shares of the total goodwill recognized. Many accountants criticize recording goodwill on the retirement of a partner on the same theoretical grounds as they criticize recording unrecognized goodwill on the admission of a new partner. Nevertheless, partnership accounting sometimes uses all the recognition of goodwill at this event.

For example, if $65,000 is paid to Alt and only Alt's share of unrecognized goodwill is to be recorded, the partnership makes the following entries at the time of Alt's retirement:

(22)	Goodwill	10,000	
	Alt, Capital		10,0000
	Recognize Alt's share of goodwill.		

(23)	Alt, Capital	65,000	
	Cash		65,000
	Retirement of Alt.		

3. Buyout Price Less than Partner's Capital Credit

Sometimes, the buyout price is less than a partner's capital credit. This could result if liquidation values of net assets are less than their book values or it may occur because the dissociating partner wishes to leave the partnership badly enough to accept less than his or her current capital balance. For example, Alt agrees to accept $50,000 as the buyout price for his partnership interest. The partnership should evaluate its net assets to determine if any impairments or write-downs should be recognized. If no revaluations of the net assets are necessary, then the $5,000 difference ($50,000 cash paid less $55,000 capital credit) is distributed as a capital adjustment to Blue and Cha in their respective profit and loss ratio.

Summary of Key Concepts	Accounting for partnerships recognizes the unique aspects of this form of business organization. Most states have enacted the major provisions of the Uniform Partnership Act of 1997 (UPA 1997). This act includes the rights and responsibilities of the partners, both with third parties and among the partners, and the rights of third parties, such as creditors, against the partnership. A partnership agreement is very important because many of the sections of the UPA 1997 can be waived with a formal partnership agreement. The partnership should also file a Statement of Partnership Authority with the secretary of the state and the clerk of the county in which the partnership business takes place. The UPA 1997 includes sections stating that the partnership is an entity distinct from its partners, that partners are agents of the partnership, that partners are personally liable for the partnership obligations that exceed the partnership's assets, that partnership profits or losses are shared equally, and that a partner may dissociate, in which case that partner no longer may share in the management of the partnership.

Partnerships use a wide variety of profit or loss distribution methods and accountants must ensure that the partnership agreement is followed closely. Most partnerships continue on in business when a partner dissociates (leaves the partnership) by purchasing the dissociated partner's interest at a buyout price based on the value of the partnership were it to wind up its business. Several methods of accounting are used to account for changes in partnership membership. Some partnerships use a net asset revaluation approach, sometimes including recognizing goodwill. The other major accounting approach used to account for changes in membership is the bonus method, which uses a reclassification of partner capital. Partnerships provide four financial statements: the statement of income, the balance sheet, the statement of cash flows, and a statement of partners' capital that presents the changes in the partners' capital accounts during the period.

Key Terms

admission of a new partner, *718*	net asset revaluation, *719*	statement of partners' capital, *718*
bonus method, *719*	new partner's proportion of the partnership's book value, *722*	Statement of Partnership Authority, *708*
book value of a partnership, *720*	partners' accounts, *712*	transferable interest, *709*
buyout price, *718*	partner's dissociation, *709*	Uniform Partnership Act of 1997 (UPA 1997), *707*
entity concept, *708*	profit distribution plans, *713*	
goodwill recognition, *719*		

Appendix **15A** Tax Aspects of a Partnership

The Internal Revenue Service views the partnership form of organization as a temporary aggregation of some of the individual partners' rights. The partnership is not a separate taxable entity. Therefore, the individual partners must report their share of the partnership income or loss on their personal tax returns, whether withdrawn or not. This sometimes creates cash flow problems for partners who leave their share of income in the partnership and permit the partnership to use the income for growth. In such cases, the partners must pay income tax on income that was not distributed to them. However, this tax conduit feature also offers special tax features to the individual partners. For example, charitable contributions made by the partnership are reported on the partners' individual tax returns. Also, any tax-exempt income earned by the partnership is passed through to the individual partners.

This pass-through benefits individual partners when the business has an operating loss. The individual partners can recognize their shares of the partnership loss on their own tax returns, thereby offsetting other taxable income. If the business is incorporated, the loss does not pass through to the stockholders.

TAX BASIS OF ASSET INVESTMENTS

For capital investments, the accounting basis and the tax basis are computed differently. For tax purposes, a partnership must value the assets invested in the partnership at the tax basis of the individual partner who invests the assets. For example, assume that partner A contributes a building to the AB Partnership. The building originally cost $6,000 and has been depreciated $2,000, leaving a book value of $4,000. The building has a market value of $10,000. For tax purposes, the partnership records the building at $4,000, the adjusted basis of partner A.

This tax valuation differs from the amount that is recognized under generally accepted accounting principles. A basic concept in GAAP is to value asset transfers between separate reporting entities at their respective fair market values. In this case, the partnership records the building at its $10,000 fair value for accounting purposes. Most partnerships maintain their accounting records and financial statements using GAAP, and they use a separate adjusting schedule at the end of each period to report the results for tax purposes on Form 1065, the partnership tax information form.

In addition to asset transfers, a partnership may also assume the liabilities associated with an asset. For example, if the building was subject to a $2,000 mortgage, which the AB Partnership assumed with the building, partner A benefits because the other partners have assumed a portion of the mortgage that A originally owed entirely.

A partner's tax basis in a partnership is the sum of the following:

The partner's tax basis of any assets contributed to the partnership.

Plus the partner's share of other partners' liabilities assumed by the partnership.

Less the amount of the partner's liabilities assumed by the other partners.

To illustrate, A contributes the building discussed, which has an adjusted tax basis of $4,000 ($6,000 cost less $2,000 depreciation) and is subject to a mortgage of $2,000. The building's market value is

$10,000. B contributes machinery that has a book value of $15,000 and a market value of $20,000 and is subject to a note payable of $5,000. The partners agree to share equally in the liabilities assumed by the AB Partnership. The tax basis of each partner in the partnership is calculated as follows:

	Partner A	Partner B
Tax basis of assets contributed	$4,000	$15,000
Partner's share of other partner's liabilities assumed by partnership:		
Partner A: (1/2 of $5,000)	2,500	
Partner B: (1/2 of $2,000)		1,000
Partner's liabilities assumed by other partners:		
Partner A: (1/2 of $2,000)	(1,000)	
Partner B: (1/2 of $5,000)		(2,500)
Tax basis of partner's interest	$5,500	$13,500

The tax basis of each partner is used for tax recognition of gains or losses on subsequent disposals of the partner's investment in the partnership.

For GAAP purposes, each partner's investment is based on the fair value of the assets less liabilities assumed. Thus, in the preceding case, partner A's accounting basis is $8,000 ($10,000 market value of the building less $2,000 mortgage), and partner B's accounting basis is $15,000 ($20,000 market value of the equipment less $5,000 note payable). Any asset disposal gain or loss in the accounting financial statements is based on the valuations made using GAAP. A separate schedule of tax bases for each of the partners is typically maintained in case the information is required for a partner's individual tax return.

S CORPORATIONS

An S corporation is a corporate entity that elects to be taxed in the same manner as a partnership, with the shareholders including their share of corporate income or loss in their personal returns, whether or not the income has been distributed as dividends. This eliminates the double taxation of corporate income: first, as taxable income to the corporation, and second, as taxable dividend income to the shareholder. The S corporation form provides the shareholders with the liability limitation of an investment in a corporation. The Internal Revenue Service has certain qualifying criteria for S corporation status: (1) a maximum of 75 shareholders, all of whom must be either U.S. citizens or permanent resident aliens, is permitted; (2) only one class of stock may be issued; and (3) no more than 25 percent of the corporation's gross income can be derived from passive investment activities.

A limited liability company (LLC) is a relatively new form of corporate entity governed by the laws of the state in which it is formed. The LLC provides liability protection to its investors as well as the pass-through taxation benefits of partnerships and S corporations. However, each state has its own distinct set of laws governing LLCs, while the IRS has just one set of definitions for an S corporation. Over time, the LLC form of entity may gain in use.

Appendix 15B Joint Ventures

A joint venture usually is a business entity owned and operated by a small group of investors as a separate and specific business project organized for the mutual benefit of the ownership group. Many joint ventures are short-term associations of two or more parties to fulfill a specific project, such as the development of real estate, joint oil or gas drilling efforts, the financing of a joint production center, or the financing of a motion picture effort. Many international efforts to expand production or markets involve joint ventures either with foreign-based companies or with foreign governments. A recent phenomenon is the formation of research joint ventures in which two or more corporations agree to share the costs and eventual research accomplishments of a separate research laboratory. The venturers might not have equal ownership interests; a venturer's share could be as low as 5 or 10 percent or as high as 90 or 95 percent. Many joint ventures of only two venturers, called 50 percent–owned ventures, divide the ownership share equally.

A joint venture may be organized as a corporation, partnership, or undivided interest. A corporate joint venture is usually formed for long-term projects such as the development and sharing of technical knowledge among a small group of companies. The incorporation of the joint venture formalizes the legal relationships between the venturers and limits each investor's liability to the amount of the investment in the venture. The venture's stock is not traded publicly, and the venturers usually have other business transactions between them. Accounting for a corporate joint venture is guided by **APB Opinion No. 18**, "The Equity Method of Accounting for Investments in Common Stock" (APB 18), which requires that investors use the equity method to account for their investments in the common stock of corporate joint ventures.

When one corporation has control over another, the controlled corporation is considered a subsidiary rather than a corporate joint venture, even if it has a small number of other owners. A subsidiary should be consolidated by the controlling owner, and a noncontrolling interest recognized for the interests of other owners.

A partnership joint venture is accounted for as any other partnership. All facets of partnership accounting presented in the chapter apply to these partnerships, each of which has its own accounting records. Some joint ventures are accounted for on the books of one of the venturers; however, this combined accounting does not fully reflect the fact that the joint venture is a separate reporting entity. Each partner, or venturer, maintains an investment account on its books for its share of the partnership venture capital. The investment in the partnership account is debited for the initial investment and for the investor's share of subsequent profits. Withdrawals and shares of losses are credited to the investment account. The balance in the investment account should correspond to the balance in the partner's capital account shown on the joint venture partnership's statements.

In 1971, the AICPA issued **Accounting Interpretation No. 2**, "Investments in Partnerships and Ventures" (AIN 2 of APB 18), which stated that many of the provisions of **APB 18** are appropriate for accounting for investments in partnerships and unincorporated joint ventures. In particular, intercompany profits should be eliminated and the investor-partners should record their shares of the venture's income or loss in the same manner as with the equity method. For financial reporting purposes, if one of the investor-venturers in fact controls the joint venture, that venturer should consolidate the joint venture into its financial statements. If all investor-venturers maintain joint control, then the one-line equity method should be used to report the investment in the joint venture.

Accounting for unincorporated joint ventures that are undivided interests usually follows the method of accounting used by partnerships. An *undivided interest* exists when each investor-venturer owns a proportionate share of each asset and is proportionately liable for its share of each liability. Some established industry practices, especially in oil and gas venture accounting, provide for a pro rata recognition of a venture's assets, liabilities, revenue, and expenses. For example, assume that both A Company and B Company are 50 percent investors in a joint venture, called JTV, for the purposes of oil exploration. The JTV venture has plant assets of $500,000 and long-term liabilities of $200,000. Therefore, both A Company and B Company have an investment of $150,000 ($300,000 × .50). Under the equity method, the investment is reported in A and B companies' balance sheets as a $150,000 investment in joint venture.

International accounting standards, used outside the United States, require pro rata recognition, often termed "proportionate consolidation," in which the balance sheet of each company reports its share of the assets and liabilities of JTV. In this case, assets of $250,000 ($500,000 × .50) and liabilities of $100,000 ($200,000 × .50) are added to the present assets and liabilities of each investor-venturer. The proportionate share of the assets and liabilities should be added to similar items in the investor's financial statements. The same pro rata method is also used for the joint venture's revenue and expenses. A comparison of the equity method and the proportionate consolidation for venturer A Company is presented in Figure 15–3.

Joint ventures provide flexibility to their investors as to management, operations, and the division of profits or losses. However, companies need to be aware of **FASB Interpretation No. 46**, "Consolidation of Variable Interest Entities: An Interpretation of ARB No. 51" (FIN 46), which was issued in 2003. In situations that an investor does not have a majority stock ownership, there may exist contractual or other agreements specifying allocation of the entity's profits or losses. **FIN 46** specifies that consolidation of a variable interest entity (VIE) is required if an investor will absorb a majority of the entity's expected losses or receive a majority of the entity's expected return. Therefore, an equity investor not having a controlling financial interest may be determined to be the primary beneficiary of the VIE and thus be required to fully consolidate that entity.

Real estate development is often carried out through joint ventures. Accounting for noncontrolling interests in real estate joint ventures is guided by the AICPA's **Statement of Position 78-9**, "Accounting for Investments in Real Estate Ventures" (SOP 78-9). **SOP 78-9** recommends that the

FIGURE 15–3
Comparative
Balance Sheets for
Reporting a Joint
Venture

	Balance Sheets of A Company		
	Before Joint Venture	Equity Method	Proportionate Consolidation
Current Assets	$250	$100	$100
Property, Plant, and Equipment	400	400	650
Investment in Joint Venture	-0-	150	-0-
Total	$650	$650	$750
Current Liabilities	$100	$100	$100
Long-Term Debt	300	300	400
Stockholders' Equity	250	250	250
Total	$650	$650	$750

equity method be used to account for noncontrolling investments in corporate or noncorporate real estate ventures.

A joint venture also makes additional footnote disclosures to present additional details about the joint venture's formation and operation, the methods of accounting it uses, and a summary of its financial position and earnings.

Another form of business association is the syndicate. Syndicates are usually short term and have a defined single purpose, such as developing a financing proposal for a corporation. Syndicates are typically very informal; nevertheless, the legal relationships between the parties should be clearly specified before beginning the project.

Questions

Q15-1 Why is the partnership form of business organization sometimes preferred over the corporate or sole proprietorship forms?

Q15-2 What is the Uniform Partnership Act of 1997 and what is its relevance to partnership accounting?

Q15-3 What types of items are typically included in the partnership agreement?

Q15-4 Define the following features of a partnership: (*a*) separate business entity, (*b*) agency relationship, and (*c*) partner's joint and several liability.

Q15-5 Under what circumstances would a partner's capital account have a debit, or deficiency, balance? How is the deficiency usually eliminated?

Q15-6 A partnership agreement specifies that profits will be shared in the ratio of 4:6:5. What percentage of profits will each partner receive? Allocate a profit of $60,000 to each of the three partners.

Q15-7 The Good-Nite partnership agreement includes a profit distribution provision for interest on capital balances. Unfortunately, the provision does not state the specific capital balance to be used in computing the profit share. What choices of capital balances are available to the partners? What is the preferred capital balance to be used in an interest allocation? Why?

Q15-8 Are salaries to partners a partnership expense? Why or why not?

Q15-9 Does a partner leaving the partnership require the partnership to dissolve and wind up its business? Explain how the partnership may purchase the dissociated partner's interest in the partnership.

Q15-10 What is the book value of a partnership? Does book value also represent the partnership's market value?

Q15-11 Present the arguments for and against the bonus method of recognizing the admission of a new partner.

Q15-12 In which cases of admission of a new partner does the new partner's capital credit equal the investment made? In which cases of admission of a new partner is the new partner's capital credit less than or more than the amount of the investment?

Q15-13 Aabel, a partner in the ABC Partnership, receives a bonus of 15 percent of income. If income for the period is $20,000, what is Aabel's bonus, assuming the bonus is computed as a percentage of income before the bonus? What is the bonus if it is computed as a percentage of income *after* deducting the bonus?

Q15-14 Caine, a new partner in the ABC Partnership, has invested $12,000 for a one-third interest in a partnership with a prior capital of $21,000. What is the ABC Partnership's implied fair value? If the partners agree to recognize goodwill for the difference between the book value and fair value, present the entries the ABC Partnership should make upon Caine's admission.

Q15-15A S. Horton contributes assets with a book value of $5,000 to a partnership. The assets have a market value of $10,000 and a remaining liability of $2,000 that the partnership assumes. If the liability is shared equally with the other three partners, what is the basis of Horton's contribution for tax purposes? For GAAP purposes?

Q15-16B What is a joint venture? How are corporate joint ventures accounted for on the books of the investor companies?

Cases

C15-1 Partnership Agreement

Judgment

J. Nitty and G. Gritty are considering the formation of a partnership to operate a crafts and hobbies store. They have come to you to obtain information about the basic elements of a partnership agreement. Partnership agreements usually specify an income and loss–sharing ratio. The agreements may also provide for such additional income and loss–sharing features as salaries, bonuses, and interest allowances on invested capital.

Required

a. Discuss why a partnership agreement may need features in addition to the income and loss–sharing ratio.

b. Discuss the arguments in favor of recording salary and bonus allowances to partners as expenses included in computing net income.

c. What are the arguments against recording salary and bonus allowances to partners as partnership expenses?

d. Some partnership agreements contain a provision for interest on invested capital in distributing income to the individual partners. List the additional provisions that should be included in the partnership agreement so the interest amounts can be computed.

C15-2 Comparisons of Bonus, Goodwill, and Asset Revaluation Methods

Communication

Bill, George, and Anne are partners in the BGA Partnership. A difference of opinion exists among the partners as to how to account for the admission of Newt, a new partner. The three present partners have the following positions:

Bill wants to use the bonus method.

George believes the goodwill method is best.

Anne wants to revalue the existing tangible assets.

You have been called in to advise the three partners.

Required

Prepare a memo discussing the three different methods of accounting for the admission of a new partner, including consideration of the effects on partnership capital in the year Newt is admitted, and the effects on the capital balances in future years.

C15-3 Uniform Partnership Act Issues

(*Note*: Obtain a copy of the Uniform Partnership Act of 1997 [UPA 1997] for answering this case question. The UPA 1997 can be obtained from your university's general library, law library, or the Internet.)

Research

You are in a group that is considering forming a partnership for the purpose of purchasing a coffee shop located near your campus. The coffee shop offers freshly brewed coffee and rolls in the morning and soup and sandwiches the remainder of the day. During your preliminary discussions, several issues have emerged for which your group needs additional information.

Required

Research and provide a written summary for the following:

a. Does, in fact, every partner have the right to serve as an agent of the partnership and bind the partnership by that individual partner's actions in carrying out the partnership business?

b. If a new partner is admitted after the partnership operates for a time, what is the new partner's liability for partnership obligations arising before his or her admission? What is the new partner's liability for obligations of the partnership incurred after his or her admission?

c. Should all partners be able to examine the accounting records (the partnership's books) at any time?

d. What happens if the term of the partnership is set at one year and the partners decide to continue doing business? Is a new partnership agreement necessary at that time?

e. What happens if an individual partner wishes to leave the partnership? Can that person just announce to the other partners that he or she no longer wishes to be in the partnership and will not be liable for any future partnership obligations? What are the rights of the other partners in this matter?

f. What items do you believe should be in the partnership agreement that would be prepared before actually agreeing to form the partnership?

C15-4 **Reviewing the Annual Report of a Limited Partnership**

Although few partnerships provide publicly available financial reports, some limited partnerships do provide their financial reports. These limited partnerships usually have a general partner or other major affiliate that has offered securities to the public, such as those offered by a real estate invest-

Analysis ment trust.

Using the SEC's EDGAR (www.sec.gov), obtain the annual report for Riverside Park Associates LP for the year ended December 31, 2004. The form the entity filed is a 10-KSB, which is the small business annual filing, submitted on March 18, 2005.

Required

Answer each of the following questions from the information you obtain by analyzing the annual report of Riverside Park Associates LP.

a. Describe the business in which the limited partnership is engaged.

b. Identify the general partner of the limited partnership and describe the business relationships between the general partner and its major affiliates.

c. What percentage of the total number of outstanding units is owned by the general partner and its affiliates on December 31, 2004?

d. What amounts are presented for the net balances in the partners' capital accounts as presented on the December 31, 2004, balance sheet? Discuss how a partnership can have deficit balances for its partnership capital.

e. Compare and discuss the net loss per limited partnership unit with the distributions per limited partnership unit for the years 2003 and 2004 as reported on the statements of operations. How can distributions exceed the net loss for these two periods?

f. Who provides property management for the limited partnership? Are the costs of this service included in the determination of partnership income/loss? Explain.

g. What other types of services are provided to the partnership by the general partner and its affiliates?

h. What is the profit allocation ratio between the general partner and the limited partners?

C15-5 **Defining Partners' Authority**

Adam, Bob, and Cathy are planning to form a partnership to create a business that will retail cell phones in a new shopping center just completed in their city. They have been able to reach agreement on many issues, but Cathy is still concerned that Adam might become a little irresponsible and use

Understanding his position as a partner, and the partnership's name, in business transactions that Cathy would not approve of for the partnership. Cathy feels that Adam has superb marketing skills that will benefit the business, but she wonders what Adam may do in regard to transactions with third parties on behalf of the partnership.

Required

Prepare a memo to Cathy discussing the rights of each partner to engage in transactions on behalf of the partnership and how a partnership can restrict a partner's authority to engage in specific types of transactions.

Exercises **E15-1** **Multiple-Choice on Initial Investment [AICPA Adapted]**

Select the correct answer for each of the following questions.

1. On May 1, 20X1, Cathy and Mort formed a partnership and agreed to share profits and losses in the ratio of 3:7, respectively. Cathy contributed a parcel of land that cost her $10,000. Mort contributed

$40,000 cash. The land was sold for $18,000 immediately after formation of the partnership. What amount should be recorded in Cathy's capital account on formation of the partnership?

a. $18,000.

b. $17,400.

c. $15,000.

d. $10,000.

2. On July 1, 20X1, James and Short formed a partnership. James contributed cash. Short, previously a sole proprietor, contributed property other than cash, including realty subject to a mortgage, which the partnership assumed. Short's capital account at July 1, 20X1, should be recorded at:

a. Short's book value of the property at July 1, 20X1.

b. Short's book value of the property less the mortgage payable at July 1, 20X1.

c. The fair value of the property less the mortgage payable at July 1, 20X1.

d. The fair value of the property at July 1, 20X1.

3. A partnership is formed by two individuals who were previously sole proprietors. Property other than cash that is part of the initial investment in the partnership is recorded for financial accounting purposes at the:

a. Proprietors' book values or the fair value of the property at the date of the investment, whichever is higher.

b. Proprietors' book values or the fair value of the property at the date of the investment, whichever is lower.

c. Proprietors' book values of the property at the date of the investment.

d. Fair value of the property at the date of the investment.

4. Mutt and Jeff formed a partnership on April 1 and contributed the following assets:

	Mutt	Jeff
Cash	$150,000	$ 50,000
Land		310,000

The land was subject to a $30,000 mortgage, which the partnership assumed. Under the partnership agreement, Mutt and Jeff will share profit and loss in the ratio of one-third and two-thirds, respectively. Jeff 's capital account at April 1 should be:

a. $300,000.

b. $330,000.

c. $340,000.

d. $360,000.

5. On July 1, Mabel and Pierre formed a partnership, agreeing to share profits and losses in the ratio of 4:6, respectively. Mabel contributed a parcel of land that cost her $25,000. Pierre contributed $50,000 cash. The land was sold for $50,000 on July 1, four hours after formation of the partnership. How much should be recorded in Mabel's capital account on the partnership formation?

a. $10,000.

b. $20,000.

c. $25,000.

d. $50,000.

E15-2 Division of Income—Multiple Bases

The partnership agreement of Angela and Dawn has the following provisions:

1. The partners are to earn 10 percent on the average capital.

2. Angela and Dawn are to earn salaries of $25,000 and $15,000, respectively.

3. Any remaining income or loss is to be divided between Angela and Dawn using a 70:30 ratio.

Angela's average capital is $50,000 and Dawn's is $30,000.

Required

Prepare an income distribution schedule assuming the income of the partnership is (*a*) $80,000, and (*b*) $20,000. If no partnership agreement exists, what does the UPA 1997 prescribe as the profit or loss distribution percentages?

E15-3   Division of Income—Interest on Capital Balances

Left and Right are partners. Their capital accounts during 20X1 were as follows:

Left, Capital				Right, Capital			
8/23	6,000	1/1	30,000	3/5	9,000	1/1	50,000
		4/3	8,000			7/6	7,000
		10/31	6,000			10/7	5,000

Partnership net income is $50,000 for the year. The partnership agreement provides for the division of income as follows:

1. Each partner is to be credited 8 percent interest on his or her average capital.
2. Any remaining income or loss is to be divided equally.

Required

Prepare an income distribution schedule.

E15-4   Distribution of Partnership Income and Preparation of a Statement of Partners' Capital

The income statement for the Apple-Jack Partnership for the year ended December 31, 20X5, follows:

APPLE-JACK PARTNERSHIP
Income Statement
For the Year Ended December 31, 20X5

Net Sales	$300,000
Cost of Goods Sold	(190,000)
Gross Margin	$110,000
Operating Expenses	(30,000)
Net Income	$ 80,000

Additional Information for 20X5

1. Apple began the year with a capital balance of $40,800.
2. Jack began the year with a capital balance of $112,000.
3. On April 1, Apple invested an additional $15,000 into the partnership.
4. On August 1, Jack invested an additional $20,000 into the partnership.
5. Throughout 20X5, each partner withdrew $400 per week in anticipation of partnership net income. The partners agreed that these withdrawals are not to be included in the computation of average capital balances for purposes of income distributions.

Apple and Jack have agreed to distribute partnership net income according to the following plan:

	Apple	Jack
1. Interest on average capital balances	6%	6%
2. Bonus on net income before the bonus but after interest on average capital balances	10%	
3. Salaries	$25,000	$30,000
4. Residual (if positive)	70%	30%
Residual (if negative)	50%	50%

Required

a. Prepare a schedule that discloses the distribution of partnership net income for 20X5. Show supporting computations in good form. Round to the nearest dollar.

b. Prepare the statement of partners' capital at December 31, 20X5.

c. How would your answer to part *a* change if all of the provisions of the income distribution plan were the same except that the salaries were $30,000 to Apple and $35,000 to Jack?

E15-5   Matching Partnership Terms with Their Descriptions
Required
Match the descriptions of terms on the left with the terms on the right. A term may be used once, more than once, or not at all.

Descriptions of Terms	Terms
1. Item that occurs when the new partner's investment exceeds the new partner's capital credit.	A. General partner
2. Partner who cannot actively participate in the management of the partnership.	B. Note payable to a partner
3. The allocation of partnership profits and losses when nothing is stated in the partnership agreement.	C. Recognition of neither bonus nor goodwill
4. Item that occurs when the new partner's investment equals the new partner's capital credit and no change occurs in the old partners' capital balances.	D. Drawing account E. Limited partner F. Bonus to old partners
5. Cost not deducted to determine the partnership's net income for the period.	G. Interest on capital accounts
6. Partner who actively participates in the partnership management and who is personally liable for the partnership's debts.	H. Partnership income or loss shared equally I. New partner's goodwill recognized
7. Item that occurs when the new partner's capital credit exceeds the new partner's investment and no change occurs in the old partners' capital balances.	J. Old partners' goodwill recognized
8. Account that increases when a partner takes assets out of the partnership in anticipation of partnership net income.	K. Partnership agreement L. Bonus to new partner M. Capital account
9. Account that increases for the fair value of noncash assets invested by a partner.	
10. Related-party transaction that must be disclosed in the notes to the financial statements.	
11. Item that occurs when the new partner's investment equals the new partner's capital credit and an increase occurs in the old partners' capital balances.	
12. Item that occurs when the new partner's capital credit exceeds the new partner's investment and a decrease occurs in the old partners' capital balances.	
13. Recognition of an intangible asset upon a new partner's admission to the partnership that results in increases in the old partners' capital balances.	
14. Account closed to the capital account at year-end.	
15. Deduction of interest expense on this payable to determine the partnership's net income.	

E15-6   Admission of a Partner

In the GMP partnership, the capital balances of Mary, Gene, and Pat, who share income in the ratio of 6:3:1, are:

Mary	$240,000
Gene	120,000
Pat	40,000

Required

a. If no goodwill or bonus is recorded, how much must Elan invest for a one-third interest?

b. Prepare journal entries for the admission of Elan if she invests $80,000 for a one-fifth interest and goodwill is recorded.

c. Prepare journal entries for the admission of Elan if she invests $200,000 for a 20 percent interest. Total capital will be $600,000.

d. Elan is concerned that she may be held liable for the partnership liabilities existing on the day she is admitted to the GMP partnership. She found nothing in the partnership agreement on this item. What does the UPA 1997 state with regard to the liability of a new partner for partnership obligations incurred prior to admission?

E15-7   Admission of a Partner

Jeff and Kristie, partners in the J & K partnership, have capital balances of $100,000 and $40,000 and share income in a ratio of 4:1, respectively. Brad is to be admitted into the partnership with a 20 percent interest in the business.

Required

Record Brad's admission for each of the following independent situations:

a. Brad invests $60,000, and goodwill is to be recorded.

b. Brad invests $60,000. Total capital is to be $200,000.

c. Brad purchases the 20 percent interest by paying Jeff $22,000 and Kristie $11,000. Brad is assigned 20 percent of each of the other partners' capital accounts.

d. Brad invests $32,000. Total capital is to be $172,000.

e. Brad invests $32,000, and goodwill is to be recorded.

E15-8   Multiple-Choice Questions on the Admission of a Partner

The following balance sheet is for the partnership of Alex, Betty, and Claire, and relates to questions 1 and 2:

Cash	$ 20,000
Other Assets	180,000
	$200,000
Liabilities	$ 50,000
Alex, Capital (40%)	37,000
Betty, Capital (40%)	65,000
Claire, Capital (20%)	48,000
Total Liabilities and Capital	$200,000

(*Note:* Figures shown parenthetically reflect agreed profit and loss–sharing percentages.)
Select the correct answer for each of the following questions.

1. If the assets are fairly valued on this balance sheet and the partnership wishes to admit Denise as a new one-sixth-interest partner without recording goodwill or bonus, Denise should contribute cash or other assets of:

   a. $40,000.

   b. $36,000.

   c. $33,333.

   d. $30,000.

2. If assets on the initial balance sheet are fairly valued, Alex and Betty give their consent, and Denise pays Claire $51,000 for her interest, the revised capital balances of the partners would be:

   a. Alex, $38,000; Betty, $66,500; Denise, $51,000.

   b. Alex, $38,500; Betty, $66,500; Denise, $48,000.

   c. Alex, $37,000; Betty, $65,000; Denise, $51,000.

   d. Alex, $37,000; Betty, $65,000; Denise, $48,000.

3. On December 31, 20X4, Alan and Dave are partners with capital balances of $80,000 and $40,000, and they share profit and losses in the ratio of 2:1, respectively. On this date Scott invests $36,000 cash for a one-fifth interest in the capital and profit of the new partnership. The partners agree that the implied partnership goodwill is to be recorded simultaneously with the admission of Scott. The total implied goodwill of the firm is:

   a. $4,800.
   b. $6,000.
   c. $24,000.
   d. $30,000.

4. Boris and Richard are partners who share profits and losses in the ratio of 6:4, respectively. On May 1, 20X9, their respective capital accounts were as follows:

Boris	$60,000
Richard	50,000

   On that date, Lisa was admitted as a partner with a one-third interest in capital and profits for an investment of $40,000. The new partnership began with a total capital of $150,000. Immediately after Lisa's admission, Boris's capital should be:

   a. $50,000.
   b. $54,000.
   c. $56,667.
   d. $60,000.

5. At December 31, Rod and Sheri are partners with capital balances of $40,000 and $20,000, and they share profits and losses in the ratio of 2:1, respectively. On this date, Pete invests $17,000 in cash for a one-fifth interest in the capital and profit of the new partnership. Assuming that the bonus method is used, how much should be credited to Pete's capital account on December 31?

   a. $12,000.
   b. $15,000.
   c. $15,400.
   d. $17,000.

6. The capital accounts of the partnership of Ella, Nick, and Brandon follow with their respective profit and loss ratios:

Ella	$139,000	(.500)
Nick	209,000	(.333)
Brandon	96,000	(.167)

   Tony was admitted to the partnership when he purchased directly, for $132,000, a proportionate interest from Ella and Nick in the net assets and profits of the partnership. As a result, Tony acquired a one-fifth interest in the net assets and profits of the firm. Assuming that implied goodwill is not to be recorded, what is the combined gain realized by Ella and Nick upon the sale of a portion of their interests in the partnership to Tony?

   a. $0.
   b. $43,200.
   c. $62,400.
   d. $82,000.

7. Fred and Ralph are partners who share profits and losses in the ratio of 7:3, respectively. Their respective capital accounts are as follows:

Fred	$35,000
Ralph	30,000

They agreed to admit Lute as a partner with a one-third interest in the capital and profits and losses, upon an investment of $25,000. The new partnership will begin with total capital of $90,000. Immediately after Lute's admission, what are the capital balances of Fred, Ralph, and Lute, respectively?

a. $30,000, $30,000, $30,000.

b. $31,500, $28,500, $30,000.

c. $31,667, $28,333, $30,000.

d. $35,000, $30,000, $25,000.

8. If A is the total capital of a partnership before the admission of a new partner, B is the total capital of the partnership after the investment of a new partner, C is the amount of the new partner's investment, and D is the amount of capital credit to the new partner, then there is:

a. A bonus to the new partner if $B = A + C$ and $D < C$.

b. Goodwill to the old partners if $B > (A + C)$ and $D = C$.

c. Neither bonus nor goodwill if $B = A - C$ and $D > C$.

d. Goodwill to the new partner if $B > (A + C)$ and $D < C$.

E15-9   Withdrawal of a Partner

In the LMK partnership, Luis's capital is $40,000, Marty's is $50,000, and Karl's is $30,000. They share income in a 4:1:1 ratio, respectively. Karl is retiring from the partnership.

Required

Prepare journal entries to record Karl's withdrawal according to each of the following independent assumptions:

a. Karl is paid $38,000, and no goodwill is recorded.

b. Karl is paid $42,000, and only his share of the goodwill is recorded.

c. Karl is paid $35,000, and all implied goodwill is recorded.

d. Prepare a one-paragraph note summarizing the guidance the UPA 1997 offers on computing the buyout price for a partner who is retiring from the partnership.

E15-10   Retirement of a Partner

On January 1, 20X1, Eddy decides to retire from the partnership of Cobb, Davis, and Eddy. The partners share profits and losses in the ratio of 3:2:1, respectively. The following condensed balance sheets present the account balances immediately before and, for six independent cases, after Eddy's retirement.

	Balances prior to Eddy's Retirement	Balances after Eddy's Retirement					
Accounts		Case 1	Case 2	Case 3	Case 4	Case 5	Case 6
Assets:							
Cash	$ 90,000	$ 10,000	$ 16,000	$ 25,000	$ 16,000	$ 50,000	$ 90,000
Other Assets	200,000	200,000	200,000	200,000	200,000	220,000	200,000
Goodwill	10,000	10,000	14,000	10,000	34,000	10,000	10,000
Total Assets	$300,000	$220,000	$230,000	$235,000	$250,000	$280,000	$300,000
Liabilities and Capital:							
Liabilities	$ 60,000	$ 60,000	$ 60,000	$ 60,000	$ 60,000	$ 60,000	$ 60,000
Cobb, Capital	80,000	74,000	80,000	83,000	92,000	110,000	80,000
Davis, Capital	90,000	86,000	90,000	92,000	98,000	110,000	160,000
Eddy, Capital	70,000	-0-	-0-	-0-	-0-	-0-	-0-
Total Liabilities and Capital	$300,000	$220,000	$230,000	$235,000	$250,000	$280,000	$300,000

Required

Prepare the necessary journal entries to record Eddy's retirement from the partnership for each of the six independent cases.

Problems P15-11 Admission of a Partner

Debra and Merina sell electronic equipment and supplies through their partnership. They wish to expand their computer lines and decide to admit Wayne to the partnership. Debra's capital is $200,000, Merina's capital is $160,000, and they share income in a ratio of 3:2, respectively.

Required

Record Wayne's admission for each of the following independent situations:

a. Wayne directly purchases half of Merina's investment in the partnership for $90,000.

b. Wayne invests the amount needed to give him a one-third interest in the capital of the partnership if no goodwill or bonus is recorded.

c. Wayne invests $110,000 for a one-fourth interest. Goodwill is to be recorded.

d. Debra and Merina agree that some of the inventory is obsolete. The inventory account is decreased before Wayne is admitted. Wayne invests $100,000 for a one-fourth interest.

e. Wayne directly purchases a one-fourth interest by paying Debra $80,000 and Merina $60,000. The land account is increased before Wayne is admitted.

f. Wayne invests $80,000 for a one-fifth interest in the total capital of $440,000.

g. Wayne invests $100,000 for a one-fifth interest. Goodwill is to be recorded.

P15-12 Division of Income

C. Eastwood, A. North, and M. West are manufacturers' representatives in the architecture business. Their capital accounts in the ENW partnership for 20X1 were as follows:

C. Eastwood, Capital				A. North, Capital				M. West, Capital			
9/1	8,000	1/1	30,000	3/1	9,000	1/1	40,000	8/1	12,000	1/1	50,000
		5/1	6,000			7/1	5,000			4/1	7,000
						9/1	4,000			6/1	3,000

Required

For each of the following independent income-sharing agreements, prepare an income distribution schedule.

a. Salaries are $15,000 to Eastwood, $20,000 to North, and $18,000 to West. Eastwood receives a bonus of 5 percent of net income after deducting his bonus. Interest is 10 percent of ending capital balances. Eastwood, North, and West divide any remainder in a 3:3:4 ratio, respectively. Net income was $78,960.

b. Interest is 10 percent of weighted-average capital balances. Salaries are $24,000 to Eastwood, $21,000 to North, and $25,000 to West. North receives a bonus of 10 percent of net income after deducting the bonus and her salary. Any remainder is divided equally. Net income was $68,080.

c. West receives a bonus of 20 percent of net income after deducting the bonus and the salaries. Salaries are $21,000 to Eastwood, $18,000 to North, and $15,000 to West. Interest is 10 percent of beginning capital balances. Eastwood, North, and West divide any remainder in an 8:7:5 ratio, respectively. Net income was $92,940.

P15-13 Determining a New Partner's Investment Cost

The following condensed balance sheet is presented for the partnership of Der, Egan, and Oprins, who share profits and losses in the ratio of 4:3:3, respectively.

Cash	$ 40,000	Accounts Payable	$150,000
Other Assets	710,000	Der, Capital	260,000
		Egan, Capital	180,000
		Oprins, Capital	160,000
Total Assets	$750,000	Total Liabilities and Capital	$750,000

Assume that the partnership decides to admit Snider as a new partner with a one-fourth interest.

Required

For each of the following independent cases, determine the amount that Snider must contribute in cash or other assets.

a. No goodwill or bonus is to be recorded.

b. Goodwill of $30,000 is to be recorded and allocated to the prior partners.

c. A bonus of $24,000 is to be paid by Snider and allocated to the prior partners.

d. The prior partners, Der, Egan, and Oprins, agree to give Snider $10,000 of goodwill upon admission to the partnership.

e. Other assets are revalued for an increase of $20,000, and goodwill of $40,000 is recognized and allocated to the prior partners at the time of the admission of Snider.

f. The partners agree that total resulting capital should be $820,000 and no goodwill should be recognized.

g. Other assets are revalued down by $20,000 and a bonus of $40,000 is paid to Snider at the time of admission.

P15-14 Division of Income

Champion Play Company is a partnership that sells sporting goods. The partnership agreement provides for 10 percent interest on invested capital, salaries of $24,000 to Luc and $28,000 to Dennis, and a bonus for Luc. The 20X3 capital accounts were as follows:

Luc, Capital				Dennis, Capital			
8/1	15,000	1/1	50,000	7/1	10,000	1/1	70,000
		4/1	5,000			9/1	22,500

Required

For each of the following independent situations, prepare an income distribution schedule.

a. Interest is based on weighted-average capital balances. The bonus is 5 percent and is calculated on net income after deducting the bonus. In 20X3, net income was $64,260. Any remainder is divided between Luc and Dennis in a 3:2 ratio, respectively.

b. Interest is based on ending capital balances after deducting salaries, which the partners normally withdraw during the year. The bonus is 8 percent and is calculated on net income after deducting the bonus and salaries. Net income was $108,700. Any remainder is divided equally.

c. Interest is based on beginning capital balances. The bonus is 12.5 percent and is calculated on net income after deducting the bonus. Net income was $76,950. Any remainder is divided between Luc and Dennis in a 4:2 ratio, respectively.

P15-15 Withdrawal of a Partner under Various Alternatives

The partnership of Ace, Jack, and Spade has been in business for 25 years. On December 31, 20X5, Spade decided to retire from the partnership. The partnership balance sheet reported the following capital balances for each partner at December 31, 20X5:

Ace, Capital	$150,000
Jack, Capital	200,000
Spade, Capital	120,000

The partners allocate partnership income and loss in the ratio 20:30:50.

Required

Record Spade's withdrawal under each of the following independent situations.

a. Jack acquired Spade's capital interest for $150,000 in a personal transaction. Partnership assets were not revalued, and partnership goodwill was not recognized.

b. Assume the same facts as in part *a* except that partnership goodwill applicable to the entire business was recognized by the partnership.

c. Spade received $180,000 of partnership cash upon retirement. Capital of the partnership after Spade's retirement was $290,000.

   d. Spade received $60,000 of cash and partnership land with a fair value of $120,000. The carrying amount of the land on the partnership books was $100,000. Capital of the partnership after Spade's retirement was $310,000.

   e. Spade received $150,000 of partnership cash upon retirement. The partnership recorded the portion of goodwill attributable to Spade.

   f. Assume the same facts as in part *e* except that partnership goodwill attributable to all the partners was recorded.

   g. Due to limited cash in the partnership, Spade received land with a fair value of $100,000 and a note payable for $50,000. The carrying amount of the land on the partnership books was $60,000. Capital of the partnership after Spade's retirement was $360,000.

P15-16   **Multiple-Choice Questions—Initial Investments, Division of Income, Admission and Retirement of a Partner [AICPA Adapted]**

Select the correct answer for each of the following questions.

1. When property other than cash is invested in a partnership, at what amount should the noncash property be credited to the contributing partner's capital account?

   a. Contributing partner's tax basis.

   b. Contributing partner's original cost.

   c. Assessed valuation for property tax purposes.

   d. Fair value at the date of contribution.

2. William and Martha drafted a partnership agreement that lists the following assets contributed at the partnership's formation:

	Contributed by	
	William	**Martha**
Cash	$20,000	$30,000
Inventory		15,000
Building		40,000
Furniture and Equipment	15,000	

The building is subject to a $10,000 mortgage, which the partnership has assumed. The partnership agreement also specifies that profits and losses are to be distributed evenly. What amounts should be recorded as capital for William and Martha at the formation of the partnership?

	William	**Martha**
a.	$35,000	$85,000
b.	$35,000	$75,000
c.	$55,000	$55,000
d.	$60,000	$60,000

3. Smith and Duncan are partners with capital balances of $60,000 and $20,000, respectively. Profits and losses are divided in the ratio of 60:40. Smith and Duncan decided to form a new partnership with Johnson, who invested land valued at $15,000 for a 20 percent capital interest in the new partnership. Johnson's cost of the land was $12,000. The partnership elected to use the bonus method to record the admission of Johnson into the partnership. Johnson's capital account should be credited for:

   a. $12,000.

   b. $15,000.

   c. $16,000.

   d. $19,000.

4. On April 30, 20X5, Apple, Blue, and Crown formed a partnership by combining their separate business proprietorships. Apple contributed $50,000 cash. Blue contributed property with

a $36,000 carrying amount, a $40,000 original cost, and $80,000 fair value. The partnership accepted responsibility for the $35,000 mortgage attached to the property. Crown contributed equipment with a $30,000 carrying amount, a $75,000 original cost, and $55,000 fair value. The partnership agreement specifies that profits and losses are to be shared equally but is silent regarding capital contributions. Which partner has the largest April 30, 20X5, capital account balance?

a. Apple.

b. Blue.

c. Crown.

d. All capital account balances are equal.

Information for Questions 5 and 6

The Moon-Norbert Partnership was formed on January 2, 20X5. Under the partnership agreement, each partner has an equal initial capital balance accounted for under the goodwill method. Partnership net income or loss is allocated 60 percent to Moon and 40 percent to Norbert. To form the partnership, Moon originally contributed assets costing $30,000 with a fair value of $60,000 on January 2, 20X5, and Norbert contributed $20,000 in cash. Partners' drawings during 20X5 totaled $3,000 by Moon and $9,000 by Norbert. Moon-Norbert's net income for 20X5 was $25,000.

5. Norbert's initial capital balance in Moon-Norbert is:

   a. $20,000.

   b. $25,000.

   c. $40,000.

   d. $60,000.

6. Moon's share of Moon-Norbert's net income is:

   a. $15,000.

   b. $12,500.

   c. $12,000.

   d. $7,800.

7. In the Crowe-Dagwood partnership, Crowe and Dagwood had a capital ratio of 3:1 and a profit and loss ratio of 2:1, respectively. They used the bonus method to record Elman's admittance as a new partner. What ratio should be used to allocate, to Crowe and Dagwood, the excess of Elman's contribution over the amount credited to Elman's capital account?

   a. Crowe and Dagwood's new relative capital ratio.

   b. Crowe and Dagwood's new relative profit and loss ratio.

   c. Crowe and Dagwood's old capital ratio.

   d. Crowe and Dagwood's old profit and loss ratio.

8. Blue and Green formed a partnership in 20X4. The partnership agreement provides for annual salary allowances of $55,000 for Blue and $45,000 for Green. The partners share profits equally and losses in a 60:40 ratio. The partnership had earnings of $80,000 for 20X5 before any allowance to partners. What amount of these earnings should be credited to each partner's capital account?

	Blue	Green
a.	$40,000	$40,000
b.	$43,000	$37,000
c.	$44,000	$36,000
d.	$45,000	$35,000

9. When Jill retired from the partnership of Jill, Bill, and Hill, the final settlement of her interest exceeded her capital balance. Under the bonus method, the excess:

   a. Was recorded as goodwill.

   b. Was recorded as an expense.

c. Reduced the capital balances of Bill and Hill.

d. Had no effect on the capital balances of Bill and Hill.

P15-17 Partnership Formation, Operation, and Changes in Ownership

The partnership of Jordan and O'Neal began business on January 1, 20X7. Each partner contributed the following assets (the noncash assets are stated at their fair values on January 1, 20X7):

	Jordan	O'Neal
Cash	$ 60,000	$ 50,000
Inventories	80,000	-0-
Land	-0-	130,000
Equipment	100,000	-0-

The land was subject to a $50,000 mortgage, which the partnership assumed on January 1, 20X7. The equipment was subject to an installment note payable that had an unpaid principal amount of $20,000 on January 1, 20X7. The partnership also assumed this note payable. Jordan and O'Neal agreed to share partnership income and losses in the following manner:

	Jordan	O'Neal
Interest on beginning capital balances	3%	3%
Salaries	$12,000	$12,000
Remainder	60%	40%

During 20X7, the following events occurred:

1. Inventory was acquired at a cost of $30,000. At December 31, 20X7, the partnership owed $6,000 to its suppliers.
2. Principal of $5,000 was paid on the mortgage. Interest expense incurred on the mortgage was $2,000, all of which was paid by December 31, 20X7.
3. Principal of $3,500 was paid on the installment note. Interest expense incurred on the installment note was $2,000, all of which was paid by December 31, 20X7.
4. Sales on account amounted to $155,000. At December 31, 20X7, customers owed the partnership $21,000.
5. Selling and general expenses, excluding depreciation, amounted to $34,000. At December 31, 20X7, the partnership owned $6,200 of accrued expenses. Depreciation expense was $6,000.
6. Each partner withdrew $200 each week in anticipation of partnership profits.
7. The partnership's inventory at December 31, 20X7, was $20,000.
8. The partners allocated the net income for 20X7 and closed the accounts.

Additional Information

On January 1, 20X8, the partnership decided to admit Hill to the partnership. On that date, Hill invested $99,800 of cash into the partnership for a 20 percent capital interest. Total partnership capital after Hill was admitted totaled $450,000.

Required

a. Prepare journal entries to record the formation of the partnership on January 1, 20X7, and to record the events that occurred during 20X7.

b. Prepare the income statement for the Jordan-O'Neal Partnership for the year ended December 31, 20X7.

c. Prepare a balance sheet for the Jordon-O'Neal Partnership at December 31, 20X7.

d. Prepare the journal entry for the admission of Hill on January 1, 20X8.

P15-18A Initial Investments and Tax Bases [AICPA Adapted]

The DELS partnership was formed by combining individual accounting practices on May 10, 20X1. The initial investments were as follows:

	Current Value	Tax Basis
Delaney:		
Cash	$ 8,000	$ 8,000
Building	60,000	32,000
Mortgage payable, assumed by DELS	36,000	36,000
Engstrom:		
Cash	9,000	9,000
Office furniture	23,000	17,000
Note payable, assumed by DELS	10,000	10,000
Lahey:		
Cash	12,000	12,000
Computers and printers	18,000	21,000
Note payable, assumed by DELS	15,000	15,000
Simon:		
Cash	21,000	21,000
Library (books and periodicals)	7,000	5,000

Required

a. Prepare the journal entry to record the initial investments, using GAAP accounting.

b. Calculate the tax basis of each partner's capital if Delaney, Engstrom, Lahey, and Simon agree to assume equal amounts for the payables.

P15-19 Formation of a Partnership and Allocation of Profit and Loss

Haskins and Sells formed a partnership on January 2, 20X3. Each had been a sole proprietor before forming their partnership.

Part I

Each partner's contributions follow. The amounts under the cost column represent the amounts reported on the books of each sole proprietorship immediately before the formation of the partnership.

	Cost	Fair Value
Haskins:		
Cash	$ 45,000	$ 45,000
Inventories (FIFO)	48,000	49,000
Trade accounts receivable	40,000	40,000
Allowance for uncollectible accounts	(1,500)	(2,000)
Building	550,000	600,000
Accumulated depreciation	(200,000)	(230,000)
Mortgage on building assumed by partnership	(175,000)	(175,000)
Sells:		
Cash	$ 10,000	$ 10,000
Trade accounts receivable	30,000	30,000
Allowance for uncollectible accounts	(2,000)	(2,500)
Inventories (FIFO)	15,000	13,500
Note receivable due in 6 months	50,000	50,000
Temporary Investments	100,000	81,500
Customer lists	-0-	60,000

Required

Using the preceding information, prepare a classified balance sheet as of January 2, 20X3, for the Haskins and Sells Partnership. Assume that $25,000 of the mortgage is due in 20X3 and that the customer lists are accounted for as an intangible asset to be amortized over a five-year period.

Part II

During 20X3, the Haskins and Sells Partnership reported the following information:

Revenues	$650,000
Cost of goods sold	320,000
Selling, general, and administrative expenses	70,000
Salaries paid to each partner (not included in selling, general, and administrative expenses):	
Haskins	90,000
Sells	70,000
Bonus paid to Haskins (not included in selling, general, and adinistrative expenses)	10% of net income
Withdrawals made during the year in addition to salaries:	
Haskins	10,000
Sells	5,000
Residual profit and loss–sharing ratio:	
Haskins	20%
Sells	80%

Required

a. Prepare an income statement for the Haskins and Sells Partnership for the year ended December 31, 20X3.

b. Prepare a schedule that shows how to allocate the partnership net income for 20X3.

c. What are the partners' capital balances that will appear on the December 31, 20X3, balance sheet?

d. Assume that the distribution of partnership net income remains the same (i.e., Haskins will continue to receive a 10 percent bonus and salaries will continue to be $90,000 and $70,000 to Haskins and Sells, respectively) and that the residual profit and loss–sharing ratio will continue to be 20:80. What would partnership net income have to be for each partner to receive the same amount of income?

Supplemental Problems for this chapter are available as part of the *Online Learning Center* on the textbook's Website.

Partnerships: Liquidation

Because of the normal risks of doing business, the majority of partnerships begun in any one year fail within three years and require dissolution and liquidation. The ending of a partnership's business is often an emotional event for the partners. The partners may have had high expectations and invested a large amount of personal resources and time in the business. The end of the partnership often is the end of those business dreams. Accountants usually assist in the winding down and liquidation process and must recognize the legitimate rights of and any amounts due to the many parties involved in the partnership: individual partners, creditors of the partnership, customers, and others doing business with the partnership.

The Uniform Partnership Act of 1997 has 71 sections, 7 of which deal specifically with the dissolution and winding up of a partnership. Several sections discuss the specific rights of creditors of the partnership. Creditors have first claim to the partnership's assets. After the creditors are fully satisfied, any remaining assets are distributed to the partners based on the balances in their capital accounts. This chapter presents the concepts that accountants must know if they offer professional services to partnerships undergoing winding down and liquidation.

OVERVIEW OF PARTNERSHIP LIQUIDATIONS

The major provisions of the Uniform Partnership Act of 1997 (UPA 1997) have been adopted by most states and that act is used for the illustrations in this chapter. The chapter first presents the UPA 1997's major provisions regarding events and processes associated with partnership liquidations. After this overview, the chapter illustrates the winding up process in both a lump-sum liquidation and an installment liquidation.

Dissociation, Dissolution, Winding Up, and Liquidation of a Partnership

Dissociation

Dissociation is the legal description of the withdrawal of a partner, including the following:

1. A partner's death.
2. A partner's voluntary withdrawal (i.e., a retirement).
3. A judicial determination, including: (*a*) the partner engaged in wrongful conduct that materially and negatively affected the partnership, (*b*) the partner willfully committed a material breach of the partnership agreement, (*c*) the partner became a debtor in bankruptcy, and (*d*) an individual partner has become incapable of performing his or her duties under the partnership agreement.

Not all dissociations result in a partnership liquidation. Many partner dissociations involve only a buyout of the withdrawing partner's interest rather than a winding up and liquidation of the partnership's business.

Dissolution

Dissolution is the dissolving of a partnership. Events that cause dissolution and winding up of the partnership business are presented in section 801 of the UPA 1997, as follows:

1. In a partnership at will, a partner's express notice to leave the partnership. An at will partnership is one in which there is, at most, only an oral understanding among the partners, and there is no definite term or specific task undertaking. A partnership agreement can eliminate this event as a cause for partnership dissolution by including, for example, a provision for a buyout of that partner's interest in the partnership.

2. In a partnership for a definite term or specific undertaking, dissolution takes place: (*a*) when after a partner's death or wrongful dissociation, at least half of the remaining partners decide to wind up the partnership business, (*b*) when all of the partners agree to wind up the partnership business, or (*c*) when the term or specific undertaking has expired or been completed.

3. An event that makes it unlawful to carry on a substantial part of the partnership business.

4. A judicial determination that: (*a*) the economic purpose of the partnership is unlikely to be achieved, (*b*) a partner has engaged in conduct relating to the partnership business that makes it impracticable to carry on the partnership business, or (*c*) it is not reasonably practicable to carry on the partnership business in conformity with the partnership agreement.

On dissolution, the partnership begins the winding up of the partnership's business.

Winding Up and Liquidation

Winding up and liquidation of the partnership begins after the dissolution of the partnership. The partnership continues for the limited purpose of winding up the business and completing work in process. The winding up process includes the transactions necessary to liquidate the partnership, such as the collection of receivables, including any receivables from partners, conversion of the noncash assets to cash, payment of the partnership's obligations, and the distribution of any remaining net balance to the partners, in cash, according to their capital interests. If the partnership agreement does not provide for a special liquidation ratio, then profits or losses during the liquidation process are distributed in the normal profit and loss ratio that was used during the operation of the partnership.

Loans from Partners   Note that under the UPA 1997, liabilities to partners for loans they made to the partnership have the same status as liabilities to the partnership's third party creditors. Thus, under the UPA 1997, there is no offset of liabilities to partners with the partners' capital accounts. These partnership obligations to the individual partners must be paid during the winding up of the partnership.

Deficits in Partners' Capital Accounts   As part of the liquidation process, each partner with a deficit in his or her capital account must make a contribution to the partnership to remedy that capital deficit. The partnership makes a liquidating distribution, in cash, to each partner with a capital credit balance. The UPA 1997 specifies cash for these liquidating distributions. If a partner fails to make a required contribution to remedy his or her capital deficit, all other partners must contribute, in the proportion to which those partners share partnership losses, the additional amount necessary to pay the partnership's obligations.

Statement of Partnership Realization and Liquidation

To guide and summarize the partnership liquidation process, a ***statement of partnership realization and liquidation*** may be prepared. The statement, often called a "statement of liquidation," is the basis of the journal entries made to record the liquidation. It presents, in workpaper form, the effects of the liquidation on the balance sheet accounts of the partnership. The statement shows the conversion of assets into cash, the allocation of any gains or losses to the partners, and the distribution of cash to creditors and partners. This statement is a basic feature of accounting for a partnership liquidation and is presented and illustrated in the remainder of the chapter.

LUMP-SUM LIQUIDATIONS

A *lump-sum liquidation* of a partnership is one in which all assets are converted into cash within a very short time, creditors are paid, and a single, lump-sum payment is made to the partners for their capital interests. Although most partnership liquidations take place over an extended period, as illustrated later, the lump-sum liquidation is an excellent focal point for presenting the major concepts of partnership liquidation.

Realization of Assets

Typically, a partnership experiences losses on the disposal of its assets. A partnership may have a "Going out of Business" sale in which its inventory is marked down well below normal selling price to encourage immediate sale. Often, the remaining inventory may be sold to companies that specialize in acquiring assets of liquidating businesses. The partnership's furniture, fixtures, and equipment may also be offered at a reduced price or sold to liquidators.

The partnership usually collects the accounts receivable. Sometimes the partnership offers a large cash discount for the prompt payment of any remaining receivables whose collection may otherwise delay terminating the partnership. Alternatively, the receivables may be sold to a *factor,* a business that specializes in acquiring accounts receivables and immediately paying cash to the seller of the receivables. The partnership records the sale of the receivables as it would any other asset. Typically, the factor acquires only the best of a business's receivables at a price below face value, but some factors are willing to buy all receivables and pay a significantly lower price than face value.

The assets of the partnership, including any receivables from the partners and any contributions required of partners to remedy their capital deficits, are applied to pay the partnership's creditors. The UPA 1997 specifies that liabilities to individual partners, for example, liabilities resulting from loans made to the partnership from a partner, have the same status as liabilities to third party creditors; outside creditors do not have any priority over a partner who has made a loan to the partnership. It is very important that loans between the partnership and partners are fully documented, such as with promissory notes, to indicate clearly that the transaction is a loan and not a capital contribution or withdrawal. These loans carry interest until paid unless otherwise agreed to by the partnership and the individual partner. Loans to or from partners must be settled during the winding up process. Any remaining amount is then paid, in cash, to the partners in accordance with their rights to liquidating distributions. Section 807 of the UPA 1997 states that the liquidating distributions to the partners are to be made in cash.

Expenses of Liquidation

The liquidation process usually begins with scheduling the partnership's known assets and liabilities. The names and addresses of creditors and the amounts owed to each are specified. As diligent as the effort usually is, additional, unscheduled creditors may become known during the liquidation process. The liquidation process also involves some expenses, such as additional legal and accounting costs. The partnership may also incur costs of disposing of the business, such as special advertising and costs of locating specialized equipment dealers. These expenses are allocated to partners' capital accounts in the profit and loss distribution ratio.

Illustration of Lump-Sum Liquidation

The following illustration presents the liquidation of the ABC Partnership, whose partners, Alt, Blue, and Cha, decide to terminate the business on May 1, 20X5. The AB Partnership was formed on January 1, 20X1. Cha was admitted into the partnership on January 1, 20X3, and the name of the business was changed to the ABC Partnership. For purposes of this illustration, assume that Alt remained in the partnership and, in 20X4, the partners agreed to a realignment of their profit and loss–sharing percentages to more closely conform with each partner's efforts. The profit and loss–sharing percentages after realignment in 20X4 were as follows: Alt, 40 percent, Blue, 40 percent, and Cha, 20 percent. A condensed trial balance of the company on May 1, 20X5, the day the partners decide to liquidate the business, follows:

ABC PARTNERSHIP
Trial Balance
May 1, 20X5

Cash	$ 10,000	
Noncash Assets	90,000	
Liabilities		$ 42,000
Alt, Capital (40%)		34,000
Blue, Capital (40%)		10,000
Cha, Capital (20%)		14,000
Total	$100,000	$100,000

The basic accounting equation, Assets − Liabilities = Owners' equity, applies to partnership accounting. In this case, owners' equity is the sum of the partners' capital accounts, as follows:

$$\text{Assets} \quad - \text{Liabilities} = \text{Owners' equity}$$
$$\$100,000 - \quad \$42,000 \quad = \quad \$58,000$$

The following three cases illustrate the partnership liquidation concepts used most commonly. Each case begins with the May 1, 20X5, trial balance of the ABC Partnership. The amount of cash realized from the disposal of the noncash assets is different for each of the three cases, and the effects of the different realizations are shown in the statement of partnership realization and liquidation presented for each case.

Case 1. Partnership Solvent and No Deficits in Partners' Capital Accounts

The noncash assets are sold for $80,000 on May 15, 20X5, at a $10,000 loss. The partnership's creditors are paid their $42,000 on May 20, and the remaining $48,000 cash is distributed to the partners on May 30, 20X5.

The statement of realization and liquidation for Case 1 is presented in Figure 16–1. Note that parentheses are used to indicate credit amounts in the workpapers used throughout this chapter. The statement includes only balance sheet accounts across the columns, with all

FIGURE 16–1   Case 1. Partnership Solvent; No Deficits in Partners' Capital Accounts

ABC PARTNERSHIP
Statement of Partnership Realization and Liquidation
Lump-Sum Liquidation

				Capital Balance		
	Cash	Noncash Assets	Liabilities	Alt, 40%	Blue, 40%	Cha, 20%
Preliquidation balances, May 1	10,000	90,000	(42,000)	(34,000)	(10,000)	(14,000)
Sales of assets and distribution of $10,000 loss	80,000	(90,000)		4,000	4,000	2,000
	90,000	-0-	(42,000)	(30,000)	(6,000)	(12,000)
Payment to creditors	(42,000)		42,000			
	48,000	-0-	-0-	(30,000)	(6,000)	(12,000)
Lump-sum payment to partners	(48,000)			30,000	6,000	12,000
Postliquidation balances	-0-	-0-	-0-	-0-	-0-	-0-

Note: Parentheses indicate credit amount.

noncash assets presented together as a single total. Once a business has entered liquidation, the balance sheet accounts are the only relevant ones; the income statement is for a going concern. The liquidation process is presented in the order of occurrence in the rows of the workpaper. Thus, the workpaper includes the entire realization and liquidation process and is the basis for the journal entries to record the liquidation.

Other important observations are as follows:

1. The preliquidation balances are obtained from the May 1, 20X5, trial balance.
2. The $10,000 loss is distributed directly to the partners' capital accounts.
3. Creditors, including individual partners who have made any loans to the partnership, are paid before any cash is distributed to partners.
4. Payments to partners are made for their capital credit balances.
5. The postliquidation balances are all zero, indicating the accounts are all closed and the partnership is fully liquidated and terminated.

The statement of partnership realization and liquidation is the basis for the following journal entries to record the liquidation process:

May 15, 20X5

(1)	Cash	80,000	
	Alt, Capital	4,000	
	Blue, Capital	4,000	
	Cha, Capital	2,000	
	Noncash Assets		90,000
	Realization of all noncash assets of the ABC Partnership and distribution of $10,000 loss using profit and loss ratio.		

May 20, 20X5

(2)	Liabilities	42,000	
	Cash		42,000
	Pay creditors.		

May 30, 20X5

(3)	Alt, Capital	30,000	
	Blue, Capital	6,000	
	Cha, Capital	12,000	
	Cash		48,000
	Lump-sum payments to partners.		

Case 2. Partnership Solvent and Deficit Created in Partner's Capital Account

A deficit in a partner's capital account can occur if the credit balance of that capital account is too low to absorb his or her share of losses. A capital deficit may be created at any time in the liquidation process. Such deficits may be remedied by either of the following two means:

1. The partner invests cash or other assets to eliminate the capital deficit.
2. The partner's capital deficit is distributed to the other partners in their resulting loss–sharing ratio.

The approach used depends on the solvency of the partner with the capital deficit. A partner who is personally solvent and has sufficient net worth to eliminate the capital deficit must make an additional investment in the partnership to cover the deficit. On the other hand, if the partner is personally insolvent—that is, personal liabilities exceed personal assets—section 807 of the UPA 1997 requires the remaining partners to absorb the insolvent partner's deficit by allocating it to their capital accounts in their resulting loss-sharing ratio.

The following lump-sum distribution illustrates these points:

1. The three partners' personal financial statements are as follows:

	Alt	Blue	Cha
Personal assets	$150,000	$12,000	$42,000
Personal liabilities	(86,000)	(16,000)	(14,000)
Net worth (deficit)	$ 64,000	$ (4,000)	$28,000

Blue is personally insolvent; Alt and Cha are personally solvent.

2. The partnership's noncash assets are sold for $35,000 on May 15, 20X5, and the $55,000 loss is allocated to the partners' capital accounts.
3. The partnership's creditors are paid $42,000 on May 20, 20X5.
4. Because Blue is personally insolvent, Blue's capital deficit of $12,000 is allocated to the other partners.
5. The remaining $4,000 cash is distributed as a lump-sum payment on May 30, 20X5.

The statement of partnership realization and liquidation for Case 2 is presented in Figure 16–2.

The following observations emerge from this illustration:

1. The $55,000 loss on the realization of noncash assets is allocated in the partners' loss–sharing ratio of 40 percent for Alt, 40 percent for Blue, and 20 percent for Cha. Blue's $22,000 share of the loss on disposal creates a $12,000 deficit in his capital account. Blue is personally insolvent and is unable to make an additional investment to remove the capital deficit.
2. The partnership's creditors are paid before any distributions are made to the partners.

FIGURE 16–2 Case 2. Partnership Solvent; Deficit Created in Personally Insolvent Partner's Capital Account

ABC PARTNERSHIP
Statement of Partnership Realization and Liquidation
Lump-Sum Liquidation

				Capital Balance		
	Cash	Noncash Assets	Liabilities	Alt, 40%	Blue, 40%	Cha, 20%
Preliquidation balances, May 1	10,000	90,000	(42,000)	(34,000)	(10,000)	(14,000)
Sales of assets and distribution of $55,000 loss	35,000	(90,000)		22,000	22,000	11,000
	45,000	-0-	(42,000)	(12,000)	12,000	(3,000)
Payment to creditors	(42,000)		42,000			
	3,000	-0-	-0-	(12,000)	12,000	(3,000)
Distribution of deficit of insolvent partner:					(12,000)	
40/60 × $12,000				8,000		
20/60 × $12,000						4,000
	3,000	-0-	-0-	(4,000)	-0-	1,000
Contribution by Cha to remedy capital deficit	1,000					(1,000)
	4,000	-0-	-0-	(4,000)	-0-	-0-
Lump-sum payment to partners	(4,000)			4,000		
Postliquidation balances	-0-	-0-	-0-	-0-	-0-	-0-

Note: Parentheses indicate credit amount.

3. Blue's $12,000 deficit is distributed to Alt and Cha in their resulting loss-sharing ratio. Note that the UPA 1977 specifies the loss-sharing ratio be used for this allocation. Alt absorbs two-thirds (40/60) of Blue's deficit, and Cha absorbs one-third (20/60).

4. The distribution of Blue's deficit creates a deficit in Cha's capital account. Cha must contribute $1,000 to remedy her capital deficit.

5. A lump-sum payment is made to Alt for his $4,000 capital credit.

6. All postliquidation balances are zero, indicating the completion of the liquidation process.

Case 3. Partnership Is Insolvent and Deficit Created in Partner's Capital Account

A partnership is insolvent when existing cash and cash generated by the sale of the assets is not sufficient to pay the partnership's liabilities. In this case, the individual partners are liable for the remaining unpaid partnership liabilities. The following illustration presents an insolvent partnership and a deficit in one of the partner's capital accounts.

1. Alt and Cha are personally solvent, and Blue is personally insolvent as in Case 2.

2. The noncash assets are sold for $20,000 on May 15, 20X5.

3. The partnership's creditors are paid $42,000 on May 20, 20X5.

The statement of partnership realization and liquidation for Case 3 is presented in Figure 16–3. The following observations are made from this illustration:

1. The $70,000 loss is allocated to the partners in their loss–sharing ratio. This allocation creates a deficit of $18,000 in Blue's capital account.

2. Because Blue is personally insolvent, his $18,000 deficit is distributed to Alt and Cha in their loss-sharing ratio of 40:60 for Alt and 20:60 for Cha. The distribution of Blue's deficit results in a $6,000 deficit for Alt and a $6,000 deficit for Cha.

3. Alt and Cha make additional capital contributions to remedy their respective capital deficits of $6,000 and $6,000.

4. The $42,000 partnership cash now available is used to pay the partnership's creditors.

5. The postliquidation balances are zero, indicating completion of the partnership liquidation.

FIGURE 16–3 **Case 3. Partnership Insolvent; Deficit Created in Personally Insolvent Partner's Capital Account**

ABC PARTNERSHIP Statement of Partnership Realization and Liquidation Lump-Sum Liquidation						
				Capital Balance		
	Cash	Noncash Assets	Liabilities	Alt, 40%	Blue, 40%	Cha, 20%
Preliquidation balances, May 1	10,000	90,000	(42,000)	(34,000)	(10,000)	(14,000)
Sales of assets and distribution of $70,000 loss	20,000	(90,000)		28,000	28,000	14,000
	30,000	-0-	(42,000)	(6,000)	18,000	-0-
Distribution of deficit of insolvent partner:					(18,000)	
40/60 × $18,000				12,000		
20/60 × $18,000						6,000
	30,000	-0-	(42,000)	6,000	-0-	6,000
Contribution by Alt and Cha to remedy capital deficit	12,000			(6,000)		(6,000)
	42,000	-0-	(42,000)	-0-	-0-	-0-
Payment to creditors	(42,000)		42,000			
Postliquidation balances	-0-	-0-	-0-	-0-	-0-	-0-

Note: Parentheses indicate credit amount.

In Case 3, Alt and Cha each made additional capital contributions to eliminate their capital deficits. Whenever a partner must remedy another partner's capital deficit, the partner making the remedy has cause to bring suit against the failing partner. Blue's failure in the amount of $12,000 in Case 2, and $18,000 in Case 3, required Alt and Cha to remedy Blue's deficit. Alt and Cha can sue Blue and be included in the list of Blue's personal liabilities. Although Blue is personally insolvent, Alt and Cha may obtain a partial recovery of their amounts.

INSTALLMENT LIQUIDATIONS

An *installment liquidation* typically requires several months to complete and includes periodic, or installment, payments to the partners during the liquidation period. Most partnership liquidations take place over an extended period in order to obtain the largest possible amount from the realization of the assets. The partners typically receive periodic payments during the liquidation because they require funds for personal purposes.

Installment liquidations involve the distribution of cash to partners before complete liquidation of the assets occurs. The accountant must be especially cautious when distributing available cash because future events may change the amounts to be paid to each partner. For this reason, the following practical guides are used to assist the accountant in determining safe installment payments to the partners:

1. Distribute no cash to the partners until all liabilities and actual and potential liquidation expenses have been paid or provided for by reserving the necessary cash.

2. Anticipate the worst, or most restrictive, possible case before determining the amount of cash installment each partner receives:

   a. Assume that all remaining noncash assets will be written off as a loss; that is, assume that nothing will be realized on asset disposals.

   b. Assume that deficits created in the partners' capital accounts will be distributed to the remaining partners; that is, assume that deficits will not be eliminated by additional partner capital contributions.

3. After the accountant has assumed the worst possible cases, the remaining credit balances in capital accounts represent safe distributions of cash that may be distributed to partners in those amounts.

Illustration of Installment Liquidation

The same illustration used in the lump-sum liquidation of the ABC Partnership is now used to illustrate liquidation in installments. Alt, Blue, and Cha decide to liquidate their business over a period of time and to receive installment distributions of available cash during the liquidation process.

ABC Partnership's condensed trial balance on May 1, 20X5, the day the partners decide to liquidate the business, follows. Each partner's profit and loss–sharing percentage is also shown.

ABC PARTNERSHIP **Trial Balance** **May 1, 20X5**		
Cash	$ 10,000	
Noncash Assets	90,000	
Liabilities		$ 42,000
Alt, Capital (40%)		34,000
Blue, Capital (40%)		10,000
Cha, Capital (20%)		14,000
Total	$100,000	$100,000

The following describes this case.

1. The partners' net worth statements on May 1, 20X5, are as follows:

	Alt	Blue	Cha
Personal assets	$150,000	$12,000	$42,000
Personal liabilities	(86,000)	(16,000)	(14,000)
Net worth (deficit)	$ 64,000	$ (4,000)	$28,000

Blue is personally insolvent; Alt and Cha are personally solvent.

2. The noncash assets are sold as follows:

Date	Book Value	Proceeds	Loss
5/15/X5	$55,000	$45,000	$10,000
6/15/X5	30,000	15,000	15,000
7/15/X5	5,000	5,000	

3. The creditors are paid $42,000 on May 20.
4. The partners agree to maintain a $10,000 cash reserve during the liquidation process to pay for any liquidation expenses.
5. The partners agree to distribute the available cash at the end of each month; that is, installment liquidations will be made on May 31 and June 30. The final cash distributions to partners will be made on July 31, 20X5, the end of the liquidation process.

Figure 16–4 presents the statement of partnership realization and liquidation for the installment liquidation of the ABC Partnership.

Transactions during May 20X5

The events during May 20X5 result in a distribution of $5,000 to the partners. The procedure to arrive at this amount is as follows:

1. The sale of $55,000 of assets results in a loss of $10,000, which is distributed to the three partners in their loss–sharing ratio.
2. Payments of $42,000 are made to the partnership's creditors for the known liabilities.
3. Available cash is distributed to the partners on May 31, 20X5.

To determine the safe payment of cash to be distributed to partners, the accountant must make some assumptions about the future liquidation of the remaining assets. Under the assumption of the worst possible situation, the remaining $35,000 of assets will result in a total loss. Before making a cash distribution to the partners, the accountant prepares a ***schedule of safe payments to partners*** using the worst-case assumptions. Figure 16–5 presents the schedule of safe payments to partners as of May 31, 20X5.

The schedule of safe payments begins with the partners' capital balances as of May 31. The logic of using just the capital accounts comes from the accounting equation: Assets − Liabilities = Partners' capital balances. Thus, for example, if there was an increase in a liability that reduced the net assets, the equality of the accounting equation would also result in a decrease in the total of partners' capital balances. Because the partners' capital accounts are the focus of the payments to partners, it is unnecessary to include the assets and liabilities in the schedule of safe payments to partners. The schedule includes all the information necessary for partners to know how much cash they will receive at each cash distribution date.

Alt, Blue, and Cha agree to withhold $10,000 for possible liquidation expenses. In addition, the noncash assets have a remaining balance of $35,000 on May 31. A worst-case assumption is a complete loss on the noncash assets and $10,000 of liquidation expenses,

FIGURE 16–4 **Installment Liquidation Workpaper**

ABC PARTNERSHIP
Statement of Partnership Realization and Liquidation
Installment Liquidation

	Cash	Noncash Assets	Liabilities	Capital Balance Alt, 40%	Blue, 40%	Cha, 20%
Preliquidation balances, May 1	10,000	90,000	(42,000)	(34,000)	(10,000)	(14,000)
May 20X5:						
Sale of assets and distribution of $10,000 loss	45,000	(55,000)		4,000	4,000	2,000
	55,000	35,000	(42,000)	(30,000)	(6,000)	(12,000)
Payment to creditors	(42,000)		42,000			
	13,000	35,000	-0-	(30,000)	(6,000)	(12,000)
Payment to partners (Schedule 1, Figure 16–5)	(3,000)			3,000		
	10,000	35,000	-0-	(27,000)	(6,000)	(12,000)
June 20X5:						
Sale of assets and distribution of $15,000 loss	15,000	(30,000)		6,000	6,000	3,000
	25,000	5,000	-0-	(21,000)	-0-	(9,000)
Payment to partners (Schedule 2, Figure 16–5)	(15,000)			11,000		4,000
	10,000	5,000	-0-	(10,000)	-0-	(5,000)
July 20X5:						
Sale of assets at book value	5,000	(5,000)				
	15,000	-0-	-0-	(10,000)	-0-	(5,000)
Payment of $7,500 in liquidation costs	(7,500)			3,000	3,000	1,500
	7,500	-0-	-0-	(7,000)	3,000	(3,500)
Distribution of deficit of insolvent partner:					(3,000)	
40/60 × $3,000				2,000		
20/60 × $3,000						1,000
	7,500	-0-	-0-	(5,000)	-0-	(2,500)
Payment to partners	(7,500)			5,000		2,500
Postliquidation balances, July 31	-0-	-0-	-0-	-0-	-0-	-0-

Note: Parentheses indicate credit amount.

totaling $45,000 of charges to be distributed to the partners' capital accounts. The capital accounts of Alt, Blue, and Cha would be charged for $18,000, $18,000, and $9,000, respectively, for their shares of the $45,000 assumed loss. These assumptions result in a pro forma deficit in Blue's capital account. This is not an actual deficit that must be remedied! It is merely the result of applying the worst-case assumptions.

Continuing such worst-case planning, the accountant assumes that Blue is insolvent (which happens to be true in this example) and distributes the pro forma deficit in Blue's capital account to Alt and Cha in their *loss–sharing ratio* of 40:60 to Alt and 20:60 to Cha. The resulting credit balances indicate the amount of cash that may be safely distributed to the partners. The May 31 cash distribution is shown in Figure 16–4. The available cash of $3,000 is distributed to Alt. The ending balances should satisfy the equality of assets and equities of the accounting equation. If the equality has been destroyed, an error has occurred that must be corrected before proceeding further. As of May 31, after the installment distribution, the accounting equation is:

$$\text{Assets} - \text{Liabilities} = \text{Owners' equity}$$
$$\$45,000 - \$0 = \$45,000$$

FIGURE 16–5 Schedule of Safe Payment to Partners for an Installment Liquidation

		Partner	
	Alt 40%	**Blue 40%**	**Cha 20%**
Schedule 1, May 31, 20X5			
Computation of distribution of cash available on May 31, 20X5:			
Capital balances, May 31, before cash distribution	(30,000)	(6,000)	(12,000)
Assume full loss of $35,000 on remaining noncash assets and $10,000			
in possible future liquidation expenses	18,000	18,000	9,000
	(12,000)	12,000	(3,000)
Assume Blue's potential deficit must be absorbed by Alt and Cha:		(12,000)	
40/60 × $12,000	8,000		
20/60 × $12,000			4,000
	(4,000)	-0-	1,000
Assume Cha's potential deficit must be absorbed by Alt	1,000		(1,000)
Safe payment to partners, May 31	(3,000)	-0-	-0-
Schedule 2, June 30, 20X5			
Computation of distribution of cash available on June 30, 20X5:			
Capital balances, June 30, before cash distribution	(21,000)	-0-	(9,000)
Assume full loss of $5,000 on remaining noncash assets and $10,000 in			
possible future liquidation expenses	6,000	6,000	3,000
	(15,000)	6,000	(6,000)
Assume Blue's potential deficit must be absorbed by Alt and Cha:		(6,000)	
40/60 × $6,000	4,000		
20/60 × $6,000			2,000
Safe payment to partners, June 30	(11,000)	-0-	(4,000)

Note: Parentheses indicate credit amount.

Transactions during June 20X5

Figure 16–4 continues with transactions for June 20X5, as follows:

1. Noncash assets of $30,000 are sold on June 15 for a $15,000 loss, which is distributed to the partners in their loss–sharing ratio, resulting in a zero capital balance for Blue.

2. On June 30, 20X5, available cash is distributed as an installment payment to the partners.

The schedule of safe payments to partners as of June 30, 20X5, in Figure 16–5 shows how the amounts of distribution are calculated. A worst-case plan assumes that the remaining noncash assets of $5,000 must be written off as a loss and that the $10,000 cash in reserve will be completely used for liquidation expenses. This $15,000 pro forma loss is allocated to the partners in their loss–sharing ratio, which creates a $6,000 deficit in Blue's capital account. Continuing the worst-case scenario, it is assumed Blue will not eliminate this debit balance. Therefore, the $6,000 potential deficit is allocated to Alt and Cha in their resulting loss–sharing ratio of 40:60 to Alt and 20:60 to Cha. The resulting credit balances in the partners' capital accounts show the amount of cash that can be distributed safely. Only $15,000 of the available cash is distributed to Alt and Cha on June 30, as shown in Figure 16–4.

Transactions during July 20X5

The last part of Figure 16–4 shows the completion of the liquidation transactions during July 20X5:

1. The remaining assets are sold at their book value of $5,000.
2. Actual liquidation costs of $7,500 are paid and allocated to the partners in their loss–sharing ratio, creating a deficit of $3,000 in Blue's capital account. The remaining $2,500 of the $10,000 reserved for the expenses is released for distribution to the partners.
3. Because Blue is personally insolvent and cannot contribute to the partnership, the $3,000 deficit is distributed to Alt and Cha in their loss–sharing ratio. Note that this is an actual deficit, not a pro forma deficit.
4. The $7,500 of remaining cash is paid to Alt and Cha to the extent of their capital balances. After this last distribution, all account balances are zero, indicating the completion of the liquidation process.

Cash Distribution Plan

At the beginning of the liquidation process, accountants commonly prepare a *cash distribution plan*, which gives the partners an idea of the installment cash payments each will receive as cash becomes available to the partnership. The actual installment distributions are determined using the statement of realization and liquidation, supplemented with the schedule of safe payments to partners as presented in the preceding section of the chapter. The cash distribution plan is a pro forma projection of the application of cash as it becomes available.

Loss Absorption Power

A basic concept of the cash distribution plan at the beginning of the liquidation process is *loss absorption power (LAP)*. An individual partner's LAP is defined as the maximum loss that the partnership can realize before that partner's capital account balance is extinguished. The loss absorption power is a function of two elements, as follows:

$$LAP = \frac{\text{Partner's capital account balance}}{\text{Partner's loss share}}$$

For example, on May 1, 2005, Alt has a capital account credit balance of $34,000 and a 40 percent share in the losses of ABC Partnership. Alt's LAP is

$$LAP = \frac{\$34,000}{.40} = \$85,000$$

This means that $85,000 in losses on disposing of noncash assets or from additional liquidation expenses would eliminate the credit balance in Alt's capital account, as follows:

$$\$85,000 \times .40 = \$34,000$$

Illustration of Cash Distribution Plan

The following illustration is based on the ABC Partnership example. A trial balance of its balance sheet accounts on May 1, 20X5, the day the partners decide to liquidate the business, is prepared.

ABC PARTNERSHIP **Trial Balance** **May 1, 20X5**		
Cash	$ 10,000	
Noncash Assets	90,000	
Liabilities		$ 42,000
Alt, Capital (40%)		34,000
Blue, Capital (40%)		10,000
Cha, Capital (20%)		14,000
Total	$100,000	$100,000

The partners ask for a cash distribution plan as of May 1, 20X5, to determine the distributions of cash as it becomes available during the liquidation process. Such a plan always provides for payment to the partnership's creditors before any distributions may be made to the partners. Figure 16–6 presents the cash distribution plan as of May 1, the beginning date of the liquidation process.

The important observations from this illustration are as follows:

1. Each partner's loss absorption power is computed as the partner's preliquidation capital balance divided by that partner's *loss–sharing percentage*. Alt has the highest LAP ($85,000), Cha has the next highest ($70,000), and Blue has the lowest ($25,000). Each partner's LAP is the amount of loss that would completely eliminate his or her net capital credit balance. Alt is the least vulnerable to a loss, and Blue is the most vulnerable.

2. The least vulnerable partner is the first to receive any cash distributions after providing for creditors. Alt is the only partner to receive cash until his LAP is decreased to the level of the next highest partner, Cha. To decrease Alt's LAP by $15,000 requires the payment of $6,000 ($15,000 × .40) to Alt. After payment of $6,000 to Alt, his new loss absorption power will be the same as Cha's, calculated as Alt's remaining capital balance of $28,000 divided by his loss-sharing percentage of 40 percent ($28,000 ÷ .40 = $70,000).

FIGURE 16–6   **Cash Distribution Plan for Liquidating Partnership**

	Loss Absorption Power			Capital Balance		
ABC PARTNERSHIP **Cash Distribution Plan** **May 1, 20X5**	**Alt**	**Blue**	**Cha**	**Alt**	**Blue**	**Cha**
Loss-sharing percentages				40%	40%	20%
Preliquidation capital balances, May 1, 20X5				(34,000)	(10,000)	(14,000)
Loss absorption power (LAP)						
(Capital balance / Loss ratio)	(85,000)	(25,000)	(70,000)			
Decrease highest LAP to next-highest LAP:						
Decrease Alt by $15,000						
(cash distribution: $15,000 × .40 = $6,000)	15,000			6,000		
	(70,000)	(25,000)	(70,000)	(28,000)	(10,000)	(14,000)
Decrease LAPs to next-highest level:						
Decrease Alt by $45,000						
(cash distribution: $45,000 × .40 = $18,000)	45,000			18,000		
Decrease Cha by $45,000						
(cash distribution: $45,000 × .20 = $9,000)			45,000			9,000
	(25,000)	(25,000)	(25,000)	(10,000)	(10,000)	(5,000)
Decrease LAPs by distributing cash in the loss-sharing percentages	40%	40%	20%			
Summary of Cash Distribution Plan						
Step 1: First $42,000 to creditors						
Step 2: Next $10,000 to liquidation expenses						
Step 3: Next $6,000 to Alt				6,000		
Step 4: Next $45,000 to Alt and Cha in their respective loss ratios				18,000		9,000
Step 5: Any additional distributions in the partners' loss-sharing ratios				40%	40%	20%

Note: Parentheses indicate credit amount.

3. Alt's and Cha's LAPs are now equal, and they will receive cash distributions until the LAP of each decreases to the next highest level, the $25,000 of Blue. Multiplying the loss absorption power of $45,000 ($70,000 − $25,000) by the two partners' loss-sharing ratios shows how much of the next available cash can be safely paid to each partner. Alt and Cha will receive cash distributions according to their loss-sharing ratios. As the next $27,000 of cash becomes available, it will be distributed to Alt and Cha in the ratio of 40:60 to Alt and 20:60 to Cha.

4. Finally, when all three partners have the same LAPs, any remaining cash is distributed according to their loss-sharing ratios.

The summary of the cash distribution plan on the bottom of Figure 16–6 is provided to the partners. From this summary, partners are able to determine the relative amounts each will receive as cash becomes available to the partnership.

Figure 16–7 presents the capital balances for each of the partners in the ABC Partnership during the installment liquidation period from May 1, 20X5, through July 31, 20X5. The installment payments to partners are computed on the statement of partnership realization and liquidation (Figure 16–4) using a schedule of safe distributions to partners (Figure 16–5). Figure 16–7 shows that the actual distributions of available cash conform to the cash distribution plan prepared at the beginning of the liquidation process.

FIGURE 16–7
Confirmation of Cash Distribution Plan

	ABC PARTNERSHIP **Capital Account Balances** **May 1, 20X5, through July 31, 20X5**		
		Partner	
	Alt **40%**	**Blue** **40%**	**Cha** **20%**
Preliquidation balances, May 1	(34,000)	(10,000)	(14,000)
May loss of $10,000 on disposal of assets	4,000	4,000	2,000
	(30,000)	(6,000)	(12,000)
May 31 distribution of $3,000 available cash to partners:			
First $3,000 (of $6,000 priority to Alt)	3,000		
	(27,000)	(6,000)	(12,000)
June loss of $15,000 on disposal of assets	6,000	6,000	3,000
	(21,000)	-0-	(9,000)
June 30 distribution of $15,000 available cash to partners:			
Next $3,000 (to complete Alt's $6,000 priority)	3,000		
Remaining $12,000:			
40/60 to Alt	8,000		
20/60 to Cha			4,000
	(10,000)	-0-	(5,000)
Liquidation cost of $7,500	3,000	3,000	1,500
	(7,000)	3,000	(3,500)
Distribution of Blue's actual deficit	2,000	(3,000)	1,000
	(5,000)	-0-	(2,500)
Final payment of $7,500 to partners on July 31, 20X5:			
40/60 to Alt	5,000		
20/60 to Cha			2,500
Postliquidation balances, July 31	-0-	-0-	-0-

Note: Parentheses indicate credit amount.

ADDITIONAL CONSIDERATIONS

Incorporation of a Partnership

As a partnership continues to grow, the partners may decide to incorporate the business to have access to additional equity financing, to limit their personal liability, to obtain selected tax advantages, or to achieve other sound business purposes. At the incorporation, the partnership is terminated, and the assets and liabilities are revalued to their market values. The gain or loss on revaluation is allocated to the partners' capital accounts in the profit and loss–sharing ratio.

Capital stock in the new corporation is then distributed in proportion to the partners' capital accounts. The separate business entity of the partnership should now close its accounting records and the corporation, as a new business entity, should open its own new accounting records to record the issuance of its capital stock to the prior partners of the partnership.

The ABC Partnership's trial balance on May 1, 20X5, as shown previously, is used to illustrate incorporation of a partnership. Instead of liquidating the partnership as shown throughout the chapter, assume the partners agree to incorporate it.

The new corporation is to be called the Peerless Products Corporation. At the time of conversion from a partnership to a corporation, all assets and liabilities should be appraised and valued at their market values. Any gain or loss must be distributed to the partners in their profit and loss–sharing ratios. Assume that the noncash assets have an $80,000 market value. The $10,000 loss to market value is allocated to the partners' capital accounts before the incorporation, as follows:

(4)	Alt, Capital	4,000	
	Blue, Capital	4,000	
	Cha, Capital	2,000	
	Noncash Assets		10,000
	Recognize loss on reduction of assets to market values.		

Of course, in practice, specific asset accounts are used instead of the general classification of noncash assets. Gains on asset revaluations also may occur when a successful partnership elects to incorporate.

The partnership's net assets have a fair value of $48,000 ($90,000 of assets less $42,000 of liabilities). The corporation issues 4,600 shares of $1 par common stock in exchange for the assets and liabilities of the ABC Partnership. The entry made by the Peerless Products Corporation to acquire the partnership's assets and liabilities in exchange for the issuance of the 4,600 shares of stock is:

(5)	Cash	10,000	
	Noncash Assets	80,000	
	Liabilities		42,000
	Common Stock		4,600
	Paid-In Capital in Excess of Par		43,400
	Issuance of stock for partnership's assets and liabilities.		

The partners make the following entry on the partnership's books:

(6)	Investment in Peerless Products Stock	48,000	
	Liabilities	42,000	
	Cash		10,000
	Noncash Assets		80,000
	Receipt of stock in Peerless Products in exchange for partnership's net assets.		

Recall that the noncash assets were reduced to their fair values in entry (4). To distribute the stock to the partners and close the partnership's books, the final entry is as follows:

(7)	Alt, Capital	30,000	
	Blue, Capital	6,000	
	Cha, Capital	12,000	
	Investment in Peerless Products Stock		48,000
	Distribution of Peerless Products stock to partners.		

Summary of Key Concepts

The process of terminating and liquidating a partnership is often a traumatic time for partners. The Uniform Partnership Act of 1997 provides guidance for the liquidation process and specifies the legal rights of the partners and of partnership creditors.

Dissociation of a partner is his or her withdrawal, either voluntarily or involuntarily, from the partnership. Dissolution of the partnership is a change in the relationship between the partners. Not all dissolutions require termination, which is the cessation of normal business functions, or liquidation, with the disposal of assets, payment of liabilities, and distribution of remaining cash to partners. Termination and liquidation often can be avoided by carefully preparing the partnership agreement to allow continuation of the business when a partner retires. Liquidation may be voluntary or involuntary. The most common reasons for involuntary liquidation are court decrees or bankrupt partnerships.

Liquidation can involve a single lump-sum payment to partners. Most liquidations, however, take several months and involve installment payments to partners during the liquidation process. Liquidations are facilitated by the preparation of the statement of partnership realization and liquidation, a workpaper summarizing the liquidation process and serving as a basis for the journal entries to record the events. Installment payments to partners are determined on a worst-case basis using a schedule of safe payments to partners, which assumes that all noncash assets will be written off and that partners with debit balances in their capital accounts will not be able to remedy the deficiencies.

A cash distribution plan provides information to partners about the installment payments they will receive as cash becomes available to the partnership. The plan is prepared at the beginning of the liquidation process. Actual cash distributions during the liquidation process are determined with the statement of partnership realization and liquidation. The concept of loss absorption power (LAP) is central to the development of the cash distribution plan. Loss absorption power is the amount of partnership loss required to eliminate a given partner's capital credit balance. The loss absorption power is determined by dividing a partner's net capital credit balance by his or her loss–sharing percentage.

Key Terms

cash distribution plan, *766*
dissociation (of a partner), *755*
dissolution (of a partnership), *756*

installment liquidation, *762*
loss absorption power (LAP), *766*
lump-sum liquidation, *757*

schedule of safe payments to partners, *763*
statement of partnership realization and liquidation, *756*

Appendix **16A** Partners' Personal Financial Statements

At the beginning of the liquidation process, partners are usually asked for personal financial statements to determine each partner's personal solvency. Guidelines for preparing personal financial statements are found in **Statement of Position 82-1**, "Personal Financial Statements" (SOP 82-1).[1]

---

[1] *Accounting Standards Division of AICPA (Statement of Position 82-1),* "Accounting and Financial Reporting for Personal Financial Statements" (New York: AICPA, 1982).

FIGURE 16–8
**Personal Statement
of Financial
Condition**

C. ALT
Statement of Financial Condition
May 1, 20X5 and 20X4

	Year	
	20X5	20X4
Assets		
Cash	$ 4,000	$ 2,500
Receivables	3,500	4,000
Investments:		
Marketable securities	5,000	4,000
ABC Partnership	34,000	26,000
Cash surrender value of life insurance	3,100	3,000
Residence	84,000	76,000
Personal effects	16,400	12,500
Total assets	$150,000	$128,000
Liabilities and Net Worth		
Charge accounts	$ 2,000	$ 3,000
Income taxes—current-year balance	1,200	800
10 percent note payable	6,000	10,000
Mortgage payable	60,000	62,000
Estimated income taxes on the difference between the estimated current values of assets and liabilities and their tax bases	16,800	12,200
Net worth	64,000	40,000
Total liabilities and net worth	$150,000	$128,000

Personal financial statements consist of the following:

1. Statement of financial condition, or personal balance sheet, which presents the person's assets and liabilities at a point in time.
2. Statement of changes in net worth, or personal income statement, which presents the primary sources of changes in the person's net worth.

In addition to presenting a person's assets and liabilities, the statement of financial condition should include an estimate of the income taxes incurred as if all the assets were converted and the liabilities extinguished. The person's net worth would then be computed as assets less liabilities less estimated taxes (see Figure 16–8). In general, the accrual basis of accounting should be used to determine the person's assets and liabilities, and comparative statements are usually provided. However, unlike a balance sheet of a business that is based on historical cost, the assets in the personal statement of financial condition are stated at their estimated current values. The liabilities are stated at the lower of the discounted value of future cash payments or the current cash settlement amount. Included immediately below the liabilities are the estimated taxes that would be paid if all the assets were converted to cash and all the liabilities were paid.

Assets and liabilities are presented in their order of liquidity and maturity, not as current and noncurrent. **SOP 82-1** provides guidelines for determining the current value of a person's assets and liabilities. The primary valuation methods are discounted value of future cash flows, current market prices of marketable securities or other investments, and appraisals of properties. An investment in a separate business entity (e.g., a partnership) should be reported as a one-line, combined amount valued at the net investment's market value. The liabilities are stated at their discounted cash flow value or current liquidation value. The accountant uses applicable tax laws, carryover provisions, and other regulations to compute the estimated tax liability from the assumed conversion of assets and the assumed extinguishment of liabilities.

The statement of changes in net worth presents the major sources of income. It recognizes both realized and unrealized income. A commercial business's income statement may not recognize holding gains on some marketable securities, but such gains are recognized on an individual's statement of changes in net worth.

ILLUSTRATION OF PERSONAL FINANCIAL STATEMENTS

The following illustration presents Alt's personal financial condition as of May 1, 20X5, the day the partners decide to liquidate the ABC Partnership. Alt's net worth on this date is as follows:

Personal assets	$150,000
Personal liabilities	(86,000)
Net worth	$ 64,000

Statement of Financial Condition

Alt's statement of financial condition on May 1, 20X5, is presented in Figure 16–8 along with the prior year's statement. The 20X5 statement illustrates the following:

1. Receivables due to Alt from other people have a present value of $3,500.

2. Alt has two investments, one of which is his interest in the ABC Partnership, valued at estimated current market value, which in this case also equals its book value of $34,000. The marketable security investments are shown at market value.

3. The cash surrender value of life insurance is presented net of any loans payable on the policies.

4. Alt's residence and personal effects are presented at their appraised values.

5. Liabilities are presented at their estimated current liquidation value or the discounted value of the future cash flows.

6. The estimated income taxes on the difference between the estimated current values of assets and liabilities and their tax bases represent the amount of income tax Alt would be liable for if all assets were converted to cash and all liabilities were paid.

7. Net worth is the difference between the estimated current value of Alt's assets and liabilities, including estimated tax.

Statement of Changes in Net Worth

Alt's statement of changes in net worth, shown in Figure 16–9, illustrates the following:

1. The statement separates the realized and unrealized changes in net worth. Realized changes are cash flows to or from Alt that have already taken place. Unrealized changes are equivalent to holding gains or losses. They have not yet been converted to cash. For example, Alt received $3,000 from the ABC Partnership during the year ended May 1, 20X5. In addition, Alt's partnership interest increased by $8,000 during the year.

2. Alt had $42,200 of realized increases in net worth during the year ended May 1, 20X5. The primary source was a salary of $36,900 from full-time employment outside the ABC Partnership.

3. The major realized decrease in net worth during the year ended May 1, 20X5, was for personal expenditures of $18,800.

4. Unrealized increases of $17,600 during the year were primarily from an increase in the value of Alt's personal residence ($8,000) and an increase in the investment value of his partnership interest in the ABC Partnership ($8,000). Unrealized holding gains of $1,600 are available in Alt's investments in marketable securities.

5. The change in the estimated tax liability is an unrealized decrease because this amount is due only if Alt converts these assets to cash.

6. The net unrealized changes in net worth are added to the net realized changes in net worth to obtain the total change in Alt's net worth for each year. Alt's net worth increased by $13,000 during the year ended May 1, 20X4, and by $24,000 during the year ended May 1, 20X5.

Footnote Disclosures

Sufficient footnote disclosures should accompany the two personal financial statements. The footnotes should describe the following:

1. The methods used to value the major assets.

2. The names and the nature of businesses in which the person has major investments.

FIGURE 16–9
Personal Statement of Changes in Net Worth

C. ALT
Statement of Changes in Net Worth
For the Years Ended May 1, 20X5 and 20X4

	Year Ended May 1	
	20X5	20X4
Realized increases in net worth:		
Salary	$ 36,900	$ 34,900
Dividends and interest income	800	400
Distribution from ABC Partnership	3,000	1,000
Cash surrender value of life insurance	100	100
Gains on sales of marketable securities	1,400	1,200
	$ 42,200	$ 37,600
Realized decreases in net worth:		
Income taxes	$ 8,200	$ 7,800
Interest expense	1,400	700
Real estate taxes	2,400	2,200
Insurance payments (including $100 for increase in cash surrender value of life insurance)	400	300
Personal expenditures	18,800	18,600
	$(31,200)	$(29,600)
Net realized increase in net worth	$ 11,000	$ 8,000
Unrealized increases in net worth:		
Marketable securities	$ 1,600	$ 400
ABC Partnership	8,000	5,000
Residence	8,000	4,000
	$ 17,600	$ 9,400
Unrealized decreases in net worth:		
Increase in estimated income taxes on the difference between the estimated current values of assets and liabilities and their tax bases	(4,600)	(4,400)
Net unrealized increase in net worth	$ 13,000	$ 5,000
Net increase in net worth:		
Realized and unrealized	$ 24,000	$ 13,000
Net worth at beginning of period	40,000	27,000
Net worth at end of period	$ 64,000	$ 40,000

3. The methods and assumptions used to compute the estimated tax bases and a statement that the tax provision in an actual liquidation will probably differ from the estimate because the actual tax burden will then be based on actual realizations determined by market values at the point of liquidation.

4. Maturities, interest rates, and other details of any receivables and debt.

5. Any other information needed to present fully the person's net worth.

Questions

Q16-1 What are the major causes of a dissolution? What are the accounting implications of a dissolution?

Q16-2 During a partnership liquidation, do a partnership's liabilities to individual partners have a lower priority than the partnership's obligations to other, third party creditors? Explain.

Q16-3 X, Y, and Z are partners. The partnership is liquidating, and Partner Z is personally insolvent. What implications may this have for Partners X and Y?

Q16-4 May an individual partner simply decide to leave a partnership? Does the partnership have any legal recourse against that partner? Explain.

Q16-5 Contrast a lump-sum liquidation with an installment liquidation.

Q16-6 How is a deficit in a partner's capital account eliminated if he or she is personally insolvent?

Q16-7 The DEF Partnership has total assets of $55,000. Partner D has a capital credit of $6,000, Partner E has a capital deficit of $20,000, and Partner F has a capital credit of $8,000. Is the DEF Partnership solvent or insolvent?

Q16-8 Assume that, because of a new law recently passed, the types of significant transactions in which a partnership engages are no longer lawful. Two of the five partners wish to have a winding up and termination of the partnership. Can these two partners require the partnership to terminate? Explain.

Q16-9 How are a partner's personal payments to partnership creditors accounted for on the partnership's books?

Q16-10 What is the purpose of the schedule of safe payments to partners?

Q16-11 In what ratio are losses during liquidation assigned to the partners' capital accounts? Is this ratio used in all instances?

Q16-12 The installment liquidation process uses a worst-case assumption in computing the payments to partners. What does this *worst-case assumption* mean?

Q16-13 Define *loss absorption power* and explain its importance in the determination of cash distributions to partners.

Q16-14 Partner A has a capital credit of $25,000. Partner B's capital credit is also $25,000. Partners A and B share profits and losses in a 60:40 ratio, respectively. Which partner will receive the first payment of cash in an installment liquidation?

Q16-15* Explain the process of incorporating a partnership.

Cases

C16-1 Cash Distributions to Partners

The partnership of A. Bull and T. Bear is in the process of termination. The partners have disagreed on virtually every decision and have decided to liquidate the present business, with each partner taking his own clients from the partnership. Bull wants cash distributed as it becomes available; Bear wants no cash distributed until all assets are sold and all liabilities are settled. You are called in to aid in the termination and liquidation process.

Analysis

Required
How would you respond to each of the partners' requests?

C16-2 Cash Distributions to Partners

Adam and Bard agreed to liquidate their partnership. You have been asked to assist them in this process, and you prepare the following balance sheet for the date of the beginning of the liquidation. The loss–sharing percentages are in parentheses next to the capital account balances.

Analysis

Cash	$ 40,000
Loan Receivable from Adam	10,000
Other Assets	200,000
Total	$250,000
Accounts Payable	$ 30,000
Loan Payable to Bard	100,000
Adam, Capital (50%)	80,000
Bard, Capital (50%)	40,000
Total	$250,000

Bard is demanding that the loan from him be paid before any cash is distributed to Adam. Adam believes the available cash should be paid to him until his capital account is reduced to $40,000, the same as Bard's. Adam will then pay the loan receivable to the partnership with the cash received. You have been asked to reconcile the argument.

*Indicates that the item relates to "Additional Considerations."

Required

How would you advise in this case?

C16-3

Judgment

Incorporation of a Partnership

After successfully operating a partnership for several years, the partners have proposed to incorporate the business and admit another investor. The original partners will purchase at par an amount of preferred stock equal to the book values of their capital interests in the partnership and common stock for the amount of the market value, including unrecognized goodwill, of the business that exceeds book value. The new investor will make an investment, at a 5 percent premium over par value, in both preferred and common stock equal to one-third of the total number of shares purchased by the original partners. The corporation will acquire all the partnership's assets, assume the liabilities, and employ the original partners and the new investor.

Required

a. Discuss the differences in accounts used and valuations expected in comparing the balance sheets of the proposed corporation and the partnership.

b. Discuss the differences that would be expected in a comparison of the income statements of the proposed corporation and the partnership.

C16-4

Research

Sharing Losses during Liquidation

Hiller, Luna, and Welsh are attempting to form a partnership to operate a travel agency. They have agreed to share profits in a ratio of 4:3:2 but cannot agree on the terms of the partnership agreement relating to possible liquidation. Hiller believes that it is best not to get into any arguments about potential liquidation at this time because the partnership will be a success and it is not necessary to think negatively at this point in time. Luna believes that in the event of liquidation, any losses should be shared equally because each partner would have worked equally for the partnership's success, or lack thereof. Welsh believes that any losses during liquidation should be distributed in the ratio of capital balances at the beginning of any liquidation because then the losses will be distributed based on a capital ability to bear the losses.

You have been asked to help resolve the differences and to prepare a memo to the three individuals including the following items.

Required

a. Specify the procedures for allocating losses among partners stated in the Uniform Partnership Act of 1997 to be used if no partnership agreement terms are agreed upon regarding liquidation. (You may wish to access a copy of the Uniform Partnership Act of 1997 for this requirement.)

b. Critically assess each partner's viewpoint, discussing the pros and cons of each.

c. Specify another option for allocating potential liquidation losses not included in the positions currently taken by the three individuals. Critically assess the pros and cons of your alternative.

C16-5

Application

Analysis of a Court Decision on a Partnership Liquidation

The *Mattfield v. Kramer Brothers* court case presents a number of the interesting legal issues that often arise from the dissolution of a partnership. The case was heard in the Supreme Court of the State of Montana in 2005 and decided on May 31, 2005, as Case 03-796. The decision of the court includes a summary of the disputes and lower court decisions.

The Montana State Supreme Court's decision is available at the FindLaw site. The easiest way to obtain the script of the decision is to Google the search term "Mattfield v. Kramer Brothers" and then follow the link to the Court's 2005 decision. The legal briefs from each side that were presented to the Supreme Court may be obtained at the State Law Library of Montana site by making a Google search using "State of Montana Law Library" or use the URL of http://courts.mt.gov/library Click on Cases, and then search using case number 03-796, or a text term such as Mattfield. The briefs will then be made available.

Required

Obtain a copy of the Montana Supreme Court decision in the *Mattfield v. Kramer Brothers* case. Then answer each of the following questions regarding the case.

a. Prepare a short summary of the history of the Kramer Brothers Co-Partnership from formation through the appeal to the Montana Supreme Court.

b. What type of partnership agreement existed? Recommend several provisions that you feel should have been included in a formal, written partnership agreement of the partnership.

c. At the time the case was appealed to the Supreme Court, did Bill Kramer still have an economic interest in the partnership? Explain.

d. What legal recourse did the other partners have at the time Don Kramer dissociated from the partnership in 1994?

e. In February 1997, why did Don Kramer's attorney, Floyd Brower, request copies of Ray Kramer's and Doug Kramer's personal tax returns?

f. Select and discuss two key points regarding partnership liquidations that are illustrated by this case and that you feel are important.

Exercises   E16-1   **Multiple-Choice Questions on Partnership Liquidations**
Select the correct answer for each of the following questions.

Information for Questions 1, 2, and 3
The balance sheet for the partnership of Joan, Charles, and Thomas, whose shares of profits and losses are 40, 50, and 10 percent, is as follows:

Cash	$ 50,000	Accounts Payable	$150,000
Inventory	360,000	Joan, Capital	160,000
		Charles, Capital	45,000
		Thomas, Capital	55,000
Total Assets	$410,000	Total Liabilities and Equities	$410,000

1. If the inventory is sold for $300,000, how much should Joan receive upon liquidation of the partnership?

   a. $48,000.
   b. $100,000.
   c. $136,000.
   d. $160,000.

2. If the inventory is sold for $180,000, how much should Thomas receive upon liquidation of the partnership?

   a. $28,000.
   b. $32,500.
   c. $37,000.
   d. $55,000.

3. The partnership will be liquidated in installments. As cash becomes available, it will be distributed to the partners. If inventory costing $200,000 is sold for $140,000, how much cash should be distributed to each partner at this time?

	Joan	Charles	Thomas
a.	$56,000	$70,000	$14,000
b.	$16,000	$20,000	$ 4,000
c.	$32,000	$ -0-	$ 8,000
d.	$20,000	$ -0-	$20,000

4. In accounting for partnership liquidation, cash payments to partners after all creditors' claims have been satisfied, but before the final cash distribution, should be according to:

   a. The partners' relative profit and loss–sharing ratios.

   b. The final balances in partner capital accounts.

   c. The partners' relative share of the gain or loss on liquidations.

   d. Safe payments computations.

5. After all noncash assets have been converted into cash in the liquidation of the Adam and Kay Partnership, the ledger contains the following account balances:

	Debit	Credit
Cash	$47,000	
Accounts Payable		$32,000
Loan Payable to Adam		15,000
Adam, Capital	7,000	
Kay, Capital		7,000

   Available cash should be distributed with $32,000 going to accounts payable and then:

   a. $15,000 to the loan payable to Adam.

   b. $7,500 each to Adam and Kay.

   c. $8,000 to Adam and $7,000 to Kay.

   d. $7,000 to Adam and $8,000 to Kay.

Information for Questions 6 and 7

F, A, S, and B are partners sharing profits and losses equally. The partnership is insolvent and is to be liquidated. The status of the partnership and each partner is as follows:

	Partnership Capital Balance	Personal Assets (exclusive of partnership interest)	Personal Liabilities (exclusive of partnership interest)
F	$(15,000)	$100,000	$40,000
A	(10,000)	30,000	60,000
S	20,000[a]	80,000	5,000
B	30,000[a]	1,000	28,000
Total	$ 25,000[a]		

[a]Deficit

6. The partnership creditors:

   a. Must first seek recovery against S because she is personally solvent and has a negative capital balance.

   b. Will *not* be paid in full regardless of how they proceed legally because the partnership assets are less than the partnership liabilities.

   c. Will have to share A's interest in the partnership on a pro rata basis with A's personal creditors.

   d. Have first claim to the partnership assets before any partner's personal creditors have rights to the partnership assets.

7. The partnership creditors should seek recovery of their claims:

   a. From the partnership, including additional contributions from F and S.

   b. From the personal assets of either F or A.

   c. From the personal assets of either S or B.

   d. From the personal assets of any of the partners for all or some of their claims.

E16-2 Multiple-Choice Questions on Partnership Liquidation [AICPA Adapted]

Select the correct answer for each of the following questions.

1. On January 1, 20X7, the partners of Casey, Dithers, and Edwards, who share profits and losses in the ratio of 5:3:2, respectively, decided to liquidate their partnership. On this date the partnership condensed balance sheet was as follows:

Assets		Liabilities and Capital	
Cash	$ 50,000	Liabilities	$ 60,000
Other Assets	250,000	Casey, Capital	80,000
		Dithers, Capital	90,000
		Edwards, Capital	70,000
Total	$300,000	Total	$300,000

On January 15, 20X7, the first cash sale of other assets with a carrying amount of $150,000 realized $120,000. Safe installment payments to the partners were made on the same date. How much cash should be distributed to each partner?

	Casey	Dithers	Edwards
a.	$15,000	$51,000	$44,000
b.	$40,000	$45,000	$35,000
c.	$55,000	$33,000	$22,000
d.	$60,000	$36,000	$24,000

2. In a partnership liquidation, the final cash distribution to the partners should be made in accordance with the:

   a. Partners' profit and loss–sharing ratio.
   b. Balances of the partners' capital accounts.
   c. Ratio of the capital contributions by the partners.
   d. Ratio of capital contributions less withdrawals by the partners.

Information for Questions 3 through 5

The balance sheet for the Art, Blythe, and Cooper Partnership is as follows. Figures shown parenthetically reflect agreed profit and loss–sharing percentages.

Assets		Liabilities and Capital	
Cash	$ 20,000	Liabilities	$ 50,000
Other Assets	180,000	Art, Capital (40%)	37,000
		Blythe, Capital (40%)	65,000
		Cooper, Capital (20%)	48,000
Total	$200,000	Total	$200,000

3. If the firm, as shown on the balance sheet, is dissolved and liquidated by selling assets in installments and if the first sale of noncash assets having a book value of $90,000 realizes $50,000 and

all cash available after settlement with creditors is distributed, the respective partners would receive (to the nearest dollar):

	Art	Blythe	Cooper
a.	$8,000	$ 8,000	$ 4,000
b.	$6,667	$ 6,667	$ 6,666
c.	$ -0-	$13,333	$ 6,667
d.	$ -0-	$ 3,000	$17,000

4. If the facts are as in question 3 except that $3,000 cash is to be withheld, the respective partners would then receive (to the nearest dollar):

	Art	Blythe	Cooper
a.	$6,800	$ 6,800	$ 3,400
b.	$5,667	$ 5,667	$ 5,666
c.	$ -0-	$11,333	$ 5,667
d.	$ -0-	$ 1,000	$16,000

5. If each partner properly received some cash in the distribution after the second sale, if the cash to be distributed amounts to $12,000 from the third sale, and if unsold assets with an $8,000 book value remain, ignoring questions 3 and 4, the respective partners would receive:

	Art	Blythe	Cooper
a.	$ 4,800	$ 4,800	$ 2,400
b.	$ 4,000	$ 4,000	$ 4,000
c.	37/150	65/150	48/150
	of	of	of
	$12,000	$12,000	$12,000
d.	$ -0-	$ 8,000	$ 4,000

6. The following condensed balance sheet is presented for the partnership of Arnie, Bart, and Kurt, who share profits and losses in the ratio of 4:3:3, respectively:

Assets		Liabilities and Capital	
Cash	$100,000	Liabilities	$150,000
Other Assets	300,000	Arnie, Capital	40,000
		Bart, Capital	180,000
		Kurt, Capital	30,000
Total	$400,000	Total	$400,000

The partners agreed to dissolve the partnership after selling the other assets for $200,000. On dissolution of the partnership, Arnie should receive:

a. $0.

b. $40,000.

c. $60,000.

d. $70,000.

E16-3 Computing Alternative Cash Distributions to Partners

Bracken, Louden, and Menser, who share profits and losses in a ratio of 4:3:3, respectively, are partners in a home decorating business that has not been able to generate the type of income hoped for by the partners. They have decided to liquidate the business and have sold all the assets except for their decorating equipment. All partnership liabilities have been settled and all the partners are personally insolvent. The decorating equipment has a book value of $40,000, and the partners have capital account balances as follows:

Bracken, capital	$25,000
Louden, capital	5,000
Menser, capital	10,000

Required

Determine the amount of cash each partner will receive as a liquidating distribution if the decorating equipment is sold for the amount stated in each of the following independent cases:

a. $30,000.

b. $21,000.

c. $7,000.

E16-4 Lump-Sum Liquidation

Matthews, Mitchell, and Michaels are partners in the BG Land Development Company and share losses in a 5:3:2 ratio. The balance sheet on June 30, 20X1, when they decide to liquidate the business, is as follows:

Assets		Liabilities and Equities	
Cash	$ 20,000	Accounts Payable	$ 30,000
Noncash Assets	150,000	Mitchell, Loan	10,000
		Matthews, Capital	80,000
		Mitchell, Capital	36,000
		Michaels, Capital	14,000
Total Assets	$170,000	Total Liabilities and Equities	$170,000

The noncash assets are sold for $110,000.

Required

a. Prepare a statement of partnership realization and liquidation.

b. Prepare the required journal entries to account for the liquidation of the BG Land Development Company.

E16-5 Schedule of Safe Payments to Partners

Several years ago, Tom and Ann formed the Home Supply Company, a partnership. Last year, they admitted Ron as a partner and recognized goodwill at that time. However, after failing to gain a sufficient market of continuing customers, they recently agreed to liquidate the business. The balance sheet, with profit and loss–sharing percentages just prior to liquidation, is as follows:

THE HOME SUPPLY COMPANY
Balance Sheet
As of August 1, 20X8

Assets		Liabilities and Equities	
Cash	$ 16,000	Accounts Payable	$ 48,000
Receivables	58,000	Tom, Loan	16,000
Inventory	64,000	Note Payable	10,000
Goodwill	24,000	Tom, Capital (40%)	26,000
		Ann, Capital (30%)	45,000
		Ron, Capital (30%)	17,000
Total Assets	$162,000	Total Liabilities and Equities	$162,000

The loan from Tom was made to provide working capital for the partnership to operate during the last two months.

During August 20X8, the first month of the liquidation, the partnership collected $30,000 of the receivables and decided to write off $12,000 of the remaining receivables. Sales of one-half of the book value of the inventory realized a gain of $6,000. The partners estimate that the costs of liquidating the business are expected to be $4,000 for the remainder of the liquidation process.

Required
Prepare a schedule of safe payments to partners as of August 31, 20X8, to show how the available cash should be distributed to the partners.

E16-6 **Schedule of Safe Payments to Partners**

Partners Maness and Joiner have decided to liquidate their business. The ledger shows the following account balances:

Cash	$ 25,000	Accounts Payable	$15,000
Inventory	120,000	Maness, Capital	65,000
		Joiner, Capital	65,000

Maness and Joiner share profits and losses in a 8:2 ratio. During the first month of liquidation, half the inventory is sold for $40,000, and $10,000 of the accounts payable is paid. During the second month, the rest of the inventory is sold for $30,000, and the remaining accounts payable are paid. Cash is distributed at the end of each month, and the liquidation is completed at the end of the second month.

Required
Prepare a statement of partnership realization and liquidation with a schedule of safe payments for the two-month liquidation period.

E16-7 **Alternative Profit and Loss–Sharing Ratios in a Partnership Liquidation**

Nelson, Osman, Peters, and Quincy have decided to terminate their partnership because of recurrent arguments among the partners. The partnership's balance sheet at the time they decide to wind up is as follows:

Cash	$ 17,000	Accounts Payable	$ 12,000
Noncash Assets	190,000	Nelson, Capital	15,000
		Osman, Capital	75,000
		Peters, Capital	75,000
		Quincy, Capital	30,000
Total Assets	$207,000	Total Liabilities and Equities	$207,000

During the winding up of the partnership, the other assets are sold for $100,000 and the accounts payable are paid. Osman and Peters are personally solvent, but Nelson and Quincy are personally insolvent.

Required
Determine the amount of cash each partner will receive from the final distributions of the partnership for each of the following independent cases of profit and loss ratios.

a. The partners share profits and losses in the ratio of 3:3:2:2, respectively.

b. The partners share profits and losses in the ratio of 3:1:3:3, respectively.

c. The partners share profits and losses in the ratio of 3:1:2:4, respectively.

E16-8 Cash Distribution Plan

Adams, Peters, and Blake share profits and losses for their APB Partnership in a ratio of 2:3:5, respectively. When they decide to liquidate, the balance sheet is as follows:

Assets		Liabilities and Equities	
Cash	$ 40,000	Liabilities	$ 50,000
Adams, Loan	10,000	Adams, Capital	55,000
Other Assets	200,000	Peters, Capital	75,000
		Blake, Capital	70,000
Total Assets	$250,000	Total Liabilities and Equities	$250,000

Liquidation expenses are expected to be negligible. No interest accrues on loans with partners after termination of the business.

Required

Prepare a cash distribution plan for the APB Partnership.

E16-9 Confirmation of Cash Distribution Plan

Refer to the data in Exercise 16-8. During the liquidation process for the APB Partnership, the following events occurred:

1. During the first month of liquidation, noncash assets with a book value of $85,000 were sold for $65,000, and $21,000 of the liabilities were paid.

2. During the second month, the remaining noncash assets were sold for $79,000. The loan receivable from Adams was collected, and the rest of the creditors were paid.

3. Cash is distributed to partners at the end of each month.

Required

Prepare a statement of partnership realization and liquidation with a schedule of safe payments to partners for the liquidation period.

E16-10 Incorporation of a Partnership

When Alice and Betty decided to incorporate their partnership, the trial balance was as follows:

	Debit	Credit
Cash	$ 8,000	
Accounts Receivable (net)	22,400	
Inventory	36,000	
Equipment (net)	47,200	
Accounts Payable		$ 17,200
Alice, Capital (60%)		62,400
Betty, Capital (40%)		34,000
Total	$113,600	$113,600

The partnership's books will be closed, and new books will be used for A & B Corporation. The following additional information is available:

1. The estimated fair values of the assets follow:

Accounts Receivable	$21,600
Inventory	32,800
Equipment	40,000

2. All assets and liabilities are transferred to the corporation.
3. The common stock is $10 par. Alice and Betty receive a total of 7,100 shares.
4. The partners' profit and loss–sharing ratio is shown in the trial balance.

Required

a. Prepare the entries on the partnership's books to record (1) the revaluation of assets, (2) the transfer of the assets to the A & B Corporation and the receipt of the common stock, and (3) the closing of the books.

b. Prepare the entries on A & B Corporation's books to record the assets and the issuance of the common stock.

E16-11A **Multiple-Choice on Personal Financial Statements [AICPA Adapted]**

Select the correct answer for each of the following questions.

1. On December 31, 20X7, Judy is a fully vested participant in a company-sponsored pension plan. According to the plan's administrator, Judy has at that date the nonforfeitable right to receive a lump sum of $100,000 on December 28, 20X8. The discounted amount of $100,000 is $90,000 at December 31, 20X7. The right is not contingent on Judy's life expectancy and requires no future performance on Judy's part. In Judy's December 31, 20X7, personal statement of financial condition, the vested interest in the pension plan should be reported at:

a. $0.
b. $90,000.
c. $95,000.
d. $100,000.

2. On December 31, 20X7, Mr. and Mrs. McManus owned a parcel of land held as an investment. The land was purchased for $95,000 in 20X0, and was encumbered by a mortgage with a principal balance of $60,000 at December 31, 20X7. On this date the fair value of the land was $150,000. In the McManuses' December 31, 20X7, personal statement of financial condition, at what amount should the land investment and mortgage payable be reported?

	Land Investment	Mortgage Payable
a.	$150,000	$60,000
b.	$ 95,000	$60,000
c.	$ 90,000	$ -0-
d.	$ 35,000	$ -0-

3. Rich Drennen's personal statement of financial condition at December 31, 20X6, shows net worth of $400,000 before consideration of employee stock options owned on that date. Information relating to the stock options is as follows:

- Options are to purchase 10,000 shares of Oglesby Corporation stock.
- Options exercise price is $10 a share.
- Options expire on June 30, 20X7.
- Market price of the stock is $25 a share on December 31, 20X6.
- Assume that exercise of the options in 20X7 would result in ordinary income taxable at 35 percent.

After giving effect to the stock options, Drennen's net worth at December 31, 20X6, would be:

a. $497,500.
b. $550,000.
c. $562,500.
d. $650,000.

4. Nancy Emerson owns 50 percent of the common stock of Marks Corporation. She paid $25,000 for this stock in 20X3. At December 31, 20X8, it was ascertained that her 50 percent stock ownership in Marks had a current value of $185,000. Marks's cumulative net income and cash dividends declared for the five years ended December 31, 20X8, were $300,000 and $30,000

respectively. In Nancy's personal statement of financial condition at December 31, 20X8, what amount should be reported as her net investment in Marks?

a. $25,000.

b. $160,000.

c. $175,000.

d. $185,000.

5. In a personal statement of financial condition, which of the following should be reported at estimated current values?

	Investments in Closely Held Business	Investments in Leaseholds
a.	Yes	Yes
b.	Yes	No
c.	No	No
d.	No	Yes

6. Personal financial statements should include which of the following statements?

	Financial Condition	Changes in Net Worth	Cash Flows
a.	No	Yes	Yes
b.	Yes	No	No
c.	Yes	Yes	No
d.	Yes	Yes	Yes

7. A business interest that constitutes a large part of an individual's total assets should be presented in a personal statement of financial condition as:

a. A single amount equal to the proprietorship equity.

b. A single amount equal to the estimated current value of the business interest.

c. A separate list of the individual assets and liabilities, at cost.

d. Separate line items of both total assets and total liabilities, at cost.

8. Personal financial statements should report assets and liabilities at:

a. Historical cost.

b. Historical cost and, as additional information, at estimated current values at the date of the financial statements.

c. Estimated current values at the date of the financial statements.

d. Estimated current values at the date of the financial statements and, as additional information, at historical cost.

9. The following information pertains to marketable equity securities owned by Kent:

	Fair Value at December 31		
Stock	20X3	20X2	Cost in 20X0
City Manufacturing Inc.	$95,500	$93,000	$89,900
Tri Corporation	3,400	5,600	3,600
Zee Inc.		10,300	15,000

The Zee stock was sold in January 20X3 for $10,200. In Kent's personal statement of financial condition at December 31, 20X3, what amount should be reported for marketable equity securities?

a. $93,300.

b. $93,500.

c. $94,100.

d. $98,900.

10. Personal financial statements should report an investment in life insurance at the:

a. Face amount of the policy less the amount of premiums paid.

b. Cash value of the policy less the amount of any loans against it.

c. Cash value of the policy less the amount of premiums paid.

d. Face amount of the policy less the amount of any loans against it.

11. Mrs. Taft owns a $150,000 insurance policy on her husband's life. The cash value of the policy is $125,000, and there is a $50,000 loan against the policy. In the Tafts' personal statement of financial condition at December 31, 20X3, what amount should be shown as an investment in life insurance?

a. $150,000.

b. $125,000.

c. $100,000.

d. $75,000.

E16-12A **Personal Financial Statements**

Leonard and Michelle have asked you to prepare their statement of changes in net worth for the year ended August 31, 20X3. They have prepared the following comparative statement of financial condition based on estimated current values as required by SOP 82-1:

LEONARD AND MICHELLE
Statement of Financial Condition
August 31, 20X3 and 20X2

		20X3		20X2
Assets				
Cash		$ 3,600		$ 6,700
Marketable securities		4,900		16,300
Residence		94,800		87,500
Personal effects		10,000		10,000
Cash surrender value of life insurance		3,200		5,600
Investment in farm business:				
Farm land	$ 42,000		$32,100	
Farm equipment	22,400		9,000	
Note payable on farm equipment	(10,000)		-0-	
Net investment in farm		54,400		41,100
Total assets		$170,900		$167,200
Liabilities and Net Worth				
Credit card		$ 2,400		$ 1,500
Income taxes payable		11,400		12,400
Mortgage payable on residence		71,000		76,000
Estimated income taxes on the difference between the estimated current values of assets and liabilities and their tax bases		19,700		16,500
Net worth		66,400		60,800
Total liabilities and net worth		$170,900		$167,200

Additional Information

1. Leonard and Michelle's total salaries during the fiscal year ended August 31, 20X3, were $44,300; farm income was $6,700; personal expenditures were $43,500; and interest and dividends received were $1,400.

2. Marketable securities purchased in 20X1 at a cost of $11,000 and with a current market value of $11,000 on August 31, 20X2, were sold on March 1, 20X3, for $10,700. No additional marketable securities were purchased or sold during the fiscal year.

3. The values of the residence and farm land are based on year-end appraisals.

4. On August 31, 20X3, Leonard purchased a used combine at a cost of $14,000. He made a $4,000 down payment and signed a five-year, 10 percent note payable for the $10,000 balance owed. No other farm equipment was purchased or sold during the fiscal year.

5. The cash surrender value of the life insurance policy increased during the fiscal year by $1,600. However, Leonard borrowed $4,000 against the policy on September 1, 20X2. Interest at 15 percent for the first year of this loan was paid when due on August 31, 20X3.

6. Federal income taxes of $12,400 were paid during the 20X3 fiscal year.

7. Mortgage payments made during the year totaled $9,000, which included payments of principal and interest.

Required

Using the comparative statement of financial condition and additional information provided, prepare the statement of changes in net worth for the year ended August 31, 20X3. (*Hint:* It will be helpful to use T-accounts to determine several realized and unrealized amounts. An analysis of the cash, personal effects, and credit card accounts should not be required to properly complete the statement.)

Problems P16-13   Lump-Sum Liquidation

The Carlos, Dan, and Gail (CDG) Partnership has decided to liquidate as of December 1, 20X6. A balance sheet as of December 1, 20X6, appears below:

CDG PARTNERSHIP
Balance Sheet
At December 1, 20X6

Assets

Cash	$ 25,000
Accounts Receivable (net)	75,000
Inventories	100,000
Property, Plant, and Equipment (net)	300,000
Total Assets	$500,000

Liabilities and Capital

Liabilities:		
Accounts Payable		$270,000
Capital:		
Carlos, Capital	$120,000	
Dan, Capital	50,000	
Gail, Capital	60,000	
Total Capital		230,000
Total Liabilities and Capital		$500,000

Additional Information

1. The personal assets (excluding partnership capital interests) and personal liabilities of each partner as of December 1, 20X6, follow:

	Carlos	Dan	Gail
Personal assets	$250,000	$300,000	$350,000
Personal liabilities	(230,000)	(240,000)	(325,000)
Personal net worth	$ 20,000	$ 60,000	$ 25,000

2. Carlos, Dan, and Gail share profits and losses in the ratio 20:40:40, respectively.
3. All of the noncash assets were sold on December 10, 20X6, for $260,000.

Required

a. Prepare a statement of realization and liquidation for the CDG Partnership on December 10, 20X6.

b. Prepare a schedule of the net worth of each of the three partners as of December 10, 2006, after the liquidation of the partnership is completed.

P16-14   **Installment Liquidation**

The trial balance of the MON Partnership on April 30, 20X1, follows. The profit and loss percentages are shown in the trial balance:

	Debit	Credit
Cash	$ 15,000	
Accounts Receivable (net)	85,000	
Inventory	82,000	
Plant Assets (net)	120,000	
Accounts Payable		$ 90,000
Mane, Capital (60%)		80,000
Ondo, Capital (20%)		72,000
Norris, Capital (20%)		60,000
Total	$302,000	$302,000

The partnership is being liquidated. Liquidation activities are as follows:

	May	June	July
Accounts receivable collected	$40,000	$28,000	$ 13,000
Noncash assets sold:			
Book value	44,000	35,000	123,000
Selling price	50,000	30,000	80,000
Accounts payable paid	65,000	25,000	
Liquidation expenses:			
Paid during month	3,500	3,000	2,500
Anticipated for remainder of liquidation process	6,000	4,000	

Cash is distributed at the end of each month, and the liquidation is completed by July 31, 20X1.

Required

Prepare a statement of partnership realization and liquidation for the MON Partnership with schedules of safe payments to partners.

P16-15   Installment Liquidation [AICPA Adapted]

On January 1, 20X1, partners Art, Bru, and Chou, who share profits and losses in the ratio of 5:3:2, respectively, decide to liquidate their partnership. The partnership trial balance at this date is as follows:

	Debit	Credit
Cash	$ 18,000	
Accounts Receivable	66,000	
Inventory	52,000	
Machinery and Equipment (net)	189,000	
Accounts Payable		$ 53,000
Art, Capital		88,000
Bru, Capital		110,000
Chou, Capital		74,000
Total	$325,000	$325,000

The partners plan a program of piecemeal conversion of assets to minimize liquidation losses. All available cash, less an amount retained to provide for future expenses, is to be distributed to the partners at the end of each month. A summary of the liquidation transactions is as follows:

January 20X1

1. $51,000 was collected on accounts receivable; the balance is uncollectible.
2. $38,000 was received for the entire inventory.
3. $2,000 liquidation expenses were paid.
4. $50,000 was paid to creditors, after offset of a $3,000 credit memorandum received on January 11, 20X1.
5. $10,000 cash was retained in the business at the end of the month for potential unrecorded liabilities and anticipated expenses.

February 20X1

6. $4,000 liquidation expenses were paid.
7. $6,000 cash was retained in the business at the end of the month for potential unrecorded liabilities and anticipated expenses.

March 20X1

8. $146,000 was received on sale of all items of machinery and equipment.
9. $5,000 liquidation expenses were paid.
10. No cash was retained in the business.

Required

Prepare a statement of partnership liquidation for the partnership with schedules of safe payments to partners.

P16-16   Cash Distribution Plan

The partnership of Pen, Evan, and Torves has asked you to assist in winding up its business affairs. You compile the following information.

1. The trial balance of the partnership on June 30, 20X1, is:

	Debit	Credit
Cash	$ 6,000	
Accounts Receivable (net)	22,000	
Inventory	14,000	
Plant and Equipment (net)	99,000	
Accounts Payable		$ 17,000
Pen, Capital		55,000
Evan, Capital		45,000
Torves, Capital		24,000
Total	$141,000	$141,000

2. The partners share profits and losses as follows: Pen, 50 percent; Evan, 30 percent; and Torves, 20 percent.
3. The partners are considering an offer of $100,000 for the accounts receivable, inventory, and plant and equipment as of June 30. The $100,000 will be paid to creditors and the partners in installments, the number and amounts of which are to be negotiated.

Required

Prepare a cash distribution plan as of June 30, 20X1, showing how much cash each partner will receive if the offer to sell the assets is accepted.

P16-17 ### Installment Liquidation

Refer to the facts in Problem 16-16. The partners have decided to liquidate their partnership by installments instead of accepting the offer of $100,000. Cash is distributed to the partners at the end of each month. A summary of the liquidation transactions follows:

July

1. $16,500 collected on accounts receivable; balance is uncollectible.
2. $10,000 received for the entire inventory.
3. $1,000 liquidation expense paid.
4. $17,000 paid to creditors.
5. $8,000 cash retained in the business at the end of the month.

August

6. $1,500 in liquidation expenses paid.
7. As part payment of his capital, Torves accepted an item of special equipment that he developed, which had a book value of $4,000. The partners agreed that a value of $10,000 should be placed on this item for liquidation purposes.
8. $2,500 cash retained in the business at the end of the month.

September

9. $75,000 received on sale of remaining plant and equipment.
10. $1,000 liquidation expenses paid. No cash retained in the business.

Required

Prepare a statement of partnership realization and liquidation with supporting schedules of safe payments to partners.

P16-18 ### Installment Liquidation

The DSV Partnership decided to liquidate the partnership as of June 30, 20X5. The balance sheet of the partnership as of this date is presented as follows:

DSV PARTNERSHIP
Balance Sheet
At June 30, 20X5

Assets		
Cash		$ 50,000
Accounts Receivable (net)		95,000
Inventories		75,000
Property, Plant, and Equipment (net)		500,000
Total Assets		$720,000
Liabilities and Partners' Capitals		
Liabilities:		
Accounts Payable		$405,000
Partners' Capitals:		
D, Capital	$100,000	
S, Capital	140,000	
V, Capital	75,000	
Total Capital		315,000
Total Liabilities and Capital		$720,000

Additional Information

1. The personal assets (excluding partnership loan and capital interests) and personal liabilities of each partner as of June 30, 20X5, follow:

	D	S	V
Personal assets	$250,000	$450,000	$300,000
Personal liabilities	(270,000)	(420,000)	(240,000)
Personal net worth	$ (20,000)	$ 30,000	$ 60,000

The DSV Partnership was liquidated during the months of July, August, and September. The assets sold and the amounts realized follow:

Month	Assets Sold	Carrying Amount	Amount Realized
July	Inventories	$ 50,000	$ 45,000
	Accounts receivable (net)	60,000	40,000
	Property, plant, and equipment	400,000	305,000
August	Inventories	$ 25,000	$ 18,000
	Accounts receivable (net)	10,000	4,000
September	Accounts receivable (net)	$ 25,000	$ 10,000
	Property, plant, and equipment	100,000	45,000

Required

Prepare a statement of partnership realization and liquidation for the DSV Partnership for the three-month period ended September 30, 20X5. D, S, and V share profits and losses in the ratio 50:30:20, respectively. The partners wish to distribute available cash at the end of each month after reserving $10,000 of cash at the end of July and August to meet unexpected liquidation expenses. Actual liquidation expenses incurred and paid each month amounted to $2,500. Support each cash distribution to the partners with a schedule of safe installment payments.

P16-19   **Cash Distribution Plan**

Refer to the information contained in Problem 16-18. Assume the following amounts of cash were received during the months of July, August, and September from the sale of DSV Partnership's noncash assets:

July	$390,000
August	22,000
September	55,000

The partnership wishes to keep $10,000 of cash on hand at the end of July and August to pay for unexpected liquidation expenses.

It paid liquidation expenses of $2,500 at the end of each month, July, August, and September.

Required

a. Prepare a statement, as of June 30, 20X5, showing how cash will be distributed among partners as it becomes available.

b. Prepare schedules showing how cash is distributed at the end of July, August, and September, 20X5.

P16-20 Matching

Match the terms on the left with the descriptions on the right. Each description may be used only once.

Terms	Descriptions of Terms
1. Dissolution	A. Sale of the partnership assets, payment of the partnership creditors, and the distribution of any remaining assets to partners.
2. Partner's loss absorption power	B. Allocation to other partners in their profit and loss–sharing ratio if the partner is personally insolvent.
3. Liquidation	C. Schedule that shows how cash is to be distributed as it becomes available during liquidation process.
4. Statement of partnership realization and liquidation	D. Computed by dividing a partner's capital balance by that partner's loss–sharing ratio.
5. Installment liquidation	E. Revaluation of a partnership's assets and liabilities to their market values.
6. Cash distribution plan	F. Change in the legal relationship between partners.
7. Incorporation of a partnership	G. End of the normal business function of the partnership.
8. Partner's deficit in capital	H. Liquidation in which all assets are converted into cash over a short time period, enabling all creditors to be paid, with any remaining cash being distributed according to the partner's capital balance.
9. Lump-sum liquidation	I. Cash payments to partners computed on the assumption that all noncash assets will be sold for nothing.
10. Safe payments to partners	J. Presents, in workpaper form, the effects of the liquidation process on the balance sheet accounts of the partnership.
	K. Liquidation in which cash is periodically distributed to partners during the liquidation process.

P16-21 Partnership Agreement Issues [AICPA Adapted]

A partnership involves an association between two or more persons to carry on a business as co-owners for profit. Items 1 through 10 relate to partnership agreements.

The statement of facts for parts A and B are followed by numbered sentences that state legal conclusions relating to those facts. Determine whether each legal conclusion is correct by using the letter Y for yes or N for no.

Part A

Adams, Webster, and Coke were partners in the construction business. Coke decided to retire and found Black, who agreed to purchase his interest. Black was willing to pay Coke $20,000 and promised to assume Coke's share of all firm obligations.

Required

1. Unless the partners agree to admit Black as a partner, she could not become a member of the firm.
2. The retirement of Coke would cause a dissolution of the firm.
3. The firm's creditors are third party beneficiaries of Black's promise to Coke.
4. Coke would be released from all liability for the firm's debts if Black purchased his interest and promised to pay Coke's share of firm debts.
5. If the other partners refused to accept Black as a partner, Coke could retire, thereby causing a dissolution.

Part B

Carson, Crocket, and Kitt were partners in the importing business. They needed additional capital to expand and located an investor named White, who agreed to purchase a one-quarter interest in the partnership by contributing $50,000 in capital to the partnership. Before White became a partner, several large creditors had previously loaned money to the partnership. The partnership subsequently failed, and the creditors are now attempting to assert personal liability against White.

Required

6. White is personally liable on all of the firm's debts contracted subsequent to his entry into the firm.

7. Creditors of the first partnership automatically become creditors of the new partnership continuing the business.

8. Creditors of the old firm that existed prior to White's entry can assert rights against his capital contribution.

9. White has personal liability for firm debts existing prior to his entry into the firm.

10. White must remain in the partnership for at least one year to be subject to personal liability.

Supplemental Problems for this chapter are available as part of the *Online Learning Center* on the textbook's Website.

Chapter **Seventeen**

Governmental Entities: Introduction and General Fund Accounting

In the early 2000s, the combined annual spending of federal, state, and local governments exceeded $4.0 trillion. Governmental purchases of goods and services constitute approximately 20 percent of the total gross national product of the United States.[1]

The first part of this chapter introduces the accounting and reporting requirements for state and local governmental units. The major concepts of governmental accounting are discussed and illustrated first. The last part of this chapter presents a comprehensive illustration of accounting for the general fund of a city. The comprehensive illustration reviews and integrates the concepts presented in the first part of the chapter. Chapter 18 continues the comprehensive illustration to complete the discussion on state and local governmental accounting and reporting.

Each of the 50 states follows relatively uniform accounting standards; however, some states have unique statutory provisions for selected items. Local governments are political subdivisions of state government. The 87,000-plus local governmental units in the United States are classified as (1) general-purpose local governments, such as counties, cities, towns, villages, and townships; (2) special-purpose local governments, such as soil conservation districts; and (3) authorities and agencies, such as the New York Port Authority and local housing authorities. Authorities and agencies differ from other governmental units because they typically do not have taxing power and may sell only revenue bonds, not general obligation bonds.

Governmental entities have operating objectives different from those of commercial entities; therefore, governmental accounting is different from accounting for commercial enterprises. The major differences between governmental and for-profit entities are as follows:

1. Governmental accounting must recognize that governmental units collect resources and make expenditures to fulfill societal needs. Society expects governmental units to develop and maintain an infrastructure of highways, streets, and sewer and sanitation systems, as well as to provide public protection, recreation, and cultural services.

2. Except for some proprietary activities such as utilities, governmental entities do not have a general profit motive. Police and fire departments do not have a profit motive; instead these units must be evaluated on their abilities to provide for society's needs.

3. Governmental operations have legal authorization for their existence, conduct revenue-raising through the power of taxation, and have mandated expenditures they must make to provide their services. The governmental accounting system must make it possible to determine and demonstrate compliance with finance-related legal and contractual

---

[1] Annual reports of the national income and product accounts, including aggregate revenues and expenditures of governmental entities, are presented in the *Survey of Current Business,* published periodically by the U.S. Department of Commerce.

provisions. Governmental units are subject to extensive regulatory oversight through laws, grant restrictions, bond indentures, and a variety of other legal constraints.

4. Governmental entities use comprehensive budgetary accounting, which serves as a significant control mechanism and provides the basis for comparing actual operations against budgeted amounts. The budget is a legally established statutory control vehicle.

5. The primary emphasis in governmental fund accounting is to measure and report on management's stewardship of the financial resources committed to the objectives of the governmental unit. Accountability for the flow of financial resources is a chief objective of governmental accounting. The managers of the governmental unit must be able to show that they are in compliance with the many legal regulations governing its operations.

6. Governmental entities typically are required to establish separate funds to carry out their various missions. Each fund is an independent accounting and fiscal entity and is responsible for using its own resources to accomplish its specific responsibilities.

7. Many fund entities do not record fixed assets or long-term debt in their funds. These fund entities record the purchase of assets such as equipment and buildings as expenditures of the period. A separate record of the fixed assets and long-term debt is maintained within the governmental unit.

HISTORY OF GOVERNMENTAL ACCOUNTING

Before 1984, the development of accounting principles for local governmental units was directed by the Municipal Finance Officers Association (MFOA). In 1934, the National Committee on Municipal Accounting, a committee of the MFOA, published the first statement on local governmental accounting. The report was entitled *A Tentative Outline—Principles of Municipal Accounting.* In 1968, the National Committee on Governmental Accounting, the successor committee, published *Governmental Accounting, Auditing, and Financial Reporting (GAAFR).* Some governmental accountants call it the "blue book" after the color of its cover. The GAAFR is periodically updated to include the most recent governmental financial reporting standards.

In 1974, the American Institute of Certified Public Accountants (AICPA) published an industry audit guide, *Audits of State and Local Governmental Units,* in which it stated that "except as modified in this guide, they [GAAFR] constitute generally accepted accounting principles."[2] In March 1979, the National Council on Governmental Accounting (NCGA) issued its **Statement No. 1**, "Governmental Accounting and Financial Reporting Principles" (NCGA 1), which established a set of accounting principles for governmental reporting.

In 1984, the Financial Accounting Foundation created a companion group to the Financial Accounting Standards Board. The Governmental Accounting Standards Board (GASB) is now responsible for maintaining and developing accounting and reporting standards for state and local governmental entities. In **GASB Statement No. 1**, "Authoritative Status of NCGA Pronouncements and AICPA Industry Audit Guide" (GASB 1), released in July 1984, the GASB stated that all NCGA statements and interpretations issued and in effect on that date were accepted as generally accepted accounting principles for governmental accounting. In 1985, the GASB published a codification of the existing GAAP for state and local governments entitled *Codification of Governmental Accounting and Financial Reporting Standards.* The first section of the codification is virtually identical to **NCGA 1** as amended by subsequent NCGA statements. Section 2 presents the financial reporting issues for governmental entities. Sections 3 and 4 present specific balance sheet and operating statement topics. The GASB continues to publish updated codifications periodically. The codification is an authoritative source for accounting and financial reporting principles for governmental units.

---

[2] Committee on Governmental Accounting and Auditing, *Audits of State and Local Governmental Units,* American Institute of Certified Public Accountants, New York, 1974, pp. 8–9.

A very significant change in the governmental reporting model for governmental units was required by **GASB Statement 34**, "Basic Financial Statements—and Management's Discussion and Analysis—for State and Local Governments" (GASB 34), issued in 1999. **GASB 34** established government-wide financial statements to be prepared on the accrual basis of accounting and an array of fund-based financial statements. This standard also required several new footnote and schedule disclosures that increase the transparency of governmental reporting. The GASB continues to issue new standards to meet the information needs of citizens, creditors, and other users of the financial reports of governmental units.

Accounting for governmental units is given the general description of fund accounting to distinguish it from accounting for commercial entities. This chapter presents an overview of fund accounting and illustrates accounting in the general fund, typically the most important part of most governmental units. Chapter 18 presents the accounting for the remaining funds of a governmental entity and the financial statements required of government units.

MAJOR CONCEPTS OF GOVERNMENTAL ACCOUNTING

Governmental accounting is different from commercial accounting. Governmental entities use a fund-based accounting system in which some of the funds use a modified-accrual accounting method as opposed to the accrual method used by commercial entities. Also, the financial statements of governmental entities have a foundation in the individual funds but aggregate to a government-wide level. The following section discusses the major concepts for governmental accounting.

Elements of Financial Statements

In 2006, the GASB published a proposed Concepts Statement entitled, "Elements of Financial Statements," that defined each of the seven elements of financial statements of state and local governments. Each definition uses the central focus of a *resource,* which is an item having a present capacity to provide, directly or indirectly, services for the governmental entity. This present service capacity may be in the form of direct provision of services as well as those items having the ability to affect cash flows in the future.

The five elements of a statement of financial condition are:

1. *Assets* are resources the entity presently controls.
2. *Liabilities* are present obligations to sacrifice resources or future resources that the entity has little or no discretion to avoid.
3. A *deferred outflow of resources* is a consumption of net resources that is applicable to a future reporting period.
4. A *deferred inflow of resources* is an acquisition of net resources that is applicable to a future reporting period.
5. *Net assets* are the residual of all other elements presented in a statement of financial condition.

The two elements of the resource flows statements are:

6. An *outflow of resources* is a consumption of net resources that is applicable to the current reporting period.
7. An *inflow of resources* is an acquisition of net resources that is applicable to the current reporting period.

The central focus of present service capacity for defining the elements of governmental financial statements is different from the focus used by the FASB in its Statement of Financial Accounting Concepts No. 6, "Elements of Financial Statements." The FASB developed its definitions of the elements of financial statements based on the usefulness of financial reporting information in making economic decisions for allocating scarce resources among alternative uses.

The GASB felt that its concepts statement provides a framework that will enhance consistency in setting future governmental accounting standards and serve as guidance for preparers and auditors when evaluating transactions that are not explicitly included in existing governmental accounting standards.

Expendability of Resources versus Capital Maintenance Objectives

The major differences between commercial and governmental accounting and reporting are due to the objectives of the entities. In commercial, profit-seeking enterprises, the emphasis is on the measurement of the flow of *all economic resources* of the firm. The accrual method of accounting is used to match the revenues and expenses during a period, with the purpose of measuring profitability. The company's balance sheet contains both current and noncurrent assets and liabilities, and the change in retained earnings reflects the company's ability to maintain its capital investment.

In contrast, the major measurement focus for the governmental funds of a government entity is on changes in *current financial resources* available to provide services to the public in accordance with the government entity's legally adopted budget. The modified accrual method of accounting is used to measure the revenues that are available to finance current expenditures and the expenditures made during the period. The balance sheet reports only current assets, current liabilities, and a fund balance. Operating authorization for a fiscal period's transactions is initiated by the passage of a budget by the legislative governing body. Managers of governmental units must be fiscally accountable to show that resources are expended in compliance with the legal and financial restrictions placed on the governmental entity by its legislative body.

In 2006, the Governmental Accounting Standards Board (GASB) published a White Paper that identified a number of key differences between financial reporting for governments and for-profit businesses.[3] The White Paper made the argument that users of governmental financial reports and users of business financial reports require substantially different financial and economic information in order to evaluate fiscal and operational performance. The White Paper expands on the differences stated in the list above and presents the GASB's perspective on the need for separate governmental accounting and financial reporting standards.

Definitions and Types of Funds

Fund accounting must recognize the unique aspects of governmental operations. Governmental units must provide a large range of services, such as fire and police protection, water and sewerage, legal courts, and construction of public buildings and other facilities. In addition, governmental units receive their resources from many different sources and must make expenditures in accordance with legal restrictions.

The operations of a governmental unit must also be broken down into periodic reporting intervals of fiscal years because the management of these public operations may change as a result of elections or new appointments. Thus, governmental accounting must recognize the many different purposes, the different sources of revenue, the mandated expenditures, and the fiscal periodicity of the governmental unit. To accomplish the objectives of the governmental unit, the unit establishes a variety of *funds* as fiscal and accounting entities of the governmental unit. A fund is a separate accounting group with accounts to record the transactions and prepare the financial statements of a defined part of the governmental entity that is responsible for specific activities on objectives. Each fund records those transactions affecting its assets, related liabilities, and residual fund balance.

Different funds are established for the specific functions that a government must provide. Most funds obtain resources from taxes on property, income, or commercial sales; they also may obtain resources as grants from other governmental agencies, from fines or licenses, and from charges for services. Each fund must make its expenditures in accordance with its specified purposes. For example, a fund established for fire protection cannot be used to

---

[3] Governmental Accounting Standards Board, *Why Governmental Accounting and Financial Reporting Is—And Should Be—Different*, GASB, Norwalk, CT, 2006.

provide school buses for the local school. The fire department may make expenditures only as directly related to its function of providing fire protection.

Each fund has its own asset and liability accounts and its own revenue and expenditures accounts. The term *expenditures* refers to decreases in net financial resources available under the current financial resources measurement focus. Expenditures are made in accordance with the budget established by the governmental unit's governing body, and the internal control structure of a vouchers payable system is generally used prior to payments to external vendors. Upon receipt and acceptance of the goods or services from the external vendor, the journal entry to recognize the approved expenditure is a debit to expenditures and a credit to vouchers payable. The increase in the payables decreases the net financial resources available. The payment of the vouchers payable must then be approved by the government's governing body.

Separate fund-based financial statements must be prepared for each fiscal period. In this manner, governing bodies or other interested parties may assess the fiscal and operating performance of each fund in fulfillment of the specific purposes for which each fund was established.

Governmental accounting systems are established on a fund basis in three major categories: governmental, proprietary, and fiduciary. Figure 17–1 presents an overview of each of the funds and provides a brief description of the types of activities accounted for in each fund.

Governmental Funds

Five *governmental funds* are used to provide basic governmental services to the public. These are: (1) general fund, (2) special revenue funds, (3) capital projects funds, (4) debt service funds, and (5) permanent funds (see Figure 17–1). The number of governmental funds maintained by the governmental entity is based on its legal and operating requirements. Each governmental entity creates only one general fund, but it may create more than one of each of the other types of governmental funds based on the entity's specific needs. For example, some governmental entities establish a separate capital projects fund for each major capital project.

Proprietary Funds

Some activities of a governmental unit, such as the operation of a public swimming pool or a municipal water system, are similar to those of commercial enterprises. The objective of the governmental unit is to recover its costs in these operations through a system of user charges. The two *proprietary funds* typically used by governmental entities are (6) enterprise funds and (7) internal service funds (see Figure 17–1). Accounting and reporting for a proprietary fund is similar to accounting for a commercial operation. The balance sheet of each proprietary fund reports all assets, including long-term capital assets, and all liabilities, including long-term liabilities. Chapter 18 presents a complete discussion of proprietary funds.

Fiduciary Funds

Four *fiduciary funds* are provided for a governmental unit. Three are trust funds that account for financial resources maintained in trust by the government. These three are (8) pension and other employee benefit trust funds, (9) investment trust funds, and (10) private-purpose trust funds. The fourth fiduciary fund, (11) agency funds, is used to account for resources held by the government solely in a custodial capacity (see Figure 17–1). Note that the permanent fund, which is a governmental fund, includes resources that are legally restricted so that the governmental entity must maintain the principal and can use only the earnings from the fund's resources to benefit the government's programs for all of its citizens. The private-purpose trust funds include trusts under which the principal may or may not be expendable but for which the trust agreement specifies the principal, if expendable, and the earnings may be used only for the benefit of specific individuals, organizations, or other governments. Examples of fiduciary funds are presented in Chapter 18.

FIGURE 17–1 **Fund Structure**

Governmental Funds	
1. General fund	Accounts for all financial resources except for those required to be accounted for in another fund. Includes transactions for general governmental services provided by the executive, legislative, and judicial operations of the governmental entity.
2. Special revenue fund	Accounts for the proceeds of revenue sources that are legally restricted for specified purposes. Includes resources and expenditures for operations, such as public libraries, when a separate tax is levied for their support.
3. Capital projects fund	Accounts for financial resources for the acquisition or construction of major capital projects that benefit many citizens, such as parks and municipal buildings. This fund is in existence only during the acquisition or construction of the facilities and is closed once the project is completed.
4. Debt service fund	Accounts for the accumulation of resources for, and the payment of, general long-term debt principal and interest. This fund is used for servicing the long-term debt of the government.
5. Permanent fund	Accounts for resources that are legally restricted such that only earnings, but not principal, may be used in support of governmental programs.
Proprietary Funds	
6. Enterprise fund	Accounts for operations of governmental units that charge for services provided to the general public. Includes those activities financed in a manner similar to private business enterprises where the intent of the governing body is to recover the costs of providing goods or services to the general public on a continuing basis through user charges. Also includes those operations that the governing body intends to operate at a profit. Examples include sports arenas, municipal electric utilities, and municipal bus companies.
7. Internal service fund	Accounts for the financing of goods or services provided by one department or agency to other departments or agencies of the governmental unit. The services are usually provided on a cost-reimbursement basis and are offered only to other governmental agencies, not the general public. Examples are municipal motor vehicle pools, city print shops, and central purchasing operations.
Fiduciary Funds and Similar Component Units	
8. Pension (and other employee benefit) trust fund	Accounts for resources required to be held in trust for the members and beneficiaries of pension plans, other post-employment benefit plans, or other employee benefit plans.
9. Investment trust fund	Accounts for the external portion of investment pools reported by the sponsoring government.
10. Private-purpose trust fund	Accounts for all other trust arrangements under which the fund's resources are to be used to benefit specific individuals, private organizations, or other governments, as specified in the trust agreement.
11. Agency fund	Accounts for assets held by a governmental unit in an agency capacity for employees or for other governmental units. An example is the city employees' payroll withholding for health insurance premiums.

FINANCIAL REPORTING OF GOVERNMENTAL ENTITIES

A governmental unit may have a variety of boards, commissions, authorities, or other component units under its control. The financial statements of a governmental entity are presented for the ***reporting entity***, which consists of:

1. The primary governmental unit, such as a state government, a general-purpose local government, or a special-purpose local government that has a separately elected government body.

2. Organizations for which the primary unit has financial accountability.

3. Other organizations that have a significant relationship with the primary government and need to be included in the primary government's financial statements to avoid misleading

or incomplete financial representations. (More on these "other organizations" will be presented in Chapter 18.)

GASB Statement No. 14, "The Financial Reporting Entity" (GASB 14) states that financial accountability exists for those component units if the primary government unit appoints a majority of an organization's governing body and

(*a*) is able to impose its will on the organization, or

(*b*) possesses a financial benefit or assumes a financial burden for the organization.

The *governmental financial reporting model* is specified in **GASB Statement No. 34**, "Basic Financial Statements—and Management's Discussion and Analysis—for State and Local Governments" (GASB 34). Figure 17–2 presents the names of the financial statements and the other information specified by **GASB 34**. The reporting model has two integrated levels of financial statements.

1. The first level is the *fund-based financial statements* because governments continue to use fund-based accounting to record transactions in accordance with the legal or budgetary requirements established by their governing body. These fund-based financial statements demonstrate fiscal accountability of the management of the funds.

2. The second level is the *government-wide financial statements*. After preparing the fund-based financial statements, the governmental unit prepares reconciliation schedules to go from the governmental fund financial statements to the government-wide financial statements. In addition to the governmental funds, the reporting entity includes other funds in the government-wide financial statements. The governmental entity's capital assets, such as buildings and equipment, and long-term debt are also included in the government-wide financial statements. The government-wide financial statements demonstrate the operational accountability of the management of the governmental unit.

This chapter and the first part of Chapter 18 focus on the fund-based-financial statements. After completing our discussion of each fund type in Chapter 18, the government-wide financial statements are presented.

Fund Financial Statements: Governmental Funds

The financial reporting of the governmental funds should separately report the major funds, not all funds. The general fund is always specified as a major fund and is presented in its own column. The other governmental funds are considered major when both of the

FIGURE 17–2
The Government Reporting Model

1. Management's Discussion and Analysis (MD&A) (Required Supplementary Information)
2. Government-wide Financial Statements
   a. Statement of Net Assets
   b. Statement of Activities
3. Fund Financial Statements
   a. Governmental Funds
      1. Balance Sheet
      2. Statement of Revenues, Expenditures, and Changes in Fund Balance
   b. Proprietary Funds
      1. Statement of Net Assets (or Balance Sheet)
      2. Statement of Revenues, Expenses, and Changes in Fund Net Assets
      3. Statement of Cash Flows
   c. Fiduciary Funds
      1. Statement of Fiduciary Net Assets
      2. Statement of Changes in Fiduciary Net Assets
4. Notes to the Financial Statements
5. Required Supplementary Information (RSI)
   a. Budgetary Comparison Schedules
   b. Information about Infrastructure Assets

following criteria are met: (1) total assets, liabilities, revenues, or expenditures of that individual governmental fund are at least 10 percent of the governmental category, *and* (2) total assets, liabilities, revenues, or expenditures of the individual governmental fund are at least 5 percent of the total for all governmental and enterprise funds combined. The government unit has the ability to classify any specific fund as major even if the fund does not meet the two criteria, if the government believes that separately reporting that fund will be useful to users of the financial statements. The nonmajor funds are aggregated and reported in a single column. Two financial statements are required for each governmental fund: (1) balance sheet, and (2) statement of revenues, expenditures, and changes in fund balance.

Balance Sheet for Governmental Funds

The format of the balance sheet, with added parenthetical guidance for learning assistance, for each of the governmental funds is:

Balance Sheet for Governmental Funds		
Assets (financial resources available for current use; presented in order of liquidity)		$X,XXX
Total Assets		$X,XXX
Liabilities and Fund Balances		
Liabilities (due and expected to be paid from current financial resources; presented in order of due date)		$ XXX
Fund Balances		
Reserved (not available for appropriation for expenditures)	$ X	
Unreserved (amount of net current financial resources available for expenditure)	XX	XX
Total Liabilities and Fund Balances		$X,XXX

The five governmental funds use the ***current financial resources measurement focus***. Under this method, the asset section of the balance sheet reports only financial assets such as cash or other assets that will convert into cash (e.g., receivables) in the normal course of operations over the near future. Some governments report inventories or other prepayments because these save the entity from the incurrence of future outflows of current financial resources. Long-term capital items such as equipment or buildings are not reported on the fund-based balance sheet because these amounts are no longer currently available for expenditure. However, the long-term capital assets of the governmental entity are scheduled and reported in the government-wide financial statements, as illustrated in Chapter 18.

The liability section of the balance sheet reports only those liabilities that have become due and that will require current financial resources to liquidate, such as vouchers payable or the current portion of long-term debt. A short-term debt often used in governmental funds is tax-anticipation notes. These notes represent loans obtained using future taxes as collateral for the notes. Most states restrict these borrowings to those taxes that have been levied but not yet collected. These notes payable are paid from the first tax collections of the tax levy to which the notes are related. The principal of long-term debt not due within the next year is not reported on the balance sheet because it will not be settled in the near term with current financial resources. However, the governmental unit's long-term debt is scheduled and is reported in the government-wide financial statements.

The third section of the balance sheet for the five governmental funds reports the net fund balance, which is the amount of the difference between reported assets and reported liabilities. The fund balance is typically divided into two portions: (*a*) Unreserved, which is the amount of current financial resources still available for expenditure, and (*b*) Reserved, which is the portion of the fund balance that is not available for the next period's budget. The various types of reserves of fund balances are presented later in this chapter.

Statement of Revenues, Expenditures, and Changes in Fund Balance for Governmental Funds

This is often called the *operating statement* of the governmental funds, but the financial statements for the governmental funds use the full title. The statement of revenues, expenditures, and changes in fund balance has four major sections:

1. *Operating section.* The top section includes the revenues less expenditures for the period, with the difference shown as the excess (or deficiency) of revenues over expenditures.

2. *Other financing sources or uses.* This section includes nonrevenue items such as bond issue proceeds and interfund transfers. (Note that issuance of bonds and debt refundings of governmental long-term debt are shown in the other financing sources and uses section although the long-term debt is not shown on the fund's balance sheet.)

3. *Special and extraordinary items.* This section presents extraordinary items that are both unusual and infrequent, such as losses due to a hurricane. Special items are transactions or events within the control of management that are either unusual or infrequent in occurrence. An example of a special item would be the one-time sale of county park land.

4. *Fund balance.* The bottom portion presents both the beginning and the ending fund balance.

The format of the statement of revenues, expenditures, and changes in fund balance, with added parenthetical guidance, is:

Statement of Revenues, Expenditures, and Changes in Fund Balance	
Revenues (recognized when both measurable and available; presented by source of revenue)	$XX,XXX
Expenditures (approved decreases in net financial resources; presented by function and character)	X,XXX
Excess of Revenues over Expenditures	$ XXX
Other Financing Sources or Uses (other increases or decreases in net financial resources available, such as bond issue proceeds and interfund transfers)	XX
Special Items and Extraordinary Items	(X)
Net Change in Fund Balance	$ XX
Fund Balance—Beginning	XXX
Fund Balance—Ending (reconciles to total fund balance on balance sheet)	$ XXX

Under the current financial resources measurement focus, revenues are recognized when they become both measurable and available to finance expenditures of the fiscal period. Profit-seeking businesses measure revenue by the accrual basis as it is earned, but the current financial resources measurement focus requires that the expected timing of the revenue-related inflow be evaluated. Availability means that the transaction will result in financial resources collectible within the current period or soon thereafter in order to be used to pay liabilities of the current period.

The expenditure portion of the operating statement reports reductions in available current financial assets. Expenditures are recognized when approved services or goods are received by the governmental entity. Vouchers Payable or some other payable is credited when the expenditure is recognized. The increase in liabilities decreases the net financial resources still available for spending to meet the public purposes established by the governing body. Expenditures also include amounts to purchase capital assets such as trucks or buildings. These are expenditures because they result in a net outflow of current financial assets. Note, however, that once the expenditure has been made for a capital asset, that amount is no longer currently available to spend. Thus, although an expenditure is recognized for the purchase of a capital asset, the capital asset (e.g., truck) is not reported on the balance sheet.

Other financing sources and uses, the second section of the operating statement under the current financial resources measurement focus, reports changes in current financial resources from nonrevenue items, such as sales of bonds or interfund transfers with other funds of the governmental entity. Note that the proceeds from a sale of bonds are reported in the operating statement under the current financial resources focus, but the long-term bond payable is not reported in the liabilities on the fund's balance sheet. Interfund transfers are discussed in depth later in this chapter.

The special items section presents unusual or infrequent items that affect the fund balance but are not revenue or expenditure items. Finally, the fund balance section presents the change in the fund balance to obtain the ending fund balance. The ending fund balance amount should reconcile to the total fund balance shown on the balance sheet.

After each governmental fund prepares its financial statements, a combined balance sheet and a combined operating statement are prepared. These combined statements include all the governmental funds. The format for the combined government funds statements is multicolumnar, with a separate column for each of the major governmental funds and a separate column for the aggregated nonmajor (small) governmental funds. The columns are then added together horizontally and a total column for each line item in the governmental funds is presented.

MEASUREMENT FOCUS AND BASIS OF ACCOUNTING (MFBA)

The *basis of accounting* refers to the timing of recognizing a transaction for financial reporting purposes. For example, the cash basis recognizes revenue or expenditures when cash is received or paid. The accrual basis recognizes revenue or expenditures when the transaction or event takes place. The *modified accrual basis* is a hybrid system that includes some aspects of accrual accounting and some aspects of cash basis accounting. The modified accrual basis is used in funds that have a flow of *current financial resources measurement focus*. This measurement focus is on the flow of current financial resources and the proper expendability of the resources for designated purposes and determination of the available resources remaining to be expended. Expenditures recognized under the modified accrual basis are the amounts that would normally be liquidated with expendable available financial resources. The five governmental funds have this focus.

The accrual basis is used in funds that have a flow of *economic resources measurement focus*. This measurement focus is concerned with all economic resources available to a fund during a particular time period, thereby allowing for a comparison of revenues and expenses and a focus on maintenance of capital. The proprietary funds and fiduciary funds have this focus.

In addition, as is presented in Chapter 18, the government-wide financial statements are based on the accrual basis. This necessitates a reconciliation schedule for those items accounted for under the modified accrual basis for governmental fund accounting to obtain the accrual basis amount that is reported on the government-wide financials. The reconciliation schedule is discussed in more detail in Chapter 18.

Basis of Accounting—Governmental Funds

The current financial resources measurement focus and the modified accrual basis of accounting are used for the governmental funds financial statements. The modified accrual basis is applied as follows:

1. *Revenue* is recorded in the accounting period in which it is both measurable and available to finance expenditures made during the current fiscal period.
2. *Expenditures* are recognized in the period in which the liabilities are both measurable and incurred and are payable out of current financial resources.

Measurable means that the amount of the revenue or expenditure can be objectively determined. *Available* means due or past due and receivable within the current period and collected within the current period or expected to be collected soon enough thereafter to be used to pay current-period liabilities. The definition of "soon enough thereafter" has been stated for property taxes as a period of not more than 60 days after the end of the current fiscal period.

Recognition of Revenue

The accrual method of accounting recognizes revenues from exchange transactions (sales of goods or services) and from nonexchange transactions in which the government gives or receives value without directly receiving or giving equal value in exchange. In **GASB Statement 33**, "Accounting and Financial Reporting for Nonexchange Transactions" (GASB 33), issued in 1998, the GASB classified nonexchange transactions into four categories. **GASB 33** was written from the viewpoint of the accrual basis, and modifications are required to this statement when using the modified accrual basis of accounting. How revenues are recognized depends on the category. The four categories are discussed next.

1. *Derived tax revenues*, resulting from assessments on exchange transactions. Examples are income taxes and sales taxes.

   a. The *asset (cash or receivable) is recognized* when the underlying transaction occurs or resources are received, whichever comes first.

   b. *Revenue recognition* depends on the accounting basis used to measure the transaction. Under accrual accounting (proprietary and fiduciary funds), revenue is recognized when the underlying exchange transaction occurs. Under modified accrual accounting (governmental funds), revenue is recognized when the underlying exchange has occurred and the resources are available.

Resources received prior to the exchange transaction would be reported as deferred revenue (reported as a liability) until the revenue recognition requirement is met for the fund receiving the resources.

2. *Imposed nonexchange revenues*, resulting from assessments on nongovernmental entities, including individuals. Examples include property taxes and fines.

   a. The *asset (cash or receivable) is recognized* when the government has an enforceable legal claim to the resources or the resources are received, whichever comes first.

   b. *Revenue recognition* is made in the period when use of the resources for current expenditures is first permitted or required, or at the time the asset is recorded if no time restriction on the fund's use of the resources exists.

Resources received or recorded as receivables prior to the period in which they can be recognized as revenue should be reported as deferred revenues.

The next two categories have additional eligibility requirements that the providers of financial resources often impose. These eligibility requirements must be met before the transaction can be completed; that is, before the receiving governmental unit can recognize an asset and the associated revenue. The four types of eligibility requirements are typically (1) required characteristics of the recipient as specified by the provider of the financial resources (e.g., the receiving entity must be a school district), (2) time requirements for expending the resources (e.g., the resources must all be expended within a specific fiscal period), (3) reimbursements for only those costs determined to be allowable and incurred in conformity with a program's requirements, and (4) contingencies in which the recipient has met all actions required by the provider. If the recipient has met all of the eligibility requirements imposed by the provider, then the provider should recognize the liability (or decrease in assets) and expense, and the recipient should recognize the receivable (or increase in assets) and revenue at the time the eligibility requirements have been met. The two categories are as follows:

3. *Government-mandated nonexchange transactions*, resulting from one governmental unit's provision of resources to a governmental unit at another level and the requirement

that the recipient use the resources for a specific purpose. An example of this type is federal programs that state or local governments are required to perform.

4. *Voluntary nonexchange transactions,* resulting from legislative or contractual agreements, other than exchanges. Examples include certain grants and private donations.

GASB Statement No. 36, "Recipient Reporting for Certain Shared Nonexchange Revenues" (GASB 36), issued in 2000, amended **GASB 33** for government-mandated and voluntary nonexchange situations in which a providing government provides part of its own derived tax units to recipients. Typically, the providing government provides the recipients with a periodic report of the amount of shared revenues the recipients should anticipate. **GASB 36** states that if the notification from the providing government is not available in a timely manner, the recipient governments should use a reasonable estimate of the amount to be accrued and not wait until the actual receipt of the cash resources.

The following examples present the accounting, under the modified accrual basis of accounting, as used in preparing the governmental funds financial statements.

1. *Property taxes.* Property taxes involve a series of steps that guide the recognition of the property tax asset and the property tax revenue. A typical process is as follows:

Year 1:

Step 1: Levy filed for enforceable claims to property taxes for year 1 (often is January 1).

Step 2: Assessment notice presenting assessed value as of levy date is mailed to each property owner and any appeals are heard.

Step 3: Property tax bills for year 1 mailed to each property owner (Property tax on each property based on assessed value multiplied by the tax rate. The tax rate is determined based on the requirements specified in the levy request filed by each unit of government within the taxing district.)

Year 2:

Step 4: First installment of property taxes for year 1 are due.

Step 5: Second (and last) installment of property taxes for year 1 are due.

The levy creates an enforceable claim to the future collection of property taxes and a property tax receivable should be recorded at that date along with a deferred property tax revenue credit. As presented above, the property tax bill is mailed to each property owner in one fiscal period and the property taxes applicable to that fiscal period are then collected in the next fiscal period. There normally is a legally imposed time restriction on the use of the property tax resources until, in this example, year 2 at which time the resources become available for expenditure. In this example, property tax revenue would not be recognized until year 2 when the time restriction is extinguished. The year 2 entry would include a debit to deferred property tax revenue and a credit to property revenue. While this example presents the levy date in year 1 and the collection in year 2, some governmental entities do make the levy and the collection within the same fiscal period. The key to the timing of recognizing revenue from property taxes is to determine the fiscal period in which the use of the resources for current expenditures is permitted, not necessarily when the property taxes are levied or collected.

NCGA Interpretation No. 3, "Revenue Recognition—Property Taxes" (NCGA 3) specifies that property taxes must be collectible within a maximum of 60 days after the end of the current fiscal period to in order to be recognized as revenue in the current period. Taxes collectible 60 days or more after the current period ends are recorded as deferred revenue for the current period and then accounted for as next period's revenue.

Revenue from another governmental unit or tax-exempt entity in lieu of taxes, such as a payment by a university to a city for police and fire protection, should be accrued and recorded as revenue when it becomes billable.

Revenue from property taxes should be recorded *net* of any uncollectibles or abatements. The Property Taxes Receivable account is debited for the full amount of the taxes levied, with estimated uncollectibles recorded separately in an allowance account reported as a contra account to the receivable.

2. *Interest on investments and delinquent taxes.* Interest on investments or delinquent property taxes is accrued in the period in which the interest is earned and available to finance expenditures in the period. The governmental funds may temporarily invest available cash in interest-generating financial instruments such as certificates of deposit and federal or state securities. Governmental entities should carefully determine the credit risks and market risks of possible investments to minimize their potential loss. Governmental funds report their own current and long-term financial investments and any accrued interest receivable as assets of the funds.

3. *Income taxes and sales taxes.* These derived tax revenues are recognized as assets under the modified accrual basis of accounting in the period in which the tax is imposed or when the resources are received, whichever comes first. These taxes must be available to finance expenditures made during the current fiscal period before recognition as revenue for the period. Income tax revenue should be reported net of any anticipated refunds to taxpayers. Sales taxes collected by another governmental unit (e.g., the state government) but not yet distributed should be accrued prior to receipt by the governmental unit to which they will be distributed (e.g., a city) if the taxes are both measurable and available for expenditure. Measurability in this case is based on an estimate of the sales taxes to be received, and availability is based on the ability of the governing entity (the city) to obtain current resources through credit by using future sales tax collections as collateral for the loan.

4. *Miscellaneous revenue.* Miscellaneous revenues such as license fees, fines, parking meter revenue, and charges for services are generally recorded when the cash is received because these cannot be predicted accurately. Often states take custody of private property when its legal owner cannot be found, as with unclaimed estates or abandoned bank accounts. The property is said to *escheat* (or revert) to the state government. The government should record the property as revenue at its fair market value less a liability for any anticipated claims from possible heirs or other claimants. States generally record the net revenue in the general fund, but some states prefer to account for these resources in a separate, private-purpose trust fund.

5. *Grants, entitlements, and shared revenue.* These are resources received from other governmental units. *Grants* are contributions from another governmental unit to be used for a specified purpose, activity, or facility. *Entitlements* are payments local governments are entitled to receive as determined by the federal government. *Shared revenue* is levied by one governmental unit but shared with others on some predetermined basis (e.g., revenue from taxes on the retail sale of gasoline collected by the state). Grants are recognized as revenue in the period in which all eligibility requirements have been met. This may be at the point the grant is authorized, but, in practice, some governmental units wait until the cash is received because the grant may be withdrawn by the grantor. Some grants are made to reimburse a governmental unit for expenditures made in accordance with legal requirements. The revenue from such grants should be recognized only when the expenditure is made and all other eligibility requirements have been met. For example, a state government might agree to provide a grant for a local government's purchase of fire-fighting vehicles. Typically, the local government must meet all the requirements of the grant before it receives the monies from the state government. In these cases, the local government would record the grant revenue at the time it is received. In a few cases, such as a state grant of reimbursement for the purchase of the firefighting vehicles, the local government may receive grant monies before all the steps of the required expenditure are completed. In those few cases, the local government may be required to record the receipt of the grant monies as an unearned revenue (liability) until all the requirements have been met and the grant is expendable—at which time the unearned revenue is reclassified as earned revenue.

Proceeds from the sale of bonds are not revenue! These proceeds are reported as other financing sources on the statement of revenues, expenditures, and changes in fund balance.

Although bond sales do increase the resources available for expenditure, bonds must be repaid, whereas revenue of the governmental unit does not need to be repaid.

Recognition of Expenditures

Under the modified accrual basis of accounting, expenditures are recorded in the period in which the related liability is both measurable and incurred. Specific examples are as follows:

1. Costs for personal services, such as wages and salaries, are generally recorded in the period paid because they are normal, recurring expenditures of a governmental unit.
2. Goods and services obtained from outside the governmental entity are recorded as expenditures in the period in which they are received.
3. Capital outlays for equipment, buildings, and other long-term facilities are recorded as expenditures in the period of acquisition.
4. Interest on long-term debt is recorded in the period in which it is legally payable.

Basis of Accounting—Proprietary Funds

The two major proprietary funds are the internal service fund and the enterprise fund. Proprietary funds are established for governmental operations that have a management focus of income determination and capital maintenance; therefore, the accrual method used by for-profit–seeking corporate entities is used to account for these funds. Proprietary funds record their own long-term assets, and depreciation is recognized on these assets. Long-term debt is recorded and interest is accrued as it is for commercial operations.

Basis of Accounting—Fiduciary Funds

The accrual basis of accounting is used for all fiduciary funds. Agency funds are those resources for which the governing unit is the temporary custodian. Agency funds have only assets and liabilities; no fund equity, revenue, or expenditures are used. An example of an agency fund is a county's billing and collecting taxes on behalf of other governmental entities, such as a city and a school district. After collection is completed on the "tax roll," the county properly distributes the taxes in accordance with each governmental entity's approved levy.

For fiduciary trust funds, the economic resources measurement focus and the accrual basis of accounting are used. Note that the fiduciary trust funds include those funds in which both the principal and income may be used for the benefit of specific individuals, organizations, or other governments, in accordance with the terms under which the trust fund was established. Agency and trust funds are discussed in depth in Chapter 18.

BUDGETARY ASPECTS OF GOVERNMENTAL OPERATIONS

Budgets are used in governmental accounting to assist in management control and to provide the legal authority to levy taxes, collect revenue, and make expenditures in accordance with the budget. Budgets establish the objectives and priorities of governing units.

For state governments, budgets are proposed by governors and debated by the legislative bodies. After passage, the budget usually becomes part of the fiscal period's state law. For local governments, the mayor or the major administrator may propose the budget. Public hearings and discussions of the budget are then held by governing boards such as the city council, county board, or township board prior to the adoption of the final budget.

A governmental unit may have several types of budgets, including the following:

1. *Operating budgets.* Operating budgets specify expected revenue from the various sources provided by law. The operating budget includes expected expenditures for various line items, such as payrolls of employees, supplies, and goods and services to be obtained

from outside the governing unit. Operating budgets are used in the general fund, special revenue funds, and sometimes the debt service funds.

2. *Capital budgets.* A capital budget is prepared to provide information about proposed construction projects such as new buildings or street projects. Capital budgets are used in the capital projects funds.

Although budgets may be prepared for proprietary funds, these budgets do not serve as a primary control vehicle. Budgets in the proprietary funds are advisory in much the same way budgets are used in commercial entities.

Recording the Operating Budget

Budgets are such an important control vehicle that those governmental funds with legally adopted annual operating budgets should enter their budgets into the formal accounting records, although capital budgets are not normally entered. Recording the operating budgets permits better management control and facilitates a year-end comparison of budgeted and actual amounts. This comparison is part of the required supplementary information for the government reporting model for the funds that must have operating budgets. A budget-to-actual comparison provides an assessment of management's stewardship of the governmental entity and allows citizens and others to determine whether the governmental entity remained within its operating budgetary limits.

To help understand the process of accounting for operating budgets, this text uses the technique illustrated in *Governmental Accounting, Auditing, and Financial Reporting* (GAAFR),[4] in which the budgetary accounts are identified with all capital letters. Capitalization of the budgetary accounts clearly separates the budgetary nominal accounts from the operating accounts of the governmental unit. Although budgetary accounts are not capitalized in actual practice, this convention is helpful in learning the following material.

The recording of the operating budget for the general fund is shown with the following example. Assume that at January 1, 20X1, the first day of the new fiscal period, the city council of Barb City approves the operating budget for the general fund, providing for $900,000 in revenue and $850,000 in expenditures. Approval of the budget provides the legal authority to levy the local property taxes and to appropriate resources for the expenditures. The term *appropriation* is the legal description of the authority to expend resources. The entry made in the general fund's accounting records on this date is as follows:

January 1, 20X1

(1)	ESTIMATED REVENUES CONTROL	900,000	
	APPROPRIATIONS CONTROL		850,000
	BUDGETARY FUND BALANCE—UNRESERVED		50,000
	Record general fund budget for year.		

Note the word CONTROL used as part of the account titles. In governmental accounting, control accounts often are used in the major journals, with subsidiary accounts recording the detail behind each control account. This method is similar to a commercial entity's using a control account for its accounts receivable and then using subsidiary ledgers for the specific customer transactions. Throughout this chapter, the control account level is illustrated to focus on the major issues. In practice, detailed accounting is maintained for each separate classification of revenue and appropriation, either in the major journal or in a subsidiary ledger. The AICPA uses both control-level accounts and budgetary accounts on the Uniform CPA Examination, although it does not capitalize the letters of the budgetary accounts used in the exam.

The ESTIMATED REVENUES CONTROL account is an *anticipatory asset;* that is, the governmental unit anticipates receiving resources from the revenue sources listed in

---

[4] *Governmental Accounting, Auditing, and Financial Reporting* is updated periodically by the Governmental Finance Officers Association (Chicago).

the budget. The APPROPRIATIONS CONTROL account is an *anticipatory liability;* that is, the governmental unit anticipates incurring expenditures and liabilities for the budgeted amount. The excess of estimated revenues over anticipated expenditures is the budget surplus and is recorded to BUDGETARY FUND BALANCE—UNRESERVED. Some approved budgets have budget deficits in which expected expenditures exceed anticipated revenue. These budgets are recorded with a debit to BUDGETARY FUND BALANCE—UNRESERVED.

Recording the budget in the governmental entity's books makes the budget a formal accounting control mechanism for the fiscal period. In addition, having the budget in the accounting records provides the necessary information for the budgetary comparison schedules that are part of the required supplementary information (RSI) footnotes required by the government reporting model in **GASB 34**. At the end of the year, after the appropriate financial statements have been prepared, all the budgetary accounts are closed.

ACCOUNTING FOR EXPENDITURES

The governmental funds use a variety of controls over expenditures to ensure that each expenditure is made in accordance with any legal restrictions on the fund.

The Expenditure Process

The expenditure process in governmental accounting comprises the following sequential steps: appropriation, encumbrance, expenditure, and disbursement.

Step 1. Appropriation

The budget provides the appropriating authority to make future expenditures. Operating budgets are prepared for the general, special revenue, and often the debt service funds. The capital projects fund prepares capital budgets.

The appropriation was recorded in the budget entry made previously in entry (1) for the general fund of Barb City. Recall that a total of $850,000 in anticipated expenditures was approved in the budget.

Step 2. Encumbrance

An *encumbrance* is a reservation of part of the budgetary appropriation and is recognized at the time an order is placed for goods or services. Encumbrances are a unique element of governmental accounting. Their purpose is to ensure that the expenditures within a period do not exceed the budgeted appropriations. The appropriation level was established by the approved budget and sets the legal maximum that may be expended for each budgeted item. The managers of the governmental unit must be sure that they do not exceed this budgetary authority. Thus, encumbrances provide a control system and safeguard for governmental unit administrators.

When an order is placed for goods or services to be received from outside the governmental unit, the budgeted appropriation is encumbered for the estimated cost of the order. Encumbrances are of greatest use when an order is placed and a period of time expires before delivery. Payroll costs, immaterial costs, and costs for goods acquired from within the governmental entity typically are not encumbered because these are normal and recurring and the managers of the governmental unit are able to predict these costs based on past experiences and other administrative controls, such as employment agreements.

A sensible approach should be used with an encumbrance system. For example, it is not necessary to establish an individual encumbrance when an employee orders a pad of paper. Rather, a blanket purchase order with a maximum dollar amount, for example, a total of $500, should be prepared and encumbered, and then it can serve as the control for small, routine supply purchases. Encumbrances provide the unit administrators an important accounting control to fulfill their responsibilities to manage within an approved budget.

To illustrate encumbrance accounting, assume that on August 1, 20X1, Barb City completed a purchase order (PO) from an outside vendor for goods that are estimated to cost $15,000. The entry to record this application of part of the budgeted appropriation authority for the period is as follows:

August 1, 20X1

(2)	ENCUMBRANCES	15,000	
	BUDGETARY FUND BALANCE—RESERVED FOR ENCUMBRANCES		15,000
	Record order for goods estimated to cost $15,000.		

Note that the ENCUMBRANCES account is a budgetary account that is reserving part of the appropriation authority of the budget. For detailed accounting, governmental entities often maintain a subsidiary ledger including accounts for specific types of encumbrances to correspond to each specific type of appropriation. For purposes of this illustration, the single title ENCUMBRANCES is used to indicate a control-level account to focus attention on the major aspects of governmental accounting. In practice, very detailed account titles and classification numbers are used to fully account for each type of transaction. It is important to note that the BUDGETARY FUND BALANCE—RESERVED FOR ENCUMBRANCES is a *reservation (or restriction) of the budgetary fund balance*, not an actual liability.

Step 3. Expenditure

An expenditure and a corresponding liability are recorded when the governmental entity receives the goods or services ordered in step 2. When the goods are received, the encumbrance entry is reversed for the amount encumbered and the expenditure is recorded for the actual cost to the governmental entity. Although the actual cost is typically very close to the encumbered amount, some differences may exist because of partially completed orders, less expensive replacements, or unforeseen costs. Assume that the goods are received on September 20, 20X1, at an actual cost of $14,000. The entries to reverse the encumbrance for the goods and to record the actual expenditures are as follows:

September 20, 20X1

(3)	BUDGETARY FUND BALANCE—RESERVED FOR ENCUMBRANCES	15,000	
	ENCUMBRANCES		15,000
	Reverse encumbrances for goods received.		
(4)	Expenditures	14,000	
	Vouchers Payable		14,000
	Receive goods at cost of $14,000.		

At any time, the remaining appropriating authority available to the fund managers can be determined by the following equation:

Appropriating
authority $= \text{APPROPRIATIONS} - (\text{ENCUMBRANCES} + \text{Expenditures})$
remaining
available

Step 4. Disbursement

A **disbursement** is the payment of cash for expenditures. Disbursements usually must be approved by the governing board or council as an additional level of control over expenditures.

Virtually all governmental entities use a comprehensive voucher system to control cash outflows. The governing board receives a schedule of vouchers to be approved for payment by vote of the board. This is usually one of the early agenda items in any board or council meeting as a vote is taken to "pay all bills." Checks are then written and delivered to the supplier of the goods. If the Barb City council approved the voucher at its October 8 meeting and a check was prepared in the amount of $14,000 and mailed on October 15, 20X1, the following entry records the disbursement:

October 15, 20X1

(5)	Vouchers Payable	14,000	
	Cash		14,000
	Payment of voucher for goods received.		

Classification of Expenditure Transactions and Accounts

Governmental accounting places many controls over expenditures, and much of the financial reporting focuses on the various aspects of an expenditure. Expenditures should be classified by fund, character, function (or program), organizational unit, activity, and principal classes of objects. Figure 17–3 describes the major expenditure classifications.

Many governmental units have a comprehensive chart of accounts with specific coding digits that provide the basis for classifying each expenditure. For example, an expenditure journal entry might specify the expenditure account to be charged as number 421.23-110. The chart of accounts shows that the 421.23 account is for public safety: police—crime control and investigation—patrol, as follows:

420. Public safety
  421. Police
    421.2 Crime control and investigation
      421.23 Patrol

The -110 suffix indicates that this expenditure is for personal services in the form of salaries and wages for regular employees. It is not unusual for some accounting systems to have 11- to 14-digit accounts classifying each individual transaction. The level of specificity in the chart of accounts depends on the particular governing entity's information needs. Classifying information with such specificity allows the governing entity to maintain complete database control over the expenditure information, which it can use at any time in aggregate or relational analysis. For the examples in this chapter, only the expenditure control level is presented; in practice, a complete specification of the expenditure is made.

Outstanding Encumbrances at the End of the Fiscal Period

In the previous Barb City example, the goods were received within the same fiscal period in which they were ordered. What happens if the goods are ordered in one fiscal year and received in the next year? In this case, the encumbrance is not reversed before the end of the fiscal period.

Accounting for these outstanding encumbrances depends on the governmental unit's policy. The government may allow outstanding encumbrances to lapse; that is, the governmental unit is not required to honor these encumbrances carried over to the new year, and the new year's budget must rebudget them. In virtually all cases, the encumbrances will be rebudgeted and honored; however, this policy specifically recognizes the legal authority of the new governing board to determine its own expenditures. A second method is to carry over the encumbrances as nonlapsing spending authority. This method recognizes the practical aspects of encumbrances outstanding at the end of a fiscal period. Either method may be used in governmental accounting.

To illustrate the differences between the lapsing and nonlapsing methods of accounting for encumbrances, assume the following:

1. On August 1, 20X1, $15,000 of goods are ordered and an appropriate entry is made to record the encumbrance.
2. The goods have not been received on December 31, 20X1, the end of the fiscal period.
3. The goods are received on February 1, 20X2, at an actual cost of $14,000.

FIGURE 17–3
Major Expenditure Classifications for Governmental Funds

Classification	Description
Fund	The fund is identified to show the specific source of the expenditure. For example, the general fund would be noted for expenditures from that fund.
Character	Character classifications are based primarily on the period the expenditures are anticipated to benefit. Four major character classifications are current, capital outlay, debt service, and intergovernmental.
Function (or program)	Functions are group-related activities directed at accomplishing a major service or regulatory responsibility. Standard classifications of function include general governmental; public safety; highway and streets; sanitation; health and welfare; culture and recreation; and education.
Organizational unit	Classifying by organization unit maintains accountability by each unit director. The organization unit is determined by the governmental unit's organization chart. For example, public safety could be broken down into police, fire, corrections, protective inspection (such as plumbing and electrical code inspections), and other protection (such as flood control, traffic engineering, and examination of licensed occupations).
Activity	Activities within a function are recorded to maintain a record of the efficiency of each activity. For example, the police function could be broken down into the following activities: police administration, crime control and investigation, traffic control, police training, support service (such as communication services and ambulance services), special detail services, and police station and building maintenance. Each of these activities could be broken down further, if desired.
Object class	Object class is a grouping of types of items purchased or services obtained. For example, operating expenditures include personal services, purchased and contractual services, and commodities. Each of these objects could be further broken down, depending on the information needs of the governing entity. For example, purchased services could include utility services, cleaning services (such as custodial, lawn care, and snow plowing), repair and maintenance services, rentals, construction services, and other purchased services, such as insurance or printing.

Figure 17–4 presents a comparison of the journal entries that would be required under each of the two methods of accounting for unfilled encumbrances at year-end.

Outstanding Encumbrances Lapse at Year-End

The closing entries on December 31, 20X1, close the remaining budgetary encumbrances and establish a reserve of the actual fund balance on the December 31, 20X1, balance sheet. Although the 1994 GAAFR recommends that a reserve for lapsing encumbrances be reported on the balance sheet, the GASB codification allows the alternative of only footnote disclosure of lapsing open orders at year-end that are expected to be honored in the next fiscal period. If only footnote disclosure is used, the governmental unit would not have the second closing entry, which establishes the reserve of the actual fund balance on the balance sheet.

At the beginning of 20X2, the new governing board must decide whether to honor the outstanding encumbrances by including them in the 20X2 budgeted appropriations. If the governing board decides to honor the outstanding purchase orders, an entry is made on January 1, 20X2, to establish budgetary control over the expenditure. A "fresh start" new spending authority is established, and the sequence of entries continues as if this is a new order and purchase completed during 20X2.

FIGURE 17–4 **Comparison of Accounting for Lapsing and Nonlapsing Encumbrances at Year-End**

Item	Outstanding Encumbrances Lapse at Year-End			Outstanding Encumbrances Do Not Lapse at Year-End		
December 31, 20X1						

Close remaining budgetary encumbrances	BUDGETARY FUND BALANCE—
	  RESERVED FOR
	  ENCUMBRANCES
		15,000		BUDGETARY FUND BALANCE—
				  RESERVED FOR
				  ENCUMBRANCES
					15,000	

	ENCUMBRANCES		15,000	ENCUMBRANCES		15,000

Reserve actual fund balance for outstanding encumbrances at end of 20X1 expected to be honored in 20X1	Fund Balance—Unreserved
	  Fund Balance—Reserved
	   for Encumbrances
		15,000	15,000	Fund Balance—Unreserved
				  Fund Balance—Reserved
				   for Encumbrances
					15,000	15,000

January 1, 20X2						

Reverse prior year encumbrance reserve	Fund Balance—Reserved
	  for Encumbrances
	   Fund Balance—Unreserved
		15,000	15,000			

Establish budgetary control over encumbrances renewed from prior period	ENCUMBRANCES
	  BUDGETARY FUND
	   BALANCE—RESERVED
	   FOR ENCUMBRANCES
		15,000	15,000			

Reclassify reserve from prior year				Fund Balance—Reserved for
				  Encumbrances
				   Fund Balance—Reserved
				    for Encumbrances—20X1
					15,000	15,000

February 1, 20X2						

Receive goods and remove budgetary reserve for encumbrances	BUDGETARY FUND BALANCE—
	  RESERVED FOR
	  ENCUMBRANCES
	   ENCUMBRANCES
		15,000	15,000			

Record actual expenditure for goods received	Expenditures
	  Vouchers Payable
		14,000	14,000	Expenditures—20X1
				  Vouchers Payable
					14,000	14,000

December 31, 20X2						

Close expenditures account	Fund Balance—Unreserved
	  Expenditures
		14,000	14,000	Fund Balance—Reserved
				  for Encumbrances—20X1
				   Expenditures—20X1
				   Fund Balance—Unreserved
					15,000	14,000
						1,000

If the new governing board decides not to honor outstanding encumbrances, the following entry is made on January 1, 20X2, to record the cancellation of the open encumbrance:

	January 1, 20X2		
(6)	Fund Balance—Reserved for Encumbrances	15,000	
	Fund Balance—Unreserved		15,000

Eliminate reserve for outstanding encumbrances not being renewed.

If the governmental unit used only footnote disclosure for open encumbrances at the end of 20X1, no entry is required. The governmental unit simply cancels the order with the external vendor.

Outstanding Nonlapsing Encumbrances at Year-End

Some governing units carry over the appropriations authority from prior periods as nonlapsing encumbrances. In this case, the budget for the second fiscal period does *not* show these carryovers. Some governmental accountants believe this method is realistic for many situations in which orders placed with outside vendors cannot easily be canceled.

The 20X1 year-end closing entries presented in Figure 17–4 show the required reservation of the actual fund balance. Note that these are the same two entries made under the lapsing method with balance sheet recognition of the reserve of the fund balance. The differences between the two methods become apparent during the second fiscal period. Under the nonlapsing method, it is important to identify separately expenditures made from spending authority carried over from prior periods. Typically this is done in a reclassification entry on the first day of the second fiscal period, which dates the Fund Balance—Reserved for Encumbrances. No budgetary entry is made in the second year because the appropriation authority comes from the first year's budget. When the goods are received, the expenditures account is also dated to indicate that the expenditure authority emanated from 20X1.

At the end of 20X2, the Expenditures—20X1 account is closed directly to the Fund Balance—Reserved for Encumbrances—20X1. Note that the $1,000 difference between the actual $14,000 cost and the $15,000 reserved amount is closed to Fund Balance—Unreserved because the actual cost is less than the amount encumbered from the prior year's appropriation authority. If the actual cost is more than the reserve, the difference must be approved as part of the appropriation authority for 20X2.

Key Observation from the Illustration

Regardless of the specific method of accounting for unlapsed encumbrances, it is important to note that in this case, the statement of revenues, expenditures, and changes in fund balance will report no expenditures in 20X1 but $14,000 of expenditures in 20X2. The method of accounting for open encumbrances at year-end is based on the governmental unit's budgetary policy, and both methods are found in practice. The comprehensive example presented later in this chapter uses the lapsing method because of its widespread use.

Expenditures for Inventory

Most governmental units maintain a small amount of inventory in office supplies. A first issue is to determine which of two methods should be followed to account for the expenditure of inventories. The first method recognizes the entire expenditure for inventory in the period the supplies are acquired. This is called the *purchase* method. The second method is the *consumption* method; it recognizes expenditures for only the amount of inventory used in the period. The specific method to follow depends on the governing unit's policy and how inventory expenditures are included in the budget.

A second issue is whether to show inventory as an asset on the balance sheet of the governmental funds. Inventory is not an expendable asset; that is, it may not be spent as the governing entity wishes. **NCGA 1** states that inventory should be shown on the balance sheets for governmental funds if the amount of inventory is material. Immaterial inventories need not be shown on the balance sheet. If the inventory is material, it is presented as an asset on the balance sheet; an amount equal to the inventory also should be shown as a reservation of the fund balance, indicating that that amount is no longer expendable.

Figure 17–5 presents the entries to account for inventories under both the purchase method and the consumption method. The illustration assumes that Barb City acquires $2,000 of inventory on November 1, 20X1, having held no inventory previously. On December 31, 20X1, the end of Barb City's fiscal year, a physical count shows $1,400 still in stock. During 20X2, $900 of this inventory is used, resulting in a $500 remaining balance of supplies on December 31, 20X2.

FIGURE 17–5 **Comparison of Accounting for Inventories—Purchase versus Consumption Method**

Item	Purchase Method of Accounting		Consumption Method of Accounting	
November 1, 20X1				
Record acquisition of $2,000 of inventory.	Expenditures	2,000	Expenditures	2,000
	Vouchers Payable	2,000	Vouchers Payable	2,000
December 31, 20X1				
Recognize ending inventory of $1,400.	Inventory of Supplies	1,400	Inventory of Supplies	1,400
	Fund Balance—Reserved for Inventories	1,400	Expenditures	1,400
			Fund Balance—Unreserved	1,400
			Fund Balance—Reserved for Inventories	1,400
December 31, 20X2				
Record remaining inventory of $500, with $900 of supplies having been consumed during 20X2.	Fund Balance—Reserved for Inventories	900	Expenditures	900
	Inventory of Supplies	900	Inventory of Supplies	900
			Fund Balance—Reserved for Inventories	900
			Fund Balance—Unreserved	900

Purchase Method of Accounting for Inventories

Under the purchase method, the entire amount of inventory acquired is charged to Expenditures in the period acquired. On December 31, 20X1, the end of the fiscal year, an adjusting entry is made to recognize the $1,400 remaining inventory as an asset and to restrict the fund balance for the nonexpendable portion applicable to inventories.

The expenditure of $2,000 is closed into Fund Balance—Unreserved for 20X1 in a closing entry made at the end of the fiscal year. The December 31, 20X1, balance sheet includes the inventory of supplies as an asset in the amount of $1,400, and Fund Balance—Reserved for Inventories is shown as a fund balance reserve for $1,400. The 20X1 operating statement shows a $2,000 expenditure for supplies.

At the end of 20X2, an adjusting entry is made to recognize the use of the $900 of supplies of the $1,400 remaining from the 20X1 purchase. This entry reduces the reservation of the fund balance and decreases inventory. At the end of 20X2, Inventory of Supplies is $500, and Fund Balance—Reserved for Inventories is $500, for the remaining unused supplies.

In summary, the $2,000 expenditure is recognized in the period in which the supplies are purchased. No expenditures are recognized in subsequent periods although some of the supplies are used in those periods.

Consumption Method of Accounting for Inventories

Under the consumption method, expenditures for a period are reported only for the amount consumed. In this case, the budget for the period should be based on the expected amount of use so the budgeted and actual amounts compared at the end of the year are on the same basis.

A net expenditure of $600 ($2,000 − $1,400) for supplies used is reported in 20X1, the year the supplies were acquired. With $500 of inventory remaining at the end of 20X2, an expenditure of $900 is reported in the 20X2 operating statement to show the amount of supplies consumed during 20X2. The consumption method relates the expenditures with the use of the inventory.

A comparison of selected account balances under the purchase method and consumption method shows the different amounts reported under these two methods:

	Purchase Method	**Consumption Method**
20X1:		
Expenditures	$2,000	$ 600
Inventory of Supplies	1,400	1,400
20X2:		
Expenditures	-0-	900
Inventory of Supplies	500	500

Note that the choice of methods has no effect on the balance sheet amounts; the only effect is on the period in which the expenditures for inventory are reported.

Both inventory methods are used in practice. The method used by a specific governmental unit depends on its budgeting policy. If the governmental unit includes all inventory acquisitions in its appropriations for the period, the purchase method should be used. If the governmental unit includes only the expected amount of inventory to be used during a period in that period's appropriations, the consumption method should be used.

Accounting for Fixed Assets

Governmental entities may acquire equipment that has an economic life of more than one year. Accounting for this acquisition depends on which fund expends the resources for the acquisition. The governmental funds are concerned with the expendability and control over available resources and account for the acquisitions of equipment as expenditures. In the governmental funds, the entire amount of the cost of the acquisition of equipment and other capital assets is recognized as an expenditure in the year the asset is acquired. No capital assets are recorded in the general fund; they are treated as expenditures of the period.

The proprietary funds are concerned with capital maintenance and account for acquisitions of capital assets in the same manner as commercial entities. Thus, the accounting for the purchase of a capital asset differs in the five governmental funds from the accounting used in the proprietary funds.

For example, assume that Barb City acquires a truck. The acquisition is made from the resources of, and is accounted for in, the general fund. The encumbrance is $12,000, but the actual cost is $12,500 because of minor modifications required by the city.

The general fund makes the following entries to account for the acquisition of the truck:

(7)	ENCUMBRANCES	12,000	
	BUDGETARY FUND BALANCE—RESERVED		
	FOR ENCUMBRANCES		12,000
	Order truck at estimated cost of $12,000.		

(8)	BUDGETARY FUND BALANCE—RESERVED		
	FOR ENCUMBRANCES	12,000	
	ENCUMBRANCES		12,000
	Cancel reserve for truck received.		

(9)	Expenditures	12,500	
	Vouchers Payable		12,500
	Receive truck at actual cost of $12,500.		

The truck is not recorded as an asset in the general fund; it is an expenditure in this fund. Sales of capital assets are recorded as a debit to Cash (or receivable) and a credit to Other Financing Sources—Sales of General Capital Assets for the amount received from the sale. If the amount from the sale is immaterial, the government entity may elect to record the credit to other revenues. A schedule of the acquisition or sale of capital assets by any governmental fund should be maintained, but that record is only for the government-wide financial statements, which do report the assets of a government unit.

Works of Art and Historical Treasures

For the purposes of government-wide financial statements, governments should capitalize works of art, historical treasures, and similar types of assets at their historical costs at acquisition or at their fair values at the date of the contribution. For example, if the general fund expended $10,000 for a work of art, it reports an expenditure for that amount. However, when preparing the government-wide financial statements, the cost of the work of art is reported as an asset of the government. If the assets are donated, contribution revenue is recognized in the government-wide financial statements.

The GASB provided practical guidance to the general rule of capitalizing works of art and historical treasures. For example, many collections have a very large number of items collected over long periods of time, and it is virtually impossible to determine the cost or fair value at the times of acquisition. A provision in **GASB 34** states that the government is not required but is still encouraged to capitalize a collection of art or historical treasures if the government meets all three of the following provisions: (1) holds the collection for public exhibition, education, or research, (2) protects and preserves the collection, and (3) has an organizational policy that requires the proceeds from sales of collection items to be used to acquire other items for collections. If contributed items are not capitalized, the government-wide financial statements report both a program expense and a contribution revenue for the fair market value of the item at the time of its donation.

Capitalized collections that are exhaustible, such as displays of works whose useful lives are reduced due to display, or used for education or research, should be depreciated over their estimated useful lives. Collections or individual items whose lives are inexhaustible are not depreciated.

Long-Term Debt and Capital Leases

Commercial, profit-seeking businesses recognize long-term debt and capital leases as noncurrent liabilities. The debt or capital lease is entered into to earn income, and the liability is recognized under the flow of economic resources measurement focus model. However, accounting for long-term liabilities in governmental funds is directly affected by the flow of current financial resources measurement focus model.

The governmental funds, which include the general fund, record the proceeds from a bond issue as a debit to Cash and a credit to Bond Issue Proceeds, an other-financing source. Bond issue proceeds are not revenue because the bonds must be repaid. Other financing sources are shown in the middle section of the statement of revenues, expenditures, and other changes in fund balances. Bonds are not reported on the governmental funds' balance sheets but only on the government-wide financial statements.

Capital leases are accounted for in a manner similar to long-term debt. If a proprietary fund (e.g., internal service or enterprise fund) enters into a capital lease, the lease is accounted for using methods similar to those used by commercial, profit-seeking entities, with the recording of an asset and a lease liability. However, if a governmental fund (e.g., general fund) enters into a capital lease, the capital lease is accounted for in a manner similar to a bond's accounting.

Investments

Some governmental entities maintain investments in stock or bond securities. The purpose of these investments typically is to obtain an investment return on available resources. **GASB Statement No. 31**, "Accounting and Financial Reporting for Certain Investments and for External Investment Pools" (GASB 31), established a general rule of fair market valuation for certain investments held by a governmental entity. The following investments are to be valued at fair value, if determinable, in the asset section of the balance sheet for the governmental entity: (1) investments in debt securities; (2) investments in equity securities (other than those accounted for under the equity method as provided for in **APB 18**[5]), including

---

[5] **APB Opinion No. 18,** "The Equity Method of Accounting for Investments in Common Stock," March 1971.

option contracts, stock warrants, and stock rights; (3) investments in open-end mutual funds; (4) investment pools in which a governmental entity combines with other investors; and (5) interest-earning investment contracts in which the value is affected by market (interest rate) changes. The periodic changes in the fair value of investments should be recognized as an element of investment income in the operating statement (or other statement of activities) of the governmental entity and reported along with any realized gains or losses resulting from investments. The GASB continues to examine the accounting and reporting for newer types of investments. For example, some governmental entities are using derivatives to manage their investment risks. The GASB's general guidance for derivatives is to use fair-value reporting, including recognizing the periodic changes in fair value. If, however, the derivative is effectively hedging the risk it was created to offset, then the periodic changes in fair value may be deferred and reported only in the balance sheet.

INTERFUND ACTIVITIES

A basic concept in governmental accounting is that each fund is a separate entity and has separate sources of resources, sometimes including the power to levy and collect taxes. The revenues of each fund must then be expended in accordance with the budget and restrictions established by law. Because a single governmental entity has a number of separate funds, it sometimes becomes necessary to transfer resources from one fund to another. *Interfund activities* are resource flows between fund entities. In a consolidated financial statement for a commercial entity, intercompany transactions are eliminated to report only the effect of transactions with external entities. Governmental accounting, on the other hand, requires the separate maintenance and reporting of interfund items. The governing body must approve any interfund transfers and transactions to provide a public record and to prevent distortion of fund uses. Many governmental entities include interfund activities anticipated during a fiscal year in the operating budgets for the year. Budgetary entries for interfund activities are illustrated in the comprehensive example of Sol City presented later in this chapter. Interfund transfers must be accounted for carefully to ensure that the legal and budgetary restrictions are followed and that resources intended for one fund are not used in another.

GASB 34 established four types of interfund activities, as follows: (1) interfund loans, (2) interfund services provided and used, (3) interfund transfers, and (4) interfund reimbursements. A discussion of the four interfund items follows; they are illustrated in Figure 17–6.

(1) Interfund Loans

State law may allow lending or borrowing activities between funds. The loans must be repaid, usually within one year or before the end of the fiscal period. Loans and advances are not shown on a fund's statement of revenues, expenditures, and changes in fund balance; however, all outstanding loans or advances must be shown on the balance sheet as payables or receivables. Interest usually is not charged on interfund financing arrangements. If interest is charged, it is accounted for in the funds in the same manner as for other interest income or expense.

Some governmental entities distinguish between short-term and long-term financing arrangements by using the term "Advances to (or from)" to denote a long-term agreement and "Due to (or from)" for a short-term agreement.

The illustration of an interfund financing transaction in Figure 17–6 assumes that Barb City's general fund loans the internal service fund $4,000 for two months. The general fund reports a receivable for the amount of the loan until the loan is repaid.

(2) Interfund Services Provided and Used

These interfund activities are transactions that would be treated as revenue, expenditures, or expenses if they involved parties external to the governmental unit. These interfund

FIGURE 17–6 **Interfund Transactions and Transfers**

Item	Entry in General Fund			Entry in Other Fund		
1. Interfund loan				INTERNAL SERVICE FUND:		
	Due from Internal Service Fund	4,000		Cash	4,000	
	Cash		4,000	Due to General Fund		4,000
	Cash	4,000		Due to General Fund	4,000	
	Due from Internal Service Fund		4,000	Cash		4,000
				INTERNAL SERVICE FUND:		
2. Interfund service provided and used	Expenditures	100		Due from General Fund	100	
	Due to Internal Service Fund		100	Charge for Services		100
				Cash	100	
	Due to Internal Service Fund	100		Due from General Fund		100
	Cash		100			
				CAPITAL PROJECTS FUND:		
3. Interfund transfer	Other Financing Uses— Transfer Out to Capital Projects Fund	10,000		Cash	10,000	
	Cash		10,000	Other Financing Sources—Transfer In from General Fund		10,000
				CAPITAL PROJECTS FUND:		
4. Interfund reimbursement	Cash	3,000		Expenditures	3,000	
	Expenditures		3,000	Cash		3,000

activities are still reported as revenue, expenditures, or expenses but are different because they are entirely within the governmental unit. These interfund activities are often normal and recurring items, usually involving at least one proprietary fund. Three examples are as follows:

1. The general fund purchases goods or services from an internal service or enterprise fund.
2. Payments are made to the general fund from the enterprise fund for fire and police protection.
3. A transfer of resources from the general fund to the pension trust fund is made to pay for the city's cost of pension benefits for its employees. This is a cost associated with employee services provided to the city and is therefore an expenditure of the general fund.

Usually these transfers involve the recognition of a receivable or payable because of the time lag between the purchase of the services and the disbursement of funds. A "Due to (or from)" account is used for short-term interfund receivables and payables rather than a formal Vouchers Payable account.

The illustration of this type of interfund activity in Figure 17–6 assumes that Barb City's general fund uses an auto from the city motor pool. The motor pool operates as an internal service fund. The general fund is billed $100 based on mileage and pays the bill 30 days later.

(3) Interfund Transfers

The general fund often transfers resources into another fund to be used by the receiving fund for its own operations; occasionally, the general fund receives resources from other funds. These interfund transfers are not expected to be repaid. Such transfers are not fund revenues or expenditures but are instead called "interfund transfers." These transfers are classified under "Other Financing Sources or Uses" in the operating financial statements of the funds. The reason that the receiving fund does not recognize these transfers as revenue is that the issuing fund has already properly recognized these resources as revenue. Thus, the recording of these transfers as other financing sources eliminates the possibility of double counting the same resources as revenue in two different funds of the combined governmental entity. Examples include the following:

1. A transfer of resources, such as cash or other assets, is made from the general fund to an enterprise fund or internal service fund that has an operating deficit that must be eliminated.
2. A transfer of resources from the general fund to a capital projects fund is made to help finance new construction.
3. A transfer of resources from the general fund to the debt service fund is made to pay principal and interest.

The illustration of an interfund transfer in Figure 17–6 assumes that the general fund of Barb City agrees to provide $10,000 to the capital projects fund toward the construction of a new library. The Transfer Out account in the general fund is closed to its Unreserved Fund Balance at the end of the fiscal period. The capital projects fund also closes its Transfer In account at the end of the fiscal period to its Unreserved Fund Balance. These interfund transfers are not expected to be repaid.

(4) Interfund Reimbursements

A reimbursement transaction is for the reimbursement of a fund's expenditure or expense that was initially made from the fund but that is properly chargeable to another fund. These initial payments are sometimes made either because of improper classification to the wrong fund or for expediency within the governmental entity. The reimbursement from one fund to another is recorded as a reduction of the expenditure in the fund initially recording the expenditure and a recording of the expenditure in the proper fund for the appropriate amount. Two examples are as follows:

1. An expenditure properly chargeable to the special revenue fund is initially recorded and paid by the general fund, and the general fund subsequently is reimbursed by the special revenue fund.
2. The general fund records and pays for an expenditure to provide preliminary architectural work on the planning for a new sports arena. The sports arena enterprise fund later reimburses the general fund.

The illustration of an interfund reimbursement in Figure 17–6 assumes that the general fund of Barb City recorded a $3,000 expenditure for a bill from outside consultants that is later discovered to be properly chargeable to the capital projects fund. Upon notification, the capital projects fund reimbursed the general fund and properly recorded the expenditure in its fund.

OVERVIEW OF ACCOUNTING AND FINANCIAL REPORTING FOR THE GENERAL FUND

Figure 17–7 presents an overview of the accounting for the general fund, including accounting for the interfund activities on the general fund's operating statement, the statement of revenues, expenditures, and changes in fund balance. Note that the interfund loans are reported only on the fund's balance sheet.

COMPREHENSIVE ILLUSTRATION OF ACCOUNTING FOR THE GENERAL FUND

The following example illustrates the accounting for the general fund of Sol City for the January 1, 20X2, to December 31, 20X2, fiscal year. The entries are presented by topic, not necessarily in chronological order. The balance sheet for the general fund as

FIGURE 17–7
Overview of General Fund

Item	Description
Measurement focus	Flow of current financial resources—expendability.
Accounting basis	Modified accrual.
Budgetary basis	Operating budget.
Financial statements	1. Balance sheet.
	2. Statement of revenues, expenditures, and changes in fund balance.
Balance Sheet	
Current assets	Includes current financial resources such as cash, certificates of deposit, accrued property taxes receivable and estimated allowance for uncollectible taxes. Interfund loans receivable are included as assets.
	Material inventories reported.
Long-term productive assets (buildings, etc.)	Fixed assets not reported in general fund.
Current liabilities	Vouchers payable is primary current liability. Interfund loans payable also included as liabilities.
Long-term debt	Governmental unit long-term debt not reported in general fund.
Fund balance	Unreserved fund balance and reservations of fund balance (e.g., encumbrances and inventories).
Statement of Revenues, Expenditures, and Changes in Fund Balance	
Revenue	Recorded when measurable and available under the modified accrual method of accounting. Interfund services provided and used also included in revenues (or expenditures).
Expenditures	Recognized in period when measurable and fund liability arises.
Other financing sources and uses	Includes bond issue proceeds and interfund transfers.
Changes in fund balance	Reconciles changes in fund balance during period, including changes in reservations of fund balance.

of December 31, 20X1, presented in Figure 17–8, represents the opening balances for fiscal 20X2.

Adoption of the Budget

The city council adopts the budget for fiscal 20X2 as presented in Figure 17–9. Charles Alt, an alderman of Sol City, voted in favor of adopting the budget. The budget summarizes the four major functions of the city: general government, streets and highways, public safety (fire and police), and sanitation. In the complete budget used by the city council, the expenditures in each of the four functions are broken down into the following categories: personal services, supplies, other services and charges, and capital outlay. The public safety budget includes a budgeted capital outlay of $50,000 for a new fire truck.

Among the city's accounting policies are the following:

1. *Consumption method for inventories.* The city budgets the supplies inventory on the consumption method, including only the costs of expected inventory use during the year.
2. *Lapsing method of accounting for encumbrances.* The city uses the lapsing method for accounting for any encumbrances outstanding at the end of fiscal periods. The

FIGURE 17–8
General Fund
Balance Sheet at the
Beginning of 20X2

SOL CITY		
General Fund Balance Sheet		
December 31, 20X1		
Assets:		
Cash		$ 50,000
Property Taxes Receivable—Delinquent	$100,000	
Less: Allowance for Uncollectibles—Delinquent	(5,000)	95,000
Inventory of Supplies		14,000
Total Assets		$159,000
Liabilities and Fund Balance:		
Vouchers Payable		$ 30,000
Fund Balance:		
Reserved for Encumbrances	$ 11,000	
Reserved for Inventories	14,000	
Unreserved	104,000	129,000
Total Liabilities and Fund Balance		$159,000

APPROPRIATIONS CONTROL for fiscal 20X2 includes a reappropriation of the $11,000 of outstanding encumbrances as of December 31, 20X1.

3. *Use of control accounts.* The city uses a comprehensive system of control accounts for its major journals. The following accounts have extensive subsidiary ledgers that correspond to the entries made in the journal: ESTIMATED REVENUES CONTROL, APPROPRIATIONS CONTROL, ENCUMBRANCES, and Expenditures. The specific details supporting each of these control accounts are maintained in the subsidiary records. For purposes of focusing on the major aspects of governmental accounting, the Sol City illustration includes the control-level entries only.

FIGURE 17–9
General Fund
Operating Budget
for Fiscal 20X2

SOL CITY		
General Fund Operating Budget		
For Period of January 1, 20X1, to December 31, 20X2		
Estimated Revenue:		
Property Taxes	$775,000	
Grants	55,000	
Sales Taxes	25,000	
Miscellaneous	20,000	
Total Estimated Revenue		$875,000
Appropriations:		
General Government	$200,000	
Streets and Highways	75,000	
Public Safety	400,000	
Sanitation	150,000	
Total Appropriations		(825,000)
Excess of Estimated Revenue over Appropriations		$ 50,000
Other Financing Uses:		
Transfer out to Capital Projects Fund	$ (20,000)	
Transfer out to Initiate Internal Service Fund	(10,000)	
Total Other Financing Uses		(30,000)
Excess of Estimated Revenue and Interfund Transfers over Appropriations and Interfund Transfers		$ 20,000

4. *Budgeted interfund activities.* The city includes in the budget all anticipated interfund activities during the fiscal year. The general fund is expected to have the following interfund transfers:

OTHER FINANCING USES:	
Transfer Out to Capital Projects Fund	$20,000
Transfer Out to Internal Service Fund	10,000

The interfund transfer out to the capital projects fund is to pay for the city's share of a municipal courthouse addition project, and the transfer out to the internal service fund is to initiate the internal service fund.

The following entries are made to record the budget and to renew the lapsing encumbrances from the prior period:

January 1, 20X2

(10)	ESTIMATED REVENUES CONTROL	875,000	
	APPROPRIATIONS CONTROL		825,000
	ESTIMATED OTHER FINANCING USES—TRANSFER OUT TO CAPITAL PROJECTS		20,000
	ESTIMATED OTHER FINANCING USES—TRANSFER OUT TO INTERNAL SERVICE		10,000
	BUDGETARY FUND BALANCE—UNRESERVED		20,000
	Record budget for fiscal 20X2.		
(11)	Fund Balance—Reserved for Encumbrances	11,000	
	Fund Balance—Unreserved		11,000
	Reverse prior-year encumbrances reserve.		
(12)	ENCUMBRANCES	11,000	
	BUDGETARY FUND BALANCE—RESERVED FOR ENCUMBRANCES		11,000
	Renew encumbrances from prior period as included in budgeted appropriations in 20X2.		

(*Note:* The technique of capitalizing the account titles of all budgetary accounts continues through the comprehensive illustration. This technique is used in the text to assist differentiation of the budgetary from the operating accounts. In practice, the budgetary accounts are not capitalized.)

Property Tax Levy and Collection

Most municipalities obtain resources from property taxes, which should be recorded as a receivable when an enforceable legal claim arises. Revenue is recorded if the property taxes are measurable and available for current expenditures. Recall that the 60-day rule for property taxes allows the recognition of revenue for the current fiscal period if the property taxes are expected to be collected within 60 days of the end of the current fiscal period. A deferred revenue account is credited if the property taxes are not available for current expenditures. For Sol City, the property taxes are due and available for use within the fiscal period and therefore are recorded as revenue as of the levy date. Note that a provision for uncollectibles must be recorded, and this provision is a reduction of property tax revenue, not a bad debts expense as in commercial accounting. Governmental funds have no such account as bad debts expense. The receivables are classified as current, collectible within this period, or delinquent, for past-due accounts.

The entries in Sol City's general fund for the transactions relating to property taxes are as follows:

(13)	Property Taxes Receivable—Current		785,000	
		Allowance for Uncollectible Taxes—Current		10,000
		Revenue—Property Tax		775,000
	Property taxes levied for this fiscal year with a reduction from revenues for the estimated uncollectibles.			
(14)	Cash		791,000	
		Property Taxes Receivable—Current		695,000
		Property Taxes Receivable—Delinquent		96,000
	Collect portion of property taxes including $96,000 of past due accounts.			
(15)	Allowance for Uncollectible Taxes—Delinquent		4,000	
		Property Taxes Receivable—Delinquent		4,000
	Write off remaining $4,000 of delinquent property taxes.			
(16)	Allowance for Uncollectible Taxes—Delinquent		1,000	
	Allowance for Uncollectible Taxes—Current		5,000	
		Revenues—Property Tax		6,000
	Revise estimate of uncollectibles from $10,000 to $5,000 and close remaining $1,000 balance of allowance account for delinquent accounts.			
(17)	Property Taxes Receivable—Delinquent		90,000	
	Allowance for Uncollectible Taxes—Current		5,000	
		Property Taxes Receivable—Current		90,000
		Allowance for Uncollectible Taxes—Delinquent		5,000
	Reclassify remaining receivables and allowance account from current to delinquent.			

Other Revenue

Other sources of income are grants from other governmental units, a portion of the sales tax collected on retail sales made within the city, and miscellaneous revenue from parking meters, fines, and licenses. Grants from other governmental units should be recognized as revenue when the grants become available and measurable. The city's policy is to recognize these grants as the monies are received because the grants may be withdrawn by the grantor at any time up to the actual transmittal of the monies. In our example, the city receives only 60 percent of the expected grant that had been budgeted at $55,000. Sales tax revenue may be accrued if the city can make a good estimate of the amount to be received and if the sales tax revenue is available for current expenditures. The city's policy is to recognize the sales taxes when received. Miscellaneous revenue is recognized as received.

The entries to record the other sources of income are as follows:

(18)	Cash		33,000	
		Revenue—Grant		33,000
	Receive only 60 percent of expected grant.			
(19)	Cash		32,000	
		Revenue—Sales Tax		32,000
	Receive sales tax revenue from state.			

(20)	Cash	18,000	
	Revenue—Miscellaneous		18,000
	Receive miscellaneous revenue from fines, license fees, minor disposals of equipment, and other sources.		

Expenditures

The appropriations were recorded in the budget entry [entry (10)] with a renewal of the encumbrances carried over from the prior period under the lapsing method of accounting for encumbrances [entries (11) and (12)]. Orders for goods and services from outside vendors are encumbered, and a voucher system is used. Recall that a governmental entity typically does not encumber internal payroll.

The entries for the encumbrances, expenditures, and disbursements made in Sol City's general fund during the year are as follows:

(21)	ENCUMBRANCES	210,000	
	BUDGETARY FUND BALANCE—RESERVED FOR ENCUMBRANCES		210,000
	Encumber for purchase orders for goods and services ordered from outside vendors.		
(22)	BUDGETARY FUND BALANCE—RESERVED FOR ENCUMBRANCES	5,000	
	ENCUMBRANCES		5,000
	Reverse encumbrance for portion of order that is not deliverable because item has been discontinued.		
(23)	BUDGETARY FUND BALANCE—RESERVED FOR ENCUMBRANCES	190,000	
	ENCUMBRANCES		190,000
	Reverse reserve for partial order of goods received.		
(24)	Expenditures	196,000	
	Vouchers Payable		196,000
	Receive goods at actual cost of $196,000 that had been encumbered for $190,000. Difference due to increase in cost of items. Includes supplies for inventory.		
(25)	BUDGETARY FUND BALANCE—RESERVED FOR ENCUMBRANCES	11,000	
	ENCUMBRANCES		11,000
	Reverse reserve for goods received that were ordered in prior year.		
(26)	Expenditures	9,000	
	Vouchers Payable		9,000
	Receive goods ordered in prior year. Actual cost is $9,000 on encumbered amount of $11,000. Difference due to price reduction as part of special sale.		
(27)	Expenditures	550,000	
	Vouchers Payable		550,000
	Payroll costs to employees for period.		
(28)	Vouchers Payable	730,000	
	Cash		730,000
	Vouchers approved by city council and paid during period.		

Acquisition of Capital Asset

The budget for the fire department includes $50,000 for a new fire truck. This capital outlay is accounted for as any other expenditure of available resources. The resources for the fire truck are encumbered when the order is placed with the truck manufacturer. The entries in the general fund for the fire truck acquisition are as follows:

(29)	ENCUMBRANCES	50,000	
	BUDGETARY FUND BALANCE—RESERVED FOR ENCUMBRANCES		50,000
	Order fire truck at estimated cost of $50,000.		

(30)	BUDGETARY FUND BALANCE—RESERVED FOR ENCUMBRANCES	50,000	
	ENCUMBRANCES		50,000
	Reverse reserve for fire truck received.		

(31)	Expenditures	58,000	
	Vouchers Payable		58,000
	Receive fire truck at actual cost of $58,000 due to approved additional items required to meet new fire code.		

(32)	Vouchers Payable	58,000	
	Cash		58,000
	Voucher approved and disbursement made for fire truck.		

Interfund Activities

The anticipated interfund items are included in the budget for the fiscal period. They include the estimated transfer out of $10,000 to initiate the internal service fund and the estimated transfer out of $20,000 for capital improvements to a capital projects fund. In addition to these transfers, the general fund also has an interfund transaction with the internal service fund for services received in the amount of $1,000, and it lends the enterprise fund $3,000.

The following entries in the general fund record the general fund's side of the interfund activities during the year. Chapter 18 continues the comprehensive example of Sol City and presents the entries for these interfund transactions and transfers in each of the related funds so that both sides of accounting for interfund items are illustrated for the Sol City example:

(33)	Other Financing Uses—Transfer Out to Internal Service Fund	10,000	
	Due to Internal Service Fund		10,000
	Recognize the transfer out and associated liability to the internal service fund as included in the budget.		

(34)	Other Financing Uses—Transfer Out to Capital Projects Fund	20,000	
	Due to Capital Projects Fund		20,000
	Recognize the transfer out and associated liability to the capital projects fund as included in the budget.		

(35)	Due to Internal Service Fund	10,000	
	Cash		10,000
	Pay cash to internal service fund for payable from interfund transfer out previously recognized.		

(36)	Due to Capital Projects Fund	20,000	
	Cash		20,000
	Pay cash to capital projects fund for payable from interfund transfer out previously recognized.		

(37)	Expenditures	1,000	
	Due to Internal Service Fund		1,000
	Recognize payable for interfund supplies provided and used (received from the internal service fund).		

(38)	Due to Internal Service Fund	1,000	
	Cash		1,000
	Pay cash to eliminate payable.		

(39)	Due from Enterprise Fund	3,000	
	Cash		3,000
	City Council approves loan to enterprise fund to be repaid in 90 days.		

Adjusting Entries

Certain adjusting entries are required to state correctly the balance sheet items for the year. Assume that a physical count of the inventory shows an ending balance of $17,000 on December 31, 20X2. This is a net increase of $3,000 from the beginning balance of $14,000.

The policy of the general fund is to recognize inventory as an asset and to report a reserve against fund balance for the ending balance. Recall that the city is using the consumption method of accounting for inventories. The entries required to adjust the ending balance of the supplies inventory are as follows:

(40)	Inventory of Supplies	3,000	
	Expenditures		3,000
	Adjust ending inventory to $17,000 and reduce expenditures to net amount consumed during the period.		

(41)	Fund Balance—Unreserved	3,000	
	Fund Balance—Reserved for Inventories		3,000
	Adjust the reserve for inventories from beginning balance of $14,000 to its ending balance of $17,000.		

Closing Entries

The final set of entries closes the nominal accounts. The format presented first reverses the budget entry and then closes the operating revenues and expenditures. Some governmental entities close the accounts in a slightly different order by closing budgeted revenue against actual revenue and budgeted appropriations against actual expenditures. The specific order of closing the accounts has no impact on the final effect; all budgetary accounts and nominal operating accounts must be closed at year-end.

A preclosing trial balance is presented in Figure 17–10. Recall that the city is using the lapsing method of accounting for encumbrances open at the end of the fiscal year. The closing entries for the general fund of Sol City for fiscal 20X2 follow:

December 31, 20X2

(42)	APPROPRIATIONS CONTROL	825,000	
	ESTIMATED OTHER FINANCING USES— TRANSFER OUT TO CAPITAL PROJECTS	20,000	
	ESTIMATED OTHER FINANCING USES— TRANSFER OUT TO INTERNAL SERVICES	10,000	
	BUDGETARY FUND BALANCE—UNRESERVED	20,000	
	ESTIMATED REVENUES CONTROL		875,000
	Close budgetary accounts.		

(43)	BUDGETARY FUND BALANCE—RESERVED FOR ENCUMBRANCES	15,000	
	ENCUMBRANCES		15,000
	Close remaining encumbrances by reversing remaining budgetary balance.		

(44)	Fund Balance—Unreserved	15,000	
	Fund Balance—Reserved for Encumbrances		15,000
	Reservation of fund balance for encumbrances that lapse but are expected to be honored in 20X3.		

FIGURE 17–10
Preclosing Trial Balance for General Fund

SOL CITY General Fund Preclosing Trial Balance December 31, 20X2		
	Debit	**Credit**
Cash	$ 102,000	
Property Taxes Receivable—Delinquent	90,000	
Allowance for Uncollectible Taxes—Delinquent		$ 5,000
Due from Enterprise Fund	3,000	
Inventory of Supplies	17,000	
Vouchers Payable		55,000
Fund Balance—Reserved for Inventories		17,000
Fund Balance—Unreserved		112,000
Revenue—Property Tax		781,000
Revenue—Grant		33,000
Revenue—Sales Tax		32,000
Revenue—Miscellaneous		18,000
Expenditures	811,000	
Other Financing Uses—Transfer Out to Capital Projects Fund	20,000	
Other Financing Uses—Transfer Out to Internal Service Fund	10,000	
ESTIMATED REVENUES CONTROL	875,000	
APPROPRIATIONS CONTROL		825,000
ESTIMATED OTHER FINANCING USES— TRANSFER OUT TO CAPITAL PROJECTS		20,000
ESTIMATED OTHER FINANCING USES— TRANSFER OUT TO INTERNAL SERVICE		10,000
ENCUMBRANCES	15,000	
BUDGETARY FUND BALANCE—RESERVED FOR ENCUMBRANCES		15,000
BUDGETARY FUND BALANCE—UNRESERVED		20,000
Total	$1,943,000	$1,943,000

(45)	Revenue—Property Tax	781,000	
	Revenue—Grant	33,000	
	Revenue—Sales Tax	32,000	
	Revenue—Miscellaneous	18,000	
	Expenditures		811,000
	Other Financing Uses—Transfer Out to Capital Projects Fund		20,000
	Other Financing Uses—Transfer Out to Internal Service Fund		10,000
	Fund Balance—Unreserved		23,000
	Close operating statement accounts.		

A reconciliation of the Fund Balance—Unreserved account is used to determine its ending balance of $120,000, as follows:

Fund Balance—Unreserved			
		Bal. 1/1/X2	104,000
(41)	3,000	(11)	11,000
		Bal. Preclosing	112,000
(44)	15,000	(45)	23,000
		Bal. 12/31/X2	120,000

General Fund Financial Statement Information

The governmental funds financial statements present the financial amounts from the general fund as a major fund. For purposes of illustration, the following two statements are prepared for the general fund to be included in the governmental funds statements presented in Chapter 18. The balance sheet for the general fund is presented in Figure 17–11. The statement of revenues, expenditures, and changes in fund balance is presented in Figure 17–12.

The balance sheet includes the supplies inventory for $17,000 and the associated reservation of fund balance, reflecting that this portion of the fund balance is not expendable. The $3,000 receivable from the interfund loan transaction with the enterprise fund is shown as a current asset. The outstanding encumbrances of $15,000 are a reservation of fund balance indicating that a portion of the year's appropriation has been used but that the ordered goods or services have not yet been received.

The statement of revenues, expenditures, and changes in fund balance presents the following sections:

1. *Operating section.* Revenues less expenditures, resulting in an excess of revenues over expenditures for the period. Expenditures include the interfund services provided and used, and separate reporting of outlays for capital assets.

2. *Other financing sources (uses).* This section includes interfund transfers and nonrevenue proceeds such as bond issues.

3. *Reconciliation of fund balance.* The ending balance in fund balances, including both reserved and unreserved, is reconciled for (*a*) the results of operations, (*b*) other financing sources or uses, and (*c*) special or extraordinary items in the period.

Revenues should be classified by major sources, and expenditures by character and major functions. Although the entries presented in the illustrations for Sol City did not break down the expenditures by function (general government, streets and highways, public safety, and sanitation), this breakdown is done in the actual governmental accounting process so each expenditure can be classified by both function and object (personal services, supplies, and other services and charges). The amounts presented in the expenditures section in Figure 17–12 are the assumed amounts from a comprehensive accounting system. Total expenditures do reconcile to the expenditures recorded in the Sol City illustration.

FIGURE 17–11
General Fund
Balance Sheet
Information at the
End of the Fiscal
Period

SOL CITY General Fund Balance Sheet Information December 31, 20X2		
Assets:		
Cash		$102,000
Property Taxes Receivable—Delinquent	$ 90,000	
Less: Allowance for Uncollectibles—Delinquent	(5,000)	85,000
Due from Enterprise Fund		3,000
Inventory of Supplies		17,000
Total Assets		$207,000
Liabilities and Fund Balance:		
Vouchers Payable		$ 55,000
Fund Balance:		
Reserved for Encumbrances	$ 15,000	
Reserved for Inventories	17,000	
Unreserved	120,000	152,000
Total Liabilities and Fund Balance		$207,000

FIGURE 17–12
General Fund
Statement
of Revenues,
Expenditures and
Changes in Fund
Balance Information
for Fiscal 20X2

SOL CITY Statement of Revenues, Expenditures, and Changes in Fund Balance Information General Fund For the Year Ended December 31, 20X2		
Revenues:		
Property Taxes	$781,000	
Grants	33,000	
Sales Taxes	32,000	
Miscellaneous	18,000	
Total Revenues		$864,000
Expenditures:		
General Government	$206,000	
Streets and Highways	71,000	
Public Safety	335,000	
Sanitation	141,000	
Capital Outlay:		
Public Safety	58,000	
Total Expenditures		811,000
Excess of Revenues Over Expenditures		$ 53,000
Other Financing Sources (Uses):		
Transfer Out to Capital Projects Fund	$ (20,000)	
Transfer Out to Internal Service Fund	(10,000)	
Total Other Financing Sources (Uses)		(30,000)
Net Change in Fund Balances		$ 23,000
Fund Balance, January 1		129,000
Fund Balance, December 31		$152,000

The statement of revenues, expenditures, and changes in fund balance presents the total fund balance, including both reserved and unreserved. Note that in this example, Sol City reported no extraordinary items or special items. Special items would include significant transactions or other events within the control of management that were either unusual in nature or infrequent in occurrence. An example of a special item could be a one-time sale of some city park land. If the city did have a special item or extraordinary item, it would be reported below the other financing sources (uses) section.

Summary of Key Concepts

Accounting for state and local governmental units requires the use of fund accounting to recognize properly the variety of services and objectives of the governmental unit. Funds are separate fiscal and accounting entities established to segregate, control, and account for resource flows. Three types of funds are used by governmental units: governmental funds, of which the general fund is usually the most important; proprietary funds; and fiduciary funds. The basis of accounting for each fund depends on the fund's objective. The current financial resources measurement focus and the modified accrual basis of accounting are used for the governmental fund financial statements. The economic resources measurement focus and accrual basis of accounting are used for the government-wide statements, the proprietary fund statements, and the fiduciary fund statements.

Under the modified accrual basis, revenue is recognized when it is both measurable and available for financing expenditures of the period. A major source of revenue is property tax levies, but other sources may include sales taxes; grants from other governmental units; and fines, licenses, or permits. Note that in the five governmental funds, the estimated uncollectible property taxes are a reduction of the property tax revenue, not an expense as in commercial accounting. Expenditures are recognized in the period in which the related liability is both measurable and incurred. The expenditure process usually begins with a budget, which establishes the spending authority for the fund. Encumbrances are used for purchases outside the governmental entity to recognize the use of a portion of the spending authority for the period and to avoid overspending the expenditure authority. Encumbrances outstanding at the end of a fiscal period are reported as a reserve of the fund balance and may be accounted for as lapsing or nonlapsing. Another type of fund balance reserve is a reserve for inventories, which is used if the amount of inventory is material.

The general fund is responsible for offering many of the usual services of governmental units. Fire and police protection, the local government's administrative and legislative functions, and many other basic governmental services are administered through the general fund. The general fund will provide balance sheet information and statement of revenues, expenditures, and changes in fund balances information to the governmental funds financial statements.

The government reporting model, as established by GASB 34, specifies that both fund financial statements and government-wide financial statements must be presented for most governmental units. Some funds, such as the general fund, use the modified accrual basis of accounting to recognize revenue and expenditure transactions. Furthermore, no long-term capital assets or general long-term debt is recorded in the general fund. However, a reconciliation schedule will be required to go from the fund financial statements to the government-wide financial statements. The government-wide financial statements use the accrual basis of accounting and report all capital assets and all long-term debt. Government-wide financial statements are presented in Chapter 18 after the conclusion of that chapter's discussion of the remaining funds.

Interfund activities must be evaluated carefully to ensure that the legal and budgetary controls of the governmental unit are not violated. Four types of interfund activities exist: (1) interfund loans, (2) interfund services provided and used, (3) interfund transfers, and (4) interfund reimbursements. Outstanding interfund loans are presented as receivables or payables on the fund's balance sheet information. Interfund services provided and used are reported as part of the revenues and expenditures on the operating statements. Interfund transfers are reported separately in the other financing sources (uses) section of the operating statement. Interfund reimbursements are not reported separately on the fund's financial statements.

Key Terms

appropriation, *807*	encumbrance, *808*	government-wide financial statements, *799*
basis of accounting, *802*	expenditure, *797*	
budgets, *806*	fiduciary funds, *797*	interfund activities, *817*
current financial resources measurement focus, *800, 802*	fund-based financial statements, *799*	modified accrual basis, *802*
		proprietary funds, *797*
	funds, *796*	reporting entity, *798*
disbursement, *809*	governmental financial reporting model, *799*	reservation (or restriction) of the budgetary fund balance, *809*
economic resources measurement focus, *802*	governmental funds, *797*	

Questions

Q17-1   What is a fund? How does a fund receive resources?

Q17-2   What are the 11 funds generally used by local and state governments? Briefly state the purpose of each fund.

Q17-3   Compare the modified accrual basis with the accrual accounting basis.

Q17-4   Which of the two, the modified accrual basis or the accrual basis, is used for funds for which expendability is the concern? Why?

Q17-5   When are property taxes recognized as revenue in the general fund?

Q17-6   How are taxpayer-assessed income and sales taxes recognized in the general fund? Why?

Q17-7   What is meant by "budgetary accounting"? Explain the accounting for expected revenue and anticipated expenditures.

Q17-8   Are all expenditures encumbered?

Q17-9   Why do some governmental units not report small amounts of supply inventories in their balance sheets?

Q17-10   What are the main differences between the lapsing and nonlapsing methods of accounting for encumbrances outstanding at the end of the fiscal year? What are the differences in accounting between the lapsing and nonlapsing methods when accounting for the actual expenditure in the subsequent year?

Q17-11 When is the expenditure for inventories recognized under the purchase method? Under the consumption method?

Q17-12 Explain the difference between an interfund services provided and used and an interfund transfer. Give examples of each.

Q17-13 Where is an interfund transfer reported on the general fund's financial statements?

Q17-14 The general fund agrees to lend the enterprise fund $2,000 for three months. How is this interfund loan reported on the financial statements of the general fund?

Q17-15 Explain how an expenditure may be classified by (1) function, (2) activity, and (3) object within the financial statements of a governmental unit.

Cases

C17-1 Budget Theory

Understanding

Governmental accounting gives substantial recognition to budgets, with budgets being recorded in the accounts of the governmental unit.

Required

a. What is the purpose of a governmental accounting system, and why is the budget recorded in the accounts of a governmental unit? Include in your discussion the purpose and significance of appropriations.

b. Describe when and how a governmental unit (1) records its budget and (2) closes out the budgetary accounts.

C17-2 Municipal versus Financial Accounting

Wilma Bates is executive vice president of Mavis Industries Inc., a publicly held industrial corporation. She has just been elected to the city council of Gotham City. Before assuming office, she asks you to explain the major differences that exist in accounting and financial reporting for a large city when compared to accounting and reporting for a large industrial corporation.

Judgment

Required

a. Describe the major differences that exist in the purpose of accounting and financial reporting and in the type of financial reports of a large city when compared to a large industrial corporation.

b. Why are inventories often ignored in accounting for local governmental units? Explain.

C17-3 Revenue Issues

Communication

The bookkeeper for the community of Spring Valley has asked for your assistance on the following items.

Required

Prepare a memo discussing the proper accounting and financial reporting in the general fund for each of the following items.

a. Property taxes receivable are recognized at the levy date. One percent of the levy is not expected to be collected.

b. Property taxes are collected in advance of the year in which they are expendable.

c. Sales tax revenues are received from the state but the city is still owed another $15,000 by the state that will not be received until the next month.

d. An unexpected state grant is received to finance the purchase of fire prevention equipment. One-half of the grant is expended in this fiscal period, and the remainder is expected to be expended in the next fiscal period.

e. Interest is earned on short-term investments made from the general fund's resources.

f. A gift from a local citizen was given to be used for a new city park once the park has been completed. If the park is not constructed within two years, the gift must be returned to the grantor. It is expected that the park will be completed in the next fiscal period.

C17-4 **Discovery Case**

Research

This case provides learning opportunities using available databases and/or the Internet to obtain contemporary information about governmental accounting standards.

Required

Obtain a copy of GASB Statement 34, "Basic Financial Statements—and Management's Discussion and Analysis—for State and Local Governments." Possible sources are the GASB's Website at www.gasb.org, a printed copy of the original standard obtained from a library or other source, or the GASB's Governmental Accounting Research System (GARS), a computer-based database. Read through the preface and summary of the standard and then prepare a one- to two-page memo summarizing the major points presented for GASB 34.

C17-5 **Examining the General Fund Disclosures in a Comprehensive Annual Financial Report (CAFR)**

Analysis

This case focuses on the general fund of a governmental unit.

Required

Using the Comprehensive Annual Financial Report (CAFR) for a governmental entity chosen by your instructor, answer the following questions that relate to the overall government and the governmental funds:

a. Find the budgetary comparison schedules for the general fund. Using these schedules, what were the estimated revenues and appropriations for the most recent fiscal year?

b. Using the same information as in question (*a*), list the amounts of any transfers in and transfers out that were budgeted for the most recent year.

c. Based on the notes following the financial statements, what is the policy of the general fund with respect to outstanding encumbrances at the end of the fiscal year?

d. On the balance sheet of the general fund at the end of the most recent fiscal year, what is the total amount reported for assets and for fund balance? Of the total amount reported for fund balance, how much is unreserved?

e. On the balance sheet of the general fund at the end of the most recent fiscal year, what is the amount reported for inventories? If inventories are reported, does the government use the purchase method or the consumption method?

f. Based on the notes following the financial statements, what is the government's revenue recognition policy with respect to property taxes in the general fund? What percentage of the property tax levy is estimated to be uncollectible?

g. Read the section of the CAFR that contains management's discussion and analysis. What reasons were given for the increase or decrease in general fund revenues for the most recent year?

h. Examine the statement of revenues, expenditures, and changes in fund balance for the most recent year. Compare the change in fund balance for the general fund with the amount of change in fund balance that was budgeted for the year. Were the government's general fund actual results better or worse than expected?

i. After revenue from taxes, what was the next most significant source of revenue for the general fund for the most recent year?

j. Has the general fund engaged in any interfund loans and advances? If yes, show the amounts that are owed to or by the general fund as of the end of the most recent year.

Exercises **E17-1** **Multiple-Choice Questions on the General Fund [AICPA Adapted]**

Select the correct answer for each of the following questions.

1. One of the differences between accounting for a governmental (not-for-profit) unit and a commercial (for profit) enterprise is that a governmental unit should:

   a. *Not* record depreciation expense in any of its funds.
   b. Always establish and maintain complete self-balancing accounts for each fund.
   c. Use only the cash basis of accounting.
   d. Use only the modified accrual basis of accounting.

2. Belle Valley incurred $100,000 of salaries and wages for the month ended March 31, 20X2. How should this be recorded on that date?

	Debit	Credit
a. Expenditures—Salaries and Wages	100,000	
Vouchers Payable		100,000
b. Salaries and Wages Expense	100,000	
Vouchers Payable		100,000
c. Encumbrances—Salaries and Wages	100,000	
Vouchers Payable		100,000
d. Fund Balance	100,000	
Vouchers Payable		100,000

3. Which of the following expenditures is normally recorded on the accrual basis in the general fund?

    a. Interest.

    b. Personal services.

    c. Inventory items.

    d. Prepaid expenses.

4. Which of the following accounts of a governmental unit is credited when taxpayers are billed for property taxes?

    a. Estimated Revenue.

    b. Revenue.

    c. Appropriations.

    d. Fund Balance—Reserved for Encumbrances.

5. Fixed assets purchased from general fund revenue were received. What account, if any, should have been debited in the general fund?

    a. No journal entry should have been made in the general fund.

    b. Fixed Assets.

    c. Expenditures.

    d. Fund Balance—Unreserved.

6. The initial transfer of cash from the general fund in order to establish an internal service fund would require the general fund to credit Cash and debit:

    a. Accounts Receivable—Internal Service Fund.

    b. Transfers Out.

    c. Budgetary Fund Balance—Reserved for Encumbrances.

    d. Expenditures.

E17-2 Matching for General Fund Transactions [AICPA Adapted]

For each general fund transaction listed in items 1 through 12, select the appropriate recording for the transaction listed next to letters A through O. A letter may be selected once, more than once, or not at all.

Transactions	Recording of Transactions
1. An interfund transfer out was made to the capital projects fund.	A. Credit revenues
	B. Debit expenditures
2. Approved purchase orders were issued for supplies.	C. Debit encumbrances
	D. Debit inventories
3. The above-mentioned supplies were received and the related invoices were approved.	E. Debit interfund services provided and used
	F. Credit Budgetary Fund Balance—Unreserved
	G. Debit Appropriations Control

(continued)

(continued)

Transactions	Recording of Transactions
4. Salaries and wages were incurred.	H. Credit Property Taxes Receivable—Current
5. Cash was transferred to establish an internal service fund.	I. Credit Appropriations Control
6. The property tax levy was passed by the city council and tax bills were sent to property owners.	J. Credit residual equity transfer out K. Debit interfund transfer out L. Credit interfund transfer out
7. Property taxes for the current year were collected.	M. Debit Estimated Revenues Control N. Debit Budgetary Fund Balance—Unreserved
8. Appropriations were recorded on adoption of the budget.	O. Debit computer equipment
9. Estimated revenues were recorded on adoption of the budget.	
10. There was an excess of estimated inflows over estimated outflows.	
11. Invoices for computer equipment were received.	
12. Received billing from water and sewer fund (enterprise fund) for using city water and sewer.	

E17-3 **Multiple-Choice Questions on Budgets, Expenditures, and Revenue [AICPA Adapted]**

Select the correct answer for each of the following questions.

1. Which of the following steps in the acquisition of goods and services occurs first?

    a. Appropriation.

    b. Encumbrance.

    c. Budget.

    d. Expenditure.

2. What account is used to earmark the fund balance to recognize the contingent obligations of goods ordered but not yet received?

    a. Appropriations.

    b. Encumbrances.

    c. Obligations.

    d. Fund Balance—Reserved for Encumbrances.

3. When the Estimated Revenues Control account of a governmental unit is closed out at the end of the fiscal year, the excess of estimated revenues over estimated appropriations is:

    a. Debited to Fund Balance—Unreserved.

    b. Debited to Fund Balance—Reserved for Encumbrances.

    c. Debited to Budgetary Fund Balance—Unreserved.

    d. Credited to Fund Balance—Reserved for Encumbrances.

4. The Carson City general fund issued purchase orders of $630,000 to vendors and supplies. Which of the following entries should be made to record this transaction?

	Debit	Credit
a. Encumbrances	630,000	
Budgetary Fund Balance—Reserved for Encumbrances		630,000
b. Expenditures	630,000	
Vouchers Payable		630,000
c. Expenses	630,000	
Accounts Payable		630,000
d. Budgetary Fund Balance—Reserved for Encumbrances	630,000	
Encumbrances		630,000

5. The following balances are included in the subsidiary records of Dogwood's Parks and Recreation Department on March 31, 20X2:

Appropriations—Supplies	$7,500
Expenditures—Supplies	4,500
Encumbrances—Supply Orders	750

How much does the department have available for additional purchases of supplies?

   a. $0.

   b. $2,250.

   c. $3,000.

   d. $6,750.

6. The board of commissioners of the City of Elgin adopted its budget for the year ending July 31, 20X2, which indicated revenue of $1,000,000 and appropriations of $900,000. If the budget is formally integrated into the accounting records, what is the required journal entry?

   a. Memorandum entry only

   b. Appropriations Control   900,000
      Budgetary Fund Balance—Unreserved   100,000
         Estimated Revenues Control   1,000,000

   c. Estimated Revenues Control   1,000,000
         Appropriations Control   900,000
         Budgetary Fund Balance—Unreserved   100,000

   d. Revenue Receivable   1,000,000
         Expenditures Payable   900,000
         Budgetary Fund Balance—Unreserved   100,000

7. Which of the following accounts of a governmental unit is credited when the budget is recorded?

   a. Encumbrances.

   b. Budgetary Fund Balance—Reserved for Encumbrances.

   c. Estimated Revenue Control.

   d. Appropriations Control.

8. Which of the following accounts of a governmental unit is debited when supplies previously ordered are received?

   a. Encumbrances.

   b. Budgetary Fund Balance—Reserved for Encumbrances.

   c. Vouchers Payable.

   d. Appropriations Control.

9. Which of the following situations will increase the fund balance of a governmental unit at the end of the fiscal year?

   a. Appropriations are less than expenditures and budgetary fund balance is reserved for encumbrances.

   b. Appropriations are less than expenditures and encumbrances.

   c. Appropriations are more than expenditures and encumbrances.

   d. Appropriations are more than estimated revenue.

10. Which of the following accounts of a governmental unit is credited to close it out at the end of the fiscal year?

   a. Appropriations Control.

   b. Revenue—Property Tax.

   c. Budgetary Fund Balance—Reserved for Encumbrances.

   d. Encumbrances.

E17-4 **Multiple-Choice Questions on the General Fund**

Select the correct answer for each of the following questions.

1. The primary focus in accounting and reporting for governmental funds is on:

   a. Income determination.
   b. Flow of financial resources.
   c. Capital maintenance.
   d. Transfers relating to proprietary activities.

2. The governmental fund measurement focus is on the determination of:

	Income	Financial Position	Flow of Financial Resources
a.	Yes	Yes	No
b.	No	Yes	No
c.	No	No	Yes
d.	No	Yes	Yes

3. A Budgetary Fund Balance—Reserved for Encumbrances in excess of a balance of Encumbrances Control indicates:

   a. An excess of vouchers payable over encumbrances.
   b. An excess of purchase orders over invoices received.
   c. A recording error.
   d. An excess of appropriations over encumbrances.

4. The Encumbrances Control account of a governmental unit is debited when:

   a. Goods are received.
   b. A voucher payable is recorded.
   c. A purchase order is approved.
   d. The budget is recorded.

5. The following pertains to property taxes levied by Cedar City for the calendar year 20X6:

Expected collections during 20X6	$500,000
Expected collections during the first 60 days of 20X7	100,000
Expected collections during the remainder of 20X7	60,000
Expected collections during January 20X8	30,000
Estimated to be uncollectible (3/1/X7 through 1/1/X8)	10,000
Total levy	$700,000

   What amount should Cedar report for 20X6 as revenues from property taxes?

   a. $700,000.
   b. $600,000.
   c. $690,000.
   d. $500,000.

6. Oak City issued a purchase order for supplies with an estimated cost of $5,000. When the supplies were received, the accompanying invoice indicated an actual price of $4,950. What amount should Oak debit (credit) to Budgetary Fund Balance—Reserved for Encumbrances after the supplies and invoice are received?

   a. $5,000.
   b. $(50).
   c. $4,950.
   d. $50.

7. For the budgetary year ending December 31, 20X6, Johnson City's general fund expects the following inflows of resources:

Property taxes, licenses, and fines	$9,000,000
Transfer in from internal service fund	500,000
Transfer in from debt service fund	1,000,000

In the budgetary entry, what amount should Johnson record for estimated revenues?

    a. $9,000,000.

    b. $9,500,000.

    c. $10,500,000.

    d. $10,000,000.

8. Encumbrances outstanding at year-end in a state's general fund should be reported as a:

    a. Liability in the general fund.

    b. Fund balance designation in the general fund.

    c. Fund balance reserve in the general fund.

    d. Liability in the general long-term debt account group.

9. Interperiod equity is an objective of financial reporting for governmental entities. According to the Governmental Accounting Standards Board, is interperiod equity fundamental to public administration? Is it a component of accountability?

	Fundamental to Public Administration	Component of Accountability
a.	Yes	Yes
b.	No	No
c.	Yes	No
d.	No	Yes

10. Which of the following statements is correct regarding comparability of governmental financial reports?

    a. Comparability is not relevant in governmental financial reporting.

    b. Differences between financial reports should be due to substantive differences in underlying transactions or the governmental structure.

    c. Selection of different alternatives in accounting procedures or practices account for the differences between financial reports.

    d. Similarly designated governments perform the same functions.

E17-5 **Encumbrances at Year-End**

Fargo ordered new office equipment for $12,500 on April 20, 20X1. The office equipment had not been received by June 30, 20X1, the end of Fargo's fiscal year.

Required

a. Assume that outstanding encumbrances lapse at year-end.

    (1) Prepare the entries required on June 30, 20X1.

    (2) Assuming that the city council accepts outstanding encumbrances in its budget for the next fiscal period (20X2), prepare entries on July 1, 20X1.

    (3) Prepare entries on July 24, 20X1, when the equipment was received with an invoice for $12,750.

b. Assume that outstanding encumbrances are nonlapsing.

    (1) Prepare the entries required on June 30, 20X1.

    (2) Prepare the entry required on July 1, 20X1, to identify the expenditure with 20X1.

    (3) Prepare the entry on July 24, 20X1, when the equipment was received with an invoice for $12,750.

    (4) Prepare the closing entry on June 30, 20X2, assuming the expenditure is netted against 20X2 expenditures.

E17-6 **Accounting for Inventories of Office Supplies**

Georgetown purchased supplies on August 8, 20X2, for $3,600. At the fiscal year-end on September 30, the inventory of supplies was $2,800.

Required

a. Assume that Georgetown uses the consumption method of accounting for inventories.

  (1) Prepare the entry for the purchase on August 8, 20X2.

  (2) Prepare the entries required on September 30, 20X2, including the closing of the Expenditures account.

  (3) Assuming the supplies were used during 20X3, prepare the entries on September 30, 20X3.

b. Assume that Georgetown uses the purchase method of accounting for inventories.

  (1) Prepare the entry for the purchase on August 8, 20X2.

  (2) Prepare the entries required on September 30, 20X2, including the closing of the Expenditures account.

  (3) Assuming the supplies were used during 20X3, prepare the entry on September 30, 20X3.

E17-7 **Accounting for Prepayments and Capital Assets**
Required

Prepare journal entries for the Iron City general fund for the following, including any adjusting and closing entries on December 31, 20X1:

a. Acquired a three-year fire insurance policy for $5,400 on September 1, 20X1.

b. Ordered new furniture for the city council meeting room on September 17, 20X1, at an estimated cost of $15,600. The furniture was delivered on October 1, its actual cost was $15,200, its estimated life is 10 years, and it has no residual value.

c. Acquired supplies on November 4, 20X1, for $1,800. Iron City uses the consumption method of accounting. Supplies on hand on December 31, 20X1, were $1,120.

E17-8 **Computation of Revenues Reported on the Statement of Revenues, Expenditures, and Changes in Fund Balance for the General Fund**

Gilbert City had the following transactions involving resource inflows into its general fund for the year ended June 30, 20X8:

1. The general fund levied $2,000,000 of property taxes in July 20X7. The city estimated that 2 percent of the levy would be uncollectible and that $100,000 of the levy would not be collected until after August 31, 20X8.

2. On April 1, 20X8, the general fund received $50,000 repayment of an advance made to internal service fund. Interest on the advance of $1,500 was also received.

3. During the year ended June 30, 20X8, the general fund received $1,800,000 of the property taxes levied in transaction (1).

4. The general fund received $250,000 in grant monies from the state to be used solely for the acquisition of computer equipment. During March 20X8, the general fund acquired computer equipment using $235,000 of the grant. The city has not yet determined the use of the remainder of the grant.

5. During the year ended June 30, 20X8, the general fund received $125,000 from the state as its portion of the sales tax. At June 30, 20X8, the state owed the general fund an additional $25,000 of sales taxes. The general fund does not expect to have the $25,000 available until early August 20X8.

6. In July 20X7, the general fund borrowed $800,000 from a local bank using the property tax levy as collateral. The loan was repaid in September 20X7, with the proceeds of property tax collections.

7. In February 20X8, a terminated debt service fund transferred $30,000 to the general fund. The $30,000 represented excess resources left in the debt service fund after a general long-term debt obligation had been paid in full.

8. On July 1, 20X7, the general fund estimated that it would receive $75,000 from the sale of liquor licenses during the fiscal year ended June 30, 20X8. For the year ended June 30, 20X8, $66,000 was received from liquor license sales.

9. The general fund received $15,000 in October 20X7, from one of the city's special revenue funds. The amount received represented a reimbursement for an expenditure of the special revenue fund that was paid by the city's general fund.

10. In July 20X7, the general fund collected $80,000 of delinquent property taxes. These property taxes were classified as delinquent on June 30, 20X7. In the entry to record the property tax levy in July 20X6, the general fund estimated that it would collect all property tax revenues by July 31, 20X7.

Required

Prepare a schedule showing the amount of revenue that should be reported by Gilbert's general fund on the statement of revenues, expenditures, and changes in fund balance for the year ended June 30, 20X8.

E17-9 **Computation of Expenditures Reported on the Statement of Revenues, Expenditures, and Changes in Fund Balance for the General Fund**

Benson City had the following transactions involving resource outflows involving its general fund for the year ended June 30, 20X8:

1. During March 20X8, the general fund transferred $150,000 to a capital projects fund to help pay for the construction of a new police station.

2. During August 20X7, the general fund ordered computer equipment at an estimated cost of $200,000. The equipment was received in September 20X7, and an invoice for $202,000 was paid.

3. In November 20X7, the city authorized the establishment of an internal service fund for the maintenance of city owned vehicles. The general fund was authorized to transfer $500,000 to the internal service fund in late November. Of this amount, $200,000 will be repaid by the internal service fund in two years with interest at 6 percent; the remaining $300,000 represents a permanent transfer to the internal service fund.

4. In May 20X8, the general fund made a $15,000 payment to one of the city's special revenue funds. The amount paid represented a reimbursement to the special revenue fund for expending $15,000 of its resources on behalf of the general fund.

5. During the year ended June 30, 20X8, the general fund received bills from the city's water department totaling $12,000. Of this amount, the general fund paid all but $500 by June 30, 20X8.

6. During the year ended June 30, 20X8, the general fund acquired supplies costing $35,000 and paid the salaries and wages of its employees totaling $900,000. The general fund uses the purchase method of accounting for its supplies. At June 30, 20X8, unused supplies in the general fund amounted to $5,000.

7. At June 30, 20X8, outstanding encumbrances for goods ordered in the general fund amounted to $25,000. Outstanding encumbrances do not lapse at the end of the fiscal year.

8. On March 15, 20X8, the general fund repaid a loan to a local bank. The amount paid was $265,000, of which $250,000 represented the principal borrowed. The general fund borrowed the money in July 20X7 and used collections of the property tax levy to repay the loan.

9. For the year ended June 30, 20X8, the general fund transferred $95,000 to the city's pension trust fund. The amount transferred represented the employer's contribution to the pension trust on behalf of the employees of the general fund.

10. During May 20X8, the general fund decided to lease several copying machines instead of purchasing them. The lease arrangement was properly accounted for as an operating lease. By June 30, 20X8, the general fund had made lease payments of $10,000 to the owner of the machines.

Required

Prepare a schedule showing the amount of expenditures that should be reported by Benson's general fund on the statement of revenues, expenditures, and changes in fund balance for the year ended June 30, 20X8.

E17-10 **Closing Entries and Balance Sheet**

The preclosing trial balance at December 31, 20X1, for Lone Wolf's general fund follows.

	Debit	Credit
Cash	$ 90,000	
Property Taxes Receivable—Delinquent	100,000	
Allowance for Uncollectibles—Delinquent		$ 7,200
Due from Other Funds	14,600	
Vouchers Payable		65,000
Due to Other Funds		8,400
Fund Balance—Unreserved		119,000
Property Tax Revenue		1,130,000
Miscellaneous Revenue		40,000
Expenditures	1,140,000	
Other Financing Uses—Transfer Out	25,000	
Estimated Revenues Control	1,200,000	
Appropriations Control		1,145,000
Estimated Other Financing Uses—Transfer Out		25,000
Encumbrances	32,000	
Budgetary Fund Balance—Reserved for Encumbrances		32,000
Budgetary Fund Balance—Unreserved		30,000
Total	$2,601,600	$2,601,600

Lone Wolf uses the purchase method of accounting for inventories and the lapsing method of accounting for encumbrances.

Required

a. Prepare the closing entries for the general fund.

b. Prepare a general fund–only balance sheet at December 31, 20X1.

E17-11 **Statement of Revenues, Expenditures, and Changes in Fund Balance**

Refer to the preclosing trial balance in Exercise 17-10. Assume that the balances on December 31, 20X0, were as follows:

Fund Balance—Reserved for Encumbrances	$28,000
Fund Balance—Unreserved	91,000

Required

Prepare a general fund–only statement of revenues, expenditures, and changes in fund balance for fiscal 20X1.

E17-12 **Matching Questions Involving Interfund Transactions and Transfers in the General Fund**

The general fund of Mattville had several interfund activities during the fiscal year ended June 30, 20X9. These interfund activities are presented in the left-hand column of the following table. A list of the types of interfund activities that occur in state and local governmental accounting is provided on the right. For each general fund transaction/transfer, select a letter from the list on the right that best describes the interfund activity.

General Fund Transactions and Transfers	Type of Interfund Transactions and Transfers
1. Received bills from an internal service fund for using city-owned vehicles.	A. Interfund loan
2. Transferred cash to start an enterprise fund. The enterprise fund does not have to return the cash to the general fund.	B. Interfund service provided and used
3. Received cash from a special revenue fund that was discontinued.	C. Interfund transfer
4. Transferred cash to a capital projects fund to help construct a building.	D. Interfund reimbursement
5. Transferred cash to a debt service fund to pay interest and principal of general long-term debt.	
6. Transferred cash to the pension trust fund representing the employer's contribution toward the pension of general fund employees.	
7. Transferred resources to an enterprise fund. It is expected that these resources will be repaid with interest.	
8. Transferred cash to a special revenue fund. The special revenue fund incurred and paid expenditures on behalf of the general fund.	
9. Received cash from an internal service fund. The cash received represented repayment of an advance made during the previous year.	
10. Received bills from an enterprise fund for using public parking facilities.	

Problems   P17-13   General Fund Entries [AICPA Adapted]

The following information was abstracted from the accounts of the general fund of the City of Noble after the books had been closed for the fiscal year ended June 30, 20X2.

	Postclosing Trial Balance, June 30, 20X1	Transactions July 1, 20X1–June 30, 20X2 Debit	Transactions July 1, 20X1–June 30, 20X2 Credit	Postclosing Trial Balance, June 30, 20X2
Cash	$700,000	$1,820,000	$1,852,000	$668,000
Taxes Receivable	40,000	1,870,000	1,828,000	82,000
Total	$740,000			$750,000
Allowance for Uncollectible Taxes	$ 8,000	8,000	10,000	$ 10,000
Vouchers Payable	132,000	1,852,000	1,840,000	120,000
Fund Balance:				
Reserved for Encumbrances			70,000	70,000
Unreserved	600,000	70,000	20,000	550,000
Total	$740,000			$750,000

Additional Information

The budget for the fiscal year ended June 30, 20X2, provided for estimated revenue of $2,000,000 and appropriations of $1,940,000. Encumbrances of $1,070,000 were made during the year.

Required

Prepare proper journal entries to record the budgeted and actual transactions for the fiscal year ended June 30, 20X2. Include closing entries.

P17-14 **General Fund Entries [AICPA Adapted]**

The following trial balances were taken from the accounts of Omega City's general fund before the books had been closed for the fiscal year ended June 30, 20X2:

	Trial Balance July 1, 20X1	Trial Balance June 30, 20X2
Cash	$400,000	$ 700,000
Taxes Receivable	150,000	170,000
Allowance for Uncollectible Taxes	(40,000)	(70,000)
Estimated Revenues Control	—	3,000,000
Expenditures	—	2,900,000
Encumbrances	—	91,000
Total	$510,000	$6,791,000
Vouchers Payable	$ 80,000	$ 408,000
Due to Other Funds	210,000	142,000
Fund Balance—Reserved for Encumbrances	60,000	—
Fund Balance—Unreserved	160,000	220,000
Revenue from Taxes	—	2,800,000
Miscellaneous Revenues	—	130,000
Appropriations Control	—	2,980,000
Budgetary Fund Balance—Reserved for Encumbrances	—	91,000
Budgetary Fund Balance—Unreserved	—	20,000
Total	$510,000	$6,791,000

Additional Information

1. The estimated taxes receivable for the year ended June 30, 20X2, were $2,870,000, and the taxes collected during the year totaled $2,810,000. Miscellaneous revenue of $130,000 was also collected during the year.

2. Encumbrances in the amount of $2,700,000 were recorded. In addition, the $60,000 of lapsed encumbrances from the 20X1 fiscal year was renewed.

3. During the year, the general fund was billed $142,000 for services performed on its behalf by other city funds (debit Expenditures).

4. An analysis of the transactions in the Vouchers Payable account for the year ended June 30, 20X2, is as follows:

	Debit (Credit)
Current expenditures (liquidating all encumbrances to date except for renewed 20X1 commitment)	$(2,700,000)
Expenditures applicable to previous year	(58,000)
Vouchers for payments to other funds	(210,000)
Cash payments during year	2,640,000
Net change	$ (328,000)

5. On May 10, 20X2, encumbrances were recorded for the purchase of next year's supplies at an estimated cost of $91,000.

Required

On the basis of the data presented, reconstruct the original detailed journal entries that were required to record all transactions for the fiscal year ended June 30, 20X2, including the recording of the current year's budget. Do not prepare closing entries for June 30, 20X2.

P17-15   General Fund Closing Entries and Statements

The unadjusted trial balance for the general fund of Quincy on June 30, 20X2, follows:

	Debit	Credit
Cash	$ 100,000	
Property Taxes Receivable—Delinquent	108,000	
Allowance for Uncollectibles—Delinquent		$ 8,400
Due from Data Processing Fund	10,000	
Estimated Revenues Control	1,450,000	
Other Financing Uses—Transfer Out	50,000	
Encumbrances	23,000	
Expenditures	1,385,000	
Vouchers Payable		44,000
Due to Printing Service Fund		2,600
Property Tax Revenue		1,390,000
Grant Revenue		40,000
Miscellaneous Revenue		32,000
Appropriations Control		1,400,000
Estimated Other Financing Uses—Transfer Out		50,000
Budgetary Fund Balance—Reserved for Encumbrances		23,000
Fund Balance—Unreserved		136,000
Total	$3,126,000	$3,126,000

Additional Information

1. Quincy uses the lapsing method for outstanding encumbrances. Fund Balance Reserved for Encumbrances on June 30, 20X1, was $28,300. The encumbrances were renewed.
2. Fund Balance—Unreserved, June 30, 20X1, was $107,700.
3. Quincy uses the consumption method of accounting for inventories. No supplies were on hand on June 30, 20X1. Supplies on hand on June 30, 20X2, cost $8,000.

Required

a. Prepare adjusting and closing entries for the general fund.
b. Prepare a balance sheet for the general fund as of June 30, 20X2.
c. Prepare a statement of revenues, expenditures, and changes in fund balance for fiscal 20X2, for the general fund.

P17-16   General Fund Entries and Statements

The postclosing trial balance of the general fund of the town of Pine Ridge on December 31, 20X1, is as follows:

	Debit	Credit
Cash	$111,000	
Property Taxes Receivable—Delinquent	90,000	
Allowance for Uncollectibles—Delinquent		$ 9,000
Vouchers Payable		31,000
Fund Balance—Reserved for Encumbrances		21,000
Fund Balance—Unreserved		140,000
Total	$201,000	$201,000

Additional Information Related to 20X2

1. Estimated revenue: property taxes, $1,584,000 from a tax levy of $1,600,000 of which 1 percent was estimated uncollectible; sales taxes, $250,000; and miscellaneous, $43,000. Appropriations totaled

$1,840,000; and estimated transfers out $37,000. Appropriations included outstanding purchase orders from 20X1 of $21,000. Pine Ridge uses the lapsing method for outstanding encumbrances.

2. Cash receipts: property taxes, $1,590,000, including $83,000 from 20X1; sales taxes, $284,000; licenses and fees, $39,000; and a loan from the motor pool, $10,000. The remaining property taxes from 20X1 were written off, and those remaining from 20X2 were reclassified.

3. Orders were issued for $1,800,000 in addition to the acceptance of the $21,000 outstanding purchase orders from 20X1. A total of $48,000 of purchase orders still was outstanding at the end of 20X2. Actual expenditures were $1,788,000, including $42,000 for office furniture. Vouchers paid totaled $1,793,000.

4. Other cash payments and transfers were as follows:

Loan to central stores	$13,000
Transfer out	37,000

Required

a. Prepare entries to summarize the general fund budget and transactions for 20X2.

b. Prepare a preclosing trial balance.

c. Prepare closing entries for the general fund.

d. Prepare a balance sheet for the general fund as of December 31, 20X2.

e. Prepare a statement of revenues, expenditures, and changes in fund balance for 20X2 for the general fund.

P17-17   Matching Governmental Terms with Descriptions

Match the terms on the left with the descriptions on the right. A description may be used once or not at all.

Terms	Descriptions of Terms
1. Proprietary funds	A. Trust and agency funds.
2. Modified accrual method	B. Fiscal and accounting entities of a government.
	C. Basis of accounting used by proprietary funds.
3. Estimated revenues	D. Example of this transaction when the general fund uses the services
4. Appropriations	of an internal service fund.
5. Encumbrances	E. Expenditures for inventories representing the amount of inventories
6. Expenditures	consumed during the period.
7. Budgetary fund balance—unreserved	F. General, special revenue, debt service, capital projects funds, and permanent funds.
8. Consumption method for supplies inventories	G. Legal authority to make expenditures.
	H. Budgeted resource inflows.
	I. Revenues recognized when they are both measurable and available to finance expenditures made during the current period.
9. Nonlapsing encumbrances	J. Internal service and enterprise funds.
10. Interfund services provided or used	K. Expenditures for inventories representing the amount of inventories acquired during the current period.
11. Governmental funds	L. Reports government unit's infrastructure assets.
12. Interfund transfers	M. Recorded when the general fund orders goods and services.
13. Fiduciary funds	N. Appropriation authority that carries over to the next fiscal year for
14. Funds	these orders.
15. Government-wide financials	O. Appropriation authority that does not carry over to the next fiscal year for these orders.
16. Accrual method	P. Type of transaction that occurs when the general fund makes a cash transfer to establish an internal service fund.
	Q. Account debited in the general fund when an invoice is received for computer equipment.
	R. Account that would indicate a budget surplus or deficit in the general fund.

P17-18 **Identification of Governmental Accounting Terms**

For each of the following numbered statements, write the term(s) that is (are) described in the statement.

1. This is the set of financial statements that presents the governmental unit's infrastructure assets and long-term debt.

2. At the present time, this body has the authority to prescribe generally accepted accounting principles for state and local governmental entities.

3. This is a fiscal and an accounting entity with a self-balancing set of accounts recording cash and other financial resources with all related liabilities and residual equities or balances and changes therein that are segregated for the purpose of carrying on specific activities or attaining certain objectives in accordance with special regulations, restrictions, or limitations.

4. This type of interfund activity is accounted for as an expenditure or revenue.

5. These are the proprietary funds.

6. These are assets of the governmental unit and include roads, municipal buildings, sewer systems, sidewalks, and so forth.

7. These are the fiduciary funds.

8. This basis is used in funds that have a flow of financial resources measurement focus.

9. This is the measurement focus of government-wide financials.

10. This gives the governmental entity the legal right to collect property taxes.

11. These are the governmental funds.

12. This is subtracted from Property Taxes Receivable—Current to get the revenue from property taxes for the year.

13. This account is credited in the budget entry for the general fund if expected resource inflows exceed expected resource outflows.

14. This account is debited when the general fund records a purchase order for goods or services.

15. This method of accounting for supplies inventories in the general fund reports expenditures for supplies for only the amount used during the year.

16. This account is debited in the general fund when a transfer out is made to another fund.

17. This account is debited in the general fund when it records a billing from another fund for services that were provided to the general fund.

18. This is reported on the general fund balance sheet when assets exceed liabilities and reserved fund balance.

19. This account is debited in the general fund when fixed assets are acquired. Assume that a purchase order to acquire the fixed assets was not recorded.

20. This is the legal term that allows the general fund to make expenditures.

21. Under this method of accounting for encumbrances outstanding at year-end, expenditures are dated in the following year when the orders are received.

P17-19 **Questions on General Fund Entries [AICPA Adapted]**

The DeKalb City Council approved and adopted its budget for 20X2. The budget contained the following amounts:

Estimated revenues	$700,000
Appropriations	660,000
Authorized transfer out to the library debt service fund	30,000

During 20X2, various transactions and events occurred that affected the general fund.

Required

For items 1 through 39, indicate whether the item should be debited (D) or credited (C) or whether it is not affected (N).

Items 1 through 5 involve recording the adopted budget in the general fund.

1. Estimated Revenues.
2. Budgetary Fund Balance.
3. Appropriations.
4. Estimated Transfer Out.
5. Expenditures.

Items 6 through 10 involve recording the 20X2 property tax levy in the general fund. It was estimated that $5,000 would be uncollectible.

6. Property Tax Receivable.
7. Bad Debts Expense.
8. Allowance for Uncollectibles—Current.
9. Revenues.
10. Estimated Revenues.

Items 11 through 15 involve recording, in the general fund, encumbrances at the time purchase orders are issued.

11. Encumbrances.
12. Budgetary Fund Balance—Reserved for Encumbrances.
13. Expenditures.
14. Vouchers Payable.
15. Purchases.

Items 16 through 20 involve recording, in the general fund, expenditures that had been previously encumbered in the current year.

16. Encumbrances.
17. Budgetary Fund Balance—Reserved for Encumbrances.
18. Expenditures.
19. Vouchers Payable.
20. Purchases.

Items 21 through 25 involve recording, in the general fund, the transfer out of $30,000 made to the library debt service fund. (No previous entries were made regarding this transaction.)

21. Interfund Services Provided and Used.
22. Due from Library Debt Service Fund.
23. Cash.
24. Other Financing Uses—Transfer Out.
25. Encumbrances.

Items 26 through 35 involve recording, in the general fund, the closing entries (other than encumbrances) for 20X2.

26. Estimated Revenues.
27. Budgetary Fund Balance.
28. Appropriations.

29. Estimated Transfer Out.

30. Expenditures.

31. Revenues.

32. Other Financing Uses—Transfer Out.

33. Allowance for Uncollectibles—Current.

34. Bad Debt Expense.

35. Depreciation Expense.

Items 36 through 39 involve recording, in the general fund, the closing entry relating to the $12,000 of outstanding encumbrances at the end of 20X2 and an adjusting entry to reflect the intent to honor these commitments in 20X3.

36. Encumbrances.
37. Budgetary Fund Balance—Reserved for Encumbrances.
38. Fund Balance—Unreserved.
39. Fund Balance—Reserved for Encumbrances.

P17-20 Questions on Fund Items [AICPA Adapted]

The following information relates to actual results from Central Town's general fund for the year ended December 31, 20X1:

	Revenues	Expenditures and Transfers
Property tax collections:		
Current year taxes collected	$630,000	
Prior year taxes due 12/1/X0, collected 2/1/X1	50,000	
Current year taxes due 12/1/X1, collection expected by 2/15/X2	70,000	
Other cash receipts	190,000	
General government expenditures:		
Salaries and wages		$160,000
Other		100,000
Public safety and welfare expenditures:		
Salaries and wages		350,000
Other		150,000
Capital outlay		140,000
Transfer out to debt service fund		30,000

- Other cash receipts include a county grant of $100,000 for a specified purpose, of which $80,000 was expended; $50,000 in fines; and $40,000 in fees.
- General Government Expenditures—Other includes employer contributions to the pension plan and $20,000 in annual capital lease payments for computers over three years; the fair value and present value at lease inception is $50,000.
- Capital outlay is for police vehicles.
- Debt service represents annual interest payments due December 15 of each year on $500,000 face value, 6 percent, 20-year term bonds.

Capital Projects Fund

Central's council approved $750,000 for construction of a fire station to be financed by $600,000 in general obligation bonds and a $150,000 state grant. Construction began during 20X1, but the fire station was not completed until April 20X2. During 20X1, the following transactions were recorded:

State grant	$150,000
Bond proceeds	610,000
Expenditures	500,000
Unpaid invoices at year-end	30,000
Outstanding encumbrances at year-end, which do not lapse and are to be honored the following year	25,000

The unreserved fund balance in the capital projects fund at January 1, 20X1, was $110,000.

Required

For questions *a* through *i,* determine the December 31, 20X1, year-end amounts to be recognized in the particular fund. If the item is not reported in a particular fund but is reported on the government-wide financial statements, then specify the amount that would be reported on the government-wide financials. Select your answer from the following list of amounts below. An amount may be selected once, more than once, or not at all.

a. What amount was recorded for property tax revenues in the general fund?

b. What amount was recorded for other revenues in the general fund?

c. What amount was reported for capital leases of computers in the government-wide statement of net assets?

d. What amount was reported for the new police vehicles in the government-wide statement of net assets?

e. What amount was reported for the debt service interest payment in the debt service fund?

f. What was the total amount recorded for function expenditures in the general fund?

g. What amount was recorded for revenues in the capital projects fund?

h. What amount was reported for construction in progress in the government-wide statement of net assets?

i. What amount was reported as the Fund Balance—Unreserved at December 31, 20X1, in the capital projects fund?

Amounts
1. $0
2. $30,000
3. $50,000
4. $55,000
5. $60,000
6. $140,000
7. $150,000
8. $170,000
9. $190,000
10. $315,000
11. $345,000
12. $370,000
13. $500,000
14. $525,000
15. $630,000
16. $700,000
17. $710,000
18. $760,000

P17-21 Identifying Types of Revenue Transactions

Required

Using the requirements of GASB Statement No. 33, "Accounting and Financial Reporting for Non-exchange Transactions," classify each of the following independent transactions for the community of Fair Lake into the proper category of revenue as presented in the right-hand column.

Transactions	Types of Revenue
1. Property taxes were levied by the general fund.	A. Derived tax revenue
2. The electric utility (enterprise) fund billed the general fund for power usage.	B. Imposed nonexchange revenue
3. The city received a state grant for training its police force in additional security measures of public property.	C. Government-mandated nonexchange transaction
4. The city estimated its share of locally generated sales taxes that it expects to receive within the next month.	D. Voluntary nonexchange transaction
5. The city collected various fines it imposed during the period.	E. None of the above
6. The city sold excess office equipment from its municipal headquarters.	
7. The city received resources from the state that must be used to pay for local welfare costs.	
8. The city received a bequest from a local citizen to buy children's recreational items for the city park.	
9. The city collects its share of the local hotel taxes for which the proceeds are legislatively required to be used for a new community convention center.	
10. The state reimburses the city for specific costs related to extra security training of the city's fire department employees.	
11. The city receives its share of funds for environmental improvement resources under a state-required program.	
12. The city receives resources from the federal government to acquire new fire-prevention equipment. The equipment has not yet been acquired.	
13. The city receives grant monies under a state program encouraging cities to make their infrastructure assets wheelchair-accessible.	
14. A company that manufactures road-repaving materials gives the city a grant for the company to conduct a research project on the durability of various types of road repair materials.	

P17-22 Journal Entries for the General Fund

The general fund of Elm City began 20X3 with the following balance sheet:

Assets		
Cash		$35,000
Property Taxes Receivable—Delinquent	$10,000	
Less: Allowance for Uncollectible Taxes—Delinquent	(2,000)	8,000
Inventory of Supplies		2,500
Total Assets		$45,500

(continued)

(continued)

Liabilities and Fund Balance

Vouchers Payable		$10,000
Due to Water Utility Enterprise Fund		1,000
Fund Balance:		
Reserved for Encumbrances	$ 5,000	
Reserved for Inventories	2,500	
Unreserved	27,000	34,500
Total Liabilities and Fund Balance		$45,500

Elm City uses the purchase method of accounting for supplies inventories. The city's encumbrances at year-end are nonlapsing.

The following events occurred during the year ended December 31, 20X3, in the general fund:

1. Elm City's budget for the general fund for 20X3 follows:

Estimated Revenues	$150,000
Appropriations	125,000
Estimated Other Financing Uses—	
Transfer Out to Debt Service	20,000

2. A computer, ordered in 20X2 at a cost of $5,000, was received. Its actual cost was $4,900.

3. Of the delinquent property taxes, $8,000 was collected during the first 60 days of 20X3. Interest of $200 was also collected for late payment. All of the late interest was earned in 20X3. The remaining delinquent taxes were written off as uncollectible.

4. Property taxes were levied for 20X3 in the amount of $115,000. Of the levy, 2 percent was estimated to be uncollectible. During 20X3, $100,000 of property taxes was collected.

5. The general fund received $4,000 of sales taxes from the state in April. The amount received was Elm's share of sales taxes that the state collected in 20X2. The state plans to revise its distribution date for sales taxes in 20X4 so that Elm will receive its share of sales taxes in January.

6. Two police cars were ordered at a cost of $45,000.

7. The police cars were received; their actual cost was $42,000.

8. Cash in the amount of $35,000 was received from fines and licenses.

9. The city's water utility fund billed the general fund $12,000 for using water. The general fund paid $11,000 to the water utility fund during 20X3.

10. The general fund transferred $20,000 to the debt service fund, which used the transfer to pay matured interest on general obligation bonds.

11. Computer software costing $2,000 was ordered in 20X3, but the order was not received by December 31, 20X3.

12. Elm estimated that the general fund's share of the sales tax collected by the state amounted to $3,000 on December 31, 20X3. The state plans to remit the sales taxes to Elm in January 20X4. Elm will use the amount received to pay for expenditures incurred during 20X3.

13. Expenditures for salaries, supplies, and various other items amounted to $70,000 during 20X3. The general fund paid vouchers of $115,000 during 20X3.

14. On December 31, 20X3, Elm estimated that $5,000 of the uncollected property taxes would not be received 60 days before the end of the year.

15. Uncollected property taxes were reclassified as delinquent at December 31, 20X3.

16. On December 31, 20X3, Elm determined that unused supplies amounted to $3,500.

17. Closing entries were made for the year.

Required

Using the information given, prepare all journal entries for Elm City's general fund for the year ended December 31, 20X3. Number your entries to correspond with the numbers of the events described in the problem. Explanations for entries are not necessary.

P17-23 **Preparation of a Balance Sheet and a Statement of Revenues, Expenditures, and Changes in Fund Balance for the General Fund**

Use the information in problem 17-22 for Elm City's general fund.

Required

a. Prepare a statement of revenues, expenditures, and changes in fund balance for the general fund of Elm City for the year ended December 31, 20X3. Assume that expenditures for 20X3 consisted of the following:

General government	$55,000
Streets and highways	25,000
Public safety	30,000
Sanitation	14,000

b. Prepare a balance sheet for the general fund of Elm City at December 31, 20X3.

Supplemental Problems for this chapter are available as part of the *Online Learning Center* on the textbook's Website.

Chapter Eighteen

Governmental Entities: Special Funds and Government-wide Financial Statements

In addition to the general fund, discussed in Chapter 17, governments have a number of other funds. This chapter presents the accounting and financial reporting requirements for (1) the four remaining governmental funds, (2) the two proprietary funds, and (3) the fiduciary funds. A local government uses as many of these funds as necessary for its operations or as required by law. The typical fund organization for a local government is presented in Figure 18–1. In practice, the funds and account groups are often identified with the acronyms from the first letters of their titles, as follows:

Governmental Funds

GF	General fund
SRF	Special revenue funds
DSF	Debt service funds
CPF	Capital projects funds
PF	Permanent funds

Proprietary Funds

EF	Enterprise funds
ISF	Internal service funds

Fiduciary Funds

PTF	Pension trust funds
ITF	Investment trust funds
P-PTF	Private-purpose trust funds
AF	Agency Funds

A government should establish those funds required by law and the specific operating and management needs of the government entity. Unnecessary, additional funds add unneeded complexity and do not enhance the operational efficiency of the government. A general rule followed in many governmental entities is that all activities should be accounted for in the general fund unless specifically required by law or the different measurement focus used for proprietary and fiduciary funds. This rule does not prohibit the creation of additional funds but places a reasonable restraint on the proliferation of additional funds. The structure of funds discussed in this chapter is the typical one used in most state and local governmental systems.

One event may require entries in several funds. For example, the construction of a new municipal building through the issuance of general obligation bonds may require entries in

FIGURE 18-1
Funds for a
Governmental
Entity

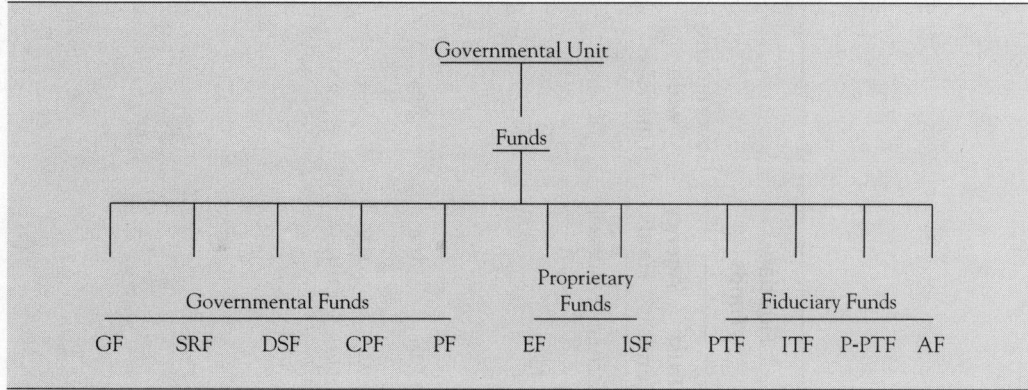

both a capital project fund and a debt service fund. In addition, interfund activities require entries in two or more funds.

The governmental funds use the modified accrual basis of accounting, and the proprietary and fiduciary funds use the accrual basis of accounting. Governmental entities recognize estimated uncollectible amounts as a reduction of revenue, not as an expense. The five governmental funds do not report long-term assets or long-term debt, but the government-wide statements do report them. Investments are reported in the appropriate funds and are valued at their fair market values at each balance sheet date. The government entity's financial report includes both fund-based and government-wide financial statements. The government-wide statements are prepared using the accrual basis of accounting that requires a reconciliation schedule between what is reported in the governmental funds and what is reported for those funds in the government-wide financial statements.

Some governmental units have pension trust funds for their employees. Accounting and reporting for pension trust funds is quite complex and beyond the scope of an advanced financial accounting course. Pension trust funds are covered briefly in the "Additional Considerations" section of this chapter.

This chapter continues the example of Sol City started in Chapter 17 where the entries and financial reports for the general fund were presented for 20X2. Sol City uses the lapsing method of accounting for encumbrances and the consumption method for inventories and records all expected budgetary accounts including anticipated interfund transactions. The techniques of capitalizing all budgetary accounts and recording journal entries at the control level are continued from Chapter 17. The final section of this chapter presents comprehensive financial reports for Sol City.

Figure 18-2 presents an overview of the major accounting and financial standards for the individual funds. This figure can be used as a continual reference point during study of Chapter 18.

GOVERNMENTAL FUNDS WORKSHEETS

The five governmental funds will report two **fund-based financial statements**: the balance sheet and the statement of revenues, expenditures, and changes in fund balance. Rather than present each of the separate governmental funds' financial statements in the chapter, worksheets for the preparation of the governmental funds' financial statements are presented. Figure 18-3 presents the individual fund information that will be used to prepare the governmental funds' balance sheet. Figure 18-4 presents the individual governmental funds information that will be used to prepare the governmental funds' statement of revenues, expenditures, and changes in fund balance. The amounts for the general fund are taken from the information in Chapter 17. The amounts for the other funds will be developed throughout this chapter. These two worksheets are used throughout the discussion of the governmental funds and are the basis for preparing the governmental funds' financial statements that will

FIGURE 18–2 Overview of Accounting and Financial Reporting for Governments

	Governmental Funds					Proprietary Funds		Fiduciary Funds		Government-wide Financials
	General Fund	Special Revenue Funds	Capital Projects Funds	Debt Service Funds	Permanent Funds	Enterprise Funds	Internal Service Funds	Trust Funds	Agency Funds	
Basis of accounting	Modified accrual	Modified accrual	Modified accrual	Modified accrual	Modified accrual	Accrual	Accrual	Accrual	Accrual	Accrual
Budgetary basis recorded: (Budgetary accounts are typically used when a legally adopted annual operating budget is passed)	Operating budget often recorded	Operating budget often recorded	Capital budget usually not recorded	Not required	Not required	No	No	No		
Long-term productive assets (buildings, equipment, etc.) reported	No	No	No	No	No	Yes	Yes	Yes	No	Yes
Long-term debt reported	No	No	No	No	No	Yes	Yes	Yes	No	Yes
Encumbrances recorded	Yes	Yes	Possibly	Possibly	Possibly	No	No	No	No	
Financial Statements										
Balance sheet	X	X	X	X	X					
Statement of net assets						X	X			X
Statement of revenues, expenditures, and changes in fund balance	X	X	X	X	X					
Statement of revenues, expenses, and changes in fund net assets						X	X			
Statement of activities										X
Statement of cash flows						X	X			
Statement of fiduciary net assets								X	X	
Statement of changes in fiduciary net assets								X	X	

FIGURE 18–3 Worksheet for the Balance Sheet for the Governmental Funds

	Governmental Funds					Total Governmental Funds	Enterprise Fund	Total Governmental and Enterprise
	General	Special Revenue	Capital Projects	Debt Service	Permanent			
Assets								
Current								
Cash	102,000	15,000	16,000	2,000	13,000			
Property Taxes (net of allowances)	85,000	1,000		3,000				
Due From Enterprise Fund	3,000							
Inventory of Supplies	17,000							
Noncurrent								
Investment in Government Bonds					90,000			
Total Assets	207,000	16,000	16,000	5,000	103,000	347,000	140,000	487,000
Liabilities and Fund Balances								
Vouchers Payable	55,000	3,000						
Contract Payable—Retainage			10,000					
Total Liabilities	55,000	3,000	10,000	-0-	-0-	68,000	112,000	180,000
Fund Balances								
Reserved for:								
Encumbrances	15,000	6,000						
Inventories	17,000							
Debt Service				5,000				
Permanent Fund					103,000			
Unreserved, reported in:								
General Fund	120,000							
Special Revenue Fund		7,000						
Capital Projects Fund			6,000					
Debt Service Fund								
Total Fund Balances	152,000	13,000	6,000	5,000	103,000	279,000		
Total Liabilities and Fund Balances	207,000	16,000	16,000	5,000	103,000	347,000		
Major Fund Tests on Total Assets:								
10% Test of Total Governmental or Enterprise		4.61%	4.61%	1.44%	29.68%		100.00%	
5% Test of Governmental Plus Enterprise		3.29%	3.29%	1.03%	21.15%		28.75%	
Major Fund Test (Yes or No)	Yes	No	No	No	Yes		Yes	
Major Fund Tests on Total Liabilities:								
10% Test of Total Governmental or Enterprise		4.41%	14.71%	0.00%	0.00%		100.00%	
5% Test of Governmental Plus Enterprise		1.67%	5.56%	0.00%	0.00%		62.22%	
Major Fund Test (Yes or No)	Yes	No	Yes	No	No		Yes	

FIGURE 18–4 Worksheet for the Statement of Revenues, Expenditures, and Changes in Fund Balances for the Governmental Funds

	Governmental Funds					Total Governmental Funds	Enterprise Fund	Total Governmental and Enterprise
	General	Special Revenue	Capital Projects	Debt Service	Permanent			
Revenues								
Property Taxes	781,000	62,000		33,000				
Sales Taxes	32,000							
Grants	33,000		10,000					
Miscellaneous	18,000				8,000			
Total Revenues	864,000	62,000	10,000	33,000	8,000	977,000	37,000	1,014,000
Expenditures								
Current								
General Government	206,000							
Streets and Highways	71,000							
Public Safety	335,000							
Sanitation	141,000							
Culture and Recreation		49,000			5,000			
Miscellaneous								
Debt Service								
Principal Retirement				20,000				
Interest Charges				10,000				
Capital Outlay	58,000		124,000					
Total Expenditures/Expenses	811,000	49,000	124,000	30,000	5,000	1,019,000	35,000	1,054,000
Excess (deficiency) of Revenues over Expenditures	53,000	13,000	(114,000)	3,000	3,000	(42,000)		
Other Financing Sources (Uses)								
Proceeds of Bond Issue			102,000					
Transfers In			20,000	2,000				
Transfers Out	(30,000)		(2,000)					
Total Other Financing Sources and Uses	(30,000)	-0-	120,000	2,000	-0-	92,000		
Special Item								
Contribution					100,000	100,000		
Net Change in Fund Balances	23,000	13,000	6,000	5,000	100,000	150,000		
Fund Balances—Beginning	129,000	-0-	-0-	-0-	103,000	129,000		
Fund Balances—Ending	152,000	13,000	6,000	5,000	103,000	279,000		
Major Fund Tests on Total Revenues:								
10% Test of Total Governmental or Enterprise		6.35%	1.02%	3.38%	0.82%		100.00%	
5% Test of Governmental and Enterprise		6.11%	0.99%	3.25%	0.79%		3.65%	
Major Fund Test (Yes or No)	Yes	No	No	No	No		No	
Major Fund Tests on Total Expenditures/Expenses:								
10% Test of Total Governmental or Enterprise		4.81%	12.17%	2.94%	0.49%		100.00%	
5% Test of Governmental and Enterprise		4.65%	11.76%	2.85%	0.47%		3.32%	
Major Fund Test (Yes or No)	Yes	No	Yes	No	No		No	

be presented later in the chapter. The worksheets also include a major funds test that will be discussed later in the chapter. Thus, the two worksheets will be developed through the following discussions in this chapter.

SPECIAL REVENUE FUNDS

Current governmental resources may be restricted for specific purposes, such as construction of the state highway system, maintenance of public parks, or operation of the public school system, city libraries, and museums. The necessary revenue often comes from special tax levies or federal or state governmental grants. Some minor revenue may be earned through user charges, but these charges are usually not sufficient to fully fund the service. *Special revenue funds* are used to account for such restricted resources. The governmental entity usually has a separate special revenue fund for each different activity of this type. Thus, a city may have several special revenue funds.

Accounting for special revenue funds is the same as for the general fund. The modified accrual basis of accounting is used, no fixed assets or depreciation are recorded, the operating budget is typically recorded in the accounts, and no long-term debt is recorded.

Special revenue fund accounting is not illustrated in the chapter because the principles for the special revenue fund are the same as those for the general fund as covered in Chapter 17. For purposes of the governmental funds statements, assume that $62,000 of property taxes were collected for the special revenue fund and that $49,000 was expended for the designated culture and recreation purposes for which the special revenue fund was established. The focus of this chapter is on the unique or interesting aspects of governmental accounting and financial reporting. Figure 18–3 presents the assumed numbers for the special revenue fund's balance sheet, and Figure 18–4 presents the revenues ($62,000) and expenditures ($49,000) assumed for the special revenue fund.

CAPITAL PROJECTS FUNDS

Capital projects funds account for the acquisition or construction of major capital facilities or improvements that benefit the public. Examples are the construction of libraries, civic centers, fire stations, courthouses, bridges, major streets, and city municipal buildings. A separate capital projects fund is created at the time the project is approved and ceases at its completion. Each project or group of related projects usually is accounted for in a separate capital projects fund.

Accounting for capital projects funds is similar to accounting for the general fund. The modified accrual basis of accounting is used, no fixed assets or depreciation are recorded in the capital projects funds, and no long-term debt is recorded in these funds. Capital projects funds, however, typically do not have annual operating budgets. A capital budget is prepared as a basis for selling bonds to finance a project, and the capital budget is the control mechanism for the length of the project. The capital budget for the project may, or may not, be formally recorded in the accounts. Theoretically, encumbrances are part of the budgetary system and should flow from the appropriating authority of the budget. However, encumbrances may be recorded even if the capital project budget is not recorded. Encumbrances maintain an ongoing accounting record of the expenditure commitments that have been made on a project. The reserve for encumbrances reported on the periodic balance sheet for the capital projects fund can be determined from the information in the recorded budgetary encumbrance accounts.

The capital projects fund records capital outlays as expenditures. Thus, no fixed assets are recorded in this fund. A record of the construction in progress, however, may be maintained in memorandum format.

Illustration of Transactions

On January 1, 20X2, Sol City establishes a capital projects fund to account for a capital addition to the municipal courthouse. The expected cost of the addition is $120,000. A $100,000,

10 percent general obligation bond issue is sold at 102 for total proceeds of $102,000. The bond is a five-year serial bond with equal amounts of $20,000 to be paid each year until the debt is extinguished. The bond proceeds are not revenue to the capital projects fund; they are reported in the other financing sources section of the statement of revenues, expenditures, and changes in fund balance. Any debt issue costs such as underwriting fees or attorney fees should be reported as expenditures when the related liability is incurred. Sol City chose not to formally enter the project budget into the accounts but does use an encumbrance system for control over project expenditures.

The capital projects fund is not entitled to the $2,000 premium on the sale of bonds. This premium is transferred as a transfer out to the debt service fund immediately upon receipt. The debt service fund records the receipt of the transfer as a transfer in (see entry [15] later in this chapter). The premium is viewed as an adjustment of the interest rate, not as a part of the funds expendable by the capital projects fund. If bonds are sold at a discount, either the amount expended for the improvement must be decreased or the general fund must make up the difference to the face value of the bonds.

In addition, a federal grant for $10,000 is received as financial support for part of the capital addition, and the capital projects fund receives an interfund transfer in of $20,000 from the city's general fund. Recall that an interfund transfer is an interfund transaction in which resources are moved from one fund, usually from the general fund, to another fund to be used for the operations of the receiving fund. The general fund records this transfer of $20,000 as an interfund transfer out (see entry [34] in Chapter 17). The following entries are recorded for the 20X2 fiscal year.

Capital Projects Revenue and Bond Proceeds

The sale of the bonds and receipt of the federal grant and operating transfer in are recorded as follows:

(1)	Cash	102,000	
	Other Financing Sources—Bond Issue		100,000
	Other Financing Sources—Bond Premium		2,000
	Issue $100,000 of bonds at 102.		
(2)	Other Financing Uses—Transfer Out to Debt Service Fund	2,000	
	Cash		2,000
	Forward bond premium to debt service fund.		
(3)	Cash	10,000	
	Revenue—Federal Grant		10,000
	Receive federal grant to be applied to courthouse addition.		
(4)	Due from General Fund	20,000	
	Other Financing Sources—Transfer In from General Fund		20,000
	Establish receivable for interfund transfer in from general fund.		
(5)	Cash	20,000	
	Due from General Fund		20,000
	Receive transferred resources from general fund.		

Entry (3) recognizes the $10,000 grant from the federal government as revenue when the grant is received. Some grants from the federal government are termed "expenditure-driven" grants, for which revenue can be recognized only as expenditures are incurred in conformity with the grant agreement. For these expenditure-driven grants, the local governmental unit credits a deferred revenue account instead of revenue at the time of receipt of the grant and then recognizes the revenue from the grant as approved expenditures are made by debiting the deferred revenue account and crediting revenue from the grant.

Capital Projects Fund Expenditures

The following encumbrances, expenditures, and disbursements are recorded in 20X2.

(6)	ENCUMBRANCES	110,000	
	BUDGETARY FUND BALANCE—RESERVED FOR ENCUMBRANCES		110,000
	Issue construction contract for $110,000.		

(7)	BUDGETARY FUND BALANCE—RESERVED FOR ENCUMBRANCES	110,000	
	ENCUMBRANCES		110,000
	Project is completed. Reverse reserve for encumbrances.		

(8)	Expenditures	118,000	
	Contract Payable		108,000
	Contract Payable—Retained Percentage		10,000
	Actual construction cost of courthouse addition is $118,000. Additional cost is approved. Contract terms include retained percentage of $10,000 until full and final acceptance of project.		

(9)	Expenditures	6,000	
	Vouchers Payable		6,000
	Additional items for courthouse addition.		

(10)	Vouchers Payable	6,000	
	Contract Payable	108,000	
	Cash		114,000
	Pay current portion of construction contract and vouchers.		

In entry (8), Contract Payable is credited for $108,000 for the current portion due, and Contract Payable—Retained Percentage is credited for $10,000. In entry (10), the $108,000 current portion of the contract liability is paid in full. A normal practice of governmental units is to have a retained percentage of the total amount due under a construction contract held back to ensure that the contractor fully completes the project to the satisfaction of the governmental unit. For example, a city may stipulate that 10 percent of the total contract price is retained until the project is fully completed and accepted. This retainage payable is released and paid upon final acceptance of the project by the governmental unit.

Closing Entries in the Capital Projects Fund

The nominal accounts are closed with the following entries:

(11)	Revenue—Federal Grant	10,000	
	Fund Balance—Unreserved	114,000	
	Expenditures		124,000
	Close operating accounts of revenue and expenditures.		

(12)	Other Financing Sources—Bond Issue	100,000	
	Other Financing Sources—Bond Premium	2,000	
	Fund Balance—Unreserved		102,000
	Close other financing sources.		

(13)	Other Financing Sources—Transfer In from General Fund	20,000	
	Other Financing Uses—Transfer Out to Debt Service Fund		2,000
	Fund Balance—Unreserved		18,000
	Close interfund transfers.		

No encumbrances are outstanding as of the end of the fiscal year. At this point, the Unreserved Fund Balance account has a credit balance of $6,000. Upon completion and final approval of a capital project, the remaining fund balance is transferred either to the general fund or to the debt service fund, depending on the policy of the governmental unit. The transfer is a transfer out for the capital projects fund and a transfer in for the receiving fund because it involves the one-time transfer of the remaining resources in the capital projects fund. In the preceding example, Sol City decided that the fund should remain open through the first part of the next fiscal year in case any minor modifications of the new courthouse addition are required. If no further modifications are required, and the courthouse addition project is officially accepted, the $10,000 in the Contract Payable—Retained Percentage account is paid to the contractor. Any remaining resources in the capital projects fund are then transferred and the capital projects fund is closed.

Financial Statement Information for the Capital Projects Fund

The financial statement information for the capital projects funds is presented in Figure 18–3 for the balance sheet and in Figure 18–4 for the statement of revenues, expenditures, and changes in fund balances. The Sol City capital projects fund was created on January 1, 20X2, the date the capital addition was approved and the serial bonds were sold. Figure 18–3 shows that the only asset remaining in this fund on December 31, 20X2, is $16,000 of cash, which includes the $10,000 for the contract payable–retainage. Figure 18–4 for the capital projects fund column presents the $102,000 of proceeds from the bond issue, which is reported among other financing sources, with a reduction for the transfer of the $2,000 premium to the debt service fund, and the transfer in of $20,000, netting out the large excess of expenditures over revenue in the amount of $114,000. The statement of revenues, expenditures, and changes in fund balance reconciles to the $6,000 fund balance at the end of the fiscal period.

DEBT SERVICE FUNDS

Debt service funds account for the accumulation and use of resources for the payment of general long-term debt principal and interest. A government may have several types of general long-term debt obligations, as follows:

1. *Serial bonds.* The most common form of debt issued by governments is in the form of serial bonds. The bonds are repaid in installments over the life of the debt. A serial bond is called "regular" if the installments are equal and "irregular" if they are not equal.

2. *Term bonds.* This form of debt is less frequent now than in the past. The entire principal of the debt is due at the maturity date.

3. *Special assessment bonds.* Special assessment bonds are secured by tax liens on the property located within the special assessment tax district. The governmental unit may also become obligated in some manner to assume the payment of the debt in the event of default by the property owners. Special assessment bonds may be used to finance capital projects, or to acquire other assets, such as ambulances or fire engines, necessary to operate the governmental unit. Special assessment bonds sold to acquire enterprise fund assets, however, should be accounted for within the enterprise fund. The special assessment feature simply states the source of financing and means of repayment.

4. *Notes and warrants.* These consist of debt typically issued for one or two years. These debts are usually secured by specific tax revenue, which may be used only to repay the debt. Property tax anticipation warrants are an example.

5. *Capital leases.* Governmental units must record capital leases in accordance with generally accepted accounting principles. These leases then become long-term liabilities of the governmental unit.

Some governmental units service long-term debt directly from the general fund, thereby eliminating the need for a debt service fund as a separate fiscal, accounting, and reporting entity. However, if a governmental entity has several long-term general obligations outstanding, it may be required by bond indentures or other regulations to establish a separate debt service fund for each obligation to account for the proper servicing of each debt obligation.

The accounting and financial reporting for debt service funds are the same as for the general fund. The modified accrual basis of accounting is used, and only that portion of the long-term debt that has matured and is currently payable is recorded in the debt service funds.

Interest payable on long-term debt is not accrued; interest is recognized as a liability only when it comes due and payable. The "when due" recognition of interest matches the debt service expenditures with the resources accumulated to repay the debt. This approach prevents an understatement of the debt service fund balance. For example, if interest is accrued before it is actually due, the fund balance may show a deficit because of the excess of liabilities over assets. The function of the debt service fund is to accumulate resources to pay debt principal and interest as they become due. Thus, the when-due recognition of interest is consistent with the fund's objectives.

Illustration of Transactions

Sol City establishes a debt service fund to service the $100,000, five-year, 10 percent serial bond issued on January 1, 20X2, to finance the capital project courthouse addition. The bond initially sold at a premium of $2,000. The resources to pay the bond principal and interest as they become due will be obtained from a property tax levy specifically for debt service.

Adoption of Debt Service Fund Budget

Debt service funds are not required to adopt annual operating budgets because the fund's expenditures are generally mandated by bond agreements and an operating budget may be viewed as unnecessarily redundant. Nevertheless, there is no restriction against having an operating budget for the debt service fund as part of a comprehensive budgeting system for a governmental entity, as illustrated here.

The annual operating budget for the debt service fund is adopted at the time the fund is created to service the serial bonds sold for the courthouse addition. Appropriations of $30,000 are budgeted to pay $20,000 of maturing principal and $10,000 of interest for the year. Sol City budgets all expected interfund transactions, and the anticipated interfund transfer in of the $2,000 premium on the serial bonds sold is part of the entry to record the budget:

(14)	ESTIMATED REVENUES CONTROL	30,000	
	ESTIMATED OTHER FINANCING SOURCES—TRANSFER IN	2,000	
	APPROPRIATIONS CONTROL		30,000
	BUDGETARY FUND BALANCE		2,000
	Adopt budget for 20X2.		

The budgetary accounts ESTIMATED REVENUES CONTROL and APPROPRIATIONS CONTROL are used to account for servicing serial bonds.

Debt Service Fund Revenue and Other Financing Sources

The debt service fund obtains revenue from a specified property tax levy in this example. The bond premium received from the capital projects fund is recognized as a transfer in. Note that the capital projects fund records this transfer as an interfund transfer out (see entry [2] earlier in this chapter). The entries to record the receipt of the bond premium and the levy and collection of taxes are as follows:

(15)	Cash	2,000	
	Other Financing Sources—Transfer In from Capital Projects Fund		2,000
	Receive bond premium from capital projects fund.		
(16)	Property Taxes Receivable	35,000	
	Allowance for Uncollectible Taxes		5,000
	Revenue—Property Tax		30,000
	Levy property taxes and provide for allowance for uncollectible taxes. Estimated uncollectible property taxes reduce Revenue.		

(17)	Cash	30,000	
	Property Taxes Receivable		30,000
	Receive portion of property taxes.		

(18)	Property Taxes Receivable—Delinquent	5,000	
	Allowance for Uncollectible Taxes	5,000	
	Property Taxes Receivable		5,000
	Revenue—Property Tax		3,000
	Allowance for Uncollectible Taxes—Delinquent		2,000
	Reclassify remaining property taxes as delinquent and reduce allowance for uncollectible taxes from $5,000 to $2,000.		

Debt Service Fund Expenditures

The primary expenditures of the debt service fund are for the first annual payment of principal and for interest on the serial bonds payable. An encumbrance system is typically not used for matured principal and interest because the debt agreement serves as the expenditure control mechanism:

(19)	Expenditures—Principal	20,000	
	Matured Bonds Payable		20,000
	Recognize matured portion of serial bond:		
	$100,000 ÷ 5 years		

(20)	Expenditures—Interest	10,000	
	Matured Interest Payable		10,000
	Recognize interest due this period:		
	$100,000 × .10 × 1 year		

(21)	Matured Bonds Payable	20,000	
	Matured Interest Payable	10,000	
	Cash		30,000
	Pay first year's installment plus interest on bond.		

Closing Entries in the Debt Service Fund

The nominal accounts are closed as follows:

(22)	APPROPRIATIONS CONTROL	30,000	
	BUDGETARY FUND BALANCE	2,000	
	ESTIMATED REVENUES CONTROL		30,000
	ESTIMATED OTHER FINANCING SOURCES—TRANSFER IN		2,000
	Close budgetary accounts.		

(23)	Revenue—Property Tax	33,000	
	Expenditures—Principal		20,000
	Expenditures—Interest		10,000
	Fund Balance—Reserved for Debt Service		3,000
	Close operating revenue and expenditures.		

(24)	Other Financing Sources—Transfer In from Capital Projects Fund	2,000	
	Fund Balance—Reserved for Debt Service		2,000
	Close interfund transfer.		

If the debt service fund services term bonds, a different budgetary account system is used. The following budgetary entry would be made for term bonds for the periods prior to the maturity date:

	REQUIRED CONTRIBUTIONS	XXX	
	REQUIRED EARNINGS	X	
	BUDGETARY FUND BALANCE		XXX

The budgetary amounts are determined based on a computation of the contributions needed each period to be invested, earning a given return to accumulate to the amount required for the payment of the bonds. The debt service fund may then receive resources from the general fund or from a tax levy, which it would invest until the term bonds became due. In the period the term bonds reach maturity, the debt service fund pays the matured principal and interest from its available resources. The debt service fund may make temporary investments of excess cash in order to maximize the return from its resources. These investments are reported as an asset of the debt service fund. Most temporary investments are made in low-risk U.S. Treasury securities or in certificates of deposit from larger banks. Interest income is accrued as earned. The investments are valued in accordance with **GASB Statement No. 31**, "Accounting for Financial Reporting for Certain Investments and for External Investment Pools" (GASB 31). The general valuation standard in **GASB 31** is fair value for most investments made by a governmental entity. However, an exception is allowed for governmental entities other than external investment pools, so that market investments may be reported at amortized cost, provided the investment has a remaining maturity of one year or less from the date of purchase. Unrealized gains or losses on investments are combined with realized gains or losses and are reported on the governmental entity's operating statements as net investment income or loss.

Financial Statement Information for the Debt Service Fund

The financial statement information for the debt service fund for the governmental funds is presented in Figure 18–3 for the balance sheet and in Figure 18–4 for the governmental funds statement of revenues, expenditures, and changes in fund balance.

PERMANENT FUNDS

Permanent funds are in the governmental funds group and are established in those cases in which the fund principal must be preserved but the income from these permanent funds is required to be used for the benefit of the government's programs or its general citizenry. The modified accrual basis of accounting is used to measure income. The financial reports for the permanent funds are the same as for all other governmental funds.

Illustration of Transactions

On January 1, 20X2, Sol City receives a $100,000 bequest from a long-term city resident. The will stipulates that the $100,000 be invested and the income be used to provide for maintenance and improvement of the city park. Note that a private-purpose fund, which would be a fiduciary fund, is one in which the government is required to use the principal or earnings for the benefit of specific individuals, private organizations, or other designated governments, as stated in the trust agreement. This bequest is for the benefit of the general citizenry, however, and is established as a permanent fund that is a governmental fund. The entries in this permanent fund during 20X2 are as follows:

(25)	Cash	100,000	
	Contributions		100,000
	Accept permanent fund resources.		

This contribution will be reported separately after other financing sources and uses at the bottom of the statement of revenues, expenditures, and changes in fund balance.

Investment and Interest

The fund's resources are used to acquire $100,000 face value, high-grade, 8 percent governmental securities at 90 to yield an effective interest rate of 10 percent. Interest income is accrued under the modified accrual method, which means that the revenue recognition may be for only that amount of interest that is both measurable and available to finance expenditures made during the current fiscal period. Therefore, only the $8,000 of accrued interest receivable is available for expenditures this period, and the discount amortization would not be shown in the modified accrual basis financial statements.

(26)	Investment in Bonds	90,000	
	Cash		90,000
	Acquire $100,000 face value government securities at 90.		

(27)	Accrued Interest Receivable	8,000	
	Interest Revenue		8,000
	Accrue interest:		
	$8,000 = $100,000 \times .08$, nominal (coupon) rate		

(28)	Cash	8,000	
	Accrued Interest Receivable		8,000
	Collect accrued interest on securities.		

Expenditures

The permanent trust fund expends $5,000 during the period for maintenance of the city park and recognizes the following entry:

(29)	Expenditures	5,000	
	Cash		5,000
	Expenditures made for maintenance of the city park.		

The balance sheet information for the permanent fund as of December 31, 20X2, is presented in Figure 18–3. The entire amount of the fund balance for the permanent fund is classified as reserved because the principal must be preserved and the income in this fund is required to be used for specified purposes. The information for the statement of revenues, expenditures, and changes in fund balance for the permanent fund is presented in Figure 18–4. Note that the $100,000 contribution is not part of operations but is reported at the bottom of the operating statement.

GOVERNMENTAL FUNDS FINANCIAL STATEMENTS

GASB Statement No. 34, "Basic Financial Statements—and Management's Discussion and Analysis—for State and Local Governments" (GASB 34), requires two financial statements for the governmental funds. The first is the governmental funds balance sheet presented in Figure 18–5, and the second is the governmental statement of revenues, expenditures, and changes in fund balance presented in Figure 18–6. The worksheets in Figures 18–3 and 18–4 are the basis for preparing these two statements, but the fund financial statements for the governmental funds separately report only major governmental funds, not necessarily individually each of the five governmental funds. The general fund is always considered a major fund, but some of the other governmental funds may not be considered major funds, and these nonmajor funds are aggregated and reported in a single column as other governmental funds. **GASB 34** specifies that the general fund is always a major fund. In addition, **GASB 34** establishes criteria that also encompass the enterprise funds. To determine which of the other governmental or specific enterprise funds are major, **GASB 34** specifies that *both* of the following criteria must be met:

1. *10 percent criterion:* Total assets, liabilities, revenues, or expenditures/expenses of that individual governmental or enterprise fund are at least 10 percent of the corresponding total (assets, liabilities, revenues, or expenditures/expenses) for all funds of that category or type (i.e., total governmental funds or total enterprise funds).

FIGURE 18–5   Governmental Funds Balance Sheet

SOL CITY
Balance Sheet
Governmental Funds
December 31, 20X2

	General	Capital Projects	Permanent	Other Governmental Funds	Total Governmental Funds
Assets					
Current					
Cash	$102,000	$16,000	$ 13,000	$17,000	$148,000
Property Taxes (net of allowances)	85,000			4,000	89,000
Due from Enterprise Fund	3,000				3,000
Inventory of Supplies	17,000				17,000
Noncurrent					
Investment in Government Bonds			90,000		90,000
Total Assets	$207,000	$16,000	$103,000	$21,000	$347,000
Liabilities and Fund Balances					
Vouchers Payable	55,000			3,000	$ 58,000
Contract Payable—Retainage		$10,000			10,000
Total Liabilities	$ 55,000	$10,000		$ 3,000	$ 68,000
Fund Balances					
Reserved for:					
Encumbrances	$ 15,000			$ 6,000	$ 21,000
Inventories	17,000				17,000
Debt Service				5,000	5,000
Permanent Fund			$103,000		103,000
Unreserved, reported in:					
General Fund	120,000				120,000
Special Revenue Fund				7,000	7,000
Capital Projects Fund		$ 6,000			6,000
Total Fund Balances	$152,000	$ 6,000	$103,000	$18,000	$279,000
Total Liabilities and Fund Balances	$207,000	$16,000	$103,000	$21,000	$347,000

2. *5 percent criterion:* Total assets, liabilities, revenues, or expenditures/expenses of the individual governmental fund or enterprise fund are at least 5 percent of the corresponding total for all governmental *plus* enterprise funds combined.

Note that the major fund reporting requirements apply to a governmental or enterprise fund only if the same element (e.g., assets, liabilities, revenues, or expenditures/expenses) exceeds both the 10 percent and the 5 percent criteria. These major funds tests are presented at the bottom of Figure 18–3 and Figure 18–4. To prepare the tests, information is also required for the enterprise funds. The underlying transactions for Sol City's enterprise fund are presented in the next section of this chapter. The information for the total assets, liabilities, revenues, and expenses of Sol City's enterprise fund is taken from the enterprise fund's financial statement information. For right now, the information for the enterprise fund is presented solely to discuss the major funds tests. More detail on the enterprise fund will be presented immediately after the following discussion of the two major funds tests.

10 Percent Criterion Tests

To compute the 10 percent criterion tests for the five governmental funds, the denominators of the four tests (assets, liabilities, revenues, and expenditures) are the totals from the five governmental funds. For example, Figure 18–3 shows the total assets of the

FIGURE 18–6   **Governmental Funds Statement of Revenues, Expenditures, and Changes in Fund Balance**

SOL CITY
Statement of Revenues, Expenditures, and Changes in Fund Balance
Governmental Funds
For the Year Ended December 31, 20X2

	General	Capital Projects	Permanent	Other Governmental Funds	Total Governmental Funds
Revenues					
Property Taxes	$781,000			$95,000	$ 876,000
Sales Taxes	32,000				32,000
Grants	33,000	$ 10,000			43,000
Miscellaneous	18,000		$ 8,000		26,000
Total Revenues	$864,000	$ 10,000	$ 8,000	$95,000	$ 977,000
Expenditures					
Current					
General Government	$206,000				$ 206,000
Streets and Highways	71,000				71,000
Public Safety	335,000				335,000
Sanitation	141,000				141,000
Culture and Recreation			$ 5,000	$49,000	54,000
Debt Service					
Principal Retirement				20,000	20,000
Interest Charges				10,000	10,000
Capital Outlay	58,000	$ 124,000			182,000
Total Expenditures	$811,000	$ 124,000	$ 5,000	$79,000	$1,019,000
Excess (deficiency) of Revenues over Expenditures	$ 53,000	$(114,000)	$ 3,000	$16,000	$ (42,000)
Other Financing Sources (Uses)					
Proceeds of Bond Issue		$ 102,000			$ 102,000
Transfers In		20,000		$ 2,000	22,000
Transfers Out	$(30,000)	(2,000)			(32,000)
Total Other Financing Sources and Uses	$(30,000)	$ 120,000	$ -0-	$ 2,000	$ 92,000
Contributions, Special Items and Extraordinary Items:					
Contribution			$100,000		$ 100,000
Net Change in Fund Balances	$ 23,000	$ 6,000	$103,000	$18,000	$ 150,000
Fund Balances—Beginning	129,000	-0-	-0-	-0-	129,000
Fund Balances—Ending	$152,000	$ 6,000	$103,000	$18,000	$ 279,000

governmental funds as $347,000. Note again that the general fund is always a major fund, so no percentages need be computed for that fund. The 10 percent asset test shows that the permanent fund meets the 10 percent criterion for total assets (29.68% = $103,000 ÷ $347,000). Continuing down to the liabilities, only the capital projects fund meets the 10 percent criterion for total liabilities (14.71% = $10,000 ÷ $68,000). Information in Figure 18–4 indicates that none of the nongeneral governmental funds meets the 10 percent criterion for revenues. For expenditures, the capital projects fund meets the 10 percent criterion for total expenditures (12.17% = $124,000 ÷ $1,019,000). Thus, the only two nongeneral governmental funds that meet the 10 percent criterion tests for a major fund are (1) the permanent fund (for total assets) and (2) the capital projects fund (for both total liabilities and for total expenditures).

5 Percent Criterion Tests

To compute the 5 percent criterion tests, the second group of major fund tests, the GASB specifies that the denominator of each of the four tests (assets, liabilities, revenues, and expenditures/expenses) is the combined total of each of these items for the five governmental funds plus the enterprise funds. For example, Figure 18–3 shows the combined total assets for the 5 percent asset test is $487,000 ($347,000 from the governmental funds plus $140,000 from the enterprise fund). For the nongeneral governmental funds, the permanent fund is the only one that meets the 5 percent criterion for total assets (21.15% = $103,000 ÷ $487,000). For total liabilities, the capital projects fund meets the 5 percent criterion (5.56% = $10,000 ÷ $180,000). Figure 18–4 shows that for revenues, the special revenue fund meets the 5 percent criterion (6.11% = $62,000 ÷ $1,014,000). For expenditures/expenses, only the capital projects fund meets the 5 percent criterion (11.76% = $124,000 ÷ $1,054,000).

Note that a governmental fund other than the general fund must meet both the 10 percent and the 5 percent criterion tests for at least one of the four financial statement items to be classified as a major fund. Thus, the following governmental funds are classified as major funds: (1) the general fund—always a major fund, (2) the capital projects fund (for liabilities and expenditures), and (3) the permanent fund (for assets). As shown in Figures 18–5 and 18–6, the governmental funds financial statements present detail on these three funds. The two nonmajor funds, special revenue and debt service, are aggregated into a single Other Governmental Funds column. However, management of the governmental unit may elect to provide separate disclosure on any nonmajor fund that it believes is important for users of the financial statements to fully understand. **GASB 34** requires that a total for all governmental funds be provided. Note that enterprise funds are not governmental-type funds.

Governmental units are permitted to disclose, on the governmental funds' balance sheet, designations of unreserved funds. A designation is not a legal reservation or restriction but is similar to an appropriation of retained earnings for a commercial entity. The designation represents management's plans for the intended use of the resources and is a communication to users of the financial statements. However, designations are not permitted to be reported on the government-wide financial statements.

GASB 34 requires a reconciliation schedule to convert from the modified accrual basis of accounting used for the governmental funds to the accrual basis of accounting used for reporting in the two government-wide financial statements. This reconciliation schedule is presented later in the chapter within the discussion of preparing the government-wide financial statements for the entire government entity.

ENTERPRISE FUNDS

Governments sometimes offer goods or services for sale to the public. The amounts charged to customers are intended to recover all or most of the cost of these goods or services. For example, a city may operate electric, gas, and water utilities; transportation systems such as buses, trains, and subways; airports; sports arenas; parking lots and garages; and public housing. Such operations are accounted for in *enterprise funds*, which differ from special revenue funds in that the costs of enterprise fund activities are recovered by user charges. Therefore, the primary difference between establishing a special revenue fund and an enterprise fund is the source of revenue.

Enterprise funds are proprietary funds, and the basis of accounting is the same as for commercial entities. The accrual method is used to measure revenue and expenses. Proprietary funds report fixed assets, which are depreciated, and long-term debt, if issued, and they focus on income determination and capital maintenance. The financial statements for proprietary funds are very similar to those for commercial entities: (1) the statement of net assets (balance sheet), (2) the statement of revenues, expenses, and changes in fund net assets (income statement), and (3) the statement of cash flows.

Budgeting in the proprietary funds also has the same role as in commercial entities. A budget may be prepared for management planning purposes; however, the budget is normally not entered into the accounts.

Illustration of Transactions

Sol City has a municipal water utility that it operates as an enterprise fund. The trial balance of the water utility as of January 1, 20X2, the first day of the 20X2 fiscal year, is presented here:

SOL CITY
Trial Balance for Water Utility Enterprise Fund
January 1, 20X2

Cash	$ 9,000	
Machinery and Equipment	94,000	
Buildings	40,000	
Accumulated Depreciation—Machinery and Equipment		$ 15,000
Accumulated Depreciation—Buildings		2,000
Bonds Payable, 5%		100,000
Net Assets:		
Invested in Capital Assets, Net of Related Debt		17,000
Unrestricted		9,000
Totals	$143,000	$143,000

One difference between balance sheet accounts for commercial entities and those for proprietary funds is the absence of a stockholders' equity section in governmental accounting. The general public is the theoretical owner of all governmental assets. Furthermore, no stock certificates are issued; therefore, a net assets section is used instead of common stock and additional paid-in capital. **GASB 34** requires the separate disclosure of the net assets invested in capital assets, net of related debt, which reports the book value (cost basis less accumulated depreciation) invested in capital assets such as land, buildings, machinery, equipment, and other tangible and intangible assets having expected useful lives exceeding one year. These resources are not readily available for other, unrestricted uses as are the current assets. The related debt is that directly associated with the capital assets and is typically long-term in nature. For our example, assume the $100,000 of bonds payable is related to the $117,000 of net capital assets ($134,000 cost less $17,000 of accumulated depreciation). Other interesting differences are the large relative amounts of fixed assets and long-term debt because enterprise funds typically require large investments in productive assets in order to provide the necessary level of service to the public, and these investments are usually financed by long-term revenue bonds.

The water utility sells its product to the residents of Sol City based on a user charge. In addition to water revenue, the water utility receives a $3,000 short-term interfund loan from the general fund and obtains its office supplies from the city's centralized purchasing operation, which is accounted for as an internal service fund. During the year, the water utility acquires a new pump costing $6,000.

Enterprise Fund Revenues

The water utility provides service during the period and bills its customers for the amount of water used. The utility estimates that 7.5 percent of its billings will not be collected. Note that revenues are reported net of uncollectibles. These transactions are recorded as follows:

(30)	Accounts Receivable	40,000	
	Allowance for Uncollectibles		3,000
	Revenue—Water Sales		37,000
	Bill customers for water used as indicated by meter readings.		
	Estimate $3,000 of billings will be uncollectible.		

(31)	Cash	32,000	
	Accounts Receivable		32,000
	Collect portion of accounts receivable.		

Capital Asset Acquisition

The water utility acquires a new pump during the year.

(32)	Equipment	6,000	
	Vouchers Payable		6,000
	Receive new pump for wellhouse.		

(33)	Vouchers Payable	6,000	
	Cash		6,000
	Pay voucher for new pump.		

Interfund Activities

Several interfund transactions occur during the year. First, in an interfund financing transaction, the water utility receives $3,000 from the general fund as a short-term loan to be repaid within 90 days. The general fund records this as a short-term receivable, Due from Enterprise Fund (see entry [39] in Chapter 17). Second, the utility acquires its office supplies from the internal service fund in an interfund services provided and used transaction. The internal service fund reports this as a revenue transaction (see entry [47] later in this chapter):

(34)	Cash	3,000	
	Due to General Fund		3,000
	Recognize payable for loan from general fund.		

(35)	Supplies Inventory	3,000	
	Due to Internal Service Fund		3,000
	Receive office supplies from centralized purchasing department at a cost of $3,000.		

(36)	Due to Internal Service Fund	2,000	
	Cash		2,000
	Approve payment of $2,000 to centralized purchasing department for supplies received.		

Enterprise Fund Expenses

The water utility fund incurs $9,000 of operating expenses during the period. In addition, several adjusting journal entries are required at the end of the fiscal year to recognize additional expenses. Note that these adjusting entries are similar to those of a commercial entity:

(37)	General Operating Expenses	9,000	
	Vouchers Payable		9,000
	Incur operating expenses during year.		

(38)	Vouchers Payable	6,000	
	Cash		6,000
	Pay approved vouchers for operating expenses.		

(39)	General Operating Expenses	3,000	
	Supplies Inventory		3,000
	Adjust for $3,000 of supplies consumed.		

(40)	Depreciation Expense	18,000	
	Accumulated Depreciation—Buildings		3,000
	Accumulated Depreciation—Machinery and Equipment		15,000
	Recognize depreciation expense for year.		

(41)	Interest Expense	5,000	
	Accrued Interest Payable		5,000
	Accrue interest on bond payable: $100,000 × .05 × 1 year		

Closing and Reclassification Entries in the Enterprise Fund

The nominal accounts are closed, the period's profit or loss is determined, and, at the close of the fiscal year, the government reclassifies the various components of net assets based on the year-end amount of net assets invested in capital assets, net of related debt:

(42)	Revenue—Water Sales	37,000	
	General Operating Expenses		12,000
	Depreciation Expense		18,000
	Interest Expense		5,000
	Profit and Loss Summary		2,000
	Close nominal accounts into profit and loss summary.		

(43)	Profit and Loss Summary	2,000	
	Net Assets—Unrestricted		2,000
	Close profit and loss summary into net assets.		

	Net Assets—Invested in Capital Assets, Net of Related Debt	12,000	
	Net Assets—Unrestricted		12,000
	To reclassify net assets as of end of fiscal period:		

12/31/X1 balance: $ 5,000 = $105,000 capital assets − $100,000 of related debt
1/1/X1 balance: 17,000 = $117,000 capital assets − $100,000 of related debt

$12,000 = Decrease during period in net assets
invested in capital assets, net of related debt

Financial Statements for the Proprietary Funds

Three financial statements are required for the proprietary funds. If a governmental entity has more than one enterprise fund, each must be individually assessed by both the 10 percent criterion and the 5 percent criterion tests to determine whether it is a major fund. Sol City has only one enterprise fund. Figure 18–7 presents the statement of net assets for the enterprise proprietary fund and for the internal service proprietary fund that will be discussed in the next section of this chapter. Figure 18–8 presents the statement of revenues, expenses, and changes in fund net assets for Sol City's two proprietary funds. Figure 18–9 presents the statement of cash flows for these two proprietary funds.

The statement of net assets in Figure 18–7 is similar to that required for commercial entities. Proprietary funds report their own fixed assets, investments, and long-term liabilities. **GASB 34** specifies that the net assets section for the proprietary funds, which is presented below liabilities, be separated into three components: (1) invested in capital assets, net of related debt; (2) restricted because of restrictions beyond the government's control, such as externally imposed restrictions or legal requirements; and (3) unrestricted. **GASB Statement 46**, "Net Assets Restricted by Enabling Legislation" (GASB 46), issued in 2004, amended **GASB 34** with regard to net assets restricted by legally enforceable actions such as enabling legislation, which specifies that a government use resources only for the purposes as specified in the enabling legislation. **GASB 46** provides guidance for reporting the net assets so restricted and accounting for changes when new enabling legislation replaces the prior legislation. The key point is that **GASB 46** confirms the **GASB 34** requirement for separate disclosure of net assets restricted by legal requirements. For our example, there are no

FIGURE 18–7
**Proprietary Funds
Statement of Net
Assets**

	SOL CITY Statement of Net Assets Proprietary Funds December 31, 20X2	
	Enterprise Fund	**Internal Service Fund**
Assets		
Current Assets:		
Cash	$ 30,000	$ 4,000
Accounts Receivable (net)	5,000	
Due from Other Funds		1,000
Inventory of Supplies		6,000
Total Current Assets	$ 35,000	$11,000
Noncurrent Assets:		
Capital Assets:		
Machinery and Equipment	$100,000	$ 3,000
Less Accumulated Depreciation	(30,000)	(1,000)
Buildings	40,000	
Less Accumulated Depreciation	(5,000)	
Total Noncurrent Assets	$105,000	$ 2,000
Total Assets	$140,000	$ 13,000
Liabilities		
Current Liabilities:		
Vouchers Payable	$ 3,000	$ 6,000
Accrued Interest Payable	5,000	
Due to Other Funds	4,000	
Total Current Liabilities	$ 12,000	$ 6,000
Noncurrent Liabilities:		
Bonds Payable, 5%	100,000	
Total Liabilities	$112,000	$ 6,000
Net Assets		
Invested in Capital Assets, Net of Related Debt	$ 5,000	$ 2,000
Unrestricted	23,000	5,000
Total Net Assets	$ 28,000	$ 7,000

externally imposed or legal restrictions on net assets. The amount of the net assets invested in capital assets, net of related debt, is computed as capital assets less accumulated depreciation, less outstanding principal of related debt. For purposes of this example, assume that the information in Figure 18–7 shows that the enterprise fund has $5,000 of net assets invested in capital assets, net of related debt ($105,000 − $100,000), and the internal service fund has $2,000 invested in capital assets, net of related debt ($2,000 − $0).

The statement of revenues, expenses, and changes in fund net assets is similar to the income statement for commercial entities. A separation of operating and nonoperating revenues and expenses is made to provide more information value regarding the operations of the proprietary funds. Contributions and transfers in or out are reported below the income (loss) line in the statement of revenues, expenses, and changes in fund net assets. Contributions would include any capital asset transfers from a governmental fund to a proprietary fund. For example, the general fund may transfer equipment to an enterprise fund. Note that the governmental funds describe the interfund transfers as other financing sources or uses, but the proprietary funds use only the terms *transfer in* or *transfer out* to describe these nonoperating interfund transactions.

FIGURE 18–8
Proprietary Funds
Statement of
Revenues, Expenses,
and Changes in
Fund Net Assets

	SOL CITY Statement of Revenues, Expenses, and Changes in Fund Net Assets Proprietary Funds For the Year Ended December 31, 20X2	
	Enterprise Fund	**Internal Service Fund**
Operating Revenues:		
Charges for Services	$37,000	$ 4,000
Total Operating Revenues	$37,000	$ 4,000
Operating Expenses:		
General Operating	$12,000	$ 4,000
Cost of Goods Sold		2,000
Depreciation	18,000	1,000
Total Operating Expenses	$30,000	$ 7,000
Nonoperating Revenue (Expenses):		
Interest Expense	$ 5,000	
Total Nonoperating Expense	$ 5,000	$ -0-
Income (Loss) before Contributions and Transfers	$ 2,000	$(3,000)
Transfer In		10,000
Change in Net Assets	$ 2,000	$ 7,000
Net Assets—Beginning	26,000	-0-
Net Assets—Ending	$28,000	$ 7,000

The statement of cash flows for enterprise funds is specified by **GASB Statement No. 9**, "Reporting Cash Flows of Proprietary and Nonexpendable Trust Funds and Governmental Entities that Use Proprietary Fund Accounting" (GASB 9). This standard provides a format that differs somewhat from the three-section format of the statement of cash flows for commercial entities. Because of the large number of capital asset acquisition and financing transactions in proprietary funds, the GASB specified four sections of the statement of cash flows, as follows:

1. *Cash flows from operating activities.* This first section includes all transactions from providing services and delivering goods. **GASB 34** requires the use of the direct method of computing cash flows from operating activities. It includes cash flows from interfund operating transactions and reimbursements from other funds.

2. *Cash flows from noncapital financing activities.* This second section includes activities such as borrowing or repaying money for purposes other than to acquire, construct, or improve capital assets. It includes cash for financing activities received from, or paid to, other funds except that which is specifically specified for capital asset use.

3. *Cash flows from capital and related financing activities.* This third section includes all activities clearly related to, or attributable to, the acquisition, disposition, construction, or improvement of capital assets. This section also includes the interest paid on borrowings for capital assets.

4. *Cash flows from investing activities.* This fourth section includes all investing activities, interest and dividend revenue, and acquisition and disposition of debt or equity instruments.

In addition to the statement of cash flows, proprietary funds are also required to provide a supplementary schedule that reconciles the cash flow from operating activities with the operating income or loss reported on the statement of revenues, expenses, and changes in fund net assets.

FIGURE 18–9 **Proprietary Funds Statement of Cash Flows**

	Enterprise Fund	Internal Service Fund
SOL CITY		
Statement of Cash Flows		
Proprietary Funds		
For the Year Ended December 31, 20X2		
Cash Flows from Operating Activities		
Receipts from Customers	$32,000	$ 3,000
Cash Payments for Goods and Services	(6,000)	(6,000)
Cash Paid to Internal Service Fund for Supplies	(2,000)	
Net Cash Provided (Used) by Operating Activities	$24,000	$(3,000)
Cash Flows from Noncapital Financing Activities		
Cash Received from General Fund for Noncapital Loan	$ 3,000	$ 7,000
Net Cash Provided by Noncapital Financing Activities	$ 3,000	$ 7,000
Cash Flows from Capital and Related Financing Activities		
Acquisition of Capital Asset	$ (6,000)	$(3,000)
Cash Received from General Fund for Capital Activity		3,000
Net Cash Provided (Used) for Capital Financing Activities	$ (6,000)	$ -0-
Cash Flows from Investing Activities	$ -0-	$ -0-
Net Increase in Cash	$21,000	$ 4,000
Balances—Beginning of Year	9,000	-0-
Balances—End of Year	$30,000	$ 4,000
Reconciliation of Operating Income to Net Cash Provided by Operating Activities:		
Operating Income	$ 7,000	$(3,000)
Adjustments to Reconcile Operating Income to Net Cash Provided (Used) by Operating Activities:		
Depreciation	18,000	1,000
Change in Assets and Liabilities:		
Increase in Net Accounts Receivable	(5,000)	
Increase in Due from Other Funds from Billings		(1,000)
Increase in Inventory of Supplies		(6,000)
Increase in Vouchers Payable	3,000	6,000
Increase in Due to Internal Service Fund	1,000	
Net Cash Provided (Used) by Operating Activities	$24,000	$(3,000)

INTERNAL SERVICE FUNDS

Internal service funds account for the financing of goods or services provided by one department or agency to other departments or agencies on a cost-reimbursement basis. These services are not available to the general public, making the internal service fund different from the enterprise fund. Examples are motor vehicle pools, central computer facilities, printing shops, and centralized purchasing and storage facilities. Separate internal service funds are established for each of these functions maintained by the local governmental unit.

Accounting and financial reporting for internal service funds are the same as for enterprise funds or for commercial entities. The accrual basis is used to measure revenue and expenses, and the balance sheet may include fixed assets, which are depreciated, and long-term debt, if issued. The statement of revenue, expenses, and changes in fund net assets reports the fund's income for the period. The statement of cash flows is also required.

Illustration of Transactions

Sol City decides to establish a centralized purchasing and storage function as an internal service fund. This centralized purchasing department provides office supplies to all other funds of the local government on a user-charge basis. After acquiring the necessary supplies, the centralized purchasing department makes the following sales:

Buying Fund	Selling Price	Cost to Internal Service Fund
General fund	$1,000	$ 500
Enterprise fund	3,000	1,500

The following entries are made during the year to record the activities of the centralized purchasing and storage department.

Establishment of Internal Service Fund and Acquisition of Inventories

The fund is started with a transfer in from the general fund in the amount of $10,000, which the internal service fund then uses to acquire inventory and equipment. The general fund records this interfund transfer as a transfer out (see entry [33] in Chapter 17):

(44)	Cash	10,000	
	Transfer In		10,000
	Receive interfund transfer in from general fund to initiate centralized purchasing and storage function.		
(45)	Inventory	8,000	
	Vouchers Payable		8,000
	Acquire inventory of supplies.		
(46)	Machinery and Equipment	3,000	
	Vouchers Payable		3,000
	Acquire equipment.		

Internal Service Fund Revenue

The revenue of the internal service fund is earned by selling supplies to other funds and billing them for the value of the supplies. The billing rate is typically established at more than the operating costs of the internal service fund so that the fund may acquire replacement assets or new assets:

(47)	Due from General Fund	1,000	
	Due from Enterprise Fund	3,000	
	Charges for Services		4,000
	Recognize revenue from providing supplies to general fund and enterprise fund.		
(48)	Cash	3,000	
	Due from General Fund		1,000
	Due from Enterprise Fund		2,000
	Collect portion of receivables.		

The general fund records the $1,000 for supplies as an interfund expenditures transaction (see entry [37] in Chapter 17). The enterprise fund records the $3,000 as an interfund inventory purchase transaction (see entry [35] earlier in this chapter).

Internal Service Fund Expenses

The internal service fund incurs $4,000 of operating expenses, including payroll, during the period. In addition, cost of goods sold of $2,000 and $1,000 of depreciation expense are recognized in adjusting entries. The $9,000 of vouchers paid include a voucher in the amount of $3,000 for the equipment acquired in entry (46) above:

(49)	General Operating Expenses	4,000	
	Vouchers Payable		4,000
	Incur operating expenses.		
(50)	Vouchers Payable	9,000	
	Cash		9,000
	Pay approved vouchers.		
(51)	Cost of Goods Sold	2,000	
	Inventory		2,000
	Recognize cost of supplies sold.		
(52)	Depreciation Expense	1,000	
	Accumulated Depreciation		1,000
	Depreciation of equipment.		

Closing Entries in the Internal Service Fund

The closing and reclassifying entries for the internal service fund follow. "Profit and Loss Summary" is used here in the closing process; however, some governmental units use the account called Excess of Net Revenues over Costs to perform the same function.

(53)	Charges for Services	4,000	
	Profit and Loss Summary	3,000	
	Cost of Goods Sold		2,000
	General Operating Expenses		4,000
	Depreciation Expense		1,000
	Close revenue and expenses.		
(54)	Transfer In	10,000	
	Profit and Loss Summary		3,000
	Net Assets—Unrestricted		7,000
	Close profit and loss summary and transfer in to net assets.		
	Net Assets—Unrestricted	2,000	
	Net Assets—Invested in Capital Assets, Net of Related Debt		2,000
	To reclassify net assets as of end of fiscal period:		
	$2,000 = $2,000 net capital assets − $0 related debt		

Financial Statements for Internal Service Funds

The financial statements required for internal service funds are the same as those required for the enterprise fund. Figure 18–7 presents the statement of net assets, and Figure 18–8 presents the statement of revenues, expenses, and changes in fund net assets for the internal service fund. Figure 18–9 presents the statement of cash flows for the internal service fund.

TRUST FUNDS

Trust funds account for resources held by a government unit in a trustee capacity. The governmental unit acts as a fiduciary for monies or properties held on behalf of individuals, employees, or other governmental agencies. The trust fiduciary funds cannot be used to support

FIGURE 18–10
Fiduciary Funds
Statement of
Fiduciary Net Assets

	SOL CITY Statement of Fiduciary Net Assets Fiduciary Funds December 31, 20X2	
	Private-Purpose Funds	**Agency Funds**
Assets		
Cash	$ 1,600	$1,000
Investments, at Fair Value:		
Municipal Bonds	26,200	
Total Assets	$27,800	$1,000
Liabilities		
Due to Insurance Company		$1,000
Total Liabilities	$ -0-	$1,000
Net Assets Held in Trust	$27,800	

the government's own programs but are for the benefit of specific individuals, organizations, or other governmental units. The three main types of fiduciary trust funds are: (1) pension and other employee benefit trust funds, (2) investment trust funds, and (3) private-purpose trust funds.

The accrual basis of accounting is used for the fiduciary funds, and the financial statements required for fiduciary funds are the statement of fiduciary net assets (Figure 18–10), and the statement of changes in fiduciary net assets (Figure 18–11). The statement of fiduciary net assets includes all trusts and agency funds. The statement of changes in fiduciary net assets includes only the trust funds because agency funds do not have a net asset balance; their assets must equal their liabilities. Agency funds are discussed after trust funds.

An example of a private-purpose trust fund is illustrated in the next section of this chapter. Public employee pension funds are discussed in the "Additional Considerations" section at the end of the chapter.

FIGURE 18–11
Fiduciary Funds
Statement of
Changes in
Fiduciary Net Assets

	SOL CITY Statement of Changes in Fiduciary Net Assets Fiduciary Funds For the Year Ended December 31, 20X2 Private-Purpose Fund	
Additions		
Contributions		$50,000
Investment Earnings:		
Increase in Fair Value of Investments	$1,200	
Interest	600	
Total Investment Earnings		1,800
Total Additions		$51,800
Deductions		
Benefits		$23,000
Administrative Costs		1,000
Total Deductions		$24,000
Change in Net Assets		$27,800
Net Assets—Beginning of Year		-0-
Net Assets—End of Year		$27,800

Illustration of Private-Purpose Trust Fund

On January 1, 20X2, Sol City receives a $50,000 donation from Charles Alt, a citizen of Sol City. The terms of the trust agreement specify that the city is to use about $25,000 each year for the next two years to help alleviate the cost of transporting senior citizens to and from the senior citizens' center. The city accepts the donation and, as allowed by the trust agreement, invests $25,000 in highly rated bonds. The remaining $25,000 is deposited in a bank account that earns 4 percent interest. The terms of the trust agreement allow the city to deduct $1,000 per year for its administrative costs of managing the trust and the transportation services. During the first year, 20X2, $23,000 is paid out of the fund for transportation services. The fund pays out the remaining resources in 20X3.

(55)	Cash	50,000	
	Additions—Contributions		50,000
	The city accepts a private-purpose trust fund of $50,000.		
(56)	Investment in Bonds	25,000	
	Cash		25,000
	The city invests half of the trust funds, as allowed by the trust agreement.		
(57)	Cash	600	
	Additions—Interest		600
	Interest earned during the year on the monies deposited in the bank is recognized from bank statements. The balance in the cash account decreased during the year as transportation costs were paid.		
(58)	Deductions—Transportation Benefits	23,000	
	Cash		23,000
	Transportation costs during the year are paid.		
(59)	Deductions—Administration Costs	1,000	
	Cash		1,000
	The $1,000 of administrative costs allowed to the city are recognized and paid.		

An adjusting journal entry is made on December 31, 20X2, to revalue the investment in bonds to their fair market values, as follows:

(60)	Investment in Bonds	1,200	
	Additions—Investment Revalued		1,200
	The fair value of the investment in bonds increased by $1,200 by the end of the year.		

Note that this private-purpose trust fund had an expendable principal as well as earnings. The requirement for a private-purpose trust fund is that its resources may be used only for specific individuals, organizations, or other governmental units as specified by the donor. Some private-purpose trust funds specify that the principal is nonexpendable and that only the earnings may be used for the private purpose. A private-purpose trust fund is differentiated from a permanent fund, which is part of the governmental funds, in the following manner. A permanent fund must maintain its principal, but the earnings are used to support the government's programs that benefit all citizens. A private-purpose trust fund must be used only for the specific purposes specified by the donor or grantor of the trust fund and is not available to support the government's general programs.

Figure 18–10 reports the statement of fiduciary net assets for the fiduciary funds for Sol City, including the private-purpose fund and agency fund. Figure 18–11 presents the statement of changes in fiduciary net assets for the private-purpose trust fund. Agency funds are presented in the next section of the chapter.

AGENCY FUNDS

Agency funds account for resources held by a governmental unit as an agent for individuals, private organizations, other funds, or other governmental units. Examples are tax collection funds that collect property taxes and then distribute them to local governmental units and employee benefit funds for such items as dental insurance or charitable contributions that employees authorize as withholdings from their paychecks.

The accrual basis of accounting is used to account for agency funds. Because agency funds are custodial in nature, assets always equal liabilities and there is no fund equity. The financial statement for agency funds is the statement of fiduciary net assets as presented in Figure 18–10. Note that there cannot be any net asset balance for agency funds; therefore, no statement of changes in fiduciary net assets is required for agency funds.

Illustration of Transactions in an Agency Fund

Sol City has established an agency fund to account for employees' share of health insurance, which is deducted from the employees' monthly paychecks and then forwarded to the insurance company on a quarterly basis. For purposes of this example, a total of $9,000 was deducted from the employees' paychecks, and $8,000 was paid to the insurance company in 20X2. The remaining $1,000 will be paid to the insurance company in the first quarter of 20X3.

Agency Fund Receipts and Disbursements

The receipts and disbursements in the agency fund during 20X2 are as follows:

(61)	Cash	9,000	
	Due to Insurance Company		9,000
	Employees' contributory share of health insurance deducted from payroll checks.		
(62)	Due to Insurance Company	8,000	
	Cash		8,000
	Pay liability to insurance company for employees' share of insurance cost.		

THE GOVERNMENT REPORTING MODEL

GASB 34 specifies the reporting model for governmental entities. All general-purpose units such as states, counties, and municipalities must provide all financial statements required in **GASB 34**. These statements are both the fund-based financial statements presented earlier in this chapter plus the government-wide financial statements that will be discussed in a following section of this chapter. Some special-purpose government units such as cemetery associations that are engaged in a single governmental activity are not required to provide the government-wide financial statements but still must provide fund-based financial statements.

Four Major Issues

Issue 1: What Organizations Comprise the Reporting Entity?

The first issue to address is the determination of the *reporting entity* for which the statements will be provided. The primary government is part of the reporting entity, but this issue concerns what other boards, commissions, agencies, or authorities should be included with the reporting entity. **GASB 34** defines the reporting entity as (*a*) the primary government, such as a city, county, or state, (*b*) an organization for which the primary government is financially accountable, and (*c*) any organization that has a significant relationship with the primary government and should be included to avoid misleading or incomplete financial statements.

Issue 2: What Constitutes Financial Accountability?

GASB Statement No. 14, "The Financial Reporting Entity" (GASB 14), states that financial accountability of the primary government for the component organization is evidenced by either *board appointment* or *fiscal dependence*. Financial accountability is evidenced when the primary government appoints a majority of the organization's governing board. Thus, the primary government has effective control over the organization, which in turn may provide specific benefits to, or may impose specific financial burdens on, the primary government. Financial accountability may also exist if the organization has a separately elected or appointed board but fiscally depends on the primary government for the financial resources required to operate.

The primary government's ability to impose its will on an organization is evidenced by such things as its ability (1) to remove appointed members of the organization's governing board, (2) to approve or modify the organization's budget or approve rates or fee changes, (3) to veto or overrule the decisions of the organization's governing body, or (4) to appoint, hire, reassign, or dismiss those persons responsible for the organization's day-to-day operations. The potential for an organization to impose specific burdens on the primary government is evidenced by such things as the primary government's legal obligation or its assumption of the obligation to finance the deficits, or otherwise provide financial support to, the organization, or the primary government's obligation in some manner for the debt of the organization. These criteria indicate that when the primary governmental unit is financially accountable for legally separate organizations, those organizations should be included in the primary government's financial statements as ***component units***.

Issue 3: What Other Organizations Should Be Included in the Reporting Entity?

GASB 14 specifies a third category of organizations to be evaluated to determine if they are part of the reporting entity with the primary government. These are legally separate, tax-exempt entities for which the primary government is *not* financially accountable. **GASB Statement No. 39**, "Determining Whether Certain Organizations Are Component Units" (GASB 39), amended parts of **GASB 14** to more fully define what other organizations should be included in a government's reporting entity. In general, a legally separate, tax-exempt organization is reported as a component unit of the primary government if *all three* of the following characteristics are met:

1. The resources of the separate organization are held for the benefit of the primary government, its component units, or the persons served by the primary government or its component units.
2. The primary government, or its component units, is entitled to, or can use, a majority of the economic resources of the separate organization.
3. The economic resources that the primary government, or its component units, can use are significant to the primary government.

Examples of other organizations that should be included in the reporting entity include university foundations and university alumni associations.

Issue 4: How Should the Financial Results of the Component Units Be Reported?

The fourth issue is how to report the financial results of component units. A choice between two methods must be made: (1) ***discrete presentation*** in a separate column of the primary government's financial statements, or (2) ***blended presentation*** by combining the organization's results into the primary government's financial results.

Most component units are discretely presented; however, the blending method should be used when the component unit is so intertwined with the primary government that, in essence, they are the same governmental unit. Blending should be used when either (1) the component unit's governing body is substantively the same as the primary government's governing body or (2) the component unit provides services entirely, or almost entirely, to the primary government or almost exclusively benefits the primary government. Some of these organizations are similar to the internal services fund. Component units may use governmental fund accounting or proprietary fund accounting, depending on their types of activities. Neither discretely presenting nor blending should change the measurement basis of the type of accounting used by the component unit; however, a general fund of a blended component unit should be reported as a special revenue fund for the primary government.

For purposes of the Sol City example, assume that the city has a separate library board responsible for managing the city library. The mayor appoints the library board, which must have its budget and tax levy approved by the mayor and council. In this case, the library is a component unit that will be discretely presented in a separate column of Sol City's two government-wide financial statements.

Government Financial Reports

Governments must present a *comprehensive annual financial report* (CAFR) that contains (*a*) an introductory section with organizational information, (*b*) a financial section with management's discussion and analysis (MD&A), both fund-based and government-wide financial statements, and the required supplementary information (RSI), and (*c*) a statistical section that presents historical information, usually 10-year trends, and other performance information. The elements of the financial section of the CAFR are:

1. Management's discussion and analysis (required supplementary information, RSI)
2. Government-wide financial statements
   a. Statement of net assets (Figure 18–12)
   b. Statement of activities (Figure 18–13)
3. Fund financial statements
   a. Governmental funds
      (1) Balance sheet (Figure 18–5)
      (2) Statement of revenues, expenditures, and changes in fund balances (Figure 18–6)
      (3) Reconciliation schedules (Figures 18–14 and 18–15)
   b. Proprietary funds
      (1) Statement of net assets (Figure 18–7)
      (2) Statement of revenues, expenses, and changes in fund net assets (Figure 18–8)
      (3) Statement of cash flows (Figure 18–9)
   c. Fiduciary funds
      (1) Statement of fiduciary net assets (Figure 18–10)
      (2) Statement of changes in fiduciary net assets (Figure 18–11)
4. Notes to the financial statements
5. Required supplementary information
   a. Budgetary comparison schedules (Figure 18–16)
   b. Information about infrastructure assets

The GASB has continued to develop the reporting standards for the statistical section to make it more useful and comparative for users of the annual report. In 2004, the GASB issued **GASB Statement 44**, "Economic Condition Reporting: The Statistical Section—An Amendment of NCGA Statement 1" (GASB 44), which specifies the types of information that should be reported in each of the five sections of the statistical section: (1) financial trends information, (2) revenue capacity information, (3) debt capacity information, (4) demographic and economic information, and (5) operating information. The intent of this statement is to further improve the understandability and usefulness of this section by

FIGURE 18–12   **Government-wide Statement of Net Assets**

	Primary Government			
	Governmental Activities	Business-type Activities	Total	Component Unit
SOL CITY **Statement of Net Assets** **December 20X2**				
Assets				
Cash and Cash Equivalents	$ 152,000	$ 30,000	$ 182,000	$ 3,000
Receivables, Net	89,000	5,000	94,000	
Internal Balances	4,000	(4,000)	-0-	
Inventories	23,000		23,000	1,000
Investment in Government Bonds	91,000		91,000	
Capital Assets:				
Land and Infrastructure	3,000,000		3,000,000	
Depreciable Assets, Net	1,202,000	105,000	1,307,000	870,000
Total Assets	$4,561,000	$136,000	$4,697,000	$874,000
Liabilities				
Vouchers Payable	$ 64,000	$ 3,000	$ 67,000	
Accrued Interest Payable		5,000	5,000	
Contract Payable—Retainage	10,000		10,000	
Noncurrent Liabilities:				
Due in More Than 1 Year	80,000	100,000	180,000	$120,000
Total Liabilities	$ 154,000	$108,000	$ 262,000	$120,000
Net Assets				
Invested in Capital Assets, Net of Related Debt	$4,122,000	$ 5,000	$4,127,000	$750,000
Restricted for:				
Debt Service	5,000		5,000	
Permanent Funds	103,000		103,000	
Unrestricted	177,000	23,000	200,000	4,000
Total Net Assets	$4,407,000	$ 28,000	$4,435,000	$754,000

also requiring the governmental unit to add information about the sources of the data and the major assumptions used and expand explanations for any unusual information presented. Thus, the statistical section is an important part of the CAFR.

The fund-based financial statements were discussed previously in the chapter. The following discussion centers on the government-wide financials and the required supplementary information (RSI).

Government-wide Financial Statements

The *government-wide financial statements* include (1) the statement of net assets and (2) the statement of activities. **GASB 34** requires that government-wide financial statements be prepared on the *economic resources measurement focus* with the accrual basis of accounting. Note that the fiduciary funds (e.g., private—purpose trust funds and agency funds) are *not* included in the two government-wide financial statements because fiduciary funds are not available to support government programs.

Statement of Net Assets

Figure 18–12 presents the statement of net assets for Sol City. Some important points regarding this statement of net assets follow:

1. *Format.* The format of the statement is Assets − Liabilities = Net assets. This focuses attention on the net assets of the government entity.

2. *Columnar presentation.* The columns used are for the governmental activities and business-type activities of the primary government, with the component unit, the city library, discretely presented in its own column. It is important to note that **GASB 34** specifies that the internal service fund be included as part of the governmental activities. This is because internal service funds provide service only to the governmental entity, not to external parties. The enterprise funds are presented as business-type activities of the primary government. This is because the enterprise funds do typically offer services to the public, thus they are more business-oriented.

3. *Assets.* Reported assets include all types of assets of the governmental entity, including infrastructure such as roads, sewers, and so on. These capital assets are not reported in the governmental funds that, under the current financial resources measurement focus, record costs of capital assets as expenditures of the period. **GASB 34** requires that all capital and infrastructure assets be reported on the government-wide financial statements. Capital assets, such as buildings and equipment, will be depreciated and that depreciation will be presented as an expense on the government-wide statement of activities. Infrastructure assets are, by their definition, long-lived assets that can be maintained for a much longer time than capital assets. Roads can be paved over, bridges can be repaired, and water and sewer systems can be maintained.

Because of the difficulty in determining any reasonable estimated useful life for the infrastructure assets, **GASB 34** provides for two methods to account for the depreciating attribute of these infrastructure assets.

a. *Report estimated depreciation expense.* The first method requires governments to estimate depreciation expense and report that estimated expense on the government-wide statement of activities.

b. *Modified approach.* The second approach allows governments to avoid the requirement to estimate depreciation expense on infrastructure assets that are part of a network or subsystem of a network as long as the government manages those assets using an asset management system and the government can document that the assets are preserved approximately at, or above, a condition level established by the government. Under the modified approach, the government entity annually expenses actual repair and renewal costs associated with the infrastructure assets. Additions and improvements are added to the cost basis of the infrastructure asset. Required footnote disclosures include: (1) an estimate of the amount required to maintain or preserve the infrastructure assets, along with the actual costs for each of the last five years, and (2) the presentation of condition assessments of the infrastructure assets for the last three years to show that these assets are indeed being maintained.

Many governments use the modified approach rather than the estimated depreciation expense method. Regardless of the method used for the depreciation element, the government must report the infrastructure assets in the asset section of the government-wide statement of net assets.

Note that Sol City distinguishes between its infrastructure assets and its buildings and equipment. Sol City has chosen to use the modified approach in recognizing the depreciating factors in its infrastructure assets. Thus, the depreciation expense reported on the statement of activities is only from the Depreciable Assets category, which includes items such as buildings and equipment. The asset, Internal Balances, represents interfund receivables/payables between the governmental activities and the business-type activities. In the Sol City example, the enterprise fund owes a total of $4,000 to other funds: $3,000 to the general fund for a loan, and $1,000 to the internal fund for supplies purchases. Note again that the internal fund is considered a governmental activity because the internal fund provides services and supplies only to other entities within the government's reporting entity.

The asset, Internal Balances, represents interfund receivables/payables between the primary government's funds comprising the governmental activities (governmental funds plus internal service funds) and the funds comprising the business-type activities (the enterprise funds). These internal balances cancel out each other for the total column. **GASB Statement No. 37**, "Basic Financial Statements—and Management's Discussion and Analysis—for State and Local Governments: Omnibus" (GASB 37), issued in 2001, eliminated the requirement for capitalizing construction-period interest on capital assets used in governmental activities. Thus, on the government-wide financial statements, this interest is now shown as an indirect expense of the period in which it is incurred.

4. *Categories of Net Assets.* Net assets are separated into three categories: (*a*) invested in capital assets, net of related debt, (*b*) restricted by external requirements of creditors, grantors, contributors, or other government entities, and any restrictions imposed by law, and (*c*) unrestricted. Note that restricted and unrestricted do not mean the same things as reserved and unreserved as used for the fund-based financial statements.

Statement of Activities

The statement of activities for Sol City is presented in Figure 18–13. Important observations regarding this statement of activities follow:

1. *Accrual basis.* The full accrual basis of accounting is used to measure revenues and expenses for the government-wide statements. A reconciliation between the modified accrual basis of accounting for the governmental funds and the accrual basis of the government-wide statements is required.

2. *Format.* The format of the statement of activities is based on the functions or programs of the government entity. Program revenues are categorized by type, and the net expenses (revenues) are shown separately for each of the governmental and business-type activities. The internal service fund is blended into the governmental activities. The enterprise funds are presented in the Business-Type Activities column. Fiduciary funds are not reported on the statement of activities. Again note that the component unit, the city library, is discretely presented in its own column.

3. *Expenses.* The expenses include depreciation of the capital assets and expenses for any infrastructure assets. However, the expenses would not include any expenditures in the governmental funds that were made for long-term capital assets. For government-wide statements, these expenditures must be included as increases to long-term capital assets on the balance sheet.

4. *General revenues.* General revenues are reported separately on the bottom of the statement. These are revenues that are not directly tied to any specific program. **GASB 34** requires that contributions to permanent endowments, special items, and extraordinary items be reported in this section for the government-wide statements. Special items are events within the control of management that are either unusual in nature or infrequent in occurrence. Sol City has no special or extraordinary items, and the only contribution to a permanent endowment was the $100,000 contribution received by the permanent fund. Note that the amount of ending net assets reported in this statement articulates with the amount of ending net assets presented on the statement of net assets.

Reconciliation Schedules

GASB 34 requires that two *reconciliation schedules* be presented to reconcile the net change in the total amounts reported on the governmental funds statements with the amounts reported on the government-wide statements. These reconciliation schedules may be presented as part of the governmental funds statements or in an accompanying schedule on the page immediately following the governmental fund financial statement it supports. The two required reconciliation schedules are as follows:

1. *Reconciliation schedule for Statement of Net Assets.* The first reconciliation schedule, the reconciliation between the fund balances reported for the governmental funds to the net assets for the government-wide financials, is presented in Figure 18–14. This schedule describes the adjustments necessary to move from the modified accrual basis used in the governmental funds to the accrual basis used for the government-wide statements. For example,

FIGURE 18–13 Government-wide Statement of Activities

Functions/Programs	Expenses	Program Revenues — Charges for Services	Program Revenues — Operating Grants and Contributions	Program Revenues — Capital Grants and Contributions	Net (Expenses) Revenue and Changes in Net Assets — Primary Government — Governmental Activities	Net (Expenses) Revenue and Changes in Net Assets — Primary Government — Business-Type Activities	Total	Component Unit
Primary Government								
Governmental Activities:								
General Government	$212,000	$ 4,000	$23,000	$20,000	$ (165,000)		$ (165,000)	
Streets and Highways	71,000				(71,000)		(71,000)	
Public Safety	335,000				(335,000)		(335,000)	
Sanitation	141,000				(141,000)		(141,000)	
Culture and Recreation	54,000				(54,000)		(54,000)	
Depreciation of Capital Assets	120,000				(120,000)		(120,000)	
Interest on Long-term Debt	10,000				(10,000)		(10,000)	
Total Governmental Activities	$943,000	$ 4,000	$23,000	$20,000	$ (896,000)		$ (896,000)	
Business-Type Activities:								
Water	$ 38,000	$40,000				$ 2,000	$ 2,000	
Total Business-Type Activities	$ 38,000	$40,000				$ 2,000	$ 2,000	
Total Primary Government	$981,000	$44,000	$23,000	$20,000	$ (896,000)	$ 2,000	$ (894,000)	
Component Unit								
Library	$ 6,000	$ 6,000						$ (6,000)
Total Component Unit	$ 6,000	$ 6,000	$ -0-					$ (6,000)
General Revenues:								
Taxes:								
Property Taxes, Levied for General Purposes					$ 781,000		$1,035,000	
Property Taxes, Levied for Special Purposes					62,000			
Property Taxes, Levied for Debt Service					33,000			
Sales Taxes					32,000			
Investment Earnings					9,000			
Miscellaneous Revenues					18,000			
Contribution					100,000			$ 12,000
Transfers between Governmental and Business-Type Funds					-0-			
Total General Revenues, Special Items, and Transfers					$1,035,000	$ 2,000	$1,035,000	$ 12,000
Change in Net Assets					$ 139,000	2,000	$ 141,000	$ 6,000
Net Assets—Beginning					4,268,000	26,000	4,294,000	748,000
Net Assets—Ending					$4,407,000	$28,000	$4,435,000	$754,000

FIGURE 18–14
Reconciliation
Schedule for the
Statement of Net
Assets

SOL CITY Reconciliation of the Balance Sheet of Governmental Funds to the Statement of Net Assets December 31, 20X2	
Fund balances reported in the governmental funds	$ 279,000
Amounts reported for the governmental activities in the statement of net assets are different because:	
Capital assets used in governmental activities are not financial resources and therefore are not reported in the governmental funds.	4,200,000
Internal service funds are used by management to charge the costs of certain activities, such as centralized purchasing and storage functions, to individual funds. The assets and liabilities of the internal service fund are included in governmental activities in the statement of net assets.	7,000
Long-term liabilities, including bonds payable, are not due and payable in the current period and therefore are not reported in the funds.	(80,000)
Interest on bonds in the permanent fund is recognized in that fund under the modified accrual basis, but must be adjusted to the accrual basis for the government-wide financial statements.	1,000
Net assets of governmental activities	$4,407,000

the balance sheets of the government funds do not include infrastructure and capital assets. These costs are recognized as expenditures in the periods in which they are made. However, the government-wide statement of net assets must report the balance sheet date cost less depreciation of these infrastructure and capital assets. In addition, the government-wide statements must include the accounts of the internal service funds, which are separately reported from the governmental funds in the fund-based financial statements.

2. *Reconciliation schedule for Statement of Activities.* The second reconciliation schedule, the reconciliation between the net change in fund balances reported in the governmental funds' statement of revenues, expenditures, and changes in fund balance to the change in net assets reported in the government-wide financials, is presented in Figure 18–15. For example, interest revenue on the investment in bonds in the permanent fund was presented in that fund under the modified accrual basis for the amount of $8,000. However, under the accrual basis, the interest revenue would be computed based on the effective interest rate, with amortization of the discount, in the amount of $9,000 ($90,000 × .10). The difference of $1,000 is an adjustment both to the change in net assets and to the net assets.

Budgetary Comparison Schedule

GASB 34 requires that a ***budgetary comparison schedule*** be presented as required supplementary information for the general fund and for each special revenue fund that has a legally adopted annual budget. This schedule may be presented as a separate financial statement after the governmental funds financials or in the footnotes of the annual report. The budgetary comparison schedule for Sol City's general fund is presented in Figure 18–16.

Important observations regarding the budgetary comparison schedule follow:

1. **GASB 34** requires that both the original budget and the final budget be presented. The original budget is the first budget for the fiscal period adopted by the government entity. Through the year, many government entities will modify the original budget because of new events or changes in expectations. These changes must go through the legislative process of the government, such as the city council. For our example, no changes were made to the formal budget during the year.

2. The budgetary comparison schedule should be presented on the same format with the same terminology and classifications as the original budget.

FIGURE 18–15
Reconciliation
Schedule for
the Statement
of Revenues,
Expenditures, and
Changes in Fund
Balances

SOL CITY Reconciliation of the Statement of Revenues, Expenditures, and Changes in Fund Balances of Governmental Funds to the Statement of Activities For the Year Ended December 31, 20X2	
Net change in fund balances—governmental funds	$150,000
Governmental funds report capital outlays as expenditures. However, in the statement of activities, the costs of those assets are capitalized and depreciated over their estimated useful lives. This is the amount by which capital outlays in the governmental funds ($182,000) exceeded depreciation of the governmental assets ($119,000).	63,000
Bond proceeds provide current financial resources for the governmental funds. However, the issuance of debt increases long-term liabilities in the statement of net assets. Repayment of debt principal is an expenditure in the governmental funds, but the repayment reduces the long-term liabilities in the statement of net assets. This is the amount by which bond proceeds ($102,000) exceeded the net repayments of principal ($20,000).	(82,000)
Revenues in the statement of activities are recorded on the accrual basis. Interest revenue in the governmental funds is recorded on the modified accrual basis. This is the amount that accrual interest exceeded the interest recognized in the permanent funds.	1,000
Internal service funds are used by management to charge the costs of certain services, such as a centralized purchasing function, to individual funds. The net revenue (expense) of the internal service funds is reported with governmental activities.	7,000
Change in net assets of governmental activities	$139,000

3. A separate column for the variance between the final budget and the actual amounts is encouraged but not required. It is presented here to provide a complete presentation of the possible disclosures of a governmental entity.

GASB Statement No. 41, "Budgetary Comparison Schedules—Perspective Differences" (GASB 41), amended **GASB 34** for state and local governments that have significantly different structures for budgetary purposes from the fund structures in **GASB 34**. These differences are termed perspective differences. A government with significant budgetary perspective differences such that the government cannot provide budgetary comparisons for the fund structure of the general fund and each special revenue fund is then required to present a budgetary comparison schedule in its required supplementary information based on the fund, program, or organizational structure that government uses for its legally adopted budget.

Management's Discussion and Analysis

GASB 34 specifies that the Management's Discussion and Analysis (MD&A) be included in the ***required supplementary information*** (RSI) of the government-wide financial statements. The MD&A is presented before the financial statements and provides an analytical overview of the government's financial and operating activities.

The MD&A discusses current-period operations and financial position and then compares those with the prior-periods. The purpose of this RSI item is to provide users of the financial statements an objective discussion of whether the government's financial position has improved or deteriorated during the year. **GASB 37** states that the MDA should be limited to the items specified in **GASB 34** rather than be used to present an abundance of other topics not specifically required. The GASB believes that additional discussions beyond those required might result in information that is not objective and cannot be directly analyzed. Governments that wish to provide additional information may do so in other supplementary information such as footnotes or transmittal letters.

Certain Financial Statement Note Disclosures

A number of footnote disclosures are required in government-wide financial statements, as specified in various governmental accounting and reporting standards. **GASB Statement 38**,

FIGURE 18–16 Budgetary Comparison Schedule

SOL CITY
Budgetary Comparison Schedule
General Fund
For the Year Ended December 31, 20X2

	Budgeted Amount		Actual Amounts (Budgetary Basis)	Variance with Final Budget Positive (Negative)
	Original	Final		
Budgetary fund balance, January 1	$ 129,000	$129,000	$ 129,000	$ -0-
Resources (inflows):				
Property taxes	775,000	775,000	781,000	6,000
Grants	55,000	55,000	33,000	(22,000)
Sales taxes	25,000	25,000	32,000	7,000
Miscellaneous	20,000	20,000	18,000	(2,000)
Amounts available for appropriation	$ 875,000	$875,000	$ 864,000	$ (11,000)
Charges to appropriations (outflows):				
General government	$ 200,000	$200,000	$ 206,000	$ (6,000)
Streets and highways	75,000	75,000	71,000	4,000
Public safety	400,000	400,000	393,000	7,000
Sanitation	150,000	150,000	141,000	9,000
Nondepartmental:				
Transfers out to other funds	30,000	30,000	30,000	-0-
Total charges to appropriations	$ 855,000	$855,000	$ 841,000	$ 14,000
Budgetary fund balance, December 31	$ 149,000	$149,000	$ 152,000	$ 3,000

"Certain Financial Statement Note Disclosures" (GASB 38), was issued in June 2001 and stated that the required footnotes should be modified for the following:

1. In the summary of significant accounting policies, provide descriptions of the activities accounted for in the major funds, internal service fund type, and fiduciary fund types. This change is a result of **GASB 34**'s focus on major funds rather than all funds.

2. Delete the requirement to disclose the accounting policy for encumbrances in the summary of significant accounting policies (i.e., the lapsing or nonlapsing method).

3. Disclose the period of availability used for recording revenues in governmental funds.

4. Disclose debt service requirements to maturity, separately identifying principal and interest for each of the subsequent five years and in five-year increments thereafter and changes in variable-rate debt. In addition, governments should disclose the future minimum payments for each of the five succeeding years for capital and noncancelable operating leases.

5. Provide a schedule of changes in short-term debt during the year along with the purposes for which the debt was issued.

6. Add a disclosure of actions taken to address any significant violations of finance-related legal or contractual provisions to the footnote describing these significant violations.

7. Disclose details of the payable and receivable amounts for interfund balances and the purposes of the interfund transfers. In addition, disclosures should be made regarding the amounts of interfund transfers during the period along with a description and amount of significant transfers that are not expected to occur on a routine basis.

8. Provide details of the components of accounts payable so that the financial statement users can understand the timeliness and payment priorities of payables.

9. Provide details about significant individual accounts when their nature is obscured by aggregation. For example, more disclosure could be made for receivables that contain a myriad of different credit risks or liquidity attributes.

Other Financial Report Items

Governments may choose to provide additional information beyond that required as discussed previously. For example, some government entities present comprehensive annual financial reports (CAFRs), which include additional statistical information about the sources of revenues, property tax levies and property values, demographic statistics, and other miscellaneous statistics that management of the governmental entity believes will aid users of the financial report. Some governmental entities may additionally disclose financial statements for individual funds or combined by fund type. Some governments may go beyond the required footnote disclosures and provide additional schedules and information. As with commercial enterprises, it is up to the management of the governmental entity to determine how much additional disclosure it wishes to provide in its annual report.

Interim Reporting

Governmental entities generally are not required to publish interim reports, although many prepare monthly or quarterly reports to determine the current progress of compliance with legal and budgetary limitations and to plan for changes in events or developments that were not foreseen when the annual budget was prepared. Interim reports are a valuable internal management control instrument; they typically are not made available to the general public.

Auditing Governmental Entities

Most governmental entities are audited annually because of state or federal requirements or because long-term creditors demand audited statements as part of the debt agreements. The audit of a governmental entity is different from the audit of a commercial entity. The auditor not only must express an opinion on the fairness of the audited entity's financial statements in conformity with applicable accounting principles but also must assess the audited entity's compliance with legal or contractual provisions of state law, debt covenants, terms of grants from other governmental entities, and other restrictions on the governmental unit.

The Single Audit Act of 1984 is a federal law specifying the audit requirements for all state and local governments receiving federal financial assistance. The audit act requires auditors to determine whether (1) the financial statements fairly present the government's financial condition, (2) the governmental entity has an internal control system to provide reasonable assurance that it is managing federal financial assistance programs in compliance with applicable laws and regulations, and (3) the governmental entity has complied with laws and regulations that may have a material effect on each federal program. The auditors issue not only the standard audit report but also special reports on items (2) and (3) above.

The Single Audit Act does not apply to all governmental entities receiving federal assistance. For fiscal years ending after December 31, 2003, governmental entities that expend $500,000 or more in federal awards in a year must have either a single or a program-specific audit for that year. A governmental entity is eligible for a program-specific audit only if the federal award is expended under a single federal program and that federal program's laws, regulations or grant agreements do not require the governmental entity to have a financial statement audit. Otherwise a single audit is required. Governmental entities that expend less that $500,000 in federal awards in a year are exempt from the single audit requirement for that year. However, their records must be available for review or audit by officials from the federal agency, the pass-through entity providing the award, or the Government Accountability Office (GAO).

ADDITIONAL CONSIDERATIONS

Special-Purpose Governmental Entities

The accounting and financial reporting standards for general-purpose governments such as states, counties, and municipalities are discussed in this chapter and Chapter 17. However, a number of governments are *special-purpose governments*, which are legally separate entities. They may be component units of a general-purpose government or stand-alone governments apart from a general-purpose government. Special-purpose governments include governmental entities such as cemetery districts, levee districts, park districts, tollway authorities, and school districts. Some of these special-purpose government entities may be engaged in governmental activities that generally are financed through taxes, intergovernmental revenues, and other nonexchange revenues. These activities are usually reported in governmental or internal service funds. Some of these entities are engaged in business-type activities that are financed by fees charged for goods or services. These activities are usually reported in enterprise funds. **GASB 34** establishes specific reporting requirements for each of the following types of special-purpose governments:

1. Engaged in more than one governmental program or in both governmental and business-type activities: These governmental entities must provide both fund financial statements and government-wide financial statements as presented earlier in this chapter and in Chapter 17.
2. Engaged in a single governmental program (such as cemetery districts or drainage districts): These governmental entities may present a simplified set of government-wide and fund-based financial statements, often combining these two statements.
3. Engaged in only business-type activities: These governmental entities must present only the financial statements required for enterprise funds. Many public universities and public hospitals will be included in this category.
4. Engaged in only fiduciary-type activities: These governmental entities are not required to present the government-wide financials but must provide only the financial statements required for fiduciary funds. This category includes special-purpose governments responsible for managing pension funds.

Regardless of the category of special-purpose government entity, all governments must include in their financial reports the Management's Discussion and Analysis, the footnotes, and any required supplementary information.

Financial Reporting for Pensions and OPEB Plans

Most states and many local governments provide a variety of pensions and other postemployment benefits (OPEB) to their employees. OPEBs include postemployment health care, life insurance, and other nonpension benefits for persons after retirement from the governmental unit. The GASB has a series of standards that prescribe the employer's accounting for these costs and the financial reporting by the entity that maintains the plans. In some cases, the governmental unit administers its own plans, such as a state-based pension plan covering all state employees in a specific employment category, while in other cases the governmental unit uses a multi-employer plan, such as a firefighter's retirement plan that includes firefighters from a number of cities.

Two standards present the accounting and financial reporting requirements for the entity that administer the plan's assets. The first is **GASB Statement No. 25**, "Financial Reporting for Defined Benefit Pension Plans and Note Disclosures for Defined Contribution Plans" (GASB 25), which established the financial reporting standards for pension plans. The second is **GASB Statement No. 43**, "Financial Reporting for Postemployment Benefit Plans Other than Pension Plans" (GASB 43), which provided financial reporting standards for OPEB plans. The general principles in these two standards are similar. The entity that administers the plans must provide two categories of information in its financial reporting: (*a*) current financial information about plan assets and financial activities, and (*b*) actuarially determined information about the funded position of the plan and the plan's progress in accumulating sufficient financial resources to provide benefits when due. The two financial statements required of the plan are: (*a*) a statement of plan net assets that provides information about the fair value and composition of the plan's assets and information about the plan's liabilities; and (*b*) a statement of changes in plan net assets that provides information on the period's changes in the net assets of the plan. The accrual method of accounting is required and informative footnotes must be provided.

Employer Accounting for Pensions and OPEB Plan Benefits

Two GASB statements present the standards for the employer's measurement and display of accounting for the expenditures/expenses for the benefits and any related liabilities (or assets) for the difference between the expenditure/expenses recognition and the amount funded by the employer. The first is **GASB Statement No. 27**, "Accounting for Pensions by State and Local Governmental Employers" (GASB 27), which presents the standards for pensions. The second is **GASB Statement No. 45**, "Accounting and Financial Reporting by Employers for Postemployment Benefits Other than Pensions" (GASB 45). The general principles for measurement, recognition, and display in these two standards are similar. The accrual method of accounting is typically used for the government-wide financial statements to measure the expenses of the employer for pension costs for its employees and for the costs of other postemployment benefits for its employees. Actuarial assumptions are required under the accrual method. The state and local government employers must report the expense/expenditures and related liabilities (or assets) for both their pension benefits and for their OPEBs.

Although **GASB 27** and **GASB 45** have many of the same measurement and display standards, there are some differences due to the differences in the nature of the specific benefits given by the employer. Accountants responsible for accounting for these two sets of postemployment benefits readily acknowledge that some plans and benefits can be quite complex and require detailed study of the specific requirements in the related GASB statements.

Accounting for Termination Benefits

Finally, termination benefits are sometimes offered by governmental entities when an employee is involuntarily terminated (i.e., fired or laid off) or voluntarily terminates in order to accept early-retirement benefits. These termination benefits may include health care–related programs, job transition costs, early retirement incentives, and other similar types of items. The accounting and reporting requirements for these benefits are presented in **GASB Statement No. 47**, "Accounting for Termination Benefits" (GASB 47). In the case of employees who voluntarily terminate, the employer recognizes a liability and expense when the employee accepts the offer and the amount can be estimated. The general measurement principle is that the dollar amount recognized should be the discounted present value of the estimated future payments.

Governmental entities may develop a plan for a reduction in their work force that involves the involuntary termination of some employees. A liability and an expense should be recognized when the plan of termination is approved by the governing body, the plan has been communicated to the employees, and the amount can be estimated. For the government-wide financial statements, the accrual method is used to recognize the discounted present value of the estimated future payments.

Governmental entities have found that they must offer employees benefits similar to those offered in the private sector in order to attract and employ persons who would otherwise seek employment with business firms in the private sector. Thus, as the private sector changes what it offers employees, governmental entities will have to adjust what they offer to their employees.

Summary of Key Concepts

This chapter completes the discussion of accounting and financial reporting principles used by local and state governments. Governments may use five governmental fund types, two proprietary fund types, and four fiduciary fund types (including agency funds). The governmental funds use the modified accrual basis of accounting; the other funds use the accrual basis of accounting.

The government reporting model is specified in **GASB 34**. Both fund-based financial statements and government-wide financial statements are required. The government-wide statements are based on the accrual basis and present both long-term capital assets, including infrastructure assets, and long-term debt. Government entities must include required supplementary information (RSI) in their annual financial reports as specified by **GASB 34**. This RSI includes reconciliation schedules and a budgetary comparison schedule.

Key Terms

Appendix 18A Other Governmental Entities—Public School Systems and the Federal Government

In addition to local and state governmental entities, two other governmental entities—public schools and the federal government—have pervasive influences on the lives of citizens. This appendix presents a brief overview of the basic accounting and financial reporting requirements for these two governmental entities.

PUBLIC SCHOOL SYSTEMS

In the United States today, more than 50 million students attend approximately 14,000 public elementary and secondary school systems employing about 2.5 million teachers and expending more than $100 billion annually. Many others attend one of the myriad of private schools formed by religious or other groups.

Accounting and Financial Reporting for Public School Systems

Accounting for public schools is similar to accounting for local or state governments. The modified accrual basis of accounting is used for most funds, and the financial statements for a school district are similar to those of a local government. More than half of school district revenue is obtained from local property taxes; the remaining sources are fees for services, state education aid, and federal grants to education. Most school districts have an elected school board that serves as a public policy-making body for the school system.

    The fund structure for a school district is similar to the fund structure for a local or state government. School district funds include the general fund, special revenue funds, capital projects funds, debt service funds, enterprise funds, internal service funds, and trust and agency funds.

    The school district's general fund resources are expended for costs directly associated with the education process: teachers' salaries, books and supplies, and other costs. Special revenue funds may include specific funds for operations, building, and maintenance (OBM) of the physical facilities of the school district, as well as the transportation special revenue fund, which is responsible for acquiring and maintaining the buses for transporting children to and from the schools.

    Public school systems have a public hearing on the annual budget, which is then approved by the school board or other governing body. The budget specifies the revenue from the three basic sources: local property taxes and fees, state school aid, and federal sources. The expenditures are broken down into the following three dimensions: *program,* such as gifted, vocational, elementary, secondary, and adult/continuing education; *function,* such as guidance counselors, instructional staff, school administration, and student transportation; and *object,* such as salaries, employee benefits, purchased services, and supplies and materials.

    The department of education of each state receives the annual reports from that state's school districts. Typically these financial statements must be audited by independent auditors. Many school districts are legally separate, fiscally independent, special-purpose government entities engaged in both governmental and business-type activities. These school districts have their own legally mandated budget process and tax levy authority, and they do not depend financially on another government entity. In these cases, school districts present their financial statements in accordance with **GASB 34**, which requires government-wide financial statements as well as fund financial statements. **GASB 34** also requires management's discussion and analysis, footnotes, and required supplementary information. School districts that are fiscally dependent and component units of a primary government entity, such as the city government in which the school is located, present their financial information within the primary government's financial statements, usually discretely presented in a column separate from the financial data of the primary government. Other statements required are the same as for other governmental units. In addition, the comprehensive annual financial report for a school district includes a variety of other disclosures relevant to the school district, such as the cost per student, the debt capacity of the district, and the assessed valuation of all property included in the school district.

Federal Government Accounting

An accounting structure for the federal government has been part of the U.S. statutes since 1789. The following individuals or entities have significant roles in the federal budgeting and expending process:

Executive Branch	Legislative Branch
President	Congress
Office of Management and Budget (OMB)	Government Accountability Office (GAO)
Secretary of the Treasury	Congressional Budget Office (CBO)
Federal agencies	

The fiscal period for the U.S. federal government is from October 1 to September 30 of the next calendar year. The President of the United States directs that the annual budget be prepared by the director of the Office of Management and Budget, who is a member of the president's staff. The director of the OMB then consults with the various federal agencies and the Secretary of the Treasury and prepares the budget that the president presents to Congress. The Congressional Budget Office then evaluates the executive budget and may propose that Congress present one of its own. After the legislative process runs its course and the budget is approved, Congress provides the authority for the executive branch to obtain revenue through taxation or other charges. The primary agency responsible for obtaining revenue is the Internal Revenue Service, which is an agency of the Department of the Treasury.

The appropriation-expenditure process is a little different for the federal government than for local government units. The federal budget provides the appropriation authority for the federal government. This appropriation authority is then allocated to the various agencies through a process of apportionments made by the Office of Management and Budget. The apportionment is then divided among the agency's programs and activities by a process of allotments. The agency then makes obligations by incurring costs for services provided. These obligations are then liquidated through the preparation of vouchers, which are submitted to the Department of the Treasury for payment.

The Department of Treasury annually issues the "Financial Report of the United States Government," which includes the auditor's report from the comptroller general of the United States. The financial report presents information on the federal government and its agencies, including a stewardship report and a statement of net cost by agency. The financial report is available on the Department of Treasury's Website.

Audits of Federal Agencies

The comptroller general of the United States is the head of the Government Accountability Office (GAO). The GAO is an agency of the legislative branch of the federal government and works with the Department of the Treasury, an executive department, to develop and maintain the federal government's accounting system. The GAO reviews the accounting systems of each executive agency each year from both a financial and a compliance perspective. The compliance part of the audit ensures that the agency fulfilled all legal and budgetary restrictions. Exceptions are reported to Congress, which then communicates them to the executive branch, thus completing the cycle that began when the executive branch first proposed the annual budget to Congress.

Questions

Q18-1   In what circumstances would a governmental unit use a special revenue fund rather than a general fund?

Q18-2   Which governmental funds use operating budgets? Which use capital budgets?

Q18-3   How is interest on long-term debt accounted for in the debt service fund?

Q18-4   What are the major differences between a special revenue fund and an enterprise fund?

Q18-5   What is the basis of accounting in the proprietary funds? Why?

Q18-6   What financial statements must be prepared for the governmental funds? For the enterprise funds?

Q18-7 How are the proceeds from a bond issue accounted for in governmental funds? Where are these proceeds reported on the governmental funds' statement of revenues, expenditures, and changes in fund balance?

Q18-8 What are the primary differences between a permanent fund (governmental) and a private-purpose trust fund (fiduciary)?

Q18-9 Not all governmental funds need to be separately presented on the governmental funds financial statements. What are the two tests for determining major governmental funds for which separate disclosure is required?

Q18-10 How are contributions to governmental funds as well as special or extraordinary items reported on the governmental funds' statement of revenues, expenditures, and changes in fund balance?

Q18-11 Do agency funds have a net fund balance? Why or why not?

Q18-12 What are component units of a government, and how are these component units reported on the government-wide financial statements?

Q18-13 Reconciliation schedules are a required disclosure in the government-wide financial statements. What are the purpose and content of these reconciliation schedules?

Q18-14 GASB 34 requires a budgetary comparison schedule for each governmental fund that has a legally adopted budget. Briefly describe this budgetary comparison schedule.

Q18-15 How are infrastructure and other long-term assets as well as general long-term debt reported on the government-wide financial statements?

Cases

C18-1   Basis of Accounting and Reporting Issues

Judgment

The accounting system of Barb City is organized and operated on a fund basis. Among the types of funds used are a general fund, a special revenue fund, and an enterprise fund.

Required

a. Explain the basic differences in revenue recognition between the accrual basis of accounting and the modified accrual basis of accounting in relation to governmental accounting.

b. What basis of accounting should be used for each of the following funds: (1) general fund, (2) special revenue fund, and (3) enterprise fund?

C18-2   Capital Projects, Debt Service, and Internal Service Funds

Understanding

The funds of Lake City include a debt service fund, a capital projects fund, and an internal service fund.

Required

a. Explain the use of capital projects funds. Include what they account for, the basis of accounting used, unusual entries and accounts, and financial statements.

b. Explain the use of debt service funds. Include what they account for, the basis of accounting used, unusual entries and accounts, and financial statements.

c. Explain the use of internal service funds. Include what they account for, the basis of accounting used, unusual entries and accounts, and financial statements.

C18-3   Discovery

This case provides learning opportunities using available databases and/or the Internet to obtain contemporary information about the topics in advanced financial accounting. Note that the Internet is dynamic and the specific Website listed may change addresses. In that case, use a good search engine to locate the current address for the Website.

Research

Required

Access the Department of Treasury's Website and scroll through until you locate the most recent "Financial Report of the United States Government" (http://fms.treas.gov/fr/index.html). Look over the report, especially the comptroller general's statement and the auditor's report, and then prepare a one- to two-page memo summarizing the major information items reported in the Financial Report of the United States Government.

C18-4   Becoming Familiar with a Local Government's Comprehensive Annual Financial Report (CAFR)

Using the Internet, find the comprehensive annual financial report (CAFR) of a local government selected by your instructor. At a minimum, a CAFR will include (1) management's discussion and analysis (MDA), (2) the basic financial statements—government-wide and fund-based financial statements, (3) notes to the basic financial statements, (4) other required supplementary information (RSI), and (5) the external auditor's opinion on the basic financial statements.

Required

Using the CAFR chosen by your instructor, answer the following questions that relate to the overall government and to the governmental funds:

a. Read the section of the report that contains management's discussion and analysis. Is your government a general purpose government? If yes, what types of services does your government provide?

b. What type of opinion was given by the external auditor on the basic financial statements? What responsibility did the auditor take with regard to MDA and the other RSI?

c. Examine the financial statements for the funds. List the fund types used by your government.

d. From reading the notes that follow the government-wide and fund-based financial statements, what is the measurement focus and basis of accounting used by the governmental funds?

e. List the financial statements of the government that use the economic resources measurement focus and the accrual basis of accounting.

f. In addition to the general fund, list your government's other major governmental and proprietary funds.

g. Examine the government-wide financial statements. List any component units over which your government has fiscal accountability.

h. Examine the balance sheet of the governmental funds. What are the total assets and the total fund balance as of the most recent balance sheet date? How much of the total fund balance is reserved?

i. Examine the statement of revenues, expenditures, and changes in fund balance for the most recent year. How much of the total revenue came from taxes?

j. Examine the statement of revenues, expenditures, and changes in fund balance for the most recent year. How are expenditures classified?

k. Examine the statement of revenues, expenditures, and changes in fund balance for the most recent year. How much of the other financing sources resulted from transfers in?

l. Examine the statement of revenues, expenditures, and changes in fund balance for the most recent year. List any special items reported. What was the increase or decrease in fund balance for the year?

Exercises **E18-1** **Multiple-Choice Questions on Government Financial Reporting**

Select the correct answer for each of the following questions.

1. The government-wide financial statements use the:

   a. Economic resources measurement focus and the accrual basis of accounting.

   b. Current financial resources measurement focus and the accrual basis of accounting.

   c. Economic resources measurement focus and the modified accrual basis of accounting.

   d. Current financial resources measurement focus and the modified accrual basis of accounting.

2. The financial statements for the governmental funds use the:

   a. Economic resources measurement focus and the accrual basis of accounting.

   b. Current financial resources measurement focus and the accrual basis of accounting.

   c. Economic resources measurement focus and the modified accrual basis of accounting.

   d. Current financial resources measurement focus and the modified accrual basis of accounting.

3. According to GASB Statement No. 34, infrastructure fixed assets:

   a. Must be capitalized and depreciated.

   b. Must be capitalized but governments do *not* have to depreciate them.

   c. May be capitalized and depreciated.

   d. Must be reported using the modified approach.

4. On which of the following government-wide financial statements would you find all liabilities of a state or local government?

    a. Statement of net assets.

    b. Statement of financial condition.

    c. Statement of activities.

    d. Statement of financial position.

5. On which of the following financial statements would you find all of the capital assets of a local government?

    a. Statement of net assets.

    b. Statement of financial condition.

    c. Statement of activities.

    d. Statement of financial position.

6. For which fund category is a statement of cash flows prepared?

    a. Governmental.

    b. Proprietary.

    c. Fiduciary.

    d. None of the above.

Use the information below to answer questions 7 through 9.

The Village of Hampton reported the following data for its governmental activities for the year ended June 30, 20X5:

Item	Amount
Cash and cash equivalents	$ 1,880,000
Receivables	459,000
Capital assets	14,250,000
Accumulated depreciation	1,750,000
Accounts payable	650,000
Long-term liabilities	5,350,000

Additional data:
  All of the long-term debt was used to acquire capital assets.
  Cash of $654,000 is restricted for debt service.

7. On the statement of net assets prepared at June 30, 20X5, what amount should be reported for total net assets?

    a. $8,839,000.

    b. $7,804,000.

    c. $7,150,000.

    d. $8,189,000.

8. On the statement of net assets prepared at June 30, 20X5, what amount should be reported for net assets, invested in capital assets net of related debt?

    a. $8,839,000.

    b. $7,804,000.

    c. $7,150,000.

    d. $8,189,000.

9. On the statement of net assets prepared at June 30, 20X5, what amount should be reported for net assets, unrestricted?

    a. $1,685,000.

    b. $1,689,000.

    c. $1,035,000.

    d. $1,031,000.

10. Which of the following funds can be major funds assuming the appropriate tests are met?

   a. The parking meter special revenue fund and the water utility enterprise fund.

   b. The fire station capital projects fund and a property tax agency fund.

   c. The fire station bonds debt service fund and the city teachers pension trust fund.

   d. The local symphony permanent fund and the Edwina Williams private-purpose trust fund.

11. Where in the basic financial statements would you find a description of the measurement focus and the basis of accounting used in the government-wide financial statements?

   a. In the statement of net assets.

   b. In the statement of activities.

   c. In management's discussion and analysis.

   d. In the notes to the financial statements.

12. Where in the financial section of a CAFR would you find an analysis of the balances and transactions of individual funds?

   a. In the government-wide financial statements.

   b. In the fund financial statements.

   c. In management's discussion and analysis.

   d. In the notes to the financial statements.

E18-2 Multiple-Choice Questions on Governmental Funds [AICPA Adapted]

Select the correct answer for each of the following questions.

1. On December 31, 20X1, Tiffin Township paid a contractor $2,000,000 for the total cost of a new firehouse built in 20X1 on township-owned land. Financing was by means of a $1,500,000 general obligation bond issue sold at face amount on December 31, 20X1, with the remaining $500,000 transferred from the general fund. What should be reported on Tiffin's financial statements for the capital projects fund?

   a. Revenue, $1,500,000; Expenditures, $1,500,000.

   b. Revenue, $1,500,000; Other Financing Sources, $500,000; Expenditures, $2,000,000.

   c. Revenue, $2,000,000; Expenditures, $2,000,000.

   d. Other Financing Sources, $2,000,000; Expenditures, $2,000,000.

2. A debt service fund of a municipality is an example of which of the following types of funds?

   a. Fiduciary.

   b. Governmental.

   c. Proprietary.

   d. Internal service.

3. Revenue of a special revenue fund of a governmental unit should be recognized in the period in which the:

   a. Revenue becomes available and measurable.

   b. Revenue becomes available for appropriation.

   c. Revenue is billable.

   d. Cash is received.

4. Taxes collected and held by a municipality for a school district would be accounted for in a(n):

   a. Enterprise fund.

   b. Intragovernmental (internal) service fund.

   c. Agency fund.

   d. Special revenue fund.

5. Interest expense on bonds payable should be recorded in a debt service fund:

   a. At the end of the fiscal period if the interest due date does not coincide with the end of the fiscal period.

   b. When bonds are issued.

   c. When legally payable.

   d. When paid.

6. Which of the following funds does *not* have a fund balance?

   a. General fund.

   b. Agency fund.

   c. Special revenue fund.

   d. Capital projects fund.

E18-3   Multiple-Choice Questions on Proprietary Funds [AICPA Adapted]

Select the correct answer for each of the following questions.

1. Which of the following accounts could be included in the statement of net assets of an enterprise fund?

	Reserve for Encumbrances	Revenue Bonds Payable	Net Assets
a.	No	No	Yes
b.	No	Yes	Yes
c.	Yes	Yes	No
d.	No	No	No

2. Customers' meter deposits that cannot be spent for normal operating purposes would most likely be classified as restricted cash in the balance sheet of which fund?

   a. Internal service.

   b. Private-purpose trust.

   c. Agency.

   d. Enterprise.

3. Which fund is not an expendable fund?

   a. Capital projects.

   b. General.

   c. Special revenue.

   d. Internal service.

4. If a governmental unit established a data processing center to service all agencies within the unit, the data processing center should be accounted for as a(n):

   a. Capital projects fund.

   b. Internal service fund.

   c. Agency fund.

   d. Trust fund.

5. Recreational facilities run by a governmental unit and financed on a user-charge basis would be accounted for in which fund?   .

   a. General.

   b. Trust.

   c. Enterprise.

   d. Capital projects.

6. The Underwood Electric Utility Fund, which is an enterprise fund, had the following during its 20X1 fiscal year, ending at December 31, 20X1:

Prepaid insurance paid in December 20X1	$ 43,000
Depreciation for 20X1	129,000

   What amount should be reflected in the statement of revenues, expenses, and changes in fund net assets of the Underwood Electric Utility Fund for these items?

   a. $(43,000).

   b. $0.

   c. $129,000.

   d. $172,000.

7. Which of the following funds of a governmental unit uses the same basis of accounting as an enterprise fund?

   a. Special revenue.

   b. Internal service.

   c. Permanent trust.

   d. Capital projects.

8. Fixed assets utilized in a city-owned utility are accounted for in which of the following?

	Enterprise Fund	General Fund
a.	No	No
b.	No	Yes
c.	Yes	No
d.	Yes	Yes

9. Which of the following funds of a governmental unit would account for long-term debt in the accounts of the fund?

   a. Special revenue.

   b. Capital projects.

   c. Internal service.

   d. General.

E18-4 Multiple-Choice Questions on Various Funds

Use the information below to answer questions 1 and 2:

On August 1, 20X6, the City of Rockhaven received $1,000,000 from a prominent citizen to establish a private-purpose trust fund. The donor stipulated that the cash be permanently invested and that the earnings from the investments be spent to support local artists. During the year ended June 30, 20X7, $50,000 of dividends were received from stock investments and $35,000 of interest was earned from bond investments. At June 30, $5,000 of the interest earned was not yet received. During the year ended June 30, 20X7, $75,000 was spent by the trust fund to support local artists.

1. For the year ended June 30, 20X7, the trust fund should report investment earnings of:

   a. $80,000.

   b. $50,000.

   c. $85,000.

   d. $35,000.

2. For the year ended June 30, 20X7, the trust fund should report the $75,000 spent to support local artists as a(n):

   a. Deduction.

   b. Contra contribution.

   c. Transfer out.

   d. Direct adjustment from fund balance.

3. Which of the following statements is (are) correct about agency funds?

   I. Agency funds should report investment earnings only when they are both measurable and available.

   II. Agency funds are reported on the proprietary funds' statement of cash flows.

   a. I only.

   b. II only.

   c. I and II.

   d. Neither I nor II.

Use the following information to answer questions 4 through 8.

On July 2, 20X6, the Village of Westbury established an internal service fund to service the data processing needs of the other village departments. The internal service fund received a transfer of $600,000 from the general fund and a $100,000 long-term advance from the water utility enterprise fund to acquire computer equipment. During July of 20X6, computer equipment costing $650,000 was acquired. The following events occurred during the year ended June 30, 20X7:

Charges for services to other departments for data processing services rendered	$100,000
Operating expenses (exclusive of depreciation expense)	45,000
Depreciation expense	40,000
Interest expense on the advance	5,000

At June 30, 20X7, all but $7,000 of the billings were collected, and all operating expenses and the interest expense were paid except for $3,000 of operating expenses.

4. For the year ended June 30, 20X7, what was the income of Westbury's internal service fund?

   a. $13,000.

   b. $6,000.

   c. $3,000.

   d. $10,000.

5. At June 30, 20X7, what total assets amount would appear on the internal service fund balance sheet?

   a. $700,000.

   b. $710,000.

   c. $713,000.

   d. $708,000.

6. Assume that the mayor's office and the police department were billed $55,000 for data processing work during the year ended June 30, 20X7. What account should be debited in the general fund to record these billings?

   a. Other Financing Use—Transfers Out.

   b. Expenditures.

   c. Due to Internal Service Fund.

   d. Operating Expenses.

7. Assume that the water utility, an enterprise fund, was billed $25,000 for data processing work during the year ended June 30, 20X7. What account should be debited in the enterprise fund to record these billings?

   a. Operating expenses.

   b. Other Financing Use—Transfers Out.

   c. Expenditures.

   d. Due to Internal Service Fund.

8. Assume that the income for Westbury's internal service fund was $10,000 for the year ended June 30, 20X7. What net assets should be reported on the internal service fund's statement of net assets at June 30, 20X7?

   a. $713,000.

   b. $610,000.

   c. $710,000.

   d. $613,000.

E18-5   Multiple-Choice Questions on Financial Reporting Issues for Government-wide and Fund-Based Financial Statements

Select the correct answer for each of the following questions.

1. Which of the following statements is correct?

   I. In the government-wide financial statements, internal service fund activities are reported in the governmental activities column.

   II. The total fund balance for the governmental funds that is reported on the governmental funds balance sheet will not equal the total net assets of governmental activities that is reported on the government-wide statement of net assets.

   a. I only.

   b. II only.

    c. I and II.

    d. Neither I nor II.

2. For the year ended June 30, 20X5, the internal service funds of Stanton Township reported an increase in net assets of $300,000 and ending net assets at June 30, 20X5, of $4,500,000. On the reconciliation of the balance sheet of the governmental funds to the statement of net assets as of June 30, 20X5, what amount should be added?

    a. $300,000.

    b. $4,200,000.

    c. $4,500,000.

    d. $4,800,000.

3. For the year ended June 30, 20X5, the enterprise funds of Stanton Township reported an increase in net assets of $300,000 and ending net assets at June 30, 20X5, of $4,500,000. The enterprise fund also reported net assets—unrestricted of $1,200,000 at June 30, 20X5, on its statement of net assets. On the reconciliation of the balance sheet of the governmental funds to the statement of net assets as of June 30, 20X5, what amount should be added?

    a. $4,200,000.

    b. $5,700,000.

    c. $4,800,000.

    d. $0.

4. Which of the following is true regarding permanent funds?

    a. Permanent funds use modified accrual accounting.

    b. The principal of permanent funds cannot be expended.

    c. Dividend and interest income from permanent fund investments are used to benefit the government and its citizens.

    d. All of the above.

Use the information below to answer questions 5 through 7.

A water and sewer enterprise fund provided you with the following information for the year ended June 30, 20X5:

Customer receipts	$ 500,000
Dividends received from investments in common and preferred stock	25,000
Proceeds from issuance of revenue bonds (used for plant construction)	1,000,000
Proceeds of short-term notes (used to pay operating expenses)	30,000
Capital grant received from state (used for wastewater plant addition)	300,000
Paid interest on revenue bonds	40,000
Paid interest on short-term notes	1,000
Proceeds received from sale of Dell common stock	20,000
Acquired investments in corporate bonds	8,000
Made capital expenditures	600,000
Operating expenses paid	350,000
Depreciation expense for period	50,000

Answer the following questions about the amounts reported on the statement of cash flows for the water and sewer enterprise fund.

5. What amount should be reported for cash flows provided by operating activities?

    a. $150,000.

    b. $175,000.

    c. $134,000.

    d. $100,000.

6. What amount should be reported for cash flows provided by investing activities?

    a. $12,000.

    b. $45,000.

    c. $17,000.

    d. $37,000.

7. What amount should be reported for cash flows provided by capital and related financing activities?

    a. $700,000.

    b. $360,000.

    c. $660,000.

    d. $400,000.

8. Mary Smith donated cash of $1,000,000 to Elizabeth City with the stipulation that the contribution be invested and that earnings from the investment be spent for salaries for the City's symphony orchestra. The contribution was received on June 30, 20X4, and the cash received was invested in bonds on July 1, 20X4. The bonds were acquired at face value and pay interest at 6 percent on January 1 and July 1. At June 30, 20X5, the fair value of the bonds was $995,000. During the year ended June 30, 20X5, $20,000 was provided to the symphony orchestra to help pay salaries. On the statement of fiduciary net assets at June 30, 20X5, what would be the amount reported for net assets held in trust for the symphony orchestra?

    a. $1,060,000.

    b. $1,055,000.

    c. $1,025,000.

    d. $1,035,000.

E18-6 Capital Projects Fund Entries

York established a capital projects fund for the construction of a walkway over Kish Avenue from the courthouse to the parking garage. The estimated cost is $300,000. The county commission agreed to provide a $100,000 grant. A 9 percent, $200,000 bond issue was sold at 102.5. The York City Council awarded a construction contract for $275,000 on March 1, 20X1. The walkway was completed on November 10, 20X1; its actual cost was $282,000. The city council approved payment of the extra cost. The walkway was carpeted at a cost of $7,400. On December 15, 20X1, the city council gave the final approval to pay for the walkway. The fund balance was transferred to the debt service fund.

Required
Prepare entries for the capital projects fund to record the following:

a. Receipt of the county grant, sale of the bonds, and transfer of the bond premium.

b. Issue of the construction contract, actual cost, carpeting, and payment.

c. Closing of the nominal accounts.

d. Transfer of the balance to the debt service fund.

E18-7 Debt Service Fund Entries and Statement

York established a debt service fund to account for the financial resources used to service the bonds issued to finance the walkway (see Exercise 18-6). The 9 percent, $200,000 bond issue was sold at 102.5 on January 1, 20X1. It is a 10-year serial bond issue. The resources to pay the interest and annual principal will be from a property tax levy.

Additional Information

1. The operating budget for 20X1 included estimated revenue of $38,000 and appropriations of $20,000 for principal and $18,000 for interest and an estimated transfer in of $5,000 from the capital projects fund.

2. The property tax levy was for $40,000, and an allowance for uncollectibles of $4,000 was established. Collections totaled $36,000. The remaining taxes were reclassified as delinquent, and the allowance was reduced to $1,000. The bond premium was received from the capital projects fund.

3. The current portion of the serial bonds and the interest due this year were recorded and paid. Other expenses charged to the debt service fund totaled $1,800, and $1,500 was paid.

4. A transfer in of $10,600 was received from the capital projects fund.

5. The nominal accounts were closed.

Required

a. Prepare entries for the debt service fund for 20X1.

b. Prepare a statement of revenues, expenditures, and changes in fund balance for 20X1 for the debt service fund.

E18-8 **Enterprise Fund Entries and Statements**

Augusta has a municipal water and gas utility district (MUD). The trial balance on January 1, 20X1, was as follows:

	Debit	Credit
Cash	$ 92,000	
Accounts Receivable	25,000	
Inventory of Supplies	8,000	
Land	120,000	
Plant and Equipment	480,000	
Accumulated Depreciation		$ 80,000
Vouchers Payable		15,000
Bonds Payable, 6%		500,000
Net Assets:		
Invested in Capital Assets, Net		
of Related Debt		20,000
Unrestricted		110,000
Total	$725,000	$725,000

Additional Information for 20X1

1. Charges to customers for water and gas were $420,000; collections were $432,000.

2. A loan of $30,000 for two years was received from the general fund.

3. The water and gas lines were extended to a new development at a cost of $75,000. The contractor was paid.

4. Supplies were acquired from central stores (internal service fund) for $12,400. Operating expenses were $328,000, and interest expense was $30,000. Payment was made for the interest and the payable to central stores, and $325,000 of the vouchers were paid.

5. Adjusting entries were as follows: for estimated uncollectible accounts receivable, $6,300; depreciation expense, $32,000; supplies expense, $15,200.

Required

a. Prepare entries for the MUD enterprise fund for 20X1, and prepare closing entries.

b. Prepare a statement of net assets for the fund for December 31, 20X1.

c. Prepare a statement of revenues, expenses, and changes in fund net assets for 20X1. Assume that the $500,000 of the 6 percent bonds is related to the net capital assets of land and of plant and equipment.

d. Prepare a statement of cash flows for 20X1.

E18-9 **Interfund Transfers and Transactions**

During 20X8, the following transfers and transactions between funds took place in the City of Matthew.

1. A $12,000 transfer was made on March 1 from the general fund to establish a building maintenance internal service fund. Matthew uses transfer accounts to account for this type of transfer.

2. On April 1, the general fund made an $8,000, six-month loan to the building maintenance service fund.

3. On April 15, $2,400 was transferred from the general fund to the debt service fund to pay interest.

4. On May 5, the Matthew transportation service fund billed the general fund $825 for April services.

Required

a. Prepare journal entries for the general fund and the other fund involved that should be recorded at the time of each transfer or transaction.

b. For each transfer or transaction, prepare the appropriate closing entries for the general fund and the other fund involved for the year ended June 30, 20X8.

E18-10   Internal Service Fund Entries and Statements

Bellevue City's printing shop had the following trial balance on January 1, 20X2:

	Debit	Credit
Cash	$ 24,600	
Due from Other Funds	15,600	
Inventory of Supplies	9,800	
Furniture and Equipment	260,000	
Accumulated Depreciation		$ 50,000
Vouchers Payable		12,000
Net Assets:		
Invested in Capital Assets		
(no related debt)		210,000
Unrestricted		38,000
Total	$310,000	$310,000

Additional Information for 20X2

1. During 20X2, the printing shop acquired supplies for $96,000, furniture for $1,500, and a copier for $3,200.

2. Printing jobs billed to other funds amounted to $292,000; cash received from other funds, $287,300; costs of printing jobs, $204,000, including $84,000 of supplies; operating expenses, $38,000, including $8,400 of supplies; depreciation expense, $23,000; and vouchers paid, $243,000.

Required

a. Prepare entries for the printing shop for 20X2, including closing entries.

b. Prepare a statement of net assets for the fund on December 31, 20X2. No debt is related to the year-end amount of the fund's capital assets.

c. Prepare a statement of revenues, expenses, and changes in fund net assets for 20X2.

d. Prepare a statement of cash flows for 20X2.

E18-11   Multiple-Choice Questions on Government-wide Financial Statements

Items 1 and 2 are based on the following:

Mountain View City is preparing its government-wide financial statements for the year. As of the year end, the city has determined the following information for its capital assets, exclusive of its infrastructure assets:

Cost of capital assets acquired by governmental funds	$1,450,000
Accumulated depreciation on the capital assets	120,000
Outstanding debt related to the capital assets	780,000

1. On the government-wide statement of net assets for the year-end, what amount should be reported for capital assets in the Governmental Activities column?

   a. $550,000.

   b. $780,000.

   c. $1,330,000.

   d. $1,450,000.

2. On the government-wide statement of net assets for the year-end, what amount should be reported in the net assets section for the capital assets?

    a. $550,000.

    b. $780,000.

    c. $1,330,000.

    d. $1,450,000.

3. In accordance with GASB 34, "Basic Financial Statements—and Management's Discussion and Analysis—for State and Local Governments," which of the following statements is correct regarding the reporting of internal service funds?

    I. The internal service fund should be discretely presented as part of the business-type activities of the government.

    II. The internal service fund should be blended into the governmental activities.

    a. I only.

    b. II only.

    c. I and II.

    d. Neither I nor II.

Items 4 and 5 are based on the following:

During the year, the City of Vero Beach sold bonds in its capital projects fund. The 6 percent, $500,000 par bonds were sold for 102. The effective interest rate was 5 percent.

4. How should the bonds be reported in the reconciliation schedule for the statement of revenues, expenditures, and changes in fund balance?

    a. A decrease of $500,000 for the par value of the bonds.

    b. A decrease of $30,000 for the interest paid on the bonds.

    c. A decrease of $510,000 for the selling price of the bonds.

    d. Not shown in this reconciliation schedule.

5. How should an interest adjustment be shown in the reconciliation of the balance sheet of governmental funds to the statement of net assets for the year?

    a. A decrease of $30,000.

    b. A decrease of $25,000.

    c. A decrease of $5,000.

    d. Not shown in this reconciliation schedule.

6. For which of the following should the accrual basis of accounting be used to measure financial performance?

	General Fund	Internal Service Fund	Government-wide Financial Statements
a.	Yes	Yes	Yes
b.	Yes	No	Yes
c.	No	No	No
d.	No	Yes	Yes

7. The City of Hastings has a separately elected school board that administers the city's schools. The city council must approve the school district's budget and tax levy. The school district's financial results should be reported in Hastings's financial statements in which way?

    a. Included only as schedules in the footnotes of Hastings's financial reports.

    b. Blended into Hastings's financial reports.

    c. Discretely presented in Hastings's financial reports.

    d. Not required to be presented in Hastings's financial reports.

8. Glen Valley City has properly adopted the modified approach to account for its infrastructure assets. Which of the following statements is correct about accounting for these infrastructure assets on the government-wide statement of activities?

    I. Depreciation expense should be computed based on the assets' estimated useful lives and reported under the governmental activities column of the city's statement of activities.

II. The amount of the expenditures made for the infrastructure assets, except for additions and improvements, should be expensed in the period incurred.

    a. I only.

    b. II only.

    c. I and II.

    d. Neither I nor II.

9. A statement of cash flows is required for

	General Fund	Enterprise Fund	Government-wide Entity
a.	Yes	Yes	Yes
b.	No	Yes	Yes
c.	No	Yes	No
d.	Yes	No	No

10. Which of the following is reported as a restriction of net assets in the net assets section of the statement of net assets?

    a. A reservation of the fund balance in the general fund for $10,000 of encumbrances.

    b. A requirement in the permanent funds that the $100,000 principal of a bequest be maintained.

    c. A governing board decision that $15,000 of general fund resources should be reserved for planning for a city park.

    d. A governing board allocation of $4,000 to establish an internal services fund.

Problems

P18-12   Capital Projects Fund Entries and Balance Sheet [AICPA Adapted]

The following information pertains to Elizabeth Township's construction and financing of a new administration center:

Estimated cost of project	$9,000,000
Project financing:	
State entitlement grant	3,000,000
General obligation bonds:	
Face amount	6,000,000
Stated interest rate	6%
Issue date	December 1, 20X6
Maturity date	10 years into the future

During Elizabeth's year ended June 30, 20X7, the following events affected the capital projects fund established to account for this project:

July 1, 20X6	The capital projects fund borrowed $300,000 from the general fund for preliminary expenses.
July 9, 20X6	The fund received an invoice for engineering and planning costs of $200,000 from Dunn Associates. The invoice was paid on July 16.
December 1, 20X6	The bonds were sold at 101. Total proceeds were retained by the capital projects fund.
December 1, 20X6	The entitlement grant was formally approved by the state.
April 30, 20X7	A $7,000,000 contract was executed with Craft Construction Company, the general contractors, for the major portion of the project. The contract provides that Elizabeth will withhold 4% of all billings pending satisfactory completion of the project.
May 9, 20X7	$1,000,000 of the state grant was received.
June 10, 20X7	The $300,000 borrowed from the general fund was repaid.
June 30, 20X7	Progress billing of $1,200,000 was received from Craft.

Elizabeth uses encumbrance accounting for budgetary control. Unencumbered appropriations lapse at the end of the year.

Required

a. Prepare journal entries in the administration center capital projects fund to record the preceding transactions.

b. Prepare the June 30, 20X7, closing entries for the administration center capital projects fund.

c. Prepare the administration center capital projects fund balance sheet at June 30, 20X7.

P18-13 **Adjusting Entries for General Fund [AICPA Adapted]**

On June 30, 20X2, the end of the fiscal year, the Wadsworth Park District prepared the following trial balance for the general fund:

	Debit	Credit
Cash	$ 47,250	
Taxes Receivable—Current	31,800	
Allowance for Uncollectibles—Current		$ 1,800
Temporary Investments	11,300	
Inventory of Supplies	11,450	
Buildings	1,300,000	
Estimated Revenues Control	1,007,000	
Appropriations Control		1,000,000
Revenue—State Grants		300,000
Bonds Payable		1,000,000
Vouchers Payable		10,200
Expenditures	848,200	
Debt Service from Current Funds	130,000	
Capital Outlays (Equipment)	22,000	
Revenue—Taxes		1,008,200
Fund Balance—Unreserved		81,800
Budgetary Fund Balance—Unreserved		7,000
Total	$3,409,000	$3,409,000

An examination of the records disclosed the following information:

1. The recorded estimate of losses for the current year taxes receivable was considered to be adequate.

2. The local governmental unit gave the park district 20 acres of land to be used for a new community park. The unrecorded estimated value of the land was $50,000. In addition, a state grant of $300,000 was received, and the full amount was used in payment of contracts pertaining to the construction of the park buildings. Purchases of playground equipment costing $22,000 were paid from general funds.

3. Five years ago, a 4 percent, 10-year sinking fund bond issue in the amount of $1,000,000 for constructing park buildings was sold; it is still outstanding. Interest on the issue is payable at maturity. Budgetary requirements of a contribution of $130,000 to the debt service fund were met. Of this amount, $100,000 represents the fifth equal contribution for principal repayment.

4. Outstanding purchase orders not recorded in the accounts at year-end totaled $2,800.

5. A physical inventory of supplies at year-end revealed $6,500 of the supplies on hand.

6. Except where indicated to the contrary, all recordings were made in the general fund.

Required

Prepare the adjusting entries to correct the general fund records.

P18-14   **Adjusting Entries for General Fund [AICPA Adapted]**

You have been engaged to examine the financial statements of Fairfield for the year ended June 30, 20X2. You discover that all transactions were recorded in the general fund. The general fund trial balance as of June 30, 20X2, was:

	Debit	Credit
Cash	$ 16,800	
Short-term Investments	40,000	
Accounts Receivable	11,500	
Taxes Receivable—Current Year	30,000	
Tax Anticipation Notes Payable		$ 50,000
Appropriations Control		400,000
Expenditures	382,000	
Estimated Revenues Control	320,000	
Revenue		360,000
General Property	85,400	
Bonds Payable	52,000	
Fund Balance—Unreserved		207,700
Budgetary Fund Balance—Unreserved	80,000	
Total	$1,017,700	$1,017,700

Your audit disclosed the following additional information:

1. The accounts receivable and revenue include $1,500 due to the city's water utility for the sale of its scrap.

2. The balance in Taxes Receivable—Current Year is now considered delinquent, and the town estimates that $24,000 will be uncollectible.

3. On June 30, 20X2, the town retired, at face value, 6 percent general obligation serial bonds totaling $40,000. The bonds were issued five years ago, at face value of $200,000. Interest paid during the year ended June 30, 20X2, was charged to Bonds Payable.

4. During the year, supplies totaling $128,000 were purchased and charged to Expenditures. The town conducted a physical inventory of supplies on hand for June 30, 20X2, which disclosed that supplies totaling $84,000 had been used. Fairfield uses the consumption method of accounting for inventories.

5. Expenditures for the year ended June 30, 20X2, included $11,200 applicable to purchase orders issued in the prior year. Outstanding purchase orders as of June 30, 20X2, not recorded in the accounts amounted to $17,500. Fairfield used the nonlapsing method.

6. On June 28, 20X2, the State Revenue Department informed the town that its share of a state-collected, locally shared tax would be $34,000.

7. During the year, equipment with a book value of $7,900 was removed from service and sold for $4,600. In addition, new equipment costing $90,000 was purchased. The transactions were recorded in General Property.

8. During the year, the town received a donation of 100 acres of land for use as an industrial park. The land had a value of $125,000. No recording of this donation has been made.

Required

a. Prepare a formal reclassification and adjusting journal entries for the general fund as of June 30, 20X2.

b. Prepare closing entries for the general fund as of June 30, 20X2.

P18-15   **Entries for Funds [AICPA Adapted]**

The following transactions represent practical situations frequently encountered in accounting for municipal governments. Each transaction is independent of the others.

1. The Green Acre City Council adopted a general operating budget in which revenue is estimated at $695,000 and anticipated expenditures are $650,000.

2. Taxes of $160,000 are levied for the special revenue fund of Hiawatha. One percent is estimated to be uncollectible.

3. On July 25, 20X2, office supplies estimated to cost $2,390 are ordered by Ivyton, which operates on the calendar-year basis and does not use a perpetual inventory system. The supplies are received on August 9, 20X2, accompanied by an invoice for $2,500.

4. On October 10, 20X2, the general fund of Junction City repaid to the utility fund a loan of $1,000 plus $40 interest. The loan had been made earlier in the fiscal year.

5. A prominent citizen died and left 10 acres of undeveloped land to Kezar Falls for a future school site. The donor's cost of the land was $55,000. The fair market value of the land at the date of death was $90,000.

6. On March 1, 20X2, Lakeland issued 6 percent special assessment bonds, payable March 1, 20X7, at face value of $90,000. The city is obligated in the event the property owners default. Interest is payable annually. Lakeland, which operates on the calendar-year basis, will use the proceeds to finance a curbing project. On October 29, 20X2, the cost of the completed project was $84,000. The contract had not been encumbered or paid.

7. A citizen of Montague donated common stock valued at $32,000 to the city. Under the terms of an agreement, the principal amount is not to be expended. Income from the stock must be used for college scholarships. On December 14, 20X2, dividends of $1,100 are received.

8. On February 1, 20X3, the City of Northstar, which operates on a calendar-year basis, issued 6 percent general obligation bonds with a face value of $300,000. Interest is payable annually on February 1. Total proceeds were $308,000; the premium was transferred to the debt service fund for ultimate payment of principal. The bond issue was floated to finance the construction of an addition to the city hall, estimated to cost $300,000. On December 30, 20X3, the addition was completed at a cost of $297,000, all of which was paid.

Required
For each of the transactions described, prepare the necessary journal entries for all funds involved. Indicate the fund in which each entry would be made by using the following format:

Fund	Journal Entry

P18-16 Entries for Funds [AICPA Adapted]

Olivia Village was recently incorporated and began financial operations on July 1, 20X2, the beginning of its fiscal year. The following transactions occurred during this first fiscal year, July 1, 20X2, to June 30, 20X3:

1. The village council adopted a budget for general operations for the fiscal year ending June 30, 20X3. Revenue was estimated at $400,000. Legal authorizations for budgeted expenditures totaled $394,000.

2. Property taxes were levied in the amount of $390,000; 2 percent of this amount was estimated to prove uncollectible. These taxes are available as of the date of levy to finance current expenditures.

3. During the year, a village resident donated marketable securities valued at $50,000 to the village under the terms of a trust agreement. Those terms stipulated that the principal amount be kept intact. The use of revenue generated by the securities is restricted to financing college scholarships for needy students. Revenue earned and received on these marketable securities amounted to $5,500 through June 30, 20X3.

4. A general fund transfer of $5,000 was made to establish an internal service fund to provide for a permanent investment in inventory.

5. The village decided to install lighting in the village park through a special assessment project authorized to do so at a cost of $75,000. The city is obligated if the property owners default on their special assessments. Special assessment bonds were issued in the amount of $72,000, and the first year's special assessment of $24,000 was levied against the village's property owners. The remaining $3,000 for the project will be contributed from the village's general fund.

6. The special assessments for the lighting project are due over a three-year period, and the first year's assessments of $24,000 were collected. The $3,000 transfer from the village's general fund was received by the lighting capital projects fund.

7. A contract for $75,000 was let for the installation of the lighting. The capital projects fund was encumbered for the contract. On June 30, 20X3, the contract was completed and the contractor was paid.

8. During the year, the internal service fund purchased various supplies at a cost of $1,900.

9. Cash collections recorded by the general fund during the year were as follows:

Current property taxes	$386,000
Licenses and permit fees	7,000

The allowance for estimated uncollectible taxes is adjusted to $4,000.

10. The village council decided to build a village hall at an estimated cost of $500,000 to replace space occupied in rented facilities. The village does not record project authorizations. It was decided that general obligation bonds bearing interest at 6 percent would be issued. On June 30, 20X3, the bonds were issued at face value of $500,000, payable in 20 years. No contracts have been signed for this project, and no expenditures have been made, nor has an annual operating budget been prepared.

11. A fire truck was purchased for $15,000 and the voucher was approved and paid by the general fund. This expenditure was previously encumbered for $15,000.

Required

Prepare journal entries to record properly each of these transactions in the appropriate fund or funds of Olivia Village for the fiscal year ended June 30, 20X3.

Use the following funds: general fund, capital projects fund, internal service fund, and private-purpose trust fund. Each journal entry should be numbered to correspond to the transactions. Do not prepare closing entries for any fund. Your answer sheet should be organized using the following format:

Fund	Journal Entry

P18-17 Entries to Adjust Account Balances [AICPA Adapted]

You have been assigned by the town of Papillion to examine its June 30, 20X1, balance sheet. You are the first CPA to be engaged by the town, and you find that acceptable methods of municipal accounting have not been employed. The town clerk stated that the books had not been closed and presented the following preclosing trial balance of the general fund as of June 30, 20X1:

	Debit	Credit
Cash	$150,000	
Taxes Receivable—Current Year	59,200	
Allowance for Uncollectibles—Current		$ 18,000
Taxes Receivable—Delinquent	8,000	
Allowance for Uncollectibles—Delinquent		10,200
Estimated Revenues Control	310,000	
Appropriations Control		348,000
Donated Land	27,000	
Expenditures—Building Addition Constructed	50,000	
Expenditures—Serial Bonds Paid	16,000	
Other Expenditures	280,000	
Special Assessment Bonds Payable		100,000
Revenue		354,000
Accounts Payable		26,000
Fund Balance—Unreserved		82,000
Budgetary Fund Balance—Unreserved	38,000	
Total	$938,200	$938,200

Additional Information

1. The estimated losses of $18,000 for current-year taxes receivable were determined to be a reasonable estimate. The delinquent taxes allowance account should be adjusted to $8,000, the amount of the remaining delinquent taxes.

2. Included in the Revenue account is a credit of $27,000, representing the value of land donated by the state as a grant-in-aid for construction of a municipal park.

3. Operating supplies ordered in the prior fiscal year and chargeable to that year were received, recorded, and consumed in July 20X0. The outstanding purchase orders for these supplies, which were not recorded in the accounts on June 30, 20X0, amounted to $8,800. The vendors' invoices for these supplies totaled $9,400. Appropriations lapse one year after the end of the fiscal year for which they are made.

4. Outstanding purchase orders on June 30, 20X1, for operating supplies totaled $2,100. These purchase orders were not recorded on the books.

5. The special assessment bonds were sold in June 20X1 to finance a street-paving project. No contracts have been signed for this project, and no expenditures have been made from the capital projects fund. The city is obligated for the bonds if the property owners default.

6. The balance in the Revenue account includes credits for $20,000 for a note issued to a bank to obtain cash in anticipation of tax collections and for $1,000 for the sale of scrap iron from the town's water plant. The note was still outstanding on June 30, 20X1. The operations of the water plant are accounted for in the water fund.

7. The Expenditures—Building Addition Constructed account balance is the cost of an addition to the town hall building. This addition was constructed and completed in June 20X1. The general fund recorded the payment as authorized.

8. The Expenditures—Serial Bonds Paid account reflects the annual retirement of general obligation bonds issued to finance the construction of the town hall. Interest payments of $7,000 for the bond issue are included in other expenditures.

Required

a. Prepare the formal adjusting and closing journal entries for the general fund for the fiscal year ended June 30, 20X1.

b. The preceding information disclosed by your examination was recorded only in the general fund even though other funds were involved. Prepare the formal adjusting journal entries for any other funds involved.

P18-18 **Capital Projects Fund Entries and Statements**

During the fiscal year ended June 30, 20X3, West City Council authorizes construction of a new city hall building and the sale of serial bonds to finance the construction. The following transactions, related to financing and constructing the city hall, occur during fiscal 20X3:

1. On August 1, 20X2, West issues $5,000,000 of serial bonds for $5,080,000. Interest is payable annually, and the first retirement of $500,000 is due on July 31, 20X7. The premium is transferred to the debt service fund.

2. The old city hall, which had a recorded cost of $650,000, is torn down. The cost of razing the old building is $45,000, net of salvage value. This cost was included in the capital budget but was not encumbered. The cost is vouchered and paid.

3. West signs a contract with Roth Construction Company to build the city hall for $4,500,000. The contract cost is to be encumbered. Construction is to be completed during fiscal 20X4.

4. Roth Construction Company bills West $2,000,000 for construction completed during fiscal 20X3. Ten percent of the billings will be retained until final acceptance of the new city hall. The billing less the retainage was paid during the fiscal year.

Required

a. For each of these transactions, prepare the necessary journal entries for all the funds involved. Indicate the fund in which the entry is made by giving its initials in the left margin: CPF (capital projects fund) or DSF (debt service fund). Give the closing entries for the capital projects fund.

b. Prepare a balance sheet for the capital projects fund at June 30, 20X3.

c. Prepare a statement of revenues, expenditures, and changes in fund balance for the capital projects fund for the fiscal year ended June 30, 20X3.

P18-19 **Recording Entries in Various Funds [AICPA Adapted]**

The following information relates to Vane City during the year ended December 31, 20X8:

1. On October 31, 20X8, to finance the construction of a city hall annex, Vane issued 8 percent, 10-year general obligation bonds at their face value of $800,000. A contractor's bid of $750,000 was accepted for the construction of the annex. By year-end, one-third of the contract was completed at a cost of $246,000, all of which was paid on January 5, 20X9.

2. Vane collected $109,000 from hotel room taxes, restricted for tourist promotion, in a special revenue fund. The fund incurred and paid $81,000 for general promotions and $22,000 for a motor vehicle. Estimated revenues for 20X8 were $112,000, while appropriations were expected to be $108,000.

3. General fund revenues of $313,500 for 20X8 were transferred to a debt service fund and used to repay $300,000 of 9 percent, 15-year term bonds, which matured in 20X8, and to repay $13,500 of matured interest. The bond proceeds were used to construct a citizens' center.

4. At December 31, 20X8, Vane was responsible for $83,000 of outstanding encumbrances in its general fund. The city uses the nonlapsing method to account for its outstanding encumbrances.

5. Vane uses the purchases method to account for supplies in the general fund. At December 31, 20X8, an inventory indicated that the supplies inventory was $42,000. At December 31, 20X7, the supplies inventory was $45,000.

Required

For each numbered item, make all the journal entries for the year ended December 31, 20X8, in all funds affected. Before each journal entry, identify the fund in which the journal entry is made. *Do not make any adjusting/closing entries for items (1), (2), and (3).*

P18-20 **Matching Questions Involving Various Funds**

The numbered items listed on the left consist of a variety of transactions that occur in a municipality. The lettered items on the right consist of various ways to record the transactions. Select the appropriate method for recording each transaction. Some transactions have more than one correct answer. Some responses under Recording of Transactions may be used once, more than once, or not at all.

Transactions	Recording of Transactions
1. Term bond proceeds of $100,000 were received by the capital projects fund.	A. Debit expenditures in the general fund
2. Equipment costing $50,000 was acquired by the water utility, an enterprise fund.	B. Debit general operating expenses in the general fund
	C. Debit equipment in the enterprise fund
3. Land with a fair value of $500,000 was donated to the city to be used as a municipal park.	D. Debit equipment in the general fund
	E. Debit building in the capital projects fund
4. Central stores, an internal service fund, received a transfer in of $750,000 from the general fund.	F. Debit general operating expenses in the enterprise fund
	G. Debit expenditures in the capital projects fund
5. General obligation serial bonds of $250,000 matured and were paid by the debt service fund.	H. Credit building in the capital projects fund
	I. Debit expenditures in the debt service fund
6. Expenditures of $5,000,000 were incurred by the capital projects fund to construct a new city hall annex. The project was started and completed within the fiscal year.	J. Credit revenue in the private-purpose trust fund
	K. Credit revenue in the capital projects fund
	L. Credit other financing sources in the capital projects fund
7. The water utility, an enterprise fund, billed the mayor's office $200 for water usage.	M. Credit transfers in in the internal services fund
8. The mayor's office received the billing in item 7.	N. Debit revenue in the agency fund
9. The tax agency fund received $250,000 of tax revenues that are to be distributed to the school districts within the municipality.	O. Credit due to other governmental units in the agency fund
	P. Credit revenue in the agency fund
	Q. Credit revenue in the enterprise fund
10. Salaries and wages of $25,000 were incurred by the water utility enterprise fund.	R. Reported only on the government-wide financial statements

P18-21   Questions on Fund Transactions [AICPA Adapted]

The following information relates to Dane City during its fiscal year ended December 31, 20X2:

1. On October 31, 20X2, to finance the construction of a city hall annex, Dane issued 8 percent, 10-year general obligation bonds at their face value of $600,000. Construction expenditures during the period equaled $364,000.

2. Dane reported $109,000 from hotel room taxes, restricted for tourist promotion, in a special revenue fund. The fund paid $81,000 for general promotions and $22,000 for a motor vehicle.

3. Dane transferred 20X2 general fund revenues of $104,500 to a debt service fund and used them to repay $100,000 of 9 percent, 15-year term bonds, and to pay $4,500 of interest. The bonds were used to acquire a citizens' center.

4. At December 31, 20X2, as a consequence of past services, city firefighters had accumulated entitlements for compensated absences of $86,000. General fund resources available at December 31, 20X2, are expected to be used to settle $17,000 of this amount, and $69,000 is expected to be paid out of future general fund resources.

5. At December 31, 20X2, Dane was responsible for $83,000 of outstanding general fund encumbrances, including the $8,000 for supplies that follow.

6. Dane uses the purchases method to account for supplies. The following information relates to supplies:

Inventory—1/1/X2	$ 39,000
—12/31/X2	42,000
Encumbrances outstanding—1/1/X2	6,000
—12/31/X2	8,000
Purchase orders during 20X2	190,000
Amount credited to vouchers payable during 20X2	181,000

Required

For items 1 through 10, determine the amounts based solely on the preceding information.

1. What is the amount of 20X2 general fund transfers out?

2. How much should be reported in 20X2 general fund liabilities from entitlements for compensated absences?

3. What is the 20X2 reserved amount of the general fund balance?

4. What is the 20X2 capital projects fund balance?

5. What is the 20X2 fund balance on the special revenue fund for tourist promotion?

6. What is the amount of 20X2 debt service fund expenditures?

7. What amount should be included in the government-wide financial statements for the cost of long-term assets acquired in 20X2?

8. What amount stemming from the 20X2 transactions and events decreased the long-term debt liabilities reported in the government-wide financial statements?

9. Using the purchases method, what is the amount of 20X2 supplies expenditures?

10. What was the total amount of 20X2 supplies encumbrances?

P18-22   Matching Questions Involving the Statement of Cash Flows for a Proprietary Fund

The numbered items on the left consist of a variety of transactions that occurred in the water utility enterprise fund of Jeffersen City for the year ended June 30, 20X9. Items A, B, C, and D on the right represent the four categories of cash flows that are reported on the statement of cash flows for proprietary funds. Item E is for transactions that are not reported on the statement of cash flows. Assume that the direct method is used for disclosing cash flows from operating activities. For each transaction, select the appropriate letter to indicate where that transaction should be disclosed on the statement of cash flows or whether that item would not be reported on the statement of cash flows.

Transactions	Categories of Disclosure
1. Received $5,000,000 from revenue bonds to be used for construction of water treatment plant.	A. Operating activities
	B. Noncapital financing activities
2. Paid $500,000 of salaries to employees of the water utility.	C. Capital and related financing activities
	D. Investing activities
3. Received $1,000,000 state grant restricted for construction of water treatment plant.	E. Not reported on the statement of cash flows
4. Collected $2,500,000 of accounts receivable from households for use of city water.	
5. Depreciation expense for the year amounted to $300,000.	
6. Received $75,000 state grant restricted to the maintenance of fixed assets.	
7. Paid $250,000 of interest on the revenue bonds issued in item 1.	
8. Borrowed $125,000 from a local bank on revenue anticipation notes payable.	
9. Paid $5,000 of interest on the notes payable in item 8.	
10. Spent $1,200,000 of the revenue bonds for construction of the water treatment plant.	
11. Paid $5,000 fire insurance premium on June 30, 20X9, for next year's insurance coverage.	
12. Uncollected accounts receivable amounted to $135,000 on June 31, 20X9.	
13. Acquired $250,000 of state bonds as an investment of idle funds.	
14. Received $7,500 of interest on the state bonds in item 13.	
15. Received a $375,000 contribution from the city's general fund to be used for the construction of water treatment plant.	

P18-23   **Matching Questions Involving the Statement of Revenues, Expenditures, and Changes in Fund Balance for a Capital Projects Fund and a Debt Service Fund**

The numbered items on the left consist of a variety of transactions and events that occurred in the capital projects and debt service funds of Walton City for the year ended June 30, 20X9. Items A, B, and C on the right represent three categories that are reported of the statement of revenues, expenditures, and changes in fund balance for capital projects and debt service funds. Item D is for transactions that are not reported on the statement of revenues, expenditures, and changes in fund balance for either debt service or capital projects funds. For each transaction, select the appropriate letter to indicate where that transaction should be reported on the statement of revenues, expenditures, and changes in fund balance or whether that item would not be reported on the statement.

Transactions/Events	Categories of Disclosure
1. The capital projects fund received the proceeds of general obligation bonds to be used for construction of a new courthouse. 2. The capital projects fund accepted the lowest bid for the construction of the courthouse. 3. The capital projects fund received resources from the city's general fund to be used in the construction of the courthouse. 4. The bonds in item 1 were rold at a premium. The capital projects fund transferred the premium to the debt service fund. Indicate how this transaction should be reported by the capital projects fund. 5. During the year ended June 30, 20X9, courthouse construction was completed. 6. In addition to the resources provided by the general obligation bonds and the general fund, the capital projects fund also received a state grant that it used to construct the courthouse. 7. The general fund of the city transferred a portion of the property tax collections to the debt service fund to be used to pay the principal and interest of the general obligation bonds issued in item 1. 8. The debt service fund acquired investments with part of the resources provided by the general fund. 9. Interest was earned on the investments acquired in item 8. 10. The debt service fund received the bond premium from the capital projects fund. 11. The debt service fund paid semiannual interest on the general obligation bonds on March 1, 20X9. 12. The debt service fund used a local bank to be its fiscal agent with regard to the recordkeeping activities related to the general obligation bonds issued in item 1. The bank charged a fee for this service. 13. As of June 30, 20X9, unmatured interest for four months was due on the general obligation bonds issued in item 1. Resources to pay this interest will be transferred to the debt service fund in the next fiscal year.	A. Revenues B. Expenditures C. Other financing sources and uses D. Not reported on the statement of revenues, expenditures, and changes in fund balance

P18-24   Question on Fund Transactions [AICPA Adapted]

Items 1 through 10 in the left-hand column represent various transactions pertaining to a municipality that uses encumbrance accounting. Items 11 through 20, also listed in the left-hand column, represent the funds and accounts used by the municipality. To the right of these items is a list of possible accounting and reporting methods.

Required

a. For each of the municipality's transactions (items 1 through 10), select the appropriate method for recording the transaction. A method of recording the transactions may be selected once, more than once, or not at all.

b. For each of the municipality's funds, accounts, and other items (items 11 to 20), select the appropriate method of accounting and reporting. An accounting and reporting method may be selected once, more than once, or not at all.

Transactions	Recording of Transactions
1. General obligation bonds were issued at par. 2. Approved purchase orders were issued for supplies. 3. Supplies in item 2 were received and the related invoices were approved.	A. Credit Appropriations Control B. Credit Budgetary Fund Balance—Unreserved C. Credit Expenditures Control

(*continued*)

4. General fund salaries and wages were incurred.
5. The internal service fund had interfund billings.
6. Revenues were earned from a previously awarded grant.
7. Property taxes were collected in advance.
8. Appropriations were recorded on adoption of the budget.
9. Short-term financing was received from a bank, secured by the city's taxing power.
10. There was an excess of estimated inflows over estimated outflows.

D. Credit Deferred Revenues
E. Credit Interfund Revenues
F. Credit Tax Anticipation Notes Payable
G. Credit Other Financing Sources
H. Credit Other Financing Uses
I. Debit Appropriations Control
J. Debit Deferred Revenues
K. Debit Encumbrances Control
L. Debit Expenditures Control

Funds and Accounts	Accounting and Reporting
11. Enterprise fund fixed assets.	A. Accounted for in a fiduciary fund
12. Capital projects fund.	B. Accounted for in a proprietary fund
13. Permanent fund.	C. Accounts for permanent endowments that can be used for government programs
14. Infrastructure fixed assets.	D. Reported as an other financing use
15. Enterprise fund cash.	E. Accounted for in a special assessment fund
16. General fund.	F. Accounts for major construction activities
17. Agency fund cash.	G. Accounts for property tax revenues
18. Transfer out from the general fund to the internal service fund.	H. Accounts for payment of interest and principal on tax-supported debt
19. Special revenue fund (a major fund).	I. Accounts for revenues from earmarked sources to finance designated activities
20. Debt service fund (a major fund).	J. Reported in government-wide statements

P18-25 Major Fund Tests

The City of Somerset has the following fund information:

Fund	Assets	Liabilities	Revenues	Expenditures (Expenses)
General	$1,320,400	$ 878,300	$4,620,000	$4,550,000
Special revenue	27,000	19,000	327,000	328,000
Capital project—library	450,000	38,000	460,000	418,000
Capital project—arena	28,000	16,000	41,000	55,800
Debt service	41,000	-0-	331,000	290,000
Permanent	246,000	-0-	11,000	18,000
Enterprise—electric	2,640,000	1,800,700	289,000	245,000
Enterprise—water	1,356,000	1,100,000	329,000	298,000

Required

Apply the criteria specified in GASB 34 to determine which of these funds meets the major fund reporting criteria.

P18-26 Reconciliation Schedules

The City of Sycamore is preparing its financial reports for the year and has requested that you prepare the reconciliation schedules to accompany its government-wide financial statements based on the following information:

1. The fund balances reported in the five governmental funds as of the end of the fiscal year total $888,400. The fund balances in governmental funds at the beginning of the year totaled $379,000.

2. The city has estimated its depreciation on capital assets to be $187,000 for the period. The city expended a total of $287,000 in capital outlays from the governmental funds. At year-end, the capital assets, net of depreciation, totaled $4,329,000. The internal service fund reported $18,000 of net capital assets. Total accumulated depreciation at year-end was $1,208,000.

3. The internal service fund reports $178,000 in total assets and $141,000 in total liabilities. The internal service fund reported $48,000 of revenues and $39,000 of expenses during the year.

4. The debt service fund paid $40,000 in interest during the year. Bonds with a face value of $500,000 and a coupon rate of 8 percent were sold at the beginning of the year at $460,000 for an effective interest rate of 10 percent. Interest is paid annually on the last day of the fiscal year. The bonds were sold to provide current financial resources for the governmental funds.

5. The permanent fund recorded interest received of $4,000 under the modified accrual basis of measurement. If the accrual basis of measurement had been used in the fund, an additional $1,000 of interest revenue would have been earned.

Required

a. Prepare a reconciliation schedule of the balance sheet of the governmental funds to the statement of net assets.

b. Prepare a reconciliation schedule of the statement of revenues, expenditures, and changes in fund balance of governmental funds to the statement of activities.

P18-27 **True/False Questions**

1. The budgetary comparison schedule in the government-wide financial statements requires only the final budget for the period and the actual amounts for the period.

2. The accrual basis of accounting is used in the government-wide financial statements.

3. A component unit of a primary government is a unit that is related to the primary government but is not financially accountable to the primary government.

4. The statement of net assets in the government-wide financial statements requires the net assets to be segregated as follows: reserved net assets (for items such as encumbrances and inventories) and unreserved net assets.

5. A major governmental fund that must be separately disclosed in the government-wide financial statements would be a fund that composed 5 percent of the total of the governmental funds.

6. Permanent governmental funds account for resources that have a principal that must be maintained and whose earnings are available for any government program that benefits all citizens.

7. The government unit's infrastructure and other fixed assets are reported on the government-wide statement of net assets.

8. The internal service fund is a proprietary fund and is not, therefore, shown in the Governmental Activities column of the government-wide statement of net assets.

9. In the reconciliation schedule for the statement of net assets, to reconcile from the net assets reported in the governmental funds to the net assets of governmental activities, capital assets used in governmental activities would be added.

10. In the reconciliation schedule for the statement of revenues, expenditures, and changes in fund balance, to reconcile from the net change in fund balances—governmental funds to the change in net assets of governmental activities, bond proceeds would be added back.

11. In the government-wide statement of activities, transfers between governmental and business-type funds must be reported as part of the change in net assets.

12. In the government-wide statement of activities, depreciation of fixed assets would equal the amount of the expenditures for assets made in the governmental funds.

13. The Management's Discussion and Analysis is a recommended but voluntary disclosure in the government-wide financial statements.

14. The government-wide statement of net assets includes the fiduciary funds of the government unit.

15. The format of the government-wide statement of activities is based on the programs of the government entity rather than the type of revenues of the government entity.

P18-28 **Determining Whether a Special Revenue Fund Is a Major Fund**

The City of Elmtree is preparing its financial statements for the year ended December 31, 20X2, and has asked for your assistance in determining whether its special revenue fund is a major or a nonmajor fund for the financial statements of its governmental funds. The city has provided the following information:

Items	Totals for Governmental Funds	Totals for Governmental and Enterprise Funds
Assets	$50,000,000	$80,000,000
Liabilities	22,000,000	37,000,000
Revenues	70,000,000	95,000,000
Expenditures/expenses	60,000,000	82,000,000

The special revenue fund reported the following amounts at December 31, 20X2 (assets and liabilities), and for the year ended December 31, 20X2 (revenues and expenditures):

Assets	$4,100,000
Liabilities	3,900,000
Revenues	6,700,000
Expenditures	6,500,000

Required
Determine whether the special revenue fund of Elmtree is a major fund for the 20X2 financial statements of the city's governmental funds.

P18-29 **Preparation of a Statement of Net Assets for a Governmental Entity**

Gibson City reported the following items at December 31, 20X2. It has no component units and does not depreciate its infrastructure fixed assets. All bonds—general obligation bonds and revenue—were issued to acquire capital assets. As of December 31, 20X2, net assets of $25,000 were restricted for road maintenance in special revenue funds, and net assets of $30,000 were restricted for debt service. Cash of $5,000 was restricted in business-type activities for plant maintenance.

	Governmental Activities	Business-Type Activities
Assets:		
Cash and cash equivalents	$ 68,000	$28,000
Taxes receivable (net)	52,000	
Accounts receivable (net)		12,000
Due from governmental activities		5,000
Inventories	10,000	7,000
Investments	25,000	15,000
Capital assets:		
Land	100,000	50,000
Infrastructure	60,000	
Other depreciable assets (net)	75,000	45,000
Liabilities:		
Vouchers payable	32,000	4,000
Accrued interest payable	1,500	2,000
Due to business-type activities	5,000	
Revenue bonds payable		80,000
General obligation bonds payable	60,000	

Required
Using the information provided, prepare in good form a statement of net assets for Gibson City at December 31, 20X2.

Kaplan CPA
Review

KAPLAN

CPA EDUCATION

Kaplan CPA Review Simulation on Governmental Accounting and Reporting

Access to the online CPA Simulation can be attained by visiting the text's Website at www.mhhe.com/baker7e.

Situation

The City of Clarksville (Clarksville) is incorporated and has a December 31 year-end. The budget is approved by the City Council (Council) annually. For internal reporting purposes, Clarksville uses the modified accrual basis of accounting to record its general fund transactions. For external reporting purposes, Clarksville prepares a comprehensive annual financial report that includes both government-wide and fund-based financial statements.

The city has a policy that any amounts to be received within 60 days are viewed as currently being available.

At the beginning of Year One, the Council authorized the construction of a new recreation center. The estimated cost of the recreation center is $25 million. Clarksville plans to finance the construction by (1) combining bond proceeds with a state grant, and (2) making a transfer from the general fund.

Topics Included in the Simulation

a. Assigning transactions in a proprietary fund to the appropriate classification on the statement of cash flows.

b. Evaluating the accuracy of recorded amounts in the governmental funds for recording budgets, the levy of taxes, and the collections of taxes.

c. Assigning nonexchange transactions to their correct categories of recognition.

d. Accounting for the construction of the new recreation center: issuance of the bonds, receipt of the state grant, accounting for the interfund transfer, and accounting for interest on the bonds.

e. Comparing fund-based reporting of the construction of the recreation center to that reportable on the government-wide financial statements.

f. Comparing the reporting of an acquisition of a capital asset on the fund-based financial statements with that on the government-wide financial statements.

g. Researching required disclosures in the comprehensive annual financial report for infrastructure assets under the modified approach.

Supplemental Problems for this chapter are available as part of the *Online Learning Center* on the textbook's Website.

Chapter **Nineteen**

Not-for-Profit Entities

This chapter presents the accounting and financial reporting principles used by both governmental (public) and nongovernmental (private) colleges and universities, health care providers such as hospitals and nursing homes, voluntary health and welfare organizations such as the Red Cross and United Way, and other not-for-profit organizations such as professional or fraternal associations.

The accounting and financial reporting for governmental, nonprofit entities is controlled by the Governmental Accounting Standards Board (GASB). Accounting and financial reporting for nongovernmental, nonprofit entities is controlled by the Financial Accounting Standards Board (FASB). Thus, it is important to determine the role the government has in the organization.

FINANCIAL REPORTING FOR PRIVATE, NOT-FOR-PROFIT ENTITIES

Private, not-for-profit entities follow the accounting and reporting standards established by the FASB. Several FASB standards and statements are particularly relevant for private, not-for-profit entities.

Private, not-for-profit entities must report their net assets in accordance with **Financial Accounting Concepts Statement No. 6**, "Elements of Financial Statements" (FAC 6). **FAC 6** specifies three mutually exclusive classes of net assets (assets less liabilities), as follows:

1. *Unrestricted net assets.* This class of net assets is not restricted by a donor. These assets are used for the entity's general operations. Unrestricted net assets include all assets and liabilities that do not have externally imposed restrictions on their use.

2. *Temporarily restricted net assets.* This net asset class reports net assets that have donor-imposed time or purpose restrictions, typically detailed in the contribution agreement between the donor and the organization. A *time restriction* means that the assets will not be available for use until after a specific time has passed. *Term endowments* that have limited lives are included in temporarily restricted net assets. A *purpose restriction* means that the resources may be used only for specified purposes. For example, the donor may specify that the contribution be used in a specific program or for specified building and equipment acquisitions.

3. *Permanently restricted net assets.* This class of net assets includes permanently restricted contributions such as regular endowments for which the principal must be preserved into perpetuity.

It is very important to properly account for, and report, each class of net assets. Some not-for-profit entities use a fund structure to account for each type of net asset class because of the accounting discipline that fund accounting provides. These entities would have funds such as the general fund, specific-purpose fund, building fund, endowment fund, and so on. Other not-for-profit entities maintain only an accounting record to show the amounts in each net asset class. The specific identification of any restricted asset must be made when the asset comes into the entity, generally by donation or bequest. The gifting agreement must be examined fully to determine whether the gift has any donor-imposed restrictions on its principal and/or on the income generated from the principal. Revenue is recorded in only one net asset class when the contribution is made. Then, as restrictions are eliminated or met, the resources are released and transferred from the restricted net asset class to the unrestricted net asset class.

For example, if C. Alt donates $40,000 to a not-for-profit organization to be used specifically for a research program, the following entry is made in the *temporarily restricted class of net assets* because of the donor-imposed use restriction:

(1)	Cash	40,000	
	Contribution Revenue		40,000
	Receipt of $40,000 donor-restricted contribution for a specified research program.		

Note that the contribution revenue is recorded in the temporarily restricted net asset class when the restricted contribution is received.

Then, when the research program costs are approved in the unrestricted net asset class, a reclassification entry is made in the temporarily restricted net asset class to record the transfer of the resources from the temporarily restricted class to the unrestricted net asset class. Note that the reclassification entry is not an expense of the restricted class.

(2)	Reclassification from Temporarily Restricted Net Assets—Satisfaction of Program Restriction	40,000	
	Cash		40,000
	Reclassification of temporarily restricted resources to the unrestricted fund upon satisfaction of the use restriction.		

Entries are then made in the unrestricted net asset class to show the receipt of the cash and the reclassification for satisfaction of the program restriction. The reclassification is not a revenue in the unrestricted net asset class because the revenue from the contribution has already been recognized once in the temporarily restricted net asset class. A key concept is that revenue should be recognized only once and only by the appropriate receiving net asset class. The entries in the *unrestricted net asset class* follow:

(3)	Cash	40,000	
	Reclassification into Unrestricted Net Assets—Satisfaction of Program Restriction		40,000
	Receipt of resources from the temporarily restricted net asset class due to satisfaction of use restriction.		
(4)	Expenses	40,000	
	Cash		40,000
	Expenses for research program.		

Some not-for-profit entities use the terms "net assets released from restriction" instead of "reclassification." The purpose is the same; the resources are released from a restricted net asset class and assigned or transferred to another net asset class.

It is very important to note that the restricted net asset classes, either temporarily or permanently, do not report expenses on the organization's statement of activities. The restricted net asset classes (temporarily or permanently) report restricted contribution revenue and any restricted investment income/losses but cannot report any expenses. Expenses are reported *only* in the unrestricted net asset class. Thus, the reclassification entry records the transfer of the resources from a restricted net asset class to the unrestricted net asset class. The reclassification and transfer is made when a appropriate evidence is provided to the restricted net asset class that the cash can be released due to the satisfaction of the temporary restriction or that the permanent restriction is no longer valid. The reclassification entry ensures that the resources are being spent by the unrestricted net asset class in accordance with the donor's wishes.

Important FASB Standards for Not-for-Profit Entities

The FASB has issued five standards that have direct applicability to private, not-for-profit entities: **FASB 93**, which guides depreciation; **FASB 116**, which guides accounting for contributions; **FASB 117**, which establishes financial display requirements; **FASB 124**, which establishes the accounting for investments; and **FASB 136**, which guides the accounting for transfers of assets to a not-for-profit organization that raises or holds contributions for others.

FASB Statement No. 93, "Recognition of Depreciation by Not-for-Profit Organizations" (FASB 93), requires that private, not-for-profit entities must show depreciation. Depreciation must be recognized on long-lived tangible assets, other than works of art or historical treasures that have cultural, aesthetic, or historical value that is worth preserving perpetually and whose holders have the ability to preserve that value and are so doing. The depreciation is reported as an expense for the period. **FASB 93** requires disclosure of the following items: (1) depreciation for the period, (2) the total of each of the major classes of depreciable assets, (3) the accumulated depreciation at the balance sheet date, and (4) the method used to compute depreciation for the major classes of depreciable assets.

FASB Statement No. 116, "Accounting for Contributions Received and Contributions Made" (FASB 116), establishes the guidelines for private, not-for-profit entities to account for contributions. Contributions can be of cash, other assets, or a promise to give (a pledge). The general rule is that contributions received are measured at their fair value and are recognized as revenues or gains in the period received. The contributions are reported as unrestricted support or, if there are donor-imposed restrictions, as restricted support. A private, not-for-profit entity does not need to recognize contributions of works of art, historical treasures, and similar assets if the donated items are added to collections that (1) are held for public exhibition, education, or research, (2) are protected, cared for, and preserved, and (3) have an organizational policy in existence that proceeds from the sales of collection items are to be used to acquire other items for collections.

Contributions of services are recognized as a revenue, with an equivalent amount recorded as an expenditure, if the services received (1) create or enhance nonfinancial assets or (2) require specialized skills, are provided by individuals possessing those skills, and typically need to be purchased if not provided by donation. Examples of contributed services are specialized skills provided by accountants, architects, doctors, teachers, and other professionals. Some religious-based colleges record revenue, with an offsetting amount to an expense, for the fair value of contributed lay teaching services. This recognition is made to report the full cost of the teaching mission of these private colleges.

FASB Statement No. 124, "Accounting for Certain Investments Held by Not-for-Profit Organizations" (FASB 124), is discussed before **FASB 117**, which is presented in the next paragraph. **FASB 124** extended to not-for-profit organizations the basic standard of fair value for investments that was presented in **FASB 115** on investments. **FASB 124** specifies that fair value should be the measurement basis for investments in all debt securities and in equity securities that have readily determinable fair values (other than those equity securities that are accounted for under the equity method in accordance with **APB 18**). Note that **FASB 124** requires that debt securities be valued at fair value. Investment income for the period includes interest or dividends and the changes in fair value. Changes in the fair value of investments in temporarily restricted or permanently restricted net assets are recognized in accordance with donor restrictions as to the income. Otherwise, investment income is reported as a change in unrestricted net assets.

FASB Statement No. 117, "Financial Statements of Not-for-Profit Organizations" (FASB 117), specifies the financial display standards for private, not-for-profit entities. The three major financial statements are (1) a statement of financial position, (2) a statement of activities, and (3) a statement of cash flows. The unique features of the statement of financial position and the statement of activities for not-for-profit organizations are presented in greater detail in the following discussions. While some flexibility exists in the presentation of financial statements under **FASB 117**, a major feature of the statement of financial position is the combined presentation of all assets and equities in a single, simplified statement. In addition, the net assets are separated into those that are (1) unrestricted, (2) temporarily restricted, and (3) permanently restricted.

FASB Statement No. 136, "Transfers of Assets to a Not-for-Profit Organization or Charitable Trust that Raises or Holds Contributions for Others" (FASB 136), issued in 1999, establishes the accounting for contributions made to foundations or other similar organizations that raise resources for not-for-profit entities. **FASB 136** defines three parties to the typical contribution process. The *donor* is the initial provider of the resources. The *recipient organization* receives the assets from the donor. The *beneficiary* is the entity that eventually receives the assets through the recipient organization, as specified by the donor.

Many not-for-profit, private colleges and universities have a foundation that is responsible for raising financial support from alumni and other donors. Typically, these foundations are institutionally related to the college or university and use its assets for the benefit of the college or university. In most cases, at the time the assets are contributed by the donor to the foundation (the recipient organization), the foundation records an increase in assets and a contribution revenue for the fair value of the donation. Usually these assets are temporarily restricted until the foundation transfers them to the college or university. When the foundation does transfer the assets to the university (the beneficiary), the foundation records an expense and a decrease in its assets. In college or university accounting, the college or university normally has an interest in the net assets of the foundation and, at the time of the donation to the foundation, the college or university will recognize the change in its interest in the university foundation, usually as a temporarily restricted net asset, unless the donor specified a permanent restriction on the donation. Then, when the college or university actually receives the assets, it increases the specific assets received and decreases its interest in the net assets of the foundation. The institutionally related foundation recognizes the contribution revenue when it receives the donation.

Some recipient organizations, such as United Way, do fund-raising that will benefit a number of not-for-profit organizations. Donors may name the specific recipient of their gifts or the donor may give to United Way without a restriction as to where the gift should be used. When the donor specifies the beneficiary, United Way recognizes an increase in its assets and records a liability to the specified beneficiary. The organization specified by the donor records an increase in its net assets, usually as a receivable, and records contribution revenue at the time of the donation. When United Way transfers the assets to the specified beneficiaries, United Way decreases its liabilities and its assets. For unrestricted donations for which United Way may determine the best uses of the resources, it records an increase in its assets and records the unrestricted gifts as contribution revenue. Then, when the assets are distributed, United Way records the expense and the decrease in its assets, and the beneficiary records contribution revenue for the fair value of the assets transferred.

Therefore, the key issues are the relationship between the recipient organization and the beneficiary and whether the donor placed any use restrictions on the donation. If the donor does not specify a beneficiary and the recipient organizations and beneficiary are not institutionally related, the beneficiary cannot recognize an increase in its net assets until it actually receives the assets and records contribution revenue at that time. If the donor does specify a beneficiary or the recipient organizations and the beneficiary are institutionally related, the beneficiary recognizes the fair value of the donation when it is made to the recipient organization. Finally, in the case of nonfinancial assets such as artwork, the recipient organization may choose whether to record the fair value of these nonfinancial assets in its books. However, all financial assets must be recorded at their fair values.

In 2005 and continuing forward, the FASB has studied how to properly account for the acquisition or purchase of a business or nonprofit activity by a not-for-profit organization. The FASB's early decisions on this topic state that the not-for-profit organization should value the identifiable net assets obtained at their fair values and then record goodwill for the extent of the consideration given in excess of the fair value of the identifiable net assets. This is the same approach as the general principle for business combinations. The topic of business combinations will continue to be a topic of study by the FASB and future board publications on accounting and reporting business combinations should be expected.

COLLEGES AND UNIVERSITIES

There are more than 3,000 colleges and universities in the United States. Some offer two-year programs, some offer four-year programs, and others offer a wide selection of both undergraduate and graduate programs. Public and private institutions provide a large variety of liberal arts, science, and professional programs for our society. Public colleges and universities receive a significant portion of their operating resources from state governments. Private, not-for-profit colleges and universities receive most of their resources from tuition and fees.

Special Conventions of Revenue and Expenditure Recognition

Both public and private colleges and universities follow several conventions of recognizing revenue and expenses, as follows:

1. *Tuition and fee remissions/waivers and uncollectible accounts.* Tuition and fees are important revenue sources for colleges and universities. In college and university accounting, the full amount of the standard rate for tuition and fees is recognized as revenue. The accounting for university-sponsored scholarships, fellowships, tuition and fee remissions or waivers depends on whether the recipient provides any services to the university. For example, if a student receives a university-sponsored scholarship that does not require any employment-type of work to be given to the university, the university accounts for this as a deduction from revenue. On the other hand, if the student must provide employment-type work to the university, the university accounts for the scholarship as an expense. Another example is the tuition remission (reduction) often given to graduate students who accept teaching assistantships. The university records revenue for the graduate student's tuition at the standard rate and then records the tuition remission as an expense of the year in which the graduate student is a teaching assistant.

2. *Tuition and fee reimbursements for withdrawals from coursework.* Students withdrawing from classes after the beginning of the class term may be able to collect a reimbursement or return of some of the tuition and fees paid at the beginning of the term. Colleges and universities account for these reimbursements of tuition and fees as a reduction of revenue. When the check to the student is approved, the university debits revenue from tuition and fee reimbursements and credits cash or accounts payable.

3. *Academic terms that span two fiscal periods.* Some academic terms may begin in one fiscal year of the university and be completed in another. This is often true for summer school sessions. For example, many universities end their fiscal years on June 30 of each year. The 1994 College and University Audit Guide, published by the AICPA, recommended that colleges and universities account for the tuition and fees as revenue in the fiscal year in which the term is predominantly conducted, along with all expenses incurred to finance that term. However, more recent practices by the National Association of College and University Business Officers (NACUBO) recommend the use of the accrual basis of accounting, which requires that the tuition revenue and costs be allocated proportionately to the two fiscal years based on the relative portions of the academic term. Many colleges and universities are electing to follow the NACUBO recommendation.

For example, if tuition and fees are collected at the beginning of summer school, in which two weeks are offered in the first fiscal year and the remaining six weeks are offered in the second fiscal year, the AICPA audit guide's approach would result in recording the collections as a debit to Cash and a credit to Deferred Revenue for the entire amount of the collections. The deferred revenue and any deferred expenses would then he recognized as revenue and expenses of the next fiscal period, in which most of the term is conducted. Under the NACUBO approach, revenue would be recognized in the first fiscal period for two-eighths of the tuition and fees and the remaining six-eighths of the collections would be recorded as a deferred revenue. The NACUBO method also would recognize the related expenses that correspond with the first two weeks of the summer session in the first fiscal period. The remaining six-eighths of the revenue, and the related expenses, would be recognized in the second fiscal period for the last six weeks of the summer session. NACUBO feels its approach follows the principles of accrual accounting.

Board-Designated Funds

The governing board, sometimes termed *regents* or *trustees,* may designate unrestricted current fund resources for specific purposes in future periods. These *board-designated funds* are internal designations similar to appropriations of retained earnings for a commercial entity. The governing board may make any designations at its own volition. For example, it might designate $50,000 of future spending in the unrestricted current fund for the development of a foreign student counseling office. Such designations are usually reported in the footnotes to the financial statements, but they may also be shown as allocations of part of the fund balance in the unrestricted current fund balance sheet. However, **FASB 117** specifies that these board-designated funds may not be reported as restricted net assets because only external, donor-imposed restrictions can result in restricted net assets.

Public Colleges and Universities

The accounting and reporting for public colleges and universities is specified by the GASB. **GASB Statement No. 35**, "Basic Financial Statements—and Management's Discussion and Analysis—for Public Colleges and Universities" (GASB 35), issued in 1999, that requires that these institutions follow the standards for governmental entities as specified in **GASB 34**. Most public institutions will be special-purpose government entities engaged in only business-type activities. This is so because most public colleges and universities do not have their own taxing authority. These special-purpose governmental entities present only the financial statements required for enterprise funds and then are included as component units of the state government. However, some community colleges do have their own taxing authority, and these are special-purpose government entities engaged in both governmental- and business-type activities. These community colleges provide both fund-based financial statements and government-wide financial statements.

Private Colleges and Universities

The FASB specifies the accounting and financial reporting standards for private colleges and universities. Although many private colleges and universities are not-for-profit entities, some private colleges, such as the University of Phoenix, are profit-seeking. Accounting for profit-seeking educational entities is similar to accounting for any commercial entity and is not covered in this chapter.

The three financial statements required for private, not-for-profit colleges and universities are the (1) statement of financial position, (2) statement of activities, and (3) statement of cash flows. Private colleges and universities are free to select any account structure that best serves their management and financial reporting needs, but some choose to use fund accounting similar to that of governmental entities. Fund accounting creates an accounting discipline and provides an accounting vehicle to track revenues and expenses related to specific programs. Figure 19–1 presents an overview of the accounting and financial reporting of colleges and universities. The financial reporting for public, special-purpose governmental entities is presented in Chapters 17 and 18 of this textbook.

The statement of financial position for Sol City College, a private, not-for-profit college, is presented in Figure 19–2. This statement presents all assets and equities in a single statement. Note that the net assets are separated into three categories: (1) unrestricted, (2) temporarily restricted, and (3) permanently restricted. The unrestricted category includes all assets, including property, plant, and equipment, whose use is not restricted by the provider or donor. Temporarily restricted assets include those that the donor has designated for specific use or for use in subsequent periods. Term endowments, funds donated for support of special

FIGURE 19–1 Overview of the Accounting and Reporting of Colleges and Universities

	Public, Special-Purpose Governmental Entities		Private Entities	
	Engaged in Both Governmental and Business-Type Activities	Engaged in Only Business-Type Activities	Not-for-Profit	Profit-Seeking
Accounting and reporting standards	GASB	GASB	FASB	FASB
Accounting structure	Funds	Funds	Not required to, but many use fund-based structure	Account-based, same as for commercial businesses
Distinguishing features	Separate governmental entity with own taxing authority	Generally reported as a component unit of a state government	Net assets classified into three classes: 1. Unrestricted net assets 2. Temporarily restricted net assets 3. Permanently restricted net assets	Same as for profit-seeking businesses
Financial statements	Both fund-based and government-wide financial statements, as presented in Chapters 17 and 18	Same as for an enterprise fund, as presented in Chapter 18	Three basic financial statements: 1. Statement of Financial Position 2. Statement of Activities 3. Statement of Cash Flows	Same as for profit-seeking businesses

FIGURE 19–2
Statement of Financial Position for a Private College

SOL CITY COLLEGE Statement of Financial Position June 30, 20X2 and 20X1		
	20X2	**20X1**
Cash	$ 579,000	$ 514,000
Investments, at Fair Value	10,763,000	9,536,000
Deposits with Trustees	125,000	122,000
Accounts Receivable	161,000	182,000
Less: Allowance for Uncollectibles	(13,000)	(14,000)
Loans to Students, Faculty, and Staff	275,000	190,000
Inventories	45,000	40,000
Prepaid Expenses	14,000	10,000
Property, Plant, and Equipment (net)	20,330,000	19,970,000
Total Assets	$32,279,000	$30,550,000
Accounts Payable	$ 70,000	$ 53,000
Accrued Liabilities	10,000	8,000
Students' Deposits	15,000	18,000
Deferred Credits	15,000	10,000
Annuities Payable	1,080,000	1,155,000
Notes Payable	50,000	—
Bonds Payable	1,300,000	1,200,000
Mortgage Payable	200,000	100,000
Deposits Held in Custody	55,000	45,000
Total Liabilities	$ 2,795,000	$ 2,589,000
Net Assets:		
Unrestricted	$20,221,000	$20,294,000
Temporarily Restricted by Donors	5,363,000	4,307,000
Permanently Restricted by Donors	3,900,000	3,360,000
Total Net Assets	$29,484,000	$27,961,000
Total Liabilities and Net Assets	$32,279,000	$30,550,000

activities, and those donated for unrestricted (or other) use in future periods are included as temporarily restricted net assets. Permanently restricted assets typically include only the principal balance of permanent endowments.

The statement of activities presented in Figure 19–3 presents separately the revenues and expenses of the unrestricted, temporarily restricted, and permanently restricted net asset categories. It also shows the transfer of assets between the three categories of net assets during the period. For example, contributions received in 20X1 and available for use in 20X2 are shown as a transfer from temporarily restricted to unrestricted net assets in the statement of activities for 20X2. Auxiliary enterprises include activities such as a student union bookstore, cafeterias, and residence halls.

The statement of cash flows presented in Figure 19–4 is similar to that used for commercial entities. Either the direct or indirect method may be used to compute cash flows from operating activities. Activities in the restricted funds are noted separately from those in the unrestricted funds.

HEALTH CARE PROVIDERS

The health care environment is currently undergoing a revolution. Rapidly increasing costs of providing medical care are forcing hospitals to merge at an increasing rate in order to consolidate the types of services offered. The cost of new technology is also requiring health care providers to reevaluate their missions to the communities they serve.

FIGURE 19–3   **Statement of Activities for a Private College**

SOL CITY COLLEGE
Statement of Activities
For the Year Ended June 30, 20X2

	Unrestricted	Temporarily Restricted	Permanently Restricted	Total
Revenues, Gains, and Other Support:				
Tuition and Fees	$ 1,290,000			$ 1,290,000
Government Appropriations	650,000	$ 40,000		690,000
Government Grants and Contracts	20,000	300,000		320,000
Contributions	425,000	1,063,000	$ 495,000	1,983,000
Auxiliary Enterprises	1,100,000			1,100,000
Investment Income	265,000	139,000	15,000	419,000
Gain on Investments		69,000	25,000	94,000
Net Assets Transferred or Released from Restriction:				
Program Use Restriction	601,000	(601,000)		
Transferred to Restricted Funds	(101,000)	101,000		
Expired Term Endowment	50,000	(50,000)		
Transferred to Endowment		(5,000)	5,000	
Total Revenue, Gains, and Other Support	$ 4,300,000	$1,056,000	$ 540,000	$ 5,896,000
Expenditures and Other Deductions:				
Instruction	$ 1,725,000			$ 1,725,000
Research	250,000			250,000
Public Service	77,000			77,000
Academic Support	125,000			125,000
Student Services	100,000			100,000
Scholarships and Fellowships	95,000			95,000
Institutional Support	275,000			275,000
Operation and Maintenance	110,000			110,000
Depreciation Expense	500,000			500,000
Interest Expense	106,000			106,000
Auxiliary Enterprises	915,000			915,000
Other Operating Costs	95,000			95,000
Total Expenses	$ 4,373,000	$ -0-	$ -0-	$ 4,373,000
Change in Net Assets	$ (73,000)	$1,056,000	$ 540,000	$ 1,523,000
Net Assets at Beginning of Year	20,294,000	4,307,000	3,360,000	27,961,000
Net Assets at End of Year	$20,221,000	$5,363,000	$3,900,000	$29,484,000

Although the major focus of this chapter section is on hospitals, the accounting and financial reporting guidelines for hospitals are the same as those used by all health care providers included within the scope of the AICPA's audit and accounting guide for Health Care Organizations.[1] The audit and accounting guide applies to the following health care entities:

1. Clinics, medical group practices, individual practice associations, individual practitioners, emergency care facilities, laboratories, surgery centers, and other ambulatory care organizations.
2. Continuing-care retirement communities (CCRCs).
3. Health maintenance organizations (HMOs) and similar prepaid health care plans.
4. Home health agencies.
5. Hospitals.

[1] The AICPA periodically revises its audit and accounting guides for specialized industries.

FIGURE 19–4
Statement of Cash
Flows for a Private
College

SOL CITY COLLEGE
Statement of Cash Flows
For the Year Ended June 30, 20X2

Cash flows from Operating Activities:			
Change in Net Assets			$1,523,000
Adjustments to Reconcile Changes in Net Assets to Net Cash Provided by Operating Activities:			
Depreciation		$ 500,000	
Increase in Deposits with Trustees		(3,000)	
Decrease in Accounts Receivable		20,000	
Increase in Loans to Students, Faculty, and Staff		(85,000)	
Increase in Inventories		(5,000)	
Increase in Prepaid Expenses		(4,000)	
Increase in Accounts Payable		17,000	
Increase in Accrued Liabilities		2,000	
Decrease in Students' Deposits		(3,000)	
Increase in Deferred Credits		5,000	
Restricted Contributions and Investment Income:			
Contributions, Grants, and Investment Income in Permanently Restricted Funds	$(1,611,000)		
Contributions, Grants, and Investment Income in Temporarily Restricted Funds	(535,000)		
Total Restricted Contributions and Investment Income	$(2,146,000)	(2,146,000)	
Total Adjustments		$(1,702,000)	(1,702,000)
Net Cash Provided by Operating Activities			$ (179,000)
Cash Flows from Investing Activities:			
Acquisition of Property, Plant, and Equipment		$ (920,000)	
Sale of Used Equipment		60,000	
Net Acquisition of Investments		(65,000)	
Flows Related to Restricted Items:			
Net Acquisition of Temporarily Restricted Investments	$ (112,000)		
Net Acquisition of Permanently Restricted Investments	(1,050,000)		
Net Cash Flow Related to Restricted Items	$(1,162,000)	(1,162,000)	
Net Cash Provided by Investing Activities			(2,087,000)
Cash Flows from Financing Activities:			
Decrease in Annuities Payable		$ (75,000)	
Increase in Notes Payable		50,000	
Increase in Bonds Payable		100,000	
Increase in Mortgage Payable		100,000	
Increase in Deposits Held in Custody		10,000	
Flows Related to Restricted Items:			
Contributions, Grants, and Investment Income in Temporarily Restricted Funds	$ 1,611,000		
Contributions, Grants, and Investment Income in Permanently Restricted Funds	535,000		
Cash Flows Related to Restricted Items	$ 2,146,000	$ 185,000	
Net Cash Provided by Financing Activities			2,331,000
Net Change in Cash			$ 65,000
Cash at the Beginning of the Year			514,000
Cash at the End of the Year			$ 579,000

6. Nursing homes that provide skilled, intermediate, and less intensive levels of health care.

7. Drug and alcohol rehabilitation centers and other rehabilitation facilities.

The AICPA audit guide serves as an important authoritative source in selecting accounting and financial reporting procedures for health care providers. The hospital financial statements illustrated in this chapter incorporate the disclosure standards of **FASB 117**, as presented and amplified in the AICPA's Audit and Accounting Guide for Health Care Organizations.

Hospital Accounting

Hospitals may be classified as (1) investor-owned businesses, (2) not-for-profit entities that cover their costs by generating fees from their activities, or (3) governmental entities. Private-sector hospitals use the FASB's accounting guidelines and requirements; public-sector (governmental) hospitals follow the GASB's accounting guidance. Investor-owned hospitals seek additional financial resources through the sale of stocks and the issuance of large amounts of debt. These profit-seeking hospitals provide the same types of financial reports as commercial entities. Not-for-profit hospitals present their financial results using a specific format required by the FASB. Not-for-profit hospitals are often affiliated with a religious group or a civic association. Governmental hospitals are managed by or affiliated with a government unit. Governmental hospitals follow the GASB's accounting and reporting requirements and are considered special-purpose entities engaged in business-type activities. As such, they present financial statements that are required for enterprise funds as presented in Chapter 18 of this textbook. Governmental hospitals then are included in the government entity's government-wide financial statements.

Two professional associations, the American Hospital Association (AHA) and the Hospital Financial Management Association (HFMA), are active in developing and improving hospital management, accounting, and financial reporting. Publications of both organizations can be useful to individuals seeking additional information on hospital accounting and reporting practices.

In this chapter, it is assumed that the hospital is a separate, not-for-profit reporting entity and is not a component unit of any government. The focus of this chapter is on not-for-profit hospitals because of the large number of such hospitals and because of their special accounting and financial reporting issues.

Hospital Fund Structure

Although not required to do so, many hospitals have used a fund accounting structure for accounting purposes. In general, operating activities are carried on in the general fund, and a series of restricted funds can be used to account for assets whose use has been restricted by the donor. If separate funds are not maintained, then all transactions are recorded in the general fund, and memorandum records show restricted amounts in the general fund. The presentation of financial statement information under **FASB 117** requires a distinction between those net assets that are unrestricted, temporarily restricted, and permanently restricted. The discussion of accounting and financial reporting for hospitals that follows assumes that unrestricted net assets are accounted for in the general fund and that one or more separate funds are used to account for temporarily restricted and permanently restricted net assets.

All transactions involving the use of unrestricted net assets are recorded in the general fund. As such, the general fund is the hospital's primary operating fund. Assets that were restricted as to the period of use or that must be used for particular purposes are accounted for in restricted funds until the restriction is satisfied. When the restriction is satisfied, the assets are transferred (reclassified) from the restricted fund to the general (unrestricted) fund. Any expenses that are incurred in satisfying the restrictions are reported as expenses in the general fund.

Restricted funds account for assets received from donors or other third parties who have imposed certain restrictions on their use. The restricted funds are often termed "holding" funds because they must hold the restricted assets and transfer expendable resources to the general fund for expenditure. Figure 19–5 presents an overview of the fund structure and the typical financial reporting for hospitals.

General Fund

The ***general fund*** accounts for the resources received and expended in the hospital's primary health care mission. The basis of accounting is the accrual method in order to measure fully all expenses of providing services during the period. Depreciation is included in the operating expenses. Fixed assets are included in the fund based on the theory that the governing board may use these assets in any manner desired.

FIGURE 19–5
Overview of
Hospital Accounting
and Reporting

			Fund Groups		
			Restricted		
	General	Specific Purpose	Time Restricted	Plant Replacement and Expansion	Endowment
Distinguishing features		Resources restricted for specific operating purposes.	Resources not available until date specified by donor.	Resources restricted for additions to plant assets.	Principal preserved as specified by donor.
Financial statements			Balance Sheet		
			Statement of Operations		
			Statement of Changes in Net Assets		
			Statement of Cash Flows		

The governing board may establish *board-designated resources* within the general fund. For example, the board may designate resources for the expansion of the hospital, for retirement of debt, or for other purposes. Funds designated in this manner are considered to be part of the unrestricted funds, but this designation provides information on the intended use of the resources.

Donor Restricted Funds All *restricted funds* account for resources whose use is restricted by the donor. For financial reporting purposes, a distinction is made between temporarily and permanently restricted funds. The major *temporarily restricted* funds are (1) specific-purpose funds, (2) time-restricted funds, and (3) plant replacement and expansion funds. *Permanently restricted* funds are assets that must be held into perpetuity and generally are included in an endowment fund. Hospitals may also have restricted loan funds and annuity and life income funds; however, few hospitals use these funds, and they are not discussed in this chapter.

Specific-purpose funds are restricted for *specific operating purposes*. For example, a donor may specify that a donation of $25,000 may be used only for maternity care. The donation is held in the specific-purpose fund until the maternity expenditure is approved in the general fund. Once approved, the specific-purpose fund transfers the resources to the general fund.

Time-restricted funds account for assets received or pledged by donors for use in future periods. The donor's restriction is satisfied by the passage of time. A pledge received in 20X1 to contribute a stated amount in 20X2 to be used for unrestricted purposes is included in the time-restricted fund in the balance sheet prepared at December 31, 20X1.

Plant replacement and expansion restricted funds account for contributions to be used only for additions to fixed assets. When the general fund approves or makes the appropriate expenditures for the fixed assets, the plant replacement and expansion fund transfers the resources to the general fund.

Endowment funds account for resources when the principal must be preserved. The income from these resources is usually available for either a restricted or a general purpose. Endowments may be either permanent or term. Term endowments are for limited time periods, for example, 5 or 10 years, or until a specific event occurs, such as the death of the donor. After the term expires, the governing board uses the principal of the fund in accordance with the gift agreement.

Financial Statements for a Not-for-Profit Hospital

Separate, not-for-profit hospitals issue four basic financial statements: (1) the balance sheet, (2) the statement of operations, (3) the statement of changes in net assets, and (4) the statement of cash flows. Comparative data for prior fiscal periods are normally presented within each statement. Each of the four statements is demonstrated in the comprehensive illustration presented later in this chapter.

Balance Sheet

The *balance sheet* presents the total assets, liabilities, and net assets of the organization as a whole.

Receivables Receivables may include amounts due from patients, third-party payors, other insurers of health care, pledges or grants, and interfund transactions. Receivables should be reported at the anticipated realizable amount. Thus, the realizable amounts may include reductions due to contractual agreements with third-party payors or provider practices, such as allowing courtesy discounts to medical staff members and employees. An allowance for uncollectibles is recognized for estimated bad debts. Note that not-for-profit hospitals recognize estimated uncollectibles from providing services as bad debts expense. Charity care occurs when health care services are provided to a patient who has demonstrated, in accordance with the hospital's established criteria, an inability to pay. In these cases, charity care does not qualify for recognition as either receivables or revenue in the hospital's financial statements. The determination of a charity care case may not be able to be made when the patient is admitted, but at some point the hospital must be able to determine that the person does meet the necessary qualifications for charity care before reducing the amount owed. Receivables from pledges of future contributions are reported in the period the pledge is made, net of an allowance for uncollectible amounts.

Investments Investments are initially recorded at cost if purchased or at fair value at the date of receipt if received as a gift. Subsequently, for investor-owned, *profit-seeking hospitals,* equity and debt securities are reported in accordance with **FASB Statement No. 115**, "Accounting for Certain Investments in Debt and Equity Securities" (FASB 115). **FASB 115** establishes three portfolios of investments: trading securities, available-for-sale securities, and hold-to-maturity debt securities. The accounting and reporting of the investment differ according to the category. For *nonprofit hospitals,* equity securities with readily determinable fair values and all investments in debt securities are measured at fair value, in accordance with **FASB Statement No. 124**, "Accounting for Certain Investments Held by Not-for-Profit Organizations" (FASB 124). The Audit and Accounting Guide for Health Care Organizations states that the investment return (including realized and unrealized gains and losses) not restricted by donors should be classified as changes in unrestricted net assets in the hospital's statement of operations. The investment return designated for current operations is included above the operation performance indicator line (Excess of Revenues, Gains, and Other Support over Expenses) reflecting operations; the investment return in excess of amounts designated for current operations is reported in the statement of operations below the operating performance indicator line. Investment returns restricted by donors or by law are reported as changes in net assets in the appropriate restricted funds. For *governmental health care entities,* **GASB Statement No. 31**, "Accounting and Financial Reporting for Certain Investments and for External Investment Pools" (GASB 31), specifies the general rule of fair value accounting for investments.

For these three types of hospitals, investments in stock accounted for under the equity method are reported in accordance with **APB Statement No. 18**, "The Equity Method of Accounting for Investments in Common Stock" (APB 18). Some hospitals receive income from trusts that donors have established with fiduciaries, such as banks. If the hospital does not own the trust or its investments, the independent trusts are not an asset of the hospital and are not reported on the hospital's balance sheet. Footnote disclosure may be made of major independent endowments or trust agreements that benefit the hospital.

Plant Assets Property, plant, and equipment is reported with any accumulated depreciation. Depreciation is recorded in the general fund because the use of assets is part of the cost of providing medical services. The assets are reported in the general fund because they are available for use in any manner deemed necessary by the governing board.

Assets Whose Use Is Limited Separate disclosure should be made for assets that have restrictions placed on their use by the donor or that have been designated by the board of directors for special use. Such funds may come from a variety of sources. For example, grant monies received for cancer research are reported as funds restricted for specific purposes and classified as temporarily restricted until used in support of research. Funds contributed to assist in constructing a new children's wing of the hospital are reported as restricted for plant replacement and expansion and classified as temporarily restricted until used in construction. Funds received for permanent investment in the principal of an endowment fund are reported as permanently restricted. Only those funds whose use is restricted by the donor are classified as restricted; thus, assets set aside for identified purposes by the governing board and over which the board retains control are not classified as restricted but are regarded as *assets whose use is limited*.

Long-Term Debt The hospital must also account for its long-term debt and pay the principal and interest as it becomes due. The debt is shown in the balance sheet. This practice differs from that used by most governmental entities that establish a separate debt service fund to service debt.

Net Assets The hospital segregates its net assets into (1) ***unrestricted net assets*** available for use at the discretion of the hospital staff and board of directors, (2) ***temporarily restricted net assets*** available for use when specific events established by the donor are satisfied, and (3) ***permanently restricted net assets*** that have been restricted by the donor as to their use.

Statement of Operations

The results of not-for-profit hospitals' operations are reported in a *statement of operations*, also often termed "the statement of activities." This statement includes the revenues, expenses, gains and losses, and other transactions affecting the unrestricted net assets during the period. Note that only those transactions in the general fund are reported on the statement of operations. Transactions affecting only the restricted funds are *not* shown on the statement of operations; rather, they are reported on the statement of changes in net assets. Gains and losses from transactions that are peripheral or ancillary to the provision of health care services are reported separately from net patient service revenue. The statement of operations should report an operating *performance indicator*, which reports the results of the hospital's operating activities for the period. This performance indicator should include both operating income (loss) for the period and other income available for current operations. **FASB 117** requires that net assets released from restrictions for use in operations be included before the performance indicator line on the statement of activities, generally termed "above the line." This is so because the transfer of net assets from the restricted group of assets for use in the entity's operations in the unrestricted group of net assets can then be matched with the expenses incurred to fulfill the operating restriction. The title of the performance indicator should be descriptive, such as the "Excess of Operating Revenues, Gains, and Other Support over Operating Expenses."

Other changes in the unrestricted net assets during the period should be reported after the performance indicator, generally termed "below the line." These changes include investment return in excess of amounts designated for current operations as defined by **FASB 124**. For example, a hospital's board of directors could reserve a portion of the investment return from the revaluation of investments for use in future periods, thus making them unavailable for current operations. The AICPA's audit guide for hospitals indicates that the investment return from other than trading securities should be presented below the operating performance line, and the investment return from trading securities should be presented above the operating line. However, an audit guide is lower than a FASB standard in the hierarchy of generally accepted accounting principles. Other changes reported below the operating performance indicator line would include transfers from restricted net assets of resources used for the purchase of property and equipment. Note that the statement of operations must separately report those items related to the acquisition of property or equipment from those related to operating activities.

A separate, third statement, entitled the *statement of changes in net assets,* is used to report items affecting the temporarily restricted and permanently restricted net assets. This third statement is covered in this chapter following discussion of the statement of operations.

Net Patient Service Revenue   Net patient service revenue represents the hospital's revenue from inpatient and outpatient care excluding charity care and contractual adjustments. Net patient service revenue represents the billings for services provided and the earning capacity of the hospital. Many hospitals are required to perform a certain amount of charity care for which they recognize no revenue. The charity cases are imposed by terms of certain federal medical care grant programs. Charity care helps ensure that indigent persons living in the region served by the hospital may obtain adequate medical services. When charity care is provided, no revenue is recognized, but disclosure of the estimated amount of charity care is presented in the footnotes to the financial statements.

Contractual Adjustments   Contractual adjustments constitute a major deduction from gross patient service revenue. Contractual adjustments result from the involvement of third-party payors in the medical reimbursement process. Insurance companies or government units (especially the federal government) reimburse less than the full standard rate for medical services provided to patients covered by insurance- or by government-provided services such as Medicare. These third-party payors may stipulate limits on the amount of costs they will pay. A hospital may have a standard rate for a specific service but may contract with the third-party payor to accept a lower amount for that service. For example, Medicare establishes specific reimbursement rates for various services, termed a "diagnosis-related group" (DRG). The hospital makes a contractual adjustment from its normal service charge, and this adjustment is a deduction from gross Patient Service Revenue.

Income from Ancillary Programs   Income from ancillary programs represents the income earned from nonpatient sources such as television rentals, cafeteria sales, sales in hospital-operated gift shops, parking fees, and tuition on hospital-provided educational programs. The income reported typically represents the net earnings from such operations rather than the gross receipts.

Interfund Transfers   It is not appropriate to hold assets in a restricted fund when the donor-specified requirements have been satisfied. For example, when contributions received to purchase plant and equipment are used to purchase new assets or when contributions received for use in educational programs are used for that purpose, the funds should be transferred from the restricted fund to the general fund. For financial reporting purposes, this transfer between funds is reported as "net assets released" in the statement of operations and is shown as an addition to the general fund. If the interfund transfer to the general fund is to be used for operations, the general fund reports it above the operating performance indicator line in the statement of operations. If the interfund transfer to the general fund is to be used for acquiring long-term assets, the general fund reports it below the performance indicator line in the statement of operations.

General Fund Expenses   The major expenses in the general fund are for nursing services, other professional services, depreciation, bad debts, and the general and administrative costs of the hospital. These costs are recognized on the accrual basis of accounting, similar to commercial entities. Hospitals that self-insure for malpractice costs should recognize an expense and a liability for malpractice costs in the period during which the incidents that give rise to the claims occur if it is probable that liabilities have been incurred and the amounts of the losses can be reasonably estimated. Any expenses related to fundraising should be classified separately.

Donations   Hospitals often receive a wide variety of services from volunteers. For example, retired physicians or pharmacists may voluntarily work part-time in their professional roles. In addition, the hospital may receive donations of supplies or equipment. The rules on accounting for donations and contributions to hospitals are as follows:

1. *Donated services.* Because it is often difficult to place a value on donated services, their values are usually not recorded. However, if the following conditions exist, the estimated value of the donated services is reported as an expense and a corresponding amount is

reported as contributions. **FASB 116** specifies that a contribution of services should be recognized if the services received (*a*) create or enhance nonfinancial assets or (*b*) require specialized skills, are provided by individuals possessing those skills, and would typically need to be purchased if not provided by donations.

2. *Donated assets.* Donated assets are reported at fair market value at the date of the contribution:

   a. Donated assets are reported as contributions in the statement of operations, if unrestricted. For example, a donation of medical supplies is recorded as a contribution in the general fund in the period received.

   b. Donated assets that are restricted in use by the donor are recognized as contribution revenue in the temporarily restricted or permanently restricted fund at the time of receipt. Note that contribution revenue is recognized in the appropriate restricted fund at the time the restricted donation is received. When the restriction no longer applies, the donated assets are transferred to the general fund. For example, when the general fund purchases assets with resources that have been restricted for that purpose, the transfer is made from the restricted fund as a debit to Net Assets Released from Restriction and a credit to Cash. The general fund accounts for the transfer of cash with a debit to Cash and a credit to Net Assets Released from Restriction, which is reported in the general fund's statement of operations.

   If the hospital does not use a fund structure for restricted assets, the contribution of restricted assets is accounted for as a debit to Cash and a credit to Net Assets Restricted, which is reported on the hospital's balance sheet. However, the statement of operations of the general fund does not report the donated assets until the restriction is no longer applicable and the assets have become available for use in the general fund. At the time the assets become available for use in the general fund, the general fund reports the transfer of the assets for use in the operations of the hospital on the statement of operations for the general fund and reclassifies the assets from the restricted net asset class to the unrestricted net asset class.

Appropriate expense accounts are charged as the donated assets are consumed. For example, donated supplies such as medicines, linen, and disposable medical items are charged to an expense as used from inventory. For donated physical plant or equipment having an estimated economic life of more than one year, depreciation is charged to each period in which the plant or equipment is used.

Statement of Changes in Net Assets

The third of the four financial statements for a not-for-profit hospital is termed the *statement of changes in net assets*. It presents the changes in all three categories of net assets: unrestricted, temporarily restricted, and permanently restricted. Donor-restricted contributions are reported in the appropriate category of restricted net assets. Net assets released from restrictions are shown as deductions from restricted net assets and as transfers to the unrestricted net assets. This release could be due to the completion of a time restriction, the fulfillment of a use restriction, or the satisfaction of any other donor-specified restriction.

Statement of Cash Flows

The fourth, and final, financial statement for a not-for-profit hospital is the *statement of cash flows*. Its format is similar to that for commercial entities and is presented as part of the comprehensive illustration in the next section of this chapter.

Comprehensive Illustration of Hospital Accounting and Financial Reporting

Sol City Community Hospital, a not-for-profit hospital operated by a community group, provides medical care for the region surrounding Sol City. The hospital has established the following funds: (1) general, (2) specific-purpose, (3) time-restricted, (4) plant replacement and expansion, and (5) endowment.

Entries to record transactions in each of the funds during the 20X2 fiscal year, ending December 31, 20X2, are presented in the next section of the chapter. First the financial statements for the period are presented, and then the transactions from which these statements resulted are discussed. The balance sheet for both the general and the restricted funds is presented in Figure 19–6. Note that the balance sheet is presented in what is generally termed an *aggregated style* rather than a *columnar* or *layered style* that would separately show the financial position of each fund. The selection of display formats is the choice of the hospital's governing board, but the aggregated format for the entity as a whole is more in keeping with the recommendations of **FASB 117**. An analysis of the composition of the net assets held as temporarily and permanently restricted at December 31, 20X2 and 20X1, provides the following amounts:

	Dec. 31, 20X2	Net Change	Dec. 31, 20X1
Temporarily restricted:			
Plant Replacement and Expansion Fund			
Cash	$ 50,000	$(150,000)	$200,000
Pledges receivable	15,000	(105,000)	120,000
Investments	140,000	122,000	18,000
Net assets	$ 205,000	$(133,000)	$338,000
Specific-Purpose Fund			
Cash	$ 3,000	$ 1,000	$ 2,000
Investments	20,000	-0-	20,000
Net assets	$ 23,000	$ 1,000	$ 22,000
Time-Restricted Fund			
Cash	$ 2,000	$ -0-	$ 2,000
Contributions receivable	-0-	(12,000)	12,000
Investments	196,000	-0-	196,000
Net assets	$ 198,000	$ (12,000)	$210,000
Permanently restricted:			
Endowment Fund			
Cash	$ 25,000	$ 15,000	$ 10,000
Investments	1,190,000	400,000	790,000
Net assets	$1,215,000	$ 415,000	$800,000

The specific-purpose fund and the time-restricted fund contain resources that will be available for operations as the restrictions are met.

The statement of operations is presented in Figure 19–7, the statement of changes in net assets is presented in Figure 19–8, and the statement of cash flows is presented in Figure 19–9. Each of these statements is discussed after presentation of the journal entries for 20X2 for Sol City Community Hospital.

General Fund

The transactions in the general fund for 20X2 are presented in accordance with their relative degree of importance in the hospital's operations. The first series of entries presented are for the revenues generated from patient care and the associated operating expenses for the period.

Net Patient Care Revenue The hospital provides patient services of $2,600,000 measured by standard rates. From this amount, $240,000 is deducted for contractual adjustments with third-party payors, which results in a net patient revenue of $2,360,000:

FIGURE 19–6
Balance Sheet for
a Not-for-Profit
Hospital

SOL CITY COMMUNITY HOSPITAL
Balance Sheet
December 31, 20X2 and 20X1

	20X2	20X1
Assets		
Current:		
Cash	$ 295,000	$ 14,000
Receivables	460,000	400,000
Less: Estimated Uncollectibles	(40,000)	(30,000)
Contributions and Pledges Receivable	-0-	12,000
Inventories	50,000	60,000
Prepaid Expenses	15,000	20,000
Total Current Assets	$ 780,000	$ 476,000
Assets Limited as to Use:		
Cash Restricted as to Use for Plant Expansion and Endowment	$ 75,000	$ 210,000
Pledges Receivable Restricted for Plant Expansion and Replacement	15,000	120,000
Investments Restricted as to Use for Plant Expansion and Endowment	1,330,000	808,000
Total Limited Assets	$1,420,000	$1,138,000
Investments (at fair value)	$ 681,000	$ 716,000
Property, Plant, and Equipment	$3,375,000	$3,200,000
Less: Accumulated Depreciation	(1,150,000)	(1,000,000)
Net Property, Plant, and Equipment	$2,225,000	$2,200,000
Total Assets	$5,106,000	$4,530,000
Liabilities and Net Assets		
Current:		
Notes Payable to Bank	$ 65,000	$ 70,000
Current Portion of Long-Term Debt	50,000	60,000
Accounts Payable	50,000	90,000
Accrued Expenses	30,000	25,000
Estimated Malpractice Costs Payable	30,000	-0-
Advances from Third Parties	160,000	125,000
Deferred Revenue	5,000	5,000
Total Current Liabilities	$ 390,000	$ 375,000
Long-Term Debt:		
Mortgage Payable	1,050,000	1,100,000
Total Liabilities	$1,440,000	$1,475,000
Net Assets:		
Unrestricted	$2,025,000	$1,685,000
Temporarily Restricted by Donors	426,000	570,000
Permanently Restricted by Donors	1,215,000	800,000
Total Net Assets	$3,666,000	$3,055,000
Total Liabilities and Net Assets	$5,106,000	$4,530,000

(5)	Accounts Receivable	2,600,000	
	Patient Services Revenue		2,600,000
	Gross charges at standard rates.		

(6)	Contractual Adjustments	240,000	
	Accounts Receivable		240,000
	Deduction from gross revenue for contractual adjustments.		

FIGURE 19–7
Statement of
Operations for
a Not-for-Profit
Hospital

SOL CITY COMMUNITY HOSPITAL Statement of Operations For the Year Ended December 31, 20X2	
Unrestricted Revenue, Gains, and Other Support:	
Net Patient Service Revenue	$2,360,000
Ancillary Programs	30,000
Unrestricted Gifts Used in Operations	93,000
Disposal of Hospital Assets	5,000
Donated Services	10,000
Investment Income Designated for Current Operations	10,000
Net Assets Released from Restrictions for Use in Operations	192,000
Total Revenue, Gains, and Other Support	$2,700,000
Expenses:	
Nursing Services	$ 800,000
Other Professional Services	630,000
General Services	700,000
Fiscal Services	100,000
Administrative Services	80,000
Medical Malpractice Costs	30,000
Bad Debts	60,000
Depreciation	200,000
Total Expenses	$2,600,000
Excess of Operating Revenues over Operating Expenses	$ 100,000
Other Items:	
Investment Return in Excess of Amounts Designated for Current Operations	15,000
Net Assets Released from Restrictions Used for Acquisition of Equipment	225,000
Increase in Unrestricted Net Assets	$ 340,000

FIGURE 19–8
Statement of
Changes in Net
Assets for a Not-
for-Profit Hospital

SOL CITY COMMUNITY HOSPITAL Statement of Changes in Net Assets For the Year Ended December 31, 20X2	
Unrestricted Net Assets:	
Excess of Operating Revenues over Operating Expenses	$ 100,000
Investment Return in Excess of Amounts Designated for Current Operations	15,000
Net Assets Released from Equipment Acquisition Restrictions	225,000
Increase in Unrestricted Net Assets	$ 340,000
Temporarily Restricted Net Assets:	
Contributions	$ 200,000
Investment Gains	73,000
Net Assets Released from:	
Program Use Restrictions	(180,000)
Equipment Acquisition Restrictions	(225,000)
Passage of Time	(12,000)
Decrease in Temporarily Restricted Net Assets	$ (144,000)
Permanently Restricted Net Assets:	
Contributions	$ 415,000
Increase in Permanently Restricted Net Assets	$ 415,000
Increase in Net Assets	$ 611,000
Net Assets at Beginning of Year	3,055,000
Net Assets at End of Year	$3,666,000

FIGURE 19–9   **Statement of Cash Flows for a Not-for-Profit Hospital (Indirect Method)**

SOL CITY COMMUNITY HOSPITAL
Statement of Cash Flows
For the Year Ended December 31, 20X2

Cash Flows from Operating Activities:			
Change in Total Net Assets			$ 611,000
Adjustments to Reconcile Changes in Net Assets			
to Net Cash Provided by Operating Activities:			
Depreciation		$ 200,000	
Investment Unrealized Holding Gain (not			
available for current operations)		(15,000)	
Contribution of Property, Plant, and Equipment		(25,000)	
Gain on Disposal of Equipment		(5,000)	
Increase in Advances from Third Parties		35,000	
Increase in Malpractice Costs		30,000	
Increase in Accrued Expenses		5,000	
Decrease in Accounts Payable		(40,000)	
Increase in Receivables, Net		(50,000)	
Decrease in Pledges Receivable—Current		12,000	
Decrease in Prepaid Expenses		5,000	
Decrease in Inventories		10,000	
Restricted Contributions and Investment Income:			
Contribution for Permanent Endowment	$(415,000)		
Contributions Restricted for Plant Acquisition	(60,000)		
Investment Income Restricted for Plant Acquisition	(7,000)		
Total Restricted Contributions and Investment Income		(482,000)	
Total Adjustments			(320,000)
Net Cash Provided by Operating Activities			$ 291,000
Cash Flows from Investing Activities:			
Sale of Used Hospital Assets			$ 55,000
Sale of Investments			50,000
Acquisition of Plant, Property, and Equipment			(250,000)
Flows Related to Restricted Items:			
Purchase of Investments in Endowment and Plant Replacement Funds	$(522,000)		
Remainder of Contributions to Endowment Fund Restricted to Investing	(15,000)		
Remainder of Contributions to Plant Fund Restricted to Plant Purchases	(50,000)		
Cash Transferred from Plant Fund for Plant Expansion	200,000		
Total Investing Flows Related to Restricted Items			(387,000)
Net Cash Used by Investing Activities			$(532,000)
Cash Flows from Financing Activities:			
Paid Notes Payable			$ (5,000)
Paid Current Portion of Long-Term Debt			(60,000)
Proceeds from Restricted Contributions:			
Contributions Restricted for Permanent Endowment		$ 415,000	
Contributions Restricted for Acquiring Fixed Assets		172,000	
Total Restricted Proceeds			587,000
Net Cash Provided by Financing Activities			$ 522,000
Net Increase in Cash			$ 281,000
Cash at the Beginning of Year			14,000
Cash at the End of Year (unrestricted)			$ 295,000

Revenue from Ancillary Programs   The hospital receives income in 20X2 from providing nonpatient services that include operating a cafeteria and gift shop and from vending machine commissions.

(7)	Cash	30,000	
	Revenue from Cafeteria Sales		20,000
	Revenue from Gift Shop Sales		4,000
	Revenue from Vending Machine Commissions		6,000
	Income from ancillary services.		

Operating Expenses The hospital incurs $2,600,000 in operating expenses for nursing and other professional care, for general and administrative expenses, for bad debts expense, and for depreciation. Not-for-profit hospitals account for estimated uncollectibles from provided services as an operating expense. Fiscal Services Expense includes interest expense on the hospital's debt. The hospital recognized $30,000 in estimated malpractice costs that are probable and reasonably estimated. Cash payments are made for $2,125,000 of the total operating expenses, and the remainder is consumption of Prepaid Assets, Allowance for Uncollectibles, Depreciation, and increases in liabilities. The hospital receives donated services valued at $10,000, which are recognized in entry (9):

(8)	Nursing Services Expense	800,000	
	Other Professional Services Expense	620,000	
	General Services Expense	700,000	
	Fiscal Services Expense	100,000	
	Administrative Services Expense	80,000	
	Medical Malpractice Costs	30,000	
	Bad Debts Expense	60,000	
	Depreciation Expense	200,000	
	Cash		2,125,000
	Allowance for Uncollectibles		60,000
	Inventories		90,000
	Prepaid Expenses		5,000
	Accumulated Depreciation		200,000
	Accounts Payable		50,000
	Accrued Expenses		30,000
	Estimated Medical Malpractice Costs Payable		30,000
	Record operating expenses.		
(9)	Other Professional Services Expense	10,000	
	Donated Services—Revenue		10,000
	Receive donated services.		

Entry (9) records the fair value of donated services both as a debit for the operating expense and as a credit for operating revenue. Therefore, donated services do not affect the bottom line of the hospital's statement of revenue and expenses, but they do affect the amounts shown for the expenses and revenue sections of the statement.

Contribution Revenue During 20X2, Sol City Community Hospital received unrestricted cash gifts in the amount of $63,000 and donated medicines and medical supplies with a market value of $30,000:

(10)	Cash	63,000	
	Contributions—Unrestricted		63,000
	Unrestricted contributions received.		
(11)	Inventory	30,000	
	Contributions—Unrestricted		30,000
	Donated supplies received.		

Other Revenues and Gains Also during 20X2, income of $10,000 was earned in the unrestricted fund and is available for current operations. In addition, a gain of $5,000 was realized on the sale of equipment:

(12)	Cash	10,000	
	Investment Income—Designated for Current Operations		10,000
	Investment earnings available for current operations.		
(13)	Cash	55,000	
	Accumulated Depreciation	50,000	
	Property, Plant, and Equipment		100,000
	Gain on Disposal of Equipment		5,000
	Sale of hospital equipment. The cash will be		
	used in the operations of the hospital.		

Net Assets Released from Restriction Assets were released for unrestricted use from a variety of sources in 20X2, as follows:

Amount	From Restricted Fund	Description
$120,000	Specific-Purpose Fund	Resources for education and research
60,000	Specific-Purpose Fund	Income from endowment investment
200,000	Plant Expansion and Replacement	Resources to acquire equipment
25,000	Plant Expansion and Replacement	Donated assets placed into use
12,000	Time-Restricted Fund	Collection of pledges receivable

Entries in the unrestricted fund to record these transactions are presented here:

(14)	Cash	120,000	
	Net Assets Released from Program Use Restrictions		120,000
	Record payment for reimbursement of operating		
	expenses incurred in accordance with restricted gift.		
(15)	Cash	60,000	
	Net Assets Released from Program Use Restrictions		60,000
	Receipt of endowment earnings from specific-purpose fund		
	upon approval and completion of specified purpose.		
(16)	Cash	200,000	
	Net Assets Released from Equipment Acquisition Restriction		200,000
	Transfer from temporarily restricted plant		
	replacement and expansion fund for use in		
	acquiring plant assets.		
(17)	Property, Plant, and Equipment	25,000	
	Net Assets Released from Equipment Acquisition Restriction		25,000
	Transfer from temporarily restricted plant		
	replacement and expansion fund of donated		
	assets placed in service.		
(18)	Cash	12,000	
	Net Assets Released from Passage of Time		12,000
	Transfer from temporarily restricted funds		
	restricted for use in 20X2.		

Each of the transfers from temporarily restricted funds involves one or more journal entries in those funds. These amounts are not included among 20X2 contributions or income in the unrestricted fund because they were recorded as contributions or income at the time of receipt in the temporarily restricted or permanently restricted funds. The transfer of donated equipment initially is recorded in the temporarily restricted plant fund until the hospital begins using the asset. At the time the assets are placed in service, the value of the donated equipment is transferred to the unrestricted fund.

Other Transactions in the General Fund The remaining transactions during the 20X2 fiscal year affect the balance sheet accounts. Transactions affecting only the asset accounts include collecting receivables, acquiring inventory, selling an investment, and purchasing additional physical plant assets, as follows:

(19)	Cash	2,250,000	
	Allowance for Uncollectibles	50,000	
	Accounts Receivable		2,300,000
	Collect some receivables and write off $50,000 as uncollectible.		
(20)	Inventories	50,000	
	Cash		50,000
	Acquire inventories.		
(21)	Cash	50,000	
	Investments		50,000
	Sell investment at cost.		
(22)	Property, Plant, and Equipment	250,000	
	Cash		250,000
	Purchase new plant with cash of $50,000 from sale of investments and $200,000 from transfer in from temporarily restricted plant replacement and expansion fund.		

Transactions affecting the current liability accounts include paying current liabilities and recording the receipt of cash in advance of billings from third parties. The hospital reclassified the portion of the long-term mortgage that is currently due. The hospital also revalues, to fair value, the general fund's investment securities.

FASB 124 requires that not-for-profit organizations value their investment securities, other than those equity investments accounted for under **APB 18**, at fair market value at each balance sheet date. The total investment income during a period is from dividends, interest, and realized and unrealized holding gains. For a not-for-profit hospital, after the total investment income is determined, the portion of investment income designated for current operations is reported above the operating performance indicator line on the hospital's statement of activities. The investment return in excess of the amount designated for current operations is separately reported below the operating performance indicator line on the hospital's statement of activities. The not-for-profit entity's management is permitted to establish a policy as to the separation of total investment return for current operations or for other purposes. This policy should be described in the footnotes of the hospital's financial statements. For our example, assume that Sol City Community Hospital's board of directors has a policy to set aside the recognition of unrealized holding gains of unrestricted investments for possible future operations. Therefore, the entire $15,000 of unrealized holding gain recognized on the hospital's year-end revaluation of its investment securities is separated and reported below the operating performance indicator line on the hospital's statement of activities.

(23)	Notes Payable to Bank	5,000	
	Current Portion of Long-Term Debt	60,000	
	Accounts Payable	90,000	
	Accrued Expenses	25,000	
	Cash		180,000
	Pay liabilities outstanding at beginning of period.		

(24)	Cash	35,000	
	Advances from Third Parties		35,000
	Increase in cash received from third parties for deposits in advance of service billings.		

(25)	Mortgage Payable	50,000	
	Current Portion of Long-Term Debt		50,000
	Reclassify current portion of long-term debt.		

(26)	Investments	15,000	
	Unrealized Holding Gain on Investment Securities		15,000
	Revalue securities to fair value and report as not designated for current operations.		

Closing entries, required for all nominal accounts, are not presented because the focus is on other aspects of hospital accounting and because the closing process for hospitals is the same as for any other accounting entity. As presented in Figure 19–8, the statement of changes in net assets includes a reconciliation of net assets between the beginning of the year and the year-end.

The statement of cash flows (Figure 19–9) is a required statement. Either the direct or the indirect method may be used to display net cash flows from operations. Under the direct method, the specific inflows and outflows from operations are presented. Under the indirect method, the statement begins with the change in net assets as presented on the statement of changes in net assets. It then presents the adjustments necessary to reconcile the net amount shown on the statement of changes in net assets with the cash flow that is provided by operating activities. Figure 19–9 presents the indirect method because of its popularity and wide use by hospitals. The statement of cash flows is similar to that required of commercial, profit-seeking entities. The three categories of operating activities, investing activities, and financing activities are the same as for commercial entities. There is an important feature, however, for the statement of cash flows for a nonprofit hospital. A nonprofit hospital's cash flow statement reconciles to the change in cash and cash equivalents that is reported as a current asset on the hospital's balance sheet. This cash amount does not include the cash balances in the restricted accounts not available for operations (the plant fund and the endowment fund in the Sol City Community Hospital example). For example, Sol City Community Hospital received a cash contribution to the endowment fund in the amount of $415,000 in transaction (40) (presented later in this chapter). The $415,000 must first be subtracted from the change in net assets in the operating section of the statement of cash flows because the endowment fund does not constitute operating activities. The $415,000 is reported as an increase in financing activities on the statement of cash flows. Of the $415,000 received, $400,000 was used to acquire investments (transaction [41] presented later in this chapter) and this amount is included in the $522,000 as an investing activity on the statement of cash flows. The $15,000 of contributions not used to acquire investments in 20X2 is reported on the statement of cash flows as an investing activity, "Remainder of contributions to endowment fund restricted to investing." This is so because the amount of financing resources from the restricted endowment fund must equal the amount of investing resources from that restricted fund. Thus, the statement of cash flows reconciles only to the change in cash and cash equivalents shown as a current asset on the hospital's balance sheet.

In addition to the primary financial statements for the present fiscal period, with comparatives for the prior period, hospitals are required to present extensive footnotes similar to those of a commercial entity. A specific footnote disclosure is required to report the estimated value of charity care services provided by the hospital during the period.

Temporarily Restricted Funds

Sol City Community Hospital uses three funds to account for temporarily restricted funds. The specific-purpose fund is for contributions designated for a particular use by the donor other than plant replacement and expansion. The time-restricted fund is for contributions pledged or received in advance that will be available for unrestricted use in the future. The plant replacement and expansion fund is for contributions to be used in acquiring additional land, buildings, and equipment.

Specific-Purpose Fund

The specific-purpose fund is used to account for contributions received for which a donor-specific use has been designated. For the most part, such contributions support particular operating activities of the hospital, such as educational or research programs, or provide a particular type of service to patients. The specific-purpose fund does not directly spend the resources; it holds the restricted resources until the general fund satisfies the terms of the restriction, usually by making the appropriate operating cost or by having the restricted cost approved by the governing board, upon which the resources are transferred from the specific-purpose fund to the general fund to pay for the operating cost.

The specific-purpose restricted fund typically invests its cash and receives interest or dividends from its investments. A variety of investment transactions can affect the fund balance. Nevertheless, the specific fund is only a holding fund for temporarily restricted resources until they are released for use by the hospital.

The following entries record the transactions in Sol City Community Hospital's specific-purpose fund during the 20X2 fiscal year and are reflected in the balance sheet in Figure 19–6 and the statement of changes in net assets in Figure 19–8.

Additions to Specific-Purpose Fund   The specific-purpose fund receives $6,000 of interest income from its investment of funds from a restricted gift to support the hospital's research activity. Restricted gifts of $115,000 are received in response to a community fund-raising effort. The restricted gifts are allocated based on the donors' specifications. In addition, endowment fund earnings in the amount of $60,000 were deposited directly in the temporarily restricted fund:

(27)	Cash	6,000	
	Investment Income—Research		6,000
	Interest on investment of research gift resources.		
(28)	Cash	115,000	
	Contributions—Education		60,000
	Contributions—Research		55,000
	Receive restricted gifts.		
(29)	Cash	60,000	
	Investment Income—Endowment Earnings		60,000
	Earnings of endowment fund deposited in temporarily restricted funds until released for specified purposes.		

Entry (29) shows the earnings generated by the permanently restricted endowment fund's investments as reported by the temporarily restricted fund. **FASB 124** specifies that dividend, interest, and other investment income should be reported in the period earned as increases in unrestricted net assets unless there are donor-imposed restrictions on the use of the assets. However, in the case of Sol City Community Hospital, the earnings are reported as investment income of the temporarily restricted fund because of a donor-imposed restriction on those earnings. After clearance is given, the resources are then transferred to the general fund to be expended for the donor-specified purposes. If the donor-restricted investment income is permanently restricted, the income is reported in the permanently restricted net assets.

Gains or losses from valuation adjustments to fair value or from sales of securities must also be applied in accordance with any donor restrictions. For example, if the donor specifies that a specific investment be held for perpetuity, any valuation or sales transaction gain or loss on that investment is reported in the permanently restricted net asset class. The important point is to follow any restrictions imposed by the donor or applicable laws. If no restrictions are applicable, the investment income and gains or losses are reported in the unrestricted net asset class.

Deductions from Specific-Purpose Fund The specific-purpose fund is notified that the general fund fulfilled the terms of agreements for specific restricted grants totaling $120,000. In addition to the $120,000, the specific-purpose fund also transferred $60,000 from endowment income to the general fund.

(30)	Net Assets Released from Program Use		
	Restriction—Education	61,000	
	Net Assets Released from Program Use		
	Restriction—Research	59,000	
	Net Assets Released from Program Use		
	Restriction—Endowment Income	60,000	
	Cash		180,000
	Funds released from temporary restriction.		

This interfund transaction was also recorded in the general fund (see entries [14] and [15] earlier in the chapter).

Time-Restricted Fund

Under **FASB 116**, procedures for recording contributions were changed. Earlier recognition of contribution revenue generally is now required for most not-for-profit organizations, including hospitals. Because of the critical nature of contributions to the operations of voluntary health and welfare organizations, a thorough treatment of this topic is included later in the chapter as part of the discussion of voluntary health and welfare organizations. For purposes of illustration in the hospital setting, it is assumed that in 20X1 the hospital received pledges for $12,000 to be collected in 20X2. During 20X2, the $12,000 in pledges was collected and immediately transferred to the general fund for unrestricted use (see entry [18] earlier in the chapter).

(31)	Cash	12,000	
	Pledges Receivable		12,000
	Collection of prior period pledge.		

(32)	Net Assets Released from Time Restrictions	12,000	
	Cash		12,000
	Funds released from time restrictions.		

Plant Replacement and Expansion Fund

The plant replacement and expansion fund, sometimes called the "plant fund," is used to account for restricted resources given to the hospital to be used only for additions or major modifications to the physical plant. This fund is used as a holding fund until the expenditures for plant assets are approved in the general fund by the governing board. The resources are then transferred to the general fund.

A primary source of resources for the plant replacement and expansion fund is from fund-raising efforts in the communities served by the hospital. Hospitals often ask potential donors to sign pledges specifying a giving level for a period of time, for example, $100 per month for the next 12 months. The pledges become receivables of the fund and typically require a substantial allowance for uncollectibles. The fund records contribution revenue at the time the pledge is received.

The entries recorded in Sol City Community Hospital's plant replacement and expansion fund during 20X2 are presented next and are reflected in the balance sheet in Figure 19–6.

Additions to Plant Fund Increases in the plant replacement and expansion fund during the period are a donation of equipment with a fair value of $25,000 that is recorded in the restricted plant fund until the equipment is placed into service; a donation of $60,000 for use to acquire additional equipment; and the receipt of $7,000 of interest on the plant fund's investments restricted to the purchase of plant. Entries to record these events follow:

(33)	Property, Plant, and Equipment		25,000	
	Contributions—Plant			25,000
	Receive donated equipment with fair value of $25,000.			
(34)	Cash		60,000	
	Contributions—Plant			60,000
	Receive restricted gifts for use to acquire equipment.			
(35)	Cash		7,000	
	Investment Income—Plant			7,000
	Receive interest on fund's investments.			

Deductions from Plant Fund Deductions from the plant fund during the year are two interfund transfers to the general fund. The first is the transfer of $25,000 of donated equipment that is placed into service, and the second is the transfer of $200,000 to the general fund for expenditures for fixed assets. These two interfund transfers are also recorded in the general fund (see entries [16] and [17] earlier in the chapter):

(36)	Net Assets Released—Plant Acquisition		25,000	
	Property, Plant, and Equipment			25,000
	Transfer donated equipment to general fund at time of placement into service.			
(37)	Net Assets Released—Plant Acquisition		200,000	
	Cash			200,000
	Transfer cash to general fund for use in acquiring plant assets.			

Other Transactions in Plant Funds Other transactions affecting only the asset or liability accounts of the plant funds represent a collection of pledges made by individual donors during the last capital fund-raising drive as well as the acquisition of additional investments in the fund. Entries for these transactions are presented here:

(38)	Cash		105,000	
	Pledges Receivable			105,000
	Collect pledges receivable.			
(39)	Investments		122,000	
	Cash			122,000
	Increase investments.			

Endowment Fund

An endowment fund is a collection of cash, securities, or other assets. The use of its assets may be permanently restricted, temporarily restricted, or unrestricted based on the donor's wishes. Generally, endowment funds are established by donors to permanently restrict the capital of the donation and specify the use(s) of any income from those investments. The classification of an endowment fund is based, however, on the terms of the donor's contribution. If the endowment fund is temporarily restricted for a stated period of time after which the principal becomes available for the specified uses, it is normally described as a *term endowment.* If an endowment fund is permanently restricted into perpetuity, it is normally described as a *regular* or *permanent endowment.*

Sol City Community Hospital has a permanently restricted endowment fund to account for resources for which the donors have specified that the principal must be maintained in perpetuity. The income from the investments in the endowment fund is recorded in the appropriate fund based on the donor's specifications. If the investment income is restricted, it is recorded in the appropriate restricted fund. If no donor-imposed restriction is present, the investment income should be recorded and reported in the unrestricted net asset fund.

The balance sheet in Figure 19–6 and the statement of changes in net assets in Figure 19–8 include the entries in Sol City Community Hospital's endowment fund for 20X2.

Additions to Endowment Fund The endowment fund earns $60,000 interest and dividends from its permanent investments that are deposited directly in the temporarily restricted fund (see entry [29]). In addition, a total of $415,000 in new permanent endowments is received and $400,000 is used to acquire additional investments:

(40)	Cash	415,000	
	Contributions—Permanent Endowment		415,000
	Receive additional endowments.		
(41)	Investments	400,000	
	Cash		400,000
	Acquire additional investments.		

Summary of Hospital Accounting and Financial Reporting

The major operating activities of a hospital take place in the general fund. The restricted funds are holding funds that transfer resources to the general fund for expenditures upon satisfaction of their respective restrictions. The accrual basis of accounting is used in the general fund to fully measure the revenue and costs of providing health care. Patient services revenue is reported at gross amounts measured at standard billing rates. A deduction for contractual adjustments is then made to arrive at net patient services revenue. Other revenue is recognized for ongoing nonpatient services, such as cafeteria sales and television rentals, and donated supplies and medicines. Charity care services are presented only in the footnotes; no revenue is recognized for them. Operating expenses in the general fund include depreciation, bad debts, and the value of recognized donated services that are in support of the basic services of the hospital. Not all donated services are recognized. Donated property and equipment are typically recorded in a restricted fund, such as the plant fund, until placed into service, at which time they are transferred to the general fund. Donated assets are recorded at their fair market values at the date of gift.

The financial statements of a hospital are (1) the balance sheet, (2) the statement of operations, (3) the statement of changes in net assets, and (4) the statement of cash flows.

VOLUNTARY HEALTH AND WELFARE ORGANIZATIONS

Voluntary health and welfare organizations (VHWOs) provide a variety of social services. Examples of such organizations are United Way, the American Heart Association, the March of Dimes, the American Cancer Society, the Red Cross, and the Salvation Army. These organizations solicit funds from the community at large and typically provide their services for no fee, or they may charge a nominal fee to those with the ability to pay.

As in the case of hospitals, accounting and financial reporting principles for VHWOs have undergone major change with the publication of **FASB 116** and **FASB 117**. Additional information on VHWOs may be obtained from a variety of sources. The AICPA Audit Guide for Not-for-Profit Organizations requires the use of generally accepted accounting principles for VHWOs. VHWOs are typically audited, and the audited financial statements are made available to contributors and to others interested in knowing about the financial condition of the organization and how the resources are being used. The federal government normally provides tax-exempt status to these organizations. Another source for accounting and reporting guidelines for VHWOs is the *Standards of Accounting and Financial Reporting for Voluntary Health and Welfare Organizations*, published by the combined group of the National Health Council, the National Assembly of National Voluntary Health and Social Welfare Organizations, and the United Way of America. The standards book, known as "The Black Book," for the color of its cover, represents an effort to incorporate accounting and financial reporting standards as well as the actual experiences of the largest VHWOs in the United States in one manual.

Accounting for a VHWO

The accrual basis of accounting is required for VHWOs in order to measure fully the resources available to the organization. Depreciation is reported as an operating expense each period because the omission of depreciation would result in an understatement of the costs of providing the organization's services. Therefore, accounting for VHWOs is similar to other not-for-profit organizations except for special financial statements that report on the important aspects of VHWOs. An overview of the accounting and financial reporting principles for a VHWO is presented in this section.

Even though not required to do so, VHWOs have been free to use fund accounting in their accounting and reporting processes. In the past, the typical VHWO has been portrayed as using a fund structure with (1) a current unrestricted fund, (2) a current restricted fund, (3) a land, building, and equipment fund, and (4) an endowment fund. Many VHWOs are considerably smaller in size and scope of activity than hospitals and may find it convenient to convert from the traditional fund structure to a single accounting entity or a fund structure that distinguishes between unrestricted, temporarily restricted, and permanently restricted assets. The journal entries for Voluntary Health and Welfare Service presented in this section assume the use of a single fund or accounting entity. When appropriate, designations have been added to the journal entry captions to show which of the three classes of assets (unrestricted, temporarily restricted, or permanently restricted) is affected. Thus, the entries could be used equally well if separate funds were established for each of the three asset classifications. Journal entries are presented in the following discussion for only a portion of the transactions of Voluntary Health and Welfare Service in 20X2.

Financial Statements for a VHWO

A VHWO must provide the following financial statements: (1) statement of financial position, (2) statement of activities, (3) statement of cash flows, and (4) statement of functional expenses.

The financial statements are designed primarily for those who are interested in the organization as "outsiders," not members of management. These include contributors, beneficiaries of services, creditors and potential creditors, and related organizations. A clear distinction should be maintained between restricted resources and those resources available for expenditure for the organization's major missions. As outlined in **FASB Concepts Statement No. 6**, "Elements of Financial Statements" (FAC 6), net assets of not-for-profit organizations are divided into three mutually exclusive classes: permanently restricted net assets, temporarily restricted net assets, and unrestricted net assets. Restricted resources are subject to externally imposed constraints, not internal or board-designated decisions that may be changed by the governing board of the VHWO. In addition, readers of the general-purpose financial statements should be able to clearly evaluate management's performance in accomplishing the objectives of the VHWO.

Statement of Financial Position for a VHWO

Figure 19–10 presents a statement of financial position for a VHWO. The format used is similar to that used in the hospital illustration. Although it is not required by existing standards, the assets and liabilities are segregated into current and noncurrent classifications.

FIGURE 19–10
Statement of
Financial Position
for a Voluntary
Health and Welfare
Organization

VOLUNTARY HEALTH AND WELFARE SERVICE
Statement of Financial Position
December 31, 20X2 and 20X1

	20X2	20X1
Assets		
Current:		
Cash	$ 68,000	$ 47,600
Short-Term Investments	39,000	48,000
Accounts Receivable	1,200	1,000
Inventories	6,400	8,300
Net Pledges Receivable	78,400	61,600
Prepaid Expenses	8,000	7,200
Total Current Assets	$201,000	$173,700
Cash Restricted for Long-Term Use	1,000	-0-
Long-Term Investments	383,000	351,900
Property, Plant, and Equipment	125,500	121,600
Total Assets	$710,500	$647,200
Liabilities and Net Assets		
Current:		
Accounts Payable	$ 16,100	$ 12,400
Accrued Expenses	4,800	4,300
Total Current Liabilities	$ 20,900	$ 16,700
Noncurrent:		
Mortgage Payable	$ 21,000	$ 23,000
Capital Leases	8,000	7,000
Total Liabilities	$ 49,900	$ 46,700
Net Assets:		
Unrestricted	$498,200	$437,800
Temporarily Restricted by Donors	22,900	24,100
Permanently Restricted by Donors	139,500	138,600
Total Net Assets	$660,600	$600,500
Total Liabilities and Net Assets	$710,500	$647,200

The net assets section of the statement of financial position for VHWOs must be segregated into unrestricted, temporarily restricted, and permanently restricted, as illustrated. Major balance sheet accounts are as follows.

Pledges from Donors   Pledges may be unconditional or conditional promises to give. Conditional promises to give, which depend on the occurrence of a specified future and uncertain event, are recognized only after the conditions on which they depend are substantially met (i.e., when the conditional promise becomes unconditional). The pledges may be unrestricted, temporarily restricted, or permanently restricted based on the circumstances of the pledge and the donor's specifications.

For the VHWO example, the current unrestricted fund includes net *pledges receivable* of $78,400 in 20X2. The accrual basis of accounting recognizes the receivable and associated revenue when the unconditional pledge is received. If the contribution is available to support current-period activities, there is no restriction. An adequate allowance for uncollectibles for the pledges receivable is recognized by a debit to Contributions, as a direct reduction from the contribution revenue account, and a credit to Allowance for Uncollectible Pledges, which is a contra account to the pledges receivable asset account. Note that VHWOs do not have a bad debts expense account; the revenue account is charged directly for estimated uncollectible amounts. Pledges or other contributions applicable to future periods should be reported in temporarily restricted net assets as "Contributions—Temporarily Restricted" to show that these resources are not currently available for the entity's operations. Further accuracy could be attained by identifying the temporary restriction as "Contributions—Temporarily Restricted—Time Restrictions." Conditional pledges are not recognized until the conditions on which they depend have been substantially met.

The following illustrates the entries used in accounting for a portion of the pledges received by Voluntary Health and Welfare Service in 20X2. Note that this discussion is for only a part of the pledges, not all of the pledges received in the year, nor does the following discussion attempt to reconcile to the $78,400 balance in net pledges receivable at the end of the year. It shows the accounting for the pledges from only one of the organization's several pledge campaigns during the year.

A special pledge campaign resulted in $100,000 of new pledges received. Of this total, $5,000 is to be received in the current period but is to be held for use for unrestricted purposes in the following period. Experience shows that 20 percent of pledges are uncollectible for this organization. An allowance for uncollectibles is recognized in the amount of $20,000. Note that both the current and deferred pledges are reported as contribution revenue in the period the unconditional pledges are received and that provisions for estimated uncollectibles are then recorded as reductions of contribution revenue.

(42)	Pledges Receivable—Unrestricted	95,000	
	Pledges Receivable—Temporarily Restricted	5,000	
	Contributions—Unrestricted		95,000
	Contributions—Temporarily Restricted		5,000
	Receive pledges and recognize receivables.		
(43)	Contributions—Unrestricted	19,000	
	Contributions—Temporarily Restricted	1,000	
	Allowance for Uncollectible Pledges—Unrestricted		19,000
	Allowance for Uncollectible Pledges—Restricted		1,000
	Provide for estimated uncollectible pledges as a reduction of contributions.		

Note that there is no separate bad debt expense recognition. Instead, the contributions accounts are reduced for the estimated amount of uncollectible pledges. **FASB 116** states that unconditional promises to give that are expected to be collected in less than one year may be measured at net realizable value (net settlement value). Pledged contributions expected to be collected in the future beyond one year should be valued at their present value of the estimated future cash flows. Subsequent increases in the present value of the future cash flows due to the reduction of the present value discount are accounted for as contribution income in the appropriate fund for which the pledge was received.

All $5,000 of the funds pledged for use the following year and $85,000 of unrestricted pledges are collected in the current period, requiring an adjustment to both unrestricted and temporarily restricted contribution revenue. Temporarily restricted contribution revenue is increased by $1,000 to the full $5,000 received, and $9,000 is added to unrestricted contribution revenue due to collections of $85,000 in pledges versus the initial estimate of $76,000 ($95,000 × .80). Of the remaining balance, $3,000 is written off as uncollectible, and the remainder is carried over to the following period:

(44)	Cash—Unrestricted	85,000	
	Cash—Temporarily Restricted	5,000	
	Allowance for Uncollectible Pledges—Unrestricted	9,000	
	Allowance for Uncollectible Pledges—Restricted	1,000	
	Pledges Receivable—Unrestricted		85,000
	Pledges Receivable—Temporarily Restricted		5,000
	Contribution Revenue—Unrestricted		9,000
	Contribution Revenue—Temporarily Restricted		1,000
	Collect pledges including $10,000 above initial estimate of collectibility.		

(45)	Allowance for Uncollectible Pledges—Unrestricted	3,000	
	Pledges Receivable—Unrestricted		3,000
	Write off uncollectible pledges in unrestricted net asset class.		

In the following period when the $5,000 is available for unrestricted use, the balance is reclassified as unrestricted. Some organizations would use the terms "net assets released" instead of "reclassification," but the terms are synonymous, and both terms are used in this chapter to show their equality.

(46)	Cash—Unrestricted	5,000	
	Reclassification of Contributions to Unrestricted		5,000
	Reclassify time restricted funds to unrestricted.		
(47)	Reclassification of Contributions from Temporarily Restricted	5,000	
	Cash—Temporarily Restricted		5,000
	Reclassify time restricted funds from temporarily restricted.		

FASB 116 also prescribes appropriate treatment for unconditional pledges to be received over a longer period of time. In general, contribution revenue is recognized at the present value of future cash receipts. As is the normal practice in utilizing present value procedures in the corporate sector, the present value is used to record contributions to be received in the following accounting periods. For example, if a donor agrees to contribute $10,000 per year at the end of each of the next five years, the stream of the payments is discounted at an appropriate rate (e.g., 8 percent), and the present value is recognized at the time the pledge is received:

(48)	Pledges Receivable—Temporarily Restricted	39,927	
	Contributions—Temporarily Restricted		39,927
	Receipt of pledge.		

At the end of the first year when the first payment of $10,000 is received, that amount is reclassified from temporarily restricted to unrestricted, and the increase in present value of the contributions receivable is recognized as an increase in temporarily restricted contributions and contributions receivable:

(49)	Cash—Unrestricted	10,000	
	Reclassification of Contributions to Unrestricted		10,000
	Reclassify time-restricted funds to unrestricted.		
(50)	Reclassification of Contributions from Temporarily Restricted	10,000	
	Pledges Receivable—Temporarily Restricted		10,000
	Reclassify time-restricted funds from temporarily restricted.		
(51)	Pledges Receivable—Temporarily Restricted	3,194	
	Contributions—Temporarily Restricted		3,194
	Increase in the present value of contributions receivable.		

Investments   Investments may be purchased or donated to the organization. Purchased investments should be recorded at cost. Securities donated to the organization should be recorded at their fair market values at the dates of the gifts. Subsequently, equity investments (other than **APB 18** equity investments) and all investments in bonds are reported at market value. Appreciation gains (or reductions in value) are separately identified as unrealized gains (losses) in the organization's statement of activity in accordance with **FASB 124**. Transfers of investments from one portfolio to another should be made at market value, with any gains or losses in valuation recorded.

Investment earnings or losses should be reported as unrestricted, temporarily restricted, or permanently restricted, depending on how they are to be used. For example, the donor of a donor-restricted endowment fund may not specify any limitations on the uses of the income or losses from the fund. In that case, the income or losses on the investments are reported on the statement of activities as changes in unrestricted net assets. However, if the donor stipulates the treatment of the income or losses from the donor-restricted endowment fund, that treatment must be followed. In some cases, the donor may impose some time or dollar requirement on the earnings, such as requiring that the income for the first five years be added to the permanent endowment or that only income above some dollar amount can be transferred to an unrestricted fund while the income below that amount must be added to the principal of the permanent endowment. The key point is that the not-for-profit association must follow the donor's specifications as presented in the contribution agreement between the donor and the not-for-profit association and any applicable law regarding a not-for-profit association's management of restricted resources.

Land, Buildings, and Equipment Land, buildings, and equipment, depreciation expense, and the accumulated depreciation on the fixed assets generally are reported as unrestricted unless restricted by the donor. The VHWO may have an accounting policy of retaining long-lived, restricted buildings and equipment in the restricted net asset class even though the assets are used in the operations of the entity. As the buildings and equipment are used in the operations, an allowance for depreciation is reclassified from the restricted net asset class to the unrestricted net asset class. This provides for depreciation and maintains the net book value of the restricted buildings and equipment in the restricted net asset class. The basis of fixed assets is cost, and donated assets are recorded at their fair market values at the dates of the gifts. Donations of fixed assets that will be sold by the organization in the near future are equivalent to other contributions and should be separately reported as unrestricted assets until sold. For example, assume that the VHWO receives land as a donation. The VHWO plans to sell the land and use the proceeds from the sale in supporting the entity's program services. The land should be recorded at fair value as an unrestricted asset and reported as land held for resale, until sold.

A VHWO may use any one of the methods of depreciation available to commercial entities. Not-for-profit entities are not required to depreciate assets such as works of art or other historically valuable assets in instances in which the not-for-profit entity has made a commitment to preserve the value of the art or historically valuable assets, and has shown the capacity to do so.

Liabilities Liabilities are recorded in the normal manner under the accrual model. In most situations, liabilities will be reported as part of the unrestricted net assets. For example, the mortgage payment made by Voluntary Health and Welfare Service in 20X2 was recorded as a $2,000 debit to Mortgage Payable and a $2,000 credit to Cash. In this illustration, property, plant, and equipment is classified as an unrestricted asset. In some cases, mortgage payments on assets classified as restricted are made from unrestricted funds. The following entries are needed in the latter case:

(52)	Reclassification to Restricted Assets	2,000	
	Cash (Unrestricted)		2,000
	Mortgage payment made from unrestricted assets.		
(53)	Mortgage Payable—Restricted Assets	2,000	
	Reclassification from Unrestricted Assets		2,000
	Reduction of carrying value of mortgage.		

Net Assets Separate disclosure should be provided for the amounts of net assets designated as unrestricted, temporarily restricted, and permanently restricted. The VHWO's governing board also may show its intent to use unrestricted resources for specific needs in the future by creating one or more board-designated captions. For example, the $498,200 of unrestricted

FIGURE 19–11 Statement of Activities for a Voluntary Health and Welfare Organization

VOLUNTARY HEALTH AND WELFARE SERVICE
Statement of Activities
For the Year Ended December 31, 20X2

	Unrestricted	Temporarily Restricted	Permanently Restricted	Total
Revenues, Gains, and Other Support:				
Contributions	$627,000	$42,300	$ 9,900	$679,200
Legacies and Bequests	15,000			15,000
Collections through Affiliates	2,800			2,800
Allocated from Federated Fund-Raising Effort	45,300			45,300
Memberships	6,100			6,100
Program Fees	700			700
Sale of Materials	200			200
Investment Income	36,400	500		36,900
Gain on Investments	12,000		1,000	13,000
Donated Services	3,000			3,000
Net Assets Released from Restriction:				
Program Use Restrictions	25,000	(25,000)		
Passage of Time	8,100	(8,100)		
Equipment Acquisition	10,900	(10,900)		
Endowment Transfers	10,000		(10,000)	
Total Revenues, Gains, and Other Support	$802,500	$ (1,200)	$ 900	$802,200
Program Services and Operating Costs:				
Research	$274,300			$274,300
Public Health Education	92,000			92,000
Professional Training	106,000			106,000
Community Services	98,600			98,600
Management and General	91,700			91,700
Fund-Raising	64,500			64,500
Payments to National Offices	15,000			15,000
Total Expenses	$742,100	$ -0-	$ -0-	$742,100
Change in Net Assets	$ 60,400	$ (1,200)	$ 900	$ 60,100
Net Assets at Beginning of Year	437,800	24,100	138,600	600,500
Net Assets at End of Year	$498,200	$22,900	$139,500	$660,600

net assets at December 31, 20X2, shown in Figure 19–10 could be separated into board designated and undesignated. Board-designated purposes might be for purchases of new equipment, research, construction of new facilities, or other asset acquisitions. While the statement of financial position could reflect the designation of resources, the governing board may change these at any time.

Statement of Activities

Figure 19–11 presents the major operating statement for Voluntary Health and Welfare Service, the statement of activities. The overall structure of the statement of activities for voluntary health and welfare organizations and other not-for-profit entities should be very similar as a result of **FASB 117**. As for other types of nonprofit entities, a number of organizations have issued standards relating to VHWOs. Both the National Health Council's "black book" of standards for VHWOs and the AICPA Audit Guide for Not-for-Profit Organizations contain recommendations for accounting for VHWOs. Several of the unique aspects of VHWOs are discussed next.

Public Support Historically, a distinction has been made in the sources of funding received by VHWOs. Nonprofit organizations generally provide services to those who cannot afford to pay for the benefits received or support programs for which little compensation is received.

For VHWOs, the primary source of funds is likely to be contributions from individuals or organizations who do not derive any direct benefit from the VHWO for their gifts. The magnitude of funds received and the diversity of contributors are important in evaluating the effectiveness of VHWOs. Four sources of resources included in the 20X2 statement of activities for Voluntary Health and Welfare Service in Figure 19–11 are considered to fall in the category of support. They include contributions, legacies and bequests, collections through affiliates (other organizations in the same community or with similar goals), and contributions received from the federated (national or regional) organization's fund-raising efforts.

A recent change has occurred in accounting for support received from special events. In the past, the costs of providing the event were deducted from the total proceeds generated and the net amount was reported as support. Under the guidelines of **FASB 117**, total proceeds from a sponsored event such as a dance gala or marathon are reported as support from special events, and the costs of sponsoring the event are reported as fund-raising costs. Even though many of the necessary items are contributed for such activities, the costs of sponsoring an event can be rather substantial. The frequency of such events undoubtedly was a factor in the change in the tax laws that now require nonprofit organizations sponsoring a special event to provide participants with a statement detailing the portion of the cost of a ticket or other contribution that may be treated as a charitable contribution for tax purposes.

Revenues Funds received in exchange for services provided or other activities are classified as revenues. Although the majority of a VHWO's resources are obtained from public support, funds also are received from memberships, fees charged to program participants, sales of supplies and services, and investment income.

Gains Investments and other assets may be sold from time to time, and the difference between the sale price and the carrying value is included in the statement of activities as a gain or loss. Much of the time, gains received from sales of investments are reinvested in anticipation of future earnings; nevertheless, all gains and losses should be included in the statement of activities for the period.

Donated Materials and Services A VHWO often relies heavily on ***donated materials and services***. Donated materials should be recorded at fair value when received. If the donated materials are used in one of the VHWO's program services, their recorded value should be reported as an expense in the period used. If the donated materials simply pass through the VHWO to its charitable beneficiaries, the VHWO is acting as an agent, and the materials are not recorded as a contribution or an expense.

Donated services are an essential part of a VHWO. Because of the difficulty of valuing these services, they often are not recorded as contributions. However, if donated services are significant, the VHWO should recognize them if the services (1) create or enhance nonfinancial assets, or (2) require specialized skills, are provided by individuals possessing those skills, and typically need to be purchased if not provided by donation. If these conditions are satisfied, the value of donated services should be reported as part of the public support and as an expense in the period in which the services are provided. As an example of donated services, assume that a CPA donates audit services with an estimated value of $3,000. The VHWO makes the following entry in the current unrestricted fund to recognize the donated services:

(54)	Expenses—Supporting Services	3,000	
	Support—Donated Services		3,000
	CPA donates audit.		

Donated services that are directly related to restricted assets should be reported in the restricted net assets class. For example, an architect may provide donated services for the planning of the construction of a new building that is restricted for a specific purpose. In this case, the value of the donated services is capitalized to the construction in progress in the restricted net asset class and becomes part of the basis of the new building.

Expenses The statement of activities should contain information about the major costs of providing services to the public, fund-raising, and general and administrative costs in order to provide contributors and others information that is useful in assessing the VHWO's effectiveness. Those costs of providing goods and services to beneficiaries, customers, or members in fulfilling the primary VHWO mission are referred to as *program service costs.* A VHWO's statement of activities normally should include the total costs of providing each of the major classes of program services. As shown in Figure 19–11, the primary activities for Voluntary Health and Welfare Service are research, public health education, professional training, and community services. **FASB 117** requires that all not-for-profit entities report total entity expenses in the unrestricted fund, even those financed by restricted fund resources. No expenses will be reported by restricted funds: the restricted fund will report a transfer out for the amount expended and the unrestricted fund will report a transfer in.

Information also is presented in the statement of activities on the costs of other activities needed for the organization to operate effectively but that may not be directly assignable to a particular program. These costs generally are reported either as management and general administrative costs or as fund-raising costs. Management and general activities include the costs of maintaining the general headquarters, recordkeeping, business management, and other management and administrative activities not directly assignable to program services or fund-raising activities. Fund-raising activities include the costs of special mailings, compiling potential donor lists, conducting campaigns through contacts with foundations and governmental agencies, and other similar costs. In those organizations whose membership contributions are an important source of funds, separate disclosure of the costs of soliciting members and providing special benefits to those who are members should be made.

Depreciation costs for 20X2 totaled $9,500. An allocation is made to each of the program services and supporting services based on square footage used or some other reasonable basis. For example, an allocation of the $9,500 of depreciation, based on square footage occupied, to each of the program and supporting services is recorded with the following entry:

(55)			
	Research—Depreciation	4,300	
	Public Health—Depreciation	1,000	
	Professional Training—Depreciation	2,000	
	Community Services—Depreciation	1,200	
	Management and General—Depreciation	500	
	Fund-Raising—Depreciation	500	
	Accumulated Depreciation		9,500
	Record depreciation for 20X2.		

Costs of Informational Materials That Include a Fund-Raising Appeal   Not-for-profit entities often prepare informational materials that include a direct or indirect message soliciting funds. The issue is how to record the cost of these materials. Should these costs be a program expense or a fund-raising expense? Many VHWOs prefer to classify such costs as program rather than fund-raising to highlight the fulfillment of their basic service mission and to present a better ratio of program expenses to total expenses. Users of the general-purpose financial statements are concerned with the amounts that VHWO organizations spend to solicit contributions, as opposed to the amounts spent for program services. If a not-for-profit entity cannot show that a program or management function has been conducted in conjunction with the appeal for funds, the entire cost of the informational materials or activities should be reported as a fund-raising expense. However, if it can demonstrate that a bona fide program or management function has been conducted in conjunction with the appeal for funds, then the ***costs of informational materials*** are allocated between programs and fund-raising. Evidence of a bona fide program intent in a brochure would be an appeal designed to motivate its audience to action other than providing financial support to the organization. The informational content of a brochure might include a description of the symptoms of a disease and the actions an individual should take if one or more of the symptoms occur. Thus, the content of the message and the intended audience are significant factors.

Statement of Cash Flows

The third required financial statement for VHWOs is the statement of cash flows, as presented in Figure 19–12. The format of this statement is similar to that for hospitals as discussed earlier in the chapter. Note that under the indirect approach, the statement begins with the change in net assets and reconciles to the net cash provided by operating activities.

Statement of Functional Expenses

The fourth statement required of all VHWOs is the ***statement of functional expenses***. This statement details the items reported in the expenses section of the statement of activities in Figure 19–11. Figure 19–13 is a standard format for the statement of functional expenses. The expense categories are presented across the columns. The rows provide the specific nature of the items composing these expense categories from the various funds.

Bad Debts Expense is from estimated uncollectibles directly related to program services and operations, including membership fees. Note that any estimated uncollectible pledges are deducted directly from contribution revenue.

The statement of functional expenses includes depreciation of $9,500 for the year, allocated among the various programs and supporting services. Total expenses of $742,100 in Figure 19–11 are analyzed and reconciled on the statement of functional expenses in Figure 19–13.

FIGURE 19–12
Statement of
Cash Flows for a
Voluntary Health
and Welfare
Organization

VOLUNTARY HEALTH AND WELFARE SERVICE		
Statement of Cash Flows		
For the Year Ended December 31, 20X2		
Change in Net Assets		$60,100
Adjustments to Reconcile Changes in Net Assets to Net Cash		
Provided by Operating Activities:		
Depreciation	$ 9,500	
Gain on Sale of Investments	(13,000)	
Decrease in Short-Term Investments	9,000	
Increase in Accounts Receivable	(200)	
Increase in Contributions Receivable (net)	(16,800)	
Decrease in Inventories	1,900	
Increase in Prepaid Expenses	(800)	
Increase in Accounts Payable	3,700	
Increase in Accrued Expenses	500	
Contributions Restricted for Equipment Acquisition	(10,900)	
Endowment Contributions Restricted for Acquisition		
of Investments	(9,900)	(27,000)
Net Cash Provided by Operating Activities		$33,100
Cash Flows from Investing Activities:		
Purchase of Property, Plant, and Equipment	$(13,400)	
Proceeds from Sale of Investments	40,000	
Purchase of Investments	(59,100)	
Investment Gain Restricted to Purchase of Investments	(1,000)	
Net Cash Used by Investing Activities		(33,500)
Cash Flows from Financing Activities:		
Mortgage Payments	$ (2,000)	
Capital Lease Agreements	1,000	
Contributions Restricted to Acquiring Fixed Assets	10,900	
Endowment Gain Restricted to Acquiring Investments	1,000	
Contributions Restricted for Permanent Endowment	9,900	
Net Cash Used in Financing Activities		20,800
Net Increase in Cash		$20,400
Cash at the Beginning of Year		47,600
Cash at the End of Year		$68,000

FIGURE 19–13   Statement of Functional Expenses for a Voluntary Health and Welfare Organization

VOLUNTARY HEALTH AND WELFARE SERVICE
Statement of Functional Expenses
Year Ended December 31, 20X2
(with comparative totals for 20X1)

	Program Services					Supporting Services			Total Program and Supporting Services Expenses	
	Research	Public Health Education	Professional Training	Community Services	Total	Management and General	Fund-Raising	Total	20X2	20X1
Salaries	$ 49,000	$58,200	$ 51,100	$53,800	$212,100	$66,100	$34,100	$100,200	$312,300	$347,000
Employee Benefits	2,800	2,900	2,900	2,900	11,500	4,100	1,000	5,100	16,600	16,800
Payroll Taxes, etc.	2,400	3,100	2,600	2,900	11,000	3,600	1,800	5,400	16,400	15,500
Total Salaries and Related Expenses	$ 54,200	$64,200	$ 56,600	$59,600	$234,600	$73,800	$36,900	$100,700	$345,300	$379,300
Professional Fees	200	1,000	5,200	1,600	8,000	3,000	1,500	4,500	12,500	12,000
Supplies	400	600	1,000	1,000	3,000	2,100	3,000	5,100	8,100	7,900
Telephone	400	1,400	1,200	4,300	7,300	2,500	7,200	9,700	17,000	16,800
Bad Debts and Other	400	3,200	900	2,800	7,300	2,600	6,000	8,600	15,900	14,300
Occupancy	1,000	3,400	6,000	9,000	19,400	3,000	1,000	4,000	23,400	20,500
Rental of Equipment	200	800	3,400	400	4,800	600	100	700	5,500	4,800
Printing and Publications	600	11,200	6,500	1,400	19,700	900	7,400	8,300	28,000	23,000
Travel	1,600	2,000	10,800	4,200	18,600	1,100	200	1,300	19,900	21,500
Conferences and Meetings	800	1,800	10,500	1,600	14,700	1,400	600	2,000	16,700	16,300
Awards and Grants	209,300	1,200	600	10,300	221,400				221,400	157,500
Postage and Shipping	900	200	1,300	1,200	3,600	200	100	300	3,900	4,200
Total Expenses Before Depreciation	$270,000	$91,000	$104,000	$97,400	$562,400	$91,200	$64,000	$155,200	$717,600	$678,100
Depreciation of Buildings and Equipment	4,300	1,000	2,000	1,200	8,500	500	500	1,000	9,500	6,500
Total Functional Expenses	$274,300	$92,000	$106,000	$98,600	$570,900	$91,700	$64,500	$156,200	$727,100	$684,600
Payments to National Office									15,000	12,000
Total Expenses									$742,100	$696,600

Summary of Accounting and Financial Reporting for VHWOs

The accounting and financial reporting requirements for VHWOs are specified in **FASB 116**, **FASB 117**, and the AICPA Audit Guide for Not-for-Profit Organizations. The accrual basis of accounting is used. Primary activities of the VHWO are reported in the unrestricted asset class. Resources restricted by the donor for specific operating purposes or future periods are reported as temporarily restricted assets. Assets contributed by the donor with permanent restrictions are reported as permanently restricted assets.

A VHWO provides four financial statements: (1) a statement of financial position, (2) a statement of activities, (3) a cash flow statement, and (4) a statement of functional expenses. The statement of functional expenses is required of all VHWOs to provide an analysis of all of the organization's expenses, including depreciation. Expenses are broken down into types, such as salaries, supplies, and travel, and are summarized by individual program services and individual supporting services.

OTHER NOT-FOR-PROFIT ENTITIES

There are many types of not-for-profit entities in addition to colleges and universities, hospitals, and voluntary health and welfare organizations. Our society depends heavily on such organizations for religious, educational, social, and recreational needs. Examples of other not-for-profit organizations (ONPOs) include the following:

Cemetery organizations	Private and community foundations
Civic organizations	Private elementary and secondary schools
Fraternal organizations	Professional associations
Labor unions	Public broadcasting stations
Libraries	Religious organizations
Museums	Research and scientific organizations
Other cultural institutions	Social and country clubs
Performing arts organizations	Trade associations
Political parties	Zoological and botanical societies

Accounting for ONPOs

The issuance of **FASB 116** and **FASB 117** has done much to bring the financial reporting standards of hospitals, voluntary health and welfare organizations, and other not-for-profit organizations into agreement. In addition to the two FASB statements, the AICPA Audit Guide for Not-for-Profit Organizations provides guidance for accounting and financial reporting standards for ONPOs.

ONPOs vary significantly in size and scope of operations. While accrual accounting is required for all ONPOs, some small organizations operate on a cash basis during the year and convert to an accrual basis at year-end. Other ONPOs have thousands or even millions of members and hold assets worth substantial sums of money. From the viewpoint of asset management and control procedures, such organizations may be virtually identical to a large business entity. The fact that they are not in business to earn profits from selling goods and services continues to distinguish some aspects of financial reporting for ONPOs from that of business entities, however.

In the past, it has been assumed that fund accounting would be used by ONPOs in a manner similar to accounting for VHWOs. With the adoption of **FASB 116** and **FASB 117**, it is likely that the procedures used by ONPOs and VHWOs will move away from the traditional funds used and account for all transactions in a single entity or by establishing separate accounts for unrestricted, temporarily restricted, and permanently restricted net assets.

Financial Statements of ONPOs

The principal purpose of the financial statements of an ONPO is to explain how the available resources have been used to carry out the organization's activities. Therefore, the statements should disclose the nature and source of the resources acquired, any restrictions on the resources, and the principal programs and their costs; they should also provide information on the organization's ability to continue to carry out its objectives. An ONPO must provide the following financial statements: (1) a statement of financial position, (2) a statement of activities, and (3) a statement of cash flows. Although the statement of functional expenses is not required of ONPOs, it may be appropriate to prepare a statement providing information on expenses by function for each major program when an ONPO is involved in a broad range of activities or conducts activities that are very distinct from one another.

Statement of Financial Position for an ONPO

Figure 19–14 presents a statement of financial position for Ellwood Historical Society, a nonprofit organization that renovates and preserves historical buildings in Sol City. The society has its own governing board and is not associated with a government. The illustrated statement of financial position is a very simple one in light of the well-defined mission of the organization.

Land, Buildings, and Equipment   Land, buildings, and equipment owned by the ONPO and used in its activities generally are recorded at historical cost and depreciated in the normal manner. Operating assets that are donated should be recorded at fair market value at the date of contribution. Unless the donor restricts the use of the asset, land, buildings, and equipment should be included in unrestricted net assets reported on the statement of financial position.

Inexhaustible Collections   Libraries, museums, art galleries, and similar entities often have collections of works of art or other historical treasures that are held for public viewing or for research. Some organizations recognize such works of art or other historical treasures as assets, but most do not. Moreover, when individual works of art or historical treasures are recorded, the Financial Accounting Standards Board in **FASB Statement No. 93**, "Recognition of Depreciation by Not-for-Profit Organizations" (FASB 93), concluded not-for-profit

FIGURE 19–14
Statement of
Financial Position
for an Other
Not-for-Profit
Organization

ELLWOOD HISTORICAL SOCIETY Statement of Financial Position June 30, 20X2 and 20X1		
	20X2	**20X1**
Cash	$ 32,000	$ 16,800
Accounts Receivable	17,500	1,500
Contributions Receivable	48,000	30,000
Inventories	3,000	1,000
Prepaid Expenses	6,500	6,500
Cash Restricted for Long-Term Investments	2,000	-0-
Long-Term Investments (at fair value)	184,000	87,000
Property, Plant, and Equipment (net)	242,000	246,000
Total Assets	$535,000	$388,800
Accounts Payable	$ 28,000	$ 28,000
Mortgage Payable	178,000	187,000
Net Assets:		
Unrestricted	179,000	130,800
Temporarily Restricted by Donors	48,000	43,000
Permanently Restricted by Donors	102,000	-0-
Total Liabilities and Net Assets	$535,000	$388,800

FIGURE 19–15
Statement of
Activities for an
Other Not-for-
Profit Organization
(ONPO)

ELLWOOD HISTORICAL SOCIETY Statement of Activities For the Year Ended June 30, 20X2				
	Unrestricted	**Temporarily Restricted**	**Permanently Restricted**	**Total**
Revenues, Gains, and Other Support:				
Contributions	$130,000	$78,000	$100,000	$308,000
Donated Services	3,000			3,000
Membership Dues	16,000			16,000
Admissions	12,000			12,000
Investment Income	12,200	2,600	12,000	26,800
Gain on Investments	5,000			5,000
Net Assets Released from Restriction:				
Program Use Restrictions	62,600	(62,600)		
Equipment Acquisition	13,000	(13,000)		
Endowment Transfers	10,000		(10,000)	
Total Revenues, Gains, and Other Support	$263,800	$ 5,000	$102,000	$370,800
Program Services and Support:				
Community Education	$139,400			$139,400
Research	24,200			24,200
Auxiliary Activities	19,000			19,000
General and Administrative	20,000			20,000
Fund-Raising	13,000			13,000
Total Expenses	$215,600	$ -0-	$ -0-	$215,600
Change in Net Assets	$ 48,200	$ 5,000	$102,000	$155,200
Net Assets at Beginning of Year	130,800	43,000	-0-	173,800
Net Assets at End of Year	$179,000	$48,000	$102,000	$329,000

organizations are not required to record depreciation on those collections. Specific rules for disclosure of the costs of items purchased and funds generated from the sale of such items are presented in **FASB 116**.

Statement of Activities

A statement of activities for Ellwood Historical Society, presented in Figure 19–15, reports the support, revenue, expenses, transfers, and changes in fund balance during the fiscal period.

The format for the statement of activities is comparable to the statement of activities for a VHWO. For the Ellwood Historical Society, contributions are the primary source of support. However, both membership dues and admissions provide a greater source of revenue than they do in the voluntary health and welfare setting. Memberships often provide free admission or admission at reduced rates in the case of a museum, art gallery, or library. Thus, memberships and admissions may be interrelated in these organizations. Other types of organizations may have very different sources of funds and major expense categories. The financial statement captions and presentation should be adjusted to focus on these attributes in such cases.

As with VHWOs, depreciation charges for the period have been apportioned to the ONPO's primary programmatic activities and reported as expenses in the unrestricted assets section of the statement of activities. Disclosure should be made of the depreciation charges for the period and the balance of accumulated depreciation in the financial statements or footnotes to the ONPO's financial statements to assist financial statement readers in assessing the ONPO's operating effectiveness and financial position.

Assets released from restriction during the period are shown as reclassifications in the statement of activities. Thus, a contribution of $21,000 for research on Civil War activities

FIGURE 19–16
Statement of Cash
Flows for an Other
Not-for-Profit
Organization

ELLWOOD HISTORICAL SOCIETY
Statement of Cash Flows
For the Year Ended June 30, 20X2

Change in Net Assets		$155,200
Adjustments to Reconcile Changes in Net Assets to Net Cash		
Provided by Operating Activities:		
Depreciation	$ 17,000	
Gain on Sale of Equipment	(5,000)	
Increase in Accounts Receivable	(16,000)	
Increase in Contributions Receivable	(18,000)	
Increase in Inventories	(2,000)	
Contribution for Permanent Endowment	(100,000)	
Contribution Restricted for Plant	(13,000)	
Permanently Restricted Endowment Income	(2,000)	(139,000)
Net Cash Provided by Operating Activities		$ 16,200
Cash Flows from Investing Activities:		
Purchase of Property, Plant, and Equipment	$ (16,000)	
Proceeds from Sale of Investments	3,000	
Purchase of Additional Investments	(100,000)	
Investment Income Restricted for Investments	(2,000)	
Proceeds from Sale of Equipment	8,000	
Net Cash Used by Investing Activities		(107,000)
Cash Flows from Financing Activities:		
Contributions Restricted for Permanent Endowment	$100,000	
Investment Income Restricted for Permanent Endowment	2,000	
Contributions Restricted for Acquiring Fixed Assets	13,000	
Mortgage Payments	(9,000)	
Net Cash Provided by Financing Activities		106,000
Net Increase in Cash		$ 15,200
Cash at Beginning of Year		16,800
Cash at End of Year		$ 32,000

would be included in the $78,000 reported as temporarily restricted contributions in Figure 19–15. If $19,500 of the contribution is spent during 20X2, that amount is part of the $62,600 reclassified from temporarily restricted to unrestricted assets (net assets released from program use restrictions) in 20X2. The $19,500 expense incurred in conducting the research is included in the $24,200 total reported as research expense in 20X2.

Statement of Cash Flows

Figure 19–16 presents the statement of cash flows for Elmwood Historical Society. It begins with the net change in assets for the combined entity taken from the statement of activities. Adjustments are made for noncash revenues and expenses and changes in account balances to arrive at cash provided by operating activities. Net cash flows from investing activities and financing activities are added (deducted) in arriving at the net increase (decrease) in cash for the period. The net cash flow for the period is added to the beginning cash balance in unrestricted assets to arrive at the balance at the end of the period.

Summary of Accounting and Financial Reporting for ONPOs

Accounting for ONPOs is similar to that for VHWOs. The accrual basis of accounting is used for financial reporting purposes. A statement of financial position, a statement of activities, and a statement of cash flows are required for financial reporting purposes. When a large number of programs or a number of very different types of programs are part of the operations of an ONPO, it may be desirable to prepare a statement of expenses by functional area or major program as well. As a result of **FASB 116** and **FASB 117**, the reporting requirements of ONPOs are substantially the same as VHWOs.

Summary of Key Concepts	Colleges and universities may be public or private. The accounting and financial reporting standards for public (governmental) colleges and universities are specified by the GASB, as provided in GASB 34 and GASB 35. Accounting and reporting for private colleges and universities are specified by the FASB. Five FASB standards are important for not-for-profit entities. FASB 93 specified that depreciation must be charged to operations and that the balance of net assets be reported. FASB 116 and FASB 136 presented the standards for accounting for contributions. FASB 117 presented the display standards for not-for-profit entities. FASB 124 specified the accounting for investments held by not-for-profit entities. Private colleges and universities must provide three financial statements: (1) a statement of financial position, (2) a statement of activities, and (3) a statement of cash flows. The net assets must be separated into three categories: (1) unrestricted, (2) temporarily restricted, and (3) permanently restricted, based on restrictions imposed by donors, law, or contract.

Health care providers, voluntary health and welfare organizations (VHWOs), and other not-for-profit organizations (ONPOs) use the accrual basis of accounting and account for a majority of transactions in the unrestricted assets class. The restricted funds of a health care provider and other not-for-profit entities are reported as temporarily or permanently restricted, depending on the terms established by the donor. Such funds are classified as restricted until the conditions of the restrictions are met and the resources are reclassified to the unrestricted net asset category. Hospitals deduct contractual adjustments from gross billings in arriving at net patient services revenue in the statement of operations. Donated medical supplies and medicines are included as revenue in the period of receipt. Nonprofit hospitals provide a statement of financial position, a statement of operations, a statement of changes in net assets, and a statement of cash flows. The statement of operations for a hospital must present a performance indicator, called something such as "Excess of revenues over expenses," that includes both operating income and other income such as investment income from trading securities in the general fund's investment portfolio. Below this operating indicator, hospitals present unrealized gains or losses on the general fund's other-than-trading securities, amounts for net assets released from restrictions used for purchase of property and equipment, and other nonoperating items.

VHWOs and ONPOs recognize contribution revenue, investment income, and gains and losses on investments for unrestricted, temporarily restricted, and permanently restricted asset classes. Contributions are reported in the unrestricted asset class unless they are intended for future periods or for specific-purpose use, in which case they are included as contributions in the temporarily or permanently restricted asset classes. When restrictions on temporarily restricted contributions are satisfied, a reclassification to unrestricted assets is shown in the statement of activities, and any expenses associated with the release from restricted funds are included in expenses for unrestricted assets for the period. Earnings of permanently restricted funds that are available for temporarily restricted or unrestricted purposes are shown as income in those net asset classes in the statement of activities for the period as well.

VHWOs and ONPOs prepare a statement of financial position, a statement of activities, and a statement of cash flows. VHWOs also must prepare a statement of functional expenses. Because of differences in the types and scope of activities of the various organizations, the statements may have differences in account titles and items included; however, many of the prior differences in financial presentation between not-for-profit organizations were eliminated by the requirements of FASB 116 and FASB 117.

Key Terms	assets whose use is limited, *932*	general fund, *929*	statement of functional expenses, *955*
	board-designated resources, *930*	performance indicator, *932*	temporarily restricted net assets, *932*
	costs of informational materials, *954*	permanently restricted net assets, *932*	unrestricted net assets, *932*
	donated materials and services, *953*	pledges receivable, *948*	
		restricted funds, *930*	
		specific operating purposes, *930*	

Questions

Q19-1 How are tuition scholarships reported by a private college or university?

Q19-2 What are the classifications of net assets reported in the statement of financial position by private colleges? Identify the types of assets assigned to each classification.

Q19-3 What are the major differences in financial reporting for a public university and a private university?

Q19-4 What is the basis of accounting in a hospital's general fund? In its restricted funds?

Q19-5 How are donated services accounted for by a hospital? How does it account for donated equipment and donated medical supplies?

Q19-6 A donor contributes $15,000 to a hospital to be used for operating costs in the intensive care unit. How does it account for this contribution? How does it account for the expenditure of the $15,000?

Q19-7 What are the components of a hospital's net patient service revenue?

Q19-8 Where is a gain on the sale of hospital properties recorded by a hospital? How is the gain reported in the hospital's financial statements?

Q19-9 Is depreciation accounted for by a hospital? Why or why not?

Q19-10 What is the basis of accounting for the unrestricted assets of a VHWO? What is the basis for the restricted assets?

Q19-11 Where are fixed assets recorded for a VHWO? Is depreciation recorded for a VHWO?

Q19-12 An individual contributes $10,000 to a VHWO for restricted use in a public health education service. How does the VHWO account for this contribution? How does it account for the expenditure of the $10,000?

Q19-13 Explain the accounting for pledges from donors to a VHWO.

Q19-14 Why do VHWOs not report all pledges received in the period in the unrestricted assets section of the statement of activities? Identify what is not included.

Q19-15 How do VHWOs account for donated services?

Q19-16 Describe the statement of functional expenses. What organizations must prepare this statement?

Q19-17 An alumna of a sorority donates $12,000 to it for restricted use in its community service activity. How is the contribution accounted for by this ONPO? How is the expenditure of the $12,000 accounted for?

Q19-18 Are donated services received by an ONPO accounted for in the same manner as those received by hospitals? Why or why not?

Q19-19 What is the market value unit method of accounting for investments?

Q19-20 Should a rotary club, an ONPO, report depreciation expense? Why or why not?

Q19-21 Describe the statement of activities for an ONPO. Compare it with the statement of activities for a VHWO.

Q19-22 Give two examples of contributions to an ONPO that should be reported as temporarily restricted and two that should be reported as permanently restricted.

Cases

C19-1 **Accounting for Donations**

Judgment

Hospitals, voluntary health and welfare organizations, and other not-for-profit organizations often rely heavily on donations of volunteers' time as well as equipment, supplies, or other assets.

Required

a. Specify the criteria to be used to determine the accounting for donated services to (1) hospitals, (2) voluntary health and welfare organizations, and (3) other not-for-profit organizations. Discuss the reasons for any differences in the accounting criteria used.

b. How are donations of capital assets, such as equipment, accounted for by hospitals? Is depreciation recorded on these donations? Why or why not?

c. How are cash contributions accounted for by (1) hospitals, (2) voluntary health and welfare organizations, and (3) other not-for-profit organizations?

C19-2 **Public Support to an Other Not-for-Profit Organization**

Understanding

Leslie Dawnes has just been elected treasurer of the local professional association of registered nurses. The association provides public health messages for the community as well as services for members. Leslie is now preparing financial statements for the year and comes to you for advice on accounting for the proceeds from a major fund drive that occurred during the year. The nursing association received $25,000 in unrestricted donations and $15,000 in restricted donations that are restricted to public health advertisements. A total of $6,000 has been incurred for public health advertising since the restricted donations were received.

The former treasurer accounted for the $40,000 of donations as revenue in the unrestricted fund. Leslie believes that this may not be correct because it does not disclose the restricted nature of the donations for the public health messages.

Required

a. Discuss the accounting and financial statement disclosure to be used to account for the $25,000 of unrestricted donations to the professional association.

b. How should the $15,000 of restricted contributions have been accounted for at the time of the donation? How should they have been reported on this year's financial statements?

C19-3 Discovery

Analysis

The purpose of these cases is to provide learning opportunities using available databases and/or the Internet to obtain contemporary information about the topics in advanced financial accounting. Note that the Internet is dynamic and that addresses of specific Websites may change. In that case, use a good search engine to locate the Website's current address.

Required

Access the Website for the American Red Cross (www.redcross.org) and scroll through until you locate the most recent annual report. It may be under the Publications button of the header bar. Review the report and then prepare a one- to two-page memo summarizing the major information items included in it. Be sure to examine each of the financial statements to determine the following:

a. The components and amounts of each of the three net asset classes shown on the statement of financial position.

b. The major sources of operating revenues and the categories and amounts of operating expenses, including the amount of the fund-raising costs for the organization, shown on the statement of activities.

c. The costs of the principal program services as shown on the statement of functional expenses.

d. The sources and uses of net cash flows as shown on the statement of cash flows.

C19-4 Conditional Gift to a Not-for-Profit Organization

Betty Gardner is the treasurer for the Central Illinois chapter of a national not-for-profit organization, the Alzheimer's Association. Some of the money raised by the chapter is sent to the national organization to support research into Alzheimer's disease. The chapter also provides information about the disease and sponsors support programs for families of patients within the community. The chapter has just received a significant pledge from Victor Wyatt, who has offered to contribute $20,000 a year for the next five years on the condition that the Central Illinois chapter sponsor a series of annual educational programs about Alzheimer's disease. If it does not do so, he will direct future contributions elsewhere.

Research FARS

The donor has already contributed the first $20,000, and the chapter has made the arrangements for the first educational workshop, which will take place in six weeks, shortly after the chapter's fiscal year-end.

Betty Gardner is aware that the chapter intends to continue the educational workshops and has asked you, as a public accountant who volunteers to audit the chapter's financial statements each year, to research the appropriate accounting for Mr. Wyatt's $20,000 contribution and $80,000 pledge in the chapter's financial statements for the current fiscal year.

Required

Obtain the most current accounting standards for accounting for conditional gifts to not-for-profit organizations. You can obtain access to accounting standards through the Financial Accounting Research System (FARS), your library, or some other source. Write a memo to Betty reporting on your research findings. Support your recommendations with citations and quotations from the authoritative financial reporting standards.

C19-5 Accounting for Contributions to and Activities of a Not-for-Profit Organization

Gerry Finley, a manager in a public accounting firm, has volunteered to audit the financial statements of the Community Chest, a not-for-profit organization that raises funds to assist people in central Illinois who are homeless or have low incomes. In reviewing the statement of activities, he notices the revenue item Auction Extravaganza. The Community Chest treasurer indicates that this amount is the net proceeds for this event, which is the organization's largest fund-raising event for the year.

Research FARS

The Auction Extravaganza combines a black-tie dinner, entertainment, and an auction of numerous donated items. Supporters buy tickets to the event and bid on the auction items. The treasurer informs Gerry that the dollar amount reported in the statement of activities is the total raised from ticket sales and from the auction, net of the expenses incurred for the event. These expenses include advertising and part of the cost of the dinner. The expenses, however, are comparatively low because a local hotel donates the ballroom and part of the cost of the dinner. A local auctioneer volunteers her time for the auction, the state university's music department provides the entertainment, and local businesses donate all auction items.

Required

Obtain the most current accounting standards for accounting for conditional gifts to not-for-profit organizations. You can obtain access to accounting standards through the Financial Accounting Research System (FARS), your library, or some other source. Gerry has asked you, as a staff accountant in his firm, to research the appropriate accounting for the Auction Extravaganza. Write him a memo reporting on your research findings. Support your recommendations with citations and quotations from the authoritative financial reporting standards.

C19-6 **An Analysis of the Financial Statements for the American Red Cross, a Voluntary Health and Welfare Organization**

Analysis   The questions below can be answered by reading the most recent annual report of the American Red Cross (ARC). This report can be accessed by going to www.redcross.org.

a. Why does the U.S. Army Audit Agency audit the financial statements of the American Red Cross?

b. For the most recent year, what was the ratio of program services expenses to total expenses? According to the Better Business Bureau, a ratio of program expenses to total expenses of 60 percent is considered acceptable. How does the ratio for the ARC compare with this benchmark?

c. What is the ARC's policy with respect to recognizing contribution revenue? Of the total contributions receivable at June 30 of the most recent year, what amount is temporarily restricted?

d. Of the total amount of unrestricted net assets at June 30 of the most recent year, what is the amount that is undesignated by the board of governors?

e. What interest rate is used to determine the present value for contributions that are receivable in years after June 30 of the current year?

f. For the most recent year ended June 30, what was the amount of net assets reclassified due to satisfaction of purpose and/or time restrictions?

g. Of all the program services provided, which one had the highest total cost for salaries and wages and employee benefits?

h. How does the ARC define temporarily restricted net assets?

i. How much contributed service revenue was reported for the most recent year?

j. At June 30 of the most recent year, what was the amount of conditional contributions? Did the ARC report these contributions in revenue for the current year?

k. Of the total amount of unrestricted investment income reported for the current year, what amount came from dividends and interest?

l. The ARC makes estimated income tax payments during each year for unrelated business income. State two sources of unrelated business income for the current year (you do not have to give dollar amounts for the income).

m. What does the ARC report when donor-imposed purpose restrictions are accomplished or donor-imposed time restrictions expire?

n. Assume the ARC received a cash contribution during the current year that was restricted by the donor for disaster relief. Also assume that the amount donated was spent in the current year for disaster relief. Specify whether the ARC would report this donation on its statement of activities for the current year: (1) as an increase in unrestricted net assets when the donation was received, or (2) as an increase in temporarily restricted net assets when the donation was received and as a reclassification of net assets from temporarily restricted to unrestricted when the donation was used.

o. Assume the ARC received a donation of equipment from a donor in the current year and the donor did not place any restrictions on the donated assets. Specify how the ARC would report this donation in its statement of activities for the current year: (1) as an increase in unrestricted net assets when the equipment was received, or (2) as an increase in temporarily restricted net assets when the equipment was received and as a reclassification of net assets from temporarily restricted to unrestricted when the equipment is depreciated.

C19-7 **An Analysis of the Financial Statements of the University of Notre Dame, a Private University**

Analysis The questions below can be answered by reading the most recent annual report of the University of Notre Dame. This report can be accessed by going to www.nd.edu.

a. For the most recent year, how much cash was contributed by donors to the university for the acquisition of buildings and equipment?

b. On the statement of changes in unrestricted net assets, how does the university decide what information is disclosed in the nonoperating section?

c. On the statement of changes in unrestricted net assets for the most recent year, how much of the net assets released were for operations?

d. What is the university's accounting policy for its art collection?

e. What interest rate is used to determine the present value of multiyear pledges?

f. On the statement of financial position at June 30 for the most recent year, how much of the amount reported for contributions receivable is unrestricted?

g. At June 30 of the most recent year, what amount of unrestricted net assets is designated by the board?

h. True or false: Operating expenses on the statement of changes in unrestricted net assets for the most recent year are reported by functional categories.

i. During the most recent year, how many individual donors made contributions to support the university?

j. True or false: Land, buildings, and equipment, net of accumulated depreciation, are reported in unrestricted net assets on the university's statement of financial position.

k. For the most recent year, what was the total investment return on investments reported in all three net asset categories? How much of this amount represented an increase in unrestricted net assets?

l. True or false: The President's Circle consists of donors who make annual unrestricted contributions of at least $50,000.

m. For the 10-year period ending with the most recent year, what was the endowment pool's annualized return?

n. On the statement of financial position at June 30 of the most recent year, what amount of investments in endowments is reported in the permanently restricted net asset class?

o. Where is the university's endowment ranked in American higher education?

Exercises **E19-1** **Multiple-Choice Questions on Colleges and Universities [AICPA Adapted]**

Select the correct answer for each of the following questions.

1. For the summer session of 20X2, Pacific University assessed its students $1,700,000 (net of refunds) covering tuition and fees for educational and general purposes. However, only $1,500,000 was expected to be realized because scholarships totaling $150,000 were granted to students, and tuition remissions of $50,000 were allowed to faculty members' children attending Pacific. What amount should Pacific include as revenues from student tuition and fees?

a. $1,500,000.

b. $1,550,000.

c. $1,650,000.

d. $1,700,000.

2. Tuition remissions for graduate student teaching assistantships should be classified by a university as:

	Revenue	Expenditures
a.	No	No
b.	No	Yes
c.	Yes	Yes
d.	Yes	No

3. For the fall semester of 20X1, Dover University assessed its students $2,300,000 for tuition and fees. The net amount realized was only $2,100,000 because of the following revenue reductions:

Refunds occasioned by class cancellations and student withdrawals	$ 50,000
Tuition remissions granted to faculty members' families	10,000
Scholarships and fellowships	140,000

How much should Dover report for the period for revenue from tuition and fees?

a. $2,100,000.

b. $2,150,000.

c. $2,250,000.

d. $2,300,000.

Items 4 through 6 are based on the following information pertaining to Global University, a private institution, as of June 30, 20X1, and for the year then ended:

Unrestricted net assets comprised $7,500,000 of assets and $4,500,000 of liabilities (including deferred revenues of $150,000). Among the receipts recorded during the year were unrestricted gifts of $550,000 and restricted grants totaling $330,000, of which $220,000 was expended during the year for current operations and $110,000 remained unexpended at the close of the year.

Volunteers from the surrounding communities regularly contribute their services to Global and are paid nominal amounts to cover their travel costs. During the year, the amount for travel paid to these volunteers aggregated $18,000. The gross value of services performed by them, determined by reference to equivalent wages available in that area for similar services, amounted to $200,000. Global University normally purchases these types of contributed services, and the university believes the contributed services enhance its assets.

4. At June 30, 20X1, Global's unrestricted net asset balance was:

a. $7,500,000.

b. $3,150,000.

c. $3,000,000.

d. $2,850,000.

5. For the year ended June 30, 20X1, what amount should be included in Global's revenue for the unrestricted gifts and restricted grants?

a. $550,000.

b. $660,000.

c. $770,000.

d. $880,000.

6. For the year ended June 30, 20X1, what amount should Global record as contribution revenue for the volunteers' services?

a. $218,000.

b. $200,000.

c. $18,000.

d. $0.

E19-2   Multiple-Choice Questions on Hospital Accounting [AICPA Adapted]

Select the correct answer for each of the following questions.

Data for Questions 1 through 3

Under Dodge Hospital's established rate structure, the hospital would have earned patient service revenue of $5,000,000 for the year ended December 31, 20X3. However, Dodge did not expect to collect this amount because of contractual adjustments of $500,000 to third-party payors. In May 20X3, Dodge purchased bandages from Hunt Supply Company at a cost of $1,000. However, Hunt notified Dodge that the invoice was being canceled and that the bandages were being donated. On December 31, 20X3, Dodge had board-designated assets consisting of $40,000 in cash and investments of $700,000.

1. For the year ended December 31, 20X3, how much should Dodge report as net patient service revenue?

    a. $4,500,000.

    b. $5,000,000.

    c. $5,500,000.

    d. $5,740,000.

2. For the year ended December 31, 20X3, Dodge should record the donation of bandages as:

    a. A $1,000 reduction in operating expenses.

    b. A decrease in net assets released from restrictions.

    c. An increase in unrestricted revenue, gains, and other support.

    d. A memorandum entry only.

3. How much of Dodge's board-designated assets should be included in unrestricted net assets?

    a. $0.

    b. $40,000.

    c. $700,000.

    d. $740,000.

4. Donated medicines that normally would be purchased by a hospital should be recorded at fair value and should be credited directly to:

    a. Unrestricted revenue.

    b. Expense of medicines.

    c. Fund balance.

    d. Deferred revenue.

5. Which of the following would normally be included as revenue of a not-for-profit hospital?

    a. Unrestricted interest income from an endowment fund.

    b. An unrestricted gift.

    c. Tuition received from an educational program.

    d. All of the above.

6. An unrestricted gift pledge from an annual contributor to a not-for-profit hospital made in December 20X1 and paid in March 20X2 would generally be credited to:

    a. Contribution revenue in 20X1.

    b. Contribution revenue in 20X2.

    c. Other income in 20X1.

    d. Other income in 20X2.

7. An organization of high school seniors assists patients at Lake Hospital. These students are volunteers who perform services that the hospital would not otherwise provide, such as wheeling patients in the park and reading to patients. Lake has no employer–employee relationship with these volunteers, who donated 5,000 hours of service to Lake in 20X2. At the minimum wage, these services would amount to $18,750, while it is estimated that the fair value of these services was $25,000. In Lake's 20X2 statement of operations, what amount should be reported as donated services?

    a. $25,000.

    b. $18,750.

    c. $6,250.

    d. $0.

8. Which of the following would be included in the unrestricted funds of a not-for-profit hospital?

    a. Permanent endowments.

    b. Term endowments.

    c. Board-designated funds originating from previously accumulated income.

    d. Funds designated by the donor for plant expansion and replacement funds.

9. During the year ended December 31, 20X1, Greenacre Hospital received the following donations stated at their respective fair values:

Essential specialized employee-type services from members of a religious group	$100,000
Medical supplies from an association of physicians that were restricted for indigent care and were used for such purpose in 20X1	30,000

How much total revenue from donations should Greenacre report its 20X1?

a. $0.

b. $30,000.

c. $100,000.

d. $130,000.

10. Johnson Hospital's property, plant, and equipment (net of depreciation) consists of the following:

Land	$ 500,000
Buildings	10,000,000
Movable equipment	2,000,000

What amount should be reported as restricted assets?

a. $0.

b. $2,000,000.

c. $10,500,000.

d. $12,500,000.

11. Depreciation should be recognized in the financial statements of:

a. Proprietary (for-profit) hospitals only.

b. Both proprietary and not-for-profit hospitals.

c. Both proprietary and not-for-profit hospitals only when they are affiliated with a college or university.

d. All hospitals, as a memorandum entry not affecting the statement of revenue and expenses.

12. On March 1, 20X1, J. Rowe established a $100,000 endowment fund, the income from which is to be paid to Central Hospital for general operating purposes. Central does not control the fund's principal. The donor appointed Sycamore National Bank as trustee of this fund. What journal entry is required by Central to record the establishment of the endowment?

		Debit	Credit
a.	Cash	100,000	
	Nonexpendable Endowment Fund		100,000
b.	Cash	100,000	
	Endowment Fund Balance		100,000
c.	Nonexpendable Endowment Fund	100,000	
	Endowment Fund Balance		100,000
d.	Memorandum entry only	—	—

E19-3 Entries for a Hospital's Unrestricted (General) Fund

The following are transactions and events of the general fund of Sycamore Hospital, a not-for-profit entity, for the 20X6 fiscal year ending December 31, 20X6.

1. A total of $6,200,000 in patient services was provided.

2. Operating expenses total $5,940,000, as follows:

Nursing services	$2,070,000
Other professional expenses	1,250,000
Fiscal services	225,000
General services	1,510,000
Bad debts	125,000
Administration	260,000
Depreciation	500,000

Accounts credited for operating expenses other than depreciation:

Cash	$4,785,000
Allowance for Uncollectibles	125,000
Accounts Payable	210,000
Inventories	240,000
Donated Services	80,000

3. Contractual adjustments of $220,000 are allowed as deductions from gross patient revenue.
4. A transfer of $180,000 is received from specific-purpose funds. This transfer is for payment of approved operating costs in accordance with the terms of the restricted gift.
5. A transfer of $200,000 is received from the temporarily restricted plant fund to fund the purchase of new equipment for the hospital.
6. Sycamore Hospital receives $155,000 of unrestricted gifts.
7. Accounts receivable are collected except for $75,000 written off.
8. A valuation of the investment securities portfolio of the general fund reports a $70,000 increase in the market value from the beginning of the period. The board designated this entire income for other than current operations.

Required

a. Prepare journal entries in the general fund for each of the transactions and events.

b. Prepare the statement of operations for the general, unrestricted fund of Sycamore Hospital.

E19-4 Entries for Other Hospital Funds

The following are selected transactions of the specific-purpose fund, the plant fund, and the endowment fund of Toddville Hospital, a not-for-profit entity:

1. The endowment fund received new permanent endowments totaling $150,000 and new term endowments totaling $120,000.
2. The plant replacement and expansion fund received pledges of $1,500,000 for the new wing. Uncollectibles were estimated at 10 percent.
3. The specific-purpose fund received gifts of $50,000 for research and $30,000 for education.
4. Interest and dividends received on investments follow:

Endowment fund (permanent)	$100,000
Plant fund	45,000
Specific-purpose fund (research)	31,000

This year's interest and dividends in the endowment fund are permanently restricted by a donor-imposed requirement.

5. The specific-purpose fund was notified that the general fund fulfilled the agreements related to restricted gifts as follows:

Research	$55,000
Education	32,000

Cash of $70,000 was transferred to the general fund, with the balance to be sent later.

6. The following investments were made:

Endowment fund	$270,000
Plant fund	160,000
Specific-purpose fund	75,000

Required

Prepare journal entries for the transactions in the specific-purpose fund, plant fund, and endowment fund, as appropriate.

E19-5   Multiple-Choice Questions on Voluntary Health and Welfare Organization Accounting [AICPA Adapted]

Select the correct answer for each of the following questions.

1. Which basis of accounting should a voluntary health and welfare organization use?

   a. Cash basis for all funds.

   b. Modified accrual basis for all funds.

   c. Accrual basis for all funds.

   d. Accrual basis for some funds and modified accrual basis for other funds.

Data for Questions 2 and 3

Town Service Center is a voluntary health and welfare organization funded by contributions from the general public. During 20X6, unrestricted pledges of $800,000 were received, half of which were payable in 20X6, with the other half payable in 20X7 for use in 20X7. It was estimated that 10 percent of these pledges would be uncollectible. In addition, Helen Ladd, a social worker on Town's permanent staff, earning $30,000 annually for a normal workload of 1,500 hours, contributed an additional 600 hours of her time to Town at no charge.

2. How much should Town report as unrestricted contribution revenue for 20X6 with respect to the pledges?

   a. $0.

   b. $360,000.

   c. $720,000.

   d. $800,000.

3. How much should Town record in 20X6 for contributed service expenses?

   a. $0.

   b. $1,200.

   c. $10,000.

   d. $12,000.

4. A voluntary health and welfare organization received a pledge in 20X1 from a donor specifying that the amount pledged be used in 20X3. The donor paid the pledge in cash in 20X2. The pledge should be accounted for as:

   a. Contribution revenue in 20X3.

   b. Contribution revenue in 20X2.

   c. Contribution revenue in 20X1.

   d. Contribution revenue in the period in which the funds are spent.

5. Turner Fund, a voluntary health and welfare organization funded by contributions from the general public, received unrestricted pledges of $300,000 during 20X4. It was estimated that 10 percent of these pledges would be uncollectible. By the end of 20X4, $240,000 of the pledges had been collected. It was expected that $35,000 more would be collected in 20X5 and that the balance of $25,000 would be written off as uncollectible. What amount should Turner include as contribution revenue in 20X4?

    a. $300,000.

    b. $275,000.

    c. $270,000.

    d. $240,000.

Data for Questions 6 through 9

On January 1, 20X2, State Center Health Agency, a voluntary health and welfare organization, received a bequest of a $200,000 certificate of deposit maturing on December 31, 20X6. The contributor's only stipulations were that the certificate be held to maturity and the interest revenue received annually be used to purchase books for the children to read in the preschool program run by the agency. Interest revenue each of the years was $9,000, and the full $9,000 was spent for books each year. When the certificate was redeemed, the board of trustees adopted a formal resolution designating $150,000 of the proceeds for future purchase of playground equipment for the preschool program.

6. What should be reported by the temporarily restricted fund in the 20X2 statement of activities?

    a. Legacies and bequests of $200,000.

    b. Investment income of $9,000.

    c. Transfers to unrestricted fund of $9,000.

    d. All of the above.

7. What amounts should be reported in the 20X2 statement of activities for the unrestricted fund?

    a. Legacies and bequests of $200,000.

    b. Investment income of $9,000.

    c. Transfers from the restricted fund of $9,000.

    d. Contributions of $209,000.

8. What should be reported in the 20X6 statement of activities for the unrestricted fund?

    a. Transfers from restricted fund of $209,000.

    b. Board-designated funds of $150,000.

    c. Playground equipment of $150,000.

    d. Transfers to plant and equipment fund of $150,000.

9. What should be reported in the December 31, 20X6, statement of financial position for the unrestricted fund?

    a. Liability for purchase of playground equipment, $150,000.

    b. Due to plant and equipment fund, $150,000.

    c. Board-designated funds, $150,000.

    d. Temporarily restricted funds, $200,000.

E19-6   **Entries for Voluntary Health and Welfare Organizations**

The following are the 20X2 transactions of the Midwest Heart Association, which has the following funds and fund balances on January 1, 20X2:

Unrestricted net assets	$281,000
Temporarily restricted net assets	87,000
Permanently restricted (endowment) net assets	219,000

1. Unrestricted pledges total $700,000, of which $150,000 is for 20X3. Uncollectible pledges are estimated at 8 percent.

2. Restricted use grants total $150,000.

3. A total of $520,000 of current pledges are collected, and $30,000 of remaining uncollected current pledges are written off.

4. Office equipment is purchased for $15,000.

5. Unrestricted funds are used to pay the $3,000 mortgage payment due on the buildings.

6. Interest and dividends received are $27,200 on unrestricted investments and $5,400 on temporarily restricted investments. An endowment investment with a recorded value of $5,000 is sold for $6,000, resulting in a realized transaction gain of $1,000. A donor-imposed restriction specified that gains on sales of endowment investments must be maintained in the permanently restricted endowment fund.

7. Depreciation is recorded and allocated as follows:

Community services	$12,000
Public health education	7,000
Research	10,000
Fund-raising	15,000
General and administrative	9,000

8. Other operating costs of the unrestricted current fund are:

Community services	$250,600
Public health education	100,000
Research	81,000
Fund-raising	39,000
General and administrative	61,000

9. Clerical services donated during the fund drive total $2,400. These are not part of the expenses reported in item 8. It has been determined that these donated services should be recorded.

Required

a. Prepare journal entries for the transactions in 20X2.

b. Prepare a statement of activities for 20X2.

E19-7 Determination of Contribution Revenue

Atwater Health Services, a voluntary health and welfare organization, has provided support for families with low income in the town of Atwater for approximately 20 years. In 20X6, Atwater Health Services conducted a major funding campaign to help replace facilities that are no longer adequate and to generate operating and endowment funds.

The community of Atwater ran a number of special events, and the chamber of commerce made the fund-raising campaign a major activity for 20X6. In 20X6, the following gifts and pledges were received:

1. The family of I. B. Plentiful donated a lot adjacent to the current building for future use as a playground and parking lot. The family had purchased the lot for $22,000 several years ago. It had a current value of $42,000 at the date contributed.

2. A number of new pledges were received and many were partially or fully paid in 20X6. The following information was compiled:

Unrestricted pledges for use in 20X6	$120,000
Unrestricted pledges for use in 20X7	70,000
Pledges to support screening tests for children's hearing abilities	90,000
Pledge to assist in construction of addition to building; donor agrees to make eight annual payments of $50,000 each	400,000
	$680,000

3. Also during 20X6, $45,000 was spent in providing vision tests for grade school children. A total of $38,000 of funds collected in 20X4 and 20X5 for this purpose were used to help pay for the costs of providing the tests free of charge to all children in the community.

Required

a. Prepare the journal entries for 20X6 for these activities, including receipt of the first installment on the pledge for building construction, which was received at the end of 20X6. Atwater currently earns an 8 percent return on its investments. The present value of the seven future payments of $50,000 is $260,318.

b. Prepare the journal entry or entries recorded at the end of 20X7 upon receipt of the second payment on the pledge for building construction.

E19-8   **Multiple-Choice Questions on Other Nonprofit Organizations [AICPA Adapted]**

Select the correct answer for each of the following questions.

1. On January 2, 20X2, a nonprofit botanical society received a gift of an exhaustible fixed asset with an estimated useful life of 10 years and no salvage value. The donor's cost of this asset was $20,000, and its fair market value at the date of the gift was $30,000. What amount of depreciation of this asset should the society recognize in its 20X2 financial statements?

a. $3,000.

b. $2,500.

c. $2,000.

d. $0.

2. In 20X1, a nonprofit trade association enrolled five new member companies, each of which was obligated to pay nonrefundable initiation fees of $1,000. These fees were receivable by the association in 20X1. Three of the new members paid the initiation fees in 20X1, and the other two new members paid their initiation fees in 20X2. Annual dues (excluding initiation fees) received by the association from all members have always covered the organization's costs of services provided to its members. It can be reasonably expected that future dues will cover all costs of the organization's future services to members. Average membership duration is 10 years because of mergers, attrition, and economic factors. What amount of initiation fees from these five new members should the association recognize as revenue in 20X1?

a. $5,000.

b. $3,000.

c. $500.

d. $0.

3. Roberts Foundation received a nonexpendable endowment of $500,000 in 20X3 from Multi Enterprises. The endowment assets were invested in publicly traded securities. Multi did not specify how gains and losses from dispositions of endowment assets were to be treated. No restrictions were placed on the use of dividends received and interest earned on fund resources. In 20X4, Roberts realized gains of $50,000 on sales of fund investments and received total interest and dividends of $40,000 on fund securities. The amount of these capital gains, interest, and dividends available for expenditure by Roberts's unrestricted current fund is:

a. $0.

b. $40,000.

c. $50,000.

d. $90,000.

4. In July 20X2, Ross donated $200,000 cash to a church with the stipulation that the revenue generated from this gift be paid to him during his lifetime. The conditions of this donation are that after Ross dies, the principal may be used by the church for any purpose voted on by the church elders. The church received interest of $16,000 on the $200,000 for the year ended June 30, 20X3, and the interest was remitted to Ross. In the church's June 30, 20X3, annual financial statements:

a. $200,000 should be reported as temporarily restricted net assets in the balance sheet.

b. $184,000 should be reported as revenue in the activity statement.

c. $216,000 should be reported as revenue in the activity statement.

d. Both a and c.

5. The following expenditures were among those incurred by a nonprofit botanical society during 20X4:

Printing of annual report	$15,000
Unsolicited merchandise sent to encourage contributions	35,000

What amount should be classified as fund-raising costs in the society's activity statement?

a. $0.

b. $5,000.

c. $35,000.

d. $40,000.

6. Trees Forever, a community foundation, incurred $5,000 in expenses during 20X3 putting on its annual fund-raising talent show. In the statement of activities of Trees Forever, the $5,000 should be reported as:

a. A contra asset account.

b. A contra revenue account.

c. A reduction of fund-raising costs.

d. Part of fund-raising costs.

7. In 20X3, the board of trustees of Burr Foundation designated $100,000 from its current funds for college scholarships. Also in 20X3, the foundation received a bequest of $200,000 from an estate of a benefactor who specified that the bequest was to be used for hiring teachers to tutor handicapped students. What amount should be accounted for as temporarily restricted funds?

a. $0.

b. $100,000.

c. $200,000.

d. $300,000.

Information for 8 through 10

United Together, a labor union, had the following receipts and expenses for the year ended December 31, 20X2:

Receipts:	
Per capita dues	$680,000
Initiation fees	90,000
Sales of organizational supplies	60,000
Nonexpendable gift restricted by donor for loan purposes for 10 years	30,000
Nonexpendable gift restricted by donor for loan purposes in perpetuity	25,000
Expenses:	
Labor negotiations	500,000
Fund-raising	100,000
Membership development	50,000
Administrative and general	200,000

Additional Information

The union's constitution provides that 10 percent of the per capita dues be designated for the strike insurance fund to be distributed for strike relief at the discretion of the union's executive board.

8. In United Together's statement of activities for the year ended December 31, 20X2, what amount should be reported under the classification of revenue from unrestricted funds?

a. $740,000.

b. $762,000.

c. $770,000.

d. $830,000.

9. In United Together's statement of activities for the year ended December 31, 20X2, what amount should be reported under the classification of program services?

    a. $500,000.

    b. $550,000.

    c. $600,000.

    d. $850,000.

10. In United Together's statement of activities for the year ended December 31, 20X2, what amounts should be reported under the classifications of temporarily and permanently restricted net assets?

    a. $0 and $55,000, respectively.

    b. $55,000 and $0, respectively.

    c. $30,000 and $25,000, respectively.

    d. $25,000 and $30,000, respectively.

E19-9   Statement of Activities for an Other Nonprofit Organization

The following is a list of selected account balances in the unrestricted operating fund for the Pleasant School:

	Debit	Credit
Unrestricted Net Assets, July 1, 20X1		$ 420,000
Tuition and Fees		1,200,000
Contributions		165,000
Auxiliary Activities Revenue		40,000
Investment Income (for current operations)		32,000
Other Revenue		38,000
Instruction	$1,050,000	
Auxiliary Activities Expenses	37,000	
Administration	250,000	
Fund-Raising	28,000	
Transfer from Temporarily Restricted Assets		130,000
Transfer from Permanently Restricted Assets		12,000

Required

Prepare a statement of activities for the unrestricted operating fund of the Pleasant School for the year ended June 30, 20X2.

Problems   P19-10   Financial Statements for a Private, Not-for-Profit College

Friendly College is a small, privately supported liberal arts college. The college uses a fund structure; however, it prepares its financial statements in conformance with FASB 117.

Partial balance sheet information as of June 30, 20X2, is given as follows:

Unrestricted Items:		
Cash	$210,000	
Accounts Receivable (student tuition and fees,		
less allowance for doubtful accounts of $9,000)	341,000	
State Appropriation Receivable	75,000	
Accounts Payable		$ 45,000
Deferred Revenue		66,000
Unrestricted Net Assets		515,000
Restricted Items:		
Cash	$ 7,000	
Investments	60,000	
Temporarily Restricted Net Assets		$ 67,000

The following transactions occurred during the fiscal year ended June 30, 20X3:

1. On July 7, 20X2, a gift of $100,000 was received from an alumnus. The alumnus requested that half the gift be restricted to the purchase of books for the university library and the remainder be used for the establishment of an endowed scholarship fund. The alumnus further requested that the income generated by the scholarship fund be used annually to award a scholarship to a qualified disadvantaged student. On July 20, 20X2, the board of trustees resolved that the funds of the newly established scholarship endowment fund would be invested in savings certificates. On July 21, 20X2, the savings certificates were purchased.

2. Revenue from student tuition and fees applicable to the year ended June 30, 20X3, amounted to $1,900,000. Of this amount, $66,000 was collected in the prior year, and $1,686,000 was collected during the year ended June 30, 20X3. In addition, on June 30, 20X3, the university had received cash of $158,000 representing deferred revenue fees for the session beginning July 1, 20X3.

3. During the year ended June 30, 20X3, the university had collected $349,000 of the outstanding accounts receivable at the beginning of the year. The balance was determined to be uncollectible and was written off against the allowance account. On June 30, 20X3, the allowance account was increased by $3,000 to $11,000.

4. During the year, interest charges of $6,000 were earned and collected on late student fee payments.

5. During the year the state appropriation was received. An additional unrestricted appropriation of $50,000 was made by the state but had not been paid to the university as of June 30, 20X3.

6. An unrestricted gift of $25,000 cash was received from alumni of the university.

7. During the year, restricted investments of $21,000 were sold for $26,000. Temporarily restricted investment interest income amounting to $1,900 was received.

8. During the year, unrestricted operating expenses of $1,777,000 were recorded, not including year-end accruals or transfers from other categories of net assets. On June 30, 20X3, $59,000 of these expenses remained unpaid.

9. Restricted current funds of $13,000 were released and spent for authorized operating purposes during the year.

10. The accounts payable on June 30, 20X2, were paid during the year.

11. During the year, $7,000 interest was earned and received on the savings certificates purchased in accordance with the board of trustees' resolutions, as discussed in transaction 1.

Required

a. Prepare a comparative balance sheet for Friendly College as of June 30, 20X2, and June 30, 20X3.
b. Prepare a statement of activities for Friendly College for the year ended June 30, 20X3.

P19-11 **Balance Sheet for a Hospital**
Brookdale Hospital hired an inexperienced controller early in 20X4. Near the end of 20X4, the board of directors decided to conduct a major fund-raising campaign. They wished to have the December 31, 20X4, statement of financial position for Brookdale fully conform with current generally accepted principles for hospitals. The trial balance prepared by the controller at December 31, 20X4, is as follows:

	Debit	Credit
Cash	$ 100,000	
Investment in Short-Term Marketable Securities	200,000	
Investment in Long-Term Marketable Securities	300,000	
Interest Receivable	15,000	
Accounts Receivable	55,000	
Inventory	35,000	
Land	120,000	
Buildings and Equipment	935,000	
Allowance for Depreciation		$ 260,000
Accounts Payable		40,000
Mortgage Payable		320,000
Fund Balance		1,140,000
Total	$1,760,000	$1,760,000

Additional Information

1. Your analysis of the contributions receivable as of December 31, 20X4, determined that there were unrecognized contributions for the following:

For unrestricted use	$ 40,000
For use in cancer research	10,000
For purchase of equipment	20,000
For permanently restricted endowment principal	30,000
Total	$100,000

2. Short-term investments at year-end consist of $150,000 of unrestricted funds and $50,000 of funds restricted for future cancer research. All of the long-term investments are held in the permanently restricted endowment fund.

3. Land is carried at its current market value of $120,000. The original owner purchased the land for $70,000, and at the time of donation to the hospital, the land had an appraised value of $95,000.

4. Buildings were purchased 11 years ago for $600,000 and had an estimated useful life of 30 years. Equipment costing $150,000 was purchased 7 years ago and had an expected life of 10 years. The controller had improperly increased the reported values of the buildings and equipment to their current fair value of $935,000 and had incorrectly computed the accumulated depreciation.

5. The board of directors voted on December 29, 20X4, to designate $100,000 of unrestricted funds invested in short-term investments for use in developing a drug rehabilitation center.

Required

Prepare in good form a balance sheet for Brookdale Hospital at December 31, 20X4.

**P19-12   Entries and Statement of Activities for an Other Nonprofit Organization
[AICPA Adapted]**

A group of civic-minded merchants in Eldora organized the "Committee of 100" for the purpose of establishing the Community Sports Club, a nonprofit sports organization for local youth. Each of the committee's 100 members contributed $1,000 toward the club's capital and, in turn, received a participation certificate. In addition, each participant agreed to pay dues of $200 a year for the club's operations. All dues have been collected in full by the end of each fiscal year ending March 31. Members who have discontinued their participation have been replaced by an equal number of new members through transfer of the participation certificates from the former members to the new ones. Following is the club's trial balance for April 1, 20X2:

	Debit	Credit
Cash	$ 9,000	
Investments (at market, equal to cost)	58,000	
Inventories	5,000	
Land	10,000	
Building	164,000	
Accumulated Depreciation—Building		$130,000
Furniture and Equipment	54,000	
Accumulated Depreciation—Furniture and Equipment		46,000
Accounts Payable		12,000
Participation Certificates (100 at $1,000 each)		100,000
Cumulative Excess of Revenue over Expenses		12,000
Total	$300,000	$300,000

Transactions for the year ended March 31, 20X3, were as follows:

Collections from participants for dues	$20,000
Snack bar and soda fountain sales	28,000
Interest and dividends received	6,000
Additions to voucher register:	
House expenses	17,000
Snack bar and soda fountain	26,000
General and administrative	11,000
Vouchers paid	55,000
Assessments for capital improvements not yet incurred (assessed on March 20, 20X3; none collected by March 31, 20X3; deemed 100% collectible during year ending March 31, 20X4)	10,000
Unrestricted bequest received	5,000

Adjustment Data

1. Investments are valued at market, which amounted to $65,000 on March 31, 20X3. There were no investment transactions during the year.

2. Depreciation for year:

Building	$4,000
Furniture and equipment	8,000

3. Allocation of depreciation:

House expenses	$9,000
Snack bar and soda fountain	2,000
General and administrative	1,000

4. Actual physical inventory on March 31, 20X3, was $1,000 and pertains to the snack bar and soda fountain.

Required

a. Record the transactions and adjustments in journal entry form for the year ended March 31, 20X3. Omit explanations.

b. Prepare the appropriate all-inclusive statement of activities for the year ended March 31, 20X3.

P19-13 Entries and Statements for General Fund of a Hospital

The postclosing trial balance of the general fund of Serene Hospital, a not-for-profit entity, on December 31, 20X1, was as follows:

	Debit	Credit
Cash	$ 125,000	
Accounts Receivable	400,000	
Allowance for Uncollectibles		$ 50,000
Due from Specific-Purpose Fund	40,000	
Inventories	95,000	
Prepaid Expenses	20,000	
Investments	900,000	
Property, Plant, and Equipment	6,100,000	

(continued)

Accumulated Depreciation		1,500,000
Accounts Payable		150,000
Accrued Expenses		55,000
Deferred Revenue—Reimbursement		75,000
Bonds Payable		3,000,000
Fund Balance—Unrestricted		2,850,000
Total	$7,680,000	$7,680,000

During 20X2 the following transactions occurred:

1. The value of patient services provided was $6,160,000.
2. Contractual adjustments of $330,000 from patients' bills were approved.
3. Operating expenses totaled $5,600,000, as follows:

Nursing services	$1,800,000
Other professional services	1,200,000
Fiscal services	250,000
General services	1,550,000
Bad debts	120,000
Administration	280,000
Depreciation	400,000

Accounts credited for operating expenses other than depreciation:

Cash	$4,580,000
Allowance for Uncollectibles	120,000
Accounts Payable	170,000
Accrued Expenses	35,000
Inventories	195,000
Prepaid Expenses	30,000
Donated Services	70,000

4. Received $75,000 cash from specific-purpose fund for partial reimbursement of $100,000 for operating expenditures made in accordance with a restricted gift. The receivable increased by the remaining $25,000 to an ending balance of $65,000.
5. Payments for inventories and prepaid expenses were $176,000 and $24,000, respectively.
6. Received $85,000 income from endowment fund investments.
7. Sold an X-ray machine that had cost $30,000 and had accumulated depreciation of $20,000 for $17,000.
8. Collected $5,800,000 in receivables and wrote off $132,000.
9. Acquired investments amounting to $60,000.
10. Income from board-designated investments was $72,000.
11. Paid the beginning balance in Accounts Payable and Accrued Expenses.
12. Deferred Revenue—Reimbursement increased $20,000.
13. Received $140,000 from the plant replacement and expansion fund for use in acquiring fixed assets.
14. Net receipts from the cafeteria and gift shop were $63,000.

Required

a. Prepare journal entries to record the transactions for the general fund. Omit explanations.
b. Prepare comparative balance sheets for only the general fund for 20X2 and 20X1.
c. Prepare a statement of operations for the unrestricted, general fund for 20X2.
d. Prepare a statement of cash flows for 20X2.

P19-14 Statements for Current Funds of a Voluntary Health and Welfare Organization [AICPA Adapted]

Following are the adjusted current funds trial balances of Community Association for Handicapped Children, a voluntary health and welfare organization, on June 30, 20X4:

COMMUNITY ASSOCIATION FOR HANDICAPPED CHILDREN
Adjusted Current Funds Trial Balances
June 30, 20X4

	Unrestricted		Restricted	
	Debit	Credit	Debit	Credit
Cash	$ 40,000		$ 9,000	
Bequest Receivable			5,000	
Pledges Receivable	12,000			
Accrued Interest Receivable	1,000			
Investments (at market)	100,000			
Accounts Payable and Accrued Expenses		$ 50,000		$ 1,000
Deferred Revenue		2,000		
Allowance for Uncollectible Pledges		3,000		
Fund Balances, July 1, 20X3:				
Designated		12,000		
Undesignated		26,000		
Restricted				23,000
Transfers of Expired Endowment Fund Principal		20,000	20,000	
Contributions		300,000		15,000
Membership Dues		25,000		
Program Service Fees		30,000		
Investment Income		10,000		
Deaf Children's Program Expenses	120,000			
Blind Children's Program Expenses	150,000			
Management and General Services	45,000		4,000	
Fund-Raising Services	8,000		1,000	
Provision for Uncollectible Pledges	2,000			
Total	$478,000	$478,000	$39,000	$39,000

Required

a. Prepare a statement of activities for the year ended June 30, 20X4.

b. Prepare a statement of financial position as of June 30, 20X4.

P19-15 Comparative Journal Entries for a Government Entity and a Voluntary Health and Welfare Organization [AICPA Adapted]

Following are four independent transactions or events that relate to a local government and a voluntary health and welfare organization:

1. A disbursement of $25,000 was made from the general fund unrestricted assets for the cash purchase of new equipment.

2. An unrestricted cash gift of $100,000 was received from a donor.

3. Investments in common stocks with a total carrying value of $50,000 were sold by a permanently restricted endowment fund for $55,000 before any dividends were earned on these stocks. The gain is donor-restricted to remain in the permanently restricted fund.

4. General obligation bonds payable with a face amount of $1,000,000 were sold at par, with the proceeds required to be used solely for construction of a new building. This building was completed at a total cost of $1,000,000, and the total amount of bond issue proceeds was disbursed toward this cost. Disregard interest capitalization.

Required

a. For each of these transactions or events, prepare journal entries without explanations, specifying the affected funds and showing how these transactions or events should be recorded by a local government whose debt is serviced by general tax revenue.

b. For each of these transactions or events, prepare journal entries without explanations, specifying the affected funds and showing how these transactions or events should be recorded by a voluntary health and welfare organization.

P19-16   Matching Effects of Transactions on a Hospital's Financial Statements [AICPA Adapted]

DeKalb Hospital, a large not-for-profit organization, has adopted an accounting policy that does not imply a time restriction on gifts of long-lived assets.

For each of the six items presented, select the best answer from the Answer List.

Transactions	Answer List
1. DeKalb's board designates $1,000,000 to purchase investments whose income will be used for capital improvements.	A. Increase in unrestricted revenues, gains, and other support
2. Income from investments in item 1, which was not previously accrued, is received.	B. Decrease in an expense
3. A benefactor provided funds for building expansion.	C. Increase in temporarily restricted net assets
4. The funds in item 3 are used to purchase a building in the fiscal period following the period in which the funds were received.	D. Increase in permanently restricted net assets
5. An accounting firm prepared DeKalb's annual financial statements without charge.	E. No required reportable event
6. DeKalb received investments subject to the donor's requirement that investment income be used to pay for outpatient services.	

P19-17   Balance Sheet for a Hospital

The following information is contained in the funds that are used to account for the transactions of the Hospital of Havencrest, which is operated by a religious organization. The balances in the accounts are as of June 30, 20X8, the end of the hospital's fiscal year.

	General Fund	Specific-Purpose Fund	Plant Replacement and Expansion Fund	Endowment Fund
Cash	$ 30,000	$32,000	$140,000	$ 20,000
Accounts Receivable	25,000			
Allowance for Uncollectibles	(5,000)			
Inventories	50,000			
Prepaid Expenses	10,000			
Long-Term Investments	100,000		60,000	500,000
Property, Plant, and Equipment	300,000			
Accumulated Depreciation	(140,000)			
Accounts Payable	45,000			
Accrued Expenses	17,000			
Deferred Revenue	11,000			
Current Portion—Long-Term Debt	24,000			
Mortgage Payable	125,000			

Additional Information

The $32,000 in the specific-purpose fund is restricted for research activities to be conducted by the hospital.

Required

Prepare a balance sheet for Havencrest at June 30, 20X8.

P19-18 Matching of Transactions to Effects on Statement of Changes in Net Assets for a Hospital

Match the transactions on the left with the effects of the transactions on the statement of changes in net assets for a private, not-for-profit hospital.

Transactions	Effects of Transactions on Statement of Changes in Net Assets
1. Patients billed for services rendered.	A. Increases unrestricted net assets
2. Realized a gain from the sale of securities that are permanently invested.	B. Decreases unrestricted net assets
3. Recorded depreciation expense for the year.	C. Increases temporarily restricted net assets
4. Designated assets for plant expansion.	D. Decreases temporarily restricted net assets
5. Contributions restricted for research activities received.	E. Increases permanently restricted net assets
6. Contributions restricted for equipment acquisition.	F. Decreases permanently restricted net assets
7. Acquired equipment with all of the contributions received in item 6.	G. Does not affect the statement of changes in net assets
8. Earned endowment income. The donor placed no restrictions on the investment earnings.	
9. Expended 50 percent of the contributions restricted for research in item 5.	
10. Received cash contribution from donor who stipulated the contribution be permanently invested.	
11. Acquired investments with cash received in item 10.	
12. Received tuition revenue from hospital nursing program and cash from sales of goods in the hospital gift shop.	

P19-19 Matching of Transactions to Effects on Statement of Activities for a Voluntary Health and Welfare Organization

Match the transactions on the left with the effects of the transactions on the statement of activities for a voluntary health and welfare organization. A transaction may have more than one effect.

Transactions	Effects of Transactions on Statement of Activities
1. Received cash contributions restricted by donors for research.	A. Increases unrestricted net assets
2. Incurred fund-raising costs.	B. Decreases unrestricted net assets
3. Recorded depreciation expense for the year.	C. Increases temporarily restricted net assets
4. Designated assets for plant expansion.	D. Decreases temporarily restricted net assets
5. Realized a gain from the sale of securities that were permanently restricted. The donor specified that any gains from sales of these securities must be preserved and invested in other permanently restricted investments.	E. Increases permanently restricted net assets
6. Earned endowment income. The donor specified that the income be used for community service.	F. Decreases permanently restricted net assets
7. Received a multiyear pledge, with cash being received this year and for the next four years. Donors did not place any use restrictions on how the pledges were to be spent.	G. Is not reported on the statement of activities
8. Earned income from investments of assets that the board designated in item 4.	
9. Received pledges from donors who placed no time or use restrictions on how the pledges were to be spent.	

(continued)

10. Received cash contributions restricted by donors for equipment.

11. Acquired equipment with all of the contributions received in item 10.

12. Expended 75 percent of the contributions received in item 1 for research.

P19-20   **Net Asset Identification for Transactions Involving a Private University**

Buckwall University (BU), a private university, had the following transactions during the year ended June 30, 20X8:

1. Assessed students $2,000,000 for tuition for the winter semester, starting in January 20X8.

2. Received $1,000,000 from the federal government to be distributed to qualified students as loans and grants.

3. Recognized depreciation expense of $200,000 on university buildings and equipment for the fiscal year.

4. Received $1,500,000 in alumni contributions restricted to the construction of a new library building. Construction of the library is expected to begin in September 20X8.

5. Invested the contributions received in item 4 in equity securities that had a market value of $1,650,000 on June 30, 20X8.

6. Received $75,000 of investment revenue from investments in a term endowment. The donor stipulated that the investment revenue be used to fund scholarships for qualified entering freshmen.

7. Used $60,000 of the investment revenue in item 6 to fund scholarships during the year ended June 30, 20X8.

8. Designated $250,000 of cash to be used for refurbishing the steam tunnels used for heating the university during the winter.

9. Received from an alumnus a contribution of artwork with a fair value of $3,750,000. The donor has stipulated that the artwork be preserved, that it not be sold, and that it be on public view in the university museum. The university has a policy of recording donations of works of art and historical treasures.

10. Acquired debt securities at a cost of $400,000 during the year. Required by the governing board to keep these investments intact for the next five years and use interest revenue from the securities for funding summer research grants to faculty of BU.

11. Received during the year ended June 30, 20X8, interest revenue from the debt securities in item 10, which amounted to $18,000, of which $12,000 was used for research grants.

Required

For each of the numbered transactions, indicate the net asset class affected by the transaction for the year ended June 30, 20X8. The three net asset classes are (1) unrestricted, (2) temporarily restricted, and (3) permanently restricted. Your answer should also specify the dollar amount and whether the asset class increased or decreased.

P19-21   **Questions on Voluntary Health and Welfare Organization [AICPA Adapted]**

Items 1 through 6 represent various transactions pertaining to Crest Haven, a voluntary health and welfare organization, for the year ended December 31, 20X2. The information presented also includes a list of how transactions could affect the statement of activities (List A Effects) and the statement of cash flows (List B Effects). Crest Haven follows both FASB 116 and 117.

Transactions

1. Pledges of $500,000 were made by various donors for the acquisition of new equipment. The equipment will be acquired in 20X3.

2. Dividends and interest of $40,000 were received from endowment investments. The donors have stipulated that the earnings from endowment investments be used for research in 20X3.

3. Cash donations of $350,000 were received from donors who did not stipulate how the donations were to be used.

4. Investments of $250,000 were acquired from cash donated in 20X0 by a donor who stipulated that the cash donation be invested permanently.

5. Depreciation expense of $75,000 was recorded for 20X2.

6. Of the amount pledged in transaction 1, $300,000 was received.

Required

Indicate how Crest Haven should report each transaction on (1) the statement of activities and (2) the statement of cash flows prepared for the year ended December 31, 20X2. Crest Haven reports separate columns for changes in unrestricted, temporarily restricted, and permanently restricted net assets on its statement of activities. In addition, Crest Haven uses the direct method of reporting its cash flows from operation activities. The items in List A Effects and List B Effects may be used once, more than once, or not at all.

Example

Cash paid to employees and suppliers: List A = D   List B = I

Statement of Activities List A Effects	Statement of Cash Flows List B Effects
A. Increases unrestricted net assets	H. Increases cash flows from operating activities
B. Increases temporarily restricted net assets	I. Decreases cash flows from operating activities
C. Increases permanently restricted net assets	J. Increases cash flows from investing activities
D. Decreases unrestricted net assets	K. Decreases cash flows from investing activities
E. Decreases temporarily restricted net assets	L. Increases cash flows from financing activities
F. Decreases permanently restricted net assets	M. Decreases cash flows from financing activities
G. Is not reported on the statement of activities	N. Transaction not reported on the statement of cash flows

P19-22 **Contributions to a Hospital [AICPA Adapted]**

Alpha Hospital, a large not-for-profit organization, has adopted an accounting policy that does not imply a time restriction on gifts of long-lived assets.

Required

For items 1 through 6, indicate the effect of the transaction on Alpha's financial statements by selecting the appropriate letter.

Transactions	Effect
1. Alpha's board designates $1,000,000 to purchase investments whose income will be used for capital improvements.	A. Increase in unrestricted revenues, gains, and other support
2. Income from investments in item 1, which was not previously accrued, is received.	B. Decrease in expense
3. A benefactor provides funds for a building expansion.	C. Increase in temporarily restricted net assets
4. The funds in item 3 are used to purchase a building in the fiscal period following the period the funds were received.	D. Increase in permanently restricted net assets
5. An accounting firm prepares Alpha's annual financial statements without charge to Alpha.	E. No required reportable event
6. Alpha receives investments subject to the donor's requirement that investment income be used to pay for outpatient services.	

P19-23 **Evaluating Items for a Hospital's Statement of Operations**

Smallville Community Hospital, a not-for-profit hospital, has a number of items to be evaluated to determine their proper placement on the hospital's statement of operations (either above the performance measure of Excess of Revenues over Expenses or below the performance measure). It is possible that an item need not be reported on the hospital's statement of operations.

Required

Select the proper letter from the Where Reported column to match each item in the left-hand column. If an item is presented in two or more places on the statement of operations, provide the correct answer for each placement.

Items	Where Reported
1. Bad debts expense.	A. Above the performance measure line
2. Donated supplies used in patient care.	B. Below the performance measure line
3. Unrestricted investment interest income.	C. Not reported on the statement of operations
4. Gain on sale of hospital assets.	
5. Net assets released from restriction for acquisition of equipment.	
6. Net assets released from restriction for use in hospital operations.	
7. Gain on sale of permanently restricted endowment investments that the donor requires to be permanently restricted.	
8. Investment interest income that donor restricted for use in medical care education programs, which the hospital plans to begin next year.	
9. Pledges for a new hospital building wing to be constructed next year.	
10. Revenue from cafeteria sales.	
11. Donations of specialized, professional-quality services.	
12. Depreciation expense on hospital equipment.	
13. Resources designated by the hospital board of directors to be set aside for the new hospital wing.	
14. Gift of new heart-monitoring equipment received.	
15. Charity care provided by the hospital in accordance with its state charter.	
16. Contractual adjustment to the normal service charge for persons covered by an insurance company's health insurance.	
17. Proceeds of a bond issue for the new wing.	
18. Purchase of new operating tables for the operating rooms.	
19. Recognition of unrealized holding gain for change in market value of investment securities. Income is in excess of amounts designated for current operations.	

P19-24   ### True-False Questions about Not-for-Profit Accounting and Reporting

Determine whether each of the following is true or false. Assume that each organization is a private, nonprofit entity.

1. A statement of functional expenses is required for a musical arts association that is a not-for-profit organization.

2. Pledges received by a research organization should result in recording revenue net of estimated uncollectible pledges.

3. A college should account for a donor-restricted contribution to support student scholarships for the next three years as contribution revenue in its unrestricted net assets.

4. A hospital should record an insurance provider's contractual adjustment on a patient bill as an operating expense for the period in which the services were provided to the patient.

5. A university should account for its governing board's designation of resources for the development of a fine arts academic program as a transfer to a temporarily restricted net asset class.

6. An environmental watch organization received a donor-restricted donation for the purchase of equipment. The organization properly accounted for the donation when it was received. When the equipment is acquired, the organization should record "net assets released" from temporarily restricted net assets and an addition to unrestricted net assets.

7. A hospital used donated supplies for its patient services during the year. The hospital should not record the donation because it incurred no cost to obtain the supplies.

8. An organization earned investment income on its endowment fund that is permanently donor restricted for use in a specific organizational program. The investment income should be recorded directly into the temporarily restricted net asset class.

9. A hospital has a portfolio of securities that decreased in fair market value during the year. Because the securities were not sold during the year, the change in market value should not be recognized on the hospital's statement of operations.

10. A not-for-profit art museum receives for public display a donation of historical artifacts that the museum will care for and preserve. If any item in the collection is ever sold, the museum has agreed to use the proceeds for additional items for the collection. The museum is not required to record the contribution revenue and increase in collection assets.

11. All of a hospital's building and equipment should be recorded in its restricted building fund.

12. A local accountant donated significant professional services to a local fraternal organization, which should recognize the value of the donated services as both a contribution revenue and an operating expense.

13. A hospital has estimated uncollectibles on patient accounts that should be reported as a reduction of net patient service revenue.

14. A college received a conditional pledge based on the occurrence of a future event. The school should record the contribution at its fair value if it is determined that the future event is possible.

15. A hospital that received a donation restricted for a cancer awareness education program properly recorded the donation as contribution revenue in the temporarily restricted net asset class. The cost of the program that the hospital offered should be recorded as an expense in the temporarily restricted net asset class to offset the contribution revenue for the program.

16. A voluntary health and welfare organization received a contribution that the donor specified could not be spent until the next year. Because the organization had received it in this year, the donation should be recorded as a debit to Cash and a credit to Deferred Revenue in the unrestricted net asset class.

17. Hospitals are required to use fund accounting, which specifies which funds are unrestricted, which are temporarily restricted, and which are permanently restricted.

18. Hospitals are required to report a performance measure in their statement of operations to separate the operating income from the nonoperating income.

19. A hospital's building fund transfers resources to the general fund for the purchase of new equipment. The building fund should record this as an expense of the period of the transfer, and the general fund should record this as an income of the period of the transfer.

20. A voluntary health and welfare organization conducted a major fund-raising effort that involved significant expenses. Because the expenses were incurred to obtain contribution revenue, the fund-raising costs should be accounted for as a direct reduction of contribution revenue to obtain the net contribution revenue reported on the organization's statement of activities.

P19-25   **Statement of Activities for a Voluntary Health and Welfare Organization**

The following information pertains to United Ways, a private voluntary health and welfare organization, for the year ended December 31, 20X3.

Balances in net assets at January 1, 20X3:	
Unrestricted	$3,000,000
Temporarily restricted	5,000,000
Permanently restricted	6,000,000

The following transactions occurred during the year ended December 31, 20X3:

1. Received cash donations of $500,000 from donors who did not place any time or purpose restrictions on their donations.

2. Received $1,000,000 of pledges from donors to be received in 20X4; it was estimated that 5 percent of the pledges would not be collected. Donors did not place any restrictions on the use of their pledges.

3. Earned investment income of $200,000 on endowment investments that donors permanently restricted for research activities.

4. Designated $225,000 of the $500,000 of cash donations received in 20X3 for computer acquisitions.

5. Spent $150,000 of the $200,000 of investment income earned on endowment investments on research during the year ended December 31, 20X3. (This amount is included in the $250,000 shown below for research expenses.)

6. Acquired $100,000 of equipment from donations made in 20X2 that donors had restricted for that purchase. The governing board of United Ways reports acquisitions of capital assets as unrestricted.

7. Received donated audit services that would have cost $15,000 from the organization's accounting firm.

8. The organization learned that the fair value of endowment investments was $600,000 higher at the end of 20X3 than it had been at the beginning of 20X3. United Ways did not acquire or sell any endowment investments during 20X3. Gains and losses on endowment investments are treated as permanently restricted.

9. Incurred program and supporting services expenses during 20X3 as follows (depreciation expense for 20X3 has been properly allocated to the functional expenses):

Research	$250,000
Public health education	100,000
Community services	150,000
Management and general (does not include the audit that was donated)	125,000
Fund-raising	115,000

Required

Prepare a statement of activities in good form for United Way for the year ended December 31, 20X3.

P19-26 Reporting Transactions on the Statement of Cash Flows for Private, Not-for-Profit Entities

Following is a list of transactions and events that may occur in private, not-for-profit entities. Indicate where each transaction or event should be reported on the entity's statement of cash flows. Assume that the indirect method of reporting operating activities is used. If a transaction or event is reported as an adjustment to the change in net assets in the operating activities section, your answer should indicate whether the adjustment is added to or subtracted from the change in net assets. If a transaction or event is reported in more than one section on the statement of cash flows, you should include all sections in your answer.

Sample Question

A hospital recorded depreciation expense for the year of $50,000.

Answer

Report the depreciation expense of $50,000 as an addition to the change in net assets in the operating activities section.

Transactions and Events

1. A hospital's accounts receivable from patients increased $100,000 during the year.

2. A college received from a donor a $200,000 contribution restricted to acquiring fixed assets.

3. A voluntary health and welfare organization received $25,000 from a donor who stipulated that the amount be invested permanently.

4. A hospital's accounts payable for the purchase of medical supplies increased $20,000 during the year.

5. A botanical society borrowed $70,000 from the First National Bank on a long-term note payable.

6. A professional trade association invested $50,000 to acquire investments in bonds that it intends to keep until their maturity.

7. A college received investment income of $45,000 from endowment investments. The donor stipulated that the income be used for the acquisition of fixed assets.

8. A hospital spent $850,000 to acquire equipment.

9. A college made loans of $100,000 to students and faculty.

10. A zoological society made a payment of $30,000 to a local bank to repay the principal of a short-term note payable.

11. A college's accrued interest receivable related to student and faculty loans increased $5,000 during the year.

12. A performing arts organization had an increase of $12,000 in deferred revenue for the year.

13. A college received $100,000 for the repayment of principal on loans made to students and faculty.

14. A hospital's prepaid assets increased $2,500 during the year.

15. A hospital's endowment investments increased in value by $35,000 during the year.

Kaplan CPA Review

CPA EDUCATION

Kaplan CPA Review Simulation on University and College Accounting and Reporting

Access to the online CPA Simulation can be attained by visiting the text's Website at www.mhhe.com/baker7e.

Situation

Jones University starts the current year with net assets of $1.5 million: $800,000 in unrestricted net assets, $500,000 in temporarily restricted net assets, and $200,000 in permanently restricted net assets. Unless otherwise stated, assume that Jones University is a private, not-for-profit organization.

Topics Included in the Simulation

a. The required financial statements for a private, not-for-profit university versus the required financial statements for a public, not-for-profit university.

b. Accounting and reporting for transactions resulting in changes in unrestricted net assets, such as construction, and donations of money, property, and services.

c. Accounting for pledges, investments, and restricted donations.

d. Accounting for financial aid to students.

e. Accounting for future vacation costs of administration and staff.

f. Research on a conditional pledge.

Supplemental Problems for this chapter are available as part of the *Online Learning Center* on the textbook's Website.

Corporations in Financial Difficulty

A life cycle exists for businesses as for individuals. The business press often carries stories of companies in financial difficulty, including large companies such as K-Mart, United Airlines, Bethlehem Steel, Enron, and WorldCom. On average, there are 35,000 business filings in the U.S. bankruptcy courts each year. About 60 percent of these are filed under Chapter 7 as liquidations, and the remaining 40 percent are filed under Chapter 11 as reorganizations. Untold thousands of other companies use alternate courses of action, such as debt restructuring and agreements with creditors in order to work themselves out of financial difficulty.

Companies get into financial difficulty for a large variety of reasons. A company may suffer from continued losses from operations, overextended credit to customers, poor management of working capital, failure to react to changes in economic conditions, inadequate financing, and a host of other reasons for not sustaining a viable economic position. A company's liquidity problems often become cumulative. Failing to make a sufficient level of sales, a company cannot obtain adequate financing, then begins to miss debt payments, and the vicious cycle of financial difficulty is under way. At this point, outside creditors may decide to exercise their claims and demand payment of their receivables. The debtor company has a number of alternative courses open to it. It may try to reach an agreement with its creditors to postpone required payments, it may turn its assets over to its creditors for liquidation, or it may take the legal remedy of bankruptcy.

A company may petition the courts for bankruptcy for other reasons, such as to protect itself from an onslaught of legal suits. Several companies have also attempted to void union contracts by petitioning for bankruptcy. The courts are still defining the exact limits of bankruptcy, and each case must be decided individually.

Insolvency is defined as a condition in which a company is unable to meet debts as the debts mature. The insolvent company is unable to meet its liabilities. Before 1978, creditors had to show that the debtor was insolvent before they could petition for relief in a bankruptcy court. Because of changes in the bankruptcy law in 1978, insolvency is no longer a necessary precondition for bankruptcy.

A company in financial difficulty has a large number of alternatives, of which bankruptcy is only a final course. This chapter presents the range of major actions typically used by a company experiencing financial problems.

COURSES OF ACTION

Bankruptcy is the final step for a financially distressed business. Prior to that, however, management usually tries to work closely with the company's creditors to provide for their claims while attempting to ensure the firm's continuing existence. A variety of nonjudicial arrangements with creditors is available. If these fail, the company usually ends up in a judicial action under the direction of a bankruptcy court.

Nonjudicial Actions

Formal agreements between the company and its creditors are legally binding but are not administered by a court. The major nonjudicial action is debt restructuring as illustrated in Appendix 20A.

Debt Restructuring Arrangements

Arrangements between a debtor company and one or more of its creditors are common for companies in temporary financial difficulty. The debtor may solicit an extension of due dates of its debt, ask for a decrease of the interest rate on the debt, or ask for a modification of other terms of the debt contract. Creditors are usually willing to extend concessions to a debtor rather than risk the legal expense and ill will from legal action against a previously valuable debtor. Many banks, for example, prefer to continue to work with a customer who is in temporary financial difficulty rather than force that customer into bankruptcy. Experience has shown that banks eventually realize a larger portion of their receivables and continue to have a future customer if they assist the debtor with financial problems by restructuring the debt. The debtors' accounting for these **troubled debt restructurings** is presented in **FASB Statement No. 15**, "Accounting by Debtors and Creditors for Troubled Debt Restructurings" (FASB 15). The creditor's accounting for impairments in the values of notes and loans is presented in **FASB Statement No. 114**, "Accounting by Creditors for Impairment of a Loan" (FASB 114), issued in May 1993 and superseding **FASB 15** for the creditor's accounting of troubled debt restructurings. In addition, **FASB Statement No. 118**, "Accounting by Creditors for Impairment of a Loan—Income Recognition and Disclosures" (FASB 118), was issued in October 1994 and makes minor changes to **FASB 114** for creditor accounting for the income from impaired loans. Examples of an impairment and a troubled debt restructuring are presented in Appendix 20A.

Another form of debt restructuring arrangement is the *composition agreement*. In this case, creditors agree to accept less than the face amount of their claims. The advantage to the creditors is that they receive an immediate cash payment and usually negotiate the timing of the remaining cash payments. Although creditors receive less than the full amount, they are assured of receiving most of their receivables. Composition agreements typically involve all creditors, although some may not be willing to agree to the composition. In some cases, the consenting group of creditors agrees to allow the dissenting creditors to be paid in full if it is highly probable the debtor can eventually return to profitable operations.

Creditors' Committee Management

Under **creditors' committee management**, the creditors may agree to assist the debtor in managing the most efficient payment of creditors' claims. Most creditors' committees are advisory and counsel closely with the debtor because the creditors do not want to assume additional liabilities and problems of actual operation of the debtor. Forming a creditors' committee is a nonjudicial action usually initiated with a *plan of settlement* proposed by the debtor. The plan of settlement is a detailed document that includes a schedule of payments listing the specific debts and the anticipated payments. The creditors then work closely with the debtor to enact the plan.

In some extreme cases, creditors may decide to assume operating control of the debtor company. The creditors appoint a trustee who assumes management responsibility for the debtor company. The trustee reports to the creditors with recommendations for the eventual settlement of claims. The trustee may attempt to work out a payment schedule or may recommend bankruptcy as the best alternative. The advantage of the creditors' committee management in these extreme cases is that creditors have operating control of the debtor and receive a full report of the debtor's financial condition. The disadvantage of assuming operating control to the creditors is that they incur an increased risk if the debtor enters bankruptcy because, as managers before the bankruptcy, they may be held responsible. The advantage to the debtor is that the creditors are attempting to assist the debtor out of its financial difficulty and may return operating control once the financial problems are solved without resorting to legal action.

Transfer of Assets

Some debtors in financial difficulty may transfer assets, such as receivables or other financial instruments, in an effort to obtain quick cash. For example, debtors in need of cash may factor their trade receivables at a discount, and the contract may specify that the receivables are sold "with recourse" or "without recourse." The "with recourse" provision means that the debtor must accept the return of any uncollectible receivables that were initially transferred. The accounting issue is to determine whether these transfers should be accounted for as sales of the receivables or as a financing arrangement between the debtor company and the factor company. **FASB Statement No. 140**, "Accounting for Transfers and Servicing of Financial Assets and Extinguishment of Liabilities" (FASB 140), provides the accounting and reporting guidelines for these transfers. **FASB 140** specifies that a transfer of financial assets is considered a sale only if the transferor (the debtor company) has surrendered control over the transferred assets. Surrendering control means that the transferred assets have been isolated from the transferor, that the transferee (i.e., recipient) obtains the right to pledge or exchange the transferred assets, and that the transferor does not maintain effective control over the transferred assets such as through an agreement allowing the transferor to repurchase or redeem the transferred assets.

Judicial Actions

Bankruptcy is a judicial action administered by bankruptcy courts and bankruptcy judges using the guidance provided in Title 11 of the United States Bankruptcy Code (Bankruptcy Code). This Bankruptcy Code provides the essential structure for bankruptcy proceedings, but periodically, amendments to this Bankruptcy Code have been made by the U.S. Congress. For example, the Bankruptcy Reform Act of 1994 (Reform Act of 1994) attempts to improve the efficiency and administration of bankruptcy cases while increasing creditors' legal protections. The Reform Act of 1994 also created a National Bankruptcy Review Commission to periodically investigate, analyze, and review bankruptcy issues and to improve the Bankruptcy Code. The Bankruptcy Abuse Prevention and Consumer Protection Act of 2005 (Bankruptcy Reform Act of 2005) made several changes for business filings, but most of the act pertains to personal filings. For example, the Bankruptcy Reform Act of 2005 makes it more difficult for persons to file for bankruptcy under Chapter 7 liquidations, and it changed Chapter 11 for personal filings to require the payment of debts such as credit card balances and other common forms of consumer debt. Personal bankruptcy filings are beyond the scope of this chapter; however, individuals considering filing for bankruptcy should first seek appropriate legal guidance.

The Bankruptcy Code is composed of eight chapters, numbered as follows:

Chapter 1	General Provisions
Chapter 3	Case Administration
Chapter 5	Creditors, the Debtor, and the Estate
Chapter 7	Liquidation
Chapter 9	Adjustment of Debts of a Municipality
Chapter 11	Reorganization
Chapter 12	Adjustment of Debts of a Family Farmer with Regular Annual Income
Chapter 13	Adjustment of Debts of an Individual with Regular Income

Chapters 1, 3, and 5 present the definitions and operating provisions of the Bankruptcy Code. Chapters 7 and 11 deal with corporations. Chapter 9 deals with municipal governments and Chapters 12 and 13 with individual bankruptcies.

Either the debtor or its creditors may decide that a judicial action is best in the individual circumstances. The debtor may file a *voluntary petition* seeking judicial protection in the form of an ***order of relief*** against the initiation or continuation of legal claims by the creditors against the debtor. Alternatively, creditors may file an *involuntary petition* against the debtor. Certain conditions must exist before creditors may file a petition. First, the debtor is generally not paying debts as they become due or within the last 120 days has had a custodian appointed by other creditors, by the debtor, or by some other agency to take possession of the debtor's assets. Second, if more than 12 creditors exist, 3 or more must combine to file the petition, and these must have aggregate unsecured claims of at least $5,000. The debtor is permitted to file an answer to an involuntary petition.

Once a petition has been filed, the bankruptcy court evaluates the company and determines whether present management should continue to manage the company or the court should appoint a trustee. Appointments of trustees are common when creditors make allegations of management fraud or gross management incompetence.

The Bankruptcy Code provides for two major alternatives under the protection of the bankruptcy court. These two alternatives are often known by the chapters of the Bankruptcy Code. The first is *reorganization under Chapter 11*, in which the debtor is provided judicial protection for a rehabilitation period during which it can eliminate unprofitable operations, obtain new credit, develop a new company structure with sustainable operations, and work out agreements with its creditors. The second alternative is a *liquidation under Chapter 7* of the Bankruptcy Code. A Chapter 7 liquidation is often administered by a trustee appointed by the court. The debtor's assets are sold and its liabilities extinguished as the business is liquidated. The major difference between a reorganization and a liquidation is that the debtor continues as a business after a reorganization, whereas the business does not survive a liquidation. Both of these alternatives are illustrated next.

CHAPTER 11 REORGANIZATIONS

Chapter 11 of the Bankruptcy Code allows for legal protection from creditors' actions during a time needed to reorganize the debtor company and return its operations to a profitable level. The bankruptcy court administers reorganizations and often appoints trustees to direct the reorganization. Reorganizations are typically described by the four Ps of reorganization. A company in financial distress *petitions* the bankruptcy court for *protection* from its creditors. If granted protection, the company receives an order of relief to suspend making any payments on its prepetition debt. The company continues to operate while it prepares a *plan of reorganization*, which serves as an operating guide during the reorganization. The *proceeding* includes the actions that take place from the time the petition is filed until the company completes the reorganization.

The petition must discuss the alternative of liquidating the debtor and distributing the expected receipts to the creditors. The plan of reorganization is the essence of any reorganization. The plan must include a complete description of the expected debtor actions during the reorganization period and the way these actions will be in the best interest of the debtor and its creditors. A *disclosure statement* is transmitted to all creditors and other parties eligible to vote on the plan of reorganization. The disclosure statement includes information that would enable a reasonable investor or creditor to make an informed judgment about the worthiness of the plan and how it will affect that person's financial interest in the debtor company. The bankruptcy court then evaluates the responses to the plan from creditors and other parties and either confirms the plan of reorganization or rejects it. Confirmation of the plan implies that the debtor, or an appointed trustee, will fully follow the plan. The reorganization period may be as short as a few months or as long as several years. Most reorganizations require more than one year; however, the time span of the proceeding depends on the complexity of the reorganization.

Statement of Position No. 90-7, "Financial Reporting by Entities in Reorganization under the Bankruptcy Code" (SOP 90-7),[1] provides guidance for financial reporting for companies in reorganization. The financial statements issued by a company during Chapter 11 proceedings should distinguish transactions and events directly associated with the reorganization from those associated with ongoing operations. Companies in reorganization are required to present balance sheets, income statements, and statements of cash flows, but

---

[1] *Statement of Position No. 90-7*, "Financial Reporting by Entities in Reorganization under the Bankruptcy Code" (New York: American Institute of Certified Public Accountants, 1990).

SOP 90-7 requires these three statements to clearly reflect the unique circumstances related to the reorganization.

The balance sheet of a company in reorganization has the following special attributes:

1. Prepetition liabilities subject to compromise as part of the reorganization proceeding should be reported separately from liabilities not subject to compromise. Liabilities subject to compromise include unsecured debt and other payables that were incurred before the company entered reorganization. Liabilities that are not subject to change by the reorganization plan include fully secured liabilities incurred before reorganization and all liabilities incurred after the company enters its petition for reorganization relief.

2. The liabilities should be reported at the expected amount to be allowed by the bankruptcy court. If no reasonable estimation is possible, the claims should be disclosed in the footnotes.

The income statement of a company in reorganization has the following special requirements:

1. Income statement amounts directly related to the reorganization, such as legal fees and losses on disposals of assets, should be reported separately as reorganization items in the period incurred. However, any gains or losses on discontinued operations, or extraordinary items, should be reported separately according to **APB Opinion 30**, "Reporting the Results of Operations" (APB 30).

2. Some of the interest income earned during reorganization is a result of not requiring the debtor to pay debt and thus investing the available resources in interest-bearing sources. Such interest income should be reported separately as a reorganization item. The extent to which reported interest expense differs from the contractual interest on the company's debt should be disclosed, either parenthetically on the face of the income statement or within the footnotes.

3. Earnings per share is disclosed as are any anticipated changes to the number of common shares or common stock equivalents outstanding as a result of the reorganization plan.

The statement of cash flows of a company in reorganization has the following special features:

1. **SOP 90-7** prefers the direct method of presenting cash flows from operations, but if the indirect method is used, the company must also disclose separately the operating cash flows associated with the reorganization.

2. Cash flows related to the reorganization should be reported separately from those from regular operations. For example, excess net interest received as a result of the company's not paying its debts during reorganization should be reported separately.

Fresh Start Accounting

The basic view of a reorganization is that it is a fresh start for the company. However, it is difficult to determine whether a Chapter 11 reorganization results in a new entity for which fresh start accounting should be used or if it results in a continuation of the prior entity. **SOP 90-7** states that fresh start reporting should be used as of the confirmation date of the plan of reorganization if both the following conditions occur:[2]

1. The reorganization value of the assets of the emerging entity immediately before the date of confirmation is less than the total of all postpetition liabilities and allowed claims.

2. Holders of existing voting shares immediately before confirmation receive less than 50 percent of the voting shares of the emerging entity. This implies that the prior shareholders have lost control of the emerging company.

Fresh start accounting results in a new reporting entity. First, the company is required to compute the reorganization value of the emerging entity's assets. ***Reorganization value***

---

[2] *Statement of Position No. 90-7*, para. 36.

represents the fair value of the entity before considering liabilities and approximates the amount a willing buyer would pay for the entity's assets. The reorganization value is then allocated to the assets using the allocation of value method in **FASB Statement No. 141**, "Business Combinations" (FASB 141). A reorganization value in excess of amounts assignable to identifiable assets is reported as an intangible asset called Reorganization Value in Excess of Amounts Allocable to Identifiable Assets. This excess is then accounted for in conformity with **FASB Statement No. 142**, "Goodwill and Other Intangible Assets" (FASB 142). Intangibles with a finite life are amortized over that life span while intangibles with an indefinite useful life are reviewed annually for impairment to determine whether the carrying value exceeds its fair value. The emerging company's liabilities are recorded at the present values of the amounts to be paid. Any retained earnings or deficits are eliminated. A set of final operating statements is prepared just prior to emerging from reorganization. In essence, the company is a new reporting entity after reorganization.

Companies Not Qualifying for Fresh Start Accounting

Those companies not meeting the two conditions for fresh start accounting should determine whether their assets are impaired in value. In addition, they should report liabilities at the present values of the amounts to be paid, with any gain or loss on the revaluation of the liabilities recorded in accordance with **APB 30** as to extraordinary or ordinary events.

Many companies decide to restructure their operations as part of the reorganization plan. Those companies not qualifying for fresh start accounting account for restructuring costs, such as the costs of closing a plant and reducing the work force, combining some of the remaining operations, and so on in accordance with **FASB Statement No. 146**, "Accounting for Costs Associated with Exit or Disposal Activities" (FASB 146). This statement establishes the recognition of a liability for a cost associated with an exit or disposal activity when the liability is incurred, not at the earlier time the company makes a commitment to an exit plan.

The accounting for long-lived assets should be performed in accordance with **FASB Statement No. 144**, "Accounting for Impairment or Disposal of Long-Lived Assets" (FASB 144). The long-lived assets are divided between (1) those to be held and used and (2) those to be disposed of by sale. An impairment loss on long-lived assets to be held and used is recognized only if the asset's carrying value is less than the estimated discounted cash flows from operations of the asset over its estimated useful life. The amount of the impairment loss is the difference between the asset's carrying amount and its fair value. Goodwill is not considered part of the long-lived assets to be tested for impairment under **FASB 144**. Note that **FASB 142** guides the accounting for any impairment of goodwill.

Individual long-lived assets that will be disposed of by sale are revalued to their lower of carrying amount or fair value less the selling costs. In addition, once the use of a long-lived asset is discontinued and set aside for disposal by sale, depreciation is stopped. A management decision to dispose of a component of the entity is accounted for as a discontinued segment under **APB 30**.

FASB 15 does not apply to troubled debt restructurings in which debtors restate their liabilities generally under the purview of the bankruptcy court. **FASB 15** applies only to specific debt restructuring transactions. This exception is not an issue in the immediate settlement of debt in which the debtor's gain or loss is the difference between the fair value of the consideration given and the carrying value of the debt. The gain or loss is the same under **FASB 15** as under a general restatement of liabilities in a reorganization. However, in cases of modification of terms in a reorganization involving a general restatement of liabilities, the debtor's restructuring gain is computed as the difference between the carrying value of the debt and the new principal after restructuring of the debt. The future cash flows from interest payments are not included in the computation of the new principal. Thus, in most cases of debt restructuring of companies in reorganization proceedings, the debtor's gain from the debt restructuring is greater than it would have been under **FASB 15**.

Plan of Reorganization

The plan of reorganization is typically a detailed document with a full discussion of all major actions to be taken during the reorganization period. In addition to these major actions, management also continues to manufacture and sell products, collect receivables, and pursue other day-to-day operations. Most plans include detailed discussions of the following:

1. Disposing of unprofitable operations, through either sale or liquidation.
2. Restructuring of debt with specific creditors.
3. Revaluation of assets and liabilities.
4. Reductions or eliminations of claims of original stockholders and issuances of new shares to creditors or others.

The plan of reorganization must be approved by at least half of all creditors, who must hold at least two-thirds of the dollar amount of the debtor's total outstanding debt, although the court may still confirm a plan that the necessary number of creditors do not approve, provided the court finds that the plan is in the best interests of all parties and is equitable and fair to those groups not voting approval.

Illustration of a Reorganization

A balance sheet for Peerless Products Corporation on December 31, 20X6, is presented in Figure 20–1. On January 2, 20X7, Peerless's management petitions the bankruptcy court for a Chapter 11 reorganization to obtain relief from debt payments and time to rehabilitate the company and return to profitable operations.

The following time line presents the dates relevant for this example:

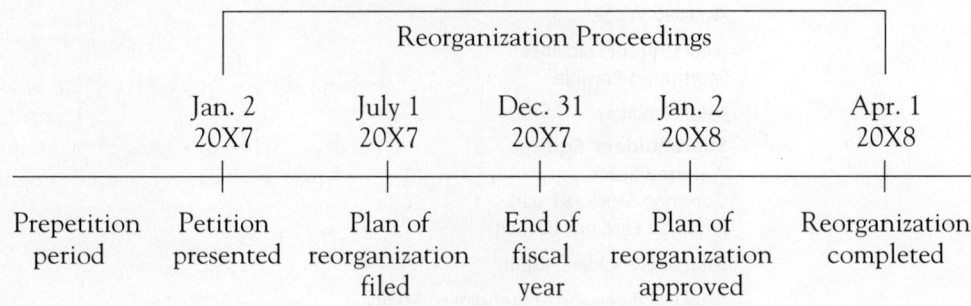

The bankruptcy court accepts the petition, and Peerless Products prepares its plan of reorganization. The plan is filed on July 1, 20X7, and the disclosure statement is sent to all creditors and other affected parties. On December 31, 20X7, the company presents its financial statements for the 20X7 fiscal period in which it was in Chapter 11 proceedings. The bankruptcy court approves the reorganization plan on January 2, 20X8, and the reorganization is completed by April 1, 20X8.

Peerless Products files the plan of reorganization presented in Figure 20–2, with audited financial statements and other disclosures requested by the bankruptcy court.

Prior to the approval of the plan of reorganization, Peerless Products continues to operate under the protection of the granted petition of relief. The company makes only court-approved payments on the prepetition liabilities. The only court-approved payment on prepetition liabilities is a $2,000 payment on the mortgage payable. On December 31, 20X7, the company issues financial statements for the fiscal year. **SOP 90-7** prescribes the reporting guidelines for companies in reorganization proceedings. A most important reporting concern is that the reorganization amounts be reported separately from other operating amounts. Peerless Products prepares the following financial statements as of December 31, 20X7: balance sheet (Figure 20–3), income statement (Figure 20–4), and statement of cash flows

FIGURE 20–1
Balance Sheet on the Date of Corporate Insolvency

PEERLESS PRODUCTS CORPORATION
Balance Sheet
December 31, 20X6

Assets

Cash					$ 2,000
Marketable Securities					8,000
Accounts Receivable			$ 20,000		
Less: Allowance for Uncollectible Accounts			(2,000)		18,000
Inventory					45,000
Prepaid Assets					1,000
Total Current Assets					$ 74,000

Property, Plant, and Equipment:

	Cost	Accumulated Depreciation	Undepreciated Cost	
Land	$ 10,000	$ -0-	$ 10,000	
Plant	75,000	20,000	55,000	
Equipment	40,000	4,000	36,000	
Total	$125,000	$24,000	$101,000	101,000
Total Assets				$175,000

Liabilities

Accounts Payable		$ 26,000
Notes Payable:		
Partially Secured	$ 10,000	
Unsecured, 10% interest	80,000	90,000
Accrued Interest		3,000
Accrued Wages		14,000
Total Current Liabilities		$133,000
Mortgages Payable		50,000
Total Liabilities		$183,000

Shareholders' Equity

Preferred Stock	$ 40,000	
Common Stock ($1 par)	10,000	
Retained Earnings (Deficit)	(58,000)	
Total Shareholders' Equity		(8,000)
Total Liabilities and Shareholders' Equity		$175,000

FIGURE 20–2
Plan of Reorganization

PEERLESS PRODUCTS CORPORATION
Plan of Reorganization
Under Chapter 11 of the Bankruptcy Code
(Filed July 1, 20X7)

a. The accounts payable of $26,000 will be provided for as follows: (1) $6,000 will be eliminated, (2) $4,000 will be paid in cash, (3) $12,000 of the payables will be exchanged for subordinated debt, and (4) $4,000 of the payables are to be exchanged for 4,000 shares of newly issued common stock.

b. The partially secured notes payable of $10,000 will be provided for as follows: (1) $2,000 will be paid in cash and (2) the remaining $8,000 will be exchanged for senior debt secured by a lien on equipment.

c. The unsecured notes payable of $80,000 will be provided for as follows: (1) $12,000 is to be eliminated, (2) $14,000 is to be paid in cash, (3) $49,000 is to be exchanged to senior debt secured by a lien against fixed assets, and (4) $5,000 is to be exchanged into 5,000 shares of newly issued common stock.

d. The accrued interest of $3,000 will be provided for as follows: (1) $2,000 will be eliminated and (2) the remaining $1,000 will be paid in cash.

e. The accrued wages of $14,000 will be provided for as follows: (1) $12,000 will be paid in cash and (2) the remaining $2,000 will be exchanged into 2,000 shares of newly issued common stock.

f. The preferred shareholders will receive 8,000 shares of newly issued common stock in exchange for their preferred stock.

g. The present common stockholders will receive 1,000 shares of newly issued common stock in exchange for their present common stock

FIGURE 20–3
Balance Sheet for a Company in Reorganization Proceedings

PEERLESS PRODUCTS CORPORATION		
(Debtor-in-Possession)		
Balance Sheet		
December 31, 20X7		
Assets		
Cash		$ 40,000
Income Tax Refund Receivable		12,000
Marketable Securities		8,000
Accounts Receivable	$ 6,000	
Less: Allowance for Uncollectibles	(1,000)	5,000
Inventory		37,000
Total Current Assets		$102,000
Property, Plant, and Equipment	$104,000	
Less: Accumulated Depreciation	(26,000)	78,000
Total Assets		$180,000
Liabilities		
Liabilities Not Subject to Compromise:		
Current Liabilities (postpetition):		
Short-Term Borrowings	$ 15,000	
Accounts Payable—Trade	10,000	
Noncurrent Liability:		
Mortgage Payable, Fully Secured	48,000	
Total Liabilities Not Subject to Compromise		$ 73,000
Liabilities Subject to Compromise (prepetition):		
Accounts Payable	$ 26,000	
Notes Payable, Partially Secured	10,000	
Notes Payable, Unsecured	80,000	
Accrued Interest	3,000	
Accrued Wages	14,000	
Total Liabilities Subject to Compromise		133,000
Total Liabilities		$206,000
Shareholders' Equity		
Preferred Stock	$ 40,000	
Common Stock ($1 par)	10,000	
Retained Earnings (deficit)	(76,000)	
Total Shareholders' Equity		(26,000)
Total Liabilities and Shareholders' Equity		$180,000

(Figure 20–5). Note that "Debtor-in-Possession" indicates that Peerless Products continues to manage its own assets rather than having them managed by a court-appointed trustee.

On January 2, 20X8, the bankruptcy court approves the plan of reorganization, as filed. Peerless Products Corporation carries out the plan as shown in the recovery analysis presented in Figure 20–6.

An important concept for determining the appropriate accounting for entities in reorganization is the determination of reorganization value. *Reorganization value* is the fair value of the entity's assets. Typical methods of determining reorganization value are discounting future cash flows or appraisals. After extensive analysis, a reorganization value of $195,000 is determined for Peerless Products' assets. Recall that fresh start accounting is appropriate only when both of the following conditions occur: (1) Reorganization value is less than total postpetition liabilities and allowed claims and (2) holders of existing shares of voting stock immediately before the plan of reorganization is approved retain less than 50 percent of the

FIGURE 20–4
Income Statement for a Company in Reorganization Proceedings

PEERLESS PRODUCTS CORPORATION		
(Debtor-in-Possession)		
Income Statement		
For the Year Ended December 31, 20X7		
Revenue:		
Sales		$120,000
Cost and Expenses:		
Cost of Goods Sold	$110,000	
Selling, Operating, and Administrative	21,000	
Interest (contractual interest $6,000)	3,000	134,000
Loss before Reorganization Items and Income Tax Benefit		$(14,000)
Reorganization Items:		
Loss on Disposal of Assets	$(10,000)	
Professional Fees	(8,000)	
Interest Earned on Accumulated Cash Resulting from Chapter 11 Proceeding	2,000	
Total Reorganization Items		(16,000)
Loss before Income Tax Benefit		$(30,000)
Income Tax Benefit		12,000
Net Loss		$(18,000)

voting shares of the emerging entity. To determine the first condition for Peerless Products, a comparison is made on the date the plan of reorganization is approved:

Postpetition liabilities	$ 73,000
Liabilities deferred pursuant to Chapter 11 proceedings	133,000
Total postpetition liabilities and allowed claims	$206,000
Reorganization value	(195,000)
Excess of liabilities over reorganization value	$ 11,000

Note that the first condition for fresh start accounting is present. The second condition for fresh start accounting also occurs, as shown in Figure 20–6. The common shareholders immediately before the plan of reorganization is approved hold only 5 percent of the common stock of the emerging entity. Therefore, fresh start accounting is used for Peerless Products. If both conditions for fresh start accounting are not met, the emerging company is not a new reporting entity.

After intensive study of risk-equivalent companies, the profit potential of the emerging company, and the present value of future cash flows, the capital structure of the emerging company is established as follows:

Postpetition current liabilities	$ 25,000
Postpetition mortgage payable	48,000
Senior debt	57,000
Subordinated debt	12,000
Common stock (new)	20,000
Total postreorganization capital structure	$162,000

Note that for purposes of the illustration, the newly issued common stock is no-par stock; therefore, no additional paid-in capital is carried forward to the emerging entity. If the

FIGURE 20–5
Statement of
Cash Flows for
a Company in
Reorganization
Proceedings

PEERLESS PRODUCTS CORPORATION	
(Debtor-in-Possession)	
Statement of Cash Flows	
For the Year Ended December 31, 20X7	
Cash Flows Provided by Operating Activities:	
Cash Received from Customers	$ 133,000
Cash Paid to Suppliers and Employees	(109,000)
Interest Paid	(3,000)
Net Cash Provided by Operating Activities before Reorganization Items	$ 21,000
Operating Cash Flows Used by Reorganization Activities:	
Professional Fees	$ (8,000)
Interest Received on Cash Accumulated Due to Chapter 11 Proceeding	2,000
Net Cash Used by Reorganization Items	$ (6,000)
Net Cash Provided by Operating Activities and Reorganization Items	$ 15,000
Cash Flows Provided by Investing Activities:	
Proceeds from Sale of Assets Due to Chapter 11 Proceeding	$ 10,000
Net Cash Provided by Investing Activities	$ 10,000
Cash Flows Provided by Financing Activities:	
Net Borrowings under Short-Term Financing Plan	$ 15,000
Principal Payments on Prepetition Debt Authorized by Court (Mortgage Payable)	(2,000)
Net Cash Provided by Financing Activities	$ 13,000
Net Increase in Cash	$ 38,000
Cash at January 1, 20X7	2,000
Cash at December 31, 20X7	$ 40,000

assigned value of the newly issued stock is greater than its par value, an additional paid-in capital account is credited for the excess. The $162,000 of postreorganization capital is the reorganization value of $195,000 less the $33,000 paid out for the prepetition liabilities as part of the plan of reorganization.

Peerless Products prepares entries to record the execution of the plan of reorganization as it transpires between January 1, 20X8, and April 1, 20X8. Figure 20–7 presents a worksheet illustrating the effects of executing the plan of reorganization on Peerless Products's balance sheet accounts. The first journal entry (1) records the debt restructuring and the gain on the discharge of debt:

January 1, 20X8–April 1, 20X8

(1)	Liabilities Subject to Compromise	133,000	
	Cash		33,000
	Senior Debt		57,000
	Subordinated Debt		12,000
	Common Stock (new)		11,000
	Gain on Debt Discharge		20,000
	Record debt discharge.		

The second journal entry (2) records the exchange of stock for stock. The prior preferred shareholders receive 8,000 shares of newly issued common stock. The prior common shareholders receive 1,000 shares of the newly issued common stock:

January 1, 20X8–April 1, 20X8

(2)	Preferred Stock	40,000	
	Common Stock (old)	10,000	
	Common Stock (new)		9,000
	Additional Paid-In Capital		41,000
	Record exchange of stock for stock.		

FIGURE 20–6   Recovery Analysis for Plan of Reorganization

PEERLESS CORPORATION
Plan of Reorganization
Recovery Analysis

Claims/Interest	Elimination of Debt and Equity		Surviving Debt	Recovery Cash	Recovery Senior Debt	Recovery Subordinated Debt	Common Stock %	Common Stock Value	Total Recovery $	Total Recovery %
Postpetition Liabilities			(73,000)						(73,000)	100%
Claims/Interest:										
Accounts Payable	(26,000)	6,000		(4,000)		(12,000)	20%	(4,000)	(20,000)	77
Notes Payable, partially secured	(10,000)			(2,000)	(8,000)				(10,000)	100
Notes Payable unsecured	(80,000)	12,000		(14,000)	(49,000)		25	(5,000)	(68,000)	85
Accrued interest	(3,000)	2,000		(1,000)					(1,000)	33
Accrued wages	(14,000)			(12,000)			10	(2,000)	(14,000)	100
Total	(133,000)	20,000								
Preferred Shareholders	(40,000)	32,000					40	(8,000)	(8,000)	
Common Shareholders	(10,000)	9,000					5	(1,000)	(1,000)	
Retained Earnings Deficit	76,000	(76,000)								
Total	(180,000)	(15,000)		(33,000)	(57,000)	(12,000)	100%	(20,000)	(195,000)	

Note: Parentheses indicate credit amount.

FIGURE 20–7 **Effect of Plan of Reorganization on Company's Balance Sheet**

	Pre-confirmation	Adjustments to Record Confirmation of Plan			Company's Reorganized Balance Sheet
		Debt Discharge	Exchange of Stock	Fresh Start	
Assets					
Cash	$ 40,000	$ (33,000)			$ 7,000
Income Tax Refund Receivable	12,000				12,000
Marketable Securities	8,000			$ 2,000	10,000
Accounts Receivable (net)	5,000				5,000
Inventory	37,000			(4,000)	33,000
Total	$ 102,000				$ 67,000
Property, Plant, and Equipment (net)	78,000			7,000	85,000
Reorganization Value in Excess of Amounts Allocable to Identifiable Assets				10,000	10,000
Total Assets	$ 180,000	$ (33,000)		$ 15,000	$ 162,000
Liabilities					
Liabilities Not Subject to Compromise:					
Current Liabilities:					
Short-Term Borrowings	$ (15,000)				$ (15,000)
Accounts Payable	(10,000)				(10,000)
Noncurrent Liability:					
Mortgage Payable	(48,000)				(48,000)
Total	$ (73,000)				$ (73,000)
Liabilities Subject to Compromise	(133,000)	$133,000			
Senior Debt		(57,000)			(57,000)
Subordinated Debt		(12,000)			(12,000)
Total Liabilities	$(206,000)	$ 64,000			$(142,000)
Shareholders' Equity					
Preferred Stock	$ (40,000)		$40,000		
Common Stock (old)	(10,000)		10,000		
Common Stock (new)		$ (11,000)	(9,000)		$ (20,000)
Additional Paid-In Capital			(41,000)	$ 41,000	
Retained Earnings (deficit)	76,000	(20,000)		20,000	
				(76,000)	-0-
Total Shareholders' Equity	$ 26,000	$ (31,000)	-0-	$(15,000)	$ (20,000)
Total Liabilities and Shareholders' Equity	$(180,000)	$ 33,000	-0-	$(15,000)	$(162,000)

Note: Parentheses indicate credit amount.

The third and last journal entry (3) records the fresh start adjustments of the assigned values of the assets of the emerging entity and the elimination of any retained earnings, or deficit. A comparison between the book values and fair values of the company follows. The fair values are determined according to the procedures in **FASB Statement No. 144**, "Accounting for the Impairment or Disposal of Long-Lived Assets" (FASB 144), issued in 2001. An ***impairment loss*** is measured by the amount that the carrying value of a long-lived asset (or asset group) exceeds its fair value. Note that Reorganization Value in Excess of Amounts Allocable to Identifiable Assets is debited for an amount not assignable to other assets. The reorganization value excess is reported as an intangible asset and accounted for according to **FASB Statement No. 142**, "Goodwill and Other Intangible Assets" (FASB 142). **FASB 142** specifies that intangibles with finite useful lives should be amortized over their lives.

However, for intangible assets determined to have an indefinite life, no amortization should be taken. Instead these indefinite life intangibles shall be tested for impairment at least annually to determine whether the asset is impaired and a loss should be recognized for a reduction in the asset's carrying amount.

Note that if prior to entering reorganization Peerless had goodwill that was judged to be impaired, it would recognize any impairment loss on the debtor-in-possession income statement. Typically, a company in reorganization proceedings is not expected to have goodwill because it is related to excess earnings potential. A case-by-case examination must be made, however, to determine whether the company's recognized goodwill was impaired.

	Book Value	Fair Value	Difference
Cash	$ 7,000	$ 7,000	$ -0-
Income tax refund receivable	12,000	12,000	-0-
Marketable securities	8,000	10,000	2,000
Accounts receivable (net)	5,000	5,000	-0-
Inventory	37,000	33,000	(4,000)
Property, plant, and equipment	78,000	85,000	7,000
Reorganization value in excess of amounts allocable to identifiable assets	-0-	10,000	10,000
Totals	$147,000	$162,000	$15,000

The entry to record the fresh start revaluation of assets and elimination of the deficit follows:

April 1, 20X8

(3)	Marketable Securities	2,000	
	Property, Plant, and Equipment	7,000	
	Reorganization Value in Excess of Amounts Allocable to Identifiable Assets	10,000	
	Gain on Debt Discharge	20,000	
	Additional Paid-In Capital	41,000	
	Inventory		4,000
	Retained Earnings—Deficit		76,000
	Record fresh start accounting and eliminate deficit.		

The last column in Figure 20–7 presents the postreorganization, new reporting entity's balance sheet.

Some reorganizations are unsuccessful, and the debtor must be liquidated. The major reason for unsuccessful reorganizations is continuing losses from operations and no reasonable likelihood of rehabilitation. Another common reason is the inability to consummate a reorganization plan because of the failure to dispose of an unprofitable subsidiary, a material default of the plan by either the debtor or a creditor, or the inability to effect part of the plan as a result of changes in the economic environment. The debtor company then moves from reorganization into liquidation; the latter is the topic of the next section of the chapter.

CHAPTER 7 LIQUIDATIONS

Liquidations are administered by the bankruptcy courts in the interests of the corporation's creditors and shareholders. The intent in liquidation is to maximize the net dollar amount recovered from disposal of the debtor's assets. Bankruptcy courts appoint accountants, attorneys, or experienced business managers as trustees to administer the liquidation. The liquidation process is often completed within 6 to 12 months, during which the trustees must make periodic reports to the bankruptcy court. The entire liquidation process is governed by the Bankruptcy Code, which describes the specific procedures to be followed and reports to be made. A very important aspect of liquidation is determining the legal rights of each creditor and establishing priorities for those rights.

CLASSES OF CREDITORS

The Bankruptcy Code specifies three classes of creditors whose claims have the following priorities: (1) secured creditors, (2) creditors with priority, and (3) unsecured creditors. The priority of claims determines the order and source of payment to each creditor.

Secured Creditors

Secured creditors have liens, or security interests, on specific assets, often called "collateral." A creditor with such a legal interest in a specific asset has the highest priority claim on that asset. For example, in Figure 20–8, Peerless Products' $50,000 mortgage payable is secured by the company's land and plant. On December 31, 20X6, the land and plant have a combined net book value of $65,000 and a fair value of $55,000. The mortgage holders have first claim to the proceeds from the sale of the land and plant. Therefore, when the land and plant are sold for $55,000, $50,000 of the proceeds is used to discharge the Mortgage Payable account and the remaining $5,000 is available to the next-lower class of creditor.

Creditors with Priority

As defined by the Bankruptcy Code, *creditors with priority* are unsecured creditors, that is, those having no collateral claim against specific assets, who have priority over other unsecured creditors. Creditors with priority are the first to be paid from any proceeds available to unsecured creditors. For businesses, the Bankruptcy Code presents the following as liabilities with priority:

1. Costs of administering the bankruptcy, including accounting and legal costs for experts appointed by the bankruptcy court.
2. Liabilities arising in the ordinary course of business during the bankruptcy proceedings.
3. Wages, salaries, or commissions, including severance and sick pay earned within 180 days of the date the petition was filed, but limited to $10,000 for each individual.
4. Contributions to employee benefit plans for the last 180 days remaining after elimination of compensation in item 3 but constrained by the remainder of the limit of $10,000 per individual.
5. Deposits of customers who made partial payments for the purchase or lease of goods or services that were not delivered. Priority is given to the first $1,800 per individual; any excess deposit is added to the unsecured claims.
6. Unsecured tax claims of governmental units, including income taxes, property taxes, excise taxes, and other taxes.

These six groups of creditors are paid from assets available to unsecured creditors. Any remaining monies are then distributed to the general unsecured creditors.

General Unsecured Creditors

The lowest priority is given to claims by *general unsecured creditors*. These creditors are paid only after secured creditors and unsecured creditors with priority are satisfied to the extent of any legal limits. Often the general unsecured creditors receive less than the full amount of their claim. The amounts to be paid to these creditors are usually stated as a percentage of the total claim, such as 55 cents on the dollar, or whatever the specific percentage is. The payment to general unsecured creditors is often termed a "dividend." It is not uncommon for these dividends to be as low as 20 to 25 percent of the total remaining unsecured claims.

FIGURE 20–8   Accounting Statement of Affairs

PEERLESS PRODUCTS CORPORATION
Statement of Affairs
December 31, 20X6

Book Values			Estimated Current Values	Estimated Amount Available to Unsecured Claims	Estimated Gain or (Loss) on Realization
Assets					
	(1)	Assets pledged with fully secured creditors:			
$ 10,000		Land	$15,000		$ 5,000
55,000		Plant (net)	40,000		(15,000)
			$55,000		
		Less: Mortgage Payable	(50,000)	$ 5,000	
	(2)	Assets pledged with partially secured creditors:			
8,000		Marketable Securities	$ 9,000		1,000
		Less: Notes Payable	(10,000)		
	(3)	Free assets:			
2,000		Cash	$ 2,000	2,000	
18,000		Accounts Receivable (net)	18,000	18,000	
45,000		Inventory	26,000	26,000	(19,000)
1,000		Prepaid Assets	-0-	-0-	(1,000)
36,000		Equipment (net)	12,000	12,000	(24,000)
		Estimated amount available		$ 63,000	
		Less: Creditors with priority		(18,000)	
		Net estimated amount available to unsecured creditors (41 cents on the dollar: $45,000/$110,000)		$ 45,000	
		Estimated deficiency to unsecured creditors		65,000	
$175,000					$(53,000)
		Total unsecured debt (from liabilities)		$110,000	

				Estimated Amount Unsecured
Liabilities and Stockholders' Equity				
	(1)	Fully secured creditors:		
$ 50,000		Mortgage Payable	$50,000	
	(2)	Partially secured creditors:		
10,000		Notes Payable—Partially Secured	$10,000	
		Less: Marketable Securities	(9,000)	$ 1,000
	(3)	Creditors with priority:		
-0-		Estimated liquidation expenses	$ 4,000	
14,000		Accrued wages	14,000	
			$18,000	
	(4)	Remaining unsecured creditors:		
26,000		Accounts Payable		26,000
80,000		Notes Payable—Unsecured		80,000
3,000		Accrued Interest		3,000
	(5)	Stockholders' equity:		
40,000		Preferred Stock		
10,000		Common Stock		
(58,000)		Retained Earnings (Deficit)		
$175,000		(Carry up to asset section)		$110,000

"Preference payments" made by the debtor to one creditor to the detriment of all other creditors within 90 days before the bankruptcy petition was filed may usually be recovered from the specific creditor and returned to the cash available for all creditors. Sometimes a member of the debtor's management may assure a creditor that the debtor will pay any claim to that specific creditor. This often occurs during the latter phases of financial difficulty, just before filing a petition for bankruptcy. These management assurances are not binding and do not increase the level of the legal claim against the debtor's assets. The priority of the claims is determined solely in accordance with the Bankruptcy Code.

Statement of Affairs

The *accounting statement of affairs* is the basic accounting report made at the beginning of the liquidation process to present the expected realizable amounts from disposal of the assets, the order of creditors' claims, and the expected amount that unsecured creditors will receive as a result of the liquidation. A different report, also entitled the "statement of affairs," is a list of questions the debtor must answer as part of the bankruptcy petition. The following discussion is about the accounting report, not the legal questionnaire.

The statement of affairs is not a going-concern report; it is an important planning report for the anticipated liquidation of a company. The statement of affairs presents the book values of the debtor company's balance sheet accounts, the estimated fair market values of the assets, the order of the claims, and the estimated deficiency to the general unsecured creditors. Common stockholders rarely receive any monies from a liquidating company. The statement of affairs is a planning instrument: The actual liquidation process is recorded on the debtor's books as the transactions occur.

Assume that rather than reorganizing, Peerless decided on December 31, 20X6, to enter Chapter 7 bankruptcy on that date. The following illustration begins with the December 31, 20X6, statement of affairs for Peerless Products shown in Figure 20–8:

1. The report presents the balance sheet accounts in order of priority for liquidation. Current versus noncurrent accounts no longer have importance for Peerless Products.

2. The report presents estimated current fair values and expected gains or losses on the disposal of the assets. These are only estimates at the point the bankruptcy petition is filed. Actual gains or losses will be recorded as realized.

3. In this example, fully secured creditors are expected to have their entire claims of $50,000 satisfied with the proceeds from the disposal of the secured asset. The mortgage payable is expected to be fully satisfied with the proceeds of $55,000 from the sale of the land and plant. The remaining $5,000 will then be available to satisfy unsecured claims.

4. The claims of partially secured creditors will not be completely satisfied from the sale of the collateral asset. Marketable securities having an estimated fair value of $9,000 are used to secure notes payable of $10,000. The first $9,000 of the notes payable is satisfied; the remaining $1,000 is added to the general unsecured liabilities.

5. Free assets are available to unsecured creditors. The first unsecured creditors are those with priority as defined by the Bankruptcy Code. Peerless Products has accrued wages of $14,000 payable to its employees, none of whom has more than $2,000 due. In addition, the company expects to incur $4,000 of expenses to administer the liquidation.

6. All remaining claims are added to the general unsecured liabilities. The total of unsecured claims is $110,000. Only $45,000 is expected to be available to meet these claims. Therefore, the estimated dividend to general unsecured creditors is 41 cents on the dollar ($45,000/$110,000). The estimated deficiency to unsecured creditors is $65,000.

7. The stockholders will not receive anything upon liquidation of Peerless Products. Stock is a residual claim to be settled only after all creditors' claims are fully settled. Stockholders typically do not receive anything from a bankruptcy liquidation.

The statement of affairs is a planning instrument prepared only at the beginning of the bankruptcy process. It provides important information to creditors and the bankruptcy court as to the expected monies available to each class of creditors. Once the bankruptcy is underway, the debtor records the transactions on its accounting records as they occur.

ADDITIONAL CONSIDERATIONS

Presented now are the accounting and reporting practices for trustees who act as fiduciaries for the creditors' committee or for the bankruptcy court. Trustees' reports are different from the traditional financial statements because the trustees' legal rights and responsibilities differ from those of the debtor company's management.

Also included is a brief presentation on the bankruptcy provisions applicable to individuals. The area of individual bankruptcies is undergoing constant change, and thus the presentation is only a general guide.

Trustee Accounting and Reporting

Bankruptcy courts appoint trustees to manage a company under Chapter 11 reorganization in cases of management fraud, dishonesty, incompetence, or gross mismanagement. The trustee then attempts to rehabilitate the business. In Chapter 7 liquidations, the trustee normally has the responsibility to expeditiously liquidate the bankrupt company and pay creditors in conformity with the legal status of their secured or unsecured interests. In some cases under Chapter 7, the court appoints a trustee to operate the company for a short time in an effort to obtain a better price for the company in entirety rather than selling it piecemeal.

Trustees examine the proofs of all creditors' claims against the debtor's bankruptcy estate, that is, the debtor's net assets. Sometimes the trustee receives title to all assets as a *receivership*, becomes responsible for the actual management of the debtor, and must direct a plan of reorganization or liquidation. A trustee who takes title to the debtor's assets in a liquidation must make a periodic financial report to the bankruptcy court, reporting on the progress of the liquidation and on the fiduciary relationship held. When the trustee accepts the assets, the trustee usually establishes a set of accounting records to account for the receivership. The trustee's accounting records include a liability of the trustee which is created to recognize the debtor's interest in the assets accepted by the trustee. This new account is credited for the book value of the assets accepted and is usually named for the debtor company in receivership. The trustee does not transfer the debtor's liabilities, because these remain the legal responsibility of the debtor company. The general form of the trustee's opening entry, accepting the assets of the debtor company, is as follows:

Assets	XXX	
Debtor Company—In Receivership		XXX

The actual entry details the individual asset accounts and includes the debtor's company name.

Statement of Realization and Liquidation

A monthly report, called a *statement of realization and liquidation*, is prepared for the bankruptcy court. It shows the results of the trustee's fiduciary actions beginning at the point the trustee accepts the debtor's assets. The statement has three major sections: assets, supplementary items, and liabilities. The debtor's liabilities are not transferred to the trustee, but the trustee may incur new liabilities that must be reported in the statement of realization and liquidation.

The assets section of the statement is divided into the following four groups:

Assets	
Assets to be realized	Assets realized
Assets acquired	Assets not realized

The assets to be realized are those received from the debtor company. The assets acquired are those subsequently acquired by the trustee. The assets realized are those sold by the trustee; the assets not realized are those remaining under the trustee's responsibility as of the end of the period. Cash is usually not reported in the statement of realization and liquidation because a separate cash flow report is typically made.

The supplementary items section of the report consists of the following two items:

Supplementary Items	
Supplementary charges	Supplementary credits

Supplementary charges include the trustee's administration fees and any cash expenses paid by the trustee. Supplementary credits may include any unusual revenue items.

Although the trustee does not record the debtor's liabilities, the trustee settles some of the debtor's payables and may incur new payables during the receivership. The liabilities section of the statement is divided as follows:

Liabilities	
Liabilities liquidated	Liabilities to be liquidated
Liabilities not liquidated	Liabilities incurred

The liabilities liquidated are creditors' claims settled during the period. The liabilities not liquidated are those outstanding at the end of the reporting period. The liabilities to be liquidated are those debts remaining on the books of the debtor company for whose liquidation the trustee is responsible as of the date of appointment. Finally, the liabilities incurred are new obligations incurred by the trustee.

Illustration of Trustee Accounting and Reporting

On December 31, 20X6, D. Able was appointed trustee in charge of liquidating Peerless Products Corporation. Able will be allowed to operate the company for a short period of time to determine whether the company can be sold in entirety as opposed to piecemeal. During this time, the trustee must reduce the current short-term debts of Peerless Products. If a sale in entirety is infeasible, Able is directed to liquidate the company. Able accepts the assets on December 31, 20X6, and makes several transactions during January 20X7. The transactions and the entries made on Peerless's books and on the trustee's books are presented in Figure 20–9 and discussed in the following pages.

1. Entry (4) records the transfer of assets from Peerless Products to D. Able. Able recognizes the assets at their book values as reported by Peerless. Accounts receivable are dated as "old" to note that these were part of the transferred assets. The credit for $175,000 to Peerless Products Corporation—In Receivership is a liability of the trustee. On Peerless's books, the reciprocal account, D. Able—Receiver, is a receivable. Note that no liabilities are transferred. These remain on Peerless's books because they are legal responsibilities of the corporation.

2. The trustee's transactions are recorded in the normal manner in entries (5) through (8). The only difference is the differentiation between "old" accounts, which were part of the assets transferred, and "new" accounts, which result from the trustee's transactions.

3. The trustee pays $20,000 of Peerless's accounts payable and pays $10,000 for the partially secured note payable. In entry (9), the debit of $30,000 is made to the liability account Peerless Products Corporation—In Receivership. Peerless makes a corresponding entry to reduce its accounts payable and notes payable and to reduce the receivable, D. Able—Receiver.

4. The remaining entries (10) through (14) complete the transactions, adjust the books, and close the books at the end of the first period of receivership. Operations resulted in a net income of $4,000 for the period. The closing entry transfers the net income to the

FIGURE 20–9 Trustee and Debtor Company Entries during Liquidation

Trustee D. Able's Books

	Debit	Credit
(4) Cash	2,000	
Marketable Securities	8,000	
Accounts Receivable (old)	20,000	
Inventory	45,000	
Prepaid Assets	1,000	
Property, Plant, and Equipment	125,000	
Allowance for Uncollectibles (old)		2,000
Accumulated Depreciation		24,000
Peerless Products Corporation—In Receivership		175,000
Transfer of Peerless's net assets to trustee.		
(5) Inventory	20,000	
Accounts Payable (new)		20,000
Purchases of inventory on account by trustee, $20,000.		
(6) Accounts Receivable (new)	85,000	
Sales		85,000
Sales on account by trustee, $85,000.		
(7) Cost of Sales	50,000	
Inventory		50,000
Cost of sales is $50,000, including all inventory transferred from Peerless Products Corporation.		
(8) Cash	56,000	
Accounts Receivable (old)		12,000
Accounts Receivable (new)		44,000
Receivables collected by trustee:		
Old receivables	$12,000	
New receivables	44,000	
(9) Peerless Products Corporation—In Receivership	30,000	
Accounts Payable (new)	4,000	
Operating Expenses	13,000	
Trustee's Expenses	5,000	
Cash		52,000
Disbursements by trustee:		
Old accounts payables	$30,000	
New accounts payables	4,000	
Operating expenses	13,000	
Trustee's expenses	5,000	

Peerless Products Corporation's Books

	Debit	Credit
D. Able—Receiver	175,000	
Allowance for Uncollectibles	2,000	
Accumulated Depreciation	24,000	
Cash		2,000
Marketable Securities		8,000
Accounts Receivable		20,000
Inventory		45,000
Prepaid Assets		1,000
Property, Plant, and Equipment		125,000
(No entry)		
(No entry)		
(No entry)		
(No entry)		
Accounts Payable	20,000	
Notes Payable	10,000	
D. Able—Receiver		30,000

(continued)

(10) Cash 9,000

    Marketable Securities 8,000

    Gain on Sale of Securities 1,000

    Sales of marketable securities for $9,000.

(No entry)

Adjusting entries at end of the period:

(11) Uncollectibles Expense 3,000

Depreciation Expense 10,000

    Allowance for Uncollectibles (old) 1,000

    Allowance for Uncollectibles (new) 2,000

    Accumulated Depreciation 10,000

    Provision for bad debts:

      Old receivables $1,000

      New receivables 2,000

    Recognize depreciation expense of $10,000 for period.

(No entry)

(12) Allowance for Uncollectibles (old) 2,000

    Accounts Receivable (old) 2,000

    Old receivables of $2,000 are written off.

(No entry)

(13) Prepaid Costs Expense 1,000

    Prepaid Assets 1,000

    Recognize prepaid costs of $1,000 expired during period.

(No entry)

Closing entry at end of the period:

(14) Sales 85,000

Gain on Sale of Securities 1,000

    Cost of Sales 50,000

    Operating Expenses 13,000

    Trustee's Expenses 5,000

    Prepaid Costs Expense 1,000

    Uncollectibles Expense 3,000

    Depreciation Expense 10,000

    Peerless Products Corporation—In Receivership 4,000

D. Able—Receiver

Retained Earnings 4,000

FIGURE 20–10
Receiver's
Statement of
Realization and
Liquidation

PEERLESS PRODUCTS CORPORATION
D. Able, Receiver
Statement of Realization and Liquidation
December 31, 20X6, to January 31, 20X7

Assets

Assets to Be Realized		**Assets Realized**	
Old receivables (net)	$ 18,000	Old receivables	$ 12,000
Marketable securities	8,000	New receivables	44,000
Old inventory	45,000	Marketable securities	9,000
Prepaid assets	1,000	Sales of inventory	85,000
Depreciable assets (net)	101,000		
Assets Acquired		**Assets Not Realized**	
New receivables	85,000	Old receivables (net)	5,000
New inventory purchased	20,000	New receivables (net)	39,000
		New inventory	15,000
		Depreciable assets (net)	91,000

Supplementary Items

Supplementary Charges		**Supplementary Credits**	
Operating expenses paid	$ 13,000		
Receiver's expenses	5,000		
Net gain from operations	4,000		

Liabilities

Debts Liquidated		**Debts to Be Liquidated**	
Old current payables	$ 30,000	Old current payables	$133,000
New current payables	4,000	Mortgage payable	50,000
Debts Not Liquidated		**Debts Incurred**	
Old current payables	103,000	New current payables	20,000
New current payables	16,000		
Mortgage payable	50,000		
	$503,000		$503,000

receivership account on the trustee's books. A corresponding entry on Peerless's books increases the receiver's account and the retained earnings account.

The entries are the basis of the statement of realization and liquidation for the month of January 20X7. This statement is reported to the bankruptcy court to show the current state of the liquidation process and to report on the fiduciary responsibility of D. Able, the trustee. The statement of realization and liquidation for Peerless Products Corporation, as reported by Able, is shown in Figure 20–10.

Following are observations concerning this statement:

1. The statement begins with an accounting of the assets received from Peerless Products Corporation and those acquired by the trustee. The assets realized section reports the proceeds of the sale of assets. For example, the marketable securities were sold for $9,000, which is $1,000 more than their book value. Sales of inventory are also reported for the amount of the total proceeds. This is the traditional approach used most often in practice, although an alternative sometimes found recognizes the disposal of the assets at their book values, with the profit or gain element recognized as a supplementary credit. Either method, using gross proceeds or book value, is allowed in practice. The assets not realized section shows the ending book values of remaining assets as of January 31, 20X7. Cash is not included on the statement because it is already a realized asset. Cash is reported in a separate statement by the trustee.

2. Supplementary items include $13,000 of operating expenses paid, receiver's expenses of $5,000, and the net gain of $4,000 as a balancing item. It is important to note that cost allocations are not included in the supplementary items. For example, the trustee recognized

depreciation expense of $10,000, bad debt expense of $3,000, and expiration of prepaid assets of $1,000. These do not appear directly in the statement, but they are shown indirectly. For example, under assets to be realized, depreciable assets, net, are reported as $101,000 while under the assets not realized, the depreciable assets, net, are shown as $91,000. The $10,000 difference is the depreciation expense for the period. Bad debts expense and prepaid expense are treated in a similar way.

3. The last part of the statement is a report on the liabilities. The trustee is responsible for liquidating the preexisting debts of $183,000 and has incurred additional debt of $20,000 during the month. A total of $34,000 of debts has been liquidated, leaving $169,000 still to be liquidated.

4. The statement balances at a total of $503,000, indicating that all items are reported.

The trustee provides a statement of realization and liquidation to the bankruptcy court on a monthly basis. In addition, a short cash flow statement that summarizes the cash receipts and cash disbursements during the period is provided.

The fact that various bankruptcy courts are accepting alternative forms of the statement of realization may create some consternation for accountants providing professional services in several judicial districts. For example, should assets realized be shown at their gross proceeds, or should a net amount be shown with the gain or loss in supplementary items? The report format presented in this chapter is the traditional approach accepted by a large majority of courts. Some courts, however, are currently experimenting with other forms of trustee reporting. The experiments now taking place in trustee reporting may eventually lead to a new report that will be a modification of the present statement. Until then, accountants serving as trustees or advising trustees should ascertain from the specific bankruptcy court administering the estate which reporting form to use.

Summary of Key Concepts

Various nonjudicial actions are available to companies in financial difficulty. A debtor may restructure its existing debt by agreeing to settle its obligation at less than current value or to modify some of the terms of the debt agreement. The debtor's payable may be settled with the transfer of equity or assets, or the terms of the debt may be modified. In some cases, creditors may form a committee to manage the debtor's business. In this nonjudicial action, the debtor agrees to comply with the creditors. The creditors' committee may attempt to rehabilitate the business or may find that liquidation is the best course of action.

Two judicial remedies are available under the Bankruptcy Code. The first is Chapter 11 reorganization, in which the debtor is given some relief from creditors' claims and can attempt to rehabilitate the business and return it to profitable operations. A trustee is sometimes appointed by the bankruptcy court to advise the debtor. SOP 90-7 requires that financial statements produced during reorganization proceedings clearly separate the reorganization items from operating items. In addition, SOP 90-7 prescribes the two conditions that must occur before fresh start accounting may be used by firms emerging from reorganization proceedings: (1) The postpetition liabilities, plus prepetition liabilities allowed as claims by the court, must be greater than the reorganization value assigned to the company's assets and (2) the holders of voting shares immediately prior to confirmation of the plan of reorganization must hold less than 50 percent of the voting shares of the emerging company. Fresh start accounting includes the revaluation of assets and the elimination of any retained earnings, or deficit.

The second judicial remedy is a Chapter 7 liquidation. At the beginning of a judicial action, a statement of affairs is prepared as a planning document to show the expected amounts that will be realized on the liquidation of the business and the order of the creditors' claims against the debtor's assets. During liquidation, the debtor's assets are sold, and the creditors' claims are settled in the order of priority defined by the Bankruptcy Code. Secured claims are satisfied with proceeds of the sale of the corresponding collateral; unsecured claims with priority are then settled. Any remaining cash is distributed to the general unsecured creditors.

Trustees are sometimes appointed by bankruptcy courts to administer the reorganization or liquidation process. A trustee provides a statement of realization and liquidation to the bankruptcy court to report on the progress of the judicial action and on the fiduciary actions of the trustee. The statement presents the assets transferred to the trustee, the additional assets acquired by the trustee, and the ending balance of unrealized assets still to be converted into cash. The statement also reports on the debtor's liabilities discharged by the trustee as well as the additional liabilities incurred by the trustee. Some minor variations of the statement format are found in bankruptcy courts.

Key Terms

accounting statement of affairs, *1005*	impairment loss, *1001*	reorganization value, *993*
creditors' committee management, *990*	liquidation under Chapter 7, *992*	secured creditors, *1003* statement of realization and
creditors with priority, *1003*	order of relief, *991*	liquidation, *1006*
fresh start accounting, *993*	plan of reorganization, *992*	troubled debt
general unsecured creditors, *1003*	receivership, *1006* reorganization under Chapter 11, *992*	restructurings, *990*

Appendix 20A Accounting for Impaired Loans and Debt Restructuring Arrangements

CREDITOR ACCOUNTING FOR IMPAIRED LOANS

FASB 114 presents the creditor's accounting and disclosure standards for impaired loans, including notes receivable. A loan is defined as being impaired when it is probable that the creditor will not be able to collect all amounts due under the loan agreement. The determination that a loan is impaired may be made during the creditor's normal loan review procedures or may be based on other current information and events. Impaired loans are measured based on the present value of expected future cash flows, discounted at the loan's effective interest rate at the point of origination of the loan. Alternatively, if the loan is collateral dependent, that is, the creditor determines that foreclosure is probable, the loan value should be measured by using the fair value of the collateral. The creditor should make the best estimates of total future cash flows from the loan based on reasonable assumptions and projections.

The entry to recognize the reduction in value of impaired loans will debit either Bad Debts Expense or the Allowance for Uncollectibles if adequate provision for uncollectible loans has been made already. The credit is to the Valuation Allowance for Impaired Loans account, which is used as a contra-loan receivable to reduce the carrying value of the loan to its present value of the future cash flows. The creditor recognizes interest revenue on the impaired loans using the effective interest method that computes the interest revenue as the effective interest rate multiplied by the present value of the loan outstanding during the period. The valuation allowance account is then adjusted for subsequent changes in the loan's present value.

The following example demonstrates the creditor accounting for impaired loans:

1. On December 31, 20X5, Creditor Company has an unsecured current loan receivable of $30,000 from Peerless Products Corporation due on December 31, 20X6. The loan is documented with a note bearing interest at 10 percent per year. The interest is currently in default in the amount of $3,000, which represents the interest for 20X5.

2. During its periodic loan review cycle, Creditor determines that as of December 31, 20X5, it is probable that the loan from Peerless Products will not be collected in full. The best estimate of the amount that will be collected on December 31, 20X6, is $23,000.

The first step is to determine whether the loan is impaired by comparing its carrying value with the present value of the estimated total future cash flows. The present value is computed as the estimated total future cash flows discounted at the loan's original effective interest rate, which is 10 percent in this case. For this example, there was no premium or discount on the original loan, and thus the effective rate equals the loan's stated rate:

Carrying value of the loan:		
Principal	$ 30,000	
Accrued interest	3,000	
Carrying value		$33,000
Present value of total future cash flows:		
Estimated total future cash flows	$ 23,000	
Present value factor for 10%, 1 year	×.90909	
Present value of future cash flows		20,909
Creditor loss on impaired loan		$12,091

The entries Creditor makes to recognize the impaired loan receivable follow:

December 31, 20X5

(15)	Bad Debt Expense	12,091	
	Valuation Allowance for Impaired Loans		12,091
(16)	Impaired Notes Receivable	30,000	
	Notes Receivable		30,000

Entry (15) revalues the carrying value of the loan principal and interest down to its present value of $20,909. The company could have debited an Allowance for Uncollectibles if an adequate provision had already been made. Entry (16) is the entry to reclassify the notes from the current loan portfolio to the impaired loan portfolio. The December 31, 20X5, balance sheet reports the impaired loan in the asset section as follows:

Impaired Note Receivable, including accrued interest of $3,000	$33,000
Less: Valuation Allowance for Impaired Loan	−12,091
Present Value of Impaired Loans	$20,909

It is important to note that Peerless Products will not make any entries for the impaired loan. Indeed, it is very doubtful that Peerless will even know that Creditor has revalued its note.

On December 31, 20X6, the end of the next year, Creditor will recognize interest revenue using the effective interest method, as follows:

(17)	Accrued Interest Receivable ($30,000 × .10)	3,000	
	Valuation Allowance for Impaired Loans		909
	Interest Revenue ($20,909 PV × .10)		2,091

Note that the balance in the valuation allowance account is now $13,000 ($12,091 plus $909). The final entry recognizes the collection of the note. If Creditor actually receives only the $23,000 it had estimated, the entry is as follows:

(18)	Cash	23,000	
	Valuation Allowance for Impaired Loans	13,000	
	Impaired Notes Receivable		30,000
	Accrued Interest Receivable		6,000

If Creditor receives the full amount of the original principal ($30,000) plus the two years of accrued interest receivable ($6,000 = $3,000 per year × 2), it makes the following entry to record the collection and eliminate the balance in the valuation allowance account against either the bad debts expense or the allowance for uncollectibles, depending on what account was used in entry (15) to recognize the impairment:

(18b)	Cash	36,000	
	Valuation Allowance for Impaired Loans	13,000	
	Impaired Notes Receivable		30,000
	Accrued Interest Receivable		6,000
	Bad Debts Expense (or Allowance for Uncollectibles)		13,000

The key points from **FASB 114** are that the creditor must recognize an impairment when it becomes probable that the creditor will be unable to collect all amounts due according to the loan agreement's contractual terms. The maturity value of the original loan is preserved in the accounts by using a contra-valuation allowance account to decrease the impaired loan to its impaired value. Impairment should be measured using the present value of the estimated total future cash flows from the loan, discounted at the original effective interest rate of the impaired loan. Alternatively, if the creditor expects to foreclose on collateralized property, the fair value of the collateral should be used to determine the impaired loan's value. The debtor does not record any reductions in the value of the note receivable on its books because there has not been any legal agreement for reducing the basis of the loan. The impairment on the creditor's books is based on the best estimates of future collections, and any changes in circumstances affecting the creditor's estimates should be treated for accounting purposes as a change in estimate.

TROUBLED DEBT RESTRUCTURING

FASB 15 prescribes the debtor's accounting for troubled debt restructurings while **FASB 114** presents the standards for the creditor's accounting for these restructurings. Not all renegotiations of debt covenants are covered by these standards; the restructuring must be a concession granted by a creditor to a debtor in financial difficulties. Renegotiations between a debtor and a creditor because of changes in the competitive general economic environment are not troubled debt restructurings and are not included in these standards.

The most common form of troubled debt restructuring is a modification of the debt terms to alleviate the debtor's short-term cash needs. For example, the creditor may reduce the current interest rate, forgive some of the accrued interest or principal, or modify some other term of the debt agreement. Another common form of troubled debt restructuring is the creditor's acceptance of assets or equity with a fair value less than the amount of the debt because the creditor believes it is the best alternative to maximize recoverability of the receivable from the debtor in financial difficulty. For example, the creditor may accept land with a fair value of $50,000 in exchange for extinguishing a $65,000 debt because the creditor believes the $50,000 is the maximum amount it will be able to collect. The key issue is how to account for and report the troubled debt restructuring on the books of the creditor and the debtor companies.

For the Debtor

Under **FASB 15**, the debtor compares the debt's carrying value with the total future cash flows related to the debt or with the fair value of the consideration exchanged in extinguishment of that debt. This comparison is made to determine whether a gain or loss should be recognized on the transaction as follows:

$$\text{Restructuring difference (debtor)} = CV - TFCF \text{ } or \text{ } CV - FV$$

where

CV = Carrying value of the debt

$TFCF$ = Total future cash flows

FV = Fair value of noncash items

The debt's carrying value is the debt's book value on the books of the creditor or debtor plus accrued interest as of the date of the restructuring. If the debtor and creditor agree to extinguish the current debt through an immediate payment of cash, transfer of noncash assets, or transfer of an equity interest, a *restructuring difference* is computed as the difference between the carrying value of the debt and the fair value of the consideration exchanged. The debtor recognizes a gain and the creditor a loss for the amount of the restructuring difference. The debtor's legal fees and other direct costs incurred are accounted for in the following manner: If an equity interest is transferred, the fees and direct costs incurred reduce the amount recorded for the equity interest; in other restructurings, the fees and direct costs are deducted in measuring the gain on the restructuring.

In a debt restructuring involving a modification of terms, the total future cash flows are the aggregate of all cash payments after the restructuring takes place as specified in the restructuring agreement. Any immediate cash payments or transfers of assets or equity reduce the debt's book value prior to computing a gain or loss. The following decision rules are then used:

1. $CV \leq TFCF$: *No gain or loss; future interest.* If the debt's carrying value is less than or equal to the total future cash flows, no gain or loss is shown, and the debtor's future effective interest expense on this debt is the restructuring difference between the carrying value and the future cash flows.

2. $CV > TFCF$: *Debtor gain; no future interest.* If the debt's carrying value is greater than the total future cash flows, the debtor recognizes a restructuring gain for the amount of the restructuring difference. In this case, the debt's current book value is greater than the total amount of cash that will

be paid, so the book value obviously must be reduced. Once a gain has been recognized, the debtor reports no future interest expense on this debt.

For the Creditor

Under **FASB 114**, the creditor accounts for a troubled debt restructuring as an impairment of a loan as presented earlier in this chapter. The major difference between the debtor's and the creditor's measurement methods is that the creditor must determine the present value of the estimated total future cash flows to compare with the carrying value of the loan, as follows:

$$\text{Restructuring difference (creditor)} = CV - PV\,(TFCF)\ or\ CV - FV$$

where

$\qquad\qquad CV = $ Carrying value of the debt, including both principal and accrued interest

$\quad PV(TFCF) = $ Present value of total future cash flows

$\qquad\qquad FV = $ Fair value of property

Remember that the present value is computed using the loan's *original* effective interest rate. If the creditor recognizes an impairment, a contra-valuation allowance account is credited for the reduction from the carrying value of the debt down to its present value. A creditor typically provides for uncollectibles with an allowance for uncollectibles, and the creditor's impairment loss is charged against the allowance. If the creditor has not anticipated adequately for uncollectibles, the impairment loss is recognized as an increase in Bad Debts Expense for the period.

Illustration of Troubled Debt Restructurings

The following illustration demonstrates the accounting for various forms of a troubled debt restructuring. This example is independent of the earlier illustration of creditor recognition of loan impairment. Peerless Products Corporation is financially distressed and is evaluating a variety of restructuring alternatives. Following are observations about Peerless Products:

1. On December 31, 20X6, the company has an unsecured current liability of $30,000 to the Creditor Company, on which $3,000 interest has been accrued and is unpaid.

2. Peerless Products has been negotiating with Creditor to restructure the current debt of $33,000 ($30,000 + $3,000). The three alternatives are discussed next.

Alternative 1: Transfer of Cash in Full Settlement of Debt

The first alternative is the immediate transfer of $27,000 in full settlement of the carrying value of the debt. The restructuring difference between the carrying value of the debt and total cash flow of the restructuring agreement is computed as follows:

Carrying value of the debt:		
Principal	$30,000	
Accrued interest (10% for 1 year)	3,000	$33,000
Cash flows		(27,000)
Restructuring difference (debtor = creditor)		$ 6,000

The total cash flows of $27,000 are less than the $33,000 carrying value of the debt. If the creditor agrees to the restructuring, the debtor recognizes a restructuring gain of $6,000, and the creditor recognizes a restructuring loss in the same amount. The creditor needs no present value computation for the immediate cash flow alternative.

The entry required for Peerless Products, the debtor company, is as follows:

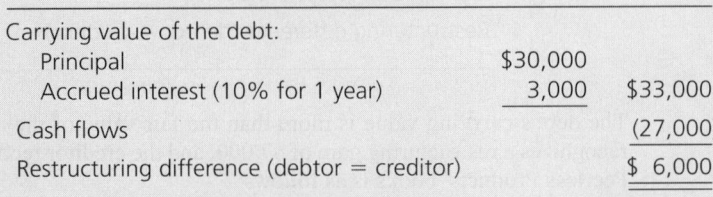

December 31, 20X6

(19)	Notes Payable	30,000	
	Accrued Interest Payable	3,000	
	Cash		27,000
	Gain on Restructuring of Debt		6,000
	Restructure and settle debt.		

The gain on the restructuring of debt is reported on the debtor's income statement according to the criteria in **APB 30**, "Reporting the Results of Operations—Reporting the Effects of Disposal of a Segment of a Business, and Extraordinary, Unusual and Infrequently Occurring Events and Transactions" (APB 30). If the gain is material, is of unusual nature, and has an infrequency of occurrence, it is reported as an extraordinary item. Note that **FASB Statement No. 145**, "Rescission of FASB Statements No. 4, 44, and 64, Amendment of FASB Statement No. 13, and Technical Corrections" (FASB 145), issued in 2002, rescinded **FASB 4** that had required extinguishment of debt gains generally to be reported as extraordinary items. Thus, these gains are now typically reported as part of continuing operations.

The entry required for Creditor is as follows:

December 31, 20X6

(20)	Cash	27,000	
	Allowance for Uncollectibles	6,000	
	Notes Receivable		30,000
	Accrued Interest Receivable		3,000
	Restructure and settle receivable.		

If Creditor had not provided adequately for uncollectible receivables, the bad debts account would be debited instead of the Allowance for Uncollectibles.

Alternative 2: Transfer of Noncash Assets in Settlement of Debt

In the second alternative, Peerless Products agrees to transfer inventory with a book value of $45,000 and a fair value of $26,000 to Creditor in full settlement of the $33,000 debt. When noncash assets are transferred in a restructuring agreement, the assets must be revalued to their fair values *before* determining the restructuring difference. The gain or loss on the debtor's income statement is typically shown as an operating item resulting from the disposal of assets. Therefore, Peerless Products recognizes a loss on disposal of its inventory for the $19,000 decline in its inventory from its book value of $45,000 to its fair value of $26,000. The revaluation is typically made in the journal entry summarizing the troubled debt restructuring.

The restructuring difference is computed as follows:

Carrying value of the debt:		
Principal	$30,000	
Accrued interest	3,000	$33,000
Fair value of assets transferred		(26,000)
Restructuring difference (debtor = creditor)		$ 7,000

The debt's carrying value is more than the fair value of the assets transferred; therefore, the debtor recognizes a restructuring gain of $7,000, and the creditor recognizes a $7,000 loss. The entry made on Peerless Products' books is as follows:

December 31, 20X6

(21)	Notes Payable	30,000	
	Accrued Interest Payable	3,000	
	Loss on Disposal of Inventory	19,000	
	Inventory		45,000
	Gain on Restructuring of Debt		7,000
	Restructure and settle debt.		

The $19,000 loss on the disposal of inventory reduces the Inventory account from its $45,000 book value to its $26,000 fair value before the restructuring difference is computed. The debt's $33,000 carrying value is extinguished by the $26,000 fair value of the inventory. Therefore, the debtor company recognizes a restructuring gain of $7,000.

The entry on the creditor's books is as follows:

December 31, 20X6

(22)			
	Inventory	26,000	
	Allowance for Uncollectibles	7,000	
	Notes Receivable		30,000
	Accrued Interest Receivable		3,000
	Restructure and settle receivable.		

The noncash asset is recorded at its fair value. Allowance for Uncollectibles is charged for the difference between the $26,000 value received and the $33,000 book value of the debt.

The creditor may also accept the debtor's common stock or other equity as settlement of the debt. The stock is recorded at its fair value, and the restructuring difference is computed as in the case of the transfer of a noncash asset. It may seem unusual that a creditor would accept the stock of a company that is experiencing financial difficulty, but the creditor may believe that the company is viable and that the stock is a reasonable long-term investment.

Alternative 3: Modification of Terms

A common technique of debt restructuring is to modify some of the terms of the original debt contract. Modification of terms may include the following:

1. Reduction of the stated interest rate for the remainder of the original debt.
2. Extension of the maturity date of the original debt at a lower rate of interest.
3. Reduction of part of the face amount of the original debt.
4. Reduction in the accrued interest.

The debtor's accounting for a modification of debt terms is included in **FASB 15**. The restructuring difference is computed as the difference between the carrying value of the debt and the total future estimated cash flows under the new terms. If the debt's carrying value is more than the total future estimated cash flows, the debtor recognizes a gain for the restructuring difference. If the carrying value of the debt is less than the total future cash flows, no gain or loss is recognized and the debtor's new effective interest rate is determined based on the amount of the restructuring difference. The following cases illustrate these points.

Case A. Carrying Value of Debt More than Modified Total Future Cash Flows—Debtor Gain and Creditor Loss (Expense) Recognized

Peerless Products, the debtor, owes $30,000 principal plus $3,000 accrued interest to Creditor. On December 31, 20X6, the two entities agree to the following modification of terms on the debt contract:

1. Forgive accrued interest of $3,000.
2. Reduce the interest rate from 10 percent to 5 percent.
3. Extend the maturity for one additional year to December 31, 20X7.

The restructuring difference as of the date of the modification of terms is as follows:

		Debtor	Creditor
Carrying value of the debt:			
Principal	$30,000		
Interest	3,000		
Carrying value of the debt	$33,000	$33,000	$33,000
Total future estimated cash flows:			
Total future principal	$30,000		
Total future contractual interest ($30,000 × .05 × 1 year)	1,500		
Total future estimated cash flows	$31,500	(31,500)	
Present value factor, 10%, 1 year	×.90909		
Present value of total future cash flows	$28,636		(28,636)
Restructuring difference		$ 1,500	$ 4,364

For the debtor, the debt's $33,000 carrying value is more than the $31,500 total future estimated cash flows, and the debtor recognizes a $1,500 restructuring gain. Because of this recognition, **FASB 15** states that the debtor will not recognize any interest expense on the debt in future periods. Therefore, although the restructuring agreement calls for contractual interest of 5 percent for a one-year period, the debtor includes this amount in the debt's remaining book value as of the restructuring date.

The entry required for Peerless Products, the debtor, on December 31, 20X6, the date of the modification of terms agreement, is as follows:

December 31, 20X6

(23)	Accrued Interest Payable	3,000	
	Notes Payable (10%)	30,000	
	Restructured Debt Payable (5%)		31,500
	Gain on Restructuring of Debt		1,500
	Restructuring of terms of debt.		

The total future cash flows of $31,500 are recorded as restructured debt, and the original debt and accrued interest are written off.

When Peerless Products repays the debt on December 31, 20X7, it makes the following entry:

December 31, 20X7

(24)	Restructured Debt Payable (5%)	31,500	
	Cash		31,500
	Pay restructured debt.		

Although the terms of the restructuring agreement specify a contractual interest rate of 5 percent, no interest expense is recorded.

The creditor must recognize a loss (expense or charge Allowance for Uncollectibles) in the amount of $4,364, the restructuring difference between the carrying value of the debt and the present value of estimated total future cash flows. Under **FASB 114**, the creditor recognizes future interest revenue using the effective interest method. The entries are as follows:

December 31, 20X6

(25)	Allowance for Uncollectibles	4,364	
	Accrued Interest Receivable		3,000
	Valuation Allowance for Impaired Loans		1,364
(26)	Impaired Notes Receivable (5%)	30,000	
	Notes Receivable (10%)		30,000

Note that the December 31, 20X6, balance sheet reports the following:

Impaired Notes Receivable	$30,000	
Less: Valuation Allowance for Impaired Loans	(1,364)	
Present Value of Impaired Notes Receivable		$28,636

The creditor's entries on December 31, 20X7, are as follows:

(27)	Cash	1,500	
	Valuation Allowance for Impaired Loans	1,364	
	Interest Revenue		2,864

$1,500 = $30,000 × .05 contractual interest rate
$2,864 = $28,636 present value × .10 effective interest rate

(28)	Cash	30,000	
	Impaired Notes Receivable		30,000

Case B. Carrying Value of Debt Less than Modified Total Future Cash Flows: No Gain Recognized by the Debtor Peerless Products, the debtor, and Creditor agree to the following modification of terms for the debt of $30,000 and $3,000 of accrued interest:

1. Forgive $500 of accrued interest.
2. Reduce contracted interest from 10 percent to 5 percent.
3. Extend maturity for one additional year to December 31, 20X7.

The first step is to determine the restructuring difference on December 31, 20X6, the date of the troubled debt restructuring:

		Debtor	Creditor
Carrying value of the debt:			
Principal	$30,000		
Interest	3,000		
Carrying value of the debt	$33,000	$33,000	$33,000
Total future estimated cash flows:			
Total future principal	$30,000		
Remaining accrued interest not forgiven	2,500		
Total future contractual interest			
($30,000 × .05 × 1 year)	1,500		
Total future estimated cash flows	$34,000	(34,000)	
Present value factor, 10%, 1 year	×.90909		
Present value of total future cash flows	$30,909		(30,909)
Restructuring difference		$ (1,000)	$ 2,091

The debtor will not recognize a gain in this case because the $33,000 carrying value of the debt is less than the total future estimated cash flows resulting from the restructuring. The entry required on Peerless Products' books on December 31, 20X6, the restructuring date, is as follows:

December 31, 20X6

(29)	Accrued Interest Payable	3,000	
	Notes Payable (10%)	30,000	
	Restructured Debt Payable (5%)		33,000
	Restructuring of terms of debt.		

Note that under this approach, the restructured debt payable (5 percent) is stated at the carrying value of the old note ($30,000) plus all accrued interest ($3,000) even though the creditor forgave $500 of the accrued interest as part of the restructuring. Because the total future estimated cash flows ($34,000) exceed the carrying value of the debt ($33,000), no adjustments are made to the total amount of the carrying value of the debt. The restructured payable is stated at $33,000, and a total of $1,000 of interest expense will be recognized over the term to maturity of the restructured debt, representing the difference between the total $34,000 of future cash flows and the $33,000 carrying value of the restructured debt.

On December 31, 20X7, Peerless Products must pay a total of $34,000, which includes $33,000 to extinguish the restructured debt and $1,000 of interest expense. The entry on December 31, 20X7, is as follows:

December 31, 20X7

(30)	Interest Expense	1,000	
	Restructured Debt Payable (5%)	33,000	
	Cash		34,000
	Pay restructured debt and interest expense.		

The debtor's actual interest rate for the restructured debt may be found by solving the present value formula for the interest rate, as follows:

$$\text{Present value} = \text{Present value factor} \times \text{Future amount}$$

where the present value is the present book value of debt; the present value factor (PVF) is the factor from the "present value of $1" table for one period, which is the term of the debt; and the future value is the total future cash flows. Therefore,

$$\$33,000 = \text{PVF} \times \$34,000$$

and

$$\text{PVF} = \$33,000/\$34,000 = .9705$$

In a present value of $1 table, the factor .9705 is found for one year in the 3 percent column. Therefore, the interest rate is approximately 3 percent. For this one-year example, the interest rate may be approximated by a more direct manner, as follows:

$$\frac{\$1,000}{\$33,000} = .0303, \text{ or } 3.03 \text{ percent interest rate}$$

Although the restructuring agreement shows the contractual interest rate as 5 percent, the interest expense reported on the debtor's income statement is reported at an effective interest rate of 3.03 percent. The difference between the 5 percent and the 3.03 percent becomes part of the restructured debt principal. For notes payable of more than one year in length, the computed effective rate of interest is used to determine the amount of interest expense to be reported for each year.

The creditor's entries are as follows:

December 31, 20X6

(31)	Allowance for Uncollectibles	2,091	
	Accrued Interest Receivable		500
	Valuation Allowance for Impaired Loans		1,591
(32)	Impaired Notes Receivable (5%)	30,000	
	Notes Receivable (10%)		30,000

December 31, 20X7

(33)	Cash	4,000	
	Valuation Allowance for Impaired Loans	1,591	
	Accrued Interest Receivable		2,500
	Interest Revenue		3,091

$4,000 = $30,000 × .05 contractual interest rate plus accrued interest not forgiven of $2,500

$3,091 = $30,909 present value × .10 effective interest rate

(34)	Cash	30,000	
	Impaired Notes Receivable		30,000

Other Considerations

Some restructuring agreements contain provisions for contingent payments. For example, the agreement may specify that the debtor must pay an additional amount if its future net income exceeds a certain level. At the time of the restructuring agreement, contingent amounts should be included in the estimated total future cash payments by both the debtor and creditor if the conditions established in **FASB Statement No. 5**, "Accounting for Contingencies" (FASB 5), for a recognition of a loss contingency have been met. This standard requires contingencies to be recognized as payables in the first period in which it is probable that a liability has been incurred and the amount can be reasonably estimated.

At the time of a debt restructuring, the debtor is required to make supplementary footnote disclosures in its financial reports describing the major features of the restructuring plan, the aggregate gain on restructuring the payables and any related income tax effects, the net gain or loss on transfers of assets in accordance with the plan, and the per-share effects of the aggregate gain on restructuring of the payables net of related income tax effects. For periods after the restructuring, the debtor must disclose amounts that are contingently payable and the terms under which these contingencies become payable.

Creditors must disclose, either in the financial statements or in the notes, specific information about impaired loans. These disclosures include the recorded investment in the loans for which impairment has been recognized and the total valuation allowance related to those loans. In addition, the creditor must disclose both the beginning and ending balances for the period in the Allowance for Uncollectibles, including any direct write-downs during the period and any recoveries recorded during the period. Finally, the creditor must disclose its income recognition policy and the amount of interest income recognized in the period.

Questions

Q20-1   What are the nonjudicial actions available to a financially distressed company? What judicial actions are available?

Q20-2   What is the difference between a Chapter 7 action and a Chapter 11 bankruptcy action?

Q20-3   Under what circumstances may an involuntary petition for relief be filed? Who files this petition?

Q20-4   What is usually included in the plan of reorganization filed as part of a Chapter 11 reorganization?

Q20-5   Explain the use of the account Reorganization Value in Excess of Amount Assigned to Identifiable Assets during a Chapter 11 reorganization.

Q20-6   What conditions must occur for a company in reorganization to use fresh start accounting?

Q20-7   What financial statements must be filed by a company during a Chapter 11 reorganization?

Q20-8   What are the rights of creditors with priority in a Chapter 7 liquidation?

Q20-9   Describe the statement of affairs used in planning an anticipated liquidation.

Q20-10*   What are the financial reporting responsibilities of a trustee who accepts the debtor company's assets in a Chapter 7 liquidation?

Q20-11*   How are the sales of assets reported on the statement of realization and liquidation?

Q20-12A   What is a troubled debt restructuring? Are all debt restructurings accounted for in the same manner?

Q20-13A   Summarize the procedures for determining whether a gain or loss from debt restructuring is reported.

Q20-14A   Explain the two steps involved with accounting for the transfer of noncash assets in settlement of a restructured debt.

Q20-15A   How is a gain from a troubled debt restructuring reported on the debtor's financial statements? How is a loss reported on the creditor's financial statements?

Q20-16A   Under what circumstances will a gain be shown by a debtor in a modification of terms of the debt agreement?

Q20-17A   How is interest expense computed by the debtor after a modification of terms in which the carrying value of the debt is less than the modified total future cash flows?

Cases

C20-1A   **Restructuring of Debt**

Elec-Tric Inc. is experiencing financial difficulties and is seeking ways to settle a $100,000 debt with one of its creditors. The creditor is willing to accept $70,000 in cash or accept land that cost Elec-Tric Inc. $20,000 but was recently appraised at $90,000. The company's controller wishes to settle the debt by transferring the land, but its president believes the debt should be settled by transferring the $70,000 in cash.

Judgment

Required

Discuss the accounting procedures and financial statement disclosures to be used by Elec-Tric Inc. to account for and report the settlement of the debt with the (*a*) transfer of the land and (*b*) transfer of the $70,000 cash.

C20-2   **Creditors' Alternatives**

Communication

The creditors of the Lost Hope Company have had several meetings with the company's management to discuss the company's financial difficulties. Lost Hope currently has a significant deficit in Retained Earnings and has defaulted on several of its debt issues. The options currently open to the creditors

---

* Indicates that the item relates to "Additional Considerations."

are to (1) form a creditors' committee, (2) work with the company in a Chapter 11 reorganization, or (3) go through a Chapter 7 liquidation. The creditors have come to you to seek your advice on the advantages and disadvantages of each of the three options from their viewpoint.

Required

Discuss the advantages and disadvantages to the creditors of each of the three options available. Include a discussion of the probable recovery of each of the creditors' claims and the time period of that recovery.

C20-3   **Research Related to Bankruptcy**

Research

You are working on a report regarding bankruptcies. You need to locate more information and have heard that the U.S. bankruptcy courts have a Website that would be useful. Locate the Website using a search engine. (*Hint:* A helpful search term may be "U.S. Bankruptcy Courts.") Locate the following information, and incorporate it into a one- to two-page report.

a. How are bankruptcy judges assigned to specific cases? (You might look under the frequently asked questions, FAQs, for guidance on this question.)

b. (1) How can a business obtain the appropriate filing forms for a voluntary petition for bankruptcy?
   (2) Briefly summarize the types of information required on the voluntary petition.

c. Locate and summarize the following bankruptcy statistics:

   (1) First determine total business filings and then determine the number of filings by type (i.e., Chapter 7, Chapter 11, and so on) for the most recent calendar year ending on December 31.

   (2) Determine the number of filings by type for businesses in your specific federal judicial district. (*Hint:* Some circuits have several district courts, so select the one you feel is most appropriate based on the location of your educational institution.) Briefly discuss how the number of filings in your federal judicial district compare with those filed in other districts.

C20-4A   **Debt Restructuring**

Easy Riding, Inc., customizes luxury recreational vehicles with features such as marble flooring, deluxe upholstery, custom woodwork, and so on. For several years, Easy Riding was extremely profitable and expanded its operations rapidly through borrowing. However, an economic downturn has occurred, and the company is finding it difficult to meet its maturing debt obligations, including a $5 million loan payable to the First Commerce Bank scheduled to be repaid in six months.

As the company's principal creditor, First Commerce believes that Easy Riding is well positioned to return to profitability when the economy recovers; however, the bank is also concerned that a prolonged downturn could result in the company's bankruptcy. As a result of these concerns, First Commerce has agreed to restructure its loan agreement with Easy Riding.

Research
FARS

The terms of the loan restructure reduce the principal of the loan by 25 percent, extend the principal repayment by five years, and reduce the interest rate on the loan to 2 percent, which is substantially lower than the bank's current lending rates. Easy Riding's controller has determined that the total amount that it will pay under these modified terms is less than the current carrying amount of this loan and, therefore, plans to report a gain of $875,000 in its income statement for the current year.

Martin Wheeler, the manager in charge of Easy Riding's audit, has reviewed the documentation for the debt restructure agreement. He notes that the agreement also provides that Easy Riding will repay the original, rather than the reduced, principal amount of the loan if the company's earnings per share exceeds $2.50 in each of the last two years of the loan term.

Required

Martin asks you, as an accountant assigned to the Easy Riding audit, to research the appropriate accounting treatment for the debt restructuring. You can obtain access to accounting standards through the Financial Accounting Research System (FARS), your library, or some other source. Write a memo to him reporting on the results of your research. Support your recommendations with citations and quotations from the authoritative financial reporting standards.

C20-5*   **Selection of Bankruptcy Trustee and Trustee's Responsibilities**

Research

The United States trustee in each of the federal judicial districts is a federal official appointed by the U.S. attorney general to oversee the administration of bankruptcy cases and private trustees in specific cases. You seek information on the selection of a trustee and the trustee's responsibilities in a Chapter 7 bankruptcy filing.

a. Access Title 11 of the United States Bankruptcy Code and locate the material for a Chapter 7 filing. Summarize the procedure by which an interim trustee is appointed to a bankruptcy case. Then briefly summarize how a trustee may be elected by the creditors.

b. Summarize the duties of the trustee under Chapter 7 of the Bankruptcy Code.

C20-6   The Bankruptcy of WorldCom

Analysis

WorldCom Inc. was one of the largest companies to file for bankruptcy. This case requires the analysis of WorldCom's December 31, 2002, 10-K filed with the Securities and Exchange Commission. The 10-K can be obtained through EDGAR (www.sec.gov), Edgarscan (edgarscan.pwcglobal.com), or some other publicly available source. (*Note:* After its emergence from bankruptcy, WorldCom was merged into MCI, Inc.; however, that did not affect WorldCom's financial reporting for periods prior to the merger.)

Required

Provide answers to the following questions, referencing the section(s) of the 10-K where you found the information.

a. At what date and under which chapter of the Bankruptcy Code did WorldCom file for bankruptcy?

b. Briefly discuss several reasons why WorldCom filed for bankruptcy at that time.

c. Describe the major accounting irregularities of WorldCom prior to its bankruptcy.

d. After the bankruptcy filing, WorldCom performed an extensive review and restatement of its consolidated financial statements for the two years prior to the bankruptcy. List the major categories and amounts of these restatements for each of the two years.

e. Describe the company's financial accounting and reporting during the reorganization period. Include in your answer a brief discussion of the meaning of the title "Debtors-In-Possession" at the top of each of the company's financial statements during the reorganization period.

f. Briefly discuss the form of accounting the company used as it emerged from bankruptcy.

Exercises   E20-1   Multiple-Choice Questions on Chapter 11 Reorganizations [AICPA Adapted]

Select the correct answer for each of the following questions.

1. A client has joined other creditors of Jet Company in a composition agreement seeking to avoid the necessity of a bankruptcy proceeding against Jet. Which statement describes the composition agreement?

   a. It provides for the appointment of a receiver to take over and operate the debtor's business.

   b. It must be approved by all creditors.

   c. It provides that the creditors will receive less than the full amount of their claims.

   d. It provides a temporary delay, not to exceed six months, in the debtor's obligation to repay the debts included in the composition.

2. Hardluck Inc. is insolvent. Its liabilities exceed its assets by $13 million. Hardluck is owned by its president, Blank, and members of her family. Blank, whose assets are estimated at less than $1 million, guaranteed the loans of the corporation. A consortium of banks is the principal creditor of Hardluck, having lent it $8 million, the bulk of which is unsecured. The banks have decided to seek reorganization of Hardluck, and Blank has agreed to cooperate. Regarding the proposed reorganization:

   a. Blank's cooperation is necessary since she must sign the petition for a reorganization.

   b. If a petition for bankruptcy is filed against Hardluck, Blank will also have her personal bankruptcy status resolved and relief granted.

   c. Only a duly constituted creditors' committee may file a plan of reorganization of Hardluck.

   d. Hardluck will remain in possession unless a request is made to the court for the appointment of a trustee.

3. Among other provisions, a Chapter 11 plan of reorganization must:

   a. Rank claims according to their liquidation priorities.

   b. Not impair claims of secured creditors.

   c. Provide adequate means for the plan's execution.

   d. Treat all claims alike.

4. A condition that must exist for the filing of an involuntary bankruptcy petition is:

   a. The debtor must have debts of at least $10,000.

   b. If the debtor has 12 or more creditors, a majority of the creditors must sign the petition.

   c. If the debtor has 12 or more creditors, only one creditor need sign the petition, but that creditor must be owed at least $5,000.

   d. If the debtor has 12 or more creditors, the required number of creditors signing the petition must be owed at least $5,000 in total.

5. The plan of reorganization must be approved by:

   a. At least one-third of all creditors who hold at least half of the total debt.

   b. At least half of all creditors who hold at least half of the total debt.

   c. At least half of all creditors who hold at least two-thirds of the total debt.

   d. At least two-thirds of all creditors who hold at least two-thirds of the total debt.

E20-2 Recovery Analysis for a Chapter 11 Reorganization

The plan of reorganizing for Taylor Companies, Inc., was approved by the court, stockholders, and creditors on December 31, 20X1. The plan calls for a general restructuring of all debt of Taylor. The liability and capital accounts of the company on December 31, 20X1, are as follows:

Accounts Payable (postpetition)	$ 30,000
Liabilities Subject to Compromise:	
Accounts Payable	80,000
Notes Payable, 10%, unsecured	150,000
Interest Payable	40,000
Bonds Payable, 12%	200,000
Common Stock, $1 par	100,000
Additional Paid-In Capital	200,000
Retained Earnings (deficit)	(178,000)
Total	$622,000

A total of $30,000 of accounts payable has been incurred since the company filed its petition for relief under Chapter 11. No other liabilities have been incurred since the petition was filed. No payments have been made on the liabilities subject to compromise that existed on the petition date.

Under the terms of the reorganization plan:

1. The accounts payable creditors existing at the date the petition was filed agree to accept $72,000 of net accounts receivable in full settlement of their claims.

2. The holders of the 10 percent notes payable of $150,000 plus $16,000 of interest payable agree to accept land having a fair value of $125,000 and a book value of $85,000.

3. The holders of the 12 percent bonds payable of $200,000 plus $24,000 of interest payable agree to cancel accrued interest of $18,000, accept cash payment of the remaining $6,000 of interest, and accept a secured interest in the equipment of the company in exchange for extending the term of the bonds for an additional year at no interest.

4. The common shareholders agree to reduce the deficit by changing the par value of the stock to $2 per share and eliminating any remaining deficit after recognition of all gains or losses from the debt restructuring transactions specified in the plan of reorganization. The deficit will be eliminated by reducing additional paid-in capital.

Required

a. Prepare a recovery analysis for the plan of reorganization, concluding with the total recovery of each liability and capital component of Taylor Companies.

b. Prepare the journal entries to account for the discharge of the debt and the restructuring of the common equity in fulfillment of the plan of reorganization.

E20-3 Multiple-Choice Questions on Chapter 7 Liquidations

Select the correct answer for each of the following questions.

1. Lear Company ceased doing business and is in bankruptcy. Among the claimants are employees seeking unpaid wages. The following statements describe the possible status of such claims in a bankruptcy proceeding. Which is the *incorrect* statement?

   a. They are entitled to priority.

   b. If a priority is afforded such claims, it cannot exceed $5,000 per wage earner.

   c. Such claims include wages earned within 180 days before the filing of the bankruptcy petition, but not to exceed $10,000 in amount per wage earner.

   d. The amounts of excess wages not entitled to a priority are mere unsecured claims.

2. The highest priority for payment of unsecured claims in a bankruptcy proceeding is:

   a. Administrative expenses of the bankruptcy.

   b. Unpaid federal income taxes.

   c. Wages of each employee up to $10,000 earned within 180 days before the petition.

   d. Wages owed to an insolvent employee.

3. The order of payments for unsecured priority claims in a Chapter 7 bankruptcy case is such that:

   a. Tax claims of governmental units are paid before claims for administrative expenses incurred by the trustee.

   b. Tax claims of governmental units are paid before claims of employees for wages.

   c. Claims of employees for wages are paid before administrative expenses incurred by the trustee.

   d. Claims incurred between the filing of an involuntary petition and appointment of a trustee are paid before the claims for contributions to employee benefit plans.

4. Narco is in serious financial difficulty and is unable to meet current unsecured obligations of $30,000 to some 14 creditors who are demanding immediate payment. Narco owes Johnson $5,000, and Johnson has decided to file an involuntary petition against Narco. Which of the following is necessary in order for Johnson to file validly?

   a. Johnson must be joined by at least two other creditors.

   b. Narco must have committed a fraudulent act within one year of the filing.

   c. Johnson must allege and subsequently establish that Narco's liabilities exceed Narco's assets upon fair valuation.

   d. Johnson must be a secured creditor.

5. Your client is insolvent under the federal bankruptcy law. Under the circumstances:

   a. So long as the client can meet current debts or claims by its most aggressive creditors, a bankruptcy proceeding is *not* possible.

   b. Such information—that is, insolvency—need *not* be disclosed in the financial statements reported on by your CPA firm so long as you are convinced that the problem is short-lived.

   c. A transfer of assets to a creditor less than 90 days before filing a petition may be a voidable transfer.

   d. Your client *cannot* file a voluntary petition for bankruptcy.

E20-4 Chapter 7 Liquidation

The carrying values and estimated fair values of the assets of Penn Inc. are as follows:

	Carrying Value	Fair Value
Cash	$ 16,000	$ 16,000
Accounts Receivable	60,000	50,000
Inventory	90,000	65,000
Land	100,000	80,000
Building (net)	220,000	160,000
Equipment (net)	250,000	100,000
Total	$736,000	$471,000

Debts of Penn Inc. are as follows:

Accounts Payable	$ 95,000
Wages Payable (all have priority)	9,500
Taxes Payable	14,000
Notes Payable (secured by receivables and inventory)	190,000
Interest on Notes Payable	5,000
Bonds Payable (secured by land and building)	220,000
Interest on Bonds Payable	11,000
Total	$544,500

Required

a. Prepare a schedule to calculate the net estimated amount available for general unsecured creditors.

b. Compute the percentage dividend to general unsecured creditors.

c. Prepare a schedule showing the amount to be paid each of the creditor groups upon distribution of the $471,000 estimated to be realizable.

E20-5A Multiple-Choice Questions on Debt Restructuring [AICPA Adapted]

Select the correct answer for each of the following questions:

1. On January 1, 20X1, Kalb Company purchased at par 500 of the $1,000 face value, 8 percent bonds of Lane Corporation as a long-term investment. The bonds mature on January 1, 20X9, and pay interest semiannually on July 1 and January 1. Lane incurred heavy losses from operations for several years and defaulted on the July 1, 20X4, and January 1, 20X5, interest payments. Because of the permanent decline in market value of Lane's bonds, Kalb wrote down its investment to $400,000 on December 31, 20X4. Pursuant to Lane's plan of reorganization effected on January 1, 20X5, Kalb received 5,000 shares of $100 par value, 8 percent cumulative preferred stock of Lane in exchange for the $500,000 face value bond investment. The quoted market value of the preferred stock was $70 per share on January 1, 20X5. What amount of loss should be included in the determination of Kalb's net income for 20X5?

    a. $0.

    b. $50,000.

    c. $100,000.

    d. $150,000

2. Carling Inc. is indebted to Dow Finance Company under a $600,000, 10 percent, five-year note dated January 1, 20X1. Interest, payable annually on December 31, was paid on the December 31, 20X1 and 20X2, due dates. However, during 20X3, Carling experienced severe financial difficulties and is likely to default on the note and interest unless some concessions are made. On December 31, 20X3, Carling and Dow signed an agreement restructuring the debt as follows:

Interest for 20X3 was reduced to $30,000, payable March 31, 20X4.
Interest payments each year were reduced to $40,000 per year for 20X4 and 20X5.
The principal amount was reduced to $400,000.

    What is the amount of gain that Carling should report on the debt restructuring in its income statement for the year ended December 31, 20X3?

    a. $120,000.

    b. $150,000.

    c. $200,000.

    d. $230,000.

3. For a troubled debt restructuring involving only modification of terms, it is appropriate for a debtor to recognize a gain when the carrying amount of the debt:

    a. Exceeds the total future cash payments specified by the new terms.

    b. Is less than the total future cash payments specified by the new terms.

> *c.* Exceeds the present value specified by the new terms.
>
> *d.* Is less than the present value specified by the new terms.

4. Hull Company is indebted to Apex under a $500,000, 12 percent, three-year note dated December 31, 20X1. Because of Hull's financial difficulties developing in 20X3, Hull owed accrued interest of $60,000 on the note at December 31, 20X3. Under a troubled debt restructuring, on December 31, 20X3, Apex agreed to settle the note and accrued interest for a tract of land having a fair value of $450,000. Hull's acquisition cost of the land is $360,000. Ignoring income taxes, on its 20X3 income statement, Hull should report as a result of the troubled debt restructuring:

	Other Income	Gain on Extinguishment of Debt
a.	$200,000	$ 0
b.	$140,000	$ 0
c.	$ 90,000	$ 50,000
d.	$ 90,000	$110,000

E20-6A Impairment Entries by Debtor and Creditor

On January 2, 20X7, Tristar Bank determined it was probable that a $400,000 note receivable from Johnson Corporation was unlikely to be paid in full at maturity. The note had been issued December 31, 20X2, and will mature on December 31, 20X8. The note pays interest of 8 percent per year each December 31. After reviewing all available evidence at January 2, 20X7, Tristar Bank determined it was probable that Johnson Corporation would pay back only $250,000 of the principal at maturity. As a result, Tristar Bank decided that the loan was immediately impaired. Interest at 8 percent on the original value of the note will continue to be paid until maturity.

Required

Prepare the journal entries (if any) by Tristar Bank and Johnson Corporation at January 2, 20X7, December 31, 20X7, and December 31, 20X8.

E20-7A Settlement of a Debt: Debtor's and Creditor's Entries

On December 15, 20X5, Thom Corporation informed Linco Company that Thom would be unable to repay its $80,000 note due on December 31 to Linco. Linco agreed to accept title to Thom's delivery equipment in full settlement of the note. The equipment's carrying value was $30,000 and its fair value was $35,000. Thom's tax rate is 35 percent.

Required

Prepare journal entries on the debtor's and creditor's books on December 15, 20X5.

E20-8A Creditor's Entries for a Modification of Terms [AICPA Adapted]

On December 31, 20X2, Clark Company entered into a debt-restructuring agreement with Astro Company, which was experiencing financial difficulties. Clark restructured a $90,000 note receivable as follows:

> Reduced the principal obligation to $50,000.
> Forgave all $9,000 of accrued interest.
> Extended the maturity date from December 31, 20X2, to December 31, 20X4.
> Reduced the interest rate from 10 percent to 5 percent.

Interest was payable annually on December 31, 20X3, and 20X4. In accordance with the agreement, Astro made payments to Clark on December 31, 20X3, and 20X4. Present value factors are as follows:

Present value of a single sum, two years at 5 percent	.90703
Present value of a single sum, two years at 10 percent	.82645
Present value of an ordinary annuity of two years at 5 percent	1.85941
Present value of an ordinary annuity of two years at 10 percent	1.73554

Required

Prepare journal entries on Clark Company for December 31, 20X2, December 31, 20X3, and December 31, 20X4, that are related to the restructured debt.

E20-9*   **Statement of Realization and Liquidation**

A trustee has been appointed for Pace Inc., which is being liquidated under Chapter 7 of the Bankruptcy Code. The following transactions occurred after the assets were transferred to the trustee:

1. Sales on account by the trustee were $75,000. Cost of goods sold were $60,000, consisting of all the inventory transferred from Pace.

2. The trustee sold all $12,000 worth of marketable securities for $10,500.

3. Receivables collected by the trustee:

Old:	$21,000 of the $38,000 transferred
New:	$47,000

4. Recorded $16,000 depreciation on the plant assets of $96,000 transferred from Pace.

5. Disbursements by the trustee:

Old current payables:	$22,000 of the $48,000 transferred
Trustee's expenses:	$4,300

Required

Prepare a statement of realization and liquidation according to the traditional approach illustrated in the chapter.

Problems   P20-10   **Chapter 11 Reorganization**

During the recent recession, Polydorous Inc. accumulated a deficit in retained earnings. Although still operating at a loss, the company posted better results during 20X1. Polydorous is having trouble paying suppliers on time and paying interest when it is due. The company files for protection under Chapter 11 of the Bankruptcy Code and has the following liabilities and stockholders' equity accounts at the time the petition is filed:

Accounts Payable	$160,000
Interest Payable	20,000
Notes Payable, 10%, unsecured	340,000
Preferred Stock	100,000
Common Stock, $5 par	150,000
Retained Earnings (deficit)	(80,000)
Total	$690,000

A plan of reorganization is filed with the court, which approves it after review and after obtaining creditor and investor votes. The plan of reorganization includes the following actions:

1. The prepetition accounts payable will be restructured according to the following: (*a*) $40,000 will be paid in cash; (*b*) $20,000 will be eliminated; and (*c*) the remaining $100,000 will be exchanged for a five-year, secured note payable paying 12 percent interest.

2. The interest payable will be restructured as follows: $10,000 of the interest will be eliminated, and the remaining $10,000 will be paid in cash.

3. The 10 percent, unsecured notes payable will be restructured as follows: (*a*) $60,000 of the notes will be eliminated; (*b*) $10,000 of the notes will be paid in cash; (*c*) $240,000 of the notes will be exchanged for a five-year, 12 percent secured note; and (*d*) the remaining $30,000 will be exchanged for 3,000 shares of newly issued common stock having a par value of $10.

4. The preferred shareholders will exchange their stock for 5,000 shares of newly issued $10 par common stock.

5. The common shareholders will exchange their stock for 2,000 shares of newly issued $10 par common stock.

After extensive analysis, the company's reorganization value is determined to be $510,000 prior to any payments of cash required by the reorganization plan. An additional $10,000 in current liabilities have been incurred since the petition was filed. After the reorganization is completed, the capital structure of the company will be as follows:

Current liabilities (postpetition)	$ 10,000
Notes payable, 12%, secured	340,000
Common stock ($10 par)	100,000
Postreorganization capital structure	$450,000

An evaluation of the fair values of the assets was made after the company completed its reorganization, immediately prior to the point the company emerged from the proceedings. The following information is available:

	Book Value	Fair Value
Cash	$ 30,000	$ 30,000
Accounts receivable (net)	140,000	110,000
Inventory	25,000	18,000
Property, plant, and equipment (net)	445,000	262,000
Total	$640,000	$420,000

Required

a. Prepare a plan of reorganization recovery analysis for the liability and stockholders' equity accounts of Polydorous Inc. on the day the plan of reorganization is approved. (*Hint:* The liabilities on the plan's approval day are $530,000, which is $520,000 from prepetition payables plus $10,000 in additional accounts payable incurred postpetition.)

b. Prepare an analysis showing whether the company qualifies for fresh start accounting as it emerges from the reorganization.

c. Prepare journal entries for execution of the plan of reorganization with its general restructuring of debt and capital.

d. Prepare the balance sheet for the company on completion of the plan of reorganization.

P20-11 ### Chapter 7 Liquidation, Statement of Affairs

Name Brand Company is to be liquidated under Chapter 7 of the Bankruptcy Code. The balance sheet on July 31, 20X1, is as follows:

Assets	
Cash	$ 5,000
Marketable Securities	30,000
Accounts Receivable (net)	105,000
Inventory	160,000
Prepaid Insurance	7,000
Land	80,000
Plant and Equipment (net)	412,000
Franchises	72,000
Total	$871,000

(continued)

(continued)

Equities

Accounts Payable	$265,000
Wages Payable	20,000
Taxes Payable	12,000
Interest Payable	37,000
Notes Payable	280,000
Mortgages Payable	220,000
Common Stock ($20 par)	240,000
Retained Earnings (deficit)	(203,000)
Total	$871,000

Additional Information

1. Marketable securities consist of 1,000 shares of Wooly Inc. common stock. The market value per share of the stock is $22. The stock was pledged against a $28,000, 10 percent note payable that has accrued interest of $1,400.

2. Accounts receivable of $50,000 are collateral for a $40,000, 12 percent note payable that has accrued interest of $4,000.

3. Inventory with a book value of $79,000 and a current value of $75,000 is pledged against accounts payable of $105,000. The appraised value of the remainder of the inventory is $76,000.

4. Only $1,500 will be recovered from prepaid insurance.

5. Land is appraised at $110,000 and plant and equipment at $340,000.

6. It is estimated that the franchises can be sold for $30,000.

7. All the wages payable qualify for priority.

8. The mortgages are on the land and on a building with a book value of $162,000 and an appraised value of $150,000. The accrued interest on the mortgages is $14,600.

9. Estimated legal and accounting fees for the liquidation are $13,000.

Required

a. Prepare a statement of affairs as of July 31, 20X1.

b. Compute the estimated percentage settlement to unsecured creditors.

P20-12 **Chapter 7 Liquidation, Statement of Affairs [AICPA Adapted]**

Tower Inc. advises you that it is facing bankruptcy proceedings. As the company's CPA, you are aware of its condition. Tower's balance sheet on December 31, 20X1, and supplementary data are presented here.

Assets

Cash	$ 2,000
Accounts Receivable (net)	70,000
Inventory, Raw Materials	40,000
Inventory, Finished Goods	60,000
Marketable Securities	20,000
Land	13,000
Buildings (net)	90,000
Machinery (net)	140,000
Prepaid Expenses	5,000
Total Assets	$440,000

Liabilities and Capital

Accounts Payable	$ 80,000
Notes Payable	135,000
Wages	15,000
Mortgages Payable	130,000
Common Stock	100,000
Retained Earnings (deficit)	(20,000)
Total Liabilities and Capital	$440,000

Additional Information

1. Cash includes a $500 travel advance that has been expended.

2. Accounts receivable of $40,000 have been pledged in support of bank loans of $30,000. Credit balances of $5,000 are netted in the accounts receivable total.

3. Marketable securities consist of government bonds costing $10,000 and 500 shares of Dawson Company stock. The market value of the bonds is $10,000, and the stock is $18 per share. The bonds have $200 of accrued interest due. The securities are collateral for a $20,000 bank loan.

4. Appraised value of raw materials and finished goods is $30,000 and $50,000, respectively. For an additional cost of $10,000, the raw materials could realize $70,000 as finished goods.

5. The appraised value of fixed assets is $25,000 for land, $110,000 for buildings, and $75,000 for machinery.

6. Prepaid expenses will be exhausted during the liquidation period.

7. Accounts payable include $15,000 of withheld payroll taxes and $6,000 owed to creditors who have been reassured by the president of Tower that they will be paid. There are unrecorded employer's payroll taxes in the amount of $500.

8. Wages payable are not subject to any limitations under bankruptcy laws.

9. Mortgages payable consist of $100,000 on land and buildings and $30,000 for a chattel mortgage on machinery. Total unrecorded accrued interest for these mortgages amounts to $2,400.

10. Estimated legal fees and expenses in connection with the liquidation are $10,000.

11. The probable judgment on a pending damage suit is $50,000.

12. You have not rendered an invoice for $5,000 for last year's audit, and you estimate a $1,000 fee for liquidation work.

Required

a. Prepare a statement of affairs. (The Book Value column should reflect adjustments that properly should have been made as of December 31, 20X1, in the normal course of business.)

b. Compute the estimated settlement per dollar of unsecured liabilities.

P20-13 **Financial Statements for a Firm in Chapter 11 Proceedings**
On January 2, 20X2, Hobbes Company files a petition for relief under Chapter 11 of the Bankruptcy Code. Hobbes had disastrous operating performance during the recent recession and needs time to reestablish profitable operations. The trial balance on January 2, 20X2, is as follows:

	Debit	Credit
Cash	$ 15,000	
Accounts Receivable (net)	65,000	
Inventory	102,000	
Property, Plant, and Equipment	620,000	
Accumulated Depreciation		$140,000
Accounts Payable		138,000
Notes Payable, 10%		170,000
Bonds Payable, 12%		250,000
Interest Payable		47,000
Preferred Stock		50,000
Common Stock, $1 par		50,000
Additional Paid-In Capital		75,000
Retained Earnings (deficit)	118,000	
Total	$920,000	$920,000

The following information applies to the 20X2 fiscal year, ending December 31, 20X2. Hobbes is in reorganization proceedings for the entire year, and the plan of reorganization has not been approved as of December 31, 20X2. The debtor remained in possession of the company during the year.

Income Data for 20X2

1. Sales revenue of $246,000 is generated during the year.

2. Cost of goods sold is $170,000 as a result of cost reduction programs installed during the year.

3. Selling, operating, and administrative expenses are $50,000 for the year.

4. Interest expense is $4,000. Contractual interest would have been $51,000 for the year.

5. Reorganization items include $15,000 in fees paid to professionals and $3,000 of interest earned on cash accumulated as a result of the Chapter 11 proceedings.

6. The income tax of $5,000 on operating income was paid during the year.

7. Discontinued operations included a loss on operations, net of tax, of $16,000, and a gain on the sale of assets, net of tax, of $9,000. The sale of the assets was administered by the court under the Chapter 11 proceedings.

Cash Flow Data for 20X2

1. A total of $264,000 is received from customers. This includes $18,000 received on the accounts receivable that were outstanding prior to filing the petition.

2. A total of $206,000 is paid to suppliers, employees, and others for operations.

3. The current interest expense of $4,000 on postpetition debt is paid during the year.

4. Professional fees of $15,000 are paid, and interest on cash accumulations of $3,000 is received.

5. Net cash used by discontinued operations, excluding the sale of assets, is $3,000.

6. The proceeds from the sale of the discontinued assets is $18,000. This sale was administered by the bankruptcy court.

7. Hobbes borrowed $10,000 in short-term debt as part of a financing plan administered by the court.

8. The court authorized a payment of $10,000 on the bonds payable. The ending cash balance of $72,000 represents an increase of $57,000 during the year.

Other Data for 20X2

1. Through careful working capital management, the ending inventory is reduced to $88,000. Continued reduction is expected in 20X3.

2. The property, plant, and equipment, net of accumulated depreciation, at the end of 20X2 totaled $460,000.

3. In addition to the $10,000 short-term borrowings that are part of the court-approved financing plan, Hobbes has postpetition accounts payable of $7,000.

Required

a. Prepare the income statement for Hobbes for the year ending December 31, 20X2.

b. Prepare the statement of cash flows for the company for the year ending December 31, 20X2.

c. Prepare the balance sheet for the company as of December 31, 20X2.

Supplemental Problems for this chapter are available as part of the *Online Learning Center* on the textbook's Website.

Index

Mautz, R., 630n
McCaw Cellular Communications, 49
McDonnell Douglas, 2
McFarland, R., 630n
MCI, 2
MDA (management discussion and
analysis), 694–695
in government financial statements, 886
Measurement focus and basis of
accounting (MFBA), 802–806
Mergers, 6. *See also* Business
combinations; Consolidation *entries*
MFBA (measurement focus and basis of
accounting), 802–806
MFOA (Municipal Finance Officers
Association), 794
Minority interest. *See* Noncontrolling
interest
Miramax Films, 92
MNEs (multinational enterprises). *See*
Financial statement remeasurement;
Financial statement translation;
Foreign currencies; Foreign
currency forward exchange
financial instruments
Modified accrual basis, 802
Modified equity method for intercorporate
investments, 71
Moviefone, 92
Multilevel ownership, 435–440
Multinational enterprises (MNEs). *See*
Financial statement remeasurement;
Financial statement translation;
Foreign currencies; Foreign
currency forward exchange
financial instruments
Municipal Finance Officers Association
(MFOA), 794
Mutual holdings, 435, 440–445

N

NAFTA (North American Free Trade
Agreement), 501
National Assembly of National Voluntary
Health and Social Welfare
Organizations, 947
National Committee on Governmental
Accounting, 794
National Committee on Municipal
Accounting, 794
National Conference of Commissioners on
Uniform State Laws (NCCUSL), 707
National Council on Governmental
Accounting (NCGA)
Interpretation No. 3 ("Revenue
Recognition—Property
Taxes"), 804
Statement No. 1 ("Governmental
Accounting and Financial
Reporting Principles"), 794
National Health Council, 947
NCCUSL (National Conference of
Commissioners on Uniform State
Laws), 707

NCGA. *See* National Council on
Governmental Accounting (NCGA)
Negative goodwill, 18–19, 146
Net assets
on not-for-profit hospital
balance sheet, 932
voluntary health and welfare
organizations and, 951–952
"Net Assets Restricted by Enabling
Legislation" (GASB 46), 870
Net income, consolidated. *See*
Consolidated net income
New Deal legislation, 680
New Line Cinema, 92
New partner's proportion of partnership's
book value, 722
New York Stock Exchange (NYSE),
574, 679
Nikkeiren, 574
Nippon Keidanren, 573–574
Noncontrolling interest, 11, 102–103,
196–198
consolidated net income and, 196–197
consolidated retained earnings and,
197–198
workpaper format and, 198
Noncontrolling ownership, 6–7
Noncurrent assets, intercorporate transfers
of. *See* Intercorporate transfers, of
noncurrent assets
Nonequity interests in other companies,
65–66
North American Free Trade Agreement
(NAFTA), 501
Northwest Airlines, 5
"The Norwalk Agreement" (FASB), 573
Not-for-profit entities, 919–961
colleges and universities, 923–926
FASB standards for, 921–923
financial reporting for, 919–923
hospitals. *See* Hospital accounting
voluntary health and welfare
organizations. *See* Voluntary
health and welfare organizations
(VHWOs)
Notional amount, 513
NYSE (New York Stock Exchange),
574, 679

O

OCI (other comprehensive income),
579–580
Off-balance sheet financing, 104
Omissions, on subsidiary's books, 146
One-line consolidations, 66, 139
OPEBs (other postemployment benefits),
889–890
Operating budgets, 807–808
Operating expenses of hospitals, 939
Operating losses, interim income taxes
and, 653
Operating statement, of governmental
funds, 801–802
Option contracts, 538–539

Order of relief, 991
Organizational structure. *See also* Business
entities, expansion of
business objectives and, 2
ethical considerations for, 2–3
financial reporting and, 6–7
Other comprehensive income (OCI),
579–580
consolidation of less-than-wholly
owned subsidiaries and,
210–216
adjusting entries and, 212
consolidation procedures and,
212–213, 214, 215
consolidation workpaper and, 211–
212, 213, 216
investor's share of, 68
Other not-for-profit organizations
(ONPOs), 957–960
financial statements of, 958–960
Other postemployment benefits (OPEBs),
889–890
Ownership, beneficial, 689
Oxley, Michael, 691

P

Pacific Stock Exchange (PSE), 538
Pacific Telesis, 4
Parent company, 2, 10, 49, 92. *See also*
Subsidiaries
consolidated financial statements for.
See Consolidated financial
statements
ownership of. *See* Changes in parent
company ownership
Parent company theory of accounting,
107–110
Parent-subsidiary relationships, 10
Partners, personal financial statements of,
770–773
Partners' accounts, 712
Partnership(s), 706–736
book value of, 720
definition of, 707
determination of new partner's
investment cost, 732–733
dissociations and, 733–735, 755
dissolution of, 756
equity investments in, 63–65
financial statements of, 718
formation of, 707–708, 710–711
incorporation of, 769–770
limited, 709–710
liquidation of. *See* Partnership
liquidations
new partner investment in, 722–731
new partner purchase of interest in,
720–722
partners' accounts and, 712
profit and loss allocation to partners in,
713–718
standards for reporting interests
in, 65
tax aspects of, 736–737

ACCOUNTING

FIFTH EDITION

Charles T. Horngren
Stanford University

Walter T. Harrison Jr.
Baylor University

Linda Smith Bamber
University of Georgia

Prentice Hall International, Inc.

To Betsy Willis and Becky Jones for their wisdom on learning and teaching over a 10-year period and to Michael Bamber for his insight on business practices and ethical issues in management accounting.

This edition may be sold only in those countries to which it has been consigned by Prentice Hall International. It is not to be re-exported and it is not for sale in the U.S.A., Mexico, or Canada.

Executive Editor:	Deborah Hoffman
Developmental Editor:	Jeannine Ciliotta
Assistant Editor:	Kasey Sheehan
Director of Development:	Steve Deitmer
Editor-in-Chief:	P.J. Boardman
Senior Editorial Assistant:	Jane Avery
Media Project Manager:	Nancy Welcher
Executive Marketing Manager:	Beth Toland
Senior Production Editor:	Anne Graydon
Managing Editor (Production):	Sondra Greenfield
Production Manager:	Arnold Vila
Associate Director, Manufacturing:	Vincent Scelta
Text Permissions Coordinator:	Suzanne Grappi
Design Manager:	Pat Smythe
Interior Design:	Blair Brown, Christine Cantera
Cover Design and Illustration:	Blair Brown
Infographic Illustrations:	Kenneth Batelman
Manager, Multimedia Production:	Christy Mahon
Photo Researcher:	Abby Reip
Photo Permissions Coordinator:	Michelina Viscusi
Composition:	Progressive Information Technologies
Full-Service Project Management:	Progressive Publishing Alternatives
Printer/Binder:	R.R. Donnelley, Willard

10 9 8 7 6 5 4 3 2 1

ISBN 0-13-093409-7

About the Authors

Charles T. Horngren is the Edmund W. Littlefield Professor of Accounting, Emeritus, at Stanford University. A graduate of Marquette University, he received his MBA from Harvard University and his Ph.D. from the University of Chicago. He is also the recipient of honorary doctorates from Marquette University and DePaul University.

A Certified Public Accountant, Horngren served on the Accounting Principles Board for six years, the Financial Accounting Standards Board Advisory Council for five years, and the Council of the American Institute of Certified Public Accountants for three years. For six years, he served as a trustee of the Financial Accounting Foundation, which oversees the Financial Accounting Standards Board and the Government Accounting Standards Board.

Horngren is a member of the Accounting Hall of Fame.

A member of the American Accounting Association, Horngren has been its President and its Director of Research. He received its first annual Outstanding Accounting Educator Award.

The California Certified Public Accountants Foundation gave Horngren its Faculty Excellence Award and its Distinguished Professor Award. He is the first person to have received both awards.

The American Institute of Certified Public Accountants presented its first Outstanding Educator Award to Horngren.

Horngren was named Accountant of the Year, Education, by the national professional accounting fraternity, Beta Alpha Psi.

Professor Horngren is also a member of the Institute of Management Accountants, where he has received its Distinguished Service Award. He was a member of the Institute's Board of Regents, which administers the Certified Management Accountant examinations.

Horngren is the author of other accounting books published by Prentice-Hall: *Cost Accounting: A Managerial Emphasis*, Tenth Edition, 2000 (with George Foster and Srikant Datar); *Introduction to Management Accounting*, Twelfth Edition (with Gary L. Sundem and William Stratton); *Introduction to Financial Accounting*, Eighth Edition, 2002 (with Gary L. Sundem and John A. Elliott); and *Financial Accounting*, Fourth Edition, 2001 (with Walter T. Harrison, Jr.).

Horngren is the Consulting Editor for the Charles T. Horngren Series in Accounting.

Walter T. Harrison, Jr. is Professor of Accounting at the Hankamer School of Business, Baylor University. He received his B.B.A. degree from Baylor University, his M.S. from Oklahoma State University, and his Ph.D. from Michigan State University.

Professor Harrison, recipient of numerous teaching awards from student groups as well as from university administrators, has also taught at Cleveland State Community College, Michigan State University, the University of Texas, and Stanford University.

A member of the American Accounting Association and the American Institute of Certified Public Accountants, Professor Harrison has served as Chairman of the Financial Accounting Standards Committee of the American Accounting Association, on the Teaching/Curriculum Development Award Committee, on the Program Advisory Committee for Accounting Education and Teaching, and on the Notable Contributions to Accounting Literature Committee.

Professor Harrison has lectured in several foreign countries and published articles in numerous journals, including *The Accounting Review, Journal of Accounting Research, Journal of Accountancy, Journal of Accounting and Public Policy, Economic Consequences of*

Financial Accounting Standards, *Accounting Horizons*, *Issues in Accounting Education*, and *Journal of Law and Commerce*. He is coauthor of *Financial Accounting*, Fourth Edition, 2001 (with Charles T. Horngren and *Accounting, Fifth Edition*, 2002 (with Charles T. Horngren and Linda S. Bamber) published by Prentice Hall. Professor Harrison has received scholarships, fellowships, research grants or awards from PriceWaterhouseCoopers, Deloitte & Touche, the Ernst & Young Foundation, and the KPMG Foundation.

Linda Smith Bamber is Professor of Accounting at the J.M. Tull School of Accounting at the University of Georgia. She graduated summa cum laude from Wake Forest University, where she was a member of Phi Beta Kappa. She is a certified public accountant. For her performance on the CPA examination, Professor Bamber received the Elijah Watt Sells Award in addition to the North Carolina Bronze Medal. Before returning to graduate school, she worked in cost accounting at RJR Foods. She then earned an MBA from Arizona State University, and a Ph.D. from The Ohio State University.

Professor Bamber has received numerous teaching awards from The Ohio State University, the University of Florida, and the University of Georgia, including selection as Teacher of the Year at the University of Florida's Fisher School of Accounting.

She has lectured in Canada and Australia in addition to the U.S., and her research has appeared in numerous journals, including *The Accounting Review*, *Journal of Accounting Research*, *Journal of Accounting and Economics*, *Journal of Finance*, *Contemporary Accounting Research*, *Auditing: A Journal of Practice and Theory*, *Accounting Horizons*, *Issues in Accounting Education*, and *CPA Journal*. She provided the annotations for the *Annotated Instructor's Edition* of Horngren, Foster, and Datar's *Cost Accounting: A Managerial Emphasis*, Seventh, Eighth, and Ninth Editions.

A member of the Institute of Management Accounting, the American Accounting Association (AAA), and the AAA's Management Accounting Section and Financial Accounting and Reporting Section, Professor Bamber has chaired the AAA New Faculty Consortium Committee, served on the AAA Council, the AAA Research Advisory Committee, the AAA Corporate Accounting Policy Seminar Committee, the AAA Wildman Medal Award Committee, the AAA Nominations Committee, and has chaired the Management Accounting Section's Membership Outreach Committee. She served as Associate Editor of *Accounting Horizons*, and is serving as editor of *The Accounting Review* from 1999 to 2002.

ACCOUNTING

CHARLES T. HORNGREN SERIES IN ACCOUNTING

AUDITING: AN INTEGRATED APPROACH, 8th ed.
Arens/Loebbecke

GOVERNMENTAL AND NONPROFIT ACCOUNTING:
THEORY AND PRACTICE, 6th ed.
Freeman/Shoulders

FINANCIAL ACCOUNTING, 4th ed.
Harrison/Horngren

COST ACCOUNTING: A MANAGERIAL EMPHASIS, 10th ed.
Horngren/Foster/Datar

ACCOUNTING, 5th ed.
Horngren/Harrison/Bamber

CASES IN FINANCIAL REPORTING, 3rd ed.
Hirst/McAnally

INTRODUCTION TO FINANCIAL ACCOUNTING, 8th ed.
Horngren/Sundem/Elliott

INTRODUCTION TO MANAGEMENT ACCOUNTING, 12th ed.
Horngren/Sundem/Stratton

BUDGETING, 7th ed.
Welsch/Hilton/Gordon

> *This is what I especially like about this textbook. There are always ways of checking yourself to make sure you are understanding what you are reading. I am really impressed with the book. It is so well put together that all the subjects seem to flow together and offer a complete knowledge of the accounting world.*
>
> **—Lisa Cronauer, student, Saint Leo University**

> *[This textbook is] easy to understand and made me feel that accounting could possibly be my major. . . . This textbook [is] a valuable learning tool that will aid me in the future.*
>
> **—Carrie Hupp, student, Middle Tennessee State University**

Teaching accounting today means helping students navigate a changing business world. It means helping them succeed in the classroom and in their careers. Whether this is the first or only accounting course students take, learning the fundamentals of accounting can help them make better decisions, evaluate real-world situations, and understand the value of "crunching the numbers."

In *Accounting, fifth ed.*, publisher, authors, faculty, and students target a common goal: improving student success and understanding of accounting concepts. This edition provides:

- The most motivational text and writing style
- The best assessment and reinforcement tools
- The widest assortment of technology resources
- The best free student resources
- The best service and support for faculty

We believe *Accounting, fifth ed.*, offers the best possible system for student success, and we invite you to learn more about it. We welcome your comments and suggestions.

CHARLES T. HORNGREN ◉ **WALTER T. HARRISON, JR.** ◉ **LINDA SMITH BAMBER**
STANFORD UNIVERSITY   **BAYLOR UNIVERSITY**   **UNIVERSITY OF GEORGIA**

Chapter Opening Vignettes and On Location! Videos

The chapter-opening vignettes thrust students into the real world of accounting—where business decisions affect the future of actual organizations. Vignettes provide the real business context for chapter topics. Companies include Target, NetGenesis, Lucent and MCI WorldCom, McDonald's, AOL Time Warner, and more.

Many of the chapter-opening vignettes are linked to our unique, custom-created *On Location! Videos*. Each 5- to 10-minute video provides a "plant tour" introducing students to the business professionals who are using accounting information to enhance the success of their organizations. *NEW* **segments** include Cisco, Nantucket Nectars, Teva Sandals, Oracle, and others.

You probably recognize the bulls'-eye logo. You may even do your shopping at a **Target, Mervyn, Marshall Field, Dayton,** or **Hudson** store. All these companies are part of the retail empire known as **Target Corporation.** It is a pacesetter in retailing: Target stores are currently the place to find the latest fashions at the best prices. Target is also a pacesetter in philanthropy and community relations. Through its Five Percent Club, the company donates 5% of its taxable income to support charities in the communities where it operates. In 2000, Target gave more than $1 million every week to local communities. The company, which employs about 189,000 people nationwide, is considered a good employer. *Working Mother* magazine has recognized Target as a "Top Work Place for Women." Target sells its merchandise through nearly 900 stores in 44 states, and through its Web site on the Internet. It is one of the largest mass-merchandise retailers in the United States, ringing up sales of over $33 billion in the year ended January 31, 2000.

NEW Featured Company: Target

The fifth edition includes the **Target Annual Report** both as an appendix within the text and as a separate booklet shrinkwrapped with each copy. We also highlight Target in Chapter 5 and in financial statement cases throughout the book.

NEW e-Accounting Boxes

Nothing has changed business more in recent years than the Internet. Horngren/Harrison/Bamber's new e-Accounting boxes focus on the accounting issues affecting companies doing business on the World Wide Web, such as CDNow, Priceline.com, and DHL.

 **e-Accounting**

Varsitybooks.com: A Textbook Case on the Fulfillment Cost Conundrum

Order the fifth edition of *Accounting* from **Varsitybooks.com** and the company arranges for **Baker & Taylor**—book distributors—to ship it to you immediately. Varsitybooks doesn't have a warehouse or any inventory, but it does have to pay Baker & Taylor for this convenient arrangement. How does the fledgling dot.com account for these costs?

As you know from personal experience, e-commerce has revolutionized business. It has bent certain accounting rules in the process. One such rule is that the cost of goods sold to customers is usually considered the "cost of goods sold." Yet, on-line powerhouses like Amazon.com and eToys, Inc. count some of this cost as "sales and marketing expenses because they never own the inventory." By listing these "fulfillment costs" as marketing expense, new-age companies don't have to subtract the costs from their gross profit. This seemed like a good idea to Varsitybooks, and its managers announced to their auditor, **KPMG**, that they wanted to do the same.

After all, Varsitybooks argued, mail-order companies have always done this. And the practice would allow the new agers to keep from reporting razor-thin profit margins. For instance, if the SEC tightens the rules and makes Amazon.com account for fulfillment cost as "cost of sales," gross profit margins for the last quarter of 1999 would go from 15% to −3%. The company's sales and net profit or net loss amounts would remain the same, but analysts looked at the gross profit figure to see how well a company can make money from basic business operations.

Small wonder that this approach is controversial! Varsitybooks.com fired KPMG when the auditors objected to it. They hired **PricewaterhouseCoopers** instead, but in the end Varsitybooks had to follow the traditional accounting procedures anyway. The auditors knew best after all.

Source: Based on Shannon Henry, "An E-Tail Identity Crisis," *The Washington Post*, May 4, 2000, p. E01. Anonymous, "Web Retailers' 'Gross Profit' Questioned; E-commerce; The SEC may make some firms account f distribution costs, possibly turning their profits into losses," *The Los Angeles Times*, February 19, 2000, p. 2.

Exhibits 5-10 and 5-11 tell an interesting s
at a low gro

Work It Out Boxes

These exercises allow students to work out problems related to text concepts. Answers are provided for immediate reinforcement.

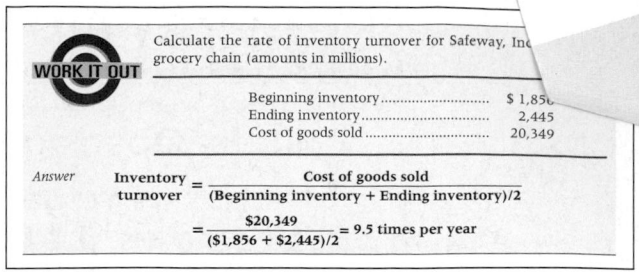

Calculate the rate of inventory turnover for Safeway, Inc., grocery chain (amounts in millions).

Beginning inventory	$ 1,856
Ending inventory	2,445
Cost of goods sold	20,349

Answer

$$\text{Inventory turnover} = \frac{\text{Cost of goods sold}}{(\text{Beginning inventory} + \text{Ending inventory})/2}$$

$$= \frac{\$20,349}{(\$1,856 + \$2,445)/2} = 9.5 \text{ times per year}$$

Think It Over Boxes

These exercises ask students to reflect on and apply concepts they've just learned. Again, answers are provided for immediate reinforcement.

How much did Proctor & Gamble (P&G) borrow from the bank? $98,000 or $100,000? How much will they pay back?

Answers

P&G borrowed $98,000, the amount of cash the company received. They will pay back $100,000 at maturity.

Decision Guidelines with *NEW* Excel Application Problems

Why should English or engineering majors care about accounting? Easy! **Decision Guidelines** are designed to show *when, why, and how* all managers—not just accountants—use accounting information to make good business decisions. Many of the Decision Guidelines now include **optional Excel Application Problems** for a hands-on approach. Excel is the single piece of applications software every business professional must master. These problems give students a step-by-step guide to creating Excel templates to solve accounting and financial dilemmas.

DECISION GUIDELINES

Merchandising Operations and the Accounting Cycle

DECISION	GUIDELINES
How do merchandising operations differ from service operations?	• Merchandisers buy and sell *merchandise inventory* • Service entities perform a *service*.

Balance sheet:

• Merchandiser has *inventory*, an asset.
• Service business has no inventory.

Income Statement:

Merchandiser

Sales revenue	$ XXX
− Cost of goods sold	(X)
= Gross profit	XX
− Operating expenses	(X)
= Net income	$ X

Service Business

Service revenue	$XX
− Operating expenses	(X)
= Net income	$ X

Statements of Owner's Equity:

How do a merchandiser's financial statements differ from the financial statements of a service business?

No difference

Which type of inventory system to use?

• *Perpetual system* shows the amount of *inventory* on hand (the asset) and the cost of goods sold (the expense) at all times.
• *Periodic system* shows the correct balances of inventory and cost of goods sold only after a physical count of the inventory, which occurs at least once each year.

How do the adjusting and closing processes of merchandisers and service entities differ?

Very little. The merchandiser may have to adj... Inventory account for spoilage an...

NEW "Lessons Learned"

At the end of each chapter, this feature gives students the key "takeaway" lessons from the chapter that they should retain in preparation for testing.

LESSONS LEARNED

1. ***Use sales and gross profit to evaluate a company.*** The major revenue of a merchandising business is *sales revenue,* or *sales*. The major expense is *cost of goods sold*. Net sales minus cost of goods sold is *gross profit*, or *gross margin*. This amount measures the business's success or failure in selling its products at a higher price than it paid for them.

2. ***Account for the purchase and sale of inventory.*** The merchandiser's major asset is inventory. In a merchandising entity, the accounting cycle is from cash to inventory as the inventory is purchased for resale, and back to cash as the inventory is sold. The *invoice* is the business document generated by a purchase or sale transaction. Most merchandising entities allow customers to *return* unsuitable

4. ***Prepare a merchandise*** income statement may ap step format. A single-step i sections—one for revenue and a single income amou income statement has s income from operations. F

5. ***Use the gross profit percen*** ***ratio to evaluate a busine*** merchandiser are the *gross* sales revenue) and the *r* goods sold/average inven sures u

UNIQUE Concept Links

To keep previously covered material fresh in students' minds, concept links appear in the margins of the text. They explain how earlier topics are relevant to the new material being introduced. For students who need to go back and review, the margin links include a page cross reference.

Running Glossary

Is terminology important to student success? You bet! All key terms are boldface within the text at introduction, with a definition in the margin.

MORE Internet Exercises

Internet Exercises now appear in every chapter, and include such companies as eBay, Intuit Inc., Southwest Airlines, General Motors, FedEx, and Amazon.com. To do these exercises, students go first to the book Web site, and then use hotlinks to the company sites to complete the work.

www.prenhall.com/horngren

NEW CyberCoach

At three points in each chapter, the CyberCoach icon directs the student to exercises on the text Web site at ***www.prenhall.com/horngren***

- At the beginning of each chapter, to see if they have mastered concepts covered in the previous chapter. *(Readiness Assessment)*
- At mid-chapter, to see if they have learned chapter topics up to this point. *(Mid-Chapter Assessment)*
- At the end of each chapter, to see if they have mastered the chapter as a whole. *(End-of-Chapter Assessment)*

With CyberCoach, students can check their answers and monitor their progress as they learn. Now they're better prepared for class, for homework assignments, and for examinations.

In addition to CyberCoach, the fifth edition offers other unique, targeted student self-evaluation materials, plus a full program of assignment exercises, problems, and cases for each chapter.

Daily Exercises

These unique, single-concept exercises appear in the end-of-chapter assignment material. Daily Exercises serve as warm-ups or confidence builders. Each is linked to the text material so that students may refer back for additional assistance. Each is also cited in the margin at the appropriate point in the text.

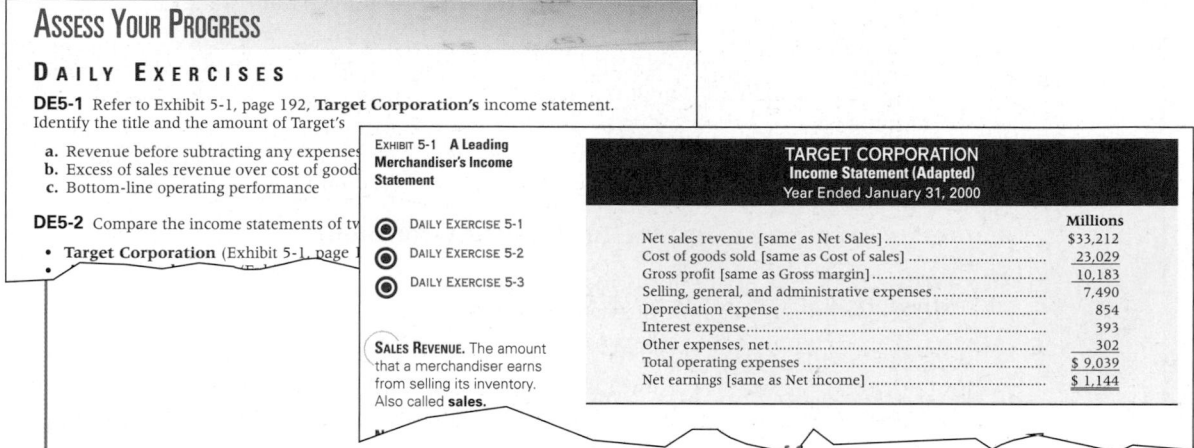

ASSESS YOUR PROGRESS

DAILY EXERCISES

DE5-1 Refer to Exhibit 5-1, page 192, **Target Corporation's** income statement. Identify the title and the amount of Target's

a. Revenue before subtracting any expenses
b. Excess of sales revenue over cost of goods
c. Bottom-line operating performance

DE5-2 Compare the income statements of tw

• **Target Corporation** (Exhibit 5-1, page

EXHIBIT 5-1 A Leading Merchandiser's Income Statement

◉ DAILY EXERCISE 5-1
◉ DAILY EXERCISE 5-2
◉ DAILY EXERCISE 5-3

SALES REVENUE. The amount that a merchandiser earns from selling its inventory. Also called **sales.**

TARGET CORPORATION
Income Statement (Adapted)
Year Ended January 31, 2000

	Millions
Net sales revenue [same as Net Sales]	$33,212
Cost of goods sold [same as Cost of sales]	23,029
Gross profit [same as Gross margin]	10,183
Selling, general, and administrative expenses	7,490
Depreciation expense	854
Interest expense	393
Other expenses, net	302
Total operating expenses	$ 9,039
Net earnings [same as Net income]	$ 1,144

Enhanced PH ReEnforcer Tutorial Software*

This Windows-based tutorial software enables students to test their understanding of key concepts through a variety of exercises, with immediate feedback. A "Quick Tour" tutorial provides an overview of the program. New and enhanced exercise types include:

- *Multiple Choice Questions*
- *Financial Statement Analysis Questions* (Students manipulate a financial statement by entering transactions.)
- *T-account Problems* (Students complete journal entries, then select the T-accounts, and then enter numbers.)
- *General Problems* (Students integrate accounting terms into their vocabulary by writing journal entries, using terms from the text.)

Enhanced PHAS General Ledger Tutorial*

This Windows-based software reinforces accounting procedures through hands-on activity. Problem templates allow students to enter their own problems and complete the entire accounting cycle: journalize, post, print multiple reports, and close. A "Quick Tour" overviews the program and offers online help.

The software is free to students when downloaded from the text Web site. Students may also purchase a CD-ROM containing the software packaged to their book.

# TARGET STUDENT SUCCESS: WHAT'S NEW IN THIS EDITION

Every topic, every sentence, every word in every chapter has been carefully reviewed to

- **Streamline the exposition** to make text clearer and more direct.
- **Enhance readability** to make the text as accessible as possible to students taking accounting for the first time.
- **Place exhibits** as close to the introductory text reference as possible to make them easier for students to use and learn from.
- **Integrate e-commerce, Internet, and technology** information and examples wherever possible.
- **Add new real-company examples,** including hi-tech companies like Lucent Technologies and Cisco Systems, MCI WorldCom, Dell Computer, and dot.coms like Priceline.com, and Amazon.com.

Here are the major chapter changes:

Chapter 1: Accounting and the Business Environment

- *NEW* Chapter vignette: Texas Tobacco Lawyers
- *NEW* Continuing example of sole proprietorship: Gay Gillen eTravel
- *NEW* e-Accounting box: Microstrategy: A Cautionary Tale for the New Economy

Chapter 2: Recording Business Transactions

- *NEW* Chapter vignette: e-Retailers
- *NEW* e-Accounting box: The Seven Trillion Dollar Mistake (the Pentagon's accounting problems)

Chapter 3: Measuring Business Income: The Adjusting Process

- *NEW* e-Accounting box: Grossing up the Revenue: Priceline.com and Ventro
- *NEW* Decision Guidelines Excel exercise

Chapter 4: Completing the Accounting Cycle

- *NEW* Vignette: NetGenesis
- *NEW* e-Accounting box: A Forced Debt Ratio for South Korea's Companies
- *NEW* Decision Guidelines Excel exercise

Chapter 5: Merchandising Operations and the Accounting Cycle

- *NEW* Vignette: Target (annual report company), also used throughout chapter
- *NEW* e-Accounting box: Varsitybooks.com: A Textbook Case on the Fulfillment Cost Conundrum
- *NEW* Comparison of service entities vs. merchandisers for ease of understanding

Chapter 6: Accounting Information Systems

- *NEW* e-Accounting box: Accounting Pioneers on the Virtual Frontier (virtual/online accountants)

Chapter 7: Internal Control, Managing Cash, and Making Ethical Judgments

- *NEW* e-Accounting box: The Barings Bank Debacle
- *NEW* section on Internal Controls for e-Commerce

Chapter 8: Accounts and Notes Receivable

- *NEW* Vignette: NYJets/Oracle
- *NEW* e-Accounting box: Merchant Beware: Credit Cards Boom with Online Sales . . . But So Does Fraud

Chapter 9: Merchandise Inventory

- *NEW* Vignette: Deckers Outdoor (Teva)
- *NEW* e-Accounting box: It's a Bird . . . It's a Plane . . . It's a Warehouse! DHL Worldwide Express
- *NEW* Decision Guidelines Excel exercise

Chapter 10: Plant Assets and Intangible Assets

- *NEW* e-Accounting box: Singapore International Airlines: Ratcheting Up the Value of Tangibles and Intangibles
- Intangibles: expanded and updated section to reflect fact that intangibles are sometimes now more important than tangibles.

Chapter 11: Current Liabilities and Payroll

- *NEW* e-Accounting box: A Taxing Dilemma: Sales Tax Liability and the Internet
- Simplified and revised section on Contingent Liabilities with new and current example of Sun Microsystems and Microsoft lawsuit

Chapter 12: Partnerships

- *NEW* Vignette: Arthur Andersen
- *NEW* e-Accounting box: The Limited But Lively Life of a Dot.Com Partnership
- Updated and expanded section on S Corporations

Chapter 13: Corporations: Paid-in Capital and the Balance Sheet

- *NEW* e-Accounting box: UPS Delivers the Dough at Record-breaking IPO
- *NEW* Work It Out boxes using IHOP

Chapter 14: Retained Earnings, Treasury Stock, and the Income Statement

- *NEW* Vignette: America OnLine and TimeWarner
- *NEW* e-Accounting box: Stock Buybacks Catch On in Europe
- Streamlined and revised: Recording Stock Dividends, Stock Splits, Treasury Stock

Chapter 15: Long-Term Liabilities

- *NEW* Vignette on Internet startups and online information
- *NEW* e-Accounting box: Borrowers OnLine: Click Here to Lend Us $6 Billion
- Extensive example material using Amazon.com and eBay throughout chapter
- Internet startups like Vista.com

Chapter 16: Investments and International Operations

- *NEW* Vignette: McDonald's
- *NEW* e-Accounting box: Avon Products Inc.: Staying Up When the Currency Goes Down
- Streamlined coverage of Accounting for International Operations, with new examples such as Infosys and Nokia

Chapter 17: The Statement of Cash Flows

- *NEW* Vignette: drkoop.com's and MotherNature.com's cash flow problems
- *NEW* e-Accounting box: Cash Crunch Turns CDNow into CDThen

# TARGET STUDENT SUCCESS: THE TEACHING AND LEARNING PACKAGE

ACCOUNTING, FIFTH ED., OFFERS A COMPLETE TEACHING AND LEARNING PACKAGE TO PROVIDE STUDENTS AND INSTRUCTORS WITH THE BEST AIDS TO SUCCESS. AND DEPENDING ON HOW YOU TEACH YOUR COURSE, WE OFFER ACCOUNTING, FIFTH ED., IN SEVERAL VERSIONS: HARD COVER CHAPTERS 1–26; PAPERBACKS CHAPTERS 1–13 AND CHAPTERS 12–26; AND A NEW! HARDCOVER CHAPTERS 1–18, THE FINANCIAL ACCOUNTING CHAPTERS.

Instructor Resources

- Annotated Instructor's Edition
- Instructor's Manual and Video Guide
- Solutions Manual with Transparencies
- Four-Color Teaching Transparencies
- Test Item File
- Prentice Hall Test Manager
- *NEW Free* Instructor's CD-ROM (contains all print and technology resources on CD-ROM)
- Accounting and Taxation Services Hotline (call your PH representative for hotline number and e-mail address)
- Prentice Hall Accounting Faculty Directory (call your PH representative for information)

Student Resources

- *NEW Free* Target Annual Report
- *NEW* Student CD-ROM (contains all PowerPoint slides, tutorial, and general ledger software)
- *NEW Free e-BIZ: The Prentice Hall Guide to e-Business and e-Commerce in Accounting*
- *Free How to Study Accounting* Guidebook
- *NEW The Wall Street Journal* discount subscription offer
- *NEW* MoviesDoorToDoor.com by Mark Beasley and Frank Buckless
- Working Papers
- Study Guides
- Practice Sets

Technology Resources

- *NEW Free* Standard Online Distance Learning Course (WebCT, Blackboard, Pearson CourseCompass)
- *NEW* Premium Online Distance Learning Course (WebCT, Blackboard, Pearson CourseCompass)
- *NEW Free* myPHLIP companion Web site available at www.prenhall.com/horngren
- *Enhanced Free* ReEnforcer Tutorial Software*
- *Free* General Ledger Software*
- *Enhanced Free* Excel Spreadsheet Templates with Excel Tutorial
- *Free* Powerpoint Slides/Ready Notes*
- *NEW Free* "Getting Started with Peachtree" Guidebook
- *NEW Free* "Getting Started with QuickBooks" Guidebook
- *NEW Free* "Getting Started with Simply Accounting" Guidebook
- *NEW* Peachtree Software
- *NEW* Mastering Accounting CD-ROM
- *On Location!* Videos with *NEW segments on* Cisco, Nantucket Nectars (The Juice Guys!), Teva Sandals, Oracle, Amy's Ice Cream, and more
- PHACTS Tutorial Videos
- Accounting Made Easy CD-ROM (available in two CDs)

*All may be downloaded at no charge from the text Web site by adopters. These items are also available on our Student CD-ROM, at a nominal price, with text purchase.

TARGET STUDENT SUCCESS: ONLINE AND INTEGRATED COURSE SOLUTIONS

Online Courses

Are you interested in offering a complete and fully functional online course? Would you like to take advantage of existing technology to better communicate with your students, post supplementary course materials, or conduct online testing and grading?

As the leading college textbook publisher, Prentice Hall has formed close alliances with each of the leading online platform providers—Blackboard, WebCT, and our own Pearson CourseCompass.

Two Levels of Content

We offer two levels of content for most of our online principles of accounting courses:

Standard Courses

(Free with New Text Purchase)
Standard Courses include traditional online course features: online testing, course management and page tracking, communication (i.e., bulletin board, chat rooms, and e-mail), course information, calendar, Powerpoints, Gradebook, etc. Test questions for faculty use, along with sample quizzes and tests for students, are **pre-loaded** for ease of use. Both may be edited by an instructor.

Premium Courses

(Available at a Nominal Price with New Text Purchase)
Prentice Hall offers many distinctive features for our textbook adopters—**including the highest possible service** from our platform partners. For several of our online courses, including Horngren/Harrison/Bamber *Accounting*, fifth ed., the Premium course provides:

- **Rich, Prentice Hall custom-created** course and lecture materials
- **Custom-created PowerPoint slides with audio** to assist students in understanding key concepts
- **Unique video segments** for each text chapter feature an accounting faculty member experienced in conducting online courses, who shares insights with students that help them (1) better prepare to read the chapter and then (2) review the key concepts and takeaway lessons prior to taking an exam.

Each of these features is designed to personalize the course and enhance student understanding of the material.

myPHLIP

Welcome to myPHLIP — your personal guide to the FREE online resources for your book

Featuring one-click access to all the new materials created by our award-winning team of educators, myPHLIP provides a personalized view of the great new resources available:

- **myPHLIP pages**—your personal access page unites all your myPHLIP texts.
- **Notes**—add personal notes to our resources.
- **Messages**—send messages to individual students, or all students linked to your course.
- **Student Resources**—such as our PowerPoints, videos, and spreadsheets
- **Business Headlines**—provide links to articles in today's business news!
- **Search**—search all PHLIP resources for relevant articles and exercises.
- **Instructor Manual**—tips and suggestions for integrating PHLIP resources into your course.

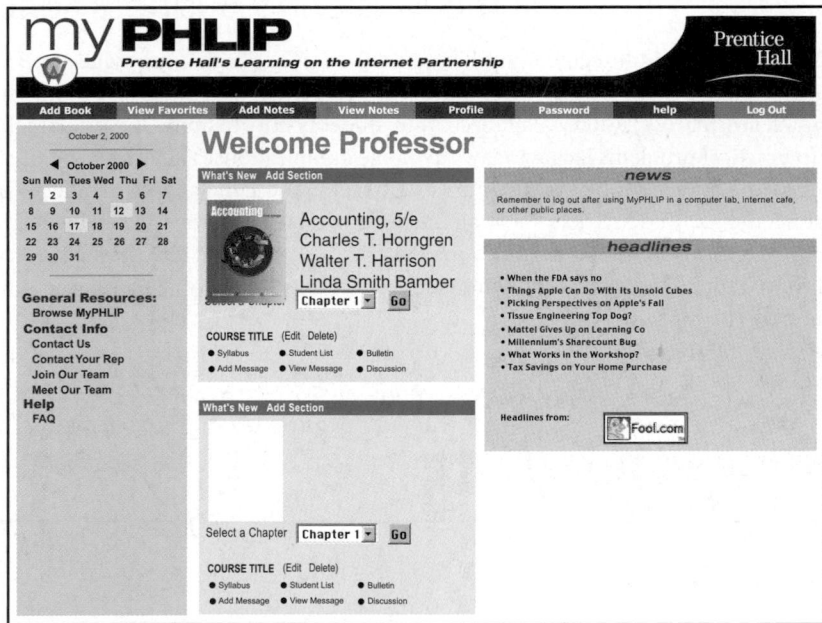

And of course you and your students will still have access to the original PHLIP resources you have trusted throughout the years to provide the best business education support available:

For Instructors

- In the News current events articles
- Teaching Resources
- Online faculty support
- Research Area
- Internet Resources
- What's New on your myPHLIP Web site

For the Student

1. In the News current events articles
2. Research Area
3. Internet Resources
4. Online Study Guide
5. Talk to the Tutor virtual office hours
6. Writing Resource Center
7. Career Center

MoviesDoorToDoor.com: How Accounting Helped Make the Difference

Mark Beasley and Frank Buckless, both of North Carolina State University

MoviesDoorToDoor.com is the fictional story of three college friends who sense a unique business opportunity. Although none of them majored in accounting, the book shows how accounting information is a key component of the major business decisions they make for their start-up business—one that enables customers to select and order videotape rentals via the Internet, which are then delivered direct to the customer's home. The book can be a supplementary reading assignment or a team project.

 ## The Mastering Business Series

Mastering Business is a multisegment, multimedia CD-ROM series that uses video and interactive exercises. The series covers all the core business disciplines. Through dramatic situations and rigorous exercises, the **Mastering Accounting** CD-ROM will teach your students how to apply the fundamental concepts of accounting to practical problems facing today's dynamic organizations. The Mastering Business series has been developed around an e-business startup, CanGo. By seeing the same people handle a variety of situations in each of the segments, students learn how all the areas of a business are affected by decisions such as making a new product, going public, and starting a new marketing campaign. The Mastering Accounting CD-ROM may be shrinkwrapped to this text for a nominal fee. Go to www.prenhall.com/accountingconnection for more details.

 # ACKNOWLEDGMENTS

Special thanks to

Student reviewers who provided us with quotable assessments of the book:
Patricia Colarusso, Luzerne County Community College
Lisa Cronauer, Saint Leo University
Carla Hillhouse, Middle Tennessee State University
Carrie Hupp, Middle Tennessee State University
JoAnne Jones, Macomb Community College
Pam Walsh, Oakland Community College

Professor Michael Bamber of the University of Georgia for help and support in preparing text and assignments

Professor Lynn Mazzola of Nassau Community College for her help in checking assignment material and reading the text of Chapters 19–26

Students Chaundolyn Johnson and Grant Rumsey, at the University of Georgia, for their help in checking assignments for Chapters 19–26

Professor Jean Hawkes of William Jewell College for revising the instructor's edition annotations

Writer Nancy Brandwein for the new e-Accounting boxes

Supplement Authors/Reviewers

Instructor's Manual and Video Guides

Betsy Willis, Baylor University
Becky Jones, Baylor University

Video Guides by Beverly Amer, Northern Arizona University

Study Guide

Stephen C. Schaefer, Contra Costa Community College

Allan D. Campbell, Saint Leo University

Mastering Accounting CD

Active Learning Technologies

Working Papers

Ellen Sweatt, Georgia Perimeter College

Anthony Dellarte, Luzerne County Community College

Solutions Manual and Solutions Transparencies

Charles T. Horngren, Stanford University
Walter T. Harrison, Baylor University

Linda Smith Bamber, University of Georgia

Technical Reviewers:

Robert Bauman, Allan Hancock College
Becky Jones, Baylor University
Betsy Willis, Baylor University
Thomas Hoar, Houston Community College

Lynn Mazzola, Nassau Community College
Blake Willis
Chaundolyn Johnson
Grant Rumsey

Test Item File

Alice B. Sineath, Forsyth Technical Community College

Sharie L. Dow, Saint Leo University Center for Online Learning

WIN PH Custom Test Manager

Alice B. Sineath and Engineering Software Associates

Student Resource CD-ROM

Instructor's Resource CD-ROM

PowerPoint Presentations by Olga Quintana, University of Miami
PHAS General Ledger by Lanny Nelms and Jean Insinga

PH ReEnforcer by Albert Oddo, Niagra Univeristy
Spreadsheet Templates by Albert Fisher, Community College of Southern Nevada

On Location Videos

Beverly Amer, Northern Arizona University

Companion Website PHLIP/COMPANION WEBSITE

Randy Kidd, Penn Valley Community College

OnLine Courses (WebCT, Blackboard, Pearson Course Compass)

Michele Bevan, Anthony Fortini, and Maryann Pionegro Carol, with special thanks to Nancy Welcher at Prentice Hall Business Publishing for her technical assistance.

Reviewers of ACCOUNTING, Fifth Ed.

Hicks E. Anderson Jr., Montreat College
Thomas Badley, Baker College
David S. Baglia, Grove City College
Robert C. Brush, Cecil Community College
David T. Collins, Bellarmine College
Joan E. Cook, Milwaukee Area Technical College
Kenneth P. Couvillion, San Joaquin Delta College
Ann S. DeCapite, Coastal Carolina College
Anthony J. Dellarte, Luzerne Community College
Joan Demko, Wor-Wic Community College
Mari Suzanne duToit, Okaloosa-Walton Community College
James J. Formosa, Nashville State Technical College
Sally W. Gilfillan, Longwood College
Shirley Glass, Macomb Community College
Janet L. Grange, Chicago State University
Susan S. Hamlen, State University of New York at Buffalo
Ken Harmon, Middle Tennessee State University
Steven Jackson, University of Southern Maine
Fred R. Jex, Macomb Community College
Peg Johnson, Metropolitan Community College

Thomas K. Y. Kam, Hawaii Pacific University
John E. Karayan, California State Polytechnic University, Pomona
Lynn R. Krausse, Bakersfield College
Steven P. Landry, University of Hawaii at Hilo
Suzanne Lowensohn, Barry University
Angelo Luciano, Columbia College-Chicago
Susan Murphy, Monroe Community College
Michael Palma, Gwinnett Technical Institute
William D. Parrish, Delgado Community College
James E. Racic, Lakeland Community College
Rodney R. Ridenour, Montana State University-Bozeman
E. Thomas Robinson, University of Alaska-Fairbanks
Barbara E. Roper, Chicago State University
Gerald W. Rosson, Lynchburg College
Robin D. Turner, Dabney S. Lancaster Community College
Scott Wallace, Blue Mountain Community College
Idalene Williams, Metropolitan Community College
Kitty Williams, Georgia Southern University
Lori S. Zulauf, Slippery Rock University

Focus Group Participants

Richard Ahrens, Los Angeles Pierce College
Charles Alvis, Winthrop University
Juanita Ardevany, Los Angeles Valley College
Patricia Ayres, Arapahoe Community College
David S. Baglia, Grove City College
Carl Ballard, Central Piedmont Community College
Maria Barillas, Phoenix College
James F. Benedum, Milwaukee Area Technical College
Dorcus Berg, Wingate College
Angela Blackwood, Belmont Abbey College
Gary R. Bower, Community College of Rhode Island
Jack Brown, Los Angeles Valley College
Virginia Brunell, Diablo Valley College
James Carriger, Ventura College
Stan Carroll, New York City Technical College
Janet Cassagio, Nassau Community College
Lester Chadwick, University of Delaware
Stanley Chu, Borough of Manhattan Community College
Kerry Colton, Aims Community College
Shaun Crayton, New York City Technical College
Susan Crosson, Santa Fe Community College
Donald Daggett, Mankato State University
Joneal W. Daw, Los Angeles Valley College
Lyle E. Dehning, Metropolitan State College
Wanda DeLeo, Winthrop University
Jim Donnelly, Bergen Community College
Bruce England, Massasoit Community College
Dave Fellows, Red Rocks Community College
Mike Foland, Southwestern Illinois College
Roger Gee, San Diego Mesa College
Martin Ginsberg, Rockland Community College
Earl Godfrey, Gardner Webb University
Edward S. Goodhart, Shippensburg University
Janet L. Grange, Chicago State University
Jean Gutmann, University of Southern Maine
Ralph W. Hernandez, New York City Technical College
Carl High, New York City Technical College
Mary Hill, University of North Carolina - Charlotte
Jean Insinga, Middlesex Community College
Fred R. Jex, Macomb Community College
Bernard Johnson, Santa Monica College
Diane G. Kanis, Bergen Community College

John Keelan, Massachusetts Bay Community College
Mary Thomas Keim, California State University - Bakersfield
Shirly A. Kleiner, Johnson County Community College
Cynthia Kreisner, Austin Community College
Raymond L. Larson, Appalachian State University
Cathy Larson, Middlesex Community College
Linda Lessing, SUNY College of Technology - Farmingdale
Angela Letourneau, Winthrop University
Frank Lordi, Widener University
Audra Lowray, New York City Technical College
Grace Lyons, Bergen Community College
Edward Malmgren, University of North Carolina - Charlotte
Paola Marocchi, New York City Technical College
Larry McCarthy, Slippery Rock University
Linda Spotts Michael, Maple Woods Community College
Greg Mostyn, Mission College
Kitty Nessmith, Georgia Southern University
Lee Nicholas, University of Northern Iowa
Terry Nunnelly, University of North Carolina - Charlotte
Alfonso R. Oddo, Niagara University
Margie Sinclair-Parish, Lewis & Clark Community College
Al Partington, Los Angeles Pierce College
Lynn Mazzola Paluska, Nassau Community College
Juan Perez, New York City Technical College
Ronald Pierno, University of Missouri
Geraldine Powers, Northern Essex Community College
Harry Purcell, Ulster County Community College
John Ribezzo, Community College of Rhode Island
Rosemarie Ruiz, York University
Stephen Schaefer, Contra Costa College
Parmar Sejal, Bergen Community College
Lynn Shoaf, Belmont Abbey College
Walter J. Silva, Roxbury Community College
Leon Singleton, Santa Monica College
David Skougstad, Metropolitan State College
Donna Sum, Prairie State College
Paul Sunko, Olive-Harvey College
Mary Ann Swindlehurst, Carroll Community College
Chandra Taylor, New York City Technical College
Phillip Thornton, Metropolitan State College
John L. Vaccaro, Bunker Hill Community College

Brief Contents

Contents

ACCOUNTING

Prologue: Careers in Accounting

Every organization uses accounting. The corner store keeps accounting records to measure its success selling groceries. The largest corporations need accounting to keep track of their locations, employees, and transactions. And all the dot.coms must account for their transactions. Why is accounting so important? Because it helps an organization the same way a model helps an architect construct a building. Accounting helps the manager understand the organization without drowning in its details.

Accounting offers exciting career opportunities. Accounting careers are usually divided into two areas: private accounting and public accounting.

PRIVATE ACCOUNTING

Private accountants work for a single business, such as a local department store, the **McDonald's** restaurant chain, or **Eastman Kodak Company.** Charitable organizations, educational institutions, and government agencies also employ private accountants. The chief accounting officer usually carries the title of controller, treasurer, or chief financial officer (CFO). This person often has the status of a vice president. Accountants who have met certain professional requirements in the area of management accounting are designated as *certified management accountants (CMAs)*.

Private accountants perform a wide variety of services:

- *Budgeting* sets sales and profit goals and develops detailed plans (called *budgets*) for achieving those goals. Some of the most successful companies in the United States have been pioneers in the field of budgeting—**Procter & Gamble** and **General Electric,** for example.
- *Information systems design* identifies the organization's information needs, both internal and external. Systems designers develop and implement information systems to meet those needs.
- *Cost accounting* analyzes a business's costs to help managers control expenses. Cost accounting records guide managers in pricing their products and services to achieve greater profits. Also, cost accounting information shows when a product is not profitable and should be dropped.
- *Internal auditing* is performed by a business's own accountants. Large organizations—**Motorola, Bank of America,** and **3M** among them—maintain a staff of internal auditors. These accountants evaluate the firm's accounting and management systems to improve operating efficiency and to ensure that employees follow company policies.

PUBLIC ACCOUNTING

Public accountants serve the general public and collect professional fees for their work, much as doctors and lawyers do. Public accountants are a small fraction (about 10%) of all accountants. Accountants who have met certain professional requirements in law, auditing, and accounting are designated as *certified public accountants (CPAs)*.

Like private accountants, public accountants provide valuable services:

- *Consulting* describes the wide scope of advice CPAs provide to help managers run a business. As accountants look deep into an organization, they find many ways to improve the business's operations. Accountants help their clients recruit executives, reorganize the business, and plan mergers with other companies.
- *Assurance* is the service of providing a professional statement that certain information is accurate. CPAs *audit*, or examine, the financial statements of companies and attest to the accuracy and completeness of the data in the statements. Auditors also examine companies' Web sites and provide statements that the information is accurate.
- *Tax accounting* has two aims: complying with the tax laws and minimizing the company's tax bill. Reducing the company's tax bill is an important management consideration. CPAs advise companies and individuals on what type of investments to make and how to structure transactions.

Some public accountants pool their talents and work together within a single firm. Most of their professional employees are CPAs. CPA firms vary greatly in size. Most are small businesses, but many are large partnerships. Exhibit P-1 gives data on the largest U.S. accounting firms.

Exhibit P-2 shows the accounting positions within public accounting firms and other organizations. Note the upward movement of accounting personnel, as indicated by the arrows. In particular, note how accountants may move from positions in public accounting firms to similar or higher positions in industry and government. This is a frequently traveled career path. Because accounting deals with all facets of an organization—such as purchasing, manufacturing, marketing, and distribution—it provides an excellent opportunity for gaining broad business experience.

During this term, you will learn how to use accounting to make business decisions. Consider a career in accounting as you work through this first course.

Rank (2000)	Firm Location	Net Revenue (in millions)	Partners	Number of Offices	Revenue per Partner (in millions)
1	Andersen Worldwide* New York	$7,824	2,117	92	$3.7
2	PricewaterhouseCoopers New York	$6,750	2,938	189	$2.3
3	Ernst & Young New York	$6,375	2,546	87	$2.5
4	Deloitte & Touche Wilton, Connecticut	$5,300	1,913	101	$2.8
5	KPMG New York	$4,656	1,800	136	$2.6
6	H&R Block Tax Services Kansas City, Missouri	$1,267	3,361	8,923	$0.4
7	Century Business Services** Cleveland, Ohio	$460	N/A	798	N/A
8	RSM McGladrey Bloomington, Minnesota	$381	369	65	$1.1
9	Grant Thornton Chicago	$375	274	48	$1.5
10	BDO Seidman Chicago	$298	335	42	$0.9

* During 2000, Andersen Worldwide separated into two firms: Arthur Andersen and Accenture.
** Unlike the other firms, Century Business Services is not a partnership.
Source: Adapted from *Accounting Today* (March 13–April 2, 2000), Special Supplement.

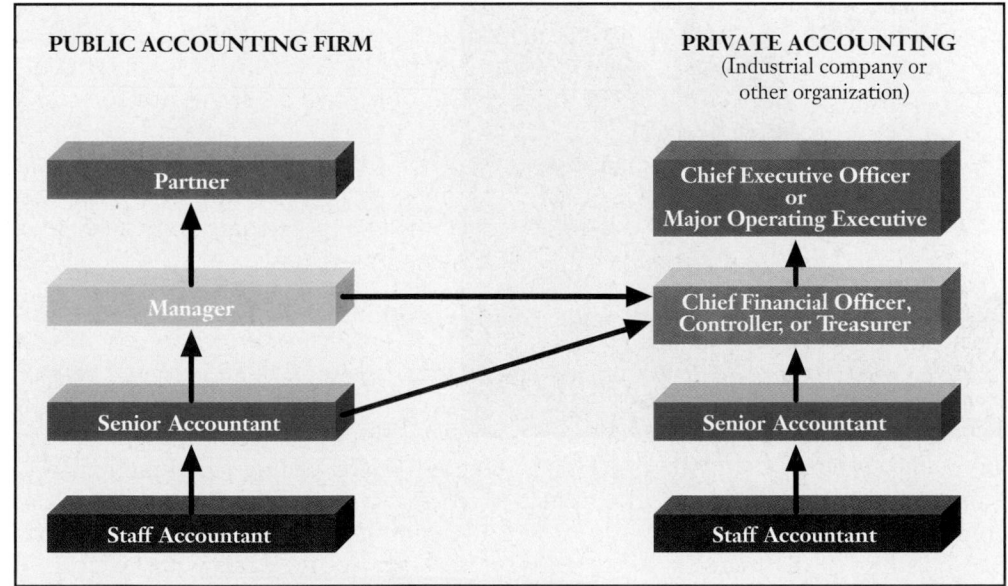

Accounting and the Business Environment

LEARNING OBJECTIVES

*After studying this chapter,
you should be able to*

1. Use accounting vocabulary

2. Apply accounting concepts and
   principles to business situations

3. Use the accounting equation to
   describe an organization's
   financial position

4. Use the accounting equation to
   analyze business transactions

5. Prepare and use the financial
   statements

6. Evaluate the performance of a
   business

www.prenhall.com/horngren

Readiness Assessment

Every three months, five Texas lawyers receive $25 million for their work in a lawsuit against the large tobacco companies. These attorneys proved in court that the tobacco companies withheld information that could have helped people make better decisions about whether to smoke. So far the attorneys have collected more than $400 million from the cigarette makers. With this new-found income, they are helping build a new law center for Baylor University, their college alma mater. How do the attorneys account for this legal income? How do they account for the donations to Baylor? The legal agreements require the tobacco companies to pay billions to the states and to their attorneys. How do the cigarette makers, such as **Philip Morris** and **American Brands,** account for these payments?

As you work through this book, you will learn how to account for the attorneys' earnings and for the tobacco companies' expenses. In this chapter, you'll see how one of the attorneys, Harold Nix, uses accounting to manage his practice. We begin the study of accounting with a small single-person business, known as a proprietorship. Many attorneys practice law alone as a proprietorship. Others, such as the "Texas tobacco lawyers," work in partnerships with other attorneys. The large tobacco companies are corporations, the most complex form of business organization. As you study accounting principles, you will also learn to account for the affairs of partnerships and corporations.

Let's begin our study by learning exactly what accounting is.

ACCOUNTING: THE BASIS FOR BUSINESS DECISIONS

Objective 1
Use accounting vocabulary

Accounting is the information system that measures business activities, processes that information into reports, and communicates the results to decision makers. Accounting is not the same as bookkeeping. *Bookkeeping* is a procedure in accounting, just as arithmetic is a procedure in mathematics. Accounting is often called "the language of business." The better you understand this language, the better your business decisions will be, and the better you can manage the financial aspects of living. Personal financial planning, education expenses, loans, car payments, income taxes, and investments are based on the information system that we call accounting.

ACCOUNTING. The information system that measures business activities, processes that information into reports, and communicates the results to decision makers.

A key product of an accounting system is a set of financial statements. **Financial statements** report on a business in monetary terms. Is my business making a profit? Should I hire assistants? Am I earning enough money to pay my rent? Answers to business questions like these are based on accounting information.

Today people use computers to do detailed bookkeeping—in households, businesses, and organizations of all types. Exhibit 1-1 illustrates the role of accounting in business. The process starts and ends with people making decisions.

FINANCIAL STATEMENTS. Documents that report on a business in monetary amounts, providing information to help people make informed business decisions.

Decision Makers: The Users of Accounting Information

Decision makers need information. The more important the decision, the greater the need for information. Virtually all businesses and most individuals keep accounting records to aid in making decisions.

INDIVIDUALS   People such as you use accounting information to manage bank accounts, evaluate job prospects, make investments, and decide whether to rent or buy a house. Harold Nix, one of the Texas tobacco lawyers, uses accounting information to manage his law office.

BUSINESSES   Business managers use accounting information to set goals for their organizations, to evaluate progress toward those goals, and to take corrective action if necessary. Decisions based on accounting information may include which building to purchase, how much merchandise to keep on hand, and how much cash to borrow.

EXHIBIT 1-1 The Accounting System: The Flow of Information

INVESTORS Investors provide the money a business needs to begin operations. To decide whether to invest in a company, potential investors evaluate what income they can expect from their investment. This means analyzing the financial statements of the business and keeping up with developments in the business press—for example, *The Wall Street Journal* and *Business Week.*

CREDITORS Before making a loan, creditors (lenders) such as banks determine the borrower's ability to meet scheduled payments. This evaluation includes a report on the borrower's financial position and a prediction of future operations, both of which are based on accounting information. To borrow from a bank before striking it rich, Harold Nix probably had to document his income and financial position.

GOVERNMENT REGULATORY AGENCIES Most organizations face government regulation. For example, the *Securities and Exchange Commission (SEC),* a federal agency, requires businesses to disclose certain financial information to the investing public.

TAXING AUTHORITIES Local, state, and federal governments levy taxes on individuals and businesses. Income tax is figured using accounting information. Businesses determine the sales tax they owe from accounting records that show how much they have sold.

NONPROFIT ORGANIZATIONS Nonprofit organizations—such as churches, hospitals, government agencies, and colleges—use accounting information in much the same way that profit-oriented businesses do.

OTHER USERS Employees and labor unions make wage demands based on employers' reported income. Consumer groups and the general public are also interested in the amount of income businesses earn. Newspapers report "improved profit pictures" for companies as the nation emerges from economic downturns. Such news, based on accounting information, has an effect on our standard of living.

Financial Accounting and Management Accounting

Users of accounting information may be categorized as *external users or internal users.* This distinction allows us to classify accounting into two fields—financial accounting and management accounting.

 Financial accounting focuses on information for people outside the firm. Creditors and outside investors, for example, are not part of the day-to-day management of the company. Government agencies and the general public are external users of a firm's accounting information. Chapters 2–18 of this book deal primarily with financial accounting.

FINANCIAL ACCOUNTING. The branch of accounting that focuses on information for people outside the firm.

Management accounting focuses on information for internal decision makers, such as top executives, department heads, college deans, and hospital administrators. Chapters 19–26 cover management accounting.

The Authority Underlying Accounting

In the United States, a private organization called the **Financial Accounting Standards Board (FASB)** determines how accounting is practiced. The FASB works with a governmental agency, the Securities and Exchange Commission (SEC), the American Institute of Certified Public Accountants (AICPA), and the Institute of Management Accountants (IMA), two large professional organizations of accountants. **Certified public accountants,** or **CPAs,** are accountants who are licensed to serve the general public rather than one particular company. **Certified management accountants,** or **CMAs,** are licensed accountants who work for a single company. The rules that govern public accounting information are called generally accepted accounting principles (GAAP). Exhibit 1-2 diagrams the relationships among the various accounting organizations.

MANAGEMENT ACCOUNTING. The branch of accounting that focuses on information for internal decision makers of a business.

FINANCIAL ACCOUNTING STANDARDS BOARD (FASB). The private organization that determines how accounting is practiced in the United States.

CERTIFIED PUBLIC ACCOUNTANT (CPA). A licensed accountant who serves the general public rather than one particular company.

CERTIFIED MANAGEMENT ACCOUNTANT (CMA). A licensed accountant who works for a single company.

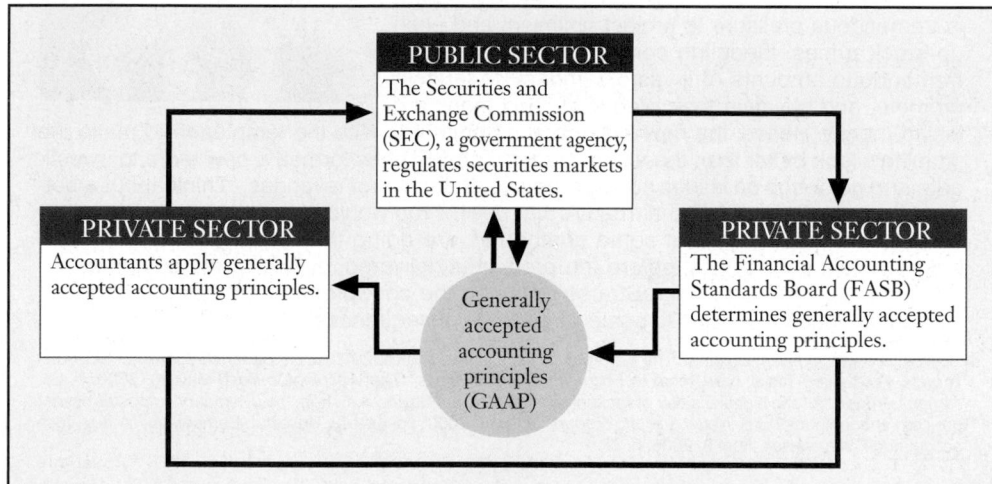

EXHIBIT 1-2 Key Accounting Organizations

Ethics in Accounting and Business

Ethical considerations pervade all areas of accounting and business. Consider a current situation: Tobacco companies are defendants in a large number of lawsuits. The managers of **Philip Morris, RJR Nabisco,** and **American Brands** have reason to downplay these lawsuits for fear investors will stop buying their stock and banks will stop lending them money. Should Philip Morris, RJR Nabisco, and American Brands disclose this sensitive information? Accounting guidelines require companies to describe such lawsuits in their financial statements. And each company's auditor is required to state whether the information each company reports to the public is adequate.

By what criteria do accountants address such ethical questions? The AICPA, other professional accounting organizations, and most large companies have codes of ethics that bind members and employees to high standards of ethical conduct.

Standards of Professional Conduct

The AICPA's Code of Professional Conduct for Accountants was adopted by its members to provide guidance to CPAs in their work. Ethical standards in accounting are designed to produce accurate information for decision making. The preamble to the Code states: "[A] certified public accountant assumes an obligation of self-discipline above and beyond the requirements of laws and regulations . . . [and] an unswerving commitment to honorable behavior. . . ."

The opening paragraph of the Standards of Ethical Conduct of the Institute of Management Accountants (IMA) states: "Management accountants have an

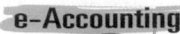

MicroStrategy: A Cautionary Tale for the New Economy

MicroStrategy illustrates both the tremendous rise of e-commerce and the accounting temptations that go with it. MicroStrategy was founded ten years ago as a data-mining software company, and the Internet helped its revenues soar. The company became a darling of Wall Street. In 12 months, the stock rose from $7.34 to $333 and turned its CEO, 35-year-old Michael Saylor, into one of the nation's youngest billionaires. Then boom: On March 20, 2000, MicroStrategy announced a change in accounting practices and the stock lost 60% of its value in one day. Suddenly 1999's profit of $12.6 million turned into a loss of around $40 million. Seems that MicroStrategy had been booking revenue for software contracts even though the revenue would be earned over a multi-year period.

In the frenzy accompanying the rise of e-commerce—estimated to reach $4 trillion by 2003—there is tremendous pressure to project optimism and push up stock prices. Fledgling companies are spending tremendous amounts of investors' money to launch, promote, and maintain their Web sites, and many are losing money. Hence, the new wizards of e-commerce face the temptation to make the financials look better than the actual results. The SEC has formed a new team to investigate and get tough on issues such as the overstatement of revenues. "Think about a bottle of fine wine," says SEC chairman Arthur Levitt: "You wouldn't pop the cork on that bottle before it was ready. But some companies are doing this—recognizing revenues before a sale is complete, before the product is delivered, or [while] the customer still [can] void . . . the sale." MicroStrategy popped the cork prematurely, and in so doing, alerted its dot.com cousins to some real-world consequences.

Sources: Based on Adam Zagorin, "The E-numbers game," *Time,* April 3, 2000, p. 66. Sandra Sugawara, "SEC Unit Targets Accounting Tricks; New Team to Focus on Cooked Books," *The Washington Post,* May 26, 2000, p. E5. James Lardner, "A tech highflier's day of reckoning: How Michael Saylor went from 'boy visionary' to poster boy for dot-com shenanigans," *U.S. News & World Report,* April 10, 2000, pp. 42–43. Robert J. Samuelson, "A high-tech accounting?" *Newsweek,* April 3, 2000, p. 37.

obligation to the organizations they serve, their profession, the public, and themselves to maintain the highest standards of ethical conduct." The requirements are similar to those in the AICPA code.

Most corporations also set standards of ethical conduct for their employees. For example, **The Boeing Company,** a leading manufacturer of aircraft, has a highly developed set of business conduct guidelines. In the introduction to those guidelines, the chairperson of the board and the chief executive officer state: "We owe our success as much to our reputation for integrity as we do to the quality and dependability of our products and services. This reputation is fragile and can easily be lost."

TYPES OF BUSINESS ORGANIZATIONS

A business takes one of three forms of organization. In some cases, accounting procedures depend on which form the organization takes. You should understand the differences among the three: proprietorships, partnerships, and corporations.

PROPRIETORSHIP. A business with a single owner.

PROPRIETORSHIPS A **proprietorship** has a single owner, called the proprietor, who is generally also the manager. Suppose the law office of Harold Nix started out as a proprietorship. Proprietorships tend to be small retail establishments or individual professional businesses, such as those of physicians, attorneys, and accountants. From the accounting viewpoint, each proprietorship is distinct from its proprietor: The accounting records of the proprietorship do *not* include the proprietor's personal financial records.

PARTNERSHIPS A **partnership** joins two or more individuals together as co-owners. Each owner is a partner. Mr. Nix's law firm will become a partnership if Nix takes on a partner. Many retail establishments, as well as some professional organizations of physicians, attorneys, and accountants, are partnerships. Most partnerships are small or medium-sized, but some are gigantic, exceeding 2,000 partners. Accounting treats the partnership as a separate organization, distinct from the personal affairs of each partner.

CORPORATIONS A **corporation** is a business owned by **stockholders,** or shareholders, people who own stock (shares of ownership) in the business. A business becomes a corporation when the state approves its articles of incorporation. A corporation is a legal entity, an "artificial person" that conducts its business in its own name. Like the proprietorship and the partnership, the corporation is an organization with an existence separate from its owners.

Corporations differ significantly from proprietorships and partnerships in one very important way. If a proprietorship or a partnership cannot pay its debts, lenders can take the owners' personal assets—cash and belongings—to satisfy the business's obligations. But if a corporation goes bankrupt, lenders cannot take the personal assets of the stockholders. This *limited personal liability* of stockholders for corporate debts partly explains why corporations are the dominant form of business organization: People can invest in corporations with limited personal risk.

Another factor in corporate growth is the division of ownership into individual shares. **The Coca-Cola Company,** for example, has 3.5 billion shares of stock owned by many stockholders. An investor with no personal relationship either to the corporation or to any other stockholder can become a co-owner by buying 30, 100, 5,000, or any number of shares of its stock.

Exhibit 1-3 summarizes the differences among the three types of business organization.

PARTNERSHIP. A business with two or more owners.

CORPORATION. A business owned by stockholders; it begins when the state approves its articles of incorporation. A corporation is a legal entity, an "artificial person," in the eyes of the law.

STOCKHOLDER. A person who owns stock in a corporation. Also called a **shareholder.**

EXHIBIT 1-3 **Comparison of the Three Forms of Business Organization**

	Proprietorship	Partnership	Corporation
1. Owner(s)	Proprietor—there is only one owner	Partners—there are two or more owners	Stockholders—there are generally many owners
2. Life of the organization	Limited by the owner's choice, or death	Limited by the owners' choices, or death	Indefinite
3. Personal liability of the owner(s) for the business's debts	Proprietor is personally liable	Partners are personally liable	Stockholders are not personally liable
4. Accounting status of the organization	The proprietorship is separate from the proprietor	The partnership is separate from the partners	The corporation is separate from the stockholders

ACCOUNTING CONCEPTS AND PRINCIPLES

Accounting follows certain guidelines. The rules that govern how accountants measure, process, and communicate financial information fall under the heading **GAAP,** which stands for **generally accepted accounting principles.** GAAP is the "law" of accounting—rules for conducting behavior in a way acceptable to the majority of people.

GAAP rests on a conceptual framework written by the FASB: *The primary objective of financial reporting is to provide information useful for making investment and lending decisions.* To be useful, information must be relevant, reliable, and comparable. We begin the discussion of GAAP by introducing basic accounting concepts and principles.

Objective 2
Apply accounting concepts and principles to business situations

GENERALLY ACCEPTED ACCOUNTING PRINCIPLES (GAAP). Accounting guidelines, formulated by the Financial Accounting Standards Board, that govern how accountants measure, process, and communicate financial information.

The Entity Concept

The most basic concept in accounting is that of the **entity.** An accounting entity is an organization or a section of an organization that stands apart as a separate economic unit. In accounting, boundaries are drawn around each entity so as not to confuse its affairs with those of other entities.

Consider Harold Nix, one of the Texas lawyers. Think back to when Nix was starting out as a young lawyer, fresh out of law school. Suppose he began his law practice with $5,000 obtained from a bank loan. Following the entity concept, Nix would account for the $5,000 separately from his personal assets, such as his clothing, house, and automobile. To mix the $5,000 of business cash with his personal assets would make it difficult to measure the financial position of Nix's business.

Consider **Toyota,** a huge organization with several divisions. Toyota management evaluates each division as a separate accounting entity. If sales in the Lexus division are dropping, Toyota can find out why. If sales figures from all divisions of the company are combined, management will not know that Lexus sales are going down. Thus, the entity concept also applies to the parts of a large organization—in fact, *to any economic unit that needs to be evaluated separately.*

The Reliability (Objectivity) Principle

Accounting records and statements are based on the most reliable data available so that they will be accurate and useful. This guideline is the *reliability principle,* also called the *objectivity principle.* Reliable data are verifiable. They may be confirmed by any independent observer. For example, Harold Nix's $5,000 bank loan is supported by a promissory note. This is objective evidence of the loan. Ideally, accounting records are based on information that flows from activities documented by objective evidence. Without the reliability principle, accounting data might be based on whims and opinions.

Suppose you want to open a stereo shop. For a store location, you transfer a small building to the business. You believe the building is worth $155,000. To confirm its cost to the business, you hire two real estate appraisers, who value the building at $147,000. Which is the more reliable estimate of the building's value, your estimate of $155,000 or the $147,000 professional appraisal? The appraisal of $147,000 is more reliable because it is supported by an independent, objective observation. The business should record the building cost as $147,000.

The Cost Principle

The *cost principle* states that acquired assets and services should be recorded at their actual cost (also called *historical cost*). Even though the purchaser may believe the price is a bargain, the item is recorded at the price paid in the transaction and not at the "expected" cost. Suppose your stereo shop purchases equipment from a supplier who is going out of business. Assume that you get a good deal and pay only $2,000 for equipment that would have cost you $3,000 elsewhere. The cost principle requires you to record the equipment at its actual cost of $2,000, not the $3,000 that you believe the equipment is worth.

The cost principle also holds that the accounting records should maintain the historical cost of an asset for as long as the business holds the asset. Why? Because cost is a reliable measure. Suppose your store holds the stereo equipment for six months. During that time, stereo prices rise, and the equipment can be sold for $3,500. Should its accounting value—the figure "on the books"—be the actual cost of $2,000 or the current market value of $3,500? According to the cost principle, the accounting value of the equipment remains at actual cost, $2,000.

The Going-Concern Concept

Another reason for measuring assets at historical cost is the *going-concern concept,* which holds that the entity will remain in operation for the foreseeable future. Most firm resources—such as supplies, land, buildings, and equipment—are acquired to use rather than to sell. Under the going-concern concept, accountants assume that the business will remain in operation long enough to use existing resources for their intended purpose.

To understand the going-concern concept better, consider the alternative, which is to go out of business. A store that is holding a Going-Out-of-Business Sale is trying to sell all its holdings. In that case, instead of historical cost, the relevant measure is current market value. Going out of business, however, is the exception rather than the rule.

The Stable-Monetary-Unit Concept

In the United States, we record transactions in dollars because the dollar is the medium of exchange. British accountants record transactions in pounds sterling, and the Japanese record transactions in yen. The value of a dollar or a Mexican peso changes over time. A rise in the price level is called *inflation*. During inflation, a dollar will purchase less milk, less toothpaste, and less of other goods. When prices are stable—when there is little inflation—a dollar's purchasing power is also stable.

Accountants assume that the dollar's purchasing power is stable. The *stable-monetary-unit concept* is the basis for ignoring the effect of inflation in accounting. It allows us to add and subtract dollar amounts as though each dollar has the same purchasing power as any other dollar at any other time.

 DAILY EXERCISE 1-1

You are considering the purchase of land for future expansion. The seller is asking $50,000 for land that cost her $35,000. An appraisal shows a value of $47,000. You first offer $44,000. The seller counter-offers with $48,000, and you agree on a price of $46,000. What dollar value for this land is reported on your financial statements? Which accounting concept or principle guides your answer?

Answer: According to the *cost principle*, assets and services should be recorded at their actual cost. You paid $46,000 for the land. Therefore, $46,000 is the cost to report on your financial statements.

THE ACCOUNTING EQUATION

Financial statements tell how a business is performing and where it stands. They are the final product of the accounting process. But how do we produce the financial statements? The basic tool of accounting is the **accounting equation.** It presents the resources of the business and the claims to those resources.

Assets and Liabilities

Assets are the economic resources of a business that are expected to be of benefit in the future. Cash, office supplies, merchandise, furniture, land, and buildings are assets.

Claims to those assets come from two sources. **Liabilities** are *outsider* claims, which are economic obligations—debts—payable to outsiders. These outside parties are called *creditors*. For example, a creditor who has loaned money to a business has a claim—a legal right—to a part of the assets until the business pays the debt. *Insider* claims to the business's assets are called **owner's equity,** or **capital.** These are the claims held by the owners of the business. Owners have a claim to the entity's assets because they have invested in the business.

The accounting equation shows the relationship among assets, liabilities, and owner's equity. Assets appear on the left-hand side of the equation. The legal and economic claims against the assets—the liabilities and owner's equity—appear on the right-hand side of the equation. As Exhibit 1-4 shows, the two sides must be equal:

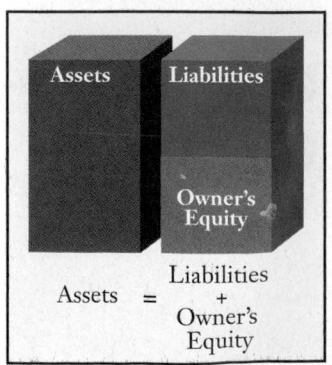
(Economic Resources)   *(Claims to Economic Resources)*

ASSETS   =   LIABILITIES + OWNER'S EQUITY

Let's take a closer look at the elements that make up the accounting equation. Suppose you run Top Cut Meats, which supplies beef to **McDonald's** and other restaurants. Some customers pay you in cash when you deliver the meat. Cash is an asset. Other customers buy on credit and promise to pay you within a certain time after delivery. This promise is also an asset because it is an economic resource that will benefit you in the future, when you receive the cash. To Top Cut Meats, this promise is an **account receivable.** A *written* promise for future collection is called a **note receivable.** McDonald's promise to pay you for the meat it purchases on credit creates a debt for McDonald's. This liability is an **account payable** of McDonald's— the debt is not written. Instead, it is backed by the reputation and the credit standing of McDonald's. A written promise of future payment is called a **note payable.** All receivables are assets. All payables are liabilities.

Owner's Equity

Owner's equity is the amount of an entity's assets that remain after the liabilities are subtracted.

$$\text{ASSETS} - \text{LIABILITIES} = \text{OWNER'S EQUITY}$$

The purpose of business is to increase owner's equity through **revenues,** which are increases in owner's equity earned by delivering goods or services to customers. Revenues increase owner's equity because they increase the business's assets or decrease its liabilities. As a result, the owner's share of business assets increases. Exhibit 1-5 shows that owner investments and revenues increase the owner's equity of the business.

EXHIBIT 1-5
Transactions That Increase or Decrease Owner's Equity

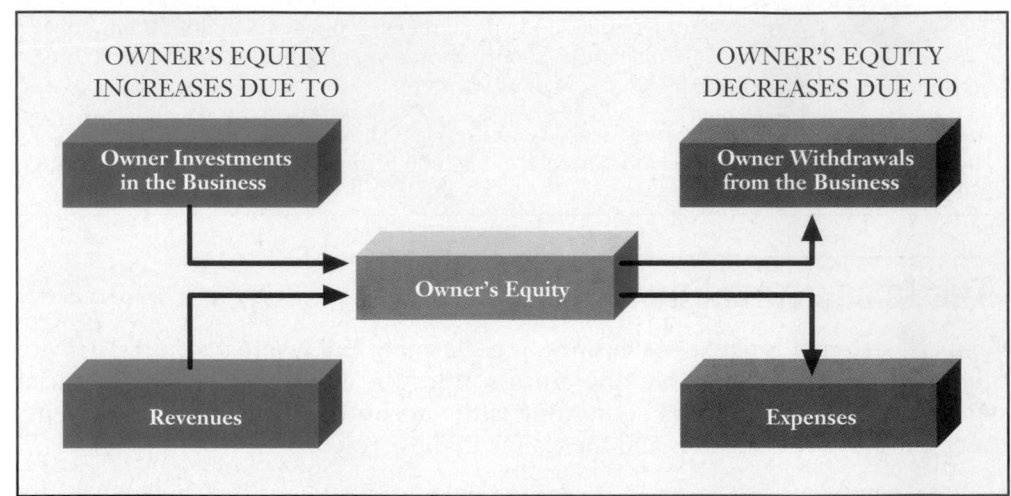

DAILY EXERCISE 1-2

OWNER WITHDRAWALS. Amounts removed from the business by an owner.

EXPENSE. Decrease in owner's equity that occurs from using assets or increasing liabilities in the course of delivering goods or services to cus-tomers.

DAILY EXERCISE 1-3

DAILY EXERCISE 1-4

Exhibit 1-5 also indicates the types of transactions that decrease owner's equity. **Owner withdrawals** are amounts removed from the business by the owner. Withdrawals are the opposite of owner investments. **Expenses** are decreases in owner's equity that occur from using assets or increasing liabilities in the course of delivering goods and services to customers. Expenses are the cost of doing business and are the opposite of revenues. Expenses include

- office rent
- salaries of employees
- newspaper advertisements
- utility payments

- interest on loans
- insurance
- property taxes

WORK IT OUT

1. If the assets of a business are $174,300 and the liabilities total $82,000, how much is the owner's equity?
2. If the owner's equity in a business is $22,000 and the liabilities are $36,000, how much are the assets?

Answers: To answer both questions, use the accounting equation:

1.

ASSETS	–	LIABILITIES	=	OWNER'S EQUITY
$174,300	–	$82,000	=	$92,300

2.

ASSETS	=	LIABILITIES	+	OWNER'S EQUITY
$58,000	=	$36,000	+	$22,000

ACCOUNTING FOR BUSINESS TRANSACTIONS

In accounting terms, a **transaction** is any event that *both* affects the financial position of the business entity *and* can be recorded reliably. Many events can affect a company, including (1) elections, (2) economic booms and downturns, (3) purchases and sales of merchandise inventory, (4) payment of rent, and (5) collection of cash from customers. But an accountant records only those events with effects that can be measured reliably. Which of these events would an accountant record? The answer is events (3), (4), and (5), because their dollar amounts can be measured reliably. The accountant would not record events (1) and (2) because the dollar effects of elections and economic trends cannot be measured reliably.

TRANSACTION. An event that affects the financial position of a particular entity and can be recorded reliably.

To illustrate accounting for a business, let's use Gay Gillen eTravel. Gillen operates a travel agency that offers service in two ways. Some customers phone or e-mail Gay Gillen eTravel. Other customers do business with the travel agency strictly online. On-line customers plan and pay for their trips through the Gillen Web site. The Web site is linked to airlines, hotels, and cruise lines, so clients can obtain the latest information 24 hours a day, 7 days a week. Gillen's Web site allows the agency to transact more business than would be possible through phone calls, fax, or e-mail. As a result, Gillen is able to operate with fewer employees, and this saves on operating expenses. She passes along the cost savings to clients by charging them lower commissions. It is a win/win situation for both parties. Gillen provides more service and generates a nice profit. Customers save on travel costs.

Now let's analyze Gillen eTravel's transactions.

TRANSACTION 1: STARTING THE BUSINESS Gay Gillen invests $30,000 of her own money to begin the business. Specifically, she deposits $30,000 in a bank account entitled Gay Gillen eTravel. The effect of this transaction on the accounting equation of the Gay Gillen eTravel business entity is

Objective 4
Use the accounting equation to analyze business transactions

Assets	=	Liabilities	+	Owner's Equity	Type of Owner's Equity Transaction
Cash				Gay Gillen, Capital	
(1) +30,000				+30,000	*Owner investment*

For every transaction, the amount on the left side of the equation must equal the amount on the right side. The first transaction increases both the assets (in this case, Cash) and the owner's equity of the business (Gay Gillen, Capital). To the right of the transaction, we write "Owner investment" to keep track of the reason for the effect on the owner's equity.

TRANSACTION 2: PURCHASE OF LAND Gillen purchases land for an office location, paying cash of $20,000. The effect of this transaction on the accounting equation is

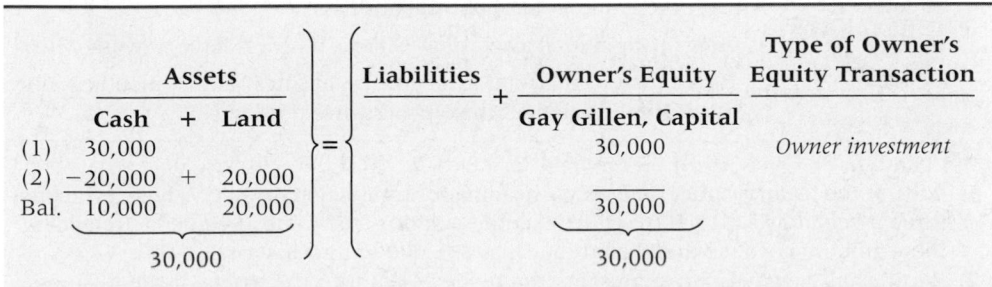

	Assets		=	Liabilities	+	Owner's Equity	Type of Owner's Equity Transaction
	Cash	+ Land				Gay Gillen, Capital	
(1)	30,000					30,000	*Owner investment*
(2)	−20,000	+ 20,000					
Bal.	10,000	20,000				30,000	
	30,000					30,000	

 DAILY EXERCISE 1-5

 DAILY EXERCISE 1-6

The cash purchase of land increases one asset, Land, and decreases another asset, Cash, by the same amount. After the transaction is completed, Gillen's business has cash of $10,000, land of $20,000, no liabilities, and owner's equity of $30,000. Note that the sums of the balances (abbreviated Bal.) on both sides of the equation must always be equal.

TRANSACTION 3: PURCHASE OF OFFICE SUPPLIES Gillen buys stationery and other office supplies, agreeing to pay $500 within 30 days. This transaction increases both the assets and the liabilities of the business. Its effect on the accounting equation is

	Assets				Liabilities	+	Owner's Equity
	Cash	+ Office Supplies +	Land		Accounts Payable	+	Gay Gillen, Capital
Bal.	10,000		20,000	=			30,000
(3)		+500			+500		
Bal.	10,000	500	20,000		500		30,000
		30,500				30,500	

Office Supplies is an asset, not an expense, because the supplies can be used in the future. The liability created by this transaction is an account payable. Recall that a *payable* is a liability.

TRANSACTION 4: EARNING OF SERVICE REVENUE Gay Gillen eTravel earns service revenue by providing travel services for clients. She earns $5,500 revenue and collects this amount in cash. The effect on the accounting equation is an increase in the asset Cash and an increase in Gay Gillen, Capital, as follows:

	Assets				Liabilities +	Owner's Equity	Type of Owner's Equity Transaction
	Cash +	Office Supplies +	Land		Accounts Payable +	Gay Gillen, Capital	
Bal.	10,000	500	20,000	=	500	30,000	
(4)	+5,500	—				+5,500	*Service revenue*
Bal.	15,500	500	20,000		500	35,500	
		36,000				36,000	

⊙ DAILY EXERCISE 1-7

This revenue transaction caused the business to grow, as shown by the increases in total assets and in the sum of total liabilities plus owner's equity. A company that sells goods to customers is a merchandising business. Its revenue is called *sales revenue*. By contrast, Gay Gillen and Harold Nix, the attorney, perform services for clients; their revenue is called *service revenue*.

WORK IT OUT

Gillen's travel business has now completed four business transactions. Answer these questions about the business:

1. How much in total assets does Gillen's business have to work with?
2. How much of the total assets of the business does Gillen actually own? How much does the business owe outsiders?

Answers

1. Look at the balances under the Assets heading for transaction 4. Gillen's business owns three assets: Cash ($15,500), Office Supplies ($500), and Land ($20,000). By adding these amounts, we see that the business has $36,000 in total assets.
2. Recall that *owner's equity* represents the owner's claim to the assets of the business. Gillen's owner's equity is $35,500.
   Liabilities are the amounts that a business owes to outsiders. After transaction 4, the company owes $500 in liabilities.

TRANSACTION 5: EARNING OF SERVICE REVENUE ON ACCOUNT Gillen performs services for clients who do not pay immediately. In return for her travel services, Gillen receives clients' promises to pay $3,000 within one month. This promise is an asset to Gillen, an account receivable because she expects to collect the cash in the future. In accounting, we say that Gillen performed this service *on account*. When the business performs service for a client, the business earns revenue whether it receives cash now or expects to collect the cash later. This $3,000 of service revenue increases the wealth of Gillen's business just like the $5,500 of revenue that she collected immediately in transaction 4. Gillen records an increase in the asset Accounts Receivable and an increase in owner's equity as follows:

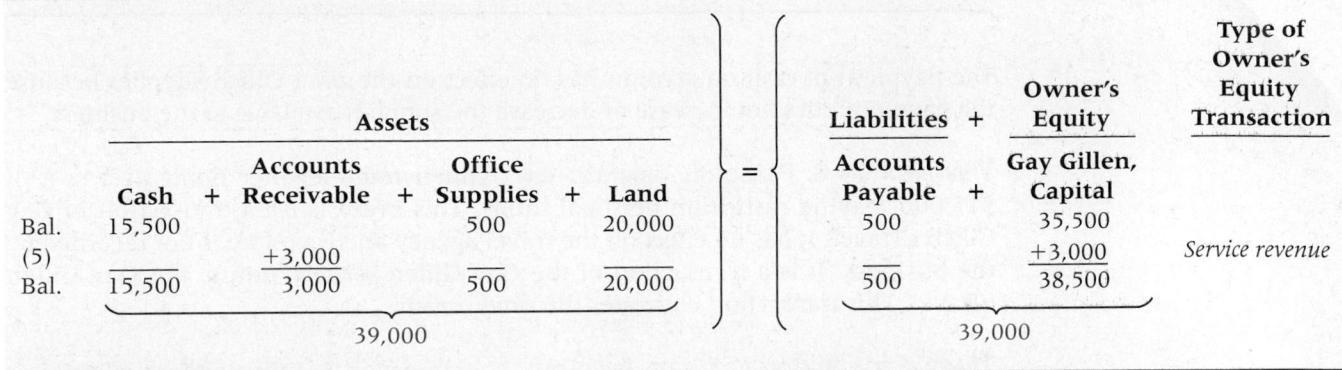

		Assets				=	Liabilities	+	Owner's Equity		Type of Owner's Equity Transaction
	Cash	+	Accounts Receivable	+	Office Supplies	+	Land	=	Accounts Payable	+	Gay Gillen, Capital	
Bal.	15,500				500		20,000		500		35,500	
(5)			+3,000								+3,000	*Service revenue*
Bal.	15,500		3,000		500		20,000		500		38,500	
				39,000							39,000	

TRANSACTION 6: PAYMENT OF EXPENSES During the month, Gillen pays $3,100 in cash expenses: lease expense on a computer, $400; office rent, $1,100; employee salary, $1,200 (part-time assistant); and utilities, $400. The effects on the accounting equation are:

	Assets							=	Liabilities	+	Owner's Equity	Type of Owner's Equity Transaction
	Cash	+	Accounts Receivable	+	Office Supplies	+	Land	=	Accounts Payable	+	Gay Gillen, Capital	
Bal.	15,500		3,000		500		20,000		500		38,500	
	− 400										− 400	*Lease expense, computer*
(6)	− 1,100										− 1,100	*Rent expense, office*
	− 1,200										− 1,200	*Salary expense*
	− 400										− 400	*Utilities expense*
Bal.	12,400		3,000		500		20,000		500		35,400	
				35,900							35,900	

Because expenses have the opposite effect of revenues, they cause the business to shrink, as shown by the smaller balances of total assets and owner's equity.

Each expense should be recorded in a separate transaction. They are listed together here for simplicity. We could record the cash payment in a single amount for the sum of the four expenses, $3,100 ($400 + $1,100 + $1,200 + $400). In all cases, the "balance" of the equation holds, as we know it must.

Businesspeople, Gay Gillen included, run their businesses to have more revenues than expenses. An excess of total revenues over total expenses is called **net income, net earnings,** or **net profit.** If total expenses exceed total revenues, the result is a **net loss.**

TRANSACTION 7: PAYMENT ON ACCOUNT Gillen pays $300 to the store from which she purchased $500 worth of office supplies in transaction 3. In accounting, we say that she pays $300 *on account*. The effect on the accounting equation is a decrease in the asset Cash and a decrease in the liability Accounts Payable as shown at the top of page16.

NET INCOME. Excess of total revenues over total expenses. Also called **net earnings** or **net profit.**

NET LOSS. Excess of total expenses over total revenues.

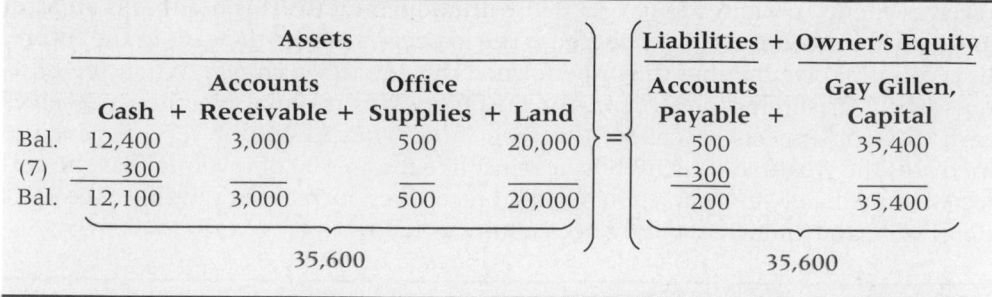

	Assets				Liabilities + Owner's Equity	
	Cash +	Accounts Receivable +	Office Supplies +	Land	Accounts Payable +	Gay Gillen, Capital
Bal.	12,400	3,000	500	20,000	500	35,400
(7)	− 300				−300	
Bal.	12,100	3,000	500	20,000	200	35,400
		35,600				35,600

The payment of cash on account has no effect on the asset Office Supplies because the payment does not increase or decrease the supplies available to the business.

TRANSACTION 8: PERSONAL TRANSACTION Gillen remodels her home at a cost of $15,000, paying cash from personal funds. This event is *not* a transaction of Gay Gillen eTravel. It has no effect on the travel agency and therefore is not recorded by the business. It is a transaction of the Gay Gillen *personal* entity, not Gay Gillen eTravel. This transaction illustrates the *entity concept.*

TRANSACTION 9: COLLECTION ON ACCOUNT In transaction 5, Gillen performed services for a client on account. The business now collects $1,000 from the client. We say that Gillen collects the cash *on account.* Gillen will record an increase in the asset Cash. Should she also record an increase in service revenue? No, because she already recorded the revenue when she earned it in transaction 5. The phrase "collect cash on account" means to record an increase in Cash and a decrease in the asset Accounts Receivable. The effect on the accounting equation of Gay Gillen eTravel is:

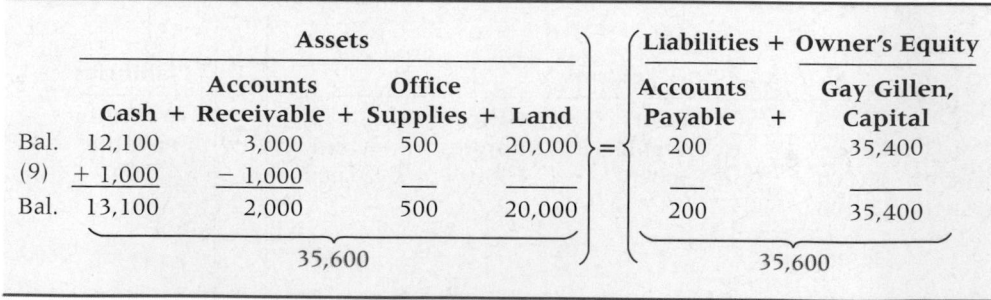

	Assets				Liabilities + Owner's Equity	
	Cash +	Accounts Receivable +	Office Supplies +	Land	Accounts Payable +	Gay Gillen, Capital
Bal.	12,100	3,000	500	20,000	200	35,400
(9)	+ 1,000	− 1,000				
Bal.	13,100	2,000	500	20,000	200	35,400
		35,600				35,600

DAILY EXERCISE 1-8

Total assets are unchanged from the preceding transaction's total. Why? Because Gillen merely exchanged one asset for another. Also, total liabilities and owner's equity are unchanged.

TRANSACTION 10: SALE OF LAND An individual approaches Gillen about selling land owned by the travel agency. Gillen and the other person agree to a sale price of $9,000, which is equal to Gillen's cost of the land. Gillen's business sells the land and receives $9,000 cash. The effect on the accounting equation of the travel agency is as follows:

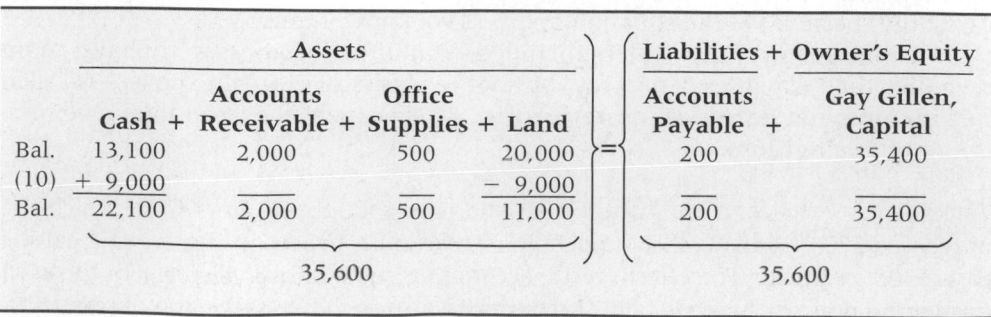

	Assets				Liabilities + Owner's Equity	
	Cash +	Accounts Receivable +	Office Supplies +	Land	Accounts Payable +	Gay Gillen, Capital
Bal.	13,100	2,000	500	20,000	200	35,400
(10)	+ 9,000			− 9,000		
Bal.	22,100	2,000	500	11,000	200	35,400
		35,600				35,600

TRANSACTION 11: WITHDRAWING OF CASH Gillen withdraws $2,100 cash ~~~ business for personal use. The effect on the accounting equation is

		Assets				Liabilities	+	Equ... Type of ...ner's Equity ...nsaction
	Cash	+	**Accounts Receivable**	+	**Office Supplies**	+	**Land**	=	**Accounts Payable**	+	**Gay Gillen...r Capital**
Bal.	22,100		2,000		500		11,000		200		35,400	
(11)	− 2,100										− 2,100	Owner
Bal.	20,000		2,000		500		11,000		200		33,300	...wal

33,500   33,500

Gillen's withdrawal of $2,100 cash decreases the asset Cash and also the owner's equity of the business. *The withdrawal does not represent a business expense because the cash is used for personal affairs.* We record this decrease in owner's equity as Withdrawals or as Drawings. The double underlines below each column indicate a final total.

EVALUATING BUSINESS TRANSACTIONS

Exhibit 1-6 on page 18 summarizes the 11 preceding transactions. Panel A lists the details of the transactions, and Panel B presents the analysis. As you study the exhibit, note that every transaction maintains the equality

ASSETS = LIABILITIES + OWNER'S EQUITY

THE FINANCIAL STATEMENTS

After analyzing transactions, we need a way to present the results. We look now at the *financial statements,* the formal reports of an entity's financial information. The primary financial statements are the

- income statement
- statement of owner's equity
- balance sheet
- statement of cash flows

INCOME STATEMENT The **income statement** presents a summary of an entity's revenues and expenses for a specific period of time, such as a month or a year. The income statement, also called the **statement of earnings** or **statement of operations,** is like a video—it presents a moving financial picture of business operations during the period. The income statement holds one of the most important pieces of information about a business—its *net income,* or revenues minus expenses. If expenses exceed revenues, there is a net loss for the period.

STATEMENT OF OWNER'S EQUITY The **statement of owner's equity** presents a summary of the changes that occurred in the entity's *owner's equity* during a specific time period, such as a month or a year. Increases in owner's equity arise from investments by the owner and from net income earned during the period. Decreases result from owner withdrawals and from a net loss for the period. Net income or net loss come directly from the income statement. Owner investments and withdrawals are capital transactions between the business and its owner, so they do not affect the income statement.

BALANCE SHEET The **balance sheet** lists all the entity's assets, liabilities, and owner's equity as of a specific date, usually the end of a month or a year. The balance sheet is like a snapshot of the entity. For this reason, it is also called the **statement of financial position.**

STATEMENT OF CASH FLOWS The **statement of cash flows** reports the amount of cash coming in (cash receipts) and the amount of cash going out (*cash payments* or

INCOME STATEMENT. Summary of an entity's revenues, expenses, and net income or net loss for a specific period. Also called the **statement of earnings** or the **statement of operations.**

STATEMENT OF OWNER'S EQUITY. Summary of the changes in an entity's owner's equity during a specific period.

BALANCE SHEET. List of an entity's assets, liabilities, and owner's equity as of a specific date. Also called the **statement of financial position.**

STATEMENT OF CASH FLOWS. Reports cash receipts and cash payments during a period.

EXHIBIT 1-6 Analy.. ansactions

PANEL A

...000 cash in the business.
... for land.
(1) Giller... office supplies on account.
(2) Paid ...500 cash from clients for service revenue earned.
(3) Bo.. travel service for clients on account, $3,000.
(4) ..h expenses: computer lease, $400; office rent, $1,100; employee salary, $1,200; utilities, $400.
(5) $300 on the account payable created in transaction 3.
(6) ...modeled Gillen's personal residence. This is *not* a transaction of the business.
... Collected $1,000 on the account receivable created in transaction 5.
.0) Sold land for cash at its cost of $9,000.
(11) Withdrew $2,100 cash for personal expenses.

PANEL B—Analysis of Transactions

	Cash	+	Accounts Receivable	+	Office Supplies	+	Land				Accounts Payable	+	Gay Gillen, Capital	Type of Owner's Equity Transaction
(1)	+30,000												+30,000	Owner investment
Bal.	30,000												30,000	
(2)	−20,000						+20,000							
Bal.	10,000						20,000						30,000	
(3)					+500						+500			
Bal.	10,000				500		20,000				500		30,000	
(4)	+ 5,500												+ 5,500	Service revenue
Bal.	15,500				500		20,000				500		35,500	
(5)			+3,000										+ 3,000	Service revenue
Bal.	15,500		3,000		500		20,000				500		38,500	
	− 400							=					− 400	Lease expense, computer
(6)	− 1,100												− 1,100	Rent expense, office
	− 1,200												− 1,200	Salary expense
	− 400												− 400	Utilities expense
Bal.	12,400		3,000		500		20,000				500		35,400	
(7)	− 300										−300			
Bal.	12,100		3,000		500		20,000				200		35,400	
(8)	Not a transaction of the business													
(9)	+ 1,000		−1,000											
Bal.	13,100		2,000		500		20,000				200		35,400	
(10)	+ 9,000						− 9,000							
Bal.	22,100		2,000		500		11,000				200		35,400	
(11)	− 2,100												− 2,100	Owner withdrawal
Bal.	20,000		2,000		500		11,000				200		33,300	

Assets   **Liabilities +**   **Owner's Equity**

33,500   33,500

disbursements) during a period. Business activities result in a net cash inflow (receipts greater than payments) or a net cash outflow (payments greater than receipts). The statement of cash flows shows the net increase or net decrease in cash during the period and the cash balance at the end of the period. (We cover the statement of cash flows in greater depth in Chapter 17.)

Financial Statement Headings

Each financial statement has a heading giving the name of the business (in our discussion, Gay Gillen eTravel), the name of the particular statement, and the date or time period covered by the statement. A balance sheet taken at the end of year 20X1 would be dated December 31, 20X1. A balance sheet prepared at the end of March 20X3 is dated March 31, 20X3.

An income statement or a statement of owner's equity that covers an annual period ended in December 20X5 is dated "Year Ended December 31, 20X5." A monthly income statement or statement of owner's equity for September 20X4 has in its heading "Month Ended September 30, 20X4," "For the Month Ended September 30, 20X4," or "For the Month of September 20X4." Income is meaningless unless identified with a particular time period.

Software programs such as Quick Books and Peachtree have streamlined the preparation of the financial statements. These statements can now be produced instantaneously after the financial records are entered into the computer. Of course, any errors in the financial records will show up in the financial statements. So the person who analyzes the data controls the accuracy of the financial statements.

Relationships Among the Financial Statements

Objective 6
Evaluate the performance of a business

Exhibit 1-7 illustrates all four financial statements. Their data come from the transaction analysis in Exhibit 1-6, which covers the month of April 20X1. Study the exhibit carefully. Specifically, observe the following in Exhibit 1-7:

1. The *income statement* for the month ended April 30, 20X1
   a. Reports all revenues and all expenses during the period. Expenses are listed in decreasing order of amount, with the largest expense first.
   b. Reports *net income* of the period if total revenues exceed total expenses, as in the case of Gay Gillen eTravel's operations for April. If total expenses exceed total revenues, a *net loss* is reported instead.
2. The *statement of owner's equity* for the month ended April 30, 20X1
   a. Opens with the owner's capital balance at the beginning of the period.
   b. Adds *investments by the owner* and adds net income (or subtracts net loss, as the case may be). Net income or net loss come directly from the income statement (see arrow ① in Exhibit 1–7).
   c. Subtracts withdrawals by the owner. Parentheses indicate a subtraction.
   d. Ends with the owner's capital balance at the end of the period.
3. The *balance sheet* at April 30, 20X1
   a. Reports all assets, all liabilities, and owner's equity at the end of the period.
   b. Reports that total assets equal the sum of total liabilities plus total owner's equity.
   c. Reports the owner's ending capital balance, taken directly from the statement of owner's equity (see arrow ②).
4. The *statement of cash flows* for the month ended April 30, 20X1
   a. Reports cash flows from three types of business activities (*operating, investing,* and *financing activities*) during the month.
   - *Operating activities* are cash receipts from revenues and cash payments of expenses.
   - *Investing activities* are the results of purchasing and selling the long-term assets that the business uses for operations.
   - *Financing activities* are the cash receipts from people who finance the organization (the owner and the lenders), and also payments back to those people.
   Each category of cash-flow activities includes both cash receipts, which are positive amounts, and cash payments, which are negative amounts (denoted by parentheses). Each category results in a net cash inflow or a net cash outflow for the period. We discuss these categories in detail in later chapters.
   b. Reports a net increase in cash during the month and ends with the cash balance at April 30, 20X1. This is the amount of cash to report on the balance sheet (see arrow ③).

EXHIBIT 1-7
**Financial Statements of
Gay Gillen eTravel**

GAY GILLEN ETRAVEL
Income Statement
Month Ended April 30, 20X1

Revenue		
Service revenue		$8,500
Expenses:		
Salary expense	$1,200	
Rent expense, office	1,100	
Lease expense, computer	400	
Utilities expense	400	
Total expenses		3,100
Net income		$5,400

①

GAY GILLEN ETRAVEL
Statement of Owner's Equity
Month Ended April 30, 20X1

Gay Gillen, capital, April 1, 20X1	$ 0	
Add: Investments by owner	30,000	
Net income for the month	5,400	
	35,400	
Less: Withdrawals by owner	(2,100)	
Gay Gillen, capital, April 30, 20X1	$33,300	

②

GAY GILLEN ETRAVEL
Balance Sheet
April 30, 20X1

Assets		Liabilities	
Cash	$20,000	Accounts payable	$ 200
Accounts receivable	2,000		
Office supplies	500	**Owner's Equity**	
Land	11,000	Gay Gillen, capital	33,300
		Total liabilities and	
Total assets	$33,500	owner's equity	$33,500

③

GAY GILLEN ETRAVEL
Statement of Cash Flows*
Month Ended April 30, 20X1

Cash flows from **operating** activities:		
Receipts:		
Collections from customers ($5,500 + $1,000)		$ 6,500
Payments:		
To suppliers ($1,100 + $400 + $400 + $300)	$ (2,200)	
To employees	(1,200)	(3,400)
Net cash inflow from operating activities		3,100
Cash flows from **investing** activities:		
Acquisition of land	$(20,000)	
Sale of land	9,000	
Net cash outflow from investing activities		(11,000)
Cash flows from **financing** activities:		
Investment by owner	$ 30,000	
Withdrawal by owner	(2,100)	
Net cash inflow from financing activities		27,900
Net increase in cash		20,000
Cash balance, April 1, 20X1		0
Cash balance, April 30, 20X1		$20,000

*Chapter 17 explains how to prepare this statement.

The Decision Guidelines feature summarizes the chapter in terms of decisions businesspeople must make. Decision Guidelines appear in each chapter of this book. They serve as useful summaries of the decision-making process in business.

DECISION GUIDELINES

Major Business Decisions

DECISION	GUIDELINES
How to organize the business?	If a single owner—a *proprietorship*.
	If two or more owners, but not incorporated—a *partnership*.
	If the business issues stock to stockholders—a *corporation*.
What to account for?	Account for the business, a separate entity apart from its owner *(entity concept)*.
	Account for transactions and events that affect the business and can be measured objectively *(reliability principle)*.
How much to record for assets and liabilities?	Actual historical amount *(cost principle)*.
How to organize the various effects of a transaction?	The accounting equation:
	$$\text{Assets} = \text{Liabilities} + \text{Owner's Equity}$$
How to measure profits and losses?	Income statement:
	$$\text{Revenues} - \text{Expenses} = \text{Net Income (or Net Loss)}$$
Did owner's equity increase or decrease?	Statement of owner's equity:
	Beginning capital
	+ Owner investments
	+ Net income (or − Net loss)
	− Owner withdrawals
	= Ending capital
Where does the business stand financially?	Balance sheet (accounting equation):
	$$\text{Assets} = \text{Liabilities} + \text{Owner's Equity}$$
Where did the business's cash come from? Where did cash go?	Statement of cash flows
	Operating activities Net cash inflow (or outflow)
	+ *Investing activities* Net cash inflow (or outflow)
	+ *Financing activities* Net cash inflow (or outflow)
	= Net increase (decrease) in cash

REVIEW ACCOUNTING AND THE BUSINESS ENVIRONMENT

SUMMARY PROBLEM

Jill Smith opens an apartment-location business near a college campus. She is the sole owner of the proprietorship, which she names Campus Apartment Locators. During the first month of operations, July 20X1, she engages in the following transactions:
a. Smith invests $35,000 of personal funds to start the business.
b. She purchases on account office supplies costing $350.
c. Smith pays cash of $30,000 to acquire a lot next to the campus. She intends to use the land as a future building site for her business office.
d. Smith locates apartments for clients and receives cash of $1,900.
e. She pays $100 on the account payable she created in transaction (b).
f. She pays $2,000 of personal funds for a vacation.
g. She pays cash expenses for office rent, $400, and utilities, $100.
h. The business sells office supplies to another business for its cost of $150.
i. Smith withdraws cash of $1,200 for personal use.

www.prenhall.com/horngren
End-of-Chapter Assessment

1. Analyze the preceding transactions in terms of their effects on the accounting equation of Campus Apartment Locators. Use Exhibit 1-6 as a guide, but show balances only after the last transaction.
2. Prepare the income statement, statement of owner's equity, and balance sheet of the business after recording the transactions. Use Exhibit 1-7 as a guide.

Solution

Requirement 1

PANEL A—Details of transactions

(a) Smith invested $35,000 cash to start the business.
(b) Purchased $350 of office supplies on account.
(c) Paid $30,000 to acquire land as a future building site.
(d) Earned service revenue and received cash of $1,900.
(e) Paid $100 on account.
(f) Paid for a personal vacation, which is not a transaction of the business.
(g) Paid cash expenses for rent, $400, and utilities, $100.
(h) Sold office supplies for cost of $150.
(i) Withdrew $1,200 cash for personal use.

PANEL B—Analysis of transactions:

			Assets				Liabilities	+	Owner's Equity	Type of Owner's Equity Transaction
	Cash	+	Office Supplies	+	Land		Accounts Payable	+	Jill Smith, Capital	
(a)	+35,000								+35,000	Owner investment
(b)			+350				+350			
(c)	−30,000				+30,000					
(d)	+ 1,900								+ 1,900	Service revenue
(e)	− 100						−100			
(f)	Not a transaction of the business									
(g)	− 400								− 400	Rent expense
	− 100								− 100	Utilities expense
(h)	+ 150		−150							
(i)	− 1,200								− 1,200	Owner withdrawal
Bal.	5,250		200		30,000		250		35,200	

35,450 = 35,450

Requirement 2   **Financial Statements of Campus Apartment Locators**

CAMPUS APARTMENT LOCATORS
Income Statement
Month Ended July 31, 20X1

Revenue:		
Service revenue...............		$1,900
Expenses:		
Rent expense...................	$400	
Utilities expense	100	
Total expenses		500
Net income.........................		$1,400

CAMPUS APARTMENT LOCATORS
Statement of Owner's Equity
Month Ended July 31, 20X1

Jill Smith, capital, July 1, 20X1	$ 0	
Add: Investment by owner	35,000	
Net income for the month	1,400	
	36,400	
Less: Withdrawals by owner	(1,200)	
Jill Smith, capital, July 31, 20X1	$35,200	

CAMPUS APARTMENT LOCATORS
Balance Sheet
July 31, 20X1

Assets		Liabilities	
Cash	$ 5,250	Accounts payable	$ 250
Office supplies	200		
Land	30,000	**Owner's Equity**	
		Jill Smith, capital	35,200
		Total liabilities and	
Total assets	$35,450	owner's equity	$35,450

LESSONS LEARNED

1. **Use accounting vocabulary.** Accounting is an information system for measuring, processing, and communicating financial information. As the "language of business," accounting helps a wide range of decision makers.

2. **Apply accounting concepts and principles to analyze business situations.** *Generally accepted accounting principles (GAAP)* guide accountants in their work. Accountants use the entity concept to keep the business's records separate from other economic units. Other important guidelines are the *reliability principle*, the *cost principle*, the *going-concern concept*, and the *stable-monetary-unit concept*.

3. **Use the accounting equation to describe an organization's financial position.** In its most common form, the accounting equation is

    Assets = Liabilities + Owner's Equity

4. **Use the accounting equation to analyze business transactions.** A transaction is any event that both affects the financial position of a business entity and can be reliably recorded. Transactions affect a business's assets, liabilities, and owner's equity.

5. **Prepare and use the financial statements.** The *financial statements* communicate information for decision making by an entity's managers, owners, and creditors and by government agencies. The *income statement* summarizes the entity's operations in terms of revenues earned and expenses incurred during a specific period. The *statement of owner's equity* reports the changes in owner's equity during the period. The *balance sheet* lists the entity's assets, liabilities, and owner's equity at a specific time. The *statement of cash flows* reports the cash receipts and the cash payments during the period.

6. **Evaluate the performance of a business.** High net income indicates success in business; net loss indicates a bad business year.

ACCOUNTING VOCABULARY

Accounting has a special vocabulary and it is important that you understand the following terms. They are explained in the chapter and also in the glossary at the end of the book.

account payable (p. 12)
account receivable (p. 12)
accounting (p. 5)
accounting equation (p. 11)
asset (p. 11)
balance sheet (p. 17)
capital (p. 11)
certified management accountant (CMA) (p. 7)
certified public accountant (CPA) (p. 7)
corporation (p. 9)

entity (p. 10)
expense (p. 12)
financial accounting (p. 6)
Financial Accounting Standards Board (FASB) (p. 7)
financial statements (p. 5)
generally accepted accounting principles (GAAP) (p. 9)
income statement (p. 17)
liability (p. 11)
management accounting (p. 7)
net earnings (p. 15)

net income (p. 15)
net loss (p. 15)
net profit (p. 15)
note payable (p. 12)
note receivable (p. 12)
owner's equity (p. 11)
owner withdrawals (p. 12)
partnership (p. 9)
proprietorship (p. 8)
revenue (p. 12)
shareholder (p. 9)
statement of cash flows (p. 17)

statement of earnings (p. 17) statement of operations (p. 17) stockholder (p. 9)
statement of financial position statement of owner's equity transaction (p. 13)
(p. 17) (p. 17)

QUESTIONS

1. Distinguish between accounting and bookkeeping.
2. Identify five users of accounting information, and explain how they use it.
3. What organization formulates generally accepted accounting principles? Is this organization a government agency?
4. Why are ethical standards important in accounting? Which organization directs its standards toward independent auditors? Which organization directs its standards more toward management accountants?
5. Why is the entity concept so important to accounting?
6. Briefly describe the reliability principle.
7. What role does the cost principle play in accounting?
8. If *assets = liabilities + owner's equity*, then how can liabilities be expressed?
9. Explain the difference between an account receivable and an account payable.

10. Give a more descriptive title for the balance sheet. What feature of the balance sheet gives this financial statement its name?
11. Give another title for the income statement. Which financial statement is like a snapshot of the entity at a specific time? Which financial statement is like a video of the entity's operations during a period of time?
12. What information does the statement of owner's equity report?
13. Give a synonym for the owner's equity of a proprietorship.
14. What piece of information flows from the income statement to the statement of owner's equity? What information flows from the statement of owner's equity to the balance sheet? What balance sheet item is explained by the statement of cash flows?

ASSESS YOUR PROGRESS

DAILY EXERCISES

Applying accounting concepts and principles
(Obj. 2)

DE1-1 Suppose you are starting a business, Montvale Delivery Service, that will provide delivery services for law firms in your city. In organizing the business and setting up its accounting records, consider the following:

1. In keeping the books of the business, you must decide the amount to record for assets purchased and liabilities incurred. At what amount should you record assets and liabilities? Which accounting concept or principle provides guidance?
2. Should you account for your personal assets and personal liabilities along with the assets and the liabilities of the business, or should you keep the two sets of records separate? Why? Which accounting concept or principle provides guidance?

Explaining assets, liabilities, owner's equity
(Obj. 1)

DE1-2 Shortly after starting Gifts for You, you realize the need for a bank loan in order to purchase office equipment. In evaluating your loan request, the banker asks about the assets and liabilities of your business. In particular, he wants to know the amount of your owner's equity. In your own words, explain the differences among *assets, liabilities,* and *owner's equity.* Give the mathematical relationship among assets, liabilities, and owner's equity.

Explaining revenues, expenses
(Obj. 1)

DE1-3 Gay Gillen eTravel has been open for one year, and Gillen wants to know the amount of the business's profit (net income) or net loss for the year. First, she must identify the revenues earned and the expenses incurred during the year. What are *revenues* and *expenses?* How do revenues and expenses enter into the determination of net income or net loss? Review the definitions on page 12 and Exhibit 1-7 on page 20.

Using the accounting equation
(Obj. 3)

DE1-4 You begin Montvale Delivery Service by investing $2,000 of your own money in a business bank account. Before starting operations, you borrow $8,000 cash by signing a note payable to Summit Bank. Write the business's accounting equation (page 12) after completing these transactions.

Using the accounting equation
(Obj. 3)

DE1-5 Brenda Trujillo owns Town East Travel, near the campus of Birmingham College. The business has cash of $5,000 and furniture that cost $12,000. Debts include accounts payable of $1,000 and a $6,000 note payable. How much equity does Trujillo have in the business? Using Trujillo's figures, write the accounting equation (page 11) of the travel agency.

Analyzing transactions
(Obj. 4)

DE1-6 Review transaction 2 of Gay Gillen eTravel, on page 13. In that transaction, Gillen's business purchased land for $20,000. To buy the land, Gillen was obligated to pay for it. Why, then, did she record no liability in this transaction?

Analyzing transactions
(Obj. 4)

DE1-7 Study Gay Gillen's transaction 4 on page 14. Gillen recorded revenues she earned from providing travel planning services for clients. Suppose the amount of revenue earned in transaction 4 was $3,500 instead of $5,500. How much are the business's cash and total assets after the transaction? How much is Gay Gillen, Capital?

DE1-8 Review transaction 9 of Gay Gillen eTravel, on page 16. Gillen collected cash from a client for whom she had provided travel services earlier. Why did the travel agency not record any revenue in transaction 9?

Analyzing transactions (Obj. 4)

DE1-9 Return to Gay Gillen's first business transaction on page 13. Gillen deposited $30,000 in a business bank account to start her company (assume Gillen started on April 2, 20X1). Prepare the travel agency's balance sheet on April 2, 20X1, immediately after the first transaction. The figures are given on page 13, and Exhibit 1-7 (page 20), shows the format of the balance sheet.

Preparing a balance sheet (Obj. 5)

Note: This exercise shows that financial statements can be prepared at any time. Usually, however, they are prepared at the end of the accounting period.

DE1-10 Examine Exhibit 1-6 on page 18. The exhibit summarizes the transactions of Gay Gillen eTravel for the month of April 20X1. Suppose Gillen has completed only the first seven transactions and needs a bank loan on April 21, 20X1. The vice president of the bank requires financial statements to support all loan requests.

Preparing the financial statements (Obj. 5)

Prepare the income statement, statement of owner's equity, and balance sheet that Gay Gillen would present to the banker after completing the first seven transactions on April 21, 20X1. Exhibit 1-7, page 20, shows the format of these financial statements.

DE1-11 Gay Gillen wishes to know how well her business performed during April. The income statement in Exhibit 1-7, page 20, helps answer this question. Write the formula for the income statement as an equation: $X - Y = Z$. What are X, Y, and Z?

Format of the income statement (Obj. 5)

DE1-12 Examine Exhibit 1-7 on page 20. The exhibit gives the financial statements of Gay Gillen eTravel at the end of the company's first month of operations. Focus on the arrows that show the flow of information from statement to statement, and then answer these questions:

Using the financial statements (Obj. 5)

1. Which statement measures net income or net loss? Into which other statement does net income flow? That is, where is net income's final resting place in the financial statements?
2. Which statement lists the assets, liabilities, and owner's equity of the business? Which of these elements is most directly affected by net income?

DE1-13 Return to Exhibit 1-7 on page 20, which gives the financial statements of Gay Gillen eTravel, at April 30, 20X1. Suppose Gay Gillen's travel agency paid Salary Expense of $2,500 for April instead of the actual amount of $1,200.

Evaluating performance (Obj. 6)

1. What would be the amount of the business's net income or net loss for April?
2. What would be the amount of Gay Gillen's capital at April 30?
3. What would be the ending amount of cash at April 30?

DE1-14 Exhibit 1-7, page 20, gives the statement of cash flows of Gay Gillen eTravel for the month of April. Study the exhibit and answer these questions to solidify your understanding of the accounting process and the financial statements:

Using the statement of cash flows (Obj. 5)

1. The statement of cash flows is organized in terms of three categories of *activities*. What are the three main categories of cash-flow activities?
2. Why do you think collections from customers is an operating activity? Why is the acquisition of land an investing activity? Why is the business's receipt of cash from the investment by the owner a financing activity? Answer in your own words.
3. How does the statement of cash flows relate to the balance sheet?

DE1-15 Montvale Delivery Service has just completed operations for the year ended December 31, 20X3. This is the third year of operations for the company. As the proprietor, you want to know how well the business performed during the year. You also wonder where the business stands financially at the end of the year. To address these questions, you have assembled the following data:

Preparing the income statement (Obj. 5)

Salary expense	$32,000	Insurance expense	$ 4,000
Accounts payable	8,000	Service revenue	101,000
Owner, capital,		Accounts receivable	17,000
December 31, 20X2	13,000	Supplies expense	1,000
Supplies	2,000	Cash	16,000
Withdrawals by owner	36,000	Fuel expense	6,000
Rent expense	8,000		

Prepare the income statement of Montvale Delivery Service for the year ended December 31, 20X3. Follow the format shown in Exhibit 1-7, page 20.

DE1-16 Use the data in Daily Exercise 1-15 to prepare the statement of owner's equity of Montvale Delivery Service for the year ended December 31, 20X3. Follow the format in Exhibit 1-7. Compute net income from the data in Daily Exercise 1-15.

Preparing the statement of owner's equity (Obj. 5)

DE1-17 Use the data in Daily Exercise 1-15 to prepare the balance sheet of Montvale Delivery Service at December 31, 20X3. The year-end balance sheet will show where the business stands financially at the end of the year. Follow the format in Exhibit 1-7. Owner's equity (Owner, capital) at December 31, 20X3, is $27,000.

Preparing the balance sheet (Obj. 5)

Note: Daily Exercise 1-18 should be used in conjunction with Daily Exercises 1-15, 1-16, and 1-17.

Evaluating performance
(Obj. 6)

DE1-18 Review the Montvale Delivery Service financial statements that you prepared for Daily Exercises 1-15, 1-16, and 1-17. Use the statements to evaluate the business's performance by answering these questions:

1. The income statement gives the results of operations. Did the business earn a profit or suffer a loss? The owner had hoped to earn at least $40,000. Will he be pleased or disappointed?
2. The statement of owner's equity reveals whether the owner's capital increased or decreased during the year—and why. Did Montvale Delivery Service's equity increase or decrease? Is this a good sign or a bad sign about the company? State your reason.
3. The balance sheet reports the financial position of the business. Which are greater, total assets or total liabilities? By how much? What is the name of the difference between assets and liabilities? Is the financial position of Montvale Delivery Service strong or weak? Give your reason.

EXERCISES

Explaining the income statement
and the balance sheet
(Obj. 1)

E1-1 Lisa Malesovas publishes a travel magazine. In need of cash, she asks Community Bank & Trust for a loan. The bank's procedures require borrowers to submit financial statements to show likely results of operations for the first year and likely financial position at the end of the first year. With little knowledge of accounting, Malesovas doesn't know how to proceed. Explain to her the information provided by the balance sheet and the income statement. Indicate why a lender would require this information.

Business transactions
(Obj. 2)

E1-2 For each of the following items, give an example of a business transaction that has the described effect on the accounting equation:

a. Increase an asset and increase a liability.
b. Increase one asset and decrease another asset.
c. Decrease an asset and decrease owner's equity.
d. Decrease an asset and decrease a liability.
e. Increase an asset and increase owner's equity.

Transaction analysis
(Obj. 2)

E1-3 Sterling Design, a proprietorship (Eric Sterling, owner), experienced the following events. State whether each event (1) increased, (2) decreased, or (3) had no effect on the total assets of the business. Identify any specific asset affected.

a. Sterling Design received a cash investment from the owner.
b. Cash purchase of land for a building site.
c. Paid cash on accounts payable.
d. Purchased machinery and equipment for a manufacturing plant; signed a promissory note in payment.
e. Performed service for a customer on account.
f. Sterling withdrew cash from the business for personal use.
g. Received cash from a customer on account receivable.
h. Sterling used personal funds to purchase a swimming pool for his home.
i. Sold land for a price equal to the cost of the land; received cash.
j. Borrowed money from the bank.

Accounting equation
(Obj. 3)

E1-4 Compute the missing amount in the accounting equation for each entity:

	Assets	Liabilities	Owner's Equity
Company A	$?	$61,800	$34,400
Company B	65,900	?	34,000
Company C	81,700	79,800	?

Accounting equation
(Obj. 4, 5)

E1-5 Oracle Corporation started 19X9 with total assets of $5,819 million and total liabilities of $2,861 million. At the end of 19X9, Oracle's total assets stood at $7,260 million, and total liabilities were $3,565 million.

Required

1. Did the owners' equity of Oracle Corporation increase or decrease during 19X9? By how much?
2. Identify two possible reasons for the change in owners' equity of Oracle during the year.

E1-6 Telemarketing Associates' balance sheet data at May 31, 20X2, and June 30, 20X2, follow:

Accounting equation
(Obj. 4, 5)

	May 31, 20X2	June 30, 20X2
Total assets	$150,000	$195,000
Total liabilities	109,000	131,000

Required

Following are three assumptions about investments and withdrawals by the owner of the business during June. For each assumption, compute the amount of net income or net loss of the business during June 20X2.

1. The owner invested $5,000 in the business and made no withdrawals.
2. The owner made no additional investments in the business but withdrew $11,000 for personal use.
3. The owner invested $41,000 in the business and withdrew $6,000 for personal use.

E1-7 Indicate the effects of the following business transactions on the accounting equation. Transaction (a) is answered as a guide.

Transaction analysis
(Obj. 4)

  a. Received cash of $18,000 from the owner, who was investing in the business.
    Answer: Increase asset (Cash)
              Increase owner's equity (Capital)
  b. Paid $700 cash to purchase office supplies.
  c. Performed legal service for a client on account, $3,000.
  d. Purchased on account office furniture at a cost of $500.
  e. Received cash on account, $900.
  f. Paid cash on account, $250.
  g. Sold land for $12,000, which was our cost of the land.
  h. Performed legal service for a client and received cash of $680.
  i. Paid monthly office rent of $500.

E1-8 Lance Huber opens a medical practice. During the first month of operation, May, the business, entitled Lance Huber, M.D., experienced the following events.

Transaction analysis; accounting equation
(Obj. 2, 4)

May 6	Huber invested $90,000 in the business by opening a bank account in the name of Lance Huber, M.D.
9	Huber paid $55,000 cash for land. He plans to build an office building on the land.
12	He purchased medical supplies for $2,000 on account.
15	Huber officially opened for business.
15–31	During the rest of the month, he treated patients and earned service revenue of $7,000, receiving cash.
15–31	He paid cash expenses: employees' salaries, $1,400; office rent, $1,000; utilities, $300.
28	He sold supplies to another physician for the cost of those supplies, $500.
31	He paid $1,500 on account.

Required

Analyze the effects of these events on the accounting equation of the medical practice of Lance Huber, M.D. Use a format similar to that of Exhibit 1-6, with headings for Cash; Medical Supplies; Land; Accounts Payable; and Lance Huber, Capital.

E1-9 The analysis of the transactions that Sinclair Leasing completed during its first month of operations follows. The company buys equipment that it leases out to earn revenue. The owner of the business made only one investment to start the business and no withdrawals.

Business organization, transactions, and net income
(Obj. 1, 2, 3, 4)

	Cash	+	Accounts Receivable	+	Lease Equipment	=	Accounts Payable	+	Owner Capital
(a)	+50,000								+50,000
(b)	− 750				+ 750				
(c)					+100,000		+100,000		
(d)			+800						+ 800
(e)	− 2,000								− 2,000
(f)	+ 6,600								+ 6,600
(g)	−10,000						− 10,000		
(h)	+ 150		−150						

Required

1. Describe each transaction of Sinclair Leasing.
2. If these transactions fully describe the operations of Sinclair Leasing during the month, what was the amount of net income or net loss?

Business organization, balance sheet

(Obj. 1, 2, 5)

E1-10 The balances of the assets and liabilities of TELETAX as of September 30, 20X2, follow. Also included are the revenue and expense figures of this tax-preparation business for September.

Delivery service revenue	$9,100	Office equipment	$15,500
Accounts receivable	6,900	Supplies...................................	600
Accounts payable......................	1,750	Note payable	8,000
M. Dalton, capital	?	Rent expense	500
Salary expense..........................	2,000	Cash	950

Required

1. What type of business organization is TELETAX? How can you tell?
2. Prepare the balance sheet of TELETAX as of September 30, 20X2.
3. What does the balance sheet report—financial position or operating results? Which financial statement reports the other information?

Income statement

(Obj. 2, 5)

E1-11 The assets, liabilities, owner's equity, revenues, and expenses of Venecor Import Service at December 31, 20X3, the end of its first year of business, have the following balances. During the year, T. Venecor, the owner, invested $15,000 in the business.

Office furniture........................	$ 45,000	Note payable	$30,000
Utilities expense	6,800	Rent expense	24,000
Accounts payable.....................	3,300	Cash	3,600
T. Venecor, capital....................	27,100	Office supplies.........................	4,800
Service revenue	161,200	Salary expense	49,000
Accounts receivable.................	9,000	Salaries payable.......................	2,000
Supplies expense	4,000	Property tax expense	1,200

Required

1. Prepare the income statement of Venecor Import Service for the year ended December 31, 20X3. What is the result of Venecor's operations for 20X3?
2. What was the amount of the proprietor's withdrawals during the year?

Evaluating the performance of a real company

(Obj. 6)

E1-12 In this exercise you will practice using the actual data of a well-known company. The 19X9 annual report of **Toys "Я" Us** reported net sales revenue of $11,170 million. Total expenses for the year were $11,302 million. Toys "Я" Us ended the year with total assets of $7,899 million, and the company owed debts totaling $4,275 million at year end.

During the preceding year, 19X8, Toys "Я" Us earned net income of $490 million. At year-end 19X8, Toys "Я" Us reported total assets of $7,963 million and total liabilities of $3,535 million.

Required

1. Compute Toys "Я" Us's net income for 19X9. Did net income increase or decrease from 19X8 to 19X9, and by how much?
2. Did Toys "Я" Us's owners' equity increase or decrease during 19X9? By how much?
3. Toys "Я" Us management strives for a steady increase in net income and owners' equity. How would you rate Toys "Я" Us's performance for 19X9—excellent, fair, or poor? Give your reason.

Preparing a statement of cash flows

(Obj. 5)

E1-13 During 19X8, **Lands' End, Inc.**, the catalog merchant located in Dodgeville, Wisconsin, experienced the following cash flows (adapted):

	Millions
Collections from customers	$1,257
Payments to suppliers and employees..	1,284
Purchases of assets...	35
Dividend payments to owners (same as withdrawals by owner)	10
Cash balance, beginning of year..	93

Required

Prepare the statement of cash flows of Lands' End, Inc., for the year. Follow the format of the statement of cash flows in Exhibit 1-7, page 20.

CHALLENGE EXERCISE

E1-14 Compute the missing amounts for each of the following companies. For each company, you will need to prepare a statement of owner's equity.

Using the financial statements (Obj. 5)

	Circle Co.	Triangle Co.	Square Co.
Beginning:			
Assets	$105,000	$ 50,000	$110,000
Liabilities	50,000	20,000	60,000
Ending:			
Assets	$160,000	$ 70,000	$?
Liabilities	70,000	35,000	80,000
Owner's Equity:			
Investments by owner	$?	$ 0	$ 10,000
Withdrawals by owner	100,000	40,000	70,000
Income Statement:			
Revenues	$430,000	$230,000	$400,000
Expenses	320,000	?	300,000

PROBLEMS

(Group A)

P1-1A Blake Dubis practiced law with a partnership for five years after graduating from law school. Recently he resigned his position to open his own law office, which he operates as a proprietorship. The name of the new entity is Blake Dubis, Attorney. Dubis experienced the following events during the organizing phase of his new business and its first month of operations. Some of the events were personal and did not affect his law practice. Others were business transactions and should be accounted for by the business.

Entity concept, transaction analysis, accounting equation (Obj. 2, 4)

Feb. 4	Dubis received $90,000 cash from his former law-firm partners.
5	Dubis deposited $80,000 cash in a new business bank account entitled Blake Dubis, Attorney.
6	Dubis paid $300 cash for letterhead stationery for his new law office.
7	Dubis purchased office furniture for his law office. He agreed to pay the account payable, $7,000, within six months.
10	Dubis sold 500 shares of IBM stock, which he and his wife had owned for several years, receiving $75,000 cash from his stockbroker.
11	Dubis deposited the $75,000 cash from sale of the IBM stock in his personal bank account.
12	A representative of a large company telephoned Dubis and told him of the company's intention to transfer its legal business to the new entity of Blake Dubis, Attorney.
18	Dubis finished court hearings on behalf of a client and submitted his bill for legal services, $5,000. Dubis expected to collect from this client within two weeks.
25	Dubis paid office rent, $1,000.
28	Dubis withdrew $1,000 cash from the business for personal living expenses.

Required

1. Classify each of these events as one of the following:
   a. A business transaction to be accounted for by the proprietorship of Blake Dubis, Attorney.
   b. A business-related event but not a transaction to be accounted for by the proprietorship of Blake Dubis, Attorney.
   c. A personal transaction not to be accounted for by the proprietorship of Blake Dubis, Attorney.
2. Analyze the effects of the above events on the accounting equation of the proprietorship of Blake Dubis, Attorney. Use a format similar to that in Exhibit 1-6.

P1-2A The bookkeeper of Trésoro Publishing Co. prepared the company's balance sheet while the accountant was ill. The balance sheet contains numerous errors. In particular, the bookkeeper knew that the balance sheet should balance, so he plugged in the owner's equity amount needed to achieve this balance. The owner's equity amount, however, is not correct. All other amounts are accurate, but some are out of place.

Balance sheet (Obj. 2, 5)

TRÉSORO PUBLISHING CO.
Balance Sheet
Month Ended July 31, 20X3

Assets		Liabilities	
Cash..................................	$12,000	Accounts receivable	$ 3,000
Office supplies	1,000	Service revenue	68,000
Land	44,000	Property tax expense	800
Salary expense...............	2,500	Accounts payable	9,000
Office furniture..............	8,000		
Note payable..................	16,000	**Owner's Equity**	
Rent expense..................	4,000	Owner's equity..........................	6,700
Total assets....................	$87,500	Total liabilities	$87,500

Required

1. Prepare the correct balance sheet, and date it correctly. Compute total assets, total liabilities, and owner's equity.
2. Identify the accounts that should *not* be presented on the balance sheet and state why you excluded them from the correct balance sheet you prepared for requirement 1.

Balance sheet, entity concept
(Obj. 2, 3, 5)

P1-3A Olivia Casinelli is a realtor. She buys and sells properties on her own, and she also earns commissions as a real estate agent for buyers and sellers. She organized her business as a proprietorship on November 24, 20X4. Consider the following facts as of November 30, 20X4.

a. Casinelli owed $55,000 on a note payable for some undeveloped land that had been acquired by her business for a total price of $100,000.
b. Casinelli's business had spent $20,000 for a Century 21 real estate franchise, which enti-tled her to represent herself as a Century 21 agent. Century 21 is a national affiliation of independent real estate agents. This franchise is a business asset.
c. Casinelli owed $60,000 on a personal mortgage on her personal residence, which she acquired in 20X1 for a total price of $150,000.
d. Casinelli had $8,000 in her personal bank account and $22,000 in her business bank account.
e. Casinelli owed $1,800 on a personal charge account with the Neiman-Marcus store.
f. Casinelli acquired business furniture for $17,000 on November 25. Of this amount, her business owed $6,000 on open account at November 30.
g. Office supplies on hand at the real estate office totaled $1,000.
  (1) Prepare the balance sheet of the real estate business of Olivia Casinelli, Realtor, at November 30, 20X4.
  (2) Identify the personal items that would not be reported on the balance sheet of the business.

Business transactions and
analysis
(Obj. 4)

P1-4A Mandarin Enterprises was recently formed. The balance of each item in the company's accounting equation is shown for October 10 and for each of the nine following business days.

	Cash	Accounts Receivable	Supplies	Land	Accounts Payable	Owner's Equity
Oct. 10	$ 4,000	$4,000	$1,000	$ 8,000	$4,000	$13,000
11	13,000	4,000	1,000	8,000	4,000	22,000
12	6,000	4,000	1,000	15,000	4,000	22,000
15	6,000	4,000	3,000	15,000	6,000	22,000
16	5,000	4,000	3,000	15,000	5,000	22,000
17	7,000	2,000	3,000	15,000	5,000	22,000
18	15,000	2,000	3,000	15,000	5,000	30,000
19	12,000	2,000	3,000	15,000	2,000	30,000
22	11,000	2,000	4,000	15,000	2,000	30,000
23	3,000	2,000	4,000	15,000	2,000	22,000

Required

Assuming that a single transaction took place on each day, briefly describe the transaction that most likely occurred on each day, beginning with October 11. Indicate which accounts were increased or decreased and by what amount. No revenue or expense transactions occurred on these dates.

P1-5A Presented below are (a) the assets and liabilities of Starmate Talent Search as of December 31, and (b) the revenues and expenses of the company for the year ended on that date. The items are listed in alphabetical order.

Income statement, statement of owner's equity, balance sheet (Obj. 5)

Accounts payable	$ 19,000	Land	$ 60,000
Accounts receivable	12,000	Note payable	85,000
Advertising expense	13,000	Property tax expense	4,000
Building	170,000	Rent expense	23,000
Cash	14,000	Salary expense	63,000
Equipment	20,000	Salary payable	1,000
Insurance expense	2,000	Service revenue	178,000
Interest expense	9,000	Supplies	3,000

The owner's beginning balance, Brian Sartor, Capital, was $150,000, and during the year Sartor withdrew $40,000 for personal use.

Required

1. Prepare Starmate's income statement for the year ended December 31 of the current year.
2. Prepare the company's statement of owner's equity for the year ended December 31.
3. Prepare the company's balance sheet at December 31.
4. Answer these questions about the company:
   a. Was the result of operations for the year a profit or a loss? How much?
   b. Did Sartor drain off all the earnings for the year, or did he build the company's capital during the period? How will his actions affect the company's ability to borrow in the future?
   c. How much in total economic resources does the company have as it moves into the new year? How much does the company owe? What is the dollar amount of Sartor's equity interest in the business at the end of the year?

P1-6A Helen Ingersoll owns and operates an interior design studio called Ingersoll Interiors. The following amounts summarize the financial position of her business on August 31, 20X2:

Transaction analysis, accounting equation, financial statements (Obj. 4, 5)

	Assets				= Liabilities +	Owner's Equity
	Cash +	Accounts Receivable +	Supplies +	Land =	Accounts Payable +	Helen Ingersoll, Capital
Bal.	2,250	1,500		12,000	8,000	7,750

During September 20X2, the following events occurred.

a. Ingersoll inherited $20,000 and deposited the cash in the business bank account.
b. Performed services for a client and received cash of $700.
c. Paid off the beginning balance of accounts payable.
d. Purchased supplies on account, $1,000.
e. Collected cash from a customer on account, $1,000.
f. Invested personal cash of $1,000 in the business.
g. Consulted on the interior design of a major office building and billed the client for services rendered, $2,400.
h. Recorded the following business expenses for the month:
   (1) Paid office rent, $900.
   (2) Paid advertising, $100.
i. Sold supplies to another business for $150 cash, which was the cost of the supplies.
j. Withdrew cash of $1,100 for personal use.

Required

1. Analyze the effects of the preceding transactions on the accounting equation of Ingersoll Interiors. Adapt the format of Exhibit 1-6.
2. Prepare the income statement of Ingersoll Interiors for the month ended September 30, 20X2. List expenses in decreasing order by amount.
3. Prepare the entity's statement of owner's equity for the month ended September 30, 20X2.
4. Prepare the balance sheet of Ingersoll Interiors at September 30, 20X2.

P1-1B Sharon Marsh practiced law with a partnership for ten years after graduating from law school. Recently she resigned her position to open her own law office, which she operates as a proprietorship. The name of the new entity is Sharon Marsh, Attorney. Marsh experienced the following events during the organizing phase of her new business and its first month of operation. Some of the events were personal and did not affect the law practice. Others were business transactions and should be accounted for by the business.

July 1	Marsh sold 1,000 shares of Eastman Kodak stock, which she had owned for several years, receiving $68,000 cash from her stockbroker.
2	Marsh deposited the $68,000 cash from sale of the Eastman Kodak stock in her personal bank account.
3	Marsh received $170,000 cash from her former law-firm partners.
5	Marsh deposited $100,000 cash in a new business bank account entitled Sharon Marsh, Attorney.
6	A representative of a large company telephoned Marsh and told her of the company's intention to transfer its legal business to the new entity of Sharon Marsh, Attorney.
7	Marsh paid $450 cash for letterhead stationery for her new law office.
9	Marsh purchased office furniture for the law office, agreeing to pay the account payable, $9,500, within three months.
23	Marsh finished court hearings on behalf of a client and submitted her bill for legal services, $3,000. She expected to collect from this client within one month.
30	Marsh paid office rent, $1,900.
31	Marsh withdrew $5,500 cash from the business for personal living expenses.

Required

1. Classify each of these events as one of the following:
   a. A business transaction to be accounted for by the proprietorship of Sharon Marsh, Attorney.
   b. A business-related event but not a transaction to be accounted for by the proprietorship of Sharon Marsh, Attorney.
   c. A personal transaction not to be accounted for by the proprietorship of Sharon Marsh, Attorney.

2. Analyze the effects of the preceding events on the accounting equation of the proprietorship of Sharon Marsh, Attorney. Use a format similar to Exhibit 1-6.

P1-2B The bookkeeper of Haynes Editorial Service prepared the balance sheet of the company while the accountant was ill. The balance sheet contains numerous errors. In particular, the bookkeeper knew that the balance sheet should balance, so he plugged in the owner's equity amount to achieve this balance. The owner's equity amount, however, is not correct. All other amounts are accurate, but some are out of place.

HAYNES EDITORIAL SERVICE
Balance Sheet
Month Ended October 31, 20X7

Assets		Liabilities	
Cash	$ 5,400	Notes receivable	$14,000
Insurance expense	300	Interest expense	2,000
Land	31,500	Office supplies	800
Salary expense	3,300	Accounts receivable	2,600
Office furniture	6,700	Note payable	21,000
Accounts payable	3,000		
Utilities expense	2,100	**Owner's Equity**	
		Owner's equity	11,900
Total assets	$52,300	Total liabilities	$52,300

Required

1. Prepare the correct balance sheet, and date it correctly. Compute total assets, total liabilities, and owner's equity.
2. Identify the accounts that should *not* be presented on the balance sheet and state why you excluded them from the correct balance sheet you prepared for requirement 1.

P1-3B Nik Tahari is a realtor. He buys and sells properties on his own, and he also earns commission as a real estate agent for buyers and sellers. He organized his business as a proprietorship on March 10, 20X2. Consider the following facts as of March 31, 20X2:

a. Tahari had $15,000 in his personal bank account and $7,000 in his business bank account.
b. Office supplies on hand at the real estate office totaled $1,000.
c. Tahari's business had spent $15,000 for an Electronic Realty Associates (ERA) franchise, which entitled Tahari to represent himself as an ERA agent. ERA is a national affiliation of independent real estate agents. This franchise is a business asset.
d. Tahari owed $34,000 on a note payable for some undeveloped land that had been acquired by his business for a total price of $60,000.
e. Tahari owed $65,000 on a personal mortgage on his personal residence, which he acquired in 20X1 for a total price of $90,000.
f. Tahari owed $950 on a personal charge account with Sears.
g. Tahari had acquired business furniture for $12,000 on March 26. Of this amount, Tahari's business owed $6,000 on open account at March 31.

Required

1. Prepare the balance sheet of the real estate business of Nik Tahari, Realtor, at March 31, 20X2.
2. Identify the personal items that would not be reported on the balance sheet of the business.

P1-4B Royal Gulf Oil Company was recently formed. The balance of each item in the company's accounting equation follows for April 4 and for each of the nine business days given:

Business transactions and analysis (Obj. 4)

	Cash	Accounts Receivable	Supplies	Land	Accounts Payable	Owner's Equity
Apr. 4	$2,000	$7,000	$ 800	$11,000	$3,800	$17,000
9	6,000	3,000	800	11,000	3,800	17,000
14	4,000	3,000	800	11,000	1,800	17,000
17	4,000	3,000	1,100	11,000	2,100	17,000
19	5,000	3,000	1,100	11,000	2,100	18,000
20	3,900	3,000	1,100	11,000	1,000	18,000
22	9,900	3,000	1,100	5,000	1,000	18,000
25	9,900	3,700	400	5,000	1,000	18,000
26	9,300	3,700	1,000	5,000	1,000	18,000
28	4,200	3,700	1,000	5,000	1,000	12,900

Required

Assuming that a single transaction took place on each day, describe briefly the transaction that most likely occurred on each day, beginning with April 9. Indicate which accounts were increased or decreased and by what amount. No revenue or expense transactions occurred on these dates.

P1-5B The amounts of (a) the assets and liabilities of Aspen Supply Co. as of December 31, 20X4, and (b) the revenues and expenses of the company for the year ended on that date follow. The items are listed in alphabetical order.

Income statement, statement of owner's equity, balance sheet (Obj. 5)

Accounts payable....................	$12,000	Note payable...........................	$ 31,000
Accounts receivable................	3,000	Property tax expense.............	2,000
Building..................................	56,000	Rent expense..........................	14,000
Cash.......................................	7,000	Salary expense........................	38,000
Equipment..............................	21,000	Service revenue......................	108,000
Interest expense......................	4,000	Supplies..................................	7,000
Interest payable......................	1,000	Utilities expense....................	3,000
Land.......................................	8,000		

The owner's beginning balance, Linda Elkins, Capital, was $43,000, and during the year Elkins withdrew $32,000 for personal use.

Required

1. Prepare the income statement of Aspen Supply Co. for the year ended December 31, 20X4.
2. Prepare the company's statement of owner's equity for the year ended December 31, 20X4.
3. Prepare the company's balance sheet at December 31, 20X4.
4. Answer these questions about the company.
   a. Was the result of operations for the year a profit or a loss? How much?
   b. Did Elkins drain off all the earnings for the year, or did she build the company's capital during the period? How would her actions affect the company's ability to borrow in the future?

c. How much in total economic resources does the company have as it moves into the new year? How much does the company owe? What is the dollar amount of Elkins's equity interest in the business at the end of the year?

Transaction analysis, accounting equation, financial statements (Obj. 4, 5)

P1-6B Joel Clark owns and operates an interior design studio called Clark Design Studio. The following amounts summarize the financial position of his business on April 30, 20X5:

	Assets				= Liabilities +	Owner's Equity
		Accounts			Accounts	Joel Clark,
	Cash +	Receivable +	Supplies +	Land =	Payable +	Capital
Bal.	1,720	3,240		24,100	5,400	23,660

During May 20X5, the following events occurred.

 a. Clark received $12,000 as a gift and deposited the cash in the business bank account.
 b. Paid off the beginning balance of accounts payable.
 c. Performed services for a client and received cash of $1,100.
 d. Collected cash from a customer on account, $750.
 e. Purchased supplies on account, $720.
 f. Consulted on the interior design of a major office building and billed the client for services rendered, $5,000.
 g. Invested personal cash of $1,700 in the business.
 h. Recorded the following business expenses for the month:
  (1) Paid office rent, $1,200.
  (2) Paid advertising, $660.

 i. Sold supplies to another interior designer for $80 cash, which was the cost of the supplies.
 j. Withdrew cash of $1,400 for personal use.

Required

 1. Analyze the effects of the preceding transactions on the accounting equation of Clark Design Studio. Adapt the format of Exhibit 1-6.
 2. Prepare the income statement of Clark Design Studio for the month ended May 31, 20X5. List expenses in decreasing order by amount.
 3. Prepare the statement of owner's equity of Clark Design Studio for the month ended May 31, 20X5.
 4. Prepare the balance sheet of Clark Design Studio at May 31, 20X5.

APPLY YOUR KNOWLEDGE

DECISION CASES

Using financial statements to evaluate a request for a loan (Obj. 1, 2, 6)

Case 1. The proprietors of two businesses, L. L. Sams Company and Melinda Garcia Career Services, have sought business loans from you. To decide whether to make the loans, you have requested their balance sheets.

L. L. SAMS COMPANY
Balance Sheet
August 31, 20X4

Assets			Liabilities		
Cash.......................................	$	9,000	Accounts payable....................	$	12,000
Accounts receivable...............		14,000	Note payable...........................		18,000
Merchandise inventory..........		85,000	Total liabilities........................		30,000
Store supplies		500			
Furniture and fixtures............		9,000	**Owner's Equity**		
Building..................................		80,000	L. L. Sams, capital...................		181,500
Land.......................................		14,000	Total liabilities		
Total assets.............................		$211,500	and owner's equity		$211,500

MELINDA GARCIA CAREER SERVICES
Balance Sheet
August 31, 20X4

Assets		Liabilities	
Cash	$ 11,000	Accounts payable	$ 6,000
Accounts receivable	7,000	Note payable	168,000
Office supplies	1,000	Total liabilities	174,000
Office furniture	56,000		
Land	169,000	**Owner's Equity**	
		Melinda Garcia, capital	70,000
		Total liabilities and	
Total assets	$244,000	owner's equity	$244,000

Required

1. Solely on the basis of these balance sheets, to which entity would you be more comfortable lending money? Explain fully, citing specific items and amounts from the balance sheets.
2. In addition to the balance sheet data, what other information would you require? Be specific.

Case 2. Camp Trinity conducts summer camps for children with disabilities. Samuel and Margaret Shields operate the camp near Leander, Texas. Because of the nature of its business, the camp experiences many unusual transactions. Evaluate each of the following transactions in terms of its effect on Camp Trinity's income statement and balance sheet.

Transaction analysis, effects on the financial statements (Obj. 4)

1. A camper suffered an injury that was not covered by insurance. Camp Trinity paid $900 for the child's medical care. How does this transaction affect the camp's income statement and balance sheet?
2. Camp Trinity sold land adjacent to the camp for $190,000, receiving cash of $70,000 and a note receivable for $120,000. When purchased five years earlier, the land cost Camp Trinity $100,000. How should the camp account for the sale of the land?
3. One camper's father is a physician. Camp Trinity allows this child to attend camp in return for the father's serving part-time in the camp infirmary for the two-week term. The standard fee for a camp term is $1,000. The physician's salary for this part-time work would be $1,000. How should Camp Trinity account for this arrangement?
4. A tornado damaged the camp dining hall. The cost to repair the damage will be $12,000 over and above what the insurance company will pay.

ETHICAL ISSUES

Ethical Issue 1. The chapter-opening story relates to the billions of dollars the tobacco companies have paid because of smoking-related illnesses. In particular, **Philip Morris,** a leading cigarette manufacturer, paid over $3 billion in 1998.

Required

1. Suppose you are the chief financial officer (CFO) responsible for the financial statements of Philip Morris. What ethical issue would you face as you consider what to report in your company's annual report about the cash payments? What is the ethical course of action for you to take in this situation?
2. What are some of the negative consequences to Philip Morris for not telling the truth? What are some of the negative consequences to Philip Morris for telling the truth?

Ethical Issue 2. The board of directors of Silvertron Corporation is meeting to discuss the past year's results before releasing financial statements to the public. The discussion includes this exchange: Amanda Blume, company president: "Well, this has not been a good year! Revenue is down and expenses are up—way up. If we don't do some fancy stepping, we'll report a loss for the third year in a row. I can temporarily transfer some land that I own into the company's name, and that will beef up our balance sheet. Kent, can you shave $500,000 from expenses? Then we can probably get the bank loan that we need."

Kent Kohler, company chief accountant: "Amanda, you are asking too much. Generally accepted accounting principles are designed to keep this sort of thing from happening."

Required

1. What is the fundamental ethical issue in this situation?
2. Discuss how Amanda Blume's proposals violate generally accepted accounting principles. Identify the specific concept or principle involved.

FINANCIAL STATEMENT CASE

Identifying items from a company's financial statements (Obj. 4)

This and similar cases in later chapters focus on the financial statements of a real company—**Target Corporation,** the upscale discount chain. As you work each problem, you will build your confidence in understanding and using the financial statements of real companies.

Refer to Target Corporation's financial statements in Appendix A at the end of the book.

Required

1. How much in cash (including cash equivalents) did Target Corporation have on January 29, 2000?
2. What were the company's total assets at January 29, 2000? At January 30, 1999?
3. Write the company's accounting equation at January 29, 2000, by filling in the dollar amounts:

ASSETS = LIABILITIES + STOCKHOLDERS' EQUITY

4. Identify total revenue for the year ended January 29, 2000 (fiscal year 1999). How much did total revenue increase or decrease in fiscal year 1999?
5. How much net income or net loss did Target experience for fiscal year 1999 and for fiscal year 1998? Was fiscal year 1999 a good year or a bad year compared to 1998? State your reasons.

TEAM PROJECTS

Project 1. You are opening a pet kennel. Your purpose is to earn a profit, so you will need to establish the business. Assume you organize as a proprietorship.

1. Make a detailed list of ten factors you must consider to establish the business.
2. Identify ten or more transactions that your business will undertake to open and operate the kennel.
3. Prepare the kennel's income statement, statement of owner's equity, and balance sheet at the end of the first month of operations before you have had time to pay all the business's bills. Use made-up figures and include a complete heading for each financial statement. Date the balance sheet as of August 31, 20XX.
4. Discuss how you will evaluate the success of your business and how you will decide whether to continue its operation.

Project 2. You are promoting a rock concert in your area. Your purpose is to earn a profit, so you will need to establish the business. Assume you organize as a proprietorship.

Required

1. Make a detailed list of ten factors you must consider to establish the business.
2. Describe ten of the items your business must arrange in order to promote and stage the rock concert.
3. Prepare your business's income statement, statement of owner's equity, and balance sheet on August 31, 20XX, immediately after the rock concert and before you have had time to pay all the business's bills and to collect all receivables. Use made-up amounts, and include a complete heading for each financial statement. For the income statement and the statement of owner's equity, assume the period is the three months ended August 31, 20XX.
4. Assume that you will continue to promote rock concerts if the venture is successful. If it is unsuccessful, you will terminate the business within three months after the concert. Discuss how you will evaluate the success of your venture and how you will decide whether to continue in business.

INTERNET EXERCISE

eBay

Hoover's Online, The Business Network offers information about companies, industries, people, and products. For researching a company, this site is a good place to start gathering basic information.

1. Go to **http://www.hoovers.com** and then use the "Search" scroll bar to select *Company*. In the next box type eBay and then click on *Go*. For **eBay Inc.** click on *Capsule*.
   a. Read the written description of the company and briefly summarize its contents.
   b. Review the other site information and comment on one item of interest.
2. Go to the top of the page and click on the *Financials* tab. Under "Free Financial Information" click on *Annual Financials*.

a. For the three most recent years, list the amounts reported for "Revenue" and "Total Net Income." Is eBay growing and expanding? Is eBay a profitable company?

b. For the most recent year, list amounts reported for "Total Assets," "Total Liabilities," and "Total (Owner's) Equity." Does the accounting equation hold true? Are assets primarily financed by debt or owner's equity?

3. Go to the top of the page and click on the *Company Capsule* tab. Click on the URL for eBay (www.ebay.com) and then click on *Browse* to explore the world's largest online marketplace. Comment on one item you found of interest.

Recording Business Transactions

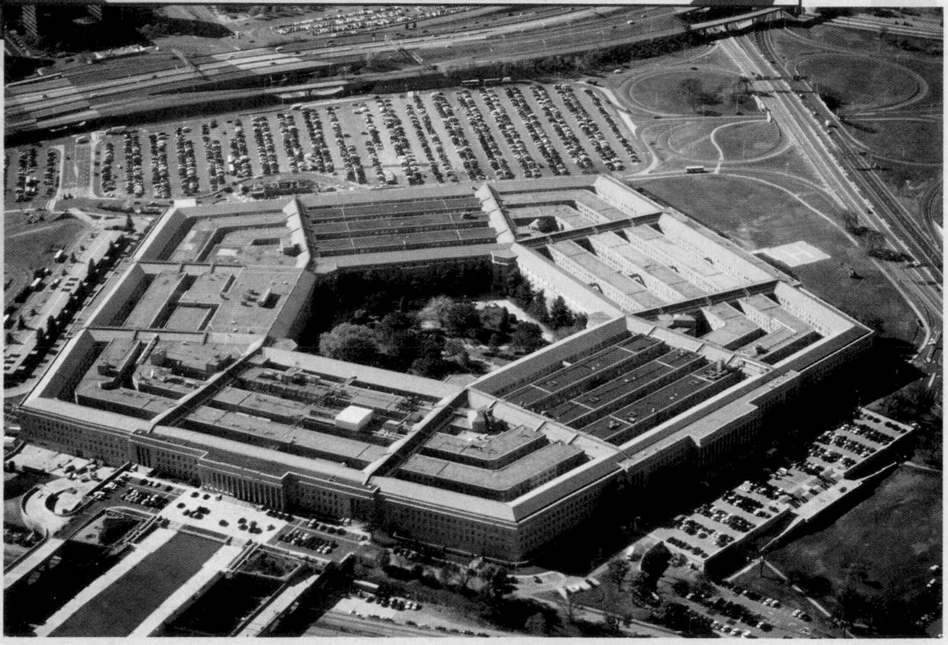

2

ACCOUNTING

After studying this chapter, you should be able to

1. Define and use key accounting terms

2. Apply the rules of debit and credit

3. Record transactions in the journal

4. Post from the journal to the ledger

5. Prepare and use a trial balance

6. Set up a chart of accounts for a business

7. Analyze transactions without a journal

Forget about e-retailers putting **Wal-Mart** out of business. Their task now is simply to stay alive. Time is running out because many e-retailers have yet to turn a profit. They are spending so much on advertising they may soon run out of cash. In fact, during the fourth quarter of 1999, only four e-retailers — **priceline.com, Drugstore.com, Value America,** and **eBay** — increased their gross profit margins.

How do these companies monitor their financial progress, or lack of it? Managers don't roll dice to decide whether to launch a new product or whether the business is profitable. They keep accounting records like those we illustrate in this chapter. Accounting helps to measure profits and losses.

Chapter 1 introduced transaction analysis and the financial statements but did not show how the financial statements are prepared. Chapters 2, 3, and 4 cover the accounting process that results in the financial statements.

Chapter 2 discusses the processing of accounting information as it is done in practice. Throughout this and the next two chapters, we continue to illustrate accounting procedures with service businesses, such as Gay Gillen eTravel, a CPA, a law practice, or a sports franchise like the **Atlanta Braves.** In Chapter 5, we move into merchandising businesses such as **Macy's** and **Wal-Mart.** All these businesses use the basic accounting system we illustrate in this book.

THE ACCOUNT

The basic summary device of accounting is the **account,** the detailed record of the changes that have occurred in a particular asset, liability, or owner's equity during a period of time. For convenient access to the information, accounts are grouped in a record called the **ledger.** This is what we mean when we say "keeping the books" and "auditing the books." A ledger usually takes the form of a computer listing.

Accounts are grouped in three broad categories, according to the accounting equation ⇒ :

ASSETS = LIABILITIES + OWNER'S EQUITY

WORK IT OUT

Suppose you bought a $20,000 Pontiac Grand Am and had to borrow $12,000 to pay for it. Can you write your personal accounting equation for this transaction?

Answer

	Assets	=	Liabilities	+	Owner's Equity
	$20,000	=	$12,000	+	$8,000

Assets

Assets are economic resources that benefit the business and will continue to do so in the future. Most firms use the following asset accounts.

CASH   The Cash account is a record of the cash effects of a business's transactions. Cash includes money and any medium of exchange that a bank accepts at face value, such as bank account balances, paper currency, coins, certificates of deposit, and checks. Successful companies such as **Wal-Mart** have plenty of cash. Many e-retailers may go bankrupt due to a shortage of cash.

NOTES RECEIVABLE   A business may sell its goods or services in exchange for a *promissory note,* which is a written pledge that the customer will pay a fixed amount of money by a certain date. The Notes Receivable account is a record of the promissory notes the business expects to collect in cash. A note receivable offers more security for collection than an account receivable.

ACCOUNTS RECEIVABLE   A business may sell its goods or services in exchange for an oral or implied promise of future cash receipt. Such sales are made on credit ("on account"). The Accounts Receivable account contains these amounts. Most

Objective 1
Define and use key accounting terms

ACCOUNT. The detailed record of the changes that have occurred in a particular asset, liability, or owner's equity during a period. The basic summary device of accounting.

LEDGER. The book of accounts.

◂◂ In Chapter 1, p. 11, we learned that the accounting equation is the basic tool in all of accounting. It measures the assets of the business and the claims to those assets.

sales in the United States and in other developed countries are made on account receivable.

PREPAID EXPENSES   A business often pays certain expenses, such as rent and insurance, in advance. A *prepaid expense* is an asset because the prepayment provides a future benefit for the business. The ledger has a separate asset account for each prepaid expense. Prepaid Rent, Prepaid Insurance, and Office Supplies are prepaid expense accounts.

LAND   The Land account is a record of the cost of land a business owns and uses in its operations. Land held for sale is accounted for separately—in an investment account.

BUILDING   The cost of a business's buildings—office, warehouse, store, and the like—appear in the Buildings account. The e-retailers need little in the way of buildings because of the electronic nature of their business. Wal-Mart, on the other hand, owns buildings in many locations. Buildings held for sale are separate assets accounted for as investments.

EQUIPMENT, FURNITURE, AND FIXTURES   A business has a separate asset account for each type of equipment—Computer Equipment, Office Equipment, and Store Equipment, for example. The Furniture and Fixtures account shows the cost of this asset. Computers and the related software are the most important assets of e-retailers.

Liabilities

Recall that a *liability* is a debt. A business generally has fewer liability accounts than asset accounts because a business's liabilities are summarized in a few accounts.

NOTES PAYABLE   The Notes Payable account is the opposite of the Notes Receivable account. Notes Payable represents amounts the business must pay because it signed promissory notes to borrow money or to purchase goods or services.

ACCOUNTS PAYABLE   The Accounts Payable account is the opposite of Accounts Receivable. The oral or implied promise to pay off debts arising from credit purchases appears in the Accounts Payable account. Such a purchase is said to be made on account. All companies, including **CBS, Coca-Cola,** and **eBay** have accounts payable.

ACCRUED LIABILITIES   An *accrued liability* is a liability for an expense that has not been paid. Accrued liability accounts are added as needed. Taxes Payable, Interest Payable, and Salary Payable are liability accounts of most companies.

Owner's Equity

The owner's claim to the assets of the business is called *owner's equity.* In a proprietorship or a partnership, owner's equity is split into separate accounts for the owner's capital balance and the owner's withdrawals.

CAPITAL   The Capital account shows the owner's claim to the assets of the business. Consider Gay Gillen eTravel. After the travel agency's total liabilities are subtracted from its total assets, the remainder is the owner's capital. The Capital balance equals the owner's investments in the business plus the business's net income and minus any net losses and owner withdrawals. ◄◄

➤ See the statement of owner's equity in Chapter 1, Exhibit 1-7.

WITHDRAWALS   When Gay Gillen withdraws cash or other assets from the business for her personal use, the travel agency's assets and owner's equity decrease. The amounts taken out of the business appear in a separate account entitled Gay Gillen, Withdrawals, or Gay Gillen, Drawing. If withdrawals were recorded directly in the Capital account, the amount of owner withdrawals would not be highlighted and decision making would be more difficult. The Withdrawals account *decreases* owner's equity.

REVENUES   The increase in owner's equity created by delivering goods or services to customers or clients is called *revenue*. The ledger contains as many revenue accounts as needed. Gay Gillen eTravel needs a Service Revenue account for amounts earned by providing travel services for clients. If a business lends money to an outsider, it needs an Interest Revenue account for the interest earned on the loan. If the business rents a building to a tenant, it needs a Rent Revenue account.

EXPENSES   Expenses use up assets or create liabilities in the course of operating a business. Expenses have the opposite effect of revenues; they *decrease* owner's equity. A business needs a separate account for each type of expense, such as Salary Expense, Rent Expense, Advertising Expense, and Utilities Expense. Businesses of all sizes strive to minimize their expenses in order to maximize net income — whether it's **General Electric** or Gay Gillen eTravel.

Exhibit 2-1 shows how asset, liability, and owner's equity accounts can be grouped in the ledger.

⊙ DAILY EXERCISE 2-1

EXHIBIT 2-1
The Ledger (Asset, Liability, and Owner's Equity Accounts)

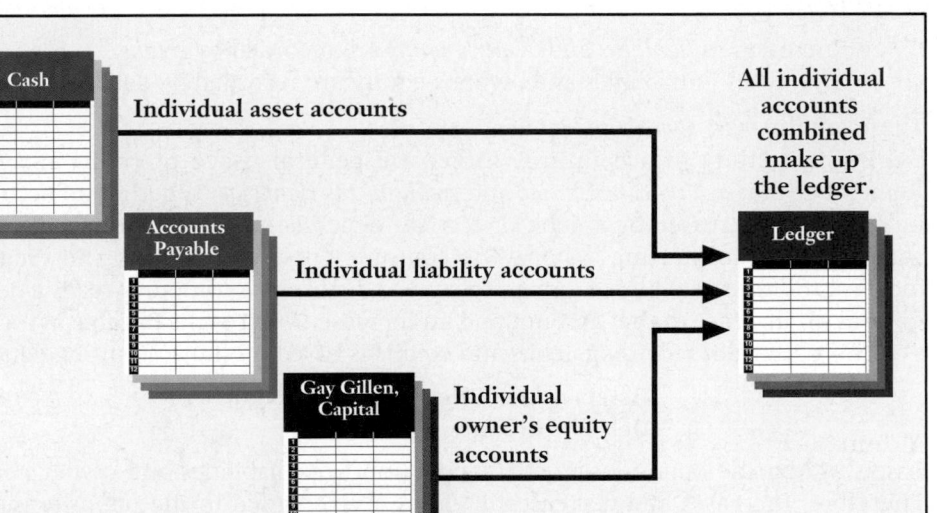

DOUBLE-ENTRY ACCOUNTING

Accounting is based on a *double-entry system*, which means that we record the *dual effects* of a business transaction. *Each transaction affects at least two accounts.* For example, Gay Gillen's $30,000 cash investment in her travel agency increased both the Cash account and the Capital account of the business. It would be incomplete to record only the increase in the entity's cash without recording the increase in its owner's equity.

Consider a cash purchase of supplies. What are the dual effects of this transaction? The purchase (1) decreases cash and (2) increases supplies. A purchase of supplies on credit (1) increases supplies and (2) increases accounts payable. All transactions have at least two effects on the entity.

The T-Account

The most widely used account format is called the *T-account* because it takes the form of the capital letter "T." The vertical line in the T-account divides the account into its left and right sides. The account title rests on the horizontal line. For example, the Cash account of a business appears in the following T-account format:

CASH
(Left side)	(Right side)
Debit	*Credit*

DEBIT. The left side of an account.

CREDIT. The right side of an account.

The left side of the account is called the **debit** side, and the right side is called the **credit** side. The words *debit* and *credit* can be confusing because they are new. To become comfortable using them, remember that

Debit = Left side   Credit = Right side

Even though *left side* and *right side* are more descriptive, the terms *debit* and *credit* are deeply entrenched in business.[1] Debit and credit are abbreviated as follows:

• **Dr = Debit**   • **Cr = Credit**

Increases and Decreases in the Accounts

The account category determines how increases and decreases in it are recorded. For any given account, all increases are recorded on one side, and all decreases are recorded on the other side.

Objective 2
Apply the rules of debit and credit

- Increases in *assets* are recorded on the left (*debit*) side of the account.
- Decreases in assets are recorded on the right (credit) side.

Conversely,

- Increases in *liabilities* and *owner's equity* are recorded by *credits*.
- Decreases in liabilities and owner's equity are recorded by debits.

These are the *rules of debit and credit.*

In your study of accounting, forget the general usage of credit and debit. Remember that *debit means left side* and *credit means right side*. Whether an account is increased or decreased by a debit or a credit depends on the type of account. In a computerized accounting system, the computer interprets debits and credits as increases or decreases by account category. For example, a computer reads a debit to Cash as an increase to that account and an increase to Accounts Payable as a credit.

This pattern of recording debits and credits is based on the accounting equation:

⊙ DAILY EXERCISE 2-2

Assets = Liabilities + Owner's Equity
Debits = Credits

Assets are on the opposite side of the equation from liabilities and owner's equity. Therefore, increases and decreases in assets are recorded in the opposite manner from those in liabilities and owner's equity. And liabilities and owner's equity, which are on the same side of the equal sign, are treated in the same way. Exhibit 2-2 shows the relationship between the accounting equation and the rules of debit and credit.

EXHIBIT 2-2
The Accounting Equation and the Rules of Debit and Credit

Accounting Equation:	Assets	=	Liabilities	+	Owner's Equity
Rules of Debit and Credit:	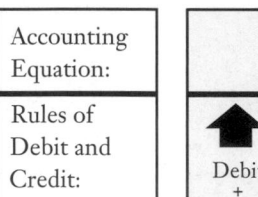		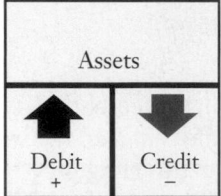		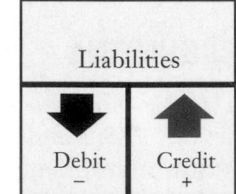

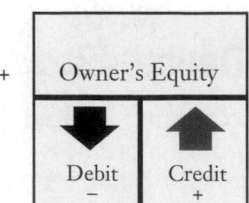

To illustrate the ideas diagrammed in Exhibit 2-2, reconsider the first transaction from Chapter 1. Gay Gillen invested $30,000 in cash to begin her travel agency. The business received $30,000 cash from Gillen and gave her the owner's equity in the business. We are accounting for the business entity, Gay Gillen eTravel. Which accounts of the business are affected? By what amounts? On what side (debit or credit)? The answer: The business's Assets and Capital would increase by $30,000, as the following T-accounts show.

ASSETS	=	LIABILITIES	+	OWNER'S EQUITY
CASH				**GAY GILLEN, CAPITAL**
Debit for Increase, 30,000				Credit for Increase, 30,000

---

[1]The words *debit* and *credit* have a Latin origin (*debitum* and *creditum*). Luca Pacioli, the Italian monk who wrote about accounting in the 15th century, popularized these terms.

The amount remaining in an account is called its *balance*. The first transaction gives Cash a $30,000 debit balance and Gay Gillen, Capital a $30,000 credit balance.

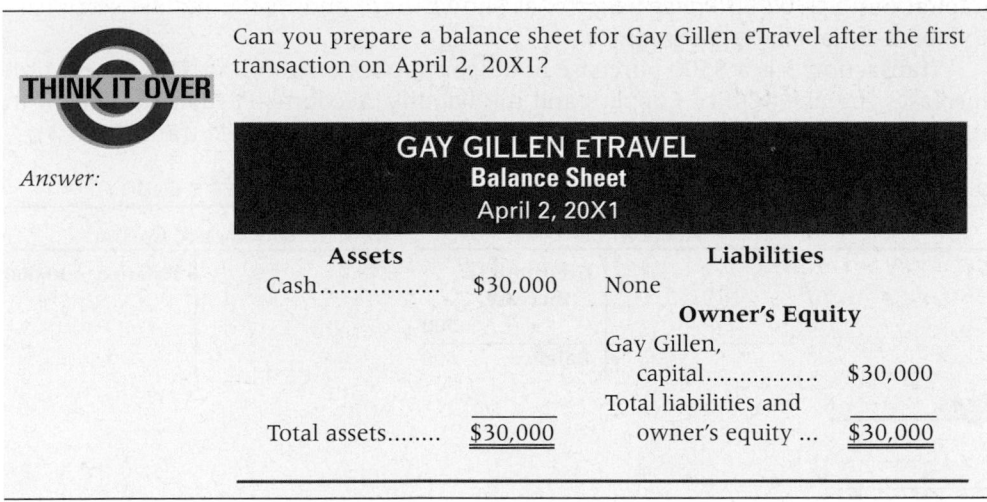

THINK IT OVER

Can you prepare a balance sheet for Gay Gillen eTravel after the first transaction on April 2, 20X1?

Answer:

GAY GILLEN ETRAVEL
Balance Sheet
April 2, 20X1

Assets		Liabilities	
Cash..................	$30,000	None	
		Owner's Equity	
		Gay Gillen,	
		capital.................	$30,000
		Total liabilities and	
Total assets........	$30,000	owner's equity ...	$30,000

Notice that Assets = Liabilities + Owner's Equity *and* that total debit amounts = total credit amounts. Exhibit 2-3 illustrates the accounting equation and Gay Gillen eTravel's first three transactions.

EXHIBIT 2-3 **The Accounting Equation and the First Three Transactions of the Business Entity, Gay Gillen eTravel**

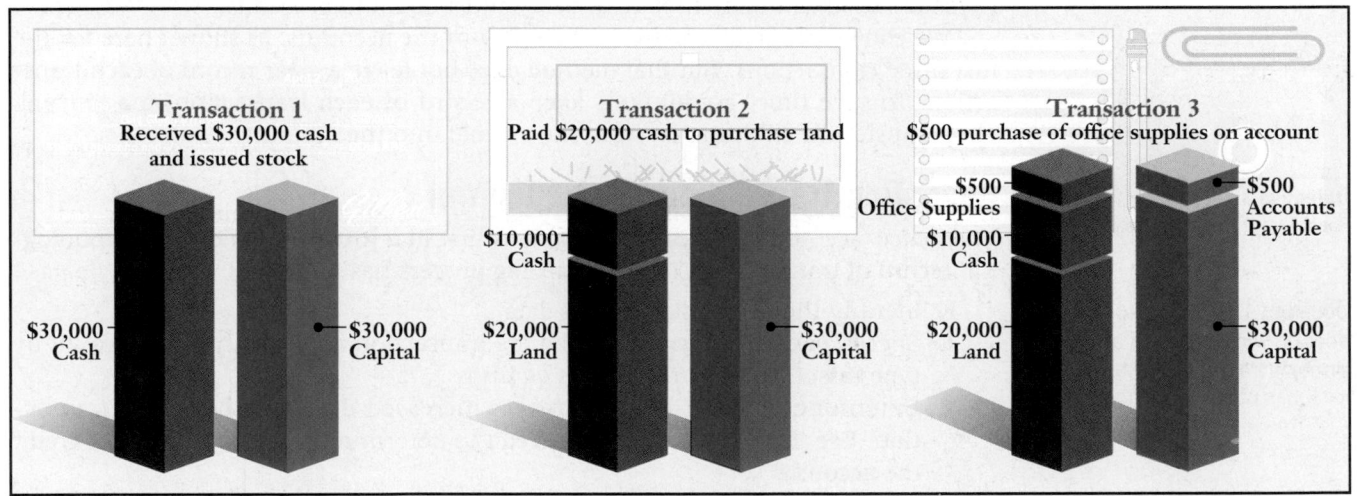

The second transaction is a $20,000 cash purchase of land. This transaction affects two assets: Cash and Land. It decreases (credits) Cash and increases (debits) Land, as shown in the T-accounts:

ASSETS	=	LIABILITIES	+	OWNER'S EQUITY

CASH		
Balance	30,000	Credit for Decrease, 20,000
Balance	10,000	

GAY GILLEN, CAPITAL	
	Balance 30,000

LAND	
Debit for Increase, 20,000	
Balance 20,000	

After this transaction, Cash has a $10,000 debit balance ($30,000 debit amount minus $20,000 credit amount), Land has a debit balance of $20,000, and Gay Gillen, Capital has a $30,000 credit balance, as shown here and in the middle section of Exhibit 2-3 (labeled transaction 2).

Transaction 3 is a $500 purchase of office supplies on account. This transaction increases the asset Office Supplies and the liability Accounts Payable, as shown in the following accounts and in the right side of Exhibit 2-3 (labeled transaction 3):

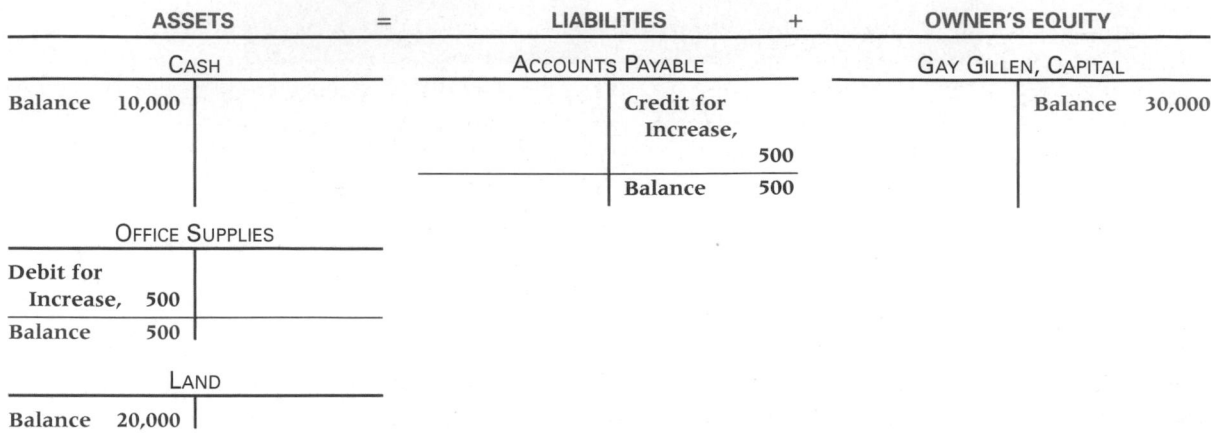

We create accounts as needed. The process of creating a new T-account in preparation for recording a transaction is called *opening the account.* For transaction 1, we opened the Cash account and the Gay Gillen, Capital account. For transaction 2, we opened the Land account and for transaction 3, Office Supplies and Accounts Payable. For each transaction, total debits must equal total credits.

We could record all transactions directly in the accounts, as shown here for the first three transactions. But that method does not leave a clear record of each transaction. To save time, accountants keep a record of each transaction in a journal. They transfer the information from the journal into the accounts.

Recording Transactions in the Journal

Objective 3
Record transactions in the journal

JOURNAL. The chronological accounting record of an entity's transactions.

In practice, accountants record transactions first in a **journal,** which is a chronological record of transactions. The journalizing process has four steps:

1. Identify the transaction and its data.
2. Specify each account affected by the transaction and classify each account by type (asset, liability, or owner's equity).
3. Determine whether each account is increased or decreased by the transaction. Use the rules of debit and credit to determine whether to debit or credit the account.
4. Enter the transaction in the journal, including a brief explanation for the journal entry. The debit side of the entry is entered first and the credit side last.

Step 4, "Enter the transaction in the journal," means to record the transaction in the journal. This step is also called "making the journal entry" or "journalizing the transaction."

These four steps are the same in a computerized accounting system or in a manual system. In step 4, however, the journal entry is generally entered into the computer by account number, and the account name is then listed automatically.

Let's apply the four steps to journalize the first transaction of Gay Gillen eTravel–the receipt of Gillen's $30,000 cash investment in the business.

Step 1. The data appear on Gillen's bank deposit slip and on her $30,000 check, which she deposits in the business bank account. See Exhibit 2-3.

Step 2. The accounts affected by the transaction are *Cash* and *Gay Gillen, Capital.* Cash is an asset account. Gay Gillen, Capital is an owner's equity account.

Step 3. Both accounts increase by $30,000. Therefore, we debit Cash, the asset account, and we credit Gay Gillen, Capital, the owner's equity account.

Step 4. The journal entry is

Journal			Page 1
Date	Accounts and Explanation	Debit	Credit
Apr. 2[a]	Cash[b]	30,000[d]	
	Gay Gillen, Capital[c].......................................		30,000[e]
	Received initial investment from owner.[f]		

The journal entry includes (a) the date of the transaction; (b) the title of the account debited (placed flush left); (c) the title of the account credited (indented); the dollar amounts of the (d) debit (left) and (e) credit (right), and (f) a short explanation of the transaction. Note that dollar signs are omitted in the money columns. It is understood that the debit and credit amounts are in dollars.

To journalize a transaction, first pinpoint the obvious effects on the accounts. For example, cash effects are easy to identify. Did cash increase or decrease? Then find the transaction's effects on other accounts.

The journal holds information that the ledger accounts do not provide. Each journal entry shows the complete effect of a business transaction. Consider Gay Gillen's initial investment. The Cash account shows a single figure, the $30,000 debit. We know that every transaction must also have a credit, so in what account will we find the corresponding $30,000 credit? In this illustration, we know that the Capital account holds this figure. But imagine the difficulty of linking debits and credits for hundreds of transactions without a separate record of each transaction. The journal solves this problem and presents the full story for each transaction. Exhibit 2-4 shows how Journal page 1 looks after Gillen has recorded the first transaction.

EXHIBIT 2-4   **The Journal**

Journal			Page 1
Date	Accounts and Explanation	Debit	Credit
Apr. 2	Cash	30,000	
	Gay Gillen, Capital..		30,000
	Received initial investment from owner.		

WORK IT OUT

Prepare the journal entry to record a $1,600 payment on account.

1. Identify the accounts.
2. Are these accounts increased or decreased? Should they be debited or credited?
3. Make the journal entry, with an explanation.

Answers

1. The company paid $1,600 on account. The accounts affected are Cash and Accounts Payable.
2. Cash (an asset) decreases by $1,600. Accounts Payable (a liability) decreases by $1,600. To account for a decrease in an asset, we record a credit. For a decrease in a liability, we use a debit. Review Exhibit 2-2.
3. The journal entry is   Accounts Payable 1,600
                                          Cash..   1,600
                                      Made payment on account.

Objective 4
Post from the journal to the ledger

Copying Information (Posting) from the Journal to the Ledger

Posting means copying the amounts from the journal to the accounts in the ledger. Debits in the journal are posted as debits in the ledger, and credits in the journal are credits in the ledger. The initial investment transaction of Gay Gillen eTravel is posted to the ledger in Exhibit 2-5. Here we ignore the date of the transaction to focus on the accounts and their dollar amounts.

POSTING. Copying amounts from the journal to the ledger.

EXHIBIT 2-5
Journal Entry and Posting to the Ledger

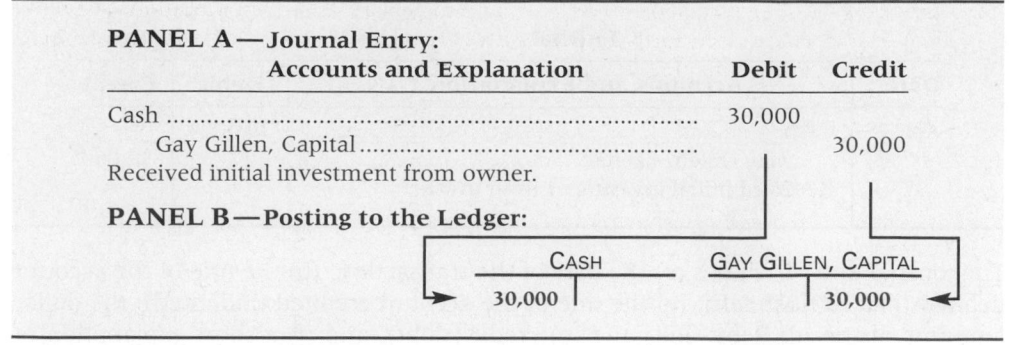

PANEL A—Journal Entry:

Accounts and Explanation	Debit	Credit
Cash	30,000	
Gay Gillen, Capital.....................................		30,000
Received initial investment from owner.		

PANEL B—Posting to the Ledger:

CASH		GAY GILLEN, CAPITAL	
30,000			30,000

THE FLOW OF ACCOUNTING DATA

Exhibit 2-6 summarizes the flow of accounting data from a business transaction through the accounting system to the ledger. In the pages that follow, we account for six of Gay Gillen eTravel's early transactions. Keep in mind that we are accounting for the travel agency. We are *not* accounting for Gay Gillen's *personal* transactions.

EXHIBIT 2-6 **Flow of Accounting Data from the Journal to the Ledger**

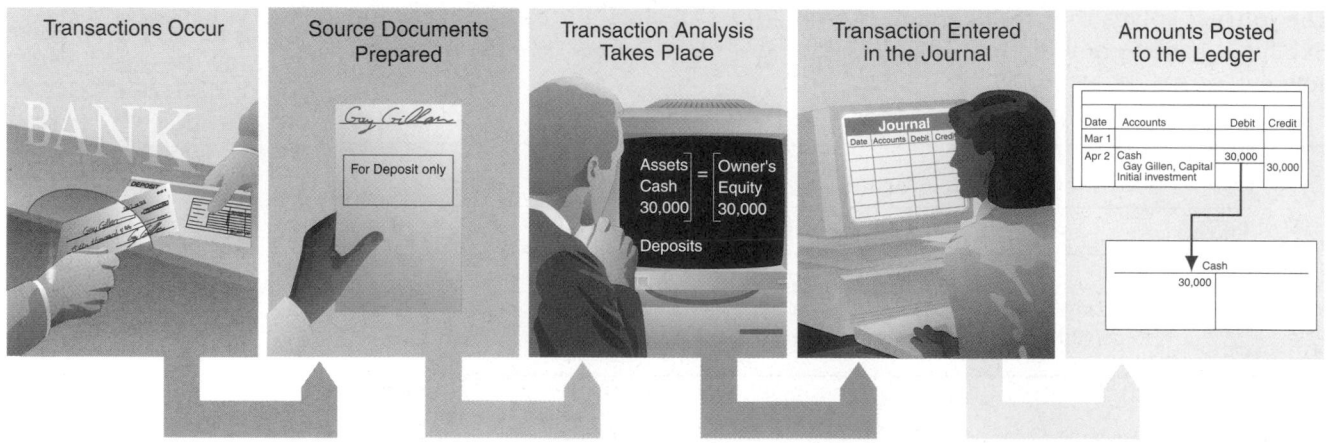

Transaction Analysis, Journalizing, and Posting to the Accounts

1. *Transaction Analysis*   The business received $30,000 cash that Gay Gillen invested to begin her travel agency. The business increased its asset cash, so we debit Cash. The business also increased its owner's equity; to record this increase, credit Gay Gillen, Capital.

Accounting Equation

ASSETS	=	LIABILITIES	+	OWNER'S EQUITY
Cash				Gay Gillen, Capital
+50,000	=	0	+	+30,000

Journal Entry

Cash..	30,000	
Gay Gillen, Capital.............		30,000
Received investment from owner.		

The journal entry records the same information that you learned by using the accounting equation in Chapter 1. Both accounts—Cash and Gay Gillen, Capital—increased because the business received $30,000 cash and gave Gillen $30,000 of capital (owner's equity) in the business.

Ledger Accounts

CASH		GAY GILLEN, CAPITAL	
(1) 30,000		(1) 30,000	

2. *Transaction Analysis* Gillen paid $20,000 cash for land to be used as an office location. The purchase decreased the business's cash; therefore, credit Cash. The entity's asset, land, increased, so we debit the Land account.

Accounting Equation

ASSETS		=	LIABILITIES	+	OWNER'S EQUITY
Cash	Land				
−20,000	+20,000	=	0	+	0

Journal Entry

Land 20,000
    Cash 20,000
Paid cash for land.

This transaction increased one asset, land, and decreased another asset, cash. The *net* effect on total assets was zero, and there was no effect on liabilities or owner's equity. (The term *net* in business means an amount after a subtraction.)

Ledger Accounts

	CASH				LAND	
(1)	30,000	(2)	20,000	(2)	20,000	

⊙ DAILY EXERCISE 2-3

3. *Transaction Analysis* Gillen purchased $500 in office supplies on account payable. The asset office supplies increased, so we debit Office Supplies. The purchase also increased the liability accounts payable; to record this increase, credit Accounts Payable.

Accounting Equation

ASSETS	=	LIABILITIES	+	OWNER'S EQUITY
Office Supplies		Accounts Payable		
+500	=	+500	+	0

Journal Entry

Office Supplies 500
    Accounts Payable 500
Purchased office supplies on account.

Ledger Accounts

	OFFICE SUPPLIES		ACCOUNTS PAYABLE	
(3)	500		(3)	500

4. *Transaction Analysis* Gillen paid $300 on the account payable created in transaction 3. The payment decreased the asset cash; therefore, credit Cash. The payment also decreased the liability accounts payable, so we debit Accounts Payable.

Accounting Equation

ASSETS	=	LIABILITIES	+	OWNER'S EQUITY
Cash		Accounts Payable		
−300	=	−300	+	0

Journal Entry

Accounts Payable 300
    Cash 300
Paid cash on account.

Ledger Accounts

	CASH				ACCOUNTS PAYABLE		
(1)	30,000	(2)	20,000	(4)	300	(3)	500
		(4)	300				

5. *Transaction Analysis* Gay Gillen remodeled her home with personal funds and a loan from Nations Bank. This is not a transaction of the travel agency, so we make no journal entry on its books.

6. *Transaction Analysis* Gillen withdrew $2,100 cash for personal living expenses. The withdrawal decreased the entity's cash; therefore, credit Cash. The transaction also decreased owner's equity. Decreases in a proprietorship's owner's equity that result from owner withdrawals are debited to a separate account, Withdrawals. Therefore, debit Gay Gillen, Withdrawals.

Accounting Equation	ASSETS	=	LIABILITIES	+	OWNER'S EQUITY
	Cash				Gay Gillen, Withdrawals
	−2,100	=	0		−2,100

Journal Entry

Gay Gillen, Withdrawals	2,100	
Cash		2,100

Withdrawal of cash by owner.

Ledger Accounts

CASH				GAY GILLEN, WITHDRAWALS	
(1)	30,000	(2)	20,000	(6)	2,100
		(4)	300		
		(6)	2,100		

Each journal entry posted to the ledger is keyed by date or by transaction number. In this way, any transaction can be traced from the journal to the ledger and back to the journal. This linking allows you to locate any information you may need for decision making.

Accounts After Posting

We next show how the accounts look when the preceding transactions have been posted. The accounts are grouped under their headings.

Each account has a balance, denoted *Bal.* An account balance is the difference between the account's total debits and its total credits. For example, the balance in the Cash account is the difference between the total debits, $30,000, and the total amount of the credits, $22,400 ($20,000 + $300 + $2,100). Thus, the cash balance is $7,600. The balances are residual amounts left over after the journal entries have been posted to the accounts. We set an account balance apart from the transaction amounts by a horizontal line. The final figure in an account, below the horizontal line, is the balance after the transactions have been posted.

ASSETS				=	LIABILITIES			+	OWNER'S EQUITY		
CASH					ACCOUNTS PAYABLE				GAY GILLEN, CAPITAL		
(1)	30,000	(2)	20,000	(4)	300	(3)	500			(1)	30,000
		(4)	300			Bal.	200			Bal.	30,000
		(6)	2,100								
Bal.	7,600										

OFFICE SUPPLIES			GAY GILLEN, WITHDRAWALS		
(3)	500		(6)	2,100	
Bal.	500		Bal.	2,100	

LAND		
(2)	20,000	
Bal.	20,000	

If the sum of an account's debits is greater than the sum of its credits, that account has a debit balance, as the Cash account does. If the sum of its credits is greater, that account has a credit balance, as for Accounts Payable.

Objective 5

Prepare and use a trial balance

TRIAL BALANCE. A list of all the accounts with their balances.

The Trial Balance

A **trial balance** is a list of all the accounts with their balances—assets first, followed by liabilities and then owner's equity—taken from the ledger. Before computers, the trial balance provided a check on accuracy by showing whether total debits

equal total credits. The trial balance is now a useful summary of all the accounts and their balances. A trial balance may be taken whenever the postings are up to date. The most common time is at the end of the accounting period. Exhibit 2-7 is the trial balance of Gay Gillen eTravel after the first six transactions.

EXHIBIT 2-7
Trial Balance

 DAILY EXERCISE 2-4

GAY GILLEN ETRAVEL
Trial Balance
April 30, 20X1

Account Title	Balance	
	Debit	Credit
Cash	$ 7,600	
Office supplies	500	
Land	20,000	
Accounts payable		$ 200
Gay Gillen, capital		30,000
Gay Gillen, withdrawals	2,100	
Total	$30,200	$30,200

Correcting Trial Balance Errors

In a trial balance, total debits and total credits should be equal. If they are not, there must be an accounting error. Computerized accounting systems eliminate most errors because the journal amounts are posted precisely as they have been journalized. But computers cannot *eliminate* all errors because humans sometimes input the wrong data.

Out-of-balance conditions are detected by computing the difference between total debits and total credits on the trial balance. Then perform one or more of the following actions:

1. Search the trial balance for a missing account. For example, suppose the accountant omitted Gay Gillen, Withdrawals, from the trial balance in Exhibit 2-7. The total amount of the debits would be $28,100 ($30,200 − $2,100). Trace each account from the ledger to the trial balance, and you will locate the missing account.

2. Divide the difference between total debits and total credits by 2. A debit treated as a credit, or vice versa, doubles the amount of error. Suppose Gay Gillen's accountant posted a $300 credit as a debit. Total debits contain the $300, and total credits omit the $300. The out-of-balance amount is $600. Dividing the difference by 2 identifies the $300 amount of the transaction. Then search the journal for a $300 transaction and trace to the account affected.

3. Divide the out-of-balance amount by 9. If the result is evenly divisible by 9, the error may be a *slide* (example: writing $300 as $30) or a *transposition* (example: treating $61 as $16). Suppose Gillen printed her $2,100 Withdrawal as $21,000 on the trial balance—a slide-type error. Total debits would differ from total credits by $18,900 ($21,000 − $2,100 = $18,900). Dividing $18,900 by 9 yields $2,100, the correct amount of withdrawals. Trace this amount through the ledger until you reach the Gay Gillen, Withdrawals account with a balance of $2,100. Computer-based systems avoid such errors.

A warning: Do not confuse the trial balance with the balance sheet. A trial balance is an internal document seen only by the company's owners, managers, and accountants. The company reports its balance sheet, a formal financial statement, to the public.

The Seven Trillion Dollar Mistake

"If we can send missiles to a bull's-eye at a . . . training camp in Afghanistan, we ought to be able to set up an accounting system at the Defense Department. . . ."

This is what Senator Charles Grassley (R-Iowa) said in 1998 after embezzlements at U.S. military installations were allowed to occur because of weaknesses in the Pentagon's accounting system.

A year later, precision was still lacking at the Department of Defense. Pentagon money managers required almost $7 trillion of accounting adjustments to make their books balance. Each adjustment represents an accountant's correction of a discrepancy. The lesson of the $7 trillion mistake is this: Computers don't keep books; people do.

These bookkeeping errors affect all our pocketbooks. Without sound costing data, military managers simply can't make good decisions—like whether to close a base or keep it open. The public never knows the real cost of defense programs such as the missile defense shield or the cost of health care for military retirees. With more reliable accounting data, we would know how to vote on these issues.

Sources: Based on: Julia Malone, "Auditors cite failings in 11 of 24 agencies," *The Atlanta Constitution,* March 31, 2000, p. A; 20. John M. Donnelly, "Pentagon's Finances Just Don't Add Up; Audit: Hundreds of computer systems fail to keep running totals of income and outgo. Last year, the Defense Department's bookkeeping errors totaled more than the entire federal budget," *The Los Angeles Times,* March 5, 2000, p. 8. Ralph Vartabedian, "Thefts Reveal Flawed Pentagon Contract System," *The Los Angeles Times,* September 28, 1998, p. 1.

MID-CHAPTER

SUMMARY PROBLEM

www.prenhall.com/horngren

Mid-Chapter Assessment

On August 1, 20X5, Liz Shea opens Shea's Research Service. She is the owner of the proprietorship. During the entity's first ten days of operations, the business completes these transactions:

a. To begin operations, Shea deposits $40,000 of personal funds in a bank account entitled Shea's Research Service. The business receives the cash and gives Shea capital (owner's equity).

b. Shea pays $30,000 cash for a small building to be used as an office for the business.

c. Shea purchases office supplies for $500 on account.

d. Shea pays cash of $6,000 for office furniture.

e. Shea pays $150 on the account payable she created in transaction (c).

f. Shea withdraws $1,000 cash for personal use.

Required

1. Give the accounting equation for each transaction. Then journalize these transactions and post to the accounts. Key the journal entries by letter.

2. Show all the T-accounts after posting.

3. Prepare the trial balance of Shea's Research Service at August 10, 20X5.

Solution

Requirement 1

a. *Accounting Equation*

ASSETS	=	LIABILITIES	+	OWNER'S EQUITY
Cash				Liz Shea, Capital
+40,000	=	0	+	$40,000

Journal Entry

```
Cash .............................................................  40,000
     Liz Shea, Capital ...........................             40,000
Received investment from owner.
```

Ledger Accounts

CASH		LIZ SHEA, CAPITAL	
(a) 40,000			(a) 40,000

b. *Accounting Equation*

ASSETS		=	LIABILITIES	+	OWNER'S EQUITY
Cash	Building				
−30,000	+30,000	=	0	+	0

Journal Entry

```
Building ........................................................  30,000
     Cash ......................................................             30,000
Purchased building.
```

Ledger Accounts

CASH			BUILDING	
(a) 40,000	(b) 30,000		(b) 30,000	

c. *Accounting Equation*

ASSETS	=	LIABILITIES	+	OWNER'S EQUITY
Office Supplies		Accounts Payable		
+500	=	+500	+	0

Journal Entry

```
Office Supplies ............................................  500
     Accounts Payable.............................             500
Purchased office supplies on account.
```

Ledger Accounts

OFFICE SUPPLIES		ACCOUNTS PAYABLE	
(c) 500			(c) 500

d. *Accounting Equation*

ASSETS		=	LIABILITIES	+	OWNER'S EQUITY
	Office				
Cash	Furniture				
−6,000	+6,000	=	0	+	0

Journal Entry

```
Office Furniture .........................................  6,000
     Cash .................................................             6,000
Purchased office furniture.
```

Ledger Accounts

CASH		OFFICE FURNITURE	
(a) 40,000	(b) 30,000	(d) 6,000	
	(d) 6,000		

e. *Accounting Equation*

ASSETS	=	LIABILITIES	+	OWNER'S EQUITY
Cash		Accounts Payable		
−150	=	−150	+	0

Journal Entry

```
Accounts Payable........................................  150
     Cash .................................................             150
Paid cash on account.
```

Ledger Accounts

CASH		ACCOUNTS PAYABLE	
(a) 40,000	(b) 30,000	(e) 150	(c) 500
	(d) 6,000		
	(e) 150		

f. *Accounting Equation*

ASSETS	=	LIABILITIES	+	OWNER'S EQUITY
Cash				Liz Shea, Withdrawals
−1,000	=	0		−1,000

Journal Entry

Liz Shea, Withdrawals 1,000
      Cash   1,000

Ledger Accounts

CASH				LIZ SHEA, WITHDRAWALS	
(a)	40,000	(b)	30,000	(f)	1,000
		(d)	6,000		
		(e)	150		
		(f)	1,000		

Requirement 2

ASSETS

CASH			
(a)	40,000	(b)	30,000
		(d)	6,000
		(e)	150
		(f)	1,000
Bal.	2,850		

OFFICE FURNITURE		
(d)	6,000	
Bal.	6,000	

OFFICE SUPPLIES		
(c)	500	
Bal.	500	

BUILDING		
(b)	30,000	
Bal.	30,000	

LIABILITIES

ACCOUNTS PAYABLE			
(e)	150	(c)	500
		Bal.	350

OWNER'S EQUITY

LIZ SHEA, CAPITAL			
		(a)	40,000
		Bal.	40,000

LIZ SHEA, WITHDRAWALS		
(f)	1,000	
Bal.	1,000	

Requirement 3

SHEA'S RESEARCH SERVICE
Trial Balance
August 10, 20X5

	Balance	
Account Title	Debit	Credit
Cash...	$ 2,850	
Office supplies	500	
Office furniture	6,000	
Building......................................	30,000	
Accounts payable		$ 350
Liz Shea, capital.........................		40,000
Liz Shea, withdrawals	1,000	
Total..	$40,350	$40,350

DETAILS OF JOURNALS AND LEDGERS

To focus on the main points of journalizing and posting, we purposely omitted certain essential data. In practice, the journal and the ledger provide additional details that create a "trail" through the accounting records. For example, a supplier may bill us twice for the same item that we purchased on account. To prove we paid the bill, we would search the accounts payable records to find our payment. To see how this process works, let's take a closer look at the journal and the ledger.

DETAILS IN THE JOURNAL Exhibit 2-8, Panel B, presents the journal. The journal page number appears in the upper right corner, and the journal displays the following information:

1. The *date* when the transaction occurred, April 2, 20X1, for the first transaction.
2. The *account title* and explanation of the transaction.

EXHIBIT 2-8 **Journalizing and Posting**

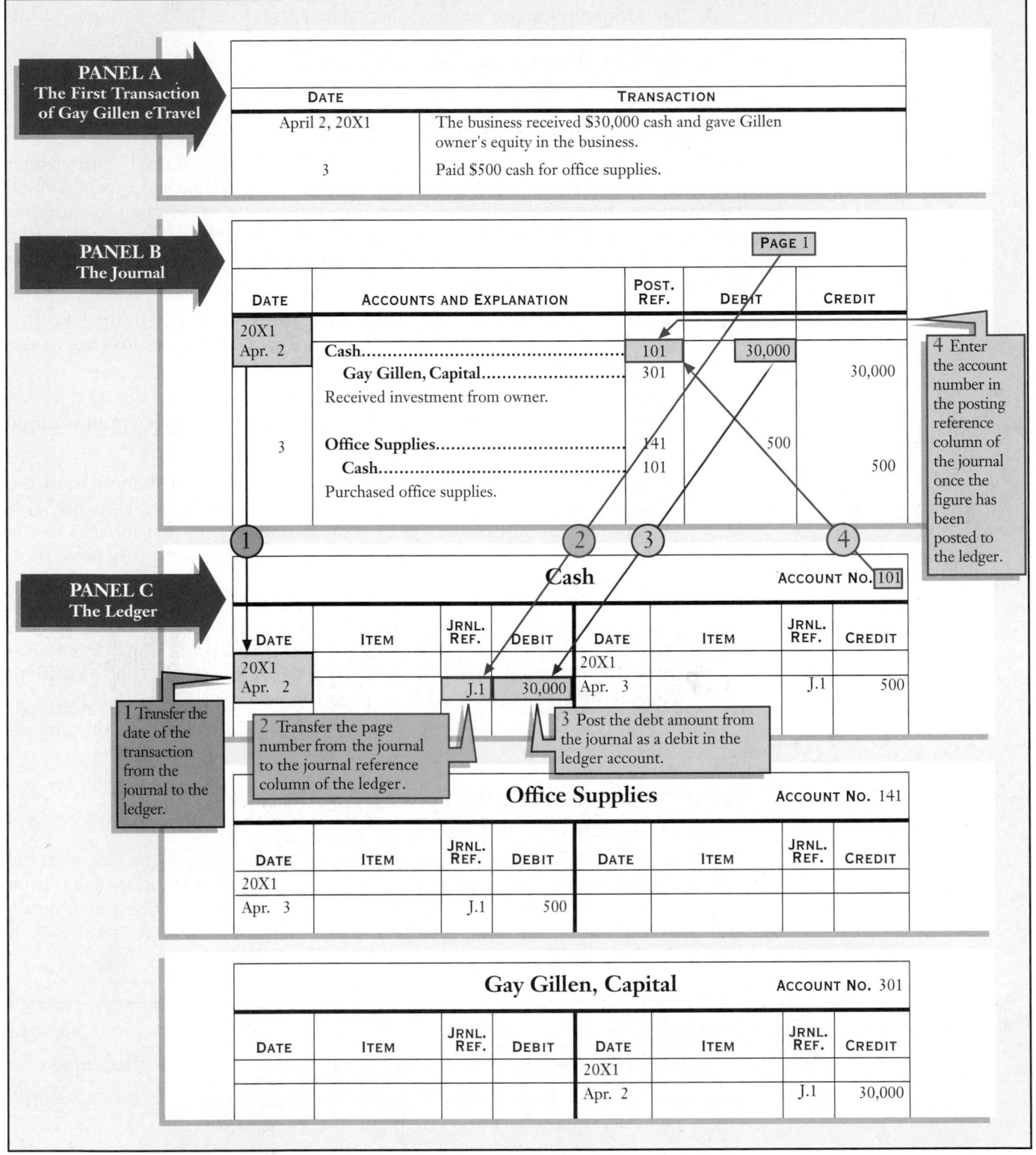

3. The *posting reference,* abbreviated Post. Ref. Use of this column will become clear when we discuss the details of posting.

4. The *debit* column, which shows the dollar amount debited.

5. The *credit* column, which shows the dollar amount credited.

DETAILS IN THE LEDGER Exhibit 2-8, Panel C, presents the T-accounts affected by the first transaction: Cash and Gay Gillen's Capital account. The account number appears at the upper right corner of each account. Each account has a separate column for

1. The date.
2. The item column, which can be used for any special notation.
3. The journal reference column, abbreviated Jrnl. Ref. The importance of this column will become clear when we discuss the mechanics of posting.
4. The debit column, with the amount debited.
5. The credit column, with the amount credited.

Posting from the Journal to the Ledger

We know that posting means copying information from the journal to the ledger accounts. But how do we handle the additional details that we have just seen? Exhibit 2-8 illustrates the steps in full detail. Panel A lists the first transaction of the business entity, Gay Gillen eTravel; Panel B presents the journal; and Panel C shows the ledger.

The posting process includes four steps. After recording the transaction in the journal:

Arrow ①—Copy (post) the transaction **date** from the journal to the ledger.

Arrow ②—Copy (post) the journal page number from the journal to the ledger. We use several abbreviations:

Jrnl. Ref. means Journal Reference. **J.1** refers to Journal page 1.

This step indicates where the information in the ledger came from: Journal page 1.

Arrow ③—Copy (post) the dollar amount of the debit **($30,000)** from the journal as a debit to the same account (Cash) in the ledger. Likewise, post the dollar amount of the credit (also **$30,000**) from the journal to the appropriate account in the ledger. Now the ledger accounts have their correct amounts.

Arrow ④—Copy (post) the account number **(101)** from the ledger back to the journal. This step indicates that the $30,000 debit to Cash has been posted to the Cash account in the ledger. Also, copy the account number **(301)** for Gay Gillen, Capital, back to the journal to show that the $30,000 amount of the credit has been posted to the ledger.

Post. Ref. is the abbreviation for Posting Reference. After posting, you can prepare the trial balance.

The Four-Column Account Format: An Alternative to the T-Account Format

The ledger accounts illustrated in Exhibit 2-8 appear in the T-account format, with the debit on the left and the credit on the right. The T-account clearly separates debits from credits and is used for teaching purposes in situations that do not have much detail. Another standard format has four amount columns, as illustrated for the Cash account in Exhibit 2-9.

EXHIBIT 2-9
Account in Four-Column Format

Account Cash					Account No. 101	
		Jrnl.			**Balance**	
Date	**Item**	**Ref.**	**Debit**	**Credit**	**Debit**	**Credit**
20X1						
Apr. 2		J.1	30,000		30,000	
3		J.1		500	29,500	

The first pair of amount columns are for the debit and credit amounts posted from individual entries, as just discussed. The second pair of amount columns are for the account balance. This four-column format keeps a running balance in the account. For this reason, it is used more often in practice than the two-column format. In Exhibit 2-9, Cash has a debit balance of $30,000 after the first transaction and a debit balance of $29,500 after the second transaction.

Chart of Accounts in the Ledger

As you know, the ledger contains the business's accounts grouped under these headings:

- Balance sheet accounts: Assets, Liabilities, and Owner's Equity
- Income statement accounts: Revenues and Expenses

Organizations use a **chart of accounts** to list all the accounts they use along with their account numbers. These account numbers are used as posting references, illustrated by arrow 4 in Exhibit 2-8.

Accounts are identified by account numbers with two or more digits. Assets are often numbered beginning with 1, liabilities with 2, owner's equity with 3, revenues with 4, and expenses with 5. The second, third, and higher digits in an account number indicate the position of each account within the category. For example, Cash may be account number 101, which is the first asset account. Accounts Receivable may be account number 111, the second asset account. Accounts Payable may be number 201, the first liability account. All accounts are numbered by this system. Organizations with many accounts use lengthy account numbers.

The chart of accounts for Gay Gillen eTravel, appears in Exhibit 2-10. Notice the gap in account numbers between 111 and 141. Gillen realizes that at some later dates she may need to add another category of receivables—for example, Notes Receivable, which she might number 121.

Objective 6
Set up a chart of accounts for a business

CHART OF ACCOUNTS. List of all the accounts and their account numbers in the ledger.

BALANCE SHEET ACCOUNTS:

Assets	Liabilities	Owner's Equity
101 Cash	201 Accounts Payable	301 Gay Gillen, Capital
111 Accounts Receivable	231 Notes Payable	311 Gay Gillen, Withdrawals
141 Office Supplies		
151 Office Furniture		
191 Land		

INCOME STATEMENT ACCOUNTS (PART OF OWNER'S EQUITY):

Revenues	Expenses
401 Service Revenue	501 Rent Expense
	502 Salary Expense
	503 Utilities Expense

EXHIBIT 2-10
Chart of Accounts— Gay Gillen eTravel

Appendix B gives two expanded charts of accounts that you will find helpful as you work through this course. The first chart lists the typical accounts of a large *service* proprietorship, such as Gay Gillen eTravel after a period of growth. The second chart is for a *merchandising* corporation, one that sells a product rather than a service. The third chart gives some accounts that a *manufacturing* company uses. You will use these accounts in Chapters 19–26. Study the service proprietorship now, and refer to the other charts of accounts as needed later.

The Normal Balance of an Account

An account's **normal balance** appears on the side of the account—debit or credit—where we record *increases*. That is, the normal balance is on the side that is positive. For example, Cash and other assets usually have a debit balance (the debit side is positive and the credit side negative), so the normal balance of assets is on the debit side. Assets are called *debit-balance accounts*. Conversely, liabilities and owner's equity usually have a credit balance, so their normal balances are on the credit side. They are called *credit-balance accounts*. Exhibit 2-11 illustrates the normal balances of assets, liabilities, and owner's equity.

An account that normally has a debit balance may occasionally have a credit balance. That indicates a negative amount of the item. For example, Cash will have a temporary credit balance if the entity overdraws its bank account. Similarly, the

 DAILY EXERCISE 2-5

NORMAL BALANCE. The account balance that appears on the side of the account—debit or credit—where we record increases.

EXHIBIT 2-11
Normal Balances of the Balance Sheet Accounts

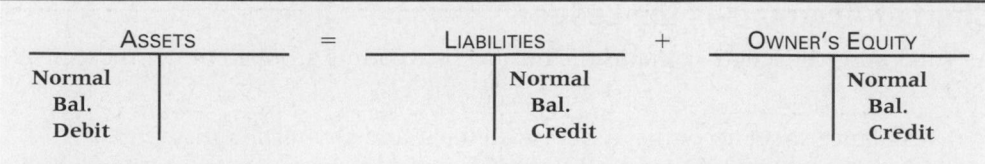

ASSETS	=	LIABILITIES	+	OWNER'S EQUITY
Normal Bal. Debit		Normal Bal. Credit		Normal Bal. Credit

liability Accounts Payable—normally a credit-balance account—will have a debit balance if the entity overpays its account. In other instances, an odd balance may indicate an accounting error. For example, a credit balance in Office Supplies, Office Furniture, or Buildings indicates an error because negative amounts of these assets cannot exist.

As we saw earlier, owner's equity contains the Capital account and the Withdrawals account. In total, these accounts show a normal credit balance. An individual owner's equity account with a normal credit balance, such as Gay Gillen, Capital, represents an *increase* in owner's equity. An owner's equity account that has a normal debit balance, such as Gay Gillen, Withdrawals, represents a *decrease* in owner's equity.

EXPANDING THE ACCOUNTING EQUATION TO ACCOUNT FOR REVENUES AND EXPENSES

DAILY EXERCISE 2-15

Owner's equity also includes Revenues and Expenses because revenues and expenses make up net income or net loss, which flows into owner's equity. As we have noted, *revenues* are increases in owner's equity that result from delivering goods or services to customers in the course of operating the business. *Expenses* are decreases in owner's equity that occur from using assets or increasing liabilities in the course of operations. Therefore, the accounting equation may be expanded as shown in Exhibit 2-12. Revenues and expenses appear in parentheses to highlight the fact that their net effect—revenues minus expenses—equals net income, which increases owner's equity. If expenses are greater than revenues, the net effect of operations is a net loss, which decreases owner's equity.

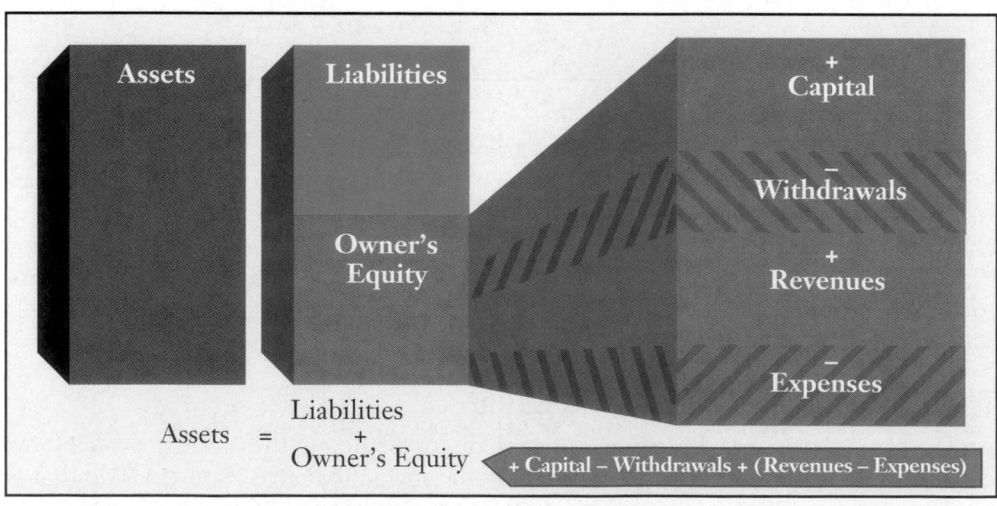

We can now express the rules of debit and credit in final form, as shown in Exhibit 2-13, Panel A. Panel B shows the *normal* balances of the five types of accounts: *Assets; Liabilities;* and *Owner's Equity* and its subparts, *Revenues and Expenses.* All of accounting is based on these five types of accounts.

You should not proceed until you have learned the rules of debit and credit and the normal balances of the five types of accounts.

PANEL A—Rules of Debit and Credit:

	ASSETS			LIABILITIES			CAPITAL	
	Debit for Increase	Credit for Decrease	=	Debit for Decrease	Credit for Increase	+	Debit for Decrease	Credit for Increase

PANEL B—Normal Balances:

		WITHDRAWALS	
Assets	Debit	Debit for Increase	Credit for Decrease
Liabilities...	Credit		
Owner's equity—overall	Credit	REVENUES	
Capital..	Credit	Debit for Decrease	Credit for Increase
Withdrawals...............................	Debit		
Revenues......................................	Credit		
Expenses	Debit	EXPENSES	
		Debit for Increase	Credit for Decrease

DAILY EXERCISE 2-6

Compute the missing amounts in each of the following T-accounts.

WORK IT OUT

1.
CASH

Bal. 10,000	
20,000	13,000
	cd 17000
Bal. *30000?*	*300 0*
	bd 17000

2. ACCOUNTS RECEIVABLE

Bal. 12,800	
45,600	?
Bal. 23,500	

3. ANNIE TODD, CAPITAL

	Bal. ?
22,000	56,000
	15,000
	Bal. 73,000

Answers

1. The ending balance (X) for Cash is:

$$X = \$10,000 + \$20,000 - \$13,000$$
$$X = \$17,000$$

2. We are given the beginning and ending balances. We can compute the credit entry (X) as follows for Accounts Receivable:

$$\$12,800 + \$45,600 - X = \$23,500$$
$$\$58,400 - \$23,500 = X$$
$$X = \$34,900$$

3. The Capital account has an ending credit balance of $73,000. We can figure the beginning credit balance (X), as follows:

$$X + \$56,000 + \$15,000 - \$22,000 = \$73,000$$
$$X = \$73,000 - \$56,000 - \$15,000 + \$22,000$$
$$X = \$24,000$$

EXPANDED PROBLEM INCLUDING REVENUES AND EXPENSES

Let's account for the revenues and expenses of the law practice of Jeff Hatton, Attorney, for the month of July 20X1. We follow the same steps illustrated earlier in this chapter: Analyze the transaction, journalize, post to the ledger, and prepare the trial balance.

Transaction Analysis, Journalizing, and Posting

1. *Transaction Analysis* — Jeff Hatton invested $10,000 cash in a business bank account to open his law practice. The business received the cash and gave Hatton owner's equity. The business's asset cash is increased; therefore, debit Cash. The owner's equity of the business increased, so credit Jeff Hatton, Capital.

	Accounting Equation	ASSETS	=	LIABILITIES	+	OWNER'S EQUITY

Accounting Equation	ASSETS = LIABILITIES + OWNER'S EQUITY
	Cash +10,000 = 0 + Jeff Hatton, Capital 10,000

Accounting Equation

ASSETS = **LIABILITIES** + **OWNER'S EQUITY**

Cash +10,000	=	0	+	Jeff Hatton, Capital 10,000

Journal Entry

Cash 10,000
    Jeff Hatton, Capital   10,000
Received investment from owner.

Ledger Accounts

CASH		JEFF HATTON, CAPITAL	
(1) 10,000			(1) 10,000

2. *Transaction Analysis*

Hatton performed service for a client and collected $3,000 cash. The asset cash is increased, so debit Cash. The revenue account Service Revenue is increased; credit Service Revenue.

Accounting Equation

ASSETS = **LIABILITIES** + **OWNER'S EQUITY** + **REVENUES**

Cash +3,000	=	0			+	Service Revenue 3,000

Journal Entry

Cash 3,000
    Service Revenue   3,000
Performed service and received cash.

Ledger Accounts

CASH		SERVICE REVENUE	
(1) 10,000			(2) 3,000
(2) 3,000			

3. *Transaction Analysis*

Hatton performed service for a client and billed the client for $500 on account receivable. This means the client owes the business $500, and Hatton expects to collect the $500 later. The asset accounts receivable is increased; therefore, debit Accounts Receivable. Service revenue is increased; credit Service Revenue. Remember that revenues are credit-balance accounts.

Accounting Equation

ASSETS = **LIABILITIES** + **OWNER'S EQUITY** + **REVENUES**

Accounts Receivable +500	=	0			+	Service Revenue 500

Journal Entry

Accounts Receivable 500
    Service Revenue   500
Performed service on account.

Ledger Accounts

ACCOUNTS RECEIVABLE		SERVICE REVENUE	
(3) 500			(2) 3,000
			(3) 500

4. *Transaction Analysis*

Hatton earned $700 service revenue by performing legal service for a client. The client paid Hatton $300 cash immediately. Hatton billed the remaining $400 to the client on account receivable. The assets cash and accounts receivable are increased; therefore, debit both of these asset accounts. Service revenue is increased; credit Service Revenue for the sum of the two debit amounts.

Accounting Equation

ASSETS = **LIABILITIES** + **OWNER'S EQUITY** + **REVENUES**

Cash	Accounts Receivable					Service Revenue
+300	+400	=	0		+	700

Journal Entry	Cash..	300	
	Accounts Receivable..	400	
	Service Revenue		700
	Performed service for cash and on account.		

Note: Because this transaction affects more than two accounts at the same time, the entry is called a *compound entry.* **No matter how many accounts a compound entry affects—there may be any number—total debits must equal total credits.**

● DAILY EXERCISE 2-7

Ledger Accounts

CASH		ACCOUNTS RECEIVABLE		SERVICE REVENUE	
(1) 10,000		(3) 500		(2) 3,000	
(2) 3,000		(4) 400		(3) 500	
(4) 300				(4) 700	

5. *Transaction Analysis* Hatton paid the following cash expenses: office rent, $900; employee salary, $1,500; and utilities, $500. The asset cash is decreased; therefore, credit Cash for the sum of the three expense amounts. The following expenses are increased: Rent Expense, Salary Expense, and Utilities Expense. Each expense account should be debited separately. Remember that expenses are debit-balance accounts, the opposite of revenues.

Accounting Equation

ASSETS	=	LIABILITIES	+	OWNER'S EQUITY	–	EXPENSES		
						Rent Expense	Salary Expense	Utilities Expense
Cash −2,900	=	0				−900	−1,500	−500

Journal Entry

Rent Expense	900	
Salary Expense	1,500	
Utilities Expense..	500	
Cash		2,900
Paid cash expenses.		

Note: In practice, the business would record these three transactions separately. To save space, we can record them together in a compound journal entry.

Ledger Accounts

CASH				RENT EXPENSE	
(1) 10,000	(5)	2,900		(5) 900	
(2) 3,000					
(4) 300					

SALARY EXPENSE		UTILITIES EXPENSE	
(5) 1,500		(5) 500	

6. *Transaction Analysis* Hatton received a telephone bill for $120 and will pay this expense next week. There is no cash payment now. Utilities expense is increased, so debit this expense. The liability accounts payable is increased, so credit Accounts Payable.

Accounting Equation

ASSETS	=	LIABILITIES	+	OWNER'S EQUITY	–	EXPENSES	
		Accounts Payable				Utilities Expense	
0	=	+120			–	120	

Journal Entry

Utilities Expense...	120	
Accounts Payable		120
Received utility bill.		

Ledger Accounts

ACCOUNTS PAYABLE		UTILITIES EXPENSE	
	(6) 120	(5) 500	
		(6) 120	

7. *Transaction Analysis*   Hatton collected $200 cash from the client established in transaction 3. The asset cash is increased, so debit Cash. The asset accounts receivable is decreased; credit Accounts Receivable.

Accounting Equation

ASSETS		=	LIABILITIES	+	OWNER'S EQUITY
Cash	Accounts Receivable				
+200	−200	=	0	+	0

Journal Entry

Cash 200
    Accounts Receivable.........................   200
Received cash on account.

Note: This transaction has no effect on revenue; the related revenue was accounted for in transaction 3.

Ledger Accounts

	CASH				ACCOUNTS RECEIVABLE		
(1)	10,000	(5)	2,900	(3)	500	(7)	200
(2)	3,000			(4)	400		
(4)	300						
(7)	200						

8. *Transaction Analysis*   Hatton paid the telephone bill that was received and recorded in transaction 6. The asset cash is decreased; credit Cash. The liability accounts payable is decreased; therefore, debit Accounts Payable.

Accounting Equation

ASSETS	=	LIABILITIES	+	OWNER'S EQUITY
Cash		Accounts Payable		
−120	=	−120	+	0

Journal Entry

Accounts Payable 120
    Cash   120
Paid cash on account.

Note: This transaction has no effect on expense because the related expense was recorded in transaction 6.

Ledger Accounts

	CASH				ACCOUNTS PAYABLE		
(1)	10,000	(5)	2,900	(8)	120	(6)	120
(2)	3,000	(8)	120				
(4)	300						
(7)	200						

9. *Transaction Analysis*   Hatton withdrew $1,100 cash for personal use. The asset cash decreased; credit Cash. The withdrawal decreased owner's equity; therefore, debit Jeff Hatton, Withdrawals.

Accounting Equation

ASSETS	=	LIABILITIES	+	OWNER'S EQUITY
Cash				Jeff Hatton, Withdrawals
−1,100	=	0		−1,100

Journal Entry

Jeff Hatton, Withdrawals 1,100
    Cash   1,100
Withdrew cash for personal use.

⦿ DAILY EXERCISE 2-8

⦿ DAILY EXERCISE 2-9

⦿ DAILY EXERCISE 2-10

⦿ DAILY EXERCISE 2-11

Ledger Accounts

	CASH				JEFF HATTON, WITHDRAWALS	
(1)	10,000	(5)	2,900	(9)	1,100	
(2)	3,000	(8)	120			
(4)	300	(9)	1,100			
(7)	200					

Ledger Accounts After Posting

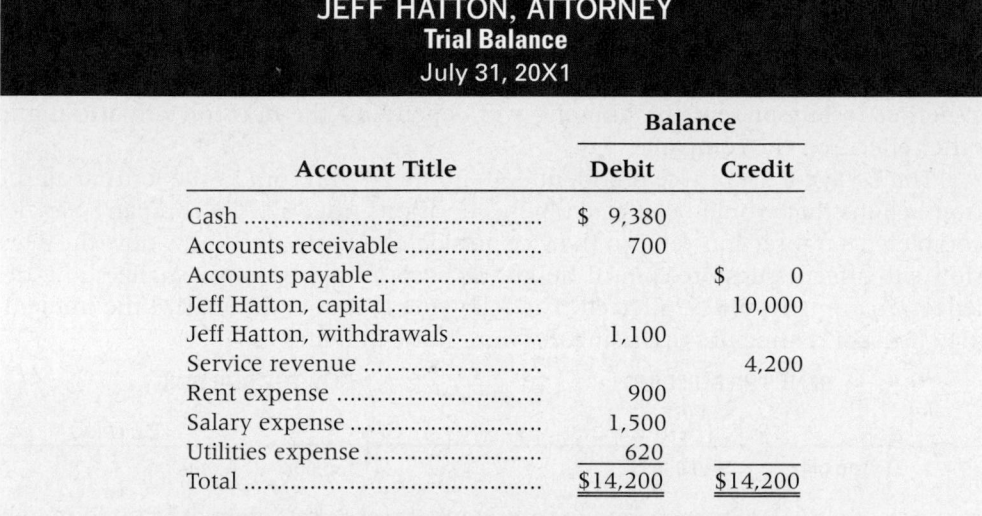

ASSETS	LIABILITIES	OWNER'S EQUITY	REVENUE	EXPENSES

CASH

(1)	10,000	(5)	2,900
(2)	3,000	(8)	120
(4)	300	(9)	1,100
(7)	200		
Bal.	9,380		

ACCOUNTS RECEIVABLE

(3)	500	(7)	200
(4)	400		
Bal.	700		

ACCOUNTS PAYABLE

(8)	120	(6)	120
		Bal.	0

JEFF HATTON, CAPITAL

		(1)	10,000
		Bal.	10,000

JEFF HATTON, WITHDRAWALS

(9)	1,100		
Bal.	1,100		

SERVICE REVENUE

		(2)	3,000
		(3)	500
		(4)	700
		Bal.	4,200

RENT EXPENSE

(5)	900		
Bal.	900		

SALARY EXPENSE

(5)	1,500		
Bal.	1,500		

UTILITIES EXPENSE

(5)	500		
(6)	120		
Bal.	620		

Trial Balance

The trial balance lists the balance of each account.

JEFF HATTON, ATTORNEY
Trial Balance
July 31, 20X1

Account Title	Balance Debit	Balance Credit
Cash	$ 9,380	
Accounts receivable	700	
Accounts payable		$ 0
Jeff Hatton, capital		10,000
Jeff Hatton, withdrawals	1,100	
Service revenue		4,200
Rent expense	900	
Salary expense	1,500	
Utilities expense	620	
Total	$14,200	$14,200

⊙ DAILY EXERCISE 2-12

⊙ DAILY EXERCISE 2-13

⊙ DAILY EXERCISE 2-14

Now you have seen how to record business transactions, post to the ledger accounts, and prepare a trial balance. Solidify your understanding of the accounting process by reviewing the Decision Guidelines below.

DECISION GUIDELINES

Analyzing and Recording Transactions

DECISION	GUIDELINES
• Has a transaction occurred?	If the event affects the entity's financial position and can be reliably recorded—*Yes* If either condition is absent—*No*
• Where to record the transaction?	In the *journal,* the chronological record of transactions
• What to record for each transaction?	Increases and/or decreases in all the accounts affected by the transaction
• How to record an increase/decrease in a (an)	Rules of debit and credit:

	Increase	Decrease
Asset	**Debit**	**Credit**
Liability	**Credit**	**Debit**
Owner's Equity	**Credit**	**Debit**
Revenue	**Credit**	**Debit**
Expense	**Debit**	**Credit**

DECISION GUIDELINES (CONT.)

DECISION	GUIDELINES
• Where to store all the information for each account?	In the *ledger,* the book of accounts and their balances
• Where to list all the accounts and their balances?	In the *trial balance*
• Where to report the results of operations?	In the income statement (Revenues − Expenses = Net income or Net loss)
• Where to report financial position?	In the balance sheet (Assets = Liabilities + Owner's equity)

USING ACCOUNTING INFORMATION FOR QUICK DECISION MAKING

Objective 7
Analyze transactions without a journal

◉ DAILY EXERCISE 2-16

Often businesspeople make decisions without taking the time to follow all the steps in an accounting system. For example, suppose Drugstore.com needs more warehouse space to meet customer demand. The company can purchase a warehouse building for $700,000, or it can rent a building at an overall cost of $100,000. Whether to buy or rent the building will depend on the decision's financial and other effects on the company.

The Drugstore.com vice president does not need to record in the journal all the transactions that would be affected by his decision. After all, the company has not completed a transaction yet. But the vice president does need to know how the decision will affect Drugstore.com. If he knows accounting, he can visualize how the ledger accounts would be affected. The following accounts summarize the immediate effects of renting or purchasing the warehouse building.

RENT THE BUILDING				BUY THE BUILDING		
CASH		RENT EXPENSE		CASH		BUILDING
100,000		100,000		700,000		700,000

Immediately the Drugstore.com vice president can see that buying the building will require more cash. But he can also see that he will obtain the building as an asset. This may motivate him to borrow cash and buy the building. A low cash balance may lead to renting.

Companies do not actually keep their records in this short-cut fashion. But a decision maker who needs information immediately can quickly analyze the effect of a set of transactions on the company's financial statements.

REVIEW THE RECORDING OF BUSINESS TRANSACTIONS

SUMMARY PROBLEM

www.prenhall.com/horngren
End-of-Chapter Assessment

The trial balance of Tomassini Computer Service Center on March 1, 20X2, lists the entity's assets, liabilities, and owner's equity on that date.

	Balance	
Account Title	Debit	Credit
Cash	$26,000	
Accounts receivable	4,500	
Accounts payable		$ 2,000
Larry Tomassini, capital...............		28,500
Total..	$30,500	$30,500

During March, the business engaged in the following transactions:
a. Borrowed $45,000 from the bank and signed a note payable in the name of the business.
b. Paid cash of $40,000 to a real estate company to acquire land.
c. Performed service for a customer and received cash of $5,000.
d. Purchased supplies on credit, $300.
e. Performed customer service and earned revenue on account, $2,600.
f. Paid $1,200 on account.
g. Paid the following cash expenses: salaries, $3,000; rent, $1,500; and interest, $400.
h. Received $3,100 on account.
i. Received a $200 utility bill that will be paid next week.
j. Withdrew $1,800 for personal use.

Required

1. Open the following accounts, with the balances indicated, in the ledger of Tomassini Computer Service Center. Use the T-account format.
- Assets—Cash, $26,000; Accounts Receivable, $4,500; Supplies, no balance; Land, no balance
- Liabilities—Accounts Payable, $2,000; Note Payable, no balance
- Owner's Equity—Larry Tomassini, Capital, $28,500; Larry Tomassini, Withdrawals, no balance
- Revenues—Service Revenue, no balance
- Expenses—(none have balances) Salary Expense, Rent Expense, Utilities Expense, Interest Expense

2. For each transaction, give the accounting equation. Then journalize the transaction. Key journal entries by transaction letter.
3. Post to the ledger.
4. Prepare the trial balance of Tomassini Computer Service Center at March 31, 20X2.

Solution

Requirement 1

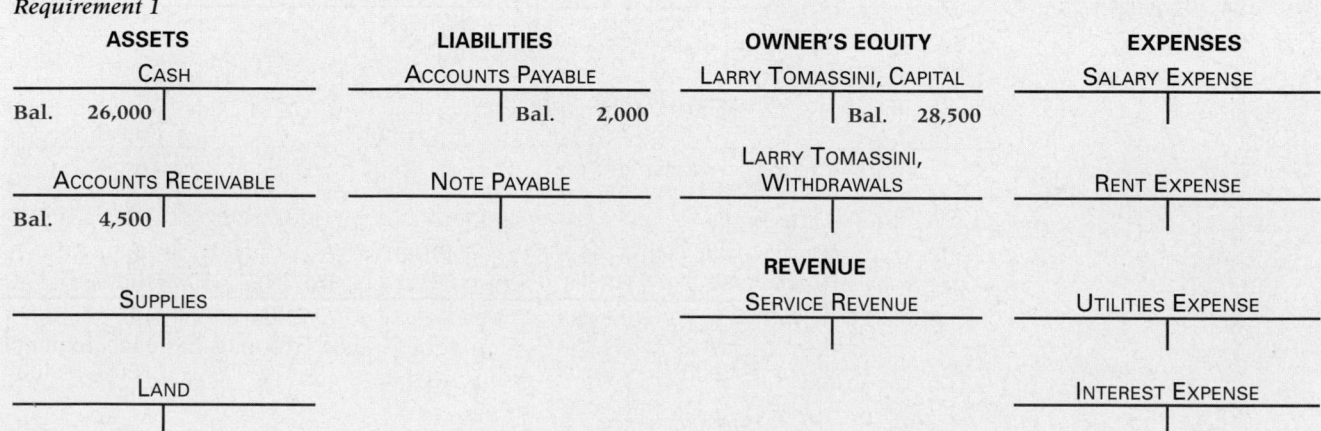

ASSETS	LIABILITIES	OWNER'S EQUITY	EXPENSES
CASH	ACCOUNTS PAYABLE	LARRY TOMASSINI, CAPITAL	SALARY EXPENSE
Bal. 26,000	Bal. 2,000	Bal. 28,500	
ACCOUNTS RECEIVABLE	NOTE PAYABLE	LARRY TOMASSINI, WITHDRAWALS	RENT EXPENSE
Bal. 4,500			
SUPPLIES		REVENUE	UTILITIES EXPENSE
		SERVICE REVENUE	
LAND			INTEREST EXPENSE

Requirement 2

a. *Accounting Equation*

ASSETS	=	LIABILITIES	+	OWNER'S EQUITY
Cash		Note Payable		
+45,000	=	+45,000	+	0

Journal Entry

Cash 45,000
    Note Payable.................................. 45,000
Borrowed cash on note payable.

b. *Accounting Equation*

ASSETS		=	LIABILITIES	+	OWNER'S EQUITY
Cash	Land				
−40,000	+40,000	=	0	+	0

Journal Entry

Land 40,000
    Cash 40,000
Purchased land.

c. *Accounting Equation*

ASSETS	=	LIABILITIES	+	OWNER'S EQUITY	+	REVENUES
Cash						Service Revenue
+5,000	=	0			+	5,000

Journal Entry

Cash	5,000	
Service Revenue		5,000
Performed service and received cash.		

d. *Accounting Equation*

ASSETS	=	LIABILITIES	+	OWNER'S EQUITY
Supplies		Accounts Payable		
+300	=	+300	+	0

Journal Entry

Supplies	300	
Accounts Payable		300
Purchased supplies on account.		

e. *Accounting Equation*

ASSETS	=	LIABILITIES	+	OWNER'S EQUITY	+	REVENUES
Accounts Receivable						Service Revenue
+2,600	=	0			+	2,600

Journal Entry

Accounts Receivable	2,600	
Service Revenue		2,600
Performed service on account.		

f. *Accounting Equation*

ASSETS	=	LIABILITIES	+	OWNER'S EQUITY
Cash		Accounts Payable		
−1,200	=	−1,200	+	0

Journal Entry

Accounts Payable	1,200	
Cash		1,200
Paid on account.		

g. *Accounting Equation*

ASSETS	=	LIABILITIES	+	OWNER'S EQUITY	−	EXPENSES		
						Salary Expense	Rent Expense	Interest Expense
Cash								
−4,900	=	0				−3,000	−1,500	−400

Journal Entry

Salary Expense	3,000	
Rent Expense	1,500	
Interest Expense	400	
Cash		4,900
Paid expenses.		

h. *Accounting Equation*

ASSETS		=	LIABILITIES	+	OWNER'S EQUITY
Cash	Accounts Receivable				
+3,100	−3,100	=	0	+	0

Journal Entry

Cash	3,100	
Accounts Receivable		3,100
Received cash on account.		

i. *Accounting Equation*

ASSETS	=	LIABILITIES	+	OWNER'S EQUITY	−	EXPENSES
		Accounts Payable				Utilities Expense
0	=	+200			−	200

Journal	Utilities Expense.....................................	200	
Entry	Accounts Payable		200
	Received utility bill.		

j. *Accounting Equation*

ASSETS	=	LIABILITIES	+	OWNER'S EQUITY
				Larry Tomassini,
Cash				Withdrawals
−1,800	=	0		−1,800

Journal	Larry Tomassini, Withdrawals.................	1,800	
Entry	Cash		1,800
	Owner withdrawal.		

Requirement 3

	ASSETS					LIABILITIES				OWNER'S EQUITY				EXPENSES	

ASSETS

CASH

Bal.	26,000	(b)	40,000
(a)	45,000	(f)	1,200
(c)	5,000	(g)	4,900
(h)	3,100	(j)	1,800
Bal.	31,200		

ACCOUNTS RECEIVABLE

Bal.	4,500	(h)	3,100
(e)	2,600		
Bal.	4,000		

SUPPLIES

(d)	300		
Bal.	300		

LAND

(b)	40,000		
Bal.	40,000		

LIABILITIES

ACCOUNTS PAYABLE

(f)	1,200	Bal.	2,000
		(d)	300
		(i)	200
		Bal.	1,300

NOTE PAYABLE

		(a)	45,000
		Bal.	45,000

OWNER'S EQUITY

LARRY TOMASSINI, CAPITAL

		Bal.	28,500

LARRY TOMASSINI, WITHDRAWALS

(j)	1,800		
Bal.	1,800		

REVENUE

SERVICE REVENUE

		(c)	5,000
		(e)	2,600
		Bal.	7,600

EXPENSES

SALARY EXPENSE

(g)	3,000		
Bal.	3,000		

RENT EXPENSE

(g)	1,500		
Bal.	1,500		

INTEREST EXPENSE

(g)	400		
Bal.	400		

UTILITIES EXPENSE

(i)	200		
Bal.	200		

Requirement 4

TOMASSINI COMPUTER SERVICE CENTER
Trial Balance
March 31, 20X2

	Balance	
Account Title	Debit	Credit
Cash..	$31,200	
Accounts receivable.............................	4,000	
Supplies	300	
Land..	40,000	
Accounts payable		$ 1,300
Note payable...		45,000
Larry Tomassini, capital		28,500
Larry Tomassini, withdrawals...............	1,800	
Service revenue		7,600
Salary expense......................................	3,000	
Rent expense...	1,500	
Interest expense	400	
Utilities expense	200	
Total..	$82,400	$82,400

LESSONS LEARNED

1. **Define and use key accounting terms.** Accounts can be viewed in the form of the letter "T." The left side of each T-account is its *debit* side. The right side is its *credit* side. The *ledger,* which contains a record for each account, groups and numbers accounts by category in the following order: assets, liabilities, and owner's equity (and its subparts, revenues and expenses).

2. **Apply the rules of debit and credit.** *Assets* and *expenses* are increased by debits and decreased by credits. *Liabilities, owner's equity,* and *revenues* are increased by credits and decreased by debits. An account's *normal balance* is the side of the account—debit or credit—in which increases are recorded. Thus, the normal balance of assets and expenses is a debit, and the normal balance of liabilities, owner's equity, and revenues is a credit. The Withdrawals account, which decreases owner's equity, normally has a debit balance. Revenues, which are increases in owner's equity, have a normal credit balance. Expenses, which are decreases in owner's equity, have a normal debit balance.

3. **Record transactions in the journal.** The recording process begins by entering each transaction in the *journal,* a chronological list of all the entity's transactions.

4. **Post from the journal to the ledger.** *Posting* means copying the amounts from the journal to the *ledger* accounts. Posting references are used to trace amounts back and forth between journal and ledger.

5. **Prepare and use a trial balance.** *The trial balance* is a summary of all the account balances in the ledger. When *double-entry accounting* is done correctly, the total debits and the total credits in the trial balance are equal.

6. **Set up a chart of accounts for a business.** A chart of accounts lists all the accounts in the ledger and their account numbers.

7. **Analyze transactions without a journal.** Decision makers must often make decisions without a complete accounting system. They can analyze the transactions without a journal.

ACCOUNTING VOCABULARY

account   (p. 39)
chart of accounts   (p. 55)
credit   (p. 42)

debit   (p. 42)
journal   (p. 44)
ledger   (p. 39)

normal balance   (p. 55)
posting   (p. 45)
trial balance   (p. 48)

QUESTIONS

1. Name the basic summary device of accounting. What letter of the alphabet does it resemble? Name its two sides.
2. Is the following statement true or false? Debit means decrease and credit means increase. Explain your answer.
3. What are the three *basic* types of accounts? Name two additional types of accounts. Which of the three basic types are these two additional types of accounts most closely related to?
4. Briefly describe the flow of accounting information.
5. Indicate the normal balance of the five types of accounts.

Account Type	Normal Balance
Assets	
Liabilities	
Capital	
Revenues	
Expenses	

6. What does posting accomplish? Why is it important? Does it come before or after journalizing?
7. Label each of the following transactions as increasing owner's equity (+), decreasing owner's equity (−), or as having no effect on owner's equity (0). Write the appropriate symbol in the space provided.

_____**a.** Investment by owner
_____**b.** Revenue transaction
_____**c.** Purchase of supplies on credit
_____**d.** Expense transaction
_____**e.** Cash payment on account
_____ **f.** Withdrawal by owner
_____**g.** Borrowing money on a note payable
_____**h.** Sale of service on account

8. Rearrange the following accounts in their logical sequence in the ledger:

Notes Payable   Cash
Accounts Receivable   Jane East, Capital
Sales Revenue   Salary Expense

9. What is the meaning of this statement? Accounts Payable has a credit balance of $1,700.
10. Why do accountants prepare a trial balance?
11. What is a compound journal entry?
12. The accountant for Bower Construction Company mistakenly recorded a $500 purchase of supplies on account as a $5,000 purchase. He debited Supplies and credited Accounts Payable for $5,000. Does this error cause the trial balance to be out of balance? Explain your answer.
13. What is the effect on total assets of collecting cash on account from customers?
14. What is the advantage of analyzing transactions without the use of a journal? Describe how this analysis works.

Assess Your Progress

DAILY EXERCISES

DE2-1 There are three broad categories of accounts: assets, liabilities, and owner's equity.

1. Owner's equity is more complex than assets and liabilities. What is the definition of *owner's equity?* Suppose your assets total $8,000 and your liabilities are $5,000. How much is your owner's equity?
2. Identify two categories of transactions that *increase* owner's equity. Name two categories of transactions that *decrease* owner's equity. This concept is discussed beginning on page 40.
3. Give a short (one- or two-word) synonym for an *asset* and a *liability.* Then list several individual assets and several specific liabilities.

Using key terms
(Obj. 1)

DE2-2 Review basic accounting definitions by completing the following crossword puzzle.

Using key terms
(Obj. 1)

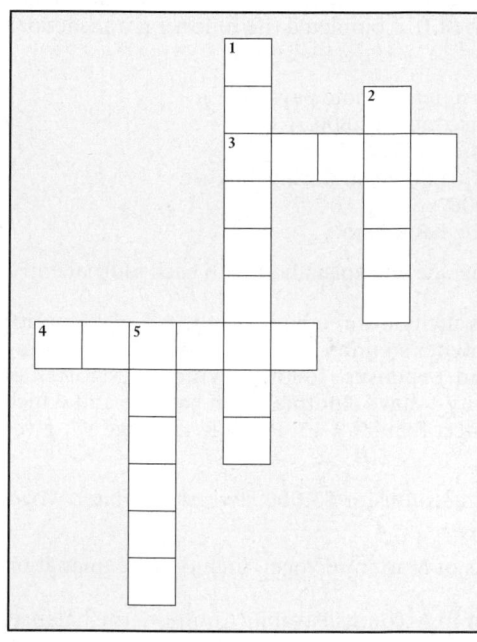

Across:
3. Economic resource of an entity.
4. Records an increase in a liability or owner's equity.

Down:
1. A debt.
2. Records an increase in an asset or an expense.
5. Assets − Liabilities = Owner's _____.

DE2-3 Rolfe Schmidt opened an architectural firm and immediately paid $60,000 for equipment to be used in the business. Was Schmidt's payment an expense of the business? If not, what did he acquire? Explain your reasoning after reviewing the definitions of *assets* on page 39 and *expenses* on page 41.

Explaining an asset versus an expense
(Obj. 1)

DE2-4 Understanding basic concepts is essential for success in accounting. Tighten your grip on the accounting process by filling in the blanks to review the definitions of key terms.

Using key terms
(Obj. 1)

Erika Darby, an introductory accounting student, is describing the accounting process for a friend who is a philosophy major. Erika states, "The basic summary device in accounting is the **account,** which can be represented by the letter _____. The left side of an account is called the _____ side, and the right side is called the _____ side.

"We record transactions first in a _____. Then we post (copy the data) to the accounts in the _____. It is helpful to list all the accounts with their balances on a _____ _____."

DE2-5 Accounting has its own vocabulary and basic relationships. Match the accounting terms at left with the corresponding definition at right.

Using accounting terms
(Obj. 1)

___ 1. Ledger	A. Record of transactions
___ 2. Posting	B. Always an asset
___ 3. Normal balance	C. Left side of an account
___ 4. Payable	D. Side of an account where increases are recorded
___ 5. Journal	E. Copying data from the journal to the ledger
___ 6. Receivable	F. Using up assets in the course of operating a business
___ 7. Capital	G. Always a liability
___ 8. Debit	H. Revenues − Expenses
___ 9. Expense	I. Grouping of accounts
___ 10. Net income	J. Owner's equity in the business

DE2-6 Josh Birbary, a recent graduate, is tutoring Trevor Grant, who is taking introductory accounting. Josh explains to Trevor that *debits* are used to record increases in accounts and *credits* record decreases. Trevor is confused and seeks your advice.

- When are credits increases? When are credits decreases?
- When are debits increases? When are debits decreases?

Exhibit 2-13, page 57, gives the rules of debit and credit.

DE2-7 Lee Jackson opened a medical practice in Cincinnati, Ohio. Record the following transactions in the journal of Lee Jackson, M.D. Include an explanation with each journal entry.

June 1 Jackson invested $25,000 cash in a business bank account to start his medical practice. The business received the cash and gave Jackson owner's equity in the business.

2 Purchased medical supplies on account, $10,000.

2 Paid monthly office rent of $4,000.

3 Recorded $5,000 revenue for service rendered to patients. Received cash of $1,000 and sent bills to patients for the remainder.

DE2-8 After operating for a month, Lee Jackson, M.D., completed the following transactions during the latter part of July:

July 15 Borrowed $20,000 from the bank, signing a note payable.

22 Performed service for patients on account, $2,800.

30 Received cash on account from patients, $1,000.

31 Received a utility bill, $200, which will be paid during August.

31 Paid monthly salary to nurse, $3,000.

31 Paid interest expense of $200 on the bank loan.

Journalize the transactions of Lee Jackson, M.D. Include an explanation with each journal entry.

DE2-9 The accounting records of all businesses include three basic categories of accounts: assets, liabilities, and owner's equity. In turn, owner's equity is divided into the following categories: capital, withdrawals, revenues, and expenses. Identify which categories of accounts—including the subparts of owner's equity—have a normal debit balance and which categories of accounts have a normal credit balance. Exhibit 2-13, Panel B, on page 57, gives the normal balance in each category of account.

DE2-10 Marianne Vogel purchased supplies on account for $3,000. Two weeks later, Vogel paid half on account.

1. Journalize the two transactions on the books of Marianne Vogel. Include an explanation for each transaction.
2. Open the Accounts Payable account and post to Accounts Payable. Compute the balance, and denote it as *Bal.*
3. How much does Vogel owe after both transactions? In which account does this amount appear?

DE2-11 Peter Nguyen performed legal service for a client who could not pay immediately. Nguyen expected to collect the $5,000 the following month. Later, Nguyen received $2,700 cash from the client.

1. Record the two transactions on the books of Peter Nguyen, Attorney. Include an explanation for each transaction.
2. Open these accounts: Cash; Accounts Receivable; Service Revenue. Post to all three accounts. Compute each account's balance, and denote as *Bal.*
3. Answer these questions based on your analysis:
   a. How much did Nguyen earn? Which account shows this amount?
   b. How much in total assets did Nguyen acquire as a result of the two transactions? Show the amount of each asset.

Note: Daily Exercise 2-12 should be used in connection with Daily Exercise 2-7.

DE2-12 Use the June transaction data for Lee Jackson, M.D., given in Daily Exercise 2-7.

1. Open the following T-accounts of Lee Jackson, M.D.: Cash; Accounts Receivable; Medical Supplies; Accounts Payable; Lee Jackson, Capital; Service Revenue; Rent Expense.
2. After making the journal entries in Daily Exercise 2-7, post from the journal to the ledger. No dates or posting references are required. Compute the balance of each account, and denote it as *Bal.*
3. Prepare the trial balance, complete with a proper heading, at June 3, 20X8. Use the trial balance on page 52 as a guide.

DE2-13 Intel Corporation, famous for the Pentium© processor, reported the following summarized data at December 31, 19X9. Accounts appear in no particular order; dollar amounts are in billions.

Revenues	$29	Other liabilities	$11
Other assets	40	Cash	4
Accounts payable	1	Expenses	22
Capital	25		

Prepare the trial balance of Intel Corporation at December 31, 19X9. List the accounts in their proper order, as on page 52.

DE2-14 Jeff Hatton, Attorney, prepared the business's trial balance on page 61. Suppose Hatton made two errors in preparing the trial balance, as follows:

Correcting a trial balance (Obj. 5)

> **Error 1—Hatton erroneously listed his capital balance of $10,000 as a debit rather than as a credit.**
>
> **Error 2—Hatton erroneously listed Service Revenue as a credit balance of $42,000 rather than the correct amount of $4,200.**

Consider each error separately.

1. For each error, compute the incorrect trial balance totals for total debits and total credits.
2. Refer to the discussion of correcting trial balance errors on page 49 and show how to correct each error.

DE2-15 Metrolink Apartment Finder Service helps college students locate apartments because Dundalk Community College has no student housing on campus. Wayne Gibbs, the owner of Metrolink, is setting up the business's chart of accounts after making an initial investment of cash in the business.

Setting up a chart of accounts (Obj. 6)

Gibbs will perform apartment locator services for clients on account. His office will need some supplies, a computer (equipment), and furniture. Gibbs has borrowed money by signing a note payable to the bank. The business will also purchase on account some of the things it needs.

Expenses of the business will include rent, utilities, and advertising.

Prepare the chart of accounts for Metrolink Apartment Finder Service, including three-digit account numbers. Use Exhibit 2-10, page 55, as a guide.

DE2-16 Marta Fraser established Bodyfit, a health club, with an initial cash investment of $100,000. The business immediately purchased equipment on account for $45,000. Marta needs to know her account balances immediately and doesn't have time to journalize the transactions.

Analyzing transactions without a journal (Obj. 7)

1. Open the following T-accounts on the books of Bodyfit. Cash; Equipment; Accounts Payable; Marta Fraser, Capital.
2. Record the first two transactions of Bodyfit directly in the T-accounts without using a journal.
3. Compute the balance in each account and show that total debits equal total credits.

EXERCISES

E2-1 Your employer, Digitech Enterprises, has just hired an office manager who does not understand accounting. Digitech's trial balance lists Cash of $43,000. Write a short memo to the office manager, explaining the accounting process that produced this listing on the trial balance. Mention *debits, credits, journal, ledger, posting,* and *trial balance.*

Using accounting vocabulary (Obj. 1)

E2-2 ◄ *Link Back to Chapter 1 (Accounting Equation).* **The Coca-Cola Company** is famous worldwide for its soft drinks. At the end of 1999, Coca-Cola had total assets of $22 billion and liabilities totaling $12 billion.

Using debits and credits with the accounting equation (Obj. 1, 2)

Required

1. Write the company's accounting equation, and label each element as a debit amount or a credit amount.
2. Coca-Cola's total revenues for 1999 were $20 billion, and total expenses for the year were $18 billion. How much was Coca-Cola's net income (or net loss) for 1999? Write the equation to compute Coca-Cola's net income, and indicate which element is a debit amount and which element is a credit amount. Does net income represent a net debit or a net credit? Does net loss represent a net debit or a net credit? Review Exhibit 1-7, page 20, if needed.
3. During 1999, the owners of Coca-Cola withdrew $1 billion in the form of dividends (same as owner Withdrawals). Did the dividends represent a debit amount or a credit amount?

4. Considering both Coca-Cola's net income (or net loss) and dividends for 1999, by how much did the company's owners' equity increase or decrease during 1999? Was the increase in owners' equity a debit amount or a credit amount?

Analyzing and journalizing transactions (Obj. 2, 3)

E2-3 Analyze the following transactions in the manner shown for the December 1 transaction of Miramar Electronics. Also record each transaction in the journal. Explanations are not required.

Dec. 1   Paid utilities expense of $700. (*Analysis:* The expense, Utilities Expense, is increased; therefore, debit Utilities Expense. The asset, Cash, is decreased; therefore, credit Cash.)

1	Utilities Expense	700	
	Cash..........................		700

5	Purchased office furniture on account, $800.
10	Performed service on account for a customer, $1,600.
12	Borrowed $7,000 cash, signing a note payable.
19	Sold for $29,000 land that had cost this same amount.
24	Purchased building for $140,000; signed a note payable.
27	Paid the liability created on December 5.

Applying the rules of debit and credit (Obj. 2)

E2-4 Refer to Exercise 2-3 for the transactions of Miramar Electronics.

Required

1. Open the following T-accounts with their December 1 balances: Cash, debit balance $6,000; Land, debit balance $29,000; Martha Cross, Capital, credit balance $35,000.
2. Record the transactions of Exercise 2-3 directly in the T-accounts affected. Use the dates as posting references. Journal entries are not required.
3. Compute the December 31 balance for each account, and prove that total debits equal total credits.

Journalizing transactions (Obj. 3)

E2-5 New Balance Spa engaged in the following transactions during March 20X3, its first month of operations:

Mar. 1   Joy Liebermann invested $55,000 of cash to start the business.
2   Purchased office supplies of $200 on account.
4   Paid $40,000 cash for a building to use as an office in the very near future.
6   Performed service for customers and received cash, $3,000.
9   Paid $100 on accounts payable.
17   Performed service for customers on account, $1,600.
23   Received $1,200 cash from a customer on account.
31   Paid the following expenses: salary, $1,200; rent, $500.

Required

Record the preceding transactions in the journal of New Balance Spa. Key transactions by date and include an explanation for each entry, as illustrated in the chapter. Use the following accounts: Cash; Accounts Receivable; Office Supplies; Building; Accounts Payable; Joy Liebermann, Capital; Service Revenue; Salary Expense; Rent Expense.

Posting to the ledger and preparing a trial balance (Obj. 4, 5)

E2-6 Refer to Exercise 2-5 for the transactions of New Balance Spa.

Required

1. After journalizing the transactions of Exercise 2-5, post the entries to the ledger, using T-account format. Key transactions by date. Date the ending balance of each account Mar. 31.
2. Prepare the trial balance of New Balance Spa at March 31, 20X3.

Describing transactions and posting (Obj. 2, 3)

E2-7 The journal of Freebin & Associates includes the following transaction entries for May 20X6.

Required

1. Describe each transaction.
2. Post the transactions to the ledger using the following account numbers: Cash, 110; Accounts Receivable, 120; Supplies, 130; Accounts Payable, 210; Note Payable, 230; Leonard Freebin, Capital, 310; Service Revenue, 410; Rent Expense, 510; Advertising Expense, 520; Utilities Expense, 530. Use dates, journal references, and posting references as illustrated in Exhibit 2-8. You may write the account numbers as posting references directly in your book unless directed otherwise by your instructor.
3. Compute the balance in each account after posting. Prepare Freebin & Associates' trial balance at May 31, 20X6.

Journal　Page 5

Date	Accounts and Explanation	Post. Ref.	Debit	Credit
May 2	Cash..		20,000	
	Leonard Freebin, Capital................			20,000
5	Cash..		15,000	
	Note Payable			15,000
9	Supplies		270	
	Accounts Payable			270
11	Accounts Receivable......................		2,630	
	Service Revenue			2,630
14	Rent Expense...............................		3,200	
	Cash			3,200
22	Accounts Payable..........................		270	
	Cash			270
25	Advertising Expense......................		350	
	Cash			350
27	Cash..		1,400	
	Accounts Receivable			1,400
31	Utilities Expense		220	
	Accounts Payable			220

E2-8 The first five transactions of Flores Security Company have been posted to the company's accounts as follows:

Journalizing transactions (Obj. 3)

CASH				SUPPLIES		EQUIPMENT		LAND	
(1)	62,000	(3)	56,000	(2)	400	(5)	6,000	(3)	56,000
(4)	7,000	(5)	6,000						

ACCOUNTS PAYABLE		NOTE PAYABLE		TONY FLORES, CAPITAL	
(2)	400	(4)	7,000	(1)	62,000

Required

Prepare the journal entries that served as the sources for the five transactions. Include an explanation for each entry as illustrated in the chapter.

E2-9 Prepare the trial balance of Flores Security Company at April 30, 20X4, using the account data from Exercise 2-8.

Preparing a trial balance (Obj. 5)

E2-10 The accounts of Beaulieu Company follow with their normal balances at December 31, 20X4. The accounts are listed in no particular order.

Preparing a trial balance (Obj. 5)

Account	Balance
Pierre Beaulieu, capital.......................	$48,800
Advertising expense............................	650
Accounts payable................................	4,300
Sales commission revenue..................	26,000
Land..	29,000
Supplies expense	300
Cash	5,000
Salary expense...................................	6,000
Building...	65,000
Rent expense	2,000
Pierre Beaulieu, withdrawals..............	6,000
Utilities expense.................................	400
Accounts receivable	9,500
Note payable......................................	45,000
Supplies	250

Required

Prepare the company's trial balance at December 31, 20X4, listing accounts in proper sequence, as illustrated in the chapter. For example, Supplies comes before Building and Land. List the expense with the largest balance first, the expense with the next largest balance second, and so on.

E2-11 The trial balance of Atlantis Enterprises at March 31, 20X9, does not balance:

Cash	$ 4,500	
Accounts receivable	2,000	
Supplies	600	
Land	66,000	
Accounts payable		$23,000
Paige Dylan, capital		41,600
Service revenue		9,700
Salary expense	1,700	
Rent expense	800	
Utilities expense	300	
Total	$75,900	$74,300

Investigation of the accounting records reveals that the bookkeeper

a. Recorded a $400 cash revenue transaction by debiting Accounts Receivable. The credit entry was correct.
b. Posted a $1,000 credit to Accounts Payable as $100.
c. Did not record utilities expense or the related account payable in the amount of $200.
d. Understated Paige Dylan, Capital, by $700.

Required

Prepare the correct trial balance at March 31, complete with a heading; journal entries are not required.

E2-12 Open the following T-accounts of Cole Gates, CPA: Cash; Accounts Receivable; Office Supplies; Office Furniture; Accounts Payable; Cole Gates, Capital; Cole Gates, Withdrawals; Service Revenue; Salary Expense; Rent Expense.

Record the following transactions directly in the T-accounts without using a journal. Use the letters to identify the transactions. Compute the balance of each account.

a. Gates opened an accounting firm by investing $12,400 cash and office furniture valued at $5,400.
b. Paid monthly rent of $1,500.
c. Purchased office supplies on account, $700.
d. Paid employee's salary, $1,800.
e. Paid $400 of the account payable created in transaction (c).
f. Performed accounting service on account, $1,600.
g. Withdrew $7,000 for personal use.

E2-13 After recording the transactions in Exercise 2-12, prepare the trial balance of Cole Gates, CPA, at May 31, 20X7.

E2-14 Moseley Supply began when Lynette Moseley invested $75,000 cash in a business bank account. During the first week, the business purchased supplies on credit for $8,000 and paid $12,000 cash for equipment. Moseley later paid $5,000 on account.

Required

1. Open the following T-accounts: Cash; Supplies; Equipment; Accounts Payable; Lynette Moseley, Capital.
2. Record the four transactions described above directly in the T-accounts without using a journal.
3. Compute the balance in each account, and show that total debit balances equal total credit balances after you have recorded all the transactions. The T-accounts on page 48 provide a guide for your answer.

Continuing Exercise Exercise 2-15 is the first exercise in a sequence that begins an accounting cycle. The cycle is completed in Chapter 5.

E2-15 Amos Faraday completed these transactions during the first half of December:

Dec.	2	Invested $14,000 to start a consulting practice, Amos Faraday, Consultant.
	2	Paid monthly office rent, $500.
	3	Paid cash for a Dell computer, $2,000. The computer is expected to remain in service for five years.
	4	Purchased office furniture on account, $3,600. The furniture should last for five years.
	5	Purchased supplies on account, $300.
	9	Performed consulting service for a client on account, $1,700.
	12	Paid utility expenses, $200.
	18	Performed service for a client and received cash for the full amount of $800.

1. Open T-accounts in the ledger: Cash; Accounts Receivable; Supplies; Equipment; Furniture; Accounts Payable; Amos Faraday, Capital; Amos Faraday, Withdrawals; Service Revenue; Rent Expense; Utilities Expense; and Salary Expense.
2. Journalize the transactions. Explanations are not required.
3. Post to the T-accounts. Key all items by date, and denote an account balance as *Bal.* Formal posting references are not required.
4. Prepare a trial balance at December 18. In the Continuing Exercise of Chapter 3, we will add transactions for the remainder of December and prepare a trial balance at December 31.

Challenge Exercises

E2-16 The owner of Midwest Catering Services needs to compute the following summary information from the accounting records:

Computing financial statement amounts without a journal (Obj. 7)

a. Net income for the month of March.
b. Total cash paid during March.
c. Cash collections from customers during March.
d. Cash paid on a note payable during March.

The quickest way to compute these amounts is to analyze the following accounts:

Account	Balance Feb. 28	Mar. 31	Additional Information for the Month of March
a. Owner, Capital	$ 9,000	$15,000	Withdrawals, $7,000
b. Cash	7,000	2,000	Cash receipts, $61,000
c. Accounts Receivable	24,000	26,000	Revenues on account, $76,000
d. Note Payable	11,000	16,000	New borrowing on a note payable, $7,500

The net income for March can be computed as follows:

OWNER, CAPITAL			
		Feb. 28 Bal.	9,000
March Withdrawals	7,000	March Net Income	X = $13,000
		March 31 Bal.	15,000

Use a similar approach to compute the other three items.

E2-17 Tara Hale has trouble keeping her debits and credits equal. During a recent month, she made the following errors:

Analyzing accounting errors (Obj. 2, 3, 4, 5)

a. In journalizing a receipt of cash for service revenue, Hale debited Cash for $1,800 instead of the correct amount of $800. Hale credited Service Revenue for $1,800, the incorrect amount.
b. Hale recorded a $120 purchase of supplies on account by debiting Supplies and crediting Accounts Payable for $210.
c. In preparing the trial balance, Hale omitted a $40,000 note payable.
d. Hale posted a $700 utility expense as $70. The credit posting to Cash was correct.
e. In recording a $400 payment on account, Hale debited Supplies and credited Accounts Payable.

Required

1. For each of these errors, state whether the total debits equal total credits on the trial balance.
2. Identify any accounts with misstated balances, and indicate the amount and direction of the error (such as account balance too high or too low).

PROBLEMS

(Group A)

P2-1A ◄ *Link Back to Chapter 1 (Balance Sheet, Income Statement)*. The owner of Cantor Polling Service is selling the business. She offers the trial balance shown here to prospective buyers. Your best friend is considering buying Cantor Polling Service. He seeks your advice in interpreting this information. Specifically, he asks whether this trial balance is the same as a balance sheet and an income statement. He also wonders whether Cantor is a sound business. After all, the company's accounts are in balance.

Analyzing a trial balance (Obj. 1)

CANTOR POLLING SERVICE
Trial Balance
December 31, 20X8

Cash	$ 12,000	
Accounts receivable	27,000	
Prepaid expenses	4,000	
Land	63,000	
Accounts payable		$ 35,000
Note payable		32,000
Kendra Cantor, capital		30,000
Kendra Cantor, withdrawals	48,000	
Service revenue		116,000
Rent expense	26,000	
Advertising expense	3,000	
Wage expense	23,000	
Supplies expense	7,000	
Total	$213,000	$213,000

Required

Write a short note to answer your friend's questions. To aid his decision, state how he can use the information on the trial balance to compute Cantor's net income or net loss for the current period. State the amount of net income or net loss in your note. Refer to Exhibit 1-7, page 20, if needed.

Analyzing and journalizing transactions
(Obj. 2, 3)

P2-2A Silverstar Cinemas owns movie theaters in the shopping centers of a major metropolitan area. Its owner, Joseph Reese, engaged in the following business transactions:

April 1	Reese invested $500,000 personal cash in the business by depositing that amount in a bank account entitled Silverstar Cinemas. The business gave Reese owner's equity in the company.
2	Paid $400,000 cash to purchase a theater building.
5	Borrowed $220,000 from the bank. Reese signed a note payable to the bank in the name of Silverstar Cinemas.
10	Purchased theater supplies on account, $1,700.
15	Paid $800 on account.
15	Paid property tax expense on theater building, $1,200.
16	Paid employee salaries, $2,800, and rent on equipment, $1,800.
17	Withdrew $6,000 from the business for personal use.
30	Received $20,000 cash from ticket sales and deposited that amount in the bank. (Label the revenue as Sales Revenue.)

Silverstar uses the following accounts: Cash; Supplies; Building; Accounts Payable; Notes Payable; Joseph Reese, Capital; Joseph Reese, Withdrawals; Sales Revenue; Salary Expense; Rent Expense; Property Tax Expense.

Required

1. Analyze each business transaction of Silverstar Cinemas, as shown for the April 1 transaction:

   Apr. 1   The asset Cash is increased. Increases in assets are recorded by debits; therefore, debit Cash. The owner's equity of the entity is increased. Increases in owner's equity are recorded by credits; therefore, credit Joseph Reese, Capital.

2. Journalize each transaction. Explanations are not required.

Journalizing transactions, posting to T-accounts, and preparing a trial balance
(Obj. 2, 3, 4, 5)

P2-3A Terence Larkin opened a law office on September 3 of the current year. During the first month of operations, the business completed the following transactions:

Sep. 3	Larkin transferred $43,000 cash from his personal bank account to a business account entitled Terence Larkin, Attorney. The business gave Larkin owner's equity in the business.
4	Purchased supplies, $200, and furniture, $1,800, on account.
6	Performed legal services for a client and received $4,000 cash.
7	Paid $15,000 cash to acquire land for a future office site.
10	Defended a client in court, billed the client, and received her promise to pay the $800 within one week.
14	Paid for the furniture purchased September 4 on account.
15	Paid secretary's salary, $600.
17	Received partial collection from client on account, $500.

Sep. 20   Prepared legal documents for a client on account, $800.
     28   Received $1,500 cash for helping a client sell real estate.
     30   Paid secretary's salary, $600.
     30   Paid rent expense, $500.
     30   Withdrew $2,900 for personal use.

Required

Open the following T-accounts: Cash; Accounts Receivable; Supplies; Furniture; Land; Accounts Payable; Terence Larkin, Capital; Terence Larkin, Withdrawals; Service Revenue; Salary Expense; Rent Expense.

1. Record each transaction in the journal, using the account titles given. Key each transaction by date. Explanations are not required.
2. Post the transactions to the ledger, using transaction dates as posting references in the ledger. Label the balance of each account *Bal.,* as shown in the chapter.
3. Prepare the trial balance of Terence Larkin, Attorney, at September 30 of the current year.

P2-4A The trial balance of the accounting practice of Jill Case, CPA, is dated February 14, 20X3:

Journalizing transactions, posting to accounts in four-column format, and preparing a trial balance (Obj. 2, 3, 4, 5)

JILL CASE, CPA
Trial Balance
February 14, 20X3

Account Number	Account	Debit	Credit
11	Cash	$ 2,000	
12	Accounts receivable	9,500	
13	Supplies	800	
14	Land	18,600	
21	Accounts payable		$ 3,000
31	Jill Case, capital		26,500
32	Jill Case, withdrawals	1,200	
41	Service revenue		7,200
51	Salary expense	3,600	
52	Rent expense	1,000	
	Total	$36,700	$36,700

During the remainder of February, Case completed the following transactions:

Feb. 15   Case collected $3,500 cash from a client on account.
     16   Performed tax services for a client on account, $700.
     20   Paid on account, $1,000.
     21   Purchased supplies on account, $100.
     21   Withdrew $1,200 for personal use.
     21   Paid for a wooden deck for private residence, using personal funds, $9,000.
     22   Received cash of $5,100 for consulting work just completed.
     28   Paid rent, $800.
     28   Paid employees' salaries, $1,800.

Required

1. Record the transactions that occurred during February 15–28 in page 3 of the journal. Include an explanation for each entry.
2. Open the ledger accounts listed in the trial balance, together with their balances at February 14. Use the four-column account format illustrated in the chapter (Exhibit 2-9). Enter *Bal.* (for previous balance) in the Item column, and place a check mark (✓) in the journal reference column for the February 14 balance in each account. Post the transactions to the ledger using dates, account numbers, journal references, and posting references.
3. Prepare the trial balance of Jill Case, CPA, at February 28, 20X3.

P2-5A ↩ *Link Back to Chapter 1 (Income Statement).* The trial balance for Chapel Lawn Service at the top of the next page does not balance.
    The following errors were detected:

Correcting errors in a trial balance (Obj. 2, 5)

a. The cash balance is understated by $700.
b. The cost of the land was $43,000, not $46,000.
c. A $200 purchase of supplies on account was neither journalized nor posted.
d. The balance of Utilities Expense is overstated by $70.
e. Rent expense of $200 was erroneously posted as a credit rather than a debit.

CHAPEL LAWN SERVICE
Trial Balance
June 30, 20X2

Cash	$ 3,000	
Accounts receivable	10,000	
Supplies	900	
Equipment	5,100	
Land	46,000	
Accounts payable		$ 5,000
Note payable		22,000
Rob Rylander, capital		31,600
Rob Rylander, withdrawals	2,000	
Service revenue		6,500
Salary expense	2,100	
Rent expense	1,000	
Advertising expense	500	
Utilities expense	400	
Total	$71,000	$65,100

    f. The balance of Advertising Expense is $600, but it was listed as $500 on the trial balance.
    g. A $300 debit to Accounts Receivable was posted as $30.
    h. A $4,300 credit to Service Revenue was not posted.
    i. A $900 debit to the Withdrawals account was posted as a debit to Rob Rylander, Capital.

Required

1. Prepare the correct trial balance at June 30. Journal entries are not required.
2. Prepare the company's income statement for the month ended June 30, 20X2, in order to determine Chapel Lawn Service's net income or net loss for the month. Refer to Exhibit 1-7, page 20, if needed.

Recording transactions directly in T-accounts; preparing a trial balance
(Obj. 2, 5, 7)

P2-6A Allen Musser started a consulting service and during the first month of operations (June 20X3) completed the following selected transactions:

    a. Musser began the business with an investment of $5,000 cash and a building valued at $60,000. The business gave Musser owner's equity in the business.
    b. Borrowed $30,000 from the bank; signed a note payable.
    c. Purchased office supplies on account, $2,100.
    d. Paid $18,000 for office furniture.
    e. Paid employee's salary, $2,200.
    f. Performed consulting service on account for client, $5,100.
    g. Paid $800 of the account payable created in transaction (c).
    h. Received a $600 bill for advertising expense that will be paid in the near future.
    i. Performed consulting service for customers and received cash, $1,600.
    j. Received cash on account, $1,200.
    k. Paid the following cash expenses:
        (1) Rent on land, $700.   (2) Utilities, $400.
    l. Withdrew $7,500 for personal use.

Required

1. Open the following T-accounts: Cash; Accounts Receivable; Office Supplies; Office Furniture; Building; Accounts Payable; Note Payable; Allen Musser, Capital; Allen Musser, Withdrawals; Service Revenue; Salary Expense; Advertising Expense; Rent Expense; Utilities Expense.
2. Record each transaction directly in the T-accounts without using a journal. Use the letters to identify the transactions.
3. Prepare the trial balance of Musser Consulting Service at June 30, 20X3.

Note: Problem 2-7A should be used in conjunction with Problem 2-6A.

Preparing the financial statements
(Obj. 5)

P2-7A ◄ *Link Back to Chapter 1 (Income Statement, Statement of Owner's Equity, Balance Sheet).* Refer to Problem 2-6A. After completing the trial balance in Problem 2-6A, prepare the following financial statements for Musser Consulting Service:

1. Income statement for the month ended June 30, 20X3.
2. Statement of owner's equity for the month ended June 30, 20X3.
3. Balance sheet at June 30, 20X3.

Draw arrows to link the statements. If needed, use Exhibit 1-7, page 20, as a guide for preparing the financial statements.

PROBLEMS

P2-1B ← *Link Back to Chapter 1 (Balance Sheet, Income Statement).* The owner of Biokinetic Engineering is selling the business. He offers the following trial balance to prospective buyers. Your best friend is considering buying Biokinetic. She seeks your advice in interpreting this information. Specifically, she asks whether this trial balance is the same as a balance sheet and an income statement. She also wonders whether Biokinetic is a sound business. After all, the company's accounts are in balance.

Analyzing a trial balance
(Obj. 1)

BIOKINETIC ENGINEERING Trial Balance December 31, 20X4		
Cash	$ 7,000	
Accounts receivable	6,000	
Prepaid expenses.............................	4,000	
Land...	51,000	
Accounts payable		$ 31,000
Note payable		20,000
Avery Patella, capital......................		33,000
Avery Patella, withdrawals..............	21,000	
Service revenue...............................		72,000
Wage expense	28,000	
Rent expense...................................	14,000	
Advertising expense........................	18,000	
Supplies expense.............................	7,000	
Total	$156,000	$156,000

Required

Write a short note to answer your friend's questions. To aid her decision, state how she can use the information on the trial balance to compute Biokinetic's net income or net loss for the current period. State the amount of net income or net loss in your note. Refer to Exhibit 1-7, page 20, if needed.

P2-2B Deborah Fedro practices medicine under the business title Deborah Fedro, M.D. During June, her medical practice engaged in the following transactions:

Analyzing and journalizing transactions
(Obj. 2, 3)

June 1   Fedro deposited $55,000 cash in the business bank account. The business gave Fedro owner's equity in the business.

     5   Paid monthly rent on medical equipment, $700.

     9   Paid $22,000 cash to purchase land for an office site.

   10   Purchased supplies on account, $1,200.

   19   Borrowed $20,000 from the bank for business use. Fedro signed a note payable to the bank in the name of the business.

   22   Paid $1,000 on account.

   30   Revenues earned during the month included $6,000 cash and $5,000 on account.

   30   Paid employees' salaries ($2,400), office rent ($1,500), and utilities ($400).

   30   Withdrew $10,000 from the business for personal use.

Fedro's business uses the following accounts: Cash; Accounts Receivable; Supplies; Land; Accounts Payable; Notes Payable; Deborah Fedro, Capital; Deborah Fedro, Withdrawals; Service Revenue; Salary Expense; Rent Expense; Utilities Expense.

Required

1. Analyze each transaction of Deborah Fedro, M.D., as shown for the June 1 transaction:

June 1   The asset Cash is increased. Increases in assets are recorded by debits; therefore, debit Cash. The owner's equity is increased. Increases in owner's equity are recorded by credits; therefore, credit Deborah Fedro, Capital.

2. Journalize each transaction. Explanations are not required.

P2-3B Rodney Troon opened a law office on December 2 of the current year. During the first month of operations, the business completed the following transactions:

Dec. 2	Troon deposited $50,000 cash in the business bank account Rodney Troon, Attorney.
3	Purchased supplies, $500, and furniture, $2,600, on account.
4	Performed legal service for a client and received cash, $1,500.
7	Paid cash to acquire land for a future office site, $22,000.
11	Prepared legal documents for a client on account, $900.
15	Paid secretary's salary, $570.
16	Paid for the furniture purchased December 3 on account.
18	Received $1,800 cash for helping a client sell real estate.
19	Defended a client in court and billed the client for $800.
29	Received partial collection from client on account, $400.
31	Paid secretary's salary, $570.
31	Paid rent expense, $700.
31	Withdrew $2,200 for personal use.

Required

Open the following T-accounts: Cash; Accounts Receivable; Supplies; Furniture; Land; Accounts Payable; Rodney Troon, Capital; Rodney Troon, Withdrawals; Service Revenue; Salary Expense; Rent Expense.

1. Record each transaction in the journal, using the account titles given. Key each transaction by date. Explanations are not required.
2. Post the transactions to the ledger, using transaction dates as posting references in the ledger. Label the balance of each account *Bal.*, as shown in the chapter.
3. Prepare the trial balance of Rodney Troon, Attorney, at December 31 of the current year.

P2-4B The trial balance of the law practice of Brent Busch, Attorney, at November 15, 20X3, follows.

BRENT BUSCH, ATTORNEY
Trial Balance
November 15, 20X3

Account Number	Account	Debit	Credit
11	Cash	$ 3,000	
12	Accounts receivable	8,000	
13	Supplies	600	
14	Land	35,000	
21	Accounts payable		$ 4,600
31	Brent Busch, capital		40,000
32	Brent Busch, withdrawals	2,300	
41	Service revenue		7,100
51	Salary expense	1,800	
52	Rent expense	1,000	
	Total	$51,700	$51,700

During the remainder of November, Busch completed the following transactions:

Nov. 16	Collected $6,000 cash from a client on account.
17	Performed tax service for a client on account, $1,700.
21	Used personal funds to pay for the renovation of private residence, $55,000.
22	Purchased supplies on account, $800.
23	Withdrew $2,100 for personal use.
23	Paid on account, $2,600.
24	Received $1,900 cash for legal work just completed.
30	Paid rent, $700.
30	Paid employees' salaries, $2,100.

Required

1. Record the transactions that occurred during November 16–30 on page 6 of the journal. Include an explanation for each entry.
2. Post the transactions to the ledger, using dates, account numbers, journal references, and posting references. Open the ledger accounts listed in the trial balance together with their balances at November 15. Use the four-column account format illustrated in the chapter

(Exhibit 2-9). Enter *Bal.* (for previous balance) in the Item column, and place a check mark (✓) in the journal reference column for the November 15 balance of each account.

3. Prepare the trial balance of Brent Busch, Attorney, at November 30, 20X3.

P2-5B ◄ *Link Back to Chapter 1 (Income Statement).* The trial balance for Ballard Financial Services does not balance. The following errors were detected:

Correcting errors in a trial balance (Obj. 2, 5)

a. The cash balance is understated by $400.
b. Rent expense of $350 was erroneously posted as a credit rather than a debit.
c. An $8,300 credit to Service Revenue was not posted.
d. A $600 debit to Accounts Receivable was posted as $60.
e. The balance of Utilities Expense is understated by $60.
f. A $1,300 debit to the Withdrawal account was posted as a debit to Meredith Ballard, Capital.
g. A $100 purchase of supplies on account was neither journalized nor posted.
h. The balance of Advertising Expense is $300, but it is listed as $400 on the trial balance.
i. Office furniture should be listed in the amount of $1,300.

BALLARD FINANCIAL SERVICES
Trial Balance
March 31, 20X1

Cash	$ 6,200	
Accounts receivable	2,000	
Supplies	500	
Office furniture	2,300	
Land	46,000	
Accounts payable		$ 2,700
Note payable		18,300
Meredith Ballard, capital		29,500
Meredith Ballard, withdrawals	3,700	
Service revenue		4,900
Salary expense	1,300	
Rent expense	500	
Advertising expense	400	
Utilities expense	200	
Total	$63,100	$55,400

Required

1. Prepare the correct trial balance at March 31. Journal entries are not required.
2. Prepare Ballard Financial Services' income statement for the month ended March 31, 20X1, to determine whether the business had a net income or a net loss for the month. Refer to Exhibit 1-7, page 20, if needed.

P2-6B Vince Serrano started Serrano Catering Service, and during the first month of operations (January 20X7), he completed the following selected transactions:

Recording transactions directly in T-accounts; preparing a trial balance (Obj. 2, 5, 7)

a. Serrano began the business with an investment of $23,000 cash and a van (automobile) valued at $13,000. The business gave Serrano owner's equity in the business.
b. Borrowed $25,000 from the bank; signed a note payable.
c. Paid $32,000 for food-service equipment.
d. Purchased supplies on account, $400.
e. Paid employee's salary, $1,300.
f. Received $800 for a catering job performed for customers.
g. Received an $800 bill for advertising expense that will be paid in the near future.
h. Paid $100 of the account payable created in transaction (d).
i. Performed service at a wedding on account, $3,300.
j. Received cash on account, $1,100.
k. Paid the following cash expenses:
　　(1) Rent, $1,000.　　(2) Insurance, $600.
l. Withdrew $2,600 for personal use.

Required

1. Open the following T-accounts: Cash; Accounts Receivable; Supplies; Food-Service Equipment; Automobile; Accounts Payable; Note Payable; Vince Serrano, Capital; Vince Serrano, Withdrawals; Service Revenue; Salary Expense; Rent Expense; Advertising Expense; Insurance Expense.
2. Record the transactions directly in the T-accounts without using a journal. Use the letters to identify the transactions.
3. Prepare the trial balance of Serrano Catering Service at January 31, 20X7.

Note: Problem 2-7B should be used in conjunction with Problem 2-6B.

Preparing the financial statements
(Obj. 5)

P2-7B ← *Link Back to Chapter 1 (Income Statement, Statement of Owner's Equity, Balance Sheet).* Refer to Problem 2-6B. After completing the trial balance in Problem 2-6B, prepare the following financial statements for Serrano Catering Service:

1. Income statement for the month ended January 31, 20X7.
2. Statement of owner's equity for the month ended January 31, 20X7.
3. Balance sheet at January 31, 20X7.

Draw arrows to link the statements. If needed, use Exhibit 1-7, page 20, as a guide for preparing the financial statements.

APPLY YOUR KNOWLEDGE

DECISION CASES

Using the accounting equation
Obj. 2)

Case 1. Answer the following questions. Consider each question separately.

1. Explain the advantages of double-entry bookkeeping over single-entry bookkeeping to a friend who is opening a used book store.
2. When you deposit money in your bank account, the bank credits your account. Is the bank misusing the word *credit* in this context? Why does the bank use the term *credit* to refer to your deposit, and not *debit?*
3. Your friend asks, "When revenues increase assets and expenses decrease assets, why are revenues credits and expenses debits and not the other way around?" Explain to your friend why revenues are credits and expenses are debits.

Recording transactions directly in T-accounts, preparing a trial balance, and measuring net income or loss
(Obj. 2, 5, 7)

Case 2. You have been requested by a friend named Belinda Nathews to give advice on the effects that certain transactions will have on her business. Time is short, so you cannot journalize the transactions. Instead, you must analyze the transactions without the use of a journal. Nathews will continue the business only if she can expect to earn monthly net income of $5,000. The following transactions have occurred during March:

a. Nathews deposited $8,000 cash in a business bank account to start the company.
b. Borrowed $6,000 cash from the bank and signed a note payable due within one year.
c. Paid $300 cash for supplies.
d. Paid cash for advertising in the local newspaper, $700.
e. Paid the following cash expenses for one month: secretary's salary, $1,400; office rent, $800; utilities, $300; interest, $50.
f. Earned service revenue on account, $5,300.
g. Earned service revenue and received $3,500 cash.
h. Collected cash from customers on account, $1,200.

Required

1. Open the following T-accounts: Cash; Accounts Receivable; Supplies; Notes Payable; Belinda Nathews, Capital; Service Revenue; Salary Expense; Rent Expense; Advertising Expense; Utilities Expense; Interest Expense.
2. Record the transactions directly in the accounts without using a journal. Key each transaction by letter.
3. Prepare a trial balance at March 31, 20X9. List expenses with the largest amount first, the next largest amount second, and so on. The business name is Nathews Apartment Locators.
4. Compute the amount of net income or net loss for this first month of operations. Would you recommend that Nathews continue in business?

ETHICAL ISSUE

Brave Hearts, a charitable organization in Panama City, Florida, has a standing agreement with De Leon State Bank. The agreement allows Brave Hearts to overdraw its cash balance at the bank when donations are running low. In the past, Brave Hearts managed funds wisely and rarely used this privilege. Jacob Henson has recently become the president of Brave Hearts. To expand operations, Henson acquired office equipment and spent large amounts on fundraising. During Henson's presidency, Brave Hearts has maintained a negative bank balance of approximately $6,000.

Required

What is the ethical issue in this situation? State why you approve or disapprove of Henson's management of Brave Hearts' funds.

FINANCIAL STATEMENT CASE

This problem helps you develop skill in recording transactions by using a company's actual account titles. Refer to the **Target Corporation** financial statements in Appendix A. Assume that Target completed the following selected transactions during October 2001:

Journalizing transactions for a company
(Obj. 2, 3)

Oct. 5   Earned sales revenue on account, $110,000.
     9   Borrowed $500,000 by signing a note payable (long-term debt).
     12   Purchased equipment and paid cash, $50,000.
     17   Paid $100,000, a current maturity of a long-term debt, plus interest expense of $8,000.
     19   Earned sales revenue and immediately received cash of $86,000.
     22   Collected half the cash on account that was earned on October 5.
     28   Received a home-office electricity bill for $3,000, which will be paid in November (this is an administrative expense).

Required

Journalize these transactions, using the following account titles taken from the Target financial statements: Cash; Retained Securitized Receivables (same as Accounts Receivable), Equipment; Accounts Payable; Current Portion of Long-Term Debt; Long-Term Debt; Sales (Revenue), Selling, General and Administrative Expense; Interest Expense. Explanations are not required.

TEAM PROJECT

Contact a local business and arrange with the owner to learn what accounts the business uses.

Required

1. Obtain a copy of the business's chart of accounts.
2. Prepare the company's financial statements for the most recent month, quarter, or year. You may use either made-up account balances or balances supplied by the owner.

If the business has a large number of accounts within a category, combine related accounts and report a single amount on the financial statements. For example, the company may have several cash accounts. Combine all cash amounts and report a single Cash amount on the balance sheet.

     You will probably encounter numerous accounts that you have not yet learned. Deal with these as best you can. The chart of accounts given in Appendix B at the end of the book will be helpful.

     Keep in mind that the financial statements report the balances of the accounts listed in the company's chart of accounts. Therefore, the financial statements must be consistent with the chart of accounts.

INTERNET EXERCISE

The accounting process illustrated in this chapter may be simplified with the aid of financial software. **Intuit Inc.** is a leader in e-finance and develops and supports Quicken®, the leading personal finance software; Turbo Tax®, the best-selling tax preparation software; and QuickBooks®, the most popular small business accounting software.

Intuit Inc.

1. Go to **http://www.quicken.com** and read the "Top News" headlines. In the "Get Quotes & Research" section type <u>INTU</u>, the stock symbol of Intuit Inc., and then click on *Go*. Review the information provided and comment on one item of interest.
2. In the left-hand column, click on *Financial Statements*. Amounts are reported in thousands.
   a. For the three most recent fiscal years, list the amounts reported for "Total Revenues" and "Net Incomes." For each of these amounts, comment on the results from 1997 to 1999. Is the trend favorable or unfavorable? In 1999, Intuit started to promote its Internet financial support services. Has this marketing strategy been profitable for Intuit?
   b. For the three most recent years, list the amounts reported for "Property and Equipment, Net" and "Total Assets." What percentage of total assets does property and equipment comprise? Would you expect this for an e-finance company?
   c. For property and equipment, what is the normal balance? Is the amount reported from before or after posting to the ledger?
3. It is important to understand the accounting process even though financial software is available. Explain why this is true.
4. Select one other feature of this Web site to explore. Comment on what you found and whether you consider this feature useful.

3 Measuring Business Income: The Adjusting Process

LEARNING OBJECTIVES

After studying this chapter, you should be able to

1. Distinguish accrual-basis accounting from cash-basis accounting

2. Apply the revenue and matching principles

3. Make adjusting entries at the end of the accounting period

4. Prepare an adjusted trial balance

5. Prepare the financial statements from the adjusted trial balance

www.prenhall.com/horngren

Readiness Assessment

Disappointed by blind dates and personal ads, Andrea McGinty started her own dating service. She also found a lucrative career. When McGinty's fiancé walked out on her five weeks before the wedding, it was back to the singles scene. Wouldn't it be nice if a dating service could arrange prescreened lunch dates for busy professionals like herself? "Lunch is over in an hour, and you don't have to kiss goodnight," she dreamed.

McGinty made her dream a reality. Her company, **It's Just Lunch,** now has thousands of customers. McGinty charges $1,000 to arrange 12 dates. "These are people who work long hours in fast-track careers. They need help with their social lives," says McGinty.

The business is a money-making machine, netting over $2 million of profit in a recent year.

Source: Adapted from Suzanne Oliver, "Yuppie Yenta," *Forbes* (March 25, 1996), pp. 102–103.

What do we mean when we say that **It's Just Lunch** *nets* over $2 million per year? The business earns net income, or profit, of more than $2 million, as reported on its income statement. The business's revenues consist of service-revenue fees earned by arranging lunch dates for clients. What are its expenses? Advertising, computer data searches, mailings to clients, and office expenses (such as employee salaries, rent, and supplies). It's Just Lunch operates in much the same way as **Gay Gillen eTravel,** the business studied in Chapters 1 and 2.

Whether the business is **It's Just Lunch,** Gillen's travel agency, or **IBM,** the profit motive increases the owner's drive to carry on the business. In this chapter, we'll consider how important net income is to a business.

FINANCIAL STATEMENTS AND ADJUSTING ENTRIES

How does a business know whether it is profitable? At the end of each accounting period, the entity prepares its financial statements. The period may be a month, three months, or a full year. **It's Just Lunch** is typical. The company reports on a quarterly basis every three months—with annual financial statements at the end of each year.

Whatever the length of the period, the main product of the accounting system is the financial statements. And the most important single amount in these statements is net income or net loss—the profit or loss—for the period. Net income captures much information: total revenues minus total expenses for the period.

An important step in financial statement preparation is the trial balance that we covered in Chapter 2. To measure its income, a business must bring the records up to date at the end of the period. This process is called *adjusting the books,* and it consists of making special journal entries called *adjusting entries.* This chapter focuses on these adjusting entries to show how to measure business income.

The accounting profession has concepts and principles to guide the measurement of business income. Chief among these are accrual-basis accounting, the accounting period, the revenue principle, and the matching principle. In this chapter, we apply these (and other) concepts and principles to measure income and prepare the financial statements of Gay Gillen eTravel for the month of April.

Accrual-Basis Accounting Versus Cash-Basis Accounting

There are two ways to do accounting:

- **Accrual-basis accounting** records the effect of every business transaction as it occurs. Most businesses use the accrual basis, and that is the method covered in this book.
- **Cash-basis accounting** records only cash receipts and cash payments. It ignores receivables, payables, and depreciation. Only very small businesses use cash-basis accounting.

Objective 1
Distinguish accrual-basis accounting from cash-basis accounting

ACCRUAL-BASIS ACCOUNTING.
Accounting that records the impact of a business event as it occurs, regardless of whether the transaction affected cash.

CASH-BASIS ACCOUNTING.
Accounting that records transactions only when cash is received or paid.

Suppose **Drugstore.com** purchased $2,000 of supplies on account from **Johnson & Johnson,** the health-care products company. On the accrual basis, Drugstore.com records the asset Supplies and the liability Accounts Payable as follows:

Supplies	2,000	
Accounts Payable		2,000
Purchased supplies on account.		

Under the accrual basis, Drugstore.com's balance sheet reports the asset Supplies and the liability Accounts Payable.

In contrast, cash-basis accounting ignores this transaction because Drugstore.com paid no cash. The cash basis records only cash receipts and cash payments. *Cash receipts are treated as revenues, and cash payments are handled as expenses.* Therefore, under the cash basis, Drugstore.com would record a $2,000 cash payment as an expense rather than as an asset. This is faulty accounting: Drugstore.com acquired supplies, which are assets because they provide future benefit to the company.

Now let's see how differently the accrual basis and the cash basis account for a revenue. Suppose Drugstore.com sold goods on account. Under the accrual basis, Drugstore.com records a $10,000 sale as follows:

Accounts Receivable..................	10,000	
Sales Revenue..................		10,000
Sold goods on account.		

The balance sheet then reports the asset Accounts Receivable, and the income statement reports Sales Revenue. We have a complete picture of the transaction.

Under the cash basis, Drugstore.com would not even bother to record a sale *on account* because there is no cash receipt. Instead, it would wait until cash is received and then record the cash as revenue. As a result, cash-basis accounting never reports accounts receivable from customers. It shows the revenue in the wrong accounting period, when cash is received. Revenue should be recorded when it is earned, and that is how the accrual basis operates.

Exhibit 3-1 illustrates the difference between the accrual basis and the cash basis. Keep in mind that the accrual basis is the correct way to do accounting. Panel A of the exhibit illustrates a revenue, and Panel B covers an expense.

EXHIBIT 3-1
Accrual-Basis Accounting Versus Cash-Basis Accounting

DAILY EXERCISE 3-1

DAILY EXERCISE 3-2

PANEL A (a revenue)—Collect $3,000 cash on January 1. The $3,000 of revenue is to be earned evenly during January, February, and March.

		Jan.	Feb.	Mar.
Accrual-basis accounting:	Service revenue...................	$1,000	$1,000	$1,000
Cash-basis accounting:	Service revenue...................	$3,000		

PANEL B (an expense)—Prepay $6,000 for TV advertising to be run during October, November, and December.

		Oct.	Nov.	Dec.
Accrual-basis accounting:	Advertising expense.............	$2,000	$2,000	$2,000
Cash-basis accounting:	Advertising expense.............	$6,000		

The Accounting Period

The only way to know for certain how successfully a business has operated is to close its doors, sell all its assets, pay the liabilities, and return any leftover cash to the owners. This process, called *liquidation,* is the same as going out of business. It is not practical to measure business income in this manner. Instead, businesses need periodic reports on their situation. Accountants slice time into small segments and prepare financial statements for specific periods.

The basic accounting period is one year, and virtually all businesses prepare annual financial statements. For about 60% of large companies in a recent survey, the annual accounting period runs the calendar year from January 1 through December 31. Other companies use a *fiscal year,* which can end on any date other than December 31. The year-end date is usually the low point in business activity for the year. Retailers are a notable example. For instance, **J.C. Penney Company** uses a fiscal year ending on January 31 because the low point in Penney's business activity falls after the Christmas sales. J.C. Penney does more than 30% of its yearly sales during November and December, but only 5% in January.

Managers and investors cannot wait until the end of the year to gauge a company's progress. Companies therefore prepare financial statements for *interim* periods. Managers want financial information often, so monthly statements are common. A series of monthly statements can be combined for quarterly and semiannual periods. Most of the discussions in this book are based on an annual accounting period, but the procedures and statements can be applied to interim periods as well.

The Revenue Principle

The **revenue principle** tells accountants (1) *when* to record revenue by making a journal entry, and (2) the *amount* of revenue to record. ➥ When we speak of "recording" something in accounting, we mean "make an entry in the journal." That is where the accounting process starts.

The general principle guiding *when* to record revenue says to record revenue once it has been earned—but not before. In most cases, revenue is earned when the business has delivered a completed good or service to the customer. The business has done everything required by the sale agreement, including transferring the item to the customer. Exhibit 3-2 shows two situations that provide guidance on when to record revenue. The first situation illustrates when *not* to record revenue—because the client merely states her plans. Situation 2 illustrates when revenue should be recorded—after Gay Gillen has performed a service for the client.

Objective 2
Apply the revenue and matching principles

REVENUE PRINCIPLE. The basis for recording revenues; tells accountants when to record revenue and the amount of revenue to record.

◀ Revenue, defined in Chapter 1, p. 12, is the increase in owner's equity from delivering goods and services to customers in the course of operating a business.

EXHIBIT 3-2 **Recording Revenue: The Revenue Principle**

◉ DAILY EXERCISE 3-3

The general principle guiding the *amount* of revenue says to record revenue equal to the cash value of the goods or the service transferred to the customer. Suppose that in order to obtain a new client, Gillen Travel performs accounting service for the price of $500. Ordinarily, Gillen would have charged $600 for this service. How much revenue should Gillen record? The answer is $500, because that was the cash value of the transaction. Gillen will not receive the full value of $600, so that is not the amount of revenue to record. She will receive only $500 cash, so that is the amount of revenue she has earned.

The Matching Principle

The **matching principle** is the basis for recording expenses. ◄◄ Recall that expenses—such as rent, utilities, and advertising—are the costs of operating a business. Expenses are the costs of assets that are used up and liabilities that are increased in the earning of revenue. The matching principle directs accountants to (1) identify all expenses incurred during the accounting period, (2) measure the expenses, and (3) match the expenses against the revenues earned during that same span of time. To match expenses against revenues means to subtract expenses from revenues in order to compute net income or net loss. Exhibit 3-3 illustrates the matching principle.

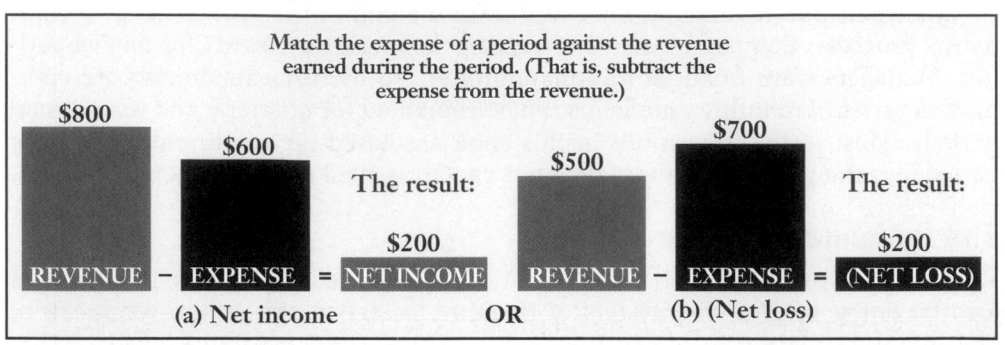

Match the expense of a period against the revenue earned during the period. (That is, subtract the expense from the revenue.)

(a) Net income OR (b) (Net loss)

There is a natural link between revenues and some types of expenses. Accountants first identify a period's revenues and the expenses that can be linked to particular revenues. For example, a business that pays sales commissions to its sales personnel will have commission expense only if the employees make sales. *Cost of goods sold* is another example. If there are no sales of Ford automobiles, **Ford Motor Company** has no cost of goods sold.

Other expenses are not so easy to link with particular sales. For example, monthly rent expense occurs regardless of the revenues earned during the period. The matching principle directs accountants to identify those expenses with a particular time period, such as a month or a year. If Gay Gillen eTravel employs a secretary at a monthly salary of $1,900, the business will record salary expense of $1,900 for each month.

How does Gay Gillen account for a transaction that begins in April but ends in May? How does she bring the accounts up to date for preparing the financial statements? To answer these questions, accountants use the time-period concept.

The Time-Period Concept

Managers, investors, and creditors make decisions daily and need periodic readings on the state of the business. The **time-period concept** ensures that accounting information is reported at regular intervals. It interacts with the revenue principle and the matching principle. To measure income accurately, companies update the revenue and expense accounts immediately before the end of the period. **US Airways** provides an example of an expense accrual. At December 31, 1999, US Airways recorded employee compensation of $341 million that the company owed its workers for unpaid services performed before year end. The company's accrual entry, adapted and in millions of dollars, was

1999
Dec. 31   Salary Expense............................   341
                    Salary Payable   341
              Accrued salary expense.

This entry serves two purposes. First, it assigns the expense to the proper period. Without the accrual entry at December 31, total expenses of 1999 would be understated, and as a result, net income would be overstated. The expense would incorrectly fall in 2000 when US Airways pays the next payroll. Second, the accrual entry

records the liability for the balance sheet at December 31, 1999. Without the accrual entry, total liabilities would be understated.

At the end of an accounting period, companies also accrue revenues that have been earned but not collected. The remainder of the chapter discusses how to make the adjusting entries to show these transactions and bring the accounts up to date.

ADJUSTING THE ACCOUNTS

At the end of the period, the accountant prepares the financial statements. The end-of-period process begins with the trial balance, which lists the accounts and their balances after the period's transactions have been recorded in the journal and posted to the accounts. We saw how to prepare the trial balance in Chapter 2.

Exhibit 3-4 is the trial balance of Gay Gillen eTravel at April 30, 20X1. This *unadjusted trial balance* includes some new accounts that we will explain in this section. It lists most of the revenues and expenses of the travel agency for the month of April. These trial balance amounts are incomplete because they omit certain revenue and expense transactions that affect more than one accounting period. That is why the trial balance is *unadjusted.* In most cases, however, we refer to it simply as the trial balance, without the label "unadjusted."

Objective 3
Make adjusting entries at the end of the accounting period

EXHIBIT 3-4
Unadjusted Trial Balance

GAY GILLEN eTRAVEL Unadjusted Trial Balance April 30, 20X1		
Cash	$24,800	
Accounts receivable	2,250	
Supplies	700	
Prepaid rent	3,000	
Furniture	16,500	
Accounts payable		$13,100
Unearned service revenue		450
Gay Gillen, capital		31,250
Gay Gillen, withdrawals	3,200	
Service revenue		7,000
Salary expense	950	
Utilities expense	400	
Total	$51,800	$51,800

Under cash-basis accounting, there is no need for adjustments to the accounts because all April cash transactions have already been recorded. However, the accrual basis requires adjusting entries at the end of the period in order to produce correct balances for the financial statements. To see why, consider the Supplies account in Exhibit 3-4.

Gay Gillen eTravel uses supplies in providing travel services for clients during the month. This reduces the quantity of supplies on hand and thus constitutes an expense, just like salary or rent. It is not worth the effort to record supplies expense more than once a month. It takes time to make daily or weekly journal entries. So how does Gillen account for supplies expense?

By the end of the month, the Supplies balance of $700 on the unadjusted trial balance (Exhibit 3-4) is not correct. The unadjusted balance represents the amount of supplies on hand at the start of the month plus any supplies purchased during the month. This balance fails to take into account the supplies used *(supplies expense)* during the accounting period. It is necessary, then, to subtract the month's expenses from the amount of supplies listed on the trial balance. The resulting new adjusted balance will measure the cost of supplies that are still on hand at April 30, say $400. This is the correct amount of Supplies to report on the balance sheet—$400. The adjusting entry will bring the supplies account up to date.

Adjusting entries assign revenues to the period in which they are earned and expenses to the period in which they are incurred. Adjusting entries also update the asset and liability accounts. They are needed to (1) properly measure the period's

ADJUSTING ENTRY. Entry made at the end of the period to assign revenues to the period in which they are earned and expenses to the period in which they are incurred. Adjusting entries help measure the period's income and bring the related asset and liability accounts to correct balances for the financial statements.

income on the income statement, and (2) bring related asset and liability accounts to correct balances for the balance sheet. Adjusting entries, which are the key to accrual-basis accounting, are made before the financial statements are prepared. The end-of-period process of updating the accounts is called *adjusting the accounts, making the adjusting entries,* or *adjusting the books.*

A large company uses accounting software to print out a trial balance. For example, **Occidental Petroleum (OXY),** a large oil company, has accounting software that prints a monthly trial balance. The accountants then analyze the amounts on the trial balance. This analysis results in the adjusting entries that OXY makes. The trial balance has now become the *adjusted* trial balance. This chapter shows the adjusting process as it moves from the trial balance to the adjusted trial balance. Two basic types of adjustments are *prepaids* and *accruals.*

PREPAIDS (DEFERRALS) AND ACCRUALS

In a *prepaid* adjustment, the cash transaction occurs before the related expense or revenue is recorded. Prepaids are also called *deferrals* because the recording of the expense or the revenue is deferred until after cash is paid or received. *Accrual*-type adjustments are the opposite of prepaids. For accruals, we record the expense or revenue before the related cash settlement.

Adjusting entries can be further divided into five categories:

1. Prepaid expenses   4. Accrued revenues
2. Depreciation of plant assets   5. Unearned revenues
3. Accrued expenses

The core of this chapter is the discussion of these five types of adjusting entries on pages 88–96. Study this material carefully because it is the most challenging topic in all of introductory accounting.

Prepaid Expenses

PREPAID EXPENSE. Advance payments of expenses. A category of current assets that typically expire or are used up in the near future. Examples include prepaid rent, prepaid insurance, and supplies.

Prepaid expenses are advance payments of expenses. The category includes prepayments that typically expire or that will be used up in the near future. Prepaid rent and prepaid insurance are examples. They are called "prepaid" expenses because they are paid in advance. Salary expense and utilities expense, among others, are typically *not* prepaid because they are not paid in advance. All companies, large and small, must make adjustments regarding prepaid expenses. For example, **McDonald's Corporation,** the restaurant chain, must contend with such prepayments as rents, packaging supplies, and insurance. Keep in mind that prepaid expenses are assets, not expenses.

PREPAID RENT Landlords usually require tenants to pay rent in advance. This prepayment creates an asset for the renter, who has purchased the future benefit of using the rented item. Suppose Gay Gillen eTravel prepays three months' office rent on April 1, 20X1. If the lease specifies monthly rental amounts of $1,000, the entry to record the payment for three months is a debit to the asset account, Prepaid Rent, as follows:

Apr. 1	Prepaid Rent ($1,000 × 3) 3,000	
	Cash	3,000
	Paid three months' rent in advance.	

After posting, Prepaid Rent appears as follows:

ASSETS

PREPAID RENT
Apr. 1	3,000

The trial balance at April 30, 20X1, lists Prepaid Rent as an asset with a debit balance of $3,000. Throughout April, the Prepaid Rent account maintains this beginning balance, as shown in Exhibit 3-4. But $3,000 is *not* the amount to report for Prepaid Rent on the travel agency's balance sheet at April 30. Why?

At April 30, Prepaid Rent should be adjusted to remove from its balance the amount of the asset that has been used up, which is one month's worth of the pre-payment. By definition, the amount of an asset that has expired is *expense.* The adjusting entry transfers one-third, or $1,000 ($3,000 × 1/3), of the debit balance from Prepaid Rent to Rent Expense. The debit side of the entry records an increase in Rent Expense, and the credit records a decrease in the asset Prepaid Rent:

Apr. 30   Rent Expense ($3,000 × 1/3).............   1,000
                  Prepaid Rent   1,000
            To record rent expense.

After posting, Prepaid Rent and Rent Expense appear as follows:

ASSETS		EXPENSES	
PREPAID RENT		RENT EXPENSE	
Apr. 1 3,000	Apr. 30 1,000	Apr. 30 1,000	
Bal. 2,000		Bal. 1,000	

Correct asset → Total accounted ← Correct expense
amount: $2,000   for: $3,000   amount: $1,000

The full $3,000 has been accounted for: Two-thirds measures the asset, and one-third measures the expense. Recording this expense illustrates the matching principle.

The same analysis applies to prepayment of three months of insurance premiums. The only difference is in the account titles, which would be Prepaid Insurance and Insurance Expense instead of Prepaid Rent and Rent Expense. In a computerized system, the adjusting entry crediting the prepaid account and debiting the expense account could be established to recur automatically in each accounting period until the prepaid account has a zero balance.

The chapter appendix shows an alternative treatment of prepaid expenses. The end result on the financial statements is the same as illustrated here.

SUPPLIES   Supplies are accounted for in the same way as prepaid expenses. On April 2, Gay Gillen paid cash of $700 for office supplies:

Apr. 2   Supplies   700
                  Cash...   700
            Paid cash for supplies.

Assume that Gillen purchased no additional supplies during April. The April 30 trial balance, therefore, lists Supplies with a $700 debit balance, as shown in Exhibit 3-4. But Gillen's April 30 balance sheet should *not* report supplies of $700. Why?

During April, Gillen used supplies in performing services for clients. The cost of the supplies used is the measure of *supplies expense* for the month. To measure supplies expense during April, Gillen counts the supplies on hand at the end of the month. This is the amount of the asset (the economic resource) still available to the business. Assume the count at April 30 indicates that supplies costing $400 remain. Subtracting the $400 of supplies on hand at the end of April from the cost of supplies available during April ($700) measures supplies expense during the month ($300).

Cost of asset available during the period	−	Cost of asset on hand at the end of the period	=	Cost of asset used (expense) during the period
$700	−	$400	=	$300

The April 30 adjusting entry to update the Supplies account and to record the supplies expense for the month debits the expense and credits the asset, as follows:

Apr. 30   Supplies Expense ($700 − $400)   300
                  Supplies   300
            To record supplies expense.

After posting, the Supplies and Supplies Expense accounts appear as follows:

ASSETS				EXPENSES		
SUPPLIES				SUPPLIES EXPENSE		
Apr. 2	700	Apr. 30	300	Apr. 30	300	
Bal.	400			Bal.	300	

Correct asset amount: $400 → Total accounted for: $700 ← Correct expense amount: $300

The Supplies account then enters the month of May with a $400 balance, and the adjustment process is repeated at the end of May.

 **WORK IT OUT** At the beginning of the month, Supplies were $5,000. During the month, the company purchased $7,800 of supplies. At month's end, $3,600 of supplies were still on hand.

1. What was the cost of supplies used during the month?
2. What is the ending balance of Supplies? Where is this item reported?
3. Make the adjusting entry to update the Supplies account at the end of the month.

Answers

1.

Beginning balance	$ 5,000
+Purchases	7,800
=Supplies available	12,800
−Ending balance	(3,600)
=Expense (supplies used during the period).........	$ 9,200

2. The ending balance of Supplies is $3,600. This is the amount that should be reported on the *balance sheet*.

3. Supplies Expense 9,200
      Supplies   9,200

Depreciation of Plant Assets

The logic of the accrual basis is probably best illustrated by how businesses account for plant assets. **Plant assets** are long-lived tangible assets—such as land, buildings, furniture, machinery, and equipment—used in the operations of the business. As one accountant said, "All assets but land are on a march to the junkyard." That is, all plant assets except land decline in usefulness as they age. This decline is an expense to the business. Accountants systematically spread the cost of each plant asset, except land, over the years of its useful life. This allocation of a plant asset's cost to expense over its useful life is called **depreciation.**

SIMILARITY TO PREPAID EXPENSES   The concept underlying accounting for plant assets is the same as for prepaid expenses. In a sense, plant assets are merely prepaid expenses that expire over a number of periods. With both prepaid expenses and plant assets, the business purchases an asset that wears out. As the asset is used, its cost is transferred from the asset account to the expense account. The major difference between prepaid expenses and plant assets is the length of time it takes for the asset to expire. Prepaid expenses usually expire within a year, while most plant assets remain useful for a number of years.

Consider Gay Gillen eTravel. Suppose that on April 3 Gillen purchased furniture on account for $16,500 and made this journal entry:

Apr. 3   Furniture.. 16,500
           Accounts Payable   16,500
           Purchased office furniture on account.

PLANT ASSET. Long-lived tangible assets—such as land, buildings, and equipment—used in the operations of a business.

DEPRECIATION. The allocation of a plant asset's cost to expense over its useful life.

After posting, the Furniture account appears as follows:

ASSETS

FURNITURE

Apr. 3 16,500	

Gillen believes the furniture will remain useful for five years and will be worthless at the end of its life. One way to compute the amount of depreciation for each year is to divide the cost of the asset ($16,500 in our example) by its expected useful life (five years). This procedure—called the straight-line method—computes annual depreciation of $3,300 ($16,500/5 years = $3,300 per year). Depreciation for the month of April is $275 ($3,300/12 months = $275 per month).

THE ACCUMULATED DEPRECIATION ACCOUNT Depreciation expense for April is recorded by the following entry:

Apr. 30	Depreciation Expense—Furniture............................	275	
	Accumulated Depreciation—Furniture		275
	To record depreciation on furniture.		

Accumulated Depreciation is credited instead of Furniture because the original cost of a plant asset (the furniture) should remain in the asset account as long as the business uses the asset. Accountants and managers can then refer to the Furniture account to see how much the asset cost. This information may be useful in a decision about whether to replace the furniture and how much to pay.

The amount of depreciation is an estimate. The Accumulated Depreciation account holds the cumulative sum of all depreciation expense recorded for the asset. The balance of the Accumulated Depreciation account increases over the life of the asset.

Accumulated Depreciation is a contra asset account, which means an asset account with a normal credit balance. A **contra account** has two distinguishing characteristics:

- A contra account has a companion account.
- A contra account's normal balance (debit or credit) is opposite that of the companion account.

In this case, Accumulated Depreciation is the contra account that accompanies Furniture. It appears in the ledger directly after Furniture. Furniture has a debit balance, and therefore Accumulated Depreciation, a contra asset, has a credit balance. *All contra asset accounts have credit balances.*

A business carries an accumulated depreciation account for each depreciable asset. If a business has a building and a machine, for example, it will carry the accounts Accumulated Depreciation—Building and Accumulated Depreciation—Machine.

After the depreciation entry has been posted, the Furniture, Accumulated Depreciation, and Depreciation Expense accounts of Gay Gillen eTravel, appear as follows:

ASSETS	**CONTRA ASSET**	**EXPENSES**
FURNITURE	ACCUMULATED DEPRECIATION—FURNITURE	DEPRECIATION EXPENSE—FURNITURE
Apr. 3 16,500	Apr. 30 275	Apr. 30 275
Bal. 16,500	Bal. 275	Bal. 275

ACCUMULATED DEPRECIATION. The cumulative sum of all depreciation expense recorded for an asset.

CONTRA ACCOUNT. An account that always has a companion account and whose normal balance is opposite that of the companion account.

BOOK VALUE (OF A PLANT ASSET). The asset's cost minus accumulated depreciation.

BOOK VALUE   The balance sheet shows the relationship between Furniture and Accumulated Depreciation. The balance of Accumulated Depreciation is subtracted from the balance of Furniture. The resulting net amount of a plant asset (cost minus accumulated depreciation) is called its **book value,** or *net book value,* as shown at top of next page for Furniture:

Plant Assets:	
Furniture..	$16,500
Less: Accumulated depreciation..............	(275)
Book value	$16,225

Suppose Gillen eTravel also owns a building that cost $48,000 and on which annual depreciation is $2,400 ($48,000/20 years). The amount of depreciation for one month would be $200 ($2,400/12), and the following entry records depreciation for April:

⊙ DAILY EXERCISE 3-8

Apr. 30	Depreciation Expense—Building..............................	200	
	Accumulated Depreciation—Building............		200
	To record depreciation on building.		

The balance sheet at April 30 reports Gillen's plant assets as shown in Exhibit 3-5.

Exhibit 3-5
Plant Assets on the Balance Sheet of Gay Gillen eTravel (April 30)

Plant Assets:		
Furniture...	$16,500	
Less: Accumulated depreciation..............	(275)	$16,225
Building	48,000	
Less: Accumulated depreciation..............	(200)	47,800
Book value of plant assets...........................		$64,025

Exhibit 3-6 shows how **Johnson & Johnson**—maker of Band-Aids, Tylenol, and other health-care products—displayed Property, Plant, and Equipment in its annual report. Johnson & Johnson has real-estate holdings around the world; they are reported in line 1 of Exhibit 3-6. Line 2 includes the cost of buildings and the related equipment (air conditioners and elevators) in those buildings. The company's manufacturing machinery, office equipment, and furniture are given in line 3, and line 4 reports the cost of assets that are under construction.

Exhibit 3-6
Johnson & Johnson's Reporting of Property, Plant, and Equipment

	Millions
(1) Land and land improvements	$ 344
(2) Buildings and building equipment	2,611
(3) Machinery and equipment..........................	4,217
(4) Construction in progress	1,003
	8,175
Less: Accumulated depreciation........................	(2,979)
	$5,196

Johnson & Johnson's cost of plant assets was $8,175 million (cost principle). Of the total cost, Johnson & Johnson has depreciated a total of $2,979 million (matching principle). The book value of J&J's plant assets is therefore $8,175 − $2,979 = $5,196 million.

Now let's return to Gay Gillen eTravel.

Accrued Expenses

ACCRUED EXPENSE. An expense that the business has incurred but not yet paid.

Businesses often incur expenses before they pay for them. Consider an employee's salary. The employer's salary expense and salary payable grow as the employee works, so the liability is said to *accrue*. Another example is interest expense on a note payable. Interest accrues as the clock ticks. The term **accrued expense** refers to an expense the business has incurred but has not yet paid. Accrued expenses can be viewed as the opposite of prepaid expenses.

It is time-consuming to make weekly journal entries to accrue expenses. Consequently, the accountant waits until the end of the period. Then an adjusting entry brings each expense (and related liability) up to date just before the financial statements are prepared.

Remember the key difference between a prepaid expense and an accrued expense: A prepaid expense is paid first and expensed later. An accrued expense is expensed first and paid later. Prepaids and accruals are opposites.

SALARY EXPENSE   Most companies pay their employees at set times. Suppose Gay Gillen pays her employee a monthly salary of $1,900, half on the 15th and half on the last day of the month. Here is a calendar for April with the two paydays circled:

			APRIL			
S	M	T	W	T	F	S
					1	2
3	4	5	6	7	8	9
10	11	12	13	14	(15)	16
17	18	19	20	21	22	23
24	25	26	27	28	29	(30)

Assume that if either payday falls on the weekend, Gillen pays the employee on the following Monday. During April, Gillen paid her employee's first half-month salary of $950 on Friday, April 15, and recorded the following entry:

Apr. 15   Salary Expense 950
                  Cash 950
          To pay salary.

After posting, the Salary Expense account is

EXPENSES

SALARY EXPENSE

Apr. 15	950

The trial balance at April 30 (Exhibit 3-4) includes Salary Expense, with its debit balance of $950. This unadjusted balance of $950 is Gillen's salary expense for only the first half of April. Because April 30, the second payday of the month, falls on a Saturday, the second half-month amount of $950 will be paid on Monday, May 2. However, Gillen must record salary expense for the second half of April. Because of the need to accrue salary expense at April 30, Gillen makes an adjusting entry for additional Salary Expense and Salary Payable of $950 as follows:

Apr. 30   Salary Expense 950
                  Salary Payable 950
          To accrue salary expense.

This is the accrual basis of accounting in action. After posting, the Salary Expense and Salary Payable accounts are updated to April 30:

EXPENSES   **LIABILITIES**

SALARY EXPENSE   SALARY PAYABLE

Apr. 15	950			Apr. 30	950
Apr. 30	950			Bal.	950
Bal.	1,900				

The accounts at April 30 now contain complete salary information for the month of April. The expense account has a full month's salary, and the liability account shows the portion that the business still owes at April 30. Gillen will record the payment of this liability on Monday, May 2.

 **WORK IT OUT**

Weekly salaries for a five-day workweek total $3,500, payable on a Friday. This month, November 30 falls on a Tuesday.

1. Which accounts require adjustment at November 30?
2. Make the adjusting entry.

Answers

1. Salary Expense and Salary Payable.
2.   Salary Expense ($3,500 × 2/5) 1,400
                Salary Payable   1,400
         To accrue salary expense.

Accrued Revenues

ACCRUED REVENUE. A revenue that has been earned but not yet collected in cash.

Some expenses occur before the cash payment, and we must record an accrued expense. Likewise, businesses may also earn revenue before they receive the cash. This calls for an **accrued revenue,** which is a revenue that has been earned but not yet collected in cash.

Assume that Gay Gillen eTravel is hired on April 15 by **Procter & Gamble** to perform travel services on a continuing basis. Under this agreement, Gillen will receive $500 monthly, with the first cash receipt on May 15. During April, she will earn half a month's fee, $250, for work performed April 15 through April 30. On April 30, she makes the following adjusting entry to accrue the revenue earned during April 15–30:

         Apr. 30   Accounts Receivable ($500 × 1/2)   250
                          Service Revenue................................   250
                    To accrue service revenue............................

We see from the unadjusted trial balance in Exhibit 3-4 that Accounts Receivable has an unadjusted balance of $2,250. Service Revenue's unadjusted balance is $7,000. Posting the April 30 adjusting entry has the following effects on these two accounts:

ASSETS		REVENUES	
ACCOUNTS RECEIVABLE		SERVICE REVENUE	
	2,250		7,000
Apr. 30	250	Apr. 30	250
Bal.	2,500	Bal.	7,250

This adjusting entry illustrates the revenue principle. Without the adjustment, Gillen's financial statements would be incomplete and misleading—they would understate Accounts Receivable and Service Revenue by $250 each. All accrued revenues are accounted for similarly—by debiting a receivable and crediting a revenue.

Now we turn to a different category of adjusting entries.

Unearned Revenues

UNEARNED REVENUE. A liability created when a business collects cash from customers in advance of doing work. The obligation is to provide a product or a service in the future. Also called **deferred revenue.**

Some businesses collect cash from customers in advance of doing work for them. Receiving cash in advance creates a liability called **unearned revenue** or **deferred revenue.** This liability arises from receiving cash in advance of providing a product or a service. Only when the job is completed will the business have *earned* the revenue.

Suppose **Baldwin Piano Company** engages Gillen to provide travel services, agreeing to pay her $450 monthly, beginning immediately. Baldwin makes the first payment on April 20. Gillen records the cash receipt and the related increase in liabilities as follows:

         Apr. 20   Cash   450
                          Unearned Service Revenue...............   450
                    Collected revenue in advance.

After posting, the liability account Unearned Service Revenue appears as follows:

LIABILITIES

UNEARNED SERVICE REVENUE		
	Apr. 20	450

Unearned Service Revenue is a liability account because it represents Gillen's obligation to perform service for the client. The April 30 unadjusted trial balance (Exhibit 3-4) lists Unearned Service Revenue with a $450 credit balance prior to the adjusting entries. During the last ten days of the month—April 21 through April 30—Gillen will have *earned* one-third (10 days divided by April's total 30 days) of the $450, or $150. Therefore, Gillen makes the following adjustment to decrease the liability, Unearned Service Revenue, and to record an increase in Service Revenue, as follows:

Apr. 30	Unearned Service Revenue ($450 × 1/3)	150	
	Service Revenue		150
	To record service revenue that was collected in advance.		

This adjusting entry shifts $150 of the total amount of unearned service revenue from the liability account to the revenue account. After posting, the balance of Service Revenue is increased by $150, and the balance of Unearned Service Revenue is reduced by $150, to $300. Now, both accounts have the correct balances at April 30:

LIABILITIES

UNEARNED SERVICE REVENUE				
Apr. 30	150	Apr. 20	450	
		Bal.	300	

REVENUES

SERVICE REVENUE			
			7,000
		Apr. 30	250
		Apr. 30	150
		Bal.	7,400

Correct liability amount: $300	→	Total accounted for: $450	←	Correct revenue amount: $150

All types of revenues collected in advance are accounted for in the same way.

 DAILY EXERCISE 3-11

An unearned revenue to one company is a prepaid expense to the company that made the payment. For example, suppose that **Xerox Corporation** paid **American Airlines** $1,800 two months in advance for the air travel expenses of Xerox executives. To Xerox, the payment is Prepaid Travel Expense. To American Airlines, the receipt of cash creates Unearned Service Revenue. After the executives take the trip, American Airlines records the revenue and Xerox records travel expense.

Remember: An unearned revenue is a liability, not a revenue.

 **WORK IT OUT**

Consider the tuition you pay your college or university. Assume that one semester's tuition costs $500 and that you make a single payment at the start of the term. Can you make the journal entries to record the tuition transactions on your own books and on the books of your college or university?

Answer

	Your Books			**Your College's Books**		
Start of Semester	Prepaid Tuition	500		Cash..........................	500	
	Cash		500	Unearned Tuition		
	Paid semester tuition.			Revenue................		500
				Collected revenue in advance.		
End of Semester	Tuition Expense.................	500		Unearned Tuition		
	Prepaid Tuition..............		500	Revenue	500	
	To record tuition expense.			Tuition Revenue ...		500
				To record tuition revenue that was collected in advance.		

Exhibit 3-7 summarizes the timing of prepaid- and accrual-type adjusting entries. The chapter appendix shows an alternative treatment for unearned revenues.

EXHIBIT 3-7 Prepaid- and Accrual-Type Adjustments

PREPAIDS—The cash transaction occurs initially.

	Initially		Later	
Prepaid Expenses	Pay cash and record an asset: Prepaid Expense .... XXX Cash	XXX	Record an expense and decrease the asset: Expense...................................... XXX Prepaid Expense	XXX
Unearned Revenues	Receive cash and record unearned revenue: Cash................................. XXX Unearned Revenue	XXX	Record a revenue and decrease unearned revenue: Unearned Revenue .... XXX Revenue	XXX

ACCRUALS—The cash transaction occurs later.

	Initially		Later	
Accrued Expenses	Accrue an expense and the related payable: Expense .... XXX Payable..............................	XXX	Pay cash and decrease the payable: Payable...................................... XXX Cash..	XXX
Accrued Revenues	Accrue a revenue and the related receivable: Receivable................................ XXX Revenue.................................	XXX	Receive cash and decrease the receivable: Cash .... XXX Receivable	XXX

Source: The authors thank Darrel Davis and Alfonso Oddo for suggesting this exhibit.

www.prenhall.com/horngren
Mid-Chapter Assessment

Summary of the Adjusting Process

The adjusting process has two purposes:

1. Measure net income or net loss on the *income statement.* Every adjusting entry affects either a *Revenue* or an *Expense.*
2. Update the *balance sheet.* Every adjusting entry affects either an *Asset* or a *Liability.*

No adjusting entry debits or credits Cash because the cash transactions are recorded before the end of the period. Exhibit 3-8 summarizes the adjusting entries.

EXHIBIT 3-8
Summary of Adjusting Entries

	Type of Account	
Category of Adjusting Entry	**Debited**	**Credited**
Prepaid expense	Expense	Asset
Depreciation	Expense	Contra asset
Accrued expense	Expense	Liability
Accrued revenue	Asset	Revenue
Unearned revenue	Liability	Revenue

Source: Adapted from material provided by Beverly Terry.

Exhibit 3-9 summarizes the adjusting entries of Gay Gillen eTravel at April 30. Panel A briefly describes the data for each adjustment, Panel B gives the adjusting entries, and Panel C shows the accounts after they have been posted. The adjustments are keyed by letter.

THE ADJUSTED TRIAL BALANCE

Objective 4
Prepare an adjusted trial balance

This chapter began with the trial balance before any adjusting entries—the unadjusted trial balance (Exhibit 3-4). After the adjustments are journalized and posted, the accounts appear as shown in Exhibit 3-9, Panel C. A useful step in preparing the

PANEL A—Information for Adjustments at April 30, 20X1

(a) Prepaid rent expired, $1,000.
(b) Supplies on hand, $400.
(c) Depreciation on furniture, $275.
(d) Accrued salary expense, $950.

(e) Accrued service revenue, $250
(f) Service revenue earned that was collected in advance, $150.

PANEL B—Adjusting Entries

(a)	Rent Expense	1,000	
	Prepaid Rent		1,000
	To record rent expense.		
(b)	Supplies Expense	300	
	Supplies		300
	To record supplies used.		
(c)	Depreciation Expense—Furniture	275	
	Accumulated Depreciation—Furniture		275
	To record depreciation on furniture.		
(d)	Salary Expense	950	
	Salary Payable		950
	To accrue salary expense.		
(e)	Accounts Receivable	250	
	Service Revenue		250
	To accrue service revenue.		
(f)	Unearned Service Revenue	150	
	Service Revenue		150
	To record revenue that was collected in advance.		

PANEL C—Ledger Accounts

ASSETS

CASH
Bal. 24,800

ACCOUNTS RECEIVABLE
2,250
(e) 250
Bal. 2,500

SUPPLIES
700 | (b) 300
Bal. 400

PREPAID RENT
3,000 | (a) 1,000
Bal. 2,000

FURNITURE
Bal. 16,500

ACCUMULATED DEPRECIATION—FURNITURE
(c) 275
Bal. 275

LIABILITIES

ACCOUNTS PAYABLE
Bal. 13,100

SALARY PAYABLE
(d) 950
Bal. 950

UNEARNED SERVICE REVENUE
(f) 150 | 450
Bal. 300

OWNER'S EQUITY

GAY GILLEN, CAPITAL
Bal. 31,250

GAY GILLEN, WITHDRAWALS
Bal. 3,200

REVENUE

SERVICE REVENUE
7,000
(e) 250
(f) 150
Bal. 7,400

EXPENSES

RENT EXPENSE
(a) 1,000
Bal. 1,000

SALARY EXPENSE
950
(d) 950
Bal. 1,000

SUPPLIES EXPENSE
(b) 300
Bal. 300

DEPRECIATION EXPENSE—FURNITURE
(c) 275
Bal. 275

UTILITIES EXPENSE
Bal. 400

---

financial statements is to list the accounts, along with their adjusted balances, on an **adjusted trial balance.** This document has the advantage of listing all the accounts and their adjusted balances in a single place. Exhibit 3-10 shows the preparation of the adjusted trial balance.

Exhibit 3-10 is a *work sheet.* We will discuss the work sheet in detail in Chapter 4. For now, simply note how clearly this format presents the data. The information in

ADJUSTED TRIAL BALANCE. A list of all the accounts with their adjusted balances.

Grossing up the Revenue: Priceline.com and Ventro

Suppose you're going to Australia. You want a cheap air ticket, and **Priceline.com** lets you "name your price" for airline tickets and hotel rooms. Your bid of $975 is accepted,

and Priceline pockets the spread between your price and the amount that Priceline pays the airline company. What should Priceline claim as revenue—the fee Priceline earns or the full price of your ticket?

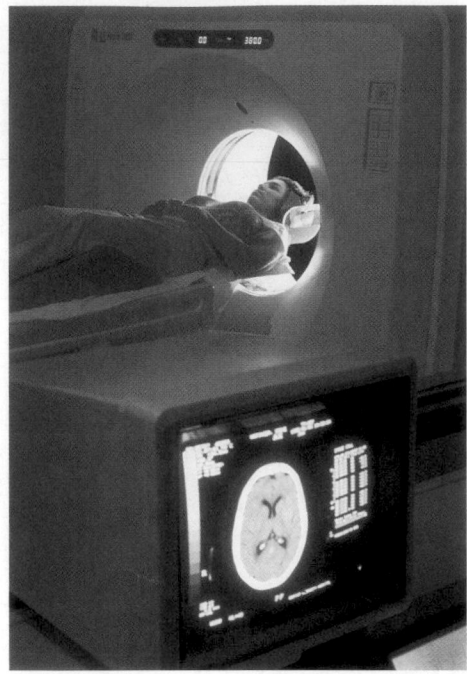

Priceline.com and other Internet service companies are claiming the entire value of the products sold through their sites. The SEC and the FASB call this practice "grossing up" revenue. Dot.com companies do it to show a profit when they're actually operating at a loss. The practice draws investors and pushes up stock prices. Grossing up may be legal, but the SEC and the FASB are considering placing restrictions on it.

Ventro, which handles the sale of specialty medical products over the Internet, is one company that would be adversely affected by such a restriction. Ventro's $29 million in grossed-up revenue for 1999 was expected to more than quadruple to $140 million in 2000. The company argues that its accounting

method is sound since the company assumes various revenue risks: shelling out money if a product is returned, bearing credit risk if the customer won't pay, and taking title to the products sold. Yet Ventro never takes actual products into its own inventory and only takes title to the products during the time it takes to ship them. Ventro's suppliers are happy to absorb refund costs and Ventro's blue-chip customers rarely pose credit problems. If the accounting rulemakers decide that grossing up is okay, expect to see the value of business-to-business sites like Ventro soar.

Sources: Based on: Elizabeth McDonald, "Plump from Web Sales, Some Dot.Coms Face Crash Diet of Restriction on Booking Revenue," *Wall Street Journal,* February 28, 2000, p. C4. Jeremy Kahn, "Presto chango! Sales are huge!" *Fortune,* March 20, 2000, pp. 90–96.

DAILY EXERCISE 3-12

DAILY EXERCISE 3-13

DAILY EXERCISE 3-14

DAILY EXERCISE 3-15

DAILY EXERCISE 3-16

the Account Title column and in the Trial Balance columns is copied directly from the trial balance. The two Adjustments columns list the debit and credit adjustments directly across from the appropriate account title. Each adjusting debit is identified by a letter that refers to the adjusting entry. For example, the debit labeled (a) on the work sheet refers to the debit adjusting entry of $1,000 to Rent Expense in Panel B of Exhibit 3-9. For adjusting credits, the corresponding credit—labeled (a)—refers to the $1,000 credit to Prepaid Rent.

The Adjusted Trial Balance columns give the adjusted account balances. Each amount in these columns is computed by combining the amounts from the unadjusted trial balance plus or minus the adjustments. For example, Accounts Receivable starts with a debit balance of $2,250. Adding the $250 debit amount from adjusting entry (e) gives Accounts Receivable an adjusted debit balance of $2,500. Supplies begins with a debit balance of $700. After the $300 credit adjustment, its adjusted balance is $400. More than one entry may affect a single account, as is the case for Service Revenue. If an account is unaffected by the adjustments, it will show the same amount on both the unadjusted and the adjusted trial balances. In this example, the balances of Cash, Furniture, Accounts Payable, Capital, and Withdrawals do not change.

EXHIBIT 3-10 **Preparation of Adjusted Trial Balance**

GAY GILLEN ETRAVEL
Preparation of Adjusted Trial Balance
April 30, 20X1

Account Title	Trial Balance Debit	Trial Balance Credit	Adjustments Debit		Adjustments Credit		Adjusted Trial Balance Debit	Adjusted Trial Balance Credit
Cash	24,800						24,800	
Accounts receivable	2,250		(e)	250			2,500	
Supplies	700				(b)	300	400	
Prepaid rent	3,000				(a)	1,000	2,000	
Furniture	16,500						16,500	
Accumulated depreciation					(c)	275		275
Accounts payable		13,100						13,100
Salary payable					(d)	950		950
Unearned service revenue		450	(f)	150				300
Gay Gillen, capital		31,250						31,250
Gay Gillen, withdrawals	3,200						3,200	
Service revenue		7,000			(e)	250		7,400
					(f)	150		
Rent expense			(a)	1,000			1,000	
Salary expense	950		(d)	950			1,900	
Supplies expense			(b)	300			300	
Depreciation expense			(c)	275			275	
Utilities expense	400						400	
	51,800	51,800		2,925		2,925	53,275	53,275

Account Title	Adjusted Trial Balance Debit	Adjusted Trial Balance Credit	
Cash	24,800		
Accounts receivable	2,500		
Supplies	400		
Prepaid rent	2,000		
Furniture	16,500		**Balance Sheet** (Exhibit 3-14)
Accumulated depreciation		275	
Accounts payable		13,100	
Salary payable		950	
Unearned service revenue		300	
Gay Gillen, capital		31,250	**Statement of Owner's Equity** (Exhibit 3-13)
Gay Gillen, withdrawals	3,200		
Service revenue		7,400	
Rent expense	1,000		
Salary expense	1,900		**Income Statement** (Exhibit 3-12)
Supplies expense	300		
Depreciation expense	275		
Utilities expense	400		
	53,275	53,275	

Objective 5
Prepare the financial statements
from the adjusted trial balance

PREPARING THE FINANCIAL STATEMENTS

The April financial statements of Gay Gillen eTravel can be prepared from the adjusted trial balance. Exhibit 3-11 shows how the accounts are distributed from the adjusted trial balance to three of the four main financial statements. As we have seen in Chapters 1–3, the income statement (Exhibit 3-12) comes from the revenue and expense accounts. The statement of owner's equity (Exhibit 3-13) shows why the owner's capital changed during the period. The balance sheet (Exhibit 3-14) reports the assets, liabilities, and owner's equity.

The financial statements are best prepared in the order shown: the income statement first, followed by the statement of owner's equity, and then the balance sheet.

EXHIBIT 3-12
Income Statement

GAY GILLEN ETRAVEL
Income Statement
Month Ended April 30, 20X1

Revenue:		
Service revenue		$7,400
Expenses:		
Salary expense	$1,900	
Rent expense....................	1,000	
Utilities expense	400	
Supplies expense...............	300	
Depreciation expense.........	275	
Total expenses		3,875
Net income		$3,525

EXHIBIT 3-13
Statement of Owner's Equity

GAY GILLEN ETRAVEL
Statement of Owner's Equity
Month Ended April 30, 20X1

Gay Gillen, capital, April 1, 20X1...............	$31,250
Add: Net income	3,525
	34,775
Less: Withdrawals..	(3,200)
Gay Gillen, capital, April 30, 20X1..............	$31,575

EXHIBIT 3-14
Balance Sheet

GAY GILLEN ETRAVEL
Balance Sheet
April 30, 20X1

Assets			Liabilities		
Cash		$24,800	Accounts payable		$13,100
Accounts			Salary payable		950
receivable		2,500	Unearned service		
Supplies		400	revenue		300
Prepaid rent		2,000	Total liabilities		14,350
Furniture	$16,500				
Less:					
Accumulated			**Owner's Equity**		
depreciation	(275)	16,225	Gay Gillen, capital...............		31,575
			Total liabilities and		
Total assets		$45,925	owner's equity.................		$45,925

The essential features of all financial statements are these:

Heading

- Name of the entity
- Title of the statement
- Date, or period, covered by the statement

Body of the statement

It is customary to list expenses in descending order by amount on the income statement, as shown in Exhibit 3-12. However, Miscellaneous Expense, a catchall account for expenses that do not fit another category, is usually reported last.

RELATIONSHIPS AMONG THE THREE FINANCIAL STATEMENTS

The arrows in Exhibits 3-12, 3-13, and 3-14 illustrate the relationships among the income statement, the statement of owner's equity, and the balance sheet. ➤ Consider why the income statement is prepared first and the balance sheet last.

◀ The relationships among the financial statements were introduced in Chapter 1, p. 20.

1. The income statement reports net income or net loss (revenues minus expenses). Because revenues and expenses are owner's equity accounts, their net amount is transferred to the statement of owner's equity. Note that net income in Exhibit 3-12, $3,525, increases owner's equity in Exhibit 3-13. A net loss would decrease owner's equity.
2. Capital is a balance sheet account, so the ending balance in the statement of owner's equity is transferred to the balance sheet. This amount is the final balancing element of the balance sheet. To solidify your understanding of this relationship, trace the $31,575 figure from Exhibit 3-13 to Exhibit 3-14.

You may be wondering why the total assets on the balance sheet ($45,925 in Exhibit 3-14) do not equal the total debits on the adjusted trial balance ($53,275 in Exhibit 3-11). Likewise, the total liabilities and owner's equity ($45,925 in Exhibit 3-14) do not equal the total credits on the adjusted trial balance ($53,275 in Exhibit 3-11). The reason for these differences is that Accumulated Depreciation and Owner's Withdrawals are contra accounts. Recall that contra accounts are *subtracted* from their companion accounts on the balance sheet. But on the adjusted trial balance, contra accounts are *added* as a debit or a credit in their respective columns.

WORK IT OUT Examine Gillen eTravel's adjusted trial balance in Exhibit 3-10. Suppose Gillen forgot to record the $950 accrual of salary expense at April 30. What net income would the travel agency then report for April? What total assets, total liabilities, and total owner's equity would the balance sheet report at April 30?

Answer: Omitting the salary accrual would produce these effects:

1. Net income (Exhibit 3-12) would have been $4,475 ($3,525 + $950).
2. Total assets would have been unaffected by the error—$45,925 (Exhibit 3-14).
3. Total liabilities (Exhibit 3-14) would have been $13,400 ($14,350 − $950).
4. Owner's equity (Gay Gillen, capital) would have been $32,525 ($31,575 + $950) (Exhibit 3-14).

ETHICAL ISSUES IN ACCRUAL ACCOUNTING

Like other aspects of business, accounting poses ethical challenges. At the most fundamental level, accountants must be honest in their work. Only with honest and complete information, including accounting data, can people expect to make wise decisions. An example will illustrate.

It's Just Lunch has done well as a business. Andrea McGinty is an excellent businesswoman. The company has opened offices in most major cities in the United States. Suppose It's Just Lunch wishes to open an office in Nashville, Tennessee, and needs to borrow $100,000 for prepaid rent, office equipment, and so on. Assume It's Just Lunch understated expenses in order to inflate net income as reported on the company's income statement. A banker could be tricked into lending the company money. Then if It's Just Lunch could not repay the loan, the bank would lose money—all because the banker relied on incorrect accounting information.

Accrual accounting provides several opportunities for unethical accounting. It would be easy for a dishonest businessperson to overlook an accrued expense or depreciation expense at the end of the period. Failing to make these adjustments would overstate net income and paint an overly favorable picture of the company's financial situation.

The cash basis of accounting poses fewer ethical challenges because either the company has the cash, or it does not. Therefore, the amount of cash a company reports is rarely disputed. By contrast, adjusting entries for accrued expenses, accrued revenues, and depreciation often must be estimated. Whenever there is an estimate, the accountant must deal with the temptation to make the company look different from its true condition. Fortunately, accounting has a good reputation for honesty.

The Decision Guidelines feature provides a map of the adjusting process that leads to the financial statements.

DECISION GUIDELINES

Measuring Business Income: The Adjusting Process

DECISION	GUIDELINES
Which basis of accounting better measures business income (revenues − expenses)?	*Accrual basis*, because it provides more complete reports of operating performance and financial position
How to measure revenues?	Revenue principle
How to measure expenses?	Matching principle
Where to start with the measurement of income at the end of the period?	Unadjusted trial balance, usually referred to simply as the *trial balance*
How to update the accounts for preparation of the financial statements?	*Adjusting entries* at the end of the accounting period
What are the categories of adjusting entries?	Prepaid expenses Accrued revenues Depreciation of plant assets Unearned revenues Accrued expenses

How do the adjusting entries differ from other journal entries?	1. Adjusting entries are usually made only at the end of the accounting period.
	2. Adjusting entries never affect cash.
	3. All adjusting entries debit or credit.
	  • At least one *income statement* account (a revenue or an expense), and
	  • At least one *balance sheet* account (an asset or a liability)

Where are the accounts with their adjusted balances summarized?	*Adjusted trial balance*, which becomes the basis for preparing the financial statements

EXCEL APPLICATION PROBLEM

Goal: Create an Excel spreadsheet that contains an income statement, statement of owner's equity, and balance sheet, complete with the formula relationships among all three statements.

Scenario: The three financial statements are related. The relationships show up when net income changes. Using Exhibits 3-12, 3-13, and 3-14, replicate the Income Statement, Statement of Owner's Equity, and Balance sheet for Gay Gillen eTravel. When you are finished, you will change just two related variables, but see the effect ripple through all the statements you have created.

1. Change service revenue from $7,400 to $10,900 and cash from $24,800 to $28,300. (Remember, every transaction requires at least one debit entry and one credit entry.) What is the new net income figure?
2. What is the new balance for Gay Gillen, Capital, April 30, 20X1?
3. Did any other amounts change? If so, which ones?

Step-by-step:

1. Open a new Excel spreadsheet.
2. Create a boldfaced heading for your spreadsheet that contains the following:

a. Chapter 3 Decision Guidelines
b. Gay Gillen eTravel

3. Refer to Exhibit 3-12. Prepare the Income Statement as it appears in the text near the top of your spreadsheet, formatting and using formulas as appropriate. When finished, put a border around the Income Statement.
4. Refer to Exhibit 3-13. In your spreadsheet, prepare the Statement of Owner's Equity as it appears in the text to the right of the Income Statement. Be sure "Net Income" is a cell reference to your Income Statement's Net Income. Format and use formulas as appropriate. When finished, put a border around the Statement of Owner's Equity.
5. Refer to Exhibit 3-14. Prepare the Balance Sheet as it appears in the text below the income statement in your spreadsheet. Be sure "Gay Gillen, Capital" is a cell reference to the ending capital balance in your Statement of Owner's Equity. When finished, put a border around the Balance Sheet.
6. Make the two changes in scenario question 1. Save your file to disk and print a copy for comparison against Exhibits 3-12, 3-13, and 3-14 in the textbook.

REVIEW THE ADJUSTING PROCESS

SUMMARY PROBLEM

The trial balance of State Service Company pertains to December 31, 20X3, which is the end of its year-long accounting period. Data needed for the adjusting entries include

a. Supplies on hand at year end, $2,000.
b. Depreciation on furniture and fixtures, $20,000.
c. Depreciation on building, $10,000.
d. Salaries owed but not yet paid, $5,000.
e. Accrued service revenue, $12,000.
f. Of the $45,000 balance of unearned service revenue, $32,000 was earned during the year.

www.prenhall.com/horngren

End-of-Chapter Assessment

Required

1. Open the ledger accounts with their unadjusted balances. Show dollar amounts in thousands as done for Accounts Receivable:

ACCOUNTS RECEIVABLE
370

2. Journalize State Service Company's adjusting entries at December 31, 20X3. Key entries by letter, as in Exhibit 3-9.
3. Post the adjusting entries.
4. Write the trial balance on a work sheet, enter the adjusting entries, and prepare an adjusted trial balance, as shown in Exhibit 3-10.
5. Prepare the income statement, the statement of owner's equity, and the balance sheet. Draw arrows linking these three financial statements.

STATE SERVICE COMPANY
Trial Balance
December 31, 20X3

Cash	$ 198,000	
Accounts receivable	370,000	
Supplies	6,000	
Furniture and fixtures	100,000	
Accumulated depreciation—furniture and fixtures		$ 40,000
Building	250,000	
Accumulated depreciation—building		130,000
Accounts payable		380,000
Salary payable		
Unearned service revenue		45,000
Owner's capital		293,000
Owner's withdrawals	65,000	
Service revenue		286,000
Salary expense	172,000	
Supplies expense		
Depreciation expense—furniture and fixtures		
Depreciation expense—building		
Miscellaneous expense	13,000	
Total	$1,174,000	$1,174,000

Solution

Requirements 2 and 3 (amounts in thousands)

ASSETS

CASH

Bal.	198		

ACCOUNTS RECEIVABLE

	370		
(e)	12		
Bal.	382		

SUPPLIES

	6	(a)	4
Bal.	2		

FURNITURE AND FIXTURES

Bal.	100		

ACCUMULATED DEPRECIATION—FURNITURE AND FIXTURES

			40
		(b)	20
		Bal.	60

BUILDING

Bal.	250		

ACCUMULATED DEPRECIATION—BUILDING

			130
		(c)	10
		Bal.	140

LIABILITIES

ACCOUNTS PAYABLE

		Bal.	380

SALARY PAYABLE

		(d)	5
		Bal.	5

UNEARNED SERVICE REVENUE

(f)	32		45
		Bal.	13

OWNER'S EQUITY

OWNER'S CAPITAL

		Bal.	293

OWNER'S WITHDRAWALS

Bal.	65		

REVENUE

SERVICE REVENUE

			286
		(e)	12
		(f)	32
		Bal.	330

EXPENSES

SALARY EXPENSE

	172		
(d)	5		
Bal.	177		

SUPPLIES EXPENSE

(a)	4		
Bal.	4		

DEPRECIATION EXPENSE—FURNITURE AND FIXTURES

(b)	20		
Bal.	20		

DEPRECIATION EXPENSE—BUILDING

(c)	10		
Bal.	10		

MISCELLANEOUS EXPENSE

Bal.	13		

Requirement 2

20X3

a. Dec. 31   Supplies Expense ($6,000 − $2,000)   4,000

         Supplies   4,000

     To record supplies used.

b.   31   Depreciation Expense—Furniture and Fixtures   20,000

         Accumulated Depreciation—Furniture and Fixtures   20,000

     To record depreciation expense on furniture and fixtures.

c.   31   Depreciation Expense—Building   10,000

         Accumulated Depreciation—Building   10,000

     To record depreciation expense on building.

d.   31   Salary Expense   5,000

         Salary Payable   5,000

     To accrue salary expense.

e.   31   Accounts Receivable   12,000

         Service Revenue   12,000

     To accrue service revenue.

f.   31   Unearned Service Revenue   32,000

         Service Revenue   32,000

     To record service revenue that was collected in advance.

Requirement 4

STATE SERVICE COMPANY
Preparation of Adjusted Trial Balance
December 31, 20X3
(amounts in thousands)

Account Title	Trial Balance Debit	Trial Balance Credit	Adjustments Debit	Adjustments Credit	Adjusted Trial Balance Debit	Adjusted Trial Balance Credit
Cash	198				198	
Accounts receivable	370		(e) 12		382	
Supplies	6			(a) 4	2	
Furniture and fixtures	100				100	
Accumulated depreciation— furniture and fixtures		40		(b) 20		60
Building	250				250	
Accumulated depreciation—building		130		(c) 10		140
Accounts payable		380				380
Salary payable				(d) 5		5
Unearned service revenue		45	(f) 32			13
Owner's capital		293				293
Owner's withdrawals	65				65	
Service revenue		286		(e) 12 (f) 32		330
Salary expense	172		(d) 5		177	
Supplies expense			(a) 4		4	
Depreciation expense— furniture and fixtures			(b) 20		20	
Depreciation expense—building			(c) 10		10	
Miscellaneous expense	13				13	
	1,174	1,174	83	83	1,221	1,221

STATE SERVICE COMPANY
Income Statement
Year Ended December 31, 20X3
(amounts in thousands)

Revenue:		
Service revenue		$330
Expenses:		
Salary expense..	$177	
Depreciation expense—furniture and fixtures	20	
Depreciation expense—building................................	10	
Supplies expense	4	
Miscellaneous expense	13	
Total expenses..		224
Net income		$106

STATE SERVICE COMPANY
Statement of Owner's Equity
Year Ended December 31, 20X3
(amounts in thousands)

Capital, January 1, 20X3............................	$293
Add: Net income	106
	399
Less: Withdrawals	(65)
Capital, December 31, 20X3	$334

STATE SERVICE COMPANY
Balance Sheet
December 31, 20X3
(amounts in thousands)

Assets			**Liabilities**		
Cash...................................		$198	Accounts payable		$380
Accounts receivable.........		382	Salary payable		5
Supplies		2	Unearned service revenue ..		13
Furniture and fixtures	$100		Total liabilities		398
Less: Accumulated					
depreciation..............	(60)	40			
			Owner's Equity		
Building...........................	$250				
Less: Accumulated			Owner's capital...................		334
depreciation..............	(140)	110	Total liabilities and		
Total assets......................		$732	owner's equity................		$732

LESSONS LEARNED

1. **Distinguish accrual-basis accounting from cash-basis accounting.** In *accrual-basis accounting*, business events are recorded as they occur. In *cash-basis accounting*, only those events that affect cash are recorded. Some small organizations use cash-basis accounting, but the generally accepted method is the accrual basis.

2. **Apply the revenue and matching principles.** Businesses divide time into definite periods—such as a month, a quarter, or a year—to report the entity's financial statements. The year is the basic *accounting period*, but companies prepare financial statements as often as they need the information. The *revenue principle* helps accountants determine when to record revenue and the amount of revenue to record. Revenue is recorded after it has been earned, and not before. The *matching principle* directs accountants to match expenses against revenues earned during a particular period of time.

3. **Make adjusting entries at the end of the accounting period.** Adjusting entries are a result of the accrual basis of accounting. Made at the end of the period, these entries update the accounts for preparation of the financial statements. Adjusting entries are divided into five categories: *prepaid expenses, depreciation, accrued expenses, accrued revenues,* and *unearned revenues.*

4. **Prepare an adjusted trial balance.** To prepare the *adjusted trial balance,* accountants enter the adjusting entries next to the *unadjusted trial balance* and compute each account's balance.

5. **Prepare the financial statements from the adjusted trial balance.** The adjusted trial balance can be used to prepare the financial statements. Income, shown on the *income statement,* increases the owner's capital, which also appears on the *statement of owner's equity.* The ending balance of capital is the last amount reported on the *balance sheet.*

ACCOUNTING VOCABULARY

accrual-basis accounting (p. 83)
accrued expense (p. 92)
accrued revenue (p. 94)
Accumulated Depreciation (p. 91)
adjusted trial balance (p. 97)
adjusting entry (p. 87)

book value (of a plant asset) (p. 91)
cash-basis accounting (p. 83)
contra account (p. 91)
deferred revenue (p. 94)
depreciation (p. 90)
matching principle (p. 86)

plant asset (p. 90)
prepaid expense (p. 88)
revenue principle (p. 85)
time-period concept (p. 86)
unearned revenue (p. 94)

QUESTIONS

1. Distinguish accrual-basis accounting from cash-basis accounting.
2. How long is the basic accounting period? What is a fiscal year? What is an interim period?
3. What two questions does the revenue principle help answer?
4. Briefly explain the matching principle.
5. What is the purpose of making adjusting entries?
6. Why are adjusting entries made at the end of the accounting period?
7. Name five categories of adjusting entries, and give an example of each.
8. Do all adjusting entries affect the net income or net loss of the period? Include the definition of an adjusting entry.
9. Why must the balance of Supplies be adjusted at the end of the period?
10. On January 1, ABC Company pays $1,800 for an insurance policy that covers three years. At the end of the first year, the balance of its Prepaid Insurance account contains two elements. What are the two elements, and what is the correct amount of each?
11. The title Prepaid Expense suggests that this account is an expense. If it is, explain why. If it is not, what type of account is it?
12. What is a contra account? Identify the contra account introduced in this chapter, along with the account's normal balance.
13. The balance sheet reports plant assets at book value of $135,000 and accumulated depreciation of $65,000. What does *book value* of a plant asset mean? What was the cost of the plant assets?
14. Why is an unearned revenue a liability? Give an example.
15. What purposes does the adjusted trial balance serve?
16. Explain the relationship among the income statement, the statement of owner's equity, and the balance sheet.

ASSESS YOUR PROGRESS

DAILY EXERCISES

DE3-1 Study Exhibit 3-1, and the related discussion on pages 83 and 84. Suppose **Drugstore.com** is preparing its income statement. Identify the amount of revenue Drugstore.com would report on its January income statement under (a) cash-basis accounting and (b) accrual-basis accounting. How much advertising expense would Drugstore.com report for December under the (a) cash basis and (b) accrual basis?

Accrual accounting versus cash-basis accounting for revenues (Obj. 1)

DE3-2 **It's Just Lunch,** the business featured at the beginning of this chapter, uses computer databases to help its clients meet each other. Suppose It's Just Lunch paid $2,900 for a Dell computer. Review pages 00 and 00, and then describe how It's Just Lunch would account for the $2,900 expenditure under (a) the cash basis and (b) the accrual basis. State in your own words why the accrual basis is more realistic for this situation.

DE3-3 **Intel Corporation** produces the Pentium© processor that is featured in many computers. Demand for Pentium© processors is very strong. Suppose Intel has completed production of 2,000 processor units that it expects to sell to IBM. Assume that Intel's cost to manufacture each processor is $140 and that Intel sells each processor for $375.

Apply the revenue principle to determine (1) when Intel should record revenue for this situation, and (2) the amount of revenue Intel should record for the sale of 2,000 Pentium© processors.

DE3-4 Return to the **Intel Corporation** situation described in Daily Exercise 3-3. Suppose that Intel has sold 2,000 Pentium© processors to IBM. What will Intel record in order to apply the matching principle? Give the name of the expense that Intel will record, and specify its amount.

DE3-5 **Storage USA** operates approximately 475 miniwarehouses across the United States. The company's headquarters are in Memphis, Tennessee. During 1998, Storage USA earned rental revenue of $217 million and collected cash of $223 million from customers. Total expenses for 1998 were $162 million, of which Storage USA paid $153 million.

1. Using the data supplied here, apply the revenue principle and the matching principle to compute Storage USA's net income for 1998.
2. Identify the information that you did not use to compute Storage USA's net income. Give the reason for not using the information.

DE3-6 At December 31, 1999, **US Airways** recorded Salary Expense and Salary Payable of $341 million, as shown on page 86. Suppose US Airways paid $350 million to its employees on January 3, 2000, the company's next payday after the end of the 1999 year.

1. Consider the salary expense that US Airways accrued at December 31, 1999, and the related payment on January 3, 2000. Assuming no other expenses in this category, how much Salary Expense would US Airways report on its 1999 income statement? How much Salary Expense would the company report on its year 2000 income statement?
2. Journalize US Airways' entry for payment of the payroll on January 3, 2000. Include the date and an explanation for the entry.

DE3-7 Answer the following questions.

1. Prepaid expenses are discussed beginning on page 88. Focus on the accounting for pre-paid rent. Assume that Gay Gillen's initial $3,000 prepayment of rent on April 1 (page 88) was for 12 months rather than three. Give Gay Gillen's adjusting entry to record rent expense at April 30. Include the date of the entry and an explanation. Then post to the two accounts involved, and show their balances at April 30.
2. Refer to the supplies example on pages 88–90. Assume that Gillen's travel agency has $200 of supplies on hand (rather than $400) at April 30. Give the adjusting entry, complete with date and explanation, at April 30. Post to the accounts and show their balances at April 30.

DE3-8 ◄ *Link Back to Chapters 1 and 2 (Income Statement and Balance Sheet).* **It's Just Lunch** uses computers for data searches. Suppose that on May 1 the company paid cash of $36,000 for Gateway computers that are expected to remain useful for two years. At the end of two years, the value of the computers is expected to be zero.

1. Make journal entries to record (a) purchase of the computers on May 1 and (b) depreciation on May 31. Include dates and explanations, and use the following accounts: Computer Equipment; Accumulated Depreciation—Computer Equipment; and Depreciation Expense—Computer Equipment.
2. Post to the accounts listed in requirement 1, and show their balances at May 31.
3. What is the equipment's book value at May 31?
4. Which account(s) listed in requirement 1 will It's Just Lunch report on the income statement for the month of May? Which account(s) will appear on the balance sheet at May 31? Show the amount to report for each account.

DE3-9 Suppose Gay Gillen borrowed $20,000 on October 1 by signing a note payable to Community One Bank. Gillen's interest expense for each month is $100. The loan agreement requires Gillen to pay October interest at the end of December, along with the interest that will accrue for November and December.

1. Make the same adjusting entry to record interest expense and interest payable at October 31, at November 30, and at December 31. Date each entry and include its explanation.
2. Post all three entries to the Interest Payable account. You need not take the balance of the account at the end of each month.

3. On which financial statement and under what category will Gillen report the interest payable? How much interest payable will Gillen report at October 31 and at November 30?

DE3-10 Return to the situation of Daily Exercise 3-9. Suppose you are accounting for the same transactions on the books of Community One Bank, which lent the money to Gay Gillen eTravel. Perform all three requirements of Daily Exercise 3-9 for Community One Bank using its own accounts: Interest Receivable and Interest Revenue. (For requirements 2 and 3, use the Interest Receivable account.)

Accruing and receiving cash from interest revenue
(Obj. 3)

DE3-11 Write a paragraph to explain why unearned revenues are liabilities rather than revenues. In your explanation, use the following actual example: **Southern Living Magazine** collects cash from subscribers in advance and later mails the magazines to subscribers over a one-year period. Explain what happens to the unearned subscription revenue over the course of a year as Southern Living mails the magazines to subscribers. Where (into what account) does the unearned subscription revenue go as Southern Living mails magazines to subscribers? Give the adjusting entry that Southern Living makes to record the earning of $20,000 of Subscription Revenue. Include an explanation for the entry, as illustrated in the chapter.

Explaining unearned revenues
(Obj. 3)

DE3-12 Study the T-accounts in Exhibit 3-9, Panel C, on page 97. Focus on the Prepaid Rent account. Which amount in the Prepaid Rent account appeared on the *unadjusted* trial balance (Exhibit 3-10, page 99)? Which amount in the Prepaid Rent account will appear on the *adjusted* trial balance? Which amount will be reported on the balance sheet at April 30? Why will the balance sheet report this amount? Under what balance sheet category will Prepaid Rent appear?

Contrasting the unadjusted and the adjusted trial balances
(Obj. 4)

DE3-13 In the Adjustments columns of Exhibit 3-10, page 99, two adjustments affected Service Revenue.

Using the adjusted trial balance
(Obj. 4)

1. Make journal entries for the two adjustments. Date each entry and include an explanation.
2. The journal entries you just made affected three accounts: Accounts Receivable; Unearned Service Revenue; and Service Revenue. Show how Gay Gillen eTravel will report all three accounts in its financial statements at April 30. For each account, identify its (a) financial statement, (b) category on the financial statement, and (c) balance.

DE3-14 Write a business memorandum to your supervisor explaining the difference between the unadjusted amounts and the adjusted amounts in Exhibit 3-10, page 99. Use Accounts Receivable in your explanation. If necessary, refer to the discussion of Accrued Revenues that begins on page 94.

Explaining the adjusted trial balance
(Obj. 4)

Business memos are formatted as follows:

Date:	_____
To:	_____
From:	_____
Subject:	Difference between the *unadjusted* and the *adjusted* amounts on an adjusted trial balance

DE3-15 Refer to the adjusted trial balance in Exhibit 3-10, page 99.

Preparing the balance sheet
(Obj. 5)

1. Focus first on the *unadjusted* amounts. Compute the amount of **total assets** that Gay Gillen would have reported on the balance sheet at April 30 if she had *not* made the adjusting entries at the end of the period. Also compute unadjusted **total liabilities.**
2. Now focus on the *adjusted* figures. Compute Gillen's total assets and total liabilities at April 30. Compare your totals to the balance sheet in Exhibit 3-14, page 100. Are they the same?
3. Why does a business need to make adjusting entries at the end of the period?

DE3-16 Refer to the adjusted trial balance in Exhibit 3-10 page 99.

Preparing the income statement
(Obj. 5)

1. Focus first on the *unadjusted* amounts. Compute the amount of **total revenues** that Gay Gillen eTravel would have reported on the income statement for the month of April if she had *not* made the adjusting entries at the end of the period. Also compute unadjusted **total expenses.** Finally, determine the amount of **net income** Gillen would have reported if she had not adjusted the accounts.
2. Now focus on the *adjusted* figures. Compute Gillen's total revenues, total expenses, and net income for April. Compare your totals to the income statement in Exhibit 3-12, page 100. Are they the same?
3. Why does a business need to make adjusting entries at the end of the period?

EXERCISES

Cash basis versus accrual basis
(Obj. 1)

E3-1 Homewood Suites had the following selected transactions during January:

Jan. 1   Prepaid rent for three months, $2,700.
    5   Paid electricity expenses, $400.
    9   Received cash for the day's room rentals, $1,400.
  14   Paid cash for six television sets, $3,000.
  23   Served a banquet, receiving a note receivable, $1,600.
  31   Made the adjusting entry for rent (from Jan. 1).
  31   Accrued salary expense, $900.

Show how each transaction would be handled using the accrual basis. Give the amount of revenue or expense for January. Journal entries are not required. Use the following format for your answer, and show your computations:

Amount of Revenue (Expense) for January		
Date	Revenue or (Expense)	Accrual-Basis Amount

Applying accounting concepts and principles
(Obj. 2)

E3-2 Identify the accounting concept or principle (there may be more than one) that gives the most direction on how to account for each of the following situations:

a. The owner of a business desires monthly financial statements to measure the progress of the entity on an ongoing basis.
b. Expenses of the period total $6,700. This amount should be subtracted from revenue to compute the period's income.
c. Expenses of $1,200 must be accrued at the end of the period to measure income properly.
d. A customer states her intention to switch health clubs. Should the new health club record revenue based on this intention? Give the reason for your answer.

Applying accounting concepts
(Obj. 2)

E3-3 Write a memo to your supervisor explaining in your own words the need for adjusting entries at the end of the period. Cite two accounts that need to be adjusted. Adapt the format for a business memo that is given with Daily Exercise 3-14.

Allocating prepaid expense to the asset and the expense
(Obj. 2, 3)

E3-4 Compute the amounts indicated by question marks for each of the following situations for Prepaid Insurance. For situations A and B, journalize the needed entry. Consider each situation separately.

	Situation			
	A	B	C	D
Beginning Prepaid Insurance.........	$ 450	$500	$ 900	$ 600
Payments for Prepaid Insurance during the year	1,400	?	1,100	?
Total amount to account for	?	?	2,000	1,500
Ending Prepaid Insurance..............	250	400	?	700
Insurance Expense.......................	?	$900	$1,200	$ 800

Journalizing adjusting entries
(Obj. 3)

E3-5 Journalize the entries for the following adjustments at January 31, the end of the accounting period.

a. Employee salaries owed for Monday and Tuesday of a five-day workweek; weekly payroll, $15,000.
b. Unearned service revenue earned, $800.
c. Depreciation, $3,200.
d. Prepaid insurance expired, $300.
e. Interest revenue accrued, $4,400.

Analyzing the effects of adjustments on net income
(Obj. 3)

E3-6 Suppose the adjustments required in Exercise 3-5 were not made. Compute the overall overstatement or understatement of net income as a result of the omission of these adjustments.

Journalizing adjusting entries
(Obj. 3)

E3-7 Journalize the adjusting entry needed at December 31 for each of the following independent situations.

a. On July 1, when we collected $10,000 rent in advance, we debited Cash and credited Unearned Rent Revenue. The tenant was paying for one year's rent in advance.

b. The business owes interest expense of $400, which it will pay early in the next period.

c. Interest revenue of $700 has been earned but not yet received. The business holds a $20,000 note receivable.

d. Salary expense is $1,500 per day—Monday through Friday—and the business pays employees each Friday. This year December 31 falls on a Wednesday.

e. The unadjusted balance of the Supplies account is $3,100. The cost of supplies on hand is $1,200.

f. Equipment was purchased last year at a cost of $10,000. The equipment's useful life is four years. Record the year's depreciation.

g. On September 1, when we prepaid $1,200 for a two-year insurance policy, we debited Prepaid Insurance and credited Cash.

E3-8 The accounting records of Lane Ginsburg, Architect, include the following unadjusted balances at March 31: Accounts Receivable, $1,000; Supplies, $600; Salary Payable, $0; Unearned Service Revenue, $400; Service Revenue, $4,700; Salary Expense, $1,200; Supplies Expense, $0. Ginsburg's accountant develops the following data for the March 31 adjusting entries:

Recording adjustments in T-accounts (Obj. 3)

a. Service revenue accrued, $650.

b. Unearned service revenue that has been earned, $200.

c. Supplies on hand, $100.

d. Salary owed to employee, $600.

Open T-accounts for each and record the adjustments directly in the accounts, keying each adjustment amount by letter. Show each account's adjusted balance. Journal entries are not required.

E3-9 The adjusted trial balance of Signet Repair Company is incomplete. Enter the adjustment amounts directly in the adjustment columns of the text. Service Revenue is the only account affected by more than one adjustment.

Adjusting the accounts (Obj. 3, 4)

	SIGNET REPAIR COMPANY Preparation of Adjusted Trial Balance May 31, 20X2						
	Trial Balance		Adjustments		Adjusted Trial Balance		
Account Title	Debit	Credit	Debit	Credit	Debit	Credit	
Cash	3,000				3,000		
Accounts receivable	4,500				7,400		
Supplies	1,040				800		
Office furniture	32,300				32,300		
Accumulated depreciation		14,040				14,400	
Salary payable						900	
Unearned service revenue		900				690	
Capital		26,360				26,360	
Owner's withdrawals	6,000				6,000		
Service revenue		9,630				12,740	
Salary expense	2,690				3,590		
Rent expense	1,400				1,400		
Depreciation expense					360		
Supplies expense					240		
	50,930	50,930			55,090	55,090	

E3-10 Make journal entries for the adjustments that would complete the preparation of the adjusted trial balance in Exercise 3-9. Date the entries and include explanations.

Journalizing adjustments (Obj. 3, 4)

E3-11 Refer to the adjusted trial balance in Exercise 3-9. Prepare Signet Repair Company's income statement and statement of owner's equity for the month ended May 31, 20X2, and its balance sheet on that date. Draw arrows linking the three statements.

Preparing the financial statements (Obj. 5)

E3-12 The accountant for Kay Fuston, Publisher, has posted adjusting entries (a)–(e) to the accounts at December 31, 20X2. Selected balance sheet accounts and all the revenues and expenses of the entity follow in T-account form.

Preparing the financial statements (Obj. 5)

ACCOUNTS RECEIVABLE			SUPPLIES			ACCUMULATED DEPRECIATION— EQUIPMENT			ACCUMULATED DEPRECIATION—BUILDING	
23,000		4,000	(a)	1,000				5,000			33,000
(e)	7,000						(b)	2,000	(c)	5,000

SALARY PAYABLE			SERVICE REVENUE	
	(d)	1,500		105,000
			(e)	7,000

SALARY EXPENSE			SUPPLIES EXPENSE			DEPRECIATION EXPENSE— EQUIPMENT		DEPRECIATION EXPENSE— BUILDING	
28,000		(a)	1,000		(b)	2,000	(c)	5,000	
(d)	1,500								

Required

1. Prepare the income statement of Kay Fuston, Publisher, for the year ended December 31, 20X2. List expenses in order from the largest to the smallest.
2. Were 20X2 operations successful? Give the reason for your answer.

Preparing the statement of owner's equity
(Obj. 5)

E3-13 Quikwash Laundromat began the year with capital of $155,000. On July 12, Kent Carmichael (the owner) invested $12,000 cash in the business. On September 26, he transferred to the company land valued at $70,000. The income statement for the year ended December 31, 20X5, reported a net loss of $28,000. During this fiscal year, Carmichael withdrew $1,500 monthly for personal use.

Required

1. Prepare the laundromat's statement of owner's equity for the year ended December 31, 20X5.
2. Did the owner's equity of the business increase or decrease during the year? What caused this change?

Continuing Exercise. *Exercise 3-14 continues the Amos Faraday, Consultant, situation begun in Exercise 2-15 of Chapter 2.*

Adjusting the accounts, preparing an adjusted trial balance, and preparing the financial statements
(Obj. 3, 4, 5)

E3-14 Refer to Exercise 2-15 of Chapter 2. Start from the trial balance and the posted T-accounts that Amos Faraday, Consultant, prepared for his business at December 18, as follows:

AMOS FARADAY, CONSULTANT
Trial Balance
December 18, 20XX

Account	Debit	Credit
Cash	$12,100	
Accounts receivable	1,700	
Supplies	300	
Equipment	2,000	
Furniture	3,600	
Accounts payable		$ 3,900
Amos Faraday, capital		14,000
Amos Faraday, withdrawals	—	
Service revenue		2,500
Rent expense	500	
Utilities expense	200	
Salary expense		
Total	$20,400	$20,400

Later in December, the business completed these transactions, as follows:

Dec. 21 Received $900 in advance for client service to be performed evenly over the next 30 days.

21 Hired a secretary to be paid $1,500 on the 20th day of each month. The secretary begins work immediately.

26 Paid $300 on account.

28 Collected $600 on account.

30 Withdrew $1,600 for personal use.

Required

1. Open these additional T-accounts: Accumulated Depreciation—Equipment; Accumulated Depreciation—Furniture; Salary Payable; Unearned Service Revenue; Depreciation Expense—Equipment; Depreciation Expense—Furniture; Supplies Expense.
2. Journalize the transactions of December 21–30.
3. Post to the T-accounts, keying all items by date.
4. Prepare a trial balance at December 31. Also set up columns for the adjustments and for the adjusted trial balance, as illustrated in Exhibit 3-10.
5. At December 31, Faraday gathers the following information for the adjusting entries:
   a. Accrued service revenue, $400.
   b. Earned a portion of the service revenue collected in advance on December 21.
   c. Supplies on hand, $100.
   d. Depreciation expense—equipment, $50; furniture, $60.
   e. Accrued expense for secretary's salary—10 days worked.

   Make these adjustments directly in the adjustments columns, and complete the adjusted trial balance at December 31. Throughout the book, to avoid rounding errors, we base adjusting entries on 30-day months and 360-day years.

6. Journalize and post the adjusting entries. Denote each adjusting amount as *Adj.* and an account balance as *Bal.*
7. Prepare the income statement and the statement of owner's equity of Amos Faraday, Consultant, for the month ended December 31, and prepare the balance sheet at that date.

Challenge Exercises

E3-15 Morris Chang Enterprises aids Chinese students upon their arrival in the United States. Paid by the Chinese government, Morris Chang collects some service revenue in advance. In other cases, he receives cash after performing relocation services. At the end of August—a particularly busy period—Morris Chang's books show the following:

Computing the amount of revenue (Obj. 3)

	July 31	August 31
Accounts receivable......................	$1,900	$2,500
Unearned service revenue..............	1,200	300

During August, Morris Chang Enterprises received cash of $7,000 from the Chinese government. How much service revenue did the business earn during August? Show your work.

E3-16 For the situation of Exercise 3-15, assume the service revenue of Morris Chang Enterprises was $5,900 during August. How much cash did the business collect from the Chinese government that month? Show your work.

Computing cash amounts (Obj. 3)

PROBLEMS

(Group A)

P3-1A Normandy Psychiatric Group had the following selected transactions during January:

Cash basis versus accrual basis (Obj. 1, 2)

Jan. 1 Prepaid insurance for January through March, $600.
4 Performed medical service on account, $1,000.
5 Purchased office furniture on account, $150.
8 Paid advertising expense, $450.
11 Purchased office equipment for cash, $800.
19 Performed medical service and received cash, $700.
24 Collected $400 on account for January 4 service.
26 Paid account payable from January 5.
29 Paid salary expense, $900.
31 Recorded adjusting entry for January insurance expense (see Jan. 1).
31 Debited unearned revenue and credited revenue to adjust the accounts, $600.

Required

1. Show how each transaction would be handled using the accrual basis of accounting. Give the amount of revenue or expense for January. Journal entries are not required. Use the following format for your answer, and show your computations:

Amount of Revenue (Expense) for January		
Date	**Revenue (Expense)**	**Accrual-Basis Amount**

2. Compute January net income or net loss under the accrual basis of accounting.
3. State why the accrual basis of accounting is preferable to the cash basis.

Applying accounting principles
(Obj. 1, 2)

P3-2A As the controller of Lake Cypress Lumber Company, you have hired a new bookkeeper, whom you must train. He objects to making an adjusting entry for accrued salaries at the end of the period. He reasons, "We will pay the salaries soon. Why not wait until payment to record the expense? In the end, the result will be the same." Write a business memo to explain to the bookkeeper why the adjusting entry for accrued salary expense is needed. The format of a business memo follows.

Date:	_____
To:	New Bookkeeper
From:	(Student Name)
Subject:	Why the adjusting entry for salary expense is needed

Journalizing adjusting entries
(Obj. 3)

P3-3A Journalize the adjusting entry needed on December 31, end of the current accounting period, for each of the following independent cases affecting Arvin Marketing Associates.

a. Each Friday, Arvin pays its employees for the current week's work. The amount of the payroll is $6,000 for a five-day workweek. The current accounting period ends on Thursday.
b. Arvin has received notes receivable from some clients for professional services. During the current year, Arvin has earned accrued interest revenue of $170, which will be collected next year.
c. The beginning balance of Supplies was $3,800. During the year, the entity purchased supplies costing $5,530, and at December 31, the inventory of supplies on hand is $2,970.
d. Arvin designed a marketing campaign, and the client paid Arvin $36,000 at the start of the project. Arvin recorded this amount as Unearned Service Revenue. The campaign will run for several months. Arvin estimates that the company has earned three-fourths of the total fee during the current year.
e. Depreciation for the current year includes: Office Furniture, $5,500; Building, $3,790. Make a compound entry, as illustrated in Chapter 2.
f. Details of Prepaid Insurance are shown in the account:

PREPAID INSURANCE			
Jan. 1	Bal.	900	
April 30		2,700	

Arvin pays insurance each year on April 30. At December 31, part of the last payment is still in force.

Analyzing and journalizing adjustments
(Obj. 3)

P3-4A Platt Investment Brokers' unadjusted and adjusted trial balances at December 31, 20X7, follow at the top of page 115.

Required

Journalize the adjusting entries that account for the differences between the two trial balances.

Journalizing and posting adjustments to T-accounts; preparing the adjusted trial balance
(Obj. 3, 4)

P3-5A The trial balance of Liberty Duplicating Services at August 31, 20X6, year and the data needed for the month-end adjustments follow at the bottom of page 115.

Adjustment data:

a. Unearned service revenue still unearned at August 31, $1,670.
b. Prepaid rent still in force at August 31, $620.
c. Supplies used during the month, $700.
d. Depreciation for the month, $400.
e. Accrued advertising expense at August 31, $610. (Credit Accounts Payable.)
f. Accrued salary expense at August 31, $550.

Required

1. Open T-accounts for the accounts listed in the trial balance, inserting their August 31 unadjusted balances.
2. Journalize the adjusting entries and post them to the T-accounts. Key the journal entries and the posted amounts by letter.
3. Prepare the adjusted trial balance.
4. How will the company use the adjusted trial balance?

PLATT INVESTMENT BROKERS
Adjusted Trial Balance
December 31, 20X7

Account Title	Trial Balance		Adjusted Trial Balance	
	Debit	Credit	Debit	Credit
Cash.................................	4,120		4,120	
Accounts receivable...........	5,260		14,090	
Supplies	1,200		280	
Prepaid insurance	2,600		2,330	
Office furniture..................	21,630		21,630	
Accumulated depreciation		8,220		10,500
Accounts payable..............		6,420		6,420
Salary payable				960
Interest payable				480
Note payable.....................		12,000		12,000
Unearned commission revenue		1,840		1,160
Claire Platt, capital............		13,510		13,510
Claire Platt, withdrawals ...	29,370		29,370	
Commission revenue.........		66,890		76,400
Depreciation expense			2,280	
Supplies expense			920	
Utilities expense	4,960		4,960	
Salary expense...................	26,660		27,620	
Rent expense	12,200		12,200	
Interest expense.................	880		1,360	
Insurance expense			270	
	108,880	108,880	121,430	121,430

LIBERTY DUPLICATING SERVICES
Trial Balance
August 31, 20X6

	Debit	Credit
Cash...	$ 7,100	
Accounts receivable.........................	19,780	
Prepaid rent	2,420	
Supplies	1,180	
Furniture	19,740	
Accumulated depreciation..............		$ 3,630
Accounts payable............................		3,310
Salary payable.................................		
Unearned service revenue		2,790
Milton Hupp, capital.......................		35,510
Milton Hupp, withdrawals..............	5,350	
Service revenue		15,700
Salary expense.................................	3,800	
Rent expense		
Depreciation expense		
Advertising expense	1,570	
Supplies expense		
Total	$60,940	$60,940

P3-6A The adjusted trial balance of Mastercraft Marble Cutters at December 31, 20X8, follows.

MASTERCRAFT MARBLE CUTTERS Adjusted Trial Balance December 31, 20X8		
Cash	$ 2,340	
Accounts receivable	50,490	
Prepaid rent	1,350	
Supplies	970	
Equipment	75,690	
Accumulated depreciation—equipment		$ 22,240
Office furniture	24,100	
Accumulated depreciation—office furniture		3,670
Accounts payable		13,600
Unearned service revenue		4,520
Interest payable		2,130
Salary payable		930
Note payable		45,000
B. Masters, capital		32,380
B. Masters, withdrawals	48,000	
Service revenue		204,790
Depreciation expense—equipment	11,300	
Depreciation expense—office furniture	2,410	
Salary expense	87,800	
Rent expense	12,000	
Interest expense	4,200	
Utilities expense	3,770	
Insurance expense	3,150	
Supplies expense	1,690	
Total	$329,260	$329,260

Required

1. Prepare Mastercraft's 20X8 income statement and statement of owner's equity and year-end balance sheet. List expenses in decreasing order on the income statement and show total liabilities on the balance sheet. Draw arrows linking the three financial statements.
2. a. Which financial statement reports Mastercraft's results of operations? Were 20X8 operations successful? Cite specifics from the financial statements to support your evaluation.
   b. Which statement reports the company's financial position? Does Mastercraft's financial position look strong or weak? Give the reason for your evaluation.

P3-7A Consider the unadjusted trial balance of ReliaMark Insurers at October 31, 20X2, and the related month-end adjustment data.

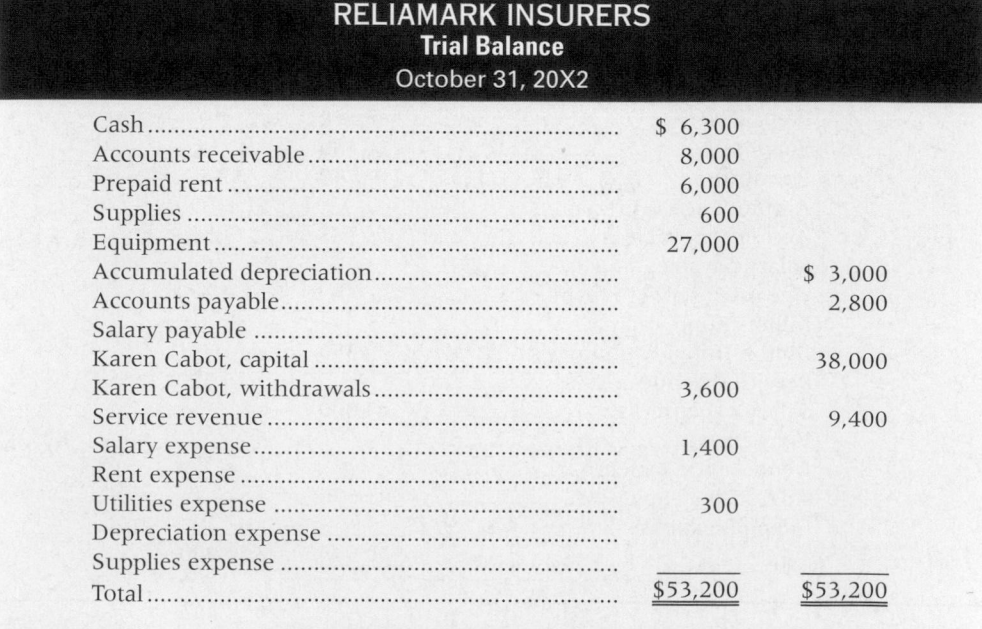

RELIAMARK INSURERS Trial Balance October 31, 20X2		
Cash	$ 6,300	
Accounts receivable	8,000	
Prepaid rent	6,000	
Supplies	600	
Equipment	27,000	
Accumulated depreciation		$ 3,000
Accounts payable		2,800
Salary payable		
Karen Cabot, capital		38,000
Karen Cabot, withdrawals	3,600	
Service revenue		9,400
Salary expense	1,400	
Rent expense		
Utilities expense	300	
Depreciation expense		
Supplies expense		
Total	$53,200	$53,200

Adjustment data:

a. Accrued service revenue at October 31, $2,000.
b. Prepaid rent expired during the month. The unadjusted prepaid balance of $6,000 relates to the period October 20X2 through January 20X3.
c. Supplies on hand October 31, $200.
d. Depreciation on equipment for the month. The equipment's expected useful life is five years.
e. Accrued salary expense at October 31 for one day only. The five-day weekly payroll is $2,000.

Required

1. Write the trial balance on a work sheet, using Exhibit 3-10 as an example, and prepare the adjusted trial balance of ReliaMark Insurers at October 31, 20X2. Key each adjusting entry by letter.
2. Prepare the income statement and the statement of owner's equity for the month ended October 31, 20X2, and the balance sheet at that date. Draw arrows linking the three financial statements.

PROBLEMS

(Group B)

P3-1B Valleydale Bone and Joint Clinic completed the following selected transactions during May:

Cash basis versus accrual basis (Obj. 1, 2)

May	2	Prepaid insurance for May through July, $800.
	4	Paid gas bill, $550.
	5	Performed services on account, $1,000.
	9	Purchased office equipment for cash, $1,400.
	12	Received cash for services performed, $900.
	14	Purchased office equipment on account, $300.
	28	Collected $500 on account from May 5.
	29	Paid salary expense, $1,100.
	30	Paid account payable from May 14.
	31	Recorded adjusting entry for May insurance expense (see May 2).
	31	Debited unearned revenue and credited revenue in an adjusting entry, $700.

Required

1. Show how each transaction would be handled using the accrual basis of accounting. Give the amount of revenue or expense for May. Journal entries are not required. Use the following format for your answer, and show your computations:

Amount of Revenue (Expense) for May

Date	Revenue (Expense)	Accrual-Basis Amount

---

2. Compute May net income or net loss under the accrual basis of accounting.
3. Why is the accrual basis of accounting preferable to the cash basis?

P3-2B Write a business memo to a new bookkeeper to explain the difference between the cash basis of accounting and the accrual basis. Mention the roles of the revenue principle and the matching principle in accrual-basis accounting. The format of a business memo follows.

Applying accounting principles (Obj. 1, 2)

Date:	_____
To:	New Bookkeeper
From:	(Student Name)
Subject:	Difference between the cash basis and the accrual basis

P3-3B Journalize the adjusting entry needed on December 31, end of the current accounting period, for each of the following independent cases affecting Coronado Heating and Cooling.

Journalizing adjusting entries (Obj. 3)

a. Details of Prepaid Rent are shown in the account:

PREPAID RENT

Jan.	1	Bal.	600
Mar. 31			2,400

Coronado pays office rent annually on March 31. At December 31, part of the last payment is still an asset.

b. Coronado pays its employees each Friday. The amount of the weekly payroll is $2,000 for a five-day workweek, and the daily salary amounts are equal. The current accounting period ends on Monday.

c. Coronado has loaned out money, receiving notes receivable. During the current year, the entity has earned accrued interest revenue of $737, which it will collect next year.

d. The beginning balance of Supplies was $2,680. During the year, the entity purchased supplies costing $6,180, and at December 31, the cost of supplies on hand is $2,150.

e. Coronado is servicing the air-conditioning system in a large building, and the owner of the building paid Coronado $12,900 as the annual service fee. Coronado recorded this amount as Unearned Service Revenue. Enrique Coronado, the owner, estimates that the company has earned one-fourth the total fee during the current year.

f. Depreciation for the current year includes Equipment, $3,850; Trucks, $10,320. Make a compound entry, as illustrated in Chapter 2.

Analyzing and journalizing adjustments
(Obj. 3)

P3-4B Olen Chemical Servicing's unadjusted and adjusted trial balances at April 30, 20X1, follow.

Account Title	Trial Balance Debit	Trial Balance Credit	Adjusted Trial Balance Debit	Adjusted Trial Balance Credit
Cash	6,180		6,180	
Accounts receivable	5,990		6,700	
Interest receivable			300	
Note receivable	4,100		4,100	
Supplies	980		290	
Prepaid rent	2,480		720	
Building	66,450		66,450	
Accumulated depreciation		16,010		17,290
Accounts payable		6,920		6,920
Wages payable				320
Unearned service revenue		670		110
Paul Olen, capital		58,790		58,790
Paul Olen, withdrawals	3,600		3,600	
Service revenue		9,570		10,840
Interest revenue				300
Wage expense	1,600		1,920	
Rent expense			1,760	
Depreciation expense			1,280	
Insurance expense	370		370	
Supplies expense			690	
Utilities expense	210		210	
	91,960	91,960	94,570	94,570

OLEN CHEMICAL SERVICING
Adjusted Trial Balance
April 30, 20X1

Required

Journalize the adjusting entries that account for the differences between the two trial balances.

Journalizing and posting adjustments to T-accounts; preparing the adjusted trial balance
(Obj. 3, 4)

P3-5B The trial balance of Great Lakes Investments at December 31, 20X2, and the data needed for the month-end adjustments follow at the top of the next page.

Adjustment data:

a. Prepaid rent still in force at December 31, $600.
b. Supplies used during the month, $640.
c. Depreciation for the month, $900.
d. Accrued advertising expense at December 31, $320. (Credit Accounts Payable.)
e. Accrued salary expense at December 31, $180.
f. Unearned commission revenue still unearned at December 31, $1,150.

GREAT LAKES INVESTMENTS
Trial Balance
December 31, 20X2

Cash	$ 2,200	
Accounts receivable	14,100	
Prepaid rent	3,100	
Supplies	780	
Furniture	22,710	
Accumulated depreciation		$11,640
Account payable		1,940
Salary payable		
Unearned commission revenue		2,290
Gina Pulver, capital		25,060
Gina Pulver, withdrawals	2,900	
Commission revenue		7,750
Salary expense	2,160	
Rent expense		
Depreciation expense		
Advertising expense	730	
Supplies expense		
Total	$48,680	$48,680

Required

1. Open T-accounts for the accounts listed in the trial balance, inserting their December 31 unadjusted balances.
2. Journalize the adjusting entries and post them to the T-accounts. Key the journal entries and the posted amounts by letter.
3. Prepare the adjusted trial balance.
4. How will the company use the adjusted trial balance?

P3-6B The adjusted trial balance of Marineland Travel Designers at December 31, 20X6, follows.

Preparing the financial statements from an adjusted trial balance (Obj. 5)

MARINELAND TRAVEL DESIGNERS
Adjusted Trial Balance
December 31, 20X6

Cash	$ 1,320	
Accounts receivable	4,920	
Supplies	2,300	
Prepaid rent	1,600	
Office equipment	20,180	
Accumulated depreciation—office equipment		$ 4,350
Office furniture	37,710	
Accumulated depreciation—office furniture		4,870
Accounts payable		4,740
Interest payable		830
Unearned service revenue		620
Note payable		13,500
Ken Sorley, capital		26,090
Ken Sorley, withdrawals	29,000	
Service revenue		120,910
Depreciation expense—office equipment	6,680	
Depreciation expense—office furniture	2,370	
Salary expense	39,900	
Rent expense	17,400	
Interest expense	3,100	
Utilities expense	2,670	
Insurance expense	3,810	
Supplies expense	2,950	
Total	$175,910	$175,910

Required

1. Prepare Marineland's 20X6 income statement and statement of owner's equity and year-end balance sheet. List expenses in decreasing order on the income statement and show total liabilities on the balance sheet. Draw arrows linking the three financial statements.
2. **a.** Which financial statement reports Marineland's results of operations? Were operations successful during 20X6? Cite specifics from the financial statements to support your evaluation.
   b. Which statement reports the company's financial position? Does Marineland's financial position look strong or weak? Give the reason for your evaluation.

P3-7B The unadjusted trial balance of Christine Salomon, at July 31, 20X2, and the related month-end adjustment data follow.

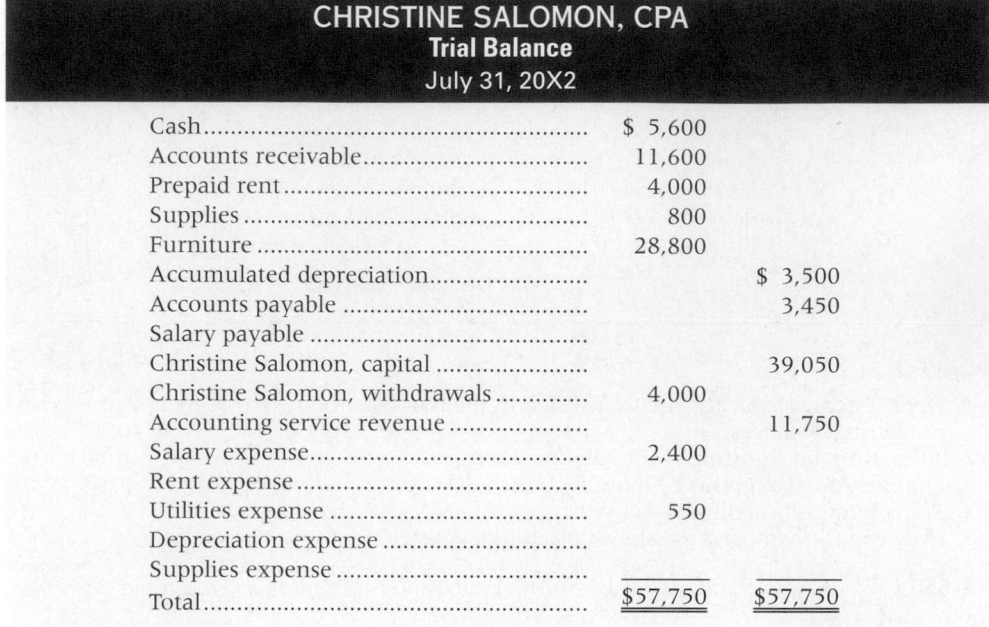

CHRISTINE SALOMON, CPA **Trial Balance** July 31, 20X2		
Cash..	$ 5,600	
Accounts receivable................................	11,600	
Prepaid rent...	4,000	
Supplies...	800	
Furniture...	28,800	
Accumulated depreciation.......................		$ 3,500
Accounts payable		3,450
Salary payable		
Christine Salomon, capital		39,050
Christine Salomon, withdrawals..............	4,000	
Accounting service revenue.....................		11,750
Salary expense.......................................	2,400	
Rent expense..		
Utilities expense	550	
Depreciation expense		
Supplies expense		
Total..	$57,750	$57,750

Adjustment data:

a. Accrued accounting service revenue at July 31, $900.
b. Prepaid rent expired during the month. The unadjusted prepaid balance of $4,000 relates to the period July through October.
c. Supplies on hand at July 31, $400.
d. Depreciation on furniture for the month. The estimated useful life of the furniture is four years.
e. Accrued salary expense at July 31 for one day only. The five-day weekly payroll is $1,000.

Required

1. Using Exhibit 3-10 as an example, write the trial balance on a work sheet and prepare the adjusted trial balance of Christine Salomon, CPA, at July 31, 20X2. Key each adjusting entry by letter.
2. Prepare the income statement and the statement of owner's equity for the month ended July 31, 20X2, and the balance sheet at that date. Draw arrows linking the three financial statements.

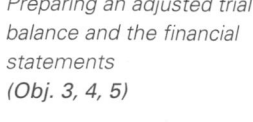

Apply Your Knowledge

Decision Cases

Case 1. Benjamin O'Henry has owned and operated O'Henry's Data Services since its beginning ten years ago. From all appearances, the business has prospered. In the past few years, you have become friends with O'Henry and his wife through your church. Recently, O'Henry mentioned that he has lost his zest for the business and would consider selling it for the right price. You are interested in buying this business and obtain its most recent monthly unadjusted trial balance, which follows.

O'HENRY'S DATA SERVICES
Unadjusted Trial Balance
November 30, 20XX

Cash	$ 9,700	
Accounts receivable	7,900	
Prepaid expenses	2,600	
Furniture, fixtures, and equipment	151,300	
Accumulated depreciation		$ 15,600
Accounts payable		3,800
Salary payable		
Unearned service revenue		6,700
Benjamin O'Henry, capital		137,400
Benjamin O'Henry, withdrawals	2,000	
Service revenue		14,300
Rent expense		
Salary expense	3,400	
Utilities expense	900	
Depreciation expense		
Supplies expense		
Total	$177,800	$177,800

Revenues and expenses vary little from month to month, and November is a typical month. Your investigation reveals that the unadjusted trial balance does not include the effects of monthly revenues of $2,100 and monthly expenses totaling $2,750. If you were to buy O'Henry's Data Services, you would hire a manager who would require a monthly salary of $3,000.

Required

1. The most you would pay for the business is 20 times the monthly net income *you could expect to earn* from it. Compute this possible price.
2. The least O'Henry will take for the business is his ending capital. Compute this amount.
3. Under these conditions, how much should you offer O'Henry? Give your reason.

Case 2. Suppose a new management team is in charge of Sunpool, Inc., an appliance manufacturer. Assume Sunpool's new top managers rose through the ranks in the sales and marketing departments and have little appreciation for the details of accounting. Consider the following conversation between these two managers:

Explaining why adjusting entries are needed
(Obj. 3)

Morgan Gummelt, President:	"I want to avoid the hassle of adjusting the books every time we need financial statements. Sooner or later we receive cash for all our revenues, and we pay cash for all our expenses. I can understand cash transactions, but all these accruals confuse me. If I cannot understand *our own accounting,* I'm fairly certain the average person who invests in our company cannot understand it either. Let's start recording only our cash transactions. I bet it won't make any difference to anyone."
Sarah Mead, Chief Financial Officer:	"Sounds good to me. This will save me lots of headaches. I'll implement the new policy immediately."

Write a business memo to the company president giving your response to the new policy. Identify at least five individual items (such as specific accounts) in the financial statements that will be reported incorrectly. Will outside investors care? Adapt the format of a business memo given with Daily Exercise 3-14.

ETHICAL ISSUE

The net income of Simon & Hobbs, a department store, decreased sharply during 2000. Carol Simon, owner of the store, anticipates the need for a bank loan in 2001. Late in 2000, Simon instructs the store's accountant to record a $10,000 sale of furniture to the Simon family, even though the goods will not be shipped from the manufacturer until January 2001. Simon also tells the accountant *not* to make the following December 31, 2000, adjusting entries:

Salaries owed to employees...........................	$900
Prepaid insurance that has expired..............	400

Required

1. Compute the overall effects of these transactions on the store's reported income for 2000.
2. Why is Simon taking this action? Is her action ethical? Give your reason, identifying the parties helped and the parties harmed by Simon's action.
3. As a personal friend, what advice would you give the accountant?

FINANCIAL STATEMENT CASE

Journalizing and posting transactions and tracing account balances to the financial statements (Obj. 3, 5)

Target Corporation—like all other businesses—makes adjusting entries prior to year end in order to measure assets, liabilities, revenues, and expenses properly. Examine Target's balance sheet, and pay particular attention to Other Current Assets (which includes Prepaid Expenses) and Accrued Liabilities (which includes Salary Payable and Interest Payable).

1. Open T-accounts for Other Current Assets (Prepaid Expenses), Accrued Liabilities, and Accumulated Depreciation. Insert Target's balances (in millions) at January 30, 1999. (Example: Other Current Assets (Prepaid Expenses), $619)
2. Journalize the following transactions for the current year, ended January 29, 2000. Key entries by letter. Explanations are not required.
   Cash transactions (amounts in millions):
   a. Paid prepaid expenses, $2,113.
   b. Paid the January 30, 1999, accrued liabilities.
   Adjustments at January 29, 2000 (amounts in millions):
   c. Prepaid expenses expired, $2,104. (Debit Administrative Expense)
   d. Accrued liabilities, $1,520. (Debit Selling Expense.)
   e. Depreciation expense, $157.
3. Post to the Other Current Assets (Prepaid Expenses) account the Accrued Liabilities account and the Accumulated Depreciation account. Then these accounts should agree with the corresponding amounts reported in the January 29, 2000, balance sheet. Check to make sure they do agree with Target's actual balances.

TEAM PROJECT

Return to the chapter-opening story, which describes Andrea McGinty's business, **It's Just Lunch.** Suppose your group is opening an It's Just Lunch office in your area. You must make some important decisions—where to locate, how to advertise, and so on—and you must also make some accounting decisions. For example, what will be the end of your business's accounting year? How often will you need financial statements to evaluate operating performance and financial position? Will you use the cash basis or the accrual basis? When will you account for the revenue that the business earns? How will you account for the expenses?

Required

Write a report (or prepare an oral presentation, as directed by your professor) to address the following considerations:

1. Will you use the cash basis or the accrual basis of accounting? Give a complete explanation of your reasoning.
2. How often do you want financial statements? Why? Discuss how you will use each financial statement.
3. What kind of revenue will you earn? When will you record it as revenue? How will you decide when to record the revenue?
4. Prepare a made-up income statement for It's Just Lunch for the Year ended December 31, 1998. List all the business's expenses, starting with the most important (largest dollar amount) and working through the least important (smallest dollar amount). Try to come as close as you can to the actual figures, as follows: Net revenues, $20,175,920; Net income, $2,018,516.
5. Using made-up dollar amounts, prepare all the adjusting entries your business will need at the end of the year. Identify the date of your adjustments.

1. **It's Just Lunch** customers may meet their dates at one of the many **Darden** restaurants. Go to **http://www.darden.com** and list at least three of the Darden restaurant chains.
2. In the left-hand column click on *The Numbers* followed by *Annual Report and Financials.* Select the HTML version of the *most recent annual report.* Click on *next* to reach the table of contents. Use the Consolidated Balance Sheets to answer the following questions.
   a. Does the Darden Restaurants company use cash-basis or accrual-basis accounting? How can you tell?
   b. For the two most recent years list the amounts reported for "Cash and cash equivalents" and for "Land, Buildings and Equipment." For each of these accounts, identify whether it requires an adjustment at the end of the accounting period.
3. Use the Consolidated Statements of Earnings to answer the following questions.
   a. For the three most recent fiscal years list the amounts reported for "Sales." Comment on whether the three-year trend of sales is favorable or unfavorable. Sales is what type of an account? Which principle of accounting is relevant for recording these amounts?
   b. For the three most recent fiscal years list the amounts reported for "Total Cost of Sales." Total Cost of Sales is what type of account? Were all of these amounts paid in cash? Which principle of accounting is relevant for recording these amounts?
   c. For the three most recent fiscal years list the amounts reported for "Net Earnings (Loss)." Is the three-year trend of net income favorable or unfavorable? What title does the text use to refer to net earnings?

**Darden
Corporation**

Go to the "Deferrals (Unearned Revenues and Prepaid Expenses)" episode on the *Mastering Accounting* CD-ROM for an interactive, video-enhanced exercise explaining the principles of income statements and timing of recorded transactions to CanGo managers to help them interpret financial reports.

APPENDIX TO CHAPTER 3

ALTERNATIVE TREATMENT OF PREPAID EXPENSES AND UNEARNED REVENUES

Chapters 1–3 illustrate the most popular way to account for prepaid expenses and unearned revenues. This appendix illustrates an alternative—and equally appropriate—approach.

Prepaid Expenses

Prepaid expenses are advance payments of expenses. Prepaid Insurance, Prepaid Rent, Prepaid Advertising, and Prepaid Legal Cost are prepaid expenses. Supplies that will be used up in the current period or within one year are also accounted for as prepaid expenses.

When a business prepays an expense—rent, for example—it can debit an *asset* account (Prepaid Rent), as illustrated on page 88:

Aug. 1	Prepaid Rent	XXX	
	Cash		XXX

Alternatively, it can debit an *expense* account to record this cash payment:

Aug. 1	Rent Expense	XXX	
	Cash		XXX

Regardless of the account debited at the time of the prepayment, the business must adjust the accounts at the end of the period to report the correct amounts of the expense and the asset.

Prepaid Expense Recorded Initially as an Expense

Prepaying an expense creates an asset, as explained on page 88. However, the asset may be so short-lived that it will expire in the current accounting period—within one year or less. Thus, the accountant may decide to debit the prepayment to an expense account at the time of payment. A $6,000 cash payment for rent (one year, in advance) on August 1 may be debited to Rent Expense:

20X6			
Aug. 1	Rent Expense	6,000	
	Cash		6,000

At December 31, only five months' prepayment has expired (for August through December), leaving seven months' rent still prepaid. In this case, the accountant must transfer 7/12 of the original prepayment of $6,000, or $3,500, to the asset account Prepaid Rent. At December 31, 20X6, the business still has the benefit of the prepayment for January through July of 20X7. The adjusting entry at December 31 is

Adjusting Entries		
20X6		
Dec. 31 Prepaid Rent ($6,000 × 7/12)................	3,500	
Rent Expense................................		3,500

After posting, the two accounts appear as follows (where CP = cash payment entry; Adj = adjusting entry):

PREPAID RENT			
20X6			
Dec. 31 Adj.	3,500		
Dec. 31 Bal.	3,500		

RENT EXPENSE			
20X6		20X6	
Aug. 1 CP	6,000	Dec. 31 Adj.	3,500
Dec. 31 Bal.	2,500		

The balance sheet at the end of 20X6 reports Prepaid Rent of $3,500, and the income statement for 20X6 reports Rent Expense of $2,500, regardless of whether the business initially debits the prepayment to an asset account or to an expense account.

Unearned (Deferred) Revenues

Unearned (deferred) revenues arise when a business collects cash before earning the revenue. Unearned revenues are liabilities because the business that receives cash owes the other party goods or services to be delivered later.

Unearned (Deferred) Revenue Recorded Initially as a Revenue

Receipt of cash in advance creates a liability, as recorded on page 000. Another way to account for the receipt of cash is to credit a *revenue account*. If the business has earned all the revenue within the same period, no adjusting entry is needed at the end of the period. However, if the business earns only part of the revenue at the end of the period, it must make an adjusting entry.

Suppose on October 1, 20X2, a law firm records as revenue the receipt of cash for a nine-month fee of $7,200 received in advance. The cash receipt entry is

20X2			
Oct. 1	Cash..	7,200	
	Legal Revenue		7,200

At December 31, the attorney has earned only 3/9 of the $7,200, or $2,400, for the months of October, November, and December. Accordingly, the firm makes an adjusting entry to transfer the unearned portion (6/9 of $7,200, or $4,800) from the revenue account to a liability account, as follows:

Adjusting Entries		
20X2		
Dec. 31 Legal Revenue ($7,200 × 6/9)...............	4,800	
Unearned Legal Revenue..............		4,800

The adjusting entry transfers the unearned portion (6/9, or $4,800) of the original amount to the liability account because the law firm still owes legal service to the client during January through June of 20X3. After posting, the total amount ($7,200) is properly divided between the liability account ($4,800) and the revenue account ($2,400), as follows (where CR = Cash receipt entry and Adj. = Adjusting entry).

UNEARNED LEGAL REVENUE			LEGAL REVENUE				
	20X2		**20X2**			**20X2**	
	Dec. 31 Adj. 4,800		Dec. 31 Adj	4,800		Oct. 1 CR	7,200
	Dec. 31 Bal. 4,800					Dec. 31 Bal.	2,400

The attorney's 20X2 income statement reports legal revenue of $2,400, and the balance sheet at December 31, 20X2, reports the unearned legal revenue of $4,800 as a liability, regardless of whether the business initially credits a liability account or a revenue account.

ASSESS YOUR PROGRESS

APPENDIX EXERCISES

E3A-1 At the beginning of the year, supplies of $1,190 were on hand. During the year, Laser Printing Company paid $5,400 cash for supplies. At the end of the year, the count of supplies indicates the ending balance is $860.

Recording supplies transactions two ways
(Obj. A1)

Required

1. Assume that Laser Printing records supplies by initially debiting an *asset* account. Therefore, place the beginning balance in the Supplies T-account, and record the preceding entries directly in the accounts without using a journal.
2. Assume that Laser Printing records supplies by initially debiting an *expense* account. Therefore, place the beginning balance in the Supplies Expense T-account, and record the preceding entries directly in the accounts without using a journal.
3. Compare the ending account balances under both approaches. Are they the same?

E3A-2 At the beginning of the year, Laser Printing Company owed customers $2,750 for unearned service collected in advance. During the year, Laser Printing received advance cash receipts of $7,000. At year end, the liability for unearned revenue is $3,700.

Recording unearned revenues two ways
(Obj. A2)

Required

1. Assume that Laser Printing records unearned revenues by initially crediting a *liability* account. Open T-accounts for Unearned Service Revenue and Service Revenue, and place the beginning balance in Unearned Service Revenue. Journalize the cash collection and adjusting entries, and post their dollar amounts. As references in the T-accounts, denote a balance by *Bal.*, a cash receipt by *CR*, and an adjustment by *Adj.*
2. Assume that Laser Printing records unearned revenues by initially crediting a *revenue* account. Open T-accounts for Unearned Service Revenue and Service Revenue, and place the beginning balance in Service Revenue. Journalize the cash collection and adjusting entries, and post their dollar amounts. As references in the T-accounts, denote a balance by *Bal.*, a cash receipt by *CR*, and an adjustment by *Adj.*
3. Compare the ending balances in the two accounts.

APPENDIX PROBLEM

P3A-1 Diebolt Sales and Service completed the following transactions during 20X4:

Oct. 1 Paid $4,500 store rent covering the six-month period ending March 31, 20X5.
Dec. 1 Collected $3,200 cash in advance from customers. The service revenue will be earned $800 monthly over the period ending March 31, 20X5.

Recording prepaid rent and rent revenue collected in advance two ways
(Obj. A1, A2)

Required

1. Journalize these entries by debiting an asset account for Prepaid Rent and by crediting a liability account for Unearned Service Revenue. Explanations are unnecessary.
2. Journalize the related adjustments at December 31, 20X4.
3. Post the entries to the ledger accounts, and show their balances at December 31, 20X4. Posting references are unnecessary.
4. Repeat requirements 1–3. This time, debit Rent Expense for the rent payment and credit Service Revenue for the collection of revenue in advance.
5. Compare the account balances in requirements 3 and 4. They should be equal.

4 Completing the Accounting Cycle

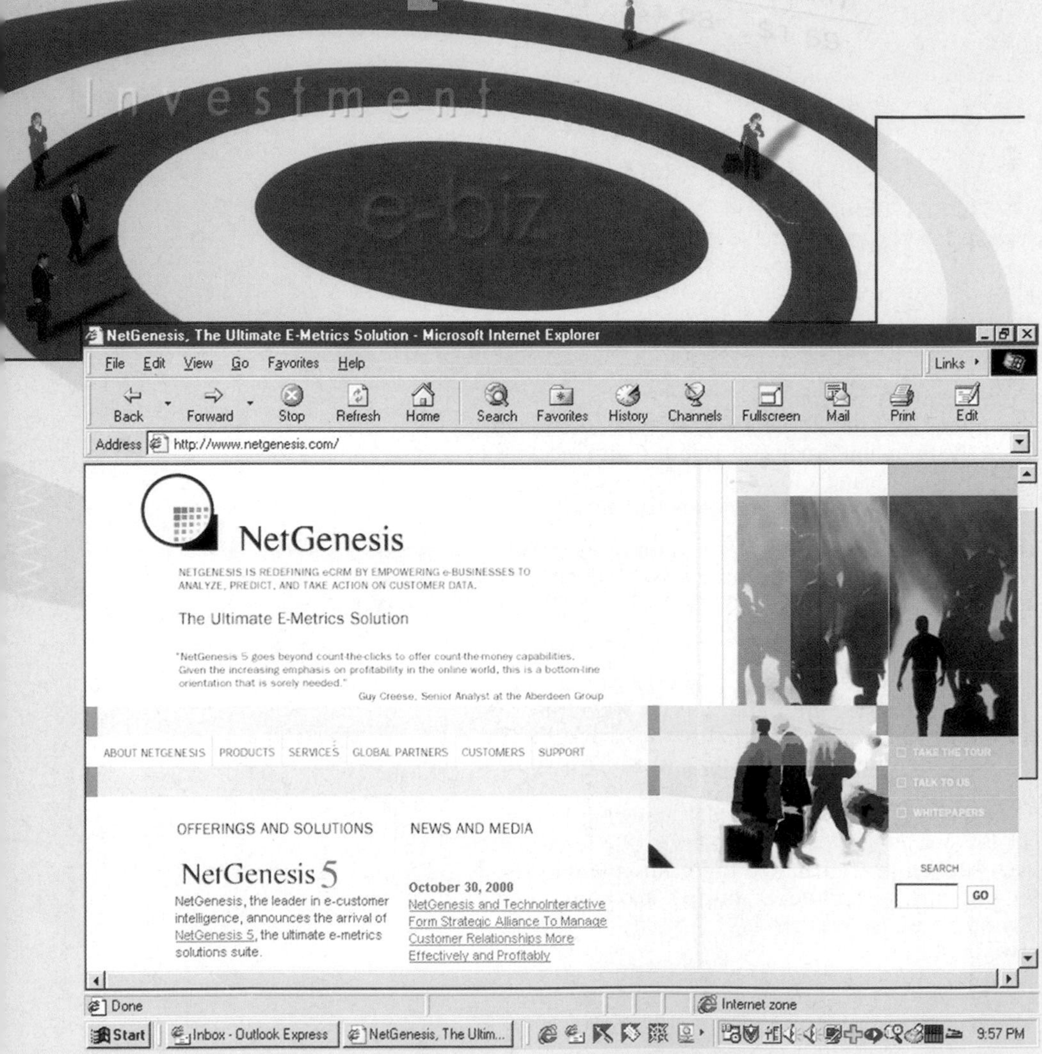

www.prenhall.com/horngren

LEARNING OBJECTIVES

After studying this chapter, you should be able to

1. Prepare an accounting work sheet

2. Use the work sheet to complete the accounting cycle

3. Close the revenue, expense, and withdrawal accounts

4. Classify assets and liabilities as current or long-term

5. Use the current and debt ratios to evaluate a business's ability to pay its debts

---

NetGenesis, The Ultimate E-Metrics Solution - Microsoft Internet Explorer

File   Edit   View   Go   Favorites   Help   Links

Back   Forward   Stop   Refresh   Home   Search   Favorites   History   Channels   Fullscreen   Mail   Print   Edit

Address http://www.netgenesis.com/

NetGenesis

NETGENESIS IS REDEFINING eCRM BY EMPOWERING e-BUSINESSES TO ANALYZE, PREDICT, AND TAKE ACTION ON CUSTOMER DATA.

The Ultimate E-Metrics Solution

"NetGenesis 5 goes beyond count the clicks to offer count the money capabilities. Given the increasing emphasis on profitability in the online world, this is a bottom-line orientation that is sorely needed."

Guy Creese, Senior Analyst at the Aberdeen Group

ABOUT NETGENESIS   PRODUCTS   SERVICES   GLOBAL PARTNERS   CUSTOMERS   SUPPORT

☐ TAKE THE TOUR
☐ TALK TO US
☐ WHITEPAPERS

OFFERINGS AND SOLUTIONS   NEWS AND MEDIA

NetGenesis 5

NetGenesis, the leader in e-customer intelligence, announces the arrival of NetGenesis 5, the ultimate e-metrics solutions suite.

October 30, 2000
NetGenesis and TechnoInteractive Form Strategic Alliance To Manage Customer Relationships More Effectively and Profitably

SEARCH
[   ] GO

Done   Internet zone

Start   Inbox - Outlook Express   NetGenesis, The Ultim...   9:57 PM

www.prenhall.com/horngren

Readiness Assessment

Matt Cutler is 27 years old and the co-founder of **NetGenesis,** which sells software to help other companies understand their customers better. He started NetGenesis in 1994 and in February 2000 he took the company public. That means Cutler and his co-founder sold some shares of NetGenesis stock (the ownership in the company) to the public. By May 2000, NetGenesis was worth about $350 million. When asked how a business downturn would affect NetGenesis, Matt replied: "Any organization successful in dealing with rapid change in an upswing will be able to deal with a downswing." The key is to be able to deal with rapid change.

The way for Matt to convince people that NetGenesis is a sound company is the same way that **Procter and Gamble, Xerox Corporation,** and **Sony** do it. Earn a profit year after year, and build up more assets than liabilities. In this chapter, we complete the accounting cycle that produces the financial statements investors use for their decision making.

Source: *Wall Street Journal,* May 22, 2000, p. R18.

In Chapter 3, we prepared the financial statements of Gay Gillen eTravel from an adjusted trial balance. That approach works well for quick decision making, but organizations of all sizes take the accounting process a step further. At the end of each period, after making the adjusting entries, they close their books. Whether the company is **NetGenesis, Xerox,** or Gay Gillen eTravel, the closing process follows the same basic pattern. Closing the books marks the end of the *accounting cycle* for a given period.

Accountants often use a document known as the *work sheet.* There are many different types of work sheets in business—as many, in fact, as there are needs for summary data. Work sheets are valuable because they summarize lots of data.

THE ACCOUNTING CYCLE

The **accounting cycle** is the process by which companies produce their financial statements for a specific period of time. For a new business, the cycle begins with setting up (opening) the ledger accounts. **NetGenesis** opened its doors in January 1994, and the first step in the accounting cycle was to open the accounts. After a business has operated for one period, the account balances carry over from period to period. Therefore, the accounting cycle starts with the beginning account balances. Exhibit 4-1 outlines the complete accounting cycle of NetGenesis, Gillen eTravel, and every other business. The boldface items in Panel A indicate the new concepts we introduce in this chapter.

The accounting cycle includes work performed at two different times:

- During the period—Journalizing transactions
  Posting to the ledger
- End of the period—Adjusting the accounts, including journalizing and posting the adjusting entries
  Closing the accounts, including journalizing and posting the closing entries
  Preparing the financial statements (income statement, statement of owner's equity, and balance sheet)

The end-of-period work also readies the accounts for the next period. In Chapters 3 and 4, we cover the end-of-period accounting for a service business such as Gay Gillen eTravel. Chapter 5 shows how a merchandising entity adjusts and closes its books.

Companies prepare financial statements on a monthly or a quarterly basis. Steps 1–6a in Exhibit 4-1 are adequate for statement preparation. Steps 6b–7 can be performed monthly or quarterly, but are necessary only at the end of the year.

Accounting Cycle. Process by which companies produce an entity's financial statements for a specific period.

Exhibit 4-1 The Accounting Cycle

PANEL A

During the Period	End of the Period

1. Start with the account balances in the ledger at the beginning of the period.
2. Analyze and journalize transactions as they occur.
3. Post journal entries to the ledger accounts.
	4. Compute the unadjusted balance in each account at the end of the period.
	5. Enter the trial balance on the work sheet, and complete the work sheet (optional).
	6. Using the adjusted trial balance or the full work sheet as a guide,
	   a. Prepare the financial statements.
	   b. Journalize and post the adjusting entries.
	   c. Journalize and post the closing entries.
	7. Prepare the **postclosing trial balance.** This trial balance becomes step 1 for the next period.

PANEL B

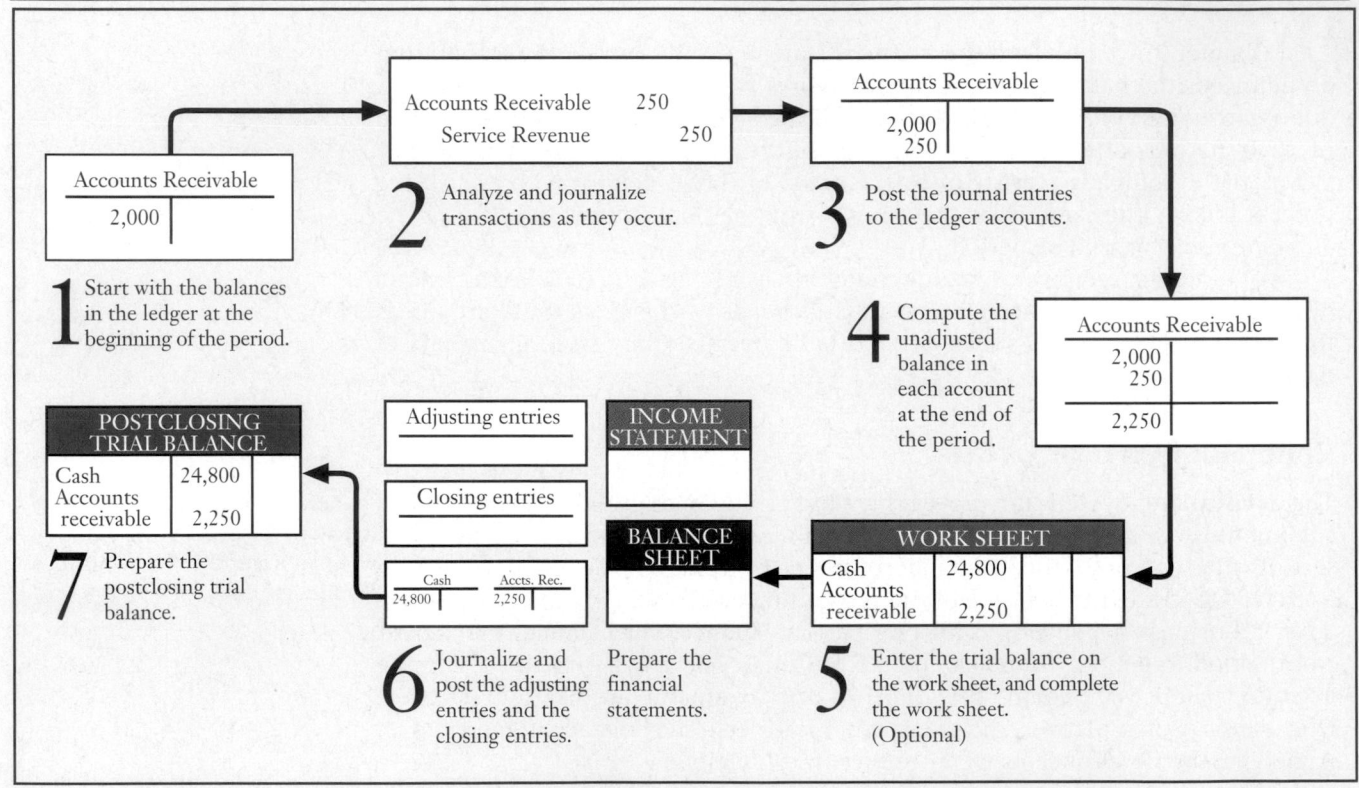

THE WORK SHEET

WORK SHEET. A columnar document designed to help move data from the trial balance to the financial statements.

Accountants often use a **work sheet**—a document with several columns—to help summarize and move data from the trial balance to the financial statements. The work sheet is not part of the ledger or the journal, and it is not a financial statement. It is merely a summary device that aids the accounting process. Listing all the accounts and their unadjusted balances helps identify accounts that need adjustment.

Exhibits 4-2 through 4-6 illustrate the development of a typical work sheet for the business of Gay Gillen eTravel. The heading at the top names the business, identifies the document, and states the accounting period.

A step-by-step description of its preparation follows.

Steps introduced in Chapter 3 to prepare the adjusted trial balance:

1. Enter the account titles and their unadjusted ending balances in the Trial Balance columns of the work sheet, and total the amounts (Exhibit 4-2).

2. Enter the adjustments in the Adjustments columns, and total the amounts (Exhibit 4-3). Total debits must equal total credits.

3. Compute each account's adjusted balance by combining the trial balance and adjustment figures. Enter the adjusted amounts in the Adjusted Trial Balance columns (Exhibit 4-4). Then compute the total for each column. Total debits should equal total credits.

Steps introduced in this chapter:

4. Extend the asset, liability, and owner's equity amounts from the Adjusted Trial Balance to the Balance Sheet columns. Extend the revenue and expense amounts to the Income Statement columns. Total the statement columns (Exhibit 4-5). For a change, total debits will not equal total credits.

5. Compute net income or net loss as the difference between total revenues and total expenses on the income statement. Enter net income or net loss as a balancing amount on the income statement and on the balance sheet, and compute the final column totals (Exhibit 4-6). Now all pairs of debit and credit columns should hold equal totals.

Let's examine these steps in greater detail.

1. *Enter the account titles and their unadjusted balances in the Trial Balance columns of the work sheet, and total the amounts.* Total debits must equal total credits, as shown in Exhibit 4-2. The account titles and unadjusted balances come directly from the ledger accounts before the adjusting entries are prepared. Accounts are grouped on the work sheet by category (assets, liabilities, owner's equity, revenues, and expenses) and are usually listed in the order they appear in the ledger (Cash first, Accounts Receivable second, and so on).

Accounts may have zero balances (for example, Depreciation Expense). All accounts are listed on the trial balance because they appear in the ledger.

2. *Enter the adjusting entries in the Adjustments columns, and total the amounts.* Exhibit 4-3 includes the April adjusting entries. These are the same adjustments that we used in Chapter 3 to prepare the adjusted trial balance.

● DAILY EXERCISE 4-1

We can identify the accounts that need to be adjusted by scanning the trial balance. Cash needs no adjustment because all cash transactions are recorded as they occur during the period. Consequently, Cash's balance is up to date.

Accounts Receivable is listed next. Has Gay Gillen earned revenue she has not yet recorded? The answer is yes. At April 30, Gillen has earned $250 that she has not yet recorded because the cash will be received during May. Gillen debits Accounts Receivable and credits Service Revenue on the work sheet in Exhibit 4-3. A letter is used to link the debit and the credit of each adjusting entry.

By moving down the trial balance, Gillen identifies the remaining accounts that need adjustment. Supplies is next. The business has used supplies during April, so Gillen debits Supplies Expense and credits Supplies. The other adjustments are analyzed and entered on the work sheet as in Chapter 3.

Listing the accounts in proper sequence aids the process of identifying accounts that need to be adjusted. But suppose some accounts are omitted from the trial balance. An account title can always be written below the first column totals—51,800. Assume that Supplies Expense was accidentally omitted and thus did not appear on the trial balance. The accountant can write Supplies Expense beneath the amount totals and enter the debit adjustment—$300—on the Supplies Expense line. After the adjustments are entered on the work sheet, the amount columns are totaled.

3. *Compute each account's adjusted balance by combining the trial balance and adjustment figures. Enter the adjusted amounts in the Adjusted Trial Balance columns.* Exhibit 4-4 shows the work sheet with the adjusted trial balance columns completed. For example, the Cash balance is up to date, so it receives no adjustment. Accounts Receivable's adjusted balance of $2,500 is computed by adding the trial balance amount of $2,250 to the $250 debit adjustment. Supplies' adjusted balance is determined by subtracting the $300 credit adjustment from the unadjusted debit balance of $700. An account may receive more than one adjustment, as Service Revenue does. The column totals must maintain the equality of debits and credits.

● DAILY EXERCISE 4-2

Exhibit 4-2 **Trial Balance**

GAY GILLEN ETRAVEL
Accounting Work Sheet
For the Month Ended April 30, 20X1

Account Title	Trial Balance Dr.	Trial Balance Cr.	Adjustments Dr.	Adjustments Cr.	Adjusted Trial Balance Dr.	Adjusted Trial Balance Cr.	Income Statement Dr.	Income Statement Cr.	Balance Sheet Dr.	Balance Sheet Cr.
Cash	24,800									
Accounts receivable	2,250									
Supplies	700									
Prepaid rent	3,000									
Furniture	16,500									
Accumulated depreciation										
Accounts payable		13,100								
Salary payable										
Unearned service revenue		450								
Gay Gillen, capital		31,250								
Gay Gillen, withdrawals	3,200									
Service revenue		7,000								
Rent expense										
Salary expense	950									
Supplies expense										
Depreciation expense										
Utilities expense	400									
	51,800	51,800								
Net income										

Write the account titles and their unadjusted ending balances in the Trial Balance columns of the work sheet, and total the amounts.

4. *Extend (that is, copy) the asset, liability, and owner's equity amounts from the Adjusted Trial Balance to the Balance Sheet columns. Copy the revenue and expense amounts to the Income Statement columns. Total the statement columns.* Every account is either a balance sheet account or an income statement account. The asset, liability, and owner's equity accounts go to the balance sheet, and the revenues and expenses go to the income statement. Debits on the adjusted trial balance remain debits in the statement columns, and credits remain credits. Each account's balance should appear in only one statement column, as shown in Exhibit 4-5.

DAILY EXERCISE 4-3

First, total the *income statement columns,* as follows:

INCOME STATEMENT

- Debits (Dr.) Total expenses = $3,875   }   Difference = $3,525, a net income
- Credits (Cr.) Total revenues = $7,400   }   because revenues exceed expenses

Then total the *balance sheet* columns:

BALANCE SHEET

- Debits (Dr.) Total assets and withdrawals   = $49,400   }   Difference = $3,525,
- Credits (Cr.) Total liabilities, owner's equity, = $45,875   }   a net income because
           and accumulated depreciation   }   total assets are greater

5. *Compute net income or net loss as the difference between total revenues and total expenses on the income statement. Enter net income as the balancing amount on the income statement and as the balancing amount on the balance sheet. Then compute the adjusted column totals.* Exhibit 4-6 presents the completed accounting work sheet, which shows net income of $3,525, computed as follows:

DAILY EXERCISE 4-4

Revenue (total credits on the income statement).....................	$7,400
Less: Expenses (total debits on the income statement)..............	(3,875)
Net income...	$3,525

Net income of $3,525 is entered in the debit column of the income statement to balance with the credit column of the income statement, which totals $7,400. The net income amount is then extended to the credit column of the balance sheet, because an excess of revenues over expenses increases capital, and increases in capital are recorded by a credit. In the closing process, net income will find its way into the Capital account.

If expenses exceed revenues, the result is a net loss. In that event, Net Loss is printed on the work sheet. The loss amount should be entered in the *credit* column of the income statement (to balance out) and in the *debit* column of the balance sheet (to balance out). After completion, total debits equal total credits in the Income Statement columns and in the Balance Sheet columns. The balance sheet columns are totaled at $49,400.

SUMMARY PROBLEM

www.prenhall.com/horngren

Mid-Chapter Assessment

The trial balance of State Service Company at December 31, 20X1, the end of its fiscal year, is as follows.

STATE SERVICE COMPANY Trial Balance December 31, 20X1		
Cash	$ 198,000	
Accounts receivable	370,000	
Supplies	6,000	
Furniture and fixtures	100,000	
Accumulated depreciation—furniture and fixtures		$ 40,000
Building	250,000	
Accumulated depreciation—building		130,000
Accounts payable		380,000
Salary payable		
Unearned service revenue		45,000
Capital		293,000
Withdrawals	65,000	
Service revenues		286,000
Salary expense	172,000	
Supplies expense		
Depreciation expense—furniture and fixtures		
Depreciation expense—building		
Miscellaneous expense	13,000	
Total	$1,174,000	$1,174,000

Data needed for the adjusting entries include:
a. Supplies on hand at year end, $2,000.
b. Depreciation on furniture and fixtures, $20,000.
c. Depreciation on building, $10,000.
d. Salaries owed but not yet paid, $5,000.
e. Accrued service revenue, $12,000.
f. Of the $45,000 balance of Unearned Service Revenue, $32,000 was earned during 20X1.

Required

Prepare the accounting work sheet of State Service Company for the year ended December 31, 20X1. Key each adjusting entry by the letter corresponding to the data given.

Solution

STATE SERVICE COMPANY
Work Sheet
Year Ended December 31, 20X1

Account Title	Trial Balance Dr.	Trial Balance Cr.	Adjustments Dr.	Adjustments Cr.	Adjusted Trial Balance Dr.	Adjusted Trial Balance Cr.	Income Statement Dr.	Income Statement Cr.	Balance Sheet Dr.	Balance Sheet Cr.
Cash	198,000				198,000				198,000	
Accounts receivable	370,000		(e) 12,000		382,000				382,000	
Supplies	6,000			(a) 4,000	2,000				2,000	
Furniture and fixtures	100,000				100,000				100,000	
Accumulated depreciation—furniture and fixtures		40,000		(b) 20,000		60,000				60,000
Building	250,000				250,000				250,000	
Accumulated depreciation—building		130,000		(c) 10,000		140,000				140,000
Accounts payable		380,000				380,000				380,000
Salary payable				(d) 5,000		5,000				5,000
Unearned service revenue		45,000	(f) 32,000			13,000				13,000
Capital		293,000				293,000				293,000
Withdrawals	65,000				65,000				65,000	
Service revenue		286,000		(e) 12,000 (f) 32,000		330,000		330,000		
Salary expense	172,000		(d) 5,000		177,000		177,000			
Supplies expense			(a) 4,000		4,000		4,000			
Depreciation expense—furniture and fixtures			(b) 20,000		20,000		20,000			
Depreciation expense—building			(c) 10,000		10,000		10,000			
Miscellaneous expense	13,000				13,000		13,000			
	1,174,000	1,174,000	83,000	83,000	1,221,000	1,221,000	224,000	330,000	997,000	891,000
Net income							106,000			106,000
							330,000	330,000	997,000	997,000

COMPLETING THE ACCOUNTING CYCLE

Objective 2

Use the work sheet to complete the accounting cycle

The work sheet helps organize the data for the computation of the net income or net loss for the period. The work sheet aids in preparing the financial statements, recording the adjusting entries, and closing the accounts.

Preparing the Financial Statements

The work sheet shows the amount of net income or net loss for the period, but we still must prepare the financial statements. ➤ The sorting of accounts to the balance sheet and the income statement eases the preparation of the statements. The work sheet also provides the data for the statement of owner's equity. Exhibit 4-7 presents the April financial statements for Gay Gillen eTravel (based on data from the work sheet in Exhibit 4-6). Most accountants prepare the financial statements immediately after completing the work sheet.

◄ The financial statements can be prepared directly from the adjusted trial balance; see p. 99. This is why completion of the work sheet is optional.

Recording the Adjusting Entries

The actual adjustment of the accounts requires journal entries and posting to the ledger accounts. Panel A of Exhibit 4-8 gives the adjusting entries of Gay Gillen eTravel at April 30. Panel B shows the postings to the accounts; *Adj.* denotes an amount posted from an adjusting entry. The adjusting entries can be recorded in the journal when they are entered on the work sheet. Only the revenue and expense accounts are presented in the exhibit in order to focus on the closing process.

EXHIBIT 4-7
**April Financial Statements of
Gay Gillen eTravel**

GAY GILLEN ETRAVEL
Income Statement
Month Ended April 30, 20X1

Revenue:		
Service revenue		$7,400
Expenses:		
Salary expense	$1,900	
Rent expense	1,000	
Utilities expense	400	
Supplies expense	300	
Depreciation expense—furniture	275	
Total expenses		3,875
Net income		$3,525

GAY GILLEN ETRAVEL
Statement of Owner's Equity
Month Ended April 30, 20X1

Gay Gillen, capital, April 1, 20X1	$31,250
Add: Net income	3,525
	34,775
Less: Withdrawals	(3,200)
Gay Gillen, capital, April 30, 20X1	$31,575

GAY GILLEN ETRAVEL
Balance Sheet
April 30, 20X1

Assets			Liabilities		
Cash		$24,800	Accounts payable		$13,100
Accounts receivable		2,500	Salary payable		950
Supplies		400	Unearned service		
Prepaid rent		2,000	revenue		300
Furniture	$16,500		Total liabilities		14,350
Less:					
Accumulated			**Owner's Equity**		
depreciation	(275)	16,225	Gay Gillen, capital		31,575
			Total liabilities and		
			owner's equity		
Total assets		$45,925			$45,925

CLOSING THE ACCOUNTS. Step in
the accounting cycle at the
end of the period. Closing the
accounts consists of journalizing and posting the closing
entries to set the balances of
the revenue, expense, and
withdrawal accounts to zero
for the next period.

Many companies journalize and post the adjusting entries (as in Exhibit 4-8)
only once annually—at the end of the year. Accountants can use the work sheet to
prepare monthly or quarterly statements without journalizing and posting the
adjusting entries.

Closing the Accounts

Closing the accounts is the end-of-period process that prepares the accounts for
the next period. Closing the accounts consists of journalizing and posting the closing
entries. Closing zeroes out the balances of the revenue and expense accounts in
order to clearly measure the net income of each period separately from all other
periods.

Recall that the income statement reports only one period's net income. For
example, net income for **NetGenesis Corp.** for 2001 relates exclusively to 2001. At
December 31, 2001, the NetGenesis accountants close the company's revenue and
expense accounts for that year. Because the revenue and expense account balances

EXHIBIT 4-8 **Journalizing and Posting the Adjusting Entries**

PANEL A—Journalizing: **Page 4**

Adjusting Entries

Apr. 30	Accounts Receivable...............................	250	
	Service Revenue		250
30	Supplies Expense...................................	300	
	Supplies..		300
30	Rent Expense...	1,000	
	Prepaid Rent		1,000
30	Depreciation Expense..............................	275	
	Accumulated Depreciation		275
30	Salary Expense	950	
	Salary Payable..................................		950
30	Unearned Service Revenue	150	
	Service Revenue		150

PANEL B—Posting the Adjustments to the Revenue and Expense Accounts:

REVENUE		EXPENSES		

SERVICE REVENUE

			7,000
	Adj.	250	
	Adj.	150	
	Bal.	7,400	

RENT EXPENSE

Adj.	1,000	
Bal.	1,000	

SALARY EXPENSE

		950	
Adj.	950		
Bal.	1,900		

SUPPLIES EXPENSE

Adj.	300	
Bal.	300	

DEPRECIATION EXPENSE

Adj.	275	
Bal.	275	

UTILITIES EXPENSE

	400	
Bal.	400	

Adj. = Amount posted from an adjusting entry   Bal. = Balance

relate to a particular accounting period and are therefore closed at the end of the period (December 31, 2001), the revenue and expense accounts are called **temporary (nominal) accounts.** For example, Gay Gillen's balance of Service Revenue at April 30, 20X1, is $7,400. This balance relates exclusively to the month of April and must be zeroed out before Gillen records revenue for May.

The owner's Withdrawal account—although not a revenue or an expense—is also a temporary account because it measures withdrawals for only one period. The Withdrawals account is also closed.

To better understand the closing process, contrast the nature of the temporary accounts with the nature of the **permanent (real) accounts**—the asset, liability, and capital accounts. The asset, liability, and owner's capital accounts are *not* closed at the end of the period because their balances are not used to measure income. Consider Cash, Accounts Receivable, Accounts Payable, and Gay Gillen, Capital. These accounts do not represent business *activity* for a single period and thus are not closed at the end of the period. Their balances carry over to become the beginning balances of the next period. For example, the Cash balance at December 31, 20X1, becomes the beginning balance for 20X2.

Closing entries transfer the revenue, expense, and owner withdrawal balances from their respective accounts to the capital account. As you know,

TEMPORARY ACCOUNTS. The revenue and expense accounts that relate to a particular accounting period and are closed at the end of the period. For a proprietorship, the owner withdrawal account is also temporary. Also called **nominal accounts.**

PERMANENT ACCOUNTS. Accounts that are *not* closed at the end of the period— asset, liability, and capital accounts. Also called **real accounts.**

CLOSING ENTRIES. Entries that transfer the revenue, expense, and owner withdrawal balances from these respective accounts to the capital account.

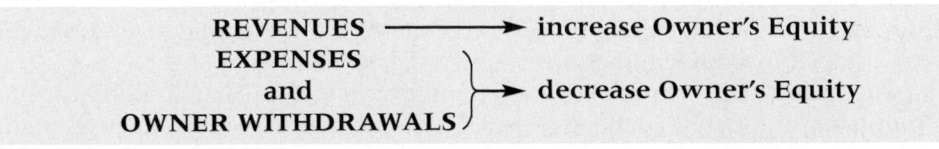

Posting the closing entries causes the Capital account to absorb the balances in all temporary accounts.

EXHIBIT 4-9 **Journalizing and Posting the Closing Entries**

PANEL A—Journalizing   **Page 5**

Closing Entries

①	Apr. 30	Service Revenue..	7,400	
②		Income Summary		7,400
	30	Income Summary..	3,875	
		Rent Expense....................................		1,000
		Salary Expense		1,900
		Supplies Expense..............................		300
		Depreciation Expense........................		275
		Utilities Expense		400
③	30	Income Summary ($7,400 − $3,875)............	3,525	
		Gay Gillen, Capital...............................		3,525
④	30	Gay Gillen, Capital	3,200	
		Gay Gillen, Withdrawals.....................		3,200

PANEL B—Posting

RENT EXPENSE

Adj.	1,000		
Bal.	1,000	Clo.	1,000

SALARY EXPENSE

	950		
Adj.	950		
Bal.	1,900	Clo.	1,900

SUPPLIES EXPENSE

Adj.	300		
Bal.	300	Clo.	300

DEPRECIATION EXPENSE

Adj.	275		
Bal.	275	Clo.	275

UTILITIES EXPENSE

	400		
Bal.	400	Clo.	400

② ③

INCOME SUMMARY

Clo.	3,875	Clo.	7,400
Clo.	3,525	Bal.	3,525

① ④

SERVICE REVENUE

			7,000
		Adj.	250
		Adj.	150
Clo.	7,400	Bal.	7,400

GAY GILLEN, WITHDRAWALS

Bal.	3,200	Clo.	3,200

GAY GILLEN, CAPITAL

Clo.	3,200		31,250
		Clo.	3,525
		Bal.	31,575

Adj. = Amount posted from an adjusting entry   Clo. = Amount posted from a closing entry   Bal. = Balance

INCOME SUMMARY. A temporary "holding tank" account into which revenues and expenses are transferred prior to their final transfer to the capital account.

As an intermediate step, the revenues and the expenses are transferred first to an account entitled **Income Summary,** which collects the total debit for the sum of all expenses and the total credit for the sum of all revenues of the period. The Income Summary account is like a "holding tank." The balance of Income Summary is then transferred to capital.

The steps in closing the accounts of a proprietorship such as Gay Gillen eTravel are as follows (the circled numbers are keyed to Exhibit 4-9).

① Debit each *revenue* account for the amount of its credit balance. Credit Income Summary for the total of the revenues. This entry transfers total revenues to the *credit* side of Income Summary.

② Credit each *expense* account for the amount of its debit balance. Debit Income Summary for the total of the expenses. This entry transfers total expenses to the *debit* side of Income Summary. It is not necessary to make a separate closing entry for each expense. In one closing entry, record one debit to Income Summary and a separate credit to each expense account.

③ To close net income, debit Income Summary for the amount of its *credit balance* (if there is a *net income*), and credit the Capital account. If there is a *net loss*, Income Summary has a *debit balance*. In that case, credit Income Summary for the amount of the loss, and debit Capital. This closing entry transfers net income or net loss from Income Summary to the Capital account.

④ Credit the *Withdrawals* account for the amount of its debit balance. Debit the Capital account of the proprietor. This entry transfers the amount of owner withdrawals during the period to the *debit* side of the Capital account. *Withdrawals do not affect net income or net loss because withdrawals are not an expense.*

 DAILY EXERCISE 4-5

These steps are best illustrated with an example. Suppose Gay Gillen closes the books at the end of April. Exhibit 4-9 presents the complete closing process for Gillen's travel agency. Panel A gives the closing journal entries, and Panel B shows the accounts after the closing entries have been posted.

Each expense account holds its adjusted balance. For example, Rent Expense has a $1,000 debit balance. Service Revenue has a credit balance of $7,400 before closing. These amounts come directly from the adjusted balances in Exhibit 4-8, Panel B.

- Closing entry ① in Exhibit 4-9 transfers Service Revenue's balance to the Income Summary account. This entry zeroes out Service Revenue for April and transfers total revenue to the credit side of Income Summary.
- Closing entry ② zeroes out the expenses and moves their total ($3,875) to the debit side of Income Summary. At this point, Income Summary contains all of April's revenues and expenses. Income Summary's credit balance shows the month's net income ($3,525).
- Closing entry ③ closes the Income Summary account by transferring net income ($3,525) to the credit side of Gay Gillen, Capital.[1]
- The last closing entry, entry ④, moves the owner withdrawals to the debit side of Gay Gillen, Capital, leaving a zero balance in Withdrawals.

The closing entries set all the revenues, the expenses, and the Withdrawals account back to zero. Now the owner's Capital account includes the full effects of April's revenues, expenses, and withdrawals, plus the beginning Capital balance. The Gay Gillen, Capital account has an ending balance of $31,575. Trace this ending Capital balance to the statement of owner's equity and also to the balance sheet in Exhibit 4-7.

DAILY EXERCISE 4-6

DAILY EXERCISE 4-7

DAILY EXERCISE 4-8

DAILY EXERCISE 4-9

CLOSING A NET LOSS What would the closing entries be if Gillen's travel agency had suffered a net *loss* during April? Suppose expenses totaled $7,700 and all other factors were unchanged (revenues were $7,400, so Gillen's business suffered a net loss of $300 for April). Only closing entries ② and ③ would change. Closing entry ② would transfer expenses of $7,700 to the debit side of Income Summary, as follows:

INCOME SUMMARY			
Clo.	7,700	Clo.	7,400
Bal.	300		

Closing entry ③ would then credit Income Summary to close this account and to transfer the net loss to Gay Gillen, Capital:

③ Apr. 30   Gay Gillen, Capital 300

               Income Summary..............   300

After posting, these two accounts would appear as follows:

INCOME SUMMARY				GAY GILLEN, CAPITAL			
Clo.	7,700	Clo.	7,400	Clo.	300		31,250
Bal.	300	Clo.	300				

---

[1]The Income Summary account is a convenience for combining the effects of the revenues and expenses before transferring their income effect to Capital. It is not necessary to use the Income Summary account in the closing process. In an alternative procedure, revenues and expenses are closed directly to Capital.

EXHIBIT 4-10
Postclosing Trial Balance

 DAILY EXERCISE 4-10

Finally, the Withdrawals balance would be closed to Capital, as before. The double underline in an account means that the account has a zero balance; nothing more will be posted to it in the current period.

The closing process is fundamentally mechanical and is completely automated in a computerized system. Accounts are identified as either temporary or permanent. The temporary accounts are closed automatically by selecting that option from the software menu. Posting also occurs automatically.

Postclosing Trial Balance

The accounting cycle ends with the **postclosing trial balance** (Exhibit 4-10). It lists the accounts and their adjusted balances after closing. This step shows where the business stands as it moves into the next accounting period. The postclosing trial balance is dated as of the end of the period.

GAY GILLEN ETRAVEL Postclosing Trial Balance April 30, 20X1		
Cash	$24,800	
Accounts receivable	2,500	
Supplies	400	
Prepaid Rent	2,000	
Furniture	16,500	
Accumulated depreciation		$ 275
Accounts payable		13,100
Salary Payable		950
Unearned service revenue		300
Gay Gillen, capital		31,575
Total	$46,200	$46,200

The postclosing trial balance resembles the balance sheet. It contains the ending balances of the permanent accounts—the balance sheet accounts: the assets, liabilities, and capital. No temporary accounts—revenues, expenses, or withdrawal accounts—are included because their balances have been closed. The ledger is up to date and ready for the next period's transactions.

Reversing entries are special journal entries that ease the burden of accounting for transactions that key off the adjustments at the end of the period. Reversing entries are optional, and for that reason, we cover them in the appendix at the end of this chapter.

CLASSIFYING ASSETS AND LIABILITIES

Assets and liabilities are classified as either *current* or *long-term* to indicate their relative liquidity. **Liquidity** measures how quickly an item can be converted to cash. Cash is the most liquid asset. Accounts receivable is relatively liquid because the business expects to collect the money in the near future. Supplies are less liquid than receivables, and furniture and buildings are even less liquid.

Managers and owners are interested in liquidity because business difficulties often arise from a shortage of cash. How quickly can the business convert an asset to cash and pay a debt? How soon must a liability be paid? These are questions of liquidity. A classified balance sheet helps to answer questions such as these.

Assets

CURRENT ASSETS **Current assets** are assets that are expected to be converted to cash, sold, or consumed during the next 12 months or within the business's normal operating cycle. The **operating cycle** is the time span during which (1) cash is used to acquire goods and services, (2) these goods and services are sold to customers, and (3) the business collects cash. For most businesses, the operating cycle is a few months. A few types of businesses have operating cycles longer than a year. Cash, Accounts Receivable, Notes Receivable due within a year or less, and Prepaid Expenses are current assets. Merchandising entities such as **Intel, Sears,** and **IBM** have an additional current asset, Inventory. This account shows the cost of the goods the business is holding for sale to customers.

LONG-TERM ASSETS   **Long-term assets** are all assets other than current assets. One category of long-term assets is **plant** (or **fixed**) **assets,** another name for Property, Plant, and Equipment. Land, Buildings, Furniture and Fixtures, and Equipment are fixed assets. Of these, Gay Gillen eTravel has only Furniture.

Other categories of long-term assets include Long-Term Investments in Stock, and Other Assets (a catchall category). We discuss these categories in later chapters.

Liabilities

Managers and owners are interested in the due dates of an entity's liabilities. Liabilities that must be paid the quickest create the greatest strain on cash. Therefore, the balance sheet lists liabilities in the order in which they are due to be paid. Knowing how much of a business's liabilities is current and how much is long-term helps creditors assess the likelihood of collecting cash from the entity. Balance sheets have two liability classifications, *current liabilities* and *long-term liabilities.*

CURRENT LIABILITIES   **Current liabilities** are debts that must be paid with cash or with goods and services within one year or within the entity's operating cycle if the cycle is longer than a year. Accounts Payable, Notes Payable due within one year, Salary Payable, Unearned Revenue, and Interest Payable owed on notes payable are current liabilities.

LONG-TERM LIABILITIES   All liabilities that are not current are classified as **long-term liabilities.** Many notes payable are long-term—payable after one year or the entity's operating cycle. Some notes payable are paid in installments, with the first installment due within one year, the second installment due the second year, and so on. In that case, the first installment is a current liability, and the remaining installments long-term liabilities. For example, a $100,000 note payable to be paid $10,000 per year over ten years would include a current liability of $10,000 for next year's payment and a long-term liability of $90,000.

Thus far we have presented the *unclassified* balance sheet of Gay Gillen eTravel. Our purpose was to focus on the main points of assets, liabilities, and owner's equity without the details of *current* assets, *current* liabilities, and so on. Exhibit 4-11 presents Gillen's classified balance sheet.

EXHIBIT 4-11 **Classified Balance Sheet of Gay Gillen eTravel**

GAY GILLEN ETRAVEL
Balance Sheet
April 30, 20X1

Assets			Liabilities		
Current assets:			**Current liabilities:**		
Cash		$24,800	Accounts payable		$13,100
Accounts receivable		2,500	Salary payable		950
Supplies		400	Unearned service revenue		300
Prepaid rent		2,000	Total current liabilities		14,350
Total current assets		29,700	Long-term liabilities (None)		0
Fixed assets:			Total liabilities		14,350
Furniture	$16,500				
Less: Accumulated			**Owner's Equity**		
depreciation	(275)	16,225	Gay Gillen, capital		31,575
			Total liabilities and		
Total assets		$45,925	owner's equity		$45,925

Gillen classifies each asset and each liability as current or long-term. She could have labeled fixed assets as *long-term assets.*

Compare Gillen's *classified* balance sheet in Exhibit 4-11 with the *unclassified* balance sheet in Exhibit 4-7. The classified balance sheet reports more information—totals for current assets and current liabilities, which do not appear on the unclassified balance sheet. Gillen has no long-term liabilities, so there are none to report on either balance sheet.

 **THINK IT OVER** Why is the classified balance sheet in Exhibit 4-11 more useful than an unclassified balance sheet (Exhibit 4-7) to (a) Gay Gillen and (b) a banker considering whether to lend $10,000 to Gillen?

Answer: A classified balance sheet indicates to (a) Gillen and (b) a banker

- Which of Gillen's liabilities, and the dollar amounts, Gillen must pay within the next year
- Which of Gillen's assets are the most liquid and thus available to pay the liabilities
- Which assets and liabilities (and amounts) are long-term

A Real Classified Balance Sheet

Exhibit 4-12 is an actual classified balance sheet of **PepsiCo, Inc.** Dollar amounts are reported in millions to avoid clutter. You should be familiar with all but a few of PepsiCo's account titles. Among the Current Assets are Short-term investments, which are investments that PepsiCo expects to sell within one year. These assets are very liquid, which explains why they are reported before the receivables.

EXHIBIT 4-12
PepsiCo's Classified Balance Sheet

PEPSICO, INC.
Balance Sheet (Adapted)
December 31, 1999

ASSETS	*(In millions)*
Current Assets	
Cash and cash equivalents...	$ 964
Short-term investments, at cost	92
	1,056
Accounts and notes receivable, net	1,704
Inventories...	899
Prepaid expenses and other current assets..................	514
Total Current Assets..	4,173
Property, plant and equipment, net of	
Accumulated depreciation of $3,550........................	5,266
Intangible assets, net	4,735
Investments in other companies	2,846
Other assets	531
Total Assets...	$17,551
LIABILITIES AND SHAREHOLDERS' EQUITY	
Current Liabilities	
Short-term borrowings..	$ 233
Accounts payable and other current liabilities	3,399
Income taxes payable	156
Total Current Liabilities...	3,788
Long-term debt..	2,812
Other liabilities	4,070
Shareholders' equity..	6,881
Total Liabilities and Shareholders' Equity.................	$17,551

 DAILY EXERCISE 4-12

PepsiCo reports Property, Plant, and Equipment, *net,* of $5,266 million. *Net* means the amount of the assets after subtracting Accumulated Depreciation. At

December 31, 1999, Accumulated Depreciation of PepsiCo's property, plant, and equipment totaled $3,550 million. Another way for PepsiCo to report property, plant, and equipment would be (in millions)

Property, Plant, and Equipment, at cost..............	$8,816
Less: Accumulated Depreciation..........................	(3,550)
Property, Plant and Equipment, net....................	$5,266

PepsiCo also reports **Intangible Assets.** Intangibles are assets, such as patents, trademarks, and goodwill, which have no physical form. Intangibles are valuable because of the rights they provide the owner. PepsiCo's trademarks (Pepsi and Tropicana drinks, Lay's chips, and Aquafina) are worth a lot.

All of PepsiCo's liabilities should be familiar to you. We can compute total liabilities two ways, as follows (in millions):

- Add: Total Current liabilities, Long-Term Debt, and Other Liabilities
    ($3,788 + $2,812 + $4,070) $10,670
- Total Liabilities = Total Assets − Shareholders' (Owners') Equity
    ($17,551 − $6,881) $10,670

Both computations are valid. When all the liability amounts are available, as on PepsiCo's balance sheet, you can add them up. When some data are missing, you can still compute total liabilities by using the accounting equation: Assets = Liabilities + Shareholders' Equity (same as Owners' Equity).

BALANCE SHEET FORMATS

The balance sheet of PepsiCo in Exhibit 4-12 lists the assets at the top and the liabilities and owners' equity below. This arrangement is known as the *report format*. The balance sheet of Gay Gillen eTravel presented in Exhibit 4-7 lists the assets at the left and the liabilities and the owner's equity at the right. That arrangement is known as the *account format*.

Either format is acceptable. A recent survey of 600 companies indicated that 73% (436 companies) use the report format and only 27% (164 companies) use the account format.

ACCOUNTING RATIOS

The purpose of accounting is to provide information for decision making. Chief users of accounting information are managers, business owners, and creditors. A creditor considering lending money must predict whether the borrower can repay the loan. If the borrower already has a lot of debt, the probability of repayment is lower than if the borrower doesn't owe much money. To assess a company's financial position, decision makers use ratios computed from the company's financial statements.

Current Ratio

One of the most widely used financial ratios is the **current ratio,** which compares an entity's current assets to its current liabilities:

$$\text{Current ratio} = \frac{\text{Total current assets}}{\text{Total current liabilities}}$$

The current ratio measures the ability to pay current liabilities with current assets. A company prefers to have a high current ratio, which means that the business has plenty of current assets to pay current liabilities. An increasing current ratio from period to period indicates improvement in the ability to pay current debts.

A rule of thumb: A very strong current ratio is 2.00, which indicates that the company has $2.00 in current assets for every $1.00 in current liabilities. A company with a current ratio of 2.00 would probably have little trouble paying its

INTANGIBLE ASSETS. Assets, such as patents, trademarks, and goodwill, which have no physical form.

Objective 5
Use the current and debt ratios to evaluate a business's ability to pay its debts

CURRENT RATIO. Current assets divided by current liabilities. Measures the company's ability to pay current liabilities from current assets.

current liabilities. Most successful businesses operate with current ratios between 1.50 and 2.00. A current ratio of 1.00 is considered low.

Compute PepsiCo's current ratio at December 31, 1999. Use the company's balance sheet in Exhibit 4-12 and show dollar amounts in millions.

Answer: $$\text{Current} = \frac{\text{Total current assets}}{\text{Total current liabilities}} = \frac{\$4,173}{\$3,788} = 1.10$$

How much in current assets does PepsiCo have for every dollar the company owes in current liabilities?

Answer: $1.10

Is PepsiCo's current ratio high or low? Is this ratio value risky?

Answer: PepsiCo's current ratio is low, which makes it look risky. However, PepsiCo operates successfully with a low current ratio because the company sells food products that people buy in both good times and hard times. Thus far, PepsiCo has had no trouble paying its debts.

Debt Ratio

DEBT RATIO. Ratio of total liabilities to total assets. Tells the proportion of a company's assets that it has financed with debt.

A second aid to decision making is the **debt ratio,** which is the ratio of total liabilities to total assets:

$$\text{Debt ratio} = \frac{\text{Total liabilities}}{\text{Total assets}}$$

The debt ratio indicates the proportion of a company's assets that are financed with debt. This ratio measures a business's overall ability to pay both current and long-term debts—total liabilities. The debt ratio measures debt-paying ability differently than the current ratio.

A low debt ratio is safer than a high debt ratio. Why? Because a company with a small amount of liabilities has low required payments. Such a company is unlikely to get into financial difficulty. By contrast, a business with a high debt ratio may have trouble paying its liabilities, especially when sales are low and cash is scarce. When a company fails to pay its debts, the creditors can take the business away from its owner. The largest retail bankruptcy in history, **Federated Department Stores,** the parent company of Bloomingdale's, was due largely to high debt during an economic recession in the retail industry. Federated was unable to weather the downturn and had to declare bankruptcy.

A rule of thumb: A debt ratio below 0.60, or 60%, is considered safe for most businesses. A debt ratio above 0.80, or 80%, borders on high risk. Most companies have debt ratios in the range of 0.60–0.80.

We saw that PepsiCo has a low current ratio, but PepsiCo nevertheless operates successfully (profits are high, cash is plentiful, and the company grows steadily). Now compute PepsiCo's debt ratio from the company's balance sheet in Exhibit 4-12. Show dollar amounts in millions.

Answer: $$\text{Debt ratio} = \frac{\text{Total liabilities}}{\text{Total assets}} = \frac{\$10,670*}{\$17,551} = 0.61, \text{ or } 61\%$$

For each dollar of its total assets, how much does PepsiCo owe in total liabilities?

Answer: $0.61

What percentage of PepsiCo's total assets is financial with debt?

Answer: 0.61, or 61%

If you owed $0.61 for every dollar of your total assets, would you worry about your ability to pay your debts?

Managing Both the Current Ratio and the Debt Ratio

In general, a *high* current ratio is preferable to a low current ratio. *Increases* in the current ratio indicate improving financial position. By contrast, a low debt ratio is preferable to a high debt ratio. Improvement is indicated by a *decrease* in the debt ratio.

 DAILY EXERCISE 4-13

 DAILY EXERCISE 4-14

Financial ratios aid decision making. It is unwise, however, to place too much confidence in a single ratio. A company may have a high current ratio, which indicates financial strength. It may also have a high debt ratio, which suggests weakness. Which ratio gives the more reliable signal? Experienced lenders and investors examine a large number of ratios over several years to spot trends and turning points. They also consider other factors, such as the company's cash flow and its trend of net income.

As you progress through your study of accounting, we will introduce key ratios used for decision making. Chapter 18 summarizes all the ratios discussed in this book and provides an overview of the more common ratios used in decision making.

e-Accounting

A Forced Debt Ratio for South Korea's Companies

Samsung. Daewoo. Hyundai. Just five years ago these companies were the economic engines driving South Korea's economy. Now they are mired in debt. When the Asian currency crisis hit South Korea in 1997, investors fled and companies had to borrow money. The bigger the company, the more debt they had to take on. According to the **Bank of Korea,** the average debt ratio of Korea's manufacturing companies was 71% in 1999.

According to the government of President Kim Dae Jung, the only way for the giant family-run companies to move toward financial stability is to meet a hard and fast debt ratio target of 67%. Carmaking giant Daewoo was struggling to meet payments on $47 billion in debt— equivalent to the entire national debt of Poland or Malaysia. The Korean government strong-armed Daewoo into selling off the pieces of the company. President Kim's reform plan may save some companies from going bust, but it may hurt others.

Source: Based on Howard W. French, "Dismantling of yesterday's economic engines," *New York Times,* September 3, 1999, p. C1. Jane L. Lee, "Korea moves anew to reform top 5 chaebols; this time, control by families could diminish," *Wall Street Journal,* August 26, 1999, p. A13. Anonymous, "Government under fire for strict debt ratio target," *Business Korea,* December 1999, pp. 18–19.

Now study the Decision Guidelines feature, which summarizes what you have learned in this chapter.

DECISION GUIDELINES

Completing the Accounting Cycle

DECISION	GUIDELINES
How (where) to summarize the effects of all the entity's transactions and adjustments throughout the period?	Accountant's *work sheet* with columns for • Trial balance • Income statement • Adjustments • Balance sheet • Adjusted trial balance
What is the last *major* step in the accounting cycle?	*Closing entries* for the *temporary accounts:* • Revenues ⎫ • Expenses ⎬ Income statement accounts • Owner's withdrawals
Why close out revenues, expenses, and owner withdrawals?	Because these *temporary accounts* have balances that relate only to one accounting period and do *not* carry over to the next period.
Which accounts do not get closed out?	*Permanent (balance sheet) accounts:* • Assets • Owner's capital • Liabilities The balances of these accounts *do* carry over to the next period.
How do businesses classify their assets and liabilities for reporting on the balance sheet?	*Current* (within one year or the entity's operating cycle if longer than a year) *Long-term* (not current)
How do decision makers evaluate a company?	There are many ways, such as the company's net income or net loss on the income statement. Another way to evaluate a company is based on the company's *financial ratios*. Two key ratios: $$\text{Current ratio} = \frac{\text{Total current assets}}{\text{Total current liabilities}}$$ The *current ratio* measures the entity's ability to pay its current liabilities with its current assets. $$\text{Debt ratio} = \frac{\text{Total liabilities}}{\text{Total assets}}$$ The *debt ratio* shows the proportion of the entity's assets that are financed with debt. The debt ratio measures the entity's overall ability to pay its liabilities.

EXCEL APPLICATION PROBLEM

Goal: Create an Excel spreadsheet to calculate the current ratio and debt ratio for Target and use the results to answer questions about the company.

Scenario: You are deciding whether to buy the stock in **Target.** You know that the current ratio and the debt ratio measure whether a company has the assets to cover its liabilities.

Your task is to create a simple spreadsheet to calculate the current ratio and the debt ratio for the company. Data may be found in Target's annual report (Web site: www.target-corp.com). When done, answer these questions:

1. Does the company have an acceptable current ratio? How can you tell?
2. Does the company have an acceptable debt ratio? How can you tell?

3. What is the trend (up or down) for the ratios? Is the trend positive or negative? Why?

Step-by-step:

1. Locate the following current and prior years' information for Target (found on the "Consolidated Statements of Financial Position"):
   a. Current Assets
   b. Total Assets
   c. Current Liabilities
   d. Long-Term Liabilities (computed on the spreadsheet)
   e. Total Liabilities (computed on the spreadsheet)
   f. Total Shareholders' Investment (Owners' Equity)
   g. Total Liabilities and Shareholders' Investment
2. Open a new Excel spreadsheet.

EXCEL APPLICATION PROBLEM (CONT.)

Step-by-step *(cont.)*

3. Create a boldfaced heading for your spreadsheet that contains the following:
   a. Chapter 4 Decision Guideline
   b. The Current Ratio and the Debt ratio
   c. Target
   d. Today's date
4. Two rows down from your worksheet heading, create a column heading titled "TARGET (in millions)." Make it bold and underline the heading.
5. One row down from Target's column heading, create a row with the following bold, underlined column titles:
   a. Account
   b. FYxx (xx = the most recent fiscal year, for example, 00)
   c. FYyy (yy = the prior fiscal year, for example, 99)
6. Starting with the "Account" column heading, enter the data found in 1, above. You should have seven rows of data, with row descriptions (for example, "Current Assets"). Format the columns as necessary.
7. Skip a row at the end of your data, and then create a row titled "Current Ratio" and another row titled "Debt Ratio."
8. Enter the formula for each ratio in the "Fyxx" and "FYyy" columns. You should have four formulas. Make both rows bold.
9. Save your work to disk, and print a copy for your files.

REVIEW THE ACCOUNTING CYCLE

SUMMARY PROBLEM

Refer to the data in the Mid-Chapter Summary Problem (State Service Company, page 132–133).

www.prenhall.com/horngren

End-of-Chapter Assessment

Required

1. Journalize and post the adjusting entries. (Before posting to the accounts, enter into each account its balance as shown in the trial balance. For example, enter the $370,000 balance in the Accounts Receivable account before posting its adjusting entry.) Key adjusting entries by *letter*, as shown in the work sheet solution to the Mid-Chapter Summary Problem. You can take the adjusting entries straight from the work sheet on page 133.
2. Journalize and post the closing entries. (Each account should carry its balance as shown in the adjusted trial balance.) To distinguish closing entries from adjusting entries, key the closing entries by *number*. Draw arrows to illustrate the flow of data, as shown in Exhibit 4-9. Indicate the balance of the Capital account after the closing entries are posted.
3. Prepare the income statement for the year ended December 31, 20X1. List Miscellaneous Expense last among the expenses, a common practice.
4. Prepare the statement of owner's equity for the year ended December 31, 20X1. Draw an arrow linking the income statement to the statement of owner's equity.
5. Prepare the classified balance sheet at December 31, 20X1. Use the report form. All liabilities are current. Draw an arrow linking the statement of owner's equity to the balance sheet.

Solution

Requirement 1

Adjusting Entries

a. Dec. 31		Supplies Expense	4,000	
		Supplies		4,000
b.	31	Depreciation Expense—Furniture and Fixtures	20,000	
		Accumulated Depreciation—Furniture and Fixtures		20,000
c.	31	Depreciation Expense—Building	10,000	
		Accumulated Depreciation—Building		10,000
d.	31	Salary Expense	5,000	
		Salary Payable		5,000
e.	31	Accounts Receivable	12,000	
		Service Revenue		12,000
f.	31	Unearned Service Revenue	32,000	
		Service Revenue		32,000

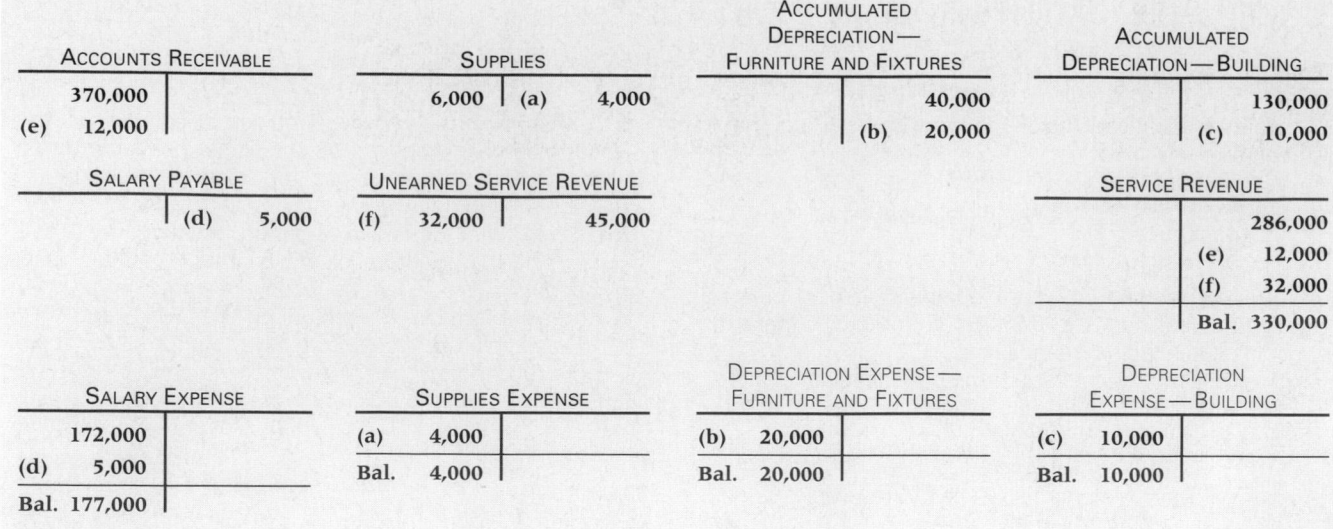

ACCOUNTS RECEIVABLE
370,000	
(e) 12,000	

SUPPLIES
6,000	(a) 4,000

ACCUMULATED DEPRECIATION— FURNITURE AND FIXTURES
	40,000
(b)	20,000

ACCUMULATED DEPRECIATION—BUILDING
	130,000
(c)	10,000

SALARY PAYABLE
	(d) 5,000

UNEARNED SERVICE REVENUE
(f) 32,000	45,000

SERVICE REVENUE
	286,000
(e)	12,000
(f)	32,000
	Bal. 330,000

SALARY EXPENSE
172,000	
(d) 5,000	
Bal. 177,000	

SUPPLIES EXPENSE
(a) 4,000	
Bal. 4,000	

DEPRECIATION EXPENSE— FURNITURE AND FIXTURES
(b) 20,000	
Bal. 20,000	

DEPRECIATION EXPENSE—BUILDING
(c) 10,000	
Bal. 10,000	

Requirement 2

Closing Entries

1. Dec. 31	Service Revenue	330,000	
	Income Summary		330,000
2.	31	Income Summary	224,000	
		Salary Expense		177,000
		Supplies Expense		4,000
		Depreciation Expense—Furniture and Fixtures........		20,000
		Depreciation Expense—Building...............................		10,000
		Miscellaneous Expense..		13,000
3.	31	Income Summary ($330,000 − $224,000)...........................	106,000	
		Capital		106,000
4.	31	Capital...	65,000	
		Withdrawals		65,000

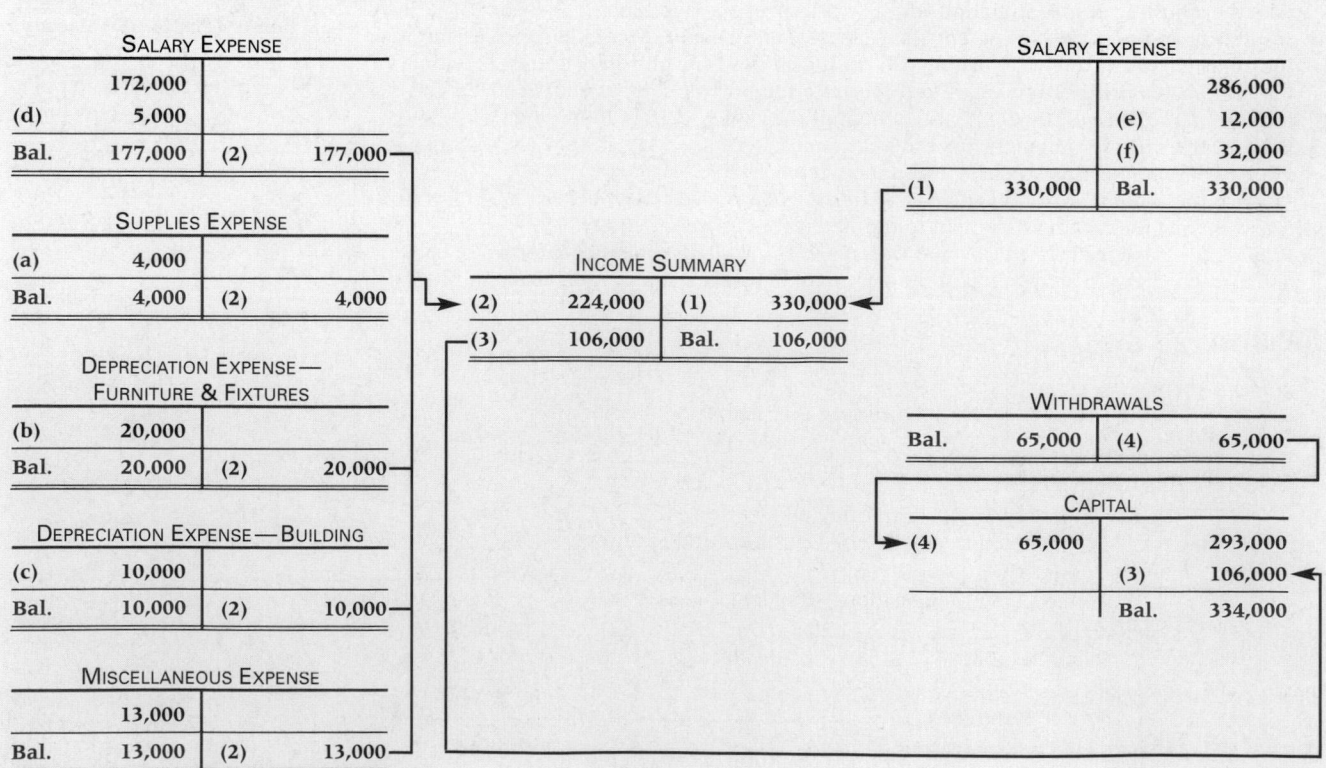

SALARY EXPENSE
172,000			
(d) 5,000			
Bal. 177,000	(2)	177,000	

SUPPLIES EXPENSE
(a) 4,000			
Bal. 4,000	(2)	4,000	

DEPRECIATION EXPENSE— FURNITURE & FIXTURES
(b) 20,000			
Bal. 20,000	(2)	20,000	

DEPRECIATION EXPENSE—BUILDING
(c) 10,000			
Bal. 10,000	(2)	10,000	

MISCELLANEOUS EXPENSE
13,000			
Bal. 13,000	(2)	13,000	

INCOME SUMMARY
(2) 224,000	(1)	330,000	
(3) 106,000	Bal.	106,000	

SALARY EXPENSE
		286,000	
	(e)	12,000	
	(f)	32,000	
(1) 330,000	Bal.	330,000	

WITHDRAWALS
Bal. 65,000	(4)	65,000	

CAPITAL
(4) 65,000		293,000	
	(3)	106,000	
	Bal.	334,000	

Requirement 3

STATE SERVICE COMPANY
Income Statement
Year Ended December 31, 20X1

Revenue:		
Service revenue		$330,000
Expenses:		
Salary expense	$177,000	
Depreciation expense—furniture and fixtures	20,000	
Depreciation expense—building	10,000	
Supplies expense	4,000	
Miscellaneous expense	13,000	
Total expenses		224,000
Net income		$106,000

Requirement 4

STATE SERVICE COMPANY
Statement of Owner's Equity
Year Ended December 31, 20X1

Capital, January 1, 20X1	$293,000
Add: Net income	106,000
	399,000
Less: Withdrawals	(65,000)
Capital, December 31, 20X1	$334,000

Requirement 5

STATE SERVICE COMPANY
Balance Sheet
December 31, 20X1

Assets

Current assets:		
Cash		$198,000
Accounts receivable		382,000
Supplies		2,000
Total current assets		582,000
Long-term assets:		
Furniture and fixtures	$100,000	
Less: Accumulated depreciation.	(60,000)	40,000
Building	$250,000	
Less: Accumulated depreciation.	(140,000)	110,000
Total assets		$732,000

Liabilities

Current liabilities:		
Accounts payable		$380,000
Salary payable		5,000
Unearned service revenue		13,000
Total current liabilities		398,000

Owner's Equity

Capital		334,000
Total liabilities and owner's equity....		$732,000

LESSONS LEARNED

1. **Prepare an accounting work sheet.** The *accounting cycle* is the process by which accountants produce the financial statements for a specific period of time. The cycle starts with the beginning account balances. During the period, the business journalizes transactions and posts them to the ledger accounts. At the end of the period, the trial balance is prepared, and the accounts are adjusted in order to measure the period's net income or net loss. A *work sheet* summarizes the effects of all the period's activity.

2. **Use the work sheet to complete the accounting cycle.** The work sheet is a convenient device for completing the accounting cycle. It has columns for the trial balance, the adjustments, the adjusted trial balance, the income statement, and the balance sheet. It aids the adjusting process, and it is the place where the period's net income or net loss is first computed. The work sheet also provides the data for the financial statements and the *closing entries*. However, the accounting cycle can also be completed from the less elaborate adjusted trial balance.

3. **Close the revenue, expense, and withdrawal accounts.** Revenues, expenses, and withdrawals represent increases and decreases in owner's equity for a specific period. At the end of the period, their balances are closed out to zero. For this reason, they are called *temporary accounts*. Assets, liabil-

ities, and capital are not closed because they are the *permanent accounts*. Their balances at the end of one period become the beginning balances of the next period. The final accuracy check of the period is the *postclosing trial balance*.

4. **Classify assets and liabilities as current or long-term.** The balance sheet reports *current* and *long-term assets* and *current* and *long-term liabilities*. It can be presented in *report format* or *account format*.

5. **Use the current and debt ratios to evaluate a business's ability to pay its debts.** Two decision-making aids are the *current ratio* (total current assets divided by total current liabilities) and the *debt ratio* (total liabilities divided by total assets).

ACCOUNTING VOCABULARY

accounting cycle (p. 127)
closing the accounts (p. 134)
closing entries (p. 135)
current asset (p. 138)
current liability (p. 139)
current ratio (p. 141)
debt ratio (p. 142)
fixed asset (p. 139)

Income Summary (p. 136)
intangible assets (p. 141)
liquidity (p. 138)
long-term asset (p. 139)
long-term liability (p. 139)
nominal account (p. 135)
operating cycle (p. 139)

permanent account (p. 135)
plant asset (p. 139)
postclosing trial balance (p. 138)
real account (p. 135)
reversing entry (p. 138)
temporary account (p. 135)
work sheet (p. 128)

QUESTIONS

1. Identify the steps in the accounting cycle. Distinguish those that occur during the period from those that are performed at the end.
2. Why is the work sheet a valuable accounting tool?
3. Why must the adjusting entries be journalized and posted if they have already been entered on the work sheet?
4. Which types of accounts are closed?
5. What purpose is served by closing the accounts?
6. Distinguish between permanent accounts and temporary accounts; indicate which type is closed at the end of the period. Give five examples of each type of account.
7. Is Income Summary a permanent account or a temporary account? When and how is it used?
8. Give the closing entries for the following accounts (balances in parentheses): Service Revenue ($5,900); Salary Expense ($1,100); Income Summary (credit balance of $2,000); Asa Warner, Withdrawals ($2,300).
9. Why are assets classified as current or long-term? On what basis are they classified? Where do the classified amounts appear?

10. Indicate which of the following accounts are current assets and which are long-term assets: Prepaid Rent, Building, Furniture, Accounts Receivable, Merchandise Inventory, Cash, Note Receivable (due within one year), Note Receivable (due after one year).
11. In what order are assets and liabilities listed on the balance sheet?
12. Identify an outside party that would be interested in whether a liability is current or long-term. Why would this party be interested in this information?
13. A friend tells you that the difference between a current liability and a long-term liability is that the two types are payable to different types of creditors. Is your friend correct? Define these two categories of liabilities.
14. Show how to compute the current ratio and the debt ratio. Indicate what ability each ratio measures, and state whether a high value or a low value is safer for each.

ASSESS YOUR PROGRESS

DAILY EXERCISES

Explaining items on the work sheet
(Obj. 1)

DE4-1 ◄ *Link Back to Chapter 3 (Adjusting Entries).* Return to the trial balance in Exhibit 4-2, on the acetate between pages 130 and 131. In your own words, explain why at April 30 the following accounts must be adjusted:

a. Supplies
b. Prepaid rent
c. Accumulated depreciation
d. Salary payable
e. Unearned service revenue

Explain why these accounts do *not* need to be adjusted at April 30:

f. Cash
g. Furniture

Explaining items on the work sheet (Obj. 1, 2)

DE4-2 ◄ *Link Back to Chapters 1, 2, and 3 (Definitions of Accounts).* Examine the Adjusted Trial Balance columns of Exhibit 4-4, on the acetate between pages 130 and 131. Explain what the following items mean at April 30:

a. Accounts receivable
b. Supplies
c. Prepaid rent
d. Furniture
e. Accumulated depreciation

f. Accounts payable
g. Unearned service revenue
h. Service revenue
i. Rent expense

DE4-3 Study the completed work sheet (Exhibit 4-6) on the acetates between pages 130 and 131. How is the work sheet in Exhibit 4-2 similar to the adjusted trial balance in Chapter 3? How does the work sheet differ from the adjusted trial balance of Chapter 3 (Exhibit 3-10, page 99)?

Comparing the work sheet and the adjusted trial balance (Obj. 1, 2)

DE4-4 Consider the Income Statement columns and the Balance Sheet columns of the work sheet in Exhibit 4-6, on the acetates between pages 130 and 131. Answer the following questions:

Using the work sheet and closing entries (Obj. 2, 3)

1. What balance does the Owner's Capital account have—debit or credit?
2. Which Income Statement account has the same type of balance as the Capital account?
3. Which Income Statement accounts have the opposite type of balance?
4. What do we call the difference between the total dollar amounts in the debit and credit columns of the Income Statement? Into what account is the difference figure closed?

DE4-5 Examine Exhibits 4-2 and 4-4 on the acetates between pages 130 and 131. Answer this question about closing entries:

Identifying accounts that need to be closed (Obj. 3)

Exhibit 4-2, the (unadjusted) Trial Balance, lists all the accounts of the business entity Gay Gillen eTravel. Draw a horizontal line to separate the accounts that do *not* get closed out at the end of the period from those accounts that *do* get closed out. Identify the categories of accounts that *do* and do *not* get closed (assets, liabilities, and so on).

DE4-6 Study Exhibit 4-5 on the acetates between pages 130 and 131.

Making closing entries (Obj. 3)

1. Journalize the closing entries for
   a. Owner's withdrawals
   b. Service revenue
   c. All the expenses (make a single closing entry for all the expenses)
   d. Income Summary
2. Set up all the T-accounts affected by requirement 1 and insert their adjusted balances (denote as *Bal.*) at April 30. Also set up a T-account for Income Summary. Post the closing entries to the accounts, denoting posted amounts as *Clo.*
3. What is the ending balance of
   a. Gay Gillen, Capital?
   b. All the other accounts for which you set up T-accounts?

DE4-7 This exercise should be used in conjunction with Daily Exercise 4-6.

Analyzing the overall effect of the closing entries on the owner's capital account (Obj. 3)

1. Return to Exhibit 4-5 on the acetates between pages 130 and 131. Without making any closing entries or using any T-accounts, compute the ending balance of Gay Gillen, Capital.
2. Trace Gay Gillen's ending capital balance to its two appropriate places in Exhibit 4-7 (page 134). In which financial statements do you find Gay Gillen, Capital? Where on each statement?

DE4-8 Oracle Corporation, the world's second largest software company, reported the following items adapted from its financial statements at May 31, 1999 (amounts in millions):

Making closing entries (Obj. 3)

Cash	$1,786	Sales and marketing expense	$2,622
Service revenue	5,139	Other assets	477
Accounts payable	284	Interest expense	21
Accounts receivable	2,238	Long-term liabilities	382

Make Oracle's closing entries, as needed, for these accounts.

DE4-9 This exercise should be used in conjunction with Daily Exercise 4-8. Use the data in Daily Exercise 4-8 to set up T-accounts for those accounts that **Oracle Corporation** closed out at May 31, 1999. Insert these account balances prior to closing, post the closing entries to these accounts, and show each account's final balance after closing. Denote a balance as *Bal.* and a closing entry amount as *Clo.* For posting to the T-accounts, you may ignore the Income Summary account.

Posting closing entries (Obj. 3)

DE4-10 After closing its accounts at May 31, 1999, **Oracle Corporation** had the following account balances (adapted) with amounts given in millions:

Preparing a postclosing trial balance (Obj. 3)

Property	$ 988	Long-term liabilities	$ 518
Cash	1,786	Other assets	825
Service revenue	0	Accounts receivable	2,479
Owners' equity	3,695	Total expenses	0
Other current assets	1,182	Accounts payable	284
Short-term notes payable	4	Other current liabilities	2,759

Prepare Oracle's postclosing trial balance at May 31, 1999. List accounts in proper order, as shown in Exhibit 4-10, page 138.

Classifying assets and liabilities as current or long-term (Obj. 4)

DE4-11 Lands' End had sales of $1,320 million during the year ended January 31, 2000, and total assets of $456 million at January 31, 2000, the end of the company's fiscal year. The financial statements of Lands' End reported the following (amounts in millions):

Land and buildings	$ 103	Sales revenue	$1,320
Accounts payable	75	Inventory	162
Total expenses	1,073	Receivables	18
Accumulated depreciation	117	Interest expense	2
Accrued liabilities (such as		Equipment	176
Salary payable)	44	Prepaid expenses	22

1. Identify the assets (including contra assets) and liabilities.
2. Classify each asset and each liability as current or long-term.

Classifying assets and liabilities as current or long-term (Obj. 4)

DE4-12 ◄ *Link Back to Chapter 3 (Book Value).* Examine **PepsiCo's** balance sheet in Exhibit 4-12 on page 140. Identify or compute the following amounts for PepsiCo at December 31, 1999.

a. Total current assets
b. Total current liabilities
c. Book value of Property, Plant, and Equipment
d. Total long-term assets
e. Total long-term liabilities

Computing and using the current ratio and the debt ratio (Obj. 5)

DE4-13 This exercise should be used in conjunction with Daily Exercise 4-10. Use the postclosing trial balance that you prepared for Daily Exercise 4-10 to compute **Oracle Corporation's** current ratio and debt ratio.

1. How much in *current* assets does Oracle have for every dollar of *current* liabilities that it owes?
2. What percentage of Oracle's total assets are financed with debt?
3. What percentage of Oracle's total assets do the owners of the company actually own free and clear of debt?

Computing and evaluating the current ratio and the debt ratio (Obj. 5)

DE4-14 Use Gay Gillen eTravel's classified balance sheet in Exhibit 4-11, page 139, to compute the current ratio and the debt ratio of Gillen's business at April 30.

1. How do Gillen's ratios compare to those of **PepsiCo,** which are presented in the Work It Out feature on page 142 and the Think It Over feature on pages 142–143? Based solely on these ratios, which business looks stronger? Why?
2. Do these two ratios tell the complete story of a company's financial position? What other factors should a lender consider in evaluating a business's ability to pay its debts?

EXERCISES

Preparing a work sheet (Obj. 1)

E4-1 The trial balance of Pfeiffer Pack-n-Mail Service follows at the top of the next page.

Additional information at September 30, 20X6:

a. Accrued service revenue, $600.
b. Depreciation, $40.
c. Accrued salary expense, $500.
d. Prepaid rent expired, $800.
e. Supplies used, $1,650

Required

Complete Pfeiffer's work sheet for September 20X6. How much was net income for September?

Journalizing adjusting and closing entries (Obj. 2, 3)

E4-2 Journalize the adjusting and closing entries in Exercise 4-1.

Posting adjusting and closing entries (Obj. 2, 3)

E4-3 Set up T-accounts for those accounts affected by the adjusting and closing entries in Exercise 4-1. Post the adjusting and closing entries to the accounts; denote adjustment amounts by *Adj.,* closing amounts by *Clo.,* and balances by *Bal.* Double underline the accounts with zero balances after you close them, and show the ending balance in each account.

PFEIFFER PACK-N-MAIL SERVICE
Trial Balance
September 30, 20X6

Cash	$ 3,560	
Accounts receivable	3,440	
Prepaid rent	1,200	
Supplies	3,390	
Equipment	32,600	
Accumulated depreciation		$ 1,840
Accounts payable		3,600
Salary payable		
Gail Pfeiffer, capital		36,030
Gail Pfeiffer, withdrawals	2,000	
Service revenue		7,300
Depreciation expense		
Salary expense	1,800	
Rent expense		
Utilities expense	780	
Supplies expense		
Total	$48,770	$48,770

Preparing a postclosing trial balance   *(Obj. 2, 3)*

E4-4 After completing Exercises 4-1, 4-2, and 4-3, prepare the postclosing trial balance in Exercise 4-1.

E4-5 ← *Link Back to Chapter 2 (Adjusting Entries).* TelSurf accounting records include the following account balances:

Adjusting and closing the accounts
(Obj. 2, 3)

	December 31,	
	20X1	**20X2**
Prepaid insurance	$1,400	$1,600
Unearned service revenue	4,100	3,700

During 20X2, TelSurf recorded these transactions and adjusting entries:

a. Collected $17,000 cash in advance for service revenue to be earned later.
b. Made the year-end adjustment to record the earning of $17,400 service revenue that had been collected in advance.
c. Paid the annual insurance premium of $4,400.
d. Made the year-end adjustment to record insurance expense for the year. You must compute this amount.

Required

1. Set up T-accounts for Prepaid Insurance, Insurance Expense, Unearned Service Revenue, and Service Revenue. Insert beginning and ending balances for Prepaid Insurance and Unearned Service Revenue.
2. Journalize entries a–d above, and post to the T-accounts. Explanations are not required. Ensure that the ending balances for Prepaid Insurance and Unearned Service Revenue agree with the December 31, 20X2, balances given here for those accounts.
3. Make the closing entries for the above accounts, as needed. Post to the accounts to bring their balances to zero. You need not post to the Income Summary account.

E4-6 From the following selected accounts of Hyundai Energy at June 30, 20X4, prepare the entity's closing entries:

Identifying and journalizing entries
(Obj. 3)

Liu Hyundai, capital	$ 21,600	Interest expense	$ 2,200
Service revenue	101,100	Accounts receivable	14,000
Unearned revenues	1,350	Salary payable	850
Salary expense	12,500	Depreciation expense	10,200
Accumulated depreciation	35,000	Rent expense	5,900
Supplies expense	1,700	Liu Hyundai, withdrawals	40,000
Interest revenue	700	Supplies	1,400

What is Hyundai's ending capital balance at June 30, 20X4?

E4-7 The accountant for MissouriOne.com has posted adjusting entries (a) through (e) to the following selected accounts at December 31, 20X8. All the revenue, expense, and owner's equity accounts—plus a few of the assets and liabilities—of the entity are listed here in T-account form.

ACCOUNTS RECEIVABLE		SUPPLIES		ACCUMULATED DEPRECIATION—FURNITURE		ACCUMULATED DEPRECIATION—BUILDING	
126,000		4,000 │ (b) 2,000			5,000		33,000
(a) 9,500					(c) 1,100		(d) 6,000

SALARY PAYABLE		FELIX ROHR, CAPITAL		FELIX ROHR, WITHDRAWALS		SERVICE REVENUE	
	(e) 700		52,400	61,400			211,000
							(a) 9,500

SALARY EXPENSE		SUPPLIES EXPENSE		DEPRECIATION EXPENSE—FURNITURE		DEPRECIATION EXPENSE—BUILDING	
26,000		(b) 2,000		(c) 1,100		(d) 6,000	
(e) 700							

Required

1. Journalize MissouriOne.com's closing entries at December 31, 20X8.
2. Determine Felix Rohr's ending capital balance at December 31, 20X8.

E4-8 From the following accounts of Lubricon Chemical Company, prepare the entity's statement of owner's equity for the year ended December 31, 20X2.

MATTHEW KNOWLES, CAPITAL		MATTHEW KNOWLES, WITHDRAWALS		INCOME SUMMARY	
Dec. 31 142,000	Jan. 1 436,000	Mar. 31 39,000 │ Dec. 31 142,000		Dec. 31 285,000 │ Dec. 31 428,000	
	Mar. 9 28,000	Jun. 30 27,000		Dec. 31 143,000	
	Dec. 31 143,000	Sep. 30 39,000			
		Dec. 31 37,000			

E4-9 The trial balance and income statement amounts from the April work sheet of H.B. Fuller Polling Company follow:

Account Title	Unadjusted Trial Balance		Income Statement	
Cash	$ 5,200			
Supplies	2,400			
Prepaid rent	1,100			
Computer equipment	51,100			
Accumulated depreciation		$ 6,200		
Accounts payable		4,600		
Salary payable				
Unearned service revenue		4,400		
Long-term note payable		10,000		
H.B. Fuller, capital		25,800		
H.B. Fuller, withdrawals	1,000			
Service revenue		14,800		$19,100
Salary expense	3,000		$ 3,800	
Rent expense	1,200		1,400	
Depreciation expense			300	
Supplies expense			400	
Utilities expense	800		800	
	$65,800	$65,800	6,700	19,100
Net income or net loss			?	
			$19,100	$19,100

Required

1. Journalize the adjusting and closing entries of H.B. Fuller Polling Company at April 30.
2. How much net income or net loss did Fuller have for April? How can you tell?

E4-10 Refer to Exercise 4-9.

Preparing a classified balance sheet
(Obj. 4, 5)

Required

1. After solving Exercise 4-9, use the data in that exercise to prepare the classified balance sheet of H.B. Fuller Polling Company at April 30 of the current year. Use the report format.
2. Compute Fuller Polling's current ratio and debt ratio at April 30. One year ago, the current ratio was 1.20 and the debt ratio was 0.30. Indicate whether Fuller's ability to pay its debts has improved or deteriorated or hasn't changed much during the current year.

Continuing Exercise. *This exercise continues the Amos Faraday, Consultant, situation begun in Exercise 2-15 of Chapter 2 and continued in Exercise 3-14 of Chapter 3.*

E4-11 Refer to Exercise 3-14 of Chapter 3. Start from the posted T-accounts and the adjusted trial balance that Amos Faraday, Consultant, prepared for his business at December 31:

Closing the books, preparing a classified balance sheet, and evaluating a business
(Obj. 3, 4, 5)

AMOS FARADAY, CONSULTANT
Adjusted Trial Balance
December 31, 20XX

Account	Adjusted Trial Balance	
	Debit	Credit
Cash	$11,700	
Accounts receivable	1,500	
Supplies	100	
Equipment	2,000	
Accumulated depr.—equipment		$ 50
Furniture	3,600	
Accumulated depr.—furniture		60
Accounts payable		3,600
Salary payable		500
Unearned service revenue		600
Amos Faraday, capital		14,000
Amos Faraday, withdrawals	1,600	
Service revenue		3,200
Rent expense	500	
Utilities expense	200	
Salary expense	500	
Depreciation expense—equipment	50	
Depreciation expense—furniture	60	
Supplies expense	200	
Total	$22,010	$22,010

Required

1. Journalize and post the closing entries at December 31. Denote each closing amount as *Clo.* and an account balance as *Bal.*
2. Prepare a classified balance sheet at December 31.
3. If your instructor assigns it, complete the accounting work sheet at December 31.

Challenge Exercise

E4-12 Data for the unadjusted trial balance of Links Resorts at December 31, 20X2, follow:

Computing financial statement amounts
(Obj. 2, 4)

Cash	$ 3,000	Horst Schulz, capital	$49,100
Other current assets	9,400	Horst Schulz, withdrawals	51,800
Property, plant, and equipment	66,200	Service revenue	93,600
Accumulated depreciation	21,800	Salary expense	42,700
Accounts payable	6,100	Depreciation expense	
Salary payable		Supplies expense	
Unearned service revenue	5,300	Insurance expense	
		Utilities expense	2,800

Adjusting data at the end of the year include the following:

a. Unearned service revenue that has been earned, $3,600.
b. Accrued service revenue, $8,100
c. Supplies used in operations, $600.

d. Accrued salary expense, $1,400.
e. Insurance expense, $1,800.
f. Depreciation expense, $2,900.

Horst Schulz, the owner, has received an offer to sell the company. He needs to know the following information within one hour: Net income for the year covered by these data.

Required

Without opening any accounts, making any journal entries, or using a work sheet, provide Schulz with the requested information. Prepare an income statement, and show all computations.

(Group A) PROBLEMS

Preparing a work sheet (Obj. 1)

P4-1A The trial balance of Cohen Construction Co. at June 30, 20X3, follows.

COHEN CONSTRUCTION CO. Trial Balance June 30, 20X3		
Cash..	$ 21,200	
Accounts receivable............................	37,820	
Supplies...	17,660	
Prepaid insurance..............................	2,300	
Equipment...	32,690	
Accumulated depreciation—equipment		$ 26,240
Building..	42,890	
Accumulated depreciation—building....		10,500
Land...	28,300	
Accounts payable		22,690
Interest payable		
Wages payable		
Unearned service revenue....................		10,560
Note payable, long-term......................		22,400
Lynn Cohen, capital		79,130
Lynn Cohen, withdrawals	4,200	
Service revenue..................................		20,190
Depreciation expense—equipment		
Depreciation expense—building...........		
Wage expense....................................	3,200	
Insurance expense..............................		
Interest expense		
Utilities expense	1,110	
Advertising expense	340	
Supplies expense		
Total...	$191,710	$191,710

Additional data at June 30, 20X3:

a. Depreciation: equipment, $630; building, $370.
b. Accrued wage expense, $240.
c. Supplies on hand, $14,370
d. Prepaid insurance expired during June, $500.

e. Accrued interest expense, $180.
f. Unearned service revenue earned during June, $4,970.
g. Accrued advertising expense, $100 (credit Accounts Payable).
h. Accrued service revenue, $1,100.

Required

Complete Cohen Construction's work sheet for June. Key adjusting entries by letter.

P4-2A The *adjusted* trial balance of Gallo Shipping & Handling at June 30, 20X9, after all adjustments, follows.

Preparing financial statements
from an adjusted trial balance;
journalizing the adjusting and
closing entries
(Obj. 2, 3, 5)

GALLO SHIPPING & HANDLING
Adjusted Trial Balance
June 30, 20X9

Cash	$ 12,350	
Accounts receivable	26,470	
Supplies	31,290	
Prepaid insurance	3,200	
Equipment	135,800	
Accumulated depreciation—equipment		$ 16,480
Building	34,900	
Accumulated depreciation—building		16,850
Land	30,000	
Accounts payable		38,400
Interest payable		1,490
Wages payable		770
Unearned service revenue		2,300
Note payable, long-term		97,000
Linda Gallo, capital		58,390
Linda Gallo, withdrawals	45,300	
Service revenue		139,860
Depreciation expense—equipment	7,300	
Depreciation expense—building	3,970	
Wage expense	21,470	
Insurance expense	3,100	
Interest expense	8,510	
Utilities expense	4,300	
Supplies expense	3,580	
Total	$371,540	$371,540

Adjusting data at June 30, 20X9, which have all been incorporated into the *adjusted* trial balance figures:

a. Prepaid insurance expired during the year, $2,200.
b. Accrued interest expense, $540.
c. Accrued service revenue, $940.
d. Unearned service revenue earned during the year, $7,790.
e. Accrued wage expense, $770.
f. Depreciation for the year: equipment, $7,300; building, $3,970.
g. Supplies used during the year, $3,580.

Required

1. Journalize the adjusting entries that would lead to the adjusted trial balance shown here. Also journalize the closing entries.
2. Prepare Gallo's income statement and statement of owner's equity for the year ended June 30, 20X9, and the classified balance sheet on that date. Use the account format for the balance sheet.
3. Compute Gallo's current ratio and debt ratio at June 30, 20X9. One year ago, the current ratio stood at 1.41 and the debt ratio was 0.71. Did Gallo's ability to pay debts improve or deteriorate during fiscal year 20X9?

P4-3A The unadjusted T-accounts of Fidelity Sound Studio, at December 31, 20X2, and the related year-end adjustment data follow at the top of the next page.

Taking the accounting cycle
through the closing entries
(Obj. 2, 3)

Adjustment data at December 31, 20X2:
a. Unearned service revenue earned during the year, $5,000.
b. Supplies on hand, $1,000.
c. Depreciation for the year, $9,000.
d. Accrued salary expense, $1,000.
e. Accrued service revenue, $2,000.

Required

1. Enter the trial balance on a work sheet, and complete the work sheet. Key each adjusting entry by the letter corresponding to the data given. List all the accounts, including those with zero balances. Leave a blank line under Service Revenue.
2. Prepare the income statement, the statement of owner's equity, and the classified balance sheet in account format.
3. Journalize the adjusting and closing entries.
4. Did Fidelity Sound Studio have a good or a bad year during 20X2? Give the reason for your answer.

T-Accounts

CASH		ACCOUNTS RECEIVABLE		SUPPLIES		EQUIPMENT	
Bal. 15,000		Bal. 36,000		Bal. 9,000		Bal. 99,000	

ACCUMULATED DEPRECIATION		ACCOUNTS PAYABLE		SALARY PAYABLE		UNEARNED SERVICE REVENUE	
	Bal. 13,000		Bal. 6,000				Bal. 5,000

NOTE PAYABLE, LONG-TERM				BETSY WILLIS, CAPITAL		BETSY WILLIS, WITHDRAWALS	
	Bal. 60,000				Bal. 36,000	Bal. 62,000	

SERVICE REVENUE				SALARY EXPENSE		SUPPLIES EXPENSE	
	Bal. 182,000			Bal. 53,000			

DEPRECIATION EXPENSE		INTEREST EXPENSE		RENT EXPENSE		INSURANCE EXPENSE	
		Bal. 6,000		Bal. 15,000		Bal. 7,000	

Completing the accounting cycle (Obj. 2, 3)

P4-4A This problem should be used in conjunction with Problem 4-3A. It completes the accounting cycle by posting to T-accounts and preparing the postclosing trial balance.

Required

1. Using the Problem 4-3A data, post the adjusting and closing entries to the T-accounts, denoting adjusting amounts by *Adj.,* closing amounts by *Clo.,* and account balances by *Bal.,* as shown in Exhibit 4-9. You must set up a T-account for Income Summary. Double underline all accounts with a zero ending balance.
2. Prepare the postclosing trial balance.

Completing the accounting cycle (Obj. 2, 3, 4)

P4-5A The trial balance of Allianz Publishing at August 31, 20X9, and the data needed for the month-end adjustments follow:

ALLIANZ PUBLISHING
Trial Balance
August 31, 20X9

Account Number	Account Title	Debit	Credit
11	Cash	$ 23,800	
12	Accounts receivable	15,560	
13	Prepaid rent	1,290	
14	Supplies	900	
15	Equipment	15,350	
16	Accumulated depreciation—equipment		$ 12,800
17	Building	89,900	
18	Accumulated depreciation—building		28,600
21	Accounts payable		4,240
22	Salary payable		
23	Unearned service revenue		8,900
31	Lou Kraft, capital		71,920
32	Lou Kraft, withdrawals	4,800	
41	Service revenue		27,300
51	Salary expense	1,100	
52	Rent expense		
53	Utilities expense	410	
54	Depreciation expense—equipment		
55	Depreciation expense—building		
56	Advertising expense	650	
57	Supplies expense		
	Total	$153,760	$153,760

Adjustment data:

a. Unearned commission revenue still unearned at August 31, $6,500.
b. Prepaid rent still in force at August 31, $1,050.
c. Supplies used during the month, $340.
d. Depreciation on equipment for the month, $370.
e. Depreciation on building for the month, $130.
f. Accrued salary expense at August 31, $460.

Required

1. Open the accounts listed in the trial balance and insert their August 31 unadjusted balances. Also open the Income Summary account, number 33. Use four-column accounts. Date the balances of the following accounts as of August 1: Prepaid Rent, Supplies, Equipment, Accumulated Depreciation—Equipment, Building, Accumulated Depreciation—Building, Unearned Service Revenue, and Lou Kraft, Capital.
2. Enter the trial balance on a work sheet and complete the work sheet of Allianz Publishing for the month ended August 31, 20X9. See the trial balance on page 156.
3. Prepare the income statement, the statement of owner's equity, and the classified balance sheet in report format.
4. Using the work sheet data that you prepare, journalize and post the adjusting and closing entries. Use dates and posting references. Use 7 as the number of the journal page.
5. Prepare a postclosing trial balance.

P4-6A The accounts of Martinez Political Consulting at December 31, 20X6, follow:

Preparing a classified balance sheet in report format (Obj. 4, 5)

Accounts payable	$ 5,100	Angel Martinez, capital,	
Accounts receivable	6,600	December 31, 20X5	$59,800
Accumulated depreciation—		Angel Martinez, withdrawals	50,400
building	37,800	Note payable, long-term	27,800
Accumulated depreciation—		Other assets	3,600
computers	11,600	Other current liabilities	4,700
Advertising expense	2,200	Prepaid insurance	1,100
Building	104,400	Prepaid rent	6,600
Cash	16,500	Salary expense	24,600
Service revenue	93,500	Salary payable	3,900
Computers	22,700	Supplies	2,500
Depreciation expense	1,300	Supplies expense	5,700
Insurance expense	800	Unearned service	
Interest payable	600	revenue	5,400
Interest expense	1,200		

Required

1. All adjustments have been journalized and posted, but the closing entries have not yet been made. Prepare the company's classified balance sheet in report format at December 31, 20X6. Show totals for total assets, total liabilities, and total liabilities and owner's equity.
2. Compute Martinez's current ratio and debt ratio at December 31, 20X6. At December 31, 20X5, the current ratio was 1.52 and the debt ratio was 0.39. Did Martinez's ability to pay debts improve or deteriorate during 20X6?

P4-7A ◄━ *Link Back to Chapter 2 (Accounting Errors).* The accountant for Liberty Landscaping encountered the following situations while adjusting and closing the books at December 31. Consider each situation independently.

Analyzing errors and journalizing adjusting and closing entries (Obj. 3)

a. A $500 credit to Accounts Receivable was posted as a debit.
   (1) At what stage of the accounting cycle will this error be detected?
   (2) Describe the technique for identifying the amount of the error.

b. The $16,000 balance of Equipment was entered as $1,600 on the trial balance.
   (1) What is the name of this type of error?
   (2) Assume that this is the only error in the trial balance. Which will be greater, the total debits or the total credits, and by how much?
   (3) How can this type of error be identified?

c. The accountant failed to make the following adjusting entries at December 31:
   (1) Accrued property tax expense, $200.
   (2) Supplies expense, $1,090.
   (3) Accrued interest revenue on a $50,000 note receivable, $1,650.
   (4) Depreciation of equipment, $400.
   (5) Earned service revenue that had been collected in advance, $1,100.
   Compute the overall net income effect of these omissions.

d. Record each of the adjusting entries identified in item c.

PROBLEMS

(Group B)

P4-1B The trial balance of Reneé Greenspan Productions at May 31, 20X2, follows at the top of the next page.

Preparing a work sheet (Obj. 1)

RENEÉ GREENSPAN PRODUCTIONS
Trial Balance
May 31, 20X2

Cash	$ 4,370	
Notes receivable	10,340	
Interest receivable		
Supplies	560	
Prepaid insurance	1,790	
Furniture	27,410	
Accumulated depreciation—furniture		$ 1,480
Building	53,900	
Accumulated depreciation—building		34,560
Land	18,700	
Accounts payable		14,730
Interest payable		
Salary payable		
Unearned service revenue		8,800
Note payable, long-term		18,700
Reneé Greenspan, capital		29,990
Reneé Greenspan, withdrawals	3,800	
Service revenue		16,970
Interest revenue		
Depreciation expense—furniture		
Depreciation expense—building		
Salary expense	2,170	
Insurance expense		
Interest expense		
Utilities expense	1,130	
Advertising expense	1,060	
Supplies expense		
Total	$125,230	$125,230

Additional data at May 31, 20X2:

a. Depreciation: furniture, $480; building, $460.
b. Accrued salary expense, $420.
c. Supplies on hand, $410.
d. Prepaid insurance expired during May, $390.
e. Accrued interest expense, $220.

f. Unearned service revenue earned during May, $4,400.
g. Accrued advertising expense, $60 (credit Accounts Payable).
h. Accrued interest revenue, $170.

Required

Complete Greenspan's work sheet for May. Key adjusting entries by letter.

Preparing financial statements from an adjusted trial balance; journalizing the adjusting and closing entries
(Obj. 2, 3, 5)

P4-2B The *adjusted* trial balance of Chase Webmaster Service at April 30, 20X2, after all adjustments, follows at the top of the next page. Adjusting data at April 30, 20X2, which have all been incorporated into the *adjusted* trial balance figures above, consist of

a. Accrued service revenue, $2,200.
b. Depreciation for the year: equipment, $6,900; building, $3,710.
c. Accrued wage expense, $830.
d. Unearned service revenue earned during the year, $4,180.

e. Supplies used during the year, $5,880.
f. Prepaid insurance expired during the year, $5,110.
g. Accrued interest expense, $1,280.

Required

1. Journalize the adjusting entries that would lead to the adjusted trial balance shown here. Also journalize the closing entries.
2. Prepare Chase's income statement and statement of owner's equity for the year ended April 30, 20X2, and the classified balance sheet on that date. Use the account format for the balance sheet.
3. Compute Chase's current ratio and debt ratio at April 30, 20X2. One year ago, the current ratio stood at 1.61 and the debt ratio was 0.72. Did Chase's ability to pay debts improve or deteriorate during fiscal year 20X2?

CHASE WEBMASTER SERVICE
Adjusted Trial Balance
April 30, 20X2

Cash	$ 14,570	
Accounts receivable	43,740	
Supplies	3,690	
Prepaid insurance	2,290	
Equipment	63,930	
Accumulated depreciation—equipment		$ 28,430
Building	74,330	
Accumulated depreciation—building		18,260
Land	20,000	
Accounts payable		19,550
Interest payable		2,280
Wages payable		830
Unearned service revenue		3,660
Note payable, long-term		69,900
Monica Chase, capital		77,140
Monica Chase, withdrawals	27,500	
Service revenue		98,550
Depreciation expense—equipment	6,900	
Depreciation expense—building	3,710	
Wage expense	32,810	
Insurance expense	5,110	
Interest expense	8,170	
Utilities expense	4,970	
Supplies expense	6,880	
Total	$318,600	$318,600

Taking the accounting cycle through the closing entries (Obj. 2, 3)

P4-3B The unadjusted T-accounts of Lisa Tenney, M.D., at December 31, 20X2, and the related year-end adjustment data follow.

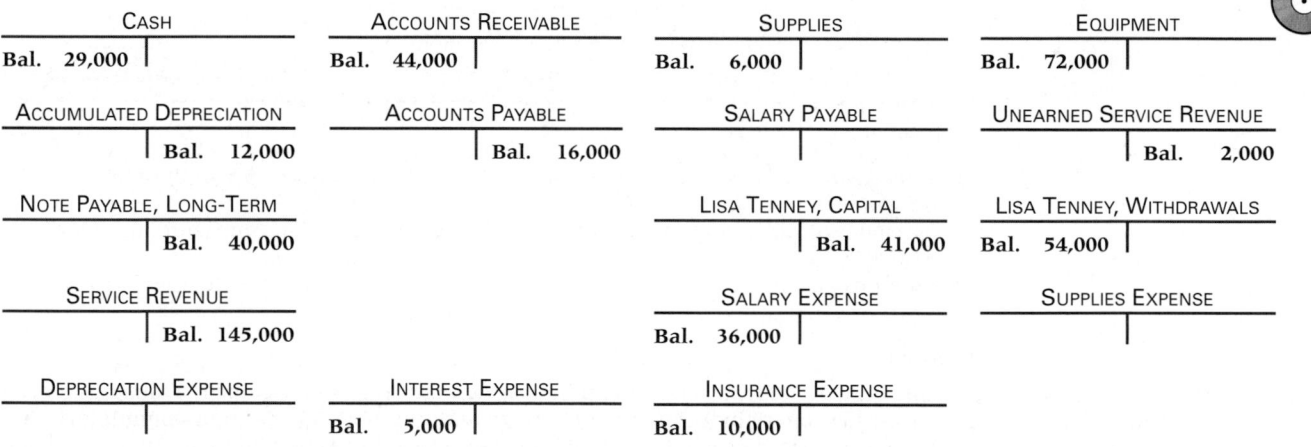

Adjustment data at December 31, 20X2:

a. Depreciation for the year, $5,000.
b. Supplies on hand, $2,000.
c. Accrued service revenue, $4,000.
d. Unearned service revenue earned during the year, $2,000.
e. Accrued salary expense, $4,000.

Required

1. Enter the trial balance on a work sheet, and complete the work sheet. Key each adjusting entry by the letter corresponding to the data given. List all the accounts, including those with zero balances. Leave a blank line under Service Revenue.
2. Prepare the income statement, the statement of owner's equity, and the classified balance sheet in account format.
3. Journalize the adjusting and closing entries.
4. Did Tenney have a good or a bad year during 20X2? Give the reason for your answer.

P4-4B This problem should be used in conjunction with Problem 4-3B. It completes the accounting cycle by posting to T-accounts and preparing the postclosing trial balance.

Completing the accounting cycle (Obj. 2, 3)

Required

1. Using the Problem 4-3B data, post the adjusting and closing entries to the T-accounts, denoting adjusting amounts by *Adj.*, closing amounts by *Clo.*, and account balances by *Bal.*, as shown in Exhibit 4-9. You must set up a T-account for Income Summary. Double underline all accounts with a zero ending balance.
2. Prepare the postclosing trial balance.

P4-5B The trial balance of Uniworld Language Services at October 31, 20X0, follows. The data needed for the month-end adjustments also follow.

	UNIWORLD LANGUAGE SERVICES Trial Balance October 31, 20X0		
Account Number	Account Title	Debit	Credit
11	Cash..	$ 4,900	
12	Accounts receivable..............................	15,310	
13	Prepaid rent...	2,200	
14	Supplies	840	
15	Equipment..	26,830	
16	Accumulated depreciation—equipment..		$ 3,400
17	Building..	68,300	
18	Accumulated depreciation—building......		12,100
21	Accounts payable		7,290
22	Salary payable		
23	Unearned service revenue.....................		5,300
31	Chris Stott, capital		84,490
32	Chris Stott, withdrawals........................	3,900	
41	Service revenue....................................		12,560
51	Salary expense......................................	1,840	
52	Rent expense...		
53	Utilities expense	1,020	
54	Depreciation expense—equipment		
55	Depreciation expense—building..............		
56	Supplies expense		
	Total...	$125,140	$125,140

Adjusting data:

a. Unearned service revenue still unearned at October 31, $800.
b. Prepaid rent still in force at October 31, $2,000.
c. Supplies used during the month, $770.
d. Depreciation on equipment for the month, $250.
e. Depreciation on building for the month, $580.
f. Accrued salary expense at October 31, $310.

Required

1. Open the accounts listed in the trial balance, inserting their October 31 unadjusted balances. Also open the Income Summary account, number 33. Use four-column accounts. Date the balances of the following accounts October 1: Prepaid Rent, Supplies, Equipment, Accumulated Depreciation—Equipment, Building, Accumulated Depreciation—Building, Unearned Service Revenue, and Chris Stott, Capital.
2. Enter the trial balance on a work sheet and complete the work sheet of Uniworld Language Services for the month ended October 31, 20X0.
3. Prepare the income statement, the statement of owner's equity, and the classified balance sheet in report format.
4. Using the work sheet data that you prepare, journalize and post the adjusting and closing entries. Use dates and posting references. Use 12 as the number of the journal page.
5. Prepare a postclosing trial balance.

P4-6B The accounts of Justin Leonard, Architect, at December 31, 20X3, are listed on the following page:

Required

1. All adjustments have been journalized and posted, but the closing entries have not yet been made. Prepare the company's classified balance sheet in report format at December 31, 20X3. Show totals for total assets, total liabilities, and total liabilities and owner's equity.

Accounts payable	$34,700	Insurance expense	$ 600
Accounts receivable	41,500	Interest payable	300
Accumulated depreciation—		Interest receivable	900
building	47,300	Note payable, long-term	3,200
Accumulated depreciation—		Note receivable, long-term	6,900
equipment	7,700	Other assets	2,300
Advertising expense	900	Other current liabilities	1,100
Building	55,900	Prepaid insurance	600
Cash	3,400	Prepaid rent	4,700
Depreciation expense	1,900	Salary expense	17,800
Justin Leonard, capital,		Salary payable	2,400
December 31, 20X2	50,700	Service revenue	71,100
Justin Leonard,		Supplies	3,800
withdrawals	31,200	Supplies expense	4,600
Equipment	43,200	Unearned service revenue	1,700

2. Compute Leonard's current ratio and debt ratio at December 31, 20X3. At December 31, 20X2, the current ratio was 1.28 and debt ratio was 0.42. Did Leonard's ability to pay debts improve, deteriorate, or change very little during 20X3?

P4-7B ◂ *Link Back to Chapter 2 (Accounting Errors).* The accountant of Iowa Packing Company encountered the following situations while adjusting and closing the books at February 28. Consider each situation independently.

Analyzing errors and journalizing adjusting and closing entries (Obj. 3)

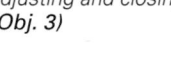

a. A $1,400 debit to Supplies was posted as $4,100.
   (1) At what stage of the accounting cycle will this error be detected?
   (2) What is the name of this type of error? Explain how to identify the error.
b. The $1,300 balance of Computer Software was entered as $13,000 on the trial balance.
   (1) What is the name of this type of error?
   (2) Assume that this is the only error in the trial balance. Which will be greater, the total debits or the total credits, and by how much?
   (3) How can this type of error be identified?
c. The accountant failed to make the following adjusting entries at February 28:
   (1) Depreciation of equipment, $700.
   (2) Earned service revenue that had been collected in advance, $2,700.
   (3) Accrued service revenue, $1,400.
   (4) Insurance expense, $360.
   (5) Accrued interest expense on a note payable, $520.
   Compute the overall net income effect of these omissions.
d. Record each of the adjusting entries identified in item c.

APPLY YOUR KNOWLEDGE

DECISION CASES

Case 1. One year ago, Alex Fleming founded Jack-of-All-Trades Job Search, and the business has prospered. Fleming comes to you for advice. He wishes to know how much net income his business earned during the past year. He also wants to know what the entity's total assets, liabilities, and capital are. The accounting records consist of the T-accounts in the ledger, which were prepared by an accountant who has moved. The ledger at December 31 appears at the top of the next page.

Completing the accounting cycle to develop the information for a bank loan (Obj. 3, 4)

Fleming indicates that at year end customers owe him $1,600 accrued service revenue, which he expects to collect early next year. These revenues have not been recorded. During the year, he collected $4,130 service revenue in advance from customers, but the business has earned only $2,500 of that amount. Rent expense for the year was $2,400, and he used up $2,100 of the supplies. Fleming estimates that depreciation on equipment was $5,900 for the year. At December 31, he owes his employee $1,200 accrued salary.

Fleming expresses concern that his withdrawals during the year might have exceeded the business's net income. To get a loan to expand the business, Fleming must show the bank that his capital account has grown from its original $25,000 balance. Has it? You and Fleming agree that you will meet again in one week.

Required

Prepare the work sheet and the financial statements to answer Fleming's questions.

CASH		ACCOUNTS RECEIVABLE		PREPAID RENT		SUPPLIES	
Dec. 31 5,830		Dec. 31 12,360		Jan. 2 2,800		Jan. 2 2,600	

EQUIPMENT		ACCUMULATED DEPRECIATION				ACCOUNTS PAYABLE	
Jan. 2 43,600							Dec. 31 18,540

SALARY PAYABLE		UNEARNED SERVICE REVENUE		ALEX FLEMING, CAPITAL		ALEX FLEMING, WITHDRAWALS	
			Dec. 31 4,130		Jan. 2 25,000	Dec. 31 43,420	

SERVICE REVENUE				SALARY EXPENSE		DEPRECIATION EXPENSE	
	Dec. 31 80,740			Dec. 31 17,000			

RENT EXPENSE		UTILITIES EXPENSE		SUPPLIES EXPENSE	
		Dec. 31 800			

Finding an error in the work sheet
(Obj. 1)

Case 2. You are preparing the financial statements for the year ended October 31, 20X5, for Zadell Software Company.

- You began with the trial balance of the ledger, which balanced, and then made the required adjusting entries.
- To save time, you omitted preparing an adjusted trial balance.
- After making the adjustments on the work sheet, you extended the balances from the trial balance, adjusted for the adjusting entries, and computed amounts for the income statement and the balance sheet columns.

Required

a. When you added the total debits and the total credits on the income statement, you found that the credits exceeded the debits by $45,000. Did the business have a profit or a loss?

b. You took the balancing amount from the income statement columns to the debit column of the balance sheet and found that the total debits exceeded the total credits in the balance sheet. The difference between the total debits and the total credits on the balance sheet is $90,000. What is the cause of this difference? (Except for these errors, everything else is correct.)

ETHICAL ISSUE

◄ *Link Back to Chapter 3 (Revenue Principle).* Forbes Painting Company wishes to expand and has borrowed $2 million. As a condition for making this loan, the bank requires that Forbes maintain a current ratio of at least 1.50.

Business has been good but not great. Expansion costs have brought the current ratio down to 1.40 at December 15. Jacob Forbes, owner of the company, is considering what might happen if the business reports a current ratio of 1.40 to the bank. One course of action for Forbes is to record in December some revenue that the business will earn in January of next year. The contract for this job has been signed.

Required

1. Journalize the revenue transaction, and indicate how recording this revenue in December would affect the current ratio.
2. State whether it is ethical to record the revenue transaction in December. Identify the accounting principle relevant to this situation.
3. Propose a course of action that is ethical for Forbes.

FINANCIAL STATEMENT CASE

Using a balance sheet
(Obj. 4, 5)

This problem, based on the balance sheet of **Target Corporation** in Appendix A, will familiarize you with some of the assets and liabilities of that company. Use the Target balance sheet to answer the following questions.

Required

1. Which balance sheet format does Target Corporation use?
2. Name the company's largest current asset and largest current liability at January 29, 2000.
3. Compute Target's current ratios and debt ratios at January 30, 1999, and at January 29, 2000. Target treats Convertible Preferred Stock as a liability. Did the ratio values improve, worsen, or hold steady during the fiscal year ended January 29, 2000? Refer to the income statement to explain your evaluation of the ratio values.
4. Under what category does Target report land, buildings, fixtures, and equipment?
5. What was the cost of the company's plant assets at January 29, 2000? What was the amount of accumulated depreciation? What was the book value of the plant assets?

TEAM PROJECT

Doug Maltbee formed a lawn service business as a summer job. To start the business on May 1, he deposited $1,000 in a new bank account in the name of the proprietorship. The $1,000 consisted of a $600 loan from his father and $400 of his own money. Doug rented lawn equipment, purchased supplies, and hired fellow students to mow and trim his customer's lawns.

At the end of each month, Doug mailed bills to his customers. On August 31, he was ready to dissolve the business and return to Louisiana State University for the fall semester. Because he was so busy, he kept few records other than his checkbook and a list of amounts owed to him by customers.

At August 31, Doug's checkbook shows a balance of $690, and his customers still owe him $500. During the summer, he collected $4,250 from customers. His checkbook lists payments for supplies totaling $400, and he still has gasoline, weedeater cord, and other supplies that cost a total of $50. He paid his employees $1,900, and he still owes them $200 for the final week of the summer.

Doug rented some equipment from Scholes Machine Shop. On May 1, he signed a six-month lease on mowers and paid $600 for the full lease period. Scholes will refund the unused portion of the prepayment if the equipment is in good shape. In order to get the refund, Doug has kept the mowers in excellent condition. In fact, he had to pay $300 to repair a mower.

To transport employees and equipment to jobs, Doug used a trailer that he bought for $300. He figures that the summer's work used up one-third of the trailer's service potential. The business checkbook lists a payment of $460 for cash withdrawals by Doug during the summer. Doug paid his father back during August.

Required

1. Prepare the income statement of Maltbee Lawn Service for the four months May through August.
2. Prepare the classified balance sheet of Maltbee Lawn Service at August 31.
3. Was Maltbee's summer work successful? Give the reason for your answer.

INTERNET EXERCISE

Southwest Airlines Company started in 1971 with three planes and now has more than 300 planes that fly into 55 different cities. In years when many other airlines reported net losses, Southwest Airlines' low-cost, no-frills flights resulted in profits.

Southwest Airlines

1. Go to **http://www.Southwest.com,** click on *About SWA*, and read "A Brief History of Southwest Airlines." Who is the CEO of Southwest Airlines? Why can Southwest Airlines offer lower fares than other airlines?
2. In the left-hand column click on *History* and read the information provided. What is the Triple Crown? How often has Southwest Airlines won this award? Comment on one other item that you found of interest.
3. Go to **http://www.Forbes.com** to get the latest financial information. In the "Stock" section type <u>LUV</u>, the stock symbol of Southwest Airlines Co., and then click on *Go*. In the left-hand column, click on "Company Info" and read the information provided. Comment on one item that makes Southwest Airlines different from other airlines.
4. In the left-hand column, click on "Financials." Menu selections are presented in the left-hand column.
   a. For the most recent year, list the amount reported for "Passenger revenue." Is this account closed at the end of the accounting period?
   b. For the two most recent years, list the amounts reported for "Cash/Equivalents," "Total current assets," "Total assets," "Total current liabilities," and "Total liabilities."
   c. Is the balance sheet presented in a classified format? How can you tell?
   d. Is Cash/Equivalents closed at the end of the accounting period? Why or why not?
   e. For the two most recent years, calculate Southwest's current ratio and debt ratio. Do these values look strong or weak?

APPENDIX TO CHAPTER 4

REVERSING ENTRIES: AN OPTIONAL STEP

Reversing entries are special types of entries that ease the burden of accounting for transactions that key off the adjustments at the end of the period. Reversing entries are used most often in conjunction with accrual-type adjustments such as accrued salary expense and accrued service revenue. *Generally accepted accounting principles do not require reversing entries. They are used only for convenience and to save time.*

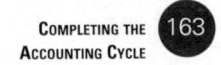

ACCOUNTING FOR ACCRUED EXPENSES

To see how reversing entries work, return to Gay Gillen's unadjusted trial balance at April 30 (Exhibit 4-2, page 130). Salary Expense has a debit balance of $950 for salaries paid during April. At April 30, the business still owes its employee an additional $950 for the last half of the month, so Gillen makes this adjusting entry:

Adjusting Entries

Apr. 30	Salary Expense	950	
	Salary Payable		950

After posting, the accounts are updated at April 30.[2]

SALARY PAYABLE		
	Apr. 30 Adj.	950
	Apr. 30 Bal.	950

SALARY EXPENSE		
Paid during April CP	950	
Apr. 30 Adj.	950	
Apr. 30 Bal.	1,900	

After the adjusting entry,

- The April income statement reports salary expense of $1,900.
- The April 30 balance sheet reports salary payable of $950.

The $1,900 debit balance of Salary Expense is closed at April 30, 20X1, with this closing entry:

Closing Entries

Apr. 30	Income Summary	1,900	
	Salary Expense		1,900

After posting, Salary Expense has a zero balance as follows:

SALARY EXPENSE				
Paid during April CP	950			
Apr. 30 Adj.	950			
Apr. 30 Bal.	1,900	Apr. 30 Clo.	1,900

Zero balance

Assume for this illustration that on May 5, the next payday, Gillen will pay the $950 of accrued salary left over from April 30 plus $100 of salary for the first few days of May. Gillen's next payroll payment will be $1,050 ($950 + $100).

ACCOUNTING WITHOUT A REVERSING ENTRY

On May 5, the next payday, Gillen pays the payroll of $1,050 and makes this journal entry:

May 5	Salary Payable	950	
	Salary Expense	100	
	Cash		1,050

This method of recording the cash payment is correct. However, it wastes time because Gillen must refer to the adjusting entries of April 30. Otherwise, she does not know the amount of the debit to Salary Payable (in this example, $950). Searching the preceding period's adjusting entries takes time and, in business, time is money. To save time, accountants use reversing entries.

---

[2]Entry explanations used throughout this discussion are

Adj. = entry	CP = Cash payment entry—a credit to Cash
Bal. = Balance	CR = Cash receipt entry—a debit to Cash
Clo. = Closing entry	Rev. = Reversing entry

MAKING A REVERSING ENTRY

A **reversing entry** switches the debit and the credit of a previous adjusting entry. *A reversing entry, then, is the exact opposite of a prior adjusting entry.* The reversing entry is dated the first day of the period that follows the adjusting entry.

To illustrate reversing entries, recall that on April 30, Gillen made the following adjusting entry to accrue Salary Payable:

Adjusting Entries

Apr. 30	Salary Expense	950	
	Salary Payable		950

The reversing entry simply reverses the debit and the credit of the adjustment:

Reversing Entries

May 1	Salary Payable	950	
	Salary Expense		950

Observe that the reversing entry is dated the first day of the new period. It is the exact opposite of the April 30 adjusting entry. Ordinarily, the accountant who makes the adjusting entry also prepares the reversing entry at the same time. Gillen dates the reversing entry as of the first day of the next period, however, so that it affects only the new period. Note how the accounts appear after Gillen posts the reversing entry:

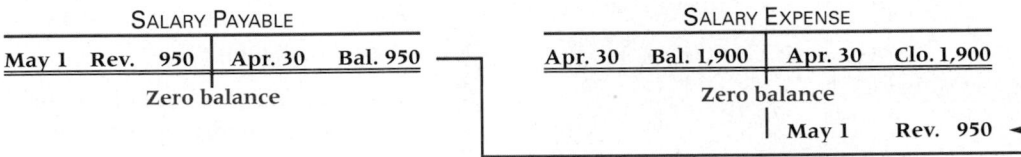

The arrow shows the transfer of the $950 credit balance from Salary Payable to Salary Expense. This credit balance in Salary Expense does not mean that the entity has negative salary expense, as you might think. Instead, the odd credit balance in the Salary Expense account is merely a temporary result of the reversing entry. The credit balance is eliminated on May 5, when Gillen pays the payroll and debits Salary Expense in the customary manner:

May 5	Salary Expense	1,050	
	Cash		1,050

Then this cash payment entry is posted as follows:

SALARY EXPENSE					
May 5	CP	1,050	May 1	Rev.	950
May 5	Bal.	100			

Now Salary Expense has its correct debit balance of $100, which is the amount of salary expense incurred thus far in May. The $1,050 cash disbursement also pays the liability for Salary Payable so that Salary Payable has a zero balance, which is correct.

ASSESS YOUR PROGRESS

APPENDIX PROBLEM

P4A-1 Refer to the data in Problem 4-5A, page 156.

Using reversing entries

Required

1. Open accounts for Salary Payable and Salary Expense. Insert their unadjusted balances at August 31, 20X9.
2. Journalize adjusting entry (f) and the closing entry for Salary Expense at August 31. Post to the accounts.
3. On September 5, Allianz Publishing paid the next payroll amount of $580. Journalize this cash payment, and post to the accounts. Show the balance in each account.
4. Using a reversing entry, repeat requirements 1–3. Compare the balances of Salary Payable and Salary Expense computed using a reversing entry with those balances computed without the reversing entry (as they appear in your answer to requirement 3).

5 Merchandising Operations and the Accounting Cycle

LEARNING OBJECTIVES

*After studying this chapter,
you should be able to*

1. Use sales and gross profit to evaluate a company

2. Account for the purchase and sale of inventory

3. Adjust and close the accounts of a merchandising business

4. Prepare a merchandiser's financial statements

5. Use the gross profit percentage and the inventory turnover ratio to evaluate a business

6. Compute cost of goods sold

www.prenhall.com/horngren

Readiness Assessment

You probably recognize the bulls'-eye logo. You may even do your shopping at a **Target, Mervyn, Marshall Field, Dayton,** or **Hudson** store. All these companies are part of the retail empire known as **Target Corporation.** It is a pacesetter in retailing: Target stores are currently the place to find the latest fashions at the best prices. Target is also a pacesetter in philanthropy and community relations. Through its Five Percent Club, the company donates 5% of its taxable income to support charities in the communities where it operates. In 2000, Target gave more than $1 million every week to local communities. The company, which employs about 189,000 people nationwide, is considered a good employer. *Working Mother* magazine has recognized Target as a "Top Work Place for Women." Target sells its merchandise through nearly 900 stores in 44 states, and through its Web site on the Internet. It is one of the largest mass-merchandise retailers in the United States, ringing up sales of over $33 billion in the year ended January 31, 2000.

Chapter 5 marks a new direction for this book. In Chapters 1–4, we studied accounting through the lens of Gay Gillen eTravel, which earns revenue by providing travel services for clients. **Yahoo!, Sprint,** physicians, and lawyers are other examples of service entities.

We now shift gears and focus on merchandising operations like **Target** stores, **Drugstore.com,** and **Best Buy** electronics centers. They earn their revenues by selling products rather than services. These companies are identified by the goods they sell—their *merchandise inventory,* or simply *inventory.*

This chapter demonstrates the central role of inventory in a business that sells merchandise. **Inventory** includes all goods that the company owns and expects to sell in the normal course of operations. We illustrate accounting for the purchase and sale of inventory, and we also illustrate how to adjust and close the books of a merchandiser. The chapter covers two ratios investors and creditors use to evaluate companies. Before launching into merchandising, let's compare service entities, with which you are familiar, to merchandising companies.

Chapters 1–4 have used both service entities and merchandisers to illustrate key accounting concepts. Chapter 5 jumps into the world of merchandising with both feet. As you make this transition, the following summarized financial statements will show how the two types of companies are similar and different. Observe that Merchandising Co.'s income statement reports Sales Revenue, Cost of Goods Sold, and Gross Profit. Merchandising Co.'s balance sheet reports Inventory. Service Co. reports none of these items. All the new merchandising items are italicized for easy reference.

INVENTORY. All the goods that the company owns and expects to sell in the normal course of operations.

SERVICE CO.* Income Statement Year Ended June 30, 20XX		**MERCHANDISING CO.**** Income Statement Year Ended June 30, 20XX	

Service revenue	$XXX →	*Sales* revenue......................	$XXX
Expenses: ────────────→		*Cost of goods sold*	X
Salary expense	X	*Gross profit*	XX
Depreciation expense....	X └→	Operating *expenses:*	
Income tax expense	X	Salary expense	X
Net income.......................	$ X	Depreciation expense...	X
		Income tax expense	$ X
		Net income.......................	$ X
*Such as Gay Gillen eTravel		**Such as Target Corporation	

SERVICE CO. Balance Sheet June 30, 20XX		**MERCHANDISING CO.** Balance Sheet June 30, 20XX	
Assets		**Assets**	
Current assets:		Current assets:	
Cash...........................	$X	Cash	$X
Short-term investments	X	Short-term investments	X
Accounts receivable, net	X	Accounts receivable, net	X
Prepaid expenses................	X	*Inventory*	X
		Prepaid expenses................	X

WHAT ARE MERCHANDISING OPERATIONS?

Objective 1
Use sales and gross profit to evaluate a company

EXHIBIT 5-1
A Leading Merchandiser's Income Statement

◉ DAILY EXERCISE 5-1

◉ DAILY EXERCISE 5-2

◉ DAILY EXERCISE 5-3

SALES REVENUE. The amount that a merchandiser earns from selling its inventory. Also called **sales.**

NET SALES. Sales revenue less sales discounts and sales returns and allowances.

COST OF GOODS SOLD. The cost of the inventory that the business has sold to customers. Also called **cost of sales.**

Exhibit 5-1 shows the income statement of **Target Corporation.** The six high-lighted items are unique to merchandisers.

TARGET CORPORATION Income Statement (Adapted) Year Ended January 31, 2000	
	Millions
Net sales revenue [same as Net sales]	$33,212
Cost of goods sold [same as Cost of sales]	23,029
Gross profit [same as Gross margin]...	10,183
Selling, general, and administrative expenses...........................	7,490
Depreciation expense	854
Interest expense..	393
Other expenses, net..	302
Total operating expenses	$ 9,039
Net earnings [same as Net income]	$ 1,144

Sales Revenue, Cost of Goods Sold, and Gross Profit

The amount that a business earns from selling merchandise inventory is called **sales revenue,** often abbreviated as **sales.** (**Net sales** equals sales revenue minus any returns and discounts.) The major revenue of a merchandising entity is sales revenue, which results from delivering inventory to customers. The major expense of a merchandiser is **cost of goods sold,** also called **cost of sales.** It represents the entity's cost of the goods (the inventory) sold to customers.

While the inventory is held by a business, the inventory is an asset. When the inventory is sold, the inventory's cost becomes an expense to the seller. When Target sells you a shirt, the shirt's cost is expensed as cost of goods sold on Target's books.

Net sales revenue minus cost of goods sold is called **gross profit** or **gross margin**.

Net sales revenue (abbreviated as Sales)	−	Cost of goods sold (same as Cost of sales)	=	Gross profit (same as Gross margin)

GROSS PROFIT. Excess of net sales revenue over cost of goods sold. Also called **gross margin**.

or, more simply,

Sales − Cost of sales = Gross profit

Gross profit is a measure of business success. A sufficiently high gross profit is vital to a merchandiser. Target's operations were quite successful during the year ended January 31, 2000. Target's gross profit was over $10 billion.

The following example will clarify the nature of gross profit. Suppose Target's cost to purchase a man's shirt is $30 and Target sells the shirt for $50. Target's gross profit per shirt is $20, computed as follows:

Sales revenue earned by selling one shirt........	$50
Less: Cost of goods sold for the shirt (what the shirt cost Target)	(30)
Gross profit on the sale of one shirt................	$20

The gross profit reported on Target Corporation's income statement, $10,183 million, is the sum of the gross profits on all the shirts and other products the company sold during its fiscal year.

The Operating Cycle of a Merchandising Business

A merchandising entity buys inventory, sells the goods to customers, and uses the cash to purchase more inventory and repeat the cycle. Exhibit 5-2 diagrams the operating cycle for *cash sales* and for *sales on account*.

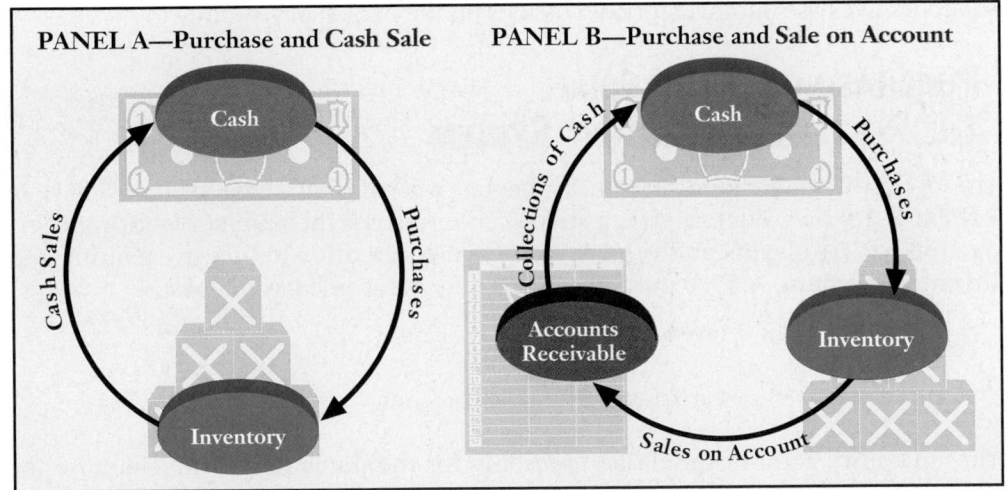

EXHIBIT 5-2
Operating Cycle of a Merchandiser

For a cash sale—Panel A—the cycle is from cash to inventory, and back to cash. For a sale on account—Panel B—the cycle is from cash to inventory to accounts receivabfle and back to cash. In all lines of business, managers try to shorten the cycle in order to keep assets active. The faster the sale of inventory and the collection of cash, the higher the profits.

Inventory Systems: Perpetual and Periodic

There are two main types of inventory accounting systems:

- the periodic system
- the perpetual system

The **periodic inventory system** is used by businesses that sell relatively inexpensive goods. A grocery store without optical-scanning cash registers does not keep a

PERIODIC INVENTORY SYSTEM. An inventory accounting system in which the business does not keep a continuous record of the inventory on hand. Instead, at the end of the period the business makes a physical count of the on-hand inventory and uses this information to prepare the financial statements.

daily running record of every loaf of bread and every can of pineapple that it sells. The cost of recordkeeping would be overwhelming. Instead, grocers count their inventory periodically—at least once a year—to determine the quantities on hand. The inventory amounts are used to prepare the annual financial statements. Businesses such as restaurants and small retail stores also use the periodic inventory system. The end-of-chapter appendix covers this system, which is becoming less popular as more businesses keep their inventory records by computer.

PERPETUAL INVENTORY SYSTEM. The accounting inventory system in which the business keeps a running record of inventory and cost of goods sold.

Under the **perpetual inventory system,** the business maintains a running record of inventory and cost of goods sold. This system achieves control over expensive goods such as automobiles, jewelry, and furniture. The loss of one item would be significant, and this justifies the cost of a perpetual system. Computers increase a company's ability to control its merchandise. But even under a perpetual system, the business counts inventory on hand at least once a year. The physical count establishes the correct amount of ending inventory and serves as a check on the perpetual records.

The following chart compares the periodic and perpetual systems:

PERPETUAL INVENTORY SYSTEM
- Keeps a running record of all goods bought and sold.
- Inventory counted at least once a year.
- Used for all types of goods.

PERIODIC INVENTORY SYSTEM
- Does *not* keep a running record of all goods bought and sold.
- Inventory counted at least once a year.
- Used for *inexpensive* goods.

Computerized Inventory Systems

A computerized inventory system can keep accurate, up-to-date records of the number of units purchased, the number of units sold, and the quantities on hand. Inventory systems are often integrated with accounts receivable and sales. For example, Target's computers keep up-to-the-minute records, so managers can call up current inventory information at any time. In a perpetual system, the "cash register" at a Target store is a computer terminal that records the sale and also updates inventory records. Bar codes are scanned by a laser as part of the perpetual inventory system. The lines of the bar coding represent coded data that keep track of each item. Because most businesses use bar codes, we base our inventory discussions on the perpetual system.[1]

PURCHASING MERCHANDISE: THE PERPETUAL INVENTORY SYSTEM

Objective 2
Account for the purchase and sale of inventory

The cycle of a merchandising entity begins with the purchase of inventory, as Exhibit 5-2 shows. For example, a stereo center records the purchase of **Sony** compact disc (CD) players and other inventory acquired for resale, by debiting the Inventory account. A $500 purchase on account is recorded as follows:

June 14	Inventory...	500	
	Accounts Payable		500
	Purchased inventory on account.		

The Inventory account should be used only for the purchases of merchandise for resale. Purchases of other assets are recorded in other accounts. For example, the purchase of supplies is debited to Supplies, not to Inventory.

The Purchase Invoice: A Basic Business Document

Business documents give tangible evidence of transactions. In this section, we trace the steps that **Austin Sound Center,** in Austin, Texas, takes to order, receive, and pay for inventory. Many companies buy and sell their goods electronically—with no invoices, no checks, and so on. Here we use actual documents to illustrate what takes place behind the scenes.

---

[1]For instructors who prefer to concentrate on the periodic inventory system, an overview starts on page 188 and a comprehensive treatment of that system begins on page 211. Follow Appendix Objectives A2–A5 instead of Chapter Objectives 2 through 4.

1. Suppose Austin Sound wants to stock **JVC** brand CD players and speakers. Austin Sound prepares a *purchase order* and faxes it to JVC.

2. On receipt of the purchase order, JVC's computer scans its warehouse for the inventory that Austin Sound ordered. JVC ships the equipment and sends the invoice to Austin the same day. The **invoice** is the seller's request for cash from the purchaser. It is also called the *bill*.

3. Often the purchaser receives the invoice before the inventory arrives. Austin Sound does not pay immediately. Instead, Austin waits until the inventory arrives in order to ensure that it is the correct type and quantity ordered, and in good condition. After the inventory is inspected and approved, Austin Sound pays JVC the invoice amount.

> **INVOICE.** A seller's request for cash from the purchaser.

Exhibit 5-3 is an updated copy of an actual invoice from JVC to Austin Sound Center.

- From Austin Sound's perspective, this document is a *purchase invoice*.
- To JVC, it is a *sales invoice*.

EXHIBIT 5-3 **An Invoice**

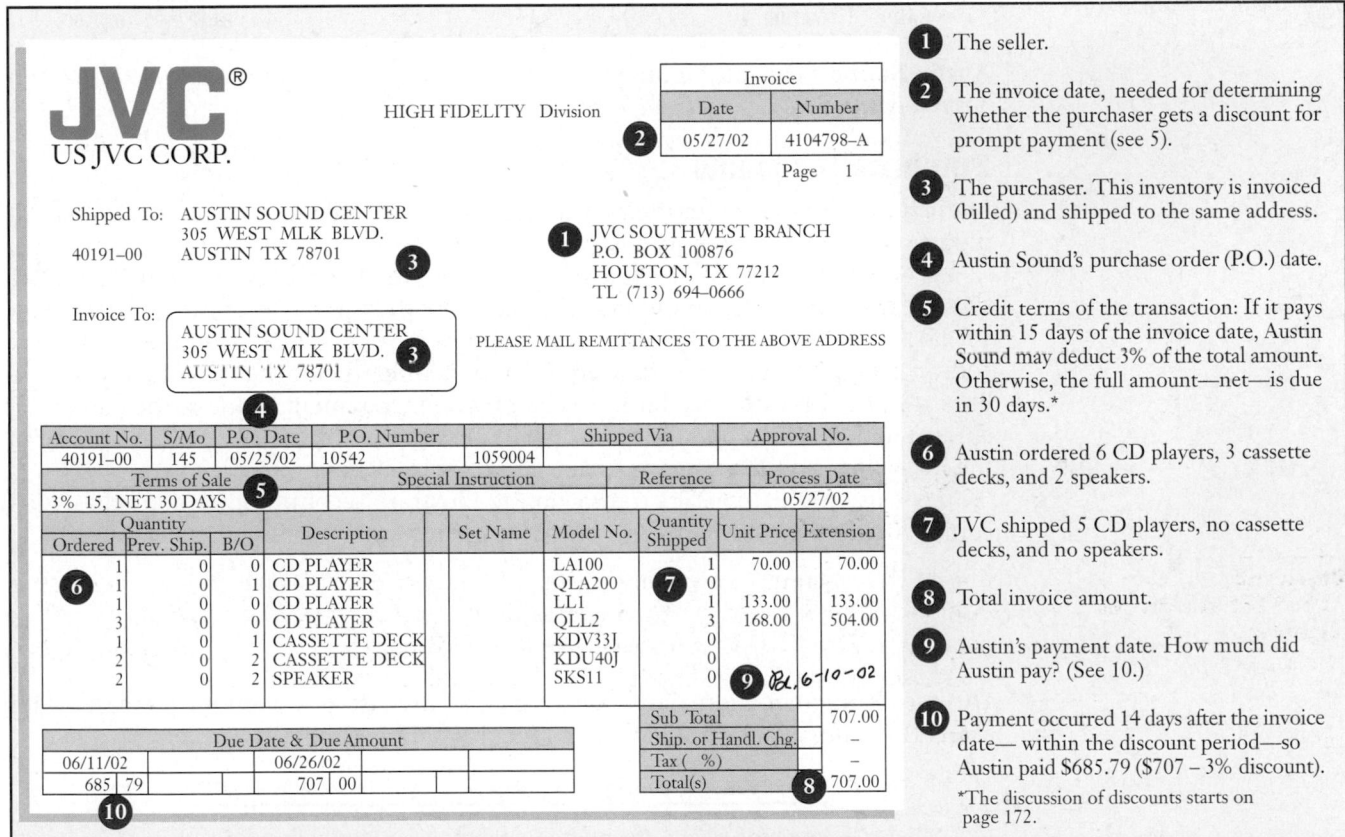

① The seller.

② The invoice date, needed for determining whether the purchaser gets a discount for prompt payment (see ⑤).

③ The purchaser. This inventory is invoiced (billed) and shipped to the same address.

④ Austin Sound's purchase order (P.O.) date.

⑤ Credit terms of the transaction: If it pays within 15 days of the invoice date, Austin Sound may deduct 3% of the total amount. Otherwise, the full amount—net—is due in 30 days.*

⑥ Austin ordered 6 CD players, 3 cassette decks, and 2 speakers.

⑦ JVC shipped 5 CD players, no cassette decks, and no speakers.

⑧ Total invoice amount.

⑨ Austin's payment date. How much did Austin pay? (See ⑩.)

⑩ Payment occurred 14 days after the invoice date— within the discount period—so Austin paid $685.79 ($707 – 3% discount).

*The discussion of discounts starts on page 172.

Purchase Returns and Allowances

Most businesses allow their customers to *return* merchandise that is defective, damaged in shipment, or otherwise unsuitable. But if the buyer chooses to keep the damaged goods, the seller may deduct an *allowance* from the amount the buyer owes. Both purchase returns and purchase allowances decrease the amount that the buyer must pay the seller.

Suppose the $70 CD player purchased by Austin Sound (top line of section 6 in Exhibit 5-3) was not the CD player Austin ordered. Austin returns the merchandise to the seller and records the purchase return as follows:

June 3	Accounts Payable	70.00	
	Inventory		70.00
	Returned inventory to seller.		

Now assume that one of the CD players was damaged in shipment to Austin Sound. The damage is minor, and Austin decides to keep the CD player in exchange for a $10 allowance from JVC. To record this purchase allowance, Austin Sound makes this entry:

June 4	Accounts Payable............................	10.00	
	Inventory		10.00
	Received a purchase allowance.		

The return and the allowance have two effects:

1. They decrease Austin Sound's liability, which is why we debit Accounts Payable.
2. They decrease Austin Sound's net cost of the goods, so we credit Inventory.

Assume that Austin Sound has not yet paid its debt to JVC. After the return ($70) and the allowance ($10) transactions are posted, Austin Sound's accounts will show these balances:

⊙ DAILY EXERCISE 5-4

⊙ DAILY EXERCISE 5-5

⊙ DAILY EXERCISE 5-6

INVENTORY					ACCOUNTS PAYABLE				
May 27	707.00	June 3	70.00		June 3	70.00	May 27	707.00	
		June 4	10.00		June 4	10.00			
Bal.	627.00						Bal.	627.00	

Austin Sound's cost of the *inventory* is $627, and Austin Sound owes JVC $627 on *account payable*.

Purchase Discounts

Many businesses also offer their customers purchase discounts. A purchase discount reduces the cost of inventory.

JVC's credit terms of 3% 15, NET 30 DAYS can also be expressed as 3/15 n/30. This means that Austin Sound may deduct 3% of the total debt if Austin pays within 15 days of the invoice date. Otherwise, the full amount—NET—is due in 30 days. Terms of simply n/30 mean that no discount is offered and that payment is due 30 days after the invoice date. Terms of *eom* mean that payment is due at the end of the current month. But a purchase after the 25th of the month can be paid at the end of the following month.

Let's use the Exhibit 5-3 transaction to illustrate accounting for a purchase discount. Austin Sound records this purchase on account as follows:

May 27	Inventory......................................	707.00	
	Accounts Payable		707.00
	Purchased inventory on account.		

The accounting equation shows that a credit purchase of inventory increases both assets (Inventory) and liabilities (Accounts Payable), as follows:

ASSETS	=	LIABILITIES	+	OWNER'S EQUITY
Inventory	=	Accounts Payable		
$707	=	$707	+	0

Austin Sound paid within the discount period, so its cash payment entry is

⊙ DAILY EXERCISE 5-7

June 10	Accounts Payable............................	707.00	
	Cash ($707.00 × 0.97)..........		685.79
	Inventory ($707.00 × 0.03)..		21.21
	Paid within discount period.		

After paying the account, Austin Sound's assets and liabilities both decrease, as follows:

	ASSETS			=	LIABILITIES	+	OWNER'S EQUITY
	Cash	+	Inventory	=	Accounts Payable		
	−$685.29		−$21.21	=	−$707	+	0
	−$707						

Note the credit to Inventory. After Austin Sound has taken its discount, this inventory costs Austin Sound $685.79 ($707.00 – Purchase discount of $21.21), as shown in the Inventory account:

INVENTORY			
May 27	707.00	June 10	21.21
Bal.	685.79		

But if Austin Sound pays this invoice after the discount period, it must pay the full amount of $707. In that case, the payment entry is

June 29   Accounts Payable 707.00
                Cash 707.00
           Paid after discount period.

INVENTORY		
May 27	707 .00	

WORK IT OUT

On September 15, Austin Sound purchases $1,000 of merchandise on account, with terms 2/10, n/30. Austin returns $100 of merchandise for credit on September 20, then makes payment in full on September 25. Journalize these transactions.

Answer: Three separate journal entries are needed here. The initial purchase entry is

Purchase: Sep. 15   Inventory 1,000
                              Accounts Payable 1,000

The second entry records the return of inventory, as follows:

Return: Sep. 20   Accounts Payable 100
                            Inventory 100

The third entry records the payment of $882, as follows: Original amount, $1,000, minus the $100 return equals the net payable of $900. Now subtract the 2% discount ($900 × 0.02 = $18) to arrive at the final payment of $882.

Payment: Sep. 25   Accounts Payable 900
                              Cash 882
                              Inventory 18

Transportation Cost: Who Pays?

The transportation cost of moving inventory from seller to buyer can be significant. The purchase agreement specifies FOB terms to indicate who pays the shipping charges. *FOB* means *free on board.* FOB governs (1) when legal title to the goods passes from seller to buyer, and (2) who pays the freight.

- Under FOB *shipping point* terms, title passes when the inventory leaves the seller's place of businesss—the shipping point. The buyer owns the goods while they are in transit and therefore the buyer pays the transportation cost.
- Under FOB *destination* terms, title passes when the goods reach the destination, so the seller pays the transportation cost.

Exhibit 5-4 summarizes FOB terms.

EXHIBIT 5-4
FOB Terms

Factors to Consider	FOB Shipping Point	FOB Destination
When does the title to the goods pass to the buyer?	At the shipping point	At the destination
Who pays the transportation cost?	Buyer	Seller

FREIGHT IN FOB shipping point terms are most common, so the buyer generally pays the freight. A freight cost that the buyer pays on an inventory purchase is called *freight in*. In accounting, the cost of an asset includes all costs incurred to bring the asset to its intended use. For inventory, cost therefore includes the

- *Net cost* after all discounts and returns have been subtracted, plus
- *Freight* (transportation, or shipping) costs to be paid

To record the payment for freight in, the buyer debits Inventory and credits Cash or Accounts Payable for the amount. Suppose Austin Sound receives a $60 shipping bill directly from the freight company. Austin Sound's entry to record payment of the freight charge is

June 1	Inventory..	60	
	Cash		60
	Paid a freight bill.		

The freight charge increases the final cost of the inventory to $687, as follows:

	INVENTORY					
May 27	Purchase	707.00	June 3	Return	70.00	
June 1	Freight	60.00	June 4	Allowance	10.00	
Bal.	Net cost	687.00				

Any discounts would be computed only on the account payable to the seller, not on the transportation costs, because the freight company offers no discount.

Under FOB shipping point terms, the seller sometimes prepays the transportation cost as a convenience and lists this cost on the invoice. The buyer debits Inventory for the combined cost of the inventory and the shipping cost because both costs apply to the merchandise. A $5,000 purchase of goods, coupled with a related freight charge of $400, would be recorded as follows:

March 12	Inventory..	5,400	
	Accounts Payable		5,400
	Purchased on account including freight.		

If the buyer pays within the discount period, the discount will be computed on the $5,000 merchandise cost, not on the $5,400. For example, a 2% discount would be $100 ($5,000 × 0.02).

FREIGHT OUT The cost of freight charges paid to ship goods sold to customers is called *freight out*. Freight out is delivery expense paid by the seller. Delivery expense is an operating expense for the seller. It is debited to the Delivery Expense account.

This Work It Out example is exactly like the preceding one, but with freight in added to illustrate the accounting for shipping cost. On September 15, Austin Sound purchased $1,000 of merchandise, with *$80 freight added,* for an invoice total of $1,080. Austin returns $100 of the goods for credit on September 20 and pays the account payable in full on September 25. Journalize these transactions.

Answer

Purchase:	Sept. 15	Inventory ($1,000 + $80)...................................	1,080	
		Accounts Payable		1,080
Return:	Sept. 20	Accounts Payable	100	
		Inventory		100
Payment:	Sept. 25	Accounts Payable ($1,080 − $100).....................	980	
		Inventory [($1,000 − $100) × 0.02]..........		18
		Cash ($1,000 + $80 − $100 − $18)..........		962

The buyer does *not* get a discount on the cost of freight in.

Detailed Accounting for Purchase Returns and Allowances, Discounts, and Transportation Costs

Some businesses keep detailed records of purchase returns and allowances, discounts, and transportation costs. For example, Austin Sound receives defective CD players from an off-brand manufacturer. In recording purchase returns, Austin Sound can credit a special account, Purchase Returns and Allowances, which serves as a running record of defective merchandise.

The Purchase Returns and Allowances account carries a credit balance and is a contra account to Inventory. Freight In can be debited for transportation costs. Then, for reporting on the financial statements, these accounts can be combined with the Inventory account to determine the total cost of inventory (amounts assumed):

Inventory		$35,000
Less: Purchase discounts	$(700)	
Purchase returns and allowances	(800)	(1,500)
Net purchases of inventory		33,500
Freight in		2,100
Total cost of inventory		$35,600

SELLING INVENTORY AND RECORDING COST OF GOODS SOLD

After a company buys inventory, the next step in the operating cycle is to sell the goods. We shift now to the selling side and follow **Austin Sound Center** through a sequence of selling transactions. A sale earns a reward, Sales Revenue. A sale also requires a sacrifice in the form of an expense, Cost of Goods Sold, as the seller gives up the asset Inventory.

After making a sale on account, Austin Sound may experience any of the following:

- A sales return: The customer may return goods to Austin Sound.
- A sales allowance: Austin Sound may grant a sales allowance to reduce the amount of cash collected from the customer.
- A sales discount: If the customer pays within the discount period—under terms such as 2/10 n/30—Austin Sound collects the discounted amount.
- Freight out: Austin Sound may have to pay delivery expense to transport the goods to the buyer's location.

Let's begin with a cash sale.

Cash Sale

Sales of retailers, such as grocery stores and restaurants, are often for cash. Cash sales of $3,000 would be recorded by debiting Cash and crediting Sales Revenue as follows:

Jan. 9	Cash	3,000	
	Sales Revenue		3,000
	Cash sale.		

To update the inventory records, the business also must decrease the Inventory balance. Suppose these goods cost the seller $1,900. An accompanying entry is needed to transfer the $1,900 cost of the goods—not their selling price of $3,000—from the Inventory account to Cost of Goods Sold as follows:

Jan. 9	Cost of Goods Sold	1,900	
	Inventory		1,900
	Recorded the cost of goods sold.		

Cost of goods sold (also called cost of sales) is the largest single expense of most merchandisers. ➡ The Cost of Goods Sold account keeps a current balance throughout the period as transactions are journalized and posted.

◄ The recording of cost of goods sold along with sales revenue is an example of the matching principle (Chapter 3, p. 86).

After posting, the Cost of Goods Sold account holds the cost of the merchandise sold ($1,900 in this case):

INVENTORY		COST OF GOODS SOLD	
Purchases 50,000	Jan. 9 1,900	⟷ Jan. 9	1,900
(amount			
assumed)			

The computer automatically records the cost of goods sold entry when the cashier keys in the code number of the inventory that is sold. Optical scanners perform this task in most stores.

Sale on Account

Most sales in the United States are made on account (on credit). A $5,000 sale on account is recorded by a debit to Accounts Receivable and a credit to Sales Revenue, as follows:

Jan. 11	Accounts Receivable............................	5,000	
	Sales Revenue............................		5,000
	Sale on account.		

If we assume that these goods cost the seller $2,900, the accompanying cost of goods sold entry is

Jan. 11	Cost of Goods Sold..............................	2,900	
	Inventory		2,900
	Recorded the cost of goods sold.		

When the cash comes in, the seller records the related cash receipt on account as follows:

Jan. 19	Cash..	5,000	
	Accounts Receivable		5,000
	Collection on account.		

Offering Sales Discounts and Sales Returns and Allowances

SALES RETURNS AND ALLOWANCES. Decreases in the seller's receivable from a customer's return of merchandise or from granting the customer an allowance from the amount owed to the seller. A contra account to Sales Revenue.

SALES DISCOUNT. Reduction in the amount receivable from a customer, offered by the seller as an incentive for the customer to pay promptly. A contra account to Sales Revenue.

We just saw that purchase purchase returns and allowances and purchase discounts decrease the cost of inventory purchases. In the same way, **sales returns and allowances** and **sales discounts,** which are contra accounts to Sales Revenue, decrease the net amount of revenue earned on sales.

Credit-balance account	Debit-balance accounts		Credit subtotal (*not* a separate account)
Sales Revenue −	Sales Returns and Allowances −	Sales Discounts =	Net sales revenue[2]

This equation calculates net sales. Note that sales discounts can be given on both goods and services.

Companies keep close watch on their customers' paying habits and on their own sales of defective and unsuitable merchandise. They maintain separate accounts for Sales Discounts and Sales Returns and Allowances. Now let's examine a sequence of JVC sale transactions. Assume **JVC** is selling to Austin Sound.

On July 7, JVC sells stereo components for $7,200 on credit terms of 2/10 n/30. These goods cost JVC $4,700. JVC's entries to record this credit sale and the related cost of the goods sold are

July 7	Accounts Receivable................................	7,200	
	Sales Revenue................................		7,200
	Sale on account.		
July 7	Cost of Goods Sold	4,700	
	Inventory		4,700
	Recorded the cost of goods sold.		

[2]Often abbreviated as Net sales.

Assume that the buyer returns goods that sold for $600. JVC records the sales return and the related decrease in Accounts Receivable as follows:

July 12	Sales Returns and Allowances	600	
	Accounts Receivable		600
	Received returned goods.		

JVC receives the returned merchandise and updates the inventory records. JVC must also decrease Cost of Goods Sold as follows (these goods cost JVC $400):

July 12	Inventory	400	
	Cost of Goods Sold		400
	Placed goods back in inventory.		

Suppose JVC grants a $100 sales allowance for damaged goods. Austin Sound then subtracts $100 from the amount it will pay JVC. JVC journalizes this transaction by debiting Sales Returns and Allowances and crediting Accounts Receivable as follows:

July 15	Sales Returns and Allowances	100	
	Accounts Receivable		100
	Granted a sales allowance for damaged goods.		

No inventory entry is needed for a sales allowance transaction because the seller receives no returned goods from the customer. Instead, JVC will simply receive less cash from the customer.

After the preceding entries are posted, all the accounts have up-to-date balances. Accounts Receivable has a $6,500 debit balance, as follows:

ACCOUNTS RECEIVABLE

July 7	Sale	7,200	July 12	Return	600
			15	Allowance	100
Bal.		6,500			

On July 17, the last day of the discount period, JVC collects $4,000 of this receivable. Assume JVC allows customers to take discounts on all amounts JVC receives within the discount period. JVC's cash receipt is $3,920 [$4,000 − ($4,000 × 0.02)], and the collection entry is

July 17	Cash	3,920	
	Sales Discounts ($4,000 × 0.02)	80	
	Accounts Receivable		4,000
	Cash collection within the discount period.		

DAILY EXERCISE 5-8

DAILY EXERCISE 5-9

DAILY EXERCISE 5-10

Suppose that JVC collects the remainder, $2,500, on July 28. That date falls after the discount period, so there is no sales discount. To record this collection on account, JVC makes this entry:

July 28	Cash ($6,500 − $4,000)	2,500	
	Accounts Receivable		2,500
	Cash collection within the discount period.		

Now, JVC's Accounts Receivable balance is zero, as follows:

ACCOUNTS RECEIVABLE

July 7	Sale	7,200	July 12	Return	600
			15	Allowance	100
			17	Collection	4,000
			28	Collection	2,500
Bal.		−0−			

SUMMARY PROBLEM

Brun Sales Company engaged in the following transactions during June of the current year:

June 3 Purchased inventory on credit terms of 1/10 net eom (end of month), $1,610.
    9 Returned 40% of the inventory purchased on June 3. It was defective.
  12 Sold goods for cash, $920 (cost, $550).
  15 Purchased goods of $5,000. Credit terms were 3/15 net 30.
  16 Paid a $260 freight bill on goods purchased.
  18 Sold inventory on credit terms of 2/10 n/30, $2,000 (cost, $1,180).
  22 Received damaged goods from the customer of the June 18 sale, $800 (cost, $480).
  24 Borrowed money from the bank to take advantage of the discount offered on the June 15 purchase. Signed a note payable to the bank for the net amount.
  24 Paid supplier for goods purchased on June 15, less the discount.
  28 Received cash in full settlement of the account from the customer who purchased inventory on June 18, less the return on June 22.
  29 Paid the amount owed on account from the purchase of June 3, less the June 9 return.

Required

1. Journalize the preceding transactions. Explanations are not required.
2. Set up T-accounts and post the journal entries to show the ending balances in the Inventory and the Cost of Goods Sold accounts.
3. Assume that the note payable signed on June 24 requires the payment of $95 interest expense. Was borrowing funds to take the cash discount a wise or unwise decision?

Solution

Requirement 1

June 3	Inventory	1,610	
	Accounts Payable		1,610
9	Accounts Payable ($1,610 × 0.40)	644	
	Inventory		644
12	Cash	920	
	Sales Revenue		920
12	Cost of Goods Sold	550	
	Inventory		550
15	Inventory	5,000	
	Accounts Payable		5,000
16	Inventory	260	
	Cash		260
18	Accounts Receivable	2,000	
	Sales Revenue		2,000
18	Cost of Goods Sold	1,180	
	Inventory		1,180
22	Sales Returns and Allowances	800	
	Accounts Receivable		800
22	Inventory	480	
	Cost of Goods Sold		480
24	Cash [$5,000 − 0.03($5,000)]	4,850	
	Note Payable		4,850
24	Accounts Payable	5,000	
	Inventory ($5,000 × 0.03)		150
	Cash ($5,000 × 0.97)		4,850
28	Cash [($2,000 − $800) × 0.98]	1,176	
	Sales Discounts [($2,000 − $800) × 0.02]	24	
	Accounts Receivable ($2,000 − $800)		1,200
29	Accounts Payable ($1,610 − $644)	966	
	Cash		966

Requirement 2

INVENTORY			
June 3	1,610	June 9	644
15	5,000	12	550
16	260	18	1,180
22	480	24	150
Bal.	4,826		

COST OF GOODS SOLD			
June 12	550	June 22	480
18	1,180		
Bal.	1,250		

Requirement 3

The decision to borrow funds was wise because the discount ($150) exceeded the interest paid ($95). Thus the entity was $55 better off as a result of its decision.

ADJUSTING AND CLOSING THE ACCOUNTS OF A MERCHANDISER

Objective 3
Adjust and close the accounts of a merchandising business

A merchandising business adjusts and closes the accounts the same way a service entity does. If a work sheet is used, the trial balance is entered, and the work sheet is completed to determine net income or net loss. The work sheet aids the adjusting and closing processes and helps the accountant prepare the financial statements.

Adjusting Inventory Based on a Physical Count

In theory, the Inventory account stays current at all times. However, the actual amount of inventory on hand may differ from what the books show. Theft losses and damage occur. Accounting errors can require adjustments. For this reason, virtually all businesses, like the bookstore chain **Barnes & Noble,** take a physical count of inventory at least once a year. The most common time for a business to count its inventory is at the end of the fiscal year, before the financial statements are prepared. The business then adjusts the Inventory account on the basis of the physical count.

Exhibit 5-5, **Austin Sound's** trial balance at December 31, 20X2, lists a $40,500 balance for inventory. With no shrinkage—due to theft or error—the business should have on hand inventory costing $40,500. But on December 31, when Charles Ernest, the owner of Austin Sound, counts the merchandise in the store, the total cost of the goods on hand comes to only $40,200. Austin Sound then records the $300 of inventory shrinkage with this adjusting entry:

Dec. 31	Cost of Goods Sold	300	
	Inventory ($40,500 − $40,200)		300

This entry brings Inventory and Cost of Goods Sold to their correct balances. Austin Sound's December 31, 20X2, adjustment data, including the correct inventory information [item (b)], are given at the bottom of Exhibit 5-5 on page 180.

The physical count can indicate that more inventory is present than the books show. Austin Sound may have made a purchase it did not record. This would be entered the standard way: Debit Inventory and credit Cash or Accounts Payable.

If the reason for the excess inventory cannot be identified, the business adjusts the accounts by debiting Inventory and crediting Cost of Goods Sold. To illustrate a merchandiser's adjusting and closing process, let's use Austin Sound's December 31, 20X2, trial balance in Exhibit 5-5. All the new accounts—Inventory, Cost of Goods Sold, and the contra accounts—are highlighted for emphasis.

Additional data at December 31, 20X2.
  a. Interest revenue earned but not yet collected, $400.
  b. Inventory on hand, $40,200.
  c. Supplies on hand, $100.
  d. Prepaid insurance expired during the year, $1,000.
  e. Depreciation, $600.
  f. Unearned sales revenue earned during the year, $1,300.
  g. Accrued wage expense, $400.
  h. Accrued interest expense, $200.

EXHIBIT 5-5 Trial Balance

AUSTIN SOUND CENTER
Trial Balance
December 31, 20X2

Cash	$ 2,850	
Accounts receivable	4,600	
Note receivable, current	8,000	
Interest receivable		
Inventory	40,500	
Supplies	650	
Prepaid insurance	1,200	
Furniture and fixtures	33,200	
Accumulated depreciation		$ 2,400
Accounts payable		47,000
Unearned sales revenue		2,000
Wages payable		
Interest payable		
Note payable, long-term		12,600
C. Ernest, capital		25,900
C. Ernest, withdrawals	54,100	
Sales revenue		168,000
Sales discounts	1,400	
Sales returns and allowances	2,000	
Interest revenue		600
Cost of goods sold	90,500	
Wage expense	9,800	
Rent expense	8,400	
Depreciation expense		
Insurance expense		
Supplies expense		
Interest expense	1,300	
Total	$258,500	$258,500

Preparing and Using the Work Sheet

The Exhibit 5-6 work sheet is similar to the work sheets we have seen so far, but there are a few differences. This work sheet does not include adjusted trial balance columns. ◄ In most accounting systems, a single operation combines trial balance amounts with the adjustments and extends the adjusted balances directly to the income statement and balance sheet columns. Therefore, to reduce clutter, the adjusted trial balance columns are omitted here.

➤ This work sheet is slightly different from the one introduced in the Chapter 4 acetates following p. 130—it contains four pairs of columns, not five.

ACCOUNT TITLE COLUMNS The trial balance lists a number of accounts without balances. Ordinarily, these accounts are affected by the adjusting process. Examples include Interest Receivable, Wages Payable, and Depreciation Expense. The accounts are listed in the order they appear in the ledger. If additional accounts are needed, they can be entered at the bottom of the work sheet, above net income.

TRIAL BALANCE COLUMNS Examine the Inventory account in the trial balance. Inventory has a balance of $40,500 before the physical count at the end of the year. Cost of Goods Sold's balance is $90,500 before any adjustment. Any difference between the Inventory amount on the trial balance ($40,500) and the correct amount based on the physical count ($40,200) is unexplained and should be debited or credited to Cost of Goods Sold.

EXHIBIT 5-6 Accounting Work Sheet

AUSTIN SOUND CENTER
Accounting Work Sheet
Year Ended December 31, 20X2

Account Title	Trial Balance Debit	Trial Balance Credit	Adjustments Debit		Adjustments Credit		Income Statement Debit	Income Statement Credit	Balance Sheet Debit	Balance Sheet Credit
Cash	2,850								2,850	
Accounts receivable	4,600								4,600	
Note receivable, current	8,000								8,000	
Interest receivable			(a)	400					400	
Inventory	**40,500**				(b)	300			**40,200**	
Supplies	650				(c)	550			100	
Prepaid insurance	1,200				(d)	1,000			200	
Furniture and fixtures	33,200								33,200	
Accumulated depreciation		2,400			(e)	600				3,000
Accounts payable		47,000								47,000
Unearned sales revenue		2,000	(f)	1,300						700
Wages payable					(g)	400				400
Interest payable					(h)	200				200
Note payable, long-term		12,600								12,600
C. Ernest, capital		25,900								25,900
C. Ernest, withdrawals	54,100								54,100	
Sales revenue		168,000			(f)	1,300		169,300		
Sales discounts	1,400						1,400			
Sales returns and allowances	2,000						2,000			
Interest revenue		600			(a)	400		1,000		
Cost of goods sold	**90,500**		(b)	300			90,800			
Wage expense	9,800		(g)	400			10,200			
Rent expense	8,400						8,400			
Depreciation expense			(e)	600			600			
Insurance expense			(d)	1,000			1,000			
Supplies expense			(c)	550			550			
Interest expense	1,300		(h)	200			1,500			
	258,500	258,500		4,750		4,750	116,450	170,300	143,650	89,800
Net income							53,850			53,850
							170,300	170,300	143,650	143,650

DAILY EXERCISE 5-11

ADJUSTMENTS COLUMNS The adjustments are similar to those discussed in Chapters 3 and 4. The adjustments may be entered in any order desired. The debit amount of each entry should equal the credit amount, and total debits should equal total credits. You should review the adjusting data in Exhibit 5-5 to reassure yourself that the adjustments are correct.

INCOME STATEMENT COLUMNS The income statement columns on the work sheet in Exhibit 5-6 contain adjusted amounts for the revenues and the expenses. Sales Revenue, for example, has an adjusted balance of $169,300.

The income statement column subtotals indicate whether the business had a net income or a net loss.

- Net income: Total credits > Total debits
- Net loss: Total debits > Total credits

Austin Sound's total credits of $170,300 exceed the total debits of $116,450, so the company earned a net income.

Insert the *net income* amount in the debit column to bring total debits into agreement with total credits. Insert a *net loss* amount in the credit column to equalize total debits and total credits. Net income or net loss is then extended to the opposite column of the balance sheet.

BALANCE-SHEET COLUMNS The only new item in the balance sheet columns is Inventory. The balance listed in Exhibit 5-6 is the ending amount of $40,200, as determined by the physical count of goods on hand at the end of the period.

PREPARING THE FINANCIAL STATEMENTS OF A MERCHANDISER

Objective 4
Prepare a merchandiser's financial statements

Exhibit 5-7 presents **Austin Sound's** financial statements.

EXHIBIT 5-7
Financial Statements of Austin Sound Center

DAILY EXERCISE 5-12

DAILY EXERCISE 5-13

AUSTIN SOUND CENTER
Income Statement
Year Ended December 31, 20X2

Sales revenue		$169,300	
Less: Sales discounts	$(1,400)		
Sales returns and allowances	(2,000)	(3,400)	
Net sales revenue			$165,900
Cost of goods sold			90,800
Gross profit			75,100
Operating expenses:			
Wage expense		$ 10,200	
Rent expense		8,400	
Insurance expense		1,000	
Depreciation expense		600	
Supplies expense		550	20,750
Operating income			54,350
Other revenue and (expense):			
Interest revenue		$ 1,000	
Interest expense		(1,500)	(500)
Net income			$ 53,850

AUSTIN SOUND CENTER
Statement of Owner's Equity
Year Ended December 31, 20X2

C. Ernest, capital, December 31, 20X1	$25,900
Add: Net income	53,850
	79,750
Less: Withdrawals	(54,100)
C. Ernest, capital, December 31, 20X2	$25,650

AUSTIN SOUND CENTER
Balance Sheet
December 31, 20X2

DAILY EXERCISE 5-14

Assets			Liabilities		
Current:			Current:		
Cash		$ 2,850	Accounts payable		$47,000
Accounts receivable		4,600	Unearned sales		
Note receivable		8,000	revenue		700
Interest receivable		400	Wages payable		400
Inventory		40,200	Interest payable		200
Prepaid insurance		200	Total current		
Supplies		100	liabilities		48,300
Total current assets		56,350	Long-term:		
Plant:			Note payable		12,600
Furniture and fixtures	$33,200		Total liabilities		60,900
Less: Accumulated					
depreciation	(3,000)	30,200	**Owner's Equity**		
			C. Ernest, capital		25,650
			Total liabilities and		
Total assets		$86,550	owner's equity		$86,550

To solidify your understanding of how the financial statements are prepared, you should trace the amounts in the work sheet (Exhibit 5-6) to the statements in Exhibit 5-7.

INCOME STATEMENT   The income statement reports **operating expenses,** which are those expenses other than cost of goods sold that are incurred in the entity's major line of business. Austin Sound's operating expenses include wage expense, rent, depreciation, insurance, and supplies expense.

Many companies report their operating expenses in two categories:

- *Selling expenses* are expenses related to marketing the company's products— sales salaries; sales commissions; advertising; depreciation, rent, and utilities on store buildings; and delivery expense.
- *General expenses* include office expenses, such as the salaries of the company president and office employees; depreciation, rent, utilities, and property taxes on the home office building.

Target Corporation (Exhibit 5-1) groups selling, general, and administrative expenses together for reporting on the income statement.

Gross profit minus operating expenses plus any other operating revenues equals **operating income,** or **income from operations.** Many people view operating income as an important indicator of performance because it measures the results of the entity's major ongoing activities.

The last section of Austin Sound's income statement is **other revenue and expense.** This category reports revenues and expenses that are outside the main operations of the business. Examples include gains and losses on the sale of plant assets (not inventory) and gains and losses on lawsuits. Accountants have traditionally viewed Interest Revenue and Interest Expense as "other" items because they arise from loaning and borrowing money. These financing activities are outside the operating scope of selling merchandise. Target (Exhibit 5-1) lists Interest expense among the operating expenses, also a common practice.

The bottom line of the income statement is net income:

Net income = Total revenues and gains − Total expenses and losses

We often hear the term *bottom line* used to refer to a final result. *Bottom line* originated from the position of net income on the income statement.

STATEMENT OF OWNER'S EQUITY   A merchandiser's statement of owner's equity looks exactly like that of a service business. In fact, you cannot determine whether the entity sells merchandise or services from looking at the statement of owner's equity.

BALANCE SHEET   If the business is a merchandiser, the balance sheet shows inventory as a major current asset. Service businesses usually have no inventory at all or minor amounts of inventory.

Journalizing the Adjusting and Closing Entries

Exhibit 5-8 presents Austin Sound's adjusting entries, which are similar to those you have seen previously, except for the inventory adjustment [entry (b)]. ➡ The closing entries in the exhibit also follow the pattern illustrated in Chapter 4.

The *first closing entry* debits the revenue accounts for their ending balances. The offsetting credit of $170,300 transfers the sum of total revenues to Income Summary. This amount comes directly from the credit column of the income statement on the work sheet (Exhibit 5-6).

The *second closing entry* includes credits to Cost of Goods Sold, to the contra revenue accounts (Sales Discounts and Sales Returns and Allowances), and to all the expense accounts. The offsetting $116,450 debit to Income Summary represents the amount of total expenses plus the contra revenues, which come from the debit column of the income statement on the work sheet.

The *last two closing entries* close net income from Income Summary to the Capital account and also close the owner Withdrawals into the Capital account.

OPERATING EXPENSES. Expenses, other than cost of goods sold, that are incurred in the entity's major line of business. Examples include rent, depreciation, salaries, wages, utilities, and supplies expense.

OPERATING INCOME. Gross profit minus operating expenses plus any other operating revenues. Also called **income from operations.**

OTHER REVENUE. Revenue that is outside the main operations of a business, such as a gain on the sale of plant assets.

OTHER EXPENSE. Expense that is outside the main operations of a business, such as a loss on the sale of plant assets.

↞ The closing entries also close the Cost of Goods Sold expense account. See Chapter 4, pp. 135, 136.

EXHIBIT 5-8
Adjusting and Closing Entries for a Merchandiser

⊙ DAILY EXERCISE 5-15

⊙ DAILY EXERCISE 5-16

Journal

Adjusting Entries

a.	Dec. 31	Interest Receivable		400	
		Interest Revenue			400
b.	31	Cost of Goods Sold		300	
		Inventory			300
c.	31	Supplies Expense ($650 – $100)		550	
		Supplies			550
d.	31	Insurance Expense		1,000	
		Prepaid Insurance			1,000
e.	31	Depreciation Expense		600	
		Accumulated Depreciation			600
f.	31	Unearned Sales Revenue		1,300	
		Sales Revenue			1,300
g.	31	Wage Expense		400	
		Wages Payable			400
h.	31	Interest Expense		200	
		Interest Payable			200

Closing Entries

1.	Dec. 31	Sales Revenue		169,300	
		Interest Revenue		1,000	
		Income Summary			170,300
2.	31	Income Summary		116,450	
		Sales Discounts			1,400
		Sales Returns and Allowances			2,000
		Cost of Goods Sold			90,800
		Wage Expense			10,200
		Rent Expense			8,400
		Depreciation Expense			600
		Insurance Expense			1,000
		Supplies Expense			550
		Interest Expense			1,500
3.	31	Income Summary ($170,300 – $116,450)		53,850	
		C. Ernest, Capital			53,850
4.	31	C. Ernest, Capital		54,100	
		C. Ernest, Withdrawals			54,100

Study Exhibits 5-6, 5-7, and 5-8 carefully because they illustrate the entire end-of-period process that leads to the financial statements.

Here is an easy way to remember the closing process. First, look at the work sheet. Then:

1. Debit all income statement accounts with a credit balance. Credit Income Summary for the total.

2. Credit all income statement accounts with a debit balance. Debit Income Summary for the total.

3. Take the balance in the Income Summary account. A debit balance indicates a net loss; credit Income Summary for that amount, and debit Capital. If Income Summary has a credit balance, there is a net income; debit Income Summary for that amount, and credit Capital.

4. Withdrawals has a debit balance. Credit Withdrawals to close its balance, and debit Capital for the same amount.

Income Statement Formats: Multi-Step and Single-Step

We have seen that the balance sheet appears in two formats:

- the report format (assets on top, . . . , owner's equity at bottom)
- the account format (assets at left, liabilities and owner's equity at right)

→ There are also two basic formats for the income statement:

- the multi-step format
- the single-step format

The multi-step format is by far the more popular.

← For a review of balance sheet formats, see Chapter 4, p. 141.

Multi-Step Income Statement

The **multi-step format** shows subtotals to highlight significant relationships. In addition to net income, it also presents gross profit and income from operations. This format communicates a merchandiser's results of operations especially well because gross profit and income from operations are important to investors. Exhibit 5-1 shows the multi-step format. The income statements presented thus far in this chapter have also been multi-step. Austin Sound's multi-step income statement for the year ended December 31, 20X2, appears in Exhibit 5-7.

MULTI-STEP INCOME STATEMENT. Format that contains subtotals to highlight significant relationships. In addition to net income, it presents gross profit and operating income.

Single-Step Income Statement

The **single-step format** groups all revenues together and then lists and deducts all expenses together without drawing any subtotals. **IBM** and **Wal-Mart** use this format. The single-step format clearly distinguishes revenues from expenses as Exhibit 5-9 shows. This format works well for service entities because they have no gross profit to report.

SINGLE-STEP INCOME STATEMENT. Format that groups all revenues together and then lists and deducts all expenses together without drawing any subtotals.

EXHIBIT 5-9
Single-Step Income Statement

AUSTIN SOUND CENTER
Income Statement
Year Ended December 31, 20X2

Revenues:	
Net sales (net of sales discounts, $1,400, and returns and allowances, $2,000)	$165,900
Interest revenue	1,000
Total revenues	166,900
Expenses:	
Cost of goods sold	90,800
Wage expense	10,200
Rent expense	8,400
Interest expense	1,500
Insurance expense	1,000
Depreciation expense	600
Supplies expense	550
Total expenses	113,050
Net Income	$ 53,850

Most published financial statements are highly condensed. Appendix A at the end of the book gives the income statement of Target Corporation. Of course, condensed statements can be supplemented with desired details.

TWO KEY RATIOS FOR DECISION MAKING

Merchandise inventory is the most important asset for a merchandising business. To manage the firm, owners and managers focus on the best way to sell the inventory. They use several ratios to evaluate operations, among them gross profit percentage and rate of inventory turnover.

Objective 5
Use the gross profit percentage and the inventory turnover ratio to evaluate a business

The Gross Profit Percentage

A key decision-making tool for a merchandiser is related to gross profit, which is net sales minus cost of goods sold. Merchandisers strive to increase the **gross profit percentage,** which is computed as follows:

GROSS PROFIT PERCENTAGE. Gross profit divided by net sales revenue. A measure of profitability. Also called **gross margin percentage.**

$$\text{Gross profit percentage} = \frac{\text{Gross profit}}{\text{Net sales revenue}} = \frac{\$75,100}{\$165,900} = 0.453 = 45.3\%$$

The gross profit percentage (also called the *gross margin percentage*) is one of the most carefully watched measures of profitability. A 45% gross margin means that each dollar of sales generates 45 cents of gross profit. On average, the goods cost the seller 55 cents. For most firms, the gross profit percentage changes little from year to year. A small increase may signal an important rise in income, and vice versa for a decrease.

Exhibit 5-10 compares **Austin Sound's** gross margin to that of both **Target** and **Wal-Mart.**

EXHIBIT 5-10
Gross Profit on $1 of Sales for Three Merchandisers

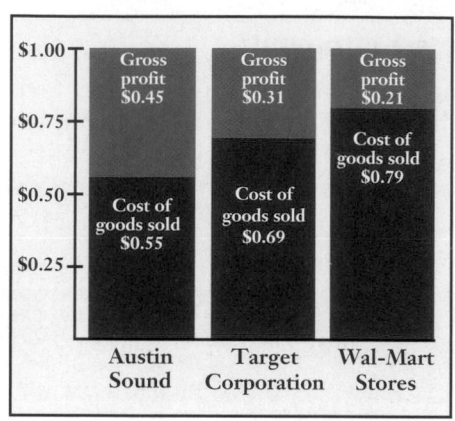

The Rate of Inventory Turnover

INVENTORY TURNOVER. Ratio of cost of goods sold to average inventory. Measures the number of times a company sells its average level of inventory during a year.

Owners and managers strive to sell inventory as quickly as possible because it generates no profit until it is sold. The faster the sales occur, the higher the income. The slower the sales, the lower the income. Ideally, a business could operate with zero inventory. Most businesses, however, including retailers such as Target and Austin Sound, must keep goods on hand. **Inventory turnover,** the ratio of cost of goods sold to average inventory, indicates how rapidly inventory is sold. It is computed as follows:

$$\begin{aligned}\frac{\text{Inventory}}{\text{turnover}} &= \frac{\text{Cost of goods sold}}{\text{Average inventory}} = \frac{\text{Cost of goods sold}}{(\text{Beginning inventory} + \text{Ending inventory})/2} \\ &= \frac{\$90,800}{(\$38,600^* + \$40,200)/2} = \frac{2.3 \text{ times per year}}{(\text{every } 159 \text{ days})}\end{aligned}$$

*Taken from balance sheet at the end of the preceding period.

 DAILY EXERCISE 5-17

 DAILY EXERCISE 5-18

Inventory turnover is usually computed for an annual period, and the relevant cost-of-goods sold figure is the amount for the entire year. Average inventory is computed from the beginning and ending balances. Austin Sound's beginning inventory would be taken from the business's balance sheet at the end of the preceding year. A high turnover rate is preferable, and an increase in the turnover rate usually means higher profits.

Inventory turnover varies from industry to industry. Grocery stores, for example, turn their goods over much faster than automobile dealers do. Drug stores have a higher turnover rate than furniture stores. Retailers of electronic products, such as Austin Sound, have an average turnover of 3.6 times per year. A turnover rate of 2.3 times per year suggests that Austin Sound is not very successful. Exhibit 5-11 compares the inventory turnover rate of Austin Sound, Target, and Wal-Mart Stores.

Varsitybooks.com: A Textbook Case on the Fulfillment Cost Conundrum

Order the fifth edition of *Accounting* from **Varsitybooks.com** and the company arranges for **Baker & Taylor**—book distributors—to ship it to you immediately. Varsitybooks doesn't have a warehouse or any inventory, but it does have to pay Baker & Taylor for this convenient arrangement. How does the fledgling dot.com account for these costs?

As you know from personal experience, e-commerce has revolutionized business. It has bent certain accounting rules in the process. One such rule is that the cost of goods sold to customers is usually considered the "cost of goods sold." Yet, on-line powerhouses like Amazon.com and eToys, Inc. count some of this cost as "sales and marketing expenses because they never own the inventory." By listing these "fulfillment costs" as marketing expense, new-age companies don't have to subtract the costs from their gross profit. This seemed like a good idea to Varsitybooks, and its managers announced to their auditor, **KPMG**, that they wanted to do the same.

After all, Varsitybooks argued, mail-order companies have always done this. And the practice would allow the new agers to keep from reporting razor-thin profit margins. For instance, if the SEC tightens the rules and makes Amazon.com account for fulfillment cost as "cost of sales," gross profit margins for the last quarter of 1999 would go from 15% to −3%.

Small wonder that this approach is controversial! Varsitybooks.com fired KPMG when the auditors objected to it. They hired **PricewaterhouseCoopers** instead, but in the end Varsitybooks had to follow the traditional accounting procedures anyway. The auditors knew best after all.

Source: Based on Shannon Henry, "An E-Tail Identity Crisis," *The Washington Post*, May 4, 2000, p. E01. Anonymous, "Web Retailers' "Gross Profit" Questioned; E-commerce; The SEC may make some firms account for distribution costs, possibly turning their profits into losses," *The Los Angeles Times*, February 19, 2000, p. 2.

Exhibits 5-10 and 5-11 tell an interesting story. Wal-Mart sells a lot of inventory at a low gross profit percentage. Wal-Mart earns its profits by turning its inventory over rapidly—7.0 times during the year. Target sells slightly more upscale merchandise and therefore turns its inventory over only 6.3 times per year.

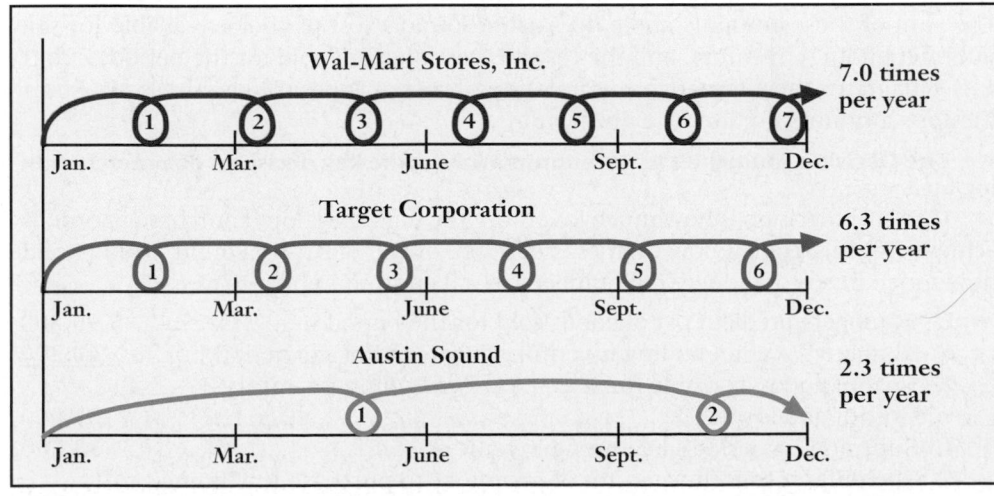

EXHIBIT 5-11
Rate of Inventory Turnover for Three Merchandisers

WORK IT OUT

Calculate the rate of inventory turnover for **Safeway, Inc.,** the large grocery chain (amounts in millions).

Beginning inventory.............	$ 1,856
Ending inventory.................	2,445
Cost of goods sold.................	20,349

Answer

$$\text{Inventory turnover} = \frac{\text{Cost of goods sold}}{(\text{Beginning inventory} + \text{Ending inventory})/2}$$

$$= \frac{\$20,349}{(\$1,856 + \$2,445)/2} = \textbf{9.5 times per year}$$

THE PERIODIC SYSTEM: MEASURING COST OF GOODS SOLD AND INVENTORY PURCHASES

Objective 6
Compute cost of goods sold

The perpetual inventory accounting system we have illustrated provides up-to-date records of inventory and cost of goods sold. That system aids both day-to-day decisions and the preparation of the financial statements. However, managers have other information needs that the perpetual system does not meet. For example, buyers for **Target** and **Austin Sound** must know how much inventory to purchase in order to reach their sales goals.

Computation of cost of goods sold from the periodic inventory system helps managers determine how much inventory to purchase. This alternative computation is used so often in accounting that your education would be incomplete without it. (The appendix at the end of the chapter covers the periodic inventory system in more detail.)

EXHIBIT 5-12

Measuring Austin Sound's Cost of Goods Sold in the Periodic Inventory System

⊙ DAILY EXERCISE 5-19

⊙ DAILY EXERCISE 5-20

⊙ DAILY EXERCISE 5-21

Beginning inventory..................................	$ 38,600
+ **Net purchases**...	87,200*
+ Freight in	5,200
= Cost of goods available for sale.................	131,000
− Ending inventory.......................................	(40,200)
= Cost of goods sold	$ 90,800
*Computation of **Net purchases**:	
Purchases..	$ 91,400
− Purchase discounts	(3,000)
− Purchase returns and allowances	(1,200)
= Net purchases	$ 87,200

NET PURCHASES. Purchases less purchase discounts and purchase returns and allowances.

Exhibit 5–12 gives the alternative computation of Austin Sound's cost of goods sold for 20X2. Austin Sound began the year with inventory of $38,600. During the year, it purchased more goods, also paying freight charges. Note that **net purchases** equals purchases minus purchase discounts and purchase returns and allowances. The sum of these amounts make up Austin Sound's cost of goods available for sale. Subtract ending inventory, and the result is cost of goods sold for the period. Exhibit 5–13 diagrams the alternative computation of cost of goods sold, with Austin Sound Center's amounts used for the illustration.

The Decision Guidelines feature summarizes some key decisions of a merchandising business.

One such decision is how much inventory the business should purchase in order to achieve its goals. Here is how Charles Ernest, the owner of Austin Sound, would decide how much inventory to buy (all numbers are taken from Exhibit 5-12):

1. Managers predict Cost of goods sold for the period.......................	$ 90,800
2. Managers predict Ending inventory at the end of the period........	40,200
3. Cost of goods available for sale = Sum of Ending inventory + Cost of goods sold	131,000
4. Subtract the period's beginning inventory	(38,200)
5. The difference is the amount of inventory to purchase (including Freight in) during the coming year	$ 92,000

	INVENTORY		
Beginning balance	38,600		
Net purchases	87,200		
Freight in	5,200	Cost of goods sold	90,800
Ending balance	40,200		

This T-account shows that the *perpetual* and the *periodic* inventory systems compute the same amounts for ending inventory and for cost of goods sold:

- The *perpetual* system accumulates the balances of Inventory and Cost of Goods Sold throughout the period.
- The *periodic* system determines the correct amounts for Inventory and Cost of Goods Sold only at the end of the period.

Source: The authors thank Betsy Willis for suggesting this exhibit.

DECISION GUIDELINES

Merchandising Operations and the Accounting Cycle

DECISION	GUIDELINES
How do merchandising operations differ from service operations?	• Merchandisers buy and sell *merchandise inventory* • Service entities perform a *service*.

Balance sheet:

DECISION	GUIDELINES
How do a merchandiser's financial statements differ from the financial statements of a service business?	• Merchandiser has *inventory,* an asset. • Service business has no inventory.

Income Statement:

Merchandiser

Sales revenue	$ XXX
− Cost of goods sold	(X)
= Gross profit	XX
− Operating expenses	(X)
= Net income	$ X

Service Business

Service revenue	$XX
− Operating expenses	(X)
= Net income	$ X

Statements of Owner's Equity:

No difference

DECISION	GUIDELINES
Which type of inventory system to use?	• *Perpetual system* shows the amount of *inventory* on hand (the asset) and the cost of goods sold (the expense) at all times. • *Periodic system* shows the correct balances of inventory and cost of goods sold only after a physical count of the inventory, which occurs at least once each year.
How do the adjusting and closing processes of merchandisers and service entities differ?	Very little. The merchandiser may have to *adjust* the Inventory account for spoilage and theft. The merchandiser must *close* the Cost of Goods Sold account. Service entities have no inventory to adjust or cost of goods sold to close.

DECISION GUIDELINES (CONT.)

How to format the merchandiser's income statement?

Multi-step Format		Single-step Format	
Sales revenue	$ XXX	*Revenues:*	
− Cost of goods sold	(X)	Sales revenue	$ XXX
= Gross profit	$ XX	Other revenues.....................	X
− Operating expenses..............	(X)	Total revenues	XXXX
+ Other revenues.....................	X	*Expenses:*	
= Net income	$ XX	Cost of goods sold...............	(X)
		Operating expenses	(X)
		Total expenses......................	XX
		Net income	$ XX

How to evaluate inventory operations?

Two key ratios: $\text{Gross profit percentage*} = \dfrac{\text{Gross profit}}{\text{Net sales revenue}}$

$\text{Inventory turnover*} = \dfrac{\text{Cost of goods sold}}{\text{Average inventory}}$

*In most cases—the higher, the better

How to determine the amount of cost of goods sold?

Can use the *cost of goods sold* model (assumed amounts):

Beginning inventory.............................	$100
+ Net purchases and freight in	800
= Cost of goods available	900
− Ending inventory	(200)
= Cost of goods sold	$700

REVIEW MERCHANDISING OPERATIONS

SUMMARY PROBLEM

The following trial balance and additional data are related to Jan King Distributing Company.

JAN KING DISTRIBUTING COMPANY
Trial Balance
December 31, 20X3

Cash	$ 5,670	
Accounts receivable	37,100	
Inventory	60,500	
Supplies	3,930	
Prepaid rent	6,000	
Furniture and fixtures	26,500	
Accumulated depreciation		$ 21,200
Accounts payable..................................		46,340
Salary payable.......................................		
Interest payable		
Unearned sales revenue.......................		3,500
Note payable, long-term		35,000
Jan King, capital		23,680
Jan King, withdrawals	48,000	
Sales revenue.......................................		346,700
Sales discounts.....................................	10,300	
Sales returns and allowances...............	8,200	
Cost of goods sold	171,770	
Salary expense......................................	82,750	
Rent expense	7,000	
Depreciation expense...........................		
Utilities expense...................................	5,800	
Supplies expense..................................		
Interest expense...................................	2,900	
Total	$476,420	$476,420

Additional data at December 31, 20X3:

a. Supplies used during the year, $2,580.

b. Prepaid rent in force, $1,000.

c. Unearned sales revenue still not earned, $2,400.

d. Depreciation. The furniture and fixtures' estimated useful life is 10 years, and they are expected to be worthless when they are retired from service.

e. Accrued salaries, $1,300.

f. Accrued interest expense, $600.

g. Inventory on hand, $65,800.

Required

1. Enter the trial balance on a work sheet and complete the work sheet.
2. Journalize the adjusting and closing entries at December 31. Post to the Income Summary account as an accuracy check on the entries affecting that account. The credit balance closed out of Income Summary should equal net income computed on the work sheet.
3. Prepare the company's multi-step income statement, statement of owner's equity, and balance sheet in account format. Draw arrows linking the statements.
4. Compute the inventory turnover for 20X3. Inventory at December 31, 20X2, was $61,000. Turnover for 20X2 was 2.1 times. Would you expect Jan King Distributing Company to be more profitable or less profitable in 20X3 than in 20X2? Give your reason.

Solution

Requirement 1

JAN KING DISTRIBUTING COMPANY
Accounting Work Sheet (Perpetual Inventory System)
Year Ended December 31, 20X3

Account Title	Trial Balance Debit	Trial Balance Credit	Adjustments Debit	Adjustments Credit	Income Statement Debit	Income Statement Credit	Balance Sheet Debit	Balance Sheet Credit
Cash............................	5,670						5,670	
Accounts receivable	37,100						37,100	
Inventory	60,500		(g) 5,300				65,800	
Supplies.......................	3,930			(a) 2,580			1,350	
Prepaid rent................	6,000			(b) 5,000			1,000	
Furniture and fixtures....................	26,500						26,500	
Accumulated depreciation.............		21,200		(d) 2,650				23,850
Accounts payable		46,340						46,340
Salary payable				(e) 1,300				1,300
Interest payable...........				(f) 600				600
Unearned sales revenue....................		3,500	(c) 1,100					2,400
Note payable, long-term.................		35,000						35,000
Jan King, capital..........		23,680						23,680
Jan King, withdrawals	48,000						48,000	
Sales revenue		346,700		(c) 1,100		347,800		
Sales discounts	10,300				10,300			
Sales returns and allowances	8,200				8,200			
Cost of goods sold........	171,770			(g) 5,300	166,470			
Salary expense	82,750		(e) 1,300		84,050			
Rent expense...............	7,000		(b) 5,000		12,000			
Depreciation expense....................			(d) 2,650		2,650			
Utilities expense	5,800				5,800			
Supplies expense.........			(a) 2,580		2,580			
Interest expense	2,900		(f) 600		3,500			
	476,420	476,420	18,530	18,530	295,550	347,800	185,420	133,170
Net income..................					52,250			52,250
					347,800	347,800	185,420	185,420

Requirement 2

Adjusting Entries

20X3

Dec. 31	Supplies Expense		2,580	
	Supplies			2,580
31	Rent Expense		5,000	
	Prepaid Rent			5,000
31	Unearned Sales Revenue ($3,500 − $2,400)		1,100	
	Sales Revenue			1,100
31	Depreciation Expense ($26,500/10)		2,650	
	Accumulated Depreciation			2,650
31	Salary Expense		1,300	
	Salary Payable			1,300
31	Interest Expense		600	
	Interest Payable			600
31	Inventory ($65,800 − $60,500)		5,300*	
	Cost of Goods Sold			5,300

*Excess of inventory on hand over the balance in the Inventory account. This adjustment brings Inventory to its correct balance.

Closing Entries

20X3

Dec. 31	Sales Revenue		347,800	
	Income Summary			347,800
31	Income Summary		295,550	
	Sales Discounts			10,300
	Sales Returns and Allowances			8,200
	Cost of Goods Sold			166,470
	Salary Expense			84,050
	Rent Expense			12,000
	Depreciation Expense			2,650
	Utilities Expense			5,800
	Supplies Expense			2,580
	Interest Expense			3,500
31	Income Summary ($347,800 − $295,550)		52,250	
	Jan King, Capital			52,250
31	Jan King, Capital		48,000	
	Jan King, Withdrawals			48,000

INCOME SUMMARY

Clo.	295,550	Clo.	347,800
Clo.	52,250	Bal.	52,250

Requirement 3

JAN KING DISTRIBUTING COMPANY
Income Statement
Year Ended December 31, 20X3

Sales revenue		$347,800	
Less: Sales discounts	$(10,300)		
Sales returns and allowances	(8,200)	(18,500)	
Net sales revenue			329,300
Cost of goods sold			166,470
Gross profit			162,830
Operating expenses:			
Salary expense		$ 84,050	
Rent expense		12,000	
Utilities expense		5,800	
Depreciation expense		2,650	
Supplies expense		2,580	107,080
Income from operations			55,750
Other expense:			
Interest expense			3,500
Net income			$ 52,250

JAN KING DISTRIBUTING COMPANY
Statement of Owner's Equity
Year Ended December 31, 20X3

Jan King, capital, December 31, 20X2	$23,680
Add: Net income	52,250
	75,930
Less: Withdrawals	(48,000)
Jan King, capital, December 31, 20X3	$27,930

JAN KING DISTRIBUTING COMPANY
Balance Sheet
December 31, 20X3

Assets			Liabilities		
Current:			Current:		
Cash		$ 5,670	Accounts payable		$ 46,340
Accounts receivable		37,100	Salary payable		1,300
Inventory		65,800	Interest payable		600
Supplies		1,350	Unearned sales revenue		2,400
Prepaid rent		1,000	Total current liabilities		50,640
Total current assets		110,920	Long-term:		
Plant:			Note payable		35,000
Furniture and					
fixtures	$26,500		Total liabilities		85,640
Less:					
Accumulated					
depreciation	(23,850)	2,650	**Owner's Equity**		
			Jan King, capital		27,930
			Total liabilities and owner's		
Total assets		$113,570	equity		$113,570

Requirement 4

$$\text{Inventory turnover} = \frac{\text{Cost of goods sold}}{\text{Average inventory}} = \frac{\$166,470}{(\$61,000 + \$65,800)/2} = 2.6 \text{ times}$$

The increase in the rate of inventory turnover from 2.1 to 2.6 suggests higher profits in 20X3 than in 20X2.

LESSONS LEARNED

1. **Use sales and gross profit to evaluate a company.** The major revenue of a merchandising business is *sales revenue,* or *sales.* The major expense is *cost of goods sold.* Net sales minus cost of goods sold is *gross profit,* or *gross margin.* This amount measures the business's success or failure in selling its products at a higher price than it paid for them.

2. **Account for the purchase and sale of inventory.** The merchandiser's major asset is inventory. In a merchandising entity, the accounting cycle is from cash to inventory as the inventory is purchased for resale, and back to cash as the inventory is sold. The *invoice* is the business document generated by a purchase or sale transaction. Most merchandising entities allow customers to *return* unsuitable merchandise and also offer *discounts* for early payment. They grant *allowances* for damaged goods that the buyer chooses to keep. Returns and Allowances and Discounts are contra accounts to Sales Revenue.

3. **Adjust and close the accounts of a merchandising business.** The end-of-period adjusting and closing process of a merchandising business is similar to that of a service business. In addition, a merchandiser adjusts inventory for theft losses, damage, and accounting errors.

4. **Prepare a merchandiser's financial statements.** The income statement may appear in *single-step format* or *multi-step format.* A single-step income statement has only two sections—one for revenues and the other for expenses—and a single income amount for net income. A multi-step income statement has subtotals for gross profit and income from operations. Both formats are widely used.

5. **Use the gross profit percentage and the inventory turnover ratio to evaluate a business:** Two key decision aids for a merchandiser are the *gross profit percentage* (gross profit/net sales revenue) and the *rate of inventory turnover* (cost of goods sold/average inventory). Increases in these measures usually signal an increase in profits.

6. **Compute cost of goods sold.** *Cost of goods sold* is the cost of the inventory that the business has sold. It is the largest single expense of most merchandising businesses. Cost of goods sold is the sum of the cost of goods sold amounts recorded during the period. In a periodic inventory system, Cost of goods sold = Beginning inventory + Purchases + Freight in − Ending inventory.

ACCOUNTING VOCABULARY

cost of goods sold   (p 168)
cost of sales   (p. 168)
gross margin   (p. 169)
gross margin percentage   (p. 185)
gross profit   (p. 169)
gross profit percentage   (p. 185)
income from operations   (p. 183)
inventory   (p. 167)
inventory turnover   (p. 186)
invoice   (p. 171)

multi-step income statement   (p. 185)
net purchases   (p. 188)
net sales   (p. 168)
operating expenses   (p. 183)
operating income   (p. 183)
other expense   (p. 183)
other revenue   (p. 183)
periodic inventory system   (p. 169)

perpetual inventory system   (p. 170)
sales   (p. 168)
sales discount   (p. 176)
sales returns and allowances   (p. 176)
sales revenue   (p. 168)
single-step income statement   (p. 185)

QUESTIONS

1. Gross profit is often mentioned in the business press as an important measure of success. What does gross profit measure, and why is it important?
2. Describe the operating cycle for (a) the purchase and cash sale of inventory, and (b) the purchase and sale of inventory on account.
3. Identify ten items of information on an invoice.
4. Indicate which accounts are debited and credited for (a) a credit purchase of inventory and the subsequent cash payment, and (b) a credit sale of inventory and the subsequent cash collection. Assume no discounts, returns, allowances, or freight.
5. Inventory costing $1,000 is purchased and invoiced on July 28 under terms of 3/10 n/30. Compute the payment amount on August 6. How much would the payment be on August 9? What explains the difference? What is the latest acceptable payment date under the terms of sale?
6. Name the new contra accounts introduced in this chapter.
7. Why is the title Cost of Goods Sold especially descriptive? What type of account is Cost of Goods Sold?

8. Beginning inventory is $5,000, net purchases total $30,000, and freight in is $1,000. If ending inventory is $8,000, what is the cost of goods sold?
9. You are beginning the adjusting and closing process at the end of your company's fiscal year. Does the trial balance carry the final ending amount of inventory? Why or why not?
10. Give the adjusting entry for inventory if shrinkage is $9,100.
11. Name and describe two formats for the income statement, and identify the type of business to which each format best applies.
12. Which financial statement reports sales discounts and sales returns and allowances? Show how they are reported, using any reasonable amounts in your illustration.
13. Does a merchandiser prefer a high or a low rate of inventory turnover? Explain.
14. In general, what does a decreasing gross profit percentage, coupled with an increasing rate of inventory turnover, suggest about a business's pricing strategy?

ASSESS YOUR PROGRESS

DAILY EXERCISES

DE5-1 Refer to Exhibit 5-1, page 168, **Target Corporation's** income statement. Identify the title and the amount of Target's

a. Revenue before subtracting any expenses
b. Excess of sales revenue over cost of goods sold
c. Bottom-line operating performance

Using sales, gross profit, and net income to evaluate a company (Obj. 1)

DE5-2 Compare the income statements of two merchandisers:

- **Target Corporation** (Exhibit 5-1, page 168)
- **Austin Sound Center** (Exhibit 5-7, page 182)

For every item on the Target income statement, give the title and the amount of the same item on Austin Sound's income statement. You can ignore Target's four individual *expenses* and the related total of $9,039 million.

Using sales, cost of goods sold, gross profit, and net income (Obj. 1)

DE5-3 Refer to Target's income statement in Exhibit 5-1. Give some alternative titles for the following items:

- Net sales revenue
- Gross profit
- Cost of goods sold
- Net earnings

Using merchandising terminology (Obj. 1)

DE5-4 You may have shopped at a **Gap** store. Suppose Gap purchases 2,000 pairs of slacks on account for $45,000. Credit terms are 2/10 n/30. As part of this shipment, the supplier, Miralu Products of Hong Kong, shipped $8,000 worth of defective merchandise, which Gap rejected and sent back. Gap then paid the balance within the discount period.
Journalize the following transactions for Gap:

a. Purchase of inventory.
b. Return of defective goods.
c. Payment within the discount period.

Recording purchase, purchase return, and cash payment transactions (Obj. 2)

DE5-5 **Toys "Я" Us** purchases inventory from a variety of suppliers, including **Mattel, Hasbro,** and **Tonka.** Suppose Toys "Я" Us buys $150,000 worth of **Lego** toys on credit terms of 3/15 n/45. Unfortunately, the goods are damaged in shipment, so Toys "Я" Us returns $20,000 (original amount, before any discounts) of the merchandise to Lego.
     How much must Toys "Я" Us pay Lego

a. After the discount period?
b. Within the discount period?

Accounting for the purchase of inventory—quantity discount (Obj. 2)

DE5-6 Refer to the **Toys "Я" Us** situation in Daily Exercise 5-5 and journalize the following transactions on the books of Toys "Я"Us. Explanations are not required.

a. Original purchase of the goods on May 6, 20X1.
b. Return of the damaged goods on May 13.
c. Payment on May 15. Before journalizing this transaction, it is helpful to post the first two transactions to the Accounts Payable T-account.

Recording purchase, purchase return, and cash payment transactions (Obj. 2)

DE5-7 Suppose a **Lord & Taylor** store purchases $140,000 of women's sportswear on account from **Liz Claiborne, Inc.** Credit terms are 2/10 net 30. Lord & Taylor pays electronically, and Liz Claiborne receives the money on the tenth day.
     Journalize Lord & Taylor's (a) purchase and (b) payment transactions. What was Lord & Taylor's net cost of this inventory?

Note: Daily Exercise 5-8 covers this same situation for the seller.

Recording purchase transactions (Obj. 2)

DE5-8 **Liz Claiborne, Inc.,** sells $140,000 of women's sportswear to a **Lord & Taylor** store under credit terms of 2/10 net 30. Liz Claiborne's cost of the goods is $82,000, and Claiborne receives the appropriate amount of cash from Lord & Taylor on the tenth day.
     Journalize Liz Claiborne's (a) sale, (b) cost of goods sold, and (c) cash receipt. How much gross profit did Liz Claiborne earn on this sale?

Note: Daily Exercise 5-7 covers the same situation for the buyer.

Recording sales, cost of goods sold, and cash collections (Obj. 2)

Recording sale, sales return, and cash collection entries
(Obj. 2)

DE5-9 Refer to the **Gap/Miralu Products** situation in Daily Exercise 5-4. Record the three transactions on the books of the seller, Miralu Products. Assume Miralu keeps its records in U.S. dollars and that the goods cost Miralu $22,500. Miralu's transactions are

a. Sale of inventory and the related cost of goods sold.
b. The $8,000 sales return and the related receipt of defective goods (cost, $4,000) from the purchaser.
c. Collection of cash within the discount period.

Computing net sales and gross profit
(Obj. 2)

DE5-10 **Intel Corporation,** famous for the Pentium© processor that powers many personal computers, offers sales discounts to the computer companies to which Intel sells its products. Intel also allows its customers to return defective processors. Suppose that during a recent period, Intel made sales of $600,000 on credit terms of 2/10 net 30. Assume that Intel received sales returns of $12,000. Later, Intel collected cash within the discount period. Cost of goods sold for the period was $255,000 after all sales returns.

For this particular period, compute Intel's

a. Net sales revenue   **b.** Gross profit

Adjusting the accounts of a merchandiser
(Obj. 3)

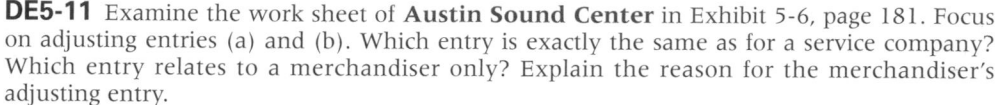

DE5-11 Examine the work sheet of **Austin Sound Center** in Exhibit 5-6, page 181. Focus on adjusting entries (a) and (b). Which entry is exactly the same as for a service company? Which entry relates to a merchandiser only? Explain the reason for the merchandiser's adjusting entry.

Using a merchandiser's financial statements
(Obj. 4)

DE5-12 Examine the financial statements of **Austin Sound Center** in Exhibit 5-7, page 182. Identify every item, including subtotals and totals, that relates exclusively to a merchandiser and will not appear in the financial statements of a service entity.

Note: An early-payment discount, similar to a sales discount, can relate to a service entity because a service business can allow its customers to take a discount for early payment.

Preparing a merchandiser's income statement
(Obj. 4)

DE5-13 **Dell Computer Corporation** reported these figures in its January 31, 2000, financial statements (adapted, and in millions):

Cash	$ 3,809	Other assets (long-term)	$ 3,025
Total operating expenses	3,552	Other current liabilities	1,654
Accounts payable	3,538	Property and equipment, net	765
Owners' equity	5,308	Net sales revenue	25,265
Long-term liabilities	971	Other current assets	873
Inventory	391	Accounts receivable	2,608
Cost of goods sold	20,047		

Prepare Dell's multi-step income statement for the year ended January 31, 2000.

Preparing a merchandiser's balance sheet
(Obj. 4)

DE5-14 Use the data in Daily Exercise 5-13 to prepare **Dell Computer's** classified balance sheet at January 31, 2000. Use the report format with all headings, and list accounts in proper order.

Making closing entries
(Obj. 3)

DE5-15 Refer to the work sheet of **Austin Sound Center** in Exhibit 5-6, page 181. Based solely on the Income Statement columns of the work sheet, make two closing entries, as follows:

• Journalize the closing entry for the *first account* listed that must be closed at the end of the period.
• Journalize the closing entry for the *last account* listed on the work sheet (not net income, which is not an account).

All closing entries for revenues and expenses follow the pattern of the closing entries you just made. Now make the final two closing entries of Austin Sound Center:

• Journalize the closing entry for the Owner's Withdrawals account.
• Journalize the closing entry for net income.

Set up a T-account for the Owner's Capital account, and insert the balance from the work sheet. Then post your closing entries to the Capital account. Its ending balance should be the same as the amount reported on Austin Sound's balance sheet in Exhibit 5-7 on page 182. Is it?

DE5-16 Refer to the income statement of **Target Corporation** in Exhibit 5-1, page 168.

Closing the accounts (Obj. 3)

1. Identify every account on Target's income statement that the company will close out at the end of the year. Make two closing entries for these accounts at January 31, 2000:
   - Close the revenue
   - Close the expenses

2. Target's balance sheet reports the following selected accounts:
   - Inventory
   - Accounts payable
   - Land
   - Long-term debt
   - Other assets
   - Owners' equity

Which of these accounts does Target close, if any? Give your reason.

DE5-17 Refer to the **Dell Computer** situation in Daily Exercise 5-13. Compute Dell's gross profit percentage and rate of inventory turnover for 2000. One year earlier, at January 31, 1999, Dell's inventory balance was $320 million.

Computing the gross profit percentage and the rate of inventory turnover (Obj. 5)

DE5-18 Lands' End, the catalog merchant, reported the following for the year ended January 31, 2000 (as adapted, with amounts in millions):

Contrasting accounting income and cash flows (Obj. 4)

Cash collections from customers	$1,323	Cash payments to suppliers	$ 682
		Net sales revenue	1,320
Selling, general, and administrative expenses	529	Cost of sales	727

As an investor, you wonder which was greater, Lands' End's (a) gross profit, or (b) the company's excess of cash collections from customers over cash payments to suppliers? Compute both amounts to answer this question.

DE5-19 At January 31, 1999, **Target Corporation** had merchandise inventory of $3,475 million. During the following year, Target purchased inventory costing $23,352 million, including freight in. At January 31, 2000, Target's inventory stood at $3,798 million.

Computing cost of goods sold in a periodic inventory system (Obj. 6)

1. Compute Target's cost of goods sold as in the periodic inventory system.
2. Compare your cost-of-goods-sold figure to Exhibit 5-1, page 000. The two amounts should be equal. Are they?

DE5-20 Les Fleurs, a boutique in Paris, France, had the following accounts in its accounting records at December 31, 20X2 (amounts in French francs, denoted as "F"):

Computing net sales, cost of goods sold and gross profit in a periodic inventory system (Obj. 6)

Purchases	F250,000	Freight in	F	8,000
Sales discounts	4,000	Purchase returns		7,000
Inventory:		Sales		400,000
December 31, 20X1	20,000	Purchase discounts		3,000
December 31, 20X2	30,000	Sales returns		8,000

Compute the following for Les Fleurs during 20X2:

1. Net sales revenue   2. Cost of goods sold   3. Gross profit

DE5-21 Gap Inc., reported Cost of Goods Sold totaling $6,775 million. Ending inventory was $1,462 million, and beginning inventory was $1,056 million. How much inventory did Gap purchase during the year?

Computing inventory purchases (Obj. 6)

EXERCISES

Evaluating a company's revenues, gross profit, operating income, and net income (Obj. 1)

E5-1 Toys "Я" Us reported the following:

TOYS "Я" US, INC.
Statements of Earnings (adapted)

(In millions)	Fiscal Years Ended January 31, 2000	January 31, 1999
Net sales	$11,862	$11,170
Costs and expenses:		
Cost of sales	8,321	8,191
Other expenses	3,262	3,111
Net earnings (net loss)	$ 279	$ (132)

TOYS "Я" US, INC.
Balance Sheets (partial, adapted)

Assets (In millions)	January 31, 2000	January 31, 1999
Current Assets:		
Cash and cash equivalents	$ 584	$ 410
Accounts and other receivables	182	204
Merchandise inventories	2,027	1,902
Prepaid expenses and other current assets	80	81
Total Current Assets	$2,873	$2,597

Required

1. Is Toys "Я" Us a merchandising entity, a service business, or both? How can you tell? List the items in the Toys "Я" Us financial statements that influence your answer.
2. Compute Toys "Я" Us's gross profit for fiscal years 2000 and 1999. Did the gross profit increase or decrease in 2000? Is this a good sign or a bad sign about the company?
3. Write a brief memo to investors advising them of Toys "Я" Us's trend of sales, gross profit, and net income. Indicate whether the outlook for Toys "Я" Us is favorable or unfavorable, based on this trend. Use the following memo format:

Date:	_____
To:	Investors
From:	Student Name
Subject:	Trend of sales, gross profit and net income for Toys " Я " Us

Journalizing purchase and sales transactions (Obj. 2)

E5-2 Journalize, without explanations, the following transactions of Lane's Fine Gifts during the month of September:

Sept. 3   Purchased $1,900 of inventory on account under terms of 2/10 n/eom (end of month) and FOB shipping point.

     7   Returned $300 of defective merchandise purchased on September 3.

     9   Paid freight bill of $30 on September 3 purchase.

   10   Sold inventory on account for $3,100. Payment terms on the remainder were 2/15 n/30. These goods cost Lane's Fine Gifts $1,700.

   12   Paid amount owed on credit purchase of September 3, less the discount and the return.

   16   Granted a sales allowance of $800 on the September 10 sale.

   23   Received cash from September 10 customer in full settlement of her debt, less the allowance and the discount.

Journalizing transactions from a purchase invoice (Obj. 2)

E5-3 As the proprietor of Stevens Goodyear Tire Co., you receive the following invoice from a supplier:

BELTLINE TIRE WHOLESALE DISTRIBUTORS, INC.
2600 Commonwealth Avenue
Boston, Massachusetts 02215

Invoice date: May 14, 20X3

Payment terms: 2/10 n/30

Sold to: Stevens Goodyear Tire Co.
4219 Crestwood Parkway
Lexington, Mass. 02173

Quantity Ordered	Description	Quantity Shipped	Price	Amount
4	P135–X4 Radials	4	$37.14	$ 148.56
8	L912 Belted-bias	8	41.32	330.56
14	R39 Truck tires	10	50.02	500.20
	Total			$979.32

Due date:	Amount:
May 24, 20X3	$959.73
May 25 through June 13, 20X3	$979.32

Paid:

Required

1. Stevens received the invoice on May 15. Record the May 15 purchase on account. Carry to the nearest cent throughout.
2. The R39 truck tires were ordered by mistake and were therefore returned to Beltline. Journalize the return on May 19.
3. Record the May 22 payment of the amount owed.

E5-4 On April 30, De Boulle Jewelers purchased inventory of $8,000 on account from Intergem Jewels, a jewelry importer. Terms were 3/15 net 45. On receiving the goods, De Boulle checked the order and found $800 of unsuitable merchandise. De Boulle returned $800 of the merchandise to Intergem on May 4.

Journalizing purchase transactions (Obj. 2)

To pay the remaining amount owed, De Boulle borrowed the net amount of the invoice from the bank. On May 14, De Boulle signed a short-term note payable to the bank and immediately paid the borrowed funds to Intergem. On June 14, De Boulle paid the bank the net amount of the invoice, which De Boulle had borrowed plus 1% monthly interest (round to the nearest dollar).

Required

Record the indicated transactions in the journal of De Boulle Jewelers. Explanations are not required.

E5-5 Refer to the business situation in Exercise 5-4. Journalize the transactions of Intergem Jewels. Intergem's gross profit is 40%, so cost of goods sold is 60% of sales. Explanations are not required.

Journalizing sales transactions (Obj. 2)

E5-6 The Home Depot is one of the largest retailers in the United States. For a recent year, The Home Depot's accounting records carried the following accounts (adapted, with amounts in millions) at January 31, 2000:

Making closing entries (Obj. 3)

Receivables	$ 587	Selling expense	$ 6,832
Interest revenue	37	Sales revenue............................	38,434
Accounts payable............	1,993	Interest expense........................	28
Cost of goods sold	27,023	Merchandise inventories	5,489
Other expense	1,597	General and administrative	
Owner withdrawals	255	expense	671

Required

1. Journalize all of The Home Depot's closing entries at January 31, 2000. Use an Owner Capital account.

2. Set up T-accounts for the Income Summary account and the Owner Capital account. Post to these accounts and take their ending balances. One year earlier, at January 31, 1999, the Owner Capital balance was $8,740 million.

Using work sheet data to make the closing entries (Obj. 3)

E5-7 The trial balance and adjustments columns of the work sheet of Northstar Auto Supply at March 31, 20X2 follow.

Account Title	Trial Balance		Adjustments	
	Debit	Credit	Debit	Credit
Cash...	2,000			
Accounts receivable............................	8,500		(a) 6,100	
Inventory...	36,100			(b) 4,290
Supplies	13,000			(c) 8,600
Equipment..	42,470			
Accumulated depreciation...................		11,250		(d) 2,250
Accounts payable...............................		9,300		
Salary payable				(e) 1,200
Note payable, long-term......................		7,500		
Jack Potter, capital............................		33,920		
Jack Potter, withdrawals.....................	45,000			
Sales revenue...................................		233,000		(a) 6,100
Sales discounts.................................	2,000			
Cost of goods sold.............................	111,600		(b) 4,290	
Selling expense.................................	21,050		(c) 5,200	
			(e) 1,200	
General expense	10,500		(c) 3,400	
			(d) 2,250	
Interest expense................................	2,750			
Total..	294,970	294,970	22,440	22,440

Compute the adjusted balance for each account that must be closed. Then journalize Northstar's closing entries at March 31, 20X2. How much was Northstar's net income or net loss?

Preparing a multi-step income statement   (Obj. 4)

E5-8 Use the data in Exercise 5-7 to prepare the multi-step income statement of Northstar Auto Supply for the year ended March 31, 20X2.

Using the gross profit percentage and the rate of inventory turnover to evaluate profitability (Obj. 5)

E5-9 Refer to Exercise 5-8. After completing Northstar's income statement for the year ended March 31, 20X2, compute these ratios to evaluate Northstar's performance:

- Gross profit percentage
- Inventory turnover (Ending inventory one year earlier, at March 31, 20X1, was $30,500.)

Compare your figures with the 20X1 gross profit percentage of 48% and the inventory turnover rate of 3.16 for 20X1. Does the two-year trend suggest that Northstar's profits are increasing or decreasing?

Preparing a merchandiser's multi-step income statement to evaluate the business (Obj. 4, 5)

E5-10 Selected amounts from the accounting records of Barringer Boats, Ltd., are listed in alphabetical order.

Accounts payable	$16,200	Owner's equity,	
Accumulated depreciation	18,700	December 31, 20X0	$126,070
Cost of goods sold	99,300	Sales discounts.................	9,000
General expenses	23,500	Sales returns	4,600
Interest revenue	1,500	Sales revenue	204,000
Inventory, December 31, 19X9	21,000	Selling expenses	37,800
Inventory, December 31, 20X0	19,400	Unearned sales revenue....	6,500

Required

1. Prepare the business's multi-step income statement for the year ended December 31, 20X0.
2. Compute the rate of inventory turnover for the year. Last year the turnover rate was 3.8 times. Does this two-year trend suggest improvement or deterioration in inventory turnover?

E5-11 Prepare Barringer Boats, Ltd.'s single-step income statement for 20X0, using the data from Exercise 5-10. Compute the gross profit percentage, and compare it with last year's gross profit percentage of 50%. Does this two-year trend in the gross profit percentage suggest better or worse profitability during the current year?

Preparing a single-step income statement to evaluate the business
(Obj. 4, 5)

E5-12 General Motors (GM) is a business empire, with both automotive operations and financial services. During 1999, GM's automotive operations made sales of $153 billion and had cost of goods sold totaling $127 billion. GM's automotive assets totaled $126 billion at December 31, 1999. Total automotive liabilities were $115 billion. During 1999, GM's automotive operations paid $123 billion for inventory and collected $152 billion from customers.

Comparing gross profit and cash flows
(Obj. 4)

Required

As an investor, you wonder which was greater, (a) GM's gross profit on automotive sales or (b) GM's excess of cash collections from customers over cash payments to suppliers. Compute both amounts to answer this question.

E5-13 The periodic inventory records of Barringer Boats, Ltd. include these accounts at December 31, 20X0:

Computing cost of goods sold in a periodic inventory system
(Obj. 6)

Purchases of inventory	$98,600
Purchase discounts	3,000
Purchase returns and allowances	2,000
Freight in	4,100
Inventory	19,400

One year ago, at December 31, 19X9, Barringer's inventory balance stood at $21,000.

Required

Compute Barringer's cost of goods sold for 20X0 as in the periodic inventory system.

E5-14 Supply the missing income statement amounts in each of the following situations:

Computing inventory and cost of goods sold amounts in a periodic inventory system (Obj. 6)

Sales	Sales Discounts	Net Sales	Beginning Inventory	Net Purchases	Ending Inventory	Cost of Goods Sold	Gross Profit
$98,300	(a)	$92,800	$32,500	$66,700	$39,400	(b)	$33,000
62,400	$2,100	(c)	27,450	43,000	(d)	$44,100	(e)
91,500	1,800	89,700	(f)	44,900	22,900	59,400	(g)
(h)	3,000	(i)	40,700	(j)	48,230	72,500	39,600

E5-15 For the year ended December 31, 20X1, Lighthouse Designs, a retailer of home-related products, reported net sales of $338 million and cost of goods sold of $154 million. The company's balance sheet at December 31, 20X0 and 20X1, reported inventories of $103 million and $129 million, respectively. How much were Lighthouse Designs' net purchases during 20X1?

Computing an actual company's net purchases
(Obj. 6

Continuing Exercise. *This exercise completes the Amos Faraday, Consultant, situation from Exercise 2-15 of Chapter 2, Exercise 3-14 of Chapter 3, and Exercise 4-11 of Chapter 4.*

E5-16 Amos Faraday's consulting practice includes a great deal of systems consulting business. Faraday has begun selling accounting software. During January, the business completed these transactions:

Jan. 2 Completed a consulting engagement and received cash of $7,200.
2 Prepaid three months' office rent, $1,500.
7 Purchased accounting software inventory on account, $4,000.
16 Paid employee salary, $1,400.
18 Sold accounting software on account, $1,100 (cost $700).
19 Consulted with a client for a fee of $900 on account.
21 Paid on account, $2,000.
24 Paid utilities, $300.
28 Sold accounting software for cash, $600 (cost $400).
31 Recorded these adjusting entries:
    Accrued salary expense, $1,400.
    Accounted for expiration of prepaid rent.
    Depreciation of office furniture, $200.

Required

1. Open the following selected T-accounts in the ledger: Cash; Accounts Receivable; Accounting Software Inventory; Prepaid Rent; Accumulated Depreciation; Accounts Payable; Salary Payable; Amos Faraday, Capital; Income Summary; Service Revenue; Sales Revenue; Cost of Goods Sold; Salary Expense; Rent Expense; Utilities Expense; and Depreciation Expense.
2. Journalize and post the January transactions. Key all items by date. Compute each account balance, and denote the balance as *Bal.* Journalize and post the closing entries. Denote each closing amount as Clo. After posting all closing entries, prove the equality of debits and credits in the ledger.
3. Prepare the January income statement of Amos Faraday, Consultant. Use the single-step format.

(Group A) PROBLEMS

P5-1A Wal-Mart Stores, Inc., is the largest retailer in the world, with almost 4,000 stores. A key Wal-Mart advantage is its sophisticated perpetual inventory accounting system.

Required

You are the manager of a Wal-Mart store in Nashville, Tennessee. Write a one-paragraph business memo to a new employee explaining how the company accounts for the purchase and sale of merchandise inventory. Use the following heading for your memo:

Date:	_____
To:	New Employee
From:	Store Manager
Subject:	Wal-Mart's accounting system for inventories

P5-2A Assume the following transactions occurred between **Johnson & Johnson (J&J),** the healthcare products company, and **CVS Drugstores,** during February of the current year:

Feb. 6 Johnson & Johnson sold $8,000 worth of merchandise to CVS on terms of 2/10 n/30, FOB shipping point. J&J prepaid freight charges of $500 and included this amount in the invoice total. (J&J's entry to record the freight payment debits Accounts Receivable and credits Cash.) These goods cost J&J $6,100.
10 CVS returned $900 of the merchandise purchased on February 6. J&J accounted for the $900 sales return and placed the goods back in inventory (cost, $590).
15 CVS paid $3,000 of the invoice amount owed to J&J for the February 6 purchase, less the discount. This payment included none of the freight charge.
27 CVS paid the remaining amount owed to J&J for the February 6 purchase.

Required

Journalize these transactions, first on the books of CVS and second on the books of Johnson & Johnson.

P5-3A Preakness Wholesale Grocery engaged in the following transactions during May:

Journalizing purchase and sale transactions
(Obj. 2)

May 3 Purchased office supplies for cash, $300.
   7 Purchased inventory on credit terms of 3/10 net eom, $2,000.
   8 Returned half the inventory purchased on May 7. It was not the inventory ordered.
   10 Sold goods for cash, $450 (cost, $250).
   13 Sold inventory on credit terms of 2/15 n/45, $3,900 (cost, $1,800).
   16 Paid the amount owed on account from the purchase of May 7, less the discount and the return.
   17 Receive defective inventory as a sales return from May 13 sale, $900. Preakness's cost of the inventory received was $600.
   18 Purchased inventory of $4,000 on account. Payment terms were 2/10 net 30.
   26 Borrowed $3,920 from the bank to take advantage of the discount offered on the May 18 purchase. Signed a note payable to the bank for this amount.
   28 Received cash in full settlement of the account from the customer who purchased inventory on May 13, less the discount and the return.
   29 Purchased inventory for cash, $2,000, plus freight charges of $160.

Required

1. Journalize the preceding transactions on the books of Preakness Wholesale Grocery.
2. The note payable signed on May 26 requires Preakness to pay $30 interest expense. Was the decision to borrow funds in order to take advantage of the cash discount wise or unwise? Support your answer by comparing the discount to the interest paid.

P5-4A House of India Restaurant's trial balance pertains to December 31, 20X9.

Preparing a merchandiser's work sheet
(Obj. 3)

HOUSE OF INDIA RESTAURANT Trial Balance December 31, 20X9		
Cash	$ 1,270	
Accounts receivable	4,430	
Inventory	73,900	
Prepaid rent	4,400	
Fixtures	22,100	
Accumulated depreciation		$ 8,380
Accounts payable		6,290
Salary payable		
Interest payable		
Note payable, long-term		18,000
Reshma Desai, capital		55,920
Reshma Desai, withdrawals	39,550	
Sales revenue		170,150
Cost of goods sold	67,870	
Salary expense	24,700	
Rent expense	7,700	
Advertising expense	4,510	
Utilities expense	3,880	
Depreciation expense		
Insurance expense	2,770	
Interest expense	1,660	
Total	$258,740	$258,740

Additional data at December 31, 20X9:

a. Total rent expense for the year, $10,200.
b. Store fixtures have an estimated useful life of ten years and are expected to be worthless when they are retired from service.
c. Accrued salaries at December 31, $900.
d. Accrued interest expense at December 31, $360.
e. Inventory on hand at December 31, $72,700.

Required

Complete House of India's accounting work sheet for the year ended December 31, 20X9. Key adjusting entries by letter.

P5-5A Refer to the data in Problem 5-4A.

1. Journalize the adjusting and closing entries.
2. Determine the December 31 balance of Reshma Desai, Capital.

P5-6A ←← *Link Back to Chapter 4 (Classified Balance Sheet)*. Selected accounts of Mother Earth Organic Products are listed along with their balances before closing at May 31, 20X9.

Accounts payable	$ 16,900	Interest expense	$ 400
Accounts receivable	33,700	Interest payable	1,100
Accumulated depreciation—		Inventory: May 31	45,500
equipment	38,000	Note payable, long-term	45,000
P. Debruge, capital,		Salary payable	2,800
April 30	73,900	Sales discounts	10,400
P. Debruge, withdrawals	9,000	Sales returns and allowances	18,000
Cash	7,800	Sales revenue	701,000
Cost of goods sold	362,000	Selling expenses	137,900
Equipment	146,000	Supplies	5,100
General expenses	116,700	Unearned sales revenue	13,800

Required

1. Prepare the business's *multi-step* income statement for the month ended May 31, 20X9.
2. Prepare Mother Earth's classified balance sheet in *report format* at May 31, 20X9. Show your computation of the May 31 balance of P. Debruge, Capital.

P5-7A ←← *Link Back to Chapter 4 (Classified Balance Sheet)*.

Required

1. Use the data of Problem 5-6A to prepare a *single-step* income statement for the month ended May 31, 20X9.
2. Prepare Mother Earth's classified balance sheet in *report format* at May 31, 20X9. Show your computation of the May 31 balance of P. Debruge, Capital.

P5-8A The trial balance and adjustments columns of the work sheet of Purcell Music Company include the following accounts and balances at November 30, 20X4:

Account Title	Trial Balance Debit	Trial Balance Credit	Adjustments Debit	Adjustments Credit
Cash	24,000			
Accounts receivable	14,500		(a) 4,000	
Inventory	36,330		(b) 1,010	
Supplies	2,800			(c) 2,400
Furniture	39,600			
Accumulated depreciation		4,900		(d) 2,450
Accounts payable		12,600		(f) 1,000
Salary payable				
Unearned sales revenue		13,570	(e) 6,700	
Note payable, long-term		15,000		
H. Purcell, capital		60,310		
H. Purcell, drawing	42,000			
Sales revenue		174,000		(a) 4,000
				(e) 6,700
Sales returns	6,300			
Cost of goods sold	72,170			(b) 1,010
Selling expense	28,080		(f) 1,000	
General expense	13,100		(c) 2,400	
			(d) 2,450	
Interest expense	1,500			
Total	280,380	280,380	17,560	17,560

Required

1. Inventory on hand one year ago, at November 30, 20X3, was $32,650. Without entering the preceding data on a formal work sheet, prepare the company's multi-step income statement for the year ended November 30, 20X4.
2. Compute the gross profit percentage and the rate of inventory turnover for 20X4. For 20X3, Purcell's gross profit percentage was 55%, and inventory turnover was 1.91 times during the year. Does the two-year trend in these ratios suggest improvement or deterioration in profitability?

(Computing cost of goods sold and gross profit in a periodic inventory system; evaluating the business (Obj. 5, 6))

P5-9A The accounting records of Copeland Appliance list the following at November 30, 20X1:

Purchases of inventory	$132,000	Inventory: November 30, 20X0	$41,700
Selling expenses	8,800	November 30, 20X1	41,500
Furniture	37,200	Cash	3,700
Purchase returns and allowances	900	Freight in	1,600
Salary payable	300	Accumulated depreciation	
Jim Copeland, capital	52,800	—furniture	13,600
Sales revenue	199,600	Purchase discounts	600
Sales returns and allowances	3,200	Sales discounts	2,100
Accounts payable	9,500	General expenses	19,300

Required

1. Show the computation of Copeland's net sales, cost of goods sold, and gross profit for the year ended November 30, 20X1. Compute cost of goods sold as in the periodic inventory system.
2. Jim Copeland, owner of the company, strives to earn a gross profit percentage of 30%. Did he achieve this goal?
3. Did the rate of inventory turnover reach the industry average of 3.5 times per year?

PROBLEMS

(Group B)

P5-1B **Optic Nerve** is a regional chain of optical shops in the southwestern United States. The company offers a large selection of eyeglass frames, and Optic Nerve stores provide while-you-wait service. The company has launched a vigorous advertising campaign to promote two-for-the-price-of-one frame sales.

Explaining the perpetual inventory system (Obj. 2)

Required

Optic Nerve expects to grow rapidly and to increase its level of inventory. As the chief accountant of this company, you wish to install a perpetual inventory system. Write a one-paragraph business memo to the company president to explain how that system would work. Use the following heading for your memo:

Date:	_____
To:	Company President
From:	Chief Accountant
Subject:	How a perpetual inventory system works

P5-2B Assume the following transactions occurred between **Eckerd Drug Stores** and **Johnson & Johnson (J&J)**, the healthcare products company, during June of the current year:

Accounting for the purchase and sale of inventory (Obj. 2)

June 8	Johnson & Johnson sold $6,000 worth of merchandise to Eckerd Drug Stores on terms of 2/10 n/30, FOB shipping point. J&J prepaid freight charges of $200 and included this amount in the invoice total. (J&J's entry to record the freight payment debits Accounts Receivable and credits Cash.) These goods cost J&J $2,100.
11	Eckerd returned $600 of the merchandise purchased on June 8. J&J accounted for the $600 sales return and placed the goods back in inventory (J&J's cost, $250).
17	Eckerd paid $2,000 of the invoice amount owed to J&J for the June 8 purchase, less the discount. This payment included none of the freight charge.
26	Eckerd paid the remaining amount owed to J&J for the June 8 purchase.

Required

Journalize these transactions, first on the books of Eckerd Drug Stores and second on the books of Johnson & Johnson.

P5-3B Larkspur Lighting Company engaged in the following transactions during July:

July 2	Purchased inventory for cash, $800.
5	Purchased store supplies on credit terms of net eom, $450.
8	Purchased inventory of $3,000, plus freight charges of $230. Credit terms are 3/15 n/30.
9	Sold goods for cash, $1,200. Larkspur's cost of these goods was $700.
11	Returned $200 of the inventory purchased on July 8. It was damaged.
12	Purchased inventory on credit terms of 3/10 n/30, $3,330.
14	Sold inventory on credit terms of 2/10 n/30, $9,600 (cost $5,000).
16	Paid utilities expense, $275.
20	Received returned inventory from the July 14 sale, $400. Larkspur shipped the wrong goods by mistake. Larkspur's cost of the inventory received was $250.
21	Borrowed the amount owed on the July 8 purchase. Signed a note payable to the bank for $2,946, which takes into account the return of inventory on July 11.
21	Paid supplier for goods purchased on July 8 less the discount and the return.
23	Received $6,860 cash in partial settlement of his account from the customer who purchased inventory on July 14. Granted the customer a 2% discount and credited his account receivable for $7,000.
30	Paid for the store supplies purchased on July 5.

Required

1. Journalize the preceding transactions on the books of Larkspur Lighting Company.
2. Compute the amount of the receivable at July 31 from the customer to whom Larkspur sold inventory on July 14. What amount of cash discount applies to this receivable at July 31?

P5-4B Fresh Market Grocery's trial balance pertains to December 31, 20X1.

FRESH MARKET GROCERY
Trial Balance
December 31, 20X1

Cash	$ 2,910	
Accounts receivable	6,560	
Inventory	101,760	
Store supplies	1,990	
Prepaid insurance	3,200	
Store fixtures	63,900	
Accumulated depreciation		$ 37,640
Accounts payable		29,770
Salary payable		
Interest payable		
Note payable, long-term		37,200
Elaine Lorens, capital		63,120
Elaine Lorens, withdrawals	36,300	
Sales revenue		286,370
Cost of goods sold	161,090	
Salary expense	46,580	
Rent expense	14,630	
Utilities expense	6,780	
Depreciation expense		
Insurance expense	5,300	
Store supplies expense		
Interest expense	3,100	
Total	$454,100	$454,100

Additional data at December 31, 20X1:

a. Insurance expense for the year, $6,090.
b. Store fixtures have an estimated useful life of ten years and are expected to be worthless when they are retired from service.
c. Accrued salaries at December 31, $1,260.
d. Accrued interest expense at December 31, $870.
e. Store supplies on hand at December 31, $760.
f. Inventory on hand at December 31, $94,780.

Required

Complete Fresh Market's accounting work sheet for the year ended December 31, 20X1. Key adjusting entries by letter.

P5-5B Refer to the data in Problem 5-4B at the bottom of the facing page.

Required

1. Journalize the adjusting and closing entries of Fresh Market Grocery.
2. Determine the December 31 balance of Elaine Lorens, Capital.

Journalizing the adjusting and closing entries of a merchandising business (Obj. 3)

P5-6B ◄═ *Link Back to Chapter 4 (Classified Balance Sheet).* Selected accounts of Genesis Electronics are listed along with their balances before closing at July 31, 20X2.

Preparing a multi-step income statement and a classified balance sheet (Obj. 3, 4)

Accounts payable	$127,300	Interest payable	$ 3,000
Accounts receivable	46,200	Inventory: July 31	187,300
Accumulated depreciation—		Note payable, long-term	160,000
store equipment	16,400	Salary payable	6,100
A. L. Genesis, capital,		Sales discounts	8,300
June 30	69,100	Sales returns and allowances	17,900
A. L. Genesis, withdrawals	11,000	Sales revenue	556,600
Cash	24,300	Selling expense	84,600
Cost of goods sold	360,900	Store equipment	126,000
General expense	75,800	Supplies	4,300
Interest expense	1,200	Unearned sales revenue	9,300

Required

1. Prepare the entity's *multi-step* income statement for the month ended July 31, 20X2.
2. Prepare Genesis's classified balance sheet in *report format* at July 31, 20X2. Show your computation of the July 31 balance of A.L. Genesis, Capital.

P5-7B ◄═ *Link Back to Chapter 4 (Classified Balance Sheet).*

Preparing a single-step income statement and a classified balance sheet (Obj. 4)

Required

1. Use the data of Problem 5-6B to prepare Genesis Electronics' *single-step* income statement for July 31, 20X2.
2. Prepare Genesis's classified balance sheet in *report format* at July 31, 20X2. Show your computation of the July 31 balance of A. L. Genesis, Capital.

P5-8B The trial balance and adjustments columns of the work sheet of **Carolina Crystal Company** follow.

Using work sheet data to prepare financial statements and evaluate the business; multi-step income statement (Obj. 4, 5)

	Trial Balance		Adjustments	
Account Title	**Debit**	**Credit**	**Debit**	**Credit**
Cash	7,300			
Accounts receivable	4,360		(a) 1,400	
Inventory	9,630		(b) 2,100	
Supplies	10,700			(c) 7,940
Equipment	99,450			
Accumulated depreciation		29,800		(d) 9,900
Accounts payable		13,800		
Salary payable				(f) 200
Unearned sales revenue		3,780	(e) 2,600	
Note payable, long-term		10,000		
Claire Burke, capital		58,360		
Claire Burke, drawing	35,000			
Sales revenue		212,000		(a) 1,400
				(e) 2,600
Sales returns	3,100			
Cost of goods sold	95,600			(b) 2,100
Selling expense	40,600		(c) 7,940	
			(f) 200	
General expense	21,000		(d) 9,900	
Interest expense	1,000			
Total	327,740	327,740	24,140	24,140

Required

1. Inventory on hand at September 30, 20X2, was $9,250. Without completing a formal accounting work sheet, prepare the company's multi-step income statement for the year ended September 30, 20X3.

2. Compute the gross profit percentage and the inventory turnover for 20X3. For 20X2, Carolina's gross profit percentage was 50% and the inventory turnover rate was 7.8 times. Does the two-year trend in these ratios suggest improvement or deterioration in profitability?

Computing cost of goods sold and gross profit in a periodic inventory system; evaluating the business (Obj. 5, 6)

P5-9B The accounting records of Vanguard Security Systems at June 30, 20X2 list the following:

Cash	$ 13,600	Inventory: June 30, 20X1	$23,800
Purchases of inventory.............	98,100	June 30, 20X2	28,500
Freight in	4,300	Equipment	44,700
Sales revenue	199,100	Purchase discounts...................	1,300
Purchase returns		Accumulated depreciation—	
and allowances....................	1,400	equipment...........................	6,900
Salary payable..........................	1,800	Sales discounts.........................	3,400
Luke Stover, capital..................	36,000	General expenses......................	16,300
Sales returns and allowances ...	12,100	Accounts payable.....................	23,800
Selling expenses.......................	29,800		

Required

1. Show the computation of Vanguard Security Systems' net sales, cost of goods sold, and gross profit for the year ended June 30, 20X2. Compute cost of goods sold as in the periodic inventory system.

2. Luke Stover, owner of the business, strives to earn a gross profit percentage of 44%. Did he achieve this goal?

3. Did the rate of inventory turnover reach the industry average of 4.0 times per year?

APPLY YOUR KNOWLEDGE

DECISION CASES

Using the financial statements to decide on a business expansion (Obj. 4, 5)

Case 1. ← *Link Back to Chapter 4 (Classified Balance Sheet, Current Ratio, Debt Ratio).* David Wheelis owns Heights Pharmacy, which has prospered during its second year of operation. In deciding whether to open another pharmacy in the area, Wheelis has prepared the current financial statements of the business (on page 209). Wheelis read in an industry trade journal that a successful pharmacy meets all of these criteria:

a. Gross profit percentage is at least 60%.
b. Current ratio is at least 2.0.
c. Debt ratio is no higher than 0.50.
d. Inventory turnover rate is at least 3.40. (Heights Pharmacy's inventory one year ago, at December 31, 20X0, was $19,200.)

Basing his opinion on the entity's financial statement data, Wheelis believes the business meets all four criteria. He intends to go ahead with the expansion plan and asks your advice on preparing the pharmacy's financial statements in accordance with generally accepted accounting principles. When you point out that the statements are not properly prepared, he assures you that all amounts are correct. However, he admits that some items may be listed in the wrong place.

Required

1. Compute the four ratios based on the Heights Pharmacy financial statements prepared by Wheelis. Does the business appear to be ready for expansion?

2. Prepare a correct multi-step income statement, a correct statement of owner's equity, and a correct classified balance sheet in report format.

3. On the basis of the corrected financial statements, compute correct measures of the four ratios listed in the trade journal.

4. Make a recommendation about whether Wheelis should undertake the expansion.

HEIGHTS PHARMACY
Income Statement
Year Ended December 31, 20X1

Sales revenue		$195,000
Gain on sale of land		24,600
Total revenue		219,600
Cost of goods sold		85,200
Gross profit		134,400
Operating expenses:		
Salary expense	$18,690	
Rent expense	12,000	
Interest expense	6,000	
Depreciation expense	4,900	
Utilities expense	2,330	
Supplies expense	1,400	
Total operating expense		45,320
Income from operations		89,080
Other expense:		
Sales discounts ($3,600)		
and returns ($7,100)		10,700
Net income		$78,380

HEIGHTS PHARMACY
Statement of Owner's Equity
Year Ended December 31, 20X1

D. Wheelis, capital, December 31, 20X0	$ 30,000
Add increases in owner's equity:	
Net income	78,380
D. Wheelis, capital, December 31, 20X1	$108,380

HEIGHTS PHARMACY
Balance Sheet
December 31, 20X1

Assets

Current:		
Cash		$ 5,320
Accounts receivable		9,710
Inventory		30,100
Supplies		2,760
Store fixtures		63,000
Total current assets		110,890
Other:		
Withdrawals		65,000
Total assets		$175,890

Liabilities

Current:		
Accumulated depreciation—store fixtures		$ 6,300
Accounts payable		10,310
Salary payable		900
Total current liabilities		17,510
Other:		
Note payable due in 90 days		50,000
Total liabilities		67,510

Owner's Equity

D. Wheelis, capital		108,380
Total liabilities and owner's equity		$175,890

Case 2. The employees of Ewald Systems made an error when they performed the inventory count at year end, October 31, 20X8. Part of one warehouse was not counted, and therefore its inventory was not included in the company's total ending inventory.

Required

1. Indicate the effect of the inventory error on ending inventory, cost of goods sold, gross profit, and net income for the year ended October 31, 20X8.
2. Will the error affect cost of goods sold, gross profit, and net income in 20X9? If so, what will the effects be?

ETHICAL ISSUE

Greg Ogden Belting Company makes all sales of industrial conveyor belts under terms of FOB shipping point. The company usually receives orders for sales approximately one week before shipping inventory to customers. For orders received late in December, Greg Ogden, the owner, decides when to ship the goods. If profits are already at an acceptable level, Ogden delays shipment until January. If profits for the current year are lagging behind expectations, Ogden ships the goods during December.

Required

1. Under Ogden's FOB policy, when should the company record a sale?
2. Do you approve or disapprove of Ogden's manner of deciding when to ship goods to customers and record the sales revenue? If you approve, give your reason. If you disapprove, identify a better way to decide when to ship goods. (There is no accounting rule against Ogden's practice.)

FINANCIAL STATEMENT CASE

This case uses both the income statement (statement of income) and the balance sheet of **Target Corporation,** in Appendix A. It will help you understand the closing process of a business with inventories.

Required

1. Journalize Target's closing entries for fiscal year 1999. You may be unfamiliar with certain revenues and expenses, but treat them as either revenues or expenses. *Net credit revenue* is interest revenue. *Provision for income taxes* is another name for income tax expense and the *extraordinary charge* is like an expense. Close the Income Summary account to the Retained Earnings account. For this purpose, Retained Earnings is similar to the Owner's Capital account.
2. What amount was closed to Retained Earnings? How is this amount labeled on the income statement?
3. Compute Target's gross profit percentage and inventory turnover rate for fiscal year 1999.

TEAM PROJECT

With a small team of classmates, visit one or more actual merchandising businesses in your area. Interview a responsible official of the company to learn about its inventory policies and accounting system. Obtain answers to the following questions, write a report, and be prepared to make a presentation to the class if your instructor so directs:

Required

1. What merchandise inventory does the business sell?
2. From whom does the business buy its inventory? Is the relationship with the supplier new or longstanding?
3. What are the FOB terms on inventory purchases? Who pays the freight, the buyer or the seller? Is freight a significant amount or is freight cost low? What percentage of total inventory cost is the freight?
4. What are the credit terms on inventory purchases—2/10 n/30, or other? Does the business pay early to get purchase discounts? If so, why? If not, why not?
5. How does the business actually pay its suppliers? Does it mail a check or pay electronically? What is the actual payment procedure?
6. Which type of inventory accounting system does the business use—perpetual or periodic? Is this system computerized?
7. How often does the business take a physical count of its inventory? When during the year is the count taken? Describe the count procedures followed by the company.
8. Does the owner or manager use the gross profit percentage and the rate of inventory turnover to evaluate the business? If not, show the manager how to use these ratios in decision making.
9. Ask any other questions your group considers appropriate.

You can now compare prices for consumer electronics, personal computers, and entertainment software online by visiting the **Best Buy** and **Circuit City** Web sites. You can also compare their financial information online. Let's see how these companies compare.

Required

1. Go to **http://www.hoovers.com** and then use the "Search" scroll bar to select *Company*. In the next box type *BBY*, the stock symbol for Best Buy, and click on *Go*. For Best Buy Co., Inc., click on *capsule* and read the written description of the company. In what parts of the country are Best Buy stores located?

2. Go to the top of the page and click on the *Financials* tab. Under "Free Financial Information," click on *Annual Financials*.

   a. For the two most recent fiscal years, list the amounts reported for "Revenue," "Cost of Goods Sold," "Gross Profit Margin" percentage, "Total Net Income," and "Inventories."

   b. For the most recent year, calculate the rate of inventory turnover. Explain what this ratio indicates for Best Buy.

3. In the "Search for" box at the top of page, type *CC*, the stock symbol for Circuit City, and click on *Go*. For Circuit City Stores, Inc., click on *capsule* and read the written description of the company. What is Circuit City's rank among major appliance and electronics chains? Which company is the leader?

4. Gather the same information requested in (2a) and (2b) above for Circuit City.

5. Which company is more profitable? Why?

APPENDIX TO CHAPTER 5

ACCOUNTING FOR MERCHANDISE IN A PERIODIC INVENTORY SYSTEM

After studying this appendix to Chapter 5, you should be able to:

A2. Account for purchase and sale of inventory

A3. Compute cost of goods sold

A4. Adjust and close the accounts of a merchandising business

A5. Prepare a merchandiser's financial statement

PURCHASING MERCHANDISE

Some businesses find it uneconomical to invest in a computerized (perpetual) inventory system. These types of business use a periodic system.

Recording Purchases of Inventory

All inventory systems use the Inventory account. But in a periodic system, purchases, purchase discounts, purchase returns and allowances, and transportation costs are recorded in separate accounts. Let's account for **Austin Sound Center's** purchase of the **JVC** goods in Exhibit 5A-1. The following entries record the purchase and payment on account within the discount period:

> **Objective A2**
> Account for the purchase and sale of inventory

May 27	Purchases	707.00	
	Accounts Payable		707.00
	Purchased inventory on account.		
June 10	Accounts Payable	707.00	
	Cash ($707.00 × 0.97)		685.79
	Purchase Discounts ($707.00 × 0.03)		21.21
	Paid on account.		

Recording Purchase Returns and Allowances

Suppose that, prior to payment, **Austin Sound** returned to **JVC** goods costing $70 and also received from JVC a purchase allowance of $10. Austin Sound would record these transactions as follows:

June 3	Accounts Payable	70.00	
	Purchase Returns and Allowances		70.00
	Returned inventory to seller.		

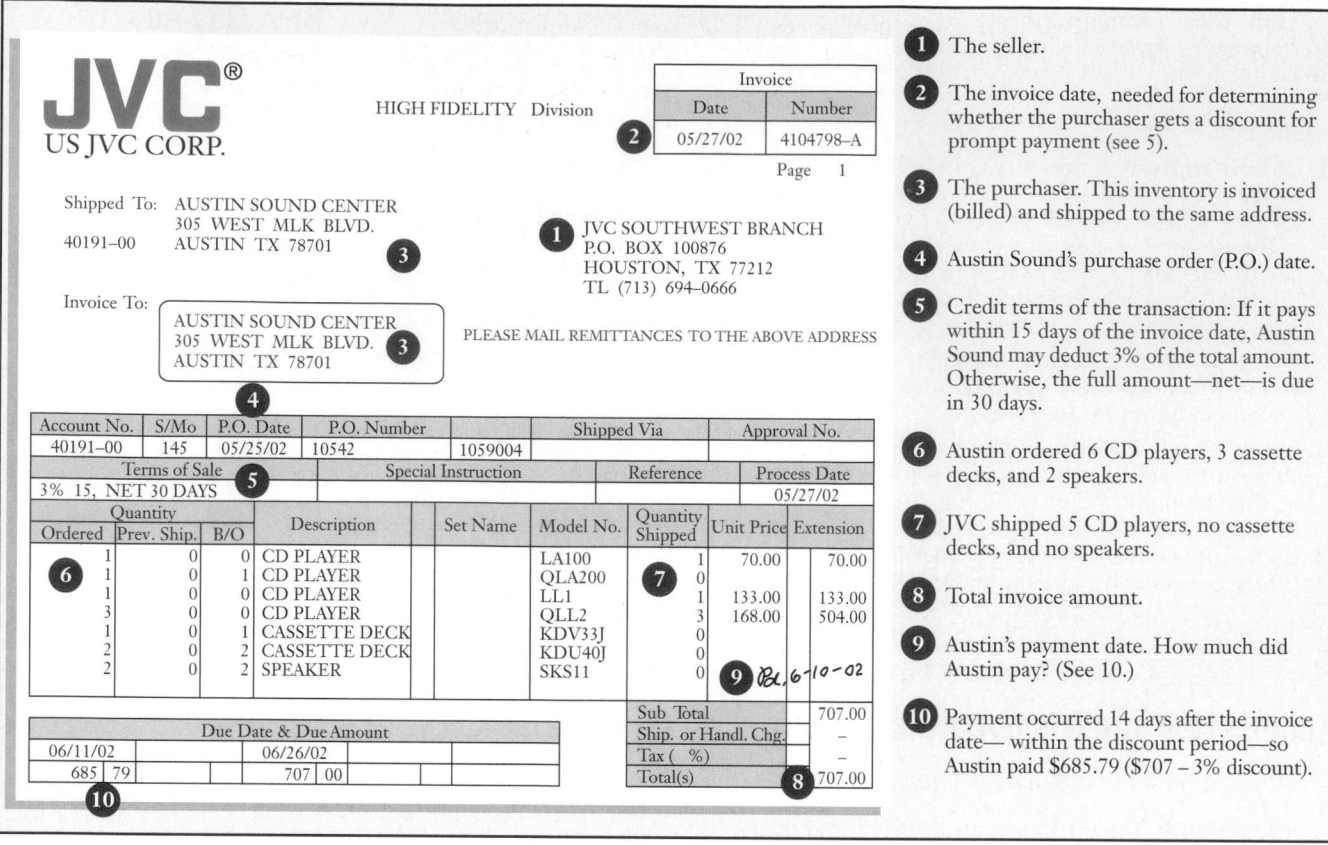

| | | | The seller. |

The following notes accompany the invoice:

1. The seller.

2. The invoice date, needed for determining whether the purchaser gets a discount for prompt payment (see 5).

3. The purchaser. This inventory is invoiced (billed) and shipped to the same address.

4. Austin Sound's purchase order (P.O.) date.

5. Credit terms of the transaction: If it pays within 15 days of the invoice date, Austin Sound may deduct 3% of the total amount. Otherwise, the full amount—net—is due in 30 days.

6. Austin ordered 6 CD players, 3 cassette decks, and 2 speakers.

7. JVC shipped 5 CD players, no cassette decks, and no speakers.

8. Total invoice amount.

9. Austin's payment date. How much did Austin pay? (See 10.)

10. Payment occurred 14 days after the invoice date— within the discount period—so Austin paid $685.79 ($707 – 3% discount).

June 4	Accounts Payable	10.00	
	Purchase Returns and Allowances..............		10.00
	Received a purchase allowance.		

During the period, the business records the cost of all inventory bought in the Purchases account. The balance of Purchases is a *gross* amount because it does not include subtractions for discounts, returns, or allowances. **Net purchases** is the remainder computed by subtracting the contra accounts from Purchases:

NET PURCHASES. Purchases less purchase discounts and purchase returns and allowances.

> **Purchases** (*debit* **balance account**)
> − **Purchase Discounts** (*credit* **balance account**)
> − **Purchase Returns and Allowances** (*credit* **balance account**)
> = **Net purchases** (a *debit* **subtotal, not a separate account**)

Recording Transportation Costs

Under the periodic system, costs to transport purchased inventory from seller to buyer are debited to the freight in account, as shown for a $60 freight bill:

June 1	Freight In..	60.00	
	Cash		60.00
	Paid a freight bill.		

RECORDING THE SALE OF INVENTORY

Recording sales is streamlined in the periodic system. With no running record of inventory to maintain, we can record a $3,000 sale as follows:

June 5	Accounts Receivable...	3,000	
	Sales Revenue...		3,000
	Sale on account.		

No accompanying entry to Inventory and Cost of Goods Sold is required. Also, discounts and returns and allowances are recorded as shown for the perpetual system on pages 176–177, but with no entry to Inventory and Cost of Goods Sold.

Cost of goods sold (also called **cost of sales**) is the largest single expense of most businesses that sell merchandise, such as **Gap Inc.**, and **Austin Sound**. It is the cost of the inventory the business has sold to customers. In a periodic system, cost of goods sold must be computed as in Exhibit 5A-2.

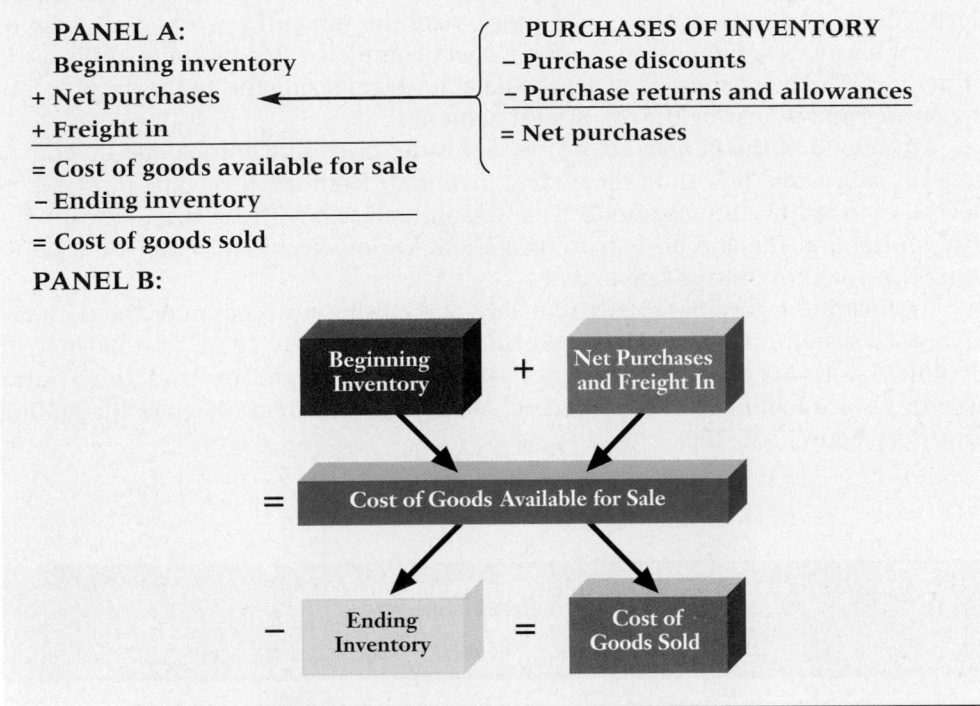

PANEL A:

Beginning inventory
+ Net purchases
+ Freight in
= Cost of goods available for sale
– Ending inventory
= Cost of goods sold

PURCHASES OF INVENTORY
– Purchase discounts
– Purchase returns and allowances
= Net purchases

PANEL B:

AUSTIN SOUND CENTER
Income Statement
Year Ended December 31, 20X2

PANEL A—Detailed Gross Profit Section

Sales revenue		$169,300	
Less: Sales discounts	$ (1,400)		
Sales returns and allowances	(2,000)	(3,400)	
Net sales			$165,900
Cost of goods sold:			
Beginning inventory		$38,600	
Purchases	$91,400		
Less: Purchase discounts	$(3,000)		
Purchase returns and allowances	(1,200)	(4,200)	
Net purchases		87,200	
Freight in		5,200	
Cost of goods available for sale		131,000	
Less: Ending inventory		(40,200)	
Cost of goods sold			90,800
Gross profit			$ 75,100

PANEL B—Gross Profit Section
(Streamlined in Annual Reports to Outsiders)

Net sales	$165,900
Cost of goods sold	90,800
Gross profit	$ 75,100

Exhibit 5A-3 on page 213 summarizes the first half of this appendix by showing Austin Sound's net sales revenue, cost of goods sold—including net purchases and freight in—and gross profit on the income statement for the periodic system. (All amounts are assumed.)

ADJUSTING AND CLOSING THE ACCOUNTS

A merchandising business adjusts and closes the accounts much as a service entity does. The steps of this end-of-period process are the same: If a work sheet is used, the trial balance is entered and the work sheet completed to determine net income or net loss. The work sheet provides the data for journalizing the adjusting and closing entries and preparing the financial statements.

At the end of the period, before any adjusting or closing entries, the Inventory account still holds the cost of the ending inventory from the preceding period. It is necessary to remove this beginning balance and replace it with the cost of the inventory on hand at the end of the current period. Various techniques may be used to bring the inventory records up to date.

To illustrate a merchandiser's adjusting and closing process under the periodic inventory system, let's use **Austin Sound's** December 31, 20X2, trial balance in Exhibit 5A-4. All the new accounts—Inventory, Freight In, and the contra accounts—are highlighted for emphasis. Additional data item (h) gives the ending inventory figure, $40,200.

EXHIBIT 5A-4
Trial Balance

AUSTIN SOUND CENTER Trial Balance December 31, 20X2		
Cash	$ 2,850	
Accounts receivable	4,600	
Note receivable, current............................	8,000	
Interest receivable.....................................		
Inventory	38,600	
Supplies...	650	
Prepaid insurance	1,200	
Furniture and fixtures................................	33,200	
Accumulated depreciation		$ 2,400
Accounts payable.......................................		47,000
Unearned sales revenue.............................		2,000
Wages payable..		
Interest payable..		
Note payable, long-term		12,600
C. Ernest, capital		25,900
C. Ernest, withdrawals...............................	54,100	
Sales revenue...		168,000
Sales discounts	1,400	
Sales returns and allowances.....................	2,000	
Interest revenue...		600
Purchases	91,400	
Purchase discounts.....................................		3,000
Purchase returns and allowances..............		1,200
Freight in	5,200	
Wage expense	9,800	
Rent expense	8,400	
Depreciation expense.................................		
Insurance expense		
Supplies expense..		
Interest expense...	1,300	
Total	$262,700	$262,700

Additional data at December 31, 20X2

a. Interest revenue earned but not yet collected, $400.
b. Supplies on hand, $100.
c. Prepaid insurance expired during the year, $1,000.
d. Depreciation, $600.
e. Unearned sales revenue earned during the year, $1,300.
f. Accrued wage expense, $400.
g. Accrued interest expense, $200.
h. Inventory on hand, $40,200.

Preparing and Using the Work Sheet in a Periodic System

The Exhibit 5A-5 work sheet is similar to the work sheets we have seen so far, with a few differences. ⟹ In most accounting systems, a single operation combines trial balance amounts with the adjustments and extends the adjusted balances directly to the income statement and balance sheet columns. Therefore, to reduce clutter, the adjusted trial balance columns are omitted.

◄ This work sheet is slightly different from the one introduced in the Chapter 4 acetates following page 128—it contains four pairs of columns, not five.

Exhibit 5A-5 **Accounting Work Sheet**

	AUSTIN SOUND CENTER							
	Accounting Work Sheet (Periodic Inventory System)							
	Year Ended December 31, 20X2							
	Trial Balance		Adjustments		Income Statement		Balance Sheet	
Account Title	Debit	Credit	Debit	Credit	Debit	Credit	Debit	Credit
Cash..................................	2,850						2,850	
Accounts receivable...........	4,600						4,600	
Note receivable, current....	8,000						8,000	
Interest receivable			(a) 400				400	
Inventory...........................	38,600				38,600	40,200	40,200	
Supplies	650			(b) 550			100	
Prepaid insurance..............	1,200			(c) 1,000			200	
Furniture and fixtures.......	33,200						33,200	
Accumulated depreciation		2,400		(d) 600				3,000
Accounts payable		47,000						47,000
Unearned sales revenue		2,000	(e) 1,300					700
Wages payable...................				(f) 400				400
Interest payable				(g) 200				200
Note payable, long-term....		12,600						12,600
C. Ernest, capital		25,900						25,900
C. Ernest, withdrawals	54,100						54,100	
Sales revenue		168,000		(e) 1,300		169,300		
Sales discounts	1,400				1,400			
Sales returns and allowances	2,000				2,000			
Interest revenue		600		(a) 400		1,000		
Purchases..........................	91,400				91,400			
Purchase discounts		3,000				3,000		
Purchase returns and allowances		1,200				1,200		
Freight in..........................	5,200				5,200			
Wage expense....................	9,800		(f) 400		10,200			
Rent expense.....................	8,400				8,400			
Depreciation expense			(d) 600		600			
Insurance expense.............			(c) 1,000		1,000			
Supplies expense			(b) 550		550			
Interest expense	1,300		(g) 200		1,500			
	262,700	262,700	4,450	4,450	160,850	214,700	143,650	89,800
Net income					53,850			53,850
					214,700	214,700	143,650	143,650

ACCOUNT TITLE COLUMNS The trial balance lists a number of accounts without balances. Ordinarily, these accounts are affected by the adjusting process. Examples include Interest Receivable, Interest Payable, and Depreciation Expense. The accounts are listed in the order they appear in the ledger. If additional accounts are needed, they are written in at the bottom, above net income.

TRIAL BALANCE COLUMNS Examine the Inventory account, $38,600 in the trial balance. This $38,600 is the cost of the beginning inventory. The work sheet is designed to replace this outdated amount with the new ending balance, which in our example is $40,200 [additional data item (h) in Exhibit 5A-4].

ADJUSTMENTS COLUMNS The adjustments are similar to those discussed in Chapters 3 and 4. They may be entered in any order desired. The debit amount of each entry should equal the credit amount, and total debits should equal total credits. You should review the adjusting data in Exhibit 5A-5 to reassure yourself that the adjustments are correct.

INCOME STATEMENT COLUMNS The income statement columns contain adjusted amounts for the revenues and the expenses. Sales Revenue, for example, is $169,300, which includes the $1,300 adjustment.

You may be wondering why the two inventory amounts appear in the income statement columns. The reason is that both beginning inventory and ending inventory enter the computation of cost of goods sold. *Placement of beginning inventory ($38,600) in the work sheet's income statement Debit column has the effect of adding beginning inventory in computing cost of goods sold. Placing ending inventory ($40,200) in the Credit column decreases cost of goods sold.*

Purchases and Freight In appear in the Debit column because they are added in computing cost of goods sold. Purchase Discounts and Purchase Returns and Allowances appear as Credits because they are subtracted in computing cost of good sold—$90,800 on the income statement in Exhibit 5A-6.

The income statement column subtotals on the work sheet indicate whether the business earned net income or incurred a net loss. If total credits are greater, the result is net income, as shown in Exhibit 5A-5. If total debits are greater, a net loss has occurred.

BALANCE SHEET COLUMNS The only new item on the balance sheet is inventory. The balance listed is the ending amount of $40,200, which is determined by a physical count of inventory on hand at the end of the period.

Objective A5
Prepare a merchandiser's financial statements

Preparing the Financial Statements of a Merchandiser

Exhibit 5A-6 presents Austin Sound's financial statements. The *income statement* through gross profit repeats Exhibit 5A-3. This information is followed by the **operating expenses,** expenses other than cost of goods sold that are incurred in the entity's major line of business. Wage expense is Austin Sound's cost of employing workers. Rent is the cost of obtaining store space. Insurance helps to protect the inventory. Store furniture and fixtures wear out; the expense is depreciation. Supplies expense is the cost of stationery, mailing, and the like, used in operations. Many companies report their operating expenses in two categories.

- *Selling expenses* are those expenses related to marketing the company's products—sales salaries, sales commissions, advertising, depreciation, rent, and utilities, delivery expense, and so on.
- *General expenses* include office expenses, such as the salaries of office employees, and depreciation, rent, utilities, and property taxes on the home office building.

Gross profit minus operating expenses and plus any other operating revenues equals **operating income,** or **income from operations.** Many businesspeople view operating income as the most reliable indicator of a business's success because it measures the results of the entity's major ongoing activities.

The last section of Austin Sound's income statement is **other revenue and expenses,** which is handled the same way in both inventory systems. This category reports revenues and expenses that are outside the company's main line of business.

AUSTIN SOUND CENTER
Income Statement
Year Ended December 31, 20X2

Sales revenue			$169,300
Less: Sales discounts		$ (1,400)	
Sales returns and allowances		(2,000)	(3,400)
Net sales revenue			$165,900
Cost of goods sold:			
Beginning inventory			$ 38,600
Purchases		$91,400	
Less: Purchases discounts	$(3,000)		
Purchase returns and allowances	(1,200)	(4,200)	
Net purchases			87,200
Freight in			5,200
Cost of goods available for sale			131,000
Less: Ending inventory			(40,200)
Cost of goods sold			90,800
Gross profit			75,100
Operating expenses:			
Wage expense			10,200
Rent expense			8,400
Insurance expense			1,000
Depreciation expense			600
Supplies expense			550	20,750
Income from operations			54,350
Other revenue and (expense):			
Interest revenue			1,000
Interest expense			(3,400)	(500)
Net income			$53,850

AUSTIN SOUND CENTER
Statement of Owner's Equity
Year Ended December 31, 20X2

C. Ernest, capital, December 31, 20X1	$25,900
Add: Net income	53,850
	79,750
Less: Withdrawals	(54,100)
C. Ernest, capital, December 31, 20X2	$25,650

AUSTIN SOUND CENTER
Balance Sheet
December 31, 20X2

Assets			**Liabilities**		
Current:			Current:		
Cash	$ 2,850		Accounts payable	$47,000	
Accounts receivable	4,600		Unearned sales revenue	700	
Note receivable	8,000		Wages payable	400	
Interest receivable	400		Interest payable	200	
Inventory	40,200		Total current liabilities	48,300	
Prepaid insurance	200		Long-term:		
Supplies	100		Note payable	12,600	
Total current assets	56,350		Total liabilities	60,900	
Plant:					
Furniture and fixtures	$33,200		**Owner's Equity**		
Less: Accumulated			C. Ernest, capital	25,650	
depreciation	(3,000)	30,200	Total liabilities and		
Total assets	$86,550		owner's equity	$86,550	

Journalizing Adjusting and Closing Entries

Exhibit 5A-7 presents Austin Sound's adjusting entries. These entries follow the same pattern illustrated in Chapter 4 for a service entity.

EXHIBIT 5A-7
Adjusting and Closing Entries

		Journal		
		Adjusting Entries		
a.	Dec. 31	Interest Receivable	400	
		Interest Revenue		400
b.	31	Supplies Expense ($650 – $100)	550	
		Supplies		550
c.	31	Insurance Expense	1,000	
		Prepaid Insurance		1,000
d.	31	Depreciation Expense...	600	
		Accumulated Depreciation		600
e.	31	Unearned Sales Revenue	1,300	
		Sales Revenue..		1,300
f.	31	Wage Expense	400	
		Wages Payable		400
g.	31	Interest Expense	200	
		Interest Payable		200
		Closing Entries		
1.	Dec. 31	Sales Revenue...	169,300	
		Interest Revenue	1,000	
		Income Summary		170,300
2.	31	Cost of Goods Sold...	135,200	
		Inventory (beginning balance)		38,600
		Purchases		91,400
		Freight In		5,200
3.	31	Inventory (ending balance)..................................	40,200	
		Purchase Discounts.......................................	3,000	
		Purchase Returns and Allowances	1,200	
		Cost of Goods Sold.......................................		44,400
4.	31	Income Summary...	116,450	
		Sales Discounts		1,400
		Sales Returns and Allowances......................		2,000
		Cost of Goods Sold ($135,200 – $44,400)		90,800
		Wage Expense...		10,200
		Rent Expense		8,400
		Depreciation Expense		600
		Insurance Expense..		1,000
		Supplies Expense		550
		Interest Expense		1,500
5.	31	Income Summary ($170,300 – $116,450)	53,850	
		C. Ernest, Capital		53,850
6.	31	C. Ernest, Capital...	54,100	
		C. Ernest, Withdrawals		54,100

The exhibit also gives Austin Sound's closing entries. The first closing entry closes the revenue accounts. Closing entries 2 and 3 are new. Entry 2 closes the beginning balance of the Inventory account ($38,600), along with Purchases and Freight In, into the Cost of Goods Sold account. Entry 3 sets up the ending balance of Inventory ($40,200) with a debit and also closes the Purchases contra accounts to Cost of Goods Sold.[1] Now Inventory and Cost of Goods Sold have their correct ending balances as follows:

INVENTORY						
Jan. 1	Bal.	38,600	Dec. 31	Clo.	38,600
Dec. 31	Clo.	40,200			

COST OF GOODS SOLD			
Beg. Inventory	38,600	Pur. discounts	3,000
Purchases	91,400	Pur. returns and	
Freight in	5,200	allowances	1,200
		End. inventory	40,200
Bal.	90,800		

[1]Some accountants make the inventory entries as adjustments rather than as part of the closing process. The adjusting-entry approach adds these adjustments (shifted out of the closing entries):

The entries to the Inventory account deserve additional explanation. Recall that before the closing process, Inventory still had the period's beginning balance. At the end of the period, this balance is one year old and must be replaced with the ending balance in order to prepare the financial statements at December 31, 20X2. Closing entries 2 and 3 give Inventory its correct ending balance of $40,200.

Closing entry 4 then closes the Sales contra accounts and Cost of Goods Sold along with the other expense accounts into Income Summary. Closing entries 5 and 6 complete the closing process. All data for the closing entries are taken from the income statement columns of the work sheet.

Study Exhibits 5A-5, 5A-6, and 5A-7 carefully because they illustrate the entire end-of-period process that leads to the financial statements. As you progress through this book, you may want to refer to these exhibits to refresh your understanding of the adjusting and closing process for a merchandising business.

Net sales, cost of goods sold, operating income, and net income are unaffected by the choice of inventory system. You can prove this by comparing Austin Sound's financial statements given in Exhibit 5A-6 with the corresponding statements in Exhibit 5-7. The only differences appear in the cost-of-goods-sold section of the income statement, and those differences are unimportant. In fact, virtually all companies report cost of goods sold in streamlined fashion, as shown for **Target Corporation** in Exhibit 5-1 and for **Austin Sound** in Exhibit 5-7.

REVIEW PERIODIC INVENTORY SYSTEM

APPENDIX SUMMARY PROBLEM

The following trial balance pertains to Jan King Distributing Company:

JAN KING DISTRIBUTING COMPANY
Trial Balance (Periodic Inventory System)
December 31, 20X3

Cash	$ 5,670	
Accounts receivable	37,100	
Inventory	60,500	
Supplies	3,930	
Prepaid rent	6,000	
Furniture and fixtures	26,500	
Accumulated depreciation		$ 21,200
Accounts payable		46,340
Salary payable		
Interest payable		
Unearned sales revenue		3,500
Note payable, long-term		35,000
Jan King, capital		23,680
Jan King, withdrawals	48,000	
Sales revenue		346,700
Sales discounts	10,300	
Sales returns and allowances	8,200	
Purchases	175,900	
Purchase discounts		6,000
Purchase returns and allowances		7,430
Freight in	9,300	
Salary expense	82,750	
Rent expense	7,000	
Depreciation expense		
Utilities expense	5,800	
Supplies expense		
Interest expense	2,900	
Total	$489,850	$489,850

Additional data at December 31, 20X3:
- **a.** Supplies used during the year, $2,580.
- **b.** Prepaid rent in force, $1,000.
- **c.** Unearned sales revenue still not earned, $2,400. The company expects to earn this amount during the next few months.
- **d.** Depreciation. The furniture and fixtures' estimated useful life is ten years, and they are expected to be worthless when they are retired from service.
- **e.** Accrued salaries, $1,300.
- **f.** Accrued interest expense, $600.
- **g.** Inventory on hand, $65,800.

Required

1. Enter the trial balance on an accounting work sheet and complete the work sheet.
2. Journalize the adjusting and closing entries at December 31. Post to the Income Summary account as an accuracy check on the entries affecting that account. The credit balance closed out of Income Summary should equal net income computed on the work sheet.
3. Prepare the company's multi-step income statement, statement of owner's equity, and balance sheet in account format. Draw arrows linking the statements.

Solution

Requirement 1

JAN KING DISTRIBUTING COMPANY
Accounting Work Sheet (Periodic Inventory System)
Year Ended December 31, 20X3

Account Title	Trial Balance Debit	Trial Balance Credit	Adjustments Debit	Adjustments Credit	Income Statement Debit	Income Statement Credit	Balance Sheet Debit	Balance Sheet Credit
Cash	5,670						5,670	
Accounts receivable	37,100						37,100	
Inventory	60,500				60,500	65,800	65,800	
Supplies	3,930			(a) 2,580			1,350	
Prepaid rent	6,000			(b) 5,000			1,000	
Furniture and fixtures	26,500						26,500	
Accumulated depreciation		21,200		(d) 2,650				23,850
Accounts payable		46,340						46,340
Salary payable				(e) 1,300				1,300
Interest payable				(f) 600				600
Unearned sales revenue		3,500	(c) 1,100					2,400
Note payable, long-term		35,000						35,000
Jan King, capital		23,680						23,680
Jan King, withdrawals	48,000						48,000	
Sales revenue		346,700		(c) 1,100		347,800		
Sales discounts	10,300				10,300			
Sales returns and allowances	8,200				8,200			
Purchases	175,900				175,900			
Purchase discounts		6,000				6,000		
Purchase returns and allowances		7,430				7,430		
Freight in	9,300				9,300			
Salary expense	82,750		(e) 1,300		84,050			
Rent expense	7,000		(b) 5,000		12,000			
Depreciation expense			(d) 2,650		2,650			
Utilities expense	5,800				5,800			
Supplies expense			(a) 2,580		2,580			
Interest expense	2,900		(f) 600		3,500			
	489,850	489,850	13,230	13,230	374,780	427,030	185,420	133,170
Net income					52,250			52,250
					427,030	427,030	185,420	185,420

Adjusting Entries

20X3

Dec. 31	Supplies Expense	2,580	
	Supplies		2,580
31	Rent Expense	5,000	
	Prepaid Rent		5,000
31	Unearned Sales Revenue ($3,500 − $2,400)	1,100	
	Sales Revenue		1,100
31	Depreciation Expense ($26,500/10)	2,650	
	Accumulated Depreciation		2,650
31	Salary Expense	1,300	
	Salary Payable		1,300
31	Interest Expense	600	
	Interest Payable		600

Closing Entries

20X3

Dec. 31	Sales Revenue	347,800	
	Income Summary		347,800
31	Cost of Goods Sold	245,700	
	Inventory (beginning balance)		60,500
	Purchases		175,900
	Freight In		9,300
31	Inventory	65,800	
	Purchase Discounts	6,000	
	Purchase Returns and Allowances	7,430	
	Cost of Goods Sold		79,230
31	Income Summary	295,550	
	Sales Discounts		10,300
	Sales Returns and Allowances		8,200
	Cost of Goods Sold ($245,700 − $79,230)		166,470
	Salary Expense		84,050
	Rent Expense		12,000
	Depreciation Expense		2,650
	Utilities Expense		5,800
	Supplies Expense		2,580
	Interest Expense		3,500
31	Income Summary ($347,800 − $295,550)	52,250	
	Jan King, Capital		52,250
31	Jan King, Capital	48,000	
	Jan King, Withdrawals		48,000

INCOME SUMMARY			
Clo.	295,550	Clo.	347,800
Clo.	52,250	Bal.	52,250

JAN KING DISTRIBUTING COMPANY
Income Statement
Year Ended December 31, 20X3

Sales revenue			$347,800
Less: Sales discounts		$(10,300)	
Sales returns and allowances		(8,230)	(18,500)
Net sales revenue			$329,300
Cost of goods sold:			
Beginning inventory		$ 60,500	
Purchases	$175,900		
Less: Purchase discounts	$(6,000)		
Purchase returns and allowances	(7,430)	(13,430)	
Net purchases		162,470	
Freight in		9,300	
Cost of goods available for sale		232,270	
Less: Ending inventory		(65,800)	
Cost of goods sold			166,470
Gross profit			162,830
Operating expenses:			
Salary expense		84,050	
Rent expense		12,000	
Utilities expense		5,800	
Depreciation expense		2,650	
Supplies expense		2,580	107,080
Income from operations			55,750
Other expense:			
Interest expense			3,500
Net income			$ 52,250

JAN KING DISTRIBUTING COMPANY
Statement of Owner's Equity
Year Ended December 31, 20X3

Jan King, capital, December 31, 20X2	$23,680
Add: Net income	52,250
	75,930
Less: Withdrawals	(48,000)
Jan King, capital, December 31, 20X3	$27,930

JAN KING DISTRIBUTING COMPANY
Balance Sheet
December 31, 20X3

Assets			Liabilities		
Current:			Current:		
Cash		$ 5,670	Accounts payable		$ 46,340
Accounts receivable		37,100	Salary payable		1,300
Inventory		65,800	Interest payable		600
Supplies		1,350	Unearned sales revenue		2,400
Prepaid rent		1,000	Total current liabilities		50,640
Total current assets		110,920	Long-term:		
Plant:			Note payable		35,000
Furniture and fixtures	$26,500				
Less:			Total liabilities		85,640
Accumulated depreciation	(23,850)	2,650	**Owner's Equity**		
			Jan King, capital		27,930
			Total liabilities and owner's		
Total assets		$113,570	equity		$113,570

ASSESS YOUR PROGRESS

APPENDIX EXERCISES

E5A-1 Journalize, without explanations, the following transactions of Lane's Fine Gifts during June:

Journalizing purchase and sale transactions
(Obj. A2)

June 3 Purchased $700 of inventory under terms of 2/10 n/eom (end of month) and FOB shipping point.
   7 Returned $300 of defective merchandise purchased on June 3.
   9 Paid freight bill of $30 on June 3 purchase.
   10 Sold inventory for $3,200. Payment terms were 2/15 n/30.
   12 Paid amount owed on credit purchase of June 3, less the discount and the return.
   16 Granted a sales allowance of $800 on the June 10 sale.
   23 Received cash from June 10 customer in full settlement of her debt, less the allowance and the discount.

E5A-2 As the proprietor of Stevens Goodyear Tire Company you receive the following invoice from a supplier:

Journalizing transactions from a purchase invoice
(Obj. A2)

BELTLINE TIRE WHOLESALE DISTRIBUTORS, INC.
2600 Commonwealth Avenue
Boston, Massachusetts 02215

Invoice date: May 14, 20X3

Payment terms: 2/10 n/30

Sold to: Stevens Goodyear Tire Co.
4219 Crestwood Parkway
Lexington, Mass. 02173

Quantity Ordered	Description	Quantity Shipped	Price	Amount
4	P135–X4 Radials	4	$37.14	$ 148.56
8	L912 Belted-bias	8	41.32	330.56
14	R39 Truck tires	10	50.02	500.20
	Total			$979.32

Due date:	Amount:
May 24, 20X3	$959.73
May 25 through June 13, 20X3	$979.32

Paid:

Required

1. Stevens received the invoice on May 15. Record the May 15 purchase on account. Carry to the nearest cent throughout.
2. The R39 truck tires were ordered by mistake and were therefore returned to Beltline. Journalize the return on May 19.
3. Record the May 22 payment of the amount owed.

E5A-3 On April 30, De Boulle Jewelers purchased inventory of $8,000 on account from Intergem Jewels, a jewelry importer. Terms were 3/15 net 45. On receiving the goods, De Boulle checked the order and found $800 of unsuitable merchandise. Therefore, De Boulle returned $800 of merchandise to Intergem on May 4.

Journalizing purchase transactions
(Obj. A2)

To pay the remaining amount owed, De Boulle borrowed the net amount of the invoice from the bank. On May 14, De Boulle signed a short-term note payable to the bank and immediately paid the borrowed funds to Intergem. On June 14, De Boulle paid the bank the net amount of the invoice, which De Boulle had borrowed, plus 1% monthly interest (round to the nearest dollar).

Required

Record the indicated transactions in the journal of De Boulle Jewelers. Explanations are not required.

E5A-4 Refer to the business situation in Exercise 5A-3. Journalize the transactions of Intergem Jewels. Explanations are not required.

Note: Exercises 5-13 (page 201), 5-14 (page 201), and 5-15 (page 201) also pertain to the periodic inventory system.

APPENDIX PROBLEMS

P5A-1 The following transactions occurred between Abba Medical Supply and a Hillcrest Drug store during November of the current year:

Nov. 6   Abba Medical Supply sold $6,200 worth of merchandise to Hillcrest on terms of 2/10 n/30, FOB shipping point. Abba prepaid freight charges of $300 and included this amount in the invoice total. (Abba's entry to record the freight payment debits Accounts Receivable and credits Cash.)

   10   Hillcrest returned $900 of the merchandise purchased on November 6. Abba issued a credit memo for this amount.

   15   Hillcrest paid $3,000 of the invoice amount owed to Abba for the November 6 purchase. This payment included none of the freight charge.

   27   Hillcrest paid the remaining amount owed to Abba for the November 6 purchase.

Required

Journalize these transactions, first on the books of the Hillcrest Drug store and second on the books of Abba Medical Supply.

P5A-2 Preakness Wholesale Grocery engaged in the following transactions during May of the current year:

May 3   Purchased office supplies for cash, $300.
   7   Purchased inventory on credit terms of 3/10 net eom, $2,000.
   8   Returned half the inventory purchased on May 7. It was not the inventory ordered.
   10   Sold goods for cash, $450.
   13   Sold inventory on credit terms of 2/15 n/45, $3,900.
   16   Paid the amount owed on account from the purchase of May 7, less the discount and the return.
   17   Received defective inventory returned from May 13 sale, $900.
   18   Purchased inventory of $4,000 on account. Payment terms were 2/10 net 30.
   26   Borrowed $3,920 from the bank to take advantage of the discount offered on May 18 purchase. Signed a note payable to the bank for this amount.
   26   Paid supplier for goods purchased on May 18, less the discount.
   28   Received cash in full settlement of the account from the customer who purchased inventory on May 13, less the discount and the return.
   29   Purchased inventory for cash, $2,000, plus freight charges of $160.

Required

1. Journalize the preceding transactions. Explanations are not required.
2. The note payable signed on May 26 requires the payment of $30 interest expense. Was the decision to borrow funds in order to take advantage of the cash discount wise or unwise? Support your answer by comparing the discount to the interest paid.

P5A-3 Larkspur Lighting Company engaged in the following transactions during July of the current year:

July 2   Purchased inventory for cash, $800.
   5   Purchased store supplies on credit terms of net eom, $450.
   8   Purchased inventory of $3,000, plus freight charges of $230. Credit terms are 3/15 n/30.
   9   Sold goods for cash, $1,200.
   11   Returned $200 of the inventory purchased on July 8. It was damaged.
   12   Purchased inventory on credit terms of 3/10 n/30, $3,330.
   14   Sold inventory on credit terms of 2/10 n/30, $9,600.
   16   Paid utilities expense, $275
   20   Received a sales return from July 14 sale, $400. Larkspur shipped the wrong goods by mistake.
   21   Borrowed the amount owed on the July 8 purchase. Signed a note payable to the bank for $2,946, which takes into account the return of inventory on July 11.
   21   Paid supplier for goods purchased on July 8 less the discount and the return.
   23   Received $6,860 cash in partial settlement of the account from the customer who purchased inventory on July 14. Granted the customer a 2% discount and credited this account receivable for $7,000.
   30   Paid for the store supplies purchased on July 5.

Required

1. Journalize the preceding transactions. Explanations are not required.
2. Compute the amount of the receivable at July 31 from the customer to whom Larkspur sold inventory on July 14. What amount of cash discount applies to this receivable at July 31?

P5A-4 The year-end trial balance of Latham Sales Company pertains to March 31, 20X4.

Preparing a merchandiser's accounting work sheet, financial statements, and adjusting and closing entries (Obj. A3, A4, A5)

LATHAM SALES COMPANY
Trial Balance
March 31, 20X4

Cash...	$ 7,880	
Note receivable, current.............................	12,400	
Interest receivable		
Inventory...	130,050	
Prepaid insurance.......................................	3,600	
Notes receivable, long-term	62,000	
Furniture...	6,000	
Accumulated depreciation		$ 4,000
Accounts payable		12,220
Sales commission payable		
Sales payable		
Unearned sales revenue		9,610
Ben Latham, capital		172,780
Ben Latham, withdrawals	66,040	
Sales revenue		440,000
Sales discounts	4,800	
Sales returns and allowances	11,300	
Interest revenue		8,600
Purchases...	233,000	
Purchase discounts		3,100
Purchase returns and allowances..............		7,600
Freight in...	10,000	
Sales commission expense	78,300	
Salary expense	24,700	
Rent expense...	6,000	
Utilities expense	1,840	
Depreciation expense.................................		
Insurance expense......................................		
Total...	$657,910	$657,910

Additional data at March 31, 20X4:

a. Accrued interest revenue, $1,030.
b. Insurance expense for the year, $3,000.
c. Furniture has an estimated useful life of six years. Its value is expected to be zero when it is retired from service.
d. Unearned sales revenue still unearned, $7,400.
e. Accrued salaries, $1,200.
f. Accrued sales commission expense, $1,700.
g. Inventory on hand, $133,200.

Required

1. Enter the trial balance on an accounting work sheet, and complete the work sheet for the year ended March 31, 20X4.
2. Prepare the company's multi-step income statement and statement of owner's equity for the year ended March 31, 20X4. Also prepare its classified balance sheet at that date. Long-term notes receivable should be reported on the balance sheet between current assets and plant assets in a separate section labeled Investments.
3. Journalize the adjusting and closing entries at March 31, 20X4.
4. Post to the Ben Latham, Capital account and to the Income Summary account as an accuracy check on the adjusting and closing process.

Note: Problems 5-9A (page 205) and 5-9B (page 208) also pertain to the periodic inventory system.

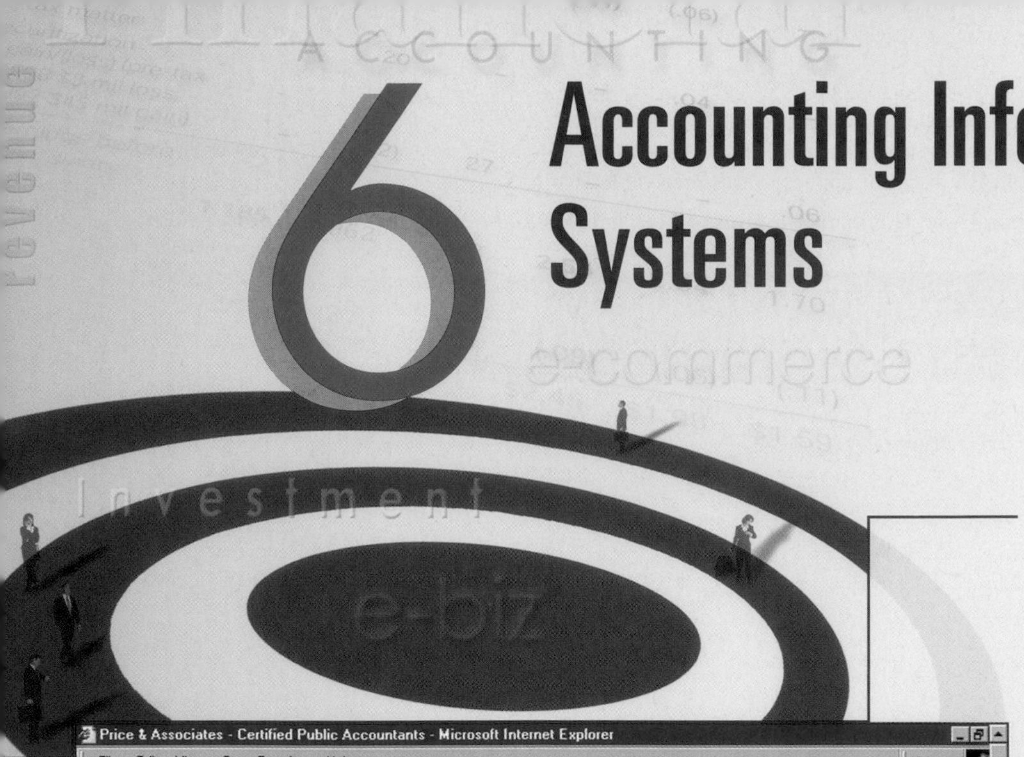

6

Accounting Information Systems

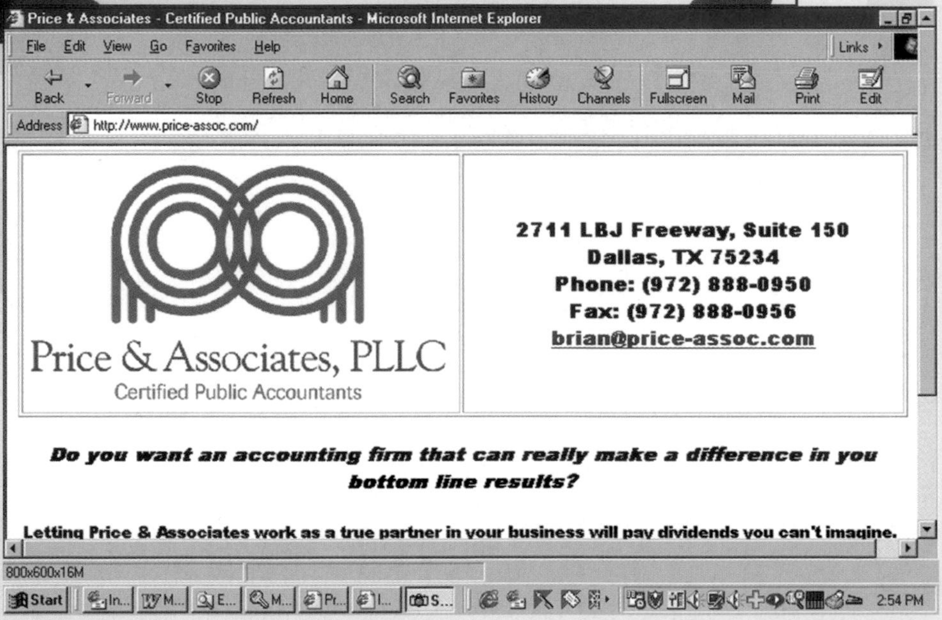

e-commerce

e-biz

Price & Associates - Certified Public Accountants - Microsoft Internet Explorer

File   Edit   View   Go   Favorites   Help

Back   Forward   Stop   Refresh   Home   Search   Favorites   History   Channels   Fullscreen   Mail   Print   Edit

Address http://www.price-assoc.com/

Price & Associates, PLLC
Certified Public Accountants

2711 LBJ Freeway, Suite 150
Dallas, TX 75234
Phone: (972) 888-0950
Fax: (972) 888-0956
brian@price-assoc.com

Do you want an accounting firm that can really make a difference in you bottom line results?

Letting Price & Associates work as a true partner in your business will pay dividends you can't imagine.

800x600x16M

Start   In...   M...   E...   M...   Pr...   I...   S...   2:54 PM

LEARNING OBJECTIVES

After studying this chapter, you should be able to

1. Describe the features of an effective accounting information system
2. Understand how both computerized and manual accounting systems work
3. Understand how spreadsheets are used in accounting
4. Use the sales journal, the cash receipts journal, and the accounts receivable subsidiary ledger
5. Use the purchases journal, the cash payments journal, and the accounts payable subsidiary ledger

www.prenhall.com/horngren

Readiness Assesment

With QuickBooks and Peachtree taking over, you'd think accountants would be worried about the future. After all, why does a business need an accountant when there's a virtual one on a disk? But the reverse is true. The new developments in software and Web applications are creating lots of new career opportunities in accounting.

Many entrepreneurs don't know how to do more than boot up their software, and they don't have time to learn how to use it. Many won't pay a full-time accountant to do their books. Enter the Accounting Software Consultant. Brian Price of **Price and Associates** has built a $400,000 business by consulting on small business accounting software. Price's clients range from mom-and-pop businesses that bring in $100,000–$200,000 a year to a $2 million services firm. The typical engagement for his firm brings in $1,100 of revenue. For a flat fee, Price installs QuickBooks or other software and provides five hours of training. Of course, five hours is never enough, so clients end up buying additional training time for $65 to $100 an hour.

The best part for Price is that clients then can do the bookkeeping. This frees Price to do the more creative work: analyzing financial information and helping clients make decisions based on the information.

Source: Adapted from Jeff Stimpson, "The new consultant," *The Practical Accountant,* September 1999, pp. 325–42.

Every organization needs an accounting system. An **accounting information system** is the combination of personnel, records, and procedures that a business uses to provide financial data. We have already been using an accounting information system in this text. It consists of two basic components: a general journal and a general ledger.

Every accounting system has these components, but this simple system can efficiently handle only a few transactions per period. Businesses cope with heavy transaction loads in two ways: computerization and specialization. We *computerize* to do the accounting faster and more reliably. *Specialization* comes when we group similar transactions to speed the process. We explore special journals in the second half of this chapter.

ACCOUNTING INFORMATION SYSTEM. The combination of personnel, records, and procedures that a business uses to provide financial data.

EFFECTIVE ACCOUNTING INFORMATION SYSTEMS

Objective 1
Describe the features of an effective accounting information system

Good personnel are critical to the success of any operation. Employees must be both competent and honest. And several design features can make the accounting system run more efficiently. A good system—whether computerized or manual—includes control, compatibility, flexibility, and a favorable cost/benefit relationship.

Features of Effective Systems

Managers need *control* over operations. *Internal controls* are the methods and procedures used to authorize transactions and safeguard assets. For example, in companies such as **Coca-Cola, America Online,** and **Kinko's,** managers control cash disbursements to avoid theft through unauthorized payments. **VISA, MasterCard,** and **Discover** keep records of their accounts receivable to ensure that they receive collections on time.

A *compatible* system is one that works smoothly with the business's operations, personnel, and organizational structure. An example is **Bank of America,** which is organized as a network of branch offices. Bank of America's top managers want to know revenues in each region where the bank does business. They also want to analyze loans in different geographic regions. If revenues in California are lagging, managers can concentrate their efforts in that state. They may relocate some branch offices or hire new personnel.

Organizations evolve. They develop new products, sell off unprofitable operations and acquire new ones, and adjust employee pay scales. Changes in the business often call for changes in the accounting system. A well-designed system is *flexible* if it accommodates changes without a complete overhaul. Consider **Monsanto Company's** acquisition of the pharmaceuticals firm **Searle** including Searle's Nutrasweet division. Monsanto's accounting system was flexible enough to fold Searle/Nutrasweet financial statements into those of Monsanto.

Achieving control, compatibility, and flexibility costs money. Managers strive for a system that offers maximum benefits at a minimum cost—that is, a favorable *cost/benefit relationship*. Most small companies use off-the-shelf computerized accounting packages, and the very smallest businesses might not computerize at all. But large companies, such as the brokerage firm **Edward Jones,** have specialized needs for information. For them, custom programming is a must. The benefits—in terms of information tailored to the company's needs—far outweigh the costs. The result? Better decisions.

Components of a Computerized System

Three components form the heart of a computerized accounting system: hardware, software, and company personnel. Each component is critical to the system's success.

Hardware is the electronic equipment: It includes computers, disk drives, monitors, printers, and the network that connects them. Most modern accounting systems require a **network,** the system of electronic linkages that allows different computers to share the same information. In a networked system, many computers can be connected to the main computer, or **server,** which stores the program and the data. With the right network, a **PricewaterhouseCoopers** auditor in London can access the data of a client located in Sydney, Australia. The result is a speedier audit for the client.

Software is the set of programs that drive the computer to perform the work desired. Accounting software accepts, edits (alters), and stores transaction data and generates the reports managers use to run the business. Many software packages operate independently from the other computing activities of the system. For example, a company that is only partly computerized may use software programs to account for employee payrolls and sales and accounts receivable. Other parts of the accounting system may not be automated.

For large enterprises, like **Hershey Foods** and **Caterpillar Tractor,** the accounting software is integrated within the overall company **database,** or computerized storehouse of information. Many business databases include accounting and nonaccounting data. In negotiating a union contract, the **Union Pacific Railroad** often needs to examine the relationship between the employment history and salary levels of company employees. Union Pacific's database provides the data managers need to negotiate effectively. During negotiations, both parties carry laptop computers to analyze the effects of decisions on the spot.

HOW COMPUTERIZED AND MANUAL ACCOUNTING SYSTEMS WORK

Computerized accounting systems have replaced manual systems in many organizations—even in small businesses such as your neighborhood pharmacy. As we discuss the stages of data processing, observe the differences between a computerized system and a manual system. The three stages of data processing (inputs, processing, outputs) are shown in Exhibit 6-1.

DAILY EXERCISE 6-1

HARDWARE. Electronic equipment that includes computers, disk drives, monitors, printers, and the network that connects them.

NETWORK. The system of electronic linkages that allows different computers to share the same information.

SERVER. The main computer in a network, where the program and data are stored.

 DAILY EXERCISE 6-2

 DAILY EXERCISE 6-3

SOFTWARE. Set of programs or instructions that drive the computer to perform the work desired.

DATABASE. A computerized storehouse of information.

Objective 2
Understand how both computerized and manual accounting systems work

EXHIBIT 6-1
The Three Stages of Data Processing

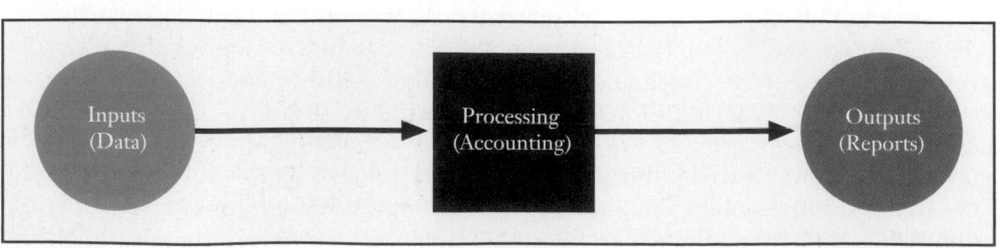

Inputs represent data from source documents, such as sales receipts, bank deposit slips, fax orders, and other telecommunications. Inputs are usually grouped by type. For example, a firm would enter cash-sale transactions separately from credit sales and purchase transactions.

In a manual system, *processing* includes journalizing transactions, posting to the accounts, and preparing the financial statements. A computerized system also processes, but without the intermediate steps (journal, ledger, and trial balance).

Outputs are the reports used for decision making, including the financial statements (income statement, balance sheet). Business owners are making better decisions—and prospering—because of the reports produced by their accounting system. Exhibit 6-2 is an overview of a computerized system. Start with data inputs in the lower left corner.

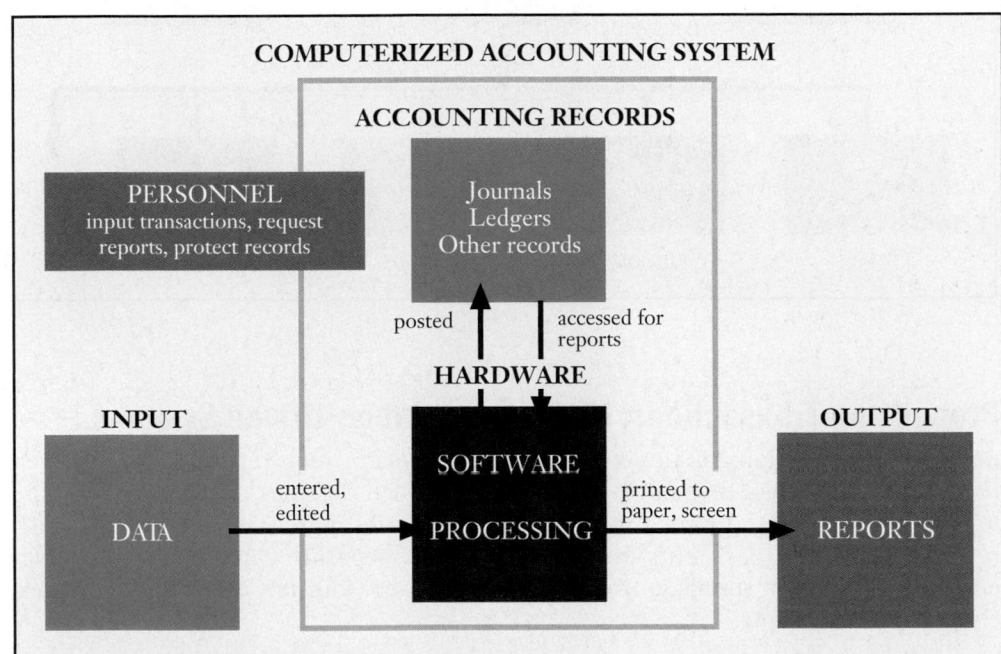

EXHIBIT 6-2
Overview of a Computerized Accounting System

Designing a System: The Chart of Accounts

Design of the accounting system begins with the chart of accounts. ➡ In the accounting system of a large, complex company such as **Eastman Kodak,** account numbers take on added importance. It is efficient to represent a complex account title, such as Accumulated Depreciation—Photographic Equipment, with a concise account number (for example, 12570).

◀ Recall from Chapter 2 that the chart of accounts lists all the accounts and their account numbers.

Recall that asset accounts generally begin with the digit 1, liabilities with the digit 2, owner's equity accounts with the digit 3, revenues with 4, and expenses with 5. Exhibit 6-3 diagrams one structure for computerized accounts. Assets are divided into current assets, fixed assets (property, plant, and equipment), and other assets. Among the current assets, we illustrate only three general ledger accounts: Cash in Bank (Account No. 111), Accounts Receivable (No. 112), and Prepaid Insurance (No. 115).

The account numbers in Exhibit 6-3 get longer and more detailed as you move from top to bottom. For example, Customer A's account number is 1120001: 112 represents Accounts Receivable, and 0001 refers to Customer A.

Computerized accounting systems rely on account *number ranges* to translate accounts and their balances into properly organized financial statements and other reports. For example, accounts numbered 101–399 (assets, liabilities, and owner's equity) are sorted to the balance sheet, while accounts numbered 401–599 (revenues and expenses) go to the income statement.

DAILY EXERCISE 6-4

EXHIBIT 6-3
Structure for Computerized Accounts

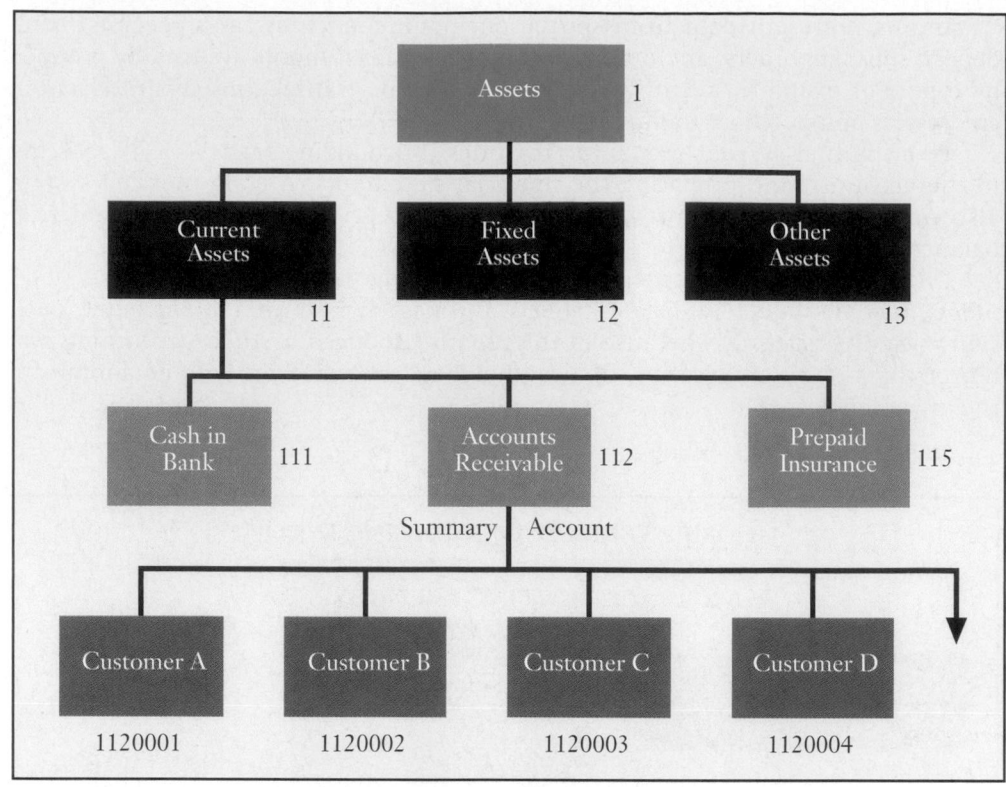

Processing Transactions: Manual and Menu-Driven Systems

Recording transactions in an actual accounting system requires an additional step that we have skipped thus far. A business of any size classifies transactions by type for efficient handling. In a manual system, credit sales, purchases on account, cash receipts, and cash payments are treated as four separate categories, with each entered into its own special journal. (We discuss these journals in detail later in this chapter.) For example:

- Credit sales are recorded in a special journal called a *sales journal.*
- Cash receipts are entered into a *cash receipts journal.*
- Credit purchases of inventory and other assets are recorded in a *purchases journal.*
- Cash payments are entered in a *cash payments journal.*
- Transactions that do not fit any of the special journals, such as the adjusting entries at the end of the period, are recorded in the *general journal,* which serves as the "journal of last resort."

MENU. A list of options for choosing computer functions.

ON-LINE PROCESSING. Computerized processing of related functions, such as the recording and posting of transactions, on a continuous basis.

BATCH PROCESSING. Computerized accounting for similar transactions in a group or batch.

Computerized systems are organized by function, or task. Access to functions is arranged in terms of menus. A **menu** is a list of options for choosing computer functions. In a *menu-driven* system, you first access the most general group of functions, called the *main menu.* You then choose from one or more submenus until you finally reach the function you want.

Exhibit 6-4 illustrates one type of menu structure. The row at the top of the exhibit shows the main menu. The computer operator (or accountant) has chosen the General option (short for General Ledger), highlighted by the cursor. This action opened a submenu of four items—Transactions, Posting, Account Maintenance, and Closing. The Transactions option was then chosen (highlighted).

Posting in a computerized system can be performed continuously as transactions are being recorded (**on-line processing**) or later for a group or batch of similar transactions (**batch processing**). In either case, posting is automatic. Batch processing of accounting data allows accountants to check the entries for accuracy before posting them. In effect, data are "parked" in the computer to await posting, which simply updates the account balances.

Accounting Pioneers on the Virtual Frontier

As you saw in the chapter-opening story, computer and Internet technology are remaking the bookkeeping and tax aspects of accounting. There are "virtual" software consultants, and now there are "virtual" or "on-line" accountants. Slogans like "Real Accounting in a Virtual World" and "Outsourced Accounting Services for a Wired World" are advertising

- basic bookkeeping
- full-service outsourcing
- real-time accounting
- 24-hour access to accounting data

TADOnline, founded by Lance and Deanna Gildea in San Diego, is one such service. TAD starts clients out scanning their invoices, bank statements, and other documents into the computer. Scanned documents are transmitted to TAD, and within minutes, TAD updates the client's accounts. Customers then use a Web browser to sign in to a home page prepared by TAD, where they can view, print, and download reports, checks, and other information. Soon clients will be able to get real-time access to their accounting data through a new Web-based service.

For clients—typically small- to mid-sized businesses—the key benefits of TADOnline are price and reliability. In some cases, TAD's monthly fees are half what it would cost to hire a bookkeeper—and TAD doesn't call in sick or take vacations. A big plus for the "virtual accountants" is being able to live wherever they please, regardless of where clients are located. For TAD's Lance and Deanna Gildea, that means San Diego half the year and scenic Vashon Island, Washington, for the other half.

Source: Adapted from Antoinette Alexander, "Pioneers on the virtual frontier," *Accounting Technology,* Jan./Feb. 2000, pp. 18–24.

EXHIBIT 6-4   **Main Menu of a Computerized Accounting System**

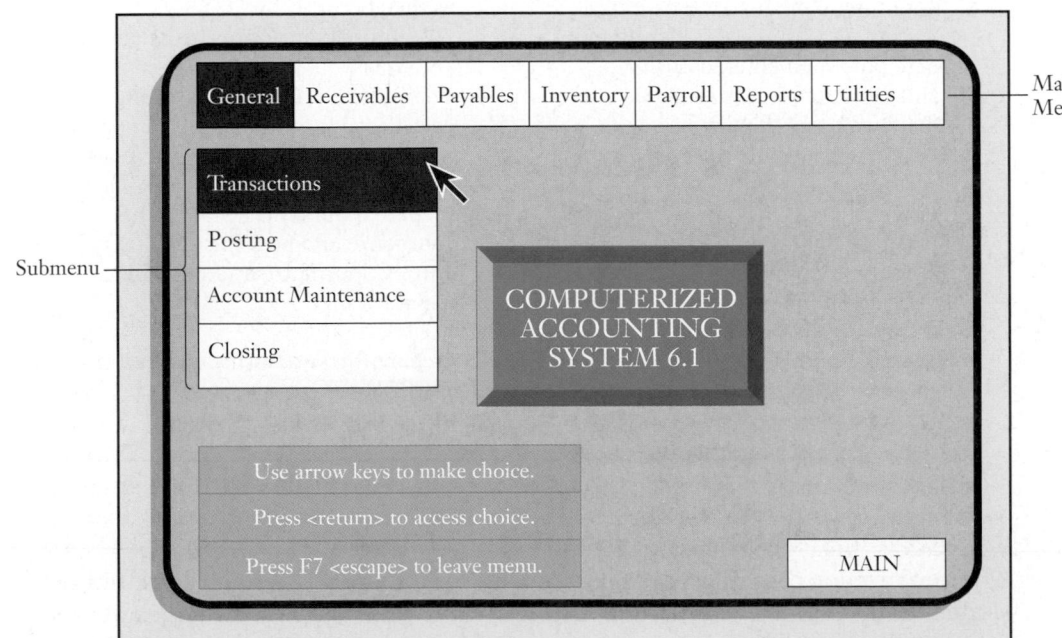

Outputs—accounting reports—are the final stage of data processing. In a computerized system, financial statements can be printed automatically. For example, the Reports option in the main menu gives the operator various report choices, which are expanded in the Reports submenu of Exhibit 6-5. In the exhibit, the operator is working with the financial statements, and specifically the balance sheet, as shown by the highlighting.

EXHIBIT 6-5
Reports Submenu of a Computerized Accounting System

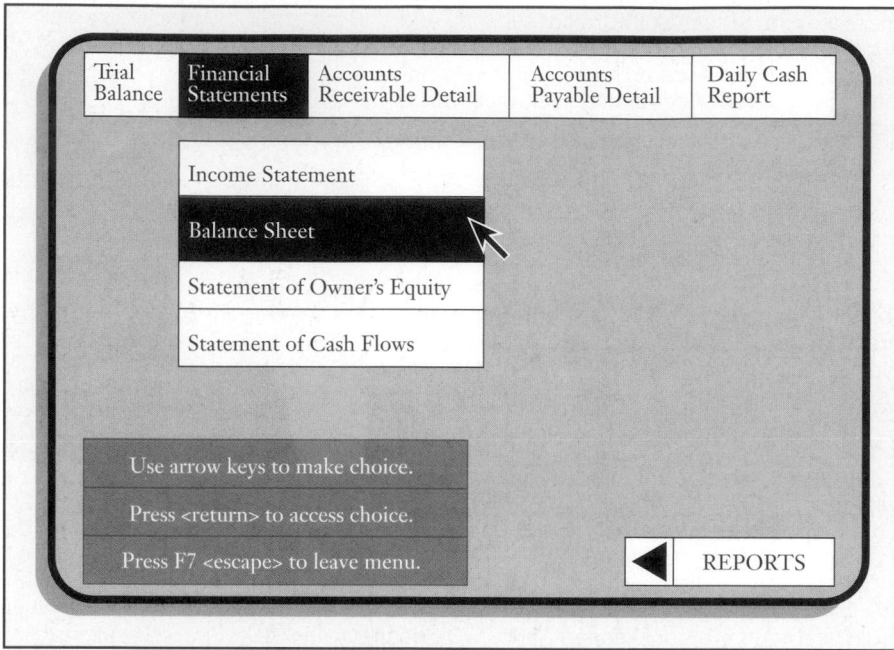

Exhibit 6-6 summarizes the accounting cycle in a computerized system and in a manual system. Compare and contrast the two types of systems.

EXHIBIT 6-6
Comparison of the Accounting Cycle in a Computerized and a Manual System

Computerized System	Manual System
1. Start with the account balances in the ledger at the beginning of the period.	1. Same.
2. Classify transactions by type. Access appropriate menus for data entry.	2. Analyze and journalize transactions as they occur.
3. Automatic posting of transactions as a batch or when entered on-line.	3. Post journal entries to the ledger accounts.
4. Unadjusted balances available immediately after each posting.	4. Compute the unadjusted balance in each account at the end of the period.
5. The trial balance, if needed, can be accessed as a report.	5. Enter the trial balance on the work sheet, and complete the work sheet.
6. Enter and post the adjusting entries. Print the financial statements. Run automatic closing procedure after backing up the period's accounting records.	6. Prepare the financial statements. Journalize and post the adjusting entries. Journalize and post the closing entries.
7. The next period's opening balances are created automatically as a result of closing.	7. Prepare the postclosing trial balance. This trial balance becomes step 1 for the next period.

MODULE. Separate compatible units of an accounting package that are integrated to function together.

Integrated Accounting Software: Spreadsheets

Computerized accounting packages are organized by **modules,** separate but integrated units that are compatible and that function together. Changes affecting one module will affect others. For example, entering and posting a credit-sale

transaction will update two modules: Accounts Receivable/Sales and Inventory/Cost of Goods Sold. Accounting packages, such as QuickBooks and Peachtree, come as an integrated system.

You may be preparing your homework assignments manually. Imagine preparing a work sheet for **General Motors** (GM). Each adjustment changes the company's financial statement totals. Consider computing GM's revenue amounts by hand. The task would be overwhelming. For even a small business with only a few departments, the computations are tedious, time-consuming, and therefore expensive. Also, errors are likely.

Spreadsheets are computer programs that link data by means of formulas and functions. These electronic work sheets were invented to update budgets. Spreadsheets are organized as a rectangular grid composed of *cells,* each defined by a row number and a column number. A cell can contain words (called labels), numbers, or formulas (relationships among cells). The *cursor,* or electronic highlighter, indicates which cell is active. When the cursor is placed over any cell, information can be entered there for processing.

Exhibit 6-7 shows a simple income statement on a spreadsheet screen. The labels were entered in cells A1 through A4. The dollar amount of revenues was entered in cell B2 and expenses in cell B3. A formula was placed in cell B4 as follows: =B2−B3. This formula subtracts expenses from revenues to compute net income in cell B4. If revenues in cell B2 increase to $170,000, net income in B4 automatically increases to $80,000. No other cells will change.

Objective 3
Understand how spreadsheets are used in accounting

SPREADSHEET. A computer program that links data by means of formulas and functions; an electronic work sheet.

EXHIBIT 6-7
A Spreadsheet Screen

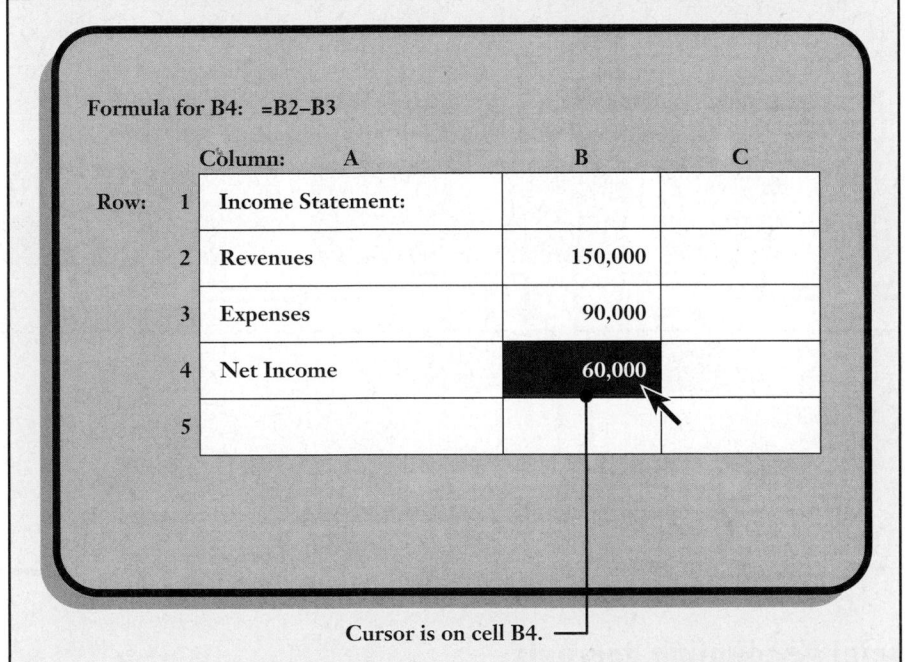

Formula for B4: =B2−B3

Column:	A	B	C
Row: 1	Income Statement:		
2	Revenues	150,000	
3	Expenses	90,000	
4	Net Income	60,000	
5			

Cursor is on cell B4.

Spreadsheets are ideally suited to preparing a budget, which summarizes the financial goals of a business. Consider **Procter & Gamble,** whose Health-Care Sector has an annual advertising budget of several hundred million dollars. Suppose Procter & Gamble allocates $50 million for its Crest Complete toothbrush. Procter & Gamble's advertising expenses will increase. The company will also forecast an increase in sales revenue, cost of goods sold, and other expenses. A spreadsheet computes all these changes in response to the advertising. It lets Procter & Gamble's managers track the profitability of each product. Armed with current data, the managers can make informed decisions. The result is higher profits.

We can add or delete whole rows and columns of data and move blocks of numbers and words on a spreadsheet. The power of a spreadsheet is apparent when enormous amounts of data must be analyzed. Change only one number, and you save hours of manual recalculation. Exhibit 6-8 shows the basic arithmetic operations in popular spreadsheet programs such as Excel.

Exhibit 6-8
Basic Arithmetic Operations in Excel Spreadsheets

DAILY EXERCISE 6-5

Operation	Symbol
Addition	+
Subtraction	−
Multiplication	*
Division	/
Addition of a range of cells	=SUM(beginning cell:ending cell)
Examples:	
Add the contents of cells A2 through A9	=SUM(A2:A9)
Divide the contents of cell C2 by the	
contents of cell D1	=C2/D1

www.prenhall.com/horngren
Mid-Chapter Assessment

SPECIAL JOURNALS

Exhibit 6-9 diagrams a typical accounting system for a merchandising business. The remainder of this chapter describes some of the more important aspects of that system.

EXHIBIT 6-9 **Overview of an Accounting System with Special Journals for a Merchandising Business**

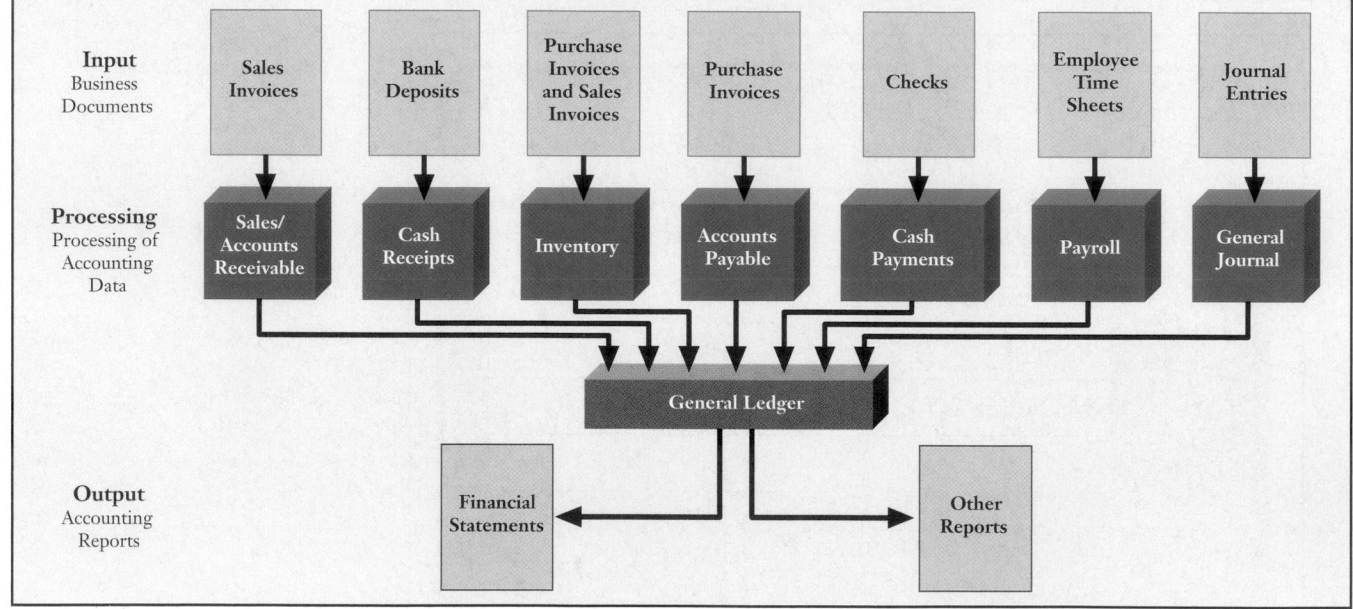

Special Accounting Journals

GENERAL JOURNAL. Journal used to record all transactions that do not fit one of the special journals.

The journal entries illustrated so far in this book have been made in the **general journal.** This journal is used to record all transactions that do not fit one of the special journals. In practice, it is not efficient to record all transactions in the general journal, so we use special journals. A **special journal** is an accounting journal designed to record one specific type of transaction.

SPECIAL JOURNAL. An accounting journal designed to record one specific type of transaction.

Both manual and computerized systems organize transaction entries by type using special journals and accounting modules. In a computerized system, accountants input data through various modules, such as the Accounts Receivable module for credit sales. In a manual system, they enter transaction data in special journals. But the underlying accounting principles are the same in both manual and computerized systems.

In all likelihood, you will be working with a computerized system. We would rather you *not* view the process as a black box. To help you understand the basic accounting, over the next several pages we take you through the steps in a manual system.

Most of a business's transactions fall into one of five categories, so accountants use five different journals to record these transactions. This system reduces the time and cost otherwise spent journalizing. The five categories of transactions, the related journal, and the posting abbreviations are as follows:

Transaction	Special Journal	Posting Abbreviation
1. Sale on account	Sales journal	S
2. Cash receipt	Cash receipts journal	CR
3. Purchase on account	Purchases journal	P
4. Cash payment	Cash payments journal	CP
5. All others	General journal	J

DAILY EXERCISE 6-6

Adjusting and closing entries are entered in the general journal. Transactions are recorded in either the general journal or a special journal, but not in both.

Using the Sales Journal

Most merchandisers sell at least some of their inventory on account. These credit sales are entered in the **sales journal.** Credit sales of assets other than inventory—for example, buildings—occur infrequently and are recorded in the general journal.

Exhibit 6-10 illustrates a sales journal (Panel A) and the related posting to the ledgers (Panel B) of **Austin Sound Center,** introduced in Chapter 5. Each entry in the Accounts Receivable/Sales Revenue column of the sales journal in Exhibit 6-10 is a debit (Dr.) to Accounts Receivable and a credit (Cr.) to Sales Revenue, as the heading above this column indicates. For each transaction, the accountant enters the date, invoice number, customer account, and transaction amount. This streamlined way of recording sales on account saves a vast amount of time that, in a manual system, would be spent entering account titles and dollar amounts in the general journal.

In recording credit sales in previous chapters, we did not keep a record of the names of credit-sale customers. In practice, the business must know the amount receivable from each customer. How else can the company keep track of who owes it money, when collection is due, and how much?

Consider the first transaction in Panel A. On November 2, Austin Sound sold stereo equipment on account to Maria Galvez for $935. The invoice number is 422. All this information appears on a single line in the sales journal. No explanation is necessary. The transaction's presence in the sales journal means it is a credit sale, debited to Accounts Receivable—Maria Galvez and credited to Sales Revenue. To gain additional information about the transaction, we would look up the actual invoice.

Recall from Chapter 5 that Austin Sound uses a *perpetual* inventory system. At the time of recording the sale, Austin Sound also records the cost of the goods sold and the decrease in inventory. Many computerized accounting systems are programmed to read both the sales amount (from the bar code on the package of the item sold) and the cost of goods sold. A separate column of the sales journal holds the cost of goods sold and inventory amount—$505 for the sale to Maria Galvez. If Austin Sound used a *periodic* inventory system, it would not record cost of goods sold and the decrease in inventory at the time of sale. The sales journal would need only one column to debit Accounts Receivable and to credit Sales Revenue for the amount of the sale.

POSTING TO THE GENERAL LEDGER   The ledger we have used so far is the **general ledger,** which holds the accounts reported in the financial statements. We will soon introduce other ledgers.

Posting from the sales journal to the general ledger can be done only once each month. In Exhibit 6-10 (Panel A), November's credit sales total $4,319. This column has two headings, Accounts Receivable and Sales Revenue. When the $4,319 is posted to these accounts in the general ledger, their account numbers are written beneath the total in the sales journal. In Panel B of Exhibit 6-10, the account number for Accounts Receivable is 112 and the account number for Sales Revenue is

Objective 4
Use the sales journal, the cash receipts journal, and the accounts receivable subsidiary ledger

SALES JOURNAL. Special journal used to record credit sales.

DAILY EXERCISE 6-7

DAILY EXERCISE 6-8

GENERAL LEDGER. Ledger of accounts that are reported in the financial statements.

EXHIBIT 6-10   Sales Journal (Panel A) and Posting to the Ledgers (Panel B)

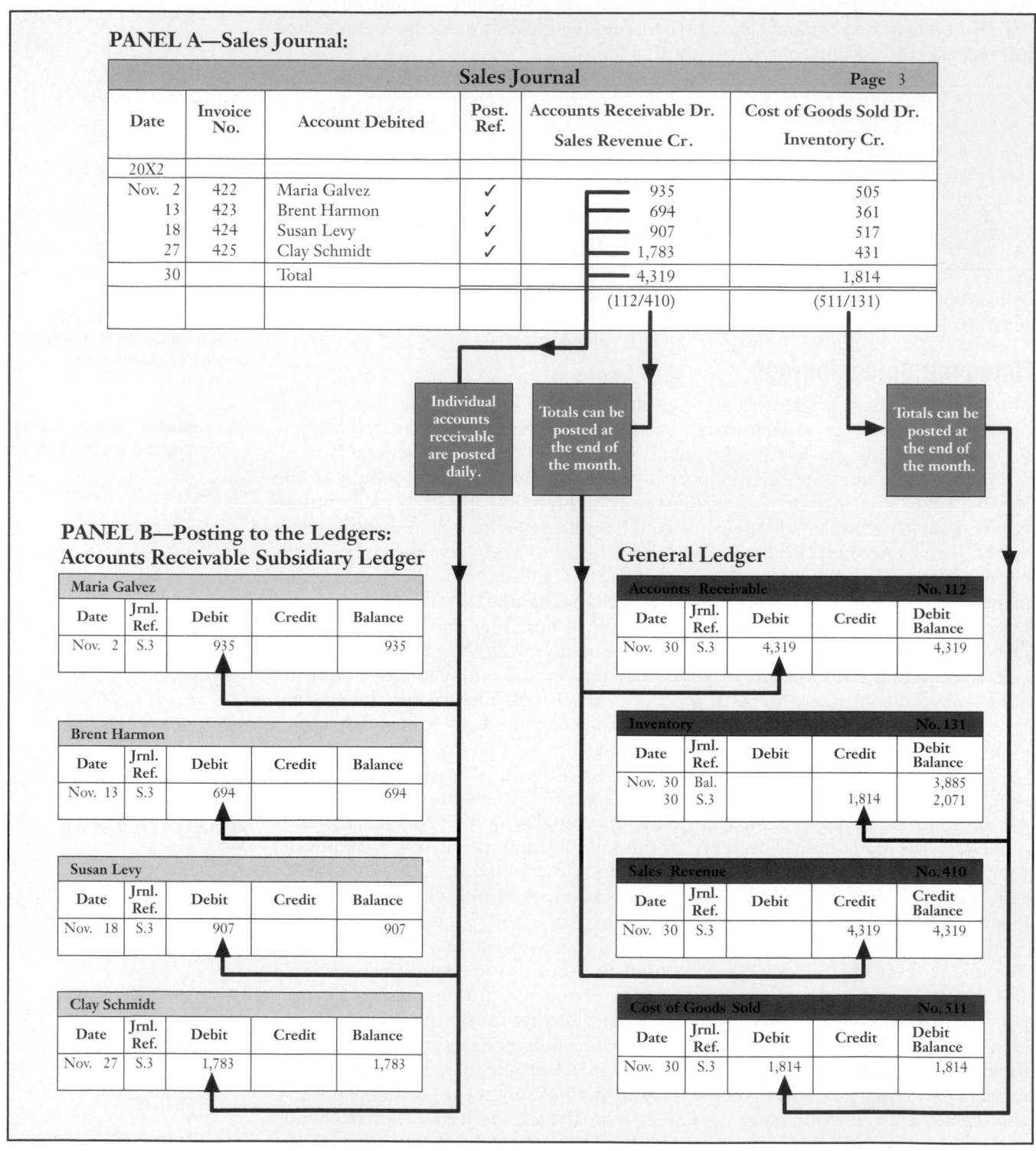

PANEL A—Sales Journal:

				Accounts Receivable Dr.	Cost of Goods Sold Dr.
Sales Journal					**Page** 3
Date	Invoice No.	Account Debited	Post. Ref.	Accounts Receivable Dr. Sales Revenue Cr.	Cost of Goods Sold Dr. Inventory Cr.
20X2					
Nov. 2	422	Maria Galvez	✓	935	505
13	423	Brent Harmon	✓	694	361
18	424	Susan Levy	✓	907	517
27	425	Clay Schmidt	✓	1,783	431
30		Total		4,319	1,814
				(112/410)	(511/131)

Individual accounts receivable are posted daily.

Totals can be posted at the end of the month.

Totals can be posted at the end of the month.

PANEL B—Posting to the Ledgers:
Accounts Receivable Subsidiary Ledger

General Ledger

Maria Galvez

Date	Jrnl. Ref.	Debit	Credit	Balance
Nov. 2	S.3	935		935

Accounts Receivable — No. 112

Date	Jrnl. Ref.	Debit	Credit	Debit Balance
Nov. 30	S.3	4,319		4,319

Brent Harmon

Date	Jrnl. Ref.	Debit	Credit	Balance
Nov. 13	S.3	694		694

Inventory — No. 131

Date	Jrnl. Ref.	Debit	Credit	Debit Balance
Nov. 30	Bal.			3,885
30	S.3		1,814	2,071

Susan Levy

Date	Jrnl. Ref.	Debit	Credit	Balance
Nov. 18	S.3	907		907

Sales Revenue — No. 410

Date	Jrnl. Ref.	Debit	Credit	Credit Balance
Nov. 30	S.3		4,319	4,319

Clay Schmidt

Date	Jrnl. Ref.	Debit	Credit	Balance
Nov. 27	S.3	1,783		1,783

Cost of Goods Sold — No. 511

Date	Jrnl. Ref.	Debit	Credit	Debit Balance
Nov. 30	S.3	1,814		1,814

410. Printing these account numbers beneath the credit-sales total in the sales journal signifies that the $4,319 has been posted to the two accounts.

The debit to Cost of Goods Sold and the credit to Inventory for the monthly total of $1,814 can also be posted at the end of the month. After posting, these accounts' numbers are entered beneath the total to show that Cost of Goods Sold and Inventory have been updated.

POSTING TO THE ACCOUNTS RECEIVABLE SUBSIDIARY LEDGER The $4,319 sum of the November debits to Accounts Receivable does not identify the amount receivable from any specific customer. A business may have thousands of customers. For example, the **Consumers Digest Company,** a Chicago-based firm that publishes the bimonthly magazine *Consumers Digest,* has 1.2 million customer accounts—one for each subscriber.

To streamline operations, businesses place the accounts of their individual credit customers in a subsidiary ledger, called the Accounts Receivable ledger. A **subsidiary ledger** is a record of accounts that provides supporting details on individual balances, the total of which appears in a general ledger account. The customer accounts are arranged in alphabetical order.

Amounts in the sales journal are posted to the subsidiary ledger *daily* to keep a current record of the amount receivable from each customer. Daily posting allows the business to answer customer inquiries promptly. Suppose Maria Galvez telephones Austin Sound on November 3 to ask how much money she owes. The subsidiary ledger readily provides that information, $935 in Exhibit 6-10, Panel B.

When each transaction amount is posted to the subsidiary ledger, a check mark or some other notation is entered in the posting reference column of the sales journal (see Exhibit 6-10, Panel A).

SUBSIDIARY LEDGER. Record of accounts that provides supporting details on individual balances, the total of which appears in a general ledger account.

JOURNAL REFERENCES IN THE LEDGERS   When amounts are posted to the ledgers, the journal page number is printed in the account to identify the source of the data. All transaction data in Exhibit 6-10 originated on page 3 of the sales journal, so all journal references in the ledger accounts are S.3. The "S." indicates sales journal.

Trace all the postings in Exhibit 6-10. The most effective way to learn about accounting systems and special journals is to study the flow of data. The arrows indicate the direction of the information. The arrows also show the links between the individual customer accounts in the subsidiary ledger and the Accounts Receivable account. The Accounts Receivable debit balance in the general ledger should equal the sum of the individual customer balances in the subsidiary ledger, as follows:

General Ledger

Accounts Receivable debit balance...............	$4,319

Subsidiary Ledger: Customer Accounts Receivable

Customer	Balance
Maria Galvez	$ 935
Brent Harmon	694
Susan Levy	907
Clay Schmidt	1,783
Total accounts receivable.............................	$4,319

Accounts Receivable in the general ledger is a **control account.** Its balance equals the sum of the balances of a group of related accounts in a subsidiary ledger. The individual customer accounts are subsidiary accounts. They are said to be "controlled" by the Accounts Receivable account in the general ledger.

Additional data can be recorded in the sales journal. For example, a company may add a column to record sales terms, such as 2/10 n/30. The design of the journal depends on managers' needs for information.

CONTROL ACCOUNT. An account whose balance equals the sum of the balances in a group of related accounts in a subsidiary ledger.

THINK IT OVER

Suppose Austin Sound had 400 credit sales for the month. How many postings to the general ledger would be made from the sales journal? (Ignore Cost of Goods Sold and Inventory.) How many would there be if all sales transactions were routed through the general journal?

Answer: There are only two postings from the sales journal to the general ledger: one to Accounts Receivable and one to Sales Revenue. There would be 800 postings from the general journal: 400 to Accounts Receivable and 400 to Sales Revenue. This difference clearly shows the benefit of using a sales journal.

Using Documents as Journals

Many small businesses streamline their accounting systems by using their business documents as the journals. This practice avoids the need for special journals and saves money. For example, Austin Sound could keep sales invoices in a loose-leaf binder and let the invoices serve as the sales journal. At the end of the period, the accountant simply totals the sales on account and posts the total as a debit to Accounts Receivable and a credit to Sales Revenue. The accountant can also post directly from the invoices to customer accounts in the accounts receivable ledger.

Using the Cash Receipts Journal

CASH RECEIPTS JOURNAL. Special journal used to record cash receipts.

Cash transactions are common in most businesses. To record repetitive cash receipt transactions, accountants use the **cash receipts journal.**

Exhibit 6-11, Panel A, illustrates the cash receipts journal. The related posting to ledgers is shown in Panel B. The exhibit illustrates November transactions for Austin Sound Center.

Every transaction recorded in this journal is a cash receipt, so the second column (after the date) is for debits to the Cash account. The next column is for debits to Sales Discounts on collections from customers. In a typical merchandising business, the main sources of cash are collections on account and cash sales.

The cash receipts journal has credit columns for Accounts Receivable and Sales Revenue. The journal also has a credit column for Other Accounts, which lists sources of cash other than cash sales and collections on account. This Other Accounts column is also used to record the names of customers from whom cash is received on account.

In Exhibit 6-11, cash sales occurred on November 6, 19, and 28. Observe the debits to Cash and the credits to Sales Revenue ($517, $853, and $1,802). Each sale entry is accompanied by a separate entry that debits Cost of Goods Sold and credits Inventory for the cost of the merchandise sold. The column for this entry is at the far right side of the cash receipts journal.

On November 11, Austin Sound borrowed $1,000 from First Bank. Cash is debited, and Note Payable to First Bank is credited in the Other Accounts column because no specific credit column is set up to account for borrowings. For this transaction, we print the account title, Note Payable to First Bank, in the Other Accounts/Account Title column. This entry records the source of cash.

On November 25, Austin Sound collected $762 of interest revenue. The account credited, Interest Revenue, is printed in the Other Accounts column. The November 11 and 25 transactions illustrate a key fact about business. Different entities have different types of transactions; they design their special journals to meet their particular needs for information. In this case, the Other Accounts credit column is the catchall used to record all nonroutine cash receipt transactions.

DAILY EXERCISE 6-9

On November 14, Austin Sound collected $900 from Maria Galvez. Referring to Exhibit 6-10, we see that on November 2, Austin Sound sold merchandise for $935 to Galvez. The terms of sale allowed a $35 discount for prompt payment, and she paid within the discount period. Austin's cash receipt is recorded by debiting Cash for $900 and Sales Discounts for $35, and by crediting Accounts Receivable for $935. The customer's name appears in the Other Accounts/Account Title column.

Total debits should equal total credits in the cash receipts journal. This equality holds for each transaction and for the monthly totals. For the month, total debits ($6,134 + $35 = $6,169) equal total credits ($1,235 + $3,172 + $1,762 = $6,169). The debit to Cost of Goods Sold and the credit to Inventory are separate.

POSTING TO THE GENERAL LEDGER Column totals can be posted monthly. To indicate their posting, the account number is written below the column total in the cash receipts journal. Note the account number for Cash (101) below the column total $6,134, and trace the posting to Cash in the general ledger. Likewise, the other column totals also are posted to the general ledger.

The column total for *Other Accounts* is *not* posted. Instead, these credits are posted individually. In Exhibit 6-11, the November 11 transaction reads "Note Payable to

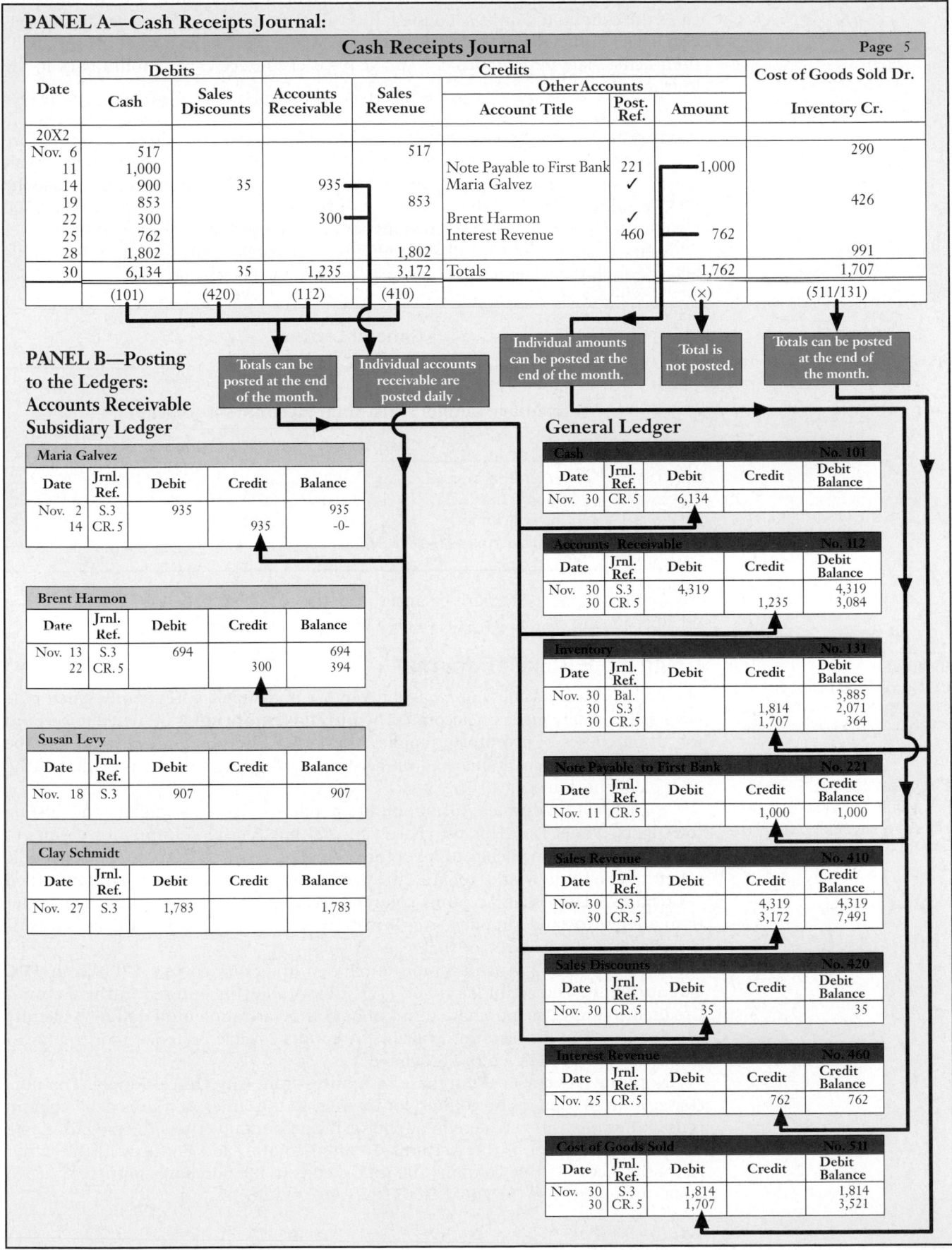

First Bank." This account's number (221) in the Post. Ref. column indicates that the transaction amount was posted individually. The letter x below the column indicates the column total was *not* posted. Individual amounts can be posted to the general ledger at the end of the month. But their date in the ledger accounts should be their actual date in the journal, to make it easier to trace each amount back to the journal.

POSTING TO THE SUBSIDIARY LEDGER   Amounts from the cash receipts journal are posted to the subsidiary accounts receivable ledger daily to keep the individual balances up to date. The postings to the accounts receivable ledger are credits. Trace the $935 posting to Maria Galvez's account. It reduces her balance to zero. The $300 receipt from Brent Harmon reduces his accounts receivable balance to $394.

After posting, the sum of the individual balances in the accounts receivable ledger equals the general ledger balance in Accounts Receivable.

General Ledger

Accounts Receivable debit balance...............	$3,084 ←

Subsidiary Ledger: Customer Accounts Receivable

Customer	Balance
Brent Harmon	$ 394
Susan Levy	907
Clay Schmidt	1,783
Total accounts receivable............................	$3,084 ←

Austin Sound's list of account balances from the subsidiary ledger helps it follow up on slow-paying customers. This helps a business manage cash.

Using the Purchases Journal

Objective 5
Use the purchases journal, the cash payments journal, and the accounts payable subsidiary ledger

PURCHASES JOURNAL. Special journal used to record all purchases of inventory, supplies, and other assets on account.

A merchandising business purchases inventory and supplies frequently. Such purchases are usually made on account. The **purchases journal** is designed to account for all purchases of inventory, supplies, and other assets *on account*. It can also be used to record expenses incurred on account. Cash purchases are recorded in the cash payments journal.

Exhibit 6-12 illustrates Austin Sound's purchases journal (Panel A) and posting to ledgers (Panel B).[1] This purchases journal has special columns for credits to Accounts Payable and debits to Inventory, Supplies, and Other Accounts. A periodic inventory system would replace the Inventory column with a column titled "Purchases." The Other Accounts columns accommodate purchases of items other than inventory and supplies. Accounts Payable is credited for all transactions recorded in the purchases journal.

On November 2, Austin Sound purchased inventory costing $700 from **JVC Corporation.** The creditor's name (JVC Corporation) is entered in the Account Credited column. The purchase terms of 3/15 n/30 are also entered to help identify the due date and the discount available. Accounts Payable is credited for the transaction amount, and Inventory is debited.

Note the November 9 purchase of fixtures from City Office Supply. The purchases journal contains no column for fixtures, so the Other Accounts debit column is used. Because this was a credit purchase, the accountant enters the creditor name (City Office Supply) in the Account Credited column and Fixtures in the Other Accounts/Account Title column. The total credits in the purchases journal ($2,876) equal the total debits ($1,706 + $103 + $1,067 = $2,876).

---

[1]This is the only special journal that we illustrate with the credit column placed to the left and the debit columns to the right. This arrangement of columns focuses on Accounts Payable (which is credited for each entry to this journal).

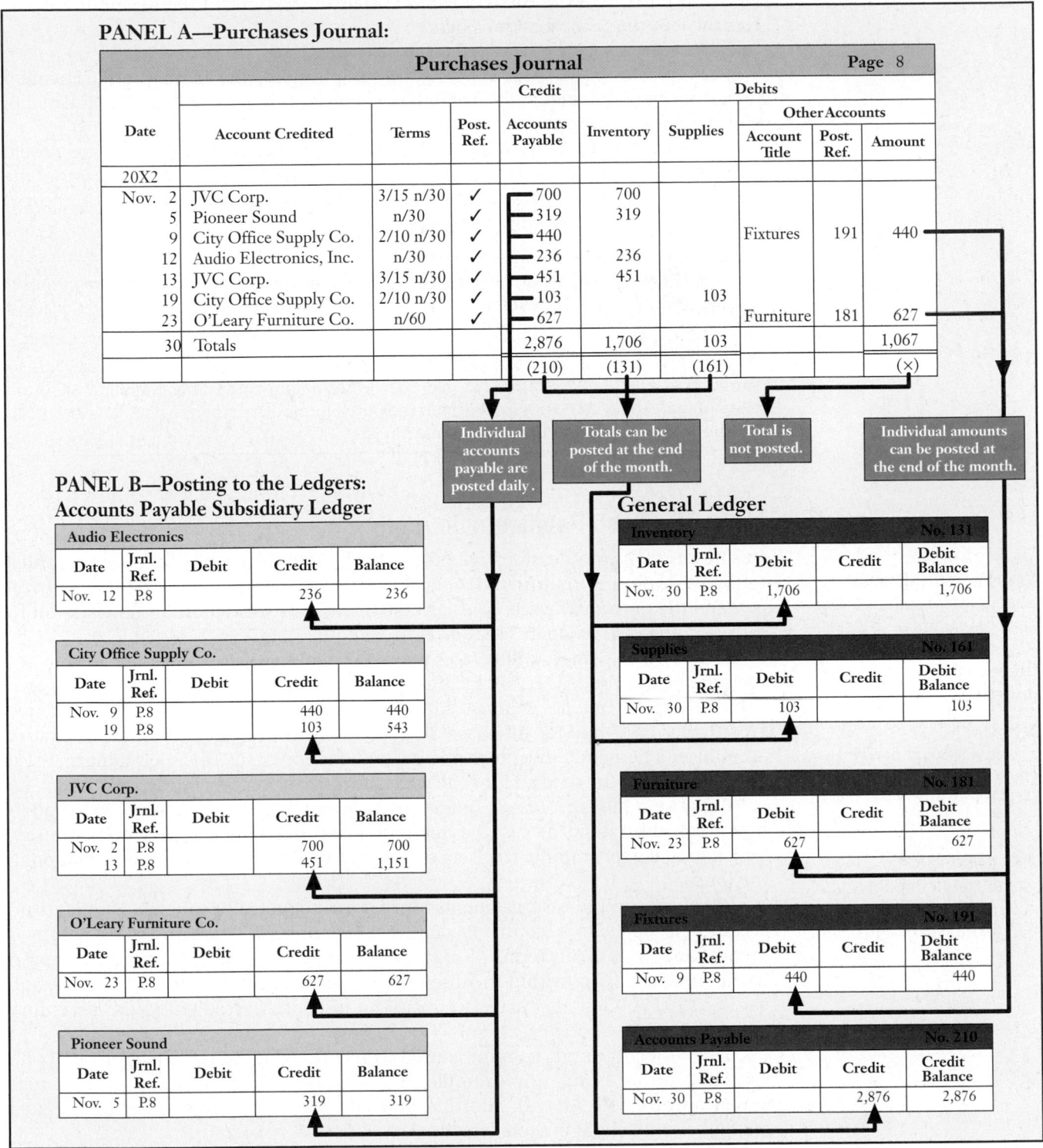

PANEL A—Purchases Journal:

| | | | | Credit | Debits | | | | |
Date	Account Credited	Terms	Post. Ref.	Accounts Payable	Inventory	Supplies	Account Title	Post. Ref.	Amount
20X2									
Nov. 2	JVC Corp.	3/15 n/30	✓	700	700				
5	Pioneer Sound	n/30	✓	319	319				
9	City Office Supply Co.	2/10 n/30	✓	440			Fixtures	191	440
12	Audio Electronics, Inc.	n/30	✓	236	236				
13	JVC Corp.	3/15 n/30	✓	451	451				
19	City Office Supply Co.	2/10 n/30	✓	103		103			
23	O'Leary Furniture Co.	n/60	✓	627			Furniture	181	627
30	Totals			2,876	1,706	103			1,067
				(210)	(131)	(161)			(×)

Individual accounts payable are posted daily.

Totals can be posted at the end of the month.

Total is not posted.

Individual amounts can be posted at the end of the month.

PANEL B—Posting to the Ledgers:
Accounts Payable Subsidiary Ledger

General Ledger

Audio Electronics

Date	Jrnl. Ref.	Debit	Credit	Balance
Nov. 12	P.8		236	236

City Office Supply Co.

Date	Jrnl. Ref.	Debit	Credit	Balance
Nov. 9	P.8		440	440
19	P.8		103	543

JVC Corp.

Date	Jrnl. Ref.	Debit	Credit	Balance
Nov. 2	P.8		700	700
13	P.8		451	1,151

O'Leary Furniture Co.

Date	Jrnl. Ref.	Debit	Credit	Balance
Nov. 23	P.8		627	627

Pioneer Sound

Date	Jrnl. Ref.	Debit	Credit	Balance
Nov. 5	P.8		319	319

Inventory   No. 131

Date	Jrnl. Ref.	Debit	Credit	Debit Balance
Nov. 30	P.8	1,706		1,706

Supplies   No. 161

Date	Jrnl. Ref.	Debit	Credit	Debit Balance
Nov. 30	P.8	103		103

Furniture   No. 181

Date	Jrnl. Ref.	Debit	Credit	Debit Balance
Nov. 23	P.8	627		627

Fixtures   No. 191

Date	Jrnl. Ref.	Debit	Credit	Debit Balance
Nov. 9	P.8	440		440

Accounts Payable   No. 210

Date	Jrnl. Ref.	Debit	Credit	Credit Balance
Nov. 30	P.8		2,876	2,876

ACCOUNTS PAYABLE SUBSIDIARY LEDGER To pay debts efficiently, a company must know how much it owes particular creditors. The Accounts Payable account in the general ledger shows only a single total for the amount owed on account. It does not indicate the amount owed to each creditor. Companies keep an accounts payable subsidiary ledger that is similar to the accounts receivable subsidiary ledger used in conjunction with credit sales.

The accounts payable subsidiary ledger lists the creditors in alphabetical order, along with the amounts owed to them. Exhibit 6-12, Panel B, shows Austin Sound's accounts payable subsidiary ledger, which includes accounts for Audio Electronics,

City Office Supply, and others. After the daily posting is done, the total of the individual balances in the subsidiary ledger equals the balance in the Accounts Payable control account in the general ledger.

POSTING FROM THE PURCHASES JOURNAL   Posting from the purchases journal is similar to posting from the sales journal and the cash receipts journal. Exhibit 6-12, Panel B, illustrates the posting process.

Individual accounts payable in the *accounts payable subsidiary ledger* are posted daily, and column totals and other amounts can be posted to the *general ledger* at the end of the month. In the ledger accounts, P.8 indicates the source of the posted amounts—that is, purchases journal page 8.

THINK IT OVER   Contrast the number of *general ledger* postings from the purchases journal in Exhibit 6-12 with the number that would be required if the general journal were used to record the same seven transactions.

Answer: Use of the purchases journal requires only five *general ledger* postings—$2,876 to Accounts Payable, $1,706 to Inventory, $103 to Supplies, $440 to Fixtures, and $627 to Furniture. Without the purchases journal, there would have been 14 postings, two for each of the seven transactions.

Using the Cash Payments Journal

CASH PAYMENTS JOURNAL.
Special journal used to record cash payments by check. Also called the **check register** or **cash disbursements journal.**

Businesses make most cash payments by check. All payments by check are recorded in the **cash payments journal.** Other titles of this special journal are the *check register* and the *cash disbursements journal.* Like the other special journals, it has columns for recording cash payments that occur frequently.

Exhibit 6-13, Panel A, illustrates the cash payments journal, and Panel B shows the postings to the ledgers of Austin Sound. This cash payments journal has two debit columns—one for Other Accounts and one for Accounts Payable. It has two credit columns—one for purchase discounts, which are credited to the Inventory account in a perpetual inventory system, and one for Cash. This special journal also has columns for the date and for the check number of each cash payment.

Suppose a business makes numerous cash purchases of inventory. What additional column would its cash payments journal need? A column for Inventory, which would appear under the Debits heading, would streamline the information in the journal.

All entries in the cash payments journal include a credit to Cash. Payments on account are debits to Accounts Payable. On November 15, Austin Sound paid JVC on account, with credit terms of 3/15 n/30 (for details, see the first transaction in Exhibit 6-12). Paying within the discount period, Austin took the 3% discount and paid $679 ($700 less the $21 discount). The discount is credited to the Inventory account.

The Other Accounts column is used to record debits to accounts for which no special column exists. For example, on November 3, Austin Sound paid rent expense of $1,200. As with all other journals, the total debits ($3,461 + $819 = $4,280) should equal the total credits ($21 + $4,259 = $4,280).

DAILY EXERCISE 6-10

DAILY EXERCISE 6-11

DAILY EXERCISE 6-12

POSTING FROM THE CASH PAYMENTS JOURNAL   Posting from the cash payments journal is similar to posting from the cash receipts journal. Individual creditor amounts are posted daily, and column totals and Other Accounts can be posted at the end of the month. Exhibit 6-13, Panel B, illustrates the posting process.

Observe the effect of posting to the Accounts Payable account in the general ledger. The first posted amount in the Accounts Payable account (credit $2,876) originated in the purchases journal, page 8 (P.8). The second posted amount (debit $819) came from the cash payments journal, page 6 (CP.6). The resulting credit balance in Accounts Payable is $2,057. Also, see the Cash account; after posting, its debit balance is $1,875.

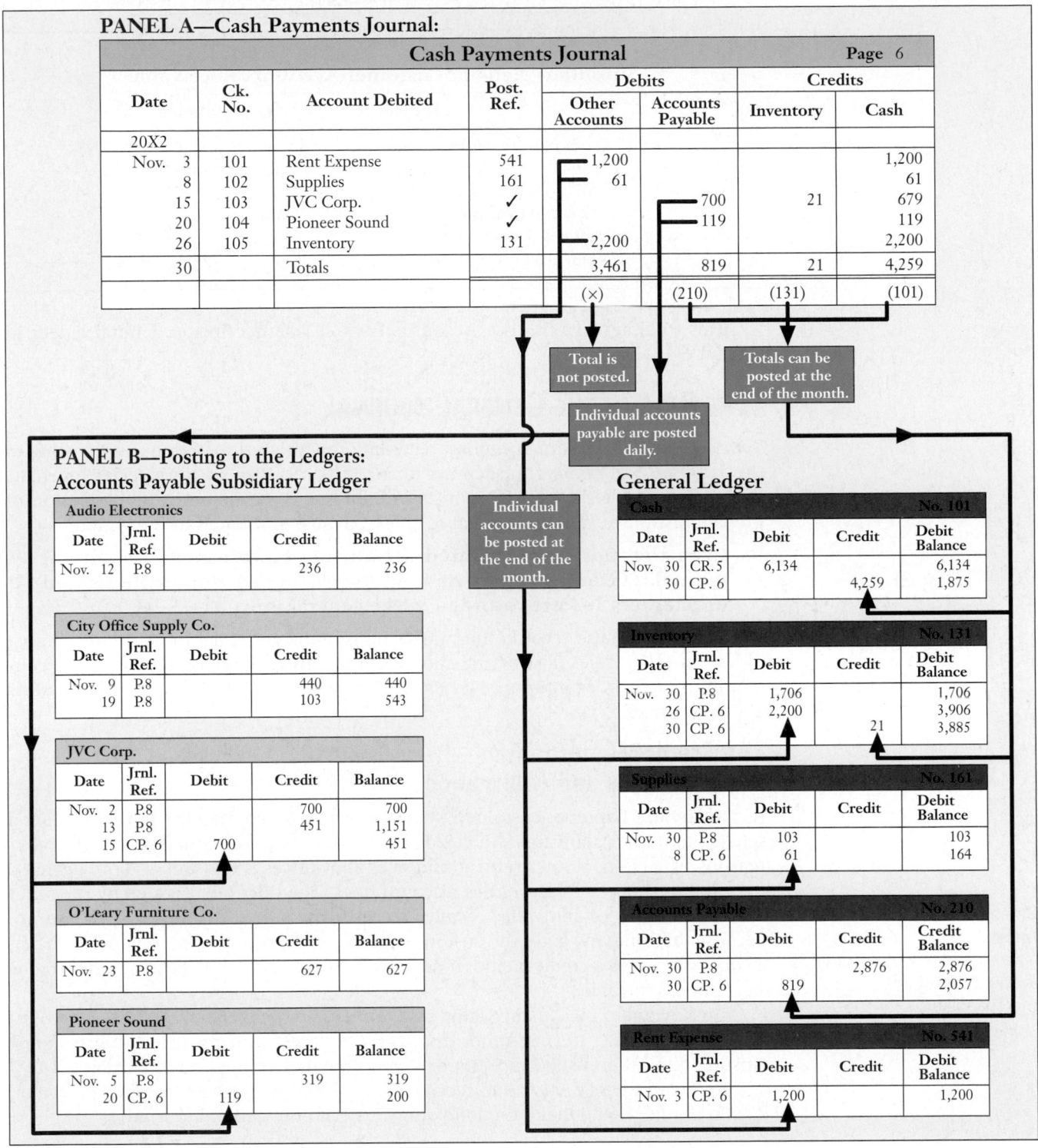

Amounts in the Other Accounts column are posted individually (for example, Rent Expense—debit $1,200). When each amount in the Other Accounts column is posted to the general ledger, the account number is entered in the Post. Ref. column of the journal. The letter x below the column signifies that the total is *not* posted.

To review their accounts payable, companies list the individual creditor balances in the accounts payable subsidiary ledger, as follows:

General Ledger

Accounts Receivable credit balance.............. $2,057 ◄

Subsidiary Ledger: Customer Accounts Receivable

Creditor	Balance
Audio Electronics	$ 326
City Office Supply	543
JVC Corp	451
O'Leary Furniture	627
Pioneer Sound..	200
Total accounts payable	$2,057 ◄

This total agrees with the Accounts Payable balance in the general ledger in Exhibit 6-13.

THE ROLE OF THE GENERAL JOURNAL

Special journals save much time in recording repetitive transactions and posting to the ledgers. But some transactions do not fit into any of the special journals. Examples include the depreciation of buildings and equipment, the expiration of prepaid insurance, and the accrual of salary payable at the end of the period.

Even the most sophisticated accounting system needs a general journal. The adjusting entries and the closing entries we illustrated in Chapters 3–5 are recorded in the general journal.

Accountants also record other transactions in the general journal. Many companies record their sales returns and allowances and their purchase returns in the general journal. Let's examine the *credit memorandum,* the document for sales returns and allowances.

The Credit Memorandum—Recording Sales Returns and Allowances

CREDIT MEMORANDUM OR CREDIT MEMO. A document issued by a seller to credit a customer account for returned merchandise.

As we saw in Chapter 5, customers sometimes return merchandise to the seller, and sellers grant sales allowances to customers because of product defects and for other reasons. The effect of sales returns and sales allowances is the same—both decrease net sales in the same way a sales discount does. The document issued by the seller for a sales return or allowance is called a **credit memorandum,** or **credit memo,** because the company gives the customer credit for the returned merchandise. When a company issues a credit memo, it debits Sales Returns and Allowances and credits Accounts Receivable.

On November 27, Austin Sound sold four stereo speakers for $1,783 on account to Clay Schmidt. Later, Schmidt discovered a defect and returned the speakers. Austin Sound then issued to Schmidt a credit memo like the one in Exhibit 6-14.

To record the *sale return* and receipt of the defective speakers from the customer, Austin Sound would make the following entries in the general journal:

General Journal — Page 9

Date	Accounts	Post Ref.	Debit	Credit
Dec. 1	Sales Returns and Allowances	430	1,783	
	Accounts Receivable—Clay Schmidt............	112/✓		1,783
	Credit memo no. 27.			
Dec. 1	Inventory	131	431	
	Cost of Goods Sold	511		431
	Received defective goods from customer.			

EXHIBIT 6-14
**Credit Memorandum Issued by
Austin Sound Center**

<table>
<tr><td colspan="2">**Credit Memorandum**</td><td>No. 27</td></tr>
<tr><td colspan="3"></td></tr>
<tr><td>Austin Sound Center
305 West Martin Luther King Blvd.
Austin, Texas 78701</td><td colspan="2">Date   December 1, 20X2</td></tr>
<tr><td colspan="3">Customer Name _____ Clay Schmidt</td></tr>
<tr><td colspan="3">538 Rio Grande, Apt.236</td></tr>
<tr><td colspan="3">Austin, Texas 78703</td></tr>
<tr><td colspan="3">Reason for Credit   Defective merchandise returned</td></tr>
</table>

Description	Amount
4 Trailblazer JU170456 Speakers	$1,783

Focus on the first entry. The debit side of the entry is posted to Sales Returns and Allowances. Its account number (430) is written in the posting reference column. The credit side of the entry requires two $1,783 postings, one to Accounts Receivable, the control account in the general ledger (account number 112), and the other to Clay Schmidt's account in the accounts receivable subsidiary ledger. These credit postings explain why the document is called a *credit memo*. The account number (112) denotes the posting to Accounts Receivable in the general ledger. The check mark (✓) denotes the posting to Schmidt's account in the subsidiary ledger. A business with a high volume of sales returns, such as a department store chain, may use a special journal for sales returns and allowances.

The second entry records Austin Sound's receipt of the defective inventory from the customer. The speakers cost Austin Sound $431, and Austin Sound, like all other merchandisers, records its inventory at cost. Now let's see how Austin Sound records the return of the defective speakers to JVC, from which Austin Sound purchased them.

The Debit Memorandum—Recording Purchase Returns and Allowances

Purchase returns occur when a business returns goods to the seller. The procedures for handling purchase returns are similar to those for handling sales returns. The purchaser gives the merchandise back to the seller and receives either a cash refund or replacement goods.

When a business returns merchandise to the seller, it may also send a business document known as a **debit memorandum,** or **debit memo.** This document states that the buyer no longer owes the seller for the goods. The buyer debits Accounts Payable and credits Inventory for the cost of the goods returned to the seller.

Many businesses record their purchase returns in the general journal. Austin Sound would record its return of defective speakers to JVC as follows:

DEBIT MEMORANDUM OR DEBIT MEMO. A document issued by a buyer when returning merchandise. The memo informs the seller that the buyer no longer owes the seller for the amount of the returned purchases.

	General Journal			Page 9
Date	**Accounts**	**Post Ref.**	**Debit**	**Credit**
Dec. 2	Accounts Payable—JVC Corp.	210/✓	431	
	Inventory	131		431
	Debit memo no. 16.			

Balancing the Ledgers

At the end of the period, after all postings, equality should exist between

1. *General ledger:*

   Total debits = Total credits of all account balances

2. *General ledger and Accounts receivable subsidiary ledger:*

   $$\begin{matrix} \textbf{Balance} \\ \textbf{Accounts Receivable} \\ \textbf{control account} \end{matrix} = \begin{matrix} \textbf{Sum of individual customer account} \\ \textbf{balances in the Accounts receivable} \\ \textbf{subsidiary ledger} \end{matrix}$$

3. *General ledger and Accounts payable subsidiary ledger:*

   $$\begin{matrix} \textbf{Balance of Accounts} \\ \textbf{Payable control account} \end{matrix} = \begin{matrix} \textbf{Sum of individual creditor account} \\ \textbf{balances in the Accounts payable} \\ \textbf{subsidiary ledger} \end{matrix}$$

The process of ensuring that these equalities exist is called *balancing the ledgers,* or *proving the ledgers.* It is an important control procedure because it helps ensure the accuracy of the accounting records.

Blending Computers and Special Journals in an Accounting Information System

Computerizing special journals requires no drastic change in system design. Systems designers create a special screen for each accounting application (module)—credit sales, cash receipts, credit purchases, and cash payments. The special screen for credit sales would ask the computer operator to enter the following information: date, customer number, customer name, invoice number, and the dollar amount of the sale. These data can generate debits to the subsidiary accounts receivable and files from which the monthly customer statements that show account activity and ending balance are generated. For purchases on account, additional computer files keep the subsidiary ledger information on individual vendors.

The Decision Guidelines feature provides guidelines for some of the major decisions accountants must make as they use an information system.

DECISION GUIDELINES

Using Special Journals and Control Accounts

DECISION	GUIDELINES
What are the main components of an accounting system?	**Journals** • General journal • Special journals **Ledgers** • General ledger • Subsidiary ledgers Accounts receivable Accounts payable
Where to record • Sales on account? • Cash receipts? • Purchases on account? • Cash payments? • All other transactions?	**Journals** • Sales journal • Cash receipts journal • Purchases journal • Cash payments journal • General journal

How does the general ledger relate to the subsidiary ledgers?

GENERAL LEDGER

ACCOUNTS RECEIVABLE	ACCOUNTS PAYABLE
X,XXX		XX

SUBSIDIARY LEDGERS

ACCOUNTS RECEIVABLE FROM: ACCOUNTS PAYABLE TO:

ARNOLD	BARNES	AGNEW	BLACK
XX	XX	X	X

DECISION GUIDELINES (CONT.)

Using Special Journals and Control Accounts

DECISION	GUIDELINES
When to post from the journals to • General ledger? • Subsidiary ledgers? How to achieve control over • Accounts receivable? • Accounts payable?	—Monthly (or more often, if needed) —Daily Balance the ledgers, as follows:

General Ledger		Subsidiary Ledger
Accounts receivable	=	Sum of individual *customer* account balances
Accounts payable	=	Sum of individual *creditor* account balances

Review Accounting Information Systems

SUMMARY PROBLEM

Riggs Company completed the following selected transactions during March:

www.prenhall.com/horngren
End-of-Chapter Assessment

Mar. 4   Received $500 from a cash sale to a customer (cost, $319).

    6   Received $60 on account from Brady Lee. The full invoice amount was $65, but Lee paid within the discount period to gain the $5 discount.

    9   Received $1,080 on a note receivable from Beverly Mann. This amount includes the $1,000 note receivable plus interest revenue.

  15   Received $800 from a cash sale to a customer (cost, $522).

  24   Borrowed $2,200 by signing a note payable to Interstate Bank.

  27   Received $1,200 on account from Lance Albert. Collection was received after the discount period lapsed.

Required

The general ledger showed the following balances at February 28: Cash, $1,117; Accounts Receivable, $2,790; Note Receivable—Beverly Mann, $1,000; and Inventory, $1,819. The accounts receivable subsidiary ledger at February 28 contained debit balances as follows: Lance Albert, $1,840; Melinda Fultz, $885; Brady Lee, $65.

1. Record the transactions in the cash receipts journal, page 7.
2. Compute column totals at March 31. Show that total debits equal total credits in the cash receipts journal.
3. Post to the general ledger and the accounts receivable subsidiary ledger. Use complete posting references, including the following account numbers: Cash, 11; Accounts Receivable, 12; Note Receivable—Beverly Mann, 13; Inventory, 14; Note Payable—Interstate Bank, 22; Sales Revenue, 41; Sales Discounts, 42; Interest Revenue, 46; and Cost of Goods Sold, 51. Insert a check mark (✓) in the posting reference column for each February 28 account balance.
4. Show that the total of the customer balances in the subsidiary ledger equals the general ledger balance in Accounts Receivable.

Solution

Requirements 1 and 2

Cash Receipts Journal

| | Debits | | Credits | | | | | Cost of Goods |
| | | | | | Other Accounts | | | Sold Debit |
Date	Cash	Sales Discounts	Accounts Receivable	Sales Revenue	Account Title	Post. Ref.	Amount	Inventory Credit
Mar. 4	500			500				319
6	60	5	65		Brady Lee	✓		
9	1,080				Note Receivable—			
					Beverly Mann	13	1,000	
					Interest Revenue	46	80	
15	800			800				522
24	2,200				Note Payable—			
					Interstate Bank	22	2,200	
27	1,200		1,200		Lance Albert	✓		
31	5,840	5	1,265	1,300	Total		3,280	841
	(11)	(42)	(12)	(41)			(✓)	(51/14)

Total Dr. = 5,845   Total Cr. = 5,845

Requirement 3

Accounts Receivable Ledger

Lance Albert

Date	Jrnl. Ref.	Debit	Credit	Balance
Feb. 28	✓			1,840
Mar. 27	CR.7		1,200	640

Melinda Fultz

Date	Jrnl. Ref.	Debit	Credit	Balance
Feb. 28	✓			885

Brady Lee

Date	Jrnl. Ref.	Debit	Credit	Balance
Feb. 28	✓			65
Mar. 6	CR.7		65	—

General Ledger

Cash   **No. 11**

Date	Jrnl. Ref.	Debit	Credit	Balance
Feb. 28	✓			1,117
Mar. 31	CR.7	5,840		6,957

Accounts Receivable   **No. 12**

Date	Jrnl. Ref.	Debit	Credit	Balance
Feb. 28	✓			2,790
Mar. 31	CR.7		1,265	1,525

Note Receivable—Beverly Mann   **No. 13**

Date	Jrnl. Ref.	Debit	Credit	Balance
Feb. 28	✓			1,000
Mar. 9	CR.7		1,000	—

Inventory   **No. 14**

Date	Jrnl. Ref.	Debit	Credit	Balance
Feb. 28	✓			1,819
Mar. 31	CR.7		841	978

Note Payable—Interstate Bank   **No. 22**

Date	Jrnl. Ref.	Debit	Credit	Balance
Mar. 24	CR.7		2,200	2,200

Sales Revenue   **No. 41**

Date	Jrnl. Ref.	Debit	Credit	Balance
Mar. 31	CR.7		1,300	1,300

Sales Discounts   **No. 42**

Date	Jrnl. Ref.	Debit	Credit	Balance
Mar. 31	CR.7	5		5

Interest Revenue   **No. 46**

Date	Jrnl. Ref.	Debit	Credit	Balance
Mar. 9	CR.7		80	80

Cost of Goods Sold   **No. 51**

Date	Jrnl. Ref.	Debit	Credit	Balance
Mar. 31	CR.7	841		841

Requirement 4

General Ledger

Accounts Receivable debit balance	$1,525 ◄

Accounts Receivable Subsidiary Ledger: Customer Accounts Receivable

Customer	Balance
Lance Albert	$ 640
Melinda Fultz	885
Total accounts receivable	$1,525 ◄

LESSONS LEARNED

1. **Describe the features of an effective accounting information system.** An effective *accounting information system* has (1) control over operations; (2) compatibility with the particular features of the business; (3) flexibility in response to changes in the business; and (4) a favorable cost/benefit relationship.

2. **Understand how both computerized and manual accounting systems work.** Computerized accounting systems process inputs faster than manual systems. The key components of a system are *hardware, software,* and company personnel. Both computerized and manual accounting systems require transactions to be classified by type.

   Computerized accounting systems use a *menu* structure to organize accounting functions. Computerized systems are integrated so that the different modules are updated together. Manual systems use special journals for sales, cash receipts, purchases, and cash payments.

3. **Understand how spreadsheets are used in accounting.** *Spreadsheets* are electronic work sheets whose grid points, or cells, are linked by formulas. Numerical relationships remain whenever changes are made to the spreadsheet. Spreadsheets aid in detailed computations, such as budgeting.

4. **Use the sales journal, the cash receipts journal, and the accounts receivable subsidiary ledger.** Many accounting systems use special journals to record transactions by category. Credit sales are recorded in a *sales journal,* and cash receipts in a *cash receipts journal.* The accounts receivable *subsidiary ledger* lists each customer and the amount receivable from that customer. It is the main device for ensuring that the company collects from customers.

5. **Use the purchases journal, the cash payments journal, and the accounts payable subsidiary ledger.** Credit purchases in a manual system are recorded in a *purchases journal,* and cash payments in a *cash payments journal.* The accounts payable subsidiary ledger helps the company stay current in its payments to suppliers.

ACCOUNTING VOCABULARY

accounting information system (p. 227)
batch processing (p. 230)
cash disbursements journal (p. 242)
cash payments journal (p. 242)
cash receipts journal (p. 238)
check register (p. 242)
control account (p. 237)

credit memorandum or credit memo (p. 244)
database (p. 228)
debit memorandum or debit memo (p. 245)
general journal (p. 234)
general ledger (p. 235)
hardware (p. 228)
menu (p. 230)
module (p. 232)

network (p. 228)
on-line processing (p. 230)
purchases journal (p. 240)
sales journal (p. 235)
server (p. 228)
software (p. 228)
special journal (p. 234)
spreadsheet (p. 233)
subsidiary ledger (p. 237)

QUESTIONS

1. Describe the four criteria for an effective accounting system.
2. Distinguish batch computer processing from on-line computer processing.
3. What accounting categories correspond to the account numbers 1, 2, 3, 4, and 5 in a typical computerized accounting system?
4. Why might the number 112 be assigned to Accounts Receivable and the number 1120708 to Bill Thomas, a customer?
5. Describe the function of menus in a computerized accounting system.
6. How do formulas in spreadsheets speed the process of budget preparation and revision?
7. Name four special journals used in accounting systems. For what type of transaction is each designed?
8. Describe the two advantages that special journals have over recording all transactions in the general journal.
9. What is a control account, and how is it related to a subsidiary ledger? Name two common control accounts.
10. DeLay Company's sales journal has one amount column headed Accounts Receivable Dr. and Sales Revenue Cr. In this journal, 86 transactions are recorded. How many posting references appear in the journal? What does each posting reference represent?
11. The accountant for T-Questa Company posted all amounts correctly from the cash receipts journal to the general ledger. However, he failed to post three credits to customer accounts in the accounts receivable subsidiary ledger. How would this error be detected?
12. At what two times is posting done from a special journal? What items are posted at each time?
13. What is the purpose of balancing the ledgers?
14. Posting from the journals of Lexite Sales is complete. But the total of the individual balances in the accounts payable subsidiary ledger does not equal the balance in the Accounts Payable control account in the general ledger. Does this discrepancy necessarily indicate that the trial balance is out of balance? Explain.

Assess Your Progress

DAILY EXERCISES

DE6-1 Suppose you have just invested your life savings in a **Baskin Robbins** franchise. The business is growing fast, and you need a better accounting information system. Consider the features of an effective system, as discussed on pages 227–228. Which do you regard as most important? Why? Which feature must you consider if your financial resources are limited?

Features of an effective information system (Obj. 1)

DE6-2 Match each component of a computerized accounting system with its meaning.

Components of a computerized accounting system (Obj. 1)

Component		Meaning
A. Server	_____	Electronic linkages that allow different computers to share the same information
B. Hardware	_____	Electronic equipment
C. Software	_____	Programs that drive a computer
D. Network	_____	Main computer in a networked system

DE6-3 Complete the crossword puzzle that follows.

Accounting system vocabulary (Obj. 1)

Down:

1. Managers need _____ over operations in order to authorize transactions and safeguard assets
3. Programs that drive a computer
4. Electronic computer equipment
5. A _____ible information system accommodates changes as the organization evolves
6. The opposite of debits

Across:

2. Electronic linkage that allows different computers to share the same information
3. Main computer in a networked system
7. Cost-_____ relationship must be favorable

DE6-4 Use account numbers 11–16, 21, 22, 31, 32, 41, 51, and 52 to correspond to the following selected accounts from the general ledger of Entreé Home Furnishings. List the accounts and their account numbers in proper order, starting with the most liquid current asset.

Setting up a chart of accounts (Obj. 2)

Depreciation expense	Madeline Jacobs, capital	Accounts receivable
Cash	Cost of goods sold	Note payable, long-term
Madeline Jacobs, withdrawals	Accounts payable	Store fixtures
Prepaid insurance	Inventory	
Accumulated depreciation	Sales revenue	

DE6-5 Refer to the spreadsheet screen in Exhibit 6-7, page 233. Suppose cells B1 through B4 are your business's actual income statement for the current year. You wish to develop your financial plan for the coming year. Assume that you expect revenues to increase by 15% and expenses to increase by 10%. Write the formulas in cells C2 through C4 to compute the amounts of expected revenues, expenses, and net income for the coming year.

Using a spreadsheet (Obj. 3)

DE6-6 Use the following abbreviations to indicate the journal in which you would record transactions a–n.

Using the journals (Obj. 4, 5)

J = General journal	P = Purchases journal
S = Sales journal	CP = Cash payments journal
CR = Cash receipts journal	

Transactions:

_____	a. Cash purchase of inventory.	_____	g. Cash sale of inventory.
_____	b. Collection of dividend revenue earned on an investment.	_____	h. Payment of rent.
_____	c. Prepayment of insurance.	_____	i. Depreciation of computer equipment.
_____	d. Borrowing money on a long-term note payable.	_____	j. Purchases of inventory on account.
_____	e. Purchase of equipment on account.	_____	k. Collection of accounts receivable.
_____	f. Cost of goods sold along with a credit sale.	_____	l. Expiration of prepaid insurance.
		_____	m. Sale on account.
		_____	n. Payment on account.

Using the sales journal and the related ledgers
(Obj. 4)

DE6-7 ◄← *Link Back to Chapter 5 (Gross Profit).* Use the sales journal and the related ledger accounts in Exhibit 6-10, page 236, to answer these questions about **Austin Sound Center.**

1. How much gross profit did Austin Sound earn on credit sales during November? For this answer, ignore sales discounts and sales returns and allowances.
2. What amount did Austin Sound post to the Sales Revenue account? When did Austin Sound post to the Sales Revenue account? Assume a manual accounting system.
3. After these transactions, how much does Susan Levy owe Austin Sound? Where do you obtain this information? Be specific.
4. If there were no discounts, how much would Austin Sound hope to collect from all its customers? Where is this amount stored in a single figure?

Using accounts receivable records
(Obj. 4)

DE6-8

1. Where does the total amount receivable from all the customers appear? Be specific.
2. A key control feature of **Austin Sound Center's** accounting system lies in the agreement between the detailed customer receivable records and the summary total in the general ledger. Use the data in Exhibit 6-10, page 236, to prove that Austin Sound's accounts receivable records are accurate.
3. A business that sells on account must have good accounts receivable records to ensure collection from customers. What is the name of the detailed record of amounts collectible from individual customers?

Using cash receipts data
(Obj. 4)

DE6-9 The cash receipts journal of **Austin Sound Center** appears in Exhibit 6-11, page 239, along with the company's various ledger accounts. Use the data in Exhibit 6-11 to answer the following questions that Charles Ernest, owner of the business, might face.

1. How much were cash sales during November?
2. How much did Austin Sound borrow during November? Where else could you look to determine whether Austin Sound has paid off part of the loan?
3. How much were total cash receipts during November?
4. How much cash did Austin Sound collect on account from customers? How much in total discounts did customers earn by paying quickly? How much did Austin Sound's accounts receivable decrease because of collections from customers during November?

Using the purchases journal and the cash payments journal
(Obj. 5)

DE6-10 Refer to **Austin Sound Center's** purchases journal (Exhibit 6-12, page 241) and cash payments journal (Exhibit 6-13, page 243). Charles Ernest, the owner, has raised the following questions about the business.

1. At November 30, after all purchases and all cash payments, how much does Austin Sound owe **JVC Corporation?** How much in total does Austin Sound owe on account?
2. How much did total credit purchases of inventory, supplies, fixtures, and furniture increase Austin Sound's accounts payable during November?
3. How much of the accounts payable did Austin Sound pay off during November? What amount of cash did Austin Sound pay on account? Explain the difference.

Using the purchases journal and the cash payments journal
(Obj. 5)

DE6-11 ◄← *Link Back to Chapters 1 and 2 (Recording transactions).* Use **Austin Sound's** purchases journal (Exhibit 6-12, page 241) and cash payments journal (Exhibit 6-13, page 243) to address these real-world questions faced by Charles Ernest, owner of the business.

1. Why did Austin Sound debit Rent Expense for the rent payment on November 3?
2. How much were Austin Sound's total purchases of inventory during November? How much were net purchases of inventory? What explains the difference between total purchases and net purchases? Which account holds these amounts?
3. Suppose it is December 1 and Ernest wishes to pay the full amount that Austin Sound owes on account. Examine the purchases journal (page 241) to determine whether Ernest can take any purchase discounts, and also consider the cash payments journal. Then make a general journal entry to record payment of the correct amount on December 1. Include an explanation.

DE6-12 Answer the following questions about the November transactions of Austin Sound Center. You will need to refer to Exhibits 6-10 through 6-13, which begin on page 236.

Using all the journals
(Obj. 4, 5)

1. How did Austin Sound purchase furniture—for cash or on account? Indicate the basis for your answer.
2. From whom did Austin Sound purchase supplies on account? How much in total does Austin Sound owe this company on November 30? Can Austin Sound take a discount when Austin Sound pays? Why or why not?
3. How much cash does Austin Sound have on hand at November 30? How much inventory does Austin Sound have after all transactions are recorded, including the cash receipts journal (Exhibit 6-11, page 239)? Indicate which exhibit provides each answer.
4. Determine Austin Sound's gross sales revenue and net sales revenue for November. Indicate which ledger provides the data for your answer.
5. Did Austin Sound's interest revenue for November result from a cash receipt or from an accrual of interest? How can you tell?

EXERCISES

E6-1 Assign account numbers (from the list that follows) to the accounts of AudioBasket. Identify the headings, which are *not* accounts and would not be assigned an account number.

Assigning account numbers
(Obj. 2)

Assets	Mark Lancaster, Capital
Current Assets	Mark Lancaster, Withdrawals
Accounts Receivable	Revenues
Note Payable, Long-Term	Depreciation Expense

Numbers from which to choose:

100	111	281
200	121	311
300	161	321
400	171	331
500	211	531

E6-2 The following accounts of Kim Fisher Company show some of the company's adjusted balances before closing:

Using a trial balance
(Obj. 2)

Total assets	$?	Long-term liabilities	$?
Current assets	31,600	Kim Fisher, capital	8,600
Plant assets	63,400	Kim Fisher, withdrawals	2,000
Total liabilities	?	Total revenues	28,000
Current liabilities	41,100	Total expenses	21,000

Compute the missing amounts. You must also compute ending owner's equity.

E6-3 Equipment listed on a spreadsheet has a cost of $400,000; this amount is located in cell B9. The number of years of the asset's useful life is found in cell C3. Write the spreadsheet formula to express annual depreciation expense for the equipment.

Using a spreadsheet to compute depreciation
(Obj. 3)

E6-4 The values of the following items are stored in the cells of a Kovar Associates spreadsheet:

Computing financial statement amounts with a spreadsheet
(Obj. 3)

Item	Cell
Total assets	B14
Current assets	B6
Fixed assets	B9
Total liabilities	C13
Current liabilities	C8
Long-term liabilities	C10

Write the spreadsheet formula to calculate the company's

a. Current ratio　　　**b.** Total owner's equity　　　**c.** Debt ratio

E6-5 The sales and cash receipts journals of Keester.com include the following entries:

Sales Journal

Date	Account Debited	Post. Ref.	Accounts Receivable Dr. Sales Revenue Cr.	Cost of Goods Sold Dr. Inventory Cr.
May 7	L. Ewald	✓	930	550
10	T. Ross	✓	4,100	1,970
10	E. Lovell	✓	690	410
12	B. Goebel	✓	5,470	3,340
31	Total		11,190	6,270

Cash Receipts Journal

	Debits			Credits				
					Other Accounts			**Cost of Goods Sold Dr.**
Date	Cash	Sales Discounts	Accounts Receivable	Sales Revenue	Account Title	Post. Ref.	Amount	Inventory Cr.
May 16					L. Ewald	✓		
19					E. Lovell	✓		
24	300			300				190
30					T. Ross	✓		

Keester.com makes all credit sales on terms of 2/10 n/30. Complete the cash receipts journal for those transactions indicated. Also, total the journal and show that total debits equal total credits. Each cash receipt was for the appropriate amount of the receivable.

E6-6 The cash receipts journal of EnvisioNet follows.

Cash Receipts Journal   Page 7

	Debits			Credits			
					Other Accounts		
Date	Cash	Sales Discounts	Accounts Receivable	Sales Revenue	Account Title	Post. Ref.	Amount
Jan. 2	794	16	810		Annan Corp.	(e)	
9	491		491		Kamm, Inc.	(f)	
19	4,480				Note Receivable	(g)	4,000
					Interest Revenue	(h)	480
30	314	7	321		J. T. Franz	(i)	
31	4,235			4,235			
31	10,314	23	1,622	4,235	Totals		4,480
	(a)	(b)	(c)	(d)			(j)

EnvisioNet's general ledger includes the following selected accounts, along with their account numbers:

Number	Account	Number	Account
111	Cash	511	Sales revenue
112	Accounts receivable	512	Sales discounts
113	Note receivable	513	Sales returns
119	Land	521	Interest revenue

E6-7 A customer account in the accounts receivable ledger of Vitria Paint Company follows.

Identifying transactions from postings to the accounts receivable subsidiary ledger
(Obj. 4)

Jo Mei Chang

Date		Jrnl. Ref.	Dr.	Cr.	Balance Dr.	Balance Cr.
Nov. 3	....				403	
6	....	S.5	1,180		1,583	
14	....	J.8		191	1,392	
27	....	CR.9		703	689	

Required

Describe the three posted transactions.

E6-8 During April, Nike/Time completed the following *credit purchase* transactions:

April 5	Purchased supplies, $1,106, from Disch Corporation
11	Purchased inventory, $3,600, from Conn Corp. Nike/Time uses a perpetual inventory system.
19	Purchased equipment, $14,300, from Saturn Co.
22	Purchased inventory, $2,210, from Milan, Inc.

Record these transactions first in the general journal—with explanations—and then in the purchases journal. Omit credit terms and posting references. Which procedure for recording transactions is quicker? Why?

Recording purchase transactions in the general journal and in the purchases journal
(Obj. 5)

E6-9 The purchases journal of Hans Bauman Company follows.

Posting from the purchases journal; balancing the ledgers
(Obj. 5)

							Other Accounts Dr.		
Date	Account Credited	Terms	Post. Ref.	Account Payable Cr.	Inventory Dr.	Supplies Dr.	Acct. Title	Post. Ref.	Amt. Dr.
Sep. 2	Lancer Technologies	n/30		800	800				
5	Saturn Office Supply	n/30		175		175			
13	Lancer Technologies	2/10 n/30		1,151	1,151				
26	Faver Equipment Company	n/30		916			Equipment		916
30	Totals			3,042	1,951	175			916

Purchases Journal — **Page 7**

Required

1. Open ledger accounts for Inventory, Supplies, Equipment, and Accounts Payable. Post to these accounts from the purchases journal. Use dates and posting references in the accounts.
2. Open accounts in the accounts payable subsidiary ledger for Faver Equipment Company, Lancer Technologies, and Saturn Office Supply. Post from the purchases journal. Use dates and journal references in the ledger accounts.
3. Balance the Accounts Payable control account in the general ledger with the total of the balances in the accounts payable subsidiary ledger.

E6-10 During August, Silicon Valley Sporting Goods had the following transactions:

Aug. 1 Paid $490 on account to Rabin Associates, net of a $10 discount for an earlier purchase of inventory.

5 Purchased inventory for cash, $4,300.

9 Paid $375 for supplies.

15 Purchased inventory on credit from Monroe Corporation, $774.

16 Paid $4,062 on account to LaGrange Company; there was no discount.

21 Purchased furniture for cash, $960.

26 Paid $3,910 on account to VisioNet Software for an earlier purchase of inventory. The discount was $90.

30 Made a semiannual interest payment of $800 on a long-term note payable. The entire payment was for interest.

Required

1. Prepare a cash payments journal similar to the one illustrated in this chapter. Omit the check number (Ck. No.) and posting reference (Post. Ref.) columns.
2. Record the transactions in the journal. Which transaction should not be recorded in the cash payments journal? In what journal does it belong?
3. Total the amount columns of the journal. Determine that total debits equal total credits.

E6-11 ◄ *Link Back to Chapter 5 (Recording Purchases, Sales, and Returns).* The following documents describe two business transactions.

Invoice		
Date:	May 14, 20X0	
Sold to:	BiWheel Bicycle Shop	
Sold by:	Schwinn Company	
Terms:	2/10 n/30	

Items Purchased	Bicycles	
Quantity	Price	Total
8	$95	$760
1	70	70
5	60	300
Total		$1,130

Debit Memo		
Date:	May 20, 20X0	
Issued to:	Schwinn Company	
Issued by:	BiWheel Bicycle Shop	

Items Returned	Bicycles	
Quantity	Price	Total
1	$95	$ 95
1	70	70
Total		$165
Reason:	Damaged in shipment	

Required

Use the general journal to record these transactions and BiWheel's cash payment on May 21. Record the transactions first on the books of BiWheel Bicycle Shop and, second, on the books of **Schwinn Company,** which makes and sells bicycles. Both BiWheel and Schwinn use a perpetual inventory system as illustrated in Chapter 5. Schwinn's cost of the bicycles sold to BiWheel was $690. Schwinn's cost of the returned merchandise was $80. Round to the nearest dollar. Explanations are not required. Set up your answer in the following format:

Date	BiWheel Journal Entries	Schwinn Journal Entries

Challenge Exercise

E6-12 ◄ *Link Back to Chapter 5 (Cost of Goods Sold, Gross Profit).*

1. **Austin Sound Center's** special journals in Exhibits 6-10 through 6-13 (pages 236–243) provide the owner with much of the data needed for preparation of the financial statements. Austin Sound uses the *perpetual* inventory system, so the amount of cost of goods sold is simply the ending balance in that account. Charles Ernest, the owner, needs to know the business's gross profit for November. Compute the gross profit.
2. Suppose Austin Sound uses the *periodic* inventory system. In that case, the business must compute cost of goods sold by the following formula:

Cost of goods sold:

Beginning inventory .... $ X*
+ Net purchases XXX
= Cost of goods available for sale .... X,XXX
− Ending inventory .... (XX)
= Cost of goods sold .... $ XX

*$0 for Austin Sound at November 1.

Perform this calculation of cost of goods sold for Austin Sound. Does this computation of cost of goods sold agree with your answer to requirement 1?

PROBLEMS

(Group A)

P6-1A The following spreadsheet shows the income statement of Tradex Technologies:

Using a spreadsheet to prepare an income statement and evaluate operations (Obj. 3)

	Column	
Row Number	A	B
7	Revenues:	
8	Service revenue ⟶	
9	Rent revenue ⟶	
10		_____
11	Total revenue ⟶	
12		
13	Expenses:	
14	Salary expense ⟶	
15	Supplies expense ⟶	
16	Rent expense ⟶	
17	Depreciation expense ⟶	
18		_____
19	Total expenses ⟶	
20		_____
21	Net income ⟶	
22		======

Required

1. Write the word *number* in the cells (indicated by arrows) where numbers will be entered.
2. Write the appropriate formula in each cell that will need a formula. Choose from these symbols.

+	add	*	multiply
−	subtract	/	divide

= SUM(beginning cell:ending cell)

3. Last year, Tradex used this spreadsheet to prepare the company's budgeted income statement—which shows the company's net income goal—for the current year. It is now one year later, and Tradex has prepared its actual income statement for the year. State how the owner of the company can use this income statement in decision making.

P6-2A The general ledger of Ariba Genetics includes the following selected accounts:

Using the sales, cash receipts, and general journals (Obj. 4)

Cash	11	Sales Revenue	41
Accounts Receivable	12	Sales Discounts	42
Inventory	13	Sales Returns and Allowances	43
Notes Receivable	15	Interest Revenue	47
Supplies	16	Cost of Goods Sold	51
Land	18		

All credit sales are on the company's standard terms of 2/10 n/30. Transactions in July that affected sales and cash receipts were as follows:

July 2 Sold inventory on credit to Intelysis, Inc., $2,400. Ariba's cost of these goods was $1,400.

3 As an accommodation to a competitor, sold supplies at cost, $85, receiving cash.

7 Cash sales for the week totaled $1,890 (cost, $1,640).

9 Sold merchandise on account to A. L. Prince, $7,320 (cost, $5,110).

10 Sold land that cost $10,000 for cash of $10,000.

11 Sold goods on account to Sloan Electric, $5,104 (cost, $3,520).

12 Received cash from Intelysis in full settlement of its account receivable from July 2.

14 Cash sales for the week were $2,106 (cost, $1,530).

15 Sold inventory on credit to the partnership of Wilkie & Blinn, $3,650 (cost, $2,260).

18 Received inventory sold on July 9 to A. L. Prince for $600. The goods shipped were unsatisfactory. These goods cost Ariba $440.

20 Sold merchandise on account to Sloan Electric, $629 (cost, $450).

21 Cash sales for the week were $990 (cost, $690).

22 Received $4,000 cash from A. L. Prince in partial settlement of his account receivable.

25 Received cash from Wilkie & Blinn for its account receivable from July 15.

25 Sold goods on account to Olsen Co., $1,520 (cost, $1,050).

27 Collected $5,125 on a note receivable, of which $125 was interest.

28 Cash sales for the week totaled $3,774 (cost, $2,460).

29 Sold inventory on account to R. O. Bankston, $242 (cost, $170).

30 Received goods sold on July 25 to Olsen Co. for $40. The inventory was damaged in shipment. The salvage value of these goods was $10. Record the inventory at its salvage value.

31 Received $2,720 cash on account from A. L. Prince.

Required

1. Ariba records sales returns and allowances in the general journal. Use the appropriate journal to record the preceding transactions in a sales journal (omit the Invoice No. column), a cash receipts journal, and a general journal.
2. Total each column of the cash receipts journal. Show that total debits equal total credits.
3. Show how postings would be made from the journals by writing the account numbers and check marks in the appropriate places in the journals.

Correcting errors in the cash receipts journal (Obj. 4)

P6-3A The following cash receipts journal of Trilogy Buying Cooperative contains five entries. All five entries are for legitimate cash receipt transactions, but the journal contains some errors in recording the transactions. In fact, only one entry is correct, and each of the other four entries contains one error.

	Debits		**Credits**					**Cost of Goods**
					Other Accounts			**Sold Debit**
Date	**Cash**	**Sales Discounts**	**Accounts Receivable**	**Sales Revenue**	**Account Title**	**Post. Ref.**	**Amount**	**Inventory Credit**
2/6		7,200		7,200				2,900
7	429	22			Paul Dalton	✓	451	
14	8,200				Note Receivable	15	7,700	
					Interest Revenue	45	500	
18				330				150
24	1,100		770					
28	9,729	7,222	770	7,530	Totals		8,651	3,050
	(11)	(42)	(12)	(41)			(x)	(51/13)

Cash Receipts Journal — Page 22

Total Dr. = $16,951   Total Cr. = $16,951

Required

1. Identify the correct entry.
2. Identify the error in each of the other four entries.
3. Using the following format, prepare a corrected cash receipts journal.

Cash Receipts Journal — Page 22

	Debits		Credits					
					Other Accounts			Cost of Goods Sold Debit
Date	Cash	Sales Discounts	Accounts Receivable	Sales Revenue	Account Title	Post. Ref.	Amount	Inventory Credit
2/6								
7					Paul Dalton	✓		
14					Note Receivable	15		
					Interest Revenue	45		
18								
24								
28	16,929	22	1,221	7,530	Totals		8,200	3,050
	(11)	(42)	(12)	(41)			(x)	(51/13)

Total Dr. = $16,951   Total Cr. = $16,951

P6-4A The general ledger of Sun Network.com includes the following accounts:

Using the purchases, cash payments, and general journals (Obj. 5)

Cash	111	Furniture	187
Inventory	131	Accounts Payable	211
Prepaid Insurance	161	Rent Expense	564
Supplies	171	Utilities Expense	583

Transactions in December that affected purchases and cash payments were as follows:

Dec. 2 Purchased inventory on credit from **Microsoft,** $4,000. Terms were 2/10 n/30.
3 Paid monthly rent, debiting Rent Expense for $2,000.
5 Purchased supplies on credit terms of 2/10 n/30 from Ross Supply, $450.
8 Paid electricity utility bill, $588.
9 Purchased furniture on account from A-1 Office Supply, $4,100. Payment terms were net 30.
10 Returned the furniture to A-1 Office Supply. It was the wrong color.
11 Paid Microsoft the amount owed on the purchase of December 2.
12 Purchased inventory on account from Wynne, Inc., $4,400. Terms were 3/10 n/30.
13 Purchased inventory for cash, $655.
14 Paid a semiannual insurance premium, debiting Prepaid Insurance, $1,200.
16 Paid our account payable to Ross Supply, from December 5.
18 Paid gas and water utility bills, $196.
21 Purchased inventory on credit terms of 1/10 n/45 from Software, Inc., $5,200.
21 Paid account payable to Wynne, Inc., from December 12.
22 Purchased supplies on account from Office Sales, Inc., $274. Terms were net 30.
26 Returned to Software, Inc., $1,200 of the inventory purchased on December 21.
31 Paid Software, Inc., the net amount owed from December 21 less the return on December 26.

Required

1. Sun Network.com records purchase returns in the general journal. Use the appropriate journal to record the preceding transactions in a purchases journal, a cash payments journal (omit the Check No. column), and a general journal.
2. Total each column of the special journals. Show that total debits equal total credits in each special journal.
3. Show how postings would be made from the journals by writing the account numbers and check marks in the appropriate places in the journals.

P6-5A Fairchild Fidelity Co., which uses the perpetual inventory system and makes all credit sales on terms of 2/10 n/30, completed the following transactions during May:

Using all the journals, posting, and balancing the ledgers (Obj. 4, 5)

May 2 Issued invoice no. 913 for sale on account to K. D. Forbes, $2,000. Fairchild's cost of this inventory was $900.
3 Purchased inventory on credit terms of 3/10 n/60 from Chicosky Co., $2,467.
5 Sold inventory for cash, $1,077 (cost, $480).
5 Issued check no. 532 to purchase furniture for cash, $2,185.

May 8   Collected interest revenue of $1,775.

9   Issued invoice no. 914 for sale on account to Bell Co., $5,550 (cost, $2,310).

10   Purchased inventory for cash, $1,143, issuing check no. 533.

12   Received cash from K. D. Forbes in full settlement of her account receivable from the sale on May 2.

13   Issued check no. 534 to pay Chicosky Co. the net amount owed from May 3. Round to the nearest dollar.

13   Purchased supplies on account from Manley, Inc., $441. Terms were net end-of-month.

15   Sold inventory on account to M. O. Brown, issuing invoice no. 915 for $665 (cost, $240).

17   Issued credit memo to M. O. Brown for $665 for defective merchandise returned to us by Brown. Also accounted for receipt of the inventory.

18   Issued invoice no. 916 for credit sale to K. D. Forbes, $357 (cost, $127).

19   Received $5,439 from Bell Co. in full settlement of its account receivable from May 9. Bell earned a discount by paying early.

20   Purchased inventory on credit terms of net 30 from Sims Distributing, $2,047.

22   Purchased furniture on credit terms of 3/10 n/60 from Chicosky Co., $645.

22   Issued check no. 535 to pay for insurance coverage, debiting Prepaid Insurance for $1,000.

24   Sold supplies to an employee for cash of $54, which was Fairchild's cost.

25   Issued check no. 536 to pay utilities, $453.

28   Purchased inventory on credit terms of 2/10 n/30 from Manley, Inc., $675.

29   Returned damaged inventory to Manley, Inc., issuing a debit memo for $675.

29   Sold goods on account to Bell Co., issuing invoice no. 917 for $496 (cost, $220).

30   Issued check no. 537 to pay Manley, Inc., in full on account from May 13.

31   Received cash in full on account from K. D. Forbes on credit sale of May 18. There was no discount.

31   Issued check no. 538 to pay monthly salaries of $2,347.

Required

1. For Fairchild Fidelity, open the following general ledger accounts using the account numbers given:

Cash	111	Sales Revenue	411
Accounts Receivable	112	Sales Discounts	412
Supplies	116	Sales Returns and Allowances	413
Prepaid Insurance	117	Interest Revenue	419
Inventory	118	Cost of Goods Sold	511
Furniture	151	Salary Expense	531
Accounts Payable	211	Utilities Expense	541

2. Open these accounts in the subsidiary ledgers: Accounts receivable subsidiary ledger—Bell Co., M. O. Brown, and K. D. Forbes; accounts payable subsidiary ledger—Chicosky Co., Manley, Inc., and Sims Distributing.

3. Enter the transactions in a sales journal (page 7), a cash receipts journal (page 5), a purchases journal (page 10), a cash payments journal (page 8), and a general journal (page 6), as appropriate.

4. Post daily to the accounts receivable subsidiary ledger and to the accounts payable subsidiary ledger. On May 31, post to the general ledger.

5. Total each column of the special journals. Show that total debits equal total credits in each special journal.

6. Balance the total of the customer account balances in the accounts receivable subsidiary ledger against Accounts Receivable in the general ledger. Do the same for the accounts payable subsidiary ledger and Accounts Payable in the general ledger.

(Group B)   P R O B L E M S

Using a spreadsheet to prepare a partial balance sheet and evaluate financial positions (Obj. 3)

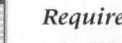

P6-1B The following spreadsheet on page 261 shows the assets of the Clarus Consulting balance sheet:

Required

1. Write the word *number* in the cells (indicated by arrows) where numbers will be entered.

2. Write the appropriate formula in each cell that will need a formula. Choose from these symbols:

```
+    add                              *    multiply
−    subtract                         /    divide
=    SUM(beginning cell:ending cell)
```

	Column	
Row Number	**A**	**B**
2	Assets:	
3	Current assets:	
4	Cash ⟶	
5	Receivables ⟶	
6	Inventory ⟶	_____
7		
8	Total current assets ⟶	
9		
10	Equipment ⟶	
11	Accumulated depreciation ⟶	
12		_____
13	Equipment, net ⟶	
14		_____
15	Total assets ⟶	
16		=====

3. Last year Clarus used this spreadsheet to prepare the company's budgeted balance sheet for the current year. The budgeted balance sheet shows the company's goal for total current assets at the end of the year. It is now one year later, and Clarus has prepared its actual year-end balance sheet. State how the owner of the company can use this balance sheet in decision making.

P6-2B The general ledger of Remedy Corporation includes the following selected accounts:

Using the sales, cash receipts, and general journals (Obj. 4)

Cash...	111	Sales Revenue...............................	411
Accounts Receivable......................	112	Sales Discounts	412
Notes Receivable...........................	115	Sales Returns and Allowances	413
Inventory..	131	Interest Revenue...........................	417
Equipment......................................	141	Gain on Sale of Land.....................	418
Land...	142	Cost of Goods Sold........................	511

All credit sales are on the company's standard terms of 2/10 n/30. Transactions in November that affected sales and cash receipts were as follows:

Nov. 2 Sold inventory on credit to Grant Thornton $800. Remedy's cost of these goods was $314.
6 As an accommodation to another company, sold new equipment for its cost of $770, receiving cash in this amount.
7 Cash sales for the week totaled $2,107 (cost, $1,362).
8 Sold merchandise on account to McNair Co., $2,830 (cost, $1,789).
9 Sold land that cost $22,000 for cash of $40,000. The difference is a gain.
11 Sold goods on account to Nickerson Builders, $6,099 (cost, $3,853).
11 Received cash from Grant Thornton in full settlement of his account receivable from November 2.
13 Cash sales for the week were $1,995 (cost, $1,286).
15 Sold inventory on credit to Montez and Montez, a partnership, $800 (cost, $517).
18 Received inventory sold on November 8 to McNair Co. for $120. The goods we shipped were unsatisfactory. These goods cost Remedy $73.
19 Sold merchandise on account to Nickerson Builders, $3,900 (cost, $2,618).
20 Cash sales for the week were $2,330 (cost, $1,574).
21 Received $1,200 cash from McNair Co. in partial settlement of its account receivable. There was no discount.
22 Received cash from Montez and Montez for its account receivable from November 15.
22 Sold goods on account to Diamond Co., $2,022 (cost, $1,325).
25 Collected $4,200 on a note receivable, of which $200 was interest.

Nov. 27   Cash sales for the week totaled $2,970 (cost, $1,936).
27   Sold inventory on account to Littleton Corporation, $2,290 (cost, $1,434).
28   Received goods sold on November 22 to Diamond Co. for $680. The goods were damaged in shipment. The salvage value of these goods was $96. Record the inventory at its salvage value.
30   Received $1,510 cash on account from McNair Co. There was no discount.

Required

1. Use the appropriate journal to record the preceding transactions in a sales journal (omit the Invoice No. column), a cash receipts journal, and a general journal. Remedy Corporation records sales returns and allowances in the general journal.
2. Total each column of the cash receipts journal. Determine that total debits equal total credits.
3. Show how postings would be made from the journals by writing the account numbers and check marks in the appropriate places in the journals.

Correcting errors in the cash receipts journal
(Obj. 4)

P6-3B The following cash receipts journal contains five entries. All five entries are for legitimate cash receipt transactions, but the journal contains some errors in recording the transactions. In fact, only one entry is correct, and each of the other four entries contains one error.

Cash Receipts Journal   Page 16

| | Debits | | Credits | | | | | Cost of Goods Sold Debit |
| | | | | | Other Accounts | | | |
Date	Cash	Sales Discounts	Accounts Receivable	Sales Revenue	Account Title	Post. Ref.	Amount	Inventory Credit
7/3	582	18	600		Alliance Chemicals	✓		
9			346	346	Carl Ryther	✓		
10	22,000			22,000	Land	19		
19	73							44
30	1,060			1,133				631
31	23,715	18	946	23,479	Totals			675
	(11)	(42)	(12)	(41)			(x)	(51/13)

Total Dr. = $23,733   Total Cr. = $24,425

Required

1. Identify the correct entry.
2. Identify the error in each of the other four entries.
3. Using the following format, prepare a corrected cash receipts journal.

Cash Receipts Journal   Page 16

| | Debits | | Credits | | | | | Cost of Goods Sold Debit |
| | | | | | Other Accounts | | | |
Date	Cash	Sales Discounts	Accounts Receivable	Sales Revenue	Account Title	Post. Ref.	Amount	Inventory Credit
7/3					Alliance Chemicals	✓		
9					Carl Ryther	✓		
10					Land	19		
19								
30								
31	24,061	18	946	1,133	Totals		22,000	675
	(11)	(42)	(12)	(41)			(x)	(51/13)

Total Dr. = $24,079   Total Cr. = $24,079

P6-4B The general ledger of Commerce One includes the following accounts:

Using the purchases, cash payments, and general journals
(Obj. 5)

Cash	111	Equipment	189
Inventory	131	Accounts Payable	211
Prepaid Insurance	161	Rent Expense	562
Supplies	171	Utilities Expense	565

Transactions in January that affected purchases and cash payments were as follows:

Jan. 4   Paid monthly rent, debiting Rent Expense for $1,350.
     5   Purchased inventory on credit from Sylvania Co., $5,000. Terms were 2/15 n/45.
     6   Purchased supplies on credit terms of 2/10 n/30 from Harmon Sales, $800.
     7   Paid gas and water utility bills, $406.
   10   Purchased equipment on account from Lancer Co., $1,050. Payment terms were 2/10 n/30.
   11   Returned the equipment to Lancer Co. It was defective.
   12   Paid Sylvania Co. the amount owed on the purchase of January 5.
   12   Purchased inventory on account from Lancer Co., $1,100. Terms were 2/10 n/30.
   14   Purchased inventory for cash, $1,585.
   15   Paid an insurance premium, debiting Prepaid Insurance, $2,416.
   17   Paid electricity utility bill, $165.
   19   Paid our account payable to Harmon Sales, from January 6.
   20   Paid account payable to Lancer Co., from January 12.
   21   Purchased supplies on account from Master Supply, $754. Terms were net 30.
   22   Purchased inventory on credit terms of 1/10 n/30 from Linz Brothers, $3,400.
   26   Returned inventory purchased for $500 on January 22, to Linz Brothers.
   31   Paid Linz Brothers the net amount owed from January 22, less the return on January 26.

Required

1. Use the appropriate journal to record the preceding transactions in a purchases journal, a cash payments journal (omit the Check No. column), and a general journal. Commerce One records purchase returns in the general journal.
2. Total each column of the special journals. Show that total debits equal total credits in each special journal.
3. Show how postings would be made from the journals by writing the account numbers and check marks in the appropriate places in the journals.

P6-5B Contour Publishing, which uses the perpetual inventory system and makes all credit sales of 2/10 n/30, had these transactions during March:

Using all the journals, posting, and balancing the ledgers
(Obj. 4, 5)

Mar. 2   Issued invoice no. 191 for sale on account to L. E. Wooten, $2,350. Contour's cost of this inventory was $1,390.
     3   Purchased inventory on credit terms of 3/10 n/60 from Delwood Plaza, $5,900.
     4   Sold inventory for cash, $1,413 (cost, $820).
     5   Issued check no. 473 to purchase furniture for cash, $1,087.
     8   Collected interest revenue of $2,440.
     9   Issued invoice no. 192 for sale on account to Cortez Co., $6,250 (cost, $3,300).
   10   Purchased inventory for cash, $776, issuing check no. 474.
   12   Received $2,303 cash from L. E. Wooten in full settlement of her account receivable, net of the discount, from the sale of March 2.
   13   Issued check no. 475 to pay Delwood Plaza net amount owed from March 3.
   13   Purchased supplies on account from Havrilla Corp., $689. Terms were net end-of-month.
   15   Sold inventory on account to J. R. Wakeland, issuing invoice no. 193 for $743 (cost, $410).
   17   Issued credit memo to J. R. Wakeland for $743 for defective merchandise returned to us by Wakeland. Also accounted for receipt of the inventory.
   18   Issued invoice no. 194 for credit sale to L. E. Wooten, $1,825 (cost, $970).
   19   Received $6,125 from Cortez Co. in full settlement of its account receivable from March 9.
   20   Purchased inventory on credit terms of net 30 from Jasper Sales, $2,150.
   22   Purchased furniture on credit terms of 3/10 n/60 from Delwood Plaza, $775.
   22   Issued check no. 476 to pay for insurance coverage, debiting Prepaid Insurance for $1,345.
   24   Sold supplies to an employee for cash of $86, which was Contour's cost.
   25   Issued check no. 477 to pay utilities, $388.
   28   Purchased inventory on credit terms of 2/10 n/30 from Havrilla Corp., $421.
   29   Returned damaged inventory to Havrilla Corp., issuing a debit memo for $421.
   29   Sold goods on account to Cortez Co., issuing invoice no. 195 for $567 (cost, $314).
   30   Issued check no. 478 to pay Havrilla Corp. on account from March 13.

Mar. 31   Received cash in full on account from L. E. Wooten on credit sale of March 18. There was no discount.

31   Issued check no. 479 to pay monthly salaries of $2,600.

Required

1. For Contour Publishing, open the following general ledger accounts using the account numbers given:

Cash	111	Sales Revenue	411
Accounts Receivable	112	Sales Discounts	412
Supplies	116	Sales Returns and Allowances	413
Prepaid Insurance	117	Interest Revenue	419
Inventory	118	Cost of Goods Sold	511
Furniture	151	Salary Expense	531
Accounts Payable	211	Utilities Expense	541

2. Open these accounts in the subsidiary ledgers. Accounts receivable subsidiary ledger: Cortez Co., J. R. Wakeland, and L. E. Wooten. Accounts payable subsidiary ledger: Delwood Plaza, Havrilla Corp., and Jasper Sales.

3. Enter the transactions in a sales journal (page 8), a cash receipts journal (page 3), a purchases journal (page 6), a cash payments journal (page 9), and a general journal (page 4), as appropriate.

4. Post daily to the accounts receivable subsidiary ledger and to the accounts payable subsidiary ledger. On March 31, post to the general ledger.

5. Total each column of the special journals. Show that total debits equal total credits in each special journal.

6. Balance the total of the customer account balances in the accounts receivable subsidiary ledger against Accounts Receivable in the general ledger. Do the same for the accounts payable subsidiary ledger and Accounts Payable in the general ledger.

APPLY YOUR KNOWLEDGE

DECISION CASES

Designing a special journal (Obj. 4, 5)

Case 1. AccuTrac Software creates and sells cutting-edge networking software. AccuTrac's quality control officer estimates that 20% of the company's sales and purchases of inventory are returned for additional debugging. AccuTrac needs special journals for

- Sales returns and allowances
- Purchase returns and allowances

Required

1. Design the two special journals. For each journal, include a column for the appropriate business document.

2. Enter one transaction in each journal, using the **Austin Sound** transaction data illustrated on pages 236–243. Show all posting references, including those for column totals.

Reconstructing transactions from amounts posted to the accounts receivable subsidiary ledger (Obj. 4)

Case 2. A fire destroyed certain accounting records of DuPont Science Corp. The owner, François DuPont, asks for your help in reconstructing the records. *He needs to know the beginning and ending balances of Accounts Receivable and the credit sales and cash receipts on account from customers during March.* All of DuPont's sales are on credit, with payment terms of 2/10 n/30. All cash receipts on account reached DuPont within the 10-day discount period, except as noted. Round all amounts to the nearest dollar. The only accounting record preserved from the fire is the accounts receivable subsidiary ledger, which appears on page 265.

ETHICAL ISSUE

On a recent trip to Ireland, Ian O'Shea, sales manager of Elán, Inc., took his wife along at company expense. Martha Gibney, vice president of sales and O'Shea's boss, thought his travel and entertainment expenses seemed excessive. Gibney approved the reimbursement, however, because she owed O'Shea a favor. Gibney, well aware that the company president reviews all expenses recorded in the cash payments journal, had the accountant record O'Shea's wife's expenses in the *general* journal as follows:

Sales Promotion Expense	3,500	
Cash		3,500

Garcia Sales

Date	Item	Jrnl. Ref.	Debit	Credit	Balance
Apr. 1	Balance				440
3		CR.8		440	-0-
25		S.6	3,655		3,655
29		S.6	1,123		4,778

Leewright, Inc.

Date	Item	Jrnl. Ref.	Debit	Credit	Balance
Apr. 1	Balance				2,378
15		S.6	2,635		5,518
29		CR.8		2,883*	2,635

*Cash receipt did not occur within the discount period.

Sally Jones

Date	Item	Jrnl. Ref.	Debit	Credit	Balance
Apr. 1	Balance				1,096
5		CR.8		1,096	-0-
11		S.6	396		396
21		CR.8		396	-0-
24		S.6			5,108

Jacques LeHavre

Date	Item	Jrnl. Ref.	Debit	Credit	Balance
Apr. 8	Balance	S.6	2,378		2,378
16		S.6	903		3,281
18		CR.8		2,378	903
19		J.5		221	682
27		CR.8		682	-0-

Ethical Issue (continued)

Required

1. Does recording the transaction in the *general* journal rather than in the cash payments journal affect the amounts of cash and total expenses reported in the financial statements?
2. Why did O'Shea want this transaction recorded in the *general* journal?
3. What is the ethical issue in this situation? What role does accounting play in this issue?

TEAM PROJECTS

Project 1: Preparing a Business Plan for a Merchandising Entity. As you work through Part 2 of this book (Chapters 7–12), you will be examining in detail the current assets, current liabilities, and plant assets of a business. Most of the organizations that form the context for business activity in the remainder of the book are merchandising entities. Therefore, in a group or individually—as directed by your instructor—develop a plan for beginning and operating an audio/video store or other type of business. Develop your plan in as much detail as you can. Remember that the business manager who attends to the most details delivers the best product at the lowest price for customers!

Project 2: Preparing a Business Plan for a Service Entity. List what you have learned thus far in the course. On the basis of what you have learned, refine your plan for promoting a rock concert (from Team Project 2 in Chapter 1) to include everything you believe you must do to succeed in this business venture.

INTERNET EXERCISE

The Internet has opened new consulting opportunities for the accounting profession. The government has regulations and forms available on-line. Individual accountants have Web sites explaining the services they offer. Accounting organizations provide information to members at low cost through the Internet.

AICPA

1. Go to **http://www.AICPA.org** and read the information displayed. (Note: Make certain the URL uses the .org suffix for organizations rather than the .com suffix for companies.) What is the AICPA? How many accountants belong to this organization? What do the initials AICPA stand for?
2. In the left-hand column are links to a variety of accounting information. Click on *Students* and then *becoming a CPA*. List two characteristics of what earnings the CPA certification indicates.
3. In the left-hand column, click on *Pubs* and then the *current issue* of the "Journal of Accountancy." Scan one of the articles. List the title and author of the article and comment on one item of interest.
4. In the left-hand column, click on *CPA Links.*

   a. Click on *Accounting Associations.* Many of these associations offer scholarships and student memberships. What is Beta Alpha Psi?
   b. Go back to the CPA Links menu and click on *State Boards of Accountancy.* This board grants certificates and licenses to practice public accounting in that state. Click on the link to your state board of accountancy and comment on one item of interest.

7 Internal Control, Managing Cash, and Making Ethical Judgments

LEARNING OBJECTIVES

After studying this chapter, you should be able to

1. Define internal control

2. Identify the characteristics of an effective system of internal control

3. Prepare a bank reconciliation and the related journal entries

4. Apply internal controls to cash receipts

5. Apply internal controls to cash payments

6. Use a budget to manage cash

7. Make ethical judgments in business

Darlyne Lopez was a cashier at the Waco, Texas, office of the brokerage firm **Merrill Lynch.** Only after Lopez had an auto accident that landed her in the hospital did the Merrill Lynch office manager receive complaints from customers who had not received credit for their deposits. The result: Merrill Lynch uncovered a five-year-old embezzlement scheme.

The court found that Lopez stole over $600,000 in a "rob-Peter-to-pay-Paul" scheme. She transferred customer deposits into her own account and then concealed the missing amounts with deposits from other customers. Thus, customer accounts appeared to be in balance as long as Lopez manipulated the computerized records. But her replacement was unable to explain the missing deposits. All the evidence pointed in the direction of the absent employee. Lopez was sentenced to jail, and the Merrill Lynch office manager belatedly understood why his dedicated cashier never took a vacation.

What went wrong at **Merrill Lynch?** Darlyne Lopez controlled not only the cash received from customers, but also part of her company's computerized accounting records. By manipulating the records, she hid her theft for several years. Evidently, no one checked her work. Several procedures we discuss in this chapter will explain how Merrill Lynch could have prevented the embezzlement.

To protect people's money and avoid situations like the one at Merrill Lynch, the Foreign Corrupt Practices Act requires companies under SEC jurisdiction to maintain a system of internal control, whether or not they have foreign operations. This chapter discusses *internal control*—the organizational plan managers use to protect company assets. The chapter applies control techniques mainly to cash (the most liquid asset) and provides a framework for making ethical judgments in business. Later chapters discuss how managers control other assets.

INTERNAL CONTROL

A key responsibility of managers is to control operations. Owners and top managers set a company's goals, managers lead the way, and employees carry out the plan. **Internal control** is the organizational plan and all the related measures that an entity adopts to

1. Safeguard the assets the business uses in its operations,
2. Encourage adherence to company policies,
3. Promote operational efficiency (obtain the best outcome at the lowest cost), and
4. Ensure accurate and reliable accounting records.

INTERNAL CONTROL. Organizational plan and all the related measures adopted by an entity to safeguard assets, encourage adherence to company policies, promote operational efficiency, and ensure accurate and reliable accounting records.

 DAILY EXERCISE 7-1

Internal controls are most effective when employees at all levels adopt the organization's goals and ethical standards. Top managers need to communicate these goals and standards to workers. Lee Iacocca, former president of **Chrysler Corporation,** instilled goals in Chrysler employees by spending time with assembly-line workers. (Japanese firms pioneered this style of participative management.) The result? Defects decreased, and Chrysler products became more competitive.

Exhibit 7-1 presents an excerpt from **Target Corporation's** Report of Management. The company's top managers take responsibility for the financial statements and for the related system of internal control. Let's examine in more detail how companies create an effective system of internal control.

An Effective Internal Control System

Whether the business is **First Fidelity, Target Corporation,** or a local department store, an effective system of internal controls has the following characteristics.

Report of Management

Management is responsible for the consistency, integrity and presentation of the information in the Annual Report.

To fulfill our responsibility, we maintain comprehensive systems of internal control designed to provide reasonable assurance that assets are safeguarded and transactions are executed in accordance with established procedures.

Robert J. Ulrich
Chairman of the Board and
Chief Executive Officer
February 28, 2000

Douglas A. Scovanner
Executive Vice President and
Chief Financial Officer

COMPETENT, RELIABLE, AND ETHICAL PERSONNEL Employees should be *competent, reliable,* and *ethical.* Paying top salaries to attract top-quality employees, training them to do their job well, and supervising their work all help a company build a competent staff.

ASSIGNMENT OF RESPONSIBILITIES In a business with a good internal control system, no important duty is overlooked. Each employee is assigned certain responsibilities. A model of this *assignment of responsibilities* appears in the corporate organizational chart in Exhibit 7-2. Notice that the company has a vice president of finance and accounting. Two other officers, the treasurer and the controller, report to that vice president. The treasurer is responsible for cash management. The **controller** is the chief accounting officer.

Within this organization, the controller may be responsible for approving invoices (bills) for payment, and the treasurer may actually sign the checks. Working under the controller, one accountant may be responsible for payroll,

CONTROLLER. The chief accounting officer of a company.

EXHIBIT 7-2   **A Corporate Organization Chart**

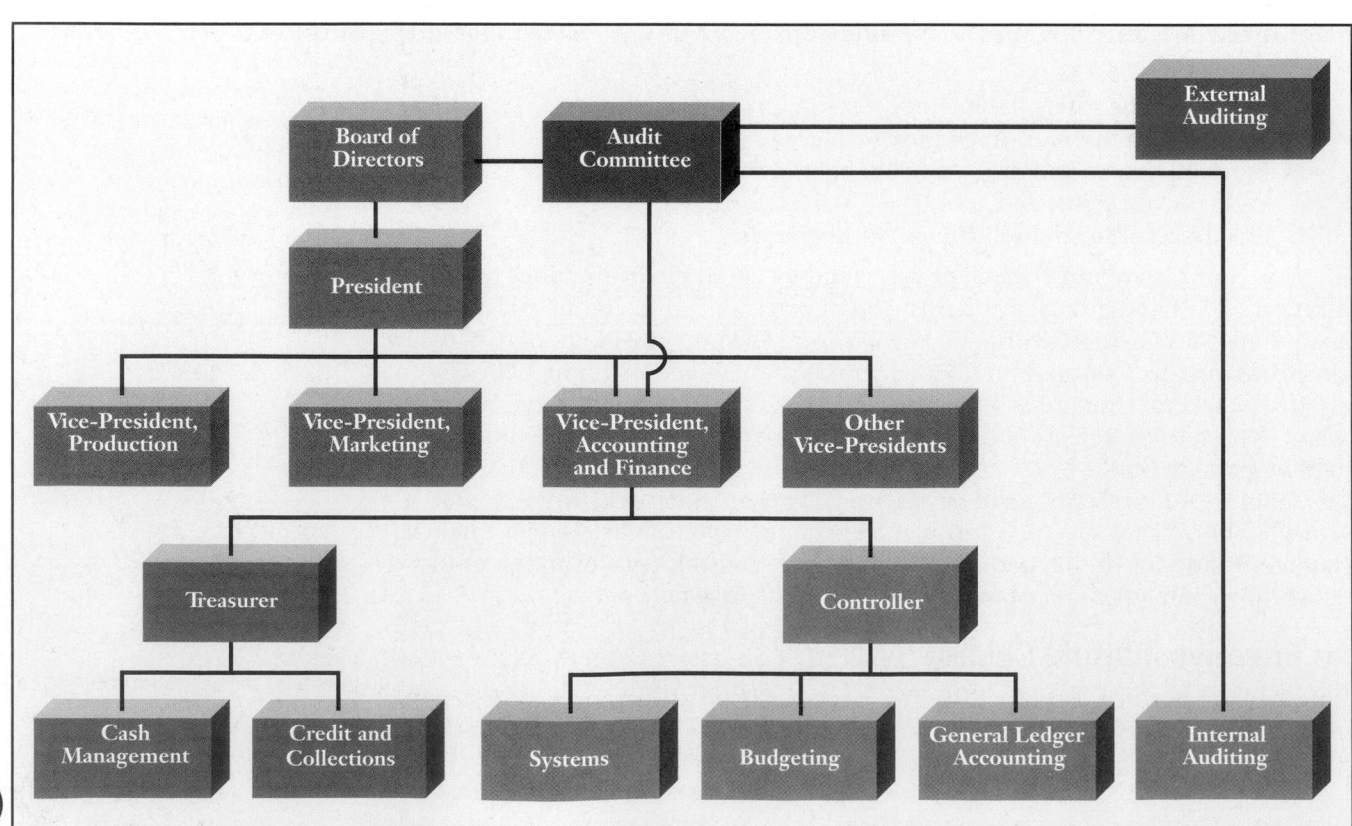

The Barings Bank Debacle: What Your Internal Auditor Tells You Might Save Your Company

On February 26, 1995, one fresh-faced 28-year-old trader brought a venerable 233-year-old British bank to its knees. Nick Leeson, a trader for **Barings Bank,** had bought $27

billion worth of securities on Japan's Nikkei stock market. When the Nikkei plunged, Barings lost $27 billion and collapsed. All fingers pointed to Leeson. How could a conservative bank allow this to happen? It soon became clear that nobody was supervising Leeson's trades.

Leeson worked in Barings' Singapore office from 1992 to the time of the collapse. Barings fell because it lacked internal controls. Leeson was allowed to execute *cross trades,* transactions in which he acted as both buyer and seller. Leeson's transactions were not at "arms' length," where the seller tries to get the highest price, and the buyer tries to pay the lowest price. Without arms' length trading, the amount of the transaction could be anything Leeson entered into the system. Amazingly, the bank did not require Leeson to give up his job as head of selling when he became head of buying.

From the start, Leeson lost money in Singapore, but he hid the losses—$296 million in 1994 alone. What did Leeson's bosses think of his performance that year? They thought he made a $46 million profit for the bank, and proposed paying him a bonus of $720,000.

Months before the collapse, Barings knew of Leeson's dual role. Internal auditors warned of "significant general risk" because Leeson controlled both the buying and the selling sides of transactions. But Barings' higher-ups viewed Leeson as a golden boy, and they ignored the audit report—with disastrous consequences.

Source: Based on Lillian Chew, "Not just one man," *http://www.risk.ifci.ch/137560.htm.* Robert D. Allen, "Managing internal audit conflicts," *Internal Auditor,* August 1996, p. 58. Anonymous, "The collapse of Barings: A fallen star," *Economist,* March 4, 1995, p. 19.

---

another accountant for depreciation. All duties should be clearly defined and assigned to individuals who bear responsibility for carrying them out.

 DAILY EXERCISE 7-2

PROPER AUTHORIZATION An organization generally has written rules to outline its procedures. Any deviation from policy requires *proper authorization.* For example, an assistant manager of a retail store must approve customer checks for amounts above a certain limit. Likewise, a dean or department chair of a college and university must authorize a junior to enroll in courses restricted to seniors.

SEPARATION OF DUTIES Smart management divides responsibility for transactions between two or more people or departments. *Separation of duties* limits the chances for fraud and promotes the accuracy of the accounting records. This crucial component of the internal control system can be divided into four parts:

1. *Separation of operations from accounting.* Accounting should be completely separate from the operating departments, such as manufacturing and sales. This

allows reliable records to be kept. What would happen if the sales personnel controlled the company's revenue records? Sales figures would probably be inflated, and top managers wouldn't know how much the company actually sold. Notice how accounting and marketing (sales) are separate in Exhibit 7-2.

2. *Separation of the custody of assets from accounting.* Temptation and fraud are reduced if accountants do not handle cash and if cashiers do not have access to the accounting records. If one employee has both cash-handling and accounting duties, that person can steal cash and conceal the theft by making a bogus entry on the books. We see this component of internal control in Exhibit 7-2. The treasurer has custody of the cash, and the controller accounts for the cash. Neither person has both responsibilities. Darlyne Lopez was able to apply one customer's cash deposit to another customer's account at **Merrill Lynch.** Apparently, Lopez, a cashier, controlled some data that went into the accounting system.

3. *Separation of authorization of transactions from custody of related assets.* Persons who authorize transactions should not handle the related asset. For example, the same person should not authorize a payment and also sign the check to pay the bill. Otherwise the person can authorize payments to him- or herself and then sign the checks. When these duties are separated, only legitimate bills get paid.

4. *Separation of duties within the accounting function.* Different people should perform the various accounting duties to minimize errors and the opportunities for fraud. For example, different accountants should be responsible for recording cash receipts and cash payments. The employee who processes cash payments should have nothing to do with the approval process.

 DAILY EXERCISE 7-3

 DAILY EXERCISE 7-6

THINK IT OVER Ralph works at the Galaxy Theater. Occasionally, he must both sell tickets and take them as customers enter the theater. Standard procedure requires that Ralph tear the tickets, give half to the customer, and keep the other half. To control cash receipts, the theater manager compares each night's cash receipts with the number of ticket stubs on hand.

1. How could Ralph steal cash receipts and hide the theft? What additional steps should the manager take to strengthen the control over cash receipts?
2. What is the internal control weakness in this situation? Explain the weakness.

Answers

1. Ralph could
   - Issue no ticket and keep the customer's cash.

   - Destroy some tickets and keep the customers' cash.

   Management could
   - Physically count the number of people watching a movie and compare that number to the number of ticket stubs retained.
   - Account for all ticket stubs by serial number. Missing serial numbers raise questions.

2. The internal control weakness is the lack of separation of duties. Ralph receives cash and also controls the tickets.

AUDIT. An examination of a company's financial statements and the accounting system.

INTERNAL AND EXTERNAL AUDITS To guarantee the accuracy of their accounting records, most companies undergo periodic audits. An **audit** is an examination of the company's financial statements and the accounting system.

It is not economically feasible for auditors to examine all transactions, so they must rely on the accounting system to produce accurate records. To evaluate the company's accounting system, auditors examine its system of internal controls. Auditors often spot weaknesses in the system because they are objective in their outlook. The company's managers, on the other hand, are immersed in day-to-day operations and may overlook their own weaknesses.

Audits can be internal or external. Exhibit 7-2 shows *internal auditors* as employees of the business. Throughout the year, the internal auditors examine various segments of the organization to ensure that employees are following company policies and that operations are running efficiently.

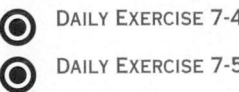
External auditors are entirely independent of the business. They are hired to determine that the company's financial statements are prepared in accordance with generally accepted accounting principles. Both internal and external auditors are independent of the operations they examine, and both suggest improvements that help the business run efficiently.

DOCUMENTS AND RECORDS   Business *documents and records* vary from invoices and purchase orders to special journals and subsidiary ledgers. Documents should be prenumbered. A gap in the numbered sequence draws attention.

Prenumbering sale receipts discourages theft by cashiers because the copies retained by the cashiers list the amount of the sale. These figures can be checked against the actual amount of cash received. If the receipts are not prenumbered, a cashier can destroy the sale receipt and pocket the cash received.

In a bowling alley a key document is the score sheet. The manager can compare the number of games scored with the amount of cash received. By multiplying the number of games by the price per game and comparing the result with each day's cash receipts, the manager can see whether the business is collecting all the revenue.

ELECTRONIC DEVICES AND COMPUTER CONTROLS   Accounting systems are relying less and less on documents and more and more on digital storage devices. Computers shift the internal controls to the people who write the programs. Programmers then become the focus of internal controls because they can write programs that transfer company assets to themselves.

Businesses use electronic devices to protect assets and control operations. Retailers such as **Target Stores, Macy's,** and **Dillard's** control inventory by attaching an electronic sensor to merchandise. The cashier removes the sensor when a sale is made. If a customer tries to remove an item from the store with the sensor attached, an alarm is activated. According to **Checkpoint Systems,** which manufactures the sensors, these devices reduce theft by as much as 50%.

OTHER CONTROLS   Businesses keep cash and important business documents (such as contracts and titles to property) in *fireproof vaults. Burglar alarms* protect buildings and other property.

Retailers receive most of their cash from customers on the spot. To safeguard cash, they use *point-of-sale terminals* that serve as a cash register and also record each transaction entered into the machine. Several times each day, a supervisor removes the cash for deposit in the bank.

Employees who handle cash are in an especially tempting position. Many businesses purchase *fidelity bonds* on cashiers. The bond is an insurance policy that reimburses the company for any losses due to employee theft. Before issuing a fidelity bond, the insurance company investigates the employee's past record.

Mandatory vacations and *job rotation* require that employees be trained to do a variety of jobs. **General Electric, Eastman Kodak,** and other large companies move employees from job to job—often at six-month intervals. This improves morale by giving employees a broad view of the business and helps them decide where they want to specialize. Knowing that someone else will be doing their job next month also keeps employees honest. Had Merrill Lynch moved Darlyne Lopez from job to job and required her to take a vacation, her embezzlement would probably have been detected much earlier.

Internal Controls for e-Commerce

e-Commerce creates some new risks. Buying and selling over the Internet can give hackers access to confidential information unavailable in face-to-face transactions. Confidentiality is a significant challenge for dotcoms. Pitfalls include

1. Stolen credit-card numbers
2. Computer viruses and Trojan horses
3. Impersonation of companies

To convince people to buy on-line, companies must ensure security of data.

Stolen credit-card numbers. Suppose you buy several CDs from **EMusic.com.** To make the purchase, your credit-card number must travel through cyberspace. Amateur hacker Carlos Salgado, Jr., used his home computer to steal 100,000 credit-card numbers with a combined limit exceeding $1 billion from an Internet service provider. Salgado was caught when he tried to sell the credit-card numbers to an undercover FBI agent.

Computer viruses and Trojan horses. A **computer virus** is a malicious program that (a) reproduces itself, (b) gets included into program code without consent, and (c) performs actions that can be destructive. A **Trojan horse** works like a virus, but it does not reproduce. Viruses can destroy or alter data, make bogus calculations, and infect word-processing and spreadsheet files. The International Computer Security Association reports that 99.3% of firms it surveyed found a virus somewhere in their system.

Suppose the U.S. Department of Defense solicits bids for the design of a missile defense system. **Raytheon, Lockheed-Martin,** and **General Dynamics** bid on the contract. A hacker infects Raytheon's system and alters two small details of Raytheon's design. In evaluating the three bids, Pentagon engineers label the Raytheon design as flawed even though Raytheon has designed the best system for the lowest price. The American public winds up paying too much—all because of a trickster's prank.

Impersonation. Hackers sometimes create bogus Web sites, such as AOL4Free.com. The neat-sounding Web site attracts lots of visitors, and the hackers are able to solicit confidential data from unsuspecting people. The hackers then use the data for a variety of illicit purposes.

FIREWALLS AND ENCRYPTION Information traveling the Internet is secure, but the server holding the information may be insecure. A server is a computer that performs a particular function (for example, data storage or printing) in a network. Two standard techniques companies use to secure e-commerce data are encryption and firewalls.

Encryption is the primary method of achieving confidentiality in e-commerce. Plain-text messages are rearranged by some mathematical process. The encrypted message cannot be read by anyone who does not know the process. A simple accounting example is the use of check-sum digits for customer account numbers. Each account number is set up so that the last digit is the sum of the previous digits, for example Customer Number 2237, where $2 + 2 + 3 = 7$. Any account number that fails this test triggers an error message.

Firewalls limit access to a local network. The intent is to keep intruders out. Often firewalls work between two networks, such as between a local network and the Internet. Firewalls enable members of the local network to access the Internet but keep nonmembers out of the network. Usually several firewalls are built into the local network so that hackers must work their way around more than one. Think of a fortress with multiple walls protecting the king's chamber in the center. At the point of entry, passwords, PINs (personal identification numbers), fingerprints, and signatures are used. More sophisticated firewalls are used deeper in the network.

The Limitations of Internal Control

Unfortunately, most internal control measures can be overcome. Two or more employees working as a team—*colluding*—can beat an internal control system and defraud the firm. Consider Galaxy Theater. Ralph and another employee could put together a scheme in which the ticket seller pockets the cash from ten customers and the ticket taker admits ten customers without tickets. To prevent this situation, the manager must take additional control measures, such as matching the number of people in the theater against the number of ticket stubs retained. But that would take time away from other duties. The stricter the internal control system, the more expensive and time-consuming it becomes.

A system of internal control that is too complex can strangle the business with red tape. How tight should controls be? Managers must make sensible judgments. Investments in internal control must be judged in light of the costs and benefits.

The Bank Account as a Control Device

Cash is the most liquid asset because it is the medium of exchange. Cash often consists of electronic impulses in a bank's accounting system with no accompanying paper checks or deposit slips. Cash is easy to conceal, easy to move, and relatively easy to steal. As a result, most businesses create specific controls to safeguard cash.

Keeping cash in a *bank account* is important because banks have established practices for safeguarding cash. Banks also provide depositors with detailed records of their transactions. To take full advantage of these control features, the business should deposit all cash receipts in the bank account and make all cash payments through it (except petty cash transactions, which we examine later in this chapter).

The documents used to control a bank account include the

- signature card
- bank statement
- deposit ticket
- bank reconciliation
- check

SIGNATURE CARD Banks require each person authorized to transact business through an account to sign a *signature card*. The bank compares the signatures on documents against the signature card to protect against forgery.

DEPOSIT TICKET Banks supply standard forms such as *deposit tickets*. The customer fills in the dollar amount and the date of deposit. As proof of the transaction, the customer retains either (1) a duplicate copy of the deposit ticket, or (2) a deposit receipt, depending on the bank's practice.

CHECK To draw money from an account, the depositor writes a **check,** which is a document instructing the bank to pay the designated person or business a specified amount of money. There are three parties to a check: the *maker,* who signs the check; the *payee,* to whom the check is paid; and the *bank* on which the check is drawn. Most checks are serially numbered and preprinted with the name of the maker and the bank.

Exhibit 7-3 shows a check drawn on the bank account of Business Research, Inc. The check has two parts, the check itself and the *remittance advice,* an optional attachment that tells the payee the reason for the payment. The maker (Business Research) retains a duplicate copy of the check for its cash payments journal.

> **CHECK.** Document that instructs a bank to pay the designated person or business a specified amount of money.

EXHIBIT 7-3 **Check with Remittance Advice**

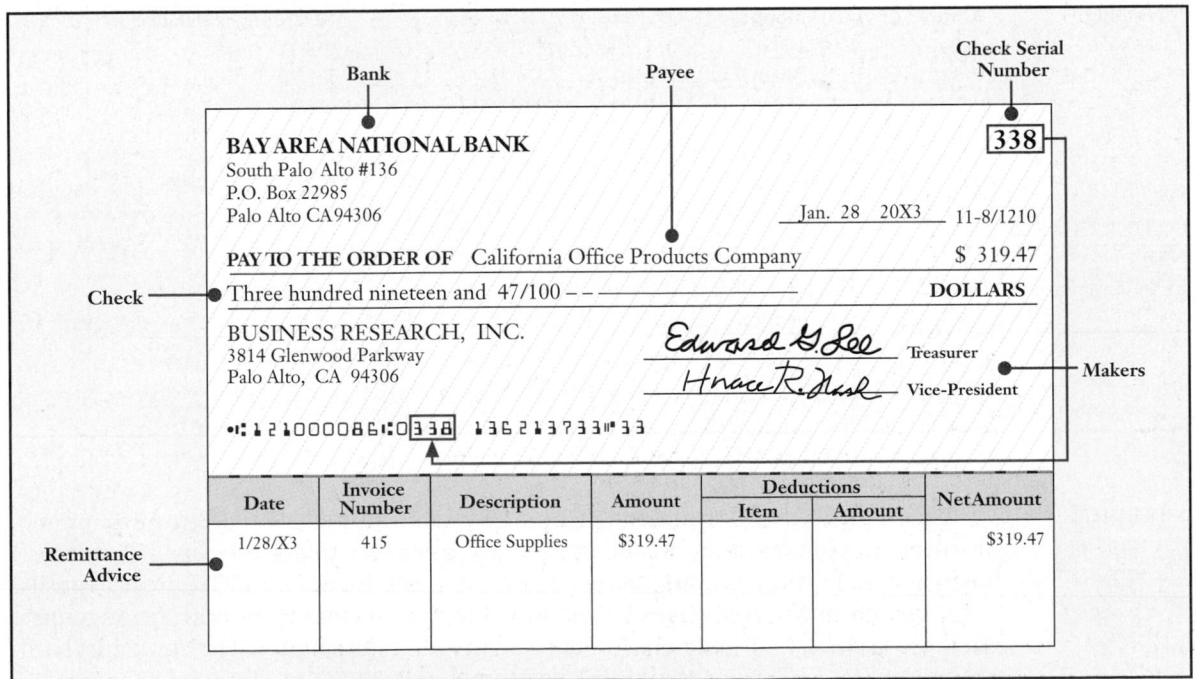

BANK STATEMENT Banks send monthly bank statements to depositors. A **bank statement** is the document the bank uses to report what it did with the depositor's cash. The statement shows the bank account's beginning and ending cash balances for the period and lists the month's cash transactions conducted through the bank. Included with the statement are the maker's *canceled checks*, those checks the bank has paid on behalf of the depositor. The bank statement also lists any deposits and other changes in the account. Deposits appear in chronological order and checks in a logical order (usually by check serial number), along with the date each check cleared the bank. Exhibit 7-4 is the bank statement of Business Research, Inc., for the month ended January 31, 20X3.

EXHIBIT 7-4 **Bank Statement**

ACCOUNT STATEMENT

BAY AREA NATIONAL BANK
SOUTH PALO ALTO #136 P.O. BOX 22985 PALO ALTO, CA 94306

Business Research, Inc.
3814 Glenwood Parkway
Palo Alto, CA 94306

CHECKING ACCOUNT 136–213733

CHECKING ACCOUNT SUMMARY AS OF 01/31/X3

BEGINNING BALANCE	TOTAL DEPOSITS	TOTAL WITHDRAWALS	SERVICE CHARGES	ENDING BALANCE
6,556.12	4,352.64	4,963.00	14.25	5,931.51

CHECKING ACCOUNT TRANSACTIONS

DEPOSITS	DATE	AMOUNT
Deposit	01/04	1,000.00
Deposit	01/04	112.00
Deposit	01/08	194.60
EFT—Collection of rent	01/17	904.03
Bank Collection	01/26	2,114.00
Interest	01/31	28.01

CHARGES	DATE	AMOUNT
Service Charge	01/31	14.25
Checks:		

CHECKS

Number	Date	Amount
656	01/06	100.00
332	01/12	3,000.00
333	01/12	150.00
334	01/10	100.00
335	01/06	100.00
336	01/31	1,100.00

DAILY BALANCE

Date	Balance	Date	Balance
12/31	6,556.12	01/17	5,264.75
01/04	7,616.12	01/20	4,903.75
01/06	7,416.12	01/26	7,017.75
01/08	7,610.72	01/31	5,931.51
01/10	7,510.72		
01/12	4,360.72		

OTHER CHARGES	DATE	AMOUNT
NSF	01/04	52.00
EFT—Insurance	01/20	361.00

MONTHLY SUMMARY

Withdrawals: 8   Minimum Balance: 4,360.72   Average Balance: 6,085.19

Electronic funds transfer (EFT) is a system that relies on electronic communications to transfer cash. More and more businesses today rely on EFT for cash transactions. It is cheaper for a company to pay employees by EFT (direct deposit). Many people make mortgage, rent, and insurance payments by prior arrangement with their bank and never write checks for those payments. The monthly bank statement lists EFT deposits and EFT payments.

The Bank Reconciliation

There are two records of a business's cash: (1) its Cash account in its own general ledger (Exhibit 7-5), and (2) the bank statement, which shows the actual amount of cash the business has in the bank.

EXHIBIT 7-5
Cash Records of Business Research, Inc.

 DAILY EXERCISE 7-9

General Ledger:

ACCOUNT   Cash   No. 111

Date	Item	Jrnl. Ref.	Debit	Credit	Balance
20X3					
Jan. 1	Balance	✓			6,556.12
2	Cash receipt	CR. 9	1,112.00		7,668.12
7	Cash receipt	CR. 9	194.60		7,862.72
31	Cash payments	CP. 17		6,160.14	1,702.58
31	Cash receipt	CR. 10	1,591.63		3,294.21

Cash Payments:

Check No.	Amount	Check No.	Amount
332	$3,000.00	338............	$ 319.47
333	510.00	339............	83.00
334	100.00	340............	203.14
335	100.00	341............	458.53
336	1,100.00		
337	286.00	Total...........	$6,160.14

The books and the bank statement can show different amounts, yet both be correct. The difference arises because of a time lag in recording certain transactions. When a firm writes a check, it immediately credits its Cash account. The bank, however, does not subtract the amount of the check from the business's balance until the bank receives the check and pays it. This step may take days, even weeks, if the payee waits to cash the check. Likewise, the business immediately debits Cash for all cash receipts, but it may take a day or so for the bank to add these amounts to the business's bank balance.

To ensure accuracy of the financial records, the firm's accountant must explain all differences between the firm's own cash records and the bank statement figures on a certain date. The result of this process is a document called the **bank reconciliation,** which is prepared by the company (not by the bank). Properly done, the bank reconciliation ensures that all cash transactions have been accounted for and that the bank and book records of cash are correct. Knowing where cash comes from, how it is spent, and the balance of cash available is vital to success in business.

Here are some common items that cause differences between the bank balance and the book balance:

1. Items recorded by the company but not yet recorded by the bank
   a. **Deposits in transit** (outstanding deposits). The company has recorded these deposits, but the bank has not.
   b. **Outstanding checks.** The company has issued these checks and recorded them on its books, but the bank has not yet paid them.
2. Items recorded by the bank but not yet recorded by the company
   a. **Bank collections.** Banks sometimes collect money for their depositors. Many businesses have customers pay directly to the company bank account. This practice, called a *lock-box system,* reduces theft and places the business's cash in circulation faster than if the cash is collected and deposited by company personnel. An example is a bank's collecting cash and interest on a note receivable for the depositor.
   b. *Electronic funds transfers.* The bank may receive or pay cash on behalf of the depositor. The bank statement will list the EFTs.

BANK RECONCILIATION. Document explaining the reasons for the difference between a depositor's cash records and the depositor's cash balance in its bank account.

DEPOSIT IN TRANSIT. A deposit recorded by the company but not yet by its bank.

OUTSTANDING CHECK. A check issued by the company and recorded on its books but not yet paid by its bank.

BANK COLLECTION. Collection of money by the bank on behalf of a depositor.

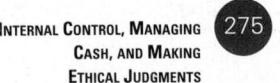

c. *Service charge.* This is the bank's fee for processing the depositor's transactions. Banks base the service charge on the account balance or on the number of transactions. The depositor learns the amount of the service charge from the bank statement.

d. *Interest revenue on checking account.* Depositors earn interest if they keep enough cash in their account. The bank notifies depositors of this interest on the bank statement.

e. Nonsufficient funds (NSF) checks are worthless checks received from customers. To understand how NSF checks (sometimes called *hot checks*) are handled, consider the route a check takes. Exhibit 7-6 diagrams the paths that two checks take in the bank clearing process. The first diagram tracks the path of a good check. The second diagram shows what happens to an NSF (hot) check.

NSF checks are cash *receipts* that turn out to be worthless. The payee may learn of NSF checks through the bank statement, which lists the NSF check as a charge (subtraction). See the $52 item near the bottom of Exhibit 7-4. Because an NSF check is worthless, the customer still owes Business Research $52 in Exhibit 7-4. As a result, Business Research has a receivable from the customer who wrote the NSF check.

> **NONSUFFICIENT FUNDS (NSF) CHECK.** A "hot" check, one for which the maker's bank account has insufficient money to pay the check.

EXHIBIT 7-6   **The Paths That Two Checks Take**

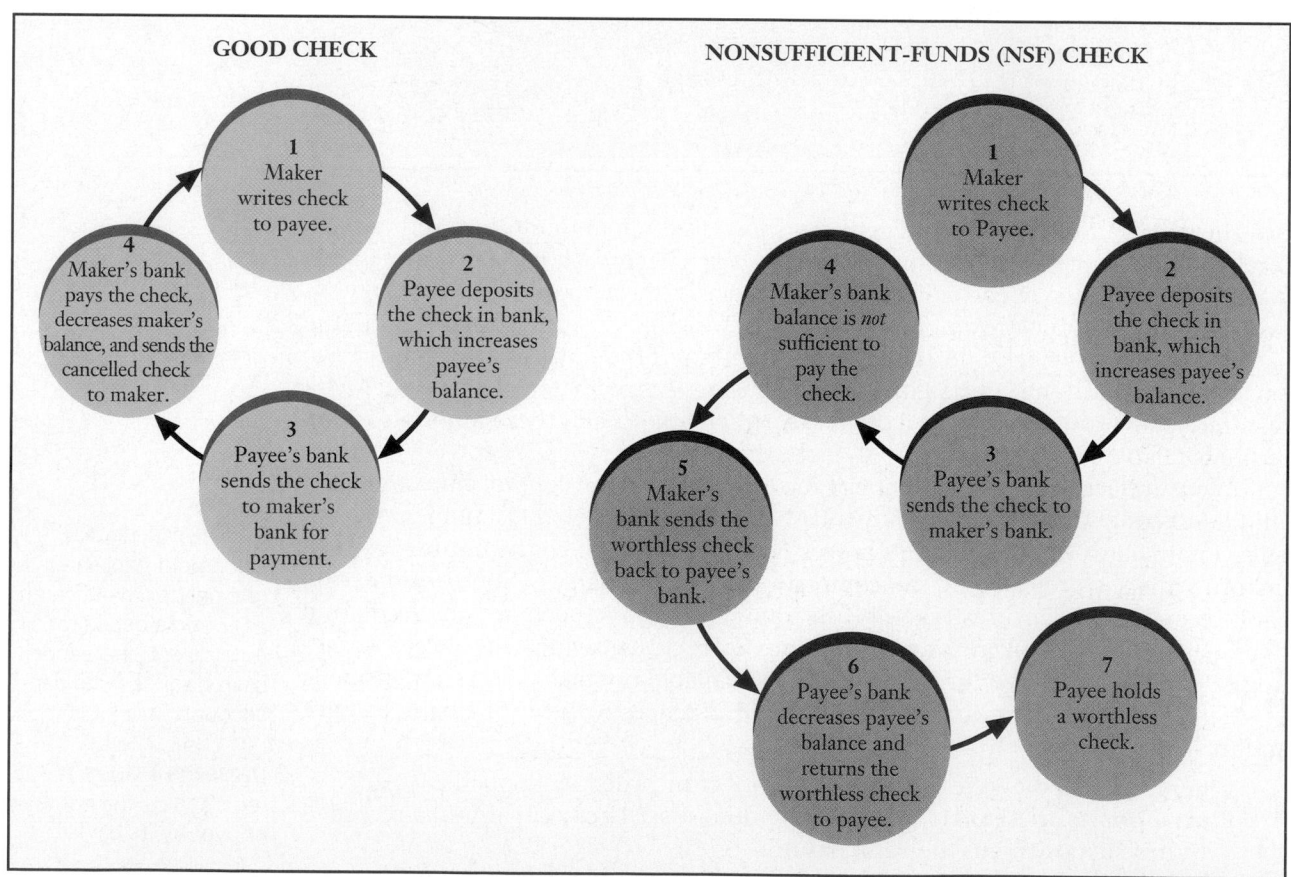

f. *Checks collected, deposited, and returned to payee by the bank for reasons other than NSF.* Banks return checks to the payee if (1) the maker's account has closed, (2) the date is "stale" (some checks state "void after 30 days"), (3) the signature is not authorized, (4) the check has been altered, or (5) the check form is improper (for example, a counterfeit). Accounting for all returned checks is the same as for NSF checks.

g. *The cost of printed checks.* This charge is handled like a service charge.

3. Errors by the company or the bank. For example, a bank may improperly charge (decrease) the bank balance of Business Research, Inc., for a check drawn by another company, perhaps Business Research Associates. Or a company may miscompute its bank balance on its own books. Error correction will be part of the bank reconciliation.

PREPARING THE BANK RECONCILIATION   The steps in preparing the bank reconciliation are as follows:

Objective 3

Prepare a bank reconciliation and the related journal entries

1. Start with two figures, the balance shown on the bank statement (*balance per bank*) and the balance in the company's Cash account (*balance per books*). These two amounts will probably disagree because of the differences discussed earlier.
2. Add to, or subtract from, the *bank* balance those items that appear on the books but not on the bank statement:
   a. Add *deposits in transit* to the bank balance. Deposits in transit show up as cash receipts on the books but not as deposits on the bank statement.
   b. Subtract *outstanding checks* from the bank balance. Outstanding checks show up as cash payments on the books but not as paid checks on the bank statement. Outstanding checks are usually the most numerous items on a bank reconciliation.
3. Add to, or subtract from, the *book* balance those items that appear on the bank statement but not on the company books:
   a. Add to the book balance (1) *bank collections,* (2) *EFT cash receipts,* and (3) *interest revenue* earned on money in the bank. These items show up as cash receipts on the bank statement but not on the books.
   b. Subtract from the book balance (1) *EFT cash payments,* (2) *service charges,* (3) *cost of printed checks,* and (4) *NSF checks received, and other bank charges* (for example, stale-date checks). These items show up as subtractions on the bank statement but not as cash payments on the books.
4. Compute the *adjusted bank balance* and the *adjusted book balance.* The two adjusted balances should be equal.
5. Journalize each item in step 3—those items listed on the *Book* portion of the bank reconciliation. These transactions must be recorded on the company books because they affect cash.
6. Correct all book errors and notify the bank of any errors it has made.

BANK RECONCILIATION ILLUSTRATED   The bank statement in Exhibit 7-4 indicates that the January 31 bank balance of Business Research, Inc., is $5,931.51. However, the company's Cash account has a balance of $3,294.21, as shown in Exhibit 7-5. The following reconciling items explain why the bank balance and the book balance differ:

1. The January 31 deposit of $1,591.63 (deposit in transit) does not appear on the bank statement. See the last item in the Company's Cash Account (Exhibit 7-5).
2. The bank erroneously charged to the Business Research, Inc., account a $100 check—number 656—written by Business Research Associates (a bank error).
3. Five company checks issued late in January and recorded in the cash payments journal have not been paid by the bank. The following checks are outstanding:

Check No.	Date	Amount
337	Jan. 17	$286.00
338	26	319.47
339	27	83.00
340	28	203.14
341	30	458.53

These checks are listed under cash payments in Exhibit 7-5.

4. The bank received $904.03 by EFT on behalf of Business Research, Inc. (an EFT receipt).
5. The bank collected on behalf of the company a note receivable, $2,114 (including interest revenue of $214). Business Research has not recorded this cash receipt (a bank collection).

6. The bank statement shows interest revenue of $28.01, which the company has earned on its cash balance (interest revenue).
7. Check number 333 for $150 paid to Brown Company on account was recorded as a cash payment of $510, creating a $360 understatement of the Cash balance in the books (a book error).

◉ DAILY EXERCISE 7-7

8. The bank service charge for the month was $14.25 (service charge).
9. The bank statement shows an NSF check for $52, which was received from customer L. Ross (NSF check).

◉ DAILY EXERCISE 7-10

10. Business Research pays insurance expense monthly by EFT. The company has not yet recorded this $361 payment (an EFT payment).

Exhibit 7-7 is the bank reconciliation based on the preceding data. Panel A lists the reconciling items, which are keyed by number to the reconciliation in Panel B.

EXHIBIT 7-7 **Bank Reconciliation**

PANEL A — Reconciling Items

1. Deposit in transit, $1,591.63.
2. Bank error, add $100 to bank balance.
3. Outstanding checks; no. 337, $286; no. 338, $319.47; no. 339, $83; no. 340, $203.14; no. 341, $458.53.
4. EFT receipt of rent revenue, $904.03.
5. Bank collection, $2,114, including interest revenue of $214.

6. Interest earned on bank balance, $28.01.
7. Book error, add $360 to book balance.
8. Bank service charge, $14.25.
9. NSF check from L. Ross, $52.
10. EFT payment of insurance expense, $361.

PANEL B — Bank Reconciliation

BUSINESS RESEARCH, INC.
Bank Reconciliation
January 31, 20X3

Bank			Books		
Balance, January 31		$5,931.51	Balance, January 31		$3,294.21
Add:			Add:		
1. Deposit of January 31 in transit		1,591.63	4. EFT receipt of rent revenue		904.03
2. Correction of bank error— Business Research Associates check 656 erroneously charged against company account		100.00	5. Bank collection of note receivable, including interest revenue of $214		2,114.00
		7,623.14	6. Interest revenue earned on bank balance		28.01
			7. Correction of book error— overstated amount of check no. 333		360.00
					6,700.25
Less:					
3. Outstanding checks					
No. 337	$286.00		Less:		
No. 338	319.47		8. Service charge	$ 14.25	
No. 339	83.00		9. NSF check	52.00	
No. 340	203.14		10. EFT payment of insurance expense	361.00	
No. 341	458.53	(1,350.14)			(427.25)
Adjusted bank balance		$6,273.00	Adjusted book balance		$6,273.00

↑ **Amounts agree.** ↑

Each reconciling item is treated in the same way in every situation. Here is a summary of how to treat the various reconciling items:

BANK BALANCE—ALWAYS	BOOK BALANCE—ALWAYS
• *Add* deposits in transit.	• *Add* bank collections, interest revenue, and EFT receipts.
• *Subtract* outstanding checks.	• *Subtract* service charges, NSF checks, and EFT payments.
• *Add* or *subtract* corrections of bank errors.	• *Add* or *subtract* corrections of book errors.

JOURNALIZING TRANSACTIONS FROM THE RECONCILIATION The bank reconciliation does not place entries in the journals or the ledgers. The reconciliation is an accountant's tool, separate from the company's books.

The bank reconciliation acts as a control device. It signals the company to record transactions for all the reconciling items listed in the Books section of the reconciliation. The company has not yet recorded these items. For example, the bank collected the note receivable for the company, but the company has not yet recorded this cash receipt. In fact, the company learned of the cash receipt only when it received the bank statement.

THINK IT OVER

Why doesn't the company need to record the reconciling items on the Bank side of the reconciliation?

Answer: Those items have already been recorded on the company books.

On the basis of the reconciliation in Exhibit 7-7, Business Research, Inc., makes the following journal entries. They are dated January 31 to bring the Cash account to the correct balance on that date. Numbers in parentheses correspond to the reconciling items listed in Exhibit 7-7, Panel A.

DAILY EXERCISE 7-8

(4) Jan. 31	Cash	904.03		
	Rent Revenue.........		904.03	
	Receipt of monthly rent.			
(5)	31	Cash	2,114.00	
	Notes Receivable.....		1,900.00	
	Interest Revenue		214.00	
	Note receivable collected by bank.			
(6)	31	Cash	28.01	
	Interest Revenue		28.01	
	Interest earned on bank balance.			
(7)	31	Cash	360.00	
	Accounts Payable			
	—Brown Co.........		360.00	
	Correction of check no. 333.			

(8) 31	Miscellaneous Expense[1]	14.25		
	Cash..............................		14.25	
	Bank service charge.			
(9) 31	Accounts Receivable			
	—L. Ross.........................	52.00		
	Cash..............................		52.00	
	NSF check returned by bank.			
(10) 31	Insurance Expense...........	361.00		
	Cash..............................		361.00	
	Payment of monthly insurance.			

These entries bring the company's books up to date.

The entry for the NSF check (entry 9) needs explanation. Upon learning that L. Ross's $52 check was not good, Business Research credits Cash to bring the Cash account up to date. Business Research still has a receivable from Ross, so the company debits Accounts Receivable—L. Ross and pursues collection from him.

DAILY EXERCISE 7-11

WORK IT OUT

The bank statement balance is $4,500 and shows a service charge of $15, interest earned of $5, and an NSF check for $300. Deposits in transit total $1,200; outstanding checks are $575. The bookkeeper recorded as $152 a check of $125 in payment of an account payable.

1. What is the adjusted bank balance?

2. Prepare the journal entries needed to update the company's (not the bank's) books.

Answers

1. $5,125 ($4,500 + $1,200 − $575)

2. Journal entries on the books:

Miscellaneous Expense	15		Accounts Receivable	300	
Cash....................................		15	Cash..............................		300
Cash	5		Cash ($152 − $125)............	27	
Interest Revenue................		5	Accounts Payable...........		27

---

[1]Note: Miscellaneous Expense is debited for the bank service charge because the service charge pertains to no particular expense category.

How Owners and Managers Use the Bank Reconciliation

The bank reconciliation is a powerful control device in the hands of a business owner or manager, as the following example illustrates.

Randy Vaughn is a CPA in Houston, Texas. He owns several apartment complexes that his aunt manages. His accounting practice leaves little time to devote to his apartments. Vaughn's aunt signs up tenants, collects the monthly rent, arranges custodial work, hires and fires employees, writes the checks, and performs the bank reconciliation. In short, she does it all. This concentration of duties in one person is terrible from an internal control standpoint. Vaughn's aunt could be stealing from him, and as a CPA he is aware of this possibility.

Vaughn trusts his aunt because she is a member of the family. Nevertheless, he exercises some loose controls over her management of his apartments. Vaughn periodically drops by his properties to see whether the custodial staff is keeping them in good condition.

To control cash, Vaughn uses the bank statement and the bank reconciliation. On an irregular basis, he examines the bank reconciliations. He matches every paid check to the journal entry on the books. Vaughn would know immediately if his aunt is writing checks to herself. Vaughn sometimes prepares his own bank reconciliation to see whether he agrees with his aunt's work. To keep his aunt on her toes, Vaughn lets her know that he periodically audits her work.

Vaughn has a simple method for controlling cash receipts. He knows the occupancy level of his apartments. He also knows the monthly rent he charges. He multiplies the number of apartments—say 20—by the monthly rent (which averages $500 per unit) to arrive at expected monthly rent revenue of $10,000. By tracing the $10,000 revenue to the bank statement, Vaughn can tell that his rent money went into his bank account.

Control activities such as these are critical in small businesses. With only a few employees, a separation of duties may not be feasible. The owner must oversee the operations of the business, or the assets will slip away, as they did for Merrill Lynch in the chapter opening story.

 DAILY EXERCISE 7-12

 DAILY EXERCISE 7-13

MID-CHAPTER

SUMMARY PROBLEM

www.prenhall.com/horngren

Mid-Chapter Assessment

The Cash account of Zuboff Associates at February 28, 20X3, is as follows:

CASH			
Feb. 1	Bal. 3,995	Feb. 3	400
6	800	12	3,100
15	1,800	19	1,100
23	1,100	25	500
28	2,400	27	900
Feb. 28	Bal. 4,095		

Zuboff Associates received the bank statement—shown on facing page—on February 28, 20X3 (as always, negative amounts are in parentheses):

Bank Statement for February 20X3		

Beginning balance		$3,995
Deposits:		
Feb. 7	$ 800	
15	1,800	
24	1,100	3,700
Checks (total per day):		
Feb. 8	$ 400	
16	3,100	
23	1,100	(4,600)
Other items:		
Service charge		(10)
NSF check from M. E. Crown		(700)
Bank collection of note receivable for the company.........		1,000*
EFT—monthly rent expense		(330)
Interest on account balance		15
Ending balance		$3,070

*Includes interest of $119.

Additional data: Zuboff deposits all cash receipts in the bank and makes all payments by check.

Required

1. Prepare the bank reconciliation of Zuboff Associates at February 28, 20X3.
2. Record the entries based on the bank reconciliation.

Solution

Requirement 1

ZUBOFF ASSOCIATES
Bank Reconciliation
February 28, 20X3

Bank:		
Balance, February 28, 20X3...		$3,070
Add: Deposit of February 28 in transit		2,400
		5,470
Less: Outstanding checks issued on Feb. 25 ($500)		
and Feb. 27 ($900)...		(1,400)
Adjusted bank balance, February 28, 20X3		$4,070
Books:		
Balance, February 28, 20X3...		$4,095
Add: Bank collection of note receivable, including		
interest of $119		1,000
Interest earned on bank balance......................................		15
		5,110
Less: Service charge	$ 10	
NSF check	700	
EFT—Rent expense...	330	(1,040)
Adjusted book balance, February 28, 20X3		$4,070

Requirement 2

Feb. 28	Cash	1,000			Feb. 28	Accounts Receivable—		
	Note Receivable					M. E. Crown......................	700	
	($1,000 − $119)...		881			Cash		700
	Interest Revenue......		119			NSF check returned by bank.		
	Note receivable collected by bank.				28	Rent Expense	330	
28	Cash	15				Cash		330
	Interest Revenue......		15			Monthly rent expense.		
	Interest earned on bank balance.							
28	Miscellaneous Expense.......	10						
	Cash		10					
	Bank service charge.							

INTERNAL CONTROL OVER CASH RECEIPTS

Internal control over cash receipts ensures that all cash receipts are deposited in the bank and that the company's accounting record is correct. Many businesses receive cash over the counter and through the mail. Each source of cash receipts calls for its own security measures.

 DAILY EXERCISE 7-14

 DAILY EXERCISE 7-15

CASH RECEIPTS OVER THE COUNTER The point-of-sale terminal (cash register) offers management control over the cash received in a store. Consider a **Macy's** store. First, the terminal should be positioned so that customers can see the amounts the cashier enters into the computer. Company policy should require issuance of a receipt to make sure each sale is recorded by the cash register.

Second, the cash drawer opens only when the sales clerk enters an amount on the keypad, and the machine records each sale and cash transaction. At the end of the day, a manager proves the cash by comparing the total amount in the cash drawer against the machine's record of the day's sales. This step helps prevent outright theft by the clerk.

Third, pricing merchandise at "uneven" amounts—say, $3.95 instead of $4.00—means that the clerk generally must make change, which in turn means having to get into the cash drawer. This requires entering the amount of the sale on the keypad and so onto the register tape—another way to prevent fraud.

At the end of the day, the cashier or other employee with cash-handling duties deposits the cash in the bank. The tape then goes to the accounting department as the basis for an entry in the accounting records. These security measures, coupled with periodic on-site inspection by a manager, discourage theft.

CASH RECEIPTS BY MAIL All incoming mail should be opened by a mailroom employee. This person should compare the amount of the check received with the attached remittance advice (the slip of paper that lists the amount of the check). If no advice was sent, the mailroom employee should prepare one and enter the amount of each receipt on a control tape. At the end of the day, this control tape is given to a responsible official, such as the controller, for verification. Cash receipts should be given to the cashier, who combines them with any cash received over the counter and prepares the bank deposit.

Having a mailroom employee handle postal cash receipts is another application of a good separation of duties. If the accountants were to open postal cash receipts, they could easily hide a theft.

The mailroom employee forwards the remittance advices to the accounting department. These provide the data for entries in the cash books and postings to customers' accounts in the accounts receivable ledger. As a final step, the controller compares the three records of the day's cash receipts:

1. The control tape total from the mailroom
2. The bank deposit amount from the cashier
3. The debit to Cash from the accounting department

 DAILY EXERCISE 7-16

Many companies use a lock-box system to separate cash duties and establish control over cash receipts. Customers send their checks directly to an address that is essentially a bank account. Internal control over the cash is enhanced because company personnel do not handle incoming cash. The lock-box system improves efficiency because the cash goes to work for the company immediately.

 **THINK IT OVER** The bookkeeper in your company has stolen cash received from customers. The bookkeeper prepared fake documents that indicate the customers returned the merchandise. What internal control feature could have prevented this theft?

Answer: The bookkeeper should not have access to cash.

CASH SHORT AND OVER Differences sometimes exist between actual cash receipts and the day's record of cash received. Usually, these differences are small and result from honest errors. When the recorded cash balance exceeds cash on hand, a *cash short* situation exists. When actual cash exceeds the recorded cash balance, there is a *cash over* situation. Suppose the cash register tapes of Macy's indicated sales revenue of $25,000, but the cash received was $24,980. To record the day's sales, the store would make this entry:

Cash	24,980	
Cash Short and Over............	20	
Sales Revenue		25,000
Daily cash sales.		

As the entry shows, Cash Short and Over is debited when cash receipts are less than sales revenue. This account is credited when cash receipts exceed sales. A debit balance in Cash Short and Over appears on the income statement as Miscellaneous Expense, a credit balance as Other Revenue.

Exhibit 7-8 summarizes the controls over cash receipts.

EXHIBIT 7-8   **Internal Controls over Cash Receipts**

Elements of Internal Control	Internal Controls over Cash Receipts
Competent, reliable, ethical personnel	Companies carefully screen employees for undesirable traits. They commit time and effort to training programs.
Assignment of responsibilities	Specific employees are designated as cashiers, supervisors, or accountants.
Proper authorization	Only designated employees, such as department managers, can approve check receipts above a certain amount.
Separation of duties	Cashiers and mailroom employees who handle cash do not have access to the accounting records. Accountants have no opportunity to handle cash.
Internal and external audits	Internal auditors examine company transactions for agreement with management policies. External auditors examine the internal controls to determine whether the accounting system produces accurate amounts for revenues and receivables.
Documents and records	Customers receive receipts as transaction records. Bank statements list cash receipts for deposits.
Electronic devices and computer controls	Cash registers serve as transaction records. Each day's receipts are matched with customer remittance advices and with the day's deposit ticket from the bank.
Other controls	Cashiers are bonded. Cash is stored in vaults and banks. Employees are rotated among jobs and are required to take vacations.

INTERNAL CONTROL OVER CASH PAYMENTS (DISBURSEMENTS)

Objective 5
Apply internal controls to cash payments

Exercising control over cash payments is as important as controlling cash receipts.

Controls over Payment by Check

Payment by check is an important control over cash payments. First, the check provides a record of the payment. Second, to be valid, the check must be signed by an authorized official. Before signing the check, the manager should study the evidence supporting the payment. To illustrate the internal control over cash payments, let's suppose the business is buying merchandise inventory.

CONTROLS OVER PURCHASING   The purchasing process—outlined in Exhibit 7-9—starts when the sales department prepares a *purchase request* (or *requisition*). A separate purchasing department locates the goods and mails a *purchase order* to the supplier. When the supplier ships the merchandise, the supplier also mails the *invoice,* or bill. ➡ The goods arrive, and the receiving department checks the goods for damage and lists the merchandise received on a document called the *receiving report.* The accounting department combines all the foregoing documents and forwards this *payment packet* to officers for payment. The packet includes the purchase request, purchase order, invoice, and receiving report, as shown in Exhibit 7-10.

◄ We introduced purchase orders and invoices in Chapter 5.

283

EXHIBIT 7-9
Purchasing Process

Business Document	Prepared by	Send to
Purchase request (requisition)	Sales department	Purchasing department
Purchase order	Purchasing department	Outside company that sells the needed merchandise (supplier or vendor)
Invoice (bill)	Outside company that sells the needed merchandise (supplier or vendor)	Accounting department
Receiving report	Receiving department	Accounting department
Payment packet	Accounting department	Officer who signs the check

EXHIBIT 7-10
Payment Packet

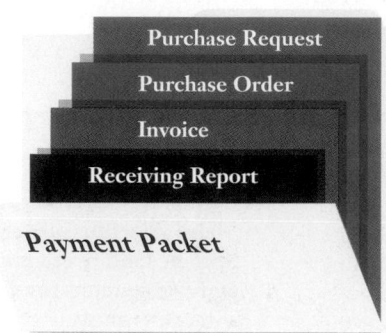

CONTROLS OVER APPROVAL OF PAYMENTS   Before approving the payment, the controller or the treasurer should examine the packet to ascertain that the accounting department has performed the following control steps:

1. The invoice is compared with a copy of the purchase order and purchase request to ensure that the business pays only for the goods that it ordered.
2. The invoice is compared with the receiving report to ensure that cash is paid only for the goods actually received.
3. The mathematical accuracy of the invoice is proved.

DAILY EXERCISE 7-17

To avoid document alteration, some firms use machines that stamp the amount on the check in indelible ink. After payment, the check signer punches a hole through the payment packet. This hole makes it hard to run the documents through for a duplicate payment.

Technology is streamlining cash payment procedures. Evaluated Receipts Settlement (ERS) compresses the approval process into a single step: compare the receiving report to the purchase order. If the two documents match, that proves **Kinko's** received the paper it ordered, and then Kinko's pays **Hammermill Paper,** the supplier. ERS requires fewer employees and saves on accounting expense.

An even more streamlined process bypasses people and documents altogether. In Electronic Data Interchange (EDI), **Wal-Mart's** computers communicate directly with the computers of suppliers like **Goodyear Tire, Rubbermaid,** and **Procter & Gamble.** When Wal-Mart's inventory of auto tires reaches a low level, the computer sends a purchase order to Goodyear. Goodyear ships the tires and invoices Wal-Mart electronically. Then an electronic fund transfer (EFT) sends the cash from Wal-Mart to Goodyear.

These streamlined procedures depend on the mutual trust of the companies involved. They know each other well and operate ethically. They cannot afford to do otherwise. Exhibit 7-11 summarizes the internal controls over cash payments.

Exhibit 7-11 Internal Controls over Cash Payments

Element of Internal Control	Internal Controls over Cash Payments
Competent, reliable, ethical personnel	Cash payments are entrusted to high-level employees.
Assignment of responsibilities	Specific employees approve purchase documents for payment. Executives examine approvals, then sign checks.
Proper authorization	Large expenditures must be authorized by the company owner or board of directors.
Separation of duties	Computer operators and other employees who handle checks have no access to the accounting records. Accountants have no opportunity to handle cash.
Internal and external audits	Internal auditors examine company transactions for agreement with management policies. External auditors examine the internal controls over cash payments and the accounting records.
Documents and records	Suppliers issue invoices. Bank statements list cash payments. Checks are renumbered in sequence to account for payments.
Electronic devices, computer controls, and other controls	Blank checks are stored in a vault and controlled by a responsible official. Machines stamp the amount on a check in indelible ink. Paid invoices are punched to avoid duplicate payment.

THINK IT OVER Talon Computer Concepts processes payroll checks for small businesses. Clients give their employee time cards to Talon, and Talon programmers write the software to meet the clients' payrolls. Talon computer operators deliver the checks to clients for distribution to employees. Identify two employee functions of Talon's cash payment system that should be separated. Give your reason.

Answer: The *programmers* should not also be computer *operators*. Persons who both program and operate computers can write the program to process checks to themselves and then pocket the printed checks.

Controlling Petty Cash Payments

It is uneconomical for a business to write a separate check for an executive's taxi fare, floppy disks needed right away, or the delivery of a package across town. To meet these needs, companies keep a small amount of cash on hand to pay for such minor amounts. This fund is called **petty cash.**

Even though amounts paid through the petty cash fund are small, the business needs to set up controls such as the following:

1. Designate an employee to administer the fund as its custodian.
2. Keep a specific amount of cash on hand.
3. Support all fund payments with a petty cash ticket.
4. Replenish the fund through normal cash payment procedures.

The petty cash fund is opened when a payment is approved for a predetermined amount and a check for that amount is issued to Petty Cash. Assume that on February 28, the business decides to establish a petty cash fund of $200. The custodian cashes the check and places the currency and coin in the fund, which may be a cash box, safe, or other device. The petty cash custodian is responsible for controlling the fund. Starting the fund is recorded as follows:

Feb. 28	Petty Cash	200	
	Cash in Bank		200
	To open the petty cash fund.		

For each petty cash payment, the custodian prepares a *petty cash ticket* like the one illustrated in Exhibit 7-12.

PETTY CASH. Fund containing a small amount of cash that is used to pay for minor expenditures.

Exhibit 7-12
Petty Cash Ticket

```
┌──────────────────────────────────────────────────────────────┐
│                      PETTY CASH TICKET                         │
│  Date   Mar. 25, 20X6                            No.   47       │
│  Amount   $23.00                                               │
│  For    Box of floppy diskettes                               │
│  Debit   Office Supplies, Acct. No. 145                        │
│  Received by   Lewis Wright      Fund Custodian   MAR          │
└──────────────────────────────────────────────────────────────┘
```

IMPREST SYSTEM. A way to account for petty cash by maintaining a constant balance in the petty cash account, supported by the fund (cash plus payment tickets) totaling the same amount.

Observe that signatures (or initials) identify the recipient of petty cash and the fund custodian. Requiring both signatures reduces unauthorized payments. The custodian keeps all the petty cash tickets in the fund. The sum of the cash plus the total of the ticket amounts should equal the opening balance at all times—in this case, $200. Also, the Petty Cash account keeps its prescribed $200 balance at all times. Maintaining the Petty Cash account at this balance, supported by the fund (cash plus tickets totaling the same amount), is a characteristic of an **imprest system.** In an imprest system, the amount of cash for which the custodian is responsible is clearly identified. This is the system's main internal control feature.

Payments reduce the amount of cash in the fund, so periodically the fund must be replenished. Suppose that on March 31, the fund has $118 in cash and $82 in tickets. A check for $82 is issued, made payable to Petty Cash. The fund custodian cashes this check and puts the money in the fund to return its actual cash to $200. The petty cash tickets identify the accounts to be debited, as shown in the entry to record replenishment of the fund:

Mar. 31	Office Supplies	23	
	Delivery Expense	17	
	Miscellaneous Selling Expense	42	
	Cash in Bank		82
	To replenish the petty cash fund.		

DAILY EXERCISE 7-18

If this cash payment exceeds the sum of the tickets—that is, if the fund comes up short, Cash Short and Over is debited for the missing amount. If the sum of the tickets exceeds the payment, Cash Short and Over is credited. Replenishing the fund does *not* affect the Petty Cash account. Petty Cash keeps its $200 balance at all times.

Petty Cash is debited only when the fund is started (see the February 28 entry) or when its amount is changed. Suppose the business decides to raise the fund amount from $200 to $250. This step would require a $50 debit to Petty Cash.

Objective 6
Use a budget to manage cash

USING A BUDGET TO MANAGE CASH

BUDGET. A quantitative expression of a plan that helps managers coordinate the entity's activities.

Owners and managers control their organizations with the help of budgets. A **budget** is a quantitative expression of a plan that helps managers coordinate the entity's activities. Cash receives the most attention in the budgeting process because all transactions ultimately affect cash.

How does **MCI WorldCom** decide when to invest in new telecommunications equipment? How will the company decide how much to spend? Similarly, by what process do you decide how much to spend on your education? On an automobile? All these decisions depend to some degree on the information that a cash budget provides. A cash budget helps a business manage its cash by expressing the plan for the receipt and payment of cash during a future period.

To prepare for the future, a company must determine how much cash it will need and then figure out how to obtain the needed cash. Preparation of a cash budget includes four steps:

1. Start with the entity's cash balance at the beginning of the period. This is the amount of cash left over from the preceding period.
2. Add the budgeted cash receipts and subtract the budgeted cash payments, including

a. Revenue and expense transactions
   b. Asset acquisition and sale transactions
   c. Liability and stockholders' equity transactions

3. The beginning balance plus the expected receipts minus the expected payments equals the expected cash balance at the end of the period.

4. Compare the expected cash balance to the desired, or *budgeted,* cash balance at the end of the period. Owners and managers know the minimum amount of cash they need (the budgeted balance) to keep the entity running. If there is excess cash, they can invest more than originally planned. If the expected cash balance falls below the budgeted amount, the company must raise more money to reach the desired cash balance.

Exhibit 7-13 shows a hypothetical cash budget for **Gap Inc.,** for the year ended January 31, 20X2. Study it carefully, because at some point in your career or personal affairs you will use a cash budget.

EXHIBIT 7-13
Cash Budget (Hypothetical)

 DAILY EXERCISE 7-19

GAP INC. Cash Budget (Hypothetical) Year Ended January 31, 20X2		
		(In millions)
(1) Cash balance, February 1, 20X1		$ 203
Estimated cash receipts:		
(2) Collections from customers	$ 2,858	
(3) Interest and dividends on investments	6	
(4) Sale of store fixtures	5	2,869
		3,072
Estimated cash payments:		
(5) Purchases of inventory	$(1,906)	
(6) Operating expenses	(561)	
(7) Expansions of existing stores	(206)	
(8) Opening of new stores	(349)	
(9) Payment of long-term debt	(145)	
(10) Payment to owners of the business	(219)	(3,386)
(11) Cash available (needed) before new financing		(314)
(12) Budgeted cash balance, January 31, 20X2		(200)
(13) Cash available for additional investments, or (New financing needed)		$ (514)

The cash budget has sections for cash receipts and cash payments. The budget is prepared *before* the period's transactions and can take any form that helps people make decisions. The cash budget is an internal document, so it is not bound by generally accepted accounting principles.

Gap Inc.'s hypothetical cash budget in Exhibit 7-13 begins with the company's actual cash balance at the beginning of the period. At February 1, 20X1, Gap had cash of $203 million (line 1). The budgeted cash receipts and payments are expected to create a need for additional financing during the year (line 13).

Assume that managers of Gap wish to maintain a cash balance of at least $200 million (line 12). Because the year's activity is expected to leave the company with a *negative* cash balance of $314 million (line 11), Gap's managers must arrange $514 million of financing (line 13). *Add* lines 11 and 12 to arrive at the amount of new financing needed.

 DAILY EXERCISE 7-20

Suppose line 11 of Exhibit 7-13 showed cash available of $250 million. What would Gap Inc. do, borrow additional money, or have an excess to invest?

Answer: Gap would have an additional $50 million to invest ($250 million available − $200 million needed = excess of $50 million).

International transactions add to the complexity of managing cash. When a U.S. company buys goods internationally, it may pay cash in a foreign currency, such as Canadian dollars or Mexican pesos. Foreign currencies change in value from day to day. In settling up, a company may have a gain or a loss on the foreign currency. We show how to account for foreign currency transactions in Chapter 16.

REPORTING CASH ON THE BALANCE SHEET

Cash is the first current asset listed on the balance sheet. Businesses often have many bank accounts and petty cash funds, but they usually combine all cash amounts into a single total called "Cash and Cash Equivalents."

Cash equivalents include liquid assets such as time deposits and certificates of deposit, which are interest-bearing accounts that can be withdrawn with no penalty. Although they are slightly less liquid than cash, these assets are sufficiently similar to be reported along with cash. The balance sheet of **Intel Corporation** recently reported the following:

INTEL CORPORATION Balance Sheet (Adapted) December 31; 1999	
	(In millions)
Assets	
Current assets:	
Cash and cash equivalents	$ 3,695
Short-term investments	8,093
Accounts receivable.........................	3,700
Inventories	1,478
Other current assets	853
Total current assets............................	$17,819

Source: Intel Corporation. *Annual Report 1999,* p. 19.

Intel's cash balance means that $3,695 million is available for use as needed. Cash that is restricted should not be reported as a current asset. For example, banks require customers to keep a *compensating balance* on deposit in order to borrow from the bank. The compensating balance is restricted and therefore is not included in the cash amount on the balance sheet.

ETHICS AND ACCOUNTING

A *Wall Street Journal* article described a Russian entrepreneur who claimed he was getting ahead in business by breaking laws. "Older people have an ethics problem," he said. "By that I mean they *have* ethics." Conversely, Roger Smith, former chairman of **General Motors,** said, "Ethical practice is, quite simply, good business." Smith has been around long enough to see the danger in unethical behavior. Sooner or later unethical conduct comes to light. Moreover, ethical behavior wins out in the end because it is the right thing to do.

Corporate and Professional Codes of Ethics

Most large companies have a code of ethics to encourage employees to behave ethically and responsibly. But codes of ethics are not enough by themselves. Senior management must set a high ethical tone. They must make it clear that the company will not tolerate unethical conduct by employees.

As professionals, accountants are expected to maintain higher standards than society in general. Their ability to do business depends entirely on their reputation. Most independent accountants are members of the American Institute of Certified Public Accountants and must abide by the *AICPA Code of Professional Conduct.* Accountants who are members of the Institute of Management Accountants are bound by the *Standards of Ethical Conduct for Management Accountants.*

Ethical Issues in Accounting

Objective 7
Make ethical judgments in business

In many situations, the ethical choice is easy. For example, stealing cash is both unethical and illegal. In our chapter opening story, the cashier's actions landed her in jail. In other cases, the choices are more difficult. But in every instance, ethical judgments boil down to a personal decision: What should I do in a given situation? Let's consider three ethical issues in accounting. The first two are easy to resolve. The third is more difficult.

SITUATION 1   Sonja Kleberg is preparing the income tax return of a client who has had a particularly good year—higher income than expected. On January 2, the client pays for newspaper advertising and asks Sonja to backdate the expense to the preceding year. The tax deduction would help the client more in the year just ended than in the current year. Backdating would decrease taxable income of the earlier year and lower the client's tax payments. After all, there is a difference of only two days between January 2 and December 31. This client is important to Kleberg. What should she do?

> **She should refuse the request because the transaction took place in January of the new year.**

What control device could prove that Kleberg behaved unethically if she backdated the transaction in the accounting records? An IRS audit and documents and records—the date of the cash payment could prove that the expense occurred in January rather than in December.

SITUATION 2   Jack Mellichamp's software company owes $40,000 to Bank of America. The loan agreement requires Mellichamp's company to maintain a current ratio (current assets divided by current liabilities) of 1.50 or higher. ➤ It is late in the year, and the bank will review Mellichamp's situation early next year. At present, the company's current ratio is 1.40. At this level, Mellichamp is in violation of his loan agreement. He can increase the current ratio to 1.53 by paying off some current liabilities right before year end. Is it ethical to do so?

 For a review of the current ratio, see Chapter 4.

> **Yes, because the action is a real business transaction.**

However, paying off the liabilities is only a delaying tactic. It will hold off the creditors for now, but the business still must improve its underlying operations.

SITUATION 3   Emilia Gomez, an accountant for the Democratic Party, discovers that her supervisor, Myles Packer, made several errors last year. Campaign contributions received from foreign citizens, which are illegal, were recorded as normal. It is not clear whether the errors were deliberate or accidental. Gomez knows that Packer evaluates her job performance. What should Gomez do? She is uncertain.

DAILY EXERCISE 7-21

> To make her decision, Gomez could follow the framework outlined in the Decision Guidelines feature on the next page.

DECISION GUIDELINES

Framework for Making Ethical Judgments

Weighing tough ethical judgments requires a decision framework. Answering these six questions will guide you through tough decisions. Apply them to Emilia Gomez's situation.

QUESTION	DECISION GUIDELINE
1. What are the facts?	**1.** *Determine the facts.* They are given on page 289.
2. What is the ethical issue, if any?	**2.** *Identify the ethical issues.* The root work of ethical is *ethics,* which Webster's dictionary defines as the "the discipline dealing with what is good and bad and with moral duty and obligation." Gomez's ethical dilemma is to decide what she should do with the information she has uncovered.
3. What are the options?	**3.** *Specify the alternatives.* For Emilia Gomez, three reasonable alternatives include (a) reporting the errors to Packer, (b) reporting the errors to Packer's boss, and (c) doing nothing.
4. Who is involved in the situation?	**4.** *Identify the people involved.* Individuals who could be affected include Gomez, Packer, the Democratic Party, and Gomez's co-workers who observe her behavior.
5. What are the possible consequences?	**5.** *Assess the possible outcomes.* **a.** If Gomez reports the errors to Packer, he may penalize her, or he may reward her for careful work. Reporting the errors preserves her integrity and will probably lead to returning the money to the donors. But the Democratic Party could suffer embarrassment if this situation is made public. **b.** If Gomez reports to Packer's boss, her integrity is preserved. Her relationship with Packer will be strained. If Packer's boss has colluded with Packer in recording the campaign contribution, Gomez could be penalized. If the error is corrected and outsiders notified, the Democratic Party will be embarrassed. Others observing this situation would be affected by the outcome. **c.** If Gomez does nothing, she avoids a confrontation with Packer or his boss. They may or may not discover the error. If they discover it, they may or may not correct it. They may criticize Gomez for not bringing the error to their attention. Colleagues might learn of the situation.
6. What shall I do?	**6.** *Make the decision.* The choice is difficult. Gomez must balance the likely effects on the various people against the dictates of her own conscience. Gomez should report the errors. Ordinarily, Packer should be the first person contacted. If Packer fails to act in an honest way, then Gomez should inform Packer's boss. Senior management should always protect the messenger of accurate news, whether good or bad.

Ethics and External Controls

There is another dimension to most ethical issues: *external controls,* the discipline placed on business conduct by outsiders who interact with the company.

- In situation 1, for example, Sonja Kleberg could give in to the client's request to backdate the advertising expense. But this action would be both dishonest and illegal. These external controls arise from the business's interaction with the taxing authorities. An IRS audit of Kleberg's client could uncover her action.
- In situation 2, the external controls arise from Jack Mellichamp's relationship with the bank that lent money to his software company. As long as the loan agreement is in effect, the company must maintain a current ratio of 1.50 or higher. Paying off current liabilities to improve the current ratio would be a short-term solution to Mellichamp's problem. Over the long run, his business must generate more current assets through operations.

- The primary external control in situation 3 results from U.S. laws and their enforcement through the legal system. Campaign contributions are public information, and sooner or later the public will learn that the Democratic Party received illegal campaign contributions. It would be in the party's best interest to admit its mistake and correct the errors as quickly as possible—by returning the illegal contributions to the donors.

REVIEW INTERNAL CONTROL AND CASH

SUMMARY PROBLEM

Grudnitski Company established a $300 petty cash fund. James C. Brown is the fund custodian. At the end of the first week, the petty cash fund contains the following:

a. Cash: $171 **b.** Petty cash tickets:

www.prenhall.com/horngren
End-of-Chapter Assessment

No.	Amount	Issued to	Signed by	Account Debited
44	$14	B. Jarvis	B. Jarvis and JCB	Office Supplies
45	9	S. Bell	S. Bell	Miscellaneous Expense
47	43	R. Tate	R. Tate and JCB	—
48	33	L. Blair	L. Blair and JCB	Travel Expense

Required

1. Identify the four internal control weaknesses revealed in the given data.
2. Prepare the general journal entries to record:
  a. Establishment of the petty cash fund.
  b. Replenishment of the fund. Assume that petty cash ticket no. 47 was issued for the purchase of office supplies.
3. What is the balance in the Petty Cash account immediately before replenishment? Immediately after replenishment?

Solution

Requirement 1

The four internal control weaknesses are

a. Petty cash ticket no. 46 is missing. Coupled with weakness (b), this omission raises questions about the administration of the petty cash fund and about how the petty cash funds were used.
b. The $171 cash balance means that $129 has been disbursed ($300 − $171 = $129). However, the total amount of the petty cash tickets is only $99 ($14 + $9 + $43 + $33). The fund, then, is $30 short of cash ($129 − $99 = $30). Was petty cash ticket no. 46 issued for $30? The data in the problem offer no hint that helps answer this question. In practice, management would investigate the problem.
c. The petty cash custodian (JCB) did not sign petty cash ticket no. 45. This omission may have been an oversight on his part. However, it raises the question of whether he authorized the payment. Both the fund custodian and the recipient of cash should sign the ticket.
d. Petty cash ticket no. 47 does not indicate which account to debit. What did Tate do with the money, and what account should be debited? With no better choice available, debit Miscellaneous Expense.

Requirement 2

Petty cash journal entries:
a. Entry to establish the petty cash fund: **b.** Entry to replenish the fund:

Petty Cash............................	300		Office Supplies ($14 + $43).............	57	
Cash in Bank............		300	Miscellaneous Expense....................	9	
			Travel Expense................................	33	
			Cash Short and Over.......................	30	
			Cash in Bank........................		129

Requirement 3

The balance in Petty Cash is *always* its specified balance, in this case $300.

LESSONS LEARNED

1. **Define internal control.** *Internal control* is the organizational plan and all the related measures an entity uses to safeguard assets, encourage adherence to company policies, promote operational efficiency, and ensure accurate and reliable accounting records.

2. **Identify the characteristics of an effective system of internal control.** An effective internal control system includes these features: competent, reliable, and ethical personnel; clear-cut assignment of responsibilities; proper authorization; separation of duties; internal and external audits; documents and records; and electronic devices and computer controls.

3. **Prepare a bank reconciliation and the related journal entries.** The *bank account* helps control and safeguard cash. Businesses use the *bank statement* and the *bank reconciliation* to account for banking transactions.

4. **Apply internal controls to cash receipts.** To control cash receipts over the counter, companies use point-of-sale terminals that customers can see, and require that cashiers provide customers with receipts. The machine records each sale and cash transaction.

   To control cash receipts by mail, a mailroom employee should be charged with opening the mail, comparing the enclosed amount with the remittance advice, and preparing a control tape. This is an essential separation of duties—the accounting department should not open the mail. At the end of the day, the controller compares the three records of the day's cash receipts: the control tape total from the mailroom, the bank deposit amount from the cashier, and the debit to Cash from the accounting department.

5. **Apply internal controls to cash payments.** To control payments by check, checks should be issued and signed only when a *payment packet* including the purchase request, purchase order, invoice (bill), and receiving report (with all appropriate signatures) has been prepared. To control petty cash payments, the custodian of the fund should require a completed petty cash ticket for all disbursements.

6. **Use a budget to manage cash.** A budget is a quantitative expression of a plan to help managers coordinate the entity's activities. First, a company must determine how much cash it will need. Then it budgets cash receipts and payments for the upcoming period. By comparing the ending budgeted cash balance to the amount needed, managers can determine whether they need to borrow or will have extra cash to invest.

7. **Make ethical judgments in business.** To make ethical decisions, people should follow six steps: (1) Determine the facts. (2) Identify the ethical issues. (3) Specify the alternatives. (4) Identify the people involved. (5) Assess the possible outcomes. (6) Make the decision.

ACCOUNTING VOCABULARY

audit (p. 270)
bank collection (p. 275)
bank reconciliation (p. 275)
bank statement (p. 274)
budget (p. 286)
check (p. 273)
computer virus (p. 272)

controller (p. 268)
deposit in transit (p. 275)
electronic funds transfer (EFT) (p. 274)
encryption (p. 272)
firewalls (p. 272)
imprest system (p. 286)

internal control (p. 267)
nonsufficient funds (NSF) check (p. 276)
outstanding check (p. 275)
petty cash (p. 285)
Trojan horse (p. 272)

QUESTIONS

1. Which feature of effective internal control is the most fundamental? Why?
2. Identify seven features of an effective system of internal control.
3. Separation of duties may be divided into four parts. What are they?
4. Are internal control systems designed to be foolproof and perfect? What is a fundamental constraint in planning and maintaining systems?
5. Briefly state how each of the following serves as an internal control measure over cash: bank account, signature card, deposit ticket, and bank statement.
6. Each of the following items affects the bank reconciliation. Next to each item, enter the appropriate letter from the following possible treatments: (a) bank side of reconciliation—add the item; (b) bank side of reconciliation—subtract the item; (c) book side of reconciliation—add the item; (d) book side of reconciliation—subtract the item.
   ____ Deposit in transit
   ____ Bank collection
   ____ Customer check returned because of un-authorized signature
   ____ Book error that increased balance of Cash account

   ____ Outstanding check
   ____ NSF check
   ____ Bank service charge
   ____ Cost of printed checks
   ____ Bank error that decreased bank balance
7. What purpose does a bank reconciliation serve?
8. A company has six bank accounts, two petty cash funds, and three certificates of deposit that can be withdrawn on demand. How many cash amounts would this company likely report on its balance sheet?
9. What role does a cash register play in an internal control system?
10. Describe internal control procedures for cash received by mail.
11. What documents make up the payment packet? Describe three procedures that use the payment packet to ensure that each payment is appropriate.
12. What balance does the Petty Cash account have at all times? Does this balance always equal the amount of cash in the fund? When are the two amounts equal? When are they unequal?
13. Describe how a budget helps a company manage its cash.
14. Why should accountants adhere to a higher standard of ethical conduct than many other members of society?

DAILY EXERCISES

DE7-1 Give the title of the chief finance officer and the title of the chief accounting officer in an organization. What are the responsibilities of each person? How does separating their duties provide good internal control?

Aspects of internal control
(Obj. 1)

DE7-2 Internal controls are designed to safeguard assets, encourage employees to follow company policies, promote operational efficiency, and ensure accurate records. Which goal is most important? Which goal must the internal controls accomplish for the business to survive? Give your reason.

Definition of internal control
(Obj. 1)

DE7-3 Explain in your own words why separation of duties is often described as the cornerstone of internal control for safeguarding assets. Describe what can happen if the same person has custody of an asset and also accounts for the asset.

Characteristics of an effective system of internal control
(Obj. 2)

DE7-4 Examine the organization chart in Exhibit 7-2, page 268. What is the main duty of the internal auditors? To whom do the internal auditors report? Why don't the internal auditors report directly to the treasurer?

Characteristics of an effective system of internal control
(Obj. 2)

DE7-5 How do external auditors differ from internal auditors? How does an external audit differ from an internal audit? How are the two types of audits similar?

Characteristics of an effective system of internal control
(Obj. 2)

DE7-6 Review the characteristics of an effective system of internal control that begin on page 267. Then identify two things that **Merrill Lynch** in the chapter-opening story could have done to make it harder for Darlyne Lopez, the cashier, to steal from the company and hide the theft. Explain how each new measure taken by Merrill Lynch would have accomplished its goal.

Characteristics of an effective system of internal control
(Obj. 2)

DE7-7 Make a simple diagram with three boxes and two arrows to show the relationships among (a) the bank statement, (b) the bank reconciliation, and (c) the accounting records. Use the arrows to show the flow of data.

Bank reconciliation
(Obj. 3)

DE7-8 Answer the following questions about the bank reconciliation:

1. What is the difference between a bank statement and a bank reconciliation?
2. Is the bank reconciliation a journal, a ledger, an account, or a financial statement? If none of these, what is it?
3. Which side of the bank reconciliation generates data for new journal entries in the company's accounting records?

Aspects of a bank reconciliation
(Obj. 3)

DE7-9 Compare Business Research, Inc.'s Cash account in Exhibit 7-5, page 275, with the bank statement that the company received in Exhibit 7-4, page 274.

1. Trace each cash receipt from the Cash account (Exhibit 7-5) to a deposit on the bank statement (Exhibit 7-4). Which deposit is in transit on January 31? Give its date and dollar amount.
2. Trace each Business Research check from the cash payments record in Exhibit 7-5 to the bank statement in Exhibit 7-4. List all outstanding checks by check number and dollar amount.
3. On which side of the bank reconciliation do deposits in transit and outstanding checks appear—the bank side or the book side? Are they added or subtracted on the bank reconciliation?

Identifying reconciling items from bank documents
(Obj. 3)

DE7-10 The Cash account of Theraband Equipment reported a balance of $2,280 at May 31. Included were outstanding checks totaling $900 and a May 31 deposit of $200 that did not appear on the bank statement. The bank statement, which came from Park Cities Bank, listed a May 31 balance of $3,270. Included in the bank balance was a May 30 collection of $300 on account from Kelly Brooks, a Theraband customer who pays the bank directly. The bank statement also shows a $20 service charge and $10 of interest revenue that Theraband earned on its bank balance. *Prepare Theraband's bank reconciliation at May 31.*

Preparing a bank reconciliation
(Obj. 3)

DE7-11 After preparing Theraband Equipment's bank reconciliation in Daily Exercise 7-10, make Theraband's general journal entries for transactions that arise from the bank reconciliation. Include an explanation with each entry.

Recording transactions from a bank reconciliation
(Obj. 3)

DE7-12 Who in an organization should prepare the bank reconciliation? Should it be someone with cash-handling duties, someone with accounting duties, or someone with both duties? Does it matter? Give your reason.

Internal controls and the bank reconciliation   (Obj. 2, 3)

DE7-13 Barry Cruise owns Cruise Vacation Planners. He fears that a trusted employee has been stealing from the company. This employee receives cash from customers and also prepares the monthly bank reconciliation. To check up on the employee, Cruise prepares his own bank reconciliation, as follows:

CRUISE VACATION PLANNERS
Bank Reconciliation
August 31, 20X7

Bank		Books	
Balance, August 31	$3,000	Balance, August 31	$2,500
Add: Deposit in transit.............	400	Add: Bank collection	800
		Interest revenue	10
Less: Outstanding checks..........	(1,100)	Less: Service charge..................	(30)
Adjusted bank balance	$2,300	Adjusted book balance................	$3,280

Does it appear that the employee has stolen from the company? If so, how much? Explain your answer. Which side of the bank reconciliation shows the company's true cash balance?

DE7-14 Consider the men's sportswear department of a **Macy's** department store. What could a dishonest salesperson do if he had access to the record of transactions conducted through his cash register? How does Macy's keep employees from behaving in this manner?

DE7-15 Ted Carter sells furniture at Dupree Home & Garden in Huntsville, Alabama. Company procedure requires Carter to write a customer receipt for all sales. The receipt forms are prenumbered. Carter is having personal financial problems and takes $500 that he received from a customer. To hide his theft, Carter simply destroys the company copy of the sales receipt he gave the customer. What will alert Gerald Dupree, the owner, that something is wrong? What will this knowledge lead Dupree to do?

DE7-16 Review the internal controls over cash receipts by mail, discussed on page 282. Briefly describe how the final step in the process, performed by the controller, establishes that **(1)** the cash receipts went into the bank; and **(2)** the business's customers received credit for their payments.

How does a lock-box system protect cash from theft?

DE7-17 Answer the following questions about internal control over cash payments.

1. Payment of cash payments by check carries two basic controls over cash. What are they?
2. Suppose a purchasing agent receives the goods that he purchases and also approves payment for the goods. How could a dishonest purchasing agent cheat his company? How do companies avoid this internal control weakness?

DE7-18

1. Describe how an *imprest* petty cash system works. What is the main control feature of an imprest system?
2. Atlantic Press Publishers maintains an imprest $400 petty cash fund, which is under the control of Brenda Chavez. At November 30, the fund holds $220 cash and petty cash tickets for travel expense, $80; office supplies, $60; and delivery expense, $40.
   Journalize (a) establishment of the petty cash fund on November 1, and (b) replenishment of the fund on November 30.
3. Draw a T-account for Petty Cash, and post to the account. What is Petty Cash's account balance at all times?

DE7-19

1. Return to **Gap Inc.'s** hypothetical cash budget in Exhibit 7-13, page 287. Suppose Gap postpones the opening of new stores until 20X3. In that case, how much additional financing will Gap need for the year ended January 31, 20X2?
2. Now suppose Gap postpones both existing-store expansions and new-store openings until 20X3. How much new financing will Gap need, or how much cash would Gap have available for additional investment during the year ended January 31, 20X2?

DE7-20 Florida Progreso Growers is a major food cooperative. The company begins 2002 with cash of $6 million. Florida Progreso estimates cash receipts during 2002 will total $147 million. Planned disbursements for the year will require cash of $158 million. To meet daily cash needs, Florida Progreso must maintain a cash balance of at least $5 million.

Prepare Florida Progreso's cash budget for 2002.

DE7-21 Peter Larson, an accountant for BSI Consulting, discovers that his supervisor, Rose Kwan, made several errors last year. Overall, the errors overstated BSI's net income by 20%. It is not clear whether the errors were deliberate or accidental. What should Larson do?

Making an ethical judgment
(Obj. 7)

EXERCISES

E7-1 Consider this adaptation of a *Wall Street Journal* article:

Correcting an internal control weakness
(Obj. 2)

TOKYO—Toshima Corp., a Japanese trading company, said unauthorized trades by its former head of copper trading caused losses that may total $1.8 billion. Toshima learned of the damage when Yuji Takeda confessed to making unauthorized trades that led to losses over a 10-year period. Mr. Takeda concealed the losses by falsifying Toshima's books and records.

What internal control weakness at Toshima allowed this loss to grow so large? How could the company have avoided and/or limited the size of the loss?

E7-2 The following situations describe two cash receipts situations and two equipment purchase situations. In each pair, one situation's internal controls are significantly better than the other's. Evaluate the internal controls in each situation as strong or weak, and give the reason for your answers.

Identifying internal control strengths and weaknesses
(Obj. 1)

Cash Receipts:

a. Cash received by mail goes straight to the accountant, who debits Cash and credits Accounts Receivable to record collections from customers. The accountant then deposits the cash in the bank.

b. Cash received by mail goes to the mail room, where a mail clerk opens envelopes and totals the cash receipts for the day. The mail clerk forwards customer checks to the cashier for deposit in the bank and forwards the remittance slips to the accounting department for posting credits to customer accounts.

Equipment Purchases:

a. Centennial Homes policy calls for construction supervisors to request the equipment needed for construction jobs. The home office then purchases the equipment and has it shipped to the construction site.

b. Wayside Construction Company policy calls for project supervisors to purchase the equipment needed for construction jobs. The supervisors then submit the paid receipts to the home office for reimbursement. This policy enables supervisors to get the equipment they need quickly and keep construction jobs moving along.

E7-3 The following situations suggest a strength or a weakness in internal control. Identify each as *strength* or *weakness,* and give the reason for your answer.

Identifying internal control strengths and weaknesses.
(Obj. 2)

a. Cash received over the counter is controlled by the sales clerk, who rings up the sale and places the cash in the register. The sales clerk matches the total recorded on the control tape stored in the register to each day's cash sales.

b. The vice president who signs checks does not examine the payment packet because the accounting department has matched the invoice with other supporting documents.

c. Top managers delegate all internal control measures to the accounting department.

d. The accounting department orders merchandise and approves invoices for payment.

e. The operator of a computer has no other accounting or cash-handling duties.

E7-4 Identify the missing internal control characteristic in the following situations:

Identifying internal controls
(Obj. 2)

a. When business is brisk, Stop-n-Go and many other retail stores deposit cash in the bank several times during the day. The manager at one store wants to reduce the time employees spend delivering cash to the bank, so he starts a new policy. Cash will build up over Saturdays and Sundays, and the total two-day amount will be deposited on Sunday evening.

b. While reviewing the records of Discount Pharmacy, you find that the same employee orders merchandise and approves invoices for payment.

c. Business is slow at Fun City Amusement Park on Tuesday, Wednesday, and Thursday nights. To reduce expenses, the owner decides not to use a ticket taker on those nights. The ticket seller (cashier) is told to keep the tickets as a record of the number sold.

d. The manager of a discount store wants to speed the flow of customers through check-out. She decides to reduce the time cashiers spend making change, so she prices merchandise at round dollar amounts—such as $8.00 and $15.00—instead of the customary amounts—$7.95 and $14.95.

e. Grocery stores such as **Safeway** and **Meier's** purchase large quantities of merchandise from a few suppliers. At another grocery store, the manager decides to reduce paperwork. He eliminates the requirement that a receiving department employee prepare a receiving report, which lists the quantities of items actually received from the supplier.

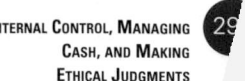

E7-5 The following questions pertain to internal control. Consider each situation separately.

a. Many managers think that safeguarding assets is the most important objective of internal control systems, while auditors emphasize internal control's role in ensuring reliable accounting data. Explain why managers are more concerned about safeguarding assets and auditors are more concerned about the quality of the accounting records.

b. Separation of duties is an important consideration if a system of internal control is to be effective. Why is this so?

c. Cash can be a relatively small item on the financial statements. Nevertheless, internal control over cash is very important. Why is this true?

d. Ling Ltd. requires that all documents supporting a check be canceled (stamped Paid) by the person who signs the check. Why do you think this practice is required? What might happen if it were not?

E7-6 The following items could appear on a bank reconciliation:

a. Book error: We debited Cash for $200. The correct debit was $2,000.
b. Outstanding checks.
c. Bank error: The bank charged our account for a check written by another customer.

d. Service charge.
e. Deposits in transit.
f. NSF check.
g. Bank collection of a note receivable on our behalf.

Required

Classify each item as (1) an addition to the book balance, (2) a subtraction from the book balance, (3) an addition to the bank balance, or (4) a subtraction from the bank balance.

E7-7 Bill Westphal's checkbook lists the following:

Date	Check No.	Item	Check	Deposit	Balance
9/1					$ 525
4	622	JD's Art Café	$ 19		506
9		Dividends received		$ 116	622
13	623	General Tire Co.	43		579
14	624	Exxon Oil Co.	58		521
18	625	Cash	50		471
26	626	Redeemer Presbyterian Church	75		396
28	627	Bent Tree Apartments	275		121
30		Paycheck		1,800	1,921

Westphal's September bank statement shows the following:

Balance				$525
Add: Deposits				116
Debit checks:	No.	Amount		
	622	$19		
	623	43		
	624	68*		
	625	50		(180)
Other charges:				
Printed checks			$ 8	
Service charge			12	(20)
Balance				$441

*This is the correct amount for check number 624.

Required

Prepare Westphal's bank reconciliation at September 30.

E7-8 Mario Bocelli operates four Quik Pak convenience stores. He has just received the monthly bank statement at October 31 from City National Bank, and the statement shows an ending balance of $2,750. Listed on the statement are an EFT rent collection of $400, a service charge of $12, two NSF checks totaling $74, and a $9 charge for printed checks. In reviewing his cash records, Bocelli identifies outstanding checks totaling $467 and an October 31 deposit in transit of $1,788. During October, he recorded a $290 check for the salary of a part-time employee by debiting Salary Expense and crediting Cash for $29. Bocelli's Cash account shows an October 31 cash balance of $4,027. *Prepare the bank reconciliation at October 31.*

Preparing a bank reconciliation
(Obj. 3)

E7-9 Using the data from Exercise 7-8, make the journal entries Bocelli should record on October 31. Include an explanation for each entry.

Making journal entries from a bank reconciliation
(Obj. 3)

E7-10 A grand jury indicted the manager of a Hickory Stick restaurant for stealing cash from the company. Over a 3-year period, the manager allegedly took almost $100,000 and attempted to cover the theft by manipulating the bank reconciliation.

Applying internal controls to the bank reconciliation
(Obj. 2, 3)

What is the most likely way that a person would manipulate a bank reconciliation to cover a theft? Be specific. What internal control arrangement could have avoided this theft?

E7-11 At the check-out of **Best Buy** stores, cash registers display the amount of each sale, the cash received from the customer, and any change returned to the customer. The registers also produce a customer receipt but keep no internal record of transactions. At the end of the day, clerks count the cash in the register and give it to the cashier for deposit in the company bank account.

Evaluating internal control over cash receipts
(Obj. 4)

Write a memo to convince the store manager that there is an internal control weakness over cash receipts. Identify the weakness that gives an employee the best opportunity to steal cash, and state how to prevent such a theft.

E7-12 Record the following selected transactions of Rosetree Florist in general journal format (explanations are not required):

Petty cash, cash short and over
(Obj. 5)

April 1 Established a petty cash fund with a $300 balance.
2 Journalized the day's cash sales. Cash register tapes show a $2,869 total, but the cash in the register is $2,873.
10 The petty cash fund has $119 in cash and $161 in petty cash tickets that were issued to pay for Office Supplies ($111), Delivery Expense ($13), and Entertainment Expense ($37). Replenished the fund and recorded the expenses.

E7-13 Operation Recycle in Seattle created a $500 imprest petty cash fund. During the first month of use, the fund custodian authorized and signed petty cash tickets as follows:

Accounting for petty cash
(Obj. 5)

Petty Cash Ticket No.	Item	Account Debited	Amount
1	Delivery of pledge cards to donors	Delivery Expense	$22.19
2	Mail package	Postage Expense	52.80
3	Newsletter	Supplies Expense	34.14
4	Key to closet	Miscellaneous Expense	2.85
5	Wastebasket	Miscellaneous Expense	13.78
6	Computer diskettes	Supplies Expense	85.37

Required

1. Make the general journal entries that **(a)** first create the petty cash fund and **(b)** show its replenishment. Include explanations.
2. Describe the items in the fund immediately before replenishment.
3. Describe the items in the fund immediately after replenishment.

E7-14 Suppose **Sprint Corporation,** the long-distance telephone company, is preparing its cash budget for 20X4. The company ended 20X3 with $135 million, and top management foresees the need for a cash balance of at least $137 million to pay all bills as they come due in 20X4.

Preparing a cash budget
(Obj. 6)

Collections from customers are expected to total $11,813 million during 20X4, and payments for the cost of services and products should reach $6,166 million. Operating expense payments are budgeted at $2,744 million.

During 20X4, Sprint expects to invest $1,826 million in new equipment, $275 million in the company's cellular division, and to sell older assets for $116 million. Debt payments scheduled for 20X4 will total $597 million. The company forecasts net income of $890 million for 20X4 and plans to pay $338 million to its owners.

Required

Prepare Sprint's cash budget for 20X4. Will the budgeted level of cash receipts leave Sprint with the desired ending cash balance of $137 million, or will the company need additional financing?

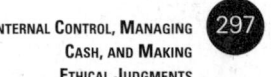

Evaluating the ethics of conduct
by government legislators
(Obj. 7)

E7-15 Approximately 300 current and former members of the U.S. House of Representatives—on a regular basis—wrote a quarter million dollars of checks on the House bank without having the cash in their accounts. In effect, the delinquent check writers were borrowing money from each other on an interest-free, no-service-charge basis. The House closed its bank after the events became public.

Required

Suppose you are a new congressional representative from your state. Apply the ethical judgment framework outlined in the Decision Guidelines feature on page 290 to decide whether you would write NSF checks on a regular basis through the House bank.

Challenge Exercise.

E7-16 ← *Link Back to Chapter 4 (Current Ratio and Debt Ratio).* Among its many products, Continental Paper Company makes paper for shopping bags, canned-food labels, and magazines. Ruth Majer, the Chief Budget Officer, is responsible for Continental's cash budget for 20X5. The budget helps Majer determine the amount of long-term borrowing needed to end the year with a cash balance of $300 million. Majer has assembled budget data for 20X5. Not all of the following items are used in preparing the cash budget. Receipts are positive amounts; payments are in parentheses.

	(In millions)
Acquisition of other companies	$ (1,168)
Actual cash balance, December 31, 20X4	340
Borrowing	?
Budgeted total assets before borrowing	23,977
Budgeted total current assets before borrowing	5,873
Budgeted total current liabilities before borrowing	4,863
Budgeted total liabilities before borrowing	16,180
Budgeted total stockholder's equity before borrowing	7,797
Collections from customers	19,467
Payments to owners	(237)
Investments by owners	516
Net income	1,153
Other cash receipts	111
Payment of long-term and short-term debt	(950)
Payment of operating expenses	(2,349)
Purchases of inventory	(14,345)
Purchase of property and equipment	(1,518)

Required

1. Prepare the cash budget to determine the amount of borrowing Continental Paper needs during 20X5.
2. Compute Continental Paper's expected current ratio and debt ratio at December 31, 20X5, both before and after borrowing on long-term debt. Assume you are the chief loan officer at a bank. Based on these figures, and on the budgeted levels of assets and liabilities, would you lend the requested amount to Continental Paper? Give the reason for your decision.

(Group A) PROBLEMS

Identifying the characteristics
of an effective internal control
system (Obj. 1, 2)

P7-1A An employee of Suntech Oil Company recently stole thousands of dollars of the company's cash. The company has installed a new system of internal controls. As a consultant for Suntech Oil Company, write a memo to the president explaining how a separation of duties helps to safeguard assets.

P7-2A The following situations have an internal control weakness.

a. Roberson Computer Programs is a software company that specializes in programs with accounting applications. The company's most popular program prepares the journal, accounts receivable subsidiary ledger, and general ledger. In the company's early days, the owner and eight employees wrote the computer programs, sold the products to stores such as ComputerWorld, and performed general management and accounting. As the company has grown, the number of employees has increased dramatically. Recently, the development of a new software program stopped while the programmers redesigned Roberson's accounting system. Roberson's accountants could have performed this task.

b. Emma Blue, a widow with no known sources of outside income, has been a trusted employee of Stone Products Company for 15 years. She performs all cash-handling and accounting duties, including opening the mail, preparing the bank deposit, accounting for all aspects of cash and accounts receivable, and preparing the bank reconciliation. She has just purchased a new Mercedes and a new home in an expensive suburb. Juan Perez, owner of the company, wonders how she can afford these luxuries.

c. Harriet Laman employs three professional interior designers in her design studio. She is located in an area with a lot of new construction, and her business is booming. Ordinarily, Laman does all the purchasing of draperies, fabrics, and labor needed to complete jobs. During the summer she takes a long vacation, and in her absence she allows each designer to purchase materials and labor. On her return, Laman observes that expenses are much higher and net income much lower than in the past.

d. Discount stores such as **Target** and **Sam's** receive a large portion of their sales revenue in cash, with the remainder in credit-card sales. To reduce expenses, one store manager ceases purchasing fidelity bonds on the cashiers.

e. The office supply company from which Champs Sporting Goods purchases cash receipt forms recently notified Champs that the last shipped receipts were not prenumbered. Alex Champ, the owner, replied that he never uses the receipt numbers.

Required

1. Identify the missing internal control characteristics in each situation.
2. Identify the business's possible problem.
3. Propose a solution to the internal control problem.

P7-3A The cash receipts and the payments of Veralux Interiors for March 20X5 follow:

Using the bank reconciliation as a control device
(Obj. 3)

Cash Receipts (Posting reference is CR)		Cash Payments (Posting reference is CP)	
Date	**Cash Debit**	**Check No.**	**Cash Credit**
Mar. 4	$2,716	1413	$1,465
9	544	1414	1,004
11	1,655	1415	450
14	896	1416	8
17	367	1417	775
25	890	1418	88
31	2,038	1419	4,126
Total	$9,106	1420	970
		1421	200
		1422	2,267
		Total	$11,353

The Cash account of Veralux Interiors shows the following on March 31, 20X5:

Cash					
Date	**Item**	**Jrnl. Ref.**	**Debit**	**Credit**	**Balance**
Mar. 1	Balance				12,188
31		CR. 10	9,106		21,294
31		CP. 16		11,353	9,941

On March 31, 20X5, Veralux Interiors received the bank statement at the top of the next page.

Additional data for the bank reconciliation:

a. The EFT deposit was a receipt of rent. The EFT debit was payment of insurance.
b. The NSF check was received late in February from Mark Anthony.
c. The $1,000 bank collection of a note receivable on March 31 included $122 interest revenue.
d. The correct amount of check number 1419, a payment on account, is $4,216. (The Veralux Interiors accountant mistakenly recorded the check for $4,126.)

Bank Statement for March 20X5			

Beginning balance		$12,188	
Deposits and other Credits:			
Mar. 1..	$ 625 EFT		
5..	2,716		
10..	544		
11..	1,655		
15..	896		
18..	367		
25..	890		
31..	1,000 BC	8,693	
Checks and other Debits:			
Mar. 8..	$ 441 NSF		
9..	1,465		
13..	1,004		
14..	450		
15..	8		
19..	340 EFT		
22..	775		
29..	88		
31..	4,216		
31..	25 SC	(8,812)	
Ending balance		$12,069	

Explanations: BC—bank collection, EFT—electronic funds transfer,
NSF—nonsufficient funds check, SC—service charge.

Required

1. Prepare the bank reconciliation of Veralux Interiors at March 31, 20X5.
2. Describe how a bank account and the bank reconciliation help Veralux managers control the business's cash.

Preparing a bank reconciliation and the related journal entries (Obj. 3)

P7-4A The May 31 bank statement of Payne Stationers has just arrived from First State Bank. To prepare the Payne bank reconciliation, you gather the following data.

a. The May 31 bank balance is $21,110.82.
b. The bank statement includes two charges for returned checks from customers. One is an NSF check in the amount of $67.50 received from Sarah Batten, a student, recorded on the books by a debit to Cash, and deposited on May 19. The other is a $195.03 check received from Lena Masters and deposited on May 21. It was returned by Masters' bank with the imprint "Unauthorized Signature."
c. The following Payne checks are outstanding at May 31:

Check No.	Amount
616	$403.00
802	74.25
806	36.60
809	161.38
810	229.05
811	48.91

d. Payne Stationers collects from a few customers by EFT. The May bank statement lists a $200 deposit for a collection on account from customer Jack Oates.
e. The bank statement includes two special deposits: $899.14, which is the amount of dividend revenue the bank collected from General Electric Company on behalf of Payne, and $16.86, the interest revenue Payne earned on its bank balance during May.
f. The bank statement lists a $6.25 subtraction for the bank service charge.
g. On May 31, the Payne treasurer deposited $381.14, but this deposit does not appear on the bank statement.
h. The bank statement includes a $410.00 deduction for a check drawn by Marimont Freight Company. Payne promptly notified the bank of its error.
i. Payne's Cash account shows a balance of $20,101.55 on May 31.

Required

1. Prepare the bank reconciliation for Payne Stationers at May 31.
2. Record the entries necessary to bring the book balance of Cash into agreement with the adjusted book balance on the reconciliation. Include an explanation for each entry.

P7-5A East Coast Heating makes all sales on credit. Cash receipts arrive by mail. Kenneth Sartain opens envelopes and separates the checks from the accompanying remittance advices. Sartain forwards the checks to another employee, who makes the daily bank deposit but has no access to the accounting records. Sartain sends the remittance advices, which show cash received, to the accounting department for entry in the accounts. Sartain's only other duty is to grant sales allowances to customers. (Recall that a *sales allowance* decreases the amount receivable.) When Sartain receives a customer check for less than the full amount of the invoice, he records the sales allowance and forwards the document to the accounting department.

Identifying internal control weakness in cash receipts
(Obj. 4)

Required

You are a new employee of East Coast Heating. Write a memo to the company president identifying the internal control weakness in this situation. State how to correct the weakness.

P7-6A On April 1, Sealy Electronics creates a petty cash fund with an imprest balance of $400. During April, Elise Nelson, the fund custodian, signs the petty cash tickets:

Accounting for petty cash transactions
(Obj. 5)

Petty Cash Ticket Number	Item	Amount
101	Office supplies	$86.89
102	Cab fare for executive	25.00
103	Delivery of package across town	37.75
104	Dinner money for sales manager entertaining a customer	80.00
105	Inventory	85.70
106	Decorations for office party	19.22
107	Six boxes of floppy disks	44.37

On April 30, prior to replenishment, the fund contains these tickets plus $17.36. The accounts affected by petty cash payments are Office Supplies Expense, Travel Expense, Delivery Expense, Entertainment Expense, and Freight In.

Required

1. Explain the characteristics and the internal control features of an imprest fund.
2. Make the general journal entries to (a) create the fund and (b) replenish it. Include explanations. Also, briefly describe what the custodian does on April 1 and April 30.
3. Make the May 1 entry to increase the fund balance to $500. Include an explanation, and briefly describe what the custodian does.

P7-7A Suppose you are preparing your personal cash budget for the year 20X2. During 20X2, assume you expect to earn $3,600 from your summer job and $1,500 for work in the college cafeteria. Also, your family always gives you gifts totaling around $800 during the year. A scholarship from your home church adds $1,000 each year while you are in college.

Preparing a personal cash budget
(Obj. 6)

Your family pays your college costs except for room and board. Planned expenditures for 20X2 include apartment rent of $150 per month for 12 months and annual food costs of $4,800. Gas and other auto expenses usually run about $50 per month. You need to have a little fun, so entertainment will eat up $100 per month.

You need to keep a little cash in reserve for auto repairs and other emergencies, so you maintain a cash reserve of $300 at all times. To start 20X2, you have this cash reserve plus $200.

Will you need a loan during 20X2? To answer this question, prepare your personal cash budget for the year based on the data given.

P7-8A Lesa Krause, Chief Financial Officer of Datek Enterprises, is responsible for the company's budgeting process. Suppose Krause's staff is preparing the Datek cash budget for 20X9. A key input to the budgeting process is last year's statement of cash flows, which provides the data at the top of the next page for 20X8 (in millions). Cash receipts appear as positive amounts; cash payments are negative amounts, denoted within parentheses.

Preparing a cash budget
(Obj. 6)

DATEK ENTERPRISES			
Cash-Flow Data for 20X8			
Cash and Cash Equivalents			
Beginning of year 20X8	$ 764	Purchases of plant assets	$ (614)
End of year 20X8	792	Borrowings	160
Collections from customers	8,089	Long-term debt repayments	(1)
Interest revenue collected	24	Cash received for	
Purchases of inventory	(5,597)	investments by owners	30
Operating expenses paid	(1,859)	Payments to owners	(183)

Required

1. Prepare the Datek cash budget for 20X9. Date the budget "20X9" and denote the beginning and ending cash balances as "beginning" and "ending." Round to the nearest million dollars. Assume the company expects 20X9 to be similar to 20X8, but with the following changes:
   a. In 20X9, the company expects a 7% increase in collections from customers and a 5% increase in purchases of inventory.
   b. Krause plans for Datek to end the year with a cash balance of $400 million.
2. Based on the cash budget you prepared, how much additional cash does it appear that Datek will have available for other investments during 20X9?

Making an ethical judgment (Obj. 7)

P7-9A Tri State Bank in Cairo, Illinois, has a loan receivable from Cortez Manufacturing Company. Cortez is six months late in making payments to the bank, and Milton Reed, a Tri State vice president, is helping Cortez restructure its debt. Reed learns that Cortez is depending on landing a manufacturing contract from Peters & Sons, another Tri State client. Reed also serves as Peters' loan officer at the bank. In this capacity, he is aware that Peters is considering declaring bankruptcy. No one outside Peters & Sons knows this. Reed has been a great help to Cortez Manufacturing, and Cortez's owner is counting on him to carry the company through this difficult restructuring. To help the bank collect on this large loan, Reed has a strong motivation to help Cortez survive.

Apply the ethical judgment framework from the chapter to help Reed plan his next action.

(Group B) PROBLEMS

Identifying the characteristics of an effective internal control system (Obj. 1, 2)

P7-1B Caldwell-Bailey Development Company prospered during the lengthy economic expansion of the 1990s. Business was so good that the company used very few internal controls. A recent decline in the local real estate market caused Caldwell-Bailey to experience a shortage of cash. Dave Matthews, the company owner, is looking for ways to save money.

As a consultant for the company, write a memo to convince Matthews of the company's need for a system of internal control. Be specific in explaining how an internal control system could save the company money. Include the definition of internal control, and briefly discuss each characteristic of an effective internal control system, beginning with competent, reliable, and ethical personnel.

Correcting internal control weaknesses (Obj. 2, 4, 5)

P7-2B Each of the following situations has an internal control weakness.

a. Aimee Atkins has been an employee of Mary V's Bridal Salon for many years. Because the business is relatively small, Atkins performs all accounting duties, including opening the mail, preparing the bank deposit, and preparing the bank reconciliation.

b. Most large companies have internal audit staffs that continuously evaluate the business's internal control. Part of the auditor's job is to evaluate how efficiently the company is running. For example, does the company purchase inventory from the least expensive wholesaler? After a particularly bad year, Design Company eliminates its internal audit department to reduce expenses.

c. CPA firms, law firms, and other professional organizations use paraprofessional employees to perform routine tasks. For example, an accounting paraprofessional might examine documents to assist a CPA in conducting an audit. In the CPA firm of Lee & Dunham, Joseph Lee, the senior partner, turns over a significant portion of his own audit work to his paraprofessional staff.

d. In evaluating the internal control over cash payments, an auditor learns that the purchasing agent is responsible for purchasing diamonds for use in the company's manufacturing process, approving the invoices for payment, and signing the checks.

e. Blake Lemmon owns an engineering firm. His staff consists of 12 engineers, and he manages the office. Often, his work requires him to travel. He notes that when he returns from business trips, the engineering jobs in the office have not progressed much. When he is away, his senior employees take over office management and neglect their engineering duties. One employee could manage the office.

Required

1. Identify the missing internal control characteristic in each situation.
2. Identify the business's possible problem.
3. Propose a solution to the internal control problem.

P7-3B The cash receipts and the cash payments of Good Eats Café for April 20X4 are as follows:

Using the bank reconciliation as a control device
(Obj. 3)

Cash Receipts (Posting reference is CR)		Cash Payments (Posting reference is CP)	
Date	**Cash Debit**	**Check No.**	**Cash Credit**
Apr. 2	$ 4,174	3113	$ 891
8	407	3114	147
10	559	3115	1,930
16	2,187	3116	664
22	1,854	3117	1,472
29	1,060	3118	1,000
30	337	3119	632
Total	$10,578	3120	1,675
		3121	100
		3122	2,413
		Total	$10,924

The Cash account of Good Eats Café shows the following at April 30, 20X4:

Cash					
Date	**Item**	**Jrnl. Ref.**	**Debit**	**Credit**	**Balance**
Apr. 1	Balance				5,911
30		CR. 6	10,578		16,489
30		CP. 11		10,924	5,565

On April 30, 20X4, Good Eats received the bank statement shown on the top of page 304. Additional data for the bank reconciliation:

a. The EFT deposit was a receipt of rent. The EFT debit was an insurance payment.
b. The unauthorized-signature check was received from S. M. Holt.
c. The $1,368 bank collection of a note receivable included $185 interest revenue.
d. The correct amount of check number 3115, a payment on account, is $1,390. (Good Eats' accountant mistakenly recorded the check for $1,930.)

Required

1. Prepare the Good Eats Café bank reconciliation at April 30, 20X4.
2. Describe how a bank account and the bank reconciliation help Good Eats managers control the business's cash. See the bank statement at the top of page 304.

P7-4B The August 31 bank statement of Beeson Nursery has just arrived from United Bank. To prepare the Beeson bank reconciliation, you gather the following data:

Preparing a bank reconciliation and the related journal entries
(Obj. 3)

a. Beeson's Cash account shows a balance of $3,998.14 on August 31.
b. The bank statement includes two charges for returned checks from customers. One is a $395.00 check received from Lakeland Express and deposited on August 20, returned by Lakeland's bank with the imprint "Unauthorized Signature." The other is an NSF check for $146.67 received from Veracruz, Inc. This check was deposited on August 17.
c. Beeson pays rent expense ($750) and insurance expense ($290) each month by EFT.

(continued near the middle of page 304)

Bank Statement for April 20X4		
Beginning balance..........................		$ 5,911
Deposits and other Credits:		
Apr. 1..	$ 326 EFT	
4..	4,174	
9..	407	
12..	559	
17..	2,187	
22..	1,368 BC	
23..	1,854	10,875
Checks and other Debits:		
Apr. 7..	$ 891	
13..	1,390	
14..	903 US	
15..	147	
18..	664	
21..	219 EFT	
26..	1,472	
30..	1,000	
30..	20 SC	(6,706)
Ending balance..............................		$10,080

Explanations: EFT—electronic funds transfer, BC—bank collection, US—unauthorized signature, SC—service charge.

d. The Beeson checks below are outstanding at August 31.

Check No.	Amount
237	$ 46.10
288	141.00
291	578.05
293	11.87
294	609.51
295	8.88
296	101.63

e. The bank statement includes a deposit of $1,191.17, collected by the bank on behalf of Beeson Nursery. Of the total, $1,011.81 is collection of a note receivable, and the remainder is interest revenue.

f. The bank statement shows that Beeson earned $38.19 of interest on its bank balance during August. This amount was added to Beeson's account by the bank.

g. The bank statement lists a $10.50 subtraction for the bank service charge.

h. On August 31, the Beeson treasurer deposited $316.15, but this deposit does not appear on the bank statement.

i. The bank statement includes a $300.00 deposit that Beeson did not make. The bank erroneously credited the Beeson account for another bank customer's deposit.

j. The August 31 bank balance is $5,116.22.

Required

1. Prepare the bank reconciliation for Beeson Nursery at August 31.

2. Record the journal entries necessary to bring the book balance of Cash into agreement with the adjusted book balance on the reconciliation. Include an explanation for each entry.

Identifying internal control weakness in cash receipts
(Obj. 4)

P7-5B SpreadMax, Inc., makes all sales of its spreadsheet software on credit. Cash receipts arrive by mail. Nick Vaughn opens envelopes and separates the checks from the accompanying remittance advices. Vaughn forwards the checks to another employee, who makes the daily bank deposit but has no access to the accounting records. Vaughn sends the remittance advices, which show the cash received, to the accounting department for entry in the accounts. Vaughn's only other duty is to grant sales allowances to customers. (Recall that a *sales allowance* decreases the amount receivable.) When he receives a customer check for less than the full amount of the invoice, he records the sales allowance and forwards the document to the accounting department.

Required

You are a new employee of SpreadMax, Inc. Write a memo to the company president identifying the internal control weakness in this situation. State how to correct the weakness.

P7-6B Suppose that on June 1, Alpha Audio-Video opens a district office in Omaha and creates a petty cash fund with an imprest balance of $350. During June, Carol McColgin, fund custodian, signs the following petty cash tickets:

Accounting for petty cash transactions (Obj. 5)

Petty Cash Ticket Number	Item	Amount
1	Postage for package received	$ 18.40
2	Decorations and refreshments for office party	13.19
3	Two boxes of floppy disks	20.82
4	Printer cartridges	27.13
5	Dinner money for sales manager entertaining a customer	50.00
6	Plane ticket for executive business trip to Memphis	169.00
7	Delivery of package across town	6.30

On June 30, prior to replenishment, the fund contains these tickets plus cash of $42.37. The accounts affected by petty cash payments are Office Supplies Expense, Travel Expense, Delivery Expense, Entertainment Expense, and Postage Expense.

Required

1. Explain the characteristics and the internal control features of an imprest fund.
2. Make the general journal entries to (a) create the fund and (b) replenish it. Include explanations. Also, briefly describe what the custodian does on these dates.
3. Make the entry on July 1 to increase the fund balance to $500. Include an explanation, and briefly describe what the custodian does.

P7-7B Suppose you are preparing your personal cash budget for 20X2. During 20X2, assume that you can expect to earn $3,000 from your summer job and $2,000 for work in the college cafeteria. Also, your family always gives you gifts totaling around $300 during the year. A scholarship from your home church adds $500 each year while you are in college.

Preparing a personal cash budget (Obj. 6)

Assume your family pays your college costs except for room and board. Planned expenditures for 20X2 include apartment rent of $175 per month for 12 months and annual food costs of $5,000. Gas and other auto expenses usually run about $50 per month. You need to have a little fun, so entertainment will eat up $125 per month.

You need some cash in reserve for auto repairs and other emergencies, so you maintain a cash reserve of $500 at all times. To start 20X2, you have this cash reserve plus $100.

Will you need a loan during 20X2? To answer this question, prepare your personal cash budget for the year based on the data given.

P7-8B Len Filer, Chief Financial Officer of Toys.com, is responsible for the company's budgeting process. Filer's staff is preparing the company's cash budget for 20X1. A key input to the budgeting process is last year's statement of cash flows, which provides the data in the table (in millions) for 20X0. Cash receipts appear as positive amounts; cash payments are negative amounts, denoted within parentheses.

Preparing a cash budget (Obj. 6)

TOYS.COM
Cash-Flow Data for 20X0

Cash and Cash Equivalents

Beginning of year 20X0.............	$ 370	Purchases of plant assets.............	$(535)
End of year 20X0.......................	203	Borrowings	292
Collections from customers	9,414	Long-term debt repayments	(9)
Interest revenue collected..........	17	Cash received for	
Purchases of inventory	(6,750)	investments by owners	16
Operating expenses paid............	(2,431)	Payments to owners	(200)

Required

1. Prepare the Toys.com cash budget for 20X1. Date the budget "20X1" and denote the beginning and ending cash balances as "beginning" and "ending." Round to the nearest million dollars. Assume the company expects 20X1 to be the same as 20X0, but with the following changes:
   a. In 20X1, the company expects a 9% increase in collections from customers and an 8% increase in purchases of inventory.
   b. Filer plans for the company to end the year with a cash balance of $400 million.

2. Based on the cash budget you prepared, how much additional financing will Toys.com need beyond the borrowings already scheduled for 20X1?

Making an ethical judgment
(Obj. 7)

P7-9B Beth Youngdale is vice president of Stateline Loan Associates in Yellowstone, Wyoming. Active in community affairs, Youngdale serves on the board of directors of Baker Publishing Company. Baker is expanding and relocating its plant. At a recent meeting, board members decided to buy 15 acres of land on the edge of town. The owner of the property, Jack Fletcher, is a customer of Stateline Loan. Fletcher is completing a divorce, and Youngdale knows that Fletcher is eager to sell his property. In view of Fletcher's difficult situation, Youngdale believes he would accept almost any offer for the land. Realtors have appraised the property at $5 million.

Apply the ethical judgment framework from the Decision Guidelines feature (page 290) to help Youngdale decide what her role should be in Baker's attempt to buy the land from Fletcher.

APPLY YOUR KNOWLEDGE

DECISION CASES

Using the bank reconciliation to detect a theft
(Obj. 3)

Case 1. Flexall Plastics Company has poor internal control over its cash transactions. Genevieve Gilbreath, the owner, suspects Sam Knicks, the cashier, of stealing. Here are some details of the business's cash position at September 30.

a. The Cash account shows a balance of $17,502. This amount includes a September 30 deposit of $3,794 that does not appear on the September 30 bank statement.

b. The September 30 bank statement shows a balance of $14,124. The bank statement lists a $200 credit for a bank collection, an $8 debit for the service charge, and a $36 debit for an NSF check. The Flexall accountant has not recorded any of these items on the books.

c. At September 30, the following checks are outstanding:

Check No.	Amount
154	$116
256	150
278	353
291	190
292	206
293	145

d. The cashier handles all incoming cash and makes bank deposits. He also reconciles the monthly bank statement. Here is his September 30 reconciliation:

Balance per books, September 30.............			$17,502
Add: Outstanding checks........................			260
Bank collection			200
			17,962
Less: Deposits in transit	$3,794		
Service charge...............................	8		
NSF check	36		3,838
Balance per bank, September 30..............			$14,124

Gilbreath asks you to determine whether the cashier has stolen cash from the business and, if so, how much. She also asks how the cashier concealed the theft. Perform your own bank reconciliation using the format illustrated in the chapter. There are no bank or book errors. Gilbreath also wants your input on changes that will improve Flexall's internal controls.

Correcting an internal control weakness
(Obj. 1, 5)

Case 2. This case is based on an actual situation. A-1 Construction Company, headquartered in Terre Haute, Indiana, built a Rest Easy Motel 35 miles east of Terre Haute. The construction foreman, whose name was Monty, hired the 40 workers needed to complete the project. Monty had the construction workers fill out the necessary tax forms, and sent the employment documents to the home office, which opened a payroll file for each employee.

Work on the motel began on April 1 and ended September 1. Each week, Monty filled out a time card of the hours worked by each employee during the week. Monty faxed the time sheets to the home office, which prepared the payroll checks on Friday morning. Monty drove to the home office after lunch on Friday, picked up the payroll checks, and returned to the construction site. At 5 P.M. on Friday, Monty distributed the payroll checks to the workers.

a. Describe in detail the main internal control weakness in this situation. Specify what negative result(s) could occur because of the internal control weakness.

b. Describe what you would do to correct the internal control weakness.

ETHICAL ISSUE

Internal control over cash payments; ethical considerations (Obj. 5, 7)

Jill Hudson owns apartment buildings in Oklahoma. Each property has a manager who collects rent, arranges for repairs, and runs advertisements in the local newspaper. The property managers transfer cash to Hudson monthly and prepare their own bank reconciliations. The manager in Tulsa has been stealing large sums of money. To cover the theft, he understates the amount of the outstanding checks on the monthly bank reconciliation. As a result, each monthly bank reconciliation appears to balance. However, the balance sheet reports more cash than Hudson actually has in the bank. In negotiating the sale of the Tulsa property, Hudson is showing the balance sheet to prospective investors.

Required

1. Identify two parties other than Hudson who can be harmed by this theft. In what ways can they be harmed?
2. Discuss the role accounting plays in this situation.

FINANCIAL STATEMENT CASE

Internal controls and cash (Obj. 1, 3)

Study the responsibility statement (labeled Report of Management) and the audit opinion (labeled Report of Independent Auditors) of **Target Corporation,** financial statements given at the end of Appendix A. Answer the following questions about the company's internal controls and cash position.

Required

1. What is the name of Target's outside auditing firm (independent auditors)? What office of this firm signed the audit report? How long after the Target year end did the auditors issue their opinion?
2. Who bears primary responsibility for the financial statements? How can you tell?
3. Does it appear that the Target internal controls are adequate? How can you tell?
4. What standard of auditing did the outside auditors use in examining the Target financial statements? By what accounting standards were the statements evaluated?
5. By how much did Target's cash balance (including cash equivalent) change during the year ended January 29, 2000? What were the beginning and ending cash balances?

TEAM PROJECT

You are promoting a rock concert in your area. Each member of your team will invest $10,000 of their hard-earned money in this venture. It is April 1, and the concert is on June 30. Your promotional activities begin immediately, and ticket sales start on May 1. You expect to sell all the business's assets, pay all the liabilities, and distribute all remaining cash to the group members by July 31.

Required

Write an internal control manual that will help safeguard the assets of the business. The starting point of the manual is to assign responsibilities among the group members. Authorize individuals, including group members and any outsiders that you need to hire, to perform specific jobs. Separate duties among the group and any employees.

INTERNET EXERCISE

Telemate.Net Software, Inc.

Corporate managers face internal control and ethical challenges with Internet access at the fingertips of many employees. Is it okay for an employee to log on to make a quick personal stock trade? What about sending personal e-mail, checking sports team scores, playing games, visiting chat rooms, or shopping online? These dilemmas face corporate America every day.

1. Discuss several internal control issues that may concern management regarding personal use of the Internet by employees during working hours.
2. Do any special issues arise for company e-mail?
3. Many web sites can trace and identify the company making visits. Do any special issues arise as to which Web sites are accessed by company employees?
4. Expanded Internet use has created a new industry to monitor Web site visits and the duration of employee time online. Go to **http://www.telemate.net/** and read the information displayed. What services does this company provide?
5. Go to **http://www.Forbes.com.** Under "Stocks" type *TMNT,* the stock symbol for **Telemate.Net Software, Inc.,** and then click on *Go.* In the left-hand column, click on *Financials.* Use the latest financial information to answer the following questions:
   a. Is the demand for the services and products of Telemate.Net Software, Inc., increasing? How can you tell?
   b. For the most recent year was Telemate.Net Software, Inc., profitable?
   c. How much did Cash/Equivalents increase (decrease) during the current year? Compute Telemate's current ratio at the most recent financial statement date.

APPENDIX TO CHAPTER 7

THE VOUCHER SYSTEM

The voucher system for recording cash payments improves internal control over cash payments by formalizing the process of approving and recording invoices for payment. The voucher system uses (1) vouchers, (2) a voucher register (similar to a purchases journal), (3) an unpaid voucher file, (4) a check register (similar to a cash payments journal), and (5) a paid voucher file. The improvement in internal control comes from recording all payments through the voucher register. In a voucher system, all expenditures must be approved before payment can be made. This approval takes the form of a voucher. The larger the business, the more likely it is to need strict control over payments. The voucher system helps supply this control.

VOUCHER. Instrument authorizing a cash payment.

A **voucher** is a document authorizing a cash payment. The accounting department prepares vouchers. Exhibit 7A-1 illustrates the voucher of Bliss Wholesale Company. In addition to places for writing in the *payee, due date, terms, description,* and *invoice amount,* the voucher includes a section for designated officers to sign their approval for payment. The back of the voucher has places for recording the *account debited, date paid,* and *check number.* You should locate these eight items in Exhibit 7A-1.

EXHIBIT 7A-1 **Voucher**

Voucher No. 326			
BLISS WHOLESALE COMPANY			
Payee Address	Van Heusen, Inc.		
	4619 Shotwell Avenue		
	Brooklyn, NY 10564		
Due Date	March 7		
Terms	2/10, n/30		

Date	Invoice No.	Description	Amount
Mar. 1	6380	144 men's shirts stock no. X14	$1,764

Approved *Jane Trent* Controller Approved *Bob Kraft* Treasurer

Front of Voucher

Voucher No. 326
Payee Van Heusen, Inc.
Invoice Amount $1,800
Discount 36
Net Amount $1,764
Due Date Mar. 7
Date Paid Mar. 6
Check No. 694

Account Distribution			
Account Debited	Acct. No.	Amount	
Inventory	105	1,800	
Store Supplies	145		
Salary Expense	538		
Advertising Expense	542		
Utilities Expense	548		
Delivery Expense	544		
Total		$1,800	

Back of Voucher

Exhibit 7A-2 lists the various business documents used to ensure that the company receives the goods it ordered and pays only for the goods it receives. Exhibit 7A-3 shows how a voucher added to the other documents can provide the evidence for a cash payment. The amounts on all these documents should agree.

Exhibit 7A-2
Purchasing Process

Business Document	Prepared by	Sent to
Purchase request	Sales department	Purchasing department
Purchase order	Purchasing department	Outside company that sells the needed merchandise (supplier or vendor)
Invoice	Outside company that sells the needed merchandise (supplier or vendor)	Accounting department
Receiving report	Receiving department	Accounting department
Voucher	Accounting department	Officer who signs the check

Exhibit 7A-3
Voucher Packet

8

Accounts and Notes Receivable

www.prenhall.com/horngren

Readiness Assessment

In the **New York Jets** locker room, pregame reviews have taken on a whole new look. Gone are the old-style playbooks with *X-and-O* diagrams of opponents' alignments. In their place is an exciting world of multimedia.

Desktop computers turn football formations into live animation. With help from **Oracle Corporation,** Carl Banks, the Jets' director of player development, has turned passive training into an interactive success. Using Developer/2000 and multimedia software, Banks has developed a state-of-the-art teaching model that gives the Jets a competitive edge. Banks states: "By the time [the players] hit the practice field, [they] lose the ability to visualize *X's* and *O's* as actual plays. Oracle [helps] create a learning environment that increases [players'] retention by as much as 250%."

Oracle is the word's second largest software company. With annual revenues exceeding $8.0 billion, the company offers its products and services in more than 145 countries around the world.

Source: Adapted from Oracle Corporation's Web site.

With exciting new products and services like Developer/2000, **Oracle** is growing rapidly. Revenues are increasing, and so are the company's receivables. Accounts receivable (also called trade receivables) are the company's largest asset. Receivables present an accounting challenge: How much of its receivables will the company be able to collect in cash? This chapter shows how to answer this and other questions about receivables. It also covers notes receivable, a more formal type of receivable supported by a written promise.

Like most other assets, accounts receivable can represent good news or bad news: Good news because receivables represent a claim to the customer's cash; bad news when the business fails to collect the cash.

A *receivable* arises when a business (or person) sells goods or services to a second business (or person) on credit. The receivable is the seller's claim against the buyer for the amount of the transaction. Each credit transaction involves at least two parties:

- The **creditor** sells goods or a service and obtains a receivable, which is an asset.
- The **debtor** makes the purchase and has a payable, which is a liability.

This chapter focuses on accounting for receivables by the seller (the creditor).

RECEIVABLES: AN INTRODUCTION

The Types of Receivables

Receivables are monetary claims against businesses and individuals. The two major types of receivables are accounts receivable and notes receivable. A business's *accounts receivable* are the amounts to be collected from customers. Accounts receivable, which are *current assets,* are also called *trade receivables.*

The Accounts Receivable account in the general ledger serves as a *control account.* It summarizes the total amounts receivable from all customers. Companies also keep a *subsidiary ledger* of accounts receivable with a separate account for each customer, illustrated at the top of the next page. *Notes receivable* are more formal than accounts receivable. The debtor for a note receivable promises in writing to pay the creditor a definite sum at a future date—the *maturity* date. A written document known as a *promissory note* serves as evidence of the receivable. The note may require the debtor to pledge *security* for the loan: This means the borrower promises that the lender can claim certain assets if the borrower fails to pay the amount due at maturity.

Notes receivable due within one year or less are current assets. Notes due beyond one year are *long-term receivables.* Some notes receivable are collected in periodic installments. The portion due within one year is a current asset, and the

CREDITOR. The party to a credit transaction who sells goods or a service and obtains a receivable.

DEBTOR. The party to a credit transaction who makes a purchase and has a payable.

RECEIVABLES. Monetary claims against a business or individual.

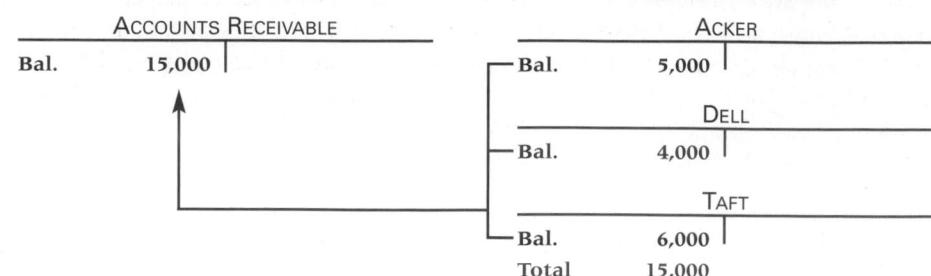

remaining amount is a long-term asset. **General Motors** may hold a $6,000 note receivable from you, but only the $2,000 you owe this year is a current asset to GM. The remaining $4,000 is a long-term receivable.

Other receivables is a miscellaneous category that includes loans to employees and subsidiary companies. Usually, these are long-term receivables, but they are current assets if due within one year or less. Long-term notes receivable and other receivables are often reported on the balance sheet, as illustrated in Exhibit 8-1. Receivables are highlighted for emphasis.

EXHIBIT 8-1 **Balance Sheet with Receivables Highlighted for Emphasis**

EXAMPLE COMPANY
Balance Sheet
Date

Assets			Liabilities		
Current:			Current:		
Cash..		$X,XXX	Accounts payable		$X,XXX
Accounts receivable...........................	$X,XXX		Notes payable, short-term...................		X,XXX
Less: Allowance for			Accrued current liabilities...................		X,XXX
uncollectible accounts	(XXX)	X,XXX	Total current liabilities........................		X,XXX
Notes receivable, short-term		X,XXX			
Inventories		X,XXX			
Prepaid expenses		X,XXX			
Total...		X,XXX	Long-term:		
Investments and long-term receivables:			Notes payable, long-term		X,XXX
Investments in other companies		X,XXX	Total liabilities		X,XXX
Notes receivable, long-term		X,XXX			
Other receivables...............................		X,XXX			
Total...		X,XXX	**Owner Equity**		
Plant assets:					
Property, plant, and equipment		X,XXX	Capital...		X,XXX
Total assets		$X,XXX	Total liabilities and owner equity............		$X,XXX

Establishing Internal Control over Collection of Receivables

Businesses that sell on credit receive most cash receipts by mail. Internal control over collections of cash on account is an important part of the overall internal control system (see Chapter 7). A critical element of internal control is the separation of cash-handling and cash-accounting duties. Consider the following case.

> **Butler Supply Co. is a family-owned office supply business that takes pride in the loyalty of its workers. Most company employees have been with the Butlers for years. The company makes 90% of its sales on account.**
>
> **The office staff consists of a bookkeeper and a supervisor. The bookkeeper maintains the accounts receivable subsidiary ledger. He also makes the daily bank deposit. The supervisor prepares monthly financial statements and special reports.**

Can you identify the internal control weakness here? The bookkeeper has access to the accounts receivable subsidiary ledger, and also has custody of the cash. The bookkeeper could steal a customer check and write off the customer's account as uncollectible.[1] Unless the supervisor or some other manager reviews the bookkeeper's work, the theft may go undetected. In a small business like Butler Supply Co., such a review may never be performed.

How can this control weakness be corrected? The supervisor could open incoming mail and make the daily bank deposit. *The bookkeeper should not be allowed to handle cash.* Only the remittance advices would go to the bookkeeper to indicate which customer accounts to credit. By removing cash-handling duties from the bookkeeper, the company strengthens internal control.

Using a bank lock box achieves the same result. Customers send payments directly to Butler Supply's bank, which deposits the cash into the company's bank account. ➤➤

 DAILY EXERCISE 8-2

◀ We examined the lock-box system in detail in Chapter 7, p. 275.

Managing the Collection of Receivables: The Credit Department

Most companies have a department to evaluate customers who apply for credit. The extension of credit requires a balancing act. The company doesn't want to lose sales to good customers who need time to pay. It also wants to avoid selling to deadbeats.

 DAILY EXERCISE 8-3

For good internal control over the collections of receivables, it is critical that the credit department have no access to cash. For example, if a credit employee handles cash, he can pocket money received from a customer. He can then label the customer's account as uncollectible, and the accounting department will write off the account receivable, as discussed in the next section. The company stops billing the customer, and the credit employee has covered up the embezzlement. For this reason, a sharp separation of duties is important indeed.

The Decision Guidelines feature identifies the main issues in controlling, managing, and accounting for receivables. These guidelines serve as a framework for the remainder of the chapter.

DECISION GUIDELINES

Controlling, Managing, and Accounting for Receivables

The main issues in *controlling* and *managing* the collection of receivables, plus a plan of action, are as follows:

ISSUE	ACTION
Extend credit only to customers most likely to pay.	Run a credit check on prospective customers.
Separate cash-handling, credit, and accounting duties to keep employees from stealing the cash collected from customers.	Design the internal control system to separate duties.
Pursue collection from customers to maximize cash flow.	Keep a close eye on collections from customers.

The main issues in *accounting* for receivables, and the related plan of action, are as follows:

ISSUE	ACTION
Measure and report receivables on the balance sheet at their *net realizable value,* the amount we expect to collect. This is necessary to report assets accurately.	Estimate the amount of uncollectible receivables.
Measure and report the expense associated with failure to collect receivables, which we call *uncollectible-account expense,* on the income statement. This helps to report net income at a reasonable amount.	Report receivables at their net realizable value (accounts receivable minus the allowance for uncollectibles). Measure the expense of failing to collect from customers.

---

[1]The bookkeeper would need to forge the endorsements on the checks and deposit them in a bank account he controls.

ACCOUNTING FOR UNCOLLECTIBLE ACCOUNTS (BAD DEBTS)

Selling on credit creates both a benefit and a cost.

- *The benefit:* The business increases revenues and profits by making sales to good customers who cannot pay cash immediately.
- *The cost:* The company will be unable to collect from some customers, and that creates an expense, which is called **uncollectible-account expense, doubtful-account expense,** or **bad-debt expense.**

Uncollectible-account expense varies from company to company. In certain businesses, a six-month-old receivable of $1 is worth only 67 cents, and a five-year-old receivable of $1 is worth only 4 cents. The older the receivable, the less valuable it is because of the increasing likehood that the customer will not pay. For **Oracle Corporation,** featured in the chapter opening story, each $1 of accounts receivable is worth 91 cents.

For a firm that sells on credit, uncollectible-account expense is as much a part of doing business as salary expense and utilities expense. Uncollectible-Account Expense—an operating expense—must be measured, recorded, and reported. To do so, accountants use the allowance method or, in certain limited cases, the direct write-off method (which we discuss on page 318).

The Allowance Method

Accountants in firms with large credit sales use the **allowance method** to measure bad debts. This method does not wait to see which customers the business will not collect from. Instead, it records collection losses on the basis of estimates. In this sense, the allowance method can be viewed as an *indirect* approach.

Rather than try to guess which accounts will go bad, managers estimate the total bad-debt expense for the period on the basis of the company's experience. The business records Uncollectible-Account Expense for the estimated amount and sets up **Allowance for Uncollectible Accounts** (or **Allowance for Doubtful Accounts**), a contra account to Accounts Receivable. This allowance account shows the amount of receivables the business expects *not* to collect.

Subtracting the uncollectible allowance amount from Accounts Receivable yields the net amount the company does expect to collect, as shown here (using Oracle Corporation's actual figures, in millions):

Balance sheet (partial):

Accounts receivable	$2,455
Less: Allowance for uncollectible accounts	(217)
Accounts receivable, net	$2,238

Customers owe Oracle $2,455 million, of which Oracle expects to collect $2,238 million. Oracle estimates it will not collect $217 million of these accounts receivable.

Another way to report receivables follows the pattern actually used by Oracle and other companies, as adapted from the Oracle balance sheet (in millions):

Accounts receivable, net of allowance for uncollectible accounts of $217	$2,238

The income statement can report Uncollectible-Account Expense (Doubtful-Account Expense) among the operating expenses, as follows (assumed figures):

Income statement (partial):

Expenses:	
Uncollectible-account expense	$4,000

UNCOLLECTIBLE-ACCOUNT EXPENSE. Cost to the seller of extending credit. Arises from the failure to collect from credit customers. Also called **doubtful-account expense,** or **bad-debt expense.**

ALLOWANCE METHOD. A method of recording collection losses on the basis of estimates, instead of waiting to see which customers the company will not collect from.

ALLOWANCE FOR UNCOLLECTIBLE ACCOUNTS. A contra account, related to accounts receivable, that holds the estimated amount of collection losses. Also called **Allowance for Doubtful Accounts.**

DAILY EXERCISE 8-4

Estimating Uncollectibles

The more accurate the estimate of uncollectibles, the more reliable the financial statements. How are bad-debt estimates made? Companies examine their past records. There are two basic ways to estimate uncollectibles:

Objective 2
Use the allowance method to account for uncollectibles by the percent-of-sales and aging methods

- Percentage-of-sales method
- Aging-of-accounts method

Both approaches work with the allowance method.

PERCENT-OF-SALES METHOD The **percent-of-sales method** computes uncollectible-account expense as a percentage of net credit sales. This method is also called the **income statement approach** because it focuses on the amount of expense to be reported on the income statement. Uncollectible-account expense is recorded as an adjusting entry at the end of the period. Assume it is December 31, 20X3, and the accounts have these balances *before the year-end adjustments:*

PERCENT-OF-SALES METHOD. A method of estimating uncollectible receivables that calculates uncollectible-account expense. Also called the **income statement approach.**

ACCOUNTS RECEIVABLE		ALLOWANCE FOR UNCOLLECTIBLE ACCOUNTS	
120,000			500

Customers owe the business $120,000, and the Allowance for Uncollectible Accounts is only $500. The $500 balance is left over from the preceding period. Prior to any adjustments, the net receivable amount is $119,500 ($120,000 − $500), which is more than the business expects to collect from customers.

Based on prior experience, the credit department estimates that uncollectible-account expense is 1.5% of net credit sales, which were $500,000 for 20X3. The adjusting entry to record uncollectible-account expense for the year and to update the allowance is

```
20X3
   Dec. 31        Uncollectible-Account Expense
                  ($500,000 × 0.015) ...........................................   7,500
                        Allowance for Uncollectible Accounts.......         7,500
                  Recorded expense for the year.
```

The accounting equation shows that the transaction to record the expense decreases the business's assets by the amount of the expense:

ASSETS	=	LIABILITIES	+	OWNER'S EQUITY	−	EXPENSES
−7,500	=	0			−	7,500

Now the accounts are ready for reporting in the 20X3 financial statements.

ACCOUNTS RECEIVABLE		ALLOWANCE FOR UNCOLLECTIBLE ACCOUNTS	
120,000			500
			7,500
			8,000

DAILY EXERCISE 8-5

Customers still owe the business $120,000, but now the allowance for uncollectible accounts is realistic. The balance sheet will report accounts receivable at the net amount of $112,000 ($120,000 − $8,000). The income statement will report the period's uncollectible-account expense of $7,500, along with the other operating expenses for the period.

AGING-OF-ACCOUNTS The second popular approach for estimating uncollectibles is the **aging-of-accounts method.** This method is also called the **balance sheet approach** because it focuses on accounts receivable. Individual accounts receivable from specific customers are analyzed according to the length of time they have been receivable from the customer.

Computerized accounting packages now routinely age the accounts receivable. The computer sorts customer accounts by number and date of invoice. For example,

AGING-OF-ACCOUNTS METHOD. A way to estimate bad debts by analyzing individual accounts receivable according to the length of time they have been receivable from the customer. Also called the **balance-sheet approach.**

EXHIBIT 8-2 Aging the Accounts Receivable of Schmidt Builders Supply

| | Age of Account | | | | |
Customer Name	1–30 Days	31–60 Days	61–90 Days	Over 90 Days	Total Balance
T-Bar-M Co.	$20,000				$ 20,000
Chicago Pneumatic Parts..	10,000				10,000
Sarasota Pipe Corp.		$13,000	$10,000		23,000
Oneida, Inc.			3,000	$1,000	4,000
Other accounts*	39,000	12,000	2,000	2,000	55,000
Totals..	$69,000	$25,000	$15,000	$3,000	112,000
Estimated percent uncollectible.............................	× 0.1%	× 1%	× 5%	× 90%	
Allowance for Uncollectible Accounts balance.......	$ 69 +	$ 250 +	$ 750 +	$2,700 +	$ 3,769

*Each of the "Other accounts" would appear individually.

the credit department of Schmidt Builders Supply groups its accounts receivable into 30-day periods, as Exhibit 8-2 shows.

Schmidt's accounts receivable total $112,000. Of this amount, the aging schedule estimates that Schmidt will *not* collect $3,769. The allowance for uncollectible accounts is not up-to-date *before the year-end adjustment,* as follows (note the $1,100 balance in the allowance):

ACCOUNTS RECEIVABLE	ALLOWANCE FOR UNCOLLECTIBLE ACCOUNTS
112,000		1,100

The aging method is designed to bring the balance of the allowance account to the needed amount as determined by the aging schedule in Exhibit 8-2 (see the lower-right corner for the final result—a needed credit balance of $3,769.)

To update the allowance, Schmidt makes this adjusting entry:

```
20X3
Dec. 31    Uncollectible-Account Expense...............................    2,669
                Allowance for Uncollectible Accounts
                ($3,769 − $1,100).........................................                2,669
           Recorded expense for the year.
```

Again, the recording of the expense decreases the business's assets by the amount of the expenses. The accounting equation for the expense transaction is

ASSETS	=	LIABILITIES	+	OWNER'S EQUITY	−	EXPENSES
−2,669	=	0			−	2,669

Now the balance sheet can report receivables at the amount that Schmidt expects to collect from customers, $108,231 ($112,000 − $3,769), as follows:

Net accounts receivable, 108,231

The *net* amount of accounts receivable—$108,231 in this case—is called *net realizable value* because it is the amount Schmidt expects to realize (collect in cash) from the receivables.

USING THE PERCENT-OF-SALES AND AGING METHODS TOGETHER   In practice, companies use the percent-of-sales and the aging-of-accounts methods together.

- For *interim statements* (monthly or quarterly), companies use the percent-of-sales method because it is easier. This method focuses on the amount of uncollectible-account *expense*. But that is not enough.
- At the end of the year, these companies use the aging method to ensure that Accounts Receivable is reported at *expected realizable value*. The aging method focuses on the amount of the receivables—the *asset*—that is uncollectible.
- Using the two methods together provides good measures of both the expense and the asset. Exhibit 8-3 summarizes and compares the two methods.

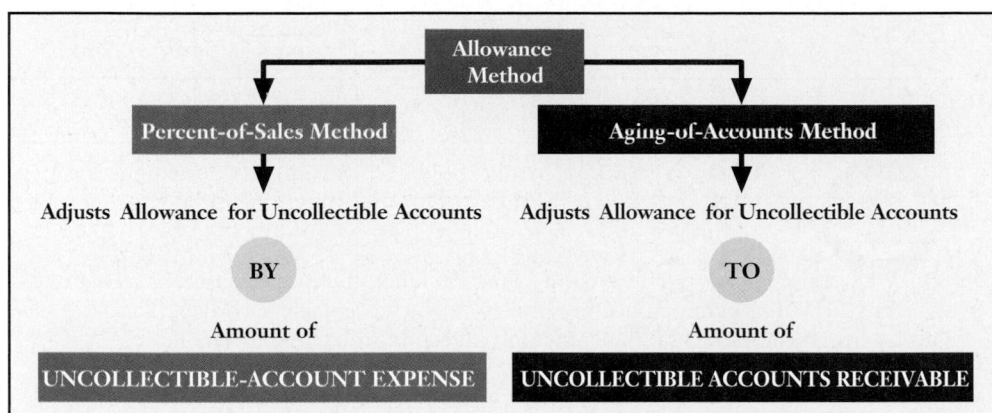

EXHIBIT 8-3
Comparing the Percent-of-Sales and Aging Methods

⊚ DAILY EXERCISE 8-6

⊚ DAILY EXERCISE 8-7

Writing Off Uncollectible Accounts

Early in 20X4, Schmidt Builders Supply collects on most of its $112,000 accounts receivable and records the cash receipts as follows:

```
20X4
Jan.–Mar.   Cash .................................................... 92,000
                  Accounts Receivable ...........................        92,000
            Collected on account.
```

Cash increases, and Accounts Receivable decrease by the same amount. Total assets are unchanged.

| | | | OWNER'S |
ASSETS	=	LIABILITIES	+	EQUITY
+92,000				
−92,000	=	0	+	0

Suppose that, after repeated attempts to collect from customers, Schmidt's credit department determines that Schmidt cannot collect a total of $1,200 from customers Abbott ($900) and Smith ($300). Schmidt's accountant then writes off Schmidt's receivables from the two delinquent customers with this entry:

```
20X4
Mar. 31     Allowance for Uncollectible Accounts ............ 1,200
                  Accounts Receivable—Abbott .............          900
                  Accounts Receivable—Smith ...............          300
            Wrote off uncollectible accounts.
```

The accounting equation shows that the write-off of the uncollectible receivables has no impact on total assets or liabilities or equity.

| | | | OWNER'S |
ASSETS	=	LIABILITIES	+	EQUITY
+1,200				
−1,200	=	0	+	0

DAILY EXERCISE 8-8

 DAILY EXERCISE 8-9

Study the write-off entry carefully. It affects no expense account, so it *does not affect net income.* The write-off has no effect on net receivables either, as shown for Schmidt Builders Supply in Exhibit 8-4.

EXHIBIT 8-4 **Net Receivables Are the Same Before and After the Write-Off of Uncollectible Accounts**

	Before Write-Off	After Write-Off	
Accounts Receivable ($112,000 − $92,000) ..	$20,000	($20,000 − $1,200)	$18,800
Less: Allowance for uncollectible accounts ...	(3,769)	(3,769 − $1,200)	(2,569)
Accounts receivable, net	$16,231	← same →	$16,231

THINK IT OVER

If the write off of uncollectible accounts affects no expense or net receivables, then why go to the trouble of writing off the uncollectible accounts of a specific customer?

Answer: The business has decided that the customer's account is worthless. Therefore, eliminate this account from the receivable records. That alerts the credit department not to waste time pursuing collection from this customer.

Objective 3

Use the direct write-off method to account for uncollectibles

DIRECT WRITE-OFF METHOD. A method of accounting for uncollectible receivables, in which the company waits until the credit department decides that a customer's account receivable is uncollectible, and then debits Uncollectible-Account Expense and credits the customer's Account Receivable.

 DAILY EXERCISE 8-10

 DAILY EXERCISE 8-11

The Direct Write-Off Method

There is another way to account for uncollectible receivables. Under the **direct write-off method,** the company waits until it decides that it will never collect from the customer. Then the accountant writes off the customer's account receivable by debiting Uncollectible-Account Expense and crediting the customer's Account Receivable, as follows (using assumed data):

20X7			
Jan. 2	Uncollectible-Account Expense	2,000	
	Accounts Receivable—Jones		2,000
	Wrote off a bad account.		

This method is defective for two reasons:

1. It does not set up an allowance for uncollectibles. As a result, it always reports the receivables at their full amount, which is more than the business expects to collect. Assets are therefore overstated on the balance sheet.
2. It may not match the uncollectible-account expense of each period against the revenue of the period. In this example, the company made the sale to Jones in 20X6 and should have recorded the uncollectible-account expense during 20X6 to measure net income properly. By recording the expense in 20X7, the company overstates net income in 20X6 and understates net income in 20X7.

Don't confuse the direct write-off method with the allowance method. The two methods of accounting for uncollectible receivables are totally different, and a company adopts one method or the other. The direct write-off method is acceptable only when the amount of uncollectible receivables is very low. It works well for retailers such as **Wal-Mart, Lands' End,** and **Gap,** which carry almost no receivables.

Recovery of Accounts Previously Written Off

When an account receivable is written off as uncollectible, the receivable does not die: The customer still has an obligation to pay. However, the company stops pursuing collection and writes off the account as uncollectible.

Some companies turn delinquent receivables over to an attorney and recover some of the cash. This is called the recovery of a bad account. Let's see how to record the recovery of an account that we wrote off earlier. Recall that on March 31, 20X4, Schmidt Builders Supply wrote off the $900 receivable from customer Lou Abbott (see page 317). It is now January 4, 20X5, and Schmidt unexpectedly receives $900 from Abbott. To account for this recovery. Schmidt makes two journal entries to (1) reverse the earlier write-off and (2) record the cash collection, as follows:

(1) Accounts Receivable—Abbott	900	
Allowance for Uncollectible Accounts		900
Reinstated Abbott's account receivable.		
(2) Cash	900	
Accounts Receivable—Abbott		900
Collected on account.		

CREDIT-CARD, BANKCARD, AND DEBIT-CARD SALES

Credit-Card Sales

Credit-card sales are common in retailing. Customers present credit cards like **American Express** and **Discover** to pay for purchases. The credit-card company then pays the seller the transaction amount and bills the customer, who then pays the credit-card company.

Credit cards offer customers the convenience of buying without having to pay cash immediately. An American Express customer receives a monthly statement from American Express, detailing each of his or her transactions. The customer can write one check to cover the entire month's credit-card purchases.

Retailers also benefit from credit-card sales. They do not have to check a customer's credit rating. The company that issued the card has already done so. Retailers do not have to keep accounts receivable records, and they do not have to collect cash from customers.

These benefits do not come free. The seller receives less than 100% of the face value of the sale. The credit-card company takes a fee of 1–5% on the sale. Suppose you have lunch at the Russian Tea Room, and pay the bill—$100—with a Discover card. The Russian Tea Room's entry to record the $100 sale, subject to the credit-card company's 3% discount, is

Accounts Receivable—Discover	97	
Credit-Card Discount Expense	3	
Sales Revenue		100
Recorded credit-card sales.		

On collection of the discounted value, the Russian Tea Room records the following:

Cash	97	
Accounts Receivable—Discover		97
Collected from Discover.		

Bankcard Sales

Most banks issue their own cards, known as *bankcards*, which operate much like credit cards. **VISA** and **MasterCard** are the two main bankcards. When an **Exxon** station makes a sale and takes a VISA card, the station receives cash at the point of the sale. The cash received is less than the full amount of the sale because the bank deducts its fee. Suppose the Exxon station sells $150 of fuel to a family vacationing in its motor home. The station takes a VISA card, and the bank that issued the card charges a 2% fee. The Exxon station records the bankcard sale as follows:

Cash	147	
Bankcard Discount Expense ($150 × 0.02)	3	
Sales Revenue		150
Recorded a bankcard sale.		

⊙ DAILY EXERCISE 8-12

Debit-Card Sales

Debit cards are fundamentally different from credit cards and bankcards. Using a debit card to buy groceries is like paying with cash, except that the customer doesn't have to carry cash or write a check.

At **Safeway** (or **Kroger** or **Wal-Mart**), the buyer "swipes" the card through a special terminal, and the buyer's bank balance is automatically decreased. Safeway's Cash account is increased immediately—without having to deposit a check and wonder if it will clear the bank. With a debit card there is no third party, such as VISA or MasterCard, so there is no Credit-Card Discount Expense.

e-Accounting

Merchant Beware: Credit Cards Boom with Online Sales ... But So Does Fraud

The TV ad blends e-commerce and credit cards: A cloistered nun is shown with all the comforts of the outside world, compliments of **Amazon.com** and **VISA.** Currently 97%

of all Web payments are made via credit cards. At the end of every month, e-tailers send up to 2.5% of their revenues to credit-card companies. **VISA, MasterCard, American Express,** and their cousins earn millions in transaction fees.

Who takes the hit when customers deny credit-card charges they actually made (chargebacks) or when criminals commit "identity theft" and make purchases with stolen card numbers? It's the online merchants.

Lack of face-to-face transactions has led to an increase in chargebacks for online sales. The online merchant never touches the card, and the online consumer never signs a ticket. The result: There is no paper trail to prove that the cardholder actually okayed the charge. Anonymity also paves the way for identity theft. Online travel company **Expedia, Inc.,** was recently victimized by criminals who used stolen credit-card numbers to buy airplane tickets. The Bellevue, Washington, company lost $6 million on the fraud.

Source: Based on Marcia Savage, "Online fraud: New twist on old issue," *Computer Reseller News*, March 27, 2000, p. 28. Leslie Beyer, "The Internet revolution," *Credit Card Management*, November 1999, Mercedes M. Cardona, "Visa teams up with e-tailers to acquire online dominance," *Advertising Age*, December 6, 1999, p. 4. Patricia A. Murphy, "The murky world of 'Net chargebacks," *Credit Card Management*, February 2000, pp. 54–60.

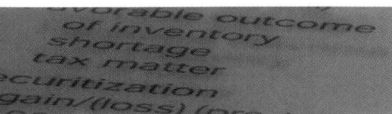

MID-CHAPTER

www.prenhall.com/horngren

Mid-Chapter Assessment

SUMMARY PROBLEM

CPC International, Inc., produces Skippy peanut butter, Hellmann's mayonnaise, and Mazola corn oil. Suppose CPC's balance sheet at December 31, 20X2, reported the following:

	Millions
Notes and accounts receivable [total]...............	$549.9
Allowance for uncollectible accounts...............	(12.5)

Required

1. How much of the December 31, 20X2, balance of the receivable did CPC expect to collect? Stated differently, what was the expected realizable value of these receivables?

2. Journalize, without explanations, 20X3 entries for CPC International, assuming
   a. Total estimated Uncollectible-Account Expense was $19.2 million for the first three quarters of the year, based on the percent-of-sales method.
   b. Write-offs of accounts receivable totaled $23.6 million.
   c. December 31, 20X3, aging of receivables, which indicates that $15.3 million of the total receivables of $582.7 million is uncollectible. Post all three entries to Allowance for Uncollectible Accounts.
3. Show how CPC International's receivables and related allowance will appear on the December 31, 20X3, balance sheet.

   What is the expected realizable value of receivables at December 31, 20X3? How much is uncollectible-account expense for 20X3?

Solution

Requirement 1

	(In millions)
Expected realizable value of receivables ($549.9 − $12.5)	$537.4

Requirement 2

	(In millions)	
(a) Uncollectible-Account Expense.......................................	19.2	
Allowance for Uncollectible Accounts.......................		19.2
(b) Allowance for Uncollectible Accounts	23.6	
Accounts Receivable..		23.6
(c) Uncollectible-Account Expense ($15.3 − $8.1)..............	7.2	
Allowance for Uncollectible Accounts.......................		7.2

ALLOWANCE FOR UNCOLLECTIBLE ACCOUNTS

20X3 Write-offs	23.6	Dec. 31, 20X2 Bal.	12.5
		20X3 Expense	19.2
		Bal. before adj.	8.1
		Dec. 31, 20X3 Adj.	7.2
		Dec. 31, 20X3 Bal.	15.3

Requirement 3

	(In millions)
Notes and accounts receivable...	$582.7
Less: Allowance for uncollectible accounts	(15.3)
Notes and accounts receivable, net..	$567.4
Uncollectible-account expense for 20X3 ($19.2 + $7.2).......	$26.4

NOTES RECEIVABLE: AN OVERVIEW

As we pointed out earlier in this chapter, notes receivable are more formal arrangements than accounts receivable. The debtor signs a promissory note, which serves as evidence of the debt. Before launching into the accounting for notes receivable, let's define the special terms used for them.

- **Promissory note:** A written promise to pay a specified amount of money at a particular future date.
- **Maker of the note (debtor):** The person or business that signs the note and promises to pay the amount required by the note agreement; the maker of the note is the *debtor*.

- **Payee of the note (creditor):** The person or business to whom the maker promises future payment; the payee of the note is the *creditor.*
- **Principal amount,** or **principal:** The amount loaned out by the payee and borrowed by the maker of the note.
- **Interest:** The revenue to the payee for loaning money, and the expense of borrowing for the maker.
- **Interest period:** The period of time during which interest is to be computed. It extends from the original date of the note to the maturity date. Also called the **note period, note term,** or simply **time.**
- **Interest rate:** The percentage rate that is multiplied by the principal amount to compute the amount of interest on the note. Interest rates are almost always stated for a period of one year. A 9% note means that the amount of interest for *one year* is 9% of the principal amount of the note.
- **Maturity date:** The date when final payment of the note is due. Also called the **due date.**
- **Maturity value:** The sum of the principal plus interest due at the maturity date.

Exhibit 8-5 illustrates a promissory note. Study it carefully.

EXHIBIT 8-5   **A Promissory Note**

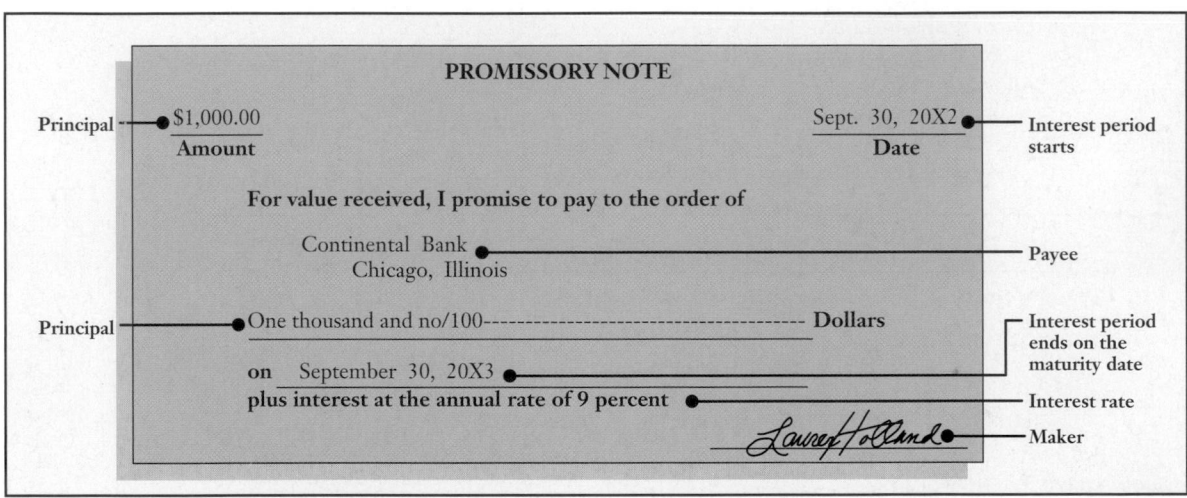

Identifying a Note's Maturity Date

Some notes specify the maturity date, as shown in Exhibit 8-5. Other notes state the period of the note in days or months. When the period is given in months, the note's maturity date falls on the same day of the month as the date the note was issued. For example, a six-month note dated February 16 matures on August 16.

When the period is given in days, the maturity date is determined by counting the days from the date of issue. A 120-day note dated September 14, 20X2, matures on January 12, 20X3, as shown here:

Month	Number of Days	Cumulative Total
Sep. 20X2	$30 - 14 = 16$	16
Oct. 20X2	31	47
Nov. 20X2	30	77
Dec. 20X2	31	108
Jan. 20X3	12	120

In counting the days remaining for a note, remember to count the maturity date and to omit the date the note was issued.

Computing Interest on a Note

The formula for computing the dollar amount of interest on a note is

Principal	×	Interest rate	×	Time	=	Amount of interest

⊙ DAILY EXERCISE 8-13

Using the data in Exhibit 8-5, Continental Bank computes its interest revenue for one year on its note receivable as

Principal	×	Interest rate	×	Time	=	Amount of interest
$1,000		0.09		1 yr.		$90

The maturity value of the note is $1,090 ($1,000 principal + $90 interest). The time element is 1 because interest is computed over a one-year period.

When the interest period of a note is stated in months, we compute the interest based on the 12-month year. Interest on a $2,000 note at 15% for three months is computed as

Principal	×	Interest rate	×	Time	=	Amount of interest
$2,000		0.15		3/12		$75

When the interest period is stated in days, we sometimes compute interest based on a 360-day year rather than on a 365-day year.[2] The interest on a $5,000 note at 12% for 60 days can be computed as

Principal	×	Interest rate	×	Time	=	Amount of interest
$5,000		0.12		60/360		$100

Keep in mind that interest rates are stated as an annual rate. Therefore, the time in the formula for computing interest should also be expressed in terms of a year.

Practice calculating interest on

1. A $30,000, 12 1/2%, 180-day note
2. An $8,000, 9%, 6-month note

Answers

1. ($30,000 × 0.125 × 180/360) = $1,875   **2.** ($8,000 × 0.09 × 6/12) = $360

ACCOUNTING FOR NOTES RECEIVABLE

Recording Notes Receivable

Consider the loan agreement shown in Exhibit 8-5. After Lauren Holland signs the note, Continental Bank gives her $1,000 cash. At maturity, Holland pays the bank $1,090 ($1,000 principal plus $90 interest). The bank's entries are

Objective 4
Account for notes receivable

⊙ DAILY EXERCISE 8-14

Sep. 30, 20X2	Note Receivable—L. Holland..................................	1,000	
	Cash		1,000
	Loaned out money.		
Sep. 30, 20X3	Cash	1,090	
	Note Receivable—L. Holland.........................		1,000
	Interest Revenue ($1,000 × 0.09 × 1)		90
	Collected note receivable.		

---

[2]A 360-day year eliminates some rounding, which is consistent with our use of whole-dollar amounts throughout this book.

Some companies sell merchandise in exchange for notes receivable. Suppose that on October 20, 20X3, **General Electric** sells household appliances for $15,000 to Dorman Builders. Dorman signs a 90-day promissory note at 10% annual interest. General Electric's entries to record the sale and collection from Dorman are

Oct. 20, 20X3	Note Receivable—Dorman Builders	15,000	
	Sales Revenue		15,000
	Made a sale.		
Jan. 18, 20X4	Cash	15,375	
	Note Receivable—Dorman Builders...................		15,000
	Interest Revenue ($15,000 × 0.10 × 90/360)		375
	Collected note receivable.		

⊙ DAILY EXERCISE 8-15

A company may accept a note receivable from a trade customer who fails to pay an account receivable within the customary 30–60 days. The customer signs a promissory note—that is, becomes the **maker of the note**—and gives it to the creditor, who becomes the **payee.** Suppose Interlogic, Inc., cannot pay Hoffman Supply. Hoffman may accept a one-year, $2,400 note receivable, with 9% interest, from Interlogic on October 1, 20X1. Hoffman's entry is

MAKER OF A NOTE. The person or business that signs the note and promises to pay the amount required by the note agreement; the debtor.

PAYEE OF A NOTE. The person or business to whom the maker of a note promises future payment; the creditor.

Oct. 1, 20X1	Note Receivable—Interlogic, Inc.................................	2,400	
	Accounts Receivable—Interlogic, Inc.................		2,400
	Received a note on account.		

Accruing Interest Revenue

Notes receivable may be outstanding at the end of an accounting period. The interest revenue earned on the note during the year is part of that year's earnings. Recall that interest revenue is earned over time, not just when cash is received. ◄

➤ We saw in Chapter 3 on p. 94 that accrued revenue creates an asset because the revenue has been earned but not received.

Let's continue with the Hoffman Supply note receivable from Interlogic, Inc. Hoffman Supply's accounting period ends December 31. How much of the total interest revenue does Hoffman earn in 20X1? How much does it earn in 20X2?

Hoffman will earn three months' interest in 20X1—for October, November, and December. In 20X2, Hoffman will earn nine months' interest—for January through September. At December 31, 20X1, Hoffman Supply will make the following adjusting entry to accrue interest revenue:

Dec. 31, 20X1	Interest Receivable ($2,400 × 0.09 × 3/12).................	54	
	Interest Revenue		54
	Accrued interest revenue.		

Then, on the maturity date, Hoffman Supply records collection of principal and interest as follows:

Sep. 30, 20X2	Cash [$2,400 + ($2,400 × 0.09)]................................	2,616	
	Note Receivable—Interlogic, Inc.		2,400
	Interest Receivable ($2,400 × 0.09 × 3/12)		54
	Interest Revenue ($2,400 × 0.09 × 9/12)		162
	Collected note receivable on which interest has been accrued previously.		

⊙ DAILY EXERCISE 8-16

⊙ DAILY EXERCISE 8-17

The entries for interest earned in 20X1 and for collection in 20X2 assign the correct amount of interest to each year. This follows the revenue principle.

A company holding a note receivable may need the cash before the note matures. There is a procedure for selling the note, called discounting a note receivable. The chapter appendix covers this topic.

Dishonored Notes Receivable

DISHONOR OF A NOTE. Failure of a note's maker to pay a note receivable at maturity. Also called **default on a note.**

If the maker of a note does not pay at maturity, the maker is said to **dishonor,** or **default on,** the note. Because the term of the note has expired, the note agreement is no longer in force. However, the payee still has a claim against the debtor and usually transfers the note receivable amount to Accounts Receivable. The payee records the amount of interest revenue the payee has earned on the note and debits Accounts Receivable for the maturity value of the note.

Rubinstein Jewelers has a six-month, 10% note receivable for $1,200 from Mario Adair, and on the February 3 maturity date, Adair defaulted. Rubinstein Jewelers will record the default as follows:

Feb. 3	Accounts Receivable—M. Adair		
	[$1,200 + ($1,200 × 0.10 × 6/12)]	1,260	
	Note Receivable—M. Adair		1,200
	Interest Revenue ($1,200 × 0.10 × 6/12)		60
	Recorded a dishonored note receivable.		

Rubinstein will pursue collection from Adair as an account receivable. If the account receivable later proves uncollectible, Rubinstein will then write off the account as previously discussed. Note that all notes receivable bear interest until they are proved dead.

Reporting Receivables on the Balance Sheet

Objective 5
Report receivables on the balance sheet

Let's look at how some well-known companies report their receivables and related allowances for uncollectibles on the balance sheet. All receivables and the related allowance accounts appear on the balance sheet, but terminology may vary. **Intel Corporation,** maker of the Pentium® processor, reports accounts receivable under Current Assets (in millions):

Accounts receivable, net of allowance for doubtful accounts of $67.... $3,700

The net realizable value of Intel's accounts receivable is $3,700 million. To compute Intel's total amount receivable, add the allowance to the net receivable: $67 + $3,700 = $3,767. Customers actually owe Intel $3,767 million, of which the company expects to collect $3,700 million.

General Electric Company reports a single amount—net realizable value—for receivables in the balance sheet and uses a note to give the details (adapted with amounts in millions):

Current receivables (note 10)	$8,743
Note 10: Current Receivables:	
Aircraft Engines.............................	$ 1,541
Appliances	285
Power Systems...............................	3,350
Other	3,887
	9,063
Less: Allowance for losses..............	(320)
	$8,743

WORK IT OUT

1. How much did customers owe General Electric (GE)?
2. How much did GE expect to collect?
3. How much did GE expect *not* to collect?

Answers

1. $9,063 million 2. $8,743 million 3. $320 million

DAILY EXERCISE 8-18

DAILY EXERCISE 8-19

Computers and Accounts Receivable

Accounting for receivables by a large company like **M&M Mars** requires tens of thousands of postings to customer accounts each month for credit sales and cash collections. Manual accounting methods cannot keep up.

As we saw in Chapter 6, Accounts Receivable can be set up on a computerized system. The order entry and shipping systems interface with the billing system, which credits Sales Revenue and debits Accounts Receivable. The computer then creates a sale invoice for each customer. At the same time, the computer prints out the sales for the period. Finally, computerized posting to the general ledger and accounts receivable subsidiary ledger occurs.

Objective 6
Use the acid-test ratio and days' sales in receivables to evaluate a company's financial position

USING ACCOUNTING INFORMATION FOR DECISION MAKING

The balance sheet lists assets in order of liquidity (closeness to cash):

- Cash comes first because it is the medium of exchange.
- Short-term investments (covered in a later chapter) come next because they can be sold for cash whenever the owner wishes.
- Current receivables are less liquid than short-term investments because the receivables must be collected.
- Merchandise inventory is less liquid than receivables because the goods must be sold.

The balance sheet of **Oracle Corporation,** as adapted, provides an example in Exhibit 8-6. Focus on the current assets at May 31, 1999. Oracle reports no inventory because the company earns revenue by providing services, not by selling products.

EXHIBIT 8-6
Oracle Corporation Balance Sheet

Oracle Corporation Balance Sheet (partial, adapted) May 31, 1999 and May 31, 1998	(In millions)	
	May 31,	
Assets	1999	1998
Current assets:		
Cash and cash equivalents	$1,786	$1,274
Short-term investments	777	645
Trade receivables net of allowance for doubtful accounts of $217 in 1999 and $196 in 1998	2,238	1,857
Prepaid expenses	405	339
Other current assets	241	208
Total current assets	$5,447	$4,323
Liabilities		
Current liabilities:		
Total current liabilities	$3,046	$2,484

Acid-Test (or Quick) Ratio

ACID-TEST RATIO. Ratio of the sum of cash plus short-term investments plus net current receivables, to total current liabilities. Tells whether the entity could pay all its current liabilities if they came due immediately. Also called the quick ratio.

Owners and managers use ratios for decision making. In Chapter 4, we discussed the current ratio, which measures the ability to pay current liabilities with current assets. A more stringent measure of ability to pay current liabilities is the **acid-test (or quick) ratio.** The acid-test ratio reveals whether the entity can pay all its current liabilities if they come due immediately:

For Oracle Corporation (Exhibit 8-6)
(Dollar amounts in millions)

$$\text{Acid-test ratio} = \frac{\text{Cash} + \begin{array}{c}\text{Short-term}\\\text{investments}\end{array} + \begin{array}{c}\text{Net current}\\\text{receivables}\end{array}}{\text{Total current liabilities}} \quad \frac{\$1,786 + \$777 + \$2,238}{\$3,046} = 1.58$$

The higher the acid-test ratio, the more able the business is to pay its current liabilities. Oracle's acid-test ratio of 1.58 means that Oracle has $1.58 of quick assets to pay each $1 of current liabilities—an extremely strong position.

What is an acceptable acid-test ratio? The answer depends on the industry. **Wal-Mart** operates smoothly with an acid-test ratio of 0.18. Several things make this possible: Wal-Mart has almost no current receivables. The acid-test ratios for most department stores cluster about 0.80, while travel agencies average 1.10. In general, an acid-test ratio of 1.00 is considered safe.

WORK IT OUT

Use the data in Exhibit 8-6 to compute Oracle Corporation's current ratio at May 31, 1999. Then compare Oracle's current ratio and acid-test ratio. Why is the current ratio higher?

Answer:

$$\text{Current ratio} = \frac{\text{Total current assets}}{\text{Total current liabilities}} = \frac{\$5{,}447}{\$3{,}046} = 1.79$$

$$\text{Acid-test ratio} = 1.58$$

The current ratio is higher because it includes all current assets and not just cash, short-term investments, and receivables.

Days' Sales in Receivables

After making a credit sale, the next step is to collect the receivable. **Days' sales in receivables,** also called the **collection period,** indicates how many days it takes to collect the average level of receivables. The shorter the collection period, the more quickly the organization can use cash for operations. The longer the collection period, the less cash is available to pay bills and expand. Days' sales in receivables can be computed in two steps, as follows:[3]

DAYS' SALES IN RECEIVABLES. Ratio of average net accounts receivable to one day's sales. Tells how many days' sales it takes to collect the average level of receivables. Also called the **collection period.**

For Oracle Corporation (Exhibit 8-6) (Dollar amounts in millions)

1. $$\text{One day's sales} = \frac{\text{Net sales (or Total revenues)}}{365 \text{ days}} = \frac{\$8{,}827^*}{365} = \$24.2 \text{ per day}$$

2. $$\text{Days' sales in average accounts receivable} = \frac{\text{Average net accounts receivable}}{\text{One day's sales}} = \frac{\left(\text{Beginning net receivables} + \text{Ending net receivables}\right) \div 2}{\text{One day's sales}}$$

$$= \frac{(\$1{,}857 + \$2{,}238)/2}{\$24.2} = 85 \text{ days}$$

*Taken from Oracle Corporation's 1999 income statement, which is not reproduced here.

The length of the collection period depends on the credit terms of the company's revenues. For example, sales on net 30 terms should be collected within approximately 30 days. When there is a discount, such as 2/10 net 30, the collection period may be shorter. Terms of net 45 or net 60 result in longer collection periods.

We discussed sales discounts in Chapter 5, p. 172.

Investors and creditors do not evaluate a company on the basis of one or two ratios. Instead, they perform a thorough analysis of all the information available. Then they stand back from the data and ask, "What is our overall impression of this company?"

DAILY EXERCISE 8-20

DAILY EXERCISE 8-21

THINK IT OVER

AMR Corporation, the parent company of American Airlines, had a collection period of only 24 days during 1999. Why was it so short?

Answer: Generally, people pay for airline tickets before they travel. This causes the airlines' days' sales in receivables to be very low.

The Decision Guidelines feature summarizes some key decisions people must make in order to manage and evaluate receivables.

[3]Days' sales in average receivables can also be computed in this one step:

$$\text{Days' sales in average receivables} = \frac{\text{Average net receivables}}{\text{Net sales}} \times 365$$

DECISION GUIDELINES

Accounting for Receivables Transactions

DECISION	GUIDELINES
Accounts Receivable	
How much of our receivables will we collect?	Less than the full amount of the receivables because we will be unable to collect from some customers.
How to report receivables at their net realizable value?	1. Use the *allowance method* to account for uncollectible receivables. Set up the allowance for Uncollectible Accounts.
	2. Estimate uncollectibles by the
	a. *Percent-of-sales method* (income statement approach)
	b. *Aging-of-accounts method* (balance sheet approach)
	3. Write off uncollectible receivables as they are deemed uncollectible.

4. $\dfrac{\text{Net accounts}}{\text{receivable}} = \dfrac{\text{Accounts}}{\text{Receivable}} - \dfrac{\text{Allowance for}}{\text{Uncollectible Accounts}}$

Is there another way to account for uncollectible receivables?	The *direct write-off method* uses no Allowance for Uncollectibles Accounts. It simply debits Uncollectible-Account Expense and credits a customer's Account Receivable to write it off when uncollectible. This method is acceptable only when uncollectibles are insignificant.
Notes Receivable	
What two other accounts are related to notes receivable?	Notes receivable are related as follows:
	• Notes receivable earn *Interest Revenue*.
	• Interest revenue that has not been collected is debited to *Interest Receivable*.
How to compute the interest on a note receivable?	Amount of interest = Principal × Interest rate × Time
Receivables in General	
What two key decision aids use receivables to evaluate a company's financial position?	• Acid-test ratio $= \dfrac{\overset{\text{Short-term}}{\text{Cash} + \text{investments}} + \overset{\text{Net current}}{\text{receivables}}}{\text{Total current liabilities}}$
	• $\dfrac{\text{Day's sales in}}{\text{average receivables}} = \dfrac{\begin{array}{c}\text{Average net}\\\text{accounts receivable}\end{array}}{\text{One day's sales}}$

How to report receivables on the balance sheet?	Accounts (or Notes) Receivable .... $XXX
	Less: Allowance for uncollectible accounts .... (X)
	Accounts (or notes) receivable, net .... $ XX

REVIEW ACCOUNTS AND NOTES RECEIVABLE

SUMMARY PROBLEM

Suppose First Fidelity, Inc., engaged in the following transactions:

20X4

Apr.	1	Loaned $8,000 to Bland Co. Received a six-month, 10% note.
Oct.	1	Collected the Bland note at maturity.
Dec.	1	Loaned $6,000 to Flores, Inc., on a 180-day, 12% note.
Dec.	31	Accrued interest revenue on the Flores note.

20X5

May	30	Collected the Flores note at maturity.

First Fidelity's accounting period ends on December 31.

Required

Explanations are not needed.
1. Record the 20X4 transactions on April 1 through December 1 on First Fidelity's books.
2. Make the adjusting entry needed on December 31, 20X4.
3. Record the May 30, 20X5, collection of the Flores note.

Solution

Requirement 1

20X4

Apr. 1	Note Receivable—Bland Co.	8,000	
	Cash...		8,000
Oct. 1	Cash ($8,000 + $400)	8,400	
	Note Receivable—Bland Co.		8,000
	Interest Revenue ($8,000 × 0.10 × 6/12)		400

Requirement 2

20X4

Dec. 1	Note Receivable—Flores, Inc.	6,000	
	Cash...		6,000
31	Interest Receivable	60	
	Interest Revenue ($6,000 × 0.12 × 30/360)		60

Requirement 3

20X5

May 30	Cash ($6,000 + $360)	6,360	
	Note Receivable—Flores, Inc.		6,000
	Interest Receivable		60
	Interest Revenue ($6,000 × 0.12 × 150/360)		300

LESSONS LEARNED

1. **Design internal controls for receivables.** Companies that sell on credit receive most customer collections in the mail. Good *internal control* over mailed-in cash receipts means separating cash-handling duties from cash-accounting duties.

2. **Use the allowance method to account for uncollectibles by the percent-of-sales and aging-of-accounts methods.** Uncollectible receivables are accounted for by the allowance method or the direct write-off method. The *allowance method* matches expenses against revenue and also results in a more realistic measure of net accounts receivable. The *percent-of-sales method* and the *aging-of-accounts method* are the two main approaches to estimating bad debts under the allowance method.

3. **Use the direct write-off method to account for uncollectibles.** The *direct write-off method* is easy to apply, but it fails to match bad debt expense to the corresponding revenue. Also, Accounts Receivable are reported at their full amount, which is misleading because it suggests that the company expects to collect all its accounts receivable.

4. **Account for notes receivable.** *Notes receivable* are formal credit agreements. Interest earned by the creditor is computed by multiplying the note's principal amount by the interest rate times the length of the interest period.

5. **Report receivables on the balance sheet.** All accounts receivable, notes receivable, and allowance accounts appear in the balance sheet. Companies use various formats to report these assets at net realizable value.

6. **Use the acid-test ratio and days' sales in receivables to evaluate a company's financial position.** The *acid-test ratio* measures the company's ability to pay current liabilities from the most liquid current assets. *Days' sales in receivables* indicates how long it takes to collect the average level of receivables.

ACCOUNTING VOCABULARY

acid-test ratio (p. 326)
aging-of-accounts method (p. 315)
Allowance for Doubtful Accounts (p. 314)
Allowance for Uncollectible Accounts (p. 314)
allowance method (p. 314)
bad-debt expense (p. 314)
balance sheet approach (p. 315)
collection period (p. 327)

contingent liability (p. 344)
creditor (p. 311)
days' sales in receivables (p. 327)
debtor (p. 311)
default on a note (p. 324)
direct write-off method (p. 318)
discounting a note receivable (p. 343)
dishonor of a note (p. 324)
doubtful-account expense (p. 314)

due date (p. 322)
income statement approach (p. 315)
interest (p. 322)
interest period (p. 322)
interest rate (p. 322)
maker of a note (p. 324)
maturity date (p. 322)
maturity value (p. 322)
note period (p. 322)
note term (p. 322)

payee of a note   (p. 324)
percent-of-sales method   (p. 315)
principal   (p. 322)
principal amount   (p. 322)

promissory note   (p. 321)
quick ratio   (p. 326)
receivables   (p. 311)
time   (p. 322)

uncollectible-account expense
   (p. 314)

QUESTIONS

1. Name the two parties to a receivable/payable transaction. Which party has the receivable? Which has the payable? Which has the asset? The liability?
2. List the two main categories of receivables. State how receivables are classified for reporting on the balance sheet.
3. Name the two methods of accounting for uncollectible receivables. Which method is easier to apply? Which method is consistent with generally accepted accounting principles?
4. Identify the accounts debited and credited to account for uncollectibles under (a) the allowance method, and (b) the direct write-off method.
5. What is another term for Allowance for Uncollectible Accounts? What are two other terms for Uncollectible-Account Expense?
6. Identify and briefly describe the two ways to estimate bad-debt expense and uncollectible accounts, using the allowance method.

7. Use the terms *maker, payee, principal amount, maturity date, promissory note,* and *interest* in an appropriate sentence or two describing a note receivable.
8. Name three situations in which a company might receive a note receivable. For each situation, show the account debited and the account credited to record receipt of the note.
9. When the maker of a note dishonors the note at maturity, what accounts does the payee debit and credit?
10. Why does the payee of a note receivable usually need to make adjusting entries for interest at the end of the accounting period?
11. Show three ways to report Accounts Receivable of $100,000 and Allowance for Uncollectible Accounts of $2,800 on the balance sheet or in the related notes.
12. Why is the acid-test ratio a more stringent measure of the ability to pay current liabilities than the current ratio?
13. Which measure of days' sales in receivables is preferable, 30 or 40? Give your reason.

ASSESS YOUR PROGRESS

DAILY EXERCISES

Accounts receivable records (Obj. 1)

DE8-1   Examine the Accounts Receivable T-accounts on page 312, and answer these questions:

1. Which account (and which amount) will appear on the company's balance sheet? Suppose the company has cash of $2,000. Show how the balance sheet will report cash and the other item on page 312.
2. Who are Acker, Dell, and Taft? What do their accounts indicate that these three persons are obligated to do?

Internal control over the collection of receivables   (Obj. 1)

DE8-2   Return to the Accounts Receivable T-accounts on page 312. Suppose Nathan Forester is the accountant responsible for these records. What duty will a good internal control system withhold from Forester? Why?

Internal control over the credit department   (Obj. 1)

DE8-3   What duty must be withheld from a company's credit department in order to safeguard its cash? If this duty is granted to the credit department, what can a dishonest credit department employee do to hurt the company?

Applying the allowance method to account for uncollectibles (Obj. 2)

DE8-4   The allowance method of accounting for uncollectible receivables uses two accounts in addition to Accounts Receivable. Identify the two accounts and indicate which financial statement reports each account. Which of these is a contra account? Make up reasonable amounts to show how to report the contra account under its companion account on the balance sheet.

Applying the allowance method (percent-of-sales) to account for uncollectibles (Obj. 2)

DE8-5   During its first year of operations, SBC Communications had net sales of $600,000, all on account. Industry experience suggests that SBC's bad debts will amount to 2% of net sales. At December 31, 20X3, SBC's accounts receivable total $90,000. The company uses the allowance method to account for uncollectibles.

1. Journalize SBC's uncollectible-account expense using the percent-of-sales method.
2. Show how SBC should report accounts receivable on its balance sheet at December 31, 20X3. Follow the reporting format illustrated in the middle of page 314.

Applying the allowance method (percent-of-sales) to account for uncollectibles (Obj. 2)

DE8-6   ◄ *Link Back to Chapter 5 (Recording Sales Transactions).* This exercise continues the situation of Daily Exercise 8-5, in which SBC Communications ended the year 20X3 with accounts receivable of $90,000 and an allowance for uncollectible accounts of $12,000.

During 20X4, SBC Communications completed the following transactions:

1. Net credit sales, $800,000 (ignore cost of goods sold).
2. Collections on account, $690,000.
3. Write-offs of uncollectibles, $15,000.
4. Uncollectible-account expense, 1.8% of net credit sales.

Journalize the foregoing 20X4 transactions for SBC Communications.

DE8-7 Use the solution to Daily Exercise 8-6 to answer these questions about SBC Communications.

Applying the allowance method (percent-of-sales) to account for uncollectibles (Obj. 2)

1. Start with Accounts Receivable's beginning balance ($90,000), and then post to the Accounts Receivable T-account. How much do SBC's customers owe the company at December 31, 20X4?
2. Start with the Allowance account's beginning balance ($12,000), and then post to the Allowance for Uncollectible Accounts T-account. How much of the receivables at December 31, 20X4, does SBC expect *not* to collect?
3. At December 31, 20X4, how much cash does SBC expect to collect on its accounts receivable?

DE8-8 ←= *Link Back to Chapter 5 (Recording Sales Transactions).* Guardian Medical Group started 20X0 with accounts receivable of $120,000 and an allowance for uncollectible accounts of $6,000. The 20X0 credit sales were $800,000, and cash collections on account totaled $720,000. During 20X0, Guardian wrote off uncollectible accounts receivable of $12,000. At December 31, 20X0, the aging of accounts receivable indicated that Guardian will *not* collect $4,000 of its accounts receivable.

Applying the allowance method (aging-of-accounts) to account for uncollectibles (Obj. 2)

Journalize Guardian's (a) credit sales (ignore cost of goods sold), (b) cash collections on account, (c) write-offs of uncollectible receivables, and (d) uncollectible-account expense for the year. Prepare a T-account for Allowance for Uncollectible Accounts to show your computation of uncollectible-account expense for the year.

DE8-9 Hot Button.com accounts include the following balances at December 31, 20X1, before the year-end adjustments:

Applying the allowance method (aging-of-accounts) to account for uncollectibles (Obj. 2)

ACCOUNTS RECEIVABLE	ALLOWANCE FOR UNCOLLECTIBLE ACCOUNTS
104,000	1,300

The aging of accounts receivable yields these data:

	Age of Accounts Receivable				
	0–30 Days	31–60 Days	61–90 Days	Over 90 Days	Total Receivables
Amount receivable	$70,000	$20,000	$10,000	$4,000	$104,000
Percent uncollectible	×1%	×2%	×5%	×50%	

Journalize Hot Button's entry to adjust the allowance account to its correct balance at December 31, 20X1.

DE8-10 Buchwald, Inc.'s experience indicates that Buchwald will fail to collect 3% of net credit sales, which totaled $100,000 during the three-month period January through March of 20X3. During this period Buchwald wrote off $4,000 of accounts receivable as uncollectible. Record Buchwald's uncollectible-account expense for January through March under

Contrasting the allowance method and the direct write-off method of accounting for uncollectibles (Obj. 2, 3)

a. The allowance method.
b. The direct write-off method. You need not identify individual customer accounts.

Which method of accounting for uncollectibles is preferred? What makes this method better?

DE 8-11 Masahiro Oguchi is an attorney in San Francisco. Oguchi uses the direct write-off method to account for his uncollectible receivables.

Applying the direct write-off method to account for uncollectibles (Obj. 3)

At May 31, Oguchi's accounts receivable were $8,000. During June, he earned service revenue of $60,000 and collected $62,000 from clients on account. He also wrote off uncollectible receivables of $500. What is Oguchi's balance of Accounts Receivable at June 30? Does he expect to collect all of this amount? Why or why not?

DE 8-12 Gas stations do a large volume of business by customer credit cards and bankcards. Suppose the **Shell** station near Lenox Square in Atlanta, Georgia, had these transactions on a busy Saturday in July:

Recording credit-card sales (Obj. 3)

American Express credit-card sales	$6,000
VISA bankcard sales	8,000

Suppose **American Express** charges merchants 4% and **VISA** charges 2%. Record these sale transactions for the Shell station.

DE 8-13 Examine the promissory note in Exhibit 8-5, page 322. Answer these questions:

1. When does interest on the note start running? When does the interest stop running?
2. Who is the debtor? Who is the creditor?
3. Which party to the note has a note receivable? Which party has a note payable? Which party has interest revenue? Which party has interest expense?
4. When must Lauren Holland pay off the note?
5. How much interest must Holland pay on the maturity date of the note? How much cash must Holland pay in total at maturity?

DE 8-14 For each of the following notes receivable, compute the amount of interest revenue earned during 20X5. Use a 360-day year.

	Principal	Interest Rate	Interest Period	Maturity Date
Note 1	$ 10,000	9%	60 days	11/30/20X5
Note 2	50,000	10%	3 months	9/30/20X5
Note 3	100,000	8%	$1\frac{1}{2}$ years	12/31/20X6
Note 4	15,000	12%	90 days	1/15/20X6

DE 8-15 Deutsche Bank lent $400,000 to Jean Nowlin on a 90-day, 8% note. Record the following transactions for Deutsche Bank (explanations are not required):

a. Lending the money on June 12.
b. Collecting the principal and interest at maturity. Specify the date. For the computation of interest, use a 360-day year.

Accruing interest receivable and
collecting a note receivable
(Obj. 4)

DE 8-16 Return to the promissory note in Exhibit 8-5, page 322. The accounting year of Continental Bank ends on December 31, 20X2. Journalize Continental Bank's (a) lending money on the note receivable at September 30, 20X2, (b) accrual of interest at December 31, 20X2, and (c) collection of principal and interest at September 30, 20X3, the maturity date of the note. Carry amounts to the nearest cent.

DE 8-17 Using your answers to Daily Exercise 8–16 for Continental Bank, and carrying amounts to the nearest cent, show how the bank will report

a. Note receivable and interest receivable on the bank's classified balance sheet at December 31, 20X2.
b. Whatever needs to be reported on the bank's income statement for the year ended December 31, 20X2.
c. Whatever needs to be reported for the note and related interest on the bank's classified balance sheet at December 31, 20X3. You may ignore Cash.
d. Whatever needs to be reported on the bank's income statement for the year ended December 31, 20X3.

DE 8-18 Examine the receivables for **Intel, General Electric,** and **Oracle** shown on page 325 and in Exhibit 8-6, page 326. Complete the table below to show the amounts (in millions of dollars) that each company will report on its balance sheet:

Company	Total Current Receivables	−	Allowance for Uncollectibles =	Net Realizable Value
Intel Corporation......................	$		$( )	$
General Electric........................				
Oracle Corporation(1999 only).				

At May 31, 1999, how much does Oracle expect to collect from its customers?

Reporting receivables and
other accounts in the financial
statements
(Obj. 5)

DE 8-19 ← *Link Back to Chapters 1–3 (Debit/Credit Balances; Income Statement).* **Sprint Corporation,** the telecommunications company, included the following items in its financial statements (adapted, in millions):

Unearned revenues...................	$ 200	Service revenue	$14,045
Allowance for doubtful		Other assets............................	355
accounts...............................	117	Cost of services sold and	
Cash	1,151	other expenses	12,861
Accounts receivable	2,581	Notes payable........................	3,281
Accounts payable	1,027		

1. How much net income did Sprint earn for the year?
2. Show how Sprint reported receivables on its classified balance sheet. Follow the reporting format shown in the middle of page 314.

DE 8-20 Vision Maker, a cable TV company, reported the following items at February 28, 20X0 (amounts in millions, with last-year's 19X9 amounts also given as needed):

Using the acid-test ratio and days' sales in receivables to evaluate an actual company (Obj. 6)

Accounts payable	$369	Accounts receivable:	
Cash	215	February 28, 20X0	$ 235
Allowance for uncollectible		February 29, 19X9	160
accounts:		Cost of goods sold	575
February 28, 20X0	15	Short-term investments	165
February 29, 19X9	7	Other current assets	93
Inventories:		Other current liabilities	145
February 28, 20X0	198	Net sales revenue	1,406
February 29, 19X9	161	Long-term assets	416
Long-term liabilities	11		

Compute Vision Maker's (a) acid-test ratio and (b) days' sales in average receivables for 20X0. Evaluate each ratio value as strong or weak. Assume Vision Maker sells on terms of net 45.

DE 8-21 ← *Link Back to Chapter 4 (Current Ratio and Debt Ratio) and Chapter 5 (Gross Profit Percentage and Inventory Turnover).* Using the data in Daily Exercise 8-20, compute for Vision Maker the following ratios for 20X0:

Computing key ratios for an actual company (Obj. 6)

a. Current ratio   c. Gross profit percentage
b. Debt ratio   d. Rate of inventory turnove

EXERCISES

E8-1 As a recent college graduate, you land your first job in the customer collections department of Sun Systems. Karla Bates, one of the owners, has asked you to propose a system to ensure that cash received by mail from customers is handled properly. Draft a short memorandum identifying the essential element in your plan, and state why it is important.

Controlling cash receipts from customers (Obj. 1)

Refer to Chapter 7 if necessary. Use this format for your memo:

Date:	_____
To:	Karla Bates
From:	Your Name
RE:	Essential element of internal control over customer collections

E8-2 ← *Link Back to Chapter 7 (Internal Control Over Cash Receipts).* Suppose **Carnation,** the instant breakfast company, is opening an office in Chicago. Timothy Mayborne, the office manager, is designing the internal control system. Mayborne proposes the following procedures for credit checks on new customers, sales on account, cash collections, and write-offs of uncollectible receivables:

Identifying and correcting an internal control weakness (Obj. 1)

- The credit department will run a credit check on all customers who apply for credit.
- Sales on account are the responsibility of the Carnation salespersons. Credit sales above a reasonable limit require the approval of the credit manager.
- Cash receipts come into the credit department, which separates the cash received from the customer remittance slips. The credit department lists all cash receipts by customer name and amount of cash received. The cash goes to the treasurer for deposit in the bank. The remittance slips go to the accounting department for posting to customer accounts. Each day's listing of cash receipts goes to the controller for comparison with the daily deposit slip and the day's listing of the total dollar amount posted to customer accounts. The three amounts must agree.

Identify the internal control weakness in this situation, and propose a way to correct it.

E8-3 On September 30, Ageless Technology had a $28,000 debit balance in Accounts Receivable. During October, the company had sales of $187,000, which included $120,000 in credit sales. October collections were $91,000. Other data include

Using the allowance method for bad debts (Obj. 2, 5)

- September 30 credit balance in Allowance for Uncollectible Accounts, $1,600.
- Uncollectible-account expense, estimated as 2% of credit sales.
- Write-offs of uncollectible receivables totaled $1,070.

Required

1. Prepare journal entries to record sales, collections, uncollectible-account expense by the allowance method (percent-of-sales method), and write-offs of uncollectibles during October.
2. Show the ending balances in Accounts Receivable, Allowance for Uncollectible Accounts, and *net* accounts receivable at October 31. How much does Ageless expect to collect?
3. Show how Ageless will report Accounts Receivable on its October 31 balance sheet. Use the format illustrated for Intel on page 325.

Using the direct write-off method for bad debts
(Obj. 3)

E8-4 Refer to Exercise 8-3.

Required

1. Record uncollectible-account expense for October using the direct write-off method.
2. What amount of accounts receivable would Ageless report on its October 31 balance sheet under the direct write-off method? Does Ageless expect to collect the full amount?

Using the aging method to estimate bad debts
(Obj. 2, 5)

E8-5 At December 31, 20X4, the accounts receivable balance of Quest Corp. is $300,000. The Allowance for Doubtful Accounts has a $3,910 credit balance. Accountants for Quest prepare the following aging schedule for its accounts receivable:

	Total Balance	Age of Accounts			
		1–30 Days	31–60 Days	61–90 Days	Over 90 Days
$300,000............................		$140,000	$78,000	$69,000	$13,000
Estimated percent uncollectible..................		0.3%	1.2%	6.0%	50%

Required

1. Journalize the adjusting entry for doubtful accounts on the basis of the aging schedule. Show the T-account for the Allowance.
2. Show how Quest Corp. will report Accounts Receivable on its December 31 balance sheet.

Reporting bad debts by the allowance method
(Obj. 2, 5)

E8-6 At December 31, 20X2, Circuit Software has an accounts receivable balance of $137,000. Sales revenue for 20X2 is $950,000, including credit sales of $450,000. For each of the following situations, prepare the year-end adjusting entry to record uncollectible-account expense. Show how the accounts receivable and the allowance for uncollectible accounts are reported on the balance sheet. Use the reporting format illustrated for Intel on page 325.

a. Allowance for Uncollectible Accounts has a credit balance of $1,600 before adjustment. Circuit estimates that uncollectible-account expense for the year is 1/2 of 1% of credit sales.
b. Allowance for Uncollectible Accounts has a debit balance of $1,700 before adjustment. Circuit estimates that $2,600 of the accounts receivable will prove uncollectible.

Computing notes receivable amounts
(Obj. 4)

E8-7 On April 30, 20X7, First National Bank of Kansas City lent $1,000,000 to Marjorie Redwine on a two-year, 9% note.

Required

1. Compute the interest during 20X7, 20X8, and 20X9 for the Redwine note receivable.
2. Which party has a
   a. Note receivable?   c. Interest revenue?
   b. Note payable?   d. Interest expense?
3. How much in total would Redwine pay First National Bank if she paid off the note early—say, on November 30, 20X7?

Recording notes receivable and accruing interest revenue
(Obj. 4)

E8-8 Record the following transactions in the journal of Glacial Enterprises, Inc.:

Nov. 1 Loaned $50,000 cash to Victor Rashad on a one-year, 8% note.
Dec. 3 Sold goods to Lendox Corp., receiving a 90-day, 11% note for $3,750.
     16 Received a $4,000, six-month, 12% note on account from CFO Co.
     31 Accrued interest revenue on all notes receivable. Use a 360-day year for interest computations.

Recording bankcard sales and a note receivable, and accruing interest revenue
(Obj. 4)

E8-9 Record the following transactions in Wachovia Company's journal:

20X3
Feb. 12 Recorded VISA bankcard sales of $55,000, less a 2% discount.
Apr.   1 Loaned $8,000 to Peter Liu on a one-year, 12% note.
Dec. 31 Accrued interest revenue on the Liu note.

20X4
Apr.   1 Collected the maturity value of the note from Liu.

E8-10 Horizon Energy Corp. sells on account. When a customer account becomes two months old, Horizon converts the account to a note receivable. During 20X2, Horizon completed these transactions:

Recording notes receivable transactions
(Obj. 4)

Aug. 29 Sold goods on account to M. Tallus, $5,400.
Nov. 1 Received a $5,400, 60-day, 10% note from M. Tallus in satisfaction of his past-due account receivable.
Dec. 31 Collected the Tallus note at maturity.

Required

Record the transactions in Horizon Energy's journal.

E8-11 Bernstein Bros., a clothing store, reported the following amounts in its 20X3 financial statements. The 20X2 figures are given for comparison.

Evaluating ratio data
(Obj. 6)

		20X3		20X2
Current assets:				
Cash		$ 3,000		$ 10,000
Short-term investments		23,000		11,000
Accounts receivable	$80,000		$74,000	
Less: Allowance for uncollectibles...	(7,000)	73,000	(6,000)	68,000
Inventory		192,000		189,000
Prepaid insurance		2,000		2,000
Total current assets............................		293,000		280,000
Total current liabilities..........................		$124,000		$127,000
Net sales...		$703,000		$732,000

Required

1. Determine whether Bernstein's acid-test ratio improved or deteriorated from 20X2 to 20X3. How does Bernstein's acid-test ratio compare with the industry average of 0.80?
2. Compare the days' sales in receivables for 20X3 with Bernstein's credit terms of net 30.

E8-12 **Wal-Mart Stores, Inc.,** is the largest retailer in the United States. Recently, Wal-Mart reported these figures (in billions of dollars):

Analyzing a company's financial statements
(Obj. 6)

	1999	1998
Net sales...	$165	$138
Receivables at end of year	1	1

The Wal-Mart financial statements include no uncollectible-account expense or allowance.

Required

1. Compute Wal-Mart's average collection period on receivables during 1999.
2. Why are Wal-Mart's receivables so low? How can Wal-Mart have $1 billion of receivables at January 31, 1999, and no significant allowance for uncollectibles?

Challenge Exercise

E8-13 Slazenger Sporting Equipment sells on store credit and manages its own receivables. Average experience each year for the past three years has been as follows:

Evaluating credit-card sales for profitability
(Obj. 2)

	Total
Sales	$350,000
Cost of goods sold.....................................	210,000
Uncollectible-account expense..................	4,000
Other expenses..	61,000

Bruce Slazenger, the owner, is considering whether to accept bankcards (**VISA, MasterCard**). Typically, accepting bankcards increases total sales and cost of goods sold by 12%. But VISA and MasterCard charge approximately 2% of bankcard sales. If Slazenger switches to bankcards, he can save $2,000 on accounting and other expenses. After the switchover to bankcards, Slazenger expects cash sales of $200,000.

Required

Should Slazenger start accepting bankcards? Show the computations of net income under the present plan and under the bankcard plan.

(Group A) PROBLEMS

Controlling cash receipts from customers
(Obj. 1)

P8-1A Newcastle Sporting Goods distributes merchandise to sporting goods stores. All sales are on credit, so virtually all cash receipts arrive in the mail. William Borrows, the company president, has just returned from a meeting with new ideas for the business. Among other things, Borrows plans to institute stronger internal controls over cash receipts from customers.

Required

Assume you are William Borrows. Write a memo to employees outlining a set of procedures to ensure that all cash receipts are deposited in the bank and that the total amounts of each day's cash receipts are posted as credits to customer accounts receivable. Use the memorandum format given in Exercise 8-1, page 333.

Accounting for uncollectibles by the direct write-off and allowance methods
(Obj. 2, 3, 5)

P8-2A On February 28, Signa, Inc., had a $75,000 debit balance in Accounts Receivable. During March, Signa made sales of $445,000, all on credit. Other data for March include

• Collections on account, $422,600.   • Write-offs of uncollectible receivables, $3,500.

Required

1. Record sales and collections on account. Then record uncollectible-account expense for March using the *direct write-off* method. Post to Accounts Receivable and Uncollectible-Account Expense and show their balances at March 31.
2. Record sales and collections on account. Then record uncollectible-account expense and write-offs of customer accounts for March using the *allowance* method. Show all March activity in Accounts Receivable, Allowance for Uncollectible Accounts, and Uncollectible-Account Expense (post to these T-accounts). The February 28 unadjusted balance in Allowance for Uncollectible Accounts was $800 (debit). Uncollectible-account expense was estimated at 2% of credit sales.
3. What amount of uncollectible-account expense would Signa, Inc., report on its March income statement under the two methods? Which amount better matches expense with revenue? Give your reason.
4. What amount of *net* accounts receivable would Signa, Inc., report on its March 31 balance sheet under the two methods? Which amount is more realistic? Give your reason.

Using the percent-of-sales and aging methods for uncollectibles
(Obj. 2, 5)

P8-3A The June 30, 20X4, balance sheet of Delforce Associates, Inc., reports the following:

Accounts Receivable	$265,000
Allowance for Uncollectible Accounts (credit balance)	7,100

At the end of each quarter, Delforce estimates uncollectible-account expense to be 2% of credit sales. At the end of the year, the company ages its accounts receivable and adjusts the balance in Allowance for Uncollectible Accounts to correspond to the aging schedule. During the second half of 20X4, Delforce completed the following transactions:

July 14	Made a compound entry to write off the following uncollectible accounts: T. J. Dooley, $766; Design Works, Inc., $2,413; and S. DeWitt, $134.
Sep. 30	Recorded uncollectible-account expense equal to 2% of credit sales of $141,400.
Nov. 22	Wrote off the following accounts receivable as uncollectible: Transnet Corp., $1,345; Webvan, Inc., $2,109; and The Avenue Group, $755.
Dec. 31	Recorded uncollectible-account expense based on the aging of accounts receivable.

		Age of Accounts			
	Total Balance	1–30 Days	31–60 Days	61–90 Days	Over 90 Days
	$256,600	$121,500	$86,000	$34,000	$15,100
Estimated percent uncollectible		0.2%	0.5%	4.0%	50.0%

Required

1. Record the transactions in the journal.
2. Open the Allowance for Uncollectible Accounts, and post entries affecting that account. Keep a running balance.
3. Most companies report two-year comparative financial statements. If Delforce's Accounts Receivable balance was $271,400 and the Allowance for Uncollectible Accounts stood at

$8,240 at December 31, 20X3, show how the company will report its accounts receivable in a comparative balance sheet for 20X4 and 20X3.

P8-4A ◄ *Link Back to Chapter 4 (Closing Entries).* Minnetonk Enterprises completed the following selected transactions during 20X1 and 20X2:

Using the percent-of-sales method for uncollectibles (Obj. 2, 5)

20X1

Dec. 31 Estimated that uncollectible-account expense for the year was 2/3 of 1% on credit sales of $450,000, and recorded that amount as expense.

   31 Made the closing entry for uncollectible-account expense.

20X2

Feb. 4 Sold inventory to Sam Vesper, $1,521, on credit terms of 2/10 n/30. Ignore cost of goods sold.

July 1 Wrote off Sam Vesper's account as uncollectible after repeated efforts to collect from him.

Oct. 19 Received $521 from Sam Vesper, along with a letter stating his intention to pay his debt in full within 30 days. Reinstated his account in full.

Nov. 15 Received the balance due from Sam Vesper.

Dec. 31 Made a compound entry to write off the following accounts as uncollectible: Kaycee Britt, $899; Tim Sands, $530; and Anna Chin, $1,272.

   31 Estimated that uncollectible-account expense for the year was 2/3 of 1% on credit sales of $585,000 and recorded the expense.

   31 Made the closing entry for uncollectible-account expense.

Required

1. Open general ledger accounts for Allowance for Uncollectible Accounts and Uncollectible-Account Expense. Keep running balances.
2. Record the transactions in the general journal, and post to the two ledger accounts.
3. The December 31, 20X2, balance of Accounts Receivable is $164,500. Show how Accounts Receivable would be reported on the balance sheet at that date.

P8-5A Windows Company received the following notes during 20X3.

Accounting for notes receivable, including accruing interest revenue (Obj. 4)

Note	Date	Principal Amount	Interest Rate	Term
(1)	Oct. 31	$11,000	12%	3 months
(2)	Nov. 19	15,000	10%	60 days
(3)	Dec. 1	12,000	9%	1 year

Required

Identify each note by number, compute interest using a 360-day year for those notes with terms specified in days or years, round all interest amounts to the nearest dollar, and present entries in general journal form. Explanations are not required.

1. Determine the due date and maturity value of each note.
2. Journalize a single adjusting entry at December 31, 20X3, to record accrued interest revenue on all three notes.
3. Journalize the collection of principal and interest on note (1).

P8-6A ◄ *Link Back to Chapter 4 (Closing Entries).* Record the following selected transactions in the general journal of Recognition Systems. Explanations are not required.

Accounting for notes receivable, dishonored notes, and accrued interest revenue (Obj. 4)

20X2

Dec. 21 Received a $2,800, 30-day, 10% note on account from Lindsey Fitzhugh.

   31 Made an adjusting entry to accrue interest on the Fitzhugh note.

   31 Made a closing entry for interest revenue.

20X3

Jan. 20 Collected the maturity value of the Fitzhugh note.

Sept. 14 Loaned $4,000 cash to Bullseye Investors, receiving a three-month, 13% note.

   30 Received a $1,675, 60-day, 16% note from Chuck Powers on his past-due account receivable.

Nov. 29 Chuck Powers dishonored his note at maturity; wrote off the note as uncollectible, debiting Allowance for Uncollectible Accounts.

Dec. 14 Collected the maturity value of the Bullseye Investors note.

Journalizing uncollectibles, notes receivable, and accrued interest revenue (Obj. 4)

P8-7A Assume that **Sherwin Williams,** the paint manufacturer, completed the following selected transactions:

20X1

Dec. 1 Sold goods to Kelly Paint Supply, receiving a $13,500, three-month, 10% note. Ignore cost of goods sold.

31 Made an adjusting entry to accrue interest on the Kelly note. Round the interest amount to the nearest dollar.

31 Made an adjusting entry to record uncollectible-account expense based on an aging of accounts receivable. The aging analysis indicates that $355,800 of accounts receivable will not be collected. Prior to this adjustment, the credit balance in Allowance for Uncollectible Accounts is $346,100.

20X2

Mar. 1 Collected the maturity value of the Kelly Paint Supply note.

July 21 Sold merchandise to Mellon Co., receiving a 60-day, 9% note for $4,000. Ignore cost of goods sold.

Sep. 19 Mellon Co. dishonored its note (failed to pay) at maturity; we converted the maturity value of the note to an account receivable.

Nov. 11 Loaned $40,000 cash to Thermo Control, Inc., receiving a 90-day, 9% note.

Dec. 2 Collected in full from Mellon Co.

31 Accrued the interest on the Thermo Control note.

Required

Record the transactions in the journal of Sherwin Williams. Explanations are not required.

Using ratio data to evaluate a company's financial position (Obj. 6)

P8-8A ◄ *Link Back to Chapter 4 (Current Ratio).* The comparative financial statements of Grapevine Securities for 20X3, 20X2, and 20X1 include the data shown here:

		(In millions)	
	20X3	**20X2**	**20X1**
Balance sheet			
Current assets:			
Cash	$ 27	$ 26	$ 22
Short-term investments	93	101	69
Receivables, net of allowance for doubtful accounts of $7, $6, and $4, respectively	146	154	127
Inventories	454	383	341
Prepaid expenses	32	31	25
Total current assets	752	695	584
Total current liabilities	$ 440	$ 446	$ 388
Income statement			
Sales revenue	$2,671	$2,505	$1,944
Cost of sales	1,380	1,360	963

Required

1. Compute these ratios for 20X3 and 20X2:
   a. Current ratio   **b.** Acid-test ratio   **c.** Days' sales in receivables

2. Write a memo explaining to top management which ratios improved from 20X2 to 20X3 and which ratios deteriorated. Which item in the financial statements caused some ratios to improve and others to deteriorate? Discuss whether this factor conveys a favorable or an unfavorable sign about the company.

(Group B) PROBLEMS

Controlling cash receipts from customers (Obj. 1)

P8-1B Molson Appliance Co., prepares crowns, dentures, and other dental appliances. All work is performed on account, with regular monthly billing to participating dentists. Eve Nations, accountant for Molson, opens the mail. Company procedure requires her to separate customer checks from the remittance slips, which list the amounts she posts as credits to customer accounts receivable. Nations deposits the checks in the bank. She computes each day's total amount posted to customer accounts and matches this total to the bank deposit slip. This procedure is intended to ensure that all receipts are deposited in the bank.

Required

As a consultant hired by Molson Appliance Co., write a memo to management evaluating the company's internal controls over cash receipts from customers. If the system is effective, identify its strong features. If the system has flaws, propose a way to strengthen the controls. Use the memorandum format given in Exercise 8-1, page 333.

P8-2B On May 31, Nortell Networks, had a $210,000 debit balance in Accounts Receivable. During June, Nortell made sales of $640,000, all on credit. Other data for June include

Accounting for uncollectibles by the direct write-off and allowance methods
(Obj. 2, 3, 5)

- Collections on account, $567,400.
- Write-offs of uncollectible receivables, $8,900.

Required

1. Record sales and collections on account. Then record uncollectible-account expense for June using the *direct write-off* method. Post to Accounts Receivable and Uncollectible-Account Expense and show their balances at June 30.
2. Record sales and collections on account. Then record uncollectible-account expense and write-offs of customer accounts for June using the *allowance* method. Show all June activity in Accounts Receivable, Allowance for Uncollectible Accounts, and Uncollectible-Account Expense (post to these T-accounts). The May 31 unadjusted balance in Allowance for Uncollectible Accounts was $2,800 (credit). Uncollectible-account expense was estimated at 2% of credit sales.
3. What amount of uncollectible-account expense would Nortell report on its June income statement under the two methods? Which amount better matches expense with revenue? Give your reason.
4. What amount of *net* accounts receivable would Nortell report on its June 30 balance sheet under the two methods? Which amount is more realistic? Give your reason.

P8-3B The June 30, 20X1, balance sheet of Clarus Consultants, Inc., reports the following:

Using the percent-of-sales and aging methods for uncollectibles
(Obj. 2, 5)

Accounts Receivable	$143,000
Allowance for Uncollectible Accounts (credit balance)	3,200

At the end of each quarter, Clarus estimates uncollectible-account expense to be 1 1/2% of credit sales. At the end of the year, the company ages its accounts receivable and adjusts the balance in Allowance for Uncollectible Accounts to correspond to the aging schedule. During the second half of 20X1, Clarus completed the following selected transactions:

Aug. 9   Made a compound entry to write off the following uncollectible accounts: Aguilar, Inc., $235; Seaton Co., $188; and T. Taylor, $706.

Sep. 30   Recorded uncollectible-account expense equal to $1\frac{1}{2}$% of credit sales of $140,000.

Oct. 18   Wrote off as uncollectible the $767 account receivable from Lintz Co. and the $430 account receivable from Navisor Corp.

Dec. 31   Recorded uncollectible-account expense based on the aging of accounts receivable.

	Age of Accounts			
Total Balance	1–30 Days	31–60 Days	61–90 Days	Over 90 Days
$136,500	$81,700	$31,100	$14,000	$9,700
Estimated percent uncollectible	0.1%	0.4%	5.0%	30.0%

Required

1. Record the transactions in the journal. Round all amounts to the nearest dollar.
2. Open the Allowance for Uncollectible Accounts, and post entries affecting that account. Keep a running balance.
3. Most companies report two-year comparative financial statements. If Clarus's Accounts Receivable balance was $118,000 and the Allowance for Uncollectible Accounts stood at $2,700 at December 31, 20X0 show how the company will report its accounts receivable on a comparative balance sheet for 20X1 and 20X0.

P8-4B ◂━ *Link Back to Chapter 4 (Closing Entries)*. Interbiz Interactive completed the following transactions during 20X1 and 20X2:

Using the percent-of-sales method for uncollectibles
(Obj. 2, 5)

20X1

Dec. 31   Estimated that uncollectible-account expense for the year was 3/4 of 1% on credit sales of $290,000, and recorded that amount as expense.

31   Made the closing entry for uncollectible-account expense.

20X2

Jan. 17   Sold inventory to Mitch Vanez, $652, on credit terms of 2/10 n/30. Ignore cost of goods sold.

June 29   Wrote off the Mitch Vanez account as uncollectible after repeated efforts to collect from him.

Aug. 6   Received $250 from Mitch Vanez, along with a letter stating his intention to pay his debt in full within 30 days. Reinstated his account in full.

Sept. 4   Received the balance due from Mitch Vanez.

Dec. 31   Made a compound entry to write off the following accounts as uncollectible: Bernard Klaus, $737; Marie Monet, $348; and Terry Fuhrman, $622.

31   Estimated that uncollectible-account expense for the year was 2/3 of 1% on credit sales of $400,000, and recorded that amount as expense. Round to the nearest dollar.

31   Made the closing entry for uncollectible-account expense.

Required

1. Open general ledger accounts for Allowance for Uncollectible Accounts and Uncollectible-Account Expense. Keep running balances.
2. Record the transactions in the general journal, and post to the two ledger accounts.
3. The December 31, 20X2, balance of Accounts Receivable is $139,000. Show how Accounts Receivable would be reported on the balance sheet at that date.

Accounting for notes receivable, including accruing interest revenue
(Obj. 4)

P8-5B Mindgames Company received the following notes during 20X3.

Note	Date	Principal Amount	Interest Rate	Term
(1)	Nov. 30	$12,000	12%	6 months
(2)	Dec. 7	9,000	10%	30 days
(3)	Dec. 23	13,000	9%	1 year

Required

Identify each note by number, compute interest using a 360-day year for those notes with terms specified in days or years, round all interest amounts to the nearest dollar, and present entries in general journal form. Explanations are not required.

1. Determine the due date and maturity value of each note.
2. Journalize a single adjusting entry at December 31, 20X3, to record accrued interest revenue on all three notes.
3. Journalize the collection of principal and interest on note (2).

Accounting for notes receivable, dishonored notes, and accrued interest revenue
(Obj. 4)

P8-6B ◂ *Link Back to Chapter 4 (Closing Entries).* Record the following selected transactions in the general journal of SAS Services. Explanations are not required.

20X4

Dec. 19   Received a $3,000, 60-day, 12% note on account from Arnold Cohen.

31   Made an adjusting entry to accrue interest on the Cohen note.

31   Made a closing entry for interest revenue.

20X5

Feb. 17   Collected the maturity value of the Cohen note.

June 1   Loaned $8,000 cash to Blues Brothers, receiving a 6-month, 11% note.

Oct. 31   Received a $1,500, 60-day, 12% note from Juan Juarez on his past-due account receivable.

Dec. 1   Collected the maturity value of the Blues Brothers note.

30   Juan Juarez dishonored his note at maturity; wrote off the note receivable as uncollectible, debiting Allowance for Uncollectible Accounts.

Journalizing uncollectibles, notes receivable, and accrued interest revenue
(Obj. 4)

P8-7B Assume that **Del Monte Foods,** famous for fruits and vegetables, completed the following selected transactions:

20X1

Nov. 1   Sold goods to **Kroger,** receiving a $20,000, three-month, 8% note. Ignore cost of goods sold.

Dec. 31   Made an adjusting entry to accrue interest on the Kroger note. Round to the nearest dollar.

31   Made an adjusting entry to record uncollectible-account expense based on an aging of accounts receivable. The aging analysis indicates that $197,400 of accounts receivable will not be collected. Prior to this adjustment, the credit balance in Allowance for Uncollectible Accounts is $189,900.

20X2

Feb.	1	Collected the maturity value of the Kroger note.
June	23	Sold merchandise to Artesian Corp., receiving a 60-day, 10% note for $9,000. Ignore cost of goods sold.
Aug.	22	Artesian Corp. dishonored (failed to pay) its note at maturity; we converted the maturity value of the note to an account receivable.
Nov.	16	Loaned $6,800 cash to Crane, Inc., receiving a 90-day, 12% note.
Dec.	5	Collected in full from Artesian Corp.
	31	Accrued the interest on the Crane, Inc., note.

Required

Record the transactions in the journal of Del Monte Foods. Explanations are not required.

P8-8B ← *Link Back to Chapter 4 (Current Ratio).* The comparative financial statements of American Dataset, for 20X3, 20X2, and 20X1 include the following selected data:

Using ratio data to evaluate a company's financial position (Obj. 6)

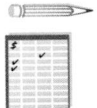

	(In millions)		
	20X3	**20X2**	**20X1**
Balance sheet			
Current assets:			
Cash...	$ 82	$ 80	$ 60
Short-term investments.......................................	140	174	122
Receivables, net of allowance for doubtful			
accounts of $6, $6, and $5, respectively	257	265	218
Inventories..	429	341	302
Prepaid expenses	21	27	46
Total current assets	929	887	748
Total current liabilities......................................	$ 503	$ 528	$ 413
Income statement			
Sales revenue	$5,189	$4,995	$4,206
Cost of sales...	2,734	2,636	2,418

Required

1. Compute these ratios for 20X3 and 20X2:
   a. Current ratio   **b.** Acid-test ratio   **c.** Days' sales in receivables
2. Write a memo explaining to top management which ratios improved from 20X2 to 20X3 and which ratios deteriorated. Which item in the financial statements caused some ratios to improve and others to deteriorate? Discuss whether this factor conveys a favorable or an unfavorable impression about American Dataset.

APPLY YOUR KNOWLEDGE

DECISION CASES

Case 1. Deutschetek Corporation performs service either for cash or on notes receivable. The business uses the direct write-off method to account for bad debts. Hilda Lyth, the owner, has prepared the company's financial statements. The most recent comparative income statements, for 20X3 and 20X2, are as follows:

Uncollectible accounts and evaluating a business (Obj. 2, 3)

	20X3	**20X2**
Total revenue	$220,000	$195,000
Total expenses..............	107,000	103,000
Net income..................	$113,000	$ 92,000

On the basis of the increase in net income, Lyth wants to expand operations. She asks you to invest $50,000 in the business. You and Lyth have several meetings, at which you learn that notes receivable from customers were $200,000 at the end of 20X1 and $400,000 at the end of 20X2. Also, total revenues for 20X3 and 20X2 include interest at 13% on the year's beginning notes receivable balance. Total expenses include uncollectible-account expense of $2,000 each year, based on the direct write-off method. Lyth estimates that uncollectible-account expense would be 5% of sales revenue if the allowance method were used.

Required

1. Prepare for Deutschetek a comparative single-step income statement that identifies service revenue, interest revenue, uncollectible-account expense, and other expenses, all computed in accordance with generally accepted accounting principles.
2. Is Deutschetek's future as promising as Lyth's income statement makes it appear? Give the reason for your answer.

Computing receivables amounts to report on the balance sheet (Obj. 5)

Case 2. This case takes the statement of cash flows a step beyond the chapter's coverage of this topic. However, you should be able to apply the principles learned thus far to solve it. Treasure Point Jewelry's statement of cash flows reported the following for the year ended June 30, 20X1.

TREASURE POINT JEWELRY
Statement of Cash Flows
Year Ended June 30, 20X1

Cash flows from operating activities:	
Collections from customers on account	$260,000
Cash flows from investing activities:	
Loaned out money on notes receivable	$ (45,000)
Collected on notes receivable	60,000

Treasure Point's balance sheet one year earlier—at June 30, 20X0—reported Accounts Receivable of $40,000 and Notes Receivable of $20,000. Credit sales for the year ended June 30, 20X1, totaled $310,000, and the company collects all of its accounts receivable because uncollectibles rarely occur.

Treasure Point Jewelry needs a loan and the owner is preparing Treasure Point's balance sheet at June 30, 20X1. To complete the balance sheet, the owner needs to know the balances of Accounts Receivable and Notes Receivable at June 30, 20X1. Supply the needed information; T-accounts are helpful.

ETHICAL ISSUE

QuiKash Finance Company is in the consumer loan business. It borrows from banks and loans out the money at higher interest rates. QuiKash's bank requires QuiKash to submit quarterly financial statements in order to keep its line of credit. QuiKash's main asset is Notes Receivable. Therefore, Uncollectible-Account Expense and Allowance for Uncollectible Accounts are important accounts.

Cameron Karr, the company's owner, wants net income to increase in a smooth pattern, rather than increase in some periods and decrease in others. To report smoothly increasing net income, Karr underestimates Uncollectible-Account Expense in some periods. In other periods, Karr overestimates the expense. He reasons that over time the income overstatements roughly offset the income understatements.

Required

Is QuiKash's practice of smoothing income ethical? Why or why not?

FINANCIAL STATEMENT CASE

Analyzing accounts receivable and uncollectibles (Obj. 2, 6)

Use the balance sheet and income statement of **Target Corporation,** in Appendix A.

1. How much did customers owe Target at January 29, 2000? Of this amount, how much did Target expect to collect? How much did Target expect *not* to collect? To answer these questions, refer to (a) Target's balance sheet (statement of financial position) and (b) the note entitled "Allowance for Doubtful Accounts" on page 22 of the Target Annual Report. *Retained securitized receivables* is Target's name for its accounts receivable.

2. During the year ended January 29, 2000, Target recorded doubtful-account expense of $147 million. The company also wrote off uncollectible receivables of $147 million. Prepare a T-account for Allowance for Doubtful Accounts. Insert the current year's beginning and ending balances as reported in the note. Then post the doubtful-account expense for the year and the write-offs for the year into the T-account. After your postings, the Allowance account should show all of Target's bad-debt activity for the current year.

3. Compute Target's acid-test ratio at January 29, 2000. If all the current liabilities came due immediately, could Target pay them?

342 CHAPTER 8

TEAM PROJECT

Bob Opper and Denise Shapp worked for several years as sales representatives for **Xerox Corporation.** During this time, they became close friends as they acquired expertise with the company's full range of copier equipment. Now they see an opportunity to put their experience to work and fulfill lifelong desires to establish their own business. Lakeside College, located in their city, is expanding, and there is no copy center within five miles of the campus. Business in the area is booming—office buildings and apartments are springing up, and the population in this section of the city is growing.

Opper and Shapp want to open a copy center, similar to a **Kinko's,** near the campus. A small shopping center across the street from the college has a vacancy that would fit their needs. Opper and Shapp each have $20,000 to invest in the business, and they forecast the need for $30,000 to renovate the store. **Xerox Corporation** will lease two large copiers to them at a total monthly rental of $4,000. With enough cash to see them through the first six months of operation, they are confident they can make the business succeed. The two work very well together, and both have excellent credit ratings. Opper and Shapp must borrow $80,000 to start the business, advertise its opening, and keep it running for its first six months.

Assume the roles of Opper and Shapp, the partners who will own Lakeside Copy Center.

1. As a group, visit a copy center to familiarize yourselves with its operations. If possible, interview the manager or another employee. Then write a loan request that Opper and Shapp will submit to a bank with the intent of borrowing $80,000 to be paid back over three years. The loan will be a personal loan to the partnership of Opper and Shapp, not to Lakeside Copy Center. The request should specify all the details of Opper's and Shapp's plan that will motivate the bank to grant the loan. Include a budgeted income statement for the first six months of the copy center's operation.

2. As a group, interview a loan officer in a bank. Have the loan officer evaluate your loan request. Write a report, or make a presentation to your class—as directed by your instructor—to reveal the loan officer's decision.

INTERNET EXERCISE

As the baby boomers age, the demand for pharmaceuticals has increased. Over the past several years **Pfizer Inc.** helped introduce three record-breaking products: Lipitor, Viagra, and Celebrex. As a result, in 1999 Pfizer became the world's number one pharmaceutical company in prescription sales.

Pfizer Inc.

1. Go to **http://www.Pfizer.com.** Click on *Investing in Pfizer* and select the *most recent annual report.* Use the pull-down menu to select *Our Global Presence.* In how many countries does Pfizer sell its products?

2. Use the pull-down menu to select the *Consolidated Balance Sheet.*
   a. To account for the uncollectible receivables, does Pfizer use the allowance method or the direct write-off method? How can you tell?
   b. For the most recent year, how much do customers owe Pfizer? How much does Pfizer expect to collect? How much does Pfizer expect not to collect?

3. Use the pull-down menu to select the *Consolidated Statement of Income.*
   a. Which expense listed includes the amount for uncollectible-account expense? How do you think Pfizer estimates its uncollectible-account expense? Do you think Pfizer wrote off any uncollectible accounts this past year?
   b. For the most recent year, research and development (R&D) expenses are what percentage of total revenues? R&D costs are a major expense for pharmaceutical companies. Explain why this is true.

4. For the two most recent years calculate the acid-test ratio. Show your work for the ratio calculations. For the most recent year comment on what the ratio indicates. Is the trend increasing or decreasing? Favorable or unfavorable? Explain why.

5. For the two most recent years calculate one day's sales using the amount reported for net sales in the numerator. For the two most recent years calculate days' sales in receivables. Please show your work for the ratio calculations. For the most recent year comment on what the days' sales in receivables ratio indicates. Is the trend increasing or decreasing? Favorable or unfavorable? Explain why.

APPENDIX TO CHAPTER 8

DISCOUNTING A NOTE RECEIVABLE

A payee of a note receivable may need the cash before the maturity date of the note. When this occurs, the payee may sell the note, a practice called **discounting a note receivable.** The price to be received for the note is determined by present-value

DISCOUNTING NOTE RECEIVABLE. Selling a note receivable before its maturity date.

→ We discuss these concepts in Chapter 15.

concepts. ←← But the transaction between the seller and the buyer of the note can take any form agreeable to the two parties. Here we illustrate one procedure used for discounting short-term notes receivable. To receive cash immediately, the seller accepts a lower price than the note's maturity value.

To illustrate discounting a note receivable, suppose **General Electric** loaned $15,000 to Dorman Builders on October 20, 20X3. GE took a note receivable from Dorman. The maturity date of the 90-day 10% Dorman note is January 18, 20X4. Suppose GE discounts the Dorman note at First City Bank on December 9, 20X3, when the note is 50 days old. The bank applies a 12% annual interest rate to determine the discounted value of the note. The bank will use a discount rate that is higher than the note's interest rate in order to earn some interest on the transaction. The discounted value, called the *proceeds*, is the amount GE receives from the bank. The proceeds can be computed in five steps, as shown in Exhibit 8A-1. GE's entry to record discounting (selling) the note on December 9, 20X3, is:

Dec. 9, 20X3	Cash	15,170	
	Note Receivable—Dorman Builders		15,000
	Interest Revenue ($15,170 − $15,000)		170
	Discounted a note receivable.		

EXHIBIT 8A-1
Discounting (Selling) a Note Receivable: GE Discounts the Dorman Builders Note

Step	Computation	
1. Compute the original amount of interest on the note receivable.	$15,000 × 0.10 × 90/360	= $375
2. Maturity value of the note = Principal + Interest	$15,000 + $375	= $15,375
3. Determine the period (number of days, months, or years) the *bank* will hold the note (the discount period).	Dec. 9, 19X3 to Jan. 18, 19X4	= 40 days
4. Compute the bank's discount on the note. This is the bank's interest revenue from holding the note.	$15,375 × 0.12 × 40/360	= $205
5. Seller's proceeds from discounting the note receivable = Maturity value of the note − Bank's discount on the note.	$15,375 − $205	= $15,170

The authors thank Doug Hamilton for suggesting this exhibit.

 DAILY EXERCISE 8-1A

When the proceeds from discounting a note receivable are less than the principal amount of the note, the payee records a debit to Interest Expense for the amount of the difference. For example, GE could discount the note receivable for cash proceeds of $14,980. The entry to record this discounting transaction is

Dec. 9, 20X3	Cash	14,980	
	Interest Expense	20	
	Note Receivable—Dorman Builders		15,000
	Discounted a note receivable.		

CONTINGENT LIABILITIES ON DISCOUNTED NOTES RECEIVABLE

CONTINGENT LIABILITY. A potential liability that will become an actual liability only if a particular event does occur.

A **contingent liability** is a potential liability that will become an actual liability only if a particular event occurs. Discounting a note receivable creates a contingent liability for the endorser. If the maker of the note (Dorman, in our example) fails to pay at maturity, then the original payee (GE) must pay the bank the amount due.[1] If Dorman pays the bank, then GE can forget the note.

DAILY EXERCISE

Discounting notes receivable (Obj. 4)

DE 8A-1 General Telecom installs telephone systems and receives its pay in the form of notes receivable. General Telecom installed a system for the city of Durango, Colorado, receiv-

---

[1]The discounting agreement can be "without recourse." That means the seller of the note has no liability if the note is dishonored at maturity. In that case, there is no contingent liability.

ing a nine-month, 8%, $500,000 note receivable on May 31, 20X1. To obtain cash quickly, General Telecom discounted the note with Rocky Mountain Bank on June 30, 20X1. The bank charged a discount rate of 9%.

Compute General Telecom's cash proceeds from discounting the note. Follow the five-step procedure outlined in Exhibit 8A-1.

EXERCISES

E8A-1A ◄ *Link Back to Chapter 5 (Recording a Sale).* Use your answers to Daily Exercise 8A-1 to journalize General Telecom's transactions as follows:

Accounting for a discounted note receivable (Obj. 4)

May 31	Sold a telecommunications system, receiving a 9-month, 8%, $500,000 note from the city of Durango. General Telecom's cost of the system was $450,000.
June 30	Received cash for interest revenue for one month. Round to the nearest dollar.
30	Discounted the note to Rocky Mountain Bank at a discount rate of 9%.

E8A-2A Rider Systems, Inc., sells on account. When a customer account becomes three months old, Rider converts the account to a note receivable and immediately discounts the note to a bank. During 20X4, Rider completed these transactions:

Recording notes receivable, discounting a note, and reporting the contingent liability in a note (Obj. 4)

Aug. 29	Sold goods on account to V. Moyer, $3,900.
Dec. 1	Received a $3,900, 60-day, 10% note from V. Moyer in satisfaction of his past-due account receivable.
1	Sold the Moyer note by discounting it to a bank for $3,600.

Required

Record the transactions in Rider Systems' journal.

PROBLEMS

P8A-1 A company received the following notes during 20X3. Notes (1), (2), and (3) were discounted on the dates and at the rates indicated.

Discounting notes receivable (Obj. 4)

Note	Date	Principal Amount	Interest Rate	Term	Date Discounted	Discount Rate
(1)	July 12	$10,000	10%	3 months	Aug. 12	15%
(2)	Aug. 4	6,000	11%	90 days	Aug. 30	13%
(3)	Oct. 21	8,000	15%	60 days	Nov. 3	18%

Required

Identify each note by number, compute interest using a 360-day year for those notes with terms specified in days, round all interest amounts to the nearest dollar, and present entries in general journal form. Explanations are not required.

1. Determine the due date and maturity value of each note.
2. Determine the discount and proceeds from the sale (discounting) of each note.
3. Journalize the discounting of notes (1) and (2).

P8A-2 A company received the following notes during 20X5. Notes (1), (2), and (3) were discounted on the dates and at the rates indicated.

Discounting notes receivable (Obj. 4)

Note	Date	Principal Amount	Interest Rate	Term	Date Discounted	Discount Rate
(1)	July 15	$6,000	10%	6 months	Oct. 15	12%
(2)	Aug. 19	9,000	12%	90 days	Aug. 30	15%
(3)	Sept. 1	8,000	15%	120 days	Nov. 2	20%

Required

Identify each note by number, compute interest using a 360-day year for those notes with terms specified in days, round all interest amounts to the nearest dollar, and present entries in general journal form. Explanations are not required.

1. Determine the due date and maturity value of each note.
2. Determine the discount and proceeds from the sale (discounting) of each note.
3. Journalize the discounting of notes (1) and (2).

Merchandise Inventory

LEARNING OBJECTIVES

After studying this chapter, you should be able to

1. Account for inventory by the perpetual and periodic systems

2. Apply inventory costing methods: specific unit cost, weighted-average cost, FIFO, and LIFO

3. Identify the income effects and the tax effects of the inventory costing methods

4. Apply the lower-of-cost-or-market rule to inventory

5. Determine the effects of inventory errors on cost of goods sold and net income

6. Estimate ending inventory by the gross profit method

www.prenhall.com/horngren

Readiness Assessment

Deckers Outdoor Corporation began when University of California at Santa Barbara student Doug Otto started making sandals. From a fledgling operation, Deckers has grown into an international company, with footwear brands Teva and Simple. The company also sells clothing lines Teva and Picante. (Teva is a play off the Hebrew word *Teh-vah* for *nature*.) Teva sandals were initially designed by a Grand Canyon river guide for river rafting. Their quality and stability touched off a small revolution in footwear.

Deckers Outdoor had sales of almost $110 million in 1999, and the company's assets totaled $73 million. As the company has grown, Doug Otto and Deckers have faced a number of accounting decisions. Which method should Deckers use to account for its inventory of sandals and clothing? How much inventory should the company purchase from suppliers? This chapter discusses how to account for and manage inventory—the asset that defines a merchandising business.

Deckers Outdoor is a **merchandising company.** This means that Deckers sells a product rather than a service. To a merchandiser, inventory is the lifeblood of the organization. Deckers' balance sheet in Exhibit 9-1 lists inventory of $18.1 million among its current assets.

A merchandiser's major expense is *cost of goods sold,* also called *cost of sales*. This is Deckers' cost of the sandals and clothing it sold. For Deckers and other merchandisers, cost of goods sold is greater than the sum of all the other expenses combined. Exhibit 9-1 shows that Deckers had cost of sales of $64.5 million during 1999.

MERCHANDISING COMPANY. A company that resells products bought from suppliers.

EXHIBIT 9-1
Financial Statements of Deckers Outdoor Corporation, Maker of Teva Sandals

DECKERS OUTDOOR CORPORATION
Income Statement (partial, adapted)
Year Ended December 31, 1999

	Millions
Net sales	$109.6
Cost of goods sold	64.5
Gross profit	45.1
Total operating expenses (can be detailed)	42.2
Net income	$ 2.9

DECKERS OUTDOOR CORPORATION
Balance Sheet (Current assets only)
December 31, 1999

Assets	Millions
Current assets:	
Cash	$ 1.6
Trade accounts receivable,	
Less Allowance of $1.8	24.4
Inventories	18.1
Prepaid expenses	4.9
Total current assets	$49.0

We begin this chapter with the basic concept of accounting for inventories. Then we examine different inventory systems (perpetual and periodic), the different inventory methods (FIFO, LIFO, and average), and several related topics.

ACCOUNTING FOR INVENTORY AND INVENTORY SYSTEMS

Basic Concepts

The basic concept of accounting for inventory is straightforward. Suppose **Deckers Outdoor Corporation** buys three pairs of sandals for $30 each, marks them up by $20, and sells two of the pairs for $50 each. Deckers' balance sheet reports the inventory that the company still holds, and the income statement reports cost of goods sold for the units sold, as follows (focus on the highlights):

Balance Sheet (partial)		Income Statement (partial)	
Current assets:	$XXX	Sales revenue	
Cash	XXX	(2 pairs @ $50)	$100
Accounts receivable	XXX	Cost of goods sold	
Inventory (1 pair @ $30)	30	(2 pairs @ $30)	60
Prepaid expenses	XXX	Gross profit	$ 40

GROSS PROFIT OR GROSS MARGIN.
Excess of sales revenue over cost of goods sold.

 DAILY EXERCISE 9-1

Objective 1
Account for inventory by the perpetual and periodic systems

➤ We described these methods in Chapter 5.

PERIODIC INVENTORY SYSTEM. An inventory accounting system in which the business does not keep a continuous record of the inventory on hand. Instead, at the end of the period, the business counts the inventory on hand and uses this information to prepare the financial statements.

PERPETUAL INVENTORY SYSTEM. An inventory accounting system in which the business keeps a running record to show the inventory on hand at all times.

As we saw in Chapter 5, **gross profit,** also called **gross margin,** is the excess of sales revenue over cost of goods sold. It is called *gross* profit because operating expenses have not yet been subtracted. Gross profit minus all the operating expenses then equals *net* income. In practice, accounting for inventory is more complex than our simple example.

There are two main types of inventory accounting systems: the periodic system and the perpetual system. ➤ The **periodic inventory system** is used by businesses that sell relatively inexpensive goods. Many small businesses use the periodic system. Stores without optical-scanning cash registers do not keep a running record of every loaf of bread and every six-pack of drinks they sell. Instead, these stores count their inventory periodically—at least once a year—to determine the quantities on hand and prepare the financial statements.

Under the **perpetual inventory system,** the business maintains a running record of inventory on hand, usually on computer. This system achieves control over goods such as automobiles, jewelry, and furniture. The loss of one item would be significant and this justifies the cost of a perpetual system. Because computers are costing less and less, many small businesses now use perpetual inventory systems.

Under both systems, the business still counts its inventory annually. The physical count establishes the amount of ending inventory and serves as a check on the records. The following chart compares the periodic and perpetual systems:

Periodic Inventory System	Perpetual Inventory System
• Does not keep a running record of inventory	• Keeps a running record of all goods
• Used for inexpensive goods	• Used for all types of goods
• Inventory counted at least once a year	• Inventory counted at least once a year

Perpetual Inventory System

Perpetual inventory records can be a computer printout like the Deckers' record shown for a line of Teva sandals in Exhibit 9-2. The quantities of goods on hand are updated daily, as inventory transactions occur. Many companies keep their perpetual records in terms of quantities only, as shown in the exhibit. When a customer orders 10 pairs of sandals, Deckers can refer to its perpetual inventory record.

In the perpetual system, the business records purchases of inventory by debiting the Inventory account. When the business makes a sale, two entries are needed: one to record the sale and the other to record the decrease in inventory on hand.

Exhibit 9-3 illustrates the accounting in a perpetual system for a single line of Teva sandals at Deckers Outdoor. Panel A gives the journal entries and the

Item: Teva Sandals			
Date	Quantity Received	Quantity Sold	Quantity on Hand
Nov. 1			10
5		6	4
7	25		29
12		13	16
26	25		41
30		21	20
Totals	50	40	20

T-accounts, and Panel B shows the resulting income statement and balance sheet. All amounts are assumed.

 DAILY EXERCISE 9-2

DAILY EXERCISE 9-3

EXHIBIT 9-3   **Recording and Reporting Inventory Transactions of Deckers Outdoor—Perpetual System** (amounts assumed)

PANEL A—Recording in the Journal and Posting to the T-accounts—Perpetual System

INVENTORY AND COST OF GOODS SOLD ACCOUNTS

1. Credit purchases of $560,000:
   Inventory 560,000
        Accounts Payable............. 560,000
2. Credit sales of $900,000 (cost $540,000):
   Accounts Receivable 900,000
        Sales Revenue.................. 900,000

   Cost of Goods Sold 540,000
        Inventory......................... 540,000
3. End-of-period entries:
   None required. Both Inventory and Cost of Goods Sold are up to date.

INVENTORY		COST OF GOODS SOLD
100,000*	540,000	540,000
560,000		
120,000		

* Beginning inventory was $100,000.

PANEL B—Reporting in the Financial Statements

Income Statement (partial)

Sales revenue	$ 900,000
Cost of goods sold..........................	540,000
Gross profit.....................................	$ 360,000

Balance Sheet (partial)

Current assets:		
Cash	$	XXX
Short-term investments		XXX
Accounts receivable		XXX
Inventories.................................		120,000
Prepaid expenses........................		XXX

In Exhibit 9-3, Panel A, the first entry to Inventory summarizes a lot of detail. The cost of the inventory, $560,000, is the *net* amount of the purchases, determined as follows (using assumed amounts):

Net Purchases	
Purchase price of the inventory (including freight in)	$600,000
− Purchase returns for unsuitable goods returned to the seller	(25,000)
− Purchase allowances granted by the seller	(5,000)
− Purchase discounts taken for early payment.............	(10,000)
= Net purchases of inventory...	$560,000

Throughout the remainder of the book, we often refer to Net Purchases simply as Purchases, as in Exhibit 9-3.

The cost of the goods purchased by Deckers Outdoor during the year was $560,000. This is based on a general principle:

$$\text{The cost of an asset} = \begin{array}{c}\textbf{The sum of all the costs}\\\textbf{incurred to bring the}\\\textbf{asset to its intended purpose,}\\\textbf{after subtracting all discounts}\end{array}$$

The buyer's cost of transporting goods from the supplier (called freight in) is part of the purchase cost of the inventory. Freight in is *not* recorded as an expense.

At the end of the period, no adjusting entries are required. Both Inventory and Cost of Goods Sold are up to date.[1]

Cost of Goods Sold (Cost of Sales) and Gross Profit

Exhibit 9-3 illustrates the measurement of cost of goods sold (cost of sales) in the perpetual inventory system. Cost of sales is simply the sum of all the amounts posted to the Cost of Goods Sold account throughout the period (see Exhibit 9-3, Panel A). There is another way to compute cost of goods sold, and it comes from the periodic inventory system. Using the periodic system, the cost-of-goods-sold computation is as follows, using the data from Exhibit 9-3:

Cost of Goods Sold	
Beginning inventory...................................	$100,000
+ Purchases (including freight in)..............	560,000
= Cost of goods available for sale...............	660,000
− Ending inventory....................................	(120,000)
= Cost of goods sold..................................	$540,000

The business began the period with $100,000 of inventory. During the period, purchases totaled $560,000. The sum of the beginning inventory plus purchases equals the **cost of goods available for sale,** $660,000. Goods available are either in ending inventory, $120,000, or were sold. Cost of goods sold was therefore $660,000 − $120,000 = $540,000.

This computation of cost of goods sold is so important that all companies use it to bring together all the inventory data of an accounting period. Even companies that use the perpetual system summarize their inventory data this way.

How Owners and Managers Use the Cost-of-Goods-Sold Model

Suppose you are in charge of a line of Teva Sandals at Deckers Outdoor. You are planning your buying of inventory for the next period, and you must decide how much inventory to purchase from your supplier in Taiwan. How will you make the decision? The amount of inventory to purchase depends on three factors:

- budgeted cost of goods sold
- budgeted ending inventory
- the beginning inventory with which you started the period

A rearrangement of the cost-of-goods-sold formula helps you decide how much to purchase for the coming year (all budgeted amounts for the next period are assumed):

COST OF GOODS AVAILABLE FOR SALE Beginning inventory plus purchases.

---

[1]An adjusting entry is needed only if the Inventory account does not agree with the physical count of goods on hand.

Computation of Budgeted Purchases	
Cost of goods sold (budgeted for the next period)	$600,000
+ Ending inventory (budgeted for the next period)	150,000
= Cost of goods available for sale, as budgeted	750,000
− Beginning inventory (actual amount left over from the prior period)	(120,000)
= Purchases (the inventory you need to buy to reach your goal)	$630,000

Business owners and managers use this formula to determine how much to spend on inventory, regardless of the inventory system used. The power of the cost-of-goods-sold model lies in the information it captures: beginning and ending inventory levels, purchases, and cost of goods sold.

Computing the Cost of Inventory

The Deckers Outdoor inventory record in Exhibit 9-2 follows the common practice of recording quantities only. The company multiplies the 20 pairs of Teva Sandals on hand by the cost of each pair to compute the ending inventory for the balance sheet, as follows:

Cost of inventory on hand	=	Quantity on hand	×	Unit cost
$600	=	20 pairs	×	$30

DETERMINING THE QUANTITY OF INVENTORY   Many businesses count their inventory on the last day of the fiscal year. If you have worked at a retail business, you will recall the process of "taking inventory." Some entities shut the business down to get a good inventory count.

A complication in counting inventory arises from consigned goods. In a **consignment** arrangement, the owner of the inventory (the *consignor*) transfers the goods to another business (the *consignee*). Then the consignee sells the inventory for the owner. The consignee does *not* own the consigned goods and therefore should not include them in its own inventory. Consignments are common in retailing. Suppose Deckers Outdoor is the consignee for a line of backpacks. Should Deckers include this consigned merchandise in its inventory? No, because Deckers does not own the goods. Instead, the backpack manufacturer—the consignor—includes the consigned goods in its inventory. *Include in inventory only what the business owns.*

CONSIGNMENT. Transfer of goods by the owner (consignor) to another business (consignee) that sells the inventory on the owner's behalf. The consignee does not take title to the consigned goods.

DETERMINING THE UNIT COST OF INVENTORY   As we've seen, *inventory cost* is the price the business pays to purchase the goods—not the selling price. Suppose Deckers Outdoor purchases a T-shirt for $10 and sells it for $15. Deckers would report the inventory at its cost of $10 per unit, not at its selling price of $15.

Inventory cost includes invoice price, less any purchase discount, plus sales tax, tariffs, transportation charges, insurance while in transit, and all other costs incurred to make the goods ready for sale. *Net purchases* means the net cost of inventory acquired for resale, after subtracting any purchase discounts and purchase returns and allowances. As we stated earlier, we use the terms *purchases* and *net purchases* interchangeably.

Periodic Inventory System

In the periodic inventory system, the business does not keep a running record of the inventory on hand. Instead, at the end of the period, the business counts the goods on hand and computes the cost of ending inventory. This inventory figure appears on the balance sheet and is used to compute cost of goods sold. The periodic system is also called the *physical system* because it relies on the actual physical count of inventory.

It's a Bird . . . It's a Plane . . . It's a Warehouse!
DHL Worldwide Express

Say "inventory" and you probably conjure up a warehouse filled with auto tires awaiting shipment. In the new world economy, however, inventory is likely to be zipping overhead via overnight air express. At 3:00 A.M. in Brussels, Belgium, you get a snapshot of just what lean inventory means: Workers at the **DHL Air Express** hub use forklifts to hoist **Dell Computers, Nokia** cell phones and **Ford** car parts onto planes bound for Finland, South Africa, and Argentina. And all these products just came off other planes: nothing sits in a warehouse.

The pressure to keep inventory levels low has fueled the profits of the air express industry. "You can't have any dead space in your supply chain," says Lynnette McIntire of **UPS.** McIntire says her customers no longer stock a month of inventory. Instead, they depend on today's deliveries for tomorrow's manufacturing.

DHL may play second fiddle to **FedEx** and **UPS** in the United States, but it rules the world of overseas business-to-business transactions. In fact, DHL invented the industry. International air shipments are growing at 18% a year, twice the rate of domestic. With over 40% of the international market, DHL Worldwide Express was named the "World's Most Global Company" by *Global Finance* magazine.

Source: Based on Andrew Tanzer, "Warehouses that fly," *Forbes,* October 18, 1999, pp. 120–124. Vanessa Drucker, "B2B boom," *Global Finance,* April 2000, pp. 46–48. Anonymous, "New offerings: DHL considers an IPO after buy-back of stake, "Daily Investing Report, *Atlanta Constitution,* December 14, 1999, p. F6. http://www.dhl-usa.com/press_display/press release dated 9/29/99.

In the periodic system (Exhibit 9-4, Panel A), the business uses a Purchases account to record the purchase of inventory. Purchases is an expense account. Throughout the period, the Inventory account carries the beginning balance left over from the end of the preceding period. Then at the end of the current period, the Inventory account is updated for the financial statements. The end-of-period entries can be made during the closing process. Exhibit 9-4 illustrates the accounting for inventory in the periodic system. Your professor may have you compare the perpetual and periodic inventory systems. The appendix to this chapter provides a side-by-side comparison.

INVENTORY COSTING METHODS

Measuring the cost of inventory is easy when $50 cost per unit remains constant. But the unit cost often changes. For example, during inflation, prices rise. A pair of Teva sandals that cost **Deckers Outdoor** $50 in January may cost $52 in June and $55 in October. Suppose Deckers sells 10,000 pairs of Tevas in December. How many of the pairs cost $50? How many cost $52 or $55? To compute the cost of goods sold and ending inventory, the accountant must assign a cost to each item sold. The four costing methods GAAP allows are

1. Specific unit cost
2. Weighted-average cost
3. First-in, first-out (FIFO) cost
4. Last-in, first-out (LIFO) cost

PANEL A—Recording in the Journal and Posting to the T-accounts—Periodic System

INVENTORY AND COST OF GOODS SOLD ACCOUNTS

1. Credit purchases of $560,000:

Purchases	560,000	
Accounts Payable..............		560,000

2. Credit sales of $900,000:

Accounts Receivable	900,000	
Sales Revenue...................		900,000

3. End-of-period entries to update Inventory and record Cost of Goods Sold:

a. Transfer the cost of beginning inventory ($100,000) to Cost of Goods Sold:

Cost of Goods Sold...........	100,000	
Inventory (beginning balance)........................		100,000

b. Record the cost of ending inventory ($120,000) based on a count:

Inventory (ending balance)	120,000	
Cost of Goods Sold........		120,000

c. Transfer the cost of purchases to Cost of Goods Sold:

Cost of Goods Sold...........	560,000	
Purchases		560,000

INVENTORY

100,000*	100,000
120,000	

COST OF GOODS SOLD

100,000	120,000
560,000	
540,000	

* Beginning inventory was $100,000.

PANEL B—Reporting in the Financial Statements

Income Statement (partial)

Sales revenue............................		$900,000
Cost of goods sold:		
Beginning inventory	$100,000	
Purchases	560,000	
Cost of goods available	660,000	
Less: Ending inventory..........	(120,000)	
Cost of goods sold		540,000
Gross profit		$360,000

Balance Sheet (partial)

Current assets:		
Cash..	$	XXX
Short-term investments.............................		XXX
Accounts receivable....................................		XXX
Inventories...		120,000
Prepaid expenses..		XXX

 DAILY EXERCISE 9-4

A company can use any of these methods. The computation of inventory cost is essentially the same under both the perpetual and the periodic systems.[1]

Specific Unit Cost

Some businesses deal in inventory items that differ from unit to unit, such as automobiles, jewels, and real estate. These businesses usually cost their inventory at the specific unit cost of the particular unit. For instance, a Chevrolet dealer may have two vehicles in the showroom—a "stripped-down" model that cost $14,000 and a "loaded" model that cost $17,000. If the dealer sells the loaded model for $19,700, cost of goods sold is $17,000, the cost of the specific unit. The gross margin on this sale is $2,700 ($19,700 − $17,000). If the stripped-down auto is the only unit left in inventory at the end of the period, ending inventory is $14,000, the dealer's cost of the specific unit on hand.

Objective 2
Apply the inventory costing methods: specific unit cost, weighted-average cost, FIFO, and LIFO

---

[1]Theoretically, there can be a difference between the last-in, first-out (LIFO) costs under the perpetual and the periodic systems. In actual practice, however, this difference does not exist. Complications with LIFO cause companies to wait until year end to compute ending inventory and cost of goods sold. Their computations for perpetual LIFO then parallel those for periodic LIFO. This topic is covered in later accounting courses.

SPECIFIC-UNIT-COST METHOD.
Inventory cost method based
on the specific cost of particular units of inventory. Also
called the **specific identification method.**

The **specific-unit-cost method** is also called the **specific identification method.** This method is not practical for inventory items that have common characteristics, such as bushels of wheat, gallons of paint, or boxes of laundry detergent.

The weighted-average cost, FIFO (first-in, first-out) cost, and LIFO (last-in, first-out) cost methods are fundamentally different from the specific-unit-cost method. These methods do not assign to inventory the specific cost of particular units. Instead, they assume different flows of costs into and out of inventory, as illustrated in Exhibit 9-5. Panel A gives the illustrative data for all three inventory cost methods.

EXHIBIT 9-5

Inventory and Cost of Goods Sold Under Three Costing Methods: *Weighted-Average (Panel B), FIFO (Panel C), LIFO (Panel D)*

 DAILY EXERCISE 9-5

 DAILY EXERCISE 9-6

 DAILY EXERCISE 9-7

PANEL A—Illustrative Data

Beginning inventory (10 units @ $10 per unit)		$ 100
Purchases:		
No. 1 (25 units @ $14 per unit)	$ 350	
No. 2 (25 units @ $18 per unit)	450	
Total purchases..		800
Cost of goods available for sale (60 units)		900
Ending inventory (20 units @ $? per unit)		(?)
Cost of goods sold (40 units @ $? per unit)...................		$?

**PANEL B—Ending Inventory and Cost of Goods Sold
(Weighted-Average Cost Method)**

Cost of goods available for sale—see Panel A (60 units @ average cost of $15* per unit)	$ 900
Ending inventory (20 units @ $15 per unit).................................	(300)
Cost of goods sold (40 units @ $15 per unit)	$ 600

$$* \frac{\text{Cost of goods available for sale, \$900}}{\text{Number of units available for sale, 60}} = \text{Average cost per unit, \$15}$$

**PANEL C—Ending Inventory and Cost of Goods Sold
(FIFO Cost Method)**

Cost of goods available for sale (60 units—see Panel A).................		$ 900
Ending inventory (cost of the *last* 20 units available):		
20 units @ $18 per unit (from purchase No. 2)............................		(360)
Cost of goods sold (cost of the *first* 40 units available):		
10 units @ $10 per unit (all of beginning inventory)..................	$ 100	
25 units @ $14 per unit (all of purchase No. 1)	350	
5 units @ $18 per unit (from purchase No. 2)............................	90	
Cost of goods sold..	$ 540	$ 540

**PANEL D—Ending Inventory and Cost of Goods Sold
(LIFO Cost Method)**

Cost of goods available for sale (60 units—see Panel A).................		$ 900
Ending inventory (cost of the *first* 20 units available):		
10 units @ $10 per unit (all of beginning inventory)..................	$(100)	
10 units @ $14 per unit (from purchase No. 1)............................	(140)	
Ending inventory		(240)
Cost of goods sold (cost of the *last* 40 units available):		
25 units @ $18 per unit (all of purchase No. 2)	$ 450	
15 units @ $14 per unit (from purchase No. 1)............................	210	
Cost of goods sold..	$ 660	$ 660

WEIGHTED-AVERAGE COST METHOD. Inventory costing method based on the weighted-average cost of inventory during the period. Weighted-average cost is determined by dividing the cost of goods available for sale by the number of units available. Also called the average-cost method.

Weighted-Average Cost

The **weighted-average cost method,** often called the *average-cost method,* is based on the weighted-average cost of inventory during the period. Weighted-average cost is determined as follows:

- Determine the weighted-average cost by dividing the cost of goods available for sale (beginning inventory plus purchases) by the number of units available (beginning inventory plus purchases).
- Compute the ending inventory and cost of goods sold by multiplying the number of units by the weighted-average cost per unit.

To illustrate the costing methods, suppose the business has 60 units of inventory available for sale during the period.

- Ending inventory consists of 20 units.
- Cost of goods sold is based on 40 units.

Panel A of Exhibit 9-5 gives the data for computing ending inventory and cost of goods sold, and Panel B shows the weighted-average cost computations.

First-In, First-Out (FIFO) Cost

Under the **first-in, first-out (FIFO) method,** the company must keep a record of the cost of each inventory unit purchased. The unit costs for ending inventory may differ from the unit costs used to compute the cost of goods sold. Under FIFO,

- The first costs into inventory are the first costs out to cost of goods sold— hence the name *first-in, first-out.*
- Ending inventory is based on the costs of the most recent purchases.

In Exhibit 9-5, the FIFO cost of ending inventory is $360. Cost of goods sold is $540. Panel A gives the data, and Panel C shows the computations.

FIRST-IN, FIRST-OUT (FIFO) INVENTORY COSTING METHOD. Inventory costing method by which the first costs into inventory are the first costs out to cost of goods sold. Ending inventory is based on the costs of the most recent purchases.

Last-In, First-Out (LIFO) Cost

The **last-in, first-out (LIFO) method** also depends on the costs of particular inventory purchases. LIFO is the opposite of FIFO. Under LIFO,

- The last costs into inventory are the first costs out to cost of goods sold.
- Ending inventory is based on the oldest costs—those of beginning inventory and plus the earliest purchases of the period.

Exhibit 9-5 shows that the LIFO cost of ending inventory is $240. Cost of goods sold is $660. Again, Panel A gives the data, and Panel D shows the computations.

Remember that the terms *FIFO* and *LIFO* do not describe which goods are left in ending inventory, but rather which goods are sold. FIFO assumes that goods purchased first are sold first; therefore, the last goods purchased are left in ending inventory. LIFO assumes that the last goods in are sold first; therefore, the first goods purchased are left in ending inventory.

LAST-IN, FIRST-OUT (LIFO) INVENTORY COSTING METHOD. Inventory costing method by which the last costs into inventory are the first costs out to cost of goods sold. This method leaves the oldest costs—those of beginning inventory and the earliest purchases of the period—in ending inventory.

The Income Effects of FIFO, LIFO, and Weighted-Average Cost

In our example, the cost of inventory rose during the accounting period from $10 per unit to $14 and finally to $18 (Exhibit 9-5, Panel A). When inventory unit costs change, the different costing methods produce different cost of goods sold and ending inventory figures, as Exhibit 9-5 shows (Panels B, C, and D).

When inventory unit costs are *increasing,*

- FIFO ending inventory is *highest* because it is priced at the most recent (highest) costs.
- LIFO ending inventory is *lowest* because it is priced at the oldest (lowest) costs.

When inventory unit costs are *decreasing,*

- FIFO ending inventory is lowest.
- LIFO ending inventory is highest.

Exhibit 9-6 on page 356 summarizes the income effects of the three inventory methods, using the data from Exhibit 9-5. Study the exhibit carefully, focusing on ending inventory, cost of goods sold, and gross profit.

	FIFO	LIFO	Weighted-Average
Sales revenue (assumed)........	$1,000	$1,000	$1,000
Cost of goods sold:			
Goods available for sale (from Exhibit 9-5)...........	$900	$900	$900
Ending inventory...............	(360)	(240)	(300)
Cost of goods sold..............	540	660	600
Gross profit...........................	$ 460	$ 340	$ 400

Summary of Income Effects—When inventory unit costs are *increasing*

FIFO:	Highest ending inventory Lowest cost of goods sold Highest gross profit	LIFO:	Lowest ending inventory Highest cost of goods sold Lowest gross profit	Weighted-average:	Results fall between the extremes of FIFO and LIFO

Summary of Income Effects—When inventory unit costs are *decreasing*

FIFO:	Lowest ending inventory Highest cost of goods sold Lowest gross profit	LIFO:	Highest ending inventory Lowest cost of goods sold Highest gross profit	Weighted-average:	Results fall between the extremes of FIFO and LIFO

 DAILY EXERCISE 9-8

 DAILY EXERCISE 9-9

Objective 3
Identify the income effects and the tax effects of the inventory costing methods

 DAILY EXERCISE 9-10

The Income Tax Advantage of LIFO

When prices are rising, the LIFO method results in the *lowest taxable income* and thus the *lowest income taxes*. Using the gross profit data of Exhibit 9-6, we have the following (using assumed data):

	FIFO	LIFO	Weighted-Average
Gross profit..	$460	$340	$400
Operating expenses (assumed)	260	260	260
Income before income tax....................	200	80	140
Income tax expense (40%).................	$ 80	$ 32	$ 56

Income tax expense is lowest under LIFO ($32) and highest under FIFO ($80). The most attractive feature of LIFO is reduced income tax payments, which is why **Lands' End, PepsiCo,** and **Wal-Mart** use the LIFO method. These companies are willing to report lower profits in order to save on taxes.

Some periods are marked by high inflation, and companies change to LIFO for its tax advantage. Exhibit 9-7, based on an American Institute of Certified Public Accountants (AICPA) survey of 600 companies, indicates that FIFO and LIFO are the most popular inventory costing methods.

EXHIBIT 9-7
Use of the various Inventory Costing Methods

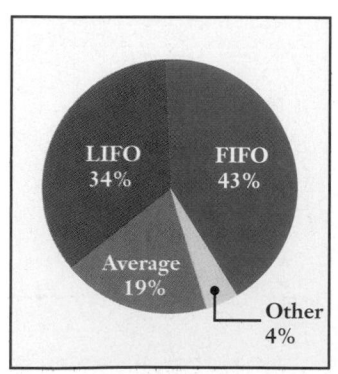

GAAP and Practical Considerations: A Comparison of Inventory Methods

To judge the three major inventory costing methods, ask three questions:
1. How well does each method measure net income on the income statement?
2. Which method reports the most up-to-date inventory amount on the balance sheet?
3. What effects do the methods have on income taxes?

MEASURING NET INCOME ON THE INCOME STATEMENT   LIFO best matches the current value of cost of goods sold with current revenue by assigning to this expense the most recent inventory costs. Therefore, LIFO produces the cost-of-goods-sold figure that is closest to what it would cost the company to replace the goods that were sold. In this sense, LIFO produces the best measure of net income. In contrast, FIFO matches the oldest inventory costs against the period's revenue—a poor match of current expense with current revenue.

CURRENT INVENTORY COST ON THE BALANCE SHEET FIFO reports the most current inventory costs on the balance sheet. LIFO can result in misleading inventory costs on the balance sheet because the oldest prices are left in ending inventory.

INCOME TAX LIFO results in the lowest income tax payments when prices are rising. Tax payments are highest under FIFO. When inventory prices are falling, tax payments are highest under LIFO and lowest under FIFO. The weighted-average cost method produces amounts between the extremes of LIFO and FIFO.

LIFO ALLOWS OWNERS TO MANAGE REPORTED INCOME—UP OR DOWN LIFO is often criticized because it allows managers to manipulate net income. When inventory prices are rising rapidly and a company wants to show less income for the year (in order to pay less taxes), managers can buy a large amount of inventory before the end of the year. Under LIFO, these high inventory costs immediately become expense—as cost of goods sold. As a result, the income statement reports a lower net income.

Conversely, if the business is having a bad year, the owner may wish to increase reported income. To do so, he or she can delay a large purchase of high-cost inventory until the next period. This high-cost inventory is not expensed as cost of goods sold in the current year. This avoids decreasing the current year's reported income. In the process, the company draws down inventory quantities below the level of the previous period, a practice known as **LIFO liquidation.**

LIFO LIQUIDATION. Situation when the LIFO inventory method is used and inventory quantities fall below the level of the previous period.

HIGHER INCOME OR LOWER TAXES? A company may want to report the highest income, and FIFO meets this need when prices are rising. But FIFO leads to the highest income taxes. When prices are falling, LIFO reports the highest income.

Which inventory method is better—LIFO or FIFO? There is no single answer to this question. Different companies have different motives for the inventory method they choose. **The Gap** uses FIFO, **Lands' End** uses LIFO, and **Pier 1 Imports** uses weighted-average cost. Still other companies use more than one method. **The Quaker Oats Company** uses all three methods.

INTERNATIONAL PERSPECTIVE Many companies manufacture their inventory in foreign countries. Companies that value inventory by the LIFO method often use another accounting method for inventories in foreign countries. Why? LIFO is allowed in the United States, but other countries are not bound by U.S. accounting practices. Australia and the United Kingdom, for example, do not permit the use of LIFO. Exhibit 9-8 lists a sampling of countries and whether or not they permit LIFO.

 DAILY EXERCISE 9-11

EXHIBIT 9-8
LIFO Use by Country

Country	LIFO Permitted?	Country	LIFO Permitted?
Australia	No	Netherlands	Yes
Canada	Yes	Singapore	No
France	Yes	Switzerland	No
Germany	Yes	United Kingdom	No
Japan	Yes	United States	Yes

MID-CHAPTER

SUMMARY PROBLEM

Suppose a division of **IBM Corporation** that handles computer components has these inventory records for January 20X6:

www.prenhall.com/horngren
Mid-Chapter Assessment

Date		Item	Quantity	Unit Cost	Sale Price
Jan.	1	Beginning inventory.........	100 units	$ 8	
	6	Purchase...........................	60 units	9	
	13	Sale	70 units		$20
	21	Purchase...........................	150 units	9	
	24	Sale	210 units		22
	27	Purchase...........................	90 units	10	
	30	Sale	30 units		25

Company accounting records reveal that operating expense for January was $1,900.

Required

1. Prepare the January income statement, showing amounts for FIFO, LIFO, and weighted-average cost. Label the bottom line "Operating income." (Round the weighted-average cost per unit to three decimal places and all other figures to whole-dollar amounts.) Show your computations, and use the periodic inventory model in Exhibit 9-6 to compute cost of goods sold.
2. Suppose you are the financial vice president of IBM. Which inventory method will you use if your motive is to (state the reason for each answer)
   a. Minimize income taxes?
   b. Report the highest operating income?
   c. Report operating income between the extremes of FIFO and LIFO?
   d. Report inventory on the balance sheet at the most current cost?
   e. Attain the best measure of net income for the income statement?

Solution

Requirement 1

IBM CORPORATION
Income Statement for Component
Month Ended January 31, 20X6

	FIFO		LIFO		Weighted-Average	
Sales revenue................................		$6,770		$6,770		$6,770
Cost of goods sold:						
Beginning inventory	$ 800		$ 800		$ 800	
Net purchases..........................	2,790		2,790		2,790	
Cost of goods						
available for sale	3,590		3,590		3,590	
Ending inventory	(900)		(720)		(808)	
Cost of goods sold....................		2,690		2,870		2,782
Gross profit		4,080		3,900		3,988
Operating expenses.....................		1,900		1,900		1,900
Operating income		$2,180		$2,000		$2,088

Computations

Sales revenue:	$(70 \times \$20) + (210 \times \$22) + (30 \times \$25)$ = $6,770	
Beginning inventory:	$100 \times \$8$	= $800
Purchases:	$(60 \times \$9) + (150 \times \$9) + (90 \times \$10)$	= $2,790
Ending inventory		
FIFO	$90* \times \$10$	= $900
LIFO	$90 \times \$8$	= $720
Weighted-average:	$90 \times \$8.975**$	= $808 (rounded from $807.75)

* Number of units in ending inventory = $100 + 60 - 70 + 150 - 210 + 90 - 30 = 90$

** $3,590/400 units† = $8.975 per unit

† Number of units available = $100 + 60 + 150 + 90 = 400$

THE PERPETUAL SYSTEM AND INVENTORY COSTING METHODS

Many companies keep their perpetual inventory records in quantities only, as illustrated in Exhibit 9-2. Other companies keep perpetual records in both quantities and dollar costs. Here we show how the inventory costing methods are applied in a *perpetual* inventory system.

FIFO

Deckers Outdoor uses the FIFO inventory method. Exhibit 9-9 shows Deckers' perpetual inventory record for a particular style of Teva sandals in both quantities and dollar costs for the month of November.

EXHIBIT 9-9 Perpetual Inventory Record—FIFO Cost for Deckers Outdoor Corporation

Item: Teva Sandals

Date	Received Qty.	Received Unit Cost	Received Total	Sold Qty.	Sold Unit Cost	Sold Total	Balance on Hand Qty.	Balance on Hand Unit Cost	Balance on Hand Total
Nov. 1							10	$30	$300
5				6	$30	$ 180	4	30	120
7	25	$31	$ 775				4	30	120
							25	31	775
12				4	30	120			
				9	31	279	16	31	496
26	25	32	800				16	31	496
							25	32	800
30				16	31	496			
				5	32	160	20	32	640
Totals	50		$1,575	40		$1,235	20	$32	$640

To prepare financial statements at November 30, Deckers can take the ending inventory cost ($640) straight to the balance sheet. Cost of goods sold for the November income statement is $1,235. Here is Deckers' cost of goods sold for the sandals during November (data taken from Exhibit 9-9):

Cost of Goods Sold (Teva sandals)—November	
Beginning inventory	$ 300
+ Purchases	1,575
= Cost of goods available for sale	1,875
− Ending inventory	(640)
= Cost of goods sold	$1,235

DAILY EXERCISE 9-12

LIFO

Few companies keep perpetual inventory records at LIFO cost. The record-keeping is expensive, and LIFO liquidations can occur during the year. To avoid these problems, LIFO companies follow different strategies than FIFO and average-cost companies. LIFO companies can keep perpetual inventory records in terms of quantities only, as illustrated in Exhibit 9-2. For financial statements, they apply LIFO costs at the end of the period. Other LIFO companies maintain perpetual inventory records at FIFO cost and then convert the FIFO amounts to LIFO costs for the financial statements. These procedures arrive at ending inventory and cost-of-goods-sold figures that parallel those from the periodic inventory system.

Weighted-Average Cost

Perpetual inventory records can be kept at weighted-average cost. Most companies using this method compute the weighted-average cost for the entire period. They apply this cost to both ending inventory and cost of goods sold. These procedures parallel those used in the periodic inventory system (Exhibit 9-5).

Examine Exhibit 9-9. What was Deckers' weighted-average unit cost during November? How much were ending inventory and cost of goods sold at weighted-average cost?

Answer

$$\text{Weighted-average unit cost} = \frac{\text{Cost of goods available for sale}}{\text{Units available for sale}}$$

$$= \frac{\text{Cost of beginning inventory} + \text{Cost of purchases}}{\text{Units of beginning inventory} + \text{Units purchased}}$$

$$= \frac{\$300 + \$1,575}{10 \text{ units} + 50 \text{ units}} = \frac{\$1,875}{60 \text{ units}} = \$31.25$$

Ending Inventory = 20 units × $31.25 = $ 625
Cost of goods sold = 40 units × $31.25 = $1,250

ACCOUNTING PRINCIPLES AND INVENTORIES

Several accounting principles have special relevance to inventories. Among them are consistency, disclosure, materiality, and accounting conservatism.

Consistency Principle

CONSISTENCY PRINCIPLE. A business should use the same accounting methods and procedures from period to period.

The **consistency principle** states that businesses should use the same accounting methods and procedures from period to period. Consistency helps investors compare a company's financial statements from one period to the next.

Suppose you are analyzing a company's net income pattern over a two-year period. The company switched from LIFO to FIFO during that time. Its net income increased dramatically but only as a result of the change in inventory method. If you did not know of the change, you might believe that the company's income increased because of improved operations.

The consistency principle does not require that all companies within an industry use the same accounting method. Nor does it mean that a company may *never* change its methods. However, a company making an accounting change must disclose the effect of the change on net income. **Sun Company, Inc.,** an oil company, disclosed the following in a note to its annual report:

EXCERPT FROM NOTE 6 OF SUN COMPANY STATEMENTS
. . . Sun changed its method of accounting for the cost of crude oil and refined product inventories . . . from . . . FIFO . . . to . . . LIFO . . . . Sun believes that the . . . LIFO method better matches current costs with current revenues . . . . The change decreased the 20X1 net loss . . . by $3 million. . . .

Disclosure Principle

The **disclosure principle** holds that a company's financial statements should report enough information for outsiders to make knowledgeable decisions about the company. In short, the company should report *relevant, reliable,* and *comparable* information about its economic affairs. With respect to inventories, the disclosure principle means disclosing the method being used to value inventories. Suppose a banker is comparing two companies—one using LIFO and the other FIFO. The FIFO company reports higher net income, but only because it uses the FIFO inventory method. Without knowledge of the accounting methods the companies are using, the banker could loan money to the wrong business.

Materiality Concept

The **materiality concept** states that a company must perform strictly proper accounting *only* for items that are significant for the business's financial statements. Information is significant—or, in accounting terminology, *material*—when its presentation in the financial statements would cause someone to change a decision because of that information. Immaterial items justify less-than-perfect accounting. Their inclusion and proper presentation would not affect a statement user's decision. The materiality concept frees accountants from having to report every last item in strict accordance with GAAP.

How does a business decide where to draw the line between the material and the immaterial? This decision depends on how large the business is. **Lucent Technologies,** the maker of cordless phones, for example, has over $38 billion in assets. Management would likely treat as immaterial a $1,000 loss of inventory due to spoilage. A loss of this amount may be immaterial to Lucent's total assets and net income, so company accountants may not report the loss separately. Will this accounting treatment affect banker's or investor's decision about Lucent? Probably not. So it doesn't matter whether the loss is reported separately or simply embedded in cost of goods sold.

Accounting Conservatism

Conservatism in accounting means reporting items in the financial statements at amounts that lead to the most cautious immediate results. What advantage does conservatism give a business? Managers must be optimistic to be good leaders. This optimism sometimes causes them to look on the bright side of operations, and they may overstate a company's income and asset values. Many accountants regard conservatism as a counterbalance to managers' optimistic tendencies. The goal is for financial statements to present realistic figures.

Conservatism appears in accounting guidelines such as

- "Anticipate no gains, but provide for all probable losses."
- "If in doubt, record an asset at the lowest reasonable amount and a liability at the highest reasonable amount."
- When there's a question, record an expense rather than an asset."

Conservatism directs accountants to decrease the accounting value of an asset if it appears unrealistically high. Assume that a company paid $35,000 for inventory that has become obsolete and whose current value is only $12,000. Conservatism dictates that the inventory be *written down* (that is, decreased) to $12,000.

Objective 4
Apply the lower-of-cost-or-market rule to inventory

Lower-of-Cost-or-Market Rule

The **lower-of-cost-or-market rule** (abbreviated as **LCM**) shows accounting conservatism in action. LCM requires that inventory be reported in the financial statements at whichever is lower—the inventory's historical cost or its market value. For inventories, *market value* generally means *current replacement cost* (that is, the cost to replace the inventory on hand). If the replacement cost of inventory falls below its historical cost, the business must write down the value of its goods. The business reports ending inventory at its LCM value on the balance sheet.

Suppose a business paid $3,000 for inventory on September 26. By December 31, its value has fallen. The inventory can now be replaced for $2,200 and the decline in value appears permanent. Market value is below cost, and the December 31 balance sheet reports this inventory at its LCM value of $2,200.

Exhibit 9-10 shows the effects of LCM on the income statement and the balance sheet. The exhibit shows that the lower of (a) cost or (b) market value is the relevant amount for valuing inventory on the balance sheet. Now examine the income statement in Exhibit 9-10. What expense absorbs the impact of the $800 inventory write-down? The entry to write down the inventory to LCM debits Cost of Goods Sold:

Cost of Goods Sold (cost, $3,000 − market, $2,200)	800	
Inventory		800

Exhibit 9-10
Lower-of-Cost-or-Market (LCM) Effects

DAILY EXERCISE 9-13

Balance Sheet

Current assets:	
Inventories, at market	
(which is lower than $3,000 cost)	**$ 2,200**

Income Statement

Sales revenue..		$20,000
Cost of goods sold:		
Beginning inventory (LCM = Cost).......................	**$ 2,800**	
Net purchases...	11,000	
Cost of goods available for sale	13,800	
Ending inventory—		
Cost = $3,000		
Replacement cost (market value) = $2,200		
LCM = Market	(2,200)	
Cost of goods sold...		11,600
Gross profit		$ 8,400

Companies often disclose LCM in notes to their financial statements, as shown here for **Cisco Systems,** the worldwide leader in networking for the Internet.

NOTE 2: STATEMENT OF SIGNIFICANT ACCOUNTING POLICIES
Inventories. Inventories are stated at the *lower of cost or market.* [Emphasis added.]

Objective 5
Determine the effects of inventory errors on cost of goods sold and net income

Effects of Inventory Errors

Businesses count their inventories at the end of the period. As the period 1 segment of Exhibit 9-11 shows, an error in the ending inventory creates errors in cost of goods sold and gross profit. Compare period 1, when ending inventory is overstated and cost of goods sold is understated, each by $5,000, with period 3, which is correct. Period 1 should look exactly like period 3.

DAILY EXERCISE 9-14

Recall that one period's ending inventory is the next period's beginning inventory. Thus, the error in ending inventory carries over into the next period; note the amounts highlighted in Exhibit 9-11.

Because ending inventory is *subtracted* in computing cost of goods sold in one period and the same amount is *added* as beginning inventory to compute next period's cost of goods sold, the error's effect cancels out at the end of the second period. The overstatement of cost of goods sold in period 2 counterbalances the understatement for period 1. Thus, the total gross profit for the two periods is correct. As a result, owner's equity at the end of period 2 is correct. These effects are summarized in Exhibit 9-12.

DAILY EXERCISE 9-15

Inventory errors cannot be ignored simply because they counterbalance, however. Suppose you are analyzing trends in the business's operations. Exhibit 9-11 shows a drop in gross margin from period 1 to period 2, followed by an increase in period 3. But that picture of operations is untrue because of the accounting error.

EXHIBIT 9-11   **Inventory Errors: An Example**

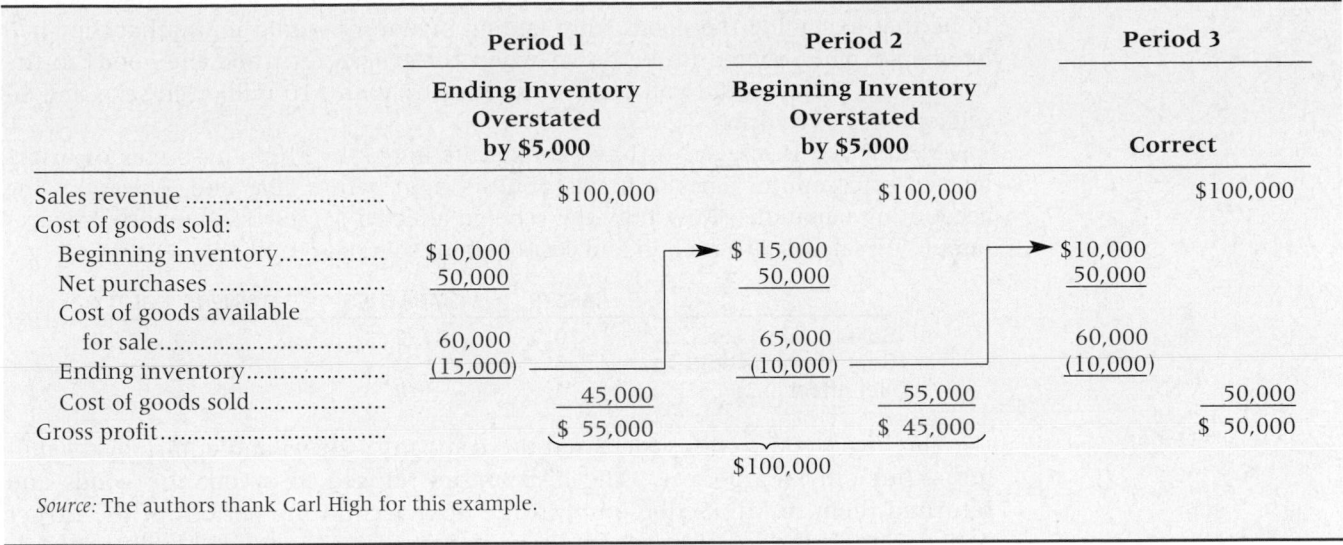

	Period 1 Ending Inventory Overstated by $5,000		Period 2 Beginning Inventory Overstated by $5,000		Period 3 Correct	
Sales revenue		$100,000		$100,000		$100,000
Cost of goods sold:						
Beginning inventory................	$10,000		$ 15,000		$10,000	
Net purchases	50,000		50,000		50,000	
Cost of goods available						
for sale................................	60,000		65,000		60,000	
Ending inventory.....................	(15,000)		(10,000)		(10,000)	
Cost of goods sold...................		45,000		55,000		50,000
Gross profit..............................		$ 55,000		$ 45,000		$ 50,000

$100,000

Source: The authors thank Carl High for this example.

EXHIBIT 9-12   **Effects of Inventory Errors**

	Period 1			Period 2		
Inventory Error	Cost of Goods Sold	Gross Profit and Net Income	Ending Owner's Equity	Cost of Goods Sold	Gross Profit and Net Income	Ending Owner's Equity
Period 1 Ending inventory *overstated*	Understated	Overstated	Overstated	Overstated	Understated	Correct
Period 1 Ending inventory *understated*	Overstated	Understated	Understated	Understated	Overstated	Correct

The correct gross profit is $50,000 for each period. Providing accurate information for decision making requires that all inventory errors be corrected.

OTHER INVENTORY ISSUES

Ethical Issues

No area of accounting has a deeper ethical dimension than inventory. Owners and managers of companies whose profits are lagging are sometimes tempted to "cook the books" to increase reported income. The increase in income may lead investors and creditors to think the business is more successful than it really is.

There are two main schemes for cooking the books. The easiest, and the most obvious, is simply to overstate ending inventory. In Exhibit 9-12, we saw how an error in ending inventory affects net income. A company can intentionally overstate its ending inventory. Such an error understates cost of goods sold and overstates net income and owner's equity, as shown in the accounting equation. The upward-pointing arrows indicate an overstatement—reporting more assets and equity than are actually present:

$$\text{ASSETS} = \text{LIABILITIES} + \text{OWNERS' EQUITY}$$
$$\uparrow \quad = \quad 0 \quad + \quad \uparrow$$

 DAILY EXERCISE 9-16

The second way of using inventory to cook the books involves sales. Sales schemes are more complex than simple inventory overstatements. **Datapoint Corporation** and **MiniScribe,** both computer-related concerns, were charged with creating fictitious sales to boost reported profits.

Datapoint is alleged to have hired drivers to transport its inventory around San Antonio so that the goods could *not* be physically counted. Datapoint's logic seemed to be that excluding the goods from ending inventory would imply that they had been sold. The scheme broke down when the trucks returned the goods to the warehouse. What would you think of a company with $10 million in sales and $4 million of sales returns?

MiniScribe is alleged to have cooked its books by shipping boxes of bricks labeled as computer parts to its distributors right before year end. The following accounting equations show how the scheme affected MiniScribe's reported figures (assuming sales of $10 million and cost of goods sold of $6 million):

	ASSETS	=	LIABILITIES	+	OWNERS' EQUITY
Sales.............................	10	=	0	+	10
Cost of goods sold......	−6	=	0	−	6
Net effect	4	=	0	+	4

The bogus transactions increased the company's assets and equity by $4 million—but only temporarily. The distributors refused to accept the goods and returned them to MiniScribe—but in the next accounting period. In the earlier period, MiniScribe recorded sales revenue and temporarily reported millions of dollars of sales and income that did not exist. The scheme boomeranged in the next period when MiniScribe had to record the sales returns. In virtually every area, accounting imposes a discipline that works to keep every business honest in its financial reporting.

Estimating Inventory

Objective 6
Estimate ending inventory by the gross profit method

Often a business must *estimate* the value of its inventory. Because of cost and inconvenience, few companies physically count inventories at the end of each month, yet they may need monthly financial statements. Suppose the company does not use the perpetual inventory system and thus cannot determine ending inventory by looking at the Inventory account. Fortunately, there is a way to estimate ending inventory for monthly or quarterly financial statements. Also, a fire may destroy inventory, and to file an insurance claim, the business must estimate the value of its loss.

GROSS PROFIT METHOD. A way to estimate inventory on the basis of the cost-of-goods-sold model: Beginning inventory + Net purchases = Cost of goods available for sale. Cost of goods available for sale − Cost of goods sold = Ending inventory. Also called the **gross margin method**.

The **gross profit method,** also known as the *gross margin method,* is a way of estimating inventory on the basis of the familiar cost-of-goods-sold model (amounts assumed for illustration):

Beginning inventory	$10
+ Purchases	50
= Cost of goods available for sale	60
− Ending inventory....................................	(20)
= Cost of goods sold..................................	$40

Rearranging *ending inventory* and *cost of goods sold* makes the model useful for estimating ending inventory and is illustrated in the following equation and in Exhibit 9-13 (amounts assumed for illustration):

Beginning inventory	$10
+ Purchases	50
= Cost of goods available for sale	60
− Cost of goods sold..................................	(40)
= Ending inventory....................................	$20

DAILY EXERCISE 9-17

Suppose a fire destroys your inventory. To collect insurance, you must estimate the cost of the ending inventory. Using your normal *gross profit percent* (that is, gross profit divided by net sales revenue), you can estimate cost of goods sold. Then subtract cost of goods sold from goods available to estimate ending inventory. Exhibit 9-13 illustrates the gross profit method.

Beginning inventory		$14,000
Purchases		66,000
Cost of goods available for sale		80,000
Estimated cost of goods sold:		
Sales revenue..	$100,000	
Less: Estimated gross profit of 40%	(40,000)	
Estimated cost of goods sold............................		(60,000)
Estimated cost of *ending inventory*.........................		$20,000

Beginning inventory is $70,000, net purchases total $298,000, and net sales are $480,000. With a normal gross profit rate of 40% of sales, how much is ending inventory?

Answer

Beginning inventory		$ 70,000
Net purchases...		298,000
Cost of goods available for sale		368,000
Estimated cost of goods sold:		
Net sales revenue	$480,000	
Less: Estimated gross profit of 40%...........	(192,000)	
Estimated cost of goods sold......................		(288,000)
Estimated cost of ending inventory		$ 80,000

Internal Control

Internal control over inventory is important because inventory is such an important asset. Successful companies take great care to protect their inventory. Elements of good internal control include

1. Physically counting inventory at least once each year
2. Storing inventory to protect it against theft, damage, and decay
3. Giving access only to personnel who have *no* access to the accounting records
4. Not stockpiling too much inventory; this avoids tying up money in unneeded items

Computerized inventory systems allow companies to minimize the amount of inventory on hand (item 4). In a competitive environment, companies cannot afford to tie up cash in too much inventory. Many manufacturing companies use *just-in-time (JIT) inventory systems,* which require suppliers to deliver materials just in time to be used in the production process.

This chapter has discussed various aspects of controlling and accounting for inventory. The Decision Guidelines feature on page 366 summarizes some basic decision guidelines that are helpful in managing a business's inventory operations.

DECISION GUIDELINES

Guidelines for Inventory Management

DECISION	GUIDELINES	SYSTEM OR METHOD
Which inventory system to use?	• Expensive merchandise • Cannot control inventory by visual inspection	→ Perpetual system
	• Can control inventory by visual inspection	→ Periodic system
Which costing method to use?	• Unique inventory items	→ Specific unit cost
	• Most current cost of ending inventory • Maximizes reported income when costs are rising	→ FIFO
	• Most current measure of cost of goods sold and net income • Minimizes income tax when costs are rising	→ LIFO
	• Middle-of-the-road approach for income tax and reported income	→ Weighted-average
How to estimate the cost of ending inventory?	• The cost-of-goods-sold model provides the framework	→ Gross profit (gross margin) method

EXCEL APPLICATION PROBLEM

Goal: Create an Excel spreadsheet that compares gross profit, ending inventory, and cost of goods sold under the LIFO, FIFO, and weighted-average methods of inventory valuation.

Scenario: John Kalinich, Chief Operations Officer at Teva Sport Sandals in Flagstaff, Arizona, has a decision to make. He's in charge of Teva's on-line store, and is responsible for the inventory sold through the Web. John must decide which inventory method to use for the business.

Your task is to create a spreadsheet and embedded graph that compares gross profit, ending inventory, and cost of goods sold under three methods: weighted-average, FIFO, and LIFO. John has provided the following data from the most recent month of operations for your use in creating the spreadsheet:

July	1	Beginning inventory	2,000 units @ $30.00 cost per unit
	6	Purchase	600 units @ $31.25 cost per unit
	17	Purchase	400 units @ $33.50 cost per unit
	28	Purchase	200 units @ $34.75 cost per unit

Sales for July: 1,800 pairs of sandals sold @ $69.00 each

After you have prepared your spreadsheet, answer these questions:

1. Which method produces the lowest cost of goods sold? Why?
2. Which method produces the lowest ending inventory? Why?
3. If John Kalinich wants to maximize gross profit for Teva, which method should he choose? Does this method do a good job of matching inventory expense (cost of goods sold) to sales revenue?

Step-by-step:

1. Open a new Excel spreadsheet.
2. Create a heading for your spreadsheet that contains the following:
   a. Chapter 9 Decision Guidelines
   b. Inventory Management
   c. Teva Sport Sandals
   d. Today's date
3. At the top of your spreadsheet, create a "Data Section" for the July data provided by John Kalinich. Set up columns for Date, Activity (Beginning Inventory, Purchases, Goods Available for Sale, Sales, and Ending Inventory), Units, Unit Cost, and Total Cost. Compute goods available for sale and ending inventory.
4. Include the calculation for "average unit cost" on a separate row in this section.
5. Next, create a section titled "Inventory Method Comparison" in bold print and underlined. Include one column for each method (weighted-average, FIFO, and LIFO). Include rows for Ending Inventory, Cost of Goods Sold, and Gross Profit. Format as necessary. Be sure your calculations are based on the Data Section figures. Do not "hard-code" any amounts in this section.
6. When done, create an embedded bar chart underneath the Inventory Method Comparison section that compares Gross Profit, Ending Inventory, and Cost of Goods Sold for all three methods. (*Hint:* Use the Chart Wizard button on the Standard Excel toolbar.)
7. Save your spreadsheet, and print a copy for your files.

REVIEW MERCHANDISE INVENTORY

SUMMARY PROBLEM

Mesa Hardware Company began 20X4 with 60,000 units of inventory that cost $36,000. During 19X8, Mesa purchased merchandise on account for $352,500 as follows:

Purchase 1 (100,000 units costing)	$ 65,000
Purchase 2 (270,000 units costing)	175,500
Purchase 3 (160,000 units costing)	112,000

www.prenhall.com/horngren

End-of-Chapter Assessment

Cash payments on account for inventory totaled $326,000 during the year.

Mesa's sales during 20X4 consisted of 520,000 units of inventory for $660,000, all on account. The company uses the FIFO inventory method.

Cash collections from customers were $630,000. Operating expenses totaled $240,500, of which Mesa paid $211,000 in cash. Mesa credited Accrued Liabilities for the remainder.

Required

1. Make summary journal entries to record Mesa Hardware's transactions for the year, assuming the company uses a perpetual inventory system.
2. Determine the FIFO cost of Mesa's ending inventory at December 31, 20X4, two ways:
   a. Use a T-account.
   b. Multiply the number of units by the unit cost.
3. Use the cost-of-goods-sold model to show how Mesa would compute cost of goods sold for 20X4 under the periodic inventory system.
4. Prepare Mesa Hardware's income statement for 20X4. Show totals for the gross profit and net income.

Solution

Requirement 1

Inventory ($65,000 + $175,500 + $112,000)	352,500	
Accounts Payable		352,500
Accounts Payable	326,000	
Cash		326,000
Accounts Receivable	660,000	
Sales Revenue		660,000
Cost of Goods Sold	339,500	
Inventory		339,500
[$36,000 + $65,000 + $175,500 + $63,000;		
(90,000 units × $0.70)]($112,000 ÷ 160,000		
units = $0.70 per unit)		
Cash	630,000	
Accounts Receivable		630,000
Operating Expenses	240,500	
Cash		211,000
Accrued Liabilities		29,500

Requirement 2

a.

INVENTORY	
36,000	339,500
352,500	
49,000	

b. Number of units in ending inventory

(60,000 + 100,000 + 270,000 + 160,000 − 520,000)	70,000
Unit cost of ending inventory at FIFO ($112,000 ÷ 160,000)	× $0.70
FIFO cost of ending inventory	$49,000

Requirement 3

Cost of goods sold (periodic inventory system):	
Beginning inventory	$ 36,000
Purchases	352,500
Cost of goods available for sale	388,500
Less: Ending inventory	(49,000)
Cost of goods sold	$339,500

Requirement 4

MESA HARDWARE COMPANY
Income Statement
Year Ended December 31, 20X4

Sales revenue	$660,000
Cost of goods sold	339,500
Gross profit	320,500
Operating expenses	240,500
Net income	$ 80,000

LESSONS LEARNED

1. *Account for inventory by the perpetual and periodic systems.* Inventory is the heart of a merchandiser's business. *Cost of goods sold* is usually the largest expense on the income statement.

   Merchandisers can choose between two inventory systems. *A periodic system* does not keep a running record of the inventory on hand. Instead, at the end of the period, the business counts the inventory and then updates its records. In a *perpetual inventory system,* the business keeps a running record to show inventory on hand at all times. A physical count of inventory is needed in both systems.

2. *Apply the inventory costing methods: specific-unit-cost, weighted-average cost, FIFO, and LIFO.* Businesses multiply inventory quantity by unit cost to determine the cost of this asset. The four inventory costing methods are *specific-unit-cost; weighted-average cost; first-in, first-out (FIFO) cost;* and *last-in, first-out (LIFO) cost.* Businesses that sell unique items use the specific-unit-cost method. Most other companies use the other methods. FIFO reports ending inventory at the most current cost. LIFO reports cost of goods sold at the most current cost. Weighted-average cost falls in the middle.

3. *Identify the income effects and the tax effects of the inventory costing methods.* When prices are rising, LIFO produces the highest cost of goods sold and the lowest income, thus minimizing income taxes. FIFO results in the highest income. The weighted-average cost method falls between the extremes of FIFO and LIFO.

4. *Apply the lower-of-cost-or-market rule to inventory.* The *lower-of-cost-or-market (LCM) rule*—an example of accounting *conservatism*—requires that businesses report inventory on the balance sheet at the lower of its cost or current replacement value. Companies can disclose LCM in notes to their financial statements.

5. *Determine the effects of inventory errors on cost of goods sold and net income.* Inventory overstatements in one period are counterbalanced by understatements in the next period, and understatements are counterbalanced by overstatements.

6. *Estimate ending inventory by the gross profit method.* The *gross profit method* estimates the cost of inventory. It comes in handy for preparing interim financial statements and for estimating the cost of inventory destroyed by fire or other disasters.

ACCOUNTING VOCABULARY

average-cost method (p. 354)
conservatism (p. 361)
consignment (p. 351)
consistency principle (p. 360)
cost of goods available for sale (p. 350)
disclosure principle (p. 361)
first-in, first-out (FIFO) inventory costing method (p. 355)
gross margin (p. 347)

gross margin method (p. 364)
gross profit (p. 347)
gross profit method (p. 364)
last-in, first-out (LIFO) inventory costing method (p. 355)
LIFO liquidation (p. 357)
lower-of-cost-or-market (LCM) rule (p. 361)
materiality concept (p. 361)
merchandising company (p. 347)

periodic inventory system (p. 347)
perpetual inventory system (p. 348)
specific identification method (p. 354)
specific-unit-cost method (p. 354)
weighted-average cost method (p. 354)

QUESTIONS

1. Suppose your company deals in expensive jewelry. Which inventory system should you use to achieve good internal control over the inventory? If your business is a hardware store that sells low-cost goods, which inventory system would you be likely to use? Why would you choose this system?

2. Identify the accounts debited and credited in the standard purchase and sale entries under (a) the perpetual inventory system, and (b) the periodic inventory system.

3. If beginning inventory is $10,000, purchases total $85,000, and ending inventory is $12,700, how much is cost of goods sold?

4. If beginning inventory is $32,000, purchases total $119,000, and cost of goods sold is $127,000, how much is ending inventory?

5. Briefly describe the four generally accepted inventory cost methods. During a period of rising prices, which method produces the highest reported income? Which produces the lowest reported income?

6. Which inventory costing method produces the ending inventory valued at the most current cost? Which method produces the cost-of-goods-sold amount valued at the most current cost?

7. What is the most attractive feature of LIFO? Does LIFO have this advantage during periods of increasing prices or during periods of decreasing prices?

8. Identify the chief criticism of LIFO.

9. Briefly describe the influence that the concept of conservatism has on accounting for inventory.

10. Manley Company's inventory has a cost of $48,000 at the end of the year, and the current replacement cost of the inventory is $51,000. At which amount should the company report the inventory on its balance sheet? Suppose the current replacement cost of the inventory is $45,000 instead of $51,000. At which amount should Manley report the inventory? What rule governs your answers to these questions?

11. Gabriel Company accidentally overstated its ending inventory by $10,000 at the end of period 1. Is gross margin of period 1 overstated or understated? Is gross margin of period 2 overstated, understated, or unaffected by the period-1 error? Is total gross margin for the two periods overstated, understated, or correct? Give the reason for your answers.

12. Identify an important method of estimating inventory amounts. What familiar model underlies this estimation method?

13. True or false? A company that sells inventory of low unit cost needs no internal controls over the goods. Any inventory loss would probably be small.

ASSESS YOUR PROGRESS

DAILY EXERCISES

DE9-1 Beakman Ventures purchased 2,000 units of inventory for $60 each and marked up the goods by $40 per unit. It then sold 1,600 units. For these transactions, show what Beakman would report on its balance sheet at December 31, 20X0 and on its income statement for the year ended December 31, 20X0. Include a complete heading for each statement.

Basic concept of accounting for inventory (Obj. 1)

DE9-2 Study Exhibit 9-3, page 349, and answer these questions:

1. What was the cost of **Deckers'** inventory purchases during the year?
2. How much were Deckers' sales for the year? How much were cost of goods sold and the gross profit? What was the cost of ending inventory?
3. Study the journal entries in Panel A of the exhibit. How can you tell from the journal entries that Deckers is using the perpetual inventory system?

Using the inventory records (Obj. 1)

DE9-3 Rugged River Outfitters purchased inventory costing $85,000 and sold half the goods for $103,000, with all transactions on account.

Journalize these two transactions under the perpetual inventory system. How much gross profit did Rugged River earn on these sales? Which statement reports the gross profit?

Accounting for inventory in the perpetual system (Obj. 1)

DE9-4 Use the data in Daily Exercise 9-3 to record Rugged River Outfitters' purchase and sale transactions under the periodic inventory system. Why can't you measure Rugged River's gross profit under the periodic system? What additional information is needed to compute cost of goods sold and the gross profit?

Accounting for inventory in the periodic system (Obj. 1)

DE9-5 Study Exhibit 9-5, page 354, and answer these questions.

1. In Panel A, are the company's inventory costs stable, increasing, or decreasing during the period? Cite specific figures to support your answer.
2. Which inventory method results in the *lowest* amount for ending inventory (give this figure)? Explain why this method produces the lowest amount for ending inventory.
3. Does this method result in the highest, or the lowest, cost of goods sold? Explain.
4. Does this method result in the highest, or the lowest, gross profit? Explain your answer.

Applying the FIFO, LIFO, and weighted-average methods (Obj. 2)

DE9-6 Study Exhibit 9-5, page 354, and answer these questions.

1. In Panel A, are the company's inventory costs stable, increasing, or decreasing during the period? Cite specific figures to support your answer.
2. Which inventory method results in the *highest* amount for ending inventory (give this figure)? Explain why this method produces the highest amount for ending inventory.
3. Does this method result in the highest, or the lowest, cost of goods sold? Explain.
4. Does this method result in the highest, or the lowest, gross profit? Explain your answer.

DE9-7 Return to Exhibit 9-5, page 354, and assume that the business sold 50 units of inventory during the period (instead of 40 units as in the exhibit). Compute ending inventory and cost of goods sold for each of the following costing methods:

a. Weighted-average   b. FIFO   c. LIFO

Follow the computational format illustrated in the exhibit.

DE9-8 Jetlink Data Systems markets ink used in inkjet printers. Jetlink started the year with 100 containers of ink (weighted-average cost of $9.14 each; FIFO cost of $9 each, LIFO cost of $8 each). During the year, Jetlink purchased 800 containers of ink at $14 and sold 700 units for $22 each, with all transactions on account.

    Journalize Jetlink's purchases, sales, and cost of goods sold transactions using the following format. Jetlink uses the perpetual inventory method to account for inkjet-printer ink.

Accounts	Debit/Credit Amounts		
	Weighted-Average*	FIFO	LIFO

* Round weighted-average unit cost to the nearest cent.

DE9-9 This exercise uses the data from Daily Exercise 9-8. It can follow Daily Exercise 9-8, or it can be solved independently. Operating expenses totaled $4,000.

    Prepare Jetlink Data Systems' income statement for the current year ended December 31 under the weighted-average, FIFO, and LIFO inventory costing methods. Include a complete statement heading, and use a format similar to that illustrated for Daily Exercise 9-8 for the three inventory methods.

DE9-10 This exercise should be used in conjunction with Daily Exercise 9-9.

    Assume Jetlink Data Systems in Daily Exercise 9-9 is a corporation subject to a 40% income tax. Compute Jetlink's income tax expense under the weighted-average, FIFO, and LIFO inventory costing methods. Which method would you select to (a) maximize reported income, or (b) minimize income tax expense? Format your answer as shown on page 356.

DE9-11 **Lands' End,** the mail-order merchant, uses the LIFO method to account for inventory. Suppose Lands' End is having an unusually good year, with net income far above expectations. Assume Lands' End's inventory costs are rising rapidly. What can Lands' End managers do immediately before the end of the year to decrease reported profits and thereby save on income taxes? Explain how this action decreases reported income.

DE9-12 Examine the perpetual inventory record in Exhibit 9-9, page 359. Answer these questions about **Deckers Outdoor's** inventory of Teva sandals.

1. Which costing method does Deckers use? Prove your answer by citing cost data from the exhibit. Focus on the November 12 sale.
2. Deckers sold all the sandals in the exhibit for $50 each. How much did Deckers report for November sales revenue, cost of goods sold, and gross profit? On which financial statement did Deckers report these figures?

DE9-13 **Deckers Outdoor** uses the perpetual inventory record for Teva sandals in Exhibit 9-9, page 359. At December 31, 1999, Scott Ash, chief financial officer of the company, applied the lower-of-cost-or-market rule to Deckers' inventories. Suppose Ash determined that the current replacement cost (current market value) of the sandals was $550. Show how Decker would report this inventory on the balance sheet and cost of goods sold on the income statement.

DE9-14 Examine **Deckers Outdoor's** financial statements in Exhibit 9-1, on page 347. Suppose Deckers' reported cost of inventory at December 31 is overstated by $3 million. What are Deckers' correct amounts for (a) inventory, (b) cost of goods sold, (c) gross profit and (d) net income (net loss)? Ignore income tax.

DE9-15 Barbara Warren, staff accountant of Shimeido Fragrance Co., learned that Shimeido's $4 million cost of inventory at the end of last year was understated by $2 million. She notified the company president of the need to alert Shimeido's lenders that last year's reported net income was incorrect. Akiro Luhara, president of Shimeido, explained to Warren that there is no need to report the error to lenders because the error will counterbalance this year. This year's error will affect this year's net income in the opposite direction of last year's error. Even with no correction, Luhara reasons that net income for both years combined will be the same whether or not Shimeido corrects its error.

Measuring the effect of an inventory error on two years' statements
(Obj. 5)

1. Was last year's reported net income of $6.3 million overstated, understated, or correct? What was the correct amount of net income last year?
2. Is this year's net income of $7 million overstated, understated, or correct? What is the correct amount of net income for the current year?
3. Whose perspective is better, Warren's or Luhara's? Give your reason. Consider the trend of reported net income both without the correction and with the correction.

DE9-16 Determine whether each of the following actions in buying, selling, and accounting for inventories is ethical or unethical. Give your reason for each answer.

Ethical implications of inventory actions
(Obj. 3, 4, 5)

1. Lake Fork Motors consciously overstated purchases to produce a high figure for cost of goods sold (low amount of net income). The real reason was to decrease the company's income tax payments to the government.
2. In applying the lower-of-cost-or-market rule to inventories, Old World Restoration Co. recorded an excessively low market value for ending inventory. This allowed the company to keep from paying income tax for the year.
3. Lamplight Fixtures Ltd. purchased lots of inventory shortly before year end to increase the LIFO cost of goods sold and decrease reported income for the year.
4. T & M Beauty Products delayed the purchase of inventory until after December 31, 20X2, in order to keep 20X2's cost of goods sold from growing too large. The delay in purchasing inventory helped net income of 20X2 to reach the level of profit demanded by the company's investors.
5. Calais Ferry Supply deliberately overstated ending inventory in order to report higher profits (net income).

DE9-17 Answer the following questions.

Estimating ending inventory by the gross profit method
(Obj. 6)

1. Asamax Insulation Company began the year with inventory of $350,000. Inventory purchases for the year totaled $1,600,000. Asamax managers estimate that cost of goods sold for the year will be $1,800,000. How much is Asamax's estimated cost of ending inventory? Use the gross profit method.
2. Cyrus Roofing, a related company, began the year with inventory of $350,000 and purchased $1,600,000 of goods during the year (the same as in requirement 1). Sales for the year are $3,000,000, and Cyrus's gross profit percentage is 40% of sales. Compute Cyrus's estimated cost of ending inventory by the gross profit method. Compare this answer to your answer in requirement 1; they should be the same. Focus on the computation of estimated cost of goods sold to explain why the two answers are the same.

EXERCISES

E9-1 Accounting records for Durall Luggage yield the following data for the year ended December 31, 20X5 (amounts in thousands):

Accounting for inventory in the perpetual system
(Obj. 1)

Inventory, December 31, 20X4..	$ 370
Purchases of inventory (on account)	3,105
Sales of inventory—80% on account; 20% for cash (cost $2,821).........	4,395
Inventory, December 31, 20X5...	?

Required

1. Journalize Durall's inventory transactions in the perpetual system. Show all amounts in thousands. Use Exhibit 9-3 on page 349 as a guide.
2. Report ending inventory, sales, cost of goods sold, and gross profit on the appropriate financial statement (amounts in thousands).
3. Show the computation of cost of goods sold in the periodic system.

E9-2 Use the data in Exercise 9-1.

Accounting for inventory in the periodic system   (Obj. 1)

Required

1. Journalize Durall's inventory transactions in the periodic system. Show all amounts in thousands, and use Exhibit 9-4, page 353, as a guide.

2. Report inventory, sales, cost of goods sold, and gross profit on the appropriate financial statement (amounts in thousands).

Budgeting inventory purchases
(Obj. 1)

E9-3 **Toys "Я" Us** is budgeting for the fiscal year ended January 31, 2000. During the preceding year ended January 31, 1999, cost of goods sold was $8,191 million. Inventory stood at $1,902 million at January 31, 1999.

During the upcoming 2000 year, suppose Toys "Я" Us expects sales and cost of goods sold to increase by 6%. The company budgets next year's ending inventory at $2,020 million.

Required

How much inventory should Toys "Я" Us purchase during the upcoming year in order to reach its budgeted figures? Round to the nearest $1 million.

Determining ending inventory and cost of goods sold by four methods
(Obj. 2)

E9-4 The inventory records of Flexon Prosthetics indicate the following at October 31:

Oct.	1	Beginning inventory	9 units @ $160
	8	Purchase	4 units @ 160
	15	Purchase	12 units @ 170
	26	Purchase	3 units @ 176

The physical count of inventory at October 31 indicates that eight units are on hand, and there are no consignment goods.

Required

Compute ending inventory and cost of goods sold, using each of the following methods. Follow the approach illustrated in Exhibit 9-5.

1. Specific unit cost, assuming four $170 units and four $160 units are on hand
2. Weighted-average cost (round weighted-average unit cost to three decimal places)
3. First-in, first-out   4. Last-in, first-out

Recording inventory transactions—perpetual system
(Obj. 1, 2)

E9-5 Use the data in Exercise 9-4 to journalize the following for the perpetual inventory system.

a. Total October purchases in one summary entry. All purchases were on credit.
b. Total October sales in a summary entry. The selling price was $300 per unit and all sales were on credit. Flexon Prosthetics uses FIFO.

Recording inventory transactions—periodic system
(Obj. 1, 2)

E9-6 Use the data in Exercise 9-4 to journalize the following for the periodic system:

a. Total October purchases in one summary entry. All purchases were on credit.
b. Total October sales in a summary entry. The selling price was $300 per unit and all sales were on credit. Flexon Prosthetics uses LIFO.
c. October 31 end-of-period entries for inventory in the periodic system. Flexon Prosthetics uses LIFO. Post to the Cost of Goods Sold T-account. Label each item in the account. What is the balance of cost of goods sold?

Computing the tax advantage of LIFO over FIFO *(Obj. 3)*

E9-7 Use the data in Exercise 9-4 to illustrate income tax advantage of LIFO over FIFO for Flexon Prosthetics. Sales revenue is $8,000, operating expenses are $1,100, and the income tax rate is 30%. How much in taxes would Flexon Prosthetics save by using the LIFO method?

Determining amounts for the income statement: periodic system *(Obj. 1)*

E9-8 Supply the missing income statement amounts for each of the following companies:

Company	Net Sales	Beginning Inventory	Net Purchases	Ending Inventory	Cost of Goods Sold	Gross Profit
Maple	$101,800	$12,500	$62,700	$19,400	(a)	$37,000
Walnut	(b)	25,450	93,000	(c)	$94,100	43,200
Pine	94,700	(d)	54,900	22,600	62,500	(e)
Magnolia	84,300	10,700	(f)	8,200	(g)	47,100

Prepare the income statement for Magnolia Company, which uses the periodic inventory system. Include a complete heading. Magnolia's operating expenses for the year were $31,600.

E9-9 ← *Link Back to Chapter 5 (Gross Profit Percentage and Inventory Turnover)*. Refer to the data in Exercise 9-8. Suppose you are a financial analyst, and a client has asked you to recommend an investment in one of these companies. Which company is likely to be the most profitable, based on its gross profit percentage and rate of inventory turnover? Write a memo outlining which company you recommend, and explain your reasoning. Use the following format for your memo:

Measuring profitability
(Obj. 3)

Date: _____	
To:	Investor
From: _____	
RE:	Investment recommendation

E9-10 Picker's Paradise carries a large inventory of guitars and other musical instruments. Because each item is expensive, Picker's uses a perpetual inventory system. Company records indicate the following for a particular line of Honeydew guitars:

Determining ending inventory and cost of goods sold in a perpetual system
(Obj. 1, 2)

Date	Item	Quantity	Unit Cost
May 1	Balance.....................	5	$95
6	Sale...........................	3	
8	Purchase..................	11	83
17	Sale...........................	4	
30	Sale...........................	1	

Required

Determine the amounts that Picker's should report for ending inventory and cost of goods sold by the FIFO method. Prepare the perpetual inventory record for the guitars, using Exhibit 9-9 as a guide.

E9-11 Homestake Industries is considering a change from the LIFO inventory method to the FIFO method. Managers are concerned about the effect of this change on income tax expense and reported net income. If the change is made, it will become effective on March 1. Inventory on hand at February 28 is $63,000. During March, Homestake managers expect sales of $295,000, net purchases between $159,000 and $182,000, and operating expenses of $83,000. Inventories at March 31 are budgeted as follows: FIFO, $85,000; LIFO, $78,000.

Change from LIFO to FIFO
(Obj. 3)

Required

Create a spreadsheet to compute estimated net income four ways: Net purchases may be $159,000 or $182,000 for March under both FIFO and LIFO. Format your answer as follows:

	A	B	C	D	E
1		**HOMESTAKE INDUSTRIES**				
2		**Estimated Income under FIFO and LIFO**				
3		**March 20XX**				
4					
5		**FIFO**	**LIFO**	**FIFO**	**LIFO**
6					
7	Sales	$295,000	$295,000	$295,000	$295,000
8					
9	Cost of goods sold				
10	Beginning inventory	63,000	63,000	63,000	63,000
11	Net purchases	159,000	159,000	182,000	182,000
12					
13	Cost of goods available				
14	Ending inventory	85,000	78,000	85,000	78,000
15					
16	Cost of goods sold				
17					
18	Gross profit				
19	Operating expenses	83,000	83,000	83,000	83,000
20					
21	Net income	$	$	$	$

Managing income taxes under
the LIFO method
(Obj. 3)

E9-12 Willitz Paper Supply is nearing the end of its best year ever. With three weeks until year end, it appears that net income for the year will have increased by 70% over last year. Bruce Willitz, the principal stockholder and president, is pleased with the year's success but unhappy about the huge increase in income taxes that the business will have to pay.

He asks you, the financial vice president, to come up with a way to decrease the business's income tax. Inventory quantities are a little lower than normal because sales have been especially strong during the last few months. Willitz Paper Supply uses the LIFO inventory method, and inventory costs have risen dramatically late in the year.

Required

Write a memorandum to Bruce Willitz to explain how Willitz Paper Supply can decrease its income taxes for the current year. Willitz is a man of integrity, so your plan must be completely honest. Adapt the memo format given for Exercise 9-9.

Identifying income, tax, and other
effects of the inventory methods
(Obj. 3)

E9-13 This exercise tests your understanding of the four inventory methods. In the space provided, write the name of the inventory method that best fits the description. Assume that the cost of inventory is rising.

———— a. Generally associated with saving income taxes.
———— b. Results in a cost of ending inventory that is close to the current cost of replacing the inventory.
———— c. Used to account for automobiles, jewelry, and art objects.
———— d. Provides a middle-ground measure of ending inventory and cost of goods sold.
———— e. Maximizes reported income.
———— f. Enables a company to buy high-cost inventory at year end and thereby decrease reported income.
———— g. Reported income and income taxes rise when the company liquidates older, low-cost, layers of inventory.
———— h. Matches the most current cost of goods sold against sales revenue.
———— i. Results in an old measure of the cost of ending inventory.

Applying the lower-of-cost-or-
market rule to inventories:
perpetual system
(Obj. 1, 4)

E9-14 Alcoa Enterprises, which uses a perpetual inventory system, has these account balances at December 31, 20X1, prior to releasing the financial statements for the year:

INVENTORY		COST OF GOODS SOLD		SALES REVENUE	
Beg. bal. 12,489					
End bal. 18,028		Bal. 113,245		Bal. 225,000	

A year ago, when Alcoa prepared its 20X0 financial statements, the replacement cost of ending inventory was $13,051. Alcoa has determined that the replacement cost (current market value) of the December 31, 20X1, ending inventory is $16,840.

Required

Prepare Alcoa Enterprises 20X1 income statement through gross profit to show how Alcoa would apply the lower-of-cost-or-market rule to its inventories. Include a complete heading for the statement.

Applying the lower-of-cost-or-
market rule to inventories:
periodic system
(Obj. 1, 4)

E9-15 Nash-Robin Food Wholesalers uses a periodic inventory system and reports inventory at the lower of FIFO cost or market. Prior to releasing its March 20X4 financial statements, Nash-Robin's preliminary income statement appears as follows:

NASH-ROBIN FOOD WHOLESALERS
Income Statement (partial)

Sales revenue		$112,000
Cost of goods sold:		
Beginning inventory	$17,200	
Net purchases	51,700	
Cost of goods available for sale	68,900	
Ending inventory	(23,800)	
Cost of goods sold		45,100
Gross profit		$ 66,900

Nash-Robin has determined that the current replacement cost of ending inventory is $19,800.

Required

Adjust the preceding income statement to apply the lower-of-cost-or market rule to Nash-Robin's inventory. Also show the relevant portion of Nash-Robin's balance sheet. The replacement cost of Nash-Robin's beginning inventory was $18,600.

E9-16 Lazlo Power Tools reported the following comparative income statement for the years ended September 30, 20X2 and 20X1.

Correcting an inventory error— two years (Obj. 5)

LAZLO POWER TOOLS Income Statements Years Ended September 30, 20X2 and 20X1			
	20X2		**20X1**
Sales revenue......................		$137,300	$121,700
Cost of goods sold:			
Beginning inventory........	$14,000		$12,800
Net purchases...................	72,000		66,000
Cost of goods available.....	86,000		78,800
Ending inventory.............	(16,600)		(14,000)
Cost of goods sold		69,400	64,800
Gross profit		67,900	56,900
Operating expenses		30,300	26,100
Net income		$ 37,600	$ 30,800

During 20X2, accountants for the company discovered that ending 20X1 inventory was overstated by $3,500. Prepare the corrected comparative income statement for the two-year period, complete with a heading for the statement. What was the effect of the error on net income for the two years combined? Explain your answer.

E9-17 Lakely Marineland began January with inventory of $47,500. The business made net purchases of $37,600 and had net sales of $60,000 before a fire destroyed the company's inventory. For the past several years, Lakely's gross profit on sales has been 40%. Use the gross profit method to estimate the cost of the inventory destroyed by the fire. Identify another purpose for which managers use the gross profit method to estimate inventory cost.

Estimating ending inventory by the gross profit method (Obj. 6)

Challenge Exercises

E9-18 For each of the following situations, identify the inventory method that you would use, or, given the use of a particular method, state the strategy that you would follow to accomplish your goal.

Inventory policy decisions (Obj. 2, 3)

a. Suppliers of your inventory are threatening a labor strike, and it may be difficult for your company to obtain inventory. This situation could increase your income taxes.
b. Inventory costs are decreasing, and your company's board of directors wants to minimize income taxes.
c. Inventory costs are increasing. Your company uses LIFO and is having a very good year. It is near year end, and you need to keep net income from increasing too much.
d. Inventory costs have been stable for several years, and you expect costs to remain stable for the indefinite future. (Give the reason for your choice of method.)
e. Company management, like those of **Polaroid** and **Hewlett-Packard,** prefers a middle-of-the-road inventory policy that avoids extremes.
f. Inventory costs are increasing, and the company prefers to report high income.

E9-19 ◄ *Link Back to Chapter 5 (Income Statement and Balance Sheet).* **Campbell Soup Company** uses a perpetual inventory system and the LIFO method to determine the cost of its inventory. During the year ended July 31, 19X9, Campbell Soup reported the following items (adapted) in its financial statements (amounts in millions)

Reporting inventory transactions on the income statement and balance sheet (Obj. 1)

Cost of goods sold............	$3,050	Revenues, total	$6,424
Other expenses................	2,650	Total assets	5,522
Owners' equity................	?	Total liabilities	5,287

Required

1. Prepare Campbell Soup Company's summary income statement for the year ended July 31, 19X9, complete with a heading.
2. Prepare Campbell Soup Company's summary balance sheet at July 31, 19X9, complete with a heading.

(Group A) PROBLEMS

*Accounting for inventory in a
perpetual system
(Obj. 1, 2)*

P9-1A **Pier 1 Imports** operates more than 800 stores. Assume you are dealing with one department in a Pier 1 store in Dallas. The company's fiscal year ends each February 28. Also assume the department began fiscal year 20X0 with an inventory of 50 units that cost $2,135. During the year, the department purchased merchandise on account as follows:

March (60 units @ $32)	$1,920
August (40 units @ $34)	1,360
October (180 units @ $35)	6,300
Total purchases...	$9,580

Cash payments on account during the year totaled $9,110.

During fiscal year 20X0, the department sold 300 units of merchandise for $13,400, of which $4,700 was for cash and the balance was on account. Pier 1 uses the weighted-average cost method for inventories.

Operating expenses for the year were $2,430. The department paid two-thirds in cash and accrued the rest.

Required

1. Make summary journal entries to record the department's transactions for the year ended February 28, 20X0. The company uses a perpetual inventory system.
2. Determine the weighted-average cost of the department's ending inventory at February 28, 20X0. Follow the computational approach illustrated in Exhibit 9-5.
3. Prepare the department's income statement for the year ended February 28, 20X0. Show totals for gross profit and net income.

*Using the cost-of-goods-sold
model to budget operations
(Obj. 1)*

P9-2A Condensed versions of a **Shell** convenience store's most recent income statement and balance sheet reported the following. The business is organized as a proprietorship, so it pays no income tax. It uses a periodic inventory system.

SHELL CONVENIENCE STORE
Income Statement
Year Ended December 31, 20X1

(Thousands)	
Sales...	$900
Cost of sales	720
Gross profit	180
Operating expenses...................	90
Net income...............................	$ 90

SHELL CONVENIENCE STORE
Balance Sheet
December 31, 20X1

(Thousands) Assets		Liabilities and Capital	
Cash	$ 40	Accounts payable	$ 30
Inventories	70	Note payable	190
Land and buildings, net.........	270	Total liabilities	220
		Owner, capital......................	160
Total assets............................	$380	Total liabilities and capital.....	$380

The owner is budgeting for 20X2. He expects sales and cost of sales to increase by 9%. To meet customer demand for the increase in sales, ending inventory will need to be $80 thousand at December 31, 20X2. The owner can lower operating expenses by doing some of the work himself. He hopes to earn a net income of $110 thousand next year.

Required

1. A key variable the owner can control is the amount of inventory he purchases. Show how to determine the amount of purchases the owner should make in 20X2.
2. Prepare the store's budgeted income statement for 20X2 to reach the target net income of $110 thousand.

*Using the perpetual and periodic
inventory systems
(Obj. 1, 2)*

P9-3A Rambler Lawn Supply began March with 50 units of inventory that cost $17 each. The sale price of each unit was $36. During March, Rambler completed these inventory transactions:

	Units	Unit Cost	Unit Sale Price
March 2 Purchase	12	$20	$37
8 Sale.....................	27	17	36
13 Sale.....................	23	17	36
	1	20	37
17 Purchase..............	24	20	37
22 Sale.....................	31	20	37
29 Purchase..............	24	21	39

Required

1. The preceding data are taken from Rambler's perpetual inventory records. Which cost method does Rambler use?
2. Determine Rambler's cost of goods sold for March under the

   a. Perpetual inventory system   b. Periodic inventory system

3. Compute gross profit for March.

P9-4A A Best Yet Electronic Center began December with 140 units of inventory that cost $75 each. During December, the store made the following purchases:

Computing inventory by three methods
(Obj. 2, 3)

Dec. 3	217 @ $79
12	95 @ 82
18	210 @ 83
24	248 @ 87

The store uses the periodic inventory system, and the physical count at December 31 indicates that ending inventory consists of 229 units.

Required

1. Determine the ending inventory and cost-of-goods-sold amounts for the December financial statements under the weighted-average, FIFO, and LIFO cost methods. Round weighted-average cost per unit to the nearest cent and all other amounts to the nearest dollar.
2. How much income tax would Best Yet save during December for this one store by using LIFO versus FIFO? The income tax rate is 40%.

P9-5A Assume the records of **Drug Emporium** include the following accounts for one of its products at December 31 of the current year:

Preparing an income statement directly from the accounts
(Obj. 2, 3)

INVENTORY

Jan. 1	Balance	300 units @ $3.00	1,215
		100 units @ 3.15	

PURCHASES

Feb. 6	800 units @ $3.15	2,520
May 19	600 units @ 3.35	2,010
Aug. 12	460 units @ 3.50	1,610
Oct. 4	800 units @ 3.95	3,160
Dec. 31—Balance		9,300

SALES REVENUE

	Dec. 31	2,600 units	11,200

Required

1. Prepare a partial income statement through gross profit under the weighted-average, FIFO, and LIFO cost methods. Round weighted-average cost to the nearest cent and all other amounts to the nearest dollar. Assume **Drug Emporium** uses a periodic inventory system.
2. Which inventory method would you use to report the highest net income?

P9-6A **Revco Drug** has been plagued with lackluster sales, and some of the company's merchandise is gathering dust. It is now December 31, 20X1. Assume the current replacement cost of a Revco store's ending inventory is $700,000 below what Revco paid for the goods, which was $3,900,000. Before any adjustments at the end of the period, assume the store's Cost of Goods Sold account has a balance of $22,400,000.

What action should Revco take in this situation, if any? Give any journal entry required. At what amount should Revco report Inventory on the balance sheet? At what amount should the company report Cost of Goods Sold on the income statement? Discuss the accounting principle or concept that is most relevant to this situation.

P9-7A The accounting records of Treviño's Mexican Restaurant show these data (in thousands):

	20X3	20X2	20X1
Net sales revenue	$210	$165	$170
Cost of goods sold:			
Beginning inventory	$ 15	$ 25	$ 40
Net purchases	135	100	90
Cost of goods available	150	125	130
Less: Ending inventory	(30)	(15)	(25)
Cost of goods sold	120	110	105
Gross profit	90	55	65
Operating expenses	74	38	46
Net income	$ 16	$ 17	$ 19

In early 20X4, internal auditors discovered that the ending inventory for 20X1 had been understated by $8 thousand and that the ending inventory for 20X3 had been overstated by $5 thousand. The ending inventory at December 31, 20X2, was correct.

Required

1. Show corrected income statements for the three years.
2. State whether each year's net income as reported here and the related owner's equity amounts are understated or overstated. Ignore income tax because Treviño's is organized as a proprietorship. For each incorrect figure, indicate the amount of the understatement or overstatement.

P9-8A Padgitt Camera Store estimates its inventory by the gross profit method when preparing monthly financial statements. For the past two years, gross profit has averaged 32% of net sales. Assume further that the company's inventory records for stores in the northwestern region reveal the following data (amounts in thousands):

Inventory, March 1	$ 292
Transactions during March:	
Purchases	6,585
Purchase discounts	149
Purchase returns	8
Sales	8,657
Sales returns	17

Required

1. Estimate the March 31 inventory using the gross profit method.
2. Prepare the March income statement through gross profit for the Padgitt Camera Store stores in the northwestern region.

P9-9A ◂ *Link Back to Chapter 5 (Merchandiser's Income Statement and Balance Sheet).* **Gap Inc.,** uses a perpetual inventory system and the FIFO method to determine the cost of its inventory. During a recent year, Gap reported the following items (as adapted) in its financial statements (amounts in millions):

Cost of goods sold	$ 6,775	Owners' equity	$?
Long-term liabilities	1,203	Property, plant, and	
Net sales revenue	11,635	equipment, net	2,715
Other assets	276	Total current assets	2,198
Other expenses	3,733	Total current liabilities	1,753

Required

1. Prepare Gap's single-step income statement for the year ended January 29, 20X0, complete with a heading.
2. Prepare Gap's balance sheet at January 29, 20X0, complete with a heading.

PROBLEMS

(Group B)

P9-1B Toys "Я" Us purchases inventory in crates of merchandise, so each unit of inventory is a crate of toys. Assume you are dealing with a single department in the Toys "Я" Us store in Santa Barbara, California. The fiscal year of Toys "Я" Us ends each January 31.

Accounting for inventory using the perpetual system (Obj. 1, 2)

Assume the department began fiscal year 20X5 with an inventory of 20 units that cost a total of $1,200. During the year, the department purchased merchandise on accounts as follows:

April (30 units @ $65)	$ 1,950
August (50 units @ $65)......................	3,250
November (110 units @ $70)................	7,700
Total purchases	$12,900

Cash payments on account during the year totaled $11,390.

During fiscal year 20X5, the department sold 180 units of merchandise for $16,400, of which $5,300 was for cash and the balance was on account. Toys "Я" Us uses the LIFO method for inventories. Department operating expenses for the year were $3,630. The department paid two-thirds in cash and accrued the rest.

Required

1. Make summary journal entries to record the department's transactions for the year ended January 31, 20X5. Toys "Я" Us uses a perpetual inventory system.
2. Determine the LIFO cost of the store's ending inventory at January 31, 20X5. Use a T-account.
3. Prepare the department's income statement for the year ended January 31, 20X5. Include a complete heading, and show totals for gross profit and net income.

P9-2B Condensed versions of a **Chevron** convenience store's most recent income statement and balance sheet reported the following figures. The business uses a periodic inventory system.

Using the cost-of-goods-sold model to budget operations (Obj. 1)

CHEVRON CONVENIENCE STORE Balance Sheet December 31, 20X4			
(Thousands)	**Assets**	**Liabilities and Capital**	
Cash..............................	$ 70	Accounts payable.............	$ 35
Inventories	35	Note payable	280
Land and buildings, net...	360	Total liabilities..................	315
		Owner, capital..................	150
Total assets......................	$465	Total liabilities and capital	$465

CHEVRON CONVENIENCE STORE Income Statement Year Ended December 31, 20X4	
	(Thousands)
Sales...	$800
Cost of sales	660
Gross profit	140
Operating expenses	80
Net income	$ 60

The owner is budgeting for 20X5. He expects sales and cost of sales to increase by 8%. To meet customer demand for the increase in sales, ending inventory will need to be $40 thousand at December 31, 20X5. The owner can lower operating expenses by doing some of the work himself. He hopes to earn a net income of $75 thousand next year.

Required

1. A key variable the owner can control is the amount of inventory he purchases. Show how to determine the amount of purchases he should make in 20X5 (amounts in thousands).
2. Prepare the store's budgeted income statement for 20X5 to reach the target net income of $75 thousand.

P9-3B A **Samsonite** outlet store began August 20X1 with 50 units of inventory that cost $40 each. The sale price of these units was $70. During August, the store completed these inventory transactions:

Using the perpetual and periodic inventory systems (Obj. 1, 2)

	Units	Unit Cost	Unit Sale Price
Aug. 3 Sale.........................	16	$40	$70
8 Purchase.................	80	41	72
11 Sale.........................	34	40	70
19 Sale.........................	9	41	72
24 Sale.........................	35	41	72
30 Purchase.................	18	42	73
31 Sale.........................	11	41	72

Required

1. The preceding data are taken from the store's perpetual inventory records. Which cost method does the store use?
2. Determine the store's cost of goods sold for August under the

    a. Perpetual inventory system   **b.** Periodic inventory system

3. Compute gross profit for August.

Computing inventory by three methods (Obj. 2, 3)

P9-4B Lafferty Framing Co. began March with 73 units of inventory that cost $23 each. During the month, Lafferty made the following purchases:

March 4................................	113 @ $26
12	81 @ 30
19	167 @ 32
25	44 @ 35

The company uses the periodic inventory system, and the physical count at March 31 includes 51 units.

Required

1. Determine the ending inventory and cost-of-goods-sold amounts for the March financial statements under (a) weighted-average cost, (b) FIFO cost, and (c) LIFO cost. Round weighted-average cost per unit to the nearest cent and all other amounts to the nearest dollar.
2. How much income tax would Lafferty Framing save during the month by using LIFO versus FIFO? The income tax rate is 35%.

Preparing an income statement directly from the accounts (Obj. 2, 3)

P9-5B The records of Heavenly Confection Co. include the following accounts at December 31 of the current year:

INVENTORY

Jan. 1	Balance (700 units @ $6.45)	4,515	

PURCHASES

Jan. 6	300 units @ $7.05	2,115	
Mar. 19	1,100 units @ 7.35	8,085	
June 22	8,400 units @ 7.50	63,000	
Oct. 4	500 units @ 8.50	4,250	
Dec. 31	Balance	77,450	

SALES REVENUE

		Dec. 31	10,100 units	138,070

Required

1. Prepare a partial income statement through gross profit under the weighted-average, FIFO, and LIFO methods. Round weighted-average cost to the nearest cent and all other amounts to the nearest dollar. Heavenly Confection uses a periodic inventory system.
2. Which inventory method would you use to minimize income tax?

P9-6B **The Army/Navy Surplus Store** has experienced lackluster sales, and some of the company's merchandise is gathering dust. It is now December 31, 20X2, and the current replacement cost of the ending inventory is $650,000 below what Army/Navy actually paid for the goods, which was $4,900,000. Before any adjustments at the end of the period, the company's Cost of Goods Sold account has a balance of $29,600,000.

What action should The Army/Navy Surplus Store take in this situation, if any? Give any journal entry required. At what amount should Army/Navy report Inventory on the balance sheet? At what amount should the company report Cost of Goods Sold on the income statement? Discuss the accounting principle or concept that is most relevant to this situation.

Applying the lower-of-cost-or-market rule to inventories
(Obj. 4)

P9-7B The Lamarque Copper Company books show the data (in thousands) on page 435. In early 20X3, internal auditors found that the ending inventory for 20X0 had been overstated by $8 thousand and that the ending inventory for 20X2 had been understated by $4 thousand. The ending inventory at December 31, 20X1, was correct.

Correcting inventory errors over a three-year period
(Obj. 5)

(Thousands)	20X2		20X1		20X0	
Net sales revenue		$360		$285		$244
Cost of goods sold:						
Beginning inventory...........	$ 65		$ 55		$ 70	
Net purchases......................	195		135		130	
Cost of goods available	260		190		200	
Less: Ending inventory.....	(70)		(65)		(55)	
Cost of goods sold		190		125		145
Gross profit...........................		170		160		99
Operating expenses		113		109		76
Net income		$ 57		$ 51		$ 23

Required

1. Show corrected income statements for the three years.
2. State whether each year's net income and owner's equity amounts are understated or overstated. Ignore income tax because Lamarque is a proprietorship. For each incorrect figure, indicate the amount of the understatement or overstatement.

P9-8B Beaucock Publishing estimates its inventory by the gross profit method when preparing monthly financial statements. The gross profit has averaged 43% of net sales. The company's inventory records reveal the following data (amounts in thousands):

Estimating ending inventory by the gross profit method; preparing the income statement
(Obj. 6)

Inventory, July 1............................	$ 367
Transactions during July:	
Purchases	3,789
Purchase discounts....................	26
Purchase returns	12
Sales	6,430
Sales returns.............................	25

Required

1. Estimate the July 31 inventory, using the gross profit method.
2. Prepare the July income statement through gross profit for Beaucock Publishing.

P9-9B ← Link Back to Chapter 5 (Merchandiser's Income Statement and Balance Sheet). **Lands' End, Inc.,** uses a perpetual inventory system and the LIFO method to determine the cost of its inventory. During a recent year, Lands' End reported the following items (adapted) in its financial statements (amounts in millions):

Reporting inventory items on the income statement and balance sheet
(Obj. 1)

Cost of goods sold......................	$ 727	Interest revenue	$ 1
Long-term liabilities	9	Owners' equity.............................	?
Net sales revenue	1,320	Property, plant, & equipment, net	166
Other assets...............................	1	Total current assets......................	289
Other expenses..........................	546	Total current liabilities.................	151

Required

1. Prepare a single-step income statement for Lands' End for the year ended January 28, 2000, complete with a heading.
2. Prepare the Lands' End balance sheet at January 28, 2000, complete with a heading.

APPLY YOUR KNOWLEDGE

DECISION CASES

Measuring the impact of a year-end purchase of inventory (Obj. 2, 3)

Case 1. Lena's Shoes is nearing the end of its first year of operations. The company made inventory purchases of $745,000 during the year, as follows:

January..................	1,000 units @ $100.00	=	$100,000
July.......................	4,000	121.25	485,000
November..............	1,000	160.00	160,000
Totals....................	6,000		$745,000

Sales for the year will be 5,000 units for $1,200,000 revenue. Expenses other than cost of goods sold and income taxes will be $200,000. The president of the company is undecided about whether to adopt the FIFO method or the LIFO method for inventories.

The company has storage capacity for 5,000 additional units of inventory. Inventory prices are expected to stay at $160 per unit for the next few months. The president is considering purchasing 1,000 additional units of inventory at $160 each before the end of the year. He wishes to know how the purchase would affect net income under both FIFO and LIFO. The income tax rate is 42%.

Required

1. To aid the decision, prepare income statements under FIFO and under LIFO, both without and with the year-end purchase of 1,000 units of inventory at $160 per unit.
2. Compare net income under FIFO without and with the year-end purchase. Make the same comparison under LIFO. Under which method does the year-end purchase affect net income?

Assessing the impact of the inventory costing methods on the financial statements (Obj. 2, 3, 4)

Case 2. The inventory costing method a company chooses can affect the financial statements and thus the decisions of the people who use those statements.

Required

1. A leading accounting researcher stated that one inventory costing method reports the most recent costs in the income statement, while another reports the most recent costs in the balance sheet. What did the researcher mean? Name the methods.
2. Conservatism is an accepted accounting concept. Would you want the management of your company to be conservative in accounting for inventory? Give your reason.
3. TriArc Co. follows conservative accounting and writes the value of its inventory of bicycles down to market, which has declined below cost. The following year, an unexpected cycling craze results in a demand for bicycles that far exceeds supply, and the market price increases above the previous cost. What effect will conservatism have on the income of TriArc during each year?

ETHICAL ISSUE

During 20X2, Darden Furniture Company changed to the LIFO method of accounting for inventory. Suppose that during 20X3, Darden changes back to the FIFO method and the following year switches back to LIFO again.

Required

1. What would you think of a company's ethics if it changes accounting methods every year?

2. What accounting principle would changing methods every year violate?
3. Who can be harmed when a company changes its accounting methods too often? How?

FINANCIAL STATEMENT CASE

Analyzing inventories (*Obj. 2*)

The notes are an important part of a company's financial statements, giving valuable details that would clutter the tabular data presented in the statements. This case will help you learn to use a company's inventory notes. Refer to the **Target** financial statements and related notes in Appendix A and answer the following questions:

Required

1. How much was the Target merchandise inventory at January 29, 2000? At January 30, 1999?
2. How does Target value its inventories? Which cost methods does the company use? Ignore the *retail method* that Target refers to.
3. By rearranging the cost-of-goods-sold formula, you can determine purchases, which are not disclosed in the Target statements. How much were the company's inventory purchases during the year ended January 29, 2000?

TEAM PROJECT

◄■ *Link Back to Chapter 5 (Gross Profit Percentage and Inventory Turnover).* Obtain the annual reports of as many companies as you have team members—one company per team member. Most companies post their financial statements on their Web sites.

Required

1. Identify the inventory method used by each company.
2. Compute each company's gross profit percentage and rate of inventory turnover for the most recent two years.
3. For the industries of the companies you are analyzing, obtain the industry averages for gross profit percentage and inventory turnover from Robert Morris Associates, *Annual Statement Studies;* Dun and Bradstreet, *Industry Norms and Key Business Ratios;* or Leo Troy, *Almanac of Business and Industrial Financial Ratios.*
4. How well does each of your companies compare to the average for its industry? What insight about your companies can you glean from these ratios?

INTERNET EXERCISE

General Motors (GM) remains the world's Number 1 maker of cars and trucks, including the Buick, Cadillac, Chevrolet, GMC, Oldsmobile, Pontiac, and Saturn brands.

1. In the past, General Motors has also been ranked Number 1 in the Fortune 500 listing. Go to **http://www.Fortune.com** and under "Lists" click on *Fortune 500.* What is GM's Fortune 500 ranking this year?
2. Click on *General Motors* and then click on the URL for GM, **www.gm.com,** and go to GM's Web site. Click on *The Company* followed by *Investor Information.* Select the *most recent annual report* and watch the video show. Use the information in the annual report to answer the following questions.
   a. Read the "Letter to Stockholders." Did GM have a good year? Give the basis for your evaluation.
   b. Refer to the "Consolidated Statements of Income for General Motors Corporation and Subsidiaries." For the two most recent years, list the amounts reported for "Total net sales and revenues" and "Cost of sales and other operating expenses." For each year, calculate gross profit. Comment on the trend of gross profit, what the trend indicates, and whether the trend is favorable or unfavorable.
   c. Refer to the "Consolidated Balance Sheets for General Motors Corporation and Subsidiaries." For the two most recent years, list the amounts reported for "Inventories." For the most recent year, calculate the rate of inventory turnover. On average, how many days does GM hold inventory before selling it?

General Motors

Go to the "Depreciation Methods and Inventory Cost Flow Assumptions" episode on the *Mastering Accounting* CD-Rom for an interactive, video-enhanced exercise focused on the different methods for depreciation and inventory. CanGo staff must prepare reports that present potential investors with the best possible financial outlook for the company.

APPENDIX TO CHAPTER 9

COMPARING THE PERPETUAL AND PERIODIC INVENTORY SYSTEMS

⦿ DAILY EXERCISE 9-4

Exhibit 9A-1 provides a side-by-side comparison of the two inventory accounting systems. It combines the material from Exhibits 9-3 and 9-4. Both systems report the same amounts for inventory, cost of goods sold, and everything else.

Answer the following questions about various features of the perpetual inventory system and the periodic inventory system.

1. Do the perpetual and periodic inventory systems result in the same or different dollar amounts for Inventory and Cost of Goods Sold? Explain.

2. a. Which inventory system records the cost of inventory purchased as an asset and the cost of inventory sold as expense?

   b. Which inventory system records the cost of inventory purchased as an expense (name the expense account) and then sets up the cost of ending inventory as an asset?

3. Suppose your company produces microchips for use in making computer circuit boards. Technology is advancing rapidly, and you need monthly financial statements to remain competitive. Which inventory system should you use?

PANEL A—Recording in the Journal and Posting to the T-accounts

Perpetual System	Periodic System

1. Credit purchases of $560,000:

Inventory..................................... 560,000
    Accounts Payable..............   560,000

2. Credit sales of $900,000 (cost $540,000):

Accounts Receivable.................. 900,000
    Sales Revenue.........................   900,000

Cost of Goods Sold 540,000
    Inventory.........................   540,000

3. End-of-period entries:

No entries required. Both Inventory and Cost of Goods Sold are up-to-date.

---

1. Credit purchases of $560,000:

Purchases.................................... 560,000
    Accounts Payable..............   560,000

2. Credit sales of $900,000:

Accounts Receivable.................. 900,000
    Sales Revenue...................   900,000

3. End-of-period entries to update Inventory and record Cost of Goods Sold:

a. Transfer the cost of beginning inventory ($100,000) to Cost of Goods Sold:

Cost of Goods Sold 100,000
    Inventory (beginning balance)   100,000

b. Record the cost of ending inventory ($120,000) based on a physical count:

Inventory (ending balance)........ 120,000
    Cost of Goods Sold............   120,000

c. Transfer the cost of purchases to Cost of Goods Sold:

Cost of Goods Sold 560,000
    Purchases...........................   560,000

INVENTORY AND COST OF GOODS SOLD ACCOUNTS

INVENTORY		COST OF GOODS SOLD	
100,000*	540,000	540,000	
560,000			
120,000			

*Beginning inventory was $100,000

INVENTORY AND COST OF GOODS SOLD ACCOUNTS

INVENTORY		COST OF GOODS SOLD	
100,000**	100,000	100,000	120,000
120,000		560,000	
		540,000	

**Beginning inventory was $100,000

PANEL B—Reporting in the Financial Statements

Perpetual System	Periodic System

Income Statement (partial)

Sales revenue.......................... $900,000
Cost of goods sold ....   540,000 ◄
Gross profit............................. $360,000

Sales revenue $900,000
Cost of goods sold:
  Beginning inventory...................... $100,000
  Purchases..   560,000
  Cost of goods available for sale...... 660,000
  Less: Ending inventory .... (120,000)
Cost of goods sold   540,000
Gross profit....................................... $360,000

Balance Sheet (partial)

Current assets:

Cash....................................... $ XXX
Accounts receivable   XXX
Inventories.......................... **120,000** ◄

Current assets:

Cash... $ XXX
Accounts receivable.....................   XXX
Inventories **120,000**

10 Plant Assets and Intangible Assets

LEARNING OBJECTIVES

After studying this chapter, you should be able to

1. Measure the cost of a plant asset
2. Account for depreciation
3. Select the best depreciation method for income tax purposes
4. Account for the disposal of a plant asset
5. Account for natural resource assets and depletion
6. Account for intangible assets and amortization

www.prenhall.com/horngren

Readiness Assessment

The Home Depot is the world's largest home improvement dealer and ranks among the largest retailers in the United States. The company has experienced major growth, and it plans to keep expanding. The Home Depot's business strategy is twofold: (1) offer high-quality merchandise at "Day-In, Day-Out" warehouse prices and (2) provide exceptional customer service.

Fiscal 1999 (the year ended January 30, 2000) marked the 13th straight year of record profits. Assets topped $17 billion. Over $10 billion of these assets are property, plant, and equipment, the subject of this chapter.

Source: The Home Depot® *1999 Annual Report.*

How did **The Home Depot** grow so rapidly? By opening new stores at a fast pace. The Home Depot's balance sheet (Exhibit 10-2) shows the effect of the company's growth. During the most recent year, total assets grew to $17.1 billion (line 13). Much of the growth shows up in Property and equipment (lines 2–10), collectively labeled *plant assets,* which we examine in this chapter. ➤

◄ We introduced plant assets in Chapter 3, page 90.

This chapter also covers *intangibles,* those assets without physical form, such as Cost in excess of the fair value of net assets acquired—better known as *goodwill.* This is the next-to-last asset reported on Home Depot's balance sheet (line 11). Finally, we discuss natural resources (such as oil, gas, timber, and gravel). The expenses that relate to plant assets, natural resources, and intangible assets are *depreciation, depletion,* and *amortization.*

Chapter 10 concludes our coverage of assets, except for investments (Chapter 16). After completing this chapter, you should understand the various assets of a business and how to account for them.

MEASURING THE COST OF PLANT ASSETS

Plant assets, or **fixed assets,** are long-lived tangible assets—for instance, land, buildings, and equipment—used to operate a business and not held for sale. Their physical form provides their usefulness. The expense associated with plant assets is called *depreciation.* ➤ Of the plant assets, land is unique. Its cost is *not* depreciated—expensed over time—because its usefulness does not decrease. Most companies report plant assets under the heading Property, plant, and equipment on the balance sheet.

Intangible assets do not have a physical form. We cannot see or touch them. They are useful only because of the special rights they carry. Patents, copyrights, and trademarks are intangible assets, and their accounting is similar to that for plant assets. Accounting for intangibles has its own terminology. Exhibit 10-1 shows that we refer to the using up of intangibles as *amortization,* which is the same concept as depreciation.

To begin our study, let's take a tour of **The Home Depot** balance sheet in Exhibit 10-2. The company holds land, buildings, and other plant assets (lines 2–8). Total cost is $11.9 billion (line 8). Home Depot has used up (depreciated) $1.7 billion of its plant assets (line 9). This is what accumulated depreciation on the balance sheet means—the used-up portion of the plant asset. The book value of these assets (cost less accumulated depreciation) is $10.2 billion (line 10). Home Depot's goodwill has a book value of $311 million (line 11).

The *cost principle* directs a business to carry an asset on the balance sheet at its cost—the amount paid for the asset. The general rule for measuring cost (repeated from Chapter 9, page 350) is

The cost of an asset = **The sum of all the costs incurred to bring the asset to its intended purpose, net of all discounts**

The *cost of a plant asset* is its purchase price plus applicable taxes, purchase commissions, and all other amounts paid to acquire the asset and make it ready for its intended use. In Chapter 9, we applied this principle to inventory. The types of costs differ for the various plant assets, so we discuss each asset individually.

PLANT ASSETS. Long-lived tangible assets, such as land, buildings, and equipment, used to operate a business. Also called **fixed assets.**

◄ We introduced the concept of depreciation in Chapter 3, page 90.

INTANGIBLE ASSETS. Assets with no physical form. Valuable because of the special rights they carry. Examples are patents and copyrights.

Objective 1
Measure the cost of a plant asset

	Asset Account on the Balance Sheet	Related Expense Account on the Income Statement
Plant Assets		
	Land	None
	Buildings, Machinery, and Equipment, Furniture and Fixtures, and Land Improvements	Depreciation
	Natural Resources	Depletion
Intangibles	....	Amortization

EXHIBIT 10-2
The Home Depot Balance Sheet (partial, adapted)

THE HOME DEPOT, INC.
Balance Sheet (Adapted, Assets Only)
Amounts in Millions
January 30, 2000

Assets

		Current Assets:	
	1	Total Current Assets	$6,390
		Property and Equipment, at cost:	
Plant assets	2	Land	3,248
	3	Buildings	4,834
	4	Furniture, fixtures, and equipment	2,279
	5	Leasehold improvements	493
	6	Construction in progress	791
	7	Capital leases	245
	8	Total cost of plant assets	11,890
	9	Less Accumulated depreciation	(1,663)
	10	Net property and equipment	10,227
Intangibles	11	Cost in excess of the fair value of net assets acquired, net of accumulated amortization of $33	311
	12	Other assets	153
	13	Total Assets	$17,081

◉ DAILY EXERCISE 10-1

Land and Land Improvements

The cost of land includes its purchase price, brokerage commission, survey and legal fees, and any back property taxes that the purchaser pays. Land cost also includes the cost of clearing the land and removing any unwanted buildings. The cost of land is not depreciated.

The cost of land does *not* include fencing, paving, sprinkler systems, and lighting. These separate plant assets—called *land improvements*—are subject to depreciation.

Suppose The Home Depot signs a $500,000 note payable to purchase land for a store site. Home Depot also pays $40,000 in back property tax, $8,000 in transfer taxes, $5,000 to remove an old building, a $1,000 survey fee, and $260,000 to pave the parking lot, all in cash. What is the cost of this land? The cost of paving the lot, $260,000, is *not* included in the Land account. The pavement is a land improvement.

Purchase price of land...............		$500,000
Add related costs:		
Back property taxes...............	$40,000	
Transfer taxes	8,000	
Removal of building..............	5,000	
Survey fee	1,000	
Total related costs.................		54,000
Total cost of land......................		$554,000

Home Depot's entries to record purchase of the land and pavement of the parking lot are as follows:

Land	554,000	
Note Payable		500,000
Cash		54,000

We would say that The Home Depot *capitalized* the cost of the land at $554,000. This means that the company debited an asset account (Land) for $554,000.

Land Improvements	260,000	
Cash		260,000

Land and Land Improvements are two entirely separate asset accounts. Land improvements include lighting, signs, fences, paving, sprinkler systems, and landscaping. These costs are debited to the Land Improvements account and then depreciated over their useful life.

 DAILY EXERCISE 10-2

Buildings

The cost of constructing a building includes architectural fees, building permits, contractors' charges, and payments for material, labor, and overhead. The time to complete a building can be months, even years. If the company constructs its own assets, the cost of the building may include the cost of interest on borrowed money. (We discuss this topic in the next section of the chapter.) When an existing building is purchased, its cost includes all the usual items, plus the cost to repair and renovate the building.

Machinery and Equipment

The cost of machinery and equipment includes its purchase price (less any discounts), plus transportation charges, insurance while in transit, sales and other taxes, purchase commission, installation costs, and the cost of testing the asset before it is used. After the asset is up and running, we cease capitalizing these costs to the Equipment account. Thereafter, insurance, taxes, and maintenance costs are recorded as expenses.

Leasehold Improvements

Leasehold improvements are similar to land improvements. Leasehold improvements are alterations to assets the company is leasing. For example, The Home Depot leases store buildings, warehouses, and vehicles. The company customizes leased assets by painting its logo on trucks and buildings.

These improvements are assets of The Home Depot even though the company does not own the truck or building. Leasehold improvements appear on the company's balance sheet (see line 5 of Home Depot's balance sheet on page 388). Leasehold improvements should be amortized (depreciated) over the term of the lease.

Construction in Progress and Capital Leases

The Home Depot's balance sheet includes two additional categories of plant assets: Construction in progress (line 6) and Capital leases (line 7).

CONSTRUCTION IN PROGRESS *Construction in progress* is an asset, such as a warehouse, that the company is constructing for its own use. The construction is incomplete and the warehouse is not ready for use. However, the construction costs are assets because the warehouse, when completed, will render future benefits for the company.

CAPITAL LEASES A *capital lease* is a lease arrangement similar to the installment purchase of an asset. Companies report assets leased through capital leases as assets even though they do not own them. After all, their lease payments secure the use of the asset over the term of the lease. For example, The Home Depot has long-term capital leases on some of its store buildings. The Home Depot reports the cost of these plant assets under Capital leases on the balance sheet.

 DAILY EXERCISE 10-3

A capital lease is different from an *operating lease,* which is an ordinary rental agreement, such as your dorm room or apartment lease or the rental of a **Hertz** automobile. The renter records rent expense for each payment under an operating lease.

Capitalizing the Cost of Interest

The Home Depot constructs some of its plant assets and finances the construction with borrowed money. The Home Depot pays interest that it includes as part of the cost of a self-constructed asset. Including interest in the asset's total cost is called *capitalizing interest.* To **capitalize a cost** means to debit an asset (versus an expense) account.

CAPITALIZE A COST. To record a cost as part of an asset's cost, rather than as an expense.

Suppose on July 2, 20X2, The Home Depot borrows $1,000,000 on a two-year, 10% note payable to build a warehouse. The interest cost for 20X2 on this note payable is $50,000 ($1,000,000 $\times$ .10 $\times$ 6/12). Assume all of this interest cost should be capitalized as part of the cost of the building. The Home Depot's entry for the construction cost is

```
20X2
July–Dec.    Building.....................................................    1,000,000
                 Cash ..................................................                  1,000,000
             Incurred construction cost.
```

The Home Depot's entry to capitalize the interest paid at year end is as follows:

 DAILY EXERCISE 10-4

```
20X2
Dec. 31      Building.....................................................    50,000
                 Cash ..................................................                  50,000
             Paid interest on construction loan.
```

A Lump-Sum (Basket) Purchase of Assets

Businesses often purchase several assets as a group, or in a "basket," for a single amount. For example, a company may pay one price for land and an office building. For accounting purposes the company must identify the cost of each asset. The total cost is divided among the assets according to their relative sales (or market) values. This allocation technique is called the *relative-sales-value method.*

Suppose **Xerox Corporation** purchases land and a building in Kansas City for a midwestern sales office. The combined purchase price of land and building is $2,800,000. An appraisal indicates that the land's market (sales) value is $300,000 and that the building's market (sales) value is $2,700,000.

First, figure the ratio of each asset's market value to the total market value of both assets combined. Suppose the total appraised value is $2,700,000 + $300,000 = $3,000,000. Thus, the land, valued at $300,000, is 10% of the total market value. The building's appraised value is 90% of the total. The cost of each asset is determined as follows:

Asset	Market (Sales) Value	Percentage of Total Value			Total Purchase Price		Cost of Each Asset
Land	$ 300,000	$300,000/$3,000,000	=	10% $\times$	$2,800,000	=	$ 280,000
Building	2,700,000	$2,700,000/$3,000,000	=	90% $\times$	2,800,000	=	2,520,000
Total	$3,000,000			100%			$2,800,000

If Xerox pays cash, the entry to record the purchase of the land and building is

```
Land........................................................    280,000
Building....................................................    2,520,000
    Cash ...................................................                  2,800,000
```

WORK IT OUT

How would a business divide a $120,000 lump-sum purchase price for land, building, and equipment with estimated market values of $40,000, $95,000, and $15,000, respectively? Round decimals to three places.

Answer

Asset	Market (Sales) Value	Percentage of Total Value				Total Purchase Price		Cost of Each Asset
Land.............	$ 40,000	$40,000/$150,000	=	26.7%	×	$120,000	=	$ 32,040
Building.......	95,000	$95,000/$150,000	=	63.3%	×	120,000	=	75,960
Equipment...	15,000	$15,000/$150,000	=	10.0%	×	120,000	=	12,000
Total.............	$150,000			100.0%				$120,000

 DAILY EXERCISE 10-5

Capital Expenditures

When a company makes a plant asset expenditure, it must decide whether to debit an asset account or an expense account. In this context, *expenditure* refers to a cash or a credit purchase of goods or services related to the asset. Examples of such expenditures range from **General Motors'** purchase of robots for an assembly plant to a motorist's replacing the windshield on a Chevrolet.

Expenditures that increase the asset's capacity or efficiency or extend its useful life are called **capital expenditures.** For example, the cost of a major overhaul that extends a taxi's useful life is a capital expenditure. Repair work that generates a capital expenditure is called a **major repair,** or an **extraordinary repair.** The amount of the capital expenditure, said to be capitalized, is debited to an asset account. For an extraordinary repair on a taxi, we would debit the asset account Automobiles.

Other expenditures that do not extend the asset's capacity, which merely maintain the asset or restore it to working order, are called *expenses*. These costs are matched against revenue. Examples include the costs of repainting a taxi, repairing a dented fender, and replacing tires. These costs are debited to an expense account. For the **ordinary repairs** on the taxi, we would debit Repair Expense.

The distinction between capital and maintenance expenditures is often a matter of opinion. Does the cost extend the life of the asset (a capital expenditure), or does it only maintain the asset in good order (an expense)? When in doubt, companies tend to debit an expense, for two reasons. First, many expenditures are minor and most companies have a policy of debiting expense for all expenditures below a specific minimum, such as $1,000. Second, the income tax motive favors debiting all borderline expenditures to expense in order to create an immediate tax deduction. Exhibit 10-3 illustrates the distinction between capital expenditures and expenses for several delivery-truck expenditures.

CAPITAL EXPENDITURE. Expenditure that increases the capacity or efficiency of an asset or extends its useful life. Capital expenditures are debited to an asset account.

MAJOR REPAIR OR EXTRAORDINARY REPAIR. Repair work that generates a capital expenditure.

ORDINARY REPAIR. Repair work that is debited to an expense account.

DEBIT AN ASSET ACCOUNT FOR CAPITAL EXPENDITURES	DEBIT REPAIR AND MAINTENANCE EXPENSE FOR AN EXPENSE
Extraordinary repairs:	*Ordinary repairs:*
Major engine overhaul	Repair of transmission or engine
Modification of truck body for new use	Oil change, lubrication, and so on
Addition to storage capacity of truck	Replacement tires or windshield
	Paint job

EXHIBIT 10-3
Delivery-Truck Expenditures— Capital Expenditure or Expense

Treating a capital expenditure as an expense, or vice versa, creates errors in the financial statements. Suppose a company makes a capital expenditure and erroneously expenses this cost. A capital expenditure should have been debited to an asset account. This accounting error overstates expenses and understates net income on the income statement. On the balance sheet, the Equipment account is understated, and so is owner's equity, as follows:

Income Statement

Revenues................	CORRECT
Expenses.................	OVERSTATED
Net income	UNDERSTATED

Balance Sheet

Current assets.............	CORRECT	Total liabilities	CORRECT
Plant assets	UNDERSTATED	Owner's equity..............................	UNDERSTATED
Total assets.................	UNDERSTATED	Total liabilities and equity	UNDERSTATED

 DAILY EXERCISE 10-6

Capitalizing the cost of an ordinary repair creates the opposite error. Expenses are then understated, and net income is overstated. The balance sheet overstates assets and owner's equity.

MEASURING PLANT ASSET DEPRECIATION

→ See Chapter 3, page 86, for a discussion of the matching principle.

The allocation of a plant asset's cost to expense over the asset's useful life is called *depreciation*. Depreciation accounting matches the asset's cost (expense) against the revenue earned by the asset, as the matching principle directs. ◄ Exhibit 10-4 shows depreciation for the purchase of a Boeing 737 jet by **United Airlines.**

EXHIBIT 10-4
Depreciation and the Matching of Expense with Revenue

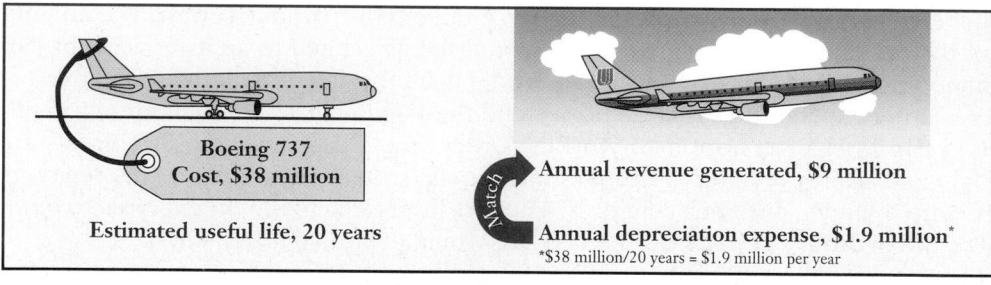

Boeing 737
Cost, $38 million

Estimated useful life, 20 years

Annual revenue generated, $9 million

Annual depreciation expense, $1.9 million*
*$38 million/20 years = $1.9 million per year

Suppose **The Home Depot** buys a computer for use in its accounting system. Home Depot believes it will get four years of service from the computer, and it will then be worthless. Using the straight-line depreciation method, The Home Depot expenses one-quarter of the asset's cost in each of its four years of use.

Let's contrast what depreciation accounting is with what it is *not*.

1. *Depreciation is not a process of valuation*. Businesses do not record depreciation based on the market (sales) value of their plant assets at the end of each year. Instead, businesses allocate an asset's cost to expense during the period of its use.
2. *Depreciation does not mean that the business sets aside cash to replace an asset when it is used up*. Establishing a cash fund is entirely separate from depreciation, and depreciation does not represent cash.

Causes of Depreciation

All assets but land wear out. For some plant assets, physical *wear and tear* and the elements cause depreciation. For example, physical deterioration wears out the trucks that move Home Depot merchandise from warehouses to company stores. The store fixtures used to display merchandise are also subject to physical wear and tear.

Assets such as computers, software, and airplanes may be *obsolete* before they deteriorate. An asset is obsolete when another asset can do the job better or more efficiently. Thus, an asset's useful life may be much shorter than its physical life.

Accountants usually depreciate computers over a short period—perhaps two to four years—even though the computers will continue working much longer. Whether wear and tear or obsolescence causes depreciation, the asset's cost is depreciated over its expected useful life.

Measuring Depreciation

Depreciation of a plant asset is based upon the asset's

1. Cost   2. Estimated useful life   3. Estimated residual value

Cost is a known amount. The other two factors must be estimated.

Estimated useful life is the length of the service period expected from the asset. Useful life may be expressed in years, units of output, miles, or another measure. For example, the useful life of a building is stated in years. The useful life of a bookbinding machine is the number of books the machine can bind—that is, its expected units of output. A delivery truck's useful life can be measured in miles. Companies make such estimates from past experience, industry information, and government publications.

Estimated residual value—also called **scrap value** or **salvage value**—is the expected cash value of an asset at the end of its useful life. For example, a machine's useful life may be seven years. After seven years, the company expects to sell the machine as scrap metal. The cash the business thinks it can sell the machine for is its estimated residual value. Estimated residual value is *not* depreciated because the business expects to receive this amount from disposing of the asset. If there's no residual value, then it depreciates the full cost of the asset. Cost minus residual value is called the **depreciable cost** of the asset.

ESTIMATED USEFUL LIFE. Length of the service period expected from an asset. May be expressed in years, units of output, miles, or another measure.

ESTIMATED RESIDUAL VALUE. Expected cash value of an asset at the end of its useful life. Also called **scrap value,** or **salvage value.**

DEPRECIABLE COST. The cost of a plant asset minus its estimated residual value.

Depreciation Methods

Objective 2
Account for depreciation

Three major methods exist for computing depreciation:

- straight-line
- units-of-production
- declining-balance

These methods allocate different amounts of depreciation to each period. However, they all result in the same total amount of depreciation over the life of the asset. Exhibit 10-5 gives the data we will use to illustrate the depreciation computations for a Home Depot truck. We cover the three most widely used methods. We omit the sum-of-years'-digits method because only around 1% of all companies use it.

Data Item	Amount
Cost of truck	$41,000
Less: Estimated residual value	(1,000)
Depreciable cost	$40,000
Estimated useful life:	
Years	5 years
Units of production	100,000 units [miles]

EXHIBIT 10-5
Data for Depreciation Computations for a Home Depot Truck

STRAIGHT-LINE METHOD   In the **straight-line (SL) method,** an equal amount of depreciation is assigned to each year of asset use. Depreciable cost is divided by useful life in years to determine the annual amount of depreciation. The equation for SL depreciation, applied to the Home Depot truck data from Exhibit 10-5, is

STRAIGHT-LINE (SL) DEPRECIATION METHOD. Depreciation method in which an equal amount of depreciation expense is assigned to each year of asset use.

$$\text{Straight-line depreciation per year} = \frac{\text{Cost} - \text{Residual value}}{\text{Useful life, in years}}$$

$$= \frac{\$41,000 - \$1,000}{5}$$

$$= \$8,000$$

The entry to record one year's depreciation is

$$
\begin{array}{lll}
\text{Depreciation Expense} & 8{,}000 & \\
\quad \text{Accumulated Depreciation} & & 8{,}000
\end{array}
$$

This truck was purchased on January 1, 20X1, and let's assume The Home Depot's fiscal year ends on December 31. A *straight-line depreciation schedule* is given in Exhibit 10-6. The final column in the exhibit shows the asset's *book value*, which is its cost less accumulated depreciation. Book value is also called *carrying amount* or *carrying value*. ←

➤ We introduced book value in Chapter 3, page 91.

As an asset is used, accumulated depreciation increases, and the book value decreases. Compare the Accumulated Depreciation and the Book Value columns of Exhibit 10-6. An asset's final book value is its *residual value* ($1,000 in Exhibit 10-6). At the end of its useful life, the asset is said to be *fully depreciated*.

EXHIBIT 10-6
Straight-Line Depreciation Schedule for a Home Depot Truck

| Date | Asset Cost | Depreciation for the Year | | | Accumulated Depreciation | Asset Book Value |
		Depreciation Rate	Depreciable Cost	Depreciation Expense		
1-1-20X1	$41,000					$41,000
12-31-20X1		0.20* ×	$40,000 =	$8,000	$ 8,000	33,000
12-31-20X2		0.20 ×	40,000 =	8,000	16,000	25,000
12-31-20X3		0.20 ×	40,000 =	8,000	24,000	17,000
12-31-20X4		0.20 ×	40,000 =	8,000	32,000	9,000
12-31-20X5		0.20 ×	40,000 =	8,000	40,000	1,000

*1/5 year = 0.20 per year

An asset with cost of $10,000, useful life of five years, and residual value of $2,000 was purchased on January 1. What is the SL depreciation for the first year? For the second year? For the fifth year?

Answer:

$$
\frac{\text{SL depreciation}}{\text{per year}} = \frac{\text{Cost} - \text{Residual value}}{\text{Useful life, in years}}
$$

$$
= \frac{\$10{,}000 - \$2{,}000}{5} = \frac{\$1{,}600 \text{ per year}}{\text{every year}}
$$

UNITS-OF-PRODUCTION (UOP) METHOD In the **units-of-production (UOP) method,** a fixed amount of depreciation goes with each *unit of output* produced by the asset. Depreciable cost is divided by useful life, in units of production. This per-unit expense is then multiplied by the number of units produced each period to compute depreciation for that period. The UOP depreciation equation for the Home Depot truck data in Exhibit 10-5 is

UNITS-OF-PRODUCTION (UOP) DEPRECIATION METHOD.
Depreciation method by which a fixed amount of depreciation is assigned to each unit of output produced by an asset.

$$
\frac{\text{Units-of-production depreciation}}{\text{per unit of output}} = \frac{\text{Cost} - \text{Residual value}}{\text{Useful life, in units of production}}
$$

$$
= \frac{\$41{,}000 - \$1{,}000}{100{,}000 \text{ miles}}
$$

$$
= \$0.40 \text{ per mile}
$$

This the truck is expected to be driven 20,000 miles during the first year, 30,000 during the second, 25,000 during the third, 15,000 during the fourth, and 10,000 during the fifth. The amount of UOP depreciation each period varies with the number of units the asset produces. The UOP schedule for this asset is shown in Exhibit 10-7.

Date	Asset Cost	Depreciation for the Year				Accumulated Depreciation	Asset Book Value
		Depreciation Per Unit	Number of Units		Depreciation Expense		
1-1-20X1	$41,000						$41,000
12-31-20X1		$0.40	× 20,000	=	$ 8,000	$ 8,000	33,000
12-31-20X2		0.40	× 30,000	=	12,000	20,000	21,000
12-31-20X3		0.40	× 25,000	=	10,000	30,000	11,000
12-31-20X4		0.40	× 15,000	=	6,000	36,000	5,000
12-31-20X5		0.40	× 10,000	=	4,000	40,000	1,000

WORK IT OUT

The asset in the preceding Work It Out produced 3,000 units in the first year, 4,000 in the second, 4,500 in the third, 2,500 in the fourth, and 2,000 units in the last year. Its total estimated useful life is 16,000 miles. What is UOP depreciation for each year?

Answer

$$\frac{\text{Depreciation}}{\text{per unit}} = \frac{\text{Cost} - \text{Residual value}}{\text{Useful life, in units of production}} = \frac{\$10,000 - \$2,000}{16,000 \text{ miles}} = \$0.50 \text{ per mile}$$

Yr. 1: $1,500 (3,000 × $0.50) Yr. 4: $1,250 (2,500 × $0.50)
Yr. 2: $2,000 (4,000 × $0.50) Yr. 5: $1,000 (2,000 × $0.50)
Yr. 3: $2,250 (4,500 × $0.50)

DOUBLE-DECLINING BALANCE METHOD An **accelerated depreciation method** writes off more of the asset's cost near the start of its useful life than the straight-line method does. The main accelerated depreciation method, **double-declining-balance (DDB),** multiplies the asset's decreasing book value by a constant percentage that is 2 times the straight-line depreciation rate. DDB amounts can be computed in four steps:

1. Compute the straight-line depreciation rate per year. A five-year truck has a straight-line depreciation rate of 1/5, or 20% per year. A ten-year asset has a straight-line rate of 1/10, or 10% per year, and so on.
2. Compute the DDB rate: Multiply the straight-line rate by 2. The DDB rate for a ten-year asset is 20% per year (10% × 2 = 20%). For a five-year asset, such as the Home Depot truck, the DDB rate is 40% (20% × 2 = 40%).
3. Compute DDB depreciation for each year. Multiply the asset's book value (cost less accumulated depreciation) at the beginning of each year by the DDB rate. You should ignore the asset's residual value in computing depreciation, except for the last year. The first-year depreciation for the truck in Exhibit 10-5 is

ACCELERATED DEPRECIATION METHOD. A depreciation method that writes off more of the asset's cost near the start of its useful life than the straight-line method does.

DOUBLE-DECLINING-BALANCE (DDB) DEPRECIATION METHOD. An accelerated depreciation method that computes annual depreciation by multiplying the asset's decreasing book value by a constant percent that is 2 times the straight-line rate.

$$\frac{\text{DDB depreciation}}{\text{for the first year}} = \frac{\text{Asset book value}}{\text{at the begining} \times \text{DDB rate}}{\text{of the year}}$$

| $16,400 | = | $41,000 | × | 0.40 |

The same approach is used to compute DDB depreciation for all later years, except for the final year, as follows.

4. Determine the final year's depreciation, the amount needed to reduce the asset's carrying amount to its residual value. In the DDB depreciation schedule in Exhibit 10-8 (on page 396), the last year's depreciation is $4,314— book value of $5,314 less the $1,000 residual value.

EXHIBIT 10-8
Double-Declining-Balance Depreciation Schedule for a Home Depot Truck

Date	Asset Cost	Depreciation for the Year			Accumulated Depreciation	Asset Book Value
		DDB Rate	Asset Book Value	Depreciation Expense		
1-1-20X1	$41,000					$41,000
12-31-20X1		0.40 ×	$41,000 =	$16,400	$16,400	24,600
12-31-20X2		0.40 ×	24,600 =	9,840	26,240	14,760
12-31-20X3		0.40 ×	14,760 =	5,904	32,144	8,856
12-31-20X4		0.40 ×	8,856 =	3,542	35,686	5,314
12-31-20X5				4,314*	40,000	1,000

*Last-year depreciation is the amount needed to reduce asset book value to the residual value ($5,314 − $1,000 = $4,314).

The DDB method differs from the other methods in two ways:

- The asset's residual value is ignored at the start. In the first year, depreciation is computed on the asset's full cost.
- The final year's depreciation is the amount needed to bring the asset's carrying amount to residual value. The final-year depreciation amount is like a "plug" figure.

Many companies change to the straight-line method during the next-to-last year of the asset's life. Under this plan, annual depreciation for 20X4 and 20X5 is $3,928. Look at Exhibit 10-8. Depreciable cost at the end of 20X3 is $7,856 (book value of $8,856 less residual value of $1,000). Depreciable cost can be spread evenly over the last two years of the asset's life ($7,856 ÷ 2 remaining years = $3,928 per year).

What is DDB depreciation for each year for the asset in the Work It Out on page 394?

Answer: DDB rate = 1/5 × 2 = 40%

Yr. 1: $4,000 ($10,000 × 40%)
Yr. 2: $2,400 [($10,000 − $4,000 = $6,000) × 40%]
Yr. 3: $1,440 [($6,000 − $2,400 = $3,600) × 40%]
Yr. 4: $160 ($3,600 − $1,440 − $2,000*)

*An asset's cost is not depreciated below its residual value.

Comparing Depreciation Methods

Let's compare the depreciation methods we've just discussed. Annual depreciation varies by method, but the total is the same for all methods—$40,000.

DAILY EXERCISE 10-7

DAILY EXERCISE 10-8

	Amount of Depreciation Per Year		
			Accelerated Method
Year	Straight-Line	Units-of-Production	Double-Declining-Balance
1	$ 8,000	$ 8,000	$16,400
2	8,000	12,000	9,840
3	8,000	10,000	5,904
4	8,000	6,000	3,542
5	8,000	4,000	4,314
Total	$40,000	$40,000	$40,000

STRAIGHT-LINE   A business should match an asset's expense against the revenue that asset produces. For an asset that generates revenue evenly over time, the straight-line method follows the matching principle. Each period the asset is used, an equal amount of depreciation is recorded.

UNITS-OF-PRODUCTION   The units-of-production method best fits an asset that wears out because of physical use rather than obsolescence. Depreciation is expensed only when the asset is used, and more asset use causes greater depreciation.

DOUBLE-DECLINING-BALANCE   The accelerated method (DDB) works best for assets that produce more revenue in their early years. The greater expense in the earlier periods is matched against those periods' greater revenue. This is the mark of an accelerated depreciation method.

COMPARISONS   Exhibit 10-9 graphs annual depreciation for the three methods.

- The graph of *straight-line* depreciation is flat because annual depreciation is the same in all periods.
- Units-of-production depreciation follows no pattern because annual depreciation varies depending on the use of the asset. The greater the use, the greater the amount of depreciation.
- Accelerated depreciation is greatest in the asset's first year and less in the later years.

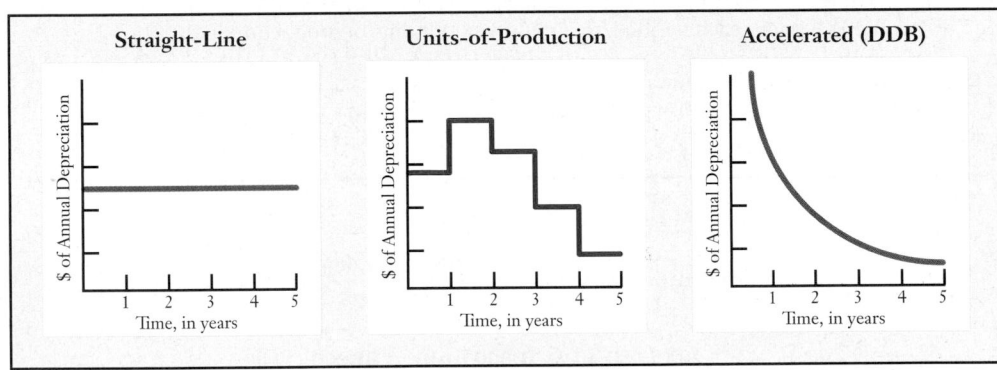

EXHIBIT 10-9
Depreciation Patterns Through Time

A recent survey of 600 companies, conducted by the American Institute of CPAs, indicated that the straight-line method is most popular. Exhibit 10-10 shows the percentages of companies that use each depreciation method.

EXHIBIT 10-10
Use of Depreciation Methods

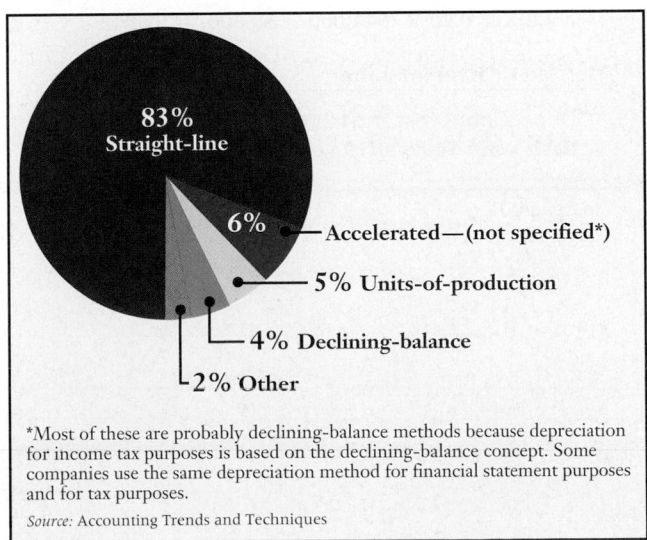

83%
Straight-line

6% Accelerated—(not specified*)

5% Units-of-production

4% Declining-balance

2% Other

*Most of these are probably declining-balance methods because depreciation for income tax purposes is based on the declining-balance concept. Some companies use the same depreciation method for financial statement purposes and for tax purposes.
Source: Accounting Trends and Techniques

SUMMARY PROBLEM

Not Just Copies purchased equipment on January 1, 20X5, for $44,000. Its expected useful life is ten years or 100,000 units of production, and its residual value is $4,000. Under three depreciation methods, the annual depreciation and the balance of accumulated depreciation at the end of 20X5 and 20X6 are as follows:

	Method A		Method B		Method C	
Year	Annual Depreciation Expense	Accumulated Depreciation	Annual Depreciation Expense	Accumulated Depreciation	Annual Depreciation Expense	Accumulated Depreciation
20X5	$1,200	$1,200	$8,800	$ 8,800	$4,000	$4,000
20X6	5,600	6,800	7,040	15,840	4,000	8,000

Required

1. Identify the depreciation method used in each instance, and show the equation and computation for each. (Round amounts to the nearest dollar.)
2. Assume continued use of the same method through year 20X7. Determine the annual depreciation expense, accumulated depreciation, and book value of the equipment for 20X5 through 20X7 under each method, assuming 12,000 units of production in 20X7.

Solution

Requirement 1

Method A: Units-of-Production

$$\text{Depreciation per unit} = \frac{\$44,000 - \$4,000}{100,000 \text{ units}} = \$0.40$$

20X5: $0.40 × 3,000 units = $1,200
20X6: $0.40 × 14,000 units = $5,600

Method B: Double-Declining-Balance

$$\text{Rate} = \frac{1}{10 \text{ years}} \times 2 = 10\% \times 2 = 20\%$$

20X5: 0.20 × $44,000 = $8,800
20X6: 0.20 × ($44,000 − $8,800) = $7,040

Method C: Straight-Line

Depreciable cost = $44,000 − $4,000 = $40,000
Each year: $40,000/10 years = $4,000

Method A: Units-of-Production

Year	Annual Depreciation Expense	Accumulated Depreciation	Book Value
Start			$44,000
20X5	$1,200	$ 1,200	42,800
20X6	5,600	6,800	37,200
20X7	4,800	11,600	32,400

Method B: Double-Declining-Balance

Year	Annual Depreciation Expense	Accumulated Depreciation	Book Value
Start			$44,000
20X5	$8,800	$ 8,800	35,200
20X6	7,040	15,840	28,160
20X7	5,632	21,472	22,528

Method C: Straight-Line

Year	Annual Depreciation Expense	Accumulated Depreciation	Book Value
Start			$44,000
20X5	$4,000	$ 4,000	40,000
20X6	4,000	8,000	36,000
20X7	4,000	12,000	32,000

Computations for 20X7:

Units-of-production	$0.40 × 12,000 units = $4,800
Double-declining-balance	0.20 × $28,160 = $5,632
Straight-line	$40,000/10 years = $4,000

OTHER ISSUES IN ACCOUNTING FOR PLANT ASSETS

Plant assets are complex because of their long lives. Depreciation affects income taxes, and companies may have gains or losses when they sell their plant assets. This section covers these topics.

Depreciation and Income Taxes

Most companies use the straight-line depreciation method for their financial statements. But they keep separate depreciation records for income taxes. For tax purposes, most companies use an accelerated method.

> **Objective 3**
> Select the best depreciation method for income tax purposes

Suppose you manage a **Home Depot** store. The IRS allows the DDB depreciation method, and most managers prefer that to straight-line depreciation. Why? Because it provides the most depreciation expense as quickly as possible. The accelerated depreciation method decreases immediate tax payments. You can then invest the cash you save to earn more income. This is a common strategy.

To understand the relationships between cash flow (cash provided by operations), depreciation, and income tax, recall our earlier depreciation of the Home Depot truck: First-year depreciation is $8,000 under straight-line and $16,400 under double-declining-balance. Now let's assume that DDB is permitted for income tax reporting, and let's apply DDB to the Home Depot truck as before. This store has $400,000 in cash sales and $300,000 in cash operating expenses during the truck's first year and an income tax rate of 30%. The cash-flow analysis appears in Exhibit 10-11 on page 400.

 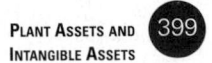

DAILY EXERCISE 10-9

		Income Tax Rate (30%)	
		SL	Accelerated
(1)	Cash revenues	$400,000	$400,000
(2)	*Cash* operating expenses	300,000	300,000
(3)	Cash provided by operations before income tax	100,000	100,000
(4)	Depreciation expense (a noncash expense)	8,000	16,400
(5)	Income before income tax	92,000	83,600
(6)	Income tax expense (30%)	27,600	25,080
(7)	Net income	$ 64,400	$ 58,520
	Cash-flow analysis:		
(8)	Cash provided by operations before income tax	$100,000	$100,000
(9)	Income tax expense	27,600	25,080
(10)	Cash provided by operations	$ 72,400	$ 74,920
(11)	Extra cash available for investment if DDB is used ($74,920 − $72,400)		$ 2,520

Exhibit 10-11 reveals some important relationships. Compare the amount of cash provided by operations before income tax (line 3). Both columns show $100,000. If there were no income taxes, the cash provided by operations would be the same for all depreciation methods. Depreciation is a noncash expense (it requires no outlay of cash) and thus does not affect cash from operations.

But depreciation is a tax-deductible expense. The higher the depreciation (line 4), the lower the income and the lower the tax payment. Therefore, accelerated depreciation helps conserve cash for use in the business. Exhibit 10-11 indicates that the business will have $2,520 more cash to invest at the end of the first year if it uses accelerated depreciation (line 11). The additional investment will earn a return and increase the company's net income.

A special depreciation method called the *modified accelerated cost recovery system (MACRS)* is used only for income tax purpose. Under MACRS, assets are segmented into classes by asset life, as shown in Exhibit 10-12. Depreciation for the first three classes is computed by the double-declining-balance method. Depreciation for 20-year assets is computed by the 150%-declining-balance method. Under 150% DB, the annual depreciation rate is computed by multiplying the straight-line rate by 1.50 (rather than by 2, as for DDB). For a 20-year asset, the straight-line rate is 0.05 × (1/20 = 0.05), so the annual MACRS depreciation rate is 0.075 (0.05 × 1.50 = 0.075). Finally, as the exhibit shows, most real estate is depreciated by the straight-line method.

EXHIBIT 10-12
Selected Details of the Modified Accelerated Cost Recovery System (MACRS) Depreciation Method

Class Identified by Asset Life (years)	Representative Assets	Depreciation Method
3	Race horses	DDB
5	Automobiles, light trucks	DDB
10	Equipment	DDB
20	Certain real estate	150% DB
27 1/2	Residential rental property	SL
39	Nonresidential rental property	SL

Depreciation for Partial Years

Companies purchase plant assets whenever they need them. They don't wait until the beginning of a period. Therefore, companies must develop policies to compute depreciation for partial years. Suppose **Towels 'n Things** in St. Louis purchases a building on April 1 for $500,000. The building's estimated life is 20 years, and its estimated residual value is $80,000. How does Towels 'n Things compute depreciation for the year ended December 31?

Many companies compute partial-year depreciation by first computing a full year's depreciation. They then multiply the full-year amount by the fraction of the year that they held the asset. Assuming the straight-line method, the year's depreciation for the Towels 'n Things building is $15,750, computed as follows:

$$\text{Full year depreciation:} \quad \frac{\$500,000 - \$80,000}{20 \text{ years}} = \$21,000$$

$$\text{Partial-year depreciation:} \quad \$21,000 \times 9/12 = \$15,750$$

What if the company bought the asset on April 18? One widely used policy is to record no depreciation on assets purchased after the 15th of the month and to record a full month's depreciation on an asset bought on or before the 15th. In that case, the year's depreciation would be $14,000 for eight months ($21,000 \times 8/12 = \$14,000$).

How is partial-year depreciation computed under the other depreciation methods? Suppose Towels 'n Things acquired the building on October 4 and uses the double-declining-balance method. For a 20-year asset, the DDB rate is 10% ($1/20 = 5\%$; $5\% \times 2 = 10\%$). The annual depreciation computations for 20X1, 20X2, and 20X3 are shown in Exhibit 10-13.

EXHIBIT 10-13 **Annual DDB Depreciation for Partial Years**

Date	Asset Cost	DDB Rate	Asset Book Value, Beginning		Fraction of the Year		Depreciation Expense	Accumulated Depreciation	Asset Book Value, Ending
			Depreciation for the Year						
10- 4-20X1	$500,000								$500,000
12-31-20X1		$1/20 \times 2 = 0.10$ ×	$500,000	×	3/12	=	$12,500	$ 12,500	487,500
12-31-20X2		0.10 ×	487,500	×	12/12	=	48,750	61,250	438,750
12-31-20X3		0.10 ×	438,750	×	12/12	=	43,875	105,125	394,875

Most companies use computerized systems to account for fixed assets. The system will automatically calculate the depreciation expense for each period.

 DAILY EXERCISE 10-10

Changing the Useful Life of a Depreciable Asset

Estimating the useful life of each plant asset poses an accounting challenge. As the asset is being used, the business may refine its estimate on the basis of experience and new information. The **Walt Disney Company** made such a change, called a *change in accounting estimate*. Disney refigured depreciation for the revised useful lives of several theme-park assets. The following note in Disney's financial statements reports this change in accounting estimate:

> **Note 5**
> . . . [T]he Company extended the estimated useful lives of certain theme park . . . assets based upon . . . engineering studies. The effect of this change was to decrease depreciation by approximately $8 million (an increase in net income of approximately $4.2 million. . .).

Accounting changes like these are common because no one has perfect foresight. Generally accepted accounting principles require the business to report the nature, reason, and effect of the accounting change on net income, as the Disney example shows. For a change in accounting estimate, the remaining book value of the asset is spread over its remaining useful life. The new useful life may be longer or shorter than the original useful life.

Assume that a Disney World hot dog stand cost $40,000 and that the company originally believed the asset had an eight-year life with no residual value. Using the straight-line method, the company would record depreciation of $5,000 each year ($40,000/8 years = $5,000).

Suppose Disney used the asset for two years. Accumulated depreciation reached $10,000, leaving a remaining depreciable book value (cost *less* accumulated depreciation *less* residual value) of $30,000 ($40,000 − $10,000). Suppose Disney management believes the hot dog stand will remain useful for an additional ten years. The company would revise the annual depreciation amount as follows:

Asset's remaining depreciable book value	÷	(New) Estimated useful life remaining	=	(New) Annual depreciation
$30,000	÷	10 years	=	$3,000

The yearly depreciation entry based on the new useful life is

DAILY EXERCISE 10-11

Depreciation Expense—Hot Dog Stand..............................	3,000	
Accumulated Depreciation—Hot Dog Stand		3,000

The equation for revised straight-line depreciation is

$$\text{Revised SL depreciation} = \frac{\text{Cost } - \text{ Accumulated depreciation } - \text{ New residual value}}{\text{Estimated remaining useful life in years}}$$

Using Fully Depreciated Assets

A *fully depreciated asset* is an asset that has reached the end of its *estimated* useful life. No more depreciation is recorded for the asset. If the asset is no longer suitable for its purpose, it is disposed of. However, the company may be unable to replace the asset. Or the asset may remain useful. In any event, companies sometimes continue using fully depreciated assets. The asset account and its accumulated depreciation remain on the books, even though no additional depreciation is recorded.

THINK IT OVER

A fully depreciated asset has a cost of $80,000 and zero residual value. What is the asset's accumulated depreciation?

Answer: $80,000 (same as the asset's cost).

Now suppose the asset's residual value is $10,000. How much is accumulated depreciation?

Answer: $70,000 ($80,000 − $10,000).

Disposing of Plant Assets

Objective 4
Account for the disposal of a plant asset

Eventually, an asset ceases to serve its purpose. The asset may have become worn out or obsolete. In general, a company disposes of a plant asset by selling it or exchanging it. If the asset cannot be sold or exchanged, then it is junked. Whatever the method of disposal, the business should bring depreciation up-to-date to measure the asset's final book value properly.

To record the disposal, credit the asset account and debit its accumulated depreciation to remove these accounts from the books. Suppose the final year's depreciation expense has just been recorded for a machine that cost $6,000 with no residual value. The machine's accumulated depreciation thus totals $6,000. This asset cannot be sold or exchanged, so it is junked. The entry to record its disposal is

Accumulated Depreciation—Machinery	6,000	
Machinery..		6,000

To dispose of fully depreciated machine.

MACHINERY		ACCUMULATED DEPRECIATION—MACHINERY	
6,000	6,000	6,000	6,000

Now both accounts have a zero balance, as shown in the T-accounts at the right.

If assets are junked before being fully depreciated, the company records a loss equal to the asset's book value. Suppose Home Depot fixtures that cost $4,000 are junked at a loss. Accumulated depreciation is $3,000, and book value is therefore $1,000. Disposal of these store fixtures generates a loss equal to the book value of the asset, as follows:

```
Accumulated Depreciation—Store Fixtures ..................... 3,000
Loss on Disposal of Store Fixtures....................................... 1,000
        Store Fixtures .......................................................          4,000
    To dispose of store fixtures.
```

All losses, including this Loss on Disposal of Store Fixtures, decrease net income. Along with expenses, losses are reported on the income statement.

SELLING A PLANT ASSET   Suppose Clarkson Eyecare sells furniture (a plant asset) on September 30, 20X4, for $5,000 cash. The furniture cost $10,000 when purchased on January 1, 20X1, and has been depreciated on a straight-line basis. Clarkson estimated a ten-year useful life and no residual value. Prior to recording the sale of the furniture, accountants must update its depreciation. Because Clarkson uses the calendar year as its accounting period, partial-year depreciation must be recorded for the asset's expense from January 1, 20X4, to the sale date on September 30. The straight-line depreciation entry at September 30, 20X4, is

```
Sep. 30    Depreciation Expense ($10,000/10 years × 9/12) ..............    750
                Accumulated Depreciation—Furniture ....................            750
            To update depreciation.
```

After this entry is posted, the Furniture account and the Accumulated Depreciation—Furniture account appear as follows. The furniture book value is $6,250 ($10,000 − $3,750).

FURNITURE		ACCUMULATED DEPRECIATION—FURNITURE	
Jan. 1, 20X1 10,000		Dec. 31, 20X1 1,000	
		Dec. 31, 20X2 1,000	
		Dec. 31, 20X3 1,000	
		Sep. 30, 20X4 750	
		Balance 3,750	

Book Value = $6,250

Suppose Clarkson sells the furniture for $5,000 cash. The loss on the sale is $1,250, determined as follows:

Cash received from sale of the asset		$5,000
Book value of asset sold:		
Cost...	$10,000	
Less: Accumulated depreciation up to date of sale..............	(3,750)	6,250
Gain (loss) on sale of the asset...		($1,250)

Clarkson's entry to record sale of the furniture for $5,000 cash is

```
Sep. 30    Cash  .................................................................................. 5,000
            Accumulated Depreciation—Furniture ........................... 3,750
            Loss on Sale of Furniture ................................................. 1,250
                Furniture ..............................................................            10,000
            To sell furniture.
```

When recording the sale of a plant asset, the business must remove the balances in the asset account (Furniture, in this case) and its accumulated depreciation account and also record a gain or a loss if the amount of cash received differs from the asset's book value. In our example, cash of $5,000 is less than the book value of the furniture, $6,250. The result is a loss of $1,250.

If the sale price had been $7,000, Clarkson Eyecare would have had a gain of $750 (Cash, $7,000—asset book value, $6,250). The entry to record this transaction would be

```
Sep. 30    Cash ..................................................    7,000
              Accumulated Depreciation—Furniture ............    3,750
                 Furniture................................................              10,000
                 Gain on Sale of Furniture ........................                  750
              To sell furniture.
```

DAILY EXERCISE 10-12

A gain is recorded when an asset is sold for a price (sale proceeds) greater than the asset's book value. A loss is recorded when the sale price is less than book value.

- **Gain = Sale proceeds > Book value**
- **Loss = Sale proceeds < Book value**

Gains increase net income, and losses decrease net income. All gains and losses are reported on the income statement.

EXCHANGING PLANT ASSETS   Businesses often exchange (trade in) their old plant assets for newer, more efficient assets. For example, **Domino's Pizza** may trade in a five-year-old delivery car for a newer model. To record the exchange, Domino's must remove from the books the balances for the old asset and its accumulated depreciation exactly as we did for the disposal of furniture in the preceding section.

In many cases, the business simply carries forward the book value of the old asset plus any cash payment as the cost of the new asset. For example, assume Domino's old delivery car cost $9,000 and has accumulated depreciation of $8,000. The car's book value is $1,000. Domino's trades in the old auto and pays cash of $10,000. Domino's should first record depreciation on its old auto up to the date of the exchange. This updates the asset's book value. Then the business records the exchange transaction with this journal entry:

```
Delivery Auto (new)..........................................    11,000
Accumulated Depreciation (old).........................     8,000
     Delivery Auto (old) ...................................              9,000
     Cash........................................................             10,000
To trade in old delivery car for new auto.
```

Domino's cost of the new car is $11,000 (cash paid $10,000, plus the book value of the old auto, $1,000).

ACCOUNTING FOR NATURAL RESOURCES

Objective 5
Account for natural resource
assets and depletion

Natural resources such as iron ore, petroleum (oil), natural gas, and timber are plant assets of a special type. Natural resources are like inventories in the ground (oil) or on top of the ground (timber). Natural resource assets are expensed through *depletion*. **Depletion expense** is that portion of the cost of natural resources used up in a particular period. Depletion expense is computed in the same way as units-of-production depreciation:

DEPLETION EXPENSE. The portion of a natural resource's cost used up in a particular period. Depletion expense is computed in the same way as units-of-production depreciation.

$$\frac{\text{Depletion}}{\text{per unit}} = \frac{\text{Cost} - \text{Residual value}}{\text{Estimated total units of natural resource}}$$

An oil well may cost $100,000 and contain an estimated 10,000 barrels of oil. The well has no residual value. The depletion rate would thus be $10 per barrel ($100,000/10,000 barrels). If 3,000 barrels are extracted during the year, depletion expense is $30,000 (3,000 barrels × $10 per barrel). The depletion entry for the year is

```
Depletion Expense (3,000 barrels × $10)...............    30,000
     Accumulated Depletion—Oil .......................             30,000
```

If 4,500 barrels are removed the next year, that period's depletion is $45,000 (4,500 barrels × $10 per barrel). Accumulated Depletion is a contra account similar to Accumulated Depreciation.

Natural resource assets can be reported on the balance sheet as follows:

Property, Plant, and Equipment:		
Land		$120,000
Buildings	$800,000	
Equipment	160,000	
	960,000	
Less: Accumulated depreciation	(410,000)	550,000
Oil	$380,000	
Less: Accumulated depletion	(80,000)	300,000
Property, plant, and equipment, net		$970,000

 DAILY EXERCISE 10-13

 **WORK IT OUT** Ladue Paper Products pays $500,000 for land that contains an estimated 500,000 board feet of lumber. The land can be sold for $100,000 after the timber has been cut. If Ladue Paper harvests 200,000 board feet in the year of purchase, how much depletion should be recorded?

Answer: **(Cost − Residual) ÷ Total = Depletion rate × Production = Depletion**
($500,000 − $100,00) ÷ 500,000 = $0.80 per foot × 200,000 = $160,000

ACCOUNTING FOR INTANGIBLE ASSETS

Objective 6
Account for intangible assets and amortization

As we saw earlier in the chapter, *intangible assets* are long-lived and have no physical form. Instead, these assets are special rights from patents, copyrights, trademarks, and so on.

In today's technology-driven economy, intangibles are surpassing tangible assets in value. The electronic economy rewards brand and customer loyalty. Consider on-line auction pioneer **eBay**. The company has no physical products or equipment, but it helps people buy and sell everything from Batman toys to bathroom tiles. In 1999, eBay served 10 million customers and earned $225 billion in revenues with fewer than 150 employees.

Alas, accountants typically deal with historical costs rather than future value. A company's intellectual capital is difficult to measure. But when one company buys another, we get a glimpse of the value of the acquired company's intellectual capital. For example, **America Online** announced it would acquire **Time Warner.** AOL said it would exchange $146 billion worth of stock and agree to pay $38 billion of future liabilities for Time Warner's net tangible assets of only $9 billion. Why? Because Time Warner's intangible assets were worth $190 billion. Intangibles can account for as much as 85% of a company's perceived value, so companies must find ways to account for intangibles just as they do for their inventory and equipment.

The acquisition cost of a patent is debited to Patents, an asset account. The intangible is expensed through **amortization,** the systematic reduction of the asset's carrying value on the books. Amortization applies to intangible assets exactly as depreciation applies to plant assets and depletion applies to natural resources. Depreciation, depletion, and amortization are conceptually the same.

AMORTIZATION. The systematic reduction of the asset's carrying value on the books. Expense that applies to intangibles in the same way depreciation applies to plant assets and depletion applies to natural resources.

Amortization is generally computed on a straight-line basis over the asset's estimated useful life—up to a maximum of 40 years, according to generally accepted accounting principles. But obsolescence often shortens an intangible's useful life. Amortization expense for an intangible asset can be written off directly against the asset account rather than held in an accumulated amortization account. The residual value of most intangible assets is zero.

Assume that **Sealy Mattress Company** purchases a patent on a special manufacturing process. Legally, the patent may run for 20 years. Sealy realizes, however, that new technologies will limit the process's life to 4 years. If the patent cost $80,000, each year's amortization expense is $20,000 ($80,000/4). Sealy's balance sheet reports the patent at its acquisition cost less accumulated amortization to date. After 1 year, the patent has a $60,000 balance ($80,000 − $20,000), after 2 years a $40,000 balance ($80,000 − $40,000), and so on.

Specific Intangibles

PATENTS **Patents** are federal government grants giving the holder the exclusive 20-year right to produce and sell an invention. The invention may be a product or a process—for example, **Sony** compact disc players and the **Dolby** noise-reduction process. Like any other asset, a patent may be purchased. Suppose **General Electric Company (GE)** pays $170,000 to acquire a patent on January 1, and GE believes its expected useful life is only five years. Amortization expense is $34,000 per year ($170,000/5 years). Acquisition and amortization entries for this patent are

Jan. 1	Patents	170,000	
	Cash		170,000
	To acquire a patent.		
Dec. 31	Amortization Expense—Patents ($170,000/5)	34,000	
	Patents..		34,000
	To amortize the cost of a patent.		

COPYRIGHTS **Copyrights** are exclusive rights to reproduce and sell a book, musical composition, film, or other work of art. Copyrights also protect computer software programs, such as **Microsoft** Windows® and the Excel spreadsheet. Issued by the federal government, copyrights extend 50 years beyond the author's (composer's, artist's, or programmer's) life.

The cost of obtaining a copyright from the government is low, but a company may pay a large sum to purchase an existing copyright. For example, **Simon & Schuster,** the publisher, may pay the author of a popular novel $1 million for the book's copyright. The useful life of a copyright is usually no longer than two or three years, so most copyrights have short lives.

TRADEMARKS, BRAND NAMES **Trademarks** and **trade names** (or **brand names**) are assets that represent distinctive identifications of products or services. The "eye" symbol is the trademark of the **CBS** television network. You are probably also familiar with **NBC's** peacock. Seven-Up, Pepsi, and Egg McMuffin are everyday trade names. Advertising slogans that are legally protected include **United Airlines'** "Fly the friendly skies" and **Avis Rent A Car's** "We try harder."

The cost of a trademark or trade name is amortized over its useful life, not to exceed 40 years. The cost of advertising and promotion is not a part of the asset's cost, but rather an advertising expense.

FRANCHISES, LICENSES **Franchises** and **licenses** are privileges granted by a private business or a government to sell a product or service under specified conditions. The **Green Bay Packers** football organization is a franchise granted by the National Football League. **McDonald's** restaurants and **Holiday Inns** are popular business franchises. The acquisition costs of a franchise or license is amortized over its useful life, subject to the 40-year maximum.

GOODWILL The term *goodwill* in accounting has a very different meaning from the everyday term, "goodwill among men." In accounting, **goodwill** is the excess of the cost to purchase another company over the market value of the other company's net assets (assets minus liabilities). **Wal-Mart** has now expanded into Mexico. Suppose Wal-Mart acquired Mexana Company at a cost of $10 million. The sum of the market values of Mexana's assets was $9 million and its liabilities totaled $1 million, so Mexana's net assets totaled $8 million. In this case, Wal-Mart paid $2 million for goodwill, computed as follows:

Purchase price paid for Mexana Company		$10 million
The market value of Mexana Company's assets................	$9 million	
Less: Mexana Company's liabilities	(1 million)	
Market value of Mexana Company's net assets		8 million
Excess is called *goodwill*		$ 2 million

Wal-Mart's entry to record the purchase of Mexana Company, including the goodwill that Wal-Mart purchases would be

Assets (Cash, Receivables, Inventories, Plant Assets, all at market value)	9,000,000	
Goodwill	2,000,000	
Liabilities		1,000,000
Cash		10,000,000
Purchased Mexana Company.		

Note that Wal-Mart acquired all of Mexana's assets *and* all of Mexana's liabilities.

Goodwill has some special features:

1. Goodwill is recorded only when it is purchased in the acquisition of another company. A company's favorable location, superior product, or outstanding reputation may create goodwill for a company, but that entity never records goodwill for its own business. Instead, goodwill is recorded *only* by the acquiring entity when it buys another company.

2. According to generally accepted accounting principles (GAAP), goodwill is amortized over a period not to exceed 40 years. In reality, the goodwill of many entities actually increases in value. Nevertheless, GAAP requires that the cost of all intangible assets be amortized as expense.

 DAILY EXERCISE 10-14

DAILY EXERCISE 10-15

 e-Accounting

Singapore International Airlines: Ratcheting Up the Value of Tangibles and Intangibles

During the Asian recession of 1997–1998, **Singapore International Airlines (SIA)** was able to keep its profitability high. The secret to the airline's success has always been the impeccable quality of its assets, tangible and intangible: its fleet of 90 planes and its service. It recently spent $300 million for first-class seats that recline 180% and personal TV screens in all seats.

An airline's ground service is as important as its planes. You might be surprised to know that **American Airlines'** reservation system—Sabre—was valued at 60% of the company's assets, far more than American's fleet of planes. And **Singapore Airlines Terminal Services Group (SATS)** is so profitable that the company is taking it public. The company credits SATS for its success in reducing the adverse effects of the Asian economic downturn. "Ongoing investment in staff training continues to be a decisive, motivating factor in our success," says CEO Karmit Singh. The company's YES! campaign trains everyone—from baggage handlers to security personnel—to act like frontline staff. No wonder business travelers have chosen Singapore International Airlines as the "best airline" for eleven years running.

Source: Based on Leonard Hill, "Two for the money," *Air Transport World*, May 2000, pp. 59–63. Perry Flint, "SIA's global tilt," *Air Transport World*, May 2000, pp. 50–55. Anonymous, "Business travelers select Singapore Airlines No. 1," *Houston Chronicle*, January 23, 2000, p. 5. Ben Dolven, "Profitable romance," *Far Eastern Economic Review*, December 30, 1999–January 6, 2000, pp. 78–79. Staff Reports, Companies may be unwittingly ignoring the bulk of their asset value," *Investor Relations Business*, December 13, 1999, p. 4.

Special Issues

INTERNATIONAL ACCOUNTING FOR GOODWILL Companies in The Netherlands (such as **Royal Dutch Shell** and **Phillips**), in Great Britain (such as **British Petroleum** and **British Airways**), and in other European nations do not have to record goodwill when they purchase another business. Instead, they may record the cost of goodwill as a decrease in owner's equity. These companies never have to amortize the cost of goodwill, so their net income is higher than a U.S. company's net income would be. As a result, U.S. companies often cry "foul" when bidding against a European firm to acquire another business. Americans claim the Europeans can pay higher prices because their income never takes a hit for amortization expense.

THINK IT OVER

How could companies around the world be placed on the same accounting basis?

Answer: If all companies worldwide followed the same accounting rules, they would be reporting income and other amounts computed similarly. But this is not the case. A company must follow the accounting rules of its own nation, and there are differences, as the goodwill situation illustrates.

◉ DAILY EXERCISE 10-16

RESEARCH AND DEVELOPMENT COSTS Accounting for research and development (R&D) costs is one of the toughest issues the accounting profession has faced. R&D is the lifeblood of companies such as **Procter & Gamble, General Electric, Intel,** and **Boeing** because it is vital to the development of new products and processes. The cost of R&D activities is one of these companies' most valuable (intangible) assets. But, in general, they do not report R&D assets on their balance sheets.

GAAP requires companies to expense R&D costs as they incur those costs. Only in certain circumstances may the company capitalize an R&D asset. Consider a company that incurs R&D costs under a contract guaranteeing it will recover the costs from the customer. In this case, the company records R&D cost as an asset. But this is the exception. Otherwise, the Financial Accounting Standards Board (FASB) requires that R&D cost be expensed as incurred.

ETHICAL ISSUES: PLANT ASSETS AND INTANGIBLES

The main ethical issue in accounting for plant assets and intangibles is whether to capitalize or to expense a particular cost. In this area, companies have split personalities. On the one hand, they all want to save on taxes. This motivates them to expense all costs in order to decrease their taxable income. On the other hand, most companies also want their financial statements to look as good as possible, with high net income and high reported amounts for assets.

In most cases, a cost that is capitalized or expensed for tax purposes must be treated the same way for reporting to stockholders and creditors in the financial statements. What, then, is the ethical path? Accountants should follow the general guidelines for capitalizing a cost: Capitalize all costs that provide a future benefit for the business, and expense all other costs, as outlined in the Decision Guidelines box that follows.

➥ We discussed accounting conservatism in Chapter 9, page 361.

Many companies have gotten into trouble by capitalizing costs they should have expensed. They made their financial statements look better than the facts warranted. But there are very few cases of companies getting into trouble by following the general guidelines, or even by erring on the side of expensing questionable costs. This is another example of accounting conservatism in action. It works. ◄◄

DECISION GUIDELINES

Accounting for Plant Assets and Related Expenses

DECISION	GUIDELINES
Capitalize or expense a cost?	General rule: Capitalize all costs that provide *future benefit* for the business. Expense all costs that provide *no future benefit*.
Capitalize or expense: • Cost associated with a new asset? • Cost associated with an existing asset?	Capitalize all costs that bring the asset to its intended use. Capitalize only those costs that add to the asset's usefulness or its useful life. Expense all other costs as maintenance or repairs.
• Interest cost incurred to finance the asset's acquisition?	Capitalize interest cost only on assets constructed by the business for its own use. Expense all other interest cost.
Which depreciation method to use: • For financial reporting? • For income tax?	Use the method that best matches depreciation expense against the revenues produced by the asset. Use the method that produces the fastest tax deductions (MACRS). A company can use different depreciation methods for financial reporting and for income tax purposes. In the United States, this practice is considered both legal and ethical.

REVIEW PLANT ASSETS

SUMMARY PROBLEM

The following figures appear in the Answers to the Mid-Chapter Summary Problem, requirement 2, on page 339.

	Method B: Double-Declining-Balance			Method C: Straight-Line		
Year	Annual Depreciation Expense	Accumulated Depreciation	Book Value	Annual Depreciation Expense	Accumulated Depreciation	Book Value
Start			$44,000			$44,000
20X5	$8,800	$ 8,800	35,200	$4,000	$ 4,000	40,000
20X6	7,040	15,840	28,160	4,000	8,000	36,000
20X7	5,632	21,472	22,528	4,000	12,000	32,000

Not Just Copies purchased equipment on January 1, 20X5. Management has depreciated the equipment by using the double-declining-balance method. On July 1, 20X7, the company sold the equipment for $27,000 cash.

Required

1. Suppose the income tax authorities permit a choice between the two depreciation methods shown. Which method would you select for income tax purposes? Why?
2. Record Not Just Copies' depreciation for 20X7 and the sale of the equipment on July 1, 20X7.

www.prenhall.com/horngren

End-of-Chapter Assessment

Solution

Requirement 1

For tax purposes, most companies select the accelerated method because it results in the most depreciation in the earliest years of the equipment's life. Accelerated depreciation minimizes taxable income and income tax payments in the early years of the asset's life, thereby maximizing the business's cash at the earliest possible time.

LESSONS LEARNED

1. **Measure the cost of a plant asset.** Plant assets are long-lived tangible assets, such as land, buildings, and equipment, used in the operation of a business. The cost of a plant asset is the purchase price plus all taxes, purchase commissions, and all other amounts paid to acquire the asset and to prepare it for its intended use.

2. **Account for depreciation.** Businesses may account for depreciation (the allocation of a plant asset's cost to expense over its useful life) by four methods: *straight-line, units-of-production, double-declining-balance,* or *sum-of-the-years'-digits*. The SYD method is not used much.

3. **Select the best depreciation method for income tax purposes.** Most companies use an accelerated depreciation method for income tax purposes. Accelerated depreciation results in higher expenses, lower taxable income, and lower tax payments early in the asset's life.

4. **Account for the disposal of a plant asset.** Before disposing of a plant asset, the company must update the asset's depreciation. Disposal is then recorded by removing the book balances from both the asset and its accumulated depreciation account. Sales often result in a gain or loss, which is reported on the income statement.

5. **Account for natural resource assets and depletion.** The cost of natural resources, a special category of long-lived assets, is expensed through *depletion*. Depletion is computed on a units-of-production basis.

6. **Account for intangible assets and amortization.** *Intangible assets* have no physical form. They give their owners special rights. The major types of intangible assets are patents, copyrights, trademarks, franchises and licenses, leaseholds, and goodwill. The cost of intangibles is expensed through *amortization,* which is the same as depreciation.

ACCOUNTING VOCABULARY

accelerated depreciation method (p. 395)
amortization (p. 405)
brand names (p. 407)
capital expenditure (p. 391)
capitalize a cost (p. 390)
copyright (p. 406)
depletion expense (p. 404)
depreciable cost (p. 393)
double-declining-balance (DDB) depreciation method (p. 395)

estimated residual value (p. 393)
estimated useful life (p. 393)
extraordinary repair (p. 391)
fixed assets (p. 387)
franchises (p. 407)
goodwill (p. 407)
intangible asset (p. 387)
licenses (p. 407)
major repair (p. 391)
ordinary repair (p. 391)
patent (p. 406)

plant assets (p. 387)
salvage value (p. 393)
scrap value (p. 393)
straight-line (SL) depreciation method (p. 393)
trademark (p. 407)
trade name (p. 407)
units-of-production (UOP) depreciation method (p. 394)

QUESTIONS

1. To what types of long-lived assets do the following expenses apply: depreciation, depletion, and amortization?

2. Describe how to measure the cost of a plant asset. Would an ordinary cost of repairing the asset after it is placed in service be included in the asset's cost?

3. When assets are purchased as a group for a single price and no individual asset cost is given, how is each asset's cost determined?

4. Distinguish a capital expenditure from an expense.

5. Define depreciation. Present the common misconceptions about depreciation.

6. Explain the concept of accelerated depreciation. Which of the depreciation methods results in the most depreciation in the first year of the asset's life?

7. The level of business activity fluctuates widely for Harwood Delivery Service, reaching its peak around Christmas each year. At other times, business is slow. Which depreciation method is most appropriate for Harwood's fleet of minivans? Explain your answer.

8. Which type of depreciation method is best from an income tax standpoint? Why?

9. Describe how to compute depreciation for less than a full year and how to account for depreciation for less than a full month.

10. Describe how to determine whether a company experiences a gain or a loss when it sells an old plant asset.

11. What expense applies to natural resources? By which depreciation method is this expense computed?

12. How do intangible assets differ from most other assets? Why are they assets at all? What expense applies to intangible assets?
13. Your company has just purchased another company for $400,000. The market value of the other company's net assets is $325,000. What is the $75,000 excess called? What type of asset is it? What is the maximum period over which its cost is amortized under generally accepted accounting principles?
14. Oracle Corporation is a world leader in the development of software. The company's past success has created vast amounts of business goodwill. Would you expect to see this goodwill reported on Oracle's financial statements? Why or why not?

ASSESS YOUR PROGRESS

DAILY EXERCISES

DE10-1 Examine the balance sheet of **The Home Depot** in Exhibit 10-2 at the beginning of this chapter. Answer these questions about the company:

Cost and book value of a company's plant assets (Obj. 1)

1. When does The Home Depot's fiscal year end? Why does the company's fiscal year end on this date?
2. What is The Home Depot's largest category of assets—current assets, property and equipment, or other category?
3. What was The Home Depot's cost of property and equipment at January 30, 2000? What was the book value of property and equipment on this date?

DE10-2 Page 388 of this chapter lists the costs included for the acquisition of land. First is the purchase price of the land, which is obviously included in the cost of the land. The reasons for including the related costs are not so obvious. For example, the removal of a building looks more like an expense. State why the costs listed are included as part of the cost of the land. After the land is ready for use, will these costs be capitalized or expensed?

Measuring the cost of a plant asset (Obj. 1)

DE10-3 A lessee (who is renting an asset such as a building) makes periodic lease payments to the lessor (who owns the building). The lessee does not have a legal title to the building. Nevertheless, under certain conditions the lessee may account for the building as though the lessee owned an asset. How can a capital lease be fundamentally like an asset to the lessee?

Understanding leases (Obj. 1)

DE10-4 Suppose Florida Power, the utility company, is constructing power-generating equipment for use in its operations. To finance construction, Florida Power borrows $800,000 on notes payable on January 2, 20X3. During 20X3, Florida Power incurs interest cost equal to 9% of its construction loan. All of the company's interest cost should be capitalized to the Equipment account.

Capitalizing interest cost (Obj. 1)

1. Make the journal entry to pay Florida Power's interest cost at December 31, 20X3.
2. At December 31, 20X3, what is the balance in the Equipment account? Prepare a T-account for Equipment to answer this question.

DE10-5 Return to the Work It Out feature on page 391. Suppose at the time of your acquisition, the land has a current market value of $80,000, the building's market value is $60,000, and the equipment's market value is $20,000. Journalize the lump-sum purchase of the three assets for a total cost of $100,000. You sign a note payable for this amount.

Lump-sum purchase of assets (Obj. 1)

DE10-6 Vantas Airways repaired one of its Boeing 767 aircraft at a cost of $750,000, which Vantas paid in cash. Vantas erroneously capitalized this cost as part of the cost of the plane.

Capitalizing versus expensing plant asset costs (Obj. 1)

1. Journalize both the incorrect entry the accountant made to record this transaction and the correct entry that the accountant should have made.
2. Show the effects of the accounting error on Vantas Airways' income statement and balance sheet, using the format illustrated on page 392.

DE10-7 At the beginning of the year, Vantas Airways purchased a used Boeing MD-11 aircraft at a cost of $36,000,000. Vantas expects the plane to remain useful for five years (5 million miles) and to have a residual value of $6,000,000. Vantas expects the plane to be flown 750,000 miles the first year and 1,250,000 miles the last year.

Computing depreciation by three methods—first year only (Obj. 2)

1. Compute Vantas' first-year depreciation on the plane using the following methods:
   a. Straight-line   **b.** Units-of-production   **c.** Double-declining-balance
2. Show the airplane's book value at the end of the first year under each depreciation method.

DE10-8 At the beginning of 20X1, Vantas Airways purchased a used Boeing MD-11 aircraft at a cost of $36,000,000. Vantas expects the plane to remain useful for five years (5 million miles) and to have a residual value of $6,000,000. Vantas expects the plane to be flown 750,000 miles the first year and 1,250,000 miles the fifth year. Compute Vantas's fifth-year depreciation on the plane using the following methods:

Computing depreciation by three methods—final year only (Obj. 2)

a. Straight-line
b. Units-of-production
c. Double-declining-balance (you must compute depreciation for all five years)

Selecting the best depreciation method for income tax purposes (Obj. 3)

DE10-9 This exercise uses the Vantas Airways' data from Daily Exercise 10-7. Assume Vantas Airways is trying to decide which depreciation method to use for income tax purposes.

1. Which depreciation method offers the tax advantage for the first year? Describe the nature of the tax advantage.
2. How much income tax will Vantas save for the first year of the airplane's use as compared to using the straight-line depreciation method? Vantas' income tax rate is 40%.

Partial-year depreciation (Obj. 2)

DE10-10 On March 31, 20X2, Vantas Airways purchased a used Boeing MD-11 aircraft at a cost of $36,000,000. Vantas expects the plane to remain useful for five years (5,000,000 miles) and to have a residual value of $6,000,000. Vantas expects the plane to be flown 800,000 miles during the remainder of the first year ended December 31, 20X2. Compute Vantas' depreciation on the plane for the year ended December 31, 20X2, using the following methods:

a. Straight-line   b. Units-of-production   c. Double-declining-balance

Computing and recording depreciation after a change in useful life of the asset (Obj. 2)

DE10-11 Return to the example of the **Disney World** hot dog stand on pages 401–402. Suppose that after using the hot dog stand for four years, the company determines that the asset will remain useful for only two more years. Record Disney's depreciation on the hot dog stand for year 5 by the straight-line method.

Recording a gain or loss on disposal under two depreciation methods (Obj. 4)

DE10-12 Return to the **Home Depot** delivery-truck depreciation example in Exhibits 10-6 and 10-8. Suppose The Home Depot sold the truck on December 31, 20X2, for $23,000 cash, after using the truck for two full years. Depreciation for 20X2 has already been recorded.

1. Make a separate journal entry to record The Home Depot's sale of the truck under
   a. Straight-line depreciation (Exhibit 10-6)
   b. Double-declining-balance depreciation (Exhibit 10-8)
2. Why is there such a big difference between the gain or loss on disposal under the two depreciation methods?

Accounting for the depletion of a company's natural resources (Obj. 5)

DE10-13 Chevron, the giant oil company, holds huge reserves of oil and gas assets. At the end of 20X0, Chevron's cost of mineral assets totaled approximately $18 billion, representing 2.4 billion barrels of oil and gas reserves in the ground.

1. Which depreciation method do Chevron and other oil companies use to compute their annual depletion expense for the minerals removed from the ground?
2. Suppose Chevron removed 0.6 billion barrels of oil during 20X1. Record Chevron's depletion expense for 20X1.
3. At December 31, 20X0, Chevron's Accumulated Depletion account stood at $11.5 billion. If Chevron did not add any new oil and gas reserves during 20X1, what would be the book value of the company's oil and gas reserves after recording depletion at December 31, 20X1?

Accounting for goodwill (Obj. 6)

DE10-14 Media-related companies have little in the way of tangible plant assets. Instead, their main asset is goodwill. When one media company buys another, goodwill is often the most costly asset acquired. Flannahan Newsprint paid $700,000 to acquire *The Thrifty Nickel,* an advertising paper headquartered in Texas. At the time of Flannahan's acquisition, *The Thrifty Nickel's* balance sheet reported total assets of $1,150,000 and liabilities of $600,000. The fair market value of *The Thrifty Nickel's* assets was $990,000.

1. How much goodwill did Flannahan purchase as part of the acquisition of *The Thrifty Nickel?*
2. Make Flannahan's summary journal entry to record the acquisition of *The Thrifty Nickel.*
3. What is the maximum useful life of the goodwill under GAAP? If Flannahan amortizes the goodwill over the maximum useful life, how much amortization expense will Flannahan record each year?

Analyzing a company's goodwill (Obj. 6)

DE10-15 Examine the balance sheet of **The Home Depot** in Exhibit 10-2 at the beginning of this chapter. Answer these questions about the company:

1. What account title does The Home Depot use for goodwill?
2. What was the book value of The Home Depot's goodwill at January 30, 2000? What was the amount of accumulated amortization on the goodwill? What was The Home Depot's cost of its goodwill on this date?
3. One year earlier, on January 30, 1999, The Home Depot had Goodwill at a cost of $329 million, less Accumulated Amortization of $21 million, for a book value of $308 million. During the year ended January 30, 2000, The Home Depot sold no companies and thus sold none of its goodwill. Use your answer to requirement 2 to compute the cost of the goodwill The Home Depot purchased during the year ended January 30, 2000.

Accounting for patents and research and development cost (Obj. 6)

DE10-16 This exercise summarizes the accounting for patents, which like copyrights and trademarks, provide the owner with a special right. It also covers research and development.

Questor Applications paid $875,000 to research and develop a new software program. Questor also paid $300,000 to acquire a patent on the new software. After readying the software for production, Questor's sales revenue for the first year totaled $1,500,000. Cost of goods sold was $200,000 and selling expenses were $400,000. All these transactions occurred during 20X3. Questor expects the patent to have a useful life of three years.

1. Prepare Questor Applications' income statement for the year ended December 31, 20X3, complete with a heading.
2. Considering the makeup of Questor's expenses, what should the company's outlook for future profits be on the new software program?

EXERCISES

E10-1 Delmar Mining Company purchased land, paying $77,000 cash as a down payment and signing a $120,000 note payable for the balance. In addition, Delmar paid delinquent property tax of $2,000, title insurance costing $2,500, and a $5,400 charge for leveling the land and removing an unwanted building. The company constructed an office building on the land at a cost of $799,000. It also paid $51,000 for a fence around the boundary of the property, $10,400 for the company sign near the entrance to the property, and $6,000 for special lighting of the grounds. Determine the cost of the company's land, land improvements, and building. Which of the assets will Delmar depreciate?

Determining the cost of plant assets
(Obj. 1)

E10-2 Weidman Belts, Inc. manufactures conveyor belts in St. Louis, Missouri. Early in January 20X3, Weidman constructed its own factory building with borrowed money. The 9% loan was for $600,000. During the year, Weidman spent the loan amount on construction of the building. At year end, Weidman paid the interest for one year.

Measuring the cost of an asset; capitalizing interest
(Obj. 1)

Required
1. How much should Weidman record as the cost of the building in 20X3?
2. Record all of Weidman's transactions during 20X3.

E10-3 The Williamsburg Equestrian Center bought three valuable saddles in a $10,000 lump-sum purchase. An independent appraiser valued the saddles as follows:

Allocating cost to assets acquired in a lump-sum purchase
(Obj. 1)

Saddle	Appraised Value
1	$3,350
2	5,400
3	4,250

Williamsburg paid half in cash and signed a note payable for the remainder. Record the purchase in the journal, identifying each saddle's individual cost in a separate Saddle account. Round decimals to three places.

E10-4 Classify each of the following expenditures as a capital expenditure or an expense related to machinery: (a) major overhaul to extend useful life by three years; (b) ordinary recurring repairs to keep the machinery in good working order; (c) lubrication of the machinery before it is placed in service; (d) periodic lubrication after the machinery is placed in service; (e) purchase price; (f) sales tax paid on the purchase price; (g) transportation and insurance while machinery is in transit from seller to buyer; (h) installation; (i) training of personnel for initial operation of the machinery; (j) special reinforcement to the machinery platform; and (k) income tax paid on income earned from the sale of products manufactured by the machinery.

Distinguishing capital expenditures from expenses
(Obj. 1)

E10-5 Leslie Peres has just slept through the class in which Professor Dobbins explained the concept of depreciation. Because the next test is scheduled for Wednesday, Peres telephones Kim Barnes to get her notes from the lecture. Barnes's notes are concise: "Depreciation— Sounds like Greek to me." Peres next tries Tim Lake, who says he thinks depreciation is what happens when an asset wears out. Lee McPherson is confident that depreciation is the process of building up a cash fund to replace an asset at the end of its useful life. Explain the concept of depreciation for Peres. Evaluate the explanations of Lake and McPherson. Be specific.

Explaining the concept of depreciation
(Obj. 2)

E10-6 De Plain International bought a delivery truck on January 2, 20X1, for $15,000. The truck was expected to remain in service four years and to last 100,000 miles. At the end of its useful life, De Plain officials estimated that the truck's residual value would be $3,000. The truck traveled 34,000 miles the first year, 28,000 the second year, 18,000 the third year, and 20,000 the fourth year. Prepare a schedule of *depreciation expense* per year for the truck under the three depreciation methods. After two years under the double-declining-balance method, the company switched to the straight-line method. Show your computations.

Which method tracks the wear and tear on the truck most closely? Which method would De Plain prefer to use for income tax purposes? Explain in detail why De Plain prefers this method.

Determining depreciation amounts by three methods
(Obj. 2, 3)

E10-7 Taylor Marshall Co. paid $165,000 for equipment that is expected to have a seven-year life. The residual value of equipment is approximately 10% of the asset's cost.

Select the appropriate MACRS depreciation method for income tax purposes. Then determine the extra amount of cash that Marshall Co. can invest by using MACRS depreciation, versus straight-line, during the first two years of the equipment's life. Ignore any interest Marshall can earn by investing the extra cash.

E10-8 Relax-the-Back Mattress Store purchased a building for $775,000 and depreciated it on a straight-line basis over a 40-year period. The estimated residual value was $100,000. After using the building for 15 years, Relax-the-Back realized that wear and tear on the building would force the company to replace it before 40 years. Starting with the 16th year, Relax-the-Back began depreciating the building over a revised total life of 30 years and increased the estimated residual value to $200,000. Record depreciation expense on the building for years 15 and 16.

E10-9 On January 2, 20X3, Kloss Furniture Warehouse purchased showroom fixtures for $9,500 cash, expecting the fixtures to remain in service five years. Kloss has depreciated the fixtures on a double-declining-balance basis, with a $1,000 estimated residual value. On September 30, 20X4, Kloss sold the fixtures for $4,950 cash. Record both the depreciation expense on the fixtures for 20X4 and the sale of the fixtures on September 30, 20X4.

E10-10 Lasseter Transportation, based in Natchez, Mississippi, is a large trucking company that operates throughout the southern United States. Lasseter uses the units-of-production (UOP) method to depreciate its trucks because UOP depreciation best measures wear and tear. Lasseter trades in used trucks often to keep driver morale high and to maximize fuel efficiency. Consider these facts about one Mack truck in the company's fleet.

When acquired in 20X1, the tractor/trailer rig cost $385,000 and was expected to remain in service for ten years or 1,000,000 miles. Estimated residual value was $100,000. The truck was driven 75,000 miles in 20X1, 120,000 miles in 20X2, and 210,000 miles in 20X3. After 40,000 miles in 20X4, the company traded in the Mack truck for a less-expensive Freightliner. Lasseter paid cash of $80,000. Determine Lasseter's cost of the new truck. Journal entries are not required.

E10-11 El Dorado Drilling paid $298,500 for the right to extract ore from a 200,000-ton mineral deposit. In addition to the purchase price, El Dorado also paid a $500 filing fee, a $1,000 license fee to the state of Wyoming, and $60,000 for a geological survey of the property. Because the company purchased the rights to the minerals only, the company expected the asset to have zero residual value when fully depleted. During the first year, El Dorado removed 42,000 tons of ore. Make journal entries to record (a) purchase of the minerals (debit Mineral Asset), (b) payment of fees and other costs, and (c) depletion for the first year.

E10-12 *Part 1.* Westmark Printing Co., which manufactures high-speed printers, has recently paid $1.37 million for a patent on a new laser printer. Although it gives legal protection for 20 years, the patent is expected to provide Westmark with a competitive advantage for only 8 years. Assuming the straight-line method of amortization, make journal entries to record (a) the purchase of the patent, and (b) amortization for year 1.

Part 2. After using the patent for 4 years, Westmark learns at an industry trade show that another company is designing a more efficient printer. On the basis of this new information, Westmark decides, starting with year 5, to amortize the remaining cost of the patent over 2 remaining years, giving the patent a total useful life of 6 years. Record amortization for year 5.

E10-13 Campbell Soup Company's 19X9 statement of cash flows includes the following (adapted):

	Millions
	19X9
Cash Flows from Investing Activities:	
Payments to acquire other businesses..............	$105

Campbell's Note 16 to the balance sheet includes the following for Intangible Assets:

	Millions	
	19X9	19X8
Purchase price in excess of net assets of businesses acquired.......................................	$1,697	$1,655
Less: Accumulated amortization	(219)	(179)

Required

1. What title does Campbell Soup Company use to describe its goodwill? How well does Campbell's title agree with the text definition of goodwill?
2. How much did Campbell Soup Company pay to acquire other businesses during 19X9? How much of the purchase price was for goodwill? How much did Campbell pay for the other assets of the businesses it acquired, such as receivables, inventory, property, and equipment?

E10-14 PepsiCo, Inc., has aggressively acquired other companies, such as **Frito-Lay,** famous for its snack foods. Assume that PepsiCo purchased Adelaide Bakeries for $12 million cash. The market value of Adelaide's assets is $15 million, and it has liabilities of $10 million.

Measuring and recording goodwill *(Obj. 6)*

Required

1. Compute the cost of the goodwill purchased by PepsiCo.
2. Record the purchase of Adelaide Bakeries by PepsiCo.
3. Record PepsiCo's amortization of goodwill for year 1, assuming the straight-line method and a useful life of ten years.

CHALLENGE EXERCISES

E10-15 Papillon Knits is a catalog merchant in France similar to **L. L. Bean** and **Lands' End** in the United States. The company's assets consist mainly of inventory, a warehouse, and automated shipping equipment. Assume that early in year 1, Papillon purchased equipment at a cost of $4.5 million francs (F4.5 million). Management expects the equipment to remain in service five years. Because the equipment is so specialized, estimated residual value is negligible. Papillon uses the straight-line depreciation method. Through an accounting error, Papillon accidentally expensed the entire cost of the equipment at the time of purchase. The company is family-owned and operated as a partnership, so it pays no income tax.

Capitalizing versus expensing; measuring the effect of an error *(Obj. 1)*

Required

Prepare a schedule to show the overstatement or understatement in the following items at the end of each year over the five-year life of the equipment.

1. Total current assets   2. Equipment, net   3. Net income

E10-16 General Motors Corporation's comparative balance sheet reported these amounts (in millions of dollars):

Reconstructing transactions from the financial statements *(Obj. 2, 4)*

	December 31,	
	19X9	**19X8**
Property:		
Land, plant, and equipment	$ 59,777	$ 59,565
Less accumulated depreciation	(34,363)	(34,641)
Net land, plant, and equipment	25,414	24,924
Unamortized special tools	7,365	7,298
Net property	$ 32,779	$ 32,222

GM's income statement for 19X9 reported the following expenses (in millions):

Depreciation	$4,155
Amortization of special tools	2,492

Unamortized special tools refers to the remaining asset balance after amortization expense has been subtracted. GM does not use an accumulated amortization account for special tools.

Required

1. There were no disposals of special tools during 19X9. Compute the cost of new acquisitions of special tools. Use a T-account for Special Tools.
2. Assume that during 19X9, GM sold land, plant, and equipment for $215 million and that this transaction produced a gain of $15 million. What was the book value of the assets sold?

PROBLEMS

(Group A)

P10-1A Metropolitan Glass Company incurred the following costs in acquiring land and a garage, making land improvements, and constructing and furnishing an office building:

Identifying the elements of a plant asset's cost *(Obj. 1, 2)*

a.	Purchase price of 3 1/2 acres of land, including a building that will be used as a garage for company vehicles (land market value is $700,000; building market value is $100,000)	$640,000
b.	Delinquent real estate taxes on the land to be paid by Metropolitan	3,700
c.	Landscaping (additional dirt and earth moving)	5,175
d.	Title insurance on the land acquisition	1,000
e.	Fence around the boundary of the land	44,100
f.	Building permit for the office building	200
g.	Architect's fee for the design of the office building	32,000
h.	Company signs near the approaches to the company property	20,950
i.	Renovation of the garage	27,500
j.	Concrete, wood, and materials used to construct the office building	814,000
k.	Masonry, carpentry, roofing, and other labor to construct the office building	734,000
l.	Interest cost on construction loan for the office building	3,400
m.	Parking lots and concrete walks on the property	17,450
n.	Lights for the parking lot, walkways, and company signs	8,900
o.	Salary of construction supervisor (90% to office building; 6% to fencing, parking lot, and concrete walks; and 4% to garage renovation)	55,000
p.	Furniture for the office building	123,500
q.	Transportation of furniture from seller to the office building	1,100
r.	Landscaping (trees and shrubs)	9,100

Metropolitan Glass depreciates buildings over 40 years, land improvements over 20 years, and furniture over 8 years, all on a straight-line basis with zero residual value.

Required

1. Set up columns for Land, Land Improvements, Office Building, Garage, and Furniture. Show how to account for each of Metropolitan's costs by listing the cost under the correct account. Determine the total cost of each asset.
2. All construction was complete and the assets were placed in service on March 29. Record depreciation for the year ended December 31. Round to the nearest dollar.

Recording plant asset transactions, exchange, and disposal (Obj, 1, 2, 4)

P10-2A Lee & Smythe surveys American television-viewing trends. The company's balance sheet reports the following assets under Property and Equipment: Land, Buildings, Office Equipment, Communication Equipment, and Televideo Equipment, with a separate accumulated depreciation account for each depreciable asset. During 20X2, Lee & Smythe completed the following transactions:

May 3 Purchased communication and televideo equipment from the Gallup polling organization. Total cost was $80,000 paid in cash. An independent appraisal valued the communication equipment at $90,000 and the televideo equipment at $10,000.

July 30 Traded in old office equipment with book value of $11,000 (cost of $96,000) for new equipment with a cash cost of $88,000. The seller gave Lee & Smythe a trade-in allowance of $20,000 on the old equipment, and Lee & Smythe paid the remainder in cash.

Sep. 1 Sold a building that had cost $475,000 (accumulated depreciation of $353,500 through December 31 of the preceding year. Depreciation is computed on a straight-line basis. The building has a 30-year useful life and a residual value of $47,500. Lee & Smythe received $150,000 cash and a $450,000 note receivable.

Dec. 31 Recorded depreciation as follows:
Communication equipment and televideo equipment are depreciated by the double-declining-balance method over a five-year life with zero residual value. Office equipment is depreciated straight-line over seven years with $9,000 residual value. Record depreciation on the equipment acquired on May 3 and on July 30 separately.

Required

Record the transactions in the journal of Lee & Smythe.

Explaining the concept of depreciation (Obj. 2)

P10-3A The board of directors of Ameritech Satellite Technology is having its regular quarterly meeting. Accounting policies are on the agenda, and depreciation is being discussed. A new board member, an attorney, has some strong opinions about two aspects of depreciation policy. Clay Fitzhugh argues that depreciation must be coupled with a fund to replace company assets. Otherwise, there is no substance to depreciation, he argues. Fitzhugh also challenges the three-year depreciable life of company computers. He states that the computers will last much longer and should be depreciated over at least five years.

Required

Write a memo to explain the concept of depreciation to Fitzhugh and to answer his arguments. Format your memo as follows:

P10-4A On January 2, 20X1, Machinery Unlimited purchased a used trailer at a cost of $63,000. Before placing the trailer in service, the company spent $2,200 painting it, $800 replacing tires, and $4,000 overhauling the chassis. Machinery Unlimited management estimates that the trailer will remain in service for six years and have a residual value of $14,200. The trailer's annual mileage is expected to be 18,000 miles in each of the first four years and 14,000 miles in each of the next two years. In deciding which depreciation method to use, Brett Vivecek, the general manager, requests a depreciation schedule for each of the depreciation methods (straight-line, units-of-production, and double-declining-balance).

Computing depreciation by three methods and the cash-flow advantage of accelerated depreciation for tax purposes (Obj. 2, 3)

Required

1. Prepare a depreciation schedule for each depreciation method, showing asset cost, depreciation expense, accumulated depreciation, and asset book value. For the units-of-production method, round depreciation per mile to three decimal places.
2. Machinery Unlimited reports to creditors in the financial statements using the depreciation method that maximizes reported income in the early years of asset use. For income tax purposes, however, the company uses the depreciation method that minimizes income tax payments in those early years. Consider the first year that Machinery Unlimited uses the trailer. Identify the depreciation methods that meet the general manager's objectives, assuming the income tax authorities permit the use of any of the methods.
3. Cash provided by operations before income tax is $150,000 for the trailer's first year. The combined federal and state income tax rate is 40%. For the two depreciation methods identified in requirement 2, compare the net income and cash provided by operations (cash flow). Show which method gives the net-income advantage and which method gives the cash-flow advantage.

P10-5A *Note:* This problem uses the statement of cash flows, but all items are self-explanatory. **Curtiss-Wright Corporation** is a medium-sized manufacturer of high-tech parts used in commercial and military aircraft. The following excerpts come from Curtiss-Wright's 19X9 financial statements:

Analyzing plant asset transactions from a company's financial statements (Obj. 2, 4)

CURTISS-WRIGHT CORPORATION
Balance Sheet (Adapted)

(In thousands) Assets	December 31, 19X9	19X8
Current assets:		
Cash and cash equivalents	$ 9,547	$ 5,809
Short-term investments	25,560	66,444
Receivables, net...	70,729	60,912
Inventories	60,584	54,048
Other current assets	13,950	11,360
Total current assets..	180,370	198,573
Property, plant, and equipment, at cost.............	242,000	237,215
Less: Accumulated depreciation........................	(147,422)	(162,704)
Property, plant, and equipment, net..................	94,578	74,511
Other assets...	112,178	79,656
Total assets	$387,126	$352,740

CURTISS-WRIGHT CORPORATION
Statements of Cash Flows (Excerpts, Adapted)

(In thousands) Cash Flows from Investing Activities	For the Years Ended December 31, 19X9	19X8
Cash receipts from sales of plant assets	$ 2,586	$ 950
Payments for property, plant, and equipment..............	(19,883)	(10,642)

Required

Answer these questions about Curtiss-Wright's plant assets.

1. At December 31, 19X9, what was Curtiss-Wright's cost of its plant assets? What was the amount of accumulated depreciation? What was the book value of the plant assets? Does book value measure how much Curtiss-Wright could sell the assets for? Explain.
2. Curtiss-Wright's depreciation expense for 19X9 was $12,864 thousand. Why is the amount of depreciation expense so different from accumulated depreciation at December 31, 19X9?
3. How much did Curtiss-Wright pay to purchase plant assets during 19X9? Prepare a T-account showing the 19X8 and 19X9 balances of Property, Plant, and Equipment cost. Post to the T-account the cost of plant assets purchased during 19X9. Then compute the cost of plant assets *sold* during 19X9. Finally, determine whether Curtiss-Wright bought or sold more plant assets during the year.

Accounting for intangibles, natural resources, and the related expenses (Obj. 5, 6)

P10-6A *Part 1.* **United Telecommunications, Inc.** (United Telecom) provides communication services in Florida, North Carolina, New Jersey, Texas, and other states. The company's balance sheet reports the asset Cost of Acquisitions in Excess of the Fair Market Value of the Net Assets of Subsidiaries. Assume that United Telecom purchased this asset as part of the acquisition of another company, which had these figures:

Book value of assets	$575,000
Market value of assets	906,000
Liabilities	405,000

Required

1. What is another title for the asset Cost of Acquisitions in Excess of the Fair Market Value of the Net Assets of Subsidiaries?
2. Make the journal entry recording United Telecom's purchase of the other company for $1,650,000 cash. Use the account titled Goodwill.
3. Assume United Telecom amortizes Cost of Acquisitions in Excess of the Fair Market Value of the Net Assets of Subsidiaries over 20 years. Record straight-line amortization for one year. Use the account titled Goodwill.

Part 2. **Continental Pipeline Company** operates a pipeline that provides natural gas to Atlanta, Washington, D.C., Philadelphia, and New York City. The company's balance sheet includes the asset Oil and Gas Properties.

Suppose Continental paid $7 million cash for oil and gas reserves with an estimated 500,000 barrels of oil. Assume the company paid $350,000 for additional geological tests of the property and $110,000 to prepare the surface for drilling. Prior to production, the company signed a $65,000 note payable to have a building constructed on the property. The building will be abandoned when the oil is depleted, so its cost is debited to the Oil Properties account and included in depletion charges. During the first year of production, Continental removed 77,000 barrels of oil, which it sold on credit for $19 per barrel. Operating expenses related to this project totaled $185,000 for the first year, all paid in cash.

Required

1. Record all of Continental's transactions, including depletion, for the year.
2. Prepare the company's income statement for this oil and gas project for the first year. Evaluate the profitability of the project.

Reporting plant asset transactions in the financial statements—a review (Obj. 1, 2, 4)

P10-7A At the end of 1998, **Sprint Corporation,** the telecommunications company, had total assets of $33.3 billion and total liabilities of $20.9 billion. Included among the assets were property, plant, and equipment with a cost of $32.1 billion and accumulated depreciation of $13.1 billion.

Assume that Sprint completed the following selected transactions during 1999: The company earned total revenues of $19.9 billion and incurred total expenses of $20.8 billion, which included depreciation of $3.7 billion. During the year, Sprint paid $6.1 billion for new property, plant, and equipment, and sold old plant assets for $0.2 billion. The cost of the assets sold was $1.1 billion, and their accumulated depreciation was also $1.1 billion.

Required

1. Show how Sprint Corporation would report property, plant, and equipment on the balance sheet at December 31, 1999.
2. How much of the plant assets that Sprint sold during 1999 had been depreciated? Did Sprint have a gain or a loss on the sale of plant assets? What was the amount of the gain or loss?
3. How much was Sprint's owner's equity at December 31, 1998?
4. Did Sprint report net income or net loss on its 1999 income statement? Compute the amount.

PROBLEMS

P10-1B Bobby Jones Golf Company incurred the following costs in acquiring land, making land improvements, and constructing and furnishing its own sales building.

a.	Purchase price of four acres of land, including a building that will be used for a garage (land market value is $280,000; building market value is $40,000)	$300,000
b.	Landscaping (additional dirt and earth moving)	8,100
c.	Fence around the boundary of the land	17,650
d.	Attorney fee for title search on the land	770
e.	Delinquent real estate taxes on the land to be paid by Bobby Jones	5,900
f.	Company signs at front of the company property	4,475
g.	Building permit for the sales building	350
h.	Architect's fee for the design of the sales building	22,500
i.	Masonry, carpentry, roofing, and labor to construct the sales building	709,000
j.	Concrete, wood, and other materials used to construct the sales building	214,000
k.	Renovation of the garage building	36,900
l.	Interest cost on construction loan for sales building	9,000
m.	Landscaping (trees and shrubs)	6,400
n.	Parking lot and concrete walks on the property	29,750
o.	Lights for the parking lot, walkways, and company signs	7,300
p.	Salary of construction supervisor (85% to sales building; 9% to fencing, parking lot, and concrete walks; and 6% to garage building)	40,000
q.	Furniture for the sales building	107,100
r.	Transportation and installation of furniture	2,270

Bobby Jones depreciates buildings over 40 years, land improvements over 20 years, and furniture over 8 years, all on a straight-line basis with zero residual value.

Required

1. Set up columns for Land, Land Improvements, Sales Building, Garage Building, and Furniture. Show how to account for each of Bobby Jones's costs by listing the cost under the correct account. Determine the total cost of each asset.
2. All construction was complete and the assets were placed in service on May 2. Record depreciation for the year ended December 31. Round to the nearest dollar.

P10-2B Westway Freight Co. provides local freight service in Lincoln, Nebraska. The company's balance sheet includes the following assets under Property, Plant, and Equipment: Land, Buildings, and Motor-Carrier Equipment. Westway has a separate accumulated depreciation account for each of these assets except land. Assume that Westway Freight Co. completed the following transactions:

Jan. 2 Traded in motor-carrier equipment with book value of $47,000 (cost of $130,000) for similar new equipment with a cash cost of $176,000. Westway received a trade-in allowance of $70,000 on the old equipment and paid the remainder in cash.

July 1 Sold a building that cost $550,000 and that had accumulated depreciation of $247,500 through December 31 of the preceding year. Depreciation is computed on a straight-line basis. The building has a 30-year useful life and a residual value of $55,000. Westway received $100,000 cash and a $600,000 note receivable.

Oct. 26 Purchased land and a building for a single price of $300,000. An independent appraisal valued the land at $115,000 and the building at $230,000.

Dec. 31 Recorded depreciation as follows:

    Motor-carrier equipment has an expected useful life of six years and an estimated residual value of 5% of cost. Depreciation is double-declining-balance.

    Depreciation on buildings is straight-line. The new building has a 40-year useful life and a residual value equal to 12% of its cost.

Required

Record the transactions in Westway Freight's journal.

P10-3B The board of directors of Wentzville Corporation is reviewing the 20X1 annual report. A new board member—a professor—questions the company accountant about the depreciation amounts. The professor wonders why depreciation expense has decreased from $200,000 in 19X9 to $184,000 in 20X0 to $172,000 in 20X1. He states that he could understand the decreasing annual amounts if the company had been selling properties each year, but that has not occurred. Further, growth in the city is increasing the values of property. Why is the company recording depreciation when property values are increasing?

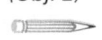

Required

Write a paragraph or two to explain the concept of depreciation and answer the professor's questions. Which depreciation method does Wentzville appear to be using?

P10-4B On January 3, 20X1, Dobb Automotive Company paid $224,000 for equipment used in manufacturing automotive supplies. In addition to the basic purchase price, the company paid $700 transportation charges, $100 insurance for the equipment while in transit, $12,100 sales tax, and $3,100 for a special platform on which to place the equipment in the plant. Dobb management estimates that the equipment will remain in service five years and have a residual value of $17,000. The equipment will produce 50,000 units the first year, with annual production decreasing by 5,000 units during each of the next four years (that is, 45,000 units in year 2; 40,000 units in year 3; and so on). In trying to decide which depreciation method to use, Jacqueline Dobb has requested a depreciation schedule for each of three depreciation methods (straight-line, units-of-production, and double-declining-balance).

Required

1. For each depreciation method, prepare a depreciation schedule showing asset cost, depreciation expense, accumulated depreciation, and asset book value. For the units-of-production method, round depreciation per unit to three decimal places.
2. Dobb reports to stockholders and creditors in the financial statements using the depreciation method that maximizes reported income in the early years of asset use. For income tax purposes, the company uses the depreciation method that minimizes income tax payments in those early years. Consider the first year Dobb uses the equipment. Identify the depreciation methods that meet Dobb's objectives, assuming the income tax authorities permit the use of any of the methods.
3. Assume that cash provided by operations before income tax is $180,000 for the equipment's first year. The combined federal and state income tax rate is 40%. For the two depreciation methods identified in requirement 2, compare the net income and cash provided by operations (cash flow). Show which method gives the net-income advantage and which method gives the cash-flow advantage.

P10-5B *Note:* This problem uses the statement of cash flows, but all items are self-explanatory. **IBM** is the world's largest computer company. After a few lean years, Big Blue, as the company is called, has rebounded strongly with some new products and improving profits. The following excerpts come from IBM's 19X9 financial statements:

INTERNATIONAL BUSINESS MACHINES CORPORATION
Balance Sheet (Adapted)

(Dollars in Millions) At December 31:	19X9	19X8
Assets		
Current assets:		
Cash and cash equivalents	$ 5,043	$ 5,375
Marketable securities	788	393
Notes and accounts receivable—trade, net of allowances	20,039	18,958
Sales-type leases receivable	6,220	6,510
Other accounts receivable	1,359	1,313
Inventories	4,868	5,200
Prepaid expenses and other current assets	4,838	4,611
Total current assets	43,155	42,360
Plant, machines, and other property, at cost	39,616	44,870
Less: Accumulated depreciation	(22,026)	(25,239)
Plant, machines, and other property—net	17,590	19,631
Software	663	599
Investments and sundry assets	26,087	23,510
Total assets	$87,495	$86,100

INTERNATIONAL BUSINESS MACHINES CORPORATION
Statement of Cash Flows (Excerpts)

(Dollars in Millions) For the year ended December 31:	19X9	19X8
Cash flows from investing activities:		
Payments for plant, machines, and other property	$(5,959)	$(6,520)
Cash received from the sale of plant, rental machines, and other property	1,207	905

Required

1. At December 31, 19X9, what was IBM's cost of its plant assets? What was the amount of accumulated depreciation? What percent of the cost has been used up?
2. IBM's depreciation expense for 19X9 was $6,159 million. Why is the amount of depreciation expense so different from accumulated depreciation at December 31, 19X9?
3. How much did IBM pay to purchase plant assets during 19X9? Prepare a T-account showing the 19X8 and 19X9 balances of total Plant Assets at cost. Post the cost of plant asset purchases during 19X9. Then compute the cost of plant assets *sold* during 19X9. Finally, determine whether IBM bought or sold more plant assets during the year.
4. IBM's balance sheet reports Software. What category of asset is software?

Accounting for intangibles, natural resources, and the related expenses (Obj. 5, 6)

P10-6B *Part 1.* **Collins Foods International Inc.** is the majority owner of Sizzler Restaurants. The company's balance sheet reports the asset Cost in Excess of Net Assets of Purchased Businesses. Assume that Collins purchased this asset as part of the acquisition of another company, which carried these figures:

Book value of assets	$2.4 million
Market value of assets	2.8 million
Liabilities	2.2 million

Required

1. What is another title for the asset Cost in Excess of Net Assets of Purchased Businesses?
2. Make the journal entry to record Collins's purchase of the other company for $2.7 million cash. Use the account titled Goodwill.
3. Assume Collins amortizes Cost in Excess of Net Assets of Purchased Businesses over 20 years. Record the straight-line amortization for one year. Use the account titled Goodwill.

Part 2. **Georgia-Pacific Corporation** is one of the world's largest forest products companies. The company's balance sheet includes the assets Natural Gas, Oil, and Coal.

Suppose Georgia-Pacific paid $2.8 million cash for the right to work a mine with an estimated 100,000 tons of coal. Assume the company paid $60,000 to remove unwanted buildings from the land and $45,000 to prepare the surface for mining. Further, assume that Georgia-Pacific signed a $30,000 note payable to a company that will return the land surface to its original condition after the lease ends. During the first year, Georgia-Pacific removed 35,000 tons of coal, which it sold on account for $37 per ton. Operating expenses for the first year totaled $252,000, all paid in cash.

Required

1. Record all of Georgia-Pacific's transactions, including depletion, for the year.
2. Prepare the company's income statement for its coal operations for the first year. Evaluate the profitability of the coal operations.

Reporting plant asset transactions in the financial statements—a review (Obj. 1, 2, 4)

P10-7B At the end of 19X8, **The Coca-Cola Company** had total assets of $19.1 billion and total liabilities of $10.7 billion. Included among the assets were property, plant, and equipment with a cost of $5.7 billion and accumulated depreciation of $2.0 billion.

Coca-Cola completed the following selected transactions during 19X9: The company earned total revenues of $19.8 billion and incurred total expenses of $17.3 billion, which included depreciation of $0.8 billion. During the year, Coca-Cola paid $1.1 billion for new property, plant, and equipment and sold old plant assets, receiving cash of $0.2 billion. The cost of the assets sold was $0.1 billion; their accumulated depreciation was also $0.1 billion.

Required

1. Show how Coca-Cola would report property, plant, and equipment on the balance sheet at December 31, 19X9. What was the book value of property, plant, and equipment on that date?
2. How much of the assets that Coca-Cola sold during 19X9 had been depreciated? Did Coca-Cola have a gain or loss on the sale of plant assets during 19X9? What was the amount of the gain or loss?
3. How much was Coca-Cola's owners' equity at December 31, 19X8?
4. Did Coca-Cola report net income or net loss on its 19X9 income statement? Compute the amount.

DECISION CASES

Measuring profitability based on different inventory and depreciation methods (Obj. 2, 3)

Case 1. ← *Link Back to Chapter 9 (Inventory Methods).* Suppose you are considering investing in two businesses, Astoria Enterprises and Hilton Systems. The two companies are virtually identical, and both began operations at the beginning of the current year. During the year, each company purchased inventory as follows:

Jan.	4	10,000 units at $4 =	$	40,000
Apr.	6	5,000 units at 5 =		25,000
Aug.	9	7,000 units at 6 =		42,000
Nov.	27	10,000 units at 7 =		70,000
Totals		32,000		$177,000

During the first year, both companies sold 25,000 units of inventory.

In early January, both companies purchased equipment costing $143,000 (ten-year estimated useful life and a $20,000 residual value). Astoria uses the inventory and depreciation methods that maximize reported income (FIFO and straight-line). By contrast, Hilton uses the inventory and depreciation methods that minimize income tax payments (LIFO and double-declining-balance). Both companies' trial balances at December 31 included the following:

Sales revenue..........................	$370,000
Operating expenses	80,000

Required

1. Prepare both companies' income statements.
2. Write an investment newsletter to address the following questions for your clients: Which company appears to be more profitable? Which company has more cash to invest in promising projects? If prices continue rising in both companies' industries over the long-term, which company would you prefer to invest in? Why?

Plant assets and intangible assets (Obj. 1, 6)

Case 2. The following questions are unrelated except that they all apply to fixed assets and intangible assets:

a. The manager of Clarkson Corporation regularly debits the cost of repairs and maintenance of plant assets to Plant and Equipment. Why would she do that, since she knows she is violating generally accepted accounting principles (GAAP)?

b. It has been suggested that, because many intangible assets have no value except to the company that owns them, they should be valued at $1.00 or zero on the balance sheet. Many accountants disagree with this view. Which view do you support? Why?

c. The manager of Ladue Company regularly buys plant assets and debits the cost to Repairs and Maintenance Expense. Why would he do that, since this action violates GAAP?

ETHICAL ISSUE

Reflection Cove Apartments purchased land and a building for the lump sum of $4.1 million. To get the maximum tax deduction, Reflection Cove managers allocated 90% of the purchase price to the building and only 10% to the land. A more realistic allocation would have been 70% to the building and 30% to the land.

Required

1. Explain the tax advantage of allocating too much to the building and too little to the land.
2. Was Reflection Cove's allocation ethical? If so, state why. If not, why not? Identify who was harmed.

FINANCIAL STATEMENT CASE

Plant assets and intangible assets (Obj. 2, 3, 4, 6)

Refer to the **Target Corporation** financial statements in Appendix A, and answer the following questions.

Required

1. Which depreciation method does Target use for reporting in the financial statements? What type of depreciation method does the company probably use for income tax purposes? Why is this method preferable for tax purposes?
2. Depreciation and amortization expense is embedded in the selling, general, and administrative expense amounts listed on the income statement. The statement of cash flows gives the amount of depreciation and amortization expense. What was the amount of depreciation and amortization for fiscal year 1999? Record Target's depreciation and amortization expense for 1999.
3. The statement of cash flows reports the purchases of plant assets and the proceeds (sale prices) received on disposal of plant assets. How much were Target's plant asset acquisitions during 1999? Journalize the company's acquisition of plant assets.
4. How much cash did Target receive on the sale of plant assets during 1999? Assume the plant assets that were sold had a cost of $988 million and accumulated depreciation of $697 million. Record the sale of these plant assets. How much was the gain or loss on the sale of plant assets during the year?

TEAM PROJECT

Required

Visit a local business.

1. List all its plant assets.
2. If possible, interview the manager. Gain as much information as you can about the business's plant assets. For example, try to determine the assets' costs, the depreciation method the company is using, and the estimated useful life of each asset category. If an interview is impossible, then develop your own estimates of the assets' costs, useful lives, and book values, assuming an appropriate depreciation method.
3. Determine whether the business has any intangible assets. If so, list them and gain as much information as possible about their nature, cost, and estimated useful lives.
4. Write a detailed report of your findings and be prepared to present it to the class.

INTERNET EXERCISE

On Saturday, July 8, 2000, **FedEx** teamed up with **Amazon.com** to deliver 250,000 copies of the book *Harry Potter and the Goblet of Fire*. To deliver this unprecedented number of books, 100 regularly scheduled FedEx flights, 9,000 FedEx delivery personnel, and vehicles from 700 stations were mobilized from Amazon.com distribution centers to distribute approximately 675,000 pounds (more than 300 tons) of the book.

1. Go to **http://www.fedex.com** and in the left-hand column click on *Investor Relations*. Select the *on-line* version of the most recent annual report. Within the Annual Report menu, click on *Financial Information*. (Note: There are two links titled *Financial Information*. Use the link classified under Annual Report.) Use this information to answer the following questions.
   a. At the most recent year-end, examine *Property and Equipment, at cost*. List the four types of property and equipment reported by FedEx Corporation. What is the total cost of these assets? What is the book value? What amount of cost has already been expensed through depreciation? What is the expensed portion called?
   b. Which financial statement reports depreciation expense? For the most recent year identify the amount reported for *Depreciation and amortization expense*.

2. Refer to Note 2: Summary of Significant Accounting Policies to answer the following.
   a. Which method of depreciation does FedEx use for financial reporting purposes? For tax reporting purposes? Explain why a company uses different depreciation methods for tax reporting and for financial statement purposes. Is this ethical? Is it legal? Does this comply with the Consistency Principle?
   b. What is the range of useful lives FedEx uses for flight equipment? For computer and electronic equipment? Do these useful lives make sense?
   c. What amount of residual value does FedEx use for aircraft frames and engines? For all other property and equipment?

FedEx Corporation

Go to the "Depreciation Methods and Inventory Cost Flow Assumptions" episode on the *Mastering Accounting* CD-ROM for an interactive, video-enhanced exercise that shows how CanGo staff must choose when and how to depreciate fixed assets, such as a new warehouse the company needs.

11

Current Liabilities and Payroll

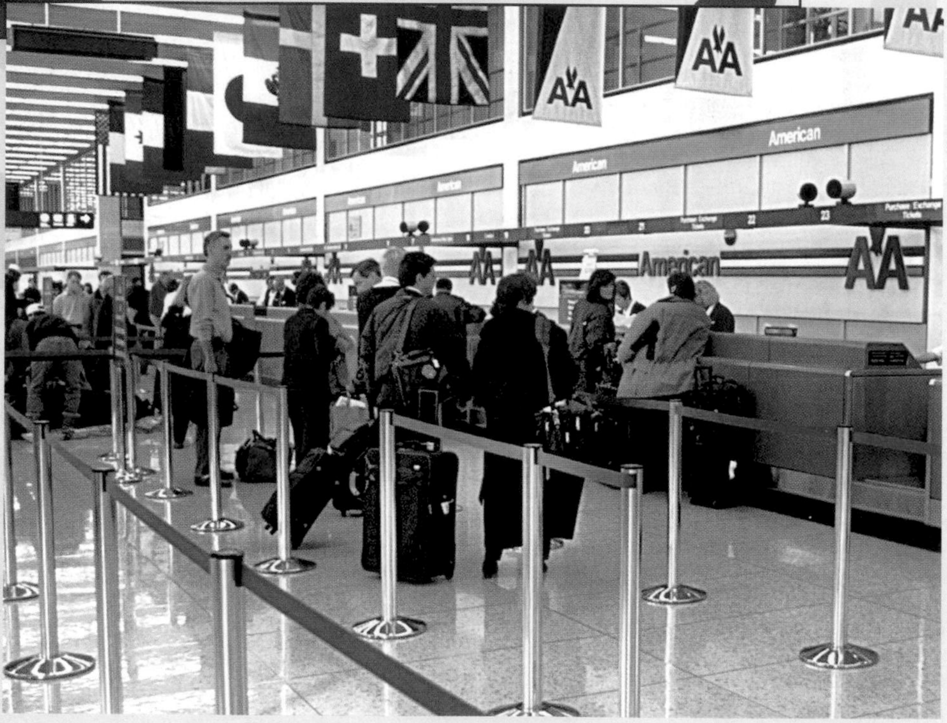

LEARNING OBJECTIVES

After studying this chapter, you should be able to

1. Account for current liabilities of known amount
2. Account for current liabilities that must be estimated
3. Compute payroll amounts
4. Record basic payroll transactions
5. Use a payroll system
6. Report current liabilities on the balance sheet

Advantage®, Mileage Plus®, and SkyMiles®—these are the frequent-flier plans of **American Airlines, United,** and **Delta.** American was the first to capitalize on this mode of creating loyal customers. Boy, does it work!

When Ron and Lisa Schmidt fly on American Airlines, they get a mile of frequent-flier credit for every mile they fly. They also get mileage credit when they pay their VISA bill, whether it's for gas at the pump or carpet in their home. Had Ron and Lisa been able to fly American on a recent trip to Florida, they would have gotten VIP treatment. But flying on Delta landed them back in ordinary no-frills coach. Of course, it works both ways. Delta's frequent fliers don't automatically get kid-glove treatment when they fly American or United.

The mileage credit granted to frequent fliers adds up to quite an accounting challenge for the airlines. It's both promotion expense and a major liability. For each mile of credit granted to the Schmidts, American Airlines books a liability for their free travel in the future. How do the airlines estimate this payable—called Air Traffic Liability? The answer is "Very carefully, because they must report this liability on their balance sheets."

In this chapter, we explain how to account for all types of current liabilities. The first half of the chapter concentrates on current liabilities, and the second half on payrolls, which generate some specific current liabilities. Exhibit 11-1 shows how **AMR Corporation,** the parent company of American Airlines, reported its current liabilities at March 31, 2000. Recall that *current liabilities* are obligations due within one year or within the company's normal operating cycle if it is longer than one year. Obligations due beyond that period are classified as *long-term liabilities.* ➡

◀◀ We discussed current liabilities and long-term liabilities in Chapter 4, p. 139.

CURRENT LIABILITIES OF KNOWN AMOUNT

Current liabilities fall into two categories: liabilities of a known amount and liabilities that must be estimated. We look first at current liabilities of known amount.

Objective 1
Account for current liabilities of known amount

Accounts Payable

Amounts owed to suppliers for products or services purchased on open account are *accounts payable.* We have seen many accounts payable illustrations in preceding chapters. For example, most businesses purchase inventory and office supplies on account. **AMR Corporation** reported Accounts payable of $1,231 million at March 31, 2000 (see line 1 of Exhibit 11-1).

Let's see how AMR's accounts payable get onto the company's balance sheet. One of AMR's common transactions is the credit purchase of its inventory of food to be served on flights. AMR's accounts payable and inventory systems are integrated. When the food inventory dips below a certain level, the computer automatically prepares a purchase request for more food. The order is placed and the goods are received. AMR makes the following journal entry to buy the inventory of account (amount assumed):

Inventory	600	
Accounts Payable		600
Purchase on account.		

The computer thus increases Inventory and Accounts Payable. Then for payments, the computer debits Accounts Payable and credits Cash, as follows:

Accounts Payable	400	
Cash		400
Paid on account.		

EXHIBIT 11-1
How AMR Reports Its Current Liabilities

AMR CORPORATION (PARENT COMPANY OF AMERICAN AIRLINES) Balance Sheet (partial; adapted) March 31, 2000		
	Liabilities	**(In Millions)**
	Current Liabilities	
1	Accounts payable	$1,231
2	Accrued liabilities payable	1,818
3	Air traffic liability	2,758
4	Current maturities of long-term debt	241
5	Current obligations under capital leases	231
6	Total current liabilities	$6,279

WORK IT OUT

After AMR Corporation buys inventory and pays the account payable in the two preceding transactions, how much does AMR owe the other company? Stated differently, how much is AMR's account payable to the supplier?

Answer: $200 ($600 − $400)

AMR Corporation completes thousands of transactions such as these. AMR's $1,231 million balance of Accounts Payable (Exhibit 11-1) is the sum of all the amounts AMR still owes on account.

Short-Term Notes Payable

SHORT-TERM NOTE PAYABLE. Promissory note payable due within one year, a common form of financing.

Short-term notes payable are a common form of financing. They are promissory notes that must be paid within one year. Companies often issue short-term notes payable to borrow cash or to purchase inventory. The following entries are typical for a short-term note payable:

20X1			
Sep. 30	Inventory	8,000	
	Note Payable, Short-Term		8,000
	Purchased inventory on a one-year, 10% note.		
20X1			
Dec. 31	Interest Expense ($8,000 × 0.10 × 3/12)	200	
	Interest Payable		200
	Accrued interest expense at year end.		

The balance sheet at December 31, 20X1, will report the Note Payable of $8,000 and Interest Payable of $200 as current liabilities. The 20X1 income statement will report interest expense of $200, as illustrated.

Balance Sheet December 31, 20X1		**Income Statement Year Ended December 31, 20X1**	
Liabilities		**Expenses**	
Current liabilities:		Interest expense	$200
Note payable, short-term	$8,000		
Interest payable	200		

The following entry records payment of the note at maturity:

```
20X2
Sep. 30   Note Payable, Short-Term .....................................   8,000
          Interest Payable ....................................................      200
          Interest Expense ($8,000 × 0.10 × 9/12)..............      600
               Cash [$8,000 + ($8,000 × 0.10)] .................             8,800
          Paid a note and interest at maturity.
```

◉ DAILY EXERCISE 11-1

◉ DAILY EXERCISE 11-2

◉ DAILY EXERCISE 11-3

The cash payment entry must separate the total interest on the note ($800) between

- the interest expense of 20X1 ($200), and
- the interest expense of 20X2 ($600).

This way, each year's financial statements report the correct amounts for *that* year.

Short-Term Notes Payable Issued at a Discount

There is another way to set up a borrowing arrangement. It is called **discounting a note payable.** The lender subtracts the interest amount from the note's face value, and the borrower receives the net amount. At maturity, the borrower pays back the full face value, which includes all the interest.

Suppose **Procter & Gamble** discounts a $100,000, 60-day note payable to its bank at 12%. P&G will receive $98,000—that is, the $100,000 face value less interest of $2,000 ($100,000 × 0.12 × 60/360). Assume that this transaction occurs on November 25, 20X1. Procter & Gamble's entry to record discounting the note follows.[1]

DISCOUNTING A NOTE PAYABLE. A borrowing arrangement in which the bank subtracts the interest amount from a note's face value. The borrower receives the net amount.

```
20X1
Nov. 25   Cash ($100,000 − $2,000*) ...................................   98,000
               Note Payable, Short-Term.............................             98,000
          Discounted a $100,000, 60-day, 12% note payable.
          *Discount = $100,000 × 0.12 × 60/360 = $2,000.
```

THINK IT OVER

How much did Procter & Gamble actually borrow from the bank—$98,000 or $100,000? How much will P&G pay back? How much interest expense will P&G record for the borrowing arrangement?

Answers: Procter & Gamble borrowed $98,000, the amount of cash the company received. P&G will pay back $100,000 at maturity. P&G's interest expense will be $2,000 ($100,000 paid back − $98,000 borrowed).

Procter & Gamble must record accrued interest at year end as it would for any note payable. P&G's adjusting entry at December 31 records interest for 36 days, as follows:

```
20X1
Dec. 31   Interest Expense ($100,000 × 0.12 × 36/360)......   1,200
               Note Payable .................................................             1,200
          Accrued interest expense at year end.
```

After the year-end adjustment, the Note Payable account carries its current balance of $99,200.

	NOTE PAYABLE	
	Nov. 25	98,000
	Dec. 31	1,200
	Bal.	99,200

---

[1] Another set of journal entries can be used to record the discounting of a note payable. The alternate method uses a separate Discount on Note Payable account and obscures the true nature of the borrowing arrangement.

At maturity, the business records the final amount of interest expense on the note:

20X2
Jan. 24   Interest Expense ($100,000 × 0.12 × 24/360)   800
            Note Payable   800
        To record interest expense.

On the note's maturity date, the Note Payable account holds the maturity value of $100,000.

NOTE PAYABLE		
	Nov. 25, 20X1	98,000
	Dec. 31, 20X1	1,200
	Jan. 24, 20X2	800
	Bal.	100,000

The final entry pays off the note at maturity.

◉ DAILY EXERCISE 11-4

20X2
Jan. 24   Note Payable, Short-Term   100,000
            Cash...   100,000
        To pay note at maturity.

Sales Tax Payable

Most states levy a sales tax on retail sales. Only Delaware, Montana, New Hampshire, and Oregon do not have a sales tax. Retailers collect the sales tax in addition to the price of the item sold. The retailers owe the state the sales tax, so, the account Sales Tax Payable is a current liability. For example, **ShowBiz Pizza Time, Inc.** (operator of family restaurants and entertainment centers, such as Chuck E. Cheese), reported sales tax payable of $737,712 as a current liability.

Suppose one Saturday's sales at a ShowBiz Pizza Time totaled $10,000. The business collected an additional 5% in sales tax, which would equal $500 ($10,000 × 0.05). The business would record that day's sales as follows:

Cash ($10,000 × 1.05)   10,500
    Sales Revenue...   10,000
    Sales Tax Payable ($10,000 × 0.05)   500
To record cash sales and the related sales tax.

CASH		SALES TAX PAYABLE		SALES REVENUE	
10,500			500		10,000

Companies forward the collected sales tax to the taxing authority at regular intervals. Then they debit Sales Tax Payable and credit Cash.

Many companies do not credit Sales Tax Payable for each sale. Instead, they record sales revenue and sales tax together. Then, prior to paying the tax, they make an adjusting entry to bring Sales Revenue and Sales Tax Payable to their correct balances.

Suppose a **Kinko** store earned service revenue of $100,000 during July, subject to sales tax of 6%. Kinko's summary entry to record the month's revenue could be as follows:

July 31   Cash ($100,000 × 1.06)   106,000
            Service Revenue...   106,000
        Revenue for the month.

The entry to adjust Service Revenue and Sales Tax Payable to their correct balances would then be

July 31   Service Revenue [$106,000 − ($106,000 ÷ 1.06)].....   6,000
            Sales Tax Payable   6,000
        To record sales tax.

Now both accounts are ready for the financial statements:

SERVICE REVENUE		SALES TAX PAYABLE	
6,000	106,000		6,000
	100,000		

A Taxing Dilemma: Sales Tax Liability and the Internet

e-Commerce offers two big pluses: shopping from home in your pajamas and no sales tax. Say you live in New York City and purchase a CD from a music store. You pay the retail price of $15.99, plus sales tax of 8.25%. The sales tax is a current liability, payable to the State of New York. A purchase of the same CD from **Amazon.com** will be $1.32 cheaper. Fortunately for on-line (and mail-order) consumers, the Supreme Court ruled that only the U.S. Congress can require retailers who don't have a physical location in the state to charge sales taxes.

We consumers are always happy to pay less for a product, but we may be wise to consider the long-term effects of the e-commerce sales tax loophole. By 2003 state and local governments may lose $20 billion in tax revenues if Internet sales are exempted. The sales tax you pay builds roads and pays your governor, the mayor, and other state and local employees, such as firefighters and teachers. In addition, if e-commerce takes over, there may be no downtowns left in San Antonio or Tacoma—just boarded up businesses and empty strip malls.

If you are civic-minded, you can voluntarily pay your "use tax," which is imposed in the state in which you use the goods that you purchase. Most consumers don't pay this tax, but states may start collecting it if Congress continues to exempt dot.coms from sales tax. Expect to hear more on this issue. And if you're starting your own dot.com, see **EcommerceTax.com** for up-to-the-minute news. How sales tax is treated may influence how you set up your business.

Source: Based on Peter Schrag, "loophole.com," *The Nation,* May 15, 2000, pp. 6–7. Anonymous, "United States: Offline," *The Economist,* March 25, 2000, p. 35. http://www.ecommercetax.com/doc/043000.htm.

Current Portion of Long-Term Debt

Some long-term notes payable and bonds payable are paid in installments. The **current portion of long-term debt,** or **current maturity,** is the amount of the principal payable within one year. At the end of each year, a company reclassifies (from long-term debt to a current liability) the amount that must be paid during the upcoming year.

> **CURRENT PORTION OF LONG-TERM DEBT.** Amount of the principal that is payable within one year. Also called **current maturity.**

AMR's balance sheet (Exhibit 11-1) reports Current maturities of long-term debt, the next-to-last current liability (line 4). On its full balance sheet, AMR reports Long-term debt immediately after total current liabilities. *Long-term debt* refers to notes payable that are payable later than one year beyond the balance sheet date.

The liability for the current portion of long-term debt (line 4) does *not* include any accrued interest payable. The account, Current Maturities of Long-Term Debt, represents only the *principal amount owed.* Interest Payable is a separate account for a different liability. AMR includes interest payable under the current liability caption Accrued liabilities payable (line 2).

AMR Corporation reports Current obligations under capital leases as its last current liability (line 5). This liability is similar to current maturities of long-term debt because it is next year's lease payment on leases that AMR has capitalized as an asset.

 Suppose AMR Corporation owes $600 million on long-term notes payable at December 31, 20X5. The borrowing agreement requires AMR to pay $241 million of this debt on September 30, 20X6. Show how AMR will report both current and long-term liabilities on its balance sheet at December 31, 20X5.

Answer

	(Millions)
Current liabilities:	
Current maturities of long-term debt	$241
Long-term liabilities:	
Long-term debt ($600 − $241)........................	359

Accrued Expenses (Accrued Liabilities)

ACCRUED EXPENSE. An expense that the business has not yet paid. Also called **accrued liability.**

An **accrued expense** is an expense that the business has not yet paid. Therefore, an accrued expense is also a liability. This explains why accrued expenses are also called **accrued liabilities.** Accrued expenses typically occur with the passage of time, such as interest payable on long-term debt. By contrast, an account payable results from the purchase of a good or a service. ◂◂

➤ We introduced accrued expenses in Chapter 3, p. 92.

Like most other companies, AMR Corporation reports accrued liabilities on its balance sheet (line 2 in Exhibit 11-1). The total of $1,818 million includes salaries and wages payable. This caption also includes other payroll-related liabilities, such as taxes withheld from employee paychecks, plus current liabilities for interest payable and income tax payable. AMR Corporation's Air traffic liability, discussed in the chapter opening story, is another example of an accrued liability. See line 3 of Exhibit 11-1.

We illustrate accounting for interest payable under the heading Short-Term Notes Payable on page 426. The next section, plus the second half of this chapter, covers accounting for accrued salaries, wages, and other payroll liabilities.

Payroll Liabilities

PAYROLL. A major expense. Also called **employee compensation.**

Payroll, also called **employee compensation,** is a major expense. For service organizations—such as CPA firms, physicians, and travel agents—payroll is *the* major expense. Service organizations sell their personnel's services, so employee compensation is their primary cost of doing business, just as cost of goods sold is the largest expense for a merchandising company.

Employee compensation takes different forms:

- *Salary* is pay expressed in a yearly, monthly, or weekly rate.
- *Wages* are employee pay amounts stated at an hourly figure.
- *Commissions* are compensation computed as a percentage of the sales the employee made.
- *Bonus* is an amount over and above regular compensation.

Journalizing all these forms of compensation follows the same pattern, as illustrated in Exhibit 11-2 (using assumed figures).

EXHIBIT 11-2
**Accounting for Payroll
Expenses and Liabilities**

Salary Expense (or Wage Expense or Commission Expense)..............	10,000	
Employee Income Tax Payable..		1,200
FICA Tax Payable..		800
Employee Union Dues Payable		140
Salary Payable to Employees [take-home pay]...........................		7,860
To record salary expense.		

Salary (or other payroll) expense represents employees' *gross pay* (pay before subtractions for taxes and other deductions). Salary expense creates several liabilities.

- Salary payable to employees is their net (take-home) pay.
- *Employee Income Tax Payable* is income tax that has been withheld from employee paychecks.
- *FICA Tax Payable* is the employees' Social Security tax, which also is withheld from paychecks. (FICA stands for the Federal Insurance Contributions Act, which created the Social Security tax.) The company owes these liabilities to the U.S. government.
- In Exhibit 11-2, employees authorize the company to withhold union dues. These amounts are payable to the union.

In addition to salaries and wages, companies also pay some payroll taxes and other expenses for employee fringe benefits. Accounting for these expenses is similar to the illustration in Exhibit 11-2 and is covered in more detail in the second half of this chapter.

Unearned Revenues

Unearned revenues are also called *deferred revenues, revenues collected in advance,* and *customer prepayments.* ➡ All these account titles indicate that the business has received cash from its customers before earning the revenue. For unearned revenue, the company has an obligation to provide goods or services to the customer. Let's consider an example.

⇐ As we saw in Chapter 3, p. 94, an unearned revenue is a liability because it represents an obligation to provide a good or service.

The **Dun & Bradstreet (D&B) Corporation** provides credit reports for subscribers. Finance companies pay D&B in advance to have D&B investigate the credit histories of potential customers. By receiving cash before earning the revenue, D&B incurs a liability for future service. The liability account is called Unearned Subscription Revenue (or Unearned Subscription *Income*).

Assume that D&B charges $600 for a three-year subscription. D&B's cash-receipt entry would be

20X1			
Jan. 1	Cash	600	
	Unearned Subscription Revenue..............		600
	Received cash in advance.		

After receiving the cash on January 1, 20X1, D&B owes its professional service to customers over three years. D&B's liability is

UNEARNED SUBSCRIPTION REVENUE
| | 600 |

During 20X1, D&B performs one-third of the total service and earns $200 ($600 × 1/3) of the revenue. At December 31, 20X1, D&B makes the following adjusting entry to decrease Unearned Subscription Revenue, the liability account, and to increase Subscription Revenue:

20X1			
Dec. 31	Unearned Subscription Revenue	200	
	Subscription Revenue ($600 × 1/3)		200
	Earned revenue that was collected in advance.		

After posting, the two accounts are

UNEARNED SUBSCRIPTION REVENUE			
Dec. 31	200	Jan. 1	600
		Bal.	400

SUBSCRIPTION REVENUE	
Dec. 31	200

At December 31, 20X1, D&B has earned $200 of the revenue. D&B still owes its customer $400 in total liabilities:

- $200 for the service D&B will perform during 20X2. This is a current liability.
- $200 for the service D&B will perform during 20X3. This is a long-term liability.

D&B's financial statements would report the following at the end of the first year:

DAILY EXERCISE 11-5

Balance Sheet at December 31, 20X1		Income Statement for the Year Ended December 31, 20X1	
Current liabilities:		Revenues:	
Unearned subscription revenue................................	$200	Subscription revenue	$200
Long-term liabilities:			
Unearned subscription revenue................................	$200		

CURRENT LIABILITIES THAT MUST BE ESTIMATED

Objective 2
Account for current liabilities that must be estimated

A business may know that a liability exists but not know the exact amount. It cannot simply ignore the liability. The unknown amount must be estimated, recorded in the accounts, and reported on the balance sheet.

Estimated current liabilities vary among companies. As a first example, let's look at Estimated Warranty Payable, a common liability for merchandisers.

Estimated Warranty Payable

Many companies guarantee their products against defects under *warranty* agreements. Ninety-day warranties and one-year warranties are common. The automobile companies—**Toyota, Ford,** and **BMW,** for example—accrue liabilities for their five-year, 50,000-mile warranties.

➦ For a review of the matching principle, see Chapter 3, p. 86.

The matching principle demands that the company record the *warranty expense* in the same period that the business recognizes sales revenue, regardless of when the company pays warranty claims. ◄ Offering the warranty—and incurring warranty expense—is a cost of making sales. At the time of the sale, the company does not know the exact amount of warranty expense. But the business must estimate its warranty expense and the related liability.

Assume that **Whirlpool Corporation,** which manufactures appliances for **Sears** and other companies, made sales of $200,000, subject to product warranties. Assume that in the past between 2% and 4% of the products proved defective. Whirlpool management could estimate that 3% of the products it sells this year will require warranty payments. The company would record the sales of $200,000 and the warranty expense of $6,000 ($200,000 × 0.03) in the same period as follows:

Accounts Receivable....................................	200,000	
Sales Revenue....................................		200,000
Sales on account.		
Warranty Expense	6,000	
Estimated Warranty Payable..............		6,000
To accrue warranty expense.		

Assume that Whirlpool's warranty payments total $5,800. If Whirlpool repairs the defective appliances, Whirlpool makes this journal entry:

| Estimated Warranty Payable | 5,800 | |
| Cash | | 5,800 |

To *repair* defective products sold under warranty.

If Whirlpool gives customers replacement appliances for their warranty claims, Whirlpool would instead make this entry:

| Estimated Warranty Payable | 5,800 | |
| Inventory | | 5,800 |

To *replace* defective products sold under warranty.

Whirlpool's expense on the income statement is $6,000 in all cases. The amount of the cash payment or the cost of the replacement inventory has no bearing on the amount of warranty expense for the period. After paying these warranty claims, Whirlpool's Estimated Warranty Payable account appears as follows:

ESTIMATED WARRANTY PAYABLE

| 5,800 | 6,000 |
| | Bal. 200 |

The balance sheet reports a current liability for Estimated Warranty Payable of $200.

 DAILY EXERCISE 11-6

 DAILY EXERCISE 11-7

 **WORK IT OUT**

Maxim Company made sales of $400,000 and estimated warranty repairs at 5% of the sales. Maxim's actual warranty outlays were $19,000. Record the sales (ignore cost of goods sold), the warranty expense, and the warranty payments. The beginning balance of Estimated Warranty Payable was zero. How much is Maxim's estimated warranty payable at the end of the period?

Answer

Accounts Receivable	400,000	
Sales Revenue		400,000
Warranty Expense ($400,000 × 0.05)	20,000	
Estimated Warranty Payable		20,000
Estimated Warranty Payable	19,000	
Cash		19,000

ESTIMATED WARRANTY PAYABLE

| 19,000 | 20,000 |
| | Bal. 1,000 |

Estimated Vacation Pay Liability

Most companies grant paid vacations to their employees. The employees receive this benefit when they take their vacation, but they earn the benefit by working the remainder of the year. Two-week vacations are common. To match expense with revenue, the company accrues the vacation pay expense and liability over the course of the year. Then, the company records payment during the two-week vacation period. Companies must estimate their vacation pay liability.

Suppose a company's January payroll is $100,000 and vacation pay adds 4%, or $4,000. Experience indicates that only 90% of the available vacations will be taken, so the January vacation pay estimate is $3,600 ($4,000 × 0.90). In January, the company records vacation pay as follows:

| Jan. 31 | Vacation Pay Expense | 3,600 | |
| | Estimated Vacation Pay Liability | | 3,600 |

Each month thereafter, the company makes a similar entry.

If an employee takes a two-week vacation during August, his or her $2,000 salary is recorded as follows:

Aug. 31	Estimated Vacation Pay Liability	2,000	
	Cash		2,000

Income Tax Payable (for a Corporation)

Corporations pay income tax in the same way that individuals do. Corporations file their tax returns after the end of the year, so they must estimate their income tax payable for the balance sheet. During the year, corporations make quarterly tax payments to the government. A corporation would record the payment of $100,000 of income tax expense for the third quarter as follows:

Sept. 30	Income Tax Expense	100,000	
	Cash		100,000
	To pay quarterly income tax.		

The corporation's entry to accrue $40,000 of income tax expense and payable at year end is

Dec. 31	Income Tax Expense	40,000	
	Income Tax Payable		40,000
	To accrue income tax at year end.		

The corporation will pay off this tax liability early in the next year, so Income Tax Payable is a current liability.

Contingent Liabilities

➤ We introduced contingent liabilities in the Appendix to Chapter 8, p. 344.

A *contingent liability* is not an actual liability. Instead, it is a potential liability that depends on a *future* event. ◀ For example, suppose **AMR Corporation,** the parent company of **American Airlines,** faces a possible loss if its pilots walk off the job in a threatened labor strike. The future event is the negotiation between the airline and the pilots' labor union. The airline thus faces a contingent liability, which may or may not become an actual liability.

It would be unethical for the airline to withhold knowledge of the labor negotiations from anyone considering investing in the business. Another contingent liability arises when one company *cosigns a note payable* for another company. Suppose Company A guarantees that Company B will pay a note payable owed to another party. This practice obligates Company A to pay the note and interest if Company B fails to pay. Thus, Company A has a contingent liability until the note becomes due. If Company B pays off the note, the contingent liability ceases to exist. If not, Company A's liability becomes actual.

The most important source of contingent liabilities is a lawsuit in which the company is being sued. Until the case is settled, the defendant has a contingent liability. One of the most famous lawsuits occurred when **Microsoft Corporation** was sued for matters related to the Java programming language technology. Until the court reached its decision, Microsoft reported the contingency in the notes to its financial statements. In its 1999 annual report, Microsoft included the following (excerpt):

> **Sun Microsystems, Inc. brought suit against Microsoft in the U.S. District Court for [. . .] California. Sun's complaint alleges several claims against Microsoft, all related to the [. . .] Java programming language technology.**

Contingent liabilities may be reported in two ways. In what is called a **short presentation,** the contingent liability appears in the body of the balance sheet, after total liabilities, but with no amounts given. In general, an explanatory note accompanies a short presentation. The Microsoft note is typical for a contingent liability arising from a lawsuit.

SHORT PRESENTATION. A way to report contingent liabilities in the body of the balance sheet, after total liabilities but with no amount given. An explanatory note accompanies the presentation.

 DAILY EXERCISE 11-8

ETHICAL ISSUES IN REPORTING LIABILITIES

Accounting for current liabilities poses ethical and legal challenges. Business owners and managers want their company to look as successful as possible. They like to report high levels of net income on the income statement. High net income makes

the company look profitable and helps the company raise money from investors. And high net income leads to large bonuses for managers. Owners want their balance sheet to report high asset values and low liability amounts, which make the company look safe to lenders and help the company borrow money at low interest rates.

- Low expenses ——————→ High net income
- Low liabilities ——————→ High owner's equity

Owners and managers may be tempted to overlook some accrued expenses at the end of the accounting period. For example, a company can fail to accrue warranty expense. This failure will cause total expenses to be understated and net income to be overstated on the income statement.

Contingent liabilities also pose an ethical challenge. Because contingencies are not real liabilities, they are easy to overlook. But a contingent liability can be very important. The **Microsoft** contingency is an example. Ethical business owners and managers do not play games with their accounting. Falsifying financial statements can ruin one's reputation. It can also land a person in a federal or state prison.

At this half-way point in the chapter, review what you have learned by studying the following Decision Guidelines.

DECISION GUIDELINES

Accounting for Current and Contingent Liabilities, Including Payroll

DECISION	GUIDELINES
What are the two main issues in accounting for current liabilities?	• *Recording* the liability and the asset acquired or the expense incurred • *Reporting* the liability on the balance sheet

What are the two basic categories of current liabilities?	• Current liabilities of *known amount:*
	  Accounts payable Accrued expenses
	  Short-term notes payable (accrued liabilities)
	  Sales tax payable Payroll liabilities
	  Current portion of long- Salary, wages, commission,
	    term debt and bonus payable
	  Unearned revenues
	• Current liabilities that *must be estimated:*
	  Estimated warranty payable
	  Estimated vacation pay liability
	  Income tax payable (for a corporation)

How to account for contingent (potential) liabilities?	Report contingent liabilities either • *Short* (with no dollar amount) on the balance sheet, along with an explanatory note, or • With *only* the explanatory note
What is the ethical and legal challenge in accounting for current and contingent liabilities?	To ensure that the balance sheet (and the related notes) reports the *full amount of all* the business's current and contingent liabilities

SUMMARY PROBLEM

This problem consists of three independent parts.

Required

1. A **Wendy's** hamburger restaurant made cash sales of $4,000 subject to a 5% sales tax. Record the sales and the related sales tax. Also record Wendy's payment of the tax to the state government.
2. Assume that at April 30, 20X2, **H. J. Heinz Company** reported its 6% long-term debt as follows:

Current Liabilities (in part)

Portion of long-term debt due within one year	$ 14,000,000
Interest payable ($200,000,000 × 0.06 × 5/12)	5,000,000

Long-Term Debt and Other Liabilities (in part)

Long-term debt...	$186,000,000

The company pays interest on its long-term debt on November 30 each year.

Show how Heinz Company would report its liabilities on the year-end balance sheet one year later—April 30, 20X3. Assume that the current maturity of its long-term debt is $16 million.

3. What distinguishes a contingent liability from an actual liability?

Solution

1.

Cash ($4,000 × 1.05)	4,200	
Sales Revenue		4,000
Sales Tax Payable ($4,000 × 0.05)		200
To record cash sales and related sales tax.		
Sales Tax Payable...	200	
Cash		200
To pay sales tax to the state government.		

2. H. J. Heinz Company balance sheet at April 30, 20X3:

Current Liabilities (in part)

Portion of long-term debt due within one year	$ 16,000,000
Interest payable ($186,000,000 × 0.06 × 5/12)	4,650,000

Long-Term Debt and Other Liabilities (in part)

Long-term debt...	$170,000,000

3. A contingent liability is a *potential* liability, which may or may not become an actual liability.

Objective 3
Compute payroll amounts

ACCOUNTING FOR PAYROLL

Payroll costs are so important to most businesses that they adopt special systems to account for their labor costs. This section covers the basics of accounting for payroll.

Businesses often pay employees at a base rate for a set number of hours—called *straight time*. For working any additional hours—called *overtime*—the employee receives a higher rate.

Lucy Childres is an accountant for Bobby Jones Golf Company. Lucy earns $600 per week straight time. The company work week runs 40 hours, so Lucy's hourly straight-time pay is $15 ($600/40). Her company pays her *time and a half* for overtime. That rate is 150% (1.5 times) the straight-time rate. Thus, Lucy earns $22.50 for each hour of overtime she works ($15.00 × 1.5 = $22.50). For working 42 hours during a week, she earns $645, computed as follows:

Straight-time pay for 40 hours..	$600
Overtime pay for 2 overtime hours: 2 × $22.50..............	45
Total pay...	$645

Gross Pay and Net Pay

Before withholding taxes were introduced in 1943, employees brought home all they earned. Back in 1940, Lucy Childres would have taken home the full $645 that she made. Those days are long past.

The federal government, most state governments, and even some city governments require employers to act as collection agents for employee taxes. Employers then deduct the taxes from employee checks. Insurance companies, labor unions, and other organizations may also receive pieces of employees' pay. Amounts withheld from an employee's check are called *deductions*.

Gross pay is the total amount of salary, wages, commissions, or any other employee compensation before taxes and other deductions. **Net pay**—or "take-home pay"—equals gross pay minus all deductions. As Exhibit 11-3 shows, net pay is the amount the employee actually takes home.

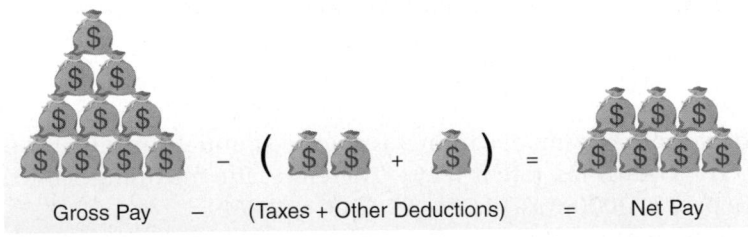

Gross Pay — (Taxes + Other Deductions) = Net Pay

EXHIBIT 11-3
Gross Pay and Net Pay

Many companies also pay employee *benefits*, another form of employee compensation. Examples include health and life insurance. Other examples include retirement pay and health insurance during the retirement years. Payroll accounting has become quite complex.

Payroll Deductions

Payroll deductions withheld from employees' pay fall into two categories: (1) *required deductions*, such as employee income tax and social security tax; and (2) *optional deductions* for union dues, insurance premiums, charitable contributions, and other amounts withheld at the employee's request. After their withholding, payroll deductions become the liability of the employer, who then must pay the outside party. For example, the employer pays the government the employee income tax withheld and pays the union the union dues withheld.

 DAILY EXERCISE 11-9

REQUIRED PAYROLL DEDUCTIONS: EMPLOYEE INCOME TAX   In the United States, the law requires most employers to withhold income tax from employees' pay. Income tax is the largest sources of national tax revenues. Employee income tax generates approximately 36% of tax receipts in the United States, 38% in Sweden, and 41% in Canada.

The amount of income tax deducted from gross pay is called **withheld income tax.** The amount withheld depends on the employee's gross pay and on the number of *withholding allowances* the employee claims.

All employees file a Form W-4 with their employer to indicate the number of allowances claimed for withholding purposes. Each allowance lowers the tax withheld from the employee's paycheck. An unmarried taxpayer can claim only one allowance; a childless married couple, up to two allowances; a married couple with one child, up to three allowances; and so on. Exhibit 11-4 shows a W-4 for R. C. Dean, who claims four allowances (line 5).

EXHIBIT 11-4 Form W-4

Form **W-4** Department of the Treasury Internal Revenue Service	**Employee's Withholding Allowance Certificate** ▶ **For Privacy Act and Paperwork Reduction Act Notice, see page 2.**	OMB No. 1545-0010 **2000**

1 Type or print your first name and middle initial	Last name	2 Your social security number
R. C.	Dean	344 ⋮ 86 ⋮ 4529

Home address (number and street or rural route)	3 ☐ Single ☒ Married ☐ Married, but withhold at higher Single rate.
4376 Palm Drive	**Note:** If married, but legally separated, or spouse is a nonresident alien, check the Single box.
City or town, state, and ZIP code	4 If your last name differs from that on your social security card, check
Fort Lauderdale, FL 33317	here. **You must call 1-800-772-1213 for a new card** . . . ▶ ☐

5	Total number of allowances you are claiming (from line **H** above **OR** from the applicable worksheet on page 2)	5	4
6	Additional amount, if any, you want withheld from each paycheck	6	$

7 I claim exemption from withholding for 2000, and I certify that I meet **BOTH** of the following conditions for exemption:
● Last year I had a right to a refund of **ALL** Federal income tax withheld because I had **NO** tax liability **AND**
● This year I expect a refund of **ALL** Federal income tax withheld because I expect to have **NO** tax liability.
If you meet both conditions, write "EXEMPT" here . . . . ▶ | 7 |

Under penalties of perjury, I certify that I am entitled to the number of withholding allowances claimed on this certificate, or I am entitled to claim exempt status.
Employee's signature
(Form is not valid
unless you sign it) ▶ *R. C. Dean*   Date ▶   7-22,1997

8 Employer's name and address (Employer: Complete lines 8 and 10 only if sending to the IRS.) Blumenthal's Crescent Square Shopping Center Fort Lauderdale, FL 33310	9 Office code (optional) 14	10 Employer identification number 83 ⋮ 19475

Cat. No. 10220Q

REQUIRED PAYROLL DEDUCTIONS: EMPLOYEE SOCIAL SECURITY (FICA) TAX The *Federal Insurance Contributions Act (FICA)*, also known as the Social Security Act, created the Social Security Tax. The Social Security program provides retirement, disability, and medical benefits. The law requires employers to withhold **Social Security (FICA) tax** from employees' pay. The FICA tax has two components:

1. Old age, survivors', and disability insurance (OASDI)
2. Health insurance (Medicare)

The amount of tax withheld from employees' pay varies from year to year. As of 2000, the OASDI portion of the tax applies to the first $76,200 of employee earnings in a year. The taxable amount of earnings is adjusted annually depending on the rate of inflation. The OASDI tax rate is 6.2%. Therefore, the maximum OASDI tax that an employee paid in 2000 was $4,724 ($76,200 × 0.062).

The Medicare portion of the FICA tax applies to all employee earnings. This tax rate is 1.45%. An employee thus pays a combined FICA tax rate of 7.65% (6.2% + 1.45%) of the first $76,200 of annual earnings, plus 1.45% of earnings above $76,200.

To ease the computational burden and focus on the concepts, we assume that the FICA tax is 8% of the first $75,000 of employee earnings each year. (Use these numbers when you complete this chapter's assignment material, unless instructed otherwise.) For each employee who earns $75,000 or more, the employer withholds $6,000 ($75,000 × 0.08) and sends that amount to the federal government. The employer records this employee tax in the account FICA Tax Payable.

Assume that Rex Jennings, an employee, earned $73,500 prior to December. Jennings' salary for December is $7,000. How much FICA tax will be withheld from his December paycheck? The computation is as follows:

Employee earnings subject to the tax in one year	$75,000
Employee earnings prior to the current pay period	−73,500
Current pay subject to FICA tax...	$ 1,500
FICA tax rate	×0.08
FICA tax to be withheld from current pay...........................	$ 120

OPTIONAL PAYROLL DEDUCTIONS As a convenience to employees, many companies make payroll deductions and disburse cash according to employee instructions. Union dues, insurance payments, payroll savings plans, and gifts to charities such as **United Way** and **Habitat for Humanity** are examples.

SOCIAL SECURITY TAX. Federal Insurance Contributions Act (FICA) tax, which is withheld from employees' pay. Also called **FICA tax.**

Many employers offer *cafeteria plans* that allow workers to select from a menu of insurance coverage. Suppose **Ford Motor Company** provides each employee with $450 of insurance coverage each month. One employee may use the monthly allowance to purchase only life insurance. Another employee may select only disability coverage. A third worker may choose a combination of life insurance and disability coverage.

Employer Payroll Taxes

Employers must bear the expense of at least three payroll taxes:

1. Employer Social Security (FICA) tax
2. State **unemployment compensation tax**
3. Federal **unemployment compensation tax.**

EMPLOYER FICA TAX   In addition to collecting the employee's Social Security tax, the employer also must pay into the program. The employer's Social Security tax is the same as the amount withheld from employee pay. Thus, the Social Security system is funded by equal contributions from employees and employers. Using our 8% and $75,000 annual pay figures, the maximum annual employer tax on each employee is $6,000 ($75,000 × 0.08). The employer records this payroll tax in the same FICA Tax Payable account that is used for the withholding from employee paychecks.

STATE AND FEDERAL UNEMPLOYMENT COMPENSATION TAXES   State and federal unemployment taxes are products of the Federal Unemployment Tax Act (FUTA). These taxes finance workmen's compensation for people who have been laid off from work. *In recent years, employers have paid a combined tax of 6.2% on the first $7,000 of each employee's annual earnings.* The proportion paid to the state is 5.4%, and 0.8% is paid to the federal government. The employer uses the accounts Federal Unemployment Tax Payable and State Unemployment Tax Payable. Exhibit 11-5 shows a typical disbursement of payroll costs by an employer company.

> **UNEMPLOYMENT COMPENSATION TAX.** Payroll tax paid by employers to the government, which uses the money to pay unemployment benefits to people who are out of work.

DAILY EXERCISE 11-10

DAILY EXERCISE 11-11

EXHIBIT 11-5
Typical Breakdown of Payroll Costs for One Employee

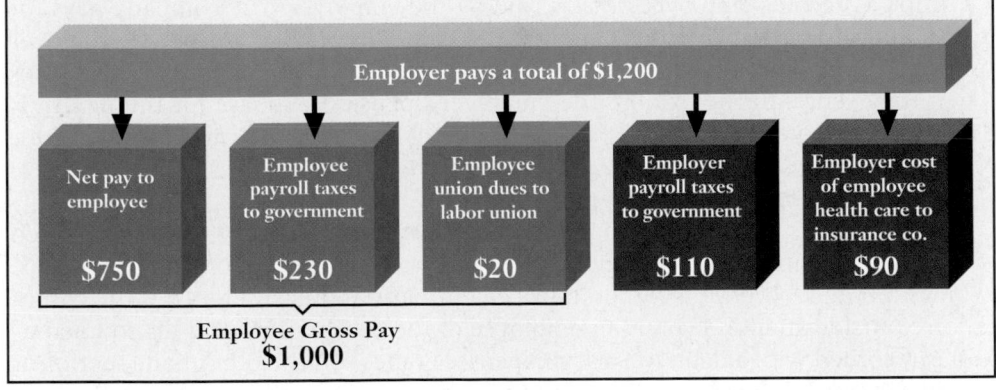

Payroll Entries

Exhibit 11-6 summarizes an employer's entries to record a monthly payroll of $10,000. All amounts are assumed for illustration only.

Entry A in Exhibit 11-6 records the employer's *salary expense*. The *gross salary* of all employees, $10,000, is their monthly pay before any deductions. The federal government imposes the income tax and the FICA tax. Most states and some cities also levy income taxes, which are accounted for in the same way. The union dues are optional. Employees' take-home (net) pay is $7,860. One important point about this payroll transaction is that the employees pay their own income and FICA taxes and union dues. The employer serves merely as collecting agent and sends these amounts to the government and the union.

Entry B records the employer's *payroll tax expense*. In addition to the employee's FICA tax ($800 in entry A), the employer also pays the $800 FICA tax

Objective 4
Record basic payroll transactions

DAILY EXERCISE 11-12

EXHIBIT 11-6 **Payroll Accounting by the Employer**

A. Salary Expense

Salary Expense (or Wage Expense or Commission Expense)	10,000	
Employee Income Tax Payable		1,200
FICA Tax Payable ($10,000 × 0.08)		800
Employee Union Dues Payable..		140
Salary Payable to Employees [take-home pay]		7,860
To record *salary expense*.		

B. Payroll Tax Expense

Payroll Tax Expense	1,420	
FICA Tax Payable ($10,000 × 0.08)		800
State Unemployment Tax Payable ($10,000 × 0.054).................		540
Federal Unemployment Tax Payable ($10,000 × 0.008)..............		80
To record employer's *payroll taxes*.		

C. Benefits Expense

Health Insurance Expense for Employees..	800	
Life Insurance Expense for Employees	200	
Pension Expense	500	
Employee Benefits Payable...		1,500
To record employee benefits payable by employer.		

Total Payroll Expense ($12,920) = Salary Expense ($10,000) + Payroll Tax Expense ($1,420)
+ Benefits Expense ($1,500)

in entry B. The other two employer payroll taxes are for state and federal unemployment. Employees do not pay the unemployment taxes. Only the employer pays them.

Entry C records employee *benefits* paid by the employer. The company pays for health and life insurance on its employees, a common practice. Also, the employer funds pensions (that is, pays cash into a pension plan) for the benefit of employees when they retire. In the exhibit, the employer's pension expense for the month is $500, and the total employer expense for benefits is $1,500. *The total payroll expense of the employer in Exhibit 11-6 is $12,920 (salary expense of $10,000 + payroll tax expense of $1,420 + benefits expense of $1,500).*

A company's payments to people who are not employees—outsiders called independent contractors—are *not* company payroll expenses. Consider two CPAs, Lyon and Franco. Lyon is a corporation's chief financial officer. Franco is the corporation's outside auditor. Lyon is an employee of the corporation, and his compensation is recorded with a debit to Salary Expense. Franco, on the other hand, performs consulting services for many clients, and the corporation debits Consulting Expense when it pays her. *Any payment for services performed by a person outside the company is a debit to an expense account other than payroll.*

 DAILY EXERCISE 11-13

 DAILY EXERCISE 11-14

 WORK IT OUT

Record the payroll and payroll taxes for the following information:

Gross salary (subject to all taxes)	$190,000
Employees' federal income tax withheld	35,800
Life insurance withheld from employees	2,000
FICA tax rate	8%
State unemployment tax rate................................	5.4%
Federal unemployment tax rate............................	0.8%

Answer

Payroll Entry:

Salary Expense	190,000	
FICA Tax Payable ($190,000 × 0.08)		15,200
Life Insurance Premium Payable		2,000
Employee Income Tax Payable		35,800
Salary Payable		137,000

Payroll Tax Entry:

Payroll Tax Expense	26,980	
FICA Tax Payable		15,200
State Unemployment Tax Payable ($190,000 × 0.054)		10,260
Federal Unemployment Tax Payable ($190,000 × 0.008)		1,520

THE PAYROLL SYSTEM

Objective 5
Use a payroll system

Good business means paying employees accurately and on time. Companies must handle both employees' and their own payroll taxes, as we have seen. Thus, companies process lots of payroll data. For accurate and timely payrolls, accountants have developed the *payroll system*.

The components of the payroll system are

- A payroll record
- A special payroll bank account
- Payroll checks
- An earnings record for each employee

Payroll Record

Each pay period the company organizes the payroll data in a special journal called the *payroll record* or *payroll journal*. This record lists each employee and the figures the business needs to record payroll amounts. The payroll record, which resembles the cash payments journal, also serves as a check register by providing a place to record each payroll check. ➡

A payroll record similar to that for **Blumenthal's** in Exhibit 11-7 is used by companies such as **Marriott Corp.,** the hotel chain. The *Gross Pay* section has columns for straight-time pay, overtime pay, and total gross pay for each employee. The *Deductions* columns vary from company to company, but every employer must deduct federal income tax and FICA tax. (State income tax is left out for convenience.) Additional column headings depend on the optional deductions the business handles. In Exhibit 11-7, the employer deducts employee payroll taxes, union dues, and gifts to **United Way,** and then sends the amounts to the proper parties. The *Net Pay* section lists each employee's net (take-home) pay and the number of the check issued to him or her. The last two columns indicate the *Account Debited* for the employee's gross pay. (The company has both office workers and salespeople.)

The payroll record in Exhibit 11-7 gives the employer the information needed to record salary expense for the pay period. Using the total amounts for columns (d) through (l), the employer records total salary expense as follows:

◄ We introduced the cash payments journal in Chapter 6, p. 242.

Dec. 31	Office Salary Expense	4,464.00	
	Sales Salary Expense	9,190.00	
	Employee Income Tax Payable		3,167.76
	FICA Tax Payable		861.94
	Employee Union Dues Payable		85.00
	Employee United Way Payable		155.00
	Salary Payable to Employees		9,384.30

 DAILY EXERCISE 11-15

Payroll Bank Account

After journalizing the payroll, the company books show a credit balance in Salary Payable to Employees for net pay of $9,384.30. (See column (i) in Exhibit 11-7.) How the business pays this liability depends on its payroll system. Many companies

Exhibit 11-7 **Blumenthal's Payroll Record**

Week ended December 31, 2000

			a	b	c	d	e	f	g	b	i	j	k	l
				Gross Pay			Deductions				Net Pay		Account Debited	
Employee Name	Hours		Straight-Time	Overtime	Total	Federal Income Tax	FICA Tax	Union Dues	United Way Charities	Total	(c – h) Amount	Check No.	Office Salary Expense	Sales Salary Expense
Chen, W. L.*	40		500.00		500.00	71.05	40.00	5.00	2.50	118.55	381.45	1621	500.00	
Dean, R. C.	46		400.00	90.00	490.00	59.94	39.20		2.00	101.14	388.86	1622		490.00
Ellis, M.	41		560.00	21.00	581.00	86.14	46.48	5.00		137.62	443.38	1623	581.00	
Trimble, E. A.†	40		1,360.00		1,360.00	463.22			15.00	478.22	881.78	1641		1,360.00
Total			12,940.00	714.00	13,654.00	3,167.76	861.94	85.00	155.00	4,269.70	9,384.30		4,464.00	9,190.00

*W. L. Chen earned gross pay of $500. His net pay was $381.45, paid with check number 1621. Chen is an office worker, so his salary is debited to Office Salary Expense.

†The business deducted no FICA tax from E. A. Trimble. She has already earned more than $75,000. Any employee whose earnings exceed this annual maximum pays no additional FICA tax during that year.

Note: For simplicity we ignore the additional tax for Medicare benefits.

pay employees from a special *payroll bank account.* The employer transfers the net pay ($9,384.30 in our illustration) from its regular bank account into the special payroll bank account. Then the company writes paychecks to employees from the payroll account. When the paychecks clear the bank, the payroll account has a zero balance. Writing paychecks from a separate bank account isolates payroll amounts for analysis and control, as we discuss later in the chapter.

Payroll Checks

Most companies pay employees by check or by electronic fund transfer (EFT). A *paycheck* is like any other check except that its attachment details the employee's payroll amounts. These figures come from the payroll record in Exhibit 11-7. Exhibit 11-8 shows payroll check number 1622, issued to R. C. Dean for net pay of $388.86 earned during the week ended December 31, 2000. To enhance your ability to use payroll data, trace all amounts on the check attachment to the payroll record in Exhibit 11-7.

EXHIBIT 11-8 **Payroll Check**

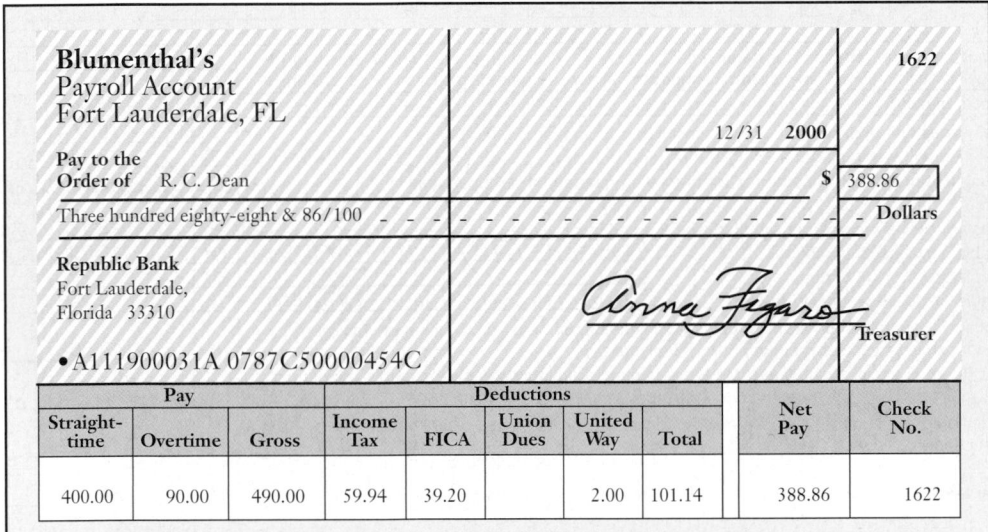

Pay			Deductions					Net Pay	Check No.
Straight-time	Overtime	Gross	Income Tax	FICA	Union Dues	United Way	Total		
400.00	90.00	490.00	59.94	39.20		2.00	101.14	388.86	1622

Increasingly, companies are paying employees by electronic funds transfer. The employee can authorize the company to make all deposits directly to his or her bank. With no check to deliver to the employee, the company saves time and money. As evidence of the deposit, most companies, including **American Airlines,** issue a voided check to employees. The employee doesn't have to receive, endorse, and deposit the paycheck.

Earnings Record

The employer must file payroll tax returns with the federal and state governments. Exhibit 11-9 (on page 444) is the Form 941 that Blumenthal's filed with the Internal Revenue Service for the quarter ended December 31, 2000. These forms must be filed no later than one month after the end of a quarter.

Line 13 of the exhibit shows that Blumenthal's payroll taxes for the quarter totaled $35,200. Line 14 indicates that during the quarter Blumenthal's paid the full tax bill, so the balance due on line 15 was zero. (There are heavy penalties for paying these taxes late.)

The employer must also provide the employee with a wage and tax statement, Form W-2, at the end of the year. Therefore, employers maintain an *earnings record* for each employee. Exhibit 11-10 (on page 445) is a five-week excerpt from the earnings record of employee R. C. Dean.

The employee earnings record is not a journal or a ledger, and it is not required by law. It is an accounting tool—like the work sheet—that the employer uses to prepare payroll tax reports to the Internal Revenue Service.

Exhibit 11-11 (on page 445) is the Wage and Tax Statement, Form W-2, for employee R. C. Dean. The employer prepares this statement and gives copies to the employee and to the Internal Revenue Service (IRS). Dean uses the W-2 to prepare

EXHIBIT 11-9   **Payroll Tax Return**

Form **941**		**Employer's Quarterly Federal Tax Return**			

(Rev. January 2000)
Department of the Treasury
Internal Revenue Service

► See separate instructions for information on completing this return.
Please type or print.

OMB No. 1545-0029

Enter state code for state in which deposits were made ONLY if different from state in address to the right ► **F:L** (see page 2 of instructions).

	T
	FF
	FD
	FP
	I
	T

Name (as distinguished from trade name)

Date quarter ended

Trade name, if any

Blumenthal's

Address (number and street)

Crescent Square Shopping Center
Fort Lauderdale, FL 33310-1234

Employer identification number

City, state, and ZIP code

If address is different from prior return, check here ►

IRS Use

```
1 1 1 1 1 1 1 1 1 1   2   3 3 3 3 3 3 3   4 4 4   5 5 5
                                                          
6   7   8 8 8 8 8 8 8   9 9 9 9   10 10 10 10 10 10 10 10 10 10
```

If you do not have to file returns in the future, check here ► ☐   and enter date final wages paid ►

If you are a seasonal employer, see **Seasonal employers** on page 1 of the instructions and check here ► ☐

1	Number of employees in the pay period that includes March 12th . ► **1**	**19**	
2	Total wages and tips, plus other compensation	**2**	113,654
3	Total income tax withheld from wages, tips, and sick pay	**3**	18,168
4	Adjustment of withheld income tax for preceding quarters of calendar year	**4**	—
5	Adjusted total of income tax withheld (line 3 as adjusted by line 4—see instructions)	**5**	18,168
6	Taxable social security wages . . . . . **6a** 110,774 × 12.4% (.124) =	**6b**	13,736
	Taxable social security tips . . . . . . **6c** × 12.4% (.124) =	**6d**	
7	Taxable Medicare wages and tips . . . **7a** 113,654 × 2.9% (.029) =	**7b**	3,296
8	Total social security and Medicare taxes (add lines 6b, 6d, and 7b). Check here if wages are not subject to social security and/or Medicare tax . . . . ► ☐	**8**	17,032
9	Adjustment of social security and Medicare taxes (see instructions for required explanation) Sick Pay $_____ ± Fractions of Cents $_____ ± Other $_____ =	**9**	—
10	Adjusted total of social security and Medicare taxes (line 8 as adjusted by line 9—see instructions)	**10**	17,032
11	**Total taxes** (add lines 5 and 10)	**11**	35,200
12	Advance earned income credit (EIC) payments made to employees	**12**	—
13	Net taxes (subtract line 12 from line 11). **If $1,000 or more, this must equal line 17, column (d) below (or line D of Schedule B (Form 941))**	**13**	35,200
14	Total deposits for quarter, including overpayment applied from a prior quarter	**14**	35,200
15	**Balance due** (subtract line 14 from line 13). See instructions	**15**	−0−
16	**Overpayment.** If line 14 is more than line 13, enter excess here ► $_____ and check if to be: ☐ Applied to next return **OR** ☐ Refunded.		

● **All filers:** If line 13 is less than $1,000, you need not complete line 17 or Schedule B (Form 941).
● **Semiweekly schedule depositors:** Complete Schedule B (Form 941) and check here . . . . ► ☐
● **Monthly schedule depositors:** Complete line 17, columns (a) through (d), and check here. . . . . ► ☐

17	**Monthly Summary of Federal Tax Liability.** Do not complete if you were a semiweekly schedule depositor.		
(a) First month liability	**(b)** Second month liability	**(c)** Third month liability	**(d)** Total liability for quarter
35,017	35,336	34,967	35,200

Sign Here   Under penalties of perjury, I declare that I have examined this return, including accompanying schedules and statements, and to the best of my knowledge and belief, it is true, correct, and complete.

Signature ► *Anna Figaro*   Print Your Name and Title ► Anna Figaro, Treasurer   Date ► 1/30/00

For Privacy Act and Paperwork Reduction Act Notice, see back of Payment Voucher.   Cat. No. 17001Z   Form **941** (Rev. 1-2000)

his income tax return. To ensure that Dean is paying income tax on all his income from that job, the IRS matches Dean's income as reported on his tax return with his earnings as reported on the W-2.

Paying the Payroll

Up to this point, we have talked about the recording of payroll expenses. We now turn to the *payment* of these liabilities. Most employers must record at least three cash payments for payrolls:

- net pay to employees
- payroll taxes to the government and other payroll deductions
- employee benefits

EXHIBIT 11-10 **Employee Earnings Record for 2000**

EMPLOYEE NAME AND ADDRESS:

DEAN, R. C.
4376 PALM DRIVE
FORT LAUDERDALE, FL 33317

SOCIAL SECURITY NO.: 344-86-4529
MARITAL STATUS: MARRIED
WITHHOLDING EXEMPTIONS: 4
PAY RATE: $400 PER WEEK
JOB TITLE: SALESPERSON

		Gross Pay				Deductions					Net Pay	
Week Ended	Hrs.	Straight-Time	Over-time	Total	To Date	Federal Income Tax	FICA Tax	Union Dues	United Way Charity	Total	Amount	Check No.
Dec. 3	40	400.00		400.00	21,340.00	42.19	32.00		2.00	76.19	323.81	1525
Dec. 10	40	400.00		400.00	21,740.00	42.19	32.00		2.00	76.19	323.81	1548
Dec. 17	44	400.00	60.00	460.00	22,200.00	54.76	36.80		2.00	93.56	366.44	1574
Dec. 24	48	400.00	120.00	520.00	22,720.00	66.75	41.60		2.00	110.35	409.65	1598
Dec. 31	46	400.00	90.00	490.00	23,210.00	59.94	39.20		2.00	101.14	388.86	1622
Total		20,800.00	2,410.00	23,210.00		1,946.72	1,856.80		104.00	3,907.52	19,302.48	

a Control number 22222 Void ☐ For Official Use Only ► OMB No. 1545-0008

b Employer identification number 83-19475	1 Wages, tips, other compensation 23,210.00	2 Federal income tax withheld 1,946.72
c Employer's name, address, and ZIP code Blumenthal's Crescent Square Shopping Center Fort Lauderdale, FL 33310-1234	3 Social security wages 23,210.00	4 Social security tax withheld 1,439.02
	5 Medicare wages and tips 23,210.00	6 Medicare tax withheld 417.78
	7 Social security tips	8 Allocated tips
d Employee's social security number 344-86-4529	9 Advance EIC payment	10 Dependent care benefits
e Employee's name (first, middle initial, last) R. C. Dean	11 Nonqualified plans	12 Benefits included in box 1
4376 Palm Drive Fort Lauderdale, FL 33317	13 See instrs. for box 13	14 Other
f Employee's address and ZIP code	15 Statutory employee ☐ Deceased ☐ Pension plan ☐	Legal rep. ☐ Deferred compensation ☐

16 State Employer's state I.D. no.	17 State wages, tips, etc.	18 State income tax	19 Locality name	20 Local wages, tips, etc.	21 Local income tax

Form **W-2** **Wage and Tax Statement** **2000**

Department of the Treasury—Internal Revenue Service
For Privacy Act and Paperwork Reduction Act Notice, see separate instructions.

Copy A For Social Security Administration—Send this entire page with Form W-3 to the Social Security Administration; photocopies are **not** acceptable.

Cat. No. 10134D

EXHIBIT 11-11
Employee Wage and Tax Statement, Form W-2

NET PAY TO EMPLOYEES When the company pays employees, it debits Salary Payable to Employees and credits Cash. Using the data in Exhibit 11-7, the company would make the following entry to record the cash payment (column (i)) for the December 31 weekly payroll:

Dec. 31	Salary Payable to Employees	9,384.30	
	Cash		9,384.30

PAYROLL TAXES TO THE GOVERNMENT AND OTHER PAYROLL DEDUCTIONS The employer must send the government two sets of payroll taxes: those withheld from employees' pay and those paid by the employer. In Exhibit 11-7, columns (d) through (g), the business would record a series of cash payment entries that can be summarized as follows (the unemployment tax amounts are assumed):

Dec. 31	Employee Income Tax Payable	3,167.76	
	FICA Tax Payable ($861.94 × 2)	1,723.88	
	Employee Union Dues Payable	85.00	
	Employee United Way Payable	155.00	
	State Unemployment Tax Payable	104.62	
	Federal Unemployment Tax Payable	15.50	
	Cash		5,251.76

⊙ DAILY EXERCISE 11-16

BENEFITS The employer might pay for employees' insurance coverage and their pension plan. If the total cash payment for these benefits is $1,927.14, the entry is

| Dec. 31 | Employee Benefits Payable | 1,927.14 | |
| | Cash | | 1,927.14 |

Many companies provide *postretirement benefits* such as medical insurance for retired workers. The companies accrue this liability during the employees' working years and then pay it off during their retirement.

Internal Control over Payroll

The internal controls over cash payments discussed in Chapter 7 apply to payroll. The large number of transactions and the complex arrangements increase the risk of a control failure. There are two main types of special controls for payroll: controls for efficiency and controls for safeguarding payroll disbursements.

CONTROLS FOR EFFICIENCY Reconciling the bank account can be time-consuming because of the large number of paychecks. For example, a March 30 paycheck would probably clear the bank before a March 31 bank statement. This check and others would be outstanding. A large number of outstanding checks for the bank reconciliation increases accounting expense. To limit the number of outstanding paychecks, many companies use two payroll bank accounts. They pay the payroll from one bank account one month and from the other payroll account the next month. This way they can reconcile each account every other month. In this system, a March 30 paycheck has until April 30 to clear the bank before the account is reconciled. Outstanding checks are almost eliminated, the bank reconciliation is streamlined, and accounting expense decreases.

Payroll transactions are ideal for computer processing. Employee payroll data are stored in a file. Each pay period, keyboarders enter the number of hours worked by each employee. The computer makes all calculations, prints the payroll record and the paychecks, and updates employee earnings records. The program also computes payroll taxes and prepares the quarterly tax reports.

CONTROLS FOR SAFEGUARDING PAYROLL DISBURSEMENTS Owners and managers of small businesses can monitor their payrolls by personal contact with employees. Large corporations cannot. These businesses must establish controls to ensure that paychecks go only to legitimate employees and for the correct amounts. A particular danger is that a paycheck may be written to a fictitious employee and cashed by a dishonest employee. To guard against this and other crimes, large businesses adopt strict internal control policies.

The duties of hiring and firing employees should be separated from the duties of payroll accounting and passing out paychecks. Requiring a photo ID also helps internal control. Issuing paychecks only to employees with badges ensures that only actual employees receive pay.

A formal timekeeping system helps ensure that employees actually worked the number of hours claimed. Having employees punch time cards at the start and end of the workday proves their attendance.

⊙ DAILY EXERCISE 11-17

As we saw in Chapter 7, the key to good internal control is separation of duties. The responsibilities of the personnel department, the payroll department, the accounting department, time-card management, and paycheck distribution should be separate.

THINK IT OVER

Centurion Homes of Omaha, Nebraska, builds houses with four construction crews. The foremen hire—and fire—workers and keep their hourly records. Each Friday morning, the foremen telephone their workers' hours to the home office, where accountants prepare the weekly paychecks. Around noon, the foremen pick up the paychecks. They return to the construction site and pay the workers at day's end. What is the internal control weakness in this situation? Propose a way to improve the internal controls.

Answer: Construction workers often have limited contact with the home office. The foremen control most of the payroll information, so they can forge the payroll records of fictitious employees and pocket their pay. To improve internal control, Centurion could hire and fire all workers through the home office. This practice would establish the identity of all workers listed in the payroll records. Another way to improve the internal controls would be to have a home-office employee distribute paychecks on a surprise basis. Any unclaimed checks would arouse suspicion. This system would probably prevent foremen from cheating the company.

REPORTING PAYROLL EXPENSE AND LIABILITIES

On the balance sheet, **IBM** and other companies report the amount of *payroll liability* owed to all parties—employees, governments, unions, and so on. Payroll liability is *not* the payroll expense for the year. The liability at year end is the amount of the expense that is still unpaid. Payroll expense appears on the income statement payroll liability on the balance sheet. On a recent balance sheet, IBM reported compensation and benefits payable of $3,840 million as a current liability as shown in Exhibit 11-12. The exhibit also presents the other current liabilities we have discussed.

Objective 6
Report current liabilities on the balance sheet

Current Liabilities	Millions
Taxes payable	$ 4,792
Short-term debt	14,230
Accounts payable	6,400
Compensation and benefits payable	3,840
Unearned revenue	4,529
Other accrued expenses and liabilities	5,787
Total current liabilities	**$39,578**

EXHIBIT 11-12
IBM Balance Sheet (partial, adapted) December 31, 1999

 DAILY EXERCISE 11-18

 DAILY EXERCISE 11-19

The following Decision Guidelines feature summarizes some of the more important payroll decisions that a business must consider.

DECISION GUIDELINES

Accounting for Payroll

DECISION	GUIDELINES
What are the key elements of a payroll accounting system?	• Employee's Withholding Allowance Certificate, Form W-4 • Payroll register • Payroll bank account and payroll checks • Employer's quarterly tax returns, such as Form 941 • Employee earnings record • Employee wage and tax statement, Form W-2
What are the key terms in the payroll area?	Gross pay (Total amount earned by the employee) − *Payroll deductions* a. Withheld income tax b. FICA (Social Security) tax—equal amount also payable by employer c. Optional deductions (insurance, savings, charitable contributions, union dues) = *Net (take-home) pay*
What is the employer's total payroll expense?	Gross pay + *Employer's payroll taxes* a. FICA (Social Security) tax—equal amount also payable by employee b. State and federal unemployment taxes + *Benefits for employees* a. Insurance (health, life, and disability) b. Pension (and other retirement) benefits c. Club memberships and other = *Employer's total payroll costs*
Where to report payroll costs?	• Payroll expenses on the income statement • Payroll liabilities on the balance sheet

REVIEW CURRENT LIABILITIES

SUMMARY PROBLEM

www.prenhall.com/horngren
End-of-Chapter Assessment

Beth Denius, Limited, a clothing store, employs one salesperson, Alan Kingsley. His straight-time salary is $360 per week. He earns time and a half for hours worked in excess of 40 per week. The owner, Beth Denius, withholds income tax (11.0%) and FICA tax (8.0%) from Kingsley's pay. She pays the following employer payroll taxes: FICA (8.0%) and state and federal unemployment (5.4% and 0.8%, respectively). In addition, Denius contributes to a pension plan an amount equal to 10% of Kingsley's gross pay.

During the week ended December 26, 20X4, Kingsley worked 48 hours. Prior to this week, Kingsley had earned $5,470.

Required

1. Compute Kingsley's gross pay and net pay for the week.
2. Record the following payroll entries that Denius would make:
   a. Expense for Kingsley's salary, including overtime pay
   b. Employer payroll taxes
   c. Expense for employee benefits
   d. Payment of cash to Kingsley
   e. Payment of all payroll taxes
   f. Payment for employee benefits
3. How much total payroll expense did Denius incur for the week? How much cash did the business spend on its payroll?

Solutions

Requirement 1

Gross pay:	Straight-time pay for 40 hours		$360.00
	Overtime pay:		
	Rate per hour ($360/40 × 1.5)	$13.50	
	Hours (48 − 40)	8	108.00
	Total gross pay		$468.00
Net pay:	Gross pay		$468.00
	Less: Withheld income tax ($468 × 0.11)	$51.48	
	Withheld FICA tax ($468 × 0.08)	37.44	88.92
	Net pay..		$379.08

Requirement 2

a.	Sales Salary Expense	468.00	
	Employee Income Tax Payable		51.48
	FICA Tax Payable..		37.44
	Salary Payable to Employee		379.08
b.	Payroll Tax Expense	66.45	
	FICA Tax Payable ($468 × 0.08)		37.44
	State Unemployment Tax Payable ($468 × 0.054)		25.27
	Federal Unemployment Tax Payable (468 × 0.008)		3.74
c.	Pension Expense ($468 × 0.10)...	46.80	
	Employee Benefits Payable...		46.80
d.	Salary Payable to Employee	379.08	
	Cash		379.08
e.	Employee Income Tax Payable...	51.48	
	FICA Tax Payable ($37.44 × 2)	74.88	
	State Unemployment Tax Payable	25.27	
	Federal Unemployment Tax Payable....................................	3.74	
	Cash		155.37
f.	Employee Benefits Payable	46.80	
	Cash		46.80

Requirement 3

- Denius incurred *total payroll expense* of $581.25 (gross salary of $468.00 + payroll taxes of $66.45 + benefits of $46.80). See entries (a) through (c).
- Denius *paid cash* of $581.25 on payroll (Kingsley's net pay of $379.08 + payroll taxes of $155.37 + benefits of $46.80). See entries (d) through (f).

LESSONS LEARNED

1. *Account for current liabilities of known amount.* Trade accounts payable, short-term notes payable, interest payable, sales tax payable, payrolls, and unearned revenues are current liabilities of known amount.

2. *Account for current liabilities that must be estimated.* Current liabilities that must be estimated include warranties payable, vacation pay, and corporations' income tax payable. *Contingent liabilities* are potential liabilities that may arise in the future.

3. *Compute payroll amounts. Payroll* accounting handles the expenses and liabilities arising from compensating employees. Employers must withhold income and FICA taxes from employees' pay and send these tax amounts to the government. In addition, many employers allow employees to pay for insurance and union dues and to make gifts to charities through payroll deductions. An employee's net pay is the gross pay less all payroll taxes and optional deductions.

4. *Record basic payroll transactions.* An *employer's* payroll expenses include FICA and unemployment taxes, which are separate from the payroll taxes borne by the employees. Also, most employers provide employees with benefits such as insurance coverage and pensions.

5. *Use a payroll system.* A *payroll system* consists of a payroll record, a payroll bank account, payroll checks, and an earnings record for each employee. Good *internal controls* over payrolls help the business to achieve efficiency and to safeguard the company's cash.

6. *Report current liabilities on the balance sheet.* The company reports on the balance sheet all current liabilities that it owes: current liabilities of known amount, including payroll liabilities, and current liabilities that must be estimated.

ACCOUNTING VOCABULARY

accrued expense (p. 430)
accrued liability (p. 430)
current portion of long-term debt (p. 429)
current maturity (p. 429)
discounting a note payable (p. 427)

employee compensation (p. 430)
FICA tax (p. 438)
gross pay (p. 437)
net pay (p. 437)
payroll (p. 430)
short presentation (p. 434)
short-term note payable (p. 426)

Social Security tax (p. 438)
unemployment compensation tax (p. 439)
withheld income tax (p. 437)

QUESTIONS

1. What distinguishes a current liability from a long-term liability? What distinguishes a contingent liability from an actual liability?
2. A company purchases a machine by signing a $21,000, one-year, 10% note payable on July 31. Interest is to be paid at maturity. What two current liabilities related to this purchase does the company report on its December 31 balance sheet? What is the amount of each current liability?
3. Explain why sales tax that is paid by consumers is a liability of the store that sold the merchandise.
4. What is meant by the term *current portion of long-term debt,* and how is this item reported in the financial statements?
5. At the beginning of the school term, what type of account is the tuition that your college or university collects from students? What type of account is the tuition at the end of the school term?
6. Patton Company warrants its products against defects for three years from date of sale. During the current year, the company made sales of $300,000. Store management estimated that warranty costs on those sales would total 6% of sales over the three-year warranty period. Ultimately, the company paid $22,000 cash on warranties. What was the company's warranty expense for the year? What accounting principle governs this answer?

7. Why is payroll expense more important to a service business such as a CPA firm than it is to a merchandising company such as **Target?**
8. Two persons are studying Allen Company's manufacturing process. One person is Allen's factory supervisor, and the other is an outside consultant who is an expert in the industry. Which person's salary is the payroll expense of Allen Company? Identify the expense account that Allen would debit to record the pay of each person.
9. What are two elements of an employer's payroll expense in addition to salaries, wages, commissions, and overtime pay?
10. What are FICA taxes? Who pays them? What are the funds used for?
11. Identify two required deductions and four optional deductions from employee paychecks.
12. Who pays state and federal unemployment taxes? What are these funds used for?
13. How much Social Security tax is withheld from the pay of an employee who earns $70,000 during the current year? How much Social Security tax is withheld if the employee earns $77,000?
14. Identify three internal controls designed to safeguard payroll cash.

ASSESS YOUR PROGRESS

DAILY EXERCISES

Accounts payable and notes payable (Obj. 1)

DE11-1 Describe the similarities and the differences between an account payable and a short-term note payable. If necessary, review notes receivable in Chapter 8.

Accounting for a note payable (Obj. 1)

DE11-2 Return to the $8,000 purchase of inventory on a short-term note payable that begins on page 426. Assume that the purchase of inventory occurred on June 30, 20X1, instead of September 30, 20X1. Journalize the company's (a) purchase of inventory, (b) accrual of interest expense on December 31, 20X1, and (c) payment of the note plus interest on June 30, 20X2.

Reporting a short-term note payable and the related interest in the financial statements (Obj. 1)

DE11-3 This exercise should be done in conjunction with Daily Exercise 11-2.

1. Refer to the data in Daily Exercise 11-2. Show what the company would report for the note payable on its balance sheet at December 31, 20X1, and on its income statement for the year ended on that date.
2. What one item will the financial statements for the year ended December 31, 20X2, report? Identify the financial statement, the item, and its amount.

Accounting for a discounted note payable (Obj. 1)

DE11-4 Accounting for a discounted note payable is illustrated for a $100,000 note at the top of page 427.

1. Why did **Procter & Gamble (P&G)** sign the note payable? What did P&G receive?
2. Suppose P&G signed the note payable on November 16, 20X1, instead of November 25, 20X1. Make P&G's adjusting entry to accrue interest expense at December 31, 20X1.
3. Show how P&G would report the note payable on its balance sheet at December 31, 20X1.
4. Journalize P&G's interest expense and payment of the note payable at maturity. Give the date.

DE11-5 The chapter opening story describes the airlines' frequent-flier programs. Suppose passengers fly 1,000,000 miles on **American Airlines** and the AAdvantage® frequent-flier program costs American $.0015 per mile. During the next six months, AAdvantage® customers use 200,000 of the miles for free trips on American Airlines.

Accounting for unearned revenue (Obj. 1)

1. Using American Airlines' actual account titles (see Exhibit 11-1), journalize American's (a) accrual of Promotion Expense and Air Traffic Liability and (b) the provision of free transportation for the AAdvantage® customers (credit Cash). Explanations are not required.
2. Post to the Air Traffic Liability T-account. How much does American Airlines owe the AAdvantage® customers after the preceding transactions?

DE11-6 **Ford,** the automaker, guarantees its automobiles for three years or 36,000 miles, whichever comes first. Suppose Ford's experience indicates that the company can expect warranty costs during the three-year period to add up to 5% of sales.

Accounting for warranty expense and estimated warranty payable (Obj. 2)

Assume that Five Points Ford in Cincinnati made sales of Ford Escorts totaling $600,000 during 20X7, its first year of operations. The company received cash for 30% of the sales and notes receivable for the remainder. Payments to satisfy customer warranty claims totaled $22,000 during 20X7.

1. Record the sales, warranty expense, and warranty payments for Five Points Ford.
2. Post to the Estimated Warranty Payable T-account. At the end of 20X7, how much in estimated warranty payable does Five Points Ford owe its customers? Why must the warranty payable amount be estimated?

DE11-7 Refer to the data given in Daily Exercise 11-6.

Applying GAAP; reporting warranties in the financial statements (Obj. 2)

What amount of warranty expense will Five Points Ford report during 20X7? Which accounting principle addresses this situation? Does the warranty expense for the year equal the year's cash payments for warranties? Explain how the accounting principle works for measuring warranty expense.

DE11-8 **Harley-Davidson, Inc.,** the motorcycle manufacturer, included the following note (adapted) in its annual report:

Interpreting a company's contingent liabilities (Obj. 2)

NOTES TO CONSOLIDATED FINANCIAL STATEMENTS

7 (In Part): Commitments and Contingencies

The Company self-insures its product liability losses in the United States up to $3 million (catastrophic coverage is maintained for individual claims in excess of $3 million up to $25 million). Outside the United States, the Company is insured for product liability up to $25 million per individual claim and in the aggregate.

---

1. Why are these *contingent* (versus real) liabilities?
2. In the United States, how can the contingent liability become a real liability for Harley-Davidson? What are the limits to the company's product liabilities in the United States? Explain how these limits work.
3. How can a contingency outside the United States become a real liability for the company? How does Harley-Davidson's potential liability differ for claims outside the United States?

DE11-9 Consider the operations of a **Wendy's** restaurant, **Toyota Motor Corporation,** and a large accounting firm. Rank these businesses in terms of the percentage of labor cost to the company's total expenses—from most important to least important. Give the reason for your ranking.

Assessing the importance of payroll expenses (Obj. 3)

Daily Exercise 11-10 begins a sequence of exercises that ends with Daily Exercise 11-12.
DE11-10 Examine the payroll situation of Lucy Childres on page 437.

Computing an employee's total pay (Obj. 3)

1. Compute Childres's total pay for working 50 hours during the first week of February.
2. Childres is single, and her income tax withholding is 9% of total pay. Her only payroll deductions are payroll taxes. Compute Childres's net pay for the week. (Use an 8% FICA tax rate.)

DE11-11 Return to the Lucy Childres payroll situation in Daily Exercise 11-10. Childres's employer, Bobby Joncs Golf Company, pays all the standard payroll taxes plus benefits for employee pensions (6% of total pay), health insurance ($60 per employee per month), and disability insurance ($8 per employee per month).

Computing total payroll expense of an employer (Obj. 3)

Compute Bobby Jones's total expense of employing Lucy Childres for the 50 hours that she worked during the first week of February. Carry amounts to the nearest cent.

DE11-12 After solving Daily Exercises 11-10 and 11-11, journalize for Bobby Jones Golf Company the following expenses related to the employment of Lucy Childres:

Making payroll entries (Obj. 4)

a. Salary expense   **b.** Employer payroll taxes   **c.** Benefits

Use Exhibit 11-6 (p. 440) to format your journal entries. Carry all amounts to the nearest cent.

Computing payroll amounts late
in the year
(Obj. 3)

DE11-13 Suppose you have worked for an accounting firm all year and you earn a monthly salary of $8,000. Your withheld income taxes consume 15% of your gross pay. In addition to payroll taxes, which are required, you elect to contribute 5% monthly to your pension plan. Your employer also deducts $200 monthly for your co-pay of the health insurance premium.

Compute your net pay for October. Use an 8% FICA tax rate on the first $75,000 of income.

DE11-14 Exhibit 11-5, page 439, shows the breakdown of an employer's total payroll cost of $1,180 for one employee. Journalize the employer's (a) salary expense (use a single Payroll Tax Payable account), (b) payroll taxes (use a single Payroll Tax Payable account), and (c) cost of health insurance. Follow the pattern of the entries in Exhibit 11-6, page 440.

DE11-15 Refer to the payroll record in Exhibit 11-7, page 442.

1. How much cash did the employees take home for their work this week?
2. How much was the company's total salary expense for the week? What accounts were debited? How much was debited to each account?
3. How much did *employees* pay this week for
   a. Withheld federal income tax?
   b. Withheld FICA tax?
4. How much expense did the *employer* have this week for
   a. Employee federal income tax?
   b. FICA tax?
5. Which employees earned less than $75,000, and which employees earned more than $75,000 this year? How can you tell?

Using a payroll system to compute total payroll expense
(Obj. 5)

DE11-16 Study the Employee Earnings Record for R. C. Dean in Exhibit 11-10, page 445. In addition to the amounts shown in the exhibit, the employer also paid all payroll taxes plus (a) an amount equal to 7% of gross pay into Dean's pension retirement account, and (b) health insurance for Dean at a cost of $140 per month.

Compute the employer's total payroll expense for employee R. C. Dean during 2000. Carry all amounts to the nearest cent.

DE11-17 ◄= *Link Back to Chapter 7 (Internal Controls)*

1. What are some of the important elements of good internal control to safeguard payroll disbursements?
2. Explain how the use of two payroll bank accounts (one account the first month, the other account the next month) makes accounting for the payroll of a large company more efficient. Identify another control for efficiency in the payroll area.

DE11-18 Study the payroll record of **Blumenthal's** in Exhibit 11-7, page 442. Assume Blumenthal's will pay this payroll on January 2, 2001. In addition to the payroll liabilities shown in the exhibit, Blumenthal's has the following liabilities at December 31, 2000:

Accounts payable..................	$44,140	Current portion of	
Employer FICA tax payable....	862	long-term debt	$20,000
Long-term debt......................	80,000	Interest payable	1,116
Unearned revenue.................	4,430	Contingent liabilities..............	—

Prepare the current liabilities section of Blumenthal's balance sheet at December 31, 2000. List current liabilities in descending order starting with the largest first. Also list each of the payroll liabilities from Exhibit 11-7, rounded to the nearest dollar. Show the total of current liabilities.

Interpreting the current liabilities
of a company
(Obj. 6)

DE11-19 Refer to **IBM Corporation's** current liabilities in Exhibit 11-12, page 447.

1. Explain in your own words each of the company's current liabilities.
2. When will IBM pay these liabilities? When is the latest date that IBM will pay the liabilities? How can you tell?

EXERCISES

E11-1 Make general journal entries to record the following transactions of Club Lanai Vacation Co. for a two-month period. Explanations are not required.

March 31   Recorded cash sales of $200,000 for the month, plus sales tax of 5% collected on behalf of the state of Arizona. Recorded sales tax in a separate account.
April   6   Sent March sales tax to the state.

Required

Journalize these transactions a second time. Record the sales tax initially in the Sales Revenue account.

E11-2 Pier 1 Imports, Inc., reported the following current liabilities (adapted, all amounts in thousands):

Analyzing current liabilities (Obj. 1)

	February 28,	
	20X2	**20X1**
Accrued payroll liabilities..................	$27,194	$25,068
Gift certificates outstanding	11,276	8,242

Required

1. The purpose of this requirement is to show how Pier 1's ending balance of accrued payroll liabilities arose from the company's transactions during the year ended February 28, 20X2. Create a T-account for accrued Payroll Liabilities. Insert the balance at February 28, 20X1 as the beginning balance. Assume that during the year ended February 28, 20X2, Pier 1 accrued payroll expense of $265,000 and paid $262,874 of this total. Post both amounts directly into the Accrued Payroll Liabilities T-account and compute its ending balance. Compare your result to Pier 1's actual ending balance. The two amounts should be the same.
2. Explain the nature of Pier 1's Gift certificates outstanding. What is another name for this account?

E11-3 Assume **The Dallas Morning News** publishing company completed the following transactions during 20X1:

Recording and reporting current liabilities (Obj. 1)

Nov. 1   Sold a six-month subscription, collecting cash of $120, plus sales tax of 5%.
Dec. 15   Remitted (paid) the sales tax to the state of Texas.
    31   Made the necessary adjustment at year end to record the amount of subscription revenue earned during the year.

Required

Journalize these transactions (explanations are not required). Then report the liability on the company's balance sheet at December 31, 20X1.

E11-4 The accounting records of Blaze Electronics included the following balances at the end of the period:

Accounting for warranty expense and the related liability (Obj. 2)

ESTIMATES WARRANTY PAYABLE	SALES REVENUE	WARRANTY EXPENSE
Beg. bal. 3,100	161,000	

In the past, Blaze's warranty expense has been 7% of sales. During the current period, the business paid $10,400 to satisfy the warranty claims of customers.

Required

1. Journalize Blaze's warranty expense for the period and the company's cash payments during the period to satisfy warranty claims. Explanations are not required.
2. What ending balance of Estimated Warranty Payable will Blaze report on its balance sheet?

E11-5 Record the following note payable transactions of Carnegie Publishing, Inc., in the company's general journal. Explanations are not required.

Recording note payable transactions (Obj. 1)

20X2
Apr. 1   Purchased equipment costing $15,000 by issuing a one-year, 8% note payable.
Dec. 31   Accrued interest on the note payable.

20X3
Apr. 1   Paid the note payable at maturity.

E11-6 On September 1, 20X4, Tic-Toc Watch Repair discounted a six-month, $12,000 note payable to the bank at 8%.

Discounting a note payable (Obj. 1)

Required

1. Prepare general journal entries to record (a) issuance of the note, (b) accrual of interest at December 31, and (c) payment of the note at maturity in 20X5. Explanations are not required.
2. Show how Tic-Toc would report the note on the December 31, 20X4, balance sheet.

E11-7 Vanguard Security Systems is a defendant in lawsuits brought against the marketing and distribution of its products. Damages of $9.1 million are claimed against Vanguard, but the company denies the charges and is vigorously defending itself. In a recent press conference, the president of the company said management does not believe that any

Reporting a contingent liability (Obj. 3)

actual liabilities resulting from the lawsuits will significantly affect the company's financial position.

Required

Write Note X to describe the contingency.

Reporting current liabilities (Obj. 6)

E11-8 ◀ *Link Back to Chapter 4 (Current Ratio).* The owner of Ciliotta Pharmacy examines the company accounting records at December 29, immediately before the end of the year:

Total current assets..................	$ 490,000
Noncurrent assets.....................	730,000
	$1,220,000
Total current liabilities..............	$ 260,000
Noncurrent liabilities................	300,000
Owner's equity	660,000
	$1,220,000

Ciliotta's borrowing agreements with creditors require the company to keep a current ratio of 2.0 or better. How much in current liabilities should Ciliotta pay off within the next two days in order to comply with its borrowing agreements?

Computing net pay (Obj. 3)

E11-9 Ken Shermac is manager of the men's department of Parisian Department Store in Birmingham. He earns a base monthly salary of $750 plus a 10% commission on his personal sales. Through payroll deductions, Shermac donates $25 per month to a charitable organization, and he authorizes Parisian to deduct $22.50 monthly for his family's health insurance. Tax rates on Shermac's earnings are 10% for income tax and 8% of the first $75,000 for FICA. During the first 11 months of the year, he earned $72,140.

Required

Compute Shermac's gross pay and net pay for December, assuming his sales for the month are $80,000.

Computing and recording gross pay and net pay (Obj. 3, 4)

E11-10 Ruby Degrate works for a Steak 'n Shake diner for straight-time earnings of $6 per hour, with time-and-a-half compensation for hours in excess of 40 per week. Degrate's payroll deductions include withheld income tax of 7% of total earnings, FICA tax of 8% of total earnings, and a weekly deduction of $5 for a charitable contribution to United Fund.

Required

Assuming she worked 50 hours during the week, (a) compute her gross pay and net pay for the week, and (b) make a general journal entry to record the store's wage expense for Degrate's work, including her payroll deductions. Explanations are not required. Round all amounts to the nearest cent.

Recording a payroll (Obj. 3, 4)

E11-11 Clarkson Eyecare incurred salary expense of $92,000 for December. The store's payroll expense includes employer FICA tax of 8% in addition to state unemployment tax of 5.4% and federal unemployment tax of 0.8%. Of the total salaries, $88,400 is subject to FICA tax, and $9,100 is subject to unemployment tax. Also, the store provides the following benefits for employees: health insurance (cost to the store, $2,062.15), life insurance (cost to the store, $351.07), and pension benefits (cost to the store, 8% of salary expense).

Required

Record Clarkson's payroll taxes and its expenses for employee benefits. Explanations are not required.

Reporting payroll expense and liabilities (Obj. 6)

E11-12 Norwest Bank has annual salary expense of $900,000. In addition, the bank incurs payroll tax expense equal to 9% of the total payroll. At December 31, the end of the bank's accounting year, Norwest owes salaries of $4,000 and FICA and other payroll tax of $1,000. The bank will pay these amounts early next year.

Required

Show what Norwest Bank will report for these facts on its income statement and year-end balance sheet.

Reporting current and long-term liabilities (Obj. 6)

E11-13 Suppose Unity Medical Group borrowed $5,000,000 on January 2, 20X1, by issuing 9% long-term debt that must be paid in five equal annual installments plus interest each January 2.

Required

Insert the appropriate amounts to show how Unity Medical Group would report its long-term debt.

	December 31,				
	20X1	**20X2**	**20X3**	**20X4**	**20X5**
Current liabilities:					
Current portion of long-term debt	$____	$____	$____	$____	$____
Interest payable	____	____	____	____	____
Long-term liabilities:					
Long-term debt.....................................	____	____	____	____	____

E11-14 Assume that **Wilson Sporting Goods** completed these selected transactions during December 20X1:

Reporting current and long-term liabilities
(Obj. 6)

a. Sales of $1,000,000 are subject to estimated warranty cost of 3.4%.

b. On December 1, Wilson signed a $200,000 note payable that requires annual payments of $20,000 plus 9% interest on the unpaid balance each December 1.

c. Champs, a chain of sporting goods stores, ordered $9,000 of tennis and golf equipment. With its order, Champs sent a check for $9,000 in advance. Wilson will ship the goods on January 3, 20X2.

d. The December payroll of $195,000 is subject to employee withheld income tax of 9%, FICA tax of 8% (employee and employer), state unemployment tax of 5.4%, and federal unemployment tax of 0.8%. On December 31, Wilson pays employees but accrues all tax amounts.

Required

Classify each liability as current or long-term, and report the amount that would appear for each item on Wilson's balance sheet at December 31, 20X1. Show total current liabilities.

Challenge Exercises

E11-15 ◄ *Link Back to Chapter 4 (Current Ratio).* The balance sheets of **PepsiCo, Inc.,** for two years reported these figures:

Analyzing current liabilities
(Obj. 1, 6)

	Billions	
	20X2	**20X1**
Total current assets....................	$ 4.6	$ 4.1
Noncurrent assets......................	14.2	13.0
	$18.8	$17.1
Total current liabilities	$ 3.7	$ 4.8
Noncurrent liabilities	9.5	7.4
Stockholders' equity	5.6	4.9
	$18.8	$17.1

Assume that during 20X2, PepsiCo reclassified $2.1 billion of current liabilities as long-term.

Required

1. Compute PepsiCo's current ratio as reported at the end of each year. Describe the trend you observe.

2. Assume that PepsiCo had not reclassified $2.1 billion of current liabilities as long-term during 20X2. Recompute the current ratio at the end of 20X2. Why do you think PepsiCo reclassified the liabilities as long-term?

E11-16 PepsiCo, Inc., reported short-term debt payable and salary payable (adapted, in millions), as follows:

Analyzing current liabilities
(Obj. 1, 6)

	December 31,	
	20X2	**20X1**
Current liabilities (partial):		
Short-term debt payable..............	$707	$228
Salary payable............................	327	334

Assume that during 20X2, PepsiCo borrowed $1,106 million on short-term debt. Also assume that PepsiCo paid $3,200 million for salaries during 20X2.

Required

1. Compute PepsiCo's payment of short-term debt during 20X2.
2. Compute PepsiCo's salary expense during 20X2.

(Group A) PROBLEMS

Journalizing liability-related transactions
(Obj. 1, 2)

P11-1A The following transactions of Leland Communications occurred during 20X4 and 20X5:

20X4

Jan. 9   Purchased equipment at a cost of $20,000, signing a six-month, 8% note payable for that amount.

29   Recorded the week's sales of $40,200, three-fourths on credit, and one-fourth for cash. Sales amounts are subject to an additional 6% state sales tax.

Feb. 5   Sent the last week's sales tax to the state.

28   Borrowed $200,000 on a four-year, 9% note payable that calls for annual installment payments of $50,000 principal plus interest.

July 9   Paid the six-month, 8% note at maturity.

Oct. 22   Discounted a $10,000, 90-day, 8% note payable to the bank, receiving cash for the net amount after interest was deducted from the note's maturity value.

Nov. 30   Purchased inventory for $3,100, signing a six-month, 10% note payable.

Dec. 31   Accrued warranty expense, which is estimated at 3% of sales of $650,000.

31   Accrued interest on all outstanding notes payable. Made a separate interest accrual entry for each note payable.

20X5

Jan. 20   Paid off the 8% discounted note payable. Made a separate entry for the interest.

Feb. 28   Paid the first installment and interest for one year on the long-term note payable.

May 31   Paid off the 10% note plus interest on maturity.

Required

Record the transactions in the company's general journal. Explanations are not required.

Identifying contingent liabilities
(Obj. 2)

P11-2A Rountree Acura is one of the largest **Acura** dealers in the Midwest. The dealership sells new and used cars and operates a body shop and a service department. Mitch McGee, the general manager, is considering changing insurance companies because of a disagreement with Hank Callendar, agent for the **Travelers Insurance Company.** Travelers is doubling Rountree's liability insurance cost for the next year. In discussing insurance coverage with you, a trusted business associate, McGee brings up the subject of contingent liabilities.

Required

Write a memorandum to inform Rountree Acura of specific contingent liabilities arising from the business. In your discussion, define a contingent liability.

Computing and recording payroll amounts
(Obj. 3, 4)

P11-3A The partial monthly records of Allstar Cycle Co. show the following figures:

Employee Earnings	
(a) Straight-time earnings	$16,431
(b) Overtime pay	?
(c) Total employee earnings	?
Deductions and Net Pay	
(d) Withheld income tax	$ 2,403
(e) FICA tax	?
(f) Charitable contributions	340
(g) Medical insurance	668
(h) Total deductions	5,409
(i) Net pay	18,540
Accounts Debited	
(j) Salary Expense	$?
(k) Wage Expense	8,573
(l) Sales Commission Expense	2,077

Required

1. Determine the missing amounts on lines (b), (c), (e), and (j).
2. Prepare the general journal entry to record Allstar's payroll for the month. Credit Payrolls Payable for net pay. No explanation is required.

P11-4A Virginia Nadair is a vice president of Palm City Bank's leasing operations in Pensacola, Florida. During 20X2, she worked for the company all year at a $5,625 monthly salary. She also earned a year-end bonus equal to 12% of her salary.

Nadair's federal income tax withheld during 20X2 was $737 per month. Also, there was a one-time federal withholding tax of $1,007 on her bonus check. State income tax withheld came to $43 per month, and there was a one-time state withholding tax of $27 on the bonus. The FICA tax withheld was 8.0% of the first $75,000 in annual earnings. Nadair authorized the following payroll deductions: United Fund contribution of 1% of total earnings and life insurance of $19 per month.

Palm City Bank incurred payroll tax expense on Nadair for FICA tax of 8% of the first $75,000 in annual earnings. The bank also paid state unemployment tax of 5.4% and federal unemployment tax of 0.8% on the first $7,000 in annual earnings. In addition, the bank provides Nadair with health insurance at a cost of $35 per month and pension benefits. During 20X2, Palm City Bank paid $7,178 into Nadair's pension program.

Computing and recording payroll amounts
(Obj. 3, 4)

Required

1. Compute Nadair's gross pay, payroll deductions, and net pay for the full year 20X2. Round all amounts to the nearest dollar.
2. Compute Palm City Bank's total 20X2 payroll cost for Nadair.
3. Prepare Palm City Bank's summary general journal entries to record its expense for the following:
   a. Nadair's total earnings for the year, her payroll deductions, and her net pay. Debit Salary Expense and Executive Bonus Compensation as appropriate. Credit liability accounts for the payroll deductions and Cash for net pay.
   b. Employer payroll taxes on Nadair. Credit liability accounts.
   c. Benefits provided to Nadair. Credit a liability account. Explanations are not required.

P11-5A The general ledger of Red Mountain Investments at June 30, 20X3, the end of the company's fiscal year, includes the following account balances before adjusting entries.

Journalizing, posting, and reporting liabilities
(Obj. 1, 2, 3, 4, 5, 6)

Accounts Payable	$105,520
Current Portion of Long-Term Debt	_____
Interest Payable	_____
Salary Payable	_____
Employee Payroll Taxes Payable	_____
Employer Payroll Taxes Payable	_____
Estimated Vacation Pay Liability	7,620
Unearned Rent Revenue	6,000
Long-Term Debt	200,000

The additional data needed to develop the adjusting entries at June 30 are as follows:

a. The long-term debt is payable in annual installments of $40,000 with the next installment due on July 31. On that date, Red Mountain will also pay one year's interest at 9%. Interest was last paid on July 31 of the preceding year. (Make the adjusting entry to shift the current installment of the long-term debt to a current liability.)
b. Gross salaries for the last payroll of the fiscal year were $5,044. Of this amount, employee payroll taxes payable were $1,088, and salary payable was $3,956.
c. Employer payroll taxes payable were $876.
d. Red Mountain estimates that vacation pay expense is 5% of gross salaries.
e. On February 1, the company collected one year's rent of $6,000 in advance.
f. At June 30, Red Mountain is the defendant in a $300,000 lawsuit, which the company expects to win. However, the outcome is uncertain. Write the note to report this contingent liability in the financial statements.

Required

1. Open the listed accounts, inserting their unadjusted June 30 balances.
2. Journalize and post the June 30 adjusting entries to the accounts opened. Key adjusting entries by letter.
3. Prepare the liability section of the balance sheet at June 30.

P11-6A Assume that the payroll records of a district sales office of **Spalding Sporting Goods** provided the following information for the weekly pay period ended December 21, 20X3.

Using a payroll record; recording a payroll
(Obj. 5)

Employee	Hours Worked	Hourly Earnings Rate	Federal Income Tax	Union Dues	United Way Contributions	Earnings Through Previous Week
Larry Fisher................	42	$28	$278	$6	$35	$77,474
Felicia Jones..............	47	8	87	4	4	23,154
Sara Opper	40	11	64	—	4	4,880
Brian Tate..................	41	22	188	6	8	74,600

Fisher and Tate are salesmen. Jones and Opper work in the office. All employees are paid time and a half for hours worked in excess of 40 per week. Round all amounts to the nearest dollar. Show your computations. Explanations are not required for journal entries.

Required

1. Enter the appropriate information in a payroll record similar to Exhibit 11-7, page 442. In addition to the deductions listed, the employer also takes out FICA tax: 8% of the first $75,000 of each employee's annual earnings.
2. Record the payroll information in the general journal.
3. Assume that the first payroll check is number 319, paid to Larry Fisher. Record the check numbers in the payroll record. Also, prepare the general journal entry to record payment of net pay to the employees
4. The employer's payroll taxes include FICA tax of 8% of the first $75,000 of each employee's earnings. The employer also pays unemployment taxes of 6.2% (5.4% for the state and 0.8% for the federal government on the first $7,000 of each employee's annual earnings). Record the employer's payroll taxes in the general journal.

Reporting current liabilities (Obj. 6)

P11-7A Following are pertinent facts about events during the current year at Innovech, Inc.:

a. On November 30, Innovech received rent of $6,600 in advance for a lease on a building. This rent will be earned evenly over three months.
b. December sales totaled $113,000, and Innovech collected an additional state sales tax of 7%. This amount will be sent to the State of Tennessee early in January.
c. Innovech owes $100,000 on a long-term note payable. At December 31, 6% interest since July 31 and $20,000 of this principal are payable within one year.
d. Sales of $430,000 were covered by Innovech's product warranty. At January 1, estimated warranty payable was $8,100. During the year, Innovech recorded warranty expense of $22,300 and paid warranty claims of $24,900.
e. On September 30, Innovech signed a six-month, 9% note payable to purchase equipment costing $30,000. The note requires payment of principal and interest at maturity.

Required

For each item, indicate the account and the related amount to be reported as a current liability on Innovech's December 31 balance sheet.

(Group B) PROBLEMS

Journalizing liability-related transactions (Obj. 1, 2)

P11-1B The following transactions of **Bethlehem Steel** occurred during 20X2 and 20X3.

20X2

Feb.	3	Purchased equipment for $10,200, signing a six-month, 9% note payable.
	28	Recorded the week's sales of $51,000, one-third for cash, and two-thirds on credit. All sales amounts are subject to a 5% state sales tax.
Mar.	7	Sent the last week's sales tax to the state.
Apr.	30	Borrowed $100,000 on a four-year, 9% note payable that calls for annual installment payments of $25,000 principal plus interest.
Aug.	3	Paid the six-month, 9% note at maturity.
Sep.	14	Discounted a $6,000, 60-day, 7% note payable to the bank, receiving cash for the net amount after interest was deducted from the note's maturity value.
Nov.	13	Recorded interest on the 7% discounted note and paid off the note at maturity.
	30	Purchased inventory at a cost of $7,200, signing a three-month, 9% note payable for that amount.
Dec.	31	Accrued warranty expense, which is estimated at 3% of sales of $260,000.
	31	Accrued interest on all outstanding notes payable. Made a separate interest accrual entry for each note payable.

20X3

Feb.	28	Paid off the 9% inventory note, plus interest, at maturity.
Apr.	30	Paid the first installment and interest for one year on the long-term note payable.

Required

Record the transactions in the company's general journal. Explanations are not required.

P11-2B Briarwood Stables provides riding lessons for girls ages 8–15. Most students are beginners, and none of the girls owns her own horse. Sally Arnold, the owner of the stable, uses horses stabled at her farm and owned by the O'Malleys. Most of the horses are for sale, but the economy has been bad for several years and sales have been slow. The O'Malleys are happy that Arnold uses their horses in exchange for boarding them. Because of a recent financial setback, Arnold cannot afford liability insurance. She seeks your advice about her business's exposure to liabilities.

Identifying contingent liabilities
(Obj. 2)

Required

Write a memorandum to inform Arnold of specific contingent liabilities arising from the business. It will be necessary to define a contingent liability because she is a professional horse trainer, not a businessperson. Propose a way for Arnold to limit her risk due to these liabilities.

P11-3B The partial monthly records of Aramark Food Service show the following figures:

Computing and recording payroll amounts
(Obj. 3, 4)

Employee Earnings

(a)	Straight-time earnings	$?
(b)	Overtime pay	5,109
(c)	Total employee earnings	?

Deductions and Net Pay

(d)	Withheld income tax	$ 9,293
(e)	FICA tax	6,052
(f)	Charitable contributions	?
(g)	Medical insurance	1,373
(h)	Total deductions	18,880
(i)	Net pay	64,813

Accounts Debited

(j)	Salary Expense	$31,278
(k)	Wage Expense	?
(l)	Sales Commission Expense	27,931

Required

1. Determine the missing amounts on lines (a), (c), (f), and (k).
2. Prepare the general journal entry to record Aramark's payroll for the month. Credit Payrolls Payable for net pay. No explanation is required.

P11-4B Jan Summers is a commercial lender at Harbor State Bank in Boston. During 20X2, she worked for the bank all year at a $5,195 monthly salary. She also earned a year-end bonus equal to 10% of her annual salary.

Computing and recording payroll amounts
(Obj. 3, 4)

Summers' federal income tax withheld during 20X2 was $822 per month. Also, there was a one-time withholding of $2,487 on her bonus check. State income tax withheld came to $61 per month, and the city of Boston withheld income tax of $21 per month. In addition, Summers paid one-time withholdings of $64 (state) and $19 (city) on the bonus. The FICA tax withheld was 8% of the first $75,000 in annual earnings. Summers authorized the following payroll deductions: United Fund contribution of 1% of total earnings and life insurance of $17 per month.

Harbor State Bank incurred payroll tax expense on Summers for FICA tax of 8% of the first $75,000 in total annual earnings. The bank also paid state unemployment tax of 5.4% and federal unemployment tax of 0.8% on the first $7,000 in annual earnings. The bank provided Summers with the following benefits: health insurance at a cost of $48 per month, and pension benefits to be paid to Summers during her retirement. During 20X2, the bank's cost of Summers' pension program was $4,083.

Required

1. Compute Summers' gross pay, payroll deductions, and net pay during 20X2. Round all amounts to the nearest dollar.
2. Compute Harbor State Bank's total 20X2 payroll cost for Summers.
3. Prepare the bank's summary general journal entries to record its expense for the following:
   a. Summers' total earnings for the year, her payroll deductions, and her net pay. Debit Salary Expense and Executive Bonus Compensation as appropriate. Credit liability accounts for the payroll deductions and Cash for net pay.
   b. Employer payroll taxes for Summers. Credit liability accounts.
   c. Benefits provided to Summers. Credit a liability account.

Explanations are not required.

P11-5B The St. Charles Consulting general ledger at September 30, 20X2, the end of the company's fiscal year, includes the following account balances before adjusting entries. Parentheses indicate a debit balance.

Accounts Payable	$ 88,240
Current Portion of Long-Term Debt	
Interest Payable	
Salary Payable	
Employee Payroll Taxes Payable	
Employer Payroll Taxes Payable	
Estimated Vacation Pay Liability	2,105
Unearned Rent Revenue	3,900
Long-Term Debt	100,000

The additional data needed to develop the adjusting entries at September 30 are as follows:

a. The long-term debt is payable in annual installments of $50,000, with the next install-ment due on January 31, 20X3. On that date, St. Charles Consulting will also pay one year's interest at 6.6%. Interest was last paid on January 31. (Make the adjusting entry to shift the current installment of the long-term debt to a current liability.)

b. Gross salaries for the last payroll of the fiscal year were $4,319. Of this amount, employee payroll taxes payable were $958, and salary payable was $3,361.

c. Employer payroll taxes payable were $890.

d. St. Charles estimates that vacation pay is 4% of gross salaries.

e. On August 1, the company collected six months' rent of $3,900 in advance.

f. At September 30, St. Charles is the defendant in a $500,000 lawsuit, which the company expects to win. However, the outcome is uncertain. Write the note to report this contin-gent liability in the financial statements.

Required

1. Open the listed accounts, inserting their unadjusted September 30 balances.
2. Journalize and post the September 30 adjusting entries to the accounts opened. Key adjusting entries by letter.
3. Prepare the liability section of St. Charles Consulting's balance sheet at September 30. Show total current liabilities.

P11-6B Assume that payroll records of a district sales office of Audi Motor Systems provided the following information for the weekly pay period ended December 26, 20X3:

Employee	Hours Worked	Weekly Earnings Rate	Federal Income Tax	Health Insurance	United Way Contributions	Earnings Through Previous Week
Clay Cooper	43	$ 400	$ 74	$ 9	$ 7	$17,060
Tim LeMann	46	480	90	5	5	22,365
Lena Marx	47	1,200	319	16	30	74,247
Karen York	40	240	32	4	2	3,413

Cooper and York work in the office, and LeMann and Marx work in sales. All employees are paid time and a half for hours worked in excess of 40 per week.

Required

For convenience, round all amounts to the nearest dollar. Show your computations. Explanations are not required for journal entries.

1. Enter the appropriate information in a payroll record similar to Exhibit 11-7. In addition to the deductions listed, the employer also takes out FICA tax: 8% of the first $75,000 of each employee's annual earnings.
2. Record the payroll information in the general journal.
3. Assume that the first payroll check is number 178, paid to Cooper. Record the check numbers in the payroll record. Also, prepare the general journal entry to record payment of net pay to the employees.
4. The employer's payroll taxes include FICA of 8% of the first $75,000 of each employee's annual earnings. The employer also pays unemployment taxes of 6.2% (5.4% for the state and 0.8% for the federal government) on the first $7,000 of each employee's annual earnings. Record the employer's payroll taxes in the general journal.

P11-7B Following are pertinent facts about events during the current year at Nevis Marine Company:

Reporting current liabilities (Obj. 6)

a. December sales totaled $404,000 and Nevis collected sales tax of 9%. The sales tax will be sent to the state of Washington early in January.

b. Nevis owes $75,000 on a long-term note payable. At December 31, 6% interest for the year plus $25,000 of this principal are payable within one year.

c. On August 31, Nevis signed a six-month, 6% note payable to purchase a machine costing $80,000. The note requires payment of principal and interest at maturity.

d. Sales of $909,000 were covered by Nevis' product warranty. At January 1, estimated warranty payable was $11,300. During the year, Nevis recorded warranty expense of $27,900 and paid warranty claims of $30,100.

e. On October 31, Nevis received rent of $2,400 in advance for a lease on a building. This rent will be earned evenly over four months.

Required

For each item, indicate the account and the related amount to be reported as a current liability on Nevis's December 31 balance sheet.

APPLY YOUR KNOWLEDGE

DECISION CASES

Case 1. SureBuilt Homes is a construction company in Fond du Lac, Wisconsin. The owner and manager, Art Waverly, oversees all company operations. He employs 15 work crews, each made up of six to ten members. Construction supervisors, who report directly to Waverly, lead the crews. Most supervisors are longtime employees, so Waverly trusts them. Waverly's office staff consists of an accountant and an office manager.

Identifying internal control weaknesses and their solution (Obj. 5)

Because employee turnover is high in the construction industry, supervisors hire and fire their own crew members. Supervisors notify the office of all personnel changes. Also, supervisors forward to the office the employee W-4 forms, which the crew members fill out. Each Thursday, the supervisors submit weekly time sheets for their crews, and the accountant prepares the payroll. At noon on Friday, the supervisors come to the office to get paychecks for distribution to the workers at 5 p.m.

SureBuilt's accountant prepares the payroll, including the payroll checks, which are written on a single payroll bank account. Waverly signs all payroll checks after matching the employee name to the time sheets submitted by the foremen. Often the workers wait several days to cash their paychecks. To verify that each construction worker is a bona fide employee, the accountant matches the employee's endorsement signature on the back of the canceled payroll check with the signature on that employee's W-4 form.

Required

1. Identify one *efficiency* weakness in SureBuilt's payroll accounting system. How can the business correct this weakness?

2. Identify one way that a supervisor can defraud SureBuilt Homes under the present system.

3. Discuss a control feature that SureBuilt Homes can use to *safeguard* against the frauds you identified in requirement 2.

Case 2. **The Boeing Company,** manufacturer of jet aircraft, is the defendant in numerous lawsuits claiming unfair trade practices. Boeing has strong incentives not to disclose these contingent liabilities. However, GAAP requires that companies report their contingent liabilities.

Unearned revenues, warranties, and contingent liabilities (Obj. 1, 2)

Required

1. Why would a company prefer *not* to disclose its contingent liabilities?

2. Describe how a bank could be harmed if a company seeking a loan did not disclose its contingent liabilities.

3. What ethical tightrope must companies walk when they report contingent liabilities?

ETHICAL ISSUE

LTV, manufacturer of aircraft and aircraft-related electronic devices, has at times borrowed heavily to finance operations. Often LTV is able to earn operating income much higher than its interest expense and is therefore quite profitable. However, when the business cycle turns down, LTV's debt burden has pushed the company to the brink of bankruptcy. Operating income is sometimes less than interest expense.

Required

Is it unethical for managers to saddle a company with a high level of debt? Or is it just risky? Who can get hurt when a company takes on too much debt? Discuss.

FINANCIAL STATEMENT CASE

Current and contingent liabilities (Obj. 1, 2)

Details about a company's current and contingent liabilities appear in a number of places in the annual report. Use **Target's** financial statements to answer the following questions.

Required

1. Give the breakdown of Target's current liabilities at January 29, 2000. Give the February 2000 entry to record the payment of accounts payable that Target owed at January 29, 2000.
2. How much was Target's long-term debt at January 29, 2000? Of this amount, how much was due within one year? How much was payable beyond one year in the future?
3. The balance sheet lists a $318 million liability for "Income Taxes Payable." Was income tax expense for the year, as reported on the income statement, equal to, less than, or greater than this amount? Why is one amount greater than the other?
4. Locate Target's report of its contingent liabilities. What event caused Target's contingent liabilities?

TEAM PROJECTS

Project 1. In recent years, the airline industry has dominated headlines. Consumers are shopping **Priceline.com** and other Internet sites for the lowest rates. The airlines have also lured customers with frequent-flyer programs, which award free flights to passengers who accumulate specified miles of travel. Unredeemed frequent-flyer mileage represents a liability that airlines must report on their balance sheets, usually as Air Traffic Liability.

Southwest Airlines, a profitable, no-frills carrier based in Dallas, has been rated near the top of the industry. Southwest controls costs by flying to smaller, less expensive airports; using only one model of aircraft; serving no meals; increasing staff efficiency; and having a shorter turnaround time on the ground between flights. The fact that most of the cities served by Southwest have predictable weather maximizes its on-time arrival record.

Required

With a partner or group, lead your class in a discussion of the following questions, or write a report as directed by your instructor.

1. Frequent-flyer programs have grown into significant obligations for airlines. Why should a liability be recorded for those programs? Discuss how you might calculate the amount of this liability. Can you think of other industries that offer similar incentives that create a liability?
2. One of Southwest Airlines' strategies for success is shortening stops at airport gates between flights. The company's chairman has stated, "What [you] produce is lower fares for the customers because you generate more revenue from the same fixed cost in that airplane." Look up *fixed cost* in the index of this book. What are some of the "fixed costs" of an airline? How can better utilization of assets improve a company's profits?

Project 2. Consider three different businesses:

a. A bank **b.** A magazine publisher **c.** A department store

Required

For each business, list all of its liabilities—both current and long-term. If necessary, study Chapter 15 on long-term liabilities. Then compare your lists to identify what liabilities the three businesses have in common. Also identify the liabilities that are unique to each type of business.

INTERNET EXERCISE

Amazon.com

In 1995, **Amazon.com** opened its virtual doors and now serves over 17 million customers in over 150 different countries.

1. Go to **http://www.hoovers.com** and use the "Search" scroll bar to select *Company*, in the next box type <u>AMZN</u>, and then click on *Go*. For Amazon.com, Inc., click on *Capsule*. Scan the paragraph description of the company. What products does Amazon.com offer online?
2. Go to the top of the page and click on the *Financials* tab. Under "Free Financial Information" click on *Annual Financials*.

a. For the two most recent years, list the amounts reported for "Total Current Assets" and "Total Current Liabilities." Calculate the current ratio. Does Amazon.com have the ability to pay its current liabilities? Which year reports a stronger ratio?

b. For the two most recent years, list the amounts reported for "Total Liabilities" and "Total Assets." Calculate the debt ratio. How is Amazon.com financing its asset growth? Founder Jeff Bezos and family own about 34% of the company. Why do you think Mr. Bezos has chosen this method to finance asset growth?

c. Of approximately 100 Internet stocks, most showed staggering increases in revenue but only five showed net income in 1999. Is Amazon.com a typical Internet stock? Why or why not?

12

Partnerships

www.prenhall.com/horngren

LEARNING OBJECTIVES

After studying this chapter, you should be able to

1. Identify the characteristics of a partnership
2. Account for the partners' investments in a partnership
3. Allocate profits and losses to the partners
4. Account for the admission of a partner to the business
5. Account for a partner's withdrawal from the firm
6. Account for the liquidation of a partnership
7. Prepare partnership financial statements

www.prenhall.com/horngren

Readiness Assessment

Once upon a time **Arthur Andersen LLP** was a stodgy accounting firm. No longer. Arthur Andersen—or "Arthur" as insiders call it—has shed its old image. For starters, the firm now earns much of its income from consulting, not accounting.

The firm is a profit-making machine, and it doesn't have to share its income with millions of stockholders the way corporations do. Arthur Andersen LLP is a partnership. That means the people who own the firm, around 2,000 of them—are all partners. Each partner's profit from the firm averages well over a half million dollars a year.

The most interesting thing about Arthur Andersen is the divorce the partners worked out. The consulting partners formed **Andersen Consulting,** a different firm. But they wanted to continue using the Andersen name, and that's where the rub came. The partners of Arthur Andersen, the original firm, demanded billions from Andersen Consulting because the consulting firm was launched from contacts with the firm's audit clients. As a compromise, the consulting firm took the name of **!Accenture.**

Is all this confusing? You bet it is. That's why the Andersen divorce was so difficult. It is a classic case for showing the fragile nature of a partnership. So, if you ever consider going into business with anyone besides your mother, choose your partners carefully. And don't forget to get the partnership agreement in writing.

The partnership form of business introduces some complexities that a proprietorship avoids. How much cash should a new partner contribute to the business? How should the partners divide profits and losses? This seems to be the most difficult issue for the partners. How should a partner who leaves the firm be compensated for his or her share of the business? This issue seems paramount to the partners of **Arthur Andersen LLP.**

A **partnership** is an association of two or more persons who co-own a business for profit. This definition comes from the Uniform Partnership Act, which nearly every state in the United States has adopted to regulate partnership practice.

Forming a partnership is easy. It requires no permission from the government and no legal procedures. When two persons decide to go into business together, a partnership is automatically formed.

A partnership brings together the assets and the experience of the partners. Business opportunities closed to an individual may open up to a partnership. Perhaps none of the Arthur Andersen partners has enough money individually to operate a large firm. But they are able to afford it together in a partnership. They pool their talents and know-how. Their partnership thus offers clients a fuller range of services than any one person can offer alone.

Partnerships come in all sizes. Many partnerships have fewer than ten partners. Some medical and law firms have 20 or more partners. The largest accounting/consulting firms have over 2,000 partners. Exhibit 12-1 lists the eight largest accounting/consulting firms in the United States, the number of partners in each firm, and their revenues in 1999.

CHARACTERISTICS OF A PARTNERSHIP

Starting a partnership is voluntary. A person cannot be forced to join a partnership, and partners cannot be forced to accept another person as a partner. Although the partnership agreement may be oral, a written agreement between the partners reduces the chance of a misunderstanding. The following characteristics distinguish partnerships from sole proprietorships and corporations.

The Written Agreement

A business partnership is like a marriage. To be successful, the partners must cooperate. But business partners do not vow to remain together for life. To make certain that each partner fully understands how the partnership operates and to lower the chances that any partner might misunderstand how the business is run, partners may draw up a **partnership agreement,** also called the **articles of**

Revenue Rank (1999)	Firm Location	Partners	Revenue Per Partner (in millions)
1	Arthur Andersen, New York	2,117	$3.7
2	PricewaterhouseCoopers, New York	2,938	$2.3
3	Ernst & Young, New York	2,546	$2.5
4	Deloitte & Touche, Wilton, Connecticut	1,913	$2.8
5	KPMG, New York	1,800	$2.6
6	RSM McGladrey, Bloomington, Minnesota	369	$1.1
7	Grant Thornton, Chicago	274	$1.5
8	BDO Seidman, Chicago	335	$0.9

Source: Adapted from *Accounting Today* (March 13–April 2, 2000), Special Supplement, and the *Wall Street Journal*, August 8, 2000, page A3.

partnership. This agreement is a contract between the partners, so transactions involving the agreement are governed by contract law. The articles of partnership should make the following points clear:

1. Name, location, and nature of the business
2. Name, capital investment, and duties of each partner
3. Method of sharing profits and losses among the partners
4. Withdrawals of assets allowed to the partners
5. Procedures for settling disputes between the partners
6. Procedures for admitting new partners
7. Procedures for settling up with a partner who withdraws from the business
8. Procedures for liquidating the partnership—selling the assets, paying the liabilities, and disbursing any remaining cash to the partners

Limited Life

DISSOLUTION. Ending of a partnership.

A partnership has a life limited by the length of time that all partners continue to own the business. If one or more **Arthur Andersen** partners withdraws from the business, the old partnership will cease to exist. A new partnership may emerge to continue the same business, but the old partnership will have been dissolved. **Dissolution** is the ending of a partnership. The addition of a new partner dissolves the old partnership and creates a new partnership. Large partnerships such as Arthur Andersen retain the firm name even after partners resign from the firm.

Mutual Agency

MUTUAL AGENCY. Every partner can bind the business to a contract within the scope of the partnership's regular business operations.

Mutual agency in a partnership means that every partner can bind the business to a contract within the scope of the partnership's regular business operations. If Jana Jones, a partner in the firm of Willis and Jones, enters into a contract with a business to provide accounting service, then the firm of Willis & Jones—not just Jones—is bound to provide that service. If Jones signs a contract to purchase lawn services for her home, however, the partnership will not be bound to pay because the lawn service is a personal matter for Jones. It is not a regular business operation of the partnership.

Unlimited Liability

UNLIMITED PERSONAL LIABILITY. When a partnership (or a proprietorship) cannot pay its debts with business assets, the partners (or the proprietor) must use personal assets to meet the debt.

Each partner has an **unlimited personal liability** for the debts of the partnership. When a partnership cannot pay its debts with business assets, the partners must use their personal assets to meet the debt. Proprietors also have unlimited personal liability for the debts of their business.

Suppose the Willis & Jones firm has had an unsuccessful year and the partnership's liabilities exceed its assets by $20,000. Willis and Jones must pay this amount with their personal assets. Because each partner has unlimited liability, if a partner is unable to pay his or her part of the debt, the other partner (or partners) must pay. If Jones can pay only $5,000 of the liability, Willis must pay $15,000.

Unlimited liability and mutual agency are closely related. A dishonest partner or a partner with poor judgment may commit the partnership to a contract under which the business loses money. In turn, creditors may force *all* the partners to pay the debt from personal assets.

Partners can avoid unlimited personal liability for partnership obligations by forming a *limited partnership*. **Arthur Andersen LLP** is a limited liability partnership, as are the other large accounting and consulting firms in Exhibit 12-1. In this form of business organization, the partners have limited liability similar to the limited liability enjoyed by the stockholders of a corporation.

Co-Ownership of Property

Any asset—cash, inventory, machinery, and so on—that a partner invests in the partnership becomes the joint property of all the partners. Also, each partner has a claim to his or her share of the business's profits.

No Partnership Income Taxes

A partnership pays no income tax on its business income. Instead, the net income of the partnership is divided and becomes the taxable income of the partners. Suppose Willis & Jones, Certified Public Accountants, earned net income of $200,000, shared equally by the partners. The firm would pay no income tax *as a business entity.* Willis and Jones, however, would each pay income tax as individuals on their $100,000 shares of partnership income.

Partners' Owner's Equity Accounts

 DAILY EXERCISE 12-1

Accounting for a partnership is much like accounting for a proprietorship. We record buying and selling goods and services and collecting and paying cash for a partnership just as we do for a proprietorship. But because a partnership has more than one owner, the partnership must have more than one owner's equity account.

Every partner in the business—whether the firm has 2 or 2,000 partners—has an individual owner's equity account. Often these accounts carry the name of the particular partner and the word *capital*. For example, the owner's equity account for Blake Willis would read "Willis, Capital." Similarly, each partner has a withdrawal account. If the number of partners is large, the general ledger may contain the single account Partners' Capital, or Owners' Equity. A subsidiary ledger can be used for individual partner accounts.

Exhibit 12-2 lists the advantages and disadvantages of partnerships (compared with proprietorships and corporations). A partnership is really a "multiple proprietorship." Most features of a proprietorship also apply to a partnership—in particular, limited life and unlimited liability.

 DAILY EXERCISE 12-2

EXHIBIT 12-2
Advantages and Disadvantages of Partnerships

Partnership Advantages	Partnership Disadvantages
Versus Proprietorships: 1. Can raise more capital. 2. Brings together the expertise of more than one person. 3. 1 + 1 > 2 in a good partnership. If the partners work well together, they can add more value than by working alone. *Versus Corporations:* 4. Less expensive to organize than a corporation, which requires a charter from the state. 5. No taxation of business income, which is taxed to the partners as individuals.	1. Partnership agreement may be difficult to formulate. Each time a new partner is admitted or a partner withdraws, the business needs a new partnership agreement. 2. Relationships among partners may be fragile. 3. Mutual agency and unlimited personal liability create personal obligations for each partner.

TYPES OF PARTNERSHIPS

There are two basic types of partnerships: general and limited.

General Partnerships

A **general partnership** is the basic form of partnership organization. Each partner is an owner of the business with all the privileges and risks of ownership. The general partners share the profits, losses, and the risks of the business. The partnership *reports* its income to governmental tax authorities (the Internal Revenue Service in the United States), but the partnership itself pays *no* income tax. The profits and losses of the partnership pass through the business to the partners, who then pay personal income tax on their income.

Limited Partnerships

A **limited partnership** has at least two classes of partners. There must be at least one *general partner*, who takes primary responsibility for the management of the business. The general partner also takes the bulk of the risk of failure in the event the partnership goes bankrupt (liabilities exceed assets). In real-estate limited partnerships, the general partner often invests little cash in the business. Instead, the general partner's contribution is his or her skill in managing the organization. Usually, the general partner is the last owner to receive a share of partnership profits and losses. But the general partner may earn all excess profits after satisfying the limited partners' demands for income.

The *limited partners* are so named because their personal obligation for the partnership's liabilities is limited to the amount they have invested in the business. Usually, the limited partners have invested the bulk of the partnership's assets and capital. They therefore usually have first claim to partnership profits and losses, but only up to a specified limit. In exchange for their limited liability, their potential for profits usually has a limit as well.

Most of the large accounting firms are organized as **limited liability partnerships,** or **LLPs,** which means that each partner's personal liability for the business's debts is limited to a certain amount. The LLP must carry a large insurance policy to protect the public in case the partnership is found guilty of malpractice. Medical, legal, and other firms of professionals can also be organized as LLPs.

S Corporations

An **S Corporation** is a corporation that is taxed in the same way that a partnership is taxed. Therefore, S corporations are often discussed in conjunction with partnerships. This form of business organization derives its name from Subchapter S of the U.S. Internal Revenue Code.

An S corporation offers its owners the benefits of a corporation—no personal liability for business debts—and of a partnership—no double taxation. An ordinary (Subchapter C) corporation is subject to double taxation. First, the corporation pays corporate income tax on its income. Then, when the corporation pays dividends to the stockholders, they pay personal income tax on their dividend income. An S corporation pays no corporate income tax. Instead, the corporation's income flows through directly to the stockholders (the owners), who pay personal income tax on their share of the S corporation's income. The one-time taxation of an S corporation's income is an important advantage over an ordinary corporation. From a tax standpoint, an S corporation operates like a partnership.

To qualify as an S corporation, a company can have no more than 75 stockholders, all of whom must be citizens or residents of the United States. Accounting for an S corporation resembles that of accounting for a partnership because the allocation of corporate income follows the same procedure used by partnerships.

The popularity of S corporations rises and falls with the passage of new legislation. When individual income tax rates exceed corporate tax rates, S corporations increase in number. When corporate tax rates fall, there is less incentive to form an S corporation. Also, new entities called limited-liability companies have formed. **Arthur Andersen Limited Liability Partnership (LLP)** is an example. An LLP offers its owners the same limited liability as a corporation, and an LLP avoids some of the restrictions that S corporations face. Currently, LLPs are more popular than S corporations.

THE PARTNERSHIP START-UP

Let's examine the start-up of a partnership. We will see how to account for the owner's equity accounts of the partners. We will also learn how they appear on the balance sheet.

Partners in a new partnership may invest assets and liabilities in the business. These contributions are entered in the books in the same way that a proprietor's

Objective 2
Account for the partners' investments in a partnership

e-Accounting

The Limited but Lively Life of a Dot.Com Partnership

Founding partners say that starting up a business is *the life*. Sleep is scant and cash is low, but hopes and energy run high. Some Internet businesses have started with nothing more than enthusiastic partners and a winning idea.

- The story of **Yahoo!** founders Jerry Yang and David Filo is now legend. In 1994, the two Stanford graduate students came up with a way to categorize Web sites. Their guide, named Yahoo!, was the first place for Web browsers to find sites easily. Now Yahoo! is a global Internet communications, commerce, and media company with over 2,000 employees. Yahoo! has a global Web network of 21 properties and offices in Europe, Asia, Latin America, Canada, and the United States.

- Founded in 1999 by 19-year-old Shawn Fanning and 20-year-old Sean Parker, **Napster** created software that lets people trade music files on the Internet for free. In almost no time, the company was turning the music industry upside down. Twenty million users downloaded the free software in just seven months, and *Fortune* magazine commended the company for pioneering one of the hottest business concepts of our time: peer-to-peer information sharing. Napster is so successful at stealing copyrighted music that the music industry threatens to put the organization out of business.

- In 1994, Todd Krizelman and Stephan Paternot, both 25 and at Cornell, came up with an on-line community where participants go to find news, discussion forums, and products—**TheGlobe.com.** Krizelman and Paternot recruited employees in the student lounge, paid them with Domino pizza, drained their own bank accounts, and lived off credit cards. Four years later, TheGlobe.com brought in $27 million in an initial public offering, and the former dorm buddies are now joint CEOs.

Sources: Based on [Yahoo!] Information from http://join.yahoo.com/chief.html and http://join.yahoo.com/overview.html. [Napster] Chuck Philips, "Company town; THE BIZ Q & A; Humming a hopeful tune at napster," *The Los Angeles Times*, July 19, 2000, p. 1. Amy Kover, "Napster: The hot idea of the year," *Fortune*, June 26, 2000, pp. 128–136. [TheGlobe.com] Stephanie Armour, "Tech grads loving life: Pizza, jeans, happy hour," June 21, 1999, *USA Today*, p. 01B

assets and liabilities are recorded. Subtraction of each partner's liabilities from his or her assets yields the amount to be credited to that partner's capital account. Often, the partners hire an independent firm to appraise their assets and liabilities at current market value at the time a partnership is formed. This outside evaluation assures an objective accounting for what each partner brings into the business.

Assume that Dave Benz and Joan Hanna form a partnership to manufacture and sell computer software. The partners agree on the following values based on an independent appraisal:

Benz's Contributions

- Cash, $10,000; inventory, $70,000; and accounts payable, $85,000 (The appraiser believes that the current market values for these items equal Benz's values.)
- Accounts receivable, $30,000, less allowance for doubtful accounts of $5,000
- Computer equipment—cost, $800,000; accumulated depreciation, $200,000; current market value, $450,000

Hanna's Contributions

- Cash, $5,000
- Computer software: cost, $18,000; market value, $100,000

The partnership records receipt of the partners' initial investments at the current market values of the assets and liabilities because, in effect, the partnership is buying the assets and assuming the liabilities at their current market values. The partnership entries are as follows:

Benz's Investment

June 1	Cash..	10,000	
	Accounts Receivable.......................................	30,000	
	Inventory..	70,000	
	Computer Equipment.......................................	450,000	
	Allowance for Doubtful Accounts..........................		5,000
	Accounts Payable		85,000
	Benz, Capital ($560,000 − $90,000)		470,000
	To record Benz's investment in the partnership.		

Hanna's Investment

June 1	Cash..		5,000
	Computer Software	100,000	
	Hanna, Capital		105,000
	To record Hanna's investment in the partnership.		

◉ DAILY EXERCISE 12-3

◉ DAILY EXERCISE 12-4

The initial partnership balance sheet reports the amounts shown in Exhibit 12-3. Note that the asset and liability sections on the balance sheet are the same for a proprietorship and a partnership.

SHARING PROFITS AND LOSSES, AND DRAWINGS

Objective 3
Allocate profits and losses to the partners

Allocating profits and losses among partners is one of the most challenging aspects of managing a partnership. If the partners have not drawn up an agreement or if the agreement does not state how the partners will divide profits and losses, then by law, the partners must share profits and losses equally. If the agreement specifies a method for sharing profits but not losses, then losses are shared in the same proportion as profits. For example, a partner who was allocated 75% of the profits would likewise absorb 75% of any losses. Partners may agree to any profit-and-loss-sharing method they desire.

Exhibit 12-3
Partnership Balance Sheet

BENZ AND HANNA
Balance Sheet
June 1, 20X5

Assets			Liabilities	
Cash............................		$ 15,000	Accounts payable	$ 85,000
Accounts receivable......	$30,000			
Less Allowance for doubtful accounts	(5,000)	25,000	**Capital**	
Inventory.....................		70,000	Benz, capital..............	470,000
Computer equipment...		450,000	Hanna, capital	105,000
Computer software.......		100,000	Total liabilities	
Total assets...................		$660,000	and capital	$660,000

In some cases, an equal division is not fair. One partner may perform more work for the business than the other partner, or one partner may make a larger capital contribution. In the preceding example, Joan Hanna might agree to work longer hours for the partnership than Dave Benz to earn a greater share of profits. Benz could argue that he should share in more of the profits because he contributed more net assets ($470,000) than Hanna did ($105,000). Hanna might contend that her computer software program is the partnership's most important asset and that her share of the profits should be greater than Benz's share. Agreeing on a fair sharing of profits and losses in a partnership may be difficult.

Sharing Based on a Stated Fraction

Partners may state a particular fraction of the total profits and losses each individual partner will share. Suppose the partnership agreement of Lou Cagle and Justin Dean allocates two-thirds of the business profits and losses to Cagle and one-third to Dean. If net income for the year is $90,000 and all revenue and expense accounts have been closed, the Income Summary account has a credit balance of $90,000:

INCOME SUMMARY

| | Bal. | 90,000 |

● DAILY EXERCISE 12-5

The entry to close this account and allocate the profit to the partners' capital accounts is

Dec. 31	Income Summary	90,000	
	Cagle, Capital ($90,000 × 2/3)............		60,000
	Dean, Capital ($90,000 × 1/3)		30,000
	To allocate net income to partners.		

Consider the effect of this entry. Does Cagle get cash of $60,000 and Dean cash of $30,000? No. The increase in the partners' capital accounts cannot be linked to any particular asset, including cash. Instead, the entry indicates that Cagle's ownership in *all* the assets of the business increased by $60,000 and Dean's by $30,000.

If the year's operations resulted in a net loss of $66,000, the Income Summary account would have a debit balance of $66,000. In that case, the closing entry to allocate the loss to the partners' capital accounts would be

Dec. 31	Cagle, Capital ($66,000 × 2/3).....................	44,000	
	Dean, Capital ($66,000 × 1/3)	22,000	
	Income Summary		66,000
	To allocate net loss to partners.		

● DAILY EXERCISE 12-6

Just as a profit of $90,000 did not mean that the partners received cash of $60,000 and $30,000, so the loss of $66,000 does not mean that the partners must contribute cash of $44,000 and $22,000. A profit or loss will increase or decrease each partner's capital account, but cash may not change hands.

Sharing Based on Capital Contributions

Profits and losses are often allocated in proportion to capital contributions in the business. Suppose that Jenny Aycock, Erika Barber, and Sue Cordoba are partners in ABC Company. Their capital accounts have the following balances at the end of the year, before the closing entries:

Aycock, Capital.........................	$ 40,000
Barber, Capital.........................	60,000
Cordoba, Capital.....................	50,000
Total capital balances..............	$150,000

Assume that the partnership earned a profit of $120,000 for the year. To allocate this amount on the basis of capital contributions, compute each partner's percentage share of the partnership's total capital balance by dividing each partner's contribution by the total capital amount. These figures, multiplied by the $120,000 profit amount, yield each partner's share of the year's profits:

Aycock:	($40,000/$150,000) × $120,000 =	$ 32,000
Barber:	($60,000/$150,000) × $120,000 =	48,000
Cordoba:	($50,000/$150,000) × $120,000 =	40,000
	Net income allocated to partners =	$120,000

The closing entry to allocate the profit to the partners' capital accounts is

Dec. 31	Income Summary	120,000	
	Aycock, Capital...................................		32,000
	Barber, Capital....................................		48,000
	Cordoba, Capital.................................		40,000
	To allocate net income to partners.		

After this closing entry, the partners' capital balances are

Aycock, Capital ($40,000 + $32,000)...................................	$ 72,000
Barber, Capital ($60,000 + $48,000)....................................	108,000
Cordoba, Capital ($50,000 + $40,000).................................	90,000
Total capital balances after allocation of net income	$270,000

Sharing Based on Capital Contributions and on Service

One partner, regardless of capital contribution, may put more work into the business than the other partners do. Even among partners who log equal service time, one person's superior experience and knowledge may command a greater share of income. To reward the harder-working or more valuable person, the profit-and-loss-sharing method may be based on a combination of contributed capital *and* service to the business. The Chicago-based law firm **Baker & McKenzie,** for example, which has nearly 500 partners, takes seniority into account in determining partner compensation.

Assume that Debbie Randolph and Nancy Scott formed a partnership in which Randolph invested $60,000 and Scott invested $40,000, a total of $100,000. Scott devotes more time to the partnership and earns the larger salary. Accordingly, the two partners have agreed to share profits as follows:

1. The first $50,000 of partnership profits is to be allocated on the basis of partners' capital contributions to the business.
2. The next $60,000 of profits is to be allocated on the basis of service, with Randolph receiving $24,000 and Scott receiving $36,000.
3. Any remaining amount is to be allocated equally.

If net income for the first year is $125,000, the partners' shares of this profit are computed as follows:

	Randolph	Scott	Total
Total net income			$125,000
Sharing of first $50,000 of net income, based on capital contributions:			
Randolph ($60,000/$100,000 × $50,000) ..	$30,000		
Scott ($40,000/$100,000 × $50,000)		$20,000	
Total..			50,000
Net income remaining for allocation...............			75,000
Sharing of next $60,000, based on service:			
Randolph	24,000		
Scott		36,000	
Total..			60,000
Net income remaining for allocation...............			15,000
Remainder shared equally:			
Randolph ($15,000 × 1/2)	7,500		
Scott ($15,000 × 1/2)		7,500	
Total...			15,000
Net income remaining for allocation...............			$ 0
Net income allocated to the partners...............	$61,500	$63,500	$125,000

On the basis of this allocation, the closing entry is

Dec. 31	Income Summary...	125,000	
	Randolph, Capital...............................		61,500
	Scott, Capital		63,500
	To allocate net income to partners.		

 DAILY EXERCISE 12-7

Sharing Based on Salaries and on Interest

Partners may be rewarded for service and capital contributions in other ways. In one sharing plan, the partners are allocated salaries plus interest on their capital balances. Assume that Randy Lewis and Gerald Clark form an oil-exploration partnership. At the beginning of the year, their capital balances are $80,000 and $100,000, respectively. The partnership agreement allocates annual salaries of $43,000 to Lewis and $35,000 to Clark. After salaries are allocated, each partner earns 8% interest on his beginning capital balance. Any remaining net income is divided equally. Partnership profit of $96,000 will be allocated as follows:

	Lewis	Clark	Total
Total net income			$96,000
First, salaries:			
Lewis	$43,000		
Clark...		$35,000	
Total			78,000
Net income remaining for allocation			18,000
Second, interest on beginning capital balances:			
Lewis ($80,000 × 0.08).....................................	6,400		
Clark ($100,000 × 0.08)		8,000	
Total			14,400
Net income remaining for allocation			3,600
Third, remainder shared equally:			
Lewis ($3,600 × 1/2)	1,800		
Cleark ($3,600 × 1/2)		1,800	
Total			3,600
Net income remaining for allocation			$ 0
Net income allocated to the partners....................	$51,200	$44,800	$96,000

 DAILY EXERCISE 12-8

In the preceding illustration, net income exceeded the sum of salary and inter-est. If the partnership profit is less than the allocated sum of salary and interest, a negative remainder will occur at some stage in the allocation process. Even so, the partners use the same method for allocation purposes. For example, assume that Lewis and Clark Partnership earned only $82,000:

	Lewis	Clark	Total
Total net income			$82,000
First, salaries:			
Lewis	$43,000		
Clark...		$35,000	
Total			78,000
Net income remaining for allocation			4,000
Second, interest on beginning capital balances:			
Lewis ($80,000 × 0.08)..................................	6,400		
Clark ($100,000 × 0.08)		8,000	
Total			14,400
Net income remaining for allocation			10,400
Third, remainder shared equally:			
Lewis ($10,400 × 1/2)	(5,200)		
Clark ($10,400 × 1/2)		(5,200)	
Total			(10,400)
Net income remaining for allocation			$ 0
Net income allocated to the partners.................	$44,200	$37,800	$82,000

A net loss would be allocated to Lewis and Clark in the same manner outlined for net income. The sharing procedure would begin with the net loss and then allo-cate salary, interest, and any other specified amounts to the partners.

THINK IT OVER

Are these salaries and interest amounts business expenses in the usual sense? Explain your answer.

Answer: No, partners do not work for their own business to earn a salary, as an employee does. They do not loan money to their own business to earn interest. Their goal is for the partnership to earn a profit. Therefore, salaries and interest in partnership agreements are simply ways of expressing the allocation of prof-its and losses to the partners. For example, the salary component of partner income rewards service to the partnership. The interest component rewards a partner's investment of cash or other assets in the business. But the partners' salary and interest amounts are *not* salary expense and interest expense in the partnership's accounting or tax records.

Partner Drawings of Cash and Other Assets

Like anyone else, partners need cash for personal living expenses. Partnership agreements usually allow partners to withdraw cash or other assets from the busi-ness. Drawings from a partnership are recorded exactly as for a proprietorship. Assume that both Randy Lewis and Gerald Clark are allowed a monthly withdrawal of $3,500. The partnership records the March withdrawals with this entry:

Mar. 31	Lewis, Drawing	3,500	
	Clark, Drawing..	3,500	
	Cash..		7,000
	Monthly partner withdrawals of cash.		

During the year, each partner's drawing account accumulates 12 such amounts, a total of $42,000 ($3,500 × 12) per partner. At the end of the period, the general ledger shows the following account balances immediately after net income has been closed to the partners' capital accounts. Assume these beginning balances for Lewis and Clark at the start of the year and that $82,000 of profit has been allocated on the basis of the preceding illustration.

LEWIS, CAPITAL		CLARK, CAPITAL	
	Jan. 1 Bal. 80,000		Jan. 1 Bal. 100,000
	Dec. 31 Net. inc. 44,200		Dec. 31 Net. inc. 37,800

LEWIS, DRAWING		CLARK, DRAWING	
Dec. 31 Bal. 42,000		Dec. 31 Bal. 42,000	

The drawing accounts must be closed at the end of the period, exactly as for a proprietorship: The closing entry credits each partner's drawing account and debits each capital account. ➡

◂ We covered this closing entry in Chapter 4, page 137.

ADMISSION OF A PARTNER

The addition of a new member or the withdrawal of an existing member dissolves the partnership. We turn now to a discussion of how partnerships dissolve—and how new partnerships arise.

Objective 4
Account for the admission of a new partner to the business

Often, a new partnership is formed to carry on the former partnership's business. In fact, the new partnership may retain the dissolved partnership's name. **PricewaterhouseCoopers LLP,** for example, is an accounting/consulting firm that retires and hires partners during the year. Thus, the former partnership dissolves and a new partnership begins many times. But the business retains its name and continues operations. Other partnerships may dissolve and then re-form under a new name. Let's look at the ways a new member may gain admission into an existing partnership.

Admission by Purchasing a Partner's Interest

A person may become a member of a partnership by gaining the approval of the other partner (or partners) for entrance into the firm *and* by purchasing a present partner's interest in the business. Let's assume that Roberta Fisher and Benitez Garcia have a partnership that carries these figures:

Cash	$ 40,000	Total liabilities	$120,000
Other assets	360,000	Fisher, capital	110,000
		Garcia, capital	170,000
Total assets	$400,000	Total liabilities and capital	$400,000

Business is going so well that Fisher receives an offer from Barry Dynak, an outside party, to buy her $110,000 interest in the business for $150,000. Fisher agrees to sell out to Dynak, and Garcia approves Dynak as a new partner. The firm records the transfer of capital interest in the business with this entry:

Apr. 16	Fisher, Capital	110,000	
	Dynak, Capital		110,000
	To transfer Fisher's equity in the business to Dynak.		

The debit side of the entry closes Fisher's capital account because she is no longer a partner in the firm. The credit side opens Dynak's capital account because Fisher's equity has been transferred to Dynak. The entry amount is Fisher's capital balance ($110,000) and not the $150,000 Dynak paid Fisher to buy into the business. The full $150,000 goes to Fisher, including the $40,000 difference between her capital balance and the price received from Dynak. In this example, the partnership receives no cash because the transaction was between Dynak and Fisher, not between Dynak and the partnership. Suppose Dynak pays Fisher less than Fisher's capital balance. The entry on the partnership books is not affected. Fisher's equity is transferred to Dynak at book value ($110,000).

The old partnership has dissolved. Garcia and Dynak draw up a new partnership agreement with a new profit-and-loss-sharing ratio and continue business operations. If Garcia does not accept Dynak as a partner, Dynak gets no voice in management of the firm. However, under the Uniform Partnership Act, the purchaser shares in the profits and losses of the firm and in its assets at liquidation.

Admission by Investing in the Partnership

A person may be admitted as a partner by investing directly in the partnership rather than by purchasing an existing partner's interest. The new partner contributes assets—for example, cash, inventory, or equipment—to the business. Assume that the partnership of Robin Ingel and Michael Jay has the following assets, liabilities, and capital:

Cash	$ 20,000	Total liabilities	$ 60,000
Other assets	200,000	Ingel, capital	70,000
		Jay, capital	90,000
Total assets	$220,000	Total liabilities and capital	$220,000

Laura Kahn offers to invest equipment and land (Other Assets) with a market value of $80,000 to persuade the existing partners to take her into the business. Ingel and Jay agree to dissolve the existing partnership and to start up a new business, giving Kahn one-third interest—[$80,000/($70,000 + $90,000 + $80,000) = 1/3]—in exchange for the contributed assets. Notice that Kahn is buying into the partnership at book value because her one-third investment ($80,000) equals one-third of the new partnership's total capital ($240,000). The entry to record Kahn's investment is

July 18	Other Assets	80,000	
	Kahn, Capital		80,000
	To admit L. Kahn as a partner with a one-third interest in the business.		

After this entry, the partnership books show

Cash	$ 20,000	Total liabilities	$ 60,000
Other assets		Ingel, capital	70,000
($200,000 + $80,000)	280,000	Jay, capital	90,000
		Kahn, capital	80,000
Total assets	$300,000	Total liabilities and capital	$300,000

⊙ DAILY EXERCISE 12-9

⊙ DAILY EXERCISE 12-10

Kahn's one-third interest in the partnership does not necessarily entitle her to one-third of the profits. The sharing of profits and losses is a separate element in the partnership agreement.

ADMISSION BY INVESTING IN THE PARTNERSHIP—BONUS TO THE OLD PARTNERS The more successful a partnership, the higher the payment the partners may demand from a person entering the business. Partners in a business that is doing quite well might require an incoming person to pay them a bonus. The bonus increases the current partners' capital accounts.

Suppose that Hiro Nagasawa and Ralph Osburn's partnership has earned above-average profits for ten years. The two partners share profits and losses equally. The partnership balance sheet carries these figures:

Cash	$ 40,000	Total liabilities	$100,000
Other assets	210,000	Nagasawa, capital	70,000
		Osburn, capital	80,000
Total assets	$250,000	Total liabilities and capital	$250,000

The partners agree to admit Glen Parker to a one-fourth interest with his cash investment of $90,000. Parker's capital balance on the partnership books is only $60,000, computed as follows:

Partnership capital before Parker is admitted ($70,000 + $80,000)	$150,000
Parker's investment in the partnership...	90,000
Partnership capital after Parker is admitted...	$240,000
Parker's capital in the partnership ($240,000 × 1/4)	$ 60,000
Bonus to the old partners ($90,000 − $60,000)	$ 30,000

In effect, Parker had to buy into the partnership at a price ($90,000) above the book value of his one-fourth interest ($60,000). Parker's investment of an extra $30,000 creates a *bonus* for the existing partners. The entry on the partnership books to record Parker's investment is

Mar. 1	Cash	90,000	
	Parker, Capital		60,000
	Nagasawa, Capital ($30,000 × 1/2)............................		15,000
	Osburn, Capital ($30,000 × 1/2)................................		15,000
	To admit G. Parker as a partner with a one-fourth interest in the business.		

Parker's capital account is credited for his one-fourth interest in the partnership. The *bonus* is allocated to the partners on the basis of their profit-and-loss ratio.

The new partnership's balance sheet reports these amounts:

Cash ($40,000 + $90,000)...	$130,000	Total liabilities........................		$100,000
Other assets..........................	210,000	Nagasawa, capital		
		($70,000 + $15,000)		85,000
		Osburn, capital		
		($80,000 + $15,000)		95,000
		Parker, capital........................		60,000
Total assets	$340,000	Total liabilities and capital		$340,000

Mia and Susan are partners with capital balances of $25,000 and $75,000, respectively. They share profits and losses in a 30:70 ratio. Mia and Susan admit Tab to a 10% interest in a new partnership when Tab invests $20,000 in the business.

1. Journalize the partnership's receipt of cash from Tab.
2. What is each partner's capital in the new partnership?

Answers

1.	Cash	20,000	
	Tab, Capital		12,000
	Mia, Capital ($8,000 × 0.30)		2,400
	Susan, Capital ($8,000 × 0.70)................................		5,600
	To admit Tab with a 10% interest in the business.		

Partnership capital before Tab is admitted ($25,000 + $75,000).............	$100,000
Tab's investment in the partnership...	20,000
Partnership capital after Tab is admitted	$120,000
Tab's capital in the partnership ($120,000 × 1/10)	$ 12,000
Bonus to the old partners ($20,000 − $12,000)	$ 8,000

2. Partners' capital balances:

Mia, capital ($25,000 + $2,400).................	$ 27,400
Susan, capital ($75,000 + $5,600)	80,600
Tab, capital	12,000
Total partnership capital.............................	$120,000

ADMISSION BY INVESTING IN THE PARTNERSHIP—BONUS TO THE NEW PARTNER A potential new partner may be so important that the existing partners offer him or her a partnership share that includes a bonus. A law firm may strongly desire a former governor or other official as a partner because of the person's reputation and connections. A restaurant owner may want to go into partnership with a famous sports personality, movie star, or model. The popular chain **Planet Hollywood,** for example, opened its first restaurant in New York City with the help of celebrity partners Sylvester Stallone, Arnold Schwarzenegger, Bruce Willis, and Don Johnson.

Suppose that Allan Page and Olivia Franco have a law partnership. The firm's balance sheet appears as follows:

DAILY EXERCISE 12-13

Cash	$140,000	Total liabilities........................	$120,000
Other assets........................	360,000	Page, capital...........................	230,000
		Franco, capital	150,000
Total assets	$500,000	Total liabilities and capital	$500,000

Page and Franco admit Martin Schiller, a former attorney general, as a partner with a one-third interest in exchange for his cash investment of $100,000. At the time of Schiller's admission, the firm's capital is $380,000 (Page, $230,000, plus Franco, $150,000). Page and Franco share profits and losses in the ratio of two-thirds to Page and one-third to Franco. The computation of Schiller's equity in the partnership is

Partnership capital before Schiller is admitted ($230,000 + $150,000)	$380,000
Schiller's investment in the partnership	100,000
Partnership capital after Schiller is admitted	$480,000
Schiller's capital in the partnership ($480,000 × 1/3)	$160,000
Bonus to the new partner ($160,000 − $100,000)	$ 60,000

In this case, Schiller bought into the partnership at a price ($100,000) below the book value of his interest ($160,000). The bonus of $60,000 went to Schiller from the other partners. The capital accounts of Page and Franco are debited for the $60,000 difference between the new partner's equity ($160,000) and his investment ($100,000). The existing partners share this decrease in capital as though it were a loss, on the basis of their profit-and-loss ratio. The entry to record Schiller's investment is

Aug. 24	Cash	100,000	
	Page, Capital ($60,000 × 2/3)..............................	40,000	
	Franco, Capital ($60,000 × 1/3)	20,000	
	Schiller, Capital...		160,000
	To admit M. Schiller as a partner with a one-third interest in the business.		

The new partnership's balance sheet reports these amounts:

Cash		Total liabilities.......................	$120,000
($140,000 + $100,000)	$240,000	Page, capital	
Other assets.........................	360,000	($230,000 − $40,000)	190,000
		Franco, capital	
		($150,000 − $20,000)	130,000
		Schiller, capital	160,000
Total assets	$600,000	Total liabilities and capital	$600,000

WORK IT OUT

John and Ron are partners with capital balances of $30,000 and $40,000, respectively. They share profits and losses in a 25:75 ratio. John and Ron admit Lou to a 20% interest in a new partnership when Lou invests $10,000 in the business.

1. Journalize the partnership's receipt of cash from Lou.
2. What is each partner's capital in the new partnership?

Answers

1. Cash 10,000
   John, Capital ($6,000 × 0.25) 1,500
   Ron, Capital ($6,000 × 0.75) 4,500
       Lou, Capital 16,000
   To admit Lou with a 20% interest in the business.

Partnership capital before Lou is admitted ($30,000 + $40,000) $70,000
Lou's investment in the partnership 10,000
Partnership capital after Lou is admitted $80,000
Lou's capital in the partnership ($80,000 × 0.20) $16,000
Bonus to the new partner ($16,000 − $10,000) .... $ 6,000

2. Partners' capital balances:
   John, capital ($30,000 − $1,500) $28,500
   Ron, capital ($40,000 − $4,500) 35,500
   Lou, capital 16,000
   Total partnership capital $80,000

WITHDRAWAL (RESIGNATION OR DEATH) OF A PARTNER

Objective 5
Account for a partner's withdrawal (resignation) from the firm

A partner may withdraw from the business for many reasons, including retirement or a dispute with the other partners. The resignation of a partner dissolves the old partnership. The partnership agreement should contain a provision to govern how to settle with a withdrawing partner. In the simplest case, illustrated on page 476, a partner may resign and sell his or her interest to another partner in a personal transaction.

The only entry needed to record this transfer of equity debits the withdrawing partner's capital account and credits the purchaser's capital account. The dollar amount of the entry is the capital balance of the withdrawing partner, regardless of the price paid by the purchaser. The accounting when one current partner buys a second partner's interest is the same as when an outside party buys a current partner's interest.

If the partner resigns in the middle of an accounting period, the partnership books should be updated to determine each partner's capital balance. The business must measure net income or net loss for the fraction of the year up to the resignation date and allocate profit or loss according to the existing ratio. After the books have been closed, the business accounts for the change in partnership capital.

The withdrawing partner may receive his or her share of the business in partnership assets other than cash. Then the question is what value to assign the partnership assets—book value or current market value? The settlement procedure may specify an independent appraisal to determine current market value. If market values have changed, the appraisal will result in revaluing the partnership assets. The partners share in any market value changes that their efforts caused.

Suppose that Keith Isaac is retiring in midyear from the partnership of Green, Henry, and Isaac. After the books have been adjusted for partial-period income but before the asset appraisal, revaluation, and closing entries, the balance sheet reports the following:

Cash...........................		$ 39,000	Total liabilities		$ 80,000
Inventory...................		44,000	Green, capital		54,000
Land		55,000	Henry, capital		43,000
Building.....................	$95,000		Isaac, capital.............		21,000
Less Accum. depr. ...	(35,000)	60,000	Total liabilities and		
Total assets.................		$198,000	capital		$198,000

An independent appraiser revalues the inventory at $38,000 (down from $44,000) and the land at $101,000 (up from $55,000). The partners share the differences between these assets' market values and their prior book values on the basis of their profit-and-loss ratio.

The partnership agreement has allocated one-fourth of the profits to Susan Green, one-half to Charles Henry, and one-fourth to Keith Isaac. (This ratio may be written 1:2:1 for one part to Green, two parts to Henry, and one part to Isaac.) For each share that Green or Isaac has, Henry has two. The entries to record the revaluation of the inventory and land are

July 31	Green, Capital ($6,000 × 1/4)		1,500	
	Henry, Capital ($6,000 × 1/2)		3,000	
	Isaac, Capital ($6,000 × 1/4)		1,500	
	Inventory ($44,000 − $38,000)			6,000
	To revalue the inventory and allocate the loss to the partners.			
31	Land ($101,000 − $55,000)		46,000	
	Green, Capital ($46,000 × 1/4)			11,500
	Henry, Capital ($46,000 × 1/2)			23,000
	Isaac, Capital ($46,000 × 1/4)			11,500
	To revalue the land and allocate the gain to the partners.			

After the revaluations, the partnership balance sheet reports the following:

Cash		$ 39,000	Total liabilities..	$80,000
Inventory......................		38,000	Green, capital ($54,000 − $1,500 + $11,500).........	64,000
Land..............................		101,000	Henry, capital ($43,000 − $3,000 + $23,000)	63,000
Building	$95,000		Isaac, capital ($21,000 − $1,500 + $11,500)............	31,000
Less Accum. depr.	(35,000)	60,000		
Total assets		$238,000	Total liabilities and capital	$238,000

The books now carry the assets at current market value, which becomes the new book value, and the capital accounts have been adjusted accordingly. As the balance sheet shows, Isaac has a claim to $31,000 in partnership assets. How is his withdrawal from the business accounted for?

Withdrawal at Book Value

If Keith Isaac withdraws by receiving cash equal to the book value of his owner's equity, the entry will be

July 31	Isaac, Capital..	31,000	
	Cash..		31,000
	To record withdrawal of K. Isaac from the business.		

DAILY EXERCISE 12-14

This entry records the payment of partnership cash to Isaac and the closing of his capital account upon his withdrawal from the business.

Withdrawal at Less than Book Value

The withdrawing partner may be so eager to leave the business that he or she is willing to take less than his or her equity. Assume that Keith Isaac withdraws from the business and agrees to receive partnership cash of $10,000 and the new partnership's note for $15,000. This $25,000 settlement is $6,000 less than Isaac's $31,000 equity in the business. The remaining partners share this $6,000 difference—which is a bonus to them—according to their profit-and-loss ratio.

Because Isaac has withdrawn from the partnership, a new agreement—and a new profit-and-loss ratio—must be drawn up. In forming a new partnership, Henry and Green may decide on any ratio that they see fit. Let's assume they agree that Henry will earn two-thirds of partnership profits and losses and Green one-third. The entry to record Isaac's withdrawal at less than book value is

July 31	Isaac, Capital	31,000	
	Cash		10,000
	Note Payable to K. Isaac		15,000
	Green, Capital ($6,000 × 1/3)		2,000
	Henry, Capital ($6,000 × 2/3)		4,000
	To record withdrawal of K. Isaac from the business.		

Isaac's account is closed, and Henry and Green may or may not continue the business as a new partnership.

 DAILY EXERCISE 12-15

Withdrawal at More than Book Value

The settlement with a withdrawing partner may allow him or her to take assets of greater value than the book value of that partner's capital. Also, the remaining partners may be so eager for the withdrawing partner to leave the firm that they pay him or her a bonus to withdraw from the business. In either case, the partner's withdrawal causes a decrease in the book equity of the remaining partners. This decrease is allocated to the partners on the basis of their profit-and-loss ratio.

The accounting for this situation follows the pattern illustrated for withdrawal at less than book value—with one exception. The remaining partners' capital accounts are debited because the withdrawing partner receives more than his or her book equity.

 DAILY EXERCISE 12-16

 Matt is withdrawing from the partnership of Matt, Lee, and Karla. The partners share profits and losses in a 1:2:3 ratio for Matt, Lee, and Karla, respectively. After the revaluation of assets, Matt's capital balance is $50,000, and the other partners agree to pay her $60,000. Journalize the payment to Matt and his withdrawal from the partnership.

Answer

Matt, Capital	50,000	
Lee, Capital [($60,000 − $50,000) × 2/5]	4,000	
Karla, Capital [($60,000 − $50,000) × 3/5]	6,000	
Cash..		60,000
To record withdrawal of Matt from the business.		

Death of a Partner

Like any other form of partnership withdrawal, the death of a partner dissolves a partnership. The partnership accounts are adjusted to measure net income or loss for the fraction of the year up to the date of death, then closed to determine the partners' capital balances on that date. Settlement with the deceased partner's estate is based on the partnership agreement. The estate commonly receives partnership assets equal to the partner's capital balance. The partnership closes the deceased partner's capital account with a debit. This entry credits a payable to the estate.

Suppose Susan Green (of the partnership on page 480) dies after all accounts have been adjusted to current market value. Green's capital balance is $64,000. Green's estate may request cash for her final share of the partnership's assets. At this time the business has only $39,000 of cash, so it must borrow. Let's assume the partnership borrows $50,000 and then pays Green's estate for her capital balance. The partnership's journal entries are

Objective 6
Account for the liquidation of a partnership

Aug. 1	Cash	50,000	
	Note Payable		50,000
	To borrow money		
Aug. 1	Green, Capital	64,000	
	Cash		64,000
	To record withdrawal of Green from the business.		

Alternatively, a remaining partner may purchase the deceased partner's equity. The deceased partner's equity is debited, and the purchaser's equity is credited. The journal entry to record this transaction follows the pattern given on page 475 for the transfer of Fisher's equity over to Dynak. The amount of this entry is the ending credit balance in the deceased partner's capital account.

LIQUIDATION OF A PARTNERSHIP

LIQUIDATION. The process of going out of business by selling the entity's assets and paying its liabilities. The final step in liquidation is the distribution of any remaining cash to the owner(s).

Admission of a new partner or withdrawal or death of an existing partner dissolves the partnership. However, the business may continue operating with no apparent change to outsiders such as customers and creditors. In contrast, business **liquidation** is the process of going out of business by selling the entity's assets and paying its liabilities. The final step in liquidation is the *distribution of the remaining cash to the owners.* Before the business is liquidated, its books should be adjusted and closed. After closing, only asset, liability, and partners' capital accounts remain open.

Liquidation of a partnership includes three basic steps:

1. Sell the assets. Allocate the gain or loss to the partners' capital accounts on the basis of the profit-and-loss ratio.
2. Pay the partnership liabilities.
3. Disburse the remaining cash to the partners on the basis of their capital balances.

In practice, the liquidation of a business can stretch over weeks or months. Selling every asset and paying every liability of the entity takes time. After the partners of **Shea & Gould,** one of New York's best-known law firms, voted to dissolve their partnership, the firm remained open for an extra year to collect bills and pay off liabilities.

To avoid excessive detail in our illustrations, we include only two asset categories—Cash and Noncash Assets—and a single liability category—Liabilities. Our examples assume that the business sells the noncash assets in a single transaction and pays the liabilities in a single transaction.

Assume that Jane Avignon, Elaine Bloch, and Mark Crane have shared profits and losses in the ratio of 3:1:1. (This ratio is equal to 3/5, 1/5, 1/5, or a 60%, 20%, 20% sharing ratio.) They decide to liquidate their partnership. After the books are adjusted and closed, the general ledger contains the following balances:

Cash	$ 10,000	Liabilities	$ 30,000
Noncash assets	90,000	Avignon, capital....................	40,000
		Bloch, capital........................	20,000
		Crane, capital	10,000
Total assets	$100,000	Total liabilities and capital	$100,000

Sale of Noncash Assets at a Gain

Assume that the Avignon, Bloch, and Crane partnership sells its noncash assets (shown on the balance sheet as $90,000) for cash of $150,000. The partnership realizes a gain of $60,000, which is allocated to the partners on the basis of their profit-and-loss-sharing ratio. The entry to record this sale and allocation of the gain is

Oct. 31	Cash	150,000	
	Noncash Assets...		90,000
	Avignon, Capital ($60,000 × 0.60)		36,000
	Bloch, Capital ($60,000 × 0.20)		12,000
	Crane, Capital ($60,000 × 0.20)...................		12,000
	To sell noncash assets at a gain.		

The partnership must next pay off its liabilities:

Oct. 31	Liabilities	30,000	
	Cash		30,000
	To pay liabilities.		

In the final liquidation transaction, the remaining cash is disbursed to the partners. *The partners share in the cash according to their capital balances. (Gains and losses on the sale of assets are shared by the partners on the basis of their profit-and-loss-sharing ratio.)* The amount of cash left in the partnership is $130,000—the $10,000 beginning balance plus the $150,000 cash sale of assets minus the $30,000 cash payment of liabilities. The partners divide the remaining cash according to their capital balances:

Oct. 31	Avignon, Capital ($40,000 + $36,000)	76,000	
	Bloch, Capital ($20,000 + $12,000)	32,000	
	Crane, Capital ($10,000 + $12,000)	22,000	
	Cash		130,000
	To pay cash in liquidation.		

A convenient way to summarize the transactions in a partnership liquidation is given in Exhibit 12-4. Remember: Upon liquidation, gains on the sale of assets are divided according to the *profit-and-loss ratio*. The final cash payment to the partners is based on *capital balances*.

 DAILY EXERCISE 12-17

 DAILY EXERCISE 12-18

EXHIBIT 12-4 **Partnership Liquidation—Sale of Assets at a Gain**

	Cash	+	Noncash Assets	= Liabilities +	Capital Avignon (60%)	+	Bloch (20%)	+	Crane (20%)
Balance before sale of assets	$ 10,000		$90,000	$30,000	$40,000		$20,000		$10,000
Sale of assets and sharing of gain	150,000		(90,000)		36,000		12,000		12,000
Balances	160,000		0	30,000	76,000		32,000		22,000
Payment of liabilities	(30,000)			(30,000)					
Balances	130,000		0	0	76,000		32,000		22,000
Payment of cash to partners	(130,000)				(76,000)		(32,000)		(22,000)
Balances	$ 0		$ 0	$ 0	$ 0		$ 0		$ 0

After the payment of cash to the partners, the business has no assets, liabilities, or owners' equity. All the balances are zero. By the accounting equation, partnership assets *must* equal partnership liabilities plus partnership capital.

Sale of Noncash Assets at a Loss

Liquidation of a business often includes the sale of noncash assets at a loss. When this occurs, the partners' capital accounts are debited as they share the loss in their profit-and-loss-sharing ratio. Otherwise, the accounting follows the pattern illustrated for the sale of noncash assets at a gain.

The liquidation of the Dirk & Cross partnership included the sale of assets at a $150,000 loss. Lorraine Dirk's capital balance of $45,000 was less than her $60,000 share of the loss. Allocation of losses to the partners created a $15,000 deficit (debit balance) in Dirk's capital account. Identify ways that the partnership could deal with the negative balance (a capital deficiency) in Dirk's capital account.

Answer: Two possibilities are

1. Dirk could contribute assets to the partnership in an amount equal to her capital deficiency.
2. Joseph Cross could absorb Dirk's capital deficiency by decreasing his own capital balance.

Objective 7
Prepare partnership financial statements

PARTNERSHIP FINANCIAL STATEMENTS

Partnership financial statements are much like those of a proprietorship. However, a partnership income statement includes a section showing the division of net income to the partners. For example, the partnership of Leslie Gray and Wayne Hayward might report its statements for the year ended December 31, 20X3, as shown in Panel A of Exhibit 12-5. A proprietorship's statements are presented in Panel B for comparison.

EXHIBIT 12-5 **Financial Statements of a Partnership and a Proprietorship**

PANEL A—Partnership

GRAY & HAYWARD CONSULTING
Income Statement
Year Ended December 31, 20X3

		Thousands
Revenues		$460
Expenses		(270)
Net income		$190
Allocation of net income:		
To Gray	$114	
To Hayward	76	$190

GRAY & HAYWARD CONSULTING
Statement of Owners' Equity
Year Ended December 31, 20X3

	Thousands	
	Gray	Hayward
Capital, December 31, 20X2	$ 50	$ 40
Additional investments	10	—
Net income	114	76
Subtotal	174	116
Drawings	(72)	(48)
Capital, December 31, 20X3	$102	$ 68

GRAY & HAYWARD CONSULTING
Balance Sheet
December 31, 20X3

Assets	Thousands
Cash and other assets	$170
Owners' Equity	
Gray, capital	$102
Hayward, capital	68
Total capital	$170

PANEL B—Proprietorship

GRAY CONSULTING
Income Statement
Year Ended December 31, 20X3

	Thousands
Revenues	$460
Expenses	(270)
Net income	$190

GRAY CONSULTING
Statement of Owners' Equity
Year Ended December 31, 20X3

	Thousands
Capital, December 31, 20X2	$ 90
Additional investment	10
Net income	190
Subtotal	290
Drawings	(120)
Capital, December 31, 20X3	$170

GRAY CONSULTING
Balance Sheet
December 31, 20X3

Assets	Thousands
Cash and other assets	$170
Owner's Equity	
Gray, capital	$170

EXHIBIT 12-6 **Reporting Net Income for a Large Partnership**

DAILY EXERCISE 12-19

DAILY EXERCISE 12-20

MAIN PRICE & ANDERS
Statements of Earnings
Year Ended August 31, 20X4

	Thousands
Fees for professional services	$2,507,690
Earnings for the year	$ 832,340
Allocation of Earnings:	
To partners active during the year—	
Resigned, retired, and deceased partners	$ 109,901
Partners active at year end	627,730
To retired and deceased partners—retirement and death benefits	18,310
Not allocated to partners—retained for specific partnership purposes	76,399
	$ 832,340
Average earnings per partner active at year end (1,340 partners)	$ 621

Large partnerships may not find it feasible to report the net income of every partner. Instead, the firm may report the allocation of net income to active and retired partners and average earnings per partner. Exhibit 12-6 shows how the accounting/consulting firm Main Price & Anders reported its earnings.

The following Decision Guidelines feature summarizes the main points of accounting for partnerships.

DECISION GUIDELINES

Accounting for Partnerships

DECISION	GUIDELINES
How to organize the business?	A partnership offers both advantages and disadvantages in comparison with proprietorships and corporations. (See Exhibit 12-2).
On what matters should the partners agree?	See the list on page 466, under the heading "The Written Partnership Agreement."
At what value does the partnership record assets and liabilities?	Current market value on the date of acquisition, because, in effect, the partnership is buying its assets at their current market value.

How are partnership profits and losses shared among the partners?	• Equally if there is no profit-and-loss-sharing agreement.
	• As provided in the partnership agreement. Can be based on the partners'
	  a. Stated fractions
	  b. Capital contributions
	  c. Service to the partnership
	  d. Salaries and interest on their capital contributions

What happens when a partner withdraws from the partnership? How are new partners admitted to the partnership?	The old partnership ceases to exist. The remaining partners may or may not form a new partnership. • *Purchase a partner's interest.* The old partnership is dissolved. The remaining partners may admit the new partner to the partnership. If not, the new partner gets no voice in the management of the firm but shares in the profits and losses. Close the withdrawing partner's Capital account, and open a Capital account for the new partner. Carry over the old partner's Capital balance to the Capital account of the new partner. • *Invest in the partnership.* Buying in at book value creates no bonus to any partner. Buying in at a price above book value creates a bonus to the old partners. Buying in at a price below book value creates a bonus for the new partner.

How to account for the withdrawal of a partner from the business?	• First, adjust and close the books up to the date of the partner's withdrawal from the business.
	• Second, appraise the assets and the liabilities at their current market value.
	• Third, account for the partner's withdrawal
	  a. At book value (no change in remaining partners' Capital balances)
	  b. At less than book value (increase the remaining partners' Capital balances)
	  c. At more than book value (decrease the remaining partners' Capital balances)

What happens if the partnership goes out of business?	Liquidate the partnership, as follows:
	  a. Adjust and close the partnership books up to the date of liquidation.
	  b. Sell the partnership's assets. Allocate gain or loss to the partner's Capital accounts based on their profit-and-loss ratio.
	  c. Pay the partnership liabilities.
	  d. Pay any remaining cash to the partners based on their Capital balances.

How do partnership financial statements differ from those of a proprietorship?	• The partnership income statement reports the allocation of net income or net loss to the partners. • The partnership balance sheet (or a separate schedule) reports the Capital balance of each partner. • The statement of cash flows is the same for a partnership as for a proprietorship.

485

SUMMARY PROBLEM

The partnership of Taylor & Uvalde is considering admitting Steven Vaughn as a partner on January 1, 20X5. The partnership general ledger includes the following balances on that date:

Cash........................	$ 9,000	Total liabilities	$ 50,000
Other assets	110,000	Taylor, capital	45,000
		Uvalde, capital.........................	24,000
Total assets...........................	$119,000	Total liabilities and capital.......	$119,000

Ross Taylor's share of profits and losses is 60%, and Thomas Uvalde's share is 40%.

Required (Items 1 and 2 Are Independent)

1. Suppose that Vaughn pays Uvalde $31,000 to acquire Uvalde's interest in the business. Taylor approves Vaughn as a partner.
    a. Record the transfer of owner's equity on the partnership books.
    b. Prepare the partnership balance sheet immediately after Vaughn is admitted as a partner.
2. Suppose that Vaughn becomes a partner by investing $31,000 cash to acquire a one-fourth interest in the business.
    a. Compute Vaughn's capital balance, and record his investment in the business.
    b. Prepare the partnership balance sheet immediately after Vaughn is admitted as a partner. Include the heading.
3. Which way of admitting Vaughn to the partnership increases its total assets? Give your reason.

Solution

Requirement 1

a. Jan. 1   Uvalde, Capital.. 24,000
                      Vaughn, Capital................................. 24,000
                      To transfer Uvalde's equity in the partnership to Vaughn.

b. The balance sheet for the partnership of Taylor and Vaughn is identical to the balance sheet given for Taylor and Uvalde in the problem, except that Vaughn's name replaces Uvalde's name in the title and in the listing of Capital accounts.

Requirement 2

a. Computations of Vaughn's capital balance:

Partnership capital before Vaughn is admitted ($45,000 + $24,000)...	$ 69,000
Vaughn's investment in the partnership....................................	31,000
Partnership capital after Vaughn is admitted............................	$100,000
Vaughn's capital in the partnership ($100,000 × 1/4)	$ 25,000

Jan. 1   Cash 31,000
                Vaughn, Capital 25,000
                Taylor, Capital [($31,000 − $25,000) × 0.60]......... 3,600
                Uvalde, Capital [($31,000 − $25,000) × 0.40] 2,400
                To admit Vaughn as a partner with a one-fourth interest in the business.

b.

TAYLOR, UVALDE, & VAUGHN
Balance Sheet
January 1, 20X5

Cash ($9,000 + $31,000)	$ 40,000	Total liabilities	$ 50,000
Other assets	110,000	Taylor, capital ($45,000 + $3,600).............	48,600
		Uvalde, capital ($24,000 + $2,400)............	26,400
		Vaughn, capital	25,000
Total assets..............................	$150,000	Total liabilities and capital......	$150,000

LESSONS LEARNED

1. **Identify the characteristics of a partnership.** A *partnership* is a business co-owned by two or more persons for profit. The characteristics of this form of business organization are its *ease of formation, limited life, mutual agency, unlimited liability,* and *no partnership income taxes.* A written *partnership agreement* establishes procedures for admission of a new partner, withdrawal of a partner, and the sharing of profits and losses among the partners.

2. **Account for the partners' investments in a partnership.** Accounting for a partnership is similar to accounting for a proprietorship. Each partner has an individual capital account and a withdrawal account.

3. **Allocate profits and losses to the partners.** Partners share net income or loss in any manner they choose. Common sharing agreements base the *profit-and-loss ratio* on a stated fraction, partners' capital contributions, and/or their service to the partnership.

4. **Account for the admission of a partner to the business.** An outside person may become a partner by purchasing a current partner's interest or by investing in the partner-ship. The new partner may pay the current partners a bonus to join. Or the new partner may receive a bonus to join.

5. **Account for a partner's withdrawal (resignation) from the firm.** When a partner withdraws, partnership assets may be reappraised. Partners share any gain or loss on the asset revaluation on the basis of their profit-and-loss ratio. The withdrawing partner may receive payment equal to, greater than, or less than his or her capital book value, depending on the agreement with the other partners.

6. **Account for the liquidation of a partnership.** In *liquidation,* a partnership goes out of business by selling the assets, paying the liabilities, and disbursing any remaining cash to the partners.

7. **Prepare partnership financial statements.** Partnership *financial statements* are similar to those of a proprietorship. The partnership income statement commonly allocates net income to the partners, and the balance sheet has a Capital account for each partner.

ACCOUNTING VOCABULARY

articles of partnership (p. 465)
dissolution (p. 466)
general partnership (p. 468)
limited liability partnership
  (p. 468)

limited partnership (p. 468)
liquidation (p. 482)
LLPs (p. 468)
mutual agency (p. 466)
partnership (p. 465)

partnership agreement (p. 465)
S Corporation (p. 468)
unlimited personal liability
  (p. 466)

QUESTIONS

1. What is another name for a partnership agreement? List eight items that the agreement should specify.
2. Ron Montgomery, who is a partner in M&N Associates, commits the firm to a contract for a job within the scope of its regular business operations. What term describes Montgomery's ability to obligate the partnership?
3. If a partnership cannot pay a debt, who must make the payment? What term describes this obligation of the partners?
4. How is the income of a partnership taxed?
5. Identify the advantages and disadvantages of the partnership form of business organization.
6. Rex Randall and Ken Smith's partnership agreement states that Randall gets 60% of profits and Smith gets 40%. If the agreement does not discuss the treatment of losses, how are losses shared? How do the partners share profits and losses if the agreement specifies no profit-and-loss-sharing ratio?

7. Do partner withdrawals of cash for personal use affect the sharing of profits and losses by the partner? If so, explain how. If not, explain why not.
8. Name two events that can cause the dissolution of a partnership.
9. When a partner resigns from the partnership and receives assets greater than his or her capital balance, how is the excess shared by the other partners?
10. Name the three steps in liquidating a partnership.
11. The partnership of Cope and Hope is in the process of liquidation. How do the partners share (a) gains and losses on the sale of noncash assets, and (b) the final cash distribution?
12. Summarize the situations in which partnership allocations are based on (a) the profit-and-loss-sharing ratio, and (b) the partners' capital balances.

DAILY EXERCISES

Partnership characteristics
(Obj. 1)

DE12-1 After studying the characteristics of a partnership, write two short paragraphs, as follows:

1. Explain the *advantages* of a partnership over a proprietorship and a corporation.
2. Explain the *disadvantages* of a partnership over a proprietorship and a corporation.

Partnership characteristics
(Obj. 1)

DE12-2 Timothy Lane and Sam Medford are forming a business to imprint T-shirts. Lane suggests that they organize as a partnership in order to avoid the unlimited personal liability of a proprietorship. According to Lane, partnerships are not very risky.

Lane explains to Medford that if the business does not succeed, each partner can withdraw from the business, taking the same assets that he or she invested at its beginning. Lane states that the main disadvantage of the partnership form of organization is double taxation: First, the partnership pays a business income tax; second, each partner also pays personal income tax on his or her share of the business's profits.

Correct the errors in Lane's explanation.

A partner's investment in a
partnership
(Obj. 2)

DE12-3 Dean Hahn invests a building in a partnership with Margo Klem. Hahn purchased the building in 20X1 for $300,000. Accumulated depreciation to the date of forming the partnership is $80,000. A real estate appraiser states that the building is now worth $285,000. Hahn wants $400,000 capital in the new partnership, but Klem objects. Klem believes that capital contribution into the partnership should be measured by the book value of his building.

Klem and Hahn seek your advice. Which value of the building is appropriate for measuring Hahn's capital, book value or current market value? State the reason for your answer. Give the partnership's journal entry to record Hahn's investment in the business.

Investments by partners
(Obj. 2)

DE12-4 Seth Green and Nate Smith are forming the partnership Sun Florida Development to develop a theme park near Panama City. Green contributes cash of $4 million and land valued at $17 million. When Green purchased the land in 20X1, its cost was $8 million. The partnership will assume Green's $3 million note payable on the land. Smith invests cash of $10 million and construction equipment that he purchased for $7 million (accumulated depreciation to date, $3 million). The equipment's market value is equal to its book value.

1. Before recording any journal entries, compute the partnership's total assets, total liabilities, and total owners' equity immediately after organizing.
2. Journalize the partnership's receipt of assets and liabilities from Green and from Smith. Record each asset at its current market value with no entry to accumulated depreciation.
3. Use your journal entries to prove the correctness of total owners' equity from requirement 1.

Partners' profits, losses, and
capital balances
(Obj. 3)

DE12-5 Examine the Benz and Hanna balance sheet in Exhibit 12-3, page 471. Note that Benz invested far more in the partnership than Hanna. Suppose the two partners fail to agree upon a profit-and-loss-sharing ratio. For the first month (June 20X5), the partnership lost $15,000.

1. How much of this loss goes to Benz? How much goes to Hanna?
2. Assume the partners withdrew no cash or other assets during June. What is each partner's capital balance at June 30? Prepare a T-account for each partner's capital to answer this question.

Partners' profits, drawings, and
capital balances; closing entries
(Obj. 3)

DE12-6 ← *Link Back to Chapter 4 (Closing Entries).* Return to the Benz and Hanna balance sheet in Exhibit 12-3, page 471. The partnership earned $115,000 during the year ended May 31, 20X6, its first year of operation. The partners share profits and losses based on their capital balances at the beginning of the year. During the first year, Benz withdrew $70,000 cash from the business and Hanna's drawings totaled $50,000.

1. Journalize the entries for (a) partner withdrawals of cash, (b) closing the business's profits into the partner's capital accounts at May 31, 20X6, and (c) closing the partners' drawing accounts.
2. Post to the partners' capital accounts after inserting their beginning amounts. What is the amount of total partnership capital at May 31, 20X6?

Allocating partnership profits
based on capital contributions
and service
(Obj. 3)

DE12-7 Lawson, Martinez, and Edwards have capital balances of $20,000, $30,000, and $50,000, respectively. The partners share profits and losses as follows:

a. The first $40,000 is divided based on the partners' capital balances.
b. The next $40,000 is based on service, equally shared by Lawson and Edwards.
c. The remainder is divided equally.

Compute each partner's share of the business's $140,000 net income for the year.

DE12-8 Lucy Fung and Ako Kiawa have capital balances of $30,000 and $40,000, respectively. The partners share profits and losses as follows:

Allocating partnership profits based on salaries and interest (Obj. 3)

a. Fung receives a salary of $15,000 and Kiawa a salary of $10,000.
b. The partners earn 7% interest on their capital balances.
c. The remainder is shared equally.

Compute each partner's share of the year's net income of $50,000.

DE12-9 Study the Ingel and Jay partnership balance sheet near the top of page 476. Claire Reynoldo pays $110,000 to purchase Michael Jay's interest in the partnership.

Admitting a partner who purchases an existing partner's interest (Obj. 4)

1. Journalize the partnership's transaction to admit Reynoldo to the partnership. What happens to the $20,000 difference between Reynoldo's payment and Jay's capital balance?
2. Must Robin Ingel accept Claire Reynoldo as a full partner? What right does Reynoldo have after purchasing Jay's interest in the partnership?

DE12-10 Return to the partnership balance sheet of Ingel and Jay near the top of page 476. Larry Welsh invests cash of $80,000 to acquire a one-third interest in the partnership.

Admitting a partner who invests in the business (Obj. 4)

1. Does Welsh's investment provide a bonus to the partners? Show calculations to support your answer.
2. Journalize the partnership's receipt of the $80,000 from Welsh.

Admitting a new partner; bonus to the existing partners (Obj. 4)

DE12-11 Study the partnership balance sheet of Nagasawa and Osburn on page 476. Suppose Christine Kliptel invests $50,000 to purchase a one-fifth interest in the new partnership of Nagasawa, Osburn, and Kliptel (NOK Partners).
Journalize the partnership's receipt of cash from Kliptel.

Preparing a partnership balance sheet (Obj. 7)

DE12-12 This exercise uses the data given in Daily Exercise 12-11. After recording the partnership's receipt of cash from Kliptel in Daily Exercise 12-11, prepare the balance sheet of the new partnership of NOK Partners at June 30, 20X2. Include a complete heading.

Admitting a new partner; bonus to the new partner (Obj. 4)

DE12-13 Refer to the partnership balance sheet of Page and Franco near the top of page 478 and the paragraph immediately following the balance sheet. Assume Everett invests $140,000 to acquire a 30% interest in the new partnership of Page, Franco, and Everett.
Journalize the partnership's receipt of cash from Everett.

DE12-14 Examine the Green, Henry, and Isaac balance sheet at the top of page 480.

Withdrawal of a partner (Obj. 5)

1. The partners share profits and losses as follows: 25% to Green, 50% to Henry, and 25% to Isaac. Suppose Susan Green is withdrawing from the business, and the partners agree that no appraisal of assets is needed. How much in assets can Green take from the partnership? Give the reason for your answer, including an explanation of why the profit-and-loss-sharing ratio is not used for this determination.
2. Henry and Isaac plan to form a new partnership to continue the business. If Green demands cash for her full settlement upon withdrawing from the business, how can Henry and Isaac come up with the cash to pay Green? Identify two ways.

Withdrawal of a partner at more than book value; asset revaluation (Obj. 5)

DE12-15 Return to the Green, Henry, and Isaac partnership balance sheet near the middle of page 480. Suppose Henry is retiring from the business and the partners agree to revalue the assets at their current market value. A real-estate appraiser issues his professional opinion that the current market value of the land is $150,000. The book values of all other assets approximate their current market value.
Journalize (a) the revaluation of the land, (b) borrowing $90,500 on a note payable in order to pay Henry, and (c) payment of $90,500 to Henry upon his retirement from the business on July 31.

Withdrawal of a partner at less than book value (Obj. 5)

DE12-16 This exercise uses the data given in Daily Exercise 12-15 with one modification. Assume Henry is retiring from the partnership and agrees to take cash of $60,500.
Journalize the payment of $60,500 to Henry upon his withdrawal from the partnership.

Liquidation of a partnership at a loss (Obj. 6)

DE12-17 Use the data in Exhibit 12-4, page 483. Suppose the partnership of Avignon, Bloch, and Crane liquidates by selling all noncash assets for $75,000.
Complete the liquidation schedule as shown in Exhibit 12-4.

DE12-18 This exercise builds on the solution to Daily Exercise 12-17. After completing the liquidation schedule in Daily Exercise 12-17, journalize the partnership's (a) sale of noncash assets for $75,000 (use a single account for Noncash Assets), (b) payment of liabilities, and (c) payment of cash to the partners. Include an explanation with each entry.

Liquidation of a partnership (Obj. 6)

DE12-19 This exercise uses the Green, Henry, and Isaac balance sheet, after revaluation of inventory and land, given in the middle of page 480. Furthermore, assume Isaac has withdrawn from the partnership at less than his book value, as recorded at the top of page 481.
Prepare the balance sheet of the new partnership of Green and Henry on July 31.

Partnership balance sheet (Obj. 7)

DE12-20 The partnership of Frost and Martin had these balances at September 30, 20X4:

Cash	$20,000	Service revenue	$140,000
Liabilities	40,000	Frost, capital	30,000
Martin, capital	10,000	Total expenses	35,000
Other assets	60,000		

Frost gets two-thirds of profits and losses, and Martin one-third.

Prepare the partnership's income statement for the year ended September 30, 20X4.

EXERCISES

E12-1 Suzanne Drake, a friend from college, approaches you about forming a partnership to export software. Since graduating, Drake has worked for the International Trade Bank, developing important contacts among government officials and business leaders in Eastern Europe. Drake believes she is in a unique position to capitalize on the growing market in Eastern Europe for American computers. With expertise in finance, you would have responsibility for accounting and finance in the partnership.

Required

Discuss the advantages and disadvantages of organizing the export business as a partnership rather than a proprietorship. Comment on how partnership income is taxed and how your taxes would change if you organized as an S corporation.

E12-2 Mason Flute has been operating an apartment-locater service as a proprietorship. He and Barrett Schraeder have decided to reorganize the business as a partnership. Flute's investment in the partnership consists of cash, $16,300; accounts receivable, $10,600, less allowance for uncollectibles, $800; office furniture, $2,700, less accumulated depreciation, $1,100; a small building, $55,000, less accumulated depreciation, $27,500; accounts payable, $3,300; and a note payable to the bank, $10,000.

To determine Flute's equity in the partnership, he and Schraeder hire an independent appraiser. This outside party provides the following market values of the assets and liabilities that Flute is contributing to the business: cash, accounts receivable, office furniture, accounts payable, and note payable—the same as Flute's book value; allowance for uncollectible accounts, $2,900; building, $71,000; and accrued expenses payable (including interest on the note payable), $1,200.

Required

Make the entry on the partnership books to record Flute's investment.

Computing partners' shares of
net income and net loss
(Obj. 3)

E12-3 Adam Meppen and Bailey Quaid form a partnership, investing $40,000 and $70,000, respectively. Determine their shares of net income or net loss for each of the following situations:

  a. Net loss is $52,000 and the partners have no written partnership agreement.

  b. Net income is $77,000, and the partnership agreement states that the partners share profits and losses on the basis of their capital contributions.

  c. Net loss is $33,000, and the partnership agreement states that the partners share profits on the basis of their capital contributions.

  d. Net income is $98,000. The first $60,000 is shared on the basis of partner capital contributions. The next $30,000 is based on partner service, with Meppen receiving 30% and Quaid receiving 70%. The remainder is shared equally.

E12-4 Adam Meppen withdrew cash of $47,000 for personal use, and Bailey Quaid withdrew cash of $53,000 during the year. Using the data from situation (d) in Exercise 12-3, journalize the entries to close (a) the income summary account, and (b) the partners' drawing accounts. Explanations are not required. What was the overall effect on partnership capital?

E12-5 Trey Falco is admitted to a partnership. Prior to his admission, the partnership books show Sean Graham's capital balance at $100,000 and Kelly Ott's capital balance at $50,000. Compute each partner's equity on the books of the new partnership under the following plans:

  a. Falco pays $92,000 for Ott's equity. Falco's payment is not an investment in the partnership, but instead goes directly to Ott.

  b. Falco invests $75,000 to acquire a one-third interest in the partnership.

  c. Falco invests $60,000 to acquire a one-fourth interest in the partnership.

E12-6 Make the partnership journal entry to record the admission of Falco under plans (a), (b), and (c) in Exercise 12-5. Explanations are not required.

Admitting a new partner (*Obj. 4*)

E12-7 After the books are closed, Echols & Schaeffer's partnership balance sheet reports capital of $60,000 for Echols and $80,000 for Schaeffer. Echols is withdrawing from the firm. The partners agree to write down partnership assets by $45,000. They have shared profits and losses in the ratio of one-third to Echols and two-thirds to Schaeffer. The partnership agreement states that a withdrawing partner will receive assets equal to the book value of his owner's equity.

Withdrawal of a partner (*Obj. 5*)

1. How much will Echols receive? Schaeffer will continue to operate the business as a proprietorship.
2. What is Schaeffer's beginning capital on the proprietorship books?

E12-8 Eve Bermuda is retiring from the partnership of Bermuda, Rye, and Augustine on May 31. The partner capital balances are Bermuda, $36,000; Rye, $51,000; and Augustine, $22,000. The partners agree to have the partnership assets revalued to current market values. The independent appraiser reports that the book value of the inventory should be decreased by $12,000, and the book value of the land should be increased by $32,000. The partners agree to these revaluations. The profit-and-loss ratio has been 5:3:2 for Bermuda, Rye, and Augustine, respectively. In retiring from the firm, Bermuda receives $25,000 cash and a $25,000 note from the partnership.

Withdrawal of a partner (*Obj. 5*)

Required

Journalize (a) the asset revaluations, and (b) Bermuda's withdrawal from the firm.

E12-9 Barry, McCall, and Flaten are liquidating their partnership. Before selling the noncash assets and paying the liabilities, the capital balances are Barry, $23,000; McCall, $20,000; and Flaten, $11,000. The partnership agreement divides profits and losses equally.

Liquidation of a partnership (*Obj. 6*)

Required

1. After selling the noncash assets and paying the liabilities, the partnership has cash of $54,000. How much cash will each partner receive in final liquidation?
2. After selling the noncash assets and paying the liabilities, the partnership has cash of $45,000. How much cash will each partner receive in final liquidation?

E12-10 Prior to liquidation, the accounting records of Deluth, Liu, and Bush included the following balances and profit-and-loss-sharing percentages:

Liquidation of a partnership (*Obj. 6*)

	Cash	+	Noncash Assets	=	Liabilities	+	Capital Deluth (40%)	+	Liu (30%)	+	Bush (30%)
Balances before sale of assets.............	$ 8,000		$57,000		$19,000		$20,000		$15,000		$11,000

The partnership sold the noncash assets for $69,000, paid the liabilities, and disbursed the remaining cash to the partners. Complete the summary of transactions in the liquidation of the partnership. Use the format illustrated in Exhibit 12-4.

E12-11 The partnership of Valahu, Leman, and Sucre is dissolving. Business assets, liabilities, and partners' capital balances prior to dissolution follow. The partners share profits and losses as follows: Marie Valahu, 25%; Pierre Leman, 45%; and Anna Sucre, 30%.

Liquidation of a partnership (*Obj. 6*)

Required

Create a spreadsheet or solve manually (see the top of page 492)—as directed by your instructor—to show the ending balances in all accounts after the noncash assets are sold for $136,000 and for $90,000. Determine the unknown amounts. Identify two ways the partners can deal with the negative ending balance in Sucre's capital account.

Challenge Exercise

E12-12 On October 31, 20X2, Steve Klatt and Russell Stover agree to combine their proprietorships as a partnership. Their balance sheets on October 31 are shown on page 492.

Partnership balance sheet (*Obj. 7*)

Required

Prepare the partnership balance sheet at October 31, 20X2.

EXERCISE 12-11 Valahu, Leman, and Sucre

	A	B	C	D	E	F
1			**VALAHU, LEMAN, AND SUCRE**			
2			**Sale of Noncash Assets**			
3			**(For $136,000)**			
4						
5		Noncash		Valahu	Leman	Sucre
6	Cash	Assets	Liabilities	Capital	Capital	Capital
7	$ 6,000	$126,000	$77,000	$12,000	$37,000	$6,000
8	136,000	(126,000)		?	?	?
9						
10	$142,000	$ 0	$77,000	$?	$?	$?
11						
12				($A8–$B7) * .25		
13						
14						
15			**(For $90,000)**			
16		Noncash		Valahu	Leman	Sucre
17	Cash	Assets	Liabilities	Capital	Capital	Capital
18	$ 6,000	$126,000	$77,000	$12,000	$37,000	$6,000
19	90,000	(126,000)		?	?	?
20						
21	$96,000	$ 0	$77,000	$?	$?	$?
22						
23				($A19–$B18) * .25		
24						

EXERCISE 12-12
Klatt and Stover

	Klatt's Business		Stover's Business	
	Book Value	Current Market Value	Book Value	Current Market Value
Assets				
Cash	$ 3,700	$ 3,700	$ 4,000	$ 4,000
Accounts receivable (net)	22,000	20,200	8,000	6,300
Inventory	51,000	46,000	34,000	35,100
Plant assets (net)	121,800	103,500	53,500	57,400
Total assets	$198,500	$173,400	$99,500	$102,800
Liabilities and Capital				
Accounts payable	$ 25,500	$ 25,500	$ 8,300	$ 8,300
Accrued expenses payable	2,200	2,200	1,400	1,400
Notes payable	55,000	55,000		
Klatt, capital	115,800	?		
Stover, capital			89,800	?
Total liabilities and capital	$198,500	$173,400	$99,500	$102,800

(Group A) PROBLEMS

Writing a partnership agreement
(Obj. 1)

P12-1A Levita Nuñez and Rosa Lupe Gaitan are discussing the formation of a partnership to import dresses from Guatemala. Nuñez is especially artistic, so she will travel to Central America to buy merchandise. Gaitan is a super salesperson and has already lined up several large stores to which she can sell the dresses.

Required

Write a partnership agreement to cover all elements essential for the business to operate smoothly. Make up names, amounts, profit-and-loss-sharing percentages, and so on as needed.

Investments by partners
(Obj. 2, 7)

P12-2A Beth Saran and Jake Gentry formed a partnership on March 15. The partners agreed to invest equal amounts of capital. Gentry invested his proprietorship's assets and liabilities (credit balances in parentheses). See the table at the top of the next page.

	Gentry's Book Value	Current Market Value
Accounts receivable............................	$12,000	$12,000
Allowance for doubtful accounts......	(740)	(1,360)
Inventory..	43,850	31,220
Prepaid expenses	3,700	3,700
Store equipment................................	36,700	26,600
Accumulated depreciation................	(9,200)	(–0–)
Accounts payable..............................	(22,300)	(22,300)

On March 15, Saran invested cash in an amount equal to the current market value of Gentry's partnership capital. The partners decided that Gentry would earn 70% of partnership profits because he would manage the business. Saran agreed to accept 30% of profits. During the period ended December 31, the partnership earned net income of $70,000. Saran's drawings were $27,000, and Gentry's drawings were $41,000.

Required

1. Journalize the partners' initial investments.
2. Prepare the partnership balance sheet immediately after its formation on March 15.
3. Journalize the December 31 entries to close the Income Summary account and the partners' drawing accounts.

P12-3A Lost Pines Escape is a partnership, and its owners are considering admitting Victor Lampe as a new partner. On July 31 of the current year, the capital accounts of the three existing partners and their shares of profits and losses are as follows:

Admitting a new partner (Obj. 4)

	Capital	Profit-and-Loss Ratio
Eric Runyan...............	$48,000	1/6
Sara Braden...............	64,000	1/3
Ken Maness...............	88,000	1/2

Required

Journalize the admission of Lampe as a partner on July 31 for each of the following independent situations:

1. Lampe pays Maness $114,000 cash to purchase Maness's interest.
2. Lampe invests $50,000 in the partnership, acquiring a one-fifth interest in the business.
3. Lampe invests $50,000 in the partnership, acquiring a one-eighth interest in the business.
4. Lampe invests $30,000 in the partnership, acquiring an 18% interest in the business.

P12-4A Rudy Trump, Monica Rivers, and Courtney Jetta have formed a partnership. Trump invested $20,000; Rivers, $40,000; and Jetta, $60,000. Trump will manage the store, Rivers will work in the store three-quarters of the time, and Jetta will not work.

Computing partners' shares of net income and net loss (Obj. 3, 7)

Required

1. Compute the partners' shares of profits and losses under each of the following plans:
   a. Net income is $87,000, and the articles of partnership do not specify how profits and losses are shared.
   b. Net loss is $47,000, and the partnership agreement allocates 45% of profits to Trump, 35% to Rivers, and 20% to Jetta. The agreement does not discuss the sharing of losses.
   c. Net income is $104,000. The first $50,000 is allocated on the basis of salaries of $34,000 for Trump and $16,000 for Rivers. The remainder is allocated on the basis of partner capital contributions.
   d. Net income for the year ended September 30, 20X4, is $86,000. The first $30,000 is allocated on the basis of partner capital contributions. The next $30,000 is based on service, with $20,000 going to Trump and $10,000 going to Rivers. Any remainder is shared equally.
2. Revenues for the year ended September 30, 20X4, were $572,000, and expenses were $486,000. Under plan (d), prepare the partnership income statement for the year.

P12-5A Custom Homes is a partnership owned by three individuals. The partners share profits and losses in the ratio of 30% to Pam Tracy, 40% to Bill Mertz, and 30% to Cameron Brucks. At December 31, 20X3, the firm has the balance sheet shown at the top of page 494. Tracy withdraws from the partnership on this date.

Withdrawal of a partner (Obj. 4, 5)

Required

Record Tracy's withdrawal from the partnership under the following plans:

Cash...............................		$ 25,000	Total liabilities	$103,000
Accounts receivable........	$ 16,000			
Less allowance for uncollectibles...........	(1,000)	15,000		
Inventory.......................		92,000	Tracy, capital...............	38,000
Equipment.....................	130,000		Mertz, capital	49,000
Less accumulated depreciation.............	(30,000)	100,000	Brucks, capital........... Total liabilities and	42,000
Total assets		$232,000	capital	$232,000

1. Tracy gives her interest in the business to Sally Schuster, her cousin.
2. In personal transactions, Tracy sells her equity in the partnership to Walt Fair and Beverly Holtz, who each pay Tracy $35,000 for half her interest. Mertz and Brucks agree to accept Fair and Holtz as partners.
3. The partnership pays Tracy cash of $9,000 and gives her a note payable for the remainder of her book equity in settlement of her partnership interest.
4. Tracy receives cash of $6,000 and a note payable for $34,000 from the partnership.
5. The partners agree that the equipment is worth $160,000 and that accumulated depreciation should remain at $30,000. After the revaluation, the partnership settles with Tracy by giving her cash of $15,000 and inventory for the remainder of her book equity.

Liquidation of a partnership (Obj. 6)

P12-6A The partnership of Jackson, Pierce, & Fenner has experienced operating losses for three consecutive years. The partners—who have shared profits and losses in the ratio of Leigh Jackson, 15%; Trent Pierce, 60%; and Bruce Fenner, 25%—are considering the liquidation of the business. They ask you to analyze the effects of liquidation under various possibilities regarding the sale of the noncash assets. They present the following condensed partnership balance sheet at December 31, end of the current year:

Cash	$ 7,000	Liabilities...........................	$ 63,000
Noncash assets	163,000	Jackson, capital...............	24,000
		Pierce, capital..................	66,000
		Fenner, capital	17,000
		Total liabilities and	
Total assets	$170,000	capital..........................	$170,000

Required

1. Prepare a summary of liquidation transactions (as illustrated in Exhibit 12-4) for each of the following situations:
   a. The noncash assets are sold for $183,000.
   b. The noncash assets are sold for $141,000.
2. Make the journal entries to record the liquidation transactions in requirement 1(b).

Liquidation of a partnership (Obj. 6)

P12-7A ← *Link Back to Chapter 4 (Closing Entries)*. ABS & Company is a partnership owned by Alberts, Beech, and Sumner, who share profits and losses in the ratio of 1:3:4. The adjusted trial balance of the partnership (in condensed form) at June 30, end of the current fiscal year, follows.

ABS & COMPANY
Adjusted Trial Balance
June 30, 20XX

Cash	$ 24,000	
Noncash assets	116,000	
Liabilities...........................		$100,000
Alberts, capital		22,000
Beech, capital...................		41,000
Sumner, capital		62,000
Alberts, drawing...............	14,000	
Beech, drawing	35,000	
Sumner, drawing	54,000	
Revenues..........................		108,000
Expenses	90,000	
Totals	$333,000	$333,000

Required

1. Prepare the June 30 entries to close the revenue, expense, income summary, and drawing accounts.
2. Insert the opening capital balances in the partners' capital accounts, post the closing entries to the capital accounts, and determine each partner's ending capital balance.
3. The partnership liquidates on June 30 by selling the noncash assets for $105,000. Using the ending balances of the partners' capital accounts computed in requirement 2, prepare a summary of liquidation transactions (as illustrated in Exhibit 12-4).

PROBLEMS

P12-1B Anne Avonlee and Gus Teamley are discussing the formation of a partnership to install payroll accounting systems. Avonlee is skilled in systems design, and she is convinced that her designs will draw large sales volumes. Teamley is a super salesperson and has already lined up several clients.

Writing a partnership agreement (Obj. 1)

Required

Write a partnership agreement to cover all elements essential for the business to operate smoothly. Make up names, amounts, profit-and-loss-sharing percentages, and so on as needed.

P12-2B On June 30, Lou Busby and Marshall Box formed a partnership. The partners agreed to invest equal amounts of capital. Busby invested his proprietorship's assets and liabilities (credit balances in parentheses).

Investments by partners (Obj. 2, 7)

	Busby Book Value	Current Market Value
Accounts receivable	$ 7,200	$ 7,200
Allowance for doubtful accounts	(–0–)	(1,050)
Inventory	22,340	24,100
Prepaid expenses	1,700	1,700
Office equipment	45,900	27,600
Accumulated depreciation	(15,300)	–0–
Accounts payable	(19,100)	(19,100)

On June 30, Box invested cash in an amount equal to the current market value of Busby's partnership capital. The partners decided that Busby would earn two-thirds of partnership profits because he would manage the business. Box agreed to accept one-third of the profits. During the remainder of the year, the partnership earned net income of $75,000. Busby's drawings were $39,100, and Box's drawings were $31,000.

Required

1. Journalize the partners' initial investments.
2. Prepare the partnership balance sheet immediately after its formation on June 30.
3. Journalize the December 31 entries to close the Income Summary account and the partners' drawing accounts.

P12-3B Cedarlake Solutions is a partnership, and its owners are considering admitting Emily Conyers as a new partner. On March 31 of the current year, the capital accounts of the three existing partners and their shares of profits and losses are as follows:

Admitting a new partner (Obj. 4)

	Capital	Profit-and-Loss Share
Nick Nelson	$ 40,000	15%
Luke Bright	100,000	30
Lela Clapton	160,000	55

Required

Journalize the admission of Conyers as a partner on March 31 for each of the following independent situations:

1. Conyers pays Clapton $219,000 cash to purchase Clapton's interest in the partnership.
2. Conyers invests $60,000 in the partnership, acquiring a one-sixth interest in the business.
3. Conyers invests $80,000 in the partnership, acquiring a one-fourth interest in the business.
4. Conyers invests $50,000 in the partnership, acquiring a 12% interest in the business.

Computing partners' shares of
net income and net loss
(Obj. 3, 7)

P12-4B Charles Lake, Liz Wood, and Hal Parks have formed a partnership. Lake invested $15,000, Wood $18,000, and Parks $27,000. Lake will manage the store, Wood will work in the store half-time, and Parks will not work in the business.

Required

1. Compute the partners' shares of profits and losses under each of the following plans:
   a. Net loss is $42,900, and the articles of partnership do not specify how profits and losses are shared.
   b. Net loss is $60,000, and the partnership agreement allocates 40% of profits to Lake, 25% to Wood, and 35% to Parks. The agreement does not discuss the sharing of losses.
   c. Net income is $92,000. The first $40,000 is allocated on the basis of salaries, with Lake receiving $28,000 and Wood receiving $12,000. The remainder is allocated on the basis of partner capital contributions.
   d. Net income for the year ended January 31, 20X4, is $210,000. The first $75,000 is allocated on the basis of partner capital contributions, and the next $36,000 is based on service, with Lake receiving $28,000 and Wood receiving $8,000. Any remainder is shared equally.

2. Revenues for the year ended January 31, 20X4, were $870,000, and expenses were $660,000. Under plan (d), prepare the partnership income statement for the year.

P12-5B Priority Accounting Firm is a partnership owned by three individuals. The partners share profits and losses in the ratio of 28% to Cary Blesh, 38% to Dick McNut, and 34% to Jen Tate. At December 31, 20X2, the firm has the following balance sheet:

Cash		$ 12,000	Total liabilities	$ 75,000
Accounts receivable	$ 22,000			
Less allowance for				
uncollectibles	(4,000)	18,000		
Building	$310,000		Blesh, capital..............	83,000
Less accumulated			McNut, capital............	50,000
depreciation	(70,000)	240,000	Tate, capital	62,000
			Total liabilities and	
Total assets		$270,000	capital.......................	$270,000

McNut withdraws from the partnership on December 31, 20X2, to establish his own consulting practice.

Required

Record McNut's withdrawal from the partnership under the following plans:

1. McNut gives his interest in the business to Rich Blynn, his nephew.
2. In personal transactions, McNut sells his equity in the partnership to Ashley Napper and Jim Lucks, who each pay McNut $40,000 for half his interest. Blesh and Tate agree to accept Napper and Lucks as partners.
3. The partnership pays McNut cash of $15,000 and gives him a note payable for the remainder of his book equity in settlement of his partnership interest.
4. McNut receives cash of $10,000 and a note for $70,000 from the partnership.
5. The partners agree that the building is worth only $250,000 and that its accumulated depreciation should remain at $70,000. After the revaluation, the partnership settles with McNut by giving him cash of $14,100 and a note payable for the remainder of his book equity.

P12-6B The partnership of Parr, Johnston, & Rake has experienced operating losses for three consecutive years. The partners—who have shared profits and losses in the ratio of Sharon Parr 10%; Alicia Johnston, 30%; and Chet Rake, 60%—are considering the liquidation of the business. They ask you to analyze the effects of liquidation under various possibilities regarding the sale of the noncash assets. They present the following condensed partnership balance sheet at December 31, end of the current year:

Cash	$ 27,000	Liabilities	$131,000
Noncash assets.....................	202,000	Parr, capital...........................	21,000
		Johnston, capital	39,000
		Rake, capital	38,000
Total assets..........................	$229,000	Total liabilities and capital ...	$229,000

Required

1. Prepare a summary of liquidation transactions (as illustrated in Exhibit 12-4) for each of the following situations:
   a. The noncash assets are sold for $208,000.
   b. The noncash assets are sold for $189,000.
2. Make the journal entries to record the liquidation transactions in requirement 1(b).

P12-7B ◄ *Link Back to Chapter 4 (Closing Entries).* VT&P is a partnership owned by Vela, Thomas, and Prago, who share profits and losses in the ratio of 5:3:2. The adjusted trial balance of the partnership (in condensed form) at September 30, end of the current fiscal year, follows.

Liquidation of a partnership (Obj. 6)

VT&P Adjusted Trial Balance September 30, 20XX		
Cash	$ 10,000	
Noncash assets	177,000	
Liabilities		$135,000
Vela, capital		57,000
Thomas, capital		44,000
Prago, capital		21,000
Vela, drawing	45,000	
Thomas, drawing	37,000	
Prago, drawing	18,000	
Revenues		211,000
Expenses	181,000	
Totals	$468,000	$468,000

Required

1. Prepare the September 30 entries to close the revenue, expense, income summary, and drawing accounts.
2. Insert the opening capital balances in the partner capital accounts, post the closing entries to the capital accounts, and determine each partner's ending capital balance.
3. The partnership liquidates on September 30 by selling the noncash assets for $147,000. Using the ending balances of the partner capital accounts computed in requirement 2, prepare a summary of liquidation transactions (as illustrated in Exhibit 12-4).

APPLY YOUR KNOWLEDGE

DECISION CASES

Case 1. Kimberly Gardner invested $20,000 and Leah Johanssen invested $10,000 in a public relations firm that has operated for ten years. Neither partner has made an additional investment. Gardner and Johanssen have shared profits and losses in the ratio of 2:1, which is the ratio of their investments in the business. Gardner manages the office, supervises the 16 employees, and does the accounting. Johanssen, the moderator of a television talk show, is responsible for marketing. Her high profile generates important revenue for the business. During the year ended December 20X4, the partnership earned net income of $87,000, shared in the 2:1 ratio. On December 31, 20X4, Gardner's capital balance was $150,000, and Johanssen's capital balance was $100,000.

Settling disagreements among partners (Obj. 3)

Required

Respond to each of the following situations.

1. What explains the difference between the ratio of partner capital balances at December 31, 20X4, and the 2:1 ratio of partner investments and profit sharing?
2. Johanssen believes that the profit-and-loss-sharing ratio is unfair. She proposes a change, but Gardner insists on keeping the 2:1 ratio. What two factors may underlie Johanssen's unhappiness?
3. During January 20X5, Gardner learned that revenues of $18,000 were omitted from the reported 20X4 income. She brings this omission to Johanssen's attention, pointing out that Gardner's share of this added income is two-thirds, or $12,000, and Johanssen's share is one-third, or $6,000. Johanssen believes that they should share this added income on the basis of their capital balances—60%, or $10,800, to Gardner and 40%, or $7,200, to herself. Which partner is correct? Why?

4. Assume that the 20X4 $18,000 omission was an account payable for an operating expense. On what basis would the partners share this amount?

Partnership issues
(Obj. 1, 5)

Case 2. The following questions relate to issues faced by partnerships.

1. The text suggests that a written partnership agreement should be drawn up between the partners in a partnership. One benefit of an agreement is that it provides a mechanism for resolving disputes between the partners. List five areas of dispute that might be resolved by a partnership agreement.
2. The statement has been made that "if you must take on a partner, make sure the partner is richer than you are." Why is this statement valid?
3. Corwin & Corwin is a law partnership. Natalie Corwin is planning to retire from the partnership and move to Israel. What options are available to Corwin to enable her to convert her share of the partnership assets to cash?

ETHICAL ISSUE

Tracy Wynn and Lee Spitz operate New England Engraving in Portsmouth, New Hampshire. The partners split profits and losses equally, and each takes an annual salary of $80,000. To even out the workload, Spitz does the buying and Wynn serves as the accountant. From time to time, they use small amounts of store merchandise for personal use. In preparing for her daughter's wedding, Wynn took engraved invitations and other goods that cost $2,700. She recorded the transaction as follows:

Cost of Goods Sold	2,700	
Inventory		2,700

1. How should Wynn have recorded this transaction?
2. Discuss the ethical dimensions of Wynn's action.

FINANCIAL STATEMENT CASE

KPMG is an international accounting firm. Summary data from the partnership's *19X7 Annual Report* follow:

(Dollars in millions except where indicated)	19X7	19X6	Years Ended June 30 19X5	19X4	19X3
Revenues					
Assurance	$1,234	$1,122	$1,064	$1,093	$1,070
Consulting	1,007	775	658	473	349
Tax	743	628	567	515	557
Total Revenues	$2,984	$2,525	$2,289	$2,081	$1,976
Operating Summary					
Revenues	$2,984	$2,525	$2,289	$2,081	$1,976
Personnel Costs	1,215	1,004	887	805	726
Other Costs	1,212	1,030	967	898	829
Income to Partners	$ 557	$ 491	$ 435	$ 378	$ 421
Statistical Data					
Average Number of Partners	1,494	1,428	1,413	1,449	1,453

Required

1. What percentages of total revenues did KPMG earn by performing assurance services (similar to audit), consulting services, and tax services during 19X3? What were the percentages in 19X7? Which type of services grew the most from 19X3 to 19X7?
2. Compute the average revenue per partner in 19X7.
3. How much net income did each KPMG partner earn, on average, in 19X7?

TEAM PROJECT

Visit a business partnership in your area, and interview one or more of the partners. Obtain answers to the following questions and ask your instructor for directions. As directed by your instructor, either (a) prepare a written report of your findings, or (b) make a presentation to your class.

Required

1. Why did you organize the business as a partnership? What advantages does the partnership form of organization offer the business? What are the disadvantages of the partnership form of organization?
2. Is the business a general partnership, or is it a limited partnership?
3. Do the partners have a written partnership agreement? What does the agreement cover? Obtain a copy if possible.
4. Who manages the business? Do all partners participate in day-to-day management, or is management the responsibility of only certain partners?
5. If there is no written agreement, what is the mechanism for making key decisions?
6. Have you ever admitted a new partner? If so, when? What are the partnership's procedures for admitting a new partner?
7. Has a partner ever withdrawn from the business? If so, when? What are the partnership's procedures for settling up with a withdrawing partner?
8. If possible, learn how the partnership divides profits and losses among the partners.
9. Ask for any additional insights the partner you interview can provide about the business.

INTERNET EXERCISE

Arthur Andersen LLP is a limited liability partnership and one of the most respected accounting/consulting firms in the world. Since 1913, Arthur Andersen has offered accounting and business solutions and helped companies view change as an opportunity to learn, think, see, and leap ahead.

Arthur Andersen LLP

1. Go to **http://www.arthurandersen.com** and watch the video. Click on *About Us*. What does Arthur Andersen LLP do to stay ahead of its competitors?
2. Under "Our Scorecard" click on *facts*. For the most recent years, Arthur Andersen LLP reported how much in revenue? Information is available on the revenues of the company, but the entire set of financial statements is not publicly available. Why not? Does Arthur Andersen LLP pay income tax? Are the partners of a limited liability partnership personally liable for the debts of the partnership?
3. Click on *Careers*. Arthur Andersen LLP provides services in how many different countries?
4. Arthur Andersen, the founder of the company, was a university professor and recruited the brightest students into his classes. He helped his students understand how to improve financial performance. Click on "start your career *here*." What characteristics is Arthur Andersen LLP currently looking for in an employee?
5. Click on *Words of Wisdom*. What words of wisdom does Arthur Andersen LLP offer?

13

Corporations: Paid-in Capital and the Balance Sheet

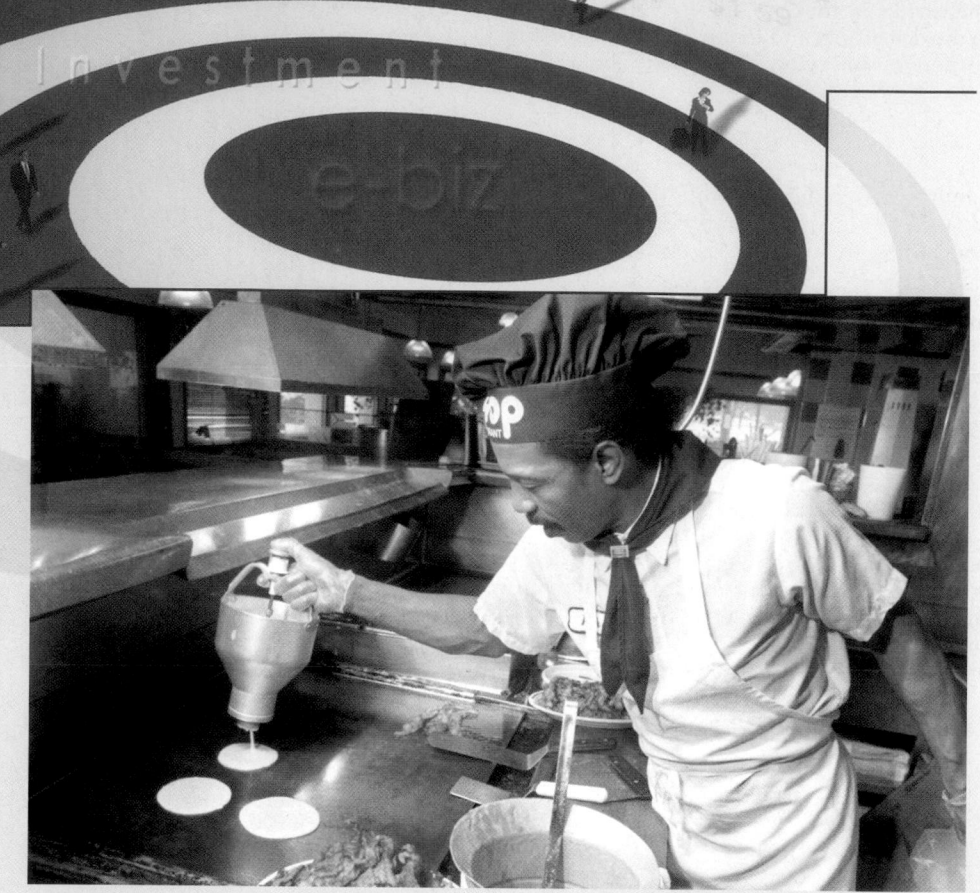

LEARNING OBJECTIVES

After studying this chapter, you should be able to

1. Identify the characteristics of a corporation

2. Record the issuance of stock

3. Prepare the stockholders' equity section of a corporation's balance sheet

4. Account for cash dividends

5. Use different stock values in decision making

6. Evaluate a company's return on assets and return on stockholders' equity

7. Account for the income tax of a corporation

Initial public offerings of stock, or IPOs as they are called, reached new highs during the late 1990s. Consider what happened to this well-known company.

IHOP Corporation operates International House of Pancakes restaurants throughout the United States and in several foreign countries. IHOP serves pancakes, sandwiches, and other casual food along the interstate highway system. The restaurant chain caters to college students and families, with late hours and reasonable prices.

IHOP began as a small company in Glendale, California. To spur growth, IHOP *went public*. This means that IHOP offered its stock to anyone who would buy it. The initial public offering of IHOP's stock was fairly successful. The company offered to sell 6.2 million shares of its stock for $10 per share. As it turned out, investors bought only 3.2 million shares. IHOP thus received $32 million (3.2 million × $10), which the company then invested to open new restaurants and upgrade old ones.

This chapter covers the issuance of stock by large corporations such as IHOP. Any company—large or small—can sell (issue) its stock to investors. All companies issue their stock for the same reasons: to raise money (cash), to obtain assets such as land and buildings, or to pay off debt. Now let's explore how corporations differ from the proprietorships and partnerships we have been studying.

CORPORATIONS: AN OVERVIEW

Objective 1
Identify the characteristics of a corporation

The corporation is the dominant form of business organization in the United States. **IHOP** is one example. Proprietorships and partnerships are more numerous, but corporations transact more business and are larger in terms of total assets and sales revenue. Most well-known companies, such as **Target** and **Intel,** are corporations. Their full names include *Corporation* or *Incorporated* (abbreviated *Corp.* and *Inc.*) to show that they are corporations—for example, Target Corporation and **Nike, Inc.**

Characteristics of a Corporation

What makes the corporate form of organization so attractive? We now examine how corporations differ from proprietorships and partnerships and the advantages and disadvantages of corporations.

SEPARATE LEGAL ENTITY A corporation is a business entity formed under state law. The state grants a **charter,** a document that gives a business the state's permission to form a corporation. Neither a proprietorship nor a partnership requires a charter, because in the eyes of the law the business is the same as the owner(s).

From a legal perspective, a corporation is a totally separate entity from its owners, who are called **stockholders** or **shareholders.** The corporation has many of the rights that a person has. For example, a corporation may buy, own, and sell property. The assets and liabilities of IHOP belong to the corporation rather than to its owners. The corporation may enter into contracts, sue, and be sued. If IHOP accidentally serves contaminated food and customers get sick, they may sue IHOP.

CONTINUOUS LIFE AND TRANSFERABILITY OF OWNERSHIP The owners' equity of a corporation is divided into shares of **stock.** Most corporations have *continuous lives* regardless of changes in the ownership of their stock. The stockholders of IHOP or any corporation may sell or trade the stock to another person, give it away, or bequeath it in a will. The transfer of the stock does not affect the continuity of the corporation. In contrast, proprietorships and partnerships terminate when their ownership changes.

NO MUTUAL AGENCY *Mutual agency* means that all owners act as agents of the business. A contract signed by one owner is binding for the whole company.

CHARTER. Document that gives the state's permission to form a corporation.

STOCKHOLDER. A person who owns the stock of a corporation. Also called **shareholder.**

STOCK. Shares into which the owners' equity of a corporation is divided.

→ We introduced the idea of mutual agency for partnerships in Chapter 12, page 466.

LIMITED LIABILITY. No personal obligation of a stockholder for corporation debts. A stockholder can lose no more on an investment in a corporation's stock than the cost of the investment.

Mutual agency operates in partnerships but *not* in corporations. ← A stockholder of IHOP Corp. cannot commit the corporation to a contract (unless he or she is also an officer in the business).

LIMITED STOCKHOLDER LIABILITY Stockholders have **limited liability** for corporation debts. That means they have no personal obligation for corporation liabilities. The most that a stockholder can lose on an investment in a corporation is the amount invested. In contrast, proprietors and partners are personally liable for all the debts of their businesses.

The combination of limited liability and no mutual agency means that persons can invest in a corporation without fear of losing all their personal wealth if the business fails. This feature enables a corporation to raise more money from a wider group of investors than proprietorships and partnerships can.

SEPARATION OF OWNERSHIP AND MANAGEMENT Stockholders own the business, but a *board of directors*—elected by the stockholders—appoints the officers to manage the business. Stockholders may invest $1,000 or $1 million in the corporation without having to manage the business or disrupt their personal affairs.

Management's goal is to maximize the firm's value for the benefit of the stockholders. However, the separation between the owners—stockholders—and management can create problems. Corporate officers may decide to run the business for their own benefit and not for the stockholders. The distance between the stockholders and management may make it difficult for stockholders to protest bad management. How else can stockholders protest? They can sell their stock in that corporation.

CORPORATE TAXATION Corporations are separate taxable entities. They pay several taxes not borne by proprietorships or partnerships, including an annual franchise tax levied by the state. The franchise tax keeps the corporate charter in force and enables the corporation to continue in business. Corporations also pay federal and state income taxes just as individuals do.

DOUBLE TAXATION. Corporations pay their own income taxes on corporate income. Then, the stockholders pay personal income tax on the cash dividends they receive from corporations.

Corporate earnings are subject to **double taxation.** First, corporations pay income taxes on corporate income. Then, stockholders pay personal income tax on the cash dividends they receive from corporations. Proprietorships and partnerships pay no business income tax. Instead, the tax falls solely on the owners.

GOVERNMENT REGULATION As we have seen, stockholders have only limited liability for corporation debts. Outsiders can look no further than the corporation for any claims that may arise against the business. To protect persons who do business with the corporation, both federal agencies and the states monitor corporations. This *government regulation* consists mainly of ensuring that corporations disclose adequate information for investors and creditors.

Exhibit 13-1 summarizes the advantages and disadvantages of the corporate form of business organization.

 DAILY EXERCISE 13-1

EXHIBIT 13-1
Advantages and Disadvantages of a Corporation

Advantages	Disadvantages
1. Can raise more money than a proprietorship or partnership	1. Separation of ownership and management
2. Continuous life	2. Corporate taxation
3. Easy transfer of ownership	3. Government regulation
4. No mutual agency of the stockholders	
5. Limited liability of the stockholders	

Organizing a Corporation

AUTHORIZATION OF STOCK. Provision in a corporate charter that gives the state's permission for the corporation to issue—that is, to sell—a certain number of shares of stock.

The process of creating a corporation begins when its organizers, called the *incorporators,* obtain a charter from the state. The charter includes the **authorization** for the corporation to issue a certain number of shares of stock for the ownership in the

corporation. The incorporators pay fees, sign the charter, and file documents with the state. The corporation then becomes a legal entity. The stockholders agree to a set of **bylaws,** which act as the constitution for the corporation.

Ultimate control of the corporation rests with the stockholders. The stockholders elect the **board of directors,** which sets policy and appoints the officers. The board elects a **chairperson,** who is the most powerful person in the corporation. The board also designates the **president,** who is in charge of day-to-day operations. Most corporations also have vice presidents of sales, manufacturing, accounting and finance, and other key areas. The president and one or more vice presidents are usually elected to the board of directors. Exhibit 13-2 shows the authority structure in a corporation.

BYLAWS. Constitution for governing a corporation.

BOARD OF DIRECTORS. Group elected by the stockholders to set policy and to appoint the officers.

CHAIRPERSON. Elected by a corporation's board of directors, the most powerful person in the corporation.

EXHIBIT 13-2 **Authority Structure in a Corporation**

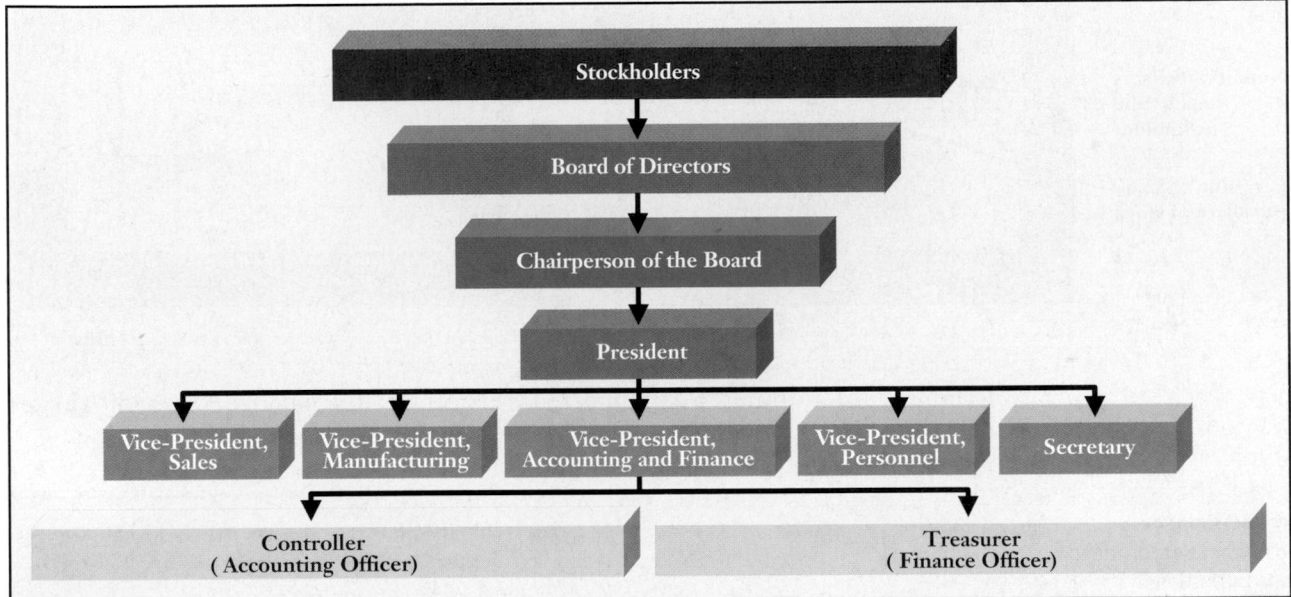

Capital Stock

A corporation issues *stock certificates* to its owners when they invest in the business. The stock represents the corporation's capital, so it is called *capital stock.* The basic unit of stock is a *share.* A corporation may issue a stock certificate for any number of shares—1, 100, or any other number—but the total number of *authorized* shares is limited by charter. Exhibit 13-3, at the top of the next page, depicts an actual stock certificate for 288 shares of **Central Jersey Bancorp** common stock. The certificate shows the company's name, the stockholder's name, the number of shares, and the par value of the stock (discussed later in this chapter).

Stock that is held by a stockholder is said to be **outstanding.** The total shares of stock outstanding represent 100% ownership of the corporation.

STOCKHOLDERS' EQUITY: THE BASICS

The balance sheet of a corporation reports assets and liabilities in the same way as a proprietorship or a partnership. However, the owners' equity of a corporation—called **stockholders' equity**—is reported differently. State laws require corporations to report the sources of their capital. The two basic sources of capital are

- **Paid-in capital** (also called **contributed capital**) represents stockholder investments in the corporation.
- **Retained earnings** is capital that the corporation has earned through profitable operations.

PRESIDENT. Chief operating officer in charge of managing the day-to-day operations of a corporation.

 DAILY EXERCISE 13-2

OUTSTANDING STOCK. Stock in the hands of of stockholders.

STOCKHOLDERS' EQUITY. Owners' equity of a corporation.

PAID-IN CAPITAL. A corporation's capital from investments by the stockholders. Also called **contributed capital.**

RETAINED EARNINGS. A corporation's capital that is earned through profitable operation of the business.

EXHIBIT 13-3 **Stock Certificate**

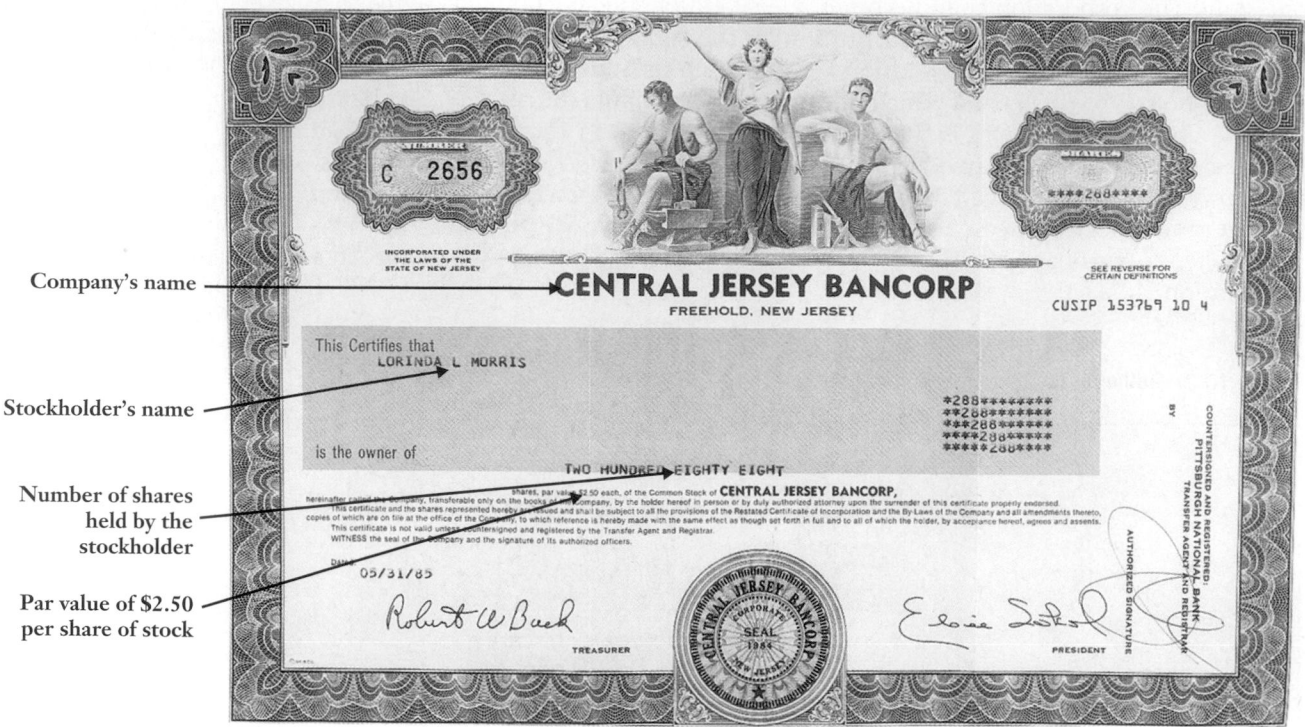

Company's name →

Stockholder's name →

Number of shares
held by the
stockholder →

Par value of $2.50
per share of stock →

Exhibit 13-4 outlines a summarized version of the balance sheet of **Target Corporation** to show how to report these categories of stockholders' equity.

EXHIBIT 13-4
Summarized Balance Sheet of Target Corporation (Amounts in Millions)

 DAILY EXERCISE 13-3

Assets	$17,143	Liabilities		$11,281
		Stockholders' Equity		
		Paid-in capital:		
		Common stock...............		806
		Retained earnings..............		5,056
		Total stockholders' equity...		5,862
		Total liabilities and		
Total assets	$17,143	stockholders' equity		$17,143

Paid-in Capital Is Received from the Stockholders

COMMON STOCK. The basic form of capital stock. In a corporation, the common stockholders are the owners of the business.

Common stock is paid-in capital because it comes from the stockholders. Target's entry to record the receipt of $20,000 cash and the issuance of Target stock is

Oct. 20	Cash	20,000	
	Common Stock..............		20,000
	Issued stock.		

This entry illustrates the fact that the issuance of stock increases both the assets and the stockholders' equity of the corporation.

Retained Earnings Are Earned from the Customers

Profitable operations generate income for the corporation, and income increases stockholders' equity through a separate account called Retained Earnings. At the end of the year, the balance of the Income Summary account (a net income or a net loss) is closed to Retained Earnings. For example, if Target's net income is $1,200 million, Income Summary will have a $1,200 million credit balance (see the T-account on p. 505). Target's closing entry will debit Income Summary to close that account. The credit side of the closing entry transfers net income to Retained

Earnings as follows (in millions of dollars):

Jan. 31   Income Summary 1,200
          Retained Earnings..   1,200
          To close *net income* to Retained Earnings.

INCOME SUMMARY		
Closing	1,200	Net income 1,200
		Balance -0-

RETAINED EARNINGS		
	Closing	1,200

The T-accounts show that net income winds up in the Retained Earnings account.

If operations produce a net *loss* rather than net income, the Income Summary account will have a debit balance. To close a $60,000 loss, the closing entry credits Income Summary and debits Retained Earnings as follows:

Dec. 31   Retained Earnings.. 60,000
          Income Summary................................   60,000
          To close *net loss* to Retained Earnings.

Prepare a T-account for Income Summary to show its debit balance of $60,000. Also prepare a T-account for Retained Earnings (no balance yet). Then post the $60,000 closing entry and take the balance for Income Summary and Retained Earnings. Where does the net loss of $60,000 end up?

Answer:

INCOME SUMMARY			
Net loss	60,000	Closing	60,000
Balance	-0-		

RETAINED EARNINGS		
Closing	60,000	

A large loss may cause a debit balance in the Retained Earnings account. This condition—called a Retained Earnings **deficit**—is reported on the balance sheet as a negative amount in stockholders' equity. **HAL, Inc.,** which owns Hawaiian Airlines, Inc., reported this deficit:

DEFICIT. Debit balance in the Retained Earnings account.

Stockholders' Equity	(In Millions)
Paid-in capital: Common stock	$ 50
Deficit..	(193)
Total stockholders' equity	$(143)

HAL's deficit was so large that it produced a negative amount of stockholders' equity. This situation is unusual for a going concern.

Corporations May Pay Dividends to the Stockholders

If the corporation has been profitable and has sufficient cash, it may distribute cash to the stockholders. Such distributions—called **dividends**—are similar to a proprietor's withdrawal of cash from a business or by a partner from a partnership. Dividends decrease both the assets and the retained earnings of the business. Most states prohibit using paid-in capital for dividends. Accountants use the term **legal capital** to refer to the portion of stockholders' equity that *cannot* be used for dividends.

DIVIDENDS. Distributions by a corporation to its stockholders.

LEGAL CAPITAL. The portion of stockholders' equity that cannot be used for dividends.

Some people think of Retained Earnings as a fund of cash. It is not, because Retained Earnings is an element of stockholders' equity. *Remember that cash dividends are paid out of assets, not out of retained earnings.*

Stockholders' Rights

The ownership of stock entitles stockholders to four basic rights, unless specific rights are withheld by agreement with the stockholders:

1. *Vote.* Stockholders participate in management by voting on matters that come before them. This is a stockholder's sole right to manage the corporation. Each share of stock carries one vote.
2. *Dividends.* Stockholders receive a proportionate part of any dividend. Each share of stock receives an equal dividend with every other share of the same class.
3. *Liquidation.* Stockholders receive their proportionate share of any assets remaining after the corporation pays its liabilities in liquidation (goes out of business).
4. *Preemption.* Stockholders can maintain their proportionate ownership in the corporation. Suppose you own 5% of a corporation's stock. If the corporation issues 100,000 new shares of stock, it must offer you the opportunity to buy 5% (5,000) of the new shares. This right, called the *preemptive right,* is usually withheld from the stockholders.

Classes of Stock

Corporations issue different types of stock. The stock of a corporation may be either common or preferred and either par or no-par.

COMMON AND PREFERRED STOCK   Every corporation issues *common stock,* the basic form of capital stock. Unless designated otherwise, the word *stock* is understood to mean "common stock." Common stockholders have the four basic rights of stock ownership, unless a right is specifically withheld. For example, some companies issue Class A common stock, which carries the right to vote. They may also issue Class B common stock, which may be nonvoting. (Classes of common stock may also be designated Series A, Series B, and so on.) There is a separate account for each class of stock.

Investors who buy common stock take the ultimate risk with a corporation. The corporation makes no promises to pay them. If the corporation succeeds, it will pay dividends to its stockholders, but if net income and cash are too low, stockholders may receive no dividends. The stock of successful corporations increases in value, and investors may sell the stock at a gain. But stock prices can decrease, leaving the investors holding worthless stock. Because common stockholders take a risk, they demand increases in stock prices, high dividends, or both. If the corporation does not deliver, the stockholders sell the stock.

Preferred stock gives its owners certain advantages over common stockholders. These benefits include the right to receive dividends before the common stockholders and the right to receive assets before the common stockholders if the corporation liquidates. Corporations pay a fixed amount of dividends on preferred stock. Investors usually buy preferred stock to earn those fixed dividends.

Owners of preferred stock also have the four basic stockholder rights, unless a right is specifically denied. The right to vote may be withheld from preferred stockholders. Companies may issue different classes of preferred stock (Class A and Class B or Series A and Series B, for example). Each class of stock is recorded in a separate account. Preferred stock is rarer than you might think. A recent survey of 600 corporations revealed that only 99 of them (16.5%) had some preferred stock outstanding (Exhibit 13-5).

All corporations have common stock. Exhibit 13-6 summarizes the similarities and differences among common stock, preferred stock, and long-term debt.

PREFERRED STOCK. Stock that gives its owners certain advantages over common stockholders, such as the right to receive dividends before the common stockholders and the right to receive assets before the common stockholders if the corporation liquidates.

EXHIBIT 13-5
Preferred Stock

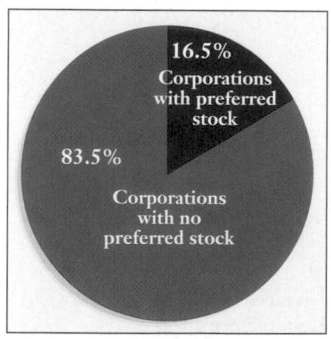

16.5%
Corporations with preferred stock

83.5%
Corporations with no preferred stock

EXHIBIT 13-6
Comparison of Common Stock, Preferred Stock, and Long-Term Debt

	Common Stock	Preferred Stock	Long-Term Debt
Investment risk	High	Medium	Low
Corporate obligation to repay principal	No	No	Yes
Dividends/Interest	Dividends	Dividends	Interest

PAR VALUE, STATED VALUE, AND NO-PAR STOCK   Stock may be par-value stock or no-par stock. **Par value** is an arbitrary amount assigned by a company to a share of its stock. Most companies set the par value of their common stock quite low to avoid legal difficulties from issuing their stock below par. Most states require companies to maintain a minimum amount of stockholders' equity for the protection of creditors, and this minimum represents the corporation's legal capital. For corporations with par-value stock, *legal capital* is usually the par value of the shares issued.

The common stock par value of **Oracle Corporation,** the software giant, is $0.01 (1 cent) per share. **Pier 1 Imports'** common carries a par value of $1 per share. Par value of preferred stock is often higher; some preferred stocks have par values of $25 and $100. Par value is used to compute dividends on preferred stock, as we shall see.

No-par stock does not have par value. **Kimberly Clark** has 20 million shares of preferred stock authorized with no par value. But some no-par stock has a **stated value,** which makes it similar to par-value stock. The stated value is an arbitrary amount that accountants treat as though it were par value.

PAR VALUE. Arbitrary amount assigned to a share of stock.

 DAILY EXERCISE 13-4

STATED VALUE. An arbitrary amount that accountants treat as though it were par value.

ISSUING STOCK

Objective 2
Record the issuance of stock

Large corporations such as **Hewlett-Packard, Coca-Cola,** and **British Petroleum Amoco** need huge quantities of money to operate. They cannot finance all their operations through borrowing. They need capital that they raise by issuing stock. Corporations may sell the stock directly to stockholders or use the services of an *underwriter,* such as the brokerage firms **Merrill Lynch** and **Morgan Stanley, Dean Witter.** An underwriter agrees to buy all the stock it cannot sell to its clients.

The price that the corporation receives from issuance of its stock is called the *issue price.* Often, the issue price far exceeds the stock's par value because the par value is intentionally set quite low. The company's profits, financial position, and future prospects determine the issue price. Investors will pay no more than market value for the stock. In the following sections, we show how to account for the issuance of stock.

Issuing Common Stock

Companies advertise their stock to attract investors. The *Wall Street Journal* is the most popular medium for the advertisements. They are called *tombstones.* Exhibit 13-7 at the top of page 508 is a reproduction of IHOP's tombstone, which appeared in the *Wall Street Journal.*

The lead underwriter of **IHOP's** public offering was **The First Boston Corporation.** Other brokerage firms and investment bankers also sold IHOP's stock to their clients. IHOP's tombstone shows that IHOP hoped to raise approximately $62 million of capital. But in the final analysis, IHOP issued only 3.2 million of the shares and received cash of approximately $32 million.

COMMON STOCK AT PAR   Suppose IHOP's common stock carried a par value of $10 per share. The stock issuance entry of 3.2 million shares would be

Jan. 31	Cash (3,200,000 × $10)	32,000,000	
	Common Stock.........................		32,000,000
	Issued common stock at par.		

COMMON STOCK AT A PREMIUM   Most corporations set par value low and issue common stock for a price above par value. The amount above par is called a *premium.* IHOP's common stock has an actual par value of $0.01 (1 cent) per share. The $9.99 difference between issue price ($10) and par value ($0.01) is a premium. This sale of stock increases the corporation's paid-in capital by the full $10, the total issue price of the stock.

A premium on the sale of stock is not gain, income, or profit to the corporation, because the entity is dealing with its own stockholders. This situation illustrates one of the fundamentals of accounting: *A company neither earns a profit nor incurs a loss when it sells its stock to, or buys its stock from, its own stockholders.*

EXHIBIT 13-7 **Announcement of Public Offering of IHOP Stock (Partial)**

Number of shares
offered to the public

Company issuing
the stock

Class of stock

Par value per share

Issue price—the amount
per share that IHOP
received for the stock

Lead U.S.
underwriter

Lead foreign
underwriter

This announcement is neither an offer to sell nor a solicitation of offers to buy any of these securities. The offering is made only by the Prospectus, copies of which may be obtained in any State in which this announcement is circulated only from such of the undersigned as may legally offer these securities in such State.

6,200,000 Shares

INTERNATIONAL HOUSE *of* PANCAKES RESTAURANT

IHOP CORP.

Common Stock
($.01 par value)

Price $10 Per Share

These securities are being offered in the United States and internationally.

United States Offering
4,960,000 Shares

The First Boston Corporation

Alex. Brown & Sons
Incorporated

Donaldson, Lufkin & Jenrette
Securities Corporation

A. G. Edwards & Sons, Inc.

Goldman, Sachs & Co.

Lehman Brothers

Montgomery Securities

PaineWebber Incorporated

Prudential Securities Incorporated

International Offering
1,240,000 Shares

Credit Suisse First Boston Limited

Prepare IHOP's classified balance sheet immediately after this issuance of stock. Assume zero balances prior to the transaction.

WORK IT OUT

Answer

IHOP CORPORATION
Balance Sheet
January 31, 20XX

Assets		Liabilities	
Current:			
Cash	$32,000,000	No liabilities	0
		Stockholders' Equity	
		Common stock..............	$32,000,000
		Total liabilities and	
Total assets	$32,000,000	stockholders' equity ..	$32,000,000

With a par value of $0.01, IHOP's entry to record the issuance of the stock is

July 31	Cash (3,200,000 × $10)	32,000,000	
	Common Stock (3,200,000 × $0.01)		32,000
	Paid-in Capital in Excess of Par—		
	Common (3,200,000 × $9.99)		31,968,000
	Issued common stock at a premium.		

● DAILY EXERCISE 13-5

Account titles that could be used in place of Paid-in Capital in Excess of Par—Common are *Additional Paid-in Capital—Common* and *Premium on Common Stock*. Since both par value and premium amounts increase the corporation's capital, they appear in the stockholders' equity section of the balance sheet.

At the end of the year, IHOP Corp. would report stockholders' equity on its balance sheet as follows, assuming that the corporate charter authorizes 40,000,000 shares of common stock and the balance of retained earnings is $26,000,000.

Stockholders' Equity

Paid-in capital:	
Common stock, $0.01 par, 40 million shares authorized, 3.2 million shares issued	$ 32,000
Paid-in capital in excess of par	31,968,000
Total paid-in capital	32,000,000
Retained earnings	26,000,000
Total stockholders' equity	$58,000,000

◉ DAILY EXERCISE 13-6

◉ DAILY EXERCISE 13-7

We determine the dollar amount reported for common stock by multiplying the total number of shares *issued* (3.2 million) by the par value per share ($0.01). The *authorization* reports the maximum number of shares of stock the company may issue under its charter.

All transactions recorded in this section include a receipt of cash by the corporation as it issues new stock to stockholders. These transactions are different from

UPS Delivers the Dough at Record-Breaking IPO

If you want stock in a company that operates in the global electronic marketplace, what comes to mind? Pioneering dot.coms like **Amazon.com** or **eBay?** Think again. There's a 97-year-old business whose workers drive old-fashioned brown trucks and run parcels up to your door. **United Parcel Service (UPS)** is a business as traditional as apple pie. UPS raised a record-breaking $5.5 billion at its IPO (initial public offering) when it went public. All this money came from investors who saw UPS as a sign of the new economy.

Why would UPS sell its stock to the public? To build a cross-border, USA/European infrastructure, UPS figured it would need to acquire and merge with foreign firms. That required a lot of money. During the first hours of trading in UPS stock, the company's share price soared 40%. By the end of a week, the UPS workforce included 10,000 new millionaires.

Source: Based on Avital Louria Hahn, "Men in brown: A growth story—UPS recasts itself for IPO," *The Investment Dealers' Digest: IDD,* December 13, 1999, p. 35. Elise Ackerman, "UPS delivers as IPO investors give the world's no. 1 package-delivery company full dot-com treatment," *U.S. News & World Report,* November 22, 1999, p. 53. Jenny Anderson, "Up, UPS and away," *Institutional Investor,* January 2000, pp. 96–98.

the vast majority of stock transactions reported each day in the financial press. In those transactions, one stockholder sells his or her stock to another investor, and the corporation makes no formal journal entry because its paid-in capital is unchanged.

NO-PAR COMMON STOCK When a company issues stock that has no par value, there can be no premium. A recent survey of 600 companies revealed 59 issues of no-par stock.

When a company issues no-par stock, it debits the asset received and credits the stock account. Glenwood Corporation, which manufactures ski equipment, issues 4,000 shares of no-par common stock for $20 per share. The stock issuance entry is

Aug. 14	Cash (4,000 × $20)	80,000	
	Common Stock		80,000
	Issued no-par common stock.		

Regardless of the stock's price, Cash is debited and Common Stock is credited for the cash received. There is no Paid-in Capital in Excess of Par for no-par stock.

Glenwood Corporation's charter authorizes Glenwood to issue 10,000 shares of no-par stock, and the company has $151,000 in retained earnings. The corporation reports stockholders' equity on the balance sheet as follows:

Stockholders' Equity

Paid-in capital:	
Common stock, no par, 10,000 shares authorized, 4,000 shares issued	$ 80,000
Retained earnings	151,000
Total stockholders' equity	$231,000

 DAILY EXERCISE 13-8

NO-PAR COMMON STOCK WITH A STATED VALUE Accounting for no-par stock with a stated value is identical to accounting for par-value stock. The premium account for no-par common stock with a stated value is Paid-in Capital in Excess of *Stated* Value—Common.

COMMON STOCK FOR ASSETS OTHER THAN CASH When a corporation issues stock and receives assets other than cash, it records the assets received at their current market value and credits the capital accounts accordingly. The assets' prior book value is irrelevant because the stockholder will demand stock equal to the market value of the asset given. Kahn Corporation issued 15,000 shares of its $1 par common stock for equipment worth $4,000 and a building worth $120,000. Kahn's entry is

Nov. 30	Equipment	4,000	
	Building	120,000	
	Common Stock (15,000 × $1)		15,000
	Paid-in Capital in Excess of Par— Common ($124,000 − $15,000)		109,000
	Issued common stock in exchange for equipment and a building.		

WORK IT OUT

Prepare the stockholders' equity section of Kahn's balance sheet immediately after this transaction. Before this issuance of stock, Kahn already had outstanding 10,000 shares of common stock that the company had issued for $8 per share. Kahn's corporate charter authorizes the issuance of 100,000 shares of common stock. Retained earnings is $519,000 and liabilities total $622,000.

Answer

Stockholders' Equity

Paid-in capital:
Common stock, $1 par, 100,000 shares authorized,
25,000 (10,000 + 15,000) shares issued .... $ 25,000
Paid-in capital in excess of par ($70,000* + $109,000).............. 179,000
Total paid-in capital 204,000
Retained earnings 519,000
Total stockholders' equity $723,000

*10,000 shares × ($8 − $1 par) = $70,000

Issuing Preferred Stock

Accounting for preferred stock follows the pattern illustrated for common stock. **Chiquita Brands International, Inc.,** famous for its bananas, has some preferred stock outstanding. Assume Chiquita issued 110,887 shares of preferred stock at par value of $1 per share. The issuance entry is

July 31   Cash 110,887
                Preferred Stock (110,887 shares × $1) 110,887
            Issued preferred stock at par.

If Chiquita had issued the preferred stock at a premium, the entry would have credited Paid-in Capital in Excess of Par—Preferred for the excess over par value. A corporation lists separate accounts for Paid-in Capital in Excess of Par on Preferred Stock and on Common Stock to differentiate the two classes of equity. The balance sheet then lists preferred stock, common stock, and retained earnings, in that order.

Ethical Considerations in Accounting for the Issuance of Stock

Issuance of stock for *cash* poses no ethical challenge. The company receives cash and issues stock, giving the stockholders certificates as evidence of their ownership.

Issuing stock for assets other than cash can pose an ethical challenge. The company issuing the stock often wishes to record a large amount for the asset received (such as land or a building) and for the stock being issued. Why? Because large asset and equity amounts make the business look prosperous and creditworthy. The motivation to look good can inject a subtle bias into the amount recorded for the assets received and the stock issued.

A company is supposed to record an asset received at its current market value. But one person's evaluation of a building can differ from another person's valuation. One person may appraise the building at a market value of $4 million. Another may honestly believe it is worth only $3 million. A company receiving the building in exchange for its stock must decide whether to record the building received and the stock issued at $3 million, $4 million, or some other amount.

The ethical course of action is to record the asset at its current fair market value, as determined by a good-faith estimate of market value from independent appraisers. It is rare for a public corporation to be found guilty of *understating* the asset values on its balance sheet, but companies have been embarrassed by *overstating* their asset values. Investors who rely on the financial statements may be able to prove that an overstatement of asset values caused them to pay too much for the company's stock. In that case, a court of law may render a judgment against the company. So companies tend to value assets conservatively (that is, on the low side) in order to avoid an overstatement of their book value.

Review of Accounting for Paid-in Capital

Let's review the first half of this chapter by showing the stockholders' equity section of MedTech.com Corporation's balance sheet in Exhibit 13-8 on page 512.

Objective 3
Prepare the stockholders' equity section of a corporation's balance sheet

Stockholders' Equity	
Paid-in capital:	
Preferred stock, 5%, $100 par, 5,000 shares	
authorized, 400 shares issued	$ 40,000
Paid-in capital in excess of par—preferred...............	14,000
Common stock, $10 par, 20,000 shares	
authorized, 4,500 shares issued	45,000
Paid-in capital in excess of par—common	72,000
Total paid-in capital..	171,000
Retained earnings..	85,000
Total stockholders' equity...................................	$256,000

Note the two sections of stockholders' equity: paid-in capital and retained earnings. Also observe the order of the equity accounts:

- Preferred stock at par value
- Paid-in capital in excess of par—preferred
- Common stock at par value
- Paid-in capital in excess of par—common
- Retained earnings (after the paid-in capital accounts)

ADDITIONAL PAID-IN CAPITAL. The paid-in capital in excess of par—common plus other accounts combined for reporting on the balance sheet.

Many companies combine several accounts, including Paid-in Capital in Excess of Par—Common, and report the sum as **Additional Paid-in Capital** on the balance sheet. However, they are careful not to include Paid-in Capital in Excess of Par—Preferred because that paid-in capital belongs to the preferred stockholders.

THINK IT OVER

Examine MedTech.com Corporation's stockholders' equity in Exhibit 13-8, and answer these questions.

1. How much did MedTech.com's preferred stockholders pay into the corporation?
2. How much did the common stockholders pay into MedTech.com?
3. What did the stockholders get for their payments into the company?

Answers

1. $54,000 ($40,000 + $14,000)
2. $117,000 ($45,000 + $72,000)

3. The stockholders received stock, which represents their ownership in the assets of the corporation.

Now review the Decision Guidelines feature to solidify your understanding of stockholders' equity as it is reported on the balance sheet.

DECISION GUIDELINES

Reporting Stockholders' Equity on the Balance Sheet

DECISION	GUIDELINES
What are the two main segments of stockholders' equity?	• Paid-in capital • Retained earnings
Which is more permanent, paid-in capital or retained earnings?	Paid-in capital is more permanent because corporations use their retained earnings for declaring dividends.
How are paid-in capital and retained earnings • Similar?	• Both represent the stockholders' equity (ownership) in the assets of the corporation.

• Different?	• Paid-in capital and retained earnings come from different sources:
	  a. *Paid-in capital* comes from the corporation's stockholders, who invested in the company.
	  b. *Retained earnings* comes from the corporation's customers. It was earned by profitable operations.

What are the main categories of paid-in capital?	• Preferred stock, plus paid-in-capital in excess of par • Common stock, plus paid-in-capital in excess of par

MID-CHAPTER

SUMMARY PROBLEM

www.prenhall.com/horngren
Mid-Chapter Assessment

1. Test your understanding of the first half of this chapter: Is each of the following statements true or false?
   a. Issuance of 1,000 shares of $5 par-value stock at $12 increases contributed capital by $7,000.
   b. The issuance of no-par stock with a stated value is fundamentally different from issuing par-value stock.
   c. A corporation issues its preferred stock in exchange for land and a building with a combined market value of $200,000. This transaction increases the corporation's owners' equity by $200,000 regardless of the assets' prior book value.
   d. A stockholder may bind the corporation to a contract.
   e. The policy-making body in a corporation is called the board of directors.
   f. The owner of 100 shares of preferred stock has greater voting rights than the owner of 100 shares of common stock.
   g. Par-value stock is worth more than no-par stock.
2. The brewery **Adolph Coors Company** has two classes of common stock. Only the Class A common stockholders are entitled to vote. The company's balance sheet included the following presentation:

Stockholders' Equity

Capital stock	
Class A common stock, voting, $1 par value, authorized and issued 1,260,000 shares	$ 1,260,000
Class B common stock, nonvoting, no par value, authorized and issued 46,200,000 shares	11,000,000
	12,260,000
Additional paid-in capital	2,011,000
Retained earnings	872,403,000
	$886,674,000

Required

1. Record the issuance of the Class A common stock. The additional paid-in capital is related to the Class A common stock. Use the Coors account titles.
2. Record the issuance of the Class B common stock. Use the Coors account titles.
3. Rearrange the Coors stockholders' equity section to correspond to the following format:

Stockholders' Equity

Paid-in capital:	
Class A common stock	$
Paid-in capital in excess of par—Class A common stock	
Class B common stock	
Total paid-in capital	
Retained earnings	
Total stockholders' equity	$

4. What is the total paid-in capital of the company?
5. How did Coors withhold the voting privilege from the Class B common stockholders?

Solutions

1. Answers to true/false statements:
   a. False   **c.** True   **e.** True   **g.** False
   b. False   **d.** False   **f.** False

(1) Cash	3,271,000	
Class A Common Stock		1,260,000
Additional Paid-in Capital		2,011,000
To record issuance of Class A common stock at a premium.		
(2) Cash	11,000,000	
Class B Common Stock		11,000,000
To record issuance of Class B common stock.		

(3) **Shareholders' Equity**
Paid-in capital:

Class A common stock, voting, $1 par value, authorized and issued 1,260,000 shares	$ 1,260,000
Paid-in capital in excess of par—Class A common stock	2,011,000
Class B common stock, nonvoting, no par value, authorized and issued 46,200,000 shares	11,000,000
Total paid-in capital	14,271,000
Retained earnings	872,403,000
Total shareholders' equity	$886,674,000

(4) Total paid-in capital is $14,271,000.
(5) The voting privilege was withheld by specific agreement with the stockholders.

ACCOUNTING FOR CASH DIVIDENDS

Corporations share the company's wealth with their stockholders through dividends. Corporations declare dividends from retained earnings and pay the dividends with cash. The corporation must have enough *retained earnings* to declare the dividend and enough *cash* to pay the dividend.

Dividend Dates

A corporation must declare a dividend before paying it. The board of directors alone has the authority to declare a dividend. The corporation has no obligation to pay a dividend until the board declares one, but once declared, the dividend becomes a legal liability of the corporation. Three relevant dates for dividends are

1. *Declaration date.* On the declaration date, the board of directors announces the intention to pay the dividend. The declaration creates a liability for the corporation. Declaration is recorded by debiting Retained Earnings and crediting Dividends Payable.
2. *Date of record.* At declaration, the corporation also announces the record date, which follows the declaration date by a few weeks. Those stockholders who own the stock on the date of record will receive the dividend when it is paid. The corporation makes no journal entry on the date of record because no transaction occurs. But much work takes place behind the scenes to identify stockholders of record on this date.
3. *Payment date.* Payment of the dividend usually follows the record date by two to three weeks. Payment is recorded by debiting Dividends Payable and crediting Cash.

Objective 4
Account for cash dividends

Dividends on Preferred and Common Stock

Declaration of a cash dividend is recorded by debiting Retained Earnings and crediting Dividends Payable as follows:[1]

June 19	Retained Earnings	XXX	
	Dividends Payable		XXX
	Declared a cash dividend.		

---

[1]In Chapters 1–4, we debited the Dividends account, which is closed to Retained Earnings. Many businesses debit Retained Earnings directly, as shown here.

Payment of the dividend, which usually follows declaration by a few weeks, is recorded by debiting Dividends Payable and crediting Cash:

⊙ DAILY EXERCISE 13-13

July 2	Dividends Payable............................ XXX	
	Cash..	XXX
	Paid the cash dividend.	

Dividends Payable is a current liability. When a company has issued both preferred stock and common stock, the preferred stockholders receive their dividends first. The common stockholders receive dividends only if the total declared dividend is large enough to pay the preferred stockholders first.

In addition to its common stock, Pine Industries, Inc., has 9,000 shares of preferred stock outstanding. Preferred dividends are paid at the annual rate of $1.75 per share. Exhibit 13-9 shows the division between preferred and common for three amounts of the total annual dividend declared by Pine Industries.

Case A: Total dividend of $150,000
    Preferred dividend (9,000 shares × $1.75 per share) .... $ 15,750
    Common dividend ($150,000 − $15,750) 134,250
    Total dividend $150,000
Case B: Total dividend of $20,000
    Preferred dividend (9,000 shares × $1.75 per share) .... $ 15,750
    Common dividend ($20,000 − $15,750) 4,250
    Total dividend .... $ 20,000
Case C: Total dividend of $8,000
    Preferred dividend (the full $8,000 goes to preferred
      because the annual preferred dividend is $15,750) .... $ 8,000
    Common dividend (none because the total dividend
      did not cover the preferred dividend for the year) 0
    Total dividend .... $ 8,000

EXHIBIT 13-9
Division of a Dividend Between Preferred Stock and Common Stock

If Pine Industries' annual dividend is large enough to cover the preferred dividend for the year (Cases A and B), the preferred stockholders receive their regular dividend, and the common stockholders receive the remainder. But if the year's dividend falls below the amount of the annual preferred dividend (Case C), the preferred stockholders receive the entire dividend, and the common stockholders receive nothing that year.

This example illustrates an important relationship between preferred stock and common stock. To an investor, the preferred stock is safer because it receives dividends first. However, the earnings potential from an investment in common stock is much greater. Preferred stockholders usually receive only the specified dividend, but there is no upper limit on the amount of common dividends.

When a company has more than one class of preferred stock or common stock, the division of dividends among the various classes of stock follows this same pattern: The most senior preferred stock gets the first dividends, and so on.

We noted that preferred stockholders enjoy the advantage of priority over common stockholders in receiving dividends. The dividend preference is stated as a percentage rate or a dollar amount. For example, preferred stock may be "6% preferred," which means that owners of the preferred stock receive an annual dividend of 6% of the par value of the stock. If par value is $100 per share, preferred stockholders receive an annual cash dividend of $6 per share (6% of $100). The preferred stock may be "$3 preferred," which means that stockholders receive an annual dividend of $3 per share regardless of the preferred stock's par value. The dividend rate on no-par preferred stock is stated in a dollar amount per share.

⊙ DAILY EXERCISE 13-14

Dividends on Cumulative and Noncumulative Preferred Stock

The allocation of dividends may be complex if the preferred stock is *cumulative.* Corporations sometimes fail to pay a dividend to their preferred stockholders. This is called *passing the dividend,* and the passed dividends are said to be *in arrears.* The owners

CUMULATIVE PREFERRED STOCK.
Preferred stock whose owners must receive all dividends in arrears before the corporation pays dividends to the common stockholders.

of **cumulative preferred stock** must receive all dividends in arrears plus the current year's dividend before the corporation pays dividends to the common stockholders.

The preferred stock of Pine Industries is cumulative. Suppose the company passed the 20X4 preferred dividend of $15,750. Before paying dividends to its common stockholders in 20X5, the company must first pay preferred dividends of $15,750 for both 20X4 and 20X5, a total of $31,500. *Preferred stock is cumulative in the eyes of the law unless it is labeled as noncumulative.* Most preferred stock is cumulative.

Assume that Pine Industries passes its 20X4 preferred dividend. In 20X5, the company declares a $50,000 dividend. The entry to record the declaration of this dividend is

Sep. 6	Retained Earnings	50,000	
	Dividends Payable, Preferred ($15,750 × 2)............		31,500
	Dividends Payable, Common		
	($50,000 − $31,500)...		18,500
	Declared a cash dividend.		

If the preferred stock is *noncumulative,* the corporation is not obligated to pay dividends in arrears. Suppose the Pine Industries preferred stock was noncumulative and the company passed the 20X4 preferred dividend of $15,750. The preferred stockholders would lose the 20X4 dividend forever. Of course, the common stockholders would not receive a 20X4 dividend either. Before paying any common dividends in 20X5, the company would have to pay the 20X5 preferred dividend of $15,750.

Having dividends in arrears on cumulative preferred stock is *not* a liability for the corporation. (A liability for dividends arises only after the board of directors declares the dividend.) Nevertheless, a corporation must report cumulative preferred dividends in arrears. This information alerts common stockholders as to how much in preferred dividends must be paid before the common stockholders will receive any dividends.

Dividends in arrears are often disclosed in notes, as follows (all dates and amounts assumed). Observe the two references to Note 3 in this section of the balance sheet. The "6%" after "Preferred stock" is the annual dividend rate.

Preferred stock, 6%, $50 par, 2,000 shares issued (Note 3)	$100,000
Retained earnings (Note 3)...	414,000

Note 3—Cumulative preferred dividends in arrears. At December 31, 20X2, dividends on the preferred stock were in arrears for 20X1 and 20X2, in the amount of $12,000 (6% × $100,000 × 2 years).

DIFFERENT VALUES OF STOCK

Objective 5
Use different stock values in decision making

There are several different *stock values* in addition to par value. Market value, liquidation value, and book value are used for various investor decisions.

Market Value

MARKET VALUE. Price for which a person could buy or sell a share of stock.

A stock's **market value,** or *market price,* is the price for which a person could buy or sell a share of the stock. The issuing corporation's net income, financial position, and future prospects and general economic conditions determine market value. The Internet and most newspapers report the market price of many stocks. Log onto any company's Web site to track its stock price. *In almost all cases, stockholders are more concerned about the market value of a stock than about any other value.* In the chapter-opening story, **IHOP's** stock had a market price of $10 when it was issued. Shortly thereafter, the stock shot up to a market price of $36, which means that the stock could be sold for, or bought for, $36 per share. The purchase of 100 shares of IHOP stock at $36 would cost $3,600 ($36 × 100), plus a commission. If you were selling 100 shares of IHOP stock, you would receive cash of $3,600 less a commission. The commission is the fee an investor pays to a stockbroker for buying or selling the stock. The price of a share of IHOP stock has fluctuated from $10 at issuance to a recent high of $25.

If you buy IHOP stock from another investor, IHOP gets no cash. The transaction is a sale between you and the other investor. IHOP records only the change in stockholder name.

Liquidation Value

Some preferred stocks have a liquidation value. The *liquidation value* is the amount the corporation agrees to pay the preferred stockholder per share if the company liquidates. Dividends in arrears are added to liquidation value in determining the payment to the preferred stockholders if the company liquidates.

Some companies report their preferred stock at its liquidation value on the balance sheet. Consider **BF Goodrich Company,** which makes chemicals and aerospace components and sells tires under the Michelin label. BF Goodrich has 2.2 million shares of convertible preferred stock that is stated at "a liquidation value of $50 per share." The balance in BF Goodrich's preferred stock account is thus $110 million (2.2 million shares × $50).

DAILY EXERCISE 13-15

Book Value

The **book value** of a stock is the amount of owners' equity on the company's books for each share of its stock. Corporations often report this amount in their annual reports. If the company has only common stock outstanding, its book value is computed by dividing total stockholders' equity by the number of shares *outstanding*. A company with stockholders' equity of $180,000 and 5,000 shares of common stock outstanding has a book value of $36 per share ($180,000/5,000 shares).

BOOK VALUE. Amount of owners' equity on the company's books for each share of its stock.

If the company has both preferred stock and common stock outstanding, the preferred stockholders have the first claim to owners' equity. Ordinarily, preferred stock has a specified liquidation value. The book value of preferred stock is its liquidation value plus any cumulative dividends in arrears on the stock. Its book value *per share* equals the sum of liquidation value and any cumulative dividends in arrears divided by the number of preferred shares *outstanding*. After the corporation figures the book value of the preferred shares, it computes the book value per share of the common. The corporation divides the common equity (total stockholders' equity minus preferred equity) by the number of common shares outstanding.

Lille Corporation's balance sheet reports the following amounts:

Stockholders' Equity	
Paid-in capital:	
Preferred stock, 6%, $10 par, 5,000 shares authorized,	
5,000 shares issued (liquidation value $13 per share)	$ 50,000
Paid-in capital in excess of par—preferred	14,000
Common stock, $1 par, 20,000 shares authorized,	
15,000 shares issued	15,000
Paid-in capital in excess of par—common	172,000
Total paid-in capital	251,000
Retained earnings	422,000
Total stockholders' equity	$673,000

Suppose that four years' (including the current year) cumulative preferred dividends are in arrears. The book-value-per-share computations are as follows:

Preferred	
Liquidation value (5,000 shares × $13)	$ 65,000
Cumulative dividends ($50,000 × 0.06 × 4)	12,000
Stockholders' equity allocated to preferred.................................	$ 77,000
Book value per share ($77,000/5,000 shares)	$ 15.40
Common	
Total stockholders' equity..	$673,000
Less stockholders' equity allocated to preferred..........................	(77,000)
Stockholders' equity allocated to common	$596,000
Book value per share ($596,000/15,000 shares)	$39.73

DAILY EXERCISE 13-16

If the preferred stock has no specified liquidation value, then we would use the sum of par value plus paid-in capital in excess of par-preferred, $64,000, plus cumulative dividends to compute the book value of the preferred stock.

BOOK VALUE AND DECISION MAKING How is book value used in decision making? Book value may figure into the negotiated purchase price of a corporation whose stock is not publicly traded. Also, a corporation may buy out a retiring executive or other stockholder by agreeing to pay the book value of the person's stock in the company.

Some investors have traditionally compared the book value of a share of a company's stock with the stock's market value. The idea was that a stock selling below its book value was underpriced and thus a good buy. The relationship between book value and market value is far from clear. Some investors believe that a company whose stock sells at a price below book value must be experiencing financial difficulty. Exhibit 13-10 contrasts the book values and ranges of market values for the common stocks of three well-known companies. For all three companies, the market value of the stock exceeds its book value—a mark of success. The market price of **Dell Computer's** stock far exceeds its book value per share.

◉ DAILY EXERCISE 13-17

EXHIBIT 13-10
Book Value and Market Value for Three Well-Known Companies

	Book Value Per Share	July 6, 2000 Stock Price
IHOP Corp.*	$11.28	$17.13
MCI WORLDCOM*	18.02	$46.44
Dell Computer**	2.06	$47.75

  * December 31, 1999.
** January 28, 2000.

Objective 6
Evaluate a company's return on assets and return on stockholders' equity

EVALUATING OPERATIONS

Investors and creditors are constantly evaluating companies' profits. Investors search for companies whose stocks are likely to increase in value. The decision often requires a comparison of companies. But **IHOP's** net income may not be comparable with the net income of a new company. IHOP's profits may run into the millions of dollars, which far exceed a new company's net income. To compare companies of different size, investors use standard profitability measures. Two of the most widely used are the rate of return on total assets and rate of return on stockholders' equity.

Rate of Return on Total Assets

The **rate of return on total assets,** or simply **return on assets,** measures a company's success in using its assets to earn income for those who are financing the business.

- Creditors have loaned money to the corporation and thus earn interest.
- Stockholders have invested in the corporation's stock and therefore own the company's net income.

The sum of interest expense and net income is the return to the two groups that have financed the corporation's assets, and this is the numerator of the return-on-assets ratio. The denominator is average total assets. Return on assets is computed as follows, using data from the 1999 annual report of IHOP Corp. (dollar amounts in thousands):

RATE OF RETURN ON TOTAL ASSETS. The sum of net income plus interest expense divided by average total assets. This ratio measures the success a company has in using its assets to earn income for the persons who finance the business. Also called **return on assets.**

$$\text{Rate of return on total assets} = \frac{\text{Net income} + \text{Interest expense}}{\text{Average total assets}}$$

$$= \frac{\$32,125 + \$19,391}{(\$443,032 + \$520,402)/2} = \frac{\$51,516}{\$481,717} = 0.107$$

Net income and interest expense are taken from the income statement. Average total assets is computed from the beginning and ending balance sheets.

What is a good rate of return on total assets? There is no single answer to this question because rates of return vary widely by industry. For example, high technology companies such as **Intel** and **Hewlett-Packard** earn higher returns than utility companies and manufacturers of consumer goods such as toothpaste. In most industries a return on assets of 10% is considered good.

Rate of Return on Common Stockholders' Equity

Rate of return on common stockholders' equity, often called **return on equity,** shows the relationship between net income and average common stockholders' equity. The numerator is net income minus preferred dividends. Preferred dividends are subtracted because the preferred stockholders have the first claim to dividends from the company's net income. The denominator is average *common stockholders' equity*—total stockholders' equity minus preferred equity. IHOP's rate of return on common stockholders' equity for 1999 is computed as follows (dollar amounts in thousands):

$$\text{Rate of return on common stockholders' equity} = \frac{\text{Net income} - \text{Preferred dividends}}{\text{Average common stockholders' equity}}$$

$$= \frac{\$32,125 - \$0}{(\$187,868 + \$226,480)/2} = \frac{\$32,125}{\$207,174} = 0.155$$

IHOP Corp. has no preferred stock, so preferred dividends are zero. With no preferred stock outstanding, average *common* stockholders' equity is the same as average *total* equity—the average of the beginning and ending amounts.

IHOP's return on equity (15.5%) is higher than its return on assets (10.7%). This indicates a financially healthy company because IHOP is earning more for its stockholders than it is paying for interest expense. Companies such as IHOP borrow at one rate (say, 7%) and invest the funds to earn a higher rate (almost 16%). Borrowing at a lower rate than the return on investments is called *using leverage.*

If return on assets is higher than return on equity, the company is in trouble because its interest expense is greater than its return on equity. Interest expense should always be lower than the amount the company earns on its investments. Investors and creditors use return on common stockholders' equity in much the same way they use return on total assets—to compare companies. The higher the rate of return, the more successful the company. IHOP's 15.5% return on common stockholders' equity would be considered good in most industries.

ACCOUNTING FOR INCOME TAXES BY CORPORATIONS

Corporations pay income tax just as individuals do, but not at the same rates. At this writing, the federal tax rate on most corporate income is 35%. Most states also levy a corporate income tax, so most corporations have a combined federal and state income tax rate of approximately 40%.

To account for income tax, the corporation measures

- Income tax expense, an expense on the income statement
- Income tax payable, a liability on the balance sheet

Accounting for income tax by a corporation follows the general principles that govern accounting for all other transactions. Let's return to **IHOP Corp.** In 20X0, suppose IHOP reported income before tax (also called pretax accounting income) of approximately $50 million on its income statement. IHOP's combined income tax rate is 40%. Assume IHOP's income tax expense and income tax payable are the same. Then IHOP would record income tax for the year as follows (amounts in millions):

20X0			
Dec. 31	Income Tax Expense ($50 × 0.40)	20	
	Income Tax Payable		20
	Recorded income tax for the year.		

RATE OF RETURN ON COMMON STOCKHOLDERS' EQUITY. Net income minus preferred dividends, divided by average common stockholders' equity. A measure of profitability. Also called **return on equity.**

◉ DAILY EXERCISE 13-18

◉ DAILY EXERCISE 13-19

Objective 7
Account for the income tax of a corporation

IHOP's 20X0 financial statements would report these figures (adapted, in millions):

Income Statement		Balance Sheet	
Income before income tax	$ 50	Current liabilities:	
Income tax expense	(20)	Income tax payable	$20
Net income	$ 30		

Early in 20X1, IHOP would pay its income tax payable when the company files its 20X0 income tax return with the Internal Revenue Service. Now, let's move to 20X1 with a more realistic income tax example. In general, income tax expense and income tax payable can be computed as follows:[2]

Income tax *expense*	=	Income before income tax (from the income statement)	×	Income tax rate		Income tax *payable*	=	Taxable income (from the income tax return filed with the IRS)	×	Income tax rate

For most companies, income tax expense and income tax payable differ. The most important difference between income tax expense and income tax payable occurs when a corporation uses the straight-line depreciation method for the financial statements and an accelerated depreciation method for the tax return. The tax depreciation method is called the *modified accelerated cost recovery system*, abbreviated as MACRS. ← For any one year, MACRS depreciation may differ from accounting depreciation on the income statement.

Continuing with the IHOP illustration, suppose for 20X1 that IHOP Corp. has

- Income before income tax of $60 million on the income statement
- Taxable income of $55 million on the company's income tax return

IHOP will record income tax for 20X1 as follows (dollar amounts in millions and an income tax rate of 40%):

20X1
Dec. 31   Income Tax Expense ($60 × 0.40)   24
           Income Tax Payable ($55 × 0.40)............   22
           Deferred Tax Liability   2
      Recorded income tax for the year.

IHOP will pay the $22 million of Income Tax Payable, a current liability, within a few months. The Deferred Tax Liability account is long-term, so IHOP will pay this debt over a number of years. IHOP's 20X1 financial statements would report these figures (adapted, in millions):

Income Statement		Balance Sheet	
Income before income tax	$60	Current liabilities:	
Income tax expense......................	(24)	Income tax payable	$22
Net income	$36	Long-term liabilities:	
		Deferred tax liability................	2*

* Assumes the beginning balance of Deferred tax liability was zero.

The Decision Guidelines feature provides an overview of the second half of the chapter.

→ We learned in Chapter 10, page 400, that the MACRS depreciation method is similar to the double-declining-balance method.

⊙ DAILY EXERCISE 13-20

_____
[2] The authors thank Jean Marie Hudson for suggesting this presentation.

DECISION GUIDELINES

Dividends, Stock Values, Evaluating Operations, & Accounting for Income Tax

DECISION	GUIDELINES
Dividends	
Whether to declare a cash dividend?	• Must have enough retained earnings to declare the dividend. • Must have enough cash to pay the dividend.
What happens with a dividend?	• The corporation's board of directors declares the dividend. Then the dividend becomes a liability of the corporation. • The date of record fixes who will receive the dividend. • Payment of the dividend occurs later.
Who receives the dividend?	• Preferred stockholders first receive their dividends at a specified rate. • Common stockholders receive the remainder.
Stock Values	
How much to pay for a stock? What unique value applies to preferred stock?	Its market value. • Liquidation value—the amount the corporation agrees to pay if the company liquidates
What is book value's role in decision making?	Sometimes used to help determine the market value of a stock that is not traded on a stock exchange.
Evaluating Operations	
How to evaluate the operations of a corporation?	Two measures that relate earnings to the amount stockholders have invested include • Rate of return on assets • Rate of return on common stockholders' equity For a healthy company, return on stockholders' equity should exceed return on assets.
Accounting for Income Tax	
What are the three main accounts?	• Income tax expense • Income tax payable, a current liability • Deferred tax liability, usually a long-term liability
How to measure • Income tax expense?	Income before income tax × Income tax rate (from the income statement)
• Income tax payable?	Taxable income × Income tax rate (from the income tax return filed with the Internal Revenue Service)
• Deferred tax liability?	Difference between income tax expense and income tax payable for any one year

EXCEL APPLICATION PROBLEM

Goal: Create an Excel spreadsheet that compares financial performance of several publicly traded stocks.

Scenario: Your task is to create an Excel spreadsheet that compares the historical performance of **The Gap** and **Abercrombie & Fitch** on three key financial measures. Embedded graphs of each financial dimension also must be created. All data used in your spreadsheet will come from Morningstar's Web site.

When done, answer these questions:

1. Which company has earned a consistently higher return on equity?
2. Which company has earned a consistently higher return on assets?
3. Increasing cash flow from operations is a good sign for investing. Which company has experienced increasing cash flows over the past five years?
4. Based on these very limited data, would you invest in either of these companies? Why or why not?

EXCEL APPLICATION PROBLEM (CONT.)

Step-by-step:
1. Locate **www.morningstar.com** on the Web.
2. Under the "Quotes & Reports" section, enter the ticker symbol for each company. Then, look under "Company Performance" and "Historical Overview." You should see a five-year summary of fiscal-year-end financial performance. Print out the Historical Overview for each company.
3. Open a new Excel spreadsheet.
4. Create a boldfaced heading for your spreadsheet that contains the following:
   a. Chapter 13 Decision Guidelines
   b. Investing in Stock
   c. Stock Performance Analysis
   d. Today's date
5. Under the heading, create a boldfaced, underlined section titled "Return on Equity %." Move down one row.

Create one column each for the last five years (for example, "1999," "1998," and so on). Create one row each for The Gap and Abercrombie & Fitch.
6. Enter the return on equity data for the past five years found on the Morningstar Historical Overview for each company.
7. Repeat steps 5 and 6 for "Return on Assets %" and "Operating Cash Flow (in millions)."
8. Using the Excel Chart Wizard, create separate graphs for Return on Equity %, Return on Assets %, and Operating Cash Flow. Resize and position each graph to the right of the data so that everything appears on one page when you print.
9. Save your work, and print your spreadsheet in landscape mode (with graphs) for your files.

REVIEW CORPORATIONS: PAID-IN CAPITAL AND THE BALANCE SHEET

SUMMARY PROBLEM

www.prenhall.com/horngren

End-of-Chapter Assessment

1. Use the following accounts and related balances to prepare the classified balance sheet of Whitehall, Inc., at September 30, 20X4. Use the account format of the balance sheet.

Common stock, $1 par, 50,000 shares authorized, 20,000 shares issued	$ 20,000	Long-term note payable	$ 73,000
		Inventory	85,000
Dividends payable	4,000	Property, plant, and equipment, net	225,000
Cash	9,000	Accounts receivable, net	23,000
Accounts payable	28,000	Preferred stock, $3.75, no-par, 10,000 shares authorized, 2,000 shares issued	24,000
Retained earnings	75,000		
Paid-in capital in excess of par—common	115,000	Accrued liabilities	3,000

2. The balance sheet of Trendline Corporation reported the following at March 31, 20X6, the end of its fiscal year. Note that Trendline reports paid-in capital in excess of par or stated value after the stock accounts.

Stockholders' Equity	
Preferred stock, 4%, $10 par, 10,000 shares authorized (liquidation value $110,000)	$100,000
Common stock, no-par, $5 stated value, 100,000 shares authorized	250,000
Paid-in capital in excess of par:	
Common stock	231,500
Retained earnings	395,000
Total stockholders' equity	$976,500

Required
1. Is the preferred stock cumulative or noncumulative? How can you tell?
2. What is the total amount of the annual preferred dividend?
3. How many shares of preferred and common stock has the company issued?

4. Compute the book value per share of the preferred and the common stock. No prior year preferred dividends are in arrears, but Trendline has not declared the current-year dividend.

Solution

WHITEHALL, INC.
Balance Sheet
September 30, 20X4

Assets		Liabilities	
Current:		Current:	
Cash	$ 9,000	Accounts payable....................	$ 28,000
Accounts receivable, net	23,000	Dividends payable..................	4,000
Inventory	85,000	Accrued liabilities	3,000
Total current assets....................................	117,000	Total current liabilities.........	35,000
Property, plant and equipment, net..............	225,000	Long-term note payable	73,000
		Total liabilities.........................	108,000
		Stockholders' Equity	
		Paid-in capital:	
		Preferred stock, $3.75, no-par,	
		10,000 shares authorized,	
		2,000 shares issued	$ 24,000
		Common stock, $1 par, 50,000	
		shares authorized, 20,000	
		shares issued	20,000
		Paid-in capital in excess of	
		par—common	115,000
		Total paid-in capital	159,000
		Retained earnings.......................	75,000
		Total stockholders' equity.......	234,000
		Total liabilities and	
Total assets..	$342,000	stockholders' equity................	$342,000

Required

1. The preferred stock is cumulative because it is not specifically labeled otherwise.
2. Total annual preferred dividend: $4,000 ($100,000 × 0.04).
3. Preferred stock issued: 10,000 shares ($100,000/$10 par value).
   Common stock issued: 50,000 shares ($250,000/$5 stated value).
4. Book values per share of preferred and common stock:

Preferred:	
Liquidation value	$110,000
Cumulative dividend for current year ($100,000 × 0.04)	4,000
Stockholders' equity allocated to preferred............................	$114,000
Book value per share ($114,000/10,000 shares)	$11.40
Common:	
Total stockholders' equity...	$976,500
Less stockholders' equity allocated to preferred.....................	(114,000)
Stockholders' equity allocated to common	$862,500
Book value per share ($862,500/50,000 shares)	$17.25

Lessons Learned

1. *Identify the characteristics of a corporation.* A corporation is a separate legal and business entity. *Continuous life,* the *ease of raising large amounts of capital and transferring ownership,* and *limited liability* are among the advantages of the corporate form of organization. An important disadvantage is *double taxation.* Corporations pay *income taxes,* and stockholders pay tax on dividends. *Stockholders* are the owners of the corporations. They elect a *board of directors,* which elects a chairperson and appoints the officers to manage the business.

2. *Record the issuance of stock.* Corporations may issue different classes of stock: *par value, no-par value, common,* and *preferred.* Stock is usually issued at a *premium*—an amount above par value.

3. *Prepare the stockholders' equity section of a corporation's balance sheet.* The balance sheet carries the capital raised through stock issuance under the heading Paid-in Capital or Contributed Capital in the stockholders' equity section.

4. **Account for cash dividends.** Only when the board of directors declares a *dividend* does the corporation incur the liability to pay dividends. Preferred stock has priority over common stock as to dividends, which may be stated as a percent of par value or as a dollar amount per share. In addition, preferred stock has a claim to dividends in arrears if it is *cumulative*.

5. **Use different stock values in decision making.** A stock's *market value* is the price for which a share may be bought or sold. *Liquidation value* and *book value*—the amount of owners' equity per share of company stock—are other values that may apply to stock.

6. **Evaluate a company's return on assets and return on stockholders' equity.** *Return on assets* and *return on stockholders' equity* are two standard measures of profitability. A healthy company's return on equity will exceed its return on assets.

7. **Account for the income tax of a corporation.** Corporations pay income tax and must account for the income tax expense and income tax payable. A difference between the expense and the payable creates another account, Deferred Tax Liability.

ACCOUNTING VOCABULARY

additional paid-in capital (p. 512)
authorization of stock (p. 502)
board of directors (p. 503)
book value (p. 517)
bylaws (p. 503)
chairperson (p. 503)
charter (p. 501)
common stock (p. 504)
contributed capital (p. 503)
cumulative preferred stock (p. 516)
deficit (p. 505)

dividends (p. 505)
double taxation (p. 502)
legal capital (p. 505)
limited liability (p. 502)
market value (p. 516)
outstanding stock (p. 503)
paid-in capital (p. 503)
par value (p. 507)
preferred stock (p. 506)
president (p. 503)
rate of return on common stockholders' equity (p. 519)

rate of return on total assets (p. 518)
retained earnings (p. 503)
return on assets (p. 518)
return on equity (p. 519)
shareholder (p. 501)
stated value (p. 507)
stock (p. 501)
stockholder (p. 501)
stockholders' equity (p. 503)

QUESTIONS

1. Identify the characteristics of a corporation.
2. Explain why corporations face a tax disadvantage.
3. How are the structures of a partnership and a corporation similar, and how are they different?
4. Dividends on preferred stock may be stated as a percent or a dollar amount. What is the annual dividend on these preferred stocks: 4%, $100 par; $3.50, $20 par; and 6%, no-par with $50 stated value?
5. Which event increases the assets of the corporation: authorization of stock or issuance of stock? Explain.
6. Suppose H. J. Heinz Company issued 1,000 shares of its 3.65%, $100 par preferred stock for $120. How much would this transaction increase the company's paid-in capital? How much would it increase Heinz's retained earnings? How much would it increase Heinz's annual cash dividend payments?
7. Give two alternative account titles for Paid-in Capital in Excess of Par—Common Stock.
8. How does issuance of 1,000 shares of no-par stock for

land and a building, together worth $150,000, affect paid-in capital? Total stockholders' equity?
9. Rank the following accounts in the order they would appear on the balance sheet: Common Stock, Preferred Stock, Retained Earnings, Dividends Payable. Also, give each account's balance sheet classification.
10. As a preferred stockholder, would you rather own cumulative or noncumulative preferred? If all other factors are the same, would the corporation rather the preferred stock be cumulative or noncumulative? Give your reason.
11. Distinguish between the market value of stock and the book value of stock. Which is more important to investors?
12. How is book value per share of common stock computed when the company has both preferred stock and common stock outstanding?
13. Why should a healthy company's rate of return on stockholders' equity exceed its rate of return on total assets?
14. Explain the difference between the income tax expense and the income tax payable of a corporation.

ASSESS YOUR PROGRESS

DAILY EXERCISES

Characteristics of a corporation
(Obj. 1)

DE13-1 Suppose you are forming Spuds, Inc., which will feature 20 different toppings for baked potatoes. You need some outside money from other investors, and you have decided to organize the business as a corporation that will issue stock to raise the needed funds. Briefly discuss your most important reason for organizing Spuds as a corporation rather than as a partnership. If you had organized as a partnership, what would be your most important reason for not organizing as a corporation?

Authority structure in a corporation
(Obj. 1)

DE13-2 Consider the authority structure in a corporation, as diagrammed in Exhibit 13-2.
1. Who is in charge of day-to-day operations?
2. Who manages the accounting?

3. Who has primary responsibility for the corporation's cash?

4. What group holds the ultimate power in a corporation?

5. Who is the most powerful person in the corporation?

DE13-3 Examine the summarized balance sheet of **Target Corporation** in Exhibit 13-4 page 504. Suppose Target were a proprietorship owned by Lee Target. How would the Target proprietorship balance sheet differ from the one given in Exhibit 13-4? How would the proprietorship balance sheet be similar to the one given in Exhibit 13-4?

Similarities and differences between the balance sheets of a corporation and a proprietorship (Obj. 1)

DE13-4 Answer the following questions about the characteristics of a corporation's stock.

Characteristics of preferred and common stock (Obj. 1)

1. What privileges do preferred stockholders enjoy that common stockholders do not have?

2. Which class of stockholders would expect to reap greater benefits from a highly profitable corporation? Why?

3. Which stockholders are the real owners of a corporation?

4. Which right clearly distinguishes a stockholder from a creditor (who has lent money to the corporation)?

DE13-5 Study **IHOP's** July 31 stock issuance entry given on page 507, and answer these questions about the nature of the IHOP transaction.

Effect of a stock issuance on net income (Obj. 2)

1. IHOP received $32,000,000 for the issuance of its stock. The par value of the IHOP stock was only $32,000. Was the excess amount of $31,968,000 a profit to IHOP? If not, what was it?

2. Suppose the par value of the IHOP stock had been $1 per share, $5 per share, or $10 per share. Would a change in the par value of the company's stock affect IHOP's net income? Give the reason for your answer.

DE13-6 **The Coca-Cola Company** reported the following on its balance sheet at December 31, 1999 (adapted, amounts in millions, except for par value):

Issuing stock and interpreting stockholders' equity (Obj. 2)

Common stock, $0.25 par value	
Authorized: 5,600 shares	
Issued: 3,466 shares	$ 867
Paid-in capital in excess of par..............	2,584
Retained earnings	20,773

1. Assume Coca-Cola issued all of its stock during 1999. Journalize the company's issuance of the stock for cash.

2. Was Coca-Cola's main source of stockholders' equity paid-in capital or profitable operations? How can you tell?

DE13-7 At December 31, 1999, **The Coca-Cola Company** reported the following on its comparative balance sheet, which included 1998 amounts for comparison (adapted, with all amounts except par value in millions):

Issuing stock and analyzing retained earnings (Obj. 2)

	December 31,	
	1999	**1998**
Common stock $0.25 par value		
Authorized: 5,600 shares		
Issued: 3,466 shares in 1999	$ 867	
3,460 shares in 1998		$ 865
Paid-in capital in excess of par................	2,584	2,158
Retained earnings	20,773	19,922

1. How much did Coca-Cola's total paid-in capital increase during 1999? What caused total paid-in capital to increase? How can you tell?

2. Journalize Coca-Cola's issuance of stock for cash during 1999.

3. Did Coca-Cola have a profit or a loss for 1999? How can you tell?

DE13-8 Brunnheimer Corporation has three classes of stock: Common, $1 par; Preferred Class A, $10 par; and Preferred Class B, no-par.

Issuing stock (Obj. 2)

Journalize Brunnheimer's issuance of

a. 1,000 shares of common stock for $30 per share

b. 1,000 shares of Class A preferred stock for a total of $32,000

c. 1,000 shares of Class B preferred stock for $14 per share

Explanations are not required.

Issuing stock to finance the purchase of assets
(Obj. 2)

DE13-9 This exercise shows the similarity and the difference between two ways to acquire plant assets.

Case A — Issue stock and buy the assets in separate transactions:

Avisa Machines, Inc., issued 10,000 shares of its $10 par common stock for cash of $700,000. In a separate transaction, Avisa Machines purchased a warehouse building for $480,000 and equipment for $220,000. Journalize the two transactions.

Case B — Issue stock to acquire the assets:

Avisa Machines issued 10,000 shares of its $10 par common stock to acquire a warehouse building valued at $480,000 and equipment worth $220,000. Journalize this transaction.

Compare the balances in all accounts after making both sets of entries. Are the account balances similar or different?

Preparing the stockholders' equity section of a balance sheet
(Obj. 3)

DE13-10 The financial statements of Arthur Binding, Inc., reported the following accounts (adapted, in millions except for par value):

Paid-in capital in excess of par	$ 17.3	Net sales	$1,081.5
Cost of goods sold.........................	588.0	Accounts payable	62.4
Common stock $0.01 par,		Retained earnings.......................	166.2
40.2 shares issued	0.4	Other current liabilities	52.3
Cash..	24.0	Operating expenses	412.9
Long-term debt.............................	7.6	Total assets..................................	?

Prepare the stockholders' equity section of the Arthur Binding balance sheet. Net income has already been closed to Retained Earnings.

Using stockholders' equity data
(Obj. 3)

DE13-11 ◄◄ *Link Back to Chapter 1 (Accounting Equation, Income Statement).* Use the Arthur Binding data in Daily Exercise 13-10 to compute Arthur's

   a. Net income   **b.** Total liabilities   **c.** Total assets

Reporting stockholders' equity on the balance sheet
(Obj. 3)

DE13-12 Varlux Corporation began operations in 20X3 with a charter that authorized the company to issue 10,000 shares of 5%, $8 par preferred stock and 100,000 shares of no-par common stock. During 20X3 through 20X8, Varlux issued 3,000 shares of the preferred stock for $25 per share and 50,000 shares of its common stock for $5 per share. At December 31, 20X8, Varlux had retained earnings of $110,000. During 20X9, Varlux earned net income of $70,000 and declared cash dividends of $15,000.

Show how Varlux Corporation reported stockholders' equity on its balance sheet at December 31, 20X9.

Accounting for cash dividends
(Obj. 4)

DE13-13 Colombia Coffee Company earned net income of $85,000 during the year ended December 31, 20X3. On December 15, Colombia declared the annual cash dividend on its 6% preferred stock (10,000 shares with total par value of $100,000) and a $0.50 per share cash dividend on its common stock (50,000 shares with total par value of $250,000). Colombia then paid the dividends on January 4, 20X4.

Journalize for Colombia Company
   a. Declaring the cash dividends on December 15
   b. Closing net income to Retained Earnings on December 31, 20X3
   c. Paying the cash dividends on January 4, 20X4

Did Retained Earnings increase or decrease during 20X3? By how much?

Dividing cash dividends between preferred and common stock
(Obj. 4)

DE13-14 Refer to the stockholders' equity of MedTech.com Corporation in Exhibit 13-8, page 512. Answer these questions about MedTech.com's dividends.

   1. How much in dividends must MedTech.com declare each year before the common stockholders receive cash dividends for the year?
   2. Suppose MedTech.com declares cash dividends of $20,000 for 20X1. How much of the dividends goes to preferred? How much goes to common?
   3. Is MedTech.com's preferred stock cumulative or noncumulative? How can you tell?
   4. Suppose MedTech.com passed the preferred dividend in 20X2 and 20X3. In 20X4, the company declares cash dividends of $9,000. How much of the dividends goes to preferred? How much goes to common?

Similarities and differences between preferred stock and common stock
(Obj. 5)

DE13-15 Indicate whether each of the following characteristics applies to preferred stock, common stock, or both.
   a. Cumulative   **d.** Stated dividend
   b. Callable   **e.** Voting rights
   c. Liquidation value   **f.** Priority to receive assets in the event of liquidation

DE13-16 Refer to the stockholders' equity of MedTech.com Corporation in Exhibit 13-8, page 512. MedTech.com's preferred stock has a liquidation value of $125 per share, and MedTech.com has not declared preferred dividends for three years (including the current year). Compute the book value of MedTech.com's (a) preferred stock and (b) common stock.

Book value per share of preferred and common stock
(Obj. 5)

DE13-17 Answer the following questions about various stock values.

Explaining the use of different stock values for decision making
(Obj. 5)

1. Suppose you are an investor considering the purchase of **Intel** common stock as an investment. You have called your stockbroker to inquire about the stock. Which stock value are you most concerned about and why?
2. How is the book value of a stock used in decision making?
3. Suppose you are the general manager of a small company that is considering going public, as **IHOP Corp.** did in the chapter-opening story. Which stock value are you most concerned about and why?

DE13-18 Answer these questions about two rates of return.

Computing and explaining return on assets and return on equity
(Obj. 6)

1. Give the formula for computing (a) rate of return on common stockholders' equity and (b) rate of return on total assets.
2. Why are preferred dividends subtracted from net income to compute return on common stockholders' equity?
3. Why is interest expense added to net income to compute return on assets?

DE13-19 **The Coca-Cola Company** has earned solid rates of return on its assets and its stockholders' equity in recent years. Coca-Cola's 1999 financial statements reported the following items—with 1998 figures given for comparison (adapted, in millions):

Computing return on assets and return on equity for a leading company
(Obj. 6)

	1999	1998
Balance sheet		
Total current assets	$ 6,480	$ 6,380
Total long-term assets	15,143	12,765
Total assets	$21,623	$19,145
Total liabilities	$12,110	$10,742
Total stockholders' equity (all common)	9,513	8,403
Total liabilities and equity	$21,623	$19,145
Income statement		
Net sales	$19,805	
Cost of goods sold	6,009	
Gross profit	13,796	
Selling, administrative, and general expenses	9,814	
Interest expense	337	
All other expenses, net	1,214	
Net income	$ 2,431	

Compute Coca-Cola's rate of return on total assets and rate of return on common stockholders' equity for 1999. Do these rates of return look high or low?

DE13-20 Harry's Hot Dogs had income before income tax of $120,000 and taxable income of $90,000 for 20X1, the company's first year of operations. The income tax rate is 40%.

Accounting for a corporation's income tax
(Obj. 7)

1. Make the entry to record Harry's income taxes for 20X1.
2. Show what Harry's Hot Dogs will report on its 20X1 income statement starting with income before income tax. Also show what Harry will report for current and long-term liabilities on its December 31, 20X1, balance sheet.

EXERCISES

E13-1 Dena Kelly and Tiffany Lewis are opening a limousine service to be named D & T Limo. They need outside capital, so they plan to organize the business as a corporation. They come to you for advice. Write a memorandum informing them of the steps in forming a corporation. Identify specific documents used in this process, and name the different parties involved in the ownership and management of a corporation.

Organizing a corporation
(Obj. 1)

E13-2 New England Systems completed the following stock issuance transactions:

April 19 Issued 1,000 shares of $1.50 par common stock for cash of $10.50 per share.
May 3 Sold 300 shares of $4.50, no-par Class A preferred stock for $12,000 cash.
11 Received inventory valued at $23,000 and equipment with market value of $11,000. Issued 3,300 shares of the $1.50 par common stock.
15 Issued 1,000 shares of 5%, no-par Class B preferred stock with stated value of $50 per share. The issue price was cash of $62 per share.

Required

1. Journalize the transactions. Explanations are not required.
2. How much paid-in capital did these transactions generate for New England Systems?

E13-3 The charter for Sartis Rugs, Inc., authorizes the company to issue 100,000 shares of $3, no-par preferred stock and 500,000 shares of common stock with $1 par value. During its start-up phase, Sartis completed the following transactions:

Aug. 6 Issued 500 shares of common stock to the promoters who organized the corporation, receiving cash of $15,000.
12 Issued 300 shares of preferred stock for cash of $18,000.
14 Issued 1,000 shares of common stock in exchange for land valued at $26,000.
31 Earned a small profit for August and closed the $13,000 net income into Retained Earnings.

Required

1. Record the transactions in the general journal.
2. Prepare the stockholders' equity section of the Sartis balance sheet at August 31.

E13-4 The balance sheet of Levitz Corporation, as adapted, reported the following stockholders' equity. Levitz has two separate classes of preferred stock, labeled Series A and Series B.

Stockholders' Equity	$ Thousands
Preferred stock, $2 par, authorized 4,000,000 shares (Note 7)	
Series A	$ 100
Series B	740
Common stock, $0.10 par, authorized 20,000,000,	
issued 9,000,000 shares	900
Capital in excess of par (sum of preferred and common)	74,580

Note 7. Preferred Stock:

	Shares Issued
Series A	50,000
Series B	370,000

Required

The Series A preferred stock was issued for $5 cash per share, the Series B preferred was issued for $10 cash per share, and the common was issued for cash of $72,370 thousand. Make the summary journal entries to record issuance of all the Levitz stock. Explanations are not required. After you record these entries, what is the total balance of Capital in Excess of Par?

E13-5 Modern Furniture Co., located in Boston, Massachusetts, imports European furniture and Oriental rugs. The corporation issued 5,000 shares of no-par common stock for $8 per share. Record issuance of the stock if the stock (a) is true no-par stock and (b) has stated value of $2 per share.

E13-6 The charter of Laurclake Corporation authorizes the issuance of 5,000 shares of Class A preferred stock, 1,000 shares of Class B preferred stock, and 10,000 shares of common stock. During a two-month period, Laurelake completed these stock-issuance transactions:

Nov. 23   Issued 2,000 shares of $1 par common stock for cash of $12.50 per share.
Dec. 2   Sold 300 shares of $4.50, no-par Class A preferred stock for $20,000 cash.
     12   Received inventory valued at $25,000 and equipment with market value of $16,000 for 3,300 shares of the $1 par common stock.
     17   Issued 1,000 shares of 5%, no-par Class B preferred stock with stated value of $50 per share. The issue price was cash of $60 per share.

Required

Prepare the stockholders' equity section of the Laurelake balance sheet for the transactions given in this exercise. Retained Earnings has a balance of $46,000.

E13-7 ReadyTech Co. recently organized. The company issued common stock to an attorney in exchange for his patent with a market value of $40,000. In addition, ReadyTech received cash both for 2,000 shares of its $50 par preferred stock at $80 per share and for 26,000 shares of its no-par common stock at $11 per share. Retained Earnings at the end of the first year was $70,000. Without making journal entries, determine the total paid-in capital created by these transactions.
Paid-in capital for a corporation
(Obj. 2)

E13-8 Gene Shattler, Inc., has the following selected account balances at June 30, 20X2. Prepare the stockholders' equity section of the company's balance sheet.
Stockholders' equity section of a balance sheet
(Obj. 3)

Common stock, no par with $1 stated value, 100,000 shares authorized and issued	$100,000	Inventory	$112,000
		Machinery and equipment	109,000
		Preferred stock, 5%, $20 par, 20,000 shares authorized, 5,000 shares issued	100,000
Accumulated depreciation— machinery and equipment	62,000	Paid-in capital in excess of par—preferred stock	88,000
Retained earnings	119,000		
Cost of goods sold	81,000		

E13-9 Qualcomm Communications has the following stockholders' equity:
Dividing dividends between preferred and common stock
(Obj. 4)

Preferred stock, 8%, $10 par, 100,000 shares authorized, 20,000 shares issued	$ 200,000
Common stock, $0.50 par, 500,000 shares authorized, 300,000 shares issued	150,000
Paid-in capital in excess of par—common	600,000
Total paid-in capital	$ 950,000
Retained earnings	150,000
Total stockholders' equity	$1,100,000

First, determine whether preferred stock is cumulative or noncumulative. Then compute the amount of dividends to preferred and to common for 20X1 and 20X2 if total dividends are $10,000 in 20X1 and $60,000 in 20X2.

E13-10 The following elements of stockholders' equity are adapted from the balance sheet of Levitz Corporation.
Computing dividends on preferred and common stock
(Obj. 4)

Stockholders' Equity	$ Thousands
Preferred stock, cumulative, $2 par (Note 7)	
Series A, 50,000 shares issued	$100
Series B, 370,000 shares issued	740
Common stock, $0.10 par, 9,000,000 shares issued	900

Note 7. Preferred Stock:

	Designated Annual Cash Dividend per Share
Series A	$0.40
Series B	1.30

The Series A preferred has preference over the Series B preferred, and the company has paid all preferred dividends through 20X3.

Required

Compute the dividends to both series of preferred stock and to common for 20X4 and 20X5 if total dividends are $0 in 20X4 and $1,100,000 in 20X5.

Book value per share of preferred and common stock
(Obj. 5)

E13-11 The balance sheet of Iota Corporation reported the following:

Preferred stock; 100 shares issued and outstanding, liquidation value $6,000	$ 4,800
Common stockholders' equity, 10,000 shares issued and outstanding	222,000
Total stockholders' equity	$226,800

Assume that Iota has paid preferred dividends for the current year and all prior years (no dividends in arrears). Compute the book value per share of the preferred stock and the common stock.

Book value per share of preferred and common stock; preferred dividends in arrears   (Obj. 5)

E13-12 Refer to Exercise 13-11. Compute the book value per share of the preferred stock and the common stock if three years' preferred dividends (including dividends for the current year) are in arrears. The preferred stock dividend rate is 6%. Round book value to the nearest cent.

Evaluating profitability
(Obj. 6)

E13-13 Weimeyer Furniture, Inc., reported these figures for 20X3 and 20X2:

	20X3	20X2
Income statement:		
Interest expense....................................	$ 17,400,000	$ 7,100,000
Net income	12,000,000	18,700,000
Balance sheet:		
Total assets	326,000,000	317,000,000
Preferred stock, $1.30, no-par, 100,000 shares issued and outstanding	2,500,000	2,500,000
Common stockholders' equity	164,000,000	157,000,000
Total stockholders' equity.......................	166,500,000	159,500,000

Compute rate of return on total assets and rate of return on common stockholders' equity for 20X3. Do these rates of return suggest strength or weakness? Give your reason.

Accounting for income tax by a corporation
(Obj. 7)

E13-14 The income statement of **Pier 1 Imports, Inc.,** reported income before income tax of $130 million during a recent year. Assume Pier 1's taxable income for the year was $100 million. The company's income tax rate was 40%.

1. Journalize Pier 1's entry to record income tax for the year.
2. Show how Pier 1 would report income tax on its income statement and on its balance sheet. Complete the income statement, starting with income before tax. For the balance sheet, assume all beginning balances were zero.

Challenge Exercise

Accounting for stockholders' equity transactions
(Obj. 2, 4)

E13-15 **Wal-Mart Stores, Inc.,** reported these comparative stockholders' equity data (adapted, with amounts in millions except par value):

	January 31,	
	20X0	**19X9**
Common stock ($0.10 par value)..............	$ 446	$ 445
Capital in excess of par value	714	435
Retained earnings......................................	25,129	20,741

During 20X0, Wal-Mart completed these transactions:

   a. Net income, $5,377
   b. Cash dividends declared and paid, $989
   c. Issuance of stock for cash, $280

Required

1. Journalize these 20X0 transactions.
2. For each stockholders' equity account, start with the January 31, 19X9, balance and work toward the balance at January 31, 20X0 to show how your journal entries accounted for the changes in the Wal-Mart accounts.

PROBLEMS

(Group A)

P13-1A Joy Shields and Lin Liu are opening a **Cracker Barrel Restaurant** in Denver, Colorado. There are no competing family restaurants in the immediate vicinity. Their fundamental decision is how to organize the business, which will manage the restaurant and country store. Shields thinks the partnership form is best for their business. Liu favors the corporate form of organization. They seek your advice.

Organizing a corporation (Obj. 1)

Required

Write a memo to Shields and Liu to make them aware of the advantages and the disadvantages of organizing the business as a corporation. Use the following format:

Date: _____	
To:	Joy Shields and Lin Liu
From:	Student Name
Subject:	Advantages and disadvantages of the corporate form of business organization

P13-2A The partnership of Duran & Nueces needed additional capital to expand into new markets, so the business incorporated as Ventura, Inc. The charter from the state of Arizona authorizes Ventura to issue 50,000 shares of 6%, $100-par preferred stock and 100,000 shares of no-par common stock. To start, Ventura completed the following transactions:

Journalizing corporation transactions and preparing the stockholders' equity section of the balance sheet (Obj. 2, 3)

Dec. 2   Issued 9,000 shares of common stock to Duran and 12,000 shares to Nueces, both for cash of $5 per share.

      10   Issued 400 shares of preferred stock to acquire a patent with a market value of $50,000.

      27   Issued 12,000 shares of common stock to other investors for cash of $96,000.

Required

1. Record the transactions in the general journal.
2. Prepare the stockholders' equity section of the Ventura, Inc., balance sheet at December 31. The ending balance of Retained Earnings is $57,100.

P13-3A Hudson Corporation was organized in 20X1. At December 31, 20X1, Hudson's balance sheet reported the following stockholders' equity:

Issuing stock and preparing the stockholders' equity section of the balance sheet (Obj. 2, 3)

Preferred stock, 6%, $50 par, 100,000 shares authorized, none issued	$ —
Common stock, $1 par, 500,000 shares authorized, 60,000 shares issued	60,000
Paid-in capital in excess of par—common	40,000
Retained earnings	25,000
Total stockholders' equity	$125,000

Required

Answer the following questions, making journal entries as needed.

1. What does the 6% mean for the preferred stock? After Hudson issues preferred stock, how much in annual cash dividends will Hudson expect to pay on 1,000 shares?
2. At what price per share did Hudson issue the common stock during 20X1?

3. Were first-year operations profitable? Give your reason.
4. During 20X2, the company completed the following selected transactions. Journalize each transaction. Explanations are not required.
   a. Issued for cash 1,000 shares of preferred stock at par value.
   b. Issued for cash 2,000 shares of common stock at a price of $3 per share.
   c. Issued 50,000 shares of common stock to acquire a building valued at $150,000.
   d. Net income for the year was $82,000, and the company declared no dividends. Make the closing entry for net income.
5. Prepare the stockholders' equity section of the Hudson Corporation balance sheet at December 31, 20X2.

Stockholders' equity section of the balance sheet (Obj. 3)

P13-4A The following summaries for Yurman Jewelry, Inc., and Northern Lights Insurance Company provide the information needed to prepare the stockholders' equity section of each company's balance sheet. The two companies are independent.

- *Yurman Jewelry, Inc.* Yurman Jewelry is authorized to issue 40,000 shares of $1 par common stock. All the stock was issued at $12 per share. The company incurred net losses of $50,000 in 20X1 and $14,000 in 20X2. It earned net income of $23,000 in 20X3 and $71,000 in 20X4. The company declared no dividends during the four-year period.
- *Northern Lights Insurance Company.* Northern Lights Insurance Company's charter authorizes the company to issue 50,000 shares of 7%, $10 par preferred stock and 500,000 shares of no-par common stock. Northern Lights Insurance issued 1,000 shares of the preferred stock at $15 per share. It issued 100,000 shares of the common stock for $400,000. The company's retained earnings balance at the beginning of 20X4 was $120,000. Net income for 20X4 was $90,000, and the company declared the specified preferred dividend for 20X4. Preferred dividends for 20X3 were in arrears.

Required

For each company, prepare the stockholders' equity section of its balance sheet at December 31, 20X4. Show the computation of all amounts. Entries are not required.

Analyzing the stockholders' equity of an actual corporation (Obj. 3, 4)

P13-5A The Procter & Gamble Company reported the following stockholders' equity, as adapted, on its balance sheet at June 30, 19X9:

Stockholders' Equity	$ Millions
Preferred stock, 6.125%—	
Authorized 600,000,000 shares; issued 1,781,000 shares	$ 1,781
Common stock—$1 stated value—	
Authorized 5,000,000,000 shares; issued 1,320,000,000	1,320
Additional paid-in capital, common...	1,337
Retained earnings..	10,778
Other	(3,158)
Total..	$12,058

Required

1. Identify the different issues of stock Procter & Gamble has outstanding.
2. Make two summary journal entries to record issuance of all the Procter & Gamble stock. Assume all the stock was issued for cash. Explanations are not required.
3. Assume preferred dividends are in arrears for fiscal year 19X9. Journalize the declaration of a $1,626 million dividend at June 30, 20X0. Use separate Dividends Payable accounts for Preferred and Common. Round to the nearest $1 million. An explanation is not required.

Preparing a corporation balance sheet; measuring profitability (Obj. 3, 6)

P13-6A ←= *Link Back to Chapter 1 (Accounting Equation).* The following accounts and related balances of Omaha Mutual, Inc., are arranged in no particular order.

Common stock, $5 par,		Retained earnings........................	$	?
100,000 shares authorized,		Inventory......................................		181,000
22,000 shares issued..............	$110,000	Property, plant, and		
Dividends payable	3,000	equipment, net		278,000
Total assets,		Prepaid expenses		13,000
November 30, 20X1...............	581,000	Goodwill, net..............................		37,000
Net income	47,200	Accrued liabilities		17,000
Common stockholders' equity,		Long-term note payable		104,000
November 30, 20X1...............	383,000	Accounts receivable, net.............		102,000
Interest expense	12,800	Preferred stock, 4%, $10 par,		
Additional paid-in capital—		25,000 shares authorized,		
common..................................	140,000	3,700 shares issued		37,000
Accounts payable	31,000	Cash...		43,000

1. Prepare the company's classified balance sheet in the account format at November 30, 20X2. Use the accounting equation to compute Retained Earnings.
2. Compute rate of return on total assets and rate of return on common stockholders' equity for the year ended November 30, 20X2.
3. Do these rates of return suggest strength or weakness? Give your reason.

P13-7A Eastern Seaboard Airline Corporation has 5,000 shares of 5%, $10 par value preferred stock and 100,000 shares of $1.50 par common stock outstanding. During a three-year period, Eastern Seaboard declared and paid cash dividends as follows: 20X1, $1,500; 20X2, $15,000; and 20X3, $23,000.

Computing dividends on preferred and common stock (Obj. 4)

Required

1. Compute the total dividends to preferred stock and to common stock for each of the three years if
   a. Preferred is noncumulative
   b. Preferred is cumulative
2. For case (1b), record the declaration of the 20X3 dividends on December 22, 20X3, and the payment of the dividends on January 14, 20X4. Use separate Dividends Payable accounts for Preferred and Common.

P13-8A The balance sheet of Hardwood Furniture, Inc., reported the following:

Analyzing the stockholders' equity of an actual corporation (Obj. 4, 5)

Stockholders' Investment [same as Stockholders' Equity]	($ Thousands)
Cumulative preferred stock...............................	$ 45
Common stock, $1 par, authorized 40,000,000 shares; issued 16,000,000 shares...............................	16,000
Additional paid-in capital.................................	217,000
Retained earnings (Deficit)...............................	(77,165)
Total stockholders' investment..........................	$155,880

Notes to the financial statements indicate that 9,000 shares of $1.45 preferred stock with a stated value of $5 per share were issued and outstanding. The preferred stock has a liquidation value of $25 per share, and preferred dividends are in arrears for two years, including the current year. The additional paid-in capital belongs to common. On the balance sheet date, the market value of the Hardwood Furniture common stock was $9.50 per share.

Required

1. Is the preferred stock cumulative or noncumulative? How can you tell?
2. What is the amount of the annual preferred dividend?
3. What is the total paid-in capital of the company?
4. What was the total market value of the common stock?
5. Compute the book value per share of the preferred stock and the common stock.

P13-9A The accounting (not the income tax) records of Solarex Energy Corporation provide the income statement for 20X4.

Computing and recording a corporation's income tax (Obj. 7)

Total revenue.....................................	$930,000
Expenses:	
Cost of goods sold	$430,000
Operating expenses........................	270,000
Total expenses before tax..............	700,000
Income before income tax................	$230,000

The operating expenses include depreciation of $50,000 computed on the straight-line method. In calculating taxable income on the tax return, Solarex uses the modified accelerated cost recovery system (MACRS). MACRS depreciation was $80,000 for 20X4. The corporate income tax rate is 35%.

Required

1. Compute taxable income for the year.
2. Journalize the corporation's income tax for 20X4.
3. Prepare the corporation's single-step income statement for 20X4.

(Group B) PROBLEMS

Organizing a corporation
(Obj. 1)

P13-1B Ted Andrews and Ron Durham are opening a **Pier 1 Imports** store in a shopping center in Taos, New Mexico. The area is growing, and no competitors are located nearby. Their basic decision is how to organize the business. Andrews thinks the partnership form is best. Durham favors the corporate form of organization. They seek your advice.

Required

Write a memo to Andrews and Durham to make them aware of the advantages and the disadvantages of organizing the business as a corporate. Use the following format for your memo:

Date:	_____
To:	Ted Andrews and Ron Durham
From:	Student Name
Subject:	Advantages and disadvantages of the corporate form of business organization

---

Journalizing corporation transactions and preparing the stockholders' equity section of the balance sheet
(Obj. 2, 3)

P13-2B The partners who own Craven & Thames wished to avoid the unlimited personal liability of the partnership form of business, so they incorporated the partnership as C & T Services, Inc. The charter from the state of Louisiana authorizes the corporation to issue 10,000 shares of 6%, $100 par preferred stock and 250,000 shares of no-par common stock. In its first month, C & T Services completed the following transactions:

Jan. 3   Issued 6,300 shares of common stock to Craven and 3,800 shares to Thames, both for cash of $10 per share.
12   Issued 1,000 shares of preferred stock to acquire a patent with a market value of $110,000.
22   Issued 1,500 shares of common stock to other investors for $15 cash per share.

Required

1. Record the transactions in the general journal.
2. Prepare the stockholders' equity section of the C & T Services, Inc., balance sheet at January 31. The ending balance of Retained Earnings is $40,300.

Issuing stock and preparing the stockholders' equity section of the balance sheet
(Obj. 2, 3)

P13-3B Zaponata Corporation was organized in 20X1. At December 31, 20X1, Zaponata's balance sheet reported the following stockholders' equity:

Preferred stock, 5%, $10 par, 50,000 shares authorized, none issued	$ —
Common stock, $2 par, 100,000 shares authorized, 10,000 shares issued	20,000
Paid-in capital in excess of par—common..............................	30,000
Retained earnings (Deficit)...	(5,000)
Total stockholders' equity...	$45,000

Required

Answer the following questions, making journal entries as needed.

1. What does the 5% mean for the preferred stock? After Zaponata issues preferred stock, how much in annual cash dividends will Zaponata expect to pay on 1,000 shares?
2. At what price per share did Zaponata issue the common stock during 20X1?
3. Were first-year operations profitable? Give your reason.
4. During 20X2, the company completed the following selected transactions. Journalize each transaction. Explanations are not required.
   a. Issued for cash 5,000 shares of preferred stock at par value.
   b. Issued for cash 1,000 shares of common stock at a price of $7 per share.
   c. Issued 20,000 shares of common stock to acquire a building valued at $120,000.
   d. Net income for the year was $50,000, and the company declared no dividends. Make the closing entry for net income.
5. Prepare the stockholders' equity section of the Zaponata Corporation balance sheet at December 31, 20X2.

P13-4B Stockholders' equity information for two independent companies, Granada Enterprises, Inc., and Traigon Corp. is as follows:

Stockholders' equity section of the balance sheet (Obj. 3)

- *Granada Enterprises, Inc.* Granada is authorized to issue 60,000 shares of $5 par common stock. All the stock was issued at $12 per share. The company incurred a net loss of $41,000 in 20X1. It earned net income of $60,000 in 20X2 and $90,000 in 20X3. The company declared no dividends during the three-year period.
- *Traigon Corp.* Traigon's charter authorizes the company to issue 10,000 shares of $2.50 preferred stock with par value of $50 and 120,000 shares of no-par common stock. Traigon issued 1,000 shares of the preferred stock at $54 per share. It issued 40,000 shares of the common stock for a total of $220,000. The company's Retained Earnings balance at the beginning of 20X3 was $64,000, and net income for the year was $90,000. During 20X3, the company declared the specified dividend on preferred and a $0.50 per share dividend on common. Preferred dividends for 20X2 were in arrears.

Required

For each company, prepare the stockholders' equity section of its balance sheet at December 31, 20X3. Show the computation of all amounts. Entries are not required.

P13-5B **Tandy Corporation,** which operates Radio Shack stores, included the following stockholders' equity on its year-end balance sheet at December 31, 19X8, with all dollar amounts, except par value per share, in millions:

Analyzing the stockholders' equity of an actual corporation (Obj. 3, 4)

Stockholders' Equity	($ Millions)
Preferred stock, 6% cumulative	$ 100
Common stock—par value $1 per share; 250,000,000	
shares authorized, 139,000,000 shares issued	139
Paid-in capital in excess of par—common...........................	110
Retained earnings...	1,693
	$2,042

Required

1. Identify the different issues of stock Tandy has outstanding.
2. Give two summary entries to record issuance of all the Tandy stock. Assume that all the stock was issued for cash. Explanations are not required.
3. Assume that preferred dividends are in arrears for 19X7 and 19X8. Record the declaration of a $50 million cash dividend on December 30, 19X9. Use separate Dividends Payable accounts for Preferred and Common. An explanation is not required.

P13-6B ←⊂ *Link Back to Chapter 1 (Accounting Equation).* The following accounts and related balances of Witt, Inc., are arranged in no particular order:

Preparing a corporation balance sheet; measuring profitability (Obj. 3, 6)

Interest expense	$ 6,100	Accounts receivable, net	$ 46,000
Property, plant, and		Paid-in capital in excess of	
equipment, net	261,000	par—common	19,000
Common stock, $1 par,		Accrued liabilities	26,000
500,000 shares authorized,		Long-term note payable.............	42,000
236,000 shares issued	236,000	Inventory....................................	81,000
Dividends payable	9,000	Prepaid expenses	10,000
Retained earnings......................	?	Common stockholders'	
Accounts payable.......................	31,000	equity, June 30, 20X1............	222,000
Trademark, net	9,000	Net income	51,000
Preferred stock, $0.10, no-par,		Total assets, June 30, 20X1........	404,000
10,000 shares authorized and		Cash..	10,000
issued	25,000		

Required

1. Prepare the company's classified balance sheet in the account format at June 30, 20X2. Use the accounting equation to compute Retained Earnings.
2. Compute rate of return on total assets and rate of return on common stockholders' equity for the year ended June 30, 20X2.
3. Do these rates of return suggest strength or weakness? Give your reason.

Computing dividends on preferred and common stock (Obj. 4)

P13-7B OnPoint Consulting, Inc., has 10,000 shares of $4.50, no-par preferred stock and 50,000 shares of no-par common stock outstanding. OnPoint declared and paid the following dividends during a three-year period: 20X1, $20,000; 20X2, $100,000; and 20X3, $215,000.

Required

1. Compute the total dividends to preferred stock and to common stock for each of the three years if
   a. Preferred is noncumulative   **b.** Preferred is cumulative
2. For case (1b), record the declaration of the 20X3 dividends on December 28, 20X3, and the payment of the dividends on January 17, 20X4. Use separate Dividends Payable accounts for Preferred and Common.

Analyzing the stockholders' equity of an actual corporation (Obj. 4, 5)

P13-8B The balance sheet of The Gonzalez Group reported the following:

Stockholders' Investment **[same as stockholders' equity]**	
Nonvoting preferred stock, no-par (liquidation value, $358,000)	$320,000
Common stock, $1.50 par value, authorized 75,000 shares; issued 36,000 shares	54,000
[Additional] paid-in capital	231,000
Retained earnings	141,000
Total stockholders' investment	$746,000

Notes to the financial statements indicate that 8,000 shares of $3.40 preferred stock with a stated value of $40 per share were issued and outstanding. Preferred dividends are in arrears for three years, including the current year. The additional paid-in capital belongs to common. On the balance sheet date, the market value of the Gonzalez common stock was $10 per share.

Required

1. Is the preferred stock cumulative or noncumulative? How can you tell?
2. What is the amount of the annual preferred dividend?
3. Which class of stockholders controls the company? Give your reason.
4. What is the total paid-in capital of the company?
5. What was the total market value of the common stock?
6. Compute the book value per share of the preferred stock and the common stock.

Computing and recording a corporation's income tax (Obj. 7)

P13-9B The accounting (not the income tax) records of Fox Security Systems, Inc., provide the income statement for 20X3.

Total revenue	$680,000
Expenses:	
Cost of goods sold	$290,000
Operating expenses	180,000
Total expenses before tax	470,000
Income before income tax	$210,000

The operating expenses include depreciation of $40,000 computed under the straight-line method. In calculating taxable income on the tax return, Fox uses the modified accelerated cost recovery system (MACRS). MACRS depreciation was $50,000 for 20X3. The corporate income tax rate is 40%.

Required

1. Compute taxable income for the year.
2. Journalize the corporation's income tax for 20X3.
3. Prepare the corporation's single-step income statement for 20X3.

DECISION CASES

Case 1. Terry Caine and Nicole Jacks have written a spreadsheet program that they believe will rival Excel and Lotus. They need additional capital to market the product, and they plan to incorporate the business. They are considering alternative capital structures for the corporation. Their primary goal is to raise as much capital as possible without giving up control of the business. The partners plan to invest the software program and receive 110,000 shares of the corporation's common stock. The partners have been offered $110,000 for the rights to the software program.

Evaluating alternative ways to raise capital
(Obj. 2, 3)

The corporation's plans for a charter include an authorization to issue 5,000 shares of preferred stock and 500,000 shares of $1 par common stock. Caine and Jacks are uncertain about the most desirable features for the preferred stock. Prior to incorporating, the partners are discussing their plans with two investment groups. The corporation can obtain capital from outside investors under either of the following plans:

- *Plan 1.* Group 1 will invest $105,000 to acquire 1,000 shares of $5, no-par preferred stock and $70,000 to acquire 70,000 shares of common stock. Each preferred share receives 50 votes on matters that come before the stockholders.
- *Plan 2.* Group 2 will invest $160,000 to acquire 1,400 shares of 6%, $100 par nonvoting, noncumulative preferred stock.

Required

Assume that the corporation is chartered.

1. Journalize the issuance of common stock to Caine and Jacks. Explanations are not required.
2. Journalize the issuance of stock to the outsiders under both plans. Explanations are not required.
3. Assume that net income for the first year is $180,000 and total dividends are $30,000. Prepare the stockholders' equity section of the corporation's balance sheet under both plans.
4. Recommend one of the plans to Caine and Jacks. Give your reasons.

Case 2. Answering the following questions will enhance your understanding of the capital stock of corporations. Consider each question independently of the others.

Characteristics of corporations' capital stock
(Obj. 2, 5)

1. Why are capital stock and retained earnings shown separately in the shareholders' equity section?
2. Chiu Wang, major shareholder of C-W, Inc., proposes to sell some land she owns to the company for common shares in C-W. What problem does C-W, Inc., face in recording the transaction?
3. Preferred shares have advantages with respect to dividends and corporate liquidation. Why would investors buy common stock when preferred stock is available?
4. What does it mean if the liquidation value of a company's preferred stock is greater than its market value?
5. If you owned 100 shares of stock in **Dell Computer Corporation** and someone offered to buy the stock for its book value, would you accept the offer? Why or why not?

ETHICAL ISSUE

Note: This case is based on an actual situation.

Jeremy Copeland paid $50,000 for a franchise that entitled him to market Success Associates software programs in the countries of the European Common Market. Copeland intended to sell individual franchises for the major language groups of western Europe—German, French, English, Spanish, and Italian. Naturally, investors considering buying a franchise from Copeland asked to see the financial statements of his business.

Believing the value of the franchise to be greater than $50,000, Copeland sought to capitalize his own franchise at $500,000. The law firm of St. Charles & LaDue helped Copeland form a corporation chartered to issue 500,000 shares of common stock with par value of $1 per share. Attorneys suggested the following chain of transactions:

a. A third party borrows $500,000 and purchases the franchise from Copeland.
b. Copeland pays the corporation $500,000 to acquire all its stock.
c. The corporation buys the franchise from the third party, who repays the loan.

In the final analysis, the third party is debt-free and out of the picture. Copeland owns all the corporation's stock, and the corporation owns the franchise. The corporation's balance sheet lists a franchise acquired at a cost of $500,000. This balance sheet is Copeland's most valuable marketing tool.

Required

1. What is unethical about this situation?
2. Who can be harmed? How can they be harmed? What role does accounting play?

FINANCIAL STATEMENT CASE

Analyzing stockholders' equity
(Obj. 2, 3)

The **Target Corporation** financial statements appear in Appendix A. Answer the following questions about Target's stock.

Required

1. How much of Target's preferred stock was outstanding at January 29, 2000? How can you tell? The statement of shareholders' investment (stockholders' equity) reports what happened to Target's preferred stock during the fiscal year ended January 29, 2000. What was it?
2. Examine Target's balance sheet. Which stockholders' equity account increased the most during the year ended January 29, 2000 (fiscal year 2000)? Did this increase occur because of new paid-in capital that Target received from stockholders during this year? If not, explain where the additional paid-in capital came from.
3. Give Target's journal entries during fiscal year 2000 to record (a) closing net income to Retained Earnings and (b) declaring cash dividends. The statement of shareholders' investment gives the details for these transactions.

TEAM PROJECT

Competitive pressures are the norm in business. **Lexus** automobiles (made in Japan) have cut into the sales of **Mercedes Benz** (a German company), **Jaguar Motors** (a British company), **General Motors'** Cadillac Division, and **Ford's** Lincoln Division (both U.S. companies). **Dell, Gateway,** and **Compaq** computers have siphoned business away from **IBM.** Foreign steelmakers have reduced the once-massive U.S. steel industry to a fraction of its former size.

Indeed, corporate downsizing has occurred on a massive scale. During the past few years, each company or industry mentioned here has pared down plant and equipment, laid off employees, or restructured operations.

Required

1. Identify all the stakeholders of a corporation and the stake each group has in the company. A *stakeholder* is a person or a group who has an interest (that is, a stake) in the success of the organization.
2. Identify several measures by which a corporation may be considered deficient and which may indicate the need for downsizing. How can downsizing help to solve this problem? Discuss how each measure can indicate the need for downsizing.
3. Debate the downsizing issue. One group of students takes the perspective of the company and its stockholders, and another group of students takes the perspective of other stakeholders of the company.

INTERNET EXERCISE

Yahoo! Inc.

Go to the "Dividends and Treasury Stock" episode on the *Mastering Accounting* CD-ROM for an interactive, video-enhanced exercise on how CanGo can boost investor confidence after poor quarterly performance reports. The episode focuses on the difference between cash and stock dividends.

1. Go to **http://finance.yahoo.com** and type in the stock symbol YHOO. Using the pull-down menu, select *Basic,* and then click on *Get Quotes.* In the chart under "Last Trade," identify how much investors were willing to pay for a share of stock on the last trade.
2. In the chart under "More Info" click on *Profile.*
   a. Review the "Business Summary." How many users does **Yahoo!** serve each month?
   b. Scroll down to review "Statistics at a Glance." What is Yahoo!'s book value per share? Compare the book value to the market value of the last trade. Which is greater?
   c. What is Yahoo!'s return on assets and return on equity? Explain what both of these ratios indicate for Yahoo! Which ratio is greater? What does this indicate?
   d. How much is Yahoo's annual dividend?
3. Go to **http://www.forbes.com** and under "Stocks" type YHOO, and then click on *Go.* In the left-hand column click on "Financials" to find the answers to the following questions.

a. As of the most recent balance sheet date, how much have shareholders paid in total for Yahoo! stock? During the most recent year, how much capital did Yahoo! raise through the issuance of stock? Yahoo! does not pay dividends. Why would shareholders be interested in purchasing stock in this company?

b. As of the most recent balance sheet date, what is Yahoo!'s reported retained earnings balance? Is this balance positive or negative? How does a company get a retained earnings deficit? Does Yahoo! have enough retained earnings to declare dividends?

c. What is the primary source of financing for Yahoo!'s assets?

14 Retained Earnings, Treasury Stock, and the Income Statement

LEARNING OBJECTIVES

After studying this chapter, you should be able to

1. Account for stock dividends

2. Distinguish stock splits from stock dividends

3. Account for treasury stock

4. Report restrictions on retained earnings

5. Identify the elements of a complex income statement

6. Prepare a statement of stockholders' equity

www.prenhall.com/horngren
Readiness Assessment

America Online (AOL), the world leader in Internet technology, and **Time Warner,** the world's largest media and entertainment company, have merged. AOL's e-commerce capability, plus Time Warner's empire—CNN and HBO, *Time* and *Sports Illustrated*, and Warner Bros., has created a powerhouse.

Wall Street is sorting out the effects on investors. Which company will dominate the new organization? Will it be AOL, or will Time Warner take the lead? How do the companies' finances figure into the plan? These questions arise as investors decide whether to buy or sell AOL and Time Warner stock. It is critical for companies to report accurate accounting information so that investors have a fair chance to make an informed decision.

AOL turned a profit for the first time in 1999 after years of losses. Time Warner's profits have been up and down. Top executives of the two companies obviously think the combined company—AOL Time Warner—can earn a healthy net income for years to come. Boot up and stay tuned to see if the profits do in fact roll in.

Exhibit 14-1 (page 542) shows an adapted version of the income statement that **AOL Time Warner Inc.** sent out to show how the *combined* company would have performed in 1999. "Pro Forma" (as if) in the title means that the income statement depicts results *as if* the two companies had merged in 1999. Overall, the result would have been a loss of $2.5 billion. Included in the net loss is a gain on the sale of cable systems.

Special gains and losses such as this often appear on a corporation's income statement. Discontinued operations and extraordinary gains and losses can also make the income statement quite complex. This chapter explains the full range of items that can appear on an income statement in the real world of accounting and finance.

The chapter also covers several stockholders' equity topics to round out your understanding of a corporation's balance sheet. Let's begin with Retained Earnings, the element of stockholders' equity that results from profitable operations. Over time, AOL Time Warner must build up a large balance of Retained Earnings. If not, the company will not survive.

RETAINED EARNINGS, STOCK DIVIDENDS, AND STOCK SPLITS

We have seen that the equity section on a corporate balance sheet is called *stockholders' equity* or *shareholders' equity*. The paid-in capital accounts and retained earnings make up the stockholders' equity section.

Retained Earnings

Retained Earnings carries the balance of the business's net income less all net losses and less any dividends accumulated over the corporation's lifetime. *Retained* means "held onto." Retained Earnings is the shareholders' stake in total assets that come from profits. A debit balance in Retained Earnings is called a *deficit*. In a recent survey, 68 of 600 companies (11%) had a retained earnings deficit (see Exhibit 14-2 on page 542).

 **WORK IT OUT**

Assume that the beginning balance of Retained Earnings was $720,000. The net loss for the year was $810,000. What will the Retained Earnings balance be after this net income?

Answer

RETAINED EARNINGS			
Dec. 31, 20X1 Net loss	810,000	Jan. 1, 20X1 Bal.	720,000
Dec. 31, 20X1 Bal. (Deficit)	90,000		

EXHIBIT 14-1
**AOL Time Warner
Income Statement
(Pro Forma, adapted)**

AOL TIME WARNER, INC.	
Pro Forma Income Statement, adapted	
(as if the two companies were already merged)	
Year Ended December 31, 1999	
	Millions
Revenues	$33,051
Gain on sale of cable systems and other gains	2,355
Cost of revenues	17,998
Selling, general, and administrative expenses	9,085
Amortization expense of goodwill and other intangibles	8,393
Interest expense and other expenses	1,825
Income (loss) before income tax	(1,895)
Income tax expense	(627)
Net income (net loss)	$ (2,522)

Source: AOL Time Warner Merger, *Joint Proxy Statement-Prospectus.*

EXHIBIT 14-2
**Retained Earnings of the
*Accounting Trends &
Techniques* 600 Companies**

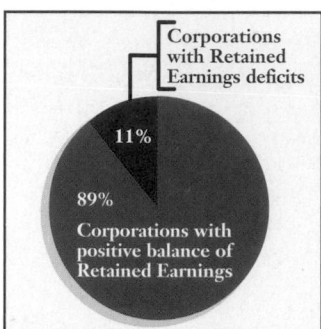

When you see a balance sheet, remember these facts about Retained Earnings:

1. *Credits to the Retained Earnings account arise only from net income.* To learn how much net income a corporation has earned and retained in the business, see Retained Earnings. Its balance is the cumulative, life-time earnings of the company minus all net losses and all dividends.
2. *The Retained Earnings account is not a reservoir of cash waiting for the board of directors to pay out in dividends.* Instead, Retained Earnings is simply one of several owners' equity accounts. Retained Earnings represents no asset in particular. In fact, the corporation may have a large balance in Retained Earnings but not have enough cash to pay a dividend. To *declare* a dividend, the company must have an adequate balance in Retained Earnings. To *pay* the dividend, it must have the cash.

Cash and Retained Earnings are two separate accounts with no particular relationship. Retained Earnings is *not* a bank account. A $5,000 balance in Retained Earnings means that $5,000 of capital has been created by profits that the corporation has reinvested in the business.

Stock Dividends

Objective 1
Account for stock dividends

STOCK DIVIDEND. A distribution by a corporation of its own stock to its stockholders.

A **stock dividend** is a distribution by a corporation of its own stock to its stockholders. Stock dividends are fundamentally different from cash dividends because stock dividends do not give any assets to the stockholders. Stock dividends

- Affect *only* stockholders' equity accounts (Retained Earnings and Common Stock).
- Have *no* effect on total stockholders' equity.

A stock dividend decreases Retained Earnings and increases Common Stock. Both accounts are elements of stockholders' equity, so total equity is unchanged. There is merely a transfer from Retained Earnings to Common Stock. No asset or liability is affected by a stock dividend.

The corporation distributes stock dividends to stockholders in proportion to the number of shares they already own. Suppose you own 300 shares of **AOL Time Warner** common stock. If AOL distributes a 10% common stock dividend, you would receive 30 (300 × 0.10) additional shares. You would now own 330 shares of the stock. All other AOL stockholders would receive additional shares equal to 10% of their prior holdings. Both you and all other AOL stockholders would be in the same relative position after the dividend as before.

REASONS FOR STOCK DIVIDENDS   Why do companies issue stock dividends? There are several reasons:

1. *To continue dividends but conserve cash.* A company may want to keep cash in the business in order to expand, pay off debts, and so on. Yet the company may wish to continue dividends in some form. Stockholders pay tax on cash dividends but not on stock dividends.

2. *To reduce the market price of its stock.* Distribution of a stock dividend may cause the market price of the company's stock to fall because of the increased supply of the stock. Suppose the market price of a share of AOL stock is $60. Doubling the number of shares of stock outstanding by issuing a stock dividend would drop the stock's market price by approximately half, to $30 per share. The objective is to make the stock less expensive and thus more attractive to a wider range of investors.

RECORDING STOCK DIVIDENDS   The board of directors announces stock dividends on the declaration date. The date of record and the distribution date then follow. (This is the same sequence of dates used for a cash dividend.) The declaration of a stock dividend does *not* create a liability because the corporation is not obligated to pay assets. (Recall that a liability is a claim on *assets*.) Instead, the corporation has declared its intention to distribute its stock. Assume that Georgia Lumber Corporation has the following stockholders' equity prior to a stock dividend:

Georgia Lumber Corporation Stockholders' Equity	
Paid-in capital:	
Common stock, $10 par, 50,000 shares authorized,	
20,000 shares issued...	$200,000
Paid-in capital in excess of par—common...............................	70,000
Total paid-in capital..	270,000
Retained earnings	85,000
Total stockholders' equity	$355,000

The entry to record a stock dividend depends on its size. Generally accepted accounting principles distinguish between

- a *large* stock dividend (25% or more of issued stock), and
- a *small* stock dividend (less than 20–25% of issued stock).

Stock dividends between 20% and 25% are rare.

Large Stock Dividends—25% or More. A *large* stock dividend significantly increases the number of shares available in the market and usually lowers the stock price. A common practice is to transfer the par value of the dividend shares from Retained Earnings to Common Stock, as shown in Exhibit 14-3 on page 544.

Small Stock Dividends—Less Than 20–25%. A *small* stock dividend is less likely to affect the price of the company's stock significantly. For this reason, generally accepted accounting principles (GAAP) requires small stock dividends to be accounted for at their market value. Retained Earnings is decreased for the market value of the dividend shares, Common Stock is credited for the stock's par value, and Paid-in Capital in Excess of Par is credited for the remainder.

Assume Georgia Lumber Corporation distributes a stock dividend when the market value of the company's common stock is $16 per share. Exhibit 14-3 illustrates the accounting if the dividend is large (a 50% dividend) or small (a 10% dividend).[1]

---

[1] A stock dividend can be recorded with two journal entries for (1) the declaration and (2) the stock distribution. Most companies record stock dividends with a single entry on the date of distribution, as we illustrate here.

Exhibit 14-3 **Accounting for Stock Dividends—Georgia Lumber Corporation**

Large Stock Dividend—for example, 50% (Accounted for at *par* value)		Small Stock Dividend—for example, 10% (Accounted for at *market* value)	
Retained Earnings	100,000	Retained Earnings (20,000 ×	
Common Stock		0.10 × $16 market value)	32,000
(20,000 shares × 0.50 ×		Common Stock	
$10 par)	100,000	(20,000 × 0.10 × $10 par)	20,000
		Paid-in Capital in Excess of Par ..	12,000

Neither a large nor a small stock dividend affects assets, liabilities, or total stockholders' equity. A stock dividend merely rearranges the stockholders' equity accounts, leaving total equity unchanged.

DAILY EXERCISE 14-1

DAILY EXERCISE 14-2

DAILY EXERCISE 14-3

THINK IT OVER

Suppose Georgia Lumber Corporation issues 1,000 shares of its $15 par common as a stock dividend when the stock's market price is $25 per share. Assume that the 1,000 shares issued are (1) 10% of the outstanding shares and (2) 100% of the outstanding shares. Which stock dividend decreases total stockholders' equity?

Answer: Neither a large stock dividend nor a small stock dividend affects total stockholders' equity.

Stock Splits

STOCK SPLIT. An increase in the number of outstanding shares of stock coupled with a proportionate reduction in the par value of the stock.

A **stock split** is an increase in the number of authorized, issued, and outstanding shares of stock, coupled with a proportionate reduction in the stock's par value. For example, if the company splits its stock 2 for 1, the number of outstanding shares is doubled and each share's par value is cut in half. A stock split, like a large stock dividend, decreases the market price of the stock—with the intention of making the stock more affordable for investors. Most leading companies in the United States— **General Electric, IBM,** and many others—have split their stock.

The market price of a share of IBM common stock has been approximately $100. Assume that the company wishes to decrease the market price to approximately $25. That is, IBM decides to split the common stock 2 for 1 to reduce the stock's market price from $100 to $50. A 2-for-1 stock split means that the company would have twice as many shares of stock outstanding after the split as it had before and that each share's par value would be cut in half. Assume that IBM had 1,875 million shares of $0.20 (20 cents) par common stock before the split:

IBM Stockholders' Equity (Adapted) Before 2-for-1 Stock Split	(In Millions)	After 2-for-1 Stock Split	(In Millions)
Common stock, $0.20 par,		Common stock, $0.10 par,	
5,000 million shares authorized,		10,000 million shares authorized,	
1,875 million shares issued	$ 375	3,750 million shares issued	$ 375
Capital in excess of par	11,387	Capital in excess of par...........................	11,387
Retained earnings	16,878	Retained earnings	16,878
Other..	(8,376)	Other..	(8,376)
Total stockholders' equity	$20,264	Total stockholders' equity	$20,264

After the 2-for-1 stock split, IBM would have 10,000 million shares authorized and 3,750 million shares (1,875 million shares × 2) of $0.10 (10 cents) par ($0.20/2) common stock outstanding. Total stockholders' equity would be exactly as before. Indeed, the balance in the Common Stock account does not even change. Only the par value of the stock and the number of shares change. Compare the figures in color in the preceding stockholders' equity presentations for IBM.

Because the stock split affects no account balances, no formal journal entry is necessary. Instead, the split is recorded in a *memorandum entry* such as the following:

Aug. 19	Split the common stock 2 for 1. Called in the $0.20 par common stock and distributed two shares of $0.10 par common stock for each old share previously outstanding.

A company may engage in a reverse split to decrease the number of shares of stock outstanding. For example, IBM could split its stock 1 for 2. After the split, par value would be $0.40 (40 cents, that is, $0.20 × 2); shares authorized would be 2,500 million (5,000 million/2); and shares issued and outstanding would be 937.5 million (1,875 million/2). Reverse splits are unusual.

● DAILY EXERCISE 14-4

● DAILY EXERCISE 14-5

Similarities and Differences Between Stock Dividends and Stock Splits

Objective 2
Distinguish stock splits from stock dividends

Both stock dividends and stock splits increase the number of shares of stock owned by each stockholder. Neither stock dividends nor stock splits change investors' cost of the stock they own.

SIMILARITIES   Consider **Avon Products, Inc.,** whose beauty products are sold in countries around the world. Assume you paid $3,000 to acquire 150 shares of Avon common stock.

- If Avon distributes a 100% stock dividend, your 150 shares increase to 300, but your total cost is still $3,000.
- If Avon distributes a 2-for-1 stock split, your shares increase to 300, but your total cost is unchanged.
- Neither a stock dividend nor a stock split creates taxable income for the investor.

DIFFERENCES   Stock dividends and stock splits differ in that

- A stock *dividend* shifts an amount from retained earnings to the stock account, leaving the par value per share unchanged.
- A stock *split* affects no account balances. A stock split changes the par value of the stock. It also increases the number of shares of stock authorized, issued, and outstanding.

● DAILY EXERCISE 14-6

Exhibit 14-4 summarizes the effects of dividends and stock splits on total stockholders' equity.

EXHIBIT 14-4
Effects of Dividends and Stock Splits on Total Stockholders' Equity

Event	Effect on Total Stockholders' Equity
Declaration of *cash* dividend	Decrease
Payment of *cash* dividend	No effect
Distribution of *stock* dividend	No effect
Stock split	No effect

Source: Adapted from material provided by Beverly Terry.

TREASURY STOCK

Objective 3
Account for treasury stock

A company's own stock that it has issued and later reacquired is called **treasury stock.**[2] In effect, the corporation holds the stock in its treasury. Corporations may purchase their own stock for several reasons:

TREASURY STOCK. A corporation's own stock that it has issued and later reacquired.

1. The company has issued all its authorized stock and needs the stock for distributions to employees under stock purchase plans.

---

[2]In this text, we illustrate the *cost* method of accounting for treasury stock because it is used most widely. Other methods are presented in intermediate accounting courses.

2. The purchase helps support the stock's market price by decreasing the supply of stock available.
3. The business is trying to increase net assets by buying its shares low and hoping to sell them for a higher price later.
4. Management wants to avoid a takeover by an outside party.

When **AOL Time Warner, General Motors,** or **Eastman Kodak** buys its own stock as treasury stock, the company gives up cash and becomes a smaller entity as a result. Now let's see how companies actually account for their treasury stock.

Purchase of Treasury Stock

We record the purchase of treasury stock by debiting Treasury Stock and crediting the asset given in exchange—usually Cash. Suppose that Jupiter Drilling Company had the following stockholders' equity before purchasing treasury stock:

JUPITER DRILLING COMPANY	
Stockholders' Equity [*Before* Purchase of Treasury Stock]	
Common stock, $1 par, 10,000 shares authorized, 8,000 shares issued	$ 8,000
Paid-in capital in excess of par—common	12,000
Retained earnings	14,600
Total stockholders' equity	$34,600

On November 22, Jupiter purchases 1,000 shares of its $1 par common as treasury stock, paying cash of $7.50 per share. Jupiter records the purchase of treasury stock as follows:

<table>
<tr><td>Nov. 22</td><td>Treasury Stock—Common (1,000 × $7.50)</td><td>7,500</td><td></td></tr>
<tr><td></td><td>Cash</td><td></td><td>7,500</td></tr>
<tr><td></td><td>Purchased 1,000 shares of treasury stock at $7.50 per share.</td><td></td><td></td></tr>
</table>

TREASURY STOCK—COMMON

7,500 |

The Treasury Stock account has a debit balance, which is the opposite of the other owners' equity accounts. Therefore, *Treasury Stock is a contra stockholders' equity account*. Treasury stock is recorded at cost, without reference to par value. The Treasury Stock account is often reported beneath Retained Earnings on the balance sheet. Treasury Stock's balance is subtracted from the sum of total paid-in capital and retained earnings, as follows:

◉ DAILY EXERCISE 14-7

JUPITER DRILLING COMPANY	
Stockholders' Equity [*After* Purchase of Treasury Stock]	
Common stock, $1 par, 10,000 shares authorized, 8,000 shares issued, 7,000 shares outstanding	$ 8,000
Paid-in capital in excess of par—common	12,000
Retained earnings	14,600
Subtotal	34,600
Less: Treasury stock, 1,000 shares at cost	(7,500)
Total stockholders' equity	$27,100

Total stockholders' equity decreases by the cost of the treasury stock. Also, shares of stock *outstanding* decrease. The number of *outstanding* shares is computed as follows:

Number of shares of stock *issued*	8,000
Less: Number of shares of treasury stock held	(1,000)
Number of shares of stock *outstanding*	7,000

Although the number of *outstanding shares* is not required to be reported on the balance sheet, this figure is important. Only outstanding shares have voting rights, receive cash dividends, and share in assets if the corporation liquidates.

 **THINK IT OVER** *Ethical Issue:* Treasury stock transactions have a serious ethical and legal dimension. A company such as **PENTAX** buying its own shares as treasury stock must be careful that its disclosures of information are complete and accurate. What would happen if PENTAX purchases treasury stock at $17 per share and one day later announces a technological breakthrough that will generate millions of dollars in new business?

Answer: PENTAX's stock price would likely rise in response to the new information. If it could be proved that PENTAX management withheld the information, a shareholder selling stock back to PENTAX could file a lawsuit against PENTAX. The stockholder would claim that with knowledge of the technological advance, he or she would have been able to sell the PENTAX stock at a higher price.

Sale of Treasury Stock

A company may sell its treasury stock at any price agreeable to the corporation and the purchaser: at cost, above cost, or below cost.

SALE AT COST   If the stock is sold for the same price the corporation paid to reacquire it, the entry is a debit to Cash and a credit to Treasury Stock for the same amount.

SALE ABOVE COST   If the sale price of treasury stock is greater than its reacquisition cost, the difference is credited to the account Paid-in Capital from Treasury Stock Transactions because the excess came from the company's stockholders. Suppose Jupiter Drilling Company resold 200 of its treasury shares for $9 per share (cost was $7.50 per share). The entry is

Dec. 7	Cash (200 × $9)..	1,800	
	Treasury Stock—Common (200 × $7.50 cost)....................		1,500
	Paid-in Capital from Treasury Stock Transactions................		300
	Sold treasury stock at $9 per share.		

TREASURY STOCK—COMMON	
7,500	1,500
6,000	

Paid-in Capital from Treasury Stock Transactions is reported with the other paid-in capital accounts on the balance sheet, beneath the Common Stock and Paid-in Capital in Excess of Par accounts as shown here:

JUPITER DRILLING COMPANY
Stockholders' Equity [*After* Purchase and Sale of Treasury Stock]

Paid-in capital:	
Common stock, $1 par, 10,000 shares authorized,	
8,000 shares issued, 7,200 shares outstanding	$ 8,000
Paid-in capital in excess of par—common...	12,000
Paid-in capital from treasury stock transactions................................	300
Retained earnings	14,600
Subtotal...	34,900
Less treasury stock, 800 shares at cost (of $7.50 per share)...............	(6,000)
Total stockholders' equity	$28,900

● DAILY EXERCISE 14-8

● DAILY EXERCISE 14-9

Compare Jupiter Drilling's total equity after the sale of the treasury stock ($28,900) to equity before the sale ($27,100). Notice that total equity increased by the full amount received from the sale of treasury stock ($1,800). Jupiter Drilling is now a larger company because of the increase in assets and stockholders' equity.

Paid-in Capital from Treasury Stock Transactions can be combined as part of Additional Paid-in Capital, as shown in the Real-World Format (Exhibit 14-6, page 551).

SALE BELOW COST   At times, the resale price of treasury stock is less than cost. The difference between these two amounts is debited to Paid-in Capital from Treasury Stock Transactions if this account has a credit balance, as in our example. If this account's balance is too small, then the company debits Retained Earnings for the remaining amount.

Treasury Stock Transactions: A Summary

Neither the purchase nor the sale of treasury stock creates a gain or a loss for the income statement, and thus treasury stock transactions have no effect on net income. Exhibit 14-5 on page 549 illustrates a sequence of assumed treasury stock transactions for Eastman Kodak Company.

e–Accounting

"Aktienrueckkauf," "Rachat des actions," "Recompra de acciones": Stock Buybacks Catch On in Europe

Stock repurchase plans—called stock buybacks—are common in the United States, but are new to Europe. Until a few years ago, European companies were either prohibited from buying back their own stock or slapped with harsh tax penalties. These companies normally invest their spare cash conservatively or plow it into the acquisition of other companies. The Europeans may turn out to be smarter than their American counterparts, who have rushed to buy back company stock. In Europe, 1999 saw only an estimated $50 billion in buybacks, whereas American companies bought back that much in the first two months of 2000.

Do buybacks really prop up the price of a stock? In one view, a buyback sends a message that a company's top managers think its stock is undervalued. After all, who knows the most about the company's backlog of sales and future prospects? But the stock prices of **Anheuser Busch, Carnival Corp.,** and Germany's **Siemens**—all of which announced big buybacks in 2000—barely budged. Analysts say that a buyback announcement may now stigmatize a company as too "old economy." It may show that a company doesn't have any new tricks up its sleeve, no interesting new investment projects on the horizon.

Source: Based on Robert O'Brien, "Deals & deal makers: Stock buybacks gain popularity, but price pops aren't guaranteed," *Wall Street Journal,* March 6, 2000, C17. David Nicklaus, "Stock buybacks have lost their magic for the area's 'Old Economy' companies." *St. Louis Post-Dispatch,* March 18, 2000, p. Biz. 1. Joan Warner, "Buyback fever hits europe," *Business Week,* May 11, 1998, p. 46. Suzanne McGee, "Buybacks catch on in Europe with mixed results," *Wall Street Journal,* January 25, 1999, p. C14. Caspar Busse and Angela Cullen, "Germany's Siemens posts surge in profit; stock buyback, U.S. spinoff are planned," *Wall Street Journal,* April 28, 2000, p. A17.

REPORTING ISSUES

Companies may retire their stock, restrict retained earnings, and vary the way they report stockholders' equity. This section covers these reporting issues.

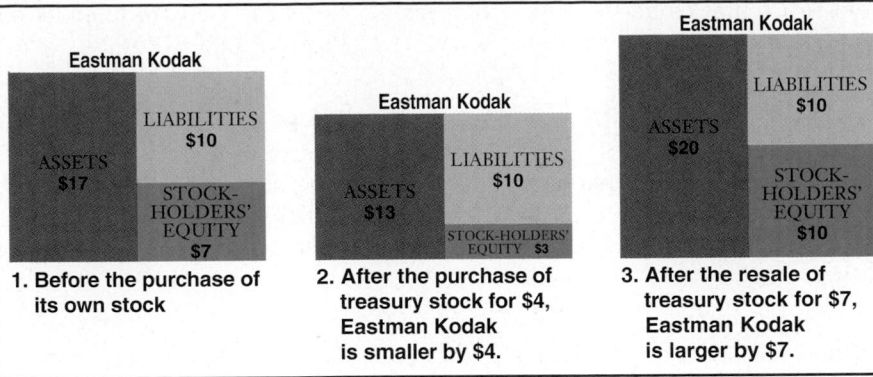

1. Before the purchase of its own stock

2. After the purchase of treasury stock for $4, Eastman Kodak is smaller by $4.

3. After the resale of treasury stock for $7, Eastman Kodak is larger by $7.

Retirement of Stock

A corporation may purchase its own stock and *retire* it by canceling the stock certificates. Retirements of preferred stock occur more often than retirements of common stock, as companies seek to avoid having to pay dividends on the preferred stock. The retired stock cannot be reissued.

Retiring stock, like purchasing treasury stock, decreases the corporation's outstanding stock. Retirement also decreases the number of shares issued. In retiring stock, the corporation removes the balances from all stock and paid-in capital accounts related to the retired shares, such as Preferred Stock and Capital in Excess of Par.

 DAILY EXERCISE 14-10

Review the first half of the chapter by studying the following Decision Guidelines feature.

DECISION GUIDELINES

Accounting for Retained Earnings, Dividends, and Treasury Stock

DECISION	GUIDELINES		
How to record:			
• Distribution of a small stock dividend? (20–25%)	Retained Earnings .... Market value		
	Common Stock	Par value	
	Paid-in Capital in Excess of Par	Excess	
• Distribution of a large stock dividend? (25% or more)	Retained Earnings .... Par value		
	Common Stock	Par value	
• Stock split?	Memorandum only: Split the common stock 2 for 1. Called in the outstanding $10 par common stock and distributed two shares of $5 par for each old share outstanding (amounts assumed).		

What are the effects of stock dividends and stock splits on:	Effects of Stock	
	Dividend	Split
• Number of shares of stock authorized?	No effect	Increase
• Shares issued?	Increase	Increase
• Shares outstanding?	Increase	Increase
• Par value per share?	No effect	Decrease
• Total assets and total liabilities?	No effect	No effect
• Total stockholders' equity?	No effect	No effect
• Common Stock account?	Increase	No effect
• Retained Earnings account?	Decrease	No effect

DECISION GUIDELINES (CONT.)

Accounting for Retained Earnings, Dividends, and Treasury Stock

DECISION	GUIDELINES

How to record:
- Purchase of treasury stock?
- Sale of treasury stock?

Treasury Stock	Cost
Cash..	Cost

At cost?

Cash	Amt received
Treasury Stock	Cost

Above cost?

Cash	Amt received
Treasury Stock	Cost
Paid-in Capital from Treasury	
Stock Transactions	Excess

Below cost?

Cash	Amt received
Paid-in Capital from Treasury	
Stock Transactions...........................	Amt up to prior bal.
Retained Earnings	Excess
Treasury Stock	Cost
or Cash	Amt received
Retained Earnings	Excess
Treasury Stock	Cost

What are the effects of the purchase and sale of treasury stock on:

- Total assets?

- Total stockholders' equity?

	Effects of	
	Purchase	**Sale**
	Decrease by full amount of payment	Increase by full amount of cash receipt
	Decrease by full amount of payment	Increase by full amount of cash receipt

---

Restrictions on Retained Earnings

Dividends, purchases of treasury stock, and retirements of stock require payments by the corporation to its stockholders. These outlays decrease the corporation's assets, so fewer assets are available to pay liabilities. A bank may agree to loan $500,000 only if the borrowing corporation limits dividend payments and the purchase of treasury stock.

LIMITS ON DIVIDENDS AND TREASURY STOCK PURCHASES   To ensure that corporations maintain a minimum level of stockholders' equity for the protection of creditors, state laws restrict the amount of treasury stock a corporation may purchase. Restrictions on dividends and treasury stock purchases often focus on the balance of retained earnings.

Companies usually report their retained earnings restrictions in notes to the financial statements. The following disclosure by RTE Corporation, a manufacturer of electronic transformers, is typical:

> **NOTES TO CONSOLIDATED FINANCIAL STATEMENTS**
>
> **NOTE F—LONG-TERM DEBT**
>
>   The . . . Company's loan agreements . . . restrict cash dividends and similar payments to shareholders. Under the most restrictive of these provisions, retained earnings of $4,300,000 were unrestricted as of December 31, 20X0.

With this restriction, the maximum dividend that RTE Corporation can pay its stock-holders is $4,300,000.

APPROPRIATIONS OF RETAINED EARNINGS **Appropriations** are restrictions on Retained Earnings that are recorded by formal journal entries. A corporation may *appropriate*—segregate in a separate account—a portion of Retained Earnings for a specific use. For example, the board of directors may appropriate part of Retained Earnings for expansion or to pay future liabilities. A debit to Retained Earnings and a credit to a separate account—Retained Earnings Appropriated for Plant Expansion—records the appropriation. Appropriated Retained Earnings appears directly above the regular Retained Earnings account on the balance sheet as shown near the bottom of Exhibit 14-6.

> **APPROPRIATION OF RETAINED EARNINGS.** Restriction of retained earnings that is recorded by a formal journal entry.

Retained earnings appropriations are rare. Most companies report any retained earnings restrictions in the notes to the financial statements, as illustrated for RTE Corporation above.

 DAILY EXERCISE 14-11

Variations in Reporting Stockholders' Equity

Accountants sometimes use formats for reporting stockholders' equity that differ from our examples. We use a detailed format to help you learn the components of stockholders' equity. Companies assume that readers of their statements already understand the details.

One of the most important skills you will learn in this course is the ability to understand the financial statements of real companies. In Exhibit 14-6, we present a side-by-side comparison of our general teaching format and the format that you are likely to encounter in real-world balance sheets. Note the following points in the real-world format:

1. The heading Paid-in Capital does not appear. It is commonly understood that Preferred Stock, Common Stock, and Additional Paid-in Capital are elements of paid-in capital.
2. Preferred stock is often reported in a single amount that combines its par value and premium.

EXHIBIT 14-6 **Formats for Reporting Stockholders' Equity**

General Teaching Format		Real-World Format	
Stockholders' equity		**Stockholders' equity**	
Paid-in capital:			
Preferred stock, 8%, $10 par,		Preferred stock, 8%, $10 par,	
30,000 shares authorized and issued	$ 300,000	30,000 shares authorized	
Paid-in capital in excess of par—preferred	10,000	and issued	$ 310,000
Common stock, $1 par, 100,000 shares		Common stock, $1 par,	
authorized, 60,000 shares issued	60,000	100,000 shares authorized,	
Paid-in capital in excess of par—common	2,140,000	60,000 shares issued	60,000
Paid-in capital from treasury stock		Additional paid-in capital	2,160,000
transactions, common	9,000	Retained earnings (Note 7)	1,565,000
Paid-in capital from retirement of		Less: Treasury stock, common	
preferred stock	4,000	(1,400 shares at cost)	(42,000)
Donated capital	7,000		$4,053,000
Total paid-in capital	2,530,000		
Retained earnings appropriated for		*Note 7—Restriction on retained earnings.*	
contingencies	400,000	At December 31, 20XX, $400,000 of retained	
Retained earnings—unappropriated	1,165,000	earnings is restricted by the company's board	
Total retained earnings	1,565,000	of directors to absorb the effect of any	
Subtotal	4,095,000	contingencies that may arise. Accordingly,	
Less: Treasury stock, common		any dividend declarations are restricted to a	
(1,400 shares at cost)	(42,000)	maximum of $1,165,000 ($1,565,000 −	
Total stockholders' equity	$4,053,000	$400,000).	

551

3. For presentation in the financial statements, all additional paid-in capital—from capital in excess of par on common stock, treasury stock transactions, and stock retirement—appears as a single amount labeled Additional Paid-in Capital. Additional Paid-in Capital belongs to the common stockholders, and so it follows Common Stock in the real-world format.

4. Often, total stockholders' equity ($4,053,000 in Exhibit 14-6) is not specifically labeled.

MID-CHAPTER

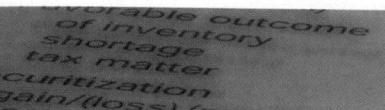

SUMMARY PROBLEM

Simplicity Pattern Co., Inc., the maker of sewing patterns, reported shareholder's equity:

Shareholders' Equity	($ Thousands)
Preferred stock, $1.00 par value	
Authorized—10,000,000 shares; Issued—None	$ —
Common Stock, 8 1/3 cents par value	
Authorized, 30,000,000 shares; Issued 13,733,229 shares...........	1,144
Capital in excess of par value...	48,122
Earnings retained in business..	89,320
	138,586
Less: Treasury stock, at cost (1,919,000 common shares)	(14,742)
	$123,844

Required

1. What was the average issue price per share of the common stock?
2. Journalize the issuance of 1,200 shares of common stock at $4 per share. Use Simplicity's account titles.
3. How many shares of Simplicity's common stock are outstanding?
4. How many shares of common stock would be outstanding after Simplicity split its common stock 3 for 1?
5. Using Simplicity account titles, journalize the distribution of a stock dividend when the market price of Simplicity common stock is $3 per share. Consider each of the following stock dividends independently:
   a. Simplicity distributes a 10% common stock dividend on the shares outstanding, computed in requirement 3.
   b. Simplicity distributes a 100% common stock dividend on the shares outstanding, computed in requirement 3.
6. Journalize the following treasury stock transactions, assuming they occur in the order given:
   a. Simplicity purchases 500 shares of treasury stock at $8 per share.
   b. Simplicity sells 100 shares of treasury stock for $9 per share.

Solution

1. Average issue price of common stock was $3.59 per share
   [($1,144,000 + $48,122,000)/13,733,229 shares = $3.59].
2. Cash (1,200 × $4) 4,800
   Common Stock (1,200 × $0.08 1/3)   100
   Capital in Excess of Par Value.......................   4,700
   Issued common stock at a premium.
3. Shares outstanding = 11,814,229 (13,733,229 shares issued minus 1,919,000 shares of treasury stock).
4. Shares outstanding after a 3-for-1 stock split = 35,442,687 (11,814,229 shares outstanding × 3).

5a. Earnings Retained in Business (11,814,229 × 0.10 × $3)	3,544,269	
Common Stock (11,814,229 × 0.10 × $0.08 1/3)		98,452
Capital in Excess of Par Value....................................		3,445,817
Distributed a 10% common stock dividend.		
b. Earnings Retained in Business (11,814,229 × $0.08 1/3)............	984,519	
Common Stock...		984,519
Distributed a 100% common stock dividend.		
6a. Treasury Stock (500 × $8)...	4,000	
Cash..		4,000
Purchased 500 shares of treasury stock at $8 per share.		
b. Cash (100 × $9)	900	
Treasury Stock (100 × $8)		800
Paid-in Capital from Treasury Stock Transactions..............		100
Sold 100 shares of treasury stock at $9 per share.		

THE CORPORATE INCOME STATEMENT: ANALYZING THE QUALITY OF EARNINGS

Objective 5
Identify the elements of a complex income statement

Now that we have covered stockholders' equity in detail, we turn to the corporate income statement. A corporation's net income (revenues plus gains minus expenses and losses) receives more attention than any other item in the financial statements. In fact, net income is probably the most important piece of information about a company. Net income measures the business's ability to earn a profit and indicates how successfully the company has operated.

Suppose you are considering investing in the stock of **AOL Time Warner, Inc.** You would examine the company's income statement. Of particular interest is the amount of net income (or net loss) that AOL Time Warner can expect to earn year after year. To understand net income, let's examine Exhibit 14-7 on page 554. It is the income statement of Allied Electronics Corporation, a small manufacturer of precision instruments.

Continuing Operations

Income from a business's continuing operations helps investors make predictions about future earnings. In Exhibit 14-7, the topmost section reports income from continuing operations. This part of the business is expected to continue from period to period. We may use this information to predict that Allied Electronics Corporation will earn income of approximately $54,000 next year.

The continuing operations section of Allied Electronics' statement includes three items needing explanation. *First*, during 20X5, the company had a $10,000 loss on restructuring operations. Restructuring costs include severance pay to laid-off workers, moving expenses for employees transferred to other locations, and environmental cleanup expenses. The restructuring loss is part of continuing operations because Allied Electronics is remaining in the same line of business. But the loss is highlighted as an "Other" item (unusual) on the income statement because its cause—restructuring—falls outside Allied's main business, which is selling electronics products.

Second, Allied had a gain on the sale of machinery, which is also outside the company's core business activity. This explains why the gain is reported separately from Allied's sales revenue, cost of goods sold, and gross profit.

Third, income tax expense has been deducted in arriving at income from continuing operations. We use a tax rate of 40% in our illustrations ($90,000 × 0.40 = $36,000).

 DAILY EXERCISE 14-12

 DAILY EXERCISE 14-13

Special Items

An income statement may include three categories of special gains and losses:

EXHIBIT 14-7   Allied Electronics Corporation's Income Statement

ALLIED ELECTRONICS CORPORATION
Income Statement
Year Ended December 31, 20X5

Continuing operations	
Net sales revenue	$500,000
Cost of goods sold	240,000
Gross profit	260,000
Operating expenses (detailed)	181,000
Operating income	79,000
Other gains (losses):	
Loss on restructuring operations	(10,000)
Gain on sale of machinery	21,000
Income from continuing operations before income tax	90,000
Income tax expense	36,000
Income from continuing operations	54,000
Special items	
Discontinued operations, income of $35,000, less income tax of $14,000	21,000
Income before extraordinary item and cumulative effect of change in depreciation method	75,000
Extraordinary flood loss, $20,000, less income tax saving of $8,000	(12,000)
Cumulative effect of change in depreciation method, $10,000, less income tax of $4,000	6,000
Net income	$ 69,000
Earnings per share	
Earnings per share of common stock (20,000 shares outstanding):	
Income from continuing operations	$2.70
Income from discontinued operations	1.05
Income before extraordinary item and cumulative effect of change in depreciation method	3.75
Extraordinary loss	(0.60)
Cumulative effect of change in depreciation method	0.30
Net income	$3.45

- Discontinued operations
- Extraordinary gains and losses
- Cumulative effect of a change in accounting principle

DISCONTINUED OPERATIONS   Most large corporations engage in several lines of business. For example, **Sears, Roebuck & Co.** best known for its retail stores, has a real-estate development company **(Homart)** and an insurance company **(Allstate).** We call each identifiable division of a company a **segment of the business.** Allstate is the insurance segment of Sears.

SEGMENT OF THE BUSINESS. One of various separate divisions of a company.

A company may sell a segment of its business. For example, **May Department Stores,** the chain that operates **Lord & Taylor, Foley's,** and **Robinsons-May** stores, sold **Payless,** its chain of shoe stores. Such a sale is not a regular source of income because the sale of a business segment is viewed as a one-time transaction. Financial analysts typically do not include income or loss on discontinued operations to predict a company's future income. The discontinued segments will generate no income in the future.

The income statement carries information on the segment that has been disposed of under the heading Discontinued operations. Income from the discontinued operation ($35,000) is taxed at the 40% rate and reported by Allied Electronics Corporation, as shown in Exhibit 14-7. A loss on discontinued operations is reported similarly, with a subtraction for the income tax *savings* on the loss.

In the normal course of business, companies dispose of old plant and equipment. Gains and losses on these asset dispositions are *not* reported as discontinued operations. Gains and losses on normal asset dispositions can be reported along with operating revenues and expenses or highlighted as "Other gains (losses)" on the income statement.

EXTRAORDINARY GAINS AND LOSSES (EXTRAORDINARY ITEMS) **Extraordinary gains and losses,** also called **extraordinary items,** are both unusual for the company and infrequent. Losses from natural disasters (floods, earthquakes, and tornadoes) and the taking of company assets by a foreign government (expropriation) are extraordinary. Gains and losses on the early retirement of debt are also extraordinary items.

EXTRAORDINARY GAINS AND LOSSES. A gain or loss that is both unusual for the company and infrequent. Also called **extraordinary items.**

Extraordinary items are reported along with their income tax effect. During 20X5, Allied Electronics Corporation lost $20,000 of inventory in a flood. This flood loss, which reduced income, also reduced Allied's income tax. The tax effect of the loss is computed by multiplying the amount of the loss by the tax rate. The tax effect decreases the net amount of the loss in the same way that the income tax reduces the amount of net income. An extraordinary loss can be reported along with its tax effect on the income statement as follows:

Extraordinary flood loss	$(20,000)
Less: Income tax saving.........................	8,000
Extraordinary flood loss, net of tax	(12,000)

Trace this item to the income statement in Exhibit 14-7. An extraordinary gain is reported in the same way as a loss, net of the income tax on the gain.

Gains and losses due to employee strikes, lawsuits, discontinued operations, and the sale of plant assets are *not* extraordinary items. They are considered normal business events. However, they are outside the business's central operations, so they are reported on the income statement as other gains and losses. Examples include the gain on sale of machinery and the restructuring loss in the Other gains (losses) section of Exhibit 14-7.

Cumulative Effect of a Change in Accounting Principle

Companies sometimes change accounting methods, such as from double-declining-balance (DDB) to straight-line depreciation, or from first-in, first-out (FIFO) to weighted-average cost for inventory. ➡ An accounting change makes it difficult to compare one period's financial statements with the statements of preceding periods.

For a review of depreciation methods, see Chapter 10. For a review of inventory methods, see Chapter 9.

Without detailed information, investors and creditors can be misled into thinking that the current year is better than the preceding year when in fact the only difference is a change in accounting. Investors must separate the effects of business operations from effects created by accounting. This leads companies to report the effect of the accounting change in a special section of the income statement. This section usually appears after extraordinary items.

Suppose Allied Electronics Corporation changes from DDB to straight-line depreciation at the beginning of 20X5. If the company had been using straight-line depreciation every year, depreciation expense would have been less in prior years, and net income would have been higher. Exhibit 14-7 reports the $6,000 cumulative effect of this accounting change. A change from straight-line to double-declining-balance usually produces a negative cumulative effect.

WORK IT OUT

Examine all the income tax amounts in Exhibit 14-7. How much was Allied Electronics' *total* income tax expense during 19X5?

Answer: **46,000 = $36,000 + $14,000 − $8,000 + $4,000**

Note that $36,000 is the company's income tax expense from continuing operations; $46,000 is *total* income tax expense.

Earnings Per Share

EARNINGS PER SHARE (EPS).
Amount of a company's net income per share of its outstanding common stock.

The final segment of a corporate income statement presents the company's earnings per share, abbreviated as EPS. EPS is the most widely used of all accounting statistics. **Earnings per share (EPS)** is the amount of a company's net income for each share of its *outstanding common stock*. It is a key measure of a business's success:

$$\text{Earnings per share} = \frac{\text{Net income} - \text{Preferred dividends}}{\substack{\text{Weighted-average number of} \\ \text{common shares outstanding}}}$$

Just as the corporation lists its different sources of income separately—from continuing operations, discontinued operations, and so on—it also lists a separate EPS figure for each element of income. Allied Electronics Corporation's EPS calculations are as follows:

Earnings per share of common stock (20,000 shares outstanding):	
Income from continuing operations ($54,000/20,000)	$2.70
Income from discontinued operations ($21,000/20,000)	1.05
Income before extraordinary item and cumulative effect of change in depreciation method ($75,000/20,000)	3.75
Extraordinary loss ($12,000/20,000)	(0.60)
Cumulative effect of change in depreciation method ($6,000/20,000)	0.30
Net income ($69,000/20,000)	$3.45

The final section of Exhibit 14-7 reports the EPS figures for Allied Electronics.

WEIGHTED-AVERAGE NUMBER OF COMMON SHARES OUTSTANDING Computing EPS is straightforward if the number of common shares outstanding does not change during the accounting period. For many corporations, however, this figure varies as the company issues new stock and purchases treasury stock during the year. Suppose **Qualcomm Corporation** had 100,000 shares outstanding from January through May, then purchased 40,000 shares as treasury stock. Qualcomm's EPS would be misleadingly high if computed using 60,000 (100,000 − 40,000) shares. To make EPS as meaningful as possible, corporations use the weighted average of the number of common shares outstanding during the period.

Let's assume that Qualcomm Corporation had these shares of common stock outstanding for the following periods:

- January through June—100,000 shares
- July through August—60,000 shares (after buying 40,000 treasury shares)
- September through December—90,000 shares (after issuing 30,000 new shares)

We compute the weighted-average number of common shares outstanding by considering the outstanding shares per month as a fraction of the year:

Number of Common Shares Outstanding	×	Fraction of Year	Period During the Year	=	Weighted-Average Number of Common Shares Outstanding
100,000	×	6/12	January through June	=	50,000
60,000	×	2/12	July through August	=	10,000
90,000	×	4/12	September through December	=	30,000
			Weighted-average number of common shares outstanding during the year	=	90,000

The weighted-average number (90,000) of common shares outstanding would then be used to compute Qualcomm's EPS.

EFFECT OF PREFERRED DIVIDENDS ON EARNINGS PER SHARE Preferred dividends also affect EPS. Recall that EPS is earnings per share of *common* stock. Recall also that dividends on preferred stock are paid first. ➨ Therefore, preferred dividends must be subtracted from income to compute EPS. If Allied Electronics Corporation had 10,000 shares of preferred stock outstanding, each with a $1.00 dividend, the annual preferred dividend would be $10,000 (10,000 × $1.00). The $10,000 would be subtracted from each of the income subtotals (lines 1, 3, and 6), resulting in the following EPS computations for the company:

◄ Chapter 13, p. 506, provides detailed information on preferred stock.

	Earnings per share of common stock (20,000 shares outstanding):	
1	Income from continuing operations ($54,000 − $10,000)/20,000.................	$2.20
2	Income from discontinued operations ($21,000/20,000)	1.05
3	Income before extraordinary item and cumulative effect of change in depreciation method ($75,000 − $10,000)/20,000...................................	3.25
4	Extraordinary loss ($12,000/20,000)	(0.60)
5	Cumulative effect of change in depreciation method ($6,000/20,000)	0.30
6	Net income ($69,000 − $10,000)/20,000	$2.95

● DAILY EXERCISE 14-14

● DAILY EXERCISE 14-15

BASIC AND DILUTED EARNINGS PER SHARE Some corporations must report two sets of EPS figures as follows.

- EPS based on outstanding common shares (*basic* EPS).
- EPS based on outstanding common shares plus the number of additional common shares that would arise from conversion of the preferred stock into common stock (*diluted* EPS). Diluted EPS is always lower than basic EPS.

THINK IT OVER What makes earnings per share so useful as a business statistic?

Answer: Earnings per share is useful because it relates a company's income to one share of stock. Stock prices are quoted at an amount per share, and investors usually consider how much they must pay for a certain number of shares. Earnings per share is used to help determine the value of a share of stock.

● DAILY EXERCISE 14-16

● DAILY EXERCISE 14-17

Combined Statement of Income and Retained Earnings

Some companies report income and retained earnings on a single statement. Exhibit 14-8 illustrates how Allied Electronics would combine its income statement and its statement of retained earnings.

EXHIBIT 14-8
Combined Statement of Income and Retained Earnings

	ALLIED ELECTRONICS CORPORATION	
	Statement of Income and Retained Earnings	
	Year Ended December 31, 20X5	
Income statement	Sales revenue	$500,000
	Cost of goods sold	240,000
	Gross profit..	260,000
	Expenses (listed individually)	191,000
	Net income for 20X5..	$ 69,000
Statement of retained earnings	Retained earnings, December 31, 20X4..............	130,000
		199,000
	Dividends for 20X5	(21,000)
	Retained earnings, December 31, 20X5..............	$178,000

Reporting Comprehensive Income

As we have seen throughout this book, all companies report net income or net loss on the income statement. Companies with certain gains and losses must also report another income figure. **Comprehensive income** is the company's change in total stockholders' equity from all sources other than from the owners. Comprehensive income includes net income plus some specific gains and losses. FASB Statement

COMPREHENSIVE INCOME.
Company's change in total stockholders' equity from all sources other than from the owners.

130 includes these components of comprehensive income (Chapter 16 explains these items):

- Unrealized gains or losses on certain investments
- Foreign-currency translation adjustments

These items do not enter into the determination of net income but instead are reported as other comprehensive income, as shown in Exhibit 14-9. Assumed figures are used for all items.

EXHIBIT 14-9
Reporting Comprehensive Income

NATIONAL EXPRESS COMPANY
Income Statement
Year Ended December 31, 20X2

Revenues...	$10,000
Expenses (summarized)	6,000
Net income..	4,000
Other comprehensive income:	
Unrealized gain on investments..............	1,000
Comprehensive income	$ 5,000

DAILY EXERCISE 14-18

Earnings per share applies only to net income and its components, as discussed earlier. Earnings per share is not reported for other comprehensive income.

The Decision Guidelines feature summarizes a corporate income statement.

DECISION GUIDELINES

Analyzing a Corporate Income Statement

DECISION	GUIDELINES	
What are the main sections of the income statement? See Exhibit 14-7 for an example.	**Continuing operations**	• Continuing operations, including other gains and losses and less income tax expense
	Special items	• Discontinued operations—gain or loss—less the income tax effect
		• Extraordinary gain or loss, less the income tax effect
		• Cumulative effect of change in accounting principle, less the income tax effect
		• Net income (or net loss)
		• Other comprehensive income (Exhibit 14-9)
What earnings per share (EPS) figures must a corporation report?	**Earnings per share**	• Earnings per share—applies only to net income (or net loss) and its components, not to other comprehensive income
		Separate EPS figures for
		• Income from continuing operations
		• Discontinued operations
		• Income before extraordinary item and cumulative effect of accounting change
		• Extraordinary gain or loss
		• Cumulative effect of accounting change
		• Net income (or net loss)

How to compute EPS for net income?

$$\text{EPS} = \frac{\text{Net income} - \text{Preferred dividends}}{\text{Weighted-average number of common shares outstanding}}$$

Prior-Period Adjustments

A company may make an error in recording revenues or expenses. After the revenue and expense accounts are closed, the Retained Earnings account holds the error. The balance of Retained Earnings is wrong until corrected. Corrections to Retained Earnings for errors of an earlier period are called **prior-period adjustments.** The prior-period adjustment (correction) either increases or decreases the beginning balance of Retained Earnings and appears on the statement of retained earnings.

PRIOR-PERIOD ADJUSTMENT. A correction to retained earnings for an error of an earlier period.

Assume De Graff Corporation recorded $30,000 of income tax expense for 20X4. The correct amount was $40,000. This error

- Understated expenses by $10,000
- Overstated net income by $10,000

In 20X5, the government required De Graff to pay the additional $10,000 in taxes for the prior year. De Graff's prior-period adjustment will decrease retained earnings as follows.

DE GRAFF CORPORATION Statement of Retained Earnings Year Ended December 31, 20X5	
Retained earnings, December 31, 20X4, as originally reported	$390,000
Prior-period adjustment—To correct error in the income tax of 20X4	(10,000)
Retained earnings, December 31, 20X4, as adjusted	380,000
Net income for 20X5	114,000
	494,000
Dividends for 20X5	(41,000)
Retained earnings, December 31, 20X5	$453,000

DAILY EXERCISE 14-19

Statement of Stockholders' Equity

Most companies report a statement of stockholders' equity, which is more comprehensive than a statement of retained earnings. The statement of stockholders' equity is formatted exactly as a statement of retained earnings but with columns for each element of equity. The **statement of stockholders' equity** reports the changes in all categories of equity during the period:

- Common stock
- Additional paid-in capital
- Retained earnings
- Treasury stock
- Total stockholders' equity

Objective 6
Prepare a statement of stockholders' equity

STATEMENT OF STOCKHOLDERS' EQUITY. Reports the changes in all categories of stockholders' equity during the period.

Exhibit 14-10 uses assumed figures for Allied Electronics Corporation to illustrate the statement of stockholders' equity. Negative amounts—debits—appear in parentheses. If the company has preferred stock, the statement needs a column for Preferred Stock.

DAILY EXERCISE 14-20

EXHIBIT 14-10 **Statement of Stockholders' Equity**

ALLIED ELECTRONICS CORPORATION Statement of Stockholders' Equity Year Ended December 31, 20X5					
	Common Stock	Additional Paid-in Capital	Retained Earnings	Treasury Stock	Total
Balance, December 31, 20X4	$ 80,000	$160,000	$130,000	$(25,000)	$345,000
Issuance of stock	20,000	65,000			85,000
Net income			69,000		69,000
Cash dividends			(21,000)		(21,000)
Stock dividends—8%	8,000	26,000	(34,000)		–0–
Purchase of treasury stock				(9,000)	(9,000)
Sale of treasury stock		13,000		4,000	17,000
Balance, December 31, 20X5	$108,000	$264,000	$144,000	$(30,000)	$486,000

SUMMARY PROBLEM

The following information was taken from the ledger of **Kraft Corporation:**

Common stock, no-par,			Discontinued operations,	
45,000 shares issued...........	$180,000		income..................................	$ 20,000
Sales revenue.........................	620,000		Prior-period adjustments—	
Extraordinary gain.................	26,000		credit to Retained Earnings	5,000
Loss due to lawsuit	11,000		Gain on sale of plant assets	21,000
General expenses...................	62,000		Cost of goods sold	380,000
Preferred stock, 8%, $100 par,			Income tax expense (saving):	
500 shares issued................	50,000		Continuing operations.........	32,000
Retained earnings, beginning,			Discontinued operations......	8,000
as originally reported	103,000		Extraordinary gain	10,000
Cumulative effect of change			Cumulative effect of change	
in inventory method (debit)	(10,000)		in inventory method........	(4,000)
Dividends................................	16,000		Treasury stock, common	
Selling expenses.....................	108,000		(5,000 shares at cost)...........	25,000

Required

Prepare a single-step income statement and a statement of retained earnings for Kraft Corporation for the current year ended December 31. Include the EPS presentation and show your computations. Kraft had no changes in its stock accounts during the year.

Solution

KRAFT CORPORATION
Income Statement
Year Ended December 31, 20XX

Revenue and gains:		
Sales revenue...		$620,000
Gain on sale of plant assets...		21,000
Total revenues and gains...		641,000
Expenses and losses:		
Cost of goods sold	$380,000	
Selling expenses...	108,000	
General expenses...	62,000	
Loss due to lawsuit...	11,000	
Income tax expense	32,000	
Total expenses and losses		593,000
Income from continuing operations...		48,000
Discontinued operations, income of $20,000, less income tax of $8,000		12,000
Income before extraordinary item and cumulative effect of change in inventory method		60,000
Extraordinary gain, $26,000, less income tax, $10,000		16,000
Cumulative effect of change in inventory method, $10,000, less income tax saving, $4,000		(6,000)
Net income		$ 70,000
Earnings per share:		
Income from continuing operations [($48,000 − $4,000)/40,000 shares]		$1.10
Income from discontinued operations ($12,000/40,000 shares)...		0.30
Income before extraordinary item and cumulative effect of change in inventory		
method [($60,000 − $4,000)/40,000 shares]		1.40
Extraordinary gain ($16,000/40,000 shares)...		0.40
Cumulative effect of change in inventory method ($6,000/40,000)...		(0.15)
Net income [($70,000 − $4,000)/40,000 shares]...		$1.65

Computations:

$$EPS = \frac{\text{Income} - \text{Preferred dividends}}{\text{Common shares outstanding}}$$

Preferred dividends: $50,000 × 0.08 = $4,000
Common shares outstanding
  45,000 shares issued − 5,000 treasury shares = 40,000 shares outstanding

KRAFT CORPORATION
Statement of Retained Earnings
Year Ended December 31, 20XX

Retained earnings balance, beginning, as originally reported..............	$103,000
Prior-period adjustment—credit..	5,000
Retained earnings balance, beginning, as adjusted	108,000
Net income for current year...	70,000
	178,000
Dividends for current year	(16,000)
Retained earnings balance, ending..	$162,000

LESSONS LEARNED

1. **Account for stock dividends.** *Retained Earnings* carries the balance of cumulative net income, less all dividends and net losses. *Cash dividends* are distributions of corporate assets. *Stock dividends* are distributions of the corporation's own stock to its stockholders.

2. **Distinguish stock splits from stock dividends.** Stock dividends shift amounts from retained earnings to paid-in capital. *Stock splits* do not change any account balance. Both increase the number of shares outstanding and lower the market price per share of stock.

3. **Account for treasury stock.** *Treasury stock* is the corporation's own stock that has been issued and reacquired, and the company is currently holding. The corporation may sell treasury stock for cost or for more or less than cost.

4. **Report restrictions on retained earnings.** Retained earnings may be *restricted* by law or contract or by the corporation itself.

5. **Identify the elements of a complex income statement.** The corporate *income statement* lists the various sources of income—*continuing operations; discontinued operations;* and *extraordinary gains and losses.* The bottom line of the income statement reports *net income* or *net loss* for the period. *Earnings-per-share* (EPS) figures also appear on the income statement, likewise divided into the different categories of income.

6. **Prepare a statement of stockholders' equity.** A statement of stockholders' equity reports the change in each stockholders' equity account.

ACCOUNTING VOCABULARY

appropriation of retained earnings (p. 551)

comprehensive income (p. 557)

earnings per share (EPS) (p. 556)

extraordinary gains and losses (p. 555)

extraordinary item (p. 555)

prior-period adjustment (p. 559)

segment of the business (p. 554)

statement of stockholders' equity (p. 559)

stock dividend (p. 542)

stock split (p. 544)

treasury stock (p. 545)

QUESTIONS

1. Identify the two main parts of stockholders' equity.
2. A friend receives a stock dividend on an investment. He believes that stock dividends are the same as cash dividends. Explain why the two are not the same.
3. What percentage distinguishes a small stock dividend from a large stock dividend? What is the main difference in accounting for small and large stock dividends?
4. To an investor, a stock split and a stock dividend have essentially the same effect. Explain the similarity and difference to the corporation between a 100% stock dividend and a 2-for-1 stock split.
5. Give four reasons why a corporation might purchase treasury stock.
6. What effect does the purchase of treasury stock have on the (a) assets, (b) issued stock, and (c) outstanding stock of the corporation?
7. What is the normal balance of the Treasury Stock account? What type of account is Treasury Stock? Where is Treasury Stock reported on the balance sheet?

8. What are two ways to report a retained earnings restriction? Which way is more common?
9. Identify four items on the income statement that generate income tax expense. What is an income tax saving, and how does it arise?
10. Why is it important for a corporation to report income from continuing operations separately from discontinued operations and extraordinary items?
11. Give two examples of extraordinary gains and losses and four examples of gains and losses that are *not* extraordinary.
12. What is the most widely used of all accounting statistics?
13. What is the earnings per share of a company with net income of $5,500, issued common stock of 12,000 shares, and treasury common stock of 1,000 shares?
14. What account is affected by all prior-period adjustments? On what financial statement are prior-period adjustments reported?

DAILY EXERCISES

Recording a small stock dividend
(Obj. 1)

DE14-1 Vartec Telecom Company has 200,000 shares of $2.50 par common stock outstanding. Vartec distributes a 5% stock dividend when the market value of its stock is $13 per share.

1. Journalize Vartec's distribution of the stock dividend on March 19. An explanation is not required.
2. What is the overall effect of the stock dividend on Vartec Telecom's total assets? On total stockholders' equity?

Recording a large stock dividend and reporting stockholders' equity
(Obj. 1)

DE14-2 Strongarm Steel Works has 30,000 shares of $1 par common stock outstanding. Strongarm issued this stock at a price of $10 per share. Strongarm declares and distributes a 50% stock dividend when the market value of its common stock is $62.50 per share.

1. Journalize Strongarm's distribution of the stock dividend on July 15. An explanation is not required.
2. Prepare the stockholders' equity section of Strongarm's balance sheet after distribution of the stock dividend. Retained Earnings had a balance of $60,000 before the dividend, and Strongarm's corporate charter authorizes the company to issue 100,000 shares of common stock.

Comparing and contrasting cash dividends and stock dividends
(Obj. 1)

DE14-3 ← *Link Back to Chapter 13 (Cash Dividends).* Compare and contrast the accounting for cash dividends and stock dividends. In the space provided, insert either "Cash dividends," "Stock dividends," or "Both cash dividends and stock dividends" to complete each of the following statements:

1. _____ decrease Retained Earnings.
2. _____ have no effect on a liability.
3. _____ increase paid-in capital by the same amount that they decrease Retained Earnings.
4. _____ decrease both total assets and total stockholders' equity, resulting in a decrease in the size of the company.
5. _____ rearrange the account balances within stockholders' equity but have no effect on total stockholders' equity.

Accounting for a stock split
(Obj. 2)

DE14-4 Examine Georgia Lumber's stockholders' equity on page 543. Suppose Georgia Lumber split its common stock 2-for-1 in order to decrease the market price of its stock. The company's stock was trading at $15 immediately before the split.

1. Prepare the stockholders' equity section of Georgia Lumber's balance sheet after the stock split.
2. Which account balances changed after the stock split? Which account balances were unchanged?

Accounting for a reverse stock split
(Obj. 2)

DE14-5 Examine Georgia Lumber's stockholders' equity on page 543. Suppose Georgia Lumber split its common stock 1 for 2 (a reverse stock split) in order to increase the market price of its stock. The company's stock was trading at $15 immediately before the split.

1. Prepare the stockholders' equity section of Georgia Lumber's balance sheet after the stock split.
2. Which account balances changed after the stock split? Which account balances were unchanged?

Using a stock split or a stock dividend to decrease the market price of a stock *(Obj. 2)*

DE14-6 Wearall Rubber Products has prospered during the past ten years, and the company's stock price shot up to $59 recently. Wearall management wishes to decrease its stock price to around $30, which will be attractive to more investors. Should Wearall issue a 100% stock dividend or split the stock? If you propose a stock split, state the split ratio that will accomplish the company's objective. Show your computations.

Accounting for the purchase of treasury stock
(Obj. 3)

DE14-7 Jupiter Drilling Company's stockholders' equity (before the purchase of treasury stock) appears on page 546. Suppose Jupiter later purchases 600 shares of its common stock as treasury stock, paying cash of $5 per share.

1. Journalize the purchase of treasury stock.
2. Prepare the stockholders' equity section of Jupiter's balance sheet immediately after the purchase of treasury stock.
3. What effect does the purchase of treasury stock always have on total stockholders' equity? How did Jupiter's purchase of treasury stock affect the company's total stockholders' equity? Give the amount.

Accounting for the sale of treasury stock
(Obj. 3)

DE14-8 Return to the Jupiter Drilling Company situation in Daily Exercise 14-7. After purchasing the 600 shares of treasury stock for $5 per share, Jupiter later sold 400 of the treasury shares for $12 per share.

1. Journalize the sale of treasury stock.
2. Prepare the stockholders' equity section of Jupiter's balance sheet immediately after the sale of treasury stock.
3. What effect does the sale of treasury stock always have on total stockholders' equity? How did Jupiter's sale of treasury stock affect the company's total stockholders' equity? Give the amount.

DE14-9 Biscoff Productions, Inc., began operations in 20X0. After issuing its common stock to the public, Biscoff completed the following treasury stock transactions during the year:

Accounting for the purchase and sale of treasury stock (above cost) (Obj. 3)

a. Purchased 2,000 shares of the company's $1 par common stock as treasury stock, paying cash of $6 per share.
b. Sold 1,000 shares of the treasury stock for cash of $8 per share.

Journalize these transactions. Explanations are not required. Show how Biscoff will report treasury stock on its December 31, 20X0, balance sheet after completing the two transactions. In reporting the treasury stock, focus solely on the Treasury Stock account. You may ignore all other accounts.

DE14-10 Study Exhibit 14-6 on page 551. Suppose the corporation retired its preferred stock. What will be the amount of the company's total stockholders' equity if the cost to retire the preferred stock is $353,000? Is the company larger or smaller after the stock retirement? Give your reason.

Accounting for the retirement of preferred stock (Obj. 3)

DE14-11 Study Exhibit 14-6, page 551. The company's board of directors is preparing to declare a cash dividend.

Interpreting a restriction of retained earnings (Obj. 4)

1. The company has plenty of cash. What is the maximum amount of cash dividends the board of directors can declare? Explain how you arrived at your answer.
2. What is the nature of the retained earnings restriction in the exhibit? Why did the company restrict (appropriate) its retained earnings? Explain.

DE14-12 List the major parts of a complex corporate income statement for Ninja Motor Corporation for the year ended December 31, 20X1. Include all the major parts of the income statement, starting with net sales revenue and ending with net income (net loss). You may ignore dollar amounts and earnings per share. Use Exhibit 14-7, page 554, as a guide.

Preparing a complex corporate income statement (Obj. 5)

DE14-13 Study the income statement of Allied Electronics Corporation in Exhibit 14-7, page 554. Answer these questions about the company's operations:

Explaining the items on a complex corporate income statement (Obj. 5)

1. How much total gross profit did Allied earn on the sale of its products—before deducting any operating expenses? Name this item and give its amount.
2. Why are the loss on restructuring and the gain on sale of machinery reported as Other gains (losses)?
3. What dollar amount of net income would most sophisticated investors predict for Allied Electronics to earn during 20X6 and beyond? Name this item, give its amount, and state your reason.

DE14-14 MCI WorldCom, Inc., reported a net loss for 19X8. The net loss included a $58 million expense from the cumulative effect of an accounting change, less income tax saving of $22 million, and an extraordinary loss of $207 million, less income tax saving of $78 million. The company's loss before the cumulative effect of the accounting change and before the extraordinary loss was $2,560 million.

Computing net loss after the effects of an accounting change and an extraordinary loss (Obj. 5)

1. Compute MCI WorldCom's net loss for 19X8.
2. Compute EPS for the final amount of the net loss. MCI WorldCom had 1,906 million shares of common stock outstanding during the year.

DE14-15 ETransmission Corporation accounting records include the following items, listed in no particular order, at December 31, 20X3.

Preparing a complex corporate income statement (Obj. 5)

Extraordinary gain	$ 5,000	Other gains (losses)	$ (2,000)
Cost of goods sold	71,000	Net sales revenue	182,000
Operating expenses	64,000	Loss on discontinued	
Accounts receivable	19,000	operations	(15,000)

Income tax of 35% applies to all items.

Prepare ETransmission Corporation's income statement for the year ended December 31, 20X3. Use Exhibit 14-7, page 554, as a guide. Omit earnings per share.

DE14-16 Return to the ETransmission Corporation data in Daily Exercise 14-15. ETransmission had 8,000 shares of common stock outstanding at December 31, 20X2. The company issued an additional 6,000 shares of common stock on August 31, 20X3. ETransmission declared and paid preferred dividends of $3,000 during 20X3.

Reporting earnings per share (Obj. 5)

Show how ETransmission Corporation reported earnings-per-share data on its 20X3 income statement.

Interpreting earnings-per-share data
(Obj. 5)

DE14-17 The **Procter & Gamble Company** has preferred stock outstanding, and the corporation issued additional common stock during the year.

1. Give the basic equation to compute earnings per share of common stock for net income.
2. List all the income items for which Procter & Gamble must report earnings-per-share data.
3. What makes earnings per share so useful as a business statistic?

Reporting comprehensive income
(Obj. 5)

DE14-18 Use the ETransmission Corporation data in Daily Exercise 14-15. In addition, ETransmission had unrealized losses of $4,000 on investments and a $2,000 foreign-currency translation adjustment (a gain) during 20X3. Start with ETransmission Corporation's net income from Daily Exercise 14-15 and show how the company could report other comprehensive income on its 20X3 income statement.

Should ETransmission Corporation report earnings-per-share data for other comprehensive income?

Reporting a prior-period adjustment   (Obj. 6)

DE14-19 Examine De Graff Corporation's statement of retained earnings on page 559. Suppose instead that De Graff had overpaid 20X4 income tax expense by $10,000. Show how De Graff would report this prior-period adjustment on the statement of retained earnings for 20X5.

Using the statement of stockholders' equity
(Obj. 6)

DE14-20 ◂ *Link Back to Chapter 1 (Accounting Equation).* Use the statement of stockholders' equity in Exhibit 14-10, page 559, to answer the following questions about Allied Electronics Corporation.

1. Make a single journal entry to record Allied's declaration and payment of cash dividends during 20X5.
2. How much cash did the issuance of common stock bring in during 20X5?
3. Was the stock dividend that Allied declared and distributed during 20X5 "large" or "small"? How can you tell?
4. What was the cost of the treasury stock that Allied purchased during 20X5? What was Allied's cost of the treasury stock that Allied sold during the year? For how much did Allied sell the treasury stock during 20X5?

Exercises

Journalizing cash and stock dividends and reporting stockholders' equity
(Obj. 1)

E14-1 Ogden Aviation Services, Inc., is authorized to issue 500,000 shares of $1 par common stock. The company issued 80,000 shares at $4 per share, and all 80,000 shares are outstanding. When the retained earnings balance was $150,000, Ogden distributed a 50% stock dividend. Later, Ogden declared and paid a $0.30 per share cash dividend.

Required

1. Journalize the distribution of the stock dividend.
2. Journalize both the declaration and the payment of the cash dividend.
3. Prepare the stockholders' equity section of the balance sheet after both dividends.

Journalizing a small stock dividend and reporting stockholders' equity
(Obj. 1)

E14-2 The stockholders' equity for Jaworski, Inc., on September 30, 20X4—end of the company's fiscal year—follows:

Stockholders' Equity	
Common stock, $8 par, 100,000 shares authorized, 50,000 shares issued	$400,000
Paid-in capital in excess of par—common	50,000
Retained earnings	140,000
Total stockholders' equity	$590,000

On May 26, the market price of Jaworski's common stock was $16 per share and the company distributed a 10% stock dividend.

Required

1. Journalize the distribution of the stock dividend.
2. Prepare the stockholders' equity section of the balance sheet after the stock dividend.

Reporting stockholders' equity after a stock split   (Obj. 2)

E14-3 Redwood Construction, Inc., had the following stockholders' equity at May 31:

Common stock, $4 par, 200,000 shares authorized,		
50,000 shares issued		$200,000
Paid-in capital in excess of par		100,000
Retained earnings		210,000
Total stockholders' equity		$510,000

On November 6, Redwood split its $4 par common stock 4 for 1. Make the necessary entry to record the stock split, and prepare the stockholders' equity section of the balance sheet immediately after the split.

E14-4 Identify the effects of the following transactions on total stockholders' equity. Each transaction is independent.

Effects of stock issuance, dividends, and treasury stock transactions
(Obj. 1, 2, 3)

a. Purchase of 1,500 shares of treasury stock (par value $0.50) at $5 per share.
b. A 50% stock dividend. Before the dividend, 5,000,000 shares of $1 par common stock were outstanding; market value was $13.75 at the time of the dividend.
c. A 10% stock dividend. Before the dividend, 500,000 shares of $1 par common stock were outstanding; market value was $7.625 at the time of the dividend.
d. Sale of 600 shares of $5 par treasury stock for $7.00 per share. Cost of the treasury stock was $2.00 per share.
e. A 3-for-1 stock split. Prior to the split, 60,000 shares of $4.50 par common were outstanding.
f. Issuance of 50,000 shares of $10 par common at $16.50.

E14-5 Journalize the following transactions of **Foot Locker,** a chain of sports stores:

Journalizing treasury stock transactions
(Obj. 3)

Feb. 4 Issued 20,000 shares of no-par common stock at $15 per share.
Apr. 22 Purchased 1,000 shares of treasury stock at $14 per share.
Aug. 22 Sold 600 shares of treasury stock at $16 per share.

E14-6 Lordstrom's, Inc., had the following stockholders' equity on November 30:

Journalizing treasury stock transactions and reporting stockholders' equity
(Obj. 3)

Stockholders' Equity		
Common stock, $5 par, 500,000 shares authorized,		
50,000 shares issued		$250,000
Paid-in capital in excess of par		150,000
Retained earnings		520,000
Total stockholders' equity		$920,000

On November 27, the company purchased 25,000 shares of treasury stock at $6 per share. Journalize the purchase of the treasury stock, and prepare the stockholders' equity section of the balance sheet at December 31.

E14-7 The agreement under which Tadashi, Inc., issued its long-term debt requires the restriction of $100,000 of the company's retained earnings balance. Total retained earnings is $250,000, and total paid-in capital is $220,000.

Reporting a retained earnings restriction
(Obj. 4)

Required

Show how to report stockholders' equity on Tadashi's balance sheet, assuming the following:

a. Tadashi discloses the restriction in a note. Write the note.
b. Tadashi appropriates retained earnings in the amount of the restriction and includes no note in its statements.
c. Tadashi's cash balance is $185,000. What is the maximum amount of dividends Tadashi can declare?

E14-8 Beauvette Corporation's accounting records include the following for 20X3:

Sales revenue	$410,000	Income tax expense—	
Operating expenses		extraordinary gain	$ 6,000
(including income tax)	106,000	Income tax saving—change	
Cumulative effect of change in		in depreciation method	3,000
depreciation method (debit)	(7,000)	Income tax saving—loss	
Cost of goods sold	245,000	on discontinued operations	20,000
Loss on discontinued operations	50,000	Extraordinary gain	15,000

Required

Prepare a multi-step income statement for 20X3. Omit earnings per share. Was 20X3 a good year, a fair year, or a bad year for Beauvette Corporation? Explain your answer in terms of the outlook for 20X4.

E14-9 Kilgore Corporation earned net income of $71,000 for the second quarter of 20X6. The ledger reveals the following figures:

Preferred stock, $5.00 per year, no-par, 1,600 shares issued and outstanding	$ 70,000
Common stock, $10 par, 52,000 shares issued........................	520,000
Treasury stock, common, 2,000 shares at cost.........................	36,000

Required

Compute Kilgore's EPS for the quarter. Kilgore Corporation had no changes in its stock accounts during the quarter.

E14-10 Bastrop, Inc., had 40,000 shares of common stock and 10,000 shares of 5%, $10 par preferred stock outstanding on December 31, 20X1. On April 30, 20X2, the company issued 9,000 additional common shares and ended 20X2 with 49,000 shares of common stock outstanding. Income from continuing operations of 20X2 was $115,400, and loss on discontinued operations (net of income tax saving) was $8,280. The company had an extraordinary gain (net of tax) of $59,400.

Required

Compute Bastrop's EPS amounts for 20X2, starting with income from continuing operations.

Preparing a statement of retained
earnings with a prior-period
adjustment
(Obj. 6)

E14-11 Light Crust, Inc., a bakery, reported a prior-period adjustment in 20X3. An accounting error caused net income of prior years to be overstated by $3.8 million. Retained earnings at December 31, 20X2, as previously reported, stood at $395.3 million. Net income for 20X3 was $111.9 million, and dividends totaled $39.8 million.

Required

Prepare the company's statement of retained earnings for the year ended December 31, 20X3.

Preparing a combined statement
of income and retained earnings
(Obj. 5, 6)

E14-12 The Parisian Hotel Company, a large hotel chain, had retained earnings of $413 million at the beginning of 20X7. The company showed these figures at December 31, 20X7:

	($ Millions)
Net income	$141
Cash dividends—preferred	2
common	85
Decrease in retained earnings due to retirement of preferred stock	11

Required

Beginning with net income, prepare a combined statement of income and retained earnings for The Parisian Hotel Company for 20X7.

E14-13 During 20X3, The Belleville Group earned income from continuing operations of $95,000. The company also sold its land development segment (discontinued operations) at a loss of $30,000 and had an extraordinary gain of $8,000 on an insurance settlement. Late in the year, Belleville sold treasury stock for $9,000 that the company had purchased for $4,000 two years earlier. At year end, Belleville had a foreign-currency translation adjustment (a loss) of $3,000.

1. Compute Belleville's net income and comprehensive income for 20X3. All amounts are net of income taxes.
2. What would be the final earnings-per-share figure that Belleville would report for 20X3? During the year, Belleville had 20,000 shares of common stock (and no preferred stock) outstanding.

E14-14 At December 31, 20X1, NEWSTATE Corp. reported the following stockholders' equity on page 567.

During 20X2, NEWSTATE completed these transactions and events (listed in chronological order):

Common stock, $5 par, 200,000 shares authorized, 120,000 shares issued..	$ 600,000
Additional paid-in capital	1,100,000
Retained earnings	1,700,000
Treasury stock, 2,500 shares at cost.................................	(78,000)
	$3,322,000

a. Declared and issued a 50% stock dividend. At the time, NEWSTATE's stock was quoted at a market price of $31 per share.
b. Sold 1,000 shares of treasury stock for $36 per share (cost of these shares was $31 per share).
c. Issued 500 shares of common stock to employees at $28 per share.
d. Net income for the year was $275,000.
e. Declared and paid cash dividends of $180,000.

Required

Prepare NEWSTATE's statement of stockholders' equity for 20X2.

Challenge Exercise

E14-15 Omni Communications, Inc., began 20X5 with 3 million shares of $1 par common stock issued and outstanding. Beginning paid-in capital in excess of par was $6 million, and retained earnings was $7 million. In February 20X5, Omni issued 100,000 shares of stock at $11 per share. In September, when the stock's market price was $12 per share, the board of directors distributed a 10% stock dividend.

Recording a small stock dividend and preparing a statement of stockholders' equity
(Obj. 1, 6)

Required

1. Make the journal entries for the issuance of stock for cash and for the distribution of the 10% stock dividend.
2. Prepare the company's statement of stockholders' equity for the year ended December 31, 20X5.

PROBLEMS

(Group A)

P14-1A Driemann Corp. completed the following transactions during the current year:

Journalizing stockholders' equity transactions
(Obj. 1, 3)

April 18	Declared a cash dividend on the 5%, $100 par preferred stock (1,000 shares outstanding). Declared a $0.20 per share dividend on the 100,000 shares of common stock outstanding. The date of record is May 2, and the payment date is May 23.
May 23	Paid the cash dividends.
June 10	Split common stock 2 for 1 by calling in the 100,000 shares of $10 par common and issuing new stock in its place.
July 30	Distributed a 10% stock dividend on the common stock. The market value of the common stock was $15 per share.
Oct. 26	Purchased 2,500 shares of the company's own common stock at $14 per share.
Nov. 8	Sold 950 shares of treasury common stock for $17 per share.

Required

Record the transactions in Driemann's general journal.

P14-2A The balance sheet of Kugel, Inc., at December 31, 20X6, reported 100,000 shares of no-par common stock authorized, with 30,000 shares issued and a Common Stock balance of $180,000. Retained Earnings had a balance of $141,500. During 20X7, the company completed the following selected transactions:

Journalizing dividend and treasury stock transactions and reporting stockholders' equity
(Obj. 1, 2, 3)

Mar. 15	Purchased 4,000 shares of the company's own common stock for the treasury at $5 per share.
Apr. 30	Distributed a 20% stock dividend on the 26,000 shares of *outstanding* common stock. The market value of Kugel common stock was $10 per share.
Oct. 8	Sold 2,800 shares of treasury common stock for $12 per share.
Dec. 19	Split the no-par common stock 2 for 1 by issuing two new no-par shares for each old no-par share previously issued. Prior to the split, the corporation had issued 35,200 shares. Stock splits affect all authorized and issued stock, including treasury stock as well as stock that is outstanding.
31	Earned net income of $117,000 during the year. Closed net income to Retained Earnings.

1. Record the transactions in the general journal. Explanations are not required.
2. Prepare the stockholders' equity section of Kugel's balance sheet at December 31, 20X7.

Increasing dividends to fight off a takeover of the corporation
(Obj. 1)

P14-3A Ecker Enterprises is ideally positioned in the clothing business. Located in Lansing, Michigan, Ecker is the only company with a distribution network for its imported goods. The company does a brisk business with specialty stores such as **Neiman Marcus, Saks Fifth Avenue,** and **Nordstrom.** Ecker's recent success has made the company a prime target for a takeover. Against the wishes of Ecker's board of directors, an investment group from Detroit is attempting to buy 51% of Ecker's outstanding stock. Board members are convinced that the Detroit investors would sell off the most desirable pieces of the business and leave little of value.

At the most recent board meeting, several suggestions were advanced to fight off the hostile takeover bid. One suggestion is to increase the stock outstanding by distributing a 100% stock dividend.

Required

As a significant stockholder of Ecker Corporation, write a short memo to explain to the board whether distributing the stock dividend would make it more difficult for the investor group to take over Ecker Corporation. Include in your memo a discussion of the effect that the stock dividend would have on assets, liabilities, and total stockholders' equity—that is, the dividend's effect on the size of the corporation.

Journalizing dividend and treasury stock transactions; reporting retained earnings and stockholders' equity
(Obj. 1, 3)

P14-4A The balance sheet of Beech Bros. Design Co. at December 31, 20X6, reported the following stockholders' equity:

Paid-in capital:	
Common stock, $10 par, 100,000 shares authorized,	
20,000 shares issued	$200,000
Paid-in capital in excess of par-common	300,000
Total paid-in capital	500,000
Retained earnings	177,000
Total stockholders' equity	$677,000

During 20X7, Beech Bros. completed the following selected transactions:

Feb. 6   Distributed a 10% stock dividend on the common stock. The market value of Beech Bros.' common stock was $24 per share.

July 29   Purchased 2,000 shares of the company's own common stock at $21 per share.

Nov. 13   Sold 400 shares of treasury common stock for $22 per share.

     27   Declared a $0.30 per share dividend on the common stock outstanding. The date of record is December 17, and the payment date is January 7, 20X8.

Dec. 31   Closed the $62,000 net income to Retained Earnings.

Required

1. Record the transactions in the general journal.
2. Prepare a retained earnings statement at December 31, 20X7.
3. Prepare the stockholders' equity section of the balance sheet at December 31, 20X7.

Preparing a detailed income statement (Obj. 5)

P14-5A The following information was taken from the records of Beaulac Excursions, Inc., at September 30, 20X1.

Interest expense	$ 11,000	General expenses	$113,000
Cost of goods sold	424,000	Preferred stock, $2, no-par,	
Cumulative effect of change in		10,000 shares authorized,	
depreciation method (expense)	(3,000)	5,000 shares issued	200,000
Loss on sale of plant assets	20,000	Retained earnings, beginning	88,000
Income from discontinued		Selling expenses	121,000
operations	8,000	Common stock, $10 par, 25,000	
Income tax expense (tax saving):		shares authorized and issued	250,000
Continuing operations	72,000	Net sales revenue	833,000
Income from discontinued		Treasury stock, common	
operations	2,000	(1,000 shares)	11,000
Extraordinary loss (tax saving)	(12,000)	Interest revenue	4,000
Cumulative effect of change in		Extraordinary loss	30,000
depreciation method (tax saving)	(1,000)		

Required

Prepare a single-step income statement, including earnings per share, for Beaulac Excursions, Inc., for the fiscal year ended September 30, 20X1. Evaluate income for the year ended September 30, 20X1, in terms of the outlook for 20X2. Assume that 20X1 was a typical year and that Beaulac managers hoped to earn income from continuing operations equal to 10% of net sales. The number of shares of common stock outstanding was unchanged during fiscal year 20X1.

P14-6A Luke Capps, accountant for Mabry Furniture Company, was injured in a boating accident. Another employee prepared the accompanying income statement for the year ended December 31, 20X3.

Preparing a corrected combined statement of income and retained earnings
(Obj. 5)

The individual *amounts* listed on the income statement are correct. However, some accounts are reported incorrectly, and others do not belong on the income statement at all. Also, income tax has not been applied to all appropriate figures. The income tax rate on discontinued operations and on the extraordinary loss, was 40%. Mabry Furniture Company issued 52,000 shares of common stock in 20X1 and held 2,000 shares as treasury stock during 20X3. Retained earnings, as originally reported at December 31, 20X2, was $361,000.

MABRY FURNITURE COMPANY Income Statement Year Ended December 31, 20X3		
Revenue and gains:		
Sales		$362,000
Gain on retirement of preferred stock		
(issued for $81,000; purchased for $71,000)		10,000
Paid-in capital in excess of par—common		80,000
Total revenues and gains		452,000
Expenses and losses:		
Cost of goods sold	$105,000	
Selling expenses	67,000	
General expenses	61,000	
Sales returns	11,000	
Dividends	7,000	
Sales discounts	6,000	
Income tax expense	20,000	
Total expenses and losses		277,000
Income from operations		175,000
Other gains and losses:		
Loss on discontinued operations	$ (3,000)	
Extraordinary flood loss	(20,000)	
Prior-period adjustment—understated		
income tax for 20X2	(14,000)	
Total other losses		(37,000)
Net income		$138,000
Earnings per share		$2.76

Required

Prepare a corrected combined statement of income and retained earnings for 20X3; include earnings per share. Prepare the income statement in single-step format.

P14-7A The capital structure of Midori Flooring, Inc., at December 31, 20X6, included 20,000 shares of $1.25 preferred stock and 44,000 shares of common stock. Common shares outstanding during 20X7 were 44,000 January through May, 50,000 June through August, and 60,500 September through December. Income from continuing operations during 20X7 was $94,100. The company discontinued a segment of the business at a gain of $6,630, and also had an extraordinary gain of $33,660. Midori's board of directors restricts $100,000 of retained earnings for contingencies.

Computing earnings per share and reporting a retained earnings restriction
(Obj. 4, 5)

Required

1. Compute Midori's earnings per share. Start with income from continuing operations. Income and loss amounts are net of income tax.
2. Show two ways of reporting Midori's retained earnings restriction. Retained earnings at December 31, 20X6, was $107,000, and Midori declared cash dividends of $29,000 during 20X7.

P14-8A Boulder Technology, Inc., reported the following statement of stockholders' equity for the year ended October 31, 20X4:

(Dollar Amounts in Millions)	Common Stock	Additional Paid-in Capital	Retained Earnings	Treasury Stock	Total
BOULDER TECHNOLOGY, INC. **Statement of Stockholders' Equity** Year Ended October 31, 20X4					
Balance, Nov. 1, 20X3	$427	$1,622	$904	$(117)	$2,836
Net income			336		336
Cash dividends			(194)		(194)
Issuance of stock (61,500,000 shares)..............	123	260			383
Stock dividend..	22	48	(70)		–0–
Sale of treasury stock		9		19	28
Balance, Oct. 31, 20X4.......................................	$572	$1,939	$976	$ (98)	$3,389

Using a statement of stockholders' equity
(Obj. 6)

Required

Answer these questions about Boulder Technology's stockholders' equity transactions.

1. What is the par value of the company's common stock?
2. At what price per share did Boulder Technology issue its common stock during the year?
3. What was the cost of treasury stock sold during the year? What was the selling price of the treasury stock sold? What was the increase in total stockholders' equity?
4. Boulder Technology's statement lists the stock transactions in the order they occurred. What was the percentage of the stock dividend? Round to the nearest percentage.

(Group B) PROBLEMS

Journalizing stockholders' equity transactions
(Obj. 1, 3)

P14-1B Taylor Tennis, Inc., completed the following selected transactions during 20X6:

Feb. 6   Declared a cash dividend on the 10,000 shares of $2.25, no-par preferred stock. Declared a $0.20 per share dividend on the 10,000 shares of common stock outstanding. The date of record is February 17, and the payment date is February 20.

Feb. 20   Paid the cash dividends.

Mar. 21   Split common stock 3 for 1 by calling in the 10,000 shares of $15 par common and issuing new stock in its place.

Apr. 18   Distributed a 50% stock dividend on the common stock. The market value of the common stock was $27 per share.

June 18   Purchased 2,400 shares of the company's own common stock at $12 per share.

Dec. 22   Sold 700 shares of treasury common stock for $16 per share.

Required

Record the transactions in the general journal.

Journalizing dividend and treasury stock transactions and reporting stockholders' equity
(Obj. 1, 2, 3)

P14-2B The balance sheet of Jade, Inc., at December 31, 20X1, reported 500,000 shares of $1 par common stock authorized with 100,000 shares issued. Paid-in Capital in Excess of Par—Common had a balance of $300,000. Retained Earnings had a balance of $57,000. During 20X2, the company completed the following selected transactions:

Feb. 15   Purchased 5,000 shares of the company's own common stock for the treasury at $4 per share.

Mar. 8   Sold 2,000 shares of treasury common stock for $7 per share.

Sep. 28   Distributed a 10% stock dividend on the *outstanding* common stock. The market value of Jade's common stock was $5 per share.

Nov. 5   Split the common stock 2 for 1 by calling in the 109,700 shares of old $1 par common stock and issuing twice as many shares of $0.50 par common. (Stock splits affect all authorized and issued stock, including treasury stock and stock that is outstanding.)

Dec. 31   Earned net income of $73,000 during the year. Closed net income to Retained Earnings.

Required

1. Record the transactions in the general journal. Explanations are not required.
2. Prepare the stockholders' equity section of the balance sheet at December 31, 20X2.

P14-3B Stouse Import Corporation is positioned ideally in its business. Located in Tucson, Arizona, Stouse is the only company between Texas and California with reliable sources for its imported gifts. The company does a brisk business with specialty stores such as **Pier 1 Imports.** Stouse's recent success has made the company a prime target for a takeover. An investment group from Hong Kong is attempting to buy 51% of Stouse's outstanding stock against the wishes of Stouse's board of directors. Board members are convinced that the Hong Kong investors would sell the most desirable pieces of the business and leave little of value.

At the most recent board meeting, several suggestions were advanced to fight off the hostile takeover bid. The suggestion with the most promise is to purchase a huge quantity of treasury stock. Stouse has the cash to carry out this plan.

Purchasing treasury stock to fight off a takeover of the corporation (Obj. 3)

Required

1. As a significant stockholder of Stouse Corporation, write a memorandum to explain to the board how the purchase of treasury stock would make it difficult for the Hong Kong group to take over Stouse. Include a discussion of the effect that purchasing treasury stock would have on stock outstanding and on the size of the corporation.
2. Suppose Stouse management is successful in fighting off the takeover bid and later sells the treasury stock at prices greater than the purchase price. Explain what effect these sales will have on assets, stockholders' equity, and net income.

P14-4B The balance sheet of Bradley Laser Corporation at December 31, 20X3, presented the following stockholders' equity:

Journalizing dividend and treasury stock transactions; reporting retained earnings and stockholders' equity (Obj. 1, 3)

Paid-in capital:	
Common stock, $1 par, 250,000 shares authorized,	
50,000 shares issued	$ 50,000
Paid-in capital in excess of par—common	350,000
Total paid-in capital	400,000
Retained earnings	99,000
Total stockholders' equity	$499,000

During 20X4, Bradley completed the following selected transactions:

Mar. 29	Distributed a 50% stock dividend on the common stock. The market value of Bradley common stock was $5 per share.
July 13	Purchased 2,000 shares of the company's own common stock at $6 per share.
Oct. 4	Sold 1,600 shares of treasury common stock for $8 per share.
Dec. 27	Declared a $0.20 per share dividend on the common stock outstanding. The date of record is January 17, 20X5, and the payment date is January 31.
31	Closed the $71,000 net income to Retained Earnings.

Required

1. Record the transactions in the general journal.
2. Prepare the retained earnings statement at December 31, 20X4.
3. Prepare the stockholders' equity section of the balance sheet at December 31, 20X4.

P14-5B The following information was taken from the records of Escobedo Corporation at June 30, 20X5:

Preparing a detailed income statement (Obj. 5)

Common stock, no-par, 22,000		Selling expenses	$ 87,000
shares authorized and issued	$350,000	General expenses	71,000
Preferred stock, 6%, $25 par,		Income from discontinued operations	1,000
20,000 shares authorized,		Cost of goods sold	279,000
4,000 shares issued	100,000	Interest expense	23,000
Cumulative effect of change in		Dividend revenue	19,000
depreciation method (income)	7,000	Treasury stock, common (2,000 shares)	28,000
Income tax expense (tax saving):		Extraordinary loss	27,000
Continuing operations	28,000	Loss on sale of plant assets	10,000
Gain on discontinued operations	400	Net sales revenue	567,000
Extraordinary loss (tax saving)	(10,800)	Retained earnings, beginning	63,000
Cumulative effect of change in			
depreciation method	3,000		

Prepare a single-step income statement, including earnings per share, for Escobedo Corporation for the fiscal year ended June 30, 20X5. Evaluate income for the year ended June 30, 20X5, in terms of the outlook for 20X6. Note that 20X5 was a typical year, and Escobedo managers hoped to earn income from continuing operations equal to 10% of net sales.

Preparing a corrected combined statement of income and retained earnings
(Obj. 5)

P14-6B Felicia Barrow, accountant for Lackland Aviation, Inc., was injured in a bicycle accident. Another employee prepared the following income statement for the fiscal year ended June 30, 20X4:

LACKLAND AVIATION
Income Statement
June 30, 20X4

Revenues and gains:		
Sales		$733,000
Gain on retirement of preferred stock (issued for		
$70,000; purchased for $59,000)		11,000
Paid-in capital in excess of par—common		100,000
Total revenues and gains		844,000
Expenses and losses:		
Cost of goods sold	$383,000	
Selling expenses	103,000	
General expenses	91,000	
Sales returns	22,000	
Prior-period adjustment—understated		
income tax for fiscal year 20X3	4,000	
Dividends	15,000	
Sales discounts	10,000	
Income tax expense—continuing operations	32,000	
Total expenses and losses		660,000
Income from operations		184,000
Other gains and losses:		
Extraordinary gain	$ 30,000	
Loss on discontinued operations	(15,000)	
Total other gains		15,000
Net income		$199,000
Earnings per share		$9.95

The individual *amounts* listed on the income statement are correct. However, some accounts are reported incorrectly, and others do not belong on the income statement at all. Also, income tax has not been applied to all appropriate figures. The income tax rate on discontinued operations and on the extraordinary gain, is 40%. Lackland issued 24,000 shares of common stock in 20X1 and held 4,000 shares as treasury stock during the fiscal year 20X4. The retained earnings balance, as originally reported at June 30, 20X3, was $209,000.

Required

Prepare a corrected combined statement of income and retained earnings for fiscal year 20X4; include earnings per share. Prepare the income statement in single-step format.

Computing earnings per share and reporting a retained earnings restriction
(Obj. 4, 5)

P14-7B The capital structure of The Martin Rehabilitation Group at December 31, 20X2, included 5,000 shares of $2.50 preferred stock and 130,000 shares of common stock. Common shares outstanding during 20X3 were 130,000 January through February; 119,000 during March; 121,000 April through October; and 128,000 during November and December. Income from continuing operations during 20X3 was $353,360. The company discontinued a segment of the business at a gain of $69,160, and also had an extraordinary loss of $49,510. The board of directors of The Martin Rehabilitation Group has restricted $300,000 of retained earnings for expansion of the company's office facilities.

Required

1. Compute Martin's earnings per share for 20X3. Start with income from continuing operations. Income and loss amounts are net of income tax.
2. Show two ways of reporting Martin's retained earnings restriction. Retained earnings at December 31, 20X2, was $127,800, and Martin declared cash dividends of $109,000 during 20X3.

P14-8B Pacer Communications, Inc., reported the following statement of stockholders' equity for the year ended September 30, 20X1:

PACER COMMUNICATIONS, INC.
Statement of Stockholders' Equity
Year Ended September 30, 20X1

(Dollar Amounts in Millions)	Common Stock	Additional Paid-in Capital	Retained Earnings	Treasury Stock	Total
Balance, October 1, 20X0	$173	$2,118	$1,706	$(18)	$3,979
Net income...			520		520
Cash dividends..			(117)		(117)
Issuance of stock (5,000,000 shares)	9	46			55
Stock dividend	18	92	(110)		–0–
Sale of treasury stock..................................		5		11	16
Balance, September 30, 20X1	$200	$2,261	$1,999	$ (7)	$4,453

Required

Using a statement of stockholders' equity
(Obj. 6)

1. What is the par value of Pacer's common stock?
2. At what price per share did Pacer issue its common stock during the year?
3. What was the cost of treasury stock sold during the year? What was the selling price of the treasury stock sold? What was the increase in total stockholders' equity from selling the treasury stock?
4. Pacer's statement of stockholders' equity lists the stock transactions in the order in which they occurred. What was the percentage of the stock dividend? Round to the nearest percentage.

APPLY YOUR KNOWLEDGE

DECISION CASES

Case 1. Ganache Industries had the following stockholders' equity amounts on June 30, 20X2:

Analyzing cash dividends and stock dividends
(Obj. 1)

Common stock, no-par, 100,000 shares issued	$ 750,000
Retained earnings...	790,000
Total stockholders' equity..	$1,540,000

In the past, Ganache has paid an annual cash dividend of $1.50 per share. Despite the large retained earnings balance, the board of directors wished to conserve cash for expansion. The board delayed the payment of cash dividends and in July distributed a 10% stock dividend. During August, the company's cash position improved. The board declared and paid a cash dividend of $1.364 per share in September.

Suppose you owned 10,000 shares of Ganache common stock, acquired three years ago, prior to the 10% stock dividend. The market price of the stock was $30 per share before any of these dividends.

Required

1. What amount of cash dividends did you receive last year—before the stock dividend? What amount of cash dividends will you receive after the dividend action?
2. How does the stock dividend affect your proportionate ownership in Ganache Industries? Explain.
3. Immediately after the stock dividend was distributed, the market value of Ganache stock decreased from $30 per share to $27.273 per share. Does this decrease represent a loss to you? Explain.

Case 2. The following accounting issues have arisen at Cooltouch Cotton, Inc.:

Reporting special items
(Obj. 3, 5)

1. Corporations sometimes purchase their own stock. When asked why they do so, Cooltouch management responds that the stock is undervalued. What advantage would Cooltouch gain by buying and selling its own undervalued stock?
2. The treasurer of Cooltouch wants to report a large loss as an extraordinary item because Cooltouch produced too much product and cannot sell it. Why do you think the treasurer wants to report the loss as extraordinary? Would that be acceptable?

3. Cooltouch earned a significant profit in the year ended November 30, 20X2, because land that it held was purchased by the State of North Carolina for a new highway. The company proposes to treat the sale of land as operating revenue. Why do you think Cooltouch is proposing this plan? Is this disclosure appropriate?

ETHICAL ISSUE

◄ *Link Back to Chapter 9 (Accounting Principles).* Gladewater Petroleum Company is an independent oil producer in Gladewater, Texas. In February, company geologists discovered a pool of oil that tripled the company's proven reserves. Prior to disclosing the new oil to the public, top managers of the company quietly bought most of Gladewater's stock as treasury stock. After the discovery was announced, Gladewater's stock price rose from $7 to $52.

Required

1. Did Gladewater managers behave ethically? Explain your answer.
2. Identify the accounting principle relevant to this situation. Review Chapter 9 if necessary.
3. Who was helped and who was harmed by management's action?

FINANCIAL STATEMENT CASE

Complex income statement, earnings per share, and dividends (Obj. 1, 5)

Use the **Target Corporation** financial statements in Appendix A to answer the following questions.

Required

1. Study Target's income statement, which the company labels "consolidated results of operations." *Consolidated* means that Target owns other companies. Target reported one "special" item of income on its income statement. What was it, and what was its amount for 1999? Was this special item a gain or a loss? How can you tell?
2. Target's preferred dividends during 1999 were $19 million. Show how Target computed Basic earnings per share of $2.55.
3. The statement of stockholders' equity, which Target labels "consolidated statement of shareholders' investment," gives details of transactions that affected stockholders' equity. Use Target's statement of shareholders' investment to answer these questions:
   a. Journalize Target's closing entry for net income of 1999.
   b. Journalize Target's declaration of dividends during 1999.
   c. How much did Target pay to repurchase its stock during 1999?
   d. During 1999, Target issued common stock to its Employee Stock Option Plan (ESOP). Assume Target received cash for the stock it issued. How much cash did Target receive?

TEAM PROJECT

Required

Obtain the annual reports (or annual report data) of five well-known companies. You can get the reports either from your college library or by mailing a request directly to the company (allow two weeks for delivery). Or you can visit the Web site for this book (http://www.prenhall.com/harrison/) or the SEC EDGAR database, which includes the financial reports of most well-known companies.

1. After selecting five companies, examine their income statements to search for the following items:
   a. Income from continuing operations
   b. Discontinued operations
   c. Extraordinary gains and losses
   d. Cumulative effects of accounting changes
   e. Net income or net loss
   f. Earnings-per-share data
2. Study the companies' balance sheets to see
   a. What classes of stock each company has issued.
   b. Which item carries a larger balance—the Common Stock account, or Paid-in Capital in Excess of Par (also labeled Additional Paid-in Capital)?
   c. What percentage of each company's total stockholders' equity is made up of retained earnings?
   d. Whether the company has treasury stock. If so, how many shares and how much is the cost?
3. Examine each company's statement of stockholders' equity for evidence of
   a. Cash dividends
   b. Stock dividends (Some companies use the term *stock split* to refer to a large stock dividend.)
   c. Treasury stock purchases and sales

4. As directed by your instructor, either write a report or present your findings to your class. You may be unable to understand *everything* you find, but neither can the Wall Street analysts! You will be amazed at how much you have learned.

INTERNET EXERCISE

In 1993, **International Business Machines (IBM)** reported a record loss of $8,101,000,000 and also stopped paying cash dividends. Today IBM is thriving as the largest provider of computer hardware in the world. It produces PCs, notebooks, mainframes, servers, and peripherals, along with software, where it is second only to **Microsoft.**

1. Go to **http://www.ibm.com** and in the left-hand column, click on *Investors*. What is the current market price of IBM stock?
2. In the left-hand column, click on *Financials* and then *Stock split information*. Describe the most recent stock split and note the date of the payment (distribution) of the split shares. What effect would this stock split have on the par value per share? on total stockholders' equity?
3. In the left-hand column, click on *Annual reports* and select the *most recent annual report*. Click on *Financial Report,* and then under "Consolidated Financial Statements (Audited)," click on *Earnings*. Does IBM report any special items on the income statement? If so, what are they and what are their amounts? For the most recent year, show how IBM computed basic earnings per share of common stock.
4. At the bottom of the screen, click on *next page* to display the "Consolidated Statement of Financial Position."
   a. How many types of stock has IBM issued? List them. What is the par value per share of the common shares? As of the most recent balance sheet date, how many common shares has IBM issued? How many shares of common stock would receive a cash dividend? (*Note:* Treat the shares in the Employee Benefits Trust the same as Treasury Stock shares. Both of these accounts contain only common shares.)
   b. As of the most recent balance sheet date, how much have shareholders paid in total for the common shares issued? What was the average issue price per common share? How much has IBM paid in total to repurchase treasury stock? What was the average price paid per treasury share? Compare the average issue price, average price paid for treasury stock, and the current market price. What conclusions can you draw about when IBM purchased the treasury stock?

IBM

Go to the "Dividends and Treasury Stock" episode on the *Mastering Accounting* CD-ROM for an interactive, video-enhanced exercise on how CanGo can boost investor confidence after poor quarterly performance reports. The episode focuses on the difference between cash and stock dividends.

15

Long-Term Liabilities

LEARNING OBJECTIVES

After studying this chapter, you should be able to

1. Account for basic bonds payable transactions by the straight-line amortization method

2. Measure interest expense by the effective-interest method

3. Account for retirement of bonds payable

4. Account for conversion of bonds payable

5. Show the advantages and disadvantages of borrowing

6. Account for lease liabilities and pension liabilities

www.prenhall.com/horngren

Readiness Assessment

What's the best way to finance an Internet startup—issue stock or borrow the money? When the stock market declines, companies find it hard to sell their stock. That may be why **International Rectifier** of El Segundo, California, and Houston-based **Quanta Services, Inc.,** looked to the bond market for cash to expand. Both are high-tech support companies: International Rectifier provides enabling technology for power management; Quanta specializes in transmission infrastructure for telecommunications and electric power.

Even **Amazon.com** resorted to borrowing by issuing convertible notes payable. Convertible bonds offer advantages for companies that need to borrow and for individuals with money to invest. By issuing convertibles, companies can borrow at lower interest rates than if they issued straight bonds. Then, if the company's stock goes up, investors can swap the bonds for stock. Convertibility gives companies a low interest rate and investors the opportunity to benefit from a strong stock market.

Accessing bond information has never been easier. Investors can log onto www.convertbond.com for data on 800 convertible bond issues plus chat rooms and search functions. Or they can go to www.investinginbonds.com for the definitions of bond terms and to explore topics such as What Are Bonds? All these newly available data may make it easier for companies to borrow.

Sources: *Forbes,* May 22, 2000, "Best of the Web," p. 86; Jennifer Ablan, "Volume of convertible bond offerings continues to rise with big deals by technology concerns," *Wall Street Journal,* July 13, 2000, p. C25.

Chapters 13 and 14 covered two ways to finance operations: contributed capital (the stock accounts and additional paid-in capital) and profitable operations (retained earnings). This chapter discusses the third way to finance a company—borrowing money on long-term liabilities. The chapter appendix provides background on the valuation of long-term liabilities.

Before launching into accounting for bonds payable, let's compare stocks and bonds.

STOCKS

1. Stock represents the *ownership* (equity) of the corporation.
2. Each shareholder is an *owner* of the corporation.
3. The corporation *may or may not* pay dividends.
4. Dividends are *not* an expense of the corporation.
5. Corporation is *not* obligated to repay stock amounts to the shareholders.

BONDS

1. Bonds represent a *liability* of the corporation.
2. Each bondholder is a *creditor* of the corporation.
3. The corporation *must* pay interest.
4. Interest is a *tax-deductible* expense of the corporation.
5. Corporation *must* repay the bonds payable at maturity.

BONDS: AN INTRODUCTION

Well-known companies such as **Amazon.com, Inc.,** and **eBay** cannot borrow billions from a single lender because no lender will risk that much money on a single company. Even smaller companies such as **Quanta Services** may find it impossible to borrow all they need from a bank. Banks and other lenders diversify their risk by making loans to numerous customers. That way if a borrower cannot repay, the bank is not devastated.

How then do corporations borrow the huge amounts they need to expand? They issue bonds payable to the public. **Bonds payable** are groups of notes payable issued to multiple lenders, called bondholders. Amazon can borrow large amounts from thousands of individual investors, each of whom buys a modest amount of Amazon bonds.

Purchasers of the bonds receive a bond certificate, which carries the issuing company's name. The certificate states the *principal,* which is the amount the

BONDS PAYABLE. Groups of notes payable (bonds) issued to multiple lenders called bondholders.

company has borrowed from the bondholder. This figure, typically stated in units of $1,000, is also called the bond's face value, maturity value, or par value. The bond obligates the issuing company to pay the holder the principal amount at a specific future date, called the maturity date, which appears on the certificate.

Bondholders lend their money to earn interest. The bond certificate states the interest rate the issuer will pay the bondholder and the dates the interest payments are due (generally twice a year). Some bond certificates name the bondholder (the investor). Exhibit 15-1 shows an actual bond certificate.

EXHIBIT 15-1 **Bond (Note) Certificate**

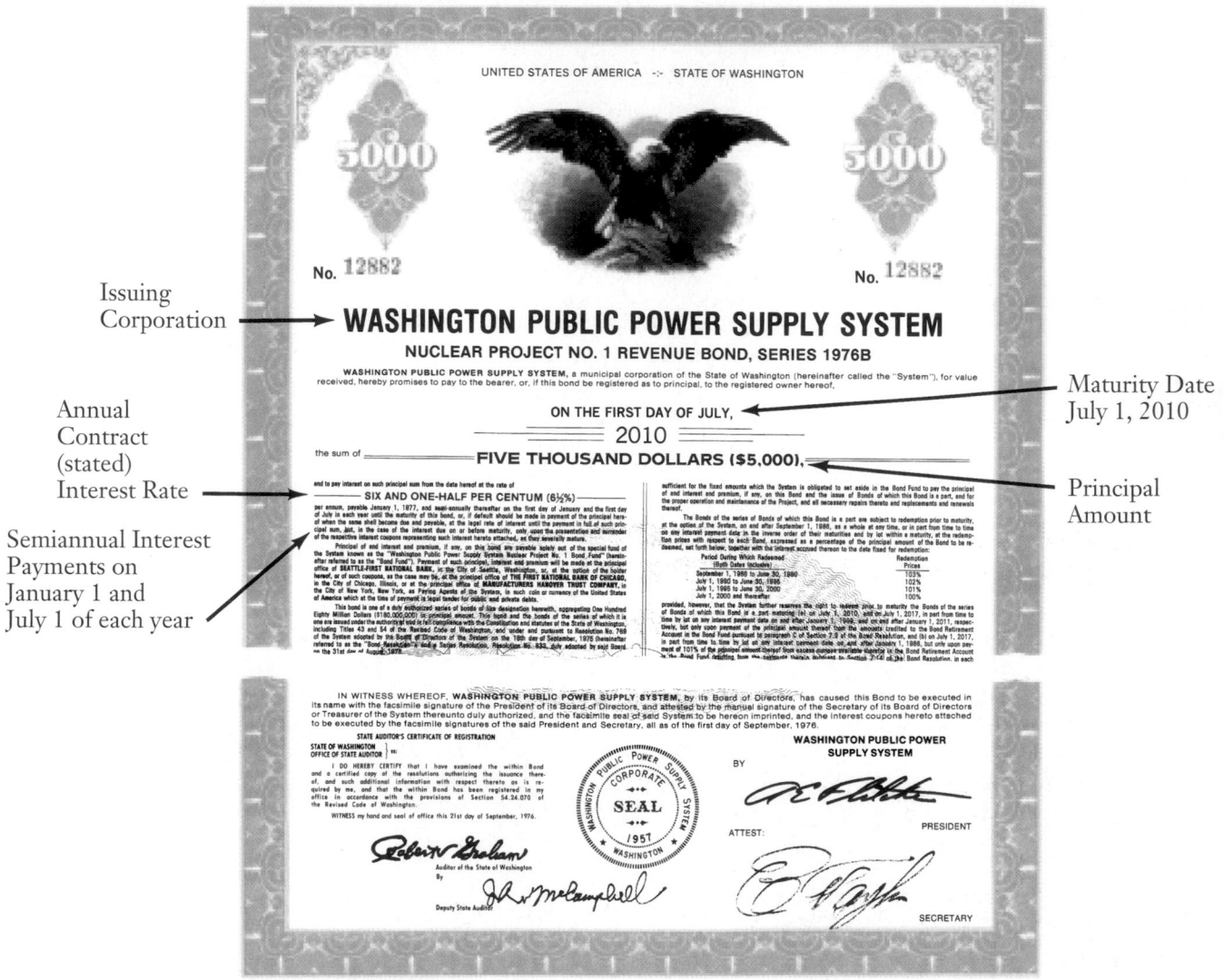

UNDERWRITER. Organization that purchases the bonds from an issuing company and resells them to its clients or sells the bonds for a commission, agreeing to buy all unsold bonds.

TERM BONDS. Bonds that all mature at the same time for a particular issue.

Issuing bonds usually requires the services of a securities firm, such as **Merrill Lynch,** to act as the *underwriter* of the bond issue. The **underwriter** purchases the bonds from the issuing company and resells them to its clients. Alternatively, the underwriter may sell the bonds for a commission, and agree to buy all unsold bonds.

Types of Bonds

All the bonds in a particular issue may mature at a specified time **(term bonds),** or they may mature in installments over a period of time **(serial bonds).** Serial bonds are like installment notes payable.

Secured, or mortgage, bonds give the bondholder the right to take specified assets of the issuer (called collateral) if the company defaults—that is, fails to pay interest or principal. Unsecured bonds, called **debentures,** are backed only by the good faith of the borrower.

Bond Prices

A bond issued at a price above its maturity (par) value is said to be issued at a **premium,** and a bond issued at a price below maturity (par) value has a **discount.** As a bond nears maturity, its market price moves toward par value. On the maturity date, the market value of a bond exactly equals its par value because the company that issued the bond pays that amount to retire the bond.

After a bond is issued, investors may buy and sell it through the bond market just as they buy and sell stocks through the stock market. The most famous bond market is the **New York Exchange,** which lists several thousand bonds. Bond prices are quoted at a percentage of their maturity value. For example, a $1,000 bond quoted at 100 is bought or sold for $1,000, which is 100% of its par value. The same bond quoted at 101 1/2 has a market price of $1,015 (101.5% of par value, or $1,000 × 1.015). Prices are quoted to one-eighth of 1%. A $1,000 bond quoted at 88 3/8 is priced at $883.75 ($1,000 × 0.88375).

Exhibit 15-2 contains price information for the bonds of **Ohio Edison Company,** taken from *The Wall Street Journal.* On this particular day, 12 of Ohio Edison's 9 1/2%, $1,000 par-value bonds maturing in the year 2006 (indicated by 06) were traded. The bonds' highest price on this day was $795 ($1,000 × 0.795). The lowest price of the day was $785 ($1,000 × 0.785). The closing price (last sale of the day) was $795. This price was 2% higher than the closing price of the preceding day. What was the bonds' closing price the preceding day? It was 77 1/2 (79 1/2 − 2).

Bonds	Volume	High	Low	Close	Net Change
OhEd 9 1/2 06	12	79 1/2	78 1/2	79 1/2	+2

EXHIBIT 15-2
Bond Price Information for Ohio Edison Company (OhEd)

Present Value[1]

A dollar received today (present value) is worth more than a dollar received in the future (future value). Why? Because you can invest today's dollar and earn income from it. Money earns income over time, a fact called the *time value of money.* Let's examine how the time value of money affects the pricing of bonds.

Assume that a bond with a face value of $1,000 reaches maturity three years from today and carries no interest. As an investor, would you pay $1,000 to purchase the bond? No, because the payment of $1,000 today to receive the same amount in the future provides you with no income on the investment. How much would you pay today in order to receive $1,000 at the end of three years? The answer is some amount *less* than $1,000. Let's suppose that $750 is a fair price. By investing $750 now to receive $1,000 later, you will earn $250 interest revenue over the three years. The issuing company sees the transaction this way: It pays you $250 interest for the use of your $750 for three years.

The amount that a person would invest *at the present time* to receive a greater amount at a future date is called the **present value.** In our example, $750 is the present value, and the $1,000 to be received three years later is the future amount.

The difference between present value and future value is interest. Present value is always less than future value. We discuss the method of computing present value in the appendix that follows this chapter. Keep the present-value concept in mind in the discussion of bond prices that follows. If your instructor so directs you, study the appendix now.

PRESENT VALUE. Amount a person would invest now to receive a greater amount at a future date.

Bond Interest Rates

Bonds are sold at market price, which is the maximum investors will pay at a given time. Market price is the bond's present value, which is the sum of the present value of the principal payment plus the present value of the cash interest payments (semi-annual, annual, or quarterly).

---

[1]The chapter appendix covers present value in more detail.

CONTRACT INTEREST RATE.
Interest rate that determines the amount of cash interest the borrower pays and the investor receives each year. Also called the **stated interest rate.**

MARKET INTEREST RATE. Interest rate that investors demand in order to loan their money. Also called the **effective interest rate.**

 DAILY EXERCISE 15-2

Two interest rates work to set the price of a bond:

- The **contract interest rate,** or **stated interest rate,** is the interest rate that determines the amount of cash interest the borrower pays—and the investors receive—each year. The contract interest rate is set by the bond contract and *does not change* during the life of the bonds. For example, Amazon.com's 10% notes payable have a contract interest rate of 10%. Thus, Amazon pays $10,000 of interest annually on each $100,000 bond. Each semiannual interest payment is $5,000 ($100,000 × 0.10 × 1/2).

- The **market interest rate,** or **effective interest rate,** is the rate that investors demand for loaning their money. The market interest rate *varies,* sometimes daily. A company may issue bonds with a contract interest rate that differs from the prevailing market interest rate. Amazon.com may issue its 10% notes when the market rate has risen to 11%. Will the Amazon bonds attract investors in this market? No, because investors can earn 11% on other bonds and notes of similar risk. Therefore, investors will purchase Amazon notes only at a price less than par value. The difference between the lower price and the notes' face value is a *discount.*

Conversely, if the market interest rate is 8%, Amazon's 10% notes will be so attractive that investors will pay more than face value for them. The difference between the higher price and face value is a *premium.* Exhibit 15-3 shows how the contract (stated) interest rate and the market interest rate interact to determine the issuance price of a bond payable.

EXHIBIT 15-3
Interaction of the Contract Interest Rate and the Market Interest Rate to Determine the Price of a Bond Payable

 DAILY EXERCISE 15-3

 DAILY EXERCISE 15-4

(Example: Bond with a Contract Interest Rate of 9%)					
Bond's Contract Interest Rate*		**Market Interest Rate****		**Issuance Price of Bonds Payable**	
9%	=	9%	⟹	Par (face, or maturity) value	
9%	<	11%	⟹	Discount (price below par)	
9%	>	7%	⟹	Premium (price above par)	

* Determines the amount of interest of each cash interest payment.
** Used to set the bond's market price.

ISSUING BONDS PAYABLE TO BORROW MONEY

Suppose **Amazon.com, Inc.,** has $50 million of 9% bonds that mature in five years. Assume that Amazon issues these bonds at par on January 1, 2002. The issuance entry is

```
2002
Jan. 1   Cash.................................................................   50,000,000
              Bonds Payable.............................................                50,000,000
         Issued bonds payable.
```

Amazon, the borrower, makes a one-time entry similar to this to record the receipt of cash and the issuance of bonds. Interest payments occur each January 1 and July 1. Amazon's entry to record the first semiannual interest payment is

```
2002
July 1   Interest Expense ($50,000,000 × 0.09 × 6/12) .....   2,250,000
              Cash ...........................................................                2,250,000
         Paid semiannual interest.
```

At maturity, Amazon.com will record payment of the bonds as follows:

 DAILY EXERCISE 15-5

```
2007
Jan. 1   Bonds Payable ...................................................   50,000,000
              Cash ...........................................................                50,000,000
         Paid off bonds payable at maturity.
```

Issuing Bonds and Notes Payable Between Interest Dates

These entries to record Amazon.com's bond transactions are straightforward because the company issued the bonds on an interest payment date (January 1). However, corporations often issue bonds between interest dates.

Suppose Amazon.com issued these bonds on March 1, 2002, rather than on January 1. The bonds were dated January 1, so interest on the bonds started accruing on January 1. On the first interest date, July 1, 2002, Amazon will pay six months' interest to whoever owns the bonds on that date. The price of this Amazon.com bond would thus be expressed as "100 plus accrued interest."

- *100* means that the price of the bond is 100% of par, or face, value, that is, $50 million. Amazon will receive $50 million from issuance of the bonds, plus
- *Accrued interest* means that to buy an Amazon.com bond, investors must also pay accrued interest from the last interest date (January 1) up to the date of issuance (March 1). Amazon will thus receive two months of accrued interest when it issues the bonds.

As we saw earlier, issuing the bonds when they were dated—on January 1, 2002—brings Amazon exactly $50 million of cash. But issuing the bonds on March 1 brings in $50 million plus accrued interest. Amazon.com's issuance entry on March 1 is

2002			
Mar. 1	Cash	50,750,000	
	Bonds Payable		50,000,000
	Interest Payable		
	($50,000,000 × 0.09 × 2/12)		750,000
	Issued bonds at par, two months after the date		
	of the bonds.		

Amazon.com has collected two months of interest in advance. Then, on July 1, Amazon pays semiannual interest and makes this entry:

2002			
July 1	Interest Expense ($50,000,000 × 0.09 × 4/12)....	1,500,000	
	Interest Payable ($50,000,000 × 0.09 × 2/12,		
	from Mar. 1)	750,000	
	Cash ($50,000,000 × 0.09 × 6/12)		2,250,000
	Paid semiannual interest.		

Amazon's T-accounts for Interest Payable and Interest Expense appear as follows after the July 1 transaction:

INTEREST PAYABLE				INTEREST EXPENSE		
July 1	750,000	Mar. 1	750,000	July 1	1,500,000	

Interest Payable has a zero balance because Amazon paid the interest that it collected in advance on March 1. Interest Expense shows a $1,500,000 balance for Amazon.com's interest expense for the four months that the bonds have been outstanding (March, April, May, and June).

From the forgoing sequence of transactions, what would Amazon.com, Inc., report if it prepared financial statements immediately after July 1?

Answer

Balance sheet: Nothing to report because Interest payable is $0

Income statement: Interest expense $1,500,000

 DAILY EXERCISE 15-6

Borrowers Online: Click Here to Lend Us $6 Billion

Original art, Uncle Lester's gold fillings, and vintage Barbie dolls are being sold on-line. Then why not bonds? Companies in need of cash are stepping into e-commerce and borrowing money on-line.

Y2K fears evaporated on January 1, 2000. A few days later, bonds made their debut in cyberspace. The U.S. government went on-line first: On January 5, its mortgage agency, **Freddie Mac,** kicked off a $6 billion bond issue. **Ford Motor** took the lead among corporate borrowers: Five days later Ford announced a three-year bond issue to borrow $1 billion.

Online bond trading offers some real advantages, such as a wider array of lenders. And online trading lets issuers see their orders filling in real time.

For all these reasons, there has been a frenzy of activity in online borrowing. But borrowers and lenders beware: The ease of selling debt online can be its undoing. Companies just *might* be seduced into borrowing more money than they can pay back.

Source: Based on Chris Wright, "Cutting through the hype of Internet bond issuance," *Corporate Finance,* April 2000, pp. 5–6. Fiona Haddock, "The seduction of on-line debt," *Global Finance,* April 2000, pp. 30–33. Antony Currie, "Bonding on the Internet," *Euromoney,* February 2000, pp. 43–50.

Issuing Bonds Payable at a Discount

Unlike stocks, bonds are often issued at a discount. We know that market conditions may force the issuing corporation to accept a discount price for its bonds. Suppose Amazon.com, Inc., issues $100,000 of its 9%, five-year bonds when the market interest rate is 9 1/2%. The market price of the bonds drops to 98, which means 98% of par value. Amazon receives $98,000 ($100,000 × 0.98) at issuance and makes the following journal entry:

```
2002
Jan. 1   Cash ($100,000 × 0.98)..................   98,000
         Discount on Bonds Payable..............    2,000
              Bonds Payable .......................           100,000
         Issued bonds payable at a discount.
```

After posting, the bond accounts have the following balances:

BONDS PAYABLE		DISCOUNT ON BONDS PAYABLE	
	100,000	2,000	

Amazon's balance sheet reports the following immediately after issuance of the bonds:

Long-term liabilities:		
Bonds payable, 9%, due 2007..................	$100,000	
Less: Discount on bonds payable..............	(2,000)	$98,000

Discount on Bonds Payable is a contra account to Bonds Payable. Subtracting the discount from Bonds Payable yields the carrying amount of the bonds. The relationship between Bonds Payable and the Discount account is similar to the relationship between Equipment and Accumulated Depreciation. Thus, Amazon.com's liability is $98,000, which is the amount the company borrowed. If Amazon were to pay off the bonds immediately, the company would pay only $98,000 because the market price of the bonds is $98,000.

INTEREST EXPENSE ON BONDS PAYABLE ISSUED AT A DISCOUNT   We earlier discussed the difference between the contract interest rate and the market interest rate. Suppose the market rate is 9 1/2% when Amazon.com issues its 9% bonds. The 1/2% interest-rate difference creates the $2,000 discount on the bonds. Investors are willing to pay only $98,000 for a $100,000, 9% bond when they can purchase similar bonds and earn 9 1/2% on the investment. Amazon borrows $98,000 cash but must pay $100,000 cash when the bonds mature five years later.

What happens to the $2,000 balance of the discount account over the life of the bond issue? The $2,000 discount is additional interest expense to Amazon. The $2,000 is a cost—beyond the stated 9% interest—that the business pays for borrowing money. The discount has the effect of raising the interest expense on the bonds to the market interest rate of 9 1/2%. For each accounting period over the life of the bonds, the discount is accounted for as interest expense through a process called amortization.

STRAIGHT-LINE AMORTIZATION OF BOND DISCOUNT   We amortize a bond discount by dividing it into equal amounts for each interest period. This method is called *straight-line amortization*. In our example, the initial discount is $2,000, and there are ten semiannual interest periods during the bonds' five-year life. Therefore, 1/10 of the $2,000 ($200) of bond discount is amortized each interest period. Amazon.com's semiannual interest entry on July 1, 2002 is recorded as follows:[2]

2002			
July 1	Interest Expense...	4,700	
	Cash ($100,000 × 0.09 × 6/12)		4,500
	Discount on Bonds Payable ($2,000/10)		200
	Paid semiannual interest and amortized discount		
	on bonds payable.		

Interest expense of $4,700 for the six-month period is the sum of

- the contract interest ($4,500, which is paid in cash), plus
- the amortization of discount ($200).

Discount on Bonds Payable is credited to amortize (reduce) its debit balance. Because Discount on Bonds Payable is a contra account, each reduction in its balance increases the carrying amount of the bonds payable. Ten amortization entries will decrease the discount balance to zero, and the carrying amount of bonds payable will have increased to the bonds' face value of $100,000. The entry to pay off the bonds at maturity is

2007			
Jan. 1	Bonds Payable..	100,000	
	Cash...		100,000
	Paid off bonds payable at maturity.		

 **DAILY EXERCISE 15-7**

---

[2]Some accountants record the payment of interest and the amortization of the discount in two separate entries, as follows:

2002			
July 1	Interest Expense...	4,500	
	Cash ($100,000 × 0.09 × 6/12)............................		4,500
	Paid semiannual interest.		
July 1	Interest Expense...	200	
	Discount on Bonds Payable ($2,000/10)		200
	Amortized discount on bonds payable.		

Issuing Bonds Payable at a Premium

The issuance of bonds at a premium is rare because to do so companies must commit to a contract interest rate that is higher than the market rate. To illustrate, let's change the Amazon example. Assume that the market interest rate is 8% when the company issues its 9%, five-year bonds. Because 9% bonds are attractive in this market, investors pay a premium price to acquire them. If the bonds are priced at 104 (104% of par value), Amazon receives $104,000 cash upon issuance. The entry is

```
2002
Jan. 1   Cash ($100,000 × 1.04) .............................   104,000
              Bonds Payable .....................................              100,000
              Premium on Bonds Payable ..............              4,000
         Issued bonds payable at a premium.
```

After posting, the bond accounts have the following balances:

BONDS PAYABLE	PREMIUM ON BONDS PAYABLE
100,000	4,000

Amazon.com's balance sheet reports the following immediately after issuance of bonds:

Long-term liabilities:		
Bonds payable, 9%, due 2004	$100,000	
Premium on bonds payable	4,000	$104,000

Premium on Bonds Payable is added to Bonds Payable to show the book value, or carrying amount, of the bonds. Amazon's liability is $104,000, which is the amount that the company borrowed. Immediate payment of the bonds would cost $104,000 because that is the market price of the bonds.

INTEREST EXPENSE ON BONDS PAYABLE ISSUED AT A PREMIUM The 1% difference between the 9% contract interest rate on the bonds and the 8% market rate creates the $4,000 premium. Amazon borrows $104,000 cash but must pay only $100,000 at maturity. The premium is like a savings of interest expense to Amazon. The premium cuts Amazon's cost of borrowing and reduces the company's interest expense to an effective interest rate of 8%, the market rate. We account for the premium much as we handled the discount. But we amortize the bond premium as a decrease in interest expense over the life of the bonds.

STRAIGHT-LINE AMORTIZATION OF BOND PREMIUM In our example, the beginning premium is $4,000, and there are ten semiannual interest periods during the bonds' five-year life. Therefore, 1/10 of the $4,000 ($400) of bond premium is amortized each interest period. Amazon.com's semiannual interest entry on July 1, 2002, is[3]

```
2002
July 1   Interest Expense ...........................................   4,100
         Premium on Bonds Payable ($4,000/10) .....    400
              Cash ($100,000 × 0.09 × 6/12) .........              4,500
         Paid semiannual interest and amortized premium
         on bonds payable.
```

● DAILY EXERCISE 15-8

Interest expense of $4,100 is the contract interest paid ($4,500) less the amount of premium amortized ($400).

---

[3]The payment of interest and the amortization of bond premium can be recorded in separate entries as follows:

```
2002
July 1   Interest Expense ................................................   4,500
              Cash ($100,000 × 0.09 × 6/12) .............................              4,500
         Paid semiannual interest.

July 1   Premium on Bonds Payable ($4,000/10) .........................    400
              Interest Expense ...................................................              400
         Amortized premium on bonds payable.
```

Consider bonds issued at a discount. Which will be greater, the cash interest paid per period or the amount of interest expense? Answer the same question for bonds issued at a premium.

Answer: For bonds issued at a *discount,* interest expense will be greater than cash interest paid, by the amount of the discount amortized each period. Remember that the company received less than face value when it issued the bonds. But at maturity the company must pay the full face value back to the bondholders. This discount increases the company's interest expense above the amount of cash interest paid each period.

For bonds issued at a *premium,* interest expense will be less than the amount of cash interest paid, by the amount of the premium amortized for the period. This is because the premium amount received at issuance decreases the interest expense below the amount of cash interest paid each period.

Reporting Bonds Payable

Bonds payable are reported on the balance sheet at their maturity amount plus any unamortized premium or minus any unamortized discount. For example, in the preceding example at December 31, Amazon.com has amortized Premium on Bonds Payable for two semiannual periods ($400 × 2 = $800). The Amazon balance sheet would show these bonds payable as follows:

Long-term liabilities:		
Bonds payable, 9%, due 2004...	$100,000	
Premium on bonds payable [$4,000 − ($2 × $400)]...........	3,200	$103,200

Over the life of the bonds, ten amortization entries will decrease the premium balance to zero. The payment at maturity will debit Bonds Payable and credit cash for $100,000.

Adjusting Entries for Interest Expense

Companies issue bonds when they need cash. The interest payments seldom occur on December 31 (or the end of the fiscal year). Nevertheless, interest expense must be accrued at the end of the period to measure income accurately. ➥ The accrual entry may often be complicated by the need to amortize a discount or a premium for a partial interest period.

Xenon Corporation issued $100,000 of its 8%, ten-year bonds at a $2,000 discount on October 1, 2002. The interest payments occur on March 31 and September 30 each year. On December 31, Xenon records interest for the three-month period (October, November, and December) as follows:

2002			
Dec. 31	Interest Expense...	2,050	
	Interest Payable ($100,000 × 0.08 × 3/12)......................		2,000
	Discount on Bonds Payable ($2,000/10 × 3/12)..............		50
	Accrued three months' interest and amortized discount on bonds payable.		

Interest Payable is credited for the three months of cash interest that have accrued since September 30. Discount on Bonds Payable is credited for three months of amortization.

Xenon's balance sheet at December 31, 2002, reports Interest Payable of $2,000 as a current liability. Bonds Payable appears as a long-term liability, presented as follows:

Long-term liabilities:		
Bonds payable, 8%, due 2009...	$100,000	
Less: Discount on bonds payable ($2,000 − $50)	(1,950)	$98,050

➥ The adjusting entry for bond interest expense follows the pattern for the adjusting entries for other accrued liabilities, as in Chapters 3 (p. 95) and 11 (p. 447), except for the addition of the amortization of the premium or discount.

Observe that the balance of Discount on Bonds Payable decreases by $50. The bonds' carrying amount therefore increases by $50. The bonds' carrying amount continues to increase over its ten-year life, reaching $100,000 at maturity, when the discount will be fully amortized.

The next semiannual interest payment occurs on March 31, 2003:

DAILY EXERCISE 15-9

DAILY EXERCISE 15-10

2003

Mar. 31	Interest Expense	2,050	
	Interest Payable	2,000	
	Cash ($100,000 × 0.08 × 6/12)		4,000
	Discount on Bonds Payable ($2,000/10 × 3/12)		50
	Paid semiannual interest, part of which was accrued, and amortized three months' discount on bonds payable.		

Amortization of a premium over a partial interest period is similar except that Premium on Bonds Payable is debited.

Take a few moments and review the first half of the chapter by studying the Decision Guidelines feature.

DECISION GUIDELINES

Accounting for Long-Term Liabilities—Part A

DECISION	GUIDELINES
Need to pay back principal amount of bonds • All at maturity? • In installments?	Type of bond to issue: • Term bonds • Serial bonds
Are the bonds secured? • Yes • No	Then they are • Mortgage, or secured, bonds • Debenture, or unsecured, bonds
How are bond prices • Quoted? • Determined?	 • As a percentage of maturity value (Example: A $500,000 bond priced at $510,000 would be quoted at 102 ($510,000 ÷ $500,000 = 1.02.) • Present value of the future principal amount to pay plus present value of the future interest payments (see chapter appendix)
What are the two interest rates used for bonds?	• *Contract (stated) interest rate* determines the amount of cash interest the borrower pays. This interest rate is set by contract and does not change during the life of the bonds. • *Market (effective) interest rate* is the rate that investors demand for loaning their money. The market interest rate determines the borrower's true rate of interest expense. This rate varies, sometimes daily.
What causes a bond to be priced at • Par (face, or maturity) value? • A premium? • A discount?	When the bonds are issued, • Contract interest rate on the bond *equals* the Market interest rate • Contract interest rate on the bond is *greater than* the Market interest rate • Contract interest rate on the bond is *less than* the Market interest rate
What is the relationship between interest expense and interest payments when bonds are issued at • Par (face, or maturity) value? • A premium? • A discount?	 • Interest expense *equals* Interest payment • Interest expense is *less than* Interest payment • Interest expense is *greater than* Interest payment
How to report bonds payable on the balance sheet?	Par (face or maturity amount) $\begin{cases} \text{+ Premium on bonds payable} \\ \text{or} \\ \text{– Discount on bonds payable} \end{cases}$

SUMMARY PROBLEM

Assume that Alabama Power Company has outstanding an issue of 9% bonds that mature on May 1, 2022. The bonds are dated May 1, 2002, and Alabama Power pays interest each April 30 and October 31.

www.prenhall.com/horngren
Mid-Chapter Assessment

Required

1. Will the bonds be issued at par, at a premium, or at a discount if the market interest rate is 8% at date of issuance? If the market interest rate is 10%?
2. Assume that Alabama Power issued $1,000,000 of the bonds at 104 on May 1, 2002.
   a. Record issuance of the bonds.
   b. Record the interest payment and amortization of premium or discount on October 31, 2002.
   c. Accrue interest and amortize premium or discount on December 31, 2002.
   d. Show how the company would report the bonds on the balance sheet at December 31, 2002.
   e. Record the interest payment on April 30, 2003.

Solution

Requirement 1

If the market interest rate is 8%, 9% bonds will be issued at a *premium*. If the market rate is 10%, the 9% bonds will be issued at a *discount*.

Requirement 2

2002

a. May 1	Cash ($1,000,000 × 1.04)...	$1,040,000	
	Bonds Payable...		1,000,000
	Premium on Bonds Payable.............................		40,000
	Issued 9%, 20-year bonds at a premium.		

b. Oct. 31	Interest Expense..	44,000	
	Premium on Bonds Payable ($40,000/40)..................	1,000	
	Cash ($1,000,000 × 0.09 × 6/12)		45,000
	Paid semiannual interest and amortized premium on bonds payable.		

c. Dec. 31	Interest Expense..	14,667	
	Premium on Bonds Payable		
	($40,000/40 × 2/6)	333	
	Interest Payable		
	($1,000,000 × 0.09 × 2/12).........................		15,000
	Accrued interest and amortized bond premium for two months.		

d. Long-term liabilities:

Bonds payable, 9%, due 2022	$1,000,000	
Premium on bonds payable		
($40,000 − $1,000 − $333)	38,667	$1,038,667

2003

e. Apr. 30	Interest Expense..	29,333	
	Interest Payable..	15,000	
	Premium on Bonds Payable ($40,000/40 × 4/6)........	667	
	Cash ($1,000,000 × 0.09 × 6/12)		45,000
	Paid semiannual interest, part of which was accrued, and amortized four months' premium on bonds payable.		

Supplement to Solution

Bond problems include many details. You may find it helpful to check your work. We verify the answers to the summary problem in the following supplement.

On April 30, 2003, the bonds have been outstanding for one year. After the entries have been recorded, the account balances should show the results of one year's cash interest payments and one year's bond premium amortization.

Fact 1:	Cash interest payments should be $90,000 ($1,000,000 × 0.09).
Accuracy check:	Two credits to Cash of $45,000 each = $90,000. Cash payments are correct.
Fact 2:	Premium amortization should be $2,000 ($40,000/40 semiannual periods × 2 semiannual periods in 1 year).
Accuracy check:	Three debits to Premium on Bonds Payable ($1,000 + $333 + $667) = $2,000. Premium amortization is correct.
Fact 3:	We can also check the accuracy of interest expense recorded during the year ended December 31, 2002.
	The bonds in this problem will be outstanding for a total of 20 years, or 240 (that is, 20 × 12) months. During 2002, the bonds are outstanding for eight months (May through December).
	Interest expense for eight months *equals* payment of cash interest for eight months minus premium amortization for eight months. Interest expense should therefore be ($1,000,000 × 0.09 × 8/12 = $60,000) minus [($40,000/240) × 8 = $1,333], or ($60,000 − $1,333 = $58,667).
Accuracy check:	Two debits to Interest Expense ($44,000 + $14,667) = $58,667. Interest expense for 2002 is correct.

Objective 2

Measure interest expense by the effective-interest method

EFFECTIVE-INTEREST METHOD OF AMORTIZATION

We presented the straight-line amortization method first to introduce the concept of amortizing bond discount and premium. However, that method has a theoretical weakness. Each period's amortization amount for a premium or discount is the same dollar amount over the life of the bonds. Over that time, however, the bonds' carrying amount continues to increase (with a discount) or decrease (with a premium). Thus, the fixed dollar amount of interest expense as a percentage of the bonds' carrying amount, making it appear that the bond issuer's interest rate changes over time. But in reality, the issuer locked in a fixed interest rate when the bonds were issued. The interest *rate* on the bonds does not change.

Generally accepted accounting principles require that interest expense be measured using the *effective-interest method* unless the difference between the straight-line method and the effective-interest method is immaterial. In that case, either method is permitted. We will see how the effective-interest method keeps interest expense at the same percentage over the bonds' life. The total amount of interest expense over the life of the bonds is the same under both methods.

Effective-Interest Method of Measuring Interest Expense — Bond Discount

Assume that **eBay Inc.** issues $100,000 of 9% bonds at a time when the market rate of interest is 10%. Assume also that these bonds mature in five years and pay interest semiannually, so there are ten semiannual interest payments. The issue price of the bonds is $96,149.[4] The discount on these bonds is $3,851 ($100,000 − $96,149). Exhibit 15-4 shows how to measure interest expense by the effective-interest method.

The *accounts* debited and credited under the effective-interest method and the straight-line method are the same. Only the *amounts* differ. We may take the amortization *amounts* directly from the table in Exhibit 15-4. We assume that the first interest payment occurs on July 1 and so we use the appropriate amounts from Exhibit 15-4, reading across the line for the first interest payment date:

DAILY EXERCISE 15-11

DAILY EXERCISE 15-12

July 1	Interest Expense (column B)	4,807	
	Discount on Bonds Payable (column C)..............		307
	Cash (column A)		4,500
	To pay semiannual interest and amortize discount on bonds payable.		

588 CHAPTER 15

---

[4]We compute this present value in the chapter appendix.

PANEL A—Bond Data

Maturity value—$100,000
Contract interest rate—9%
Interest paid—4 1/2% semiannually, $4,500 ($100,000 × 0.045)
Market interest rate at time of issue—10% annually, 5% semiannually
Issue price—$96,149

PANEL B—Amortization Table

	A	B	C	D	E
End of Semiannual Interest Period	**Interest** *Payment* **(4 1/2% of Maturity Value)**	**Interest** *Expense* **(5% of Preceding Bond Carrying Amount)**	**Discount Amortization (B − A)**	**Discount Balance (D − C)**	**Bond Carrying Amount ($100,000 − D)**
Issue Date				$3,851	$ 96,149
1	$4,500	$4,807	$307	3,544	96,456
2	4,500	4,823	323	3,221	96,779
3	4,500	4,839	339	2,882	97,118
4	4,500	4,856	356	2,526	97,474
5	4,500	4,874	374	2,152	97,848
6	4,500	4,892	392	1,760	98,240
7	4,500	4,912	412	1,348	98,652
8	4,500	4,933	433	915	99,085
9	4,500	4,954	454	461	99,539
10	4,500	4,961*	461	−0−	100,000

* Adjusted for effect of rounding.

Notes

• *Column A* The semiannual interest payments are constant—fixed by the contract interest rate and the bonds' maturity value.
• *Column B* The interest expense each period is computed by multiplying the preceding bond carrying amount by the market interest rate. This *effective interest rate* determines the interest expense each period. The amount of interest each period increases as the effective interest rate, a constant, is applied to the increasing bond carrying amount (E).
• *Column C* The excess of each interest expense amount (B) over each interest payment amount (A) is the discount amortization for the period.
• *Column D* The discount balance decreases by the amount of amortization for the period (C), from $3,851 at the issue date to zero at maturity. Balance of discount + Bonds' carrying amount = Bonds' maturity value ($100,000).
• *Column E* The bonds' carrying amount increases from $96,149 at issuance to $100,000 at maturity.

Exhibit 15-5, on page 590, Panel A, diagrams the interest expense over the life of bonds payable issued at a discount. Panel B shows how the carrying amount of the bonds rises to the maturity date. All amounts are taken from Exhibit 15-4. Focus on the highlighted items to understand the main points of the exhibit.

THINK IT OVER

Over the life of a bond issued at a *discount,* will the periodic amount of interest expense increase or decrease under the effective-interest amortization method?

Answer: The periodic amount of interest expense *increases* because the carrying amount of the bond *increases* toward maturity value. To see this, refer to columns B and E of Exhibit 15-4. The upward-sloping line in Exhibit 15-5, Panel A, illustrates the increasing amount of interest expense.

PANEL A—Interest Expense on Bonds Payable Issued at a Discount

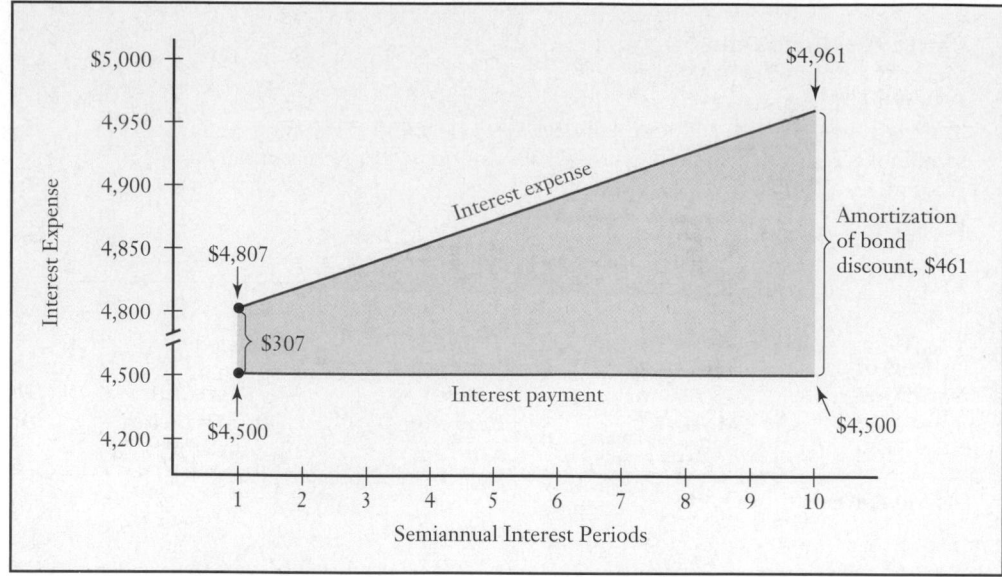

PANEL B—Carrying Amount of Bonds Payable Issued at a Discount

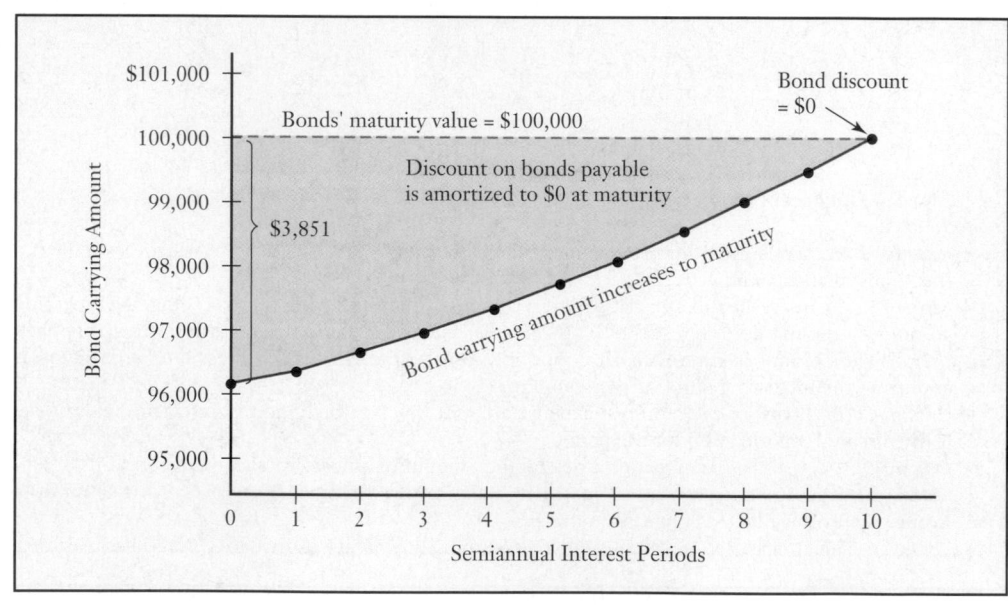

Effective-Interest Method of Measuring Interest Expense— Bond Premium

Let's modify the **eBay** bonds payable example to illustrate the interest method of measuring interest expense for a bond premium situation. Assume that **eBay** issues $100,000 of five-year, 9% bonds that pay interest semiannually. If the bonds are issued when the market interest rate is 8%, their issue price is $104,100.[5] The premium on these bonds is $4,100, and Exhibit 15-6 shows how to measure interest expense by the effective-interest method.

Assuming that the first interest payment occurs on October 31, we read across the line in Exhibit 15-6 for the first payment date and get the appropriate amounts:

Oct. 31	Interest Expense (column B)......................................	4,164	
	Premium on Bonds Payable (column C)	336	
	Cash (column A)...		4,500
	To pay semiannual interest and amortize premium on bonds payable.		

[5]Again, we compute the present value of the bonds in this chapter's appendix

PANEL A—Bond Data
Maturity value—$100,000
Contract interest rate—9%
Interest paid—4 1/2% semiannually, $4,500 ($100,000 × 0.045)
Market interest rate at time of issue—8% annually, 4% semiannually
Issue price—$104,100

PANEL B—Amortization Table

	A	B	C	D	E
End of Semiannual Interest Period	Interest *Payment* (4 1/2% of Maturity Value)	Interest *Expense* (4% of Preceding Bond Carrying Amount)	Premium Amortization (A − B)	Premium Balance (D − C)	Bond Carrying Amount ($100,000 + D)
Issue Date				$4,100	$104,100
1	$4,500	$4,164	$336	3,764	103,764
2	4,500	4,151	349	3,415	103,415
3	4,500	4,137	363	3,052	103,052
4	4,500	4,122	378	2,674	102,674
5	4,500	4,107	393	2,281	102,281
6	4,500	4,091	409	1,872	101,872
7	4,500	4,075	425	1,447	101,447
8	4,500	4,058	442	1,005	101,005
9	4,500	4,040	460	545	100,545
10	4,500	3,955*	545	−0−	100,000

* Adjusted for effect of rounding.

Notes
- *Column A* The semiannual interest payments are constant—fixed by the contract interest rate and the bonds' maturity value.
- *Column B* The interest expense each period is computed by multiplying the preceding bond carrying amount by the effective interest rate. The amount of interest decreases each period as the bond carrying amount decreases.
- *Column C* The excess of each interest payment (A) over the period's interest expense (B) is the premium amortization for the period.
- *Column D* The premium balance decreases by the amount of amortization for the period (C) from $4,100 at issuance to zero at maturity. Bonds' carrying amount − Premium balance = Bonds' maturity value ($100,000).
- *Column E* The bonds' carrying amount decreases from $104,100 at issuance to $100,000 at maturity.

THINK IT OVER

How does the method of amortizing bond premium or discount affect the amount of cash interest paid on a bond?

Answer: The amortization method has *no effect* on the amount of cash interest paid on a bond. The amount of cash interest depends on the contract interest rate stated on the bond. That interest rate, and the amount of cash interest paid, remain constant over the life of the bond. To see this, examine column A of Exhibits 15-4 and 15-6.

At year end, it is necessary to make an adjusting entry to accrue interest and amortize the bond premium for a partial period. In our example, the last interest payment occurred on October 31. The adjustment for November and December covers two months, or one-third of a semiannual period. The entry, with amounts drawn from Exhibit 15-6, line 2, is as follows:

Dec. 31	Interest Expense ($4,151 × 1/3)	1,384	
	Premium on Bonds Payable ($349 × 1/3)	116	
	Interest Payable ($4,500 × 1/3)		1,500
	To accrue two months' interest and amortize premium on bonds payable for two months.		

The second interest payment occurs on April 30 of the following year. The payment of $4,500 includes

- Interest expense for four months (January through April)
- The interest payable at December 31
- Premium amortization for four months

The payment entry is as follows:

Apr. 30	Interest Expense ($4,151 × 2/3)	2,767	
	Interest Payable	1,500	
	Premium on Bonds Payable ($349 × 2/3)	233	
	Cash		4,500
	To pay semiannual interest, some of which was accrued, and amortize premium on bonds payable for four months.		

If these bonds had been issued at a discount, procedures for these interest entries would be the same, except that Discount on Bonds Payable would be credited.

Exhibit 15-7, Panel A, diagrams the interest expense over the life of bonds issued at a premium. Panel B shows how the carrying amount of the bonds falls to maturity. All amounts are taken from Exhibit 15-6. Focus on the highlighted items.

DAILY EXERCISE 15-13

Objective 3
Account for retirement of bonds payable

THINK IT OVER

For a bond issued at a *premium*, will the periodic amount of interest expense increase or decrease? Use the effective-interest method.

Answer: The periodic amount of interest expense *decreases* because the carrying amount of the bond *decreases* toward maturity value. To see this, study columns B and E of Exhibit 15-6. The downward-sloping line in Exhibit 15-7, Panel A, illustrates the decreasing amount of interest expense.

Additional Bond Topics

Companies that issue bonds payable face additional issues, such as how to account for the retirement of bonds and convertible bonds. Two other important long-term liabilities are leases and pensions.

Retirement of Bonds Payable

Normally, companies wait until maturity to pay off, or retire, their bonds payable. All bond discount or premium has been amortized. The retirement entry debits Bonds Payable and credits Cash for the bonds' maturity value. But companies sometimes retire their bonds payable prior to maturity. The main reason for retiring bonds early is to relieve the pressure of making interest payments. Interest rates fluctuate. The company may be able to borrow at a lower interest rate and use the proceeds from new bonds to pay off the old bonds, which bear a higher interest rate.

CALLABLE BONDS. Bonds that the issuer may call or pay off at a specified price whenever the issuer wants.

Some bonds are **callable,** which means that the bonds' issuer may *call*, or pay off, those bonds at a specified price whenever the issuer so chooses. The call price is usually 100 or a few percentage points above the par value, perhaps 101 or 102. Callable bonds give the issuer the benefit of being able to take advantage of low interest rates by paying off the bonds whenever it is favorable to do so. An alternative to calling the bonds is to purchase them in the open market at their current market price. Whether the bonds are called or purchased in the open market, the journal entry is the same.

ETrade Associates has $70 million of debentures outstanding with a discount of $350,000. Lower interest rates in the market may convince management to pay off these bonds now. Assume that the bonds are callable at 103. If the market price of the bonds is 99 1/4, will ETrade call the bonds or purchase them in the open market? The market price is lower than the call price, so market price is the better choice. Retiring the bonds at 99 1/4 results in an extraordinary gain of $175,000, computed as follows:

PANEL A—Interest Expense on Bonds Payable Issued at a Premium

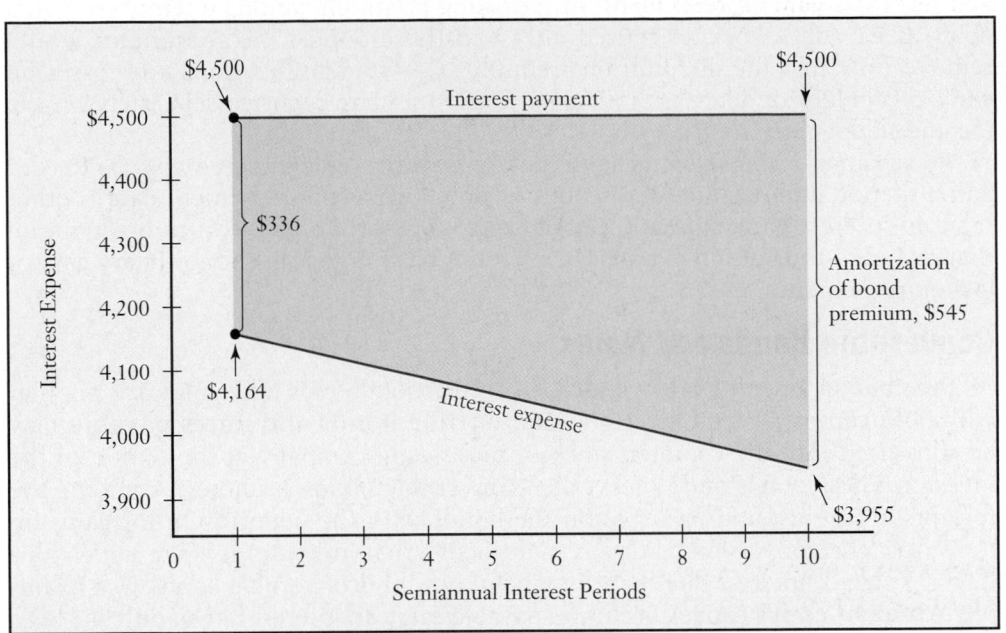

PANEL B—Carrying Amount of Bonds Payable Issued at a Premium

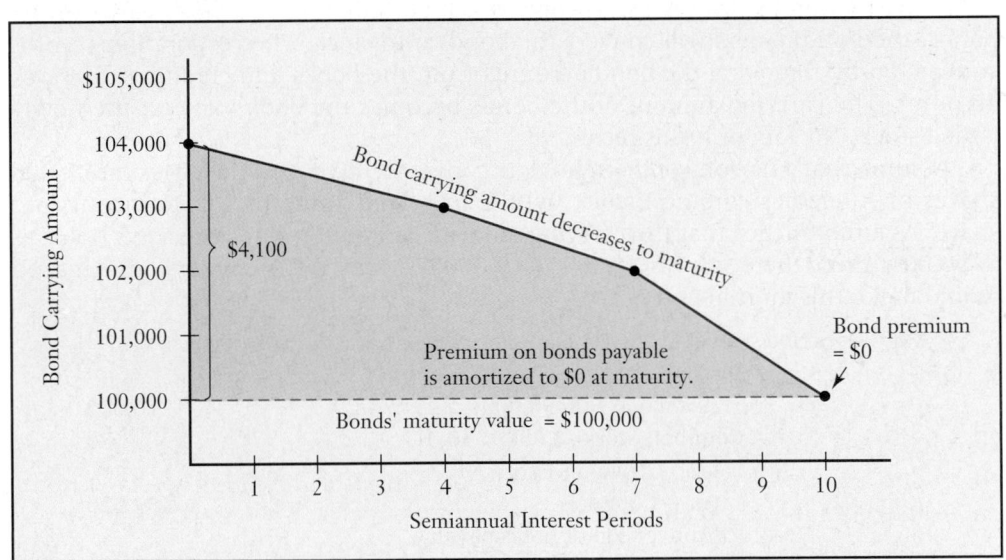

Par value of bonds being retired	$70,000,000
Less: Discount on bonds payable	(350,000)
Carrying amount of bonds payable	69,650,000
Market price ($70,000,000 × 0.9925)	69,475,000
Extraordinary gain on retirement of bonds payable	$ 175,000

The following entry records retirement of the bonds, immediately after an interest date:

June 30	Bonds Payable	70,000,000	
	Discount on Bonds Payable		350,000
	Cash ($70,000,000 × 0.9925)		69,475,000
	Extraordinary Gain on Retirement of Bonds Payable		175,000
	Retired bonds payable.		

The entry removes the bonds payable and the related discount from the accounts and records a gain on retirement. Any existing premium would be removed with a debit. If ETrade Associates retired only half these bonds, the accountant would remove only half the discount or premium. GAAP identifies gains and losses on early retirement of debts as *extraordinary,* and they are reported separately on the income statement.

In summary, when retiring bonds before maturity, follow these steps: (1) Record partial-period amortization of discount or premium, if the retirement date is other than an interest payment date. (2) Write off the portion of Discount or Premium that relates to the portion of bonds being retired. (3) Compute extraordinary gain or loss on retirement.

| Objective 4 |
Account for conversion of bonds payable

CONVERTIBLE BONDS. Bonds (or notes payable) that may be converted into the common stock of the issuing company at the option of the investor.

Convertible Bonds and Notes

As the chapter-opening story indicates, convertible bonds and notes are popular with both companies and investors. **Convertible bonds and notes payable** may be converted into the common stock of the issuing company at the option of the investor. These bonds and notes, called convertible bonds (or notes), combine the receipts of interest and principal on the bonds with the opportunity for gains on the stock. The conversion feature is so attractive that investors accept a lower contract, or stated, interest rate than they would on nonconvertible bonds. For example, **Amazon.com's** convertible notes payable carry an interest rate of only 4 3/4%. The low cash interest payments benefit Amazon.com. The issuance of convertible bonds payable is recorded like any other debt.

If the market price of Amazon.com's stock gets above the market value of the bonds, the bondholders will convert the bonds into stock. The corporation records conversion by removing the bond accounts from the books and crediting the stock accounts. The carrying amount of the bonds becomes the book value of the newly issued stock. No gain or loss is recorded.

Assume that Amazon.com noteholders convert $500,000 of the notes into 8,000 shares of Amazon's common stock, which has a par value of $0.01 (1 cent) per share. Assume further that the carrying amount of the notes on Amazon's books is $490,000; thus, there is a discount of $10,000. To record the conversion, Amazon would make this journal entry:

May 14	Notes Payable	500,000	
	Discount on Notes Payable		
	($500,000 − $490,000)		10,000
	Common Stock (8,000 × $0.01)		80
	Paid-in Capital in Excess of		
	Par—Common		489,920
	Recorded conversion of notes payable.		

 DAILY EXERCISE 15-15

The entry closes the notes (or bonds) payable account and its related discount. The carrying amount of the notes ($490,000) becomes the amount of new stockholders' equity ($489,920 + $80).

Current Portion of Long-Term Debt

Serial bonds and serial notes are payable in serials, or installments. The portion payable within one year is a current liability, and the remaining debt is long-term. At January 29, 2000, Toys "Я" Us, Inc., had $1,251 million of long-term debt maturing in various amounts in future years. Assume that the portion payable in the next year was $21 million. Therefore, $21 million was a current liability at January 29, 2000, and $1,230 million was a long-term liability. Toys "Я" Us could report the following among its liabilities at January 29, 2000:

	$ Millions
Current liabilities:	
Current maturities of long-term debt.............	$ 21
Long-term debt less current maturities..............	1,230

Mortgage Notes Payable

You have probably heard of mortgage payments. Many notes payable are mortgage notes, which actually contain two agreements:

- The *note* is the borrower's promise to pay the lender the amount of the debt.
- The **mortgage**—a security agreement related to the note—is the borrower's promise to transfer to the lender the legal title to certain assets if the debt is not paid on schedule.

MORTGAGE. Borrower's promise to transfer the legal title to certain assets to the lender if the debt is not paid on schedule.

The borrower is pledging these assets as security for the note. Often the asset pledged was acquired with the borrowed money. For example, most homeowners sign mortgage notes to purchase their residences, pledging that property as security for the loan. Businesses sign mortgage notes to acquire buildings, equipment, and other long-term assets. Mortgage notes are usually serial notes that require monthly or quarterly payments.

Advantage of Issuing Bonds Versus Stock

Objective 5
Show the advantages and disadvantages of borrowing

Businesses have different ways to acquire assets. The money to pay for the asset may be financed by the business's retained earnings, by a stock issue, or by borrowing. Each financing strategy has its advantages, as follows:

Advantages of Financing Operations by	
Issuing Stock	**Borrowing**
Creates no liabilities or interest expense. Less risky to the issuing corporation.	Does not dilute control of the corporation. Usually results in higher earnings per share because interest expense is tax-deductible.

Exhibit 15-8 shows the earnings-per-share (EPS) advantage of borrowing. ➡ Suppose that Vista.com, an Internet startup, has net income of $300,000 and 100,000 shares of common stock outstanding. Vista needs $500,000 for expansion and company management is considering two plans to finance the expansion:

◄ Earnings per share (EPS) is a company's net income per share of outstanding common stock (Chapter 14, p. 556). EPS may be the most important figure on the income statement.

- Plan 1 is to borrow $500,000 at 10% (issue $500,000 of 10% bonds payable).
- Plan 2 is to issue 50,000 shares of common stock for $500,000.

Vista management believes the new cash can be invested in operations to earn income of $200,000 before interest and taxes.

EXHIBIT 15-8   Earnings-Per-Share Advantage of Borrowing Versus Issuing Stock

	Plan 1 Borrow $500,000 at 10%	Plan 2 Issue $500,000 of Common Stock
Net income before expansion	$300,000	$300,000
Expected income on the new project before		
interest and income tax expenses	$200,000	$200,000
Less: Interest expense ($500,000 × 0.10).............	(50,000)	–0–
Project income before income tax........................	150,000	200,000
Less: Income tax expense (40%)	(60,000)	(80,000)
Project net income	90,000	120,000
Total company net income..................................	$390,000	$420,000
Earnings per share after expansion:		
Plan 1 ($390,000/100,000 shares)	$3.90	
Plan 2 ($420,000/150,000 shares)		$2.80

The EPS figure is higher if Vista.com borrows. If all goes well, Vista can earn more on the investment ($90,000) than the interest it pays on the bonds ($50,000).

DAILY EXERCISE 15-16

 DAILY EXERCISE 15-17

LEVERAGE. Earning more income on borrowed money than the related interest expense, thereby increasing the earnings for the owners of the business.

Objective 6
Account for lease and pension liabilities

LEASE. Rental agreement in which the tenant (lessee) agrees to make rent payments to the property owner (lessor) to obtain the use of the asset.

LESSEE. Tenant in a lease agreement.

LESSOR. Property owner in a lease agreement.

OPERATING LEASE. Usually a short-term or cancelable rental agreement.

CAPITAL LEASE. Lease agreement that meets any one of four criteria: (1) The lease transfers title of the leased asset to the lessee. (2) The lease contains a bargain purchase option. (3) The lease term is 75% or more of the estimated useful life of the leased asset. (4) The present value of the lease payments is 90% or more of the market value of the leased asset.

Earning more income on borrowed money than the related interest expense increases the earnings for common stockholders and is called using **leverage.** It is widely used in business to increase earnings per share of common stock.

Borrowing has its disadvantages. Interest expense may be high enough to eliminate net income and lead to a cash crisis or even bankruptcy. This has happened to lots of Internet startups. Also, borrowing creates liabilities that accrue during bad years as well as good years.

Lease Liabilities

A **lease** is a rental agreement in which the tenant **(lessee)** obtains the use of an asset and agrees to make rent payments to the property owner **(lessor).** Leasing avoids having to make the large initial cash down payment that a purchase requires. Accountants divide leases into two types: operating leases and capital leases.

OPERATING LEASES **Operating leases** may be short-term or cancelable. Many apartment leases and car-rental agreements are for a year or less. These operating leases give the lessee the right to use the asset but provide the lessee with no continuing rights to the asset. The lessor retains the usual risks and rewards of owning the leased asset. To account for an operating lease, the lessee debits Rent Expense (or Lease Expense) and credits Cash for the amount of the lease payment. The lessee's books report no leased asset and no lease liability. This is why lessees prefer operating leases over capital leases.

CAPITAL LEASES A capital lease requires the lessee to record both an asset and a lease liability. Capital leases are long-term and noncancelable. How can we distinguish a capital lease from an operating lease? A **capital lease** meets any *one* of the following criteria:

1. The lease transfers title of the leased asset to the lessee at the end of the lease term. Thus, the lessee becomes the legal owner of the leased asset.
2. The lease contains a *bargain purchase option*. The lessee can be expected to purchase the leased asset and become its legal owner.
3. The lease term is 75% or more of the estimated useful life of the leased asset. The lessee uses up most of the leased asset's service potential.
4. The present value of the lease payments is 90% or more of the market value of the leased asset. In effect, the lease payments operate as installment payments for the leased asset.

Only those leases that fail to meet all these criteria are treated as operating leases.

ACCOUNTING FOR A CAPITAL LEASE Accounting for a capital lease is like accounting for a purchase. The lessee records an asset and also records a lease liability at the beginning of the lease term. The lessee capitalizes the asset in its own financial statements, even though the lessee may never actually own the property.

Safeway, the grocery chain, operates stores in buildings that it leases from other companies. Suppose Safeway leases a store building and agrees to pay annual rentals for a 20-year period. This arrangement is similar to purchasing the building on an installment plan.

Suppose Safeway's liability under this capital lease totals $1,000,000 at the beginning of the lease term. The lease liability determines Safeway's cost of the building. If Safeway makes the first annual lease payment of $100,000 up front, Safeway makes this entry as the lease begins:

2000			
Jan. 1	Building	1,000,000	
	Lease Liability		900,000
	Cash		100,000
	Acquired building under a capital lease.		

Each year end Safeway will record depreciation expense on the building as though Safeway owned the building. The life of the building is the lease term (20 years in this example), and residual value is zero. At December 31, 2000, Safeway will report its lease liabilities on the balance sheet as follows:

Liabilities	
Current:	
Current obligation under capital lease (next year's lease payment)	$100,000
Long-term:	
Lease liability ($900,000 − $100,000)	800,000

 DAILY EXERCISE 15-18

Pension and Postretirement Benefit Liabilities

Most companies have a pension plan for their employees. A **pension** is employee compensation paid during retirement. Employees earn pensions by their service, so the company records pension expense while employees work for the company. Companies also provide postretirement benefits, mainly health insurance for retirees.

To record the company's payment into a retirement plan, the company debits Pension Expense and credits Cash. The assets of the pension plan grow. The obligation for future pension payments to employees also accumulates. At the end of each period, the company compares the fair market value of the pension plan assets with the accumulated benefit obligation of the pension plan. The *accumulated benefit obligation* is the amount of promised future pension payments to retirees.

If the plan assets exceed the accumulated benefit obligation, the plan is said to be *overfunded*. For an overfunded pension plan, the asset and obligation amounts are reported only in the notes to the financial statements. But if the accumulated benefit obligation exceeds the pension plan's assets, the plan is *underfunded*. For an underfunded plan, the company must report the excess liability amount on the balance sheet. Underfunded plans have been rare in recent years.

The pension plan of Mainstream Sales, Inc., has assets with a fair market value of $3 million on December 31, 20X3, and the accumulated pension obligation is $4 million. At December 31, 20X3, Mainstream Sales makes the following comparison:

PENSION. Employee compensation that will be received during retirement.

	Millions
Accumulated pension benefit obligation	$4
Pension plan assets	3
Pension liability to report on the balance sheet	$1

 DAILY EXERCISE 15-19

The **Decision Guidelines** feature provides a summary of the major points of the chapter's second half.

DECISION GUIDELINES

Accounting for Long-Term Liabilities—Part B

DECISION	GUIDELINES
What happens to the bonds' carrying amount when bonds payable are issued at • Par? • A premium? • A discount?	• Carrying amount *stays* at par (face, or maturity) value during the life of the bonds. • Carrying amount *falls* gradually to the bonds' maturity value on their maturity date. • Carrying amount *rises* gradually to the bonds' maturity value on their maturity date.

How to account for the retirement of bonds payable?

At maturity date:

Bonds Payable	Maturity value	
Cash		Maturity value

Before maturity date (assume a discount on the bonds and a gain on retirement):

Bonds Payable	Maturity value	
Discount on Bonds		
Payable		Balance
Cash		Amount Paid
Extraordinary Gain on		
Retirement of		
Bonds Payable		Excess

How to account for the conversion of convertible bonds payable into common stock?

Remove all the bonds payable (and related premium or discount) accounts and credit Common Stock at par, plus any excess to Paid-in Capital in Excess of Par.

What are the advantages of financing operations with
• Stock?

• Bonds (or notes) payable?

• Creates no liability or interest expense. Less risky to the issuing corporation.
• Does not dilute stock ownership or control of the corporation.
Results in higher earnings per share—under normal conditions.

How to account for
• An operating lease?
• A capital lease?

• Debit lease (or rent) expense for each lease payment.
• At the beginning of the lease period, record
  a. Asset (as though it were purchased).
  b. Lease liability—present value of future lease payments.

EXCEL APPLICATION PROBLEM

Goal: Set up an Excel spreadsheet to compare earnings per share under two financing plans: borrowing and issuing stock.

Scenario: Target is thinking about building a new distribution warehouse to serve its growing Web-based retail operations. In order to finance the warehouse, managers must recommend whether to borrow the funds for construction or issue stock. Construction costs are estimated at $5 million. If borrowing is chosen, long-term bonds payable will be issued at 8% to raise the $5 million. If stock is chosen, 80,000 shares will be issued to cover the $5 million cost. Managers expect on-line sales to increase by $700,000 in the first year. Income tax expense is 40%. Assume net income before construction is $4 million, and shares outstanding before construction total 500,000.

Your task is to create a spreadsheet that compares earnings per share under the two plans described above. After completing the spreadsheet, answer these questions:

1. Which plan generates the higher earnings per share? Why?
2. Under what circumstances would Target consider using debt to finance its new warehouse?
3. Under what circumstances would Target consider the use of equity to finance its new warehouse?
4. Which option do you recommend for Target? Why? Does your recommendation change if the interest rate on the bonds is 10% rather than 8%?

EXCEL APPLICATION PROBLEM (CONT.)

Step-by-step:

1. Open a new Excel spreadsheet.
2. Create a heading for your spreadsheet that contains the following:
   a. Chapter 15 Decision Guidelines
   b. Financing with Debt or Stock
   c. Target Corporation
   d. Today's date
3. Use Exhibit 15-8 in your textbook as a model for the layout of your spreadsheet. Label the long-term bonds as

"Plan 1," and the issuance of common stock as "Plan 2." Be sure to set up the spreadsheet so that you can change variables, such as the interest rate on the bonds, without re-typing any formulas in the body of the spreadsheet.

4. When finished, your spreadsheet should show earnings per share under both plans, and be capable of re-computing earnings per share simply by changing the interest rate on the bonds.
5. Save your work and print a copy of the worksheet (in landscape mode) for your files.

REVIEW LONG-TERM LIABILITIES

SUMMARY PROBLEM

Trademark, Inc., has outstanding an issue of 8% convertible bonds payable that mature in 2020. Suppose the bonds were dated October 1, 2000, and pay interest each April 1 and October 1.

Required

1. Complete the following effective-interest amortization table through October 1, 2002:

BOND DATA:

- Maturity value—$100,000
- Contract interest rate—8%
- Interest paid—4% semiannually, $4,000 ($100,000 × 0.04)

- Market interest rate—9% annually, 4 1/2% semiannually
- Issue price—90 3/4

www.prenhall.com/horngren

End-of-Chapter Assessment

AMORTIZATION TABLE:

	A	B	C	D	E
Semiannual Interest Date	Interest Payment (4% of Maturity Amount)	Interest Expense (4 1/2% of Preceding Bond Carrying Amount)	Discount Amortization (B − A)	Discount Balance (D − C)	Bond Carrying Amount ($100,000 − D)
10-1-00					
4-1-01					
10-1-01					
4-1-02					
10-1-02					

2. Using the amortization table, record the following transactions:
   a. Issuance of the bonds on October 1, 2000.
   b. Accrual of interest and amortization of discount on December 31, 2000.
   c. Payment of interest and amortization of discount on April 1, 2001.
   d. Conversion of one-third of the bonds payable into no-par common stock on October 2, 2002.
   e. Retirement of two-thirds of the bonds payable on October 2, 2002. Purchase price of the bonds was 102.

Solution

Requirement 1

Semiannual Interest Date	A Interest Payment (4% of Maturity Amount)	B Interest Expense (4 1/2% of Preceding Bond Carrying Amount)	C Discount Amortization (B – A)	D Discount Balance (D – C)	E Bond Carrying Amount ($100,000 – D)
10-1-00				$9,250	$90,750
4-1-01	$4,000	$4,084	$84	9,166	90,834
10-1-01	4,000	4,088	88	9,078	90,922
4-1-02	4,000	4,091	91	8,987	91,013
10-1-02	4,000	4,096	96	8,891	91,109

Requirement 2

2000

a. Oct. 1

Cash ($100,000 × 0.9075)	90,750	
Discount on Bonds Payable	9,250	
Bonds Payable		100,000

To issue 8%, 20-year bonds at a discount.

b. Dec. 31

Interest Expense ($4,084 × 3/6)	2,042	
Discount on Bonds Payable ($84 × 3/6)		42
Interest Payable ($4,000 × 3/6)		2,000

To accrue interest and amortize bond discount for three months.

2001

c. Apr. 1

Interest Expense	2,042	
Interest Payable	2,000	
Discount on Bonds Payable ($84 × 3/6)		42
Cash		4,000

To pay semiannual interest, part of which was accrued, and amortize three months' discount on bonds payable.

2002

d. Oct. 2

Bonds Payable ($100,000 × 1/3)	33,333	
Discount on Bonds Payable ($8,891 × 1/3)		2,964
Common Stock ($91,109 × 1/3)		30,369

To record conversion of bonds payable.

e. Oct. 2

Bonds Payable ($100,000 × 2/3)	66,667	
Extraordinary Loss on Retirement Bonds	7,260	
Discount on Bonds Payable ($8,891 × 2/3)		5,927
Cash ($100,000 × 2/3 × 1.02)		68,000

To retire bonds payable before maturity.

LESSONS LEARNED

1. **Account for basic bonds payable transactions by the straight-line amortization method.** A corporation may borrow money by issuing long-term notes and *bonds payable*. Bonds may be secured (*mortgage* bonds) or unsecured (*debenture* bonds).

   Bonds are typically divided into $1,000 units. Their prices are quoted at a percentage of face value. *Market interest rates* fluctuate and may differ from the contract rate on a bond. If a bond's contract rate exceeds the market rate, the bond sells at a *premium*. A contract rate below the market rate creates a bond *discount*. An investor will pay a price for a bond equal to the present value of the bond principal plus the present value of the bond interest.

   Straight-line amortization allocates an equal amount of premium or discount to each interest period.

2. **Measure interest expense by the effective-interest method.** In the *effective-interest method* of amortization, the market interest rate at the time of issuance is multiplied by the bonds' carrying amount to determine the interest expense each period.

3. **Account for retirement of bonds payable.** Companies may retire their bonds payable before maturity. Any gain or loss on early extinguishment of debt is classified as *extraordinary*.

4. Account for conversion of bonds payable. *Convertible bonds* and notes give the investor the privilege of trading the bonds in for the stock of the issuing corporation. The carrying amount of the bonds becomes the book value of the newly issued stock.

5. Show the advantages and disadvantages of borrowing. A key advantage of borrowing (versus issuing stock) is that interest expense on debt is tax-deductible. Thus, borrowing is less costly than issuing stock. Borrowing's disadvantage results from the fact that the company *must* repay the loan and its interest.

6. Account for lease and pension liabilities. A *lease* is a rental agreement between the *lessee* and the *lessor*. In an *operating lease*, the lessee debits Rent Expense and credits Cash for each lease payment. A *capital lease* is long-term, noncancelable, and similar to an installment purchase of the leased asset. In a capital lease, the lessee capitalizes the leased asset and reports a lease liability.

Companies also report a *pension liability* on the balance sheet if the pension plan's accumulated benefit obligation exceeds the market value of the pension plan assets.

ACCOUNTING VOCABULARY

bond discount   (p. 579)
bond premium   (p. 579)
bonds payable   (p. 577)
callable bonds   (p. 592)
capital lease   (p. 596)
contract interest rate   (p. 580)
convertible bonds   (p. 594)
debentures   (p. 579)
discount (on a bond)   (p. 579)

effective interest rate   (p. 580)
lease   (p. 596)
lessee   (p. 596)
lessor   (p. 596)
leverage   (p. 596)
market interest rate   (p. 580)
mortgage   (p. 595)
notes payable   (p. 594)
operating lease   (p. 596)

pension   (p. 597)
premium   (p. 579)
present value   (p. 579)
serial bonds   (p. 579)
stated interest rate   (p. 580)
term bonds   (p. 578)
underwriter   (p. 578)

QUESTIONS

1. Compute the price to the nearest dollar for the following bonds with a face value of $10,000:
   a. 93
   b. 88 3/4
   c. 101 3/8
   d. 122 1/2
   e. 100
2. In which of the following situations will bonds sell at par? At a premium? At a discount?
   a. 9% bonds sold when the market rate is 9%
   b. 9% bonds sold when the market rate is 10%
   c. 9% bonds sold when the market rate is 8%
3. Identify the accounts to debit and credit for transactions
   a. to issue bonds at *par*
   b. to pay interest
   c. to accrue interest at year end
   d. to pay off bonds at maturity.
4. Identify the accounts to debit and credit for transactions
   a. to issue bonds at a *discount*
   b. to pay interest
   c. to accrue interest at year end
   d. to pay off bonds at maturity
5. Identify the accounts to debit and credit for transactions
   a. to issue bonds at a *premium*
   b. to pay interest
   c. to accrue interest at year end
   d. to pay off bonds at maturity
6. Why are bonds sold for a price "plus accrued interest"? What happens to accrued interest when the bonds are sold by an individual?

7. How does the straight-line method of amortizing bond discount (or premium) differ from the effective-interest method?
8. A company retires ten-year bonds payable of $100,000 after five years. The business issued the bonds at 104 and called them at 103. Compute the amount of gain or loss on retirement. How is this gain or loss reported on the income statement?
9. Bonds payable with a maturity value of $100,000 are callable at 102 1/2. Their market price is 101 1/4. If you are the issuer of these bonds, how much will you pay to retire them before maturity?
10. Why are convertible bonds attractive to investors? Why are they popular with borrowers?
11. What characteristics distinguish a capital lease from an operating lease?
12. A business signs a capital lease for the use of a building, with the first lease payment due immediately. What accounts are debited and credited to begin the lease term?
13. Show how a lessee reports on the balance sheet the lease liability under a capital lease.
14. Distinguish an overfunded pension plan from an underfunded plan. Which situation requires the company to report a pension liability on the balance sheet? How is this liability computed?

ASSESS YOUR PROGRESS

DAILY EXERCISES

DE15-1 Compute the price of the following bonds:

Pricing bonds   (Obj. 1)

   a. $100,000 quoted at 94 1/2
   b. $600,000 quoted at 102 5/8
   c. $2,000,000 quoted at 77 3/4
   d. $300,000 quoted at 110 3/8

Determining bonds payable amounts
(Obj. 1)

DE15-2 **Washington Public Power Supply System (WPPSS)** borrowed money by issuing the bond payable in Exhibit 15-1 (page 578). Assume the issue price was 93 1/2.

1. How much cash did WPPSS receive when it issued the bond payable?
2. How much must WPPSS pay back at maturity? When is the maturity date?
3. How much cash interest will WPPSS pay each six months? Carry the interest amount to the nearest cent.

Bond interest rates
(Obj. 1)

DE15-3 Assume the **WPPSS** bond in Exhibit 15-1 was issued at a price of 93 1/2. Was the market interest rate at the date of issuance 6 1/2%, above 6 1/2%, or below 6 1/2%? How can you tell?

Determining bond prices at par, discount, or premium
(Obj. 1)

DE15-4 Determine whether the following bonds payable will be issued at par value, at a premium, or at a discount:

a. The market interest rate is 9%. Sicily, Inc., issues bonds payable with a stated rate of 8 1/2%.
b. Galatia Corp. issued 7 1/2% bonds payable when the market rate was 7 1/2%.
c. Cyprus Corporation issued 8% bonds when the market interest rate was 6 7/8%.
d. Tyre Company issued bonds payable that pay cash interest at the contract rate of 7%. At the date of issuance, the market interest rate was 8 1/4%.

Journalizing basic bond payable transactions
(Obj. 1)

DE15-5 Suppose **WPPSS** issued the ten-year bond in Exhibit 15-1 when the market interest rate was 6 1/2%. Assume that the fiscal year of WPPSS ends on June 30. Journalize the following transactions for WPPSS. Include an explanation for each entry.

a. Issuance of the bond payable at par on July 1, 2000.
b. Payment of cash interest on January 1, 2001. (Round to the nearest dollar.)
c. Payment of the bonds payable at maturity. (Give the date.)

Issuing bonds payable between interest dates and then paying the interest
(Obj. 1)

DE15-6 Assume **WPPSS** issued the ten-year bond in Exhibit 15-1 at par value on November 1, 2000, four months after the bond's original issue date of July 1, 2000. Assume that the fiscal year of WPPSS ends on June 30. Journalize the following transactions for WPPSS. Include an explanation for each entry.

a. Issuance of the bonds payable on November 1, 2000. (Carry amounts to the nearest cent.)
b. Payment of the first semiannual interest amount on January 1, 2001. (Carry amounts to the nearest cent.)

Issuing bonds payable at a discount; paying interest and amortizing discount by the straight-line method *(Obj. 1)*

DE15-7 Assume **WPPSS** issued the ten-year bond in Exhibit 15-1 at a price of 86 on July 1, 2000. Also assume that WPPSS's fiscal year ends on June 30. Journalize the following transactions for WPPSS. Include an explanation for each entry.

a. Issuance of the bond payable on July 1, 2000.
b. Payment of interest and amortization of bond discount on January 1, 2001. (Use the straight-line method to amortize the discount. Round interest to the nearest dollar.)

Issuing bonds payable at a premium; paying interest and amortizing premium by the straight-line method *(Obj. 1)*

DE15-8 Assume **WPPSS** issued the bond payable in Exhibit 15-1 at a price of 104 on July 1, 2000. Also assume that WPPSS's fiscal year ends on June 30. Journalize the following transactions for WPPSS. Include an explanation for each entry.

a. Issuance of the bond payable on July 1, 2000.
b. Payment of interest and amortization of bond premium on January 1, 2001. (Use the straight-line method to amortize the premium. Round interest to the nearest dollar.)

Issuing bonds payable, accruing interest, and amortizing bond discount *(Obj. 1)*

DE15-9 Return to the **WPPSS** bond in Exhibit 15-1. Assume that WPPSS issued the bond payable on July 1, 2000, at a price of 92. Also assume that WPPSS's accounting year ends on December 31. Journalize the following transactions for WPPSS. Include an explanation for each entry.

a. Issuance of the bonds on July 1, 2000.
b. Accrual of interest expense and amortization of bond discount on December 31, 2000. (Use the straight-line amortization method, and round the interest amount to the nearest dollar.)
c. Payment of the first semiannual interest amount on January 1, 2001.

Reporting interest payable and bonds payable on the balance sheet *(Obj. 1)*

DE15-10 Use the situation in Daily Exercise 15-9, and show how **WPPSS** would report interest payable and the bond payable on its balance sheet at December 31, 2000.

Issuing bonds payable and measuring interest expense by the effective-interest method
(Obj. 2)

DE15-11 Braemar Drilling, Inc., issued $650,000 of 7%, ten-year bonds payable at a price of 87 on March 31, 20X3. The market interest rate at the date of issuance was 9%, and the Braemar bonds pay interest semiannually.

1. How much cash did Braemar receive upon issuance of the bonds payable?

2. Prepare an effective-interest amortization table for the bond discount, through the first three interest payments. Use Exhibit 15-4 (page 589) as a guide, and round amounts to the nearest dollar.

3. Record Braemar's issuance of the bonds on March 31, 20X3, and on September 30, 20X3, payment of the first semiannual interest amount and amortization of the bond discount. Explanations are not required.

DE15-12 ACE Furniture, Inc., issued $400,000 of 6%, five-year bonds payable to partially finance a warehouse. At the time of issuance, the market interest rate was 8%, so ACE received cash of $368,058. ACE pays interest annually.

Preparing a complete bond amortization table and using the table for relevant information (Obj. 2)

1. Prepare ACE's effective-interest amortization table for the bonds. Use Exhibit 15-4 (page 589) as a guide, and round amounts to the nearest dollar.

2. Use the amortization table to answer these questions about ACE's bonds payable and related interest expense:

    a. At what amount will ACE report the bonds payable at the end of Year 1? At the end of Year 3?

    b. How much cash interest will ACE pay for Year 1? Year 3? Year 5?

    c. How much interest expense will ACE record for Year 1? Year 5?

DE15-13 Unix, Inc., issued $200,000 of 8%, ten-year bonds payable at at price of 110 on May 31, 20X2. The market interest rate at the date of issuance was 6%, and the Unix bonds pay interest semiannually.

Issuing bonds payable and measuring interest expense by the effective-interest method (Obj. 2)

1. How much cash did Unix receive upon issuance of the bonds payable?

2. Prepare an effective-interest amortization table for the bond premium, through the first three interest payments. Use Exhibit 15-6 (page 591) as a guide, and round amounts to the nearest dollar.

3. Record Unix's issuance of the bonds on May 31, 20X2, and, on November 30, 20X2, payment of the first semiannual interest amount and amortization of the bond premium. Explanations are not required.

DE15-14 Assume that Tradinghouse, Inc., issued the bonds payable in Exhibit 15-6 (page 591). Tradinghouse has extra cash and wishes to retire the bonds payable immediately after making the fifth semiannual interest payment. The bonds are quoted in the market at a price of 95.

Accounting for the retirement of bonds payable (Obj. 3)

1. What is Tradinghouse's carrying amount of the bonds payable on the retirement date?

2. How much cash must Tradinghouse pay to retire the bonds payable?

3. Compute Tradinghouse's gain or loss on the retirement of the bonds payable. What type of gain or loss is this?

4. Journalize Tradinghouse's transaction to retire the bonds payable.

DE15-15 ◄ *Link Back to Chapter 4 (Debt Ratio).* Blade Automotive Corp. has $1,000,000 of convertible bonds payable outstanding, with a bond premium of $60,000 also on the books. The bondholders have notified Blade that they wish to convert the bonds into stock. Specifically, the bonds may be converted into 200,000 shares of Blade's $1 par common stock.

Accounting for the conversion of bonds payable (Obj. 4)

1. What is Blade's carrying amount of its convertible bonds payable prior to the conversion?

2. Journalize, on Blade's books, the conversion of the bonds payable into common stock. No explanation is required.

3. How will the conversion affect Blade's debt ratio?

DE15-16 Northern Accounting Services of Madison, Wisconsin, needs to raise $1 million to expand company operations into Minnesota. Northern's president is considering the issuance of either

Earnings-per-share effects of financing with bonds versus stock (Obj. 5)

- Plan A: $1,000,000 of 8% bonds payable to borrow the money
- Plan B: 100,000 shares of common stock at $10 per share

Before any new financing, Northern expects to earn net income of $350,000, and the company already has 200,000 shares of common stock outstanding. Northern believes the expansion will increase income before interest and income tax by $200,000. Northern's income tax rate is 35%.

    Prepare an analysis similar to Exhibit 15-8 (page 595) to determine which plan is likely to result in the higher earnings per share. Which financing plan would you recommend for Northern?

DE15-17 Return to the financing situation of Northern Accounting Services in Daily Exercise 15-16. What other factors, besides the effect on earnings per share, should Northern consider in deciding how to raise the $1 million? Give the advantages of issuing (a) stock and (b) bonds.

Advantages and disadvantages of financing with bonds versus stock (Obj. 5)

DE15-18 Horchow, Inc., includes the following selected accounts in its general ledger at December 31, 20X3:

Reporting liabilities, including
capital lease obligations
(Obj. 6)

Notes payable, long-term.......	$100,000	Current obligation under	
Bonds payable........................	350,000	capital lease	$ 8,000
Equipment under		Accounts payable	19,000
capital lease	114,000	Long-term capital lease	
Interest payable (due		liability................................	42,000
March 1, 20X4)	7,000	Discount on bonds	
Current portion of		payable (all long-term)........	6,000
bonds payable....................	65,000		

Prepare the liabilities section of Horchow's balance sheet at December 31, 20X3, to show how Horchow would report these items. Report a total for current liabilities.

DE15-19 NM Aviation Fuel has a pension plan for its employees. NM's pension plan has an accumulated benefit obligation of $3,000,000. This means that NM would have to pay $3,000,000 now if the company had to settle the plan's pension liability today. To offset this, NM has invested in a pension fund that holds investments in stocks, bonds, and real estate.

a. The market value of the investments held by NM's pension fund is $2,400,000. Is the pension plan overfunded or underfunded? How much pension liability should NM report on its balance sheet?

b. Assume instead that the market value of the investments in NM's pension fund is $3,500,000. Is the pension plan overfunded or underfunded? How much pension liability should NM report on its balance sheet?

EXERCISES

Issuing bonds payable, paying
and accruing interest, and
amortizing discount by the
straight-line method (Obj. 1)

E15-1 On February 1, The Oasis Corp. issues 8%, 20-year bonds payable with a face value of $100,000. The bonds sell at 98 and pay interest on January 31 and July 31. The Oasis Corp. amortizes bond discount by the straight-line method. Record (a) issuance of the bonds on February 1, (b) the semiannual interest payment on July 31, and (c) the interest accrual on December 31.

Issuing bonds payable, paying
and accruing interest, and
amortizing premium by the
straight-line method (Obj. 1)

E15-2 Saturn Photo Corporation issues 8%, 20-year bonds payable with a face value of $1,000,000 on March 31. The bonds sell at 103 1/2 and pay interest on March 31 and September 30. Assume that Saturn amortizes bond premium by the straight-line method. Record (a) issuance of the bonds on March 31, (b) payment of interest on September 30, and (c) accrual of interest on December 31.

E15-3 Refer to the data for Saturn Photo Corporation in Exercise 15-2. If Saturn issued the bonds payable on June 30, how much cash would Saturn receive upon issuance of the bonds?

E15-4 Newton, Inc., issues $400,000 of 7%, 20-year bonds payable that are dated April 30. Record (a) issuance of bonds at par on May 31, and (b) the next semiannual interest payment on October 31.

Preparing an effective-interest
amortization table; recording
interest payments and interest
expense (Obj. 2)

E15-5 Assume Network Navigator Corp. is authorized to issue $500,000 of 7%, ten-year bonds payable. On January 2, when the market interest rate is 8%, the company issues $300,000 of the bonds and receives cash of $279,615. Network Navigator measures interest expense by the effective-interest method.

Required

1. Prepare an amortization table for the first four semiannual interest periods. Follow the format of Exhibit 15-4, Panel B (page 589).
2. Record the first semiannual interest payment on June 30 and the second payment on December 31.

Preparing an effective-interest
amortization table; recording
interest accrual and payment and
the related interest expense
(Obj. 2)

E15-6 On September 30, 20X2, the market interest rate is 7%. Lemmon-Blake Software, Inc., issues $200,000 of 8%, 20-year bonds payable at 110 5/8. The bonds pay interest on March 31 and September 30. Lemmon-Blake Software measures interest expense by the effective-interest method.

Required

1. Prepare an amortization table for the first four semiannual interest periods. Follow the format of Exhibit 15-6, Panel B (page 591).
2. Record issuance of the bonds on September 30, 20X2, the accrual of interest at December 31, 20X2, and the semiannual interest payment on March 31, 20X3.

E15-7 Fairfield Circuitry, Inc., issued $500,000 of 8 3/8% (0.08375), five-year bonds payable when the market interest rate was 9 1/2% (0.095). Fairfield pays interest annually at year end. The issue price of the bonds was $478,402.

Required

Create a spreadsheet model to prepare a schedule to measure interest expense on these bonds. Use the effective-interest method of amortization. Round to the nearest dollar, and format your answer as follows:

1	A	B	C	D	E	F
2						**Bond**
3		**Interest**	**Interest**	**Discount**	**Discount**	**Carrying**
4	**Date**	**Payment**	**Expense**	**Amortization**	**Balance**	**Amount**
5	1-1-X1				$ ☐	$478,402
6	12-31-X1	$ ☐	$ ☐	$ ☐		☐
7	12-31-X2					
8	12-31-X3					
9	12-31-X4					
10	12-31-X5					
		500000*.08375	+F5*.095	+C6−B6	500000−F5	+F5+D6

E15-8 Brenham Communications issued $600,000 of 8% bonds payable at 97 on October 1, 20X0. These bonds mature on October 1, 20X8, and are callable at 101. Brenham pays interest each April 1 and October 1. On October 1, 20X5, when the bonds' market price is 104, Brenham retires the bonds in the most economical way available.

Recording retirement of bonds payable (Obj. 3)

Required

Record the payment of the interest and amortization of bond discount at October 1, 20X5, and the retirement of the bonds on that date. Brenham uses the straight-line amortization method.

E15-9 Computer Diagnostics Company issued $700,000 of 8 1/2% bonds payable on July 31, 20X3, at a price of 98 1/2. After five years, the bonds may be converted into the company's common stock. Each $1,000 face amount of bonds is convertible into 40 shares of $20 par stock. The bonds' term to maturity is 15 years. On July 31, 20X9, bondholders exercised their right to convert the bonds into common stock.

Recording conversion of bonds payable (Obj. 4)

Required

1. What would cause the bondholders to convert their bonds into common stock?
2. Without making journal entries, compute the carrying amount of the bonds payable at July 31, 20X9. Computer Diagnostics uses the straight-line method to amortize bond premium and discount.
3. All amortization has been recorded properly. Journalize the conversion transaction at July 31, 20X9.

E15-10 Viewpoint Industries reported the following at September 30:

Recording early retirement and conversion of bonds payable (Obj. 3, 4)

Long-term liabilities:		
Convertible bonds payable, 9%, eight years to maturity	$400,000	
Less: Discount on bonds payable	(12,000)	$388,000

Required

1. Record retirement of half of the bonds on October 1 at the call price of 102.
2. Record conversion of the remainder of the bonds into 4,000 shares of Viewpoint's $5 par common stock on October 1. What would cause the bondholders to convert their bonds into stock?

E15-11 Talbot Electronics is considering two plans for raising $1,000,000 to expand operations. Plan A is to borrow at 9%, and plan B is to issue 100,000 shares of common stock. Before any new financing, Talbot has net income of $600,000 and 100,000 shares of common stock outstanding. Management believes the company can use the new funds to earn additional income of $420,000 before interest and taxes. The income tax rate is 35%.

Analyzing alternative plans for raising money (Obj. 5)

Required

Analyze Talbot's situation to determine which plan will result in higher earnings per share. Use Exhibit 15-8 (page 595) as a guide.

E15-12 The chief accounting officer of Royal Textile, Inc., is considering how to report long-term notes payable and pension liabilities.

Reporting long-term debt and pension liability on the balance sheet (Obj. 6)

Required

1. Royal's bookkeeper has assembled the following for long-term notes payable:

Long-Term Notes Payable	
Total..	$537,000
Less: Current portion.........................	(33,000)
Discount on notes payable	(1,000)
	$503,000

None of the discount is related to the current portion of long-term notes payable. Show how Royal's balance sheet should report these liabilities.

2. Royal's pension plan has assets with a market value of $800,000. The plan's accumulated benefit obligation is $865,000. What amount of long-term pension liability, if any, will Royal report on its balance sheet?

Journalizing capital lease and operating lease transactions (Obj. 6)

E15-13 A capital lease agreement for equipment requires Motorama Automotive Company to make ten annual payments of $7,000, with the first payment due on January 2, 20X5. Motorama's liability under the lease is $40,313.

Required

1. Journalize the following transactions of Motorama Automotive:

20X5
Jan. 2   Beginning of lease term and the first annual payment.
Dec. 31   Depreciation of equipment.

At December 31, how much lease liability will Motorama report under a capital lease?

2. Journalize the January 2, 20X5, lease payment if this is an operating lease.
At December 31, how much lease liability will Motorama report under an operating lease?

Challenge Exercises

Analyzing bond transactions (Obj. 1, 2)

E15-14 This (partial and adapted) advertisement appeared in the *Wall Street Journal*.

BEAR STEARNS

This announcement is neither an offer to sell nor a solicitation of an offer to buy any of these securities. The offering is made only by the Prospectus.

New Issue

$300,000,000

MARK IV INDUSTRIES INC.

13⅜% Subordinated Debentures due March 31, 2010
Interest payable March 31 and September 30

Price 98.50%   **March 31, 2000**

A *subordinated* debenture gives rights to the bondholder that are more restricted than the rights of other bondholders.

Required

Answer these questions about **Mark IV Industries'** debenture bonds payable:

1. Suppose Mark IV Industries issued these bonds payable at their offering price on March 31, 2000. Describe the transaction in detail, indicating who received cash, who paid cash, and how much.

2. Why is the contract interest rate on these bonds so high?

3. Compute Mark IV Industries' annual cash interest payment on the bonds.

4. Compute Mark IV Industries' annual interest expense under the straight-line amortization method.

5. Prepare an effective-interest amortization table for Mark IV Industries' first two interest payments on September 30, 2000, and March 31, 2001. Use Exhibit 15-4 (page 589) as a guide and show all amounts in thousands. The market rate of interest on the bonds is 13.65% per year.

6. Compute Mark IV Industries interest expense for the first full year ended March 31, 2001, under the effective-interest method. Use the amortization table you prepared for requirement 5.

E15-15 Refer to the bond situation of **Mark IV Industries** in Exercise 15-14. Assume Mark IV Industries issued the bonds at the advertised price and that the company uses the effective-interest amortization method and reports financial statements on a calendar-year basis.

Analyzing bond transactions (Obj. 1,2)

Required

1. Journalize the following bond transactions of Mark IV Industries. Show all amounts in thousands of dollars. Explanations are not required.

2000
Mar. 31 Issuance of the bonds.
Sep. 30 Payment of interest expense and amortization of discount on bonds payable.
Dec. 31 Accrual of interest expense and amortization of discount on bonds payable.

2. What is Mark IV Industries' carrying amount of the bonds payable at

a. September 30, 2000?
b. December 31, 2000?
c. March 31, 2001?

PROBLEMS

(Group A)

P15-1A Zefer.com issued $500,000 of ten-year, 8% bonds payable at par on May 1, 20X5. The bonds pay interest each April 30 and October 31, and the company ends its accounting year on December 31.

Analyzing bonds, recording bond transactions at par, and reporting on the financial statements (Obj. 1)

Required

1. Fill in the blanks to complete these statements:
  a. Zefer.com's bonds are priced at (express the price as a percentage) _____.
  b. When Zefer.com issued its bonds, the market interest rate was _____%.
  c. The amount of bond discount or premium for Zefer.com to account for is $_____ because the bonds were issued at _____.
2. Journalize for Zefer.com
  a. Issuance of the bonds payable on May 1, 20X5.
  b. Payment of interest on October 31, 20X5.
  c. Accrual of interest at December 31, 20X5.
  d. Payment of interest on April 30, 20X6.
3. Show what Zefer.com will report on its income statement for 20X5 and on its balance sheet at December 31, 20X5.

P15-2A The board of directors of Galaxy Production Company authorizes the issue of $8 million of 7%, ten-year bonds payable. The semiannual interest dates are May 31 and November 30. The bonds are issued on June 30, 20X5, at par plus accrued interest.

Journalizing bond transactions (at par) and reporting bonds payable on the balance sheet— bond issued between interest dates (Obj. 1)

Required

1. Journalize the following transactions:
  a. Issuance of the bonds on June 30, 20X5.
  b. Payment of interest on November 30, 20X5.
  c. Accrual of interest on December 31, 20X5.
  d. Payment of interest on May 31, 20X6.
2. Check your recorded interest expense for 20X5, using as a model the supplement to the summary problem on page 588.
3. Report interest payable and bonds payable as they would appear on the Galaxy balance sheet at December 31, 20X5.

P15-3A On March 1, 20X4, Haupstrasse Corp. issues 8 1/4%, 20-year bonds payable with a face value of $400,000. The bonds pay interest on February 28 and August 31. Haupstrasse amortizes premium and discount by the straight-line method.

Issuing bonds, amortizing by the straight-line method, and reporting on the balance sheet (Obj. 1, 2)

Required

1. If the market interest rate is 7 3/8% when Haupstrasse issues its bonds, will the bonds be priced at par, at a premium, or at a discount? Explain.

2. If the market interest rate is 8 7/8% when Haupstrasse issues its bonds, will the bonds be priced at par, at a premium, or at a discount? Explain.
3. Assume that the issue price of the bonds is 96. Journalize the following bond transactions:
   a. Issuance of the bonds on March 1, 20X4.
   b. Payment of interest and amortization of discount on August 31, 20X4.
   c. Accrual of interest and amortization of discount on December 31, 20X4.
   d. Payment of interest and amortization of discount on February 28, 20X5.
4. Check your recorded interest expense for the year ended February 28, 20X5, using as a model the supplement to the summary problem on page 588.

Analyzing a company's long-term debt and journalizing its transactions
(Obj. 2)

P15-4A Metrovan Rental Company's balance sheet reported the following data on September 30, Year 1, end of the fiscal year (amounts rounded):

Long-Term Debt:
6.00% debenture bonds payable due Year 20 with an
    effective interest rate of 8.00%, net of discount of $39,200............... $164,800

Metrovan measures interest expense by the effective-interest method.

Required

1. Answer the following questions about Metrovan's long-term debt.
   a. What is the maturity value of the 6.00% debenture bonds?
   b. What is the carrying amount of the 6.00% debenture bonds at September 30, Year 1?
   c. What is Metrovan's annual cash interest payment on the 6.00% debenture bonds?
2. Prepare an amortization table through September 30, Year 3, for the 6.00% debenture bonds. Metrovan pays interest annually on September 30.
3. Record the September 30, Year 3 interest payment and amortization of the discount on the 6.00% debenture bonds.
4. What is Metrovan's carrying amount of the 6% debenture bonds at September 30, Year 3, immediately after the interest payment?

Issuing convertible bonds at a premium, measuring interest expense by the effective-interest method, retiring bonds early, and reporting on the balance sheet
(Obj. 2, 3, 4)

P15-5A On December 31, 20X1, Diplomat Linens, Inc., issues 9%, ten-year convertible bonds with a maturity value of $500,000. The semiannual interest dates are June 30 and December 31. The market interest rate is 8%, and the issue price of the bonds is 106.8. Diplomat measures interest expense by the effective-interest method.

Required

1. Prepare an effective-interest method amortization table for the first four semiannual interest periods.
2. Journalize the following transactions:
   a. Issuance of the bonds on December 31, 20X1. Credit Convertible Bonds Payable.
   b. Payment of interest on June 30, 20X2.
   c. Payment of interest on December 31, 20X2.
   d. Retirement of bonds with face value of $100,000 on December 31, 20X3. Diplomat pays the call price of 102.
3. Prepare the balance sheet presentation of the bonds payable that are outstanding at December 31, 20X3.

Journalizing bonds payable and capital lease transactions
(Obj. 1, 6)

P15-6A Journalize the following transactions of Berkshire Properties, Inc.:

20X1
Jan. 1   Issued $400,000 of 9%, ten-year bonds payable at 97.
      1   Signed a five-year capital lease on equipment. The agreement requires annual lease payments of $20,000, with the first payment due immediately. The liability for the four remaining lease payments is $60,750.
July 1   Paid semiannual interest and amortized discount by the straight-line method on 9% bonds payable.
Dec. 31   Accrued semiannual interest expense, and amortized discount by the straight-line method on 9% bonds payable.
Dec. 31   Recorded depreciation on leased equipment.

Financing operations with debt or with stock
(Obj. 5)

P15-7A Two businesses are considering how to raise $10 million.
    Franklin Corporation is in the midst of its most successful period since it began operations in 1972. For each of the past ten years, net income and earnings per share have increased by at least 15%. The outlook for the future is equally bright, with new markets opening up and competitors unable to manufacture products of Franklin's quality. Franklin Corporation is planning a large-scale expansion.

Westchase Company has fallen on hard times. Net income has remained flat for five of the last six years, with this year falling by 10% from last year's level of profits. Top management has experienced unusual turnover, and the company lacks strong leadership. To become competitive again, Westchase Company desperately needs $10 million for expansion.

Required

1. Propose a plan for each company to raise the needed cash. Which company should borrow? Which company should issue stock? Consider the advantages and the disadvantages of raising money by borrowing and by issuing stock, and discuss them in your answer. Use the following memorandum headings to report your plans for the two companies:
   - Plan for Franklin Corporation to raise $10 million
   - Plan for Westchase Company to raise $10 million
2. How will what you learned in this problem help you manage a business?

P15-8A The accounting records of Global Hardwood, Inc., include the following items:

Reporting liabilities on the balance sheet (Obj. 6)

Capital lease liability, long-term	$ 73,000	Mortgage note payable, long-term	$116,000
Accumulated pension benefit obligation	207,000	Capital lease liability, current	11,000
Bonds payable, long-term	160,000	Pension plan assets (market value)	190,000
Premium on bonds payable (all long-term)	13,000	Bonds payable, current portion	20,000
Interest payable	14,200		

Required

Report these liabilities on Global's balance sheet, including headings and totals for current liabilities and long-term liabilities.

PROBLEMS

(Group B)

P15-1B Focalpoint.com issued $600,000 of 20-year, 9% bonds payable at par on February 1, 20X3. The bonds pay interest each January 31 and July 31, and the company ends its accounting year on December 31.

Analyzing bonds, recording bond transactions at par, and reporting on the financial statements (Obj. 1)

1. Fill in the blanks to complete these statements:
   a. Focalpoint.com's bonds are priced at (express the price as a percentage) _____.
   b. When Focalpoint.com issued its bonds, the market interest rate was _____%.
   c. The amount of bond discount or premium for Focalpoint.com to account for is $_____ because the bonds were issued at _____.
2. Journalize for Focalpoint.com
   a. Issuance of the bonds payable on February 1, 20X3.
   b. Payment of interest on July 31, 20X3.
   c. Accrual of interest at December 31, 20X3.
   d. Payment of interest on January 31, 20X4.
3. Show what Focalpoint.com will report on its income statement for 20X3 and on its balance sheet at December 31, 20X3.

P15-2B The board of directors of Tucker Communications authorizes the issue of $3 million of 9%, 20-year bonds payable. The semiannual interest dates are March 31 and September 30. The bonds are issued on April 30, 20X4, at par.

Journalizing bond transactions (at par) and reporting bonds payable on the balance sheet—bonds issued between interest dates (Obj. 1)

Required

1. Journalize the following transactions:
   a. Issuance of the bonds on April 30, 20X4.
   c. Accrual of interest on December 31, 20X4.
   b. Payment of interest on Sept. 30, 20X4.
   d. Payment of interest on March 31, 20X5.
2. Check your recorded interest expense for 20X4, using as a model the supplement to the summary problem on pages 587–588.
3. Report interest payable and bonds payable as they would appear on the Tucker balance sheet at December 31, 20X4.

P15-3B Assume that on March 31, 20X6, **Goretex Corp.** issues 8%, ten-year notes payable with a face value of $400,000. The notes pay interest on March 31 and September 30, and Goretex amortizes premium and discount by the straight-line method.

Required

1. If the market interest rate is 8 1/2% when Goretex issues its notes, will the notes be priced at par, at a premium, or at a discount? Explain.
2. If the market interest rate is 7% when Goretex issues its notes, will the notes be priced at par, at a premium, or at a discount? Explain.
3. Assume that the issue price of the notes is 101. Journalize the following note payable transactions:
   a. Issuance of the notes on April 1, 20X6.
   b. Payment of interest and amortization of premium on September 30, 20X6.
   c. Accrual of interest and amortization of premium on December 31, 20X6.
   d. Payment of interest and amortization of premium on March 31, 20X7.
4. Check your recorded interest expense for the year ended March 31, 20X7, using as a model the supplement to the summary problem on pages 587–588.

P15-4B CoStar Temp Employment, Inc.'s balance sheet reported the following data on September 30, Year 1, end of the fiscal year (amounts rounded):

Long-Term Debt

5% debenture bonds payable due Year 14, net of discount of $45,200 (effective interest rate of 8%)	$124,800

CoStar measures interest expense by the effective-interest method.

Required

1. Answer the following questions about CoStar's long-term debt:
   a. What is the maturity value of the 5% debenture bonds?
   b. What is the carrying amount of the 5% debenture bonds at September 30, Year 1?
   c. What is CoStar's annual cash interest payment on the 5% debenture bonds?
2. Prepare an amortization table through September 30, Year 3, for the 5% debenture bonds. CoStar pays interest annually on September 30.
3. Record the September 30, Year 3, interest payment and amortization of the discount on the 5% debenture bonds.
4. What is CoStar's carrying amount of the 5% debenture bonds at September 30, Year 3, immediately after the interest payment?

P15-5B On December 31, 20X1, Sportif Corp. issues 8%, ten-year convertible bonds with a maturity value of $700,000. The semiannual interest dates are June 30 and December 31. The market interest rate is 9%, and the issue price of the bonds is 94. Sportif amortizes bond premium and discount by the effective-interest method.

Required

1. Prepare an effective-interest method amortization table for the first four semiannual interest periods.
2. Journalize the following transactions:
   a. Issuance of the bonds on December 31, 20X1. Credit Convertible Bonds Payable.
   b. Payment of interest on June 30, 20X2.
   c. Payment of interest on December 31, 20X2.
   d. Retirement of bonds with face value of $100,000 December 31, 20X3. Sportif purchases the bonds at 96 in the open market.
3. Prepare a balance sheet presentation of the bonds payable that are outstanding at December 31, 20X3.

P15-6B Journalize the following transactions of Sephora Cosmetics, Inc.:

20X1
Jan. 1   Issued $1,000,000 of 7%, ten-year bonds payable at 97.
       1   Signed a five-year capital lease on machinery. The agreement requires annual lease payments of $16,000, with the first payment due immediately. The liability for the remaining lease payments is $48,590.
July 1   Paid semiannual interest and amortized discount by the straight-line method on 7% bonds payable.
Dec. 31   Accrued semiannual interest expense and amortized discount by the straight-line method on 7% bonds payable.
      31   Recorded depreciation on leased machinery.

P15-7B Research indicates that consumers prefer upscale restaurants. To capitalize on this trend, Palomino Eurobistros, Inc., is embarking on a massive expansion. Plans call for opening 20 new restaurants within the next two years. Each restaurant is scheduled to be 30% larger than the company's existing locations and feature upgraded menus. Management estimates that company operations will provide $3 million of the cash needed for expansion. Palomino must raise the remaining $1.5 million from outsiders. The board of directors is considering obtaining the $1.5 million either through borrowing or by issuing common stock.

Financing operations with debt or with stock
(Obj. 5)

Required

1. Write a memo to company management. Discuss the advantages and disadvantages of borrowing and of issuing common stock to raise the needed cash. Use the following format for your memo:

Date:	_____
To:	Management of Palomino Eurobistros, Inc.
From:	Student Name
Subject:	Advantages and disadvantages of borrowing versus issuing stock to raise $1.5 million for expansion
Advantages and disadvantages of borrowing:	
Advantages and disadvantages of issuing stock:	

2. How will what you learned in this problem help you manage a business?

P15-8B The accounting records of LeBeau Fashions, Inc., include the following items:

Reporting liabilities on the balance sheet
(Obj. 6)

Bonds payable, long-term......	$300,000	Accumulated pension benefit obligation............................	$419,000
Pension plan assets (market value).....................	382,000	Mortgage note payable, long-term...........................	93,000
Bonds payable, current portion...............................	75,000	Capital lease liability, current..............................	18,000
Capital lease liability, long-term	81,000	Mortgage note payable, current..............................	23,000
Discount on bonds payable (all long-term)	7,000	Interest payable.....................	11,000

Required

Report these liabilities on LeBeau's balance sheet, including headings and totals for current liabilities and long-term liabilities.

APPLY YOUR KNOWLEDGE

DECISION CASES

Case 1. Business is going well for DFW Designs. The board of directors of this family-owned company believes that DFW could earn an additional $1,500,000 income before interest and taxes by expanding into new markets. However, the $5 million the business needs for growth cannot be raised within the family. The directors, who strongly wish to retain family control of the company, must issue securities to outsiders. They are considering three financing plans.

Analyzing alternative ways of raising $5 million
(Obj. 5)

Plan A is to borrow at 8%. Plan B is to issue 100,000 shares of common stock. Plan C is to issue 100,000 shares of nonvoting, $3.75 preferred stock ($3.75 is the annual cash dividend paid on each share of preferred stock). DFW presently has net income of $6,000,000 and 1,000,000 shares of common stock outstanding. The company's income tax rate is 35%.

Required

1. Prepare an analysis similar to Exhibit 15-8 (page 595) to determine which plan will result in the highest earnings per share of common stock.
2. Recommend one plan to the board of directors. Give your reasons.

Case 2. ⟵ *Link Back to Chapter 4 (Debt Ratio).* The following questions are not related.

1. **IMAX Corporation** likes to borrow for longer periods when interest rates are low and for shorter periods when interest rates are high. Why is this a good business strategy?

Questions about long-term debt
(Obj. 6 and Appendix to Chapter 15)

2. IMAX needs to borrow $2 million to open new theaters. IMAX can borrow $2 million by issuing 8%, 20-year bonds at a price of 96. How much will IMAX actually be borrowing under this arrangement? How much must IMAX pay back at maturity? How will IMAX account for the difference between the amount borrowed and the amount paid back?

ETHICAL ISSUE

Python.com owes $6 million on notes payable that will come due for payment in $1.5 million installments over a four-year period. The company has used its cash to advertise heavily in the competitive dotcom business environment. The result is that cash is scarce, and Python.com's management doesn't know where next year's note payment will come from. Python.com has prepared its balance sheet at December 31, 20X4, and reports the following:

Liabilities	
Current:	
Accounts payable	$1,900,000
Salary payable and other accrued liabilites	300,000
Unearned revenue collected in advance	500,000
Income tax payable	200,000
Total current liabilities	2,900,000
Long-term:	
Notes payable	6,000,000

What is wrong with the way Python.com reported its liabilities? Why did Python.com report its liabilities this way? What is unethical about this way of reporting *these* liabilities? Who can be harmed as a result?

FINANCIAL STATEMENT CASE

Analyzing long-term debt
(Obj. 1)

The **Target Corporation** income statement, balance sheet, and statement of cash flows in Appendix A provide details about the company's long-term debt. Use those data to answer the following questions.

Required

1. How much did Target owe on long-term debt at January 29, 2000? How much was payable in the coming year?
2. Examine the statement of cash flows for 1999. Journalize the two transactions that affected long-term debt during the year. Ignore the notes payable transaction.
3. Journalize in a single entry Target's interest expense for 1999. Target paid cash of $405 million for interest, including $12 million capitalized to the Building account.

TEAM PROJECT

Note: This project uses the chapter appendix.

Bermuda Corporation leases the equipment that it uses in operations. Bermuda prefers operating leases (versus capital leases) in order to keep the lease liability off its balance sheet and maintain a low debt ratio.

Bermuda is negotiating a ten-year lease on equipment with an expected useful life of 15 years. The lease requires Bermuda to make ten annual lease payments of $20,000 each, due at the end of the period, plus a down payment that is due at the beginning of the lease term. The interest rate in the lease agreement is 10%. The leased asset has a market value of $160,000. The lease agreement specifies no transfer to title to the lessee and includes no bargain purchase option.

Write a report for Bermuda's management to explain how Bermuda should account for this lease—as an operating lease or as a capital lease. Use the following format for your report:

Date:	_____
To:	Bermuda Management
From:	Student Names
Subject:	Accounting for the company's equipment lease

1. Our nation has amassed a huge public debt. Just how huge? Go to **http://www.pub-licdebt.treas.gov/sec/sec.htm.** In the left-hand column under "The Public Debt," click on *Debt Figure.* How much is the current public debt to the penny? Is the amount of the public debt in millions, billions, or trillions of dollars?

2. Go to **http://www.investinginbonds.com.** In the left-hand column under "Bond Prices," click on *Corporate Bonds.* In the right-hand column under "Please show me bonds traded yesterday for:" use the pull-down menu to select *All Market Sectors.* Select to sort by *Price* and then click on *Search.* "Coupon" refers to the contract interest rate and "Yield" refers to the market interest rate.

   a. Refer to the bond at the *top* of the list to answer these questions. Is this bond selling at a premium, at par, or at a discount? How can you tell? Assume this entity issues a bond with a face value of $10,000. The issuing entity will receive how much cash at issuance? What is the amount of the annual interest payment? When does this bond mature? How much will the issuing entity pay at maturity?

   b. Refer to bond at the *bottom* of the list to answer these questions. Is this bond selling at a premium, at par, or at a discount? Why is this bond selling at the current price? What rate are investors demanding to loan money to this entity? What is the true rate of interest expense for the issuing entity?

3. Bonds are issued by different entities. In the left-hand column under "Investor's Guides," click on *Municipal Bonds.* Read the information displayed. Who issues municipal bonds? What do the funds raised help pay for?

4. In the left-hand column under "Bond Prices," click on *Municipal Bonds.* In the right-hand column under "Please show me bonds traded yesterday for:" use the pull-down menu to find bonds issued in your state. Select to sort by *Coupon* and then click on *Search.* What is the greatest contract (coupon) interest rate offered? What entity issued this bond?

APPENDIX TO CHAPTER 15

TIME VALUE OF MONEY: FUTURE VALUE AND PRESENT VALUE

This discussion of future value lays the foundation for present value but is not essential. For the valuation of long-term liabilities, some instructors may wish to begin at the bottom of page 616.

The term *time value of money* refers to the fact that money earns interest over time. Interest is the cost of using money. To borrowers, interest is the expense of renting money. To lenders, interest is the revenue earned from lending. We must recognize the interest. Otherwise we overlook an important part of the transaction.

Suppose you invest $4,545 in corporate bonds that pay 10% interest each year. After one year, the value of your investment has grown to $5,000. The difference between your original investment ($4,545) and the future value of the investment ($5,000) is the amount of interest revenue you will earn during the year ($455). If you ignore the interest, you would not account for the interest revenue you have earned. Interest becomes more important as the time period lengthens because the amount of interest depends on the span of time the money is invested.

Let's consider a second example, but from the borrower's perspective. Suppose you purchase a machine for your business. The cash price of the machine is $8,000, but you cannot pay cash now. To finance the purchase, you sign an $8,000 note payable. The note requires you to pay the $8,000 plus 10% interest one year from date of purchase. Is your cost of the machine $8,000, or is it $8,800 [$8,000 plus interest of $800 ($8,000 × 0.10)]? The cost is $8,000. The additional $800 is interest expense.

FUTURE VALUE

The main application of future value is the accumulated balance of an investment at a future date. In our first example, the investment earned 10% per year. After one year, $4,545 grew to $5,000, as shown in Exhibit 15A-1. If the money were invested for five years, you would have to perform five such calculations. You would also have to consider the compound interest that your investment is earning. *Compound interest* is the interest you earn not only on your principal amount, but also on the

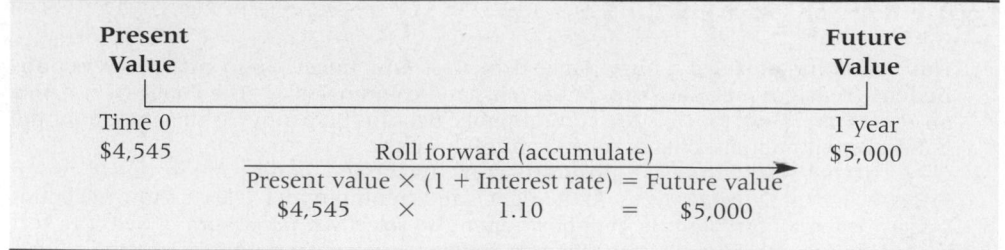

interest to date. Most business applications include compound interest. The following table shows the interest revenue earned each year at 10%:

End of Year	Interest	Future Value
0	—	$4,545
1	$4,545 × 0.10 = $455	5,000
2	5,000 × 0.10 = 500	5,500
3	5,500 × 0.10 = 550	6,050
4	6,050 × 0.10 = 605	6,655
5	6,655 × 0.10 = 666	7,321

Earning 10%, a $4,545 investment grows to $5,000 at the end of one year, to $5,500 at the end of two years, and so on. (Throughout this discussion, we round off to the nearest dollar.)

Future-Value Tables

The process of computing a future value is called *accumulating* because the future value is *more* than the present value. Mathematical tables ease the computational burden. Exhibit 15A-2, Future Value of $1, gives the future value for a single sum (a

Exhibit 15A-2 **Future Value of $1**

					Future Value of $1					
Period	**4%**	**5%**	**6%**	**7%**	**8%**	**9%**	**10%**	**12%**	**14%**	**16%**
1	1.040	1.050	1.060	1.070	1.080	1.090	1.100	1.120	1.140	1.160
2	1.082	1.103	1.124	1.145	1.166	1.188	1.210	1.254	1.300	1.346
3	1.125	1.158	1.191	1.225	1.260	1.295	1.331	1.405	1.482	1.561
4	1.170	1.216	1.262	1.311	1.360	1.412	1.464	1.574	1.689	1.811
5	1.217	1.276	1.338	1.403	1.469	1.539	1.611	1.762	1.925	2.100
6	1.265	1.340	1.419	1.501	1.587	1.677	1.772	1.974	2.195	2.436
7	1.316	1.407	1.504	1.606	1.714	1.828	1.949	2.211	2.502	2.826
8	1.369	1.477	1.594	1.718	1.851	1.993	2.144	2.476	2.853	3.278
9	1.423	1.551	1.689	1.838	1.999	2.172	2.358	2.773	3.252	3.803
10	1.480	1.629	1.791	1.967	2.159	2.367	2.594	3.106	3.707	4.411
11	1.539	1.710	1.898	2.105	2.332	2.580	2.853	3.479	4.226	5.117
12	1.601	1.796	2.012	2.252	2.518	2.813	3.138	3.896	4.818	5.936
13	1.665	1.886	2.133	2.410	2.720	3.066	3.452	4.363	5.492	6.886
14	1.732	1.980	2.261	2.579	2.937	3.342	3.797	4.887	6.261	7.988
15	1.801	2.079	2.397	2.759	3.172	3.642	4.177	5.474	7.138	9.266
16	1.873	2.183	2.540	2.952	3.426	3.970	4.595	6.130	8.137	10.748
17	1.948	2.292	2.693	3.159	3.700	4.328	5.054	6.866	9.276	12.468
18	2.026	2.407	2.854	3.380	3.996	4.717	5.560	7.690	10.575	14.463
19	2.107	2.527	3.026	3.617	4.316	5.142	6.116	8.613	12.056	16.777
20	2.191	2.653	3.207	3.870	4.661	5.604	6.727	9.646	13.743	19.461

present value), $1, invested to earn a particular interest rate for a specific number of periods. Future value depends on three factors: (1) the amount of the investment, (2) the length of time between investment and future accumulation, and (3) the interest rate.

The heading in Exhibit 15A-2 states $1. Future-value and present-value tables are based on $1 because unity (the value 1) is so easy to work with. Look at the Period column and the interest-rate columns 4–16%. In business applications, interest rates are always stated for the annual period of one year unless specified otherwise. In fact, an interest rate can be stated for any period, such as 3% per quarter or 5% for a six-month period. The length of the period is arbitrary.

For example, an investment may promise a return (income) of 3% per quarter for six months (two quarters). In that case, you would be working with 3% interest for two periods. It would be incorrect to use 6% for one period because the interest is 3% compounded quarterly, and that amount differs somewhat from 6% compounded semiannually. Take care in studying future-value and present-value problems to align the interest rate with the appropriate number of periods.

Let's use Exhibit 15A-2. The future value of $1.00 invested at 8% for one year is $1.08 ($1.00 × 1.080, which appears at the junction under the 8% column and across from 1 in the Period column). The figure 1.080 includes both the principal (1.000) and the compound interest for one period (0.080).

Suppose you deposit $5,000 in a savings account that pays annual interest of 8%. The account balance at the end of one year will be $5,400. To compute the future value of $5,000 at 8% for one year, multiply $5,000 by 1.080 to get $5,400. Now suppose you invest in a ten-year, 8% certificate of deposit (CD). What will be the future value of the CD at maturity? To compute the future value of $5,000 at 8% for ten periods, multiply $5,000 by 2.159 (from Exhibit 15A-2) to get $10,795. This future value of $10,795 indicates that $5,000 earning 8% interest compounded annually grows to $10,795 at the end of ten years. You can find any present amount's future value at a particular future date.

Future Value of an Annuity

In the preceding example, we made an investment of a single amount. Other investments, called annuities, include multiple investments of an equal periodic amount at fixed intervals over the duration of the investment. Consider a family investing for a child's education. The Dietrichs can invest $4,000 annually to accumulate a college fund for 15-year-old Helen. The investment can earn 7% annually until Helen turns 18—a three-year investment. How much will be available for Helen on the date of the last investment? Exhibit 15A-3 shows the accumulation—a total future value of $12,860.

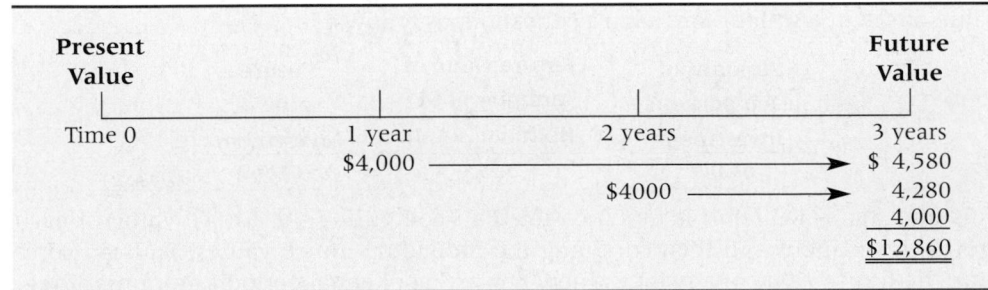

Exhibit 15A-3
Future Value of an Annuity

The first $4,000 invested by the Dietrichs grows to $4,580 over the investment period. The second amount grows to $4,280, and the third amount stays at $4,000 because it has no time to earn interest. The sum of the three future values ($4,580 + $4,280 + $4,000) is the future value of the annuity ($12,860), which can be computed as follows:

End of Year	Annual Investment	+	Interest	=	Increase for the Year	Future Value of Annuity
0	—		—		—	0
1	$4,000		—		$4,000	$ 4,000
2	4,000	+	($4,000 × 0.07 = $280)	=	4,280	8,280
3	4,000	+	($8,280 × 0.07 = $580)	=	4,580	12,860

As with the Future Value of $1 table (a lump sum), mathematical tables ease the strain of calculating annuities. Exhibit 15A-4, Future Value of Annuity of $1, gives the future value of a series of investments, each of equal amount, at regular intervals.

EXHIBIT 15A-4   **Future Value of Annuity of $1**

Future Value of Annuity of $1

Period	4%	5%	6%	7%	8%	9%	10%	12%	14%	16%
1	1.000	1.000	1.000	1.000	1.000	1.000	1.000	1.000	1.000	1.000
2	2.040	2.050	2.060	2.070	2.080	2.090	2.100	2.120	2.140	2.160
3	3.122	3.153	3.184	3.215	3.246	3.278	3.310	3.374	3.440	3.506
4	4.246	4.310	4.375	4.440	4.506	4.573	4.641	4.779	4.921	5.066
5	5.416	5.526	5.637	5.751	5.867	5.985	6.105	6.353	6.610	6.877
6	6.633	6.802	6.975	7.153	7.336	7.523	7.716	8.115	8.536	8.977
7	7.898	8.142	8.394	8.654	8.923	9.200	9.487	10.089	10.730	11.414
8	9.214	9.549	9.897	10.260	10.637	11.028	11.436	12.300	13.233	14.240
9	10.583	11.027	11.491	11.978	12.488	13.021	13.579	14.776	16.085	17.519
10	12.006	12.578	13.181	13.816	14.487	15.193	15.937	17.549	19.337	21.321
11	13.486	14.207	14.972	15.784	16.645	17.560	18.531	20.655	23.045	25.733
12	15.026	15.917	16.870	17.888	18.977	20.141	21.384	24.133	27.271	30.850
13	16.627	17.713	18.882	20.141	21.495	22.953	24.523	28.029	32.089	36.786
14	18.292	19.599	21.015	22.550	24.215	26.019	27.975	32.393	37.581	43.672
15	20.024	21.579	23.276	25.129	27.152	29.361	31.772	37.280	43.842	51.660
16	21.825	23.657	25.673	27.888	30.324	33.003	35.950	42.753	50.980	60.925
17	23.698	25.840	28.213	30.840	33.750	36.974	40.545	48.884	59.118	71.673
18	25.645	28.132	30.906	33.999	37.450	41.301	45.599	55.750	68.394	84.141
19	27.671	30.539	33.760	37.379	41.446	46.018	51.159	63.440	78.969	98.603
20	29.778	33.066	36.786	40.995	45.762	51.160	57.275	72.052	91.025	115.380

What is the future value of an annuity of three investments of $1 each that earn 7%? The answer 3.215 can be found in the 7% column and across from 3 in the Period column of Exhibit 15A-4. This amount can be used to compute the future value of the investment for Helen's education, as follows:

Amount of each periodic investment	×	Future value of annuity of $1 (Exhibit 15A-4)	=	Future value of investment
$4,000	×	3.215	=	$12,860

This one-step calculation is much easier than computing the future value of each annual investment and then summing the individual future values. You can compute the future value of any investment consisting of equal periodic amounts at regular intervals. Businesses make periodic investments to accumulate funds for plant expansion and other uses—an application of the future value of an annuity.

PRESENT VALUE

Often a person knows a future amount and needs to know the related present value. Recall Exhibit 15A-1, in which present value and future value are on opposite ends of the same time line. Suppose an investment promises to pay you $5,000 at the *end* of one year. How much would you pay *now* to acquire this investment? You would be willing to pay the present value of the $5,000 future amount.

Present value also depends on three factors: (1) the amount of payment (or receipt), (2) the length of time between investment and future receipt (or payment), and (3) the interest rate. The process of computing a present value is called *discounting* because the present value is *less* than the future value.

In our example, the future receipt is $5,000. The investment period is one year. Assume that you demand an annual interest rate of 10% on your investment. With all three factors specified, you can compute the present value of $5,000 at 10% for one year:

$$\frac{\text{Future value}}{(1 + \text{Interest rate})} = \frac{\$5,000}{1.10} = \$4,545$$

By turning the data around into a future-value problem, we verify the present-value computation:

Amount invested (present value)	$4,545
Expected earnings ($4,545 × 0.10)	455
Amount to be received one year from now (future value)	$5,000

This example illustrates that present value and future value are based on the same equation:

$$\text{Present value} \times (1 + \text{Interest rate}) = \text{Future value}$$

$$\frac{\text{Future value}}{(1 + \text{Interest rate})} = \text{Present value}$$

If the $5,000 is to be received two years from now, you will pay only $4,132 for the investment, as shown in Exhibit 15A-5.

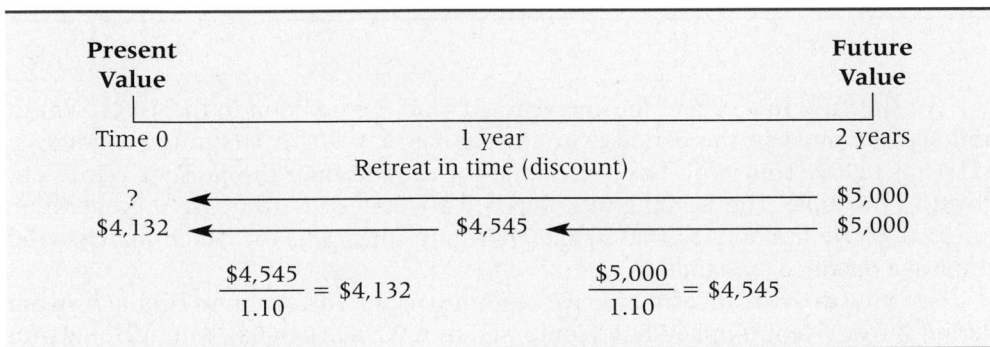

EXHIBIT 15A-5
Two-Year Investment

By turning the data around, we verify that $4,132 accumulates to $5,000 at 10% for two years:

Amount invested (present value)	$4,132
Expected earnings for first year ($4,132 × 0.10)	413
Value of investment after one year	4,545
Expected earnings for second year ($4,545 × 0.10)	455
Amount to be received two years from now (future value)	$5,000

You would pay $4,132—the present value of $5,000—to receive the $5,000 future amount at the end of two years at 10% per year. The $868 difference between the amount invested ($4,132) and the amount to be received ($5,000) is the return on the investment, the sum of the two interest receipts: $413 + $455 = $868.

Present-Value Tables

We have shown the simple formula for computing present value. However, figuring present value "by hand" for investments spanning many years is burdensome. Present-value tables ease our work. Let's reexamine our examples of present value by using Exhibit 15A-6, Present Value of $1.

EXHIBIT 15A-6 **Present Value of $1**

					Present Value of $1				
Period	4%	5%	6%	7%	8%	10%	12%	14%	16%
1	0.962	0.952	0.943	0.935	0.926	0.909	0.893	0.877	0.862
2	0.925	0.907	0.890	0.873	0.857	0.826	0.797	0.769	0.743
3	0.889	0.864	0.840	0.816	0.794	0.751	0.712	0.675	0.641
4	0.855	0.823	0.792	0.763	0.735	0.683	0.636	0.592	0.552
5	0.822	0.784	0.747	0.713	0.681	0.621	0.567	0.519	0.476
6	0.790	0.746	0.705	0.666	0.630	0.564	0.507	0.456	0.410
7	0.760	0.711	0.665	0.623	0.583	0.513	0.452	0.400	0.354
8	0.731	0.677	0.627	0.582	0.540	0.467	0.404	0.351	0.305
9	0.703	0.645	0.592	0.544	0.500	0.424	0.361	0.308	0.263
10	0.676	0.614	0.558	0.508	0.463	0.386	0.322	0.270	0.227
11	0.650	0.585	0.527	0.475	0.429	0.350	0.287	0.237	0.195
12	0.625	0.557	0.497	0.444	0.397	0.319	0.257	0.208	0.168
13	0.601	0.530	0.469	0.415	0.368	0.290	0.229	0.182	0.145
14	0.577	0.505	0.442	0.388	0.340	0.263	0.205	0.160	0.125
15	0.555	0.481	0.417	0.362	0.315	0.239	0.183	0.140	0.108
16	0.534	0.458	0.394	0.339	0.292	0.218	0.163	0.123	0.093
17	0.513	0.436	0.371	0.317	0.270	0.198	0.146	0.108	0.080
18	0.494	0.416	0.350	0.296	0.250	0.180	0.130	0.095	0.069
19	0.475	0.396	0.331	0.277	0.232	0.164	0.116	0.083	0.060
20	0.456	0.377	0.312	0.258	0.215	0.149	0.104	0.073	0.051

For the 10% investment for one year, we find the junction in the 10% column and across from 1 in the Period column. The figure 0.909 is computed as follows: $1/1.10 = 0.909$. This work has been done for us, and only the present values are given in the table. The heading in Exhibit 15A-6 states $1. To figure present value for $5,000, we multiply $5,000 by 0.909. The result is $4,545, which matches the result we obtained by hand.

For the two-year investment, we read down the 10% column and across the Period 2 row. We multiply 0.826 (computed as $0.909/1.10 = 0.826$) by $5,000 and get $4,130, which confirms our earlier computation of $4,132 (the difference is due to rounding in the present-value table). Using the table, we can compute the present value of any single future amount.

Present Value of an Annuity

Let's return to the investment example that provided the investor with only a single future receipt ($5,000 at the end of two years). Annuity investments provide multiple receipts of an equal amount at fixed intervals over the investment's duration.

Consider an investment that promises *annual* cash receipts of $10,000 to be received at the end of each of three years. Assume that you demand a 12% return on your investment. What is the investment's present value? What would you pay today to acquire the investment? The investment spans three periods, and you would pay the sum of three present values. The computation appears at the top of page 619.

The present value of this annuity is $24,020. By paying this amount today, you will receive $10,000 at the end of each of the three years while earning 12% on your investment.

Year	Annual Cash Receipt	×	Present of $1 at 12% (Exhibit 15A-6)	=	Present Value of Annual Cash Receipt
1	$10,000	×	0.893	=	$ 8,930
2	10,000	×	0.797	=	7,970
3	10,000	×	0.712	=	7,120
	Total present value of investment			=	$24,020

The example illustrates repetitive computations of the three future amounts, a time-consuming process. One way to ease the computational burden is to add the three present values of $1 (0.893 + 0.797 + 0.712) and multiply their sum (2.402) by the annual cash receipt ($10,000) to obtain the present value of the annuity ($10,000 × 2.402 = $24,020).

An easier approach is to use a present value of an annuity table. Exhibit 15A-7 shows the present value of $1 to be received at the end of each period for a given number of periods. The present value of a three-period annuity at 12% is 2.402 (the junction of the Period 3 row and the 12% column). Thus, $10,000 received annually at the end of each of three years, discounted at 12%, is $24,020 ($10,000 × 2.402), which is the present value.

EXHIBIT 15A-7   **Present Value of Annuity of $1**

Period	4%	5%	6%	7%	8%	10%	12%	14%	16%
				Present Value of Annuity of $1					
1	0.962	0.952	0.943	0.935	0.926	0.909	0.893	0.877	0.862
2	1.886	1.859	1.833	1.808	1.783	1.736	1.690	1.647	1.605
3	2.775	2.723	2.673	2.624	2.577	2.487	2.402	2.322	2.246
4	3.630	3.546	3.465	3.387	3.312	3.170	3.037	2.914	2.798
5	4.452	4.329	4.212	4.100	3.993	3.791	3.605	3.433	3.274
6	5.242	5.076	4.917	4.767	4.623	4.355	4.111	3.889	3.685
7	6.002	5.786	5.582	5.389	5.206	4.868	4.564	4.288	4.039
8	6.733	6.463	6.210	5.971	5.747	5.335	4.968	4.639	4.344
9	7.435	7.108	6.802	6.515	6.247	5.759	5.328	4.946	4.607
10	8.111	7.722	7.360	7.024	6.710	6.145	5.650	5.216	4.833
11	8.760	8.306	7.887	7.499	7.139	6.495	5.938	5.453	5.029
12	9.385	8.863	8.384	7.943	7.536	6.814	6.194	5.660	5.197
13	9.986	9.394	8.853	8.358	7.904	7.103	6.424	5.842	5.342
14	10.563	9.899	9.295	8.745	8.244	7.367	6.628	6.002	5.468
15	11.118	10.380	9.712	9.108	8.559	7.606	6.811	6.142	5.575
16	11.652	10.838	10.106	9.447	8.851	7.824	6.974	6.265	5.669
17	12.166	11.274	10.477	9.763	9.122	8.022	7.120	6.373	5.749
18	12.659	11.690	10.828	10.059	9.372	8.201	7.250	6.467	5.818
19	13.134	12.085	11.158	10.336	9.604	8.365	7.366	6.550	5.877
20	13.590	12.462	11.470	10.594	9.818	8.514	7.469	6.623	5.929

Present Value of Bonds Payable

The present value of a bond—its market price—is the present value of the future principal amount at maturity plus the present value of the future contract interest payments. The principal is a single amount to be paid at maturity. The interest is an annuity because it occurs periodically.

Let's compute the present value of the 9%, five-year bonds of **eBay Inc.** The face value of the bonds is $100,000, and they pay 4 1/2% contract (cash) interest semiannually. At issuance, the market interest rate is expressed as 10%, but it is computed at 5% semiannually. Therefore, the effective interest rate for each of the ten semiannual periods is 5%. We use 5% in computing the present value (PV) of the maturity and of the interest. The market price of these bonds is $96,149, as follows:

	Effective annual interest rate ÷ 2	Number of semiannual interest payments	
PV of principal:			
$100,000 × PV of single amount at 5%		for 10 periods	
($100,000 × 0.614—Exhibit 15A-6)..			$61,400
PV of interest:			
($100,000 × 0.045) × PV of annuity at 5%		for 10 periods	
($4,500 × 7.722—Exhibit 15A-7)..			34,749
PV (market price) of bonds..			$96,149

The market price of the eBay bonds show a discount because the contract interest rate on the bonds (9%) is less than the market interest rate (10%). We discuss these bonds in more detail on pages 588–590.

Let's consider a premium price for the eBay bonds. Assume that the market interest rate is 8% at issuance. The effective rate is 4% for each of the ten semiannual periods:

	Effective annual interest rate ÷ 2	Number of semiannual interest periods	
PV of principal:			
$100,000 × PV of single amount at 4%		for 10 periods	
($100,000 × 0.676—Exhibit 15A-6)..			$ 67,600
PV of interest:			
($100,000 × 0.045) × PV of annuity at 4%		for 10 periods	
($4,500 × 8.111—Exhibit 15A-7)..			36,500
PV (market price) of bonds			$104,100

We discuss accounting for these bonds on pages 590–592.

Capital Leases

How does a lessee compute the cost of an asset acquired through a capital lease? Consider that the lessee gets the use of the asset but does *not* pay for the leased asset in full at the beginning of the lease. A capital lease is therefore similar to an installment purchase of the leased asset. The lessee must record the leased asset at the present value of the lease liability. The time value of money must be weighed.

The cost of the asset to the lessee is the sum of any payment made at the beginning of the lease period plus the present value of the future lease payments. The lease payments are equal amounts occurring at regular intervals—that is, they are annuity payments.

Consider the 20-year building lease of **Safeway.** The lease starts on January 1, 20X4, and requires 20 annual payments of $10,000 each, with the first payment due immediately. The interest rate in the lease is 10%, and the present value of the 19 future payments at the end of each period is $83,650 ($10,000 × PV of annuity at 10% for 19 periods, or 8.365 from Exhibit 15A-7). Safeway's cost is $93,650 (the sum of the initial payment, $10,000, plus the present value of the future payments, $83,650). The entries for this capital lease are

20X4			
Jan. 1	Building...	93,650	
	Cash...		10,000
	Lease Liability (PV of the 19 lease payments)		83,650
	Acquired building under capital lease and made the first lease payment.		
Dec. 31	Depreciation Expense ($93,650/20 years)	4,683	
	Accumulated Depreciation—Building....................		4,683
	Recorded depreciation on leased building.		

Appendix Problems

P15A-1 Jerry Dyer is considering two plans for building an education fund for his children.

Computing future values of investments

    Plan A—Invest $10,000 now, to earn 8% annually for six years.
    Plan B—Invest $2,000 each year to earn 10% annually for six years.

Which plan provides the larger amount at the end of six years? At the outset, which plan would you expect to provide the larger future amount?

P15A-2 Magnuson, Inc., needs new manufacturing equipment. Two companies can provide similar equipment but under different payment plans:

Computing present-value amounts

  a. General Electric (GE) offers to let Magnuson pay $50,000 each year for five years. The payments include interest at 12% per year. What is the present value of the payments?
  b. Westinghouse will let Magnuson make a single payment of $300,000 at the end of five years. This payment includes both principal and interest at 12%. What is the present value of this payment?
  c. Magnuson will purchase the equipment that costs the least, as measured by present value. Which equipment should Magnuson select? Why?

P15-A3 The purpose of this problem is to show the relationship between the future value of 1 and the present value of 1.

Relating future-value and present-value amounts

  1. Jan Schmidt will need $10,000 at the end of ten years in order to cover a business expense due at that time. To meet this future expense, Schmidt can invest a sum today. His investment will earn 6% each year over the ten-year period. How much must Schmidt invest today (present value)?
  2. Now, let's turn this present-value situation around and view it in terms of a future value: Schmidt has $5,580 to invest today. He can earn 6% each year over a ten-year period. How much will his investment be worth at the end of ten years (future value)?

P15A-4 For each situation, compute the required amount.

Computing the future value of an investment

  1. Pentateuch Enterprises is budgeting for the acquisition of land over the next several years. Pentateuch can invest $700,000 today at 9%. How much cash will Pentateuch have for land acquisitions at the end of five years? At the end of six years?
  2. Hassell Associates is planning to invest $6,000 each year for five years. The company's investment adviser believes that Hassell can earn 6% interest without taking on too much risk. What will be the value of Hassell's investment on the date of the last deposit if Hassell can earn 6%? If Hassell can earn 8%?

P15A-5 Determine the present value of the following notes and bonds:

Computing the present values of various notes and bonds

  a. Ten-year bonds payable with maturity value of $88,000 and contract interest rate of 12%, paid semiannually. The market rate of interest is 10% at issuance.
  b. Same bonds payable as in a, but the market interest rate is 8%.
  c. Same bonds payable as in a, but the market interest rate is 12%.

P15A-6 On December 31, 20X1, when the market interest rate is 8%, Willis Realty Co. issues $400,000 of 7.25%, ten-year bonds payable. The bonds pay interest semiannually.

Computing a bond's present value, recording its issuance at a discount and interest payments

Required

  1. Determine the present value of the bonds at issuance.
  2. Assume that the bonds are issued at the price computed in requirement 1. Prepare an effective-interest method amortization table for the first two semiannual interest periods.
  3. Using the amortization table prepared in requirement 2, journalize issuance of the bonds and the first two interest payments.

P15A-7 Osaka Children's Choir needs a fleet of vans to transport the children to singing engagements throughout Japan. **Toyota** offers the vehicles for a single payment of 7,200,000 yen due at the end of four years. **Nissan** prices a similar fleet of vans for four annual payments of 1,700,000 yen each. The children's home could borrow the funds at 6%, so this is the appropriate interest rate. Which company should get the business, Toyota or Nissan? Base your decision on present value, and give your reason.

Deciding between two payment plans

P15A-8 Escort, Inc., acquired equipment under a capital lease that requires six annual lease payments of $12,000. The first payment is due when the lease begins, on January 1, 20X6. Future payments are due on January 1 of each year of the lease term. The interest rate in the lease is 16%.

Computing the cost of equipment acquired under a capital lease and recording the lease transactions

Required

  1. Compute Escort's cost of the equipment.
  2. Journalize the (a) acquisition of the equipment and (b) depreciation for 20X6.

16

Investments and International Operations

LEARNING OBJECTIVES

After studying this chapter, you should be able to

1. Account for trading investments

2. Account for available-for-sale investments

3. Use the equity method for investments

4. Understand consolidated financial statements

5. Account for long-term investments in bonds

6. Account for transactions stated in a foreign currency

www.prenhall.com/horngren

Readiness Assessment

Move over, croissants and fine wine. Here come the Golden Arches. In 1999 McDonald's invaded Disneyland-Paris and also entered Azerbaijan and Gibraltar. With restaurants in 118 countries, **McDonald's Corporation** is one of the world's best-known companies.

McDonald's 1999 Annual Report features a Chinese boy eating French fries. Can you guess where McDonald's bought those potatoes? It was in China, because the company prefers to buy raw materials close to its restaurants. The produce is fresh, and McDonald's demonstrates its commitment to the local economy. But buying potatoes in China adds a new twist to doing business. McDonald's must pay in yuan, the Chinese currency unit, rather than dollars. In Russia, McDonald's pays for potatoes in rubles, and in France, you guessed it—in francs. Where does McDonald's get yuan, rubles, and francs? That brings up accounting for international operations, one of the topics of this chapter.

Recently McDonald's split its stock and increased its cash dividend. Investors like rising stock prices and dividend increases. These topics bring up accounting for investments, the other topic of this chapter.

Throughout this course, you have become increasingly familiar with the financial statements of companies such as **Intel, Target,** and **IHOP**. This chapter continues our discussion of the real world of accounting by discussing long-term investments and international operations. We begin with investments.

Investments extend from a few shares of stock to the acquisition of an entire company. In earlier chapters, we discussed the stocks and bonds that IHOP and **Amazon.com** issued. Here we examine stocks and bonds from the perspective of the investor who bought them. Different accounting methods apply to different types of investments. We begin with stock investments and then move to bonds and notes.

STOCK INVESTMENTS: AN OVERVIEW

Some Basics

STOCK PRICES   A broker may "quote a stock price," which means to state the current market price per share. The financial community quotes stock prices in dollars and cents. Big-city newspapers carry daily information on the stocks of thousands of corporations.

Exhibit 16-1 presents information for the common stock of **McDonald's Corporation** as it appeared in the newspaper. During the previous 52 weeks, McDonald's common stock reached a high price of $49.56 and a low price of $29.81 per share. The annual cash dividend is $0.20 (20 cents) per share. During the previous day, 206,767,000 (2067670 × 100) shares of McDonald's common stock were traded. The stock price ranged from a high of $30.38 to a low of $29.63 per share. The day's closing price of $29.88 was $0.25 lower than the closing price of the preceding day.

The person or company that owns stock in a corporation is the *investor*. The corporation that issued the stock is the *investee*. If you own shares of McDonald's common stock, you are an investor and McDonald's is the investee.

CLASSIFYING INVESTMENTS   Investments are assets to the investor. The investments may be short-term or long-term. **Short-term investments**—sometimes called **marketable securities**—are current assets. To be listed on the balance sheet as short-term, investments must be liquid (readily convertible to cash). Also, the investor must intend to convert the investments to cash within one year or use them to pay a current liability.

Investments that are not short-term are classified as **long-term investments** on the balance sheet. Long-term investments include stocks and bonds

 DAILY EXERCISE 16-1

SHORT-TERM INVESTMENT. A current asset; an investment that is readily convertible to cash and that the investor intends either to convert to cash within one year or use to pay a current liability. Also called a **marketable security.**

LONG-TERM INVESTMENT. A noncurrent asset, a separate asset category reported on the balance sheet between current assets and plant assets.

EXHIBIT 16-1   Stock Price Information for McDonald's Corporation

| 52 weeks | | | | | | | | |
High	Low	Stock Symbol	Dividend	Volume 100s	High	Low	Close	Net Change
49^{56}	29^{81}	MCD	.20	2067670	30^{38}	29^{63}	29^{88}	-0^{25}

that the investor expects to hold longer than one year or that are not readily marketable—for instance, real estate held for sale. Exhibit 16-2 shows the positions of short-term and long-term investments on the balance sheet.

EXHIBIT 16-2
Reporting Investments on the Balance Sheet

ASSETS	
Current Assets	
Cash	$X
Short-term investments	X
Accounts receivable	X
Inventories	X
Prepaid expenses	X
Total current assets	$X
Long-term investments [or simply Investments]	X
Property, plant, and equipment	X
Intangible assets	X
Other assets	X

TRADING INVESTMENTS. Investments that are to be sold in the very near future with the intent of generating profits on price changes.

AVAILABLE-FOR-SALE INVESTMENTS. Stock investments other than trading securities in which the investor cannot exercise significant influence over the investee.

 DAILY EXERCISE 16-2

 DAILY EXERCISE 16-3

Objective 1
Account for trading investments

MARKET-VALUE METHOD. Used to account for all trading investments. These investments are reported at their current market value.

We report assets in the order of their liquidity, starting with cash. Long-term investments are less liquid than current assets but more liquid than property, plant, and equipment. Nevertheless, many companies report their long-term investments after property, plant, and equipment.

TRADING AND AVAILABLE-FOR-SALE INVESTMENTS   We begin our discussion of stock investments with situations in which the investor holds less than a 20% interest in the investee company. These investments in stock are classified as trading investments or as available-for-sale securities. **Trading investments** are investments that are to be sold in the very near future—days, weeks, or only a few months—with the intent of generating profits on price changes. Trading investments are therefore recorded as short-term investments and reported on the balance sheet under *current assets*, as shown in Exhibit 16-2.

Available-for-sale investments are all investments other than trading investments in which the investor cannot exercise significant influence over the investee. Available-for-sale investments are classified as current assets if the business expects to sell them within the next year or within the business's normal operating cycle if longer than a year. All other available-for-sale investments are classified as long-term (Exhibit 16-2).

The investor accounts for the two categories separately. We begin by illustrating the accounting for a trading investment. Then we show how to account for a long-term available-for-sale investment.

Accounting for Trading Investments

The **market-value method** is used to account for all trading investments because they will be sold in the near future at their current market value. Cost is used only as the initial amount to record trading investments. Assume **Intel Corporation** has excess cash for short-term investing. Suppose Intel buys 500 shares of **Ford Motor Company** stock for $50 per share on October 23, 20X5. Assume further that Intel's management hopes to sell this stock within three months. It is a trading investment. Intel's entry to record the purchase is

20X5

Oct. 23 Short-Term Investment (500 × $50)....................... 25,000

       Cash 25,000

       Purchased investment.

Ford stock pays a cash dividend of $2 per share, so Intel would receive a dividend on the investment. Intel's entry to record receipt of a cash dividend is

20X5

Nov. 14 Cash (500 × $2.00) 1,000

       Dividend Revenue 1,000

       Received cash dividend

REPORTING TRADING INVESTMENTS ON THE BALANCE SHEET Trading investments are reported on the balance sheet at current market value, not at cost. This rule requires a year-end adjustment of the trading investment from its last carrying amount to current market value. Assume that the Ford stock has decreased in value, and at December 31, 20X5, Intel's investment in Ford stock is worth $20,000 ($5,000 less than the purchase price). At year end, Intel would make the following adjustment:

20X5

Dec. 31 Loss on Trading Investment

       ($25,000 − $20,000)... 5,000

       Short-Term Investment.................................... 5,000

       Adjusted trading investment to market value.

The T-account shows the $20,000 ($25,000 − $5,000) balance of Short-Term Investment. Intel would report its trading investment on the balance sheet at December 31, 20X5, and the loss on trading investment on the 20X5 income statement, as follows:

◉ DAILY EXERCISE 16-4

Balance Sheet (partial):	**Income Statement (partial):**
ASSETS	Other gains and losses:
Current assets:	Gain (loss) on trading investment.............. $(5,000)
Short-term investments, at market value............. $20,000	

If the investment's market value had risen above $25,000, Intel would have debited Short-Term Investment and credited Gain on Trading Investment.

SELLING A TRADING INVESTMENT When a company sells a trading investment, the gain or loss on the sale is the difference between the sale proceeds and the last carrying amount of the investment. Suppose Intel sells the Ford stock for $18,000 on January 19, 20X6. Intel would record the sale as follows:

20X6

Jan. 19 Cash... 18,000

       Loss on Sale of Investment....................................... 2,000

       Short-Term Investment.................................... 20,000

       Sold investment.

◉ DAILY EXERCISE 16-5

For reporting on the income statement, Intel could combine all gains and losses ($5,000 + $2,000) on short-term investments and report a single net amount under "Other gains (losses). . . . $(7,000).

◉ DAILY EXERCISE 16-6

Accounting for Long-Term Available-for-Sale Investments

◉ DAILY EXERCISE 16-7

The *market-value method* is used to account for all available-for-sale investments in stock because the company expects to resell the stock at its market value. Available-for-sale investments are therefore reported on the balance sheet at their *current market value,* just as for trading investments.

Objective 2
Account for available-for-sale investments

Suppose **Dell Corporation** purchases 1,000 shares of **Hewlett-Packard Company** common stock at the market price of $35.75. Dell intends to hold this investment for longer than a year and classifies it as a long-term available-for-sale investment. Dell's entry to record the investment is

20X1			
Feb. 23	Long-Term Available-for-Sale Investment		
	(1,000 × $35.75)...	35,750	
	Cash...		35,750
	Purchased investment.		

Dell receives a $0.64 per share cash dividend on the Hewlett-Packard stock. Dell's entry to record receipt of the dividend is

20X1			
July 14	Cash (1,000 × $0.64)...	640	
	Dividend Revenue		640
	Received cash dividend.		

➤ For a review of stock dividends, see Chapter 14, page 542.

STOCK DIVIDEND VERSUS A CASH DIVIDEND   Receipt of a *stock* dividend is different from receipt of a cash dividend. ◄ For a stock dividend, the investor records no dividend revenue. Instead, the investor makes a memorandum entry in the accounting records to show the new number of shares of stock now held. The number of investment shares has increased, so the investor's cost per share decreases. For example, suppose Dell Corporation receives a 5% stock dividend from Hewlett-Packard. Dell would receive 50 shares (5% of 1,000 shares previously held) and make this memorandum entry in its accounting records:

⊙ DAILY EXERCISE 16-8

> MEMORANDUM—Receipt of stock dividend: Received 50 shares of Hewlett-Packard common stock in 5% stock dividend. New cost per share is $34.05 (cost of $35,750 ÷ 1,050 shares). For all future Hewlett-Packard investment transactions, Dell will use the new cost per share of $34.05.

REPORTING AVAILABLE-FOR-SALE INVESTMENTS ON THE BALANCE SHEET   Available-for-sale investments are reported on the balance sheet at their market value. This reporting requires an adjustment of the investment from its last carrying amount to current market value. Assume that the market value of Dell's investment in Hewlett-Packard common stock is $36,400 on December 31, 20X1. In this case, Dell makes the following adjustment:

20X1			
Dec. 31	Allowance to Adjust Investment to Market		
	($36,400 − $35,750)...	650	
	Unrealized Gain on		
	Available-for-Sale Investment		650
	Adjusted investment to market value.		

Allowance to Adjust Investment to Market is a companion account that is used with the Long-Term Investment account to bring the investment's carrying amount to current market value. Here the investment's cost ($35,750) plus the Allowance ($650) equals the investment carrying amount ($36,400).

LONG-TERM AVAILABLE-FOR-SALE INVESTMENT		ALLOWANCE TO ADJUST INVESTMENT TO MARKET	
35,750		650	

Investment carrying amount = Market value of $36,400 ($35,750 − $650)

In this case, the Allowance has a debit balance because the investment value (an asset) increased. If the investment's value declines, the Allowance is credited, and the investment carrying amount is cost *minus* the Allowance. When the Allowance has a credit balance, it becomes a contra account. ➤➤

The other side of the December 31 adjustment entry is a credit to Unrealized Gain on Available-for-Sale Investment. If the investment's market value declines, the company debits an Unrealized Loss. *Unrealized* means that the gain or loss resulted from a change in the investment's market value, not from the sale of the investment. A gain or loss on the sale of an investment is said to be *realized* because the company received cash from the sale. It is *cash* that turns the gain or loss into a realized gain or loss.[1] For available-for-sale investments, the Unrealized Gain (or the Unrealized Loss) account is reported on the balance sheet as part of stockholders' equity, as shown here.

◀◀ Other contra accounts are Accumulated Depreciation (Chapter 3) and Allowance for Uncollectible Accounts (Chapter 8).

Balance Sheet (partial)			
ASSETS		**STOCKHOLDERS' EQUITY**	
Total current assets	$ XXX	Common stock	$XXX
Long-term available-for-sale		Retained earnings	XXX
investments—at market value		Unrealized gain on available-for-sale	
($35,750 + $650).............................	36,400	investments	650
Property, plant, and equipment, net..............	XXX		

The Unrealized Gain (or Loss) account is reported on the balance sheet (not on the income statement) because it may take a year or longer for the company to sell this investment. When the investment is sold, the gain or loss will be realized in cash.

SELLING AN AVAILABLE-FOR-SALE INVESTMENT   The sale of an available-for-sale investment can result in a *realized* gain or loss, which we call a Gain (or Loss) on Sale of Investment to indicate that a sale transaction has occurred. For available-for-sale investments, realized gains and losses measure the difference between the amount received from the sale of the investment and the cost of the investment.

Suppose Dell Corporation sells its investment in Hewlett-Packard stock for $34,000 during 20X2. Dell would record the sale as follows:

```
20X2
May 19   Cash ...........................................      34,000
         Loss on Sale of Investment .........................   1,750
              Long-Term Available-for-Sale
              Investment (cost)...............................            35,750
         Sold investment.
```

 DAILY EXERCISE 16-9

 DAILY EXERCISE 16-10

Dell would report the Loss on Sale of Investment as an "Other gain or loss" on the income statement.[2]

Accounting for Equity-Method Investments

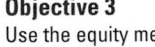 **Objective 3**
Use the equity method for investments

An investor with a stock holding between 20% and 50% of the investee's voting stock may *significantly influence* decisions on dividends, product lines, and other important matters.

For this reason, investments in the range of 20–50% of another company's stock are common. For example, **General Motors** owns nearly 40% of **Isuzu Motors Overseas Distribution Corporation,** and **Dow Jones & Company,** publisher of the *Wall Street Journal,* owns 50% of **Smart Money,** the magazine com-

---

[1]In accounting, the term *realized* usually means "made real" by a cash transaction. Suppose **Bank of America** (BOA) paid $6,000 for an investment in **General Electric** (GE) stock. If BOA sells the stock for $10,000, the bank has a realized gain of $4,000. Selling the stock for $5,000 results in a realized loss of $1,000. Whether a gain or loss is realized or unrealized is important for available-for-sale investments, but not for trading investments. It is also important for income taxes, because only realized gains are taxed.

[2]We omit the complex journal entry to adjust the Allowance account at year end. That topic is covered in intermediate accounting courses.

 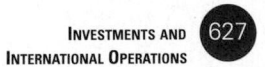

WORK IT OUT

Suppose Xenon Corporation holds the following available-for-sale securities as long-term investments at December 31, 20X3:

Stock	Cost	Current Market Value
The Coca-Cola Company	$ 85,000	$ 71,000
Eastman Kodak Company	16,000	12,000
Scott Paper Company	122,000	136,000
	$223,000	$219,000

Show how Xenon Corporation will report long-term investments and the unrealized loss on its December 31, 20X3, balance sheet.

Answer

ASSETS

Long-term available-for-sale investments, at market value............... $219,000

STOCKHOLDERS' EQUITY

Unrealized loss on available-for-sale investments
    ($223,000 − $219,000) .... $ (4,000)

---

pany. With a 20–50% investment, the investor has a voice in shaping the investee's operations.

We use the **equity method** to account for investments in which the investor owns 20–50% of the investee's stock and can significantly influence the decisions of the investee. A recent survey of 600 companies by *Accounting Trends & Techniques* indicated that 279 (46%) of the companies held investments that they accounted for by the equity method. These investee companies are often called *affiliates* or *affiliated companies*.

RECORDING THE INITIAL INVESTMENT   Investments accounted for by the equity method are recorded initially at cost. Suppose **Phillips Petroleum Company** pays $400,000 for 30% of the common stock of White Rock Corporation. Phillips may refer to White Rock Corporation as an *affiliated company*. Phillips's entry to record the purchase of this investment is as follows:

```
20X1
Jan. 6   Long-Term Equity-Method Investment..............   400,000
               Cash ........................................................              400,000
         Purchased equity-method investment.
```

ADJUSTING THE INVESTMENT ACCOUNT FOR INVESTEE NET INCOME   Under the equity method, Phillips, as the investor, applies its percentage of ownership (30%) to record its share of the investee's net income and dividends. White Rock reported net income of $250,000 for the year, and Phillips records 30% of this amount as an increase in the investment account and as equity-method investment revenue, as follows:

```
Dec. 31   Long-Term Equity-Method Investment
                ($250,000 × 0.30) ...........................................   75,000
                     Equity-Method Investment Revenue.......              75,000
          Recorded investment revenue.
```

The Investment Revenue account carries the Equity-Method label to identify its source. This labeling is similar to distinguishing Sales Revenue from Service Revenue.

EQUITY METHOD. The method used to account for investments in which the investor has 20–50% of the investee's voting stock and can significantly influence the decisions of the investee.

The investor increases the Investment account and records Investment Revenue when the investee reports income because of the close relationship between the two companies. As the investee's owners' equity increases, so does the Investment account on the investor's books.

RECEIVING DIVIDENDS ON AN EQUITY-METHOD INVESTMENT Phillips records its proportionate part of cash dividends received from White Rock. White Rock declares and pays a cash dividend of $100,000. Phillips receives 30% of this dividend and makes this journal entry:

20X2
Jan. 17 Cash ($100,000 × 0.30) 30,000
                  Long-Term Equity-Method Investment......................   30,000
            Received cash dividend on equity-method investment.

The Investment account is credited for the receipt of a dividend on an equity-method investment. Why? Because the dividend decreases both the investee's owners' equity and the investor's investment. The investor received cash for this portion of the investment and that reduced the investor's claim against the investee.

After the preceding entries are posted, Phillips's Investment account reflects its equity in the net assets of White Rock:

LONG-TERM EQUITY-METHOD INVESTMENT

20X1			20X2		
Jan. 6	Purchase	400,000	Jan. 17	Dividends received	30,000
Dec. 31	Net income	75,000			
20X2					
Jan. 17	Balance	445,000			

◉ DAILY EXERCISE 16-11

Phillips can report the long-term investment on the balance sheet and the equity-method investment revenue on the income statement as follows:

Balance sheet (partial):			Income statement (partial):	
ASSETS			Income from operations..................	$ XXX
Total current assets..................................	$	XXX	Other revenue:	
Long-term equity-method			Equity-method investment	
investments..		445,000	revenue.......................................	75,000
Property, plant, and equipment, net		XXX	Net income	$ XXX

SELLING AN EQUITY-METHOD INVESTMENT There may be a gain or loss on the sale of an equity-method investment. The gain or loss is measured as the difference between the sale proceeds and the carrying amount of the investment. Suppose Phillips sells one-tenth of the White Rock common stock for $41,000. The sale is recorded as follows:

Feb. 13 Cash.. 41,000
            Loss on Sale of Investment.. 3,500
                  Long-Term Equity-Method Investment
                  ($445,000 × 1/10)   44,500
            Sold one-tenth of investment.

◉ DAILY EXERCISE 16-12

In summary, this T-account illustrates how to account for equity-method investments:

LONG-TERM EQUITY-METHOD INVESTMENT

Cost	Share of losses
Share of income	Share of dividend received

Joint Ventures Are Accounted for by the Equity Method A *joint venture* is a separate entity owned by a small group of businesses. Joint ventures are common in risky endeavors such as oil exploration in the petroleum industry and also in the construction of nuclear power plants. **Aramco,** which stands for Arabian American Oil Company, is a joint venture half owned by Saudi Arabia. Several multinational oil companies (**Exxon, Chevron,** and others) own the remaining 50%.

A participant in a joint venture accounts for its investment by the equity method even when the investor owns less than 20% of the venture. Joint ventures are common in international business. Companies such as **British Telecom, Total** (of France) and **Toyota** partner with companies in other countries.

Objective 4
Understand consolidated financial statements

Accounting for Consolidated Subsidiaries

Most large corporations own controlling interests in other companies. A **controlling** (or **majority**) **interest** is the ownership of more than 50% of the investee's voting stock. Such an investment enables the investor to elect a majority of the investee's board of directors and thereby control the investee. The corporation that controls the other company is called the **parent company,** and the company that is controlled by another corporation is called the **subsidiary.** A well-known example is **Saturn Corporation,** which is a subsidiary of **General Motors,** the parent company. Because GM owns Saturn Corporation, the stockholders of GM control Saturn, as diagrammed in Exhibit 16-3.

Exhibit 16-3
Ownership Structure of General Motors Corporation and Saturn Corporation

Controlling Interest. Ownership of more than 50% of an investee company's voting stock. Also called majority interest.

Parent Company. An investor company that owns more than 50% of the voting stock of a subsidiary company.

Subsidiary Company. A company in which a parent company owns more than 50% of the voting stock.

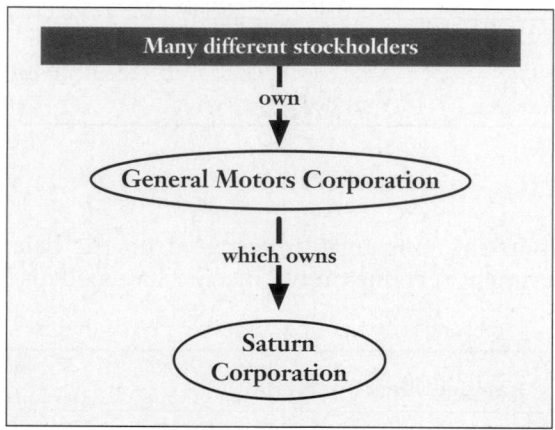

Why have subsidiaries? Why not have the corporation take the form of a single legal entity? Subsidiaries may enable the parent to save on income taxes, limit the parent's liabilities in a risky venture, and ease expansion into foreign countries. For example, **McDonald's Corporation** finds it more feasible to operate in France through a French-based subsidiary company than through the U.S. parent company. Exhibit 16-4 shows some of the subsidiaries of three large automakers.

Exhibit 16-4
Selected Subsidiaries of Three Large Automobile Manufacturers

Parent Company	Selected Subsidiaries
General Motors Corporation Total assets: $275 billion	Saturn Corporation Hughes Aircraft Company
Ford Motor Company Total assets: $276 billion	Ford Aerospace Corporation Jaguar, Ltd.
DaimlerChrysler Corporation Total assets: $176 billion	Jeep/Eagle Corporation DaimlerChrysler Rail Systems

Majority-Owned Subsidiaries *Consolidation accounting* is a method of combining the financial statements of two or more companies controlled by the same owners. This method implements the entity concept of accounting by reporting a single set of financial statements for the consolidated entity.

Most published financial reports include consolidated statements. To understand real financial statements, you need to know the basic concepts underlying consolidation accounting. **Consolidated statements** combine the balance sheets, income statements, and cash-flow statements of the parent company plus those of its majority-owned subsidiaries. The final outcome of the consolidation process is a single set of statements as if the parent and its subsidiaries were a single entity.

In consolidation accounting, the assets, liabilities, revenues, and expenses of each subsidiary are added to the parent's accounts. The consolidated financial statements report the combined account balances. For example, the balance in the Cash account of Saturn Corporation is added to the cash balance of General Motors, and the sum of the two amounts is reported on GM's balance sheet as a single amount. The consolidated financial statements bear the name of the parent company only, in this case General Motors Corporation.

Exhibit 16-5 illustrates which accounting method should be used for each stock investment according to the percentage of ownership by the investor.

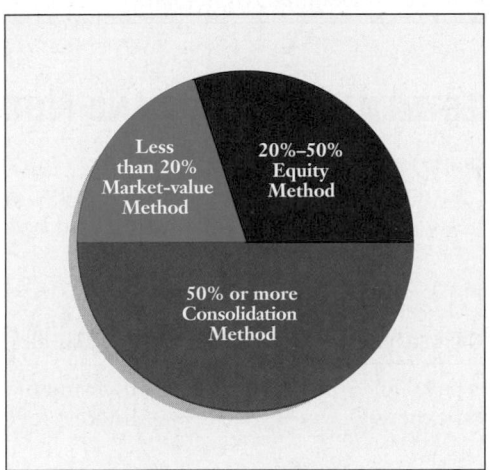

GOODWILL AND MINORITY INTEREST *Goodwill* is an intangible asset that is measured in the consolidation process. Goodwill is reported among the intangible assets on the consolidated balance sheet of the parent company. As we saw in Chapter 10, *goodwill* is the excess of the cost to acquire another company over the sum of the market value of its net assets.

A parent company may purchase less than 100% of the stock of a subsidiary company. For example, **Nokia,** the cellular telephone company, owns less than 100% of several other companies. The portions of those companies owned by outsiders is called the minority interest. **Minority interest** is the portion (less than 50%) of a subsidiary's stock that is owned by stockholders other than the parent company. Nokia Corporation, the parent company, therefore reports on its consolidated balance sheet an account titled Minority Interest. Most companies list Minority Interest among their liabilities.

Preparing consolidated financial statements is illustrated in the chapter appendix. Advanced accounting courses cover consolidation accounting in more detail.

THE INCOME OF A CONSOLIDATED ENTITY The income of a consolidated entity is the net income of the parent plus the parent's proportion of the subsidiaries' net income. Suppose Parent Company owns all the stock of Subsidiary S-1 and 60% of the stock of Subsidiary S-2. During 20X8, Parent earned net income of $330,000, S-1 earned $150,000, and S-2 had a net loss of $100,000. Parent Company would report consolidated net income of $420,000, computed as follows:

	Net Income (Net Loss)	×	Parent Stockholders' Ownership	=	Parent's Consolidated Net Income (Net Loss)
Parent Company............................	$ 330,000	×	100%	=	$330,000
Subsidiary S-1	150,000	×	100%	=	150,000
Subsidiary S-2	(100,000)	×	60%	=	(60,000)
Consolidated net income..............					$420,000

Objective 5
Account for long-term investments in bonds

LONG-TERM INVESTMENTS IN BONDS AND NOTES

Most companies invest far more in stocks than they do in bonds. The major investors in bonds are banks, pension plans, mutual funds, and insurance companies. The relationship between the issuing corporation and bondholders may be diagrammed as follows:

ISSUING CORPORATION HAS		BONDHOLDER HAS
Bonds payable	⟷	Investment in bonds
Interest expense	⟷	Interest revenue

➤ See Chapter 15, pages 583–585 for discussion of bonds payable

HELD-TO-MATURITY INVESTMENTS. Investment in bonds, notes, and other debt securities that the investor expects to hold until their maturity date.

The dollar amount of a bond transaction is the same for both the issuer and the bondholder because money passes from one to the other. However, the accounts debited and credited differ. For example, the corporation has bonds payable. To the bondholder, the bonds are an investment. The corporation's interest expense is the bondholder's interest revenue. Chapter 15 covered bonds payable ➤.

An investment in bonds is classified as short-term (a current asset) or as long-term. *Short-term investments in bonds are rare.* We focus on long-term investments in bonds that the investor intends to hold until the bonds mature. These are called **held-to-maturity investments.**

Accounting for Held-to-Maturity Investments— The Amortized-Cost Method

Bond investments are recorded at cost. Then at maturity, the investor will receive the bonds' full face value. We must amortize any discount or premium to account for interest revenue over the period the bonds will be held. The amortization of discount or premium on a bond investment follows the same pattern as for bonds payable, as in Chapter 15. Held-to-maturity investments in bonds are reported at their *amortized cost*.

➤ Straight-line amortization of premium or discount on a bond investment is calculated the same way as it is calculated for bonds payable (see Chapter 15, page 583).

Suppose an investor purchases $10,000 of 6% **CBS** bonds at a price of 95.2 (95.2% of maturity value) on April 1, 20X2. The investor intends to hold the bonds as a long-term investment until their maturity. Interest dates are April 1 and October 1. These bonds mature on April 1, 20X6, so they will be outstanding for 48 months. Let us amortize the discount by the straight-line method ➤. The following are the bondholder's entries for this long-term investment:

Apr. 1	Long-Term Investment in Bonds ($10,000 × 0.952)	9,520	
	Cash..		9,520
	Purchased bond investment.		
Oct. 1	Cash ($10,000 × 0.06 × 6/12)	300	
	Interest Revenue		300
	Received semiannual interest.		

Oct. 1 Long-Term Investment in Bonds
[($10,000 − $9,520)/48] × 6 60
    Interest Revenue 60
Amortized discount on bond investment.

At December 31, the year-end adjustments are

Dec. 31 Interest Receivable ($10,000 × 0.06 × 3/12)....................... 150
    Interest Revenue 150
Accrued interest revenue.

◉ DAILY EXERCISE 16-15

Dec. 31 Long-Term Investment in Bonds
[($10,000 − $9,520)/48] × 3 30
    Interest Revenue 30
Amortized discount on bond investment.

◉ DAILY EXERCISE 16-16

Each amortization entry (October 1 and December 31) has two effects:

1. It increases the Long-Term Investment account on its march toward maturity value.
2. It records the interest revenue earned because of the increase in the carrying amount of the investment.

The financial statements at December 31, 20X2, report the following for this investment in bonds:

Balance sheet at December 31, 20X2:
Current assets:
  Interest receivable... $ 150
  Total current assets .... X,XXX
Long-term investments in bonds ($9,520 + $60 + $30)—Note 6............ 9,610
Property, plant, and equipment .... X,XXX

Income statement for 19X2:
Other revenues:
  Interest revenue ($300 + $60 + $150 + $30) .... $ 540

◉ DAILY EXERCISE 16-17

This chapter has illustrated how to account for various types of investments. The Decision Guidelines feature summarizes the accounting by showing which method applies to each type of investment.

DECISION GUIDELINES

Accounting Method to Use for Each Type of Investment

DECISION	GUIDELINES
Investment Type	**Accounting Method**
Short-Term Investment	
Trading investment	Market value—report all gains (losses) on the income statement.
Long-Term Investment	
Investor owns less than 20% of investee stock (available-for-sale investment)	Market value—report *unrealized* gains (losses) on the balance sheet. —report *realized* gains (losses) from sale of the investment on the income statement.
Investor owns between 20 and 50% of investee stock	Equity
Investment in a joint venture	Equity
Investor owns more than 50% of investee stock	Consolidation
Long-term investment in bonds (held-to-maturity investment)	Amortized cost

www.prenhall.com/horngren

Mid-Chapter Assessment

SUMMARY PROBLEM

1. Identify the appropriate accounting method for each of the following situations:
   a. Investment in 25% of investee company's stock.
   b. Available-for-sale investment in stock.
   c. Investment in more than 50% of investee company's stock.

2. At what amount should the following available-for-sale investment portfolio be reported on the December 31 balance sheet? All the investments are less than 5% of the investee's stock.

Stock	Investment Cost	Current Market Value
Amazon.com	$ 5,000	$ 5,500
Intelysis	61,200	53,000
Procter & Gamble	3,680	6,230

Journalize any adjusting entry required by these data.

3. Investor paid $67,900 to acquire a 40% equity-method investment in the common stock of Investee. At the end of the first year, Investee's net income was $80,000, and Investee declared and paid cash dividends of $55,000. Journalize Investor's (a) purchase of the investment, (b) share of Investee's net income, (c) receipt of dividends from Investee, and (d) sale of Investee stock for $80,100.

Solution

1. (a) Equity. (b) Market value. (c) Consolidation
2. Report the investments at market value, $64,730, as follows:

Stock	Investment Cost	Current Market Value
Amazon.com	$ 5,000	$ 5,500
Intelysis	61,200	53,000
Procter & Gamble	3,680	6,230
Totals	$69,880	$64,730

Adjusting entry:

Unrealized Loss on Investments ($69,880 − $64,730)	5,150	
Allowance to Adjust Investment to Market		5,150
To adjust investments to current market value.		

3. **a.**

Long-Term Equity-Method Investment	67,900	
Cash		67,900
Purchased equity-method investment.		

b.

Long-Term Equity-Method Investment ($80,000 × 0.40)	32,000	
Equity-Method Investment Revenue		32,000
Recorded investment revenue.		

c.

Cash ($55,000 × 0.40)	22,000	
Long-Term Equity-Method Investment		22,000
Recorded receipt of cash dividend on equity-method investment.		

d.

Cash	80,100	
Long-Term Equity-Method Investment		
($67,900 + $32,000 − $22,000)		77,900
Gain on Sale of Investment		2,200
Sold investment.		

ACCOUNTING FOR INTERNATIONAL OPERATIONS

Accounting for business activities across national boundaries makes up the field of *international accounting.*

Did you know that **Coca-Cola, IBM,** and **Bank of America** earn most of their revenue outside the United States? It is common for U.S. companies to do a large part of their business abroad. **McDonald's, Toys "Я" Us,** and **Procter & Gamble** are also very active in other countries. Exhibit 16-6 shows the percentages of international sales for these companies. *International* often means outside North America.

EXHIBIT 16-6
Extent of International Business

Company	Percent of International Sales
McDonald's	62%
Toys "Я" Us	27
Procter & Gamble	49

The economic environment varies from country to country. The United States may be booming while the Pacific Rim is depressed economically. International accounting must deal with such differences.

Foreign Currencies and Foreign-Currency Exchange Rates

Each country uses its own national currency. If **Boeing,** a U.S.-owned company, sells a 747 jet to **Air France,** will Boeing receive U.S. dollars or French francs? If the transaction takes place in dollars, Air France must buy dollars to pay Boeing in U.S. currency. If the transaction takes place in francs, Boeing will receive francs, which it exchanges for dollars. In either case, a step has been added to the transaction: One company must convert domestic currency into foreign currency, or vice versa.

The price of one nation's currency can be stated in terms of another country's monetary unit. The price of a foreign currency is called the **foreign-currency exchange rate.** In Exhibit 16-7, the U.S. dollar value of a French franc is $0.14. This means that one French franc can be bought for 14 cents. Other currencies, such as the pound and the yen (also listed in Exhibit 16-7), are similarly bought and sold.

FOREIGN-CURRENCY EXCHANGE RATE. The measure of one currency against another currency.

EXHIBIT 16-7   **Foreign-Currency Exchange Rates**

Country	Monetary Unit	U.S. Dollar Value	Country	Monetary Unit	U.S. Dollar Value
Canada	Dollar	$0.68	Great Britain	Pound	$1.51
European Common Market	European currency unit	0.93	Italy	Lira	0.0004
France	Franc	0.14	Japan	Yen	0.009
Germany	Mark	0.48	Mexico	Peso	0.107

Source: The Wall Street Journal, July 21, 2000, p. C13.

We use the exchange rate to convert the price of an item stated in one currency to its price in a second currency. We call this conversion a *translation.* Suppose an item costs 200 French francs. To compute its cost in dollars, we multiply the amount in francs by the conversion rate: 200 French francs × $0.14 = $28.

Currencies are often described as "strong" or "weak." The exchange rate of a **strong currency** is rising relative to other nations' currencies. The exchange rate of a **weak currency** is falling relative to other currencies.

STRONG CURRENCY. A currency that is rising relative to other nations' currencies.

WEAK CURRENCY. A currency that is falling relative to other nations' currencies.

Foreign-Currency Transactions

As international transactions become common, more companies manage cash transactions conducted in foreign currencies. **D. E. Shipp Belting,** a family-owned company in Waco, Texas, provides an example. Shipp makes conveyor belts for several industries, including dot.coms that sell their goods on-line. **M&M Mars** which makes Snickers candy bars in Waco, is an important customer of Shipp Belting. Farmers along the Texas-Mexico border use Shipp conveyor belts to process vegetables. Some of these customers are on the Mexican side of the border, so Shipp Belting conducts some of its business in pesos, the Mexican monetary unit.

COLLECTING CASH IN A FOREIGN CURRENCY   Consider Shipp Belting's sale of conveyor belts to Artes de Mexico, a vegetable grower in Matamoros, Mexico. The sale can be conducted in dollars or pesos. If Artes de Mexico agrees to pay in dollars, Shipp avoids the foreign currency complication, and the transaction is the same as selling to M&M Mars across town. But suppose that Artes de Mexico orders conveyor belts valued at 1 million pesos (approximately $107,000). Further suppose that Artes demands to pay in pesos and that Shipp agrees to receive pesos instead of dollars.

Shipp will need to convert the pesos to dollars, so the transaction creates a new risk. What if the peso weakens (loses value) before Shipp collects from Artes? In this case, Shipp will not earn as much as expected on the sale. Let's see how to account for this transaction.

Shipp Belting sells goods to Artes de Mexico for a price of 1 million pesos on June 2. On that date, a peso was worth $0.107. One month later, on July 2, the peso has weakened against the dollar and a peso is worth only $0.102. Shipp still receives 1 million pesos from Artes because that was the price agreed upon. But the dollar value of Shipp's cash receipt is $5,000 less than the original amount, so Shipp ends up earning $5,000 less than expected. The following journal entries show how Shipp Belting would account for these transactions:

June 2	Accounts Receivable—Artes		
	(1,000,000 pesos × $0.107)	107,000	
	Sales Revenue		107,000
	Sale on account.		

○ DAILY EXERCISE 16-18

July 2	Cash (1,000,000 pesos × $0.102)	102,000	
	Foreign-Currency Loss	5,000	
	Accounts Receivable—Artes		107,000
	Collection on account.		

If Shipp had required Artes to pay at the time of the sale, Shipp would have received pesos worth $107,000. But during the 30-day collection period, Shipp was exposed to *foreign-currency exchange risk,* the risk of loss in an international transaction. In this case, Shipp experienced a $5,000 foreign-currency loss and received $5,000 less than expected, as shown in the collection entry on July 2.

PAYING CASH IN A FOREIGN CURRENCY   Purchasing from a foreign company can also expose a company to foreign-currency exchange risk. Shipp Belting buys inventory from Gesellschaft Ltd., a Swiss company. The two companies decide on a price of 20,000 Swiss francs. On August 10, when Shipp receives the goods, the Swiss franc is priced at $0.800. When Shipp pays two weeks later, on August 24, the Swiss franc has weakened against the dollar, and is now worth only $0.78. This works to Shipp's advantage. Shipp would record the purchase and payment as follows:

Aug. 10	Inventory (20,000 Swiss francs × $0.80)	16,000	
	Accounts Payable—Gesellschaft Ltd.		16,000
	Purchase on account.		

○ DAILY EXERCISE 16-19

Aug. 24	Accounts Payable—Gesellschaft Ltd.	16,000	
	Foreign-Currency Gain		400
	Cash (20,000 Swiss francs × $0.78)		15,600
	Payment on account.		

In this case, the Swiss franc weakened against the dollar, which gave Shipp a foreign-currency gain. A company with a payable stated in a foreign currency hopes that the dollar gets stronger. The company can then use fewer dollars to pay the debt and have a foreign-currency gain on the transaction.

REPORTING FOREIGN-CURRENCY GAINS AND LOSSES ON THE INCOME STATEMENT The Foreign-Currency Gain account reports gains on transactions in a currency other than the dollar. The Foreign-Currency Loss account shows losses on foreign-currency transactions. The company reports the *net amount* of these two accounts on the income statement as Other gains (losses). For example, Shipp Belting would combine the $5,000 foreign-currency loss and the $400 gain and report the net loss of $4,600 on the income statement, as follows:

Other gains (losses):
    Foreign-currency gain (loss), net ($5,000 − $400)................. $(4,600)

These gains and losses fall into the "Other" category because they arise from outside activities. Buying and selling foreign currencies are not Shipp Belting's main business.

Managers examine these gains and losses to see how well the company is doing in foreign-currency transactions. The gains and losses may offset each other, and the net result may be small. But if losses exceed gains and grow large, managers will take action to shield themselves against further loss. One possible action is hedging.

HEDGING TO AVOID FOREIGN-CURRENCY LOSSES U.S. companies can avoid foreign-currency losses by insisting that international transactions be settled in dollars. But that strategy may alienate customers. Another way for a company to protect itself is by hedging.

Hedging means to protect oneself from losing money by engaging in a counter-balancing transaction. Suppose **Lucent Technologies** is selling goods to be collected in Japanese yen. Lucent will receive a fixed number of yen in the future. If yen are losing value, they will be worth fewer dollars than the amount of Lucent's receivable. Lucent can expect a loss in this situation.

Keep in mind that Lucent Technologies has a receivable stated in Japanese yen. In other international transactions, Lucent may have accumulated payables stated in another foreign currency, say Mexican pesos. Losses on the receipt of yen may be offset by gains on the payment of pesos to the Mexican company. This is a natural foreign-currency hedge. It is inexpensive because Lucent has to take no new action to protect against foreign-currency loss.

Most companies do not have equal amounts of receivables and payables in foreign currency, so offsetting receivables and payables is imprecise. To obtain a more precise hedge, companies buy *futures contracts,* which are agreements for foreign currencies to be received in the future. Futures contracts can create a payable to exactly offset a receivable, and vice versa. Most companies that do business internationally use hedging to avoid losses.

> **HEDGING.** Protecting oneself from losing money in one transaction by engaging in a counterbalancing transaction.

Consolidation of Foreign Subsidiaries

McDonald's Corporation forms foreign subsidiaries to do business in the various foreign countries. McDonald's can establish a French subsidiary to operate in France, a Russian company to do business in that country, and so on. A U.S. company with foreign subsidiaries consolidates all subsidiaries' financial statements into its own for reporting to the public. The consolidation of a foreign subsidiary poses two accounting challenges.

1. Many countries outside the United States specify accounting treatments that differ from American accounting principles. To report to the American public, accountants must first bring the subsidiary's statements into conformity with American generally accepted accounting principles (GAAP).
2. Subsidiary statements are expressed in a foreign currency. A preliminary step in the consolidation process is to translate the subsidiary statements into dollars. Then the dollar-value statements of the subsidiary can be combined with the parent's statements in the usual manner.

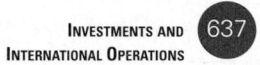

Avon Products Inc.: Staying Up When the Currency Goes Down

Cosmetics giant **Avon Products** is regularly exposed to foreign-currency crises because 66% of the company's sales occur outside the United States. As a result, the company has developed strategies for minimizing financial risk overseas.

To protect against volatile currencies, Avon tries to buy raw materials and make its products close to markets where they are sold. For instance, Avon replaced a European vendor with a local company for the lace it uses to make lingerie in Thailand.

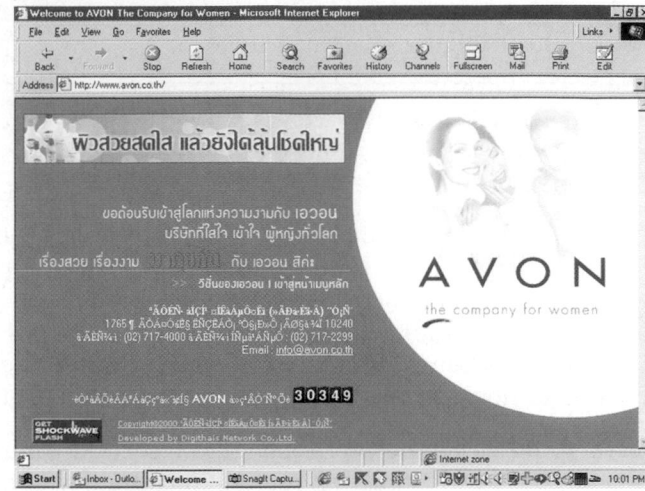

Another key strategy is to sacrifice profit for market share. Avon is willing to trade short-term losses for long-term gains. Tactics for carrying out this strategy vary from market to market. In Russia, Avon quotes prices in "currency units" tied to the U.S. dollar. When the ruble drops, prices soar. Avon may leave prices alone but give customers a hefty discount on the conversion rate of rubles for dollars, thus giving customers the incentive to buy Avon products. In Mexico, Avon slows price increases for brands aimed at the poor and middle class. To keep margins intact, the company raises prices faster on premium brands that compete with expensive imports.

Source: Based on David Whitford, "A currency drowns—Can you stay afloat?" *Fortune*, March 1, 1999, pp. 229–235. Mel Mandell, "Asia: converting crisis to opportunity," *World Trade*, April 1998, pp. 36–39. Fred R. Bleakley, "How U.S. firm copes with Asia crisis—Avon moves to protect against volatile currencies," *Wall Street Journal*, December 26, 1997, p. A2.

International Accounting Standards

In this text, we focus on accounting principles that are generally accepted in the United States. Most accounting methods are consistent throughout the world. Double-entry, the accrual system, and the basic financial statements (balance sheet, income statement, and so on) are used worldwide. But some differences exist among countries, as shown in Exhibit 16-8.

EXHIBIT 16-8 **Some International Accounting Differences**

Country	Inventories	Goodwill	Research and Development Costs
United States	Specific unit cost, FIFO, LIFO, weighted-average.	Amortized over period not to exceed 40 years.	Expensed as incurred.
Germany	LIFO is unacceptable for tax purposes and is not widely used.	Amortized over 5 years.	Expensed as incurred.
Japan	Similar to U.S.	Amortized over 5 years.	May be capitalized and amortized over 5 years.
United Kingdom (Great Britain)	LIFO is unacceptable for tax purposes and is not widely used.	Amortized over useful life or not amortized if life is indefinite.*	Expense research costs. Some development costs may be capitalized.

* Proposal being considered.

In the United States, the depreciation method used for tax purposes can differ from the method used for reporting to shareholders. By contrast, in many countries tax reporting and shareholder reporting are identical. For example, France has a "Plan Compatible," which specifies that the same chart of accounts must be used for both tax returns and reporting to shareholders. German accounting is also influenced by tax laws. Despite the common heritage of the United States and the United Kingdom, U.S. and British accounting practices vary widely. For example, LIFO is not widely used in Great Britain.

A company that sells its stock on a stock exchange must follow the accounting principles of that country. For example, **British Petroleum-Amoco (BP)** stock is traded on the New York Stock Exchange, so BP follows American GAAP for financial statements issued in the United States. **Infosys Technology** is an Indian company that sells its stock in the United States. Infosys therefore prepares U.S.-type financial statements, as does **Nokia,** which is based in Finland.

Several organizations seek worldwide harmony of accounting standards. The International Accounting Standards Committee (IASC) is headquartered in London and operates much as the Financial Accounting Standards Board in the United States. It has the support of the accounting professions in the United States, most of the British Commonwealth countries, Japan, France, Germany, the Netherlands, and Mexico. However, the IASC has no authority to require compliance and must rely on cooperation by the various national accounting professions.

 DAILY EXERCISE 16-20

Reporting Comprehensive Income

We introduced comprehensive income in Chapter 14 as required by *FASB Statement 130.* ➥ The coverage of accounting for available-for-sale investments and international operations in this chapter completes the discussion of comprehensive income. Recall that *other comprehensive income* can be reported below net income on the income statement. One of the elements of other comprehensive income is the unrealized gain or loss on available-for-sale investments. Exhibit 16-9 illustrates how to report other comprehensive income, using assumed amounts for the first year of the company.

◄ See Chapter 14, page 558, for reporting comprehensive income.

EXHIBIT 16-9
Comprehensive Income

PANEL A — Reporting Comprehensive Income

NATIONAL EXPRESS COMPANY
Income Statement
Year Ended December 31, 20X1

Revenues	$10,000
Expenses (summarized)	6,000
Net income	4,000
Other comprehensive income: Unrealized gain on available-for-sale investments	1,000
Comprehensive income	$ 5,000

PANEL B — Reporting Unrealized Gains (Losses) on Available-for-Sale Investments on the Balance Sheet

NATIONAL EXPRESS COMPANY
Balance Sheet (partial)
December 31, 20X1

Stockholders' Equity

Common stock	$ 3,000
Retained earnings	7,000
Accumulated other comprehensive income:	
Unrealized gain on available-for-sale investments	1,000
Total stockholders' equity	$11,000

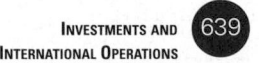

DECISION GUIDELINES

Foreign-Currency, Comprehensive Income, and Statement of Cash Flows

DECISION	GUIDELINES
When to record a • Foreign-currency gain?	• When you receive foreign currency worth *more* in U.S. dollars than the amount of the receivable recorded earlier. • When you pay foreign currency that costs *less* in U.S. dollars than the amount of the payable recorded earlier.
• Foreign-currency loss?	• When you receive foreign currency worth *less* in U.S. dollars than the amount of the receivable recorded earlier. • When you pay foreign currency that costs *more* in U.S. dollars than the amount of the payable recorded earlier.
What are the elements of comprehensive income?	• Net income, plus other comprehensive income: Unrealized gains and losses on available-for-sale investments

REVIEW INVESTMENTS AND INTERNATIONAL OPERATIONS

www.prenhall.com/horngren

End-of-Chapter Assessment

SUMMARY PROBLEM

1. Journalize the following transactions of American Corp. Explanations are not required.

20X5

Nov. 16　Purchased equipment on account for 40,000 Swiss francs when the exchange rate was $0.63 per Swiss franc.

　　27　Sold merchandise on account to a Belgian company for 700,000 Belgian francs. Each franc is worth $0.0305.

Dec. 22　Paid the Swiss company when the franc's exchange rate was $0.625.

　　31　Adjusted for the change in the exchange rate of the Belgian franc. Its current exchange rate is $0.0301.

20X6

Jan.　4　Collected from the Belgian company. The exchange rate is $0.0307.

2. In the 20X5 transactions, identify each of the following currencies as strong or weak:
a. Swiss franc　　**b.** Belgian franc　　**c.** U.S. dollar
Which currency strengthened during 20X6? Which currency weakened during 20X6?

Solution

1. Entries for transactions stated in foreign currencies:

20X5			
Nov. 16	Equipment (40,000 × $0.63)	25,200	
	Accounts Payable		25,200
27	Accounts Receivable (700,000 × $0.0305)	21,350	
	Sales Revenue		21,350
Dec. 22	Accounts Payable	25,200	
	Cash (40,000 × $0.625)..............................		25,000
	Foreign-Currency Gain		200
31	Foreign-Currency Loss		
	[700,000 × ($0.0305 − $0.0301)]	280	
	Accounts Receivable		280

```
       20X6
       Jan. 4    Cash (700,000 × $0.0307) ...................................    21,490
                     Accounts Receivable ($21,350 − $280)......                   21,070
                     Foreign-Currency Gain ........................................               420
```

2. During 20X5,
   a. Swiss franc—weak   **b.** Belgian franc—weak   **c.** U.S. dollar—strong
During 20X6, the Belgian franc strengthened and the U.S. dollar weakened.

LESSONS LEARNED

1. Account for trading investments. *Trading investments* are those the investor expects to sell within a few months. Therefore, trading investments are reported at current market value among current assets.

2. Account for available-for-sale investments. *Available-for-sale investments* are all stock investments other than trading securities. Most are classified as long-term investments and reported at current *market value.*

3. Use the equity method for investments. The *equity method* is used for 20–50% stock investments. To measure investment revenue, the investor applies its percentage of ownership to the investee's net income. Equity-method investment revenue is reported as Other revenues on the income statement.

4. Understand consolidated financial statements. Ownership of more than 50% of a company's voting stock creates a *parent-subsidiary* relationship, and the parent company uses the *consolidation method* to account for subsidiaries.

The subsidiary's financial statements are included in the parent's consolidated financial statements.

5. Account for long-term investments in bonds. *Held-to-maturity investments* are bonds the investor intends to hold until maturity. The *amortized-cost method* is used to account for held-to-maturity investments. Interest receivable is accrued and bond discount or premium is amortized. Long-term bond investments appear on the balance sheet after current assets; interest revenue from the investments appears on the income statement.

6. Account for transactions stated in a foreign currency. When foreign currency is involved in a transaction, there may be a gain or loss on the foreign currency. These gains and losses are reported on the income statement as Other gains (losses). To protect against foreign-currency losses, companies engage in *hedging*—they protect themselves from losing money by engaging in a counterbalancing transaction.

ACCOUNTING VOCABULARY

available-for-sale
  investments (p. 624)
consolidated
  statements (p. 631)
controlling interest (p. 630)
equity method for
  investments (p. 628)
foreign-currency exchange
  rate (p. 635)

hedging (p. 637)
held-to-maturity
  investments (p. 632)
long-term investment (p. 623)
majority interest (p. 630)
marketable security (p. 623)
market-value method for
  investments (p. 686)
minority interest (p. 631)

parent company (p. 630)
short-term investment (p. 623)
strong currency (p. 635)
subsidiary company (p. 630)
trading investments (p. 624)
weak currency (p. 635)

QUESTIONS

1. How are stock prices quoted in the securities market? What is the investor's cost of 1,000 shares of Ford Motor Company stock at 55.75?

2. Outline the accounting methods for the different types of investments.

3. How does an investor record the receipt of a cash dividend on an available-for-sale investment? How does this investor record receipt of a stock dividend?

4. An investor paid $11,000 for 1,000 shares of stock—a trading investment—and later received a 10% stock dividend. At December 31, the investment's market value is $11,800. Compute the gain or loss on the investment.

5. When is an investment accounted for by the equity method? Outline how to apply the equity method to purchase of the investment, the investor's proportion of the investee's net income, and receipt of a cash dividend from the investee.

6. Name the account that expresses the excess of the cost of an investment over the market value of the subsidiary's

owners' equity. What type of account is this, and where in the financial statements is it reported?

7. When a parent company buys more than 50% but less than 100% of a subsidiary's stock, a new item appears on the balance sheet. What is this category called, and under what heading do most companies report it?

8. An investor purchases Texaco bonds as a long-term investment. Suppose the face amount of the bonds is $100,000 and the purchase price is 101.3. The bonds pay interest at the stated annual rate of 8%. How much did the investor pay for the bonds? How much principal will the investor collect at maturity?

9. Buying and selling transactions stated in a foreign currency create a new complexity. What is this complexity, and what new risk does it carry?

10. What is a foreign-currency hedge? Why do companies hedge their foreign-currency transactions? State how a company with both foreign-currency receivables and payables can create a foreign-currency hedge.

11. McVey, Inc., purchased inventory from a French company, agreeing to pay 100,000 francs. On the purchase date, the franc was quoted at $0.17. When McVey paid the debt, the price of a franc was $0.18. What account does McVey debit for the $1,000 difference between the cost of the inventory and the amount of cash paid?

12. Which country does not allow the use of the LIFO method for inventories?

ASSESS YOUR PROGRESS

DAILY EXERCISES

Computing the cost of a stock investment
(Obj. 1, 2)

DE16-1 Compute the cost of each investment. Carry final figures to the nearest cent.

a. 200 shares of **Nokia** stock at 85.38.
b. 450 shares of **IBM** stock at 99.81. IBM pays a cash dividend of $0.52 per year.
c. 8,000 shares of **Nike** stock at 46.50.
d. 70 shares of **Target** stock at 52.75.

Classifying investments as current or long-term
(Obj. 1, 2)

DE16-2 ◄ *Link Back to Chapter 4 (Current Assets)*. Answer these questions about the investments held by **AOL Time Warner Corporation.**

1. Why is a trading investment always a current asset? Explain.
2. Is an available-for-sale investment a current asset or a long-term asset? What is the deciding factor?

Classifying investments as trading or available-for-sale
(Obj. 1, 2)

DE16-3 Marquette Corp. reports its annual financial statements on June 30 each year. Marquette purchased 100 shares of stock in each of three companies:

a. Investment in **Dell Computer** to be sold within the next 9–12 months.
b. Investment in **AT&T** to be sold within the next 90 days.
c. Investment in **eBay** to be sold within the next two years.

Classify each investment as (1) a current asset or a long-term asset, and (2) a trading investment or an available-for-sale investment.

Accounting for a trading investment
(Obj. 1)

DE16-4 Return to page 625, the example of **Intel Corporation's** short-term trading investment in **Ford Motor Company** stock.

1. How much did Intel pay for the short-term investment in Ford stock? Stated differently, what was Intel's cost of the Ford stock?
2. At December 31, 20X5, what was the current market value of Intel's short-term investment in Ford stock?
3. Suppose the Ford stock had increased in value to $30,000 on December 31, 20X5. Give Intel's adjusting entry at December 31, and show how Intel would report the short-term investment on its balance sheet.

Accounting for a trading investment loss
(Obj. 1)

DE16-5 Dierberg Bank completed the following transactions during 20X1 and 20X2:

20X1
Dec. 6 Purchased 1,000 shares of **Toyota** stock at a price of $92.25 per share, intending to sell the investment next month.
23 Received a cash dividend of $1.12 per share on the Toyota stock.
31 Adjusted the investment to its market value of $91 per share.
20X2
Jan. 27 Sold the Toyota stock for $88.38 per share.

1. Classify Dierberg's investment as trading or available-for-sale.
2. Journalize Dierberg's investment transactions. Explanations are not required.

Accounting for a trading investment gain
(Obj. 1)

DE16-6 Vincent Marketing Associates completed the following investment transactions during 20X6 and 20X7:

20X6
Dec. 12 Purchased 500 shares of **MCI WorldCom** stock at a price of $41.13 per share, intending to sell the investment next month.
21 Received a cash dividend of $0.23 per share on the MCI WorldCom stock.
31 Adjusted the investment to its market value of $43.13 per share.
20X7
Jan. 16 Sold the MCI WorldCom stock for $44.50 per share.

1. Classify Vincent's investment as trading or available-for-sale.
2. Journalize Vincent's investment transactions. Explanations are not required.

DE16-7 Trilogy Corp. holds a significant portfolio of short-term investments. On November 19, 20X6, Trilogy purchased a trading investment for $85,000. At December 31, 20X6, the market value of the trading investment was $83,000. Trilogy sold the investment for $90,000 on January 6, 20X7.

Compute Trilogy's gains and losses for 20X6 and 20X7.

Measuring gains and losses on a trading investment (Obj. 1)

DE16-8 **BankOne** buys 500 shares of **Chevron** stock, paying $64 per share. Suppose Chevron distributes a 10% stock dividend. Later, BankOne sells the Chevron stock for $58 per share.

1. Compute BankOne's new cost per share after receiving the stock dividend.
2. Compute BankOne's gain or loss on the sale of this available-for-sale investment.

Measuring gain or loss on the sale of an investment after receiving a stock dividend (Obj. 2)

DE16-9 BLT Financial, Inc., completed these long-term available-for-sale investment transactions during 20X7:

20X7

Jan. 14   Purchased 300 shares of **PepsiCo** stock, paying $19.75 per share. BLT intends to hold the investment for the indefinite future.

Aug. 22   Received a cash dividend of $1.25 per share on the PepsiCo stock.

Dec. 31   Adjusted the PepsiCo investment to its current market value of $5,514.

1. Journalize BLT's investment transactions. Explanations are not required.
2. Show how to report the investment and any unrealized gain or loss on BLT's balance sheet at December 31, 20X7.

Accounting for an available-for-sale investment; unrealized loss (Obj. 2)

DE16-10 Use the data given in Daily Exercise 16-9. On August 4, 20X8, BLT Financial, Inc., sold its investment in **PepsiCo** stock for $20.75 per share.

1. Journalize the sale. No explanation is required.
2. How does the gain or loss that you recorded differ from the gain or loss that was recorded at December 31, 20X7?

Accounting for the sale of an available-for-sale investment (Obj. 2)

DE16-11 Suppose on January 6, 20X2, **General Motors** paid $100 million for its 40% investment in **Isuzu.** Assume Isuzu earned net income of $15 million and paid cash dividends of $10 million during 20X2.

1. What method should General Motors use to account for the investment in Isuzu? Give your reason.
2. Journalize these three transactions on the books of General Motors. Show all amounts in millions of dollars and include an explanation for each entry.
3. Post to the Long-Term Equity-Method Investment T-account. What is its balance after all the transactions are posted?

Accounting for a 40% investment in another company (Obj. 3)

DE16-12 Use the data given in Daily Exercise 16-11. Assume that early in January 20X3, General Motors sold half its investment in Isuzu to **Toyota Motor Corporation.** The sale price was $59 million. Compute General Motors' gain or loss on the sale.

Accounting for the sale of an equity-method investment (Obj. 3)

DE16-13 Answer these questions about consolidation accounting:

1. Define a parent company. Define a subsidiary company.
2. Which company's name appears on the consolidated financial statements? How much of the subsidiary's stock must the parent own before reporting consolidated statements?
3. How do consolidated financial statements differ from the financial statements of a single company?

Understanding consolidated financial statements (Obj. 4)

DE16-14 Two accounts that arise from consolidation accounting are minority interest and goodwill.

1. What is minority interest, and which company reports it, the parent or the subsidiary? Where is minority interest reported?
2. What is goodwill, and how does it arise? Which company reports goodwill, the parent or the subsidiary? Where is goodwill reported?

Understanding goodwill and minority interest (Obj. 4)

DE16-15 **Edward Jones & Co.** owns vast amounts of corporate bonds. Suppose Edward Jones buys $1,500,000 of **MCI WorldCom** bonds at a price of 96. The MCI WorldCom bonds pay cash interest at the annual rate of 7% and mature within five years.

1. How much did Edward Jones pay to purchase the bond investment? How much will Edward Jones collect when the bond investment matures?
2. How much cash interest will Edward Jones receive each year from MCI WorldCom?
3. Will Edward Jones' annual interest revenue on the bond investment be more or less than the amount of cash interest received each year? Give your reason.
4. Compute Edward Jones' annual interest revenue on this bond investment. Use the straight-line method to amortize the discount on the investment.

Working with a bond investment (Obj. 5)

Recording bond investment transactions
(Obj. 5)

DE16-16 Return to Daily Exercise 16-15, the Edward Jones investment in **MCI WorldCom** bonds. Journalize on Edward Jones' books:

a. Purchase of the bond investment on January 2, 20X1. Edward Jones expects to hold the investment to maturity.
b. Receipt of annual cash interest on December 31, 20X1.
c. Amortization of discount on December 31, 20X1.
d. Collection of the investment's face value at the maturity date on January 2, 20X6. (Assume the receipt of 20X5 interest and amortization of discount for 20X5 have already been recorded, so you may ignore these entries.)

Recording interest revenue on a bond investment
(Obj. 5)

DE16-17 Return to the bond investment situation on page 632. Assume the investor purchased the **CBS** bond investment on June 1, 20X2, and intends to hold the bonds until maturity on June 1, 20X6. For this Daily Exercise, assume that CBS pays cash interest on June 1 and December 1 each year, rather than on April 1 and October 1 (as on page 632).

The investor made all entries as needed on December 1. Now journalize the investor's accrual of cash interest and amortization of discount on the investment at December 31, 20X2. Use the straight-line amortization method.

Accounting for transactions stated in a foreign currency
(Obj. 6)

DE16-18 Suppose **Nike Incorporated** sells athletic shoes to a Russian company on March 14. Nike agrees to accept 2,000,000 Russian rubles. On the date of sale, the ruble is quoted at $0.036. Nike collects half the receivable on April 19, when the ruble is worth $0.034. Then, on May 10, when the price of the ruble is $0.037, Nike collects the final amount.

Journalize these three transactions for Nike. Overall, how well did Nike come out in terms of a net foreign-currency gain or loss?

Accounting for transactions stated in a foreign currency
(Obj. 6)

DE16-19 Page 636 includes a sequence of **Shipp Belting** journal entries for transactions denominated in Mexican pesos. Suppose the foreign-exchange rate for a peso is $0.118 on July 2. Record Shipp Belting's collection of cash on July 2.

On page 636, Shipp Belting buys inventory for which Shipp must pay Swiss francs. Suppose a Swiss franc costs $0.82 on August 24. Record Shipp Belting's payment of cash on August 24.

International accounting differences
(Obj. 6)

DE16-20 Exhibit 16-8, page 638, outlines some differences between accounting in the United States and accounting in other countries. American companies transact more business with British companies than with any other. Contrary to what you might expect, there are several important differences between American and British accounting. In your own words, describe those differences for inventories, goodwill, and research and development.

EXERCISES

Accounting for a trading investment
(Obj. 1)

E16-1 **Nations Bank,** headquartered in Charlotte, North Carolina, holds huge portfolios of investments. Suppose Nations Bank completed the following investment transactions:

20X1
Dec. 6   Purchased 1,000 shares of **Goodyear Tire & Rubber Co.** stock for $70,000. Nations Bank plans to sell the stock at a profit next month.
     30   Received a quarterly cash dividend of $0.85 per share on the Goodyear stock.
     31   Adjusted the investment in Goodyear stock. Current market value is $67,000, and Nations Bank plans to sell the stock early in 20X2.
20X2
Jan. 14   Sold the Goodyear stock for $71,000.

Required

1. Journalize the Nations Bank investment transactions. Explanations are not required.
2. Show how Nations Bank would report its investment in the Goodyear stock on the balance sheet at December 31, 20X1.

Journalizing transactions for an available-for-sale investment
(Obj. 2)

E16-2 Journalize the following long-term available-for-sale investment transactions of Abbey-Simms Inc. Explanations are not required.

a. Purchased 400 shares (8%) of Marcor Corporation common stock at $38 per share, with the intent of holding the stock for the indefinite future.
b. Received cash dividend of $1 per share on the Marcor investment.
c. At year end, adjusted the investment account to current market value of $45 per share.
d. Sold the Marcor stock for the market price of $42 per share.

Journalizing transactions for an available-for-sale investment
(Obj. 2)

E16-3 Journalize the following investment transactions of Vemcor Manufacturing, Inc.:

Aug. 1   Purchased 500 shares (2%) of Vardaman Corporation common stock as a long-term available-for-sale investment, paying $44 per share.
Sep. 12   Received cash dividend of $1 per share on the Vardaman investment.
Nov. 23   Received 250 shares of Vardaman common stock in a 50% stock dividend. Round new cost per share to three decimal places.
Dec. 4   Unexpectedly sold the Vardaman stock for $29 per share.

E16-4 Late in the current year, Travel Consumer Corporation bought 3,000 shares of **National Geographic** common stock at $81.88, 600 shares of **AT&T Corp.** stock at $46.75, and 1,400 shares of **Hitachi** stock at $79—all as available-for-sale investments. At December 31, the *Wall Street Journal* reports National Geographic stock at $80.38, AT&T at $48.50, and Hitachi at $68.25.

Accounting for long-term investment transactions (Obj. 2)

Required

1. Determine the cost and the market value of the long-term investment portfolio at December 31.
2. Record any adjusting entry needed at December 31.
3. What two items would Travel Consumer Corporation report on its balance sheet for the information given? Make the necessary disclosures.

E16-5 Suppose **Dillard's, Inc.,** owns equity-method investments in several other department-store companies. Suppose Dillard's paid $2 million to acquire a 25% investment in Italian Imports Company. Assume that Italian Imports Company reported net income of $780,000 for the first year and declared and paid cash dividends of $500,000. Record the following in Dillard's journal: (a) purchase of the investment, (b) its proportion of Italian Imports' net income, and (c) receipt of the cash dividends.

Accounting for transactions under the equity method (Obj. 3)

E16-6 Without making journal entries, record the transactions of Exercise 16-5 directly in the **Dillard's** account, Long-Term Equity-Method Investment in Italian Imports. Assume that after all the noted transactions took place, Dillard's sold its entire investment in Italian Imports for cash of $2,600,000. How much is Dillard's gain or loss on the sale of the investment?

Measuring gain or loss on the sale of an equity-method investment (Obj. 3)

E16-7 Precision Automotive Parts paid $145,000 for a 40% investment in the common stock of Auto Chief, Inc. For the first year, Auto Chief reported net income of $84,000 and at year end declared and paid cash dividends of $16,000. On the balance sheet date, the market value of Precision's investment in Auto Chief stock was $134,000.

Applying the appropriate accounting method for investments (Obj. 3)

Required

1. Which method is appropriate for Precision Automotive to use in accounting for its investment in Auto Chief? Why?
2. Show everything that Precision would report for the investment and any investment revenue in its year-end financial statements.
3. What role does the market value of the investment play in this situation?

E16-8 On March 31, 20X3, Remke Corporation paid 92 1/4 for 7% bonds of **Dean Witter Financial Services** as a long-term held-to-maturity investment. The maturity value of the bonds will be $30,000 on September 30, 20X7. The bonds pay interest on March 31 and September 30. At December 31, the bonds' market value is 93.

Recording bond investment transactions (Obj. 5)

Required

1. What method should Remke Corporation use to account for its investment in the Dean Witter bonds?
2. Using the straight-line method of amortizing the discount, journalize all of Remke Corporation's transactions on the bonds for 20X3.
3. Show how Remke would report the bond investment on its balance sheet at December 31, 20X3.

E16-9 Journalize the following foreign-currency transactions. Explanations are not required.

Managing and accounting for foreign-currency transactions (Obj. 6)

Nov. 17 Purchased inventory on account from a Japanese company. The price was 200,000 yen, and the exchange rate of the yen was $0.0088.
Dec. 16 Paid the Japanese supplier when the exchange rate was $0.0091.
19 Sold merchandise on account to a French company at a price of 60,000 French francs. The exchange rate of the franc was $0.15.
30 Collected from the French company when the exchange rate was $0.17.

On November 18, immediately after your purchase, and on December 20, immediately after your sale, which currencies did you want to strengthen? Which currencies did in fact strengthen? Explain your reasoning in detail.

Challenge Exercises

E16-10 **AMP Incorporated,** a world leader in the manufacture of electronic connection devices, reported the stockholders' equity on its balance sheet on page 646, as adapted, at December 31.

Analyzing available-for-sale investments (Obj. 2)

Required

1. AMP's balance sheet also reports available-for-sale investments at $288 million. What was AMP's cost of the investments? What was the market value of the investments on December 31, 19X9?
2. Suppose AMP sold its available-for-sale investments in 20X0 for $259 million. Determine the gain or loss on sale of the investments.

AMP INCORPORATED	
Balance Sheet (partial, adapted)	
Millions	**19X9**
Shareholders' Equity:	
Common stock	$ 12
Other capital..	214
Unrealized gains on available-for-sale investments	22
Retained earnings...	2,330
Treasury stock, at cost	(243)
Total shareholders' equity	$2,335

Analyzing equity-method investments (Obj. 3)

E16-11 Whirlpool Corporation is a leading manufacturer of household appliances. In Brazil and Mexico, Whirlpool operates through affiliated companies, whose stock Whirlpool owns in various percentages between 20% and 50%. Whirlpool's financial statements reported these items (adapted):

	Millions	
	19X9	**19X8**
Balance Sheet (adapted)		
Equity-method investments...	$296	$286
Income Statement		
Equity-method investments revenue (losses)	(13)	4

Whirlpool's financial statements reported no sales of equity-method investments during 19X9 or 19X8. During 19X9, Whirlpool paid $42 million to purchase equity-method investments.

Required

Prepare a T-account for Equity-Method Investments to determine the amount of dividends Whirlpool Corporation received from investee companies during 19X9. Show your work.

(Group A) PROBLEMS

Accounting for trading investments (Obj. 1)

P16-1A During the second half of 20X4, the operations of Maine Lobsters, Inc., generated excess cash, which the company invested in securities, as follows:

July	2	Purchased 3,500 shares of common stock as a trading investment, paying $12.75 per share.
Aug.	21	Received semiannual cash dividend of $0.45 per share on the trading investment.
Sep.	16	Sold the trading investment for $13.50 per share.
Oct.	8	Purchased trading investments in stock for $136,000.
Dec.	31	Adjusted the trading securities to their market value of $130,000.

Required

1. Record the transactions in the journal of Maine Lobsters, Inc. Explanations are not required.
2. Post to the Short-Term Investments account, and show how to report the short-term investments on Maine Lobster's balance sheet at December 31.

Accounting for available-for-sale and equity-method investments (Obj. 2, 3)

P16-2A The beginning balance sheet of Quill.com, Inc., included the following:

Long-Term Equity-Method Investments................... $657,000

During the year the company completed the following investment transactions:

Mar.	3	Purchased 5,000 shares of LBO Software common stock as a long-term avail-able-for-sale investment, paying $9.25 per share.
	4	Purchased new long-term equity-method investment at cost of $408,000.
May	14	Received cash dividend of $0.82 per share on the LBO investment.
June	15	Received cash dividend of $27,000 from equity-method investment.
Oct.	24	Purchased long-term available-for-sale investment in Eastern Communication stock for $226,000.
Dec.	15	Received cash dividend of $31,000 from equity-method investment.
	31	Received annual reports from equity-method investee companies. Their total net income for the year was $620,000. Of this amount, Quill.com's proportion is 25%.
	31	Adjusted the available-for-sale investments to market value. The market values of Quill.com's investments are LBO, $49,100; Eastern, $221,000.

Required

1. Record the transactions in the journal of Quill.com, Inc.
2. Post entries to the Long-Term Equity-Method Investments T-account, and determine its balance at December 31. Do likewise for the Long-Term Available-for-Sale Investments T-account and the Allowance to Adjust Investments to Market T-account.
3. Show how to report the Long-Term Available-for-Sale Investments and the Long-Term Equity-Method Investments on Quill.com's balance sheet at December 31.

P16-3A Orly Chemical Company owns stock in numerous other companies. During 20X4, Orly completed the following long-term investment transactions:

Reporting investments on the balance sheet and the related revenue on the income statement (Obj. 2, 3)

20X4

May 1	Purchased 8,000 shares, which exceeds 20%, of the common stock of DeGaulle Company at total cost of $720,000.
July 1	Purchased 2,000 additional shares of DeGaulle common stock at cost of $140,000.
Sep. 15	Received semiannual cash dividend of $4.40 per share on the DeGaulle investment.
Oct. 12	Purchased 1,000 shares of TEC Corporation common stock as an available-for-sale investment paying $22.50 per share.
Dec. 14	Received semiannual cash dividend of $0.75 per share on the TEC investment.
Dec. 31	Received annual report from DeGaulle Company. Net income for the year was $360,000. Of this amount, Orly's proportion is one third.

The current market value of the TEC stock is $19,400. The market value of the DeGaulle stock is $965,000.

Required

1. For which investment is current market value used in the accounting? Why is market value used for one investment and not the other?
2. Show what Orly Chemical Company would report on its year-end balance sheet for these investments. (It is helpful to use a T-account for the investment in DeGaulle stock.)

P16-4A Financial institutions hold large quantities of bond investments. Suppose **Goldman Sachs** purchases $800,000 of 8% bonds of **Xerox Corporation** for 92 on January 31, 20X0. These bonds pay interest on January 31 and July 31 each year. They mature on July 31, 20X8.

Accounting for a bond investment; amortizing discount by the straight-line method (Obj. 5)

Required

1. Journalize Goldman Sachs' purchase of the bonds as a long-term investment on January 31, 20X0 (to be held to maturity), receipt of cash interest and amortization of discount on July 31, 20X0, and accrual of interest revenue and amortization of discount at December 31, 20X0. The straight-line method is appropriate for amortizing discount.
2. Show how to report this long-term bond investment on Goldman Sachs' balance sheet at December 31, 20X0.

P16-5A ←↩ *Link Back to Chapter 15 (Effective-Interest Amortization of Discount).* On December 31, 20X1, when the market interest rate is 10%, an investor purchases $400,000 of Yuma Inc., 9.5%, ten-year bonds at issuance. The cost of this bond investment was $387,578 and the investor expects to hold the investment to maturity.

Accounting for a bond investment; amortizing discount by the effective-interest method (Obj. 5)

Required

Journalize the purchase on December 31, 20X1, the first semiannual interest receipt on June 30, 20X2, and the year-end interest receipt on December 31, 20X2. The investor uses the effective-interest amortization method. Prepare a schedule for amortizing the discount on the bond investment through December 31, 20X2. Use Exhibit 15-4, as a guide.

P16-6A Suppose **Gap, Inc.,** completed the following transactions:

Recording foreign-currency transactions and reporting the transaction gain or loss (Obj. 6)

May 4	Sold clothing on account to a Mexican department store for $71,000. The exchange rate of the Mexican peso is $0.141, and the customer agrees to pay in dollars.
13	Purchased inventory on account from a Canadian company at a price of Canadian $65,000. The exchange rate of the Canadian dollar is $0.75, and payment will be in Canadian dollars.
20	Sold goods on account to an English firm for 89,000 British pounds. Payment will be in pounds, and the exchange rate of the pound is $1.50.
27	Collected from the Mexican company.
June 21	Paid the Canadian company. The exchange rate of the Canadian dollar is $0.72.
July 17	Collected from the English firm. The exchange rate of the British pound is $1.47.

Required

1. Record these transactions in Gap's journal, and show how to report the net foreign-currency gain or loss on the income statement. Explanations are not required.
2. How will what you learned in this problem help you structure international transactions?

(Group B) PROBLEMS

Accounting for trading investments (Obj. 1)

P16-1B During the second half of 20X2, the operations of Regency Systems generated excess cash, which the company invested in securities, as follows:

July 3	Purchased 3,000 shares of common stock as a trading investment, paying $9.25 per share.
Aug. 14	Received semiannual cash dividend of $0.32 per share on the trading investment.
Sep. 15	Sold the trading investment for $10.50 per share.
Nov. 24	Purchased trading investments for $226,000.
Dec. 31	Adjusted the trading securities to their market value of $221,000.

Required

1. Record the transactions in the journal of Regency Systems. Explanations are not required.
2. Post to the Short-Term Investment account. Then show how to report the short-term investment on the Regency Systems balance sheet at December 31.

Accounting for available-for-sale and equity-method investments (Obj. 2, 3)

P16-2B The beginning balance sheet of TalkNET On-line Incorporated included the following:

Long-Term Equity-Method Investments.............. $344,000

During the year, the company completed the following investment transactions:

Mar. 2	Purchased 2,000 shares of DLV Inc., common stock as a long-term available-for-sale investment, paying $12.25 per share.
5	Purchased new long-term equity-method investment at cost of $540,000.
Apr. 21	Received cash dividend of $0.75 per share on the DLV investment.
May 17	Received cash dividend of $47,000 from the equity-method investment.
Oct. 8	Purchased long-term available-for-sale investment in Blinn Corp. stock for $136,000.
17	Received cash dividend of $49,000 from the equity-method investment.
Dec. 31	Received annual reports from the equity-method investee companies. Their total net income for the year was $550,000. Of this amount, TalkNET On-line's proportion is 33%.
31	Adjusted the available-for-sale investments to market value. The market values of TalkNET On-line's investments are DLV, $26,800; Blinn, $134,400.

Required

1. Record the transactions in the journal of TalkNET On-line Incorporated.
2. Post entries to the Long-Term Equity-Method Investments T-account, and determine its balance at December 31. Do likewise for the Long-Term Available-for-Sale Investments T-account and the Allowance to Adjust Investments to Market T-account.
3. Show how to report the Long-Term Available-for-Sale Investments and the Long-Term Equity-Method Investments accounts on TalkNET On-line's balance sheet at December 31.

Reporting investments on the balance sheet and the related revenue on the income statement (Obj. 2, 3)

P16-3B Steinway Company owns numerous investments in the stock of other companies. Assume that Steinway completed the following long-term investment transactions:

20X2

Feb. 12	Purchased 20,000 shares, which exceeds 20%, of the common stock of Growtech, Inc., at total cost of $715,000.
July 1	Purchased 8,000 additional shares of Growtech common stock at cost of $300,000.
Aug. 9	Received annual cash dividend of $0.90 per share on the Growtech investment.
Oct. 16	Purchased 950 shares of Varnix Company common stock as an available-for-sale investment, paying $41.50 per share.
Nov. 30	Received semiannual cash dividend of $0.60 per share on the Varnix investment.
Dec. 31	Received annual report from Growtech, Inc. Net income for the year was $510,000. Of this amount, Steinway's proportion is 30%.

The current market value of the Varnix stock is $41,100. The market value of the Growtech stock is $967,000.

Required

1. For which investment is current market value used in the accounting? Why is market value used for one investment and not the other?
2. Show what Steinway Company would report on its year-end balance sheet for these investments. It is helpful to use a T-account for the investment in Growtech stock.

P16-4B Financial institutions such as insurance companies hold large quantities of bond investments. Suppose Bastrop Insurance Co. purchases $400,000 of 9% bonds of Inwood Corporation for 103 on March 1, 20X1. These bonds pay interest on March 1 and September 1 each year. They mature on March 1, 20X8.

Accounting for a bond investment; straight-line amortization of premium (Obj. 5)

Required

1. Journalize Bastrop's purchase of the bonds as a long-term investment on March 1, 20X1 (to be held to maturity). Then record Bastrop's receipt of cash interest and amortization of premium at September 1, 20X1, and the amortization of premium and accrual of interest revenue at December 31, 20X1. The straight-line method is appropriate for amortizing premium.
2. Show how to report this long-term bond investment on Bastrop Insurance Co.'s balance sheet at December 31, 20X1.

P16-5B ← *Link Back to Chapter 15 (Effective-Interest Amortization of Discount).* On December 31, 20X1, when the market interest is 8%, ChaseBank purchases $500,000 of **Michelin Corp.,** 7.4%, six-year bonds at issuance. The cost of this long-term bond investment is $486,123, and ChaseBank expects to hold the investment to maturity.

Accounting for a bond investment; effective-interest amortization of discount (Obj. 5)

Required

Journalize the purchase on December 31, 20X1, the first semiannual interest receipt on June 30, 20X2, and the year-end interest receipt on December 31, 20X2. ChaseBank uses the effective-interest amortization method. Prepare a schedule for amortizing the discount on bond investment through December 31, 20X2. Use Exhibit 15-4 as a guide.

P16-6B Manifesto Publishing Company completed the following transactions:

Recording foreign-currency transactions and reporting the transaction gain or loss (Obj. 6)

May	1	Sold inventory on account to Marconi Telegraph, an Italian public utility, for $19,000. The exchange rate of the Italian lira is $0.0007, and Marconi agrees to pay in dollars.
	10	Purchased supplies on account from a Canadian company at a price of Canadian $38,000. The exchange rate of the Canadian dollar is $0.80, and payment will be in Canadian dollars.
	17	Sold inventory on account to an English firm for 112,000 British pounds. Payment will be in pounds, and the exchange rate of the pound is $1.50.
	22	Collected from Marconi Telegraph.
June	18	Paid the Canadian company. The exchange rate of the Canadian dollar is $0.77.
	24	Collected from the English firm. The exchange rate of the British pound is $1.47.

Required

1. Record these transactions in Manifesto Publishing's journal, and show how to report the net foreign-currency gain or loss on the income statement. Explanations are not required.
2. How will what you learned in this problem help you structure international transactions?

Apply Your Knowledge

Decision Cases

Case 1. Carla Allman is the manager of Stagg Corp., whose year end is December 31. The company made two investments during the first week of January 20X2. Both investments are to be held for the indefinite future. Information about the investments follows:

Explaining the market value and equity methods of accounting for investments (Obj. 1, 2)

a. Stagg purchased 30% of the common stock of Frontenac Mfg. Co. for its book value of $250,000. During the year ended December 31, 20X2, Frontenac earned $146,000 and paid dividends totaling $53,000. At year end, the market value of the Frontenac investment is $261,000.
b. One thousand shares of the common stock of St. John Medical Corporation were purchased as an available-for-sale investment for $95,000. During the year ended December 31, 20X2, St. John paid Stagg a dividend of $3,000. St. John earned a profit of $317,000 for that period, and at year end, the market value of Stagg's investment in St. John stock was $92,000.

Allman has come to you to ask how to account for the investments. Stagg has never had such investments before. Explain the proper accounting to her by indicating that different accounting methods apply to different situations.

Required

Help Allman understand by writing a memo to

1. Describe the methods of accounting applicable to these investments.
2. Identify which method should be used to account for the investments in Frontenac Mfg. Co. and St. John Medical Corporation. Also indicate the dollar amount to report for each investment on the year-end balance sheet.

Understanding the consolidation method for investments (Obj. 4)

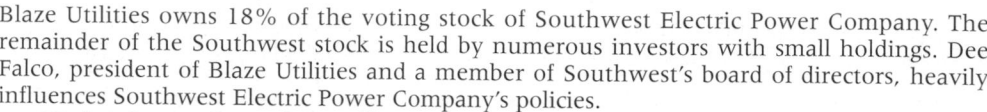

Case 2. Caesar Saled inherited some investments, and he has received the annual reports of the companies. The financial statements of the companies are puzzling to Saled, and he asks you the following questions:

1. The companies label their financial statements as *consolidated* balance sheet, *consolidated* income statement, and so on. What are consolidated financial statements?
2. The consolidated balance sheet lists the asset Goodwill. What is goodwill? Does the presence of goodwill mean that the company's stock has increased in value?

Write a memo to answer each of Saled's questions.

ETHICAL ISSUE

Blaze Utilities owns 18% of the voting stock of Southwest Electric Power Company. The remainder of the Southwest stock is held by numerous investors with small holdings. Dee Falco, president of Blaze Utilities and a member of Southwest's board of directors, heavily influences Southwest Electric Power Company's policies.

Under the market-value method of accounting for investments, Blaze's net income increases as it receives dividend revenue from Southwest Power. Blaze Utilities pays President Falco a bonus computed as a percentage of Blaze's net income. Therefore, Falco can control her personal bonus to a certain extent by influencing Southwest's dividends.

A recession occurs in 20X0 and Blaze Utilities' income is low. Falco uses her power as a board member to have Southwest pay a large cash dividend. The action requires Southwest to borrow in order to pay the dividend.

Required

1. In getting Southwest to pay the large cash dividend, is Falco acting within her authority as a member of the Southwest board of directors? Are Falco's actions ethical? Whom can her actions harm?
2. Discuss how using the equity method of accounting for investments would decrease Falco's potential for manipulating her bonus.

FINANCIAL STATEMENT CASE

Investments in stock (Obj. 3, 4)

Obtain the annual report of a company of your choosing. Answer the following questions about the company. Concentrate on the current year in the annual report you select.

Required

1. Many companies refer to other companies in which they own equity-method investments as *affiliated companies*. This signifies the close relationship between the two entities even though the investor does not own a controlling interest.

Does the company have equity-method investments? Cite the evidence. If present, what were the balances in the investment account at the beginning and the end of the current year? If the company has no equity-method investments, continue searching until you find a company with equity-method investments.

2. Scan the income statement. If equity-method investments are present, what amount of revenue (or income) did the company earn on the investments during the current year?

TEAM PROJECT

Pick a stock from the *Wall Street Journal* or other database or publication. Assume that your group purchases 1,000 shares of the stock as a short-term trading investment. Research the stock in *Value Line, Moody's Investor Record,* or other source to determine whether the company pays cash dividends and, if so, how much and at what intervals.

1. Track the stock for a period assigned by your professor. Over the specified period, keep a daily record of the price of the stock to see how well your investment has performed. Each day, search the Corporate Dividend News in the *Wall Street Journal* to keep a record of any dividends you've received. End the period of your analysis with a month end, such as September 30 or December 31.

2. Journalize all transactions that you have experienced, including the investment purchase, dividends received (both cash dividends and stock dividends), any year-end adjustment required by the accounting method that is appropriate for your investment; and the sale of your investment two ways: at a gain; and at a loss. Assume you will prepare financial statements on the ending date of your study.

3. Show what you will report on your company's balance sheet, income statement, and statement of cash flows as a result of your investment transactions.

INTERNET EXERCISE

The Coca-Cola Company is the world's largest producer of soft-drink concentrates, syrups, and juices. Its soft-drink brands include Coke, Diet Coke, Cherry Coke, Sprite, and Nestea.

The Coca-Cola Company

1. Go to **http://www.cocacola.com** and click on *Investor Relations* followed by the *most recent annual report*. Click on *operations review* and use the pull-down menu to select *Worldwide Case Volume*. What percent of Coca-Cola's worldwide case volume is from outside of North America?

2. Click on *financials* and then use the pull-down menu to select the *Consolidated Financial Statements* or the *Notes to Consolidated Financial Statements* to answer the following questions:

   a. Refer to the "Consolidated Balance Sheets." How many accounts report amounts for marketable securities? Why? For the most recent year, what amount is reported for current marketable securities? Refer to Note 8: Financial Instruments. Of the amount reported for current marketable securities, how much is held in trading securities? Available-for-sale securities? Held-to-maturity securities?

   b. The equity method is used to account for how many different investments of The Coca-Cola Company? Refer to Note 2: Bottling Investments. The Coca-Cola Company owns approximately what percent of the outstanding common shares of Coca-Cola Enterprises Inc.? What type of business is Coca-Cola Enterprises Inc.?

   c. In 1999, did Coca-Cola report equity-method income or an equity-method loss? How much? What does the equity-method income or loss represent?

3. Refer to Note 1: Organization and Summary of Significant Accounting Policies. The Coca-Cola Company operates in how many countries worldwide? What companies are included in the consolidated financial statements? Which companies are accounted for using the equity method?

APPENDIX TO CHAPTER 16

PREPARING CONSOLIDATED FINANCIAL STATEMENTS

The preparation of consolidated financial statements includes summing the statement amounts (cash, receivables, inventory, and so on) of the parent company and its majority-owned subsidiaries. This appendix shows how the consolidation method works for the balance sheet. We illustrate two cases:

- Parent Company owns all of Subsidiary's Stock (called a wholly-owned subsidiary).
- Parent Company owns less than 100% of Subsidiary's Stock.

CONSOLIDATED BALANCE SHEET— PARENT CORPORATION OWNS ALL OF SUBSIDIARY'S STOCK

Suppose Parent Corporation has purchased all the outstanding common stock of Subsidiary Corporation at its book value of $150,000. In addition, Parent Corporation loaned Subsidiary Corporation $80,000. To record these transactions, Parent Corporation and Subsidiary Corporation would make the following entries:

Parent Corporation Books[1]		Subsidiary Corporation Books	
Investment in Subsidiary Corporation	150,000	No entry	
Cash	150,000		
Note Receivable from Subsidiary	80,000	Cash	80,000
Cash	80,000	Note Payable to Parent	80,000

Each legal entity keeps its own set of books. The consolidated entity does not maintain consolidated accounts. Instead, a work sheet is used to prepare the consolidated statements. (We will see two of these work sheets here.) A major concern in consolidation accounting is this: Do not double-count—that is, do not count the same item twice in a set of consolidated financial statements.

EXPLANATION OF ELIMINATION ENTRY (A) Exhibit 16-A1 shows the work sheet for consolidating the balance sheet. Consider the elimination entry for the parent-subsidiary ownership accounts. Entry (a) credits the parent Investment account to eliminate its debit balance. It also eliminates the subsidiary stockholder's equity accounts by debiting Common Stock for $100,000 and Retained Earnings for $50,000. Because these accounts represent the same thing—Subsidiary's equity—they must be eliminated from the consolidated totals. If they are not, the same item would be counted twice.

The resulting consolidated balance sheet reports no Investment in Subsidiary account, and the consolidated totals for Common Stock and Retained Earnings are those of Parent Corporation only. The consolidated amounts appear in the final column of the consolidation work sheet.

EXPLANATION OF ELIMINATION ENTRY (B) Parent Corporation loaned $80,000 to Subsidiary Corporation, and Subsidiary signed a note payable to Parent. Therefore, Parent's balance sheet includes an $80,000 note receivable, and Subsidiary's balance sheet reports a note payable for the same amount. The parent's receivable and the subsidiary's payable represent the same resources (all entirely within the consolidated entity) and so must be eliminated. Entry (b) accomplishes this. After this work sheet entry, the consolidated amount for notes receivable is zero. The $190,000 balance of Notes Payable is the amount that the Consolidated entity owes outsiders.

EXHIBIT 16-A1 **Work Sheet for Consolidated Balance Sheet—Parent Corporation Owns All of Subsidiary's Stock**

	Parent Corporation	Subsidiary Corporation	Eliminations		Consolidated Amounts
			Debit	Credit	
Assets					
Cash	12,000	18,000			30,000
Note receivable from Subsidiary	80,000	—		(b) 80,000	—
Inventory	104,000	91,000			195,000
Investment in Subsidiary	150,000	—		(a) 150,000	—
Other assets	218,000	138,000			356,000
Total	564,000	247,000			581,000
Liabilities and Stockholders' Equity					
Accounts payable	43,000	17,000			60,000
Notes payable	190,000	80,000	(b) 80,000		190,000
Common stock	176,000	100,000	(a) 100,000		176,000
Retained earnings	155,000	50,000	(a) 50,000		155,000
Total	564,000	247,000	230,000	230,000	581,000

[1]The parent company may use either the cost method or the equity method for entries to the Investment account. Regardless of the method used, the consolidated statements are the same. Advanced accounting courses deal with this topic.

In summary, the elimination entries that we illustrate require, at most, four steps:

1. Eliminate intercompany receivables and payables.
2. Eliminate the stockholders' equity accounts of the subsidiary.
3. Eliminate the Investment in Subsidiary account.

APPENDIX PROBLEMS

P16-A1 ← *Link Back to Chapter 4 (Debt Ratio)*. This problem demonstrates the dramatic effect that consolidation accounting can have on a company's ratios. **Ford Motor Company** (Ford) owns 100% of **Ford Motor Credit Corporation** (FMCC), its financing subsidiary. Ford's main operations consist of manufacturing automotive products. FMCC mainly helps people finance the purchase of automobiles from Ford and its dealers. The two companies' individual balance sheets are adapted and summarized as follows (amounts in billions):

Analyzing consolidated financial statements (Obj. 3)

	Ford (Parent)	FMCC (Subsidiary)
Total assets	$89.6	$170.5
Total liabilities	$65.1	$156.9
Total stockholders' equity	24.5	13.6
Total liabilities and equity	$89.6	$170.5

Assume that FMCC's liabilities include $8.1 billion owed to Ford, the parent company.

Required

1. Compute the debt ratio of Ford Motor Company considered alone.
2. Determine the consolidated total assets, total liabilities, and stockholders' equity of Ford Motor Company after consolidating the financial statements of FMCC into the totals of Ford, the parent company. Remember to eliminate the subsidiary's stockholders' equity.
3. Recompute the debt ratio of the consolidated entity. Explain why it took an FASB statement to get companies to consolidate their financing subsidiaries into their own financial statements.

P16-A2 Darnell Air Corp. paid $289,000 to acquire all the common stock of Royal Dutch, Inc., and Royal Dutch owes Darnell Air $81,000 on a note payable. Immediately after the purchase on June 30, 20X3, the two companies' balance sheets were as follows:

Consolidating a wholly-owned subsidiary

	Darnell Air Corp.	Royal Dutch, Inc.
Assets		
Cash	$ 24,000	$ 20,000
Accounts receivable, net	91,000	65,000
Note receivable from Royal Dutch...............	81,000	—
Inventory	145,000	214,000
Investment in Royal Dutch.........................	289,000	—
Plant assets, net...	178,000	219,000
Total	$808,000	$518,000
Liabilities and Stockholders' Equity		
Accounts payable	$ 57,000	$ 49,000
Notes payable...	177,000	149,000
Other liabilities..	129,000	31,000
Common stock...	297,000	173,000
Retained earnings	148,000	116,000
Total	$808,000	$518,000

Required

Prepare the consolidated balance sheet for Darnell Air Corp. (It is sufficient to complete a consolidation work sheet.)

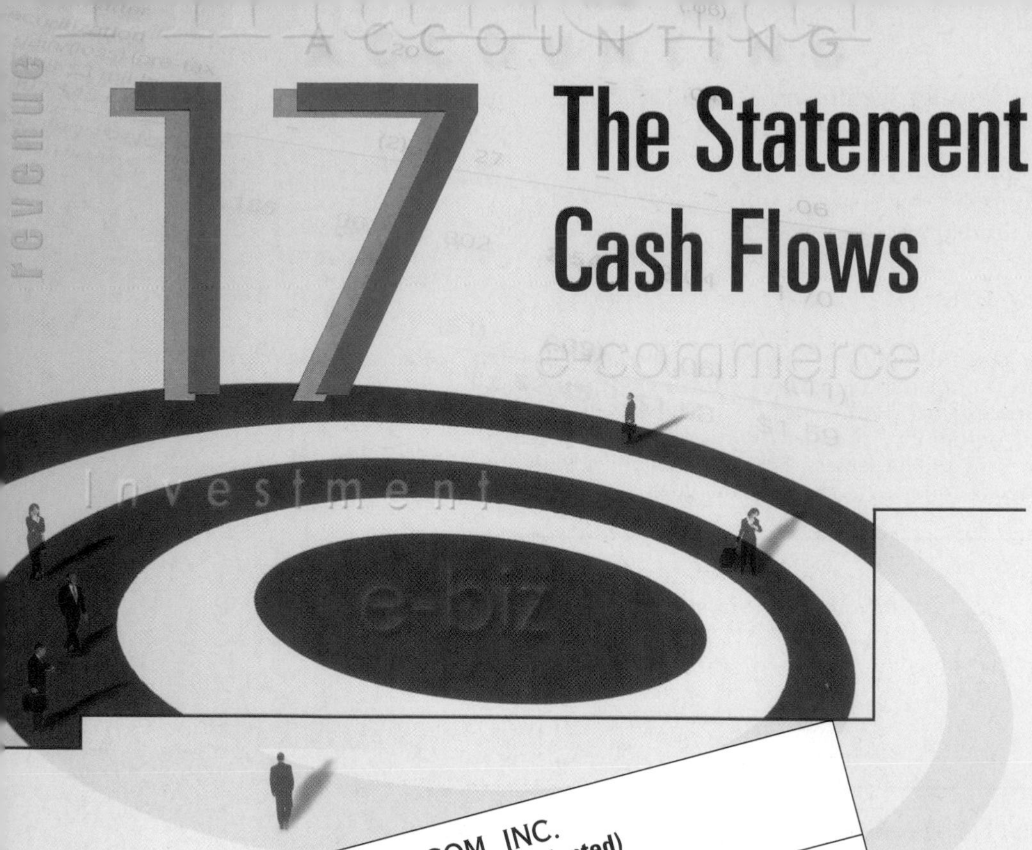

17

The Statement of Cash Flows

LEARNING OBJECTIVES

After studying this chapter, you should be able to

1. Identify the purposes of the statement of cash flows
2. Report cash flows from operating, investing, and financing activities
3. Prepare a statement of cash flows by the direct method
4. Compute the cash effects of a wide variety of business transactions
5. Prepare a statement of cash flows by the indirect method

DRKOOP.COM, INC.
Statement of Cash Flows (Adapted)
Year Ended December 31, 1999

	Thousands
Cash flows from *operating activities:*	
1 Cash receipts from customers	$13,356
2 Cash receipts from interest revenue	1,344
3 Cash payments to suppliers and employees	(72,871)
4 Other, net	5,497
5 Net cash inflow (outflow) from operating activities	(52,674)
Cash flows from *investing activities:*	
6 Purchase of property and equipment	$(9,726)
7 Net cash inflow (outflow) from investing activities	(9,726)
Cash flows from *financing activities:*	
8 New borrowing—issuing notes payable	$ 5,775
9 Issuance of common stock	88,831
10 Issuance of preferred stock	3,500
11 Net cash inflow (outflow) from financing activities	98,106
12 Increase (decrease) in cash	$35,706
13 Cash balance, beginning of year	—
14 Cash balance, end of year	$35,706

What do **drkoop.com, Inc., MotherNature.com, Inc.,** and many other dot.coms have in common? They hold the promise of revolutionizing business in the new millennium.

drkoop.com, Inc., named for former U.S. Surgeon General C. Everett Koop, operates an Internet-based health network. The company offers an interactive Web site that provides comprehensive health information and services. A year and a half after its formation, the company's Web site had attracted over 18 million users.

MotherNature.com, Inc., is an on-line retail store offering vitamins, other health products, information and powerful search capabilities. Customers can buy more than 14,000 products with the click of a mouse—24 hours a day, 7 days a week. In addition, MotherNature.com offers incentives in conjunction with physicians, HMOs, and health clubs.

Are you ready to invest in these new companies? If so, you need to take a close look at their financial statements. Neither company has ever turned a profit, and, more important, neither company is generating cash flow from operations. The cash crunch is so severe at drkoop.com that the auditors say the financial statements are okay only if the company can continue as a going concern. That *if* depends largely on the company's cash flows, which are the topic of this chapter.

The statement of cash flows, a required financial statement, reports where cash came from and how the company spent it. ➡ Like the income statement and the balance sheet, the cash-flow statement provides important information about an organization. For **drkoop.com, Inc.,** the picture is bleak because operations are generating *negative* cash flow (see line 5 of the statement on the facing page). This is a danger signal about any company because operations should be the main source of cash. Time will tell whether drkoop.com, Inc., survives.

◄◼ We learned in Chapter 1 (Exhibit 1-8) that the statement of cash flows is a required financial statement.

THE STATEMENT OF CASH FLOWS: BASIC CONCEPTS

The balance sheet reports **drkoop.com's** cash balance at the end of the period. By comparing the beginning and ending balance sheets, you can tell that the company's cash increased during 1999. But the balance sheet does not indicate *why* the cash balance changed. The income statement reports revenues, expenses and net income (or net loss)—clues about the sources and uses of cash. But neither does the income statement tell *why* cash increased or decreased.

The **statement of cash flows** (page 654) reports drkoop.com's **cash flows** (cash receipts and cash payments) during the period. It shows the *causes* of the change in cash. drkoop.com's cash is coming from investors and lenders—from borrowing and issuing stock (page 654, lines 8–10). This cannot go on forever. Soon investors will require drkoop.com to earn a profit and generate cash from operations (line 5). At some point, they will demand a return on their investment.

Examine the heading of drkoop.com's statement of cash flows (page 654). The statement covers a span of time and is dated "Year Ended December 31, 1999." Exhibit 17-1 on the following page shows the timing of the various financial statements.

STATEMENT OF CASH FLOWS. Reports cash receipts and cash payments classified according to the entity's major activities: operating, investing, and financing.

CASH FLOWS. Cash receipts and cash payments (disbursements).

Purpose of the Statement of Cash Flows

The statement of cash flows is designed to:

1. *Predict future cash flows.* It takes cash to pay the bills. Past cash receipts and cash payments are good predictors of future cash flows.
2. *Evaluate management decisions.* Wise decisions lead to profits and strong cash flows. Bad decisions bring bankruptcy. The statement of cash flows reports on the investments a company is making.
3. *Determine the company's ability to pay dividends to stockholders and principal and interest to creditors.* Stockholders are interested in receiving dividends on

Objective 1
Identify the purposes of the statement of cash flows

EXHIBIT 17-1
**Timing of the Financial
Statements**

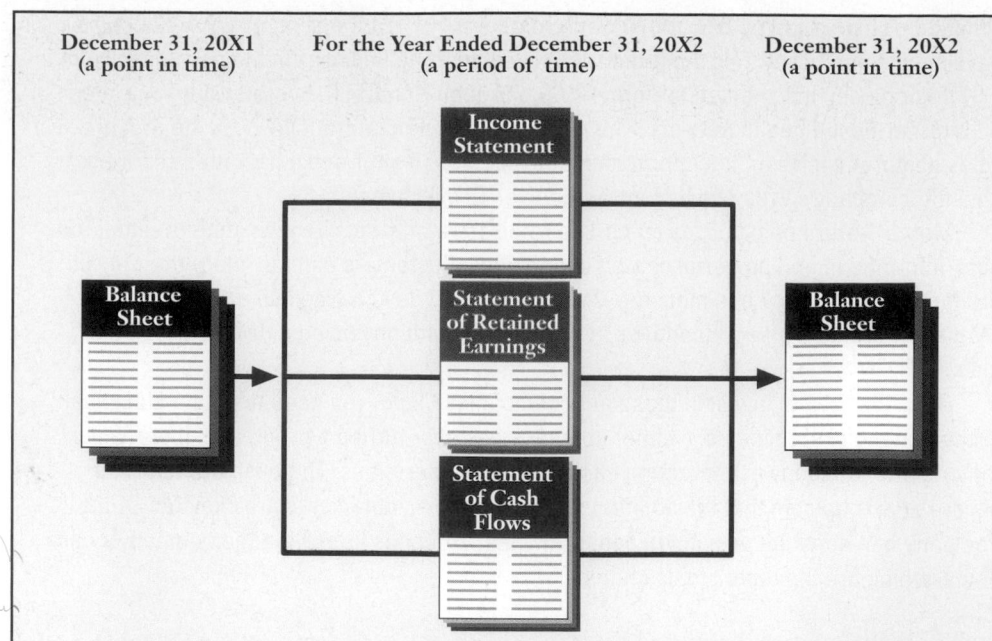

December 31, 20X1 (a point in time)	For the Year Ended December 31, 20X2 (a period of time)	December 31, 20X2 (a point in time)

handwritten margin notes:

helps management to making future financial policies as well as company cash budget

help in measurement of liquidity & dividend payments

predict company's ability use of cash in investing and financial transaction

limitations
non cash transaction ignored
ignore the basic accounts concepts
does not reveal true liquidity and working capital is ignored

 DAILY EXERCISE 17-1

their investments. Creditors want their principal and interest amounts on time. The statement of cash flows reports where the business's cash comes from and how it is being spent. Thus far, all of drkoop.com's cash is coming from investors and creditors—not from profitable operations. The outlook for dividends is not very promising.

4. *Show the relationship of net income to cash flow.* Usually, cash and net income move together. High profits lead to increases in cash, and vice versa. In 1999, drkoop.com had a net loss and cash flows from operating activities were negative, as one would expect.

Cash and Cash Equivalents

CASH EQUIVALENTS. Liquid short-term investments that can be converted into cash at will.

 DAILY EXERCISE 17-2

On financial statements, *Cash* has a broader meaning than just cash on hand and cash in the bank. It includes **cash equivalents,** which are liquid short-term investments that can be converted into cash at will. Examples are money-market investments and investments in U.S. Government Treasury bills. Businesses invest extra cash rather than let it sit idle. Here, *cash* refers to cash and cash equivalents.

Objective 2
Report cash flows from operating, investing, and financing activities

Operating, Investing, and Financing Activities

A business engages in three basic categories of business activities:

- operating activities
- investing activities
- financing activities

Operations are the most important activity. Investing activities are generally more important than financing activities because *what* a company invests in is more important than *how* the company finances the acquisition.

The statement of cash flows in Exhibit 17-2 shows how cash receipts and payments are divided into operating activities, investing activities, and financing activities for Anchor Corporation, a small manufacturer of glass products. Exhibit 17-2 shows that each set of activities includes both cash inflows (receipts) and cash outflows (payments). Outflows have parentheses to indicate that payments are subtracted. Each section of the statement reports a net cash inflow (net cash receipt) or a net cash outflow (net cash payment).

ANCHOR CORPORATION
Statement of Cash Flows
Year Ended December 31, 20X2

	Thousands	
Cash flows from operating activities:		
Receipts:		
Collections from customers	$ 271	
Interest received on notes receivable	10	
Dividends received on investments in stock	9	
Total cash receipts		$290
Payments:		
To suppliers	$(133)	
To employees	(58)	
For interest	(16)	
For income tax	(15)	
Total cash payments		(222)
Net cash inflow from operating activities		68
Cash flows from investing activities:		
Acquisition of plant assets	$(306)	
Loan to another company	(11)	
Proceeds from sale of plant assets	62	
Net cash outflow from operating activities		(255)
Cash flows from financing activities:		
Proceeds from issuance of common stock	$ 101	
Proceeds from issuance of long-term notes payable	94	
Payment of long-term notes payable	(11)	
Payment of dividends	(17)	
Net cash inflow from financing activities		167
Increase (decrease) in cash		$(20)
Cash balance, December 31, 20X1		42
Cash balance, December 31, 20X2		$ 22

Operating activities create revenues and expenses. The statement of cash flows reports the cash impacts of the revenues and expenses. The largest cash inflow from operations is the collection of cash from customers. Smaller inflows are receipts of interest and dividends. The operating outflows include cash payments to suppliers and employees and cash payments for interest and taxes. Exhibit 17-2 shows that Anchor's net cash inflow from operating activities is $68,000. A large positive cash flow from operations is a good sign. *In the long run, operations must be the main source of a business's cash.* Dot.com investors and lenders are well aware of this business truth.

OPERATING ACTIVITY. Activity that creates revenue or expense in the entity's major line of business; a section of the statement of cash flows. Operating activities affect the income statement.

Operating activities are related to the transactions that make up net income.[1]

Cash flows from operating activities require analysis of each revenue and expense on the income statement, along with the related current asset or current liability from the balance sheet.

Investing activities are the buying and selling of the long-term assets the business uses. A purchase or sale of land, a building, or equipment is an investing activity, as is the purchase or sale of a stock or bond investment. Making a loan is an investing activity because the loan creates a receivable for the lender. Collecting on the loan is also reported as an investing activity. The acquisition of plant assets

INVESTING ACTIVITY. Activity that increases and decreases the long-term assets available to the business; a section of the statement of cash flows.

[1]The authors thank Alfonso Oddo for suggesting this display.

dominates Anchor Corporation's investing activities, which produce a net cash outflow of $255,000.

Investing activities relate to the long-term asset accounts.

Investments in plant assets lay the foundation for future operations. A company that invests in plant and equipment appears stronger than one that is selling off its plant assets. Why? The latter company may be selling income-producing assets to pay the bills. Most companies need long-term assets to operate.

FINANCING ACTIVITY. Activity that obtains the funds from investors and creditors needed to launch and sustain the business; a section of the statement of cash flows.

Financing activities obtain the cash needed to launch and sustain the business. Financing activities include issuing stock, buying or selling treasury stock, borrowing money, and paying dividends to the stockholders.

Payments to creditors include *principal* payments only. The payment of *interest* is an operating activity. Financing activities of Anchor Corporation brought in net cash receipts of $167,000. One thing to watch in financing activities is whether the business is borrowing heavily. Excessive borrowing has been the downfall of many companies.

Financing activities relate to the long-term liability accounts and the owners' equity accounts.

○ DAILY EXERCISE 17-3

○ DAILY EXERCISE 17-4

○ DAILY EXERCISE 17-5

○ DAILY EXERCISE 17-6

Overall, Anchor's cash decreased by $20,000 during 20X2. The company began the year with cash of $42,000 and ended with $22,000. Each category of activities includes both cash receipts and cash payments, as shown in Exhibit 17-3 on the facing page. The exhibit lists the more common cash receipts and payments that appear on the statement of cash flows.

 **THINK IT OVER**

Examine drkoop.com's statement of cash flows on page 654, and reread the chapter-opening story. Which of the following statements explains why drkoop.com's cash outflow from operations occurred? Give your reason.

a. The company invested too heavily in new properties.
b. Payments to suppliers and employees exceeded cash receipts from customers.
c. drkoop.com did not borrow enough money to finance operations during the year.

Answer: The statement of cash flows reports that cash payments to suppliers and employees exceeded cash receipts from customers, so the answer is b.

Interest and Dividends as Operating Activities

You may be puzzled by the listing of cash receipts of interest and dividends as operating activities. After all, these cash receipts result from investing activities. Interest comes from investments in loans, and dividends come from investments in stock.

Equally puzzling is listing the payment of interest as part of operations. Interest expense results from borrowing money—a financing activity. After much debate, the FASB decided to include all these items—cash receipts of interest and dividends and the payment of interest—as part of operations. Why? Because they affect net income. Interest revenue and dividend revenue increase net income, and interest expense decreases income. Therefore, cash receipts of interest and dividends and cash payments of interest are reported as operating activities on the cash-flow statement.

In contrast, dividend payments are not operating activities. Why? Because they do not enter the computation of income. Dividend payments are financing activities on the cash-flow statement because they go to the entity's stockholders who finance the business. See the first financing activity in Exhibit 17-3.

EXHIBIT 17-3   Cash Receipts and Payments on the Statement of Cash Flows

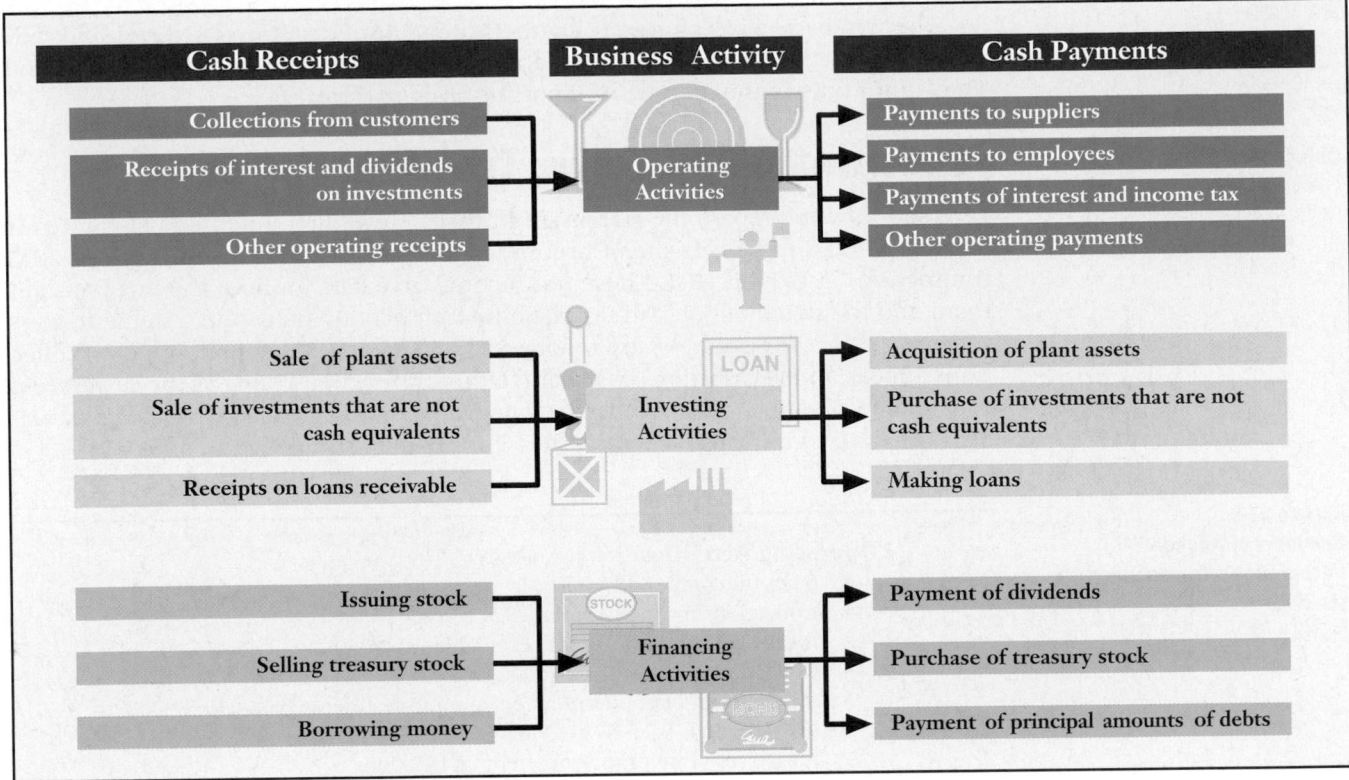

Format of the Statement of Cash Flows

The FASB approves two formats for reporting cash flows from operating activities. The **direct method,** illustrated in Exhibit 17-2, lists cash receipts from specific operating activities and cash payments for each major operating activity. The FASB has a clear preference for the direct method because it reports where cash came from and how it was spent on operating activities. The direct method is required for some insurance companies. Most governmental entities also use it.

Companies' accounting systems are designed for accrual accounting, and that makes it easy to compute cash flows from operating activities by a shortcut method. The **indirect method** starts with net income and reconciles to cash flows from operating activities. Exhibit 17-4 gives an overview of the process of converting from accrual-basis income to the cash basis for the statement of cash flows.

The direct method is easier to understand, it provides better information for decisions, and the FASB prefers it. By learning how to compute the cash-flow amounts for the direct method, you will be learning something far more important: how to determine the cash effects of business transactions. Then, after you have a firm foundation in cash-flow analysis, it is easier to learn the indirect method. If your instructor chooses to focus solely on the indirect method, you can study that

DIRECT METHOD. Format of the operating activities section of the statement of cash flows that lists the major categories of operating cash receipts (collections from customers and receipts of interest and dividends) and cash payments (payments to suppliers, to employees, for interest and income taxes).

INDIRECT METHOD. Format of the operating activities section of the statement of cash flows that starts with net income and shows the reconciliation from net income to operating cash flows. Also called the reconciliation method.

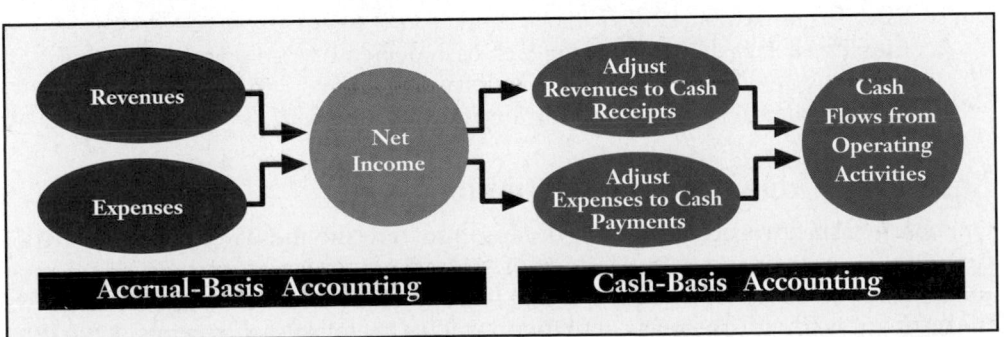

EXHIBIT 17-4
Converting from the Accrual Basis to the Cash Basis for the Statement of Cash Flows (Indirect Method)

method, which begins on page 674, with a minimum of references to earlier sections of this chapter.

The two basic ways of presenting the statement of cash flows—direct and indirect—arrive at all the same subtotals and at the same change in cash for the period. They differ only in the manner of reporting *operating activities*.

Objective 3
Prepare a statement of cash flows by the direct method

STATEMENT OF CASH FLOWS: THE DIRECT METHOD

Let's see how to prepare the statement of cash flows (direct method) illustrated in Exhibit 17-2. Suppose Anchor Corporation has assembled the summary of 20X2 transactions in Exhibit 17-5. These transactions give data for both the income statement and the statement of cash flows. Some transactions affect one statement, some the other. Sales, for example, are reported on the income statement, but cash collections appear on the cash-flow statement. Other transactions, such as the cash receipt of dividend revenue, affect both. *The statement of cash flows reports only those transactions with cash effects* (those with an asterisk in Exhibit 17-5).

EXHIBIT 17-5
Summary of Anchor Corporation's Transactions for 20X2

Operating Activities:
1. Sales on credit, $284,000
*2. Collections from customers, $271,000
3. Interest revenue on notes receivable, $12,000
*4. Collection of interest receivable, $10,000
*5. Cash receipt of dividend revenue on investments in stock, $9,000
6. Cost of goods sold, $150,000
7. Purchases of inventory on credit, $147,000
*8. Payments to suppliers, $133,000
9. Salary expense, $56,000
*10. Payments of salaries, $58,000
11. Depreciation expenses, $18,000
12. Other operating expense, $17,000
*13. Interest expense and payments, $16,000
*14. Income tax expense and payments, $15,000

Investing Activities:
*15. Cash payments to acquire plant assets, $306,000
*16. Loan to another company, $11,000
*17. Proceeds from sale of plant assets, $62,000, including $8,000 gain

Financing Activities:
*18. Proceeds from issuance of common stock, $101,000
*19. Proceeds from issuance of long-term note payable, $94,000
*20. Payment of long-term note payable, $11,000
*21. Declaration and payment of cash dividends, $17,000

* Indicates a cash-flow transaction to be reported on the statement of cash flows.

To prepare the statement of cash flows, follow three steps:
1. Identify the activities that increased or decreased cash—those items with asterisks in Exhibit 17-5.
2. Classify each cash increase and each cash decrease as an operating activity, an investing activity, or a financing activity.
3. Identify the cash effect of each transaction.

Cash Flows from Operating Activities

Operating cash flows are listed first because they are the most important source of cash for most businesses. The failure of operations to generate the bulk of cash inflows for an extended period will signal trouble for a company. Exhibit 17-2 shows that Anchor is sound; operating activities provided the most cash receipts, $290,000.

CASH COLLECTIONS FROM CUSTOMERS Cash sales bring in cash immediately, credit sales later when cash is collected. "Collections from customers" in Exhibit 17-2 include both cash sales and collections on account, $271,000.

CASH RECEIPTS OF INTEREST Interest revenue is earned on notes receivable. As the clock ticks, interest revenue accrues, but cash interest is received only on specific dates. Only the cash receipts of interest appear on the statement of cash flows— $10,000 in Exhibit 17-2.

CASH RECEIPTS OF DIVIDENDS Dividends are earned on stock investments. Dividend revenue is reported on the income statement, and this cash receipt is reported on the statement of cash flows—$9,000 in Exhibit 17-2. (Dividends *received* are part of operating activities, but dividends *paid* are a financing activity.)

PAYMENTS TO SUPPLIERS Payments to suppliers include all cash payments for inventory and most operating expenses, but not for interest, income taxes, and employee compensation expenses. *Suppliers* are entities that provide the business with inventory and essential services. For example, a clothing store's payments to **Levi, Strauss, Liz Claiborne,** and **Reebok** are payments to suppliers. A grocery store's suppliers include **Nabisco, Campbell Soup,** and **Coca-Cola.** Other suppliers provide advertising, utility, and other services. Payments to suppliers *exclude* payments to employees, payments for interest, and payments for income taxes because these are separate categories of operating cash payments. In Exhibit 17-2, Anchor Corporation's payments to suppliers are $133,000.

PAYMENTS TO EMPLOYEES Salaries, wages, commissions, and other forms of compensation require payments to employees. The statement of cash flows in Exhibit 17-2 reports cash payments of $58,000.

PAYMENTS FOR INTEREST EXPENSE AND INCOME TAX EXPENSE These cash payments are reported separately from the other expenses. In the Anchor Corporation example, interest and income tax expenses equal the cash payments. In practice, the expense and cash payment amounts may differ. The cash-flow statement reports the cash payments for interest ($16,000) and income tax ($15,000).

 DAILY EXERCISE 17-7

DEPRECIATION, DEPLETION, AND AMORTIZATION EXPENSE These expenses are *not* listed on the statement of cash flows in Exhibit 17-2 because they do not affect cash. Depreciation is recorded by debiting the expense and crediting Accumulated Depreciation. There is no debit or credit to the Cash account.

Cash Flows from Investing Activities

Investing activities are important because a company's investments determine its future. Purchases of plant assets signal expansion, which is a good sign. Low levels of investing activities indicate that the business is not replenishing its assets.

CASH PAYMENTS FOR PLANT ASSETS, INVESTMENTS, AND LOANS TO OTHER COMPANIES All these cash payments acquire a long-term asset. The first investing activity reported by Anchor Corporation on its statement of cash flows in Exhibit 17-2 is the purchase of plant assets, such as land, buildings, and equipment ($306,000). The second transaction is an $11,000 loan; Anchor obtains a note receivable. These are investing activities because the company is investing in assets for business use rather than for resale. Another transaction in this category—not shown in Exhibit 17-2— is a purchase of a stock or bond investment.

PROCEEDS FROM THE SALE OF PLANT ASSETS, INVESTMENTS, AND THE COLLECTIONS OF LOANS These transactions are the opposites of acquisitions of plant assets and investments, and making loans. They are cash receipts from investment transactions.

The sale of the plant assets needs explanation. The statement of cash flows in Exhibit 17-2 reports that Anchor Corporation received $62,000 cash on the sale of plant assets. The income statement shows an $8,000 gain on this transaction. What is the appropriate amount to show on the cash-flow statement? It is $62,000, the cash proceeds from the sale. If we assume that Anchor sold equipment that cost $64,000 and had accumulated depreciation of $10,000, the following journal entry would record the sale:

Cash	62,000	
Accumulated Depreciation	10,000	
Equipment...		64,000
Gain on Sale of Plant Assets		
(from income statement)		8,000

The analysis indicates that the book value of the equipment was $54,000 ($64,000 − $10,000). However, the book value of the asset sold is not reported on the statement of cash flows. Only the cash proceeds of $62,000 are reported on the statement. For the income statement, only the gain is reported.

Because a gain occurred, you may wonder why this cash receipt is not reported as part of operations. Operations consist of buying and selling *merchandise* or rendering services to earn revenue. Investing activities are the acquisition and disposition of assets used in operations. Therefore, the sale of plant assets and the sale of investments are cash inflows from investing activities.

 **WORK IT OUT** Suppose **Scott Paper Company** sold timber land at a $35 million gain. The land cost Scott Paper $9 million when it was purchased in 1979. What amount will Scott Paper Company report as an investing activity on the statement of cash flows?

Answer: Cash receipt of $44 million (cost of $9 million plus the gain of $35 million).

 DAILY EXERCISE 17-8

Investors and creditors are often critical of a company that sells large amounts of its plant assets. Such sales may signal an urgent need for cash. In other situations, selling off fixed assets may be good news if the company is getting rid of an unprofitable division. Whether sales of plant assets are good news or bad news should be evaluated in light of a company's net income (or net loss), financial position, and other cash flows.

Cash Flows from Financing Activities

Cash flows from financing activities include several specific items. All are related to obtaining money from investors and lenders and paying them back. Readers of financial statements want to know how the entity obtains its financing.

PROCEEDS FROM ISSUANCE OF STOCK AND NOTES PAYABLE Issuing stock (preferred and common) and notes payable are two common ways to finance operations. In Exhibit 17-2, Anchor Corporation reports that it issued common stock for cash of $101,000 and long-term notes payable for $94,000. The proceeds from issuance of notes payable can also be labeled as "Borrowing . . . $94,000."

PAYMENT OF NOTES PAYABLE AND PURCHASES OF THE COMPANY'S OWN STOCK The payment of notes payable decreases Cash, which is the opposite effect of borrowing money. Anchor Corporation paid $11,000 on its long-term notes payable. Other transactions in this category are purchases of treasury stock and payments to retire the company's stock.

PAYMENT OF CASH DIVIDENDS The payment of cash dividends decreases Cash and is therefore reported as a cash payment. Anchor's $17,000 payment in Exhibit 17-2 is an example. A dividend in another form—such as a stock dividend—has no effect on Cash and is *not* reported on the cash-flow statement.

e-Accounting

Cash Crunch Turns CDNOW into CDNOW Bertelsmann

CDNOW is one of the top 5 Web sites and the leading online music destination, with over 700,000 visitors a day and 4 million customers. Yet like its e-retailer cousins, CDNOW had been having trouble turning customers into cash. CDNOW's Web site didn't feature the sound of coins rattling in a near-empty piggybank. Yet, that sound made investors flee the cash-poor dot.com in the Spring of 2000, slashing CDNOW's stock price 80% to $4 a share. Its accounting firm, **Arthur Andersen,** expressed "substantial doubt" about the company's survival.

So what's an e-retailer to do? Unlike traditional companies, dot.coms don't issue bonds or hit up the bank for a loan. Instead, they issue stocks to get their cash. The best hope for CDNOW was to merge with or be bought by another company. That hope was realized in September 2000, when publishing giant **Bertelsmann AG,** one of the world's leading media, e-commerce, and interactive companies, completed its puchase of CDNOW. Said former CDNOW President and co-founder Jason Olim: ". . . We believe our combination with Bertelsmann is the best outcome for our shareholders, employees and customers . . . This transaction allows CDNOW to fulfill its vision of providing music fans with the ultimate music experience by being part of the Bertelsmann family . . . ." And it gives CDNOW the backing of a huge empire with no cash flow problems.

Source: Based on Charles Piller, "CDNow shares plummet on survival 'doubt'; e-Commerce: Accountants cite cash crunch at one of Web's most visited sites. Observers see signal of impending shakeout," *Los Angeles Times,* March 30, 2000, p. C1. Matt Krantz, "e-Retailers run low on fuel. Exclusive analysis: Turn profit soon or else," *USA Today,* April 26, 2000, p. 01B. Press release, Bertelsmann AG and CDNOW, Inc., July 20, 2000; September 1, 2000.

Computerized Statements

Computerized accounting systems are programmed to generate the statement of cash flows as easily as they do the balance sheet and the income statement. The amounts for the operating section can be obtained by copying cash inflows and outflows from the posted accounts. For example, the cash receipts posted to Accounts Receivable provide the information for Cash Collections from Customers. All other cash flows for operating activities, financing activities, and investing activities are handled similarly.

⊙ DAILY EXERCISE 17-9

⊙ DAILY EXERCISE 17-10

⊙ DAILY EXERCISE 17-11

MID-CHAPTER

SUMMARY PROBLEM

Drexel Corporation's accounting records include the following information for the year ended June 30, 20X3:

a. Salary expense, $104,000.

b. Interest revenue, $8,000

c. Proceeds from issuance of common stock, $31,000.

d. Declaration and payment of cash dividends, $22,000.

e. Collection of interest receivable, $7,000.

f. Payments of salaries, $110,000.

g. Credit sales, $358,000.

h. Loan to another company, $42,000.

i. Proceeds from sale of plant assets, $18,000, including $1,000 loss.

j. Collections from customers, $369,000.

k. Cash receipt of dividend revenue on stock investments, $3,000.

l. Payments to suppliers, $319,000.

m. Cash sales, $92,000.

n. Depreciation expense, $32,000.

o. Proceeds from issuance of short-term notes payable, $38,000.

p. Payments of long-term notes payable, $57,000.

q. Interest expense and payments, $11,000.

r. Loan collections, $51,000.

s. Proceeds from sale of investments, $22,000, including $13,000 gain.

t. Amortization expense, $5,000.

u. Purchases of inventory on credit, $297,000.

v. Income tax expense and payments, $16,000.

w. Cash payments to acquire plant assets, $83,000.

x. Cost of goods sold, $284,000.

y. Cash balance: June 30, 20X2—$83,000
June 30, 20X3—$?

www.prenhall.com/horngren

Mid-Chapter Assessment

Required

Prepare Drexel Corporation's income statement and statement of cash flows for the year ended June 30, 20X3. Follow the cash-flow statement format of Exhibit 17-2 and the single-step format for the income statement (grouping all revenues together and all expenses together, as shown in Exhibit 17-6, page 665).

Solution

DREXEL CORPORATION
Income Statement
Year Ended June 30, 20X3

(Ref. Letter)		Thousands	
	Revenue and gains:		
(g, m)	Sales revenue ($358 + $92).............	$450	
(s)	Gain on sale of investments............	13	
(b)	Interest revenue	8	
(k)	Dividend revenue............................	3	
	Total revenues and gains		$474
	Expenses and losses:		
(x)	Cost of goods sold...........................	$284	
(a)	Salary expense	104	
(n)	Depreciation expense	32	
(v)	Income tax expense	16	
(q)	Interest expense	11	
(t)	Amortization expense	5	
(i)	Loss on sale of plant assets	1	
	Total expenses...............................		453
	Net income..		$ 21

DREXEL CORPORATION
Statement of Cash Flows
Year Ended June 30, 20X3

(Ref. Letter)		Thousands	
	Cash flows from operating activities:		
	Receipts:		
(j, m)	Collections from customers ($369 + $92).............	$ 461	
(e)	Interest received on notes receivable	7	
(k)	Dividends received on investments in stock..........	3	
	Total cash receipts		$ 471
	Payments:		
(l)	To suppliers..	$(319)	
(f)	To employees	(110)	
(q)	For interest	(11)	
(v)	For income tax...	(16)	
	Total cash payments		(456)
	Net cash inflow from operating activities...........		15
	Cash flows from investing activities:		
(w)	Acquisition of plant assets	$ (83)	
(h)	Loan to another company	(42)	
(s)	Proceeds from sale of investments.........................	22	
(i)	Proceeds from sale of plant assets.........................	18	
(r)	Collection of loans	51	
	Net cash outflow from investing activities		(34)
	Cash flows from financing activities:		
(o)	Proceeds from issuance of short-term notes payable	$ 38	
(c)	Proceeds from issuance of common stock	31	
(p)	Payments of long-term notes payable	(57)	
(d)	Dividends paid...	(22)	
	Net cash outflow from financing activities..........		(10)
	Increase (decrease) in cash		$ (29)
(y)	Cash balance, June 30, 20X2..................................		83
(y)	Cash balance, June 30, 20X3..................................		$ 54

COMPUTING INDIVIDUAL AMOUNTS FOR THE STATEMENT OF CASH FLOWS

Objective 4
Compute the cash effects of a wide variety of business transactions

How do we compute the amounts for the statement of cash flows? We use the income statement and *changes* in the related balance sheet accounts. For the *operating* cash-flow amounts, the adjustment process follows this basic approach:

Revenue or expense from the income statement	±	Adjusted for the change in the related balance sheet account(s)	=	Amount for the statement of cash flows

This is called the T-account approach. Learning to analyze T-accounts is one of the most useful accounting skills you will acquire. It enables you to measure the cash effects of a wide variety of transactions.

The following discussions use Anchor Corporation's income statement in Exhibit 17-6, comparative balance sheet in Exhibit 17-7, and cash-flow statement in Exhibit 17-2. First, trace the ending and beginning cash balances of $22,000 and $42,000, respectively, from the balance sheet in Exhibit 17-7 to the bottom part of the cash-flow statement in Exhibit 17-2. As you see, the beginning and ending cash amounts come from the balance sheet. Now let's compute the cash flows from operating activities.

EXHIBIT 17-6
Income Statement

ANCHOR CORPORATION
Income Statement
Year Ended December 31, 20X2

	Thousands	
Revenues and gains:		
Sales revenue	$284	
Interest revenue	12	
Dividend revenue	9	
Gain on sale of plant assets	8	
Total revenues and gains		$313
Expenses:		
Cost of goods sold	$150	
Salary expense	56	
Depreciation expense	18	
Other operating expense	17	
Interest expense	16	
Income tax expense	15	
Total expenses		272
Net income		$ 41

Computing the Cash Amounts of Operating Activities

CASH COLLECTIONS FROM CUSTOMERS   Collections can be computed by converting sales revenue (an accrual-basis amount) to the cash basis. Anchor Corporation's income statement (Exhibit 17-6) reports sales of $284,000. Exhibit 17-7 shows that Accounts Receivable increased from $80,000 at the beginning of the year to $93,000 at year end, a $13,000 increase. Based on those amounts, Cash Collections equal $271,000, as shown in the Accounts Receivable T-account:

ACCOUNTS RECEIVABLE			
Beg. bal.	80,000		
Sales	284,000	Collections	271,000
End. bal.	93,000		

Another explanation: Accounts Receivable increased by $13,000, so Anchor Corporation must have received $13,000 less cash than sales revenue for the

Exhibit 17-7 **Comparative Balance Sheet**

ANCHOR CORPORATION
Comparative Balance Sheet
December 31, 20X2 and 20X1

Thousands	20X2	20X1	Increase (Decrease)	
Assets				
Current:				
Cash	$ 22	$ 42	$(20)	
Accounts receivable	93	80	13	
Interest receivable	3	1	2	Changes in current assets—**Operating**
Inventory	135	138	(3)	
Prepaid expenses	8	7	1	
Long-term receivable from another company	11	—	11	Changes in noncurrent assets—**Investing**
Plant assets, net of depreciation	453	219	234	
Total	$725	$487	$238	
Liabilities				
Current:				
Accounts payable	$ 91	$ 57	$ 34	
Salary payable	4	6	(2)	Changes in current liabilities—**Operating**
Accrued liabilities	1	3	(2)	
Long-term notes payable	160	77	83	Changes in long-term liabilities and paid-in capital—**Financing**
Stockholders' Equity				
Common stock	359	258	101	
Retained earnings	110	86	24	Changes due to net income—**Operating,** and to dividends—**Financing**
Total	$725	$487	$238	

period. The following equation shows another way to compute collections from customers.

Accounts Receivable

Beginning balance	+	Sales	−	Collections	=	Ending balance
$80,000	+	$284,000	−	X	=	$93,000
				−X	=	$93,000 − $80,000 − $284,000
				X	=	$271,000

A decrease in Accounts Receivable would mean that the company received more cash than the amount of sales revenue. This computation is the first item summarized in Exhibit 17-8.

Exhibit 17-8
Direct Method of Computing Cash Receipts from Operating Activities

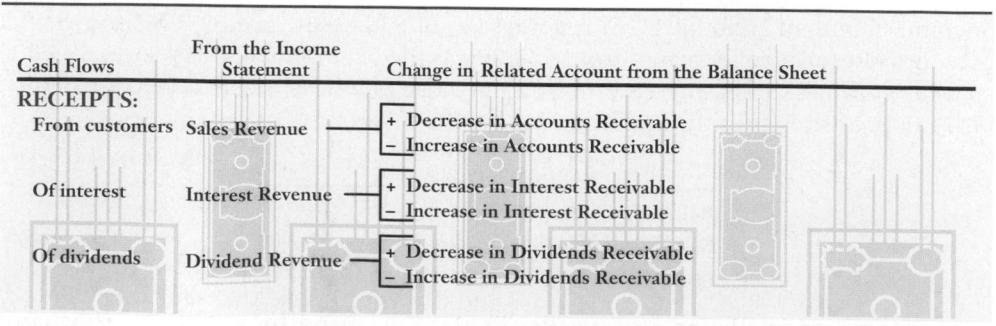

Cash Flows	From the Income Statement	Change in Related Account from the Balance Sheet
RECEIPTS:		
From customers	Sales Revenue	+ Decrease in Accounts Receivable − Increase in Accounts Receivable
Of interest	Interest Revenue	+ Decrease in Interest Receivable − Increase in Interest Receivable
Of dividends	Dividend Revenue	+ Decrease in Dividends Receivable − Increase in Dividends Receivable

Source: We thank Barbara Gerrity for suggesting this exhibit.

All collections of receivables are computed the same way. In our example, Anchor Corporation's income statement, Exhibit 17-6, reports interest revenue of $12,000. Interest Receivable's balance in Exhibit 17-7 increased $2,000. Cash receipts of interest must be $10,000 (Interest Revenue of $12,000 minus the $2,000 increase in Interest Receivable). Exhibit 17-8 summarizes the computation of cash receipts of interest.

PAYMENTS TO SUPPLIERS   This computation includes two parts, payments for inventory (related to Cost of Goods Sold) and payments for operating expenses.

Payments for inventory are computed by converting cost of goods sold to the cash basis. To do this, we analyze the Inventory and Accounts Payable accounts. To "analyze" an account means to explain each amount in the account. For companies that purchase inventory on short-term notes payable, we must also analyze Short-Term Notes Payable in the same manner as Accounts Payable. To compute Anchor Corporation's cash payments for inventory, we analyze the T-accounts (again, we are using Exhibits 17-6 and 17-7 for our numbers):

INVENTORY				ACCOUNTS PAYABLE			
Beg. inventory	138,000	Cost of goods sold	150,000	Payments for		Beg. bal.	57,000
Purchases	147,000			inventory	113,000	Purchases	147,000
End. inventory	135,000					End. bal.	91,000

The first equation details the activity in the Inventory account to compute purchases, as follows:

Inventory

Beginning inventory	+ Purchases	−	Cost of goods sold	=	Ending inventory
$138,000	+ X	−	$150,000	=	$135,000
	X				$135,000 − $138,000 + $150,000
	X				= $147,000

Now we insert the Purchases figure into Accounts Payable to compute the amount of cash paid for inventory, as follows:

Accounts Payable

Beginning balance	+ Purchases	−	Payments for inventory	=	Ending balance
$57,000	+ $147,000	−	X	=	$91,000
			−X	=	$91,000 − $57,000 − $147,000
			X	=	$113,000

Beginning and ending inventory amounts come from the balance sheet, and Cost of Goods Sold from the income statement. Exhibit 17-9 shows the general approach to compute Payments to suppliers of inventory (first item).

Payments to suppliers ($133,000 in Exhibit 17-2) equal the sum of payments for inventory ($113,000) plus payments for operating expenses ($20,000), as explained next.

DAILY EXERCISE 17-12

PAYMENTS FOR OPERATING EXPENSES   Payments for operating expenses other than interest and income tax can be computed as "plug" figures by analyzing Prepaid Expenses and Accrued Liabilities (again, all amounts come from Exhibits 17-6 and 17-7).

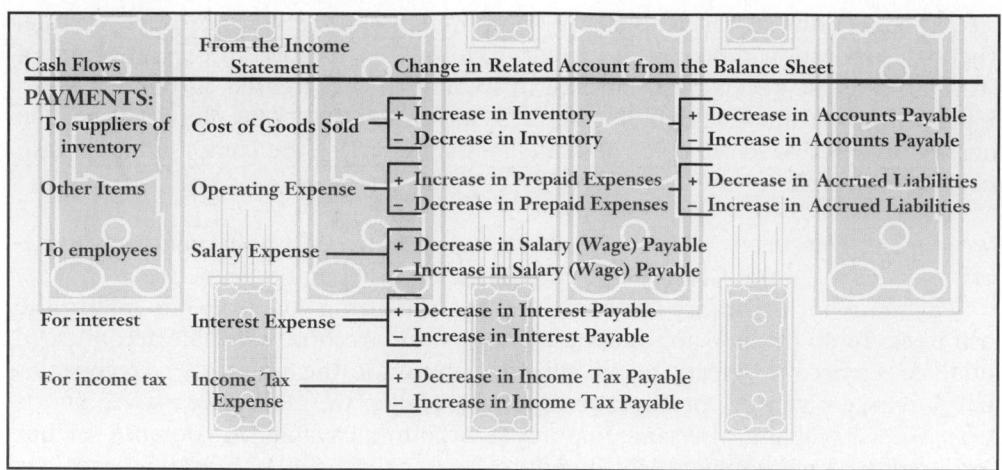

Source: We thank Barbara Gerrity for suggesting this exhibit.

T-ACCOUNTS:

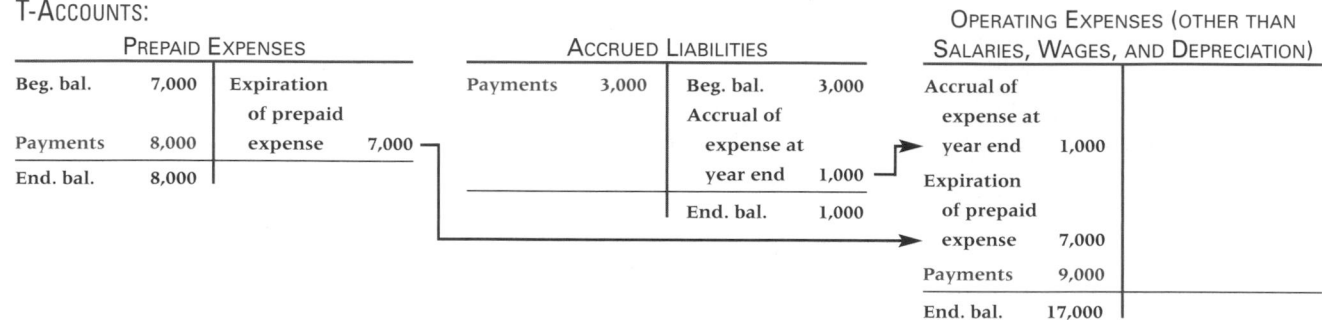

Total payments for operating expenses = $20,000
$8,000 + $3,000 + $9,000 = $20,000

EQUATIONS:

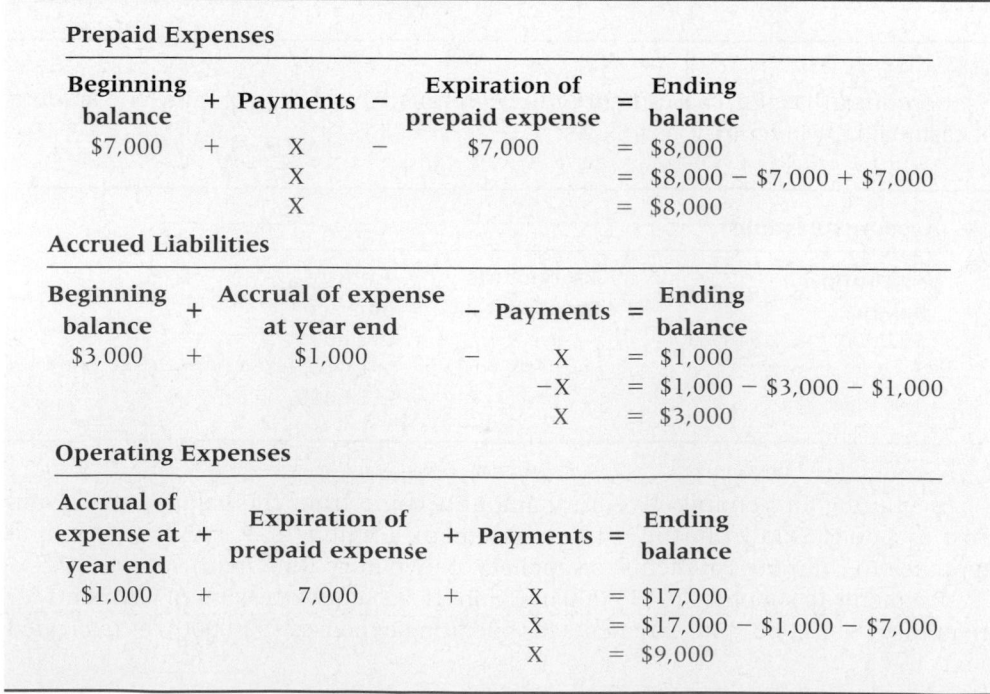

PAYMENTS TO EMPLOYEES   Companies keep separate accounts for salaries, wages, and other forms of employee compensation. It is convenient to combine all compensation amounts into one account. Anchor's calculation adjusts Salary Expense for the change in Salary Payable, as shown in the following T-account:

SALARY PAYABLE

		Beg. bal.	6,000
Payments to employees	58,000	Salary expense	56,000
		End. bal.	4,000

Salary Payable

Beginning balance	+	Salary expense	− Payments =	Ending balance	
$6,000	+	$56,000	− X =	$4,000	
			−X =	$4,000 − $6,000 − $56,000	
			X =	$58,000	

Exhibit 17-9 summarizes this computation under Payments to employees.

 DAILY EXERCISE 17-13

PAYMENTS OF INTEREST AND INCOME TAX   In our example, the expense and payment amount is the same for interest and for income tax. Therefore, no analysis is required to determine the payment amount. But if the expense and the payment differ, the payment can be computed by analyzing the related liability account. Exhibit 17-9 summarizes the procedure for interest and income tax.

Computing the Cash Amounts of Investing Activities

Investing activities affect asset accounts, such as Plant Assets, Investments, and Notes Receivable. Cash flows from investing activities can be computed by analyzing those accounts. The income statement and the beginning and ending balance sheets provide the data.

ACQUISITIONS AND SALES OF PLANT ASSETS   Companies keep separate accounts for Land, Buildings, Equipment, and other plant assets. It is helpful to combine all these accounts into a single summary. Also, we subtract accumulated depreciation from the assets' cost and get a net figure for plant assets. This approach allows us to work with a single total for plant assets.

To illustrate, observe that Anchor Corporation's balance sheet (Exhibit 17-7) reports beginning plant assets, net of depreciation, of $219,000 and an ending net amount of $453,000. The income statement (Exhibit 17-6) shows depreciation expense of $18,000 and an $8,000 gain on sale of plant assets. Further, the acquisitions of plant assets total $306,000 (see Exhibit 17-2). How much are the proceeds from the sale of plant assets? First, we compute the book value of plant assets sold, as follows:

PLANT ASSETS, NET

Beg. bal.	219,000	Depreciation	18,000
Acquisitions	306,000	Book value of assets sold	54,000
End. bal.	453,000		

Plant Assets, Net

Beginning balance	+ Acquisitions	− Depreciation	− Book value of assets sold	= Ending balance	
$219,000	+ $306,000	− $18,000	− X	= $453,000	
			−X	= $453,000 − $219,000 − $306,000 + $18,000	
			X	= $ 54,000	

Now we can compute the proceeds from the sale of plant assets, as follows:

Book value of assets sold	+ Gain	− Loss	= Sale proceeds
$54,000	+ $8,000	− $0 =	$62,000

Trace the sale proceeds ($62,000) to the statement of cash flows in Exhibit 17-2. If the sale resulted in a loss of $3,000, the sale proceeds would be $51,000

($54,000 − $3,000), and the statement would report $51,000 as a cash receipt from this investing activity. Remember:

Balance Sheet		Income Statement		Cash-Flow Statement
Book value	+	Gain	=	Proceeds
Book value	−	Loss	=	Proceeds

ACQUISITIONS AND SALES OF INVESTMENTS, AND LOANS AND LOAN COLLECTIONS The cash amounts of investment and loan transactions can be computed in the manner illustrated for plant assets. Investments are easier to analyze because there is no depreciation, as shown in the following T-account:

INVESTMENTS			
Beg. bal.*	XXX		
Purchases**	XXX	Book value of assets sold	XXX
End. bal.*	XXX		

*From the balance sheet. **From the statement of cash flows.

DAILY EXERCISE 17-14

Investments (amounts assumed for illustration only)

Beginning balance	+	Purchases	−	Book value of investments sold	=	Ending balance
$100,000	+	$50,000	−	X	=	$140,000
				−X	=	$140,000 − $100,000 − $50,000
				X	=	$10,000

Loan transactions follow the pattern described on page 665 for collections from customers. New loans increase the receivable and decrease cash. Collections decrease the receivable and increase cash, as follows:

LOANS AND NOTES RECEIVABLE			
Beg. bal.*	XXX		
New loans made**	XXX	Collections	XXX
End. bal.*	XXX		

*From the balance sheet. **From the statement of cash flows.

Loans and Notes Receivable (amounts assumed for illustration only)

Beginning balance	+	New loans made	−	Collections	=	Ending balance
$90,000	+	$10,000	−	X	=	$30,000
				−X	=	$30,000 − $90,000 − $10,000
				X	=	$70,000

Exhibit 17-10 summarizes the computation of cash flows from investing activities. We must solve for the dollar amount of each item highlighted in color. Use this exhibit as a guide when you solve the assignment material at the end of the chapter.

Computing the Cash Amounts of Financing Activities

Financing activities affect the liability and stockholders' equity accounts, such as Notes Payable, Bonds Payable, Long-Term Debt, Common Stock, Paid-in Capital in Excess of Par, and Retained Earnings. To compute the cash-flow amounts, analyze these accounts.

ISSUANCES AND PAYMENTS OF LONG-TERM NOTES PAYABLE (BORROWING) The Notes Payable, Bonds Payable, and Long-Term Debt accounts are related to borrowing, a financing activ-

EXHIBIT 17-10   **Cash Flows from Investing Activities**

Cash Receipts from Investing Activities

From sale of plant assets	Beginning plant assets (net)	+	Acquisition cost	−	Depreciation	−	Book value of assets sold	=	Ending plant assets (net)
	Cash received from sale of assets	=	Book value of assets sold	+	Gain on sale, or − Loss on sale				
From sale of investments	Beginning investments	+	Purchase cost of investments	−	Book value of investments sold	=	Ending investments		
	Cash received from sale of investments	=	Book value of investments sold	+	Gain on sale, or − Loss on sale				
From collection of loans and notes receivable	Beginning loans or notes receivable	+	New loans made	−	Collections	=	Ending loans or notes receivable		

Cash Payments for Investing Activities

For acquisition of plant assets	Beginning plant assets (net)	+	Acquisition cost	−	Depreciation	−	Book value of assets sold	=	Ending plant assets (net)
For purchase of investments	Beginning investments	+	Purchase cost of investments	−	Book value of investments sold	=	Ending investments		
For new loans made	Beginning loans or notes receivable	+	New loans made	−	Collections	=	Ending loans or notes receivable		

ity. Their balances come from the balance sheet. If either the amount of new issuances or the amount of payments is known, the other can be computed. New issuances of notes payable total $94,000 (see Exhibit 17-2). Payments of notes payable are computed from the Long-Term Notes Payable T-account, as follows (amounts from Exhibit 17-7):

LONG-TERM NOTES PAYABLE			
		Beg. bal.	77,000
Payments	11,000	Issuance of new debt	94,000
		End. bal.	160,000

Long-Term Notes Payable

Beginning balance	+	Issuance of new debt	−	Payments of debt	=	Ending balance
$77,000	+	$94,000	−	X	=	$160,000
				−X	=	$160,000 − $77,000 − $94,000
				X	=	$11,000

ISSUANCES AND RETIREMENTS OF STOCK, AND PURCHASES AND SALES OF TREASURY STOCK

These financing activities are computed from the various stock accounts. Combine Common Stock and Capital in Excess of Par into a single total as we do for plant assets. Using data from Exhibits 17-2 and 17-7, we have

COMMON STOCK			
		Beg. bal.	258,000
Retirements of stock	0	Issuance of new stock	101,000
		End. bal.	359,000

Common Stock

Beginning balance	+	Issuance of new stock	−	Retirements of stock	=	Ending balance
$258,000	+	$101,000	−	X	=	$359,000
				−X	=	$359,000 − $258,000 − $101,000
				X	=	0

Cash flows affecting Treasury Stock can be analyzed by using the T-account. Recall that Treasury Stock is a contra equity account, so it has a debit balance.

TREASURY STOCK

Beg. bal.	XXX		
Purchases of treasury stock	XXX	Cost of treasury stock sold	XXX
End. bal.	XXX		

Treasury Stock (amounts assumed for illustration only)

Beginning balance	+	Purchase of treasury stock	−	Cost of treasury stock sold	=	Ending balance
$16,000	+	$3,000	−	X	=	$5,000
				−X	=	$5,000 − $16,000 − $3,000
				X	=	$14,000

If either the cost of treasury stock purchased or sold is known, the other amount can be computed. For a sale of treasury stock, the amount to report on the cash-flow statement is the amount of cash received from the sale. Suppose a sale brought in $2,000 less cash than the $14,000 cost of the treasury stock. The statement of cash flows would report a cash receipt of $12,000 ($14,000 − $2,000).

DIVIDEND PAYMENTS   If the amount of the dividends is not given elsewhere (for example, in a statement of retained earnings), it can be computed as follows:

RETAINED EARNINGS					DIVIDENDS PAYABLE		
Dividend declarations	17,000	Beg. bal.	86,000			Beg. bal. (assumed)	0
		Net income	41,000	Dividend		Dividend	
		End. bal.	110,000	payments	17,000	declarations	17,000
						End. bal. (assumed)	0

DAILY EXERCISE 17-15

First, we compute dividend declarations by analyzing Retained Earnings. Then we solve for dividend payments with the Dividends Payable account. Anchor Corporation has no Dividends Payable account, so dividend payments are the same as declarations. The following computations show how to compute Anchor Corporation's dividend payments.

Retained Earnings

Beginning balance	+	Net income	−	Dividend declarations	=	Ending balance
$86,000	+	$41,000	−	X	=	$110,000
				−X	=	$110,000 − $86,000 − $41,000
				X	=	$17,000

Dividends Payable

Beginning balance	+	Dividend declarations	−	Dividend payments	=	Ending balance
$0	+	$17,000	−	X	=	$0
				−X	=	$0 − $17,000 − $0
				X	=	$17,000

Exhibit 17-11 summarizes the computation of cash flows from financing activities. The color highlights show amounts that must be computed. This exhibit will come in handy as you solve the assignments at the end of the chapter.

Exhibit 17-11 **Cash Flows from Financing Activities**

Cash Receipts from Financing Activities

From issuance of long-term debt (notes payable)	Beginning long-term notes payable +	Cash received from issuance of long-term notes payable −	Payment of notes payable = Ending long-term notes payable
From issuance of stock	Beginning stock +	Cash received from issuance of new stock −	Payments to retire stock = Ending stock
From sale of treasury stock	Beginning treasury stock +	Purchase cost of treasury stock −	Cost of treasury stock sold = Ending treasury stock
	Cash received from sale of treasury stock =	Cost of treasury stock sold +	Extra amount of sale above cost, or— amount of cost above sale amount

Cash Payments for Financing Activities

Of long-term debt (notes payable)	Beginning long-term notes payable +	Cash received from issuance of long-term notes payable −	Payment of notes payable = Ending long-term notes payable
To retire stock	Beginning stock +	Cash received from issuance of new stock −	Payments to retire stock = Ending stock
To purchase treasury stock	Beginning treasury stock +	Purchase cost of treasury stock −	Cost of treasury stock sold = Ending treasury stock
For dividends	Beginning retained earnings +	Net income −	Dividend declarations = Ending retained earnings
	Beginning dividends payable +	Dividend declarations −	Dividend payments = Ending dividends payable

Noncash Investing and Financing Activities

Companies make investments that do not require cash. For example, they may issue a note payable to buy land, or they may pay off a note by issuing stock. Our examples thus far have included none of these transactions. Suppose that Anchor Corporation issued $320,000 of common stock to acquire a warehouse. Anchor would make this journal entry:

> Warehouse Building 320,000
> Common Stock............... 320,000

This transaction would not appear on the cash-flow statement because Anchor paid no cash. But the importance of the warehouse and the issuance of stock requires that the transaction be reported. This is a noncash investing (buying a building) and financing (issuance of stock) transaction. Exhibit 17-12 illustrates how to report noncash investing and financing activities (all amounts are assumed). This information can be reported in a schedule that follows the cash-flow statement.

	Thousands
Acquisition of building by issuing common stock	$320
Acquisition of land by issuing note payable	72
Payment of long-term debt by giving investments to the creditor	104
Acquisition of equipment by issuing short-term note payable	37
Total noncash investing and financing activities	$533

Exhibit 17-12
Noncash Investing and Financing Activities (All Amounts Assumed)

 Daily Exercise 17-16

Reconciling Net Income to Net Cash Flow from Operating Activities

The FASB requires companies that format operating activities by the direct method to report a separate reconciliation from net income to net cash flow from operating activities. The reconciliation shows how the company's net income is related to cash flow from operating activities. Exhibit 17-13 shows the reconciliation for Anchor Corporation.

ANCHOR CORPORATION
Reconciliation of Net Income to Net Cash Inflow from Operating Activities

	Thousands	
Net income..		$41
Add (subtract) items that affect net income		
and cash flows differently:		
Depreciation	$18	
Gain on sale of plant assets...................................	(8)	
Increase in accounts receivable	(13)	
Increase in interest receivable	(2)	
Decrease in inventory...	3	
Increase in prepaid expenses..................................	(1)	
Increase in accounts payable	34	
Decrease in salary payable.....................................	(2)	
Decrease in accrued liabilities.................................	(2)	27
Net cash inflow from operating activities		$68

The end result—net cash inflow from operating activities of $68,000—is the same as for the *direct* method (see Exhibit 17-2). *The reconciliation also shows the indirect method of computing operating cash flows.*

Objective 5
Prepare a statement of cash flows
by the indirect method

STATEMENT OF CASH FLOWS: THE INDIRECT METHOD

An alternative to the direct method of computing cash flows from *operating* activities is the *indirect method,* or the **reconciliation method,** as we just saw in Exhibit 17-13. This method starts with net income from the income statement and reconciles to operating cash flows. For example, the cash-flow statement of **Hewlett-Packard** Company starts with "Net earnings," followed by "Adjustments to reconcile net earnings to net cash provided by operating activities."

The indirect method shows the link between net income and cash flow from operations better than the direct method. In fact, the vast majority of companies use the indirect method even though the FASB recommends the direct method. The main drawback of the indirect method is that it does not report the detailed operating cash flows—collections from customers and payments to suppliers, employees, and for interest and taxes.

These two methods (direct and indirect) of preparing the cash-flow statement affect only the operating activities section of the statement. No difference exists for investing or financing activities.

Exhibit 17-14 is Anchor Corporation's cash-flow statement prepared by the indirect method. Only the operating section of the statement differs from the direct method format (Exhibit 17-2). The new items Ⓐ, Ⓑ, and Ⓒ are keyed to their explanations, which are discussed in the following section. For ease of reference, we repeat Anchor Corporation's income statement and balance sheet here as Exhibits 17-15 and 17-16.

Logic Behind the Indirect Method

The indirect-method cash-flow statement begins with net income from the income statement. Additions and substractions follow. These are labeled "Add (subtract) items that affect net income and cash flows differently." The first adjustment is for depreciation.

DEPRECIATION, DEPLETION, AND AMORTIZATION EXPENSES Ⓐ   These expenses are added back to net income to compute cash flow from operations. Let's see why.
Depreciation is recorded as follows:

Depreciation Expense	18,000	
Accumulated Depreciation..............		18,000

(continued at bottom of page 675)

ANCHOR CORPORATION
Statement of Cash Flows
Year Ended December 31, 20X2

	Thousands	
Cash flows from operating activities:		
Net income		$ 41
Add (subtract) items that affect net income and cash flows differently:		
(A) Depreciation	$18	
(B) Gain on sale of plant assets	(8)	
Increase in accounts receivable	(13)	
Increase in interest receivable	(2)	
Decrease in inventory	3	
(C) Increase in prepaid expenses	(1)	
Increase in accounts payable	34	
Decrease in salary payable	(2)	
Decrease in accrued liabilities	(2)	27
Net cash inflow from operating activities		$ 68
Cash flows from investing activities:		
Acquisition of plant assets	$(306)	
Loan to another company	(11)	
Proceeds from sale of plant assets	62	
Net cash outflow from investing activities		(255)
Cash flows from financing activities:		
Proceeds from issuance of common stock	$101	
Proceeds from issuance of long-term notes payable	94	
Payment of long-term notes payable	(11)	
Payment of dividends	(17)	
Net cash inflow from financing activities		167
Increase (decrease) in cash		$ (20)
Cash balance, December 31, 20X1		42
Cash balance, December 31, 20X2		$ 22

From Exhibit 17-2

● DAILY EXERCISE 17-17

EXHIBIT 17-15
**Income Statement
(Repeated from Exhibit 17-6)**

ANCHOR CORPORATION
Income Statement
Year Ended December 31, 20X2

	Thousands	
Revenues and gains:		
Sales revenue	$284	
Interest revenue	12	
Dividend revenue	9	
Gain on sale of plant assets	8	
Total revenues and gains		$313
Expenses:		
Cost of goods sold	$150	
Salary expense	56	
Depreciation expense	18	
Other operating expense	17	
Interest expense	16	
Income tax expense	15	
Total expenses		272
Net income		$ 41

This entry neither debits nor credits Cash because depreciation has no cash effect. But depreciation expense is deducted from revenues to compute net income. Therefore, in going from net income to cash flow, we add depreciation back to net income. The addback cancels the earlier deduction.

EXHIBIT 17-16
**Comparative Balance Sheet
Repeated from Exhibit 17-7)**

ANCHOR CORPORATION
Comparative Balance Sheet
December 31, 20X2 and 20X1

Thousands	20X2	20X1	Increase (Decrease)
Assets			
Current:			
Cash	$ 22	$ 42	$(20)
Accounts receivable	93	80	13
Interest receivable	3	1	2
Inventory	135	138	(3)
Prepaid expenses	8	7	1
Long-term receivable from another company	11	—	11
Plant assets, net of depreciation	453	219	234
Total	$725	$487	$238
Liabilities			
Current:			
Accounts payable	$ 91	$ 57	$ 34
Salary payable	4	6	(2)
Accrued liabilities	1	3	(2)
Long-term notes payable	160	77	83
Stockholders' Equity			
Common stock	359	258	101
Retained earnings	110	86	24
Total	$725	$487	$238

The following example should help. Suppose a company had only two transactions, a $1,000 cash sale and depreciation expense of $300. Net income is $700 ($1,000 − $300). But cash flow from operations is $1,000. To go from net income ($700) to cash flow ($1,000), we must add back the depreciation amount ($300).

All expenses with no cash effects are added back to net income on the cash-flow statement.

Depreciation, depletion, and amortization are added back.

Likewise, revenues that do not provide cash are subtracted from net income.

➡ We saw equity-method investment revenue in Chapter 16, p. 628.

An example is equity-method investment revenue. ⬅

GAINS AND LOSSES ON THE SALES OF ASSETS Ⓑ   Sales of plant assets are investing activities on the cash-flow statement. Recall that Anchor sold equipment for $62,000, producing a gain of $8,000. The $8,000 gain is reported on the income statement and included in net income.

The cash receipt from the sale is $62,000, and that is what we report on the cash-flow statement. The $62,000 of cash received also includes the $8,000 gain on the sale. To avoid counting the gain twice, we need to remove the gain from income and report the cash receipt of $62,000 in the investing activities section of the statement. Starting with net income, we subtract the gain. This deduction removes the gain's earlier effect on income. The sale of plant assets is reported as a $62,000 cash receipt from an investing activity, as shown in Exhibit 17-14.

A loss on the sale of plant assets is also an adjustment to net income on the statement of cash flows. A loss is *added back* to income to compute cash flow from operations. The proceeds from selling the plant assets are then reported under investing activities.

**CHANGES IN THE CURRENT ASSET AND CURRENT LIABILITY ACCOUNTS © ** Most current assets and current liabilities result from operating activities. Changes in the current accounts are reported as adjustments to net income on the cash-flow statement. The following rules apply:

1. **An *increase* in a current asset other than cash is subtracted from net income to compute cash flow from operations.** Suppose Anchor Corporation makes a sale on account. Income is increased by the sale amount. Accounts Receivable increases, but Anchor receives no cash. Exhibit 17-16 reports that Anchor Corporation's Accounts Receivable increased by $13,000 during 20X2. To compute the impact of revenue on Anchor's cash flows, we must subtract the $13,000 increase in Accounts Receivable from net income (see Exhibit 17-13). The reason is this: We have *not* collected this $13,000 in cash. The same logic applies to the other current assets. If they increase during the period, subtract the increase from net income.

Remember this:[2]

Current asset other than Cash (Receivables, Inventory, Supplies) ↑	**and Cash** ↓

2. **A *decrease* in a current asset other than cash is added to net income.** Suppose Anchor's Accounts Receivable balance decreased by $4,000. Anchor's Accounts Receivable decreased and Cash increased, so decreases in Accounts Receivable and the other current assets are *added* to net income.

Symbolically,

Current asset other than Cash (Receivables, Inventory, Supplies) ↓	**and Cash** ↑

3. **A *decrease* in a current liability is subtracted from net income.** The payment of a current liability decreases both cash and the current liability, so subtract the decrease from net income. In Exhibit 17-14, the $2,000 decrease in Accrued Liabilities is *subtracted* from net income to compute net cash inflow from operating activities. This summary will help you remember that

Current liability (Accounts Payable, Salary Payable, Accrued Liabilities, Unearned Revenue) ↓	**and Cash** ↑

4. **An *increase* in a current liability is added to net income.** Anchor's Accounts Payable increased during the year. This increase can occur only if cash is not spent to pay this liability. Therefore, cash payments are less than the related expense. As a result, we have more cash. Increases in current liabilities are *added* to net income.

Current liability (Accounts Payable, Salary Payable, Accrued Liabilities, Unearned Revenue) ↑	**and Cash** ↓

Exhibit 17-17 summarizes the adjustments needed to convert net income to net cash flow from operating activities by the indirect method.

If you are studying *only* the indirect method for operating cash flows, please turn back to page 669 for investing and financing activities.

⊙ DAILY EXERCISE 17-18

⊙ DAILY EXERCISE 17-19

---

[2]The authors thank Mari S. duToit for suggesting these displays.

Net Income

Add (subtract) items
that affect net income
and cash flow differently

{
+ Depreciation, depletion, and amortization
+ Loss on disposal of a long-term asset or early
   extinguishment of note (bond) payable
− Gain on disposal of a long-term asset or early
   extinguishment of note (bond) payable
+ Decrease in current asset other than cash
− Increase in current asset other than cash
+ Increase in current liability*
− Decrease in current liability*
}

Net cash inflow (or outflow) from operating activities

* Short-term notes payable for general borrowing, and current portion of long-term notes payable,
are related to *financing* activities, not to operating activities.

Source: We thank Barbara Gerrity and Jean Marie Hudson for suggesting this exhibit.

THINK IT OVER

Examine Anchor Corporation's statement of cash flows, Exhibit 17-14, and answer these questions:

1. Does Anchor Corporation appear to be growing or shrinking? How can you tell?
2. Where did most of Anchor's cash for expansion come from?
3. Suppose Accounts Receivable decreased by $40,000 (instead of increasing by $13,000) during the current year. What then would be Anchor's cash flow from operating activities?

Answers

1. Anchor appears to be growing. The company acquired more plant assets ($306,000) than it sold during the year.
2. Most of the cash for expansion came from issuing common stock ($101,000) and from borrowing ($94,000).
3. Accounts Receivable ↓ and Cash ↑ Therefore, net cash inflow from operating activities is $121,000 ($68,000 + $40,000 + $13,000).

Using Cash-Flow Information in Investment and Credit Analysis

The chapter-opening story about **drkoop.com** and **MotherNature.com** makes it clear that cash flows are important to a company's survival. A cash shortage is usually the most pressing problem of a struggling organization. Abundant cash allows a company to expand, invest in research and development, and hire the best employees. How, then, do investors and creditors use cash-flow information for decision making?

Neither cash-flow, net income, nor balance sheet data tell investors all they need to know about a company. Decision making is much more complex than plugging a few numbers into a formula. Investors analyze **Hewlett-Packard's** financial statements, articles in the financial press, and data about the industry, to decide whether to invest in Hewlett-Packard stock. To evaluate a large loan request by **MCI WorldCom,** a bank loan officer may interview the company's top management to decide whether they are trustworthy. Both investors and creditors are mainly interested in where a company is headed. They want to make predictions about net income and future cash flows.

It has been said that cash-flow data help spot losers better than they help spot winners. This is often true. When a company's business is booming, profits are high, and cash flows are usually improving. In almost all cases, a negative cash flow from operations warrants investigation. A cash downturn in a single year is not necessarily a danger signal. But negative cash flows for two consecutive years may throw a company into bankruptcy. Without cash flow from operations, a business simply cannot survive.

You may ask, "Can't the business raise money by issuing stock or by borrowing?" The answer is no, because if operations cannot generate enough cash, then stockholders will not buy the company's stock. Bankers will not lend it money. Over the long run, if a company cannot generate cash from operations, it is doomed.

The Decision Guidelines feature provides investors and creditors with a few suggestions on how to use cash-flow information for decision making.

 DAILY EXERCISE 17-20

DECISION GUIDELINES

Investors' and Creditors' Use of Cash-Flow and Related Information

Question	Financial Statement	What to Look For
INVESTORS		
Where is most of the company's cash coming from?	Statement of cash flows	Operating activities → Good sign Investing activities → Bad sign Financing activities → Okay sign
Do high sales and profits translate into more cash?	Statement of cash flows	Usually, but cash flows from *operating* activities must be the main source of cash for long-term success.
If sales and profits are low, how is the company generating cash?	Statement of cash flows	If *investing* activities are generating the cash, the business may be in trouble because it is selling off its long-term assets. If *financing* activities are generating the cash, that cannot go on forever. Sooner or later, investors will demand cash flow from operating activities.
Is the cash balance large enough to provide for expansion?	Balance sheet	The cash balance should be growing over time. If not, the company may be in trouble.
CREDITORS		
Can the business pay its debts?	Income statement	Increasing trend of net income.
	Statement of cash flows	Cash flows from operating activities should be the main source of cash.
	Balance sheet	Current ratio, debt ratio.

REVIEW THE STATEMENT OF CASH FLOWS

SUMMARY PROBLEM

Prepare the 20X3 statement of cash flows for Robins Corporation, using the indirect method to report cash flows from operating activities. In a separate schedule, report Robin's noncash investing and financing activities.

	December 31,	
	20X3	20X2
Current assets:		
Cash and cash equivalents	$19,000	$ 3,000
Accounts receivable.....................................	22,000	23,000
Inventories	34,000	31,000
Prepaid expenses	1,000	3,000
Current liabilities:		
Notes payable (for inventory purchases)	$11,000	$ 7,000
Accounts payable	24,000	19,000
Accrued liabilities	7,000	9,000
Income tax payable	10,000	10,000

Transaction data for 20X3:

Depreciation expense	$ 7,000	Purchase of equipment....................	$98,000
Issuance of long-term note		Payment of cash dividends	18,000
payable to borrow cash.................	7,000	Net income	26,000
Issuance of common stock		Issuance of common stock to	
for cash	19,000	retire bonds payable....................	13,000
Sale of building...............................	74,000	Purchase of long-term	
Amortization expense	3,000	investment	8,000
Purchase of treasury stock...............	5,000	Issuance of long-term note	
Loss on sale of building	2,000	payable to purchase patent	37,000

Solution

ROBINS CORPORATION
Statement of Cash Flows
Year Ended December 31, 20X3

Cash flows from operating activities:		
Net income		$26,000
Add (subtract) items that affect net income		
and cash flows differently:		
Depreciation..	$ 7,000	
Amortization	3,000	
Loss on sale of building..	2,000	
Decrease in accounts receivable....................................	1,000	
Increase in inventories..	(3,000)	
Decrease in prepaid expenses	2,000	
Increase in notes payable, short-term...........................	4,000	
Increase in accounts payable...	5,000	
Decrease in accrued liabilities	(2,000)	19,000
Net cash inflow from opeating activities		45,000
Cash flows from investing activities:		
Purchase of equipment...	$(98,000)	
Sale of building...	74,000	
Purchase of long-term investment	(8,000)	
Net cash outflow from investing activities		(32,000)
Cash flows from financing activities:		
Issuance of common stock...	$ 19,000	
Payment of cash dividends	(18,000)	
Issuance of long-term note payable..	7,000	
Purchase of treasury stock..	(5,000)	
Net cash inflow from financing activities		3,000
Increase in cash and cash equivalents.....................................		$16,000
Cash balance, December 31, 20X2		3,000
Cash balance, December 31, 20X3		$19,000
Noncash investing and financing activities:		
Issuance of long-term note payable to purchase patent.........		$37,000
Issuance of common stock to retire bond payable		13,000
Total noncash investing and financing activities.................		$50,000

LESSONS LEARNED

1. **Identify the purposes of the statement of cash flows.** The *statement of cash flows* reports a business's cash receipts, payments, and change in cash for the period. It shows *why* cash increased or decreased during the period. The cash-flow statement aids prediction of future cash flows and evaluation of management decisions. Cash also includes *cash equivalents* such as liquid short-term investments.

2. **Report cash flows from operating, investing, and financing activities.** The cash-flow statement reports *operating activities, investing activities,* and *financing activities.* Operating activities create revenues and expenses in the entity's major line of business. Investing activities affect the long-term assets. Financing activities obtain the cash needed to launch and sustain the business. Each section of the statement includes cash receipts and cash payments and concludes with a net cash increase or decrease. In addition, *noncash investing and financing activities* are reported in an accompanying schedule.

3. **Prepare a statement of cash flows by the direct method.** Two formats can be used to report *operating* activities—the direct method and the indirect method. The *direct method* reports collections from customers and receipts of interest and dividends minus cash payments to suppliers, employees, and for interest and income taxes. Investing cash flows and financing cash flows are unaffected by the method used to report operating activities.

4. **Compute the cash effects of a wide variety of business transactions.** The analysis of T-accounts aids the computation of the cash effects of business transactions. The information comes from the balance sheet, the income statement, and the related accounts.

5. **Prepare a statement of cash flows by the indirect method.** The *indirect method* starts with net income and reconciles to cash flow from operations. Although the FASB permits both the indirect and the direct methods, it prefers the direct method. However, the indirect method is more widely used.

ACCOUNTING VOCABULARY

cash equivalents (p. 656)
cash flows (p. 655)
direct method (p. 659)

financing activity (p. 658)
indirect method (p. 659)
investing activity (p. 657)

operating activity (p. 657)
reconciliation method (p. 659)
statement of cash flows (p. 655)

QUESTIONS

1. Identify four purposes of the statement of cash flows.
2. Identify and briefly describe the three types of activities that are reported on the statement of cash flows.
3. What is the check figure for the statement of cash flows? (In other words, which figure do you check to make sure you've done your work correctly?) Where is it obtained, and how is it used?
4. What is the most important source of cash for most successful companies?
5. How can cash decrease during a year when income is high? How can cash increase during a year when income is low? How can investors and creditors learn these facts about the company?
6. Why are depreciation, depletion, and amortization expenses *not* reported on a cash-flow statement prepared by the direct method? Why and how are these expenses reported on a statement prepared by the indirect method?
7. Taco Grande Restaurants collected cash of $92,000 from customers and $6,000 interest on notes receivable. Cash payments included $24,000 to employees, $13,000 to suppliers, $6,000 as dividends to stockholders, and $5,000

as a loan to another company. How much was Taco Grande's net cash inflow from operating activities?
8. How should issuance of a note payable to purchase land be reported in the financial statements? Identify three other transactions that fall in this same category.
9. Which format of the cash-flow statement gives a clearer description of the individual cash flows from *operating* activities? Which format better shows the relationship between net income and *operating* cash flow?
10. An investment that cost $65,000 was sold for $80,000, resulting in a $15,000 gain. Show how to report this transaction on a statement of cash flows prepared by the indirect method.
11. Identify the cash effects of increases and decreases in current assets other than cash. What are the cash effects of increases and decreases in current liabilities?
12. Milano Corporation earned net income of $38,000 and had depreciation expense of $22,000. Also, noncash current assets decreased $13,000, and current liabilities decreased $9,000. What was Milano's net cash flow from operating activities?

ASSESS YOUR PROGRESS

DAILY EXERCISES

DE17-1 For 19X9, 19X8, and 19X7, two well-known companies reported the following (in millions):

	19X9	19X8	19X7
Safeway, Inc., the grocery chain:			
Net income...	$ 971	$ 807	$ 557
Net cash flow from operating activities..............	1,488	1,253	1,222
U.S. Airways Group, Inc.:			
Net income...	197	538	1,025
Net cash flow from operating activities..............	603	1,251	870

Which company quit paying dividends during this period? How can you tell?

Explaining cash equivalents
(Obj. 1)

DE17-2 Pepsi Co, General Electric, Qualcomm, and most other companies report the following on their balance sheets:

CURRENT ASSETS
Cash and cash equivalents........... $XXX

What is a cash equivalent (give an example), and why is it combined with cash on the balance sheet?

Distinguishing operating, investing, and financing activities
(Obj. 2)

DE17-3 Describe operating activities, investing activities, and financing activities. For each category, give an example of (a) a cash receipt and (b) a cash payment.

Journal entries for operating, investing, and financing activities
(Obj. 2)

DE17-4 ◂ *Link Back to Chapter 2 (Journal Entries).* Return to Daily Exercise 17-3. For each cash receipt and each cash payment that you identified, give the journal entry, using made-up figures.

Identifying operating, investing, and financing cash flows
(Obj. 2)

DE17-5 Storage Technology Corporation prepares its statement of cash flows by the *direct* method for operating activities. Identify the section of Storage Technology's statement of cash flows where each of the following transactions will appear. If the transaction does not appear on the cash-flow statement, give the reason.

a. Cash 14,000
     Note Payable, Long-Term   14,000

b. Salary Expense............................. 7,300
     Cash......................................   7,300

c. Cash 28,400
     Sales Revenue   28,400

d. Amortization Expense................... 6,500
     Goodwill..............................   6,500

e. Accounts Payable 1,400
     Cash......................................   1,400

f. Land 90,000
     Cash......................................   90,000

Using an actual statement of cash flows

DE17-6 Examine the statement of cash flows of **drkoop.com, Inc.,** on page 654. What is the main danger signal about the company's cash flows?

Identifying operating cash flows
(Obj. 2, 3)

DE17-7 (Daily Exercise 17-10 is an alternative exercise.) eFax.com, Inc., accountants have assembled the following data for the year ended December 31, 20X2:

Cost of goods sold	$100,000	Payment of dividends	$ 6,000
Payments to suppliers	80,000	Proceeds from issuance	
Purchase of equipment	90,000	of common stock...........................	58,000
Payments to employees	70,000	Sales revenue	210,000
Payment of note payable	30,000	Collections from customers	170,000
Proceeds from sale of land	60,000	Payment of income tax.....................	10,000
Depreciation expense......................	15,000	Purchase of treasury stock...............	5,000

Prepare the *operating* activities section of eFax.com's statement of cash flows for the year ended December 31, 20X2. eFax uses the direct method for operating cash flows.

Identifying investing cash flows
(Obj. 2, 3)

DE17-8 (Daily Exercise 17-10 is an alternative exercise.) Use the data in Daily Exercise 17-7 to prepare the *investing* activities section of eFax.com's statement of cash flows for the year ended December 31, 20X2.

DE17-9 (Daily Exercise 17-10 is an alternative exercise.) Use the data in Daily Exercise 17-7 to prepare the *financing* activities section of eFax.com's statement of cash flows for the year ended December 31, 20X2.

Identifying financing cash flows (Obj. 2, 3)

DE17-10 eFax.com, Inc., accountants have assembled the following data for the year ended December 31, 20X2.

Preparing a statement of cash flows—direct method (Obj. 3)

Cost of goods sold	$100,000	Payment of dividends	$ 6,000
Payments to suppliers	80,000	Proceeds from issuance	
Purchase of equipment	90,000	of common stock	58,000
Payments to employees	70,000	Sales revenue	210,000
Payment of note payable	30,000	Collections from customers	170,000
Proceeds from sale of land	60,000	Payment of income tax	10,000
Depreciation expense	15,000	Purchase of treasury stock	5,000

Prepare eFax.com, Inc.'s statement of cash flows for the year ended December 31, 20X2. eFax uses the *direct* method for operating activities. Use Exhibit 17-2 (page 657) as a guide.

DE17-11 Inatome Processing began 20X1 with cash of $104,000. During the year, Inatome earned service revenue of $800,000 and collected $720,000 from customers. Expenses for the year totaled $670,000, of which Inatome paid $610,000 in cash to suppliers and employees. Inatome also paid $140,000 to purchase equipment and a cash dividend of $50,000 to its stockholders during 20X1.

Preparing a statement of cash flows—direct method (Obj. 3)

1. Compute net income for the year.
2. Determine the cash balance at the end of the year.
3. Prepare the company's statement of cash flows for the year. Format operating activities by the direct method, and show the beginning and ending balances of cash.

DE17-12 Exterra Communications reported the following financial statements for 20X3:

Computing cash-flow amounts (Obj. 4)

EXTERRA COMMUNICATIONS
Income Statement
Year Ended June 30, 20X3

	Thousands
Sales revenue	$660
Cost of goods sold	$340
Depreciation expense	40
Salary expense	50
Other expense	150
Total expenses	580
Net income	$ 80

EXTERRA COMMUNICATIONS
Comparative Balance Sheet
June 30, 20X3 and 20X2

Thousands	20X3	20X2		20X3	20X2
Assets			**Liabilities**		
Current:			Current:		
Cash	$ 39	$ 16	Accounts payable	$ 53	$ 42
Accounts receivable	54	48	Salary payable	25	21
Inventory	80	84	Accrued liabilities	6	11
Prepaid expenses	3	2	Long-term notes payable	63	68
Long-term investments	85	90			
Plant assets, net	215	185	**Stockholders' Equity**		
			Common stock	40	37
			Retained earnings	289	246
Total	$476	$425	Total	$476	$425

Compute the following operating cash flows:
a. Collections from customers.   **b.** Payments for inventory.

*Computing cash-flow amounts
(Obj. 4)*

DE17-13 Use the Exterra Communications data in Daily Exercise 17-12 to compute

a. Payments of other expenses. (Use the computational approach for Operating Expense outlined in Exhibit 17-9.)
b. Payments to employees.

*Computing investing cash flows
(Obj. 4)*

DE17-14 Use the Exterra Communications data in Daily Exercise 17-12 to compute

a. Proceeds from the sale of long-term investments. (Study Exterra's income statement to see whether there was a gain or loss on the sale. Exterra purchased no investments during the year.)
b. Acquisitions of plant assets (all acquisitions were for cash). Exterra sold no plant assets during the year.

*Computing financing cash flows
(Obj. 4)*

DE17-15 Use the Exterra Communications data in Daily Exercise 17-12 to compute

a. New borrowing or payment of long-term notes payable. Exterra had only one long-term note payable transaction during the year.
b. Issuance of common stock or retirement of common stock. Exterra had only one common stock transaction during the year.
c. Payment of cash dividends (same as amount of dividends declared).

*Noncash investing and financing
transactions
(Obj. 4)*

DE17-16 Return to the Anchor Corporation income statement (Exhibit 17-6, page 665) and comparative balance sheet (Exhibit 17-7, page 666). Assume that Anchor sold no plant assets during 20X2.

1. Compute the cost of Anchor's plant asset acquisition during the year.
2. Anchor financed the plant asset by signing a long-term note payable for $83,000 and paying the remainder in cash. Journalize this transaction.
3. Show how to report Anchor's acquisition of the plant assets on the statement of cash flows and the accompanying schedule of noncash investing and financing activities.

*Identifying items for reporting
cash flows from operations—
indirect method
(Obj. 5)*

DE17-17 Laclede Shipping, Inc., is preparing its statement of cash flows for the year ended September 30, 20X2. Laclede reports cash flows from operating activities by the *indirect* method. The company's head bookkeeper has provided the following list of items for you to consider in preparing the statement of cash flows. Identify each item as an operating activity—addition to net income (O+) or subtraction from net income (O−); an investing activity (I); a financing activity (F); or an activity that is not used to prepare the cash-flow statement by the indirect method (N). Answer by placing the appropriate symbol in the blank space.

___	**a.** Decrease in accounts receivable	___	**h.** Decrease in prepaid expense
___	**b.** Purchase of equipment	___	**i.** Issuance of common stock
___	**c.** Collection of cash from customers	___	**j.** Gain on sale of building
___	**d.** Increase in accounts payable	___	**k.** Retained earnings
___	**e.** Loss on sale of land	___	**l.** Sales revenue
___	**f.** Depreciation expense	___	**m.** Payment of dividends
___	**g.** Increase in inventory	___	**n.** Decrease in accrued liabilities

*Reporting cash flows from
operating activities, indirect
method   (Obj. 5)*

DE17-18 The Tribune Herald Publishing Company began 20X2 with accounts receivable, inventory, and prepaid expenses totaling $65,000. At the end of the year, the company had a total of $78,000 for these current assets. At the beginning of 20X2, The Tribune Herald owed current liabilities of $42,000, and at year end current liabilities totaled $40,000.

Net income for the year was $55,000, after including all revenues and gains and after subtracting all expenses and losses. Included in the computation of net income were a $4,000 gain on the sale of land and depreciation expense of $9,000.

Show how The Tribune Herald should report cash flows from operating activities for 20X2. The company uses the *indirect* method. Use Exhibit 17-14 (page 675) as a guide.

*Preparing a statement of cash
flows, indirect method
(Obj. 5)*

DE17-19 Exterra Communications reported the following financial statements for 20X3:

EXTERRA COMMUNICATIONS
Income Statement
Year Ended June 30, 20X3

	Thousands
Sales revenue	$660
Cost of goods sold	$340
Depreciation expense	40
Salary expense	50
Other expenses, including income taxes	150
Total expenses	580
Net income	$ 80

EXTERRA COMMUNICATIONS
Comparative Balance Sheet
June 30, 20X3 and 20X2

Thousands	20X3	20X2		20X3	20X2
Assets			**Liabilities**		
Current:			Current:		
Cash...	$ 39	$ 16	Accounts payable	$ 53	$ 42
Accounts receivable...........	54	48	Salary payable	25	21
Inventory............................	80	84	Accrued liabilities......................	6	11
Prepaid expenses	3	2	Long-term notes payable	63	68
Long-term investments........	85	90			
Plant assets, net....................	215	185	**Stockholders' Equity**		
			Common stock.............................	40	37
			Retained earnings	289	246
Total	$476	$425	Total	$476	$425

Additional data during 20X3:

a. Exterra purchased no investments.
b. Exterra sold no plant assets.
c. Exterra had only one long-term note payable transaction.
d. Exterra had only one common stock transaction.

Prepare Exterra Communications' statement of cash flows for the year ended June 30, 20X3. Exterra uses the *indirect* method for operating activities. Use Exhibit 17-14 (page 675) as a guide.

DE17-20 ◄ *Link Back to Chapter-Opening Story.* A friend is a stockholder in **MotherNature.com** and has received the company's statement of cash flows, which follows, as adapted. Answer the following questions to help your friend understand this financial statement and its purpose.

Using an actual company's statement of cash flows (Obj. 5)

MOTHERNATURE.COM, INC.
Statement of Cash Flows (adapted)
Year Ended December 31, 1999

	Thousands
Operating Activities:	
Net loss	$(159)
Adjustments to reconcile net loss	
to net cash used in operating activities	79
Net cash used in operating activities......................	(80)
Investing Activities:	
Purchases of property and equipment	(28)
Financing Activities:	
Borrowing	89
Issuance of common stock	25
Payments of debt...	(3)
Net cash provided by financing activities	111
Increase in cash and cash equivalents.......................	$ 3
Cash and cash equivalents, beginning	1
Cash and cash equivalents, ending	$ 4

1. What does the statement of cash flows reveal that you cannot learn from the income statement and the balance sheet?
2. MotherNature.com's statement indicates that the company uses the indirect method to report cash flows from operating activities. When you see other cash-flow statements, how can you tell that the company uses the indirect method?
3. Do MotherNature.com's cash flows for 1999 look strong or weak? Give your reason. What is the main thing you should look for in evaluating a company's cash flows?

EXERCISES

Identifying the purposes of the statement of cash flows (Obj. 1)

E17-1 Morningstar Foods, a bakery partnership in South Carolina, has experienced an unbroken string of ten years of growth in net income. Nevertheless, the business is facing bankruptcy! Creditors are calling all of Morningstar's outstanding loans for immediate payment, and the cash is simply not available. Attempts to explain where Morningstar Foods went wrong make it clear that managers placed undue emphasis on net income and gave too little attention to cash flows.

Required

Write a brief memo, in your own words, to explain to the managers of Morningstar Foods the purposes of the statement of cash flows.

Identifying activities for the statement of cash flows (Obj. 2)

E17-2 Identify each of the following transactions as an operating activity (O), an investing activity (I), a financing activity (F), a noncash investing and financing activity (NIF), or a transaction that is not reported on the statement of cash flows (N). Assume that the direct method is used to report cash flows from operating activities.

___ **a.** Payment of account payable
___ **b.** Issuance of preferred stock for cash
___ **c.** Payment of cash dividend
___ **d.** Sale of long-term investment
___ **e.** Amortization of bond discount
___ **f.** Collection of account receivable
___ **g.** Issuance of long-term note payable to borrow cash
___ **h.** Depreciation of equipment
___ **i.** Purchase of treasury stock
___ **j.** Purchase of long-term investment

___ **k.** Payment of wages to employees
___ **l.** Collection of cash interest
___ **m.** Cash sale of land
___ **n.** Distribution of stock dividend
___ **o.** Acquisition of equipment by issuance of note payable
___ **p.** Payment of long-term debt
___ **q.** Acquisition of building by issuance of common stock
___ **r.** Accrual of salary expense
___ **s.** Issuance of common stock for cash

Classifying transactions for the statement of cash flows (Obj. 2)

E17-3 Indicate where, if at all, each of the following transactions would be reported on a statement of cash flows prepared by the *direct* method and the accompanying schedule of noncash investing and financing activities.

a. Salary Expense	4,300	
Cash		4,300
b. Equipment	18,000	
Cash		18,000
c. Cash	7,200	
Long-Term Investment		7,200
d. Bonds Payable	45,000	
Cash		45,000
e. Building	164,000	
Note Payable, Long-Term		164,000
f. Cash	1,400	
Accounts Receivable		1,400
g. Accounts Payable	8,300	
Cash		8,300
h. Cash	81,000	
Common Stock		12,000
Paid-in Capital in Excess of Par		69,000
i. Treasury Stock	13,000	
Cash		13,000
j. Retained Earnings	36,000	
Common Stock		36,000
k. Cash	2,000	
Interest Revenue		2,000
l. Land	87,700	
Cash		87,700
m. Dividends Payable	16,500	
Cash		16,500
n. Equipment	22,100	
Note Payable, Short-Term		22,100

E17-4 Analysis of the accounting records of Meister Corporation reveals the following:

Collection of accounts receivable.....	$128,000	Increase in current assets other than cash.....	$17,000
Payment of salaries and wages.....	34,000	Payment of dividends.....	7,000
Depreciation.....	12,000	Cash sales.....	15,000
Decrease in current liabilities.....	23,000	Loss on sale of land.....	5,000
Collection of dividend revenue.....	1,000	Acquisition of land.....	37,000
Payment of interest.....	16,000	Payment of accounts payable.....	48,000
Net income.....	21,000	Payment of income tax.....	13,000

Required

Compute cash flows from operating activities by the direct method. Use the format of the operating section of Exhibit 17-2 (page 657). Evaluate the operating cash flow of Meister Corporation. Give the reason for your evaluation.

Computing cash flows from operating activities—direct method (Obj. 3)

E17-5 Selected accounts of ASP, Inc., show the following:

Identifying items for the statement of cash flows—direct method (Obj. 3)

LONG-TERM DEBT

Payments	69,000	Beg. bal.	161,000
		Issuance of debt for cash	90,000
		End. bal.	182,000

ACCOUNTS RECEIVABLE

Beg. bal.	30,000	Cash receipts from customers	139,000
Sales revenue	120,000		
End. bal.	11,000		

INVESTMENT IN LAND

Beg. bal.	90,000	Cost of investments sold	109,000
Acquisitions	127,000		
End. bal.	108,000		

Required

For each account, identify the item or items that should appear on a statement of cash flows prepared by the direct method. State where to report the item.

E17-6 The income statement and additional data of Gillette Satellite Network, Inc., follow.

Preparing the statement of cash flows—direct method (Obj. 3)

GILLETTE SATELLITE NETWORK, INC.
Income Statement
Year Ended September 30, 20X2

Revenues:		
Sales revenue.....		$252,000
Expenses:		
Cost of goods sold.....	$115,000	
Salary expense.....	45,000	
Depreciation expense.....	29,000	
Rent expense.....	11,000	
Interest expense.....	2,000	
Income tax expense.....	9,000	211,000
Net income.....		$ 41,000

Additional data during fiscal year 20X2:

a. Collections from customers were $7,000 more than sales.
b. Payments to suppliers were $5,000 less than the sum of cost of goods sold plus rent expense.
c. Payments to employees were $1,000 more than salary expense.
d. Interest expense and income tax expense equal their cash amounts.
e. Acquisition of equipment was $135,000. Of this amount, $100,000 was paid in cash and the remainder by signing a long-term note payable. Gillette sold no equipment during fiscal year 20X2.

f. Proceeds from sale of land, $14,000.
g. Proceeds from issuance of common stock, $35,000.
h. Payment of long-term note payable, $20,000.
i. Payment of dividends, $10,000.
j. No change in cash balance. The balance at September 30, 20X1, was $18,000.

Required

1. Prepare Gillette Satellite Network's statement of cash flows and accompanying schedule of noncash investing and financing activities. Report operating activities by the *direct* method.
2. Evaluate Gillette Satellite Network's cash flows for the year. Mention all three categories of cash flows, and give the reason for your evaluation.

Computing amounts for the statement of cash flows
(Obj. 3, 4)

E17-7 Compute the following items for the statement of cash flows of Pep.com:

a. Beginning and ending Accounts Receivable are $24,000 and $19,000, respectively. Credit sales for the period total $81,000. How much are cash collections?
b. Cost of goods sold is $84,000. Beginning Inventory balance is $29,000, and ending Inventory balance is $21,000. Beginning and ending Accounts Payable are $11,000 and $8,000, respectively. How much are cash payments for inventory?

Computing investing and financing amounts for the statement of cash flows
(Obj. 4)

E17-8 Compute the following items for the statement of cash flows of Steelcase Furniture:

a. Beginning and ending Plant Assets, net, are $103,000 and $112,000, respectively. Depreciation for the period is $16,000, and acquisitions of new plant assets are $27,000. Plant assets were sold at a $1,000 gain. What were the cash proceeds of the sale?
b. Beginning and ending Retained Earnings are $45,000 and $69,000, respectively. Net income for the period is $62,000, and stock dividends are $22,000. How much are cash dividend payments?

E17-9 The accounting records of Vintage Motor Corporation reveal the following:

Cash sales	$ 9,000	Payment of accounts payable	$48,000
Loss on sale of land	5,000	Net income	33,000
Acquisition of land	37,000	Payment of income tax	13,000
Collection of dividend revenue	7,000	Collection of accounts receivable	93,000
Payment of interest	16,000	Payment of salaries and wages	34,000
Increase in current assets other than cash	17,000	Depreciation	12,000
Payment of dividends	7,000	Decrease in current liabilities	29,000

Computing cash flows from operating activities—indirect method
(Obj. 5)

Required

Compute cash flows from operating activities by the indirect method. Use the format of the operating section of Exhibit 17-14 (page 675). Then evaluate Vintage Motor's operating cash flows as strong or weak.

Classifying transactions for the statement of cash flows
(Obj. 3, 5)

E17-10 Two transactions of Transworld Express, Inc., are recorded as follows:

a. Land 290,000
        Cash 130,000
        Note Payable 160,000

b. Cash 22,000
    Accumulated Depreciation......................... 83,000
        Equipment... 92,000
        Gain on Sale of Equipment 13,000

Required

1. Indicate where, how, and in what amount to report these transactions on the statement of cash flows and accompanying schedule of noncash investing and financing activities. Transworld reports cash flows from operating activities by the *direct* method.
2. Repeat requirement 1, assuming that Transworld reports cash flows from operating activities by the *indirect* method.

Preparing the statement of cash flows by the indirect method
(Obj. 5)

E17-11 Use the income statement of Gillette Satellite Network, Inc., in Exercise 17-6, plus these additional data during fiscal year 20X2:

a. Acquisition of equipment was $135,000. Of this amount, $100,000 was paid in cash and the remainder by signing a long-term note payable. Gillette sold no equipment during fiscal year 20X2.
b. Proceeds from sale of land, $14,000.
c. Proceeds from issuance of common stock, $35,000.
d. Payment of long-term note payable, $20,000.

e. Payment of dividends, $10,000.

f. Change in cash balance, $? The balance at September 30, 20X1, was $18,000.

g. The comparative balance sheet:

GILLETTE SATELLITE NETWORK, INC.
Comparative Balance Sheet
September 30, 20X2 and 20X1

	20X2		20X1	
Current assets:				
Cash		$ 18,000		$ 18,000
Accounts receivable		65,000		72,000
Inventory		59,000		53,000
Prepaid expenses...		6,000		5,000
Total current assets		148,000		148,000
Property, plant and equipment:				
Land		–0–		14,000
Equipment	$226,000		$91,000	
Less: Accumulated depreciation....................	(70,000)	156,000	(41,000)	50,000
Total assets		$304,000		$212,000
Current liabilities:				
Accounts payable		$ 41,000		$ 28,000
Accrued liabilities..		19,000		21,000
Total current liabilities		60,000		49,000
Long-term notes payable		105,000		90,000
Stockholders' equity:				
Common stock, no-par		71,000		36,000
Retained earnings		68,000		37,000
Total liabilities and stockholders' equity............		$304,000		$212,000

Required

1. Prepare Gillette Satellite Network's statement of cash flows for the year ended September 30, 20X2, using the indirect method.

2. Evaluate Gillette Satellite Network's cash flows for the year. In your evaluation, mention all three categories of cash flows, and give the reason for your evaluation.

Computing cash flows from operating activities—indirect method (Obj. 5)

E17-12 The accounting records of Digitex Security Systems include these selected accounts:

CASH			
Mar. 1	5,000		
Receipts	451,000	Payments	448,000
Mar. 31	8,000		

ACCOUNTS RECEIVABLE			
Mar. 1	18,000		
Sales	443,000	Collections	447,000
Mar. 31	14,000		

INVENTORY			
Mar. 1	19,000		
Purchases	337,000	Cost of sales	335,000
Mar. 31	21,000		

EQUIPMENT			
Mar. 1	93,000		
Acquisition	6,000		
Mar. 31	99,000		

ACCUMULATED DEPRECIATION—EQUIPMENT		
	Mar. 1	52,000
	Depreciation	6,000
	Mar. 31	58,000

ACCOUNTS PAYABLE		
	Mar. 1	14,000
Payments 332,000	Purchases	337,000
	Mar. 31	19,000

ACCRUED LIABILITIES		
	Mar. 1	9,000
Payments 14,000	Expenses	11,000
	Mar. 31	6,000

RETAINED EARNINGS		
	Mar. 1	64,000
Quarterly dividend 18,000	Net income	23,000
	Mar. 31	69,000

Compute Digitex's net cash inflow or outflow from operating activities during March. Use the indirect method. Does Digitex have trouble collecting receivables or selling inventory? How can you tell?

Interpreting a cash-flow
statement—indirect method
(Obj. 5)

E17-13 Consider three independent cash-flow situations for Calico Textile Company:

	Case 1	Case 2	Case 3
Cash flows from operating activities:			
Net income	$ 30,000	$ 30,000	$ 30,000
Depreciation and amortization	11,000	11,000	11,000
Increase in current assets	(19,000)	(7,000)	(1,000)
Decrease in current liabilities	(6,000)	(8,000)	–0–
	$ 16,000	$ 26,000	$ 40,000
Cash flows from investing activities:			
Acquisition of plant assets	$(91,000)	$(91,000)	$(91,000)
Sale of plant assets	97,000	4,000	8,000
	$ 6,000	$(87,000)	$ (83,000)
Cash flows from financing activities:			
Net borrowing	$ 16,000	$104,000	$ 50,000
Payment of debt	(21,000)	(29,000)	(9,000)
	$ (5,000)	$ 75,000	$ 41,000
Increase (decrease) in cash	$ 17,000	$ 14,000	$ (2,000)

For each case, use the cash-flow statement to identify how Calico Textile Company generated the cash to acquire new plant assets.

Challenge Exercise

Analyzing an actual company's
statement of cash flows
(Obj. 5)

E17-14 PepsiCo's statements of cash flows (adapted) for 1999 and 1998, are reproduced on page 691.

Required

1. Which format does PepsiCo use for reporting cash flows from operating activities? How can you tell?
2. What was PepsiCo's largest source of cash during 1999? During 1998? Give each amount.
3. What was PepsiCo's largest use of cash during 1999? During 1998? Give each amount.
4. The operating activities section of the 1999 statement lists (in millions):

Accounts and notes receivable	$(149)
Accounts payable and other current liabilities	$ 636

Did these accounts' balances increase or decrease during 1999? How can you tell?
5. At December 31, 1998, PepsiCo's balance sheet (not reproduced here) reported long-term debt (similar to notes payable) of $4,028 million. Journalize PepsiCo's long-term debt transactions during 1999. Then post to the Long-Term Debt T-account to see how much long-term debt PepsiCo would owe after these transactions.

PEPSICO, INC.
Statement of Cash Flows (Adapted)
Years Ended December 31, 1999 and 1998

Millions	1999	1998
Cash Flows—Continuing Operations:		
Net income	$2,050	$1,993
Adjustments to reconcile net income to net cash provided by operations:		
Gain on sale of bottling operations	(1,000)	—
Depreciation and amortization	1,032	1,234
Other noncash charges and credits, net	847	382
Changes in:		
Accounts and notes receivable	(149)	(104)
Inventories	(186)	29
Prepaid expenses	(203)	(12)
Accounts payable and other current liabilities	636	(311)
Net Cash Provided by Continuing Operations	3,027	3,211
Cash Flows—Investing Activities:		
Investments in other companies	(430)	(4,537)
Purchases of property, plant, and equipment	(1,118)	(1,405)
Proceeds from sale of property, plant, and equipment	625	151
Other, net	(149)	772
Net Cash Used for Investing Activities	(1,072)	(5,019)
Cash Flows—Financing Activities:		
Borrowing on long-term debt	3,480	990
Payment of long-term debt	(1,123)	(2,277)
Payment of short-term debt	(1,906)	—
Borrowing on short-term debt	—	4,049
Cash dividends paid	(778)	(757)
Other, net	(975)	(1,814)
Net Cash Provided by (Used for) Financing Activities	(1,302)	191
Increase (Decrease) in Cash and Cash Equivalents	653	(1,617)
Cash and Cash Equivalents—Beginning of Year	311	1,928
Cash and Cash Equivalents—End of Year	$ 964	$ 311

Problems

(Group A)

P17-1A Top managers of Crédit Lyonnais Group are reviewing company performance for 20X4. The income statement reports a 15% increase in net income, the fifth consecutive year with an income increase above 10%. The income statement includes a nonrecurring loss without which net income would have increased by 16%. The balance sheet shows modest increases in assets, liabilities, and stockholders' equity. The assets posting the largest increases are plant and equipment because the company is halfway through a five-year expansion program. No other assets and no liabilities are increasing dramatically. A summarized version of the cash-flow statement reports the following:

Using cash-flow information to evaluate performance (Obj. 1)

Net cash inflow from operating activities	$ 310,000
Net cash outflow from investing activities	(290,000)
Net cash inflow from financing activities	$ 70,000
Increase in cash during 20X4	$ 90,000

Required

Write a memo giving top managers of Crédit Lyonnais Group your assessment of 20X4 and your outlook for the future. Focus on the information content of the cash-flow data.

Preparing the statement of cash flows—direct method (Obj. 2, 3)

P17-2A Fordham Clothing Corporation accountants have developed the following data from the company's accounting records for the year ended July 31, 20X1:

a. Loan to another company, $35,000.
b. Income tax expense and payments, $56,400.
c. Depreciation expense, $27,700.
d. Collections on accounts receivable, $673,100.
e. Loan collections, $74,400.
f. Proceeds from sale of investments, $34,700, including a $3,800 loss.
g. Payment of long-term debt by issuing preferred stock, $107,300.
h. Amortization expense, $23,900.
i. Cash sales, $146,000.
j. Proceeds from issuance of common stock, $116,900.
k. Payment of cash dividends, $50,500.
l. Cash balance: July 31, 20X0—$53,800
             July 31, 20X1—$?
m. Salary expense, $105,300.
n. Cash payments to purchase plant assets, $181,000.
o. Proceeds from issuance of short-term debt, $44,100.
p. Payments of long-term debt, $18,800.
q. Proceeds from sale of plant assets, $59,700, including a $10,600 gain.
r. Interest revenue, $12,100.
s. Cash receipt of dividend revenue on stock investments, $2,700.
t. Payments to suppliers, $673,300.
u. Interest expense and payments, $37,800.
v. Cost of goods sold, $481,100.
w. Collection of interest revenue, $3,700.
x. Acquisition of equipment by issuing short-term note payable, $35,500.
y. Payments of salaries, $104,000.
z. Credit sales, $608,100.

Required

1. Prepare Fordham's statement of cash flows for the year ended July 31, 20X1. Follow the format of Exhibit 17-2 (page 657), but do *not* show amounts in thousands. Include an accompanying schedule of noncash investing and financing activities.
2. Evaluate 20X1 in terms of cash flow. Give your reasons.

Preparing the statement of cash flows—direct method (Obj. 2, 3, 4)

P17-3A The 20X3 income statement and comparative balance sheet of Zurich Telecom, Inc., are given below.

ZURICH TELECOM, INC.
Income Statement for 20X3

Revenues:		
Sales revenue		$427,000
Interest revenue		11,700
Total revenues		438,700
Expenses:		
Cost of goods sold	$205,200	
Salary expense	76,400	
Depreciation expense	15,300	
Other operating expense	49,700	
Interest expense	24,600	
Income tax expense	16,900	
Total expenses		388,100
Net income		$ 50,600

Zurich Telecom had no noncash investing and financing transactions during 20X3. During the year, there were no sales of land or equipment, no issuances of notes payable, no retirements of stock, and no treasury stock transactions.

Required

1. Prepare the 20X3 statement of cash flows, formatting operating activities by the direct method. See the company balance sheet at the top of the next page.
2. How will what you learned in this problem help you evaluate an investment?

Preparing the statement of cash flows—indirect method (Obj. 2, 3, 5)

P17-4A Use the Zurich Telecom data from Problem 17-3A.

Required

1. Prepare the 20X3 statement of cash flows by the indirect method. If your instructor also assigned Problem 17-3A, prepare only the operating activities section.
2. How will what you learned in this problem help you evaluate an investment?

ZURICH TELECOM, INC.
Comparative Balance Sheet

	December 31, 20X3	December 31, 20X2	Increase (Decrease)
Current assets:			
Cash and cash equivalents	$ 8,700	$ 15,600	$ (6,900)
Accounts receivable	35,500	43,100	(7,600)
Interest receivable	600	900	(300)
Inventories	94,300	89,900	4,400
Prepaid expenses	1,700	2,200	(500)
Plant assets:			
Land	35,100	10,000	25,100
Equipment, net	100,900	93,700	7,200
Total assets	$276,800	$255,400	$21,400
Current liabilities:			
Accounts payable	$ 16,400	$ 17,900	$ (1,500)
Interest payable	6,300	6,700	(400)
Salary payable	2,100	1,400	700
Other accrued liabilities	18,100	18,700	(600)
Income tax payable	6,300	3,800	2,500
Long-term liabilities:			
Notes payable	55,000	65,000	(10,000)
Stockholders' equity:			
Common stock, no-par	131,100	122,300	8,800
Retained earnings	41,500	19,600	21,900
Total liabilities and stockholders' equity	$276,800	$255,400	$21,400

P17-5A Accountants for Ross Retail Company have assembled the following data for the year ended December 31, 20X4:

Preparing the statement of cash flows—indirect method (Obj. 2, 5)

Current Accounts (All Result from Operations)	December 31, 20X4	20X3
Current assets:		
Cash and cash equivalents	$49,600	$34,800
Accounts receivable	70,100	73,700
Inventories	90,600	96,500
Prepaid expenses	3,200	2,100
Current liabilities:		
Notes payable (for inventory purchases)	$36,300	$36,800
Accounts payable	72,100	67,500
Income tax payable	5,900	6,800
Accrued liabilities	28,300	23,200

Transaction data for 20X4:

Stock dividends	$ 12,600	Payment of cash dividends	$48,300
Collection of loan	10,300	Issuance of long-term debt	
Depreciation expense	19,200	to borrow cash	71,000
Acquisition of equipment	69,000	Net income	61,500
Payment of long-term debt by		Issuance of preferred stock	
issuing common stock	89,400	for cash	36,200
Acquisition of long-term		Sale of long-term investment	12,200
investment	44,800	Amortization expense	1,100
Acquisition of building by issuing		Payment of long-term debt	47,800
long-term note payable	118,000	Gain on sale of investment	3,500

Required

Prepare Ross Retail Company's statement of cash flows, using the *indirect* method for operating activities. Include a schedule of noncash investing and financing activities.

Preparing the statement of cash flows—indirect method (Obj. 2, 5)

P17-6A The comparative balance sheet of Fortis Software Co. at December 31, 20X5, reported the following:

	December 31, 20X5	December 31, 20X4
Current assets:		
Cash and cash equivalents....................................	$10,600	$15,500
Accounts receivable	28,600	29,300
Inventories...	51,600	53,000
Prepaid expenses..	4,200	3,700
Current liabilities:		
Notes payable (for inventory purchases)...............	$ 9,200	$ -0-
Accounts payable..	21,900	28,000
Accrued liabilities...	11,000	16,800

Fortis's transactions during 20X5 included the following:

Amortization expense............................	$ 5,000	Cash acquisition of building...............	$124,000
Payment of cash dividends.....................	17,000	Net income	28,600
Cash acquisition of equipment..............	55,000	Insurance of common stock	
Issuance of long-term note		for cash...	105,600
payable to borrow cash.....................	32,000	Stock dividend	13,000
Retirement of bonds payable by		Sale of long-term investment..............	6,000
issuing common stock.......................	55,000	Depreciation expense	15,000

Required

1. Prepare the statement of cash flows of Fortis Software for the year ended December 31, 20X5. Use the *indirect* method to report cash flows from operating activities. Report non-cash investing and financing activities in an accompanying schedule.
2. Evaluate Fortis Software's cash flows for the year. Mention all three categories of cash flows, and give the reason for your evaluation.

Preparing the statement of cash flows—direct and indirect methods (Obj. 3, 5)

P17-7A To prepare the statement of cash flows, accountants for Shell City Oil Corp. have summarized 20X2 activity in two accounts as follows:

CASH			
Beg. bal.	87,100	Payments of operating expenses	67,800
Issuance of common stock	34,600	Payment of long-term debt	78,900
Receipts of dividends	14,100	Payment of income tax	12,600
Sale of investments	9,900	Payments on accounts payable	101,600
Collections from customers	315,100	Payment of dividends	1,800
		Payment of salaries	67,500
		Purchase of equipment	79,900
End. bal.	50,700		

COMMON STOCK			
		Beg. bal.	103,500
		Issuance for cash	34,600
		Issuance to acquire land	62,100
		End. bal.	200,200

Required

1. Prepare Shell City's statement of cash flows for the year ended December 31, 20X2, using the *direct* method to report operating activities. Also prepare the accompanying schedule

of noncash investing and financing activities. Shell City's 20X2 income statement and selected balance sheet data follow.

2. Use these data to prepare a supplementary schedule showing cash flows from operating activities by the *indirect* method. All activity in the current accounts results from operations.

SHELL CITY OIL CORP.
Income Statement
Year Ended December 31, 20X2

Revenues and gains:		
Sales revenue....................................		$281,800
Dividend revenue		14,100
Total revenues and gains................		295,900
Expenses:		
Cost of goods sold	$103,600	
Salary expense...................................	66,800	
Depreciation expense	10,900	
Other operating expense	64,500	
Income tax expense...........................	12,600	
Total expenses..............................		258,400
Net income		$ 37,500

SHELL CITY OIL CORP.
Balance Sheet Data

	20X2 Increase (Decrease)
Current assets:	
Cash and cash equivalents................	$?
Accounts receivable..........................	(33,300)
Inventories..	5,700
Investments.......................................	(9,900)
Equipment, net..................................	69,000
Land	62,100
Current liabilities:	
Accounts payable...............................	$ 7,700
Salary payable....................................	(700)
Other accrued liabilities....................	(3,300)
Long-term debt..................................	(78,900)
Common stock	96,700
Retained earnings..............................	35,700

P17-8A Unico, Inc.'s comparative balance sheet at September 30, 20X4, included the following balances as shown at the top of the next page.

Transaction data for the year ended September 30, 20X4:

a. Net income, 85,900.
b. Depreciation expense, $8,500.
c. Acquired long-term investments, $37,300.
d. Sold land for $38,100, including a $10,900 gain.
e. Acquired equipment by issuing long-term note payable, $26,300.
f. Paid long-term note payable, $24,700.
g. Received cash of $51,900 for issuance of common stock.
h. Paid cash dividends, $64,300.
i. Acquired equipment by issuing short-term note payable, $22,000.

Preparing the statement of cash flows—indirect method (Obj. 4, 5)

Required

Prepare Unico's statement of cash flows for the year ended September 30, 20X4, using the *indirect* method to report operating activities. Also prepare the accompanying schedule of noncash investing and financing activities. All current accounts except short-term notes payable result from operating transactions.

UNICO, INC.
Balance Sheet
September 30, 20X4 and 20X3

	20X4	20X3	Increase (Decrease)
Current assets:			
Cash	$ 40,700	$ 17,600	$23,100
Accounts receivable	46,000	46,800	(800)
Inventories	121,700	116,900	4,800
Prepaid expenses	8,600	9,300	(700)
Long-term investments	51,100	13,800	37,300
Equipment, net	131,900	92,100	39,800
Land	47,100	74,300	(27,200)
	$447,100	$370,800	$76,300
Current liabilities:			
Notes payable, short-term	$ 22,000	$ -0-	$22,000
Accounts payable	61,800	70,300	(8,500)
Income tax payable	21,800	24,600	(2,800)
Accrued liabilities	23,900	33,400	(9,500)
Long-term note payable	123,000	121,400	1,600
Common stock	113,900	62,000	51,900
Retained earnings	80,700	59,100	21,600
	$447,100	$370,800	$76,300

(Group B) PROBLEMS

Using cash-flow information to evaluate performance (Obj. 1)

P17-1B Top managers of Crane Furniture, Inc., are reviewing company performance for 20X2. The income statement reports a 20% increase in net income over 20X1. However, most of the increase resulted from an extraordinary gain on insurance proceeds from storm damage to a building. The balance sheet shows a large increase in receivables. The cash-flow statement, in summarized form, reports the following:

Net cash outflow from operating activities	$(80,000)
Net cash inflow from investing activities	40,000
Net cash inflow from financing activities	50,000
Increase in cash during 20X2	$ 10,000

Required

Write a memo giving Crane managers your assessment of 20X2 operations and your outlook for the future. Focus on the information content of the cash-flow data.

Preparing the statement of cash flows—direct method (Obj. 2, 3)

P17-2B Accountants for Westpac Pharmaceuticals, Inc., have developed the following data from the company's accounting records for the year ended April 30, 20X5:

a. Credit sales, $583,900.
b. Loan to another company, $12,500.
c. Cash payments to acquire plant assets, $59,400.
d. Cost of goods sold, $382,600.
e. Proceeds from issuance of common stock, $8,000.
f. Payment of cash dividends, $48,400.
g. Collection of interest, $4,400.
h. Acquisition of equipment by issuing common stock, $41,000.
i. Payments of salaries, $93,600.
j. Proceeds from sale of plant assets, $22,400, including a $6,800 loss.
k. Collections on accounts receivable, $462,600.
l. Interest revenue, $3,800.
m. Cash receipt of dividend revenue on stock investments, $4,100.
n. Payments to suppliers, $368,500.
o. Cash sales, $180,900.
p. Depreciation expense, $59,900.
q. Proceeds from issuance of short-term debt, $19,600.
r. Payments of long-term debt, $50,000.
s. Interest expense and payments, $13,300.
t. Salary expense, $95,300.

u. Loan collections, $12,800.

v. Proceeds from sale of investments, $9,100, including a $2,000 gain.

w. Payment of short-term note payable by issuing long-term note payable, $63,000.

x. Amortization expense, $2,900.

y. Income tax expense and payments, $37,900.

z. Cash balance: April 30, 20X4—$39,300

          April 30, 20X5—$?

Required

1. Prepare Westpac's statement of cash flows for the year ended April 30, 20X5. Follow the format of Exhibit 17-2, but do *not* show amounts in thousands. Include an accompanying schedule of noncash investing and financing activities.

2. Evaluate 20X5 from a cash-flow standpoint. Give your reasons.

P17-3B The 20X5 comparative balance sheet and income statement of Dayrunner Corp. follow.

Preparing the statement of cash flows—direct method

(Obj. 2, 3, 4)

DAYRUNNER CORP.
Comparative Balance Sheet

	December 31, 20X5	December 31, 20X4	Increase (Decrease)
Current assets:			
Cash and cash equivalents..................	$ 14,200	$ 5,300	$ 8,900
Accounts receivable...........................	28,600	26,900	1,700
Interest receivable.............................	1,900	700	1,200
Inventories.......................................	83,600	87,200	(3,600)
Prepaid expenses	2,500	1,900	600
Plant assets:			
Land...	89,000	60,000	29,000
Equipment, net.................................	53,500	49,400	4,100
Total assets.......................................	$273,300	$231,400	$41,900
Current liabilities:			
Accounts payable...............................	$ 31,400	$ 28,800	$ 2,600
Interest payable	4,400	4,900	(500)
Salary payable....................................	3,100	6,600	(3,500)
Other accrued liabilities....................	13,700	16,000	(2,300)
Income tax payable............................	8,900	7,700	1,200
Long-term liabilities:			
Notes payable....................................	75,000	100,000	(25,000)
Stockholders' equity:			
Common stock, no-par......................	88,300	64,700	23,600
Retained earnings	48,500	2,700	45,800
Total liabilities and stockholders' equity..	$273,300	$231,400	$41,900

DAYRUNNER CORP.
Income Statement for 20X5

Revenues:		
Sales revenue.................................		$220,000
Interest revenue		8,600
Total revenues............................		228,600
Expenses:		
Cost of goods sold.........................	$70,600	
Salary expense...............................	27,800	
Depreciation expense	4,000	
Other operating expense	10,500	
Interest expense............................	11,600	
Income tax expense.......................	29,100	
Total expenses............................		153,600
Net income...................................		$ 75,000

Dayrunner had no noncash investing and financing transactions during 20X5. During the year, there were no sales of land or equipment, no issuances of notes payable, no retirements of stock, and no treasury stock transactions.

Required

1. Prepare the 20X5 statement of cash flows, formatting operating activities by the direct method.
2. How will what you learned in this problem help you evaluate an investment?

Preparing the statement of cash flows—indirect method (Obj. 2, 3, 5)

P17-4B Use the Dayrunner Corp. data from Problem 17-3B.

Required

1. Prepare the 20X5 statement of cash flows by the indirect method. If your instructor also assigned Problem 17-3B, prepare only the operating activities section of the statement.
2. How will what you learned in this problem help you evaluate an investment?

Preparing the statement of cash flows—indirect method (Obj. 2, 5)

P17-5B Flanagan Corporation accountants have assembled the following data for the year ended December 31, 20X3:

| | December 31, | |
Current Accounts (All Result from Operations)	20X3	20X2
Current Assets:		
Cash and cash equivalents	$67,700	$22,700
Accounts receivable	69,700	64,200
Inventories	88,600	83,000
Prepaid expenses	5,300	4,100
Current Liabilities:		
Notes payable (for inventory purchases)	$22,600	$18,300
Accounts payable	52,900	55,800
Income tax payable	18,600	16,700
Accrued liabilities	15,500	27,200

Transaction data for 20X3:

Acquisition of land by issuing long-term note payable	$107,000	Purchase of treasury stock	$14,300
Stock dividends	31,800	Loss on sale of equipment	11,700
Collection of loan	8,700	Payment of cash dividends	18,300
Depreciation expense	26,800	Issuance of long-term note payable to borrow cash	34,400
Acquisition of building	125,300	Net income	69,100
Retirement of bonds payable by issuing common stock	65,000	Issuance of common stock for cash	41,200
		Sale of equipment	58,000
Acquisition of long-term investment	31,600	Amortization expense	5,300

Required

Prepare Flanagan Corporation's statement of cash flows, using the *indirect* method for operating activities. Include a schedule of noncash investing and financing activities.

Preparing the statement of cash flows—indirect method (Obj. 2, 5)

P17-6B The comparative balance sheet of Kekst & Co. at March 31, 20X4, reported the following:

| | March 31, | |
	20X4	20X3
Current Assets:		
Cash and cash equivalents	$20,600	$ 4,000
Accounts receivable	14,900	21,700
Inventories	63,200	60,600
Prepaid expenses	1,900	1,700
Current Liabilities:		
Notes payable (for inventory purchases)	$ 4,000	$ 4,000
Accounts payable	30,300	27,600
Accrued liabilities	10,700	11,100
Income tax payable	8,000	4,700

Kekst & Co.'s transactions during the year ended March 31, 20X4, included the following:

Acquisition of land by issuing note payable	$76,000	Sale of long-term investment	$13,700
Amortization expense	2,000	Depreciation expense	9,000
Payment of cash dividend	30,000	Cash acquisition of building	47,000
Cash acquisition of equipment	78,700	Net income	77,000
Issuance of long-term note payable to borrow cash	50,000	Issuance of common stock for cash	11,000
		Stock dividend	18,000

Required

1. Prepare Kekst & Co.'s statement of cash flows for the year ended March 31, 20X4, using the *indirect* method to report cash flows from operating activities. Report noncash investing and financing activities in an accompanying schedule.
2. Evaluate Kekst & Co.'s cash flows for the year. Mention all three categories of cash flows, and give the reason for your evaluation.

P17-7B To prepare the statement of cash flows, accountants for Agilera.com, Inc., have summarized 20X3 activity in two accounts as follows:

Preparing the statement of cash flows—direct and indirect methods (Obj. 3, 5)

CASH

Beg. bal.	53,600	Payments on accounts payable	399,100
Sale of investment	21,200	Payment of dividends	27,200
Collections from customers	669,700	Payment of salaries	143,800
Issuance of common stock	47,300	Purchase of equipment	31,400
Receipts of dividends	17,100	Payment of other operating expenses	63,600
		Payment of long-term debt	41,300
		Payment of income tax	18,900
End. bal.	83,600		

COMMON STOCK

	Beg. bal.	84,400
	Issuance for cash	47,300
	Issuance to acquire land	99,100
	End. bal.	230,800

Required

1. Prepare the statement of cash flows of Agilera.com, Inc., for the year ended December 31, 20X3, using the *direct* method to report operating activities. Also prepare the accompanying schedule of noncash investing and financing activities.
2. Use the following data from Agilera.com's 20X3 income statement and (selected) balance sheet to prepare a supplementary schedule showing cash flows from operating activities by the *indirect* method. All activity in the current accounts results from operations.

AGILERA.COM, INC.
Income Statement
Year Ended December 31, 20X3

Revenues:		
Sales revenue		$706,300
Dividend revenue		17,100
Total revenues		723,400
Expenses and losses:		
Cost of goods sold	$402,600	
Salary expense	158,500	
Depreciation expense	24,300	
Other operating expense	63,600	
Income tax expense	18,900	
Total expense		667,900
Net income		$ 55,500

AGILERA.COM, INC.
Balance Sheet Data

	20X3 Increase (Decrease)
Current assets:	
Cash and cash equivalents...............	$?
Accounts receivable	36,600
Inventories..	(11,800)
Long-term investments	(21,200)
Equipment, net..................................	7,100
Land..	99,100
Current liabilities:	
Accounts payable...........................	$ (8,300)
Salary payable................................	14,700
Long-term debt.................................	(41,300)
Common stock, no-par......................	146,400
Retained earnings.............................	28,300

Preparing the statement of cash flows—indirect method (Obj. 4, 5)

P17-8B The comparative balance sheet of Shin-Etsu Chemical Company at June 30, 20X2, included the following balances:

SHIN-ETSU CHEMICAL COMPANY
Balance Sheet
June 30, 20X2 and 20X1

	20X2	20X1	Increase (Decrease)
Current assets:			
Cash	$ 31,500	$ 8,600	$ 22,900
Accounts receivable	48,800	51,900	(3,100)
Inventories......................................	68,600	60,200	8,400
Prepaid expenses............................	3,700	2,800	900
Long-term investment......................	10,100	5,200	4,900
Equipment, net................................	82,500	73,600	8,900
Land..	42,400	96,000	(53,600)
	$287,600	$298,300	$(10,700)
Current liabilities:			
Notes payable, short-term (for general borrowing)..............	$ 13,400	$ 18,100	$ (4,700)
Accounts payable	42,400	40,300	2,100
Income tax payable.........................	13,800	14,500	(700)
Accrued liabilities..........................	12,800	15,200	(2,400)
Long-term notes payable..................	47,400	94,100	(46,700)
Common stock	59,800	51,200	8,600
Retained earnings...........................	98,000	64,900	33,100
	$287,600	$298,300	$(10,700)

Transaction data for the year ended June 30, 20X2:

a. Net income, $71,200.
b. Depreciation expense, $5,400.
c. Purchased long-term investment, $4,900.
d. Sold land for $46,900, including a $6,700 loss.
e. Acquired equipment by issuing long-term note payable, $14,300.
f. Paid long-term note payable, $61,000.
g. Received cash for issuance of common stock, $3,900.
h. Paid cash dividends, $38,100.
i. Paid short-term note payable by issuing common stock, $4,700.

Required

Prepare the statement of cash flows of Shin-Etsu Chemical Company for the year ended June 30, 20X2, using the *indirect* method to report operating activities. Also prepare the accompanying schedule of noncash investing and financing activities. All current accounts except short-term notes payable result from operating transactions.

APPLY YOUR KNOWLEDGE

DECISION CASES

Case 1. The 20X2 comparative income statement and the 20X2 comparative balance sheet of Dexia Enterprises have just been distributed at a meeting of the company's board of directors. The members of the board of directors raise a fundamental question: Why is the cash balance so low? This question is especially troublesome because 20X2 showed record profits. As the controller of the company, you must answer the question.

Preparing and using the statement of cash flows to evaluate operations (Obj. 4, 5)

Required

1. Prepare a statement of cash flows for 20X2 in the format that best shows the relationship between net income and operating cash flow. The company sold no plant assets or long-

DEXIA ENTERPRISES
Comparative Income Statement
Years Ended December 31, 20X2 and 20X1

Thousands	20X2	20X1
Revenues and gains:		
Sales revenue	$452	$310
Gain on sale of equipment (sale price, $33)		18
Total revenues and gains	$452	$328
Expenses and losses:		
Cost of goods sold	$221	$162
Salary expense	48	28
Depreciation expense	46	22
Interest expense	13	20
Amortization expense on patent	11	11
Loss on sale of land (sale price, $61)		35
Total expenses and losses	339	278
Net income	$113	$ 50

DEXIA ENTERPRISES
Comparative Balance Statement
December 31, 20X2 and 20X1

Thousands	20X2	20X1
Assets		
Cash	$ 41	$ 63
Accounts receivable, net	72	61
Inventories	194	181
Long-term investments	31	–0–
Property, plant, and equipment	361	259
Accumulated depreciation	(244)	(198)
Patents	177	188
Totals	$632	$554
Liabilities and Owners' Equity		
Notes payable, short-term		
(for general borrowing)	$ 32	$101
Accounts payable	63	56
Accrued liabilities	12	17
Notes payable, long-term	147	163
Common stock, no-par	149	61
Retained earnings	229	156
Totals	$632	$554

term investments and issued no notes payable during 20X2. The changes in all current accounts except short-term notes payable arose from operations. There were *no* noncash investing and financing transactions during the year. Show all amounts in thousands.

2. Answer the board members' question: Why is the cash balance so low? In explaining the business's cash flows, identify two significant cash receipts that occurred during 20X1 but not in 20X2. Also point out the two largest cash payments during 20X2.

3. Considering net income and the company's cash flows during 20X2, was it a good year or a bad year? Give your reasons.

Using cash-flow data to evaluate an investment
(Obj. 1, 2)

Case 2. SPAR Corp. and Babcock, Inc., are asking you to recommend their stock to your clients. SPAR and Babcock earn about the same net income and have similar financial positions, so your decision depends on their cash flows, summarized as follows:

	SPAR Corp.		Babcock, Inc.	
Net cash inflows from operating activities		$90,000		$10,000
Net cash inflows (outflows) from investing activities:				
Purchase of plant assets	$(100,000)		$(20,000)	
Sale of plant assets	10,000	(90,000)	80,000	60,000
Net cash inflows (outflows) from financing activities:				
Issuance of common stock		30,000		—
Paying off long-term debt				(40,000)
Net increase in cash		$30,000		$30,000

Based on their cash flows, which company looks better? Give your reasons.

ETHICAL ISSUE

Absolute Entertainment (ET) Agency is having a bad year. Net income is only $50,000. Also, two important clients are falling behind in their payments to Absolute, and the agency's accounts receivable are ballooning. The company desperately needs a loan. The Absolute ET board of directors is considering ways to put the best face on the company's financial statements. The agency's bank closely examines cash flow from operations. Rachel McPherson, Absolute ET's controller, suggests reclassifying as *long-term* the receivables from the slow-paying clients. She explains that removing the $70,000 rise in accounts receivable will increase cash flow from operations. This may help Absolute ET get the loan.

Required

1. Using only the amounts given, compute net cash inflow from operations both with and without the reclassification of the receivables. Which way makes Absolute ET look better?

2. Under what condition would the reclassification of the receivables be ethical? Unethical?

FINANCIAL STATEMENT CASE

Using the statement of cash flows
(Obj. 2, 4)

Use the **Target Corporation** statement of cash flows along with the company's other financial statements, all in Appendix A, to answer the following questions.

Required

1. Which method does Target use to report net cash flows from *operating* activities? How can you tell?

2. Suppose Target reported net cash flows from operating activities by the direct method. Compute these amounts for the year ended January 29, 2000 (Target labels the year as "1999").

   a. Collections from customers (*Retained securitized receivables* means accounts receivable).
   b. Payments for inventory.
   c. Payments for operating expenses. (Use Selling General and Administrative Expense; Other Current Assets, which are Prepaid Expenses; and Accrued Liabilities.)

3. Evaluate 1999 in terms of net income, cash flows, balance sheet position, and overall results. Be specific.

TEAM PROJECTS

Project 1. Select a company and obtain its annual report, including all the financial statements. Focus on the statement of cash flows and the cash flows from operating activities in particular. Identify whether the company uses the direct method or the indirect method to report operating cash flows. Use the other financial statements (income statement, balance sheet, and statement of stockholders' equity) and the notes, if necessary, to prepare the company's cash flows from operating activities by the *other* method.

Project 2. Each member of the group should obtain the annual report of a different company. Select companies in different industries. Evaluate each company's trend of cash flows for the most recent two years. In your evaluation of the companies' cash flows, you may use any other information that is publicly available—for example, the other financial statements (income statement, balance sheet, statement of stockholders' equity, and the related notes) and news stories from magazines and newspapers. Rank the companies' cash flows from best to worst, and write a two-page report on your findings.

INTERNET EXERCISE

Royal Caribbean Cruises Ltd. operates the Royal Caribbean International and Celebrity Cruises brands, with 18 modern ships and a passenger capacity of 34,900.

Go to **http://www.rclinvestor.com** and click on *Annual Reports,* and then the HTML version of the *most recent annual report.* Continue until you can click on the *financial table of contents* followed by the *Consolidated Statements of Cash Flows.* Use this statement to answer the following questions.

1. Does Royal Caribbean Cruises use the direct or the indirect method to prepare the statement of cash flows? How can you tell? Which activity section is affected by this choice of method?
2. For the most recent year, list the amount of net cash inflow or outflow for each of the three major types of activities reported on the Statement of Cash Flows. Which type of activity is providing the most cash? Is this considered favorable or unfavorable?
3. For the most recent year, what amount is reported for *Net Income/(Loss)* and *Net Cash provided by Operating Activities?* Are these amounts the same? Explain why or why not.
4. For the most recent year, did Royal Caribbean Cruises purchase or sell more property and equipment? Is this considered favorable or unfavorable? What was the net amount purchased/sold? Which activity section reports this information?
5. For the most recent year, did Royal Caribbean Cruises issue or pay back more debt? What was the net amount issued/repaid? For the most recent year, did Royal Caribbean Cruises issue or purchase more common stock? What was the net amount issued/purchased? For the most recent year, what amount of cash dividends did Royal Caribbean Cruises pay out? Which activity section reports this information?
6. Does this statement of cash flows indicate a strong or weak cash position? Explain.

Royal Caribbean Cruises

Go to the "Statement of Cash Flows" episode on the *Mastering Accounting* CD-ROM for an interactive, video-enhanced exercise focused on helping CanGo managers understand the difference between direct and indirect methods and the quality of earnings when comparing net income (on paper) to actual cash flow. The difference between cash on hand and what is owed to the company on paper can affect investor confidence.

APPENDIX TO CHAPTER 17

THE WORK SHEET APPROACH TO PREPARING THE STATEMENT OF CASH FLOWS

The body of this chapter discusses the uses of the statement of cash flows in decision making and shows how to prepare the statement using T-accounts. The T-account approach works well as a learning device. In practice, however, most companies face complex situations. In these cases, a work sheet can help accountants prepare the statement of cash flows. This appendix shows how to prepare that statement using a specially designed work sheet.

The work sheet starts with the beginning balance sheet and concludes with the ending balance sheet. Two middle columns—one for debit amounts and the other for credit amounts—complete the work sheet. These columns, labeled Transaction Analysis, contain the data for the statement of cash flows. Exhibit 17A-1 presents the work sheet. Accountants can prepare the statement directly from the lower part of the work sheet (Panel B in Exhibit 17A-1). All the exhibits in this appendix are based on the Anchor Corporation data presented in the chapter.

PREPARING THE WORK SHEET—DIRECT METHOD FOR OPERATING ACTIVITIES

The direct method separates operating activities into cash receipts and cash payments. The work sheet can be prepared by following these steps:

Step 1: Panel A gives the beginning and ending balances for Cash and all other balance sheet accounts through Retained Earnings. The amounts are taken directly from the beginning and ending balance sheets in Exhibit 17-7 (page 666).

Step 2: Panel B lays out the framework of the statement of cash flows—that is, the headings for cash flows from operating, investing, and financing activities. Exhibit 17A-1 is based on the direct method and splits operating activities into Receipts and Payments.

Step 3: The bottom of the work sheet shows Net Increase in Cash or Net Decrease in Cash, as the case may be. This final amount is the difference between ending cash and beginning cash, from the balance sheet. The statement of cash flows explains why this change in cash occurred during the period.

Step 4: Analyze the period's transactions in the middle columns of the work sheet.

Step 5: Prepare the statement of cash flows directly from Panel B of the work sheet.

Transaction Analysis on the Work Sheet—Direct Method

For your convenience, we repeat the Anchor Corporation transaction data from Exhibit 17-5. These data are given below.

The transaction analysis on the work sheet appears in the form of journal entries. Only balance sheet accounts appear on the work sheet. There are no income statement accounts. Therefore, revenue transactions are entered on the work sheet as credits to Retained Earnings. For example, in transaction (a), sales on account are entered on the work sheet by debiting Accounts Receivable and crediting Retained Earnings. Cash is neither debited nor credited because credit sales do not affect cash. But all transactions should be entered on the work sheet to identify all the cash effects of the period's transactions. In transaction (c), the earning of interest revenue is entered by debiting Interest Receivable and crediting Retained Earnings. The revenue transactions that generate cash are also recorded by crediting Retained Earnings.

Operating Activities:
1. Sales on credit, $284,000
*2. Collections from customers, $271,000
3. Interest revenue on notes receivable, $12,000
*4. Collection of interest receivable, $10,000
*5. Cash receipt of dividend revenue on investments in stock, $9,000
6. Cost of goods sold, $150,000
7. Purchase of inventory on credit, $147,000

*8. Payments to suppliers, $133,000
9. Salary expense, $56,000
*10. Payments of salaries, $58,000
11. Depreciation expense, $18,000
12. Other operating expense, $17,000
*13. Interest expense and payments, $16,000
*14. Income tax expense and payments, $15,000

Investing Activities:
*15. Cash payments to acquire plant assets, $306,000
*16. Loan to another company, $11,000

*17. Proceeds from sale of plant assets, $62,000, including $8,000 gain

Financing Activities:
*18. Proceeds from issuance of common stock, $101,000
*19. Proceeds from issuance of long-term note payable, $94,000

*20. Payment of long-term note payable, $11,000
*21. Declaration and payment of cash dividends, $17,000

* Indicates a cash-flow transaction to be reported on the statement of cash flows.

ANCHOR CORPORATION
Work Sheet for Statement of Cash Flows (Direct Method)
Year Ended December 31, 20X2

	Balances	Transaction Analysis		Balances
	Dec. 31, 20X1	Debit	Credit	Dec. 31, 20X2
PANEL A—Account Titles				
Cash..	42		(v) 20	22
Accounts receivable..	80	(a) 284	(b) 271	93
Interest receivable	1	(c) 12	(d) 10	3
Inventory...	138	(g) 147	(f) 150	135
Prepaid expenses	7	(h3) 1		8
Long-term receivable from another company	—	(p) 11		11
Plant assets, net..	219	(o) 306	(k) 18	
			(q) 54	453
Totals...	487			725
Accounts payable	57	(h1) 113	(g) 147	91
Salary and wage payable...	6	(j) 58	(i) 56	4
Accrued liabilities	3	(h2) 19	(l) 17	1
Long-term notes payable	77	(t) 11	(s) 94	160
Common stock	258		(r) 101	359
Retained earnings...	86	(f) 150	(a) 284	110
		(l) 17	(c) 12	
		(i) 56	(e) 9	
		(k) 18	(q) 8	
		(m) 16		
		(n) 15		
		(u) 17		
Totals	487	1,251	1,251	725
PANEL B—Statement of Cash Flows				
Cash flows from operating activities:				
Receipts:				
Collections from customers.....................................		(b) 271		
Interest received..		(d) 10		
Dividends received		(e) 9		
Payments:				
To suppliers			(h1) 113	
			(h2) 19	
			(h3) 1	
To employees..			(j) 58	
For interest			(m) 16	
For income tax			(n) 15	
Cash flows from investing activities:				
Acquisition of plant assets			(o) 306	
Proceeds from sale of plant.....................................		(q) 62		
Loan to another company			(p) 11	
Cash flows from financing activities:				
Proceeds from issuance of common stock		(r) 101		
Proceeds from issuance of long-term note payable		(s) 94		
Payment of long-term note payable			(t) 11	
Payment of dividends			(u) 17	
		547	567	
Increase (decrease) in cash.....................................		(v) 20		
Totals		567	567	

Expense transactions are entered on the work sheet as debits to Retained Earnings. In transaction (f), cost of goods sold is entered by debiting Retained Earnings and crediting Inventory. Transaction (m) is a cash payment of interest expense. The work sheet entry debits Retained Earnings and credits Payments for Interest under operating activities. The remaining expense transactions follow a similar pattern.

NET INCREASE (DECREASE) IN CASH   The net increase or net decrease in cash for the period is the balancing amount needed to equate the total debits and total credits ($567,000) on the statement of cash flows. In Exhibit 17A-1, Anchor Corporation experienced a $20,000 decrease in cash. This amount is entered as a credit to Cash, transaction (v), at the top of the work sheet and a debit to Net Decrease in Cash at the bottom. Totaling the columns completes the work sheet.

Preparing the Statement of Cash Flows from the Work Sheet

To prepare the statement of cash flows, Exhibit 17-2 (page 657) in the text, rewrite Panel B of the work sheet and add subtotals for the three categories of activities.

PREPARING THE WORK SHEET—INDIRECT METHOD FOR OPERATING ACTIVITIES

The indirect method shows the reconciliation from net income to net cash inflow (or net cash outflow) from operating activities. Exhibit 17A-2 is the work sheet for preparing the statement of cash flows by the indirect method.

The steps for completing the work sheet by the indirect method are the same as those used in the direct method. The analysis of investing activities and financing activities uses the information presented in Exhibit 17-5 (page 660) and repeated at the bottom of page 704. As mentioned previously, there is no difference for investing activities or financing activities between the direct- and indirect-method work sheets. Therefore, the analysis that follows focuses on cash flows from operating activities. The Anchor Corporation data come from the income statement (Exhibit 17-6, page 665) and the comparative balance sheet (Exhibit 17-7, page 666).

Transaction Analysis on the Work Sheet—Indirect Method

Net income, transaction (a), is the first operating cash inflow.* Net income is entered on the work sheet as a debit to Net Income under cash flows from operating activities and a credit to Retained Earnings. Next come the additions to, and subtractions from, net income, starting with depreciation—transaction (b)—which is debited to Depreciation on the work sheet and credited to Plant Assets, Net. Transaction (c) is the sale of plant assets. The $8,000 gain on the sale is entered as a credit to Gain on Sale of Plant Assets under operating cash flows—a subtraction from net income. This credit removes the $8,000 gain in cash flow from operations because the cash proceeds from the sale were not $8,000. The cash proceeds were $62,000, so this amount is entered on the work sheet as a debit under investing activities. Entry (c) is completed by crediting the plant assets' book value of $54,000 ($62,000 − $8,000) to the Plant Assets, Net account.

Entries (d) through (j) reconcile net income to cash flows from operations for increases and decreases in the current assets other than Cash and for increases and decreases in the current liabilities. Entry (d) debits Accounts Receivable for its $13,000 increase during the year. This decrease in cash flows is credited to Increase in Accounts Receivable under operating cash flows. Entries (e) and (g) are similar for Interest Receivable and Prepaid Expenses.

The final item in Exhibit 17A-2 is the Net Increase (Decrease) in Cash—transaction (q) on the work sheet—a credit to Cash and a debit to Net Decrease in Cash, exactly as in Exhibit 17A-1. To prepare the statement of cash flows, the accountant merely rewrites Panel B of the work sheet, adding subtotals for the three categories of activities.

---

*Note that we are now using the *indirect* method. The transactions we analyze here are *not* the same as those listed on pages 704–706.

ANCHOR CORPORATION
Work Sheet for Statement of Cash Flows (Indirect Method)
Year Ended December 31, 20X2

(In thousands)

	Balances	Transaction Analysis		Balances
	Dec. 31, 20X1	Debit	Credit	Dec. 31, 20X2
PANEL A—Account Titles				
Cash	42		(q) 20	22
Accounts receivable	80	(d) 13		93
Interest receivable	1	(e) 2		3
Inventory	138		(f) 3	135
Prepaid expenses	7	(g) 1		8
Long-term receivable from another company		(l) 11		11
Plant assets, net	219	(k) 306	(b) 18	
			(c) 54	453
Totals	487			725
Accounts payable	57		(h) 34	91
Salary and wage payable	6	(i) 2		4
Accrued liabilities	3	(j) 2		1
Long-term notes payable	77	(o) 11	(n) 94	160
Common stock	258		(m) 101	359
Retained earnings	86	(p) 17	(a) 41	110
Totals	487	365	365	725
PANEL B—Statement of Cash Flows				
Cash flows from operating activities:				
Net income		(a) 41		
Add (subtract) items that affect net income and cash flow differently:				
Depreciation		(b) 18		
Gain on sale of plant assets			(c) 8	
Increase in accounts receivable			(d) 13	
Increase in interest receivable			(e) 2	
Decrease in inventory		(f) 3		
Increase in prepaid expenses			(g) 1	
Increase in accounts payable		(h) 34		
Decrease in salary and wage payable			(i) 2	
Decrease in accrued liabilities			(j) 2	
Cash flows from investing activities:				
Acquisition of plant assets			(k) 306	
Proceeds from sale of plant assets		(c) 62		
Loan to another company			(l) 11	
Cash flows from financing activities:				
Proceeds from issuance of common stock		(m) 101		
Proceeds from issuance of long-term note payable		(n) 94		
Payment of long-term note payable			(o) 11	
Payment of dividends			(p) 17	
		353	373	
Increase (decrease) in cash		(q) 20		
Totals		373	373	

NONCASH INVESTING AND FINANCING ACTIVITIES ON THE WORK SHEET Noncash investing and financing activities can also be analyzed on the work sheet. Because these types of transactions include both an investing activity and a financing activity, they require two work sheet entries. Suppose Anchor Corporation purchased a building by issuing common stock of $320,000. Exhibit 17A-3 illustrates the transaction analysis of this noncash investing and financing activity. Cash is unaffected.

Work sheet entry (t1) records the purchase of the building, and entry (t2) records the issuance of the stock. The order of these entries is unimportant.

EXHIBIT 17A-3 **Noncash Investing and Financing Activities on the Work Sheet**

	Balances Dec. 31, 20X1	Transaction Analysis		Balances Dec. 31, 20X2
ANCHOR CORPORATION Work Sheet for Statement of Cash Flows Year Ended December 31, 20X2				
		Debit	Credit	
PANEL A—Account Titles				
Cash				
Building	650,000	(t1) 320,000		970,000
Common stock..	890,000		(t2) 320,000	1,210,000
PANEL B—Statement of Cash Flows				
Noncash investing and financing transactions:				
Purchase of building by issuing common stock		(t2) 320,000	(t1) 320,000	

APPENDIX PROBLEMS

Preparing the work sheet for the statement of cash flows—direct method

P17A-1 The 20X3 comparative balance sheet and income statement of Alden Group, Inc., follow. Alden had no noncash investing and financing transactions during 20X3.

ALDEN GROUP, INC.
Comparative Balance Sheet

	December 31 20X3	20X2	Increase (Decrease)
Current assets:			
Cash and cash equivalents	$ 13,700	$ 15,600	$ (1,900)
Accounts receivable	41,500	43,100	(1,600)
Interest receivable	600•	900	(300)
Inventories	94,300	89,900	4,400
Prepaid expenses................................	1,700	2,200	(500)
Plant assets:			
Land	35,100	10,000	25,100
Equipment, net	100,900	93,700	7,200
Total assets	$287,800	$255,400	$32,400
Current liabilities:			
Accounts payable	$ 16,400	$ 17,900	$ (1,500)
Interest payable................................	6,300	6,700	(400)
Salary payable	2,100	1,400	700
Other accrued liabilities	18,100	18,700	(600)
Income tax payable	6,300	3,800	2,500
Long-term liabilities:			
Notes payable	55,000	65,000	(10,000)
Stockholder' equity:			
Common stock, no-par	131,100	122,300	8,800
Retained earnings	52,500	19,600	32,900
Total liabilities and stockholders' equity	$287,800	$255,400	$32,400

ALDEN GROUP, INC.
Income Statement for 20X3

Revenues:

Sales revenue		$438,000
Interest revenue		11,700
Total revenues		449,700

Expenses:

Cost of goods sold	$205,200	
Salary expense	76,400	
Depreciation expense	15,300	
Other operating expense	49,700	
Interest expense	24,600	
Income tax expense	16,900	
Total expenses		388,100
Net income		$ 61,600

Required

Prepare the work sheet for the 20X3 statement of cash flows. Format cash flows from operating activities by the *direct* method.

P17A-2 Using the Alden Group, Inc., data from Problem 17A-1, prepare the work sheet for Alden's 20X3 statement of cash flows. Format cash flows from operating activities by the *indirect* method.

Preparing the work sheet for the statement of cash flows— indirect method

18 Financial Statement Analysis

LEARNING OBJECTIVES

After studying this chapter, you should be able to

1. Perform a horizontal analysis of financial statements
2. Perform a vertical analysis of financial statements
3. Prepare common-size financial statements
4. Compute the standard financial ratios
5. Use ratios in decision making
6. Measure economic value added

LUCENT TECHNOLOGIES, INC.
Consolidated Statement of Income (Adapted)
Year Ended September 30, 1999

	Millions
Revenues	$38,303
Cost [of sales]	19,688
Gross profit	18,615
Operating expenses:	
Selling, general, and administrative	8,417
Research and development	4,792
Operating income	5,406
Other income (expense)	2,187
Income before income taxes	7,593
Income tax expense	2,827
Net income	$ 4,766

MCI WORLDCOM, INC.
Consolidated Statement of Operations (Adapted)
Year Ended December 31, 1999

	Millions
Revenues	$37,120
Line costs (similar to cost of sales)	15,951
Gross margin	21,169
Operating expenses:	
Selling, general, and administrative	13,281
Operating income	7,888
Other income (expense)	(910)
Income before income taxes	6,978
Income tax expense	2,965
Net income	$ 4,013

www.prenhall.com/horngren
Readiness Assessment

Analysts at the investment banking firm of **Marquardt Pennile** have identified telecommunications as a growth area and will recommend telecom stocks to their clients. Clint Herzog heads a team of analysts who are focusing on two companies: **Lucent Technologies** and **MCI WorldCom.** Lucent Technologies is best known for cordless telephones. MCI WorldCom describes itself as the preeminent Internet and data company in the world.

Herzog and his team wish to compare the performance of Lucent and MCI WorldCom. As the two companies' income statements (on the facing page) show, Lucent is more profitable than MCI WorldCom. MCI WorldCom, on the other hand, doubled revenues during 1999 and turned a loss into a nice profit. How can Herzog and his fellow analysts compare these two companies?

The way to compare companies is to use *standard* measures. Throughout this book, we have discussed financial ratios, such as the current ratio, inventory turnover, and return on equity. These ratios enable investors to compare companies that operate in different industries. Managers use the ratios to help make decisions. In this chapter, we discuss most of the basic ratios and related measures that managers use to run a company. Investors and lenders use the same tools to search for good investments and loan prospects.

THE OBJECTIVES OF FINANCIAL STATEMENT ANALYSIS

The analysis of financial statements applies some specific techniques to the data contained in the annual report. In addition to the financial statements, annual reports usually contain

1. Notes to the financial statements, including a summary of the accounting methods used
2. Management's discussion and analysis of the financial results
3. The auditor's report
4. Comparative financial data for 5–10 years

Management's discussion and analysis (MD&A) of financial results is especially important because top managers are in the best position to know how well or how poorly their company is performing. The SEC requires the MD&A from public corporations. For example, the 1999 annual report of **Lucent Technologies** includes 12 pages of MD&A. As the following excerpt shows, Lucent is acquiring companies all over the world.

Lucent Technologies, Inc.
Management's Discussion and Analysis
of Results of Operations and Financial Condition

January 1999—Acquisition of the remaining 80% interest in WaveAccess, a developer of high-speed systems for wireless data communications

September 1998—Acquisition of JNA, an Australian telecom equipment manufacturer

August 1998—Acquisition of LANNET, an Israel-based supplier of Ethernet and asynchronous transfer mode ("ATM") switching solutions

---

THINK IT OVER

Consider Lucent Technologies' January 1999 acquisition of the "remaining 80% interest in WaveAccess. . ." Then answer these questions.

1. Chapter 16 covered investments such as Lucent's acquisition of **WaveAccess.** What percentage of WaveAccess's stock does Lucent now own?
2. In the relationship between Lucent and WaveAccess, we refer to Lucent as the _____ company and to WaveAccess as the _____ company.
3. After purchasing WaveAccess, Lucent's financial statements now also include the statements of WaveAccess. Refer to Lucent's income statement (page 713) to see the word used to describe Lucent's financial statements.

Answers: 1. Lucent now owns 100% of WaveAccess.
      2. Lucent = parent company; WaveAccess = subsidiary company.
      3. *Consolidated* financial statements.

The Objectives of Financial Statement Analysis

Investors who purchase a company's stock expect to receive dividends and hope the stock's value will increase. Creditors make loans to receive cash for the interest and principal. They use financial statement analysis to (1) predict the amount of expected returns, and (2) assess the risks associated with those returns.

The tools and techniques the business community uses in evaluating financial statement information can be divided into three broad categories: horizontal analysis, vertical analysis, and ratio analysis.

HORIZONTAL ANALYSIS

Objective 1
Perform a horizontal analysis of financial statements

HORIZONTAL ANALYSIS. Study of percentage changes in comparative financial statements.

Many managerial decisions hinge on whether the dollar amounts—of sales, income, expenses, and so on—are increasing or decreasing over time. Have sales risen from last year? From two years ago? By how much? Sales may have risen by $200,000. This fact may be interesting, but considered alone it is not very useful. The *percentage change* in the net sales over time offers a more useful perspective. It is better to know that sales have increased by 20% than to know that sales rose by $200,000.

The study of percentage changes in comparative statements is called **horizontal analysis.** Computing a percentage change in comparative statements requires two steps:

1. Compute the dollar amount of the change from the base (earlier) period to the later period.
2. Divide the dollar amount of change by the base-period amount.

Horizontal analysis is illustrated for **Lucent Technologies** as follows (dollar amounts in millions):

	1999	1998	Increase (Decrease) Amount	Percent
Revenues................	$38,303	$31,806	$6,497	20.4%
Net income..............	4,766	1,035	3,731	360.5%

The percentage change in Lucent Technologies' net income during 1999 is computed as follows:

Step 1. Compute the dollar amount of change in sales from 1998 to 1999:

1999	1998	Increase
$4,766 − $1,035 =		$3,731

Step 2. Divide the dollar amount of change by the base-period amount to compute the percentage change during the later period:

$$\text{Percentage change} = \frac{\text{Dollar amount of change}}{\text{Base-year amount}}$$

$$= \frac{\$3,731}{\$1,035} = 360.5\%$$

A 360.5% increase means that net income of 1999 was 3.6 times as high as the net income of 1998. That's why technology stocks have been so popular.

Detailed horizontal analyses of comparative income statements and comparative balance sheets are shown in the two right-hand columns of Exhibits 18-1 and 18-2, the financial statements of Lucent Technologies, Inc. The income statements (statements of earnings) reveal that revenues increased by 20.4% during 1999. Expenses grew less. As a result, net income increased by a whopping 360%.

EXHIBIT 18-1
Comparative Income
Statement—Horizontal Analysis

LUCENT TECHNOLOGIES, INC.
Consolidated Statement of Income (Adapted)
Years Ended September 30, 1999 and 1998

Dollar Amounts in Millions	1999	1998	Increase (Decrease) Amount	Increase (Decrease) Percent
Revenues...	$38,303	$31,806	$6,497	20.4%
Cost [of sales]	19,688	16,715	2,973	17.8
Gross profit..	18,615	15,091	3,524	23.4
Operating expenses:				
Selling, general, administrative ..	8,417	6,867	1,550	22.6
Research and development.........	4,792	5,586	(794)	(14.2)
Operating income............................	5,406	2,638	2,768	104.9
Other income (expense).................	2,187	(126)	2,313	1,835.7
Income before income taxes	7,593	2,512	5,081	202.3
Income tax expense..........................	2,827	1,477	1,350	91.4
Net income	$ 4,766	$ 1,035	$3,731	360.5%

THINK IT OVER Identify the item on Lucent Technologies' 1999 income statement that experienced the largest percentage *increase* from 1998. Considering all other changes on the 1999 income statement, is this item of great importance? Give your reason.

Answer: Other income increased by 1,835.7%. This is relatively unimportant because (a) other income is outside the company's main operations, (b) the dollar amounts are small in comparison to revenues, and (c) other income may not repeat from year to year.

Trend Percentages

Trend percentages are a form of horizontal analysis. Trends show the direction a business is heading. How have sales changed over a five-year period? What is the trend of the company's gross profit? These questions can be answered by analyzing trend percentages over a recent period, such as the most recent five or ten years.

Trend percentages use a base year whose amounts are set equal to 100%. The amounts of each following year are expressed as a percentage of the base amount. To compute trend percentages, divide each item for following years by the corresponding amount during the base year:

$$\text{Trend \%} = \frac{\text{Any year \$}}{\text{Base year \$}}$$

continued in the middle of page 714

EXHIBIT 18-2
**Comparative Balance Sheet—
Horizontal Analysis**

⊙ DAILY EXERCISE 18-2

LUCENT TECHNOLOGIES, INC.
Consolidated Balance Sheet (Adapted)
September 30, 1999 and 1998

Dollar Amounts in Millions	1999	1998	Increase (Decrease) Amount	Increase (Decrease) Percent
Assets				
Cash and cash equivalents.............	$ 1,816	$ 1,154	$ 662	57.4%
Receivables, net..............................	10,438	7,405	3,033	41.0
Inventories....................................	6,151	4,538	1,613	35.5
Prepaid expenses	3,526	2,687	839	31.2
Total current assets....................	21,931	15,784	6,147	38.9
Property, plant, and equipment, net..........................	6,847	5,693	1,154	20.3
Prepaid pension costs	6,175	3,754	2,421	64.5
Other assets	3,822	4,132	(310)	(7.5)
Total assets.................................	$38,775	$29,363	$9,412	32.1%
Liabilities				
Accounts payable...........................	$ 2,878	$ 2,157	$ 721	33.4%
Salary and other compensation payable	2,437	2,779	(342)	(12.3)
Debt due within one year..............	2,864	2,231	633	28.4
Other current liabilities	3,599	3,718	(119)	(3.2)
Total current liabilities	11,778	10,885	893	8.2
Long-term debt.............................	4,162	2,409	1,753	72.8
Other long-term liabilities	9,251	8,360	891	10.7
Total liabilities...............................	25,191	21,654	3,537	16.3
Shareowners' Equity				
Common stock, including additional paid-in capital	7,729	6,570	1,159	17.6
Retained earnings..........................	6,099	1,422	4,677	328.9
Other equity	(244)	(283)	39	13.8
Total shareowners' equity	13,584	7,709	5,875	76.2
Total liabilities and equity.............	$38,775	$29,363	$9,412	32.1%

Lucent Technologies showed sales, cost of goods sold, and gross profit for the past five years as follows:

(In Millions)	1999	1998	1997	1996	1995
Revenues.....................	$38,303	$31,806	$27,611	$24,215	$21,718
Cost [of sales]..............	19,688	16,715	15,318	14,709	13,049
Gross profit.................	18,615	15,091	12,293	9,506	8,669

We want trend percentages for a four-year period starting with 1996. The base year is 1995. Trend percentages for revenues are computed by dividing each revenues amount by the 1995 amount of $21,718 million. Trend percentages for Cost of sales are calculated by dividing each Cost of sales amount by $13,049 (the base-year amount), and trend percentages for Gross profit are calculated by dividing each gross profit amount by $8,669 (the base-year amount). The resulting trend percentages are as follows (1995, the base year = 100%):

	1999	1998	1997	1996	1995
Revenues.....................	176%	146%	127%	111%	100%
Cost [of sales]..............	151	128	117	113	100
Gross profit.................	215	174	142	110	100

Lucent Technologies' revenues and cost of goods sold have trended upward. Gross profit has increased steadily, with the most dramatic growth during 1998 and 1999. This trend is good news for Lucent stockholders.

 DAILY EXERCISE 18-3

VERTICAL ANALYSIS

Objective 2
Perform a vertical analysis of financial statements

The horizontal analysis that we have just seen highlights changes in an item *over time*. **Vertical analysis** of a financial statement reveals the relationship of each statement item to a specified base, which is the 100% figure. Every item on the financial statement is then reported as a percentage of that base.

For an income statement, revenues (or net sales) is usually the base. Suppose under normal conditions a company's gross profit is 70% of revenues. A drop in gross profit to 60% may throw the company into a net loss on the income statement. A large decline in gross profit creates alarm. Exhibit 18-3 shows the vertical analysis of **Lucent Technologies'** income statement as a percentage of revenues. In this case,

VERTICAL ANALYSIS. Analysis of a financial statement that reveals the relationship of each statement item to the total, which is 100%.

$$\text{Vertical analysis \%} = \frac{\text{Each income statement item}}{\text{Net sales (Revenues)}}$$

So, for example, the vertical analysis percentage for Cost of sales for 1999 equals 51.4% ($19,688/$38,303 = 0.514). Exhibit 18-4 shows the vertical analysis of the balance sheet amounts as a percentage of total assets.

	1999		1998	
Dollar Amounts in Millions	**Amount**	**Percent**	**Amount**	**Percent**
Revenues...	$38,303	100.0%	$31,806	100.0%
Cost [of sales].................................	19,688	51.4	16,715	52.6
Gross profit.....................................	18,615	48.6	15,091	47.4
Operating expenses:				
Selling, general, administrative..	8,417	22.0	6,867	21.6
Research and development........	4,792	12.5	5,586	17.5
Operating income	5,406	14.1	2,638	8.3
Other income (expense)	2,187	5.7	(126)	(0.4)
Income before income taxes..........	7,593	19.8	2,512	7.9
Income tax expense	2,827	7.4	1,477	4.6
Net income....................................	$ 4,766	12.4%	$ 1,035	3.3%

LUCENT TECHNOLOGIES, INC.
Consolidated Statement of Income (Adapted)
Years Ended September 30, 1999 and 1998

EXHIBIT 18-3
Comparative Income Statement—Vertical Analysis

 DAILY EXERCISE 18-4

The vertical analysis of Lucent Technologies' income statement (Exhibit 18-3) shows no unusual relationships. The gross profit percentage was up a bit from 1998. Net income's percentage of sales increased in 1999 because Lucent controlled operating expenses and also because of the other income.

The vertical analysis of Lucent's balance sheet (Exhibit 18-4) also yields few surprises. Current assets' percentage of total assets increased a little in 1999, while current liabilities' percentage decreased. The best news on the balance sheet is the increase in stockholders' (shareowners') equity.

Lucent's financial position is strong. For example, the current ratio is 1.86 ($21,931 million/$11,778 million), and the company has little long-term debt.

EXHIBIT 18-4
**Comparative Balance Sheet—
Vertical Analysis**

LUCENT TECHNOLOGIES, INC.
Consolidated Balance Sheet (Adapted)
September 30, 1999 and 1998

Dollar Amounts in Millions	1999 Amount	1999 Percent	1998 Amount	1998 Percent
Assets				
Cash and cash equivalents..............	$ 1,816	4.7%	$ 1,154	3.9%
Receivables, net	10,438	26.9	7,405	25.2
Inventories....................................	6,151	15.9	4,538	15.5
Prepaid expenses............................	3,526	9.1	2,687	9.2
Total current assets....................	21,931	56.6	15,784	53.8
Property, plant, and equipment, net.........................	6,847	17.7	5,693	19.4
Prepaid pension costs....................	6,175	15.9	3,754	12.8
Other assets...................................	3,822	9.8	4,132	14.0
Total assets...................................	$38,775	100.0%	$29,363	100.0%
Liabilities				
Accounts payable	$ 2,878	7.4%	$ 2,157	7.3%
Salary and other compensation payable................	2,437	6.3	2,779	9.5
Debt due within one year	2,864	7.4	2,231	7.6
Other current liabilities.................	3,599	9.3	3,718	12.7
Total current liabilities................	11,778	30.4	10,885	37.1
Long-term debt	4,162	10.7	2,409	8.2
Other long-term liabilities..............	9,251	23.9	8,360	28.4
Total liabilities	25,191	65.0	21,654	73.7
Shareowner's Equity				
Common stock, including additional paid-in capital............	7,729	19.9	6,570	22.4
Retained earnings	6,099	15.7	1,422	4.8
Other equity..................................	(244)	(0.6)	(283)	(0.9)
Total shareowners' equity..............	13,584	35.0	7,709	26.3
Total liabilities and equity..............	$38,775	100.0%	$29,363	100.0%

● DAILY EXERCISE 18-5

● DAILY EXERCISE 18-6

Objective 3
Prepare common-size financial statements

COMMON-SIZE STATEMENT. A financial statement that reports only percentages (no dollar amounts); a type of vertical analysis.

COMMON-SIZE STATEMENTS

The percentages in Exhibits 18-3 and 18-4 can be presented as a separate statement that reports only percentages (no dollar amounts). Such a statement is called a **common-size statement.**

A common-size income statement reports each item as a percentage of the net sales (revenues) amount. Net sales is the *common size* for reporting amounts. In the balance sheet, the common size is total assets. A common-size statement eases the comparison of different companies because all amounts are stated in percentages.

Common-size statements may identify the need for a closer look at manager decisions. Exhibit 18-5 is the common-size income statement of **Lucent Technologies,** taken from Exhibit 18-3. Exhibit 18-5 shows research and development expense as 17.5% of revenues for 1998. The percentage drops in 1999. The result is higher net income for 1999. However, research and development (R&D) are essential for a high-tech company such as Lucent. If the company cuts back too far on R&D, that could hurt profits for years to come.

EXHIBIT 18-5
Common-Size Income Statement
of Lucent Technologies

LUCENT TECHNOLOGIES, INC.
Common-Size Statement of Income (Adapted)
Years Ended September 30, 1999 and 1998

	1999	1998
Revenues..	100.0%	100.0%
Cost [of sales]...	51.4	52.6
Gross profit...	48.6	47.4
Operating expenses:		
Selling, general, administrative..............	22.0	21.6
Research and development....................	12.5	17.5
Operating income	14.1	8.3
Other income (expense)	5.7	(0.4)
Income before income taxes......................	19.8	7.9
Income tax expense	7.4	4.6
Net income...	12.4 %	3.3 %

Percent of Revenues

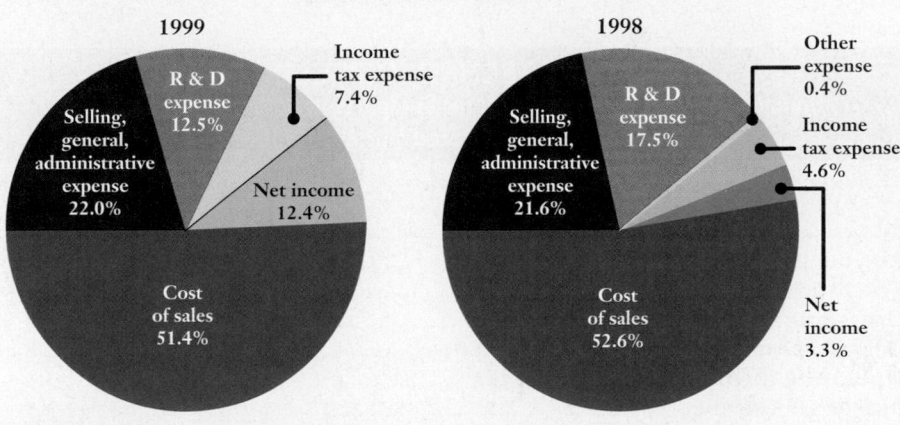

Note: Other income does not appear for 1999 because it is an income amount.
As a result, the percentages do not total to 100%.

Calculate common-size percentages for the income statement below:

Net sales..................................	$150,000
Cost of goods sold................	60,000
Gross profit	90,000
Operating expense................	40,000
Operating income	50,000
Income tax expense.............	15,000
Net income	$ 35,000

Answer:

Net sales	100%	(= $150,000 ÷ $150,000)
Cost of goods sold	40	(= $ 60,000 ÷ $150,000)
Gross margin	60	(= $ 90,000 ÷ $150,000)
Operating expense	27	(= $ 40,000 ÷ $150,000)
Operating income	33	(= $ 50,000 ÷ $150,000)
Income tax expense	10	(= $ 15,000 ÷ $150,000)
Net income.............................	23 %	(= $ 35,000 ÷ $150,000)

BENCHMARKING. The practice of comparing a company to a standard set by other companies, with a view toward improvement.

BENCHMARKING

Benchmarking is the practice of comparing a company to a standard set by other companies, with a view toward improvement.

Benchmarking Against the Industry Average

A company's financial statements show past results and help investors predict future performance. Still, that knowledge is limited to that one company. We may learn that research and development (R&D) decreased and that net income increased last year. This information is helpful, but it does not consider how businesses in the same industry have fared over the same time period. Have other companies in the same line of business also decreased R&D? Is there an industry-wide increase in net income? Managers, investors, creditors, and other interested parties need to know how one company compares with other companies in the same line of business.

Exhibit 18-6 compares the common-size income statement of **Lucent Technologies** with the average for the communications industry. This analysis compares Lucent with all other companies in its line of business. The industry averages were adapted from Robert Morris Associates' *Annual Statement Studies*. Analysts at **Merrill Lynch, Edward Jones,** and other companies specialize in a particular industry and make such comparisons in deciding which companies' stocks to buy or sell.

EXHIBIT 18-6
Common-Size Income Statement of Lucent Technologies Compared with the Industry Average

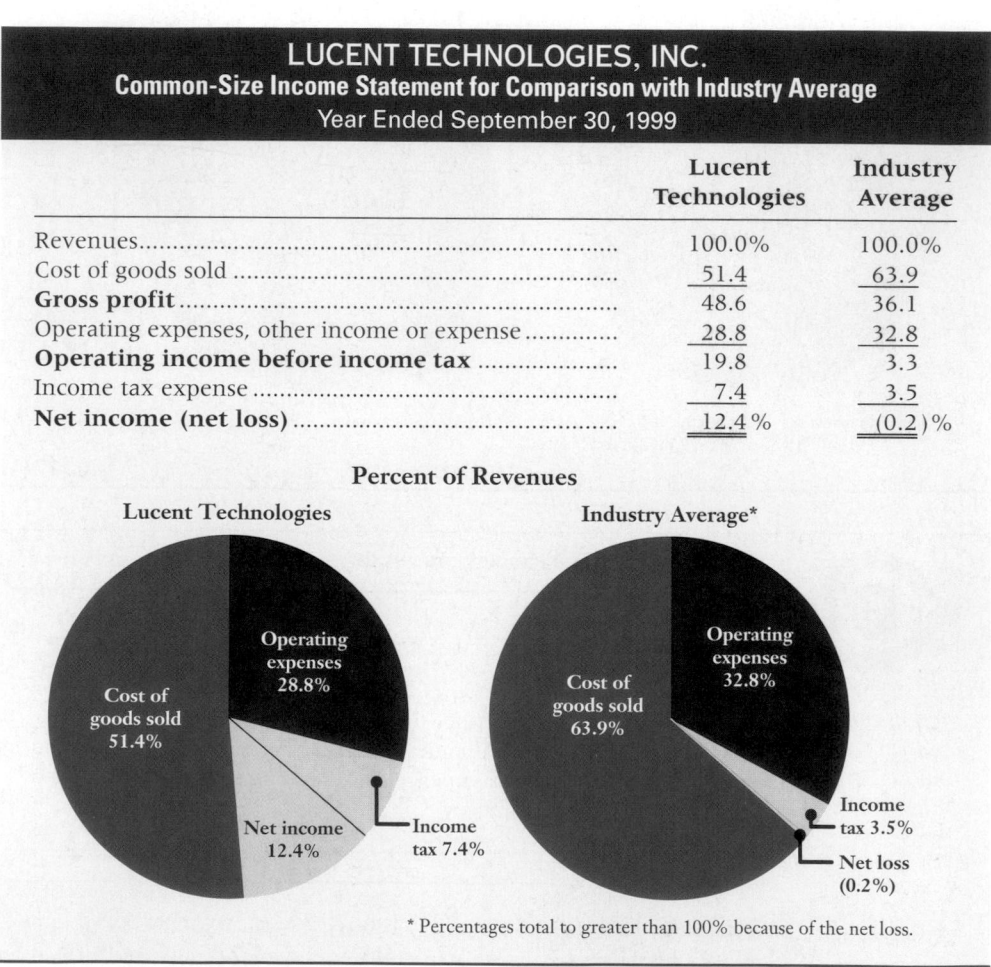

LUCENT TECHNOLOGIES, INC.
Common-Size Income Statement for Comparison with Industry Average
Year Ended September 30, 1999

	Lucent Technologies	Industry Average
Revenues	100.0%	100.0%
Cost of goods sold	51.4	63.9
Gross profit	48.6	36.1
Operating expenses, other income or expense	28.8	32.8
Operating income before income tax	19.8	3.3
Income tax expense	7.4	3.5
Net income (net loss)	12.4%	(0.2)%

Percent of Revenues

Lucent Technologies

Industry Average*

Operating expenses 28.8%
Cost of goods sold 51.4%
Net income 12.4%
Income tax 7.4%

Operating expenses 32.8%
Cost of goods sold 63.9%
Income tax 3.5%
Net loss (0.2%)

*Percentages total to greater than 100% because of the net loss.

Exhibit 18-6 shows that Lucent Technologies is much more profitable than competing companies in its industry. Its gross profit percentage is much higher, and its percentage of revenues siphoned off by operating expenses is lower, than the industry average. The company does a good job of controlling total expenses, and as a result, its net income percentage is significantly above the industry average.

Benchmarking Against Another Company

Common-size statements are also used to compare individual companies. Suppose you are a member of Clint Herzog's team at Marquardt Pennile. You are considering an investment in the stock of either **Lucent Technologies** or **MCI**

(text continues on page 720)

LUCENT TECHNOLOGIES AND MCI WORLDCOM
Common-Size Income Statement (Adapted)
Fiscal Year 1999

	Lucent Technologies	MCI WorldCom
Revenues	100.0%	100.0%
Cost of goods (or services)	51.4	43.0
Gross profit	48.6	57.0
Operating expenses	28.8	38.2
Operating income, before income tax	19.8	18.8
Income tax expense	7.4	8.0
Net income	12.4%	10.8%

Percent of Revenues

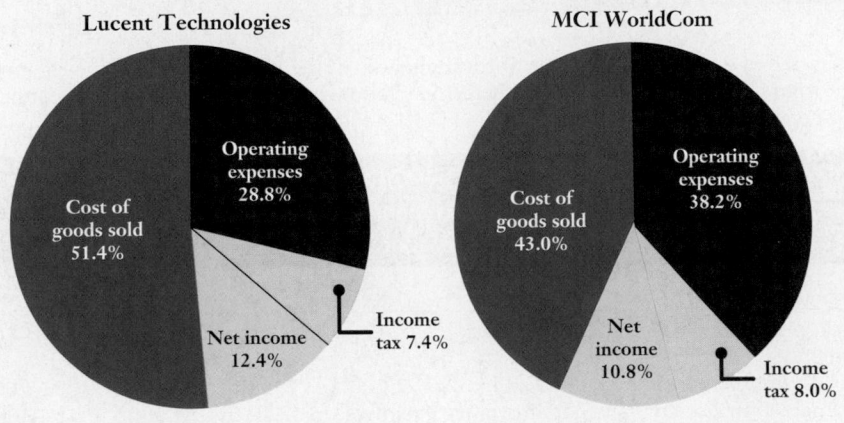

Lucent Technologies — Operating expenses 28.8%; Cost of goods sold 51.4%; Net income 12.4%; Income tax 7.4%

MCI WorldCom — Operating expenses 38.2%; Cost of goods sold 43.0%; Net income 10.8%; Income tax 8.0%

e-Accounting

Peer Performance: Benchmarking on the Web

The Internet makes many accounting functions that were once time-consuming and tedious incredibly quick and easy. The Internet also helps with benchmarking, the practice of systematically comparing your company with a leader. In April 2000, **Fourth Shift Corp.** and **Grant Thornton LLP** announced the creation of a free financial benchmarking service on the Web. The site lets manufacturers and service providers evaluate such variables as days' sales in receivables, inventory turnover, and other ratios. **BenchmarkReport. com** lists three reasons to use benchmark ratios: (1) to set goals and action programs,

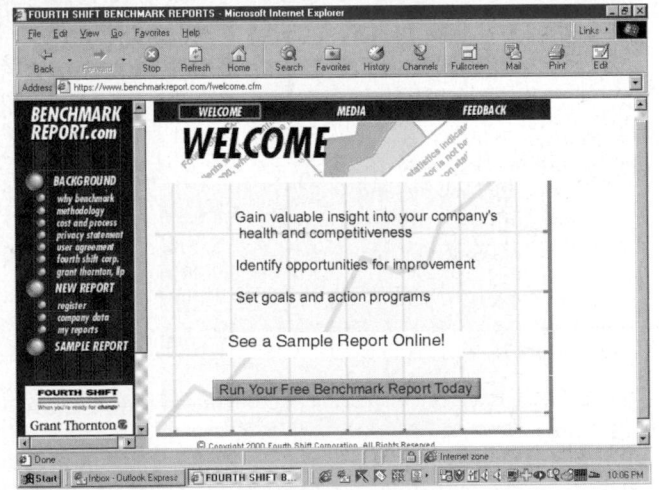

(2) to monitor performance, and (3) to share the results with others. Current and future stakeholders of the company can objectively compare a company's condition against a key competitor. Finance professionals can also use them to benchmark data.

Source: Based on Anonymous, "Online benchmarking service launched," *Electronic Buyers' News*, April 17, 2000, p. 70. Christine A. Gattenio, "Beyond lean & mean," *Electric Perspectives*, May/June 2000, pp. 40–52. And information from www.BenchmarkReport.com.

WorldCom. To compare the companies, you can convert their income statements to common size.

Exhibit 18-7 on page 719 presents the common-size income statements of Lucent Technologies and MCI WorldCom. MCI WorldCom serves as an excellent benchmark because it also operates in the communications industry. In this comparison, Lucent Technologies has the higher percentage of net income. Otherwise, the two companies are quite similar.

MID-CHAPTER

SUMMARY PROBLEM

www.prenhall.com/horngren

Mid-Chapter Assessment

Perform a horizontal analysis and a vertical analysis of the comparative income statement of TRE Corporation, which makes metal detectors. State whether 20X3 was a good year or a bad year, and give your reasons.

TRE CORPORATION
Comparative Income Statement
Months Ended December 31, 20X3 and 20X2

	20X3	20X2
Total revenues	$275,000	$225,000
Expenses:		
Cost of products sold	$194,000	$165,000
Engineering, selling, and administrative expenses	54,000	48,000
Interest expense	5,000	5,000
Income tax expense	9,000	3,000
Other expense (income)	1,000	(1,000)
Total expenses	263,000	220,000
Net earnings	$ 12,000	$ 5,000

Solution

TRE CORPORATION
Horizontal Analysis of Comparative Income Statement
Months Ended December 31, 20X3 and 20X2

			Increase (Decrease)	
	20X3	20X2	Amount	Percent
Total revenues	$275,000	$225,000	$50,000	22.2%
Expenses:				
Cost of products sold	$194,000	$165,000	$29,000	17.6
Engineering, selling, and administrative expenses	54,000	48,000	6,000	12.5
Interest expense	5,000	5,000	—	—
Income tax expense	9,000	3,000	6,000	200.0
Other expense (income)	1,000	(1,000)	2,000	—*
Total expenses	263,000	220,000	43,000	19.5
Net earnings	$ 12,000	$ 5,000	$ 7,000	140.0%

* Percentage changes are typically not computed for shifts from a negative amount to a positive amount, and vice versa.

The horizontal analysis shows that total revenues increased 22.2%. This increase was greater than the 19.5% increase in total expenses, resulting in a 140% increase in net earnings.

The vertical analysis shows that cost of products sold decreased from 73.3% to 70.5% of revenues, and engineering, selling, and administrative expenses decreased from 21.3% to 19.6%. These two items are TRE's largest expenses, so their decreases are important. The reduction in these expenses raised December 20X3 net earnings to 4.4% of sales, compared with 2.2% the preceding December. Overall, December 20X3 was much better than December 20X2.

TRE CORPORATION
Vertical Analysis of Comparative Income Statement
Months Ended December 31, 20X3 and 20X2

	20X3 Amount	20X3 Percent	20X2 Amount	20X2 Percent
Total revenues...............................	$275,000	100.0%	$225,000	100.0%
Expenses:				
Cost of products sold..................	$194,000	70.5	$165,000	73.3
Engineering, selling, and				
administrative expenses.........	54,000	19.6	48,000	21.3
Interest expense.........................	5,000	1.8	5,000	2.2
Income tax expense...................	9,000	3.3	3,000	1.4*
Other expense (income)............	1,000	0.4	(1,000)	(0.4)
Total expenses........................	263,000	95.6	220,000	97.8
Net earnings.................................	$ 12,000	4.4%	$ 5,000	2.2%

* Number rounded up.

USING RATIOS TO MAKE BUSINESS DECISIONS

Objective 4
Compute the standard financial ratios

Ratios play an important part in financial analysis. A ratio is a useful way to show the relationship of one number to another number. For example, if the balance sheet shows current assets of $100,000 and current liabilities of $50,000, the ratio of current assets to current liabilities is $100,000 to $50,000. We simplify this numerical expression to 2 to 1, which may also be written 2:1 and 2/1. Other acceptable ways of expressing this ratio include (1) "current assets are 200% of current liabilities," (2) "the business has two dollars in current assets for every one dollar in current liabilities," or simply, (3) "the current ratio is 2.0."

We often reduce the ratio fraction by writing the ratio as one figure over the other—for example, 2/1—and then dividing the numerator by the denominator. In this way, the ratio 2/1 may be expressed simply as 2. The 1 that represents the denominator of the fraction is understood, not written. Consider the ratio $175,000:$165,000. After dividing the first figure by the second, we come to 1.06:1, which we state as 1.06. The second part of the ratio, the 1, is understood.

A manager, lender, or financial analyst may use any ratio that is relevant to a particular decision. Many companies include ratios in a special section of their annual reports. **Rubbermaid, Inc.**—the manufacturer of plastic products for home, office, and industry—displays ratio data in the financial summary section of its annual report. Exhibit 18-8 shows an excerpt from that summary section.

EXHIBIT 18-8 **Financial Summary of Rubbermaid, Inc. (Dollar Amounts in Thousands Except Per-Share Amounts)**

Years Ended December 31,	20X1	20X0	19X9	19X8
Operating Results				
Net earnings...	$211,413	$164,095	$162,650	$143,520
Earnings per common share............................	$1.32	$1.02	$1.02	$0.90
Percent of sales...	10.8%	9.1%	9.8%	9.4%
Return on average shareholders' equity..............	20.0%	17.5%	19.7%	20.2%
Financial Position				
Current assets...	$829,744	$699,650	$663,999	$602,697
Current liabilities..	$259,314	$223,246	$245,500	$235,300
Current ratio...	3.20	3.13	2.70	2.56

Investment services—**Moody's, Standard & Poor's, Robert Morris Associates,** and others—report these ratios for companies and industries.

The Decision Guidelines feature on page 733 summarizes the ratios we discuss in this chapter. The ratios may be classified as follows:

1. Ratios that measure the company's ability to pay current liabilities
2. Ratios that measure the company's ability to sell inventory and collect receivables
3. Ratios that measure the company's ability to pay short-term and long-term debt
4. Ratios that measure the company's profitability
5. Ratios used to analyze the company's stock as an investment

How much can a computer help in analyzing financial statements for investment purposes? Time yourself as you perform one of the financial-ratio problems in this chapter. Multiply your efforts by, say, 100 companies that you are comparing by means of this ratio. Now consider ranking these 100 companies on the basis of four or five additional ratios.

On-line financial databases, such as **Lexis/Nexis** and the **Dow Jones NewsRetrieval Service,** offer quarterly financial figures for thousands of corporations going back as far as ten years. Assume you want to compare companies' recent earnings histories. You might have the computer compare hundreds of companies on the basis of their price/earnings ratio and rate of return on stockholders' equity. The computer could then give you the names of the 20 (or however many) companies that appear most favorable in terms of these ratios.

Measuring Ability to Pay Current Liabilities

Working capital is defined as follows:

WORKING CAPITAL. Current assets minus current liabilities; measures a business's ability to meet its short-term obligations with its current assets.

Working capital = Current assets – Current Liabilities

Working capital is widely used to measure ability to pay current liabilities with current assets. In general, the larger the working capital, the better able the business is to pay its debt. Recall that capital (owners' equity) is total assets minus total liabilities. Working capital is like a "current" version of total capital. The working-capital amount considered alone does not give a complete picture of the entity's working-capital position, however. Consider two companies with equal working capital:

	Company A	Company B
Current assets	$100,000	$200,000
Less: Current liabilities..............	(50,000)	(150,000)
Working capital........................	$ 50,000	$ 50,000

Both companies have working capital of $50,000, but Company A's working capital is as large as its current liabilities. Company B's working capital is only one-third as large as its current liabilities. Which business has the better working-capital position? Company A, because its working capital is a higher percentage of current assets and current liabilities. Two decision-making tools based on working-capital data are the *current ratio* and the *acid-test ratio*.

CURRENT RATIO. Total current assets divided by total current liabilities. Measures the ability to pay current liabilities from current assets.

CURRENT RATIO The most common ratio using current-asset and current-liability data is the **current ratio,** which is total current assets divided by total current liabilities. ⟵ Recall the makeup of current assets and current liabilities. Current assets consist of cash, short-term investments, net receivables, inventory, and prepaid expenses. Current liabilities include accounts payable, short-term notes payable, unearned revenues, and all types of accrued liabilities. The current ratio measures the company's ability to pay current liabilities with current assets.

➡ We introduced the current ratio in Chapter 4 (p. 141).

Exhibits 18-9 and 18-10 give the comparative income statement and balance sheet of Palisades Furniture, Inc., respectively. The current ratios of Palisades Furniture at December 31, 20X2 and 20X1, follow, along with the average for the retail furniture industry, a benchmark for evaluating Palisades Furniture's ratios.

	Formula	Palisades' Current Ratio		Industry Average
		20X2	20X1	
Current ratio =	$\dfrac{\text{Total current assets}}{\text{Total current liabilities}}$	$\dfrac{\$262,000}{\$142,000} = 1.85$	$\dfrac{\$236,000}{\$126,000} = 1.87$	1.80

PALISADES FURNITURE, INC.
Comparative Income Statement
Years Ended September 30, 20X2 and 20X1

Exhibit 18-9
Comparative Income Statement

	20X2	20X1
Net sales	$858,000	$803,000
Cost of goods sold	513,000	509,000
Gross profit	345,000	294,000
Operating expenses:		
Selling expenses	126,000	114,000
General expenses	118,000	123,000
Total operating expenses	244,000	237,000
Income from operations	101,000	57,000
Interest revenue	4,000	—
Interest expense	(24,000)	(14,000)
Income before income taxes	81,000	43,000
Income tax expense	33,000	17,000
Net income	$ 48,000	$ 26,000

PALISADES FURNITURE, INC.
Comparative Balance Sheet
September 30, 20X2 and 20X1

Exhibit 18-10
Comparative Balance Sheet

	20X2	20X1
Assets		
Current assets:		
Cash	$ 29,000	$ 32,000
Accounts receivable, net	114,000	85,000
Inventories	113,000	111,000
Prepaid expenses	6,000	8,000
Total current assets	262,000	236,000
Long-term investments	18,000	9,000
Property, plant, and equipment, net	507,000	399,000
Total assets	$787,000	$644,000
Liabilities		
Current liabilities:		
Notes payable	$ 42,000	$ 27,000
Accounts payable	73,000	68,000
Accrued liabilities	27,000	31,000
Total current liabilities	142,000	126,000
Long-term debt	289,000	198,000
Total liabilities	431,000	324,000
Stockholders' Equity		
Common stock, no par	186,000	186,000
Retained earnings	170,000	134,000
Total stockholders' equity	356,000	320,000
Total liabilities and stockholders' equity	$787,000	$644,000

 DAILY EXERCISE 18-9

The current ratio decreased slightly during 20X2. In general, a higher current ratio indicates a stronger financial position. A igher current ratio suggests that the business has sufficient liquid assets to maintain normal business operations. Compare Palisades Furniture's current ratio of 1.85 with the industry average of 1.80 and with the current ratios of some well-known companies:

Company	Current Ratio
Lucent Technologies..............	1.86
Wal-Mart Stores	1.26
MCI WorldCom	0.60

What is an acceptable current ratio? The answer depends on the nature of the industry. **Lucent Technologies'** current ratio of 1.86 is similar to that of Palisades Furniture, even though the two companies operate in different industries, **MCI WorldCom** has a very low current ratio. Apparently this is okay because MCI collects cash monthly from millions of long-distance customers. The norm for companies in most industries is between 1.40 and 1.70. A current ratio of 2.0 is considered very strong.

ACID-TEST RATIO. Ratio of the sum of cash plus short-term investments plus net current receivables to current liabilities. Tells whether the entity could pay all its current liabilities if they came due immediately. Also called the quick ratio.

➤ We saw in Chapter 8 (pp. 326–327) that the higher the acid-test ratio, the better able the business is to pay its current liabilities

ACID-TEST RATIO The **acid-test** (or **quick**) **ratio** tells us whether the entity could pay all its current liabilities if they came due immediately. ◄ That is, could the company pass this *acid test*? To do so, the company would have to convert its most liquid assets to cash.

To compute the acid-test ratio, we add cash, short-term investments, and net current receivables (accounts and notes receivable, net of allowances) and divide by total current liabilities. Inventory and prepaid expenses are *not* included because a business cannot convert these assets to cash immediately to pay current liabilities.

Palisades Furniture's acid-test ratios for 20X2 and 20X1 are as follows:

	Formula	Palisades' Current Ratio		Industry Average
		20X2	**20X1**	
Acid-test ratio =	$\dfrac{\text{Cash + Short-term investments + Net current receivables}}{\text{Total current liabilities}}$	$\dfrac{\$29,000 + \$0 + \$114,000}{\$142,000} = 1.01$	$\dfrac{\$32,000 + \$0 + \$85,000}{\$126,000} = 0.93$	0.60

The company's acid-test ratio improved considerably during 20X2 and is significantly better than the industry average. Compare Palisades' 1.01 acid-test ratio with those of three well-known companies:

DAILY EXERCISE 18-10

Company	Acid-Test Ratio
Lucent Technologies..............	1.04
Wal-Mart Stores	0.18
MCI WorldCom	0.39

How can leading companies such as **Wal-Mart** and **MCI WorldCom** function with such low acid-test ratios? Wal-Mart has almost no receivables. Its inventory is priced low to turn over very quickly. MCI WorldCom holds no inventory and collects cash monthly from millions of customers. The norm for the acid-test ratio ranges from 0.20 for high-tech companies to 1.00 for manufacturers of paperboard containers and certain other equipment. An acid-test ratio of 0.90 to 1.00 is safe in most industries.

THINK IT OVER

Palisades Furniture's 20X2 current ratio is 1.85, which looks strong, and its acid-test ratio is 1.01, also strong. Suppose Palisades' acid-test ratio is low, say 0.48. What would be the most likely reason for the difference between a strong current ratio and a weak acid-test ratio?

Answer: It would appear that the company is having trouble selling its inventory. The level of inventory must be relatively high, and the inventory is propping up the current ratio. The rate of inventory turnover may be low.

Measuring Ability to Sell Inventory and Collect Receivables

The ability to sell inventory and collect receivables is fundamental to business success. Recall the operating cycle of a merchandiser: cash to inventory to receivables and back to cash. In this section, we discuss three ratios that measure the company's ability to sell inventory and collect receivables.

INVENTORY TURNOVER   **Inventory turnover** is a measure of the number of times a company sells its average level of inventory during a year. ➔ In general, companies prefer a high rate of inventory turnover. An inventory turnover of 6 means that the company sells its average level of inventory six times during the year. This is generally better than a turnover of 3 or 4. But a high value can mean the business is not keeping enough inventory on hand, and that can result in lost sales if the company cannot meet a customer's need. Therefore, a business strives for the *most profitable* rate of inventory turnover, not necessarily the *highest* rate.

To compute the inventory turnover ratio, we divide cost of goods sold by the average inventory for the period. We use the cost of goods sold—not sales—in the computation because both cost of goods sold and inventory are stated *at cost*. Sales is stated at the sales value of inventory and therefore is not comparable with inventory cost.

Palisades Furniture's inventory turnover for 20X2 is

◄ We introduced inventory turnover in Chapter 5, pp. 186–188. Average inventory is computed as follows: (Beginning inventory + Ending inventory)/2.

INVENTORY TURNOVER. Ratio of cost of goods sold to average inventory. Measures the number of times a company sells its average level of inventory during a year.

Formula	Palisades' Inventory Turnover	Industry Average
Inventory turnover = $\dfrac{\text{Cost of goods sold}}{\text{Average inventory}}$	$\dfrac{\$513,000}{\$112,000} = 4.58$	2.70

Cost of goods sold appears in the income statement (Exhibit 18-9). Average inventory is figured by averaging the beginning inventory ($111,000) and ending inventory ($113,000). (See the balance sheet, Exhibit 18-10.)

Inventory turnover varies widely with the nature of the business. For example, companies that remove natural gas from the ground hold their inventory for a very short period of time and have an average turnover of 30. Palisades Furniture's turnover of 4.58 times a year is high for the retail furniture industry, which has an average turnover of 2.70. Palisades' high turnover results from its policy of keeping little inventory. The company takes customer orders and has its suppliers ship directly to customers.

Inventory turnover rates can vary greatly within a company. At **Toys "Я" Us,** diapers and formula turn over more than 12 times a year, while seasonal toys turn over less than 3 times a year. The entire Toys "Я" Us inventory turns over an average of 4 times a year.

To evaluate a company's inventory turnover, we must compare the ratio over time. A sudden sharp decline or a steady decline over a long period suggests the need for corrective action.

ACCOUNTS RECEIVABLE TURNOVER   **Accounts receivable turnover** measures a company's ability to collect cash from customers. In general, the higher the ratio, the more successfully the business collects cash. To compute the accounts receivable turnover, we divide net credit sales by average net accounts receivable. The resulting ratio indicates how many times during the year the average level of receivables was turned into cash.

ACCOUNTS RECEIVABLE TURNOVER. Ratio of net credit sales to average net accounts receivable. Measures ability to collect cash from customers.

Palisades Furniture's accounts receivable turnover ratio for 20X2 is computed as follows:

Formula	Palisades' Accounts Receivable Turnover	Industry Average
Accounts receivable turnover $= \dfrac{\text{Net credit sales}}{\text{Average net accounts receivable}}$	$\dfrac{\$858,000}{\$99,500} = 8.62$ times	22.2 times

The net credit sales figure comes from the income statement. Average net accounts receivable is figured by adding the beginning accounts receivable balance ($85,000) and the ending balance ($114,000), then dividing by 2.

Palisades' receivable turnover of 8.62 is much lower than the industry average. The explanation is this: Palisades is a home-town store that sells to local people who tend to pay their bills over a long period of time. Many larger furniture stores have tighter credit policies and collect their receivables faster.

DAYS' SALES IN RECEIVABLES Businesses must convert accounts receivable to cash. All else equal, the lower the Accounts Receivable balance, the more successful the business has been in converting receivables into cash, and the better off the business is.

The **days'-sales-in-receivables** ratio tells us how many days' sales remain in Accounts Receivable. To compute the ratio, we follow a two-step process. First, divide net sales by 365 days to figure the average sales amount for one day. Second, divide this average day's sales amount into the average net accounts receivable.

The data to compute this ratio for Palisades Furniture, Inc., for 20X2 are taken from the income statement and the balance sheet (Exhibits 18-9 and 18-10):

DAYS' SALES IN RECEIVABLES. Ratio of average net accounts receivable to one day's sales. Tells how many days' sales remain in Accounts Receivable awaiting collection.

Formula	Palisades' Days' Sales in Accounts Receivables	Industry Average
Days' Sales in Accounts Receivable:		
1. One day's sales $= \dfrac{\text{Net sales}}{365 \text{ days}}$	$\dfrac{\$858,000}{365 \text{ days}} = \$2,351$	
2. Days' sales in accounts receivable $= \dfrac{\text{Average net accounts receivable}}{\text{One day's sales}}$	$\dfrac{\$99,500}{\$2,351} = 42$ days	16 days

 DAILY EXERCISE 18-11

Days' sales in receivables can also be computed in a single step: $99,500/ (\$858,000/365 \text{ days}) = 42$ days.

Palisades' ratio tells us that 42 days' sales remained in average accounts receivable during the year. The company will increase its cash flow if it can decrease this ratio.

Measuring Ability to Pay Short-Term and Long-Term Debt

The ratios discussed so far give us insight into current assets and current liabilities. Most businesses also have long-term liabilities. Two measures of a business's ability to pay both short-term and long-term liabilities are the *debt ratio* and the *times-interest-earned ratio*.

DEBT RATIO. Ratio of total liabilities to total assets. Tells the proportion of a company's assets financed with debt.

DEBT RATIO The ratio of total liabilities to total assets—called the **debt ratio**—tells us the proportion of the company's assets financed with debt. If the debt ratio is 1, then debt has been used to finance all the assets. A debt ratio of 0.50 means that the company has financed half its assets with debt and half with owners' equity. The higher the debt ratio, the higher the strain of paying interest each year and the principal amount at maturity. The lower the ratio, the lower the business's future obligations.

Creditors view a high debt ratio with caution. If a business trying to borrow already has large liabilities, then additional debt payments may be too much for it to handle. Creditors generally charge higher interest rates on new borrowing to companies with an already high debt ratio.

Palisades Furniture's debt ratios at the end of 20X2 and 20X1 are as follows:

		Palisades' Debt Ratio		
	Formula	20X2	20X1	Industry Average
Debt ratio =	$\dfrac{\text{Total liabilities}}{\text{Total assets}}$	$\dfrac{\$431,000}{\$787,000} = 0.55$	$\dfrac{\$324,000}{\$644,000} = 0.50$	0.61

Palisades Furniture expanded operations during 20X2 by financing the purchase of property, plant, and equipment through borrowing, which is common. This expansion explains the firm's increased debt ratio. Even after the increase in 20X2, the company's debt is not very high. Robert Morris Associates reports that the average debt ratio for most companies ranges around 0.57–0.67. Palisades' 0.55 debt ratio indicates a fairly low-risk debt position.

TIMES-INTEREST-EARNED RATIO The debt ratio measures the effect of debt on the company's *financial position* (balance sheet). However, the debt ratio says nothing about the ability to pay interest expense. Analysts use a second ratio—the **times-interest-earned ratio**—to relate income to interest expense. To compute this ratio, we divide income from operations by interest expense. This ratio measures the number of times that operating income can *cover* interest expense. For this reason, the ratio is also called the **interest-coverage ratio.** A high times-interest-earned ratio indicates ease in paying interest expense; a low value suggests difficulty.

Palisades' times-interest-earned ratio follows:

> **TIMES-INTEREST-EARNED RATIO.** Ratio of income from operations to interest expense. Measures the number of times operating income can cover interest expense. Also called the **interest-coverage ratio.**

		Palisades' Times-Interest-Earned Ratio		Industry Average
	Formula	20X2	20X1	
Times-interest-earned ratio =	$\dfrac{\text{Income from operations*}}{\text{Interest expense}}$	$\dfrac{\$101,000}{\$24,000} = 4.21 \text{ times}$	$\dfrac{\$57,000}{\$14,000} = 4.07 \text{ times}$	2.00 times

* A company's income statement may not report income from operations. To estimate income from operations, you can add interest expense to income before income tax.

The company's times-interest-earned ratio increased in 20X2. This is a favorable sign, especially since liabilities rose substantially during the year. Palisades Furniture's new plant assets, we conclude, have earned more income than they have cost the business in interest expense. The company's times-interest-earned ratio of around 4.00 is much better than the 2.00 average for furniture retailers. The norm for U.S. business, as reported by Robert Morris Associates, falls in the range of 2.0–3.0 for most companies.

On the basis of its debt ratio and its times-interest-earned ratio, Palisades Furniture appears to have little difficulty *servicing its debt*—that is, paying its liabilities.

 DAILY EXERCISE 18-12

Measuring Profitability

The fundamental goal of business is to earn a profit. Ratios that measure profitability play a large role in decision making. These ratios are reported in the business press, by investment services, and in companies' annual financial reports.

RATE OF RETURN ON NET SALES In business, the term *return* is used broadly and loosely as an evaluation of profitability. Consider a ratio called the **rate of return on net sales,** or simply **return on sales.** (The word *net* is usually omitted for convenience, even though the net sales figure is used to compute the ratio.) This ratio shows the percentage of each sales dollar earned as net income. The rate-of-return-on-sales ratios for Palisades Furniture are calculated as follows:

> **RATE OF RETURN ON NET SALES.** Ratio of net income to net sales. A measure of profitability. Also called return on sales.

Formula		Palisades' Rate of Return on Sales 20X2	20X1	Industry Average
Rate of return on sales =	$\frac{\text{Net income}}{\text{Net sales}}$	$\frac{\$48{,}000}{\$858{,}000} = 0.056$	$\frac{\$26{,}000}{\$803{,}000} = 0.032$	0.008

Companies strive for a high rate of return. The higher the rate of return, the more that sales are providing income to the business and the less of sales that are absorbed by expenses. The increase in Palisades Furniture's return on sales is significant and identifies the company as more successful than the average furniture store. Compare Palisades' rate of return on sales to the rates of some other companies:

Company	Rate of Return on Sales
Lucent Technologies	0.124
General Motors	0.039
Wal-Mart Stores	0.032

As these numbers indicate, the rate of return on sales varies widely from industry to industry.

A return measure can be computed on any revenue and sales amount. Return on net sales, as we have seen, is net income divided by net sales. *Return on total revenues* is net income divided by total revenues. A company can compute a return on other specific portions of revenue as its information needs dictate.

RATE OF RETURN ON TOTAL ASSETS. The sum of net income plus interest expense divided by average total assets. This ratio measures the success a company has in using its assets to earn income for the persons who finance the business. Also called **return on assets.**

We first discussed the rate of return on total assets in Chapter 13, p. 518.

RATE OF RETURN ON TOTAL ASSETS The **rate of return on total assets,** or **return on assets (ROA),** measures a company's success in using its assets to earn a profit. Creditors have loaned money to the company, and the *interest* they receive is the return on their investment. Shareholders have invested in the company's stock, and *net income* is their return. The sum of interest expense and net income is thus the return to the two groups that have financed the company's operations, and this amount is the numerator of the return-on-assets ratio. Average total assets is the denominator. Palisades Furniture's return on total assets is computed as follows:

Formula		Palisades' 20X2 Rate of Return on Total Assets	Industry Average
Rate of return on assets =	$\frac{\text{Net income} + \text{Interest expense}}{\text{Average total assets}}$	$\frac{\$48{,}000 + \$24{,}000}{\$715{,}500} = 0.101$	0.049

Net income and interest expense are taken from the income statement (Exhibit 18-9). To compute average total assets, we take the average of beginning and ending total assets from the comparative balance sheet (Exhibit 18-10). Compare Palisades Furniture's rate of return on assets to the rates of some other companies:

Company	Rate of Return on Assets
Gap, Inc.	0.170
Lucent Technologies	0.140
Wal-Mart Stores	0.110

As you can see, the rate of return on assets varies from industry to industry.

RATE OF RETURN ON COMMON STOCKHOLDERS' EQUITY. Net income minus preferred dividends, divided by average common stockholders' equity. A measure of profitability. Also called **return on stockholders' equity** or **return on equity (ROE).**

RATE OF RETURN ON COMMON STOCKHOLDERS' EQUITY Perhaps the most widely used measure of profitability is **rate of return on common stockholders' equity,**

which is often shortened to **return on stockholders' equity,** or simply **return on equity (ROE).**

◄ We examined this ratio in detail in Chapter 13. For a review, see p. 518.

➥ This ratio shows the relationship between net income and common stockholders' investment in the company—how much income is earned for every $1 invested by the common shareholders. To compute this ratio, we first subtract preferred dividends from net income. This remainder is net income available to the common stockholders. We then divide net income available to common stockholders by the average stockholders' equity during the year. The 20X2 rate of return on common stockholders' equity for Palisades Furniture is calculated as follows:

Formula		Palisades' 20X2 Rate of Return on Common Stockholders' Equity	Industry Average
Rate of return on common stockholders' equity	$= \dfrac{\text{Net income} - \text{Preferred dividends}}{\text{Average common stockholders' equity}}$	$\dfrac{\$48{,}000 - \$0}{\$338{,}000} = 0.142$	0.093

We compute average equity by adding the beginning and ending balances, and then dividing by 2 [($356,000 + $320,000)/2 = $338,000]. Common stockholders' equity is total equity minus preferred equity.

Observe that Palisades' return on equity (14.2%) is higher than its return on assets (10.1%). This difference results from borrowing at one rate—say, 8%—and investing the funds to earn a higher rate, such as the firm's 14.2% return on stockholders' equity. This practice is called **trading on the equity,** or using **leverage.**

 Borrowing

TRADING ON THE EQUITY. Earning more income on borrowed money than the related expense, thereby increasing the earnings for the owners of the business. Also called leverage.

It is critical that a company's return on equity exceed its return on assets—for two reasons:

- The stockholders take more risk and therefore demand a higher return on equity than the company's lenders, who take less risk.
- If return on assets exceeds return on equity, that means the company's lenders are getting a better return than the company's stockholders are getting. If this continues, the stockholders will stop financing the company.

Fortunately, Palisades Furniture's return on equity (14.2%) exceeds its return on assets (10.1%). Let's compare Palisades Furniture's rate of return on equity with the rates of some leading companies:

⊙ DAILY EXERCISE 18-13

Company	Rate of Return on Common Equity
Lucent Technologies	0.45
Wal-Mart Stores......................	0.22
General Motors......................	0.34

Palisades Furniture is not as profitable as these leading companies. Lucent Technologies' high rate of return on equity explains why high-tech companies are so popular with investors.

EARNINGS PER SHARE OF COMMON STOCK *Earnings per share of common stock,* or simply **earnings per share (EPS),** is perhaps the most widely quoted of all financial statistics. ➥ EPS is the only ratio that must appear on the face of the income statement. EPS is the amount of income earned for each share of the company's outstanding *common* stock.

EARNINGS PER SHARE (EPS). Amount of a company's income earned for each share of its outstanding common stock.

Earnings per share is computed by dividing net income available to common stockholders by the number of common shares outstanding during the year. Preferred dividends are subtracted from net income because the preferred stockholders have a prior claim to their dividends. Palisades Furniture, Inc., has no preferred stock outstanding and thus has no preferred dividends. Computation of the firm's EPS for 20X2 and 20X1 follows (the company had 10,000 shares of common stock outstanding throughout 20X1 and 20X2):

◄ Recall from Chapter 14, pp. 556–557, that GAAP requires corporations to report EPS on the income statement.

		Palisades' Earnings Per Share	
	Formula	20X2	20X1
Earnings per share of common stock	$= \dfrac{\text{Net income} - \text{Preferred dividends}}{\text{Number of shares of common stock outstanding}}$	$\dfrac{\$48,000 - \$0}{10,000} = \$4.80$	$\dfrac{\$26,000 - \$0}{10,000} = \$2.60$

Palisades Furniture's EPS increased 85%. Its stockholders should not expect such a large boost in EPS every year. Most companies strive to increase EPS by 10–15% annually, and strong companies do so. But even the most successful companies have an occasional bad year.

Analyzing a Company's Stock as an Investment

Investors purchase stock to earn a return on their investment. This return consists of two parts: (1) gains (or losses) from selling the stock at a price that differs from the investors' purchase price, and (2) dividends, the periodic distributions to stockholders. The ratios we examine in this section help analysts evaluate stock in terms of market price or dividend payments.

PRICE/EARNINGS RATIO. Ratio relates the market price of a share of common stock to the company's earnings per share. Measures the value the stock market places on $1 of a company's earnings.

PRICE/EARNINGS RATIO The **price/earnings (P/E) ratio** relates the market price of a share of common stock to the company's earnings per share. This ratio appears in the *Wall Street Journal* stock listings. P/E ratios play an important part in decisions to buy, hold, and sell stocks. They indicate the market price of $1 of earnings.

Calculations for the P/E ratios of Palisades Furniture, Inc., follow. The market price of its common stock was $58 at the end of 20X2 and $35 at the end of 20X1. These prices can be obtained from a financial publication, a stockbroker, or some other source outside the accounting records.

		Palisades' Price/Earnings Ratio	
	Formula	20X2	20X1
P/E Ratio =	$\dfrac{\text{Market price per share of common stock}}{\text{Earnings per share}}$	$\dfrac{\$58.00}{\$4.80} = 12.1$	$\dfrac{\$35.00}{\$2.60} = 13.5$

● **DAILY EXERCISE 18-14**

● **DAILY EXERCISE 18-15**

A P/E ratio of 12.1 means that Palisades Furniture's stock is selling at 12.1 times earnings. Like most other ratios, P/E ratios vary from industry to industry. P/E ratios range from 8 to 10 for electric utilities (**Pennsylvania Power & Light,** for example) to 40 or more for "glamor stocks" such as **Lucent Technologies** and **Oracle Corporation,** the software company.

DIVIDEND YIELD. Ratio of dividends per share of stock to the stock's market price. Measures the percentage of the stock's market value that the company pays to stockholders as dividends.

DIVIDEND YIELD **Dividend yield** is the ratio of dividends per share of stock to the stock's market price. This ratio measures the percentage of the stock's market value that is returned annually as dividends. *Preferred* stockholders, who invest primarily to receive dividends, pay special attention to dividend yield.

Palisades Furniture paid annual cash dividends of $1.20 per share of common stock in 20X2 and $1.00 in 20X1, and market prices of the company's common stock were $58 in 20X2 and $35 in 20X1. Calculation of the firm's dividend yields on common stock is at the top of the next page.

An investor who buys Palisades Furniture common stock for $58 can expect to receive almost 2.1% of the investment annually in the form of cash dividends. Dividend yields vary widely, from 5% to 8% for older, established firms (such as **Procter & Gamble** and **General Motors**) down to the range of 0–3% for young, growth-oriented companies. **MCI WorldCom,** for example, pays no dividends. Palisades Furniture's dividend yield places the company in the second group.

BOOK VALUE PER SHARE OF COMMON STOCK. Common equity divided by the number of shares of common stock outstanding.

BOOK VALUE PER SHARE OF COMMON STOCK **Book value per share of common stock** is common equity divided by the number of shares of common stock

	Formula	Dividend Yield on Palisades' Common Stock	
		20X2	**20X1**
Dividend yield on common stock*	$= \dfrac{\text{Dividend per share of common stock}}{\text{Market price per share of common stock}}$	$\dfrac{\$1.20}{\$58.00} = 0.021$	$\dfrac{\$1.00}{\$35.00} = \$0.029$

* Dividend yields may also be calculated for preferred stock.

outstanding. Common equity equals total stockholders' equity less preferred equity. Palisades Furniture has no preferred stock outstanding. Calculations of its book value follows. Recall that 10,000 shares of common stock were outstanding at the end of years 20X2 and 20X1.

	Formula	Book Value Per Share of Palisades' Common Stock	
		20X2	**20X1**
Book value per share of common stock	$= \dfrac{\text{Total stockholders' equity} - \text{Preferred equity}}{\text{Number of shares of common stock outstanding}}$	$\dfrac{\$356,000 - \$0}{10,000} = \$35.60$	$\dfrac{\$320,000 - \$0}{10,000} = \$32.00$

Many experts argue that book value is not useful for investment analysis. It bears no relationship to *market value*. But some investors still base their decisions on book value. For example, some analysts rank stocks on the basis of the ratio of market price to book value. By this reasoning, the lower the ratio, the more attractive the stock.

⊙ DAILY EXERCISE 18-16

⊙ DAILY EXERCISE 18-17

⊙ DAILY EXERCISE 18-18

LIMITATIONS OF FINANCIAL ANALYSIS

Objective 5
Use ratios in decision making

Business decisions are made in a world of uncertainty. As useful as ratios are, they have limitations. We can liken their use in decision making to a physician's use of a thermometer. A reading of 101.6°F indicates that something is wrong with the patient, but the temperature alone does not indicate what the problem is or how to cure it.

In financial analysis, a sudden drop in a company's current ratio signals that *something* is wrong, but this change does not identify the problem or show how to correct it. The business manager must analyze the figures that go into the ratio to determine whether current assets have decreased, current liabilities have increased, or both. If current assets have dropped, is the problem a cash shortage? Are accounts receivable down? Are inventories too low?

Only by analyzing the individual items that make up the ratio can the manager determine how to solve the problem. The manager must evaluate data on all ratios in light of other information about the company and about its particular line of business, such as increased competition or a slowdown in the economy.

Legislation, international affairs, competition, scandals, and many other factors can turn profits into losses, and vice versa. To be most useful, ratios should be analyzed over a period of years to take into account a representative group of these factors. Any one year, or even any two years, may not be representative of the company's performance over the long term.

Objective 6
Measure economic value added

Economic Value Added (EVA®)— A New Measure of Performance

ECONOMIC VALUE ADDED (EVA®). Combines accounting income and finance to measure whether the company's operations have increased stockholder wealth.

The top managers of **Coca-Cola, Quaker Oats,** and other leading companies use **economic value added (EVA®)** to evaluate a company's operating performance. EVA® combines accounting and finance to measure whether the company's operations have increased stockholder wealth. EVA® can be computed as follows:

EVA® = Net income + Interest expense − Capital charge

where

$$\text{Capital charge} = \left(\begin{array}{c} \text{Short-term} \\ \text{debt} \end{array} + \begin{array}{c} \text{Long-term} \\ \text{debt} \end{array} + \begin{array}{c} \text{Stockholders'} \\ \text{equity} \end{array} \right) \times \begin{array}{c} \text{Cost of} \\ \text{capital} \end{array}$$

All amounts for the EVA® computation, except the cost of capital, are taken from the financial statements. The **cost of capital** is a weighted average of the returns demanded by the company's stockholders and lenders. The cost of capital varies with the company's level of risk. For example, stockholders would demand a higher return from a start-up computer software company than from **AT&T.** Lenders would also charge the new company a higher interest rate because of this greater risk. Thus, the new company has a higher cost of capital than AT&T. In the following discussions, we assume a value for the cost of capital (such as 10%, 12%, or 15%) to illustrate the computation of EVA®.

The idea behind EVA® is that the returns to the company's stockholders (net income) and to its creditors (interest expense) should exceed the company's capital charge. The **capital charge** is the amount that stockholders and lenders *charge* a company for the use of their money. A positive EVA® amount indicates an increase in stockholder wealth, and the company's stock price should rise. If the EVA® measure is negative, the stockholders will probably be unhappy with the company's progress and sell its stock.

Let's apply EVA® to **Lucent Technologies.** Lucent's EVA® for 1999 can be computed as follows, assuming a 12% cost of capital for the company (dollar amounts in millions):

$$\text{Lucent's EVA}^® = \begin{array}{c} \text{Net} \\ \text{income} \end{array} + \begin{array}{c} \text{Interest} \\ \text{expense} \end{array} - \left[\left(\begin{array}{c} \text{Short-term} \\ \text{debt} \end{array} + \begin{array}{c} \text{Long-term} \\ \text{debt} \end{array} + \begin{array}{c} \text{Stockholders'} \\ \text{equity} \end{array} \right) \times \begin{array}{c} \text{Cost of} \\ \text{capital} \end{array} \right]$$

$$= \$4,766 + \$406^* - [(\$2,864 + \$4,162 + \$13,584) \times 0.12]$$

$$= \$5,172 - \$20,610 \times 0.12$$

$$= \$5,172 - \$2,473$$

$$= \$2,699$$

*Included as part of Other income (expense) on the company's income statement (as adapted) in this chapter.

○ **DAILY EXERCISE 18-19**

By this measure, Lucent Technologies' operations during 1999 added $2.7 billion ($2,699 million) of value to its stockholders' wealth after meeting the company's capital charge. This performance is outstanding. Lucent's positive EVA® explains why the company's stock is popular with investors.

Efficient Markets, Management Action, and Investor Decisions

An **efficient capital market** is one in which market prices reflect the impact of all information available to the public. Market efficiency means that managers cannot fool the market with accounting gimmicks. If the information is available, the market as a whole can translate accounting data into a "fair" price for the company's stock.

Suppose you are the president of Anacomp Company. Reported earnings per share are $4, and the stock price is $40—so the P/E ratio is 10. You believe the corporation's stock is underpriced in comparison with other companies in your industry. To correct this situation, you are considering changing from accelerated to straight-line depreciation. The accounting change will increase earnings per share to $5. Will the stock price then rise to $50? Probably not. The stock price will probably remain at $40 because the market can understand the change in depreciation method, not improved operations, caused earnings to increase.

In an efficient market, the search for "underpriced" stock is fruitless unless the investor has private information. But it is unlawful to invest on the basis of *inside* information. For outside investors, an appropriate strategy seeks to manage risk, diversify investments so that you don't lose everything if one stock goes bad, and minimize transaction costs. The role of financial statement analysis is mainly to help measure the risks of various stocks. The goal is to manage the risk of the overall investment portfolio.

Managers, owners, investors, and creditors all use financial ratios to measure an entity's progress. The Decision Guidelines feature summarizes the ratios covered in this chapter. Memorize each ratio's computation and the information it provides because you will be using these ratios for the rest of your life.

COST OF CAPITAL. A weighted average of the returns demanded by a company's stockholders and lenders.

CAPITAL CHARGE. The amount that stockholders and lenders charge a company for the use of their money.

EFFICIENT CAPITAL MARKET. A capital market in which market prices reflect the impact of all information available to the public.

DECISION GUIDELINES

Using Ratios in Financial Statement Analysis

RATIO	COMPUTATION	INFORMATION PROVIDED

Measuring the company's ability to pay current liabilities:

1. Current ratio	$\dfrac{\text{Total current assets}}{\text{Total current liabilities}}$	Measures ability to pay current liabilities with current assets.
2. Acid-test (quick) ratio	$\dfrac{\text{Cash} + \text{Short-term investments} + \text{Net current receivables}}{\text{Total current liabilities}}$	Shows ability to pay all current liabilities if they come due immediately.

Measuring the company's ability to sell inventory and collect receivables:

3. Inventory turnover	$\dfrac{\text{Cost of goods sold}}{\text{Average inventory}}$	Indicates saleability of inventory—the number of times a company sells its average inventory level during a year.
4. Accounts receivable turnover	$\dfrac{\text{Net credit sales}}{\text{Average net accounts receivable}}$	Measures ability to collect cash from credit customers.
5. Days' sales in receivables	$\dfrac{\text{Average net accounts receivable}}{\text{One day's sales}}$	Shows how many days' sales remain in Accounts Receivable—how many days it takes to collect the average level of receivables.

Measuring the company's ability to pay short-term and long-term debt:

6. Debt ratio	$\dfrac{\text{Total liabilities}}{\text{Total assets}}$	Indicates percentage of assets financed with debt.
7. Times-interest-earned ratio	$\dfrac{\text{Income from operations}}{\text{Interest expense}}$	Measures the number of times operating income can cover interest expense.

Measuring the company's profitability:

8. Rate of return on net sales	$\dfrac{\text{Net income}}{\text{Net sales}}$	Shows the percentage of each sales dollar earned as net income.
9. Rate of return on total assets	$\dfrac{\text{Net income} + \text{Interest expense}}{\text{Average total assets}}$	Measures how profitably a company uses its assets.
10. Rate of return on common stockholders' equity	$\dfrac{\text{Net income} - \text{Preferred dividends}}{\text{Average common stockholders' equity}}$	Gauges how much income is earned with the money invested by common shareholders.
11. Earnings per share of common stock	$\dfrac{\text{Net income} - \text{Preferred dividends}}{\text{Number of shares of common stock outstanding}}$	Gives the amount of net income earned for each share of the company's common stock.

Analyzing the company's stock as an investment:

12. Price/earnings ratio	$\dfrac{\text{Market price per share of common stock}}{\text{Earnings per share}}$	Indicates the market price of $1 of earnings.
13. Dividend yield	$\dfrac{\text{Dividends per share of common (or preferred) stock}}{\text{Market price per share of common (or preferred) stock}}$	Shows the percentage of a stock's market value returned to stockholders as dividends each period.
14. Book value per share of common stock	$\dfrac{\text{Total stockholders' equity} - \text{Preferred equity}}{\text{Number of shares of common stock outstanding}}$	Indicates the recorded accounting amount for each share of common stock outstanding.

EXCEL APPLICATION PROBLEM

Goal: Create an Excel spreadsheet that calculates financial ratios to compare **Gap Inc.,** and **Lands' End.** Then use the results to determine which company has the stronger financial performance.

Scenario: You've recently received a $1,000 bonus from your employer, Gap Inc. You've been thinking about investing the bonus in the stock of your employer, but your parents think that Lands' End is the better investment.

Before making your purchase, your task is to create an Excel spreadsheet to compare the following ratios for Gap and Lands' End:
1. Acid-test (quick) ratio
2. Inventory turnover
3. Times-interest-earned ratio
4. Return on net sales

When done with the spreadsheet, answer the following questions:
1. Which company is in a better position to pay all current liabilities if they come due immediately?
2. Which company moves its inventory faster?
3. Which company can cover its interest expense better?
4. Which company earned more profit, as a percentage, on each sales dollar?

Step-by-step:

1. Locate the data required for each ratio in the annual reports of Gap and Lands' End. These reports may be accessed via the Web.
2. Open a new Excel spreadsheet.
3. Create a boldfaced heading for your spreadsheet that contains the following:
   a. Chapter 18 Decision Guidelines
   b. Using Ratios in Financial Statement Analysis
   c. Gap and Lands' End Comparison
   d. Today's date
4. In the first column, enter the names of all four ratios. Skip a row between each ratio name.
5. Create boldfaced, underlined column headings for Gap and Lands' End.
6. Enter the data located in step 1, using the correct ratio formulas found in the Decision Guidelines. Format all cells as necessary.
7. Save your work, and print a copy for your files.

REVIEW FINANCIAL STATEMENT ANALYSIS

SUMMARY PROBLEM

The following financial data are adapted from the annual report of **Gap Inc.,** which operates Gap, Banana Republic, and Old Navy clothing stores.

GAP INC. Five-Year Selected Financial Data					
Operating Results (in millions)	**19X9**	**19X8**	**19X7**	**19X6**	**19X5**
Net sales	$2,960	$2,519	$1,934	$1,587	$1,252
Cost of goods sold and occupancy expenses, excluding depreciation and amortization	1,856	1,496	1,188	1,007	814
Interest expense (net)	4	4	1	3	3
Income from operations	340	371	237	163	126
Income taxes	129	141	92	65	52
Net earnings	211	230	145	98	74
Cash dividends	44	41	30	23	18
Financial Position					
Merchandise inventory	366	314	247	243	193
Total assets	1,379	1,147	777	579	481
Working capital	355	236	579	129	434
Stockholders' equity	888	678	466	338	276
Current ratio	2.06:1	1.71:1	1.39:1	1.69:1	1.70:1
Average number of shares of common stock outstanding (in thousands)	144	142	142	141	145

www.prenhall.com/horngren

End-of-Chapter Assessment

Required

Compute the following ratios for 19X9–19X6, and evaluate Gap's operating results. Are operating results strong or weak? Did they improve or deteriorate during the four-year period?

a. Gross profit percentage
b. Net income as a percentage of sales
c. Earnings per share

d. Inventory turnover
e. Times-interest-earned ratio
f. Rate of return on stockholders' equity

Solution

Requirement	19X9	19X8	19X7	19X6
a. Gross profit percentage	$\dfrac{\$2,960 - \$1,856}{\$2,960}$ $= 37.3\%$	$\dfrac{\$2,519 - \$1,496}{\$2,519}$ $= 40.6\%$	$\dfrac{\$1,934 - \$1,188}{\$1,934}$ $= 38.6\%$	$\dfrac{\$1,587 - \$1,007}{\$1,587}$ $= 36.5\%$
b. Net income as a percentage of sales	$\dfrac{\$211}{\$2,960} = 7.1\%$	$\dfrac{\$230}{\$2,519} = 9.1\%$	$\dfrac{\$145}{\$1,934} = 7.5\%$	$\dfrac{\$98}{\$1,587} = 6.2\%$
c. Earnings per share	$\dfrac{\$211}{144} = \$1.47$	$\dfrac{\$230}{142} = \$1.62$	$\dfrac{\$145}{142} = \$1.02$	$\dfrac{\$98}{141} = \$0.70$
d. Inventory turnover	$\dfrac{\$1,856}{(\$366 + \$314)/2}$ $= 5.5$ times	$\dfrac{\$1,496}{(\$314 + \$247)/2}$ $= 5.3$ times	$\dfrac{\$1,188}{(\$247 + \$243)/2}$ $= 4.8$ times	$\dfrac{\$1,007}{(\$243 + \$193)/2}$ $= 4.6$ times
e. Times-interest-earned ratio	$\dfrac{\$340}{\$4} = 85$ times	$\dfrac{\$371}{\$4} = 93$ times	$\dfrac{\$237}{\$1} = 237$ times	$\dfrac{\$163}{\$3} = 54$ times
f. Rate of return on stockholders' equity	$\dfrac{\$211}{(\$888 + \$678)/2}$ $= 26.9\%$	$\dfrac{\$230}{(\$678 + \$466)/2}$ $= 40.2\%$	$\dfrac{\$145}{(\$466 + \$338)/2}$ $= 36.1\%$	$\dfrac{\$98}{(\$338 + \$276)/2}$ $= 31.9\%$

Evaluation: During this four-year period, Gap's operating results were outstanding. Operating results improved, with all ratio values but return on stockholders' equity higher in 19X9 than in 19X6. Moreover, all the performance measures indicate high levels of income and return to investors.

LESSONS LEARNED

1. **Perform a horizontal analysis of financial statements.** *Horizontal analysis* is the study of percentage changes in financial statement items from one period to the next. *Trend percentages* are a form of horizontal analysis.

2. **Perform a vertical analysis of financial statements.** *Vertical analysis* of a financial statement reveals the relationship of each statement item to a specified base, which is the 100% figure. In an income statement, net sales is the base. On a balance sheet, total assets is the 100% figure.

3. **Prepare common-size financial statements.** *Common-size statements* report only percentages, no dollar amounts. They ease the comparison of different companies and may signal the need for corrective action. *Benchmarking* is the practice of comparing a company to a standard set by other companies.

4. **Compute the standard financial ratios.** An important part of financial analysis is the use of ratios. A ratio expresses

the relationship of one item to another. The most important ratios measure a company's ability to pay current liabilities, ability to sell inventory and collect receivables, ability to pay long-term debt, its profitability, and its value as an investment.

5. **Use ratios in decision making.** Analysis of financial ratios over time helps track a company's progress. A change in the ratios over time may signal a problem. The company's managers must then find the source of this problem and correct it.

6. **Measure economic value added.** *Economic value added (EVA®)* measures whether a company's operations have increased its stockholders' wealth. EVA® is defined as the excess of net income and interest expense over the company's capital charge (the amount the company's stockholders and lenders charge for the use of their money).

ACCOUNTING VOCABULARY

accounts receivable
  turnover (p. 725)
acid-test ratio (p. 724)
benchmarking (p. 717)
book value per share of common
  stock (p. 730)

capital charge (p. 732)
common-size statement (p. 716)
cost of capital (p. 732)
current ratio (p. 722)
days' sales in
  receivables (p. 726)

debt ratio (p. 726)
dividend yield (p. 730)
earnings per share (EPS) (p. 729)
economic value added
  (EVA®) (p. 731)
efficient capital market (p. 732)

QUESTIONS

1. Name the three broad categories of analytical tools that are based on accounting information.
2. Briefly describe horizontal analysis. How do decision makers use this analytical tool?
3. What is vertical analysis, and what is its purpose? What is the purpose of common-size statements?
4. Identify two ratios used to measure a company's ability to pay current liabilities. Show how the ratios are computed.
5. Why is the acid-test ratio given that name?
6. What does the inventory turnover ratio measure?
7. Suppose the days'-sales-in-receivables ratio of Klaras Corp. increased from 36 at January 1 to 43 at December 31. Is this a good sign or a bad sign? What might Klaras management do in response to this change?
8. Snap Tool Company's debt ratio has increased from 0.50 to 0.70. Identify a decision maker to whom this increase is important, and state how the increase affects this party's decisions about the company.
9. Company A is a chain of grocery stores, and Company B is a construction company. Which company is likely to

have the higher (a) current ratio, (b) inventory turnover, and (c) rate of return on sales? Give your reasons.
10. The price/earnings ratio of **Ford Motor Company** was 8, and the price/earnings ratio of **Lucent Technologies** was 40. Which company did the stock market favor? Explain.
11. Hold all other factors constant and indicate whether each of the following situations generally signals good or bad news about a company:
    a. Increase in return on sales
    b. Decrease in earnings per share
    c. Increase in price/earnings ratio
    d. Increase in book value per share
    e. Increase in current ratio
    f. Decrease in inventory turnover
    g. Increase in debt ratio
    h. Decrease in interest-coverage ratio
12. What is EVA®, how is it computed, and how is it used in financial analysis?

ASSESS YOUR PROGRESS

DAILY EXERCISES

Horizontal analysis of revenues and gross profit
(Obj. 1)

DE18-1 **Phillips Electronics** reported the following amounts on its 1999 comparative income statement:

(In millions)	1999	1998	1997
Revenues......................	$78,596	$74,391	$72,055
Cost of sales..................	29,561	26,820	15,941

Perform a horizontal analysis of revenues and gross profit—both in dollar amounts and in percentages—for 1999 and 1998.

Using horizontal analysis for decision making
(Obj. 1)

DE18-2 Study Exhibit 18-2, the horizontal analysis of **Lucent Technologies'** balance sheet at September 30, 1999. Focus on the 41.0% increase in receivables and the 35.5% increase in inventories during 1999. Assume that Lucent's income statement reported a decrease in sales during 1999.
   Would the large percentage increases in receivables and inventories convey good news or bad news about the company? Explain your reasoning.

Trend analysis of revenues and net income
(Obj. 1)

DE18-3 **Pier 1 Imports,** reported the following revenues and net income amounts:

(In millions)	1999	1998	1997	1996	1995
Net sales	$1,139	$1,075	$947	$811	$712
Net income....................	80	78	48	10	22

1. Show Pier 1 Imports' trend percentages for revenues and net income. Start with 1995, and use 1995 as the base year.
2. Which trend looks better—net sales or net income?

Vertical analysis of the income statement

(Obj. 2)

DE18-4 Bernstein Bros. Scuba Shop has recently introduced a new ultra-light wet suit for diving. Demand for the product has been high, and Bernstein is shipping goods to many new diving shops. Bernstein's comparative income statement reports these figures for 20X2 and 20X1:

	20X2	20X1
Net sales	$204,000	$171,000
Cost of goods sold..............	61,000	50,000
Selling expenses	45,000	36,000
General expenses	18,000	17,000
Net income	$ 80,000	$ 68,000

Perform a vertical analysis of Bernstein's income statements for 20X2 and 20X1. Does the analysis reflect favorably or poorly on the company? Cite specifics in your answer.

Vertical analysis to correct a cash shortage

(Obj. 2)

DE18-5 Bernstein Bros. Scuba Shop reported the following amounts on its balance sheets at December 31, 20X2, 20X1, and 20X0:

	20X2	20X1	20X0
Cash	$ 4,000	$ 8,000	$ 9,000
Receivables, net	46,000	32,000	20,000
Inventory..	42,000	36,000	33,000
Prepaid expenses	2,000	2,000	1,000
Property, plant, and equipment, net.........	96,000	88,000	87,000
Total assets	$190,000	$166,000	$150,000

1. Sales and profits are high. Nevertheless, the company is experiencing a cash shortage. Perform a vertical analysis of Bernstein's assets at the end of each year 20X2, 20X1, and 20X0. Use the analysis to explain the reason for the cash shortage.
2. Suggest a way for Bernstein to generate more cash.

Using vertical analysis for decision making

(Obj. 2)

DE18-6 Return to Exhibit 18-4, the vertical analysis of **Lucent Technologies'** balance sheets at December 31, 1999 and 1998. Consider that Lucent's revenues and profits reached all-time highs during 1999. Focus on receivables and inventories.

1. Did receivables and inventories make up more or less of total assets in 1999 than in 1998? Give the percentages for each year.
2. Do the increases in receivables and inventories worry you? Explain your reasoning.

Common-size income statements of two leading companies

(Obj. 3)

DE18-7 **Nike, Inc.,** and **The Home Depot** are leaders in their respective industries. Compare the two companies by converting their income statements (adapted) to common size.

(In millions)	Nike	Home Depot
Net sales..	$8,777	$38,434
Cost of goods sold...	5,494	27,023
Selling and administrative expenses..............	2,427	7,579
Interest expense	44	28
Other expense	66	—
Income tax expense.......................................	295	1,484
Net income	$ 451	$ 2,320

Which company earns more net income? Which company's net income is a higher percentage of net sales? Which company is more profitable? Explain your answer.

DE18-8 Prepare a common-size analysis to compare **Nike, Inc.,** and **The Home Depot** on the makeup of their assets (amounts in millions).

Assets	Nike	Home Depot
Current assets:		
Cash and equivalents	$ 198	$ 168
Short-term investments	—	2
Accounts receivable, net	1,540	587
Inventories	1,199	5,489
Other current assets	328	144
Total current assets	3,265	6,390
Property, plant, and equipment, net	1,266	10,227
Goodwill and other intangibles	427	311
Other assets	290	153
Total assets	$5,248	$17,081

To which company are *current assets* more important? Which company places more emphasis on its *plant assets*?

Evaluating the trend in a company's current ratio
(Obj. 4, 5)

DE18-9 Examine the actual financial data of **Rubbermaid, Inc.,** in Exhibit 18-8 (page 721). Show how to compute Rubbermaid's current ratio for each year 19X8–20X1. Is the company's ability to pay its current liabilities improving or deteriorating?

Evaluating a company's acid-test ratio
(Obj. 4, 5)

DE18-10 Use the **Lucent Technologies** balance sheet data in Exhibit 18-2 (page 714).

1. Compute the company's acid-test ratio at September 30, 1999 and 1998.
2. Compare Lucent's ratio values to those of **MCI WorldCom** and **Wal-Mart** on page 724. Is Lucent's acid-test ratio strong or weak? Explain.

Computing inventory turnover and days' sales in receivables
(Obj. 4)

DE18-11 Use the **Lucent Technologies** 1999 income statement (page 713) and year-end balance sheet (page 714) to compute

a. Inventory turnover for 1999. (Round turnover to one decimal place.)
b. Days' sales in receivables during 1999. All revenues are earned on account. (Round dollar amounts to one decimal place.)

Measuring ability to pay long-term debt
(Obj. 4, 5)

DE18-12 Use the actual financial statements of **Lucent Technologies** (pages 715 and 716).

1. Compute the company's debt ratio at September 30, 1999.
2. Compute the company's times-interest-earned ratio for 1999. Interest expense for 1999 was $406 million.
3. Is Lucent Technologies' ability to pay its liabilities and interest expense strong or weak? Comment on the value of each ratio computed for requirements 1 and 2.

Measuring profitability
(Obj. 4, 5)

DE18-13 Use the financial statements of **Lucent Technologies** (pages 715 and 716) to determine or, if necessary, to compute these profitability measures for 1999:

a. Rate of return on net sales.
b. Rate of return on total assets. Interest expense for 1999 was $406 million.
c. Rate of return on common stockholders' equity.

Are these rates of return strong or weak? Explain.

Computing EPS and the price/earnings ratio
(Obj. 4)

DE18-14 The annual report of **The Home Depot** for the year ended January 31, 2000, included the following items:

Market price per share of common stock	$55.63
Preferred stock outstanding	$0
Net earnings (net income)	$2,320,000,000
Number of shares of common stock outstanding	2,244,000,000

1. Compute earnings per share (EPS) and the price/earnings ratio for The Home Depot's stock. Round to the nearest cent.
2. How much does the stock market say that $1 of The Home Depot's net income is worth?

DE18-15 During 1999, **Lucent Technologies** had earnings per share of common stock (EPS) of $1.52. The company had no preferred stock outstanding, so there were no preferred dividends. Use the income statement (Exhibit 18-3, page 715), and the formula for EPS (page 730) to compute the number of shares of common stock that Lucent had outstanding during 1999. Keep in mind that net income is in millions of dollars. Therefore, you will need to multiply the reported net income figures by 1,000,000.

Working with earnings per share (Obj. 4)

DE18-16 Use **Lucent Technologies'** balance sheet (Exhibit 18-2, page 714) to compute the book value per share of the company's common stock at September 30, 1999 and at September 30, 1998. At September 30, 1999, Lucent had 3,072 million shares of common stock outstanding. At September 30, 1998, shares outstanding were 3,022 million. Is the trend of book value per share positive or negative?

Computing book value per share of common stock (Obj. 4)

DE18-17 A skeleton of **Campbell Soup Company's** income statement (as adapted) for the year ended August 1, 19X9, appears as follows (amounts in millions):

Using ratio data to reconstruct an income statement (Obj. 4)

Income Statement

Net sales	$6,424
Cost of goods sold	(a)
Selling expenses	1,634
Administrative expenses	304
Interest expense	(b)
Other expenses	166
Income before taxes	1,097
Income tax expense	(c)
Net income	$ (d)

Use the following ratio data to complete Campbell Soup's income statement.

a. Inventory turnover is 5.174 (beginning inventory is $564; ending inventory was $615).

b. Rate of return on sales is 0.1127.

DE18-18 A skeleton of **Campbell Soup Company's** balance sheet at August 1, 19X9 (as adapted) appears as follows (amounts in millions):

Using ratio data to reconstruct a balance sheet (Obj. 4)

Balance Sheet

Cash	$ 6	Total current liabilities	$ 3,146
Receivables	(a)	Long-term debt	(e)
Inventories	615	Other long-term liabilities	811
Prepaid expenses	(b)		
Total current assets	(c)	Common stock	402
Plant assets, net	(d)	Retained earnings	4,041
Other assets	2,502	Other stockholders' equity	(4,208)
Total assets	$5,522	Total liabilities and equity	$ (f)

Use the following ratio data to complete Campbell Soup's balance sheet:

a. Debt ratio is 0.9574.   **b.** Current ratio is 0.4113.   **c.** Acid-test ratio is 0.1739.

DE18-19 Use the 1999 income statement of **MCI WorldCom,** page 710, and the following data for MCI: interest expense, $966 million; short-term and long-term debt, $21,205 million; stockholders' equity, $45,241 million.

Computing economic value added (Obj. 6)

1. Compute economic value added (EVA®) by MCI's operations during 1999. Assume the company's cost of capital is 12%. Round all amounts to the nearest million dollars.

2. Should the company's stockholders be happy with the EVA® for 1999? How did the company's stock perform?

EXERCISES

Computing year-to-year changes in working capital (Obj. 1)

E18-1 What were the amount of change and the percentage change in Berkshire Property Management's working capital during 20X2 and 20X3? Is this trend favorable or unfavorable?

	20X3	20X2	20X1
Total current assets	$408,000	$399,000	$385,000
Total current liabilities	250,000	211,000	232,000

Horizontal analysis of an income statement
(Obj. 1)

E18-2 Prepare a horizontal analysis of the following comparative income statement of Saladin Publishing. Round percentage changes to the nearest one-tenth percent (three decimal places):

SALADIN PUBLISHING
Comparative Income Statement
Years Ended December 31, 20X4 and 20X3

	20X4	20X3
Total revenue..	$460,000	$373,000
Expenses:		
Cost of goods sold.............................	$202,000	$188,000
Selling and general expenses	98,000	93,000
Interest expense	7,000	4,000
Income tax expense...........................	52,000	37,000
Total expenses	359,000	322,000
Net income	$101,000	$ 51,000

Why did net income increase by a higher percentage than total revenues during 20X4?

Computing trend percentages
(Obj. 1)

E18-3 Compute trend percentages for Traigon Corporation's net sales and net income for the following five-year period, using year 1 as the base year. Round to the nearest full percent.

(In thousands)	Year 5	Year 4	Year 3	Year 2	Year 1
Net sales..................	$1,310	$1,147	$1,065	$1,104	$1,043
Net income..............	120	114	74	81	85

Which grew faster during the period, net sales or net income?

Vertical analysis of a balance sheet
(Obj. 2)

E18-4 Artisan International has requested that you perform a vertical analysis of its balance sheet to determine the component percentages of its assets, liabilities, and stockholders' equity.

ARTISAN INTERNATIONAL
Balance Sheet
December 31, 20X3

Assets

Total current assets..	$ 99,000
Long-term investments...	35,000
Property, plant, and equipment, net.......................	217,000
Total assets	351,000

Liabilities

Total current liabilities	$ 58,000
Long-term debt	118,000
Total liabilities	176,000

Stockholders' Equity

Total stockholders' equity	175,000
Total liabilities and stockholders' equity	$351,000

Preparing a common-size income statement *(Obj. 3)*

E18-5 Prepare a comparative common-size income statement for Saladin Publishing, using the 20X4 and 20X3 data of Exercise 18-2 and rounding percentages to one-tenth percent (three decimal places).

E18-6 The financial statements of Lambert Enterprises, Inc., include the following items:

Computing five ratios
(Obj. 4)

	Current Year	Preceding Year
Balance Sheet Data		
Cash...	$ 29,000	$ 22,000
Short-term investments	11,000	26,000
Net receivables	64,000	73,000
Inventory......................................	87,000	71,000
Prepaid expenses	6,000	8,000
Total current assets.......................	197,000	200,000
Total current liabilities..................	121,000	91,000
Income Statement Data		
Net credit sales	$480,000	
Cost of goods sold.........................	260,000	

Required

Compute the following ratios for the current year: (a) current ratio, (b) acid-test ratio, (c) inventory turnover, (d) accounts receivable turnover, and (e) days' sales in average receivables.

E18-7 Cincinnati Light Company has asked you to determine whether the company's ability to pay its current liabilities and long-term debts has improved or deteriorated during 20X2. To answer this question, compute the following ratios for 20X2 and 20X1: (a) current ratio, (b) acid-test ratio, (c) debt ratio, and (d) times-interest-earned ratio. Summarize the results of your analysis in a written report.

Analyzing the ability to pay current liabilities
(Obj. 4, 5)

	20X2	20X1
Cash	$ 21,000	$ 47,000
Short-term investments..............	28,000	—
Net receivables	102,000	116,000
Inventory	226,000	263,000
Prepaid expenses.........................	11,000	9,000
Total assets	511,000	493,000
Total current liabilities	232,000	301,000
Total liabilities	261,000	273,000
Income from operations..............	174,000	160,000
Interest expense	36,000	39,000

E18-8 Compute four ratios that measure ability of Legend Data Systems, Inc., to earn profits. The company's comparative income statement follows.

Analyzing profitability
(Obj. 4, 5)

LEGEND DATA SYSTEMS, INC. Comparative Income Statement Years Ended December 31, 20X3 and 20X2		
	20X3	**20X2**
Net sales..	$178,000	$163,000
Cost of goods sold...............................	93,000	86,000
Gross profit	85,000	77,000
Selling and general expenses.............	48,000	41,000
Income from operations	37,000	36,000
Interest expense.................................	21,000	10,000
Income before income tax.................	16,000	26,000
Income tax expense............................	4,000	8,000
Net income	$ 12,000	$ 18,000

Additional data:

	20X3	20X2
Average total assets	$204,000	$191,000
Average common stockholders' equity	$96,000	$89,000
Preferred dividends	$3,000	$3,000
Shares of common stock outstanding	20,000	20,000

Did the company's operating performance improve or deteriorate during 20X3?

Evaluating a stock as an investment
(Obj. 4, 5)

E18-9 Evaluate the common stock of LeaseNet.com as an investment. Specifically, use the three stock ratios to determine whether the stock has increased or decreased in attractiveness during the past year.

	20X4	20X3
Net income	$ 58,000	$ 55,000
Dividends (half on preferred stock)	28,000	28,000
Common stockholders' equity at year end (80,000 shares)	630,000	600,000
Preferred stockholders' equity at year end	200,000	200,000
Market price per share of common stock at year end	15.12	10.88

*Using economic value added to measure corporate performance
(Obj. 6)*

E18-10 Two companies with very different economic-value-added (EVA®) profiles are **IHOP,** the restaurant chain, and **Texaco,** the giant oil company. Adapted versions of the two companies' 1999 financial statements are presented here (in millions):

	IHOP	Texaco
Balance Sheet Data		
Total assets	$520	$28,972
Interest-bearing debt	$ 41	$ 5,503
All other liabilities	253	14,022
Stockholders' equity	226	9,447
Total liabilities and equity	$520	$28,972
Income Statement Data		
Total revenue	$273	$34,975
Interest expense	19	504
All other expenses	222	33,294
Net income	$ 32	$ 1,177

Required

1. Before performing any calculations, which company do you think would represent the better investment? Give your reason.
2. Compute the EVA® for each company, and then decide which company's stock you would rather hold as an investment. Assume each company's cost of capital is 12%, and round to the nearest million dollars.

Challenge Exercises

*Using ratio data to reconstruct a company's income statement
(Obj. 2, 3, 4)*

E18-11 The following data (dollar amounts in millions) are from the financial statements of **McDonald's Corporation,** the restaurant chain.

Average stockholders' equity	$9,639
Interest expense	$436
Preferred stock	–0–
Operating income as a percent of sales	25.04%
Rate of return on sales	14.692%
Rate of return on stockholders' equity	20.21%
Income tax rate	32.45%

Required

Complete the following condensed income statement. Report amounts to the nearest million dollars.

Sales	$?
Operating expenses...............	?
Operating income	?
Interest expense....................	?
Income before tax	?
Income tax expense	?
Net income...........................	?

E18-12 The following data (dollar amounts in millions) are from the financial statements of **Wal-Mart Stores, Inc.,** the largest retailer in the world:

Using ratio data to reconstruct a company's balance sheet (Obj. 2, 3, 4)

Total liabilities	$44,515
Preferred stock	–0–
Total current assets	$24,356
Accumulated depreciation................	$8,224
Debt ratio	63.277%
Current ratio	0.94392

Required

Complete the following condensed balance sheet. Report amounts to the nearest million dollars.

Current assets		$?
Property, plant, and equipment	$?	
Less: Accumulated depreciation	?	?
Total assets		$?
Current liabilities		$?
Long-term liabilities		?
Stockholders' equity		?
Total liabilities and stockholders' equity		$?

PROBLEMS

(Group A)

P18-1A Net sales, net income, and common stockholders' equity for Keel Furniture Company for a four-year period follow.

Trend percentages, return on common equity, and comparison with the industry (Obj. 1, 4, 5)

(In thousands)	20X2	20X1	20X0	19X9
Net sales...	$782	$714	$622	$634
Net income	75	50	32	40
Ending common stockholders' equity.............	391	370	305	252

Required

1. Compute trend percentages for each item for 20X0–20X2. Use 19X9 as the base year. Round to the nearest percent.
2. Compute the rate of return on average common stockholders' equity for 20X0–20X2, rounding to three decimal places. In this industry, rates of 13% are average, rates above 16% are good, and rates above 20% are outstanding.
3. How does Keel's return on common stockholders' equity compare with the industry? Is the trend promising or not?

Common-size statements,
analysis of profitability, and
comparison with the industry
(Obj. 2, 3, 4, 5)

P18-2A CJ Home Appliance Center has asked your help in comparing the company's profit performance and financial position with the average for the home appliance industry. The general manager has given you the company's income statement and balance sheet and also the industry average data for home appliance companies.

CJ HOME APPLIANCE CENTER
Income Statement
Compared with Industry Average
Year Ended December 31, 20X1

	CJ	Industry Average
Net sales	$781,000	100.0%
Cost of goods sold	497,000	65.8
Gross profit	284,000	34.2
Operating expenses	159,000	19.7
Operating income	125,000	14.5
Other expenses	5,000	0.4
Net income	$120,000	14.1%

CJ HOME APPLIANCE CENTER
Balance Sheet
Compared with Industry Average
December 31, 20X1

	CJ	Industry Average
Current assets	$350,000	70.9%
Plant assets, net	84,000	23.6
Intangible assets, net	6,000	0.8
Other assets	20,000	4.7
Total	$460,000	100.0%
Current liabilities	$207,000	48.1%
Long-term liabilities	72,000	16.6
Stockholders' equity	181,000	35.3
Total	$460,000	100.0%

Required

1. Prepare a two-column common-size income statement and balance sheet for CJ. The first column of each statement should present CJ's common-size statement, and the second column should show the industry averages.
2. For the profitability analysis, compute CJ's (a) ratio of gross profit to net sales, (b) ratio of operating income to net sales, and (c) ratio of net income to net sales. Compare these figures with the industry averages. Is CJ's profit performance better or worse than the industry average?
3. For the analysis of financial position, compute CJ's (a) ratio of current assets to total assets, and (b) ratio of stockholders' equity to total assets. Compare these ratios with the industry averages. Is CJ's financial position better or worse than the industry averages?

P18-3A Financial statement data of Willsboro Farms, Inc., include the following items:

Cash	$ 22,000	Accounts payable	$ 94,000
Short-term investments	19,000	Accrued liabilities	38,000
Accounts receivable, net	97,000	Long-term notes payable	160,000
Inventories	141,000	Other long-term liabilities	31,000
Prepaid expenses	8,000	Net income	71,000
Total assets	657,000	Number of common shares	
Short-term notes payable	49,000	outstanding	23,000

Required

1. Compute Willsboro's current ratio, debt ratio, and earnings per share.
2. Compute the three ratios after evaluating the effect of each transaction that follows. Consider each transaction *separately.*

a. Purchased merchandise costing $26,000 on account, debiting Inventory.
b. Paid off long-term liabilities, $31,000.
c. Declared, but did not pay, a $22,000 cash dividend on common stock.
d. Borrowed $85,000 on a long-term note payable.
e. Sold short-term investments for $18,000 (cost, $11,000); assume no income tax on the gain.

Use the following format for your answer:

Requirement 1:		**Current Ratio**	**Debt Ratio**	**Earnings Per Share**
Requirement 2:	**Transaction (letter)**	**Current Ratio**	**Debt Ratio**	**Earnings Per Share**

P18-4A Comparative financial statement data of Swanner Resources, Inc., follow.

Using ratios to evaluate a stock investment
(Obj. 4, 5)

SWANNER RESOURCES, INC.
Comparative Income Statement
Years Ended December 31, 20X4 and 20X3

	20X4	20X3
Net sales	$462,000	$427,000
Cost of goods sold	289,000	278,000
Gross profit	173,000	149,000
Operating expenses	81,000	78,000
Income from operations	92,000	71,000
Interest expense	11,000	12,000
Income before income tax	81,000	59,000
Income tax expense	30,000	27,000
Net income	$ 51,000	$ 32,000

SWANNER RESOURCES, INC.
Comparative Balance Sheet
December 31, 20X4 and 20X3
(selected 20X2 amounts given for computation of ratios)

	20X4	20X3	20X2
Current assets:			
Cash	$116,000	$ 97,000	
Current receivables, net	112,000	116,000	$103,000
Inventories	104,000	122,000	101,000
Prepaid expenses	64,000	47,000	
Total current assets	396,000	382,000	
Property, plant, and equipment, net	189,000	178,000	
Total assets	$585,000	$560,000	598,000
Total current liabilities	$206,000	$223,000	
Long-term liabilities	119,000	117,000	
Total liabilities	325,000	340,000	
Preferred stockholders' equity, 6%, $100 par	100,000	100,000	
Common stockholders' equity, no par	160,000	120,000	90,000
Total liabilities and stockholders' equity	$585,000	$560,000	

Other information:

a. Market price of Swanner's common stock: $53 at December 31, 20X4, and $31.50 at December 31, 20X3.
b. Common shares outstanding: 10,000 during 20X4 and 9,000 during 20X3.

Required

1. Compute the following ratios for 20X4 and 20X3:
   a. Current ratio
   b. Inventory turnover
   c. Accounts receivable turnover
   d. Times-interest-earned ratio
   e. Return on assets
   f. Return on common stockholders' equity
   g. Earnings per share of common stock

2. Decide (a) whether Swanner's financial position improved or deteriorated during 20X4, and (b) whether the investment attractiveness of its common stock appears to have increased or decreased.
3. How will what you learned in this problem help you evaluate an investment?

Using ratio data to complete a set of financial statements (Obj. 4)

P18-5A ← *Link Back to Chapter 17 (Statement of Cash Flows).* Summarized and adapted versions of the financial statements of **Pepsi Co, Inc.,** follow (amounts in *millions*).

Income Statement
Year Ended May 31, 19X9

Net sales	$20,367
Cost of goods sold	(a)
Gross profit	(b)
Selling and general expenses	9,103
Other expense (income)	(590)
Income before income tax	(c)
Income tax expense (43.93%)	(d)
Net income	$ (e)

Balance Sheet
May 31, 19X9 and 19X8

Assets	19X9	19X8
Current:		
Cash	$ (f)	$ 311
Short-term investments	92	83
Receivables, net	1,704	2,453
Inventories	899	1,016
Prepaid expenses	(g)	499
Total current assets	(h)	4,362
Long-term assets	13,378	18,298
Total assets	$ (i)	$22,660
Liabilities		
Current liabilities	$ 3,788	$ 7,914
Long-term liabilities	(j)	8,345
Total liabilities	(k)	16,259
Stockholders' Equity		
Common stockholders' equity	(l)	6,401
Total liabilities and equity	$ (m)	$22,660

Ratio data:

a. Current ratio at May 31, 19X9 is 1.1016.
b. Inventory turnover for 19X9 was 8.562.
c. Debt ratio at May 31, 19X9 is 0.60794.
d. Increase in cash during 19X9, $653.

Required

Complete the financial statements. Start with the income statement and then complete the balance sheet last.

Using ratios to decide between two stock investments; measuring economic value added (Obj. 4, 5, 6)

P18-6A Assume that you are purchasing an investment and have decided to invest in a company in the automotive supply business. You have narrowed the choice to Bowie, Inc., and Drane Corp. and have assembled the following data.
Selected income statement data for current year:

	Bowie, Inc.	Drane Corp.
Net sales (all on credit)	$497,000	$371,000
Cost of goods sold	258,000	209,000
Income from operations	138,000	79,000
Interest expense	19,000	—
Net income	72,000	48,000

Selected balance sheet and market price data at end of current year:

	Bowie, Inc.	Drane Corp.
Current assets:		
Cash	$ 19,000	$ 22,000
Short-term investments	18,000	20,000
Current receivables, net	46,000	42,000
Inventories	100,000	87,000
Prepaid expenses	3,000	2,000
Total current assets	186,000	173,000
Total assets	328,000	265,000
Total current liabilities	98,000	108,000
Total liabilities	131,000*	108,000*
Preferred stock: 5%, $100 par	20,000	—
Common stock, $1 par (10,000 shares)		10,000
$2 par (6,000 shares)	12,000	
Total stockholders' equity	197,000	157,000
Market price per share of common stock	$81.50	$45

* Notes payable: Bowie, $86,000
     Drane, $ 1,000

Selected balance sheet data at beginning of current year:

	Bowie, Inc.	Drane Corp.
Current receivables, net	$ 48,000	$ 40,000
Inventories	88,000	93,000
Total assets	270,000	259,000
Preferred stock, 5%, $100 par	20,000	—
Common stock, $1 par (10,000 shares)		10,000
$2 par (6,000 shares)	12,000	
Total stockholders' equity	126,000	118,000

Your investment strategy is to purchase the stocks of companies that have low price/earnings ratios but appear to be in good shape financially. Assume that you have analyzed all other factors and your decision depends on the results of the ratio analysis to be performed.

Required

1. Compute the following ratios for both companies for the current year, and decide which company's stock better fits your investment strategy.
   - **a.** Current ratio
   - **b.** Acid-test ratio
   - **c.** Inventory turnover
   - **d.** Times-interest-earned ratio
   - **e.** Return on common stockholders' equity
   - **f.** Earnings per share of common stock
   - **g.** Book value per share of common stock
   - **h.** Price/earnings ratio
2. Compute each company's economic-value-added (EVA®) measure, and determine whether their EVA®s confirm or alter your investment decision. Each company's cost of capital is 13.5%. Round all amounts to the nearest $1,000.

PROBLEMS

(Group B)

P18-1B Net sales, net income, and total assets for Oaklea Corporation for a four-year period follow:

Trend percentages, return on sales, and comparison with the industry

(Obj. 1, 4, 5)

(In thousands)	20X2	20X1	20X0	19X9
Net sales	$360	$313	$266	$241
Net income	27	21	11	13
Total assets	296	254	212	166

Required

1. Compute trend percentages for each item for 20X0–20X2. Use 19X9 as the base year. Round to the nearest percent.
2. Compute the rate of return on net sales for 20X0–20X2, rounding to three decimal places. In this industry, rates above 5% are considered good, and rates above 7% are outstanding.
3. How does Oaklea's return on net sales compare with that of the industry?

Common-size statements, analysis of profitability, and comparison with the industry (Obj. 2, 3, 4, 5)

P18-2B Top managers of Geolab Exploration, Inc. have asked your help in comparing the company's profit performance and financial position with the average for the geological engineering industry. The accountant has given you the company's income statement and balance sheet and also the following data for the geological engineering industry.

GEOLAB EXPLORATION, INC. Income Statement Compared with Industry Average Year Ended December 31, 20X3		
	Geolab	**Industry Average**
Net sales	$988,000	100.0%
Cost of goods sold...............	653,000	65.9
Gross profit..........................	335,000	34.1
Operating expenses.............	257,000	28.1
Operating income.................	78,000	6.0
Other expenses....................	2,000	0.4
Net income..........................	$ 76,000	5.6%

GEOLAB EXPLORATION, INC. Balance Sheet Compared with Industry Average December 31, 20X3		
	Geolab	**Industry Average**
Current assets......................	$501,000	74.4%
Plant assets, net	127,000	20.0
Intangible assets, net	42,000	0.6
Other assets	13,000	5.0
Total....................................	$683,000	100.0%
Current liabilities.................	$246,000	35.6%
Long-term liabilities	144,000	19.0
Stockholders' equity...........	293,000	45.4
Total....................................	$683,000	100.0%

Required

1. Prepare a two-column common-size income statement and balance sheet for Geolab. The first column of each statement should present Geolab's common-size statement, and the second column should show the industry averages.
2. For the profitability analysis, compute Geolab's (a) ratio of gross profit to net sales, (b) ratio of operating income (loss) to net sales, and (c) ratio of net income (loss) to net sales. Compare these figures with the industry averages. Is Geolab's profit performance better or worse than the average for the industry?
3. For the analysis of financial position, compute Geolab's (a) ratio of current assets to total assets, and (b) ratio of stockholders' equity to total assets. Compare these ratios with the industry averages. Is Geolab's financial position better or worse than average for the industry?

Effects of business transactions on selected ratios (Obj. 4, 5)

P18-3B Financial statement data on Braum's Food Co. include the following items:

Cash	$ 47,000	Accounts payable...........................	$ 96,000
Short-term investments....................	21,000	Accrued liabilities	42,000
Accounts receivable, net..................	102,000	Long-term notes payable...............	146,000
Inventories.......................................	274,000	Other long-term liabilities	78,000
Prepaid expenses	15,000	Net income	119,000
Total assets	952,000	Number of common	
Short-term notes payable	72,000	shares outstanding	26,000

Required

1. Compute Braum's Food Co.'s current ratio, debt ratio, and earnings per share.
2. Compute the three ratios after evaluating the effect of each transaction that follows. Consider each transaction *separately.*
   a. Borrowed $76,000 on a long-term note payable.
   b. Sold short-term investments for $44,000 (cost, $66,000); assume no tax effect of the loss.
   c. Issued 14,000 shares of common stock, receiving cash of $168,000.
   d. Received cash on account, $6,000.
   e. Paid short-term notes payable, $51,000.

Use the following format for your answer:

Requirement 1:   **Current Ratio**   **Debt Ratio**   **Earnings Per Share**

Requirement 2: **Transaction (letter)** **Current Ratio**   **Debt Ratio**   **Earnings Per Share**

P18-4B Comparative financial statement data of Adolphus, Inc., follow.

Using ratios to evaluate a stock investment
(Obj. 4, 5)

ADOLPHUS, INC.
Comparative Income Statement
Years Ended December 31, 20X3 and 20X2

	20X3	20X2
Net sales	$667,000	$599,000
Cost of goods sold	358,000	283,000
Gross profit	309,000	316,000
Operating expenses	149,000	147,000
Income from operations	160,000	169,000
Interest expense	57,000	41,000
Income before income tax	103,000	128,000
Income tax expense	34,000	53,000
Net income	$ 69,000	$ 75,000

ADOLPHUS, INC.
Comparative Balance Sheet
December 31, 20X3 and 20X2
(selected 20X1 amounts given for computations of ratios)

	20X3	20X2	20X1
Current assets:			
Cash	$ 37,000	$ 60,000	
Current receivables, net	208,000	151,000	$138,000
Inventories	340,000	286,000	184,000
Prepaid expenses	5,000	20,000	
Total current assets	590,000	517,000	
Property, plant, and equipment, net	287,000	256,000	
Total assets	$877,000	$773,000	707,000
Total current liabilities	$286,000	$267,000	
Long-term liabilities	245,000	235,000	
Total liabilities	531,000	502,000	
Preferred stockholders' equity, 4%, $20 par	50,000	50,000	
Common stockholders' equity, no-par	296,000	221,000	148,000
Total liabilities and stockholders' equity	$877,000	$773,000	

Other information:

a. Market price of Adolphus's common stock: $24.50 at December 31, 20X3, and $36.25 at December 31, 20X2.

b. Common shares outstanding: 15,000 during 20X3 and 14,000 during 20X2.

Required

1. Compute the following ratios for 20X3 and 20X2:
   a. Current ratio
   b. Inventory turnover
   c. Accounts receivable turnover
   d. Times-interest-earned ratio
   e. Return on assets
   f. Return on common stockholders' equity
   g. Earnings per share of common stock
2. Decide whether (a) Adolphus' financial position improved or deteriorated during 20X3, and (b) the investment attractiveness of its common stock appears to have increased or decreased.
3. How will what you learned in this problem help you evaluate an investment?

P18-5B Summarized and adapted versions of the financial statements of **The Coca-Cola Company** follow at the top of the next page (amounts in millions).

Using ratio data to complete a set of financial statements (Obj. 4)

INCOME STATEMENT
Year Ended December 31, 19X9

Net sales	$19,805
Cost of goods sold	(a)
Gross profit	(b)
Selling and general expenses	9,814
Other expense (income)	163
Income before income tax	(c)
Income tax expense (36.34%)	(d)
Net income	$ (e)

Balance Sheet
December 31, 19X9 and 19X8

	19X9	19X8
Assets		
Current:		
Cash	$ (f)	$ 1,648
Short-term investments	201	159
Receivables, net	1,798	1,666
Inventories	1,076	890
Prepaid expenses	(g)	2,017
Total current assets	(h)	6,380
Long-term assets	15,143	12,765
Total assets	$ (i)	$19,145
Liabilities		
Current liabilities	$ 9,856	$ 8,640
Long-term liabilities	(j)	2,102
Total liabilities	(k)	10,742
Stockholders' Equity		
Common stockholders' equity	(l)	8,403
Total liabilities and equity	$ (m)	$19,145

Ratio data:

   a. Current ratio at December 31, 19X9 is 0.6575.
   b. Inventory turnover for 19X9 was 6.113.
   c. Debt ratio at December 31, 19X9 is 0.56005.
   d. Decrease in cash during 19X9, $37.

Required

Complete the financial statements. Start with the income statement. Then complete the balance sheet.

Using ratios to decide between two stock investments; measuring economic value added (Obj. 4, 5, 6)

P18-6B Assume that you are considering purchasing stock in a company in the pharmaceutical industry. You have narrowed the choice to Eckert, Inc., and Biomed, Inc., and have assembled the following data.

Selected income statement data for current year:

	Eckert, Inc.	Biomed, Inc.
Net sales (all on credit)	$519,000	$603,000
Cost of goods sold	387,000	454,000
Income from operations	72,000	93,000
Interest expense	8,000	—
Net income	32,000	56,000

Selected balance sheet and market price data at end of current year:

	Eckert, Inc.	Biomed, Inc.
Current assets:		
Cash...	$ 39,000	$ 25,000
Short-term investments......................................	13,000	6,000
Current receivables, net	164,000	189,000
Inventories...	183,000	211,000
Prepaid expenses	15,000	19,000
Total current assets	414,000	450,000
Total assets...	938,000	974,000
Total current liabilities...	338,000	366,000
Total liabilities	691,000*	667,000*
Preferred stock, 4%, $100 par..............................	25,000	
Common stock, $1 par (150,000 shares)		150,000
$5 par (20,000 shares)	100,000	
Total stockholders' equity	247,000	307,000
Market price per share of common stock..............	$55.50	$9.75

* Notes and bonds payable: Eckert, Inc., $303,000
  Biomed, Inc., $4,000

Selected balance sheet data at beginning of current year:

	Eckert, Inc.	Biomed, Inc.
Current receivables, net	$193,000	$142,000
Inventories	197,000	209,000
Total assets..	909,000	842,000
Preferred stock, 4%, $100 par..............................	25,000	
Common stock, $1 par (150,000 shares)		150,000
$5 par (20,000 shares)	100,000	
Total stockholders' equity.....................................	215,000	263,000

Your investment strategy is to purchase the stocks of companies that have low price/earnings ratios but appear to be in good shape financially. Assume that you have analyzed all other factors, and your decision depends on the results of the ratio analysis to be performed.

Required

1. Compute the following ratios for both companies for the current year and decide which company's stock better fits your investment strategy.
   a. Current ratio
   b. Acid-test ratio
   c. Inventory turnover
   d. Times-interest-earned ratio
   e. Return on common stockholders' equity
   f. Earnings per share of common stock
   g. Book value per share of common stock
   h. Price/earnings ratio
2. Compute each company's economic-value-added (EVA®) measure, and determine whether their EVA®s confirm or alter your investment decision. Each company's cost of capital is 12%. Round all amounts to the nearest $1,000.

APPLY YOUR KNOWLEDGE

DECISION CASES

Case 1. Suppose you manage Lancer.com, an e-commerce startup that lost money during the past year. Before you can set the business on a successful course, you must analyze the company and industry data for the current year to learn what is wrong. The company's data follow at the top of the next page.

Identifying action to cut losses and establish profitability (Obj. 2, 4, 5)

Required

On the basis of your analysis of these figures, suggest three courses of action Lancer.com might take to reduce its losses and establish profitable operations. Give your reasons for each suggestion.

Lancer.com Balance Sheet Data

	Lancer.com	Industry Average
Cash and short-term investments	3.0%	6.8%
Inventory	79.4	71.5
Prepaid expenses	1.0	0.0
Total current assets	83.4	78.3
Plant assets, net	12.6	15.2
Other assets	4.0	6.5
Total assets	100.0%	100.0%
Notes payable, short-term, 12%	26.2%	14.0%
Accounts payable	12.0	25.1
Accrued liabilities	7.8	7.9
Total current liabilities	46.0	47.0
Long-term debt, 11%	24.8	16.4
Total liabilities	70.8	63.4
Common stockholders' equity	29.2	36.6
Total liabilities and stockholders' equity	100.0%	100.0%

Lancer.com Income Statement Data

	Lancer.com	Industry Average
Net sales	100.0%	100.0%
Cost of sales	(74.2)	(64.8)
Gross profit	25.8	35.2
Operating expense	(35.1)	(32.3)
Operating income (loss)	(9.3)	2.9
Interest expense	(8.5)	(1.3)
Other revenue	1.1	0.3
Income (loss) before income tax	(16.7)	1.9
Income tax (expense) saving	4.4	(0.8)
Net income (loss)	(12.3)%	1.1%

Taking unethical action to improve the ratios
(Obj. 4)

Case 2. Amanda Catlin is the controller of Success Marketing, whose year end is December 31. Catlin prepares checks for suppliers in December and posts them to the appropriate accounts in that month. However, she holds on to the checks and mails them to the suppliers in January. What financial ratio(s) are most affected by the action? What is Catlin's purpose in undertaking the activity?

ETHICAL ISSUE

Lindsey Contractors' borrowing agreements make certain demands on the business. Lindsey's Long-Term Debt may not exceed Stockholders' Equity, and the current ratio may not fall below 1.50. If Lindsey fails to meet this requirement, the company's lenders can take over management of the corporation.

Current liabilities have mounted faster than current assets, causing the current ratio to fall to 1.47. Before releasing financial statements, Lindsey management is scrambling to improve the current ratio. The controller points out that an investment can be classified as either long-term or short-term, depending on management's intention. By deciding to convert an investment to cash within one year, Lindsey can classify the investment as short-term—a current asset. On the controller's recommendation, Lindsey's board of directors votes to reclassify long-term investments as short-term.

Required

1. What effect will reclassifying the investments have on the current ratio? Is Lindsey's real financial position stronger as a result of reclassifying the investments?
2. Shortly after the financial statements are released, sales improve and so then does the current ratio. As a result, Lindsey management decides not to sell the investments it had reclassified as short-term. Accordingly, Lindsey reclassifies the investments as long-term. Has management behaved unethically? Give your reason.

FINANCIAL STATEMENT CASE

Use the Summary Financial and Operating Data (Unaudited) that appears at the end of the **Target Corporation** financial statements (Appendix A) to answer the following questions.

Measuring profitability and analyzing stock as an investment (Obj. 1)

Required

1. From the Summary Financial Data, perform a five-year trend analysis of
   a. Revenues   **b.** Net earnings

   Start with 1995, and end with 1999. Use 1994 as the base year.
2. Evaluate Target's revenues and profitability trends during this five-year period.

TEAM PROJECTS

Project 1. Select an industry that interests you, and use the leading company in that industry as the benchmark. Then select two other companies in the same industry. For each category of ratios in the Decision Guidelines feature on page 731, compute at least two ratios for all three companies. Write a two-page report that compares the two companies with the benchmark company.

Project 2. Select a company and obtain its financial statements. Convert the income statement and the balance sheet to common-size, and compare the company you selected to the industry average. Robert Morris Associates' *Annual Statement Studies,* Dun & Bradstreet's *Industry Norms & Key Business Ratios,* and Prentice Hall's *Almanac of Business and Industrial Financial Ratios,* by Leo Troy, all publish common-size statements for most industries.

INTERNET EXERCISE

Home Depot serves both the do-it-yourself and the professional construction markets by stocking over 40,000 items, including lumber, floor and wall coverings, plumbing and gardening supplies, tools, and paint.

1. Go to **http://www.fortune.com** and in the left-hand column under "Lists," click on *Fortune 500.* What is Home Depot's current Fortune 500 ranking?
2. Click on *Home Depot.* Review the information displayed. Does Home Depot appear financially strong or weak? Why?
3. Click on the Industry: *Specialty Retailers.* Review the Industry Snapshot to answer the following questions.
   a. *Lowe's* is a primary competitor of Home Depot. Examine the information reported for both companies. Which company is more profitable? Why?
   b. Among all the Specialty Retailers, identify the company with the greatest "profits as % of revenues" ratio and the "profits as % of stockholders' equity" ratio. For the companies identified, what do these ratios indicate? The text refers to these ratios by what titles?
4. In the left-hand column in the "Stock/Fund Quotes:" box, type in *HD,* the stock symbol for Home Depot, and click on *Go.* At the bottom of the screen under "Financials," click on *Annual Income Statement.* For the most current years available, compute the trend percentages for "Net sales" and "Cost of Merchandise" using the earliest of the four years as the base year. Net sales have increased by what percent since the base year? Which account, Net sales or Cost of merchandise (sold) increased at a greater rate? Is this favorable or unfavorable?
5. Go to **http://www.homedepot.com** and click on Home Depot stores *opening soon.* How many Home Depot stores will be opening within the next month? Do you think future revenues for Home Depot will be increasing? Why or why not?

Home Depot

Computing ratios for two well-known companies (Obj. 4)

Go to the "Generally Accepted Accounting Principles and Audited Financial Statements" and the "Managerial Accounting and Cost Analysis" episodes on the *Mastering Accounting* CD-ROM for interactive, video-enhanced exercises that focus on CanGo's need for standardized accounting reports to prepare for an IPO and to attract investors to fund new business projects. In these episodes, CanGo managers learn the value of properly prepared financial reports.

19 Introduction to Management Accounting

LEARNING OBJECTIVES

After studying this chapter, you should be able to

1. Distinguish between financial accounting and management accounting

2. Describe the value chain and classify costs by value-chain function

3. Distinguish direct costs from indirect costs

4. Distinguish among full product costs, inventoriable product costs, and period costs

5. Prepare the financial statements of a manufacturing company

6. Identify major trends in the business environment, and use cost-benefit analysis to make business decisions

7. Use reasonable standards to make ethical judgments

Dell Computer Corporation—the direct-order computer-assembly firm—saw its net income for the year ending in January 2000 surge to nearly $1.9 billion, double its earnings only two years earlier. This phenomenal growth helped Dell pass **IBM** and become the second largest U.S. PC seller. But Dell's outlook hasn't always been so rosy. Just a few years earlier, the company posted its first-ever net loss—$36 million—after a major product recall and a shareholder lawsuit.

How did Michael Dell turn his company around? What information helped him make wise choices?

Dell knew that cost control should drive his business, because most customers prefer a good price over a specific brand name. Dell executives also had to decide how to market and distribute the computers. Should the company sell via the Internet or telephone and eliminate the middleman? Or should it sell computers through discount chains like **Sam's Club** and **Best Buy?** Should Dell focus on the U.S. market, or expand in Latin America, Europe, or the Pacific? Decisions, decisions, decisions!

Accounting information helps executives like Michael Dell make these and many other decisions. For example, the accounting system provides managers with cost and profit information broken down by

1. Type of product, such as desktop and laptop models
2. Marketing strategy, such as Internet sales versus direct-telephone sales versus sales to retailers like Best Buy
3. Geographic regions, such as U.S., Latin American, European, or Pacific operations

This kind of information helped Michael Dell steer Dell Computer in the right direction. The result? Soaring income and stock price. A $1,000 investment in Dell at the end of 1993 was worth $143,000 by January 2000.

Source: Based on Gary McWilliams, "Dell's New Push: Cheaper Laptops Built to Order," *Wall Street Journal,* June 19, 1999, p. B1; Louise Lee, "Dell Computer Profit Soars, Tops Forecasts," *Wall Street Journal,* May 21, 1997, p. A3; Toni Mack, "Michael Dell's New Religion," *Forbes,* June 6, 1994, pp. 45–46.

So far, we have focused on reporting accounting information for decision makers *outside* the organization: investors, creditors, and government authorities. We analyzed *financial accounting* reports—the income statement, the balance sheet, and the statement of cash flows. These statements report the company's *past* performance and financial position.

We now shift our focus to how accounting information helps shape the company's *future.* We will examine accounting through the eyes of the people who run the business. Decision makers *inside* a company are its managers, and accounting designed to meet their information needs is called *management accounting.* ➤

◄ We introduced the distinction between financial and management accounting in Chapter 1, p. 6.

THE FUNCTIONS OF MANAGEMENT

Managers perform two broad functions: planning and controlling (Exhibit 19-1). **Planning** means choosing goals and deciding how to achieve them. For example, one of **Dell Computer's** goals is to increase operating income. The company's managers could

1. Raise sale prices
2. Increase advertising to stimulate sales
3. Redesign the computers for faster production and servicing

Suppose Dell's managers choose alternative 3. Dell's engineers, purchasing officer, and production, marketing, and service managers work together to redesign the laptop computer to speed assembly and servicing while still meeting customer needs. Managers use the new design to budget the cost of the laptops, considering both the cost per laptop and the number of laptops they expect to

PLANNING. Choosing goals and deciding how to achieve them.

BUDGET. Quantitative expression of a plan that helps managers coordinate and implement the plan.

CONTROLLING. Evaluating the results of business operations by comparing the actual results to the plan.

sell. The **budget** is a quantitative expression of a plan that helps managers coordinate and implement the plan.

Dell's purchasing officer uses the new design and the number of laptops they expect to sell to decide how many component parts to order, and the production manager alerts the plant workers to the design changes before they begin assembling the laptops. After they implement the plan, controlling begins. **Controlling** means evaluating the results of business operations by comparing the actual results to the plan. Dell's accounting system records the number of laptops produced. The system also records the purchase prices and number of components used to assemble the laptops.

After completing the day's production, managers can compare the actual costs with the budgeted costs to evaluate the performance of the laptop operation and its employees. If actual costs fall below budgeted costs, that is good news. But if actual costs exceed budgeted amounts, managers may need to take corrective action. The operating costs provide feedback that helps managers decide whether their decision to redesign the laptop was a good decision that increased profits or a bad decision that decreased profits.

EXHIBIT 19-1 **The Functions of Management**

Managers make both shorter-term and longer-term planning and controlling decisions. In the shorter term, Dell must decide whether Internet sales will increase market share and reduce marketing costs, which will in turn increase profits. Dell's executives must also plan far into the future when they decide whether to expand in Latin America. Building a new plant in Brazil will tie up cash for years to come.

HOW IS MANAGEMENT ACCOUNTING DIFFERENT FROM FINANCIAL ACCOUNTING?

Objective 1
Distinguish between financial accounting and management accounting

Financial and management accounting both use the accrual basis, and both reflect the same underlying economic transactions. However, their focus differs. As you learned in Chapters 1–18, financial accounting focuses on preparing financial statements that allow stockholders and creditors to make informed investment decisions. These highly summarized reports, which are constrained by GAAP, focus on the company's past financial performance. In contrast, company managers need more detailed and timely information to decide how to run the company efficiently and effectively in the future.

Exhibit 19-2 summarizes the distinctions between management accounting and financial accounting. Consider points 1, 2, and 3 of the exhibit. Deciding whether to build a new production plant in Brazil relates to **Dell's** future, and the decision makers are Dell managers. Dell will budget (predict) the plant's future income and cash flows. Managers will then compare the benefits and costs of operating the plant with the benefits and costs of other investments. For example, Dell could use the money required for the Brazilian plant to develop a new workstation model. Management

EXHIBIT 19-2
Management Accounting Versus
Financial Accounting

	Management Accounting	Financial Accounting
1. Primary users	Internal—the company's managers	External—investors, creditors, and government authorities such as the IRS and SEC
2. Purpose of information	Help managers plan and control business operations	Help investors, creditors, and others make investment, credit, and other decisions
3. Focus and time dimension	Relevance and focus on the future—example: 2004 budget prepared in 2003	Reliability, objectivity, and focus on the past—example: 2001 actual performance reported in 2002
4. Type of report	Internal reports not restricted by GAAP—determined by cost-benefit analysis	Financial statements restricted by GAAP
5. Verification	No independent audit	Annual independent audit by certified public accountant
6. Scope of information	Detailed reports on parts of the company (products, departments, territories) often on a daily, weekly, or monthly basis	Summary reports primarily on the company as a whole, usually on a quarterly or annual basis
7. Behavioral implications	Concern about how reports will affect employee behavior	Concern about adequacy of disclosure; behavioral implications are secondary

accounting helps Dell executives choose the investment with the greatest expected net benefit to the company.

Now consider point 4 of Exhibit 19-2—the types of accounting reports decision makers use. There are no GAAP-type standards for preparing the information that managers use to plan and control a company's operations. Managers are thus free to tailor the company's management accounting system to provide information that will help them make better decisions. Managers weigh

- The *benefits* of the system—helping managers make better decisions that increase profit, against
- The *cost* of the system—including costs of training managers, as well as the cost to develop and run the system

Weighing costs against benefits to help make decisions is called **cost-benefit analysis.** The costs and benefits of any particular management accounting system differ from one company to the next, so different companies create different systems. For example, companies vary in the way they figure the manufacturing cost of a product, as we shall see in Chapters 20 and 21. For external reporting, though, all businesses follow GAAP and use the accrual basis of accounting. Also, externally reported financial statements are audited each year by independent certified public accountants. Internal management accounting reports are not audited, as shown in point 5 of Exhibit 19-2.

Point 6 of Exhibit 19-2 highlights another difference between management accounting and financial accounting—the scope of the information provided. Management accounting generates more detailed reports on parts of the company (products, departments, or territories) on a daily, weekly, or monthly basis. Managers need this more detailed and timely information to run the company. For example, detailed, timely information helps managers (a) identify ways to cut costs, (b) set prices that will be competitive yet yield a profit, (c) identify the most profitable products and customers so that the company can focus on key strategic profit-makers, and (d) evaluate managers' job performance. Information technology, from Web-based company Intranet systems to hand-held computers, lets managers access this information with the touch of a button or the click of a mouse.

 DAILY EXERCISE 19-1

COST-BENEFIT ANALYSIS. Weighing costs against benefits to help make decisions.

e-Accounting

Refining Dining with Data Mining

As the chefs in the kitchen slice and dice meat and veggies, the managers back at headquarters are asking the accountants to "slice and dice" the data. Using the latest in data mining technology from **Digital Equipment Corp.** and **Informix,** large restaurant operators now analyze a dizzying amount of data that extend well beyond sales, cash management, and inventory.

- **AFC,** operator and franchiser of more than 3,300 Church's, Popeye's Chicken & Biscuits, Seattle Coffee Company, and Torrefazione Italia outlets worldwide, collects customer-purchase data by item, item combination, day, and location. Information is stored in a data warehouse. Then sophisticated data mining software ferrets out patterns, trends, and even challenges and problems. Managers get information on how factors such as location affect the profitability of sales promotions and which patrons respond to which offers.
- **Red Robin International,** a 135-unit casual-dining chain based in Englewood, Colorado, relies on patterns revealed by its data warehouse to hone menus. "We do a lot of menu changes, with new items and specials," explains Howard Jenkins, Red Robin's Vice President of Information Systems. "With data mining in place, we can ask ourselves, 'If we put the items with the high margin in the middle of the menu, do we sell more versus putting [them] at the top or bottom . . . ?"
- **Pizzeria Uno** uses a more economical decision-support system to define and analyze data in response to specific queries, such as take-out versus eat-in pizza sales. A nifty tool called "80/20" identifies the 20% of customers who contribute 80% of sales, so management can adjust menus and promos to suit top patrons' preferences.

Source: Based on Anonymous, "Mining the data of dining," *Nation's Restaurant News*, May 22, 2000, pp. S22–S24.

Point 7 of Exhibit 19-2 highlights the behavioral implications of management accounting reports. Managers' actions depend on how their performance is measured, and the accounting system measures performance. For example, the manager of a **Baskin Robbins** store will care about cleanliness and cheerful service if her performance evaluation depends on the store's profit. Excellent customer service leads to higher sales, which increase profit. In contrast, if the manager is evaluated only on her ability to control costs, she will be less concerned about customer service and she may save money by cleaning the store less often. Top executives create performance evaluation plans very carefully because they understand that "you get what you measure."

SERVICE, MERCHANDISING, AND MANUFACTURING COMPANIES

SERVICE COMPANY. A company that provides intangible services, rather than tangible products.

MERCHANDISING COMPANY. A company that resells products previously bought from suppliers.

Previous chapters focused on service and merchandising firms. Now we add manufacturing companies to the mix. **Service companies** do not sell tangible products. Rather, they provide intangible services such as Web site development, hair styling, and legal advice. Labor is typically their most significant cost—often as high as 70% of total costs. Well-known service businesses include **H&R Block** (tax return preparation), **Randstad** (temporary personnel services), and **eBay** (on-line auction).

In contrast, merchandisers and manufacturers sell tangible products. **Merchandising companies** resell products previously bought from suppliers. **Amazon.com, Wal-Mart,** and **Footlocker** are merchandising companies. Consider Footlocker, which sells athletic shoes. Like other merchandisers,

Footlocker buys ready-made inventory for resale to customers. Determining Footlocker's cost of inventory is relatively easy. Cost is the price Footlocker pays for the shoes plus freight-in costs. ➡ Because merchandise inventory consists only of goods ready for sale, a merchandiser's balance sheet typically reports a single category of inventory.

➡ See Chapter 5, pages 170–177, for a review of inventory in merchandising firms.

Manufacturing companies use labor, plant, and equipment to convert raw materials into new finished products. For example, companies that supply athletic shoes to stores such as Footlocker—**New Balance** and **NIKE**—begin their manufacturing processes with raw materials (cloth, rubber, plastics). These materials are cut, glued, stitched, and formed into athletic shoes. Converting raw materials into finished products makes it more difficult to measure New Balance's inventory cost than to measure Footlocker's.

Manufacturers have three kinds of inventory:

1. **Materials inventory:** *raw materials for use in manufacturing.* For example, a shoe manufacturer's materials include leather, glue, plastic, cloth, and thread. Raw materials for Bethlehem Steel include iron ore, coal, and chemicals.

2. **Work in process inventory:** *goods that are partway through the manufacturing process, but not yet complete.* At **Dell Computer,** partially completed computers make up work in process inventory. At **Texaco,** work in process inventory is half-processed crude oil that is being refined into gasoline.

3. **Finished goods inventory:** *completed goods that have not yet been sold.* Finished goods are what the manufacturer sells to a merchandising business. For example, **Proctor & Gamble** (P&G) manufacturers Tide laundry soap and Crest toothpaste, which are finished goods that P&G sells to **Safeway** and **Kmart.** P&G's finished goods inventory then becomes the inventory of Safeway and Kmart.

Exhibit 19-3 summarizes the differences among service, merchandising, and manufacturing companies.

MANUFACTURING COMPANY. A company that uses labor, plant, and equipment to convert raw materials into new finished products.

MATERIALS INVENTORY. Raw materials for use in manufacturing.

WORK IN PROCESS INVENTORY. Goods that are partway through the manufacturing process, but not yet complete.

FINISHED GOODS INVENTORY. Completed goods that have not yet been sold.

EXHIBIT 19-3   **Service, Merchandising, and Manufacturing Companies**

	Service Companies	**Merchandising Companies**	**Manufacturing Companies**
Examples	Advertising agencies eBay H&R Block Law firms Merrill Lynch	Amazon.com Kroger The Gap Wal-Mart Wholesalers	Bethlehem Steel Cisco Systems DaimlerChrysler Dell Computer General Mills
Primary Output	Intangible services (for example, auctions, entertainment, or advice)	Tangible products purchased from suppliers	New tangible products made as workers and equipment convert raw materials (purchased from suppliers) into new finished products
Type(s) of Inventory	None	Inventory	Materials inventory Work in process inventory Finished goods inventory

THE VALUE CHAIN

Objective 2
Describe the value chain and classify costs by value-chain function

Many people describe **Dell** (or **IBM** or **Hewlett-Packard**) as a manufacturing company. Dell is perhaps more accurately described as a company that does manufacturing. Why? Because manufacturing or production is only one of its major business functions.

Companies that do manufacturing also do many other things. For example, Dell also conducts research and development to determine what kinds of new computers to introduce. It uses that information to design new computers, which it then

EXHIBIT 19-4
The Value Chain

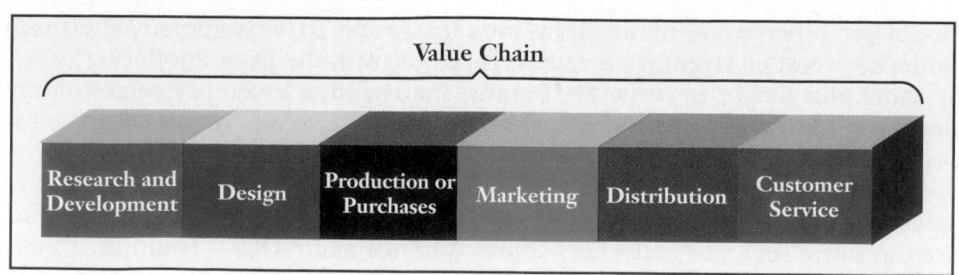

VALUE CHAIN. Sequence of activities that adds value to a firm's products or services. Includes R&D, design, production or purchases, marketing, distribution, and customer service.

RESEARCH AND DEVELOPMENT (R&D). The process of researching and developing new or improved products or services, or the processes for producing them.

DESIGN. Detailed engineering of products and services, or processes for producing them.

PRODUCTION OR PURCHASES. Resources used to produce a product or service, or to purchase finished merchandise.

MARKETING. Promotion of products or services.

DISTRIBUTION. Delivery of products or services to customers.

CUSTOMER SERVICE. Support provided for customers after the sale.

produces, markets, and distributes. These business functions collectively are called the **value chain**—the sequence of activities that adds value to a firm's products or services (Exhibit 19-4).

- **Research and development (R&D)**—the process of researching and developing new or improved products or services, or the processes for producing them. Examples: (1) identifying a need for a lighter laptop computer through market research, and (2) developing a breakthrough technology that drastically reduces the size or weight of the motherboard.
- **Design**—detailed engineering of products and services, or the processes for producing them. Example: redesigning the laptop's case and reengineering the manufacturing process to accommodate the new case.
- **Production or purchases**—Resources used to produce a product or service, or to purchase finished merchandise. Examples: (1) For a manufacturer such as Dell, the actual production of products—such as the materials, labor, and equipment used to assemble the new laptop; or (2) for a merchandiser such as **Best Buy,** the purchase of merchandise inventory (such as laptop computers) to resell to customers.
- **Marketing**—promotion of products or services. Example: an ad campaign for the new laptop.
- **Distribution**—delivery of products or services to customers. Example: delivery of the new laptop via truck to customers.
- **Customer service**—support provided for customers after the sale. Example: a hotline for owners of the new laptop.

Managers do not proceed step by step in this exact order through the value chain. Indeed, managers may form a laptop project team to work on R&D, design, production, marketing, and customer service simultaneously.

The value chain applies equally to service, merchandising, and manufacturing firms. For example, an advertising agency such as **Saatchi & Saatchi** incurs

- *Marketing* costs to obtain a new client
- *Research and development* and *design* costs to develop the new client's ad campaign
- *Customer service* costs to address the new client's concerns
- *Distribution* costs to get the ads to the media

Managers are concerned about the value chain as a whole. They must control the total costs of the entire chain. For example, Dell recently decided to spend more in product design to make its laptop easier to service and thereby reduce the costs of honoring product warranties. Even though design costs increase, the total cost of the computer—as measured by the entire value chain—is lower.

COST OBJECTS, DIRECT COSTS, AND INDIRECT COSTS

A **cost object** is anything for which managers want a separate measurement of costs. For example, **Dell Computer's** cost objects may include

- Individual products (laptop computers or desktop models)
- Alternative marketing strategies (direct-telephone sales versus Internet sales)
- Geographic segments of the business (United States, European, or Pacific)
- Departments (personnel, accounting, or information systems)

Objective 3
Distinguish direct costs from indirect costs

COST OBJECT. Anything for which managers want a separate measurement of costs.

Costs that can be specifically traced to the cost object are **direct costs.** Costs that cannot be specifically traced to the cost object are **indirect costs.**

The manager of a Dell Computer plant wants to know the cost of assembling a specific laptop. The cost of the chip in the laptop is a *direct* cost of that computer because the chip can be specifically traced to the particular laptop. In contrast, the plant manager's salary cannot be specifically traced to any one computer, so the plant manager's salary is an *indirect* cost of the laptop.

Consider another example. Suppose Dell headquarters asks for the costs incurred by a production plant. The plant now becomes the cost object. The plant manager's salary becomes a direct cost because it can be specifically traced to the plant.

Now let's focus on the most common cost object: products.

DIRECT COST. A cost th be specifically trace cost object.

INDIRECT COST. A cost that cannot be specifically traced to a cost object.

PRODUCT COSTS

Accountants use the term *product costs* for the costs of producing (or purchasing) tangible products intended for sale. We distinguish between two types of product costs: full product costs and inventoriable product costs. Managers use full product costs for certain decisions, like setting long-term sale prices for the goods and services their companies sell. However, GAAP requires accountants to use inventoriable costs for external reporting (Inventory on the balance sheet and Cost of Goods Sold on the income statement). Let's see how the two types of product costs differ.

Objective 4
Distinguish among full product costs, inventoriable product costs, and period costs

Full Product Costs

Full product costs are the costs of all resources used throughout the value chain for a product. For **New Balance,** the full product cost of a particular shoe model is the total cost incurred to research, design, manufacture, market, and distribute the model, as well as to service the customers who buy it. Before launching a new model, managers must predict the full product costs of the shoe to set a long-run average sale price that will cover all the shoe's costs, from R&D to customer service, plus return a profit. New Balance can also compare each model's sale price to its full cost to determine which models are the most profitable. Marketing can then focus on selling the more profitable models.

FULL PRODUCT COSTS. The costs of all resources used throughout the value chain for a product.

External Reporting: Inventoriable Product Costs or Period Costs?

Inventoriable product costs are product costs that are initially regarded as an asset for external financial reporting and are not expensed until the product is sold. GAAP requires a very specific definition of inventoriable product costs that includes only a *portion* of full product costs. Thus, inventoriable costs do not include costs from all elements of the value chain.

INVENTORIABLE PRODUCT COSTS. All costs of a product that are regarded as an asset for external financial reporting, and are not expensed until the product is sold. Must conform to GAAP.

Why do managers need to know the difference between full product costs and inventoriable product costs?

Answer: 1. Only inventoriable product costs are used to determine Inventory and Cost of Goods Sold amounts for the balance sheet and income statement.
2. Inventoriable product costs do not include all the costs the company must cover to earn a profit. Therefore, managers need to know the full costs of producing a product to set a long-run sale price that will cover total costs plus return a profit, and to determine which products, services, and customers are the most profitable.

Which costs are inventoriable under GAAP? The answer depends on whether the company is a merchandiser or a manufacturer.

Merchandising Companies' Inventoriable Product Costs

As we saw in Chapter 5, merchandising companies' inventoriable costs include *only* the cost of purchasing the inventory from suppliers (for example, the price

Footlocker pays **New Balance** for shoes), plus freight-in. (These are the costs in the third element of the value chain in Exhibit 19-4.) Footlocker's inventoriable cost (purchase price plus freight-in) of shoes is an asset—Inventory—in Footlocker's accounting records. This inventoriable cost remains an asset (Inventory) until the shoes are *sold*. Then it becomes an expense—Cost of Goods Sold.

In contrast, costs incurred in other elements of the value chain—such as Footlocker's employees' salaries, commissions paid to its sales staff, and distribution costs—are not inventoriable product costs. Instead, these are **period costs,** operating costs that are always expensed in the period in which they are incurred. Period costs are never part of the Inventory asset account. This contrasts with inventoriable product costs that are first considered inventory (an asset) and are not expensed (as cost of goods sold) until later when the products are sold.

Full Product Costs	
Inventoriable Product Costs (Production or Purchases)	**Period Costs (R&D, Design, Marketing, Distribution, Customer Service)**

THINK IT OVER

What would be the inventoriable costs for a service firm such as **H&R Block?**

Answer: Service firms like H&R Block have no tangible inventory of products intended for sale. Services cannot be produced today and stored up to sell later. Because service firms have no inventory, they have no inventoriable costs. Instead, they have only period costs that are expensed as incurred.

Manufacturing Companies' Inventoriable Product Costs

DAILY EXERCISE 19-5

Manufacturing firms' product costs are more complex than those for merchandising firms. Manufacturers' inventoriable costs include raw materials plus all other costs incurred in the manufacturing/production process. Let's take a closer look.

Exhibit 19-5 illustrates the major categories of inventoriable product costs for a manufacturer such as New Balance:

EXHIBIT 19-5 **Inventoriable Product Costs for a Manufacturer**

   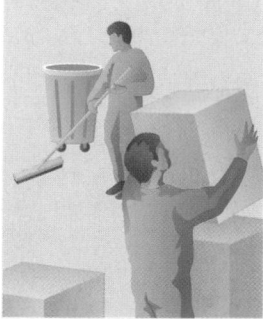 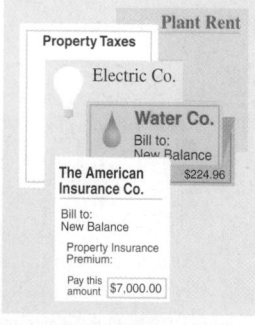

Direct Materials　　Direct Labor　　Indirect Materials　　Indirect Labor　　Other

Manufacturing Overhead

• **Direct materials** (1) must become a physical part of the finished product, and (2) their costs (invoice cost plus freight-in) must be separately and conveniently traceable to the finished product. Consider New Balance shoes—the leather uppers, the rubber and plastic soles, and the shoelaces are direct materials. They become part of the finished shoe, and we can trace the costs directly to the shoe as it moves through the production process.

- **Direct labor** is the compensation of employees who physically convert materials into the company's products. For New Balance, direct labor includes the wages of machine operators and persons who assemble the shoes. Their effort can be traced *directly* to the finished products.
- **Manufacturing overhead** includes all manufacturing costs other than direct materials and direct labor. Examples include indirect materials, indirect labor, plant utilities, plant repairs, plant maintenance, plant rent, insurance on the plant, plant property taxes, and depreciation on plant buildings and equipment. Manufacturing overhead also is called **factory overhead** or **indirect manufacturing cost.**

The key point is that manufacturing overhead includes only indirect manufacturing costs—that is, indirect costs related to the manufacturing plant. Depreciation on the plant's building and equipment is an indirect manufacturing cost, so it is part of manufacturing overhead. Likewise, insurance on the plant's building and equipment is part of manufacturing overhead. In contrast, depreciation on delivery trucks is not a manufacturing cost. Delivery is part of the distribution element of the value chain, not the production (or manufacturing) element (see Exhibit 19-4). Depreciation on delivery trucks is therefore part of distribution expense (a period expense), not part of manufacturing overhead. Similarly, auto insurance for the sales force is part of the marketing element of the value chain, not the production element. Insurance related to the sales force is part of marketing expense (a period expense), not part of manufacturing overhead.

Let's take a closer look at two major components of manufacturing overhead: indirect materials and indirect labor. First consider indirect materials. The glue and thread used in athletic shoes become physical parts of the finished product. But, compared with the cost of the leather uppers and rubber soles, the costs of glue and thread are minor. It is hard to measure the costs of those low-priced materials for a single pair of shoes. How would a supervisor figure the cost of a brushful of glue? How useful would such detailed information be? These kinds of materials, whose costs cannot conveniently be directly traced to particular finished products, are called **indirect materials.** Indirect materials are part of manufacturing overhead.

Some manufacturing labor costs are classified as **indirect labor.** Like indirect materials, indirect labor is difficult to trace to specific products. Examples include the pay of forklift operators, janitors, and plant managers. Indirect labor, like indirect materials, is part of manufacturing overhead.

To summarize, a manufacturing company computes inventoriable product costs as follows:

> Direct materials
> + Direct labor
> + Manufacturing overhead
> = Inventoriable product costs

New Balance's balance sheet will report the inventoriable cost of the finished shoes on hand at the end of the period (direct materials, direct labor, and manufacturing overhead) as an asset—Finished Goods Inventory. New Balance's income statement will report as Cost of Goods Sold the inventoriable costs of the shoes the company sold.

Remember that New Balance's inventoriable product costs include *only* the manufacturing costs—that is, only *costs incurred in the third element of the value chain in Exhibit 19-4.* Costs in other elements of the value chain—such as New Balance's cost to research and develop a new style of shoe, and to advertise and deliver shoes to customers—are *not* inventoriable product costs for external reporting. Instead, these are period costs that are expensed in the income statement in the period incurred. Period costs are never part of the Inventory asset account.

Exhibit 19-6 summarizes the differences between inventoriable and period costs for service, merchandising, and manufacturing companies. Study this exhibit carefully. When are costs like depreciation, insurance, utilities, and property taxes treated as inventoriable product costs? *Only* when those costs are related to the manufacturing plant. When those costs are related to nonmanufacturing activities like R&D or marketing, they are treated as period costs. Service companies and

DIRECT LABOR. The compensation of employees who physically convert materials into the company's products; labor costs that are directly traceable to finished products.

MANUFACTURING OVERHEAD. All manufacturing costs other than direct materials and direct labor. Also called **factory overhead** or **indirect manufacturing cost.**

 DAILY EXERCISE 19-6

INDIRECT MATERIALS. Materials whose costs cannot conveniently be directly traced to particular finished products.

INDIRECT LABOR. Labor costs that are difficult to trace to specific products.

 DAILY EXERCISE 19-7

Type of Company	Inventoriable Product Costs (Initially an asset (Inventory), and not expensed (Cost of Goods Sold) until inventory is sold)	Period Costs (Expensed in period incurred; never considered an asset)
Service companies	None	Salaries, depreciation expense, utilities, insurance, property taxes, advertising
Merchandising companies	Purchases plus freight-in	Salaries, depreciation expense, utilities, insurance, property taxes, advertising, freight-out
Manufacturing companies	Direct materials, plus direct labor, plus manufacturing overhead (including indirect materials; indirect labor; depreciation on plant and equipment; plant insurance, plant utilities, and property taxes on plant)	R&D; freight-out; depreciation expense, utilities, insurance, and property taxes on executive headquarters (separate from plant); advertising; CEO's salary

 DAILY EXERCISE 19-8

merchandisers do no manufacturing, so they always treat depreciation, insurance, utilities, and property taxes as period costs.

The difference between inventoriable product costs and period costs is important because these two kinds of cost are treated differently in the financial statements. The next section takes a closer look at how the financial statements of service companies, merchandisers, and manufacturers differ.

Objective 5
Prepare the financial statements of a manufacturing company

PRODUCT AND PERIOD COSTS IN FINANCIAL STATEMENTS

How do inventoriable product costs and period costs affect financial statements? We begin with a short review to help you see how a manufacturer's financial statements differ from those of service and merchandising companies.

Service Companies

➡ Chapter 1, p. 17, introduced income statements for service companies.

Service companies have the simplest accounting. Exhibit 19-7 shows the income statement of eNow!, a group of e-commerce consultants. ◄ The firm has no inventory and thus no inventoriable costs, so eNow!'s income statement has no Cost of Goods Sold. The statement groups all expenses (period costs) together. As for most service companies, eNow!'s largest expense is for the salaries of employees who perform the services.

EXHIBIT 19-7
Service Company Income
Statement

ENOW!
Income Statement
Month Ended December 31, 20X2

Revenues		$160,000
Expenses:		
Salary expense	$104,000	
Office rent expense	18,000	
Depreciation expense—furniture and equipment	3,500	
Marketing expense	2,500	
Training expense	2,000	(130,000)
Operating income		$ 30,000

Merchandising Companies

Exhibit 19-8 presents a bird's-eye view of how inventoriable costs and period costs affect the financial statements of merchandising companies.

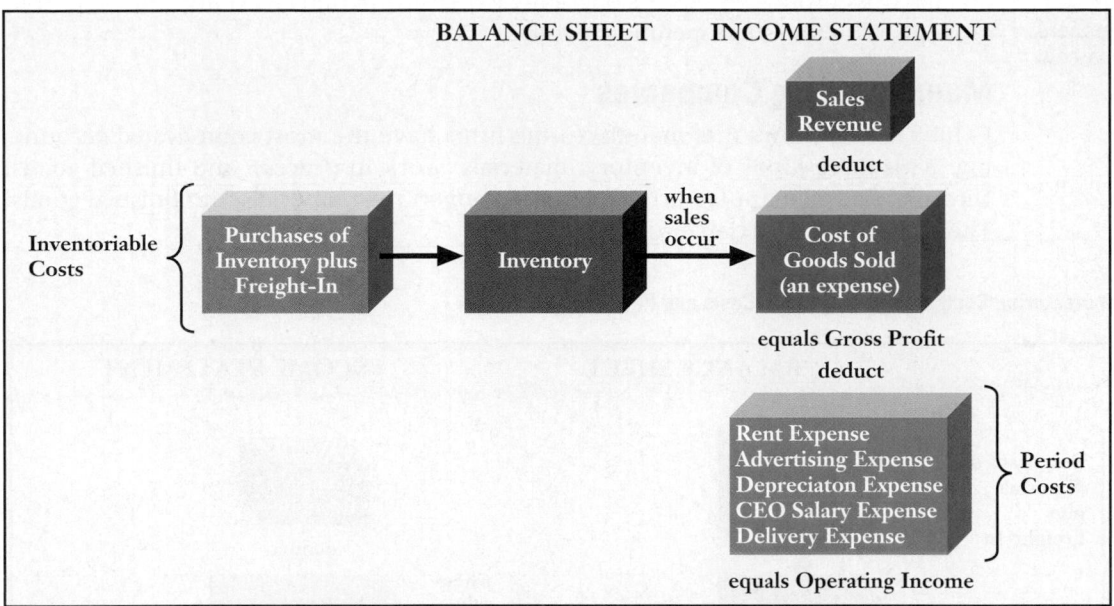

Apex Showrooms, a merchandiser of lighting fixtures, buys chandeliers and track lights ready for resale. Apex's *only* inventoriable costs are for the purchase of these goods, plus freight-in. Exhibit 19-9 shows Apex's income statement.[1]

EXHIBIT **19-9**
Merchandising Company Income Statement

⊙ DAILY EXERCISE 19-9

⊙ DAILY EXERCISE 19-10

APEX SHOWROOMS		
Income Statement		
Month Ended December 31, 20X2		
Sales revenue...		$150,000
Cost of goods sold:		
Beginning inventory	$ 9,500	
Purchases and freight-in	110,000	
Cost of goods available for sale	119,500	
Ending inventory	(13,000)	
Cost of goods sold		106,500
Gross profit		43,500
Operating expenses:..................................		
Showroom rent expense......................	5,000	
Sales salary expense............................	2,500	
Administrative expense........................	1,500	9,000
Operating income		$ 34,500

In contrast to the service company (Exhibit 19-7), the merchandiser's income statement features Cost of Goods Sold as the major expense. Merchandisers like Apex compute Cost of Goods Sold as follows:

Beginning inventory	$ 9,500	**What Apex had at the beginning of the period**
+ Purchases and freight-in	110,000	**What Apex bought during the period**
= Cost of goods available for sale	119,500	**Total available for sale during the period**
– Ending inventory	13,000	**What Apex had left at the end of the period**
= Cost of goods sold	$106,500	**What Apex sold**

[1]To highlight the roles of beginning inventory, purchases, freight-in, and ending inventory, we assume that Apex uses a periodic inventory system. However, the concepts in this chapter apply equally to companies that use perpetual inventory systems.

➡ Panel B of Exhibit 9-3, p. 349, shows a merchandiser's cost-of-goods-sold computation.

On the income statement, Cost of Goods Sold is deducted from Sales Revenue to obtain Gross profit. ◄ Apex's operating expenses (period costs) are deducted from gross profit to measure operating income.

Manufacturing Companies

Exhibit 19-10 shows that manufacturing firms have the most complicated accounting, with three kinds of inventory: materials, work in process, and finished goods. Direct labor and manufacturing overhead convert raw materials into finished goods. These are all inventoriable costs.

EXHIBIT 19-10 **Manufacturing Company: Inventoriable Costs and Period Costs**

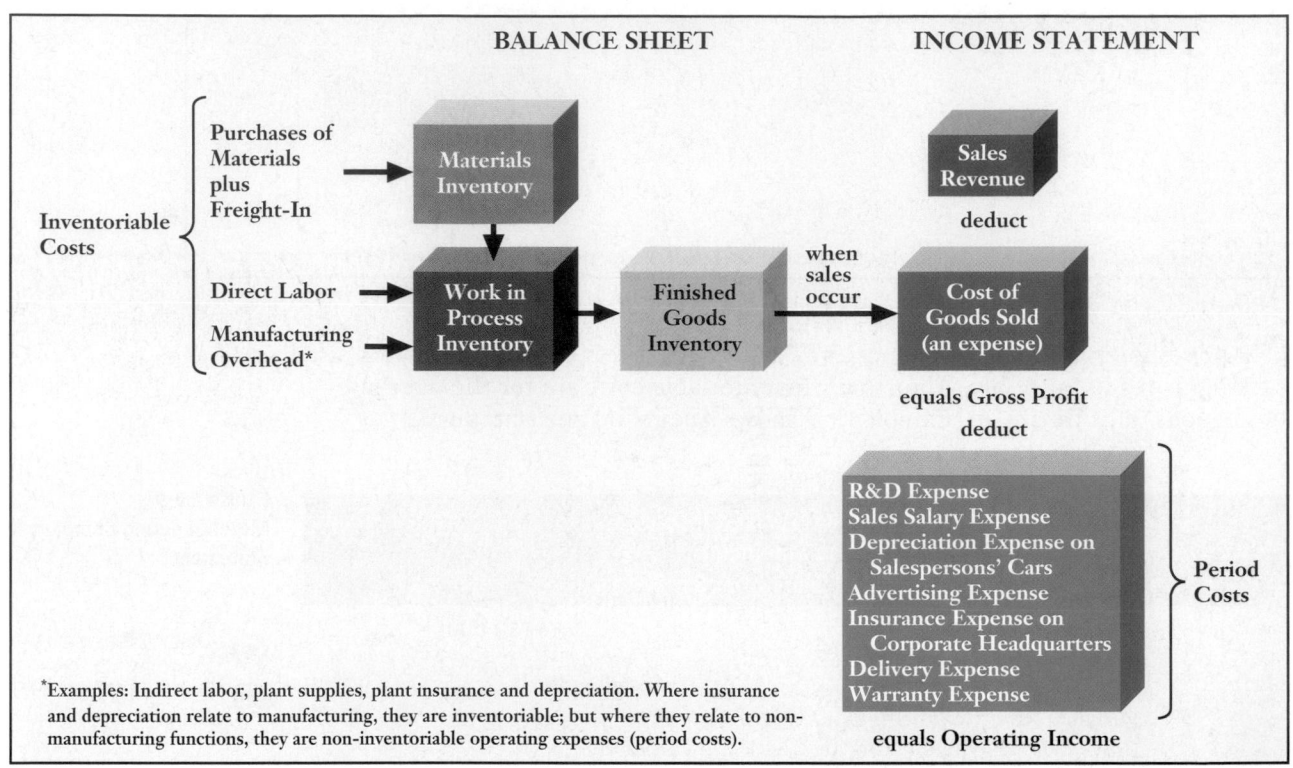

Consider Top-Flight, a manufacturer of golf equipment and athletic shoes. Compare its income statement in Exhibit 19-11 with the merchandiser's income statement in Exhibit 19-9. Both Apex and Top-Flight subtract cost of goods sold from

EXHIBIT 19-11
Manufacturing Company Income Statement

TOP-FLIGHT Income Statement Year Ended December 31, 20X2		
Sales revenue		$65,000
Cost of goods sold:...		
Beginning finished goods inventory..............	$ 6,000	
Cost of goods manufactured*	42,000	
Cost of goods available for sale	48,000	
Ending finished goods inventory...................	(8,000)	
Cost of goods sold...		40,000
Gross profit		25,000
Operating expenses:..		
Sales salary expense....................................	3,000	
Delivery expense	5,000	
Administrative expense	2,000	10,000
Operating income..		$15,000

* From the Schedule of Cost of Goods Manufactured in Exhibit 19-12.

 DAILY EXERCISE 19-11

 766 **Chapter 19**

sales revenue to obtain gross profit. Both companies subtract operating expenses from gross profit to get operating income. The only difference between the two statements is that the merchandiser (Apex) uses *purchases* in computing cost of goods sold, while the manufacturer (Top-Flight) uses the *cost of goods manufactured* in computing cost of goods sold. Otherwise, the format of a manufacturer's income statement is identical to the format of a merchandiser's income statement.

CALCULATING COST OF GOODS MANUFACTURED   Now let's see how to compute cost of goods manufactured. The **cost of goods manufactured** is the (manufacturing) cost of the goods that were *finished*—that is, the plant-related cost of the units that completed the production process this period. This is the manufacturer's counterpart to the merchandiser's purchases because it is the cost of new completed goods ready for sale that is added to beginning inventory of finished goods.

The cost of goods manufactured computation is more complex than the merchandiser's simple tally of purchases. Exhibit 19-12 shows how Top-Flight computes cost of goods manufactured during 20X2.

COST OF GOODS MANUFACTURED. The (manufacturing) cost of the goods that were *finished*—that is, the plant-related cost of the units that completed the production process this period.

⊚ DAILY EXERCISE 19-12
⊚ DAILY EXERCISE 19-13
⊚ DAILY EXERCISE 19-14
⊚ DAILY EXERCISE 19-15

EXHIBIT 19-12   Schedule of Cost of Goods Manufactured

TOP-FLIGHT
Schedule of Cost of Goods Manufactured
Year Ended December 31, 20X2

Beginning work in process inventory			**$ 2,000**
Add: Direct materials used			
Beginning materials inventory	$ 9,000		
Purchases of direct materials plus freight-in	27,000		
Available for use	36,000		
Ending materials inventory	(22,000)		
Direct materials used		$14,000	
Direct labor		19,000	
Manufacturing overhead:			
Indirect materials	$ 1,500		
Indirect labor	3,500		
Depreciation—plant building and equipment	3,000		
Plant utilities and insurance	3,500		
Property taxes on plant and equipment	500	12,000	
Total manufacturing costs incurred during year			45,000
Total manufacturing costs to account for			47,000
Less: Ending work in process inventory			(5,000)
Costs of goods manufactured			**$42,000**

The computation begins with the Work in Process Inventory balance at the beginning of the year ($2,000). To this amount, we add the three manufacturing costs incurred during the year: direct materials used ($14,000), direct labor ($19,000), and manufacturing overhead ($12,000). Adding the sum of these costs ($45,000) to the beginning Work in Process Inventory balance of $2,000 gives the total cost assigned to goods worked on during the year—$47,000. Some of these goods were completed and sent to Finished Goods Inventory during the year; others are still in process at the end of the year. Thus, we subtract the cost of goods in process at the end of the year on December 31 ($5,000) to arrive at the cost of the completed goods—that is, the cost of goods manufactured—$42,000.

Exhibit 19-13 diagrams the flow of costs through a manufacturer's inventory accounts. It reveals a similar computational format at all three stages—direct materials, work in process, and finished goods. The final amount at each stage flows into the next stage. This flow of costs through the inventory accounts can be seen in the income statement in Exhibit 19-11 and the schedule of cost of goods manufactured shown in Exhibit 19-12.

EXHIBIT 19-13
Flow of Costs Through a Manufacturer's Inventory Accounts

Direct Materials Inventory	Work in Process Inventory	Finished Goods Inventory
Beginning inventory + Purchases and freight-in	Beginning inventory + Direct materials used + Direct labor + Manufacturing overhead	Beginning inventory + Cost of goods manufactured
= Direct materials available for use − Ending inventory	= Total manufacturing costs to account for − Ending inventory	= Cost of goods available for sale − Ending inventory
= Direct materials used	= Cost of goods manu- factured	= Cost of goods sold

Source: The authors are indebted to Judith Cassidy for this presentation.

Keep in mind that cost of goods manufactured is not the same as manufacturing costs:

MANUFACTURING COSTS:	COST OF GOODS MANUFACTURED:
Direct materials used + **Direct labor** + **Manufacturing overhead** = **Manufacturing costs**	**Beginning work in process inventory** + **Manufacturing costs** − **Ending work in process inventory** = **Cost of goods manufactured**

Effects on the Balance Sheet

The only difference in the balance sheets of service, merchandising, and manufacturing companies relates to inventories. Exhibit 19-14 shows how the current asset sections of eNOW! (service company), Apex Showrooms (merchandising company), and Top-Flight (manufacturing company) might differ at the end of 20X2. eNOW! has no inventory at all, Apex has a single category of inventory, and Top-Flight has three categories of inventory (materials, work in process, and finished goods).

 DAILY EXERCISE 19-16

EXHIBIT 19-14   **Current Asset Sections of Balance Sheets**

eNOW! (Service Company)		Apex Showrooms (Merchandising Company)		Top-Flight (Manufacturing Company)		
Cash	$ 4,000	Cash	$ 4,000	Cash		$ 4,000
Accounts receivable	5,000	Accounts receivable	5,000	Accounts receivable		5,000
		Inventory (Exhibit 19-9)	13,000	Materials inventory (Exhibit 19-12)	$22,000	
				Work in process inventory (Exhibit 19-12)	5,000	
				Finished goods inventory (Exhibit 19-11)	8,000	35,000
Prepaid expenses	1,000	Prepaid expenses	1,000	Prepaid expenses		1,000
Total current assets	$10,000	Total current assets	$23,000	Total current assets		$45,000

It is important that you take time now to review the following Decision Guidelines. Make sure you have a solid understanding of all these concepts before you read further.

DECISION GUIDELINES

Building Blocks of Management Accounting

DECISION	GUIDELINES
What information should management accountants provide? What is the primary focus of management accounting?	Management accounting provides information that helps managers make better decisions; it has a • *Future* orientation • Focus on *relevance* to business decisions
How do you decide on a company's management accounting system, which is not restricted by GAAP?	Cost-benefit analysis: Design management accounting system so that benefits (from helping managers make wiser decisions) outweigh the costs of the system.

How do you distinguish among service, merchandising, and manufacturing companies? How do their balance sheets differ?	*Service companies:*
	• Provide customers with intangible services
	• Have no inventories on the balance sheet
	Merchandising companies:
	• Resell tangible products they purchased ready-made from suppliers
	• Have only one category of inventory on the balance sheet
	Manufacturing companies:
	• Apply labor, plant, and equipment to transform raw materials into new finished products
	• Have three categories of inventory on the balance sheet:
	    Materials inventory
	    Work in process inventory
	    Finished goods inventory

How do you compute cost of goods sold?

- *Service companies:* No cost of goods sold, because they don't sell tangible goods
- *Merchandising companies:*

$$
\begin{aligned}
&\quad \text{Beginning inventory}\\
&+\ \text{Purchases and freight-in}\\
&\underline{-\ \text{Ending inventory}}\\
&=\ \text{Cost of goods sold}
\end{aligned}
$$

- *Manufacturing companies:*

$$
\begin{aligned}
&\quad \text{Beginning finished goods inventory}\\
&+\ \text{Cost of goods manufactured}\\
&\underline{-\ \text{Ending finished goods inventory}}\\
&=\ \text{Cost of goods sold}
\end{aligned}
$$

How do you compute the cost of goods manufactured for a manufacturer?

$$
\begin{aligned}
&\quad \text{Beginning work in process inventory}\\
&+\ \text{Current period manufacturing costs (Direct}\\
&\quad\ \text{materials used + direct labor + manufacturing}\\
&\quad\ \text{overhead)}\\
&\underline{-\ \text{Ending work in process inventory}}\\
&=\ \text{Cost of goods manufactured}
\end{aligned}
$$

Which costs are initially treated as assets for external reporting? When are these costs expensed?

What costs are inventoriable under GAAP?

Inventoriable product costs are initially treated as assets (Inventory); these costs are not expensed (as Cost of Goods Sold) until the products are sold.

- *Service companies:* No inventoriable product costs because they do not sell tangible products
- *Merchandising companies:* Purchases and freight-in
- *Manufacturing companies:* Direct materials used, direct labor, and manufacturing overhead

SUMMARY PROBLEM

1. Show how to compute cost of goods manufactured. Use the following amounts: direct materials used ($24,000); direct labor ($9,000); manufacturing overhead ($17,000); beginning work in process inventory; ($5,000) and ending work in process inventory ($4,000).
2. For a manufacturing company, identify the following as either an inventoriable product cost or a period cost:
   a. Depreciation on plant equipment
   b. Depreciation on salespersons' automobiles
   c. Insurance on plant building
   d. Marketing manager's salary

Solution

Requirement 1

Cost of goods manufactured:

Beginning work in process inventory		$ 5,000
Add: Direct materials used	$24,000	
Direct labor	9,000	
Manufacturing overhead	17,000	
Total manufacturing costs incurred during the period		50,000
Total manufacturing costs to account for		55,000
Less: Ending work in process inventory		(4,000)
Cost of goods manufactured		$51,000

Requirement 2

(a) Inventoriable product cost; (b) Period cost; (c) Inventoriable product cost; (d) Period cost

---

THE MODERN BUSINESS ENVIRONMENT

The rest of this textbook describes management accounting tools and techniques designed to help managers make wise business decisions that lead to profits. Before we turn to these specific accounting tools, let's first consider recent trends in business that affect managers' decisions and the management accounting systems that support these decisions. These trends include the shift toward a service economy; the rise of the global marketplace; time-based competition (including electronic commerce and the just-in-time management philosophy); and total quality management.

Shift toward a Service Economy

Service companies provide health care, communication, transportation, banking, and other important benefits to society. The last century has seen our economy shift from manufacturing to service. Service companies now make up the largest sector of the U.S. economy, and employ 55% of the work force. The U.S. Bureau of the Census expects this number to increase to 60% by 2005. Even companies that do manufacturing, such as **General Electric** (GE), are shifting their focus toward selling services. It's easy to see why. In GE's jet engine business, services contribute only 30% of the revenues, but generate two-thirds of the profit.

Managers of service companies need information to make decisions. For example, banks must include the cost of servicing checking and savings accounts in the fees they charge customers. Hospitals need to know the cost of performing appendectomies to justify reimbursement from insurance companies and from Medicare.

Competing in the Global Marketplace

The costs of international trade have plummeted over the last decade, largely due to

- The Internet and the explosion of electronic commerce (e-commerce)
- Improved telecommunications, including video conferencing and e-mail
- Improved worldwide transportation, such as **UPS's** and **DHL's** worldwide overnight delivery services
- Reduced barriers to free trade, including the European Union free-trade zone (which includes more than a dozen European countries) and the North American Free Trade Agreement trading bloc (the United States, Canada, and Mexico)

These changes enable foreign companies to compete with local firms. Firms that are not world-class competitors will not survive in the global marketplace. For example, **RCA** stereos have largely been replaced by **Yamaha, Sony,** and **JVC** models. However, global markets do provide competitive companies with tremendous potential. For instance, GE's revenue is growing twice as fast in foreign countries as in the United States. Foreign operations account for over 30% of GE's revenues and nearly 40% of **Dell's** revenues. **McDonald's** has expanded in Russia and China, two countries with billions of consumers.

Manufacturers often move operations to other countries to be closer to new markets and less expensive labor. For example, **Thomson SA,** maker of GE television sets, closed the world's largest TV factory in Bloomington, Indiana, and moved the work to Mexico to save an estimated $75 million a year in labor costs. **Ford, General Motors,** and **DaimlerChrysler** are building assembly plants in Brazil to churn out cars for Brazil's car-hungry emerging middle class. Dell Computer is also considering opening a plant in Brazil. Dell's managers will go ahead with the plant if the benefits (proximity to a large untapped market and less expensive labor) outweigh the costs of building the new plant.

Globalization has several implications for management accounting:

1. Stiffer competition means managers need more accurate information to make wise decisions. For example, if **Nokia** overestimates the cost of its new cell phone, it may set prices too high and lose business to competitors.
2. Companies must decide whether to expand sales and/or production into foreign countries. To make these decisions, managers need estimates of the costs and benefits of international expansion.
3. Globalization fosters the transfer of management philosophy across international borders. For example, many U.S. companies now follow the just-in-time philosophy developed in Japan.

Time-Based Competition

Question: When did you need that order?
Response: Yesterday, of course!

The Internet, electronic commerce (e-commerce), e-mail, and express delivery services speed the pace of business in the new millennium. Customers who surf the Web and use e-mail to correspond in real time with people all over the world will not wait four weeks to receive their purchases. Companies that do not satisfy customers' demands quickly will not survive. Time is the latest competitive turf for world-class business.

Dell Computer commits to delivering your desktop computer within a week of receiving your order. Even automakers are getting in on the act: **Toyota** says it can now make a car within five days of receiving a custom order. Tom Meredith, Dell's chief financial officer, recently addressed an automakers' conference on the "Dell way" (high-quality custom-built products delivered shortly after the customer places an order). U.S. automakers, who have often kept customers waiting 30–60 days for custom orders, were all ears. To compete with Toyota, General Motors plans to cut its order-to-delivery time from 8 weeks in 1999 to no more than 11 days by 2003. How can GM do it? e-Commerce and the just-in-time management philosophy are two ways managers speed up responses to customers.

E-COMMERCE   How does Dell assemble and deliver your computer within a week after you order it? e-Commerce helps. In e-commerce, everyday business practices such as budgeting, planning, purchasing, and selling are conducted over the Internet. e-Commerce is changing the way companies do business. Companies have embraced e-commerce to survive in an increasingly competitive globally wired economy. Imagine a sales clerk who can sell to thousands of customers at once. This sales clerk instantly provides every product, option, and price the company offers. It works 24 hours a day, 365 day a year, and never takes a break or vacation. This sales clerk is an e-commerce Web site!

Business-to-business e-commerce takes this speed and efficiency to new levels. Imagine that you are sitting in your office, anywhere in the world. You enter Dell's Web site and customize your own computer. The site shows computer systems and prices your employer has pre-negotiated with Dell. After you fill your virtual shopping cart, the entire process of ordering, approval, and delivery is automated through your employer's business-to-business software.

Electronic purchases below specified dollar limits are often untouched by human hands, generate little if any paper, and avoid the time and cost of processing this paperwork. General Motors indicates that moving such purchases on-line will slash the roughly $100 it now costs to process each of the hundreds of thousands of purchase orders it issues each year.

Firms also use the Internet to tap into other companies' business processes. Companies that supply component computer parts to Dell can use the Internet to look into Dell's production process through the virtual window Dell provides each supplier. Through this customized window, each supplier sees the current demand for, and inventory levels of, the parts it supplies Dell. In addition to automating the size of the next day's order, the virtual window provides current information that helps the supplier plan, or budget, Dell's demand for their products. Access to real-time information that lets suppliers forecast Dell's demand for their products is key to Dell's ability to cut order-to-delivery times and to control costs.

In addition to reducing their own processing costs, firms that purchase on-line can often cut the prices they pay for goods and services. Competition is stiff because buyers can ask vendors throughout the world for price quotes. Firms in some industries, such as the auto industry, are cooperating to establish virtual marketplaces that link manufacturers and suppliers. A small low-cost supplier in Asia that has never before had timely information to make competitive bids needs only a password and an Internet browser to enter the on-line market and bid against every other potential supplier in the world. By joining Ford and General Motors in establishing virtual markets for their purchases, DaimlerChrysler's chairman estimates a cost saving of nearly $1,000 per vehicle. How? The big automakers expect price concessions from their suppliers not only on their own purchases, but also on purchases their suppliers make from each other. By reducing costs throughout the value chain, the automakers expect to reap substantial cost reductions.

We have seen how e-commerce provides suppliers with virtual windows into their customers' business operations, and how Internet marketplaces cut the prices businesses pay for the goods and services they purchase. e-Commerce is thus an important means of **supply-chain management,** where companies exchange information with suppliers and customers to reduce costs, improve quality, and speed delivery of goods and services from suppliers, through the company itself, and on to customers.

e-Commerce increases firms' ability (and need) to move toward a just-in-time management philosophy.

SUPPLY-CHAIN MANAGEMENT. Companies exchange information with suppliers and customers to reduce costs, improve quality, and speed delivery of goods and services from suppliers, through the company itself, and on to customers.

THE JUST-IN-TIME MANAGEMENT PHILOSOPHY   Traditionally, companies held a lot of inventory to ensure they would have enough raw materials for production and enough finished goods to fill customer orders. However, money tied up in inventory cannot be used for other purposes. Inventory held too long becomes obsolete. Storing the inventory takes space. The costs of holding inventory can easily add up to 25% of the inventory's value. The just-in-time philosophy helps managers cut these costs and speed the transformation of raw materials into new finished products by reducing the need to hold inventory. Let's see how.

Toyota generally gets credit for pioneering the **just-in-time (JIT)** management philosophy. As the name suggests, the JIT philosophy means producing *just in time* to satisfy needs. Materials are purchased and finished goods are completed only as needed to satisfy customer orders. Ideally, suppliers deliver materials for today's production in (small) batches of exactly the right quantities *just in time* to begin production, and finished units are completed *just in time* for delivery to customers.

JUST-IN-TIME (JIT). A system in which a company produces just in time to satisfy needs. Materials are purchased and finished goods are completed only as needed to satisfy customer orders.

Firms adopting JIT report sharp reductions in inventory. Reducing inventory and speeding the production process reduce **throughput time,** the time between buying raw materials and selling the finished products. For example, Dell Computer recently cut its throughput time from 31 to 17 days. Why is this important? The *Wall Street Journal* estimates that the onslaught of new technologies reduces the value of a completed PC by 1% *per week.*[2] Moving inventory quickly gives Dell pricing and manufacturing advantages over its competitors. For example, Dell can cut its prices immediately when component part costs decline. Less inventory also means that Dell can quickly incorporate new technologies.

THROUGHPUT TIME. The time between buying raw materials and selling the finished products.

Manufacturers adopting just-in-time depend on their suppliers to make on-time deliveries of perfect-quality raw materials. Thus, JIT requires close communications with suppliers. As we noted earlier, Dell has even designed special Web pages for its major suppliers that give them a "virtual window" into the Dell operations they supply. Suppliers use these windows to decide when and how much raw material to deliver to Dell.

Companies that adopt JIT must strive for perfect quality. Defects stop production lines. To avoid disrupting production, defects must be rare.

Managers considering JIT must weigh its costs against its benefits. Suppose New-Tell, a computer chip manufacturer, is considering JIT. If New-Tell adopts JIT, the company will incur costs, including employee training, searching for the most reliable suppliers, and lost sales due to initial slowing of production as it makes the transition. New-Tell estimates that these costs will total $2 million. The benefits of adopting JIT include savings on inventory and storage space, reduction in inventory obsolescence, and higher sales because of better-quality products. New-Tell estimates that these benefits will save an average of $650,000 a year for ten years.

 DAILY EXERCISE 19-18

To make this decision, New-Tell must compare the eventual benefits of adopting JIT with the immediate $2 million cost. The cost of adopting JIT comes immediately, but the benefits accrue over time. New-Tell must determine the present value today of the future benefits of adopting JIT. This is called *discounting* the future amounts to their *present values.* ➤ Let's assume that New-Tell's benefits of adopting JIT have a present value of $3,141,450.[3]

The costs of adopting JIT occur now, so the cost data are already stated at their present values. Stating all amounts at present values allows us to accurately compare the costs and benefits of adopting a JIT system. New-Tell's decision follows this rule:

◄ The Appendix to Chapter 15 discusses present-value computations, and we will cover this subject in more detail in Chapter 26.

- Present value of JIT's benefits exceed the cost of adopting JIT → Adopt JIT
- Cost of adopting JIT exceeds the present value of JIT's benefits → Do not adopt JIT

The analysis is as follows:

Present value of benefits	$3,141,450
Present value of costs	(2,000,000)
Excess of benefits over costs	$1,141,450
Decision: Invest in JIT system	

---

[2]"Compaq Stumbles as PCs Weather New Blow," *Wall Street Journal,* March 9, 1998, page B1.
[3]JIT will reduce New-Tell's costs by $650,000 per year for ten years. Using a 16% discount rate, the present value of $650,000 per year for ten years is $3,141,450 ($650,000 × 4.833 from Exhibit 15A-7 on page 619 of the appendix to Chapter 15).

Total Quality Management

TOTAL QUALITY MANAGEMENT (TQM). A philosophy of delighting customers by providing them with superior products and services. Involves improving quality and eliminating defects and waste throughout the value chain.

Today companies must deliver high-quality goods and services to remain competitive. **Hewlett-Packard** and **Ford** in the United States, **British Telecom** in the United Kingdom, and **Toyota** in Japan view **total quality management (TQM)** as key to succeeding in the global economy. The goal of total quality management is to delight customers by providing them with superior products and services. Companies achieve this goal by improving quality and by eliminating defects and waste throughout the value chain. Each business function examines its own activities and works to improve by setting higher and higher goals.

TQM emphasizes educating, training, and cross-training employees to do multiple tasks. **Motorola's** purchasing department is an example. Motorola wanted to reduce the time required to issue a purchase order. Before starting the project, a departmental team took a two-day company course called High-Commitment, High-Performance Team Training. Team members then reduced the number of steps in handling a purchase order from 17 to 6, slashing average processing time from 30 minutes to 3. The department now processes 45% more purchase orders with no added employees. Service organizations also strive to improve quality. For example, the American Institute of Certified Public Accountants is the first professional membership organization in the United States to earn the ISO 9001 international certification for quality management and assurance.

Like JIT, quality improvement programs cost money today, but the benefits usually accrue over time. Because no one can foresee the future, the exact amount of the future benefits is not known. Accountants often adjust for this uncertainty.

Consider GE. The company recently started nearly 3,000 quality-related projects at a cost of more than $200 million. The first-year cost savings from these projects totaled only $170 million. Does this mean that GE made a bad decision? Not necessarily. GE expects these projects to continue yielding benefits in the future.

DAILY EXERCISE 19-19

Suppose GE managers predict these projects will be either moderately successful or extremely successful. Assume that if the projects are moderately successful, they will yield additional benefits (cost savings) with a present value of $20 million. If the projects are extremely successful, they will yield extra benefits with a present value of $100 million. GE managers think the projects are more likely to be extremely successful, but they do not know for sure. Suppose they estimate a 60% chance that the projects will be extremely successful, and a 40% chance that they will be moderately successful.

In an uncertain environment such as GE's, managers make decisions based on expected values. We compute expected values by multiplying the dollar value of each possible outcome by the probability of that outcome, and then adding the results:

Outcome	Benefit	×	Probability	=	Expected Value (of Additional Benefit)
Extremely successful	$100 million	×	60% chance	=	$60 million
Moderately successful	20 million	×	40% chance	=	8 million
Total expected value of benefits					$68 million

What does this $68 million mean? If GE faced this exact situation ten times, it would expect to get $100 million in extra benefits six times, and only $20 million of additional benefits four times. The *average* extra benefits across the ten situations is $68 million, calculated as [(6 × $100) + (4 × $20)]/10 = $68. In effect, GE's best guess of the additional benefit is the expected value of $68 million.

The following summary shows that the total benefits expected from GE's quality projects ($238 million) exceed the $200 million cost of the projects, suggesting that GE's quality project was worthwhile:

	Total Benefits	Total Costs
Initial benefits and costs	$170 million	$200 million
Additional expected benefits	68 million	
Total	$238 million	$200 million

Even after adopting quality programs, companies cannot rest on their laurels. TQM requires that companies (and individual employees) continually look for ways to improve performance. Jack Welch, CEO of General Electric, says: "The human mind is always able to find a better way to do things." This is the **continuous improvement** philosophy.

CONTINUOUS IMPROVEMENT. A philosophy requiring employees to continually look for ways to improve performance.

How do companies improve? Many businesses find that investments in higher quality earlier in the value chain (R&D and design) generate savings in later stages (production, marketing, and customer service). Successful companies design and build quality into the product or service rather than depending on finding and fixing defects later. Carefully designed products and better employee training reduce costs of inspections, rework, and warranty claims, all of which eat into profits.

PROFESSIONAL ETHICS FOR MANAGEMENT ACCOUNTANTS

Objective 7
Use reasonable standards to make ethical judgments

A key indicator of quality is ethical behavior. As we've seen throughout this text, ethical behavior is necessary for the orderly functioning of society and business. How would you feel if parents, teachers, employers, friends, and co-workers constantly lied to you? Relationships necessary for everyday life would break down. Business would be much more difficult to conduct, and the range and quality of goods and services would decline. Because ethical behavior is so important, society enacts laws that require social responsibility. For example, it is illegal for companies to sell products that are clearly defective, such as automobiles that do not meet government safety standards.

Unfortunately, the ethical path is not always clear. You may want to act ethically and do the right thing, but the consequences can make it difficult to decide what to do. Consider the following examples:

- Sarah Baker is examining the expense reports of her staff of management accountants, who counted inventory at Top-Flight's warehouses in Arizona. She discovers that Mike Flinders has claimed but not included hotel receipts for over $1,000 of accommodation expenses. The other staff members, who also claimed $1,000, did attach hotel receipts. When asked about the receipt, Mike admits that he stayed with an old friend, not in the hotel. His wife is expecting their first child, and he believes he deserves the money he saved. After all, the company would have paid his hotel bill.
- As the accountant of Entreé Computer Co., you are aware of your company's weak financial condition. Entreé is close to signing a lucrative contract that should ensure its future. To do so, the controller states that the company *must* report a profit this year (ending December 31). He suggests: "Two customers have placed orders that are really not supposed to be shipped until early January. Ask production to fill and ship those orders on December 31, so we can record them in this year's sales."

The Institute of Management Accountants (IMA) has developed standards to help management accountants deal with these kinds of situations. An excerpt from the *Standards of Ethical Conduct for Management Accountants* appears in Exhibit 19-15. These standards require management accountants to

- Maintain their professional competence
- Preserve the confidentiality of the information they handle
- Act with integrity and objectivity

EXHIBIT 19-15
**IMA Standards of Ethical
Conduct for Management
Accountants (excerpt)**

 DAILY EXERCISE 19-20

 DAILY EXERCISE 19-21

Management accountants have an obligation to the organizations they serve, their profession, the public, and themselves to maintain the highest standards of ethical conduct. These standards include

Competence

- Maintain an appropriate level of professional competence by ongoing development of their knowledge and skills.
- Perform their professional duties in accordance with relevant laws, regulations, and technical standards.

Confidentiality

- Refrain from disclosing confidential information acquired in the course of their work except when authorized, unless legally obligated to do so.

Integrity

- Avoid actual or apparent conflicts of interest and advise all appropriate parties of any potential conflict.
- Refuse any gift, favor, or hospitality that would influence or would appear to influence their actions.
- Communicate unfavorable as well as favorable information and professional judgments or opinions.

Objectivity

- Communicate information fairly and objectively.

Source: Adapted from Institute of Management Accountants, *Standards of Ethical Conduct for Management Accountants* (Montvale, N.J.).

To resolve ethical dilemmas, the IMA also suggests discussing ethical situations with your immediate supervisor, or with an objective adviser.

There are fairly clear-cut solutions to many situations, but not to true ethical dilemmas. The IMA's *Standards of Ethical Conduct* serve as a reminder that society expects professional accountants to uphold the highest level of ethical behavior.

Let's return to the two ethical dilemmas. By asking to be reimbursed for hotel expenses he did not incur, Mike Flinders clearly violated the IMA's integrity standards (conflict of interest in which he tried to enrich himself at company expense). Because Sarah Baker discovered the inflated expense report, she would not be fulfilling her ethical responsibilities (integrity and objectivity) if she allowed the reimbursement and did not take disciplinary action.

The second dilemma, in which the controller asked you to accelerate the shipments, is less clear-cut. You should discuss the available alternatives and their consequences with others. Many people believe that following the controller's suggestion to manipulate the company's income would violate the standards of competence, integrity, and objectivity. Others would argue that because Entreé Computer already has the customer order, shipping the goods and recording the sale in December is still ethical behavior. If you refused to ship the goods in December and you simply resign without attempting to find an alternative solution, you might only hurt yourself and your family.

You have now seen cost-benefit analysis applied to several different business decisions. The general approach of weighing costs against benefits to make the best decision comes up again and again in management accounting. Study the Cost-Benefit Analysis Decision Guidelines to make sure you understand this important concept.

DECISION GUIDELINES

Cost-Benefit Analysis

DECISION	GUIDELINES
How to compete in a globally wired economy?	Embrace e-commerce and use supply chain management to compete more effectively.
How to decide whether to undertake new projects like international expansion, JIT, and TQM?	Cost-benefit analysis: Compute the benefits of the project, and compare with the costs. Undertake the project if benefits exceed costs. Abandon the project if costs exceed benefits.
How to adjust the cost-benefit analysis if the exact amount of the benefit (or cost) is not known?	Compute the *expected value* of the benefits (or costs) of each outcome as follows:

$$\begin{array}{ccc} \text{Estimated} \\ \text{amount} \end{array} \times \begin{array}{ccc} \text{Probability of} \\ \text{occurrence} \end{array} = \begin{array}{ccc} \text{Expected} \\ \text{value} \end{array}$$

Then add the expected values across all possible outcomes.

How to resolve an ethical dilemma?	Weigh the costs and benefits of alternative courses of action. Consult the IMA's *Standards of Ethical Conduct for Management Accountants* (Exhibit 19-15). Also consult the Framework for Ethical Judgments in Chapter 7.

EXCEL APPLICATION PROBLEM

Goal: Create an Excel spreadsheet to assess the costs and benefits of a new project, and use the results to answer questions about the decision.

Scenario: Dennis Popper of EZ-Rider Motorcycles has asked you to prepare an Excel spreadsheet that calculates the net benefits (expected value of benefits—total costs) of expansion into Germany. The background data for EZ-Rider's expansion project appears in the Summary Problem. When your spreadsheet is finished, you will be able to answer these questions:

1. What is the expected value of the benefits of the expansion project? What are the total costs? Does the expected value of the benefits exceed total costs? If so, what is the expected value of the net benefits?
2. What is the minimum probability of a gas price increase that would justify the expansion? What is the expected value of the net benefits at this point?

Step-by-step:

1. Open a new Excel spreadsheet.
2. Create a boldfaced heading for your spreadsheet that contains the following:
   a. Chapter 19 Decision Guidelines
   b. Cost-Benefit Analysis
   c. EZ-Rider Motorcycles
   d. Today's date
3. Move down two rows, and enter the heading "Cost Data" in Column A. Under the heading, enter the data (with descriptions) needed to calculate total costs. Compute total costs.
4. Move down two rows. In the first column, enter the boldfaced and underlined heading "PV if Stable Gas Price."
5. Under this heading, enter the present value of the project if gas prices remain stable. Copy the cell contents down 10 more rows.
6. In the next column, enter the boldfaced and underlined heading "Probability of Stable Gas Price." Spread the heading over two rows.
7. Under this heading, enter a probability of 100%. In the next 10 rows, decrement 100% by 10% each row, so that the probability is zero at the bottom.
8. In the next column, enter the boldfaced and underlined heading "PV If Gas Price Increases."
9. Under this heading, enter the present value of the project if gas prices increase. Copy the cell contents down 10 more rows.
10. In the next column, enter the boldfaced and underlined heading "Probability of Gas Price Increase." Spread the heading over two rows.
11. Under this heading, enter a probability of 0%. In the next 10 rows, increment the percentage by 10% each row, so that the probability is 100% at the bottom.
12. In the next column, enter the boldfaced and underlined heading "Expected Value of Benefits." Spread the heading over two rows. Compute the expected value for all combinations of percentages for each row.
13. In the last column, enter the boldfaced and underlined heading "Expected Value of Net Benefits." Spread the heading over two rows. Compute the next benefits for all rows.
14. Save your file to disk and print a copy for your files.

SUMMARY PROBLEM

www.prenhall.com/horngren

End-of-Chapter Assessment

Cost-benefit analysis applies to many decisions. This chapter showed how managers use cost-benefit analysis to decide whether to adopt JIT or TQM. Managers also use cost-benefit analysis for more specific decisions. This summary review problem shows how you can apply cost-benefit analysis to a more specific decision about international expansion.

EZ-Rider Motorcycles is considering whether to expand into Germany, where reunification has increased market size. Public concern over air pollution may cause the government to raise gasoline taxes. If gas prices increase, EZ-Rider expects more interest in fuel-efficient transportation such as motorcycles. Thus, EZ-Rider is considering setting up a motorcycle-assembly plant on the outskirts of Berlin.

EZ-Rider estimates it will cost $850,000 to convert an existing building to motorcycle production. The workers will need training for specific jobs, at a total cost to the company of $65,000. The CEO of EZ-Rider, Dennis Popper, would have to spend a month in Berlin to organize the business and to establish relationships. He estimates the cost of this travel at $43,000. All these costs would be incurred in the next six months.

Popper sees a 60% chance that the price of gasoline in Germany will increase significantly. If this increase occurs, he believes EZ-Rider can sell enough motorcycles over the next eight years to earn profits (before considering the costs in the preceding paragraph) with a present value of $1,624,000. However, if gas prices remain stable, Popper expects to earn profits of only about $812,000. He believes there is a 40% chance that gas prices will remain stable.

Required

1. What are the total costs of EZ-Rider's proposed expansion into Germany?
2. Compute the *expected value* of the benefits Dennis Popper expects EZ-Rider to receive if EZ-Rider expands into Germany.
3. Do the benefits outweigh the costs of expanding into Germany?

Solution

Requirement 1

The total costs are as follows:

Conversion of manufacturing plant...................	$850,000
Work force training...	65,000
Popper's trip to Berlin	43,000
Total costs..	$958,000

Requirement 2

Expected value of the benefits is computed as follows:

Benefit	×	Probability	=	Expected Value
$1,624,000	×	0.60	=	$ 974,400
812,000	×	0.40	=	324,800
				$1,299,200

The *expected value* of the benefits, or profits, is $1,299,200. This means that should EZ-Rider find itself in this exact situation many times, its average benefits in the form of profits across all the situations would be $1,299,200.

Requirement 3

Yes, the total expected benefits outweigh the costs of the expansion:

Total expected benefits of expansion (from requirement 2)....	$1,299,200
Total costs of expansion (from requirement 1).......................	958,000
Net benefits of expansion...	$ 341,200

LESSONS LEARNED

1. **Distinguish between financial accounting and management accounting.** Financial accounting information is used primarily by external groups such as investors, creditors, and government authorities; it focuses on past performance of the company as a whole; it is restricted by GAAP; and it is subject to annual independent audit. Management accounting information is used primarily by internal managers to help plan and control business operations. It focuses on the future, is restricted only by the cost of generating the information versus the benefits, often reports on parts of the company, and may be produced on a daily, weekly, or monthly basis.

2. **Describe the value chain and classify costs by value-chain function.** The *value chain* is the sequence of activities that adds value to a firm's products or services. Value-chain functions are research and development, design, production or purchases, marketing, distribution, and customer service. Managers want to control total costs throughout the value chain as a whole.

3. **Distinguish direct costs from indirect costs.** Managers need cost data on many aspects of a business to make wise decisions. A *cost object* is anything for which managers want a separate measurement of costs. Costs that can be specifically traced to the cost object are *direct costs*. Costs that cannot be specifically traced to the cost object are *indirect costs*.

4. **Distinguish among full product costs, inventoriable product costs, and period costs.** *Product costs* are costs of producing (or purchasing) tangible products intended for sale. *Full product costs* include the costs of all resources used throughout the value chain. These costs are used for internal decisions such as setting prices and do not conform to GAAP. *Inventoriable product costs* include only costs of the *production or purchases* element of the value chain, and must conform to GAAP because they are used for external financial reporting. These costs are first considered inventory (an asset), and are not expensed (as cost of goods sold) until the products are sold. *Period costs* are operating costs that are always expensed in the period in which they are incurred, and are never part of the Inventory asset account.

5. **Prepare the financial statements of a manufacturing company.** Manufacturers use three inventory accounts: *Materials Inventory, Work in Process Inventory,* and *Finished Goods Inventory.* Manufacturers compute cost of goods sold by adding the *cost of goods manufactured* to beginning finished goods inventory, and subtracting ending finished goods inventory.

6. **Identify major trends in the business environment, and use cost-benefit analysis to make business decisions.** Major trends in the business environment influencing management accounting are the shift toward a service economy, the rise of the global marketplace, time-based competition, including e-commerce and the just-in-time management philosophy, and total quality management. In making business decisions, managers compare the present value of expected future costs and benefits of alternative courses of action.

7. **Use reasonable standards to make ethical judgments.** Ethical behavior is necessary for the orderly functioning of society and business. The Institute of Management Accountants (IMA) standards require management accountants to maintain their professional competence, preserve the confidentiality of the information they handle, and act with integrity and objectivity.

ACCOUNTING VOCABULARY

budget (p. 756)
continuous improvement (p. 775)
controlling (p. 756)
cost-benefit analysis (p. 757)
cost object (p. 760)
cost of goods manufactured (p. 767)
customer service (p. 760)
design (p. 760)
direct cost (p. 761)
direct labor (p. 763)
direct materials (p. 762)
distribution (p. 760)
factory overhead (p. 761)

finished goods inventory (p. 759)
full product costs (p. 761)
indirect cost (p. 761)
indirect labor (p. 763)
indirect manufacturing cost (p. 761)
indirect materials (p. 763)
inventoriable product costs (p. 761)
just-in-time (JIT) (p. 773)
manufacturing company (p. 759)
manufacturing overhead (p. 763)
marketing (p. 760)
materials inventory (p. 759)

merchandising company (p. 758)
period costs (p. 762)
planning (p. 755)
production or purchases (p. 760)
research and development (R&D) (p. 760)
service company (p. 758)
supply-chain management (p. 772)
throughput time (p. 773)
total quality management (TQM) (p. 774)
value chain (p. 760)
work in process inventory (p. 759)

QUESTIONS

1. Explain four distinctions between management accounting and financial accounting.
2. How do manufacturing companies differ from service firms and merchandisers? What inventory accounts does each type of company use?
3. Identify the six business functions in the value chain of a manufacturing company. To which function(s) is management accounting relevant?
4. What is the manufacturer's counterpart to the merchandiser's purchases?
5. Give examples of direct materials and indirect materials for a home builder.
6. Identify at least six examples of manufacturing overhead costs.
7. Distinguish between inventoriable product costs and period costs. Which is initially an asset, and which is never an asset, only an expense?
8. What costs should managers consider in deciding on the long-term sale price of a product: inventoriable product costs or full product costs? Give your reason.
9. What is the main difference between a service company's income statement and the income statements of merchandising and manufacturing companies?

10. What is the primary difference between a merchandiser's and a manufacturer's income statement?
11. Summarize the computation of cost of goods manufactured. Use any dollar amounts.
12. List and briefly explain four recent changes in the business environment.
13. Explain two ways globalization affects management accounting.
14. Describe two ways managers respond to time-based competition.
15. Once a company decides to adopt a just-in-time philosophy, what kinds of costs and benefits should it expect?
16. The Institute of Management Accountants' *Standards of Ethical Conduct for Management Accountants* lists four broad requirements. In your own words, list and briefly explain three.

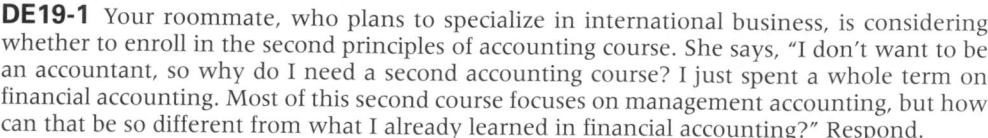

ASSESS YOUR PROGRESS

DAILY EXERCISES

Distinguishing financial from management accounting (Obj. 1)

DE19-1 Your roommate, who plans to specialize in international business, is considering whether to enroll in the second principles of accounting course. She says, "I don't want to be an accountant, so why do I need a second accounting course? I just spent a whole term on financial accounting. Most of this second course focuses on management accounting, but how can that be so different from what I already learned in financial accounting?" Respond.

Classifying costs by value-chain function (Obj. 2)

DE19-2 List the six business functions in the value chain (Exhibit 19-4, page 760). Give an example of costs that **Honda** might incur in each function for a new gas-electric hybrid car.

Classifying costs by value-chain function (Obj. 2)

DE19-3 Give an example of costs that **E*TRADE** (an online brokerage firm) might incur in each of the six business functions in the value chain. Provide another example that shows how E*TRADE might deliberately decide to spend more money on one of the six business functions in order to reduce the costs in other business functions.

Classifying costs by value-chain function (Obj. 2)

DE19-4 Classify each of **Hewlett-Packard's** costs as one of the six business functions in the value chain.

  a. Depreciation on Roseville, California, plant.
  b. Costs of a customer support center Web site.
  c. Transportation costs to deliver laser printers to retailers, like **Best Buy.**
  d. Depreciation on research lab.
  e. Cost of a prime-time TV ad featuring the new Hewlett-Packard logo.
  f. Salary of scientists at Hewlett-Packard Laboratories who are developing new printer technologies.
  g. Purchase of plastic used in printer casings.
  h. Salary of engineers who are redesigning the printer's on-off switch.
  i. Depreciation on delivery vehicles.
  j. Plant manager's salary.

Distinguishing between direct and indirect costs (Obj. 3)

DE19-5 Consider **Marvin Windows'** manufacturing plant. Give two examples of

  a. Direct materials
  b. Direct labor
  c. Indirect materials
  d. Indirect labor
  e. Other manufacturing overhead

Inventoriable vs. period costs (Obj. 4)

DE19-6 Classify each of **Georgia-Pacific's** costs as either inventoriable or period costs:

  a. Depreciation on the gypsum board plant.
  b. Purchase of lumber to be cut into boards.
  c. Life insurance on CEO.
  d. Salaries of scientists studying ways to speed forest growth.
  e. Cost of a new software package to track inventory.
  f. Cost of electricity at one of Georgia-Pacific's paper mills.
  g. Salaries of Georgia-Pacific's top executives.
  h. Cost of mold inhibitor applied to treated lumber.
  i. Cost of TV ads promoting environmental awareness.

Direct versus indirect, full versus inventoriable costs (Obj. 3, 4)

DE19-7 Listed on the following page are several terms relating to various cost definitions. Complete the following statements with one of these terms. You may use a term more than once, and some terms may not be used at all.

Cost object   Direct labor   Inventoriable product cost
Direct cost   Full product cost   Manufacturing overhead
Direct materials   Indirect cost   Period cost

a. ___ is expensed in the period incurred.
b. The product cost used for external reporting is called ___.
c. ___ includes all the elements of the value chain and is used for internal decisions such as setting long-run average selling prices.
d. ___ is initially considered an asset, and is not expensed until the related products are sold.
e. The sum of direct materials, direct labor, and manufacturing overhead is ___ for a manufacturing company.
f. ___ is all costs incurred in the plant other than direct materials and direct labor.

DE19-8 Consider **Toyota, United Parcel Service,** and **Home Depot.** For each company, answer the following questions.

1. Is this a service company, a merchandiser, or a manufacturer?
2. What is the primary output the company sells to customers?
3. What inventory accounts would this company have on its balance sheet?
4. Does this company have any inventoriable product costs? If so, how would you compute these costs?

Inventoriable costs; balance sheets of service, merchandising, and manufacturing companies (Obj. 4, 5)

DE19-9 ← *Link Back to Chapter 5.* Refer to Exhibit 19-9 on page 765. What would be Apex's beginning inventory if revenues, purchases and freight-in, and ending inventory are all the same as in Exhibit 19-9, but gross profit is $45,000 rather than $43,500?

Preparing the cost-of-goods-sold section of a merchandiser's income statement (Obj. 5)

DE19-10 ← *Link Back to Chapter 5.* Given the following information for Gemz, a fashion jewelry e-tailer, compute the cost of goods sold.

Prepare the cost-of-goods-sold section of a merchandiser's income statement (Obj. 5)

Web site maintenance.....	$1,000	Delivery expenses..........	$ 500
Freight-in	2,500	Purchases.......................	30,000
Ending inventory	5,500	Revenues.......................	60,000
Marketing expenses	6,000	Beginning inventory	3,000

DE19-11 Look at Exhibit 19-11 (page 766). What would be Top-Flight's cost of goods sold and operating income if the cost of goods manufactured were $35,000 rather than $42,000? (Other costs and revenues remain the same as in Exhibit 19-11.)

Income statement for a manufacturing company (Obj. 5)

DE19-12 Turn to Exhibit 19-12 (page 767). If direct material purchases were $35,000 rather than $27,000, what would be the cost of direct materials used and the cost of goods manufactured? (Other costs remain the same as in Exhibit 19-12.)

Computing the cost of goods manufactured (Obj. 5)

DE19-13 Jell's manufactures women's plastic sandals. Suppose the company's March records include the following items. What is Jell's total manufacturing overhead cost in March?

Computing manufacturing overhead (Obj. 5)

Ink for printing shoe boxes.....	$ 100	Company president's salary....	$15,000
Depreciation expense on		Plant foreman's salary	2,000
company cars used by		Plant janitor's salary	1,000
sales force	3,000	Oil for manufacturing	
Plant depreciation expense	10,000	equipment	25
Interest expense......................	1,500	Plastic for shoes	50,000

DE19-14 You are a new accounting intern at Mountain Gear, Inc. Your boss gives you the following information and asks you to compute direct materials used.

Computing direct materials used (Obj. 5)

Purchases of direct materials	$25,000
Freight-in..	200
Freight-out	1,000
Ending inventory of direct materials..................	1,500
Beginning inventory of direct materials..............	4,000

DE19-15 Use Exhibit 19-12 (page 767) to explain the differences between *manufacturing costs* and the *cost of goods manufactured.* How much are the *manufacturing costs?* How much is the *cost of goods manufactured?* Explain the difference between these two amounts.

Explaining the cost-of-goods-manufactured schedule (Obj. 5)

Differences among service, merchandising, and manufacturing companies' balance sheets (Obj. 5)

DE19-16 The current asset sections of the balance sheets of three companies follow. Which company is a service company? Which is a merchandiser? Which is a manufacturer? How can you tell?

X-Treme		Y-Not?		Zesto	
Cash...............................	$ 2,500	Cash	$3,000	Cash...................................	$ 2,000
Accounts receivable........	5,500	Accounts receivable	6,000	Accounts receivable..........	5,000
Inventory........................	8,000	Prepaid expenses...............	500	Materials inventory..........	1,000
Prepaid expenses............	300	Total.................................	$9,500	Work in process inventory	800
Total...............................	$16,300			Finished goods inventory .	4,000
				Total..................................	$12,800

Understanding e-commerce (Obj. 6)

DE19-17 You work for X-Rays, a company that produces and markets upscale sunglasses. One of your competitors, SunStop, has just hired eNow! Consultants to establish an on-line sales system that will enable customers to place orders via the Internet. How could this affect X-Rays, which still takes sales orders in person or over the phone? Be specific.

Understanding JIT (Obj. 6)

DE19-18 Is JIT more appropriate for **Amazon.com,** a book, music, and electronics e-tailer, or **Mouton-Rothschild,** a French winemaker specializing in fine red wines? Explain.

Expected value of the benefits of a quality program (Obj. 6)

DE19-19 Consider the cost-benefit analysis for the **GE** quality program discussed on page 774. Suppose GE's managers now estimate a 90% chance that the projects will yield an extra $20 million in benefits, and a 10% chance that the projects will yield an extra $80 million. What is the expected value of the additional benefits *now*? Assuming total costs remain $200 million, does this change your mind about whether the quality program was a worthwhile investment?

Understanding ethics (Obj. 7)

DE19-20 Explain why each of the four broad ethical standards in the Institute of Management Accountants' *Standards of Ethical Conduct for Management Accountants* (Exhibit 19-15, page 776) is necessary.

Making ethical decisions (Obj. 7)

DE19-21 The Institute of Management Accountants' *Standards of Ethical Conduct for Management Accountants* (Exhibit 19-15, page 776) require management accountants to meet standards regarding

- Competence • Confidentiality • Integrity • Objectivity

Consider the following situations. Which guidelines are violated in each situation?

a. You tell your brother that your company will report earnings significantly above financial analysts' estimates.
b. You see that others take home office supplies for personal use. As an intern, you do the same thing, assuming that this is a "perk."
c. At a conference on e-commerce, you skip the afternoon session and go sightseeing.
d. You failed to read the detailed specifications of a new general ledger package that you asked your company to purchase. After it is installed, you are surprised that it is incompatible with some of your company's older accounting software.
e. You do not provide top management with the detailed job descriptions they requested, because you fear they may use this information to cut a position from your department.

EXERCISES

Management vs. financial accounting and managers' use of information (Obj. 1)

E19-1 Listed below are several terms relating to the functions of managers and the differences between financial and management accounting. Complete the following statements with one of these terms. You may use a term more than once, and some terms may not be used at all.

Budget	Creditors	Managers	Planning
Controlling	Financial accounting	Management accounting	Shareholders

a. Financial accounting develops reports for external parties, such as ___ and ___.
b. When managers evaluate the company's performance compared to the plan, they are performing the ___ role of management.
c. Companies must follow GAAP in their ___ systems.
d. ___ are decision makers inside a company.
e. ___ provides information on a company's past performance.
f. ___ systems are not restricted by GAAP, but are chosen by comparing the costs versus the benefits of the system.
g. Choosing goals and the means to achieve them is the _____ function of management.

E19-2 Suppose the computer manufacturer Gateway, Inc., provides the following information for its costs last month (in hundreds of thousands):

Value chain, direct and indirect costs, inventoriable costs (Obj. 2, 3, 4)

Salaries of telephone salespeople ..	$ 4	Hard drives	$50
Depreciation on manufacturing plant and equipment...................	52	Rearrange production process to accommodate new robot	2
Exterior case for computer	6	Assembly-line workers' wages	10
Salaries of scientists who developed new lightweight laptop model	12	Technical support hotline for customer support after purchase..............................	3
Delivery expense via Airborne Express......................................	7	1-800 (toll-free) line for customer orders	1

Required

1. Use the following format to classify each cost according to its place in the value chain. (*Hint:* You should have at least one cost in each value-chain function.)

	Design of Products, Services, or Processes	Production					Customer Service
R&D		**Direct Materials**	**Direct Labor**	**Manufacturing Overhead**	**Marketing**	**Distribution**	

2. Compute the total costs for each value-chain category.
3. How much are the total inventoriable product costs?

E19-3 Suppose **Target** incurred the following costs at its Charleston, South Carolina, store.

Value chain, inventoriable costs (Obj. 2, 4)

Research to determine whether store should add a travel agency service.........	$ 400	Payment to consultant for advice on location of new store	$2,500
Purchases of merchandise.......	50,000	Freight-in.................................	3,000
Rearranging store layout.........	1,500	Salespersons' salaries...............	8,000
Newspaper advertisements	10,000	Customer complaint department..........................	800
Depreciation expense on delivery trucks.....................	2,000		

Required

1. Use the following format to classify each cost according to its place in the value chain.

	Design of Products, Services, or Processes	Purchases of Merchandise Inventory	Marketing	Distribution	Customer Service
R&D					

2. Compute the total costs for each value-chain category.
3. How much are the total inventoriable product costs?

E19-4 Listed below are several terms relating to service, merchandising, and manufacturing firms and their inventories. Complete the following statements with one of these terms. You may use a term more than once, and some terms may not be used at all.

Service, merchandising, and manufacturing companies and their inventories (Obj. 5)

Finished goods inventory
Manufacturing companies
Materials inventory

Inventory (merchandise)
Merchandising companies

Service companies
Work in process inventory

a. _____ do not have tangible products intended for sale.
b. _____ resell products they previously purchased ready-made from suppliers.
c. _____ produce their own inventory.
d. _____ typically have a single category of inventory.
e. _____ use their work force and equipment to transform raw materials into new finished products.
f. Swaim, a company based in North Carolina, makes furniture. Partially completed sofas are _____. Completed sofas that remain unsold in the warehouse are _____. Fabric and wood are _____.
g. For **Kellogg's,** corn, cardboard boxes, and waxed paper liners are classified as _____.

Reporting current assets
(Obj. 5)

E19-5 Consider the following selected amounts and account balances of Boyds:

Cost of goods sold	$96,000	Prepaid expenses	$ 6,000
Direct labor	47,000	Marketing expense	39,000
Direct materials	25,000	Work in process inventory	42,000
Accounts receivable	75,000	Manufacturing overhead	26,000
Cash	19,000	Finished goods inventory	72,000
Cost of goods manufactured	94,000	Materials inventory	10,000

Show how Boyds reports current assets on the balance sheet. Not all data are used. Is Boyds a service company, a merchandiser, or a manufacturer? How do you know?

Computing CGM and CGS
(Obj. 4, 5)

E19-6 Compute the 20X5 cost of goods manufactured and cost of goods sold for Strike Marine Company using the following amounts:

	Beginning of Year	End of Year		End of Year
Materials inventory	$22,000	$28,000	Insurance on plant	9,000
Work in process inventory	42,000	30,000	Depreciation—plant building and equipment	$16,000
Finished goods inventory	18,000	25,000	Repairs and maintenance—plant	4,000
Purchases of raw materials		78,000	Marketing expenses	77,000
Direct labor		82,000	General and administrative expenses	29,000
Indirect labor		15,000	Income tax expense	30,000

Preparing a manufac-
turer's I/S
(Obj. 5)

E19-7 Prepare the 20X5 income statement for the Strike Marine Company in Exercise 19-6. Assume that it sold 28,000 units of its product at a price of $14 during 20X5.

Computing GP for a manufacturer
(Obj. 5)

E19-8 Supply the missing amounts from the following computation of gross profit for Alon Plastics.

Sales revenue				$473,000
Cost of goods sold:				
Beginning finished goods inventory			$ 91,000	
Cost of goods manufactured:				
Beginning work in process inventory		$ 52,000		
Direct materials used	$64,000			
Direct labor	X			
Manufacturing overhead	51,000			
Total manufacturing costs incurred during the period		226,000		
Total manufacturing costs to account for		X		
Ending work in process inventory		(40,000)		
Costs of goods manufactured			X	
Cost of goods available for sale			X	
Ending finished goods inventory			(107,000)	
Cost of goods sold				X
Gross profit				$ X

E19-9 Listed below are several terms relating to the modern business environment. Complete the following statements with one of these terms. You may use a term more than once, and some terms may not be used at all.

Understanding the modern business environment
(Obj. 6)

E-commerce	JIT	Present value
Expected value	North American Free Trade	Shift to service economy
Future	Agreement (NAFTA)	Throughput time
Future value	Present	TQM

a. To account for uncertainty in the amounts of future costs and benefits, we compute the _____ by multiplying the probability of each outcome by the dollar value of that outcome.

b. To make a cost-benefit decision today, we must find the _____ of the costs and benefits that are incurred in the future.

c. The goal of _____ is to delight customers by providing them with superior products and services by eliminating defects and waste throughout the value chain.

d. Most of the costs of adopting JIT, expanding into a foreign market, or improving quality are incurred in the _____, but most of the benefits occur in the _____.

e. _____ is the time between buying raw materials and selling the finished products.

f. The main purpose of _____ is to loosen trade restrictions and promote trade among the United States, Canada, and Mexico.

g. Firms adopt _____ to conduct business on the Internet.

E19-10 Cool Cuts manufactures casual menswear. Eric Haynes, the CEO, is trying to decide whether to adopt just-in-time (JIT). He expects that in present-value terms, adopting JIT would save $113,000 in warehousing expenses and $67,800 in spoilage costs.

Costs and benefits of adopting JIT
(Obj. 6)

Adopting JIT will require several one-time up-front expenditures: (1) $27,000 for an employee training program, (2) $49,500 to streamline the plant's production process, and (3) $8,000 to identify suppliers that will guarantee zero defects and on-time delivery.

Required

1. What are the total costs of adopting JIT?
2. What are the total benefits of adopting JIT?
3. Should Cool Cuts adopt JIT? Why or why not?

E19-11 Mary Gonzales is the controller at Automax, a car dealership. Cory Loftus has recently been hired as bookkeeper. Cory wanted to attend a class on Excel spreadsheets, so Mary temporarily took over Cory's duties, including overseeing a fund for topping up a car's gas before a test drive. Mary found a shortage in this fund and confronted Cory when he returned to work. Cory admitted that he occasionally takes advantage of his access to this fund to pay for his own gas when his finances are low. Mary estimated that the amount involved is close to $300.

Ethics in management accounting
(Obj. 7)

Required

1. What should Mary Gonzales do?
2. Would you change your answer to the previous question if Mary Gonzales was the one recently hired as controller, while Cory Loftus was a well-liked longtime employee, and he indicated that he always eventually repaid the fund?

CHALLENGE EXERCISE

E19-12 CoverUp manufactures and sells a new line of sun-protection clothing. Unfortunately, CoverUp suffered serious hurricane damage at its home office in Miami, Florida, As a result, the accounting records for October were partially destroyed—and completely jumbled. CoverUp has hired you to help figure out the missing pieces of the accounting puzzle.

Flow of costs through manufacturing companies
(Obj. 4, 5)

Work in process inventory, October 31	$ 1,000	Accounts payable, October 1	$3,000
Finished goods inventory, October 1	4,000	Direct materials used in October	8,000
Direct labor in October	3,000	Accounts payable, October 31	4,800
Purchases of direct materials in October	9,000	Accounts receivable, October 31	6,000
Work in process inventory, October 1	0	Direct materials inventory, October 31	2,000
Revenues in October	27,000	Manufacturing overhead in October	7,000
Accounts receivable, October 1	2,000		
Gross profit in October	10,100		

(continued)

Required

Find the following amounts:

a. Cost of goods sold in October
b. Beginning direct materials inventory
c. Ending finished goods inventory

(*Hint:* You may find Exhibit 19-13 helpful.)

(Group A) PROBLEMS

Value chain, direct vs. indirect costs, inventoriable costs (Obj. 2, 3, 4)

P19-1A Suppose Dell Computer reported the following costs last month. (All costs are in millions.)

Payment to UPS for delivering PCs to customers	$ 250
Cost of hard drives used	3,300
Cost of Internet banner ads	400
Plant janitors' wages	10
Wages of workers who assemble the PCs	1,000
Cost of customer hotline for troubleshooting problems	30
Wages of forklift drivers moving parts and completed computers around the plant floor	20
Plant utilities	35
Cost of software loaded on computers	25
Depreciation on plant and equipment	250
Salaries of scientists working on next generation laptops	30
Insurance and taxes on plant property	40
Cost of oil used for conveyor belt and other plant equipment	5
Payment to engineers redesigning the exterior case	15
Wages of sales associates taking phone orders	50
Cost of circuit boards used	4,000
Total	$9,460

Required

1. Use the following format to classify each of these costs according to its place in the value chain. (*Hint:* You should have at least one cost in each value-chain function.)

	Design of Products or Processes	Production					Customer Service
R&D		Direct Materials	Direct Labor	Manufacturing Overhead	Marketing	Distribution	

2. Compute the total costs for each category.
3. How much are the total inventoriable product costs?
4. Suppose the managers of the R&D and design functions receive year-end bonuses based on meeting their own unit's target cost reductions. What are they likely to do? How might this affect costs incurred in other elements of the value chain?

Preparing financial statements for merchandising and manufacturing companies (Obj. 4, 5)

P19-2A *Part One:* On January 1, 2000, Matt Berrigan opened Boards of Paradise, a small retail store dedicated to selling snowboards, wakeboards, and skateboards. On December 31, 2000, his accounting records show the following:

Store rent	$ 6,500	Sales revenue	$87,000
Sales salaries	3,500	Store utilities	1,950
Freight-in	750	Purchases of merchandise	42,000
Inventory on December 31, 2000	8,750	Inventory on January 1, 2000	12,700
		Advertising expense	2,300

Required

Prepare an income statement for Boards of Paradise, a merchandiser.

Part Two: Boards of Paradise succeeded so well that Matt Berrigan decided to manufacture his own special brand of snowboards, to be called Paradise. At the end of December 20X3, his accounting records show the following:

Finished goods inventory, December 31, 20X3	$ 4,000	Rent on manufacturing plant	$ 11,000
Work in process inventory, December 31, 20X3	1,750	Finished goods inventory, December 31, 20X2 .	0
Direct materials inventory, December 31, 20X3	7,750	Depreciation expense on delivery truck	2,500
R&D for graphic designs	3,700	Depreciation expense on manufacturing	
Sales commissions	6,500	equipment	4,700
Utilities for plant	2,900	Work in process inventory, December 31, 20X2	0
Plant janitorial services	1,750	Sales revenue	126,450
Direct labor	23,500	Customer warranty refunds	1,500
Direct material purchases	37,000	Direct materials inventory, December 31, 20X2	15,000

Required

1. Prepare a schedule of cost of goods manufactured for Paradise Manufacturing.
2. Prepare an income statement for Paradise Manufacturing.
3. How does the format of the income statement for Paradise Manufacturing differ from the income statement of Boards of Paradise?

Part Three: Show the ending inventories that would appear on these balance sheets:

1. Boards of Paradise at December 31, 2000.
2. Paradise Manufacturing at December 31, 20X3.

P19-3A Certain item descriptions and amounts are missing from the monthly schedule of cost of goods manufactured and income statement of Southern Manufacturing Company. Fill in the missing items.

Preparing financial statements for a manufacturer
(Obj. 5)

MANUFACTURING COMPANY

April 30, 20X4

_____ work in process inventory			$ 17,000
Direct materials used:			
_____ materials _____	$ X		
_____ of materials	62,000		
_____	75,000		
_____ materials _____	(23,000)		
Direct _____		$ X	
Direct _____		68,000	
Manufacturing overhead		X	
Total _____ costs _____			X
Total _____ costs _____			175,000
_____ work in process inventory			X
_____			$148,000

MANUFACTURING COMPANY

April 30, 20X4

_____ revenue			$445,000
_____:			
Beginning _____	$ X		
_____	X		
Cost of goods _____	X		
Ending _____	(67,000)		
Cost of goods sold		X	
_____		243,000	
_____ expenses:			
Marketing expenses	X		
Administrative expenses	$ 64,000	X	
_____		$ 76,000	

P19-4A Quantx, Inc., manufactures computer disk drives. It sells these disk drives to other manufacturers, which use them in assembling computers. Quantx is having trouble with its new DVD drive. If the parts are not engineered to exact specifications, the drive does not function. About half the time, Quantx employees find these defects while the disk drive is still on the production line. These drives are immediately reworked in the plant. Otherwise, Quantx's customers do not identify the problem until they install the disk drives they've purchased from Quantx. Customers return defective drives for replacement under warranty, and they have also complained that after they install the disk drive, the drive's connector (which plugs into the computer system board) often shakes loose while the computer is being assembled. The customer must then reassemble the computer after fixing the loose connection.

Quantx CEO Jay Batson has just returned from a seminar on total quality management (TQM). He forms a team to address these quality problems. The team includes the plant engineer, the production foreman, a customer service representative, the marketing director, and the management accountant.

Three months later, the team proposes a major project to *prevent* these quality problems. Quantx's accountant Anna Hamm reports that implementing the team's proposal will require Quantx to incur the following costs over the next three months:

- $180,500 for Quantx research scientists to develop a completely new disk drive that works even with small deviations from specified part sizes.
- $70,000 for company engineers to redesign the connector so that it better tolerates rough treatment.

The project team is unsure whether this investment will pay off. If the effort fixes the problem, Hamm expects that

- A reputation for higher quality will increase sales, which in turn will increase the present value of profits by $200,042.
- Fewer disk drives will fail. The present value of the savings from fewer warranty repairs is $163,998.
- The plant will have fewer defective disk drives to rework. The present value of this savings is $100,221.

However, if this project is not successful, there will be no cost savings and no additional sales. The team predicts a 70% chance that the project will succeed, and a 30% chance that it will fail.

Required

1. If the quality improvement project succeeds, what is the dollar amount of the benefits?
2. Should Quantx undertake this project? Why or why not? Show supporting calculations.

P19-5A Problem 19-4A provided both quantitative and qualitative information about Quantx's quality project, and asked you to perform a *quantitative* analysis to help Quantx's managers decide whether to embark on the project. Now consider some *qualitative* factors in Quantx's quality improvement project.

Required

1. Why did Jay Batson create a team to address this quality problem, rather than assigning the task to one person? Consider each piece of cost/benefit information reported by management accountant Anna Hamm. Which person on the team is most likely to have contributed each item? (*Hint:* Which team member is likely to have the most information about each cost or benefit?)
2. Classify the following amounts into one of the six value-chain business functions.
   a. $180,500 cost to develop the new disk drive.
   b. $70,000 cost to redesign the connector.
   c. $163,998 for warranty repairs on disk drives.
   d. $100,221 to rework disk drives identified as defective while still in the factory.
3. This problem illustrates how Quantx can make trade-offs across business functions in the value chain. Which of the six value-chain functions are involved in the trade-offs proposed by the quality improvement team? What specific trade-offs do they propose?

P19-6A West Bank is a regional bank in California that also processes checks for smaller banks and insurance companies. This results in mounds of paperwork, because West Bank tracks which checks have been deposited and which accounts have been debited or credited. When a customer complains that a check was not deposited to its account, a West Bank clerk takes the complaint over the phone and fills out a paper form. The complaint form triggers a long search through piles of canceled checks in a warehouse to find the check in question. West Bank then compares this check to its computer and paper records.

West Bank is considering moving this process to the Web. When a customer has a question, its employee simply uses a Web browser and a password to access West Bank's databases. The customer's employee pulls up a computerized image of the check in question to verify the amount and then queries West Bank's databases to locate the mistake. If required, a credit to the customer's account can be issued immediately.

The Web-based system will require the bank to invest $74,000 in a new server and check-scanning equipment. eNow! consultants will charge $110,000 for the software and consulting fees to get the system running. The system will also require increasing the bank's Internet capacity. The present value of this cost is $20,000.

West Bank has identified two benefits of this project. First, several bank clerks freed from searching through stacks of canceled checks will be reassigned to other more responsible and interesting tasks, which will lead to cost savings with a present value of $156,000. Second, the new system's additional capacity will enable West Bank to accept more check-processing business, which should lead to additional profits with a present value of $39,600.

Required

Does a cost-benefit analysis justify the Web-based system? Explain why, showing supporting calculations.

P19-7A Consider the West Bank project described in Problem 19-6A. West Bank has revised its estimates of additional profits the bank is likely to earn. There is a 50% chance that the bank will earn $39,600 in extra profits, but also a 50% chance the bank will earn $75,000.

e-Commerce, cost-benefit analysis, expected value (Obj. 6)

Required

1. Compute the expected value of the benefits from the additional business.
2. Would you recommend that West Bank accept the proposal? Give your reason, showing supporting calculations.
3. Are there other potential benefits not listed in Problems 19-6A or 19-7A that may make the proposal more attractive to West Bank?

P19-8A Jan Hobbs is the new controller for Kromeware, a designer and manufacturer of outdoor wear. Shortly before the December 31 fiscal year end, Lashea Hare (the company president) asks Jan how things look for the year-end numbers. Lashea is not happy to learn that earnings growth may be below 10% for the first time in the company's five-year history. Lashea explains that financial analysts have again predicted a 20% earnings growth for the company and that she does not intend to disappoint them. She suggests that Jan talk to the assistant controller, who can explain how the previous controller dealt with this situation. The assistant controller suggests the following strategies:

Ethics (Obj. 7)

a. Do not record sales returns and allowances on the basis that they are individually immaterial.
b. Persuade retail customers to accelerate January orders to December.
c. Reduce the allowance for bad debts, given the company's continued strong performance.
d. Kromeware has very limited warehouse space. It regularly ships finished goods to public warehouses across the country for temporary storage, until Kromeware receives firm orders from customers. As Kromeware receives orders, it directs the warehouse to ship the goods to the nearby customer. The assistant controller suggests recording goods sent to the public warehouses as sales.
e. Postpone planned advertising expenditures from December to January.

Which of these suggested strategies are inconsistent with IMA standards? What should Jan Hobbs do if Lashea Hare insists that she follow all of these suggestions?

PROBLEMS

(Group B)

P19-1B Healthy Foods produces canned chicken á la king—chicken, mushrooms, and bell peppers in a cream sauce. The production process starts with raw chicken that workers debone. Cream sauce is prepared, the chicken is cooked, and the two are combined with the vegetables. Because chickens naturally vary in salt content, the amount of salt added varies from batch to batch.

Healthy Foods incurs the following costs (in thousands):

Value chain, direct and indirect costs, inventoriable costs (Obj. 2, 3, 4)

Plant utilities	$ 900	Production costs of "cents-off" store coupons for customers	$ 600
Depreciation on plant and equipment	2,500	Delivery truck drivers' wages	250
Payment to chef for developing new low-fat recipe	1,200	Cream	1,300
		Sales commissions	400
Salt	20	Plant janitors' wages	1,000
Replace products with expired dates upon customer complaint	50	Wages of workers who debone chicken	10,000
Rearranging plant layout to smooth production flow	1,100	Customer hotline for recipes and problems	200
Chicken	18,000	Depreciation on delivery truck	150
Mushrooms and peppers	1,000	Freight-in	1,500
		Total	$40,170

Required

1. Use the following format to classify each of these costs according to its place in the value chain. (*Hint:* You should have at least one cost in each value-chain function.)

| R&D | Design of Products or Processes | Production | | | Marketing | Distribution | Customer Service |
		Direct Materials	Direct Labor	Manufacturing Overhead			

2. Compute the total costs for each value-chain category.
3. How much are the total inventoriable product costs?
4. Suppose the managers of the R&D and design functions receive year-end bonuses based on meeting their own unit's target cost reductions. What are they likely to do? How might this affect costs incurred in other elements of the value chain?

Preparing financial statements for merchandising and manufacturing companies (Obj. 4, 5)

P19-2B *Part One:* In 20X3, Kelly Williams opened Kelly's Boutique, a small retail boutique selling makeup. On December 31, 20X4, her accounting records show the following:

Inventory on December 31, 20X4	$ 9,850
Inventory on January 1, 20X4....................	10,700
Sales revenue...	46,000
Utilities for boutique..................................	2,450
Rent for boutique	4,000
Sales commissions	1,500
Purchases of merchandise..........................	27,000

Required

Prepare an income statement for Kelly's Boutique, a merchandiser.

Part Two: Kelly's Boutique succeeded so well that Kelly Williams decided to manufacture her own brand of sun-protection makeup—CoverUp. At the end of December 20X5, her accounting records show the following:

Work in process inventory, December 31, 20X5.	$ 640	Plant janitorial services	$ 1,250
Finished goods inventory, December 31, 20X4 ..	0	Direct labor...	17,500
Finished goods inventory, December 31, 20X5 ..	5,700	Direct material purchases.....................................	30,000
Sales revenue..	97,450	Rent on manufacturing plant................................	9,000
Customer service hotline	1,000	Direct materials inventory, December 31, 20X4 .	12,000
Utilities for plant	3,400	Direct materials inventory, December 31, 20X5 .	8,750
Delivery expense...	1,500	Work in process inventory, December 31, 20X4.	0
Sales salaries..	4,500		

Required

1. Prepare a schedule of cost of goods manufactured for CoverUp Manufacturing.
2. Prepare an income statement for CoverUp Manufacturing.
3. How does the format of the income statement for CoverUp Manufacturing differ from the income statement of Kelly's Boutique?

Part Three: Show the ending inventories that would appear on these balance sheets:

1. Kelly's Boutique at December 31, 20X4.
2. CoverUp Manufacturing at December 31, 20X5.

Preparing financial statements for a manufacturer (Obj. 5)

P19-3B Certain item descriptions and amounts are missing from the monthly schedule of cost of goods manufactured and the income statement of Henriquez Manufacturing Company shown on the facing page. Fill in the missing items.

_____ MANUFACTURING COMPANY

_____ JUNE 30, 20X4

Beginning _____		$ 21,000
Direct _____:		
Beginning materials inventory	$ X	
Purchases of materials............................	51,000	
_____	82,000	
Ending materials inventory	(23,000)	
Direct _____	$ X	
Direct _____	X	
Manufacturing overhead............................	40,000	
Total _____ costs _____		166,000
Total _____ costs _____		X
Ending _____		(30,000)
_____		$ X

_____ MANUFACTURING COMPANY

_____ June 30, 20X4

Sales revenue		$ X
Cost of goods sold:		
Beginning _____	$101,000	
_____	X	
Cost of goods _____	X	
Ending _____	X	
Cost of goods sold		201,000
Gross profit...		245,000
_____ expenses:		
Marketing expense.................................	99,000	
Administrative expense...........................	X	154,000
_____ income		$ X

P19-4B Pameon manufactures fine watches. The company is having trouble with one of its watches. If the parts are not machined to exact specifications, the watch will not operate. Even a speck of dust under the crystal causes the watch to stop. About half the time, Pameon employees find the defect while the watch is still on the production line. These watches are immediately reworked in the plant. When a defect escapes detection until the customer complains, Pameon repairs the watch.

TQM, cost-benefit analysis, expected value (Obj. 6)

Pameon CEO Jon Vaucluse has just returned from a seminar on total quality management (TQM). He forms a team to address this quality problem. The team includes the plant engineer, the production foreman, the plant's watch repair specialist, the marketing director, and the management accountant.

Three months later, the team proposes a major project to *prevent* these quality problems. Pameon accountant Lily Peugot reports that implementing the team's proposal will require Pameon to incur the following costs over the next six months:

a. $52,500 to redesign the watch so it operates even with small deviations from specified part sizes.

b. $80,000 for Pameon scientists to develop a completely new watch mechanism that tolerates dust particles

The project team is unsure whether this investment will pay off. If these efforts fix the problem, Peugot expects the following to occur:

a. The plant will have no defective watches to rework. The present value of this savings is $47,450.

b. Fewer watches will fail. The present value of the savings from fewer warranty repairs is $101,440.

c. A reputation for higher quality will increase sales, which in turn will increase the present value of profits by $126,800.

However, if this project is not successful, there will be no cost savings and no additional sales. The team predicts that there is a 60% chance that the project will succeed, and a 40% chance that it will fail.

Required

1. If the quality improvement project succeeds, what is the dollar amount of the benefits?
2. Should Pameon undertake this project? Why or why not? Show supporting calculations.

Value chain, TQM
(Obj. 2, 6)

P19-5B Problem 19-4B provided both quantitative and qualitative information about Pameon's quality project, and asked you to perform a *quantitative* analysis to help Pameon's managers decide whether to embark on the quality project. Now consider some *qualitative* factors in Pameon's quality improvement project.

Required

1. Why did Jon Vaucluse create a team to address this quality problem, rather than assigning the task to one person? Consider each piece of cost/benefit information reported by management accountant Lily Peugot. Which person on the team is most likely to have contributed each item? (*Hint:* Which team member is likely to have the most information about each cost or benefit?)
2. Classify the following costs into one of the six value-chain business functions:
   a. $52,500 cost to redesign the watch.
   b. $80,000 cost to develop a completely new watch mechanism.
   c. $47,450 to rework watches identified as defective while still in the factory.
   d. $101,440 to make warranty repairs on watches returned by customers.
3. The Pameon problem illustrates how managers make trade-offs across different business functions in the value chain. Which of the six value-chain functions are involved in the trade-offs proposed by the quality improvement team? What specific trade-offs do they propose?

e-Commerce, cost-benefit analysis
(Obj. 6)

P19-6B Discount Gas Corporation wants to move its sales-order system to the Web. Under the proposed system, gas stations and other merchants will use a Web browser and, after typing in a password for the Discount Gas Web page, will be able to check the availability and current price of various products and place an order. The system processes the order electronically through links with the firm's traditional mainframe-based ordering system, without human intervention. Currently, customer service representatives take dealers' orders over the phone; they first record the information on a paper order form, then manually enter it into the firm's computer system.

CFO Steve Pronai believes that dealers will not adopt the new Web system unless Discount Gas provides financial assistance to help them purchase or upgrade their PCs. Pronai estimates this one-time cost at $800,000. Discount Gas will also have to invest $150,000 in upgrading its own computer hardware. Consultants tell Pronai that together the cost of the software and the consulting fee for installing the system will be $230,000. The Web system will enable Discount Gas to eliminate 25 clerical positions. Pronai estimates that the benefits of the new system's lower labor costs will have a present value of $1,400,000.

Required

Use a cost-benefit analysis to recommend to Steve Pronai whether or not Discount Gas should proceed with the Web-based ordering system. Give your reasons, showing supporting calculations.

e-Commerce, cost-benefit analysis, expected value
(Obj. 6)

P19-7B Consider the Discount Gas proposed entry into e-commerce in Problem 19-6B. Steve Pronai revises his estimates of the benefits from the new system's lower labor costs. He now thinks there is a 40% chance of receiving the $1,400,000 in benefits and a 60% chance the benefits will only be $920,000.

Required

1. Compute the expected benefits of the Web-based ordering system.
2. Would you recommend Discount Gas accept the proposal?
3. Before Steve Pronai makes a final decision, what other factors should he consider?

Ethics
(Obj. 7)

P19-8B Renee Abby is the new controller for Gate Software, Inc., which develops and sells educational software. Shortly before the December 31 fiscal year end, Matt Berrigan, the company president, asks Abby how things look for the year-end numbers. He is not happy to learn that earnings growth may be below 30% for the first time in the company's five-year history. Berrigan explains that financial analysts have again predicted a 30% earnings growth for the company and that he does not intend to disappoint them. He suggests that Abby talk to the assistant controller, who can explain how the previous controller dealt with this situation. The assistant controller suggests the following strategies:

a. Record as sales certain software awaiting sale that is held in a public warehouse.

b. Delay the year-end closing a few days into January of the next year, so that some of next year's sales are included as this year's sales.

c. Reduce the allowance for bad debts (and bad debts expense), given the company's continued strong performance.

d. Persuade suppliers to postpone billing until January 1.

e. Postpone routine monthly maintenance expenditures from December to January.

Which of these suggested strategies are inconsistent with IMA standards? What should Abby do if Berrigan insists that she follow all of these suggestions?

APPLY YOUR KNOWLEDGE

DECISION CASES

Case 1. Digiteck, Inc., designs and manufactures switches used in telecommunications. Digiteck's main facility is in California's Silicon Valley. Its second facility in North Carolina's Research Triangle Park services the Park's concentration of telecommunications firms. The serious flooding caused by Hurricane Floyd throughout North Carolina also affected Digiteck's facilities. Inventory was completely ruined, and the company's computer system, including all accounting records, was destroyed.

Flow of costs through manufacturing companies (Obj. 5)

Before the disaster recovery specialists clean the buildings, Annette Couch, the company controller, is anxious to salvage whatever records she can to support an insurance claim for the destroyed inventory. She is standing in what is left of the accounting department with Jay Boros, the cost accountant.

"I didn't know mud could smell so bad." Jay says, "What should I be looking for?"

"Don't worry about beginning inventory numbers," responds Annette, "we'll get them from last year's annual report. We need first-quarter cost data."

"I was working on the first-quarter results just before the hurricane hit," Jay says. "Look, my report's still in my desk drawer. But all I can make out is that for the first quarter, material purchases were $434,000 and that direct labor, manufacturing overhead, and total manufacturing costs to account for were $430,000, $245,000, and $1,300,000, respectively. Wait, and cost of goods available for sale was $1,280,000."

"Great," says Annette, "I remember that sales for the period were approximately $1.5 million. Given our gross profit of 30%, that's all you should need."

Jay is not sure about that, but decides to see what he can do with this information. The beginning inventory numbers are

- Direct materials, $109,000
- Work in process, $215,000
- Finished goods, $145,000

He remembers a schedule he learned in college that may help him get started.

Required

1. Exhibit 19-13 resembles the schedule Jay has in mind. Use it to determine the ending inventories of direct materials, work in process, and finished goods.

2. Draft an insurance claim letter for the controller, seeking reimbursement for the flood damage to inventory. Digiteck's insurance representative is Don Snowball, at Industrial Insurance Co., 1122 Main Street, Hartford, CT 06268. The policy number is #3454340-23. Digiteck's address is 5 Research Triangle Way, Raleigh, NC 27698.

Case 2. To help management accountants meet obligations to their profession, employer, the public, and themselves, the IMA has issued *Standards of Ethical Conduct for Management Accountants*. In defining ethical behavior, these standards can be applied to more than just management accounting. They are also relevant to college students. Explain at least one situation that shows how each IMA standard in Exhibit 19-15 is relevant to your experiences as a student. For example, the ethical standard of competence would suggest not cutting classes!

Ethics (Obj. 7)

ETHICAL ISSUE

◄◄ *Link Back to Chapter 7.* ComDigital, Inc., designs and manufactures chips used in digital cell phones. ComDigital is currently developing the next generation of computer chips that will allow users to receive e-mail and surf the Net using voice commands over a cell phone. Because of competition to be the first to perfect the new chip, ComDigital is investing heavily in development. Work is going slowly, and revenue growth from older chips is starting to drop. With year-end approaching, ComDigital's CEO, Jim Mann, calls a meeting with Joan

Ethics (Obj. 7)

Peters, Vice-President of Marketing, Tammy Myers, Vice-President of Finance, and Larry Case, Controller. Larry Case asks that as assistant controller, you also attend the meeting.

The CEO starts the meeting by expressing concern that with the slowdown in revenue growth and the heavy investment in new chip development, ComDigital may not meet financial analysts' earnings predictions this year. The conversation eventually turns to the new chip. Mann says the company cannot slow its R&D efforts but, since the new chip will be so profitable when it goes into production, some of the costs should be capitalized now, and then expensed later when the chip is generating revenue. VP of Finance Tammy Myers then suggests capitalizing some of these costs and charging them against revenues of chips currently being produced and sold. She argues that the new chip's R&D efforts must be providing some insights for improving the production process for existing chips. You are surprised by Controller Larry Case's silence during this discussion, as you believe these are R&D costs that GAAP requires to be expensed as incurred. The meeting ends without resolution.

Later, you learn that the CEO has told your boss to capitalize a large amount of this year's development costs for the new chip. Before talking to anyone, you decide to work through this ethical dilemma, using the following framework from Chapter 7.

1. List the facts.
2. Identify the ethical issues.
3. Specify the alternatives.
4. Identify the people involved.
5. Assess the possible consequences.
6. Make a decision.

Complete the framework.

FINANCIAL STATEMENT CASE

Identifying type of company and its cost objects, and analyzing its response to time-based competition (Obj. 4, 6)

To help determine whether current profits will continue and grow in the future, investors need information on management's plans. Investors are especially interested in how management plans to compete in the modern business environment. Let's use **Target Corporation's** annual report to consider the company's operations and management's plans. To answer the following questions, you will need to refer to the description of Target Corporation, the chairman's letter to shareholders in the company's annual report, and the financial statements.

Required

1. Is Target Corporation a service company, a merchandiser, or a manufacturer? What financial statement information supports your answer? What information outside the financial statements supports your answer?
2. What costs would Target classify as inventoriable?
3. Use Management's Discussion and Analysis in the annual report to identify some of the company's cost objects.
4. Does Target's management see time-based competition as critical to the company's success? What specific steps is it taking to meet this challenge?

TEAM PROJECT

Management accounting and e-commerce in the real world (Obj. 1, 6)

Search the Internet for a nearby company that also has a Web page. Arrange an interview with a management accountant, a controller, or other accounting/finance officer of the company. Before you conduct the interview, answer the following questions:

1. Is this a service, merchandising, or manufacturing company? What is its primary product or service?
2. Is the primary purpose of the company's Web site to provide information about the company and its products, to sell on-line, or to provide financial information for investors?
3. Are parts of the company's Web site restricted so that you need password authorization to enter? What appears to be the purpose of limiting access?
4. Does the Web site provide an e-mail link for contacting the company?

At the interview, begin by clarifying your answers to questions 1–4, and ask the following additional questions:

5. If the company sells over the Web, what benefits has the company derived? Did the company perform a cost-benefit analysis before deciding to begin Web sales?

   Or

   If the company does not sell over the Web, why not? Has the company performed a cost-benefit analysis and decided not to sell over the Web?

6. What is the biggest cost of operating the Web site?
7. Does the company make any purchases over the Internet? What percentage?

8. How has e-commerce affected the company's management accounting system? Have the management accountant's responsibilities become more or less complex? More or less interesting?
9. Does the company use Web-based accounting applications, such as accounts receivable or accounts payable?

Prepare a report describing the results of your interview.

INTERNET EXERCISE

1. Go to **http://www.forbes.com.** Under "Quotes & Research" type <u>TOY,</u> the stock symbol for **Toys "Я" Us, Inc.,** and click on *Go.* In the left-hand column click on *Company Info* and scan the information provided.
   a. Is this primarily a service, merchandising, or manufacturing company? What is the company's major product or service?
   b. Is this a global company? If so, in what countries does it operate?
2. In the left-hand column click on *Financials* and use the financial statements to answer the following questions.
   a. Review the annual balance sheet. Does this company report amounts for inventory? If so, for the most recent year what amount is reported? What major categories of cost are included in this account?
   b. Review the annual income statement. How many operating expense accounts does this company report? Of these accounts, how many contain inventoriable product costs? Period costs?
   c. Does this company report costs of goods sold? If so, for the most recent year what amount is reported? What title does the company use for this account?
3. At the top of the page in the "Quotes & Research" box type <u>HRB,</u> the stock symbol for **H&R Block, Inc.,** and click on *Go.* Follow the instructions above to answer the questions in items 1 and 2 for H&R Block, Inc.

Toys "Я" Us and H&R Block

Go to the "Managerial Accounting and Cost Analysis" episode on the *Mastering Accounting* CD-ROM for an interactive, video-enhanced exercise that focuses on CanGo's need for standardized accounting reports as it prepares for an IPO.

20

Job Costing

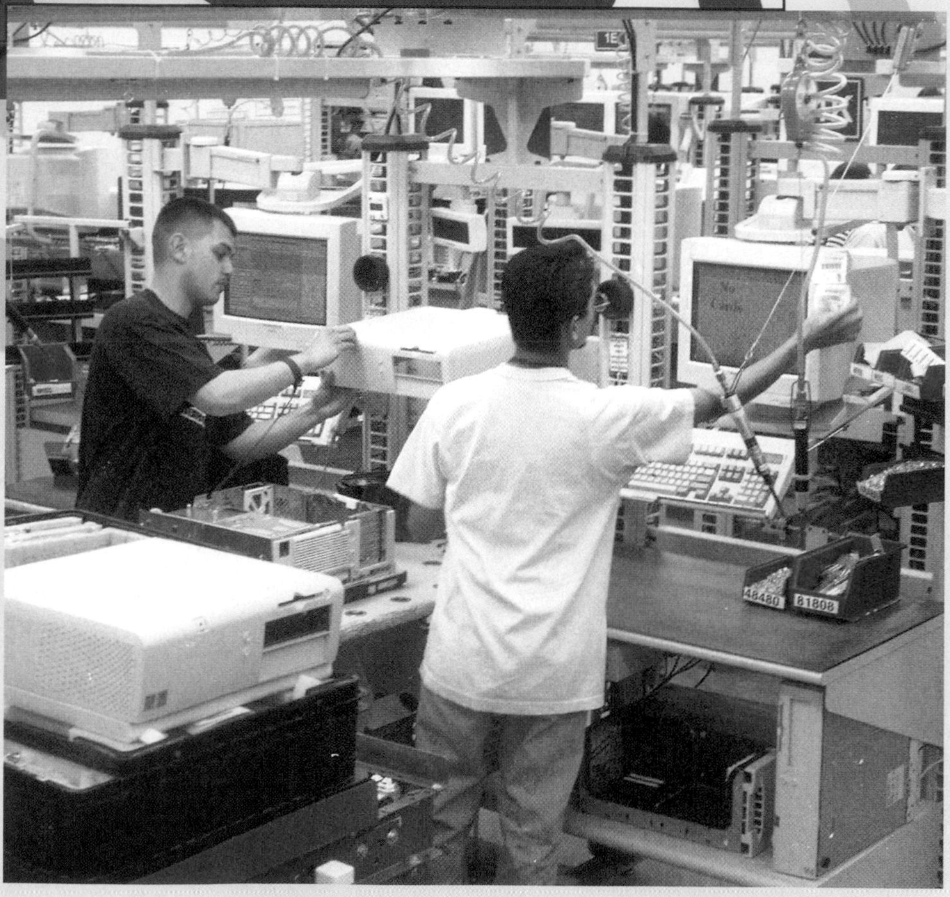

LEARNING OBJECTIVES

*After studying this chapter,
you should be able to*

1. Distinguish between job costing
   and process costing

2. Account for materials and labor
   in a manufacturer's job costing
   system

3. Account for manufacturing
   overhead in a manufacturer's
   job costing system

4. Account for noninventoriable
   costs in job costing

How did Michael Dell turn **Dell Computer** around from losses in 1993 to record profits of $1.9 *billion* for the fiscal year ending January 2000? Most companies can increase gross profit either by increasing selling prices or by reducing costs. But computer prices were falling throughout the industry, so Dell could not increase selling prices. He had no choice—Dell had to reduce manufacturing costs.

Recent estimates indicate that Dell now enjoys a 10–15% cost advantage over its competitors in the personal computer market. How did it develop this advantage? Management accounting information helped Dell and his managers decide which costs could be cut. The first step was to figure out how much it cost the company to assemble a computer.

To determine the manufacturing cost of its products, Dell uses a *job costing* system. Each computer is built to a specific customer order, called a *job*. Dell's job costing system traces direct materials (such as CD-ROMs and hard drives) and direct labor (such as assembly-line labor) to each job. Then Dell allocates indirect manufacturing overhead costs (such as depreciation on the plant) to each job. The sum of the job's direct materials, direct labor, and manufacturing overhead is its total cost.

Dell needs to know how much a product—for example, a particular computer model—costs for two main reasons:

1. *To help managers plan and control business operations, so they can:*
    - Control costs
    - Identify the most profitable products
    - Develop financial plans
    - Set selling prices for products
2. *To help managers gather information for external reporting:*
    - Cost of goods manufactured and cost of goods sold for the income statement
    - Inventory for the balance sheet

Source: McWilliams, G. "Mimicking Dell, Compaq to sell its PCs directly," *Wall Street Journal*, November 11, 1998, Page B1.

In this chapter, we will explain how **Dell Computer** and other companies use a job cost system to measure the cost of producing a product or a service. But before we get started on the details, let's pause to see where job costing fits in the big picture of cost determination for management decisions and external reporting.

In Chapter 19, you learned that managers make certain business decisions based on *full product costs* from all elements of the value chain: R&D, design, production, marketing, distribution, and customer service. Managers need to know full product costs because they must, for example, set the long-run average sale price of the products higher than the full product costs, to make a profit.

Recall that full product costs have two components: inventoriable product costs and period costs (also called noninventoriable costs). Inventoriable product costs are from the third element of the value chain in Exhibit 19-4: production for manufacturers and purchases for merchandisers. They are called inventoriable costs because in addition to serving as building blocks for computing full product costs, these are the costs GAAP requires companies to use in computing inventory and cost of goods sold for the balance sheet and income statement. Most of Chapter 20 focuses on how companies determine these inventoriable product costs. The chapter concludes with a discussion of assigning noninventoriable costs (period costs) to products and services. By adding noninventoriable costs to the inventoriable costs, managers can build up full product costs to guide internal decisions.

As you read this chapter, keep in mind that *products* are not the only cost objects. ➡ For example, managers use costs of *manufacturing processes* to identify inefficiencies and to cut costs. Knowing the costs of serving different *customers* allows managers to identify their most profitable (valuable) customers. Knowing the costs of doing business in different *geographic regions* can help managers decide which regions are more profitable and thus better candidates for expansion.

◄ For a review of cost objects, see Chapter 19, p. 760.

This chapter focuses on assigning costs to products and services because (1) products and services are the most common cost objects, and (2) managers use the costs of individual products and services to build costs of customers, geographic regions, and other cost objects.

TWO APPROACHES TO PRODUCT COSTING

Objective 1
Distinguish between job costing and process costing

 ➡ We discussed direct and indirect costs in Chapter 19, p. 761.

It is hard for companies like **Dell** to figure out how much it costs to manufacture a particular computer. Dell can trace the cost of direct materials like hard drives to the individual computers in which they are installed. But indirect costs such as depreciation on the manufacturing plant cannot be traced directly to an individual computer because Dell cannot determine exactly how much depreciation a particular computer "caused." ◄ Also, Dell makes many different computer models, and each requires different resources. How can Dell accurately measure product costs?

Unfortunately, it is impossible to determine the precise costs of producing a specific individual product. Instead, companies use product costing systems that *average* costs across products. There are two broad types of systems:

 DAILY EXERCISE 20-1

- Process costing
- Job costing

Process costing systems accumulate costs for each production process. *Job costing* systems accumulate costs for each individual job. Process costing and job costing also differ in the extent to which they average costs.

Process Costing

 **PROCESS COSTING.** System for assigning costs to large numbers of identical units that usually proceed in a continuous fashion through a series of uniform production steps or processes.

Process costing is used by companies that produce large numbers of identical units in a continuous fashion through a series of uniform production steps or processes. Consider **Pace Foods,** producer of picante sauce. Picante sauce requires two major processes: (1) chopping vegetables, and (2) mixing and bottling the sauce. Pace separately accumulates the costs for each of the two production processes. Next, the company averages the costs of the chopping process over all units passing through the process. Then it averages the costs of the mixing and bottling process over all units passing through that process. For example, if Pace spent $50,000 to mix and bottle 100,000 one-pound bottles of picante sauce, the mixing and bottling cost per bottle would be

$$\text{Cost per bottle of mixing and bottling picante sauce} = \frac{\$50,000}{100,000 \text{ bottles}} = \$0.50$$

DAILY EXERCISE 20-2

DAILY EXERCISE 20-3

To get the total cost of a bottle of picante sauce, Pace would add the $0.50 per bottle of mixing and bottling cost to the cost per bottle of vegetables and the chopping process. Each bottle of picante sauce is identical to every other bottle, so each bears the same average cost of the mixing and bottling process. In process costing, the cost assigned to each unit (bottle) is a broad average, because the costs are spread evenly over the thousands of units (bottles) passing through the production process.

Some other examples of companies that use process costing:

- Oil refining—**Texaco** produces billions of gallons of unleaded gasoline.
- Food and beverage—**Kellogg's** produces thousands of pounds of cornflakes.
- Pharmaceuticals—**Bayer** produces millions of aspirin tablets.

Exhibit 20-1 shows that process costing is not limited to manufacturers. Service companies like banks use it to determine the cost of processing customer transactions. Merchandisers, such as granaries, use process costing to determine the storage cost for each bushel of grain. We consider process costing in detail in Chapter 21.

Job Costing

 **JOB COSTING.** System for assigning costs to a specific unit or to a small batch of products or services that (1) pass through production steps as a distinct identifiable job lot, and (2) can vary considerably in terms of materials, labor, and overhead costs.

This chapter focuses on **job costing,** which assigns costs to a specific unit or to a small batch of products or services that pass through production steps as a distinct identifiable job lot. Different jobs can vary considerably in terms of materials, labor, and overhead costs, so job costing accumulates costs separately for each individual

	Service	Merchandising	Manufacturing
Job Costing	Law firms (cases) Health care (diagnoses, procedures, or patients) Public relations (campaigns)	e-tailers such as Amazon.com and Drugstore.com Mail-order catalog companies such as L.L. Bean	Commercial building construction Custom furniture
Process Costing	Banks and other financial institutions (processing customer deposit transactions)	Granaries (distribute tons of identical grains)	Paper mills Mining operations Textile mills

job. The job may be a customer order for a mail-order catalog company like **L.L. Bean,** a production order for specialized machinery for a metal fabricator, or a project such as the construction of the Olympic Stadium in Sydney, Australia. Job costing is common in industries that produce goods to customer specifications, such as

- Aircraft—in Seattle, **Boeing** produces five new 767 airplanes to complete an order from **Delta.**
- Furniture—in High Point, North Carolina, **Swaim Furniture** produces eight dining room chairs for a customer in Baltimore.
- Construction—in Atlanta, **John Wieland Homes** constructs a new home for a linebacker on the **Atlanta Falcons** football team.

Boeing, Swaim Furniture, and John Wieland Homes produce individual products or small batches of products. Dell Computer also assembles computers to specific customer orders. In each company, different jobs can vary widely in the resources and time required, and in the complexity of the production process. Because the jobs are so different, they are not assigned equal costs.

To assign job costs accurately, accountants try to determine the *drivers* of the costs. A **cost driver** is the primary factor that causes costs. When a cost driver changes, the job's total cost changes. For example, direct labor *hours* drive direct labor *costs*. If Dell Computer uses an extra half hour of direct labor to complete an order of three computers, Dell's total direct labor cost of the three computers also increases. Because Dell is in a competitive industry where selling prices are declining, cost control is the key to earning a profit on each job.

COST DRIVER. The primary factor that causes costs.

A job may consist of one unit, like the custom home built by John Wieland. Or a job may consist of a group similar units in a distinct batch, like the eight dining room chairs ordered by Swaim's customer. When a single job includes more than one unit, the manufacturer determines the average cost of each unit in that job. Suppose Swaim's total cost for the eight chairs is $800. Then Swaim's average cost per chair is

$$\text{Average cost per chair} = \frac{\$800}{8 \text{ chairs}} = \$100$$

The cost per individual unit (chair) in job costing may require averaging, just as in process costing. However, the number of units over which costs are averaged is typically much smaller in job costing. And because each job is distinct, there is less averaging of costs *across* jobs. Exhibit 20-2 summarizes key differences between job costing and process costing.

Job costing is becoming more common in manufacturing industries like electronics. Dell Computer's made-to-order assembly process is one example. Another example is contract manufacturing, where manufacturing plants (often in Mexico and Asia) produce electronic goods for a variety of customers, including **Cisco Systems, Hewlett-Packard,** and **Sony.** Most contract manufacturers make goods for several well-known companies. For example, the **Flextronics** plant in Guadalajara, Mexico, makes **Sony** Web TV set-top boxes, **PalmPilots, Hewlett-**

EXHIBIT 20-2
Differences Between Job and Process Costing

	Job Costing	**Process Costing**
Cost object	Job	Process
Outputs	Single units or small batches, with large differences between jobs	Large quantities of identical units
Extent of averaging	Less averaging—costs are averaged over the small number of units in a batch (often 1 unit)	More averaging—costs are averaged over the many identical units in the large batch

Packard printers, and **Johnson & Johnson** blood glucose monitors. Clearly, the plant must carefully track the costs of each of these separate jobs.

Job costing is not confined to manufacturers. Exhibit 20-1 shows that service organizations such as hospitals and physicians also use job costing. A hospital might consider each medical procedure a different job, while a doctor considers each individual patient a job. Professional service providers such as architects, accountants, and attorneys use job costing to determine the costs of jobs for individual clients. Merchandisers like **Amazon.com** can use job costing to determine the cost of meeting each customer order.

Job costing is most complex for manufacturers, so this chapter focuses on job costing in a manufacturing setting. The last section of the chapter applies the same principles to nonmanufacturing companies.

JOB COST RECORD Let's consider how a manufacturer, E-Z-Boy Furniture Company, could use job costing. For E-Z-Boy, each individual customer order can be treated as a different job. **Job cost records** are documents used to accumulate the costs of individual jobs. Exhibit 20-3 shows a completed job cost record for the **Macy's** New York City order of ten recliner chairs from E-Z-Boy, Job 293. The job cost record has separate sections for the costs of direct materials, direct labor, and manufacturing overhead allocated to Job 293. The total cost of the job is $1,220. The average cost of each of the ten recliners is $122 ($1,220 ÷ 10).

JOB COST RECORD. Document used to accumulate the costs of an individual job.

EXHIBIT 20-3
Job Cost Record

JOB COST RECORD

E-Z-Boy

Job No. 293

Customer Name and Address   Macy's New York City

Job Description   10 recliner chairs

Date Promised	7-31	Date Started	7-24	Date Completed	7-29

Date	Direct Materials		Direct Labor		Manufacturing Overhead Allocated		
	Requisition Numbers	Amount	Labor Time Record Numbers	Amount	Date	Rate	Amount
20X5 7-24 25 28	334 338 347	$ 90 180 230	236, 251, 258 264, 269, 273, 291 305	$150 200 50	7-29	80% of Direct Labor Cost	$320

Overall Cost Summary

Direct materials .... $ 500
Direct labor 400
Manufacturing Overhead
    Allocated 320

| Totals | | $500 | | $400 | Total Job Cost .... $1,220 |

Managers use job cost data like E-Z-Boy's job cost record in Exhibit 20-3 to plan and control manufacturing operations. Suppose managers planned to spend $450 on direct materials for Job 293. The $500 actual cost exceeds the plan by more than 10%. Managers can investigate this cost overrun to help reduce costs in the future.

 DAILY EXERCISE 20-4

The company starts a job cost record like Exhibit 20-3 when it begins working on a job. Records of jobs in process (started but not yet completed) form a subsidiary ledger for the general ledger account Work in Process Inventory. ➤ As costs are incurred for a particular job, they are added to the job cost record in the subsidiary ledger and the Work in Process Inventory in the general ledger. When the job is completed, its costs are totaled and transferred out of Work in Process Inventory into Finished Goods Inventory. When the job's output is sold, its costs are moved out of Finished Goods Inventory into Cost of Goods Sold. Exhibit 20-4 summarizes this process.

◄ For a review of ledgers and subsidiary ledgers, see Chapter 6, p. 240.

EXHIBIT 20-4   Job Costing—Flow of Costs Through the Accounts

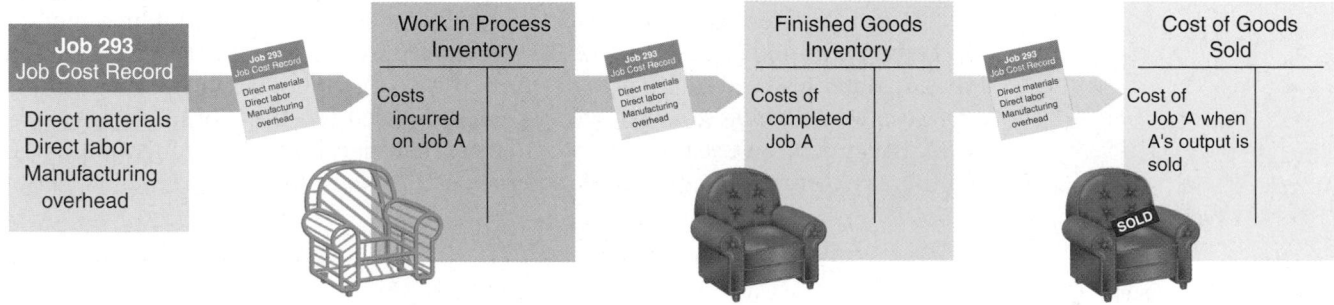

JOB COSTING ILLUSTRATED

We next illustrate accounting in a job costing system. You will see how E-Z-Boy:

1. *Accumulates* total direct material costs, direct labor costs, and manufacturing overhead costs incurred during the period for all jobs,
2. *Assigns* appropriate amounts of these costs to individual jobs such as Job 293.

On December 31, 20X4, E-Z-Boy reports the following inventories:

Materials inventory (many kinds)	$20,000
Work in process inventory (5 jobs)	29,000
Finished goods inventory (unsold recliners from 2 completed jobs)	12,000

The following data summarize transactions for the year 20X5. We will explain the accounting for these transactions, step by step.

1.	Materials purchased on account	$320,000
2.	Direct materials used for manufacturing	285,000
	Indirect materials used for manufacturing	40,000
3.	Manufacturing wages incurred	335,000
4.	Direct labor on jobs	250,000
	Indirect labor to support manufacturing	85,000
5.	Depreciation on plant and equipment	50,000
6.	Plant utilities	20,000
7.	Plant insurance	5,000
8.	Property taxes—plant	10,000
9.	Manufacturing overhead allocated to jobs	200,000
10.	Cost of goods manufactured	740,000
11.	Sales on account	996,000
	Cost of goods sold	734,000

Accounting for Materials in a Job Costing System

ACCOUNTING FOR PURCHASES   To offer an overview of the big picture of job costing, we use summary entries for the entire year 20X5. In practice, however, companies update their general ledgers more frequently.

Recall that the goals of our accounting process are to *accumulate* the total costs, and then *assign* the appropriate costs to each individual job. We begin by making the entry to *accumulate* the costs. Thus, our first entry is for purchases of materials—in this case, lumber (data from page 801):

(1) Materials Inventory.........................   320,000
        Accounts Payable..................   320,000

E-Z-Boy receives the lumber and stores it. Control over materials is established with a subsidiary *materials ledger.* This ledger holds perpetual inventory records that list the quantity and cost of all manufacturing materials on hand. Exhibit 20-5 shows a subsidiary materials ledger record for the lumber that goes into the recliner chairs.

E-Z-Boy's materials are logged in by receiving report number (abbreviated as *Rec. Report No.* in Exhibit 20-5). E-Z-Boy received 20 units of lumber, at $9 each, on July 23. Materials used in the product are recorded by materials requisition number (*Mat. Req. No.*). Exhibit 20-5 shows that E-Z-Boy used ten units of lumber on July 24. Management can use these records to trace materials into the production process and thereby control the amount of materials used in various jobs.

EXHIBIT 20-5
Materials Ledger Record

DAILY EXERCISE 20-5

MATERIALS LEDGER RECORD

E-Z-Boy

| ITEM NO. B-220 | DESCRIPTION | LUMBER/RECLINER CHAIRS |

	RECEIVED				USED				BALANCE		
DATE	REC. REPORT No.	UNITS	COST	TOTAL COST	MAT. REQ. No.	UNITS	COST	TOTAL COST	UNITS	COST	TOTAL COST
20X5 7-20									30	$9.00	$270
7-23	678	20	$9.00	$180					50	9.00	450
7-24					334	10	$9.00	$90	40	9.00	360

The general ledger has a Materials Inventory account. This account is supported by the materials subsidiary ledger that includes a separate record for each type of raw material. Exhibit 20-6 illustrates the Materials Inventory general ledger account and the subsidiary ledger for the materials E-Z-Boy uses. The balance of Materials Inventory in the general ledger ($1,170) equals the sum of the balances in the subsidiary materials ledger.

After materials are purchased, the manufacturing process begins with a document called a **materials requisition.** This is a request for materials, prepared by manufacturing personnel. In effect, they ask that the lumber be moved from storage to the manufacturing plant so work can begin. Exhibit 20-7 illustrates a materials requisition for the lumber needed to manufacture the ten recliner chairs in E-Z-Boy's Job 293.

The "Direct Materials" section in the job cost record (Exhibit 20-3) shows how the details of the materials requisitions are posted to the individual job cost records. Follow the $90 cost of the lumber from materials requisition 334 (Exhibit 20-7) to the materials ledger record (Exhibit 20-5) to the job cost record (Exhibit 20-3). Note that all the dollar amounts in Exhibits 20-3 through 20-13 show E-Z-Boy's *costs*— not the prices at which E-Z-Boy *sells* its products.

Technology simplifies the collection of data, including direct material costs. Companies such as **Dell Computer** use electronic bar codes to track material costs,

MATERIALS REQUISITION.
Request for materials, prepared by manufacturing personnel.

EXHIBIT 20-6
Materials Inventory Accounts

Exhibit 20-6: Materials Inventory Accounts

GENERAL LEDGER

MATERIALS INVENTORY
1,170

SUBSIDIARY LEDGER
MATERIALS LEDGER

LUMBER

Date	Received	Used	Balance
7-24			$360

PADDING

Date	Received	Used	Balance
7-24			$160

UPHOLSTERY FABRIC

Date	Received	Used	Balance
7-24			$390

NAILS

Date	Received	Used	Balance
7-24			$40

THREAD

Date	Received	Used	Balance
7-24			$20

OTHER MATERIALS

Date	Received	Used	Balance
7-24			$200

$1,170

TOTAL BALANCE EQUALS THE BALANCE
IN THE GENERAL LEDGER ACCOUNT.

 DAILY EXERCISE 20-6

tracing materials to individual computers by scanning bar codes on the component parts as they are installed.

DIRECT AND INDIRECT MATERIALS   Materials Inventory is debited for the costs of all materials purchased—both direct materials and indirect materials. Note that the Materials Inventory account in Exhibit 20-6 includes the costs of both direct materials (lumber, padding, and upholstery fabric) and indirect materials (nails, thread, and other materials).

When either direct or indirect materials are requisitioned from storage, Materials Inventory and the accompanying account in the subsidiary materials ledger are credited. What account is debited? The answer depends on the type of materials requisitioned. For direct materials, the debit is made directly to Work in Process Inventory. When indirect materials are used, the debit is made to a separate account called Manufacturing Overhead. ➡

Keep this distinction in mind: *Indirect manufacturing costs, such as indirect materials used, are not debited directly to Work in Process Inventory. Instead, they are accumulated in the (separate) Manufacturing Overhead account.*

◄ Recall from Chapter 19, p. 763, that manufacturing overhead includes all manufacturing costs other than direct materials and direct labor.

EXHIBIT 20-7
Materials Requisition

Exhibit 20-7: Materials Requisition

Materials Requisition No. ___334___

E-Z-Boy

Date   7-24-X5

Job No.   293

Item No.	Item	Quantity	Unit Cost	Amount
8-220	Lumber/Recliner chairs	10	$9.00	$90

DAILY EXERCISE 20-7

E-Z-Boy Furniture Company works on many jobs over the course of the year. At regular intervals, accountants collect the data from materials requisitions to make a single journal entry for all the materials that E-Z-Boy has used. The 20X5 entry for E-Z-Boy is (again, data are from page 801):

(2) Work in Process Inventory (for direct materials)	285,000	
Manufacturing Overhead (for indirect materials)	40,000	
Materials Inventory		325,000

Recall that the balance of the Work in Process Inventory account equals the total cost of all the jobs currently in process. This is the sum of the costs from all the job cost records of jobs that are still in process. For each job, E-Z-Boy takes two actions to *assign* the cost of direct materials used appropriately:

1. Debit Work in Process Inventory (in the general ledger) for the total cost of direct materials used.
2. Record the cost of the direct materials used on the individual job cost records (in the subsidiary ledger).

For example, Exhibit 20-7 shows that $90 of the direct materials relate to Job 293. Exhibit 20-8 includes this $90 on Job 293's job cost record.

EXHIBIT 20-8
Direct Materials Entry on Job Cost Record

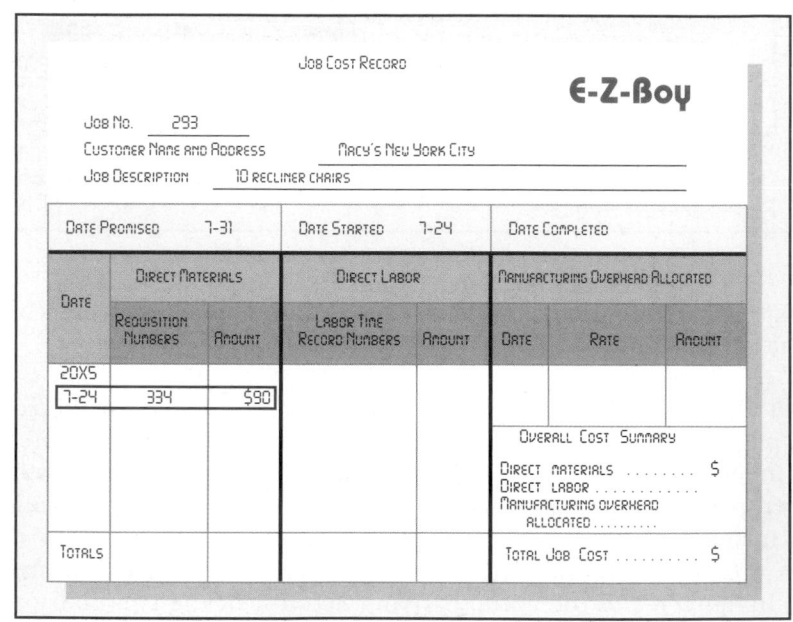

DAILY EXERCISE 20-8

By definition, the costs of indirect materials like nails and thread cannot be traced directly to individual jobs. (If they could be traced to individual jobs, they would be *direct* materials.) Thus, indirect material costs *cannot* be entered in the job cost records of specific jobs. Indirect costs are simply debited to the Manufacturing Overhead account in the general ledger.

The flow of materials costs through the T-accounts is as follows:

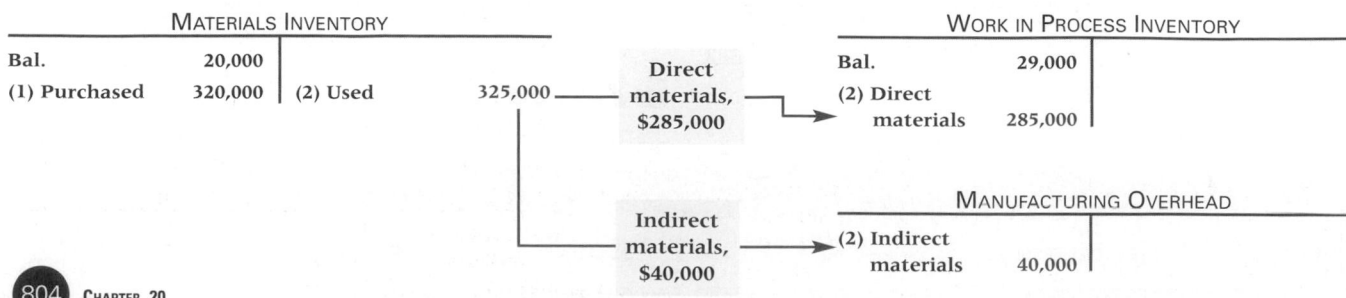

Accounting for Labor in a Job Costing System

Control over labor costs in a job costing system is established through payroll registers and time records. ➡ A **labor time record** identifies the employee, the amount of time spent on a particular job, and the labor cost charged to the job. Time records are accumulated for each job to determine its total direct labor cost. Exhibit 20-9 shows a labor time record used in a job costing system like E-Z-Boy's.

◄ Chapter 11, defined the payroll register as a special journal that lists each employee and the data to record payroll amounts.

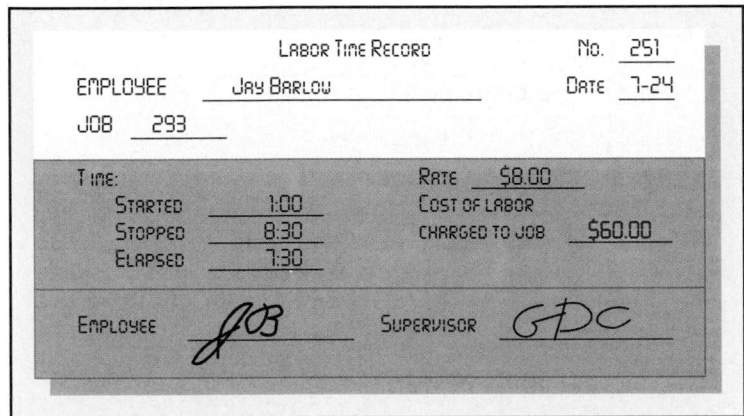

EXHIBIT 20-9
Labor Time Record

LABOR TIME RECORD. Identifies the employee, the amount of time spent on a particular job, and the labor cost charged to the job; a record that manufacturing firms commonly use to trace direct labor time to specific job cost records.

Technology can simplify collection of direct labor costs. Companies can set up computer terminals on the production floor. At various stages in the manufacturing process of **Saturn** automobiles, for example, employees insert their identification cards into the terminals. This system captures direct labor time and cost without detailed labor documents.

E-Z-Boy's entry for 20X5 *accumulates* and records the actual labor costs E-Z-Boy incurred for all jobs (data from page 801):

(3) Manufacturing Wages.. 335,000
      Wages Payable 335,000

DIRECT AND INDIRECT LABOR Similar to the distinction between direct and indirect materials costs, direct and indirect labor costs are *assigned* separately. Direct labor is debited directly to Work in Process Inventory. Indirect labor cannot be traced to a specific job so it is added to the Manufacturing Overhead account. This assignment of labor cost credits Manufacturing Wages (data from page 801):

◉ **DAILY EXERCISE 20-9**

(4) Work in Process Inventory (for direct labor) 250,000
    Manufacturing Overhead (for indirect labor) 85,000
      Manufacturing Wages 335,000

This entry brings the balance in Manufacturing Wages to zero, its transferred balance now divided between Work in Process Inventory (direct labor) and Manufacturing Overhead (indirect labor) as shown in the following T-accounts:

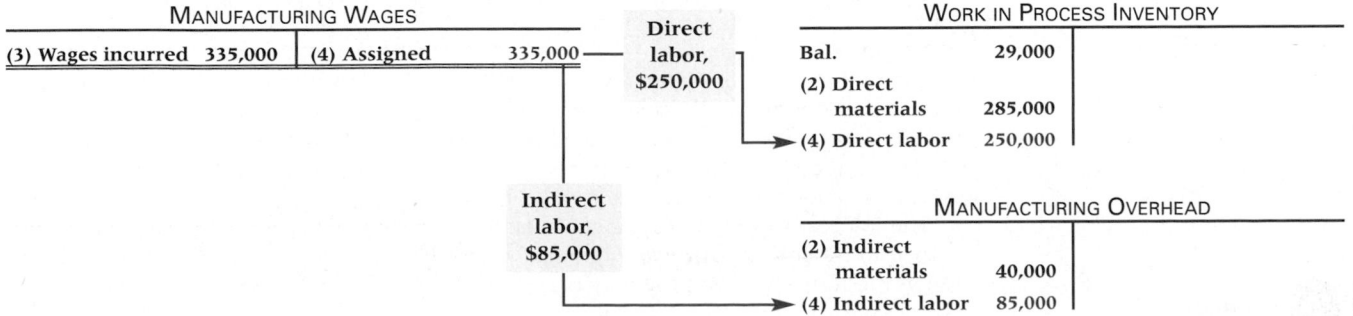

Assume that $150 of one day's direct labor cost is for Job 293. E-Z-Boy Furniture enters Job 293's direct labor on the job cost record. The $150 amount in the Direct Labor section of Exhibit 20-10 includes Jay Barlow's wages of $60 (from labor time record 251, Exhibit 20-9) and the labor costs entered on labor time records 236 and 258 (not shown).

EXHIBIT 20-10 **Direct Labor Entry on Job Cost Record**

The Work in Process Inventory account now contains the costs of direct materials and direct labor charged to Job 293—and the costs of many other jobs as well. Work in Process Inventory serves as a control account, with the job cost records giving the supporting details for each job.

To see why, keep in mind that the total direct labor debits to Work in Process Inventory equal the total direct labor costs assigned to all the individual jobs worked on during the period (and recorded on the individual job cost records). Similarly, the total direct material debits to Work in Process Inventory equal the total costs of direct materials used on all the jobs worked on during the period (and recorded on their job cost records). The job cost records thus serve as a subsidiary ledger for the general ledger balance in Work in Process Inventory.

THINK IT OVER How can the materials inventory subsidiary ledger (Exhibit 20-6), labor time records (Exhibit 20-9), and job cost records (Exhibits 20-8 and 20-10) help managers run the company more effectively and efficiently?

Answer: Managers can look at the materials inventory subsidiary ledger to see when inventories of individual materials like lumber, padding, upholstery fabric, nails, and thread are running low, so they can decide when to reorder.

Managers can use the labor time records in two ways: (1) to control employees, and (2) to control labor costs incurred on individual jobs. First, suppose an employee is paid for 7 1/2 hours of work per day. Adding across all her labor time records for each job she worked on during the day should yield a total of 7 1/2 hours worked. If not, the manager needs to find out how the employee spent any time unaccounted for. Second, managers can use labor time records to track how much time employees spend on a particular job. Managers need to ensure that employees work efficiently—if they spend longer than expected on a job, the job may not yield a profit.

The job cost record tallies materials, labor, and manufacturing overhead as they are assigned to the job. If costs exceed budget, managers must do a better job of controlling costs in the future, or else they may need to raise the sale price on similar jobs to ensure that the company remains profitable.

How Has Information Technology Changed Job Costing?

The flow of costs through the T-accounts and the journal entries applies to systems ranging from simple manual costing to sophisticated automated database systems. The main difference is in the source of data underlying the costs. In traditional systems, the sources of data include source documents such as material requisitions, labor time records, and job cost records like those we have described. These documents can be paper-based or automated.

Highly automated systems may have no physical source documents. Employees use bar codes to record materials used and scan their identification cards to record their labor time. The software immediately tracks these material and labor costs to the specific job, and updates the general ledger accounts (for example, Materials Inventory, Work in Process Inventory, Manufacturing Wages, and Manufacturing Overhead). Automated database systems may not store data in the form of separate job cost records. But when employees enter the job number, the system quickly tallies costs assigned to the job so far.

Advances in information technology may

1. Eliminate physical source documents
2. Hasten the speed with which
   a. Materials and labor costs are linked to specific jobs
   b. The general ledger accounts are updated

However, the cost flows and journal entries are identical to those we have described for E-Z-Boy.

e-Accounting

Radio-Frequency Identification System: Smart Tags for Tracking Parts and Products

How do manufacturers trace direct materials to products? The standard way to identify and follow a product through the factory and down the supply chain is the familiar bar code. Bar codes have been used for 25 years on everything from cans of beans to car bodies. Each of its stripes stands for a coded number. But the stripes are unique, like a thumbprint. If the contents or the destination of the part or product change, someone must print and attach a new bar code level.

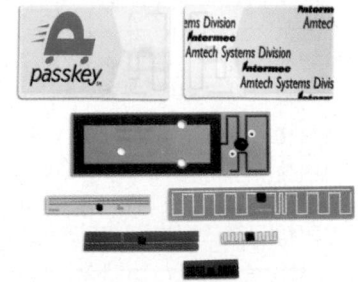

So bar codes require a lot of labor: As many as 60% of workers in warehouses spend time checking bar codes. And they must line up each item individually for scanning, even in automated identification systems.

Now there is a better method, called radio-frequency identification, or RFID, which uses electromagnetic waves. An RFID system uses a plastic tag, sometimes as small as two matches laid side by side. The tag's digital memory chip is the size of a pinhead, and it contains far more information than a bar code. And because radio is used, tagged products don't have to be aligned carefully for scanning.

In its more sophisticated "read-write" version, RFID has a stunning advantage. Without touching or removing the tag, users can alter the information on it. Workers can change the itinerary of a component on the factory floor, for example, or the destination of a shipment. The read-write tag is really a small data base that can be synchronized with a company's other data bases—and, eventually, with customers who have RFID technology.

Source: Adapted from Gene Bylinsky, "Hot new technologies for American factories," *Fortune,* June 26, 2000, pp. 288A–288K.

SUMMARY PROBLEM

www.prenhall.com/horngren

Mid-Chapter Assessment

Ecosphere Associates, Ltd. in Tucson, Arizona, produces ecospheres—self-sustaining enclosed glass spheres that include water, algae, tiny shrimp, and snails. Suppose Ecosphere has the following transactions:

a. Purchased raw materials on account, $35,000.

b. Materials costing $30,000 were requisitioned for production. Of this total, $3,000 were indirect materials.

c. Labor time records for the month show direct labor of $22,000, and indirect labor of $4,000.

Required

Prepare journal entries for each transaction.

Solution

a. Materials Inventory.............................. 35,000
        Accounts Payable   35,000

When materials are purchased on account:

- Debit (increase) the Materials Inventory asset for the *cost* of the materials, and
- Credit (increase) Accounts Payable to record the liability for the cost of the materials.

b. Work in Process Inventory.................. 27,000
    Manufacturing Overhead.................... 3,000
        Materials Inventory   30,000

When materials are requisitioned (used) in production, we record the movement of materials out of materials inventory and into production:

- Debit (increase) Work in Process Inventory for the cost of the *direct* materials (in this case, $27,000—the $30,000 total materials requisitioned less the $3,000 indirect materials)
- Debit (increase) Manufacturing Overhead for the cost of the *indirect* materials
- Credit (decrease) Materials Inventory for the cost of both direct and indirect materials moved out of the materials storage area and into production

c. Manufacturing Wages 26,000
        Wages Payable...........................   26,000

To record total labor costs actually incurred ($22,000 + 4,000):

- Debit (increase) Manufacturing Wages
- Credit (increase) Wages Payable to record the liability for wages incurred, but not paid

    Work in Process Inventory.................. 22,000
    Manufacturing Overhead.................... 4,000
        Manufacturing Wages   26,000

To assign the labor costs:

- Debit (increase) Work in Process Inventory for the cost of the *direct* labor
- Debit (increase) Manufacturing Overhead for the cost of the *indirect* labor
- Credit (decrease) Manufacturing Wages for the cost of both direct and indirect labor

---

Objective 3
Account for manufacturing overhead in a manufacturer's job costing system

ACCOUNTING FOR MANUFACTURING OVERHEAD IN A JOB COSTING SYSTEM

All manufacturing overhead costs are *accumulated* as debits to a single general ledger account—Manufacturing Overhead. We have already recorded the indirect materials (entry 2) and indirect labor (entry 4) manufacturing overhead costs. Entries 5–8 record the other manufacturing overhead costs E-Z-Boy Furniture actually incurred, as given on page 801. The account titles in parentheses indicate the specific records debited in the overhead subsidiary ledger.

(5)	Manufacturing Overhead (Depreciation—Plant and Equipment) ...	50,000	
	Accumulated Depreciation—Plant and Equipment...............		50,000
(6)	Manufacturing Overhead (Plant Utilities)...	20,000	
	Cash...		20,000
(7)	Manufacturing Overhead (Plant Insurance)	5,000	
	Prepaid Insurance—Plant		5,000
(8)	Manufacturing Overhead (Property Taxes—Plant).........................	10,000	
	Property Taxes Payable...		10,000

The actual manufacturing overhead costs (such as indirect materials, indirect labor, and depreciation, utilities, insurance and property taxes related to the plant) are debited to the Manufacturing Overhead account as they occur throughout the year. By the end of the year, the Manufacturing Overhead account has accumulated all the actual overhead costs as debits:

MANUFACTURING OVERHEAD

(2) Indirect materials	40,000
(4) Indirect labor	85,000
(5) Depreciation—plant and equipment	50,000
(6) Plant utilities	20,000
(7) Plant insurance	5,000
(8) Property taxes—plant	10,000
Total overhead cost	210,000

THINK IT OVER

How can managers use the manufacturing overhead subsidiary ledger to control overhead costs?

Answer: Managers plan the expected amount of each individual manufacturing overhead cost, such as plant-related depreciation, utilities, and insurance. Then they investigate why actual costs differ from planned costs. For example, if plant utilities are higher than expected, managers will want to know why. Did utility rates increase? Did workers waste electricity or water? Was there a delay in installing more energy-efficient machinery? Answers to these questions can help managers control (reduce) utility costs and develop more accurate estimates of future utility costs.

Now you have seen how the overhead costs are *accumulated* in the accounting records. But how are overhead costs *assigned* to individual jobs? Materials requisitions and labor time records make it easy to trace direct materials and direct labor costs to specific jobs. But as you can see from the manufacturing overhead T-account, overhead includes a variety of costs that cannot be traced to individual jobs. For example, it is impossible to say that a specific amount of the cost incurred to cool the plant is related to Job 293. Yet manufacturing overhead costs are as essential as direct materials and direct labor in producing goods, so we must find some way to assign these costs to specific jobs.

Allocating Overhead Costs to Jobs

Managers want to know the costs incurred in each job, including both direct and indirect costs. Accountants use **cost tracing** to assign direct costs (such as direct materials and direct labor) to cost objects such as jobs. They use **cost allocation** to assign manufacturing overhead and other indirect costs to cost objects. The general term **cost assignment** refers to tracing direct costs and allocating indirect costs to cost objects (jobs, in a job costing system).

COST TRACING. Assigning direct costs (such as direct materials and direct labor) to cost objects (such as jobs or production processes).

COST ALLOCATION. Assigning indirect costs (such as manufacturing overhead) to cost objects (such as jobs or production processes).

COST ASSIGNMENT. Tracing direct costs to cost objects and allocating indirect costs to cost objects.

Cost Assignment {
Direct Costs (Direct materials and direct labor) — Cost Tracing →
Indirect Costs (Manufacturing overhead) — Cost Allocation →
Cost Object (Job)

Direct material and direct labor costs are traced directly to each job, as we've seen. But managers also want to know the *total* manufacturing costs incurred on each job, including manufacturing overhead costs. Somehow, the company must allocate to each individual job its share of the wide variety of indirect manufacturing costs like depreciation and insurance on the plant and equipment, indirect materials, and indirect labor.

ALLOCATION BASE. A common denominator that links indirect costs to cost objects. Ideally, the allocation base is the primary cost driver that causes the indirect cost to be incurred.

CHOOSING AN ALLOCATION BASE The key to assigning indirect manufacturing costs to jobs is to identify a manufacturing overhead allocation base. The **allocation base** is a common denominator that links indirect manufacturing overhead costs to the cost objects. Ideally, the allocation base is the primary cost driver of manufacturing overhead costs. For example, in many companies, manufacturing overhead costs rise and fall with direct labor costs. In this case, accountants can use either direct labor costs or direct labor hours as the manufacturing overhead allocation base. The more direct labor a job uses, the more manufacturing overhead cost the job is allocated. This is a wise choice if direct labor is a driver of manufacturing overhead costs.

But direct labor is not always the best allocation base. Labor is less important in companies that have highly automated production processes, like **Saturn.** Saturn's manufacturing overhead costs are primarily machine-related. Plant depreciation, maintenance, and utilities are likely to fluctuate with the number of machine hours used. Companies with automated operations often use machine hours as the manufacturing overhead allocation base. The important point is that the cost allocation base should be the primary driver of the manufacturing overhead costs.

For simplicity, we'll assume the company uses only one allocation base to assign manufacturing overhead costs to jobs. Chapter 25 relaxes this assumption. There, we'll see how many companies use a method called *activity-based costing* to identify several different allocation bases that more accurately link indirect costs with the jobs that caused those costs. Because activity-based costing is a straightforward extension of the single allocation base method, it is important to begin by developing a solid understanding of the simpler system we describe here.

PREDETERMINED MANUFACTURING OVERHEAD RATE. Estimated manufacturing overhead rate computed at the beginning of the year, calculated as the total estimated manufacturing overhead costs divided by the total estimated quantity of the manufacturing overhead allocation base. Also called the budgeted manufacturing overhead rate.

DEVELOPING A PREDETERMINED MANUFACTURING OVERHEAD RATE The most accurate allocation cannot be made until the total amount of the manufacturing overhead cost is known, at the end of the year. But that would be much too late. Managers making decisions today cannot wait until the end of the year for product cost information. To solve this timing problem, accountants develop an estimated manufacturing overhead allocation rate at the beginning of the year. This **predetermined manufacturing overhead rate** (sometimes called the **budgeted manufacturing overhead rate**) is computed as follows:

$$\text{Predetermined manufacturing overhead rate} = \frac{\text{Total estimated manufacturing overhead costs}}{\text{Total estimated quantity of the manufacturing overhead allocation base}}$$

DAILY EXERCISE 20-11

Both the numerator and the denominator of the predetermined manufacturing overhead rate are based on *estimated* amounts. These are estimated *before* the year begins. They cannot be actual amounts because actual overhead costs and the actual quantity of the allocation base are not known until after the end of the period. Companies use this predetermined manufacturing overhead rate to allocate overhead to individual jobs.

Six Steps in Allocating Manufacturing Overhead Cost to Jobs

Companies follow six steps in allocating manufacturing overhead cost to jobs:

1. Estimate the total overhead cost for the planning period, which is usually a year. Late in 20X4, E-Z-Boy predicted overhead costs for 20X5 of $220,000.
2. Identify the manufacturing overhead (cost) allocation base. As the Manufacturing Overhead section of Exhibit 20-3 shows, E-Z-Boy selected direct labor cost.

3. Estimate the total quantity of the overhead allocation base. E-Z-Boy production managers expect to incur $275,000 of direct labor cost during 20X5.
4. Compute the predetermined manufacturing overhead rate as follows:

$$\text{Predetermined manufacturing overhead rate} = \frac{\text{Total estimated manufacturing overhead costs}}{\text{Total estimated quantity of the manufacturing overhead allocation base}}$$

$$= \frac{\text{Total estimated manufacturing overhead costs}}{\text{Total estimated direct labor costs}}$$

$$= \frac{\$220,000}{\$275,000} = 0.80 \text{ or } 80\%$$

Thus, the predetermined manufacturing overhead rate is computed as the total *estimated* manufacturing overhead cost (estimated *before* the year starts, as in step 1) divided by the total *estimated* quantity of the allocation base (also estimated *before* the year starts, as in step 3). Because the numerator and the denominator are both based on amounts that are *estimated before* the year starts, this overhead rate is *predetermined*.

5. Obtain *actual* quantities of the overhead allocation base used by individual jobs, as the year unfolds. The total actual direct labor cost of Job 293 is $400, as Exhibits 20-3 and 20-11 show.
6. Allocate manufacturing overhead cost to jobs by multiplying the *predetermined* manufacturing overhead rate (computed in step 4) by the *actual* quantity of the allocation base used by each job (from step 5). The same predetermined rate (80% of direct labor cost) is used to allocate manufacturing overhead to all jobs worked on throughout the year. Because the total direct labor cost for Job 293 is $400, and the predetermined overhead allocation rate is 80% of direct labor cost, the manufacturing overhead allocated to Job 293 is $320 ($400 × 0.80).

The complete job cost record for Job 293 in Exhibit 20-11 provides details supporting the $1,220 total cost and the $122 ($1,220 ÷ 10) unit cost of the **Macy's** order.

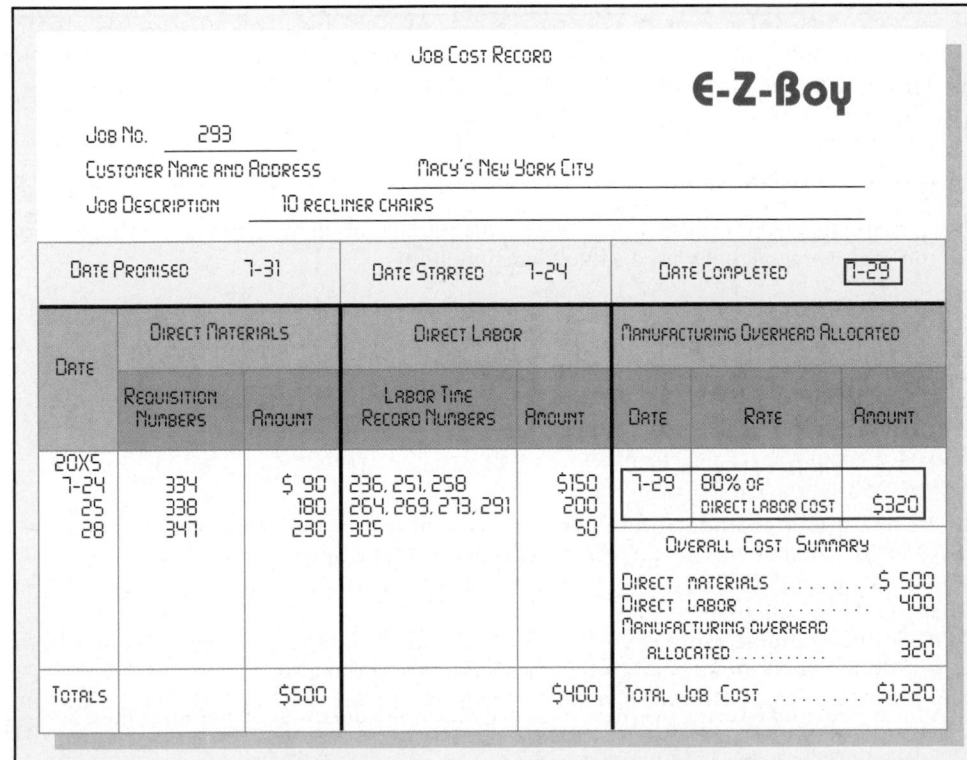

EXHIBIT 20-11
Manufacturing Overhead Entry on Job Cost Record

● DAILY EXERCISE 20-11

● DAILY EXERCISE 20-12

● DAILY EXERCISE 20-13

Of course, E-Z-Boy has made similar allocations of manufacturing overhead for each of the other jobs worked on during 20X5. The total overhead allocated to all jobs is 80% of the total $250,000 direct labor cost, or $200,000 (data from page 801). The journal entry to allocate manufacturing overhead costs to Work in Process Inventory is

(9)	Work in Process Inventory	200,000	
	Manufacturing Overhead....................		200,000

E-Z-Boy's allocation of manufacturing overhead flows through the T-accounts as follows:

MANUFACTURING OVERHEAD

(2) Indirect materials	40,000	(9) Allocated	200,000
(4) Indirect labor	85,000		
(5) Depreciation—plant and equipment	50,000		
(6) Plant utilities	20,000		
(7) Plant insurance	5,000		
(8) Property taxes— plant	10,000		
Actual overhead cost	210,000		
Bal.	10,000		

Manufacturing overhead allocated →

WORK IN PROCESS INVENTORY

Bal.	29,000		
(2) Direct materials	285,000		
(4) Direct labor	250,000		
(9) Manufacturing overhead allocated	200,000		

Note that after allocation, there is still a $10,000 debit balance in the Manufacturing Overhead account. This means that E-Z-Boy's actual overhead costs exceed the amount of overhead allocated to Work in Process Inventory. We say that E-Z-Boy's Manufacturing Overhead is *underallocated*. We'll discuss how accountants correct this problem on page 814.

WORK IT OUT

The Jarvis Company allocates manufacturing overhead cost based on machine hours. The company records the following actual costs for the year:

Indirect labor	$40,000	Rent on plant	$16,000
Plant supplies....................	20,000	Plant utilities	10,000
Machinery repair..............	14,000	Sales commissions..............	30,000
Advertising	6,000	Direct labor........................	70,000

Jarvis had budgeted 60,000 machine hours and $90,000 of manufacturing overhead costs for the year. Jarvis actually used 64,000 machine hours.

Questions

1. Compute the predetermined manufacturing overhead rate.
2. How much is actual manufacturing overhead?
3. Compute the allocated manufacturing overhead.
4. What is the ending balance in the Manufacturing Overhead account?

Answers

1. Predetermined manufacturing overhead rate based on budgeted machine hours = $90,000 ÷ 60,000 machine hours = $1.50 per machine hour.
2. Actual manufacturing overhead = $100,000 ($40,000 + $20,000 + $14,000 + $16,000 + $10,000).
3. Allocated manufacturing overhead equals the *actual* quantity of the allocation base (machine hours) multiplied by the *predetermined* overhead rate:

Allocated manufacturing overhead = 64,000 machine hours × $1.50 per machine hour = $96,000

4.

	MANUFACTURING OVERHEAD		
Actual costs (from Question 2)	100,000	Allocated costs (from Question 3)	96,000
Bal.	4,000		

There is a $4,000 debit balance in the Manufacturing Overhead account. Jarvis's Manufacturing Overhead is *underallocated* because the actual costs exceed the allocated costs by $4,000.

ACCOUNTING FOR FINISHED GOODS, SALES, AND COST OF GOODS SOLD

As each job is completed, its total cost moves out of Work in Process Inventory into Finished Goods Inventory. Sales of finished goods are recorded as they occur.

The $740,000 cost of goods manufactured (from the data on page 801) is the cost of the jobs that E-Z-Boy finished this year. E-Z-Boy credits Work in Process Inventory as the jobs leave the plant floor. The debit is to Finished Goods Inventory because the completed products move into the finished goods storage area. A summary entry for E-Z-Boy's goods completed in 20X5 is as follows:

(10)	Finished Goods Inventory	740,000	
	Work in Process Inventory..............		740,000

In turn, E-Z-Boy makes the usual entries for sales and cost of goods sold (data from page 801):

(11)	Accounts Receivable	996,000	
	Sales Revenue		996,000
	Cost of Goods Sold	734,000	
	Finished Goods Inventory..............		734,000

The key T-accounts for E-Z-Boy's manufacturing costs now show

WORK IN PROCESS INVENTORY					FINISHED GOODS INVENTORY					COST OF GOODS SOLD	
Bal.	29,000	(10)	740,000→	Cost of goods manufactured (completed this period)	Bal.	12,000	(11)	734,000→	Cost of goods sold this period →(11)	734,000	
(2)	285,000				→(10)	740,000					
(4)	250,000				Bal.	18,000					
(9)	200,000										
Bal.	24,000										

The Work in Process Inventory T-account summarizes what happens on the manufacturing plant floor. We start the period with beginning inventory of jobs that were started but not finished last period ($29,000). During the current period, the plant uses direct materials ($285,000) and direct labor ($250,000), and manufacturing overhead is allocated to the jobs passing through the plant floor ($200,000). Some jobs are completed, and their costs are transferred out to Finished Goods Inventory ($740,000). We end the period with other jobs started but not finished during this period ($24,000).

Notice also that the Work in Process T-account summarizes the Schedule of Cost of Goods Manufactured. For E-Z-Boy, the Work in Process T-account shows

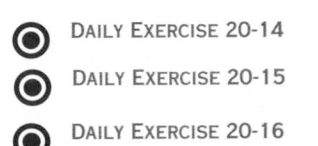

DAILY EXERCISE 20-14

DAILY EXERCISE 20-15

DAILY EXERCISE 20-16

Beginning Work in Process Inventory.....................		$ 29,000
Current manufacturing costs:		
Direct materials used	$285,000	
Direct labor	250,000	
Manufacturing overhead allocated.....................	200,000	735,000
Total manufacturing costs to account for		764,000
Ending Work in Process Inventory.......................		24,000
Cost of Goods Manufactured...............................		$740,000

DISPOSING OF UNDERALLOCATED OR OVERALLOCATED MANUFACTURING OVERHEAD

During the year, E-Z-Boy's accountants debit Manufacturing Overhead for the overhead costs the company actually incurred, and credit Manufacturing Overhead for amounts allocated to Work in Process Inventory. The total debits rarely equal the total credits. Why? Because overhead is allocated to jobs using a *predetermined* allocation rate that represents the *expected* relation between overhead costs and the allocation base. In our example, the $10,000 debit balance of Manufacturing Overhead shown on page 812 is called **underallocated manufacturing overhead** (or simply **underallocated overhead**) because the amount of manufacturing overhead allocated to Work in Process Inventory is *less* than the amount actually incurred. (**Overallocated manufacturing overhead** is just the opposite.)

Accountants dispose of underallocated and overallocated overhead at year end, when the Manufacturing Overhead account is closed. When overhead is underallocated, as in our example, a credit to Manufacturing Overhead brings the account balance to zero. What account is debited?

To see the answer, you need to understand why $10,000 of manufacturing overhead was underallocated. In our example, E-Z-Boy's accountants expected to incur 20X5 manufacturing overhead at the predetermined rate of

$$\frac{\$220,000 \ expected \ \textbf{manufacturing overhead costs}}{\$275,000 \ expected \ \textbf{direct labor cost}} = \textbf{80\%}$$

The accountants computed this 80% manufacturing overhead rate before they knew the *actual* manufacturing overhead cost and the *actual* quantity of the allocation base (direct labor cost, in this example).

Without a crystal ball to foretell the future, it would be surprising indeed if *actual* manufacturing overhead costs and *actual* quantities of the allocation base—which are not known until the end of the year—exactly match the expected amounts. At the end of 20X5, E-Z-Boy's actual manufacturing overhead rate turns out to be

$$\frac{\$210,000 \ actual \ \textbf{manufacturing overhead costs}}{\$250,000 \ actual \ \textbf{direct labor cost}} = \textbf{84\%}$$

If E-Z-Boy's accountants had a crystal ball at the beginning of the year, they would have predicted a manufacturing overhead rate of 84%. But they did not. They *underestimated* the manufacturing overhead rate, expecting it to be only 80%.

Because the predetermined manufacturing overhead rate that E-Z-Boy used to allocate overhead to each job was *less* than the actual manufacturing overhead rate, the company allocated too *little* manufacturing overhead to every job. In other words, every job worked on in 20X5 was *undercosted*. To correct this error, the cost of these jobs should be *increased*.

Ideally, E-Z-Boy would go back and increase the cost of each individual job. Many companies use software that automatically corrects each job at the end of the year. In companies without such software, accountants usually close the balance in the Manufacturing Overhead account to Cost of Goods Sold, because most of the jobs have been sold (especially in a company that follows a just-in-time philosophy).

UNDERALLOCATED (MANUFACTURING) OVERHEAD. The amount of manufacturing overhead allocated to Work in Process Inventory is *less* than the amount of manufacturing overhead costs actually incurred.

OVERALLOCATED (MANUFACTURING) OVERHEAD. The amount of manufacturing overhead allocated to Work in Process Inventory is *more* than the amount of manufacturing overhead costs actually incurred.

In this case, the jobs E-Z-Boy worked on during the year are undercosted. Because the jobs in Cost of Goods Sold are *undercosted,* the correction should increase (debit) Cost of Goods Sold, as shown in the following journal entry:

◉ DAILY EXERCISE 20-17

◉ DAILY EXERCISE 20-18

(12) Cost of Goods Sold 10,000
          Manufacturing Overhead   10,000

The T-accounts show that the Manufacturing Overhead balance is now zero:

MANUFACTURING OVERHEAD				COST OF GOODS SOLD
Actual	210,000	Allocated	200,000	734,000
		Closed	10,000	10,000

Exhibit 20-12 summarizes the accounting for manufacturing overhead:

- Before the period
- During the period
- At the end of the period

Before the Period

$$\text{Compute predetermined manufacturing overhead rate} = \frac{\text{Total estimated manufacturing overhead cost}}{\text{Total estimated quantity of allocation base}}$$

During the Period

$$\text{Allocate the overhead} = \begin{array}{c}\text{Actual quantity of the manufacturing overhead allocation base}\end{array} \times \begin{array}{c}\text{Predetermined manufacturing overhead rate}\end{array}$$

At the End of the Period

Close the Manufacturing Overhead account:

Jobs are *undercosted*   If actual > allocated → *Underallocated* manufacturing overhead
                          Need to *increase* Cost of Goods Sold

Cost of Goods Sold xxx
    Manufacturing Overhead   xxx

Jobs are *overcosted*   If actual < allocated → *Overallocated* manufacturing overhead
                         Need to *reduce* Cost of Goods Sold

Manufacturing Overhead.................. xxx
    Cost of Goods Sold...................   xxx

EXHIBIT 20-12
Summary of Accounting for Manufacturing Overhead

WORK IT OUT

Suppose E-Z-Boy's actual manufacturing overhead costs were $180,000 rather than $210,000.

Questions

1. What would the actual overhead rate have been?
2. Would manufacturing overhead have been underallocated or overallocated?
3. What journal entry would you make to close the Manufacturing Overhead account?

Answers

1. The actual manufacturing overhead rate would have been

$$\frac{\$180,000 \text{ \textit{actual} manufacturing overhead costs}}{\$250,000 \text{ \textit{actual} direct labor cost}} = 72\%$$

2. The predetermined manufacturing overhead rate (80%) is *higher* than the actual manufacturing overhead rate (72%). In this case, each job would be *overcosted*. And

(continued)

Manufacturing Overhead would be *overallocated* by $20,000, as shown in this T-account:

MANUFACTURING OVERHEAD	
Actual 180,000	Allocated $200,000

3. The jobs E-Z-Boy worked on during the year were allocated too much manufacturing overhead. Accordingly, jobs in Cost of Goods Sold were *overcosted*, so the correction should decrease (credit) Cost of Goods Sold, as shown in the following journal entry:

Manufacturing Overhead.............. 20,000
    Cost of Goods Sold............... 20,000

OVERVIEW OF JOB COSTING IN A MANUFACTURING COMPANY

Exhibit 20-13 provides an overview of the E-Z-Boy Furniture Company's job costing illustration. Each entry is keyed to one of the 12 transactions described on pages 801–815 (amounts in thousands). Take the time to study this exhibit carefully.

EXHIBIT 20-13 E-Z-Boy Furniture Company Job Costing Illustration—Flow of Costs Through Accounts (amounts in thousands)

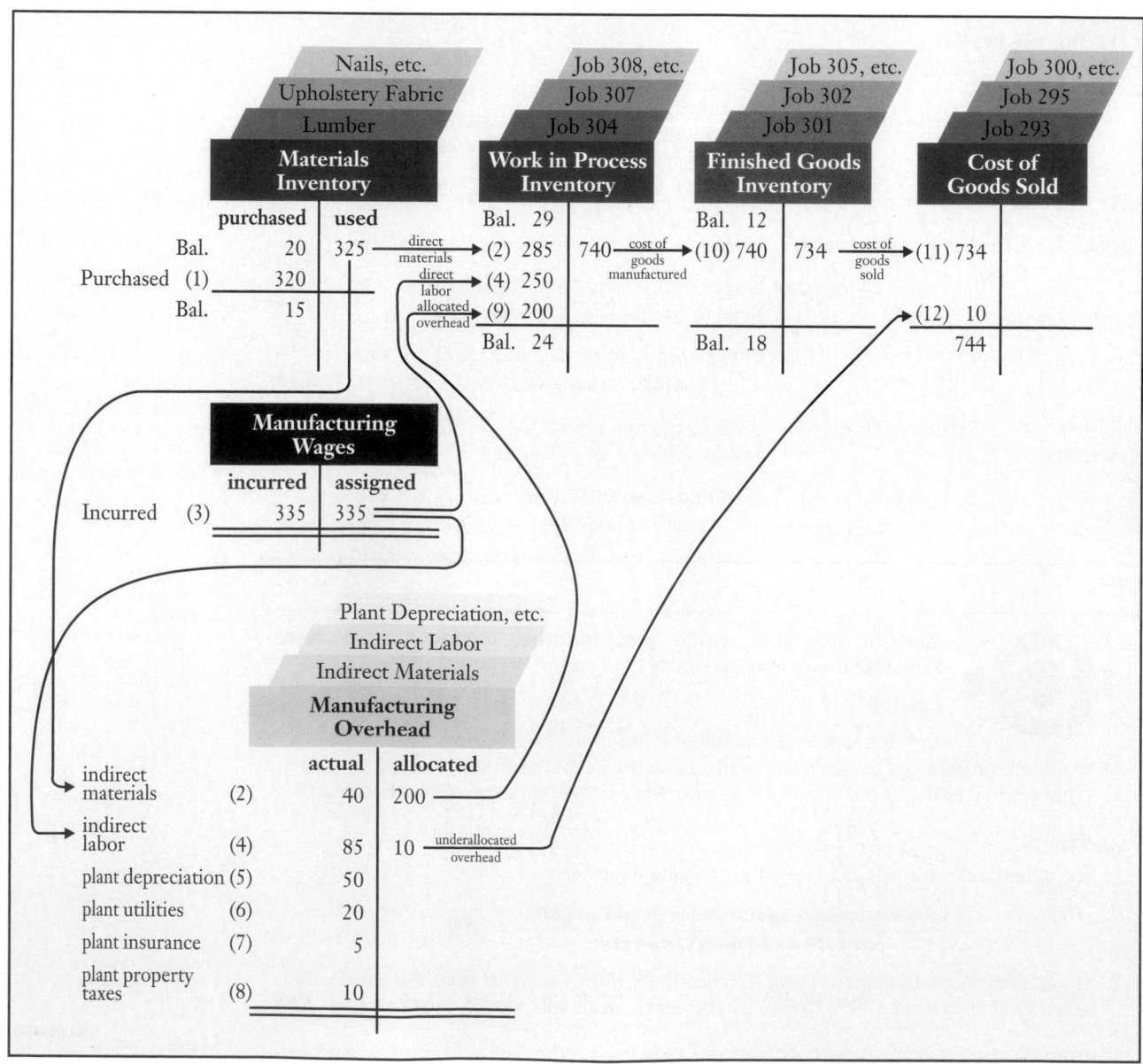

Review the flow of costs through the general ledger accounts:

- Material and labor costs are split between directs costs (traced directly to specific jobs in Work in Process Inventory) and indirect costs (added to Manufacturing Overhead).
- The Work in Process Inventory account summarizes the transactions that occurred on the floor of the manufacturing plant.
- The $740,000 credit to Work in Process (debit to Finished Goods) is the cost of goods manufactured—the manufacturer's counterpart to merchandise purchases.

Study the Manufacturing Overhead account. Actual overhead items are recorded as debits as they occur throughout the period. Credits to the Manufacturing Overhead account represent allocated overhead. E-Z-Boy also closed the $10,000 underallocated Manufacturing Overhead to Cost of Goods Sold.

The T-accounts shown in Exhibit 20-13 are general ledger control accounts. Behind the general ledger accounts appear three examples of subsidiary accounts that would underlie the general ledger control account.

◄ We discussed control accounts in Chapter 6, p. 237

INVENTORIABLE COSTS, NONINVENTORIABLE COSTS, AND JOB COSTING

Objective 4
Account for noninventoriable costs in job costing

Job costing can be complex for manufacturers, because manufacturers have

1. The most complex business operations—they use labor and overhead to transform raw materials into different finished goods
2. Three different kinds of inventory—materials, work in process, and finished goods

Job costing in manufacturing companies has traditionally focused on assigning *manufacturing* costs (*inventoriable* costs) to jobs. This is why our E-Z-Boy illustration focuses on assigning only manufacturing costs to jobs. We have not considered costs incurred in other elements of the value chain, such as R&D or marketing.

The focus on manufacturing costs stems from external reporting requirements. Generally accepted accounting principles require that the accounting records treat only inventoriable costs (manufacturing costs, for a manufacturer) as assets. Costs incurred in other elements of the value chain are treated as expenses (or period costs) for financial accounting. For this reason, the general ledger entries in this chapter have been limited to manufacturing costs.

As we noted in Chapter 19, managers often want to know the full (total) cost of a product or a job, not just the inventoriable cost. The same principles of tracing direct costs and allocating indirect costs (using predetermined allocation rates) apply to noninventoriable period costs incurred in other elements of the value chain: R&D, design, marketing, distribution, and customer service. Managers can add these noninventoriable (period) costs to inventoriable costs to build the full cost of the product or job to guide internal decisions, such as setting long-run average sale prices. However, these noninventoriable costs are assigned to products (or jobs) *only for internal decision making.* No journal entries assign noninventoriable costs to individual jobs, because noninventoriable costs are not assigned to products for external reporting.

JOB COSTING IN A NONMANUFACTURING COMPANY

Management accounting is increasingly important to service firms. Recall that a service firm has no inventoriable costs because it has no inventory. Service firms incur only noninventoriable costs. But managers of service companies still need to know the (noninventoriable) costs of different jobs to make decisions. Thus, we now illustrate the assignment of noninventoriable costs to jobs in a service firm. (A manufacturer such as E-Z-Boy or a merchandiser such as **L.L. Bean** could use the same approach to assign noninventoriable costs to individual jobs.)

Barnett Legal Associates specializes in employment law. Each client is considered a separate job. Barnett's most significant cost is direct labor—attorney time spent on clients' cases. How do service firms trace direct labor to individual jobs?

For automated services like Web site design, information technology consulting, and external auditing, employees simply enter the client number to start on the client's job. Software records the time elapsed until the employee signs off that job. When the service is not automated, employees typically fill out a computerized weekly **time record.** The software tallies the weekly total time spent on each job. Attorney Teresa Fox's time record appears in Exhibit 20-14. Fox's time record shows that she devoted 14 hours to client 367 during the week of June 10, 20X5.

TIME RECORD. Source document used primarily by employees in service activities, to trace direct labor to specific jobs.

EXHIBIT 20-14
Employee Time Record

BARNETT LEGAL ASSOCIATES
EMPLOYEE TIME RECORD
NAME TERESA FOX
WEEK OF 6/10/X5

	M	T	W	TH	F
8:00–8:30	367	520	415	367	415
8:30–9:00					
9:00–9:30					
9:30–10:00					
10:00–10:30			367		
10:30–11:00					
11:00–11:30	520				
11:30–12:00	520				
12:00–12:30					
12:30–1:00					
1:00–1:30	520	367	367	520	415
1:30–2:00			367		
2:00–2:30			415		
2:30–3:00					
3:00–3:30					
3:30–4:00					
4:00–4:30					
4:30–5:00					

WEEKLY SUMMARY:

CLIENT #	TOTAL HOURS
367	14
415	13
520	13

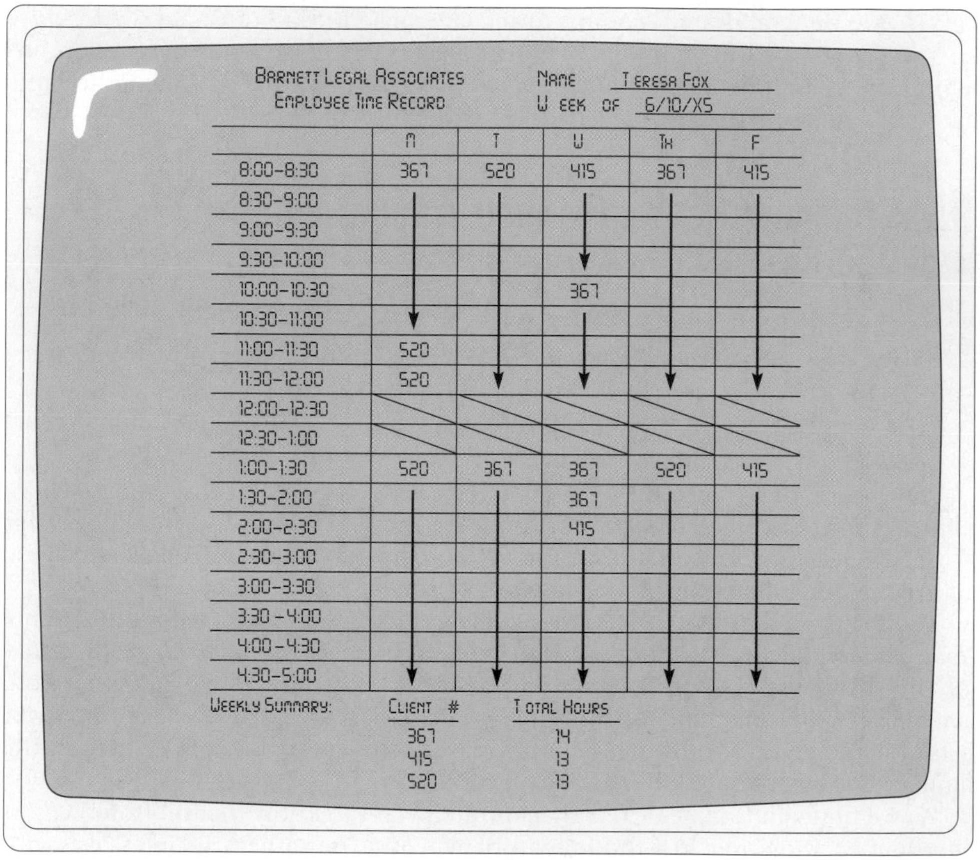

DAILY EXERCISE 20-19

Fox's salary and benefits total \$100,000 per year. Assuming a 40-hour workweek and 50 workweeks in each year, Fox has 2,000 available work hours per year (50 weeks × 40 hours per week). Barnett Legal Associates' hourly (cost) rate of employing Teresa Fox is

$$\textbf{Hourly cost rate to the employer} = \frac{\textbf{\$100,000 per year}}{\textbf{2,000 hours per year}} = \textbf{\$50 per hour}$$

Fox is the only attorney who served client 367, so the direct labor cost traced to the client is 14 hours × \$50 per hour = \$700.

Founding partner John Barnett wants to know the total costs of serving clients, not just the direct labor cost. Barnett Legal Associates also allocates indirect costs to individual jobs (clients). The law firm develops a predetermined indirect cost allocation rate, following the same six-step approach that E-Z-Boy (page 810–811) used to develop its indirect manufacturing (overhead) cost rate:

1. *Estimate the total indirect costs.*
   In December 20X4, Barnett estimates that the following indirect costs will be incurred in 20X5:

Office rent...	$200,000
Office support staff	70,000
Maintaining and updating law library for case research	25,000
Advertisements in the yellow pages...	3,000
Sponsorship of the symphony...	2,000
Total indirect costs	$300,000

2. *Identify a cost allocation base.*

   Barnett uses direct labor hours as the allocation base, because the number of hours that attorneys work on clients' cases is the main driver of indirect costs.

3. *Estimate the total quantity of the indirect cost allocation base.*

   Barnett estimates that its attorneys will work 10,000 direct labor hours in 20X5.

4. *Compute the predetermined indirect cost allocation rate.* (*Divide step 1 by step 3.*)

 DAILY EXERCISE 20-20

$$\text{Predetermined indirect cost allocation rate} = \frac{\$300,000 \text{ expected indirect costs}}{10,000 \text{ expected direct labor hours}}$$

$$= \$30 \text{ per direct labor hour}$$

5. *Obtain the actual quantity of the indirect cost allocation base used by individual jobs, as the year unfolds.*

   Exhibit 20-14 shows that client 367 required 14 direct labor hours.

6. *Allocate indirect costs to jobs by multiplying the predetermined indirect cost rate (step 4) by the actual quantity of the allocation base used by each job (step 5).*

   Client 367 is allocated indirect costs as follows:

   14 direct labor hours × $30/hour = $420

To summarize, the total costs assigned to client 367 are

Direct labor: 14 hours × $50/hour...	$ 700
Indirect costs: 14 hours × $30/hour..	420
Total costs...	$1,120

 **THINK IT OVER**

Would John Barnett want to know the total cost of each job for each of the following purposes? Why or why not?

a. Inventory valuation
b. External financial reporting
c. To determine fees charged to clients

Answers

a. No. Service firms like Barnett Legal Associates have no inventories.
b. No. Costs need not be assigned to individual clients to prepare financial statements.
c. Yes. Fees charged to clients must be high enough to cover indirect costs (and profits) as well as direct labor costs.

In summary: Noninventoriable costs are assigned to jobs only for internal decision making, not for external financial reporting.

You have now learned how to use a job cost system to assign costs to jobs. Review the Job Costing Decision Guidelines to solidify your understanding.

DECISION GUIDELINES

Job Costing

DECISION	GUIDELINES
Should I use job costing or process costing?	• *Job costing* for unique products produced in small batches • *Process costing* for identical products produced in large batches, often in a continuous flow

How to record:
- Purchase and use of materials?

Purchase:

Materials Inventory	XX	
Accounts Payable (or Cash)		XX

Use:

Work in Process (direct materials)	XX	
Manufacturing Overhead		
(indirect materials).................................	XX	
Materials Inventory		XX

- Incurrence and assignment of labor?

Incurred:

Manufacturing Wages	XX	
Wages Payable (or Cash)		XX

Assigned:

Work in Process (direct labor)....................	XX	
Manufacturing Overhead (indirect labor) ...	XX	
Manufacturing Wages......................		XX

How to determine whether utilities, insurance, property taxes, depreciation, and so on are
- Manufacturing overhead?

Utilities, insurance, property taxes, and depreciation expense are part of manufacturing overhead *only* if they are incurred in the manufacturing plant.

- Operating expenses?

If not related to manufacturing, such expenses are operating expenses. For example, if related to a sales office or store, such expenses are marketing expenses. If related to executive headquarters, they are administrative expenses. If related to delivery vehicles or distribution centers, they are distribution expenses. These are all operating expenses, not manufacturing overhead.

How to record *actual* manufacturing overhead costs?

Manufacturing Overhead...........................	XXX	
Accumulated Depreciation—		
Plant and Equipment		XX
Prepaid Insurance—Plant and Equipment		XX
Utilities Payable (or Cash)................		XX
and so on		XX

How to compute a predetermined manufacturing overhead rate?

$$\frac{\text{Total estimated manufacturing overhead cost}}{\text{Total estimated quantity of allocation base}}$$

How to record allocation of manufacturing overhead?

Work in Process Inventory..........................	XX	
Manufacturing Overhead		XX

What is the *amount* of the allocated manufacturing overhead?

$$\begin{array}{c}\textbf{Actual quantity} \\ \textbf{of the manufacturing} \\ \textbf{overhead allocation base}\end{array} \times \begin{array}{c}\textbf{Predetermined} \\ \textbf{manufacturing} \\ \textbf{overhead rate}\end{array}$$

How to close Manufacturing Overhead at the end of the period?

Close directly to Cost of Goods Sold.

Which T-account summarizes the schedule of cost of goods manufactured?

Work in Process Inventory

How do service companies trace employees' direct labor to individual jobs?

Automated software directly captures time employee spends on a client's job, or employee fills out a (usually computerized) time record.

Why do companies allocate noninventoriable costs to jobs?

Because they need total product costs for internal decisions (such as setting selling prices). For external reporting, companies assign only inventoriable costs to jobs.

SUMMARY PROBLEM

Hillis Incorporated had the following inventories at the end of 20X4:

Materials Inventory	$20,000
Work in Process Inventory	17,000
Finished Goods Inventory	11,000

www.prenhall.com/horngren

End-of-Chapter Assessment

During January 20X5, Hillis actually used 300 machine hours and recorded the following transactions:

a. Purchased materials on account, $31,000.
b. Requisitioned (placed into production) direct materials, $39,000.
c. Manufacturing labor cost incurred was $40,000.
d. Manufacturing labor was: 90% direct labor; 10% indirect labor.
e. Requisitioned indirect materials, $3,000.
f. Incurred other manufacturing overhead, $13,000 (credit Accounts Payable).
g. Allocated manufacturing overhead to production at $60 per machine hour.
h. Completed production, $99,000.
i. Sold goods on account, $172,000, cost of goods sold, $91,400.

Required

1. Record the transactions in the general journal.
2. Post the transactions and inventory balances to the following accounts:

MATERIALS INVENTORY	WORK IN PROCESS INVENTORY	FINISHED GOODS INVENTORY	COST OF GOODS SOLD

MANUFACTURING WAGES	MANUFACTURING OVERHEAD

3. Record the journal entry to close the ending balance of Manufacturing Overhead. Post your entry to the T-accounts.
4. What are the ending balances in the three inventory accounts and Cost of Goods Sold?

Solution

Requirement 1

Journal entries:

a.	Materials Inventory	31,000	
	Accounts Payable		31,000
b.	Work in Process Inventory	39,000	
	Materials Inventory		39,000
c.	Manufacturing Wages	40,000	
	Wages Payable		40,000
d.	Work in Process Inventory ($40,000 × 0.90)	36,000	
	Manufacturing Overhead ($40,000 × 0.10)	4,000	
	Manufacturing Wages		40,000
e.	Manufacturing Overhead	3,000	
	Materials Inventory		3,000
f.	Manufacturing Overhead	13,000	
	Accounts Payable		13,000
g.	Work in Process Inventory (300 × $60)	18,000	
	Manufacturing Overhead		18,000
h.	Finished Goods Inventory	99,000	
	Work in Process Inventory		99,000
i.	Accounts Receivable	172,000	
	Sales Revenue		172,000
	Cost of Goods Sold	91,400	
	Finished Goods Inventory		91,400

Requirement 2

Post the transactions:

MATERIALS INVENTORY			
Bal.	20,000	(b)	39,000
(a)	31,000	(e)	3,000
Bal.	9,000		

WORK IN PROCESS INVENTORY			
Bal.	17,000	(h)	99,000
(b)	39,000		
(d)	36,000		
(g)	18,000		
Bal.	11,000		

FINISHED GOODS INVENTORY			
Bal.	11,000	(i)	91,400
(h)	99,000		
Bal.	18,600		

COST OF GOODS SOLD			
(i)	91,400		

MANUFACTURING WAGES			
(c)	40,000	(d)	40,000

MANUFACTURING OVERHEAD			
(d)	4,000	(g)	18,000
(e)	3,000		
(f)	13,000		
Bal.	2,000		

Requirement 3

Close Manufacturing Overhead:

Cost of Goods Sold 2,000
            Manufacturing Overhead 2,000

MANUFACTURING OVERHEAD			
(d)	4,000	(g)	18,000
(e)	3,000		2,000
(f)	13,000		

COST OF GOODS SOLD			
(i)	91,400		
	2,000		
Bal.	93,400		

Requirement 4

Ending Balances:

Materials Inventory (from requirement 2)	$ 9,000
Work in Process Inventory (from requirement 2)	11,000
Finished Goods Inventory (from requirement 2)	18,600
Cost of Goods Sold (from requirement 3)	93,400

LESSONS LEARNED

1. **Distinguish between job costing and process costing.** Companies that use job costing usually produce individual products or small batches of products that pass through production steps as a distinct, identifiable job lot. Jobs can differ greatly in terms of materials, labor, and overhead. Costs are accumulated for each individual job. The *job cost record* includes direct materials, direct labor, and manufacturing overhead costs of producing the job.

    Companies that produce large numbers of identical products use process costing. Costs are accumulated for each production process, and then averaged over the many (identical) units passing through that process.

2. **Account for materials and labor in a manufacturer's job costing system.** *Direct materials* costs are traced to individual jobs and added (debited) to Work in Process Inventory. *Indirect materials* cannot be easily traced to specific jobs, so their costs are added (debited) to the Manufacturing Overhead account. *Direct labor* costs are traced to jobs and added (debited) to Work in Process Inventory. *Indirect labor* cost, such as maintenance and janitorial, is difficult to trace to individual jobs. Indirect labor costs are added (debited) to Manufacturing Overhead.

    In highly automated systems, employees use bar codes to record materials used and scan their identification cards to record their labor. The software immediately tracks these material and labor costs to the specific job and updates the general ledger accounts.

3. **Account for manufacturing overhead in a manufacturer's job costing system.** *Manufacturing overhead* is all manufacturing costs except direct materials and direct labor. Actual manufacturing overhead costs are accumulated as debits in the Manufacturing Overhead account. Manufacturing Overhead is allocated to jobs using a predetermined rate per unit of a *cost allocation* base. Ideally, the allocation base is the driver of the manufacturing overhead costs. Allocating manufacturing overhead requires a debit to Work in Process and a credit to Manufacturing Overhead. At the end of the period, software may automatically adjust each job for any underallocated or overallocated manufacturing overhead, or else the balance is closed to Cost of Goods Sold.

4. **Account for noninventoriable costs in job costing.** Service companies trace direct labor to individual jobs (clients) using software or time records. Service, merchandising, or manufacturing firms can allocate indirect costs such as marketing, office rent, and support staff salaries to jobs using predetermined indirect cost allocation rates.

ACCOUNTING VOCABULARY

allocation base (p. 810)	job cost record (p. 800)	predetermined manufacturing
budgeted manufacturing	job costing (p. 798)	overhead rate (p. 810)
overhead rate (p. 810)	labor time record (p. 805)	process costing (p. 798)
cost allocation (p. 809)	materials requisition (p. 802)	time record (p. 818)
cost assignment (p. 809)	overallocated (manufacturing)	underallocated (manufacturing)
cost driver (p. 799)	overhead (p. 814)	overhead (p. 814)
cost tracing (p. 809)		

QUESTIONS

1. Explain the basic difference between job costing and process costing.
2. Give three examples of companies that would use job costing rather than process costing, and explain why.
3. Distinguish direct materials from indirect materials and direct labor from indirect labor. Direct materials and direct labor are debited to what account when placed in production? To what account are indirect materials and indirect labor debited?
4. Give examples of direct materials and indirect materials for a caterer.
5. How can information technology simplify tracing direct materials and direct labor to specific jobs?
6. Is Manufacturing Overhead a temporary or permanent account? Explain how the account operates. What do the debits represent? What do the credits represent?
7. Is manufacturing overhead cost allocated to jobs by precisely identifying the overhead cost of each job or by an estimation? Explain.
8. Would a heavily automated manufacturing plant be more likely to use machine hours or direct labor hours as the manufacturing overhead allocation base? Explain.
9. Why do companies use predetermined rather than actual manufacturing overhead rates?
10. Transactions in what account summarize the cost of goods manufactured? Show the T-account and label the transactions.
11. Which of the following accounts have their balances brought to zero at the end of the period, and which keep their ending balances to start the next period? Materials Inventory, Manufacturing Overhead, Finished Goods Inventory, Manufacturing Wages.
12. Cost of goods sold is just one line-item in the Income Statement. What kinds of costs are included in cost of goods sold?
13. Why would an international professional services firm like **PricewaterhouseCoopers** use job costing?
14. How do professional service firms such as law firms and management consulting firms trace direct labor to individual jobs?

ASSESS YOUR PROGRESS

DAILY EXERCISES

DE20-1 Job costing and process costing differ in (a) the cost object, and (b) the number of units over which costs are averaged. Explain these two differences.

Distinguishing between job and process costing (Obj. 1)

DE20-2 Would the following companies use job costing or process costing?

  a. A manufacturer of plywood.
  b. A manufacturer of wakeboards.
  c. A manufacturer of luxury yachts.
  d. A professional services firm.
  e. A landscape garden contractor.

Distinguishing between job and process costing (Obj. 1)

DE20-3 Suppose **Olympic Paints** incurs $560,000 to produce 250,000 gallons of deck stain. What is the cost per gallon? Would Olympic Paints use job or process costing? Why?

Distinguishing between job and process costing (Obj. 1)

DE20-4 For a manufacturer that uses job costing, diagram the flow of costs through the accounts. Label each transaction. Include the following accounts in your diagram: Finished Goods Inventory, Manufacturing Wages, Cost of Goods Sold, Work in Process Inventory, Materials Inventory, Manufacturing Overhead.

Flow of costs in job costing (Obj. 2, 3)

DE20-5 ◄ *Link Back to Chapter 9 (Inventory).* Refer to E-Z-Boy's Material Ledger Record in Exhibit 20-5. Suppose material requisition #334 indicated that on July 24, 20 units of lumber (rather than ten), were used in Job 293. What is the ending balance of item B-220—Lumber/Recliner Chairs?

Accounting for materials (Obj. 2)

DE20-6 Turn to E-Z-Boy's Materials subsidiary ledger in Exhibit 20-6. Suppose that on July 24, the balance of the Upholstery Fabric account was $300 rather than $390. What is the total Materials Inventory balance?

Accounting for materials (Obj. 2)

DE20-7 Walkabout manufactures backpacks. Its plant records the following materials-related transactions:

Purchases of canvas (on account)	$70,000
Purchases of thread (on account).............	700
Material requisitions:	
Canvas..	63,000
Thread	280

What journal entries record these transactions? Post these transactions to the Material Inventory account. If the company had $28,560 of Materials Inventory at the beginning of the period, what is the ending balance of Materials Inventory?

DE20-8 Use the following T-accounts to determine direct materials used and indirect materials used.

MATERIALS INVENTORY			
Bal.	16		
Purchases	320	X	
Bal.	24		

WORK IN PROCESS INVENTORY			
Bal.	32		
Direct materials	Y	Cost of goods	
Direct labor	240	manufactured	744
Manufacturing overhead	200		
Bal.	8		

DE20-9 Art Glass reports the following labor-related transactions at its plant in Seattle, Washington.

Plant janitor's wages......................	600
Furnace operator's wages..............	900
Glass blowers' wages	76,000

Record the journal entries for the incurrence and assignment of these wages.

DE20-10 Touch Enterprises produces LCD touch screen products. The company reports the following information at December 31, 20X4. Touch began operations on January 30, 20X4.

WORK IN PROCESS INVENTORY		MANUFACTURING WAGES		MANUFACTURING OVERHEAD		FINISHED GOODS INVENTORY		MATERIALS INVENTORY	
40,000	136,000	70,000	70,000	4,000	48,000	136,000	122,000	52,000	44,000
60,000				10,000					
48,000				37,000					

1. What is the cost of direct materials used? The cost of indirect materials used?
2. What is the cost of direct labor? The cost of indirect labor?
3. What is the cost of goods manufactured?
4. What is cost of goods sold (before adjusting for any under- or overallocated manufacturing overhead)?

DE20-11 Refer to Daily Exercise 20-10.

1. What is the actual manufacturing overhead? Allocated manufacturing overhead?
2. What is the predetermined manufacturing overhead rate, as a percentage of direct labor cost?
3. Is manufacturing overhead underallocated or overallocated? By how much?

DE20-12 All-Wood Outdoor furniture reports the following costs for June 20X4. What is the balance in the Manufacturing Overhead account?

Wood	$120,000
Nails and glue	15,000
Wood preserving stain	8,000
Depreciation on saws...........................	3,000
Depreciation on delivery truck..............	2,200
Assembly-line workers' wages	56,000
Salesman's auto lease	1,400
Indirect manufacturing labor	23,000

DE20-13 Arctic-Tex produces fleece textiles woven from recycled plastic bottles. The company uses a predetermined manufacturing overhead rate to allocate overhead based on the machine hours each job requires. Arctic-Tex reports the following data for 20X5:

Computing a predetermined manufacturing overhead rate (Obj. 3)

	Expected	Actual
Manufacturing overhead.............	$715,000	$600,000
Direct labor hours........................	11,000	11,375
Direct labor costs	100,000	103,125
Machine hours	13,000	10,000

Compute Arctic-Tex's predetermined manufacturing overhead rate.

DE20-14 Refer to Daily Exercise 20-13. Arctic-Tex's Job 744 required

Accounting for overhead (Obj. 3)

a. 20 direct labor hours, at a total cost of $4,096
b. $2,140 of direct materials
c. 15 machine hours

1. Record the journal entry to allocate the manufacturing overhead to Job 744.
2. Compute the total cost of Job 744.

DE20-15 In the E-Z-Boy job cost record (Exhibit 20-11), how much manufacturing overhead cost would be allocated to Job 293 if the predetermined manufacturing overhead allocation rate is 90% of direct labor cost rather than 80%? What would be the total cost assigned to Job 293?

Accounting for overhead (Obj. 3)

DE20-16 Turn to the E-Z-Boy illustration on pages 801–814. Suppose direct material requisitions totaled $300,000 rather than $285,000. (Indirect materials used and cost of goods manufactured remain the same.) Use T-accounts to show the new ending balances of Materials Inventory and Work in Process Inventory.

Accounting for materials, labor, and work in process inventory (Obj. 2, 3)

DE20-17 In the E-Z-Boy illustration on pages 814–815, actual manufacturing overhead was $210,000. Suppose instead that the actual manufacturing overhead was $175,000.

Under/overallocated overhead (Obj. 3)

1. What would be the actual manufacturing overhead rate?
2. Is manufacturing overhead underallocated or overallocated? By how much?
3. Is Cost of Goods Sold too high or too low?

DE20-18 Refer to Daily Exercise 20-17. Make the journal entry to close out E-Z-Boy's Manufacturing Overhead account if the balance is closed to Cost of Goods Sold.

Close out under/overallocated overhead (Obj. 3)

DE20-19 In the Barnett Legal Associates example on page 818, suppose Teresa Fox's annual salary is $120,000 rather than $100,000.

Job costing in a service company (Obj. 4)

1. What would be the hourly (cost) rate to Barnett Legal Associates of employing Fox?
2. What direct labor cost would be traced to client 367?

DE20-20 Return to the original data in the Barnett Legal Associates example on pages 818–819. Suppose the Barnett attorneys expected to work a total of 8,000 direct labor hours rather than 10,000 direct labor hours.

Job costing in a service company (Obj. 4)

1. What is the indirect cost allocation rate?
2. What indirect costs will be allocated to client 367?

EXERCISES

E20-1 Listed below are several terms. Complete the following statements with one of these terms. You may use a term more than once, and some terms may not be used at all.

Distinguishing job and process costing (Obj. 1)

Cost allocation   Cost driver   Job costing   Process costing
Cost tracing   Job cost record Materials requisition

a. ___ is used by companies that produce small quantities of many different products.
b. A ___ is any factor that affects costs.
c. **Boise Cascade** pulverizes wood into pulp to manufacture cardboard. The company would use a ___ system.
d. To record costs of maintaining thousands of identical mortgage files, financial institutions like **Fleet Mortgage** would use a ___ system.
e. ___ is assigning direct costs to cost objects.
f. A ___ accumulates the costs of an individual job.
g. Companies that produce large numbers of identical products use ___ systems for product costing.

(continued)

h. The computer repair service that visits your home and repairs your computer would use a ___ system.

i. A ___ is manufacturing personnel's request that materials be moved to the production floor.

j. ___ is assigning indirect costs to cost objects.

Accounting for job costs
(Obj. 2, 3)

E20-2 Horn's Printing job cost records yielded the following information:

Job No.	Date Started		Date Finished		Date Sold		Total Cost of Job at March 31
1	February	21	March	16	March	17	$ 2,800
2	February	29	March	21	March	26	17,000
3	March	3	April	11	April	13	5,900
4	March	7	March	29	April	1	6,200
5	March	9	March	30	April	2	5,600
6	March	22	April	11	April	13	1,300
7	March	23	March	27	March	29	5,400

Required

Compute Horn's cost of (a) work in process inventory at March 31, (b) finished goods inventory at March 31, and (c) cost of goods sold for March.

Job costing journal entries
(Obj. 2, 3)

E20-3 Record the following transactions in Systems Engineering's general journal.

a. Incurred and paid Web site expenses, $6,500.

b. Incurred and paid manufacturing wages, $16,000.

c. Purchased materials on account, $13,500.

d. Used in production: direct materials, $9,000; indirect materials, $2,000.

e. Assigned $16,000 of manufacturing labor to jobs, 70% of which was direct labor and 30% of which was indirect labor.

f. Recorded manufacturing overhead: depreciation on plant, $13,000; plant insurance, $1,700; plant property tax, $4,200 (credit Property Tax Payable).

g. Allocated manufacturing overhead to jobs, 200% of direct labor cost.

h. Completed production, $27,000.

i. Sold inventory on account, $22,000; cost of goods sold, $14,000.

Identifying job costing journal entries
(Obj. 2, 3)

E20-4 Describe the lettered transactions in the following manufacturing accounts:

MANUFACTURING WAGES		MANUFACTURING OVERHEAD		COST OF GOODS SOLD	
(a)	(b)	(b)	(e)	(g)	
		(c)	(f)	(f)	
		(d)			

MATERIALS INVENTORY		WORK IN PROCESS INVENTORY		FINISHED GOODS INVENTORY	
(h)	(i)	(i)	(j)	(j)	(g)
	(c)	(b)			
		(e)			

Using the Work in Process Inventory account
(Obj. 2, 3)

E20-5 September production generated the following activity in Digital Connection's Work in Process Inventory:

WORK IN PROCESS INVENTORY	
September 1 Bal.	14,000
Direct materials used	28,000
Direct labor assigned to jobs	30,000
Manufacturing overhead allocated to jobs	11,000

Completed production, not yet recorded, consists of Jobs B-78, G-65, and Y-11, with total costs of $17,000, $26,000, and $34,000, respectively.

Required

1. Compute the cost of work in process at September 30.

2. Prepare the journal entry for production completed in September.

3. Prepare the journal entry to record the sale (on credit) of Job G-65 for $38,000. Also make the cost-of-goods-sold entry.

4. What is the gross profit on Job G-65? What other costs must this gross profit cover?

E20-6 Selected cost data for All-Flooring Co. are as follows:

Expected manufacturing overhead cost for the year...................	$119,600
Expected direct labor cost for the year	46,000
Actual manufacturing overhead cost for the year......................	104,600
Actual direct labor cost for the year...	40,500

Required

1. Compute the predetermined manufacturing overhead rate per direct labor dollar.
2. Prepare the journal entry to allocate overhead cost for the year.
3. Use a T-account to determine the amount of overallocated or underallocated manufacturing overhead.
4. Prepare the journal entry to close the balance of the manufacturing overhead account.

E20-7 Isle Awning Company in Charleston, South Carolina, uses a predetermined manufacturing overhead rate to allocate overhead to individual jobs, based on the direct labor hours required. At the beginning of 20X4, the company expected to incur the following:

Manufacturing overhead costs......................................	$500,000
Direct labor cost	$1,000,000
Machine hours...	60,000 hours
Direct labor hours	100,000 hours

At the end of 20X4, the company had actually incurred:

Direct labor cost...	$1,210,000
Depreciation on manufacturing property, plant, and equipment...	480,000
Property taxes on plant	20,000
Sales salaries	25,000
Delivery drivers' wages...	15,000
Plant janitors' wages...	10,000
Machine hours	55,000 hours
Direct labor hours...	110,000 hours

Required

1. Compute Isle Awning's predetermined manufacturing overhead rate.
2. Record the summary journal entry for *allocating* manufacturing overhead.
3. Post the manufacturing overhead transactions to the Manufacturing Overhead T-account. Is manufacturing overhead underallocated or overallocated? By how much?
4. Close the Manufacturing Overhead account to Cost of Goods Sold. Does your entry increase or decrease cost of goods sold?

E20-8 Refer to the data in Exercise 20-7. Isle Awning's accountant found an error in her 20X4 expense records. Depreciation on manufacturing property, plant, and equipment was actually $600,000, not the $480,000 she had originally reported. Unadjusted balances at the end of 20X4 include

Finished Goods Inventory	130,000
Cost of Goods Sold..	600,000

Required

1. Use a T-account to determine whether manufacturing overhead is underallocated or overallocated, and by how much.
2. Record the entry to close out the underallocated or overallocated manufacturing overhead.
3. What is the adjusted ending balance of Cost of Goods Sold?

E20-9 Terra Nova, an environmental consulting firm, specializes in advising electric utilities on compliance with recent environmental regulations. Terra Nova uses a job cost system with a predetermined indirect cost allocation rate, computed as a percentage of expected direct labor costs.

At the beginning of 20X5, managing partner Jim Bladen prepared the following plan, or budget, for 20X5:

Direct labor hours (professionals)	16,000 hours
Direct labor costs (professionals)................	$2,240,000
Office rent	350,000
Support staff salaries	860,000
Utilities..	246,000

Northern Electric is inviting several consultants to bid for work. Jim Bladen estimates that this job will require about 220 direct labor hours.

Required

1. Compute Terra Nova's (a) hourly direct labor cost rate, and (b) indirect cost allocation rate.
2. Compute the predicted cost of the Northern Electric job.
3. If Bladen wants to earn a profit that equals 20% of the job's cost, how much should he bid for the Northern Electric job?

Challenge Exercise

Accounting for manufacturing overhead
(Obj. 3)

E20-10 At the end of the 20X4 fiscal year, SeaPro's manufacturing records show the following unadjusted ending account balances:

	Work in Process Inventory	Finished Goods Inventory	Cost of Goods Sold
Direct materials...................	$100,000	$170,000	$360,000
Direct labor	80,000	250,000	600,000
Manufacturing overhead....	70,000	310,000	460,000
Total....................................	$250,000	$730,000	$1,420,000

SeaPro's accountants allocated overhead during the year using a predetermined rate of $48 per machine hour. At year end, they computed the actual rate of $52 per machine hour. The beginning balances of both Work in Process Inventory and Finished Goods Inventory were zero.

Required

1. How many machine hours did SeaPro use in 20X4?
2. Was manufacturing overhead over- or underallocated for the year? By how much?
3. Record the entry to close out the over- or underallocated overhead.

(Group A) PROBLEMS

Analyzing job cost data
(Obj. 2, 3)

P20-1A Highcountry Manufacturing builds storage systems for office and home use. Its job cost records yield the following information. The company uses a perpetual inventory system.

Job No.	Date Started	Date Finished	Date Sold	Total Cost of Job at November 30	Total Manufacturing Costs Added in December
1	10/26	11/7	11/9	$1,700	
2	11/3	11/12	11/13	1,400	
3	11/3	11/30	12/1	1,900	
4	11/17	12/24	12/27	300	$ 700
5	11/29	12/29	1/3	500	1,600
6	12/8	12/12	12/14		750
7	12/23	1/6	1/9		500
8	12/30	1/22	1/26		1,900

Required

1. Compute Highcountry's cost of (a) work in process inventory at November 30 and December 31, (b) finished goods inventory at November 30 and December 31, and (c) cost of goods sold for November and December.
2. Record summary journal entries for the transfer of completed units from work in process to finished goods for November and December.
3. Record the sale of Job 4 for $1,200.
4. What is the gross profit for Job 4? What other costs must this gross profit cover?

P20-2A Plantation Construction, Inc., is a home builder in the Southeast. Plantation uses a perpetual inventory system and a job cost system in which each house is a job. Because it constructs houses, the company uses accounts titled Construction Wages, Construction Overhead, and Supervisory Salaries (for indirect labor). The following events occurred during August:

Accounting for manufacturing transactions (Obj. 2, 3)

a. Purchased materials on account, $375,600.
b. Incurred construction wages of $189,200. Requisitioned direct materials and used direct labor in construction:

	Direct Materials	Direct Labor
House 302	$38,600	$25,300
House 303	49,100	17,400
House 304	47,400	32,000
House 305	63,900	33,700

c. Depreciation of construction equipment, $5,800.
d. Other overhead costs incurred on houses 302–305:

Indirect labor	$89,000
Equipment rentals paid in cash	17,300
Liability insurance expired	5,100

e. Allocated overhead to jobs at the predetermined overhead rate of 40% of direct labor cost.
f. Houses completed: 302, 304.
g. House sold: 304 for $152,500.

Required

1. Record the events in the general journal.
2. Open T-accounts for Work in Process Inventory and Finished Goods Inventory. Post the appropriate entries to these accounts, identifying each entry by letter. Determine the ending account balances, assuming that the beginning balances were zero.
3. Add the costs of unfinished houses, and show that this total amount equals the ending balance in the Work in Process Inventory account.
4. Add the costs of completed houses that have not yet been sold, and show that this total amount equals the ending balance in the Finished Goods Inventory account.
5. Compute the gross profit on each house that was sold. What costs must the gross profit cover for Plantation Construction?

P20-3A Digital Reproductions manufactures CDs and DVDs for computer software and entertainment companies. Digital Reproductions uses job costing and has a perpetual inventory system.

Preparing and using a job cost record (Obj. 2, 3)

On November 2, Digital Reproductions began production of 5,000 DVDs, Job 378, for Hollywood Pictures for $1.20 each. The company incurred the following costs:

Date	Time Record No.	Description	Amount
11-2	556	12 hours @ $20	$240
11-3	557	25 hours @ $18	450

Date	Materials Requisition No.	Description	Amount
11-2	36	31 lb. polycarbonate plastic @ $12	$372
11-2	37	25 lb. acrylic plastic @ $28	700
11-3	42	3 lb. refined aluminum @ $48	144

Digital Reproductions allocates overhead to jobs based on the relation between expected overhead ($537,600) and expected direct labor ($448,000). Job 378 was completed and shipped on November 3.

Required

1. Prepare a job cost record similar to Exhibit 20-3 for Job 378.
2. Journalize in summary form the requisition of direct materials and the assignment of direct labor and manufacturing overhead to Job 378.
3. Journalize completion of the job and the sale of the 5,000 DVDs.

Accounting for manufacturing overhead (Obj. 3)

P20-4A Intercraft/Burns manufactures picture frames. The primary materials (wood, plastic, and glass) and direct labor are traced directly to the products. Manufacturing costs are allocated based on machine hours. Data for the year 20X4 follow:

	Budget	Actual
Machine hours	25,000 hours	29,600 hours
Direct labor hours	42,000 hours	40,000 hours
Wood	$150,000	$148,000
Maintenance labor (repairs to equipment)	5,000	16,500
Plant supervisor's wages	30,000	32,000
Screws, nails, and glue	15,500	32,000
Plant utilities	25,000	49,575
Plastic	75,000	70,500
Glass	125,000	126,275
Freight out	35,000	44,500
Direct labor	65,000	63,000
Depreciation on plant and equipment	62,000	62,000
Advertising expenses	40,000	55,000

Required

1. Compute the predetermined manufacturing overhead rate.
2. Post actual and allocated manufacturing overhead to the Manufacturing Overhead T-account.
3. Close the under- or overallocated overhead to cost of goods sold.
4. The predetermined manufacturing overhead rate usually turns out to be inaccurate. Why don't accountants just use the actual manufacturing overhead rate?

Comprehensive accounting for manufacturing transactions (Obj. 2, 3)

P20-5A ◄— *Link Back to Chapters 2 and 19.* Citronix Systems produces components for digital network routers. Initially the company manufactured the parts for its own routers, but it gradually began selling them to other companies as well.

April 1 balances in the subsidiary ledgers were

- Materials ledger: circuit boards, $1,580; electronic parts, $1,960; indirect materials, $430.
- Work in process ledger: Job 145, $35,880.
- Finished goods ledger: relays, $5,310; switches, $8,870.

Citronix's trial balance on April 1 follows on page 383.

April transactions are summarized as follows:

a. Collections on account, $137,470.
b. Marketing and general expenses incurred and paid, $27,470.
c. Payments on account, $36,040.
d. Materials purchased on credit: circuit boards, $6,540; electronic parts, $15,830; indirect materials, $3,590.

e. Materials used in production (requisitioned):

- Job 145: circuit boards, $340.
- Job 146: circuit boards, $3,570; electronic parts, $5,980.
- Job 147: circuit boards, $1,970; electronic parts, $4,730.
- Indirect materials, $1,580.

f. Manufacturing wages incurred during April, $32,430, of which $30,520 was paid. Wages payable at March 31 were paid during April, $3,670.

g. Labor time records for the month: Job 145, $3,500; Job 146, $11,050; Job 147, $9,940; indirect labor, $7,940.

h. Other actual miscellaneous manufacturing overhead costs incurred on account, $4,630.

i. Depreciation on plant and equipment (not included in item h above), $3,450.

j. Manufacturing overhead was allocated at the predetermined rate of 70% of direct labor cost.

k. Jobs completed during the month: Job 145, 400 relays at total cost of $42,170; Job 146, 200 switches at total cost of $28,335.

l. Credit sales on account: all of Job 145 for $97,640 (cost $42,170); Job 146, 120 switches for $35,100 (cost, $17,001).

m. Closed the Manufacturing Overhead account to Cost of Goods Sold.

Required

1. Open T-accounts for the general ledger, the materials ledger, the work in process ledger, and the finished goods ledger. Insert each account balance as given, and use the reference *Bal.*
2. Record the April transactions directly in the accounts, using the letters as references. Citronix uses a perpetual inventory system.
3. Prepare a trial balance at April 30.
4. Use the work in process T-account to prepare a schedule of cost of goods manufactured for the month of April.
5. Prepare an income statement for the month of April. (*Hint:* In transaction *m* you closed any under/overallocated manufacturing overhead to Cost of Goods Sold. In the income statement, show this correction as an adjustment to Cost of Goods Sold. If manufacturing overhead is underallocated, the adjustment will increase Cost of Goods Sold. If overhead is overallocated, the adjustment will reduce Cost of Goods Sold.)

P20-6A OneClick is a Web site design and consulting firm. The firm uses a job cost system, where each client is a different "job." OneClick traces direct labor, licensing costs, and travel costs directly to each job (client). It allocates indirect costs to jobs based on a predetermined indirect cost allocation rate, computed as a percentage of direct labor costs.

At the beginning of 20X4, managing partner Lauren Pearle prepared the following budget:

Job costing in a service company (Obj. 4)

Direct labor hours (professional)..................	6,000 hours
Direct labor costs (professional)	$600,000
Support staff salaries	70,000
Computer leases	34,000
Office supplies	11,000
Office rent	35,000

In November 20X4, OneClick served several clients. Records for two clients appear here:

	Planet Foods	Deception Fragrances
Direct labor hours	675 hours	20 Hours
Licensing costs	$ 1,325	$125
Travel costs............................	$10,500	—

Required

1. Compute OneClick's predetermined indirect cost allocation rate for 20X4.
2. Compute the total cost of each job.
3. If Pearle wants to earn profits equal to 30% of sales revenue, how much (what total fee) should she charge each of these two clients?
4. Why does OneClick assign costs to jobs?

(Group B) PROBLEMS

Analyzing job cost data
(Obj. 2, 3)

P20-1B Office Solutions refurbishes photocopy machines and sells them on the Web. Its job cost records yield the following information. Office Solutions uses a perpetual inventory system.

Job No.	Date Started	Date Finished	Sold	Total Cost of Job at March 31	Total Manufacturing Cost Added in April
1	2/26	3/7	3/9	$1,400	
2	2/3	3/12	3/13	1,600	
3	3/29	3/31	4/3	1,300	
4	3/31	4/1	4/1	500	$ 400
5	3/17	4/24	4/27	500	1,500
6	4/8	4/12	4/14		700
7	4/23	5/6	5/9		1,200
8	4/30	5/22	5/26		600

Required

1. Compute Office Solutions' cost of (a) work in process inventory at March 31 and April 30, (b) finished goods inventory at March 31 and April 30, and (c) cost of goods sold for March and April.
2. Make summary journal entries to record the transfer of completed units from work in process to finished goods for March and April.
3. Record the sale of Job 5 for $3,800.
4. Compute the gross profit for Job 5. What costs must the gross profit cover?

Accounting for manufacturing
transactions
(Obj. 2, 3)

P20-2B Mountain Homes builds prefabricated log houses in Montana. The company uses a perpetual inventory system and a job cost system in which each house is a job. The following events occurred during May.

a. Purchased materials on account, $315,000.
b. Incurred manufacturing wages of $142,800. Requisitioned direct materials and used direct labor in manufacturing:

	Direct Materials	Direct Labor
House 13	$36,100	$12,300
House 14	41,700	22,500
House 15	51,000	15,000
House 16	54,000	23,800

c. Depreciation of manufacturing equipment used on different houses, $16,000.
d. Other overhead costs incurred on houses 13–16:

Indirect labor	$21,600
Equipment rentals paid in cash	8,000
Liability insurance expired	3,900

e. Allocated overhead to jobs at the predetermined rate of 30% of direct labor cost.
f. Houses completed: 13, 15, 16.
g. Houses sold: 13 for $79,000; 16 for $113,900.

Required

1. Record the preceding events in the general journal.
2. Open T-accounts for Work in Process Inventory and Finished Goods Inventory. Post the appropriate entries to these accounts, identifying each entry by letter. Determine the ending account balances, assuming that the beginning balances were zero.
3. Add the costs of unfinished houses, and show that this total amount equals the ending balance in the Work in Process Inventory account.
4. Add the costs of completed houses that have not yet been sold, and show that this total amount equals the ending balance in the Finished Goods Inventory account.
5. Compute the gross profit on each house that was sold. What costs must the gross profit cover for Mountain Homes?

P20-3B Alliance Rubber produces transmission belts that other companies use in their manufacturing processes. Alliance Rubber uses job costing and has a perpetual inventory system.

Preparing and using a job cost record
(Obj. 2, 3)

On September 22, Alliance Rubber received an order for 50 industrial-grade belts from Hoyt Corporation at a price of $110 each. The job, assigned number 449, was promised for October 10. After purchasing the materials, Alliance Rubber began production on September 30 and incurred the following costs in completing the order:

Date	Time Ticket No.	Description	Amount
9/30	1754	10 hours @ $19	$190
10/3	1805	40 hours @ $18	720

Date	Materials Requisition No.	Description	Amount
9/30	593	20 lb. rubber @ $15	$300
10/2	598	30 meters polyester fabric @ $9	270
10/3	622	12 meters steel cord @ $12	144

Alliance Rubber allocates manufacturing overhead to jobs on the basis of the relation between expected overhead ($375,000) and direct labor ($250,000). Job 449 was completed on October 3 and shipped to Hoyt on October 5.

Required

1. Prepare a job cost record similar to Exhibit 20-3 for Job 449.
2. Journalize in summary form the requisition of direct materials and the assignment of direct labor and manufacturing overhead to Job 449.
3. Journalize completion of the job and sale of the goods.

Accounting for manufacturing overhead
(Obj. 3)

P20-4B Super-Tex produces specialized textiles. The company allocates manufacturing overhead based on the machine hours each job uses. Super-Tex reports the following cost data for 20X5:

	Budget	Actual
Direct labor hours	6,000 hours	5,000 hours
Machine hours	6,900 hours	6,000 hours
Depreciation on salespersons' autos	$20,000	$20,000
Indirect materials	40,000	42,000
Depreciation on trucks used to deliver textiles to customers	12,000	11,000
Depreciation on plant and equipment	50,000	55,000
Indirect manufacturing labor	35,000	38,000
Customer service hotline	17,000	20,000
Plant utilities	13,000	15,000
Direct labor cost	60,000	80,000

Required

1. Compute the predetermined manufacturing overhead rate.
2. Post actual and allocated manufacturing overhead to the Manufacturing Overhead T-account.
3. Close the under- or overallocated overhead to cost of goods sold.
4. How can managers use accounting information to help control manufacturing overhead costs?

Comprehensive accounting for manufacturing transactions
(Obj. 2, 3)

P20-5B ◄ *Link Back to Chapters 2 and 19.* Coalton Electric manufacturers specialized parts used in power generation. Initially, the company manufactured the parts for its own use, but it gradually began selling them to public utilities as well. The trial balance of Coalton Electric's manufacturing operation on January 1 is as follows:

COALTON ELECTRIC—MANUFACTURING OPERATIONS
Trial Balance
January 1, 20XX

Cash	$ 54,000	
Accounts receivable	65,860	
Inventories:		
Materials	14,180	
Work in process	43,350	
Finished goods	56,640	
Plant assets	342,860	
Accumulated depreciation		$145,050
Accounts payable		83,920
Wages payable		5,700
Common stock		200,000
Retained earnings		142,220
Sales revenues		—
Cost of goods sold	—	
Manufacturing wages	—	
Manufacturing overhead	—	
Marketing and general expenses	—	
	$576,890	$576,890

January 1 balances in the subsidiary ledgers were

- Materials ledger: petrochemicals, $5,280; electronic parts, $7,800; indirect materials, $1,100.
- Work in process ledger: Job 86, $43,350.
- Finished goods ledger: transformers, $35,770; switches, $20,870.

January transactions are summarized as follows.

a. Payments on account, $79,330.
b. Marketing and general expenses incurred and paid, $21,660.
c. Collections on account, $187,880.
d. Materials purchased on credit: petrochemicals, $19,570; electronic parts, $28,360; indirect materials, $6,130.
e. Materials used in production (requisitioned):

- Job 86: petrochemicals, $3,800.
- Job 87: petrochemicals, $9,870; electronic parts, $5,690.
- Job 88: petrochemicals, $7,680; electronic parts, $29,920.
- Indirect materials, $6,760.

f. Manufacturing wages incurred during January, $52,080, of which $49,560 was paid. Wages payable at December 31 were paid during January, $5,700.
g. Labor time records for the month: Job 86, $4,000; Job 87, $20,880; Job 88, $16,560; indirect labor, $10,640.
h. Other actual miscellaneous manufacturing overhead costs incurred on account, $27,660.
i. Depreciation on manufacturing plant and equipment (not included in item h above), $6,710.
j. Manufacturing overhead was allocated at the predetermined rate of 120% of direct labor cost.
k. Jobs completed during the month: Job 86, one transformer at total cost of $55,950; Job 87, 400 switches at total cost of $61,496.
l. Credit sales on account: All of Job 86 for $96,490 (cost $55,950); Job 87, 300 switches for $88,030 (cost, $46,122).
m. Close Manufacturing Overhead account to Cost of Goods Sold.

Required

1. Open T-accounts for the general ledger, the materials ledger, the work in process ledger, and the finished goods ledger. Insert each account balance as given, and use the reference *Bal.*
2. Record the January transactions directly in the accounts, using the letters as references. Coalton Electric uses a perpetual inventory system.
3. Prepare a trial balance at January 31.
4. Use the work in process T-account to prepare a schedule of cost of goods manufactured for the month of January.
5. Prepare an income statement for the month of January. To calculate cost of goods sold, you may want to review Exhibit 19-11. (*Hint:* In transaction *m* you closed any under/overallocated manufacturing overhead to Cost of Goods Sold. In the income statement, show this correction as an adjustment to Cost of Goods Sold. If manufacturing overhead is underallocated, the adjustment will increase Cost of Goods Sold. If overhead is overallocated, the adjustment will reduce Cost of Goods Sold.)

P20-6B Banner.com is an Internet advertising agency. The firm uses a job cost system in which each client is a different "job." Banner.com traces direct labor, software licensing costs, and travel costs directly to each job (client). The company allocates indirect costs to jobs based on a predetermined indirect cost allocation rate, computed as a percentage of direct labor costs.

Job costing in a service company (Obj. 4)

At the beginning of 20X3, managing partner Michael Egan prepared the following budget:

Direct labor hours (professional)................	20,000 hours
Direct labor costs (professional)	$1,500,000
Support staff salaries	365,000
Rent and utilities	124,000
Supplies	16,000
Leased computer hardware	320,000

In January 20X3, Banner.com served several clients. Records for two clients appear here:

	Renolds Tennis and Golf Resort	Malaysia Cuisine
Direct labor hours	320 hours	24 hours
Software licensing costs	$1,250	$150
Travel costs..	6,000	—

Required

1. Compute Banner.com's predetermined indirect cost allocation rate for 20X3.
2. Compute the total cost of each job.
3. If Banner.com wants to earn profits equal to 20% of sales revenue, how much (what total fee) should it charge each of these two clients?
4. Why does Banner.com assign costs to jobs?

APPLY YOUR KNOWLEDGE

DECISION CASES

Costing and pricing identical products

(Obj. 2, 3)

Case 1. Coffee Central prepares gift baskets of its own blends of coffee, espresso, and coffee candies for sale to corporate clients. Each customer selects items from Coffee Central's Web site, and Coffee Central prints the customer's corporate logo on the packages. Coffee Central uses a job cost system and allocates manufacturing overhead based on direct labor cost.

One of Coffee Central's largest customers is the consulting firm Howell and Bunn. This firm sends baskets to its clients each Christmas, and also gives baskets to employees at the firm's annual holiday party. The consulting firm's managing partner, Paul Bunn, placed the client gift order in September for 650 baskets. Bunn forgot to place the December staff-party order until the beginning of December. This staff-party order was for an additional 150 baskets identical to the ones sent to clients.

Coffee Central budgeted the cost per basket for the original 650-basket order as follows:

Coffees, wrappers, basket...	$28.00
Employee time to produce items and fill the baskets (15 min.)	5.00
Manufacturing overhead	2.00
Total manufacturing cost..	$35.00

Andy Tavolo, president of Coffee Central, priced the order at $40 per basket.

In the past few months, Coffee Central has experienced price increases for both unroasted coffee and direct labor. *All other costs have remained the same.* The cost per basket for the second order was budgeted as

Coffees, wrappers, basket...	$30.00
Employee time to produce items and fill the baskets (15 min.)	6.00
Manufacturing overhead	2.40
Total manufacturing cost..	$38.40

Required

1. Do you agree with the cost analysis for the second order? Explain your answer.
2. Should the two orders be accounted for as one job or two in Coffee Central's system?
3. What sale price per basket should Tavolo set for the second order? What are the advantages and disadvantages of this price?

Case 2. Wild Berries manufactures organic fruit preserves sold primarily through health food stores and on the Web. The company closes for two weeks each December to allow employees to spend time with their families over the holiday season. Wild Berries' manufacturing overhead is mostly straight-line depreciation on its plant and air-conditioning costs for keeping the berries cool during the summer months. The company uses direct labor hours as the allocation base. President Kelly Appling has just approved new accounting software and is telling Controller Melissa Powers about her decision.

Accounting for manufacturing overhead (Obj. 3)

"I think this new software will be great," Appling says. "It will save you time in preparing all those reports."

"Yes, and having so much more information just a click away will help us make better decisions and help control costs," replies Powers. "We need to consider how we can use the new system to improve our business practices."

"And I know just where to start," says Appling. "You complain each year about having to predict the weather months in advance for estimating air-conditioning costs, and direct labor hours for the denominator of the predetermined manufacturing overhead rate, when professional meteorologists can't even get tomorrow's forecast right! I think we should calculate the predetermined overhead rate on a monthly basis."

Controller Melissa Powers is not so sure this is a good idea.

Required

1. What are the advantages and disadvantages of Appling's proposal?
2. Should Wild Berries compute its predetermined manufacturing overhead rate on an annual basis or monthly basis? Explain.

ETHICAL ISSUE

Ethics (Obj. 4)

◄ *Link back to Chapter 19.* Wave Electronics is a contract manufacturer that produces customized computer components for several well-known computer-assembly companies. Wave's latest contract with CompNow.com calls for Wave to deliver sound cards that simulate surround sound from two speakers. Wave Electronics spent several hundred thousand dollars to design the sound card to meet CompNow.com's specifications.

Wave Electronic's president Angie Harrison has stipulated a pricing policy that requires bids (selling prices) for new contracts to be based on Wave's estimated full product cost from all elements of the value chain, plus a profit margin. Upon reviewing the contract figures, Wave's controller Lilian Gomez was startled to find that the cost estimates developed by Wave's cost accountant Anthony Haywood for the CompNow.com bid were based on only the *inventoriable* costs. Gomez is upset with Haywood. She is not sure what to do next.

Required

1. How did using inventoriable cost rather than full product cost affect the amount of Wave's bid for the CompNow.com job?
2. Identify the parties involved in Lilian Gomez's ethical dilemma. What are her alternatives? How would each party be affected by each alternative? What should Gomez do next?

TEAM PROJECT

Job costing in merchandising (Obj. 3, 4)

GourmetGifts prepares cheese, bread, and fruit gift baskets for sale from the company's Web site. The company obtains these products from several vendors. Customers select items for their customized gift baskets on GourmetGifts' Web site, and then GourmetGifts assembles and decorates the baskets to order. Workers earn $21 per hour, and they prepare an average of 3 baskets per hour. For pricing, GourmetGifts determines the full "product cost" of each basket and then adds a profit margin that equals 20% of the full product cost. Indirect costs, including supervisors' and quality inspectors' wages, spoilage, Web site support, rent, and utilities, are allocated to baskets based on direct food costs.

GourmetGifts president Jennifer Wildt wants to grow the company by targeting corporate customers who would place large orders for many identical baskets. But she believes the company does not have the resources to finance such expansion. She is discussing the issue with controller Jay Boros and cost accountant Ling Chen, who has just returned from an e-commerce seminar. Chen suggests that GourmetGifts use an e-commerce software provider and use the Web to connect electronically with its main vendors. GourmetGifts could then order food items as needed for next-day delivery, avoiding the cost of holding a larger inventory and the associated spoilage. Wildt likes Chen's suggestion. Wildt also expects that filling many baskets with the same items should cut the direct labor time per basket in half. Boros and Chen calculate the following cost estimates, assuming that in addition to the 10,000 baskets currently sold to individuals, the company would sell 6,000 baskets to corporate clients.

		16,000 Baskets
Direct materials		$480,000
Direct labor		91,000
Indirect costs:		
Supervisors' and quality inspectors' wages	$64,000	
Spoilage	27,500	
Web site support	17,000	
Rent and utilities	28,000	
Total indirect costs		136,500
Total costs		$707,500

When Chen calculates the average cost per basket, all are surprised that the cost savings for the corporate sales are not as large as expected. At the estimated cost of approximately $42.03, GourmetGifts might not be able to attract corporate customers. Controller Jay Boros suggests changing the indirect cost allocation base from direct materials cost to direct labor cost. Wildt is skeptical because the firm has always used direct materials cost as the allocation base, and the last thing she wants is to have individual sales subsidize corporate sales.

Required

Form groups of three students for a role-play.

- The first person assumes the role of GourmetGifts president Jennifer Wildt. Before the meeting, prepare a written report that costs baskets sold to individuals using (a) direct materials cost, and (b) direct labor cost as the indirect cost allocation base. Also, estimate the selling price under each allocation base. Carry computations of the indirect cost allocation rate to four decimal places. Prepare arguments supporting direct materials cost as the cost allocation base.
- The second person assumes the role of cost accountant Ling Chen. Before the meeting, prepare a written report that costs baskets sold to corporate customers using (a) direct materials cost, and (b) direct labor cost as the indirect cost allocation base. Estimate the selling price under each allocation base. Carry computations of the indirect cost allocation rate to four decimal places. Prepare arguments supporting direct labor cost as the cost allocation base.
- The third person assumes the role of controller Jay Boros. Before the meeting, prepare a written report on the factors GourmetGifts should consider in identifying a cost allocation base.

During the meeting, the three team members decide which cost allocation base is best for GourmetGifts and what additional information, if any, would help in making this decision.

INTERNET EXERCISE

Dell Computer

Dell Computer Corporation entered the twenty-first century with an enviable record as the most successful company in the global computer systems industry. In terms of market share, it is the number one company in the United States, and number two in the world. One bold concept—direct customer contact—has made Dell one of the world's most successful companies.

1. Go to **http://www.dell.com/** and in the navigation bar at the top of the screen click on *About Dell* followed by *Investor Relations*. In the left-hand column, click on *Annual Reports* and then the HTML version of the most recent *Year in Review*.
   a. In the left-hand column, click on the *Five-Year Statistical Review*. Most of Dell's net revenues are generated from which region? From which product line?
   b. How can this information help managers?
2. At the top of the page, click on the *Annual Report on Form 10-K*. Scroll down until you reach the table of contents. Click on *Item: Financial Statements and Supplementary Data*. Scroll down to review the *Consolidated Statement of Income*.
   a. Which expense account(s) contain inventoriable costs? Noninventoriable costs?
   b. For what reason are noninventoriable costs assigned to products?

3. Scroll down and find *Note 13—Supplemental Consolidated Financial Information.* Refer to the information regarding inventories. (Note: In the 2000 annual report it was on page 46.)

a. For the most recent year-end, what amount was reported for Production materials inventory? Work-in-process and finished goods inventory? Which type of inventory has the greatest dollar value? What might explain this?

b. Which of these types of inventory includes direct material costs? Direct labor costs? Depreciation on the manufacturing plant?

Go to the "Alternative Income Statement Formats and Extraordinary Items" episode on the Mastering Accounting CD-ROM for an interactive, video-enhanced exercise on CanGo managers' need to consider the different income statement formats and their effect on investors.

21

Process Costing

LEARNING OBJECTIVES

*After studying this chapter,
you should be able to*

1. Distinguish between the flow of costs in process costing and job costing

2. Record process costing trans-actions

3. Compute equivalent units

4. Assign costs to units completed and to units in ending work in process inventory

5. Account for a second process-ing department by the FIFO method

6. Account for a second process-ing department by the weighted-average method

Pace Foods, a division of **Campbell Soup Co.,** leads the market in the dynamic "Mexican sauces" food category, which has surpassed ketchup in supermarket sales in the United States. The San Antonio, Texas, company mass-produces several-ton batches of mild, medium, and hot sauces in both regular and thick-and-chunky styles. Pace Foods can produce more than 150 million pounds of picante sauce and salsa a year.

Pace picante sauce is made in two processes. In the first, jalapeño peppers, onions, and other fresh vegetables are received from suppliers and then chopped into small pieces. In the second process, workers mix the vegetables with tomato products and spices. Then the picante sauce is cooked, bottled, and boxed for shipping. Inspectors test each batch to ensure purity and consistent texture and flavor.

Pace has invested in state-of-the-art manufacturing processes as well as in continuous improvement programs targeted at reducing costs and increasing the quality of the sauce. The result? Despite intense competition from major international food companies, Pace Foods has achieved steady double-digit growth.

How much does it cost **Pace Foods** to make a batch of hot picante sauce? How efficient was the cooking and bottling process last week? What is the value of the inventory of fresh vegetables in the chopping process? Like their counterparts in other manufacturing companies, managers at Pace use accounting information to answer these questions.

PROCESS COSTING: AN OVERVIEW

The two basic types of product costing systems are *job costing* and *process costing*. We saw in Chapter 20 that companies like **Dell Computer, Boeing,** and **PricewaterhouseCoopers** use job costing to determine the cost to produce custom goods and services. Job cost records accumulate the cost of each individual job.

In contrast, companies like **Pace Foods, Shell Oil,** and **Sony** use process costing to assign costs to goods that are mass-produced in a continuous sequence of steps called processes. Process industries produce large numbers of identical units (CDs, electronics like Sony Playstations or PalmPilots, and packaged foods like Hershey Kisses or Pace picante sauce). Many companies in the petroleum, food and beverage, pharmaceutical, and electronics industries use process costing.

In process industries, the flow of goods through the processes or departments is continuous and repetitive. For example, to produce picante sauce, Pace Foods has one department for chopping the vegetables and a second department for mixing and bottling. The company does not use job cost records. Instead, it accumulates costs in each department for each production period. Unit cost is computed by dividing the cost incurred in a department by the number of units produced in that department. For example, if the Chopping Department incurs $350,000 of costs to chop 1,000,000 pounds of vegetables, the unit cost of the Chopping Department is $0.35 ($350,000/1,000,000). If the Mixing & Bottling Department then incurs $500,000 to mix and bottle 1,000,000 pounds of picante sauce, the Mixing & Bottling Department's unit cost is $0.50 ($500,000/1,000,000). The *total* cost for a 1-pound bottle of chopped, mixed, and bottled picante sauce is then $0.85 ($0.35 + $0.50).

Exhibit 21-1 compares the flow of costs in

- A job costing system for Blue Ridge Fabrication, a manufacturer of custom-built machinery
- A process costing system for Pace Foods

Panel A shows that in Blue Ridge Fabrication's job costing system, there is a single Work in Process Inventory control account, supported by individual subsidiary job cost records for each job in process. Blue Ridge assigns direct materials, direct labor, and manufacturing overhead to individual jobs, as explained in Chapter 20. When the job is finished, its costs flow directly into Finished Goods Inventory, *not* from one Work in Process Inventory account into another.

EXHIBIT 21-1
Comparison of Job Costing and Process Costing

 DAILY EXERCISE 21-1

Objective 1
Distinguish between the flow of costs in process costing and job costing

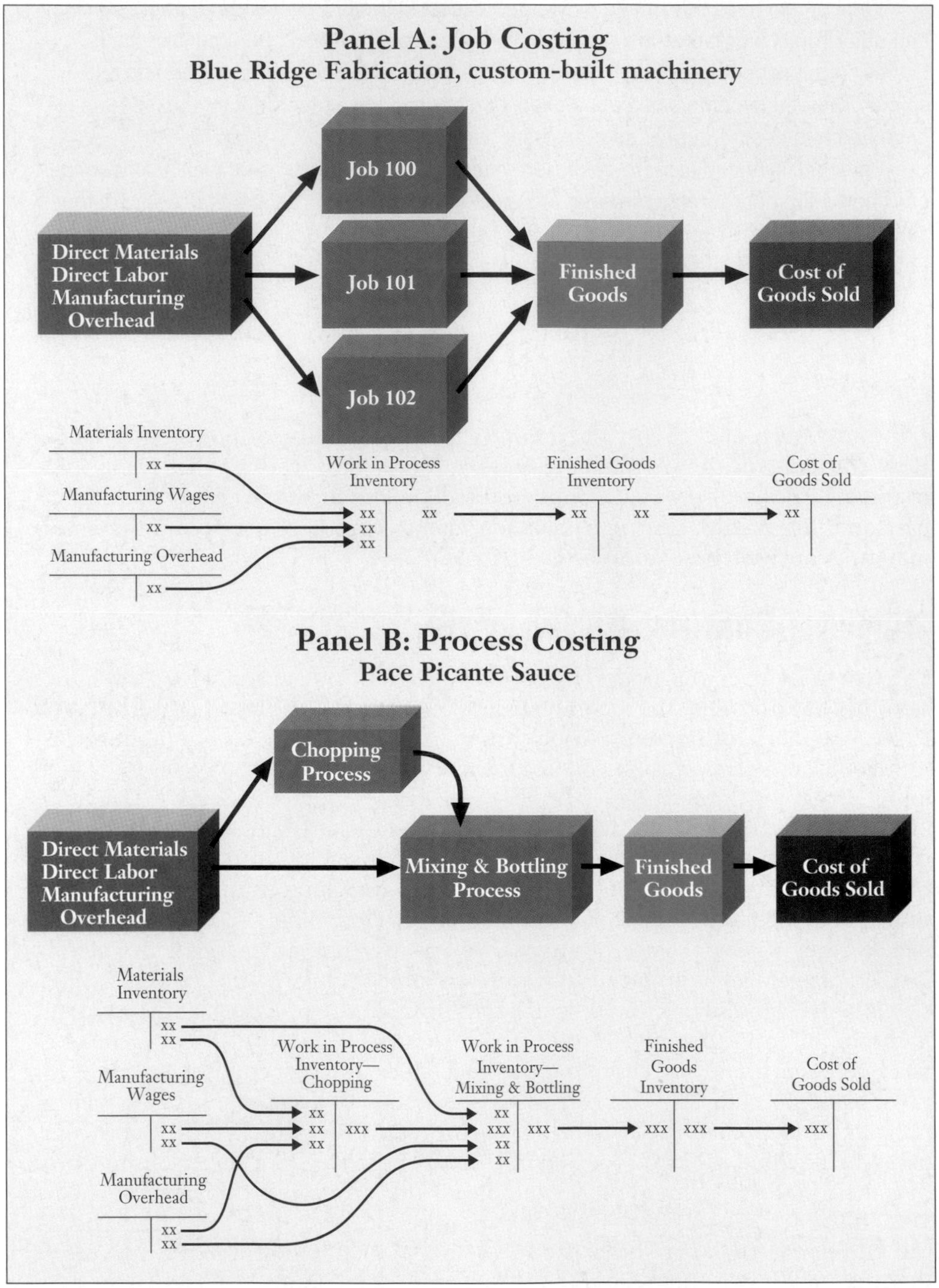

Panel A: Job Costing
Blue Ridge Fabrication, custom-built machinery

Job 100
Job 101
Job 102

Direct Materials
Direct Labor
Manufacturing
Overhead

Finished Goods

Cost of Goods Sold

Materials Inventory
xx

Manufacturing Wages
xx

Manufacturing Overhead
xx

Work in Process Inventory
xx   xx
xx
xx

Finished Goods Inventory
xx   xx

Cost of Goods Sold
xx

Panel B: Process Costing
Pace Picante Sauce

Chopping Process

Direct Materials
Direct Labor
Manufacturing
Overhead

Mixing & Bottling Process

Finished Goods

Cost of Goods Sold

Materials Inventory
xx
xx

Manufacturing Wages
xx
xx

Manufacturing Overhead
xx
xx

Work in Process Inventory— Chopping
xx   xxx
xx
xx

Work in Process Inventory— Mixing & Bottling
xx   xxx
xxx
xx
xx

Finished Goods Inventory
xxx   xxx

Cost of Goods Sold
xxx

In contrast to Blue Ridge Fabrication's individual jobs, Pace Foods uses a series of *manufacturing processes* to produce large quantities of picante sauce. Pace has two manufacturing departments: (1) Chopping, and (2) Mixing & Bottling. Exhibit 21-2 illustrates the Pace manufacturing process. In the chopping process, Pace uses labor and equipment to chop the vegetables. In the mixing and bottling process, Pace uses labor and equipment first to add tomato products, and then to mix and bottle the sauce. Companies like Pace that use a series of manufacturing processes to produce large quantities of similar products typically use process costing systems.

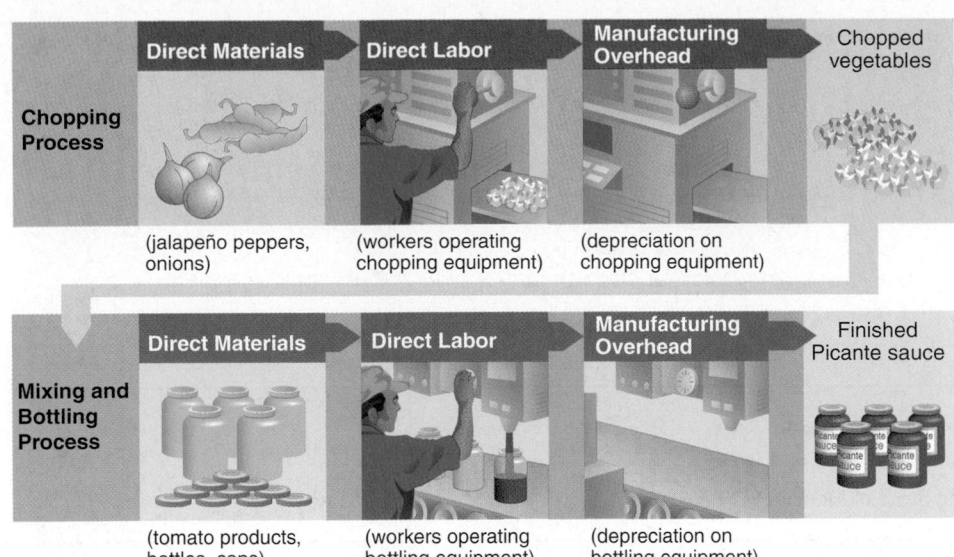

EXHIBIT 21-2
Flow of Costs in Production of Picante Sauce

⊙ DAILY EXERCISE 21-2

Notice four aspects of the process costing system in Panel B of Exhibit 21-1:

1. Each manufacturing process (chopping; mixing and bottling) has its own separate Work in Process Inventory account.

2. Direct materials, direct labor, and manufacturing overhead are assigned to each manufacturing process. For example:

	Work in Process Inventory—Chopping	**Work in Process Inventory— Mixing & Bottling**
Direct materials	Peppers, onions	Tomato products, bottles, caps
Direct labor	Wages of workers operating chopping equipment	Wages of workers operating bottling equipment
Manufacturing overhead	Depreciation on chopping equipment	Depreciation on bottling equipment

3. When the chopping process is complete, the chopped vegetables move out of the chopping process and into the mixing and bottling process. The cost of the vegetables is likewise transferred out of Work in Process Inventory— Chopping, and into Work in Process Inventory—Mixing & Bottling.

4. When the mixing and bottling process is complete, the finished picante sauce goes to finished goods storage. The costs (including costs from the Chopping Department as well as the Mixing & Bottling Department) flow into Finished Goods Inventory. Costs flow into Finished Goods Inventory only from the Work in Process Inventory of the *last* manufacturing process.

Exhibit 21-3 on page 844 summarizes the flow of costs through this process costing system (all amounts are in thousands and are assumed).

⊙ DAILY EXERCISE 21-3

RECORDING COSTS

Objective 2
Record process costing transactions

Process costing journal entries are similar to those for job costing. Accountants first *accumulate* the costs of materials purchased, and labor and actual manufacturing overhead incurred during the period (for all processes). These journal entries are identical to those made in job costing. For example, to record the purchase of materials ($11,000), and the cost of manufacturing labor ($4,000) and actual manufacturing overhead ($10,000), **Pace** would make the following journal entries (amounts in thousands):

Materials Inventory...	11	
Accounts Payable		11
Manufacturing Wages	4	
Wages Payable..		4
Manufacturing Overhead..	10	
Accumulated Depreciation—Plant..................................		2
Property Tax Payable—Plant		2
Accounts Payable, and so on		6
To purchase materials and incur direct labor and actual manufacturing overhead.		

EXHIBIT 21-3

Flow of Costs Through a Process Costing System (Amounts in Thousands)

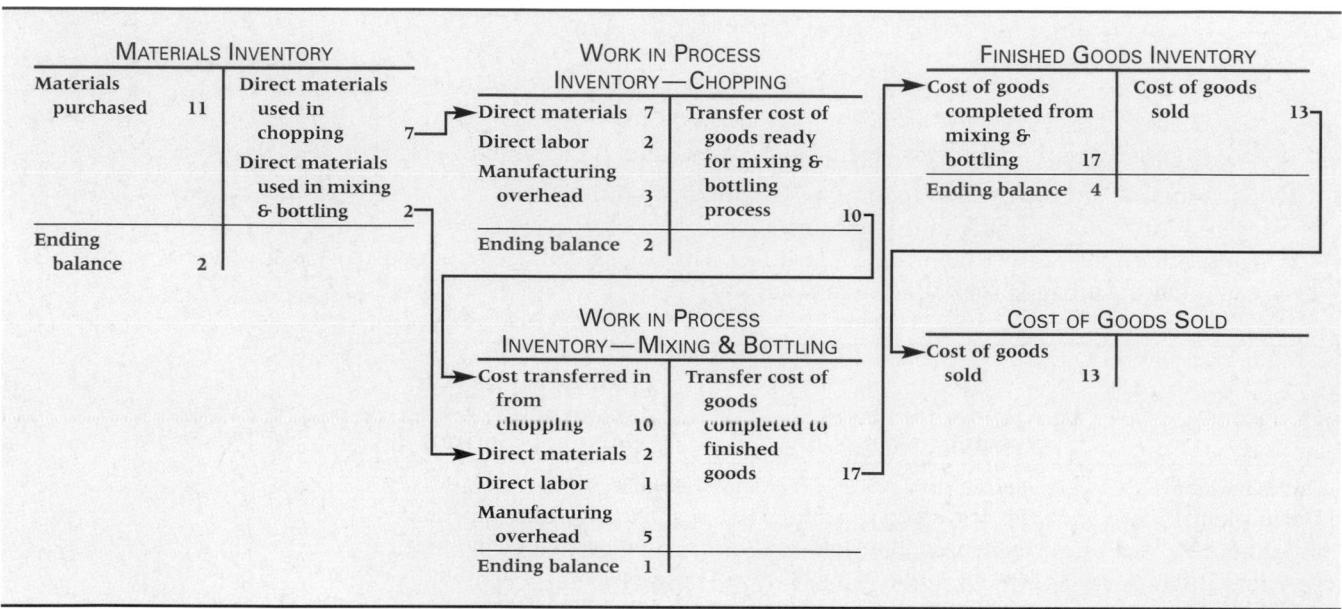

Chapter 20, p. 801, distinguishes between *accumulating* actual costs and *assigning* costs to jobs and processes.

The main difference between job costing and process costing is in *assigning* the costs of direct materials, direct labor, and manufacturing overhead. Job costing assigns costs to individual *jobs* that are transferred from Work in Process Inventory directly to Finished Goods Inventory. Process costing assigns costs to *processes*. There is a separate Work in Process Inventory account for each process. As products move from one process to the next, their costs flow from one Work in Process Inventory account to the next.

The following entries detail the flow of costs through the process costing system in Exhibit 21-3.

DAILY EXERCISE 21-4

Work in Process Inventory—Chopping...	12	
Materials Inventory		7
Manufacturing Wages..		2
Manufacturing Overhead		3
To requisition direct materials, assign direct labor cost, and allocate manufacturing overhead to the Chopping Department.		
Work in Process Inventory—Mixing & Bottling.....................................	10	
Work in Process Inventory—Chopping		10
To transfer cost out of the Chopping Department and into the Mixing & Bottling Department.		

Work in Process Inventory—Mixing & Bottling......................................	8	
Materials Inventory		2
Manufacturing Wages...		1
Manufacturing Overhead		5
To record the additional direct materials, direct labor, and		
overhead allocated to the Mixing & Bottling Department.		
Finished Goods Inventory...	17	
Work in Process Inventory—Mixing & Bottling.............................		17
To transfer the cost of goods completed out of the Mixing		
& Bottling Department and into Finished Goods Inventory.		
Cost of Goods Sold	13	
Finished Goods Inventory		13
To account for the cost of goods sold.		

Notice that in process costing

- Direct materials, direct labor, and manufacturing overhead costs are assigned to separate Work in Process Inventory accounts *for each process.*
- Costs are transferred, along with the units, from one Work in Process Inventory account to the next. Costs are not transferred to Finished Goods Inventory *until the last process is completed.*

 DAILY EXERCISE 21-5

 DAILY EXERCISE 21-6

BUILDING BLOCKS OF PROCESS COSTING

Exhibit 21-3 shows that the total cost of the first process, chopping, was $12,000 ($7,000 direct materials + $2,000 direct labor + $3,000 manufacturing overhead). Where did this $12,000 in costs go? The exhibit shows that $10,000 was transferred out of Work in Process—Chopping and into Work in Process—Mixing & Bottling, leaving a $2,000 ending balance in Work in Process—Chopping. How do we know how much of the $12,000 to assign to the chopped vegetables transferred out versus those still in ending inventory? Before we can answer this key question, we must first learn about two building blocks of process costing:

- Conversion costs
- Equivalent units

Conversion Costs

Chapter 19 introduced three kinds of manufacturing costs: direct materials, direct labor, and manufacturing overhead. Companies like **Hewlett-Packard** and **Harley-Davidson** that use automated production processes often find that direct labor costs are only a small part of total manufacturing costs. Such companies often use only two categories:

- Direct materials
- **Conversion costs** (direct labor plus manufacturing overhead)

Collapsing direct labor and manufacturing overhead into a single category simplifies the accounting. We call this category *conversion costs* because it is the cost (direct labor plus manufacturing overhead) to *convert* raw materials into new finished products.

CONVERSION COSTS. Direct labor plus manufacturing overhead.

Equivalent Units

Equivalent units measure the amount of work done during a period, expressed in terms of fully complete units of output. Assume **Calloway's** golf ball production plant has 5,000 balls in ending work in process inventory. Each ball is 80% of the way through the production process. If conversion costs are incurred evenly throughout the process, then getting 5,000 balls each 80% of the way through the process takes about the same amount of work as getting 4,000 balls (5,000 × 80%)

Objective 3
Compute equivalent units

EQUIVALENT UNITS. A measure of the amount of work done during a period, expressed in terms of fully complete units of output.

all the way through. Thus, ending work in process inventory has 4,000 equivalent units. For costs that are incurred evenly throughout the production process:

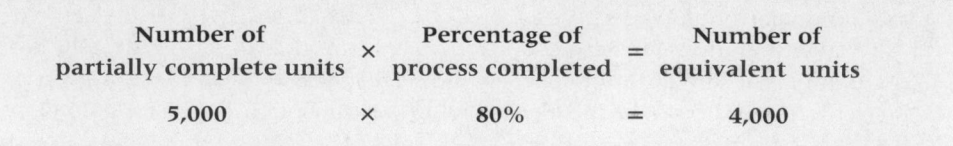

Number of partially complete units	×	Percentage of process completed	=	Number of equivalent units
5,000	×	80%	=	4,000

● DAILY EXERCISE 21-7

This formula holds only for costs that are incurred evenly throughout the production process. This is usually true for conversion costs (direct labor and manufacturing overhead). However, direct materials are often added at a particular point in the production process. Rubber is added at the very beginning of the production process and packaging materials are not added until the very end. How many equivalent units of rubber and packaging materials are in the ending inventory of 5,000 balls?

You can answer this question by looking at the time line in Exhibit 21-4:

EXHIBIT 21-4 **Calloway Production Plant Time Line**

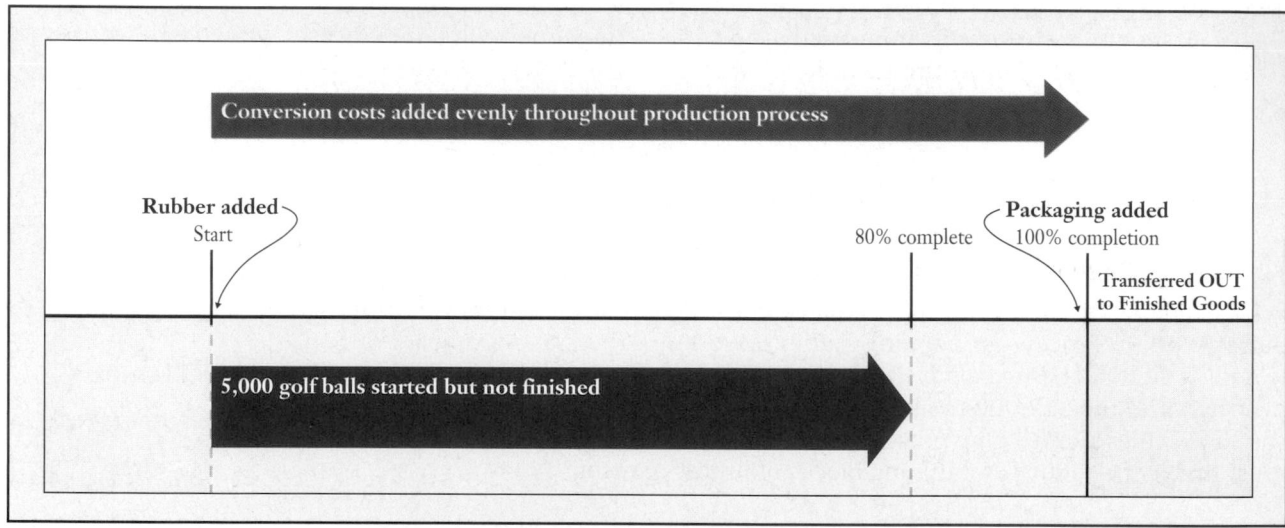

All 5,000 balls are 80% complete, so they have all passed the point where rubber is added. Thus, each ball has its full share of rubber, so the balls have 5,000 equivalent units of rubber. In contrast, the time line shows that *none* of the 5,000 balls has made it to the end of the process, where the packaging materials are added. The ending inventory therefore has *zero* equivalent units of packaging materials.

To summarize, the 5,000 balls in ending work in process inventory have

- 5,000 equivalent units of rubber
- 0 equivalent units of packaging materials
- 4,000 equivalent units of conversion costs

The point is that inputs added at different points in the process can have different equivalent units. In this case, the 5,000 physical balls have different equivalent units of rubber, packaging materials, and conversion costs.

Be careful to distinguish the *end of the production process* from the *end of the accounting period*. Goods at the end of the production process are transferred to the next process or to finished goods. For example, Calloway's completed golf balls proceed to the finished goods warehouse. By contrast, at the end of the accounting period, goods that are only partway through the production process are the ending work in process inventory. Calloway's ending work in process inventory includes 5,000 golf balls that have their rubber cores but no packaging.

PROCESS COSTING: AN ILLUSTRATION

Let's examine SeaView, a sporting goods company that manufactures swim masks. The Shaping Department shapes the body of the swim masks. The process begins with direct materials (including plastic) that labor and equipment transform into shaped masks. The direct materials are added at the beginning of the process, but conversion costs are incurred evenly throughout the shaping process. After shaping, the partially completed masks move to the Finishing Department, where the mask bodies are finished and the clear faceplates are inserted and sealed in place.

During October, the Shaping Department incurs the following costs in processing 50,000 masks:

Direct materials.................................		$140,000
Conversion costs:		
Direct labor....................................	$21,250	
Manufacturing overhead..............	46,750	68,000
Costs to account for		$208,000

If the shaping process is complete for all 50,000 masks, the costs transferred to Work in Process Inventory—Finishing are the full $208,000. The unit cost is $4.16 ($208,000/50,000 masks).

But what if only 40,000 masks are completely through the shaping process? At October 31, the Shaping Department still has 10,000 masks that are only one-quarter of the way through. How do we split the $208,000 between

- 40,000 completely shaped masks transferred to the Finishing Department
- 10,000 partially shaped masks remaining in the Shaping Department's ending work in process inventory

The answer lies in a five-step process costing procedure. We begin with the Shaping Department.

Step 1: Summarize the Flow of Physical Units

Exhibit 21-5 tracks the movement of swim masks into and out of the Shaping Department. We assume for simplicity that work began October 1, so the Work in

 DAILY EXERCISE 21-8

 DAILY EXERCISE 21-9

EXHIBIT 21-5
Step 1: Summarize the Flow of Physical Units; Step 2: Compute Output in Terms of Equivalent Units

SEAVIEW			
SHAPING DEPARTMENT			
Month of October 31, 20XX			

	Step 1	Step 2 Equivalent Units	
Flow of Production	**Flow of Physical Units**	**Direct Materials**	**Conversion Costs**
Units to account for:			
Beginning work in process, September 30	—		
Started in production during October	50,000		
Total physical units to account for.......................................	50,000		
Units accounted for:			
Completed and transferred out during October	40,000	40,000	40,000
Ending work in process, October 31	10,000	10,000	2,500*
Total physical units accounted for	50,000		
Equivalent units...		50,000	42,500

*10,000 units each 25% complete = 2,500 equivalent units

Process Inventory account had a zero balance at September 30. Of the 50,000 masks started in October, 40,000 were completely shaped and transferred out to the Finishing Department during the month. The remaining 10,000 partially shaped masks are the Shaping Department's ending work in process inventory on October 31.

Step 2: Compute Output in Terms of Equivalent Units

We compute equivalent units separately for direct materials and conversion costs because work progresses differently for materials and for conversion. The Shaping Department time line in Exhibit 21-6 shows that all direct materials are added at the beginning of the process. In contrast, conversion costs are incurred evenly throughout the process. As Exhibit 21-6 shows, 40,000 masks are complete as to both materials and conversion costs. These completed masks have incurred 40,000 equivalent units of direct materials, and 40,000 equivalent units of conversion costs.

EXHIBIT 21-6 SeaView's Shaping Department Time Line

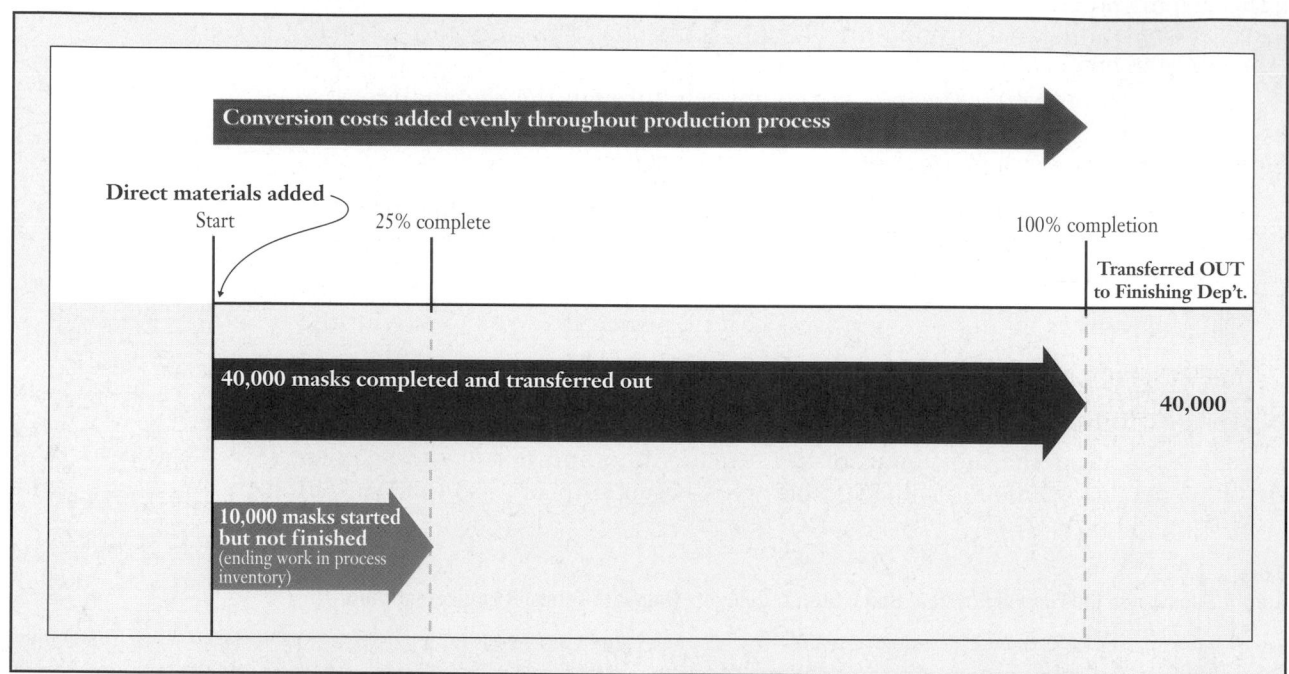

The Shaping Department has another 10,000 masks that are only 25% of the way through the process on October 31. Direct materials are added at the beginning of the process, so the time line shows that all the direct materials have been added to these 10,000 masks, even though the masks are only 25% of the way through the shaping process. The total equivalent units of direct materials include the 40,000 finished masks plus the 10,000 masks in ending (work in process) inventory that are complete as to direct materials, as shown in step 2 of Exhibit 21-5.

Shaping Department conversion costs are incurred evenly throughout the process. The time line shows that for each of the 10,000 partially completed masks, 25% of the conversion costs have been incurred by October 31. The equivalent units of conversion costs are

10,000 × 25% = 2,500 equivalent units

DAILY EXERCISE 21-10

The total equivalent units of conversion costs include the 40,000 finished masks plus the 2,500 equivalent units of conversion costs from the masks in ending work in process inventory that are only partially completed on October 31, as shown in step 2 of Exhibit 21-5.

WORK IT OUT

Suppose that direct materials were added at the *end* of SeaView's shaping process rather than at the beginning.

1. Draw a new time line similar to Exhibit 21-6.
2. Use the time line to determine the number of equivalent units of direct materials in the Shaping Department.

Answers

1. Conversion costs added evenly throughout production process

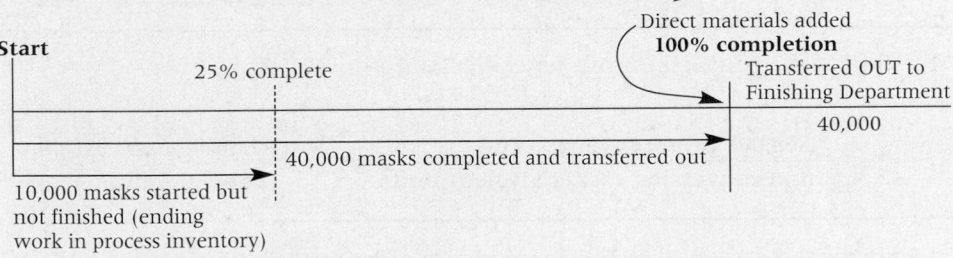

2. The time line shows that direct materials are not added until the *end* of the process, and the 10,000 masks in ending work in process inventory have not made it to the end of the shaping process. Since *no* direct materials have been added to the ending work in process inventory, materials have been added *only* to the 40,000 masks completed and transferred out. Thus, there are 40,000 equivalent units of direct materials.

Step 3: Summarize Total Costs to Account For

Exhibit 21-7 summarizes the total costs to account for in the Shaping Department (cost data are from page 847). These costs are the total debits in Work in Process Inventory—Shaping, including any beginning balance.

EXHIBIT 21-7
Step 3: Summarize Total Costs to Account For

SEAVIEW SHAPING DEPARTMENT
Month Ended October 31, 20XX

WORK IN PROCESS INVENTORY—SHAPING

	Physical Units	Dollars		Physical Units	Dollars
Beginning inventory September 30	-0-	$ -0-	Transferred out	40,000	$?
Production started:	50,000				
Direct materials		140,000			
Conversion costs:					
Direct labor		21,250			
Manufacturing overhead		46,750			
Total to account for	50,000	$208,000			
Ending inventory, October 31	10,000	$?			

The Shaping Department has 50,000 physical units and $208,000 of costs to account for. Our next task is to split these costs between the 40,000 shaped masks transferred out to the Finishing Department, and the 10,000 masks that remain in the Shaping Department's ending work in process inventory.

Step 4: Compute the Cost per Equivalent Unit

In step 2, we computed the total number of equivalent units for direct materials (50,000) and conversion costs (42,500). Because the equivalent units differ, we must compute a separate cost per unit for each category. Exhibit 21-7 shows that the direct materials cost is $140,000. Conversion cost is $68,000, which is the sum of direct labor ($21,250) and manufacturing overhead ($46,750).

To compute the direct material cost per equivalent unit, remember that the word *per* means "divided by." So the direct material cost *per* equivalent unit is the direct material cost *divided by* the number of direct material equivalent units:

$$\frac{\$140{,}000 \text{ total direct material cost}}{50{,}000 \text{ total direct material equivalent units}} = \begin{array}{c}\$2.80 \text{ direct material cost per}\\ \text{equivalent unit}\end{array}$$

We compute the conversion cost per equivalent unit similarly:

$$\frac{\$68{,}000 \text{ total conversion cost}}{42{,}500 \text{ total conversion cost equivalent units}} = \begin{array}{c}\$1.60 \text{ conversion cost per}\\ \text{equivalent unit}\end{array}$$

DAILY EXERCISE 21-11

DAILY EXERCISE 21-12

Exhibit 21-8 summarizes the computation of equivalent-unit costs.

EXHIBIT 21-8
Step 4: Compute the Cost per Equivalent Unit

SEAVIEW SHAPING DEPARTMENT
Month Ended October 31, 20XX

	Direct Materials	Conversion Costs
Beginning work in process, September 30	$ 0	$ 0
Costs added during October (from Exhibit 21-7)	$140,000	$68,000
Divide by equivalent units (from Exhibit 21-5)	÷ 50,000	÷ 42,500
Cost per equivalent unit	$2.80	$1.60

In addition to using the cost per equivalent unit in the five-step process costing procedure, managers also use this information to determine how well they have controlled costs. If the cost per equivalent unit of conversion (or direct materials) meets or beats the budgeted target cost per equivalent unit, the manager has successfully controlled the conversion (or direct materials) costs.

Objective 4
Assign costs to units completed and to units in ending work in process inventory

DAILY EXERCISE 21-13

Step 5: Assign Costs to Units Completed and to Units in Ending Work in Process Inventory

Exhibit 21-9 shows how the equivalent units computed in step 2 (Exhibit 21-5) are costed at the cost per equivalent unit computed in step 4 (Exhibit 21-8). The goal of Exhibit 21-9 is to determine how much of the $208,000 total costs incurred by the Shaping Department should be assigned to (1) the 40,000 completely shaped masks that have been transferred out to the Finishing Department, and (2) the 10,000 partially shaped masks remaining in Shaping's ending work in process inventory.

EXHIBIT 21-9
Step 5: Assign Costs to Units Completed and to Units in Ending Work in Process Inventory

SEAVIEW SHAPING DEPARTMENT
Month Ended October 31, 20XX

	Direct Materials	Conversion Costs	Total
Completed and transferred out (40,000)	[40,000 × ($2.80 + $1.60)]		= $176,000
Ending work in process inventory (10,000):			
Direct materials	[10,000 × $2.80]		= $ 28,000
Conversion costs		[2,500 × $1.60]	= 4,000
Total cost of ending work in process inventory			$ 32,000
Total cost accounted for			$208,000

First consider the 40,000 masks completed and transferred out. Exhibit 21-5 reveals 40,000 equivalent units of work for both direct materials and conversion costs. Thus, the total cost of these completed masks is (40,000 × $2.80) + (40,000 × $1.60), or simply 40,000 × $4.40 = $176,000, as shown in Exhibit 21-9.

Next consider the 10,000 masks still being shaped at the end of the month. These masks have 10,000 equivalent units of direct materials (at $2.80 per unit), so the direct material cost is 10,000 × $2.80 = $28,000. The 2,500 equivalent units of conversion work in the ending inventory at $1.60 per equivalent unit yields conversion costs of $4,000 (2,500 × $1.60). As Exhibit 21-9 shows, the total cost of the 10,000 partially completed masks in Shaping's ending (work in process) inventory is the sum of these direct material and conversion costs: $28,000 + $4,000 = $32,000.

Exhibit 21-9 has accomplished our goal of splitting the $208,000 total cost identified in step 3 (Exhibit 21-7) between

The 40,000 masks completed and transferred out to the Finishing Department...	$176,000
The 10,000 masks remaining in the Shaping Department's ending work in process inventory on October 31	32,000
Total costs of the Shaping Department	$208,000

RECORDING THE COSTS Journal entries to record October production in the Shaping Department follow (data from Exhibit 21-7):

Work in Process Inventory—Shaping	208,000	
Materials Inventory..		140,000
Manufacturing Wages		21,250
Manufacturing Overhead...		46,750
To requisition materials and assign labor and overhead cost to the Shaping Department.		

The entry to transfer the cost of the 40,000 completed masks out of the Shaping Department and into the Finishing Department is as follows (data from Exhibit 21-9):

Work in Process Inventory—Finishing	176,000	
Work in Process Inventory—Shaping......................		176,000

After these entries are posted, the Work in Process Inventory—Shaping account appears as follows:

WORK IN PROCESS INVENTORY—SHAPING

Balance, September 30	—	Transferred to Finishing	176,000
Direct materials	140,000		
Direct labor	21,250		
Manufacturing overhead	46,750		
Balance, October 31	32,000		

 DAILY EXERCISE 21-14

 **WORK IT OUT** What is the shaping cost per mask for each of the 40,000 masks completed and transferred out of the Shaping Department and into the Finishing Department? Why would SeaView's managers be interested in this information?

Answer: Shaping's cost per mask is $4.40—the $176,000 total Shaping Department cost assigned to the masks completed and transferred out (from Exhibit 21-9), divided by the total number of masks completed and transferred out of Shaping and into Finishing (40,000).

SeaView's managers would compare the cost per mask of the shaping process in October against the planned cost per mask to evaluate the efficiency of the Shaping Department's October operations. Also, the costs of the shaped masks will flow into the Finishing Department, and will become part of the total cost of the completed masks. Management can use the total cost of the masks to set selling prices and to determine which products are most profitable.

DECISION GUIDELINES

Process Costing—First Process (No Beginning Inventory)

DECISION	GUIDELINES
How do costs flow from Work in Process Inventory to Finished Goods Inventory?	Job costing → Costs flow from Work in Process Inventory directly to Finished Goods Inventory.
	Process costing → Costs flow from one Work in Process Inventory account to the next, until the last process. Costs flow from Work in Process Inventory of the last process into Finished Goods Inventory.
How many Work in Process Inventory accounts in a process costing system?	There is one Work In Process Inventory account for each separate manufacturing process.
How to account for partially complete goods?	Use equivalent units.
	If cost is incurred evenly throughout the production process:

$$\text{Equivalent units} = \text{Number of partially complete units} \times \text{Percentage of process completed}$$

DECISION	GUIDELINES
	If cost is added at a specific point in the production process:
	• If physical units have passed the point where cost is added → units are complete with respect to that cost, so equivalent units of that cost = physical units
	• If physical units have *not* passed the point where cost is added → units have not incurred any of that cost, so equivalent units of that cost = 0
Which costs require separate equivalent-unit computations?	Perform separate equivalent-unit computations for each input added at a different point in the production process. Often this requires separate computations for (1) direct materials, and (2) conversion costs.
How to compute the cost per equivalent unit?	Divide the cost by the number of equivalent units
How to split the costs of a process between • Units completed and transferred out?	Multiply the cost per equivalent unit by • Number of equivalent units of work in the physical units completed and transferred out
• Units in ending work in process inventory?	• Number of equivalent units of work in the ending work in process inventory
How to evaluate whether a manager controlled his department's costs?	If direct material and conversion cost per equivalent unit meets or beats target unit costs, the manager has controlled costs

MID-CHAPTER

SUMMARY PROBLEM

Use the five steps of process costing to identify the missing amounts X and Y in the following report prepared by Florida Tile Industries for May.

TILE-FORMING DEPARTMENT
Production Cost Report
Month Ended May 31, 20XX

	Physical Units	Total Costs
Beginning work in process, April 30	—	$ —
Started in production during May..	20,000	43,200*
Total to account for..	20,000	$43,200
Completed and transferred to Finishing Department during May.......................	16,000	$ X
Ending work in process, May 31 (25% complete as to direct materials, 55% complete as to conversion cost)...	4,000	Y
Total accounted for	20,000	$43,200

*Includes direct materials of $6,800 and conversion costs of $36,400

Solution

Step 1: Summarize the flow of physical units.

Step 2: Compute output in terms of equivalent units.

TILE-FORMING DEPARTMENT
Month Ended May 31, 20XX

	Step 1	Step 2 Equivalent Units	
Flow of Production	**Flow of Physical Units**	**Direct Materials**	**Conversion Costs**
Units to account for:			
Beginning work in process, April 30	—		
Started in production during May..	20,000		
Total physical units to account for	20,000		
Units accounted for:			
Completed and transferred out in May...	16,000	16,000	16,000
Ending work in process, May 31	4,000	1,000*	2,200*
Total physical units accounted for	20,000		
Equivalent units...		17,000	18,200

*Direct materials: 4,000 units each 25% complete = 1,000 equivalent units
Conversion costs: 4,000 units each 55% complete = 2,200 equivalent units

Step 3: Summarize total costs to account for.

TILE-FORMING DEPARTMENT
Month Ended May 31, 20XX

	Direct Materials	Conversion Costs	Total
Beginning work in process, April 30	$ 0	$ 0	$ 0
Costs added during May*...............................	6,800	36,400	43,200
Total cost to account for................................	$6,800	$36,400	$43,200

*From information in the Production Cost Report above.

Step 4: Compute the cost per equivalent unit.

TILE-FORMING DEPARTMENT
Month Ended May 31, 20XX

	Direct Materials	Conversion Costs
Beginning work in process, April 30	$ 0	$ 0
Costs added during May	$ 6,800	$36,400
Divide by equivalent units	÷17,000	÷18,200
Cost per equivalent unit	$0.40	$2.00

Step 5: Assign costs to units completed and to units in ending work in process inventory.

TILE-FORMING DEPARTMENT
Month Ended May 31, 20XX

	Direct Materials	Conversion Costs	Total
X: Units completed and transferred out (16,000)	[16,000 × ($0.40 + $2.00)]		= $38,400
Units in ending work in process inventory (4,000):			
Direct materials	[1,000 × $0.40]		= 400
Conversion costs		[2,200 × $2.00] =	4,400
Y: Total cost of ending work in process inventory			4,800
Total cost accounted for			$43,200

PROCESS COSTING FOR A SECOND DEPARTMENT

Most products require a series of processing steps. In this section, we introduce a second department—SeaView's Finishing Department—to complete the picture of process costing.

The Finishing Department receives the shaped masks, then smoothes and polishes them before inserting the faceplates at the end of the process. Thus,

- Shaped masks are transferred in from Shaping at the beginning of Finishing's process.
- Finishing's conversion costs are added evenly throughout the process.
- Finishing's direct materials (faceplates) are not added until the end of the finishing process.

Keep in mind that the label *direct materials* in the Finishing Department refers to the faceplates added *in that department* and not to the materials (the plastic) added in the Shaping Department. Likewise, *conversion cost* in the Finishing Department refers to all manufacturing costs (other than direct materials) incurred only in Finishing.

Don't confuse the Finishing Department with finished goods inventory. The Finishing Department is SeaView's second process. The masks do not become part of finished goods inventory until they have *completed* SeaView's second process, which in this case happens to be the Finishing Department.

As in many areas of accounting, there are alternative methods of accounting for process costs. We discuss two: the first-in, first-out (FIFO) method and the weighted-average method. *The FIFO and weighted-average methods differ only in their treatment of beginning work in process inventory.*

Because SeaView's Shaping Department (discussed in the first half of the chapter) had no beginning work in process inventory, we did not need to specify whether that department used the FIFO or weighted-average method. By contrast, SeaView's Finishing Department does have beginning work in process inventory. We now use the Finishing Department to illustrate the FIFO method. (The following section covers the weighted-average method.) Although the details of the FIFO and weighted average methods differ, both use the same basic five-step process costing procedure we used earlier in the chapter.

THE FIFO METHOD

The **first-in, first-out (FIFO) method** of process costing assigns to each period's equivalent units of production that period's costs per equivalent unit. ➡ Consider a batch of swim masks that were transferred out of the Shaping Department and into the Finishing Department at the end of September. These masks did not make it completely through the Finishing Department during September, so the masks are in the Finishing Department's ending (work in process) inventory at the end of September. The masks are not completed until October. Under the FIFO method, when these masks are completed in October, the total Finishing Department cost of these masks is the sum of

- September's equivalent units of Finishing's work on these masks, costed at September's cost per equivalent unit, *plus*
- October's equivalent units of Finishing's work on these masks, costed at October's cost per equivalent unit

Steps 1 and 2: Summarize the Flow of Physical Units and Compute Output in Terms of Equivalent Units

Exhibit 21-10 lists October information for SeaView's Finishing Department. Exhibit 21-11 diagrams these data on a time line to help you see what equivalent units of work the Finishing Department performed *during October*. This is important because under FIFO, the focus is on the current period—October in this example. The FIFO method determines October equivalent units of work and costs those units with October unit costs. The advantage of the FIFO method is that managers can use

Objective 5
Account for a second processing department by the FIFO method

 In Chapter 9, we saw that in the FIFO method of inventory costing, the first costs into Inventory are the first costs out to Cost of Goods Sold.

FIRST-IN, FIRST-OUT (FIFO) PROCESS COSTING METHOD. A process costing method that assigns to each period's equivalent units of production that period's costs per equivalent unit.

⊙ DAILY EXERCISE 21-15

EXHIBIT 21-10
SeaView's Finishing Department Data for October

Units:		
Beginning work in process, September 30		
(0% complete as to direct materials,		
60% complete as to conversion work)		5,000 units
Transferred in from Shaping Department		
during October		40,000 units
Completed and transferred out to Finished Goods		
Inventory during October		38,000 units
Ending work in process, October 31 (0% complete as		
to direct materials, 30% complete as to		
conversion work)		7,000 units
Costs:		
Beginning work in process, September 30		
(transferred-in costs, $22,900;		
conversion costs, $1,100)		$ 24,000
Transferred in from Shaping Department		
during October (from Exhibit 21-9)		176,000
Direct materials added during October in		
Finishing Department		19,000
Conversion costs added during October in		
Finishing Department:		
Direct labor	$ 3,710	
Manufacturing overhead	11,130	14,840

these current costs per unit to measure the efficiency of production during the month of October.

Exhibits 21-11 and 21-12 summarize the flow of physical units (step 1). The Finishing Department time line in Exhibit 21-11 is more complex than Shaping's time line in Exhibit 21-6. Why? Finishing has beginning work in process inventory (left over from the end of September), while Shaping does not. The 38,000 total masks that were completed and transferred out of the Finishing Department and into Finished Goods Inventory include

- 5,000 masks that were the Finishing Department's beginning work in process inventory. These masks were *completed* (but not started) in October.
- 33,000 masks that Finishing both *started* and *completed* during October. This number is computed as

38,000	masks completed and transferred out of the Finishing Department in October
(5,000)	masks completed from Finishing's beginning inventory
33,000	masks *started and completed during October*

The time line also shows that the 40,000 masks *transferred into* Finishing from Shaping during October (see Exhibits 21-5 and 21-6) also fall into two categories:

- 33,000 masks *started and completed* in the Finishing Department during October, plus
- 7,000 masks *started* in Finishing but not completed in October

Exhibit 21-12 uses the flow of physical units from step 1 and the time line diagram in Exhibit 21-11 to perform step 2—tabulating the Finishing Department's equivalent units of work performed in October. The Finishing Department has three categories of equivalent units. In addition to equivalent units for direct materials (faceplates) and conversion costs added in the Finishing Department, SeaView's

EXHIBIT 21-11   **SeaView's Finishing Department Time Line (FIFO)**

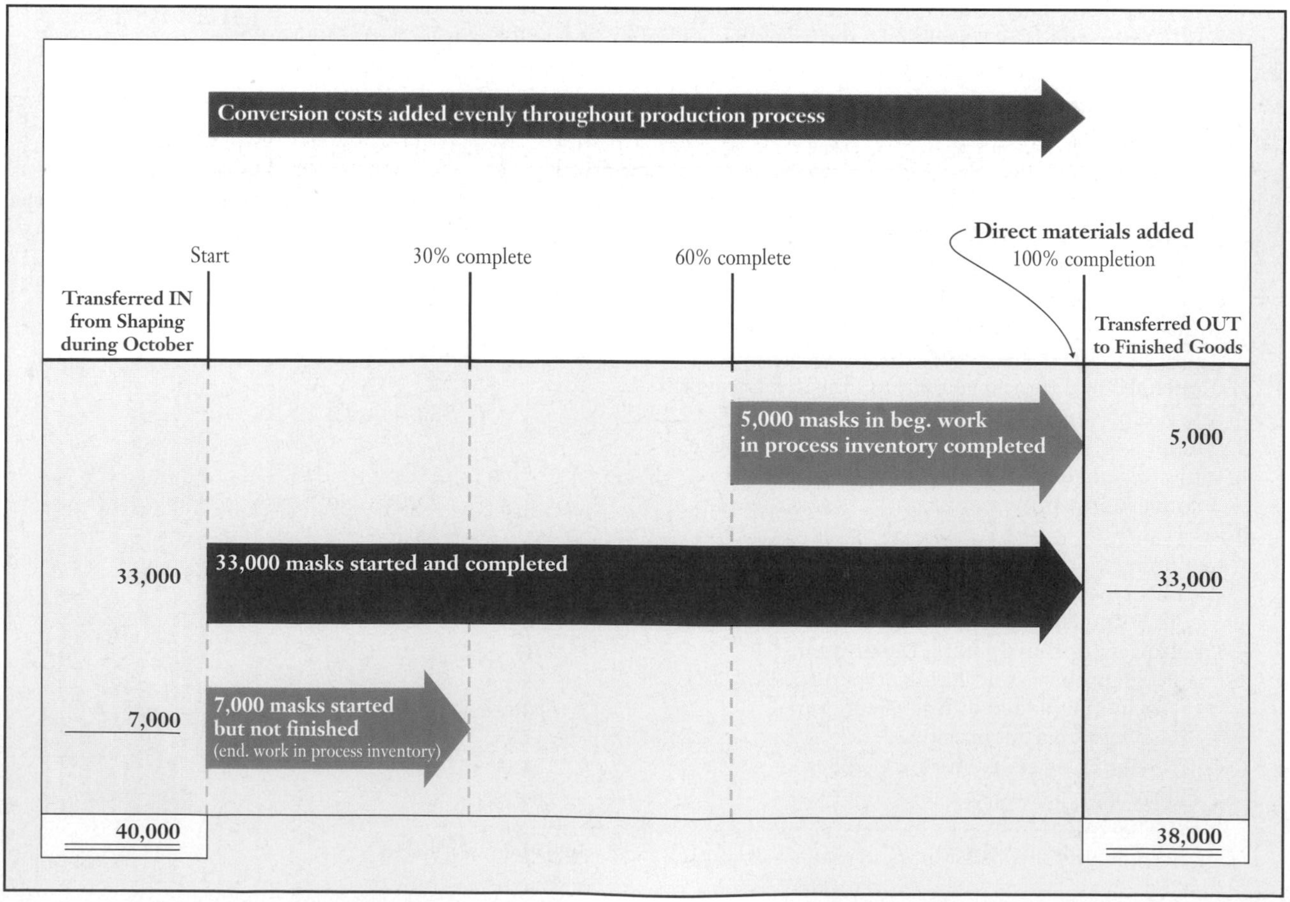

accountant must also compute equivalent units for the shaped swim masks that are *transferred in* from Shaping Department. All second and later departments in a production sequence have units (and costs) transferred in from preceding departments.

SeaView must figure out how many equivalent units of work the Finishing Department performed *during October*. SeaView's accountant looks at Exhibit 21-11 and adds the number of equivalent units of work performed to

- *Complete* the 5,000 masks in beginning inventory that were started in September,
- *Start and complete* an additional 33,000 masks, and
- *Start* (but not complete) the 7,000 masks that make up the department's work in process inventory at the end of October.

The accountant repeats these computations for each of the three categories of costs.

● DAILY EXERCISE 21-16

EQUIVALENT UNITS TRANSFERRED-IN   Let's begin with the Transferred In column of Exhibit 21-12. Keep in mind that our goal is to figure the number of equivalent units of work performed *during October.*

After the Shaping Department completes its work on the masks and transfers them out, the Finishing Department receives those units (and their accumulated costs) for final processing. Thus, transferred-in costs (from Shaping) act like costs that are added at the very beginning of the Finishing process. The time line in Exhibit 21-11 shows that the 5,000 units in Finishing's beginning inventory were *not* transferred in from Shaping *this* month. (Instead, these 5,000 units were transferred in from Shaping last month.) Consequently, beginning inventory has no transferred-in equivalent units *during October.*

Look at the time line again—it shows that the 33,000 masks the Finishing Department started and completed during October, and the 7,000 masks in Finishing's ending inventory, *were* transferred in during October. Exhibit 21-12 summarizes this equivalent-unit tabulation, showing that the total transferred-in equivalent units during October is 40,000 (33,000 + 7,000).

EXHIBIT 21-12   **FIFO, Step 1: Summarize the Flow of Physical Units; Step 2: Compute Output in Terms of Equivalent Units**

	Step 1	Step 2: Equivalent Units		
SEAVIEW FINISHING DEPARTMENT Month Ended October 31, 20XX				
Flow of Production	**Flow of Physical Units**	**Transferred In**	**Direct Materials**	**Conversion Costs**
Units to account for:				
Beginning work in process, September 30............	5,000			
Transferred in during October..............................	40,000			
Total physical units to account for	45,000			
Units accounted for:				
Completed and transferred out during October:				
From beginning work in process inventory	5,000	—	5,000*	2,000*
Started and completed during October (38,000 − 5,000)	33,000	33,000	33,000	33,000
Ending work in process, October 31	7,000	7,000	—†	2,100†
Total physical units accounted for........................	45,000			
Equivalent units		40,000	38,000	37,100

During October in the Finishing Department:
* Finish beginning inventory
    Direct materials: 5,000 units each 100% completed = 5,000 equivalent units
    Conversion costs: 5,000 units each 40% completed = 2,000 equivalent units
† Start ending inventory
    Direct materials: 7,000 units each 0% completed   = 0 equivalent units
    Conversion costs: 7,000 units each 30% completed = 2,100 equivalent units

EQUIVALENT UNITS OF DIRECT MATERIALS   Now let's turn to the direct materials added in the Finishing Department (faceplates). Direct materials are not added until the end of the finishing process, as shown in Exhibit 21-11. Exhibit 21-11 shows that during October, the 5,000 units in beginning inventory were completed, so they reached the end of the production process where the faceplates are added. The 33,000 units started and completed also reached the end of the process. However, the time line shows that the ending inventory does not yet have faceplates, so it has not incurred Finishing Department direct materials during October. Thus, Finishing added 5,000 + 33,000 = 38,000 equivalent units of materials (faceplates) during October, as shown in Exhibit 21-12.

EQUIVALENT UNITS OF CONVERSION COSTS   Finally, consider conversion costs. According to the time line, beginning inventory was 60% complete at the beginning of October. This means that during October, these 5,000 masks from the Finishing Department's beginning inventory went through the final 40% of the Finishing Department's process. This yields 5,000 × 0.40 = 2,000 equivalent units of conversion work during October. The 33,000 masks started and completed during October went through the entire Finishing Department process during October, so these units incurred 33,000 units of conversion work. Finally, the time line shows that the 7,000 masks in ending inventory that were *started* in Finishing during October made it 30% of the way through the process by October 31. The Finishing Department performed 7,000 × 0.30 = 2,100 equivalent units of conversion work on this ending inventory during October. Thus, the total conversion work performed in Finishing during October includes

2,000	units to *complete* the beginning inventory
33,000	units from masks started *and* completed during October
2,100	units to *start* the ending inventory
37,100	total equivalent units of conversion costs during October

The conversion costs column of step 2 in Exhibit 21-12 summarizes this calculation.

Steps 3 and 4: Summarize Total Costs to Account for and Compute the Cost per Equivalent Unit

Exhibit 21-13 accumulates the Finishing Department's October costs. The exhibit shows how to compute the cost per equivalent unit. The $24,000 beginning balance of work in process is kept separate from the costs incurred during the current period. That is, the $24,000 is not included in computing the cost per equivalent unit for

EXHIBIT 21-13   **FIFO, Steps 3 and 4: Summarize Total Costs to Account for and Compute the Cost per Equivalent Unit**

SEAVIEW FINISHING DEPARTMENT Month Ended October 31, 20XX				
	Transferred In	Direct Materials	Conversion Costs	Total
Beginning work in process, September 30 (from Exhibit 21-10)				$ 24,000
Costs added during October (from Exhibit 21-10)	$176,000	$ 19,000	$ 14,840	209,840
Divide by equivalent units (from Exhibit 21-12)	÷ 40,000	÷ 38,000	÷ 37,100	
Cost per equivalent unit	$4.40	$0.50	$0.40	
Total cost to account for				$233,840

work done in October because this $24,000 was incurred in *September* to start the 5,000 physical units still in process on October 1. Under FIFO, each *October* cost per equivalent unit is computed by dividing October costs by the number of equivalent units of work performed in October.

Exhibit 21-13 shows that the Finishing Department has transferred-in costs as well as direct material costs and conversion costs. **Transferred-in costs** are incurred in a previous process (the Shaping Department, in the SeaView example), and are carried forward as part of the product's cost when it moves to the next process. All second (and later) processes have transferred in costs from previous processes.

DAILY EXERCISE 21-17

TRANSFERRED-IN COSTS. Costs incurred in a previous process that are carried forward as part of the product's cost when it moves to the next process.

Step 5: Assign Costs to Units Completed and to Units in Ending Work in Process Inventory

Exhibit 21-14 shows how SeaView assigns the Finishing Department costs to

DAILY EXERCISE 21-18

- Units completed and transferred out to Finished Goods Inventory
- Units still in process in the Finishing Department's ending work in process inventory

The method illustrated in Exhibit 21-14 is identical to the approach used for the Shaping Department in Exhibit 21-9: Multiply the number of equivalent units from step 2 (Exhibit 21-12) by the cost per equivalent unit from step 4 (Exhibit 21-13).

Exhibit 21-14 shows that when computing the cost of masks completed and transferred out of Finishing, we must remember to include the costs of the beginning inventory:

- $24,000 of Finishing Department beginning inventory costs (incurred in September)
- $3,300 of costs to complete that beginning inventory in October [(5,000 equivalent units of materials added × $0.50) + (2,000 equivalent units of conversion costs added × $0.40)]

EXHIBIT 21-14 **FIFO, Step 5: Assign Costs to Units Completed and to Units in Ending Work in Process Inventory**

	Transferred In	Direct Materials	Conversion Costs	Total
SEAVIEW FINISHING DEPARTMENT Month Ended October 31, 20XX				
Units completed and transferred out to Finished Goods Inventory:				
From beginning work in process, September 30				$ 24,000
Costs added during October:				
Direct materials		[5,000 × $0.50]		2,500
Conversion costs....................................			[2,000 × $0.40]	800
Total completed from beginning inventory				27,300
Units started and completed during October	[33,000 × ($4.40 + $0.50 + $0.40)]			174,900
Total cost transferred out...............................				202,200
Ending work in process, October 31:				
Transferred-in costs	[7,000 × $4.40]			30,800
Direct materials...		—		—
Conversion costs..			[2,100 × $0.40]	840
Total ending work in process, October 31				31,640
Total cost accounted for				$233,840

The Finishing Department's journal entries are similar to those for the Shaping Department. First, recall the entry previously made to transfer the cost of shaped swim masks into the Finishing Department (page 850):

Work in Process Inventory—Finishing	176,000	
Work in Process Inventory—Shaping		176,000

The following entries record other Finishing Department activity during October (data from Exhibit 21-10):

Work in Process Inventory—Finishing	33,840	
Materials Inventory		19,000
Manufacturing Wages		3,710
Manufacturing Overhead		11,130

To requisition materials and assign conversion costs to the Finishing Department.

The entry to transfer the cost of completed units out of the Finishing Department and into Finished Goods Inventory is based on the dollar amount in Exhibit 21-14:

Finished Goods Inventory	202,200	
Work in Process Inventory—Finishing		202,200

⊙ **DAILY EXERCISE 21-19**

After posting, the key accounts appear as follows:

WORK IN PROCESS INVENTORY—SHAPING

(Exhibit 21-7)		(Exhibit 21-9)	
Balance, September 30	—	Transferred to Finishing	176,000
Direct materials	140,000		
Direct labor	21,250		
Manufacturing overhead	46,750		
Balance, October 31	32,000		

WORK IN PROCESS INVENTORY—FINISHING

(Exhibit 21-10)		(Exhibit 21-14)	
Balance, September 30	24,000	Transferred to Finished	
Transferred in from Shaping	176,000	Goods Inventory	202,200
Direct materials	19,000		
Direct labor	3,710		
Manufacturing overhead	11,130		
Balance, October 31	31,640		

FINISHED GOODS INVENTORY

Balance, September 30	—	
Transferred in from Finishing	202,000	

1. What is the average total cost per mask completed and transferred out of the Finishing Department into Finished Goods Inventory?
2. For what decisions would SeaView's managers use this cost per mask information?

Answers

1. The total costs of the masks completed and transferred out to Finished Goods Inventory is $202,200 (from Exhibit 21-14). Exhibit 21-11 shows that 38,000 masks were completed and transferred out. Thus, the average total cost per mask completed and

transferred out to Finished Goods Inventory is

$$\frac{\text{Total cost}}{\text{per mask}} = \frac{\$202,200}{38,000 \text{ masks}}$$

$$= \$5.3211 \text{ (rounded)}$$

2. SeaView's managers would use the $5.3211 cost per mask in
   • Setting the masks' sale price
   • Profitability analysis aimed at deciding which products to emphasize
   • Controlling costs and evaluating the efficiency of the production process
   • Assigning costs to Finished Goods Inventory for financial reporting

Production Cost Report

A **production cost report** summarizes a processing department's operations for the period. Exhibit 21-15 is a FIFO production cost report for SeaView's Finishing Department for October. The report combines Exhibits 21-13 and 21-14. It shows the beginning inventory, the cost transferred in during the month, and the costs added in the Finishing Department during the month. The report also shows the costs transferred out of the department, and the ending work in process inventory.

PRODUCTION COST REPORT. Summarizes a processing department's operations for a period.

How do managers use the production cost report? SeaView managers compare actual direct materials and conversion costs—particularly the equivalent unit costs in Exhibit 21-15—with expected amounts. If actual unit costs are too high, managers will investigate, with the goal of finding a way to reduce the costs. If costs are less than expected, employees may receive praise or even a bonus.

EXHIBIT 21-15 **FIFO Production Cost Report**

	Transferred In	Direct Materials	Conversion Costs	Total
SEAVIEW FINISHING DEPARTMENT Production Cost Report (FIFO Method) Month Ended October 31, 20XX				
Beginning work in process, September 30				$ 24,000
Costs added during October.............................	$176,000	$19,000	$14,840	209,840
Total cost to account for...................................				$233,840
Equivalent units...	÷40,000	÷38,000	÷37,100	
Cost per equivalent unit	$4.40	$0.50	$0.40	
Assignment of total costs:				
Units completed during October:				
From beginning work in process, September 30..				$ 24,000
Costs added during October	—	[5,000 × $0.50] = $2,500	[2,000 × $0.40] = $800	3,300
Total completed from beginning inventory...				27,300
Units started and completed during October		[33,000 × ($4.40 + $0.50 + $0.40)]		174,900
Total completed and transferred out				202,200
Ending work in process, October 31:				
Transferred-in costs	[7,000 × $4.40]			30,800
Direct materials		—		—
Conversion costs			[2,100 × $0.40]	840
Total ending work in process, October 31				31,640
Total cost accounted for				$233,840

861

Objective 6

Account for a second processing department by the weighted-average method

➡ Chapter 9, introduced the weighted-average method of inventory costing.

WEIGHTED-AVERAGE PROCESS COSTING METHOD. A process costing method that costs all equivalent units of work with a weighted average of that period's and the previous period's costs per equivalent unit.

THE WEIGHTED-AVERAGE METHOD

We now rework SeaView's Finishing Department example to demonstrate the second process costing method, weighted-average.

The FIFO method separately computes the cost per equivalent unit for each different month. The work performed in a particular month is then costed by that specific month's cost per equivalent unit. In contrast, the **weighted-average method** costs all equivalent units of work with a weighted average of that period's and the previous period's costs per equivalent unit. Exhibits 21-16 through 21-20 are the weighted-average equivalents of Exhibits 21-11 through 21-15. We apply the weighted-average method using the same five steps we used with FIFO.

Steps 1 and 2: Summarize the Flow of Physical Units and Compute Output in Terms of Equivalent Units

The weighted-average method is simpler than the FIFO method because it does not require us to separate the work and costs for beginning inventory versus units started and completed this period. Instead, all the units completed and transferred out—whether from beginning inventory or units started and completed this period—are treated identically. Each unit is assigned the same average cost per equivalent unit, using

- All costs incurred for the physical units in process this period, whether those costs were incurred this period or last
- All work performed on the physical units in process this period, whether that work was performed this period or last

Exhibit 21-16 shows the time line for SeaView's Finishing Department, using the weighted-average method. The weighted-average time line is simpler than the FIFO time line. The weighted-average method combines all 38,000 units completed

EXHIBIT 21-16   SeaView's Finishing Department Time Line (Weighted-Average)

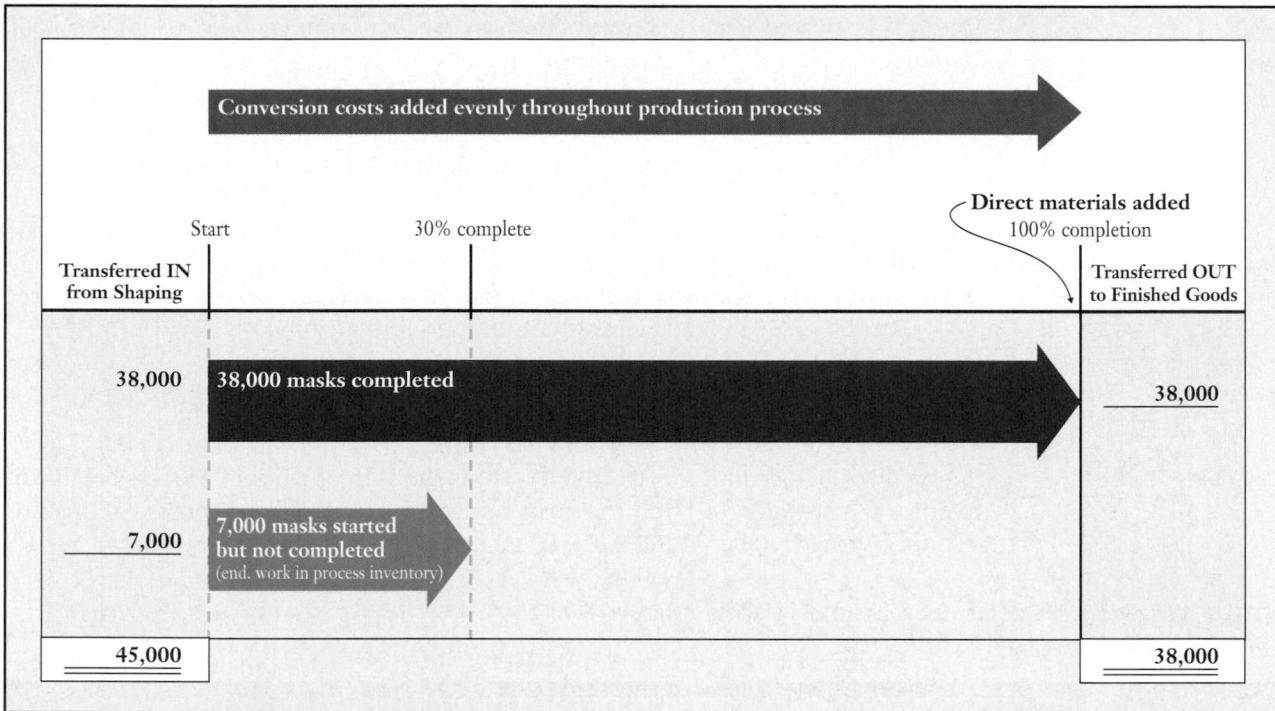

during October—whether those units are from the beginning work in process inventory, or are both started and completed in October.

Exhibits 21-10, 21-16, and 21-17 show that 38,000 masks were completed and transferred out of the Finishing Department in October (5,000 masks from beginning inventory were completed, and 33,000 masks were started and completed). The weighted-average method computes the equivalent units of all the work ever done on these units completed and transferred out—not just the work done this period. Because these 38,000 masks have been transferred to Finished Goods

◉ DAILY EXERCISE 21-20

EXHIBIT 21-17   Weighted-Average, Step 1: Summarize the Flow of Physical Units; Step 2: Compute Output in Terms of Equivalent Units

SEAVIEW FINISHING DEPARTMENT
Month Ended October 31, 20XX

	Step 1	Step 2: Equivalent Units		
Flow of Production	Flow of Physical Units	Transferred In	Direct Materials	Conversion Costs
Units to account for:				
Beginning work in process, September 30	5,000			
Transferred in during October	40,000			
Total physical units to account for	45,000			
Units accounted for:				
Completed and transferred out during October.......	38,000	38,000	38,000*	38,000*
Ending work in process, October 31	7,000	7,000	— †	2,100†
Total physical units accounted for...........................	45,000			
Equivalent units		45,000	38,000	40,100

In the Finishing Department:
* Units completed and transferred out
 Direct materials: 38,000 units each 100% completed = 38,000 equivalent units
 Conversion costs: 38,000 units each 100% completed = 38,000 equivalent units
† Start ending inventory
 Direct materials: 7,000 units each 0% completed   = 0 equivalent units
 Conversion costs: 7,000 units each 30% completed = 2,100 equivalent units

Inventory, they are complete with respect to transferred-in costs, direct materials, and conversion costs. Consequently, the masks have incurred 38,000 equivalent units of transferred-in costs, direct materials costs, and conversion costs, as shown in Exhibit 21-17.

The equivalent units for ending work in process inventory are the same under the weighted-average method as with FIFO. These 7,000 units

- have been transferred in from Shaping, so they have incurred 7,000 equivalent units of transferred-in costs
- have not reached the end of Finishing's process where faceplates are inserted; thus, they have no equivalent units of Finishing Department direct materials
- are 30% of the way through Finishing's process, so they have incurred $7,000 \times 0.30 = 2,100$ equivalent units of conversion costs

Steps 3 and 4: Summarize Total Costs to Account for and Compute the Cost per Equivalent Unit

○ DAILY EXERCISE 21-21

The total cost to account for (Exhibit 21-18) is the sum of work in process beginning inventory cost ($24,000) and the costs added to the Work in Process—Finishing account during October ($209,840). (Data are taken from Exhibit 21-10.)

EXHIBIT 21-18 **Weighted-Average, Step 3: Summarize Total Costs to Account For; Step 4: Compute the Cost per Equivalent Unit**

	Transferred In	Direct Materials	Conversion Costs	Total
SEAVIEW FINISHING DEPARTMENT				
Month Ended October 31, 20XX				
Beginning work in process, September 30 (from Exhibit 21-10)	$ 22,900	$ —	$ 1,100	$ 24,000
Costs added during October (from Exhibit 21-10)	176,000	19,000	14,840	209,840
Total cost	$198,900	$19,000	$15,940	
Divide by equivalent units (from Exhibit 21-17)	÷ 45,000	÷38,000	÷40,100	
Cost per equivalent unit	$4.42	$0.50	$0.3975	
Total cost to account for				$233,840

In the weighted-average method, step 2 computes the equivalent units of all the work ever done on the units in process this period, including work done last period to start the beginning inventory. To find the weighted-average cost per equivalent unit, we match these units with all the costs ever incurred for the units in process this period. This includes costs incurred last period to start the beginning work in process inventory, as well as costs incurred in the current period (October).

Exhibit 21-18 shows the weighted-average cost per equivalent unit for SeaView's Finishing Department. Consider conversion costs first. The Finishing Department incurred $1,100 of conversion costs in September to get the 5,000 masks in beginning inventory 60% of the way through the production process by the end of September. This $1,100 is added to the $14,840 total Finishing Department conversion cost incurred in October. We divide the sum, $15,940, by the total number of (weighted-average) equivalent units, 40,100, to obtain a weighted-average conversion cost per equivalent unit of $0.3975 (rounded). The transferred-in cost per equivalent unit and the direct materials cost per equivalent unit are computed in the same way.

○ DAILY EXERCISE 21-22

○ DAILY EXERCISE 21-23

Step 5: Assign Total Cost to Units Completed and to Units in Ending Work in Process Inventory

With the weighted-average method, the 38,000 physical units completed and transferred out of SeaView's Finishing Department are costed in one step. The 38,000 equivalent units are multiplied by the full equivalent-unit cost of $5.3175 ($4.42 +

$0.50 + \$0.3975$). The result is $202,065 (Exhibit 21-19). Equivalent units in the ending work in process inventory are also costed at the appropriate unit amounts.

EXHIBIT 21-19 **Weighted Average, Step 5: Assign Total Cost to Units Completed and to Units in Ending Work in Process Inventory**

	Transferred In	Direct Materials	Conversion Costs	Total
SEAVIEW FINISHING DEPARTMENT				
Month Ended October 31, 20XX				
Units completed and transferred out to Finished Goods Inventory..................................	[38,000 × ($4.42 + $0.50 + $0.3975)]			202,065
Ending work in process, October 31:				
Transferred in costs...	[7,000 × $4.42]			30,940
Direct materials		—		—
Conversion costs			[2,100 × $0.3975]	835*
Total ending work in process, October 31..........				31,775
Total cost accounted for...				$233,840

*Rounded.

The weighted-average production cost report in Exhibit 21-20 is similar to its FIFO counterpart, Exhibit 21-15. The weighted-average report may signal the need for action if actual unit costs or production quantities differ materially from planned amounts. But weighted-average costs per equivalent unit are not as useful for evaluating the efficiency of October production because they are affected by costs incurred in September. Even so, managers may use the weighted-average method because (1) the computations are simpler than those of the FIFO method, and (2) the difference between FIFO and weighted-average results is often insignificant.

 DAILY EXERCISE 21-24

EXHIBIT 21-20 **Weighted Average, Production Cost Report**

	Transferred In	Direct Materials	Conversion Costs	Total
SEAVIEW FINISHING DEPARTMENT				
Production Cost Report (Weighted Average Method)				
Month Ended October 31, 20XX				
Beginning work in process, September 30	$ 22,900	$ —	$ 1,100	$ 24,000
Costs added during October	176,000	19,000	14,840	209,840
Total cost to account for	$198,900	$ 19,000	$15,940	$233,840
Equivalent units	÷ 45,000	÷38,000	÷40,100	
Cost per equivalent unit	$4.42	$0.50	$0.3975	
Assignment of total costs:				
Units completed during October	[38,000 × ($4.42 + $0.50 + $0.3975)]			$202,065
Ending work in process, October 31:				
Transferred-in costs..	[7,000 × $4.42]			30,940
Direct materials...		—		—
Conversion costs			[2,100 × $0.3975]	835*
Total ending work in process, October 31..........				31,775
Total cost accounted for...				$233,840

*Rounded.

When will FIFO and weighted average give different results?

Answer: FIFO and weighted average give different results when

- There is beginning inventory. If there is no beginning inventory, FIFO and weighted average yield identical results. This is why we did not need to specify whether SeaView's Shaping Department used FIFO or weighted average—shaping had no beginning inventory.
- The cost per unit changes from one period to the next. If the cost per unit in the current period is the same as in the prior period, then FIFO and weighted average yield identical results.

FIFO and weighted average yield significantly different results only when there are large beginning inventories *and* costs change dramatically from one period to the next. This could happen, for example, in the wine-making industry, where there are significant work in process inventories, and where the cost of grapes fluctuates depending on weather and other crop conditions.

The following Decision Guidelines review key issues arising in process costing systems with multiple processes and beginning work in process inventories.

DECISION GUIDELINES

Process Costing—Second Process (with Beginning Inventory)

DECISION	GUIDELINES
At what point in a second process are transferred-in costs incurred?	Transferred in costs are typically incurred at the *beginning* of the second (or subsequent) process.
When do FIFO and weighted-average methods of process costing yield different results?	When there is beginning work in process inventory and cost per unit changes from one period to the next.
Which periods' costs are included in the cost per equivalent unit computation?	• *FIFO* → Only costs incurred in current period
	• *Weighted average* → Cost of work done in prior period to start the beginning inventory, plus all costs incurred in the current period
How to compute equivalent units using	
• FIFO method?	*FIFO* equivalent units of work done in current period equals work done to
	• *Complete* beginning inventory, plus
	• *Start* and *complete* additional units, plus
	• *Start* ending inventory
• Weighted-average method?	*Weighted-average* equivalent units of all work done on units in process equals
	• All work ever done on units completed and transferred out this period (whether work was done this period or last period), plus
	• Work done to *start* the ending inventory

REVIEW PROCESS COSTING

SUMMARY PROBLEM

This problem extends the Mid-Chapter Summary problem to a second department. During May, Florida Tile Industries reports the following in its Finishing Department:

Finishing Department Data for May

Units:	
Beginning work in process, April 30 (20% complete as to	
direct materials, 70% complete as to conversion work)	4,000 units
Transferred in from Tile-Forming Department during May	16,000 units
Completed and transferred out to Finished Goods Inventory	
during May	15,000 units
Ending work in process, May 31 (36% complete as to direct materials,	
80% complete as to conversion work)	5,000 units
Costs:	
Work in process, April 30 (transferred-in costs, $11,982;	
direct materials costs, $488; conversion costs, $5,530)	$18,000
Transferred in from Tile-Forming Department during May	
(from page 854)	38,400
Direct materials added during May	6,400
Conversion costs added during May	24,300

Required

Assign total cost to units completed and to units in ending work in process inventory for the Finishing Department in May, using
1. The FIFO method
2. The weighted-average method

Solution

Requirement 1

Steps 1 and 2: Summarize the flow of physical units; compute output in terms of equivalent units.

FINISHING DEPARTMENT (FIFO)
Month Ended May 31, 20XX

	Step 1	Step 2: Equivalent Units		
Flow of Production	**Flow of Physical Units**	**Transferred In**	**Direct Materials**	**Conversion Costs**
Units to account for:				
Beginning work in process, April 30	4,000			
Transferred in from Tile-Forming during May	16,000			
Total physical units to account for	20,000			
Units accounted for:				
Completed and transferred out during May:				
From beginning inventory	4,000	—	3,200*	1,200*
Started and completed during May				
(15,000 − 4,000)	11,000	11,000	11,000	11,000
Ending work in process, May 31	5,000	5,000	1,800†	4,000†
Total physical units accounted for	20,000			
Equivalent units		16,000	16,000	16,200

During May in the Finishing Department:
* Finish beginning inventory

        Direct materials: 4,000 units each 80% completed in May = 3,200 equivalent units.

        Conversion costs: 4,000 units each 30% completed in May = 1,200 equivalent units.

† Start ending inventory

        Direct materials: 5,000 units each 36% completed in May = 1,800 equivalent units.

        Conversion costs: 5,000 units each 80% completed in May = 4,000 equivalent units.

Steps 3 and 4: Summarize total costs to account for; compute the cost per equivalent unit.

FINISHING DEPARTMENT (FIFO)
Month Ended May 31, 20XX

	Transferred In	Direct Materials	Conversion Costs	Total
Beginning work in process, April 30				$18,000
Costs added during May	$ 38,400	$ 6,400	$ 24,300	69,100
Divide by equivalent units	÷16,000	÷16,000	÷ 16,200	
Cost per equivalent unit	$2.40	$0.40	$1.50	
Total cost to account for				$87,100

Step 5: Assign costs to units completed and to units in ending work in process inventory.

FINISHING DEPARTMENT (FIFO)
Month Ended May 31, 20XX

	Transferred In	Direct Materials	Conversion Costs	Total
Units completed and transferred out to Finished Goods Inventory:				
From beginning work in process, April 30				$18,000
Costs added during May:				
Direct materials		[3,200 × $0.40]		1,280
Conversion costs			[1,200 × $1.50]	1,800
Total completed from beginning inventory				21,080
Units started and completed during May	[11,000 × ($2.40 + $0.40 + $1.50)]			47,300
Total cost transferred out				68,380
Ending work in process, May 31:				
Transferred-in costs	[5,000 × $2.40]			12,000
Direct materials		[1,800 × $0.40]		720
Conversion costs			[4,000 × $1.50]	6,000
Total ending work in process, May 31				18,720
Total cost accounted for				$87,100

Requirement 2

Steps 1 and 2: Summarize the flow of physical units; compute output in terms of equivalent units.

FINISHING DEPARTMENT (Weighted Average)
Month Ended May 31, 20XX

	Step 1	Step 2: Equivalent Units		
Flow of Production	Flow of Physical Units	Transferred In	Direct Materials	Conversion Costs
Units to account for:				
Beginning work in process, April 30	4,000			
Transferred in from Tile-Forming during May	16,000			
Total physical units to account for	20,000			
Units accounted for:				
Completed and transferred out during May	15,000	15,000	15,000	15,000
Ending work in process, May 31	5,000	5,000	1,800*	4,000*
Total physical units accounted for	20,000			
Equivalent units		20,000	16,800	19,000

* Finish beginning inventory
   Direct materials: 5,000 units each 36% completed = 1,800 equivalent units
   Conversion costs: 5,000 units each 80% completed = 4,000 equivalent units

Steps 3 and 4: Summarize total costs to account for; compute the cost per equivalent unit.

FINISHING DEPARTMENT (Weighted Average)
Month Ended May 31, 20XX

	Transferred In	Direct Materials	Conversion Costs	Total
Beginning work in process, April 30	$11,982	$ 488	$ 5,530	$18,000
Costs added during May	38,400	6,400	24,300	69,100
Total cost	$50,382	$ 6,888	$29,830	
Divide by equivalent units	÷20,000	÷16,800	÷19,000	
Cost per equivalent unit	$2.5191	$0.41	$1.57	
Total cost to account for				$87,100

Step 5: Assign costs to units completed and to units in ending work in process inventory.

FINISHING DEPARTMENT (Weighted Average)
Month Ended May 31, 20XX

	Transferred In	Direct Materials	Conversion Costs	Total
Units completed and transferred out to Finished Goods Inventory:	[15,000 × ($2.5191 + $0.41 + $1.57)]			$67,486*
Ending work in process, May 31:				
Transferred-in costs	[5,000 × $2.5191]			12,596*
Direct materials		[1,800 × $0.41]		738
Conversion costs			[4,000 × $1.57]	6,280
Total ending work in process, May 31				19,614
Total cost accounted for				$87,100

* Rounded.

LESSONS LEARNED

1. **Distinguish between the flow of costs in process costing and job costing.** In process costing systems, costs are accumulated by processing departments and flow from one department to the next until the product is completed. In contrast, job cost systems accumulate costs for each individual job using job cost records, and the cost of a completed job flows directly to finished goods inventory.

2. **Record process costing transactions.** Journal entries in a process costing system are like those in a job cost system, with one key exception: A job cost system typically uses one Work in Process Inventory account, but a process costing system uses a separate account for each processing department. As goods move from one department to the next, the Work in Process Inventory account of the receiving department is debited and the account of the transferring department is credited. After processing is completed, the cost of the goods moves with them into Finished Goods Inventory.

3. **Compute equivalent units.** Because goods in process may be in various stages of completion, we compute *equivalent units*—the amount of work expressed in terms of fully completed units of output. Equivalent units are computed for each input that is added at a different point in the production process.

4. **Assign costs to units completed and to units in ending work in process inventory.** Accounting for a department's costs is a five-step procedure. First, the flow of physical (output) units is determined. Second, we compute equivalent units. Third, the total cost to account for is determined. Fourth, costs per equivalent unit are computed for each input that is added at a different point in the production process. Fifth, physical units are costed by multiplying equivalent units from step 2 by equivalent-unit costs from step 4.

5. **Account for a second processing department by the FIFO method.** FIFO matches equivalent units of work done in the current period with costs incurred in the current period. Equivalent units of work performed in the current month are costed at current-month unit costs. Managers compare the actual costs with planned costs to evaluate the efficiency of production.

6. **Account for a second processing department by the weighted-average method.** The *weighted-average method* costs all work to account for each month—work in process at the beginning of the month and the current month's work—with unit costs that are a weighted average of current- and prior-month costs. In contrast to FIFO, the weighted-average method computes the equivalent units of all work ever performed on units in process—whether this work was done in the current or the prior period—to obtain a weighted-average cost per equivalent unit.

ACCOUNTING VOCABULARY

conversion costs   (p. 845)
equivalent units   (p. 845)
first-in, first-out (FIFO) process
   costing method   (p. 855)

production cost report   (p. 861)
transferred-in costs   (p. 859)

weighted-average process costing
   method   (p. 862)

QUESTIONS

1. Distinguish a process costing system from a job cost system.
2. Give the type of costing system—job or process—that is better suited to account for the following products: (a) chemicals, (b) textbooks, (c) lumber, (d) specialty machinery, (e) custom lampshades.
3. Why does a process costing system use multiple Work in Process Inventory accounts but a job costing system uses only one such account?
4. Give the entries (accounts only) to record the following: (a) purchase of materials on account; (b) incurrence of labor; (c) incurrence of manufacturing overhead cost; (d) requisition of materials and assignment of labor and overhead to Work in Process Inventory—Department 1 (combine in one entry); (e) transfer of cost of work in process inventory from Department 1 to Department 2; (f) transfer of cost of completed units to finished goods; (g) cost of goods sold.
5. What is an equivalent unit? Give an example of equivalent units.
6. **Georgia-Pacific** completed and transferred 35,000 units of its product to a second department during the period. At the end of the period, another 10,000 units were in the first department's work in process inventory, 20%

complete. How many equivalent units did the first department produce during the period?
7. How are equivalent units used in Exhibits 21-8 and 21-9?
8. Why might a company have different numbers of equivalent units for direct materials and conversion costs?
9. What information does a production cost report give?
10. Using the FIFO method, compute the equivalent units for Department 2 during July:

Work in process, June 30
   (10% complete as to direct materials,
   40% complete as to conversion costs) ..   1,000 units
Transferred in from Department 1
   during July ....   25,000 units
Completed during July ....   22,000 units
Work in process, July 31
   (20% complete as to direct materials,
   70% complete as to conversion costs)...   4,000 units

11. Repeat Question 10, using the weighted-average method.
12. Under what conditions are FIFO equivalent-unit costs equal to weighted-average equivalent-unit costs?
13. "Unit costs in process costing are averages, but this is not true in job costing." Do you agree or disagree? Explain.

ASSESS YOUR PROGRESS

DAILY EXERCISES

Distinguishing between the flow of costs in job costing and process costing   (Obj. 1)

DE21-1 Use Exhibit 21-1 to help you describe, in your own words, the major difference in the flow of costs between a job costing system and a process costing system.

Flow of costs in process costing (Obj. 1)

DE21-2 Consider the SeaView example on pages 847–866. Diagram the flow of costs for the Shaping and Finishing Departments' production of swim masks, similar to Exhibit 21-2.

Flow of costs in process costing (Obj. 1)

DE21-3 In Exhibit 21-3 (page 844), suppose direct materials added in the chopping process are $20 rather than $7 (keep all amounts in thousands as in the exhibit). Assume that direct labor and manufacturing overhead amounts remain the same, as do each of the ending inventory balances.

1. Show the revised flow of costs through the Work in Process Inventory—Chopping; Work in Process Inventory—Mixing & Bottling; Finished Goods Inventory; and Cost of Goods Sold T-accounts.
2. How much are the following?
   a. Cost of goods completed and transferred out of the Chopping Department and into the Mixing & Bottling Department.
   b. Cost of goods completed and transferred out of the Mixing & Bottling Department and into Finished Goods Inventory.
   c. Cost of goods sold.

Process costing journal entries (Obj. 2)

DE21-4 Refer to your answer to Daily Exercise 21-3. Record the journal entries for the following:

1. The use of $20 rather than $7 of direct materials in the chopping process.
2. Cost of goods completed and transferred out of the Chopping Department and into the Mixing & Bottling Department.

3. Cost of goods completed and transferred out of the Mixing & Bottling Department and into Finished Goods Inventory.
4. Cost of goods sold.

DE21-5 Polar Spring produces premium bottled water. Polar Spring purchases artesian water, stores the water in large tanks, and then runs the water through two processes:

Flow of costs in process costing, cost per equivalent unit (Obj. 1, 3)

- Filtration, where workers microfilter and ozonate the water
- Bottling, where workers bottle and package the filtered water

During February, the filtration process incurs the following costs in processing 100,000 liters:

Wages of workers operating the filtration equipment	$ 5,550
Manufacturing overhead allocated to filtration	12,025
Water	50,000
Wages of workers operating ozonation equipment	6,425

Polar Spring has no beginning inventories.

1. Compute the February conversion costs in the Filtration Department.
2. If the Filtration Department completely processed 100,000 liters, what is the *total* filtration cost per liter?
3. Now assume that 80,000 liters are completely filtered and ozonated, while the remaining 20,000 are only part way through the process at the end of February. Is the cost per completely filtered and ozonated liter higher, lower, or the same as in requirement 2? Why?

DE21-6 Record the journal entries for the *use* of direct materials and direct labor, and for the allocation of manufacturing overhead to Polar Spring's filtration process, described in Daily Exercise 21-5.

Process costing journal entries (Obj. 2)

DE21-7 Colleges and universities use the equivalent-unit concept to describe the number of faculty as well as the number of students. The **University of Georgia** has about 2,000 full-time faculty and 400 part-time faculty. Assume the following:

Computing equivalent units (Obj. 3)

- A full-time faculty member teaches six courses per year
- 100 part-time faculty teach three courses per year
- 300 part-time faculty teach two courses per year

What is the "full-time equivalent" faculty—the number of equivalent units of faculty?

DE21-8 Refer to Daily Exercise 21-5. At Polar Spring, water is added at the beginning of the filtration process. Conversion costs are added evenly throughout the process, and in February 80,000 liters have been completed and transferred out of the Filtration Department, and into the Bottling Department. The 20,000 units remaining in Filtration's ending work in process inventory are 80% of the way through the filtration process. Recall that Polar Spring has no beginning inventories.

Drawing a time line, computing equivalent units (Obj. 3)

1. Draw a time line for the filtration process, similar to the one in Exhibit 21-6.
2. Compute the equivalent units of direct materials and conversion costs for the Filtration Department. (Refer to Exhibit 21-5 if necessary.)

DE21-9 Look at SeaView Shaping Department's equivalent-unit computation in Exhibit 21-5. Suppose the ending work in process inventory is 40% of the way through the shaping process, rather than 25% of the way through. Compute the equivalent units of direct materials and conversion costs.

Computing equivalent units (Obj. 3)

DE21-10 Consider the original SeaView Shaping Department equivalent-unit computations in Exhibit 21-5. Suppose plastic and chemicals are added at the beginning of the shaping process, and another direct material—a hardening agent—is added 75% of the way through the shaping process. SeaView needs to compute the equivalent units separately for each input that is added at a different point in the production process. This means that SeaView needs a separate computation of equivalent units for the hardening agent.

Drawing a time line, computing equivalent units (Obj. 3)

1. Draw a time line of the Shaping Department process showing where the different materials are added, similar to the one in Exhibit 21-6.
2. How many equivalent units of the hardening agent are incurred in the Shaping Department during October?

DE21-11 Return to the original SeaView example. Suppose direct labor is $38,250 rather than $21,250. Now what is the conversion cost per equivalent unit? (Use Exhibit 21-8 to format your answer.)

DE21-12 Return to Polar Spring's Filtration Department described in Daily Exercises 21-5 and 21-8. Using your answers to those exercises, compute the cost per equivalent unit for direct materials and for conversion costs in the Filtration Department. (Recall that there were no beginning inventories.)

DE21-13 Return to Polar Spring's Filtration Department. Use the information in Daily Exercises 21-5, 21-8, and 21-12 to fulfill the following requirements:

1. What is the cost of the 80,000 liters completed and transferred out of Polar Spring's Filtration Department?
2. What is the cost of the 20,000 liters remaining in Filtration's ending work in process inventory?

DE21-14 Use the information in Daily Exercises 21-5 and 21-13 to

1. Record the journal entry to transfer the cost of the 80,000 liters completed and transferred out of Filtration and into the Bottling Department.
2. Record all the transactions in the Work in Process Inventory—Filtration T-account. (*Hint:* Use SeaView's Work in Process Inventory—Shaping T-account on page 851 as a guide.)

DE21-15 Polar Spring produces premium bottled water. Preceding daily exercises considered Polar Spring's first process—filtration. We now consider Polar Spring's second process—bottling. In the Bottling Department, workers bottle the filtered water and pack the bottles into boxes. Conversion costs are incurred evenly throughout the bottling process, but packaging materials are not added until the end of the process.

February data from the Bottling Department follow:

Beginning work in process inventory	
(40% of the way through the process)	4,000 liters
Transferred in from Filtration*	80,000 liters
Completed and transferred out to Finished Goods	
Inventory in February..	77,000 liters
Ending work in process inventory	
(70% of the way through the bottling process).................	7,000 liters

Costs in beginning work in process inventory:		Costs added during February:	
Transferred in	$480	Transferred in*.................	$ 60,000
Direct materials	0	Direct materials	15,400
Direct labor.............................	250	Direct labor.......................	16,863
Manufacturing overhead.........	150	Manufacturing overhead..	11,242
Total beginning work in process inventory as of February 1	$880	Total costs added during February	$103,505

* Daily Exercise 21-13 showed that Polar Spring's Filtration Department completed and transferred out 80,000 liters at a total cost of $60,000.

Draw a time line for Polar Spring's Bottling Department, similar to the one in Exhibit 21-11, assuming that Polar Spring uses FIFO.

DE21-16 Use the time line you developed in Daily Exercise 21-15 to help you compute the Bottling Department's equivalent units, using the FIFO method.

DE21-17 Consider Polar Spring's Bottling Department, as described in Daily Exercise 21-15. Compute the cost per equivalent unit, using FIFO.

DE21-18 Use the information about Polar Spring's Bottling Department in Daily Exercises 21-15 through 21-17 to assign the costs to units completed and transferred out, and to ending inventory, under FIFO.

DE21-19 Refer to Polar Spring's Bottling Department and the computations you made in Daily Exercises 21-15 through 21-18.

Journal entry; T-account; second department; FIFO (Obj. 1, 2, 5)

1. Prepare the journal entry to record the cost of units completed and transferred out, using FIFO.
2. Post all transactions from Daily Exercises 21-15 through 21-18 to the Work in Process Inventory—Bottling Department T-account. What is the ending balance?

DE21-20 Using the data from Polar Spring's Bottling Department from Daily Exercise 21-15:

Drawing a time line; computing equivalent units; second department; weighted-average method (Obj. 1, 6)

1. Draw a time line similar to the one in Exhibit 21-16, using the weighted-average method.
2. Use the time line to help you compute the Bottling Department equivalent units, using the weighted-average method.

DE21-21 Using data from Polar Spring's Bottling Department in Daily Exercise 21-15 and the equivalent units computed in Daily Exercise 21-20, compute the cost per equivalent unit, using the weighted-average method.

Cost per equivalent unit; second department; weighted-average (Obj. 6)

DE21-22 Use the information on Polar Spring's Bottling Department in Daily Exercise 21-15, and the equivalent units and cost per equivalent unit you computed in Daily Exercises 21-20 and 21-21, to assign the costs to units completed and transferred out, and to ending inventory, using the weighted-average method. (*Hint:* The conversion cost per unit does not work out to an even number. Carry your computation to at least three decimal places. Should you have a "rounding error" of less than $10 in your "Total costs accounted for," assign the rounding error to the cost of units completed and transferred out.)

Assigning costs to units completed and ending inventory; second department; weighted-average method (Obj. 6)

DE21-23 Using data from Polar Spring's Bottling Department in Daily Exercise 21-15 and the cost assignments in Daily Exercise 21-22:

Journal entry, T-account; second department; weighted-average method (Obj. 1, 2, 6)

1. Prepare the journal entry to record the cost of units completed and transferred out under the weighted-average method.
2. Post all transactions from Daily Exercises 21-15 and 21-22 to the Work in Process Inventory—Bottling Department T-account. What is the ending balance?

DE21-24 ◂ *Link Back to Chapter 9 (Difference Between FIFO and Weighted Average).* For Polar Spring's Bottling Department, use your answers to Daily Exercise 21-18 and Daily Exercise 21-22 to compare the cost of the units completed and transferred out under FIFO to that under weighted-average. Compare the cost of the Bottling Department's ending work in process inventory under FIFO to that under weighted average. Did the Bottling Department cost per unit increase or decrease in February? How do you know?

Comparing FIFO and weighted-average results; second department (Obj. 5, 6)

EXERCISES

E21-1 Chesnut Furniture produces oak furniture in a three-stage process that includes milling, assembling, and finishing, in that order. Direct materials are added in the Milling and Finishing Departments. Direct labor and overhead are incurred in all three departments. The company's general ledger includes the following accounts:

Diagramming flows through a process costing system (Obj. 1)

Cost of Goods Sold	Work in Process Inventory—Finishing
Manufacturing Wages	Materials Inventory
Work in Process Inventory—Milling	Finished Goods Inventory
Work in Process Inventory—Assembling	Manufacturing Overhead

Outline the flow of costs through the company's accounts. Include a T-account for each account title given.

E21-2 Record the following process costing transactions in the general journal:

Journalizing process costing transactions (Obj. 2)

a. Purchase of raw materials on account, $8,400
b. Requisition of direct materials to
   Assembly Department, $3,800
   Finishing Department, $2,000
c. Incurrence and payment of manufacturing labor, $10,800.
d. Incurrence of manufacturing overhead costs:
   Property taxes—plant, $1,900
   Utilities—plant, $4,500
   Insurance—plant, $1,100
   Depreciation—plant, $3,400
e. Assignment of conversion costs to the Assembly Department:
   Direct labor, $4,700
   Manufacturing overhead, $2,900

f. Assignment of conversion costs to the Finishing Department:
Direct labor, $4,400
Manufacturing overhead, $6,200

g. Cost of goods completed and transferred out of Assembly and into Finishing, $10,250.

h. Cost of goods completed and transferred out of the Finishing Department into Finished Goods Inventory, $15,600.

Drawing a time line; computing equivalent units and assigning cost to completed units and ending work in process; no beginning inventory or cost transferred in (Obj. 3, 4)

E21-3 Apple Acres prepares and packages fruit juice products. Apple Acres has two departments: (1) Blending and (2) Packaging. Direct materials are added at the beginning of the blending process (raw fruit juice) and at the end of the packaging process (cartons). Conversion costs are added evenly throughout each process. Data from the month of May for the Blending Department are as follows:

Gallons:	
Beginning work in process inventory............................	0
Started production	6,000 gallons
Completed and transferred out to Packaging in May	4,500 gallons
Ending work in process inventory (30% of the way through the blending process)	1,500 gallons
Costs:	
Beginning work in process inventory............................	$ 0
Costs added during May:	
Direct materials (raw fruit juice).................................	3,600
Direct labor..	500
Manufacturing overhead...	985
Total costs added during May	$5,085

Required

1. Draw a time line for the Blending Department, similar to Exhibit 21-6.
2. Use the time line to help you compute the equivalent units for direct materials and for conversion costs.
3. Compute the total costs of the units (gallons)
   a. Completed and transferred out to the Packaging Department
   b. In the Blending Department ending work in process inventory

Journal entries, work in process T-account (Obj. 1, 2, 4)

E21-4 Return to the Blending Department for Apple Acres in Exercise 21-3.

Required

1. Present the journal entries to record the use of direct materials and direct labor, and the allocation of manufacturing overhead to the Blending Department. Also, give the journal entry to record the costs of the gallons completed and transferred out to the Packaging Department.
2. Post the journal entries to the Work in Process Inventory—Blending T-account. What is the ending balance?
3. What is the average cost per gallon transferred out of Blending and into Packaging? Why would Apple Acres' managers want to know this cost?

Computing equivalent units; assigning costs to goods completed and ending work in process inventory; first department, no beginning inventory (Obj. 2, 3, 4)

E21-5 The Assembly Department of Bentley Surge Protectors began September with no work in process inventory. During the month, production that cost $38,850 (direct materials, $8,550, and conversion costs, $30,300) was started on 21,000 units. Bentley completed and transferred to the Testing Department a total of 17,000 units. The ending work in process inventory was 50% complete as to direct materials and 80% complete as to conversion work.

Required

1. Compute the equivalent units for direct materials and conversion costs.
2. Compute the cost per equivalent unit.
3. Assign the costs to units completed and transferred out and ending work in process inventory.
4. Record the journal entry for the costs transferred out of Assembly and into Testing.
5. Post all the transactions in the Work in Process Inventory—Assembly Department T-account. What is the ending balance?

E21-6 Goodtimes is a microbrewery in Centreville, Virginia. Goodtimes has two departments—Fermenting and Packaging. Direct materials are added at the beginning of the fermenting process (barley, malt, hops) and at the end of the packaging process (bottles). Conversion costs are added evenly throughout each process. Data from the month of March for the Fermenting Department are as follows:

Drawing a time line; computing equivalent units; assigning cost to completed units and ending work in process; no beginning inventory or cost transferred in (Obj. 3, 4)

Gallons:	
Beginning work in process inventory	0
Started production	8,000 gallons
Completed and transferred out to Packaging in March	6,550 gallons
Ending work in process inventory (70% of the way through the fermenting process).......................................	1,450 gallons
Costs:	
Beginning work in process inventory	$ 0
Costs added during March:	
Direct materials	10,000
Direct labor...	1,540
Manufacturing overhead...	4,512
Total costs added during May...	$16,052

Required

1. Draw a time line for the Fermenting Department, similar to Exhibit 21-6.
2. Use the time line to help you compute the equivalent units for direct materials and for conversion costs.
3. Compute the total costs of the units (gallons)
   a. Completed and transferred out to the Packaging Department
   b. In the Fermenting Department ending work in process inventory

E21-7 Return to the Fermenting Department for Goodtimes in Exercise 21-6.

Journal entries, work in process T-account (Obj. 1, 2, 4)

Required

1. Present the journal entries to record the use of direct materials and direct labor, and the allocation of manufacturing overhead to the Fermenting Department. Also give the journal entry to record the costs of the gallons completed and transferred out to the Packaging Department.
2. Post the journal entries to the Work in Process Inventory—Fermenting T-account. What is the ending balance?
3. What is the average cost per gallon transferred out of Fermenting and into Packaging? Why would Goodtimes' managers want to know this cost?

E21-8 The following information was taken from the ledger of Newport Glass. Ending inventory is 50% complete as to direct materials but 30% complete as to conversion work.

Computing equivalent units; assigning cost to goods completed and ending work in process inventory; first department, no beginning inventory (Obj. 2, 3, 4)

WORK IN PROCESS—FORMING

	Physical Units	Dollars		Physical Units	Dollars
Beginning inventory, September 30	-0-	$ -0-	Transferred to Finishing	72,000	$?
Production started:	80,000				
Direct materials		247,000			
Conversion costs		238,080			
Ending inventory	8,000	?			

Required

Journalize the transfer of cost to the Finishing Department. (*Hint:* First compute the number of equivalent units and the cost per equivalent unit.)

E21-9 Assume that **Edy's Grand Ice Cream Co.** reports the following data from its FIFO process costing system. Insert the missing values.

Computing equivalent units in a single department that has beginning inventory, FIFO (Obj. 5)

Flow of Production	Flow of Physical Units	Equivalent Units	
		Direct Materials	Conversion Costs
Units to account for:			
Beginning work in process, March 31.................	14,000		
Started in production during April......................	X		
Total physical units to account for....................	67,000		
Units accounted for:			
Completed and transferred out during April			
From beginning work in process inventory...............	14,000	X*	X*
Started and completed during April..........................	47,000	X	X
Ending work in process, April 30..................................	X	X†	X†
Total physical units accounted for...............................	67,000		
Equivalent units...		X	X

* Finished beginning inventory
    Direct materials: 40% completed during April
    Conversion costs: 60% completed during April
† Started ending inventory
    Direct materials: 20% completed during April
    Conversion costs: 50% completed during April

Computing equivalent units, 2 departments, FIFO method (Obj. 5)

E21-10 Selected production and cost data of Clarke Chemical Co. follow for May 20X3.

Flow of Production	Flow of Physical Units	
	Mixing Department	Heating Department
Units to account for:		
Beginning work in process, April 30......................	20,000	6,000
Transferred in during May......................................	70,000	80,000
Total physical units to account for.........................	90,000	86,000
Units accounted for:		
Completed and transferred out during May		
From beginning work in process inventory........	20,000	6,000
Started and completed during May...................	60,000	70,000
Ending work in process, May 31............................	10,000	10,000
Total physical units accounted for............................	90,000	86,000

Clarke uses FIFO process costing.

Required

1. Fill in the blanks:
   a. On April 30, the Mixing Department beginning work in process inventory was 70% complete as to materials and 85% complete as to conversion costs. This means that for the beginning inventory _____% of the materials and _____% of the conversion costs were added during May.
   b. On May 31, the Mixing Department ending work in process inventory was 60% complete as to materials and 40% complete as to conversion costs. This means that for the ending inventory _____% of the materials and _____% of the conversion costs were added during May.
   c. On April 30, the Heating Department beginning work in process inventory was 40% complete as to materials and 70% complete as to conversion costs. This means that for the beginning inventory _____% of the materials and _____% of the conversion costs were added during May.
   d. On May 31, the Heating Department ending work in process inventory was 70% complete as to materials and 60% complete as to conversion costs. This means that for the ending inventory _____% of the materials and _____% of the conversion costs were added during May.

2. Use the information in the Flow of Production table and the information in Requirement 1 to compute the equivalent units for transferred-in costs, direct materials, and conversion costs for both the Mixing and the Heating Departments.

E21-11 Repeat Requirement 2 of Exercise 21-10 for Clarke Chemical's Heating Department, using the weighted-average method.

EU in a second department, WA method (Obj. 6)

E21-12 Silicon Semiconductors, Inc., experienced the following activity in its Photolithography Department during December. Materials are added at the beginning of the photolithography process.

Computing equivalent units and assigning costs to completed units and to ending work in process inventory; second department, FIFO
(Obj. 5)

Units:	
Work in process, November 30	
(80% of the way through the process)	8,000 units
Transferred in from the Polishing and Cutting Department during December	27,000 units
Completed during December	26,000 units
Work in process, December 31	
(70% of the way through the process)	9,000 units
Costs:	
Work in process, November 30	$60,116
Transferred in from the Polishing and Cutting Department during December	97,200
Direct materials added during December	74,250
Conversion costs added during December	90,650

Required

1. Draw a time line for the Photolithography Department using the FIFO method. (See Exhibit 21-11.)
2. Use the time line to help you compute the number of equivalent units of work performed by the Photolithography Department during December. Use the FIFO method.
3. Compute the costs per equivalent unit, and assign total cost to (a) units completed and transferred to Finished Goods Inventory, and (b) units in December 31 work in process inventory.

E21-13 Repeat Exercise 21-12, using the weighted-average method. (See Exhibit 21-16 for a weighted-average time line.) The November 30 balance of Work in Process Inventory—Photolithography Department ($60,116) is composed of the following amounts: transferred-in costs, $20,050; direct materials costs, $20,250; and conversion costs, $19,816.

Computing equivalent units and assigning costs to completed units and to ending work in process inventory; second department, weighted average
(Obj. 6)

Challenge Exercise

E21-14 The following data pertain to the Packaging Department of Nature's Way Supplements, for the month of July 20X3:

Using equivalent units to determine the physical flow of production (Obj. 5, 6)

	Equivalent Units		
Method	**Transferred In**	**Direct Materials**	**Conversion Costs**
FIFO	200,000	210,000	206,250
Weighted-average	210,000	210,000	208,750

Direct materials are added when the units are halfway through the packaging process. During July, 205,000 physical units were completed and transferred out.

Required

1. How many physical units were transferred in to the Packaging Department in July?
2. How many physical units were in the beginning work in process inventory?
3. How many physical units were both transferred in (started) and completed in July?
4. How many physical units were in the ending work in process inventory?
5. What percentage of the total required conversion work was done on the beginning work in process inventory during June? That is, at what percentage of completion were the beginning inventory units on July 1?

Computing equivalent units and
assigning cost to completed units
and ending work in process; no
beginning inventory or cost
transferred in
(Obj. 1, 3, 4)

P21-1A Find-it, Inc., engraves and prints address books. Production occurs in three processes: engraving, printing, and binding. The Engraving Department had no work in process on May 31. In mid-June, Find-it started production on 80,000 books. Of this number, 67,600 books were engraved during June. Direct materials are added at the beginning of the engraving process. Conversion costs are incurred evenly throughout the process. The June 30 work in process in the Engraving Department was 60% of the way through the engraving process. Direct materials costing $212,000 were placed in production in Engraving during June, and direct labor of $97,720 and manufacturing overhead of $74,872 were assigned to that department.

Required

1. Draw a time line for the Engraving Department, similar to Exhibit 21-6.
2. Use the time line to help you compute the number of equivalent units and the cost per equivalent unit in the Engraving Department for June.
3. Assign total cost in the Engraving Department to (a) units completed and transferred to Printing during June, and (b) units still in process at June 30.
4. Prepare a T-account for Work in Process Inventory—Engraving to show its activity during June, including the June 30 balance.

Computing equivalent units;
assigning cost to completed units
and ending work in process;
journalizing transactions; no
beginning inventory or cost
transferred in
(Obj. 2, 3, 4)

P21-2A Premium Paper produces the paper used by wallpaper manufacturers (**Imperial, Norwall**). Premium Paper's four-stage process includes mixing, cooking, rolling, and cutting. In the Mixing Department, wood pulp and chemicals are blended. The resulting mix is heated in the Cooking Department in much the same way food is prepared. Then the cooked mix is rolled to produce sheets. The final process, cutting, divides the sheets into large rolled units. The Mixing Department incurred the following costs during August:

WORK IN PROCESS INVENTORY—MIXING		
Aug. 1 balance	0	
Direct materials	25,872	
Direct labor	6,250	
Manufacturing overhead	17,246	

During August, the Mixing Department started and completed mixing for 2,500 rolls of paper. The department started but did not finish the mixing for an additional 700 rolls, which were 20% complete with respect to both direct materials and conversion work at the end of August.

Required

1. Draw a time line for the Mixing Department, similar to Exhibit 21-6.
2. Use the time line to help you compute the number of equivalent units and the cost per equivalent unit in the Mixing Department for August.
3. Show that the sum of (a) cost of goods transferred out of the Mixing Department, and (b) ending Work in Process Inventory—Mixing equals the total cost accumulated in the department during August.
4. Journalize all transactions affecting the company's mixing process during August, including those already posted.

EU and assigning costs to completed units and ending WIP
inventory; materials added at different points; no beginning inventory or cost transferred in
(Obj. 1, 2, 3, 4)

P21-3A Greenply produces exterior siding for homes. The Preparation Department begins with wood, which is chopped into small bits. At the end of the process, an adhesive is added. Then the wood/adhesive mixture goes on to the Compression Department, where the wood is compressed into sheets. Assume conversion costs are added evenly throughout the preparation process. Suppose that April data for the Preparation Department are as follows (in millions):

Sheets		Costs	
Beginning work in process inventory	0 sheets	Beginning work in process inventory.................	$ 0
Started production......................................	1,500 sheets	Costs added during April:	
Completed and transferred out to		Wood...	1,650
Compression in April.............................	950 sheets	Adhesives..	380
Ending work in process inventory		Direct labor..	205
(40% of the way through the		Manufacturing overhead	497
preparation process)	550 sheets	Total costs..	$2,732

Required

1. Draw a time line for the Preparation Department, similar to Exhibit 21-6.
2. Use the time line to help you compute the equivalent units for direct materials and for conversion costs. (*Hint:* Each direct material added at a different point in the production process requires its own equivalent-unit computation.)
3. Compute the total costs of the units (sheets)
   a. Completed and transferred out to the Compression Department
   b. In the Preparation Department's ending work in process inventory
4. Prepare the journal entry to record the cost of the sheets completed and transferred out to the Compression Department.
5. Post the journal entries to the Work in Process Inventory—Preparation T-account. What is the ending balance?

Computing equivalent units for a second department with beginning inventory; assigning cost to completed units and ending work in process; FIFO method (Obj. 3, 4, 5)

P21-4A Cox Carpeting manufactures broadloom carpet in seven processes: spinning, dyeing, plying, spooling, tufting, latexing, and shearing. First, fluff nylon purchased from a company such as **DuPont** or **Monsanto** is spun into yarn that is dyed the desired color. Then threads of the yarn are joined together, or plied, for added strength. The plied yarn is spooled for carpet making. Tufting is the process by which yarn is added to burlap backing. After the backing is latexed to hold it together and make it skid-resistant, the carpet is sheared to give it an even appearance and feel.

At March 31, before recording the transfer of costs out of the Dyeing Department, the Cox Carpeting general ledger included the following account for one of its lines of carpet:

WORK IN PROCESS INVENTORY—DYEING

Feb. 28 Balance	9,500
Transferred in from Spinning	23,520
Direct materials	11,760
Direct labor	8,445
Manufacturing overhead	42,900

In the Dyeing Department, direct materials (dye) are added at the beginning of the process. Conversion costs are incurred evenly throughout the process. Work in process inventory of the Dyeing Department on February 28 consisted of 75 rolls that were 50% of the way through the production process. During March, 560 rolls were transferred in from the Spinning Department. The Dyeing Department completed and transferred 500 rolls to the Plying Department in March, and 135 rolls were still in process on March 31. The ending inventory was 80% of the way through the dyeing process. Cox Carpeting uses FIFO process costing.

Required

1. Prepare a time line for the Dyeing Department, similar to Exhibit 21-11.
2. Use the time line to help you compute the equivalent units, cost per equivalent unit, and total costs to account for in the Dyeing Department for March.
3. Assign total Dyeing Department cost to (a) goods transferred from Dyeing to Plying, and (b) Work in Process Inventory—Dyeing on March 31.

P21-5A Refer to Problem 21-4A.

Preparing a production cost report and recording transactions on the basis of the report's information (Obj. 3, 4, 5)

Required

1. Prepare the March production cost report for Cox's Dyeing Department.
2. Journalize all transactions affecting the Dyeing Department during March, including the entries that have already been posted.

P21-6A EZ Lift uses three processes to manufacture lifts for personal watercraft: forming the lift's parts from galvanized steel, assembling the lift, and testing the completed lifts. The lifts are transferred to finished goods before shipment to marinas across the country.

Computing equivalent units for a second department with beginning inventory; assigning cost to completed units and ending work in process; FIFO method (Obj. 3, 4, 5)

EZ Lift's Testing Department requires no direct materials. Other process costing information follows:

Units:	
Beginning work in process (60% complete as to conversion work)...	2,000 units
Transferred in from the Assembling Department during the period...	7,000 units
Completed during the period..	4,000 units
Ending work in process (40% complete as to conversion work)........	5,000 units
Costs:	
Beginning work in process..	$111,000
Transferred in from the Assembling Department during the period...	672,000
Conversion costs added during the period...	48,000

The cost transferred into Finished Goods Inventory is the cost of the lifts transferred out of the Testing Department. EZ Lift uses FIFO process costing.

Required

1. Draw a time line for the Testing Department, similar to the one in Exhibit 21-11.
2. Use the time line to compute the number of equivalent units of work performed by the Testing Department during the period, the cost per equivalent unit, and total costs to account for.
3. Assign total cost to (a) units completed and transferred out of Testing, and (b) units in Testing's ending work in process inventory.
4. Compute the cost per unit for lifts completed and transferred out to Finished Goods Inventory. Why would management be interested in this cost?

EU for a second department with beginning inventory; assigning cost to completed units and ending WIP; WA method **(Obj. 3, 4, 6)**

P21-7A Repeat Problem 21-6A, using the weighted-average method. The $111,000 beginning balance of Work in Process—Testing includes $93,000 of transferred-in cost and $18,000 of conversion cost. (For requirement 1, use the time line in Exhibit 21-16 as a guide.)

(Group B) PROBLEMS

Computing equivalent units and assigning cost to completed units and ending work in process; no beginning inventory or cost transferred in
(Obj. 1, 3, 4)

P21-1B Quickcomm, Inc., produces components for the telecommunications industry. One part, a laser diode is manufactured in a single processing department. No laser diodes were in process on May 31, and Quickcomm started production on 10,600 units during June. Direct materials are added at the beginning of the process, but conversion costs are incurred evenly throughout the process. Completed production for June totaled 8,500 units. The June 30 work in process was 40% of the way through the production process. Direct materials costing $6,360 were placed in production during June, and direct labor of $4,900 and manufacturing overhead of $2,105 were assigned to the process.

Required

1. Draw a time line for Quickcomm, similar to Exhibit 21-6.
2. Use the time line to help you compute the number of equivalent units and the cost per equivalent unit for June.
3. Assign total cost to (a) units completed and transferred to finished goods, and (b) units still in process at June 30.
4. Prepare a T-account for Work in Process Inventory to show activity during June, including the June 30 balance.

Computing equivalent units; assigning cost to completed units and ending work in process; journalizing transactions; no beginning inventory or cost transferred in
(Obj. 2, 3, 4)

P21-2B The Southern Cotton Company produces cotton fabric in a three-stage process: cleaning, spinning, and weaving. Costs incurred in the Cleaning Department during September are summarized as follows:

WORK IN PROCESS INVENTORY—CLEANING	
Sep. 1 balance	0
Direct materials	66,500
Direct labor	4,458
Manufacturing overhead	6,950

Direct materials (raw cotton) are added at the beginning of the cleaning process, while conversion costs are incurred evenly throughout the process. September activity in the Cleaning Department included cleansing of 17,000 pounds of cotton, which were transferred to the Spinning Department. Also, work began on 2,000 pounds of cotton, which on September 30 were 70% of the way through the cleaning process.

Required

1. Draw a time line for the Cleaning Department, similar to Exhibit 21-6.
2. Use the time line to help you compute the number of equivalent units and the cost per equivalent unit in the Cleaning Department for September.
3. Show that the sum of (a) cost of goods transferred out of the Cleaning Department, and (b) ending Work in Process Inventory—Cleaning equals the total cost accumulated in the department during September.
4. Journalize all transactions affecting the company's cleaning process during September, including those already posted.

EU and assigning costs to completed units and ending WIP; materials added at different points in the production process; no beginning inventory or costs transferred in **(Obj. 1, 2, 3, 4)**

P21-3B Royal Chicken produces canned chicken à la king. The chicken à la king passes through three departments—(1) Mixing, (2) Retort (sterilization), and (3) Packing. In the Mixing Department, chicken and cream are added at the beginning of the process, the mixture is partly cooked, and then chopped green peppers and mushrooms are added at the end of the mixing process. Conversion costs are added evenly throughout the mixing process. November data from the Mixing Department are as follows:

880

Gallons		Costs	
Beginning work in process inventory	0 gallons	Beginning work in process inventory	$ 0
Started production	10,000 gallons	Costs added during November:	
Completed and transferred out to		Chicken	12,500
Retort in November............................	8,700 gallons	Cream..	4,500
		Green peppers and mushrooms	6,090
Ending work in process inventory		Direct labor...	8,002
(60% of the way through the		Manufacturing overhead	2,900
mixing process)	1,300 gallons	Total costs...	$33,992

Required

1. Draw a time line for the Mixing Department, similar to Exhibit 21-6.
2. Use the time line to help you compute the equivalent units. (*Hint:* Each direct material added at a different point in the production process requires its own equivalent-unit computation.)
3. Compute the total costs of the units (gallons)
   a. Completed and transferred out to the Retort Department
   b. In the Mixing Department's ending work in process inventory
4. Prepare the journal entry to record the cost of the gallons completed and transferred out to the Retort Department.
5. Post the transactions to the Work in Process Inventory—Mixing T-account. What is the ending balance?
6. What is the primary purpose of the work required in steps 1–3?

P21-4B Rule, Inc., manufacturers auto roof racks in a two-stage process that includes shaping and plating. Steel alloy is the basic raw material of the shaping process. The steel is molded according to the design specifications of automobile manufacturers (**Ford** and **General Motors**). The Plating Department then adds an anodized finish.

Computing equivalent units for a second department with beginning inventory; assigning cost to completed units and ending work in process; FIFO method (Obj. 3, 4, 5)

At March 31, before recording the transfer of cost from the Plating Department to Finished Goods Inventory, the Rule general ledger included the following account:

WORK IN PROCESS INVENTORY—PLATING	
Feb. 28 balance	30,200
Transferred in from Shaping	36,000
Direct materials	24,200
Direct labor	21,732
Manufacturing overhead	35,388

The direct materials (rubber pads) are added at the end of the plating process. Conversion costs are incurred evenly throughout the process. Work in process of the Plating Department on February 28 consisted of 600 racks that were 30% of the way through the production process. During March, 3,000 racks were transferred in from the Shaping Department. The Plating Department transferred 2,200 racks to Finished Goods Inventory in March, and 1,400 were still in process on March 31. This ending inventory was 50% of the way through the plating process. Rule uses FIFO process costing.

Required

1. Draw a time line for the Plating Department, similar to Exhibit 21-11.
2. Use the time line to help you compute the equivalent units, cost per equivalent unit, and total costs to account for in the Plating Department for March.
3. Assign total Plating Department cost to (a) goods transferred out of the Plating Department, and (b) Work in Process Inventory—Plating on March 31.

P21-5B Refer to Problem 21-4B.

Preparing a production cost report and recording transactions based on the report (Obj. 3, 4, 5)

Required

1. Prepare the March production cost report for the Plating Department.
2. Journalize all transactions affecting the Plating Department during March, including the entries that have already been posted.

P21-6B ToolTime uses three departments to produce screwdrivers with plastic handles. Forming the handles requires mixing the raw materials, molding, and drying.

ToolTime's Drying Department requires no direct materials. Other process costing information follows:

EU for a second department with BI; assigning cost to completed units and ending WIP; FIFO (Obj. 3, 4, 5)

Units:	
Beginning work in process (30% complete as to conversion work).....	7,000 units
Transferred in from the Molding Department during the period..........	28,000 units
Completed during the period	16,000 units
Ending work in process (20% complete as to conversion work)..........	19,000 units
Costs:	
Beginning work in process	$ 371
Transferred in from the Moldling Department during the period.........	4,760
Conversion costs added during the period...	1,947

After the drying process, the screwdrivers are completed by assembling the handles and shanks and packaging for shipment to retail outlets. The cost transferred in to the assembling phase is the cost of the plastic handles transferred out of the Drying Department. ToolTime uses FIFO process costing.

Required

1. Draw a time line of the Drying Department's process, similar to the one in Exhibit 21-11.
2. Use the time line to compute the number of equivalent units of work performed by the Drying Department during the period, the cost per equivalent unit, and the total costs to account for.
3. Assign total cost to (a) units completed and transferred to the assembly operation, and (b) units in the Drying Department's ending work in process inventory.

EU for a second department with BI; assigning cost to completed units and ending WIP; WA method (Obj. 3, 4, 6)

P21-7B Repeat Problem 21-6B, using the weighted-average method. The $371 beginning balance of Work in Process—Drying includes $140 of transferred-in cost and $231 of conversion cost. For requirement 1, use the time line in Exhibit 21-16 as a guide. From management's perspective, what are the advantages of the weighted-average method versus the FIFO method of process costing?

APPLY YOUR KNOWLEDGE

DECISION CASES

Using FIFO process cost information to evaluate production performance (Obj. 5)

Case 1. Bobby Jones operates Bobby's Cricket Farm in Baton Rouge, Louisiana. Bobby's raises about 18 million crickets a month. Most are sold to pet stores at $13 for a box of 1,000 crickets. Pet stores sell the crickets for 5–10 cents each as live feed for reptiles.

Raising crickets requires a two-step process: incubation and brooding. In the first process, incubation employees place cricket eggs on mounds of peat moss to hatch. In the second process, employees move the newly hatched crickets into large boxes filled with cardboard dividers. Depending on the desired size, the crickets spend approximately two weeks in Brooding before shipment to pet stores. In the brooding process, Bobby's crickets consume about 16 tons of food and produce 12 tons of manure.

Jones has invested $400,000 in the cricket farm and he had hoped to earn a 24% annual rate of return, which works out to a 2% monthly return on his investment. After looking at the farm's bank balance, Jones fears he is not achieving this return. To get more accurate information on the farm's performance, Jones bought new accounting software that provides process cost information. After Jones input data, the software provided the reports on the next page. However, Jones needs help interpreting these reports.

Jones does know that a unit of production is a box of 1,000 crickets. For example, in June's production cost report, the 7,000 physical units of beginning work in process inventory are 7,000 boxes (each one of the 7,000 boxes contains 1,000 immature crickets). The finished goods inventory is zero as the crickets ship out as soon as they reach the required size. Monthly operating expenses total $1,000.

Required

Bobby Jones has the following questions about the farm's performance during June.

1. What is the cost per box of crickets sold? (*Hint:* This is the cost of the boxes completed and shipped out of brooding.)
2. What is the gross profit per box?
3. How much operating income did Bobby's Cricket Farm make in June?
4. What is the return on Jones' investment of $400,000 for the month of June? (Compute this as June's operating income divided by Jones' $400,000 investment, expressed as a percentage.)
5. What monthly operating income would provide a 2% monthly rate of return? What price per box would Bobby's Cricket Farm have had to charge in June to achieve a 2% monthly rate of return?

BOBBY'S CRICKET FARM
Brooding Department
Month Ended June 30, 20XX

| | | Equivalent Units | | |
| | Flow of Physical Units | Transferred In | Direct Materials | Conversion Costs |
Flow of Production				
Units to account for:				
Beginning work in process inventory	7,000			
Transferred in during June..........................	21,000			
Total units to account for.............................	28,000			
Units accounted for:				
Completed and shipped out during June:				
From beginning inventory......................	7,000	—	1,400	4,200
Started and completed during June.........	12,000	12,000	12,000	12,000
Ending work in process, June 30	9,000	9,000	7,200	3,600
Total physical units accounted for	28,000			
Equivalent units..		21,000	20,600	19,800

BOBBY'S CRICKET FARM
Brooding Department
Production Cost Report (FIFO Method)
Month Ended June 30, 20XX

	Transferred In	Direct Materials	Conversion Costs	Total
Unit costs:				
Beginning work in process, May 31				$ 74,740
Costs added during June	$46,200	$156,560	$51,480	254,240
Divide by equivalent units	÷21,000	÷20,600	÷19,800	
Cost per equivalent unit.....................................	$2.20	$7.60	$2.60	
Total cost to account for				$328,980
Assignment of total cost:				
Units completed and shipped out:				
From beginning work in process, May 31				$ 74,740
Costs added during June:				
Direct materials...		[1,400 × $7.60]		10,640
Conversion costs..			[4,200 × $2.60]	10,920
Total completed from beginning inventory				96,300
Units transferred in from Incubation				
and completed during June		[12,000 × ($2.20 + $7.60 + $2.60)]		148,800
Total cost shipped out				245,100
Ending work in process, June 30:				
Transferred-in costs..	[9,000 × $2.20]			19,800
Direct materials..		[7,200 × $7.60]		54,720
Conversion costs...			[3,600 × $2.60]	9,360
Total ending work in process, June 30				83,880
Total cost accounted for.....................................				$328,980

Case 2. Refer to Case 1. During June, Bobby Jones made a big effort to control the farm's costs. He expects the level of costs incurred during June to continue in the future.

Using FIFO process cost information to assess profitability and make business decisions (Obj. 5)

Required

1. What is the cost per box for June production only? (*Hint:* Do not include beginning Work in Process Inventory costs.)
2. Using the June production cost per unit, what is the gross profit per box?

3. If the farm sells 18,000 boxes of crickets a month and keeps costs at the June level, will Jones earn his desired return on investment? What is the monthly return on investment using only the June data?

ETHICAL ISSUE

Effect of percentage completion of ending inventory on financial results

(Obj. 1, 3, 4)

Jay Stolz and Ben Moyer are the plant managers for Southern Lumber's particle board division. Southern Lumber has adopted a just-in-time management philosophy. Each plant combines wood chips with chemical adhesives to produce particle board to order, and all production is sold as soon as it is completed. Laura Dagosta is Southern Lumber's regional controller. All of Southern Lumber's plants and divisions send Dagosta their production and cost information. While reviewing the numbers of the two particle board plants, she is surprised that both plants estimate their ending work in process inventories at 80% complete, which is higher than usual. Dagosta calls Moyer, whom she has known for some time. He admits that to ensure their division met its profit goal and both he and Stolz made their bonus (which is based on division profit), he and Stolz agreed to inflate the percentage completion. Moyer explains, "Determining the percent complete always requires judgment. Whatever the percent complete, we'll finish the work in process inventory first thing next year."

Required

1. How would inflating the percentage completion of ending Work in Process inventory help Stolz and Moyer get their bonus?
2. The particle board division is the largest of Southern Lumber's divisions. If Dagosta does not correct the percentage completion of this year's ending work in process inventory, how will the misstatement affect Southern Lumber's financial statements?
3. Evaluate Moyer's justification, including the effect, if any, on next year's financial statements.
4. ← *Link Back to Chapter 7.* Apply the ethical framework from Chapter 7 (page 290) in considering what Dagosta should do.

TEAM PROJECT

Computing allowable cost per unit; computing cost per equivalent unit; second process; FIFO

(Obj. 3, 5)

Hermiston Food Processors in Hermiston, Oregon, processes potatoes into french fries. Production requires two processes: cutting and cooking. The cutting process begins as scalding steam explodes the potatoes' brown skins. Workers using paring knives gouge out black spots before high pressure water blasts potatoes through a pipe and into blades arranged in a quarter-inch grid. In the cooking process, the raw shoestring fries are cooked in a bleacher, dried, partially fried at 380°F and immediately flash frozen at minus 75°F before being dropped into 5-pound bags. Direct materials are added at the beginning of the cutting process (potatoes) and at the end of the cooking process (bags). Conversion costs are incurred evenly throughout each process. Hermiston uses the FIFO method of process costing.

Assume that **McDonald's** offers Hermiston $2 per 5-pound bag to supply restaurants in the Far East. If Hermiston accepts McDonald's offer, the extra cost per equivalent unit that Hermiston will incur to fill the McDonald's order equals the April cost per equivalent unit. J. R. Simlott, manager of the cooking process, must prepare a report explaining whether Hermiston should accept the offer. Simlott gathers the following information from April's cooking operations:

HERMISTON FOOD PROCESSORS	
Cooking Department	
April 20XX Activity and Costs	
Beginning work in process inventory (40% of way through process)	12,000 pounds
Raw shoestring fries started in April	129,000 pounds
French fries completed and transferred out	130,000 pounds
Ending work in process inventory (30% of way through process)	11,000 pounds
Costs to start the 12,000 pounds of beginning work in process inventory in March	$ 640
Costs added during April:	
Direct materials	6,500
Conversion costs	15,420

Lola Mendez manages the cutting process. She reports the following data for her department's April operations.

HERMISTON FOOD PROCESSORS	
Cutting Department	
April 20XX Activity and Costs	
Beginning work in process inventory (40% of way through process)	21,000 pounds
Potatoes started in April	121,000 pounds
Raw shoestring fries completed and transferred out	129,000 pounds
Ending work in process inventory (60% of way through process)	13,000 pounds
Costs to start the 21,000 pounds of beginning work in process inventory in March	$ 2,310
Costs added during April:	
Direct materials	9,680
Conversion costs	12,840

Split your team into two groups. Each group should meet separately before a meeting of the entire team.

Required

1. The first group takes the role of J. R. Simlott, manager of the cooking production process. Before meeting with the entire team, determine the maximum transferred-in cost per pound of raw shoestring fries the Cooking Department can incur from the Cutting Department if Hermiston is to make a profit on the McDonald's order. (*Hint:* You may find it helpful to prepare a time line and to use Exhibits 21-11 through 21-14 as a guide to your analysis.)
2. The second group takes the role of Lola Mendez, manager of the cutting process. Before meeting with the entire team, determine the April cost per pound of raw shoestring fries in the cutting process. (*Hint:* You may find it helpful to prepare a time line and to use Exhibits 21-11 through 21-14 as a guide to your analysis.)
3. After each group meets, the entire team should meet to decide whether Hermiston should accept or reject McDonald's offer.

INTERNET EXERCISE

Hershey Foods Corporation is the market leader in the candy business, making the well-known chocolate and candy brands Hershey's Kisses, Reese's peanut butter cups, and Kit Kat.

Hershey Foods Corporation

Required

1. Go to **http://www.hersheys.com** and, in the left-hand column, click on *Plant Tour* and then *From Bean to Bar*. Hershey identifies how many steps for making a candy bar? Review the steps. During what step are milk and sugar added? When are the nuts added? Do the nuts or the chocolate go into the mold first? Should Hershey Foods use job costing or process costing? Why?
2. How many raw material inventory accounts should Hershey maintain for its candy-bar ingredients? When are the milk and sugar ingredient costs transferred to a Work in Process Inventory account? To the Finished Goods account? To Cost of Goods Sold?
3. Assume that the processing steps each incur equal amounts of conversion costs. Assume the ingredients for 100,000 candy bars have completed step 5: blending. At this point, how many equivalents units have been added of: Milk and sugar? Nuts? Conversion costs?
4. Go to **http://www.hersheys.com/annualreport/** and read the information displayed. Did Hershey Foods have a good year financially? At the bottom of the page, use the pull-down menu to select *Assuring an Adequate Cocoa Supply*. Read the information displayed. Is Hershey concerned about maintaining an adequate supply of cocoa beans? What is the CMA?

22 Cost-Volume-Profit Analysis

e-commerce

LEARNING OBJECTIVES

After studying this chapter, you should be able to

1. Identify different cost behavior patterns

2. Use a contribution margin income statement to make business decisions

3. Compute breakeven sales and perform sensitivity analyses

4. Compute the sales level needed to earn a target operating income

5. Graph a set of cost-volume-profit relationships

6. Compute a margin of safety

7. Use the sales mix in CVP analysis

8. Compute income using variable costing and absorption costing

www.prenhall.com/horngren
Readiness Assessment

"All aboard!" shouts the conductor of the **Grand Canyon Railway** as the train departs from the Williams, Arizona, depot. The restored turn-of-the-century train features musicians in period costumes. Passengers have breakfast on the morning trip to the canyon and nibble appetizers on the afternoon trip back to Williams. The railway offers three classes of service: (1) Coach, in restored 1923 cars; (2) Club, with a mahogany bar; and (3) Chief, with an open-air rear platform.

Few of the railway's costs vary with the number of passengers because most costs are *fixed*. Track maintenance, insurance, the costs to operate the depot's railway museum, and depreciation on the locomotive and cars stay the same whether 1 or 1,000 passengers travel the scenic 65-mile route. But food and beverage costs are *variable*. They rise and fall with the number of passengers on board.

The railway's managers have to find a delicate balance. They must set ticket prices high enough to cover costs and earn a profit, but low enough to fill seats. Most costs are fixed, so the extra costs to serve each additional passenger are low. Once fixed costs are covered, most of the revenue from extra guests goes toward profits.

How do the railway's managers ensure that revenues cover costs and provide profits? How do they decide how many seats to offer in each class? How many seats must the railway fill to cover costs? **Grand Canyon's** managers perform cost-volume-profit analysis to answer these questions.

Cost-volume-profit (CVP) analysis expresses the relationships among costs, volume, and profit or loss. We begin our study by explaining how to compute *profit* in a way that is tailor-made for CVP analysis. To do this, we first need to discuss the different types of *costs*.

> **COST-VOLUME-PROFIT (CVP) ANALYSIS.** Expresses the relationships among costs, volume, and profit or loss.

VARIABLE, FIXED, AND MIXED COSTS

Chapter 20 defined a *cost driver* as any factor that affects costs. *Volume* is a common cost driver; it is often expressed as physical units produced or sold, or as sales dollars. For example, the more T-shirts **Hanes** produces, the more costs the company incurs. Nonvolume factors can also drive costs. For example, weight drives freight costs. In this chapter, we focus on volume as the cost driver. **Cost behavior** describes how costs change—if they change at all—as the cost driver changes. We examine three basic types of costs: variable, fixed, and mixed.

> **Objective 1**
> Identify different cost behavior patterns
>
> **COST BEHAVIOR.** Describes how costs change as a cost driver changes.

Variable Costs

Variable costs change in total in direct proportion to changes in the volume of activity. In the **Grand Canyon Railway** story, variable costs include food and beverages. On the morning trip from Williams, Arizona, to Grand Canyon National Park, passengers enjoy a continental breakfast of pastries, orange juice, and coffee. Let's assume this breakfast costs the railway $3 per person. On the afternoon return trip, passengers enjoy appetizers, champagne, and soft drinks. We'll say this afternoon snack costs Grand Canyon Railway $10 per person. If Grand Canyon carries 20% more passengers this month, its total food and beverage costs will increase by 20%. If the railway carries 10% fewer passengers, the total food and beverage costs will fall by 10%. But while the total amount of the food and beverage costs fluctuates with the number of passengers, the per-person costs remain constant. That is, Grand Canyon incurs $3 in breakfast costs and $10 in afternoon snack costs for each passenger, no matter how many passengers the railway carries. The key point is that *total variable costs fluctuate with the volume of activity, but the variable cost per unit remains constant.*

Exhibit 22-1 graphs Grand Canyon's $3 per-person breakfast cost and the $10 per-person afternoon snack cost. The vertical axis shows the total variable costs, while the horizontal axis plots total volume (thousands of passengers, in this case).

> **VARIABLE COSTS.** Costs that change in total in direct proportion to changes in volume of activity.

EXHIBIT 22-1   **Variable Costs**

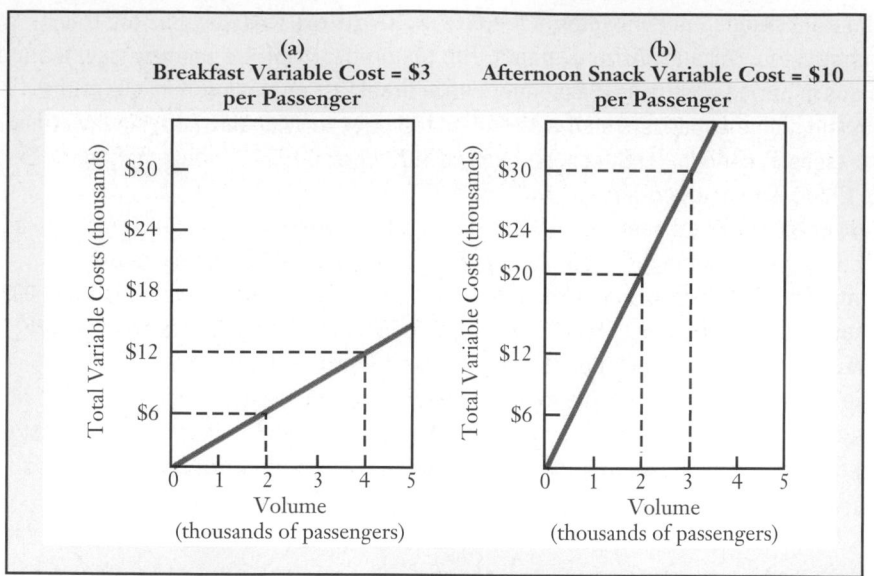

Look at the total variable breakfast costs in Exhibit 22-1(a). If there are no passengers, Grand Canyon incurs no breakfast costs. The total variable cost line begins at the bottom left corner. This point is called the *origin,* and represents zero volume and zero cost. The *slope* of the total variable cost line is the change in total variable cost (on the vertical axis) divided by the change in the total volume (on the horizontal axis). This equals the variable cost per unit. In Exhibit 22-1(a), the slope of Grand Canyon Railway's breakfast service total variable cost line is the $3 variable cost per passenger. This means that the railway spends an additional $3 on breakfast for each additional passenger. If the railroad carries 2,000 passengers, it will spend a total of $6,000 (2,000 passengers × $3 each) for breakfast service. Follow this total variable cost line to the right to see that doubling the number of passengers to 4,000 likewise doubles the total variable cost for breakfast service to $12,000 (4,000 × $3 = $12,000).

Exhibit 22-1(b) shows total variable costs for afternoon snacks and beverages. The slope of the total variable cost line for the afternoon snack service is the $10 cost of providing the refreshments for each passenger. This is much steeper than the line for breakfast service, which costs only $3 per person. So the rule is

> **The higher the variable cost per unit, the steeper the slope of the total variable cost line.**

Study Exhibit 22-1(b) to confirm that the total cost of afternoon snacks for 2,000 passengers is $20,000 (2,000 × $10). This is much higher than the breakfast cost for 2,000 passengers ($6,000), so the slope of the afternoon snack's total variable cost line is much steeper than that for breakfast. If the number of passengers increases to 3,000 (a 50% increase), then the total variable cost of providing snack service also increases by 50%—from $20,000 to $30,000 (3,000 × $10).

 DAILY EXERCISE 22-1

Fixed Costs

FIXED COST. Cost that does not change in total despite wide changes in volume.

A **fixed cost** does not change in total despite wide changes in volume. Most of Grand Canyon Railway's costs are fixed. The train makes one round-trip each day, regardless of the number of passengers. Grand Canyon's fixed costs include

- Depreciation and maintenance on the track, the locomotive, and the museum
- Entertainment costs (salaries of the strolling musicians)
- Administrative expenses (salaries of managers and accountants)

 DAILY EXERCISE 22-2

Suppose Grand Canyon has $200,000 of fixed costs per month, as shown in Exhibit 22-2. Like all graphs of fixed costs, Exhibit 22-2 shows a flat line that intersects the cost axis at the total fixed cost. This graph shows that the $200,000 monthly total fixed cost is the same for any volume of passengers. However, the *fixed cost per*

passenger depends on the number of passengers. If the railway carries 2,000 passengers, the fixed cost per passenger is $100 ($200,000 ÷ 2,000 passengers). If the number of passengers doubles to 4,000, the fixed cost per passenger is cut in half to $50 ($200,000 ÷ 4,000 passengers). Thus, the fixed cost per passenger is *inversely* proportional to the number of passengers. The key point is that *total fixed costs remain constant, but fixed cost per unit is inversely proportional to the volume of activity.*

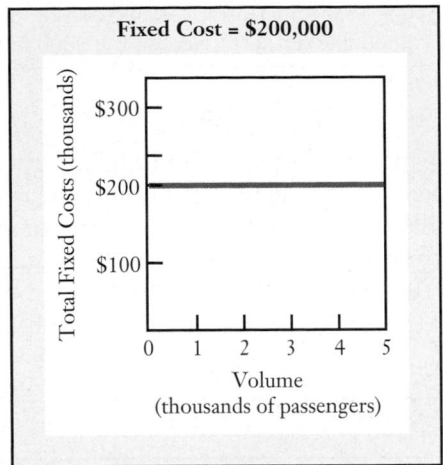

EXHIBIT 22-2
Fixed Costs

Mixed Costs

A **mixed cost** is part variable and part fixed. Suppose you start a business finding information on the Internet. Assume that **WorldCom** offers you a high-speed Internet access plan that costs $50 per month for several password accounts plus $0.05 per minute for connect time. In this plan you will pay a fixed cost of $600 per year ($50 per month × 12 months), plus $3 per hour ($0.05 per minute × 60 minutes) for connect time. Exhibit 22-3 shows the *total* (variable plus fixed) yearly costs at different volume (connect-time) levels.

MIXED COST. Cost that is part variable and part fixed.

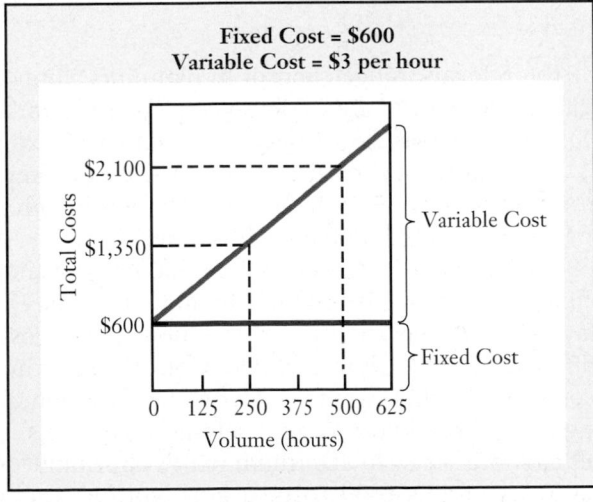

EXHIBIT 22-3
Mixed Costs

Total cost is the sum of the fixed cost plus the variable cost. If you use 250 hours of connect time, your total annual cost is $1,350 [fixed cost of $600 plus variable cost of $750 (250 hours × $3 per hour)]. If you double connect time to 500 hours, you will pay $2,100 [fixed cost of $600 plus variable cost of $1,500 (500 hours × $3 per hour)]. Even if you use no connect time, you will still pay the $600 fixed cost. Graphs of total mixed costs start at total fixed costs—not at zero as with variable costs. The slope of the total mixed cost line is the variable cost per unit.

Accountants frequently treat the fixed and variable components of mixed costs as two separate costs. They add the fixed component to other fixed costs to

 DAILY EXERCISE 22-3

determine the total cost that does not vary with the volume of goods and services produced or sold. They combine the variable component with other variable costs to compute the costs that increase in direct proportion to volume.

WORK IT OUT

In the Internet mixed cost example (Exhibit 22-3), if you double connect time from 250 to 500 hours, does your cost double? Explain.

Answer: No, total cost increases, but by less than double [($2,100 − $1,350) ÷ $1,350 = 55.6% increase]. Variable costs double (from $750 to $1,500) when you double connect time, but the $600 fixed cost does not change.

Relevant Range

RELEVANT RANGE. A band of volume within which a specific relationship exists between cost and volume.

A **relevant range** is a band of volume within which a specific relationship exists between cost and volume. Outside the relevant range, the cost changes. A fixed cost is fixed only within a given relevant range of volume (usually large) and a given time span (often a month or a year). Exhibit 22-4 shows a fixed cost of $40,000 for the volume range of 0–10,000 units. Between 10,000 and 20,000 units, fixed costs increase to $80,000, and they increase to $120,000 for volumes above 20,000 units.

EXHIBIT 22-4   **Relevant Range**

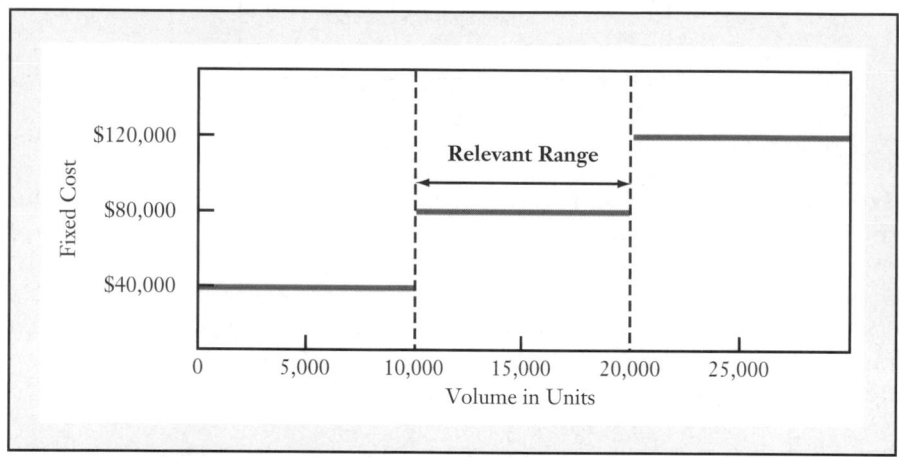

Companies use the relevant range concept in planning. Suppose a **Footlocker** store expects to sell 12,000 pairs of shoes next year. The relevant range is between 10,000 and 20,000 pairs of shoes, so managers budget fixed expenses of $80,000 (see Exhibit 22-4). If actual sales exceed 20,000 pairs, Footlocker will expand the store, which will increase rent expense. Exhibit 22-4 shows how fixed costs increase as the relevant range shifts to a higher band of volume.

Conversely, if Footlocker expects to sell only 8,000 pairs of shoes next year, the store will budget fixed costs of only $40,000. Its managers may have to cut back operating hours, lay off employees, or take other actions to cut costs.

Accountants and managers analyze cost behavior to predict how business decisions will affect costs and profits. Grand Canyon Railway managers may decide between (1) setting a higher ticket price and selling fewer seats, and (2) setting a lower price and selling more seats. To determine which alternative is likely to lead to higher profits, managers predict total costs at both volume levels. Variable costs throughout the value chain will be higher at the higher volume level. Fixed costs may or may not be higher, depending on the relevant ranges. Managers must understand how costs change with volume to predict profits from the two actions.

Objective 2
Use a contribution margin income statement to make business decisions

THE CONTRIBUTION MARGIN INCOME STATEMENT

➡ Recall from Chapter 19 that managers are concerned with the costs of the entire value chain, from R&D through manufacturing, distribution, and customer service.

The conventional income statement, illustrated for Kast-A-Ways Swimwear in Panel A of Exhibit 22-5, classifies expenses by value-chain function. ➡ Manufacturing costs of swimsuits sold are expensed as cost of goods sold. Sales revenue minus cost of goods sold equals gross profit. Most other costs (for example, marketing and

Exhibit 22-5 **Alternative Income Statement Formats**

PANEL A—Conventional Format

| KAST-A-WAYS SWIMWEAR |
| Conventional Income Statement |
| Year Ended December 31, 20X5 |

Sales revenue......................		$2,100,000
Cost of goods sold		1,320,000
Gross profit		780,000
Operating expenses:		
Marketing expense..........	$310,000	
Distribution expense	290,000	600,000
Operating income		$ 180,000

 DAILY EXERCISE 22-6

 DAILY EXERCISE 22-7

PANEL B—Contribution Margin Format

| KAST-A-WAYS SWIMWEAR |
| Contribution Margin Income Statement |
| Year Ended December 31, 20X5 |

Sales revenue		$2,100,000
Variable expenses:		
Variable manufacturing		
cost of goods sold	$840,000	
Variable marketing expense	150,000	
Variable distribution expense	210,000	1,200,000
Contribution margin		900,000
Fixed expenses:		
Fixed manufacturing expense	480,000	
Fixed marketing expense ..	160,000	
Fixed distribution expense	80,000	720,000
Operating income..................		$ 180,000

distribution costs) are grouped as "operating expenses." As explained in Chaper 5, gross profit minus operating expenses equals operating income. ➤

A conventional income statement's cost of goods sold includes both variable and fixed manufacturing costs. Variable costs include direct materials, direct labor, and variable overhead like electricity. Fixed manufacturing costs include depreciation, factory rent, and property taxes. As Panel A shows, conventional income statements do not distinguish between variable and fixed expenses.

Companies use conventional income statements for external reporting. For decision making, many managers prefer a different format. To see why, suppose CEO Linda Kast wants to predict operating income if sales increase by 10%. The conventional income statement does not help Kast predict how the change in volume will affect income because it does not separate variable costs from fixed costs. The **contribution margin income statement** in Panel B of Exhibit 22-5 groups variable and fixed expenses separately. It highlights the **contribution margin,** which is sales revenue minus all variable expenses.

The contribution margin—the excess of revenues over variable expenses—contributes to "covering" fixed expenses and to providing operating income. Think about fixed expenses. Many fixed costs are incurred before production or sales can take place. For instance, Kast-A-Ways must buy plant and equipment to produce the swimwear. The cost of the plant and machines becomes depreciation expense. As the company produces and sells swimwear, the contribution margin grows and covers this depreciation expense. After all fixed costs are recovered by the contribution margin, the contribution from additional sales provides operating income.

Compare the conventional income statement in Exhibit 22-5, Panel A, with the contribution margin income statement in Panel B. The conventional income statement subtracts cost of goods sold (including both variable and fixed manufacturing costs) from sales to obtain *gross profit.* In contrast, the contribution margin income statement subtracts all variable costs (both manufacturing and nonmanufacturing) to obtain *contribution margin.* The following chart highlights the differences between gross profit and contribution margin:

◄ See Chapter 5 for a discussion of operating income.

CONTRIBUTION MARGIN INCOME STATEMENT. Income statement that groups variable and fixed expenses separately, and highlights the contribution margin.

CONTRIBUTION MARGIN. Sales revenue minus all variable expenses.

DAILY EXERCISE 22-4

DAILY EXERCISE 22-5

CONVENTIONAL INCOME STATEMENT	CONTRIBUTION MARGIN INCOME STATEMENT
Sales revenue	**Sales revenue**
deduct Cost of Goods Sold:	**deduct Variable Expenses:**
Variable manufacturing cost of goods sold	**Variable manufacturing cost of goods sold**
Fixed manufacturing cost of goods sold	**Other (nonmanufacturing) variable expenses**
= Gross profit	**= Contribution margin**

The two major differences are

- Fixed manufacturing cost of goods sold is subtracted from sales to compute gross profit, but not to compute contribution margin.
- Variable nonmanufacturing expenses are subtracted from sales to calculate contribution margin, but not to compute gross profit.

Let's see how Linda Kast uses the contribution margin income statement to predict the company's operating income. If sales volume increases by 10%, variable costs (expenses) should also increase by 10%. Fixed costs (expenses), however, should remain the same, assuming Kast-A-Ways stays in the same relevant range:

Increase in sales (10% × $2,100,000)	$210,000
Increase in variable expenses (10% × $1,200,000)	(120,000)
Increase in contribution margin	90,000
Increase in fixed expenses	0
Increase in operating income	$ 90,000

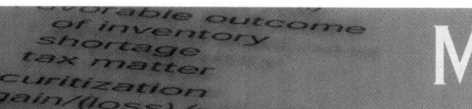 MID-CHAPTER

SUMMARY PROBLEM

www.prenhall.com/horngren
Mid-Chapter Assessment

The 20X5 contribution margin income statement of RainGear follows. RainGear's Goretex jackets sell for $45.

RAINGEAR		
Contribution Margin Income Statement		
Year Ended December 31, 20X5		
Sales revenue		$900,000
Variable expenses:		
Variable manufacturing cost of goods sold	$280,000	
Variable operating expenses	120,000	400,000
Contribution margin		500,000
Fixed expenses:		
Fixed manufacturing expenses	225,000	
Fixed operating expenses	75,000	300,000
Operating income		$200,000

Required

1. How many jackets did RainGear sell in 20X5?
2. What operating income will the company earn in 20X6 if sales volume increases by 20% and all sale prices, unit variable costs, and total fixed costs do not change? There are no beginning or ending inventories.
3. Recast the 20X5 income statement in the conventional format.

Solution

Requirement 1

RainGear sold 20,000 jackets in 20X5:

$$\text{Sales revenue} = \left(\begin{array}{c}\text{Sales price}\\\text{per jacket}\end{array}\right) \times \left(\begin{array}{c}\text{Number of}\\\text{jackets sold}\end{array}\right)$$

$$\$900,000 = \$45 \times (\text{Number of jackets sold})$$

$$\frac{\$900,000}{\$45} = \text{Number of jackets sold}$$

$$20,000 = \text{Number of jackets sold}$$

Requirement 2

Increase in sales revenue (20% × $900,000)................................	$180,000
Increase in variable expenses (20% × 400,000)	80,000
Increase in contribution margin	100,000
Increase in fixed expenses	0
Increase in operating income..	100,000
20X5 operating income..	200,000
20X6 operating income..	$300,000

Requirement 3

RAINGEAR
Conventional Income Statement
Year Ended December 31, 20X5

Sales revenue...	$900,000
Cost of goods sold ($280,000 + $225,000)......................	505,000
Gross profit	395,000
Operating expenses ($120,000 + $75,000)	195,000
Operating income	$200,000

BASIC COST-VOLUME-PROFIT (CVP) ANALYSIS

The Kast-A-Ways Swimwear example illustrates how changes in volume affect costs and profits. This is one type of cost-volume-profit (CVP) analysis. Before proceeding further, let's take a moment to consider the assumptions underlying CVP analysis.

Assumptions Underlying CVP Analysis

Cost-volume-profit analysis assumes that

1. Expenses are either variable or fixed.
2. Cost-volume-profit relationships are linear over a wide range of production and sales. Linear relationships appear on graphs as straight lines (as in Exhibits 22-1 and 22-2).
3. Sale prices, unit variable costs, and total fixed expenses will not change during the period.
4. Volume is the only cost driver. Other possible cost drivers (such as weight or size) are held constant or are insignificant.
5. The relevant range of volume is specified.
6. Inventory levels will not change.
7. The sales mix of products will not change during the period. **Sales mix** is the combination of products that make up total sales. For example, Furniture Warehouse may sell 70% household furniture and 30% office furniture.

SALES MIX. Combination of products that make up total sales.

When these conditions are met, CVP analysis is accurate. But most business conditions do not perfectly correspond to these assumptions. That is why managers regard CVP analysis as approximate rather than exact.

Basic CVP Analysis — The Breakeven Point

Objective 3
Compute breakeven sales and perform sensitivity analyses

Kay Pak is considering starting an e-tail business to sell art posters on the Internet. Pak plans to use business-to-business software that will enable her to purchase only those posters needed to satisfy her customers' demand. The posters will cost Pak $21 each, and she plans to sell them for $35 apiece. Monthly fixed costs for server leasing and maintenance, high-speed Internet access, and office rental total $7,000. We'll use this information to answer several questions about Pak's business.

BREAKEVEN POINT. The sales level at which operating income is zero: Total revenues equal total expenses.

QUESTION 1. What Is Pak's Breakeven Sales Level?

The **breakeven point** is the sales level at which operating income is zero: Total revenues equal total expenses. Sales below the breakeven point result in a loss. Sales above breakeven provide a profit.

Breakeven analysis is only one type of CVP analysis. The breakeven point is often only incidental to managers of ongoing operations who focus on the sales level needed to earn a target profit. However, when demand for an old product is declining, the breakeven point is important. It is also a useful place to start the analysis of a new product's potential.

Let's use two different methods to determine the breakeven point.

THE INCOME STATEMENT EQUATION APPROACH We start by separating total expenses into variable expenses and fixed expenses. Kay Pak's variable cost is her cost to purchase the posters. Her total variable expense equals the number of posters sold multiplied by the $21 cost per poster. Her $7,000 fixed costs include server leasing and maintenance, Internet access, and office rental.

Our next step expresses income in equation form:

> **Sales revenue − Variable expenses − Fixed expenses = Operating income**

At the breakeven point, operating income is zero, so sales revenue equals expenses. Sales revenue equals the unit sale price multiplied by the number of units sold. Variable expenses equals variable cost per unit times the number of units sold. We substitute these terms into the equation and enter the dollar amounts:

$$\text{Sales revenue} - \text{Variable expenses} - \text{Fixed expenses} = \text{Operating income}$$

$$\left(\frac{\text{Sale price}}{\text{per unit}} \times \text{Units sold}\right) - \left(\frac{\text{Variable cost}}{\text{per unit}} \times \text{Units sold}\right) - \text{Fixed expenses} = \text{Operating income}$$

($35	× Units sold) −	($21	× Units sold) −	$7,000	= $0
	($35 −	$21)	× Units sold −	$7,000	= $0
		$14	× Units sold		= $7,000
			Units sold		= $7,000/$14
			Breakeven sales in units		= 500 posters

Kay Pak must sell 500 posters to break even. Her breakeven sales level in dollars is $17,500 (500 units × $35).

It is wise to check your calculations by "proving" the breakeven point with a contribution margin income statement:

Sales revenue (500 × $35).....................................		$17,500
Less: Variable expenses (500 × $21)	$10,500	
Fixed expenses	7,000	(17,500)
Operating income.......................................		$ 0

THE CONTRIBUTION MARGIN CVP FORMULA: A SHORTCUT METHOD There is a shortcut method for CVP analysis. To use the shortcut, we must first understand more about Pak's contribution margin. Each unit sold has a **contribution margin per unit,** which equals sales revenue per unit (sale price) minus variable expense per unit.

> **Contribution margin per unit = Sales revenue per unit − Variable expense per unit**

Contribution margin can be expressed on a per-unit basis or as a ratio computed as a percentage of sales revenue. For Kay Pak's business:

	Per Unit	Percent	Ratio
Sales revenue...	$35	100	1.00
Deduct: Variable expense...........................	(21)	(60)	(0.60)
Contribution margin....................................	$14	40	0.40

Contribution margin ratio is the ratio of contribution margin to sales revenue:

CONTRIBUTION MARGIN PER UNIT. Sales revenue per unit (sale price) minus variable expense per unit.

CONTRIBUTION MARGIN RATIO. The ratio of contribution margin to sales revenue.

894

$$\text{Contribution margin ratio} = \frac{\text{Contribution margin}}{\text{Sales revenue}}$$

For Kay Pak's poster business, the contribution margin ratio is 40% ($14/$35). The contribution margin ratio tells how much a dollar of sales revenue contributes to contribution margin. Kay Pak's 40% contribution margin ratio means that each dollar of sales revenue contributes $0.40 toward fixed costs and profit, as shown in Exhibit 22-6.

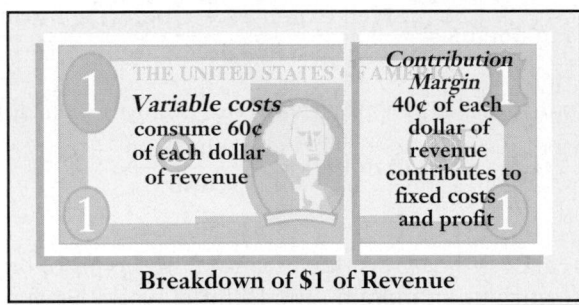

Breakdown of $1 of Revenue

Computing the Breakeven Point in Number of Units Sold. Now let's rearrange the income statement equation and use the contribution margin to develop a shortcut method for finding the number of posters Pak must sell to break even. We solve the equation for the number of units sold:

Sales revenue − **Variable expenses** − Fixed expenses = Operating income

$$\left(\frac{\text{Sale price}}{\text{per unit}} \times \text{Units sold}\right) - \left(\frac{\text{Variable cost}}{\text{per unit}} \times \text{Units sold}\right) - \text{Fixed expenses} = \text{Operating income}$$

$$\underbrace{\left(\frac{\text{Sale price}}{\text{per unit}} - \frac{\text{Variable cost}}{\text{per unit}}\right)}_{\text{Contribution margin per unit}} \times \text{Units sold} = \frac{\text{Fixed}}{\text{expenses}} + \frac{\text{Operating}}{\text{income}}$$

The sale price per unit minus the variable cost per unit equals the contribution margin per unit, so

Contribution margin per unit × Units sold = Fixed expenses + Operating income

DAILY EXERCISE 22-9

Dividing both sides of the equation by contribution margin per unit yields

$$\text{Units sold} = \frac{\text{Fixed expenses} + \text{Operating income}}{\text{Contribution margin per unit}}$$

Kay Pak can use this contribution margin CVP formula to find her breakeven point. Her fixed expenses total $7,000. Operating income is zero at the breakeven point. The contribution margin per poster is $14 ($35 sale price − $21 variable cost). Pak's breakeven computation is

$$= \frac{\$7,000 + \$0}{\$14}$$

$$= 500 \text{ posters}$$

The contribution margin CVP formula is derived from the income statement equation, so the two approaches are mathematically equivalent. Both approaches give the same answer (500 posters, in Pak's case).

Why does this shortcut method work? The formula shows that each poster Pak sells provides $14 of contribution margin. To break even, Pak must generate enough contribution margin to cover $7,000 of fixed expenses. At the rate of $14 per poster, Pak must sell 500 posters ($7,000/$14) to cover her $7,000 of fixed expenses.

Computing the Breakeven Point in Sales Dollars Using the Contribution Margin Ratio. It's easy to compute the breakeven point for a simple business, like Kay Pak's, that has only one product. The sale price per poster and the variable cost per poster are readily available. But what about companies that have hundreds of products, like **Sony** and **Procter & Gamble?**

Large companies often use the contribution margin ratio to compute breakeven points in terms of *sales dollars*, without detailed information on individual products. The contribution margin ratio approach differs from the contribution margin CVP formula we've just seen in only one way—fixed expenses plus operating income are divided by the contribution margin *ratio* to yield sales in *dollars:*

⊙ DAILY EXERCISE 22-10

$$\text{Sales in dollars} = \frac{\text{Fixed expenses + Operating income}}{\text{Contribution margin ratio}}$$

Using this ratio formula, Kay Pak's breakeven point in sales dollars is

$$\text{Sales in dollars} = \frac{\$7,000 + \$0}{0.40}$$

$$= \$17,500$$

This is the same breakeven sales revenue as shown in the proof on page 894.

Why does the contribution margin ratio formula work? Each dollar of Kay Pak's sales contributes $0.40 to fixed expenses and profit. To break even, she must generate enough contribution margin at the rate of $0.40 per sales dollar to cover the $7,000 fixed expenses ($7,000 ÷ 0.40 = $17,500).

Large companies find it easier to compute breakeven points in sales dollars using the contribution margin ratio approach because it does not require detailed information on individual products. The only information required is total fixed expenses and the contribution margin ratio. If Sony's total fixed expenses are $10 billion and its contribution margin ratio is 40%, the breakeven point in sales dollars would be

$$\text{Breakeven sales in dollars} = \frac{\$10 \text{ billion}}{0.40}$$

$$= \$25 \text{ billion}$$

CVP Sensitivity Analysis

SENSITIVITY ANALYSIS. A "what if" technique that asks what a result will be if a predicted amount is not achieved or if an underlying assumption changes.

Sensitivity analysis is a "what if" technique that asks what a result will be if a predicted amount is not achieved or if an underlying assumption changes. Let's use sensitivity analysis to see how changes in the sale price, variable costs, and fixed costs affect CVP analysis and the breakeven point.

QUESTION 2. If the Sale Price per Unit Is Changed, What Will the New Breakeven Sales Be?

Suppose the sale price per poster is $38.50 rather than $35. Variable expense per poster remains at $21, and fixed expenses stay at $7,000. What is the revised breakeven point? The per-unit contribution margin becomes $17.50 ($38.50 − $21.00), and the new contribution margin ratio is 0.4545 ($17.50 ÷ $38.50).

Using the contribution margin CVP formula:

$$\text{Sales in units} = \frac{\text{Fixed expenses + Operating income}}{\text{Contribution margin per unit}}$$

$$= \frac{\$7,000 + \$0}{\$17.50}$$

$$= 400 \text{ posters}$$

The higher sale price per unit increases the contribution margin per unit. As a result, Pak does not have to sell as many posters to break even.

Proof:

Sales revenue (400 × $38.50)...................................		$15,400
Less: Variable expenses (400 × $21)	$8,400	
Fixed expenses...	7,000	(15,400)
Operating income..		$ 0

The proof shows that Pak needs sales revenue of $15,400 to break even with a $38.50 sales price. We could also directly compute the breakeven sales in dollars using the contribution margin ratio form of the CVP formula:

$$\text{Sales in dollars} = \frac{\text{Fixed expenses} + \text{Operating income}}{\text{Contribution margin ratio}}$$

$$= \frac{\$7,000 + \$0}{0.4545}$$

$$= \$15,400 \text{ (rounded)}$$

This example shows that increasing the sale price reduces breakeven sales, both in units and in dollars. With a higher sale price, each poster contributes more toward fixed expenses, so Pak breaks even with fewer sales. Conversely, cutting the sale price would decrease the contribution margin. Then Kay Pak would have to sell more posters just to break even.

WORK IT OUT

Kay Pak believes she could dominate the e-commerce art poster business if she cut the sale price to $20. Is this a good idea?

Answer: No. The variable cost per poster is $21. If Pak sells posters for $20 each, she loses $1 on each poster. There can be no profit if the sale price does not even cover variable expenses.

QUESTION 3.   If Variable Costs Change, What Will Breakeven Sales Be?

◉ DAILY EXERCISE 22-11

Suppose Pak's variable expense per poster is $23.80 instead of $21. The sale price per poster remains $35, and fixed expenses stay at $7,000. What is the breakeven point in units and in dollars?

The new contribution margin per unit drops to $11.20 ($35.00 − $23.80), and the new contribution margin ratio falls to 0.32 ($11.20/$35.00). Breakeven sales are

$$\text{Sales in units} = \frac{\text{Fixed expenses} + \text{Operating income}}{\text{Contribution margin per unit}}$$

$$= \frac{\$7,000 + \$0}{\$11.20}$$

$$= 625 \text{ posters}$$

$$\text{Sales in dollars} = \frac{\text{Fixed expenses} + \text{Operating income}}{\text{Contribution margin ratio}}$$

$$= \frac{\$7,000 + \$0}{0.32}$$

$$= \$21,875$$

As these numbers make clear, higher variable expenses per unit reduce the contribution margin. As a result, Pak must sell more posters to break even. Conversely, a decrease in variable cost per unit would lower the breakeven point.

QUESTION 4.   If Fixed Costs Change, What Will Breakeven Sales Be?

◉ DAILY EXERCISE 22-12

Suppose the fixed costs total $10,500 instead of the original $7,000. Variable expense per poster remains at $21, and sale price stays at $35. What is Kay Pak's breakeven point in units and in dollars?

Using the contribution margin CVP formula:

$$\text{Sales in units} = \frac{\text{Fixed expenses} + \text{Operating income}}{\text{Contribution margin per unit}}$$

$$= \frac{\$10,500 + \$0}{\$14}$$

$$= 750 \text{ posters}$$

$$\text{Sales in dollars} = \frac{\text{Fixed expenses} + \text{Operating income}}{\text{Contribution margin ratio}}$$

$$= \frac{\$10,500 + \$0}{0.40}$$

$$= \$26,250$$

The $10,500 in fixed expenses is an increase of $3,500, or 50%, over the original fixed cost of $7,000. Note that fixed expenses increase by 50%, and breakeven sales also increase by 50% [(750 − 500) ÷ 500]. Pak must sell more posters to cover the higher fixed costs. However, if fixed expenses had declined, she could have sold fewer posters and still covered these (lower) costs.

Managers usually prefer a lower breakeven point to a higher one. But don't overemphasize this one aspect of CVP analysis. Managers are more interested in profits than in breakeven sales levels. Kay Pak may be willing to pay an extra $3,500 ($10,500 − $7,000) for Web banner ads if she expects the ads to stimulate enough extra sales volume to provide contribution margin to cover the extra advertising expense and to provide extra operating income.

Using CVP Analysis to Plan Profits

Managers of ongoing operations with established products and services are more interested in the sales level needed to earn a target profit than in the breakeven point. Now let's look at how managers use CVP analysis to plan profits.

Objective 4
Compute the sales level needed to earn a target operating income

 DAILY EXERCISE 22-13

QUESTION 5. How Many Units Must Be Sold to Earn a Target Operating Income?

Suppose Pak hopes to earn operating income of $4,900. Assuming fixed expenses of $7,000, variable expenses of $21 per poster, and a $35 per-poster sale price, how many posters must she sell to earn a profit of $4,900?

Until now, we have concentrated on the point at which operating income is zero. How should we consider a target operating income greater than zero? The contribution margin must be high enough to cover the fixed expenses *and* return a profit. We can still use the contribution margin CVP formula. The only difference is that target operating income is $4,900, compared to zero when we computed breakeven sales.

With a $14 ($35 − $21) contribution margin per unit:

$$\text{Sales in units} = \frac{\text{Fixed expenses} + \text{Operating income}}{\text{Contribution margin per unit}}$$

$$= \frac{\$7,000 + \$4,900}{\$14}$$

$$= \frac{\$11,900}{\$14}$$

$$= 850 \text{ posters}$$

Proof:

Sales revenue (850 × $35).....................................		$29,750
Less: Variable expenses (850 × $21)	$17,850	
Fixed expenses	7,000	(24,850)
Target operating income...		$ 4,900

This proof shows that Pak needs sales revenues of $29,750 to earn profit of $4,900. Alternatively, we can compute the dollar sales necessary to earn a $4,900 profit directly, using the contribution margin ratio form of the CVP formula:

$$\text{Sales in dollars} = \frac{\text{Fixed expenses} + \text{Operating income}}{\text{Contribution margin ratio}}$$

$$= \frac{\$7,000 + \$4,900}{0.40}$$

$$= \frac{\$11,900}{0.40}$$

$$= \$29,750$$

QUESTION 6. What Operating Income Is Expected at Various Sales Levels?

Objective 5
Graph a set of cost-volume-profit relationships

EXHIBIT 22-7
Cost-Volume-Profit Graph

⊙ DAILY EXERCISE 22-14

⊙ DAILY EXERCISE 22-16

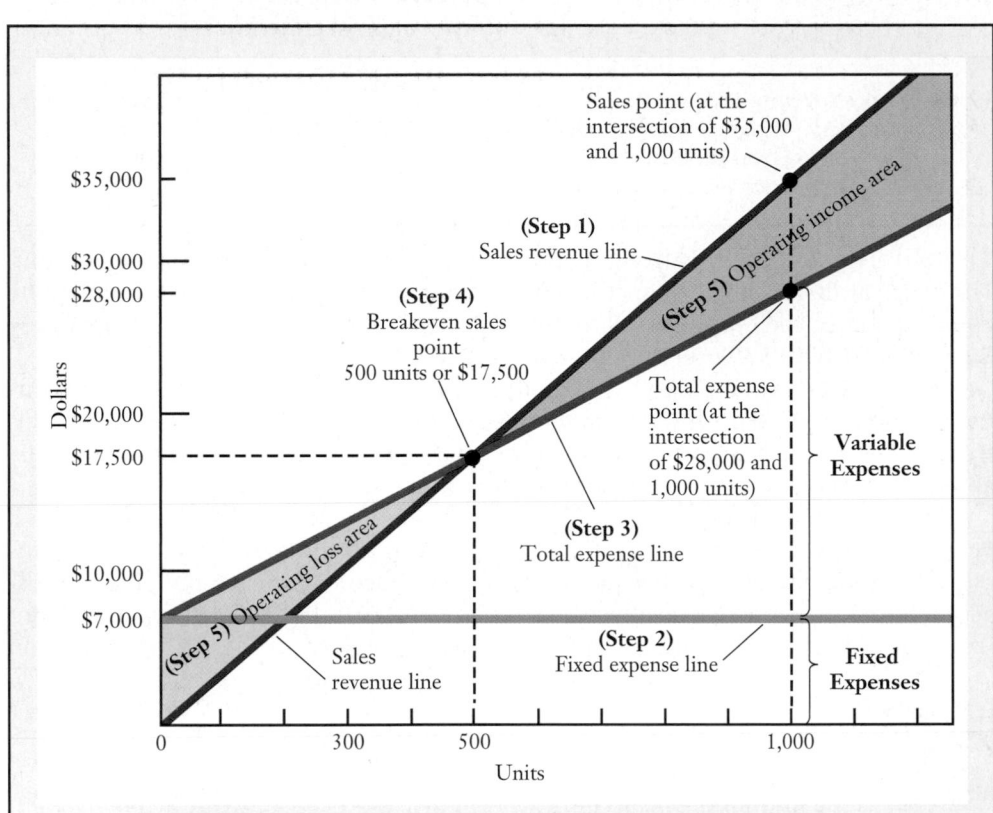

The cost-volume-profit graph in Exhibit 22-7 provides a convenient way to determine expected operating income at various sales levels. As in the cost behavior graphs earlier in this chapter (Exhibits 22-1 through 22-4), we place units on the horizontal axis and dollars on the vertical axis. We use Kay Pak's data (as originally given on page 893) and follow five steps:

Step 1. Choose a sales volume, such as 1,000 units. Plot the point for total sales revenue at that volume: 1,000 units × $35 per unit = sales of $35,000. Draw the *sales revenue line* from the origin (0) through the $35,000 point. Why does the sales revenue line start at the origin? If no posters are sold, there is no sales revenue.

Step 2. Draw the *fixed expense line,* a horizontal line that intersects the dollars axis at $7,000. Why is the fixed expense line flat? Because fixed expenses are the same ($7,000) no matter how many posters Pak sells.

Step 3. Draw the *total expense line*. Total expense is the sum of variable expense plus fixed expense. Compute variable expense at the chosen sales volume: 1,000 units × $21 per unit = variable expense of $21,000. Add variable expense to fixed expense: $21,000 + $7,000 = $28,000. Plot the total expense point ($28,000) for 1,000 units. Then draw a line through this point from the $7,000 fixed expense intercept on the dollars axis. This is the *total expense line*. Why does the total expense line start at the fixed expense line? If Pak sells no posters, she still incurs the $7,000 fixed cost for the server leasing, Internet access, and office rental, but she incurs no variable costs.

Step 4. Identify the *breakeven point*. The breakeven point is the point where the sales revenue line intersects the total expense line. This is the point where sales revenue exactly equals total expenses. The formulas we used earlier told us that Pak's breakeven point is 500 units, or $17,500 in sales. The graph shows us this information visually.

Step 5. Mark the *operating income* and the *operating loss* areas on the graph. To the left of the breakeven point, the total expense line lies above the sales revenue line. Expenses exceed sales revenue, leading to an operating loss. For example, Exhibit 22-7 shows that if Pak sells only 300 posters, she incurs an operating loss. The amount of the loss is the vertical distance between the total expense line and the sales revenue line:

Sales revenue (300 × $35)......................................		$10,500
Deduct: Variable expenses (300 × $21)	$6,300	
Fixed expenses	7,000	(13,300)
Operating income..		$ (2,800)

To the right of the breakeven point in Exhibit 22-7, the business earns a profit. The vertical distance between the sales revenue line and the total expense line equals income. The graph shows that if Pak sells 1,000 posters, she earns operating income of $7,000 ($35,000 sales revenue − $28,000 total expenses).

Why bother with a graph? Why not just use the equation approach or the contribution margin CVP formula? Graphs like Exhibit 22-7 help managers quickly estimate the profit or loss earned at different levels of sales. The equation or formula approaches only indicate income or loss for a single sales amount.

Sophisticated enterprise resource planning software like SAP, Oracle, and Peoplesoft provides detailed data that managers can use in CVP analysis. For example, after **Sears** stores lock their doors at 9:00 P.M., records for each individual transaction flow into a massive database. From a Diehard battery sold in Texas to a Trader Bay polo shirt sold in New Hampshire, the system compiles an average of 1.5 million

e-Accounting

Kozmo.com and Urbanfetch.com: Can They Continue to Deliver the Goods for Free?

It's a service made to order for couch potatoes and hectic, housebound moms. Dot.com "delivery boys" **Kozmo.com** and **Urbanfetch.com** will deliver anything from video rentals and Doritos to diapers and extra-strength Tylenol directly to your door in an hour or less. And delivery is free. Kozmo.com's friendly, spandex-suited "Kozmonauts" even tuck in a little bundle of jellybeans with your order.

Kozmo.com and Urbanfetch.com have won over both consumers and investors. Founded in 1997, Kozmo is located in five cities and plans to expand to 30 markets by the end of 2000. How can these companies make a profit, much less survive? The more people use their service, the higher their delivery costs—*variable costs*. Unlike **Amazon.com** and other e-tailers, they can't recover those costs by charging customers.

Both companies are trying various strategies to beef up revenue and keep delivery costs from sucking them dry.

- **Minimum order.** Kozmo will no longer deliver a 99¢ box of Junior Mints to the door for free; it now requires a minimum order. And Urbanfetch now requires customers to spend at least $10.
- **High-margin items.** Urbanfetch has begun stocking high-ticket items like $250 air-conditioners and PalmPilots. Its average order is $40.
- **Corporate clients.** Kozmo has a deal to deliver books, music, and toys to Amazon.com customers, and Amazon pays for the service. Urbanfetch delivers packages for **Sony Corp.** and a prominent New York law firm.

Source: Based on Andrea Petersen, "Web delivery firms adapt to turn profit," *Wall Street Journal*, June 22, 2000, p. B13. Erik Sherman, "Web delivery—in an hour," *Computerworld*, March 6, 2000, pp. 54–56. Lyle Harris, "Service while you sit, Kozmo.com fills orders fast, but selection limited." Digital Living: REPORTS FROM THE E-WORLD Buyer's Edge: YOUR THURSDAY GUIDE TO SAVING TIME and MONEY, *The Atlanta Constitution*, April 13, 2000, p. D1.

transactions a day. With the click of a mouse, managers access sale price, variable cost, and sales volume for individual products to conduct breakeven or profit planning analyses. And they can call up summary sales revenue, variable cost, and fixed cost data to perform similar analyses by individual stores or by regions.

Companies without sophisticated software systems use simple spreadsheets to answer "what if" questions such as: What will variable expenses be if sales rise by $1,000? By 200 units? If we cut fixed expenses by $20,000, how many units must we sell to earn a profit of $100,000? Spreadsheets allow managers to analyze the results of one change or several changes in the business's operations. Most software also displays CVP graphs similar to Exhibit 22-7.

OTHER CVP APPLICATIONS

Margin of Safety

The **margin of safety** is the excess of expected sales over breakeven sales. This is the drop in sales the company can absorb before incurring an operating loss. A low margin of safety is a warning. Managers use the margin of safety to evaluate current operations or to measure the risk of a new business plan.

Pak's breakeven point in our original data is 500 posters. Suppose she expects to sell 950 posters. Her margin of safety is

Objective 6
Compute a margin of safety

MARGIN OF SAFETY. Excess of expected sales over breakeven sales. Drop in sales a company can absorb before incurring an operating loss.

> **Margin of safety in units = Expected sales in units − Breakeven sales in units**
>
> = 950 posters   − 500 posters
> = 450 posters

 DAILY EXERCISE 22-15

> **Margin of safety in dollars = Margin of safety in units × Sale price per unit**
>
> = 450 posters   × $35
> = $15,750

 DAILY EXERCISE 22-17

Sales can drop by 450 posters, or $15,750, before Pak incurs a loss.

Managers can also compute the margin of safety as a percentage for any level of sales. Simply divide the margin of safety by sales. We obtain the same percentage whether we use units or dollars.

In units:

> **Margin of safety as a percentage** $= \dfrac{\text{Margin of safety in units}}{\text{Expected sales in units}}$
>
> $= \dfrac{450 \text{ posters}}{950 \text{ posters}}$
>
> = 47.4% (rounded)

In dollars:

> **Margin of safety as a percentage** $= \dfrac{\text{Margin of safety in dollars}}{\text{Expected sales in dollars}}$
>
> $= \dfrac{450 \text{ units} \times \$35}{950 \text{ units} \times \$35}$
>
> $= \dfrac{\$15,750}{\$33,250}$
>
> = 47.4% (rounded)

Sales Mix

Our CVP example has focused on a business with a single product, art posters. Companies that sell more than one product must consider *sales mix* in figuring CVP relationships. Sales mix has an important effect on profits. A company earns more income by selling high-margin products than by selling an equal number of low-margin items.

Objective 7
Use the sales mix in CVP analysis

For example, **Continental Airlines** has focused on attracting more businesspeople. Business travelers generally pay more for the same flight than leisure travelers. By increasing the proportion of higher-paying business fliers, Continental recently boosted its sales revenue per available seat-mile (available seats × miles flown) from $0.074 to $0.09. Improving sales mix by selling more high-margin tickets reduced Continental's breakeven point. Before the change, Continental had to fill 63% of its seats to break even. By attracting more business travelers, Continental only has to fill 61%.

In contrast to Continental's more favorable sales mix, **Deere and Company,** manufacturer of John Deere farm equipment, indicates that profits have decreased because of "a less favorable mix of products sold." What is a *less favorable mix* of products? It is a mix with a higher percentage of items that have below-average contribution margins.

We can use the same CVP formulas we used for a company with a single product to perform CVP analysis for a company that sells more than one product. But first, we must compute the *weighted-average contribution margin* of all products. The sales mix provides the weights.

➦ We saw another weighted-average procedure—for inventory costing—in Chapter 9 and for process costing in Chapter 21.

Suppose Kay Pak plans to sell two types of posters. Recall that the regular poster costs $21 and sells for $35. Its contribution margin is $14 ($35 − $21). The second, larger poster costs $40, and sells for $70. Its contribution margin is $30 ($70 − $40).

An established business estimates its sales mix based on experience. But Pak is starting a new venture. Suppose she expects to sell 500 regular posters and 300 large posters. This is a 5:3 sales mix. For every 5 regular posters, Pak expects to sell 3 large posters, so she expects 5/8 of the sales to be regular posters and 3/8 to be large posters. To compute breakeven sales in units, Pak arranges the data as follows:

◉ DAILY EXERCISE 22-18

◉ DAILY EXERCISE 22-20

	Regular Posters	Large Posters	Total
Sale price per unit	$35	$70	
Deduct: Variable expense per unit	(21)	(40)	
Contribution margin per unit	$14	$30	
Sales mix in units	5	3	8
Contribution margin	$70	$90	$160
Weighted-average contribution margin per unit ($160/8)			$ 20

$$\text{Sales in total units} = \frac{\text{Fixed expenses} + \text{Operating income}}{\text{Weighted-average contribution margin per unit}}$$

$$= \frac{\$7,000 + \$0}{\$20}$$

$$= 350 \text{ posters}$$

Breakeven sales of regular posters (350 × 5/8)	218.75 regular posters
Breakeven sales of large posters (350 × 3/8)	131.25 large posters

◉ DAILY EXERCISE 22-19

◉ DAILY EXERCISE 22-21

As is often the case in real situations, these computations don't yield round numbers. Since Pak cannot sell partial posters, she must sell 219 regular posters and 132 large posters to avoid a loss. Using these rounded numbers would lead to a small rounding error in our check figures, however, so the rest of our computations will use the exact results: 218.75 regular posters and 131.25 large posters.

The overall breakeven point in sales dollars is $16,844 (amounts rounded to the nearest dollar):

218.75 regular posters at $35 each	$ 7,656
131.25 large posters at $70 each	9,188
Total revenues	$16,844

We can check these amounts by preparing a contribution margin income statement (amounts rounded to the nearest dollar):

	Regular	Large	Total
Sales revenue:			
Regular (218.75 × $35)	$7,656		
Large (131.25 × $70)		$9,188	$16,844
Variable expenses:			
Regular (218.75 × $21)	4,594		
Large (131.25 × $40)		5,250	9,844
Contribution margin	$3,062	$3,938	$ 7,000
Fixed expenses			(7,000)
Operating income			$ 0

Let's review our approach:

- Compute the weighted-average contribution margin per unit. This figure expresses both types of posters in terms of a single hypothetical product that has a contribution margin of $20. From here on, the contribution margin approach follows the usual pattern.
- Divide fixed expenses (plus operating income) by the weighted-average contribution margin per unit to determine the required sales in total units.
- Separate total units (350) into regular posters (218.75) and large posters (131.25).

The breakeven proof shows that Pak's breakeven sales are $16,844. Pak could also use the contribution margin ratio formula to estimate breakeven sales in dollars. But first, she must estimate her contribution margin ratio:

Total expected contribution margin:		
Regular posters (500 × $14)	$ 7,000	
Large posters (300 × $30)	9,000	$ 16,000
Divided by total expected sales:		
Regular posters (500 × $35)	$17,500	
Large posters (300 × $70)	21,000	÷38,500
Contribution margin ratio		41.558%

Then, Pak uses the contribution margin ratio form of the CVP formula to estimate breakeven sales in dollars:

$$\text{Sales in dollars} = \frac{\text{Fixed expenses} + \text{Operating income}}{\text{Contribution margin ratio}}$$

$$= \frac{\$7,000 + \$0}{0.41558}$$

$$= \underline{\$16,844} \text{ (rounded)}$$

If Pak's actual sales mix is not 5 regular posters to 3 large posters, her actual operating income will differ from the planned amount, even if she sells exactly 800 total posters. For each total number of posters sold, there are as many different operating incomes as there are sales mixes. Similarly, there are as many different breakeven points—in total units and in sales dollars—as there are sales mixes. The sales-mix factor greatly complicates planning.

 **THINK IT OVER** Suppose Kay Pak plans to sell 800 total posters in the 5 : 3 sales mix (5 regular posters sold for every 3 large posters). She *actually* sells 800 posters—375 regular and 425 large. The unit sale prices and variable expenses are exactly as predicted, and the fixed expense is the budgeted $7,000. Can you tell, without computations, whether Pak's actual operating income is greater than, less than, or equal to her expected income?

Answer: Pak sold more of the higher-margin large posters. This favorable change in the sales mix increased her operating income.

Companies use CVP analysis to motivate their sales forces. Salespeople who know the contribution margin of each product they sell can generate more profit by emphasizing high-margin products. Many companies base sales commissions on the contribution margins produced by sales rather than on sales revenue alone.

The next section uses the building blocks of CVP analysis (contribution margin, the distinction between variable and fixed costs) to explain a costing approach that many managers use for internal decisions. Before continuing, review the CVP Analysis Decision Guidelines to make sure you understand these basic concepts.

DECISION GUIDELINES

Cost-Volume-Profit Analysis

DECISION

How do changes in the number of units affect
- total costs?

- cost per unit?

What is the difference between gross profit and contribution margin?

How to compute sales needed to break even or earn a target operating income
- in units?

- in dollars?

How to use CVP analysis to measure risk?

GUIDELINES

Total variable costs → Change in proportion to changes in volume

Total fixed costs → No change

Variable cost per unit → No change

Fixed cost per unit:
  Increases when volume drops (Fixed costs are spread over fewer units)

Decreases when volume rises (Fixed costs are spread over more units)

      Gross profit = Sales − Cost of goods sold

Contribution margin = Sales − Total variable expenses

$$\frac{\text{Fixed expense} + \text{Operating income}}{\text{Contribution margin per unit}}$$

$$\frac{\text{Fixed expense} + \text{Operating income}}{\text{Contribution margin ratio}}$$

Margin of safety = Expected sales − Breakeven sales

EXCEL APPLICATION PROBLEM

Goal: Create an Excel spreadsheet and graph to show the relationship between costs, volume, and profit, and discover the breakeven point.

Scenario: Phonetronix, Inc., is a small manufacturer of telephone and communications devices. Recently, company management decided to investigate the profitability of cellular phone production. Their proposed new phone would sell for $99.00. Variable cost per unit is $55.00, and total fixed costs are $110,000.

1. Using the data in the spreadsheet, at what volume does Phonetronix break even on production? On the graph embedded in the spreadsheet, point the cursor at the breakeven point. Does the "pop-up" value for Total Costs match Total Revenue?
2. What is the breakeven point if Phonetronix raises the price per unit to $129? Note the changes in the graph. Which direction did the breakeven point move?
3. What is the breakeven point if the price per unit is $99, but Phonetronix slashes the variable costs per phone down to $49? Note the changes in the graph. Which direction did the breakeven point move?

Step-by-Step:
1. Open a new Excel spreadsheet.
2. Create a boldfaced heading for your spreadsheet that contains the following:
   a. Chapter 22 Decision Guidelines
   b. CVP Analysis
   c. Phonetronix, Inc.
   d. Today's date
3. Move down two rows and enter the boldfaced and underlined heading "Data Section" in Column A.
4. Move down one row. Starting in Column A, enter three rows of data, with these descriptions: price, variable cost per unit, and total fixed costs. Format cells as needed as you work.
5. Move down two rows. Enter the following boldfaced and underlined column headings, in order:
   a. # Units Sold
   b. Total Revenue
   c. Total Variable Costs
   d. Total Fixed Costs
   e. Total Costs
   f. Total Profit

6. Enter # Units Sold, in 200 unit increments, starting at 100 units, and going up to 3,500 units. (*Hint:* use a formula for this.)
7. Enter the formulas for the remaining five columns.
8. Create your graph by selecting one row of titles and all data except the "Total Profit" column. Then, click on the Chart Wizard. Select the basic line graph without data values or 3D effects.
9. Title your graph "CVP Analysis," label the X-axis

"# Units Sold" and Y-axis "Dollars." Click to finish the graph. (Your X-axis values will range from "1" to "17", not the actual unit values. To see the actual values, position your cursor over the X-axis to see a pop-up box containing the values.)
10. Position the graph at the bottom of your data in the spreadsheet, and size to fit if necessary.
11. Save your file to disk, and print a copy (in color, if possible) for your files after each change.

VARIABLE COSTING AND ABSORPTION COSTING

Objective 8
Compute income using variable costing and absorption costing

Thus far, we have assigned both variable and fixed manufacturing costs to products. This approach is called **absorption costing** because products absorb fixed manufacturing costs as well as variable manufacturing costs. Supporters of absorption costing argue that companies cannot produce products without fixed manufacturing costs, so these costs are an important part of product costs.

ABSORPTION COSTING. The costing method that assigns both variable and fixed manufacturing costs to products.

For planning and decision making, many managers prefer a different approach. **Variable costing** assigns only variable manufacturing costs to products. Under variable costing, fixed manufacturing costs are considered period costs, and are expensed in the period when they are incurred. Supporters of variable costing argue that fixed manufacturing costs (such as depreciation on the plant) provide the capacity to produce during a period. Because the company incurs these fixed expenses whether or not it produces any products or services, they are period costs, not product costs.

VARIABLE COSTING. The costing method that assigns only variable manufacturing costs to products.

While variable costing often provides a more useful basis for management decisions, companies can use variable costing only for internal reports. GAAP requires that inventory be costed at the full cost to manufacture (or purchase) the goods. Consequently, published financial statements are based on absorption costing. Exhibit 22-8 clarifies the difference between variable and absorption costing.

The only difference between absorption costing and variable costing is that absorption costing considers fixed manufacturing costs as inventoriable product costs, while variable costing considers fixed manufacturing costs as period costs (expenses).

EXHIBIT 22-8
Differences Between Absorption Costing and Variable Costing

	Absorption Costing	Variable Costing
Product Costs (Capitalized as Inventory until expensed as Cost of Goods Sold)	Direct materials Direct labor Variable manufacturing overhead Fixed manufacturing overhead	Direct materials Direct labor Variable manufacturing overhead
Period Costs (Expensed in period incurred)	 Variable nonmanufacturing costs Fixed nonmanufacturing costs	Fixed manufacturing overhead Variable nonmanufacturing costs Fixed nonmanufacturing costs
Focus	External reporting— required by GAAP	Internal reporting only
Typical Income Statement Format	Conventional income statement as in Chapters 1–19	Contribution margin statement

All other costs are treated the same way under both absorption and variable costing:

- Variable manufacturing costs are inventoriable products costs.
- All nonmanufacturing costs are period costs.

Illustrating Variable Versus Absorption Costing: Sportade

To see how absorption costing and variable costing differ, let's consider the following example. Sportade manufactures a sports beverage in both liquid and powdered form. Sportade incurs the following costs for its powdered mix in March 20X5.

Direct material cost per case..	$ 6.00
Direct labor cost per case..	3.00
Variable manufacturing overhead cost per case..................	2.00
Sales commission per case..	2.50
Total fixed manufacturing overhead expenses......................	50,000
Total fixed marketing and administrative expenses..............	25,000

Sportade produced 10,000 cases of powdered mix as planned, but sold only 8,000 cases, at a price of $30 per case. There were no beginning inventories, so Sportade has 2,000 cases of powdered mix in ending finished goods inventory (10,000 cases produced − 8,000 cases sold).

What is Sportade's inventoriable product cost per case under absorption costing and variable costing?

	Absorption Costing	Variable Costing
Direct materials	$ 6.00	$ 6.00
Direct labor	3.00	3.00
Variable manufacturing overhead..............	2.00	2.00
Fixed manufacturing overhead..................	5.00*	
Total cost per case	$16.00	$11.00

$$* \frac{\$50,000 \text{ fixed manufacturing overhead}}{10,000 \text{ cases}} = \$5 \text{ per case}$$

The only difference between absorption and variable costing is that fixed manufacturing overhead is a product cost under absorption costing, but a period cost under variable costing. This is why the cost per case is $5 higher under absorption costing (total cost of $16) than under variable costing ($11).

Exhibit 22-9 shows that absorption costing income statements typically use the conventional format from Chapters 1–19: Sales minus cost of goods sold equals gross profit. Chapter 19 showed that manufacturers compute cost of goods sold by starting with beginning finished goods inventory (zero, in Sportade's case). They then add the cost of goods *manufactured,* computed by multiplying the number of units *produced* (10,000 cases) by the absorption costing product cost per unit ($16/case). They then subtract the ending finished goods inventory—the number of

Exhibit 22-9
Absorption Costing Income Statement

DAILY EXERCISE 22-21

SPORTADE		
Income Statement (Absorption Costing)		
Month Ended March 31, 20X5		
Sales revenue (8,000 × $30)		$240,000
Deduct: Cost of goods sold:		
Beginning finished goods inventory	$ 0	
Cost of goods manufactured (10,000 × $16)...................	160,000	
Cost of goods available for sale	160,000	
Ending finished goods inventory (2,000 × $16)..............	(32,000)	
Cost of goods sold..		(128,000)
Gross profit		112,000
Deduct: Operating expenses		
[(8,000 × $2.50) + $25,000]		(45,000)
Operating income		$ 67,000

units multiplied by the absorption cost per unit (2,000 cases × $16 per case in our example)—to obtain the cost of goods sold. From gross profit we subtract operating expenses (nonmanufacturing expenses) to find absorption costing operating income. The data on page 906 indicate that Sportade paid a $2.50 per-case sales commission for each case *sold,* so the total sales commission is $20,000 (8,000 cases sold × $2.50 per case). Fixed marketing and administrative costs are $25,000, somarketing and administrative expenses total $45,000 ($20,000 + $25,000).

Notice that the total cost of goods manufactured is the number of cases *produced,* multiplied by the total manufacturing cost per case. In contrast, total variable marketing expenses (for example, sales commissions) equal the variable cost per case multiplied by the number of cases *sold.*

Exhibit 22-10 shows that variable costing income statements use the contribution margin income statement format illustrated earlier in Exhibit 22-5 (Panel B). All the variable expenses are deducted from sales to get contribution margin. First, notice that the details of the (variable) cost of goods sold computation parallel those in the absorption costing income statement, *except we use the $11 variable costing product cost per case rather than the $16 absorption cost per case.*

EXHIBIT 22-10
Variable Costing Income Statement

SPORTADE Income Statement (Variable Costing) Month Ended March 31, 20X5		
Sales revenue (8,000 × $30)		$240,000
Deduct: Variable expenses:		
Variable cost of goods sold:		
Beginning finished goods inventory	$ 0	
Variable cost of goods manufactured (10,000 × $11)	110,000	
Variable cost of goods available for sale	110,000	
Ending finished goods inventory (2,000 × $11)	(22,000)	
Variable cost of goods sold	88,000	
Sales commission expense (8,000 × $2.50)	20,000	(108,000)
Contribution margin		132,000
Deduct: Fixed expenses:		
Fixed manufacturing overhead	50,000	
Fixed marketing and administrative expenses	25,000	(75,000)
Operating income		$ 57,000

To get the contribution margin, we subtract from sales both the variable cost of goods sold [$88,000 = (10,000 × $11) − (2,000 × $11)] and variable operating expenses like the sales commission (8,000 cases sold × $2.50 sales commission per case). Finally, to obtain variable costing operating income, we subtract from contribution margin all the fixed expenses ($50,000 fixed manufacturing overhead + $25,000 fixed marketing and administrative expenses).

Reconciling the Difference Between Absorption and Variable Costing Incomes

Exhibit 22-9 shows that Sportade's absorption costing operating income is $67,000. However, Exhibit 22-10 shows that variable costing yields only $57,000 of operating income. Why is operating income $10,000 lower under variable costing? To answer this question, we need to understand what happened to the $160,000 ($110,000 variable + $50,000 fixed) total manufacturing costs under each costing method.

The total manufacturing costs incurred in March are either

• Expensed in March, or
• Held back in inventory (an asset).

Exhibit 22-11 shows that of the $160,000 manufacturing costs incurred during March, absorption costing holds back $32,000 (2,000 × $16) as inventory. This $32,000 assigned to inventory is not expensed until next month, when the units are sold. Thus, only $160,000 − $32,000 = $128,000 of the manufacturing costs are expensed as cost of goods sold during March.

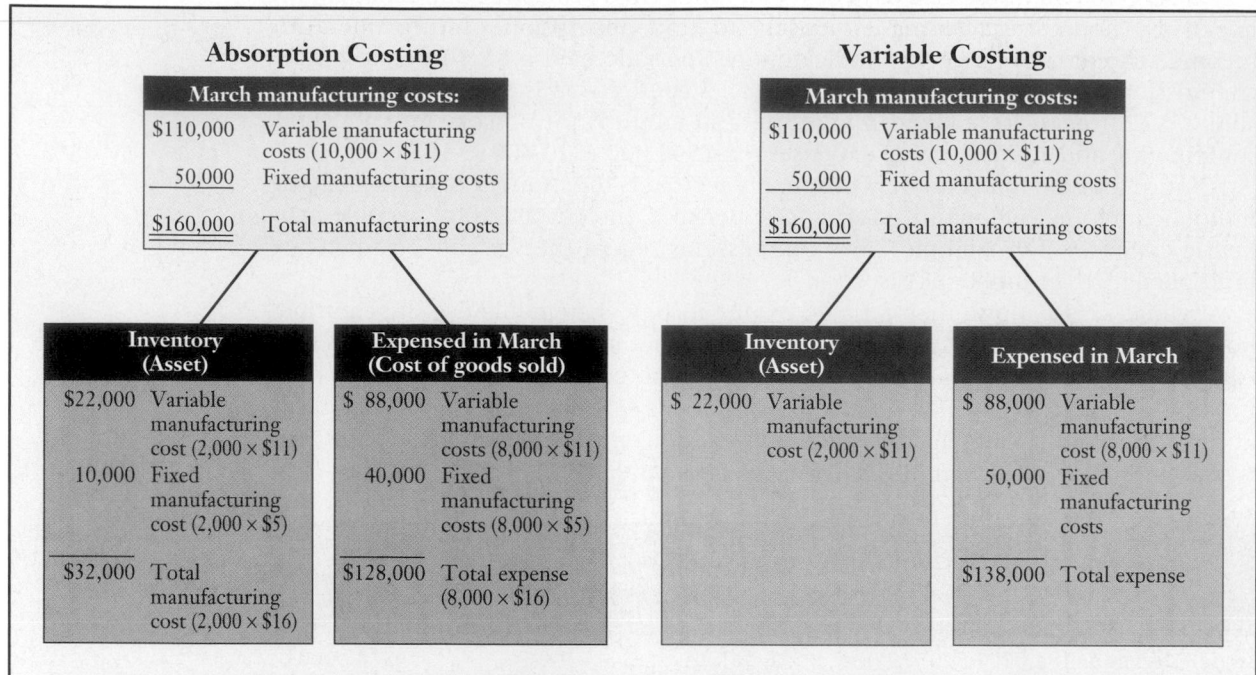

Variable costing holds back in ending inventory only $22,000 (2,000 × $11) of the total manufacturing costs. This is $10,000 ($22,000 − $32,000) *less* than absorption costing holds back in inventory. The difference arises because absorption costing assigns the $5 per case fixed manufacturing overhead costs to the 2,000 cases in ending inventory, while variable costing does not—it expenses all the fixed manufacturing overhead in the current month.

Costs that are not held back in inventory are expensed in the current period, so variable costing expenses $138,000 ($160,000 − $22,000) of manufacturing costs in March. (This $138,000 also equals the $88,000 variable cost of goods sold plus the $50,000 fixed manufacturing overhead.) This is $10,000 *more* than the $128,000 absorption costing expenses during March. *Variable costing has $10,000 more expense in March, so its income is $10,000 lower than absorption costing income.*

THINK IT OVER

Suppose Sportade has no inventory at the end of the next month, April. Will absorption costing report higher or lower operating income than variable costing for the month of April?

Answer: Absorption costing will report lower income than variable costing during April. Ending inventory in March becomes the beginning inventory of April. Absorption costing assigns a higher value to beginning inventory in April. When that beginning inventory is sold, the higher beginning inventory costs increase cost of goods sold for April, which in turn reduces income.

DAILY EXERCISE 22-24

Absorption Costing and Managers' Incentives

The general rule is this: When inventories increase (more units are produced than sold), absorption costing income is higher than variable costing income. When inventories decline (when fewer units are produced than sold), absorption costing income is lower than variable costing income. Suppose the Sportade manager receives a bonus based on absorption costing income. Will the manager want to increase or decrease production?

The manager knows that absorption costing assigns each case of Sportade $5 of fixed manufacturing overhead.

- For every case that is produced but not sold, absorption costing "hides" $5 of fixed overhead in ending inventory (an asset).

- The more cases added to inventory, the more fixed overhead is "hidden" in ending inventory at the end of the month.
- The more fixed overhead in ending inventory, the smaller the cost of goods sold, and the higher the operating income.

To maximize the bonus under absorption costing, the manager may try to increase production to build up inventory.

This incentive directly conflicts with the just-in-time philosophy, which emphasizes minimal inventory levels. ➡ Companies that have adopted just-in-time should either (1) evaluate their managers based on variable costing income, or (2) implement strict controls to prevent inventory build-up.

◄ Chapter 19 introduced the just-in-time philosophy.

Before continuing, take time to study the Absorption and Variable Costing Decision Guidelines to make sure you understand the differences between these two costing methods.

DECISION GUIDELINES

Absorption and Variable Costing

DECISION	GUIDELINE
When to use absorption costing? Variable costing?	Absorption costing must be used for external reporting. Variable costing is used only for internal reporting.
What is the difference between absorption and variable costing?	Fixed manufacturing costs are treated as • inventoriable product costs under absorption costing • period costs under variable costing

Absorption Costing	Variable Costing
Direct materials	Direct materials
+ Direct labor	+ Direct labor
+ Variable overhead	+ Variable overhead
+ Fixed overhead	—
= Product cost	= Product cost

How to compute product costs under absorption costing and variable costing?

How to determine whether absorption costing income is higher, lower, or the same as variable costing income?

If units produced > units sold:
Absorption costing income > Variable costing income

If units produced < units sold:
Absorption costing income < Variable costing income

If units produced = units sold:
Absorption costing income = Variable costing income

REVIEW CVP ANALYSIS

SUMMARY PROBLEM

Problem 1

Fleet Foot buys hiking socks for $6 a pair and sells them for $10. Management budgets monthly fixed costs of $10,000 for sales volumes between 0 and 12,000 pairs.

Required

1. Use both the income statement equation approach and the shortcut contribution margin CVP formula to compute the company's monthly breakeven sales in units.
2. Use the contribution margin ratio approach to compute the breakeven point in sales dollars.
3. Compute the monthly sales level (in units) required to earn a target operating income of $14,000. Use either the income statement equation approach or the contribution margin approach.

www.prenhall.com/horngren

End-of-Chapter Assessment

4. Prepare a graph of Fleet Foot's CVP relationships, similar to Exhibit 22-7. Draw the sales revenue line, the fixed expense line, and the total expense line. Label the axes, the breakeven point, the operating income area, and the operating loss area.

Problem 2

Suppose Fleet Foot sells a second product—heavy-duty shoelaces. Each pair costs $7 and sells for $15. Fixed costs remain $10,000 a month.

Required

1. If Fleet Foot sells 2 pairs of hiking socks for every 3 pairs of shoelaces, what is the company's breakeven sales in units? (Use the contribution margin approach.)

2. If expected sales total 11,000 units, what is Fleet Foot's margin of safety in units?

Solutions

Problem 1

Requirement 1

Income statement equation approach:

$$\text{Sales} - \text{Variable expenses} - \text{Fixed expenses} = \text{Operating income}$$

$$\left(\begin{matrix} \text{Sale price} \\ \text{per unit} \end{matrix} \times \begin{matrix} \text{Sales in} \\ \text{units} \end{matrix} \right) - \left(\begin{matrix} \text{Variable} \\ \text{cost per unit} \end{matrix} \times \begin{matrix} \text{Sales in} \\ \text{units} \end{matrix} \right) - \begin{matrix} \text{Fixed} \\ \text{expenses} \end{matrix} = \begin{matrix} \text{Operating} \\ \text{income} \end{matrix}$$

$$
\begin{aligned}
(\$10 \times \text{Sales in units}) - (\$6 \times \text{Sales in units}) - \$10{,}000 &= \$0 \\
(\$10 - \$6) \times \text{Sales in units} &= \$10{,}000 \\
\$4 \times \text{Sales in units} &= \$10{,}000 \\
\text{Sales in units} &= \$10{,}000 \div \$4 \\
\text{Breakeven sales in units} &= 2{,}500 \text{ units}
\end{aligned}
$$

Contribution margin approach:

$$\text{Sales in units} = \frac{\text{Fixed expenses} + \text{Operating income}}{\text{Contribution margin per unit}}$$

$$
\begin{aligned}
\text{Breakeven sales in units} &= \frac{\$10{,}000 + \$0}{\$10 - \$6} \\[2mm]
&= \frac{\$10{,}000}{\$4} \\[2mm]
&= 2{,}500 \text{ units}
\end{aligned}
$$

Requirement 2

$$
\begin{aligned}
\text{Breakeven sales in dollars} &= \frac{\text{Fixed expenses} + \text{Operating income}}{\text{Contribution margin ratio}} \\[2mm]
&= \frac{\$10{,}000 + \$0}{0.40^{*}} \\[2mm]
&= \$25{,}000
\end{aligned}
$$

$$^{*}\text{Contribution margin ratio} = \frac{\text{Contribution margin per unit}}{\text{Sale price per unit}} = \frac{\$4}{\$10} = 0.40$$

Requirement 3

Income statement equation approach:

$$\text{Sales} - \text{Variable expenses} - \text{Fixed expenses} = \text{Operating income}$$

$$\left(\begin{matrix} \text{Sale price} \\ \text{per unit} \end{matrix} \times \begin{matrix} \text{Sales in} \\ \text{units} \end{matrix} \right) - \left(\begin{matrix} \text{Variable} \\ \text{cost per unit} \end{matrix} \times \begin{matrix} \text{Sales in} \\ \text{units} \end{matrix} \right) - \begin{matrix} \text{Fixed} \\ \text{expenses} \end{matrix} = \begin{matrix} \text{Operating} \\ \text{income} \end{matrix}$$

$$
\begin{aligned}
(\$10 \times \text{Sales in units}) - (\$6 \times \text{Sales in units}) - \$10{,}000 &= \$14{,}000 \\
(\$10 - \$6) \times \text{Sales in units} &= \$10{,}000 + \$14{,}000 \\
\$4 \times \text{Sales in units} &= \$24{,}000 \\
\text{Sales in units} &= \$24{,}000 \div \$4 \\
\text{Sales in units} &= 6{,}000 \text{ units}
\end{aligned}
$$

Contribution margin approach:

$$\text{Sales in units} = \frac{\text{Fixed expenses} + \text{Operating income}}{\text{Contribution margin per unit}}$$

$$= \frac{\$10,000 + \$14,000}{(\$10 - \$6)}$$

$$= \frac{\$24,000}{\$4}$$

$$= 6,000 \text{ units}$$

Requirement 4

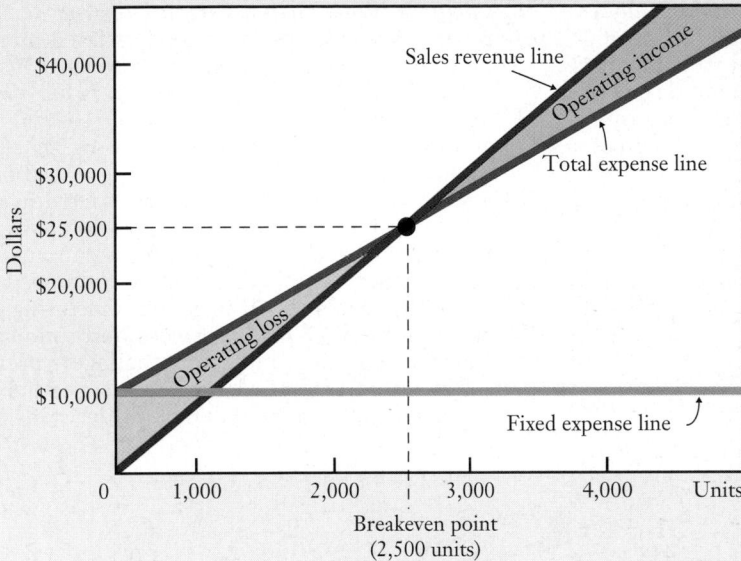

Breakeven point
(2,500 units)

Problem 2

Requirement 1

	Hiking Socks	Shoelaces	Total
Sale price per unit	$10	$15	
Deduct: Variable expense per unit	6	7	
Contribution margin per unit	$ 4	$ 8	
Sales mix in units	× 2	× 3	5
Contribution margin	$ 8	$24	$ 32
Weighted-average contribution margin per unit ($32 ÷ 5 units)			$6.40

$$\text{Breakeven sales in units} = \frac{\text{Fixed expenses} + \text{Operating income}}{\text{Weighted-average contribution margin per unit}}$$

$$= \frac{\$10,000 + \$0}{\$6.40}$$

$$= 1,563 \text{ units (rounded)}$$

Breakeven sales of hiking socks (1,563 × 2/5) .... 625 pairs of hiking socks
Breakeven sales of shoelaces (1,563 × 3/5) .... 938 pairs of shoelaces

Requirement 2

Margin of safety in units = Expected sales in units − Breakeven sales
= 11,000 − 1,563
= 9,437 units

LESSONS LEARNED

1. **Identify different cost behavior patterns.** *Cost-volume-profit (CVP) analysis* expresses the relationships among costs, volume of activity, and profit. These relationships depend on *cost behavior*. We classify costs as *variable, fixed,* or *mixed.*

2. **Use a contribution margin income statement to make business decisions.** A *contribution margin income statement* reports variable expenses and fixed expenses separately. It features the total *contribution margin,* the excess of sales revenues over variable expenses. This format helps managers predict the operating income that will result from various decisions.

3. **Compute breakeven sales and perform sensitivity analyses.** We use an equation or formula derived from the contribution margin income statement to compute a company's *breakeven point*—the sales level at which operating income is zero. We also perform sensitivity analyses to determine how changes in sale price, variable costs, or fixed costs affect the breakeven point.

4. **Compute the sales level needed to earn a target operating income.** CVP analysis also can show how many units the company must sell to earn a target operating income. The target operating income is added to the total fixed expense to determine the total contribution margin required. That amount is divided by the per-unit contribution margin to give the number of units that must be sold.

5. **Graph a set of cost-volume-profit relationships.** CVP graphs show the breakeven point and the ranges of sales volume that yield operating incomes and operating losses.

6. **Compute a margin of safety.** The *margin of safety* is the excess of expected sales over breakeven sales. The larger the margin, the lower the risk.

7. **Use the sales mix in CVP analysis.** *Sales mix* is the combination of products that make up total sales. There is a unique breakeven point for each different sales mix—the greater the proportion of higher margin items, the lower the breakeven point. Companies with multiple products use the weighted-average contribution margin per unit in computing the breakeven point.

8. **Compute income using variable costing and absorption costing.** Variable costing considers fixed manufacturing costs as period costs that are expensed in the period incurred. Absorption costing considers fixed manufacturing costs as inventoriable product costs. Variable and absorption costing yield different income figures when the number of units in inventory changes. Absorption costing assigns some of the current period's fixed manufacturing costs to ending inventory, so this portion of current period fixed manufacturing cost is not expensed until future periods when the units are sold. In contrast, variable costing always expenses all fixed manufacturing costs in the current period. **GAAP** requires absorption costing for external reporting, but many managers prefer variable costing for internal use because the separation of variable and fixed costs is helpful in making decisions.

ACCOUNTING VOCABULARY

absorption costing (p. 905)
breakeven point (p. 893)
contribution margin (p. 891)
contribution margin income statement (p. 891)
contribution margin per unit (p. 894)

contribution margin ratio (p. 894)
cost behavior (p. 887)
cost-volume-profit (CVP) analysis (p. 887)
fixed cost (p. 888)
margin of safety (p. 901)
mixed cost (p. 889)

relevant range (p. 890)
sales mix (p. 893)
sensitivity analysis (p. 896)
variable costs (p. 887)
variable costing (p. 905)

QUESTIONS

1. How do managers use cost-volume-profit analysis in planning?
2. Define the three types of cost behavior patterns.
3. Draw graphs of the three types of costs.
4. What are three questions cost-volume-profit analysis can answer?
5. How does a contribution margin income statement differ from a conventional income statement? Which is more useful for predicting how a change in sales will affect income? Why?
6. Why is the relevant range important in cost-volume-profit analysis?
7. What is the breakeven point? What is its significance to a business?
8. How does an increase in fixed expenses affect the breakeven point? How does a decrease in fixed expenses affect breakeven sales? Give the reason for each answer.

9. How does an increase in variable expenses affect the breakeven point? How does a decrease in variable expenses affect breakeven sales? Give the reason for each answer.
10. How does an increase in sale price affect the breakeven point? How does a decrease in sale price affect breakeven sales? Give the reason for each answer.
11. Briefly outline two ways to compute the sales in dollars needed to earn a target operating income.
12. What advantages does a CVP graph have over the income statement equation approach and the contribution margin approach?
13. How does the margin of safety serve as a measure of risk?
14. Briefly describe how to perform CVP analysis when a company sells more than one product.
15. How is fixed manufacturing overhead cost expensed under absorption costing? Under variable costing?

ASSESS YOUR PROGRESS

DAILY EXERCISES

DE22-1 Vandersteen builds innovative loudspeakers for music and home theater. Identify the following costs as variable or fixed:

Variable and fixed costs
(Obj. 1)

  a. Depreciation on routers used to cut wood enclosures
  b. Wood for speaker enclosures
  c. Patents on crossover relays
  d. Crossover relays
  e. Grill cloth
  f. Glue
  g. Quality inspector's salary

DE22-2 Fill in the blanks using one of the following:

Variable and fixed costs
(Obj. 1)

  • Stays the same   • Decreases   • Increases

  a. As the number of units increases, the variable cost per unit _____.
  b. As the number of units decreases, the variable cost per unit _____.
  c. As the number of units increases, the fixed cost per unit _____.
  d. As the number of units decreases, the fixed cost per unit _____.
  e. As the number of units increases, the total variable cost _____.
  f. As the number of units decreases, the total variable cost _____.
  g. As the number of units increases, the total fixed cost _____.
  h. As the number of units decreases, the total fixed cost _____.

DE22-3 Suppose World-Link offers an international calling plan that charges $3.00 per month plus $0.45 per minute for calls to China.

Mixed costs
(Obj. 1)

  1. Under this plan, what is your monthly international long-distance cost if you call China for

   a. 20 minutes?   **b.** 40 minutes?   **c.** 80 minutes?

  2. Draw a graph illustrating your total cost under this plan. Label the axes, and show your costs at 20, 40, and 80 minutes.

DE22-4 Suppose you were recently hired as an accounting intern at Optical Cable Corporation. Your boss, Bob Knechel, hands you the following information from November's operations and asks you to compute gross profit and contribution margin.

Gross profit and contribution margin
(Obj. 2)

Sales revenue...	$120,000
Sales commissions	2,500
Variable manufacturing cost of goods sold	50,000
Fixed marketing expense......................................	12,000
Research and development (fixed)........................	3,000
Fixed manufacturing cost of goods sold	20,000
Delivery expense (variable)	5,000

DE22-5 Your boss at Optical Cable (Daily Exercise 22-4) is puzzled by the difference between gross profit and contribution margin. Write a short memo explaining the primary difference between gross profit and contribution margin, using the following format:

Gross profit and contribution margin
(Obj. 2)

Date:	_____
To:	_____
From:	_____
Subject:	_____

DE22-6 Consider the Kast-A-Ways Swimwear income statements in Exhibit 22-5, page 891. How much of the total cost of goods sold consists of fixed manufacturing costs?

Cost of goods sold
(Obj. 2)

DE22-7 Blue Sky, Inc., produces climbing rope. The company incurs $100,000 of fixed expenses per month. It sells the rope for $23 per yard, and it incurs variable expenses at the rate of $9 per yard. Prepare a contribution margin income statement, assuming that Blue Sky sells 15,000 yards of rope in July.

Preparing a contribution margin income statement   *(Obj. 2)*

DE22-8 CEO John Hand thinks Blue Sky could increase its sales to 25,000 yards of rope in August if the company paid its sales force a commission of $1 per yard. What would be Blue Sky's operating income if it adopted the sales commission plan? Should Blue Sky adopt the sales commission plan? Why or why not?

DE22-9 Consider the **Grand Canyon Railway** example from the chapter opening story. Suppose the railway decides to offer only one class of service, Coach class, at an all-inclusive round-trip ticket price of $55 per passenger. Assume variable expenses of $15 per passenger. If Grand Canyon has $250,000 of fixed expenses per month, compute the number of round-trip tickets it must sell to break even:

    a. Using the income statement equation approach
    b. Using the shortcut contribution margin CVP formula

Perform a numerical proof to ensure that your answer is correct.

DE22-10 Refer to the information given in Daily Exercise 22-9.

    1. Compute **Grand Canyon Railway's** contribution margin ratio. Carry your computation to five decimal places.
    2. Use the contribution margin ratio CVP formula to determine the sales revenue Grand Canyon needs to break even.

DE22-11 Refer to the information given in Daily Exercise 22-9.

    1. Suppose **Grand Canyon Railway** cuts its round-trip ticket price from $55 to $50 in order to increase the number of passengers. Compute the new breakeven point in units (passenger round-trips) and in sales dollars.
    2. Return to the original information in Daily Exercise 22-9. Grand Canyon Railway could reduce its variable costs by eliminating champagne from the afternoon beverages. Suppose this reduces the variable expense from $15 to $12 per passenger. Compute the new breakeven point in units (passenger round-trips) and in dollars.

DE22-12 Consider the original **Grand Canyon Railway** information in Daily Exercise 22-9. Suppose Grand Canyon embarks on a cost reduction drive, and slashes fixed expenses from $250,000 per month to $200,000 per month.

    1. Compute the new breakeven point in units (passenger round-trips) and in sales dollars.
    2. Is the breakeven point higher or lower than in Daily Exercise 22-9? Explain.

DE22-13 If **Grand Canyon Railway** has a target operating income of $30,000 per month, how many round-trip tickets must the company sell? Use the original data given in Daily Exercise 22-9.

DE22-14 Using the original information in Daily Exercise 22-9, draw a graph of **Grand Canyon Railway's** cost-volume-profit relationships. Include the sales revenue line, the fixed expense line, and the total expense line. Label the axes, the breakeven point, the income area, and the loss area.

DE22-15 Consider the original **Grand Canyon Railway** information in Daily Exercise 22-9. If Grand Canyon expects to sell 7,000 round-trip tickets, compute the margin of safety.

    a. In units (round-trip tickets)   **b.** In sales dollars   **c.** As a percentage of expected sales

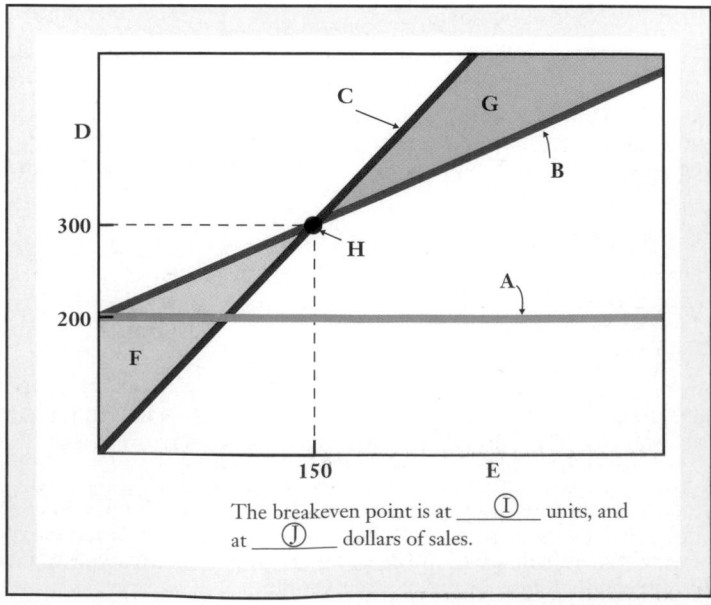

The breakeven point is at _____ units, and at _____ dollars of sales.

DE22-16 Describe what each letter stands for in the cost-volume-profit graph.

Interpreting a CVP graph (Obj. 5)

DE22-17 Consider Kay Pak's e-tail poster business. Suppose Pak expects to sell 900 posters. Use the original data on pages 894–896 to compute her margin of safety:

Computing margin of safety (Obj. 6)

a. In units (posters)   b. In sales dollars   c. As a percentage of expected sales

DE22-18 Kay Pak's e-tail poster business incurs $7,000 of fixed expenses and has the following sales and variable expenses per poster:

Sales mix and weighted-average contribution margin (Obj. 7)

	Regular Posters	Large Posters
Sale price per unit	$35	$70
Variable expense per unit	21	40

Suppose Pak estimates she will sell 10 regular posters for every 2 large posters. Compute the weighted-average contribution margin per unit. Carry your computations to five decimal places.

DE22-19 Refer to the data in Daily Exercise 22-18 and your answer. Compute

Breakeven point and sales mix (Obj. 7)

a. The total number of posters Pak must sell to break even.
b. The number of regular posters and the number of large posters she must sell to break even.
c. Compare your answer to the breakeven point calculated on page 902–903. Does the 10:2 sales mix increase or decrease the breakeven point? Why?

DE22-20 Consider the **Grand Canyon Railway** example from the chapter opening story. Suppose Grand Canyon decides to offer two classes of service: Coach class and Chief class. Assume Grand Canyon incurs $250,000 of fixed expenses per month and that it has the following ticket prices and variable expenses:

Sales mix and weighted-average contribution margin (Obj. 7)

	Coach Class	Chief Class
Sale price per ticket	$55.00	$124.00
Variable expense per passenger	15.00	24.00

If Grand Canyon Railway expects to sell five tickets in Coach class for every three tickets in Chief class, compute the weighted-average contribution margin per unit (round-trip ticket).

DE22-21 Refer to the **Grand Canyon Railway** data in Daily Exercise 22-20 and your answer. Compute

Breakeven point and sales mix (Obj. 7)

a. The total number of tickets Grand Canyon must sell to break even.
b. The number of Coach class tickets and the number of Chief class tickets the company must sell to break even.

DE22-22 Consider the Sportade example on pages 906–909. Suppose that during April, the company produces 10,000 cases of powdered drink mix, and sells 12,000 cases. Sale price, variable cost per case, and total fixed expenses remain the same as in March. Prepare the April income statement using variable costing.

Computing variable costing income (Obj. 8)

DE22-23 Refer to the Sportade example on pages 906–909, and the data and your answer to Daily Exercise 22-22.

Comparing variable and absorption costing income (Obj. 8)

1. Prepare the April income statement under absorption costing.
2. Is absorption costing income higher or lower than variable costing income? Explain why.

DE22-24 For a service company like **Grand Canyon Railway,** will absorption and variable costing give different operating income figures? Explain.

Absorption and variable costing (Obj. 8)

EXERCISES

Graphing cost behavior
(Obj. 1)

E22-1 Graph the following cost behavior patterns over a relevant range of 0–10,000 units:

a. Variable expenses of $8 per unit
b. Mixed expenses made up of fixed costs of $20,000 and variable costs of $3 per unit
c. Fixed expenses of $15,000

Preparing a contribution margin
income statement
(Obj. 2)

E22-2 Riley Watches' April income statement follows:

RILEY WATCHES		
Income Statement		
For the Month of April 20XX		
Sales revenue		$720,000
Cost of goods sold		448,000
Gross profit		272,000
Operating expenses:		
Marketing expense	$92,000	
General and administrative expense	42,000	134,000
Operating income		$138,000

Riley's cost of goods sold is a variable expense. Marketing expense is 30% fixed and 70% variable. General and administrative expense is 60% fixed and 40% variable.

Required

1. Prepare Riley's contribution margin income statement for April.
2. Compute the expected increase in operating income to the nearest $1,000 if sales increase by $50,000.

Using a contribution margin
income statement and comput-
ing breakeven sales
(Obj. 2, 3)

E22-3 For its top managers, Blue Sea Travel formats its income statement as follows:

BLUE SEA TRAVEL	
Contribution Margin Income Statement	
Three Months Ended March 31, 20XX	
Sales revenue	$ 320,000
Variable expenses	96,000
Contribution margin	224,000
Fixed expenses	210,000
Operating income	$ 14,000

Blue Sea's relevant range is between sales of $250,000 and $360,000. Prepare contribution margin income statements at those volume levels. Also, compute breakeven sales in dollars.

Computing breakeven sales by
the contribution margin approach
(Obj. 3)

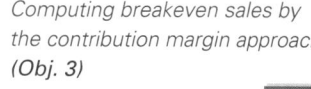

E22-4 Baker Breakfast Co. produces frozen bagels. The company has fixed expenses of $63,000, and variable expenses of $1.10 per package. Each package sells for $2.00.

Required

1. Compute the contribution margin per package and the contribution margin ratio.
2. Determine the breakeven point in units and in dollars, using the contribution margin approach.

Computing a change in
breakeven sales
(Obj. 3)

E22-5 Noodles Now fast-food restaurant has been doing such great business that owner May Chen is considering franchising her restaurant concept. She believes that customers across the country will happily pay $6 for a large bowl of noodles, veggies, and meat. Variable costs are $2.10 a bowl. Chen estimates that monthly fixed cost for franchisees would be $7,150.

Required

1. Use the contribution margin ratio approach to compute a franchisee's breakeven sales in dollars.
2. Is franchising a good idea for Chen if franchisees will want a minimum monthly operating income of $7,800, but Chen does not believe most locations could generate more than $25,000 in monthly sales?

Computing breakeven sales and
operating income or loss under
different conditions *(Obj. 3, 4)*

E22-6 West Coast Motor Freight delivers freight throughout California, Oregon, and Washington. The company has monthly fixed expenses of $490,000 and a contribution margin of 70% of revenues.

Required

1. Compute West Coast's monthly breakeven sales in dollars. Use the contribution margin ratio approach.
2. Compute West Coast's monthly operating income or operating loss if revenues are $500,000 and if they are $800,000.

E22-7 William Calhoun is considering starting a Web-based educational business, e-Prep MBA. He plans to offer a short-course review of mathematics for students entering MBA programs. The materials would be available on a password-protected Web site and students would complete the course through self-study. Calhoun would have to grade the course assignments, but most of the work is in developing the course materials, setting up the site, and marketing. Unfortunately, Calhoun's hard drive crashed before he finished his financial analysis. However, he did recover the following partial CVP chart:

Analyzing a cost-volume-profit graph
(Obj. 5)

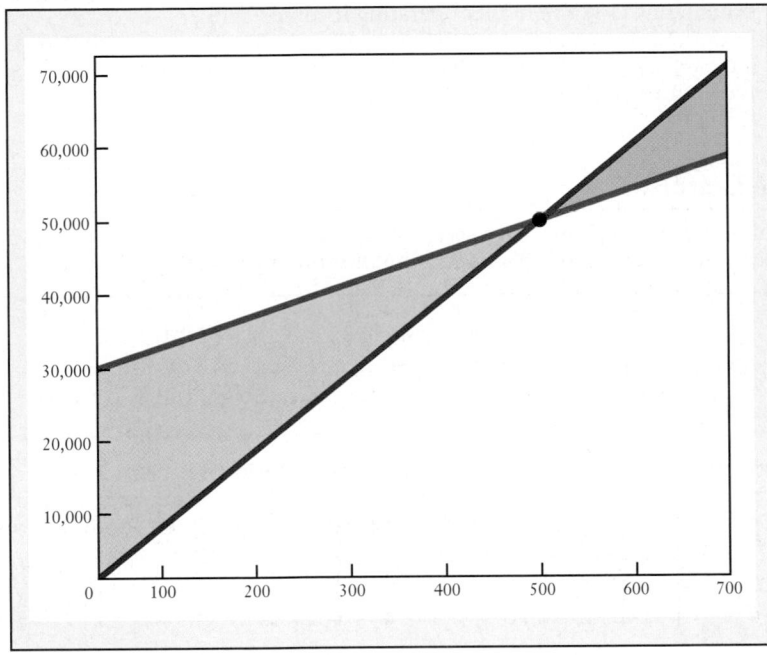

Required

1. Label each axis, sales revenue, total expenses, fixed expenses, operating income, and operating loss.
2. If Calhoun is certain he can attract 340 students to take the course, will the venture be profitable?
3. What are the breakeven sales in students and dollars?

E22-8 Suppose that Coors Field, the home of the Colorado Rockets, earns total revenue that averages $18 for every ticket sold. Assume that annual fixed expenses are $24 million, and variable expenses are $2 per ticket.

Graphing cost-volume-profit relationships
(Obj. 5)

Required

1. Prepare the ballpark's CVP graph under these assumptions. Label the axes, sales revenue line, fixed expense line, total expense line, the operating loss area, and the operating income area on the graph.
2. Show the breakeven point in dollars and in tickets.

E22-9 Waldron's drug store has a monthly target operating income of $11,000. Variable expenses are 60% of sales, and monthly fixed expenses are $9,000.

Computing breakeven and a margin of safety   (Obj. 3, 6)

Required

1. Compute the monthly margin of safety in dollars if the store achieves its income goal.
2. Express Waldron's margin of safety as a percentage of target sales.

E22-10 Three college friends open an off-campus shop named Campus Sweats. They plan to sell a standard sweatshirt for $18 and a fancier version for $22. The $18 sweatshirt costs them $10, and the $22 sweatshirt costs them $12. The friends expect to sell two fancy sweatshirts for every three standard sweatshirts. Their monthly fixed expenses are $9,680. How many of each type of sweatshirt must they sell monthly to break even? To earn $6,600?

CVP analysis with a sales mix
(Obj. 7)

Preparing absorption costing and variable costing income statements; business decision
(Obj. 2, 8)

E22-11 The 20X4 data that follow pertain to Oakley, a manufacturer of solid oak coffee tables. (Oakley has no beginning inventories in January 20X4.)

Sale price	$350	Fixed manufacturing	
Variable manufacturing		overhead	$2,000,000
expense per table...................	275	Fixed operating expense......	250,000
Sales commission		Number of tables produced ..	100,000
expense per table...................	40	Number of tables sold	85,000

Required

1. Prepare both conventional (absorption costing) and contribution margin (variable costing) income statements for Oakley.
2. Which statement shows the higher operating income? Why?
3. Oakley's marketing vice president believes a new sales promotion that costs $150,000 would increase sales to 100,000 tables. Should the company go ahead with the promotion? Give your reason.

Challenge Exercise

Computing contribution margin for one of two products
(Obj. 7)

E22-12 Solo, Inc., manufactures two styles of climbing shoe—the Mountaineer and the Pro Mountaineer. The following data pertain to the Mountaineer:

Variable manufacturing cost..............	$ 70
Variable operating cost	20
Sale price	160

Solo's monthly fixed expenses total $140,000. When Mountaineers and Pro Mountaineers are sold in the mix of 7:3, respectively, the sale of 2,000 total pairs results in an operating income of $60,000. Compute the contribution margin per pair for the Pro Mountaineers.

(Group A) PROBLEMS

Explaining the effects of different cost behavior patterns
(Obj. 1)

P22-1A Lelaine Johnson is in charge of the Los Angeles Regional Head Start program. Legislators have just cut the program's funding by 15%. Johnson cannot cut total fixed costs like the rent for the program's offices or salaries of the administrative staff. The other main costs are salaries for teachers ($30,000/yr) and teachers' aides ($12,000/yr). Johnson cannot cut the salary paid per teacher or teacher's aid.

What alternatives does Johnson have to meet the budget? Will the 15% funding cut reduce services provided by more than 15%, less than 15%, or close to 15%? Explain your reasoning.

Computing contribution margins and breakeven points
(Obj. 2, 3)

P22-2A The budgets of four companies yield the following information:

	Company			
	E	F	G	H
Target sales	$340,000	$_____	$550,000	$_____
Variable expenses	_____	100,000	280,000	104,000
Fixed expenses	_____	82,000	138,000	_____
Operating income (loss)	$ 60,000	$_____	$_____	$ 35,000
Units sold....................................	93,500	5,000	_____	_____
Contribution margin per unit....	$2	_____	$100	$12
Contribution margin ratio	_____	0.20	_____	0.60

Fill in the blanks for each company. Which company has the lowest breakeven point in sales dollars? What causes the low breakeven point?

BE and sales to earn a target Op. Inc.; CM/IS   (Obj. 2, 3, 4)

P22-3A The Royal Blue schooner sails in the U.S. Virgin Islands during the winter. The average cruise has 45 tourists on board, and each person pays $75 for a day's sail. The ship sails 80 days each year. The Royal Blue also has a crew of fifteen, each earning an average of $95 per cruise. The crew is paid only when the ship sails. The other variable expense is for refreshments, which average $14 per passenger per cruise. Annual fixed expenses total $66,000.

Required

1. Compute revenue and variable expenses for each cruise.
2. Use the income statement equation approach to compute the number of cruises the Royal Blue must make each year to break even.
3. Use the contribution margin approach to compute the number of cruises needed each year to earn $85,800. Is this profit goal realistic? Give your reason.
4. Prepare the Royal Blue contribution margin income statement for 80 cruises for the year. Report only two categories of expenses: variable and fixed.

P22-4A Studio Signatures imprints T-shirts with company logos. Studio has fixed expenses of $585,000 per year plus variable expenses of $4.20 per T-shirt. Each T-shirt sells for $12.00.

Analyzing CVP relationships (Obj. 2, 3, 4)

Required

1. Use the income statement equation approach to compute the number of T-shirts Studio must sell each year to break even.
2. Use the contribution margin ratio CVP formula to compute the dollar sales Studio needs to earn $32,500 in operating income.
3. Prepare Studio's contribution margin income statement for 20X4 for sales of 70,000 T-shirts. Cost of goods sold is 80% of variable expenses. Operating expenses make up the rest of variable expenses and all of fixed expenses.
4. The company is considering an expansion that will increase fixed expenses by 20% and variable expenses by 30 cents per T-shirt. Compute the new breakeven point in units and in dollars. Use either the income statement equation approach or the contribution margin approach.
5. Should Studio undertake the expansion? Give your reason.

P22-5A Pacific Paradise Travel is opening an office in Seattle. Fixed monthly expenses are office rent ($3,700), depreciation on office furniture ($300), utilities ($210), a special telephone line ($650), a connection with the airlines' computerized reservation service ($480), and the salary of a travel agent ($2,500). Variable expenses include commissions for the travel agent (7% of sales), advertising (8% of sales), supplies and postage (2% of sales), and usage fees for the telephone line and computerized reservation service (3% of sales).

Computing breakeven sales and sales needed to earn a target operating income; graphing CVP relationships (Obj. 1, 3, 4, 5)

Required

1. Use the contribution margin ratio CVP formula to compute Pacific Paradise's breakeven sales in dollars. If the average sale is a $700 plane ticket, how many tickets must be sold to break even?
2. Use the income statement equation approach to compute the dollar sales needed to earn a target monthly operating income of $4,160.
3. Graph the travel agency's CVP relationships. Assume that an average sale is a $700 plane ticket. Show the breakeven point, sales revenue line, fixed expense line, total expense line, operating loss area, operating income area, and the sales in units (tickets) and dollars when monthly operating income of $4,160 is earned. The graph should range from 0 to 25 units (plane tickets).
4. Assume that the average sale price decreases to $490 per ticket. Use the contribution margin approach to compute the new breakeven point in tickets sold. How does the lower sale price affect the breakeven point?

P22-6A The contribution margin income statement of Brick Oven Pizza for February 20XX follows:

Using a contribution margin income statement for breakeven analysis; sales mix, margin of safety, and changes in CVP relationships (Obj. 2, 3, 6, 7)

BRICK OVEN PIZZA
Contribution Margin Income Statement
For the Month of February 20XX

Sales revenue		$185,000
Variable expenses:		
Cost of goods sold	$32,000	
Marketing expense	25,000	
General and administrative expense	3,000	60,000
Contribution margin		125,000
Fixed expenses:		
Marketing expense	17,000	
General and administrative expense	10,500	27,500
Operating income		$ 97,500

Brick Oven sells three small pizzas for every large pizza. A small pizza sells for $8, with a variable expense of $3.75. A large pizza sells for $16, with a variable expense of $6.75.

Required

1. Determine Brick Oven's monthly breakeven point in the numbers of small pizzas and large pizzas. Prove your answer by preparing a summary contribution margin income statement at the breakeven level of sales. Show only two categories of expenses: variable and fixed.
2. Compute Brick Oven's margin of safety in dollars.
3. If Brick Oven can increase monthly sales volume by 15%, what will operating income be?

Preparing absorption and variable costing income statements and explaining the difference in income
(Obj. 8)

P22-7A ◄ *Link Back to Chapter 19 (Manufacturing Company Income Statement) and Chapter 20 (Manufacturing Overhead).* Magical Melodies manufactures music boxes, which it sells for $45 each. The company uses the FIFO inventory costing method, and it computes a new monthly fixed manufacturing overhead rate based on the actual number of music boxes produced that month. All costs and production levels are exactly as planned. The following data are from Magical Melodies' first two months in business during 20X4:

	October	November
Sales	2,000 units	2,200 units
Production	2,500 units	2,000 units
Variable manufacturing expense per music box	$15	$15
Sales commission per music box	$8	$8
Total fixed manufacturing overhead	$10,000	$10,000
Total fixed marketing and administrative expenses	$9,000	$9,000

Required

1. Compute the product cost per music box produced under absorption costing and under variable costing. Do this first for October and then for November.
2. Prepare separate monthly income statements for October and for November, using
   a. Absorption costing
   b. Variable costing
3. Is operating income higher under absorption costing or variable costing in October? In November? Explain the pattern of differences in operating income based on absorption costing versus variable costing.

(Group B) P R O B L E M S

Explaining the effects of different cost behavior patterns on the breakeven point and on likely profits
(Obj. 1)

P22-1B Techman Computer Parts is opening early next year. India Landrum, the owner, is considering two plans for obtaining the plant assets and the sales force needed for operations. Plan 1 calls for purchasing all equipment and paying the sales force straight salaries. Under plan 2, Techman would lease equipment month by month and pay the sales force low salaries but give them a big part of their pay in commissions. Discuss the effects of the two plans on variable expenses, fixed expenses, breakeven sales, and likely profits for a new business in the start-up stage. Indicate which plan you favor for Techman.

Computing contribution margins and breakeven points
(Obj. 2, 3)

P22-2B The budgets of four companies yield the following information:

	Company			
	P	**Q**	**R**	**S**
Target sales	$360,000	$600,000	$190,000	$
Variable expenses	108,000			130,000
Fixed expenses		312,000	100,000	
Operating income (loss)	$ 15,000	$	$	$160,000
Units sold		112,000	12,000	8,000
Contribution margin per unit	$6		9.50	$40
Contribution margin ratio		0.30		

Fill in the blanks for each company. Which company has the lowest breakeven point in sales dollars? What causes the low breakeven point?

BE sales and sales to earn a target Op. Inc.; CM IS *(Obj. 2, 3, 4)*

P22-3B Bahama Sunset sails a schooner from Nassau, Bahamas. The average cruise has 80 tourists on board. Each person pays $85 for a day's sail in the Atlantic. The ship sails 100 days each year.

The schooner has a crew of 12. Each crew member earns an average of $105 per cruise. The crew is paid only when the ship sails. Other variable expenses are for refreshments, which average $18 per passenger per cruise. Annual fixed expenses total $184,500.

Required

1. Compute revenue and variable expenses for each cruise.
2. Use the income statement equation approach to compute the number of cruises needed annually to break even.
3. Use the contribution margin approach to compute the number of cruises needed annually to earn $196,800. Is this profit goal realistic? Give your reason.
4. Prepare Bahama's contribution margin income statement for 100 cruises each year. Report only two categories of expenses: variable and fixed.

P22-4B Colorworks imprints calendars with company names. The company has fixed expenses of $415,000 each month plus variable expenses of $2.49 per carton of calendars. Colorworks sells each carton of calendars for $4.15.

Analyzing CVP relationships (Obj. 2, 3, 4)

Required

1. Use the income statement equation approach to compute the number of cartons of calendars Colorworks must sell each month to break even.
2. Use the contribution margin ratio CVP formula to compute the dollar amount of monthly sales Colorworks needs to earn $35,000 in operating income.
3. Prepare Colorworks' contribution margin income statement for June for sales of 450,000 cartons of calendars. Cost of goods sold is 70% of variable expenses. Operating expenses make up the rest of the variable expenses and all of the fixed expenses.
4. The company is considering an expansion that will increase fixed expenses by 40% and variable expenses by one-third. Compute the new breakeven point in units and in dollars. Use either the income statement equation approach or the contribution margin approach.
5. How would this expansion affect Colorworks' risk?

P22-5B Small World Travel is opening an office in Chicago. Fixed monthly expenses are office rent ($3,700), depreciation of office furniture ($190), utilities ($160), a special telephone line ($390), a connection with the airlines' computerized reservation service ($480), and the salary of a travel agent ($1,800). Variable expenses include commissions for the travel agent (12% of sales), advertising (9% of sales), supplies and postage (2% of sales), and usage fees for the telephone line and computerized reservation service (7% of sales).

Computing breakeven sales and sales needed to earn a target operating income; graphing CVP relationships (Obj. 1, 3, 4, 5)

Required

1. Use the contribution margin ratio CVP formula to compute the travel agency's breakeven sales in dollars. If the average sale is an $800 plane ticket, how many tickets must be sold to break even?
2. Use the income statement equation approach to compute dollar sales needed to earn monthly operating income of $3,430.
3. Graph the travel agency's CVP relationships. Assume that an average sale is an $800 plane ticket. Show the breakeven point, sales revenue line, fixed expense line, total expense line, operating loss area, operating income area, and the sales in units (tickets) and dollars when monthly operating income of $3,430 is earned. The graph should range from 0 to 20 units (plane tickets).
4. Assume that the average sale price decreases to $640 per ticket. Use the contribution margin approach to compute the new breakeven point in units (tickets). How does the lower sale price affect the breakeven point?

P22-6B The November 20X4 contribution margin income statement of Fazzio Fashion accessories store follows:

Using a contribution margin income statement for breakeven analysis; sales mix, margin of safety, and changes in CVP relationships (Obj. 2, 3, 6, 7)

FAZZIO FASHION Contribution Margin Income Statement For the Month of November 20X4		
Sales revenue		$60,000
Variable expenses:		
Cost of goods sold	$22,000	
Marketing expenses	13,000	
General and administrative expenses	7,000	42,000
Contribution margin		18,000
Fixed expenses:		
Marketing expenses	11,000	
General and administrative expenses	3,850	14,850
Operating income		$ 3,150

Fazzio Fashion sells two hats for every purse. The hats sell for $18, with a variable expense of $7 each. The purses sell for $45, with a variable cost of $22 each.

Required

1. Determine Fazzio Fashion's monthly breakeven point in the numbers of hats and purses. Prove your answer by preparing a summary contribution margin income statement at the breakeven level of sales. Show only two categories of expenses: variable and fixed.
2. Compute Fazzio Fashion's margin of safety in dollars.
3. Suppose Fazzio Fashion increases monthly sales volume by 20%. Compute operating income.

Preparing absorption and variable costing income statements and explaining the difference in income

(Obj. 8)

P22-7B ← *Link Back to Chapter 19 (Manufacturing Company Income Statement) and Chapter 20 (Manufacturing Overhead).* Spacesaver Corporation manufactures plastic storage bins, which it sells for $8 each. The company uses the FIFO inventory costing method, and it computes a new monthly fixed manufacturing overhead rate based on the actual number of bins produced that month. All costs and production levels are exactly as planned. The following data are from Spacesaver's first two months in business:

	January 20X4	February 20X4
Sales	1,000 bins	1,200 bins
Production	1,400 bins	1,000 bins
Variable manufacturing expense per bin	$4	$4
Sales commission expense per bin	$1	$1
Total fixed manufacturing overhead	$700	$700
Total fixed marketing and administrative expenses	$600	$600

Required

1. Compute the product cost per bin produced under absorption costing and under variable costing. Do this first for January and then for February.
2. Prepare separate monthly income statements for January and for February, using
   a. Absorption costing
   b. Variable costing
3. Is operating income higher under absorption costing or variable costing in January? In February? Explain the pattern of differences in operating income based on absorption costing versus variable costing.

APPLY YOUR KNOWLEDGE

DECISION CASES

Effect of changing the sales mix in CVP analysis

(Obj. 7)

Case 1. Companies like **Compaq** and **Proctor & Gamble** have recently added a new employee benefit—on-site dinner-to-go. Employees can order reheatable pre-packaged dinners during the day, and have these meals delivered to their offices at 5:00 P.M. Similar to a company cafeteria, employees pay less for these meals than they would for similar items at a for-profit take-out. Garland Enterprises, a software development company, is considering starting a similar program. The company plans to offer pre-packaged: (1) children's meals, and (2) adult dinners. Data relating to the two types of meals follows:

	Children's	Adults'
Sale price	$2.00	$5.00
Cost of food	1.00	2.75
Cost of labor to prepare food	0.50	1.25
Cost of plastic containers	0.10	0.10
Delivery expense	0.15	0.15

Other (annual) costs of offering this new service are

Chef's salary..	$20,000
Utilities expense..	5,000
Marketing the new service to the employees..............	750

Required

1. If employees purchase on average *two children's dinners for every adult dinner,* how many adult dinners and how many children's dinners must employees purchase each year for Garland to break even on the new service? (Carry your computations to five decimal places.)
2. If employees purchase on average *two adult meals for every children's dinner,* how many adult dinners and how many children's dinners must employees purchase each year for Garland to break even on the new service? (Carry your computations to five decimal places.)
3. Explain why your answers to requirements 1 and 2 differ.
4. In light of your analysis, should Garland focus on promoting the availability of adult meals or children's meals? Why?
5. Why might Garland be satisfied with breaking even on the dinner-to-go service (rather than requiring the service to earn a profit)?

Case 2. ◄ *Link Back to Chapter 19 (Just-in-Time Philosophy).* Suppose you serve on the board of directors of American Faucet, a manufacturer of bathroom fixtures that recently adopted just-in-time production. Part of your responsibility is to develop a compensation contract for Toni Moen, the Vice President of Manufacturing. To give her the incentive to make decisions that will increase the company's profits, the Board decides to give Moen a year-end bonus if American Faucet meets a target operating income.

Absorption and variable cost incentives
(Obj. 8)

Write a memo to the Chairman of the Board, Herbert Kohler, explaining whether the bonus contract should be based on absorption costing or variable costing. Use the memo format outlined in Daily Exercise 22-5.

ETHICAL ISSUE

SpringSong is a medium-sized manufacturer of squirrel-proof bird feeders. Your father, the plant manager, helped you get a summer internship working for SpringSong's CFO. Your father has told you that the company is struggling and that he is worried about his job. With a breakeven point at 80% of capacity, the company has barely been breaking even.

Assumptions of CVP analysis
(Obj. 1, 2)

As the CFO's assistant, you are attending a meeting with President Gail Ayala, Vice-President of Marketing Warren Thrasher, and CFO Shane Corwin.

"I've decided to go forward with selling on our Web site," the president announces excitedly. "We can manage the cost of setting up the Web site."

"Great," responds Thrasher. "Web sales will give us a national market. Even at our current sale price, I'm sure we can increase our sales threefold."

Corwin shows a CVP chart he has prepared and points to the operating income area. "Given our contribution margin ratio, these higher sales will mean no more sweating our quarterly income figures. The sky's the limit!"

Looking at the CVP chart, you recall studying CVP analysis and the importance of its assumptions. If SpringSong is operating at about 80% of capacity, you cannot see how a threefold increase in production can be in the relevant range. You wonder if you should raise the issue now or check your accounting textbook and make sure of the facts first. You are also reluctant to dampen the group's enthusiasm and good spirits.

Required

1. Should you raise the question of CVP analysis' assumptions during the meeting, afterward with the CFO when you have had time to do some research, or not at all? Explain.
2. The CFO asks you to draft a report explaining the role of the relevant range in CVP analysis. Address the report to President Gail Ayala, and use the memo format outlined in Daily Exercise 22-5.

FINANCIAL STATEMENT CASE

Refer to **Target Corporation's** Consolidated Results of Operations, included in the financial statements in Appendix A. Ignoring interest expense and taxes, answer the following questions:

Identifying cost behavior patterns, computing breakeven sales and margin of safety, effect of changing sales mix
(Obj. 1, 3, 6, 7)

1. Is Target Corporation's cost of sales a fixed cost or a variable cost? Is depreciation and amortization a fixed cost or a variable cost? Explain.

2. Assume that 40% of Target's selling, general, and administrative expenses are fixed costs. What is the contribution margin? (*Hint:* Use sales revenues rather than total revenues in your calculations.)
3. What is the contribution margin ratio? (Carry your computation to 5 decimal places.)
4. What is the breakeven sales in dollars?
5. Calculate the margin of safety in dollars as sales revenue less breakeven sales in dollars. What is the margin of safety as a percentage?
6. Target division's sales are growing faster than sales in either the Mervyn's or the Department Stores divisions. Since Target stores are the lowest margin division, how will this change in sales mix affect the corporation's breakeven point?

TEAM PROJECT

Variable and absorption costing, bonus contract incentives, using contribution margin statements to make decisions
(Obj. 2, 8)

Paktape Manufacturing produces filament packaging tape. In 20X4, Paktape produced and sold 15 million rolls of tape. The company has recently expanded its capacity, so it can now produce up to 30 million rolls per year. Paktape's accounting records show the following results from 20X4:

Sale price per roll	$2.00
Variable manufacturing expenses per roll	$1.00
Variable marketing and administrative expenses per roll	$0.50
Total fixed manufacturing overhead costs	$8,400,000
Total fixed marketing and administrative expenses	$600,000
Sales	15 million rolls
Production	15 million rolls

There were no beginning or ending inventories in 20X4.

In January 20X5, Paktape hired a new president, Kevin McDaniel. McDaniel has a one-year contract that specifies he will be paid 10% of Paktape's 20X5 absorption costing operating income, instead of a salary. In 20X5, McDaniel must make two major decisions:

- Should Paktape undertake a major advertising campaign? This campaign would raise sales to 25 million rolls. This is the maximum level of sales Paktape can expect to make in the near future. The ad campaign would add an additional $3.5 million in marketing and administrative costs. Without the campaign, sales will be 15 million rolls.
- How many rolls of tape will Paktape produce?

At the end of the year, Paktape Manufacturing's Board of Directors will evaluate McDaniel's performance, and decide whether to offer him a contract for the following year.

Required

Within your group, form two subgroups. The first subgroup assumes the role of Kevin McDaniel, Paktape Manufacturing's new president. The second subgroup assumes the role of Paktape Manufacturing's Board of Directors. McDaniel will meet with the Board of Directors shortly after the end of 20X5 to decide whether he will remain at Paktape. Most of your effort should be devoted to advance preparation for this meeting. Each subgroup should meet separately to prepare for the meeting between the Board and McDaniel.

Kevin McDaniel should:

1. Compute Paktape Manufacturing's 20X4 operating income.
2. Decide whether to adopt the advertising campaign. Prepare a memo to the Board of Directors explaining this decision. Use the memo format outlined in Daily Exercise 22-5. Give this memo to the Board of Directors as soon as possible (before the joint meeting).
3. Assume Paktape adopts the advertising campaign. Decide how many rolls of tape to produce in 20X5.
4. Prepare an absorption costing income statement for 20X5, ending with operating income before bonus. Then compute your bonus separately. The variable cost per unit and the total fixed expenses (with the exception of the advertising campaign) remain the same as in 20X4. Give this income statement and your bonus computation to the Board of Directors as soon as possible (before your meeting with the Board).
5. Decide whether you wish to remain at Paktape for another year. You currently have an offer from another company. The contract with the other company is identical to the one you currently have with Paktape—you will be paid 10% of absorption costing operating income instead of a salary.

The Board of Directors should:

1. Compute Paktape's 20X4 operating income.
2. Determine whether Paktape should adopt the advertising campaign.
3. Determine how many rolls of tape Paktape should produce in 20X5.

4. Evaluate McDaniel's performance, based on his decisions and the information he provided the Board. (*Hint:* You may want to prepare a variable costing income statement.)
5. Evaluate the contract's bonus provision. Are you satisfied with this provision? If so, explain why. If not, recommend how it should be changed.

After McDaniel has given the Board his memo and income statement, and after the Board has had a chance to evaluate McDaniel's performance, McDaniel and the Board should meet. The purpose of the meeting is to decide whether it is in their mutual interest for McDaniel to remain with Paktape, and if so, the terms of the contract Paktape will offer McDaniel.

INTERNET EXERCISE

Rainforest Café, Inc., is a restaurant that recreates the atmosphere of a tropical rainforest and includes a retail facility that offers an assortment of creative, signature items. Approximately 40 Rainforest Cafés are located in the United States, United Kingdom, Canada, France, Mexico, Singapore, and Hong Kong.

1. Go to **http://www.rainforestcafe.com.** Click on *Invest* and scan the information displayed. What special effects create the ambience of a tropical rainforest?
2. At the top of the screen click on *SEC Filings,* followed by *Click here to continue on to view SEC Filings,* select the *most recent annual report* (Form type 10-K), and under Item 8: Financial Statements select the *Consolidated Statements of Operations. Only* use amounts included in the computation of "Income from unit operations & licensing," to answer the following questions. Assume all assumptions underlying CVP analysis hold true. (*Note:* For easier viewing you may want to select font size 1 = smallest and click on enter.)
   a. Identify the cost behavior pattern of each account listed under "Costs and Expenses:" as fixed, mixed, or variable. Assume the primary cost driver is number of customers.
   b. Recast the income statement in the contribution margin format using amounts from the most recent year. For this computation assume 40% of the restaurant operating expenses and retail operating expenses are fixed.
   c. Compute the contribution margin ratio (rounding to the nearest whole percent). Calculate the breakeven point in sales dollars. Assume the company has set a target of $500,000 for "Income from unit operations & licensing" for next year. To reach this target how much in total revenues must Rainforest Café earn?
   d. Calculate the contribution margin and the contribution margin ratio for both restaurant sales and retail sales for the most recent year. If restaurant sales increase by $10,000 company profits will increase by what amount? After customers finish a meal the "safari guide" can suggest either dessert or a trip to the retail store. Assuming the same amount of dollars will be spent, which suggestion would generate more operating profit? Explain why.

Rainforest Café

Go to the "Cost-Volume-Profit Analysis" episode on the *Mastering Accounting* CD-ROM for an interactive, video-enhanced exercise showing CanGo managers' use of reports that predict outcomes based on estimates of cost and revenue to help make a new venture decision.

23

The Master Budget and Responsibility Accounting

LEARNING OBJECTIVES

*After studying this chapter,
you should be able to*

1. Identify the benefits of budgeting

2. Prepare an operating budget

3. Prepare the components of a financial budget

4. Use sensitivity analysis in budgeting

5. Distinguish among different types of responsibility centers

6. Prepare a performance report for management by exception

7. Allocate indirect costs to departments

The home of the:
SALAS FAMILY

In partnership with:
HABITAT WORLD

Habitat for Humanity

www.prenhall.com/horngren

Readiness Assessment

Everyone in the world should have a simple, decent, affordable place to live. That's the mission of **Habitat for Humanity International,** a worldwide nonprofit organization with nearly 2,000 local affiliates that oversee construction of homes in their own communities. Habitat International and its affiliates solicit donations of building materials, and families who will become the homeowners invest "sweat equity" alongside volunteers. The total now is more than 90,000 homes built in over 60 countries across the globe, from Australia and Bangladesh to Uganda, the United States, and Zimbabwe.

Habitat plans to build 100,000 new houses over the next five years—a tall order since it took 24 years to build the first 100,000. Founder and President Millard Fuller must plan carefully to meet this lofty goal:

- How much will it cost to support construction of 100,000 houses over the next five years?
- How can Habitat raise enough revenue to pay these expenses?
- Can Habitat raise contributions in time to fund these expenses, or will it have to borrow to finance a cash shortfall?

Fuller and his management team use *budgets* to help answer these questions. The budget is Habitat's financial roadmap: It spells out how it will obtain and spend its resources. To develop the expense budget, managers predict the funds that headquarters will transfer to affiliates for house-building and the money to be spent on educational programs. The revenue budget predicts the contributions individuals, corporations, and government grants will offer Habitat. After developing the revenue budget, Habitat's managers realized that they would not have enough money to fund the ambitious house-building goal. So Habitat is embarking on a 5-year fund-raising campaign, and is using its Web site to encourage additional on-line donations.

Habitat also uses budgets to control revenues and costs. Simply preparing the expense budget helps managers identify cost-cutting opportunities. And the budget is a benchmark for comparing actual results. Reports compare

- actual revenues to budgeted revenues for each type of donor (individuals, corporations, governments)
- actual expenses to budgeted expenses for each type of expense (funds transferred to affiliates for house-building, technology upgrades)

Managers investigate differences between actual and budgeted figures. For example, if actual revenues from individuals fall short of the budget, managers may redouble efforts to solicit funds from individuals, or they may decide to focus elsewhere, perhaps on obtaining larger donations from corporations.

WHY MANAGERS USE BUDGETS

Managers of for-profit companies as well as nonprofits like **Habitat for Humanity** play several key roles. First, they develop strategies—overall business goals like Habitat's goal to build 100,000 houses over the next five years. Next, they plan and take specific actions to achieve those goals. Finally, managers control operations by comparing actual results with plans or budgets. This performance evaluation provides valuable feedback. For example, if Habitat's expenses are higher than budgeted, managers must either cut costs or increase revenues, and these decisions will affect their future strategies and plans.

Exhibit 23-1 shows that managers develop budgets to implement the organization's strategy, and then use these budgets to plan, act, and control business operations. The process is continuous: Determine strategy, develop plans and budgets to implement the strategy, act to implement the strategy, control by comparing actual results to the budget or plan, and then use feedback from the control step to start the process again.

 DAILY EXERCISE 23-1

EXHIBIT 23-1
**Budgets, Performance
Evaluation, and the
Management Cycle**

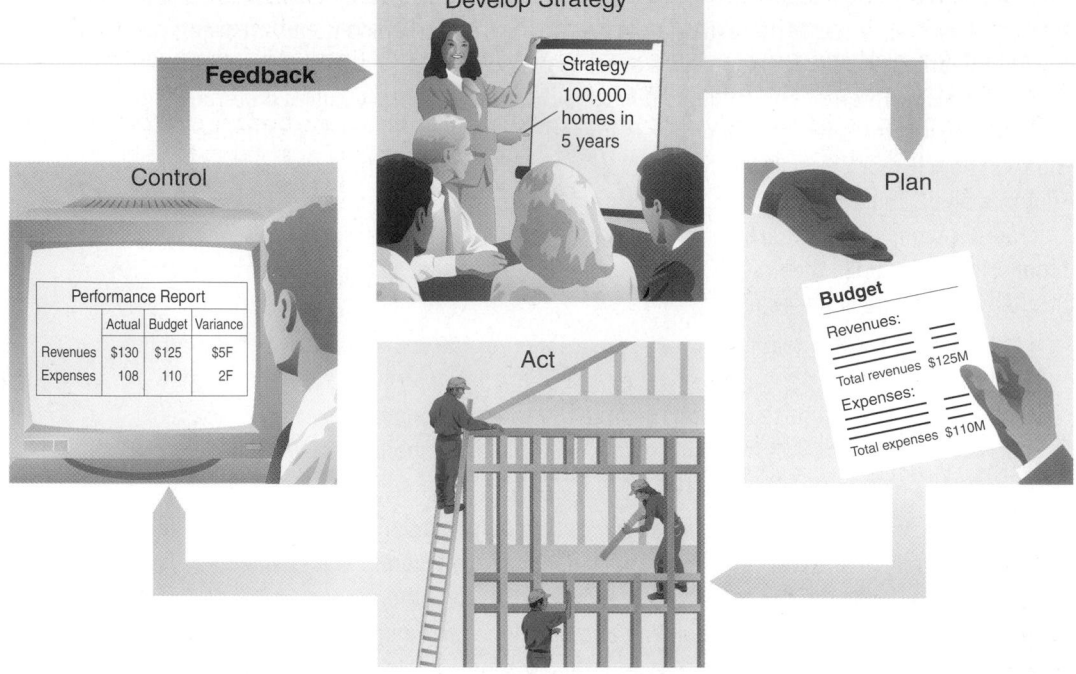

Budget Time Frames

In Chapter 19, we defined a *budget* as a quantitative expression of a plan that helps managers coordinate and implement the plan. Budgets can focus on the short-term or the long-term. Habitat developed a long-term budget to predict the costs required to reach its goal of building 100,000 houses over the next five years. **Boeing's** long-term budgets forecast demand for its planes for the next twenty years!

Other budgets have a short-term focus. Many companies budget their cash flows monthly, weekly, and daily to ensure that they have enough cash to meet their needs. They also budget revenues and expenses—and thus operating income—for months, quarters, and years. This chapter focuses on shorter-term budgets of a year or less. Chapter 26 focuses on budgets for large capital expenditures (property, plant, and equipment, for example) that naturally have a longer-term focus.

Budgeting for a Small Service Company

Let's begin by considering a budget for a small service company. Ram Dharan started a small business—an on-line service that provides travel itineraries for leisure travelers. Dharan wants to earn $275 per month to help cover his college expenses. He develops a budget to determine whether he can expect to meet this goal.

Dharan expects to sell 100 itineraries per month at a price of $3 each. Over the last six months, he paid his Internet service provider an average of $18 per month, and he spent an additional $20 per month on travel-related reference materials. He expects these monthly costs to remain about the same. Finally, he spends 5% of his sales revenues for banner ads on various other travel and leisure Web sites.

To prepare the budget, Dharan computes his total budgeted revenues and subtracts his total budgeted expenses:

RAM DHARAN TRAVEL ITINERARIES		
Budget for May 20X9		
Budgeted sales revenue (100 × $3)		$300
Less budgeted expenses:		
Internet access expense.............................	$18	
Reference materials expense.......................	20	
Advertising expense (5% × $300)..............	15	53
Budgeted operating income...........................		$247

The budget shows that if business goes according to plan, Ram Dharan will not meet his $275 per month operating income goal. He will have to increase revenue (by using word-of-mouth advertising) or cut expenses (by finding a less expensive Internet access provider) to meet his goal.

Ram Dharan is the sole proprietor of a simple business, so his budget covers the entire company's operations. While managers of large companies also prepare budgets for the organization as a whole, individual subunits prepare their own budgets, as well. For example, each of Habitat's Regional Support Centers across the United States and Area Offices in Costa Rica, Thailand, and South Africa prepare budgets. Headquarters in Americus, Georgia, uses the individual budgets to prepare the organizationwide budget.

THE BUDGET AS A MANAGEMENT TOOL

Objective 1
Identify the benefits of budgeting

Budgets are key management tools that help large organizations like **Habitat for Humanity, Boeing,** and **Sunoco** just as much as sole proprietors like Ram Dharan. Exhibit 23-2 summarizes budgeting's benefits.

EXHIBIT 23-2 **Benefits of Budgeting**

Budgets require managers to plan.

Budgets promote coordination and communication.

Budgets provide a benchmark that helps managers evaluate performance.

Budgets motivate employees to help achieve organization goals.

 DAILY EXERCISE 23-2

Benefits of Budgeting

BUDGETING REQUIRES PLANNING   Ram Dharan discovered that his expected income fell short of his target. The sooner he learns of the expected shortfall, the more time he has to plan how to increase revenues or cut expenses. The better his plan and the more time he has to execute the plan, the more likely he will meet his income target. In the chapter opening story, Habitat for Humanity's budget prompted managers to immediately initiate a major fund-raising campaign.

BUDGETING PROMOTES COORDINATION AND COMMUNICATION   The master budget coordinates the company's activities. It forces managers to consider relationships among operations across the entire value chain. Consider **Cincinnati Milacron, Inc.,** a manufacturer of machine tools and accessories. Sales managers at Cincinnati Milacron are evaluated on the basis of volume, so they prefer to accept all special orders. But some special orders cost the company more than the customer is willing to pay. The budget promotes coordination by encouraging managers to accept orders only for machines Cincinnati Milacron can manufacture at a profit.

Coordination requires effective communication. Budgets can communicate a consistent set of plans throughout the company. Suppose **Mazda's** engineers plan to redesign the Miata's brake system. By participating in the budgeting process alongside the engineers, the manufacturing vice president can see how to change the production process. He explains the plan to plant managers so they can make the changes in an orderly way.

BUDGETS PROVIDE A BENCHMARK THAT HELPS MANAGERS EVALUATE PERFORMANCE
Managers can evaluate a department or activity by comparing actual results with either the budget or past performance. The budget is usually a better benchmark because the company's operations or its markets may have changed since last year.

Suppose that **Coldwell Banker's** real-estate agents sell 10% more houses in the third quarter of 2002 than in the third quarter of 2001. Is this good performance? Not necessarily. If nationwide sales are up 20% for the quarter, Coldwell Banker's results may be disappointing. But if the overall market has declined, the 10% increase may be excellent.

Another problem with past results is that they may represent inefficient performance. Suppose that difficulties obtaining donations of material or land drove Habitat For Humanity's cost per house in Mexico to $3,500. An average cost of $3,200 the following year is better, but may still fall short of expectations if the budgeted cost is $3,000 per house.

A BUDGET MOTIVATES EMPLOYEES   Budgets motivate employees to achieve the business's goals, especially when employees believe the budget is fair. For this reason, companies often ask employees to help prepare the budgets that will be used to judge their performance.

Unrealistic budgets can hurt employee morale. Suppose Coldwell Banker's management imposed a budgeted increase of 15% in house sales for each territory. That budget may be acceptable to agents in areas with strong economies. They may work hard to achieve the increase. Agents in depressed areas may believe it is impossible to meet the budget. They may simply give up if they believe it is not possible to meet the budget. Management should allow agents in each territory a voice in the budget so budgets will be tailored to local conditions.

The Performance Report

We have seen how budgets can help managers plan. However, budgets are just as useful for controlling. To control operations, managers prepare performance reports that compare actual results to the budget. These reports help managers

- Evaluate operations
- Decide how to fix problems
- Prepare next period's budget

Suppose that Cincinnati Milacron has the performance report in Exhibit 23-3.

EXHIBIT 23-3
**Summary Income Statement
Performance Report**

	Actual	Budget	Variance (Actual–Budget)
Sales revenue	$550,000	$600,000	$(50,000)
Total expenses	510,000	520,000	10,000
Net income	$ 40,000	$ 80,000	$(40,000)

Actual sales in Exhibit 23-3 are $550,000, which is $50,000 less than budgeted sales. The actual net income is half the budgeted amount. The vice president of sales will have to explain why sales revenue was so far below the budgeted amount. The vice president, in turn, will meet with the sales staff to learn why they failed to meet the budget. There are three possible explanations:

- The budget was unrealistic.
- The sales force did a poor job of selling during the period.
- Uncontrollable factors (such as a sluggish economy) reduced sales.

Of course, all three factors may have contributed to the poor results.

Managers use performance reports like the one in Exhibit 23-3 to decide how to fix problems. If the sales department did not perform well, perhaps their compensation should be tied to sales revenue so they will be more motivated to sell. Or the company may need a new advertising campaign. Managers must decide whether to reduce budgeted sales for the next period—a decision that directly affects next period's budgeted net income.

 **THINK IT OVER** The performance report in Exhibit 23-3 shows that actual sales revenue is 8.33% less than budgeted sales revenue ($50,000 ÷ $600,000). However, actual expenses are only 1.9% less than budgeted expenses ($10,000 ÷ $520,000). Why is the percentage shortfall in expenses so much lower than the percentage shortfall in revenue?

Answer: One reason why expenses did not fall as far short of the budget is that some expenses do not increase or decrease with revenue (sales volume). For example, the vice president of sales may receive a salary of $90,000 regardless of sales revenue. Expenses such as depreciation, rent, and insurance are *fixed*. When revenue and variable expenses decline, fixed expenses remain the same. Thus, total expense does not decline as rapidly as revenue.

PREPARING THE MASTER BUDGET

The **master budget** is the set of budgeted financial statements and supporting schedules for the entire organization. This comprehensive budget includes (1) the operating budget, (2) the capital expenditures budget, and (3) the financial budget. The **operating budget** sets the expected revenues and expenses—and thus operating income—for the period. The **capital expenditures budget** presents the company's plan for purchases of property, plant, equipment, and other long-term assets. The **financial budget** projects cash inflows and outflows, the period-ending balance sheet, and the statement of cash flows. This chapter focuses on the operating budget and the financial budget. You learned about the cash budget in Chapter 7; here we will show more details behind the figures in the cash budget. Chapter 26 covers budgeting for capital expenditures.

The components of the master budget include:

1. Operating budget
   a. Sales budget
   b. Inventory budget and purchases and cost of goods sold budget
   c. Operating expenses budget
   d. Budgeted income statement
2. Capital expenditures budget
3. Financial budget
   a. Cash budget: statement of budgeted cash receipts and payments
   b. Budgeted balance sheet
   c. Budgeted statement of cash flows

The end result of the *operating* budget is the budgeted income statement, which shows expected revenues, expenses, and operating income for the period. The *financial* budget results in the budgeted statement of cash flows, which shows budgeted cash flows for operating, investing, and financing activities. The budgeted financial statements look exactly like ordinary statements. The only difference is that they list budgeted rather than actual figures. Exhibit 23-4 on the next page diagrams the master budget for a merchandising company such as **Safeway** or **J.C. Penney.**

The sales budget is the cornerstone of the master budget, because sales affect most of the other components of the master budget. After projecting sales and expenses, management can prepare the budgeted income statement. The income statement, the capital expenditures budget, and plans for raising cash and paying debts provide information for the cash budget, which feeds into the budgeted balance sheet. The budgeted statement of cash flows is usually the last step in the process.

The best way to learn about budgeting is to prepare a master budget.

MASTER BUDGET. The set of budgeted financial statements and supporting schedules for the entire organization. This comprehensive budget includes the operating budget, the capital expenditures budget, and the financial budget.

OPERATING BUDGET. Sets the expected revenues and expenses—and thus operating income—for the period.

CAPITAL EXPENDITURES BUDGET. A company's plan for purchases of property, plant, equipment, and other long-term assets.

FINANCIAL BUDGET. Projects cash inflows and outflows, the period-ending balance sheet, and the statement of cash flows.

 DAILY EXERCISE 23-3

Exhibit 23-4

Master Budget for a Merchandising Company

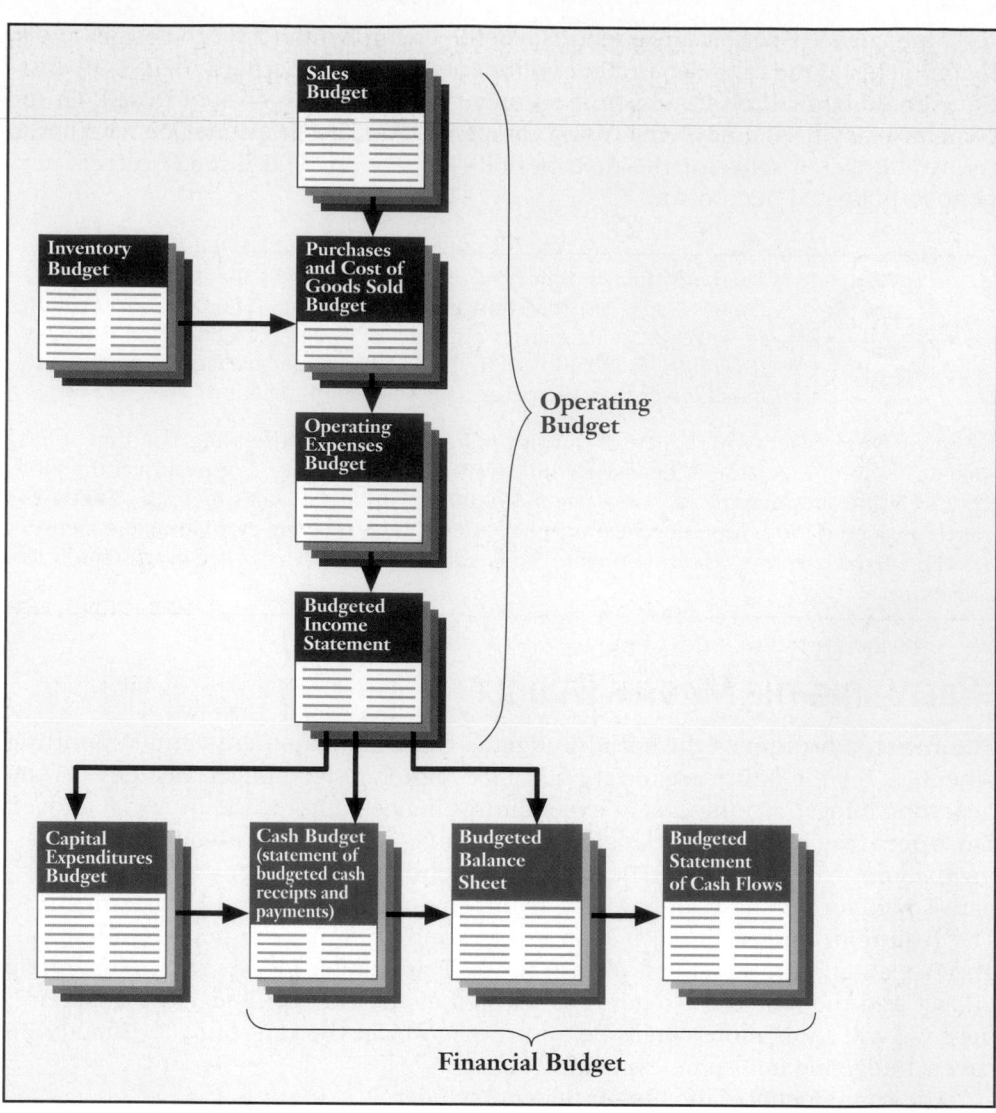

Operating Budget

Financial Budget

Whitewater Sporting Goods Master Budget

1. *You manage Whitewater Sporting Goods Store No. 18, which carries a complete line of outdoor recreation gear.* You are to prepare the store's master budget for April, May, June, and July, the main selling season. The division manager and the assistant controller (head of the Accounting Department) will arrive from headquarters next week to review the budget with you.

2. *Cash collections follow sales because the company sells on account.* When the company needs extra cash, it borrows on six-month installment notes payable.

3. *Your store's balance sheet at March 31, 20X6, the beginning of the budget period, appears in Exhibit 23-5 on the next page.* ⇦

➤ We examined the balance sheet in Chapter 5, pages 180–182.

4. *Sales in March were $40,000.* The sales force predicts these future monthly sales:

April...............	$50,000
May	80,000
June...............	60,000
July...............	50,000

Sales are 60% cash and 40% on credit. Whitewater collects all credit sales the month after the sale. The $16,000 of accounts receivable at March 31 arose from credit sales in March (40% of $40,000). Uncollectible accounts are insignificant.

5. *Whitewater maintains inventory equal to $20,000 plus 80% of the budgeted cost of goods sold for the following month.* Target ending inventory on July 31 is

EXHIBIT 23-5
Balance Sheet

WHITEWATER SPORTING GOODS STORE NO. 18
Balance Sheet
March 31, 20X6

Assets			Liabilities		
Current assets:			Current liabilities:		
Cash	$ 15,000		Accounts payable		$ 16,800
Accounts receivable	16,000		Salary and commissions		
Inventory	48,000		payable		4,250
Prepaid insurance	1,800		Total liabilities........................		21,050
Total current assets..............	80,800				
Plant assets:			**Owner's Equity**		
Equipment and fixtures	32,000		Owners' equity		78,950
Accumulated depreciation ...	(12,800)				
Total plant assets	19,200		Total liabilities		
Total assets............................	$100,000		and owners' equity		$100,000

$42,400. Cost of goods sold averages 70% of sales. (These percentages are based on past experience.) Inventory on March 31 is $48,000:

$$\text{March 31 inventory} = \$20,000 + 0.80 \times (0.70 \times \text{April sales of } \$50,000)$$
$$= \$20,000 + (0.80 \times \$35,000)$$
$$= \$20,000 + \$28,000 = \$48,000$$

Whitewater pays for inventory as follows: 50% during the month of purchase and 50% during the next month. Accounts payable consists of inventory purchases only. March purchases were $33,600, so accounts payable at the end of March total $16,800 ($33,600 × 0.50).

6. *Monthly payroll has two parts: a salary of $2,500 plus sales commissions equal to 15% of sales.* The company pays half this amount during the month and half early in the following month. Therefore, at the end of each month Whitewater reports salary and commissions payable equal to half the month's payroll. The $4,250 liability on the March 31 balance sheet is half the March payroll of $8,500:

$$\text{March payroll} = \text{Salary of } \$2,500$$
$$+ \text{Sales commissions of } \$6,000 \ (0.15 \times \$40,000)$$
$$= \$8,500$$
$$\text{March 31 salary and commissions payable} = 0.50 \times \$8,500 = \$4,250$$

7. *Other monthly expenses are as follows:*

Rent expense..	$2,000, paid as incurred
Depreciation expense, including truck............	500
Insurance expense..	200 expiration of prepaid amount
Miscellaneous expenses...................................	5% of sales, paid as incurred

8. *Whitewater plans to purchase a used delivery truck in April for $3,000 cash.*
9. *Whitewater requires each store to maintain a minimum cash balance of $10,000 at the end of each month.* The store can borrow money on 6-month notes payable of $1,000 each at an annual interest rate of 12%. Management borrows no more than the amount needed to maintain the $10,000 minimum. Notes payable require six equal monthly payments of principal, plus monthly interest on the entire unpaid principal. Borrowing and all principal and interest payments occur at the end of the month.
10. *Income taxes are the responsibility of corporate headquarters, so you can ignore tax for budgeting purposes.*

Preparing the Operating Budget

As you prepare the master budget, remember that you are developing the store's operating and financial plan for the next four months. The steps in this process may seem mechanical, but managers must think carefully about pricing, product lines, job assignments, needs for additional equipment, and negotiations with banks. Successful managers use this opportunity to make decisions that affect the future

Objective 2
Prepare an operating budget

course of business. The operating budget—the sales budget; the inventory, purchases, and cost of goods sold budgets; and the operating expenses budget—leads to the budgeted income statement.

PREPARING THE BUDGETED INCOME STATEMENT There are four steps to preparing the budgeted income statement shown in Exhibit 23-6.

EXHIBIT 23-6 **Budgeted Income Statement**

WHITEWATER SPORTING GOODS STORE NO. 18
Budgeted Income Statement
Four Months Ending July 31, 20X6

	Amount		Source
Sales revenue..................................		$240,000	Sales Budget (Exhibit 23-7)
Cost of goods sold..........................		168,000	Inventory, Purchases, and Cost of Goods Sold
Gross profit		72,000	Budget (Exhibit 23-8)
Operating expenses:			
Salary and commissions.............	$46,000		Operating Expenses Budget (Exhibit 23-9)
Rent expense	8,000		Operating Expenses Budget (Exhibit 23-9)
Depreciation expense.................	2,000		Operating Expenses Budget (Exhibit 23-9)
Insurance expense	800		Operating Expenses Budget (Exhibit 23-9)
Miscellaneous expenses	12,000	68,800	Operating Expenses Budget (Exhibit 23-9)
Operating income..........................		3,200	
Interest expense............................		225*	Cash Budget (Exhibit 23-13)
Net income		$ 2,975	

* $90 + $75 + $60

DAILY EXERCISE 23-4

DAILY EXERCISE 23-6

Step 1. **The sales budget.** Sales is the key business activity. Budgeted total sales for each product is the sale price multiplied by the expected number of units sold. The overall sales budget in Exhibit 23-7 is the sum of the budgets for the individual products. Trace the April through July total sales ($240,000) to the budgeted income statement in Exhibit 23-6.

EXHIBIT 23-7 **Sales Budget**

WHITEWATER SPORTING GOODS STORE NO. 18
Sales Budget

	April	May	June	July	April–July Total
Cash sales, 60%................	$30,000	$48,000	$36,000	$30,000	
Credit sales, 40%..............	20,000	32,000	24,000	20,000	
Total sales, 100%..............	$50,000	$80,000	$60,000	$50,000	$240,000

Step 2. **Inventory, purchases, and cost of goods sold budget.** This schedule determines cost of goods sold for the budgeted income statement, ending inventory for the budgeted balance sheet, and purchases for the cash budget. The familiar cost-of-goods-sold computation specifies the relation among these items:

$$\text{Beginning inventory} + \text{Purchases} - \text{Ending inventory} = \text{Cost of goods sold}$$

Beginning inventory is known from last month's balance sheet, budgeted cost of goods sold is a fixed percentage of sales, and budgeted ending inventory is a computed amount. You must solve for the budgeted purchases figure. To do this, take the cost-of-goods-sold computation and then move beginning inventory and ending inventory to the right side of the equation, isolating purchases on the left side:

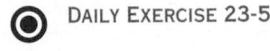
DAILY EXERCISE 23-5

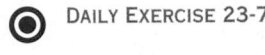
DAILY EXERCISE 23-7

$$\text{Beginning inventory} + \text{Purchases} - \text{Ending inventory} = \text{Cost of goods sold}$$

$$\text{Purchases} = \text{Cost of goods sold} + \text{Ending inventory} - \text{Beginning inventory}$$

This second equation makes sense. How much does Whitewater have to purchase? Enough to cover sales and desired ending inventory, less the amount of beginning inventory already on hand at the start of the period. Exhibit 23-8 shows Whitewater's inventory, purchases, and cost of goods sold budget.

EXHIBIT 23-8 Inventory, Purchases, and Cost of Goods Sold Budget

WHITEWATER SPORTING GOODS STORE NO. 18					
Inventory, Purchases, and Cost of Goods Sold Budget					
	April	May	June	July	April–July Total
Cost of goods sold (0.70 × sales, from Sales Budget in Exhibit 23-7)	$35,000	$ 56,000	$42,000	$35,000	$168,000
+ Desired ending inventory ($20,000 + 0.80 × Cost of goods sold for the next month)	64,800 *	53,600	48,000	42,400 ‡	
= Total inventory required	99,800	109,600	90,000	77,400	
− Beginning inventory	(48,000)†	(64,800)	(53,600)	(48,000)	
= Purchases	$51,800	$ 44,800	$36,400	$29,400	

* $20,000 + (0.80 × $56,000) = $64,800.
† Balance at March 31 (Exhibit 23-5).
‡ Given in item 5 on page 933.

Trace the total budgeted cost of goods sold from Exhibit 23-8 ($168,000) to the budgeted income statement in Exhibit 23-6. We will use the budgeted inventory and purchases amounts later.

Step 3. Operating expenses budget. Budgeted operating expenses such as sales commissions fluctuate with sales. Other expenses, such as rent and insurance, are the same each month (fixed).

Trace the April through July totals from the operating expenses budget in Exhibit 23-9 (salary and commissions of $46,000, rent expense of $8,000, and so on) to the budgeted income statement in Exhibit 23-6.

EXHIBIT 23-9 Operating Expenses Budget

WHITEWATER SPORTING GOODS STORE NO. 18					
Operating Expenses Budget					
	April	May	June	July	April–July Total
Salary, fixed amount (item 6, page 933)	$ 2,500	$ 2,500	$ 2,500	$ 2,500	
Commission, 15% of sales from Sales Budget (item 6, page 933 and Exhibit 23-7	7,500	12,000	9,000	7,500	
Total salary and commissions	10,000	14,500	11,500	10,000	$46,000
Rent expense, fixed amount (item 7, page 933)	2,000	2,000	2,000	2,000	8,000
Depreciation expense, fixed amount (item 7, page 933)	500	500	500	500	2,000
Insurance expense, fixed amount (item 7, page 933)	200	200	200	200	800
Miscellaneous expenses, 5% of sales from Sales Budget (item 7, page 933 and Exhibit 23-7)	2,500	4,000	3,000	2,500	12,000
Total operating expenses	$15,200	$21,200	$17,200	$15,200	$68,800

Step 4. Budgeted income statement. Use steps 1 through 3 to prepare the budgeted income statement in Exhibit 23-6. We explain the computation of interest expense as part of the cash budget in the next section.

Objective 3
Prepare the components of a financial budget

Preparing the Financial Budget

The second major section of the master budget that we will discuss is the financial budget. This includes the cash budget, the budgeted balance sheet, and the budgeted statement of cash flows. The **cash budget,** or **statement of budgeted cash receipts and payments,** details how the business expects to go from the beginning cash balance to the desired ending balance. ◄ Cash receipts and payments depend on revenues and expenses, which appear in the budgeted income statement. This is why the cash budget is not prepared until after the budgeted income statement.

➡ We introduced the cash budget in Chapter 7, page 286.

CASH BUDGET. Details how the business expects to go from the beginning cash balance to the desired ending balance. Also called the **statement of budgeted cash receipts and payments.**

⊙ DAILY EXERCISE 23-8

⊙ DAILY EXERCISE 23-10

PREPARING THE CASH BUDGET The cash budget has four major parts:

- Cash collections from customers (Exhibit 23-10)
- Cash payments for purchases (Exhibit 23-11)
- Cash payments for operating expenses (Exhibit 23-12)
- Capital expenditures (for example, the $3,000 capital expenditure to acquire the delivery truck)

Exhibit 23-10 shows how to compute budgeted cash collections. April's cash collections consist of two parts: (1) April's cash sales from the sales budget in Exhibit 23-7 ($30,000), plus (2) March's credit sales ($16,000 from the March 31 balance sheet, Exhibit 23-5). Trace April's $46,000 ($30,000 + $16,000) total cash collections to the cash budget in Exhibit 23-13.

EXHIBIT 23-10 **Budgeted Cash Collections**

WHITEWATER SPORTING GOODS STORE NO. 18				
Budgeted Cash Collections from Customers				
	April	May	June	July	April–July Total
Cash sales from Sales Budget (Exhibit 23-7)	$30,000	$48,000	$36,000	$30,000	
Collections of last month's credit sales, from					
Sales Budget (Exhibit 23-7)...................................	16,000 *	20,000	32,000	24,000	
Total collections..	$46,000	$68,000	$68,000	$54,000	$236,000

* March 31 accounts receivable, Exhibit 23-5.

⊙ DAILY EXERCISE 23-9

Exhibit 23-11 uses the inventory, purchases, and cost of goods sold budget from Exhibit 23-8 and payment information from item 5 to compute budgeted cash

EXHIBIT 23-11 **Budgeted Cash Payments for Purchases**

WHITEWATER SPORTING GOODS STORE NO. 18				
Budgeted Cash Payments for Purchases				
	April	May	June	July	April–July Total
50% of last month's purchases from Inventory, Purchases, and Cost of Goods Sold Budget (Exhibit 23-8)....................................	$16,800*	$25,900	$22,400	$18,200	
50% of this month's purchases from Inventory, Purchases, and Cost of Goods Sold Budget (Exhibit 23-8)....................................	25,900	22,400	18,200	14,700	
Total payments for purchases...................................	$42,700	$48,300	$40,600	$32,900	$164,500

* March 31 accounts payable, Exhibit 23-5.

payments for purchases of inventory. April's cash payments for purchases consists of two parts: (1) payment of 50% of March's purchases ($16,800 accounts payable balance from the March 31 balance sheet, Exhibit 23-5), plus (2) payment for 50% of April's purchases ($25,900 = 50% × $51,800 from Exhibit 23-8). Trace April's $42,700 ($16,800 + $25,900) cash outlay for purchases to the cash budget in Exhibit 23-13.

Exhibit 23-12 uses items 6 and 7 and the operating expenses budget (Exhibit 23-9) to compute cash payments for operating expenses. April's cash payments for operating expenses consists of four items:

Payment of 50% of March's salary and commissions (from March 31 balance sheet, Exhibit 23-5)	$ 4,250
Payment of 50% of April's salary and commissions (50% × $10,000, Exhibit 23-9)	5,000
Payment of rent expense (Exhibit 23-9)	2,000
Payment of miscellaneous expenses (Exhibit 23-9)	2,500
Total April cash payments for operating expenses.............................	$13,750

Follow April's $13,750 cash payments for operating expenses from Exhibit 23-12 to the cash budget in Exhibit 23-13.

EXHIBIT 23-12 **Budgeted Cash Payments for Operating Expenses**

WHITEWATER SPORTING GOODS STORE NO. 18 Budgeted Cash Payments for Operating Expenses					
	April	May	June	July	April–July Total
Salary and commissions:					
50% of last month's expenses, from Operating Expenses Budget (Exhibit 23-9).........	$ 4,250*	$ 5,000	$ 7,250	$ 5,750	
50% of this month's expenses, from Operating Expenses Budget (Exhibit 23-9).........	5,000	7,250	5,750	5,000	
Total salary and commissions...................................	9,250	12,250	13,000	10,750	
Rent expense, from Operating Expenses Budget (Exhibit 23-9)	2,000	2,000	2,000	2,000	
Miscellaneous expenses, from Operating Expenses Budget (Exhibit 23-9)	2,500	4,000	3,000	2,500	
Total payments for operating expenses	$13,750	$18,250	$18,000	$15,250	$65,250

* March 31 salary and commissions payable, Exhibit 23-5.

THINK IT OVER Why are depreciation expense and insurance expense from the operating expenses budget (Exhibit 23-9) *excluded* from the budgeted cash payments for operating expenses in Exhibit 23-12?

Answer: These expenses do not require cash outlays in the current period. Depreciation is the periodic write-off of the cost of the equipment and fixtures that Whitewater acquired previously. Insurance expense is the expiration of prepaid insurance.

To prepare the cash budget in Exhibit 23-13, start with the beginning cash balance and add the budgeted cash collections from Exhibit 23-10 to determine the cash available. Then subtract cash payments for purchases (Exhibit 23-11), operating expenses (Exhibit 23-12), and any capital expenditures. This yields the ending cash balance before financing.

Item 9 states that Whitewater requires a minimum cash balance of $10,000. The $1,550 budgeted cash balance before financing falls $8,450 short of the minimum required ($10,000 − $1,550). Because Whitewater borrows in $1,000 notes, the company will have to borrow $9,000 to cover April's expected shortfall. The

DAILY EXERCISE 23-11

EXHIBIT 23-13 **Cash Budget**

WHITEWATER SPORTING GOODS STORE NO. 18
Cash Budget
Four Months Ending July 31, 20X6

	April	May	June	July
Beginning cash balance	$15,000*	$10,550	$10,410	$18,235
Cash collections (Exhibit 23-10)	46,000	68,000	68,000	54,000
Cash available	$61,000	$78,550	$78,410	$72,235
Cash payments:				
Purchases of inventory (Exhibit 23-11)	$42,700	$48,300	$40,600	$32,900
Operating expenses (Exhibit 23-12)	13,750	18,250	18,000	15,250
Purchase of delivery truck (item 8, page 933)	3,000	—	—	—
Total cash payments	59,450	66,550	58,600	48,150
(1) Ending cash balance before financing	1,550	12,000	19,810	24,085
Minimum cash balance desired	10,000	10,000	10,000	10,000
Cash excess (deficiency)	$ (8,450)	$ 2,000	$ 9,810	$14,085
Financing of cash deficiency (see notes a–c):				
Borrowing (at end of month)	$ 9,000			
Principal payments (at end of month)		$(1,500)	$ (1,500)	$(1,500)
Interest expense (at 12% annually)		(90)	(75)	(60)
(2) Total effects of financing	9,000	(1,590)	(1,575)	(1,560)
Ending cash balance (1) + (2)	$10,550	$10,410	$18,235	$22,525

* March 31 cash balance, Exhibit 23-5.

Notes

a. Borrowing occurs in multiples of $1,000 and only for the amount needed to maintain a minimum cash balance of $10,000.

b. Monthly principal payments: $9,000 ÷ 6 = $1,500.

c. Interest expense:
  May: $9,000 × (0.12 × 1/12) = $90
  June: ($9,000 − $1,500) × (0.12 × 1/12) = $75
  July: ($9,000 − $1,500 − $1,500) × (0.12 × 1/12) = $60

 DAILY EXERCISE 23-12

budgeted ending cash balance equals the "ending cash balance before financing," adjusted for the total effects of the financing (a $9,000 inflow in April). Exhibit 23-13 shows that Whitewater expects to end April with $10,550 of cash ($1,550 + $9,000). The exhibit also shows the cash balance at the end of May, June, and July.

Item 9 states that Whitewater must repay the notes in six equal installments. Thus, May through July show principal repayments of $1,500 ($9,000 ÷ 6) per month. Whitewater also pays interest expense on the outstanding notes payable, at 12% per year. The June interest expense is $75 [($9,000 principal − $1,500 repayment at the end of May) × 12% × 1/12]. Interest expense for the four months totals $225 ($90 + $75 + $60). This interest expense appears on the budgeted income statement in Exhibit 23-6.

Notice that the cash balance at the end of July is $22,525. This becomes the cash balance in the July 31 budgeted balance sheet in Exhibit 23-14.

PREPARING THE BUDGETED BALANCE SHEET The next step in preparing the master budget is to complete the balance sheet. Project each asset, liability, and owners' equity account based on the plans outlined in the previous exhibits.

Study the budgeted balance sheet in Exhibit 23-14 to make certain you understand the computation of each figure. For example, on the budgeted balance sheet as of July 31, 20X6, budgeted cash equals the ending cash balance from the cash budget in Exhibit 23-13 ($22,525). Accounts receivable as of July 31 equal July's credit sales of $20,000, shown in the sales budget (Exhibit 23-7). July 31 inventory of $42,400 is July's desired ending inventory in the inventory, purchases, and cost of goods sold budget in Exhibit 23-8. Detailed computations for each of the other accounts appear in Exhibit 23-14.

EXHIBIT 23-14   Budgeted Balance Sheet

WHITEWATER SPORTING GOODS STORE NO. 18
Budgeted Balance Sheet
July 31, 20X6

Assets

Current assets:

Cash (Exhibit 23-13)	$22,525	
Accounts receivable (Sales Budget, Exhibit 23-7)	20,000	
Inventory (Inventory, Purchases, and Cost of Goods Sold Budget, Exhibit 23-8)	42,400	
Prepaid insurance (beginning balance of $1,800 − $800 for four months' expiration; Operating Expenses Budget, Exhibit 23-9)	1,000	
Total current assets		$ 85,925

Plant assets:

Equipment and fixtures (beginning balance of $32,000 + $3,000 truck acquisition; item 8, page 933)	$35,000	
Accumulated depreciation (beginning balance of $12,800 + $2,000 for four months' depreciation; Operating Expenses Budget, Exhibit 23-9)	(14,800)	
Total plant assets		20,200
Total assets...		$106,125

Liabilities

Current liabilities:

Accounts payable (0.50 × July purchases of $29,400; Inventory, Purchases, and Cost of Goods Sold Budget, Exhibit 23-8)...............................	$14,700	
Short-term note payable ($9,000 − $4,500 paid back; Exhibit 23-13)	4,500	
Salary and commissions payable (0.50 × July expenses of $10,000; Operating Expenses Budget, Exhibit 23-9)	5,000	
Total liabilities...		$ 24,200

Owners' Equity

Owners' equity (beginning balance of $78,950 + $2,975 net income; Exhibit 23-6)...		81,925
Total liabilities and owners' equity...		$106,125

PREPARING THE BUDGETED STATEMENT OF CASH FLOWS   The final step in preparing the master budget is completing the budgeted statement of cash flows. Use the information from the schedules of cash collections and payments, the cash budget, and the beginning balance of cash to project cash flows from operating, investing, and financing activities. Take time to study Exhibit 23-15, and make sure you understand the origin of each figure.

Now the *master budget* is complete. It consists of the budgeted financial statements and all supporting schedules.

THINK IT OVER   Many companies allow the manager of each department to participate in setting the budget for his or her own department. Participation can help employees accept the budget and motivate them to achieve the budget. What is the *disadvantage* of allowing managers to set budgets for their own departments? (*Hint:* Superiors often use the budget as a benchmark against which to compare actual performance.)

Answer: Managers who are evaluated by comparing their department's actual results to the budget have incentives to build *slack* into their budgets. For example, the manager might budget less sales than she really expects, and budget purchases costs higher than she expects. This increases the chance that her department's actual performance will be better than the budget, and that she will receive a good evaluation. Consequently, higher-level managers usually negotiate with lower-level managers to remove at least part of the slack lower-level managers add to the budget.

EXHIBIT 23-15
Budgeted Statement
of Cash Flows

WHITEWATER SPORTING GOODS STORE NO. 18
Budgeted Statement of Cash Flows
Four Months Ending July 31, 20X6

Cash flows from operating activities:		
Receipts:		
Collections from customers (Exhibit 23-10)...................	$ 236,000	
Total cash receipts		$236,000
Payments:		
Purchases of inventory (Exhibit 23-11)...........................	$(164,500)	
Operating expenses, excluding interest expense		
(Exhibit 23-12)...	(65,250)	
Payment of interest expense (Exhibits 23-13 and 23-6) .	(225)	
Total cash payments..		(229,975)
Net cash inflow from operating activities...........................		6,025
Cash flows from investing activities:		
Acquisition of delivery truck (item 8, page 933)................	$ (3,000)	
Net cash outflow from investing activities		(3,000)
Cash flows from financing activities:		
Proceeds from issuance of notes payable (Exhibit 23-13)...	$ 9,000	
Payment of notes payable (Exhibit 23-13).........................	(4,500)	
Net cash inflow from financing activities		4,500
Net increase in cash		$ 7,525
Cash balance, April 1, 20X6 (Exhibit 23-5)		15,000
Cash balance, July 31, 20X6 (Exhibits 23-13 and 23-14).......		$ 22,525

BUDGETING, SENSITIVITY ANALYSIS, AND INFORMATION TECHNOLOGY

The master budget models the organization's *planned* activities. The most important budget documents are the budgeted income statement (Exhibit 23-6), the cash budget (Exhibit 23-13), and the budgeted balance sheet (Exhibit 23-14). Top management analyzes these statements to ensure that all the budgeted figures are consistent with the company's goals or strategies.

Sensitivity Analysis

Actual results often differ from plans, so managers conduct sensitivity analyses to plan for various possibilities. Recall that Chapter 22 defined *sensitivity analysis* as a *what-if* technique that asks *what* a result will be *if* a predicted amount is not achieved or *if* an underlying assumption changes. ◄ *What if* the stock market crashes? How will this affect contributions to Habitat for Humanity? Will it have to postpone the planned expansion in Eastern Europe? *What* will be Whitewater Store No. 18's cash balance on July 31 *if* the period's sales are 45% cash, not 60% cash? Will Whitewater have to borrow more cash?

➡ Sensitivity analysis is introduced in Chapter 22, page 896.

Many companies use computer spreadsheet programs to prepare master budget schedules and statements. In fact, one of the earliest spreadsheet programs was developed by graduate business students specifically to perform master budget sensitivity analyses. The students realized that computers could take the drudgery out of hand-computed master budget sensitivity analyses. Managers and accountants could answer what-if questions simply by changing a number. At the press of a key, the spreadsheet prepares a revised budget that includes all the effects of the change.

Budget Management Software

Suppose the manager of Whitewater Store No. 18 uses a spreadsheet to develop the store's master budget. Then Whitewater's headquarters must "roll up" the budget data from Store No. 18, along with budgets for each of the other individual stores, to prepare the companywide master budget. This roll-up can be difficult for companies with far-flung operations, whose units may use different spreadsheets. Companies like **Sunoco** are beginning to use budget management software. Often designed to work with the company's Web-based Intranet and data warehouse (or ERP database), this software provides a companywide system that helps managers develop and analyze budgets.

Across the globe, managers can sit at their desks, log into the company's budget system, and enter their numbers. The software allows them to conduct sensitivity analyses on their own unit's data—for example, how a change in oil prices would affect the unit's budget. When the manager is satisfied with her budget, she can enter it in the companywide budget with the click of a mouse, and her unit's budget automatically "rolls up" with budgets from all other units around the world. Whether at headquarters or on the road, top executives can log into the budget system and conduct their own sensitivity analyses on individual units' budgets, or on the companywide budget. The new technology allows managers to spend less time compiling and summarizing data and more time analyzing it to ensure that the budget leads the company to achieve the goals identified at the beginning of the budget process.

e-Accounting

ERP: Enterprise Resource Planning or Enterprise Ruins Plans?

Most accountants know—though few will admit—that at least three-quarters of the best-laid budgets and corporate plans gather dust. Now some pioneering Fortune 1000 companies are reengineering their budgeting processes. To make it all happen, they're shelving their Excel spreadsheets in favor of Enterprise Resource Planning (ERP) software.

ERP software links corporate data across the entire enterprise. At **Fujitsu Computer Products of America,** an Oracle ERP program tracks the entire supply chain, including data on shipments of materials and supplies, purchases, inventory, accounts receivable, and accounts payable. An enterprise application system (EAS) program links to the ERP and allows managers to set up what-if scenarios.

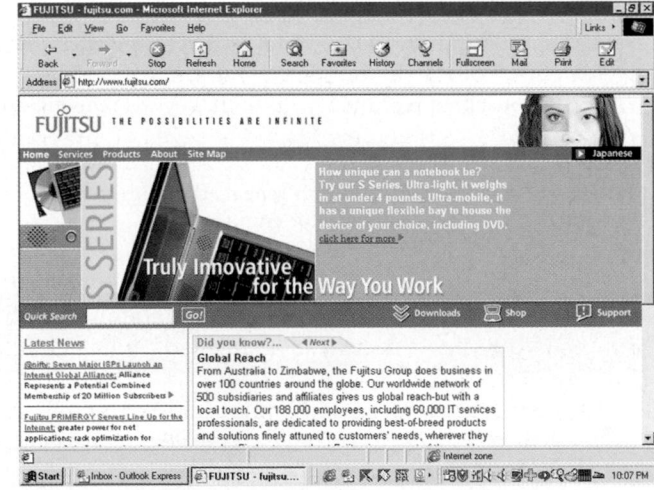

Reengineering the budget via ERP is not cheap. Fujitsu invested $40 million. **Allstate Insurance** invested $60 million. But, implemented correctly, the savings can be enormous. Allstate has saved roughly $100 million in processing costs in just 18 months.

Yet well-publicized ERP fiascoes have kept many companies from taking the plunge. In 1999 **Hershey Foods Corp.** installed an ERP system, squeezing what was originally supposed to be a 4-year project into just 30 months. Hershey rolled out its new ERP system just when retailers began ordering large amounts of candy for back-to-school; Halloween profits fell 19% due to disrupted delivery of its kisses and candies, and Hershey is still trying to regain market share. Consultants caution that implementation alone takes at least one to two years. And the reengineering process must start well before the technology is in place, with clear business goals for the ERP system.

Source: Based on Russ Banham, "Better Budgets," *Journal of Accountancy,* February 2000, pp. 37–40. J. W. Dysart, "Planning for real-time information," *Banking Strategies,* May/June 2000, pp. 6–10. Louisa Wah, "Give ERP a chance," *Management Review,* March 2000, pp. 20–24. Craig Stedman, "Failed ERP gamble haunts Hershey," *Computerworld,* November 1, 1999, pp. 1, 89.

THINK IT OVER

Consider two budget situations: (1) Whitewater Sporting Goods' marketing analysts produce a near-certain forecast for four-month sales of $4,500,000 for the company's 20 stores. (2) Much uncertainty exists about the period's sales. The most likely amount is $4,500,000, but marketing considers any amount between $3,900,000 and $5,100,000 to be possible. How will the budgeting process differ in these two circumstances?

Answer: Whitewater will prepare a master budget for the expected sales level of $4,500,000 in either case. Because of the uncertainty about sales in situation 2, executives will want a set of budgets covering the entire range of volume rather than a single level. Whitewater's managers may prepare budgets based on sales of, say, $3,900,000, $4,200,000, $4,500,000, $4,800,000, and $5,100,000. These budgets will help managers plan for sales levels throughout the forecasted range.

MID-CHAPTER

SUMMARY PROBLEM

www.prenhall.com/horngren

Mid-Chapter Assessment

Review the Whitewater Sporting Goods example in this chapter. You now think July sales might be $40,000 instead of the projected $50,000 in Exhibit 23-7. You want to perform a sensitivity analysis to see how this change in sales affects the budget.

Required

1. Revise the sales budget (Exhibit 23-7), the inventory, purchases, and cost of goods sold budget (Exhibit 23-8), and the operating expenses budget (Exhibit 23-9). Prepare a revised budgeted income statement for the four months ended July 31, 20X6.
2. Revise the schedule of budgeted cash collections (Exhibit 23-10), the schedule of budgeted cash payments for purchases (Exhibit 23-11), and the schedule of budgeted cash payments for operating expenses (Exhibit 23-12). Prepare a revised cash budget, a revised budgeted balance sheet at July 31, 20X6, and a revised budgeted statement of cash flows for the four months ended July 31, 20X6.

Note: You need not repeat the parts of the revised schedules that do not change.

Solution

Although not required, this solution repeats the budgeted amounts for April, May, and June. Revised figures appear in boldface for emphasis.

Requirement 1

WHITEWATER SPORTING GOODS STORE NO. 18
REVISED — Sales Budget

	April	May	June	July	Total
Cash sales, 60%	$30,000	$48,000	$36,000	**$24,000**	
Credit sales, 40%	20,000	32,000	24,000	**16,000**	
Total sales, 100%	$50,000	$80,000	$60,000	**$40,000**	**$230,000**

WHITEWATER SPORTING GOODS STORE NO. 18
REVISED — Inventory, Purchases, and Cost of Goods Sold Budget

	April	May	June	July	Total
Cost of goods sold (0.70 × sales, from Revised Sales Budget)..	$35,000	$56,000	$42,000	**$28,000**	**$161,000**
+ Desired ending inventory ($20,000 + 0.80 × cost of goods sold for next month).......................	64,800	53,600	**42,400**	42,400†	
= Total inventory required	99,800	109,600	**84,400**	**70,400**	
− Beginning inventory	(48,000)*	(64,800)	(53,600)	**(42,400)**	
= Purchases..	$51,800	$44,800	**$30,800**	**$28,000**	

* Balance at March 31, Exhibit 23-5.
† Given in item 5 on page 933.

942

WHITEWATER SPORTING GOODS STORE NO. 18
REVISED — Operating Expenses Budget

	April	May	June	July	Total
Salary, fixed amount	$ 2,500	$ 2,500	$ 2,500	$ 2,500	
Commission, 15% of sales from Revised Sales Budget	7,500	12,000	9,000	6,000	
Total salary and commissions	10,000	14,500	11,500	8,500	$44,500
Rent expense, fixed amount	2,000	2,000	2,000	2,000	8,000
Depreciation expense, fixed amount	500	500	500	500	2,000
Insurance expense, fixed amount	200	200	200	200	800
Miscellaneous expenses, 5% of sales from Revised Sales Budget	2,500	4,000	3,000	2,000	11,500
Total operating expenses	$15,200	$21,200	$17,200	$13,200	$66,800

WHITEWATER SPORTING GOODS STORE NO. 18
Revised Budgeted Income Statement
Four Months Ending July 31, 20X6

		Amount	Source
Sales revenue		$230,000	Revised Sales Budget
Cost of goods sold		161,000	Revised Inventory, Purchases, and Cost of Goods Sold
Gross profit		69,000	Budget
Operating expenses:			
Salary and commissions	$44,500		Revised Operating Expenses Budget
Rent expense	8,000		Revised Operating Expenses Budget
Depreciation expense	2,000		Revised Operating Expenses Budget
Insurance expense	800		Revised Operating Expenses Budget
Miscellaneous expenses	11,500	66,800	Revised Operating Expenses Budget
Operating income		2,200	
Interest expense		225	Revised Cash Budget
Net income		$ 1,975	

Requirement 2

WHITEWATER SPORTING GOODS STORE NO. 18
REVISED — Budgeted Cash Collections

	April	May	June	July	Total
Cash sales, from Revised Sales Budget	$30,000	$48,000	$36,000	$24,000	
Collections of last month's credit sales, from Revised Sales Budget	16,000*	20,000	32,000	24,000	
Total collections	$46,000	$68,000	$68,000	$48,000	$230,000

* March 31 accounts receivable, Exhibit 23-5.

WHITEWATER SPORTING GOODS STORE NO. 18
REVISED — Budgeted Cash Payments for Purchases

	April	May	June	July	Total
50% of last month's purchases, from Revised Inventory, Purchases, and Cost of Goods Sold Budget	$16,800*	$25,900	$22,400	$15,400	
50% of this month's purchases, from Revised Inventory, Purchases, and Cost of Goods Sold Budget	25,900	22,400	15,400	14,000	
Total payments for purchases	$42,700	$48,300	$37,800	$29,400	$158,200

* March 31 accounts payable, Exhibit 23-5.

WHITEWATER SPORTING GOODS STORE NO. 18
REVISED — Budgeted Cash Payments for Operating Expenses

	April	May	June	July	Total
Salary and commissions:					
50% of last month's expenses, from Revised Operating Expenses Budget	$ 4,250*	$ 5,000	$ 7,250	$ 5,750	
50% of this month's expenses, from Revised Operating Expenses Budget	5,000	7,250	5,750	4,250	
Total salary and commissions	9,250	12,250	13,000	10,000	
Rent expense, from Revised Operating Expenses Budget	2,000	2,000	2,000	2,000	
Miscellaneous expenses, from Revised Operating Expenses Budget	2,500	4,000	3,000	2,000	
Total payments for operating expenses	$13,750	$18,250	$18,000	$14,000	$64,000

* March 31 salary and commissions payable, Exhibit 23-5.

WHITEWATER SPORTING GOODS STORE NO. 18
Revised Cash Budget
Four Months Ending July 31, 20X6

	April	May	June	July
Beginning cash balance	$15,000*	$10,550	$10,410	$21,035
Cash collections (Revised Budgeted Cash Collections)	46,000	68,000	68,000	48,000
Cash available	$61,000	$78,550	$78,410	$69,035
Cash payments:				
Purchases of inventory (Revised Budgeted Cash Payments for Purchases)	$42,700	$48,300	$37,800	$29,400
Operating expenses (Revised Budgeted Cash Payments for Operating Expenses)	13,750	18,250	18,000	14,000
Purchase of delivery truck (item 8, page 933)	3,000	—	—	—
Total cash payments	59,450	66,550	55,800	43,400
(1) Ending cash balance before financing	1,550	12,000	22,610	25,635
Minimum cash balance desired	10,000	10,000	10,000	10,000
Cash excess (deficiency)	$(8,450)	$ 2,000	$12,610	$15,635
Financing of cash deficiency (see notes a–c):				
Borrowing (at end of month)	$ 9,000			
Principal payments (at end of month)		$(1,500)	$(1,500)	$(1,500)
Interest expense (at 12% annually)		(90)	(75)	(60)
(2) Total effects of financing	9,000	(1,590)	(1,575)	(1,560)
Ending cash balance (1) + (2)	$10,550	$10,410	$21,035	$24,075

* March 31 cash balance, Exhibit 23-5.

Notes

a. Borrowing occurs in multiples of $1,000 and only for the amount needed to maintain a minimum cash balance of $10,000.

b. Monthly principal payments: $9,000 ÷ 6 = $1,500.

c. Interest expense:
   May: $9,000 × (0.12 × 1/12) = $90
   June: ($9,000 − $1,500) × (0.12 × 1/12) = $75
   July: ($9,000 − $1,500 − $1,500) × (0.12 × 1/12) = $60

WHITEWATER SPORTING GOODS STORE NO. 18
Revised Budgeted Balance Sheet
July 31, 20X6

Assets

Current assets:

Cash (Revised Cash budget)	$24,075	
Accounts receivable (Revised Sales Budget)	16,000	
Inventory	42,400	
Prepaid insurance	1,000	
Total current assets		$ 83,475

Plant assets:

Equipment and fixtures	$35,000	
Accumulated depreciation	(14,800)	
Total plant assets		20,200
Total assets		$103,675

Liabilities

Current liabilities:

Accounts payable (0.50 × July purchases of **$28,000;** Revised Inventory, Purchases, and Cost of Goods Sold Budget)	$14,000	
Short-term note payable	4,500	
Salary and commissions payable (0.50 × July expenses of **$8,500;** Revised Operating Expenses Budget)	4,250	
Total liabilities		$ 22,750

Owners' Equity

Owners' equity (beginning balance of $78,950 + **$1,975** net income, Revised Budgeted Income Statement)		80,925
Total liabilities and owners' equity		$103,675

WHITEWATER SPORTING GOODS STORE NO. 18
Revised Budgeted Statement of Cash Flows
Four Months Ending July 31, 20X6

Cash flows from operating activities:

Receipts:

Collections (Revised Budgeted Cash Collections)	$230,000	
Total cash receipts		$230,000

Payments:

Purchases of inventory (Revised Budgeted Cash Payments for Purchases)	(158,200)	
Operating expenses, excluding interest expense (Revised Budgeted Cash Payments for Operating Expenses)	(64,000)	
Payment of interest expense	(225)	
Total cash payments		(222,425)
Net cash inflow from operating activities		7,575

Cash flows from investing activities:

Acquisition of delivery truck	$ (3,000)	
Net cash outflow from investing activities		(3,000)

Cash flows from financing activities:

Proceeds from issuance of notes payable	$ 9,000	
Payment of notes payable	(4,500)	
Net cash inflow from financing activities		4,500
Net increase in cash		$ 9,075
Cash balance, April 1, 20X6 (Exhibit 23-5)		15,000
Cash balance, July 31, 20X6 (Revised Cash Budget)		$ 24,075

Objective 5
Distinguish among different types
of responsibility centers

RESPONSIBILITY CENTER. A part
or subunit of an organization
whose manager is account-
able for specific activities.

RESPONSIBILITY ACCOUNTING.
A system for evaluating the
performance of each responsibility center and its
manager.

RESPONSIBILITY ACCOUNTING

You've now seen how managers set strategic goals, and then develop plans and budget resources for activities that will help reach those goals. Each manager is responsible for planning and controlling some part of the firm's activities. A **responsibility center** is a part or subunit of the organization whose manager is accountable for specific activities. Lower-level managers are often responsible for budgeting and controlling costs of a single value-chain function. For example, one manager is responsible for planning and controlling the *production* of **Pace** picante sauce at the plant, while another is responsible for planning and controlling the *distribution* of the picante sauce to customers. Lower-level managers report to higher-level managers who have broader responsibilities. For example, managers in charge of production and distribution report to senior managers responsible for profits (revenues minus costs) earned by the entire product line.

Types of Responsibility Centers

Responsibility accounting is a system for evaluating the performance of each responsibility center and its manager. Responsibility accounting reports compare plans (budgets) with actions (actual results) for each responsibility center. Superiors then evaluate how well each manager: (1) used the budgeted resources to achieve the responsibility center's goals, and thereby (2) controlled the operations for which he or she is responsible. Exhibit 23-16 illustrates four types of responsibility centers: cost centers, revenue centers, profit centers, and investment centers.

EXHIBIT 23-16
Four Types of Responsibility Centers

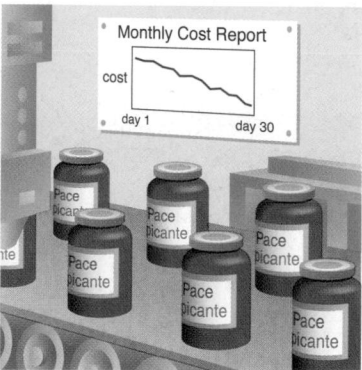

(a) A **cost center**, such as a production line for Pace picante sauce—where managers are responsible for costs

(b) A **revenue center**, such as the Midwest sales region—where managers are responsible for generating sales revenue

(c) A **profit center**, such as the Pace picante sauce line of products—where managers are responsible for generating income

(d) An **investment center**, such as Campbell Soups' soups and sauces division—where managers are responsible for income and invested capital

 DAILY EXERCISE 23-14

1. *Cost center: A responsibility center where managers are accountable for costs (expenses) only.* Manufacturing operations like the Pace picante sauce production lines are cost centers. The line foreman controls costs by ensuring that employees

work efficiently with minimal waste of ingredients. The foreman is *not* responsible for generating revenues, because he is not involved in selling the picante sauce. The plant manager evaluates the foreman on his ability to control *costs* by comparing actual costs to budgeted costs. All else being equal (for example, holding quality constant), the manager is likely to receive a more favorable performance evaluation if actual costs are less than budgeted costs.

2. *Revenue center: A responsibility center where managers are primarily accountable for revenues.* Examples include the Midwest and Southeast sales regions of businesses like **Pace Foods** and **Reebok.** Managers of revenue centers are primarily responsible for generating sales revenue, although they may also be responsible for the costs of their own sales operations. Revenue center performance reports compare actual with budgeted revenues and may also include the costs incurred by the revenue center itself. All else being equal, the manager is likely to receive a more favorable performance evaluation if actual revenues exceed the budget.

3. *Profit center: A responsibility center where managers are accountable for revenues and costs (expenses), and therefore profits.* The (higher-level) manager responsible for the entire Pace product line would be accountable for increasing sales revenue *and* controlling costs to achieve the profit goals. Other examples of profit centers include an **Outback Steakhouse** restaurant and the housewares department of a **Target** store. Profit center reports include both revenues and expenses to show the profit center's income. Superiors evaluate the manager's performance by comparing actual revenues, expenses, and profits to the budget. All else being equal, the manager is likely to receive a more favorable performance evaluation if actual profits exceed the budget.

4. *Investment center: A responsibility center where managers are accountable for investments, revenues, and costs (expenses).* Examples include the **Nutrasweet Company,** which is owned by **J.W. Childs Equity Partners,** the Saturn division of **General Motors,** and the Soups and Sauces Division (which includes Pace Foods) of **Campbell Soup.** Managers of investment centers are responsible for: (1) generating sales, (2) controlling expenses, and (3) managing the amount of investment required to earn the income (revenues minus expenses).

Top management often evaluates investment center managers based on return on investment. ➡ Chapter 18 introduced a common return on investment measure—the rate of return on total assets:

See Chapter 18, p. 728, for discussion of rate of return on total assets.

$$\frac{\text{Net income plus interest expense}}{\text{Average total assets}}$$

When evaluating a division rather than the entire company, however, the return on investment is often computed as:

$$\frac{\text{Division's operating income}}{\text{Division's average total assets}}$$

All else being equal, the manager will receive a more favorable performance evaluation if the division's actual return on investment exceeds the budgeted return on investment.

Responsibility Accounting: An Example

The simplified organization chart in Exhibit 23-17 shows how a company may assign responsibility in the fast-food industry. At the top level of O'Toole Restaurant Corporation, the Northern California district manager oversees the branch managers, who supervise the managers of the individual restaurants (called stores).

Store managers make operating decisions. They may decide the quantities of food to order, the number of employees and their schedules, and store hours.

EXHIBIT 23-17
O'Toole Restaurant Corporation Partial Organization Chart

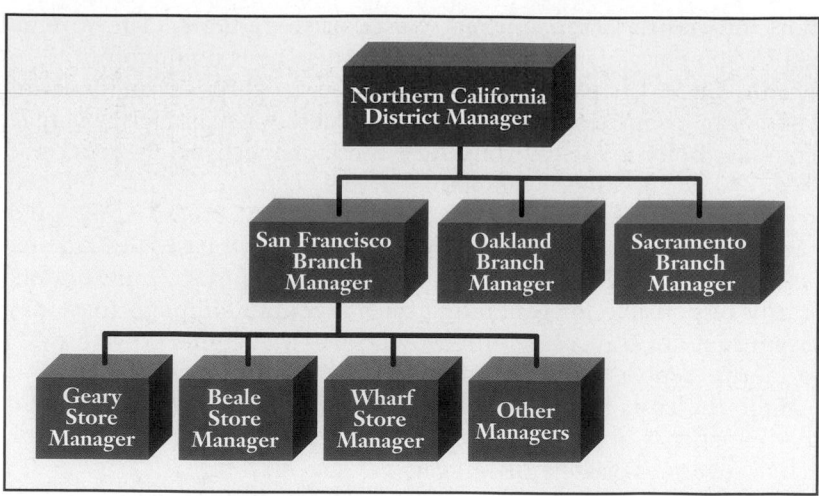

Branch managers oversee several stores, evaluate store managers' performance, and set store managers' compensation. District managers oversee several branches, evaluate branch managers' performance and compensation, set food prices, and approve sales promotions. District managers are accountable to regional managers, who answer to home-office vice presidents.

THINK IT OVER

O'Toole's store managers do not have authority to set sale prices or control advertising. Both factors affect store revenues. But the corporation nevertheless evaluates each store as a profit center instead of as a cost center. Why?

Answer: If each store were a cost center, then store managers would be motivated to cut costs to keep actual costs below the budget. Excessive cost cutting can hurt quality and service. By evaluating each store as a profit center, executives give store managers the incentive to keep stores clean and to ensure that employees provide fast and friendly service. Store managers thus are more likely to work hard to increase customer satisfaction, the foundation of long-run profitability.

◉ DAILY EXERCISE 23-15

Exhibit 23-18 provides a more detailed view of how managers use responsibility accounting performance reports to evaluate profit centers. At each level, the reports compare actual results with the budget. Examine the lowest level and move to the top. Follow how the reports are related through the three levels of responsibility.

Trace the $54,000 budgeted operating income from the Beale store manager's report to the San Francisco branch manager's report. The branch manager's report summarizes the results of all the stores he supervises. This report also includes charges the branch manager's office incurs.

Now trace the $465,000 total budgeted operating income from the San Francisco branch manager's report to the Northern California district manager's report. The district manager's report includes costs from her own district office plus a summary of each branch's operating performance.

Management by Exception

Objective 6
Prepare a performance report for management by exception

MANAGEMENT BY EXCEPTION.
Directs management's attention to important differences between actual and budgeted amounts.

Exhibit 23-18 presents variances from budget. This reporting format aids **management by exception,** which directs executives' attention to important differences between actual and budgeted amounts. Look at the district manager's report, and consider the San Francisco branch. Its actual operating income of $460,000 is very close to its budget for the current month ($465,000). Under management by exception, the district manager will not waste time investigating such a small variance. In contrast, the Oakland branch earned substantially more profit than budgeted. The district manager will want to find out why. Suppose the Oakland manager believes that a local sales promotion was especially effective. That promotion may be repeated and may also be used in other cities.

EXHIBIT 23-18   Responsibility Accounting Performance Report

O'TOOLE RESTAURANT CORPORATION
Responsibility Accounting at Various Levels
(In Thousands of Dollars)

NORTHERN CALIFORNIA DISTRICT MANAGER— Monthly Responsibility Report

Operating Income of Branches and District Manager Office Expense	Budget This Month	Budget Year to Date	Actual This Month	Actual Year to Date	Variance Favorable/ (Unfavorable) This Month	Variance Favorable/ (Unfavorable) Year to Date
District manager office expense	$ (150)	$ (600)	$ (154)	$ (620)	$(4)	$(20)
San Francisco branch	465	1,730	460	1,780	(5)	50
Oakland branch	390	1,540	475	1,855	85	315
Sacramento branch	520	2,240	468	2,061	(52)	(179)
Operating income	$1,225	$4,910	$1,249	$5,076	$24	$166

SAN FRANCISCO BRANCH MANAGER— Monthly Responsibility Report

Operating Income of Stores and Branch Manager Office Expense	Budget This Month	Budget Year to Date	Actual This Month	Actual Year to Date	Variance Favorable/ (Unfavorable) This Month	Variance Favorable/ (Unfavorable) Year to Date
Branch manager office expense	$(20)	$ (306)	$ (25)	$ (302)	$(5)	$ 4
Geary store	48	148	40	136	(8)	(12)
Beale store	54	228	61	244	7	16
Wharf store	38	160	42	170	4	10
Others	345	1,500	342	1,532	(3)	32
Operating income	$465	$1,730	$460	$1,780	$(5)	$50

BEALE STORE MANAGER— Monthly Responsibility Report

Revenues and Expenses	Budget This Month	Budget Year to Date	Actual This Month	Actual Year to Date	Variance Favorable/ (Unfavorable) This Month	Variance Favorable/ (Unfavorable) Year to Date
Revenues	$170	$690	$178	$702	$8	$12
Food expense	67	262	61	251	6	11
Paper expense	15	62	18	64	(3)	(2)
Wages expense	24	98	28	103	(4)	(5)
Depreciation expense	10	40	10	40	—	—
Total expenses	116	462	117	458	(1)	4
Operating income	$ 54	$228	$ 61	$244	$7	$16

Managers investigate large favorable variances as well as large unfavorable variances. A large favorable variance could reflect good performance. But a large favorable variance for costs such as food or wages could indicate that the store manager is skimping on the food or service.

The Northern California district manager will concentrate on improving the Sacramento branch. Its actual income of $468,000 is 10% ($52,000 ÷ $520,000) lower than its budget. The district manager may ask to see the branch manager's monthly responsibility report. That report reveals whether the income shortfall is due

 DAILY EXERCISE 23-16

 DAILY EXERCISE 23-17

to excessive branch office expenses, below-budget operating income from individual stores, or both. The two managers will work together to identify and correct problems.

Exhibit 23-18 also shows that summarized data may hide problems. Although the San Francisco branch as a whole performed well, the Geary store did not. Its actual income of $40,000 is 16.7% ($8,000 ÷ $48,000) below budget. This shortfall is offset by excellent performances by the Beale and Wharf stores. If the district manager receives only the condensed report at the top of the exhibit, she must rely on branch managers to spot and correct problems with individual stores. Some upper-level executives prefer the more detailed middle-level reports so they can keep tighter control over their responsibility centers.

Not a Question of Blame

Responsibility accounting helps top executives delegate decisions. Responsibility accounting assigns lower-level managers responsibility for their unit's actions and provides a way to evaluate the manager's and unit's performance. By allowing top managers to delegate decisions, responsibility accounting and management by exception free them to concentrate on strategic issues that affect the entire business.

Managers should not misuse responsibility accounting systems to find fault or to place blame. The question is not, Who should be blamed for an unfavorable variance? Instead, the question is, Who can best explain why a specific variance occurred? Consider again the Sacramento branch in Exhibit 23-18. Suppose that a month of unusually bad weather resulted in a 15% drop in restaurant volume. It may be that only efficient operations by the branch's stores kept the income variance as low as $52,000 (only 10% below the budget). Therefore, the Sacramento branch manager may have done a good job despite the unfavorable variance.

Objective 7
Allocate indirect costs to departments

DEPARTMENTAL ACCOUNTING

Responsibility centers are often called *departments*. Consider a retailer such as **Macy's, Lazarus,** or **Nordstrom.** Top managers of a department store want more information than just the net income of the store as a whole. They want to know each department's gross profit (sales minus cost of goods sold). They also usually want to know each department's operating income. These data can help identify the most profitable departments, so managers can decide whether to expand some departments and phase out others.

It is easy to measure gross profit for each department because the department records sales and cost of goods sold. However, it is more difficult to measure a department's operating income (gross profit minus operating expenses). Why? Many operating expenses are indirect costs that are not directly traced to the department.

➡ Chapter 19, pp. 760–761, explains how direct costs are traced.

As we noted in Chapter 19, *direct costs* are traceable to a particular department or product. ⬅ Consider Macy's Shoe Department. Clerks' wages, the cost of ads for shoes, and depreciation on display racks are all directly traceable to the Shoe Department. *Indirect costs*—all expenses other than direct costs—are not traceable to a single department. For example, Macy's Receiving Department and Stockroom serve all departments. How should Macy's allocate the cost of its Receiving Department and its Stockroom?

Allocation of Indirect Costs

➡ See Chapters 20 and 21, pp. 810–812 and 843–845, for a discussion of allocating indirect costs.

Chapters 20 and 21 explained how indirect costs are allocated to *products*. ⬅ Indirect costs are allocated to *departments* or responsibility centers using a similar process.

- Choose an allocation base for the indirect cost
- Compute an indirect cost allocation rate:

$$\frac{\text{Total indirect costs}}{\text{Total quantity of allocation base}}$$

- Allocate the indirect cost:

Quantity of allocation base used by department	×	Indirect cost allocation rate

As we noted in Chapter 20, the ideal cost allocation base is also a cost driver. Because different costs have different cost drivers, companies use several different allocation bases to allocate different indirect costs to various departments. Exhibit 23-19 lists common allocation bases for different indirect costs. Managers use their experience and judgment to choose these bases, but there is no single "correct" allocation base for each indirect cost.

EXHIBIT 23-19
Bases for Allocating Costs to Departments

 DAILY EXERCISE 23-18

Cost or Expense	Base for Allocating Cost
Direct materials	Separately traced
Merchandise inventory purchases	Separately traced
Direct labor	Separately traced
Other labor	Time spent in each department
Supervision	Time spent, or number of employees, in each department
Equipment depreciation	Separately traced, or hours used by each department
Building depreciation, property taxes	Square feet of space
Heat, light, and air conditioning	Square feet or cubic feet of space
Janitorial services	Square feet of space
Advertising	Separately traced if possible; otherwise, in proportion to sales
Materials Handling Department	Number or weight of items handled for each department
Payroll Department	Number of employees in each department
Personnel Department	Number of employees in each department
Purchasing Department	Number of purchase orders placed for each department

Consider Macy's receiving costs. Suppose Macy's decides that these costs are driven by the number of orders placed to purchase inventory. If 15% of the orders are for the Shoe Department and 20% are for the Menswear Department, then Macy's will allocate 15% of the Receiving Department costs to the Shoe Department and 20% to the Menswear Department. (The remaining Receiving Department costs will be allocated to other departments in proportion to the number of orders each issued.)

Allocating Indirect Costs to Departments: An Example

Exhibit 23-20 on the following page shows a departmental income statement for WorldPC, a retail computer store. We focus on allocating indirect operating expenses to the store's two departments: Hardware and Software.

SALARIES AND WAGES WorldPC traces salespersons' salaries and department managers' salaries directly to each department.

RENT WorldPC allocates the $600,000 rent expense based on the square feet each department occupies. The Hardware and Software Departments occupy 20,000 square feet and 5,000 square feet, respectively, so WorldPC allocates rent as follows:

 DAILY EXERCISE 23-19

Rent for entire store	$600,000
Total square feet (20,000 + 5,000)	÷ 25,000
Rent per square foot	$ 24

Hardware Department: 20,000 square feet × $24 per square foot = $480,000
Software Department: 5,000 square feet × $24 per square foot = 120,000
Total rent expense = $600,000

EXHIBIT 23-20
Departmental Income Statement

WORLDPC
Departmental Income Statement
Year Ended December 31, 20X9
(In Thousands)

		Department	
	Total	Hardware	Software
Sales revenue	$10,000	$7,000	$3,000
Cost of goods sold	6,500	4,500	2,000
Gross profit	3,500	2,500	1,000
Operating expenses:			
Salaries and wages expense	1,400	660	740
Rent expense	600	480	120
Purchasing department expense	48	36	12
Total operating expenses	2,048	1,176	872
Operating income	$ 1,452	$1,324	$ 128

PURCHASING DEPARTMENT WorldPC found that it takes just as long to complete a purchase order for inexpensive modems as for expensive "loaded" notebook computers. Consequently, the company allocates the $48,000 costs of the Purchasing Department based on the number of purchase orders processed. Hardware had 300 purchase orders, Software had 100 purchase orders.

Purchasing Department costs	$48,000
Total number of purchase orders (300 + 100)	÷ 400
Cost per purchase order	$ 120

Hardware Department: 300 purchase orders × $120 per purchase order = $36,000
Software Department: 100 purchase orders × $120 per purchase order = 12,000
Total Purchase Department cost = $48,000

WorldPC's top executives can use the departmental income statements in Exhibit 23-20 to evaluate how well each department and its manager performed in 20X9. The Hardware Department was more profitable than the Software Department. Hardware's profit margin (income divided by sales) was $1,324 ÷ $7,000 = 18.9%, while Software's profit margin was only $128 ÷ $3,000 = 4.3%. However, it is usually better to compare a department's actual results to its budget rather than to another department's results. For example, if WorldPC has just added the Software Department, performance may have exceeded expectations.

The following Decision Guidelines review budgets and how they are used in responsibility accounting. Take a moment to study these guidelines before working the summary review problem.

DECISION GUIDELINES

The Master Budget and Responsibility Accounting

DECISION	GUIDELINES
Why should a company develop a budget?	• Requires managers to plan • Promotes organization and communication • Provides a benchmark that helps managers evaluate performance • Motivates employees
In what order should you prepare the components of the master budget?	Begin with the *operating budget.* • Start with the *sales budget,* which feeds into all other budgets. • The sales and *ending inventory budgets* determine the *purchases and cost of goods sold budget.* • The sales, cost of goods sold, and *operating expense budgets* determine the *budgeted income statement.* Next, prepare the *capital expenditures budget.* Finally, prepare the *financial budget.* • Start with the *cash budget.* • The cash budget provides the ending cash balance for the *budgeted balance sheet* and the details for the *budgeted statement of cash flows.*
What if the sales forecast is uncertain?	Prepare a *sensitivity analysis* and project budgeted results at different sales levels.
How to compute budgeted purchases?	$$\text{Beginning inventory} + \text{Purchases} - \text{Ending inventory} = \text{Cost of goods sold}$$ so $$\text{Purchases} = \text{Cost of goods sold} + \text{Ending inventory} - \text{Beginning inventory}$$
What kind of a responsibility center does a given manager supervise?	Cost center: Manager is responsible for costs. Revenue center: Manager is responsible for revenues. Profit center: Manager is responsible for both revenues and costs, and therefore profits. Investment center: Manager is responsible for revenues, costs, and the amount of the investment required to earn the income.
How to evaluate managers?	Compare actual performance with the budget for the manager's responsibility center. *Management by exception* focuses only on large differences between budgeted and actual results.
How to identify the most profitable departments or product lines?	Departmental or product line income statements
How to allocate indirect costs to departments or product lines?	1. Choose an allocation base for each indirect cost. 2. Compute an indirect cost allocation rate: $$\frac{\text{Total indirect cost (\$)}}{\text{Total quantity of allocation base}}$$ 3. Allocate the indirect cost: $$\text{Quantity of allocation base used by department} \times \text{Indirect cost allocation rate}$$

SUMMARY PROBLEM

www.prenhall.com/horngren
End-of-Chapter Assessment

The Ritz-Carlton Club, an exclusive "hotel within a hotel," provides an even more luxurious atmosphere than the hotel's regular accommodations. Access is limited to guests residing on the hotel's top floors. The Club's private lounge serves complimentary continental breakfast, afternoon snacks, and evening cocktails and chocolates. The Club has its own concierge staff that provides personal service to Club guests. Guests staying in regular accommodations do not receive complimentary snacks and beverages, nor do they have a private concierge.

Ritz-Carlton Club floors are considered one department, and regular accommodations are considered a separate department.

Suppose the general manager of the new Ritz-Carlton hotel in St. Thomas, an island in the Caribbean, wants to know the costs of her hotel's Club Accommodations Department and Regular Accommodations Department. Housekeeping costs are allocated based on the number of occupied room-nights, utilities are allocated based on the number of cubic feet, and building depreciation is allocated based on the number of square feet. Assume each department reports the following information for March:

	Club Accommodations	Regular Accommodations
Number of occupied room-nights	540	7,560
Cubic feet	192,000	1,440,000
Square feet	16,000	144,000

Required

1. Given the following (assumed) total costs, what are the costs assigned to the Club Accommodations and the Regular Accommodations Departments?

Food and beverage expense	$ 12,000
Housekeeping expense	194,400
Utilities expense	97,920
Building depreciation expense	480,000
Concierage staff salaries	15,000
Total	$799,320

DAILY EXERCISE 23-20

2. What is the cost per occupied room in Club Accommodations? In Regular Accommodations?

Solution

Requirement 1

	Club Accommodations	Regular Accommodations	Total
Food and beverage expense[a]	$12,000	$ —	$ 12,000
Housekeeping expense[b]	12,960	181,440	194,400
Utilities expense[c]	11,520	86,400	97,920
Building depreciation expense[d]	48,000	432,000	480,000
Concierage staff salaries[a]	15,000	—	15,000
Total	$99,480	$699,840	$799,320

[a] Food and beverage expenses and concierge staff salaries are directly traced to the Club Accommodations Department.

[b] Housekeeping expense:

$$\text{Cost per occupied room} = \frac{\$194,400}{540 + 7,560}$$

$$= \$24/\text{room}$$

Club Accommodations: 540 rooms × $24/room = $ 12,960
Regular Accommodations: 7,560 rooms × $24/room = 181,440
Total housekeeping expense .... = $194,400

[c] Utilities expense:

$$\text{Cost per cubic foot} = \frac{\$97,920}{192,000 + 1,440,000}$$

$$= \$0.06/\text{cubic foot}$$

Club Accommodations: 192,000 cu. ft. × $0.06/cu. ft. = $11,520
Regular Accommodations:
1,440,000 cu. ft. × $0.06/cu. ft. = 86,400
Total utilities expense .... = $97,920

[d] Building depreciation expense:

$$\text{Cost per square foot} = \frac{\$480,000}{16,000 + 144,000}$$

$$= \$3/\text{square foot}$$

Club Accommodations: 16,000 sq. ft. × $3/sq. ft. = $ 48,000
Regular Accommodations: 144,000 sq. ft. × $3/sq. ft. = 432,000
Total building depreciation expense .... = $480,000

Requirement 2

	Club Accommodations	Regular Accommodations
Total costs	$99,480	$699,840
÷ Occupied rooms...........................	÷ 540	÷ 7,560
= Cost per occupied room	$184.22	$ 92.57

LESSONS LEARNED

1. **Identify the benefits of budgeting.** A budget is a quantitative expression of a plan of action that helps managers coordinate and implement the plan. Budgets require managers to plan, coordinate activities, and communicate plans throughout the company. Budgets also help managers evaluate performance and motivate employees to achieve goals.

2. **Prepare an operating budget.** The *operating budget* sets the target revenues and expenses—and thus operating income—for the period. To budget income, accountants must budget sales, inventory, purchases, cost of goods sold, and operating expenses. Sales revenue is budgeted first because other income statement elements depend on sales volume.

3. **Prepare the components of a financial budget.** A capital expenditures budget presents plans for purchasing long-term capital assets. This budget and the budgeted income statement provide data for the cash budget. Accountants use all three to prepare the budgeted balance sheet and the budgeted statement of cash flows.

4. **Use sensitivity analysis in budgeting.** Managers should make contingency plans in case actual results differ from predictions. *Sensitivity analysis* asks *what* a result will be *if* a predicted amount is not achieved or *if* an underlying assumption changes. Managers use spreadsheets or special Web-based software to study a broad range of budget possibilities.

5. **Distinguish among different types of responsibility centers.** Most companies divide operations into *responsibility centers* to establish authority for planning and controlling business operations. Four types of responsibility centers are cost centers, revenue centers, profit centers, and investment centers.

6. **Prepare a performance report for management by exception.** Performance reports show differences between budgeted and actual amounts. By focusing on important variances, managers can direct attention to areas that need improvement. This is called *management by exception.*

7. **Allocate indirect costs to departments.** First, choose an allocation base, which ideally should be a cost driver. Second, calculate an indirect cost allocation rate: Divide the indirect cost by the total quantity of the allocation base. Third, use this indirect cost allocation rate to allocate indirect costs to departments: Multiply the quantity of the allocation base used by the department times the indirect cost allocation rate.

ACCOUNTING VOCABULARY

capital expenditures budget
(p. 931)
cash budget (p. 936)
financial budget (p. 931)
management by exception
(p. 948)

master budget (p. 931)
operating budget (p. 931)
responsibility accounting
(p. 946)
responsibility center (p. 946)

statement of budgeted cash
receipts and payments
(p. 936)

QUESTIONS

1. What are four benefits of budgeting?
2. List the components of a master budget.
3. Taft Corporation installs a budgeting system in which the president sets all the goals for the company. The vice president checks up on all 90 employees to ensure that they are meeting the president's budget goals. What is the weakness in this budgeting system? How can the system be improved?
4. Why should the capital expenditures budget be prepared before the cash budget, the budgeted balance sheet, and the budgeted statement of cash flows?
5. How does a company budget inventory purchases? In your answer, show the relationships among purchases, cost of goods sold, and inventory.
6. Outline the four steps in preparing an operating budget.
7. Is sales forecasting important only to a profit-seeking business, or is it used by nonprofit organizations such as colleges and hospitals? Give your reason.
8. Why are computer spreadsheets and budget management software well suited for budgeting?

9. Which manager will control expenses better: Grant, whose performance is measured by his department's sales, or Bruns, whose performance is gauged by her department's income? Why?
10. Identify four types of responsibility centers, and give examples of each. State the information they report.
11. A company owns 50 **Burger King** restaurants in Philadelphia, Pittsburgh, and Harrisburg. In each city, a local manager oversees operations. Starting at the individual store level, describe the likely flow of information in a responsibility accounting system. What data are reported?
12. What is the objective of management by exception?
13. Identify a reasonable allocation base for the following indirect expenses: heating expense, depreciation of manufacturing equipment used by three departments, and advertising expense.
14. Why do companies allocate indirect costs to departments?

ASSESS YOUR PROGRESS

DAILY EXERCISES

Managers' use of budgets (Obj. 1)

DE23-1 What are the key roles managers play in running their business operations? How do budgets help managers with each role?

Identifying benefits of budgeting (Obj. 1)

DE23-2 Consider Ram Dharan's budget for his travel itinerary business (page 928). Explain how Dharan benefits from preparing the budget.

Ordering components of the master budget (Obj. 2, 3)

DE23-3 In what order should you prepare the following components of the master budget?

Budgeted income statement
Budgeted statement of cash flows
Budgeted balance sheet

Operating expense budget
Purchases and cost of goods sold budget
Sales budget

Cash budget
Capital expenditures budget
Inventory budget

Which are components of the operating budget? Which are components of the financial budget?

Preparing a sales budget (Obj. 2)

DE23-4 In a series of Daily Exercises, we are going to prepare parts of the master budget for Shādz, a major East Coast retailer of high-end sunglasses. We will concentrate on Shādz's budget for January and February.

Shādz expects to sell 3,000 pairs of glasses for $235 each in January, and 4,500 pairs of glasses for $240 each in February. All sales are cash only. Prepare the sales budget for January and February.

Preparing a purchases, cost of goods sold, and inventory budget (Obj. 2)

DE23-5 In Daily Exercise 23-4, Shādz expects cost of goods sold to average 65% of sales revenue, and the company expects to sell 4,300 pairs of sunglasses in March for $240 each. Shādz's target ending inventory is $10,000 plus 50% of the next month's cost of goods sold. Use this information and the sales budget from Daily Exercise 23-4 to prepare Shādz's purchases, cost of goods sold, and inventory budget for January and February.

DE23-6 Turn to the Whitewater Sporting Goods example on pages 932–940. Suppose June sales are expected to be $84,000 rather than $60,000. Revise Whitewater's sales budget.

What other components of Whitewater's master budget would be affected by this change in the sales budget?

Preparing a sales budget (Obj. 2, 4)

DE23-7 Refer to the original Whitewater Sporting Goods example on pages 932–940. Suppose cost of goods sold averages 65% of sales rather than 70%. Revise Whitewater's purchases, cost of goods sold, and inventory budget for April and May.

What other components of Whitewater's master budget would be affected by the change in the budgeted cost of goods sold?

Preparing a purchases, cost of goods sold, and inventory budget (Obj. 2, 4)

DE23-8 Turn to the original Whitewater Sporting Goods example on pages 932–940. Suppose 30% of sales are cash and 70% are credit. Revise Whitewater's sales budget and budgeted cash collections from customers for April and May.

Preparing a sales budget and cash collections budget (Obj. 2, 3, 4)

DE23-9 Refer to the original Whitewater Sporting Goods example on pages 932–940. Suppose Whitewater pays for 40% of inventory purchases in the month of the purchase and 60% during the next month. Revise Whitewater's budgeted cash payments for purchases of inventory for April and May. (*Hint:* Assume these new percentages also apply to March purchases of $33,600 given in item 5 on page 933).

Preparing a cash payments for purchases budget (Obj. 3, 4)

DE23-10 You prepared Shādz's sales budget in Daily Exercise 23-4. Now assume that Shādz's sales are 25% cash and 75% on credit. Shādz's collection history indicates that credit sales are collected as follows:

- 30% in the month of the sale
- 60% in the month after the sale
- 6% two months after the sale
- 4% are never collected

November sales totaled $391,500 and December sales were $398,250. Prepare a schedule for the budgeted cash collections for January and February.

Budgeting cash collections (Obj. 3)

DE23-11 Refer to Daily Exercise 23-10. Shādz's has $8,300 cash on hand on January 1. The company requires a minimum cash balance of $7,500. January cash collections are $531,705 (as you calculated in Daily Exercise 23-10). Total cash payments for January are $583,200. Prepare a cash budget for January. Will Shādz's need to borrow cash by the end of January?

Preparing a cash budget (Obj. 3)

DE23-12 Return to the original Whitewater Sporting Goods example on pages 932–940. Suppose Whitewater can borrow only in notes payable of $2,000 each, at an annual interest rate of 15%. The notes payable require ten equal monthly payments of the principal. Whitewater must also pay interest on the unpaid principal. Borrowing and all principal and interest payments occur at the end of the month. Answer the following questions.

1. How much will Whitewater have to borrow in April?
2. How much principal will Whitewater repay each month?
3. How much interest expense will Whitewater pay in May, June, and July?

Financing (Obj. 3)

DE23-13 How has information technology affected sensitivity analysis in budgeting?

Sensitivity analysis (Obj. 4)

DE23-14 Fill in the blanks with the phrase that best completes the sentence.

- A cost center
- An investment center
- A profit center
- A responsibility center
- A revenue center
- Higher
- Lower

a. The Maintenance Department at the **San Diego Zoo** is _____.
b. The concession stand at the San Diego Zoo is _____.
c. The Menswear Department at **Bloomingdale's,** which is responsible for buying and selling merchandise, is _____.
d. A production line at a **Palm Pilot** plant is _____.
e. _____ is any segment of the business whose manager is accountable for specific activities.
f. Gatorade, a division of **Quaker Oats** is _____.
g. The sales manager in charge of **NIKE's** northwest sales territory oversees _____.
h. Managers of cost and revenue centers are at _____ levels of the organization than are managers of profit and investment centers.

Distinguishing among different types of responsibility centers (Obj. 5)

DE23-15 In Exhibit 23-18, the first line of the district manager's report and the first line of the branch manager's report consist entirely of expenses. Describe the kinds of expenses that would be included in these categories. Explain why the store manager's report at the bottom of Exhibit 23-18 does not have a similar expense line item.

Distinguishing among responsibility centers, analyzing a performance report (Obj. 5, 6)

DE23-16 Examine the performance report in Exhibit 23-18. On which variances should the Beale store manager focus his efforts next month, according to the management by exception principle? For these variances, compute the variance as a percent of the budgeted amount, and suggest some questions that the Beale store manager may want to investigate.

Analyzing a performance report, management by exception (Obj. 6)

Not a question of blame
(Obj. 6)

DE23-17 Exhibit 23-18 shows that the Beale store had a favorable food expense variance. Does this favorable variance necessarily mean that the Beale store manager is doing a good job? Explain.

Identifying indirect cost allocation bases
(Obj. 7)

DE23-18 Listed below are several cost drivers.

Number of loads of materials moved	Number of customer complaints	Number of pages
Number of purchase orders	Number of inches	Number of square feet
Number of shipments received	Number of machine hours	Number of employees

Which of these is most likely the driver for the following costs?

a. Photocopying Department costs **f.** Material handling costs
b. Maintenance Department costs **g.** Personnel Department costs
c. Receiving Department costs **h.** Building rent and utilities
d. Customer Service Department costs **i.** Newspaper advertising costs
e. Purchasing Department costs

Allocating indirect costs to departments *(Obj. 7)*

DE23-19 Consider the WorldPC example on page 952. Suppose the Hardware Department occupies 15,000 square feet and the Software Department occupies 5,000 square feet. How would the $600,000 rent expense be allocated?

Using departmental costs
(Obj. 7)

DE23-20 ◄ *Link Back to Chapter 20 (uses of product cost information).* Study the summary review problem on pages 954–955. Why might the general manager of the new **Ritz-Carlton** hotel in St. Thomas want to know the cost per occupied room for the Club Accommodations and the Regular Accommodations?

EXERCISES

Budgeting and performance evaluation
(Obj. 1)

E23-1 John Smith owns a store that sells athletic shoes. Last year, his sales staff sold 10,000 pairs of shoes at an average sale price of $65. Variable expenses were 80% of sales revenue, and the total fixed expense was $100,000. This year the store sold more expensive product lines. Sales were 8,000 pairs at an average price of $90. The variable expense percentage and the total fixed expense were the same both years. Smith evaluates the store manager by comparing this year's income with last year's income.

Prepare a performance report for this year, similar to Exhibit 23-3. How would you improve Smith's performance evaluation system to better analyze this year's results?

Budgeting purchases, cost of goods sold, and inventory
(Obj. 2)

E23-2 i-Tote is an e-tailer of womens' accessories. Their sales budget for the nine months ended September 30 follows:

	Quarter Ended			Nine-Month Total
	March 31	**June 30**	**Sep. 30**	
Cash sales, 30%.................	$ 30,000	$ 45,000	$ 37,500	$112,500
Credit sales, 70%..............	70,000	105,000	87,500	262,500
Total sales, 100%...............	$100,000	$150,000	$125,000	$375,000

In the past, cost of goods sold has been 70% of total sales. The director of marketing and the financial vice president agree that each quarter's ending inventory should not be below $20,000 plus 10% of cost of goods sold for the following quarter. Thomas expects sales of $110,000 during the fourth quarter. The January 1 inventory was $22,000.

Prepare a purchases, cost of goods sold, and inventory budget for each of the first three quarters of the year. Compute cost of goods sold for the entire nine-month period. (Use Exhibit 23-8 as a model.)

Budgeting quarterly income for a year
(Obj. 2)

E23-3 Suresale is a real-estate firm. Suppose that its San Francisco office projects that 20X4 quarterly sales will increase by 4% in quarter 1, by 3% in quarter 2, by 5% in quarter 3, and by 6% in quarter 4. Management expects operating expenses to be 85% of revenues during each of the first two quarters, 79% of revenues during the third quarter, and 81% during the fourth. The office manager expects to borrow $100,000 on July 1, with quarterly principal payments of $10,000 beginning on September 30 and interest paid at an annual rate of 17%. Assume that fourth-quarter 20X3 sales were $3,000,000.

Prepare a budgeted income statement for each of the four quarters of 20X4 and for the entire year. Present the 20X4 budget as follows:

E23-4 Scents Unlimited is a distributor of fragrances. For each of items a through c, compute the amount of cash receipts or payments Scents will budget for September. The solution to one item may depend on the answer to an earlier item.

Computing cash receipts and payments
(Obj. 3)

a. Management expects to sell equipment that cost $12,000 at a gain of $2,000. Accumulated depreciation on this equipment is $7,000.
b. Management expects to sell 7,500 bottles in August and 8,400 in September. Each bottle sells for $16. Cash sales average 30% of total sales, and credit sales make up the rest. Three-fourths of credit sales are collected in the month of sale, with the balance collected the following month.
c. The company pays rent and property taxes of $3,500 each month. Commissions and other selling expenses average 25% of sales. Scents pays two-thirds of commissions and other selling expenses in the month incurred, with the balance paid in the following month.

E23-5 Harrison Woods, a family-owned gardening store, began October with $7,500 cash. Management forecasts that collections from credit customers will be $9,500 in October and $13,000 in November. The store is scheduled to receive $6,000 cash on a business note receivable in October. Projected cash payments include inventory purchases ($11,000 in October and $14,100 in November) and operating expenses ($3,000 each month).

Preparing a cash budget; sensitivity analysis
(Obj. 3, 4)

Harrison's bank requires a $6,500 minimum balance in the store's checking account. At the end of any month when the account balance dips below $6,500, the bank automatically extends credit to the store in multiples of $1,000. Harrison's borrows as little as possible and pays back these loans in quarterly installments of $2,000, plus 4.5% interest on the entire unpaid principal. The first payment occurs three months after the loan.

Required

1. Prepare the store's cash budget for October and November.
2. How much cash will Harrison's borrow in November if collections from customers that month total $9,300 instead of $13,000?

E23-6 Use the following information to prepare a budgeted balance sheet for Cinderella's Closet at March 31, 20X2. Show computations for the cash and owners' equity amounts.

Preparing a budgeted balance sheet
(Obj. 3)

a. March 31 inventory balance, $14,000
b. March payments for inventory, $5,900
c. March payments of accounts payable and accrued liabilities, $8,200
d. March 31 accounts payable balance, $4,900
e. February 28 furniture and fixtures balance, $34,800; accumulated depreciation balance, $26,400
f. February 28 owner's equity, $25,100
g. March depreciation expense, $600
h. Cost of goods sold, 50% of sales
i. Other March expenses, including income tax, total $5,000; paid in cash
j. February 28 cash balance, $10,300
k. March budgeted sales, $11,600
l. March 31 accounts receivable balance, one-fourth of March sales
m. March cash receipts, $14,300

E23-7 Identify each responsibility center as a cost center, a revenue center, a profit center, or an investment center.

Identifying different types of responsibility centers
(Obj. 5)

a. The bakery department of a **Kroger** supermarket reports income for the current year.
b. **Netscape Communication** is a subsidiary of **America Online, Inc.**
c. A personnel department of **State Farm Insurance Companies** prepares its budget and subsequent performance report on the basis of its expected expenses for the year.
d. The shopping section of **Garden.com** reports both revenues and expenses.
e. **Garden.com's** investor relations Web site provides operating and financial information to investors and other interested parties.
f. The manager of a **BP** service station is evaluated based on the station's revenues and expenses.
g. A charter airline records revenues and expenses for each airplane each month. The airplane's performance report shows its ratio of operating income to average book value.
h. The manager of the southwest sales territory is evaluated based on a comparison of current period sales against budgeted sales.

E23-8 D*Books.com is a New York company that sells discount books on the Web. D*Books.com has assistant managers for its adult-fiction and adult-nonfiction operations. These assistant managers report to the manager of adult books, who with the manager of children's books reports to the manager for all book sales, Beth Beverly. Beverly received the following data for November operations:

Using responsibility accounting to evaluate profit centers
(Obj. 6)

| | Adult | | |
	Nonfiction	Fiction	Children's
Revenues, budget.............	$102,000	$600,000	$1,200,000
Expenses, budget	74,000	390,000	775,000
Revenues, actual..............	107,000	630,000	1,000,000
Expenses, actual...............	65,000	400,000	690,000

Arrange the data in a performance report similar to Exhibit 23-18. Show November results, in thousands of dollars, for adult-nonfiction, adult, and books as a whole. Should Beverly investigate the performance of adult-nonfiction operations?

Allocating indirect expenses to departments
(Obj. 7)

E23-9 Johnston Fabricating incurred the following indirect costs in April:

Indirect labor expense...............................	$16,000
Equipment depreciation expense..............	22,500
Marketing expense....................................	24,000

Data for cost allocations:

| | Department | | |
	Priming	Welding	Custom Orders
Sales revenue........................	$70,000	$50,000	$80,000
Indirect labor hours	400	500	100
Machine hours......................	300	450	150
Building square feet..............	9,000	3,000	1,500
Marketing expense—allocated to departments in proportion to sales.			

Required

1. Allocate Johnston Fabricating's April indirect expenses to the three departments.
2. Compute total indirect expenses for each department.

Preparing a departmental income statement
(Obj. 7)

E23-10 Hold-It.com is an e-tailer of cedar and plastic storage containers. It has two divisions: Cedar and Plastic. The company's income statement for 20X3 appears as follows:

Sales revenue....................................	$325,000
Cost of goods sold............................	116,000
Gross profit	209,000
Operating expenses:	
Salaries expense...........................	$ 78,000
Depreciation expense...................	20,000
Advertising expense.....................	4,000
Other expenses	10,000
Total operating expenses..............	112,000
Operating income...........................	$ 97,000

Hold-It.com sales are $136,000 of cedar storage containers and $189,000 of plastic containers. Cost of goods sold is distributed $42,000 to Cedar and $74,000 to Plastic. Salaries are traced directly to departments: Cedar $36,000, and Plastic $42,000. The Cedar Department accounts for 80% of advertising. Depreciation is allocated based on the warehouse square footage occupied by each department: Cedar has 20,000 square feet and Plastic has 30,000 square feet. Other expenses are allocated based on the number of employees. Each department currently employs an equal number of employees.

Required

1. Prepare departmental income statements that show revenues, expenses, and operating income for each of the two departments.
2. Which of the expenses in the departmental performance report are the most important for evaluating Hold-It.com department managers? Give your reason.

Challenge Exercise

E23-11 You recently began a job as an accounting intern at Trailblazers Ltd. Your first task was to help prepare the cash budget for February and March. Unfortunately, the computer with the budget file crashed, and you did not have a backup or even a hard copy. You ran a program to salvage bits of data from the budget file. After entering the following data in the budget, you may have just enough information to reconstruct the budget.

Preparing a cash budget *(Obj. 3)*

Trailblazers eliminates any cash deficiency by borrowing the exact amount needed from Second State Bank, where the current interest rate is 12%. Trailblazers repays all borrowed amounts at the end of the month, as cash becomes available.

Complete the following cash budget:

TRAILBLAZERS LTD.
Cash Budget
February and March

	February	March
Beginning cash balance	$10,900	$?
Cash collections	?	74,800
Cash from sale of plant assets	0	1,800
Cash available	90,900	?
Cash payments:		
Purchase of inventory	$?	$41,000
Operating expenses	31,900	?
Total payments	82,500	?
(1) Ending cash balance before financing	?	19,500
Minimum cash balance desired	15,000	15,000
Cash excess (deficiency)	$?	$?
Financing of cash deficiency:		
Borrowing (at end of month)	$?	$?
Principal repayments (at end of month)	?	?
Interest expense	?	?
(2) Total effects of financing	?	?
Ending cash balance (1) + (2)	$?	$?

PROBLEMS

(Group A)

P23-1A Representatives of the various departments of Software Direct have assembled the following data. As the business manager, you must prepare the budgeted income statements for August and September 20X3.

Budgeting income for two months *(Obj. 2)*

a. Sales in July were $184,000. You forecast that monthly sales will increase 2% in August and 2% in September.

b. Software Direct tries to maintain inventory of $50,000 plus 20% of sales budgeted for the following month. Monthly purchases average 60% of sales. Actual inventory on July 31 is $80,000. Sales budgeted for October are $198,000.

c. Monthly salaries amount to $15,000. Sales commissions equal 6% of sales. Combine salaries and commissions into a single figure.

d. Other monthly expenses are

Rent expense	$14,000, paid as incurred
Depreciation expense	$ 3,000
Insurance expense	$ 1,000, expiration of prepaid amount
Income tax	30% of operating income

Prepare Software Direct's budgeted income statements for August and September. Show cost-of-goods sold computations. Round *all* amounts to the nearest $1,000. For example, budgeted August sales are $188,000 ($184,000 × 1.02) and September sales are $192,000 ($188,000 × 1.02).

P23-2A Refer to Problem 23-1A. Software Direct's sales are 50% cash and 50% credit. Credit sales are collected in the month after sale. Inventory purchases are paid 70% in the month of purchase and 30% the following month. Salaries and sales commissions are paid three-fourths in the month earned and one-fourth the next month. Income tax is paid at the end of the year.

The July 31, 20X3 balance sheet showed the following balances:

Cash	$20,000
Accounts payable	48,000
Salaries and commissions payable	13,500

Required

1. Prepare schedules of (a) budgeted cash collections from customers, (b) budgeted cash payments for purchases, and (c) budgeted cash payments for operating expenses. Show amounts for each month and totals for August and September. Carry your computations to the *nearest dollar*.
2. Prepare a cash budget similar to Exhibit 23-13. If no financing activity took place, what is the budgeted cash balance on September 30, 20X3?

P23-3A The Book Closet has applied for a loan. Westside Bank has requested a budgeted balance sheet at June 30, 20X5, and a budgeted statement of cash flows for June. As the controller (chief accounting officer) of The Book Closet, you have assembled the following information:

a. May 31 equipment balance, $60,600; accumulated depreciation, $11,700.
b. June capital expenditures of $15,800 budgeted for cash purchase of equipment.
c. June depreciation expense, $400.
d. Cost of goods sold, 50% of sales.
e. Other June operating expenses, including income tax, total $46,000, 75% of which will be paid in cash and the remainder accrued at June 30.
f. May 31 owners' equity, $104,800.
g. May 31 cash balance, $40,900.
h. June budgeted sales, $85,000, 30% of which is for cash. Of the remaining 70%, half will be collected in June and half in July.
i. June cash collections on May sales, $15,300.
j. June cash payments of liabilities for May inventory purchases on credit, $10,700.
k. May 31 inventory balance, $10,400.
l. June purchases of inventory, $11,000 for cash and $30,600 on credit. Half the credit purchases will be paid in June and half in July.

Required

1. Prepare the budgeted balance sheet for The Book Closet at June 30, 20X5. Show separate computations for cash, inventory, and owners' equity balances.
2. Prepare the budgeted statement of cash flows for June.
3. On the basis of this data, if you were a Westside Bank loan officer, would you grant The Book Closet a loan? Give your reason.

P23-4A Refer to Problem 23-3A. Before granting a loan to The Book Closet, Westside Bank asks for a sensitivity analysis assuming that June sales are only $65,000 rather than the $85,000 originally budgeted. (While cost of goods sold will change, assume that purchases, depreciation, and the other operating expenses will remain the same as in Problem 23-3A.)

Required

1. Prepare a revised budgeted balance sheet for The Book Closet, showing separate computations for cash, inventory, and owners' equity balances.
2. Suppose The Book Closet has a minimum desired cash balance of $15,000. Will the company borrow cash in June?
3. How would this sensitivity analysis affect Westside's loan decision?

P23-5A Is each of the following most likely a cost center, a revenue center, a profit center, or an investment center?

a. Personnel Department of **E* Trade,** the on-line broker
b. Quality Control Department of **Mayfield Dairies**
c. European subsidiary of **Coca-Cola**
d. Payroll Department of the **University of Wisconsin**

e. Lighting Department in a **Sears** store
f. Children's nursery in a church or synagogue
g. Purchasing Department of **Milliken,** a textile manufacturer
h. **Bluefly.com,** an e-tailer of womenswear

i. Service Department of an automobile dealership
j. Customer Service Department of **Procter & Gamble Co.**
k. Proposed new office of **Deutsche Bank**
l. Southwest region of **Pizza Inns, Inc.**
m. **Delta Air Lines, Inc.**
n. Order-Taking Department at **Lands' End** mail order company
o. Editorial Department of the **Wall Street Journal**
p. A **Ford Motor Company** production plant
q. Police Department of Boston
r. **Century 21 Real Estate Co.**
s. A small pet grooming business
t. Northeast sales territory for **Boise-Cascade**
u. Different product lines of **Broyhill,** a furniture manufacturer
v. **McDonald's** restaurants under the supervision of a regional manager
w. Job superintendents of a home builder

P23-6A Audio and Video is a chain of home electronics stores. Each store has a manager who answers to a city manager, who in turn reports to a statewide manager. The actual income statements of Store No. 13, all stores in the Topeka area (including Store No. 13), and all stores in the state of Kansas (including all Topeka stores) are summarized as follows for April:

Preparing a profit-center performance report for management by exception; benefits of budgeting (Obj. 1, 6)

	Store No. 13	Topeka	State of Kansas
Sales revenue	$39,800	$486,000	$3,264,500
Expenses:			
City/state manager's office expenses	$ —	$ 16,000	$ 44,000
Cost of goods sold	13,000	171,300	1,256,800
Salary expense	5,000	37,500	409,700
Depreciation expense	3,000	26,100	320,000
Utilities expense	2,700	19,300	245,600
Rent expense	1,600	16,400	186,000
Total expenses	25,300	286,600	2,462,100
Operating income	$14,500	$199,400	$ 802,400

Budgeted amounts for April were as follows:

	Store No. 13	Topeka	State of Kansas
Sales revenue	$42,000	$470,000	$3,145,000
Expenses:			
City/state manager's office expenses	$ —	$ 17,000	$ 43,000
Cost of goods sold	14,200	172,800	1,209,000
Salary expense	5,600	37,900	412,000
Depreciation expense	3,500	25,400	320,000
Utilities expense	2,100	17,000	240,000
Rent expense	1,600	15,700	181,000
Total expenses	27,000	285,800	2,405,000
Operating income	$15,000	$184,200	$ 740,000

Required

1. Prepare a report for April that shows the performance of Store No. 13, all the stores in the Topeka area, and all the stores in the state of Kansas. Follow the format of Exhibit 23-18.
2. As the city manager of Topeka, would you investigate Store No. 13 on the basis of this report? Why or why not?
3. Briefly discuss the benefits of budgeting. Base your discussion on Audio and Video's performance report.

P23-7A The Printed Page has both a Printing and a Copy Services Department. At May 31, the end of the fiscal year, the bookkeeper prepared the adjusted trial balance on page 964.

The Printed Page owns its printing equipment and leases a high-speed copier from **Xerox.** The Printed Page performs print jobs on a credit basis for established customers, but copy services are cash only. The store manager spends 60% of her time on Printing Services and 40% on Copy Services. The bookkeeper spends approximately two-thirds of

Allocating indirect costs; departmental income statements (Obj. 7)

Cash	$ 2,400	
Accounts receivable	3,300	
Prepaid expenses	1,100	
Building and office furniture	84,900	
Accumulated depreciation—building and furniture		$ 26,300
Other assets	4,700	
Accounts payable		3,200
Unearned service revenue		2,200
Owners' equity		24,800
Printing service revenue		68,750
Copy service revenue		56,250
Salary expense—machine operators	23,600	
Salary expense—store manager	22,900	
Salary expense—bookkeeper	18,300	
Lease expense—copy equipment	12,000	
Property tax expense	2,800	
Depreciation expense—building	2,000	
Depreciation expense—printing equipment	1,300	
Insurance expense	1,600	
Bad debt expense	600	
	$181,500	$181,500

his time on accounts receivable and other Printing Department transactions, and the remainder on Copy Services transactions. Insurance expense is evenly divided between the two departments. The company allocates all other expenses based on relative service revenue.

Required

1. Prepare departmental income statements.
2. Which department is more profitable? What factor contributes most to the profit differences between the two departments?

(Group B) PROBLEMS

Budgeting income for two months
(Obj. 2)

P23-1B The budget committee of Morton Restaurant Supply Co. has assembled the following data. As the business manager, you must prepare the budgeted income statements for May and June 20X2.

a. Sales in April were $31,300. You forecast that monthly sales will increase 2.4% in May and 2.4% in June.
b. Morton maintains inventory of $9,000 plus 25% of sales budgeted for the following month. Monthly purchases average 55% of sales. Actual inventory on April 30 is $14,000. Sales budgeted for July are $42,400.
c. Monthly salaries amount to $4,000. Sales commissions equal 4% of sales. Combine salaries and commissions into a single figure.
d. Other monthly expenses are

Rent expense	$3,200, paid as incurred
Depreciation expense	$ 500
Insurance expense	$ 200, expiration of prepaid amount
Income tax	20% of operating income

Prepare Morton's budgeted income statements for May and June. Show cost-of-goods-sold computations. Round *all* amounts to the nearest $100. For example, budgeted May sales are $32,100 ($31,300 × 1.024), and June sales are $32,900 ($32,100 × 1.024).

Budgeting cash receipts and payments (Obj. 3)

P23-2B Refer to Problem 23-1B. Morton's sales are 70% cash and 30% credit. Credit sales are collected in the month after sale. Inventory purchases are paid 60% in the month of purchase and 40% the following month. Salaries and sales commissions are paid half in the month earned and half the next month. Income tax is paid at the end of the year.
The April 30, 20X2 balance sheet showed the following balances:

Cash	....	$10,000
Accounts payable	....	6,200
Salary and commissions payable	....	2,800

Required

1. Prepare schedules of (a) budgeted cash collections, (b) budgeted cash payments for purchases, and (c) budgeted cash payments for operating expenses. Show amounts for each month and totals for May and June. Carry your computations to the nearest dollar.
2. Prepare a cash budget similar to Exhibit 23-13. If no financing activity took place, what is the budgeted cash balance on June 30, 20X2?

P23-3B Frank's Used Cars of Asheville, North Carolina, has applied for a loan. Bank of America has requested a budgeted balance sheet at April 30, 20X4, and a budgeted statement of cash flows for April. As the controller (chief accounting officer) of Frank's Used Cars, you have assembled the following information:

Preparing a budgeted balance sheet and budgeted statement of cash flows
(Obj. 3)

a. March 31 equipment balance, $42,500; accumulated depreciation, $31,400.
b. April capital expenditures of $41,700 budgeted for cash purchase of equipment.
c. April depreciation expense, $900.
d. Cost of goods sold, 60% of sales.
e. Other April operating expenses, including income tax, total $13,200, 25% of which will be paid in cash and the remainder accrued at April 30.
f. March 31 owners' equity, $87,000.
g. March 31 cash balance, $36,200.
h. April budgeted sales, $90,000, 60% of

which is for cash. Of the remaining 40%, half will be collected in April and half in May.
i. April cash collections on March sales, $29,700.
j. April cash payments of March 31 liabilities incurred for March purchases of inventory, $17,300.
k. March 31 inventory balance, $27,300.
l. April purchases of inventory, $9,000 for cash and $36,800 on credit. Half of the credit purchases will be paid in April and half in May.

Required

1. Prepare the budgeted balance sheet for Frank's Used Cars at April 30, 20X4. Show separate computations for cash, inventory, and owners' equity balances.
2. Prepare the budgeted statement of cash flows for April.
3. Suppose that Frank's Used Cars has become aware of more efficient (and more expensive) equipment than it budgeted for purchase in April. What is the total amount of cash available for equipment purchases in April, before financing, if the minimum desired ending cash balance is $21,000? (For this requirement, disregard the $41,700 initially budgeted for equipment purchases.)

P23-4B Refer to Problem 23-3B. Before granting a loan to Frank's Used Cars, Bank of America asks for a sensitivity analysis assuming April sales are only $60,000 rather than the $90,000 originally budgeted. (While the cost of goods sold will change, assume that purchases, depreciation, and the other operating expenses will remain the same as in Problem 23-3B.)

Preparing a budgeted balance sheet; sensitivity analysis
(Obj. 3, 4)

Required

1. Prepare a revised budgeted balance sheet for Frank's Used Cars, showing separate computations for cash, inventory, and owners' equity balances.
2. Suppose Frank's has a minimum desired cash balance of $23,000. Will the company need to borrow cash in April?
3. In this sensitivity analysis, sales declined by $33\frac{1}{3}\%$ ($30,000 ÷ $90,000). Is the decline in expenses and income more or less than $33\frac{1}{3}\%$? Explain why.

P23-5B Is each of the following most likely a cost center, a revenue center, a profit center, or an investment center?

Identifying different types of responsibility centers
(Obj. 5)

a. Shipping department of **Amazon.com**
b. Eastern district of a salesperson's territory
c. Music director of a church or synagogue
d. Catering operation of Sonny's BBQ restaurant
e. Executive director of a **United Way** agency
f. Accounts payable section of the Accounting Department at **Home Depot**
g. Proposed new office of **Coldwell Banker**, a real-estate firm

h. **Disneyland**
i. The Empire State Building in New York City
j. Branch warehouse of **Dalton Carpets**
k. Information systems director for **Habitat for Humanity**
l. Service Department of Audio Forest stereo shop
m. Investments Department of **Citibank**
n. Assembly-line supervisors at **Dell Computer**
o. American subsidiary of a Japanese manufacturer

p. Surgery unit of a privately owned hospital

q. Research and Development Department of **Cisco Systems**

r. Childrenswear department at a **Target** store

s. Typesetting Department of Northend Press, a printing company

t. Prescription Filling Department of **Drugstore.com**

u. Order-Taking Department at **L.L. Bean**

v. Personnel Department of **Goodyear Tire and Rubber Company**

w. Grounds crew at Augusta National golf course

Preparing a profit-center performance report for management by exception; benefits of budgeting (Obj. 1, 6)

P23-6B Home-Aid is a charitable organization, recently established in the Midwest, that builds low-income housing. The manager of each city's Home-Aid office reports to the state's director, who in turn reports to headquarters in Milwaukee, Wisconsin. The *actual* income statements for the Cincinnati office, the Ohio region (including the Cincinnati office) and the organization as a whole (including the Ohio region) for July 20X3 are

	Cincinnati	Ohio	Organizationwide
Revenue	$148,900	$1,647,000	$4,200,000
Expenses:			
State director/ headquarters office	$ —	$ 60,000	$ 116,000
Cost of materials	81,100	871,900	1,807,000
Salary expense	38,100	415,500	1,119,000
Depreciation expense	7,200	91,000	435,000
Utilities expense	4,200	46,200	260,000
Rent expense	2,400	34,700	178,000
Total expenses	133,000	1,519,300	3,915,000
Operating income	$ 15,900	$ 127,700	$ 285,000

Budgeted amounts for July were as follows:

	Cincinnati	Ohio	Organizationwide
Revenue	$162,400	$1,769,700	$4,450,000
Expenses:			
State director/ headquarters office	$ —	$ 65,600	$ 118,000
Cost of materials	85,500	963,400	1,972,000
Salary expense	38,800	442,000	1,095,000
Depreciation expense	7,200	87,800	449,000
Utilities expense	4,700	54,400	271,000
Rent expense	2,800	32,300	174,000
Total expenses	139,000	1,645,500	4,079,000
Operating income	$ 23,400	$ 124,200	$ 371,000

Required

1. Prepare a report for July 20X3 that shows the performance of the Cincinnati office, the Ohio region, and the organization as a whole. Follow the format of Exhibit 23-18.
2. As the director of the Ohio region manager, would you investigate the Cincinnati office on the basis of this report? Why or why not?
3. Briefly discuss the benefits of budgeting. Base your discussion on Home-Aid's performance report.

Allocating indirect costs; departmental income statements (Obj. 7)

P23-7B World Travel.com is an Internet-based travel agency. The company has a Custom Travel Department and a Group Discount Travel Department. At August 31, the end of World-Travel's fiscal year, the bookkeeper prepared the adjusted trial balance at the top of the next page.

Last September, World Travel hired a specialist in group discount travel at an annual salary of $27,000. Remaining agent salaries of $12,500 are for part-time agents who handle custom travel plans. The office manager spends 70% of her time on group discount plans and 30% on custom travel planning. The bookkeeper spends approximately two-thirds of his time on accounting for custom travel and the remainder on group discount plans. About 80% of the time spent developing and maintaining the Web site is for custom travel, and the remaining 20% is for group discount packages. Insurance expense is evenly divided between the two departments. The company allocates commissions and all other expenses based on relative service revenue.

Cash	$ 2,400	
Receivables	29,700	
Prepaid expenses	1,700	
Building and office furniture	115,600	
Accumulated depreciation—building and		
furniture		$ 28,200
Other assets	5,300	
Accounts payable		11,400
Accrued liabilities		6,900
Unearned service revenue		5,800
Owners' equity		19,200
Custom travel service revenue		88,000
Group discount travel service revenue		132,000
Salary expense—travel agents	39,500	
Commission expense—travel agents	30,800	
Salary expense—office manager	25,000	
Salary expense—bookkeeper	16,800	
Web site maintenance expense	15,000	
Property tax expense	2,200	
Depreciation expense—building and furniture	4,600	
Insurance expense	1,700	
Web advertising expense	1,200	
	$291,500	$291,500

Required

1. Prepare departmental income statements.
2. Which department is more profitable? Was the decision to hire the group specialist wise? Give your reason.

APPLY YOUR KNOWLEDGE

DECISION CASES

Case 1. Liquid Sky designs, manufactures, and sells wakeboards through water-sports specialty stores and sports superstores. In 20X5, Liquid Sky incurred the following costs that are directly traceable to its Blowout product line:

Allocating indirect costs
(Obj. 7)

Production—Molding (direct materials and direct labor)	$288,000
Production—Graphics (direct materials and direct labor)	430,000
Advertising for Blowout	100,000

In addition to these direct costs, Liquid Sky also incurred other costs that cannot be traced directly to individual product lines. These indirect costs are allocated to the different product lines. For 20X5, Liquid Sky reports the following information about its indirect costs:

	Total Indirect Costs	Allocation Base for Indirect Costs	Total Quantity of Allocation Base
Product design	$ 180,000	New designs	3 new designs
Production—Molding	1,200,000	Machine hours	6,000 machine hours
Production—Graphics	1,800,000	Labor hours	18,000 labor hours
Distribution	300,000	Shipments	1,000 shipments

(continued)

During 20X5, the whole Blowout product line required a total of one new product design, 1,000 machine hours, 3,500 labor hours, and 140 shipments. There were no beginning inventories of any kind.

Required

➤ To review *inventoriable product costs*, see Chapter 19, page 761.

1. Compute an indirect cost allocation rate for each of the four indirect costs.
2. Use the indirect cost allocation rates from requirement 1 to compute the *total costs* for the Blowout wakeboard product line, including all direct and indirect costs. Assuming Liquid Sky produced 7,000 Blowout wakeboards, what is the total cost per wakeboard?
3. ◄ At the end of 20X5, Liquid Sky's ending inventory consists solely of 600 Blowout wakeboards. What inventory value would appear on Liquid Sky's December 31, 20X5 balance sheet? (*Hint:* Round your inventoriable cost per unit to the nearest penny.)
4. A snow ski manufacturer has asked Liquid Sky to produce snowboards, which the ski manufacturer would sell under its own name. Suppose Liquid Sky decides to produce the snowboards for the snow ski manufacturer on a cost-plus-fixed-fee basis. (That is, the sale price is Liquid Sky's cost to make the snowboards plus a fixed fee of $50,000.) The rest of Liquid Sky's business is at fixed sale prices—for example, $300 for Blowout wakeboards. What cost allocation incentives would this give Liquid Sky's managers? When there are difficult allocation decisions, will Liquid Sky be tempted to allocate a bigger or smaller share of indirect costs to the snowboards? Why?
5. Liquid Sky's top management knows that the sale price of Blowout wakeboards may change over the product's life. But management wishes to identify a target sale price Liquid Sky should receive on average over the life of the product. Which of Liquid Sky's costs are relevant in setting the long-run average sale price for Blowout wakeboards? Give your reason.

Using a budgeted income statement
(Obj. 1) ✏️➡️

Case 2. Renee Willis has recently accepted the position of assistant manager at Jack and Jill, a children's clothing store in St. Louis. She has just finished her accounting courses. Jack and Jill's manager and owner, Kristy Simms, asks Renee to prepare a budgeted income statement for 20X6 based on the information she has collected. Willis' budget follows:

JACK AND JILL		
Budgeted Income Statement		
For the Year Ending July 31, 20X6		
Sales revenue		$240,000
Cost of goods sold		172,000
Gross profit		68,000
Operating expenses:		
Salary and commission expense	$46,000	
Rent expense	8,000	
Depreciation expense	2,000	
Insurance expense	800	
Miscellaneous expenses	12,000	68,800
Operating loss		(800)
Interest expense		225
Net loss		$ (1,025)

Required

Willis does not want to give Simms this budget without making constructive suggestions for steps Simms could take to improve expected performance. Write a memo to Simms outlining your suggestions. Your memo should take the following form:

Date: _____

To: **Ms. Kristy Simms, Manager**
          Jack and Jill
From: **Renee Willis**
Subject: **Jack and Jill's 20X6 budgeted income statement**

ETHICAL ISSUE

← Link Back to Chapter 7, p. 290, for Ethics, Decision Guidelines box. Guest Suites operates a regional motel chain. Each motel is operated by a manager and an assistant manager/controller. Many of the staff who run the front desk, clean the rooms, and prepare the breakfast buffet work part-time or have a second job, so turnover is high.

Budget slack (Obj. 2, 6)

Assistant manager/controller Carrie Pronai asked the new bookkeeper to help prepare the motel's master budget. The master budget is prepared once a year and submitted to company headquarters for approval. Once approved, the master budget is used to evaluate the motel's performance. These performance evaluations affect motel managers' bonuses and they also affect company decisions on which motels deserve extra funds for capital improvements.

When the budget was almost complete, Pronai asked the bookkeeper to increase amounts budgeted for labor and supplies by 15%. When asked why, Pronai responded that motel manager Clay Murry told her to do this when she began working at the motel. Murry explained that this budgetary cushion gave him flexibility in running the motel. For example, since company headquarters tightly controls capital improvement funds, Murry can use the extra money budgeted for labor and supplies to replace broken televisions or pay "bonuses" to keep valued employees. Pronai initially accepted this explanation because she had observed similar behavior at the motel where she worked previously.

Put yourself in Pronai's position. Use the ethical judgment decision guidelines in Chapter 7 (page 290) to decide how Pronai should deal with the situation.

FINANCIAL STATEMENT CASE

Budgets are an important management tool in a large company like **Target.** Refer to Target's annual report to answer the following questions:

Budgeting by quarter and segment, types of responsibility centers, performance evaluation (Obj. 3, 5, 6)

1. When preparing the master budget, would Target budget approximately the same sales and profit amounts for each quarter? Explain. (*Hint:* Quarterly results appear on page 35 of the annual report.)
2. Target Corporation distinguishes among three segments: (1) Target, (2) Mervyn's, and (3) Department Stores. Are these segments cost centers, revenue centers, profit centers, or investment centers? Explain.
3. Calculate return on assets for the Target, Mervyn's, and Department Stores segments for 1999, 1998, and 1997. Use pretax segment profit in the numerator of the return on assets computation and average segment assets in the denominator. Carry your computations to four decimal places. (*Hint:* Business segment data are presented on page 37).
4. Target changed its name from Dayton Hudson Corporation to Target Corporation in 2000. Explain why the name change makes sense in terms of requirement 3's analysis.

TEAM PROJECT

Nova Solutions provides e-commerce software for the pharmaceuticals industry. Nova is organized into several divisions. A companywide planning committee sets general strategy and goals for the company and its divisions, but each division develops its own budget.

Responsibility accounting, return on assets (Obj. 5, 6)

Rick Watson is the new division manager of Business-to-Business software. His division has two departments: Development and Sales. Patti McKeown manages the 20 or so programmers and systems specialists typically employed in Development to create and update the division's software applications. Liz Smith manages the sales department.

Nova considers the divisions to be investment centers. To earn his bonus next year, Watson must achieve a 30% return on the $3 million invested in his division. Within the Business-to-Business Division, Development is a cost center, while Sales is a revenue center.

Budgeting is in progress. Patti McKeown met with her staff and is now struggling with two sets of numbers. Alternative A is her best estimate of next year's costs. However,

NOVA SOLUTIONS — Business-to-Business Division — Development Budget 20XX		
	Alternative A	**Alternative B**
Salaries expense (including overtime and part-time)	$2,300,000	$2,530,000
Software expense...	120,000	132,000
Travel expense	65,000	71,500
Depreciation expense...	255,000	255,000
Miscellaneous expense	100,000	110,000
Total expense	$2,840,000	$3,098,500

unexpected problems can arise when writing software, and finding competent programmers is an ongoing challenge. She knows that Watson was a programmer before he earned an MBA, so he should be sensitive to this uncertainty. Consequently, she is thinking of adding another 10% to her budgeted costs (Alternative B). Her department's bonuses largely depend on whether the department meets its budgeted costs.

Liz Smith is also struggling with her sales budget. Companies have made their initial investments in business-to-business software, so it is harder to win new customers. If things go well, she believes her sales team can maintain the level of growth achieved over the last few years. This is Alternative A in the Sales Budget. However, if Smith is too optimistic, sales may fall short of the budget. If this happens, her team will not receive bonuses. Smith is therefore considering reducing the sales numbers and submitting Alternative B.

NOVA SOLUTIONS Business-to-Business Division Sales Budget 20XX		
	Alternative A	**Alternative B**
Sales revenue..................	$5,000,000	$4,500,000
Salaries expense	360,000	360,000
Travel expense.................	340,000	320,500

Split your team into three groups. Each group should meet separately before the entire team meets.

Required

1. The first group plays the role of development manager Patti McKeown. Before meeting with the entire team, determine which set of budget numbers you are going to present to Rick Watson. Write a memo supporting your decision. Use the format shown in Decision Case 2. Give this memo to the third group before the team meeting.
2. The second group plays the role of sales manager Liz Smith. Before meeting with the entire team, determine which set of budget numbers you are going to present to Rick Watson. Write a memo supporting your decision. Use the format shown in Decision Case 2. Give this memo to the third group before the team meeting.
3. The third group plays the role of division manager Rick Watson. Before meeting with the entire team, prepare a division budget based on the sales and development budgets submitted to you by McKeown and Smith. Your divisional overhead costs are approximately $390,000. Determine whether the Business-to-Business Division can meet its targeted 30% return on assets given the budgeted alternatives submitted by your department managers.

During the meeting of the entire team, the group playing Watson presents the division budget and considers its implications. Each group should take turns discussing its concerns with the proposed budget. The team as a whole should consider whether the division budget must be revised. The team should prepare a report that includes the division budget and a summary of the issues covered in the team meeting.

INTERNET EXERCISE

Starbucks

Starbucks Corporation is the number 1 specialty coffee retailer, operating more than 2,800 shops. The company also sells coffee beans to restaurants, businesses, airlines, and hotels, and offers mail order and on-line shopping.

1. Go to **http://www.Forbes.com** and under "Stocks" type SBUX, the stock symbol for Starbucks Corporation. Click on *Go*. In the left-hand column, click on *Company Info*, and scan the information provided. What one-year sales growth was reported?
2. In the left-hand column, click on *Financials*. For the most recent year identify or compute the amounts reported for total revenue, cost of goods sold, and operating expenses. Calculate operating income.
3. Is Cost of Sales a variable or fixed expense? Add the operating expenses (Store Operating Expenses, Other Operating Expenses, Depreciation, and General/Administrative Expenses) and assume that 40% of the total is fixed. Compute total variable operating expenses and total fixed operating expenses for the most recent year.

4. Consider each of the following *independent* situations regarding next year:
   a. Suppose Starbucks is anticipating a 9% increase in the number of transactions per store next year. Prepare the sales budget, cost of goods sold budget, and operating expense budget, and calculate budgeted operating income.
   b. Assume Starbucks is considering raising the price of beverages by 7 cents per cup because of a 10% increase in fixed operating costs. If the increase of 7 cents per cup increases revenues by 3%, will the increase in revenue cover the increase in costs?
   c. Suppose that due to opening new stores, Starbucks expects operating revenues to increase at the same rate as the one-year sales growth of last year. Prepare only the sales budget. Will fixed costs increase? Why or why not?
5. A Starbucks store is what type of responsibility center?

Go to the "Employee Performance Evaluation and Responsibility" episode on the *Mastering Accounting* CD-ROM for an interactive, video-enhanced exercise focused on how CanGo managers use income statements showing revenues for the whole organization and for individual subunits to assess the performance of individual product divisions.

24

Flexible Budgets and Standard Costs

LEARNING OBJECTIVES

After studying this chapter, you should be able to

1. Prepare a flexible budget for the income statement
2. Prepare an income statement performance report
3. Identify the benefits of standard costs
4. Compute standard cost variances for direct materials and direct labor
5. Analyze manufacturing overhead in a standard cost system
6. Record transactions at standard cost
7. Prepare a standard cost income statement for management

How does **McDonald's** ensure that its 26,000 restaurants deliver quality, service, cleanliness, and value to over 43 million customers worldwide each day? How do McDonald's managers use management accounting to earn a profit?

The answers are budgets, standards, and variances. McDonald's managers budget sales for each hour. The manager schedules just enough workers to handle the budgeted level of sales. During the day, the manager computes variances for sales (for example, actual sales minus budgeted sales) and for direct labor. These variances are computed *hourly*. If actual sales fall short of the budget, the manager quickly sees an unfavorable sales variance. If sales are less than budgeted, the manager can send employees home early. This helps control direct labor cost.

McDonald's also sets budgets and standards for direct materials. From Beijing to Miami, the standards for a regular McDonald's hamburger are the same: 1 bun, 1 hamburger patty, 1 pickle slice, 1/8 teaspoon dehydrated onion, 1/8 teaspoon mustard, and 1/3 ounce of ketchup. To control direct materials costs, the manager compares the number of, say, hamburger patties actually used with the number of patties that should have been used.

McDonald's uses budgets, standards, and variances to control costs so prices remain low enough that customers believe McDonald's provides good *value*. McDonald's also uses standards and variances to motivate employees to focus on *quality, service,* and *cleanliness:*

- Quality—sandwiches unsold within 10 minutes are thrown away.
- Service—customers should receive food within 90 seconds of beginning to order.
- Cleanliness—visiting inspectors score restaurants on cleanliness.

In Chapter 23, we saw how managers use budgets to quantify their plans. Executives compare actual revenues and expenses with budgeted amounts to evaluate the performance of responsibility centers and managers. This chapter explores budgeting in greater depth. The first half of the chapter shows how flexible budgets and variances help managers learn *why* actual results differed from the plan. The second half of the chapter discusses standard costs, which companies like McDonald's use to build flexible budgets.

STATIC VERSUS FLEXIBLE BUDGETS

The master budget in Chapter 23 is a **static budget**—it is prepared for one level of sales volume. The static budget does not change after it is developed, regardless of changes in volume, sale prices, or costs.

Consider Kool-Time Pools, a company that installs residential swimming pools. Kool-Time buys direct materials—gunite (a concrete derivative). It then uses labor and equipment to convert the gunite into finished outputs—installed pools. Kool-Time's static master budget forecasts that the company will install eight pools in June. However, due to an early heat wave, Kool-Time actually installed ten pools.

The comparison of June's actual results with the static budget in Exhibit 24-1 shows that Kool-Time's actual operating income is $3,000 higher than originally expected. This is a $3,000 favorable difference, or variance, in Kool-Time's June operating income. A **variance** is the difference between an actual amount and the budget. The variances in the third column of Exhibit 24-1 are favorable (F) if a higher actual amount increases operating income and unfavorable (U) if a higher actual amount decreases operating income. The variance for the number of pools installed is favorable because higher volume (ten rather than eight pools) tends to increase income.

The report in Exhibit 24-1 is hard to analyze because the static budget is based on eight pools, but actual results are for ten pools. Why did the $21,000

Objective 1
Prepare a flexible budget for the income statement

STATIC BUDGET. The budget prepared for only one level of sales volume. Also called the **master budget.**

VARIANCE. The difference between an actual amount and the budget. A variance is labeled as favorable if it increases operating income and unfavorable if it decreases operating income.

EXHIBIT 24-1   Actual Results
versus Static Budget

KOOL-TIME POOLS
Comparison of Actual Results with Static Budget
Month Ended June 30, 20X5

	Actual Results	Static Budget	Variance
Output units (pools installed)	10	8	2 F
Sales revenue	$120,000	$96,000	$24,000 F
Expenses	(105,000)	(84,000)	21,000 U
Operating income	$ 15,000	$12,000	$ 3,000 F

FLEXIBLE BUDGET. A summarized budget that can easily be computed for several different volume levels. Flexible budgets separate variable costs from fixed costs; it is the variable costs that put the "flex" in the flexible budget.

➤ Chapter 23, pp. 932–940, discusses the White-water budget process.

unfavorable expense variance occur? Did workers waste materials? Did the cost of gunite suddenly increase? How much of the additional expense arose because Kool-Time built ten rather than eight pools? Exhibit 24-1's simple comparison of actual results with the static budget does not give managers enough information to answer these questions.

Flexible budgets do help managers answer such questions. Exhibit 24-2 illustrates the difference between static and flexible budgets. Companies develop a static master budget—like the Whitewater Sporting Goods Store budget developed in Chapter 23—for a single level of sales volume. ◄ In contrast, **flexible budgets** are summarized budgets that can easily be computed for several different volume levels.

EXHIBIT 24-2   Static versus
Flexible Budgets

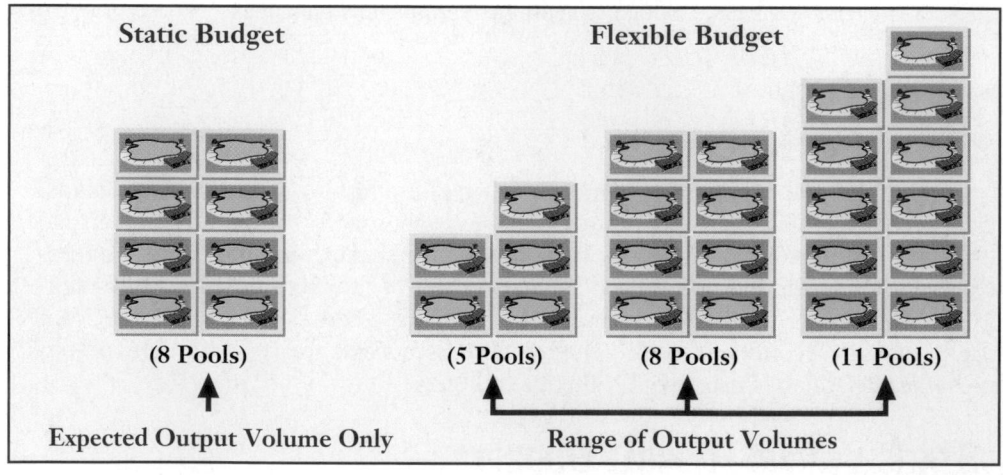

Exhibit 24-3 uses flexible budgets to show how Kool-Time's revenues and expenses should vary as sales increase from five pools to eight pools to eleven pools. The budgeted sale price per pool is $12,000. The condensed flexible budget shows

EXHIBIT 24-3   Flexible Budget

 DAILY EXERCISE 24-2

KOOL-TIME POOLS
Flexible Budget
Month Ended June 30, 20X5

	Flexible Budget per Output Unit	Output Units (Pools Installed)		
		5	8	11
Sales revenue	$12,000	$60,000	$96,000	$132,000
Variable expenses	8,000	40,000	64,000	88,000
Fixed expenses*		20,000	20,000	20,000
Total expenses		60,000	84,000	108,000
Operating income		$ 0	$12,000	$ 24,000

* Fixed expenses are given as a total amount rather than as a cost per unit.

two costs or expenses: variable and fixed. ➤ The *flexible budget formula for total cost* is:

See Chapter 22, page 887, to review the distinction between variable costs and fixed costs.

$$\text{Flexible budget total cost} = \left(\begin{array}{c} \text{Number of} \\ \text{output units} \end{array} \times \begin{array}{c} \text{Variable cost} \\ \text{per output unit} \end{array} \right) + \text{Total fixed cost}$$

Budgeted total variable costs (such as the cost of gunite and labor) increase at the rate of $8,000 per pool installed. It is these variable costs that put the "flex" in the flexible budget, because budgeted total monthly fixed costs (such as administrative salaries and depreciation on equipment) remain constant at $20,000 throughout the range of five to eleven pools. For example, Kool-Time's flexible budget cost for installing 11 pools is $108,000:

● DAILY EXERCISE 24-1

$$
\begin{aligned}
\text{Flexible budget total cost} &= \left(\begin{array}{c} \text{Number of} \\ \text{output units} \end{array} \times \begin{array}{c} \text{Variable cost} \\ \text{per output unit} \end{array} \right) + \text{Total fixed cost} \\
&= \quad (11 \text{ pools} \quad \times \quad \$8,000 \text{ per pool}) \quad + \$20,000 \\
&= \quad \$\ 88,000 \qquad\qquad\qquad\qquad + \$20,000 \\
&= \quad \$108,000
\end{aligned}
$$

Kool-Time's managers could prepare a more detailed flexible budget that lists individual variable and fixed costs separately. Each of the variable costs would increase with the number of pools installed, like the total variable costs in Exhibit 24-3, and each of the fixed costs would remain constant over the relevant range.

Managers develop flexible budgets like Exhibit 24-3 for any number of outputs, using a simple spreadsheet or more sophisticated Web-based budget management software. Kool-Time's flexible budget could include additional columns for seven, nine, or any other number of pools for which management wants to know budgeted sales revenues, costs, and profits.

However, managers must be wary: *The flexible budget total cost formula applies only to a specific relevant range*. Why? Because total monthly fixed costs and the variable cost per pool change outside this range. Kool-Time's relevant range is 0–11 pools. If the company installs 12 pools, it will have to rent additional equipment, so fixed costs will exceed $20,000. Kool-Time will also have to pay workers an overtime premium, so the variable cost per pool will be more than $8,000.

Managers prepare flexible budgets like those in Exhibit 24-3

- *Before* the period, or   - At the *end* of the period

Flexible budgets prepared *before* the period help managers *plan*. They can estimate revenues, costs, and profits, and plan for alternative levels of sales. Flexible budgets prepared at the *end* of the period help managers *control* operations. They can compare actual costs to the costs that *should have been* incurred for that level of output. For example, Kool-Time can compare the actual costs to install 10 pools with the budgeted costs (the costs that should have been incurred) to install 10 pools.

Graphing the Flexible Budget

Managers use flexible budget graphs to budget total costs at various output levels for both planning and control. Exhibit 24-4 shows budgeted total costs for the entire relevant range of 0–11 pools. The flexible budget total cost line in Exhibit 24-4 intersects the vertical axis at the amount of the total fixed cost ($20,000) Kool-Time will incur whether it installs 0 pools or 11 pools. ➤ The flexible budget's total cost line slopes upward at the rate of $8,000 per pool, which is Kool-Time's variable cost per pool. For example, the cost for one pool is $28,000 [(1 pool × $8,000 variable cost per pool) + $20,000 fixed cost]. But the *extra* cost of installing a second pool is only the additional $8,000 variable cost. The cost to install two pools is therefore $36,000 [(2 pools × $8,000 variable cost per pool) + $20,000 fixed cost].

The flexible budget cost line in Exhibit 24-4 follows the same principles as the cost-volume-profit graph's total cost line in Exhibit 22-7, page 899.

Kool-Time's managers initially expected to install eight pools per month ($84,000). The graph also shows the flexible budget costs for 5 pools ($60,000) and

EXHIBIT 24-4 **Kool-Time Pools Monthly Flexible Budget Graph**

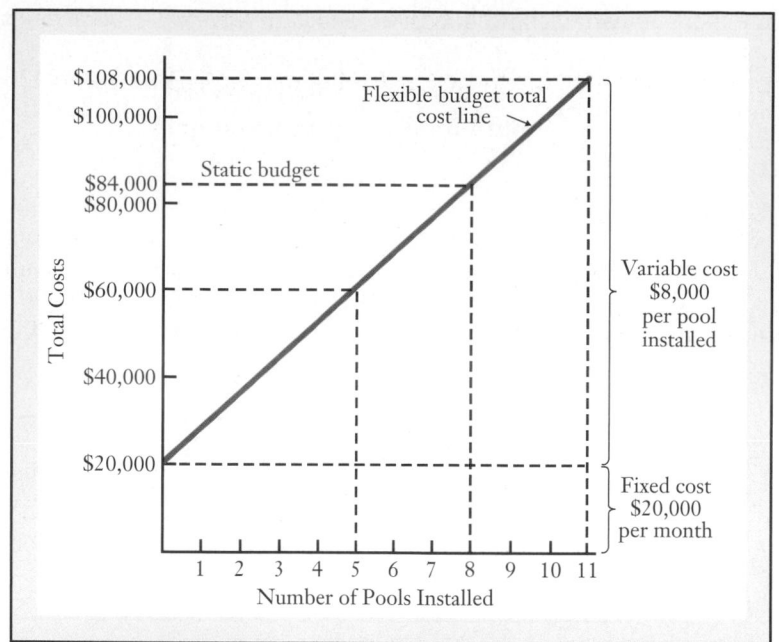

EXHIBIT 24-5 **Kool-Time Pools Graph of Actual and Budgeted Monthly Costs**

⊙ DAILY EXERCISE 24-3

⊙ DAILY EXERCISE 24-4

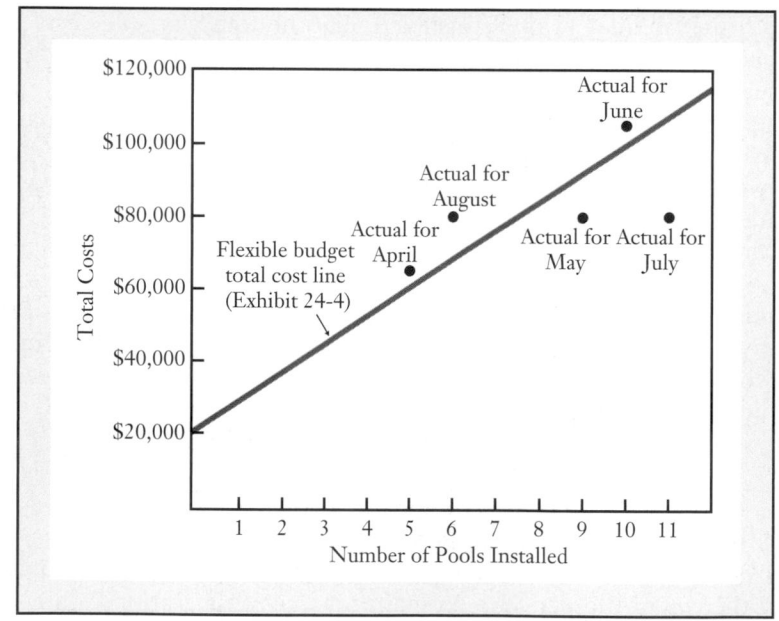

11 pools ($108,000). Managers can use the flexible budget graph in Exhibit 24-4 to plan costs for anywhere from 0 to 11 pools.

At the end of the period, managers can also use the flexible budget to help control costs. They plot actual costs on the graph, as shown in Exhibit 24-5. Consider June, when Kool-Time actually installed ten pools. The flexible budget graphs in Exhibits 24-4 and 24-5 show that *budgeted* total costs for ten pools are

Variable costs (10 × $8,000)	$ 80,000
Fixed costs	20,000
Total costs	$100,000

June's *actual* costs, or expenses, were $105,000 (Exhibit 24-1). Consequently, Exhibit 24-5 shows that June's actual costs for ten pools ($105,000) exceed the budget for ten pools ($100,000). Managers use graphs of actual versus budgeted costs to see at a glance whether actual costs are

- Higher than budgeted for the actual level of output, as in April, June, and August, or
- Lower than budgeted for the actual level of output, as in May and July

Use the graph in Exhibit 24-5 and Kool-Time's flexible budget formula (page 975) to answer the following questions:

1. How many pools did Kool-Time install in July?
2. What were Kool-Time's actual costs in July?
3. Using Kool-Time's flexible budget formula, what is the flexible budget total cost for the month of July?
4. Is Kool-Time's variance for total costs favorable or unfavorable in July?

Answers

1. Exhibit 24-5 shows that Kool-Time installed 11 pools in July.
2. Exhibit 24-5 shows that Kool-Time's actual costs in July were about $80,000.
3. Using Kool-Time's flexible budget total cost formula:

Variable costs (11 × $8,000).............	$ 88,000
Fixed costs	20,000
Total costs	$108,000

4. Kool-Time's July variance for total costs is $28,000 ($80,000 − $108,000) favorable, since actual costs are less than the budget.

The Flexible Budget and Variance Analysis

Objective 2
Prepare an income statement performance report

Managers also use flexible budgets at the *end* of the period to help explain why actual results differ from budgeted results.

Let's step back for a moment and consider managers' major planning and controlling activities:

1. Quantify the company's goals in a static master budget.
2. Take action to achieve the goals.
3. Analyze the variance between actual results and static budget amounts (the static budget variance).
4. Change actions (or plans) so that future results conform to the plan.

The flexible budget is an important tool in step 3. To analyze the variance (step 3), managers begin by asking

- How many units did we actually sell?
- How much sales revenue *should* we have received from selling this number of outputs?
- How much *should* this number of output units have cost us?

The *flexible budget for the number of units that were actually sold* helps answer the second and third questions. Of course, the number of units actually sold is not known until the end of the period. Why calculate a budget for a period that is already over? Because *the flexible budget for the number of units actually sold shows how much the company should have spent to obtain that level of output.*

Exhibit 24-6 shows how managers use this flexible budget for the number of units actually sold to divide the static budget variance into two broad categories:

- **Sales volume variance**—arises only because the number of units actually sold differs from the static budget sales.
- **Flexible budget variance**—arises because the company actually earned more or less revenue, or incurred more or less cost, than expected for the actual level of output.

Exhibit 24-6 shows that the sales volume variance is the difference between

1. The *static* (master) budget—for the number of units *expected* to be sold (8 pools, for Kool-Time), and
2. The *flexible* budget—for the number of units *actually* sold (10 pools in June)

SALES VOLUME VARIANCE. The difference arising only because the number of units actually sold differs from the static budget sales. This is computed as the difference between a static budget amount and a flexible budget amount.

FLEXIBLE BUDGET VARIANCE. The difference arising because the company actually earned more or less revenue, or incurred more or less cost, than expected for the actual level of output. This is computed as the difference between the actual amount and a flexible budget amount.

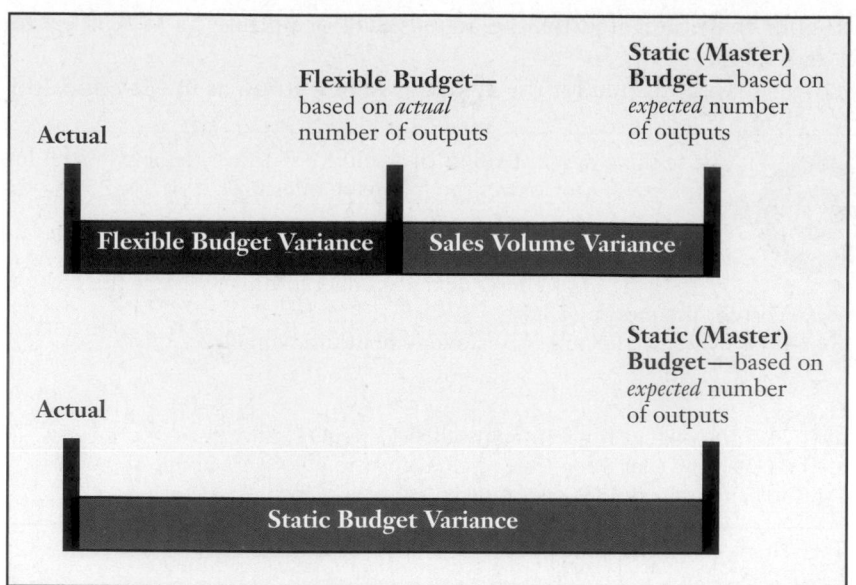

Consider Kool-Time Pool's performance report in Exhibit 24-7. The static budget amounts in column 5 are based on the static budget sales forecast developed at the *beginning* of the period—the eight pools Kool-Time *expected* to install. For these eight pools, Kool-Time's

- Budgeted sales revenue is $96,000 (8 × $12,000).
- Budgeted variable expenses (costs) are $64,000 (8 × $8,000).
- Budgeted fixed expenses (costs) are $20,000.

DAILY EXERCISE 24-5

DAILY EXERCISE 24-6

DAILY EXERCISE 24-7

In contrast to the static budget, which is developed *before* the period, the flexible budget used in the performance report is not developed until the *end* of the period. Why? Because *flexible budgets used in performance reports are based on the actual number of outputs, which is not known until the end of the period.* For Kool-Time, the flexible

EXHIBIT 24-7 **Income Statement Performance Report**

KOOL-TIME POOLS
Income Statement Performance Report
Month Ended June 30, 20X5

	(1) Actual Results at Actual Prices	(2) (1) − (3) Flexible Budget Variance	(3) Flexible Budget for Actual Number of Output Units*	(4) (3) − (5) Sales Volume Variance	(5) Static (Master) Budget*
Output units (pools installed)..............	10	–0–	10	2 F	8
Sales revenue......................................	$120,000	$ –0–	$120,000	$24,000 F	$96,000
Variable expenses...............................	83,000	3,000 U	80,000	16,000 U	64,000
Fixed expenses...................................	22,000	2,000 U	20,000	–0–	20,000
Total expenses....................................	105,000	5,000 U	100,000	16,000 U	84,000
Operating income	$ 15,000	$5,000 U	$ 20,000	$ 8,000 F	$12,000

Flexible budget variance,
$5,000 U

Sales volume variance,
$8,000 F

Static budget variance,
$3,000 F

* Budgeted sale price is $12,000 per pool, budgeted variable expense is $8,000 per pool, and budgeted total monthly fixed expenses are $20,000.

budget used in the performance report (column 3 of Exhibit 24-7) is based on the ten pools actually installed:

- Budgeted sales revenue is $120,000 (10 × $12,000).
- Budgeted variable expenses are $80,000 (10 × $8,000).
- Budgeted fixed expenses are $20,000.

The only difference between the static budget and the flexible budget used in the performance report is the number of outputs on which the budget is based (eight pools versus ten pools in the Kool-Time example). Both budgets use the same

- Budgeted sale price per unit ($12,000 per pool)
- Budgeted variable cost per unit ($8,000 per pool)
- Budgeted total fixed costs ($20,000 per month)

Holding selling price per unit, variable cost per unit, and total fixed costs constant at their budgeted amounts highlights the effects of differences in sales volume—the variance in column 4. This variance is typically the responsibility of the marketing staff. Exhibit 24-7 shows that by installing two more pools than initially expected, Kool-Time's

- Sales revenue should increase from $96,000 (8 × $12,000) to $120,000 (10 × $12,000)—a $24,000 favorable sales volume variance.
- Variable costs should increase from $64,000 (8 × $8,000) to $80,000 (10 × $8,000)—a $16,000 unfavorable sales volume variance.

Budgeted total fixed expenses are unaffected because eight pools and ten pools are within the relevant range where fixed expenses total $20,000 (0–11 pools). Consequently, installing two more pools should increase operating income by $8,000 ($24,000 F − $16,000 U).

THINK IT OVER When is there a sales volume variance for fixed expenses?

Answer: Only when the number of units actually sold falls within a different relevant range than the static budget sales volume. When actual and expected number of units sold fall in the same relevant range, there is no sales volume variance for fixed expenses.

 DAILY EXERCISE 24-8

 DAILY EXERCISE 24-9

Exhibits 24-6 and 24-7 show that the second piece of the static budget variance is the flexible budget variance—the difference between

- Actual amounts (column 1 in Exhibit 24-7) and
- Flexible budget amounts that should have been incurred *for the actual number of output units* (column 3 in Exhibit 24-7).

Kool-Time actually incurred $83,000 of variable costs to install the ten pools. This is $3,000 more than the $80,000 (10 pools × $8,000 per pool) budgeted variable cost for ten pools. The company also spent $2,000 more than budgeted on fixed expenses ($22,000 − $20,000). Consequently, the flexible budget variance for total expenses is $5,000 unfavorable ($3,000 U + $2,000 U). The $5,000 unfavorable flexible budget variance offsets much of the $8,000 favorable sales volume variance, resulting in a $3,000 favorable static budget variance (Exhibits 24-1 and 24-7).

THINK IT OVER When is there a flexible budget variance for sales revenue?

Answer: When the actual sale price differs from the budgeted sale price, the difference is a flexible budget variance for sales revenue. Suppose Kool-Time's actual sale price was $13,000 rather than $12,000 per pool. Actual sales revenue would have been $130,000 (10 × $13,000) and there would have been a $10,000 favorable flexible budget variance for sales revenue ($130,000 − $120,000).

We have now shown why simply comparing the static budget with actual results (like Exhibit 24-1) does not explain much. This is because the *actual* number of units sold may differ from the *expected* sales used to prepare the static budget. The flexible budget provides part of the information managers need to understand why actual revenues, expenses, and income differ from the budget.

Exhibit 24-7 shows how the flexible budget splits the static budget variance into the sales volume variance and the flexible budget variance. How would Kool-Time's managers use these variances? Managers use variances to help decide which business operations deserve praise or need improvement. The favorable sales volume variance reveals that strong sales caused actual income to exceed the budget by $8,000. Kool-Time may therefore reward the sales staff. On the other hand, Exhibit 24-7 shows a $5,000 unfavorable flexible budget variance for expenses. Management will want to find out why expenses were too high.

Kool-Time's higher-than-expected expenses might be due to an uncontrollable increase in the cost of gunite. Or higher costs might have resulted from more controllable factors such as employees wasting materials or working inefficiently. If so, managers can take action to reduce waste or inefficiency. The second half of this chapter explains how Kool-Time's managers probe flexible budget variances to identify the reason for the cost overrun.

Before proceeding, take some time to test your understanding of the flexible budget, static budget, and variances by reviewing the Decision Guidelines and then working the mid-chapter review problem.

DECISION GUIDELINES

Flexible Budgets

DECISION	GUIDELINES
How to estimate sales revenues, costs, and profits over the range of likely output levels?	Prepare a set of flexible budgets for different output levels.
How to prepare a flexible budget for total costs?	$$\text{Flexible budget total cost} = \left(\begin{array}{c} \text{Number} \\ \text{of output} \\ \text{units} \end{array} \times \begin{array}{c} \text{Variable} \\ \text{cost per} \\ \text{output unit} \end{array} \right) + \begin{array}{c} \text{Fixed} \\ \text{cost} \end{array}$$
How to use budgets to help control costs?	• Graph actual costs versus flexible budget costs, as in Exhibit 24-5. • Prepare an income statement performance report, as in Exhibit 24-7.
On which output level is the budget based?	Static (master) budget—*expected* number of outputs, estimated before the period Flexible budget (made at the end of the period)—*actual* number of outputs, not known until the end of the period
Why does actual income differ from budgeted income?	Prepare income statement performance report comparing actual results, flexible budget for actual number of outputs, and static (master) budget.

How much of the difference occurs because the actual number of output units sold does not equal budgeted sales?	Compute the sales volume variance (SVV) by comparing the flexible budget with the static budget.
	• Favorable SVV—Income effect if
	  Flexible budget sales revenue > Static budget sales revenue
	  Flexible budget expenses < Static budget expenses
	• Unfavorable SVV—Income effect if
	  Flexible budget sales revenue < Static budget sales revenue
	  Flexible budget expenses > Static budget expenses

How much of the difference occurs because actual revenues and costs are not what they should have been for the actual number of outputs?	Compute the flexible budget variance (FBV) by comparing actual results with the flexible budget.
	• Favorable FBV—Income effect if
	  Actual sales revenue > Flexible budget sales revenue
	  Actual expenses < Flexible budget expenses
	• Unfavorable FBV—Income effect if
	  Actual sales revenue < Flexible budget sales revenue
	  Actual expenses > Flexible budget expenses

SUMMARY PROBLEM

Exhibit 24-7 indicates that Kool-Time Pools installed ten swimming pools during June. Now assume that Kool-Time installed seven pools (instead of ten) and that the actual sale price averaged $12,500 per pool instead of $12,000. Actual variable expenses were $57,400, and actual fixed expenses were $19,000.

www.prenhall.com/horngren
Mid-Chapter Assessment

Required

1. Prepare a revised income statement performance report using Exhibit 24-7 as a guide.
2. Show that the sum of the flexible budget variance and the sales volume variance for operating income equals the static budget variance for operating income.
3. As the company owner, which employees would you praise or criticize after you analyze this performance report?

Solution

Requirements 1 and 2

KOOL-TIME POOLS
Income Statement Performance Report—Revised
Month Ended June 30, 20X5

	(1) Actual Results at Actual Prices	(2) (1) − (3) Flexible Budget Variance	(3) Flexible Budget for Actual Number of Output Units	(4) (3) − (5) Sales Volume Variance	(5) Static (Master) Budget
Output units	7	–0–	7	1 U	8
Sales revenue	$87,500	$3,500 F	$84,000	$12,000 U	$96,000
Variable expenses	57,400	1,400 U	56,000	8,000 F	64,000
Fixed expenses	19,000	1,000 F	20,000	—	20,000
Total expenses	76,400	400 U	76,000	8,000 F	84,000
Operating income..............	$11,100	$3,100 F	$ 8,000	$ 4,000 U	$12,000

Flexible budget variance, $3,100 F   Sales volume variance, $4,000 U

Static budget variance, $900 U

Requirement 3

As the company owner, you should determine the *causes* of the variances before deciding who deserves praise or criticism. It is especially important to determine who is responsible for the variance and whether the variance is due to factors the manager can control. For example, the unfavorable sales volume variance could be due to an ineffective sales staff. Or it could be due to an uncontrollable long period of heavy rain that brought work to a standstill. Similarly, the $1,000 favorable flexible budget variance for fixed expenses could be due to an employee finding a lower-cost source of rented equipment. Or the savings may have come from delaying a needed overhaul of equipment that could increase the company's costs in the long run. Smart managers use variances to raise questions and direct attention, not to fix blame.

STANDARD COSTING

Many companies—especially those that routinely produce similar or identical products—use standard costs for budgeting and control. A **standard cost** is a carefully predetermined cost that usually is expressed on a per-unit basis. In contrast, the term *budgeted cost* usually refers to a total amount. To budget a variable cost, accountants multiply a number of output units by a standard or budgeted cost per unit. Continuing

STANDARD COST. A carefully predetermined cost that usually is expressed on a per-unit basis.

our Kool-Time Pools example, the $8,000 budgeted variable cost of an installed pool is made up of *inputs,* including direct materials, direct labor, and variable overhead costs. Suppose the variable costs in Exhibit 24-3 include direct materials costs as follows:

	Flexible Budget per Output Unit (Standard Cost)	Output Units (Pools Installed)		
		5	8	11
Direct materials..............	$2,000	$10,000	$16,000	$22,000

The standard cost of direct materials is $2,000 *per pool.* Budgeted cost is the expected total cost of all pools sold during the month. As volume increases from five to eleven pools, the budgeted direct materials cost increases from $10,000 to $22,000. But the standard direct materials cost is $2,000 per pool at all three flexible budget output levels. Think of a standard cost as *a budget for a single unit of output.*

In a standard cost system, each input has both a quantity standard and a price standard. **McDonald's** has a standard for the amount of beef per hamburger and for the price paid per pound of beef. Kool-Time Pools has a standard for cubic feet of gunite per pool and for price per cubic foot of gunite.

Setting Standards

Accountants help managers set price standards. For direct labor, they take into account payroll taxes and fringe benefits as well as hourly wage rates. For overhead, accountants help identify the overhead allocation bases and then compute the overhead allocation rates.

In setting direct materials price standards, accountants consider early-payment discounts, freight-in, and receiving costs, in addition to base purchase price. World-class businesses set continuous improvement standards ◄ for direct material prices. Companies work with suppliers to cut direct material costs. For example, **Toyota** sent its own engineers to one of its bumper suppliers' plants to help the supplier cut costs. Toyota expected the supplier to pass on much of the savings in lower prices for the bumpers. E-commerce also helps managers continuously lower direct material price standards. Purchasing managers use the Internet to solicit price quotes from suppliers throughout the world. Major U.S. automakers are collaborating on an electronic market linking the automakers with their suppliers. The automakers expect price concessions from suppliers not only on their own purchases but also on purchases the suppliers make from each other through the electronic marketplace. Automakers expect these cost-cutting efforts throughout the supply chain to yield substantially lower direct material price standards.

➤ We discuss continuous improvement in Chapter 19, page 775.

Engineers and production managers usually set direct material and direct labor quantity standards, often following the continuous improvement philosophy. For example, groups of managers and workers in **Westinghouse Air Brake's** Chicago plant analyzed every moment in the production of the brakes. The goal was to (1) eliminate unnecessary work, (2) reduce the time and effort required for necessary work, and (3) set a time standard for the work. To eliminate unnecessary work, the company rearranged machines in tight U-shaped cells so production wasn't spread over a vast expanse of the factory floor. Workers no longer had to move parts all over the plant. The team conducted time-and-motion studies to streamline and reduce the physical demands of various tasks. For example, the plant installed a conveyer at waist height to minimize bending and lifting. The result? By 2000, workers had slashed the standard time to produce the slack adjustor component by 90%.

General Motors (GM) had cut average labor time per vehicle to 45.6 hours by 2000. But this far exceeds **Toyota's** average of 30.4 labor hours per vehicle. If GM workers earn an average of $45 per hour, how much cost does this extra labor add to each GM car?

Answer: $684. On average, GM workers put in an extra 15.2 hours (45.6 − 30.4) per car at an average rate of $45 per hour.

Many companies set currently attainable standards that allow normal amounts of waste and spoilage. This represents very good performance that can be achieved, but with difficulty. However, more and more companies, from **Ritz-Carlton** to **Federal Express,** are using standards based on "best practice." This is often called **benchmarking.**

Best practice may be an internal benchmark from inside the company or an external benchmark from other companies. Internal benchmarks are easy to obtain. Companies can purchase external benchmark data from consulting firms. Consider a consulting firm that develops reports comparing the costs of treating specific diagnoses (say an appendectomy) across hospitals. **Riverside Hospital** in Columbus, Ohio, can compare its cost of an appendectomy with the "best practice" cost from the report.

BENCHMARKING. Using standards based on "best practice." Best practice may be an internal benchmark from inside the company or an external benchmark from other companies.

e-Accounting

"It's 10:00, Do You Know What Your Suppliers Are Doing?"

These days it's not enough for companies to simply have their own house in order with regard to continuous improvement standards. Shrinking product cycles and increased pressure to reduce overhead have made it imperative for vendors to collaborate with suppliers to cut costs while maintaining or improving product quality. Companies are transferring the responsibility for crafting more of their product to suppliers or outside contractors. What enables vendors to keep close tabs on their suppliers is—you guessed it, the Internet.

Buzzwords abound for Web-enabled collaboration between suppliers and vendors: "seamless integration," "Web-based modeling," "electronic *keiretsu.*" It's all made possible by Internet-based software such as Extranets (secure environments for the interchange of critical data with approved business partners) or Web-based design, project management, and data-management tools.

Companies must meld product design and development all along the supply chain. The Milwaukee-based motorcycle company **Harley-Davidson, Inc.,** manages interaction with its supply base through a Supplier Advisory Council (SAC). Sixteen top suppliers sit on the council, and each member communicates with about ten other top-level suppliers, giving Harley-Davidson access to some 200 suppliers. In 1999, one of the key issues SAC addressed was understanding the cost drivers of the suppliers' production. Suppliers bidding on jobs give Harley the details behind cost breakdowns, such as process flow, run times, yield, and overhead. Says Greg Smith, a Harley-Davidson purchasing director, "We want to understand their cost drivers because they can have a huge [effect] on how we design our products."

Source: Based on Tim Stevens, "Designs in sync," http://www.iwvaluechain.com, June 12, 2000. Alorie Gilbert, "Online collaboration tools help simplify product design," *Informationweek,* April 24, 2000, pp. 130–136. Richard Vlosky and Renee J. Fontenot, "Learning to love extranets," *Marketing Management,* Fall 1999, pp. 33–55. Richard W. Oliver, "Killer KEIRETSU," *Management Review,* September 1999, pp. 10–11.

Benefits of Standard Costs

Carefully set standard costs yield several benefits (Exhibit 24-8 on the next page):

1. They help managers plan by providing the unit amounts—the building blocks—for budgeting.
2. They help managers control business operations by setting target levels of operating performance. *Management by exception* suggests that managers focus attention where actual results differ significantly from standards. ➤

Objective 3
Identify the benefits of standard costs

◄ Chapter 23, page 948, introduced management-by-exception.

EXHIBIT 24-8 **The Benefits of Standard Costs**

1. Standards help managers plan by providing unit amounts for budgeting.

2. Standards help managers control by setting target levels of operating performance.

3. Standards motivate employees by serving as benchmarks for measuring performance.

4. Standards provide unit costs that managers can use to set the sale prices of products or services.

5. Standards simplify record keeping, reducing clerical costs.

3. They help motivate employees by serving as benchmarks for measuring performance.
4. They provide unit costs managers can use to set sale prices of products or services.
5. They help simplify record keeping and so reduce clerical costs.

DAILY EXERCISE 24-10

Standard cost systems might appear to be expensive. Indeed, the company must invest in developing the standards. But standards can save data-processing costs. It is easier to value all inventories at standard costs rather than at actual costs. With standard costs, accountants avoid the expense of tracking actual unit costs and of making LIFO, FIFO, or average-cost computations.

Given these benefits, it is not surprising that companies around the globe use standard costing. U.S. surveys have shown that over 80% of responding companies use standard costing. International surveys suggest that over half the responding companies in Ireland, the United Kingdom, Sweden, and Japan use standard costing, primarily because it helps managers control costs.

Objective 4
Compute standard cost variances for direct materials and direct labor

AN EXAMPLE OF STANDARD COSTING

Let's return to our Kool-Time Pools example. To focus on the main aspects of standard costing, we assume that Kool-Time's standard costing system covers direct materials (gunite), direct labor, and manufacturing overhead but not design, marketing, or administrative expenses. We assume also that the quantity of direct materials purchased equals the quantity used.

DAILY EXERCISE 24-11

Recall that Kool-Time installed ten swimming pools during June. Exhibit 24-9 provides cost data for this actual level of output. Exhibit 24-9 also shows Kool-Time's flexible budget variances for direct materials ($3,100 U) and direct labor ($200 F). Accountants separate these variances into two components: a price variance and an efficiency variance.

Price and Efficiency Variances

A **price variance** measures how well the business keeps unit prices of material and labor inputs within standards. As the name suggests, the price variance is the *difference in prices* (actual price per unit − standard price per unit) of an input, multiplied by the *actual quantity* of the input:

PRICE VARIANCE. Measures how well the business keeps unit prices of material and labor inputs within standards. This is computed as the difference in prices (actual price per unit minus standard price per unit) of an input, multiplied by the actual quantity of the input.

$$\text{Price variance} = \begin{pmatrix} \text{Difference between} \\ \text{actual and standard} \\ \text{prices per input unit} \end{pmatrix} \times \begin{pmatrix} \text{Actual quantity} \\ \text{of input} \end{pmatrix}$$

$$\text{Price variance} = \begin{pmatrix} \text{Actual} \\ \text{price per} \\ \text{input unit} \end{pmatrix} - \begin{pmatrix} \text{Standard} \\ \text{price per} \\ \text{input unit} \end{pmatrix} \times \begin{pmatrix} \text{Actual quantity} \\ \text{of input} \end{pmatrix}$$

EXHIBIT 24-9 **Data for Standard Costing Example**

KOOL-TIME POOLS
Data for Standard Costing Example
Month of June 20X5

PANEL A—Comparison of Actual Results with Flexible Budget for 10 Swimming Pools

	Actual Results at Actual Prices	Flexible Budget for 10 Pools	Flexible Budget Variance
Variable expenses:			
Direct materials	$ 23,100*	$ 20,000†	$3,100 U
Direct labor	41,800*	42,000†	200 F
Variable overhead	9,000	8,000†	1,000 U
Marketing and administrative expenses	9,100	10,000	900 F
Total variable expenses	83,000	80,000	3,000 U
Fixed expenses:			
Fixed overhead	12,300	12,000‡	300 U
Marketing and administrative expenses	9,700	8,000	1,700 U
Total fixed expenses	22,000	20,000	2,000 U
Total expenses	$105,000	$100,000	$5,000 U

* See Panel C
† See Panel B
‡ Fixed overhead was budgeted at $12,000 per month.

PANEL B—Computation of Flexible Budget for Direct Materials, Direct Labor, and Variable Overhead for 10 Swimming Pools

	(1) Standard Quantity of Inputs Allowed for 10 Pools	(2) Standard Price per Unit of Input	(1) × (2) Flexible Budget for 10 Pools
Direct materials	1,000 cubic feet per pool × 10 pools = 10,000 cubic feet	$ 2.00	$20,000
Direct labor	400 hours per pool × 10 pools = 4,000 hours	10.50	42,000
Variable overhead	400 hours per pool × 10 pools = 4,000 hours	2.00	8,000

PANEL C—Computation of Actual Costs for Direct Materials and Direct Labor for 10 Swimming Pools

	(1) Actual Quantity of Inputs Used for 10 Pools	(2) Actual Price per Unit of Input	(1) × (2) Actual Cost for 10 Pools
Direct materials	11,969 cubic feet actually used	$1.93 actual cost/cubic foot	$23,100
Direct labor	3,800 hours actually used	$11.00 actual cost/hour	41,800

The standard price per unit of input is the *price that should have been paid per unit* of the input (per cubic foot of gunite or per direct labor hour). If the company actually pays less, the price variance is favorable. If the company actually pays more than the standard price, the price variance is unfavorable. The manager who purchases the input is responsible for the price variance. For example, the Kool-Time employee

DAILY EXERCISE 24-12

DAILY EXERCISE 24-13

EFFICIENCY VARIANCE. Measures whether the quantity of materials or labor used to make the actual number of outputs is within the standard allowed for that number of outputs. This is computed as the difference in quantities (actual quantity of input used minus standard quantity of input allowed for the actual number of outputs), multiplied by the standard price per unit of the input.

who buys the gunite is responsible for the difference between the actual and standard price for all the gunite he purchased, so the difference in price is multiplied by the *actual quantity* purchased.

An **efficiency variance** measures whether the quantity of materials or labor actually used to make the *actual number of outputs* is within the standard allowed for that number of outputs. The efficiency variance is the *difference in quantities* (actual quantity of input used − standard quantity of input allowed for the actual number of outputs), multiplied by the *standard price per unit* of the input.

$$\text{Efficiency variance} = \begin{pmatrix} \text{Difference between actual quantity of} \\ \text{inputs used and the standard quantity} \\ \text{of inputs that should have been used} \\ \text{for the actual number of outputs} \end{pmatrix} \times \begin{pmatrix} \text{Standard price} \\ \text{per input unit} \end{pmatrix}$$

$$\text{Efficiency variance} = \begin{pmatrix} \text{Actual} & & \text{Standard} \\ \text{quantity} & - & \text{quantity} \\ \text{of input} & & \text{of input} \end{pmatrix} \times \begin{pmatrix} \text{Standard price} \\ \text{per input unit} \end{pmatrix}$$

The standard quantity of inputs is the *quantity that should have been used,* or the standard quantity of inputs *allowed,* for the actual output. If the company actually uses less than the standard quantity of inputs allowed to produce the output, the efficiency variance is favorable. If the company uses more than the standard quantity, the efficiency variance is unfavorable.

Price variances show how changes in prices of raw materials and labor affect the company's profit. But price variances that reflect changes in the market prices of materials and labor are largely beyond the company's control. Because managers generally have limited control over changes in prices, *efficiency* variances are computed by multiplying the difference in quantity by the *standard* price per unit of the input. Efficiency variances thus capture the controllable aspect of how the company's *use* of materials and labor affects profits.

We can now compute Kool-Time Pool's standard cost variances for direct materials and direct labor.

Direct Materials Variances

We begin our analysis of direct materials variances by compiling the relevant data from Exhibit 24-9, as follows:

Direct Materials	Actual	Flexible Budget	Flexible Budget Variance
Cubic feet................	11,969	10,000	
Unit price................	×$1.93	×$2.00	
Total........................	$23,100	$20,000	$3,100 U

We use these data to compute the price and efficiency variances:

$$\text{Price variance} = \begin{pmatrix} \text{Actual} & & \text{Standard} \\ \text{price per} & - & \text{price per} \\ \text{input unit} & & \text{input unit} \end{pmatrix} \times \begin{matrix} \text{Actual} \\ \text{quantity} \\ \text{of input} \end{matrix}$$

$$= \begin{pmatrix} \$1.93 \text{ per} & & \$2.00 \text{ per} \\ \text{cubic foot} & - & \text{cubic foot} \end{pmatrix} \times 11{,}969 \text{ cubic feet} = \$838 \text{ F}$$

$$\text{Efficiency variance} = \begin{pmatrix} \text{Actual} & & \text{Standard} \\ \text{quantity} & - & \text{quantity} \\ \text{of input} & & \text{of input} \end{pmatrix} \times \begin{matrix} \text{Standard} \\ \text{price per} \\ \text{input unit} \end{matrix}$$

$$= \begin{pmatrix} 11{,}969 & & 10{,}000 \\ \text{cubic feet} & - & \text{cubic feet} \end{pmatrix} \times \begin{matrix} \$2.00 \text{ per} \\ \text{cubic foot} \end{matrix} = \$3{,}938 \text{ U}$$

The price variance indicates that Kool-Time's operating income will be $838 higher because the company paid less than the standard price for gunite in June. The efficiency variance indicates that Kool-Time's operating income will be $3,938 lower because workers used more gunite than the standard allowed for ten pools.

Exhibit 24-10 summarizes the direct materials variance computations. Variance analysis begins with a total variance to be explained—in this example, the $3,100 unfavorable flexible budget variance for direct materials. This variance is the sum of the price and efficiency variances:

Direct materials price variance..................................	$ 838 F
Direct materials efficiency variance	3,938 U
Direct materials flexible budget variance................	$3,100 U

EXHIBIT 24-10 **Kool-Time Pools Direct Materials Variances**

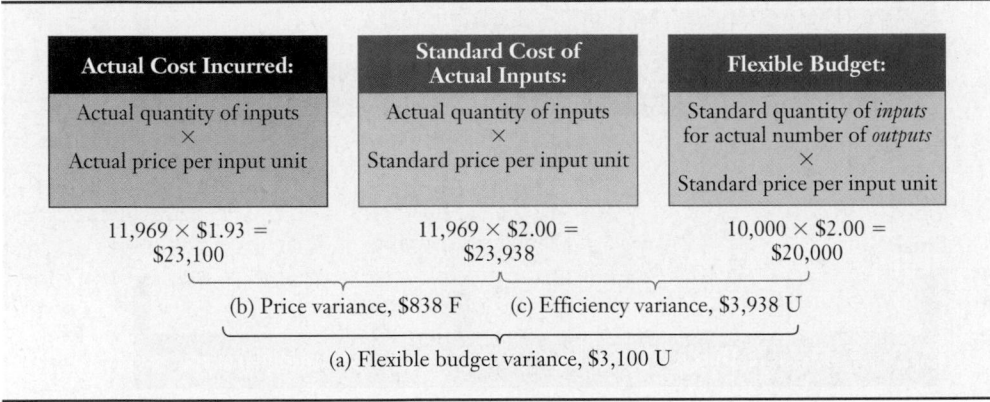

Splitting the $3,100 unfavorable direct materials flexible budget variance into price and efficiency variances explains why Kool-Time actually spent $3,100 more than it should have for gunite:

- A good price for the gunite increased profits by $838, but
- Inefficient use of the gunite reduced profits by $3,938.

Who is most likely responsible for the direct materials price variance? For the direct materials efficiency variance?

- Purchasing personnel are typically responsible for the direct materials price variance because they should know why the actual price differs from the standard price. Purchasing personnel may have negotiated a good price for gunite, thus obtaining the favorable variance. Should the gunite supplier raise prices, purchasing personnel will know why an unfavorable price variance occurred.
- Production personnel are generally responsible for the direct materials efficiency variance. Perhaps their equipment malfunctioned, causing them to use more than the standard quantity of gunite.

Common Pitfalls: Price and Efficiency Variances

Make sure you avoid three common pitfalls in computing price and efficiency variances:

1. *Static budgets like column 5 of Exhibit 24-7 play no role in computing the flexible bud-get variance or how it is split into the price and efficiency variances.* Exhibit 24-11 shows that the static budget is used *only* in computing the sales volume

variance—never in computing the flexible budget variance (or its component price and efficiency variances).

As Exhibit 24-11 shows, the price variance and the efficiency variance are components of the flexible budget variance—the difference between actual amounts and flexible budget amounts. The $838 F + $3,938 U = $3,100 U direct materials flexible budget variance is part of the $3,000 U flexible budget variance for variable expenses shown in column 2 of Exhibit 24-7. (The rest of the variable cost flexible budget variance is composed of flexible budget variances for other variable expenses, as shown in Panel A of Exhibit 24-9.)

EXHIBIT 24-11
Price, Efficiency, Flexible Budget, Sales Volume, and Static Budget Variances

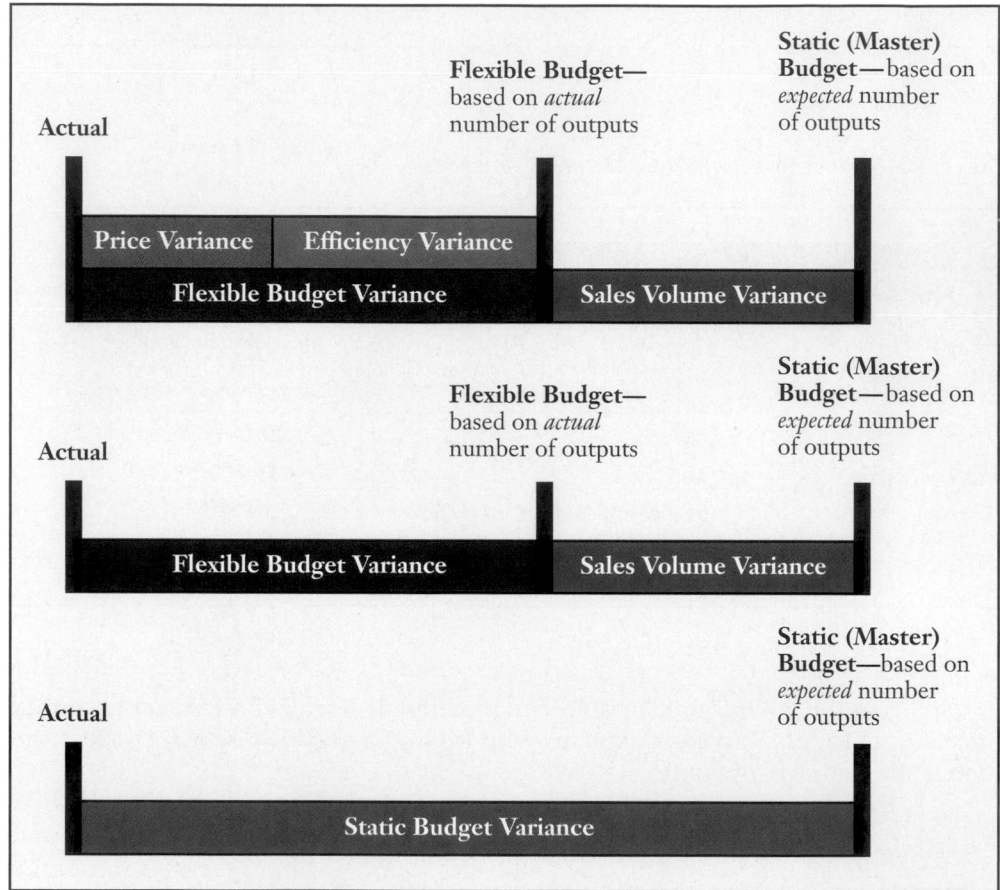

2. In the efficiency variance, the standard quantity is the *standard quantity of inputs allowed for the actual number of outputs*—the basis for the flexible budget. To compute the standard quantity of inputs allowed, first determine the actual number of outputs. For Kool-Time Pools, the actual number of outputs is ten pools. Next, compute how many inputs should have been used to produce the actual number of outputs (10 pools). Each pool should use 1,000 cubic feet of gunite, so the standard quantity of gunite allowed for ten pools is 10 × 1,000 cubic feet = 10,000 cubic feet.

   Notice that the standard quantity of inputs is *not* based on the budgeted number of outputs (8 pools). That number is the basis for the static budget, which is not used to compute price and efficiency variances.

3. In the direct materials price variance, the difference in prices is multiplied by the *actual quantity* of materials. In the direct materials efficiency variance, the difference in quantities is multiplied by the *standard price* of the materials. The following explanation can help you remember this difference.

   • The materials price variance is usually the responsibility of purchasing personnel; they purchase the actual quantity used, not just the amount of materials that should have been used (the standard quantity). So the price variance is the difference in prices multiplied by the *actual quantity* of materials they purchased.

- The materials efficiency variance is usually the responsibility of production personnel; they have no influence over the actual price paid. So the efficiency variance is computed as the difference in quantities multiplied by the *standard* price (the price that should have been paid).

Direct Labor Variances

We begin our analysis of direct labor variances by compiling the relevant data from Exhibit 24-9, as follows:

Direct Labor	Actual	Flexible Budget	Flexible Budget Variance
Hours...........................	3,800	4,000	
Hourly rate	× $11.00	× $10.50	
Total...........................	$41,800	$42,000	$200 F

We then use these data to compute the direct labor price and efficiency variances in the same way we computed the direct materials variances:

$$\text{Price variance} = \left(\begin{array}{c} \text{Actual} \\ \text{price per} \\ \text{input unit} \end{array} - \begin{array}{c} \text{Standard} \\ \text{price per} \\ \text{input unit} \end{array} \right) \times \begin{array}{c} \text{Actual quantity} \\ \text{of input} \end{array}$$

$$= \left(\begin{array}{c} \$11.00 \text{ per} \\ \text{hour} \end{array} - \begin{array}{c} \$10.50 \text{ per} \\ \text{hour} \end{array} \right) \times 3{,}800 \text{ hours} = \$1{,}900 \text{ U}$$

$$\text{Efficiency variance} = \left(\begin{array}{c} \text{Actual} \\ \text{quantity} \\ \text{of input} \end{array} - \begin{array}{c} \text{Standard} \\ \text{quantity} \\ \text{of input} \end{array} \right) \times \begin{array}{c} \text{Standard} \\ \text{price per} \\ \text{input unit} \end{array}$$

$$= (3{,}800 \text{ hours} - 4{,}000 \text{ hours}) \times 10.50/\text{hour} = \$2{,}100 \text{ F}$$

Had they looked only at the $200 favorable direct labor flexible budget variance, Kool-Time's managers may have concluded that direct labor costs were close to expectations. But this illustrates the danger in ending the analysis after computing only the flexible budget variance. "Peeling the onion" to examine the price and efficiency variances yields more insight:

- The unfavorable direct labor price variance means that Kool-Time's operating income is $1,900 lower than expected, because the company paid its employees an average of $11.00 per hour in June instead of the standard rate of $10.50. But this unfavorable variance was more than offset by
- The favorable direct labor efficiency variance. Kool-Time's operating income is $2,100 higher than expected because workers installed ten pools in 3,800 hours instead of the budgeted 4,000 hours.

As with direct materials, the direct labor price and efficiency variances sum to the flexible budget variance.

Direct labor price variance	$1,900 U
Direct labor efficiency variance........................	2,100 F
Direct labor flexible budget variance	$ 200 F

Exhibit 24-12 (next page) summarizes the direct labor variance computations.

FLEXIBLE BUDGETS AND STANDARD COSTS

989

EXHIBIT 24-12
Kool-Time Pools Direct Labor
Variances

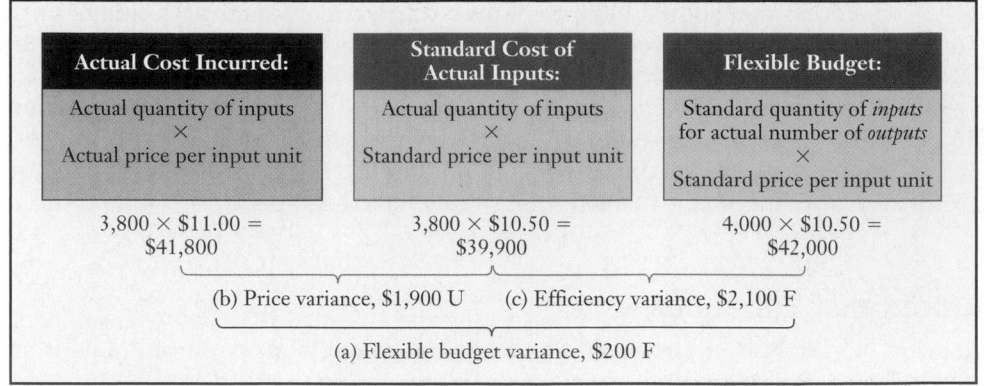

Actual Cost Incurred:	Standard Cost of Actual Inputs:	Flexible Budget:
Actual quantity of inputs × Actual price per input unit	Actual quantity of inputs × Standard price per input unit	Standard quantity of *inputs* for actual number of *outputs* × Standard price per input unit
3,800 × $11.00 = $41,800	3,800 × $10.50 = $39,900	4,000 × $10.50 = $42,000

(b) Price variance, $1,900 U   (c) Efficiency variance, $2,100 F

(a) Flexible budget variance, $200 F

THINK IT OVER

Why might an auto assembly plant experience a favorable direct labor efficiency variance? Should managers investigate favorable as well as unfavorable efficiency variances? Why?

Answer

1. The plant may have redesigned the manufacturing process to avoid wasted motion. For example, a **Dodge** van plant in Canada significantly reduced direct labor by reorganizing production so employees reach for raw materials as needed rather than carry armloads of materials across the plant floor.
2. Employees may have worked harder or more intensely than budgeted.
3. Employees may have rushed through the work and skimped on quality.

There are two reasons why managers should investigate favorable efficiency variances. First, managers want to maximize improvements that increase profits. For example, can managers capitalize on 1 and 2 to further improve labor efficiency at this or other plants? Second, managers want to prevent employees from achieving favorable variances at the expense of long-run profits through strategies like 3, which hurt the company in the long run.

 DAILY EXERCISE 24-15

Using Variances

How often should companies compute variances? Many firms monitor sales, materials quantities, and direct labor hours on a day-to-day or even hour-to-hour basis. For example, **McDonald's** restaurants compute variances for sales and direct labor each hour. Material efficiencies are computed for each shift. The Brass Products Division of **Parker Hannafin** computes variances for each job the day after workers finish the job. This allows managers to ask questions about any large variances while the job is still fresh in workers' minds. The division also prepares weekly reports showing variances by product line. The resulting database allows managers to examine variances by product (part number), by job, or by the dollar amount of the variance, with just a few keystrokes. Technology like bar coding and computerized data entry allows companies like McDonald's and Parker Hannafin to quickly compute efficiency variances. In contrast to efficiency variances, monthly computations of material and labor price variances may be sufficient if long-term contracts with suppliers or labor unions make large price variances unlikely.

Variances by themselves do not identify problems or opportunities. But large variances raise questions that deserve attention. When is a variance "large" or "significant"? The answer depends on the manager's judgment. Many managers use rules of thumb such as "investigate all variances over $10,000 or 8%, whichever is greater." For example, Parker Hannafin's Brass Products Division requires managers to investigate all variances over 5% of sales revenue and to develop a plan of action to correct any problems.

Returning to our Kool-Time Pools example, in June Kool-Time bought gunite for $1.93 per cubic foot (less than the standard price of $2.00). Kool-Time's 3.5% [($1.93 − $2.00)/$2.00] favorable direct materials price variance could arise because the purchasing officer did a good job negotiating prices with suppliers. Or perhaps the officer purchased lower-quality gunite. This is why smart managers interpret variances carefully—even a "favorable" variance can hurt long-run profits.

Kool-Time's 19.7% [(11,969 − 10,000)/10,000] unfavorable direct materials efficiency variance may indicate that the gunite was of low quality. Poor-quality materials spoil, break, or crack more often, requiring replacement. Or perhaps an uncontrollable event led to excess usage. For example, earth tremors may have cracked several pools after the gunite had hardened but before all work was completed. Workers may have used some of the extra gunite to repair the damage.

Now consider Kool-Time's direct labor flexible budget variance. Although this variance is only $200, as indicated earlier, splitting it into its two components is revealing. The 4.8% [($11.00 − $10.50)/$10.50] unfavorable price variance indicates that the company used more expensive labor than was budgeted. But those workers were more efficient. The average number of hours worked per pool (3,800 hours ÷ 10 pools = 380) was 5% less than the standard of 400 hours per pool. Kool-Time's managers may have decided to hire more experienced workers and trade off an unfavorable price variance for a favorable efficiency variance. If so, the strategy was successful—the overall effect of the decision was favorable.

These examples lead to two conclusions:

1. *Executives should be careful in using standard cost variances to evaluate performance.* First, some variances are caused by factors managers cannot control. Second, managers often make tradeoffs among variances. **Chrysler** intentionally accepted a large order for customized Dodge vans because it expected the favorable sales volume variance to more than offset the unfavorable direct labor price variance from the overtime premium and the unfavorable sales revenue price variance from extra rebates offered to the customer. Similarly, managers often trade off price variances against efficiency variances. Purchasing personnel may decide to buy higher-quality (but more-expensive) direct materials to reduce waste and spoilage. The unfavorable price variance may be more than offset by a favorable efficiency variance.

2. *Executives should consider using several measures to evaluate managers' performance.* Evaluations based on only one variance sometimes inadvertently encourage managers to take actions that make the variance look good, but hurt the company in the long run. For example, Kool-Time's managers could

   - Purchase low-quality gunite or hire less-experienced labor to get favorable price variances
   - Use less gunite or less labor (resulting in lower-quality installed pools) to get favorable efficiency variances

How can upper management discourage such actions? One approach is to base performance evaluation on *nonfinancial* measures as well, such as quality indicators like variances in the grade of gunite or labor used, or customer satisfaction measures. For example, McDonald's discourages skimping on labor by evaluating nonfinancial measures such as the difference between actual and standard time to serve drive-through customers. If the McDonald's shift manager does not have enough workers, drive-through customers may have to wait too long to get their French fries. They may take their business to **Wendy's** or **Burger King.**

MANUFACTURING OVERHEAD VARIANCES

Objective 5
Analyze manufacturing overhead in a standard cost system

Ideally, manufacturing overhead cost variances should be computed and monitored for individual overhead costs like plant-related property taxes, utilities, and insurance. However, many companies compute variances on total overhead costs. These companies often split the variances on total manufacturing overhead cost into two parts: a *flexible budget variance* and a *production volume variance*.

The *flexible budget variance* for manufacturing overhead shows whether managers are keeping the period's total overhead cost within the budget for the actual number of outputs. The *production volume variance* arises when the actual number of outputs differs from the expected number of outputs used in the static (master) budget. The two variances combine to explain the difference between actual overhead cost and the standard overhead cost that has been allocated to production (under- or overallocated overhead). Before discussing how companies compute overhead variances, let's see how they allocate manufacturing overhead.

● DAILY EXERCISE 24-16

Allocating Manufacturing Overhead in a Standard Costing System

In a standard costing system, the amount of the manufacturing overhead allocated to production is

$$\text{Manufacturing overhead allocated to production} = \text{Standard predetermined manufacturing overhead rate} \times \text{Standard quantity of the allocation base allowed for the } \textit{actual} \text{ number of outputs}$$

Let's begin by computing the first term on the right-hand side, the standard predetermined manufacturing overhead rate. Kool-Time allocates manufacturing overhead based on direct labor hours. As explained in Chapter 20, the predetermined overhead rate is the budgeted manufacturing overhead cost, divided by the budgeted quantity of the allocation base. ←

But which budget? Exhibit 24-13 shows Kool-Time's budgeted overhead costs and direct labor hours for

➤ To review the computation of the predetermined overhead rate, see Chapter 20, page 810.

- The flexible budget for actual output, which is based on actual output of 10 pools (not known until the end of the period)
- The static budget, which is based on expected output of 8 pools (known at the beginning of the period)

Notice that the $12,000 budgeted *fixed* manufacturing overhead is the same in both the static budget for 8 pools and the flexible budget for 10 pools. Why? Because fixed costs do not change throughout the relevant range of 0–11 pools. In contrast, the budgeted *variable* manufacturing overhead is higher in the flexible budget for 10 pools than in the static budget for 8 pools. Why? Because variable costs vary (in total) with the number of outputs, so Kool-Time expects to use more variable overhead items (indirect materials, indirect labor) for 10 pools than for 8 pools.

EXHIBIT 24-13
Budgeted Manufacturing Overhead Costs and Allocation Rates

KOOL-TIME POOLS		
Budget Data for the Month Ended June 30, 20X5		
	Flexible Budget for Actual Output	Static Budget for Expected Output
Output units (pools installed)	10	8
Standard direct labor hours (400 hours per pool)	4,000	3,200
Budgeted manufacturing overhead cost:		
Variable	$ 8,000	$ 6,400
Fixed	12,000	12,000
Total	$20,000	$18,400
Standard variable manufacturing overhead rate per direct labor hour		$ 6,400 ÷ 3,200 = $2.00
Standard fixed manufacturing overhead rate per direct labor hour		$12,000 ÷ 3,200 = $3.75
Standard total manufacturing overhead rate per direct labor hour		$18,400 ÷ 3,200 = $5.75

Keep in mind that managers use predetermined overhead rates because they cannot wait until the end of the year to figure the overhead costs of products. Thus, *predetermined* overhead rates use data that are available at the *beginning* of the year. Most companies base their predetermined overhead rates on amounts from the static (master) budget, which is known at the beginning of the year. (The predetermined manufacturing overhead rate cannot be based on the flexible budget for actual production because the actual number of outputs is not known until the end of the year.)

Exhibit 24-13 shows that Kool-Time's standard manufacturing overhead rates are

- Variable—$2.00 per direct labor hour ($6,400 static budget variable manufacturing overhead divided by 3,200 static budget standard direct labor hours),
- Fixed—$3.75 per direct labor hour ($12,000 static budget fixed manufacturing overhead divided by 3,200 static budget standard direct labor hours),
- Total—$5.75 per direct labor hour ($2.00 + $3.75). This is the standard predetermined manufacturing overhead rate Kool-Time uses to allocate manufacturing overhead to products.

Now that we have computed the standard predetermined manufacturing overhead rate, the next step is to identify the standard quantity of the allocation base allowed for the *actual* number of outputs. Kool-Time allocates manufacturing overhead based on direct labor hours. Kool-Time actually installed ten pools during June. Thus, the standard quantity of the allocation base (direct labor hours) allowed for the actual number of outputs (10 pools) is 4,000 direct labor hours (400 direct labor hours per pool × 10 pools actually installed). Notice that 4,000 direct labor hours is the standard number of direct labor hours for the flexible budget at the actual output level of 10 pools in Exhibit 24-13, and for the direct labor efficiency variance (Exhibit 24-12).

Thus, Kool-Time allocates manufacturing overhead as follows:

Manufacturing overhead allocated to production	=	Standard predetermined manufacturing overhead rate	×	Standard quantity of the allocation base allowed for the *actual* number of outputs
	=	$5.75 per hour		× 4,000 hours
	=	$23,000		

The total manufacturing overhead variance is the amount of under- or overallocated manufacturing overhead. This is the difference between actual and allocated manufacturing overhead, as explained in Chapter 20. ➥ Exhibit 24-14 shows that actual manufacturing overhead is $21,300.

Given $21,300 of actual manufacturing overhead and $23,000 of allocated manufacturing overhead, Kool-Time has *overallocated* overhead of $1,700. Overallocated overhead is considered a favorable variance because actual overhead costs are less than allocated costs. We now will see how Kool-Time splits this total $1,700 variance into the overhead flexible budget variance and the production volume variance.

◄ To review under- and overallocated overhead, see Chapter 20, pages 814–816.

Overhead Flexible Budget Variance

The **overhead flexible budget variance** is the difference between the actual overhead cost and the flexible budget overhead for the actual number of outputs. Kool-Time's overhead flexible budget variance for June is computed as follows (data from Exhibit 24-14):

OVERHEAD FLEXIBLE BUDGET VARIANCE. The difference between the actual overhead cost and the flexible budget overhead for the actual number of outputs.

Actual overhead cost..	$21,300
Flexible budget overhead for actual outputs (10 pools)	20,000
Overhead flexible budget variance	$ 1,300 U

Exhibit 24-14   **Data for Computing Manufacturing Overhead Variances**

	Actual Overhead Cost (Exhibit 24-9)	Flexible Budget Overhead for Actual Number of Outputs (Exhibits 24-9 and 24-13)	Standard Overhead Allocated to Production (Rates from Exhibit 24-13)
Variable overhead........	$ 9,000	$ 8,000	$2.00 × 4,000 direct labor hours = $ 8,000
Fixed overhead............	12,300	12,000	$3.75 × 4,000 direct labor hours = 15,000
Total overhead.............	$21,300	$20,000	$5.75 × 4,000 direct labor hours = $23,000

Overhead flexible budget variance, $1,300 U

Production volume variance, $3,000 F

Total manufacturing overhead variance, $1,700 F

 DAILY EXERCISE 24-17

Kool-Time actually spent $21,300 on manufacturing overhead, when the flexible budget indicated that installing 10 pools should have required only $20,000 of overhead. The unfavorable variance raises questions regarding managers' control of overhead costs.

Production Volume Variance

PRODUCTION VOLUME VARIANCE. The difference between (1) the manufacturing overhead cost in the flexible budget for actual outputs, and (2) the standard overhead allocated to production.

The **production volume variance** is the difference between (1) the manufacturing overhead cost in the flexible budget for actual outputs, and (2) the standard overhead allocated to production. Kool-Time computes its production volume variance using data from Exhibit 24-14:

Flexible budget overhead for actual outputs (10 pools)	$20,000
Standard overhead allocated to (actual) production	23,000
Production volume variance..	$ 3,000 F

The production volume variance is favorable whenever actual output (ten pools, for Kool-Time) exceeds expected output—(eight pools, Exhibit 24-13). By installing ten pools instead of eight, Kool-Time used its production capacity more fully than originally planned. If Kool-Time had installed seven or fewer pools, the production volume variance would have been unfavorable because the company would have used less production capacity than expected.

Exhibit 24-14 reveals that the *variable* overhead cost in the flexible budget for actual outputs is always the same as the standard variable overhead allocated (standard predetermined variable overhead rate × the standard quantity of the allocation base allowed for the actual number of outputs). Thus, the production volume variance is due only to fixed overhead.

How did the increase in Kool-Time's "production volume," from 8 pools (the expected static budget amount) to 10 pools (actually installed), affect June's profit? Is this amount equal to the production volume variance?

Answer: To see how the increase from 8 to 10 pools affected Kool-Time's June profits, use the contribution margin income statement approach from Chapter 22:

Increase in sales revenue (2 × $12,000).....................	$24,000
Increase in variable expenses (2 × $8,000)	16,000
Increase in contribution margin	8,000
Increase in fixed expenses	–0–
Increase in operating income.....................................	$ 8,000

Installing two more pools than initially expected increased Kool-Time's profits by $8,000, not by the $3,000 favorable "production volume variance." Thus, the production volume variance does *not* reveal how changes in production volume affect profits. The production volume variance only captures the difference between the flexible budget manufacturing overhead and the allocated manufacturing overhead. Companies use the term *production volume variance* because this variance arises only when actual production differs from expected (static budget) production.

Accounting for Standard Costs

Standard Costing Journal Entries

Objective 6
Record transactions at standard cost

Recall that manufacturing companies have three inventory accounts: Materials Inventory, Work in Process Inventory, and Finished Goods Inventory. Most companies with standard cost accounting systems record variances in separate accounts.

We use Kool-Time Pools' June transactions to demonstrate standard costing in a job costing context. Our entries are based on an important assumption: Kool-Time recognizes variances from standards as soon as possible. This means that Kool-Time records direct materials price variances when materials are purchased. It also means that Work in Process Inventory is debited (swimming pools are costed) at standard input quantities and standard prices. June's entries follow:

 DAILY EXERCISE 24-18

1. Materials Inventory (11,969 × $2.00) 23,938
   Direct Materials Price Variance...................... 838
   Accounts Payable (11,969 × $1.93) 23,100
   To record purchases of direct materials.

The credit to Accounts Payable is for the *actual quantity* of gunite purchased (11,969 cubic feet) costed at the *actual price* ($1.93 per cubic foot). In contrast, the debit to Materials Inventory is for the *actual quantity* purchased (11,969 cubic feet) costed at the *standard price* ($2 per cubic foot). Maintaining Materials Inventory at the *standard price* ($2.00) allows Kool-Time's accountants to record the direct materials price variance at time of purchase. Recall that Kool-Time's direct materials price variance was $838 favorable (page 986). A favorable variance has a credit balance in the accounts and is a contra expense, or a reduction in expense. Consequently, the $838 favorable direct materials price variance is a contra expense that increases Kool-Time's June profits.

2. Work in Process Inventory (10,000 × $2.00) 20,000
   Direct Materials Efficiency Variance....................... 3,938
   Materials Inventory (11,969 × $2.00) 23,938
   To record use of direct materials.

Kool-Time's direct materials efficiency variance was $3,938 unfavorable (page 986). An unfavorable variance has a debit balance, which increases expense. Kool-Time's $3,938 unfavorable direct materials efficiency variance is an expense that decreases June profits. Kool-Time debits Work in Process for the *standard price × standard quantity* of direct materials that should have been used for the actual output of ten pools. This maintains Work in Process Inventory at standard cost. Of course, Materials Inventory is credited for the *actual quantity* of material put into production (11,969 cubic feet) costed at the *standard price* at which journal entry 1 entered them into the Materials Inventory account.

3. Manufacturing Wages (3,800 × $10.50)................ 39,900
　　Direct Labor Price Variance 1,900
　　　　Wages Payable (3,800 × $11.00)................... 41,800
　　To record direct labor costs incurred.

By maintaining Manufacturing Wages at the *standard* price for direct labor ($10.50), Kool-Time records the direct labor price variance at the time work is performed. Of course, Wages Payable is credited for the *actual* hours worked at the *actual* wage rate.

4. Work in Process Inventory (4,000 × $10.50) 42,000
　　　　Direct Labor Efficiency Variance.................... 2,100
　　　　Manufacturing Wages (3,800 × $10.50) 39,900
　　To assign direct labor costs.

Kool-Time debits Work in Process for the standard price × standard quantity of direct labor that should have been used for ten pools, similar to the (earlier) direct materials entry #2. This maintains Work in Process Inventory at standard cost.

5. Manufacturing Overhead.. 21,300
　　　　Accounts Payable, Accumulated
　　　　Depreciation, and so on................................. 21,300
　　To record actual overhead costs incurred.
　　(See Exhibit 24-14.)

6. Work in Process Inventory (4,000 × $5.75) 23,000
　　　　Manufacturing Overhead 23,000
　　To allocate overhead. (See Exhibit 24-14.)

In standard costing, the overhead allocated to Work in Process Inventory is computed as the standard predetermined overhead rate × standard quantity of the allocation base that should have been used for the actual output (ten pools, in this case).

7. Finished Goods Inventory....................................... 85,000
　　　　Work in Process Inventory 85,000
　　To record completion of 10 pools ($20,000 of materials +
　　$42,000 of labor + $23,000 of manufacturing overhead).

8. Cost of Goods Sold 85,000
　　　　Finished Goods Inventory 85,000
　　To record the cost of sales of 10 pools.

⊙ DAILY EXERCISE 24-19

⊙ DAILY EXERCISE 24-20

9. Manufacturing Overhead.. 1,700
　　Overhead Flexible Budget Variance 1,300
　　　　Production Volume Variance 3,000
　　To record overhead variances and close the
　　Manufacturing Overhead account. (See Exhibit 24-14.)

Entry 9 closes Manufacturing Overhead. Many companies wait until the end of the fiscal year to close this account.

Exhibit 24-15 shows selected Kool-Time accounts, after posting the preceding journal entries.

Objective 7
Prepare a standard cost income statement for management

Standard Cost Income Statement for Management

Exhibit 24-16 shows Kool Time's standard cost income statement. After sales revenue, the statement shows the cost of goods sold at standard cost. Then the statement separately lists each variance, followed by the cost of goods sold at actual cost. (Recall that since Kool-Time had no raw materials, work in process, or finished goods inventories, all the variances relate to June's sales.) At the end of the period, all the variance accounts are closed to zero-out their balances. The net amount is closed to Income Summary.

The income statement shows that the net effect of this adjustment is $1,200 unfavorable. Thus, June's operating income is $1,200 lower than it would have been if all actual costs had been equal to standard amounts. Management can prepare statements with similar detail for research and development, design, marketing, distribution, and customer service costs, if they are subject to standard cost analysis.

EXHIBIT 24-15 Kool-Time Pools Flow of Costs in Standard Costing System

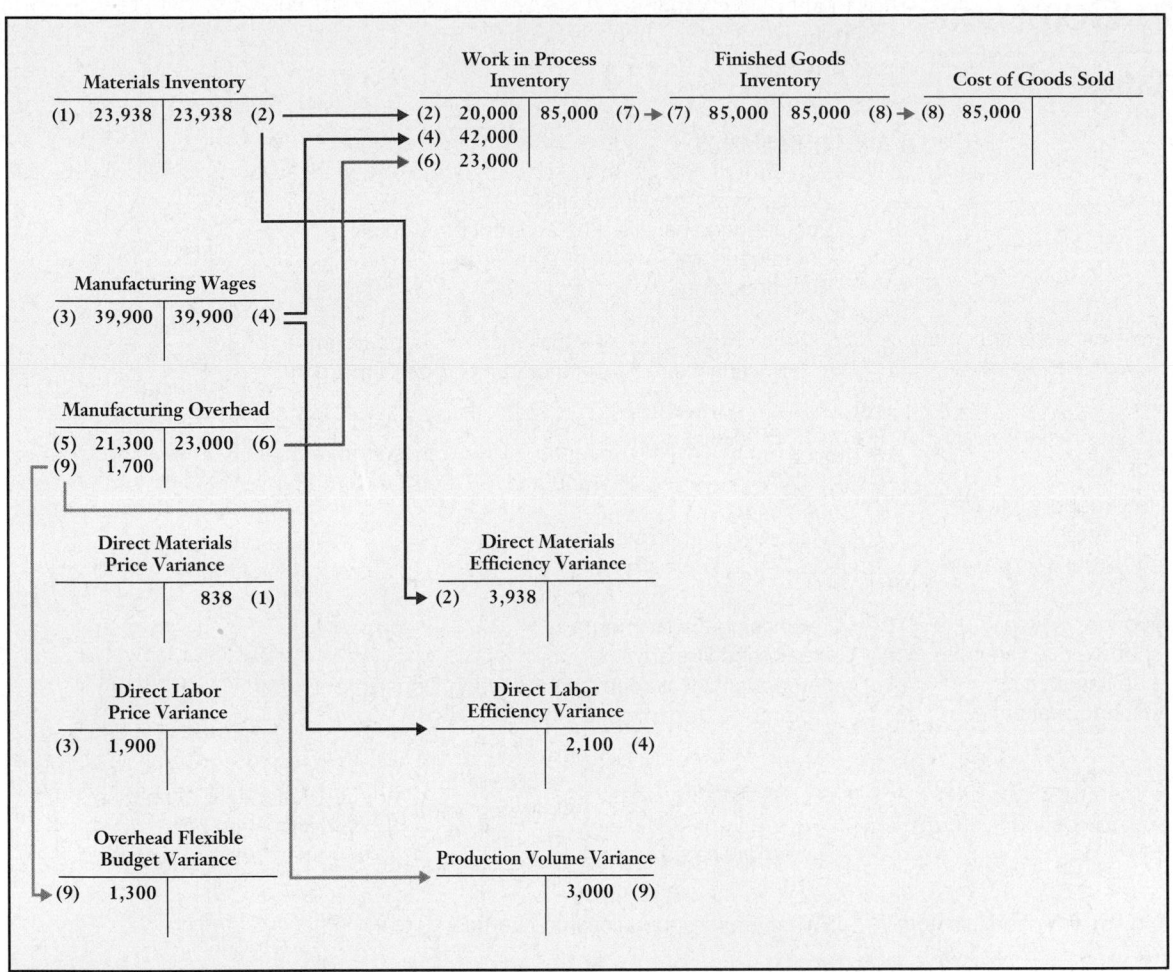

EXHIBIT 24-16
Standard Cost Income Statement

KOOL-TIME POOLS
Standard Cost Income Statement
Month Ended June 30, 20X5

Sales revenue (10 × $12,000).................................		$120,000
Cost of goods sold at standard cost.........................		85,000
Manufacturing cost variances:		
Direct materials price variance	$ (838)	
Direct materials efficiency variance..................	3,938	
Direct labor price variance................................	1,900	
Direct labor efficiency variance	(2,100)	
Manufacturing overhead flexible		
budget variance...	1,300	
Production volume variance	(3,000)	
Total manufacturing variances		1,200
Cost of goods sold at actual cost............................		86,200
Gross profit...		33,800
Marketing and administrative expenses*..............		18,800
Operating income..		$15,000

*$9,100 + $9,700 from Exhibit 24-9.

DAILY EXERCISE 24-21

Take a moment to review standard costing by studying the Decision Guidelines on the following page. Then work the summary problem.

DECISION GUIDELINES

Standard Costs

DECISION	GUIDELINES
How to set standards?	Historical performance data Engineering analysis/time-and-motion studies Continuous improvement standards Benchmarking

How to compute a price variance for materials or labor?

$$\text{Price variance} = \left(\begin{array}{c} \text{Actual price} \\ \text{per input unit} \end{array} - \begin{array}{c} \text{Standard price} \\ \text{per input unit} \end{array} \right) \begin{array}{c} \text{Actual} \\ \times \text{ quantity of} \\ \text{input} \end{array}$$

How to compute an efficiency variance for materials or labor?

$$\text{Efficiency variance} = \left(\begin{array}{c} \text{Actual} \\ \text{quantity of} \\ \text{input} \end{array} - \begin{array}{c} \text{Standard quantity} \\ \text{of input for actual} \\ \text{number of outputs} \end{array} \right) \begin{array}{c} \text{Standard} \\ \times \text{ price per} \\ \text{input unit} \end{array}$$

Who is most likely responsible for:

Sales volume variance?	Marketing Department
Sales revenue flexible budget variance?	Marketing Department
Direct material price variance?	Purchasing Department
Direct material efficiency variance?	Production Department
Direct labor price variance?	Personnel Department or Production Department
Direct labor efficiency variance?	Production Department

How to allocate manufacturing overhead in a standard costing system?

$$\begin{array}{c} \text{Manufacturing} \\ \text{overhead} \\ \text{allocated} \end{array} = \left(\begin{array}{c} \text{Standard} \\ \text{predetermined} \\ \text{manufacturing} \\ \text{overhead rate} \end{array} \right) \times \left(\begin{array}{c} \text{Standard quantity of} \\ \text{allocation base allowed} \\ \text{for actual outputs} \end{array} \right)$$

How to analyze over- or underallocated manufacturing overhead?

Split over- or underallocated overhead into

$$\text{Flexible budget variance} = \begin{array}{c} \text{Actual} \\ \text{overhead} \end{array} - \begin{array}{c} \text{Flexible budget} \\ \text{overhead} \end{array}$$

$$\text{Production volume variance} = \begin{array}{c} \text{Flexible budget} \\ \text{overhead} \end{array} - \begin{array}{c} \text{Standard overhead} \\ \text{allocated to} \\ \text{actual outputs} \end{array}$$

How to record standard costs in the accounts?

Materials Inventory: Actual quantity at standard price
Work in Process Inventory (and Finished Goods Inventory and Cost of Goods Sold): Standard quantity of inputs allowed for actual outputs, at standard price of inputs

---

REVIEW FLEXIBLE BUDGETS AND STANDARD COSTING

SUMMARY PROBLEM

Exhibit 24-9 indicates that Kool-Time Pools installed ten swimming pools in June. Suppose Kool-Time had installed seven pools instead of ten and that actual expenses were

Direct materials (gunite)...........	7,400 cubic feet @ $2.00 per cubic foot
Direct labor.............................	2,740 hours @ $10.00 per hour
Variable overhead....................	$5,400
Fixed overhead.......................	$11,900

Required

1. Given these new data, prepare two exhibits similar to Exhibits 24-9 and 24-13. Ignore marketing and administrative expenses in your first exhibit.
2. Compute price and efficiency variances for direct materials and direct labor.
3. Compute the total variance, the flexible budget variance, and the production volume variance for manufacturing overhead.
4. Prepare a June income statement through operating income for the president of Kool-Time Pools. Report all standard cost variances; assume that actual marketing and administrative expenses for the month totaled $17,700.

Solution

Requirement 1

KOOL-TIME POOLS
Revised Data for Standard Costing Example
Month of June, 20X5

PANEL A—Comparison of Actual Results with Flexible Budget for 7 Swimming Pools

	Actual Results at Actual Prices	Flexible Budget for 7 Pools	Flexible Budget Variance
Variable expenses:			
Direct materials............................	$14,800*	$14,000†	$ 800 U
Direct labor.................................	27,400*	29,400†	2,000 F
Variable overhead	5,400	5,600†	200 F
Total variable expenses.............	47,600	49,000	1,400 F
Fixed expenses:			
Fixed overhead............................	11,900	12,000 ‡	100 F
Total expenses.................................	$59,500	$61,000	$1,500 F

* See Panel C
† See Panel B
‡ Fixed overhead was budgeted at $12,000 per month.

PANEL B—Computation of Flexible Budget for Direct Materials, Direct Labor, and Variable Overhead for 7 Swimming Pools

	(1) Standard Quantity of Inputs Allowed for 7 Pools	(2) Standard Price per Unit of Input	(1) × (2) Flexible Budget for 7 Pools
Direct materials..................	1,000 cubic feet per pool × 7 pools = 7,000 cubic feet	$ 2.00	$14,000
Direct labor........................	400 hours per pool × 7 pools = 2,800 hours	10.50	29,400
Variable overhead..............	400 hours per pool × 7 pools = 2,800 hours	2.00	5,600

KOOL-TIME POOLS (*continued*)
Revised Data for Standard Costing Example
Month of June, 20X5

PANEL C—Computation of Actual Costs for Direct Materials and Direct Labor for 7 Swimming Pools

	(1) Actual Quantity of Inputs Used for 7 Pools	(2) Actual Price per Unit of Input	(1) × (2) Actual Cost for 7 Pools
Direct materials..................	7,400 cubic feet actually used	$ 2.00 actual cost/cubic foot	$14,800
Direct labor........................	2,740 hours actually used	$10.00 actual cost/hour	27,400

KOOL-TIME POOLS
Revised Budget Data for the Month Ended June 30, 20X5

	Flexible Budget for Actual Output	Static Budget for Expected Output
Output units (pools installed)......................	7	8
Standard direct labor hours (400 hours per pool)	2,800	3,200
Budgeted manufacturing overhead cost:		
Variable	$ 5,600*	$ 6,400
Fixed...	12,000†	12,000
Total...	$17,600	$18,400
Standard variable manufacturing overhead rate per direct labor hour		$ 6,400 ÷ 3,200 = $2.00
Standard fixed manufacturing overhead rate per direct labor hour		$12,000 ÷ 3,200 = $3.75
Standard total manufacturing overhead rate per direct labor hour		$18,400 ÷ 3,200 = $5.75

* Flexible budget variable overhead is computed as the standard quantity of the allocation base allowed for actual outputs (2,800 direct labor hours = 7 pools × 400 direct labor hours per pool) multiplied by the $2.00 standard variable manufacturing overhead rate per direct labor hour: 2,800 hours × $2.00 per hour = $5,600.

† Budgeted fixed overhead is *fixed* within the relevant range, so flexible budget fixed overhead is $12,000, the same as static budget fixed overhead.

Requirement 2

$$\text{Price variance} = \left(\begin{array}{c} \text{Actual price} \\ \text{per input unit} \end{array} - \begin{array}{c} \text{Standard price} \\ \text{per input unit} \end{array} \right) \times \begin{array}{c} \text{Actual} \\ \text{quantity of} \\ \text{input} \end{array}$$

Direct materials:

Price variance = ($2.00 − $2.00) × 7,400 cubic feet = $-0-

Direct labor:

Price variance = ($10.00 − $10.50) × 2,740 hours = $1,370 F

$$\text{Efficiency variance} = \left(\begin{array}{c} \text{Actual} \\ \text{quantity} \\ \text{of input} \end{array} - \begin{array}{c} \text{Standard} \\ \text{quantity of} \\ \text{input} \end{array} \right) \times \begin{array}{c} \text{Standard} \\ \text{price per} \\ \text{input unit} \end{array}$$

Direct materials:

Efficiency variance = $\left(\begin{array}{c} 7,400 \\ \text{cubic feet} \end{array} - \begin{array}{c} 7,000 \\ \text{cubic feet} \end{array} \right) \times \begin{array}{c} \$2.00 \text{ per} \\ \text{cubic foot} \end{array} = \$800$ U

Direct labor:

Efficiency variance = $\left(\begin{array}{c} 2,740 \\ \text{hours} \end{array} - \begin{array}{c} 2,800 \\ \text{hours} \end{array} \right) \times \begin{array}{c} \$10.50 \text{ per} \\ \text{hour} \end{array} = \$630$ F

Requirement 3

Total overhead variance:
Actual overhead cost ($5,400 variable + $11,900 fixed).......................... $17,300
Standard overhead allocated to production
   (2,800 standard direct labor hours × $5.75) 16,100
Total overhead variance .... $ 1,200 U
Overhead flexible budget variance:
Actual overhead cost ($5,400 + $11,900) $17,300
Flexible budget overhead for actual outputs ($5,600 + $12,000) 17,600
Overhead flexible budget variance... $ 300 F
Production volume variance:
Flexible budget overhead for actual outputs ($5,600 + $12,000) $17,600
Standard overhead allocated to (actual) production
   (2,800 standard direct labor hours × $5.75) 16,100
Production volume variance .... $ 1,500 U

Requirement 4

KOOL-TIME POOLS
Revised Standard Cost Income Statement
Month Ended June 30, 20X5

Sales revenue (7 × $12,000)....................................		$84,000
Cost of goods sold at standard cost*.......................		59,500
Manufacturing cost variances:		
Direct materials price variance	$ 0	
Direct materials efficiency variance....................	800	
Direct labor price variance.................................	(1,370)	
Direct labor efficiency variance	(630)	
Overhead flexible budget variance.....................	(300)	
Production volume variance	1,500	
Total manufacturing variances		0
Cost of goods sold at actual cost............................		59,500
Gross profit...		24,500
Marketing and administrative expenses		17,700
Operating income..		$ 6,800

*Cost of goods sold at standard cost:
Direct materials (7,000 cubic feet × $2.00 per cubic foot) $14,000
Direct labor (2,800 direct labor hours × $10.50 per direct labor hour).......... 29,400
Standard overhead allocated (2,800 direct labor hours ×
  $5.75 per direct labor hour) $16,100
Cost of goods sold at standard cost... $59,500

Lessons Learned

1. **Prepare a flexible budget for the income statement.** A *flexible budget* is a summarized budget that can easily be computed for different volume levels. Flexible budgets separate variable costs from fixed costs. These budgets show how revenues and costs vary—if at all—as the number of outputs varies within the budget range.

2. **Prepare an income statement performance report.** Static budget variances are differences between actual amounts and corresponding amounts (revenues and expenses) in the static budget. At the end of the period, accountants prepare an after-the-fact flexible budget for the actual number of outputs. Accountants use this flexible budget to divide static budget variances into two broad categories: *sales volume variances* and *flexible budget variances*.

3. **Identify the benefits of standard costs.** *Standard costs* are carefully predetermined costs that usually are expressed on a per-unit basis. Standards help managers plan and control, motivate employees, provide unit costs, and simplify record keeping.

4. **Compute standard cost variances for direct materials and direct labor.** Companies divide flexible budget variances for direct materials and direct labor into price and efficiency (quantity) variances. A *price variance* reveals the effect on total cost—and thus the effect on operating income—of paying more or less for an input than the standard allows. An *efficiency variance* reveals the effect on total cost of using more or less input than allowed by the flexible budget for the actual number of outputs.

5. **Analyze manufacturing overhead in a standard cost system.** The total variance between actual manufacturing overhead cost incurred and standard overhead cost allocated has two components: the *overhead flexible budget*

variance and the *production volume variance*. Overhead flexible budget variance is the difference between actual overhead and flexible budget overhead that should have been incurred given the actual number of outputs. Production volume variance is the difference between flexible budget overhead for actual outputs and standard overhead allocated to production.

6. **Record transactions at standard cost.** Many companies record standard costs in inventory and expense accounts.

They also record standard cost variances. At year's end, all variance accounts are closed out.

7. **Prepare a standard cost income statement for management.** The statement shows cost of goods sold at standard cost, lists all variances, and then shows the adjusted cost of goods sold—at actual cost. Operating expenses are treated similarly if they are part of the company's standard cost system.

ACCOUNTING VOCABULARY

benchmarking (p. 983)
efficiency variance (p. 986)
flexible budget (p. 974)
flexible budget variance (p. 977)
master budget (p. 973)

overhead flexible budget
  variance (p. 993)
price variance (p. 984)
production volume
  variance (p. 994)

sales volume variance (p. 977)
standard cost (p. 981)
static budget (p. 973)
variance (p. 973)

QUESTIONS

1. How does a static budget differ from a flexible budget?
2. What is the relevant range, and why must it be considered in preparing a flexible budget?
3. McLaren, Inc., prepared its static (master) budget for a sales level of 35,000 for the month. Actual sales totaled 46,000. Describe the problem of using the static budget to evaluate company performance for the month. Propose a better way to evaluate McLaren's performance.
4. What advantage does a flexible budget graph offer over a columnar flexible budget with four levels of volume?
5. What do the sales volume variance and the flexible budget variance for operating income measure?
6. Describe the benefits of a standard cost system.
7. What does a price variance measure? How is it computed?
8. What does an efficiency variance measure? How is it computed?

9. How are the price variance and the efficiency variance related to the flexible budget variance for direct materials and direct labor?
10. Describe how managers can trade off direct materials price and efficiency variances.
11. When should a cost variance be investigated?
12. What causes an overhead flexible budget variance? What information does this variance provide?
13. Scott & White, Inc., uses standard costing. The actual quantity of direct materials used to manufacture inventory, costed at standard prices, was $21,600. The direct materials efficiency variance was $1,400 favorable. Make the journal entry to record the use of materials in production.
14. How does a standard cost income statement for management differ from an income statement reported to the public?

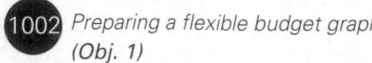

ASSESS YOUR PROGRESS

DAILY EXERCISES

Preparing flexible budgets
(Obj. 1)

DE24-1 In a series of Daily Exercises, we are going to prepare budgets and variance analyses for Digital Systems, Inc., a firm that installs household wiring for high-speed Internet connections and high-definition audio and video. For each installation, Digital Systems has budgeted direct materials costs of $500 and direct labor costs of $800. The company has budgeted fixed expenses at $8,000 per month, for 0–50 installations per month. Digital Systems' budgeted sale price is $2,500 per installation.

1. Write out Digital Systems' flexible budget total cost formula.
2. Using Exhibit 24-3 (page 974) as a guide, prepare flexible budgets for Digital Systems for
   a. 20 installations per month
   b. 30 installations per month

Preparing and using flexible budgets *(Obj. 1)*

DE24-2 Turn to the Kool-Time Pools example on page 974.

1. Using the data from Exhibit 24-3 (page 974), develop flexible budgets for three- and ten-pool levels of output.
2. Would Kool-Time's managers use the flexible budgets you developed in requirement 1 for planning or for controlling? What specific insights can Kool-Time's managers gain from the flexible budgets you prepared in requirement 1?

Preparing a flexible budget graph
(Obj. 1)

DE24-3 ➤ *Link Back to Chapter 22, Exhibit 22-7 (page 899).* Refer to Daily Exercise 24-1. Digital Systems reports the following actual results for January and February:

	January	February
Expected number of installations, per the static budget	20	30
Actual number of installations	25	20
Actual sale price per installation	$2,500	$2,800
Actual direct materials cost per installation	$ 450	$ 560
Actual direct labor cost per installation	$ 760	$ 800
Actual fixed monthly expenses	$7,000	$9,000

1. Prepare a graph of Digital Systems' monthly flexible budget total cost formula, using data from Daily Exercise 24-1. Use Exhibit 24-4 on page 976 as a guide.
2. Plot January's and February's actual costs on the flexible budget graph from requirement 1.

DE24-4 Look at Kool-Time Pools' graph of actual and budgeted monthly costs in Exhibit 24-5 on page 976.

1. How many pools did Kool-Time install in May?
2. How much were Kool-Time's actual expenses in May?
3. Using Kool-Time's flexible budget formula, what is the flexible budget total cost for the month of May?
4. What is Kool-Time's flexible budget variance for total costs? Is the variance favorable or unfavorable in May?

Interpreting flexible budget graph and formula (Obj. 1)

DE24-5 Refer to the Digital Systems data in Daily Exercises 24-1 and 24-3. Compute January and February flexible budget variances for total costs. Has Digital Systems done a better-than-expected job or a worse-than-expected job of controlling total costs in January? In February? Explain.

Computing flexible budget variances (Obj. 1)

DE24-6 Use your results from Daily Exercise 24-4 to prepare an income statement performance report for Kool-Time Pools for May. Use Exhibit 24-7 (page 978) as a guide. Assume that the actual sale price per pool remains $12,000, actual variable expenses total $59,000, and actual fixed expenses are $21,000 in May. The static budget number of pools remains eight.

Explain to Kool-Time's management why May's operating income differs from the static budget operating income.

Preparing and interpreting an income statement performance report (Obj. 2)

DE24-7 Use the data in Daily Exercises 24-1, 24-3, and 24-5 to prepare an income statement performance report for Digital Systems for January. Use Exhibit 24-7 (page 978) as a guide. Interpret the variances for Digital Systems' management.

Income statement performance report (Obj. 2)

DE24-8 Consider the Kool-Time Pools example on pages 973–980.

1. What is the relevant range for the flexible budget total cost formula?
2. Explain whether Kool-Time would have a sales volume variance for fixed expenses in Exhibit 24-7 (page 978) if
   a. Kool-Time installs 14 pools per month.
   b. Kool-Time installs 8 pools per month.

Role of fixed costs (Obj. 1, 2)

DE24-9 Fill in the blank with the phrase that best completes the sentence.

Actual number of outputs   Beginning of the period   Static budget variance
Expected number of outputs   End of the period
Sales volume variance   Flexible budget variance

a. The static budget is developed at the _____.
b. The flexible budget used in a performance report is based on the _____.
c. The master budget is based on the _____.
d. The flexible budget used in a performance report is developed at the _____.
e. The difference between actual costs and the costs that should have been incurred for the actual number of outputs is the _____.

Static budgets and flexible budgets (Obj. 2)

DE24-10 Lladró is a Spanish manufacturer of porcelain art objects. Raw materials are mixed to form clay, which is shaped into figurines. The pieces are then glazed and fired at high temperatures.

Explain how the five benefits of standard costs (pages 983–984) apply to Lladró. Be as specific as possible.

Benefits of standard costs (Obj. 3)

DE24-11 As explained in the chapter opening story, each **McDonald's** uses historical data to budget sales for each hour, and the restaurant computes hourly sales variances. If actual sales are less than budgeted, the manager can send employees home.

Sales and labor variances (Obj. 2, 4)

1. What variance does McDonald's control by sending employees home early if actual sales volume falls short of the budget? Explain.
2. What sales variance does McDonald's compute hourly?

Computing materials variances (Obj. 4)

DE24-12 In a series of Daily Exercises, we will compute variances and record journal entries for TimTam Pottery, a manufacturer of ceramic cookie jars. The company has the following standards:

Direct materials (clay)...............................	1 pound per jar, at a cost of $0.50 per pound
Direct labor	1/5 hour per jar, at a cost of $13 per hour
Static budget variable overhead.................	$60,000
Static budget fixed overhead	$20,000
Static budget direct labor hours	10,000 hours
Static budget number of cookie jars...........	50,000

TimTam allocates manufacturing overhead to production based on standard direct labor hours. Last month, TimTam reported the following actual results for the production of 60,000 jars:

Direct materials.........................	1.1 pound per jar, at a cost of $0.60 per pound
Direct labor	1/4 hour per jar, at a cost of $12 per hour
Actual variable overhead..........	$84,000
Actual fixed overhead	$18,000

Compute TimTam's variances for materials.

Computing materials efficiency variances (Obj. 4)

DE24-13 As explained in the chapter opening story, the standard direct materials for a regular **McDonald's** hamburger are

1 bun	1 pickle slice	1/4 teaspoon mustard
1 hamburger patty	1/8 teaspoon dehydrated onion	1/2 ounce ketchup

Assume that a San Diego, California, McDonald's sold 500 hamburgers yesterday and actually used the following materials:

510 buns	490 pickle slices	120 teaspoons mustard
520 hamburger patties	70 teaspoons dehydrated onion	300 ounces ketchup

Compute the direct materials efficiency variances for each material, using the following standard materials prices (all amounts assumed):

Buns.............................	$0.10 each	Dehydrated onion	$0.04 per teaspoon
Hamburger patties	0.15 each	Mustard......................	0.02 per teaspoon
Pickle slices	0.01 per slice	Ketchup......................	0.04 per ounce

Computing direct labor variances (Obj. 4)

DE24-14 Refer to the TimTam data in Daily Exercise 24-12. Compute the direct labor variances.

Interpreting materials and labor variances (Obj. 4)

DE24-15 Refer to Daily Exercises 24-12 and 24-14. For each variance, who in TimTam's organization is most likely responsible? Interpret the direct materials and direct labor variances for TimTam's management.

Standard overhead rates (Obj. 5)

DE24-16 Use the TimTam data in Daily Exercise 24-12 to compute the standard predetermined variable manufacturing overhead rate and the standard predetermined fixed manufacturing overhead rate.

Computing overhead variances (Obj. 5)

DE24-17 Refer to the TimTam data in Daily Exercises 24-12 and 24-16.

1. Compute the overhead variances. (Use Exhibit 24-14 as a guide.)
2. Is manufacturing overhead under- or overallocated? By how much?

Materials and labor journal entries (Obj. 6)

DE24-18 Refer to the information in Daily Exercises 24-12 and 24-14. Record TimTam's direct materials and direct labor journal entries.

Overhead journal entries (Obj. 6)

DE24-19 Refer to the information in Daily Exercises 24-12 and 24-17. Record TimTam's journal entries for Manufacturing Overhead, including the entry that records the overhead variances and closes the Manufacturing Overhead account.

DE24-20 Refer to the information in Daily Exercises 24-12, 24-14, and 24-17 through 24-19. TimTam sold on account each of the 60,000 jars at a sale price of $8.00 each. There were no beginning or ending inventories of any kind.

Record the journal entries for the completion and sale of the 60,000 jars.

Journal entries for goods completed and sold
(Obj. 6)

DE24-21 Use the information from Daily Exercises 24-12, 24-14, and 24-17 through 24-20 to prepare a standard cost income statement for TimTam's management, using Exhibit 24-16 as a guide. Actual marketing and administrative expenses were $88,500.

Standard cost income statement
(Obj. 7)

EXERCISES

E24-1 CompuGear sells its main product, ergonomic mouse pads, for $10 each. Its variable cost is $4 per pad. Fixed expenses are $200,000 per month for volumes up to 60,000 pads. Above 60,000 pads, monthly fixed expenses are $300,000.

Prepare a monthly flexible budget for the product, showing sales, variable expenses, fixed expenses, and operating income or loss for volume levels of 40,000, 50,000, and 70,000 pads.

Preparing a flexible budget for the income statement
(Obj. 1)

E24-2 ➡ *Link Back to Chapter 22, Exhibit 22-7 (page 899).* Graph the flexible budget total cost line for CompuGear in Exercise 24-1. Show total costs for volume levels of 40,000, 50,000, and 70,000 pads.

Graphing cost behavior
(Obj. 1)

E24-3 Beach Blanket Company managers received the following incomplete performance report:

Completing a performance report
(Obj. 2)

BEACH BLANKET COMPANY
Income Statement Performance Report
Year Ended July 31, 20X3

	Actual Results at Actual Prices	Flexible Budget Variance	Flexible Budget for Actual Number of Output Units	Sales Volume Variance	Static (Master) Budget
Output units	24,000	_____	24,000	4,000 F	_____
Sales Revenue	$192,000	_____	$192,000	$32,000 F	_____
Variable expenses	85,000	_____	80,000	20,000 U	_____
Fixed expenses	104,000	_____	100,000	–0–	_____
Total expenses	189,000	_____	180,000	20,000 U	_____
Operating income	$ 3,000	_____	$ 12,000	$12,000 F	_____

Complete the performance report. Identify the employee group that may deserve praise and the group that may be subject to criticism. Give your reasons.

E24-4 Top managers of Wang Industries predicted 20X4 sales of 145,000 units of its product at a unit price of $7. Actual sales for the year were 140,000 units at $8.50 each. Variable expenses were budgeted at $2.20 per unit, and actual variable expenses were $2.25 per unit. Actual fixed expenses of $420,000 exceeded budgeted fixed expenses by $10,000. Prepare Wang's income statement performance report in a format similar to Exercise 24-3. What variance contributed most to the year's favorable results? What caused this variance?

Preparing an income statement performance report
(Obj. 2)

E24-5 The following direct materials variance computations are incomplete:

$$\text{Price variance} = (\$? - \$12) \times 14{,}500 \text{ pounds} = \$5{,}800 \text{ U}$$
$$\text{Efficiency variance} = (? - 14{,}700 \text{ pounds}) \times \$12 = ? \text{ F}$$
$$\text{Flexible budget variance} = \$?$$

Fill in the missing values, and identify the flexible budget variance as favorable or unfavorable.

Computing price and efficiency variances for direct materials
(Obj. 4)

E24-6 Forever Frames, which uses a standard cost accounting system, manufactured 400,000 picture frames during the year, using 1,350,000 board feet of lumber purchased at $1.55 per foot. Production required 9,500 direct labor hours that cost $12.00 per hour. The materials standard was 3 board feet of lumber per frame, at a standard cost of $1.70 per foot. The labor standard was 0.025 direct labor hour per frame, at a standard cost of $11.50 per hour. Compute the price and efficiency variances for direct materials and direct labor. Does the pattern of variances suggest Forever Frames' managers have been making tradeoffs? Explain.

Price and efficiency variances for materials and labor
(Obj. 4)

E24-7 Make the journal entries to record the purchase and use of direct materials and direct labor in Exercise 24-6.

Journal entries
(Obj. 6)

E24-8 The managers of Diaz Co., a contract manufacturer of disk drives, are seeking explanations for the variances in the following report. Explain the meaning of each of Diaz's materials, labor, and overhead variances.

DIAZ CO.
Standard Costing Income Statement
Year Ended December 31, 20X4

Sales revenue		$1,200,000
Cost of goods sold at standard cost		700,000
Manufacturing cost variances:		
Direct materials price variance	$ 8,000 F	
Direct materials efficiency variance	32,000 U	
Direct labor price variance	24,000 F	
Direct labor efficiency variance	10,000 U	
Manufacturing overhead flexible budget variance	28,000 U	
Production volume variance	8,000 F	
Total manufacturing variances		30,000
Cost of goods sold at actual cost		730,000
Gross profit		470,000
Marketing and administrative expenses		418,000
Operating income		$ 52,000

E24-9 Polystar manufactures carpeting. The company charges the following standard unit costs to production on the basis of static budget volume of 30,000 linear feet of carpet per month:

Direct materials	$2.50
Direct labor	2.00
Manufacturing overhead	1.50
Standard unit cost	$6.00

Polystar uses the following monthly flexible budget overhead:

	Number of Outputs (linear feet)		
	27,000	**30,000**	**33,000**
Standard machine hours	2,700	3,000	3,300
Budgeted manufacturing overhead cost:			
Variable	$13,500	$15,000	$16,500
Fixed	30,000	30,000	30,000

Polystar actually produced 33,000 linear feet of carpet, using 3,100 machine hours. Actual variable overhead was $16,200, and fixed overhead was $30,500. Compute the total overhead variance, the overhead flexible budget variance, and the production volume variance.

E24-10 European Cuisine, Inc., revenue and expense information for the month of April follows.

Sales revenue	$440,000
Cost of good sold (standard)	242,000
Direct materials price variance	2,000 F
Direct materials efficiency variance	4,000 F
Direct labor price variance	3,000 U
Direct labor efficiency variance	2,000 F
Overhead flexible budget variance	2,500 U
Production volume variance	6,000 F

Prepare a standard cost income statement for management through gross profit. Report all standard cost variances for management's use. Has management done a good or poor job of controlling costs? Explain.

Challenge Exercise

E24-11 Laptop Solutions repairs and upgrades laptop computers. The company measures "production output" in terms of the number of laptops serviced. The company allocates overhead at the rate of $80 per laptop serviced.

Overhead variances
(Obj. 5)

	Overhead Rate per Unit
Variable	$30
Fixed	50

In June, 20X6, Laptop Solutions "produced" 5,200 serviced laptops. Its production volume variance was $10,000 favorable. Compute Laptop Solutions' budgeted fixed overhead cost per month. What monthly capacity level did Laptop Solutions use to compute the fixed overhead rate of $50 per unit?

PROBLEMS

P24-1A ➡ *Link Back to Chapter 22, Exhibit 22-7 (page 899).* Cellular Technologies manufactures capacitors for cellular base stations and other communications applications. The company's static budget income statement for October 20X4 follows. It is based on expected sales volume of 9,000 units.

Cellular Technologies' plant capacity is 9,500 units. If actual volume exceeds 9,500 units, Cellular Technologies must rent additional space. In that case, salaries will increase by 15%, rent will double, and insurance expense will increase by $1,000. Depreciation will be unaffected.

Preparing a flexible budget income statement and graphing cost behavior
(Obj. 1)

CELLULAR TECHNOLOGIES
Static Budget Income Statement
October 20X4

Sales revenue	$189,000
Variable expenses:	
Cost of goods sold	72,000
Sales commissions	9,450
Shipping expense	4,500
Fixed expenses:	
Salary expense	27,500
Depreciation expense	13,250
Rent expense	11,250
Insurance expense..................	2,750
Total expenses	140,700
Operating income	$ 48,300

Required

1. Prepare flexible budget income statements for 7,500, 9,000, and 11,000 units.
2. Graph the behavior of the company's total costs.
3. Why might Cellular Technologies' managers want to see the graph you prepared in requirement 2 as well as the columnar format analysis in requirement 1? What is the disadvantage of the graphic approach in requirement 2?

Preparing an income statement performance report *(Obj. 2)*

P24-2A Refer to Cellular Technologies, Problem 24-1A. The company sold 11,000 units during October 20X4, and its actual operating income was as follows:

CELLULAR TECHNOLOGIES
Income Statement
October 20X4

Sales revenue	$235,000
Variable expenses:	
Cost of goods sold	90,250
Sales commissions	11,250
Shipping expense	6,750
Fixed expenses:	
Salary expense	33,200
Depreciation expense	13,250
Rent expense	22,000
Insurance expense	3,700
Total expenses	180,400
Operating income	$ 54,600

Required

1. Prepare an income statement performance report for October.
2. What was the effect on Cellular Technologies' operating income of selling 2,000 units more than the static budget level of sales?
3. What is Cellular Technologies' static budget variance? Explain why the income statement performance report provides more useful information to Cellular Technologies' managers than the simple static budget variance. What insights can Cellular Technologies' managers draw from this performance report?

Preparing a flexible budget and computing standard cost variances
(Obj. 1, 3, 4, 5)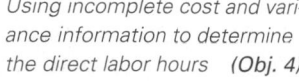

P24-3A Bronx Co. manufactures insulated hunting jackets and uses flexible budgeting and a standard cost system. Bronx allocates overhead based on yards of direct materials. The company's performance report includes the following selected data:

	Static Budget (1,000 jackets)	Actual Results (975 jackets)
Sales (1,000 jackets × $200)	$200,000	
(975 jackets × $192)		$187,200
Variable manufacturing expenses:		
Direct materials (4,000 yd × $7.90)	31,600	
(4,100 yd × $7.65)		31,365
Direct labor (5,000 hr × $6.00)	30,000	
(4,800 hr × $6.05)		29,040
Variable overhead (4,000 yd × $5.00)	20,000	
(4,100 yd × $6.40)		26,240
Fixed manufacturing expenses:		
Fixed overhead	27,000	28,500
Total cost of goods sold	108,600	115,145
Gross profit	$ 91,400	$ 72,055

Required

1. Prepare a flexible budget based on the actual number of jackets sold.
2. Compute the price variance and the efficiency variance for direct materials and for direct labor. For manufacturing overhead, compute the total variance, the flexible budget variance, and the production volume variance.
3. What is the total flexible budget variance for Bronx's manufacturing costs? Show how the total flexible budget variance is divided into materials, labor, and overhead variances.
4. Have Bronx's managers done a good job or a poor job controlling material and labor costs? Why?
5. Describe how Bronx's managers can benefit from the standard costing system.

Using incomplete cost and variance information to determine the direct labor hours (Obj. 4)

P24-4A The State of Ohio has a shop that manufactures road signs used throughout the state. The manager of the shop uses standard costs to judge performance. Recently, a clerk mistakenly threw away some of the records, and the manager has only partial data for March. The manager knows that the direct labor flexible budget variance for the month was $350 U and that the standard labor price was $8 per hour. The shop experienced an unfavorable labor price variance of $0.40 per hour. The standard direct labor hours for actual March output were 3,500.

Required

1. Find the actual number of direct labor hours worked during March. First, find the actual direct labor price per hour. Then, determine the actual direct labor hours by setting up the computation of the direct labor flexible budget variance of $350 U.
2. Compute the direct labor price and efficiency variances. Do these variances suggest the manager may have made any tradeoffs? Explain.

P24-5A SportsTime manufactures T-shirts that it sells to other companies for customizing with their own logos. SportsTime prepares flexible budgets and uses a standard cost system to control manufacturing costs. The standard unit cost of a basic white T-shirt is based on static budget volume of 40,000 T-shirts per month. The unit cost is computed as follows:

Computing and journalizing, standard cost variances (Obj. 4, 5, 6)

Direct materials (2 sq. yd @ $0.25 per sq. yd)...............		$0.50
Direct labor (3 minutes @ $0.12 per minute)		0.36
Manufacturing overhead:		
Variable (3 minutes @ $0.06 per minute)	$0.18	
Fixed (3 minutes @ $0.14 per minute)	0.42	0.60
Total cost per T-shirt...		$1.46

Transactions during May of the current year included the following:

a. Actual production and sales were 42,700 T-shirts.
b. Actual direct materials usage was 1.80 square yards per T-shirt at an actual cost of $0.20 per square yard.
c. Actual direct labor usage of 130,000 minutes cost $18,850.
d. Actual overhead cost was $28,200.

Required

1. Compute the price and efficiency variances for direct materials and direct labor.
2. Journalize the usage of direct materials and the assignment of direct labor, including the related variances.
3. For manufacturing overhead, compute the total variance, the flexible budget variance, and the production volume variance.
4. SportsTime intentionally hired more skilled workers during May. How did this decision affect the cost variances? Overall, was the decision wise?

P24-6A School Tools manufactures ring binders. During August, the company produced and sold 104,000 binders and recorded the following cost data:

Computing standard cost variances and reporting to management (Obj. 4, 5, 7)

		Standard Unit Cost	Actual Total Cost
Direct materials:			
Standard (2 parts @ $0.12 per part)		$0.24	
Actual (209,500 parts @ $0.16 per part)			$33,520
Direct labor:			
Standard (0.02 hr @ $6.00 per hr)		0.12	
Actual (1,560 hr @ $6.20 per hr)			9,672
Manufacturing overhead:			
Standard:			
Variable (0.02 machine hr @ $6.00 per hr)	$0.12		
Fixed ($24,000 for static budget volume of			
100,000 units and 3,000 machine hours)	0.24	0.36	
Actual			45,500
Total manufacturing costs		$0.72	$88,692

Required

1. Compute the price and efficiency variances for direct materials and direct labor.
2. For manufacturing overhead, compute the total variance, the flexible budget variance, and the production volume variance.
3. Prepare a standard cost income statement through gross profit to report all variances to management. Sale price of the binders to college bookstores was $1.25 each.
4. School Tools' management used more experienced workers during August. Discuss the tradeoff between the two direct labor variances.

Preparing a flexible budget
income statement and graphing
cost behavior
(Obj. 1)

P24-1B ➤ *Link Back to Chapter 22, Exhibit 22-7 (page 899).* Medix Inc., produces and sells prepackaged first-aid kits. The company's static budget income statement for August 20X3 follows. It is based on expected sales volume of 55,000 kits.

MEDIX, INC.
Static Budget Income Statement
August 20X3

Sales revenue..............................	$220,000
Variable expenses:	
Cost of goods sold....................	60,500
Sales commissions...................	16,500
Utilities expense......................	5,500
Fixed expenses:	
Salary expense........................	36,500
Depreciation expense..............	24,000
Rent expense...........................	11,500
Utilities expense......................	6,200
Total expenses...........................	160,700
Operating income......................	$ 59,300

Medix's plant capacity is 62,500 kits. If actual volume exceeds 62,500 kits, the company must expand the plant. In that case, salaries will increase by 10%, depreciation by 15%, and rent by $6,000. Fixed utilities will be unchanged by any volume increase.

Required

1. Prepare flexible budget income statements for the company, showing output levels of 55,000, 60,000, and 65,000 kits.
2. Graph the behavior of the company's total costs.
3. Why might Medix's managers want to see the graph you prepared in requirement 2 as well as the columnar format analysis in requirement 1? What is the disadvantage of the graphic approach?

Preparing an income statement
performance report
(Obj. 2)

P24-2B Refer to Medix, Inc., of Problem 24-1B. The company sold 60,000 kits during August 20X3, and its actual operating income was as follows:

MEDIX, INC.
Income Statement
August 20X3

Sales revenue..............................	$245,000
Variable expenses:	
Cost of goods sold....................	$ 66,500
Sales commissions...................	21,000
Utilities expense......................	6,000
Fixed expenses:	
Salary expense.........................	38,000
Depreciation expense..............	24,000
Rent expense...........................	10,500
Utilities expense......................	6,200
Total expenses...........................	172,200
Operating income.......................	$ 72,800

Required

1. Prepare an income statement performance report for August 20X3.
2. What accounts for most of the difference between actual operating income and static budget operating income?
3. What is Medix's static budget variance? Explain why the income statement performance report provides Medix's managers with more useful information than the simple static budget variance. What insights can Medix's managers draw from this performance report?

P24-3B Multicast Co. assembles TVs and uses flexible budgeting and a standard cost system. Multicast allocates overhead based on the number of direct materials parts. The company's performance report includes the following selected data:

Preparing a flexible budget and computing standard cost variances
(Obj. 1, 3, 4, 5)

	Static Budget (20,000 TVs)	Actual Results (22,000 TVs)
Sales (20,000 TVs × $200)	$4,000,000	
(22,000 TVs × $210)		$4,620,000
Variable manufacturing expenses:		
Direct materials (200,000 parts @ $8.00)	1,600,000	
(214,200 parts @ $7.85)		1,681,470
Direct labor (40,000 hr @ $10.00)	400,000	
(42,500 hr @ $10.25)		435,625
Variable overhead (200,000 parts @ $2.00)	400,000	
(214,200 parts @ $2.05)		439,110
Fixed manufacturing expenses:		
Fixed overhead	600,000	610,000
Total cost of goods sold	3,000,000	3,166,205
Gross profit	$1,000,000	$1,453,795

Required

1. Prepare a flexible budget based on the actual number of TVs sold.
2. Compute the price variance and the efficiency variance for direct materials and for direct labor. For manufacturing overhead, compute the total variance, the flexible budget variance, and the production volume variance.
3. What is the total flexible budget variance for Multicast's manufacturing costs? Show how the total flexible budget variance is divided into materials, labor, and overhead variances.
4. Have Multicast's managers done a good job or a poor job controlling material and labor costs? Why?
5. Describe how Multicast's managers can benefit from the standard costing system.

P24-4B The City of Jackson has a shop that manufactures park benches. The manager of the shop uses standard costs to judge performance. Recently, a clerk mistakenly threw away some of the records, and the manager has only partial data for October. The manager knows that the direct labor flexible budget variance for the month was $404 F and that the standard labor price was $7.25 per hour. A recent pay cut caused a favorable labor price variance of $0.30 per hour. The standard direct labor hours for actual October output were 3,200.

Using incomplete cost and variance information to determine the number of direct labor hours worked
(Obj. 4)

Required

1. Find the actual number of direct labor hours worked during October. First, find the actual direct labor price per hour. Then, determine the actual number of direct labor hours worked by setting up the computation of the direct labor flexible budget variance of $404 F.
2. Compute the direct labor price and efficiency variances. Do these variances suggest the manager may have made any tradeoffs? Explain.

P24-5B Pacific Products manufactures fishing waders. The company prepares flexible budgets and uses a standard cost system to control manufacturing costs. The following standard unit cost of a pair of waders is based on the static budget volume of 14,000 pairs per month:

Computing and journalizing standard cost variances
(Obj. 4, 5, 6)

Direct materials (3.0 sq. ft @ $2.00 per sq. ft)		$ 6.00
Direct labor (2 hours @ $9.40 per hour)		18.90
Manufacturing overhead:		
Variable (2 hours @ $0.65 per hour)	$1.30	
Fixed (2 hours @ $2.20 per hour)	4.40	5.70
Total cost per pair		$30.60

Data for November of the current year include the following:

a. Actual production was 13,600 pair.
b. Actual direct materials usage was 2.70 square feet per pair of waders at an actual cost of $2.15 per square foot.
c. Actual direct labor usage of 24,480 hours cost $235,008.
d. Total actual overhead cost was $79,000.

Required

1. Compute the price and efficiency variances for direct materials and direct labor.
2. Journalize the usage of direct materials and the assignment of direct labor, including the related variances.
3. For manufacturing overhead, compute the total variance, the flexible budget variance, and the production volume variance.
4. Pacific Products' management intentionally purchased superior materials for November production. How did this decision affect the other cost variances? Overall, was the decision wise?

Computing standard cost variances and reporting to management (Obj. 4, 5, 7)

P24-6B Tucker Industries produces industrial plastics. During May, the company produced and sold 42,000 sheets of plastic and recorded the following cost data:

	Standard Unit Cost	Actual Total Cost
Direct materials:		
Standard (3 lb @ $1.25 per lb)	$3.75	
Actual (134,400 lb @ $1.20 per lb)		$161,280
Direct labor:		
Standard (0.1 hr @ $6.90 per hr)	0.69	
Actual (4,400 hr @ $6.80 per hr)		29,920
Manufacturing overhead:		
Standard:		
Variable (0.2 machine hr @ $7.00 per hr) $1.40		
Fixed ($64,000 for static budget volume of 40,000 units and 8,000 machine hours) 1.60	3.00	
Actual..		118,900
Total manufacturing costs.....................................	$7.44	$310,100

Required

1. Compute the price and efficiency variances for direct materials and direct labor.
2. For manufacturing overhead, compute the total variance, the flexible budget variance, and the production volume variance.
3. Prepare a standard cost income statement through gross profit to report all variances to management. Sale price of the plastic was $10.50 per sheet.
4. Tucker intentionally purchased cheaper materials during May. Was the decision wise? Discuss the tradeoff between the two materials variances.

APPLY YOUR KNOWLEDGE

DECISION CASES

Preparing a performance report and using it to evaluate performance (Obj. 1, 2)

Case 1. Source, Inc., distributes computer games to software retailers, including dot.coms. Source's top management meets monthly to evaluate the company's performance. Controller Jennifer Lee prepared the performance report on page 1013 for the meeting.

Lee also revealed that the actual sale price of $30 per game was equal to the budgeted sale price and that there were no changes in inventories for the month.

Management is disappointed by the operating income results. CEO Mark Baker exclaims, "How can actual operating income be roughly half the static budget amount when there are so many favorable variances?"

Required

1. Prepare a more informative performance report. Be sure to include a flexible budget for the actual number of computer games bought and sold.
2. As a member of Source's management team, which variances would you want investigated? Why?
3. Baker believes that many consumers are postponing purchases of new games until after the introduction of **Microsoft's** Xbox game machine. In light of this information, how would you rate the company's performance?

Efficiency variances and setting standards (Obj. 4)

Case 2. Assume you manage your local **McDonald's** restaurant. Your restaurant is chosen to test the company's "Made-for-You" kitchen system. The system eliminates batch

SOURCE, INC.
Income Statement Performance Report
Month Ended July 31, 2001

	Actual Result	Static Budget	Variance
Sales revenue	$2,010,000	$2,490,000	$480,000 U
Variable expenses:			
Cost of goods sold	891,750	1,162,000	270,250 F
Sales commissions	87,675	124,500	36,825 F
Shipping expense	48,000	62,250	14,250 F
Fixed expenses:			
Salary expense	331,200	320,250	10,950 U
Depreciation expense	229,500	234,750	5,250 F
Rent expense	128,250	128,250	–0–
Advertising expense	95,100	82,500	12,600 U
Total expenses	1,811,475	2,114,500	303,025 F
Operating income	$ 198,525	$ 375,500	$176,975 U

production and the use of holding bins, and allows patrons to customize their orders. You think the new system is a good idea given increasing competition in the fast-food market.

Customers like the new system, and your staff appears to be adapting, but you wonder whether the new system is as efficient as the old one. Efficiency is a special concern because your performance is evaluated in part on the restaurant's efficient use of materials and labor. Assume that your superiors consider efficiency variances greater than 5% unacceptable.

You decide to look at your restaurant's hamburger sales for a typical day. You find that the restaurant used 491 lbs. of hamburger patties and 72 hours of direct labor to produce and sell 2,000 hamburgers. Assume for simplicity that the standard quantity allowed for a hamburger is a quarter pound of meat and 0.03 hours (1.8 minutes) of direct labor. Further, assume that standard costs are $2 per pound for hamburger and $9 an hour for labor.

Required

1. Compute the efficiency variances for direct labor and direct materials.
2. Provide likely explanations for the variances. Do you have reason to be concerned about your performance evaluation? Explain.
3. Write a memo to McDonald's national office explaining your concern and suggesting a remedy. Your memo should take the following form:

Date:	_____
To:	McDonald's National Office
From:	_____
Subject:	"Made-for-you" kitchen system

ETHICAL ISSUE

Terry Tubbs is a bottling machine operator for Harmony, Inc., which produces dietary supplements and homeopathic medicines. Harmony uses standard costing.

Costs and benefits of standard cost systems (Obj. 3, 4)

Tubbs enters the beginning and ending times for each job on a computer touch screen. This provides the actual direct labor hours and machine hours used to compute labor and manufacturing overhead efficiency variances. When the machine is idle due to product changeover or production-line delays, Tubbs' labor cost is recorded as indirect labor.

Tubbs has become frustrated with the maintenance department's slow response to machinery problems. Now when his machinery is not running efficiently, he clocks off the job before it is actually finished so that his efficiency does not look bad. Tubbs believes that his performance evaluation should not suffer because of the maintenance department's slow response.

1. Explain the consequences of Tubbs' behavior.
2. Is Tubbs acting ethically? Explain. What should he do?
3. In computerized information systems, including enterprise resource planning (ERP) systems, production employees directly enter data into the system. What are the implications for accountants when the data are then used in the employee's evaluation, as with Terry Tubbs?

Deciding whether to accept an order in a standard costing system
(Obj. 2, 4, 5)

Cabletronix is a contract manufacturer of electronic components, including Cisco equipment cables. Cabletronix has a number of network installers who are regular customers for the company's cables. To grow its business, Cabletronix has joined a business-to-business trading community.

Sales manager Jenny Wang informs CEO Elizabeth Pronai of a potentially promising order for 1,000 Cisco-equivalent cables on the trading community's Web site. This is a large order, and Pronai recognizes that meeting the job's three-week deadline will require a coordinated effort by the cable division and may disrupt completion of some existing orders. Still, Pronai believes the company must move in this direction to be successful.

Pronai checks with Cabletronix purchasing manager Steve Hunt, who tells her that the company has the necessary supply of wire in stock, but the connectors must be rush-ordered. Production manager Tony Alvarez suggests that he could manage the production schedule by hiring a temporary worker and using overtime. Finally, Pronai asks Wang for a sale price that would give Cabletronix a good chance of landing the order. Based on the information these managers provided, Pronai sends the following e-mail:

Subject:	Special Web Cable Order
Date:	May 15, 2005
From:	Elizabeth <EPronai@Cabletronix.com>
To:	Tony <TAlvarez@Cabletronix.com>
	Steve <SHunt@Cabletronix.com>
	Jenny <JWang@Cabletronix.com>

Thanks for your quick response to my request for information on the feasibility of meeting the special order. I have summarized our expected "actual" quantities and costs. Please consider this information and let me know whether you think we should proceed with the bid. I need a response this afternoon. We may need to meet first thing in the morning to make a final decision.

Direct materials:	
Wire (3,200 feet @ $5 a foot)	$16,000
Connectors (2,400 @ $8.50 each)	$20,400
Direct labor (350 hours @ $26 per hour)	$9,100
Variable manufacturing overhead (350 hours @ $24 per hour)	
($24 per hour is the standard variable overhead rate)	$8,400
Fixed manufacturing overhead	No change
Sale price	$60 per cable

Required

Each member of your team should play the role of one of the four members of Cabletronix's management. Team members must exchange e-mails and decide when they will meet as a group, leaving enough time for each team member to perform his or her own analysis and provide the result to CEO Elizabeth Pronai before the meeting.

Jenny Wang: Unit sales volume and the sales revenue flexible budget variance are primary determinants of your own performance evaluation as sales manager. The standard sale price is $65 a cable. Before meeting with the entire team, determine whether bidding on the order is (1) in the company's interest and (2) in your own interest. As a starting point, prepare a contribution margin income statement for the order.

➡ Chapter 22, p. 890, discusses the contribution margin income statement.

Send an e-mail presenting your recommendation (and the analysis on which the recommendation is based) to CEO Elizabeth Pronai before the team meeting.

Steve Hunt: Before meeting with the entire team, determine whether bidding on the order is (1) in the company's interest and (2) in your own interest. As a starting point, prepare a contribution margin income statement for the order.

The direct materials price variances are primary determinants of your own performance evaluation as purchasing manager. Standard prices for the materials are: wire $5 a foot, connectors $7 each. Send an e-mail presenting your recommendation (and the analysis on which the recommendation is based) to CEO Elizabeth Pronai before the team meeting.

Tony Alvarez: Before meeting with the entire team, determine whether bidding on the order is (1) in the company's interest and (2) in your own interest. As a starting point, prepare a contribution margin income statement for the order.

The direct materials efficiency variances and the direct labor variances are important determinants of your own performance evaluation as production manager. Standard quantities for the materials are 3 feet of wire and 2 connectors per cable. The direct labor standards are 0.3 hours a cable at $21 an hour. Send an e-mail presenting your recommendation (and the analysis on which the recommendation is based) to CEO Elizabeth Pronai before the team meeting.

Elizabeth Pronai: Before meeting with the entire team, determine whether bidding on the order is in the company's interest. As a starting point, prepare a contribution margin income statement for the order.

Based on the e-mail received from your managers, lead the team meeting to (1) reach a consensus on whether accepting the order is in the best interests of the company, (2) recognize any concerns the managers may have, and (3) lead the team discussion in how Cabletronix can address their concerns. After the team meeting, prepare an e-mail for distribution to managers that summarizes the team's final decision and supporting discussion.

INTERNET EXERCISE

Vail Resorts, Inc., is a holding company operating in two business segments, mountain resorts and real-estate development. For the mountain resort segment, revenues and expenses can vary widely depending on the amount of snow and other weather conditions. Assume that to plan for these differences, each year Vail Resorts prepares a flexible budget with three levels of operating activity. Use *only* operating revenues and operating expenses to answer the following questions:

1. Go to **http://www.Forbes.com** and under "Stocks," type **MTN,** the stock symbol for Vail Resorts, Inc., and click on *Go.* In the left-hand column, click on *Financials.* Assume the average mountain resort guest pays $1,000 for lodging, meals, entertainment, and lift tickets and that 30% of resort expenses are fixed costs. For the most recent year, how many guests were served? What is the variable cost per resort guest (rounded to the nearest whole dollar)?
2. Corporate expense and depreciation and amortization are fixed costs. Assume real-estate revenue and expense is not expected to change next year. Prepare a flexible budget income statement for 375,000 guests; 450,000 guests; and 525,000 guests.
3. The company understands its competition is not only other mountain resorts but also alternative leisure activities. In the left-hand column, click on *Competitors.* Identify other types of companies competing for the leisure and recreational dollar.
4. In an effort to stay competitive in the leisure and recreation industry, Vail Resorts compares its financial statistics with industry averages. In the left-hand column under "Company Info," click on *Profile.* Does Vail Resorts compare favorably or unfavorably with the industry average for net profit margin (return on sales), return on equity, current ratio, and three-year revenue growth?

Vail Resorts

Go to the "Flexible Budgeting and Variances" episode on the *Mastering Accounting* CD-ROM for an interactive, video-enhanced exercise that presents CanGo's managers with a problem. The company uses flexible budgeting and variances to determine actual costs for wages and raw materials. When managers want to know why a certain division is performing poorly, they discover that the conclusions they reach from the reports depend on who reviews the report and how data for the budget variances are analyzed.

25

Activity-Based Costing and Other Cost Management Tools

Dell Computer pioneered custom-building computers for individual orders on a just-in-time basis. But when the company reported its first-ever quarterly loss several years ago, CEO Michael Dell had to act quickly to turn the company around.

Dell decided to focus on the company's most profitable products. But which products were they? The accounting system traced direct materials and direct labor to individual product lines, but did not do a good job matching indirect costs with the specific products that caused those costs.

Dell needed a more finely tuned cost accounting system. The answer was *activity-based costing (ABC)*. Employee teams identified the ten most important indirect activities from all elements of the value chain—for example, purchases of raw materials, indirect assembly labor, and warranty service. Then, *for each activity,* the teams developed a separate indirect cost allocation rate.

The goal was to assign the cost of each activity to the product lines that caused that activity's cost. For example:

- Purchasing costs are assigned based on the number of different "part numbers" in a product.
- Indirect assembly labor is assigned based on the number of times the product is "touched."
- Warranty costs are assigned based on the number of service calls (failure rate) for the product line.

ABC costing is more accurate than simpler cost systems that combine the indirect costs of many activities into a single cost pool and then allocate these costs using a single allocation base, often direct labor or machine hours. Such a crude assignment of indirect costs can lead to a hit-or-miss pricing structure.

Has ABC worked for Dell? In 2000, Dell was earning record profits. The Controller of Dell Americas Operations says: "Activity-based costing has really allowed Dell to go to the next level of understanding of its profitability for each of the products it sells."

Given the rapidly changing costs in the computer industry, Dell uses ABC costs for pricing its computers every day. Each month, Dell reanalyzes the profitability of each product line. ABC also helps Dell's managers find ways to cut costs, especially by highlighting non-value-added activities such as inventory storage.

To thrive in a globally competitive market, **Dell Computer** must provide customers with goods or services at an attractive price, while managing costs so the company still earns a profit. This is called delivering value to the customer. This chapter will show you several methods managers use to deliver value to the customer at a profit:

- Activity-based costing
- Activity-based management and target costing
- Just-in-time systems
- Costs of quality

These methods, largely unheard of 15 years ago, are now routinely used by companies like **Dell, General Motors,** and **Toyota.** Before discussing activity-based costing and activity-based management, we first consider why companies need more detailed and accurate cost systems.

REFINING COST SYSTEMS

The Need for Refined Cost Systems

To allocate indirect costs to cost objects like departments or products, companies use average allocation rates. The broader the indirect cost pool used in the numerator of the allocation rate, and the broader the allocation base used in the denominator, the less accurate the resulting cost allocation. Similarly, the narrower the cost pools and cost allocation bases, the more refined the average rates and the more accurate the cost allocation. A simple example shows that organizations from **Dell Computer,** to **Carolina Power and Light,** to the **IRS** and the **U.S. Postal Service,** are developing more refined costing systems like ABC. Why? Because simple systems that do not match costs with the consumption of resources can assign costs inaccurately and inequitably.

David Larimer, Matt Sewell, and Marc Bryan are three college friends who decide to room together during their sophomore year. They agree to share on an equal basis the following monthly costs:

Rent and utilities............................	$570
Cable TV.......................................	50
High-speed Internet access..............	40
Groceries	240
Total monthly costs	$900

Each roommate's share is $300 ($900/3).

Things go smoothly for the first few months. But then David calls a meeting. "Since I started having dinner at Amy's each night, I shouldn't have to chip in for the groceries." Matt then pipes in: "I'm so busy studying and surfing the Net that I never have time to watch TV. I don't want to pay for the cable TV anymore." And, he continues, "Marc, since your friend Jennifer eats here most evenings, you should pay a double share of the grocery bill." Marc retorts, "If that's the way you feel, Matt, then you should pay for the Internet access, since you're the only one around here who uses it!"

What happened? The friends originally agreed to share the costs equally. But they soon discover that they are not participating equally in three costly activities: watching cable TV, surfing the Net, and eating. Equal assignment of the costs is therefore not equitable.

The roommates could use a refined approach that better matches the costs with the people who participate in each activity. This means splitting the cable TV costs between David and Marc, assigning the Internet access cost to Matt, and allocating the grocery bill 1/3 to Matt and 2/3 to Marc. Exhibit 25-1 compares the results of this refined system with the original system.

EXHIBIT 25-1   **More Refined Versus Less Refined Cost Allocation System**

	David Larimer	Matt Sewell	Marc Bryan	Total
More refined cost allocation system:				
Rent and utilities......................................	$190	$190	$190	$570
Cable TV...	25	—	25	50
High-speed Internet access.........................	—	40	—	40
Groceries	—	80	160	240
Total costs allocated.................................	$215	$310	$375	$900
Less refined original cost allocation system	$300	$300	$300	$900
Difference	$ (85)	$ 10	$ 75	$ 0

No wonder David called a meeting! The original system allocated him $300 a month, but the refined system shows that a more equitable share would be only $215. On the other hand, the new system allocates Marc $375 a month instead of $300. David was paying for resources he did not consume (Internet access and groceries), while Marc was not paying for all the resources (groceries) he and his guest consumed. We could say that David was "overcosted" and Marc was "undercosted."

Notice, however, that the total monthly costs are the same ($900) under both systems. The only difference is how that $900 is allocated among the three roommates. The amount by which David is "overcosted" ($85) must exactly equal the amounts by which Matt and Marc are "undercosted" ($10 + $75).

In a highly competitive, globally wired marketplace, companies from **Coca-Cola** to **Dell Computer** need to know how much it costs to bring each product to market. Dell needs to know what it costs to assemble and deliver a customized laptop to a client in Eugene, Oregon. Why? So Dell can set a price that covers the costs of all the resources required to assemble and deliver that specific laptop (and provide some profit), yet remain competitive with prices charged by **Gateway** and **Compaq.**

Sharpening the Focus: From Business Functions, to Departments, to Activities

Refining the cost system requires drilling down from the six broad business functions that compose the value chain, to individual departments in each function, to specific activities in those departments.

Panel A of Exhibit 25-2 lists these six broad value-chain functions for a manufacturer: R&D, design, production, marketing, distribution, customer service. In Chapter 19, we showed that companies need to know the full costs (from all elements of the value chain) to set sale prices that cover all these costs, and to determine the profitability of different products. ➥ However, remember that under GAAP, only costs incurred in the production element of the value chain are inventoriable for financial reporting. Since most companies begin refining their cost systems in the production/manufacturing function, our discussion and examples focus on this function. But managers in companies like **Dell** and **Dow Chemical** can apply the same principles to costs incurred in other elements of the value chain.

◄ For full value-chain costs discussion, see Chapter 19, pp. 759–760.

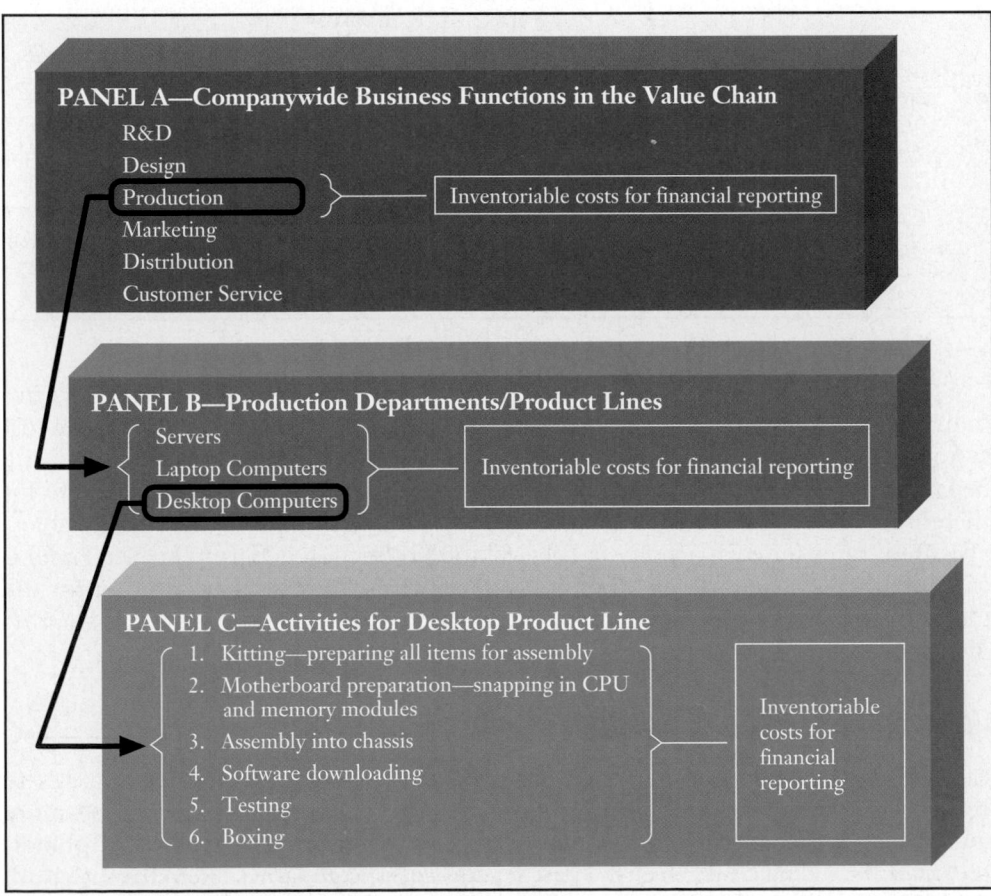

EXHIBIT 25-2
Overview of Business Functions, Departments, and Activities

Panel B of Exhibit 25-2 shows that the production function is divided into departments (servers, laptop computers, and desktop computers). Panel C then zeroes in on the desktop computer production department, and lists six common activities in assembling desktop computers. Managers need to know the costs of cost objects at each level:

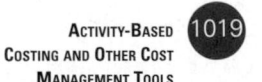

- Business functions—such as Dell Computer's production function
- Departments—such as Dell's desktop production line
- Activities—such as Dell's assembly or software downloading activities in the desktop production department

Exhibit 25-3 shows that when managers limited their focus to broad business functions, simple cost systems that allocated indirect costs using broad-based averages were often good enough to meet their needs. As increasing competition forced managers to drill down to individual departments within a function, companies often developed separate indirect cost allocation rates for each individual department. Rather than using a plantwide manufacturing overhead rate, for example, the company could develop one overhead rate for the server production department and another rate for the desktop production department.

Exhibit 25-3
Sharpening the Business Focus

Managers Focus on:	Indirect Cost Allocation System:
Broad business functions, such as production	Single functionwide indirect cost allocation rate—for example, a plantwide manufacturing overhead rate
↓	↓
Departments within a function, such as the server, laptop, and desktop computer production departments	Separate indirect cost allocation rates for each different department—for example, separate manufacturing overhead rates for the server, laptop, and desktop production departments
↓	↓
Activities within a department, such as the kitting, motherboard preparation, and assembly activities in the desktop computer production department	Specific indirect cost allocation rates for each activity within a department—for example, one indirect cost allocation rate for kitting, a separate rate for motherboard preparation, and so on. The indirect cost allocation rate for each activity uses a different cost driver.

Now managers are drilling down farther to focus on specific activities within individual departments. Exhibit 25-3 shows that companies further refine their cost systems to develop separate indirect cost allocation rates for each activity within a department. For example, rather than using one manufacturing overhead rate for the entire desktop production department, they may develop separate indirect cost allocation rates for each activity in the desktop production department. See Panel C of Exhibit 25-2: There is one allocation rate for the kitting activity, another for the motherboard preparation activity, and so on. Such a refined system is called an *activity-based costing system*.

Objective 1
Describe and develop activity-based costs (ABC)

➤ Controlling direct material and direct labor costs, see Chapter 24, pp. 984–991.

ACTIVITY-BASED COSTING (ABC).
A system that focuses on activities as the fundamental cost objects. The costs of those activities become building blocks for compiling costs as ABC links costs to the activities that cause those costs.

ACTIVITY-BASED COSTING

Chapter 24 showed how managers use standard costing and variance analysis to control direct material and direct labor costs. ◄ But most managers need more than the aggregate manufacturing overhead flexible budget variance to control indirect manufacturing costs. Over the past several years, companies like **Allied Signal, Coca-Cola,** and **Carrier Corporation** have developed refined systems like ABC to help control indirect costs.

Activity-based costing (ABC) focuses on *activities* as the fundamental cost objects. The costs of those activities become building blocks for compiling costs, as ABC links costs to the activities that cause those costs. Activity-based costing can be used with job costing or process costing. Financial institutions like **American Express** and hospitals also use ABC.

ABC systems trace direct materials and direct labor to cost objects, as described in Chapter 20. ➡ The only difference is that ABC systems make more effort to allocate *indirect costs*—such as manufacturing overhead—to the products that caused these costs.

 See Chapter 20, pp. 802–806, to review how direct materials and direct labor are traced to cost objects.

Many companies start out using a simple system that combines all the indirect costs into a single cost pool, and then allocates those costs using a single allocation base. This may not work if

1. *The allocation base is not a cost driver.* Recall that a *cost driver* is any factor whose change causes a change in a related total cost. For example, in a highly automated production process, most overhead costs are not related to direct labor, so direct labor is not the main driver of overhead costs.

⊙ DAILY EXERCISE 25-1

2. *One allocation base is insufficient.* In most companies, no *single* factor drives all indirect costs.

In either case, allocation bases that are not cost drivers lead to inaccurate product costs.

Activity-based costing reduces these problems by separately estimating the indirect costs of each activity, and then allocating those costs based on what caused the costs. Each activity's indirect cost has its own (usually unique) cost allocation base, or cost driver. For example, **Dell's** ABC system allocates indirect assembly labor costs based on the number of times workers touch a computer as it moves through assembly. A computer that requires more touches is allocated more of the indirect assembly labor activity cost than a model that requires fewer touches. Exhibit 25-4 lists common activities and related cost drivers.

EXHIBIT 25-4
Activities and Cost Drivers

Activity	Cost Driver
Materials purchasing	Number of purchase orders
Materials handling	Number of parts
Production scheduling	Number of batches
Quality inspections	Number of inspections
Photocopying	Number of pages copied
Warranty services	Number of service calls
Shipping	Number of pounds

Accountants have long known that product costs would be more accurate if companies allocated indirect costs using several cost drivers. Until recently, however, it was too expensive to develop multiple-cost-driver cost systems. However, "data warehouses" and other information technology have made ABC feasible. Optical scanning and bar coding reduce the cost of collecting activity costs and cost driver information. Powerful enterprise resource planning (ERP) systems like SAP, Oracle, and Peoplesoft now contain ABC applications. Or companies can buy specialized ABC software or develop their own. Dell began its ABC system using Excel spreadsheets.

Dell builds the manufacturing cost of each computer from the direct costs plus the indirect costs of the specific activities required to produce it. This buildup of *manufacturing costs* determines the inventoriable product cost used for *financial reporting*. However, for internal decisions such as pricing and product profitability analysis, Dell also assigns the costs of nonmanufacturing activities to products. For example, Dell assigns the costs of the warranty service activity to product lines based on the number of service calls.

Developing an Activity-Based Costing System

The main difference between ABC and traditional systems is that ABC systems have separate indirect cost allocation rates for each activity. ABC requires seven steps:

⊙ DAILY EXERCISE 25-2

1. Identify the activities.
2. Estimate the total indirect costs of each activity.
3. Identify the allocation base for each activity's indirect costs—this is the primary cost driver.

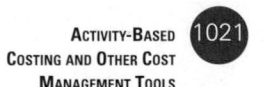

4. Estimate the total quantity of each allocation base.
5. Compute the cost allocation rate for each activity:

$$\text{Cost allocation rate for activity} = \frac{\text{Estimated total indirect costs of activity}}{\text{Estimated total quantity of cost allocation base}}$$

6. Obtain the actual quantity of each allocation base used by the cost object (for example, the quantity used by a particular product).
7. Allocate the costs to the cost object:

$$\text{Allocated activity cost} = \text{Cost allocation rate for activity} \times \text{Actual quantity of cost allocation base used by the cost object}$$

The first step in developing an activity-based costing system is identifying the activities. Analyzing all the activities required to make a product forces managers to think about how each activity might be improved—or whether the activity is necessary at all. Steps 2–7 are the same approach used to allocate manufacturing overhead, as explained in Chapter 20. The only difference is that ABC systems repeat steps 2–7 for each activity.

Traditional Versus Activity-Based Costing Systems: Chemtech

We use a streamlined example to emphasize the distinctions between ABC systems and traditional costing systems. Our example necessarily simplifies the process that would occur in a real company, which might identify more than 50 different activities.

Chemtech's Chemical Manufacturing Department produces hundreds of different chemicals. The company has focused on producing mass quantities of "commodity" chemicals for many large customers. It also manufactures small quantities of specialty chemicals for individual customers.

Last updated in 1990, the Chemical Manufacturing Department's cost system uses a single indirect cost pool and allocates manufacturing overhead at 200% of direct labor cost. Chemtech's controller, Martha Wise, gathered data for two of the department's many products:

- Aldehyde—a commodity chemical used in producing plastics
- Phenylephrine hydrochloride (PH)—a specialty chemical (A single customer uses PH in blood-pressure medications.)

	Aldehyde	Phenylephrine Hydrochloride (PH)
Number of pounds per year	7,000 lb	5 lb
Direct materials cost per pound	$5	$20
Direct labor cost per pound...................	$1	$10
Sale price per pound	$10	$70

Wise used this information to compute each product's gross profit, as shown in Exhibit 25-5.

EXHIBIT 25-5
Chemtech's Traditional Cost System—Product Cost and Gross Profit

DAILY EXERCISE 25-4

DAILY EXERCISE 25-10

	Aldehyde	PH
Sale price per pound	$10.00	$70.00
Less: Manufacturing cost per pound:		
Direct materials...	5.00	20.00
Direct labor	1.00	10.00
Manufacturing overhead (at 200% of direct labor cost)	2.00	20.00
Total manufacturing cost per pound	8.00	50.00
Gross profit per pound	$ 2.00	$20.00

The gross profit for the PH (phenylephrine hydrochloride) specialty chemical is $20 per pound—ten times as high as the gross profit for the aldehyde commodity chemical ($2). Chemtech CEO Randy Smith is surprised that PH appears so much more profitable (per pound) than aldehyde. He asks Wise to check 50 of the department's other products. Wise confirms that the gross profit per pound is ten times as high for specialty chemicals as it is for commodity chemicals. As a result, Smith wonders whether Chemtech should switch its focus to specialty chemicals.

WORK IT OUT

1. What is the *total* direct labor cost assigned to
   a. Aldehyde?
   b. PH (phenylephrine hydrochloride)?
2. What is the *total* manufacturing overhead allocated to
   a. Aldehyde?
   b. PH?

Answers

1. Total direct labor cost assigned to aldehyde is 7,000 pounds × $1 per pound = $7,000. Total direct labor cost assigned to PH is 5 pounds × $10 per pound = $50. Thus, Chemtech assigns to aldehyde 140 times as much total direct labor cost as it does to PH ($7,000 ÷ $50 = 140).
2. **Key Point:** Because Chemtech uses direct labor cost as its single allocation base, Chemtech also allocates 140 times as much total overhead to aldehyde as to PH. Total overhead allocated to aldehyde is 7,000 pounds × $2 per pound = $14,000. Total overhead allocated to PH is 5 pounds × $20 per pound = $100. Thus, the direct labor single-allocation-base system allocates 140 times as much total overhead to aldehyde as to PH ($14,000 ÷ $100). This traditional costing procedure is accurate only if aldehyde really does cause 140 times as much overhead as PH. That is, the existing system assumes that direct labor really is the primary overhead cost driver.

CEO Smith calls a meeting with the department foreman Steve Pronai and controller Wise. Smith is perplexed that the accounting numbers show specialty chemicals are more profitable (on a per-pound basis) than commodity chemicals. He expected the department would be more efficient producing a few commodity chemicals (in a few very large batches) than producing a wide variety of specialty chemicals (in many small batches). Foreman Pronai echoes Smith's concern. Pronai says it takes just as long to mix a small batch of specialty chemicals as a large batch of commodity chemicals. Finally, Smith is puzzled because Chemtech's competitors seem to be earning good profits, even though they usually undercut Chemtech's prices on commodity chemicals.

Wise fears that the problem could be Chemtech's cost accounting system. For years she had tried to get Smith to update the costing system, but Smith chose to invest in new equipment and in marketing. Now Wise has Smith's attention. Wise suggests that foreman Pronai and the plant engineer work with her to develop a pilot ABC system for part of the Chemical Manufacturing Department's operations. Exhibit 25-6 on the following page compares the original direct labor single-allocation-base system (Panel A) with the new ABC system (Panel B).

In developing their new system, Chemtech's ABC team followed the seven steps:

Step 1. Identify the activities.

Wise and her team identify three activities in the Chemical Manufacturing Department: mixing, processing, and testing. See Exhibit 25-7, page 1025, column 1.

Step 1: Identify activities

Step 2. Estimate the total indirect costs of each activity.

Pronai estimates that total mixing costs for all products will be $600,000. Estimated costs for each activity appear in Exhibit 25-7, column 2.

Step 2: Estimate indirect cost of each activity

Step 3. Identify the allocation base for each activity's indirect costs—the primary cost driver.

Workers mix ingredients separately for each batch of chemicals, so the number of batches drives mixing costs. Exhibit 25-7, column 3, lists the allocation base (cost driver) for each activity.

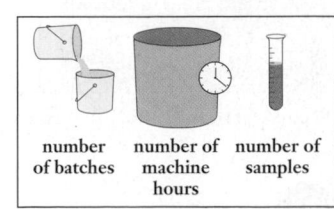

number of batches / number of machine hours / number of samples

Step 3: Identify allocation bases

EXHIBIT 25-6
Chemtech's Traditional and ABC Systems

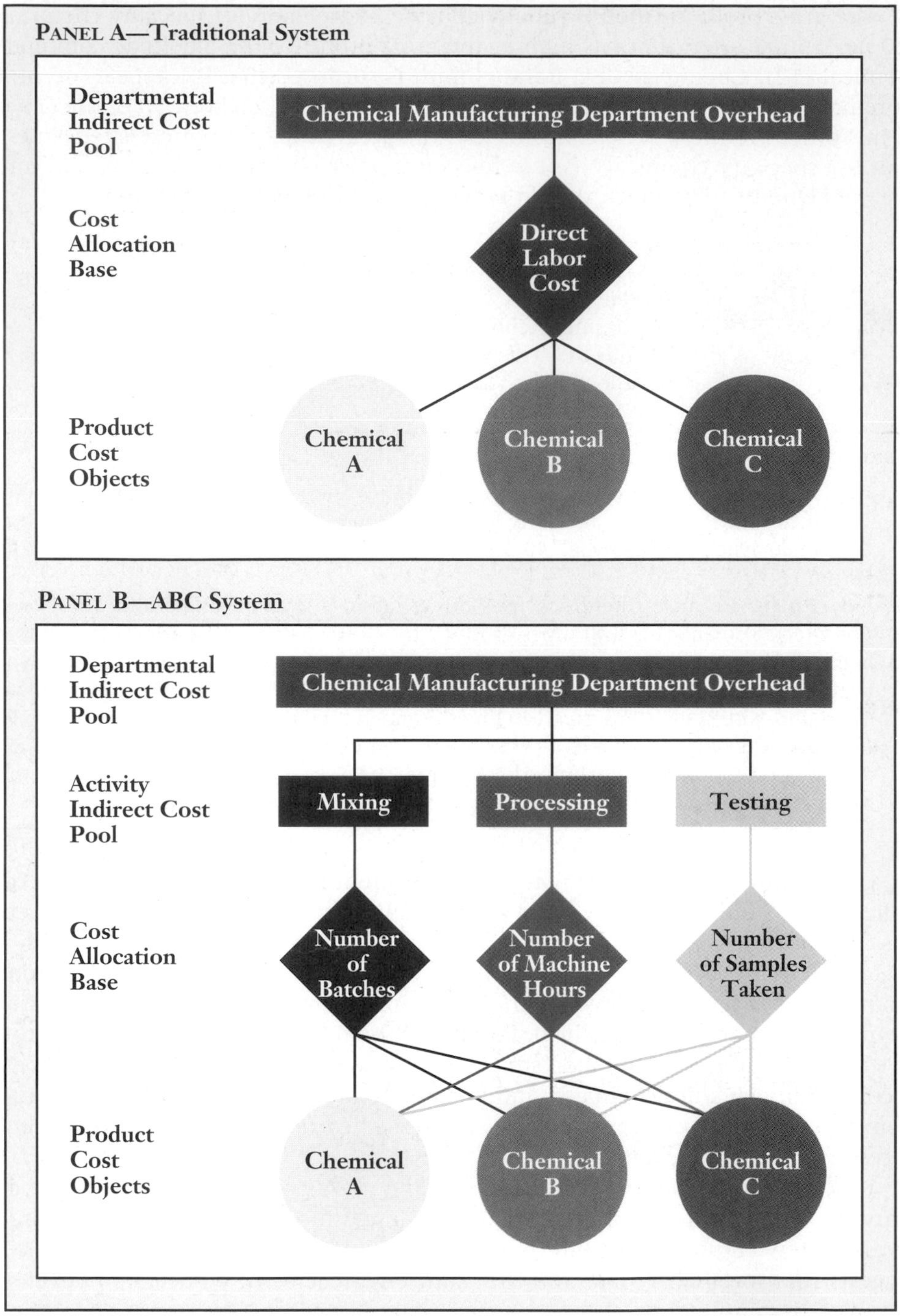

PANEL A—Traditional System

Departmental Indirect Cost Pool	Chemical Manufacturing Department Overhead
Cost Allocation Base	Direct Labor Cost
Product Cost Objects	Chemical A Chemical B Chemical C

PANEL B—ABC System

Departmental Indirect Cost Pool	Chemical Manufacturing Department Overhead
Activity Indirect Cost Pool	Mixing Processing Testing
Cost Allocation Base	Number of Batches Number of Machine Hours Number of Samples Taken
Product Cost Objects	Chemical A Chemical B Chemical C

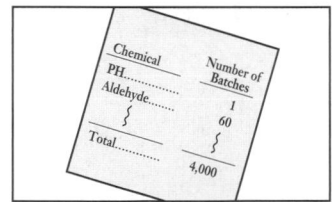

Chemical	Number of Batches
PH	1
Aldehyde	60
Total	4,000

Step 4: Estimate quantity of each allocation base

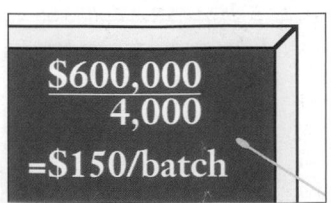

$$\frac{\$600,000}{4,000} = \$150/\text{batch}$$

Step 5: Compute allocation rates

Step 4. Estimate the total quantity of each allocation base.

Wise and Pronai estimate that the department will produce a total of 4,000 batches of chemicals. Estimated quantities of the cost driver allocation bases appear in column 4 of Exhibit 25-7.

Step 5. Compute the cost allocation rate for each activity.

Wise computes the allocation rate for mixing, as follows:

$$\frac{\text{Cost allocation rate}}{\text{for mixing}} = \frac{\$600,000}{4,000 \text{ batches}}$$

$$= \$150 \text{ per batch}$$

Column 5 of Exhibit 25-7 shows the cost allocation rate for each activity.

EXHIBIT 25-7   Chemtech's Activity-Based Costing System

(1) Activity	(2) Estimated Costs	(3) Cost Allocation Base	(4) Estimated Quantity of Cost Allocation Base	(5) Cost Allocation Rate	(6) Actual Quantity of Cost Allocation Base Used by:		(7) Allocated Activity Cost	
					Aldehyde	PH	Aldehyde	PH
Mixing	$600,000	# Batches	4,000 batches	$\frac{\$600,000}{4,000} = \$150/batch$	60 batches	1 batch	$150 × 60 = $9,000	$150 × 1 = $150
Processing	$3,000,000	# Machine hours (MH)	50,000 MH	$\frac{\$3,000,000}{50,000} = \$60/MH$	30 1/2 MH	2 MH	$60 × 30 1/2 = $1,830	$60 × 2 = $120
Testing	$600,000	# Samples	3,000 samples	$\frac{\$600,000}{3,000} = \$200/sample$	14 samples	1 sample	$200 × 14 = $2,800	$200 × 1 = $200

Step 6. Obtain the actual quantity of each allocation base used by each product.

During the year, Chemtech produces 60 batches of aldehyde and 1 batch of PH. (This total of 61 batches is only a small fraction of the 4,000 total batches Chemtech produces. The remaining batches consist of Chemtech's other chemicals.) Exhibit 25-7, column 6, shows the actual quantities of each activity's allocation base used by aldehyde and PH.

Step 6: Obtain actual quantities of each allocation base

Step 7. Allocate the costs to each product.

Wise allocates mixing costs as follows:

> **Aldehyde:** 60 batches × $150 per batch = $9,000
> **PH:** 1 batch   × $150 per batch = $ 150

Column 7 of Exhibit 25-7 shows the cost allocation for all three activities.

Wise then recomputes manufacturing overhead costs (Panel A) and gross profit (Panel B), as shown in Exhibit 25-8. For each product, Wise adds the total costs of the three activities to obtain the total manufacturing overhead allocated to each product. Panel A shows that total ABC overhead is $13,630 for aldehyde and $470 for PH. As in the original direct labor single-allocation-base system, this multiple-allocation-base ABC system allocates more *total* overhead to aldehyde, because

Step 7: Allocate costs

PANEL A — Manufacturing Overhead Per Pound

	Aldehyde	PH
Mixing (from Exhibit 25-7)	$ 9,000	$150
Processing (from Exhibit 25-7)	1,830	120
Testing (from Exhibit 25-7)	2,800	200
Total manufacturing overhead	$13,630	$470
Divide by number of pounds	÷ 7,000 lb	÷ 5 lb
Manufacturing overhead per pound	$1.95 /lb*	$94 /lb

* Rounded

PANEL B — Gross Profit Per Pound

	Aldehyde	PH
Sale price	$10.00	$ 70.00
Less: Manufacturing costs:		
Direct materials	$ 5.00	$ 20.00
Direct labor	1.00	10.00
Manufacturing overhead (from Panel A)	1.95	94.00
Total manufacturing cost	7.95	124.00
Gross profit (Loss)	$ 2.05	$(54.00)

EXHIBIT 25-8
Chemtech's Activity-Based Costing System

◉ DAILY EXERCISE 25-6

◉ DAILY EXERCISE 25-7

◉ DAILY EXERCISE 25-13

◉ DAILY EXERCISE 25-14

Chemtech produces much more aldehyde than PH. However, there is a big difference in the *ratio* of overhead allocated to aldehyde versus PH. The ABC system allocates only 29 times as much overhead to aldehyde as to PH ($13,630 ÷ $470 = 29). This is much less than in the original direct-labor-based system, which allocated 140 times as much overhead to aldehyde as to PH (see Work It Out on page 1023).

DAILY EXERCISE 25-5

After totaling the manufacturing overhead costs for each product, Wise computes the overhead cost per pound, as shown in Exhibit 25-8, Panel A. For aldehyde, Wise divides the $13,630 total manufacturing overhead by the 7,000 pounds of aldehyde produced, to get an overhead cost per pound of $1.95 (rounded). For PH, the ABC overhead cost per pound is $94.00 ($470 ÷ 5 pounds).

Compare the overhead cost per pound under the original direct-labor-based system with the ABC costs:

	Overhead Cost Per Pound	
	Traditional Direct Labor System (Exhibit 25-5)	ABC System (Exhibit 25-8)
Aldehyde..............	$ 2.00	$ 1.95
PH.........................	20.00	94.00

Which approach is more accurate? *ABC costs are more accurate because ABC takes into account the resources (mixing costs, machine time, and testing) each product actually uses.* The old direct labor single-allocation-base system allocated too much overhead to the product that uses more total direct labor (aldehyde) and too little overhead to the product that uses less total direct labor (PH). The simpler system *overcosted* aldehyde and *undercosted* PH.

DAILY EXERCISE 25-15

With more precise allocations, ABC shifts costs out of aldehyde and into PH where the costs belong. Why? Exhibit 25-7 shows that aldehyde uses more of each activity's resources than PH, but *not* 140 times as much. Column 6 shows that aldehyde uses 60 times as much mixing, about 15 times as many machine hours (processing costs), and 14 times as much testing as PH.

Although Chemtech made only 5 pounds of PH, this product still required

- Workers to mix a batch, at a mixing cost of $150
- 2 machine hours at $60 per hour
- One sample tested at a cost of $200

Spreading these costs over the 5 pounds of PH yields an overhead cost of $94 per pound, as shown in Exhibit 25-8, Panel A.

Allocating overhead based on actual *usage* of the resources increases the costs of low-volume products like PH that are produced in small batches. Why? Because costs like mixing and testing a batch are spread over the small number of units in that batch. On the other hand, mixing and testing costs are spread over the larger number of pounds for high-volume products that are produced in large batches, like aldehyde.

Controller Martha Wise is now ready to recompute product costs and gross profit using the ABC data. Exhibit 25-8, Panel B, shows that the cost per pound of aldehyde is $7.95 under the ABC system. Contrast this with the $8.00 cost per pound under Chemtech's original system (Exhibit 25-5). More important, the ABC data in Exhibit 25-8 show that specialty chemical PH costs $124 per pound, rather than the $50 per pound as indicated by the old system (Exhibit 25-5). Exhibit 25-8, Panel B shows that by selling PH for $70 per pound, Chemtech has been losing $54 on each pound—and this is *before* considering nonmanufacturing costs such as R&D, marketing, and distribution. Wise finds that most of Chemtech's other specialty chemicals show similar increases in cost under the ABC system.

The Chemtech example shows how dramatically ABC can affect product costs. In many cases, ABC systems show that companies lose money on low-volume products like Chemtech's specialty chemicals. One business consultant says: "20% of a company's products usually produce 80% of its profits." ABC spurs many companies to cut money-losing products.

ACTIVITY-BASED MANAGEMENT: USING ABC FOR DECISION MAKING

Activity-based management (ABM) refers to using activity-based cost information to make decisions that increase profits while satisfying customers' needs. We consider how Chemtech can use ABC information in three kinds of decisions: (1) pricing and product mix, (2) cost reduction, and (3) routine planning and control.

Pricing and Product Mix Decisions

Exhibit 25-9 compares key cost and gross profit information for aldehyde and PH, based on Chemtech's original cost system and then on the new ABC system. ABC shows that PH costs Chemtech $124 rather than the $50 reported by the old cost system. Chemtech is losing $54 on every pound of PH—*before* considering nonmanufacturing costs!

Objective 2
Use ABC data, and activity-based management (ABM) to make business decisions

ACTIVITY-BASED MANAGEMENT. Using activity-based cost information to make decisions that increase profits while satisfying customers' needs.

 DAILY EXERCISE 25-3

 DAILY EXERCISE 25-16

EXHIBIT 25-9
Comparison of Chemtech's Product Costs Under Original Versus ABC Systems

	Aldehyde	PH
Original cost system (from Exhibit 25-5):		
Sale price per pound	$10.00	$ 70.00
Less: Manufacturing cost per pound	8.00	50.00
Gross profit per pound	$ 2.00	$ 20.00
Activity-based cost system (from Exhibit 25-8):		
Sale price per pound	$10.00	$ 70.00
Less: Manufacturing cost per pound	7.95	124.00
Gross profit per pound	$ 2.05	$(54.00)

Chemtech may be able to use the ABC analysis to find ways to cut costs. If it cannot cut costs enough to earn a profit on PH, then it will have to consider raising the sale price. If customers will not pay a higher price, Chemtech should consider dropping PH. More generally, if the ABC system shows that commodity chemicals are more profitable than Chemtech thought, and specialty chemicals are less profitable, Chemtech may shift its product mix away from specialty chemicals toward commodity chemicals. This is the exact opposite of the strategy suggested by cost data from the original system.

Cost Reduction Decisions

Most companies adopt ABC to get more accurate product costs for pricing and product mix decisions. But managers often find that they reap even greater benefits by using ABM to pinpoint opportunities to cut costs.

VALUE ENGINEERING   With an ABC system in place, organizations can use value engineering to reduce costs. **Value engineering** means systematically evaluating activities in an effort to reduce costs while satisfying customer needs. Companies conduct value engineering using cross-functional teams: marketers identify customer needs, engineers and production personnel design more efficient processes and products, and accountants estimate how proposed changes will affect costs.

Carrier Corporation, the world's largest manufacturer of air conditioning and heating products, assembled a cross-functional team that used ABM in a value engineering drive to minimize complexity or variety in products, component parts, and manufacturing processes. The goal is to cut by half the 280 different circuit breakers and 580 different fasteners used in its products. Slashing the number of different component parts will significantly cut Carrier's ordering costs, since ABC often estimates that purchase orders cost up to $100–$200 each. It will also cut receiving,

VALUE ENGINEERING. Systematically evaluating activities in an effort to reduce costs while satisfying customer needs.

 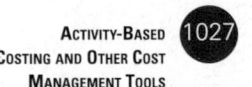

inspection, and materials-handling costs. Carrier may benefit from quantity discounts on larger orders of the remaining parts. Since experts estimate that 75–90% of a product's costs are locked in when the design is set, design changes usually present the greatest opportunities to slash costs. Even the U.S. government is getting in on the ABM act. The Internal Revenue Service recently used ABM to simplify its processes, improve the quality of its services, and cut costs.

e-Accounting

Point, Click, Buy, Sell: Businesses Cut Costs by Buying and Selling Online

The cost of processing a single purchase order for direct or indirect materials is about $175. Make that same purchase online, however, and the cost drops to as little as $10. With the electronic connection of buyers and suppliers, all authorized users in the buying organization can initiate purchases from their desktops. Companies can automate processes and access critical information across continents, business units, divisions, and departments. This incredible potential for wringing excess costs from supply chains is making business-to-business (B2B) e-commerce "the next

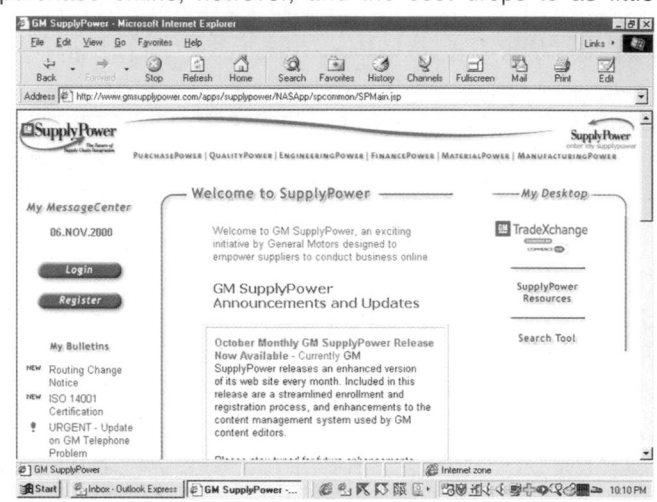

big killer app" of the World Wide Web. Analysts estimate the B2B e-commerce market will soar to $6.4 trillion in 2004.

The Big Three automakers (**Ford, General Motors,** and **Daimler-Chrysler**), recently announced they will move all business—more than $250 billion and 60,000 suppliers—to the Internet. This change will replace a bloated procurement system built on phone calls and faxes. General Motors alone issues over 100,000 purchase orders a year. Suppliers field huge sales staffs to fly on the company's dime to meet with prospects.

So moving B2B commerce to the Internet makes buying and selling more cost-efficient. Buyers and sellers get exposure to a worldwide market at the click of a mouse. Buyers conduct real-time trading to get the parts they need. Sellers auction off excess inventory. And now corporate accountants and financial managers can use their time to focus on strategic activities, such as finding the most profitable B2B relationships.

Source: Based on Russ Banham, "The B-to-B virtual bazaar," *Journal of Accountancy,* July 2000, pp. 26–30. Don Tapscot, "Manager's journal: Virtual webs will revolutionize business," *Wall Street Journal,* April 24, 2000, P. A38. Kevin P. O'Brien, "Value-chain report: Should your firm be using e-procurement?" June 12, 2000, http://www.iwvaluechain.com.

Let's return to our illustration. Chemtech assembles a cross-functional value engineering team that includes marketing manager Liz Smith, plant engineer Edward Michaels, and production foreman Steve Pronai, along with controller Martha Wise. The team analyzes each of Chemtech's three production activities: mixing, processing, and testing. For each activity, the team considers (1) how to cut costs given current production processes, and (2) how to redesign the production process to further cut costs. The team presents the following proposals to the CEO:

Mixing activity
- Group raw materials that are frequently used together, to reduce time required to assemble raw materials when mixing each batch.

- Automate the mixing process so workers can use a few mouseclicks to instruct the automated system to pipe chemicals into the mixing vat.

Processing activity
- Schedule preventive maintenance at nights and weekends to reduce emergency repairs and spoilage from breakdowns while a batch of chemicals is in-process.
- Purchase new equipment that cuts processing time in half.

Testing activity
- Improve quality control to reduce the need for testing.
- Fully automate testing.

USING ABM AND VALUE ENGINEERING TO ACHIEVE TARGET COSTS FOR TARGET PRICING

Companies like **Carrier Corporation, General Motors,** and **Compaq** are following Japanese automakers like **Toyota** and **Nissan,** and setting sale prices based on **target prices**—what customers are willing to pay for the product or service. Instead of starting with the full product cost from all elements of the value chain (as discussed in Chapter 19) and then adding a profit to determine the sale price, Exhibit 25-10 shows that target pricing does just the opposite. Target pricing starts with the price customers are willing to pay, and then subtracts the company's desired profit to determine the **target** (or allowable) **cost** to develop, produce, and deliver the product or service. Target costs are usually less than the (current) full product cost of the product or service. The target cost is really a goal the company must shoot for.

Target Pricing	Traditional Cost-Based Pricing
Target sale price (based on market research)	Full product cost (from entire value chain)
Less desired profit	Plus desired profit
Target cost	Sale price

Returning to Chemtech's ABC analysis, CEO Randy Smith decides to focus on commodity chemicals. The marketing department informs him that the market price of aldehyde is likely to fall to $9.50 per pound. Smith wants to earn a target profit equal to 20% of the sale price. In addition to the manufacturing costs in Exhibit 25-8, Chemtech incurs a total of $0.50 per pound in nonmanufacturing costs (R&D, design, marketing, distribution, and customer service).

WORK IT OUT

What is Chemtech's target cost per pound of aldehyde? Do Chemtech's current costs meet this target?

Answer

Target sale price per pound of aldehyde..............	$9.50
Desired profit ($9.50 × 20%)............................	(1.90)
Target cost per pound of aldehyde	$7.60

Chemtech's current costs do not meet the target cost.

Current total manufacturing cost (from Exhibit 25-8)..............	$7.95
Nonmanufacturing costs..	0.50
Current full product cost per pound of aldehyde	$8.45

Chemtech's current full product costs ($8.45) exceed the target cost of $7.60.

Objective 3
Use ABM and value engineering to achieve target costs for target pricing

TARGET PRICE. What customers are willing to pay for the product or service.

TARGET COST. Allowable cost to develop, produce, and deliver the product or service.

EXHIBIT 25-10
Target Pricing Versus Traditional Cost-Based Pricing

DAILY EXERCISE 25-9

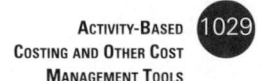

Smith decides to implement three of the cost reduction strategies Chemtech's value engineering team proposed earlier (pages 1028–1029):

- Group raw materials that are frequently used together. Total estimated savings is $150,000, and the plant's total number of batches remains unchanged at 4,000.
- Purchase equipment that cuts processing time by half. This will increase total processing costs by $1,000,000. Total machine hours will remain 50,000, but each product will require only half as many machine hours (Chemtech will use the extra machine hours to produce other profitable products).
- Improve quality control to reduce the need to test samples of each product. This action will cut total testing costs by $375,000, and cut the total number of samples tested throughout the plant by half (from 3,000 to only 1,500). Chemtech will now test only 7 (rather than 14) samples of aldehyde.

Will these changes allow Chemtech to reach the target cost? Exhibit 25-11 shows how Controller Wise starts with the original data summarized in Exhibit 25-7 and adjusts these data for the value engineering changes. Wise first recomputes the cost allocation rates for each activity: She incorporates changes in both the numerator (estimated indirect costs of the activity) and the denominator (estimated total quantity of the activity's allocation base). She then uses these new allocation rates to assign the costs of each activity to aldehyde, based on how much of each allocation base aldehyde uses after the value engineering changes.

EXHIBIT 25-11   **Recomputing Activity Costs for Aldehyde after Value Engineering Changes**

	Mixing	**Processing**	**Testing**
Estimated total indirect costs of activity:			
Mixing ($600,000 − $150,000)	$450,000		
Processing ($3,000,000 + $1,000,000)		$4,000,000	
Testing ($600,000 − $375,000)			$225,000
Estimated total quantity of each allocation base	4,000 batches	50,000 MH	1,500 samples
Compute the cost allocation rate for each activity:			
(Divide estimated indirect cost by	$450,000	$4,000,000	$225,000
estimated quantity of the allocation base)	÷ 4,000 batches	÷ 50,000 MH	÷ 1,500 samples
Cost allocation rate for each activity	= $112.50/batch	= $80/MH	= $150/sample
Actual quantity of each allocation base used by aldehyde:			
Mixing	60 batches		
Processing (30 1/2 × 50%)		15 1/4 MH	
Testing			7 samples
Allocate the costs to aldehyde:			
Mixing (60 batches × $112.50)	$6,750		
Processing (15 1/4 MH × $80)		$1,220	
Testing (7 samples × $150)			$1,050

 DAILY EXERCISE 25-8

Exhibit 25-11 shows that value engineering cuts the total manufacturing overhead costs assigned to aldehyde to $9,020 ($6,750 + $1,220 + $1,050), from $13,630 (in Exhibit 25-8). Spread over 7,000 pounds of aldehyde, this is $1.29 per pound ($9,020 ÷ 7,000, rounded). Now Wise totals the revised cost estimates for aldehyde:

Direct materials (from Exhibit 25-8)	$5.00
Direct labor (from Exhibit 25-8)	1.00
Manufacturing overhead	1.29
Total manufacturing costs	7.29
Nonmanufacturing costs	0.50
Full product cost of aldehyde	$7.79

These changes are quite an improvement from the prior full product cost of $8.45 per pound. But they are *not* enough to meet the $7.60 target cost. Chemtech

must conduct more value engineering (or accept less profit) to meet the target sale price.

Routine Planning and Control Decisions

In addition to pricing, product mix, and cost reduction decisions, Chemtech can also use ABC in routine planning and control. Companies using ABC can do activity-based budgeting, where managers budget costs of individual activities to build up the indirect cost schedules in the master budget (discussed in Chapter 23). ➡ Chemtech can also analyze manufacturing overhead variances (presented in Chapter 24) ➡ in more detail by computing variances for each of the three individual indirect activities (mixing, processing, and testing). Finally, Chemtech's managers can use ABC information to evaluate workers. For example, foreman Steve Pronai may receive a bonus if he can cut:

- the cost per sample tested (that is, cut the cost allocation rate for the testing activity) or
- the number of samples tested (that is, cut the consumption of the activity) *while maintaining product quality.*

◄ For the master budget, see Chapter 23, pp. 931–940.

◄ Analyzing manufacturing overhead variances: see Chapter 24, pp. 941–994.

ACTIVITY-BASED COSTING AND THE COST-BENEFIT TEST

The ABC concept is deceptively simple: Products cause activities, and activities consume resources. However, it is not easy for a company to develop an ABC/ABM system. In the Chemtech example in Exhibit 25-6, ABC triples the number of allocation bases—from the single allocation base (direct labor) in the original system, to three allocation bases (for mixing, processing, and testing) under ABC. ABC systems are even more complex in real-world companies that have many more activities and cost drivers.

Objective 4
Decide when ABC is most likely to pass the cost-benefit test

The Cost-Benefit Test

Like all other management tools, ABC must pass the cost-benefit test. The system should be refined enough to provide accurate product costs, but simple enough for managers to understand. ABC requires the wholehearted support of top management and operating managers, not just accountants. Dell's ABC team included representatives of all areas affected by ABC—from product engineering, to manufacturing, to customer service. Cross-functional teams increase the chance that ABC will succeed. The system will be more accurate because it incorporates a wider variety of perspectives, and managers of different functions are more likely to understand and believe costs from a system they helped build.

 DAILY EXERCISE 25-12

Activity-based costing and activity-based management pass the cost-benefit test when the benefits of adopting ABC/ABM exceed the costs. Benefits of adopting ABC/ABM are higher for companies in competitive markets because

- Accurate product cost information is essential for setting competitive sale prices that still allow the company to earn a profit.
- ABM can pinpoint opportunities for cost savings, which increase the company's profit, or are passed on to customers in lower sale prices.

ABC's benefits are higher when ABC gives managers new insights by reporting different product costs than the old system. This is likely to happen when

- The company produces many different products that use different amounts of resources. (If all products use similar amounts of resources, then a simple single-allocation-base system works fine.)
- The company has high indirect costs. (If indirect costs are immaterial, it does not matter how they are allocated.)
- The company produces high volumes of some products, and low volumes of other products. (Traditional single-allocation-base systems tend to overcost high-volume products and undercost low-volume products.)

The costs of adopting ABC are lower when the company has

- Accounting and information system expertise to develop the system.
- Information technology like bar coding, optical scanning, or "data warehouse" systems to record and compile cost driver data.

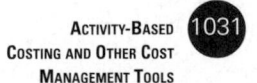

Contrast **General Motors** with **Burrito Brothers** (a fast-food take-out store in Gainesville, Florida).

General Motors	Burrito Brothers
Wide variety of different automotive products	Limited variety of similar burritos
High indirect costs	Low indirect costs
Employs experts in accounting and information systems	No accounting or information systems experts
Advanced information technology	Limited information technology

These differences help explain why General Motors was an early adopter of ABC, while Burrito Brothers has not adopted ABC.

Are real-world companies glad they adopted ABC? Usually, but not always. A recent survey has shown that 89% of the companies using ABC data say it was worth the cost.[1] Adoption is on the rise among financial companies like **American Express,** utilities like **Indianapolis Power and Light,** and nonprofits like the **U.S. Postal Service.** Organizations adopting ABC and ABM have more diverse product lines and processes, higher overhead costs, and more sophisticated information technology than nonadopters. But ABC is not a cure-all. As the controller for one Midwest manufacturer said, "ABC will not reduce cost, it will only help you understand costs better to know what to correct."

Signs That the Cost System May Be Broken

DAILY EXERCISE 25-11

Broken cars or computers simply stop running. But unlike cars and computers, even broken or outdated product cost systems continue to report "product costs." Without flashing lights or ringing bells, how can you tell whether a cost system needs repair?

Management accounting expert Robin Cooper and others suggest that a company's product cost system may need repair when

Managers don't understand costs and profits:

- In bidding for jobs, managers lose bids they expected to win, and win bids they expected to lose.
- Competitors with products similar to our high-volume products price their products below our costs, but still earn good profits.
- Employees do not believe the cost numbers reported by the accounting system.

The cost system is outdated:

- The company uses a single-allocation-base system developed long ago.
- The company has reengineered its production process, but has not changed its accounting system.

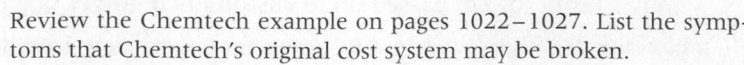
THINK IT OVER

Review the Chemtech example on pages 1022–1027. List the symptoms that Chemtech's original cost system may be broken.

Answer

1. The Chemical Manufacturing Department uses a single allocation base (direct labor cost) in a cost system developed over ten years ago.
2. Competitors that focused on high-volume commodity chemicals earned good profits, despite undercutting Chemtech's sale prices. This was puzzling because Chemtech should be especially efficient at producing large batches of commodity chemicals.
3. Cost numbers reported by the accounting system were inconsistent with employees' intuition.

To make sure you understand activity-based costing, take a few minutes to study the Decision Guidelines before working the Mid-Chapter Summary Problem.

[1]K. Krumwiede, "ABC: Why it's tried and how it succeeds," *Management Accounting* (April 1998), pp. 32–38.

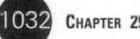

DECISION GUIDELINES

Activity-Based Costing

DECISION	GUIDELINES
How to develop an ABC system?	**1.** Identify the activities. **2.** Estimate total indirect costs of each activity. **3.** Identify the allocation base (primary cost driver) for each activity's indirect costs. **4.** Estimate the total quantity of each allocation base. **5.** Compute the cost allocation rate for each activity. **6.** Obtain the actual quantity of each allocation base used by cost object. **7.** Allocate costs to cost object.
How to compute a cost allocation rate for an activity?	$$\frac{\text{Estimated total indirect cost of activity}}{\text{Estimated total quantity of allocation base}}$$
How to allocate an activity's cost to the cost object?	$$\begin{array}{c}\text{Cost allocation}\\\text{rate for}\\\text{activity}\end{array}\times\begin{array}{c}\text{Actual quantity of}\\\text{allocation base used by}\\\text{cost object}\end{array}$$
For what kinds of decisions do managers use ABC?	Managers use ABC data in ABM to make decisions on • Pricing and product mix • Cost reduction • Routine planning and control
How to set target costs?	Target sale price (based on market research) $\underline{-\text{ less desired profit}}$ $=$ Target cost
How to achieve target costs?	Cross-functional teams use value engineering to cut costs by improving product design or production processes
What are the main benefits of ABC?	• More accurate product cost information. • More detailed information on costs of activities and drivers of those costs helps managers control costs.
When is ABC most likely to pass the cost-benefit test?	• Company is in competitive environment and needs accurate product costs. • Company makes different products that use different amounts of resources. • Company has high indirect costs. • Company produces high volumes of some products and lower volumes of other products. • Company has accounting and information technology expertise to implement system. • Old cost system appears "broken."
How to tell when a cost system needs revision?	• Managers lose bids they expected to win and win bids they expected to lose. • Competitors earn profits despite pricing high-volume products below our costs. • Employees do not believe cost numbers. • Company uses a single-allocation-base system developed long ago. • Company has reengineered the production process but not the accounting system.

www.prenhall.com/horngren

Mid-Chapter Assessment

SUMMARY PROBLEM

Indianapolis Auto Parts (IAP) has a Seat Manufacturing Department that uses activity-based costing. IAP's system has the following features:

Activity	Allocation Base	Cost Allocation Rate
Purchasing	Number of purchase orders	$60.00 per purchase order
Assembling	Number of parts	0.50 per part
Packaging	Number of finished seats	0.90 per finished seat

Each seat has 20 parts; direct materials cost per seat is $11. Suppose **Ford** has asked for a bid on 50,000 built-in baby seats that would be installed as an option on some Ford SUVs. IAP will use a total of 200 purchase orders if Ford accepts IAP's bid.

Required

1. Compute the total cost IAP will incur to purchase the needed materials and then assemble and package 50,000 baby seats. Also compute the average cost per seat.
2. For bidding, IAP adds a 30% markup to total cost. What price will the company bid for the Ford order?
3. Suppose that instead of an ABC system, IAP has a traditional product costing system that allocates all costs other than direct materials at the rate of $65 per direct labor hour. The baby-seat order will require 10,000 direct labor hours. What price will IAP bid using this system's total cost?
4. Use your answers to requirements 2 and 3 to explain how ABC can help IAP make a better decision about the bid price it will offer Ford.

Solution

Requirement 1
Total Cost of Order and Average Cost Per Seat:

Direct materials, 50,000 × $11.00...................	$ 550,000
Activity costs:	
Purchasing, 200 × $60.00...........................	12,000
Assembling, 50,000 × 20 × $0.50	500,000
Packaging, 50,000 × $0.90	45,000
Total cost of order	$1,107,000
Divide by number of seats	÷ 50,000
Average cost per seat	$ 22.14

Requirement 2
Bid Price (ABC System):

Bid price ($1,107,000 × 130%)...	$1,439,100

Requirement 3
Bid Price (Traditional System):

Direct materials, 50,000 × $11.00................	$ 550,000
Other product costs, 10,000 × $65	650,000
Total cost of order	$1,200,000
Bid price ($1,200,000 × 130%)	$1,560,000

Requirement 4
IAP's bid would be $120,900 higher using the direct labor single-allocation-base system than using ABC ($1,560,000 − $1,439,100). Assuming the ABC system more accurately captures the costs caused by the order, the traditional direct labor system overcosts the order. This leads to a higher bid price that reduces IAP's chance of winning the bid. The ABC system shows that IAP can increase its chance of winning the bid by bidding a lower price and still make a profit.

TRADITIONAL VERSUS JUST-IN-TIME PRODUCTION SYSTEMS

Objective 5
Compare a traditional production system to a just-in-time (JIT) production system

ABC and ABM often reveal the high costs of (1) buying, storing, and moving inventories, and (2) poor quality products and services. So it is not surprising that a recent study of "best practices" companies revealed most had linked their ABC/ABM systems to just-in-time (JIT) or quality initiatives. For example, **Carrier Corporation's** ABC/ABM system's evidence that materials handling was a major cost driver prompted Carrier to adopt JIT. The rest of this chapter expands on Chapter 19's introduction to JIT and quality. ➡

◀ Chapter 19, p. 773, introduced JIT.

We begin by contrasting just-in-time production systems with traditional systems.

Traditional Systems

Traditional businesses keep large inventories of raw materials, work in process, and finished goods. Why? First, to protect against poor quality. Poor quality raw materials leads companies to buy more than they need. Also, machine breakdowns and production problems *within* departments prompt managers to keep extra work in process *between* departments. Exhibit 25-12 describes the production of drill bits from bar stock (the raw material). Work in process inventory between the grinding and smoothing operations allows smoothing work to continue even if grinding machines break down.

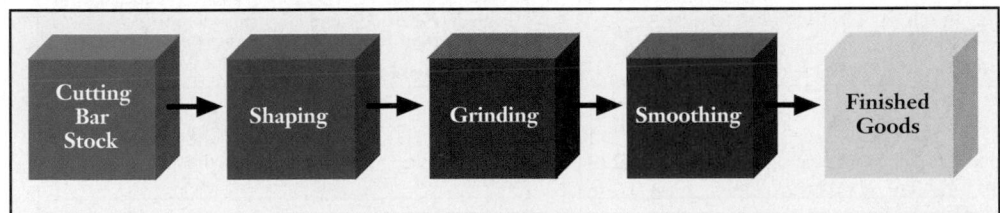

EXHIBIT 25-12
Sequence of Operations for Drill-Bit Production

A second reason for large inventories is long setup times on production equipment. Manufacturing operations can require setup times ranging from a few minutes to several hours, with correspondingly high setup costs. Companies with long setup times often make products in large batches to spread setup costs over many units. A third reason for stocking large inventories is uncertainty in deliveries from suppliers and orders from customers. Large raw material inventories protect against delayed deliveries. Large inventories of finished goods protect against lost sales if customer demand is higher than expected.

Why are large inventories a problem? First, inventories tie up cash. Companies incur interest expense or forgo interest revenue on that cash. Second, inventories often hide quality problems, production bottlenecks, and obsolescence.

Just-in-Time Systems

As the name suggests, companies with JIT systems buy materials and complete finished goods *just in time* for delivery to customers. This reduces waste. Many managers regard JIT as a *general philosophy of waste elimination* rather than a particular type of manufacturing system.

Companies that follow JIT have several common characteristics:

1. *Arrangement of production activities.* Companies following JIT arrange their equipment differently than traditional manufacturers. A traditional drill-bit manufacturer would group all the shaping machines in one area, all the grinding machines in another area, and all the smoothing machines in a third area, as illustrated in Exhibit 25-13 on the next page. After switching to JIT, the company would group the machines in self-contained production cells, or production lines, as in Panel B of Exhibit 25-13. Machines performing sequential steps may even be physically joined. The goal is continuous production without interruptions or work in process inventories.

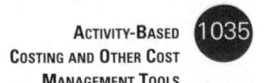

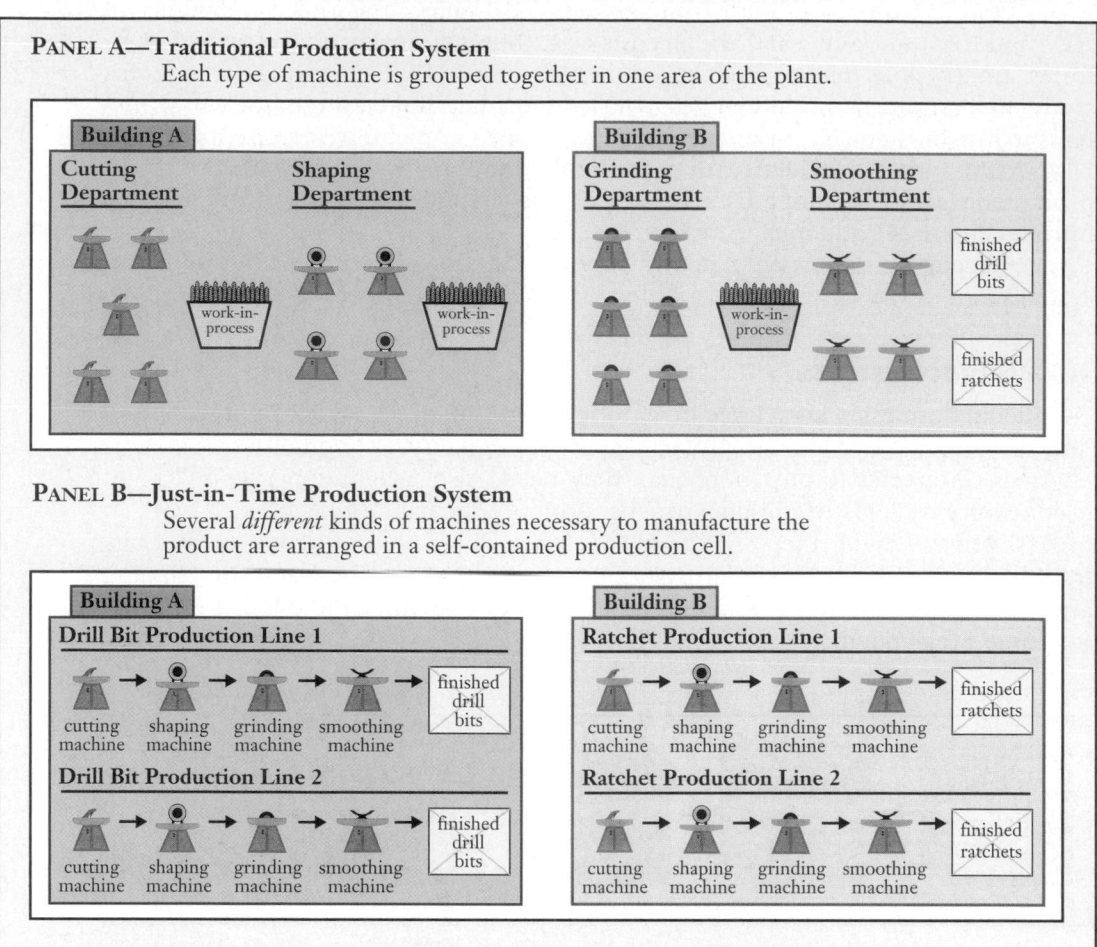

PANEL A—Traditional Production System
Each type of machine is grouped together in one area of the plant.

PANEL B—Just-in-Time Production System
Several *different* kinds of machines necessary to manufacture the product are arranged in a self-contained production cell.

Arranging machines in sequential production cells slashes production time. For example, within six years after adopting JIT, **Harley-Davidson** reduced the time to produce a motorcycle by 77%.

2. *Setup times.* JIT companies reduce setup times on machines used for more than one product. Employee training and technology helped **Toyota** cut setup times from several hours to a few minutes. This increases flexibility in scheduling production to meet customer orders, which in turn increases customer satisfaction and company profits.

3. *Employee roles.* Employees in JIT systems do more than operate a single machine. They also conduct maintenance, perform setups, inspect their own work, and operate other machines. This cross-training boosts morale and lowers costs.

4. *Production scheduling.* JIT businesses schedule production in small batches *just in time* to satisfy needs. A customer order triggers manufacturing. The final operation in the production sequence (smoothing, in our drill-bit example) "pulls" parts from the preceding operation (grinding). The grinding-machine operator pulls shaped parts from shaping, and so on. This "demand-pull" system extends back to suppliers of materials. Suppliers make frequent deliveries of defect-free materials *just in time* for production.

Purchasing and producing only what customers demand reduces inventory. As inventory declines, hidden problems are exposed. Correcting these problems before the company produces a large number of defective units saves rework and scrap costs. Also, less inventory frees floor space for more productive use. When **Hewlett-Packard** adopted JIT, the company cut its work-in-process inventory by 82%, and its production floor space by 40%.

5. *Supply chain management.* Because there are no inventory buffers, JIT requires close coordination with suppliers who will guarantee on-time delivery of defect-free materials. ➔ Chapter 19 defined *supply-chain management* as exchanging information with suppliers and customers to reduce costs, improve quality, and speed delivery of goods and services from the company's suppliers, through the company itself, and on to the company's end customers. Consider the following examples.[2]

◄ See Chapter 19, pp. 772–773, for a discussion of the JIT management philosophy.

Chrysler's Brazilian plant, which makes Dakota pickup trucks, buys a partially completed chassis from supplier **Dana Corporation's** plant 2 miles down the road. Dana assembles 320 parts onto the truck's frame, including axles, brakes, and wheels, within 108 minutes of receiving an electronic order from the Chrysler plant. Dana then delivers each partially complete chassis to the Chrysler production line, in the sequence that Chrysler specifies, so Chrysler can add the engines, transmissions, and body to complete each truck.

Wal-Mart shares its sales data to help suppliers match their production to Wal-Mart's needs. When **Procter & Gamble** delivers Crest toothpaste on a just-in-time basis to Wal-Mart's distribution center, Wal-Mart immediately unloads the toothpaste directly onto trucks headed for Wal-Mart stores. On average, the toothpaste is on the Wal-Mart shelf within 4 hours, and sold within 24 hours. "It is our objective to sell the merchandise before we pay for it" says a Wal-Mart senior vice president.

Cisco Systems, the Internet hardware maker, is working with **Federal Express** to manage Cisco's supply chain so Cisco can replace its parts warehouses with the distribution link in its value chain. A single customer order for Cisco's products may require component parts that Cisco buys from companies across the globe. Cisco currently holds these parts at a warehouse near its factory so it can ship the whole order at once. Federal Express is working with Cisco to design a system that will merge all the component parts for each individual order *en route to the customer*. The result? All parts necessary to fill a specific order should arrive from the various suppliers at the customer's door within a few hours of each other, ready for assembly at the customer's location.

Often credited for developing JIT, **Toyota** is not standing still. Toyota recently shocked competitors—who often keep customers waiting 30–60 days for custom-ordered cars—by announcing plans to custom-make vehicles within 5 days of receiving an order. How can Toyota meet this goal? By further streamlining and standardizing its production process, and by rolling out its "next generation just-in-time logistics system." Suppliers deliver parts to the assembly lines up to 24 times a day. These changes cut storage requirements by 37% and freed more space for manufacturing. In addition to saving on inventory, warehousing, and production costs, faster make-to-order times mean that Toyota dealers can cut their retail inventories, savings thousands in inventory carrying costs.

While companies like **Toyota, Carrier,** and **Dell** credit JIT for saving them millions of dollars, JIT is not without problems. With no inventory buffers, JIT adopters are vulnerable when problems strike suppliers or distributors. The Teamsters' walkout against **UPS** in the 1990s left manufacturing plants across the country starved for raw materials. More recently, **Ford** cut production of its SUVs in response to the tire shortage resulting from the **Firestone** tire recall. The electronics industry has also suffered from shortages of components. As we write this chapter, assemblers who normally obtain capacitors (parts that control the flow of electricity in telecommunications equipment) in 4 weeks are now waiting up to 40 weeks. Companies like Dell that have limited supplies of these components are hurting because their raw materials are scarce. This shortage has led one electronics executive to exclaim that just-in-time has become "just-in-trouble."

---

[2]*Sources:* "Chrysler makes manufacturing inroads at plant in Brazil," Gregory L. White, *Wall Street Journal* 8/3/98. "Wal-Mart sets supply plan as net tops forecasts," Emily Nelson, *Wall Street Journal* 11/10/99, B12. "Overnight, everything changed for FedEx; Can it reinvent itself?" Douglas A. Blackmon, *Wall Street Journal* 11/4/99, A1. "Toyota develops a way to make a car within five days of a custom order," Robert L. Simison, *Wall Street Journal* 8/6/99, A4. "Parts shortages hamper electronics makers," John E. Hillsenrath, *Wall Street Journal* 7/7/00, B5.

EXHIBIT 25-14 **Traditional Versus JIT Production Systems**

DAILY EXERCISE 25-17

Traditional Production Systems	Just-in-Time Production Systems
Arrange machines by function.	Arrange machines in sequence of operations.
Long machine setup times.	Short machine setup times.
Production workers operate a single machine.	Cross-trained workers perform many tasks.
Produce large batches.	Produce small batches.
Many suppliers.	Fewer, well-coordinated suppliers.

Exhibit 25-14 compares traditional production systems with JIT production systems. Now let's see how JIT can simplify cost accounting.

Just-in-Time Costing

Objective 6
Record manufacturing costs for a just-in-time costing system

JUST-IN-TIME (JIT) COSTING. A standard costing system that starts with output completed and then assigns manufacturing costs to units sold and to inventories. Also called **backflush costing.**

After adopting JIT, many companies simplify their cost accounting systems. **Just-in-time costing,** sometimes called **backflush costing,** is a standard costing system that starts with output completed and then assigns manufacturing costs to units sold and to inventories. There are three major differences between JIT costing and the traditional standard costing system we described in Chapter 24:

1. JIT systems do not track the cost of products from raw materials inventory, to work in process inventory, to finished goods inventory, like traditional standard costing systems do. Instead, JIT costing systems wait until the units are completed to record the cost of production.
2. Because JIT systems do not track costs attached to units in the production process, JIT systems do not need a separate Work in Process Inventory account. They combine raw materials and work in process inventories into a single account called Raw and In Process Inventory.
3. Under the JIT philosophy, workers perform many tasks. Since little labor is directly traceable to individual finished products, most companies using JIT costing do not track direct labor separately. They combine labor and manufacturing overhead costs into an account called Conversion Costs (as we saw in Chapter 21 on process costing). ◄ The Conversion Cost account is a temporary account that works just like the Manufacturing Overhead account described in Chapter 20. Actual conversion costs accumulate as debits in the Conversion Cost account, and the account is credited when conversion costs are allocated to completed units. Accountants close any under- or overallocated conversion costs to Cost of Goods Sold at the end of the year, just like under- or overallocated manufacturing overhead in Chapter 20.

➔ Chapter 21, p. 845, introduced conversion costs.

Just-in-Time Costing: An Example

To illustrate JIT costing, consider Mintel Company, which converts silicon wafers into integrated circuits for computers.

Mintel has only one direct manufacturing product cost: silicon wafers, which are labeled "raw." All other manufacturing costs, including labor and various chemicals, are indirect costs of converting the "raw" silicon wafers into the finished integrated circuits. These indirect costs are collected in the "Conversion Costs" account.

Mintel does not use a separate Work in Process Inventory account. Instead, it uses the following two inventory accounts:

- Raw and In Process Inventory, which combines direct materials with work in process
- Finished Goods Inventory, which is the usual Finished Goods account

Mintel has $100,000 of Raw and In Process Inventory and $900,000 of Finished Goods Inventory at July 31. In August, Mintel purchases $3,020,000 of direct materials (silicon wafers), and spends $18,540,000 on labor and overhead to produce

3,000,000 integrated circuits. The standard cost of the circuit is $7 ($1 direct materials and $6 conversion cost). Mintel sells 2,930,000 circuits in August.

 DAILY EXERCISE 25-18

 DAILY EXERCISE 25-19

Mintel uses JIT costing to record the August transactions.

1. Mintel purchases $3,020,000 of direct materials (silicon wafers) on account. These costs are debited (added) to Raw and In Process Inventory.

Raw and In Process Inventory	3,020,000	
Accounts Payable		3,020,000

2. Record the $18,540,000 actual conversion costs incurred. Mintel debits the Conversion Cost account. It works just like the Manufacturing Overhead account, except conversion costs also include all manufacturing labor costs.

Conversion Costs	18,540,000	
Various Accounts (such as wages payable and accumulated depreciation on property, plant, and equipment.)		18,540,000

3. Record the standard cost of goods completed. Since Mintel completed 3,000,000 circuits at a cost of $7 each, the debit (increase) to finished goods is $21,000,000 (3,000,000 completed circuits × $7). What accounts are credited? There is no work in process inventory in JIT costing, so Mintel credits

- Raw and In Process Inventory, $3,000,000 (3,000,000 completed circuits × $1 standard raw material cost per circuit) for the silicon wafers, and
- Conversion Costs, $18,000,000 (3,000,000 completed circuits × $6 standard conversion cost per completed circuit) for the labor and other indirect costs allocated to the finished circuits. This credit is similar to the way traditional systems allocate manufacturing overhead to products.

Finished Goods Inventory	21,000,000	
Raw and In Process Inventory (3,000,000 × $1)		3,000,000
Conversion Costs (3,000,000 × $6)		18,000,000

This is the essence of JIT costing. The system does not track costs as the circuits move through manufacturing operations. Instead, *completion* of the circuits triggers the accounting system to go back and pull costs from Raw and In Process Inventory and to allocate conversion costs to the finished products.

4. Record cost of goods sold in the usual manner. Mintel sold 2,930,000 circuits (2,930,000 circuits × $7 per circuit = $20,510,000).

Cost of Goods Sold	20,510,000	
Finished Goods Inventory		20,510,000

The August 31 inventory balances are

Raw and In Process Inventory ($100,000 beginning inventory + $3,020,000 purchased − $3,000,000 used in complete circuits)	$ 120,000
Finished Goods Inventory ($900,000 beginning inventory + $21,000,000 completed − $20,510,000 sold)	1,390,000
Total inventory	$1,510,000

Exhibit 25-15 shows Mintel's major accounts. Combining the raw materials inventory with work in process inventory to form the single Raw and In Process Inventory account eliminates detail. Although Mintel tracks the number of physical units in process, the company does not use material requisitions or time records to

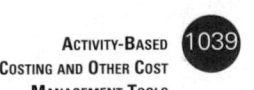

Exhibit 25-15 **Mintel's Major JIT Costing Accounts**

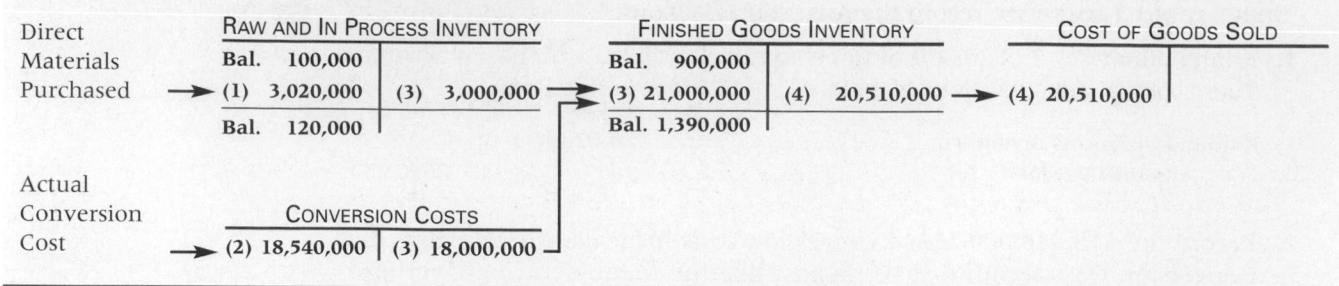

	Raw and In Process Inventory		Finished Goods Inventory		Cost of Goods Sold
Direct Materials Purchased	Bal. 100,000		Bal. 900,000		
→	(1) 3,020,000	(3) 3,000,000 →	(3) 21,000,000	(4) 20,510,000 →	(4) 20,510,000
	Bal. 120,000		Bal. 1,390,000		
Actual Conversion Cost	Conversion Costs				
→	(2) 18,540,000	(3) 18,000,000 ┘			

assign *costs* to circuits as they flow through the production process. Mintel does not assign costs to physical products until the goods are completed.

Exhibit 25-15 shows that conversion costs are underallocated by $540,000 ($18,540,000 − $18,000,000). Under- and overallocated conversion costs are treated just like under- and overallocated manufacturing overhead, and closed to Cost of Goods Sold. ◄

➡ See Chapter 20, p. 814, for a review of under- and overallocated manufacturing overhead.

Cost of Goods Sold	540,000	
Conversion Costs		540,000

> **THINK IT OVER** Activity-based costing is a more detailed and complex costing method that provides more accurate product costs. Just-in-time costing is simplified and does not track costs through the sequence of manufacturing operations. Are these two costing systems incompatible? Or can they be used together?
>
> *Answer:* ABC and JIT costing can be compatible. Mintel's $6 standard conversion cost per circuit used in JIT costing could be provided by an ABC system.

Objective 7
Contrast the four types of quality costs and use these costs to make decisions

CONTINUOUS IMPROVEMENT AND THE MANAGEMENT OF QUALITY

Companies using JIT strive for high-quality production. Because goods are produced only as needed, there are no inventories to hide inefficiencies. Poor-quality materials or defective manufacturing processes just shut down production.

Today managers know that if they fail to satisfy customers' demand for high-quality goods, their competitors will not. As we explained in Chapter 19, many companies adopt *total quality management (TQM)* to meet this challenge. ◄ The goal of TQM is to provide customers with superior products and services. Companies achieve this goal by improving quality and by eliminating defects and waste. Each business function in the value chain examines its own activities and sets higher and higher goals.

➡ See TQM discussion in Chapter 19, pp. 774–775.

Many managers invest in the front end of the value chain (R&D and design) to generate savings in the back end (production, marketing, and customer service). They strive to *design* and *build* quality into the product rather than having to *inspect* and *repair* it later. Carefully designed products reduce manufacturing time, inspections, rework, and warranty claims. The theme of total quality management is that superior work benefits the whole organization.

Types of Quality Costs

PREVENTION COSTS. Costs incurred to *avoid* poor-quality goods or services.

Business analysts have identified four types of quality-related costs: prevention costs, appraisal costs, internal failure costs, and external failure costs.

1. **Prevention costs** are incurred to *avoid* poor-quality goods or services. For example, **Deloitte & Touche** and other accounting firms invest heavily to

train personnel in auditing and consulting procedures. Highly trained accountants are more likely to follow company policies and to make fewer errors. Production workers assigned to quality teams at **General Motors** carry beepers so line workers can page when they spot a problem. The quality team then identifies and corrects the cause of the defect (for example, a misaligned robot) right away. The plant does not waste time and materials churning out defective cars.

2. **Appraisal costs** are incurred to *detect* poor-quality goods or services. For example, **Intel,** a manufacturer of integrated circuits, incurs appraisal costs when it tests its products. One procedure, called burn-in, heats circuits to a high temperature. A circuit that fails the burn-in test is also likely to fail when in customer use.

3. **Internal failure costs** occur when the company detects and corrects poor-quality goods or services *before* delivery to customers. An example is the labor of a **BMW** mechanic who reworks a faulty brake job after inspection by a supervisor.

4. **External failure costs** occur when the company does not detect poor-quality goods or services until *after* delivery to customers. If an auto-repair shop does faulty work, the customer will discover the flawed brakes. Then the shop may have to repair the body of the car as well as the brakes. External failures can ruin a company's reputation.

Exhibit 25-16 lists some examples of the four types of quality costs. Study these examples closely and you will see that most prevention costs occur in the R&D and design stages of the value chain. In contrast, most appraisal and internal failure costs occur in the production element of the value chain. External failure costs occur in the customer-service stage, or are opportunity costs of lost sales. Companies make trade-offs among these costs. Many prevention costs are incurred only periodically, while internal and external failure costs are ongoing. One expert estimates that 8¢ spent on prevention saves most manufacturers $1 in failure costs.

APPRAISAL COSTS. Costs incurred to *detect* poor-quality goods or services.

INTERNAL FAILURE COSTS. Costs incurred when the company detects and corrects poor-quality goods or services *before* delivery to customers.

EXTERNAL FAILURE COSTS. Costs incurred when the company does not detect poor-quality goods or services until *after* delivery to customers.

 DAILY EXERCISE 25-20

EXHIBIT 25-16
Examples of Quality Costs

Prevention Costs	Appraisal Costs
Training personnel	Inspection of incoming materials
Evaluating potential suppliers	Inspection at various stages of production
Improved materials	Inspection of final products or services
Preventive maintenance	Product testing
Improved equipment and processes	

Internal Failure Costs	External Failure Costs
Production loss caused by downtime	Lost profits from lost customers
Rework	Warranty costs
Scrap	Service costs at customer sites
Rejected product units	Sales returns and allowances due to quality
Disposal of rejected units	problems
	Product liability claims

Let's revisit Chemtech, the chemical processing company. Chemtech is considering spending the following amounts on a new quality program:

Inspect raw materials	$100,000
Reengineer the production process to improve product quality..............	750,000
Inspect finished goods	150,000
Supplier screening and certification	25,000
Preventive maintenance of plant and equipment	75,000

Chemtech expects this quality program to reduce the following costs:

Lost profits from lost sales due to disappointed customers..............	$800,000
Fewer sales returns to be processed..	50,000
Lost profits from lost production time due to rework	250,000
Reduced warranty costs...	125,000

Chemtech's CEO Randy Smith asks controller Martha Wise to

1. Classify each of these costs into one of the four categories (prevention, appraisal, internal failure, external failure) and total the estimated costs in each category.
2. Recommend whether Chemtech should undertake the quality program.

⊙ DAILY EXERCISE 25-21

Exhibit 25-17 classifies each cost and totals the estimated costs in each of the four categories. Wise uses these results to analyze Chemtech's two alternatives:

- Incur the prevention and appraisal costs to undertake the quality program.
- Do not undertake the quality program and incur the internal and external failure costs.

EXHIBIT 25-17 **Analysis of Chemtech's Quality Program**

Undertake the Quality Program		Do Not Undertake the Quality Program	
Prevention		**Internal Failure**	
Reengineer the production process to improve product quality	$ 750,000	Lost profits from lost production time due to rework	$ 250,000
Supplier screening and certification............	25,000	Total internal failure costs............................	$ 250,000
Preventive maintenance of plant and equipment	75,000	**External Failure**	
Total prevention costs.................................	$ 850,000	Lost profits from lost sales due to disappointed customers..........................	$ 800,000
Appraisal		Sales return processing	50,000
Inspect raw materials	$ 100,000	Warranty costs	125,000
Inspect finished goods	150,000	Total external failure costs	$ 975,000
Total appraisal costs...................................	$ 250,000		
Total costs of undertaking the quality program.................................	$1,100,000	**Total costs of not undertaking the quality program**	$1,225,000

Decision: Undertake the Quality Program

These estimates suggest that Chemtech would save $125,000 ($1,225,000 − $1,100,000) by undertaking the quality program.

Quality costs can be hard to measure. For example, design engineers may spend only part of their time on quality. Allocating their salaries to various activities is subjective. It is especially hard to measure external failure costs. The biggest external failure cost—profits lost because unhappy customers never return ($800,000)— does not even appear in the accounting records! Consequently, total quality management programs also emphasize nonfinancial measures such as number of customer complaints.

The Decision Guidelines feature summarizes key points about just-in-time and quality costs. Study these guidelines before working through the summary review problem.

DECISION GUIDELINES

Just-in-Time and Quality Costs

DECISION	GUIDELINES	
	JIT	**Traditional**
How to distinguish between just-in-time and traditional production systems?	Production cells	Like machines grouped together
	Short setup times	Longer setup times
	Smaller batches	Larger batches
	Lower inventories	Higher inventories
	An individual does wider range of tasks	An individual does fewer tasks
	Fewer, but well-coordinated suppliers	Many suppliers
How does JIT costing differ from traditional costing?	In JIT costing, **1.** Summary journal entries are not made until units are completed—costs are not separately tracked as units move through production. **2.** Raw materials and work in process are combined into a single Raw and In Process Inventory account. **3.** Labor and overhead are combined into a Conversion Cost account.	
What are the four types of quality costs?	Prevention costs Appraisal costs Internal failure costs External failure costs	
How to make trade-offs among the four types of quality costs?	Investment in prevention costs and appraisal costs reduces later internal and external failure costs.	

REVIEW ACTIVITY-BASED COSTING AND OTHER COST MANAGEMENT TOOLS

SUMMARY PROBLEM

The Flores Company manufactures cellular telephones. Flores uses a JIT costing system. The standard unit cost is $37: $24 direct materials and $13 conversion costs. Direct materials purchased on account during June totaled $2,540,000. Actual conversion costs totaled $1,295,000. Flores completed 102,000 telephones in June, and sold 98,000.

Required

1. Prepare the June journal entries for these transactions.
2. Make the entry to close the under- or overallocated conversion costs to Cost of Goods Sold.

www.prenhall.com/horngren

End-of-Chapter Assessment

Solutions

Requirement 1

Raw and In Process Inventory	2,540,000	
Accounts Payable		2,540,000
Conversion Costs	1,295,000	
Various accounts (such as payables and accumulated depreciation)		1,295,000
Finished Goods Inventory	3,774,000	
Raw and In Process Inventory (102,000 × $24)		2,448,000
Conversion Costs (102,000 × $13)		1,326,000
Cost of Goods Sold (98,000 × $37)	3,626,000	
Finished Goods Inventory		3,626,000

(Continued)

Conversion Costs	31,000	
Cost of Goods Sold		31,000

LESSONS LEARNED

1. **Describe and develop activity-based costs (ABC).** *Activity-based costing* focuses on activities as the fundamental cost objects. It uses the costs of activities as building blocks for compiling the costs of products and other cost objects. ABC uses multiple cost allocation bases to allocate activity costs.

2. **Use ABC data and ABM to make business decisions.** In ABM, managers use ABC data to make decisions that increase profits while satisfying customers' needs. Managers use ABC information to make pricing, product mix, cost reduction, and routine planning and control decisions.

3. **Use ABM and value engineering to achieve target costs for target pricing.** Target price is what customers are willing to pay for the product or service. Managers subtract desired profit from target price to obtain target cost. Target cost usually exceeds the current cost to produce the product or service, so managers use value engineering to improve design or production processes to cut costs to the target.

4. **Decide when ABC is most likely to pass the cost-benefit test.** ABC passes the cost-benefit test when the benefits (more accurate product cost information, better information for cost control) outweigh the costs of implementing the system. Companies (1) in competitive markets with (2) high indirect costs that (3) produce a wide variety of different products that make different demands on resources, and that (4) have accounting and information technology to implement the system are most likely to

pass the cost-benefit test. This is especially true if the company produces (5) high volumes of some products but low volumes of other products.

5. **Compare a traditional production system to a just-in-time (JIT) production system.** Traditional production systems have functionally arranged clusters of machines, large inventories, long setup times, and relatively inflexible employees. *Just-in-time production systems* have sequentially arranged production activities, "demand-pull" production scheduling, minimal inventories, quick setup times, cross-trained employees, and fewer but better-coordinated suppliers.

6. **Record manufacturing costs for a just-in-time costing system.** *Just-in-time costing* is a standard costing system that begins with output completed and then assigns manufacturing cost to units sold and to inventories. This differs from traditional sequential tracking standard costing that moves forward, step by step, from materials inventory, to work in process inventory, to finished goods inventory, to cost of goods sold. JIT costing is simpler because it uses a single Raw and In Process Inventory rather than separate accounts for raw materials and work in process.

7. **Contrast the four types of quality costs and use these costs to make decisions.** Four types of quality costs are *prevention, appraisal, internal failure,* and *external failure.* Managers make trade-offs among these costs, often investing more in prevention and appraisal to reduce internal and external failure costs.

ACCOUNTING VOCABULARY

activity-based costing (ABC) (p. 1020)
activity-based management (ABM) (p. 1027)
appraisal costs (p. 1041)
backflush costing (p. 1038)

external failure costs (p. 1041)
internal failure costs (p. 1041)
just-in-time (JIT) costing (p. 1038)

prevention costs (p. 1040)
target cost (p. 1029)
target price (p. 1029)
value engineering (p. 1027)

QUESTIONS

1. List three management accounting techniques that managers use to achieve their strategic goal of delivering value to customers.
2. Give two reasons why allocating manufacturing overhead based on direct labor can yield inaccurate product costs.
3. Managers often use standards and variance analysis to control direct material and direct labor costs. What accounting tool can they use to help control manufacturing overhead cost?
4. Give three examples of technology that have made gathering ABC data less expensive.
5. What kinds of decisions do managers make using ABC data?
6. What is target pricing and how does it affect cost management?

7. "Activity-based costing systems provide more accurate information than traditional systems that use a single allocation rate. Every company should adopt ABC." Do you agree? Why or why not?
8. Contrast the traditional and JIT approaches to managing machine setups.
9. Describe "demand-pull" production scheduling.
10. Do companies that implement JIT usually increase or decrease the number of suppliers they use? Why?
11. List three differences between JIT costing and traditional standard costing.
12. The just-in-time costing account Raw and In Process Inventory represents two accounts in a sequential-tracking system. What are they?
13. "Prevention costs are the most important quality costs." Explain.

DAILY EXERCISES

DE25-1 Fill in each blank with a term. You may use a term more than once. Some terms may not be used at all.

Distinctive features of activity-based costing (Obj. 1)

activity-based costing	direct labor	overcost
a cost allocation base	direct material	target costing
a cost driver	indirect	undercost
correctly cost	job costing	

a. ABC systems differ from traditional cost systems in the treatment of _____ costs.

b. Traditional costing systems that use a single overhead allocation base usually _____ high-volume products that are produced in large batches.

c. _____ uses the costs of activities as building blocks for compiling product costs.

d. _____ is any factor whose change causes a change in the related total cost.

e. Traditional cost systems that allocate manufacturing overhead based on direct labor hours or direct labor costs usually _____ direct-labor-intensive products.

DE25-2 List the seven steps in developing an ABC system. For each step, decide whether primary responsibility for the step should be assigned to

Distinctive features of activity-based costing (Obj. 1)

- The company accountant
- Production personnel (for example, the production foreman)
- Shared equally between the accountant and production personnel

(*Hint:* Think about who would likely have the most information about each step.)

DE25-3 The vice president of marketing storms into your office, exclaiming:

Activity-based management, Uses of ABC data (Obj. 2, 3)

> **Activity-based costing is worse than useless. It's endangering the future of our company! Because of your ABC cost "information," the CEO is pressuring us to (1) charge customers higher prices for customized products, (2) shift customers from customized products to standard products, and (3) require customers to accept larger deliveries than they would prefer. This completely violates our motto of "delighting the customer." Worse yet, we are being pressured to drop some of the customers we have spent a great deal of effort cultivating. This stupid ABC system will ruin us all!**

Reply to your colleague.

DE25-4 Consider Chemtech's original cost system on pages 1022–1023. Suppose Chemtech allocates manufacturing overhead at 225% of direct labor cost, instead of 200% of direct labor cost.

Allocating manufacturing overhead (Obj. 1)

1. Compute the gross profit per pound for aldehyde and for PH.
2. Compute the *total overhead* assigned to all the aldehyde and to all the PH.
3. Did the new manufacturing overhead rate change the ratio of total overhead allocated to aldehyde versus PH?

DE25-5 Suppose Chemtech's activity-based costing team identifies a fourth activity—machine setup. The foreman estimates that the total setup cost will be $270,000, and that production will require 3,000 setups. (This is less than the 4,000 total batches in Exhibit 25-7. Chemtech often eliminates a setup by running two batches of the same chemical in a row.) Aldehyde will require 35 setups, and PH will require 1 setup.

Developing an activity cost allocation rate (Obj. 1)

1. Compute the cost allocation rate for machine setups.
2. Compute the total machine setup costs allocated to aldehyde and to PH.
3. Did Chemtech's original allocation base (200% of direct labor cost) allocate setup costs appropriately? Give your reason.

DE25-6 Consider the Chemtech example on pages 1022–1027 and your analysis in Daily Exercise 25-5.

Computing activity costs and explaining changes (Obj. 1)

1. Compute the machine setup cost per pound for aldehyde and for PH.
2. Use your answer to requirement 1 to explain why switching from a traditional single-allocation-base system to an ABC system usually shifts costs away from high-volume products, toward low-volume products.

DE25-7 Use the results of Daily Exercise 25-5 and the information in Exhibit 25-8 to revise the

Using ABC to allocate indirect costs (Obj. 1)

1. Manufacturing overhead cost per pound for aldehyde and for PH
2. Gross profit per pound for aldehyde and for PH

DE25-8 Chemtech's value engineering team determines that new software for managing the mixing process will reduce mixing costs from $450,000 to $362,000. Given the other information in Exhibit 25-11, compute the new mixing activity cost allocation rate. Will this cost saving allow Chemtech to reach the target cost of $7.60 per pound?

DE25-9 Arnold Business Stationery produces engraved business stationery, which it sells for $360 per ream. The stationery currently costs Arnold's $280 per ream. A competitor has just cut the sale price of its comparable stationery to $300 per ream. Marketing believes that Arnold must cut its sale price to $300 per ream to remain competitive. Arnold currently sells 100,000 reams of engraved stationery each year. If the target profit is 25% of sales revenue, what is the target cost of a ream of stationery?

DE25-10 Daily Exercises 25-10 through 25-16 center on Soliloquy Softworks, Inc., a technology consulting firm and Microsoft Solutions Provider focused on Web site development and integration of Internet business applications. President Mary Nelson's ear is ringing after an unpleasant call from client Barry Wilner. Wilner was irate after opening his bill for Soliloquy's redesign of his company's Web site. Wilner said that Nelson's major competitor, Delta Applications, charged much more reasonable fees to another company for which Wilner serves on the board of directors.

Nelson is puzzled for two reasons. First, she is confident that her firm knows Web site design and support as well as any of Soliloquy's competitors. Nelson cannot understand how Delta Applications can undercut Soliloquy's rates and still make a profit. But Delta Applications is reputed to be very profitable. Second, just yesterday Nelson received a call from client Bob Lee. Lee was happy with the excellent service and reasonable fees Nelson charged him for adding a database-driven job posting feature to his company's Web site. Nelson was surprised by Lee's compliments because this was an unusual job for Soliloquy that required development of complex database management and control applications, and she had felt a little uneasy accepting it.

Like most consulting firms, Soliloquy traces direct labor to individual engagements (jobs). Soliloquy allocated indirect costs to engagements using a budgeted rate based on direct labor hours. Nelson is happy with this system, which she has used since she established Soliloquy in 1995.

Nelson expects to incur $180,000 of indirect costs this year, and she expects her firm to work 3,000 direct labor hours. Nelson and the other systems consultants earn $200 per hour. Clients are billed at 150% of direct labor cost. Last month Soliloquy's consultants spent 90 hours on Wilner's engagement. They also spent 90 hours on Lee's engagement.

1. Compute Soliloquy's indirect cost allocation rate.
2. Compute the total costs assigned to the Wilner and Lee engagements.
3. Compute the operating income from the Wilner and Lee engagements.

DE25-11 Review Soliloquy Softworks' situation in Daily Exercise 25-10. List all the signals or clues that indicate Soliloquy's cost system may be "broken."

DE25-12 Mary Nelson has employed your management consulting firm to help her decide whether to develop an activity-based costing system. After reviewing the information in Daily Exercises 25-10 and 25-11, draft a memo to Nelson. Make a recommendation whether her firm should develop an ABC system. Be sure to include an explanation of the costs and benefits Nelson could expect from adopting ABC. Use the following format for your memo.

Date:	_____
To:	Ms. Mary Nelson, President, Soliloquy Softworks, Inc.
From:	Student name
Subject:	Cost system recommendation

DE25-13 Mary Nelson from Daily Exercise 25-10 suspects that her allocation of indirect costs could be giving misleading results, so she decides to develop an ABC system. She identifies three activities: documentation preparation, information technology support, and training. Nelson figures that documentation costs are driven by the number of pages, information technology support costs are driven by the number of software applications used, and training costs are most closely associated with the number of direct labor hours worked. Estimates of the costs and quantities of the allocation bases follow:

Activity	Estimated Cost	Allocation Base	Estimated Quantity of Cost Driver
Documentation preparation.............	$100,000	Pages	3,125 pages
Information technology support	56,000	Applications used..............	140 applications
Training	24,000	Direct labor hours	3,000 hours
Total indirect costs...........................	$180,000		

Compute the cost allocation rate for each activity.

DE25-14 Refer to the Soliloquy Softworks example in Daily Exercises 25-10 and 25-13. The Wilner and Lee engagements used the following resources last month:

Using ABC to allocate costs and compute profit (Obj. 1)

Cost Driver	Wilner	Lee
Direct labor hours...............	90	90
Pages....................................	50	300
Applications used	1	7

1. Compute the cost assigned to the Wilner engagement and to the Lee engagement, using the ABC system.
2. Compute the operating income from the Wilner engagement and from the Lee engagement.

DE25-15 Write a memo to Mary Nelson comparing the costs of the Wilner and Lee jobs using the original direct labor single-allocation-base system (Daily Exercise 25-10) and the ABC system (Daily Exercise 25-14). Be sure to explain

Explaining results of ABC analysis (Obj. 2)

- How have the costs changed under the ABC system?
- Why have the costs changed in the direction they changed, rather than in the opposite direction?
- Do the ABC results solve Nelson's puzzle from Daily Exercise 25-10?

Your memo should follow the format outlined in Daily Exercise 25-12.

DE25-16 Write a memo to Mary Nelson (Daily Exercises 25-10 through 25-15) explaining how she can use the ABC information to make decisions about her consulting firm. Consider how she could use ABC information in

Using ABC information to make decisions (Obj. 2)

- Setting fees (prices)
- Responding to client concerns about fees
- Controlling costs

Your memo should follow the format outlined in Daily Exercise 25-12.

DE25-17 Indicate whether each of the following is characteristic of a JIT production system or a traditional production system.

Comparing JIT and traditional production systems (Obj. 5)

- a. Management works with suppliers to ensure defect-free materials.
- b. Products produced in large batches.
- c. Large stocks of finished goods protect against lost sales if customer demand is higher than expected.
- d. Suppliers make frequent deliveries of small quantities of raw materials.
- e. Long setup times.
- f. Employees do a variety of jobs, including maintenance and setups as well as operating machines.
- g. Machines are grouped into self-contained production cells or production lines.
- h. Machines are grouped according to function. For example, all cutting machines are located in one area.
- i. Suppliers can access the company's intranet.
- j. The final operation in the production sequence "pulls" parts from the preceding operation.
- k. Each employee is responsible for inspecting his or her own work.

DE25-18 Look at the Mintel Company example on pages 1038–1040. Suppose Mintel's standard cost per circuit is $1.05 for materials and $6.20 for conversion costs, and that Mintel sold 2,950,000 circuits. How would this change Mintel's journal entries, including the entry to close the Conversion Cost account? Prepare new journal entries as necessary.

Recording JIT costing journal entries (Obj. 6)

DE25-19 Hamilton Products uses a JIT system to manufacture trading pins for the 2002 Olympic Games in Salt Lake City. The standard cost per pin is $2 for raw materials and $3 for conversion costs. Last month Hamilton recorded the following data:

Number of pins completed..	4,000 pins	Raw material purchases..........	$ 8,800
Number of pins sold............	3,500 pins	Conversion costs....................	$12,660

Use JIT costing to prepare journal entries for the month, including the entry to close the Conversion Cost account.

DE25-20 Bombardier, Inc., manufactures SeaDoo personal watercraft (jet-skis). Give examples of costs Bombardier might incur in each of the four categories of quality costs:

- Prevention costs
- Appraisal costs
- Internal failure costs
- External failure costs

Be as specific as possible.

DE25-21 Porsche manufactures expensive, high-quality sports cars including the 911 and Boxster. Suppose Porsche is considering spending the following amounts on a new quality program for the 911:

Additional 20 minutes of testing for each car...	$ 500,000
Negotiating with and training suppliers to obtain higher quality materials and on-time delivery	200,000
Redesigning the 911 model to make it easier to manufacture..................	1,200,000

Porsche expects this quality program to save costs, as follows:

Reduced warranty repair costs	$150,000
Avoid inspection of raw materials	400,000
Rework avoided because of fewer defective units..............	550,000

It also expects this program to avoid lost profits from

Lost sales due to disappointed customers...........................	$800,000
Lost production time due to rework....................................	250,000

1. Classify each of these costs into one of the four categories of quality costs (prevention, appraisal, internal failure, external failure).
2. Should Porsche implement the quality program? Give your reasons.

EXERCISES

E25-1 Wheels, Inc., uses activity-based costing to account for its chrome wheel manufacturing process. Company managers have identified four manufacturing activities: materials handling, machine setup, insertion of parts, and finishing. The budgeted activity costs for 20X3 and their allocation bases are as follows:

Activity	Total Budgeted Cost	Allocation Base
Materials handling	$ 18,000	Number of parts
Machine setup	2,800	Number of setups
Insertion of parts	24,000	Number of parts
Finishing	60,000	Finishing direct labor hours
Total	$104,800	

Wheels, Inc., expects to produce 2,000 chrome wheels during the year. The wheels are expected to use 12,000 parts, require 8 setups, and consume 1,000 hours of finishing time.

Required

1. Compute the cost allocation rate for each activity.
2. Compute the indirect manufacturing cost of each wheel.

E25-2 Several years after reengineering its production process, Spokes, Inc., hired a new controller, Lindsay Bays. She developed an ABC system very similar to the one used by Spokes' chief rival, Wheels, Inc., of Exercise 25-1. Part of the reason Bays developed the ABC system was that Spokes' profits had been declining, even though the company had shifted its product mix toward the product that had appeared most profitable under the old system. Before adopting the new ABC system, Spokes had used a direct labor hour single-allocation-base system that was developed 20 years ago.

Product costing in ABC and traditional systems
(Obj. 1)

For 20X3, Spokes' budgeted ABC allocation rates are

Activity	Allocation Base	Cost Allocation Rate
Materials handling	Number of parts	$ 1.75 per part
Machine setup	Number of setups	300.00 per setup
Insertion of parts	Number of parts	4.00 per part
Finishing	Finishing direct labor hours	70.00 per hour

The number of parts is now a feasible allocation base because Spokes recently purchased bar coding technology. Spokes produces two wheel models: standard and deluxe. Budgeted data for 20X3 are as follows:

	Standard	Deluxe
Parts per wheel...	5.0	7.0
Setups per 1,000 wheels.....................................	3.0	3.0
Finishing direct labor hours per wheel	0.2	1.0
Total direct labor hours per wheel	2.0	3.0

The company's managers expect to produce 1,000 units of each model during the year.

Required

1. Compute the total budgeted indirect manufacturing cost for 20X3.
2. Compute the ABC indirect manufacturing cost per unit of each model.
3. Using Spokes' old direct labor hour single-allocation-base system, compute the (single) allocation rate based on direct labor hours. Use this rate to determine the indirect manufacturing cost per wheel for each model under the old single-allocation-base method.

E25-3 Refer to Exercise 25-2. For 20X4, Spokes' managers have decided to use the same indirect manufacturing costs per wheel that they computed in 20X3. In addition to the unit indirect manufacturing costs, the following data are budgeted for the company's standard and deluxe models for 20X4:

Using activity-based costing to make decisions
(Obj. 2)

	Standard	Deluxe
Sale price	$155.00	$215.00
Direct materials	15.00	25.00
Direct labor.....................	30.00	45.00

Because of limited machine hour capacity, Spokes can produce either 2,000 standard wheels or 2,000 deluxe wheels.

Required

1. If the managers rely on the ABC unit cost data computed in Exercise 25-2, which model will they produce? (All nonmanufacturing costs are the same for both models.)
2. If the managers rely on the single-allocation-base cost data, which model will they produce?
3. Which course of action will yield more income for Spokes?

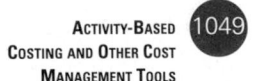

Activity-based management and target cost (Obj. 3)

E25-4 Refer to Exercise 25-2. Controller Lindsay Bays is surprised by the increase in cost of the deluxe model under ABC. Market research shows that to remain a viable product while still providing a reasonable profit, Spokes will have to meet a target cost of $165 for the deluxe wheel. A value engineering study by Spokes' employees suggests that modifications to the finishing process could cut finishing cost from $70 to $60 per hour and reduce the finishing direct labor hours per deluxe wheel from 1 hour to 0.8 hour per wheel. Direct materials would remain unchanged at $25 per wheel, as would direct labor at $45 per wheel. The materials handling, machine setups, and insertion of parts activity costs would remain the same as in Exercise 25-2. Would implementing the value engineering recommendation allow Spokes to achieve its target ABC-based cost for the deluxe wheel?

Explaining why ABC passes the cost-benefit test (Obj. 4)

E25-5 Refer to Exercise 25-2. Why might controller Lindsay Bays have expected ABC to pass the cost-benefit test? Were there any warning signs that Spokes' old direct-labor-based allocation system was "broken"?

Recording manufacturing costs in a JIT costing system (Obj. 6)

E25-6 Circuit Creations produces circuit boards. Circuit Creations uses a JIT costing system. One of the company's products has a standard direct materials cost of $6 per unit and a standard conversion cost of $20 per unit.

During 20X5, Circuit Creations produced 500,000 units and sold 480,000. It purchased $3,300,000 of direct materials and incurred actual conversion costs totaling $9,550,000.

Required

1. Prepare summary journal entries for 20X5.
2. The January 1, 20X5, balance of the Raw and In Process Inventory account was $80,000. Use a T-account to find the December 31, 20X5 balance.
3. Use a T-account to determine whether conversion cost is over- or underallocated for the year. By how much? Give the journal entry to close the Conversion Cost account.

Recording manufacturing costs in a JIT costing system (Obj. 6)

E25-7 E-Voice produces cellular phones. Suppose that E-Voice's standard cost per phone is $22 for materials and $30 for conversion costs. The following data apply to July production:

Materials purchased	$5,300,000
Conversion costs incurred	$6,120,000
Number of phones completed	200,000 phones
Number of phones sold	196,000 phones

E-Voice uses JIT costing.

Required

1. Prepare summary journal entries for July, including the entry to close the Conversion Costs account.
2. The beginning balance of Finished Goods Inventory was $100,000. Use a T-account to find the ending balance of Finished Goods Inventory.

Explaining when JIT costing is most likely to be used (Obj. 5)

E25-8 JIT costing is typically used by businesses that (1) assign standard costs to each product, and (2) have low inventories. Explain why each of these conditions makes JIT costing more feasible.

Classifying quality costs (Obj. 7)

E25-9 Abraham & Co. makes electronic components. Evan Abraham, the president, recently instructed vice president Steve Givens to develop a total quality control program. "If we don't at least match the quality improvements our competitors are making," he told Givens, "we'll soon be out of business."

Givens began by listing various "costs of quality" that Abraham incurs. The first six items that came to mind were

a. Costs incurred by Abraham customer representatives traveling to customer sites to repair defective products.
b. Lost profits from lost sales due to reputation for less than perfect quality products.
c. Costs of inspecting components in one of Abraham's production processes.
d. Salaries of engineers who are designing components to withstand electrical overloads.
e. Costs of electronic components returned by customers.
f. Costs of reworking defective components after discovery by company inspectors.

Required

Classify each item as a prevention cost, an appraisal cost, an internal failure cost, or an external failure cost.

E25-10 RPP manufactures radiation shielding glass panels. Suppose RPP is considering spending the following amounts on a new total quality management (TQM) program:

Classifying quality costs and using these costs to make decisions
(Obj. 7)

Strength-testing one item from each batch of panels..................	$50,000
Training employees in TQM	25,000
Training suppliers in TQM	35,000
Identifying preferred suppliers who commit to on-time delivery of perfect quality materials..	60,000

RPP expects the new program would save costs through the following:

Avoid lost profits from lost sales due to disappointed customers...........	$75,000
Avoid rework and spoilage...	50,000
Avoid inspection of raw materials..	40,000
Avoid warranty costs...	15,000

Required

1. Classify each item as a prevention cost, an appraisal cost, an internal failure cost, or an external failure cost.
2. Should RPP implement the new quality program? Give your reason.

Challenge Exercise

E25-11 Baxter Fabricators, Inc., completed two jobs in June 20X4. Baxter recorded the following costs assigned to the jobs by the company's activity-based costing system:

Using activity-based costing
(Obj. 1, 2)

		Allocated Cost	
Activity	**Allocation Base**	**Job 204**	**Job 609**
Materials handling	Number of parts	$ 400	$ 1,200
Lathe work	Number of turns	4,000	12,000
Milling	Number of machine hours	3,000	21,000
Grinding	Number of parts	300	1,200
Testing	Number of output units	150	3,000

Job 609 required 3,000 parts; 60,000 lathe turns; and 1,050 machine hours. All 300 of the job's output units were tested, and all units of the Job 204 were tested.

Required

1. How do you know that at least one of the costs recorded for the two jobs is inaccurate?
2. Disregard materials-handling costs. How many parts were used for Job 204? How many lathe turns did Job 204 require? How many machine hours? How many units were produced in Job 204?
3. A nearby company has offered to test all product units for $13 each. On the basis of ABC data, should Baxter accept or reject the offer? Give your reason.

PROBLEMS

(Group A)

P25-1A The Electronics Manufacturing Department of Digital Sound, Inc., in Dallas, Texas, assembles and tests electronic components used in digital music equipment. Consider the following data regarding component Q42:

Product costing in an ABC system
(Obj. 1)

Direct materials cost	$71.00
Activity costs allocated	?
Manufacturing product cost	$?

The activities required to build the component follow.

Activity	Allocation Base	Cost Allocated to Each Unit
Start station	Number of raw component chasses	1 × $1.30 = $ 1.30
Dip insertion	Number of dip insertions	? × $0.60 = 12.00
Manual insertion	Number of manual insertions	13 × $0.80 = ?
Wave solder	Number of components soldered	1 × $1.50 = 1.50
Backload	Number of backload insertions	6 × $? = 4.20
Test	Standard time each component is in test activity	0.30 × $90.00 = ?
Defect analysis	Standard time for defect analysis and repair	0.10 × $? = 5.00
Total		$?

Required

1. Fill in the blanks in both the opening schedule and the list of activities.
2. How is labor cost assigned to products under this product costing system?
3. Why might managers favor this ABC system instead of the older system, which allocated all conversion costs on the basis of direct labor?

Product costing in an ABC system
(Obj. 1, 2)

P25-2A MacArthur, Inc., manufactures CD racks and uses an activity-based costing system. MacArthur's activity areas and related data follow.

Activity	Budgeted Cost of Activity	Allocation Base	Cost Allocation Rate
Materials handling	$ 200,000	Number of parts	$ 0.30
Assembling	3,000,000	Direct labor hours	18.00
Finishing	160,000	Number of finished units	5.00

MacArthur produced two styles of CD racks in April—the standard rack and an unfinished rack, which has fewer parts per rack and requires no finishing. The totals for quantities, direct materials costs, and other data follow.

Product	Total Units Produced	Total Direct Materials Costs	Total Number of Parts	Total Assembling Direct Labor Hours
Standard CD rack	2,500	$24,000	30,000	3,000
Unfinished CD rack	3,500	27,000	36,000	2,800

Required

1. Compute the manufacturing product cost per unit of each type of CD rack.
2. Suppose that premanufacturing activities, such as product design, were assigned to the standard CD racks at $4 each and to the unfinished racks at $3 each. Similar analyses were conducted of postmanufacturing activities such as distribution, marketing, and customer service. The postmanufacturing costs were $18 per standard rack and $13 per unfinished rack. Compute the full product costs per unit.
3. Which product costs are reported in the external financial statements? Which costs are used for management decision making? Explain the difference.
4. What price should MacArthur's managers set for unfinished racks to earn a unit profit of $15?

Comparing costs from ABC versus single-rate systems; clues that ABC passes cost-benefit test
(Obj. 1, 4)

P25-3A Camden Pharmaceuticals manufactures an over-the-counter allergy medication called Breathe. Camden is trying to win market share from Sudafed and Tylenol. Camden has developed several different Breathe products tailored to specific markets. For example, the company sells large commercial containers of 1,000 capsules to health-care facilities and travel packs of 15 capsules to shops in airports, train stations, and hotels.

Camden's controller Sandra Whitney has just returned from a conference on activity-based costing. She asks Keith Miller, foreman of the Breathe product line, to help her develop an activity-based costing system. Whitney and Miller identify the following activities, related costs, and cost allocation bases:

Activity	Estimated Indirect Activity Costs	Allocation Base	Estimated Quantity of Allocation Base
Materials handling..............	$180,000	Kilos	18,000 kilos
Packaging...........................	300,000	Machine hours..............	2,000 hours
Quality assurance	112,500	Samples........................	2,250 samples
Total indirect costs	$592,500		

The commercial-container Breathe product line had a total weight of 6,000 kilos, used 1,000 machine hours, and required 200 samples. The travel-pack line had a total weight of 4,000 kilos, used 200 machine hours, and required 300 samples. Camden produced 2,500 commercial containers of Breathe and 50,000 travel packs.

Required

1. Compute the cost allocation rate for each activity.
2. Use the activity-based cost allocation rates to compute the activity costs of the commercial containers and the travel packs. (*Hint:* First compute the total activity costs allocated to each product line, and then compute the cost per unit.)
3. Camden's original single-allocation-base cost system allocated indirect costs to products at $300 per machine hour. Compute the total indirect costs allocated to the commercial containers and to the travel packs under the original system. Then compute the indirect cost per unit for each product.
4. Compare the activity-based costs per unit to the costs from the original system. How have the unit costs changed? Explain why the costs changed as they did.
5. What clues indicate that Camden's ABC system is likely to pass the cost-benefit test?

P25-4A Continuing Problem 25-3A, Camden controller Sandra Whitney is surprised that ABC reports such a higher indirect production cost per travel pack. She wonders whether Camden is making the desired profit of $1.25 per unit on this product. The current sale price is $5.75 per travel pack, direct production costs are $2.15 per pack, marketing and distribution costs are $0.90 per pack, and the indirect production costs are $1.70 per pack (from Problem 25-3A). Whitney believes that to reach estimated sales of 50,000 units, the sale price cannot exceed $5.75. If the travel pack is not providing the desired profit of $1.25 per unit, Whitney decides that the next step should be to establish a cross-functional value engineering team to identify opportunities for cost savings. If this does not provide the desired profit, Whitney doubts it will be possible to increase market share to sales of 50,000 travel packs.

Activity-based management, target cost, and value engineering (Obj. 2, 3)

Required

1. Determine the sale price that yields a profit of $1.25 per travel pack. Does this meet the $5.75 target price?
2. Whitney establishes a value engineering team. The value engineering team finds that improved supply-chain management can cut the travel pack's direct production costs from $2.15 per pack to $2.03 per pack. Further, the team believes it can cut materials-handling costs from $180,000 to $171,000. Changes in the packaging department will save $76,000 in packaging costs and 400 in machine hours. Improvements to quality assurance should reduce costs to $107,500 based on 2,150 samples. Marketing and distribution costs will remain unchanged.

    Given these cost savings, compute the indirect activity cost allocation rates for materials handling, packaging, and quality assurance?
3. If the value engineering team's suggestions are implemented, the travel pack line would require 4,000 kilos, use 180 machine hours, and require 256 samples. Compute the new indirect production cost per travel pack (including all three activities).
4. With these changes, can Camden set a sale price of $5.75 and still earn a profit of $1.25 per travel pack?

P25-5A Rugged Ways produces backpacks. The company uses JIT costing for its JIT production system.

Rugged Ways has two inventory accounts: Raw and In Process Inventory and Finished Goods Inventory. On October 1, 20X4, the account balances were Raw and In Process Inventory, $3,000; Finished Goods Inventory, $5,000.

The standard cost of a backpack is $40—$10 direct materials plus $30 conversion costs. Data for October's activity follow.

Recording manufacturing costs for a JIT costing system (Obj. 4, 6)

Number of backpacks completed............	15,000 backpacks	Direct materials purchased........................	$156,000
Number of backpacks sold	14,800 backpacks	Conversion costs incurred.........................	467,000

1. What are the major features of a JIT production system such as Rugged Ways?
2. Prepare summary journal entries for October. Under- or overallocated conversion costs are closed to Cost of Goods Sold monthly.
3. Use a T-account to determine the October 31, 20X4, balance of Raw and In Process Inventory.

Analyzing costs of quality
(Obj. 7)

P25-6A Pedals, Inc., is using a costs-of-quality approach to evaluate design engineering efforts for a new bicycle helmet. Pedal's senior managers expect the engineering work to reduce appraisal, internal failure, and external failure activities. The predicted reductions in activities over the 2-year life of the bicycle helmets follow. Also shown are the cost allocation rates for each activity.

Activity	Predicted Reduction in Activity Units	Activity Cost Allocation Rate Per Unit
Inspection of incoming materials	300	$ 40
Inspection of work in process..........................	300	20
Number of defective units discovered in-house..	1,000	50
Number of defective units discovered by customers...	400	70
Lost sales to dissatisfied customers...................	200	110

Required

1. Calculate the predicted quality cost savings from the design engineering work.
2. Pedals spent $110,000 on design engineering for the new bicycle helmet. What is the net benefit of this "preventive" quality activity?
3. What major difficulty would Pedal's managers have in implementing this costs-of-quality approach? What alternative approach could they use to measure quality improvement?

(Group B) PROBLEMS

Product costing in an ABC system
(Obj. 1)

P25-1B Nouveau Technology's Desktop PC Department, which assembles and tests printed circuit (PC) boards, reports the following data regarding PC Board XR1:

Direct materials cost	$45.00
Activity costs allocated	?
Manufacturing product cost	$?

The activities required to build the PC boards are as follows:

Activity	Allocation Base	Cost Allocated to Each Board
Start station	Number of raw PC boards	1 × $ 0.90 = $0.90
Dip insertion	Number of dip insertions	20 × $ 0.15 = ?
Manual insertion	Number of manual insertions	6 × $? = 2.40
Wave solder	Number of boards soldered	1 × $ 3.50 = 3.50
Backload	Number of backload insertions	? × $ 0.70 = 2.80
Test	Standard time each board is in test activity (hr)	0.25 × $80.00 = ?
Defect analysis	Standard time for defect analysis and repair (hr)	0.16 × $? = 8.00
Total		$?

Required

1. Fill in the blanks in both the opening schedule and the list of activities.
2. How is labor cost assigned to products under this product costing system?
3. Why might managers favor this ABC system instead of the older system that allocated all conversion costs on the basis of direct labor?

P25-2B Canyon Creek's Shelf Department manufactures bookshelves in its Santa Clarita, California, plant. The company uses activity-based costing. Its activities and related data follow.

Product costing in an ABC system
(Obj. 1, 2)

Activity	Budgeted Cost of Activity	Allocation Base	Cost Allocation Rate
Materials handling	$ 300,000	Number of parts	$ 0.50
Assembling	3,000,000	Direct labor hours	15.00
Painting	170,000	Number of painted bookshelves	6.00

Canyon Creek produced two styles of bookshelves in March—the standard bookshelf and an unpainted bookshelf, which has fewer parts and requires no painting. The totals for quantities, direct materials costs, and other data are as follows:

Product	Total Units Produced	Total Direct Materials Costs	Total Number of Parts	Total Assembling Direct Labor Hours
Standard bookshelf	5,000	$90,000	100,000	5,000
Unpainted bookshelf	1,000	15,000	15,000	900

Required

1. Compute the per-unit manufacturing product cost of standard bookshelves and unpainted bookshelves.
2. Premanufacturing activities, such as product design, were assigned to the standard bookshelves at $5 each and to the unpainted bookshelves at $3 each. Similar analyses were conducted of postmanufacturing activities such as distribution, marketing, and customer service. The post-manufacturing costs were $21 per standard bookshelf and $18 per unpainted bookshelf. Compute the full product costs per bookshelf.
3. Which product costs are reported in the external financial statements? Which costs are used for management decision making? Explain the difference.
4. What price should Canyon Creek's managers set for standard bookshelves to earn a $34.00 profit per bookshelf?

P25-3B The Software Department of Innovations, Inc., develops software for Internet applications. The market is very competitive, and Innovations' competitors continue to introduce new products at low prices. Innovations offers a wide variety of different software—from simple programs that enable new users to create personal Web pages, to complex commercial search engines. Like most software companies, Innovations' raw material costs are insignificant.

Comparing costs from ABC versus single-rate systems; clues that ABC passes cost-benefit test
(Obj. 1, 4)

Innovations has just hired Lou Zeller, a recent graduate of State University's accounting program. Zeller asks Software Department manager Ken Guess to join him in a pilot activity-based costing study. Zeller and Guess identify the following activities, related costs, and cost allocation bases.

Activity	Estimated Indirect Activity Costs	Allocation Base	Estimated Quantity of Allocation Base
Applications development...............	$3,000,000	New applications	6 new applications
Content production.........................	4,800,000	Lines of code	15 million lines
Testing	315,000	Testing hours	2,100 testing hours
Total indirect costs...........................	$8,115,000		

Innovations is planning to develop two new applications:

- MyPage—for developing personal Web pages
- Bullseye!—a commercial search engine

MyPage requires 500,000 lines of code and 100 hours of testing, while Bullseye! requires 7.5 million lines of code and 600 hours of testing. Innovations expects to produce and sell 30,000 units of MyPage and 10 units of Bullseye!

Required

1. Compute the cost allocation rate for each activity.
2. Use the activity-based cost allocation rates to compute the activity costs of MyPage and Bullseye! (*Hint:* First compute the total activity costs allocated to each product line, and then compute the cost per unit.)
3. Innovations' original single-allocation-base cost system allocated indirect costs to products at $100 per programmer hour. MyPage requires 10,000 programmer hours, while Bullseye! requires 20,000 programmer hours. Compute the total indirect costs allocated to MyPage and Bullseye! under the original system. Then compute the indirect cost per unit for each product.
4. Compare the activity-based costs per unit to the costs from the simpler original system. How have the unit costs changed? Explain why the costs changed as they did.
5. What are the clues that Innovations' ABC system is likely to pass the cost-benefit test?

Activity-based management, target cost, and value engineering (Obj. 3)

P25-4B Even though Problem 25-3B shows that MyPage's ABC costs are lower than under the simpler original cost system, Innovations' CEO Tony Millano is still concerned that the software's profitability may be less than expected. Millano asks Zeller to recommend a sale price that will yield a profit of $12 per unit, after direct production costs of $3 per unit, marketing and distribution costs of $5 per unit, and the indirect production costs of $22.50 per unit (from Problem 25-3B). Millano believes that the sale price must be $39 or less to reach estimated sales of 30,000 units. If Zeller's "cost-plus-based" recommended sale price exceeds $39, Millano authorizes him to establish a cross-functional value engineering team to squeeze out cost savings.

Required

1. Determine the sale price that yields a profit of $12 per unit. Will this meet Millano's target price?
2. Zeller establishes a value engineering team that finds new software writing routines can cut application development costs for the six new applications from $3 million to $2.7 million. This would also save $600,000 in content production and require 14 million instead of 15 million lines of code. Testing would be unaffected. The value engineering team also finds that improved supply-chain management can cut MyPage's direct production costs from $3 per unit to $2 per unit. However, marketing and distribution costs for MyPage are unchanged.

   Given these cost savings, what are the indirect activity cost allocation rates for application development, content production, and testing?
3. If the value engineering team's suggestions are implemented, MyPage would require 480,000 lines of code and the same 100 hours of testing. What is the new indirect activity (production) cost per unit (including all three activities) for MyPage?
4. With these changes, can Innovations set a sale price of $39 and still earn a profit of $12 per unit?

Recording manufacturing costs for a JIT costing system (Obj. 4, 5)

P25-5B Connection produces cellular phones. The company has a JIT production system and uses JIT costing.

Connection has two inventory accounts, Raw and In Process Inventory and Finished Goods Inventory. On August 1, 20X5, the account balances were Raw and In Process Inventory, $1,500; Finished Goods Inventory, $2,500.

Connection's standard cost per phone is $45: $30 direct materials plus $15 conversion costs. The following data pertain to August manufacturing and sales:

Number of phones completed	10,000 phones	Raw material purchased	$301,000
Number of phones sold	9,600 phones	Conversion costs incurred	$139,000

Required

1. What are the major features of a JIT production system such as Connection's?
2. Prepare summary journal entries for August. Under- and overallocated conversion costs are closed to Cost of Goods Sold at the end of each month.
3. Use a T-account to determine the August 31, 20X5, balance of Raw and In Process Inventory.

Analyzing costs of quality (Obj. 6)

P25-6B KoffeeKup is using a costs-of-quality approach to evaluate design engineering efforts for a new electric coffeemaker. The company's senior managers expect the engineering work to reduce appraisal, internal failure, and external failure activities. The predicted reductions in activities over the 2-year life of the coffeemaker follow. Also shown are the cost allocation rates for each activity.

Activity	Predicted Reduction in Activity Units	Activity Cost Allocation Rate Per Unit
Inspection of incoming materials	200	$20
Inspection of finished goods	200	30
Number of defective units discovered in-house	3,000	15
Number of defective units discovered by customers	800	35
Lost sales to dissatisfied customers	300	55

Required

1. Calculate the predicted quality cost savings from the design engineering work.
2. KoffeeKup spent $55,000 on design engineering for the new coffeemaker. What is the net benefit of this "preventive" quality activity?
3. What major difficulty would KoffeeKup's managers have had in implementing this costs-of-quality approach? What alternative approach could they use to measure quality improvement?

APPLY YOUR KNOWLEDGE

DECISION CASES

Case 1. SunSystems specializes in servers for workgroup, e-commerce, and ERP applications. The company's original job cost system has two direct cost categories—direct materials and direct labor. Overhead is allocated to jobs at the single rate of $23 per direct labor hour.

Comparing costs from ABC versus single-rate systems; using these costs to make decisions (Obj. 1, 2)

A task force headed by SunSystem's CFO recently designed an ABC system with four activities. The ABC system retains the current system's two direct cost categories. Thus, it budgets only overhead costs for each activity. Pertinent data follow.

Activity	Allocation Base	Cost Allocation Rate
Materials handling	Number of parts	$ 0.75
Machine setup	Number of setups	500.00
Assembling	Assembling hours	80.00
Shipping	Number of shipments	1,500.00

SunSystems has been awarded two new contracts, which will be produced as Job A and Job B. Budget data relating to the contracts follow.

	Job A	Job B
Number of parts.................................	15,000	2,000
Number of setups...............................	6	4
Number of assembling hours..............	1,500	200
Number of shipments	1	1
Total direct labor hours......................	8,000	600
Number of output units......................	100	10
Direct materials cost...........................	$210,000	$30,000
Direct labor cost	$160,000	$12,000

Required

1. Compute the product cost per unit for each job, using the original costing system (with two direct cost categories and a single overhead allocation rate).
2. Suppose SunSystems adopts the ABC system. Compute the product cost per unit for each job using ABC.

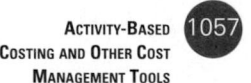

3. Which costing system more accurately assigns to jobs the costs of the resources consumed to produce them? Explain.

4. A dependable company has offered to produce both jobs for SunSystems for $5,500 per output unit. SunSystems may outsource (buy from the outside company) either Job A only, Job B only, or both jobs. Which course of action will SunSystems' managers take if they base their decision on (a) the original system? (b) ABC system costs? Which course of action will yield more income? Explain.

Activity-based management, target cost, and value engineering (Obj. 1, 2, 3)

Case 2. To remain competitive, SunSystems' management believes the company must produce Job B-type servers (from Decision Case 1) at a target cost of $5,400. SunSystems has just joined a B2B e-market site that management believes will enable the firm to cut direct material costs by 10%. SunSystems' management also believes that a value engineering team can reduce assembly time.

Compute the assembly cost saving per Job B-type server required to meet the $5,400 target cost. (*Hint:* Begin by calculating the direct material, direct labor, and allocated activity cost per server.)

ETHICAL ISSUE

ABC and ethical decisions (Obj. 1, 2)

Grace Luft is assistant controller at Allpax Packaging, Inc., a manufacturer of cardboard boxes and other packaging materials. Luft has just returned from a packaging industry conference on activity-based costing. She realizes that ABC may help Allpax meet its goal of reducing costs by 5% over each of the next three years.

Allpax Packaging's Order Department is a likely candidate for ABC. While orders are entered into a computer that updates the accounting records, clerks manually check customers' credit history and hand-deliver orders to shipping. This process occurs whether the sales order is for a dozen specialty boxes worth $60, or 10,000 basic boxes worth $8,500.

Luft believes that identifying the cost of processing a sales order would justify (1) further computerization of the order process, and (2) changing the way the company processes small orders. However, the significant cost savings would arise from elimination of two positions in the Order Department. The company's sales order clerks have been with the company many years. Luft is uncomfortable with the prospect of proposing a change that will likely result in terminating these employees.

Required

Use the IMA's ethical standards (Exhibit 19-15) to consider Luft's responsibility when cost savings come at the expense of employees' jobs.

TEAM PROJECTS

Project 1

Activity-based costing in the service sector; target costing (Obj. 1, 2, 4)

Quick Trades, Inc., began operations in 1988 as a regional discount brokerage firm. The company grew quickly because of its low trading fees. In the late 1990s, Quick Trades began offering on-line trading. Quick Trades established two types of accounts: a standard service account that provides restricted access to investment advice, and an extended service account for more active customers who maintain a minimum investment balance. Quick Trades charges customers an annual flat service fee plus a per-trade fee.

Quick Trades' CEO Mary Pownall is not happy with the company's recent profits and growth. As on-line trading has become more and more competitive, Pownall tried to increase the extended service accounts. Unfortunately, this has not helped profits. To remain competitive, she now believes that the basic per-trade fee for standard service accounts must be cut to $10. Other firms are starting to lower their per-trade charges to $10 per trade, but Pownall just does not understand how they can charge so little. Controller Joan Lipe wonders whether Quick Trades' cost accounting system may be part of the problem.

While Quick Trades has invested significantly in the latest Internet trading software, the company still uses its original accounting software. The accounting software does not trace any costs directly to customers. The company simply assigns total indirect costs to customer lines (standard service accounts and extended service accounts) based on the total number of trades processed. Lipe thinks that activity-based costing may be helpful, but Pownall wants to see how an ABC system could be helpful before investing in new accounting software.

Lipe assembles an ABC team that includes her assistant, a broker, and the information technology manager. The team begins by identifying three of Quick Trades' critical activities:

- Processing trades
- Personalized broker investment advice
- Answering customer account inquiries

The ABC team then analyzes the company's total indirect cost of $10,500,000. Classifying the components of this total indirect cost into the appropriate activity cost pools leads to the following estimates:

Assignment of Indirect Costs to Activity Cost Pools

Indirect Cost	Activity Cost Pool to Which Indirect Cost Is Assigned	Estimated Total Costs
Salaries of trade processing personnel	Trades processed	$ 1,120,000
Information technology	Trades processed	3,430,000
Brokers' salaries	Broker support	3,100,000
Investment research support	Broker support	2,300,000
Customer support staff department	Customer account inquiry	550,000
Total indirect costs		$10,500,000

The team identifies the following cost drivers for each activity pool:

Activity Cost Pool	Activity Cost Driver
Trades processed	Number of trades processed
Broker support	Number of broker contacts
Customer account inquiry	Number of account inquiry calls

The ABC team estimates that the total number of standard and extended service customers will require the following *total* resources:

Activity Cost Drivers by Customer Line

Activity Cost Driver	Total Number of Units of Activity Cost Driver Used by Standard Service Customers	Total Number of Units of Activity Cost Driver Used by Extended Service Customers	Total
Trades processed	450,000 trades	425,000 trades	875,000 trades
Broker contacts	10,000 contacts	90,000 contacts	100,000 contacts
Account inquiry calls	50,000 calls	200,000 calls	250,000 calls

Quick Trades currently has 15,000 standard service customers who average 30 trades a year, and 8,500 extended service customers who average 50 trades a year.

Split your team into two groups. Each group should meet separately before the entire team meets.

Required

Group 1: Use the original, less-refined cost system that assigns indirect costs based on the total number of trades processed and

1. Compute the indirect cost allocation rate.
2. Use the indirect cost allocation rate to determine the total indirect cost allocated to (a) the standard service customer line, and (b) the extended service customer line.
3. Compute the indirect cost per (a) standard service customer, and (b) extended service customer.
4. Based on this analysis, can CEO Mary Pownall cut the basic per-trade fee to $10 per trade (not per customer) for the standard service customer line?
5. What warning signs indicate that Quick Trades' cost accounting system may be broken? Do you believe that Lipe is correct to question the original cost system? Explain.

Group 2: Use the proposed activity-based cost (ABC) system to compute

1. The indirect activity cost allocation rates for each of the three activities.
2. The total indirect activity costs allocated to (a) the standard service customer line, and (b) the extended service customer line. (*Hint:* This is the sum of the indirect activity costs allocated to each customer line for all three activities.)

3. Compute the indirect cost per (a) standard service customer, and (b) extended service customer.
4. Can CEO Mary Pownall cut the basic per-trade fee to $10 per trade (not per customer) for the standard service customer line? Why or why not?

Team meeting: After each group has completed its individual assignments, the team as a whole should meet to compare results. The team should prepare a memo to CEO Mary Pownall that (1) explains why the costs are so different under the two cost systems, and (2) provides a recommendation along with a justification for which system Quick Trades should use for pricing decisions. Use the following format for the memo:

Memo
Date: _____
To: CEO Mary Pownall
From: ABC Team
Re: Differences between Quick Trades' present cost system and an ABC cost system

Project 2

Interviewing a company about its ABC system
(Obj. 1, 2, 4)

Form groups of four to six students. Identify a local company that has developed an activity-based costing system, and interview the accounting staff. Before the interview, learn

- The name of your company contact
- What the company produces
- Who are the company's major customers

As part of your advance preparation, decide who will ask which questions during the interview.

Required

The purpose of your interview is to learn how the company developed its ABC system. Be sure to cover the following questions. By listening carefully in the interview, you will likely think of other questions to add to this list.

1. How did the company perform each of the seven steps in developing an ABC system (see pages 1021–1022)? Who was involved in each step? Which step was most difficult? Why?
2. How many separate activities, indirect activity cost pools, and allocation bases does the company's ABC system use? Are there plans to increase or decrease the number of activities, cost pools, and allocation bases in the future?
3. Are the ABC product costs used in the general ledger, or is ABC a separate stand-alone system used primarily for management decisions? If the latter, are there plans to integrate ABC into the general ledger?
4. What spurred the company to develop an ABC system?
5. What benefits has ABC provided? Has management used the ABC data in activity-based management? If so, in what kinds of decisions has the company used ABC information? Has the ABC system lived up to expectations?
6. What problems arose in developing the ABC system? How did the company solve these problems?
7. Have the benefits of the ABC system outweighed its costs?

As directed by your instructor, report the results of your interview in

- A 3- to 5-page typed paper, or
- A 5- to 8-minute oral class presentation

Start with the background information (name of the company, contact person, company's major products and customers). Then discuss the company's ABC system, using the seven questions as a guide. If you don't have space in the paper (or time in the oral report) to cover everything, focus on the insights you found most interesting. (*Hint:* Make sure everyone in your group has a chance to critique the report. Use their suggestions to improve the report before you turn in the written report or make the oral presentation.)

INTERNET EXERCISE

K2 Inc.

K2, Inc., is a leading designer, manufacturer, and marketer of brand name sporting goods, other recreational products, and selected industrial products. The sporting goods and recreational products markets are highly competitive, with competition centering on product innovation, performance, and price. In 1999, sporting goods represented 75% of company sales.

1. Go to **http://www.k2sports.com** to watch the introduction and then click on *Go*. Pass the cursor over each colored button. What are K2's four major product lines?

2. Click on the K2 Snowboards button and watch the introduction. Review the nature of the products listed and consider the four types of quality costs. Would you expect K2 to spend more on prevention and appraisal costs to reduce external failure costs? Why or why not?

3. Go to **http://www.Forbes.com** and under "Stocks" type *KTO*, the stock symbol for K2, Inc., and click on *Go*. In the left-hand column, click on *Financials*. Of the first four operating expense accounts listed, which contain manufacturing costs? Which are used for pricing and profitability analysis? Which contain indirect costs?

4. Assume "Cost of Products" includes indirect costs for materials purchasing, materials handling, indirect assembly labor, and quality inspections for the four major product lines. Identify the primary cost drivers for each of these activities. How would K2 allocate these costs to the four major product lines?

5. Would K2 benefit from using an activity-based costing system? Why or why not? Would ABC likely pass the cost/benefit test for K2? Why or why not?

26

Special Business Decisions and Capital Budgeting

LEARNING OBJECTIVES

After studying this chapter, you should be able to

1. Identify the relevant information for a special business decision

2. Make five types of short-term special business decisions

3. Explain the difference between correct and incorrect analysis of a particular business decision

4. Use opportunity costs in decision making

5. Use four capital budgeting models to make longer-term investment decisions

6. Compare and contrast popular capital budgeting methods

www.prenhall.com/horngren
Readiness Assessment

On the slopes of **Deer Valley Ski Resort** in Park Valley, Utah—site of the 2002 Winter Olympics slalom competition—management accounting seems a world away. But the counter where you rent your skis, the chairlift that whisks you up the mountain, and the restaurant that serves you dinner are all part of the resort's recent expansion. How did Deer Valley's developers decide to spend $13 million to expand the Snow Park Lodge?

Director of Finance Jim Madsen explains that the answer is *capital budgeting*. Deer Valley has a long-term strategic expansion plan. When the resort reaches a target number of skiers per day and target level of profit, the owners expand.

Each expansion project must meet two requirements. First, the project must be profitable. Second, Deer Valley must expect to get its money back on the investment in a relatively short time. To figure out which projects meet these requirements, Deer Valley's managers compare

- The amount of the investment needed to expand the resort with
- The additional revenues expected from expansion.

How do managers make this comparison? They use two management accounting techniques:

- Net present value—to predict whether the investment will be profitable
- Payback period—to predict how long it will take to "get the money back"

In this chapter, we'll see how companies like **Deer Valley** use net present value, payback period, and other capital budgeting techniques to decide which long-term capital investments to make. Deer Valley's capital expansion project is a *long-term* special decision because it will tie up the company's resources for years to come. We'll tackle these long-term special decisions in the second half of this chapter. But first we need to consider *shorter-term* special decisions.

USING RELEVANT INFORMATION

Business managers develop and implement strategies. A **strategy** is a set of business goals and the tactics to achieve them. The main financial goals in business are to earn profits and to build a strong financial position. But managers must make many decisions about how to achieve those goals.

Decision making means choosing among alternative courses of action. Exhibit 26-1 on page 1064 illustrates the process.

Managers often choose the action that maximizes expected operating income. To do this, they analyze relevant information. **Relevant information** has two distinguishing characteristics. It is

- expected *future data* that also
- *differ among alternatives*

Suppose you are buying your first car. You are deciding whether to buy a **Toyota** or a **Saturn.** The cost of the car you want to buy, the insurance premium on this car, and the cost to maintain the car are all relevant because these costs

- will be incurred in the *future* (after you decide to buy the car), and
- will *differ between alternatives* (each car has a different cost, and the maintenance and insurance costs will also differ)

The cost of the car, the insurance, and the maintenance are *relevant* because they can affect your decision of which car to purchase.

Costs that were incurred in the past and costs that do not differ between alternatives are *irrelevant* because they do not affect your decision. For example, a campus parking sticker will cost the same whether you buy the Toyota or the Saturn, so that cost is irrelevant to your decision.

The same distinction applies to all situations—*only relevant data affect decisions.* Let's consider another application of this general principle.

Objective 1
Identify the relevant information for a special business decision

STRATEGY. A set of business goals and the tactics to achieve them.

RELEVANT INFORMATION. Expected future data that differ among alternative courses of action.

 DAILY EXERCISE 26-1

EXHIBIT 26-1   How Businesses Make Special Decisions

| Define strategies, business goals, and tactics to achieve them | → | Identify alternative courses of action | → | Gather relevant information | → | Analyze relevant information to compare alternatives | → | Choose best alternative to achieve goals |

Suppose **Pendleton Woolen Mills** is deciding whether to use pure wool or a wool blend in a new line of sweaters. Assume Pendleton predicts the following costs under the two alternatives:

| | Expected Materials and Labor Cost Per Sweater | | |
	Wool	Wool Blend	Cost Difference
Direct materials	$10	$6	$4
Direct labor	2	2	0
Total cost of direct materials and direct labor	$12	$8	$4

The cost of direct materials is relevant because this cost differs between alternatives (the wool costs $4 more than the wool blend). The labor cost is irrelevant because that cost is the same for both alternatives.

The point is worth emphasizing:

Relevant information is expected *future* data that differ among alternative courses of action.

Managers should base their decisions on expected future data rather than on historical data. Historical data supplied by the accounting system are useful guides for predictions. However, historical data by themselves are irrelevant for making decisions about the future.

THINK IT OVER   You are considering replacing your Pentium III computer with the latest model. Is the $1,500 you spent (in 2000) on the Pentium relevant to your decision about buying the new model?

Answer: The $1,500 cost of your Pentium is irrelevant. The $1,500 is a *past* (sunk) cost that has already been incurred, so it is the same whether or not you buy the new computer.

SHORT-TERM SPECIAL DECISIONS

Our approach to making decisions is called the *relevant information approach,* or the *incremental analysis approach.* This approach applies to a wide variety of special business decisions. We now consider five short-term special decisions:

- Special sales orders
- Dropping products, departments, and territories
- Product mix
- Outsourcing (make or buy)
- Selling as is or processing further

As you study these decisions, keep in mind that two keys in analyzing short-term special business decisions are

KEYS TO ANALYZING SHORT-TERM SPECIAL DECISIONS

Focus on *relevant* revenues, costs, and profits.

Use a *contribution margin approach* that separates variable costs from fixed costs.

◄ Chapter 22, page 891, explains that contribution margin equals revenues minus all variable expenses.

Special Sales Order

Objective 2
Make five types of short-term special business decisions

Suppose that **ACDelco,** a manufacturer of automobile parts, sells oil filters for $3.20 each. Assume that a mail-order company has offered ACDelco $35,000 for 20,000 oil filters, or $1.75 per filter ($35,000 ÷ 20,000 = $1.75). This sale will not affect regular business. Further, the special sales order

- Will not change fixed costs
- Will not require any additional variable nonmanufacturing expenses
- Will use manufacturing capacity that would otherwise be idle

To set the stage for the analysis, examine ACDelco's income statement in Exhibit 26-2. Suppose ACDelco made and sold 250,000 oil filters before considering the special order. Using the conventional (absorption costing) income statement on the left-hand side of Exhibit 26-2, the manufacturing cost per unit is $2 ($500,000 ÷ 250,000). This suggests that ACDelco should *not* accept the special order at a sale price of $1.75, because each oil filter costs $2 to manufacture. But appearances can be deceiving!

EXHIBIT 26-2   Conventional (Absorption Costing) Format and Contribution Margin Format Income Statements

INCOME STATEMENT				
Year Ended December 31, 20X5				
Conventional (Absorption Costing) Format		**Contribution Margin Format**		
Sales revenue	$800,000	Sales revenue		$800,000
Less manufacturing cost of goods		Less variable expenses:		
sold	500,000	Manufacturing	$300,000	
Gross profit	300,000	Marketing and		
Less marketing and administrative		administrative	75,000	375,000
expenses	200,000	Contribution margin		425,000
		Less fixed expenses:		
		Manufacturing	$200,000	
		Marketing and		
		administrative	125,000	325,000
Operating income	$100,000	Operating income		$100,000

The right-hand-side of Exhibit 26-2 shows the more helpful contribution margin income statement. Recall from Chapter 22 that contribution margin income statements separate variable expenses from fixed expenses. ➡ Managers find this contribution margin format more useful for decision making because it shows how sales volume affects costs and income. The contribution margin income statement shows that the *variable* manufacturing cost per unit is only $1.20 ($300,000 ÷ 250,000). Now let's reconsider the key question facing ACDelco: How would the special sale affect the company's operating income?

◄ Chapter 22 compares conventional and contribution margin income statements.

CORRECT ANALYSIS: CONTRIBUTION MARGIN APPROACH   The correct analysis shown in Exhibit 26-3 (page 1066) is an incremental approach that follows the two key guidelines for special business decisions:

1. Focus on relevant revenues, costs, and profits, and
2. Use a contribution margin approach.

EXHIBIT 26-3
**Incremental Analysis
of Special Sales Order**

Expected increase in revenues—	
sale of 20,000 oil filters × $1.75 each	$35,000
Expected increase in expenses—variable manufacturing costs:	
20,000 oil filters × $1.20 each	(24,000)
Expected increase in operating income	$11,000

Exhibit 26-3 shows that this special sale increases revenues by $35,000 (20,000 × $1.75). The only cost that will differ between the alternatives is the variable manufacturing cost, which is expected to increase by $24,000 (20,000 × $1.20). The other costs are irrelevant. Variable marketing and administrative expenses will be the same whether ACDelco accepts the special order or not, because no special efforts were made to get this sale. Fixed expenses are unchanged because ACDelco has enough idle capacity to produce 20,000 extra oil filters without requiring additional facilities.

 DAILY EXERCISE 26-2

 DAILY EXERCISE 26-3

To decide whether to accept the special order, ACDelco compares the additional (incremental) revenues with the additional (incremental) expenses. As long as the increase in revenues exceeds the increase in expenses, the sale contributes to profits. Management predicts that the order will increase operating income by $11,000, as shown in Exhibit 26-3, so they should accept the special order.

Thus, the guiding principle in special order decisions is

> **Special orders increase income if the revenue from the order exceeds the *extra* variable and fixed costs incurred to fill the order.**

Exhibit 26-4 gives the contribution margin income statements both without the special sales order (column 1) and with it (column 2). Column 3 shows the differences from accepting the special order, an $11,000 increase in operating income.

EXHIBIT 26-4   **Total Analysis of Special Sales Order—Income Statements without and with the Special Order**

	(1) Without Special Order (250,000 units)	(2) With Special Order (270,000 units)	(3) Difference (20,000 units) Total	Per Unit
Sales revenue	$800,000	$835,000	$35,000	$1.75
Variable expenses:				
Manufacturing...	$300,000	$324,000	$24,000	$1.20
Marketing and administrative	75,000	75,000	—	—
Total variable expenses..........................	375,000	399,000	24,000	1.20
Contribution margin	425,000	436,000	11,000	0.55
Fixed expenses:				
Manufacturing...	200,000	200,000	—	—
Marketing and administrative	125,000	125,000	—	—
Total fixed expenses...............................	325,000	325,000	—	—
Operating income	$100,000	$111,000	$11,000	$0.55

We have shown two correct ways of deciding whether to accept or reject a special sales order at a sale price less than the total cost per unit:

- An incremental analysis that quickly summarizes the differences (Exhibit 26-3)
- An analysis of total revenues, expenses, and operating income under both courses of action (Exhibit 26-4)

Which should you use? The answer depends on your question. The *incremental* analysis answers the question: What will be the *difference* in revenues, expenses, and operating income if the business accepts the special order? The *total* analysis shows the summary of differences and answers an additional question: What will be the *total* revenues, expenses, and operating income under each course of action? Managers can use either analysis to decide whether to accept or reject a special sales order.

INCORRECT ANALYSIS: IGNORING THE NATURE OF FIXED COSTS   Now consider an incorrect analysis of the special sales order decision. The conventional approach, using only the left-hand side of Exhibit 26-2, leads to an incorrect prediction of the change in expenses resulting from the sale.

Objective 3
Explain the difference between correct and incorrect analysis of a particular business decision

 DAILY EXERCISE 26-5

Total manufacturing costs	$500,000
Units produced	÷ 250,000
Manufacturing product cost per unit ($500,000 ÷ 250,000)	$2.00

A manager who follows this incorrect approach reasons that it costs $2 to make an oil filter, so it is unprofitable to sell the product for less than $2. *The flaw in this analysis arises from treating a fixed cost as though it changes in total like a variable cost does.* Manufacturing one extra oil filter will only cost $1.20—the variable manufacturing cost. *Fixed expenses are irrelevant to the decision because ACDelco will incur the fixed expenses whether or not the company accepts the special sales order.* Producing 20,000 more oil filters will not increase *total* fixed expenses. As volume increases, manufacturing costs increase at the rate of $1.20 per unit, not $2.00 per unit. In the correct (contribution margin) analysis, the variable expenses are relevant, and the fixed expenses are irrelevant.

SHORT-TERM VERSUS LONG-TERM: OTHER FACTORS TO CONSIDER   Our special sales order analysis focused on the short-term expected effect on operating income. We must also consider long-term factors. How will the special order affect ACDelco's regular customers? Will acceptance of the order at $1.75 per unit hurt ACDelco's ability to sell the oil filter at the regular price of $3.20? Will regular customers find out about the special price and balk at paying more? How will competitors react? Will this sale start a price war?

 DAILY EXERCISE 26-4

Accepting the order increases operating income by $11,000. Will potential disadvantages offset this income? The sales manager may think so and reject the order. In turning away the business, the manager would say that the company is better off passing up $11,000 now to protect its long-term market position and customer relations. Rejecting the special sales order may be an $11,000 "investment" in the company's long-term future.

To make special sales order decisions, we analyzed changes in revenues and costs among the different alternatives. We will use this same approach of analyzing differences in revenues and costs for the remaining short-term special decisions.

Dropping Products, Departments, Territories

To decide whether a company should drop a product line, a department, or a territory, let's modify our ACDelco example. We will assume that ACDelco already is operating at the 270,000-unit level, as shown in column 2 of Exhibit 26-4. Suppose the company is now considering *dropping* the air cleaner product line with $35,000 (20,000 units) in sales and total variable costs per unit of $1.50. A contribution margin income statement by product line follows:

 DAILY EXERCISE 26-6

 DAILY EXERCISE 26-7

		Product Line	
	Total (270,000 units)	Oil Filters (250,000 units)	Air Cleaners (20,000 units)
Sales revenue	$835,000	$800,000	$ 35,000
Variable expenses	405,000	375,000	30,000
Contribution margin	430,000	425,000	5,000
Fixed expenses:			
Manufacturing	200,000	185,185*	14,815*
Marketing and administrative	125,000	115,741†	9,259†
Total fixed expenses	325,000	300,926	24,074
Operating income (loss)	$105,000	$124,074	$(19,074)

* $200,000 ÷ 270,000 units = $0.74074 per unit; 250,000 units × $0.74074 = $185,185; 20,000 units ×
$0.74074 = $14,815

† $125,000 ÷ 270,000 units = $0.462963 per unit; 250,000 units × $0.462963 = $115,741; 20,000 units ×
$0.462963 = $9,259

Suppose that to measure product-line operating income, ACDelco allocates fixed expenses in proportion to the number of units sold. Dividing the fixed manufacturing expense of $200,000 by 270,000 total units yields a fixed manufacturing cost of $0.74074 per unit. Allocating this unit cost to the 250,000 units of the oil filter product line results in a fixed manufacturing cost of $185,185 for this product. The same procedure allocates $14,815 to air cleaners. Fixed marketing and administrative expenses are allocated in the same manner.

The result is an operating loss of $19,074 for air cleaners. Should ACDelco drop the air cleaner product line? The answer depends on whether or not fixed costs change.

FIXED COSTS REMAIN UNCHANGED   As in the special sales order example, we follow the two key guidelines for special business decisions: (1) focus on relevant data items, and (2) use a contribution margin approach. The relevant items are still the changes in revenues and expenses, but now we are considering a decrease in volume rather than an increase. If fixed costs will in fact remain the same whether or not the air cleaner product line is dropped, the fixed costs are not relevant to the decision. Only the revenues and variable expenses are relevant.

The preceding table shows that the air cleaner product line has a positive contribution margin of $5,000. If this product line is dropped, the company will forego this $5,000 contribution. Exhibit 26-5 verifies this amount—expected revenue decreases by $35,000, and expected variable expenses decrease by $30,000, a net $5,000 decrease in operating income (since fixed costs are unaffected). This analysis suggests that management should *not* drop air cleaners.

EXHIBIT 26-5
Dropping a Product—Fixed Costs Unchanged

Expected decrease in revenues:	
Sale of air cleaners (20,000 × $1.75)	$35,000
Expected decrease in expenses:	
Variable manufacturing expenses (20,000 × $1.50)	30,000
Expected decrease in operating income	$ 5,000

FIXED COSTS CHANGE   Don't jump to the conclusion that fixed costs never change and are always irrelevant. Suppose ACDelco had employed a foreman to oversee the air cleaner product line. The foreman's $28,000 salary can be avoided if the company stops producing air cleaners. Exhibit 26-6 shows how this additional savings affects the analysis.

 DAILY EXERCISE 26-8

In this situation, operating income will increase by $23,000 if ACDelco drops air cleaners. Here, a "fixed" cost *is* relevant, so managers must consider the change in the cost. Special decisions should take into account all costs affected by the choice of action. Managers must ask: What costs—variable *and* fixed—will change?

EXHIBIT 26-6
Dropping a Product—Fixed Costs Change

Expected decrease in revenues:		
Sale of air cleaners (20,000 × $1.75)		$35,000
Expected decrease in expenses:		
Variable manufacturing expenses (20,000 × $1.50)	$30,000	
Fixed expenses—foreman's salary	28,000	
Expected decrease in total expenses.....................................		58,000
Expected increase in operating income.................................		$23,000

As Exhibit 26-5 and 26-6 show, the key to deciding whether to drop products, departments, or territories is to compare the lost revenue against the costs that can be saved from dropping. The decision rule is

> **If the lost revenues from dropping a product, department, or territory exceed the cost savings from dropping → Do not drop.**
>
> **If the cost savings exceed the lost revenues from dropping a product, department, or territory → Drop.**

Product Mix—Which Product to Emphasize?

Companies do not have unlimited resources. They must decide which products to emphasize and which to deemphasize to maximize profits.

⊙ DAILY EXERCISE 26-9

Consider Chazz, a manufacturer of shirts and slacks. The following data suggest that shirts are more profitable than slacks:

	Per Unit	
	Shirts	**Slacks**
Sale price	$30	$60
Variable expenses	12	48
Contribution margin	$18	$12
Contribution margin ratio:		
Shirts—$18 ÷ $30	60%	
Slacks—$12 ÷ $60......................		20%

However, an important piece of information is missing—the time it takes to manufacture each product. This factor, called the **constraint,** restricts production or sale of a product. In some companies, the constraint is production capacity. The factory or labor force may be unable to produce more than a certain number of units.

Constraints vary from company to company. The constraint that limits how much the company can produce may be labor hours, machine hours, materials, or square feet of shelf space. For example, storage may be limited to 50,000 square feet of space in a warehouse. Some companies are constrained by sales. Competition may be stiff, and the business may be able to sell only so many units.

Chazz can produce either 20 pairs of slacks *or* 10 shirts per machine hour. The company can sell all the shirts and slacks it produces. The company has 2,000 machine hours of capacity. Which product should it emphasize?

To answer this question, follow the guiding principle:

CONSTRAINT. A factor that restricts production or sale of a product.

> **To maximize profits, produce the product with the highest contribution margin *per unit of the constraint.***

In our example, Chazz can sell all the slacks and shirts it makes, so production (machine hours) is the constraint. Thus, Chazz should produce the product with the highest contribution margin per machine hour.

Exhibit 26-7 first determines the contribution margin per machine hour for each product. Slacks have a higher contribution margin per machine hour ($240 = 20 pairs of slacks × $12 per pair) than shirts ($180 = 10 shirts × $18 per shirt). Chazz will earn more profit by producing slacks. Exhibit 26-7 proves this by multiplying the contribution margin per machine hour by the available number of machine hours. Chazz can earn $480,000 of contribution margin by producing slacks, but only $360,000 by producing shirts.

Exhibit 26-7
Product Mix—Which Product to Emphasize

	Shirts	Slacks
(1) Units that can be produced each hour	10	20
(2) Contribution margin per unit	× $18	× $12
Contribution margin per hour (1) × (2)	$180	$240
Capacity—number of hours	× 2,000	× 2,000
Total contribution margin at full capacity	$360,000	$480,000

Exhibit 26-7 shows that Chazz should *not* produce the product with the highest contribution margin *per unit* (shirts). The key point is that Chazz will earn more profit if it produces the product with the highest contribution margin per unit of the (machine hours) constraint—slacks.

Notice that the analysis in Exhibit 26-7 has once again followed the two guidelines for special business decisions: (1) focus on relevant data (contribution margin in this example, because only sales revenue and variable costs are relevant), and (2) use a contribution margin approach.

THINK IT OVER

Why are Chazz's fixed expenses irrelevant in the decision to produce slacks or shirts?

Answer: Chazz will use the same property, plant, and equipment to make either slacks or shirts. The fixed expenses will be the same whether the company makes slacks or shirts, so the fixed expenses are irrelevant.

Outsourcing

Manufactured goods include specialized parts. Overhead garage doors, for example, have electronic controls. **Genie,** the garage-door manufacturer, must decide whether to make the control device itself or buy from a supplier. **Swaim Furniture** may ask: Should we stain and lacquer the furniture we make or hire another company to do the finish work? These make-or-buy decisions are often called **outsourcing** decisions, because managers must decide whether to buy a component product or service, or to produce it in-house. Assuming that quality is unaffected, the heart of these decisions is *how best to use available facilities.*

Let's see how managers make outsourcing decisions. DefTone, a manufacturer of music CDs, is deciding whether to make the paper liners for the CD jewel boxes in-house, or whether to outsource them to Mūz-Art, a company that specializes in producing these paper liners. DefTone's cost to produce 250,000 liners is

OUTSOURCING. A make-or-buy decision, where managers must decide whether to buy a component product or service or to produce it in-house.

	Total Cost (250,000 liners)
Direct materials	$ 40,000
Direct labor	20,000
Variable overhead	15,000
Fixed overhead	50,000
Total manufacturing cost	$125,000
Cost per liner ($125,000 ÷ 250,000)	$0.50

Mūz-Art offers to sell DefTone the liners for $0.37 each. Should DefTone make the liners or buy them from Mūz-Art? DefTone's $0.50 cost per unit to make the liner is $0.13 higher than the cost of buying it from Mūz-Art. It appears that DefTone should outsource the liners. But the correct answer is not so simple. To make the best decision, you must compare the difference in expected future costs between the alternatives. Which costs will differ depending on whether DefTone makes or buys the liners?

By purchasing the liner, DefTone can avoid all variable manufacturing costs and reduce its fixed overhead cost by $10,000. (Fixed overhead will decrease to $40,000.) Exhibit 26-8 shows the differences in costs between the make and buy alternatives.

EXHIBIT 26-8
Outsourcing Decision

DAILY EXERCISE 26-10

DAILY EXERCISE 26-11

DAILY EXERCISE 26-12

Liner Costs	Make Liners	Buy Liners	Difference
Direct materials...............................	$ 40,000	—	$40,000
Direct labor	20,000	—	20,000
Variable overhead	15,000	—	15,000
Fixed overhead	50,000	$ 40,000	10,000
Purchase cost from Mūz-Art			
(250,000 × $0.37)	—	92,500	(92,500)
Total cost of liners.................................	$125,000	$132,500	$(7,500)
Cost per unit—250,000 liners..............	$0.50	$0.53	$(0.03)

The decision: It would cost less to make the liners than to buy them from Mūz-Art. The net savings from making 250,000 liners is $7,500, which works out to $0.03 each.

This example shows that *fixed costs are relevant to a special decision when those fixed costs differ between alternatives.* Exhibit 26-8 also shows that outsourcing decisions follow our two guidelines for special business decisions: (1) focus on relevant data (variable and fixed manufacturing costs in this case), and (2) use a contribution margin approach that separates variable costs from fixed costs. These guidelines help managers answer the fundamental question: What difference does the proposed change make?

DAILY EXERCISE 26-13

BEST USE OF FACILITIES   Suppose that buying the liners from Mūz-Art will release factory facilities that DefTone can use to make more CDs at an expected annual profit of $18,000. DefTone's managers must decide among three alternatives:

1. Use the facilities to make the liners.
2. Buy the liners and leave facilities idle.
3. Buy the liners and use facilities to make more CDs.

The alternative with the lowest *net* cost is the best use of DefTone's facilities. Exhibit 26-9 compares net cost under the three alternatives.

EXHIBIT 26-9   Best Use of Facilities

		Buy Liners	
	Make Liners	Facilities Idle	Make Additional CDs
Expected cost of obtaining 250,000 liners			
(from Exhibit 26-8)	$125,000	$132,500	$132,500
Expected profit from additional CDs	—	—	(18,000)
Expected net cost of obtaining 250,000 liners	$125,000	$132,500	$114,500

This analysis of net cost indicates that DefTone should buy the liners from Mūz-Art and use the vacated facilities to make more CDs. If the facilities remain idle, DefTone will forgo the opportunity to earn $18,000.

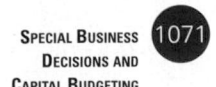

Managers making special decisions must often consider qualitative factors—that is, factors that are difficult to quantify. For example, DefTone managers may believe they can better control quality by making the liners themselves. This argues for making the liners. But Mūz-Art may be located very close to DefTone's plant. Mūz-Art may be able to achieve a higher on-time delivery rate than DefTone's own plant. This would favor buying from Mūz-Art. DefTone's managers should consider these qualitative factors as well as revenue and cost differences in making their final decision.

Outsourcing decisions are increasingly important in today's globally wired economy. In the past, make-or-buy decisions often ended up as "make," because coordination, information exchange, and paperwork problems made buying from suppliers too inconvenient. The Internet has largely eliminated these problems. Business-to-business applications allow companies to tap into suppliers' and customers' information systems and business processes, even if those suppliers and customers are located halfway around the world. Paperwork vanishes, and information required to satisfy the most stringent just-in-time delivery schedule is available in real time. As a result, companies are focusing on their core competencies and outsourcing more and more other functions.

Like **Cisco Systems, Dell,** and **Nike,** many world-class competitors have discovered that their core competency lies not in manufacturing but in research and

e-Accounting

We Brand it, You Make It: The Outsourcing Trend

Your cell phone may sport the **Motorola, Inc.,** logo, but there's a good chance it was actually made by a little-known company based in Singapore, **Flextronics International Ltd.** In May 2000, Motorola announced that it expects to outsource over $30 billion of consumer electronics production. It was the largest outsourcing agreement to date between a name-brand electronics company and a contract manufacturer. In 1998, contract manufacturing was a $60 billion industry. By 2003 it will grow to nearly $150 billion.

According to a *Purchasing* magazine survey, 81% of electronics buyers cited cost as their reason for outsourcing everything from motherboards and set-top boxes to entire products. How do contract manufacturers like Flextronics and Militpas, CA,-based **Solectron** do the job more cheaply than original equipment manufacturers (OEMs)? "We leverage our overhead," says Solectron's CFO Susan Wang. In other words, orders from multiple clients keep contract manufacturers' plants busy around the clock and cover overhead costs.

OEMs are also rushing to outsource manufacturing so they can concentrate on the activities that add value. Product development, marketing, and customer support are all areas in which OEMs can gain a competitive edge. The manufacturing process is increasingly viewed as a commodity. "OEM is an oddity as an acronym," says Pamela Gordon of Technology Forecasters, a consulting firm: "What it really means is a company whose brand name goes on the product."

Because of the importance of distinguishing their brand name, OEMs must ensure that far-flung contract manufacturers in Brazil, Mexico, or Hungary deliver quality products. Most OEMs with multi-million or -billion-dollar contract manufacturer contracts maintain a team of their own people to oversee quality control. For Motorola, the Internet will play a major role in keeping close tabs on contract manufacturers around the globe. After announcing the Flextronics deal, both companies said they plan to use Internet technology to tie themselves more closely together and streamline Motorola's supply chain.

Sources: based on Scott Thurm, "Motorola plans to outsource production to Flextronics in $30 billion agreement," *Wall Street Journal,* May 31, 2000, p. A3. Paul Gibson, "The asset paradox," *Electronic Business,* April 2000, pp. 120–126. James Carbone, "What buyers look for in contract manufacturers," *Purchasing,* March 23, 2000, pp. 32–38. John Teresko, "E-collaboration," *Industry Week,* June 12, 2000, pp. 31–36.

development and in brand marketing. Such companies outsource much of their manufacturing to contract manufacturers like **Flextronics** and **Yue Yuen Industrial Holdings,** which operate huge plants in countries where labor is less expensive, such as Mexico and Taiwan.

Cisco currently operates three plants that make its most sophisticated components, but outside suppliers directly fill 55% of Cisco's customers' orders. **Hewlett-Packard** is a leader in laser printers, but it outsources production of the laser mechanisms to **Canon.** Outsourcing doesn't stop at production. **Eastman Kodak** decided to outsource its cafeteria and security operations, and **BP Amoco** is considering outsourcing its accounting function.

Many outsourcing decisions are short-term in nature, but Cisco's decision to subcontract most of its manufacturing is a long-term one. When making decisions with long-term consequences, managers identify and analyze the relevant costs and benefits of different alternatives, as DefTone did in Exhibits 26-8 and 26-9. The only difference is that these cost and benefit calculations may extend many years into the future. In this case, managers discount these costs and benefits to their *present values,* as we explain in the second half of the chapter.

Sell As Is or Process Further?

 DAILY EXERCISE 26-14

Should a product be sold as it is, or should the product be processed further into another item? For example, suppose that the **Chevron** oil company spent $48,000 to produce 50,000 gallons of regular gasoline, as shown in Exhibit 26-10. Assume Chevron can sell this regular gasoline for $1.20 per gallon, for a total of $60,000 (50,000 × $1.20). Alternatively, Chevron could further process this regular gasoline into premium-grade gas. Suppose the additional cost to process the gas further is $0.11 per gallon, for an additional cost of $5,500 (50,000 gallons × $0.11). Assume the sale price of premium gasoline is $1.40 per gallon, for a total of $70,000 (50,000 × $1.40).

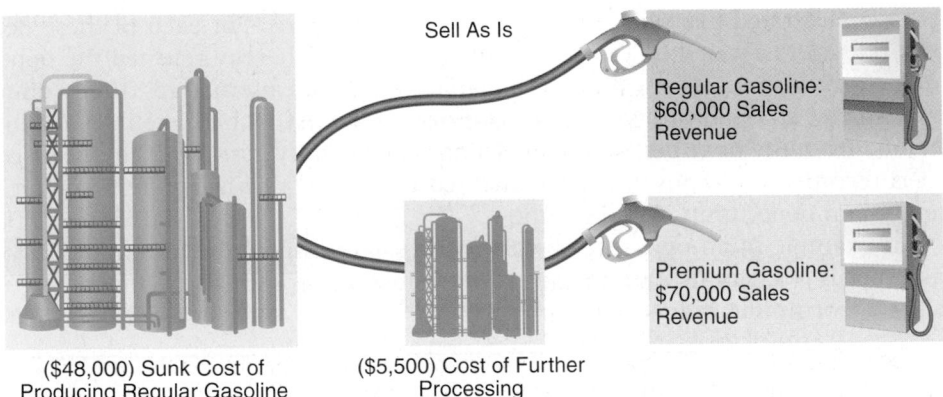

Sell As Is

Regular Gasoline: $60,000 Sales Revenue

Premium Gasoline: $70,000 Sales Revenue

($48,000) Sunk Cost of Producing Regular Gasoline

($5,500) Cost of Further Processing

EXHIBIT 26-10
Sell As Is or Process Further Decision

As in other special business decisions, managers need to know which items are relevant. The $48,000 cost of producing the 50,000 gallons of regular gasoline is *not* relevant to Chevron's sell or process further decision. Why? Because the $48,000 is a **sunk cost**—a past cost that cannot be changed regardless of which future action is taken. Exhibit 26-10 shows that the $48,000 has been incurred whether Chevron sells the regular gasoline as is or processes it further into premium gasoline.

SUNK COST. A past cost that cannot be changed regardless of which future action is taken.

Exhibits 26-10 and 26-11 show that the relevant items that differ between Chevron's (1) sell as is and (2) process further alternatives are

- Expected revenues
- Expected costs of processing further

The analysis indicates that Chevron should process the gasoline into the premium grade, because the $10,000 extra revenue ($70,000 − $60,000) outweighs the $5,500 cost of the extra processing.

Exhibit 26-11   Sell As Is or Process Further Decision

	Sell As Is	Process Further	Difference
Expected revenue from selling 50,000 gallons of regular gasoline at $1.20 per gallon	$60,000		
Expected revenue from selling 50,000 gallons of premium gasoline at $1.40 per gallon		$70,000	$10,000
Additional costs of $0.11 per gallon to convert 50,000 gallons of regular gasoline into premium gasoline		(5,500)	(5,500)
Total net revenue...	$60,000	$64,500	
Difference in net revenue...			$ 4,500

Thus, the key guideline for sell as is or process further decisions is

Process further only if the extra sales revenue (from processing further) exceeds the extra costs of additional processing.

THINK IT OVER

Some companies have obsolete inventories that cannot be sold at regular prices. How should managers decide whether to sell the units as is or to incur additional manufacturing costs to rework them?

Answer: This is a sell or process further decision. Managers should predict the additional costs of reworking the inventory. Then they should forecast the additional revenues after rework. If reworking will lead to additional revenues that exceed the additional costs, they should process further. If not, sell the units as is.

Objective 4
Use opportunity costs in decision making

OPPORTUNITY COST

OPPORTUNITY COST. The benefit that can be obtained from the next-best course of action.

We have illustrated five types of special business decisions. For each of these decisions, managers decided on one course of action—and thereby rejected the opportunity to take other actions. When the managers rejected alternatives, their companies incurred an opportunity cost. An **opportunity cost** is the benefit that can be obtained from the next-best course of action. Opportunity cost is *not* an outlay cost that is recorded in accounting. An outlay cost requires a cash payment sooner or later, but an opportunity cost does not.

An example of an opportunity cost is the salary forgone by an engineer who may quit his job with IBM to start his own business. Suppose the engineer analyzes his job opportunities as follows:

◉ DAILY EXERCISE 26-15

◉ DAILY EXERCISE 26-16

Expected Future Event	Open an Independent Business	Remain with IBM
Salary from IBM............................		$60,000
Sales revenue	$200,000	
Expenses..	120,000	
Net income	$ 80,000	$60,000

The opportunity cost of staying with IBM is the forgone $80,000 of net income from the independent business. The opportunity cost of starting a new business is the $60,000 salary from IBM.

How do managers use opportunity costs in decision making? Consider two examples.

1. *Suppose the IBM engineer has a third job opportunity—employment by* **Microsoft.** To determine the best alternative, the engineer can compare Microsoft's offer with the $80,000 opportunity cost of not opening an independent business. If the engineer's goal is to maximize his personal income, he will accept Microsoft's

offer only if it exceeds his $80,000 opportunity cost. (The IBM salary is irrelevant because opportunity cost is the benefit from the next-best course of action.)

2. *Refer to Exhibit 26-11.* Suppose **Chevron** is approached by a customer who needs 50,000 gallons of regular gasoline. The customer is willing to pay more than $1.20 per gallon. Chevron's managers can use the $64,500 ($70,000 − $5,500) opportunity cost of not further processing the gas to determine the sale price that will provide an equivalent income ($64,500 ÷ 50,000 = $1.29). If the customer offers more than Chevron's opportunity cost of $1.29 per gallon, Chevron will be better off selling the regular gasoline. If the customer offers less than $1.29, Chevron will be better off further processing the gas.

The special decisions we reviewed here usually pertain to relatively short periods of time, such as a year. In this time frame:

- Many costs are fixed and do not vary with the volume of goods or services produced. This is why short-term special business decisions use the contribution margin approach that distinguishes variable from fixed costs.
- There is no need to worry about the time value of money. Managers do not bother computing present values of revenues and expenses for short-term decisions.

In the next half of the chapter, we turn to longer-term special decisions, like **Deer Valley's** decision to build a major expansion of Snow Park Lodge. For long-term decisions:

- Few if any costs are fixed.
- Managers often take into account the time value of money.

The approach to long-term decisions will reflect these differences.

But before moving on to long-term special decisions, stop for a moment to review the Decision Guidelines that summarize key points from our discussion of short-term decisions. Then work the mid-chapter summary problems.

DECISION GUIDELINES

Short-Term Special Business Decisions

DECISION	GUIDELINE
What information is relevant to a short-term special business decision?	Relevant data: 1. are expected *future* data that 2. *differ* between alternatives.
What are two key guidelines in making short-term special business decisions?	Key guidelines: 1. focus on *relevant* data. 2. use a *contribution margin* approach that separates variable costs from fixed costs.
When will accepting a special sales order increase income?	If the revenue from the order exceeds the extra variable and fixed costs incurred to fill the order, then operating income will increase.
When will dropping a product, department, or territory increase income?	If the cost savings exceed the lost revenues from dropping a product, department, or territory, then dropping will increase operating income.
To maximize profit, which product to emphasize when there is a constraining factor?	Emphasize the product with the highest contribution margin per unit of the constraint.
How to decide whether to sell a product as is or process further?	Process further only if the extra sales revenue (from processing further) exceeds the extra costs of additional processing.
How to determine the opportunity cost of a decision?	The opportunity cost of a decision is the benefit forgone by not choosing the next-best course of action.

SUMMARY PROBLEMS

Problem 1.

Aziz, Inc., produces two styles of sunglasses, a standard model and a deluxe model, with the following data:

	Per Pair	
	Standard	Deluxe
Sale price...........................	$20	$30
Variable expenses..............	16	21

The company has 15,000 machine hours of capacity available. Seventy pairs of the standard model can be produced in an hour, compared with 30 pairs of the deluxe model. Which style should the company emphasize?

Problem 2.

Just Do It! has the following manufacturing costs for 20,000 pair of its high-tech hiking socks:

Direct materials	$ 20,000
Direct labor..	80,000
Variable overhead..	40,000
Fixed overhead...	80,000
Total manufacturing cost	$220,000
Cost per pair ($220,000 ÷ 20,000)...............	$11

Another manufacturer has offered to sell Just Do It! similar socks for $10, a total purchase cost of $200,000. By outsourcing, Just Do It! can save $50,000 of fixed overhead cost. The company can use the released facilities to make other products that will contribute $60,000 to profits. Identify and analyze the alternatives. What is the best course of action?

Solutions:
Problem 1

	Style of Sunglasses			
	Standard		Deluxe	
Sale price per pair	$	20	$	30
Variable expense per pair..		(16)		(21)
Contribution margin per pair..	$	4	$	9
Units that can be produced each machine hour		× 70		× 30
Contribution margin per machine hour	$	280	$	270
Capacity—number of hours...		× 15,000		× 15,000
Total contribution margin at full capacity......................		$4,200,000		$4,050,000

Decision: Emphasize the standard model because it has the higher contribution margin per unit of the constraint—machine hours.

Problem 2

	Make Socks	Buy Socks	
		Facilities Idle	Make Other Products
Relevant costs:			
Direct materials	$ 20,000	—	
Direct labor	80,000	—	
Variable overhead.....................	40,000	—	
Fixed overhead	80,000	$ 30,000	$ 30,000
Purchase cost from outsider (20,000 × $10)	—	200,000	200,000
Total cost of obtaining socks.........	220,000	230,000	230,000
Profit from other products	—	—	(60,000)
Net cost of obtaining 20,000 pairs of socks.............................	$220,000	$230,000	$170,000

Decision: Just Do It! should buy the socks from the outside supplier and use the released facilities to make other products.

Capital Budgeting: Payback and Accounting Rate of Return

We have seen how managers make short-term special business decisions. Now let's turn to decisions that have long-term effects on business operations.

Think back to the chapter opening story. The **Deer Valley** owners' decision to spend $13 million to expand Snow Park Lodge will tie up resources for years to come. How did the owners decide that the expansion would be a good investment? The Snow Park Lodge expansion met two conditions:

- First, the investment was part of the company's long-term plan. Deer Valley's long-term plan called for expansion when the resort served a target number of skiers per day and achieved a target level of profits.
- Second, Deer Valley's owners used capital budgeting techniques to analyze the expected financial effects of the investment.

Capital budgeting is a formal means of analyzing long-term investment decisions. The term describes budgeting for the acquisition of *capital assets*—assets used for a long period of time. Examples of capital budgeting decisions include expanding the Deer Valley resort, building a new plant, or developing a major commercial Web site for an expansion into e-commerce.

Before proceeding, you need to understand this: Capital budgeting is not an exact science. No matter how precise your calculations, they are based on predictions about an uncertain future. Because capital budgeting decisions have effects far into the future, your predictions must consider many unknown factors, such as changing consumer preferences, competition, and government regulations. The farther into the future the decision extends, the more likely that actual results will differ from predictions. Long-term decisions are thus riskier than short-term decisions.

We now discuss four popular capital budgeting decision models: payback, accounting rate of return, net present value, and internal rate of return. Three of these models compare the *net cash inflows from operations* each alternative generates. ➡ Generally accepted accounting principles are based on accrual accounting, but capital budgeting focuses on cash flows. The desirability of a capital asset depends on its ability to generate net cash inflows—that is, inflows in excess of outflows—over the asset's useful life.

CAPITAL BUDGETING. A formal means of analyzing long-term investment decisions. Describes budgeting for the acquisition of capital assets.

◀ We discussed cash flows from operating activities, often the primary source of cash, in Chapter 17, page 657.

Payback Period

Payback is the length of time it will take to recover, in net cash inflows from operations, the dollars of a capital outlay. The payback model measures how quickly managers expect to recover their investment dollars. The shorter the payback period, the more attractive the asset, all else being equal. Computing the payback period depends on whether cash flows are equal each year, or whether they differ over time. We consider each in turn.

PAYBACK. The length of time it will take to recover, in net cash inflows from operations, the dollars of a capital outlay.

PAYBACK WITH EQUAL CASH FLOWS   Tierra Firma, a manufacturer of high-quality camping gear, is considering investing $240,000 in information technology (hardware and software) to develop a portal, or interface, with a business-to-business (B2B) electronic market. The portal will enable employees throughout the company to enter the electronic market of certified suppliers, to purchase goods and services appropriate to their jobs. Accountants will be able to buy office supplies, and maintenance workers will be able to buy parts. The portal will incorporate controls on the kinds of goods and services each employee can buy, as well as preset spending limits. Tierra Firma expects the portal to save $60,000 a year for the six years of its useful life. The savings will arise from reducing the number of purchasing personnel the company employs and through lower prices on the goods and services purchased.

⊙ DAILY EXERCISE 26-17

When net cash inflows are equal each year, managers compute the payback period as follows:

⊙ DAILY EXERCISE 26-18

$$\text{Payback Period} = \frac{\text{Amount invested}}{\text{Expected annual net cash inflow}}$$

⊙ DAILY EXERCISE 26-19

In general, net cash inflows can arise from an increase in revenues, a decrease in expenses, or both. In Tierra's case, the net cash inflows result from lower expenses. Tierra computes the investment's payback as follows:

$$\text{Payback period for B2B portal} = \frac{\$240,000}{\$60,000} = 4 \text{ years}$$

Exhibit 26-12 verifies that Tierra expects to recoup the $240,000 investment in the B2B portal by the end of year 4, when the accumulated cash inflows (savings) total $240,000.

Tierra Firma is also considering investing $240,000 to develop a Web site to sell its camping gear. The company expects the Web site to generate $80,000 in cash inflows each year of its three-year life. The payback period is computed as follows:

$$\text{Payback period for Web site development} = \frac{\$240,000}{\$80,000} = 3 \text{ years}$$

Exhibit 26-12 verifies that Tierra Firma will recoup the $240,000 investment for Web site development by the end of year 3, when the accumulated net cash inflows

EXHIBIT 26-12
Payback—Equal Annual Net Cash Inflows

| | | Net Cash Inflows | | | |
| | Amount | B2B Portal | | Web site Development | |
Year	Invested	Annual	Accumulated	Annual	Accumulated
0	$240,000	—	—	—	
1	—	$60,000	$ 60,000	$80,000	$ 80,000
2	—	60,000	120,000	80,000	160,000
3	—	60,000	180,000	80,000	240,000
4	—	60,000	240,000		
5	—	60,000	300,000		
6	—	60,000	360,000		

total $240,000. Thus, the payback criterion favors Web site development because it recovers the investment more quickly.

A major criticism of the payback model is that it does not consider profitability. The payback technique can lead managers to make unwise decisions. For example, consider the two projects' useful lives. The Web site's useful life is the same as its payback period—three years. Exhibit 26-12 shows that the Web site will merely cover its cost and provide no profits. But the B2B portal has a useful life of six years. It will continue to generate net cash inflows for two years after its payback period. This will give the company an additional net cash inflow of $120,000 ($60,000 × 2 years). Unlike the Web site, the B2B portal will be profitable. After considering the assets' useful lives, the B2B portal appears to be the better investment.

PAYBACK WITH UNEQUAL ANNUAL CASH FLOWS The payback equation only works when net cash inflows are the same for each period. When periodic cash flows are unequal, you must accumulate net cash inflows until the amount invested is recovered. Suppose Tierra Firma's B2B portal will generate net cash inflows of $100,000 in Year 1, $80,000 in Year 2, $50,000 each year in Years 3–5, and $30,000 in Year 6. Exhibit 26-13 shows the payback schedule for these unequal annual cash flows.

EXHIBIT 26-13
Payback—Unequal Annual Net Cash Inflows

| | | Net Cash Inflow | |
Year	Amount Invested	Each Year	Accumulated
0	$240,000	—	—
1	—	$100,000	$100,000
2	—	80,000	180,000
3	—	50,000	230,000
3.2	—	10,000	240,000
4	—	40,000	280,000
5	—	50,000	330,000
6	—	30,000	360,000

By the end of Year 3, we have recovered $230,000. Recovery of the amount invested ($240,000) occurs during Year 4. Payback occurs in 3.2 years:

$$\text{Payback} = 3 \text{ years} + \frac{\$10,000 \text{ needed to complete recovery in Year 4}}{\$50,000 \text{ net cash inflow in year 4}} \times 1 \text{ year}$$

$$= 3 \text{ years} + 0.2 \text{ year} = 3.2 \text{ years}$$

Managers compare the payback period with the asset's useful life. The asset's payback period must be shorter than its useful life. If an asset like information technology has a payback period of five years and a useful life of three years, the company will never earn a profit from the asset.

How much shorter than the useful life the payback period must be is a business decision that varies by industry and business conditions. When the business is deciding between two or more assets, the asset with the shortest payback period is better *only if all other factors are the same*. This leads to the following decision rule:

> Invest only if payback is *shorter* than the asset's useful life. Investments with shorter payback periods are more desirable, *all else being equal*.

The payback method highlights cash flows, a key factor in business decisions. And payback is easy to understand. Managers like those at Deer Valley Resort often use the payback method to eliminate proposals that are too risky (projects with long payback periods). However, a major weakness of payback is that it ignores profitability.

 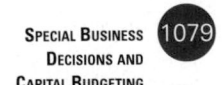

DAILY EXERCISE 26-20

ACCOUNTING RATE OF RETURN. A measure of profitability computed by dividing the average annual operating income from an asset by the average amount invested in the asset.

Accounting Rate of Return

Companies are in business to earn profits. One measure of profitability is the rate of return on investment. The **accounting rate of return** on an asset is computed as follows:

$$\text{Accounting rate of return} = \frac{\text{Average annual operating income from asset}}{\text{Average amount invested in asset}}$$

The accounting rate of return focuses on the operating income an asset generates. Operating income from an asset can be computed as net cash inflow from the asset minus depreciation on the asset. Exhibit 26-14 computes the accounting rate of return for Tierra Firma's B2B portal in the original payback example. Recall that Tierra expects the portal to generate annual net cash inflows of \$60,000. The portal's development costs \$240,000, and it has a useful life of six years with no residual value. Annual straight-line depreciation is \$40,000 (\$240,000 ÷ 6 years). Exhibit 26-14 shows that Tierra expects the portal to generate average annual operating income of \$20,000 (\$60,000 − \$40,000).

Recall from Chapter 10, page 393, that straight-line depreciation assigns an equal amount of depreciation expense to each year of an asset's life.

EXHIBIT 26-14
Accounting Rate of Return

$$\text{Accounting rate of return} = \frac{\text{Average annual operating income from asset}^{*}}{\text{Average amount invested in asset}}$$

$$= \frac{\text{Annual net cash inflow from asset} - \text{Annual depreciation on asset}}{(\text{Amount invested in asset} + \text{Residual value})/2}$$

$$= \frac{\$60{,}000 - \$40{,}000^{\dagger}}{(\$240{,}000 + \$0)/2}$$

$$= \frac{\$20{,}000}{\$120{,}000} = 0.167 = 16.7\%$$

* Operating income can also be computed as revenues minus operating expenses.

† $\$40{,}000 = \frac{\$240{,}000}{6 \text{ years}}$

The accounting rate of return is an *average*. It measures the average rate of return from using the asset over its entire life. First, consider the average annual operating income in the computation. If operating income varies by year (as in the second payback example), compute the *total* operating income over the asset's life. Then divide the total by the number of years of life to find the *average* annual operating income from the asset.

Second, consider the average amount invested. The book value of the asset decreases as it is used and depreciated. Thus, the company's investment in the asset declines over time. If the asset's residual value is zero, the average investment is half the asset's cost. Exhibit 26-14 shows that the average amount invested in Tierra's B2B portal from the original payback example is \$120,000 (\$240,000 ÷ 2).

If the asset's residual value is not zero, the average amount invested is greater than half the asset's cost. For example, assume the residual value of the portal's technology is \$30,000. Then annual depreciation declines to \$35,000 [(\$240,000 − \$30,000)/6]. The accounting rate of return is

$$\text{Accounting rate of return} = \frac{\$60{,}000 - \$35{,}000}{(\$240{,}000 + \$30{,}000)/2} = \frac{\$25{,}000}{\$135{,}000} = 0.185 = 18.5\%$$

Companies that use the accounting rate of return model set a minimum required rate of return. They invest only in assets with accounting rates of return equal to or greater than the minimum required rate. Suppose Tierra Firma requires a rate of return of at least 20 percent. Would its managers approve an investment in the B2B portal technology in Exhibit 26-14? No, because the average annual return is less than the company's minimum required rate (20%). Thus, the decision rule is:

> **Invest in assets whose expected accounting rate of return exceeds the company's required accounting rate of return.**

CAPITAL BUDGETING: DISCOUNTED CASH-FLOW MODELS

Chapter 15 introduced the concept of present value. ➡ A dollar received today is worth more than a dollar to be received in the future. Why? Because you can invest today's dollar and earn extra income. Suppose you can choose between receiving a dollar today and a dollar one year from today. If you receive $1 today and deposit it in a bank that pays 6% interest, a year from today you will have $1.06 (the original $1 plus $0.06 interest). Presumably, you would rather receive the $1 now, which will grow to $1.06 a year from today, rather than simply receive $1 a year from today. The fact that money can be invested to earn income over time is called the **time value of money,** and this explains why businesses as well as individuals would rather receive cash sooner than later.

The time value of money ➡ means that the timing of capital investments' net cash flows is important. Consider two $10,000 investments that both promise future cash inflows of $11,000. Investment 1 will bring in cash of $5,500 at the end of each of the next two years. Investment 2 will return the full $11,000 at the end of the second year. Which investment is better? Investment 1, because it brings in cash sooner. Its $5,500 net cash inflow at the end of the first year can be reinvested right away to earn additional returns.

Neither the payback period nor the accounting rate of return recognizes the time value of money. That is, these models fail to consider the *timing* of the net cash flows an asset generates. *Discounted cash-flow models*—the net present value and the internal rate of return—overcome this weakness. Over 85% of large industrial firms in the United States use discounted cash flow methods to make capital budgeting decisions. Companies that provide services, like Deer Valley Resort, also use these models.

Net Present Value

Allegra is considering producing two products, CD players and VCRs. The products require different specialized machines that each cost $1 million. Each machine has a five-year life and zero residual value. The two products have different patterns of predicted net cash inflows:

| | Annual Net Cash Inflows | |
Year	CD Players	VCRs
1	$ 305,450	$ 500,000
2	305,450	350,000
3	305,450	300,000
4	305,450	250,000
5	305,450	40,000
Total	$1,527,250	$1,440,000

Total net cash inflows are greater if Allegra invests in the CD-player project. However, the VCR project brings in cash sooner. To decide which investment is better, we use **net present value (NPV)** to bring cash inflows and outflows back to a common time period. We *discount* these expected future cash flows to their present value, using Allegra's minimum desired rate of return. We then compare the discounted cash inflows with the discounted cash outflows to decide which, if any, projects to undertake.

◄ Recall from Chapter 15, page 579, that present value is the amount a person would invest now to receive a greater amount in the future.

TIME VALUE OF MONEY. The fact that money can be invested to earn income over time.

◄ The time value of money is discussed in the Chapter 15 appendix, page 613.

NET PRESENT VALUE (NPV). The decision model that brings cash inflows and outflows back to a common time period by discounting these expected future cash flows to their present value, using a minimum desired rate of return.

Management's minimum desired rate of return on an investment is called the **discount rate.** Synonyms are **hurdle rate, required rate of return,** and **cost of capital.** The discount rate depends on the riskiness of investments. The higher the risk, the higher the discount rate. Allegra's discount rate for these investments is 14%.

NET PRESENT VALUE WITH EQUAL PERIODIC CASH FLOWS (ANNUITY) Allegra expects the CD players to generate $305,450 of new cash inflow each year. This kind of stream of equal periodic cash flows is an **annuity.** The present value of an annuity is computed by multiplying the periodic cash flow ($305,450 in this case) by the present value of an annuity of $1, obtained from the present value of an annuity table in Exhibit 26-15. The table indicates that the present value of an annuity of $1 received each year for five years, discounted at 14% per year, is $3.433. That is, the value today of receiving $1 at the end of each year for the next five years, discounted at 14%, is $3.433. Another way to think about this is that if Allegra invested $3.433 today at a 14% annual interest rate, there would be just enough money to pay out $1 at the end of each year for the next five years.

EXHIBIT 26-15 **Present Value of Annuity of $1**

Period	Present Value of Annuity of $1								
	4%	5%	6%	7%	8%	10%	12%	14%	16%
1	0.962	0.952	0.943	0.935	0.926	0.909	0.893	0.877	0.862
2	1.886	1.859	1.833	1.808	1.783	1.736	1.690	1.647	1.605
3	2.775	2.723	2.673	2.624	2.577	2.487	2.402	2.322	2.246
4	3.630	3.546	3.465	3.387	3.312	3.170	3.037	2.914	2.798
5	4.452	4.329	4.212	4.100	3.993	3.791	3.605	3.433	3.274
6	5.242	5.076	4.917	4.767	4.623	4.355	4.111	3.889	3.685
7	6.002	5.786	5.582	5.389	5.206	4.868	4.564	4.288	4.039
8	6.733	6.463	6.210	5.971	5.747	5.335	4.968	4.639	4.344
9	7.435	7.108	6.802	6.515	6.247	5.759	5.328	4.946	4.607
10	8.111	7.722	7.360	7.024	6.710	6.145	5.650	5.216	4.833
11	8.760	8.306	7.887	7.499	7.139	6.495	5.938	5.453	5.029
12	9.385	8.863	8.384	7.943	7.536	6.814	6.194	5.660	5.197
13	9.986	9.394	8.853	8.358	7.904	7.103	6.424	5.842	5.342
14	10.563	9.899	9.295	8.745	8.244	7.367	6.628	6.002	5.468
15	11.118	10.380	9.712	9.108	8.559	7.606	6.811	6.142	5.575
16	11.652	10.838	10.106	9.447	8.851	7.824	6.974	6.265	5.669
17	12.166	11.274	10.477	9.763	9.122	8.022	7.120	6.373	5.749
18	12.659	11.690	10.828	10.059	9.372	8.201	7.250	6.467	5.818
19	13.134	12.085	11.158	10.336	9.604	8.365	7.366	6.550	5.877
20	13.590	12.462	11.470	10.594	9.818	8.514	7.469	6.623	5.929

Appendix C-2 provides a more comprehensive table for the present value of an annuity of $1.

Panel A of Exhibit 26-16 uses this present value of an annuity factor (3.433) to compute the present value of the CD-player project's net cash flows. Allegra's managers multiply the $305,450 to be received each year by the present value factor for a five-year annuity of $1 discounted at 14% (3.433) to obtain the present value of the net cash inflows, $1,048,610. After subtracting the $1,000,000 investment, the net present value of the CD-player project is $48,610.

A positive net present value means that the project earns more than the target rate of return. A negative net present value means that the project fails to earn the target rate of return. This leads to the following decision rule:

Invest in projects with a positive net present value.

In Allegra's case, the CD-player project is an attractive investment. The $48,610 positive net present value means that the CD-player project earns more than Allegra's 14% target rate of return.

Exhibit 26-16   **Net Present Value**

	Present Value at 14%		Net Cash Inflow		Total Present Value
PANEL A—Net Present Value with Equal Cash Flows					
CD-Player Project					
Present value of annuity of equal annual net cash inflows for 5 years at 14%	3.433*	×	$305,450 per year	=	$1,048,610
Investment...					(1,000,000)
Net present value of the CD-player project					$ 48,610
PANEL B—Net Present Value with Unequal Cash Flows					
VCR Project					
Present value of each year's net cash inflows discounted at 14%:					
Year 1...	0.877†	×	$500,000	=	$ 438,500
Year 2...	0.769	×	350,000	=	269,150
Year 3...	0.675	×	300,000	=	202,500
Year 4...	0.592	×	250,000	=	148,000
Year 5...	0.519	×	40,000	=	20,760
Total present value of net cash inflows....................					1,078,910
Investment...					(1,000,000)
Net present value of the VCR project					$ 78,910

* Present value of annuity of $1 for 5 years at 14%, Exhibit 26-15.
† Present value of $1 in 1 year, 2 years, 3 years, and so on, at 14%, Exhibit 26-17.

Another way managers can use present value analysis is to *start* the capital budgeting process by computing the total present value of the net cash inflows from the project to determine the maximum the company can invest in the project and still earn the target rate of return. For Allegra, the present value of the net cash inflows is $1,048,610. This means that Allegra can invest a maximum of $1,048,610 in the CD-player project and still earn the 14% target rate of return. Since Allegra's managers believe they can undertake the project for $1,000,000, the project is an attractive investment.

Net Present Value with Unequal Periodic Cash Flows   In contrast to the CD-player project, the net cash inflows of the VCR project are unequal—$500,000 in Year 1, $350,000 in Year 2, and so on. Because these amounts vary by year, Allegra's managers must compute the present value of each amount separately:

Year	Present Value of $1 from Exhibit 26-17, 14% Column	Net Cash Inflow	Present Value of Net Cash Inflow
1	0.877	× $500,000 =	$438,500
2	0.769	× 350,000 =	269,150

Panel B of Exhibit 26-16 includes these present-value computations, along with similar computations for Years 3–5. The exhibit indicates that the total present value of the VCR project's net cash inflows is $1,078,910. After subtracting the $1,000,000 investment, Panel B shows that the VCR project has a total net present value of $78,910. This positive net present value means that Allegra expects the VCR project to earn more than the 14% target rate of return. Thus, the VCR project is an attractive investment.

EXHIBIT 26-17 Present Value of $1

Present Value of $1

Period	4%	5%	6%	7%	8%	10%	12%	14%	16%
1	0.962	0.952	0.943	0.935	0.926	0.909	0.893	0.877	0.862
2	0.925	0.907	0.890	0.873	0.857	0.826	0.797	0.769	0.743
3	0.889	0.864	0.840	0.816	0.794	0.751	0.712	0.675	0.641
4	0.855	0.823	0.792	0.763	0.735	0.683	0.636	0.592	0.552
5	0.822	0.784	0.747	0.713	0.681	0.621	0.567	0.519	0.476
6	0.790	0.746	0.705	0.666	0.630	0.564	0.507	0.456	0.410
7	0.760	0.711	0.665	0.623	0.583	0.513	0.452	0.400	0.354
8	0.731	0.677	0.627	0.582	0.540	0.467	0.404	0.351	0.305
9	0.703	0.645	0.592	0.544	0.500	0.424	0.361	0.308	0.263
10	0.676	0.614	0.558	0.508	0.463	0.386	0.322	0.270	0.227
11	0.650	0.585	0.527	0.475	0.429	0.350	0.287	0.237	0.195
12	0.625	0.557	0.497	0.444	0.397	0.319	0.257	0.208	0.168
13	0.601	0.530	0.469	0.415	0.368	0.290	0.229	0.182	0.145
14	0.577	0.505	0.442	0.388	0.340	0.263	0.205	0.160	0.125
15	0.555	0.481	0.417	0.362	0.315	0.239	0.183	0.140	0.108
16	0.534	0.458	0.394	0.339	0.292	0.218	0.163	0.123	0.093
17	0.513	0.436	0.371	0.317	0.270	0.198	0.146	0.108	0.080
18	0.494	0.416	0.350	0.296	0.250	0.180	0.130	0.095	0.069
19	0.475	0.396	0.331	0.277	0.232	0.164	0.116	0.083	0.060
20	0.456	0.377	0.312	0.258	0.215	0.149	0.104	0.073	0.051

Appendix C-1 provides a more comprehensive table for the present value of $1.

Use the present value of $1 table in Exhibit 26-17 to find the present value of an *annuity* of $1 for five years, discounted at 14%. Compare the result to the present value of an annuity of $1 factor from the table in Exhibit 26-15.

Answer: Exhibit 26-17 shows that at a 14% discount rate, the present value of $1 received:

In one year is	$0.877
In two years is..	0.769
In three years is	0.675
In four years is	0.592
In five years is..	0.519
Total present value of $1 received at the end of each year for five years, discounted at 14% is..............	$3.432

Except for a slight rounding error, this sum ($3.432) equals the present value of an annuity of $1 for five years discounted at 14%, shown in Exhibit 26-15 ($3.433). This shows how entries in the present value of an annuity table (Exhibit 26-15) are the sums of the present value of $1 factors from Exhibit 26-17.

Exhibit 26-16 shows that both the CD-player and the VCR projects have positive net present values. Therefore, both are attractive investments. If Allegra wants to pursue only one of the two projects, the net present value analysis in Exhibit 26-16 favors the VCR project. The VCR project should earn an additional $78,910 beyond the 14% required rate of return, while the CD-player project returns only an additional $48,610 beyond the required rate of return.

This example illustrates an important point about present-value analysis. The CD-player project promises more *total* net cash inflows. But the *timing* of the VCR cash flows—loaded near the beginning of the project—gives the VCR investment a higher net present value. The VCR project is more attractive because of the time value of money. Its dollars, which are received sooner, are worth more now than the more-distant dollars of the CD-player project.

NET PRESENT VALUE OF A PROJECT WITH RESIDUAL VALUE   Many assets yield cash inflows at the end of their useful lives. The present-value analysis must consider this residual value, discounting it to its present value when determining the total present value of the project's net cash inflows. The residual value is discounted as a single amount—not as an annuity—because it will be received only once, when the asset is sold.

 DAILY EXERCISE 26-21

Suppose Allegra expects the equipment to manufacture CD players will be worth $100,000 at the end of its five-year life. To determine the CD-player project's net present value, we discount $100,000 for five years at 14%—using the present value of $1 factor from Exhibit 26-17—and add its present value ($51,900), as shown in Exhibit 26-18.

EXHIBIT 26-18   **Net Present Value of a Project with Residual Value**

CD-Player Project	Present Value at 14%	Net Cash Inflow	Total Present Value
Present value of annuity of equal annual net cash inflows for 5 years at 14%	3.433* × $305,450 per year =		$1,048,610
Present value of residual value	0.519† × $100,000	=	51,900
Total present value of net cash inflows			1,100,510
Investment			(1,000,000)
Net present value of CD-player project			$ 100,510

* Present value of an annuity of $1 for 5 years at 14%, Exhibit 26-15.
† Present value of $1 in 5 years at 14%, Exhibit 26-17.

Compare Exhibits 26-16 and 26-18. The discounted residual value in Exhibit 26-18 raises the CD-player project's net present value to $100,510, which is higher than the VCR project. If Allegra expects the VCR equipment to have zero disposal value, then the CD-player project is now more attractive.

SENSITIVITY ANALYSIS   Great uncertainty surrounds capital budgeting decisions that affect cash flows far into the future. Allegra's managers might want to know whether their decision would be affected by

- Changing the discount rate from 14% to 12% or to 16%
- Changing the net cash flows by 10%
- Changing the residual value of the equipment

After entering the basic information for net present value analysis into spreadsheet software, managers perform sensitivity analyses with just a few keystrokes. The computer quickly displays the results.

WORK IT OUT

Suppose Allegra uses a 6% discount rate rather than the 14% rate from Exhibit 26-16. Would the net present value of the CD-player project (assuming zero residual value) be higher or lower using the 6% rate than the original 14% rate? Why?

Answer: The smaller the discount rate, the higher the present value (today) of dollars to be received in the future. Thus, discounting the cash flows at 6% rather than 14% *increases* the net present value of the CD-player project, as follows:

(Continued)

CD-Player Project	Present Value at 6%	Net Cash Inflow	Total Present Value
Present value of annuity of equal annual net cash inflows for 5 years.....................	4.212*	× $305,450 =	$1,286,555
Investment..			(1,000,000)
Net present value at 6%			286,555
Net present value at 14% (from Ex. 26-16)			(48,610)
Difference..			$ 237,945

* Present value of an annuity of $1 for 5 years at 6%, Exhibit 26-15.

Internal Rate of Return

INTERNAL RATE OF RETURN (IRR). The rate of return (based on discounted cash flows) that a company can expect to earn by investing in the project. The discount rate that makes the net present value of the project's cash flows equal to zero.

 DAILY EXERCISE 26-22

Another discounted cash-flow model for capital budgeting is the internal rate of return. The **internal rate of return (IRR)** is the rate of return (based on discounted cash flows) a company can expect to earn by investing in the project. The higher the IRR, the more desirable the project. The lower the IRR, the less desirable. The internal rate of return is the discount rate that makes the net present value of the project's cash flows equal to zero.

Exhibit 26-19 shows that Allegra's CD-player project's IRR is 16%. The 16% rate produces a net present value of zero. To see why, we follow three steps:

1. Identify the expected net cash inflows ($305,450 each year for five years) exactly as in calculating the net present value.

2. Find the discount rate that makes the total present value of the cash inflows equal to the present value of the cash outflows. This is easy when the investment consists of a single immediate cash outflow followed by a series of equal cash inflows (an annuity). Work backward to find the discount rate that makes the present value of the annuity of cash inflows equal to the amount of the investment, by solving the following equation for the annuity present-value (PV) factor:

$$\text{Investment} = \text{Expected annual net cash flow} \times \text{Annuity PV factor}$$

$$\text{Annuity PV factor} = \frac{\text{Investment}}{\text{Expected annual net cash flow}}$$

$$= \frac{\$1,000,000}{\$305,450}$$

$$= 3.274$$

3. Turn to the table presenting the present value of an annuity of $1 (Exhibit 26-15). Scan the row corresponding to the project's expected life—period 5, in our example. Choose the column with the number closest to the annuity PV factor that was calculated. The 3.274 annuity factor is in the 16% column. Therefore, the IRR of the CD-player project is 16%. Allegra expects the project to earn an annual rate of return of 16% over its life.

To decide whether the project is acceptable, compare the IRR with the minimum desired rate of return. If the IRR is equal to or greater than that minimum rate, the project is acceptable. Otherwise, it is not. That is, the decision rule is

Invest in projects whose internal rate of return exceeds the required rate of return.

If CD players were the only investment under consideration, Allegra would invest in CD players because their 16% IRR exceeds the 14% discount rate. But recall that the VCR project has a higher net present value than the CD-player project. The VCR investment also has a higher IRR. Because the VCR project has

Exhibit 26-19 **Internal Rate of Return, CD-Player Project**

	Present Value at 16%	Net Cash Inflow	Total Present Value
Present value of annuity of equal annual net cash inflows for 5 years at 16%	3.274*	× $305,450 =	$1,000,000†
Investment...			(1,000,000)
Net present value of the CD-player project			$0‡

* Present value of annuity of $1 for 5 years at 16%, Exhibit 26-15.
† Slight rounding error.
‡ The zero difference proves that the IRR is 16%.

unequal cash inflows, however, computation of the VCR's IRR requires a trial-and-error procedure that is covered in more advanced courses. (Spreadsheet software and even calculators can perform these necessary computations.)

COMPARING CAPITAL BUDGETING METHODS

Objective 6
Compare and contrast popular capital budgeting methods

Payback period, net present value, and internal rate of return are all based on *cash inflows and outflows.* Only the accounting rate of return is based on accrual accounting *revenues and expenses.* Payback is the simplest to compute, but it ignores profitability and the time value of money. The accounting rate of return considers profitability, but it also ignores the time value of money. Only net present value and internal rate of return consider the time value of money.

How do the net present value and IRR approaches compare? Net present value indicates the amount of the excess (or deficiency) of a project's present value of net cash inflows over (or under) its cost—at a specified discount rate. But net present value does not show the project's unique rate of return. The internal rate of return shows the project's rate but does not indicate the dollar difference between the project's present value and its investment cost. In many cases, the two discounted cash flow methods lead to the same investment decision.

The discounted cash-flow methods are superior because they consider both the time value of money and profitability. The time value of money enters the analysis through the discounting of future dollars to present value. Profitability is built into the discounted cash-flow methods because they consider all cash inflows and outflows over the project's life. The payback model considers only the cash flows necessary to recover the initial cash invested.

 DAILY EXERCISE 26-23

Exhibit 26-20 summarizes the strengths and weaknesses of payback, accounting rate of return, and the discounted cash-flow methods. Managers often use more than one method to gain different perspectives on risks and returns. For example, **Deer Valley's** owners could decide to pursue capital projects with positive net present values, provided that those projects have a payback of four years or less.

EXHIBIT 26-20
Capital Budgeting Methods

Method	Strengths	Weaknesses
Payback	Easy to understand Based on cash flows Highlights risks	Ignores profitability and the time value of money
Accounting rate of return	Based on profitability	Ignores the time value of money
Discounted cash flow: Net present value Internal rate of return	Based on cash flows, profitability, and the time value of money	Difficult to determine discount rate

Deer Valley's use of both payback and net present value methods is typical of U.S. companies. Surveys have shown that companies headquartered in the United States often use both payback and discounted cash-flow methods. The payback

method is most popular in Japan. Discounted cash-flow methods are more popular in Canada, Ireland, and South Korea.

THINK IT OVER

A pharmaceutical company is considering two research projects. Project A has a net present value of $232,000 and a 3 year payback period. Project B has a net present value of $237,000 and a payback period of 4.5 years. Which project do you think the managers will choose?

Answer: Many managers would choose project A. Net present value is a better guide to decision making than payback period. But managers would consider the 2.2% [($237,000 − $232,000)/$232,000] difference between the net present values to be insignificant. In contrast, the 50% [(4.5 years − 3.0 years)/3.0 years] difference between payback periods *is* significant. The uncertainty of receiving operating cash flows increases with each passing year. Managers often forgo small differences in expected cash inflows to decrease the risk of investments.

Take a moment to review the different capital budgeting methods by studying the Decision Guidelines. This will help solidify your understanding of capital budgeting before you work the summary review problem.

DECISION GUIDELINES

Capital Budgeting

DECISION	**GUIDELINE**
How to decide whether a long-term investment is worthwhile?	Investments may be worthwhile if: • Payback period is shorter than asset's useful life. • Expected accounting rate of return on asset exceeds required accounting rate of return. • Discounted cash flow methods: Net present value (NPV) is positive. Internal rate of return (IRR) exceeds required rate of return.

How to compute the payback period with
• Equal annual cash flows?

• Unequal annual cash flows?

$$\text{Payback period} = \frac{\text{Amount invested}}{\text{Expected annual net cash inflow}}$$

Accumulate cash flows until amount invested is recovered.

How to compute the accounting rate of return?

$$\frac{\text{Accounting}}{\text{rate of return}} = \frac{\text{Average annual operating income from asset}}{\text{Average amount invested in asset}}$$

$$= \frac{\text{Average annual net cash} \atop \text{inflow from asset} - \text{Annual} \atop \text{depreciation on asset}}{(\text{Amount invested in asset} + \text{Residual value})/2}$$

How to compute net present value with
• Equal annual cash flows?

$$\begin{array}{c} \text{Present value of} \\ \textit{annuity} \text{ of \$1} \\ \text{(Exhibit 26-15)} \end{array} \times \begin{array}{c} \text{Annual net cash} \\ \text{inflow or outflow} \end{array}$$

• Unequal annual cash flows?

Compute the present value of each year's net cash inflow or outflow (present value of $1 from Exhibit 26-17 × net cash inflow or outflow) and add up yearly present values.

How to compute internal rate of return with
• Equal annual cash flows?

$$\begin{array}{c} \text{Annuity PV factor} \\ \text{(Use Exhibit 26-15)} \end{array} = \frac{\text{Investment}}{\text{Expected annual net cash inflow}}$$

• Unequal annual cash flows?

Trial and error, spreadsheet software, or calculator

Which capital budgeting methods are best?

Discounted cash-flow methods (net present value and IRR) are best because they incorporate both profitability and the time value of money.

EXCEL APPLICATION PROBLEM

Goal: Create an Excel spreadsheet to compute payback period, accounting rate of return, and net present value of a machine.

Scenario: Tar-jay Corporation is considering the purchase of a new bar-coding machine for one of its warehouses. You are asked to prepare a simple analysis to determine whether the machine should be purchased. The summary problem for review at the end of the chapter provides a good outline for completing your analysis.

The bar-code machine costs $60,000. Its estimated residual value is $10,000, and it has a five-year useful life. The estimated annual net cash flow from the machine is $16,000. Tar-jay's required rate of return is 16%.
1. Compute the machine's payback period.
2. Compute the machine's accounting rate of return.
3. Compute the machine's net present value (NPV).
4. Should Tar-jay purchase the machine? Why or why not?

Step-by-step:

1. Open a new Excel spreadsheet.
2. Create a boldfaced heading for your spreadsheet that contains the following:
   a. Chapter 26 Decision Guidelines
   b. Capital Budgeting Decision
   c. Tar-jay Corporation
   d. Today's Date
3. Move down two rows and create a boldfaced and underlined "Data Section" heading. Enter the data and descriptions provided in the problem under this heading in your spreadsheet.
4. At the end of the Data Section, add a row for "Annual Depreciation on Asset." Use the "SLN" financial function to compute depreciation.
5. Move down two rows. In column A, enter the description "Payback Period (years)." Compute the payback period in column B.
6. Move down one row. In column A, enter the description "Accounting Rate of Return." Compute the accounting rate of return in column B.
7. Move down two rows, and enter "Net Present Value" as a boldfaced and underlined heading.
8. Underneath the heading, use the textbook's Summary Problem format (listed as requirement 3 on page 1090) to compute net present value. Use the "PV" financial function for the present value of an annuity. Use the "NPV" function to calculate the present value of the residual value. (Put zeroes in the first four values and the residual value cell reference in the fifth value to calculate the PV of the lump-sum residual value.)
9. Save your file to disk, and print a copy for your files.

REVIEW SPECIAL BUSINESS DECISIONS AND CAPITAL BUDGETING

SUMMARY PROBLEM

Zetamax is considering buying a new bar-coding machine for its Austin, Texas, plant. The data for the machine follow:

Cost of machine	$48,000
Estimated residual value	$ 6,000
Estimated annual net cash inflow	$13,000
Estimated useful life	5 years
Required rate of return	16%

www.prenhall.com/horngren

End-of-Chapter Assessment

Required

1. Compute the bar-coding machine's payback period.
2. Compute the bar-coding machine's accounting rate of return.
3. Compute the bar-coding machine's net present value.
4. Would you decide to buy the bar-coding machine? Give your reason.

Solution

Requirement 1

$$\text{Payback period} = \frac{\text{Amount invested}}{\text{Expected annual net cash inflow}} = \frac{\$48,000}{\$13,000} = 3.7 \text{ years}$$

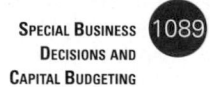

Requirement 2

$$\text{Accounting rate of return} = \frac{\text{Average annual operating income from asset}}{\text{Average amount invested in asset}}$$

$$= \frac{\substack{\text{Average annual net cash} \\ \text{inflow from asset}} - \substack{\text{Annual} \\ \text{depreciation on asset}}}{(\text{Amount invested in asset} + \text{Residual value})/2}$$

$$= \frac{\$13,000 - \$8,400^*}{(\$48,000 + \$6,000)/2}$$

$$= \frac{\$4,600}{\$27,000}$$

$$= 0.170$$

$$= 17\%$$

$$\frac{*\$48,000 - \$6,000}{5 \text{ years}} = \$8,400$$

Requirement 3

Present value of annuity of equal annual net cash inflows at 16% ($13,000 × 3.274[†])	$42,562
Present value of residual value ($6,000 × 0.476[‡])	2,856
Total present value of net cash inflows...	45,418
Investment..	(48,000)
Net present value...	$(2,582)

[†] Present value of annuity of $1 for 5 years at 16%, Exhibit 26-15.
[‡] Present value of $1 in 5 years at 16%, Exhibit 26-17.

Requirement 4

Decision: Do not buy the bar-coding machine because it has a negative net present value. The net present value model considers profitability and the time value of money. The other models ignore at least one of those factors.

LESSONS LEARNED

1. *Identify the relevant information for a special business decision.* *Relevant information* is expected future data that differ among alternative courses of action. Historical data are irrelevant per se, but they often help managers make predictions about the future.

2. *Make five types of short-term special business decisions.* Two keys to making short-term special business decisions are (1) focusing on relevant revenues and relevant costs, and (2) using a contribution margin approach that separates variable costs from fixed costs. Managers use these techniques when deciding whether to accept or reject a special sales order; whether to drop a product, department, or territory; which product to emphasize when a constraint is present; outsourcing; and whether to sell a product as is or to process it further. Managers often select the course of action that is expected to produce the most operating income.

3. *Explain the difference between correct and incorrect analysis of a particular business decision.* Correct analysis of a business decision focuses on differences in revenues and expenses. The conventional absorption costing approach may mislead managers into treating a fixed cost as a variable cost. The contribution margin approach is more useful because it highlights how sales volume affects expenses and income.

4. *Use opportunity costs in decision making.* *Opportunity cost* is the benefit that can be obtained from the next-best course of action. Opportunity cost is not an outlay cost, so it is not recorded in the accounting records.

5. *Use four capital budgeting methods to make longer-term investment decisions.* *Capital budgeting* is a formal means of analyzing long-term investment decisions. Four popular capital budgeting methods are payback, accounting rate of return, net present value, and internal rate of return. *Payback* is the length of time it will take to recover the dollars invested. The *accounting rate of return* is the average annual operating income from an asset divided by the average amount invested in that asset. *Net present value (NPV)* discounts the project's expected future cash flows by the minimum desired rate of return. The project's *internal rate of return (IRR)* is the discount rate that makes the net present value of the project's cash flows equal to zero.

6. *Compare and contrast popular capital budgeting methods.* The discounted cash-flow methods—net present value and internal rate of return—are conceptually superior to payback and accounting rate of return. Payback ignores profitability and the time value of money. Accounting rate of return ignores the time value of money. Net present value and IRR consider both profitability and the time value of money.

ACCOUNTING VOCABULARY

accounting rate of return (p. 1080)	**hurdle rate** (p. 1082)	**payback** (p. 1078)
annuity (p. 1082)	**internal rate of return**	**relevant information** (p. 1063)
capital budgeting (p. 1077)	**(IRR)** (p. 1086)	**required rate of return** (p. 1082)
constraint (p. 1069)	**net present value (NPV)** (p. 1081)	**strategy** (p. 1063)
cost of capital (p. 1082)	**opportunity cost** (p. 1074)	**sunk cost** (p. 1073)
discount rate (p. 1082)	**outsourcing** (p. 1070)	**time value of money** (p. 1081)

QUESTIONS

1. Discuss the roles of expected future data and historical data in decision analysis. On which data are special decisions based?
2. Name two key guidelines for making short-term special decisions.
3. Identify two income statement formats. Which is more useful for deciding whether to accept a special sales order? Why?
4. Identify two long-term factors managers should consider in deciding whether to accept a special sales order.
5. What is the similarity between a special sales order decision and a decision to drop a product? The difference?
6. Which cost is more likely to change in a short-term decision situation, a fixed or a variable cost? Can both costs change?
7. Outline how to decide which product to emphasize when there is a constraining factor. Give four examples of constraining factors.
8. What is an opportunity cost? How does it differ from an ordinary accounting cost?
9. Name three capital budgeting decision methods. State the strengths and the weaknesses of each method. Which method is best? Why?
10. Which capital budgeting method is (a) based on operating income, (b) based on cash flows without regard for their timing or profitability, (c) based on the time value of money.
11. How is the payback period computed for assets that generate equal annual cash inflows? How does the estimated useful life of the asset affect the payback computation?
12. How is the accounting rate of return computed when the annual amounts of operating income vary?
13. Explain why a positive net present value indicates an attractive investment project and a negative net present value indicates an unattractive project.
14. Which capital budgeting strategy is better? (a) Pick the best capital budgeting method and use it exclusively. (b) Use multiple capital budgeting methods. Explain your answer.

ASSESS YOUR PROGRESS

DAILY EXERCISES

DE26-1 You are trying to decide whether to trade in your inkjet printer for a more recent model. Your usage pattern will remain unchanged, but the old and new printers use different ink cartridges. Are the following items relevant or irrelevant to your decision?

Identifying relevant data
(Obj. 1)

a. The price of the new printer
b. The price you paid for the old printer
c. The trade-in value of the old printer
d. Paper costs
e. The difference between ink cartridges' costs

DE26-2 Consider the **ACDelco** special sales order example on pages 1065–1067. Suppose that

Accepting or rejecting a special sales order
(Obj. 2)

a. ACDelco's variable manufacturing cost is $1.45 per oil filter (instead of $1.20).
b. ACDelco would have to buy a special stamping machine that costs $9,000 to mark the customer's logo on the special-order oil filters. The machine would be scrapped when the special order is complete.

Use the incremental analysis approach from Exhibit 26-3 to determine whether you would recommend that ACDelco accept the special order under these conditions.

DE26-3 Maui Jane sunglasses sell for about $120 per pair. Suppose that the company incurs the following average costs per pair:

Deciding on a special sales order
(Obj. 2)

Direct materials	$40
Direct labor	12
Variable manufacturing overhead	8
Variable marketing expenses	4
Fixed manufacturing overhead	20*
Total costs	$84

$$* \frac{\$2,000,000 \text{ total fixed manufacturing overhead}}{100,000 \text{ pairs of sunglasses}}$$

Maui Jane has enough idle capacity to accept a one-time-only special order from Lenscrafters for 20,000 pairs of sunglasses at $76 per pair. Maui Jane will not incur any additional variable marketing expenses for the order.

How would accepting the special order affect Maui Jane's operating income?

 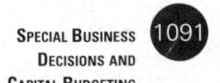

DE26-4 Consider the Maui Jane company in Daily Exercise 26-3. In addition to the special order's effect on profits, what other (longer-term qualitative) factors should Maui Jane's managers consider in deciding whether to accept Lenscrafters' special order?

Explaining the difference
between correct and incorrect
analysis for a special sales order
(Obj. 2, 3)

DE26-5 Refer to Daily Exercises 26-3 and 26-4. Maui Jane's marketing manager, Janet Sky, argues that Maui Jane should not accept Lenscrafters' special sales order because Lenscrafters' $76 offer price is less than Maui Jane's $84 cost to make the sunglasses. Sky asks you, one of Maui Jane's staff accountants, to write a memo explaining whether her analysis is correct. Use the following format:

Date:	_____
To:	Ms. Janet Sky, Marketing manager
From:	_____
Subject:	Lenscrafters' special order

DE26-6 Sam's Video in Philadelphia operates three departments: Video, Music, and Accessories. Sam's Video allocates fixed expenses (building depreciation and utilities) based on the square feet occupied by each department. Departmental operating income data for the third quarter of 20X3 are as follows:

	Department			
	Video	**Music**	**Accessories**	**Total**
Sales revenue......................	$105,000	$54,000	$100,000	$259,000
Variable expenses	60,000	35,000	75,000	170,000
Fixed expenses	25,000	15,000	30,000	70,000
Total expenses....................	85,000	50,000	105,000	240,000
Operating income (loss)	$ 20,000	$ 4,000	$ (5,000)	$ 19,000

Should Sam's Video drop any of the departments? Give your reason. (The store will remain in the same building regardless of the decision.)

Dropping a department; explaining the difference between
correct and incorrect analysis
(Obj. 2, 3)

DE26-7 Betsy Lanier is the wife of Sam Lanier, the owner of Sam's Video in Daily Exercise 26-6. Betsy is concerned. "Look at the Accessories Department's results. That department is costing us $5,000 a quarter. We would have had $10,000 more in our retirement fund if you had gotten rid of the Accessories Department like I suggested six months ago!"

Help Sam reply to Betsy. Your response should include an analysis of how dropping the Accessories Department would affect Sam's Video's operating income.

DE26-8 Consider Sam's Video from Daily Exercise 26-6. Assume that the fixed expenses assigned to each department include only

- Salaries of the department's manager
- Cost of advertising directly related to that department

Sam's Video will not incur these fixed expenses if the department is dropped. Under these circumstances, should Sam's Video drop any of the departments? Give your reason.

DE26-9 Runmaster, Inc., produces two types of exercise treadmills: Regular and Deluxe.

The exercise craze is such that Runmaster could use all its available machine hours producing either model. The two models are processed through the same production departments.

Which model should Runmaster produce? If both models should be produced, compute the mix that will maximize operating income.

	Per Unit	
	Deluxe	**Regular**
Sale price	$1,300	$750
Costs:		
Direct materials..	$ 330	$140
Direct labor	150	250
Variable manufacturing overhead*.............	375	125
Fixed manufacturing overhead*.................	150	50
Variable operating expenses........................	140	100
Total cost	1,145	665
Operating income...	$ 155	$ 85

* Allocated on the basis of machine hours.

DE26-10 U.S. Surgical Corporation in Norwalk, Connecticut, manufactures and markets surgical equipment. Lilian Gonzalez manages the company's fleet of 550 automobiles. Gonzalez has been charged with "reengineering" the fleet management function. She has an important decision to make.

Outsourcing decision for services (Obj. 1, 2)

- Should she continue to manage the fleet in-house with the five employees reporting to her? To do so, she will have to acquire new fleet management software to streamline U.S. Surgical's fleet management process.
- Should she outsource the fleet management function to Fleet Management Services, a company that specializes in managing fleets of automobiles for other companies? Fleet Management Services would take over the maintenance, repair, and scheduling of U.S. Surgical's fleet (but U.S. Surgical would retain ownership of its fleet). This alternative would require Gonzalez to lay off her five employees. However, her own job would be secure as she would be U.S. Surgical's liaison with Fleet Management Services.

Assume that Gonzalez's records show the following data concerning U.S. Surgical's fleet:

Book value of U.S. Surgical's autos, with an estimated 5-year life	$7,750,000
Annual leasing fee for new fleet management software	10,000
Annual maintenance of autos	295,500
Fleet supervisor Gonzalez's annual salary	80,000
Total annual salaries of U.S. Surgical's five other fleet management employees	175,000

Suppose that Fleet Management Services offers to manage U.S. Surgical's fleet for an annual fee of $460,000.

Which alternative will maximize U.S. Surgical's short-term operating income?

DE26-11 Refer to U.S. Surgical Corporation in Daily Exercise 26-10. What qualitative factors should Gonzalez consider before making a final decision?

Outsourcing decision for services (Obj. 2)

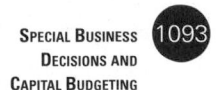

DE26-12 Etron Contract Manufacturing has been purchasing digital filters for $3 each. Etron believes it can make these filters using its excess capacity. No extra equipment or other fixed costs would be required. Etron estimates that it will need 50,000 filters and that the cost per filter would include the following:

Outsourcing decision (Obj. 1, 2)

Direct materials	$1.30
Direct labor	0.80
Variable manufacturing overhead	0.40
Fixed manufacturing overhead (allocated based on machine hours)	0.75
Total average cost per filter..............................	$3.25

Should Etron make or buy the filter?

DE26-13 Refer to Etron Contract Manufacturing in Daily Exercise 26-12. Suppose that

Outsourcing; best use of facilities (Obj. 1, 2)

- Making the filters will require Etron to hire a new part-time supervisor at a cost of $8,000.
- If Etron buys the filters, it could rent its idle facilities to another company, Alon Products, for $20,000.

Should Etron make or buy the filters?

DE26-14 Auto Components, Inc., has an inventory of 1,000 obsolete remote entry keys that are carried in inventory at a manufacturing cost of $160,000. Production supervisor Tony Ray must decide whether to

Deciding whether to sell as is or process further (Obj. 1, 2)

- Process the inventory further at a cost of $40,000, with the expectation of selling it for $65,000, or
- Scrap the inventory for a sale price of $16,000

What should Ray do? Present figures to support your decision.

DE26-15 Auto Components, Inc., from Daily Exercise 26-14 is approached by a customer who wants to buy the 1,000 obsolete keys. The customer is willing to pay more than $16,000 for the 1,000 keys.

Using opportunity costs to make decisions (Obj. 4)

1. What is Auto Components' opportunity cost of *not* processing the inventory further?
2. How can Ray use this opportunity cost to set a minimum sale price for the customer? What should be Auto Components' minimum sale price per key?

DE26-16 The concept of opportunity cost applies to all business decisions for which there are alternative courses of action. For example, in Exhibit 26-3, page 1066, the opportunity cost of rejecting the special sales order is the $11,000 of operating income that **ACDelco** would forgo if it rejects the special order.

    1. Now consider the Chazz example. In Exhibit 26-7, page 1070,
        a. What is the opportunity cost of manufacturing the shirts?
        b. What is the opportunity cost of manufacturing the slacks?

DE26-17 Sound Insurance Company of America, a property/casualty insurer based in Branchville, New Jersey, is deciding whether to purchase new accounting software. Assistant vice president Tom Selling calculated that the payback period for the $30,000 software package would be 8 years.

    What are the expected annual cash savings from the new software? Would you recommend that Sound Insurance purchase this software? Give your reason.

DE26-18 Daily Exercises 26-18 through 26-23 consider how **Deer Valley Resort** (from the chapter opening story) could use capital budgeting methods to decide whether the $13 million Snow Park Lodge expansion would be a good investment.

    Assume that Deer Valley's managers developed the following estimates concerning the expansion (all numbers assumed):

Number of additional skiers per day	100
Average number of days per year that weather conditions allow skiing at Deer Valley	150
Useful life of expansion (in years)	15
Average cash spent by each skier per day	$245
Average variable cost of serving each skier per day	$85
Cost of expansion	$13,000,000
Discount rate	12%

Assume that Deer Valley uses the straight-line depreciation method and expects the lodge expansion to have a residual value of $1 million at the end of its 15-year life.

    Compute the average annual net cash inflow from the expansion.

DE26-19 Refer to the Deer Valley Snow Park Lodge expansion project in Daily Exercise 26-18. Compute the payback period for the expansion project.

DE26-20 Refer to the Deer Valley Snow Park Lodge expansion project in Daily Exercise 26-18. What is the accounting rate of return?

DE26-21 ◄ *Link Back to Chapter 15 (Present-Value Concepts).* Refer to Daily Exercise 26-18. What is the project's net present value?

DE26-22 Refer to Daily Exercise 26-18. *Assume the expansion has zero residual value.* What is the project's internal rate of return?

DE26-23 Use your results from Daily Exercises 26-18 through 26-22 to write a memo to Deer Valley director of finance Jim Madsen. The purpose of your memo is to recommend whether Deer Valley should undertake the expansion. You should cover the strengths and weaknesses of each capital budgeting method cited in your memo. Follow the memo format outlined in Daily Exercise 26-5.

EXERCISES

E26-1 Suppose the **Baseball Hall of Fame** in Cooperstown, New York, has approached Sports-Cardz, Inc., with a special order. The Hall of Fame wishes to purchase 100,000 baseball card packs for a special promotional campaign and offers $0.95 per pack, a total of $95,000. Sports-Cardz total production cost is $1.25 per pack, as follows:

Variable costs:	
Direct materials	$0.20
Direct labor	0.14
Variable overhead	0.41
Fixed overhead	0.50
Total cost	$1.25

Sports-Cardz has enough excess capacity to handle the special order.

1. Prepare an incremental analysis to determine whether Sports-Cardz should accept the special sales order.
2. Now assume that the Hall of Fame wants special hologram baseball cards. Sports-Cardz will spend $35,000 to develop this hologram, which will be useless after the special order is completed. Should Sports-Cardz accept the special order under these circumstances?

E26-2 Top managers of New Rock Records are alarmed about their operating losses. They are considering dropping the cassette-tape product line. Company accountants have prepared the following analysis to help make this decision:

Keeping or dropping a product line (fixed costs unchanged)
(Obj. 1, 2, 3)

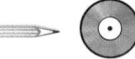

	Total	Compact Discs	Cassette Tapes
Sales revenue	$480,000	$290,000	$190,000
Variable expenses	240,000	140,000	100,000
Contribution margin	240,000	150,000	90,000
Fixed expenses:			
Manufacturing	165,000	70,000	95,000
Marketing and administrative	85,000	55,000	30,000
Total fixed expenses	250,000	125,000	125,000
Operating income (loss)	$ (10,000)	$ 25,000	$ (35,000)

Total fixed costs will not change if the company stops selling cassette tapes.

Prepare an incremental analysis to show whether New Rock should drop the cassette-tape product line. Will dropping cassette tapes add $35,000 to operating income? Explain.

E26-3 Refer to Exercise 26-2. Assume that New Rock Records can avoid $65,000 of fixed expenses by dropping the cassette-tape product line. Prepare an incremental analysis to show whether New Rock should stop selling cassette tapes.

Keeping or dropping a product line (fixed costs change) (Obj. 1, 2)

E26-4 Modern Styles sells both designer and moderately priced fashion accessories. Top management is deciding which product line to emphasize. Accountants have provided the following data:

Determining product mix (Obj. 1, 2)

	Per Item	
	Designer	Moderately Priced
Average sale price	$200	$80
Average variable expenses	85	24
Average contribution margin	115	56
Average fixed expenses (allocated)	20	10
Average operating income	$ 95	$46

The Modern Styles store in Reno, Nevada, has 10,000 square feet of floor space. If it emphasizes moderately priced goods, 650 items can be displayed in the store. If it emphasizes designer wear, only 300 designer items can be displayed. These numbers are also the average monthly sales in units.

Prepare an analysis to show which product to emphasize.

E26-5 Millenia Systems manufactures an electronic control that it uses in its final product. The electronic control has the following manufacturing costs per unit:

Outsourcing decision (Obj. 1, 2, 3)

Direct materials	$ 7.00
Direct labor	1.00
Variable overhead	1.50
Fixed overhead	5.50
Manufacturing product cost	$15.00

Another company has offered to sell Millenia the electronic control for $11 per unit. If Millenia buys the control from the outside supplier, the manufacturing facilities that will be idled cannot be used for any other purpose. Should Millenia make or buy the electronic controls? Explain the difference between correct analysis and incorrect analysis of this decision.

E26-6 Refer to Exercise 26-5. Millenia needs 90,000 electronic controls. By outsourcing them, Millenia can use its idle facilities to manufacture another product that will contribute $150,000 to operating income. Identify the *incremental* costs that Millenia will incur to acquire 90,000 electronic controls under three alternative plans. Which plan makes the best use of Millenia's facilities? Support your answer.

Sell or process further; identifying opportunity costs
(Obj. 1, 3, 4)

E26-7 Norris Creations has damaged some custom cabinets, which cost the company $10,000 to manufacture. Owner Fay Norris is considering two options for disposing of this inventory. One plan is to sell the cabinets as damaged inventory for $1,400. The alternative is to spend an additional $450 to repair the damage and expect to sell the cabinets for $2,200. What should Norris do? Support your answer with an analysis that shows expected net revenue under each alternative. Identify the opportunity cost of each alternative.

Computing payback with equal cash flows
(Obj. 5)

E26-8 Adkins Co. is considering acquiring a manufacturing plant. The purchase price is $1,457,100. The owners believe the plant will generate net cash inflows of $485,700 annually. It will have to be replaced in seven years. Use the payback method to determine whether Adkins should purchase this plant.

Computing payback with unequal cash flows
(Obj. 5)

E26-9 Sikes Hardware is adding a new product line that will require an investment of $1,454,000. Managers estimate that this investment will generate net cash inflows of $310,000 the first year, $280,000 the second year, and $240,000 each year thereafter. Compute the payback period of the investment.

Determining accounting rate of return
(Obj. 5)

E26-10 Barker Mills is shopping for new equipment. Managers are considering two investments. Equipment manufactured by Li, Inc., costs $400,000 and will last for five years, with no residual value. The Li equipment is expected to generate annual operating income of $48,000. Equipment manufactured by Veras Products is priced at $500,000 and will remain useful for six years. It promises annual operating income of $92,750, and its expected residual value is $30,000.

  Which equipment offers the higher accounting rate of return?

Computing net present value
(Obj. 5)

E26-11 ◄ *Link Back to Chapter 15 (Present-Value Concepts)*. Use the net present value method to determine whether Pine Products should invest in the following projects:

- *Project A:* Costs $295,000 and offers eight annual net cash inflows of $65,000. Pine Products requires an annual return of 14% on projects like A.
- *Project B:* Costs $435,000 and offers nine annual net cash inflows of $80,000. Pine Products demands an annual return of 12% on investments of this nature.

What is the net present value of each project? What is the maximum acceptable price to pay for each project?

Computing internal rate of return
(Obj. 5)

E26-12 Refer to Exercise 26-11. Compute the internal rate of return of each project, and use this information to identify the better investment.

Challenge Exercise

Determining product mix
(Obj. 2)

E26-13 Each morning, Ken Gaver stocks the drink case at Ken's Beach Hut in Sanibel Island, Florida. Ken's has 100 linear feet of refrigerated display space for cold drinks. Each linear foot can hold either six 12-ounce cans or four 20-ounce plastic or glass bottles. Ken's sells three types of cold drinks:

- Coca-Cola in 12-oz cans, for $1.25 per can
- Coca-Cola in 20-oz plastic bottles, for $1.50 per bottle
- SoBe in 20-oz glass bottles, for $2.00 per bottle

Ken's pays its suppliers:

- $0.25 per 12-oz can of Coca-Cola
- $0.30 per 20-oz bottle of Coca-Cola
- $0.70 per 20-oz bottle of SoBe

Ken's monthly fixed expenses include

Hut rental..............................	$ 250
Refrigerator rental	50
Gaver's salary	1,000
Total fixed expenses..............	$1,300

Ken's can sell all the drinks stocked in the display case each morning.

1. What is Ken's constraining factor? What should Gaver stock in order to maximize profits?
2. Suppose Ken's refuses to devote more than 60 linear feet to any individual product. Under this condition, how many linear feet of each drink should Gaver stock? How many units of each product will be available for sale each day?

PROBLEMS

(Group A)

P26-1A Price United Co.'s contribution margin income statement for the most recent month reports the following:

Accepting or rejecting a special sales order
(Obj. 1, 2)

Sales in units	760,000
Sales revenue	$190,000
Variable expenses:	
Manufacturing	$ 60,800
Marketing and administrative	31,200
Total variable expenses	92,000
Contribution margin	98,000
Fixed expenses:	
Manufacturing	58,000
Marketing and administrative	16,000
Total fixed expenses	74,000
Operating income	$ 24,000

Victoria Vineyards wants to buy 10,000 labels from Price. Acceptance of the order will not increase any of Price's marketing and administrative expenses. Price's plant has unused capacity to manufacture the additional labels. Victoria Vineyards has offered $0.18 per label, which is considerably below the normal sale price of $0.25.

Required

1. Prepare an incremental analysis to determine whether Price should accept this special sales order.
2. Prepare a total analysis to show Price's operating income with and without the special sales order.
3. Identify long-term factors that Price should consider in deciding whether to accept the special sales order.

P26-2A The following operating income data of Sea Cuisine highlights the losses of the fresh seafood product line:

Keeping or dropping a product line (Obj. 1, 2, 3)

		Product Line	
		Fresh	Frozen
	Total	Seafood	Seafood
Sales revenue	$857,500	$227,500	$630,000
Cost of goods sold:			
Variable	$164,000	$ 64,000	$100,000
Fixed	131,000	41,000	90,000
Total cost of goods sold	295,000	105,000	190,000
Gross profit	562,500	122,500	440,000
Marketing and administrative expenses:			
Variable	378,000	108,000	270,000
Fixed	129,500	49,500	80,000
Total marketing and administrative expenses	507,500	157,500	350,000
Operating income (loss)	$ 55,000	$ (35,000)	$ 90,000

Sea Cuisine is considering discontinuing the fresh seafood product line. The company's accountants estimate that dropping the fresh seafood line will decrease fixed cost of goods sold by $32,000 and decrease fixed marketing and administrative expenses by $15,000.

Required

1. Prepare an incremental analysis to show whether Sea Cuisine should drop the fresh seafood product line.

2. Prepare a total analysis to show Sea Cuisine's operating income with and without the fresh seafood product line. Prepare the income statement in contribution-margin format.
3. Explain the difference between correct analysis and incorrect analysis of the decision to keep or drop the fresh seafood product line.

Determining product mix
(Obj. 1, 2)

P26-3A Green's Outdoors of Harrisburg, Virginia, specializes in outdoor furniture and barbecues. Owner Linda Green is expanding the store. She is deciding which product line to emphasize. To make this decision, she assembles the following data:

	Per Unit	
	Patio Sets	Barbecues
Sale price..	$500	$300
Variable expenses.............................	240	162
Contribution margin........................	$260	$138
Contribution margin ratio...............	52 %	46 %

After renovation, the store will have 8,000 square feet of floor space. By devoting the new floor space to barbecues, Green's Outdoors can display 60 barbecues. Alternatively, Green's could display 30 patio sets. Green expects monthly sales to equal the maximum number of units displayed.

Required

1. Identify the constraining factor for Green's Outdoors.
2. Prepare an analysis to show which product line to emphasize.

Outsourcing; best use of facilities
(Obj. 1, 2)

P26-4A Afloat, Inc., manufactures swim fins. Cost data for producing 2,000 pairs of fins each year are as follows:

Direct materials.............................	$21,000
Direct labor	15,000
Variable overhead	5,600
Fixed overhead	38,400
Total manufacturing costs............	$80,000

Suppose SwimTime will sell Afloat the fins for $35 per pair. Afloat would pay $1.80 per pair to transport the fins to its warehouse.

Required

1. Afloat's accountants predict that purchasing the fins from SwimTime will enable the company to avoid $12,000 of fixed overhead. Prepare an analysis to show whether Afloat should make or buy the fins.
2. Assume that the Afloat facilities freed up by the purchase of the fins from SwimTime can be used to manufacture swim masks. The masks will contribute $35,000 to profit. Total fixed costs will be the same as if Afloat used the plant to make fins. Prepare an analysis to show which alternative makes the best use of Afloat's facilities: (a) make fins, (b) buy fins and leave facilities idle, or (c) buy fins and make masks.

Deciding whether to sell as is or process further; identifying opportunity costs
(Obj. 1, 2, 4)

P26-5A Long Petroleum Company produces a variety of petroleum products. Assume that Long has spent $300,000 to refine 60,000 gallons of petroleum distillate. Suppose Long can sell the distillate for $5.50 a gallon. Alternatively, it can process the distillate further and produce cleaner for tape heads. Assume that the additional processing will cost another $1.25 a gallon and that the cleaner can be sold for $7.50 a gallon. To make this sale, Long must pay a sales commission of $0.10 a gallon and a transportation charge of $0.15 a gallon.

Required

1. Prepare a diagram of Long's alternatives, using Exhibit 26-10, page 1073, as a guide.
2. Identify the sunk cost. Is the sunk cost relevant to Long's decision?
3. Prepare an analysis to indicate whether Long should sell the distillate or process it into tape-head cleaner. Show the expected net revenue difference between the two alternatives.
4. Identify the opportunity cost of each option. Explain how managers can use opportunity cost to make this decision.

Capital budgeting
(Obj. 5, 6)

P26-6A Waters Investments, Inc., operates a resort near Door County in the Great Lakes region of Wisconsin. The company is considering an expansion. The architectural plan calls for a construction cost of $5,200,000. Top managers of Waters believe the expansion will generate annual net cash inflows of $675,000 for ten years. Architects and engineers estimate that the new facilities will remain useful for ten years and have a residual value of $1,900,000. The company uses straight-line depreciation, and its stockholders demand an annual return of 12% on investments of this nature.

1. Compute the payback period, the accounting rate of return, and the net present value of this investment.
2. Make a recommendation to Waters management as to whether the company should invest in this project.

P26-7A Crystal's Candle Shop is considering two possible expansion plans. Plan A is to open 8 candle shops at a cost of $3,220,000. Expected annual net cash inflows are $690,000, with residual value of $350,000 at the end of seven years. Under plan B, Crystal's would open 12 candle shops at a cost of $4,200,000. This investment is expected to generate net cash inflows of $1,050,000 each year for seven years, which is the estimated useful life of the properties. Estimated residual value of the plan B candle shops is zero. Crystal's uses straight-line depreciation and requires an annual return of 14%.

Capital budgeting
(Obj. 5, 6)

Required

1. Compute the payback period, the accounting rate of return, and the net present value of each plan. What are the strengths and weaknesses of these capital budgeting models?
2. Which expansion plan should Crystal's adopt? Why?
3. Estimate the internal rate of return (IRR) for plan B. How does plan B's IRR compare with Crystal's required rate of return?

P R O B L E M S

(Group B)

P26-1B Play Day Corporation manufactures toys in Tampa, Florida. Play Day's contribution-margin income statement for the most recent month contains the following data:

Accepting or rejecting a special sales order
(Obj. 1, 2)

Sales in units	42,000
Sales revenue	$420,000
Variable expenses:	
Manufacturing	$ 84,000
Marketing and administrative	100,000
Total variable expenses	184,000
Contribution margin	236,000
Fixed expenses:	
Manufacturing	116,000
Marketing and administrative	85,000
Total fixed expenses	201,000
Operating income	$ 35,000

Sienna Studios, Inc., wishes to buy 4,000 toys from Play Day. Acceptance of the order will not increase any of Play Day's marketing and administrative expenses. The Play Day plant has unused capacity to manufacture the additional toys. Sienna has offered $8.00 per toy, which is below the normal sale price of $10.

Required

1. Prepare an incremental analysis to determine whether Play Day should accept this special sales order.
2. Prepare a total analysis to show Play Day's operating income with and without the special sales order.
3. Identify long-term factors Play Day should consider in deciding whether to accept the special sales order.

P26-2B Members of the board of directors of Energy Saver Electric, Inc., have received the following operating income data for the year just ended, shown at the top of the next page.

Members of the board are surprised that the industrial-systems product line is losing money. They commission a study to determine whether the company should drop the industrial-systems line. Company accountants estimate that dropping industrial systems will decrease fixed cost of goods sold by $95,000 and decrease fixed marketing and administrative expenses by $15,000.

Keeping or dropping a product line
(Obj. 1, 2, 3)

Required

1. Prepare an incremental analysis to show whether Energy Saver should drop the industrial-systems product line.
2. Prepare a total analysis to show Energy Saver's operating income with and without industrial systems. Prepare the income statement in contribution-margin format.
3. Explain the difference between correct analysis and incorrect analysis of the decision to keep or drop the industrial-systems product line.

	Product Line		
	Industrial Systems	Household Systems	Total
Sales revenue	$405,000	$421,000	$826,000
Cost of goods sold:			
Variable	$ 50,000	$ 55,000	$105,000
Fixed	241,000	86,000	327,000
Total cost of goods sold	291,000	141,000	432,000
Gross profit	114,000	280,000	394,000
Marketing and administrative expenses:			
Variable	86,000	92,000	178,000
Fixed	58,000	31,000	89,000
Total marketing and administrative expenses..	144,000	123,000	267,000
Operating income (loss)	$ (30,000)	$157,000	$127,000

Determining product mix (Obj. 1, 2)

P26-3B Oral-E Corp., located in Detroit, Michigan, produces two lines of electric toothbrushes: deluxe and standard models. Because Oral-E can sell all the toothbrushes it can produce, the owners are expanding the plant, and they are deciding which product line to emphasize. To make this decision, they assemble the following data.

	Per Unit	
	Deluxe Toothbrush	Standard Toothbrush
Sale price	$50	$30
Variable expenses............................	15	12
Contribution margin......................	$35	$18
Contribution margin ratio	70%	60%

After expansion, the factory will have a production capacity of 2,200 machine hours per month. The plant can manufacture either 50 standard electric toothbrushes or 20 deluxe electric toothbrushes per machine hour.

Required

1. Identify the constraining factor for Oral-E Corp.
2. Prepare an analysis to show which product line to emphasize.

Outsourcing; best use of facilities (Obj. 1, 2)

P26-4B Smooth Sailing manufactures sailboats. Assume that Smooth Sailing's cost of making 1,200 seat covers is

Direct materials	$ 7,260
Direct labor..	1,440
Variable overhead...	960
Fixed overhead..	2,400
Total manufacturing costs for 1,200 seat covers	$12,060

Suppose Sof-Seatz will sell seat covers to Smooth Sailing for $8 each. Smooth Sailing would pay $0.90 per unit to transport the seat covers to its manufacturing plant, where it would add its own Smooth Sailing logo at a cost of $0.12 per seat cover.

Required

1. Smooth Sailing's accountants predict that purchasing the seat covers from Sof-Seatz will enable the company to avoid $900 of fixed overhead. Prepare an analysis to show whether Smooth Sailing should make or buy the seat covers.
2. Assume that the Smooth Sailing facilities freed up by the purchase of seat covers from Sof-Seatz can be used to manufacture another product that will contribute $2,300 to profit. Total fixed costs will be the same as if Smooth Sailing had produced the seat covers. Prepare an analysis to show which alternative makes the best use of Smooth Sailing's facilities: (a) make seat covers, (b) buy seat covers and leave facilities idle, or (c) buy seat covers and make another product.

P26-5B Cisco Chemical Corporation has spent $320,000 to refine 84,000 gallons of acetone, which can be sold for $3.32 a gallon. Alternatively, Cisco can process the acetone further and produce 77,000 gallons of lacquer thinner that can be sold for $4.80 a gallon. The additional processing will cost $0.89 per gallon of lacquer thinner. To sell the lacquer thinner, Cisco must pay a transportation charge of $0.34 a gallon and administrative expenses of $0.16 a gallon.

Deciding whether to sell as is or process further; identifying opportunity costs *(Obj. 1, 2, 4)*

Required

1. Prepare a diagram of Cisco's decision, using Exhibit 26-10 (page 1073) as a guide.
2. Identify the sunk cost. Is the sunk cost relevant to Cisco's decision?
3. Prepare an analysis to indicate whether Cisco should sell the acetone or process it into lacquer thinner. Show the expected net revenue difference between the two alternatives.
4. Identify the opportunity cost of each alternative. Explain how managers use the notion of opportunity cost in making their decision.

P26-6B Rising Sun Developers, west of Roswell, New Mexico, is considering purchasing a water park for $1,850,000. Top managers of Rising Sun believe the new facility will generate annual net cash inflows of $420,000 for eight years. Architects and engineers estimate that the facility will remain useful for eight years and have a residual value of $300,000. The company uses straight-line depreciation, and its stockholders demand an annual return of 16% on investments of this nature.

Capital budgeting *(Obj. 5, 6)*

Required

1. Compute the payback period, the accounting rate of return, and the net present value of this investment.
2. Make a recommendation to Rising Sun management as to whether the company should invest in this project.

P26-7B TechNo operates a chain of electronics stores. The company is considering two possible expansion plans. Plan A would open eight smaller stores at a cost of $6,450,000. Expected annual net cash inflows are $860,000, with zero residual value at the end of 20 years. Under plan B, TechNo would open three larger stores at a cost of $6,420,000. This plan is expected to generate net cash inflows of $600,000 per year for 20 years, the estimated life of the store properties. Estimated residual value is $3,000,000. TechNo uses straight-line depreciation and requires an annual return of 8%.

Capital budgeting *(Obj. 5, 6)*

Required

1. Compute the payback period, the accounting rate of return, and the net present value of these two plans. What are the strengths and weaknesses of these capital budgeting models?
2. Which expansion plan should TechNo choose? Why?
3. Estimate plan A's internal rate of return (IRR). How does the IRR compare with the company's required rate of return?

Apply Your Knowledge

Decision Cases

Case 1. BKFin.com provides banks access to sophisticated financial information and analysis systems over the Web. The company combines these tools with benchmarking data access, including e-mail and wireless communications, so that banks can instantly evaluate individual loan applications and entire loan portfolios.

Outsourcing e-mail *(Obj. 1, 2)*

BKFin.com's CEO Aamer Sheikh is very happy with the company's strong growth. To better focus on client service, Sheikh is considering outsourcing some functions. CFO Isabelle Wang suggests that the company's e-mail may be the place to start. She recently attended a conference and learned that companies like **Continental Airlines, DellNet, GTE,** and **NBC** were outsourcing their e-mail function. Sheikh asks Wang to identify costs related to BKFin.com's inhouse **Microsoft** Exchange mail application, which has 2,300 mailboxes. This information follows:

Variable costs:	
E-mail license	$6 per mailbox per month
Virus protection license	$1 per mailbox per month
Other variable costs	$7 per mailbox per month
Fixed costs:	
Computer hardware costs	$85,100 per month
$6,900 monthly salary for two information technology	
staff members who work only on e-mail	$13,800 per month

Required

1. Compute the *total cost* per mailbox per month of BKFin.com's current e-mail function.
2. Suppose **Mail.com,** a leading provider of Internet messaging outsourcing services, offers to host BKFin.com's e-mail function for $8 per mailbox per month. If BKFin.com outsources its e-mail to Mail.com, BKFin.com will still need the virus protection software, its computer hardware, and one information technology staff member, who would be responsible for maintaining virus protection, quarantining suspicious e-mail, and managing content (e.g., screening e-mail for objectionable content). Should CEO Sheikh accept Mail.com's offer?
3. Suppose for an additional $5 per mailbox per month, Mail.com will also provide virus protection, quarantine, and content-management services. Outsourcing these additional functions would mean that BKFin.com would not need either an e-mail information technology staff member or the separate virus protection license. Should CEO Sheikh outsource these extra services to Mail.com?

Deciding whether to purchase a new machine
(Obj. 1, 5, 6)

Case 2. Suppose that **Intel** is considering a new computer-controlled machine for etching trenches in the surfaces of silicon wafers. The company processes these wafers into semiconductor chips. The etching machine costs $900,000, and an additional $250,000 would be required for installation. Thus $1,150,000 is the required cash outlay for the investment.

Assume the new etching machine would replace an existing machine that was purchased five years ago for $715,000. That machine has five years of useful life remaining. Intel must either keep the old machine or replace it with the new machine. The expected useful life of the new machine is five years. Suppose Intel managers believe that the new machine would save $355,000 per year in cash operating costs. However, annual maintenance cost would be $40,000 higher with the new machine than with the old.

Disposal values of the machines are as follows:

	Old Machine	New Machine
Now	$-0-	—
In five years	-0-	$150,000

Assume Intel has a minimum desired rate of return of 14% on similar investments.

Required

1. Is the $715,000 cost of the old machine relevant to the decision of whether to keep or replace the old machine? Why or why not? (*Hint:* What are the requirements for a cost to be relevant?)
2. Which of the four capital budgeting methods is best suited for making this decision? Use that method to decide which course of action is better for Intel. (*Hint:* Identify the relevant items.)

ETHICAL ISSUE/FINANCIAL STATEMENT CASE

Dropping a product line
(Obj. 2)

◄◄ *Link Back to the EPS Calculation in Chapter 14 and the IMA Ethical Guidelines in Chapter 19.* In 1996 **Target** was the third-largest retailer in the United States, with over 750 stores in 38 states. So it was big news when the company decided to stop selling cigarettes in its stores. Cigarettes often have markups of 20 to 30%. Analysts estimate that Target's decision to eliminate this product line may have cost the company up to $64 million in lost revenues and $18 million in earnings.

If Target had continued selling cigarettes and if cigarette sales had grown at the same rate as Target's other sales, Target's earnings could have been $23 million higher in 1999.

Required

1. Use Target Corporation's 1999 Annual Report to determine the company's earnings per share (EPS) before extraordinary items for 1999. (*Hint:* Look at the basic EPS calculation in the EPS footnote to the financial statements.) Estimate what EPS would have been in 1999 if Target had continued selling cigarettes.
2. As the CFO of Target, justify to the company's stockholders how the company could make a decision that reduced earnings. How do ethical considerations enter this decision? Would the IMA's Ethical Guidelines help if you had been asked to make the initial recommendation to drop this product line?

TEAM PROJECT

Identify relevant data, outsourcing, capital budgeting
(Obj. 1, 2, 5)

John Menard is the founder and sole owner of **Menard, Inc.** Analysts have estimated that his chain of home improvement stores scattered around nine midwestern states generate about $3 billion in annual sales. But how can Menard compete with giant **Home Depot?**

Suppose Menard is trying to decide whether to invest $45 million in a state-of-the-art manufacturing plant in Eau Claire, Wisconsin. Menard expects the plant would operate for 15 years, after which the plant would have no residual value. The plant would produce Menard's own line of Formica countertops, cabinets, and picnic tables.

Suppose Menard would incur the following unit costs in producing its own product lines:

| | Per Unit | | |
	Countertops	Cabinets	Picnic Tables
Direct materials	$15	$10	$30
Direct labor...	10	5	20
Variable manufacturing overhead......	5	2	7

Rather than making these products, assume Menard could buy them from outside suppliers. Suppliers would charge Menard $40 per countertop, $25 per cabinet, and $75 per picnic table.

Whether Menard makes or buys these products, assume that he expects the following annual sales:

- Countertops—487,200 at $130 each   • Cabinets—150,000 at $75 each
- Picnic tables—100,000 at $225 each

If "making" is sufficiently more profitable than outsourcing these products, then Menard will build the new plant. John Menard has asked your consulting group for a recommendation. Menard uses a 14% discount rate and the straight-line depreciation method.

Required

1. Are the following items relevant or irrelevant in Menard's decision to build a new plant that will manufacture his own products?
   a. The unit sale prices of the countertops, cabinets, and picnic tables (the sale prices that Menard charges its customers)
   b. The prices outside suppliers would charge Menard for the three products, if Menard decides to outsource the products rather than make them
   c. The $45 million to build the new plant
   d. The direct materials, direct labor, and variable overhead Menard would incur to manufacture the three product lines
   e. Menard's salary

2. Determine whether Menard should make or outsource the countertops, cabinets, and picnic tables, *assuming that the company had already built the plant and therefore has the manufacturing capacity to produce these products.* In other words, what is the annual difference in cash flows if Menard decides to make rather than outsource each of these three products?

3. In requirement 2, you computed the annual difference in cash flows if Menard decides to make rather than buy the three products. To analyze the investment in the plant relative to the alternative of outsourcing the products, use this *difference* in annual cash flows to compute the following for the investment in the new plant:
   a. Payback period   c. Net present value
   b. Accounting rate of return d. Internal rate of return

   (*Hint:* Base the benefit side of your computations on the *difference* in annual cash flows you computed in requirement 2, *not* the total expected cash flows from building the plant.)

4. Write a memo giving your recommendation to John Menard. The memo should clearly state your recommendation, along with a brief summary of the reasons for your recommendation. Use the memo format outlined in Daily Exercise 26-5.

INTERNET EXERCISE

Papa John's International Inc. has surpassed **Little Caesars** to become the number 3 pizza chain, behind **Pizza Hut** and **Domino's,** with more than 2,300 restaurants scattered across the United States and five other countries. Most restaurants offer delivery or take-out only.

Papa John's International

1. Go to **http://www.papajohns.com** and click on *Papa John's Story.* In what year did the first Papa John's restaurant open? Click on *Our Pizza Story.* What is the focus of Papa John's?

2. In the left-hand column, click on *Investor Relationships* followed by *SEC Filings* in the right-hand column. Choose the most recent annual report by clicking on Form Type *10-K.* Under Part I select *Item 1: Business.* Scan the first three pages. (Note: For easier viewing you may want to select font size 1 = smallest and click on enter.)
   a. For a company-owned restaurant, over the past fiscal year Papa John's reported how much in average sales? Average cash flow? Average operating income? What is the expected cash investment per company-owned restaurant opening next year?

b. Why is Papa John's expansion strategy to cluster restaurants in targeted markets?

3. Assume the value of the investment decreases to zero over a ten-year period of time. Use the information from 2(a) for the following computations. For one company-owned Papa John's restaurant, compute the

a. payback period

b. accounting rate of return

c. net present value assuming a 16% required rate of return

d. internal rate of return (Appendix B contains present-value tables.)

4. Does a Papa John's company-owned restaurant appear to be a good investment? Why or why not?

5. Continue to scroll down the document. How much does a franchisee pay for the right to operate a Papa John's restaurant in the United States? (Note: In the 1999 Annual Report this information was around page 7.)

6. Should a new franchisee expect to achieve the same rate of return as a company-owned Papa John's restaurant? Why or why not?

APPENDIX A

Target Corporation Annual Report

We are Target Corporation.

Annual Report 1999

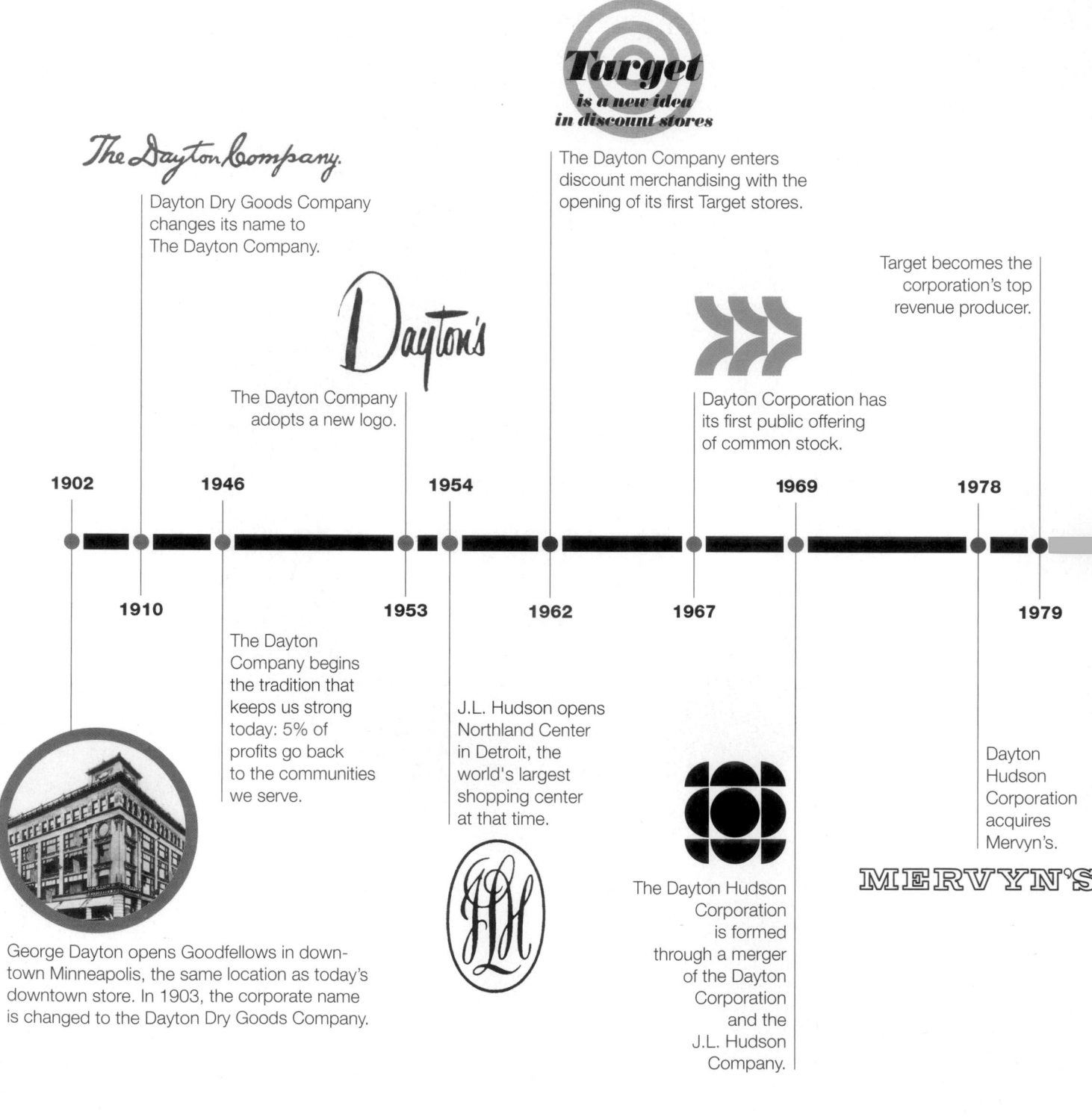

The Dayton Company.

Dayton Dry Goods Company
changes its name to
The Dayton Company.

Dayton's

The Dayton Company
adopts a new logo.

Target *is a new idea in discount stores*

The Dayton Company enters
discount merchandising with the
opening of its first Target stores.

Target becomes the
corporation's top
revenue producer.

Dayton Corporation has
its first public offering
of common stock.

1902   **1946**   **1954**   **1969**   **1978**

1910   **1953**   **1962**   **1967**   **1979**

The Dayton
Company begins
the tradition that
keeps us strong
today: 5% of
profits go back
to the communities
we serve.

J.L. Hudson opens
Northland Center
in Detroit, the
world's largest
shopping center
at that time.

The Dayton Hudson
Corporation
is formed
through a merger
of the Dayton
Corporation
and the
J.L. Hudson
Company.

Dayton
Hudson
Corporation
acquires
Mervyn's.

MERVYN'S

George Dayton opens Goodfellows in downtown Minneapolis, the same location as today's
downtown store. In 1903, the corporate name
is changed to the Dayton Dry Goods Company.

Dayton Hudson
Corporation acquires
Rivertown Trading
Company and
The Associated
Merchandising
Corporation.

Marshall Field's

Mervyn's changes
its name to
Mervyn's California.

Target launches
the industry's first
discount store credit
card, the Target
Guest Card.

First SuperTarget
stores open.

1984 **1990**   **1999**

Dayton Hudson
Corporation acquires
Marshall Field's.

1995   **1998**   **2000**

Dayton Hudson
Corporation launches its
e-commerce capability
with new store brand
web sites.

Dayton Hudson
Corporation
celebrates its
name change to
Target Corporation.

Dayton's and
Hudson's combine
to form Dayton
Hudson Department
Store Company.

TARGET CORPORATION
◎

DAYTON'S
HUDSON'S

TARGET CORPORATION

Our mission is to be the retailer of choice in

the discount, middle market and department store

retail segments. By focusing on trend leadership, excellent

guest service, exciting team member opportunities, and

community outreach, we create long-term

shareholder value.

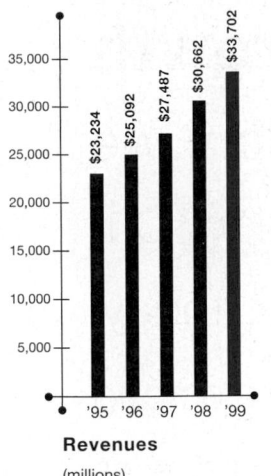

Revenues
(millions)

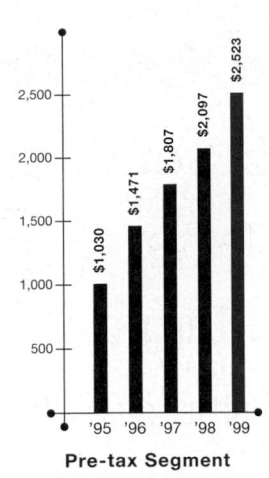

Pre-tax Segment Profit
(millions)

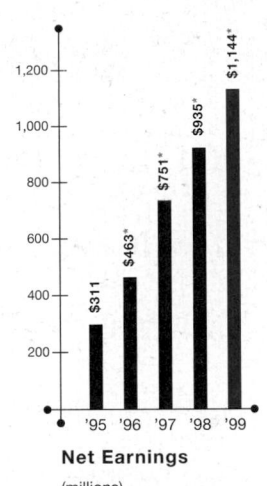

Net Earnings
(millions)

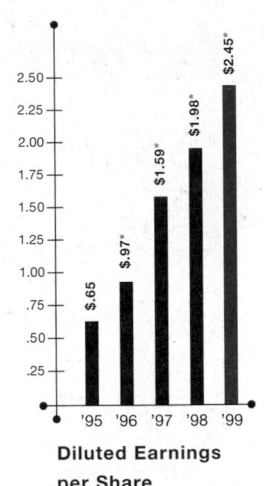

Diluted Earnings per Share

Operating Results ($ millions)	1999	1998	Change
Revenues	**$33,702**	$30,662	10%
Pre-tax segment profit	**$ 2,523**	$ 2,097	20%
Net earnings*	**$ 1,144**	$ 935	22%

Per Share Data			
Diluted earnings*	**$ 2.45**	$ 1.98	24%
Cash dividends declared	**$ .40**	$ .36	11%

At Year-End			
Common shares outstanding	**455,841,388**	441,809,806	
Retail square feet	**138,640,000**	130,172,000	
Number of stores	**1,243**	1,182	

*Includes unusual items, resulting in net after-tax charges of $44 million ($.09 per share) in 1999, $35 million ($.08 per share) in 1998, $24 million ($.05 per share) in 1997, and $92 million ($.20 per share) in 1996.

Acknowledging the strength of the Target brand and the future growth

opportunities of our largest retail division, we recently changed our name to Target Corporation. Our new name recognizes that the Target division, today, comprises more than 75 percent of the company's sales and profits, and that this contribution will continue to increase over time as we further expand our store base. Our new name also reflects our continuing commitment to leverage our resources for the benefit of the total corporation, and as a result, to improve our overall financial results and create substantial value for our shareholders.

Our performance in 1999 was driven by superior results at our Target division. Revenues for the segment increased 13 percent to $26 billion and pre-tax profit grew 28 percent to over $2 billion, establishing a new milestone in Target's history. In addition, Target's pre-tax profit as a percent of revenues equaled the reported profit margin at Wal*Mart's domestic discount/supercenter division for the year, eliminating a significant differential that existed in prior years. These outstanding results at Target in 1999, combined with record sales and profits at our Department Stores, produced our fourth consecutive year of earnings per share growth in excess of 20 percent.

We are very pleased with our performance in the past year and we are excited about the opportunities for profitable growth in 2000 and beyond. As we look forward, we remain confident that Target Corporation can continue to deliver average annual earnings per share growth of 15 percent or more over time.

New Store Growth With less than 1,000 stores in the U.S. today, Target's opportunities for domestic new store growth remain plentiful. During 1999, Target added a total of 74 new stores, increasing square footage by 9 percent. We continued to focus our efforts on markets in the Northeast and Mid-Atlantic, devoting nearly 40 percent of our new store openings to this region.

Importantly, by becoming more flexible in our site selection and store design without compromising the Target brand, we continue to have success in penetrating these markets despite difficult real estate challenges. In 1999, we entered two new markets, Boston and Pittsburgh, and in 2000, we will enter two new states, Connecticut and West Virginia, bringing the number of states in which we operate to 46.

Bob Ulrich,
Chairman and
Chief Executive Officer

Our store expansion in 2000 will also include a significant acceleration of SuperTarget store openings, reflecting our increased confidence in the sales and profit potential of this concept. We will essentially double our number of SuperTarget stores during the year, adding 15 new locations, primarily in the Midwest and South. About half of these stores will be relocations of existing discount stores, giving us the ability to capture greater market share in key metropolitan areas. With plans for at least 200 SuperTarget locations within the next ten years, we believe this strategy will generate profitable growth for many years to come.

Other Growth Opportunities At the core of Target's future growth and financial success is our differentiated merchandise strategy — with an emphasis on quality and original design, unique product, impactful presentation and value pricing. During the past year, we strengthened our merchandise assortment with the addition of new brands such as Calphalon, Stiffel, Discovery Channel toys and designs by Michael Graves and Robert Abbey. In 2000, we will continue to create excitement for our guests with new initiatives. Examples include an expanded offering of Michael Graves housewares and a new assortment of electronics; the introduction of Martex bed and bath collections; exclusive new lines of sporting goods equipment and accessories; and the expansion of our Archer Farms brand of premier food. Each of these efforts reinforces and enhances Target's brand image in the marketplace and contributes to our financial strength.

Credit is also an important contributor to our overall earnings growth. During the past five years, contribution from credit has increased at a compound annual rate of 17 percent, and both return on investment and EVA have risen sharply. While we continue to invest in credit programs at all three of our segments, the Target Guest Card is the primary driver of growth for this business. In 2000, we will continue to increase our card penetration, enhance our guest loyalty programs and leverage our credit operation to sustain our profitable growth.

In 1999, Target Corporation devoted greater resources to developing web-based strategies, reflecting our belief that the Internet and e-commerce are vital to our future. In our view, the Internet provides an important tool for communicating with our guests as well as a new distribution channel for our merchandise. Through our new business unit called target.direct, we are focused on leveraging our strengths as a well-known and trusted retailer to increase guest service and generate profitable sales. We believe our powerful marketing, our differentiated merchandise and more than 1,200 convenient store locations give us a competitive advantage in the on-line world. In 2000, we will continue to make the necessary investments in this business to attract experienced and talented team members, to improve our technology and fulfillment capability, and to provide our guests with appropriate services and merchandise selection.

Though our name has changed to reflect the growth and importance of Target, we remain committed to Dayton's, Marshall Field's, Hudson's and Mervyn's. During the past five years, Target Corporation has averaged a total return to shareholders on an annualized basis of 43 percent. During this same period, both Mervyn's and our Department Stores were key contributors to our overall strategy and financial per-formance. In 1999 alone, their combined net pre-tax cash flow again exceeded a half billion dollars. We believe that these two segments will continue to create value for Target Corporation in the years ahead.

We are excited about the future for Target Corporation and believe that we are well-positioned to build on our past performance. As we look forward, we remain confident that we will continue to deliver strong growth in sales and earnings and achieve our objective of generating at least 15 percent average annual earnings per share growth over time.

March 24, 2000

Bob Ulrich, Chairman and Chief Executive Officer

We are now

Target Corporation, a name that reflects

the powerful recognition of our largest retail brand.

Today, Target Stores makes up more than 75 percent of our

sales and profits, a percentage that will continue to grow as we

open new Target stores across the country. The Target name best

reflects our business and our company, today and in the future.

We remain a company that is committed to growth

and delivering superior returns to our

shareholders.

Target Corporation's goal is to deliver average annual earnings per share growth of 15 percent or more over time. To deliver on that pledge to shareholders we will continue to grow the Target store base; innovate to grow sales at existing stores; pursue new retail strategies; and enhance our credit programs. Our continued success depends on clearly defined brand strategies at each of our stores, great execution every day for our guests, a commitment to constant innovation and reinvention, and support of our communities.

New Store Growth Our primary growth comes from new store expansion. Target continues to open stores in new U.S. markets and increase store density in existing markets, growing retail square footage by 8 to 10 percent annually. In 2000, Target will open approximately 80 total new stores, including 15 new SuperTarget stores, essentially doubling the number of SuperTarget locations we operated at year end. Target will add locations in two new states — West Virginia and Connecticut — and expand our presence in key markets like Pittsburgh, Boston and Dallas/Fort Worth. As Target's brand becomes stronger, it allows us to add more stores in existing metropolitan markets. To provide guests with added value and convenience, all new Target stores and remodels will feature pharmacies, optical shops, one-hour photo labs and portrait studios. Our newest stores will feature an updated look with an arched entrance with more glass for a brighter, more inviting feel. We will also continue to invest in store remodels to ensure that all Target stores continue to represent the Target brand.

Our goal at SuperTarget is to bring "fashion to food."

You are now leaving Boston
But wait, we just got here!
the store you've been waiting for ⊙ TARGET

Target entered the Boston market in July 1999 with five stores, under the advertising theme, "the store you've been waiting for." Northeast and Mid-Atlantic markets are key areas for Target's expansion.

Differentiated Merchandise and Presentation Target's core merchandising strategy centers on consistent delivery of differentiation and value. We know we have to deliver excitement and value in dramatic new ways every time our guests visit our stores. The primary way we do this is by offering well-designed, trend-right merchandise at great prices, with powerful presentations in attractive stores. We are adding more exclusive product to our stores, with a greater emphasis on design and a greater depth of trend-right product.

For example, in 1999 Target completely reinvented the toy area. While we still carry traditional toy categories, we increased our offering of toys characterized by quality, craftsmanship, exclusivity and value. We carry great brand names such as Playmobil and Sanrio — and toys from the Discovery Channel. We also completely redesigned our in-store presentation of toys with new, vibrant signing and displays.

The Target "Sign of the Times" advertising campaign leverages the acceptance of the Target bullseye logo. The campaign was launched in New York City with posters, images on New York metro water towers and postings on construction sites.

In addition, our home department is evolving to become a shopping destination similar to a specialty store. In the past year we have added brands like Calphalon and Stiffel, and designs by Michael Graves and Robert Abbey. Most recently, Target introduced exclusive bedding and bath products from Martex, featuring 250-thread-count cotton sheets, duvets and plush towels. These assortments enhance Target's powerful brand image among our guests and are the heart of our strategy to offer compelling, differentiated merchandise.

Target's new toy offerings and the toy area's new signing reflect the company's commitment to constant innovation and reinvention in all merchandise areas. Target continues to add more exclusive products to its stores, with offerings like Sonia Kashuk Professional Makeup.

A-11

Better Guest Service In addition to our merchandise, we are working to differentiate Target's service as well. We know that guests want ultra-fast service with a respectful tone. That means getting in and out of the store quickly, finding merchandise in-stock, and obtaining rapid and knowledgeable answers to questions. We want to inject speed in every service area that affects the guest. Guests at Target tell us service is more important to them than any other aspect of their store experience, and therefore service is our highest priority.

Target is investing in technology and training to deliver faster, more knowledgeable service for our guests.

In addition to speed of service, ensuring that merchandise is available and in-stock is essential to delivering great guest service. To improve Target's in-stocks we have made supply chain performance a top priority.

SuperTarget Expansion SuperTarget provides us with tremendous opportunities for future growth. SuperTarget combines general merchandise with high-quality grocery items to offer a convenient one-stop shopping experience for guests. Our SuperTarget strategy is exactly the same as our general merchandise strategy: "Expect More. Pay Less." Our goal is to leverage Target's brand heritage and differentiate ourselves from other supercenters. Expanding the Archer Farms brand for the grocery side of the business — including an extensive line of Archer Farms private label grocery products that are of higher quality than most national brands — is key to this differentiation.

Target is including pharmacies in all new and remodeled Target stores, adding more than 100 pharmacies in 2000 alone. Pharmacy was one of the top performing areas at Target in 1999, producing double-digit comparable-store sales results.

In 1999, SuperTarget improved its gross margin performance, the quality of its perishable foods offering and its expense structure. As a result of these merchandising and operational improvements, we are accelerating the growth of SuperTarget, adding 15 stores in 2000. In the next ten years, we expect to open at least 200 SuperTarget stores that will generate $15 billion or more in sales. Relocations of existing Target stores provide significant opportunity for SuperTarget growth, allowing us to update our store base as it ages, and replace older stores with our newest and biggest stores. This will help fuel many years of growth for Target.

E-Commerce In early 2000, Target formed a new business unit called target.direct, which is responsible for the company's electronic retailing and direct marketing efforts. The Internet and e-commerce are a vital part of Target Corporation; target.direct will help us leverage the power of all our store brands and catalogs.

We see the Internet not only as a channel for selling merchandise, but as an important communications tool to reach guests and drive increased guest service. In 1999, we devoted more resources to building the merchandising, marketing, fulfillment and technology processes required to support this new channel. Today we operate ten websites — eight of which are full-service selling sites. The largest is target.com, an exciting site that is consistent with the Target brand, offering thousands of unique and highly differentiated items that are also available in Target Stores. In addition to buying merchandise, guests can apply for a Target Guest Card, access information on programs like Take Charge of Education, find out what's new in our stores, get a map to a specific store location, or even apply for a job.

SuperTarget offers the best in high-quality groceries and general merchandise. We plan to open more than 200 SuperTarget locations in the next ten years.

Target.com will add bridal and baby gift registries in 2000 and significantly increase the number of items for sale on-line.

We are excited about the possibilities of this medium to drive profitable sales, increase guest service and enhance the brand equity of our stores. We believe our competitive advantage in the electronic world will come from leveraging our existing strengths as a retailer, including our trusted brand names, marketing power, store presence and differentiated merchandise. We will continue investing in this area in 2000, expanding our on-line merchandise assortments and guest services.

Multiple Retail Segments Target Corporation also competes in the middle-market and traditional department store segments of the retail marketplace through Mervyn's California and Dayton's, Marshall Field's and Hudson's. Mervyn's and the Department Stores are key contributors to our overall strategy.

At our Department Stores, we remain focused on our commitment to be "The Best Store in Town" in our core Midwest markets as we strive to deliver fashion leadership and superior guest service. In 2000, we are working to enhance the shopping experience at our stores in several ways: by building stronger relationships with our guests through more personalized selling and enhanced guest loyalty programs; through a stronger commitment to newness and fashion product in our assortments; and with the creation of a more captivating store environment, with visual drama and ease of shopping. One way we are reinventing the shopping experience is through events like the Paris Flea Market and our popular "Fash Bash" fashion shows. Marketing initiatives for our department stores will continue to reinforce the strong brand heritage of our stores.

At Dayton's, Marshall Field's and Hudson's, we are committed to being "The Best Store in Town."

At Mervyn's, we are working to differentiate ourselves in the middle-market with our national and owned brands. Over the last three years, Mervyn's has added more than 125 national and market brands to the sales floor. In 1999, we made a more concerted effort to let our guests know about our brands by reinforcing our "Big Brands. Small Prices." promise in all of our marketing vehicles. We also updated our in-store presentations with more national brand shops and stronger in-store brand identification. We have introduced into our assortment more exclusive merchandise designed by individuals with national

Mervyn's California offers a strong assortment of national brands and high-quality owned brands for the middle market.

or international reputations, like craft artist Debbie Mumm and Australian painter and designer Ken Done. We also continue to upgrade and improve the quality and fashion content of our core owned brands, like Hillard & Hanson. In addition to better merchandise content, in 2000 Mervyn's will focus on improving in-stocks, guest service and merchandise presentation.

Credit Programs We offer proprietary credit in each of our business segments. Our credit portfolio is the second largest among retailers that issue their own cards and currently includes more than 30 million cards held by our guests. The growth of the Target Guest Card continues to drive increases in profit contribution from credit. Guest loyalty programs at each of our stores help us build stronger relationships with our guests and increase patronage of our stores. At Target, more than 4 million guests are enrolled in our Take Charge of Education program, where 1 percent of purchases made on the Target Guest Card are donated to a K-12 school of the guest's choice. We plan to grow credit's contribution to our results in the future by opening new accounts, enhancing guest loyalty programs and managing the business with financial discipline.

Credit programs contribute to earnings growth by driving sales at our stores and through credit's contribution to profits. The Target Guest card is now carried by more than 15 million Americans.

A Community Partner Our commitment to be an active member of the communities where we operate is also essential to our success. In 1999, we gave more than $67 million to nonprofit organizations across the country. We support the United Way with a $3 million corporate contribution — and our team members donated another $9 million to their local United Ways. In 2000, our grantmaking will exceed $80 million.

One of our greatest and most heartfelt contributions is called Target House. Dedicated in May 1999, Target House is a home-away-from-home for patients and their families undergoing treatment at St. Jude Children's Research Hospital in Memphis. Our guests help support Target House and the families it serves whenever they make pharmacy, and health and beauty product purchases at Target. In March, Target announced its intention to build a Target House annex, with an additional 44 suites, to serve even more families.

At Target House, which opened in May 1999, children who are undergoing long-term treatment at St. Jude Children's Research Hospital have a home-away-from-home for themselves and their families.

Education is important to our guests and to our company. Target has donated more than $18 million to schools across the country since our Take Charge of Education program began in 1997. More than 100,000 schools across the country participate in the program.

The Target Foundation was created in early 2000, with a continued emphasis on funding arts and social action initiatives in Minnesota. A key focus area for giving is to support immediate community needs for food, clothing and shelter. To that end, the Foundation awarded a $1 million grant to Sharing & Caring Hands, the Minneapolis nonprofit organization that serves the needs of inner city residents.

Mervyn's award-winning Community Closet program toured 15 cities in 10 states in 1999. In partnership with 82 nonprofit agencies, the Community Closet clothed 1,000 women making the transition from welfare to work. In addition, Mervyn's helped send more than 15,000 economically disadvantaged kids back to school in new clothes in 1999 through our ChildSpree program.

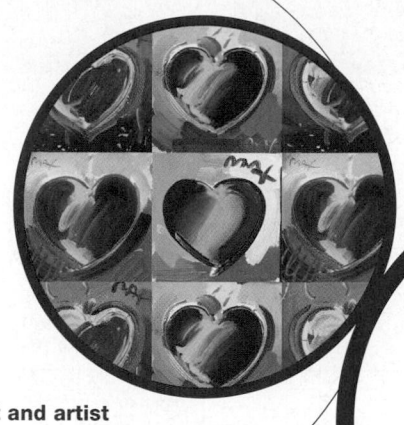

Target and artist Peter Max launched a new line of gift bags, greeting cards and wrapping paper featuring the artist's vibrant designs from the '60s to the '90s, an example of our exclusive, trend-right products.

Dayton's, Marshall Field's and Hudson's have always placed a special emphasis on supporting arts and cultural institutions. The Department Stores' "Project Imagine" showcases the arts in our communities, putting the promotional power of our stores behind arts organizations to help them achieve new levels of public awareness. Project Imagine has made possible events ranging from "Free Tuesdays" at Chicago's Museum of Contemporary Art to MacBeth at the Minnesota Opera. In recognition of the positive influence of the arts in young people's lives, the Project Imagine Scholarship was launched, awarding two scholarships per store to high school seniors.

We continue to look for innovative ways to partner with nonprofit agencies to build stronger communities across the country.

Target now offers 12 new high-style chairs from a number of designers, including Philippe Starck. Fresh design and differentiated merchandise are key to Target's merchandising strategy.

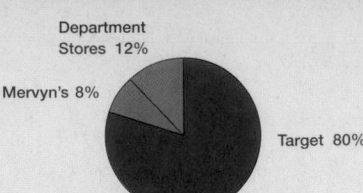

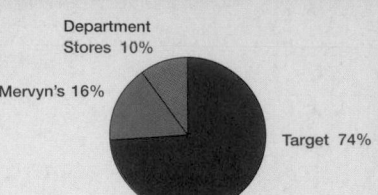

Revenues (percent of total)	Pre-tax Segment Profit (percent of total)	Retail Square Feet (percent of total)
Department Stores 9%	Department Stores 12%	Department Stores 10%
Other 1%		
Mervyn's 12%	Mervyn's 8%	Mervyn's 16%
Target 78%	Target 80%	Target 74%

Target

(dollars in millions)	1999	1998	1997
Revenues	$26,080	$23,014	$20,298
Pre-tax Segment Profit	$ 2,022	$ 1,578	$ 1,287
Stores	912	851	796
Retail Square Feet*	102,945	94,553	87,158

* In thousands, reflects total square feet less office, warehouse and vacant space.

Target (at year end) Employees: 214,000

■ =Store Occupied State
◻ =Major Market

	Retail Sq. Ft. (in thousands)	No. of Stores		Retail Sq. Ft. (in thousands)	No. of Stores		Retail Sq. Ft. (in thousands)	No. of Stores		Retail Sq. Ft. (in thousands)	No. of Stores
Alabama	117	1	Kansas	1,290	10	New Hampshire	392	3	South Dakota	391	4
Arizona	2,982	27	Kentucky	1,274	12	New Jersey	1,625	13	Tennessee	2,001	19
Arkansas	229	2	Louisiana	203	2	New Mexico	870	8	Texas	9,297	85
California	16,355	145	Maryland	2,158	18	New York	2,288	18	Utah	1,178	7
Colorado	2,533	23	Massachusetts	522	4	North Carolina	2,668	24	Virginia	2,769	23
Delaware	146	1	Michigan	4,908	46	North Dakota	437	4	Washington	2,557	24
Florida	7,442	66	Minnesota	6,024	51	Ohio	3,571	31	Wisconsin	2,599	24
Georgia	3,445	30	Mississippi	239	2	Oklahoma	817	8	Wyoming	182	2
Idaho	406	4	Missouri	1,885	17	Oregon	1,194	11			
Illinois	6,050	52	Montana	423	4	Pennsylvania	1,600	13			
Indiana	2,876	30	Nebraska	1,074	9	Rhode Island	128	1			
Iowa	1,868	17	Nevada	1,267	11	South Carolina	665	6	**Total**	**102,945**	**912**

Major Markets	No. of Stores
Greater Los Angeles	71
Chicago	38
Minneapolis/St. Paul	34
San Francisco Bay Area	28
Dallas/Ft. Worth	24
Atlanta	24
Detroit	23
Houston	21
Greater Miami	20
Phoenix	18
Denver/Boulder	15
Greater New York City	15
San Diego	14
Washington DC	14
Seattle/Tacoma	13
St. Louis	13
Tampa/St. Petersburg	12
Greater Philadelphia	12
Greater Cleveland	11
Indianapolis	11
Orlando	10
Sacramento	10
Baltimore	10

Mervyn's

(dollars in millions)	1999	1998	1997
Revenues	$4,099	$4,150	$4,219
Pre-tax Segment Profit	$ 205	$ 240	$ 280
Stores	267	268	269
Retail Square Feet*	21,635	21,729	21,810

* In thousands, reflects total square feet less office, warehouse and vacant space.

Mervyn's (at year end) Employees: 32,000

■ =Store Occupied State
◻ =Major Market

	Retail Sq. Ft. (in thousands)	No. of Stores		Retail Sq. Ft. (in thousands)	No. of Stores		Retail Sq. Ft. (in thousands)	No. of Stores		Retail Sq. Ft. (in thousands)	No. of Stores
Arizona	1,202	15	Louisiana	449	6	New Mexico	267	3	Utah	753	8
California	9,607	124	Michigan	1,162	15	Oklahoma	269	3	Washington	1,440	16
Colorado	853	11	Minnesota	1,157	9	Oregon	559	7			
Idaho	82	1	Nevada	491	7	Texas	3,344	42	**Total**	**21,635**	**267**

Major Markets	No. of Stores
Greater Los Angeles	48
San Francisco Bay Area	29
Dallas/Ft. Worth	12
San Diego	12
Phoenix	11
Detroit	9
Houston	9
Minneapolis/St. Paul	9
Seattle/Tacoma	9
Greater Salt Lake City	8
Denver/Boulder	6

Department Stores

(dollars in millions)	1999	1998	1997
Revenues	$3,074	$3,064	$2,970
Pre-tax Segment Profit	$ 296	$ 279	$ 240
Stores	64	63	65
Retail Square Feet*	14,060	13,890	14,090

* In thousands, reflects total square feet less office, warehouse and vacant space.

Department Stores (at year end) Employees: 34,000

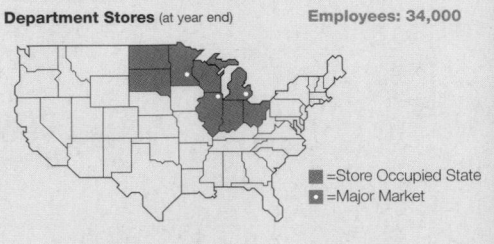

■ =Store Occupied State
◻ =Major Market

Dayton's	Retail Sq. Ft. (in thousands)	No. of Stores	**Hudson's**	Retail Sq. Ft. (in thousands)	No. of Stores	**Marshall Field's**	Retail Sq. Ft. (in thousands)	No. of Stores
Minnesota	3,040	12	Michigan	4,784	21	Illinois	4,173	17
North Dakota	297	3				Indiana	246	2
South Dakota	102	1				Ohio	618	3
Wisconsin	373	3				Wisconsin	427	2
						Total	**14,060**	**64**

Major Markets	No. of Stores
Chicago	16
Detroit	11
Minneapolis/St.Paul	10

Analysis of Operations

Our 1999 results mark the fourth consecutive year of earnings per share growth in excess of 20 percent. This exceptional growth in earnings per share was driven by substantial expansion in Target's gross margin rate.

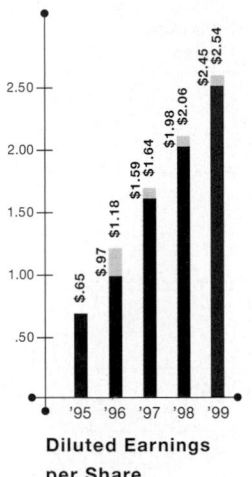

Diluted Earnings per Share

●/◒ as reported

◔ before unusual items

Earnings

Our net earnings were $1,144 million in 1999, compared with $935 million in 1998 and $751 million in 1997. Earnings per share were $2.45 in 1999, $1.98 in 1998 and $1.59 in 1997. References to earnings per share refer to diluted earnings per share. Earnings per share, dividends per share and common shares outstanding reflect our 1998 two-for-one share split and our 1996 three-for-one share split.

Management's discussion and analysis is based on our reclassified Consolidated Results of Operations as shown and discussed on page 24.

Revenues and Comparable-Store Sales

In 1999, our total revenues increased 9.9 percent and comparable-store sales increased 5.1 percent. Total revenues include retail sales and net credit revenues. Comparable-store sales are sales from stores open longer than one year. Revenue growth in 1999 and 1998 reflected Target's strong comparable-store sales growth and new store expansion. The impact of inflation was minimal and, as a result, the overall comparable-store sales increase closely approximated real growth.

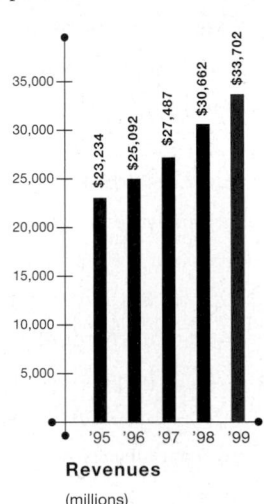

Revenues

(millions)

Earnings Analysis

(millions, except per share data)

	Earnings			Diluted Earnings per Share		
	1999	1998	1997	**1999**	1998	1997
Net earnings before unusual items	**$1,188**	$970	$775	**$2.54**	$2.06	$1.64
Mainframe outsourcing (pre-tax 1999 $5 mil, 1998 $42 mil)	**(3)**	(26)	–	**(.01)**	(.06)	–
Favorable outcome of inventory shortage tax matter	–	20	–	–	.04	–
Securitization gain/(loss) (pre-tax 1998 $3 mil loss, 1997 $45 mil gain)	–	(2)	27	–	–	.06
Net earnings before extraordinary charges	1,185	962	802	2.54	2.04	1.70
Extraordinary charges — debt repurchase	**(41)**	(27)	(51)	**(.09)**	(.06)	(.11)
Net earnings	**$1,144**	$935	$751	**$2.45**	$1.98	$1.59

Management uses net earnings before unusual items, among other standards, to measure operating performance. It supplements, and is not intended to represent a measure of performance in accordance with, disclosures required by generally accepted accounting principles. Each per share amount is calculated independently.

Revenues and Comparable-Store Sales Growth

	1999		1998	
	Revenues	**Comparable-Store Sales**	Revenues	Comparable-Store Sales
Target	**13.3%**	**6.7%**	13.4%	6.1%
Mervyn's	**(1.2)**	**(0.7)**	(1.6)	0.9
Department Stores	**0.3**	**0.8**	3.2	4.5
Total	**9.9%**	**5.1%**	11.6%	5.2%

Revenues per Square Foot

	1999	1998	1997
Target	**$264**	$253	$243
Mervyn's	**189**	191	187
Department Stores	**220**	219	211

Thirteen-month average retail square feet.

Gross Margin Rate

The gross margin rate represents gross margin as a percent of sales. In 1999, our gross margin rate increased primarily due to rate expansion at Target and the Department Stores, resulting from improved markup and markdowns at Target and improved markup at the Department Stores. This increase was partially offset by the mix impact of strong growth at Target, our lowest gross margin rate division. In 1998, our overall gross margin rate increased modestly from the prior year, primarily due to lower markdowns at Target.

The LIFO provision, included in cost of sales, is calculated based on inventory levels, markup rates and internally generated retail price indices. In 1999, the LIFO provision was a $7 million credit ($.01 per share), compared with an $18 million credit ($.02 per share) in 1998 and a $6 million charge ($.01 per share) in 1997. The 1999 LIFO credit resulted primarily from higher markup. The 1998 LIFO credit resulted primarily from higher markup and higher inventory levels.

Operating Expense Rate

Operating expense rate represents selling, general and administrative expense (including buying and occupancy, advertising, start-up and other expense) as a percent of revenues. Our operating expense rate was essentially even with the prior year, benefiting from the overall growth of Target, our lowest expense rate division, and lower bad debt expense. These factors were offset by the lack of sales leverage in 1999 at Mervyn's and the Department Stores. The operating expense rate in 1998 was essentially even with 1997.

Pre-tax Segment Profit and Percent Change from Prior Year

(millions)	1999		1998	
Target	$2,022	28%	$1,578	23%
Mervyn's	205	(14)	240	(14)
Department Stores	296	6	279	16
Total	$2,523	20%	$2,097	16%

Pre-tax Segment Profit as a Percent of Revenues

	1999	1998
Target	7.8%	6.9%
Mervyn's	5.0%	5.8%
Department Stores	9.6%	9.1%

EBITDA

EBITDA is pre-tax segment profit before depreciation and amortization.

EBITDA and Percent Change from Prior Year

(millions)	1999		1998	
Target	$2,589	25%	$2,074	20%
Mervyn's	343	(9)	378	(7)
Department Stores	429	4	414	12
Total	$3,361	17%	$2,866	15%

EBITDA as a Percent of Revenues

	1999	1998
Target	9.9%	9.0%
Mervyn's	8.4%	9.1%
Department Stores	14.0%	13.5%

Management uses pre-tax segment profit and EBITDA, among other standards, to measure operating performance. Pre-tax segment profit and EBITDA supplement, and are not intended to represent measures of performance in accordance with, disclosures required by generally accepted accounting principles.

Interest Expense

We consider payments to holders of our sold securitized receivables as "interest equivalent." In 1999, the total of interest expense and interest equivalent was $442 million, $4 million lower than 1998. The average portfolio interest rate in 1999 was 7.5 percent. In 1998, the total of interest expense and interest equivalent was $3 million lower than 1997. The average portfolio interest rate in 1998 was 7.8 percent. In both years, the reduction in interest expense and interest equivalent was due to a lower average portfolio interest rate, partially offset by higher average funded balances.

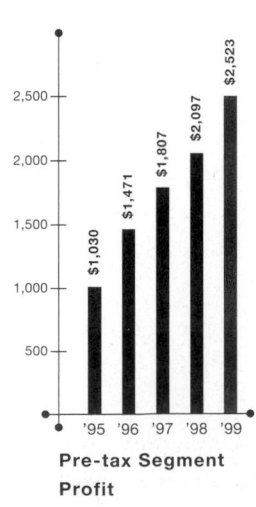

Pre-tax Segment Profit

(millions)

Pre-tax Segment Profit

Pre-tax segment profit increased 20 percent in 1999 to $2,523 million, compared with $2,097 million in 1998 and $1,807 million in 1997. Pre-tax segment profit is earnings before LIFO, securitization effects, interest, other expense and unusual items. Target provided substantially all of our pre-tax profit growth in 1999 with a 28 percent pre-tax profit increase. Target's full-year profit margin rate increased to 7.8 percent of revenues in 1999 from 6.9 percent in 1998.

During 1999, we repurchased $381 million of debt for $444 million, resulting in an after-tax extraordinary charge of $41 million ($.09 per share). The debt repurchased had a weighted-average interest rate of 9.3 percent and an average remaining life of 18 years. The replacement of this debt with lower interest rate financing will have a favorable impact on interest expense going forward. In 1998 and 1997, we repurchased $127 million and $503 million of long-term debt, resulting in after-tax extraordinary charges of $27 million ($.06 per share) and $51 million ($.11 per share), respectively.

Income Tax Rate

The effective income tax rate was 38.8 percent in 1999, and 38.2 percent and 39.5 percent in 1998 and 1997, respectively. The 1998 effective tax rate reflected the beneficial effect of $20 million ($.04 per share), resulting from the favorable outcome of our inventory shortage tax matter.

Securitized Receivables

In 1998, Target Receivables Corporation (TRC), a special-purpose subsidiary, sold to the public $400 million of securitized receivables. This issue of asset-backed securities had an expected maturity of five years and a stated rate of 5.90 percent. Proceeds from the sale were used for general corporate purposes, including funding the growth of receivables. The 1998 sale transaction and the maturity of our 1995 securitization resulted in a net pre-tax loss of $3 million (less than $.01 per share), which reduced 1998 finance charge revenues and pre-tax earnings.

In 1997, TRC sold to the public $400 million of securitized receivables, with an expected maturity of five years and a stated rate of 6.25 percent. This transaction, combined with the impact of the application of SFAS No. 125 to our 1995 securitization, resulted in a $45 million ($.06 per share) increase in finance charge revenues and pre-tax earnings.

Our Consolidated Results of Operations also include reductions of finance charge revenues and bad debt expense related to sold securitized receivables. The amounts that represent payments to holders of our sold securitized receivables are included in our pre-tax earnings reconciliation on page 37 as interest equivalent. Interest equivalent was $49 million in 1999, $48 million in 1998 and $33 million in 1997.

Mainframe Outsourcing

In 1998, we announced our plan to outsource our mainframe computer data center functions and expensed $42 million ($.06 per share) of related charges. During 1999, we completed the transition and expensed an additional $5 million ($.01 per share) related to the outsourcing. These expenses are included in selling, general and administrative expense.

Year 2000 Readiness Disclosure

We began mitigating the risks associated with the year 2000 date conversion in 1993. In 1997, we established a corporate-wide, comprehensive plan of action designed to achieve an uninterrupted transition into the year 2000. This project included three major elements: 1) information technology (IT) systems, 2) non-IT, or embedded technology, systems and 3) relationships with our key business partners. The project was divided into five phases: awareness, assessment, renovation, validation and implementation. During 1999, we completed all phases for the three elements, using both internal and external resources to implement our plan.

For our IT systems, we assessed both existing and newly implemented hardware, application software and operating systems. We also assessed non-IT systems, or embedded technology/infrastructure, risks at our stores, distribution centers and headquarters facilities. We identified our key business partners and worked closely with them to assess their readiness and mitigate the risk to us if they were not prepared for the year 2000. We installed the year 2000 ready version of Electronic Data Interchange (EDI) software and tested the software with our key vendors.

To date, we have not experienced any significant issues associated with the date rollover. We have experienced no systems failures, no unusually high levels of returned merchandise, no interruptions of data transmission using EDI software and no major disruptions in the supply of product from our vendors. We continue to test and monitor our systems and applications for such issues in order to address them promptly, should any arise.

In 1999, we expensed $16 million related to year 2000 readiness. Prior to 1999, we expensed $32 million related to year 2000 readiness. In addition, this program accelerated the timing of $15 million of planned capital expenditures. All expenditures related to our year 2000 readiness initiative were within our estimates, were funded by cash flow from operations and did not materially impact our other operating or investment plans.

Fourth Quarter Results

Due to the seasonal nature of the retail industry, fourth quarter operating results typically represent a substantially larger share of total year revenues and earnings due to the inclusion of the holiday shopping season.

Fourth quarter 1999 net earnings were $494 million, compared with $423 million in 1998. Earnings per share were $1.06 for the quarter, compared with $.90 in 1998. Total revenues increased 8.7 percent and comparable-store sales increased 3.5 percent. Our pre-tax profit increased 16 percent to $1,000 million, driven by Target's strong results.

Fourth Quarter Pre-tax Segment Profit and Percent Change from Prior Year

(millions)	1999		1998	
Target	$ 811	26%	$646	26%
Mervyn's	69	(34)	104	–
Department Stores	120	5	115	12
Total	$1,000	16%	$865	20%

Analysis of Financial Condition

Our financial condition remains strong. Cash flow from operations was $2,252 million, driven by earnings growth, strong inventory control and accounts payable leveraging. Internally generated funds continue to be the most important component of our capital resources and, along with our ability to access a variety of financial markets, provide funding for our expansion plans. We continue to fund the growth in our business through a combination of internally generated funds, debt and sold securitized receivables.

During 1999, our average total receivables serviced (which includes both retained and sold securitized receivables) increased 5 percent, or $124 million, due to growth of the Target Guest Card. Year-end total receivables serviced increased 7 percent from last year. In 1999, the number of Target Guest Card holders grew to over 15 million accounts at year end, compared with 12 million in 1998.

Inventory levels increased $323 million in 1999. This growth was more than fully funded by the $364 million increase in accounts payable over the same period.

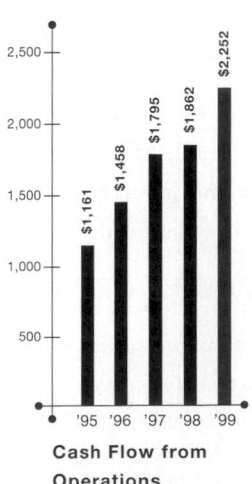

Cash Flow from Operations
(millions)

Capital expenditures were $1,918 million in 1999, compared with $1,657 million in 1998. Investment in Target accounted for 87 percent of 1999 capital expenditures and included the purchase of real estate assets of a membership-based, general merchandise retailer for approximately $125 million. Net property and equipment increased $930 million. During 1999, Target opened 61 net new stores.

Approximately 69 percent of total expenditures was for new stores, expansions and remodels. Other capital investments were for information systems, distribution and other infrastructure to support store growth, primarily at Target. Over the past five years, Target's retail square footage has grown at a compound annual rate of approximately 10 percent.

Our financing strategy is to ensure liquidity and access to capital markets, to manage the amount of floating-rate debt and to maintain a balanced spectrum of debt maturities. Within these parameters, we seek to minimize our cost of borrowing.

In January 1999, our Board of Directors authorized the repurchase of $1 billion of our common stock. We repurchased 9.4 million shares of stock during 1999 at a total cost of $588 million ($62.58 per share), net of the premium from exercised and expired put options. In March 2000, our Board of Directors authorized the repurchase of an additional $1 billion of our common stock.

Repurchases are made primarily in open market transactions, subject to market conditions. Our program also includes the sale of put options that entitle the holder to sell shares of our common stock to us, at a specified price, if the holder exercises the option. During 2000, we expect to continue to repurchase shares at a pace similar to that of 1999.

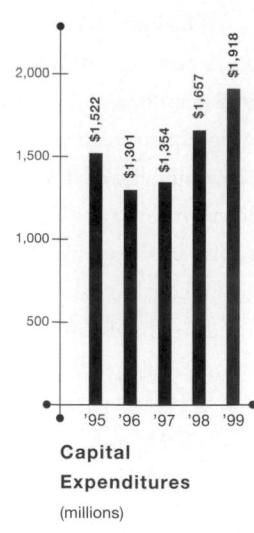

Capital Expenditures
(millions)

A key to our access to liquidity and capital markets is maintaining strong investment-grade debt ratings. During the year, our debt ratings were upgraded by Duff & Phelps. Subsequent to year-end, as reflected in the table below, our debt ratings were also upgraded by Moody's. Further liquidity is provided by $1.6 billion of committed lines of credit obtained through a group of 31 banks.

Credit Ratings

	Moody's	Standard and Poor's	Duff & Phelps
Long-term debt	A2	A-	A
Commercial paper	P-1	A-2	D-1
Sold securitized receivables	Aaa	AAA	N/A

Performance Objectives

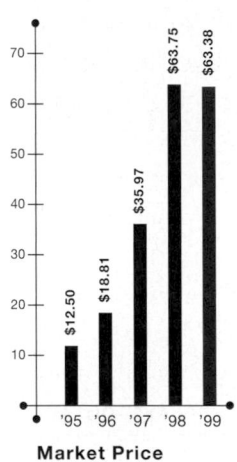

Market Price per Share
(year-end close)

Shareholder Return

Our primary objective is to maximize shareholder value over time through a combination of share price appreciation and dividend income while maintaining a prudent and flexible capital structure. Our total return to shareholders over the last five years averaged 43 percent annually, returning about $618 for each $100 invested in our stock at the beginning of this period.

Measuring Value Creation

We measure value creation internally using a form of Economic Value Added (EVA), which we define as after-tax segment profit less a capital charge for all investment employed. The capital charge is an estimate of our after-tax cost of capital adjusted for the age of our stores, recognizing that mature stores inherently have higher returns than newly opened stores. We estimate the after-tax cost of capital for our retail business is approximately 9 percent, while our credit operations' after-tax cost of capital is approximately 5 percent as a result of its ability to support higher debt levels. We expect to generate returns in excess of these costs of capital, thereby producing EVA.

EVA is used to evaluate our performance and to guide capital investment decisions. A significant portion of executive incentive compensation is tied to the achievement of targeted levels of annual EVA improvement.

Financial Objectives

We believe that managing our business with a focus on EVA helps achieve our objective of average annual earnings per share growth of 15 percent or more over time. Our financial strategy is to produce these results with strong interest coverage and prudent levels of debt, which will allow efficient capital market access to fund our growth. Earnings per share before unusual items has grown at a compound annual rate of 23 percent over the last five years.

Reflecting our strong cash flow, we ended 1999 with a retail debt ratio of 40 percent. In evaluating our debt level, we separate retail operations from credit operations due to their inherently different financial characteristics. We view the appropriate capitalization of our credit operations to be 88 percent debt and 12 percent equity, similar to ratios of comparable credit card businesses.

Debt Ratios and Interest Coverage

	1999	1998	1997
Retail	40%	41%	45%
Credit	88%	88%	88%
Total debt ratio	49%	50%	54%
Interest coverage	4.6x	4.0x	3.4x

Debt ratios and interest coverage include the impact of sold securitized receivables and off-balance sheet operating leases as if they were debt. Interest coverage represents the ratio of pre-tax earnings before unusual items and fixed charges to fixed charges (interest expense, interest equivalent and the interest portion of rent expense).

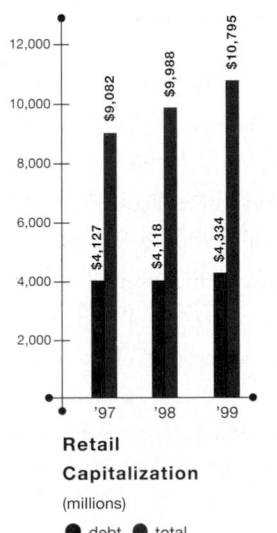

Retail Capitalization
(millions)
● debt ● total

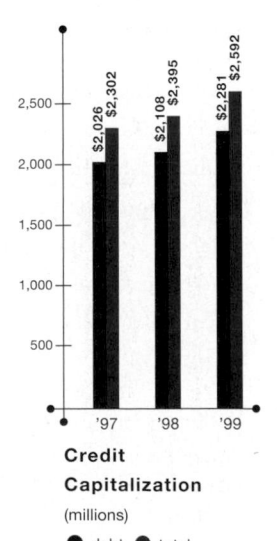

Credit Capitalization
(millions)
● debt ● total

Credit Operations

We offer proprietary credit in each of our business segments. These credit programs strategically support our core retail operations and are an integral component of each business segment. The programs contribute to our earnings growth by driving sales at our stores and through growth in credit contribution. Therefore, credit contribution, shown below, is reflected in each business segment's pre-tax profit on a receivables serviced basis. Because we service both the retained and sold securitized receivables, we manage our portfolio on a serviced basis. In contrast, our consolidated financial statements reflect only our retained securitized receivables.

In 1999, pre-tax contribution from credit increased 16 percent over the prior year, compared with a 5 percent growth in average receivables serviced. The improved credit performance reflects continued growth of the Target Guest Card, improved delinquency experience and a decrease in write-offs as a percent of receivables. In 1998 and 1997, the bad debt provision exceeded net write-offs during the year. In 1999, the bad debt provision was equal to net write-offs.

Credit Contribution

(millions)	1999	1998	1997
Revenues:			
Finance charges, late fees and other revenues	$609	$588	$510
Merchant fees	90	81	77
Total revenues	699	669	587
Expenses:			
Bad debt	147	180	190
Operations and marketing	182	169	125
Total expenses	329	349	315
Pre-tax credit contribution	**$370**	**$320**	**$272**

Merchant fees are intercompany fees charged to our retail operations on a basis similar to fees charged by third-party credit card issuers. These fees, which include deferred billing fees charged for carrying non-revenue-earning revolving balances, are eliminated in consolidation. Operations and marketing expenses include costs associated with the opening, retention and servicing of accounts.

Average Receivables Serviced

(millions)	1999	1998	1997
Target	$ 974	$ 803	$ 644
Mervyn's	718	764	812
Department Stores	719	720	707
Total average receivables serviced	$2,411	$2,287	$2,163
Total year-end receivables serviced	$2,681	$2,496	$2,424

Allowance for Doubtful Accounts

(millions)	1999	1998	1997
Allowance at beginning of year	$203	$168	$119
Bad debt provision	147	180	190
Net write-offs	(147)	(145)	(141)
Allowance at end of year	$203	$203	$168
As a percent of year-end receivables serviced	7.6%	8.1%	6.9%
As a multiple of current year net write-offs	1.4x	1.4x	1.2x

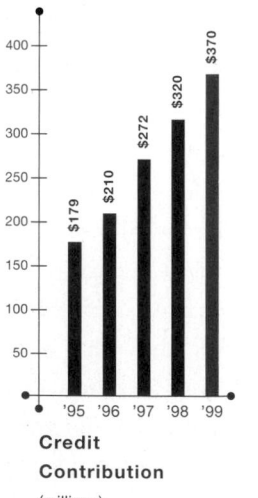

Credit Contribution
(millions)

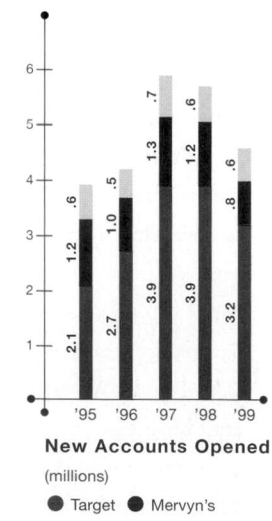

New Accounts Opened
(millions)
● Target ● Mervyn's
● Department Stores

Fiscal Year 2000

As we look forward into 2000, we believe that we will deliver another year of strong growth in revenues and earnings, driven primarily by increases in comparable-store sales and new store growth at Target. Our gross margin rate is expected to be essentially even with 1999. Our operating expense rate is expected to benefit modestly from the leveraging of fixed costs. Our credit operations are also expected to contribute to our growth in earnings as we continue to open new accounts, especially at Target, and leverage operating expenses.

In 2000, we expect to reinvest $2.5 to $3 billion in our business, through a combination of capital investment and repurchase of our shares. In the upcoming year, Target plans to open approximately 80 total new stores, including locations in two new states, West Virginia and Connecticut. Once again, our opening plans will focus on markets in the Mid-Atlantic and Northeast, and we will essentially double our number of SuperTarget locations from the 16 we operated at year-end. We expect Target's retail square footage to expand in the range of 8 to 10 percent annually for the foreseeable future. Our planned capital expenditures also include ongoing remodeling programs at all three operating segments and other capital support. Funding sources for the growth of our business include internally generated funds, debt and sold securitized receivables.

The total of interest expense and interest equivalent is expected to be moderately higher than 1999 due to higher average funded balances, partially offset by a lower average portfolio interest rate. Our $800 million of sold securitized receivables will result in approximately $50 million of interest equivalent for the year.

The effective income tax rate is expected to approximate 38.5 percent.

Forward-Looking Statements

This Annual Report, including the preceding management's discussion and analysis, contains forward-looking statements regarding our performance, liquidity and the adequacy of our capital resources. Those statements are based on our current assumptions and expectations and are subject to certain risks and uncertainties that could cause actual results to differ materially from those projected. We caution that the forward-looking statements are qualified by the risks and challenges posed by increased competition, shifting consumer demand, changing consumer credit markets, changing capital markets and general economic conditions, hiring and retaining effective team members, sourcing merchandise from domestic and international vendors, investing in new business strategies, achieving our growth objectives, and other risks and uncertainties. As a result, while we believe that there is a reasonable basis for the forward-looking statements, you should not place undue reliance on those statements. You are encouraged to review Exhibit (99)C attached to our Form 10-K Report for the year ended January 29, 2000, which contains additional important factors that may cause actual results to differ materially from those predicted in the forward-looking statements.

As we look forward into 2000, we believe that we will deliver another year of strong growth in revenues and earnings.

(millions, except per share data)	1999	1998	1997
Sales	$33,212	$30,203	$27,019
Net credit revenues	490	459	468
Total revenues	33,702	30,662	27,487
Cost of sales	23,029	21,085	18,944
Selling, general and administrative expense	7,490	6,843	6,108
Depreciation and amortization	854	780	693
Interest expense	393	398	416
Earnings before income taxes and extraordinary charges	1,936	1,556	1,326
Provision for income taxes	751	594	524
Net earnings before extraordinary charges	1,185	962	802
Extraordinary charges from purchase and redemption of debt, net of tax	41	27	51
Net earnings	$ 1,144	$ 935	$ 751
Earnings before extraordinary charges	$ 2.64	$ 2.14	$ 1.80
Extraordinary charges	(.09)	(.06)	(.12)
Basic earnings per share	$ 2.55	$ 2.08	$ 1.68
Earnings before extraordinary charges	$ 2.54	$ 2.04	$ 1.70
Extraordinary charges	(.09)	(.06)	(.11)
Diluted earnings per share	$ 2.45	$ 1.98	$ 1.59
Weighted average common shares outstanding:			
Basic	441.3	440.0	436.1
Diluted	465.7	467.3	463.7

See Notes to Consolidated Financial Statements throughout pages 24-37.

Summary of Accounting Policies

Organization Effective beginning of fiscal year 2000, Dayton Hudson Corporation changed its name to Target Corporation. We are a general merchandise retailer, comprised of three operating segments: Target; Mervyn's; and Dayton's, Marshall Field's, Hudson's (the Department Stores). Target, an upscale discount chain located in 44 states at year-end, contributed 78 percent of our 1999 total revenues. Mervyn's, a middle-market promotional department store located in 14 states in the West, South and Midwest, contributed 12 percent of total revenues. The Department Stores, traditional department stores located in eight states in the upper Midwest, contributed 9 percent of total revenues.

Consolidation The financial statements include the balances of the Corporation and its subsidiaries after elimination of material intercompany balances and transactions. All material subsidiaries are wholly owned.

Use of Estimates The preparation of our financial statements, in conformity with generally accepted accounting principles, requires management to make estimates and assumptions that affect the reported amounts in the financial statements and accompanying notes. Actual results may differ from those estimates.

Fiscal Year Our fiscal year ends on the Saturday nearest January 31. Unless otherwise stated, references to years in this report relate to fiscal years rather than to calendar years. Fiscal years 1999, 1998 and 1997 consisted of 52 weeks.

Reclassifications Within the Consolidated Results of Operations, certain reclassifications have been made to prior years' income and expense amounts to conform to the 1999 presentation. None of the reclassifications impacted our net earnings or earnings per share in any period. The reclassifications include the separate presentation of sales and net credit revenues; the application of the provisions of Staff Accounting Bulletin No. 101, "Revenue Recognition in Financial Statements"; the classification of buying and occupancy expenses in selling, general and administrative expense rather than cost of sales; and the classification of taxes other than income taxes in selling, general and administrative expense.

Revenues

Revenue from retail sales is recognized at the time of sale. Leased department sales, net of related cost of sales, are included within sales and were $31 million in 1999, $29 million in 1998, and $25 million in 1997. Net credit revenues include finance charges and late fees on internal credit sales, net of the effect of sold securitized receivables. Internal credit sales were $5.0 billion, $4.5 billion and $4.2 billion in 1999, 1998 and 1997, respectively.

Advertising Costs

Advertising costs, included in selling, general and administrative expense, are expensed as incurred and were $791 million, $745 million and $679 million for 1999, 1998 and 1997, respectively.

Impact of Year 2000

Year 2000 related costs, included in selling, general and administrative expense, were expensed as incurred. In 1999, we expensed $16 million related to year 2000 readiness. Prior to 1999, we expensed $32 million. In addition, we accelerated the timing of $15 million of planned capital expenditures, which are recorded in property and equipment at cost less accumulated depreciation.

Mainframe Outsourcing

In 1998, we announced our plan to outsource our mainframe computer data center functions and expensed $42 million ($.06 per share) of related charges. During 1999, we completed the transition and expensed an additional $5 million ($.01 per share) related to the outsourcing. These expenses are included in selling, general and administrative expense.

Start-up Expense

In first quarter 1999, we adopted SOP 98-5, "Reporting on the Costs of Start-Up Activities." The adoption did not impact total year start-up expense, which is included in selling, general and administrative expense.

Earnings per Share

Basic EPS is net earnings, less dividend requirements on the Employee Stock Ownership Plan (ESOP) preferred shares prior to their conversion to common shares, divided by the average number of common shares outstanding during the period. In January 2000, each outstanding ESOP preferred share was converted into 60 shares of our common stock. These shares are now included within weighted average common shares outstanding.

Diluted EPS assumed conversion of the ESOP preferred shares into common shares and replacement of the ESOP preferred dividends with common stock dividends, prior to the conversion of all preferred shares in January 2000. In addition, net earnings were adjusted for expense required to fund the ESOP debt service, prior to repayment of the loan in 1998. References herein to earnings per share refer to Diluted EPS.

All earnings per share, dividends per share and common shares outstanding reflect our 1998 two-for-one share split.

(millions, except per share data)	Basic EPS			Diluted EPS		
	1999	1998	1997	**1999**	1998	1997
Net earnings*	**$1,185**	$962	$802	**$1,185**	$962	$802
Less: ESOP net earnings adjustment	**(18)**	(20)	(20)	**(4)**	(8)	(13)
Adjusted net earnings*	**$1,167**	$942	$782	**$1,181**	$954	$789
Weighted average common shares outstanding	**441.3**	440.0	436.1	**441.3**	440.0	436.1
Performance shares	–	–	–	**.1**	.8	1.3
Stock options	–	–	–	**5.8**	5.5	3.9
Assumed conversion of ESOP preferred shares	–	–	–	**18.5**	21.0	22.4
Total common equivalent shares outstanding	**441.3**	440.0	436.1	**465.7**	467.3	463.7
Earnings per share*	**$ 2.64**	$2.14	$1.80	**$ 2.54**	$2.04	$1.70

*Before extraordinary charges

consolidated statements of financial position

(millions)	January 29, 2000	January 30, 1999
Assets		
Cash and cash equivalents	$ 220	$ 255
Retained securitized receivables	1,837	1,656
Inventory	3,798	3,475
Other	628	619
Total current assets	6,483	6,005
Property and equipment		
Land	2,069	1,868
Buildings and improvements	7,807	7,217
Fixtures and equipment	3,422	3,274
Construction-in-progress	526	378
Accumulated depreciation	(3,925)	(3,768)
Property and equipment, net	9,899	8,969
Other	761	692
Total assets	**$17,143**	**$15,666**
Liabilities and shareholders' investment		
Accounts payable	$ 3,514	$ 3,150
Accrued liabilities	1,520	1,444
Income taxes payable	318	207
Current portion of long-term debt and notes payable	498	256
Total current liabilities	5,850	5,057
Long-term debt	4,521	4,452
Deferred income taxes and other	910	822
Convertible preferred stock, net	–	24
Shareholders' investment		
Convertible preferred stock	–	268
Common stock	76	74
Additional paid-in-capital	730	286
Retained earnings	5,056	4,683
Total shareholders' investment	5,862	5,311
Total liabilities and shareholders' investment	**$17,143**	**$15,666**

See Notes to Consolidated Financial Statements throughout pages 24-37.

Cash Equivalents

Cash equivalents represent short-term investments with a maturity of three months or less from the time of purchase.

Retained Securitized Receivables

Through our special purpose subsidiary, Target Receivables Corporation (TRC), we transfer, on an ongoing basis, substantially all of our receivables to a trust in return for certificates representing undivided interests in the trust's assets. TRC owns the undivided interest in the trust's assets, other than the sold securitized receivables and the 2 percent of trust assets held by Retailers National Bank (RNB), a wholly owned subsidiary of the Corporation that also services the receivables. Prior to June 1998, RNB held 5 percent of trust assets. The undivided interests held by TRC and RNB, as well as related income and expenses, are reflected in each operating segment's assets and operating results based on the origin of the credit sale giving rise to the receivable.

In 1998, TRC sold to the public $400 million of securitized receivables. This issue of asset-backed securities had an expected maturity of five years and a stated rate of 5.90 percent. Proceeds from the sale were used for general corporate purposes, including funding the growth of receivables. The 1998 sale transaction and the maturity of our 1995 securitization resulted in a net loss of $3 million (less than $.01 per share), which reduced 1998 finance charge revenues and pre-tax earnings.

In 1997, TRC sold to the public $400 million of securitized receivables, with an expected maturity of five years and a stated rate of 6.25 percent. This transaction, combined with the impact of the application of SFAS No. 125 to our 1995 securitization, resulted in a $45 million ($.06 per share) increase in finance charge revenues and pre-tax earnings.

At year-end 1999, $800 million of securitized receivables had been sold to investors and TRC had borrowed $100 million through the issuance of notes payable secured by receivables.

The fair value of the retained securitized receivables, classified as available for sale, was $1,837 million and $1,656 million at year-end 1999 and 1998, respectively. The fair value of the retained securitized receivables was lower than the aggregate receivables value by $157 million and $156 million at year-end 1999 and 1998, respectively, due to our estimates of ultimate collectibility. Write-downs have been included in selling, general and administrative expense.

Inventory

Inventory and the related cost of sales are accounted for by the retail inventory accounting method using the last-in, first-out (LIFO) basis and are stated at the lower of LIFO cost or market. The cumulative LIFO provision was $53 million and $60 million at year-end 1999 and 1998, respectively.

Property and Long-lived Assets

Property and long-lived assets are recorded at cost less accumulated depreciation or amortization. Depreciation and amortization are computed using the straight-line method over estimated useful lives. Accelerated depreciation methods are generally used for income tax purposes.

Estimated useful lives by major asset category are as follows:

Asset	Life (in years)
Buildings and improvements	8 – 50
Fixtures and equipment	5 – 8
Computer hardware and software	4
Intangible assets and goodwill	3 – 20

On an ongoing basis, we evaluate our long-lived assets for impairment using undiscounted cash flow analysis.

Accounts Payable

Outstanding drafts included in accounts payable were $599 million and $519 million at year-end 1999 and 1998, respectively.

(millions)	1999	1998	1997
Operating activities			
Net earnings before extraordinary charges	$ 1,185	$ 962	$ 802
Reconciliation to cash flow:			
Depreciation and amortization	854	780	693
Deferred tax provision	75	(11)	(63)
Other noncash items affecting earnings	163	70	43
Changes in operating accounts providing/(requiring) cash:			
Retained securitized receivables	(181)	(56)	(235)
Sold securitized receivables	–	400	400
Maturity of sold securitized receivables	–	(400)	–
Inventory	(323)	(198)	(220)
Other current assets	(57)	(46)	(35)
Other assets	(65)	(65)	(33)
Accounts payable	364	336	199
Accrued liabilities	100	75	182
Income taxes payable	137	15	62
Cash flow provided by operations	2,252	1,862	1,795
Investing activities			
Expenditures for property and equipment	(1,918)	(1,657)	(1,354)
Proceeds from disposals of property and equipment	126	107	123
Acquisition of subsidiaries, net of cash received	–	(100)	–
Other	(15)	(5)	–
Cash flow required for investing activities	(1,807)	(1,655)	(1,231)
Net financing sources	445	207	564
Financing activities			
Increase/(decrease) in notes payable, net	564	(305)	(127)
Additions to long-term debt	285	600	375
Reductions of long-term debt	(600)	(343)	(690)
Principal payments received on loan to ESOP	–	8	22
Dividends paid	(195)	(178)	(165)
Repurchase of stock	(581)	–	–
Other	47	55	31
Cash flow used for financing activities	(480)	(163)	(554)
Net (decrease)/increase in cash and cash equivalents	(35)	44	10
Cash and cash equivalents at beginning of year	255	211	201
Cash and cash equivalents at end of year	$ 220	$ 255	$ 211

Amounts presented herein are on a cash basis and therefore may differ from those shown in other sections of this Annual Report. Cash paid for income taxes was $575 million, $564 million and $454 million during 1999, 1998 and 1997, respectively. Cash paid for interest (including interest capitalized) was $405 million, $393 million and $485 million during 1999, 1998 and 1997, respectively.

See Notes to Consolidated Financial Statements throughout pages 24-37.

Lines of Credit

At January 29, 2000, two committed credit agreements totaling $1.6 billion were in place through a group of 31 banks at specified rates. There were no balances outstanding at any time during 1999 or 1998 under these agreements.

Long-term Debt and Notes Payable

At January 29, 2000, $664 million of notes payable were outstanding, $564 million of which were classified as long-term debt as they were supported by our $800 million committed credit agreement that expires in 2002. The remaining $100 million of notes payable is financing secured by the Target Credit Card Master Trust Series 1996-1 Class A variable funding certificate. This certificate is debt of TRC and is classified in the current portion of long-term debt and notes payable. The average amount of secured and unsecured notes payable outstanding during 1999 was $775 million at a weighted-average interest rate of 5.5 percent.

In 1999, we issued $285 million of floating-rate notes bearing interest at initial rates between 5.32 and 5.52 percent, maturing in July through September 2001. The proceeds were used for general corporate purposes. Also during 1999, we repurchased $381 million of long-term debt with an average remaining life of 18 years and a weighted-average interest rate of 9.3 percent, resulting in an after-tax extraordinary charge of $41 million ($.09 per share).

In 1998, we issued $200 million of long-term debt at 6.65 percent, maturing in 2028 and $200 million at 5.88 percent, maturing in 2008. We also issued $200 million of long-term debt maturing in 2010, which is puttable in 2000, and we sold to a third party the right to call and remarket these securities in 2000 to their final maturity. Also during 1998, we repurchased $127 million of long-term debt, resulting in an after-tax extraordinary charge of $27 million ($.06 per share).

At year end our debt portfolio was as follows:

Long-term Debt and Notes Payable

(millions)	January 29, 2000 Rate*	Balance	January 30, 1999 Rate*	Balance
Notes payable	5.8%	$ 664	5.2%	$ 100
Notes and debentures:				
Due 1999-2003	7.8	1,682	8.1	1,544
Due 2004-2008	7.5	699	7.6	701
Due 2009-2013	7.9	472	8.1	564
Due 2014-2018	9.5	34	9.6	70
Due 2019-2023	8.5	759	8.7	1,009
Due 2024-2028	6.6	474	6.6	475
Due 2029-2037	5.9	100	5.9	100
Total notes payable, notes and debentures**	7.5%	$4,884	7.9%	$4,563
Capital lease obligations		135		145
Less: current portion		(498)		(256)
Long-term debt and notes payable		$4,521		$4,452

*Reflects the weighted-average stated interest rate as of year end.
**The estimated fair value of total notes payable and notes and debentures, using a discounted cash flow analysis based on our incremental interest rates for similar types of financial instruments, was $4,893 million at January 29, 2000 and $5,123 million at January 30, 1999.

Required principal payments on long-term debt and notes payable over the next five years, excluding capital lease obligations, are $488 million in 2000, $638 million in 2001, $756 million in 2002, $464 million in 2003 and $105 million in 2004.

Subsequent to year-end 1999, we issued $500 million of additional long-term debt bearing interest at 7.50 percent, maturing in February 2005.

Derivatives

From time to time we use interest rate swaps to hedge our exposure to interest rate risk. The fair value of the swaps is not reflected in the financial statements and any gain or loss recognized upon early termination is amortized over the life of the related debt obligation. The fair value of existing swaps is immaterial.

In 1998, the Financial Accounting Standards Board issued SFAS No. 133, "Accounting for Derivative Instruments and Hedging Activities," which is required to be adopted for fiscal years beginning after June 15, 2000. We have analyzed the impact of SFAS No. 133 on our existing and currently anticipated activities and do not believe the adoption of this new statement will have a material effect on our earnings or financial position.

(millions, except share data)	Convertible Preferred Stock	Common Stock	Additional Paid-in Capital	Retained Earnings	Loan to ESOP	Total
February 1, 1997	$271	$72	$146	$3,348	$(47)	$3,790
Consolidated net earnings	–	–	–	751	–	751
Dividends declared	–	–	–	(169)	–	(169)
Tax benefit on unallocated preferred stock dividends and options	–	–	17	–		17
Conversion of preferred stock and other	9	–	18	–	–	27
Net reduction in loan to ESOP	–	–	–	–	28	28
Stock option activity	–	1	15	–	–	16
January 31, 1998	280	73	196	3,930	(19)	4,460
Consolidated net earnings	–	–	–	935	–	935
Dividends declared	–	–	–	(182)	–	(182)
Tax benefit on unallocated preferred stock dividends and options	–	–	25	–	–	25
Conversion of preferred stock and other	(12)	–	37	–	–	25
Net reduction in loan to ESOP	–	–	–	–	19	19
Stock option activity	–	1	28	–	–	29
January 30, 1999	268	74	286	4,683	–	5,311
Consolidated net earnings	–	–	–	1,144	–	1,144
Dividends declared	–	–	–	(191)	–	(191)
Repurchase of stock	–	(1)	–	(580)	–	(581)
Issuance of stock for ESOP	–	–	81	–	–	81
Tax benefit on unallocated preferred stock dividends and options	–	–	29	–	–	29
Conversion of preferred stock	(268)	3	289	–	–	24
Stock option activity	–	–	45	–	–	45
January 29, 2000	$ –	$76	$730	$5,056	$ –	$5,862

Common Stock Authorized 3,000,000,000 shares, $.1667 par value; 455,841,388 shares issued and outstanding at January 29, 2000; 441,809,806 shares issued and outstanding at January 30, 1999.

In January 1999, our Board of Directors authorized the repurchase of $1 billion of our common stock. We repurchased 9.4 million shares of stock during 1999 at a total cost of $588 million ($62.58 per share), net of the premium from exercised and expired put options. In March 2000, our Board of Directors authorized the repurchase of an additional $1 billion of our common stock. Repurchases are made primarily in open market transactions, subject to market conditions. Our program also includes the sale of put options that entitle the holder to sell shares of our common stock to us, at a specified price, if the holder exercises the option.

We sold put options on 4.7 million shares in 1999. Options on 1.4 million shares outstanding at the end of 1999 entitled their holders to sell shares of our common stock to us at prices ranging from $63 to $74 per share on specific dates during February through June 2000. Premiums received from the sale of put options during the year were recorded in retained earnings and totaled $23 million, $7 million of which represents premiums received on put options outstanding at year end.

Preferred Stock Authorized 5,000,000 shares; no shares of Series B ESOP Convertible Preferred Stock, $.01 par value, were issued and outstanding at January 29, 2000 and 338,492 shares were issued and outstanding at January 30, 1999. In January 2000, each share of Series B ESOP Convertible Preferred Stock was converted into 60 shares of our common stock. Prior to conversion, these shares had voting rights equal to the equivalent number of common shares and were entitled to cumulative annual dividends of $56.20.

Junior Preferred Stock Rights In 1996, we declared a distribution of shares of preferred share purchase rights. Terms of the plan provide for a distribution of one preferred share purchase right for each outstanding share of our common stock. Each right will entitle shareholders to buy one six-hundredth of a share of a new series of junior participating preferred stock at an exercise price of $50.00, subject to adjustment. The rights will be exercisable only if a person or group acquires ownership of 20 percent or more of our common stock or announces a tender offer to acquire 30 percent or more of our common stock.

See Notes to Consolidated Financial Statements throughout pages 24-37.

Stock Option Plan

We have a stock option plan for key employees. Options include incentive stock options, non-qualified stock options or a combination of the two. A majority of the options vest annually in equal amounts over a four-year period. These options are cumulatively exercisable and expire no later than ten years after the date of the grant. The non-employee members of our Board of Directors also participate in our stock option plan. Their options become exercisable after one year and have a ten-year term. The typical frequency of stock option grants is once each fiscal year.

We also have a performance share and restricted share plan for key employees. The last grant was made in 1995, and all shares relating to outstanding grants were issued in 1999 pursuant to the plan. Performance shares were issued to the extent certain financial goals were met over the four-year period from the date of grant. Restricted shares were issued four years from the date of grant. Once issued, performance shares and restricted shares generally vest only upon retirement.

Options, Performance Shares and Restricted Shares Outstanding

| | Options | | | | | |
| | Total Outstanding | | Currently Exercisable | | | |
(shares in thousands)	Number of Shares	Weighted Average Exercise Price	Number of Shares	Weighted Average Exercise Price	Perform-ance Shares	Restricted Shares
February 1, 1997	14,610	$13.48	4,782	$10.88	1,264	311
Granted	2,653	33.63				
Canceled	(346)	15.02				
Exercised	(2,450)	10.27				
January 31, 1998	14,467	$17.69	4,860	$13.15	794	212
Granted	3,309	48.16				
Canceled	(173)	23.77				
Exercised	(2,023)	12.27				
January 30, 1999	15,580	$24.79	5,685	$16.49	519*	123*
Granted	1,906	67.63				
Canceled	(176)	34.91				
Exercised	(1,279)	14.03				
January 29, 2000	**16,031**	**$30.63**	**7,858**	**$20.46**	**–**	**–**

*All shares were issued in 1999 pursuant to the plan.

Options Outstanding

(shares in thousands)	Shares Outstanding at January 29, 2000	Range of Exercise Price
	5,209	$ 9.97 - $15.00
	3,424	$15.00 - $25.00
	2,246	$25.00 - $35.00
	1,211	$35.00 - $45.00
	2,032	$45.00 - $55.00
	1,909	$55.00 - $68.69
Total	16,031	$ 9.97 - $68.69

As of January 29, 2000, outstanding options had a weighted-average remaining contractual life of 7.2 years. The number of unissued common shares reserved for future grants under the stock option plans was 24,489,897 at January 29, 2000, and 4,136,969 at January 30, 1999.

We apply APB No. 25, "Accounting for Stock Issued to Employees," to account for our stock option and performance share plans. Because the exercise price of our employee stock options equals the market price of the underlying stock on the grant date, no compensation expense related to options is recognized. Performance share compensation expense was recognized based on the fair value of the shares at the end of each reporting period. If we had elected to recognize compensation cost based on the fair value of the options and performance shares at grant date as prescribed by SFAS No. 123, "Accounting for Stock-Based Compensation," net earnings would have been the pro forma amounts shown below. EPS calculated under SFAS No. 123 would be $.03 lower than reported EPS in 1999 and unchanged from reported EPS in 1998 and 1997.

Pro Forma Earnings

(millions)	1999	1998	1997
Net earnings — as reported	$1,144	$935	$751
Net earnings — pro forma	$1,132	$934	$751

The Black-Scholes method was used to estimate the fair value of the options at grant date based on the following factors:

	1999	1998	1997
Dividend yield	.6%	.7%	1.0%
Volatility	30%	30%	25%
Risk free interest rate	6.6%	4.6%	5.4%
Expected life in years	5.6	5.6	5.6
Weighted average fair value at grant date	$25.81	$16.24	$10.52

Pension and Postretirement Health Care Benefits

We have defined benefit pension plans that cover all employees who meet certain age, length of service and hours worked per year requirements. Benefits are provided based upon years of service and the employee's compensation. Retired employees also become eligible for certain health care benefits if they meet minimum age and service requirements and agree to contribute a portion of the cost.

In 1999, we adopted a change in the measurement date of our pension and postretirement health care benefits plans from December 31 to October 31. Prior periods have not been restated, as the impact of the change is not material.

Change in Benefit Obligation

(millions)	Pension Benefits		Postretirement Health Care Benefits	
	1999	1998	**1999**	1998
Benefit obligation at beginning of measurement period	$729	$610	$ 85	$ 81
Service cost	44	35	2	1
Interest cost	53	45	6	6
Actuarial loss	76	65	9	5
Acquisitions	–	26	–	–
Benefits paid	(40)	(52)	(8)	(8)
Benefit obligation at end of measurement period	$862	$729	$ 94	$ 85

Change in Plan Assets

	Pension Benefits		Postretirement Health Care Benefits	
Fair value of plan assets at beginning of measurement period	$859	$718	$ –	$ –
Actual return on plan assets	62	106	–	–
Employer contribution	100	59	8	8
Acquisitions	–	25	–	–
Benefits paid	(39)	(49)	(8)	(8)
Fair value of plan assets at end of measurement period	$982	$859	$ –	$ –

Reconciliation of Prepaid/(Accrued) Cost

	Pension Benefits		Postretirement Health Care Benefits	
Funded status	$120	$130	$(94)	$ (85)
Unrecognized actuarial loss/(gain)	51	(16)	(7)	(18)
Unrecognized prior service cost	8	2	2	3
Net prepaid/(accrued) cost	$179	$116	$(99)	$(100)

The benefit obligation and fair value of plan assets, for the pension plans with benefit obligations in excess of plan assets, were $49 and $0 as of October 31, 1999, and $34 and $0 as of December 31, 1998.

Net Pension and Postretirement Health Care Benefits Expense

(millions)	Pension Benefits			Postretirement Health Care Benefits		
	1999	1998	1997	**1999**	1998	1997
Service cost benefits earned during the period	$44	$35	$27	$2	$1	$1
Interest cost on projected benefit obligation	53	45	39	6	6	6
Expected return on assets	(72)	(58)	(48)	–	–	–
Recognized gains and losses	9	3	–	–	(1)	(2)
Recognized prior service cost	1	–	1	–	–	1
Total	$35	$25	$19	$8	$6	$6

The amortization of any prior service cost is determined using a straight-line amortization of the cost over the average remaining service period of employees expected to receive benefits under the plan.

Actuarial Assumptions

	Pension Benefits			Postretirement Health Care Benefits		
	1999	1998	1997	**1999**	1998	1997
Discount rate	7½%	7%	7¼%	7½%	7%	7¼%
Expected long-term rate of return on plans' assets	9	9	9	n/a	n/a	n/a
Average assumed rate of compensation increase	4½	4	4¼	n/a	n/a	n/a

An increase in the cost of covered health care benefits of 6 percent is assumed for 2000. The rate is assumed to remain at 6 percent in the future. The health care cost trend rate assumption has a significant effect on the amounts reported. A 1 percent change in assumed health care cost trend rates would have the following effects:

	1% Increase	1% Decrease
Effect on total of service and interest cost components of net periodic postretirement health care benefit cost	$–	$ –
Effect on the health care component of the postretirement benefit obligation	$5	$(4)

Employee Stock Ownership Plan

We sponsor a defined contribution employee benefit plan. Employees who meet certain eligibility requirements can participate by investing up to 20 percent of their compensation. We match 100 percent of each employee's contribution up to 5 percent of respective total compensation. Our contribution to the plan is invested in the ESOP. Through December 1998, ESOP preferred shares (401(k) preferred shares) were allocated to participants. In January 1999, we began providing new common shares to the ESOP to fund the employer match.

In 1989, we loaned $379 million to the ESOP at a 9 percent interest rate. Proceeds from the loan were then used by the ESOP to purchase 438,353 shares of 401(k) preferred shares. The original issue value of the 401(k) preferred shares of $864.60 per share was guaranteed by the Corporation. The loan was paid off during 1998 using dividends paid on all 401(k) preferred shares held by the ESOP. In January 2000, each 401(k) preferred share was converted into 60 shares of common stock.

Prior to the conversion of all 401(k) preferred shares to common stock, we were required to exchange at fair value each 401(k) preferred share for 60 shares of common stock and cash, if any, upon a participant's termination. The 401(k) preferred shares were classified as shareholders' investment to the extent the preferred shares were permanent equity.

Dividends earned on 401(k) preferred shares held by the ESOP were $19 million in both 1999 and 1998 and $21 million in 1997. The dividends on allocated 401(k) preferred shares were paid to participants' accounts in additional 401(k) preferred shares until June 1998. Dividends are now paid to participants in cash. Benefits expense was $78 million in 1999, $29 million in 1998 and $17 million in 1997.

Leases

Assets held under capital leases are included in property and equipment and are charged to depreciation and interest over the life of the lease. Operating leases are not capitalized and lease rentals are expensed. Rent expense on buildings, classified in selling, general and administrative expense, includes percentage rents that are based on a percentage of retail sales over stated levels. Total rent expense was $168 million, $150 million and $143 million in 1999, 1998 and 1997, respectively. Most of the long-term leases include options to renew, with terms varying from five to 30 years. Certain leases also include options to purchase the property.

Future minimum lease payments required under non-cancelable lease agreements existing at January 29, 2000, were:

Future Minimum Lease Payments

(millions)	Operating Leases	Capital Leases
2000	$ 113	$ 22
2001	105	21
2002	96	21
2003	80	19
2004	70	18
After 2004	634	124
Total future minimum lease payments	$1,098	$225
Less: interest*	(302)	(90)
Present value of minimum lease payments	$ 796	$135**

*Calculated using the interest rate at inception for each lease (the weighted average interest rate was 8.8 percent).

**Includes current portion of $10 million.

Owned and Leased Store Locations

At year end, owned, leased and "combined" (combination owned/leased) store locations by operating segment were as follows:

	Owned	Leased	Combined	Total
Target	705	92	115	912
Mervyn's	160	68	39	267
Department Stores	51	12	1	64
Total	916	172	155	1,243

Income Taxes

Reconciliation of tax rates is as follows:

Percent of Earnings Before Income Taxes

	1999	1998	1997
Federal statutory rate	35.0%	35.0%	35.0%
State income taxes,			
net of federal tax benefit	3.9	4.5	4.5
Dividends on ESOP stock	(.4)	(.5)	(.5)
Work opportunity tax credits	(.2)	(.2)	(.1)
Inventory shortage tax matter	–	(1.3)	–
Other	.5	.7	.6
Effective tax rate	38.8%	38.2%	39.5%

The components of the provision for income taxes were:

Income Tax Provision: Expense/(Benefit)

(millions)	1999	1998	1997
Current:			
Federal	$570	$497	$488
State	106	110	99
	676	607	587
Deferred:			
Federal	63	(10)	(55)
State	12	(3)	(8)
	75	(13)	(63)
Total	$751	$594	$524

The components of the net deferred tax asset/(liability) were:

Net Deferred Tax Asset/(Liability)

(millions)	January 29, 2000	January 30, 1999
Gross deferred tax assets:		
Self-insured benefits	$ 146	$ 132
Deferred compensation	130	128
Inventory	84	72
Valuation allowance	63	64
Postretirement health care obligation	41	42
Other	106	132
	570	570
Gross deferred tax liabilities:		
Property and equipment	(408)	(374)
Other	(104)	(63)
	(512)	(437)
Total	$ 58	$ 133

Inventory Shortage Tax Matter

In 1998, we received a favorable ruling from the United States Court of Appeals on a 1983 case related to the deductibility of accrued inventory shortage expense. The beneficial effect resulting from the outcome of the case was $20 million ($.04 per share) and was reflected as a reduction in the 1998 effective income tax rate. This issue has been settled for all years.

Acquisitions

In 1998, we acquired The Associated Merchandising Corporation, an international sourcing company that provides services to our operating divisions and other retailers, and we also acquired Rivertown Trading Company, a direct marketing firm. Both subsidiaries are included in the consolidated financial statements. Their revenues and operating results are included in "other" in revenues and in our pre-tax earnings reconciliation on page 37 and were immaterial in 1999 and 1998.

Commitments and Contingencies

Commitments for the purchase, construction, lease or remodeling of real estate, facilities and equipment were approximately $534 million at year-end 1999. We are exposed to claims and litigation arising out of the ordinary course of business. Management, after consulting with legal counsel, believes the currently identified claims and litigation will not have a material adverse effect on our results of operations or our financial condition taken as a whole.

Quarterly Results (Unaudited)

The same accounting policies are followed in preparing quarterly financial data as are followed in preparing annual data. The table below summarizes results by quarter for 1999 and 1998:

(millions, except per share data)	First Quarter		Second Quarter		Third Quarter		Fourth Quarter		Total Year	
	1999	1998	**1999**	1998	**1999**	1998	**1999**	1998	**1999**	1998
Total revenues	$7,158	6,402	$7,687	6,987	$7,927	7,218	$10,930	10,055	$33,702	30,662
Gross margin (a)	$2,182	1,924	$2,376	2,097	$2,441	2,172	$ 3,184	2,925	$10,183	9,118
Net earnings before extraordinary charges (c) (d)	$ 194	160	$ 228	172	$ 241	183	$ 522	447	$ 1,185	962
Net earnings (b) (c) (d)	$ 194	158	$ 224	172	$ 232	182	$ 494	423	$ 1,144	935
Basic earnings per share (b) (c) (d) (e)	$ .43	.35	$ .50	.38	$ .52	.40	$ 1.11	.95	$ 2.55	2.08
Diluted earnings per share (b) (c) (d) (e)	$ .41	.33	$ .48	.36	$ .50	.39	$ 1.06	.90	$ 2.45	1.98
Dividends declared per share (e)	$ .10	.09	$ .10	.09	$ .10	.09	$ .10	.09	$ .40	.36
Common stock price (f) High	$75.75	44.81	$72.44	52.63	$69.50	48.25	$ 75.00	63.75	$ 75.75	63.75
Low	$58.75	36.25	$57.94	42.50	$55.25	33.75	$ 60.75	42.69	$ 55.25	33.75

(a) Gross margin is sales less cost of sales. The LIFO provision, included in gross margin, is analyzed each quarter for estimated changes in year-end inventory levels, markup rates and internally generated retail price indices. A final adjustment is recorded in the fourth quarter for the difference between the prior quarters' estimates and the actual total year LIFO provision.

(b) In 1999, second, third and fourth quarter net earnings include extraordinary charges, net of tax, related to the purchase and redemption of debt of $4 million, $9 million and $28 million ($.01, $.02 and $.06 per basic and diluted share), respectively. In 1998, first, third and fourth quarter net earnings include extraordinary charges, net of tax of $2 million, $1 million and $24 million ($.01, $.00 and $.05 per basic and diluted share), respectively.

(c) Third quarter and total year 1999 net earnings before extraordinary charges, net earnings and earnings per share include a mainframe outsourcing pre-tax charge of $5 million ($.01 per share). Fourth quarter and total year 1998 net earnings before extraordinary charges, net earnings and earnings per share include a mainframe outsourcing pre-tax charge of $42 million ($.06 per basic and diluted share) and the beneficial effect of $20 million ($.04 per basic and diluted share) of the favorable outcome of our inventory shortage tax matter.

(d) Third quarter 1998 net earnings include a $3 million securitization pre-tax net loss (less than $.01 per basic and diluted share).

(e) Per share amounts are computed independently for each of the quarters presented. The sum of the quarters may not equal the total year amount due to the impact of changes in average quarterly shares outstanding and/or rounding caused by the 1998 two-for-one common share split.

(f) Our common stock is listed on the New York Stock Exchange and Pacific Exchange. At March 17, 2000, there were 13,883 shareholders of record and the common stock price was $69.50 per share.

(dollars in millions, except per share data)	1999	1998	1997	1996	1995(a)	1994
Results of operations						
Total revenues	$33,702	30,662	27,487	25,092	23,234	21,093
Net earnings (c) (d) (e)	$ 1,144	935	751	463	311	434
Financial position data						
Total assets	$17,143	15,666	14,191	13,389	12,570	11,697
Long-term debt	$ 4,521	4,452	4,425	4,808	4,959	4,488
Per common share data (b)						
Diluted earnings per share (c) (d) (e)	$ 2.45	1.98	1.59	.97	.65	.92
Cash dividend declared	$ .40	.36	.33	.32	.30	.28
Other data						
Weighted average common shares outstanding (b)	441.3	440.0	436.1	433.3	431.0	429.6
Diluted average common shares outstanding (b)	465.7	467.3	463.7	460.9	458.3	457.4
Capital expenditures	$ 1,918	1,657	1,354	1,301	1,522	1,095
Number of stores: Target	912	851	796	736	670	611
Mervyn's	267	268	269	300	295	286
Department Stores	64	63	65	65	64	63
Total stores	1,243	1,182	1,130	1,101	1,029	960
Total retail square footage (thousands)	138,640	130,172	123,058	117,989	109,091	101,163
Number of employees	281,000	256,000	230,000	218,000	214,000	194,000

(a) Consisted of 53 weeks.

(b) Earnings per share, dividends per share and common shares outstanding reflect our 1998 two-for-one common share split and our 1996 three-for-one common share split.

(c) Extraordinary charges, net of tax, related to the purchase and redemption of debt were $41 million ($.09 per share) in 1999, $27 million ($.06 per share) in 1998, $51 million ($.11 per share) in 1997 and $11 million ($.02 per share) in 1996.

(d) 1999 includes a mainframe outsourcing pre-tax charge of $5 million ($.01 per share). 1998 included a mainframe outsourcing pre-tax charge of $42 million ($.06 per share) and the beneficial effect of $20 million ($.04 per share) of the favorable outcome of our inventory shortage tax matter. 1996 included a real estate repositioning pre-tax charge of $134 million ($.18 per share).

(e) 1998 included a $3 million pre-tax net loss (less than $.01 per share) related to securitization maturity and sale transactions. 1997 included a $45 million pre-tax gain ($.06 per share) related to securitization sale transactions.

The Summary Financial and Operating Data should be read in conjunction with the Notes to Consolidated Financial Statements throughout pages 24-37.

Business Segment Comparisons

(millions)

	1999	1998	1997	1996	1995*	1994
Revenues						
Target	$26,080	$23,014	$20,298	$17,810	$15,752	$13,574
Mervyn's	4,099	4,150	4,219	4,350	4,491	4,565
Department Stores	3,074	3,064	2,970	2,932	2,991	2,954
Other	449	434	–	–	–	–
Total revenues	$33,702	$30,662	$27,487	$25,092	$23,234	$21,093
Pre-tax segment profit and earnings reconciliation						
Target	$ 2,022	$ 1,578	$ 1,287	$ 1,048	$ 721	$ 732
Mervyn's	205	240	280	272	117	198
Department Stores	296	279	240	151	192	259
Total pre-tax segment profit	$ 2,523	$ 2,097	$ 1,807	$ 1,471	$ 1,030	$ 1,189
LIFO provision credit/(expense)	7	18	(6)	(9)	(17)	19
Securitization adjustments:						
Gain/(loss)	–	(3)	45	–	–	–
Interest equivalent	(49)	(48)	(33)	(25)	(10)	–
Interest expense	(393)	(398)	(416)	(442)	(442)	(426)
Mainframe outsourcing	(5)	(42)	–	–	–	–
Real estate repositioning	–	–	–	(134)	–	–
Other	(147)	(68)	(71)	(78)	(60)	(68)
Earnings before income taxes and extraordinary charges	$ 1,936	$ 1,556	$ 1,326	$ 783	$ 501	$ 714
Assets						
Target	$12,048	$10,475	$ 9,487	$ 8,257	$ 7,330	$ 6,247
Mervyn's	2,248	2,339	2,281	2,658	2,776	2,917
Department Stores	2,149	2,123	2,188	2,296	2,309	2,392
Other	698	729	235	178	155	141
Total assets	$17,143	$15,666	$14,191	$13,389	$12,570	$11,697
Depreciation and amortization						
Target	$ 567	$ 496	$ 437	$ 377	$ 328	$ 294
Mervyn's	138	138	126	151	150	145
Department Stores	133	135	128	119	113	108
Other	16	11	2	3	3	1
Total depreciation and amortization	$ 854	$ 780	$ 693	$ 650	$ 594	$ 548
Capital expenditures						
Target	$ 1,665	$ 1,352	$ 1,155	$ 1,048	$ 1,067	$ 842
Mervyn's	108	169	72	79	273	146
Department Stores	124	127	124	173	161	96
Other	21	9	3	1	21	11
Total capital expenditures	$ 1,918	$ 1,657	$ 1,354	$ 1,301	$ 1,522	$ 1,095
Segment EBITDA						
Target	$ 2,589	$ 2,074	$ 1,724	$ 1,425	$ 1,049	$ 1,026
Mervyn's	343	378	406	423	267	343
Department Stores	429	414	368	270	305	367
Total segment EBITDA	$ 3,361	$ 2,866	$ 2,498	$ 2,118	$ 1,621	$ 1,736
Net assets**						
Target	$ 8,413	$ 7,302	$ 6,602	$ 5,711	$ 5,109	$ 4,269
Mervyn's	1,908	2,017	2,019	2,268	2,484	2,363
Department Stores	1,795	1,785	1,896	1,879	1,940	1,812
Other	428	514	169	53	96	72
Total net assets	$12,544	$11,618	$10,686	$ 9,911	$ 9,629	$ 8,516

Each operating segment's assets and operating results include the retained securitized receivables held by Target Receivables Corporation and Retailers National Bank, as well as related income and expense.

*Consisted of 53 weeks

** Net assets represent total assets (including sold securitized receivables) less non-interest bearing current liabilities.

Report of Independent Auditors

Board of Directors and Shareholders

Target Corporation

We have audited the accompanying consolidated statements of financial position of Target Corporation and subsidiaries as of January 29, 2000 and January 30, 1999 and the related consolidated results of operations, cash flows and shareholders' investment for each of the three years in the period ended January 29, 2000. These financial statements are the responsibility of the Corporation's management. Our responsibility is to express an opinion on these financial statements based on our audits.

We conducted our audits in accordance with auditing standards generally accepted in the United States. Those standards require that we plan and perform the audit to obtain reasonable assurance about whether the financial statements are free of material misstatement. An audit includes examining, on a test basis, evidence supporting the amounts and disclosures in the financial statements. An audit also includes assessing the accounting principles used and significant estimates made by management, as well as evaluating the overall financial statement presentation. We believe that our audits provide a reasonable basis for our opinion.

In our opinion, the financial statements referred to above present fairly, in all material respects, the consolidated financial position of Target Corporation and subsidiaries at January 29, 2000 and January 30, 1999 and the consolidated results of their operations and their cash flows for each of the three years in the period ended January 29, 2000 in conformity with accounting principles generally accepted in the United States.

Minneapolis, Minnesota
February 28, 2000

Ernst & Young LLP

Report of Management

Management is responsible for the consistency, integrity and presentation of the information in the Annual Report. The consolidated financial statements and other information presented in this Annual Report have been prepared in accordance with accounting principles generally accepted in the United States and include necessary judgments and estimates by management.

To fulfill our responsibility, we maintain comprehensive systems of internal control designed to provide reasonable assurance that assets are safeguarded and transactions are executed in accordance with established procedures. The concept of reasonable assurance is based upon a recognition that the cost of the controls should not exceed the benefit derived. We believe our systems of internal control provide this reasonable assurance.

The Board of Directors exercises its oversight role with respect to the Corporation's systems of internal control primarily through its Audit Committee, which is comprised of five independent directors. The Committee oversees the Corporation's systems of internal control, accounting practices, financial reporting and audits to assess whether their quality, integrity and objectivity are sufficient to protect shareholders' investments. The Committee's report appears on this page.

In addition, our consolidated financial statements have been audited by Ernst & Young LLP, independent auditors, whose report also appears on this page. As a part of its audit, Ernst & Young LLP develops and maintains an understanding of the Corporation's internal accounting controls and conducts such tests and employs such procedures as it considers necessary to render its opinion on the consolidated financial statements. Their report expresses an opinion as to the fair presentation, in all material respects, of the consolidated financial statements and is based on independent audits made in accordance with auditing standards generally accepted in the United States.

Robert J. Ulrich
Chairman of the Board and
Chief Executive Officer
February 28, 2000

Douglas A. Scovanner
Executive Vice President and
Chief Financial Officer

Report of Audit Committee

The Audit Committee met two times during fiscal 1999 to review the overall audit scope, plans for internal and independent audits, the Corporation's systems of internal control, emerging accounting issues, officer and director expenses, audit fees and retirement plans. The Committee also met individually with the independent auditors, without management present, to discuss the results of their audits. The Committee encourages the internal and independent auditors to communicate closely with the Committee.

Audit Committee results were reported to the full Board of Directors and the Corporation's annual financial statements were reviewed and approved by the Board of Directors before issuance. The Audit Committee also recommended to the Board of Directors that the independent auditors be reappointed for fiscal 2000, subject to the approval of the shareholders at the annual meeting.

February 28, 2000

Directors

LIVIO D. DESIMONE
Chairman and
Chief Executive Officer,
3M
(diversified manufacturer)
(1) (5) (6)

ROGER A. ENRICO
Chairman and
Chief Executive Officer,
PepsiCo, Inc.
(domestic and international
beverage and food company)
(1) (2) (3)

WILLIAM W. GEORGE
Chairman and
Chief Executive Officer,
Medtronic, Inc.
(therapeutic medical device
company) (1) (2) (4)

MICHELE J. HOOPER
President and
Chief Executive Officer,
Voyager Expanded Learning
(educational development
company) (1) (2) (6)

JAMES A. JOHNSON
Chairman and
Chief Executive Officer,
Johnson Capital Partners
(private investment
company) (1) (3) (4) (5)

RICHARD M. KOVACEVICH
President and
Chief Executive Officer,
Wells Fargo & Company
(banking and financial
services company) (1) (2) (6)

SUSAN A. McLAUGHLIN
President, Consumer
Services, BellSouth
Telecommunications, Inc.
(communications services
company) (1) (2) (4)

ANNE M. MULCAHY
Executive Vice President and
President,
General Markets Operations,
Xerox Corporation
(document management
company) (1) (4) (5)

STEPHEN W. SANGER
Chairman and
Chief Executive Officer,
General Mills, Inc.
(consumer food products
company) (1) (3) (5) (6)

GEORGE W. TAMKE
Former Vice Chairman and
Co-Chief Executive Officer,
Emerson Electric Co.
(industrial manufacturer) (1)

SOLOMON D. TRUJILLO
Chairman, President and
Chief Executive Officer,
US WEST, Inc.
(telecommunications
company) (1) (3) (4) (5)

ROBERT J. ULRICH
Chairman and
Chief Executive Officer,
Target Corporation and
Target Stores (1)

(1) *Executive Committee*
(2) *Audit Committee*
(3) *Compensation Committee*
(4) *Corporate Responsibility*
   Committee
(5) *Finance Committee*
(6) *Nominating Committee*

Officers

ROBERT J. ULRICH*
Chairman and
Chief Executive Officer,
Target Corporation and
Target Stores

KENNETH B. WOODROW*
Vice Chairman,
Target Corporation

LINDA L. AHLERS*
President, Dayton's
Marshall Field's and Hudson's

BART BUTZER*
President, Mervyn's

GREGG W. STEINHAFEL*
President, Target Stores

GERALD L. STORCH*
President, Financial Services
and New Businesses,
Target Corporation

LARRY V. GILPIN*
Executive Vice President,
Team, Guest and
Community Relations,
Target Corporation and
Target Stores

JAMES T. HALE*
Executive Vice President,
General Counsel and
Corporate Secretary,
Target Corporation

JOHN E. PELLEGRENE*
Executive Vice President,
Marketing,
Target Corporation and
Target Stores

DOUGLAS A. SCOVANNER*
Executive Vice President,
Finance and
Chief Financial Officer,
Target Corporation and
Target Stores

ERTUGRUL TUZCU*
Executive Vice President,
Store Operations,
Dayton's Marshall Field's and
Hudson's

TODD V. BLACKWELL*
Senior Vice President, Stores,
Mervyn's

JOHN D. GRIFFITH*
Senior Vice President,
Property Development,
Target Corporation

MAUREEN W. KYER*
Senior Vice President,
Merchandising, Mervyn's

PAUL L. SINGER*
Senior Vice President,
Technology Services and
Chief Information Officer,
Target Corporation

GAIL J. DORN
Vice President,
Communications and
Community Relations,
Target Corporation

NATE K. GARVIS
Vice President,
Government Affairs,
Target Corporation

SUSAN D. KAHN
Vice President,
Investor Relations,
Target Corporation

STEPHEN C. KOWALKE
Vice President and Treasurer,
Target Corporation

JANE P. WINDMEIER
Vice President, Finance,
Target Corporation and
Target Stores

RICHARD J. KUZMICH
President and
Chief Executive Officer,
Associated Merchandising Corp.

DALE NITSCHKE
President, target.direct

ERICA C. STREET
President, Target Brands, Inc.

JACK N. REIF
Assistant Treasurer,
Target Corporation

SARA J. ROSS
Assistant Treasurer,
Target Corporation

*Executive Officer and Corporate
Operating Committee Member*

A-41

Annual Meeting

The Annual Meeting of Shareholders is scheduled for May 17, 2000, at 9:30 a.m. CDT at The Children's Theatre, 2400 Third Avenue South, Minneapolis, Minnesota.

Shareholder Information

Quarterly and annual shareholder information, including the Form 10-Q and Form 10-K Annual Report, which are filed with the Securities and Exchange Commission, is available at no charge to shareholders. To obtain copies of these materials, you may call 612-370-6736, send an email to InvestorRelations@target.com, or write to:

Vice President, Investor Relations

Target Corporation

777 Nicollet Mall

Minneapolis, MN 55402

Our quarterly earnings release conference calls are webcast on the Internet through our website www.targetcorp.com. For additional information call investor relations at 612-370-6736.

Other information about Target Corporation is available at the same website.

Sales Information

Comments regarding the company's sales results are provided periodically throughout the year on a recorded telephone message. You may access this message by calling 612-370-6500.

Direct Stock Purchase/Dividend Reinvestment Plan

First Chicago Trust Company of New York administers a direct service investment plan that allows interested investors to purchase Target Corporation stock directly, rather than through a broker, and become a registered shareholder of the Company. The program offers many features including dividend reinvestment. For detailed information regarding this program, call First Chicago Trust toll free at 888-268-0203, or write to:

The DirectSERVICE Investment Program

c/o First Chicago Trust Company

P.O. Box 2598

Jersey City, NJ 07303-2598

Transfer Agent, Registrar and Dividend Disbursing Agent

First Chicago Trust Company of New York, a division of Equiserve

Trustee, Employee Savings 401(k) and Pension Plans

State Street Bank and Trust Company

Stock Exchange Listings

Trading symbol TGT

New York Stock Exchange and Pacific Exchange

Shareholder Assistance

For assistance regarding individual stock records, lost certificates, name or address changes, dividend or tax questions, call First Chicago Trust at 800-317-4445, or write to:

First Chicago Trust Company of New York

P.O. Box 2500

Jersey City, NJ 07303-2500.

Taking big steps, growing in size, moving forward.

(FOR BUSINESSES DISCUSSED IN CHAPTERS 1–12)

Service Proprietorship

Assets	Liabilities	Owner's Equity
Cash	Accounts Payable	Owner, Capital
Accounts Receivable	Notes Payable, Short-Term	Owner, Withdrawals
Allowance for Uncollectible Accounts	Salary Payable	**Revenues and Gains**
Notes Receivable, Short-Term	Wage Payable	Service Revenue
Interest Receivable	Employee Income Tax Payable	Interest Revenue
Supplies	FICA Tax Payable	Gain on Sale of Land (or Furniture,
Prepaid Rent	State Unemployment Tax Payable	Equipment, or Building)
Prepaid Insurance	Federal Unemployment Tax Payable	**Expenses and Losses**
Notes Receivable, Long-Term	Employee Benefits Payable	Salary Expense
Land	Interest Payable	Payroll Tax Expense
Furniture	Unearned Service Revenue	Insurance Expense for Employees
Accumulated Depreciation—Furniture	Notes Payable, Long-Term	Rent Expense
Equipment		Insurance Expense
Accumulated Depreciation—Equipment		Supplies Expense
Building		Uncollectible Account Expense
Accumulated Depreciation—Building		Depreciation Expense—Furniture
		Depreciation Expense—Equipment
		Depreciation Expense—Building
		Property Tax Expense
		Interest Expense
		Miscellaneous Expense
		Loss on Sale (or Exchange) of Land (Furniture, Equipment, or Building)

Service Partnership

Same as Service Proprietorship, except for Owners' Equity:

Owners' Equity

Partner 1, Capital
Partner 2, Capital
Partner N, Capital

Partner 1, Drawing
Partner 2, Drawing
Partner N, Drawing

Merchandising Corporation

Assets	Liabilities	Stockholders' Equity
Cash	Accounts Payable	Preferred Stock
Short-Term Investments (Trading Securities)	Notes Payable, Short-Term	Paid-in Capital in Excess of Par—Preferred
Accounts Receivable	Current Portion of Bonds Payable	Common Stock
Allowance for Uncollectible Accounts	Salary Payable	Paid-in Capital in Excess of Par—Common
Notes Receivable, Short-Term	Wage Payable	Paid-in Capital from Treasury Stock Transactions
Interest Receivable	Employee Income Tax Payable	Paid-in Capital from Retirement of Stock
Inventory	FICA Tax Payable	Retained Earnings
Supplies	State Unemployment Tax Payable	Foreign Currency Translation Adjustment
Prepaid Rent	Federal Unemployment Tax Payable	Treasury Stock
Prepaid Insurance	Employee Benefits Payable	
Notes Receivable, Long-Term	Interest Payable	
Investments in Subsidiaries	Income Tax Payable	
Investments in Stock (Available-for-Sale Securities)	Unearned Sales Revenue	
Investments in Bonds (Held-to-Maturity Securities)	Notes Payable, Long-Term	
Other Receivables, Long-Term	Bonds Payable	
Land	Lease Liability	
Land Improvements	Minority Interest	
Furniture and Fixtures		
Accumulated Depreciation—Furniture and Fixtures		
Equipment		
Accumulated Depreciation—Equipment		
Buildings		
Accumulated Depreciation—Buildings		
Organization Cost		
Franchises		
Patents		
Leaseholds		
Goodwill		

Expenses and Losses

Cost of Goods Sold
Salary Expense
Wage Expense
Commission Expense
Payroll Tax Expense
Insurance Expense for Employees
Rent Expense
Insurance Expense
Supplies Expense
Uncollectible Account Expense
Depreciation Expense—Land Improvements
Depreciation Expense—Furniture and Fixtures
Depreciation Expense—Equipment
Depreciation Expense—Buildings
Organization Expense
Amortization Expense—Franchises
Amortization Expense—Leaseholds
Amortization Expense—Goodwill
Income Tax Expense
Unrealized Holding Loss on Trading Investments
Loss on Sale of Investments
Loss on Sale (or Exchange) of Land (Furniture and Fixtures, Equipment, or Buildings)
Discontinued Operations—Loss
Extraordinary Losses

Revenues and Gains

Sales Revenue
Interest Revenue
Dividend Revenue
Equity-Method Investment Revenue
Unrealized Holding Gain on Trading Investments
Gain on Sale of Investments
Gain on Sale of Land (Furniture and Fixtures, Equipment, or Buildings)
Discontinued Operations—Gain
Extraordinary Gains

Manufacturing Corporation

Same as Merchandising Corporation, except for
Assets and Expenses:

Assets	Expenses (Contra Expenses If Credit Balance)
Inventories:	Direct Materials Price Variance
Materials Inventory	Direct Materials Efficiency Variance
Work in Process Inventory	Direct Labor Price Variance
Finished Goods Inventory	Direct Labor Efficiency Variance
	Manufacturing Overhead Flexible Budget Variance
	Manufacturing Overhead Production Volume Variance

APPENDIX C

Present-Value Tables and Future-Value Tables

This appendix provides present value tables and future-value tables (more complete than those in the Chapter 15 appendix and in Chapter 26).

EXHIBIT C-1
Present Value of $1

Present Value

Periods	1%	2%	3%	4%	5%	6%	7%	8%	9%	10%	12%
1	0.990	0.980	0.971	0.962	0.952	0.943	0.935	0.926	0.917	0.909	0.893
2	0.980	0.961	0.943	0.925	0.907	0.890	0.873	0.857	0.842	0.826	0.797
3	0.971	0.942	0.915	0.889	0.864	0.840	0.816	0.794	0.772	0.751	0.712
4	0.961	0.924	0.888	0.855	0.823	0.792	0.763	0.735	0.708	0.683	0.636
5	0.951	0.906	0.883	0.822	0.784	0.747	0.713	0.681	0.650	0.621	0.567
6	0.942	0.888	0.837	0.790	0.746	0.705	0.666	0.630	0.596	0.564	0.507
7	0.933	0.871	0.813	0.760	0.711	0.665	0.623	0.583	0.547	0.513	0.452
8	0.923	0.853	0.789	0.731	0.677	0.627	0.582	0.540	0.502	0.467	0.404
9	0.914	0.837	0.766	0.703	0.645	0.592	0.544	0.500	0.460	0.424	0.361
10	0.905	0.820	0.744	0.676	0.614	0.558	0.508	0.463	0.422	0.386	0.322
11	0.896	0.804	0.722	0.650	0.585	0.527	0.475	0.429	0.388	0.350	0.287
12	0.887	0.788	0.701	0.625	0.557	0.497	0.444	0.397	0.356	0.319	0.257
13	0.879	0.773	0.681	0.601	0.530	0.469	0.415	0.368	0.326	0.290	0.229
14	0.870	0.758	0.661	0.577	0.505	0.442	0.388	0.340	0.299	0.263	0.205
15	0.861	0.743	0.642	0.555	0.481	0.417	0.362	0.315	0.275	0.239	0.183
16	0.853	0.728	0.623	0.534	0.458	0.394	0.339	0.292	0.252	0.218	0.163
17	0.844	0.714	0.605	0.513	0.436	0.371	0.317	0.270	0.231	0.198	0.146
18	0.836	0.700	0.587	0.494	0.416	0.350	0.296	0.250	0.212	0.180	0.130
19	0.828	0.686	0.570	0.475	0.396	0.331	0.277	0.232	0.194	0.164	0.116
20	0.820	0.673	0.554	0.456	0.377	0.312	0.258	0.215	0.178	0.149	0.104
21	0.811	0.660	0.538	0.439	0.359	0.294	0.242	0.199	0.164	0.135	0.093
22	0.803	0.647	0.522	0.422	0.342	0.278	0.226	0.184	0.150	0.123	0.083
23	0.795	0.634	0.507	0.406	0.326	0.262	0.211	0.170	0.138	0.112	0.074
24	0.788	0.622	0.492	0.390	0.310	0.247	0.197	0.158	0.126	0.102	0.066
25	0.780	0.610	0.478	0.375	0.295	0.233	0.184	0.146	0.116	0.092	0.059
26	0.772	0.598	0.464	0.361	0.281	0.220	0.172	0.135	0.106	0.084	0.053
27	0.764	0.586	0.450	0.347	0.268	0.207	0.161	0.125	0.098	0.076	0.047
28	0.757	0.574	0.437	0.333	0.255	0.196	0.150	0.116	0.090	0.069	0.042
29	0.749	0.563	0.424	0.321	0.243	0.185	0.141	0.107	0.082	0.063	0.037
30	0.742	0.552	0.412	0.308	0.231	0.174	0.131	0.099	0.075	0.057	0.033
40	0.672	0.453	0.307	0.208	0.142	0.097	0.067	0.046	0.032	0.022	0.011
50	0.608	0.372	0.228	0.141	0.087	0.054	0.034	0.021	0.013	0.009	0.003

EXHIBIT C-1
(cont'd)

Present Value

14%	15%	16%	18%	20%	25%	30%	35%	40%	45%	50%	Periods
0.877	0.870	0.862	0.847	0.833	0.800	0.769	0.741	0.714	0.690	0.667	1
0.769	0.756	0.743	0.718	0.694	0.640	0.592	0.549	0.510	0.476	0.444	2
0.675	0.658	0.641	0.609	0.579	0.512	0.455	0.406	0.364	0.328	0.296	3
0.592	0.572	0.552	0.516	0.482	0.410	0.350	0.301	0.260	0.226	0.198	4
0.519	0.497	0.476	0.437	0.402	0.328	0.269	0.223	0.186	0.156	0.132	5
0.456	0.432	0.410	0.370	0.335	0.262	0.207	0.165	0.133	0.108	0.088	6
0.400	0.376	0.354	0.314	0.279	0.210	0.159	0.122	0.095	0.074	0.059	7
0.351	0.327	0.305	0.266	0.233	0.168	0.123	0.091	0.068	0.051	0.039	8
0.308	0.284	0.263	0.225	0.194	0.134	0.094	0.067	0.048	0.035	0.026	9
0.270	0.247	0.227	0.191	0.162	0.107	0.073	0.050	0.035	0.024	0.017	10
0.237	0.215	0.195	0.162	0.135	0.086	0.056	0.037	0.025	0.017	0.012	11
0.208	0.187	0.168	0.137	0.112	0.069	0.043	0.027	0.018	0.012	0.008	12
0.182	0.163	0.145	0.116	0.093	0.055	0.033	0.020	0.013	0.008	0.005	13
0.160	0.141	0.125	0.099	0.078	0.044	0.025	0.015	0.009	0.006	0.003	14
0.140	0.123	0.108	0.084	0.065	0.035	0.020	0.011	0.006	0.004	0.002	15
0.123	0.107	0.093	0.071	0.054	0.028	0.015	0.008	0.005	0.003	0.002	16
0.108	0.093	0.080	0.060	0.045	0.023	0.012	0.006	0.003	0.002	0.001	17
0.095	0.081	0.069	0.051	0.038	0.018	0.009	0.005	0.002	0.001	0.001	18
0.083	0.070	0.060	0.043	0.031	0.014	0.007	0.003	0.002	0.001		19
0.073	0.061	0.051	0.037	0.026	0.012	0.005	0.002	0.001	0.001		20
0.064	0.053	0.044	0.031	0.022	0.009	0.004	0.002	0.001			21
0.056	0.046	0.038	0.026	0.018	0.007	0.003	0.001	0.001			22
0.049	0.040	0.033	0.022	0.015	0.006	0.002	0.001				23
0.043	0.035	0.028	0.019	0.013	0.005	0.002	0.001				24
0.038	0.030	0.024	0.016	0.010	0.004	0.001	0.001				25
0.033	0.026	0.021	0.014	0.009	0.003	0.001					26
0.029	0.023	0.018	0.011	0.007	0.002	0.001					27
0.026	0.020	0.016	0.010	0.006	0.002	0.001					28
0.022	0.017	0.014	0.008	0.005	0.002						29
0.020	0.015	0.012	0.007	0.004	0.001						30
0.005	0.004	0.003	0.001	0.001							40
0.001	0.001	0.001									50

EXHIBIT C-2
Present Value of Annuity of $1

Periods	1%	2%	3%	4%	Present Value 5%	6%	7%	8%	9%	10%	12%
1	0.990	0.980	0.971	0.962	0.952	0.943	0.935	0.926	0.917	0.909	0.893
2	1.970	1.942	1.913	1.886	1.859	1.833	1.808	1.783	1.759	1.736	1.690
3	2.941	2.884	2.829	2.775	2.723	2.673	2.624	2.577	2.531	2.487	2.402
4	3.902	3.808	3.717	3.630	3.546	3.465	3.387	3.312	3.240	3.170	3.037
5	4.853	4.713	4.580	4.452	4.329	4.212	4.100	3.993	3.890	3.791	3.605
6	5.795	5.601	5.417	5.242	5.076	4.917	4.767	4.623	4.486	4.355	4.111
7	6.728	6.472	6.230	6.002	5.786	5.582	5.389	5.206	5.033	4.868	4.564
8	7.652	7.325	7.020	6.733	6.463	6.210	5.971	5.747	5.535	5.335	4.968
9	8.566	8.162	7.786	7.435	7.108	6.802	6.515	6.247	5.995	5.759	5.328
10	9.471	8.983	8.530	8.111	7.722	7.360	7.024	6.710	6.418	6.145	5.650
11	10.368	9.787	9.253	8.760	8.306	7.887	7.499	7.139	6.805	6.495	5.938
12	11.255	10.575	9.954	9.385	8.863	8.384	7.943	7.536	7.161	6.814	6.194
13	12.134	11.348	10.635	9.986	9.394	8.853	8.358	7.904	7.487	7.103	6.424
14	13.004	12.106	11.296	10.563	9.899	9.295	8.745	8.244	7.786	7.367	6.628
15	13.865	12.849	11.938	11.118	10.380	9.712	9.108	8.559	8.061	7.606	6.811
16	14.718	13.578	12.561	11.652	10.838	10.106	9.447	8.851	8.313	7.824	6.974
17	15.562	14.292	13.166	12.166	11.274	10.477	9.763	9.122	8.544	8.022	7.120
18	16.398	14.992	13.754	12.659	11.690	10.828	10.059	9.372	8.756	8.201	7.250
19	17.226	15.678	14.324	13.134	12.085	11.158	10.336	9.604	8.950	8.365	7.366
20	18.046	16.351	14.878	13.590	12.462	11.470	10.594	9.818	9.129	8.514	7.469
21	18.857	17.011	15.415	14.029	12.821	11.764	10.836	10.017	9.292	8.649	7.562
22	19.660	17.658	15.937	14.451	13.163	12.042	11.061	10.201	9.442	8.772	7.645
23	20.456	18.292	16.444	14.857	13.489	12.303	11.272	10.371	9.580	8.883	7.718
24	21.243	18.914	16.936	15.247	13.799	12.550	11.469	10.529	9.707	8.985	7.784
25	22.023	19.523	17.413	15.622	14.094	12.783	11.654	10.675	9.823	9.077	7.843
26	22.795	20.121	17.877	15.983	14.375	13.003	11.826	10.810	9.929	9.161	7.896
27	23.560	20.707	18.327	16.330	14.643	13.211	11.987	10.935	10.027	9.237	7.943
28	24.316	21.281	18.764	16.663	14.898	13.406	12.137	11.051	10.116	9.307	7.984
29	25.066	21.844	19.189	16.984	15.141	13.591	12.278	11.158	10.198	9.370	8.022
30	25.808	22.396	19.600	17.292	15.373	13.765	12.409	11.258	10.274	9.427	8.055
40	32.835	27.355	23.115	19.793	17.159	15.046	13.332	11.925	10.757	9.779	8.244
50	39.196	31.424	25.730	21.482	18.256	15.762	13.801	12.234	10.962	9.915	8.305

EXHIBIT C-2

(cont'd)

Present Value

14%	15%	16%	18%	20%	25%	30%	35%	40%	45%	50%	Periods
0.877	0.870	0.862	0.847	0.833	0.800	0.769	0.741	0.714	0.690	0.667	1
1.647	1.626	1.605	1.566	1.528	1.440	1.361	1.289	1.224	1.165	1.111	2
2.322	2.283	2.246	2.174	2.106	1.952	1.816	1.696	1.589	1.493	1.407	3
2.914	2.855	2.798	2.690	2.589	2.362	2.166	1.997	1.849	1.720	1.605	4
3.433	3.352	3.274	3.127	2.991	2.689	2.436	2.220	2.035	1.876	1.737	5
3.889	3.784	3.685	3.498	3.326	2.951	2.643	2.385	2.168	1.983	1.824	6
4.288	4.160	4.039	3.812	3.605	3.161	2.802	2.508	2.263	2.057	1.883	7
4.639	4.487	4.344	4.078	3.837	3.329	2.925	2.598	2.331	2.109	1.922	8
4.946	4.772	4.607	4.303	4.031	3.463	3.019	2.665	2.379	2.144	1.948	9
5.216	5.019	4.833	4.494	4.192	3.571	3.092	2.715	2.414	2.168	1.965	10
5.553	5.234	5.029	4.656	4.327	3.656	3.147	2.752	2.438	2.185	1.977	11
5.660	5.421	5.197	4.793	4.439	3.725	3.190	2.779	2.456	2.197	1.985	12
5.842	5.583	5.342	4.910	4.533	3.780	3.223	2.799	2.469	2.204	1.990	13
6.002	5.724	5.468	5.008	4.611	3.824	3.249	2.814	2.478	2.210	1.993	14
6.142	5.847	5.575	5.092	4.675	3.859	3.268	2.825	2.484	2.214	1.995	15
6.265	5.954	5.669	5.162	4.730	3.887	3.283	2.834	2.489	2.216	1.997	16
6.373	6.047	5.749	5.222	4.775	3.910	3.295	2.840	2.492	2.218	1.998	17
6.467	6.128	5.818	5.273	4.812	3.928	3.304	2.844	2.494	2.219	1.999	18
6.550	6.198	5.877	5.316	4.844	3.942	3.311	2.848	2.496	2.220	1.999	19
6.623	6.259	5.929	5.353	4.870	3.954	3.316	2.850	2.497	2.221	1.999	20
6.687	6.312	5.973	5.384	4.891	3.963	3.320	2.852	2.498	2.221	2.000	21
6.743	6.359	6.011	5.410	4.909	3.970	3.323	2.853	2.498	2.222	2.000	22
6.792	6.399	6.044	5.432	4.925	3.976	3.325	2.854	2.499	2.222	2.000	23
6.835	6.434	6.073	5.451	4.937	3.981	3.327	2.855	2.499	2.222	2.000	24
6.873	6.464	6.097	5.467	4.948	3.985	3.329	2.856	2.499	2.222	2.000	25
6.906	6.491	6.118	5.480	4.956	3.988	3.330	2.856	2.500	2.222	2.000	26
6.935	6.514	6.136	5.492	4.964	3.990	3.331	2.856	2.500	2.222	2.000	27
6.961	6.534	6.152	5.502	4.970	3.992	3.331	2.857	2.500	2.222	2.000	28
6.983	6.551	6.166	5.510	4.975	3.994	3.332	2.857	2.500	2.222	2.000	29
7.003	6.566	6.177	5.517	4.979	3.995	3.332	2.857	2.500	2.222	2.000	30
7.105	6.642	6.234	5.548	4.997	3.999	3.333	2.857	2.500	2.222	2.000	40
7.133	6.661	6.246	5.554	4.999	4.000	3.333	2.857	2.500	2.222	2.000	50

EXHIBIT C-3
Future Value of $1

Future Value

Periods	1%	2%	3%	4%	5%	6%	7%	8%	9%	10%	12%	14%	15%
1	1.010	1.020	1.030	1.040	1.050	1.060	1.070	1.080	1.090	1.100	1.120	1.140	1.150
2	1.020	1.040	1.061	1.082	1.103	1.124	1.145	1.166	1.188	1.210	1.254	1.300	1.323
3	1.030	1.061	1.093	1.125	1.158	1.191	1.225	1.260	1.295	1.331	1.405	1.482	1.521
4	1.041	1.082	1.126	1.170	1.216	1.262	1.311	1.360	1.412	1.464	1.574	1.689	1.749
5	1.051	1.104	1.159	1.217	1.276	1.338	1.403	1.469	1.539	1.611	1.762	1.925	2.011
6	1.062	1.126	1.194	1.265	1.340	1.419	1.501	1.587	1.677	1.772	1.974	2.195	2.313
7	1.072	1.149	1.230	1.316	1.407	1.504	1.606	1.714	1.828	1.949	2.211	2.502	2.660
8	1.083	1.172	1.267	1.369	1.477	1.594	1.718	1.851	1.993	2.144	2.476	2.853	3.059
9	1.094	1.195	1.305	1.423	1.551	1.689	1.838	1.999	2.172	2.358	2.773	3.252	3.518
10	1.105	1.219	1.344	1.480	1.629	1.791	1.967	2.159	2.367	2.594	3.106	3.707	4.046
11	1.116	1.243	1.384	1.539	1.710	1.898	2.105	2.332	2.580	2.853	3.479	4.226	4.652
12	1.127	1.268	1.426	1.601	1.796	2.012	2.252	2.518	2.813	3.138	3.896	4.818	5.350
13	1.138	1.294	1.469	1.665	1.886	2.133	2.410	2.720	3.066	3.452	4.363	5.492	6.153
14	1.149	1.319	1.513	1.732	1.980	2.261	2.579	2.937	3.342	3.798	4.887	6.261	7.076
15	1.161	1.346	1.558	1.801	2.079	2.397	2.759	3.172	3.642	4.177	5.474	7.138	8.137
16	1.173	1.373	1.605	1.873	2.183	2.540	2.952	3.426	3.970	4.595	6.130	8.137	9.358
17	1.184	1.400	1.653	1.948	2.292	2.693	3.159	3.700	4.328	5.054	6.866	9.276	10.76
18	1.196	1.428	1.702	2.026	2.407	2.854	3.380	3.996	4.717	5.560	7.690	10.58	12.38
19	1.208	1.457	1.754	2.107	2.527	3.026	3.617	4.316	5.142	6.116	8.613	12.06	14.23
20	1.220	1.486	1.806	2.191	2.653	3.207	3.870	4.661	5.604	6.728	9.646	13.74	16.37
21	1.232	1.516	1.860	2.279	2.786	3.400	4.141	5.034	6.109	7.400	10.80	15.67	18.82
22	1.245	1.546	1.916	2.370	2.925	3.604	4.430	5.437	6.659	8.140	12.10	17.86	21.64
23	1.257	1.577	1.974	2.465	3.072	3.820	4.741	5.871	7.258	8.954	13.55	20.36	24.89
24	1.270	1.608	2.033	2.563	3.225	4.049	5.072	6.341	7.911	9.850	15.18	23.21	28.63
25	1.282	1.641	2.094	2.666	3.386	4.292	5.427	6.848	8.623	10.83	17.00	26.46	32.92
26	1.295	1.673	2.157	2.772	3.556	4.549	5.807	7.396	9.399	11.92	19.04	30.17	37.86
27	1.308	1.707	2.221	2.883	3.733	4.822	6.214	7.988	10.25	13.11	21.32	34.39	43.54
28	1.321	1.741	2.288	2.999	3.920	5.112	6.649	8.627	11.17	14.42	23.88	39.20	50.07
29	1.335	1.776	2.357	3.119	4.116	5.418	7.114	9.317	12.17	15.86	26.75	44.69	57.58
30	1.348	1.811	2.427	3.243	4.322	5.743	7.612	10.06	13.27	17.45	29.96	50.95	66.21
40	1.489	2.208	3.262	4.801	7.040	10.29	14.97	21.72	31.41	45.26	93.05	188.9	267.9
50	1.645	2.692	4.384	7.107	11.47	18.42	29.46	46.90	74.36	117.4	289.0	700.2	1,084

EXHIBIT C-4
Future Value of Annuity $1

Future Value

Periods	1%	2%	3%	4%	5%	6%	7%	8%	9%	10%	12%	14%	15%
1	1.000	1.000	1.000	1.000	1.000	1.000	1.000	1.000	1.000	1.000	1.000	1.000	1.000
2	2.010	2.020	2.030	2.040	2.050	2.060	2.070	2.080	2.090	2.100	2.120	2.140	2.150
3	3.030	3.060	3.091	3.122	3.153	3.184	3.215	3.246	3.278	3.310	3.374	3.440	3.473
4	4.060	4.122	4.184	4.246	4.310	4.375	4.440	4.506	4.573	4.641	4.779	4.921	4.993
5	5.101	5.204	5.309	5.416	5.526	5.637	5.751	5.867	5.985	6.105	6.353	6.610	6.742
6	6.152	6.308	6.468	6.633	6.802	6.975	7.153	7.336	7.523	7.716	8.115	8.536	8.754
7	7.214	7.434	7.662	7.898	8.142	8.394	8.654	8.923	9.200	9.487	10.09	10.73	11.07
8	8.286	8.583	8.892	9.214	9.549	9.897	10.26	10.64	11.03	11.44	12.30	13.23	13.73
9	9.369	9.755	10.16	10.58	11.03	11.49	11.98	12.49	13.02	13.58	14.78	16.09	16.79
10	10.46	10.95	11.46	12.01	12.58	13.18	13.82	14.49	15.19	15.94	17.55	19.34	20.30
11	11.57	12.17	12.81	13.49	14.21	14.97	15.78	16.65	17.56	18.53	20.65	23.04	24.35
12	12.68	13.41	14.19	15.03	15.92	16.87	17.89	18.98	20.14	21.38	24.13	27.27	29.00
13	13.81	14.68	15.62	16.63	17.71	18.88	20.14	21.50	22.95	24.52	28.03	32.09	34.35
14	14.95	15.97	17.09	18.29	19.60	21.02	22.55	24.21	26.02	27.98	32.39	37.58	40.50
15	16.10	17.29	18.60	20.02	21.58	23.28	25.13	27.15	29.36	31.77	37.28	43.84	47.58
16	17.26	18.64	20.16	21.82	23.66	25.67	27.89	30.32	33.00	35.95	42.75	50.98	55.72
17	18.43	20.01	21.76	23.70	25.84	28.21	30.84	33.75	36.97	40.54	48.88	59.12	65.08
18	19.61	21.41	23.41	25.65	28.13	30.91	34.00	37.45	41.30	45.60	55.75	68.39	75.84
19	20.81	22.84	25.12	27.67	30.54	33.76	37.38	41.45	46.02	51.16	63.44	78.97	88.21
20	22.02	24.30	26.87	29.78	33.07	36.79	41.00	45.76	51.16	57.28	72.05	91.02	102.4
21	23.24	25.78	28.68	31.97	35.72	39.99	44.87	50.42	56.76	64.00	81.70	104.8	118.8
22	24.47	27.30	30.54	34.25	38.51	43.39	49.01	55.46	62.87	71.40	92.50	120.4	137.6
23	25.72	28.85	32.45	36.62	41.43	47.00	53.44	60.89	69.53	79.54	104.6	138.3	159.3
24	26.97	30.42	34.43	39.08	44.50	50.82	58.18	66.76	76.79	88.50	118.2	158.7	184.2
25	28.24	32.03	36.46	41.65	47.73	54.86	63.25	73.11	84.70	98.35	133.3	181.9	212.8
26	29.53	33.67	38.55	44.31	51.11	59.16	68.68	79.95	93.32	109.2	150.3	208.3	245.7
27	30.82	35.34	40.71	47.08	54.67	63.71	74.48	87.35	102.7	121.1	169.4	238.5	283.6
28	32.13	37.05	42.93	49.97	58.40	68.53	80.70	95.34	113.0	134.2	190.7	272.9	327.1
29	33.45	38.79	45.22	52.97	62.32	73.64	87.35	104.0	124.1	148.6	214.6	312.1	377.2
30	34.78	40.57	47.58	56.08	66.44	79.06	94.46	113.3	136.3	164.5	241.3	356.8	434.7
40	48.89	60.40	75.40	95.03	120.8	154.8	199.6	259.1	337.9	442.6	767.1	1,342	1,779
50	64.46	84.58	112.8	152.7	209.3	290.3	406.5	573.8	815.1	1,164	2,400	4,995	7,218

A P P E N D I X   D

Check Figures

Check Figures—Chapter 1

DE1-1	No check figure
DE1-2	No check figure
DE1-3	No check figure
DE1-4	Capital $2,000
DE1-5	Capital $10,000
DE1-6	No check figure
DE1-7	Capital $33,500
DE1-8	No check figure
DE1-9	Capital $30,000
DE1-10	Net inc. $5,400
	Capital $35,400
DE1-11	No check figure
DE1-12	No check figure
DE1-13	1. Net inc. $4,100
	2. Capital $32,000
DE1-14	No check figure
DE1-15	Net inc. $50,000
DE1-16	Capital, 12/31/X3 $27,000
DE1-17	Total assets $35,000
DE1-18	No check figure
E1-1	No check figure
E1-2	No check figure
E1-3	No check figure
E1-4	C: $1,900
E1-5	OE increased by $737 mil.
E1-6	1. Net inc. $18,000
	3. Net loss $12,000
E1-7	No check figure
E1-8	Total assets $94,800
E1-9	2. Net inc. $5,400
1-10	2. Capital $14,200
E1-11	1. Net inc. $76,200
	2. Capital $27,100
E1-12	1. Net loss for 19X9 $132 mil.
E1-13	Cash bal., end of year $21 mil.
E1-14	Circle $25,000
	Triangle $185,000
	Square $170,000
P1-1A	Total assets $90,000
P1-2A	Total assets $68,000
P1-3A	Total assets $160,000
P1-4A	No check figure
P1-5A	1. Net inc. $64,000
	3. Total assets $279,000
P1-6A	2. Net inc. $2,100
	4. Total assets $30,750
P1-1B	Total assets $105,100
P1-2B	Total assets $61,000
P1-3B	Total assets $95,000
P1-4B	No check figure
P1-5B	1. Net inc. $47,000
	3. Total assets $102,000
P1-6B	2. Net inc. $4,240
	4. Total assets $40,920
Case 1	No check figure
Case 2	No check figure
Financial Statement Case	3. Stockholders' equity $5,862 mil.
	4. Rev. increased by $3,040 mil.

Check Figures—Chapter 2

DE2-1	1. $3,000
DE2-2	No check figure
DE2-3	No check figure
DE2-4	No check figure
DE2-5	No check figure
DE2-6	No check figure
DE2-7	No check figure
DE2-8	No check figure
DE2-9	No check figure
DE2-10	3. $1,500
DE2-11	3. a. $5,000
	b. $5,000
DE2-12	Trial bal. total $40,000
DE2-13	Trial bal. total $66 bil.
DE2-14	Incorrect trial bal. total assets $24,200
DE2-15	No check figure
DE2-16	Total debits $145,000
E2-1	No check figure
E2-2	2. Net inc. $2 bil.
E2-3	No check figure
E2-4	Total debits $183,600
E2-5	No check figure
E2-6	Trial bal. total $59,700
E2-7	Trial bal. total $37,850
E2-8	No check figure
E2-9	Trial bal. total $69,400
E2-10	Trial bal. total $124,100
E2-11	Trial bal. total $76,100
E2-12	Cash bal. $1,700
E2-13	Trial bal. total $19,700
E2-14	Total debits $78,000
E2-15	4. Trial bal. total $20,400
E2-16	b. $66,000
	c. $74,000
	d. $2,500
E2-17	No check figure
P2-1A	No check figure
P2-2A	No check figure
P2-3A	3. Trial bal. total $50,300
P2-4A	3. Trial bal. total $41,600
P2-5A	1. Trial bal. total $70,500
	2. Net inc. $6,370
P2-6A	3. Trial bal. total $103,600
P2-7A	1. Net inc. $2,800
	3. Total assets $92,200
P2-1B	No check figure
P2-2B	No check figure
P2-3B	3. Trial bal. total $55,500
P2-4B	3. Trial bal. total $53,500
P2-5B	1. Trial bal. total $65,100
	2. Net inc. $10,140
P2-6B	3. Trial bal. total $66,200
P2-7B	1. Net inc. $400
	3. Total assets $59,900
Case 1	No check figure
Case 2	3. Trial bal. total $22,800
	4. Net inc. $5,550
Financial Statement Case	No check figure

Check Figures—Chapter 3

DE3-1	No check figure
DE3-2	No check figure
DE3-3	Revenue $750,000
DE3-4	Expense $280,000
DE3-5	1. $55 mil.
DE3-6	1. Salary Expense for 2000 $9 mil.
DE3-7	1. Prepaid Rent $2,750 Rent Expense $250
DE3-8	3. $34,500
DE3-9	3. Interest Payable Nov. 30 $200
DE3-10	3. Interest Receivable Nov. 30 $200
DE3-11	No check figure
DE3-12	No check figure
DE3-13	No check figure
DE3-14	No check figure
DE3-15	1. Assets $47,250 Liabilities $13,550
DE3-16	1. Net inc. $5,650
E3-1	No check figure
E3-2	No check figure
E3-3	No check figure
E3-4	A: Insur. Exp. $1,600
E3-5	No check figure
E3-6	Net income overstated by $4,300
E3-7	No check figure
E3-8	Service Rev. $5,550
E3-9	Adj. trial bal. total $55,090
E3-10	No check figure
E3-11	Net inc. $7,150 Total assets $29,100
E3-12	Net inc. $74,500
E3-13	1. End. capital $191,000
E3-14	7. net inc. $1,690 Total assets $18,790
E3-15	Revenue $8,500
E3-16	Cash collected $4,400
P3-1A	2. Net inc. $750
P3-2A	No check figure
P3-3A	c. Art Supplies Exp. $6,360 f. Insurance Exp. $2,700
P3-4A	No check figure
P3-5A	3. Adj. trial bal. total $62,500
P3-6A	1. Net inc. $78,470 Total assets $129,030
P3-7A	2. Net inc. $6,950 Total assets $44,550
P3-1B	2. Net inc. $683
P3-2B	No check figure
P3-3B	a. Rent Exp. $2,400 d. Supplies Exp. $6,710
P3-4B	No check figure
P3-5B	3. Adj. trial bal. total $50,080
P3-6B	1. Net inc. $42,030 Total assets $58,810

P3-7B	2. Net inc. $7,500
	Total assets $46,200
Case 1	Your highest price $127,000
Case 2	No check figure
Financial Statement Case	No check figure
E3A-1	Supplies $860
E3A-2	Unearned Service Rev. $3,700
P3A-1	Prepaid Rent $2,250
	Unearned Service Rev. $2,400

Check Figures—Chapter 4

DE4-1	No check figure
DE4-2	No check figure
DE4-3	No check figure
DE4-4	No check figure
DE4-5	No check figure
DE4-6	1. d. Close $3,525
	3. a. $31,575
DE4-7	1. $31,575
DE4-8	No check figure
DE4-9	No check figure
DE4-10	Trial bal. total $7,260 mil.
DE4-11	No check figure
DE4-12	c. $5,266 mil.
	d. $13,378 mil.
	e. $6,882 mil.
DE4-13	1. $1.79
	2. 49%
	3. 51%
DE4-14	1. Current ratio 2.07
	Debt ratio 0.31
E4-1	Net inc. $2,330
E4-2	No check figure
E4-3	End. bal. Gail Pfeiffer, Capital $36,360
E4-4	Trial bal. total $42,340
E4-5	No check figure
E4-6	Liu Hyundai, Capital $50,900
E4-7	2. Felix Rohr, Capital $175,700
E4-8	Matthew Knowles, Capital Dec. 31, 20X2 $465,000
E4-9	2. Net inc. $12,400
E4-10	1. Total assets $52,700
E4-11	2. Total assets $18,790
	Amos Faraday, Capital $14,090
E4-12	Net inc. $53,100
P4-1A	Net inc. $16,300
P4-2A	2. Net inc. $87,630
	Total assets $240,680
P4-3A	2. Net inc. $90,000
	Total assets $131,000
P4-4A	Trial bal. total $153,000
P4-5A	3. Net inc. $26,000
	Total assets $104,320
	5. Trial bal. total $146,220
P4-6A	1. Total assets $114,600
	2. Debt ratio 0.41
P4-7A	c. Overall, net inc. understated by $1,060
P4-1B	Net inc. $15,000
P4-2B	2. Net inc. $30,000
	Total assets $175,860
P4-3B	2. Net inc. $87,000
	Total assets $134,000
P4-4B	2. Trial bal. total $151,000
P4-5B	3. Net inc. $12,090

	Total assets $101,080
	5. Trial bal. total $117,410
P4-6B	1. Total assets $108,200
	2. Debt ratio 0.40
P4-7B	c. Overall, net inc. understated by $2,520
Case 1	1. Net inc. $55,440
	2. Total assets $58,390
Case 2	No check figure
Financial Statement Case	3. Debt ratio at 2/29/00 0.66
	5. Cost of plant assets $13,824 mil.
Team Project	Net inc. $1,500
	Total assets $1,640
P4A-1	No check figure

Check Figures—Chapter 5

DE5-1	No check figure
DE5-2	No check figure
DE5-3	No check figure
DE5-4	No check figure
DE5-5	a. $130,000
	b. $126,100
DE5-6	c. Credit cash for $126,100
DE5-7	Net cost $137,200
DE5-8	Gross profit $55,200
DE5-9	c. Debit Cash for $36,260
DE5-10	b. $321,240
DE5-11	No check figure
DE5-12	No check figure
DE5-13	Net inc. $1,666 mil.
DE5-14	Total assets $11,471 mil.
DE5-15	C. Ernest, Capital bal. $25,650
DE5-16	No check figure
DE5-17	Gross profit % 20.7%
	Invy. turnover 56.4 times
DE5-18	b. Excess of collections over payments $641 mil.
DE5-19	COGS $23,029 mil.
DE5-20	3. F150,000
DE5-21	Purchases $7,181 mil.
E5-1	2. Gross profit for 2000 $3,541 mil.
E5-2	Sept. 23 Debit Cash for $2,254
E5-3	May 22 Credit Cash for $469.54
E5-4	June 14 Credit Cash for $7,054
E5-5	May 14 Debit Cash for $6,984
E5-6	Owner Capital bal. at 12/31/00 $10,805
E5-7	Net inc. $74,860
E5-8	Net inc. $74,860
E5-9	20X2 Gross profit % 51%; Invy. turnover 3.72 times
E5-10	1. Net inc. $31,300
E5-11	Net inc. $31,300
E5-12	Excess of collections over payments $29 bil.
E5-13	COGS $99,300
E5-14	(e) $16,200 (f) $37,400 (i) $112,100
E5-15	$180 mil.
E5-16	3. Net inc. $4,900
P5-1A	No check figure
P5-2A	No check figure
P5-3A	No check figure
P5-4A	Net inc. $49,890
P5-5A	2. $66,260
P5-6A	1. Net inc. $55,600
	2. Total assets $200,100

P5-7A	1. Net inc. $55,600
	2. Total assets $200,100
P5-8A	1. Net inc. $58,710
	2. 20X4 Gross profit % 60%
	Invy. turnover 2.03 times
P5-9A	2. Gross profit % 32%
	3. Invy. turnover 3.2 times
P5-1B	No check figure
P5-2B	No check figure
P5-3B	No check figure
P5-4B	Net inc. $31,370
P5-5B	2. $58,190
P5-6B	1. Net inc. $7,900
	2. Total assets $371,700
P5-7B	1. Net inc. $7,900
	2. Total assets $371,700
P5-8B	1. Net inc. $38,760
	2. 2000 Gross profit % 56%
	Invy. turnover 8.9 times
P5-9B	2. Gross profit % 48%
	3. Invy. turnover 3.63 times
Case 1	2. Net inc. $78,380
	Total assets $104,590
Case 2	No check figure
Financial Statement Case	
	2. $1,144 mil. closed to R/E
	3. Gross profit % 30.7%
	Invy. turnover 6.3 times
E5A-1	June 23 Debit Cash for $2,352
E5A-2	May 22 Credit Cash for $469.54
E5A-3	June 14 Credit Cash for $7,054
E5A-4	May 14 Debit Cash for $6,984
P5A-1	Hillcrest: Nov. 27 Credit Cash for $2,600
P5A-2	No check figure
P5A-3	No check figure
P5A-4	1. Net inc. $88,850
	2. Total assets $218,110
	4. Ben Latham, Capital bal. $195,590

Check Figures—Chapter 6

DE6-1	No check figure
DE6-2	No check figure
DE6-3	No check figure
DE6-4	No check figure
DE6-5	No check figure
DE6-6	No check figure
DE6-7	No check figure
DE6-8	No check figure
DE6-9	4. Decrease in Accts. Rec. $1,235
DE6-10	2. $2,876
	3. Payments $798
DE6-11	2. Net Purchases $3,885
DE6-12	4. Net sales revenue $7,456
E6-1	No check figure
E6-2	No check figure
E6-3	No check figure
E6-4	No check figure
E6-5	Total Debit to cash $5,987.60
E6-6	No check figure
E6-7	No check figure
E6-8	Purchases journal: Total credit to Accts. Pay. $21,216
E6-9	3. Total Accts.Pay. $3,042
E6-10	3. Total credit to Cash $14,897
E6-11	No check figure
E6-12	1. Gross profit $3,935
P6-1A	No check figure

P6-2A	1. Cash receipts journal: Total debit to Cash $36,619
P6-3A	No check figure
P6-4A	2. Cash pay. journal: Total credit to Cash $17,237
P6-5A	6. Total Accts. Rec. $496 Total Accts. Pay. $2,692
P6-1B	No check figure
P6-2B	1. Cash recpts. journal: Total debit to Cash $58,650
P6-3B	No check figure
P6-4B	2. Cash pay. journal: Total credit to Cash $15,571
P6-5B	6. Total Accts. Rec. $567 Total Accts. Pay. $2,925
Case 1	No check figure
Case 2	Sales journal: Total $16,198 Cash recpts. journal: Total debit to Cash $7,774

Check Figures—Chapter 7

DE7-1	No check figure
DE7-2	No check figure
DE7-3	No check figure
DE7-4	No check figure
DE7-5	No check figure
DE7-6	No check figure
DE7-7	No check figure
DE7-8	No check figure
DE7-9	No check figure
DE7-10	Adj. bal. $2,570
DE7-11	No check figure
DE7-12	No check figure
DE7-13	Employee stole $980
DE7-14	No check figure
DE7-15	No check figure
DE7-16	No check figure
DE7-17	No check figure
DE7-18	3. $400
DE7-19	1. New financing needed $165 mil.
DE7-20	New financing needed $10 mil.
DE7-21	No check figure
E7-1	No check figure
E7-2	No check figure
E7-3	No check figure
E7-4	No check figure
E7-5	No check figure
E7-6	No check figure
E7-7	Adj. bal. $1,891
E7-8	Adj. bal. $4,071
E7-9	No check figure
E7-10	No check figure
E7-11	No check figure
E7-12	Apr. 10 Credit Cash for $181
E7-13	1. Credit Cash for $211.13
E7-14	New financing needed $19 mil.
E7-15	No check figure
E7-16	1. New financing needed $433 mil. 2. Current ratio after borrowing 1.30
P7-1A	No check figure 1. Adj. bal. $10,670
P7-2A	No check figure
P7-3A	1. Adj bal. $10,670
P7-4A	1. Adj. bal. $20,948.77
P7-5A	No check figure
P7-6A	Apr. 30 Credit Cash in Bank for $382.64

P7-7A	New financing needed $1,300
P7-8A	1. Cash available for additional investments $727 mil.
P7-9A	No check figure
P7-1B	No check figure
P7-2B	No check figure
P7-3B	1. Adj. bal. $6,657
P7-4B	1. Adj. bal. $3,635.33
P7-5B	No check figure
P7-6B	June 30 Credit Cash in Bank for $307.63
P7-7B	New financing needed $3,300
P7-8B	1. New financing needed $76 mil.
P7-9B	No check figure
Case 1	Cashier stole $900
Case 2	No check figure
Financial Statement Case	5. Cash decreased by $35 mil.

Check Figures—Chapter 8

DE8-1	No check figure
DE8-2	No check figure
DE8-3	No check figure
DE8-4	No check figure
DE8-5	A/R, net $78,000
DE8-6	4. Uncollect. Acct. Exp. $14,400
DE8-7	3. A/R, net $173,600
DE8-8	Allowance for U/A end. bal. $4,000
DE8-9	Debit Uncollect. Acct. Exp. $4,900
DE8-10	No check figure
DE8-11	A/R bal., June 30 $5,500
DE8-12	Debit Cash $7,840
DE8-13	5. Pay at maturity $1,090
DE8-14	Note 1 $150 Note 4 $375
DE8-15	a. Credit Cash $400,000 b. Debit Cash $408,000
DE8-16	c. Debit Cash $1,090
DE8-17	a. Note rec. $1,000 Interest rec. $22.50 d. Interest rev. $67.50
DE8-18	Net realizable value: Intel $3,700 mil. Oracle $2,238 mil.
DE8-19	1. Net inc. $1,184 mil. 2. A/R, net $2,464 mil.
DE8-20	a. 1.17 b. 48 days
DE8-21	1. 1.73 c. 0.59 d. 3.20
E8-1	No check figure
E8-2	No check figure
E8-3	2&3. A/R, net $53,000
E8-4	2. A/R $55,930
E8-5	2. A/R, net $288,004
E8-6	Debit Uncollect. Acct.Exp.: a. $2,250; B. $4,300
E8-7	1. Interest for: 20X7 $60,000 20X8 $90,000 20X9 $30,000
E8-8	Dec. 31 Debit Interest Rec. $719
E8-9	Apr. 1, 20X4 Debit Cash $8,960
E8-10	Dec. 31 Debit Cash $5,490
E8-11	1. 20X3 0.80 2. 37 days
E8-12	1. 2 days
E8-13	Net inc.: Without bankcards

	$75,000; With bankcards $93,960
P8-1A	No check figure
P8-2A	Uncollected. Acct. Exp.: 1. $3,500 2. $8,900
P8-3A	3. A/R, net: 20X4 $247,017 20X3 $263,160
P8-4A	3. A/R, net $160,301
P8-5A	1. Note 1 $11,330 Note 2 $15,250 Note 3 $13,080
P8-6A	No check figure
P8-7A	Dec. 31, 20X1 Uncollect. Acct. Exp. $9,700
P8-8A	1. Ratios for 20X3: a. 1.71; b. 0.60; c. 20 days
P8-1B	No check figure
P8-2B	Uncollect. Acct. Exp. 1. $8,900 2. $12,800
P8-3B	3. A/R, net: 20X1 $132,684 20X0 $115,300
P8-4B	3. A/R, net $135,865
P8-5B	1. Note 1 $12,720 Note 2 $9,075 Note 3 $14,170
P8-6B	No check figure
P8-7B	Dec. 31, 20X1 Uncollect. Acct. Exp. $7,500
P8-8B	1. Ratios for 20X3: a. 1.85; b. 0.95; c. 18 days
Case 1	1. Net inc.: 20X3 $106,600 20X2 $85,550
Case 2	A/R bal. $90,000 Note Rec. bal. $5,000
Financial Statement Case 3.	Acid-test ratio 0.35
DE8A-1	Proceeds $498,200
E8A-1A	June 30 Debit Cash $498,200
E8A-2A	Dec. 1 Debit Interest Exp. $300
P8A-1	2. Note 1 $9,994; Note 2 $6,023; Note 3 $8,007
P8A-2	2. Note 1 $6,111; Note 2 $8,965; Note 3 $8,129

Check Figures—Chapter 9

DE9-1	Inventory $24,000 Gross profit $64,000
DE9-2	2. Gross profit $360,000
DE9-3	Gross profit $60,500
DE9-4	No check figure
DE9-5	No check figure
DE9-6	No check figure
DE9-7	COGS: wtd-avg. $750 LIFO $800
DE9-8	COGS: wtd-avg. $9,422 LIFO $9,800
DE9-9	Net inc.: wtd-avg. $1,978; LIFO $1,600
DE9-10	Inc. tax Exp.: wtd-avg. $791; LIFO $640
DE9-11	No check figure
DE9-12	2. Gross profit $765
DE9-13	Inventory $550 COGS $1,325

DE9-14	b. COGS $67.5 mil. d. Net loss $(0.1) mil.	P9-8B	1. Est. cost of end. invy. $467 thou.	P10-5A	3. Cost of assets sold $15,098,000
DE9-15	3. Correct net inc. Last yr. $8.3 mil.; This yr. $5 mil.	P9-9B	1. Net inc. $48 mil. 2. Total assets $456 mil.	P10-6A	Part 1. 3. Amortiz. of goodwill $57,450; Part 2. 2 Net inc. $119,150

DE9-14   b. COGS $67.5 mil.
          d. Net loss $(0.1) mil.
DE9-15   3. Correct net inc.
          Last yr. $8.3 mil.;
          This yr. $5 mil.
DE9-16   No check figure
DE9-17   1. & 2. End. invy. $150,000
E9-1   2. Gross profit $1,574 thou.
E9-2   2. Gross profit $1,574 thou.
E9-3   Purchase $8,800 mil.
E9-4   COGS: wtd-avg. $3,320
          LIFO $3,368
E9-5   b. COGS $3,270
E9-6   c. COGS $3,368
E9-7   LIFO tax saving $29
E9-8   a. $64,800; d. $30,200
          f. $34,700
E9-9   Magnolia gross profit % 55.9%;
          Invy. T/O 3.9 times
E9-10   COGS $724; End. invy. $664
E9-11   Net inc. for cell B21 $75,000;
          cell C21 $68,000
E9-12   No check figure
E9-13   No check figure
E9-14   Gross profit $110,567
E9-15   Gross profit $62,900
          Inventory $19,800
E9-16   Net inc.: 20X2 $41,100
          20X1 $27,300
E9-17   Est. cost of invy. destroyed
          $49,100
E9-18   No check figure
E9-19   1. Net inc. $724 mil.
          2. Total assets $5,522 mil.
P9-1A   3. Net inc. $320
P9-2A   2. Net inc. $110 thou.
P9-3A   3. Gross profit $1,494
P9-4A   1. COGS: wtd-avg. $55,707
          FIFO $54,516
          LIFO $56,908
P9-5A   1. Gross profit:
          wtd-avg. $2,267
          FIFO $2,502
          LIFO $2,089
P9-6A   No check figure
P9-7A   1. Correct net inc.:
          20X3 $11 thou.
          20X2 $9 thou.
          20X1 $27 thou.
P9-8A   1. Est. cost of end.
          invy. $845 thou.
P9-9A   1. Net inc. $1,127 mil.
          2. Total assets $5,189 mil.
P9-1B   3. Net inc. $520
P9-2B   2. Net inc. $75 thou.
P9-3B   3. Gross profit $3,205
P9-4B   1. COGS: wtd-avg. $12,445
          FIFO $12,167
          LIFO $12,758
P9-5B   1. Gross profit:
          wtd-avg. $62,810
          FIFO $63,355
          LIFO $62,030
P9-6B   No check figure
P9-7B   1. Correct net inc.:
          20X2 $61 thou.
          20X1 $59 thou.
          20X0 $15 thou.

P9-8B   1. Est. cost of end.
          invy. $467 thou.
P9-9B   1. Net inc. $48 mil.
          2. Total assets $456 mil.
Case 1   Net inc.: FIFO with and without
          purchase $240,700;
          LIFO without purchase
          $205,900; with purchase
          $183,425
Case 2   No check figure
Financial Statement Case   Purchases
          $23,352 mil.

Check Figures—Chapter 10

DE10-1   3. Book value $10,227 mil.
DE10-2   No check figure
DE10-3   No check figure
DE10-4   2. Bal. $872,000
DE10-5   Land $50,000; Building $37,500
          Equipment $12,500
DE10-6   No check figure
DE10-7   2. Book value—SL $30,000,000;
          DDB $21,600,000
DE10-8   b. Depr. $7,500,000
          c. Depr. $–0–
DE10-9   2. Tax saved $3,360,000
DE10-10   b. Depr. $4,800,000
          c. Depr. $10,800,000
DE10-11   Depr. $10,000
DE10-12   1. a. Loss on Sale $2,000
          b. Gain on Sale $8,240
DE10-13   2. Depletion $4.5 bil.
          3. Book value $2.0 bil.
DE10-14   1. Goodwill $310,000
          3. Amort. exp. $7,750
DE10-15   2. Book value $311 mil.
          3. Goodwill purchased $15 mil.
DE10-16   1. Net loss $75,000
E10-1   Land $206,900
          Land improve. $67,400
E10-2   1. Cost $654,000
E10-3   Saddle 1 $2,580
          Saddle 2 $4,150
          Saddle 3 $3,270
E10-4   No check figure
E10-5   No check figure
E10-6   20X4 Depr.: SL $3,000;
          UOP $2,400; DDB $375
E10-7   Extra cash to invest with DDB
          $38,388
E10-8   Depr. Yr. 16 $21,458
E10-9   Gain on Sale $960
E10-10   Cost of new truck $338,175
E10-11   Depletion $75,600
E10-12   Part 2. Amortiz. $342,500
E10-13   Payment for other assets $63 mil.
E10-14   3. Amortiz. of goodwill $700,000
E10-15   Yr. 5 equip., net Correct
          Net inc. 0.9 over
E10-16   1. Acquisitions $2,559 mil.
P10-1A   2. Depr.-Land improve. $3,893;
          Office bldg. $30,621; Garage
          $2,057; Furniture $11,681
P10-2A   Dec. 31 Depr.-Commun. Equip.
          $19,200; Televideo Equip.
          $2,133; Office Equip. $10,000
P10-3A   No check figure
P10-4A   3. Net inc. advantage of SL
          $8,420; Cash flow advantage of
          DDB $5,613

P10-5A   3. Cost of assets sold
          $15,098,000
P10-6A   Part 1. 3. Amortiz. of goodwill
          $57,450;
          Part 2. 2 Net inc. $119,150
P10-7A   1. Book value $21.4 bil.
          2. Gain on sale $0.2 bil.
          3. Owners' equity $12.4 bil.
          4. Net loss $0.9 bil.
P10-1B   2. Depr.-Land improve. $2,306;
          Sales bldg. $16,481; Garage
          $1,280; Furniture $9,114
P10-2B   Dec. 31 Depr.-Motor-Carrier
          Equip. $51,000; Buildings
          $733
P10-3B   No check figure
P10-4B   3. Net inc. advantage of SL
          $30,840; Cash flow advantage of
          DDB $20,560
P10-5B   3. Cost of assets sold $11,213 mil.
P10-6B   Part 1. 3. Amortiz. of goodwill
          $105,000;
          Part 2. 2. Net inc. $15,750
P10-7B   1. Book value $4.0 bil.
          2. Gain on sale $0.2 bil.
          3. Owners' Equity $8.4 bil.
          4. Net inc. $2.5 bil.
Case 1   1. Net inc.-Astoria $149,700;
          Hilton $112,400
Case 2   No check figure
Financial Statement Case   4. Loss on
          Sale $165 mil.

Check Figures—Chapter 11

DE11-1   No check figure
DE11-2   c. Credit Cash $8,800
DE11-3   2. Interest Exp. $400
DE11-4   3. Note pay. $99,500
DE11-5   2. Air Traffic Liab. $1,200
DE11-6   2. Est. Warranty Pay. $8,000
DE11-7   No check figure
DE11-8   No check figure
DE11-9   No check figure
DE11-10   2. Net pay $684.75
DE11-11   Total exp. $1,008.65
DE11-12   No check figure
DE11-13   Net pay $5,960
DE11-14   No check figure
DE11-15   No check figure
DE11-16   Total payroll exp. $28,805.50
DE11-17   No check figure
DE11-18   Total current liab. $84,202
DE11-19   No check figure
E11-1   No check figure
E11-2   1. Accrued Payroll Liab. $27,194
E11-3   Unearned subscription rev. $80
E11-4   2. Est. Warranty Pay. $3,970
E11-5   Apr. 1, 20X3 Credit Cash $16,200
E11-6   2. Note pay, short-term $11,840
E11-7   No check figure
E11-8   Pay off $30,000
E11-9   Net pay $7,598.70
E11-10   a. Net pay $275.50
E11-11   Payroll Tax Exp. $7,636.20
E11-12   Salary Exp. $900,000
          Salary pay. $4,000
E11-13   20X1: Current portion of LT debt
          $1,000,000; Interest pay.
          $450,000
E11-14   Total current liab. $125,340

E11-15	1. Current ratio 0.85
	2. Current ratio 0.79
E11-16	1. Payments $627 mil.
	2. Salary exp. $3,193 mil.
P11-1A	No check figure
P11-2A	No check figure
P11-3A	1. b. $7,518
	c. $23,949
	e. $1,998
	j. $13,299
P11-4A	1. Net pay $58,222
	2. Total cost $89,632
P11-5A	3. Total liab. $339,312
P11-6A	3. Credit Cash $2,178
	4. Debit Payroll Tax Exp. $127
P11-7A	No check figure
P11-1B	No check figure
P11-2B	No check figure
P11-3B	1. a. $78,584
	c. $83,693
	f. $2,162
	k. $24,484
P11-4B	1. Net pay $48,780
	2. Total cost $79,153
P11-5B	3. Total liab. $202,727
P11-6B	3. Credit Cash $2,033
	4. Debit Payroll Tax Exp. $177
P11-7B	No check figure
Case 1	No check figure
Case 2	No check figure
Financial Statement Case	No check figure

Check Figures—Chapter 12

DE12-1	No check figure
DE12-2	No check figure
DE12-3	Debit Building $285,000
DE12-4	3. Total equity $32 mil.
DE12-5	2. Benz, Cap. $462,500
	Hanna, Cap. $97,500
DE12-6	2. Benz, Cap. $494,000
	Hanna, Cap. $76,000
DE12-7	Lawson $48,000; Martinez $32,000; Edwards $60,000
DE12-8	Fung $27,150
	Kiawa $22,850
DE12-9	No check figure
DE12-10	No check figure
DE12-11	Credit Kliptel, Cap. $40,000; Nagasawa, Cap. $5,000; Osburn, Cap. $5,000
DE12-12	Nagasawa, Cap. $75,000
	Osburn, Cap. $85,000
	Kliptel, Cap. $40,000
DE12-13	Debit Page, Cap. $10,667; Franco, Cap. $5,333; Credit Everett, Cap. $156,000
DE12-14	No check figure
DE12-15	a. Credit Green, Cap. $23,750; Henry, Cap. $47,500; Isaac, Cap. $23,750
DE12-16	Debit Henry, Cap. $90,500; Credit Green, Cap. $15,000; Isaac, Cap. $15,000
DE12-17	Pay Avignon $31,000; Bloch $17,000; Crane $7,000
DE12-18	No check figure
DE12-19	Green, Cap. $66,000
	Henry, Cap. $67,000
DE12-20	Net inc.: Frost $70,000; Martin $35,000

E12-1	No check figure
E12-2	Credit Flute, Cap. $82,100
E12-3	d. Net inc.: Meppen $34,818; Quaid $63,182
E12-4	Partnership capital decreased $2,000
E12-5	c. Falco, Cap. $52,500; Graham, Cap. $103,750
	Ott, Cap. $53,750
E12-6	c. Credit Falco, Cap. $52,500; Graham, Cap. $3,750; Ott, Cap. $3,750
E12-7	1. Echols receives $45,000;
	2. Schaeffer's equity $50,000
E12-8	b. Debit Bermuda, Cap. $46,000
E12-9	2. Barry gets $20,000; McCall gets $17,000; Flaten gets $8,000
E12-10	Pay Deluth $24,800;
	Liu $18,600; Bush $14,600
E12-11	Selling for $90,000—Valahu, Cap. $3,000; Leman, Cap. $20,800; Sucre, Cap. $(4,800)
E12-12	Total assets $276,200
	Klatt, Cap. $90,700
	Stover, Cap. $93,100
P12-1A	No check figure
P12-2A	2. Total assets $122,020
	Saran, Cap. $49,860
	Gentry, Cap. $49,860
P12-3A	Lampe's Cap.:
	2. $50,000
	3. $31,250
	4. $41,400
P12-4A	1. d. Net inc. to:
	Trump $33,667
	Rivers $28,667
	Jetta $23,666
P12-5A	No check figure
P12-6A	1. b. Pay: Jackson $20,700; Pierce $52,800; Fenner $11,500
P12-7A	3. Pay: Alberts $8,875; Beech $8,625; Sumner $11,500
P12-8A	No check figure
P12-9A	2. Total assets $100,000
	Busby, Cap. $40,450
	Box, Cap. $40,450
P12-3B	Conyers' Cap.:
	2. $60,000
	3. $95,000
	4. $42,000
P12-4B	1. d. Net inc. to:
	Lake $79,750
	Wood $63,500
	Parks $66,750
P12-5B	No check figure
P12-6B	1. b. Pay: Parr $19,700; Johnston $35,100; Rake $30,200
P12-7B	3. Pay: Vela $12,000; Thomas $7,000; Prago $3,000
Case 1	No check figure
Case 2	No check figure
Financial Statement Case	
	2. $1,997,323;
	3. Avg. net inc. per Partner $372,825

Check Figures—Chapter 13

| DE13-1 | No check figure |
| DE13-2 | No check figure |

DE13-3	No check figure
DE13-4	No check figure
DE13-5	No check figure
DE13-6	No check figure
DE13-7	1. Incr. in paid-in cap. $428 mil.
DE13-8	No check figure
DE13-9	Bldg. $480,000; Equip $220,000; Common Stock $100,000; PIC in Excess $600,000
DE13-10	Total S/E $183.9 mil.
DE13-11	a. Net inc. $80.6 mil.
	b. Total liab. $122.3 mil.
	c. Total assets $306.2 mil
DE13-12	Total S/E $490,000
DE13-13	R/E incr. $54,000
DE13-14	4. Pfd. gets $6,000
	Com. gets $3,000
DE13-15	No check figure
DE13-16	a. Book value-Pfd.$140;
	b. Book value-Com. $44.44
DE13-17	No check figure
DE13-18	No check figure
DE13-19	ROA 13.6%
	ROE 27.1%
DE13-20	2. Net inc. $72,000
	Inc. tax pay $36,000
	Deferred tax liab. $12,000
E13-1	No check figure
E13-2	2. Total PIC $118,500
E13-3	2. Total S/E $72,000
E13-4	Cap. in Excess of Par $74,850
E13-5	No check figure
E13-6	Total S/E $192,000
E13-7	Total S/E $486,000
E13-8	Total S/E $407,000
E13-9	Pfd. gets $22,000;
	Com. gets $38,000
E13-10	Pfd. A gets $40,000;
	Pfd. B gets $962,000;
	Com. gets $98,000
E13-11	Book value-Pdf. $60;
	Com. $22.08
E13-12	Book value-Pfd. $66.84;
	Com. $21.99
E13-13	ROA .091
	ROE .074
E13-14	2. Net inc. $78 mil.
	Inc. tax pay. $40 mil.
	Deferred tax liab. $12 mil.
E13-15	2. Bal. at Jan. 31, 20X0; Com. stk. $446 mil.; Cap. in Excess $714 mil.; R/E $25, 129 mil.
P13-1A	No check figure
P13-2A	2. Total S/E $308,100
P13-3A	5. Total S/E $413,000
P13-4A	Total S/E: Yurman $510,000; No. Lights $623,000
P13-5A	3. Div. Pay., Pfg. $218 mil.; Div. Pay., Com $1,408 mil.
P13-6A	1. Total assets $654,000; Total S/E $499,000
P13-7A	1. b. 20X2 Pfd. gets $3,500; Com. gets $11,500.
P13-8A	5. Book value-Pfd. $27.90; Com. $9.73
P13-9A	3. Net inc. $149,500
P13-1B	No check figure
P13-2B	2. Total S/E $273,800

P13-3B	5. Total S/E $272,000
P13-4B	Total S/E; Granada $829,000; Traigon $403,000
P13-5B	3. Div. Pay., Pfd. $18 mil.; Div. Pay., Com. $32 mil.
P13-6B	1. Total assets $417,000 Total S/E $309,000
P13-7B	1. b. 20X2 Pfd. gets $70,000; Com. gets $30,000
P13-8B	6. Book value-Pfd. $54.95; Com. $8.51
P13-9B	3. Net inc. $126,000
Case 1.	3. Total S/E: Plan 1 $435,000; Plan 2 $420,000
Case 2.	No check figure
Financial Statement Case	No check figure

Check Figures—Chapter 14

DE14-1	No check figure
DE14-2	2. Total S/E $360,00
DE14-3	No check figure
DE14-4	1. Total S/E $355,000
DE14-5	1. Total S/E $355,000
DE14-6	No check figure
DE14-7	2. Total S/E $31,600
DE14-8	2. total S/E $36,400
DE14-9	Bal. sheet reports Treasury stk ($6,000)
DE14-10	Total S/E $3,700,000
DE14-11	No check figure
DE14-12	No check figure
DE14-13	No check figure
DE14-14	2. EPS = $(1.43)
DE14-15	Net inc. $22,750
DE14-16	EPS for net inc. $1.98
DE14-17	No check figure
DE14-18	Comprehensive inc. $20,750
DE14-19	R/E Dec. 31, 20X5 $473,000
DE14-20	2. $85,000 4. Sold T/S for $17,000
E14-1	3. Total S/E $434,000
E14-2	2. Total S/E $590,000
E14-3	Total S/E $510,000
E14-4	d. Increase S/E $4,200
E14-5	No check figure
E14-6	Total S/E $770,000
E14-7	b. Total S/E $470,000
E14-8	Net inc. $34,000
E14-9	EPS = $1.38
E14-10	EPS for net inc. $3.51
E14-11	R/E Dec. 31, 20X3 $463.6 mil.
E14-12	R/E Dec. 31, 20X7 $456 mil.
E14-13	Comprehensive inc. $70,000
E14-14	Total S/E, Dec. 31, 20X2 $3,467,000
E14-15	2. Total S/E, Dec. 31, 20X5 $17,100,000
P14-1A	No check figure
P14-2A	2. Total S/E $452,100
P14-3A	No check figure
P14-4A	3. Total S/E $699,680
P14-5A	Net inc. $62,000; EPS for net inc. $2.17
P14-6A	Net inc. $78,200 R/E, Dec. 31, 20X3 $418,200 EPS for net inc. $1.56
P14-7A	1. EPS for net inc. $2.14

P14-8A	1. Par value = $2 2. Price per share = $6.23 4. Stk. Div. % = 4%
P14-1B	No check figure
P14-2B	2. Total S/E $524,000
P14-3B	No check figure
P14-4B	3. Total S/E $555,880
P14-5B	Net inc. $76,400 EPS for net inc. $3.52
P14-6B	Net inc. $101,000 R/E June 30, 20X4 $291,000 EPS for net inc. $5.05
P14-7B	1. EPS for net inc. $2.92
P14-8B	1. Par value = $1.80 2. Price per share - $11 3. Stk. div. % = 9.9%
Case 1.	No check figure
Case 2.	No check figure
Financial Statement Case	No check figure

Check Figures—Chapter 15

DE15-1	b. $615,750 c. $331,125
DE15-2	a. $4,675
DE15-3	No check figure
DE15-4	No check figure
DE15-5	No check figure
DE15-6	Jan 1, 2001 Interest Exp. $54.17
DE15-7	Jan. 1, 2001 Interest Exp. $198
DE15-8	Jan 1, 2001 Interest Exp. $153
DE15-9	Dec. 31, 2000 Interest Exp. $183
DE15-10	LT liab.: Bonds Payable, net $4,620
DE15-11	2. Bond carrying amt., Ending $573,963
DE15-12	2. a. Bonds pay., End of yr. 3 $385,734
DE15-13	2. Bond carrying amt., Ending $215,673
DE15-14	3. EO gain $7,281
DE15-15	2. PIC in Excess of Par $860,000
DE15-16	EPS; Plan A $2.14; Plan B $1.60
DE15-17	No check figure
DE15-18	Total current liab. $99,000
DE15-19	No check figure
E15-1	c. Dec. 31 Interest Exp. $3,375
E15-2	c. Dec. 31 Interest Exp. $19,562
E15-3	Total cash received $1,055,000
E15-4	b. Oct. 31, Interest Exp. $11,667
E15-5	1. Bond carrying amt., Ending $282,522
E15-6	1. Bond carrying amt., Ending $220,171
E15-7	Dec. 31, 20X5 Bond carrying amt. $500,000
E15-8	Oct. 1, 20X5 EO Loss $12,750
E15-9	2. July 21, 20X9 Bond carrying amt. $693,700
E15-10	2. Oct. 1 PIC in Excess of Par $174,000
E15-11	EPS: Plan A $8.15; Plan B $4.37
E15-12	1. LT Notes pay., net $503,000
E15-13	1. Dec. 31 Depreciation Exp. $4,731
E15-14	5. Mar. 31, 2001 Bond carrying amt. $295,717

E15-15	2. a. $295,605; b. $295,661; c. $295,717
P15-1A	2. Apr. 30, 20X5 Interest Exp. $13,333
P15-2A	1. d. May 31, 20X6 Interest Exp. $233,333 2. Interest Exp. For 20X5 $280,000
P15-3A	3. d. Feb. 28, 20X5 Interest Exp. $5,633 4. Interest Exp. for year ended Feb. 28, 20X5 $33,800
P15-4A	2. Sep. 30, Yr 3 Bond carrying amt $166,764
P15-5A	3. Convertible bonds pay., net $423,327
P15-6A	Dec. 31, 20X1 Depreciation Exp. $16,150
P15-7A	No check figure
P15-8A	Total current liab. $45,200 Total LT liab. $379,000
P15-1B	2. Jan. 31, 20X4 Interest Exp. $4,500
P15-2B	1. d. Mar. 31, 20X5 Interest Exp. $67,500 2. Interest exp. for 20X4 $180,000
P15-3B	3. d. Mar. 31, 20X7 Interest Exp. $7,900 4. Interest exp. for year ended Mar. 31, 20X7 $31,600
P15-4B	2. Sep. 30, yr. 3 bond carrying amt. $127,887
P15-5B	3. Convertible bonds pay., net $569,903
P15-6B	Dec. 31, 20X1 Depreciation Exp. $12,918
P15-7B	No check figure
P15-8B	Total current liab. $127,000 Total LT liab. $504,000
Case 1.	EPS: Plan A $6.72; Plan B $6.34; Plan C $6.60
Case 2.	No check figure
Financial Statement Case	No check figure

Check Figures—Chapter 16

DE16-1	a. $17,076 b. $44,914.50
DE16-2	No check figure
DE16-3	No check figure
DE16-4	3. Short-term investment $30,000
DE16-5	2. Jan 27, 20X2 Loss on Sale of Investments $2,260
DE16-6	2. Jan. 16, 20X7 Gain on Sale of Investments $685
DE16-7	20X7 Gain on sale $7,000
DE16-8	2. Loss on sale $100
DE16-9	2. Unrealized loss $411
DE16-10	1. Gain on Sale of Investment $300
DE16-11	3. Long-Term Equity-Method Investment Bal. $102 mil.
DE16-12	Gain on sale $8 mil.
DE16-13	No check figure
DE16-14	No check figure
DE16-15	4. Annual interest rev. $117,000
DE16-16	b. Interest Rev. $105,000; c. Interest Rev. $12,000

DE16-17	Interest Rev. $50 + 10
DE16-18	Overall foreign-currency Loss $1,000
DE16-19	Aug. 24 Foreign-currency Loss $400
DE16-20	No check figure
E16-1	2. Short-term investment $87,000
E16-2	d. Gain or Sale of Investment $1,600
E16-3	Dec. 4 Loss on Sale of Investment $250
E16-4	3. LT avail.-for-sale invest. $365,790; Unrealized loss $18,500
E16-5	No check figure
E16-6	Gain on sale $530,000
E16-7	2. LT Equity-Method Investment Bal. $172,200
E16-8	3. LT invest. In bonds $28,062
E16-9	Dec. 16 FC Loss $60 Dec. 30 FC Gain $1,200
E16-10	1. Cost $266 mil. 2. Loss on sale $7 mil.
E16-11	Dividends received $19 mil.
P16-1A	2. ST investment $130,000
P16-2A	3. LT avail.-for-sale invest. $270,100; LT Equity-method invest. $1,162,000
P16-3A	2. LT Equity-method invest. $936,000; Unrealized loss $3,100
P16-4A	2. LT invest. in bonds $742,902
P16-5A	Investment carrying amt. Dec. 31, 20X2 $388,355
P16-6A	FC loss, net $720
P16-1B	2. ST investment $221,000
P16-2B	3. LT avail.-for-sale invest. $161,200; LT Equity-method invest. $969,500
P16-3B	2. LT Equity-method invest. $1,142,800; Unrealized gain $1,675
P16-4B	2. LT invest. in bonds $410,572
P16-5B	Investment carrying amt. Dec. 31, 20X2 $488,051
P16-6B	FC loss, net $2,220
Case 1.	No check figure
Case 2.	No check figure
Financial Statement Case	No check figure

Check Figures—Chapter 17

DE17-1	No check figure
DE17-2	No check figure
DE17-3	No check figure
DE17-4	No check figure
DE17-5	No check figure
DE17-6	No check figure
DE17-7	Net cash inflow, oper. $10,000
DE17-8	Net cash outflow, invest $(30,000)
DE17-9	Net cash inflow, finan. $17,000
DE17-10	Net decrease in cash $(3,000)
DE17-11	2. Ending cash $24,000
DE17-12	a. $654,000; b. $325,000
DE17-13	a. $156,000; b. $46,000

DE17-14	a. $5,000; b. $70,000
DE17-15	a. $5,000; b. $3,000; c. $37,000
DE17-16	1. $252,000
DE17-17	No check figure
DE17-18	Net cash inflow, oper. $45,000
DE17-19	Net cash inflow, oper. $127 thou.
DE17-20	No check figure
E17-1	No check figure
E17-2	No check figure
E17-3	No check figure
E17-4	Net cash inflow, oper. $33,000
E17-5	No check figure
E17-6	1. Net cash inflow. oper. $81,000
E17-7	a. $86,000; b. $79,000
E17-8	a. $3,000; b. $16,000
E17-9	Net cash inflow, oper. $4,000
E17-10	No check figure
E17-11	1. Net cash inflow, oper. $81,000; No change in cash bal.
E17-12	Net cash inflow, oper. $33,000
E17-13	No check figure
E17-14	No check figure
P17-1A	No check figure
P17-2A	1. Net cash outflow, oper. $(46,000); July 31, 20X1 Cash bal. $52,300
P17-3A	1. Net cash inflow, oper. $70,600
P17-4A	1. Net cash inflow, oper. $70,600
P17-5A	Net cash inflow, oper. $95,000
P17-6A	1. Net cash inflow, oper. $47,500
P17-7A	1. Net cash inflow, oper. $79,700
P17-8A	1. Net cash inflow, oper. $59,400
P17-1B	No check figure
P17-2B	1. Net cash inflow, oper. $138,700; Apr. 30, 20X5 Cash bal. $79,600
P17-3B	1. Net cash inflow, oper. $76,600
P17-4B	1. Net cash inflow, oper. $76,600
P17-5B	Net cash inflow, oper. $92,200
P17-6B	1. Net cash inflow, oper. $97,600
P17-7B	1. Net cash inflow, oper. $61,400
P17-6B	1. Net cash inflow, oper. $76,100
Case 1.	1. Net cash inflow, oper. $148 thou.
Case 2.	No check figure
Financial Statement Case	2. a. $33,031 mil; b. $22,988 mil; c. $7,423 mil.
P17A-1	Transaction Totals: Panel A $1,510,200 Panel B $462,800
P17A-2	Transaction Totals: Panels A & B $93,200

Check Figures—Chapter 18

DE18-1	1999 Rev. increase 5.7%
DE18-2	No check figure
DE18-3	Trend %: Net sales 1999 160%
DE18-4	20X2 Net inc. 39.2% of sales
DE18-5	20X2 Cash 2.1% of total assets
DE18-6	No check figure
DE18-7	Nike net inc. 5.1% of Net sales
DE18-8	Nike Cash 3.8% of Total assets
DE18-9	20X1 Current ratio 3.20
DE18-10	1. Acid-test ratio 1999 1.04
DE18-11	a. 3.7 times b. 85 days

DE18-12	1. 0.65 2. 13.3 times
DE18-13	2. 0.152 3. 0.448
DE18-14	1. P/E ratio 54
DE18-15	3. 135,526,316 shares
DE18-16	Book value 1999 $4.42
DE18-17	a. $3,050 mil. b. $724
DE18-18	a. $541 mil. b. $1,330 mil.
DE18-19	1.EVA® $(2,995) mil.
E18-1	20X3 Work. Cap. decreased 16%
E18-2	Total rev. increase 23.3%; Net inc. increase 98.0%
E18-3	Trend %: Year 5 Net sales 126%; Net inc. 141%
E18-4	Total current assets 28.2% of total assets
E18-5	Net inc. 13.7% of total rev.
E18-6	c. 3.29 times e. 52 days
E18-7	Ratios for 20X2; a. 1.67; d. 4.83 times
E18-8	Ratios for 20X3; b. 0.162; c. 0.094
E18-9	Ratios for 20X4: a. 27.5; b. 0.012
E18-10	EVA® for IHOP $19 mil.
E18-11	Sales $13,259 mil; Net inc. $1,948 mil.
E18-12	Total assets $70,349 mil.; Current liab. $25,803 mil.
P18-1A	1. Trend %: Net sales 20X2 123% 2. Ret. On equity 20X2 0.197
P18-2A	1. Net inc. 15.4% of Net sales Current assets 76.1% of total assets
P18-3A	2. a. Current ratio 1.51; Debt ratio 0.58
P18-4A	1. Ratios for 20X4 b. 2.56; d. 8.36; f. 0.321
P18-5A	a. $8,198 mil; e. $2,050 mil.; i. $17,551 mil.
P18-6A	1. Bowie ratios: b. 0.85; c. 2.74 times; e. 0.502; h. 6.9
P18-1B	1. Trend %: Net sales 20X2 149%; 2. Ret. on sales 20X2 0.075
P18-2B	1. Net inc. 7.7% of Net sales; Current assets 73.4% of total assets
P18-3B	2. a. Current ratio 2.55; Debt ratio 0.50
P18-4B	1. Ratios for 20X3: b. 1.14; d. 2.81; f. 0.259
P18-5B	a. $4,009 mil.; e. $2,431 mil; i. $21,623 mil.
P18-6B	1. Eckert ratios: b. 0.64; c. 2.04 times; e. 0.150; h. 35.8
Case 1.	No check figure
Case 2.	No check figure
Financial Statement Case	1. Trend %: Rev. 1999 160%

Check Figures—Chapter 19

DE19-1	No check figure
DE19-2	No check figure
DE19-3	No check figure

DE19-4	No check figure
DE19-5	No check figure
DE19-6	No check figure
DE19-7	No check figure
DE19-8	No check figure
DE19-9	Beg. inv. $8,000
DE19-10	CGS $30,000
DE19-11	Op. income $22,000
DE19-12	CGM $50,000
DE19-13	Total manufacturing overhead $13,125
DE19-14	Direct materials used $27,700
DE19-15	No check figure
DE19-16	No check figure
DE19-17	No check figure
DE19-18	No check figure
DE19-19	Expected value of *additional* benefits $26 million
DE19-20	No check figure
DE19-21	No check figure
E19-1	No check figure
E19-2	Total inventoriable porduct costs $118
E19-3	Total inventoriable product costs $53,000
E19-4	No check figure
E19-5	Total current assets $224,000
E19-6	CGM $210,000
E19-7	NI $53,000
E19-8	Gross profit $251,000
E19-9	No check figure
E19-10	Excess of benefits over costs $96,300
E19-11	No check figure
E19-12	Ending finished goods inventory $4,100
P19-1A	Total inventoriable product costs $8,685
P19-2A	Paradise Manufacturing cost of goods manufactured $86,350
P19-3A	Manufacturing overhead $38,000
P19-4A	Expected value of the benefits exceeds cost by $74,483
P19-5A	No check figure
P19-4A	Expected value of the benefits exceeds cost by $74,483
P19-5A	No check figure
P19-6A	Present value of costs exceeds present value of benefits by $8,400
P19-7A	Req. 1 Expected value of benefit from additional business is $57,300
P19-8A	No check figure
P19-1B	Total inventoriable product costs $36,220
P19-2B	CoverUp Manufacturing cost of goods manufactured $63,760
P19-3B	Beginning materials inventory $31,000
P19-4B	Expected value of the benefits exceeds cost by $32,914
P19-5B	No check figure
P19-6B	Present value of benefits exceed present value of costs by $220,000
P19-7B	Req. 1 expected value of benefits is $1,112,000

P19-8B	No check figure
Case 1.	Ending material inventory $133,000
Case 2.	No check figure
Ethical Issue	No check figure
Financial Statement Case	No check figure
Team Project	No check figure

Check Figures—Chapter 20

DE20-1	No check figure
DE20-2	No check figure
DE20-3	Cost per gallon, $2.24
DE20-4	No check figure
DE20-5	Ending bal., $270
DE20-6	Ending bal., $1,080
DE20-7	Ending bal., $35,980
DE20-8	Indirect materials, $32
DE20-9	No check figure
DE20-10	Indirect labor $10,000
DE20-11	3. $3,000 underallocated
DE20-12	Bal., $49,000
DE20-13	Predetermined MOH rate, $55
DE20-14	Total cost $7,061
DE20-15	MOH Allocated $360
DE20-16	Ending bal. Materials Inventory $0
DE20-17	1. 70%
DE20-18	No check fig.
DE20-19	1. $60 per hour
DE20-20	1. $37.50 per hour
E20-1	No check figure
E20-2	CGS $25,200
E20-3	No check figure
E20-4	No check figure
E20-5	1. Ending bal. $6,000
E20-6	3. MOH is $700 overallocated
E20-7	3. MOH is $40,000 overallocated
E20-8	3. Adjusted CGS $680,000
E20-9	2. Total predicted cost $50,820
E20-10	1. 17,500 machine hours
P20-1A	1. December FGI $2,100 4. GP for Job 4 $200
P20-2A	2. FGI $74,020 5. GP House 304, $60,300
P20-3A	1. Total job cost $2,734
P20-4A	3. $29,275 underallocated
P20-5A	2. FGI $25,514 4. CGM $70-505
P20-6A	2. Planet Foods $96,200 3. Deception Fragrances $3,750
P20-1B	1. March FGI $1,300 4. GP for Job 5 $1,800
P20-2B	2. FGI $70,500 5. GP House 13 $26,910
P20-3B	1. Total job cost $2,989
P20-4B	3. $30,000 underallocated
P20-5B	2. FGI $72,014 5. Operating income $58,746
P20-6B	3. Fee charged to Malaysia $3,675
Case 1.	No check figure
Case 2.	No check figure
Ethical Issue	No check figure
Team Project	No check figure

Check Figures—Chapter 21

DE21-1	No check figure
DE21-2	No check figure
DE21-3	2c. $26

DE21-4	No check figure
DE21-5	1. cc $24,000
DE21-6	No check figure
DE21-7	2,150 full-time equivalent faculty
DE21-8	2. CCEU 96,000
DE21-9	CCEU 44,000
DE21-10	2. 40,000
DE21-11	CC per EU $2
DE21-12	CC per EU $0.25
DE21-13	1. $60,000
DE21-14	No check figure
DE21-15	73,000 liters started and completed
DE21-16	CC EU 80,300
DE21-17	CC per EU $0.35
DE21-18	Total cost transferred out $97,420
DE21-19	2. Ending Bal. $6,965
DE21-20	2. CC EU 81,900
DE21-21	CC per EU $0.348
DE21-22	Ending WIP $6,745
DE21-23	2. Ending Bal. $6,745
DE21-24	No check figure
E21-1	No check figure
E21-2	No check figure
E21-3	3b. Ending WIP $1,035
E21-4	3. Average cost per gallon transferred out $0.90
E21-5	5. Ending WIP $5,700
E21-6	3b. Ending WIP $2,624.50
E21-7	3. Average cost per gallon transferred out $2.05
E21-8	Transferred to Finishing $464,400
E21-9	53,800 Equivalent units of direct materials
E21-10	2. 67,000 Equivalent units of conversion costs in Mixing
E21-11	83,000EU of DM
E21-12	3. Ending WIP $79,200
E21-14	4. Ending WIP 5,000 units
P21-1A	Ending WIP $49,972
P21-2A	Ending WIP $2,618
P21-3A	Ending WIP $737
P21-4A	Ending WIP $18,225
P21-5A	No check figure
P21-6A	Ending WIP $500,000
P21-7A	Ending WIP $447,000
P21-1B	Ending WIP $1,890
P21-2B	Ending WIP $7,868
P21-3B	Ending WIP $3,107
P21-4B	Ending WIP $31,500
P21-5B	No check figure
P21-6B	Ending WIP $3,648
P21-7B	Ending WIP $3,078
Case 1.	3. $900
Case 2.	2. $0.60
Ethical Issue	No check figure
Team Project	Equivalent units of conversion costs in: Cooking 128,500 Cutting 128,400

Check Figures—Chapter 22

DE22-1	No check figure
DE22-2	No check figure
DE22-3	b. $21
DE22-4	CM $62,500
DE22-5	No check figure

DE22-6	$480,000
DE22-7	CM $210,000
DE22-8	CM $325,000
DE22-9	Breakeven point 6,250 tickets
DE22-10	Breakeven sales revenue $343,751 (rounded)
DE22-11	1. Breakeven sales dollars $357,150 (rounded)
DE22-12	1. Breakeven sales dollars $275,000 (rounded)
DE22-13	Required ticket sales 7,000
DE22-14	No check figure
DE22-15	Margin of safety: a. 750 round trips
DE22-16	No check figure
DE22-17	Margin of safety: a. 400 posters
DE22-18	Weighted-average CM per unit $16.66667 (rounded)
DE22-19	a. Breakeven in total units 420 posters
DE22-20	Weighted-average contribution margin per unit $62.50
DE22-21	Breakeven point: 2,500 Coach tickets 1,500 Chief tickets
DE22-22	CM $198,000
DE22-23	GP $168,000
DE22-24	No check figure
E22-1	No check figure
E22-2	Operating income $138,000
E22-3	Breakeven sales $300,000
E22-4	2. Breakeven is 70,000 units
E22-5	1. Breakeven sales $11,000
E22-6	1. Breakeven sales $700,000
E22-7	3. Breakeven sales $50,000
E22-8	Breakeven point 1,500,000 tickets
E22-9	2. margin of safety 55%
E22-10	Breakeven point: 660 standard sweatshirts 440 fancy sweatshirts
E22-11	Absorption costing income $1,025,000 Variable costing income $725,000
E22-12	Weighted-average contribution margin per unit $100
P22-1A	No check figure
P22-2A	Contribution Margin Ratio: E: 0.550 G: 0.491
P22-3A	2. Breakeven point 50 cruises 4. Operating income $39,600
P22-4A	3. Operating loss ($39,000) 4. Breakeven point 93,600 T-shirts
P22-5A	2. Target sales $15,000 4. Breakeven point 20 tickets
P22-6A	2. Margin of Safety $135,000 3. Operating income after sales increase $116,250
P22-7A	November operating income: Absorption $28,900 Variable $29,400
P22-1B	No check figure
P22-2B	Contribution margin ratio: P: 0.70 R: 0.60
P22-3B	2. Breakeven point 45 cruises 4. Operating income $225,500
P22-4B	3. Operating income $332,000 4. Breakeven sales $2,905,000

P22-5B	2. Target Sales $14,500 4. Breakeven point 15 tickets
P22-6B	2. Margin of Safety $33,270 3. Operating income after sales increase $6,750
P22-7B	February operating income: Absorption $2.240 Variable $2,300
Case 1.	1. Breakeven for: Children's meals 41,200 Adults' meals 20,600
Case 2.	No check figure
Ethical Issue	No check figure
Financial Statement Case	2. Contribution margin $5,689 million
Team Project	Absorption costing operating income $1.4 million

Check Figures—Chapter 23

DE23-1	No check figure
DE23-2	No check figure
DE23-3	No check figure
DE23-4	January sales, $705,000
DE23-5	February purchases, $686,400
DE23-6	April-July total, $264,000
DE23-7	April purchases, $46,100
DE23-8	May cash collections, $59,000
DE23-9	April total cash payments for purchases, $40,800
DE23-10	February cash collections, $848,171.25
DE23-11	Cash deficiency, $50,695
DE23-12	June interest expense, $112.50
DE23-13	No check figure
DE23-14	No check figure
DE23-15	No check figure
DE23-16	No check figure
DE23-17	No check figure
DE23-18	No check figure
DE23-19	Software department, $150,000
DE23-20	No check figure
E23-1	Income is $14,000 higher this year.
E23-2	Third-Quarter purchases, $86,450
E23-3	Net income for the year, $2,330,144.
E23-4	a. Cash receipt from sale of equipment, $7,000
E23-5	2. Cash borrowed in November, $6,000
E23-6	Ending Owners' Equity Balance, $25,300
E23-7	No check figure
E23-8	Operating Income Variance for books, $81,000 U
E23-9	2. Welding Total Indirect expense, $25,250
E23-10	Plastic Operating Income, $55,200
E23-11	March Interest Expense, $66
P23-1A	August Net Income, $27,000
P23-2A	September ending cash balance, $66,750
P23-3A	Ending Cash Balance, $24,150
P23-4A	Ending cash balance before financing, $11,150
P23-5A	No check figure
P23-6A	Kansas Operating Income Variance, $62,400 F

P23-7A	Copy Services Operating Income, $15,410
P23-1B	June Net Income, $6,400
P23-2B	June ending cash balance, $22,610
P23-3B	3. Cash available for equipment purchases, $68,900
P23-4B	Ending cash balance, $24,200
P23-5B	No check figure
P23-6B	Cincinnati office operating income variance, $7,500 U
P23-7B	Group Travel Operating Income, $54,770
Case 1.	Total cost per wakeboard, $210
Case 2.	No check figure
Ethical Issue	No check figure
Financial Statement Case	3. Mervyn's 1998 return on assets, 0.1034
Team Project	No check figure

Check Figures—Chapter 24

DE24-1	29. 20-installation operating income, $16,000
DE24-2	1. 3-pool operating loss, $8,000
DE24-3	No check figure
DE24-4	3. May flexible budget total cost, $92,000
DE24-5	Jan. FBV, $3,250 F
DE24-6	Operating income sales volume variance, $4,000 F
DE24-7	Op. Inc. SW, $6,000 F
DE24-8	No check figure
DE24-9	No check figure
DE24-10	No check figure
DE24-11	No check figure
DE24-12	Material price variance, $6,600 U
DE24-13	Total direct material efficiency variance, $6.10 U
DE24-14	DLEV, $39,000 U
DE24-15	No check figure
DE24-16	VMOHR, $6
DE24-17	PW, $4,000 F
DE24-18	No check figure
DE24-19	No check figure
DE24-20	No check figure
DE24-21	Op. inc. $69,900
E24-1	40,000-level op. inc. $40,000
E24-2	No check figure
E24-3	Op. inc. FBV, $9,000 U
E24-4	Op. inc. FBV, $193,000 F
E24-5	FBV, $3,400 U
E24-6	DMEV, $255,000 U
E24-7	No check figure
E24-8	No check figure
E24-9	Overhead flexible budget variance, $200 U
E24-10	Gross Pprofit, $206,500
E24-11	Capacity level, 5,000 units
P24-1A	11,000-unit operating income, $54,825
P24-2A	Total expenses flexible budget variance, $4,225 U
P24-3A	Production volume variance, $675 U
P24-4A	DEV, $1,000 F

P24-5A	1. Materials price variance $3,843 F
	3. Overhead flexible budget variance, $3,714 U
P24-6A	Labor price variance, $312 U
P24-1B	65,000-unit operating income, $71,050
P24-2B	Operating income flexible budget variance, $1,000 F
P24-3B	Total overhead variance, $50,890 F
P24-4B	Actual direct labor hours, 3,280
P24-5B	1. Materials price variance, $5,508 U
	3. Overhead flexible budget
P24-6B	2. MOH flexible budget variance, $3,900 F
	3. Gross profit, $130,900
Case 1.	Flexible budget variance, $43,025 F
Case 2.	Direct labor efficiency variance, $108 U
Ethical Issue	No check figure
Team Project	No check figure

Check Figures—Chapter 25

DE25-1	No check figure
DE25-2	No check figure
DE25-3	No check figure
DE25-4	Total PH overhead, $112.50
DE25-5	Total PH set-up costs, $90
DE25-6	Set-up costs per lb. of PH, $18
DE25-7	Aldehyde GP $1.60
DE25-8	Full Product cost, $7.60/lb.
DE25-9	Target cost, $225/ream
DE25-10	Lee operating income, $3,600
DE25-11	No check figure
DE25-12	No check figure
DE25-13	Information technology, $400/application
DE25-14	Wilner operating income, $6,280
DE25-15	No check figure
DE25-16	No check figure
DE25-17	No check figure
DE25-18	No check figure
DE25-19	No check figure
DE25-20	No check figure
DE25-21	Total cost of implementing program, $1,900,000
E25-1	Indirect cost per wheel, $52.40
E25-2	Deluxe model ABC Cost, $111.15
E25-3	No check figure
E25-4	Cost of deluxe wheel, $159.15
E25-5	No check figure

E25-6	Conversion cost is $450,000 overallocated
E25-7	Ending balance FG, $308,000
E25-8	No check figure
E25-9	No check figure
E25-10	Total Cost of implementing program, $170,000
E25-11	Job 204 used 750 parts
P25-1A	Manufacturing Product Cost, $132.40
P25-2A	4. Sale price, $56.20
P25-3A	2. Commercial container ABC unit cost, $88
P25-4A	3. Indirect cost, $1.52/unit
P25-5A	3. 10/31 Raw and In Process balance, $9,000
P25-6A	2. Net benefit, $8,000
P25-1B	Manufacturing Product Cost, $85.60
P25-2B	4. Sale price, $109
P25-3B	2. Bullseye! ABC unit cost $299,000
P25-4B	3. Indirect activity cost per unit, $20.30.
P25-5B	3. 8/31 Raw and In Process bal., $2,500
P25-6B	2. Net benefit, $44,500
Case 1.	Job A ABC cost per unit, $5,057.50
Case 2.	Required cost savings in assembling, $600
Ethical Issue	No check figure
Team Projects: Project 1.	Indirect cost per standard service customer: Original cost system, $360 ABC cost system, $199.33 (rounded)
Project 2.	No check figure

Check Figures—Chapter 26

DE26-1	No check figure
DE26-2	Decrease in income, $3,000
DE26-3	Increase in income, $320,000
DE26-4	No check figure
DE26-5	No check figure
DE26-6	No check figure
DE26-7	Decrease in income, $25,000
DE26-8	Increase in income, $5,000
DE26-9	Deluxe CM per unit, $305
DE26-10	Advantage to outsourcing, $20,500 per year
DE26-11	No check figure
DE26-12	Advantage to making filter, $25,000
DE26-13	Advantage to buying filters, $3,000

DE26-14	Advantage to processing further, $9,000
DE26-15	Minimum sales price, $25 per key
DE26-16	Opportunity cost of shirts, $480,000
DE26-17	Annual cash savings, $3,750
DE26-18	Annual net cash inflow, $2,400,000
DE26-19	Payback, 5.42 years
DE26-20	ARR, 22.9%
DE26-21	NPV, $3,529,400
DE26-22	IRR, 16%
DE26-23	No check figure
E26-1	2. Decrease in income, $15,000
E26-2	Decrease in income, $90,000
E26-3	Decrease in income, $25,000
E26-4	Total CM at capacity, Moderate, $36,400
E26-5	Advantage to making, $1.50/unit
E26-6	Advantage to buy and use facilities for other project, $15,000
E26-7	Advantage to further processing, $350
E26-8	Payback, 3 years
E26-9	Payback, 5.6 years
E26-10	Accounting rate of return, Veras Products, 35%
E26-11	NPV of project B, ($8.760)
E26-12	IRR of project A, 14-16%
E26-13	1. Coca-Cola in 12 oz. cans
P26-1A	1. Increase in income, $1,000
P26-2A	1. Decrease in income, $8,500
P26-3A	Total CM at capacity, patio sets, $7,800
P26-4A	1. Advantage to making, $20,000
P26-5A	3. Advantage to processing further, $30,000
P26-6A	NPV, ($774,450)
P26-7A	Plan A's NPV ($121,280)
P26-1B	1. Increase in income, $24,000
P26-2B	1. Decrease in income, $159,000
P26-3B	1. Total CM at capacity, Deluxe, $1,540,000
P26-4B	1. Advantage to making, $264
P26-5B	3. Advantage to selling as is, $16,310
P26-6B	NPV, $65,980
P26-7B	3.Plan A's IRR, about 12%
Case 1.	2. Advantage to outsourcing, $8 per mailbox
Case 2.	NPV, $9,245
Ethical Issue/Financial Statement Case	1.EPS, $2.70
Team Project	2. Annual cost savings from making, $7,872,000 3c. NPV, $3,349,824

Glossary

Absorption Costing. The costing method that assigns both variable and fixed manufacturing costs to products.

Accelerated Depreciation Method. A depreciation method that writes off more of the asset's cost near the start of its useful life than the straight-line method does.

Account. The detailed record of the changes that have occurred in a particular asset, liability, or owner's equity during a period. The basic summary device of accounting.

Account Payable. A liability backed by the general reputation and credit standing of the debtor.

Account Receivable. A promise to receive cash from customers to whom the business has sold goods or for whom the business has performed services.

Accounting. The information system that measures business activities, processes that information into reports, and communicates the results to decision makers.

Accounting Equation. The basic tool of accounting, presenting the resources of the business and the claims to those resources: Assets = Liabilities + Owner's Equity.

Accounting Information System. The combination of personnel, records, and procedures that a business uses to provide financial data.

Accounting Rate of Return. A measure of profitability computed by dividing the average annual operating income from an asset by the average amount invested in the asset.

Accounts Receivable Turnover. Ratio of net credit sales to average net accounts receivable. Measures ability to collect cash from customers.

Accrual-Basis Accounting. Accounting that records the impact of a business event as it occurs, regardless of whether the transaction affected cash.

Accrued Expense. An expense that the business has not yet paid. Also called accrued liability.

Accrued Revenue. A revenue that has been earned but not yet collected in cash.

Accumulated Depreciation. The cumulative sum of all depreciation expense recorded for an asset.

Acid-Test Ratio. Ratio of the sum of cash plus short-term investments plus net current receivables to total current liabilities. Tells whether the entity could pay all its current liabilities if they came due immediately. Also called the **quick ratio**.

Activity-Based Costing (ABC). A system that focuses on activities as the fundamental cost objects. The costs of those activities become building blocks for compiling costs as ABC links costs to the activities that cause those costs.

Activity-Based Management. Using activity-based cost information to make decisions that increase profits while satisfying customers' needs.

Additional Paid-in Capital. The paid-in capital in excess of par—common plus other accounts combined for reporting on the balance sheet.

Adjusted Trial Balance. A list of all the ledger accounts with their adjusted balances.

Adjusting Entry. Entry made at the end of the period to assign revenues to the period in which they are earned and expenses to the period in which they are incurred. Adjusting entries help measure the period's income and bring the related asset and liability accounts to correct balances for the financial statements.

Aging-of-Accounts Method. A way to estimate bad debts by analyzing individual accounts receivable according to the length of time they have been receivable from the customer. Also called the **balance-sheet approach**.

Allocation Base. A common denominator that links indirect costs to cost objects. Ideally, the allocation base is the primary cost driver that causes the indirect cost to be incurred.

Allowance for Uncollectible Accounts. A contra account, related to accounts receivable, that holds the estimated amount of collection losses. Also called **Allowance for Doubtful Accounts**.

Allowance Method. A method of recording collection losses on the basis of estimates, instead of waiting to see which customers the company will not collect from.

Amortization. The systematic reduction of the asset's carrying value on the books. Expense that applies to intangibles in the same way depreciation applies to plant assets and depletion applies to natural resources.

Annuity. A stream of equal periodic cash flows.

Appraisal Costs. Costs incurred to detect poor-quality goods or services.

Appropriation of Retained Earnings. Restriction of retained earnings that is recorded by a formal journal entry.

Asset. An economic resource that is expected to be of benefit in the future.

Audit. An examination of a company's financial statements and the accounting system.

Authorization of Stock. Provision in a corporate charter that gives the state's permission for the corporation to issue—that is, to sell—a certain number of shares of stock.

Available-for-Sale Investments. Stock investments other than trading securities in which the investor cannot exercise significant influence over the investee.

Balance Sheet. List of an entity's assets, liabilities, and owner's equity as of a specific date. Also called the **statement of financial position**.

Bank Collection. Collection of money by the bank on behalf of a depositor.

Bank Reconciliation. Document explaining the reasons for the difference between a depositor's cash records and the depositor's cash balance in its bank account.

Bank Statement. Document the bank uses to report what it did with the depositor's cash. Shows the bank account's beginning and ending balances and lists the month's cash transactions conducted through the bank.

Batch Processing. Computerized accounting for similar transactions in a group or batch.

Benchmarking. The practice of comparing a company to a standard set by other companies, with a view toward improvement.

Board of Directors. Group elected by the stockholders to set policy and to appoint the officers.

Bonds Payable. Groups of notes payable (bonds) issued to multiple lenders called bondholders.

Book Value. Amount of owners' equity on the company's books for each share of its stock.

Book Value (of a Plant Asset). The asset's cost minus accumulated depreciation.

Book Value Per Share of Common Stock. Common equity divided by the number of shares of common stock outstanding.

Breakeven Point. The sales level at which operating income is zero: Total revenues equal total expenses.

Budget. A quantitative expression of a plan that helps managers coordinate the entity's activities.

Bylaws. Constitution for governing a corporation.

Callable Bonds. Bonds that the issuer may call or pay off at a specified price whenever the issuer wants.

Capital Budgeting. A formal means of analyzing long-term investment decisions. Describes budgeting for the acquisition of capital assets.

Capital Charge. The amount that stockholders and lenders charge a company for the use of their money.

Capital Expenditure. Expenditure that increases the capacity or efficiency of an asset or extends its useful life. Capital expendtures are debited to an asset account.

Capital Expenditures Budget. A company's plan for purchases of property, plant, equipment, and other long-term assets.

Capital Lease. Lease agreement that meets any one of four criteria: (1) The lease transfers title of the leased asset to the lessee. (2) The lease contains a bargain purchase option. (3) The lease term is 75% or more of the estimated useful life of the leased asset. (4) The present value of the lease payments is 90% or more of the market value of the leased asset.

Capitalize a Cost. To record a cost as part of an asset's cost, rather than as an expense.

Cash-Basis Accounting. Accounting that records transactions only when cash is received or paid.

Cash Budget. Details how the business expects to go from the beginning cash balance to the desired ending balance. Also called the **statement of budgeted cash receipts and payments**.

Cash Equivalents. Liquid short-term investments that can be converted into cash at will.

Cash Flows. Cash receipts and cash payments (disbursements).

Cash Payments Journal. Special journal used to record cash payments by check. Also called the **check register** or **cash disbursements journal**.

Cash Receipts Journal. Special journal used to record cash receipts.

Certified Management Accountant (CMA). A licensed accountant who works for a single company.

Certified Public Accountant (CPA). A licensed accountant who serves the general public rather than one particular company.

Chairperson. Elected by a corporation's board of directors, the most powerful person in the corporation.

Chart of Accounts. List of all the accounts and their account numbers in the ledger.

Charter. Document that gives the state's permission to form a corporation.

Check. Document that instructs a bank to pay the designated person or business a specified amount of money.

Closing Entries. Entries that transfer the revenue, expense, and owner withdrawal balances from these respective accounts to the capital account.

Closing the Accounts. Step in the accounting cycle at the end of the period. Closing the accounts consists of journalizing and posting the closing entries to set the balances of the revenue, expense, and withdrawal accounts to zero for the next period.

Common-Size Statement. A financial statement that reports only percentages (no dollar amounts); a type of vertical analysis.

Common Stock. The basic form of capital stock. In a corporation, the common stockholders are the owners of the business.

Comprehensive Income. Company's change in total stockholders' equity from all sources other than from the owners.

Computer Virus. A malicious program that (a) reproduces itself, (b) gets included in program code without consent, and (c) performs actions that can be destructive.

Conservatism. Reporting the least favorable figures in the financial statements.

Consignment. Transfer of goods by the owner (consignor) to another business (consignee) that sells the inventory on the owner's behalf. The consignee does not take title to the consigned goods.

Consistency Principle. A business should use the same accounting methods and procedures from period to period.

Consolidated Statements. Financial statements of the parent company plus those of majority-owned subsidiaries as if the combination were a single legal entity.

Constraint. A factor that restricts production or sale of a product.

Contingent Liability. A potential liability that will become an actual liability only if a particular event does occur.

Continuous Improvement. A philosophy requiring employees to continually look for ways to improve performance.

Contra Account. An account that always has a companion account and whose normal balance is opposite that of the companion account.

Contract Interest Rate. Interest rate that determines the amount of cash interest the borrower pays and the investor receives each year. Also called the **stated interest rate**.

Contribution Margin Income Statement. Income statement that groups variable and fixed expenses separately, and highlights the contribution margin.

Contribution Margin per Unit. Excess of the sales revenue per unit (sale price) over the variable expense per unit.

Contribution Margin Ratio. The ratio of contribution margin to sales revenue.

Contribution Margin. Sales revenue minus all variable expenses. Also called **sales revenue per unit (sale price) minus variable expense per unit.**

Control Account. An account whose balance equals the sum of the balances in a group of related accounts in a subsidiary ledger.

Controller. The chief accounting officer of a company.

Controlling. Evaluating the results of business operations by comparing the actual results to the plan.

Controlling Interest. Ownership of more than 50% of an investee company's voting stock. Also called **majority interest.**

Conversion Costs. Direct labor plus manufacturing overhead.

Convertible Bonds. Bonds (or notes payable) that may be converted into the common stock of the issuing company at the option of the investor.

Copyright. Exclusive right to reproduce and sell a book, musical composition, film, other work of art, or computer program. Issued by the federal government, copyrights extend 50 years beyond the author's life.

Corporation. A business owned by stockholders; it begins when the state approves its articles of incorporation. A corporation is a legal entity, an "artificial person," in the eyes of the law.

Cost Allocation. Assigning indirect costs (such as manufacturing overhead) to cost objects (such as jobs or production processes).

Cost Assignment. Tracing direct costs to cost objects and allocating indirect costs to cost objects.

Cost Behavior. Describes how costs change as a cost driver changes.

Cost Driver. The primary factor that causes costs.

Cost Object. Anything for which managers want a separate measurement of costs.

Cost of Capital. A weighted average of the returns demanded by a company's stockholders and lenders.

Cost of Goods Available for Sale Beginning inventory plus purchases.

Cost of Goods Manufactured. The (manufacturing) cost of the goods that were finished—that is, the plant-related cost of the units that completed the production process this period.

Cost of Goods Sold. The cost of the inventory that the business has sold to customers. Also called **cost of sales.**

Cost Tracing. Assigning direct costs (such as direct materials and direct labor) to cost objects (such as jobs or production processes).

Cost-Benefit Analysis. Weighing costs against benefits to help make decisions.

Cost-Volume-Profit (CVP) Analysis. Expresses the relationships among costs, volume, and profit or loss.

Credit. The right side of an account.

Credit Memorandum or Credit Memo. A document issued by a seller to credit a customer account for returned merchandise.

Creditor. The party to a credit transaction who sells goods or a service and obtains a receivable.

Cumulative Preferred Stock. Preferred stock whose owners must receive all dividends in arrears before the corporation pays dividends to the common stockholders.

Current Asset. An asset that is expected to be converted to cash, sold, or consumed during the next 12 months, or within the business's normal operating cycle.

Current Liability. A debt due to be paid with cash or with goods and services within one year or within the entity's operating cycle if the cycle is longer than a year.

Current Portion of Long-Term Debt. Amount of the principal that is payable within one year. Also called **current maturity.**

Current Ratio. Total current assets divided by total current liabilities. Measures the ability to pay current liabilities from current assets.

Customer Service. Support provided for customers after the sale.

Database. A computerized storehouse of information.

Days' Sales in Receivables. Ratio of average net accounts receivable to one day's sales. Tells how many days' sales it takes to collect the average level of receivables. Also called the **collection period.**

Debentures. Unsecured bonds backed only by the good faith of the borrower.

Debit. The left side of an account.

Debit Memorandum or Debit Memo. A document issued by a buyer when returning merchandise. The memo informs the seller that the buyer no longer owes the seller for the amount of the returned purchases.

Debt Ratio. Ratio of total liabilities to total assets. Tells the proportion of a company's assets that it has financed with debt.

Debtor. The party to a credit transaction who makes a purchase and has a payable.

Deficit. Debit balance in the Retained Earnings account.

Depletion Expense. The portion of a natural resource's cost used up in a particular period. Depletion expense is computed in the same way as units-of-production depreciation.

Deposit in Transit. A deposit recorded by the company but not yet by its bank.

Depreciable Cost. The cost of a plant asset minus its estimated residual value.

Depreciation. The allocation of a plant asset's cost to expense over its useful life.

Design. Detailed engineering of products and services, or processes for producing them.

Direct Cost. A cost that can be specifically traced to a cost object.

Direct Labor. The compensation of employees who physically convert materials into the company's products; labor costs that are directly traceable to finished products.

Direct Materials. Materials that become a physical part of a finished product and whose costs are separately and conveniently traceable to the finished product.

Direct Method. Format of the operating activities section of the statement of cash flows that lists the major categories of operating cash receipts (collections from customers and receipts of interest and dividends) and cash payments (payments to suppliers, to employees, for interest and income taxes).

Direct Write-off Method. A method of accounting for uncollectible receivables, in which the company waits until the credit department decides that a customer's account receivable is uncollectible, and then debits Uncollectible-Account Expense and credits the customer's Account Receivable.

Disclosure Principle. A business's financial statements must report enough information for outsiders to make knowledgeable decisions about the company.

Discount (on a Bond). Excess of a bond's maturity (par value) over its issue price. Also called a **bond discount.**

Discount Rate. Management's minimum desired rate of return on an investment. Also called the **hurdle rate, required rate of return,** and **cost of capital**.

Discounting a Note Payable. A borrowing arrangement in which the bank subtracts the interest amount from a note's face value. The borrower receives the net amount.

Discounting Note Receivable. Selling a note receivable before its maturity date.

Dishonor of a Note. Failure of a note's maker to pay a note receivable at maturity. Also called **default on a note**.

Dissolution. Ending of a partnership.

Distribution. Delivery of products or services to customers.

Dividend Yield. Ratio of dividends per share of stock to the stock's market price. Measures the percentage of the stock's market value that the company pays to stockholders as dividends.

Dividends. Distributions by a corporation to its stockholders.

Double Taxation. Corporations pay their own income taxes on cor-porate income. Then, the stock-holders pay personal income tax on the cash dividends they receive from corporations.

Double-Declining-Balance (DDB) Depreciation Method. An accelerated depreciation method that computes annual depreciation by multiplying the asset's decreasing book value by a constant percent that is 2 times the straight-line rate.

Earnings Per Share (EPS). Amount of a company's net income per share of its outstanding common stock.

Economic Value Added (EVA®). Combines accounting income and finance to measure whether the company's operations have increased stockholder wealth.

Efficiency Variance. Measures whether the quantity of materials or labor used to make the actual number of outputs is within the standard allowed for that number of outputs. This is computed as the difference in quantities (actual quantity of input used minus standard quantity of input allowed for the actual number of outputs), multiplied by the standard price per unit of the input.

Efficient Capital Market. A capital market in which market prices reflect the impact of all information available to the public.

Electronic Funds Transfer (EFT). System that transfers cash by electronic communication rather than by paper documents.

Encryption. Rearranging plain-text messages by a mathematical process; the primary method of achieving confidentiality in e-commerce.

Entity. An organization or a section of an organization that, for accounting purposes, stands apart from other organizations and individuals as a separate economic unit.

Equity Method. The method used to account for investments in which the investor has 20–50% of the investee's voting stock and can significantly influence the decisions of the investee.

Equivalent Units. A measure of the amount of work done during a period, expressed in terms of fully complete units of output.

Estimated Residual Value. Expected cash value of an asset at the end of its useful life. Also called **scrap value,** or **salvage value**.

Estimated Useful Life. Length of the service period expected from an asset. May be expressed in years, units of output, miles, or another measure.

Expense. Decrease in owner's equity that occurs from using assets or increasing liabilities in the

course of delivering goods or services to customers.

External Failure Costs. Costs incurred when the company does not detect poor-quality goods or services until after delivery to customers.

Extraordinary gains and losses. A gain or loss that is both unusual for the company and infrequent. Also called **extraordinary items**.

Financial Accounting. The branch of accounting that focuses on information for people outside the firm.

Financial Accounting Standards Board (FASB). The private organization that determines how accounting is practiced in the United States.

Financial Budget. Projects cash inflows and outflows, the period-ending balance sheet, and the statement of cash flows.

Financial Statements. Documents that report on a business in monetary amounts, providing information to help people make informed business decisions.

Financing Activity. Activity that obtains the funds from investors and creditors needed to launch and sustain the business; a section of the statement of cash flows.

Finished Goods Inventory. Com-pleted goods that have not yet been sold.

Firewalls. Devices that enable members of a local network to access the Internet but keep nonmembers out of the network.

First-In, First-Out (FIFO) Inventory Costing Method. Inventory costing method by which the first costs into inventory are the first costs out to cost of goods sold. Ending inventory is based on the costs of the most recent purchases.

First-In, First-Out (FIFO) Process Costing Method. A process costing method that assigns to each period's equivalent units of production that period's costs per equivalent unit.

Fixed Cost. Cost that does not change in total despite wide changes in volume.

Flexible Budget. A summarized budget that can easily be computed for several different volume levels. Flexible budgets separate variable costs from fixed costs; it is the variable costs that put the "flex" in the flexible budget.

Flexible Budget Variance. The difference arising because the company actually earned more or less revenue, or incurred more or less cost, than expected for the actual level of output. This is computed as the difference between the actual amount and a flexible budget amount.

Foreign-Currency Exchange Rate. The measure of one currency against another currency.

Franchises, Licenses. Privileges granted by a private business or a government to sell a product or service under specified conditions.

Full Product Costs. The costs of all resources used throughout the value chain for a product.

General Journal. Journal used to record all transactions that do not fit one of the special journals.

General Ledger. Ledger of accounts that are reported in the financial statements.

General Partnership. A form of partnership in which each partner is an owner of the business, with all the privileges and risks of ownership.

Generally Accepted Accounting Principles (GAAP). Accounting guidelines, formulated by the Financial Accounting Standards Board, that govern how accountants measure, process, and communicate financial information.

Goodwill. Excess of the cost of an acquired company over the sum of the market values of its net assets (assets minus liabilities).

Gross Pay. Total amount of salary, wages, commissions, or any other employee compensation before taxes and other deductions.

Gross Profit. Excess of net sales revenue over cost of goods sold. Also called **gross margin**.

Gross Profit Method. A way to estimate inventory on the basis of the cost-of-goods-sold model: Beginning inventory + Net purchases = Cost of goods available for sale. Cost of goods available for sale − Cost of goods sold = Ending inventory. Also called the **gross margin method**.

Gross Profit or Gross Margin. Excess of sales revenue over cost of goods sold.

Gross Profit Percentage. Gross profit divided by net sales revenue. A measure of profitability. Also called **gross margin percentage**.

Hardware. Electronic equipment that includes computers, disk drives, monitors, printers, and the network that connects them.

Hedging. Protecting oneself from losing money in one transaction by engaging in a counterbalancing transaction.

Held-to-Maturity Investments. Investment in bonds, notes, and other debt securities that the investor expects to hold until their maturity date.

Horizontal Analysis. Study of percentage changes in comparative financial statements.

Imprest System. A way to account for petty cash by maintaining a constant balance in the petty cash account, supported by the fund (cash plus payment tickets) totaling the same amount.

Income Statement. Summary of an entity's revenues, expenses, and net income or net loss for a specific period. Also called the **statement of earnings** or the **statement of operations**.

Income Summary. A temporary "holding tank" account into which revenues and expenses are transferred prior to their final transfer to the capital account.

Indirect Cost. A cost that cannot be specifically traced to a cost object.

Indirect Labor. Labor costs that are difficult to trace to specific products.

Indirect Materials. Materials whose costs cannot conveniently be directly traced to particular finished products.

Indirect Method. Format of the operating activities section of the statement of cash flows that starts with net income and shows the reconciliation from net income to operating cash flows. Also called the **reconciliation method**.

Intangible Assets. Assets with no physical form. Valuable because of the special rights they carry. Examples are patents and copyrights.

Internal Control. Organizational plan and all the related measures adopted by an entity to safeguard assets, encourage adherence to company policies, promote operational efficiency, and ensure accurate and reliable accounting records.

Internal Failure Costs. Costs incurred when the company detects and corrects poor-quality goods or services before delivery to customers.

Internal Rate of Return (IRR). The rate of return (based on discounted cash flows) that a company can expect to earn by investing in the project. The discount rate that makes the net present value of the project's cash flows equal to zero.

Inventoriable Product Costs. All costs of a product that are regarded as an asset for external financial reporting, and are not expensed until the product is sold. Must conform to GAAP.

Inventory Profit. Difference between gross profit figured on the FIFO basis and gross profit figured on the LIFO basis.

Inventory Turnover. Ratio of cost of goods sold to average inventory. Measures the number of times a company sells its average level of inventory during a year.

Inventory. All the goods that the company owns and expects to sell in the normal course of operations.

Investing Activity. Activity that increases and decreases the long-term assets available to the business; a section of the statement of cash flows.

Invoice. A seller's request for cash from the purchaser.

Job Cost Record. Document used to accumulate the costs of an individual job.

Job Costing. System for assigning costs to a specific unit or to a small batch of products or services that (1) pass through production steps as a distinct identifiable job lot, and (2) can vary considerably in terms of materials, labor, and overhead costs.

Journal. The chronological accounting record of an entity's transactions.

Just-In-Time (JIT) Costing. A standard costing system that starts with output completed and then assigns manufacturing costs to units sold and to inventories. Also called **backflush costing**.

Just-in-Time (JIT). A system in which a company produces just in time to satisfy needs. Materials are purchased and finished goods are completed only as needed to satisfy customer orders.

Labor Time Record. Identifies the employee, the amount of time spent on a particular job, and the labor cost charged to the job; a record that manufacturing firms commonly use to trace direct labor time to specific job cost records.

Last-In, First-Out (LIFO) Inventory Costing Method. Inventory costing method by which the last costs into inventory are the first costs out to cost of goods sold. This method leaves the oldest costs—those of beginning inventory and the earliest purchases of the period—in ending inventory.

Lease. Rental agreement in which the tenant (lessee) agrees to make rent payments to the property owner (lessor) to obtain the use of the asset.

Ledger. The book of accounts.

Legal Capital. The portion of stockholders' equity that cannot be used for dividends.

Lessee. Tenant in a lease agreement.

Lessor. Property owner in a lease agreement.

Leverage. Earning more income on borrowed money than the related interest expense, thereby increasing the earnings for the owners of the business.

Liability. An economic obligation (a debt) payable to an individual or an organization outside the business.

LIFO Liquidation. Situation when the LIFO inventory method is used and inventory quantities fall below the level of the previous period.

Limited Liability. No personal obligation of a stockholder for corporation debts. A stockholder can lose no more on an investment in a corporation's stock than the cost of the investment.

Limited Liability Partnership. A form of partnership in which each partner's personal liability for the business's debts is limited to a certain amount. Also called **LLPs**.

Limited Partnership. A partnership with at least two classes of partners: a general partner and limited partners.

Liquidation. The process of going out of business by selling the entity's assets and paying its liabilities. The final step in liquidation is the distribution of any remaining cash to the owner(s).

Liquidity. Measure of how quickly an item can be converted to cash.

Long-Term Asset. An asset other than a current asset.

Long-Term Investment. A non-current asset, a separate asset category reported on the balance sheet between current assets and plant assets.

Long-Term Liability. A liability other than a current liability.

Lower-of-Cost-or-Market (LCM) Rule. Rule that an asset should be reported in the financial statements at whichever is lower—its historical cost or its market value.

Major Repair or Extraordinary Repair. Repair work that generates a capital expenditure.

Maker of a Note. The person or business that signs the note and promises to pay the amount required by the note agreement; the debtor.

Management Accounting. The branch of accounting that focuses on information for internal decision makers of a business.

Management by Exception. Directs management's attention to important differences between actual and budgeted amounts.

Manufacturing Company. A company that uses labor, plant, and equipment to convert raw materials into new finished products.

Manufacturing Overhead. All manufacturing costs other than direct materials and direct labor. Also called **factory overhead** or **indirect manufacturing cost**.

Margin of Safety. Excess of expected sales over breakeven sales. Drop in sales a company can absorb before incurring an operating loss.

Market Interest Rate. Interest rate that investors demand in order to loan their money. Also called the **effective interest rate**.

Marketing. Promotion of products or services.

Market Value. Price for which a person could buy or sell a share of stock.

Market-Value Method. Used to account for all trading investments. These investments are reported at their current market value.

Master Budget. The set of budgeted financial statements and supporting schedules for the entire organization. This comprehensive budget includes the operating budget, the capital expenditures budget, and the financial budget.

Matching Principle. The basis for recording expenses. Directs accountants to identify all expenses incurred during the period, to measure the expenses, and to match them against the revenues earned during that same span of time.

Materiality Concept. A company must perform strictly proper accounting only for items that are significant to the business's financial statements.

Materials Inventory. Raw materials for use in manufacturing.

Materials Requisition. Request for materials, prepared by manufacturing personnel.

Menu. A list of options for choosing computer functions.

Merchandising Company. A company that resells products previously bought from suppliers.

Minority Interest. A subsidiary company's equity that is held by stockholders other than the parent company.

Mixed Cost. Cost that is part variable and part fixed.

Module. Separate compatible units of an accounting package that are integrated to function together.

Mortgage. Borrower's promise to transfer the legal title to certain assets to the lender if the debt is not paid on schedule.

Multi-step Income Statement. Format that contains subtotals to highlight significant relationships. In addition to net income, it presents gross profit and operating income.

Mutual Agency. Every partner can bind the business to a contract within the scope of the partnership's regular business operations.

Net Income. Excess of total revenues over total expenses. Also called **net earnings** or **net profit**.

Net Loss. Excess of total expenses over total revenues.

Net Pay. Gross pay minus all deductions. The amount of compensation that the employee actually takes home.

Net Present Value (NPV). The decision model that brings cash inflows and outflows back to a common time period by discounting these expected future cash flows to their present value, using a minimum desired rate of return.

Net Purchases. Purchases less purchase discounts and purchase returns and allowances.

Net Sales. Sales revenue less sales discounts and sales returns and allowances.

Network. The system of electronic linkages that allows different computers to share the same information.

Nonsufficient Funds (NSF) Check. A "hot" check, one for which the maker's bank account has insufficient money to pay the check.

Normal Balance. The account balance that appears on the side of the account—debit or credit—where we record increases.

Note Payable. A written promise of future payment.

Note Receivable. A written promise for future collection of cash.

On-line Processing. Computerized processing of related functions, such as the recording and posting of transactions, on a continuous basis.

Operating Activity. Activity that creates revenue or expense in the entity's major line of business; a section of the statement of cash flows. Operating activities affect the income statement.

Operating Budget. Sets the expected revenues and expenses—and thus operating income—for the period.

Operating Cycle. Time span during which cash is paid for goods and services, which are then sold to customers from whom the business collects cash.

Operating Expenses. Expenses, other than cost of goods sold, that are incurred in the entity's major line of business. Examples include rent, depreciation, salaries, wages, utilities, and supplies expense.

Operating Income. Gross profit minus operating expenses plus any other operating revenues. Also called **income from operations**.

Operating Lease. Usually a short-term or cancelable rental agreement.

Opportunity Cost. The benefit that can be obtained from the next-best course of action.

Ordinary Repair. Repair work that is debited to an expense account.

Other Expense. Expense that is outside the

main operations of a business, such as a loss on the sale of plant assets.

Other Revenue. Revenue that is outside the main operations of a business, such as a gain on the sale of plant assets.

Outsourcing. A make-or-buy decision, where managers must decide whether to buy a component product or service or to produce it in-house.

Outstanding Check. A check issued by the company and recorded on its books but not yet paid by its bank.

Outstanding Stock. Stock in the hands of stockholders.

Overallocated (Manufacturing) Overhead. The amount of manufacturing overhead allocated to Work in Process Inventory is more than the amount of manufacturing overhead costs actually incurred.

Overhead Flexible Budget Variance. The difference between the actual overhead cost and the flexible budget overhead for the actual number of outputs.

Owner Withdrawals. Amounts removed from the business by an owner.

Owner's Equity. The claim of a business owner to the assets of the business. Also called **capital**.

Paid-in Capital. A corporation's capital from investments by the stockholders. Also called **contributed capital**.

Par Value. Arbitrary amount assigned to a share of stock.

Parent Company. An investor company that owns more than 50% of the voting stock of a subsidiary company.

Partnership Agreement. The contract between partners that specifies such items as the name, location, and nature of the business; the name, capital investment, and duties of each partner; and the method of sharing profits and losses among the partners. Also called **articles of partnership**.

Partnership. An association of two or more persons who co-own a business for profit.

Patent. A federal government grant giving the holder the exclusive right to produce and sell an invention for 20 years.

Payback. The length of time it will take to recover, in net cash inflows from operations, the dollars of a capital outlay.

Payee of a Note. The person or business to whom the maker of a note promises future payment; the creditor.

Payroll. A major expense. Also called **employee compensation**.

Pension. Employee compensation that will be received during retirement.

Percent-of-Sales Method. A method of estimating uncollectible receivables that calculates uncollectible-account expense. Also called the **income statement approach**.

Period Costs. Operating costs that are expensed in the period in which they are incurred.

Periodic Inventory System. An inventory accounting system in which the business does not keep a continuous record of the inventory on hand. Instead, at the end of the period, the business counts the inventory on hand and uses this information to prepare the financial statements.

Permanent Accounts. Accounts that are not closed at the end of the period—asset, liability, and capital accounts. Also called **real accounts**.

Perpetual Inventory System. The accounting inventory system in which the business keeps a running record of inventory and cost of goods sold.

Petty Cash. Fund containing a small amount of cash that is used to pay for minor expenditures.

Planning. Choosing goals and deciding how to achieve them.

Plant Assets. Long-lived tangible assets, such as land, buildings, and equipment, used to operate a business. Also called **fixed assets**.

Plant or Fixed Asset. Another name for property, plant, and equipment.

Postclosing Trial Balance. List of the accounts and their balances at the end of the period after journalizing and posting the closing entries. The last step of the accounting cycle, the postclosing trial balance ensures that the ledger is in balance to start the next accounting period.

Posting. Copying amounts from the journal to the ledger.

Predetermined Manufacturing Overhead Rate. Estimated manufacturing overhead rate computed at the beginning of the year, calculated as the total estimated manufacturing overhead costs divided by the total estimated quantity of the manufacturing overhead allocation base. Also called the **budgeted manufacturing overhead rate**.

Preferred Stock. Stock that gives its owners certain advantages over common stockholders, such as the right to receive dividends before the common stockholders and the right to receive assets before the common stockholders if the corporation liquidates.

Premium. Excess of a bond's issue price over its maturity (par) value. Also called **bond premium**.

Prepaid Expense. Advance payments of expenses. A category of current assets that typically expire or are used up in the near future. Examples include prepaid rent, prepaid insurance, and supplies.

Present Value. Amount a person would invest now to receive a greater amount at a future date.

President. Chief operating officer in charge of managing the day-to-day operations of a corporation.

Prevention Costs. Costs incurred to avoid poor-quality goods or services.

Price Variance. Measures how well the business keeps unit prices of material and labor inputs within standards. This is computed as the difference in prices (actual price per unit minus standard price per unit) of an input, multiplied by the actual quantity of the input.

Price/Earnings Ratio. Ratio relates the market price of a share of common stock to the company's earnings per share. Measures the value the stock market places on $1 of a company's earnings.

Prior-period Adjustment. A correction to retained earnings for an error of an earlier period.

Process Costing. System for assigning costs to large numbers of identical units that usually proceed in a continuous fashion through a series of uniform production steps or processes.

Production Cost Report. Summarizes a processing department's operations for a period.

Production or Purchases. Resources used to produce a product or service, or to purchase finished merchandise.

Production Volume Variance. The difference between (1) the manufacturing overhead cost in the flexible budget for actual outputs, and (2) the standard overhead allocated to production.

Proprietorship. A business with a single owner.

Purchases Journal. Special journal used to record all purchases of inventory, supplies, and other assets on account.

Rate of Return on Common Stockholders' Equity. Net income minus preferred dividends, divided by average common stockholders' equity. A measure of profitability. Also called **return on stockholders' equity**.

Rate of Return on Net Sales. Ratio of net income to net sales. A measure of profitability. Also called **return on sales**.

Rate of Return on Total Assets. The sum of net income plus interest expense divided by average total assets. This ratio measures the success a company has in using its assets to earn income for the persons who finance the business. Also called **return on assets**.

Receivables. Monetary claims against a business or individual.

Reconciliation Method. Another name for the indirect method.

Relevant Information. Expected future data that differ among alternative courses of action.

Relevant Range. A band of volume within which a specific relationship exists between cost and volume.

Research and Development (R&D). The process of researching and developing new or improved products or services, or the processes for producing them.

Responsibility Accounting. A system for evaluating the performance of each responsibility center and its manager.

Responsibility Center. A part or subunit of an organization whose manager is accountable for specific activities.

Retained Earnings. A corporation's capital that is earned through profitable operation of the business.

Revenue. Amounts earned by delivering goods or services to customers. Revenues increase owner's equity.

Revenue Principle. The basis for recording revenues; tells accountants when to record revenue and the amount of revenue to record.

Reversing Entry. An entry that switches the debit and the credit of a previous adjusting entry. The reversing entry is dated the first day of the period after the adjusting entry.

S Corporation. A corporation taxed in the same way as a partnership.

Sales Discount. Reduction in the amount receivable from a customer, offered by the seller as an incentive for the customer to pay promptly. A contra account to Sales Revenue.

Sales Journal. Special journal used to record credit sales.

Sales Mix. Combination of products that make up total sales.

Sales Returns and Allowances. Decreases in the seller's receivable from a customer's return of merchandise or from granting the customer an allowance from the amount owed to the seller. A contra account to Sales Revenue.

Sales Revenue. The amount that a merchandiser earns from selling its inventory. Also called **sales**.

Sales Volume Variance. The difference arising only because the number of units actually sold differs from the static budget sales. This is computed as the difference between a static budget amount and a flexible budget amount.

Segment of the Business. One of various separate divisions of a company.

Sensitivity Analysis. A "what if" technique that asks what a result will be if a predicted amount is not achieved or if an underlying assumption changes.

Serial Bonds. Bonds that mature in installments over a period of time.

Server. The main computer in a network, where the program and data are stored.

Service Company. A company that provides intangible services, rather than tangible products.

Short Presentation. A way to report contingent liabilities in the body of the balance sheet, after total liabilities but with no amount given. An explanatory note accompanies the presentation.

Short-Term Investment. A current asset; an investment that is readily convertible to cash and that the investor intends either to convert to cash within one year or use to pay a current liability. Also called a **marketable security**.

Short-Term Note Payable. Prom-issory note payable due within one year, a common form of financing.

Single-Step Income Statement. Format that groups all revenues together and then lists and deducts all expenses together without drawing any subtotals.

Social Security Tax. Federal Insurance Contributions Act (FICA) tax, which is withheld from employees' pay. Also called FICA tax.

Software. Set of programs or instructions that drive the computer to perform the work desired.

Special Journal. An accounting journal designed to record one specific type of transaction.

Specific-Unit-Cost Method. Inven-tory cost method based on the specific cost of particular units of inventory. Also called the **specific identification method**.

Spreadsheet. A computer program that links data by means of formulas and functions; an electronic work sheet.

Standard Cost. A carefully predetermined cost that usually is expressed on a per-unit basis.

Stated Value. An arbitrary amount that accountants treat as though it were par value.

Statement of Cash Flows. Reports cash receipts and cash payments classified according to the entity's major activities: operating, investing, and financing.

Statement of Owner's Equity. Summary of the changes in an entity's owner's equity during a specific period.

Statement of Stockholders' Equity. Reports the changes in all categories of stockholders' equity during the period.

Static Budget. The budget prepared for only one level of sales volume. Also called the **master budget**.

Stock. Shares into which the owners' equity of a corporation is divided.

Stock Dividend. A distribution by a corporation of its own stock to its stockholders.

Stock Split. An increase in the number of outstanding shares of stock coupled with a proportionate reduction in the par value of the stock.

Stockholder. A person who owns the stock of a corporation. Also called a **shareholder**.

Stockholders' Equity. Owners' equity of a corporation.

Straight-Line (SL) Depreciation Method. Depreciation method in which an equal amount of depreciation expense is assigned to each year of asset use.

Strategy. A set of business goals and the tactics to achieve them.

Strong Currency. A currency that is rising relative to other nations' currencies.

Subsidiary Company. A company in which a parent company owns more than 50% of the voting stock.

Subsidiary Ledger. Record of ac-counts that provides supporting details on individual balances, the total of which appears in a general ledger account.

Sunk Cost. A past cost that cannot be changed regardless of which future action is taken.

Supply-Chain Management. Companies exchange information with suppliers and customers to reduce costs, improve quality, and speed delivery of goods and services from suppliers, through the company itself, and on to customers.

Target Cost. Allowable cost to develop, produce, and deliver the product or service.

Target Price. What customers are willing to pay for the product or service.

Temporary Accounts. The revenue and expense accounts that relate to a particular accounting period and are closed at the end of the period. For a proprietorship, the owner withdrawal account is also temporary. Also called **nominal accounts**.

Term Bonds. Bonds that all mature at the same time for a particular issue.

Throughput Time. The time between buying raw materials and selling the finished products.

Time Record. Source document used primarily by employees in service activities, to trace direct labor to specific jobs.

Time Value of Money. The fact that money can be invested to earn income over time.

Time-Period Concept. Ensures that accounting information is reported at regular intervals.

Times-Interest-Earned Ratio. Ratio of income from operations to interest expense. Measures the number of times operating income can cover interest expense. Also called the **interest-coverage ratio**.

Total Quality Management (TQM). A philosophy of delighting customers by providing them with superior products and services. Involves improving quality and eliminating defects and waste throughout the value chain.

Trademarks, Trade Names, or Brand Names. Assets that represent distinctive identifications of a product or service.

Trading Investments. Investments that are to be sold in the very near future with the intent of generating profits on price changes.

Trading on the Equity. Earning more income on borrowed money than the related expense, thereby in-creasing the earnings for the owners of the business. Also called **leverage**.

Transaction. An event that affects the financial position of a particular entity and can be recorded reliably.

Transferred-in Costs. Costs incurred in a previous process that are carried forward as part of the product's cost when it moves to the next process.

Treasury Stock. A corporation's own stock that it has issued and later reacquired.

Trial Balance. A list of all the accounts with their balances.

Trojan Horse. A malicious program that works like a virus but does not reproduce.

Uncollectible-Account Expense. Cost to the seller of extending credit. Arises from the fail-

ure to collect from credit customers. Also called **doubtful-account expense**, or **bad-debt expense**.

Underallocated (Manufacturing) Overhead. The amount of manufacturing overhead allocated to Work in Process Inventory is less than the amount of manufacturing overhead costs actually incurred.

Underwriter. Organization that purchases the bonds from an issuing company and resells them to its clients or sells the bonds for a commission, agreeing to buy all unsold bonds.

Unearned Revenue. A liability created when a business collects cash from customers in advance of doing work. The obligation is to provide a product or a service in the future. Also called **deferred revenue**.

Unemployment Compensation Tax. Payroll tax paid by employers to the government, which uses the money to pay unemployment benefits to people who are out of work.

Units-of-Production (UOP) Depre-ciation Method. Depreciation method by which a fixed amount of depreciation is assigned to each unit of output produced by an asset.

Unlimited Personal Liability. When a partnership (or a proprietorship) cannot pay its debts with business assets, the partners (or the proprietor) must use personal assets to meet the debt.

Value Chain. Sequence of activities that adds value to a firm's products or services. Includes R&D, design, production or purchases, marketing, distribution, and customer service.

Value Engineering. Systematically evaluating activities in an effort to reduce costs while satisfying customer needs.

Variable Costing. The costing method that assigns only variable manufacturing costs to products.

Variable Costs. Costs that change in total in direct proportion to changes in volume of activity.

Variance. The difference between an actual amount and the budget. A variance is labeled as favorable if it increases operating income and unfavorable if it decreases operating income.

Vertical Analysis. Analysis of a fi-nancial statement that reveals the relationship of each statement item to the total, which is 100%.

Voucher. Instrument authorizing a cash payment.

Weak Currency. A currency that is falling relative to other nations' currencies.

Weighted-Average Cost Method. Inventory costing method based on the weighted-average cost of inventory during the period. Weighted-average cost is determined by dividing the cost of goods available for sale by the number of units available. Also called the **average-cost method**.

Weighted-Average Process Costing Method. A process costing method that costs all equivalent units of work with a weighted average of that period's and the previous period's costs per equivalent unit.

Withheld Income Tax. Income tax deducted from employees' gross pay.

Work in Process Inventory. Goods that are partway through the manufacturing process, but not yet complete.

Work Sheet. A columnar document designed to help move data from the trial balance to the financial statements.

Working Capital. Current assets minus current liabilities; measures a business's ability to meet its short-term obligations with its current assets.

Company Index

Subject Index

Cost of sales. *See* Cost of goods sold
Cost principle, 10, 387
Cost reduction decisions, 1027–31
Cost systems, refined, 1017–20
Cost tracing, 809
Cost-volume-profit (CVP) analysis
  breakeven point, 893–96, 896–98
  contribution margin shortcut
    formula, 894–96
  decision guidelines, 904
  defined, 887
  margin of safety, 901
  for profit planning, 898–901
  sales mix, 901–3
  sensitivity analysis, 896–98
  underlying assumptions, 893
Cost-volume-profit graph, 899
Credit-balance accounts, 55
Credit-card fraud, 320
Credit-card sales, 319
Credit department, 313
Credit memorandum, 244–45
Creditors, 11, 311. *See also* Payee of
  note
Credits, in double-entry accounting,
  42
Cumulative preferred stock, 515–16
Currency
  foreign currency, 635, 636–37,
    640
  strong currency, 635
  weak currency, 635
Current asset, 138–39
Current Asset account, 677–78
Current liability
  decision guidelines, 435
  defined, 139
  with estimation mandatory,
    432–34
  of known amount, 425–32
  measuring ability to pay, 722–25
Current Liability account, 677–78
Current maturity, 429–30
Current portion of long-term debt,
  429–30, 594
Current ratio, 141–42, 143, 722–24
Cursor, 233
Customer prepayment, 431. *See also*
  Unearned revenue
Customers, cash collections from,
  661, 665–67
Customer service, 760
Cutler, Matt, 127

D

Database, 228
Data mining, 758
Date of record, 514
Days' sales in receivables, 327, 726
Death of partner, 481–82
Debentures, 578, 579
Debit-balance accounts, 55
Debit-card sales, 319–20
Debit memorandum, 245
Debits, in double-entry accounting,
  42
Debt
  long-term, 429–30, 506, 726–27
  short-term, 726–27
Debtor, 311, 321, 324
Debt ratio, 142–43, 726–27
Decision making
  accounting information for,
    326–27
  activity-based costing for, 1027–31
  with ratios, 721–31

short-term decisions, 1064–74
using accounting information for,
  61–62
Declaration date, 514
Default on note, 324–25
Defense Department, 50
Deferred revenue, 94. *See also*
  Unearned revenue
Deficit, 505
Delivery services, 900
Dell, Michael, 755, 797
Departmental accounting, 950–52
Departmental income statement, 952
Department functions, in value
  chain, 1019–20
Depletion expense, 404, 661, 674–76
Deposits in transit, 275
Deposit ticket, 273
Depreciable asset, changing useful
  life of, 401–2
Depreciable cost, 393
Depreciation
  about, 387–88
  accelerated method of, 395
  accumulated, 91
  adjusting entries to, 90–92
  causes of, 392–93
  comparison of methods, 396–97
  defined, 90
  double-declining-balance (DDB)
    method of, 395–96, 397, 555
  income taxes and, 399–400
  matching expense with revenue,
    392
  measuring, 393
  methods of, 393–96
  for partial years, 400–401
  of plant assets, 90–92, 387–88,
    392–97
  straight-line (SL) method of,
    393–94, 397
  survey of companies, 397
  units-of-production (UOP) method
    of, 394–95
Depreciation expense, 661, 674–76
Design
  of chart of accounts, 229–30
  defined, 760
  of information systems, 2
Development costs, 408
Diluted earnings per share, 557
Direct costs, 761
Direct labor
  about, 763
  in job costing, 806–7
Direct labor variance, 989–90
Direct materials
  about, 762–63
  equivalent units of, 858
  in job costing, 803–4
  in process costing, 854
Direct materials variance, 986–87
Direct method, statement of cash
  flows, 659–62
Direct write-off method, 318
Disbursements, internal control over,
  283–86
Disclosure principle, 361
Discontinued operations, 554–55
Discount
  on bond, 579
  on bonds payable, 582–83
  detailed accounting for, 175
  on note payable, 427–28
  note receivable, 343–44
  offering on sales, 176–77
  from purchase prices, 172–73
Discounted notes receivable, contingent liabilities on, 344

Discount on Bonds Payable account,
  582–83
Discount rate, 1082
Dishonored notes receivable, 324–25
Dishonor of note, 324–25
Dissolution, of partnership, 466
Distribution, 760
Dividend dates, 514
Dividend payments, 672–73
Dividends. *See also* Cash dividends;
  Stock dividends
  in arrears, 515
  cash receipts of, 661
  on cumulative and noncumulative
    preferred stock, 515–16
  decision guidelines, 521, 549–50
  defined, 505
  limits on purchases, 550–51
  as operating activity, 658
  paid to stockholders, 505, 506
  on preferred and common stock,
    514–15
  receiving on equity-method
    investment, 629
  on small stocks, 543–44
Dividends Payable account, 514–15
Dividend yield, 730
Documents
  internal control over, 371
  using as journals, 238
Dot.com partnerships, 469
Double-declining-balance (DDB)
  depreciation method, 395–96,
    397, 555
Double-entry accounting
  about, 41
  account increases and decreases,
    42–44
  posting from journal to ledger,
    45–46
  recording transactions in journal,
    44–45
  T-accounts, 41–42
Doubtful-account expense. *See*
  Uncollectible accounts
Drawing, in partnership, 474–75
Due date, of note, 322
Duties, separation of, 269–70

E

Earnings
  quality of, 553–59
  statement of, 17, 484
Earnings per share, 556–57, 729–30
e-Commerce
  benchmarking, 719
  business-to-business (B2B), 772
  credit card fraud, 320
  delivery services, 900
  dot.com partnerships, 469
  fulfillment costs, 187
  internal controls for, 271–72
  lending and borrowing, 582
  outsourcing, 1072
  sales tax liability, 429
  service companies, 98
  stock buyouts, 663
  supplier/vendor collaboration, 983
  virtual consultants, 231
  Web-based modeling, 983
Economic value added (EVA®),
  731–32
Effective-interest method of amortization, 588–92
Effective interest rate, 580
Efficiency variance, pitfalls of, 987–89
Efficient capital market, 732
Electronic devices for internal control, 271

Electronic funds transfer (EFT), 274,
  275
Electronic *keiretsu*, 983
Employees
  compensation of, 430–31
  in just-in-time production systems,
    1036
  motivation with budgets, 930
  payments to, 661, 668
Employee Social Security (FICA) tax,
  438
Employee's Withholding Allowance
  Certificate (W-4), 438
Employer FICA tax, 439
Employer payroll taxes, 439
Employer's Quarterly Federal Tax
  Return, 444
Encryption, 272
Enterprise resource planning, 941
Entity concept, 9–10
Equipment, furniture, and fixtures, 40
Equity, trading on the, 729
Equity method, 628
Equity-method investments, 627–30
Equivalent units
  about, 846–47
  computing output in terms of,
    848–49, 855–58, 862–64
  computing per-unit cost, 849–50,
    858–59, 864
  of conversion costs, 858
  of direct materials, 858
  transferred in, 857
Errors
  correction in trial balance, 49
  effect on inventory, 362–63
Estimated residual value, 393
Estimated useful life, 393
Estimated vacation pay liability,
  433–34
Estimated warranty payable, 432–33
Ethical issues
  in accounting, 289
  in accrual accounting, 101–2
  inventory, 363–64
  in issuance of stock, 511
  judgment guidelines, 290
  plant assets and intangibles, 408
  in reporting liabilities, 434–35
Ethical standards
  in accounting and business, 7–8
  corporate and professional codes of
    ethics, 288
  for management accountants,
    775–76
EVA® (economic value added),
  731–32
Exchange rates, of foreign-currency,
  635
Expenses
  in accounting equation, 56
  defined, 12
  operating expenses, 183, 216,
    667–68
  as owner's equity, 41
  payroll reporting of, 447
  vs. inventory under absorption and
    variable costing, 908
External auditors, 271
External controls, 290–91
External failure costs, 1041
Extraordinary gains and losses, 555
Extraordinary items, 555
Extraordinary repair, 391

F

Facilities, best use of, 1071
Factory overhead, 763. *See also*
  Manufacturing overhead

Fanning, Shawn, 469
FASB (Financial Accounting Standards Board), 7, 408
Federal unemployment compensation tax, 439
FICA tax, 438, 439
Fidelity bonds, 271
FIFO. See under First-in-first-out
Filo, David, 469
Financial accounting
  about, 6
  management accounting compared to, 756–58
Financial Accounting Standards Board (FASB), 7, 408
Financial budget, 931, 936–40
Financial statement analysis
  decision guidelines, 733
  limitations of, 731–33
  objectives of, 711–12
Financial statements. See also specific statements
  adjusting entries and, 83–87
  cash equivalents on, 656
  cash on, 656
  consolidated financial statements, 651
  defined, 5
  headings, 18–19
  for manufacturing companies, 766–68
  for merchandisers, 216–17
  for merchandising companies, 216–17, 764–66
  notes to, 550–51
  for partnerships, 484–85
  perpetual inventory system reporting, 349
  preparing from adjusted trial balance, 100–101
  preparing from work sheet, 133
  product and period costs in, 764–68
  relationships among, 19–20, 101
  for service companies, 764
  types of, 17–18
Financing activity
  cash flows from, 662
  cash receipts from, 673
  computing cash amounts of, 670–73
  defined, 658
  noncash, 673
  on statement of cash flows, 658, 660
Finished goods, accounting for, 813–14
Finished goods inventory, 759
Finished Goods Inventory account, 801, 816
Fireproof vaults, 271
Firewalls, 272
First-in-first-out (FIFO) cost method
  about, 355
  change in accounting principle and, 555
  comparison with other LIFO, 356–57
  illustrated, 354
  income effects of, 355–56
  in perpetual inventory system, 359
First-in-first-out (FIFO) process costing method
  about, 855
  assigning costs, 859–61
  computing cost per equivalent unit, 858–59
  computing output in terms of equivalent units, 855–58
  production cost report, 861–62

summarizing flow of physical units, 855–58
summarizing total costs to account for, 858–59
Fixed asset, 139
Fixed costs
  about, 888–89
  ignoring nature of, 1067
  in short-term decisions, 1068–69
Flexible budget
  decision guidelines, 980
  example of, 974
  graphing, 975–77
  variance analysis and, 977–80
  vs. static budget, 973–80
Flexible budget variance, 977, 978, 991–92
FOB (free on board), 173–74
Foreign currency, 635, 636–37, 640
Foreign-currency exchange rates, 635
Foreign subsidiaries, consolidating, 637
Four-column account format, 54
Franchises, 407
Fraud, credit-card, 320
Free on board (FOB), 173–74
Freight-in costs, 174
Freight-out costs, 174
Fulfillment cost, 187
Full product costs, 761
Fully depreciated assets, 402
Future value
  about, 613–14
  of annuity, 615–16
  tables, 614–15

G

GAAP. See Generally accepted accounting principles (GAAP)
Gains and losses
  extraordinary, 555
  on foreign currency, 637
  on sale of assets, 676–77
General journal
  accounting information system role of, 244–46
  defined, 234
General ledger
  accounts receivable subsidiary ledger and, 246
  balancing, 246
  posting from cash payments journal, 242–44
  posting from cash receipts journal, 238–40
  posting from purchases journal, 242
  posting to, 235–36
Generally accepted accounting principles (GAAP)
  about, 9
  absorption costing and, 905
  inventory methods comparison, 356–57
  for research and development costs, 408
General partnership, 468
Gildea, Deanna, 231
Gildea, Lance, 231
Global marketplace competition, 771
Going-concern concept, 10–11
Goodwill
  about, 407
  international accounting for, 407–8
  minority interest and, 631
Gordon, Pamela, 1072
Government regulation, of corporation, 502

Grassley, Charles, 50
Grossing up revenue, 98
Gross margin. See Gross profit
Gross margin method, 364–65
Gross pay, 437
Gross profit
  about, 348
  contribution margin compared with, 891–92
  defined, 169
  in perpetual inventory system, 350
Gross profit method, 364–65
Gross profit percentage, 185–86
Gross salary, 439

H

Hardware, 228
Hedging, 637
Held-to-maturity investments, 632–33
Herzog, Clint, 711
Horizontal analysis, 712–15
Hurdle rate, 1082

I

Iacocca, Lee, 367
Impersonation, 272
Imprest systems, 286
Income, of consolidated entity, 631
Income from operations. See Operating income
Income statement. See also Corporate income statement
  about, 17
  absorption costing, 906, 1065
  budgeted income statement, 934, 936
  common-size income statement, 717, 719
  comparative income statement, 715, 723
  contribution margin income statement, 891–92, 1065
  departmental income statement, 952
  example of, 20
  foreign currency gains and losses on, 637
  formats, 184–85
  measuring net income on, 356
  for merchandisers, 183
  multi-step income statement, 185
  relationships of, 101
  single-step income statement, 185
  standard cost income statement, 996–97
  variable costing, 907
  with and without special sales order, 1066
  work sheet column, 181, 216
Income statement approach, 315, 316–18
Income statement equation approach, 894
Income statement performance report, 978
Income summary, 136
Income Summary account, 136–38
Income tax
  comparison of inventory methods, 357
  for corporations, 519–20
  decision guidelines for corporations, 521
  depreciation and, 399–400
  employee Social Security (FICA) tax, 438
  LIFO cost method advantage, 356
  for partnership, 467
  payments of, 669

payroll deductions, 437–39
Income tax expense, payments for, 661
Income tax payable (for corporation), 434
Indirect costs
  about, 761
  allocation of, 950–52, 1017–20
Indirect labor
  about, 763
  in job costing, 806–7
Indirect manufacturing costs, 763. See also Manufacturing overhead
Indirect materials, 763, 803–4
Indirect method, statement of cash flows, 659–60, 674–78
Inflation, 11
Information systems design, 2. See also Computerized accounting system
Information technology, impact on job costing, 807
Initial public offering (IPO), 509
Inputs, 228–29
Institute of Management Accountants (IMA)
  about, 7
  Standards of Ethical Conduct, 7–8, 775–76
Intangible asset
  accounting for, 405–6
  defined, 141, 387
Integrated accounting software, 232–34
Interest
  capitalizing cost of, 390
  cash receipts of, 661
  of note, 322
  as operating activity, 658
  partner sharing based on, 473–74
  payments of, 669
Interest-coverage ratio, 727
Interest expense
  adjusting entries for, 585–86
  on bonds payable issued at discount, 583
  on bonds payable issued at premium, 584
  effective-interest method of amortizing, 588–92
  payments for, 661
Interest Expense account, 583, 584, 585–86, 588–92
Interest period, 322
Interest rate
  of bonds, 579–80
  of notes, 322
Interest revenue, accruing for notes receivable, 324
Internal auditors, 2, 269, 270
Internal controls
  about, 267–71
  in accounting information systems, 227
  with bank account, 273–81
  for e-Commerce, 271–72
  elements of, 285
  for inventory, 365
  invoice as, 283
  limitations of, 272
  over cash payments, 283–86, 285
  over cash receipts, 282–83
  over documents, 371
  over payroll, 446–47
  over petty cash payments, 285–86

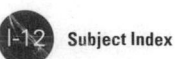